Bookman's Price Index

CUMULATIVE INDEX TO VOLUMES 68-73

ISSN 0068-0141

Bookman's Price Index

CUMULATIVE INDEX TO VOLUMES 68-73

A Consolidated Index to 90,000 Citations Describing Antiquarian Books Offered For Sale by Leading Dealers

Anne F. McGrath
Managing Editor

Richard Grazide
Editor

GALE®

THOMSON
GALE

Detroit • New York • San Diego • San Francisco • Cleveland • New Haven, Conn. • Waterville, Maine • London • Munich

THOMSON
GALE

Bookman's Price Index: Cumulative Index to Volumes 68–73

Anne F. McGrath, Managing Editor
Richard Grazide, Editor

Project Editor
Charles B. Montney

Editorial
Dana Ferguson, Nancy Franklin, Sharon McGilvray

Editorial Support Services
Wayne Fong

Data Capture
Beverly Jendrowski, Cynthia Jones, Frances Monroe, Elizabeth Pilette, Beth Richardson

Product Design
Michael Logusz

Composition and Electronic Capture
Evi Seoud

Manufacturing
Stacy L. Melson

©2004 by Gale. Gale is an imprint of The Gale Group, Inc., a division of Thomson Learning, Inc.

Gale and Design™ and Thomson Learning™ are trademarks used herein under license.

For more information, contact
The Gale Group, Inc.
27500 Drake Road
Farmington Hills, MI 48331-3535
Or you can visit our Internet site at
http://www.gale.com

ALL RIGHTS RESERVED
No part of this work covered by the copyright hereon may be reproduced or used in any form or by any means—graphic, electronic, or mechanical, including photocopying, recording, taping, Web distribution, or information storage retrieval systems—without the written permission of the publisher.

This publication is a creative work fully protected by all applicable copyright laws, as well as by misappropriation, trade secret, unfair competition, and other applicable laws. The authors and editors of this work have added value to the underlying factual material herein through one or more of the following: unique and original selection, coordination, expression, arrangement, and classification of the information.

For permission to use material from this product, submit your request via Web at http://www.gale-edit.com/permissions, or you may download our Permissions Request form and submit your request by fax or mail to:

Permissions Department
The Gale Group, Inc.
27500 Drake Road
Farmington Hills, MI, 48331-3535
Permissions hotline:
248-699-8074 or 800-877-4253, ext. 8006
Fax: 248-699-8074 or 800-762-4058.

While every effort has been made to ensure the reliability of the information presented in this publication, The Gale Group, Inc. does not guarantee the accuracy of the data contained herein. The Gale Group, Inc. accepts no payment for listing; and inclusion in the publication of any organization, agency, institution, publication, service, or individual does not imply endorsement of the editors or publisher. Errors brought to the attention of the publisher and verified to the satisfaction of the publisher will be corrected in future editions.

LIBRARY OF CONGRESS CATALOG CARD NUMBER 64-8723

ISBN 0-7876-9086-4
ISSN 0068-0141

Printed in the United States of America
10 9 8 7 6 5 4 3 2 1

Contents

This work provides speedy access to the 90,000 book titles contained in Volumes 68 through 73 of the Bookman's Price Index, *which were published between 2001 and 2003. Additional information about these titles is available in the individual volumes.*

Introduction vii
Cumulative Index to *Bookman's Price
Index, Volumes 68-73* 1

Introduction

The *Bookman's Price Index* (BPI), published since 1964, indicates the availability and price of antiquarian books in the United States, Canada, and the British Isles. Since the BPI now numbers over 70 volumes, searching for specific titles has become a time-consuming task for the user.

This volume is the tenth "cumulative index to the index." It references the entries in Volumes 68 through 73, which were published between 2001 and 2003. This work provides access to approximately 90,000 entries from the original BPI volumes.

What Is Included?

Since the primary purpose of this volume is speedy access to tens of thousands of book titles, the complete entry in the original BPI volume is not repeated here. Such repetition would necessarily negate the ability to include all this information in one volume, thus defeating its purpose of quick and easy access. This index provides sufficient information for rapid identification of a specific title including the author, date of publication, and place of publication, followed by a list of all the BPI volumes in which that book is included.

BPI's regular volumes provide extensive information so that the user can identify a rare book and get some indication of how the particular dealer arrived at its price. This information, taken from rare book dealer catalogs, includes not only the author, title, date and place of publication, publisher, edition, and price, but a thorough description of the book and notes on its condition. The description and condition information includes physical size, illustrations, binding, authors' signatures, general physical condition, specific flaws, and relative scarcity whenever this information has been given by the dealer listing the book.

Arrangement

Entries appear in a single alphabetic sequence, based on the name of the author: in cases of personal authorship, the author's last name; in cases of books produced by corporate bodies such as governments of countries or states, the name of that entity; in cases of anonymous books, the title; and in cases of anonymous classics such as *Arabian Nights*, the customary or well-known title. The editors have tried their best to duplicate the sorting rules of the original volumes, but as these rules have changed over the years that BPI has been published, this has been a difficult task. Users are advised to check the listings for possible variants to ensure they find all appropriate entries.

Extensive efforts were made to standardize the names of authors so that all titles belonging to the same author appeared together. However, in compiling the original volumes of BPI covered herein, some inconsistencies appeared in the way authors' names were presented between volumes. The editors have brought as much consistency as possible to this index, but in certain cases, changing an author's name for the sake of consistency might have made it impossible for the user to find the entry in the original BPI volume. Therefore, some latitude is necessary when searching for a specific author.

Under the author's name, works are arranged in alphabetical sequence according to the first word of the title, excepting initial articles. References to the same title are grouped together unless such grouping would have made it difficult for the user to locate the entry in the original BPI volume. Different editions of a single work are arranged according to the date of publication, with the earliest dates first. If the date of publication is the same but the place of publication is different, these entries are then organized alphabetically by the place of publication. Bearing all of this in mind, it would be advisable for users to scan the entire list of an author's works so as not to miss locating information for a specific title.

Sample Entry

The following sample illustrates the components of a typical entry:

|1| DE QUINCY, THOMAS
|2| Confessions of an English Opium Eater.
|3| Oxford: |4| 1930. |5| V. 69; 70; 73

|1| Author's Name

|2| Title

|3| Place of publication

|4| Date of publication

|5| Volumes of the BPI in which the complete descriptive entry for copies of this edition can be found.

Acknowledgments

My thanks to Charles Montney, coordinating editor at Gale Group, Inc., and to his associates Nancy Franklin, Sharon Mc-

Gilvray, and Dana Ferguson and managing editor Debra Kirby for their guiding hands throughout this project, and to Richard Grazide for his assistance in research and editing and his many hours of reviewing and correcting some 90,000 entries in order to bring consistency to the index.

Suggestions and Comments Welcome

Suggestions are always welcome. This index volume is, in part, a result of the suggestions of BPI users. The editors invite all comments, especially those that might improve the usefulness of *Bookman's Price Index*.

Please contact:

Editors
Bookman's Price Index
Gale Group, Inc.
27500 Drake Rd.
Farmington Hills, MI 48331-3535
Phone: 248-699-GALE
Toll-Free: 800-877-GALE
Fax: 248-699-8067

Anne F. McGrath
Managing Editor

A

A APPLE Pie. London: 1900. V. 73

ABC Dario di Guerra. Florence: 1915. V. 68

ABC for the Little Ones. Somerville: 1910. V. 72

A B C Nursery Rhymes and Fairy Tales. 1950. V. 73

AN A B C of Birds and Beasts Identified (With Their Diets). London: 1985. V. 73

THE A B C of Fairy Tales. London: 1900. V. 73

THE ABC of Nursery Rhymes. London: 1900. V. 72

THE ABC of Toys and Games. London: 1910. V. 72

ABC Painting Book. London: 1960. V. 72

A B C Simple Simon. Bloomsbury: 1840. V. 72; 73

A WAS An Archer. London: 1880. V. 73

AARON, CHARLES HOWARD
Leaching Gold and Silver Ores. San Francisco: 1881. V. 69

ABAGNALE, FRANK
Catch Me If You Can. New York: 1980. V. 73

ABAJIAN, JAMES DE T.
Blacks and Their Contributions to the American West: a Bibliography and Union List of Library Holdings through 1970. Boston: 1974. V. 68

ABBADIE, JAMES
The Deity of Jesus Christ Essential to the Christian Religion; a Treatise on the Divinity of Our Lord Jesus Christ. Burlington: 1802. V. 69

ABBAY, RICHARD
Castle of Knaresborough. London: 1887. V. 73

ABBE, CLEVELAND
An Account of the Progress in Meteorology in the Year 1884. Washington: 1885. V. 68

ABBEY, EDWARD
Abbey's Road. New York: 1979. V. 69; 70; 71; 73
Appalachian Wilderness. New York: 1970. V. 71
Beyond the Wall: Essays from the Outside. New York: 1984. V. 73
Black Sun. New York: 1971. V. 68; 69; 73
Black Sun. Santa Barbara: 1981. V. 71
The Brave Cowboy. New York: 1956. V. 70
The Brave Cowboy. Salt Lake City: 1993. V. 69; 73
Cactus Country. Amsterdam: 1973. V. 68; 73
Cactus Country. New York: 1973. V. 71; 73
Canyonlands Country. 1975. V. 71
Confessions of a Barbarian. Santa Barbara: 1986. V. 69
Desert Images; An American Landscape. New York: 1979. V. 72
Desert Solitaire. New York: 1968. V. 69; 70; 71; 72
Desert Solitaire. Salt Lake City: 1981. V. 68; 71
Desert Solitaire. Tucson: 1988. V. 69; 73
Fire on the Mountain. New York: 1962. V. 70
The Fool's Progress. New York: 1988. V. 68; 69; 71; 72; 73
The Fool's Progress. London: 1989. V. 68
Good News. New York: 1980. V. 69; 71; 72; 73
Hayduke Lives!. Boston: 1989-1990. V. 71; 72
Hayduke Lives!. Boston: 1990. V. 73
The Hidden Canyon. New York: 1977. V. 69; 73
Jonathan Troy. New York: 1954. V. 70
The Journey Home: Some Words in Defense of the American West. New York: 1977. V. 69
The Monkey Wrench Gang. Philadelphia & New York: 1975. V. 69; 70; 71; 72; 73
The Monkey Wrench Gang. Edinburgh: 1978. V. 70
The Monkey Wrench Gang. Salt Lake City: 1985. V. 68; 69; 70; 73
One Life at a Time, Please. New York: 1988. V. 69; 70; 73
Resist Much, Obey Little. Salt Lake City: 1985. V. 71
Slickrock. San Francisco/New York: 1971. V. 68; 69; 71; 73
Slumgullion Stew. New York: 1984. V. 68; 71
The Summer of Black Widows. New York: 1996. V. 69
Sunset Canyon. London: 1972. V. 70; 73
Vox Clamantis in Desierto. Santa Fe: 1989. V. 69; 71; 73

ABBEY, EDWIN
The Quest of the Holy Grail, a Series of Paintings. New York: 1895. V. 68

ABBEY, JOHN ROLAND
The Italian Manuscripts in the Library of Major J. R. Abbey. London: 1969. V. 70
Scenery of Great Britain and Ireland in Aquatint and Lithography 1770-1860. London: 1952. V. 69; 72

ABBEY, RITA D.
Rivertip. Flagstaff: 1977. V. 68; 73

ABBIATICO, M.
Modern Firearm Engravings. 1980. V. 73

ABBOT, ANTHONY
About the Murder of a Man Afraid of Women. New York: 1937. V. 70
Deadly Secret. London: 1943. V. 70
The Shudders. 1943. V. 68
The Shudders. New York: 1943. V. 70

ABBOT, C.
Flora Bedfordiensis...According to the System of Linnaeus. 1798. V. 69
Flora Bedfordiensis...According to the System of Linnaeus. Bedford: 1798. V. 73

ABBOT, CLAUDE COLLEER
The Correspondence of Gerard Manley Hopkins and Richard Watson Dixon. London: 1955. V. 70

ABBOT, CRAIG S.
Marianne Moore - a Descriptive Bibliography. Pittsburgh: 1977. V. 68

ABBOT, JOHN
John Abbot's Birds of Georgia. Savannah: 1997. V. 69

ABBOTT, BERENICE
Greenwich Village Today and Yesterday. New York: 1949. V. 73
The World of Atget. New York: 1964. V. 68

ABBOTT, CHARLES A.
A Treatise of the Law Relative to Merchant Ships and Seamen: In Four Parts. London: 1804. V. 70

ABBOTT, CHARLES CONRAD
In Nature's Realm. Trenton: 1900. V. 69
Travels in a Tree-Top. Philadelphia: 1894. V. 69
Upland and Meadow. New York: 1886. V. 69

ABBOTT, DOROTHY
Mississippi Writers: Reflections of Childhood and Youth. Volume I: Fiction. 1985. V. 70

ABBOTT, EARL
Instructions for Virginia and West Virginia. Charlottesville: 1962. V. 73

ABBOTT, EDITH
The One Hundred and One Country Jails of Illinois and Why They Should be Abolished. Chicago: 1916. V. 72
The Tenements of Chicago 1908-1935. Chicago: 1936. V. 68

ABBOTT, EDWIN A.
Flatland. London: 1884. V. 70

ABBOTT, G. F.
The Tale of a Tour in Macedonia. London: 1903. V. 73

ABBOTT, GEORGE
Coquette. New York: 1928. V. 70; 71
Damn Yankees. New York: 1956. V. 73
Views of the Forts of Bhurtpoore & Weire... (with) Sketches About Kurrah Mannickpore. London: 1827. V. 70

ABBOTT, JACK HENRY
In the Belly of the Beast: Letters from Prison. New York: 1981. V. 71

ABBOTT, KEITH
Rhino Ritz. Berkeley: 1979. V. 70

ABBOTT, STEPHEN
The First Regiment New Hampshire Volunteers in the Great Rebellion. Keene: 1890. V. 69

ABDILL, GEORGE B.
Rails West: A Collectors Album Of A Vanishing Era In Railroadiana. Seattle: 1960. V. 72

ABDULLA BIN ABDULKADAR
Translations from the Hakayit Abdulla (Bin Abdulkadar), Munshi. London: 1874. V. 72

ABDULLAH, ACHMED
The Thief of Bagdad. New York: 1924. V. 69

ABDULLAH, NEQINISO
The Bald Eagle: Symbol Of Oppression. New York: 1976. V. 72

ABE, K.
Jazz Giants: a Visual Retrospective. New York: 1988. V. 68

ABE, KOBO
The Box Man. New York: 1974. V. 72

ABE, T.
Keys to the Japanese Fishes Fully Illustrated in Colors. Tokyo: 1963. V. 73

A'BECKETT, GILBERT ABBOTT
The Comic Blackstone. London: 1844. V. 68
The Comic History of England. London: 1847-1848. V. 72
The Comic History of England. London: 1860. V. 69
The Comic History of England. (with) The Comic History of Rome. London: 1850. V. 68
The Comic History of Rome. London: 1851. V. 71
The Comic History of Rome. London: 1860. V. 69

ABEL, ANNIE HELOISE
Tabeau's Narrative of Loisel's Expedition to the Upper Missouri. Norman: 1939. V. 68; 73

ABELARD, PETER
Letters of Abelard and Eloisa. London: 1802. V. 69
Letters of Abelard and Heloise. London: 1718. V. 69

ABELL, WESTCOTT
The Shipwright's Trade. Cambridge: 1948. V. 70

ABEL SMITH, BRIAN
A History of the Nursing Profession. London: 1961. V. 68

ABERCONWAY, CHRISTABLE
The Story of Mr. Korah. London: 1954. V. 69

ABERCROMBIE, JOHN
Inquiries Concerning the Intellectual Powers and the Investigation of Truth. Edinburgh: 1831. V. 72

ABERCROMBIE, LASCELLES
New English Poems. London: 1931. V. 72

ABERCROMBIE, P.
Cumbrian Regional Planning Scheme, Prepared for the Cumbrian Regional Joint Advisory Scheme. 1932. V. 71

ABERCROMBIE, W. R.
Alaska: 1899. Copper River Exploring Expedition. Washington: 1900. V. 73

ABERDEEN, GEORGE GORDON, EARL OF
An Inquiry into the Principles of Beauty in Grecian Architecture.... London: 1860. V. 68

ABERDEEN, LADY
The Canadian Journal of Lady Aberdeen 1893-1898. Toronto: 1960. V. 73

ABERNATHY, JOHN R.
Catch 'Em Alive Jack-The Life and Adventures of An American Pioneer. New York: 1936. V. 71

ABERNETHY, J.
Philalethes; or, Revelation Consistent with Reason: an Attempt to Answer the Objections and Arguments Against It In Mr. Paine's Book, Entitled Age of Reason. Belfast: 1795. V. 69

ABERNETHY, JOHN
Surgical Observations on Injuries of the Head and on Miscellaneous Subjects. London: 1810. V. 70
Surgical Observations on Injuries of the Head and On Miscellaneous Subjects. London: 1811. V. 70
Surgical Observations...Local Diseases and on Aneurisms.... London: 1817. V. 71

ABERT, JAMES WILLIAM
Report of Lieut. J. W. Abert, of His Examination of New Mexico in the Years 1846-1847. Washington: 1848. V. 68
Through the Country of the Comanche Indians in the Fall of the Year 1845. San Francisco: 1970. V. 69; 71; 73
Western America in 1846-1847. San Francisco: 1966. V. 70; 73

ABERT, JOHN JAMES
Abert's New Mexico Report 1846-'47. Albuquerque: 1962. V. 71

ABINGDON, THOMAS
The Antiquities of the Cathedral Church of Worcester. London: 1717. V. 68

ABISH, WALTER
Alphabetical Africa. New York: 1974. V. 69
Minds Meet. New York: 1975. V. 69

ABITIBI POWER & PAPER CO.
Abitibi, a Story in Pictures. Montreal: 1924. V. 68

ABNEY, W. DE WIVELESLIE
A Treatise on Photography. London: 1878. V. 68

ABNEY, WILLIAM
The Art and Practice of Silver Printing. 1888. V. 71
Colour Vision. Being the Tyndall Lectures delivered in 1894 at the Royal Institution. London: 1895. V. 69

ABONYI, LAJOS
Tarloviragok. Budapest: 1907. V. 71

ABRAHAM and Isaac. 1999. V. 71

ABRAHAM, ASHLEY
Rock-Climbing in North Wales. Keswick: 1906. V. 69
Rock-Climbing in Skye. London: 1908. V. 69; 71

ABRAHAM, ASHLEY P.
Some Portraits of The Lake Poets And Their Homes. Keswick: 1920. V. 71; 72

ABRAHAM, GEORGE D.
British Mountain Climbs. London: 1945. V. 69
British Mountain Climbs. London: 1948. V. 69
The Complete Mountaineer. London: 1907. V. 69
The Complete Mountaineer. 1923. V. 68; 70; 73
Modern Mountaineering. London: 1933. V. 69
Motor Ways at Home and Abroad. London: 1928. V. 69; 71
Mountain Adventures at Home and Abroad. 1910. V. 68; 70
Mountain Adventures at Home and Abroad. London: 1910. V. 69
On Alpine Heights and British Crags. 1919. V. 68; 70
On Alpine Heights and British Crags. London: 1919. V. 69; 71
Swiss Mountain Climbs. 1911. V. 68; 70; 73
Swiss Mountain Climbs. London: 1911. V. 69

ABRAHAM, JAMES JOHNSTON
Lettsom, His Life, Times, Friends and Descendants. London: 1933. V. 68; 71; 72; 73

ABRAHAM, MAY E.
The Law Relating to Factories and Workshops (including Laundries and Docks). London: 1895. V. 71

ABRAHAMSON, W. G.
Evolutionary Ecology Across Three Trophic Levels, Goldenrods, Gallmakers and Natural Enemies. Princeton: 1997. V. 68; 71

ABRAMS, L.
Illustrated Flora of the Pacific States: Washington, Oregon and California. Stanford: 1955-. V. 71

ABRIOUX, YEVES
Ian Hamilton Finlay - a Visual Primer. London: 1992. V. 73

AN ABSTRACT of an Act for Granting an Aid to His Majesty as Well by a Land-Tax as by Several Subsidies and Other Duties Payable for One Year. London: 1696. V. 72

AN ABSTRACT of the Case and Opinions that Have Appeared in Print for and Against the Eau Brink Cut; affecting Drainage, Navigation and the Port of Lynn. By a Member of the Committee. 1794. V. 72

ABY, JOE C.
The Tales of Rube Hoffenstein. New York: 1882. V. 71

ACADIA GAS ENGINES LTD.
Catalog No. 7. Bridgewater: 192-?. V. 72

ACCADEMIA DEL CIMENTO
Sagi di Naturali Esperienze Fatte Nell'Accademia Del Cimento sotto la Protezione del Serenissimo Principe Leopoldo di Toscana e Discritte dal Segretario di essa Accademia. Florence: 1691. V. 69

ACCOMAZZO, BETTY
Arizona National Ranch Histories. Phoenix: 1980-1990. V. 69

ACCOUNT of a Voyage for the Discovery of a North-West Passage... Performed in the Year 1746 and 1747...Captain Francis Smith, Commander. London: 1748-1749. V. 70

AN ACCOUNT of the Ceremonies Observed in the Coronations of the Kings and Queens of England; viz. King James II and His Royal Consort; King William III and Queen Mary; Queen Anne; King George I; and King George II; and Queen Caroline. London: 1760. V. 69

AN ACCOUNT of the Corporation of Beccles Fen, in the County of Suffolk.... Beccles: 1826. V. 68

AN ACCOUNT of the Gospel Labours and Christian Experiences of a Faithful Minister of Christ, John Churchman.... Philadelphia: 1779. V. 68

AN ACCOUNT of the Private League Betwixt the Late King James the Second and the French King. London: 1689. V. 72

AN ACCOUNT of the Rise and Nature of the Fund Established by Parliament, for a Provision for the Widows and Children of the Ministers of the Church and of the Heads, Principals, and Masters in the Universities, of Scotland. Edinburgh: 1759. V. 69

AN ACCOUNT of the Second Commemoration of Shakespeare, Celebrated at Stratford-upon-Avon, on Friday the 23rd of April, 1830.... Leamington: 1830. V. 68

ACCUM, FREDRICK
Description of the Process of Manufacturing Coal Gas, for the Lighting of Streets, Houses and Public Buildings.... London: 1819. V. 69
Guide to the Chalybeate Spring of Thetford...With Observations on Bathing and a Sketch of the History and Present State of Thetford. 1819. V. 71
A Practical Treatise on Gas-Light.... London: 1815. V. 69

AN ACCURATE and Impartial Report of the Action for Defamation, Brought by James Tandy, Esq. Against Brabazon Morris, Esq. a Magistrate of the County of Meath. Dublin: 1807. V. 70

AN ACCURATE Description and History of the Cathedral and Metropolitical Church of St. Peter, York.... York: 1768-1770. V. 69

ACHARD, FRANZ KARL
Bestimmung der Bestandtheile Einiger Edelgesteine. Berlin: 1779. V. 68

ACHEBE, CHINUA
Anthills of the Savannah. London: 1987. V. 68
Things Fall Apart. London: 1964. V. 69

ACHERLEY, ROGER
The Britannic Constitution; or, the Fundamental Form of Government in Britain. London: 1727. V. 70

ACHESON, EDWARD
Murder to Hounds. New York: 1939. V. 69; 70

ACKERMAN, C. W.
George Eastman. Boston: 1930. V. 68

ACKERMAN, DIANE
A Natural History of the Senses. New York: 1990. V. 72

ACKERMAN, EDWARD A.
New England's Fishing Industry. Chicago: 1941. V. 68

ACKERMAN, WILLIAM K.
Historical Sketch of the Illinois Central Railroad, Together with a Brief Biographical Record of Its Incorporators and Some of Its Early Officers. Chicago: 1890. V. 68

ACKERMANN & CO.
The Youth's Own Drawing Book of Animals. London: 1820. V. 70

ACKERMANN, JACOB FIDELIS
Der Scheintod und das Rettungsverfahren. Ein Chimiatrischer Versuch. Frankfurt am Main: 1804. V. 73

ACKERMANN, RUDOLPH
Forget Me Not: a Christmas and New Year's Present for 1826. London: 1826. V. 73
The History of the Abbey Church of St. Peter's Westminster, Its Antiquities and Monuments. London: 1812. V. 68; 70
The History of the Colleges of Winchester, Eton and Westminster; with the Charter-House, the Schools of St. Paul's, Merchant Taylors, Harrow and Rugby and the Free School of Christ's Hospital. London: 1816. V. 68; 70; 72; 73
A History of the University of Cambridge. London: 1815. V. 70
The History of the University of Oxford. London: 1814. V. 72; 73
Microcosm of London. London: 1808-1810. V. 68; 72
Selection of Ornaments in Forty Pages for the Use of Sculptors, Painters, Carvers, Modellers, Parts I and II. London: 1840. V. 69

ACKERY, P. R.
Milkweed Butterflies, Their Cladistics and Biology. London: 1984. V. 70

ACKEY, MARY E.
Crossing the Plains and Early Days in California - Memories of Girlhood Days in California's Golden Age. San Francisco: 1928. V. 70

ACKROYD, PETER
Chatterton. 1987. V. 73
Chatterton. London: 1987. V. 68; 70
Dickens. London: 1990. V. 70
Dressing Up. London: 1979. V. 68
English Music. London: 1992. V. 68; 72; 73
English Music. New York: 1992. V. 68; 72
The Great Fire of London. London: 1982. V. 70
Hawksmoor. London: 1985. V. 68
Milton in America. London: 1996. V. 68
The Plato Papers. London: 1999. V. 68

ACOSTA, CRISTOVAL
Tractado de Las Drogas Medicinas de Las Indias Orientales.... Burgos: 1578. V. 72

ACRELIUS, ISRAEL
A History of New Sweden; or, The Settlements on the River Delaware. Philadelphia: 1876. V. 69

ACROSS *the Continent Via the Northern Pacific, from the Lakes and Mississippi River to the Pacific, Columbia River, Puget Sound, Alaska and the Klondike.* St. Paul. V. 73

ACTON, ELIZA
Modern Cookery for Private Families. London: 1863. V. 68; 71

ACTON, HAROLD
The Last Medici. London: 1958. V. 71
Nancy Mitford. London: 1975. V. 70
Old Lamps for New. London: 1965. V. 70
The Soul's Gymnasium. London: 1982. V. 70
Tit for Tat and Other Tales. London: 1972. V. 69; 71; 73

ADAIR, JAMES
The History of the American Indians. London: 1775. V. 71

ADAIR, JAMES MAKITTRICK
Curious Facts and Anecdotes, Not Contained in the Memoirs of Philip Thickness, Esq. Formerly Gunner of Landguard Fort, and Now Censor General of Great Britain.... London: 1790. V. 68; 73

ADAM, ALEXANDER
Roman Antiquities; or an Account of the Manners and Customs of the Romans. London: 1830. V. 71
A Summary of Geography and History, Both Ancient and Modern. London: 1824. V. 70

ADAM, MELCHIOR
Dignorum Laude Virorum, Quos Musa Vetatmori, Immortalitas, Vitae Theorlogorum, Jure-Consultorum, Politocirum, Medicorum Atque Phislosophorum Maximam Partem Germanorum.... Frankfurt: 1705. V. 68
Vitae Germanorum Medicorum; Qui Saeculo Superiori et Qui Excurrit Claruenrunt.... Heidelberg: 1620. V. 68; 73

ADAM, VICTOR
Alphabet et Chiffres Recreatifs. Paris: 1834. V. 72

ADAM, W.
The Gem of the Peak, or Matlock Bath and Its Vicinity. An Account of Derby. 1845. V. 72

ADAMIC, LOUIS
From Many Lands. New York: 1940. V. 68

ADAMS, A. LEITH
Field and Forest Rambles with Notes and Observations on the Natural History of Eastern Canada. 1873. V. 69; 70; 72; 73
Field and Forest Rambles with Notes and Observations on the Natural History of Eastern Canada. London: 1873. V. 73

ADAMS, ALICE
Rich Rewards. New York: 1980. V. 73
Second Chances. New York: 1988. V. 68
Superior Women. New York: 1984. V. 71

ADAMS, ANDY
The Log of a Cowboy. Boston: 1903. V. 71
The Log of a Cowboy. Boston: 1927. V. 69
A Texas Matchmaker. Boston: 1904. V. 69
Why the Chisholm Rail Forks. Austin: 1956. V. 69

ADAMS, ANSEL
The American Wilderness. Boston/Toronto: 1990. V. 68; 70
Images. 1923-1974. Boston: 1974. V. 73
Camera and Lens. New York: 1948. V. 68
The Eloquent Light. New York: 1980. V. 68
The Four Seasons in Yosemite National Park: A Photographic Story.... Los Angeles: 1938. V. 68
Illustrated Guide to Yosemite: the Valley, the Rim and the Central Yosemite Sierra and Mountain Photography. San Francisco: 1963. V. 68; 70
Images 1923-1974. Greenwich: 1974. V. 68; 70
Images 1923-1974. Boston/Toronto: 1981. V. 68; 70
An Introduction to Hawaii. San Francisco: 1964. V. 68
My Autobiography. Boston: 1985. V. 68
My Camera in Yosemite Valley. Yosemite: 1949. V. 68
The Negative. New York: 1948. V. 68
Photographs of the Southwest. Boston/Toronto: 1976. V. 68; 69; 72
The Portfolios. 1977. V. 68
The Print. New York: 1950. V. 68
Sierra Nevada: The John Muir Trail. Berkeley: 1938. V. 68; 70
Singular Images. Dobbs Ferry: 1974. V. 72
Taos Pueblo. Boston: 1974. V. 72
Taos Pueblo. Boston: 1977. V. 68
These We Inherit: The Parklands of America. San Francisco: 1962. V. 68
Yellowstone and the Range of Light. Boston: 1979. V. 70
Yosemite and the Range of Light. Boston/Toronto: 1979. V. 68; 69; 72
Yosemite and the Sierra Nevada. Boston: 1948. V. 68

ADAMS, ARCHIBALD
The Western Rajputana States. London: 1899. V. 72

ADAMS, ARTHUR
A Genealogy of the Lake Family of Great Egg Harbor, in Old Gloucester County in New Jersey, Descended from John Lake of Gravesend, Long Island. 1915. V. 69

ADAMS, B. Q.
R. C. Gorman, the Graphic Works. Albuquerque: 1987. V. 69

ADAMS, BERNARD
London Illustrated 1604-1851, a Survey and Index of Topographical Books and Their Plates. London: 1983. V. 69

ADAMS, C.
Fritz Scholder: Lithographs. Boston: 1975. V. 69

ADAMS, C. C.
The Variations and Ecological Distribution of the Snails of the Genus Io. Washington: 1915. V. 70

ADAMS, C. E.
Mammalian Egg Transfer. Boca Raton: 1982. V. 70

ADAMS, CHARLES
Nightcrawlers. London: 1957. V. 68

ADAMS, CHARLES FRANCIS
Memoirs of John Quincy Adams: Comprising Portions of His Diary from 1795 to 1848. Philadelphia: 1874-1877. V. 71
Railroads: Their Origin and Problems. New York: 1878. V. 70
Three Episodes of Massachusetts History: the Settlement of Boston Bay.... Boston: 1892-1893. V. 68

ADAMS, CLEVE
The Evil Star. New York: 1944. V. 70
The Private Eye. 1942. V. 73

ADAMS, DOUGLAS
Dirk Gently's Holistic Detective Agency. London: 1987. V. 68
Dirk Gently's Holistic Detective Agency. New York: 1987. V. 68
The Hitch Hiker's Guide to the Galaxy. London: 1979. V. 68
The Hitch Hiker's Guide to the Galaxy. London: 1980. V. 70; 73
The Illustrated Hitch Hiker's Guide to the Galaxy. London: 1994. V. 72; 73
Last Chance to See. London: 1990. V. 68; 71; 73
Last Chance to See. New York: 1991. V. 73
Life, The Universe and Everything. London: 1982. V. 68
The Long Dark Tea-Time of The Soul. London: 1988. V. 68; 73
Mostly Harmless. London: 1992. V. 72; 73
The Restaurant At the End of the Universe. London: 1980. V. 68
So Long, and Thanks for All the Fish. London: 1984. V. 68

ADAMS, E. B.
The Missions of New Mexico. Albuquerque: 1956. V. 69

ADAMS, EDWARD
Potee's Gal. Columbia: 1929. V. 71; 73

ADAMS, ELEANOR B.
The Missions of New Mexico 1776. Albuquerque: 1953. V. 70
The Missions of New Mexico 1776. Albuquerque: 1956. V. 72
The Missions of New Mexico 1776. Albuquerque: 1975. V. 70

ADAMS, ELIZABETH LAURA
Dark Symphony. New York: 1942. V. 72

ADAMS, F.
Eyes for the Blind; or an Insight Into the Character and Principles of James Acland. Hull: 1832. V. 69

ADAMS, F. C.
Manuel Pereira; or, the Sovereign Rule of South Carolina. Washington: 1853. V. 68; 73

ADAMS, F. COLBURN
Story Of A Trooper. New York: 1865. V. 72

ADAMS, FRANCIS
John Webb's End. Australian Bush Life. London: 1891. V. 68

ADAMS, FRANK
Pat-a-Cake and Many Other Rhymes for the Nursery. London: 1914. V. 71

ADAMS, FRANK DAWSON
The Birth and Development of the Geological Sciences. Baltimore: 1938. V. 69
The Birth and Development of the Geological Sciences. New York: 1954. V. 68

ADAMS, FREDERICK B.
Radical Literature in America, to Which is Appended a Catalogue of an Exhibition Held at the Grolier Club in New York City. Stamford: 1939. V. 70; 72

ADAMS, FREDERICK UPHAM
The Bottom of the Well. New York: 1906. V. 72

ADAMS, G. M.
The Post Near Cheyenne: A History of Fort D. A. Russell 1867-1930. Boulder: 1989. V. 72

ADAMS, GEORGE
Essays on the Microscope: Containing a Practical Description of the Most Improved Micrscopes.... London: 1798. V. 72

ADAMS, GEORGE WORTHINGTON
Doctors in Blue; the Medical History of the Union Army in the Civil War. Dayton: 1985. V. 70

ADAMS, H. G.
Beautiful Shells; Their Nature, Structure and Uses Familiarly Explained.... London: 1855. V. 68
Cyclopaedia of Female Biography.... Glasgow: 1866. V. 73
The Dictionary and Poetry of Flowers. London. V. 70
Nests and Eggs of Familiar British Birds, Described and Illustrated.... 1854. V. 70

ADAMS, H. M.
Catalogue of Books Printed on the Continent of Europe 1501-1600 in Cambridge Libraries. Cambridge: 1967. V. 68
Catalogue of Books Printed on the Continent of Europe, 1501-1600 in Cambridge Libraries. 1967-1999. V. 69

ADAMS, HANNAH
An Abridgement of the History of New England for the Use of Young Persons.... Boston: 1805. V. 73
An Alphabetical Compendium of the Various Sects Which Have Appeared in the World from the Beginning of the Christian Era to the Present Day. Boston: 1784. V. 68; 71
A View of Religions, in Two Parts. Boston: 1801. V. 69; 73

ADAMS, HAROLD
Murder. New York: 1981. V. 72

ADAMS, HENRY
Democracy. New York: 1880. V. 68; 73
Democracy. London: 1882. V. 71
The Education of Henry Adams. Washington: 1907. V. 72
A Letter to American Teachers of History. Washington: 1910. V. 68
Memoirs of Arii Taimai E Marama of Eimeo, Teriirere of Tooarai. Paris: 1901. V. 73

ADAMS, HERBERT
The Araway Oath. London: 1942. V. 72
By Order of the Five. London: 1925. V. 73
The Golf House Murder. Philadelphia: 1933. V. 69; 72; 73
The Sloane Square Mystery. London: 1925. V. 73
The Strange Murder of Hatton K.C. Philadelphia: 1933. V. 73
Welcome Home. London: 1946. V. 69; 73

ADAMS, J.
Ten Thousand Miles through Canada. 1913. V. 68

ADAMS, JAMES
Dartmoor Prison; or a Faithful Narrative of the Massacre of American Seamen. Pittsbrugh: 1816. V. 68

ADAMS, JAMES TRUSLOW
Dictionary of American History. New York: 1942. V. 71

ADAMS, JANE
Bird. London: 1997. V. 68
Cast the First Stone. London: 1996. V. 68
The Greenway. London: 1995. V. 68; 69; 71

ADAMS, JASPER
The Moral Causes of the Welfare of Nations. Charleston;: 1834. V. 73

ADAMS, JOHN
A Defence of the Constitutions...of the United States of America.... London: 1794. V. 71
The English Parnassus; Being a New Selection.... London: 1789. V. 69
The Flowers of Modern History.... London: 1788. V. 70
Sketches of the History, Genius, Disposition, Accomplishments, Employments, Customs, Virtues and Vices of the Fair Sex.... Gettysburg: 1812. V. 68; 69
Woman. Sketches of the History, Genius, Disposition, Accomplishments, Employments, Customs and Importance of the Fair Sex.... London: 1790. V. 68

ADAMS, JOHN QUINCY
A Letter to the Hon. Harrison Gray Otis, a Member of the Senate of Massachusetts, on the Present State of Our National Affairs.... Albany: 1808. V. 70
Oration on the Life and Character of...Lafayette.... Washington: 1835. V. 71

ADAMS, JOSEPH
The Angler's Guide to the Irish Fisheries. 1930. V. 69; 73
Observations on Morbid Poisons, Chronic and Acute. London: 1807. V. 72

ADAMS, JULIUS
The Challenge: A Study In Negro Leadership. New York: 1949. V. 72

ADAMS, KATHLEEN
A Book of Enchantment. New York: 1928. V. 70

ADAMS, L. E.
The Collector's Manual of British Land and Freshwater Shells. 1896. V. 72

ADAMS, OSCAR FAY
The Story of Jane Austen's Life. Boston: 1896?. V. 70; 73

ADAMS, RAMON F.
Burs Under the Saddle. A Second Look at Books and Histories of the West. Norman: 1964. V. 68; 70; 71
Charles M. Russell, the Cowboy Artist: a Biography. Pasadena: 1948. V. 68; 69; 71; 73
Come an' Get It: the Story of the Old Cowboy Cook. Norman: 1952. V. 69; 71
Cowboy Lingo. Boston: 1936. V. 69; 71
The Cowman Says It Salty. 1971. V. 68
The Cowman Says It Salty. Tucson: 1971. V. 69
A Fitting Death for Billy the Kid. Norman: 1960. V. 69; 71; 73
More Burs Under the Saddle Books and Histories of the West. Norman: 1979. V. 68
The Old Time Cowhand. New York: 1961. V. 68; 69; 73
The Rampaging Herd. 1959. V. 68
The Rampaging Herd. Norman: 1959. V. 70; 71
Six Guns and Saddle Leather. Norman: 1954. V. 69; 70; 71; 72; 73
Six Guns and Saddle Leather. Norman: 1969. V. 68; 73
Western Words-A Dictionary of the Ranch Cow Camp and Trail. Norman: 1944. V. 71

ADAMS, RANDOLPH G.
The Passports Printed by Benjamin Franklin at His Passy Press,. Ann Arbor: 1925. V. 71

ADAMS, RICHARD
The Girl in the Swing. New York: 1980. V. 72
The Iron Wolf and Other Stories. London: 1980. V. 70
Watership Down. London: 1972. V. 69
Watership Down. London/Australasia: 1974. V. 69
Watership Down. New York: 1974. V. 71
Watership Down. Harmondsworth: 1976. V. 70

ADAMS-ROGERS CO.
Bilt Well Mill Work. Indianapolis. V. 72

ADAMS, SAMPSON & CO.
The Salem Directory, Containing the City Record, the Names of the Citizens, and a Business Directory, with an Almanac for 1864. Salem: 1864. V. 73

ADAMS, SAMUEL
The Writings of Samuel Adams. New York: 1904. V. 73

ADAMS, SAMUEL HOPKINS
Our Square and the People In It. Boston: 1917. V. 71
Revelry. New York: 1926. V. 69; 71

ADAMS, TATE
The Soul Cages. Dublin: 1958. V. 72

ADAMS, THOMAS F.
Typographia; or the Printer's Instructor; a Brief Sketch of the Origin, Rise and Progress of the Typographic Art. Philadelphia: 1845. V. 68

ADAMS, W.
The King's Messengers. An Allegorical Tale. London: 1848. V. 73
Sacred Allegories. London: 1859. V. 71

ADAMS, WILLIAM
A Letter to the...Directors of Greenwich Hospital, Containing an Exposure of the Measure Resorted to, by the Medical Officers of the London Eye Infirmary.... 1817. V. 73
Club-Foot: Its Causes, Pathology, and Treatment. London: 1866. V. 70
On Contractions of the Fingers (Dupuyten's and Congenital Contractions) and on Hammer-Toe.... London: 1892. V. 70

ADAMS, WILLIAM EDGAR
The Comparative Morphology of the Carotid Body and Carotid Sinus. Springfield: 1958. V. 68

ADAMS, WILLIAM HENRY DAVENPORT
The Arctic World: Its Plants, Animals and Natural Phenomena. London: 1876. V. 73
The Bird World Described With Pen and Pencil. London: 1878. V. 68
The Forest, the Jungle and the Prairie. 1885. V. 69; 72
The Monsters of the Deep; and Curiosities of Ocean Life. London: 1875. V. 68
The Forest, the Jungle and the Prairie. 1889. V. 69; 70; 72
Nelsons' Hand-Book to the Isle of Wight: Its History, Topography and Antiquities. 1866. V. 70

ADAMS, WILLIAM TAYLOR
Our Standard-Bearer; or the Life of General Ulysses S. Grant.... Boston: 1868. V. 73

ADAMSON, A. P.
Brief History of the Thirtieth Georgia Regiment. Griffin: 1912. V. 70

ADAMSON, GEORGE
Bwana Game. The Life Story of George Adamson. 1968. V. 70; 72

ADAMSON, JOY
The Peoples of Kenya. 1975. V. 69; 70; 72

ADAMSON, R. S.
Flora of the Cape Peninsula. Cape Town and Johannesburg: 1950. V. 68

ADAMSON, STANLEY L.
Old Nursery Rhymes Dug Up at the Pyramids. London: 1890. V. 73

ADANSON, M.
Histoire Naturelle du Senegal, Coquillages.... Paris: 1757. V. 69

ADCOCK, THOMAS
Sea of Green. New York: 1989. V. 69

ADDAMS, CHARLES
My Crowd. New York: 1970. V. 71

ADDAMS, JANE
The Spirit of Youth and the City Streets. New York: 1926. V. 71
Twenty Years at Hull House with Autobiographical Notes. New York: 1910. V. 69

ADDERLEY, WILFRED T.
Three Of A Kind: Are We Constitutional Christians?. New York: 1987. V. 72

ADDEY, MARKINFIELD
The Life and Military Career of Thomas Jonathan Jackson, Lieutenant General in the Confederate Army. New York: 1863. V. 73

ADDINGTON, HENRY
Some Account of the Abbey Church of St. Peter and St. Paul, at Dorchester, Oxfordshire. Oxford: 1845. V. 72

ADDINGTON, ROBERT M.
History of Scott County, Virginia. Kingsport: 1932. V. 73

ADDINGTON, STEPHEN
A Syllabus of the History of England, to Which is Appended a Tour through the Southern Parts of Great Britain.... Philadelphia: 1806. V. 68

ADDISON, JOSEPH
Cato, a Tragedy. Florence: 1725. V. 70
A Dissertation Upon the Most Celebrated Roman Poets. London: 1718. V. 72
The Evidences of the Christian Religion, to Which are added, Several Discourses Against Atheism and Infidelity.... London: 1742. V. 73
King Trickee; or, Harlequin the Demon Beetle, the Sporting Duchess, and the Golden Casket. London: 1887. V. 70
The Life of Joseph Addison. London: 1843. V. 72
The Miscellaneous Works of Joseph Addison. London: 1830. V. 68; 70
The Old Whig Number I. On the State of the Peerage. With Remarks Upon the Plebian. (Together with: Number II). London: 1719. V. 72
Poems on Several Occasions. Glasgow: 1770. V. 73
Remarks on Several Parts of Italy, &c in the Years 1701, 1702, 1703. London: 1718. V. 70; 72
Remarks on Several Parts of Italy, &c in the Years 1701, 1702, 1703. London: 1745. V. 69; 70
The Works. London: 1811. V. 73
The Works. London: 1900-1903. V. 73

ADDISON, LANCELOT
West Barbary, or, a Short Narrative of the Revolutions of the Kingdoms of Fez and Morocco, with an Account of the Present Customs, Sacred, Civil and Domestick. Oxford: 1671. V. 68; 73

ADDISON, OTTELYN
Tom Thomson. The Algonquin Years. Toronto: 1969. V. 73

ADDISON, THOMAS
A Collection of The Published Writings of the Late Thomas Addison, M. D., Physician to Guy's Hospital. London: 1868. V. 72

ADDISON, WILLIAM
English Fairs and Markets. London: 1953. V. 72

ADDRESS des Dames de La Halle a L'Assemblee Nationale. Paris: 1791. V. 73

THE ADDRESS of the People of South Carolina, Assembled in Convention to the People of the Slaveholding States of the United States. Charleston;: 1860. V. 69

AN ADDRESS to the Electors of England. London: 1756. V. 70

AN ADDRESS To the Electors of the State of New York. New York: 1801. V. 73

AN ADDRESS to the People of the United States, On the Policy of Mantaining a Permanent Navy. Philadelphia: 1802. V. 69

AN ADDRESS to the People of the United States, Adopted at a Conference of Colored Citizens, Held at Columbia, S.C., July 20-21, 1876. Columbia: 1876. V. 68; 71

ADDY, SIDNEY OLDALL
Historical Memorials of Beauchief Abbey. Oxford and London: 1878. V. 73

ADE, GEORGE
Sho-Gun: an Original Comic Opera in Two Acts. New York: 1904. V. 69

ADELBORG, QTTILIA
Clean Peter and the Children of Grubbylea. London: 1901. V. 70
Clean Peter and the Children of Grubbylea. London: 1910. V. 71

ADELMAN, BILL
Well Involved. 1986. V. 69

ADELMAN, SEYMOUR
The Moving Pageant. A Selection of Essays. Litiz: 1977. V. 68

ADELMAN, WILLIAM J.
Bio-Physics and Physiology of Excitable Membranes. New York: 1971. V. 68

ADELMANN, HOWARD B.
Marcello Malpighi and the Evolution of Embryology. Ithaca: 1966. V. 69; 72

ADEMA, MARCEL
Apollinaire. London: 1954. V. 69

ADENEY, NOEL
No Coward Soul. London: 1956. V. 70

ADLARD, ELEANOR
Edy - Recollections of Edith Craig. London: 1949. V. 72

ADLER, ALFRED
Menschenkenntnis. (Understanding Human Nautre). Leipzig: 1927. V. 72

ADLER, JEREMY
To Cytherea!: Four Poems. 1993. V. 71

ADLER, STAN
Sagebrush Strokes, Yarns of the Southwestern Range. Bisbee: 1938. V. 69

ADLINGTON, JOHN H.
The Cyclopaedia of Law; or the Correct British Lawyer. London: 1820. V. 70

ADOLPHUS, J. H.
Voyages and Travels of Her Majesty, Caroline Queen of Great Britain.... London: 1822. V. 69

ADOLPHUS, JOHN
The Political State of the British Empire.... London: 1818. V. 70

ADORNO, ROLENA
Alvar Nunez Cabeza de Vaca: His Account, His Life and the Expedition of Panfilo de Narvaez. Lincoln: 1999. V. 71

THE ADVENTURER. London: 1754. V. 69; 73
THE ADVENTURER. London: 1770. V. 69
THE ADVENTURER. London: 1778. V. 68
THE ADVENTURER. Dublin: 1788. V. 70
THE ADVENTURER. London: 1808. V. 73

THE ADVENTURES of a Brownie. Chicago: 1908. V. 70

THE ADVENTURES of a Little Sailor Boy. London: 1860. V. 72

THE ADVENTURES OF Doctor Comicus or the Frolicks of Fortune. London: 1815. V. 73

ADVENTURES of the Beautiful Little Maid Cinderella. York: 1820. V. 73
ADVENTURES of the Beautiful Little Maid Cinderella. 1825. V. 73

ADVICE to Writers. New York: 1999. V. 72

ADYE, RALPH
The Little Bombardier and Pocket Gunner. 1801. V. 73

ADYE, STEPHEN PAYNE
A Treatise on Courts Martial. To Which is Added an Essay on Military Punishments and Rewards. London: 1786. V. 72

AELIANUS, CLAUSIUS
De Historia Animalium, Libri XVII. Lugdini: 1565. V. 70

AERONAUTICS. An Authoritative Work Dealing with the Theory and Practice of Flying. Dunellen: 1940-1941. V. 68

AESCHYLUS
The Agamemnon. London: 1877. V. 73
Fragments. Alabama: 1992. V. 73
The Oresteia. Agamemnon; The Libation-Bearers; The Furies. New York: 1961. V. 71
The Oresteia of Aeschylus. New York: 1978. V. 72; 73
The Tragedies. Norwich: 1777. V. 68; 73
The Tragedies. Oxford: 1808. V. 71

AESOPUS
Bewick's Select Fables of Aesop and Others. London: 1886. V. 69
The Bowers Movie Book: Book II: Aesop's Fables. New York: 1923. V. 69

AESOPUS continued
Aesop's Fables. London: 1813. V. 71
Aesop's Fables. London: 1848. V. 68; 71
Aesop's Fables. London: 1852. V. 72
Aesop's Fables. London: 1895. V. 72
Aesop's Fables. New York: 1911. V. 72
Aesop's Fables. London: 1912. V. 70
Aesop's Fables. New York: 1933. V. 70
Aesop's Fables. Oxford: 1933. V. 68; 69
Aesop's Fables. Garden City: 1954. V. 69
Aesop's Fables Illustrated. Edinburgh: 1830-1840. V. 69
Fables. London: 1936. V. 71
Fables. London: 1961. V. 71
Fables D'...Mises en Francais.... Lille: 1810. V. 68
Fables from Aesop and Others. 1944. V. 70
The Fables of Aesop. London: 1793. V. 68
The Fables of Aesop. London: 1894. V. 69
The Fables of Aesop. London: 1909. V. 71
The Fables of Aesop. Waltham St. Lawrence: 1926. V. 71
The Fables of Aesop and Other Eminent Mytholgists with Morals and Reflections. London: 1692. V. 72
Fables of Aesop and Other Eminent Mythologists; with Morals and Reflexions. London: 1708. V. 73
Fables of Aesop and Others. Wilmington: 1802. V. 68
The Fables of Aesop, and Others. Newcastle-upon-Tyne: 1818. V. 69
The Fables of Aesop, and Others with Designs on Wood. Newcastle: 1823. V. 71
Fables translated from Aesop, and Other Authors. London: 1760. V. 73
Fabulae Aesopi Graece & Latine (and other Works). Amsterodami: 1653. V. 69
Fabulae.... Leyden: 1632. V. 73
Fabularum Aesopiarum Libri Quinque. Amsterdam: 1667. V. 71
Select Fables of Esop and Other Fabulists. Birmingham: 1764. V. 73
A Selection of Aesop's Fables.... 1953. V. 69
Twelve Fables of Aesop. New York: 1954. V. 69

AFFAIRS In England. A Free Conference Concerning the Present Resolution of Affairs in England. London: 1689. V. 71

AN AFFECTING History of the Captivity and Sufferings of Mrs. Mary Velnet, an Italian Lady. Boston: 1804?. V. 69

THE AFFECTING Story of Jenny Wren. London: 1865. V. 69

AFLALO, FREDERICK GEORGE
British Salt Water Fishes. London: 1904. V. 69; 72; 73
The Encyclopaedia of Sport. London: 1897. V. 69
The Sportsman's Book for India. 1904. V. 69; 70; 72; 73

AFRICA and Its Explorers. London. V. 72

AFRICAN INSTITUTION, LONDON
Special Report of the Directors of the African Institution, Made at the Annual General Meeting, on the 12th of April, 1815, Respecting the Allegations Contained in a Pamphlet Entitled A Letter to William Wilberforce, Esq. by R. Thorpe Esq. &c. London: 1815. V. 72

THE AFRICAN'S Rights to Citizenship. Philadelphia: 1865. V. 69

THE AFTERNOON Lectures on English Literature. Delivered in the Theatre of the Museum of Industry, S. Stephen's Green, Dublin in May and June, 1863. London: 1863. V. 68

AFTERNOON Tea. New York: 1886. V. 72
AFTERNOON Tea. Boston: 1891. V. 73

AFTON, JEAN
Cheyenne Dog Soldiers - A Ledger Book History of Coups and Combat. Niwot: 1997. V. 72

AGAR, W. E.
Cytology with Special Reference to the Metazoan Nucleus. London: 1920. V. 68

AGARD, WALTER R.
Medical Greek and Latin at a Glance. New York: 1956. V. 68

AGASSIZ, ALEXANDER
Challenger Voyage. Zoology. Part 9. Echinoidea. 1881. V. 73
The Coral Reefs of the Tropical Pacific. Cambridge: 1903. V. 69; 73
Letters and Recollections. Boston: 1913. V. 72
Letters and Recollections. London: 1913. V. 69
Three Cruises on the United States Coast and Geodetic Survey Steamer Blake in the Gulf of Mexico, in the Caribbean Sea, and Along the Atlantic Coast of the United States of America, from 1877 to 1880. Boston: 1888. V. 71

AGASSIZ, ELIZABETH CARY
Louis Agassiz. His Life and Correspondence. London: 1885. V. 68
Louis Agassiz, His Life and Correspondence. Boston: 1886. V. 70; 72

AGASSIZ, LOUIS
A Journey in Brazil. Boston: 1868. V. 68
A Journey in Brazil. Boston: 1879. V. 70; 72
Lake Superior: Its Physical, Character, Vegetation and Animals, Compared With Those of Other and Similar Regions. Boston: 1850. V. 70
Methods of Study in Natural History. Boston: 1863. V. 68

AGATE, JAMES
The Common Touch. London: 1926. V. 70
The Contemporary Theatre 1923. London: 1924. V. 73
On an English Screen. London: 1924. V. 70

AGEE, G. W.
Rube Burrow, King of Outlaws and His Band of Train Robbers. Chicago. V. 68; 73

AGEE, JAMES
Agee on Film. Volume Two (2): Five Film Scripts by James Agee. New York: 1958. V. 69
A Death in the Family. New York: 1957. V. 69; 71; 73
Four Early Stories. West Branch: 1964. V. 72; 73
Let Us Now Praise Famous Men. Boston: 1960. V. 69; 73
Letters of James Agee to Father Flye. New York: 1962. V. 72
The Morning Watch. Rome: 1950. V. 69; 72

AGIUS DE SOLDANIS, GIOVANNI PIETRO FRANCESCO
Della Lingua Punica Presentemente Usata da Maltesi &c.... Rome: 1750. V. 68

AGNES Arlington: Life, Times, Troubles, Tribulations and Sad End of Agnes Arlington.... Baltimore/Philadelphia/NY: 1854. V. 69

AGNES, SISTER
The Story of Kendal. Kendal: 1947. V. 71
The Story of Skelsmergh. Kendal: 1949. V. 71

AGNEW, ANNA
From Under the Cloud; or Personal Reminiscences of Insanity. Cincinnati: 1887. V. 68

AGNEW, C. MORLAND
Catalogue of the Pictures Forming the Collection of Sir Charles Tennant, Bart. of 40 Grosvenor Square and the Glen Innerleithen. London: 1896. V. 69; 72

AGNEW, GEORGETTE
Elaine's Party. London: 1910. V. 69
Elaine's Party. London: 1920. V. 73

AGRICOLA, GEORGIUS
De Ortu & Causis Subterraneorum Lib. V. De Natura Eorum Quae Effluunt ex Terra Lib. IIII. Basel: 1546. V. 68
De Re Metallica. 1912. V. 69
De Re Metallica. London: 1912. V. 68
De Re Metallica. Berlin: 1928. V. 69

AGRIPPA VON NETTERSHEIM, HENRICH CORNELIUS
De Incertitudine & Vanitate Scientiarum Declamatio Invectiva.... Cologne: 1537. V. 73
Female Pre-Eminence; or the Dignity and Excellence of that Sex. London: 1670. V. 73

AGUET, ISABELLE
A Pictorial History Of The Slave Trade. Geneva: 1971. V. 72

AGUILERA, CAROLINA GARCIA
Bloody Waters. New York: 1996. V. 70

AGUTTER, WILLIAM
Christian Politics; or, the Origin of Power, and the Grounds of Subordination. London: 1792. V. 68

AHEARN, ALLEN
Collected Books: the Guide to Values 2002 Edition. New York: 2001. V. 70

AHERN, G. P.
Compilation of Notes on the Most Important Timber Tree Species of the Philippine Islands. Manila: 1901. V. 72

AHLBERG, JANET
Jeremiah in the Dark Woods. 1977. V. 69
The Jolly Christmas Postman. London: 1991. V. 71; 73
The Jolly Pocket Postman. London: 1995. V. 72
Playmates. 1984. V. 71

AI
Killing Floor. Boston: 1979. V. 71
Sin. Boston: 1986. V. 71
Vice. New York: 1999. V. 69

AICKMAN, ROBERT
Cold Hand in Mine. London: 1975. V. 72
Cold Hand in Mine. London: 1976. V. 69
Dark Entries. London: 1964. V. 73
Night Voices - Strange Stories. London: 1985. V. 72
Powers of Darkness. London: 1966. V. 69
Sub Rosa. Strange Tales. London: 1968. V. 73
We Are for the Death - Six Ghost Stories. London: 1951. V. 69

AIDE, CHARLES HAMILTON
Carr of Carrlyon. London: 1882. V. 68

AIDOO, AMA
No Sweetness Here and Other Stories. Garden City: 1971. V. 72

AIKEN, CONRAD
Among the Lost People. New York: 1934. V. 71
Blue Voyage. New York: 1927. V. 68; 71
The Charnel Rose Senlin: a Biography and Other Poems. Boston: 1918. V. 69
The Clerk's Journal, Being the Diary of a Queer Man: an Undergraduate Poem Together with a Brief Memoir. New York: 1971. V. 68
Collected Poems. New York: 1953. V. 69
Collected Poems. New York: 1970. V. 69
The Conversation or Pilgrim's Regress: A Domestic Symphony. London: 1940. V. 72
Costumes by Eros. New York: 1928. V. 71
The Divine Pilgrim. Athens: 1949. V. 71

AIKEN, CONRAD continued
Earth Triumphant. New York: 1914. V. 69
Great Circle. New York: 1933. V. 71
The Jig of Forslin. 1916. V. 70
The Jig of Forslin. Boston: 1916. V. 71
King Coffin. London: 1935. V. 71
King Coffin. New York: 1935. V. 71
Landscape West of Eden: a Poem. London: 1934. V. 68
A Letter from Li Po and Other Poems. New York: 1955. V. 71
Nocturne of Remembered Spring and Other Poems. Boston: 1917. V. 70; 71
The Pilgrimage of Festus. New York: 1923. V. 71
Preludes. Paris: 1957. V. 71
Punch. New York: 1921. V. 71
A Seizure of Limericks. New York: 1964. V. 69
Selected Poems. New York: 1929. V. 68; 70
Senlin: a Biography: a Poem. London: 1925. V. 68; 72
The Soldier. Norfolk: 1944. V. 71
Thee. 1973. V. 68
Thee. London: 1973. V. 71
Time in the Rock: Preludes to Definition. New York: 1936. V. 68
Ushant: an Essay. New York and Boston: 1952. V. 69
Ushant: an Essay. New York: 1971. V. 68

AIKIN, EDMUND
Plans, Elevation, Section and View of the Cathedral Church of St. Paul, London. London: 1813. V. 71

AIKIN, EMMA E.
Gifts. Oklahoma City: 1938. V. 73

AIKIN, JOHN
Biographical Memoirs of Medicine in Great Britian from the Revival of Literature to the Time of Harvey. London: 1780. V. 73
The Calendar of Nature.... 1787. V. 71
An Essay on the Application of Natural History to Poetry. Warrington: 1777. V. 68; 73
Essays on Song Writing.... London: 1772?. V. 69
Essays on Song Writing.... Warrington: 1774. V. 69
Letters to a Young Lady on a Course of English Poetry. London: 1807. V. 69; 70; 73
The Woodland Companion; or a Brief Description of British Trees. 1802. V. 71
The Woodland Companion; or a Description of British Trees. London: 1820. V. 70

AIKIN, LUCY
The Life of Joseph Addison. London: 1843. V. 71
Memoir of John Aikin, M.D. London: 1823. V. 69
Memoirs of the Court of King James the First. (with) Memoirs of the Court of King Charles the First. London: 1833. V. 71
Memoirs of the Court of Queen Elizabeth. London: 1818. V. 70

AIKMAN, JAMES
Natural History of Beasts, Birds and Fishes.... London: 1850. V. 68

AINSLIE, KATHLEEN
Catharine Susan and Me Goes Abroad. 1905. V. 68
Catharine Susan's Calendar for 1910. London: 1909. V. 70
Lady Tabitha and Us. London: 1903. V. 70
Me and Catharine Susan. London: 1903. V. 73
Me and Catherine Susan Earns an Honest Penny. 1907. V. 71
Mops Versus Tails. London: 1910. V. 70
Oh! Poor Amelia Jane!. 1910. V. 71
Sammy Goes A'Hunting. London: 1907. V. 69
What I Did. London: 1905. V. 72

AINSLIE, R. ST. JOHN
Sedbergh School Songs. Leeds: 1896. V. 70; 71; 73

AINSLIE, ROBERT
The Snares of the Metropolis. London: 1838. V. 71
Views in Palestine. (with) Views in the Ottoman Empire, Chiefly in Caramania, a Part of Asia Minor.... London: 1803-1804. V. 72

AINSWORTH, ED
The Cowboy in Art. New York: 1968. V. 70
Golden Checkerboard. Palm Desert: 1965. V. 68

AINSWORTH, G. C.
The Fungi, an Advanced Treatise. New York: 1965-1973. V. 68

AINSWORTH, KATHERINE
The McCallum Saga: the Story of the Founding of Palm Springs. Palm Springs: 1973. V. 68

AINSWORTH, LES
Lancashire: a Guide to Rock Climbs. London: 1969. V. 69

AINSWORTH, WILLIAM HARRISON
Beatrice Tyldesley. London: 1878. V. 73
Beau Nash, or Bath in the Eighteenth Century. London: 1881. V. 68
Cardinal Pole; or the Days of Philip and Mary. London: 1894. V. 68
The Flitch of Bacon; or the Custom of Dunmow. London: 1854. V. 73
The Lancashire Witches.... London: 1849. V. 71
Merry England; or Nobles and Serfs. London: 1874. V. 73
Old Saint Paul's: a Tale of the Plague and the Fire. London: 1841. V. 68; 70
Old Saint Paul's: a Tale of the Plague and the Fire. London: 1847. V. 73
Ovingdean Grange. London: 1860. V. 73
Rookwood: a Romance. London: 1834. V. 73
Rookwood: A Romance. London: 1851. V. 71
The Tower of London. A Historical Romance. London: 1840. V. 71
Views of the Devil's Dyke. Brighton: 1884. V. 73
Windsor Castle. An Historical Romance. London: 1843. V. 68

AINSWORTH'S Magazine: A Miscellany of Romance, General Literature, & Art. London: 1842. V. 71

AIRTH, RENNIE
Once a Spy. London: 1981. V. 73
River of Darkness. London: 1999. V. 68; 70; 71; 72; 73
River of Darkness. New York: 1999. V. 69
Snatch!. London: 1969. V. 68; 69; 70; 71; 73

AITCHEN, ROBERT
The Black Patch Pirates. London. V. 70

AITCHISON, J. E. T.
The Botany of the Afghan Delimitation Commission. 1887. V. 69

AITKEN, GEORGE A.
The Life and Works of John Arbuthnot, M.D. Oxford: 1892. V. 70; 71
The Life of Richard Steele. London: 1889. V. 69; 72

AITKEN, MICKEY
The Saga of Salubria. Weiser: 1951. V. 72

AITKEN, THOMAS
Tables, Exhibiting Superficial Measure in Yards, Feet and Inches.... London: 1838. V. 71

AITKEN, WILLIAM B.
Distinguished Families in America Descended from Wilhelmus Beekman and Jan Thomasse Van Dyke. New York: 1912. V. 69

AKENSIDE, MARK
The Pleasures of Imagination. London: 1744. V. 68; 70
The Poetical Works. With Memoir and Critical Dissertation, By The Rev. George Gilfillan. Edinburgh: 1857. V. 71; 72

AKENSON, DONALD H.
The Irish Education Experiment: the National System of Education in the 19th Century. 1973. V. 69

AKERMAN, JOHN YONGE
An Archaeological Index to Remains of Antiquity of the Celtic, Romano British and Anglo Saxon Periods. London: 1847. V. 72
Moneys Received and Paid for Secret Services of Charles II and James II. 1851. V. 69
Spring Tide; or the Angler and His Friends. 1850. V. 68; 73

AKIN, JAMES
Journal of James Akin. Norman: 1919. V. 69

AKINS, THOMAS BEAMISH
Selections from the Public Documents of the Province of Nova Scotia. Halifax: 1869. V. 69; 72
A Sketch of the Rise and Progress of the Church of England in the British North American Provinces. Halifax;: 1849. V. 73

AKIYAMA, AISABURO
Geisha Girl. Tokyo: 1933. V. 72

AKROYD, CHARLES H.
A Veteran Sportsman's Diary. Iverness: 1926. V. 73

AKURGAL, K.
The Art of the Hittites. New York: 1962. V. 69; 72

ALADDIN and the Wonderful Lamp. Chicago: 1908. V. 70
ALADDIN and the Wonderful Lamp. New York: 1935. V. 70; 73

ALADDIN COMPANY, BAY CITY, MICHIGAN
Aladdin Homes. Catalog No. 29. 1917. V. 69

ALADZAJKOV, L.
Collection and Study of Vegetables and Small Fruits from throughout Macedonia. Akopje: 1974. V. 68

ALAJALOV, CONSTANTIN
Conversation Pieces. New York: 1942. V. 71

ALASKA CONSOLIDATED MINING AND SMELTING CO.
History of Copper Mountain Mines at Coppermount, Prince of Wales Island, Alaska, U.S.A. Duluth: 1912. V. 69

ALBAUGH, WILLIAM A.
The Original Confederate Colt - the Story of the Leech and Rigdon and Rigdon-Ansley Revolvers. New York: 1953. V. 69

ALBEE, EDWARD
All Over. New York: 1971. V. 69
The American Dream. New York: 1961. V. 72; 73
Box and Quotations from Chairman Mao Tse-Tung. New York: 1969. V. 69; 73
Counting the Ways and Listening. New York: 1977. V. 69; 73
Everything in the Garden. New York: 1968. V. 69
The Lady from Dubuque. New York: 1980. V. 69; 73
Malcolm. New York: 1966. V. 68; 71
Seascape. New York: 1975. V. 69; 71
Three Tall Women: a Play in Two Acts. New York: 1995. V. 68
Who's Afraid of Virginia Woolf?. New York: 1962. V. 68; 69

ALBEE, EDWARD continued
Who's Afraid of Virginia Woolf?. 1964. V. 68
Who's Afraid of Virginia Woolf?. London: 1964. V. 72
The Wounding: An Essay on Education. Charleston: 1981. V. 72
The Zoo Story. The Death of Bessie Smith. The Sandbox. New York: 1960. V. 69

ALBEMARLE, GEORGE MONCK, 1ST DUKE OF
The Speech and Declaration of His Excellency the Lord George Monck Delivered at Whitehall Upon Tuesday the 21 of Feb. 1659. London: 1659. V. 70

ALBERONI, GIULIO
Cardinal Alberon's Scheme for Reducing the Turkish Empire to Obedience of Christian Princes.... London: 1736. V. 69

ALBERT Einstein, Philosopher Scientist. Evanston: 1949. V. 69

ALBERT, NEIL
Burning March. New York: 1994. V. 68
The February Trouble. New York: 1992. V. 68; 69; 70; 71
The January Corpse. New York: 1991. V. 68; 69; 71; 73

ALBERT, PRINCE CONSORT
The Principal Speeches and Addresses of His Royal Highness the Prince Consort. London: 1862. V. 71

ALBERTI, GIUSEPPE ANTONIO
I Giuochi Numerici Fatti Arcani Palesati.... Venezia: 1788. V. 69
Trattato Della Misura Delle Fabbriche. Venice: 1757. V. 70

ALBERTI, MICHAEL
Specimen Medicinae Theologicae, Selectiora Quaedam Themata ad Scientiam et Experientiam Medicam Praecipue Pertinentia.... Halae Magdeburgiae: 1726. V. 70

ALBERTI, RAFAEL
Pleamar (1942-1944). Buenos Aires: 1944. V. 68

ALBERTI, RAPHAEL
The Owl's Insomnia: Poems. New York: 1973. V. 69; 73

ALBERTS, DON
From Brandy Station to Manilla Bay - A Biography of General Westley Merritt. Austin: 1981. V. 72

ALBERTSON, CHRIS
Bessie. New York: 1972. V. 69; 71

ALBERTUS MAGNUS
Sermones De Tempore et de Sanctis. Ulm: 1478. V. 69

ALBERT VICTOR, PRINCE
The Cruise of Her Majesty's Ship Bacchante 1879-1882. London: 1886. V. 72

ALBERTY, WILLIAM
A Millennium of Facts in the History of Horsham and Sussex. Horsham: 1947. V. 73

ALBIN, ELEAZAR
A Natural History of English Insects. London: 1724. V. 68; 70; 73

ALBOM, MITCH
Tuesdays with Morrie. New York: 1997. V. 68; 69; 71
Tuesdays with Morrie. London: 1998. V. 68

ALBRIGHT, GEORGE LESLIE
Official Explorations for Pacific Railroads. Berkeley: 1921. V. 70

ALBRIGHT, HARDIE
All the Living. New York: 1938. V. 70

ALBRIGHT, THOMAS
Art in the San Francisco Bay Area, 1945-1950: an Illustrated History. Berkeley: 1985. V. 69; 72

THE ALBUM. New York: 1824. V. 68; 73

ALBUM Imperiale D'Haiti. New York: 1852. V. 68

ALBUM of Agricultural Statistics of the United States. Washington: 1889. V. 70

ALCAFORADO, MARIANNA
The Love Letter of a Portuguese Nun Being the Letters Written by Marianna Alcaforado to Noel Bouton de Chamilly . . . New York: 1899. V. 70
The Love Letter of a Portuguese Nun Being the Letters Written by Marianna Alcaforado to Noel Bouton de Chamilly.... Oxford: 1901. V. 70
Love Without Affection, in Five Letters from a Portuguese Nun to a French Cavalier. London: 1709. V. 73

ALCIATI, ANDREA
Diverse Impresse Accommodate a Diuerse Moralita. Lyon: 1564. V. 69
Emblemata. Lvgdvni: 1614. V. 70

ALCINA, J.
Pre-Columbian Art. New York: 1983. V. 69

ALCOCK, GEORGE W.
Fifty Years of Railway Trade Unionism. London: 1922. V. 71

ALCOHOLICS Anonymous. The Story Of How Many Thousands Of Men And Women Have Recovered From Alcoholism. New York: 1950. V. 72

ALCOHOLICS Anonymous, the Story of How Many Thousands of Men and Women Have Recovered from Alcoholism. New York: 1954. V. 69

ALCOTT, AMOS BRONSON
Observations on the Principles and Methods of Infant Instruction. Boston: 1830. V. 71; 73
Ralph Waldo Emerson. Boston: 1882. V. 69
Tablets. Boston: 1868. V. 68

ALCOTT, LOUISA MAY
Aunt Jo's Scrap-Bag. Boston: 1872. V. 71
Aunt Jo's Scrap-Bag. Cupid and Chow-Chow. Boston: 1874. V. 71
Aunt Jo's Scrap Bag. Shawl-Straps. Boston: 1873. V. 68
A Christmas Dream. Boston: 1901. V. 69
Her Life, Letters and Journals. Boston: 1889. V. 73
A Hole in the Wall. Boston: 1899. V. 68
Kitty's Class Day. Boston: 1868. V. 68
Life, Letters and Journals. Boston: 1889. V. 70
Little Men: Life at Plumfield with Jo's Boys. Boston: 1871. V. 70; 73
Little Women. Boston: 1869. V. 70; 71
Little Women. Part Second. Boston: 1869. V. 68
A Modern Mephistopheles and a Whisper in the Dark. Boston: 1890. V. 68
Moods. Boston: 1865. V. 68
Morning-Glories, and Other Stories. Boston: 1868. V. 68
A Round Dozen. New York: 1963. V. 73
Silver Pitchers and Independence. Boston: 1876. V. 71
Under the Lilacs. Boston: 1878. V. 71

ALDEN, CARROLL STORRS
Lawrence Kearny. Sailor Diplomat. Princeton: 1936. V. 69

ALDEN, ISABELLA M.
The Fortunate Calamity. Philadelphia: 1927. V. 69
An Interrupted Night. Philadelphia: 1929. V. 70

ALDEN, JOHN
The Story of a Pilgrim Family. Boston: 1890. V. 71

ALDEN, ROLAND H.
Early Naturalists in the Far West. San Francisco: 1943. V. 68

ALDEN, TIMOTHY
Alden's New Jersey Register and United States' Calendar, for...1811. Newark: 1811. V. 69
Catalogue of the Books, Tracts, Newspapers, Maps, Charts, Views, Portraits, and Manuscripts in the Library of the New York Historical Society. New York: 1813. V. 68
A Collection of American Epitaphs and Inscriptions with Occasional Notes. New York: 1814. V. 70

ALDERSON, JAMES
Observations on Sea-sickness, and on Some of the Means of Preventing It. London: 1872. V. 72

ALDERSON, R.
Lines, Written and Printed at the Request of a Friend, by Whom the Melancholy Story is Related . . . Newcastle upon Tyne: 1825. V. 71; 73

ALDERTON, G. E.
Treatise and Handbook of Orange Culture in Auckland, New Zealand. Wellington: 1884. V. 72

ALDIN, CECIL
An Artist's Models. 1930. V. 70
Cecil Aldin's Happy Family-Master Quack No. V. London: 1912. V. 73
Cecil Aldin's Letter Books. London: 1920. V. 70
Jock and Some Others. London: 1916. V. 71
The Merry Party. London: 1911. V. 73
Old Inns. London: 1921. V. 71
Pickles. London: 1909. V. 71
The Pied Piper: Cecil Aldin's Painting Books. London: 1919. V. 69
Rag's Garden Party. London: 1928. V. 68
Rough and Tumble. London: 1909. V. 72
Scarlet to M. F. H. 1933. V. 70
Time I Was Dead. Pages From My Autobiography. London: 1934. V. 73
The Twins. London: 1910. V. 73

THE ALDINE, a Typographic Art Journal. Volume IV. New York: 1872. V. 71

ALDINGTON, RICHARD
A. E. Housman and W. B. Yeats. Two Lectures. Berkshire: 1955. V. 68
All Men are Enemies. 1933. V. 70
Balls and Another Book for Suppression. 1931. V. 71
The Colonel's Daughter. London: 1931. V. 70
D. H. Lawrence. London: 1930. V. 72
A Dream in the Luxembourg. London: 1930. V. 69
Exile and Other Poems. 1923. V. 70
Fifty Romance Lyric Poems. New York: 1928. V. 68
Jane Austen. Pasadena: 1948. V. 68; 70; 73
Soft Answers. 1932. V. 70
Stepping Heavenward. Florence: 1931. V. 68; 71
A Tourist's Rome. Draguignan: 1961. V. 72
Two Stories. 1930. V. 70

ALDINI, GIOVANNI
Precis des Experiences Galvaniques Faites Recement a Londres et a Calais.... Paris: 1803. V. 73

ALDINI, TOBIA
Exactissima Descriptio Rariorum Quarundam Plantarum, Que Continentur Rome in Horto Farnesiano. Rome: 1625. V. 71

ALDIS, HARRY G.
The Printed Book. 1941. V. 72

ALDISS, BRIAN
An Age. London: 1967. V. 71
The Brightfount Diaries. London: 1955. V. 71
Cities and Stones. London: 1966. V. 71
Cracken at Critical and the Magic of the Past. 1987. V. 71
Earthworks. London: 1965. V. 71
Earthworks. New York: 1966. V. 71
Equator. London: 1958. V. 71
Farewell to a Child. Berkhamsted: 1982. V. 70
Greybeard. London: 1964. V. 71
Hothouse. London: 1962. V. 70
The Male Response. London: 1961. V. 70
The Male Response. New York: 1961. V. 71
The Pale Shadow of Science. Seattle: 1985. V. 71
The Primal Urge. New York: 1961. V. 71
The Saliva Tree and Other Strange Growths. London: 1966. V. 71

ALDRICH, GENE
Black Heritage of Oklahoma. Edmond: 1973. V. 69

ALDRICH, THOMAS BAILEY
The Stillwater Tragedy. Boston: 1880. V. 70

ALDRIDGE, REGINOLD
Ranch Notes In Kansas, Colorado, The Indian Territory and Northern Texas. London: 1885. V. 71

ALEC: a Birthday Present for Alec Guinness. London: 1994. V. 68

ALEMAN, MATHEO
The Rogue; or the First (Second) Part of the Life of Guzman de Alfarache.... London: 1623. V. 73
The Rogue, or The Life Of Guzman De Alfarache written in Spanish by Matheo Aleman, and Done Into English Anno 1623. London: 1924. V. 72

ALEMANN, M.
Am Rio-Negro Ein Zunkunftsgebiet Germanischer Niederlassung Drei Reisen nach dem Argentinischen Rio Negro-Territorum.... Berlin: 1907. V. 72

ALEMANNI, NICCOLO
De Laternanensibus Parietinis...Dissertatio Historica. Rome: 1625. V. 68

ALESSANDRO Irrigation District, California. San Francisco: 1891. V. 68

ALETHEO, THEOPHILO
Polygamia Triumphatrix id est Discurscus Politicus de Polygamia cum Notis Athanasii Vincentii Omnibus Anti-Polygamis Ubique Locorum, Terrarum, Insularum, Pagorum, Urbium, Modeste & Pie Opposita. London: 1682. V. 73

ALETHES, CLEROPHILUS
Remarks Upon F. Le Courayer's Book in Defense of the English Operations. London?: 1725. V. 72

ALEXANDER, A. E.
Colloid Science. Oxford: 1949. V. 69

ALEXANDER, ANNE TUKE
Remarks on the Theatre, and on the Late Fire at Richmond in Virginia. York: 1812. V. 71

ALEXANDER, ANNIE HECTOR FRENCH
At Bay. London: 1893?. V. 68

ALEXANDER, ARCHIBALD
Biographical Sketches of the Founder and Principal Alumni of the Log College. Princeton: 1845. V. 69
Biographical Sketches of the Founder and Principal Alumni of the Log College. Philadelphia: 1851. V. 69

ALEXANDER, C. W.
The Ashtabula Horrow! and Memoirs of Mr. Bliss and His Wife.... Philadelphia: 1877. V. 69

ALEXANDER, CHARLES BEATTY
Major William Ferguson, Member of the American Philosophical Society, Officer in the Army of the United States. New York: 1908. V. 73

ALEXANDER, CHRISTINE
A Bibliography of the Manuscripts of Charlotte Bronte. 1982. V. 70; 73

ALEXANDER, DAVID
The Death of Daddy-O. Philadelphia: 1960. V. 70

ALEXANDER, E. P.
Military Memoirs of a Confederate. New York: 1907. V. 68

ALEXANDER, FRANCESCA
The Story of Ida: Epitaph on An Etrurian Tomb. Kent: 1885. V. 71

ALEXANDER, H. G.
Seventy Years of Bird Watching. 1974. V. 68

ALEXANDER, HARTLEY B.
North American Mythology. Cambridge: 1916. V. 69
Pueblo Indian Painting. Santa Fe: 1979. V. 69
The Religious Spirit of the American Indian, as Shown in the Development of His Religious Rites and Customs. Chicago: 1910. V. 69

ALEXANDER, HELEN
Hawaiian Cook Book. Honolulu: 1943. V. 72

ALEXANDER, HENRY
The Cairngorms. Edinburgh: 1928. V. 69
The Cairngorms. Edinburgh: 1931. V. 69
The Cairngorms. Edinburgh: 1938. V. 69

ALEXANDER, HENRY CARRINGTON
The Life of Joseph Addison Alexander. New York: 1870. V. 69

ALEXANDER, JAMES
Alexander's Complete Preceptor for the Flute. New York: 1832. V. 72

ALEXANDER, JAMES E.
L'Acadie; or Seven Years' Explorations in British America. London: 1849. V. 73

ALEXANDER, JOHN H.
Mosby's Men. New York and Washington: 1907. V. 69; 70

ALEXANDER, KARL
Time After Time. New York: 1979. V. 71; 73

ALEXANDER, LLOYD
Border Haw: August Bondi. New York: 1958. V. 69

ALEXANDER, M., MRS.
Going West; or, Homes for the Homeless: a Novel. Indianapolis: 1881. V. 71

ALEXANDER, T. H.
Loot. Dallas: 1932. V. 72

ALEXANDER, W. D.
A Brief History of the Hawaiian People. New York: 1899. V. 71

ALEXANDER, WILLIAM
The History of Women . . . Dublin: 1779. V. 73
The History of Women.... London: 1782. V. 73
Johnny Gibb of Gushentneuk in the Parish of Pyketillim, with Glimpses of the Parish Politics About A.D. 1843. Edinburgh: 1881. V. 68

ALEXIE, EDWARD
Indian Killer. New York: 1996. V. 72

ALEXIE, SHERMAN
The Business of Fancy Dancing Stories and Poems. Brooklyn: 1992. V. 73
First Indian on the Moon. Brooklyn: 1993. V. 71; 73
Indian Killer. New York: 1996. V. 72
The Lone Ranger and Tonto Fistfight in Heaven. New York: 1993. V. 69; 73
The Lone Ranger and Tonto Fistfight in Heaven. London: 1994. V. 68
The Man Who Loves Salmon. Boise: 1998. V. 68
Old Shirts and New Skins. Los Angeles: 1993. V. 70; 73
One Stick Song. Brooklyn: 2000. V. 71; 73
Reservation Blues. New York: 1995. V. 68; 69; 73
The Summer at Black Widows. New York: 1996. V. 69; 73
The Toughest Indian in the World. New York: 2000. V. 72; 73

ALFIDI, RALPH J.
Computed Tomography on the Human Body. St. Louis: 1977. V. 68

ALFIERI, VITTORIO
Tragedie di Vittorio Alfieri da Asti. Florence: 1820. V. 71

ALFRED, B. W.
Flat Top Ranch-The Story of a Grassland Venture. Norman: 1957. V. 71

ALGEO, SARA M.
The Story of a Sub-Pioneer. Providence: 1935. V. 73

ALGER, HORATIO
Ben, the Luggage Boy; or, Among the Wharves. Boston: 1870. V. 69
Digging for Gold. Philadelphia: 1892. V. 68
From Farm Boy to Senator, Being the History of the Boyhood and Manhood of Daniel Webster. New York: 1882. V. 68

ALGER, WILLIAM ROUNSEVILLE
A Critical History of the Doctrine of a Future Life. With a complete Bibliography of the Subject. Philadelphia: 1864. V. 72
The Sword, The Pen and The Pulpit: with a Tribute to the Christian Genius and Memory of Charles Dickens. Boston: 1870. V. 69

AN ALGONQUIN Sampler. Chapel Hill: 1990. V. 68

ALGREN, NELSON
Chicago: City on the Make. Garden City: 1951. V. 69
The Devil's Stocking. New York: 1983. V. 69; 72
The Man with the Golden Arm. Garden City: 1949. V. 68; 69; 70; 73
Never Come Morning. New York: 1942. V. 69
A Walk on the Wild Side. New York: 1956. V. 70; 71; 72

ALI Baba and the Forty Thieves. New York: 1928. V. 73

ALI, S.
Birds of Kerala. London: 1969. V. 70
Handbook of the Birds of India and Pakistan, Together with Those of Nepal, Sikkim, Bhutan and Ceylon.... 1968-1974. V. 69; 73

ALI, S. continued
Handbook of the Birds of Indian and Pakistan, Together with Those of Bangladesh, Nepal, Bhutan and Sri Lanka. Delhi: 1983. V. 68
Systematic Study of Important Plant Families of Pakistans. First, Second, Third and Fourth Annual Reports. Karachi. V. 72

ALI, TARIQ
Pakistan. Military Rule or People's Power. London: 1970. V. 70

ALICE, GRAND DUCHESS OF HESSE, PRINCESS OF GREAT BRITAIN
Biographical Sketch and Letters. London: 1884. V. 72

ALICE in Sponsor-Land: a Chronicle of the Adventures of Alice, the Hatter, the March Hare and the Dormouse in that Twentieth Century Wonderland.... New York: 1941. V. 71

ALI KHAN, T.
Man-Eaters of Sunderbans. 1961. V. 69

ALINDER, JAMES
Carleton E. Watkins: Photographs of the Columbia River and Oregon. 1979. V. 73
Collecting Light: the Photographs of Ruth Bernhard. 1979. V. 68

ALINDER, MARY S.
Ansel Adams, Letters and Images 1916-1984. New York: 1988. V. 68

ALISON, A.
Life of John Duke of Marlborough. Edinburgh and London: 1855. V. 69

ALISON, ARCHIBALD
England in 1815 and 1845; and the Monetary Famine of 1847; or, a Sufficient and a Contracted Currency. Edinburgh and London: 1847. V. 72
Free Trade and a Fettered Currency. Edinburgh and London: 1847. V. 72

ALKEN, HENRY
The Art and Practice of Etching: with Directions for Other Methods of Light and Entertaining Engraving. London: 1849. V. 68; 69
The National Sports of Great Britain. London: 1821. V. 72

ALL About Book-Keeping. London: 1880. V. 71

THE ALL About Story Book. New York: 1929. V. 69

ALL the Talents. A Satirical Poem in Three Dialogues. London: 1807. V. 70

ALLA, OGAL
Blue Eye: A Story of the People of the Plains. Portland: 1905. V. 72

ALLAIN, MARIE FRANCOISE
One November Day in 1980 the Other Graham Greene Burst through His Shadow. London: 1983. V. 70
The Other Man. London: 1983. V. 68

ALLAIR, C. B.
Paper Dolls' Furniture: How to Make It. New York: 1857. V. 69

ALLAN, BEA
The Hookers of Kew 1785-1911. London: 1967. V. 70

ALLAN, P. B. M.
The Book-Hunter at Home. London: 1919. V. 71
The Book-Hunter at Home. London: 1922. V. 71

ALLAN, R.
The Sportsman in Ireland. 1897. V. 71

ALLAN, WILLIAM
The Army of Northern Virginia in 1862. Boston and New York: 1892. V. 69; 70
History of the Campaign of Gen. T. J. (Stonewall) Jackson in the Shenandoah Valley of Virginia, from Nov. 4, 1861 to June 17, 1862. Philadelphia: 1880. V. 69; 70

ALLARD, B. W.
Flat Top Ranch, the Story of a Grassland Venture. 1957. V. 68

ALLARD, WILLIAM ALBERT
Vanishing Breed: Photographs of the Cowboy and the West. Boston: 1982. V. 69

ALLARDICE, ROBERT BARCLAY
Agricultural Tour in the United States and Upper Canada, with Miscellaneous Notices. Edinburgh: 1842. V. 68

ALLBUT, ROBERT
London and Country Rambles with Charles Dickens. London: 1896. V. 69
London Rambles En Zigzag with Charles Dickens. London: 1890. V. 69

ALLBUTT, T. CLIFFORD
Notes on the Composition of Scientific Papers. London: 1904. V. 69

ALLDREDGE, EUGENE PERRY
Cowboys and Coyotes. Nashville: 1945. V. 69

ALLEGRETTO, MICHAEL
Death on the Rocks. New York: 1987. V. 69

ALLEINE, JOSEPH
An Alarm to Unconverted Sinners.... Elizabeth Town: 1802. V. 69

ALLEN & HANBURYS
A Reference List of Surgical Instruments and Medical Appliances, Orthopaedic and Deformity Apparatus, Hospital Furniture and Equipment, Electro-Medical and Surgical Apparatus, etc. London: 1930. V. 73

ALLEN & TICKNOR
Allen & Ticknor's Medical Catalogue. A Catalogue of Medical Books, for Sale by Allen and Ticknor. Boston;: 1833. V. 68

ALLEN, A. J.
Ten Years in Oregon. Ithaca: 1848. V. 71

ALLEN, BRASSEYA JOHNSON
Pastorals, Elegies, Odes, Epistles and other Poems. Abingdon: 1806. V. 68; 71

ALLEN, C. BRUCE
Cottage Building, or Hints for Improving the Dwellings of the Working Classes and the Labouring Pour. London: 1873. V. 68
Rudimentary Treatise. Cottage Building; or Hints for Improving the Dwellings of the Labouring Classes. London: 1849-1850. V. 69

ALLEN, C. R.
Illustrated Historical Atlas of Pictou County, Nova Scotia. Belleville: 1972. V. 73

ALLEN, CHARLES DEXTER
American Book-Plates: a Guide to Their Study with Examples. New York and London: 1894. V. 69; 71

ALLEN, DAVID O.
India Ancient and Modern.... Boston: 1856. V. 68

ALLEN, DON C.
Four Poets on Poetry. Baltimore: 1959. V. 69
The Owles Almanacke. Baltimore: 1943. V. 70

ALLEN, DOUGLAS
N. C. Wyeth: the Collected Paintings, Illustrations and Murals. New York: 1972. V. 72

ALLEN, ETHAN
Major League Baseball Technique and Tactics. New York: 1939. V. 71

ALLEN, FRANK WALKER
The Lovers of Skye. Indianapolis: 1913. V. 71

ALLEN, G. C.
The Song of Frithiof. London: 1910. V. 68

ALLEN, GEORGE
The Life of Philidor Musician and Chess-Player. Philadelphia: 1863. V. 68

ALLEN, GEORGE P.
A History and Genealogical Record of the Alling-Allens of New Haven, Connecticut, the Descendants of Roger Alling, First and John Alling, Senior from 1639.... New Haven: 1899. V. 69

ALLEN, GLOVER M.
Dogs of American Aborigines. 1920. V. 68

ALLEN, GRANT
An African Millionaire. London: 1897. V. 70
An African Millionaire. New York: 1897. V. 71
The British Barbarians - a Hill Top Novel. London and New York: 1895. V. 69; 72
Charles Darwin. London: 1885. V. 68
Charles Darwin. London: 1886. V. 73
Michael's Crag. Chicago: 1893. V. 68; 71
Miss Cayley's Adventures. London: 1899. V. 70
The Scallywag. London: 1895. V. 68
What's Bred in the Bone. London: 1891. V. 70

ALLEN, H.
A Monograh of the Bats of North America. Washington: 1893. V. 70

ALLEN, HERVEY
Anthony Adverse. New York: 1933. V. 71; 72

ALLEN, IRA
A Concise Summary of the Second Volume of the Olive Branch.... Philadelphia: 1807. V. 71
A Narrative of the Transactions Relative to the Capture of the American Ship Olive Branch. Philadelphia?: 1804. V. 68; 73
The Natural and Political History of the State of Vermont.... London: 1798. V. 71

ALLEN, J. A.
The American Museum Congo Expedition of Bats. New York: 1917. V. 70
Ontogenetic and Other Variations in Muskoxen, with Systematic Review of the Muskox Groups Recent and Extinct. New York: 1913. V. 70

ALLEN, J. ROMILLY
Celtic Art in Pagan and Christian Times. 1904. V. 70
Theory and Practice in the Design and Construction of Dock Walls. London: 1876. V. 71

ALLEN, J. S.
Industry and Prudence. London: 1950. V. 73

ALLEN, JAMES LANE
The Increasing Purpose. London: 1900. V. 68
A Kentucky Cardinal and Aftermath. London: 1901. V. 71

ALLEN, JOHN
Memories of Roundup Days. Norman: 1957. V. 71
The Physical Friend; Pointing Out the Symptoms of Every Distemper Incident to Man.... Dublin: 1777. V. 71

ALLEN, JOHN FISK
Victoria Regia; or the Great Water Lily of America. Boston: 1854. V. 69

ALLEN, JOHN HOUGHTON
Southwest. Philadelphia: 1952. V. 69

ALLEN, JOHN LOGAN
North American Exploration. Lincoln: 1997. V. 71
Passage through the Garden - Lewis and Clark and the Image of the American Northwest. Urbana: 1975. V. 73

ALLEN, JULES VERNE
Cowboy Lore. San Antonio: 1950. V. 69

ALLEN, LEE
The National League Story: the Official History. New York: 1961. V. 71

ALLEN, LEWIS M.
Printing with the Handpress. New York: 1971. V. 71

ALLEN, MERRITT PARMELEE
The Sun Trail. New York: 1943. V. 72

ALLEN, N. P.
Metallurgical Applications of the Electron Microscope. London: 1950. V. 68

ALLEN, NATHAN
The Opium Trade; Including a Sketch of Its History, Extent, Effects, Etc. as Carried on in India and China. Lowell: 1853. V. 68; 71

ALLEN, P. S.
The Begging Bear. Chicago: 1932. V. 72

ALLEN, PAUL
A History of the American Revolution. Baltimore: 1819. V. 69

ALLEN, PAULA GUNN
Coyote's Daylight Trip. Albuquerque: 1978. V. 68
The Sacred Hoop. Boston: 1986. V. 72

ALLEN, PHILIP SCHUYLER
King Arthur and His Knights - a Novel and Joyous History. Chicago: 1929. V. 70

THE ALLEN Press Bibliography...with Art Work, Sample Pages from Previous Editions. Greenbrae: 1985. V. 70; 72

ALLEN, R. P.
Birds of the Caribbean. New York: 1961. V. 72
The Flamingos: Their Life and Survival.... New York: 1956. V. 73

ALLEN, ROBERT J.
Clubs of Augustan London. Cambridge: 1933. V. 69

ALLEN, ROBERT L.
Black Awakening In Capitalist America: An Analytic History. Garden City: 1969. V. 72

ALLEN, SAMUEL A.
My Own Home and Fireside.... Philadelphia: 1846. V. 70

ALLEN, SARA WILSON
History of the Methodist Episcopal Church and Societies of Irvington, New Jersey 1845-1931. 1931. V. 69

ALLEN, STEVE
Bop Fables. New York: 1955. V. 73

ALLEN, STOOKIE
Men of Daring. New York: 1933. V. 70

ALLEN, V. C.
Rhea and Meigs Counties (Tennessee) in the Confederate War. N.P: 1908. V. 70

ALLEN, W.
Lieutenant W. Allen's Book on Ventriloquism and Latest Popular Songs.... New York: 1871. V. 69

ALLEN, W. C.
History of Halifax County. Boston: 1918. V. 71

ALLEN, WALTER C.
Hendersonia. The Music of Fletcher Henderson and His Musicians. Highland Park, NJ: 1973. V. 73

ALLEN, WILLIAM
The Works. London: 1707. V. 72

ALLEN, WILLIAM A.
Adventures With Indians and Games or Twenty Years in the Rockies. Chicago: 1903. V. 72

ALLEN, WILLIAM FRANCIS
Slave Songs of the United States. New York: 1867. V. 68

ALLEN, WOODY
Don't Drink the Water. New York: 1967. V. 68; 69; 70; 71
Everything You Always Wanted to Know About Sex But Were Afraid to Ask. New York: 1971. V. 71
The Floating Lightbulb. New York: 1982. V. 70; 72
Getting Even. New York: 1971. V. 68; 69
Getting Even. London: 1976. V. 72
God. New York: 1975. V. 69
The Illustrated Woody Allen Reader. New York: 1993. V. 71
Play It Again, Sam. New York: 1968. V. 71; 72
Play It Again, Sam. New York: 1969. V. 68; 69; 70
Side Effects. New York: 1980. V. 68; 69; 70; 72

Three Films of Woody Allen. New York: 1987. V. 68; 69
Without Feathers. New York: 1975. V. 68

ALLEN, ZACHARIAH
Defence of the Rhode Island System of the Treatment of the Indians and of Civil and Religious Liberty. Providence: 1876. V. 72

ALLENDE, ISABEL
Daughter of Fortune. New York: 1999. V. 71
Eva Luna. Franklin Center: 1988. V. 68; 73
The House of the Spirits. London: 1985. V. 68
The House of the Spirits. New York: 1985. V. 68; 69; 70; 71; 73
Of Love and Shadows. New York: 1987. V. 68; 71
Of Love and Shadows. New York: 1989. V. 69
Paula. New York: 1995. V. 69
The Stories of Eva Luna. New York: 1991. V. 72

ALLERTON, JAMES M.
Hawk's Nest, or the Last of the Cahoonshees. A Tale of the Delaware Valley and Historical Romance of 1690. Port Jervis: 1892. V. 69
Tom Quick, the Avenger; or, One Hundred for One. An Historical Tragedy in Five Acts. Port Jervis: 1888. V. 69

ALLESTREE, RICHARD
The Art of Contentment. 1719. V. 69
Forty Sermons, Whereof Twenty One are Now First Publish'd. Oxford: 1684. V. 72
The Gentleman's Calling. London: 1672. V. 73
The Gentleman's Calling. London: 1679. V. 68; 69
The Gentleman's Calling. London: 1696. V. 69; 70; 73
The Gentleman's Calling. (with) The Ladies Calling in Two Parts... Fifth Impression. London: 1682. V. 68
The Government of the Tongue. Oxford: 1693. V. 73
The Government of the Tongue. (with) The Art of Contentment. (with) The Lively Oracles Given to Us. (and) The Gentleman's Calling. (with) The Ladies Calling. (and) The Whole Duty of Man. (and) The Causes of the Decay of Christian Piety. Oxford or London: 1677. V. 70
The Ladies Calling in Two Parts. Oxford: 1673. V. 68; 69; 73
The Ladies Calling in Two Parts. Oxford: 1720. V. 73
The Works of the Learned and Pious Author of the Whole Duty of Man. Oxford: 1695. V. 73

ALLEY, JOHN
Memories of Roundup Days. Norman: 1939. V. 68

ALLEYNE, MARGARET
The Pig Who Was Too Thin. London: 1946. V. 73

ALLHANDS, J. L.
Gringo Builders. Joplin: 1931. V. 70
Uriah Lott. San Antonio: 1947. V. 69

THE ALLIES' Fairy Book. London: 1916. V. 73
THE ALLIES' Fairy Book. Philadelphia: 1916. V. 71

ALLINGHAM, MARGERY
All I Did Was This: Chapters of Autobiography.... Nashville: 1982. V. 69
The Allingham Minibus. London: 1973. V. 70; 72
Black Plumes. New York: 1941. V. 71
The China Governess. London: 1963. V. 73
Dancers in Mourning. London: 1937. V. 68
Deadly Duo. Garden City: 1949. V. 68; 69; 71; 73
The Fashion in Shrouds. New York: 1938. V. 69
Hide My Eyes. London: 1958. V. 70; 72
Kingdom of Death. New York: 1933. V. 68
The Man of Dangerous Secrets. New York: 1933. V. 70
The Mind Readers. London: 1965. V. 69; 70; 73
Mr. Campion: Criminologist. New York: 1937. V. 68
More Work for the Undertaker. London: 1948. V. 71; 72
Mystery Mile. Garden City: 1930. V. 68; 69
The Tiger in the Smoke. London: 1952. V. 69; 70
Traitor's Purse. Garden City: 1941. V. 68; 70; 72
Wanted: Someone Innocent. New York: 1946. V. 70

ALLINGHAM, WILLIAM
Ashby Manor: a Play in Two Acts. 1883. V. 73
Blackberries. London: 1890. V. 73
Choice Lyrics and Short Poems; or, Nightingale Valley. London: 1871. V. 73
Day and Night Songs. London: 1854. V. 73
Day and Night Songs. 1884. V. 73
Day and Night Songs; and The Music Master. London: 1860. V. 68; 73
Evil May-Day &c. 1882. V. 73
Evil Mayday, Etc. London: 1883. V. 70; 71
Laurence Bloomfield in Ireland; or the New Landlord. London: 1869. V. 73
The Music Master, a Love Story. London and New York: 1855. V. 73
Nightingale Valley: a Collection, Including a Great Number of the Choicest Lyrics and Short Poems in the English Language. London: 1860. V. 73
Poems. London: 1850. V. 73
Poems. Boston: 1861. V. 73
Rhymes for the Young Folk. London: 1887. V. 69
Rhymes for Young Folks. London: 1918. V. 70

ALLINSON, FRANCESCA
A Childhood. London: 1937. V. 71

ALLIONI, C.
Flora Pedemontana (Auctarium). Turin: 1785-1789. V. 69

ALLIS, EDWARD P., & COMPANY, MILWAUKEE
Catalogue and Price List of Flour Mill Machinery and Mill and Engine Supplies. 1884. V. 69

ALLIS, OSCAR H.
An Inquiry into the Difference Encountered in the Reduction of Dislocation of the Hip. Philadelphia: 1896. V. 71

ALLISON, ALFRED
The Sword and Womankind; Being a Study of the Influence of The Queen of Weapons Upon the Moral and Social Status of Women. London: 1921. V. 73

ALLISON, DAVID
History of Nova Socita. Halifax: 1916. V. 69

ALLISON, DOROTHY
Bastard Out of Carolina. New York: 1992. V. 68; 69; 70; 71; 72; 73
Lesbian Poetry. Watertown, MA: 1981. V. 71
The Women Who Hate Me. Brooklyn: 1983. V. 68; 69; 70

ALLISON, J.
Allison's Picturesque Pocket Companion and Filey Guide for Visitors. Filey: 1856. V. 73
Northern Tourist's Guide to the Lakes, of Cumberland, Westmorland and Lancashire; Wherein the Mountains, Lakes and Scenery are Correctly Described.... Penrith: 1837. V. 71

ALLISON, J. MURRAY
Official Illustrated Catalogue of the Queen's Dolls' House. Holborn: 1924. V. 69

ALLMAN, G. J.
A Monograph of the Fresh-Water Polyzoa. London: 1856. V. 71
A Monograph of the Gymnoblastic or Tubularian Hydroids. London: 1871-1872. V. 69; 73

ALLOTT, KENNETH
Poems. London: 1938. V. 70

ALLOUSE, B. E.
Birds of Iraq. Baghdad: 1960-. V. 70

ALLSOP, F. C.
Telephones; Their Construction and Fitting. London: 1892. V. 71

ALLSOPP, ALLAN
Kinder, Roches and Northern Areas. Birkenhead: 1951. V. 69

ALLSOPP, BRUCE
Decoration And Furniture. London: 1952. V. 72

ALLSOPP, FRED W.
Albert Pike - A Biography. Little Rock: 1928. V. 68; 70; 73

ALLSTON, WASHINGTON
Outlines and Sketches. Boston: 1850. V. 70
The Sylphs of the Seasons. Boston: 1813. V. 68; 70

ALLUM, TOM
Boy Beyond the Moon. Indianapolis: 1960. V. 69

ALLYN, DOUG
All Creatures Dark and Dangerous. Norfolk: 1999. V. 69
The Cheerio Killings. New York: 1989. V. 68; 71

ALLYN, ROSE
Mother Goose and Her Goslings. Chicago: 1918. V. 70

ALMACK, EDWARD
A Bibliography of the King's Book or Eikon Basilike. London: 1896. V. 73
Fine Old Bindings with Other Interesting Miscellanea in Edward Almack's Library. London: 1913. V. 70; 73

ALMBERT, JEAN LE ROND D'
Traite de l'Equilibre et du Mouvement des Fluides. Paris: 1744. V. 70

ALMEIDA, TONY DE
Jaguar Hunting in the Mato Grosso and Bolivia. 1989. V. 72

ALMESTRAND, A.
Studies on the Vegetation and Hydrochemistry of Scanian Lakes I-III. Lund: 1951. V. 68; 71

ALMON, JOHN
A Letter to the Right Honourable George Grenville, Occasioned by His Publication of the Speech He Made in the House of Commons on the Motion for Expelling Mr. Wilkes, Friday Feb. 3, 1769. London: 1769. V. 68; 72

ALMOND, CUTHBERT
The History of Ampleforth Abbey. London: 1903. V. 73

ALMOND, DAVID
Skelling. London: 1999. V. 72

ALMOND, LINDA STEVENS
Peter Rabbit and Jack the Jumper. Philadelphia: 1922. V. 69
Peter Rabbit and the Little Boy. Philadelphia: 1922. V. 69
Peter Rabbit and the Two Terrible Foxes. Philadelphia: 1925. V. 69
Peter Rabbit's Birthday. Philadelphia: 1921. V. 69
Peter Rabbit's Easter. Philadelphia: 1921. V. 69
When Peter Rabbit Went to School. Philadelphia: 1921. V. 69

ALOI, ROBERTO
L'Arredamento Moderno Terza Serie.... Milan: 1945. V. 69

ALPATOV, M. V.
Early Russian Icon Painting. Moscow: 1974. V. 69; 72

ALPHABET Cookies in ABC. Cleveland: 1928. V. 69

THE ALPHABET of Animals. London: 1880. V. 72

ALPHERAKY, SERGIUS
The Geese of Europe and Asia.... London: 1905. V. 73

THE ALPINE Club Map of Switzerland. London: 1876. V. 72

ALPINI, PROSPER
Medicina Aegyptiorum Accessit Huic Editioni Ejusdem Auctoris Liber De Balsamo et Phapontico ut et Jacobi Bontii Medicina Indorum Editio Nova. Lugduni Batavorum: 1745. V. 70
The Presage of Life and Death in Diseases.... London: 1746. V. 70; 72

ALSBERG, J. L.
Ancient Sculpture from Western Mexico. Berkeley: 1968. V. 69

ALSOP, RICHARD
The Echo. New York: 1807. V. 71

ALSOP, ROBERT
A Tribute to the Memory of Robert Alsop. London: 1879. V. 71

ALSTON, E. G.
A Hand-Book to British Columbia and Vancouver Island. London: 1870. V. 70

ALSTON, J. W.
Hints to Young Practioners in the Study of Landscape Painting.... Edinburgh: 1804. V. 70; 71

ALTER, J. CECIL
James Bridger. Salt Lake City: 1925. V. 73
James Bridger. Salt Lake City: 1945. V. 70
James Bridger. Columbus: 1951. V. 69

ALTGELD, JOHN P.
The Eight Hour Movement. 1890. V. 71
Live Questions: Including Our Penal Machinery and Its Victims. Chicago: 1890. V. 71

ALTHAUS, JULIUS
Diseases of the Nervous System. London: 1877. V. 71
Diseases of the Nervous System. New York: 1879. V. 71
A Treatise on Medical Electricity, Theoretical and Practical.... London: 1859. V. 71

ALTICK, RICHARD D.
The Shows of London. Cambridge: 1978. V. 70

ALTING, MENSONE
Descriptio Secundum Antiquos, Agri Batavi and Frisii... Sive Notitia Germaniae Inferioris.... Amsterdam: 1697-1701. V. 72

ALTMAN, P. L.
Biology Data Book. Volume II. Bethesda: 1973. V. 72
Metabolism. Bethesda: 1968. V. 68

ALTMORE, CHARLES
A Brief Memoir of The Life and Death of Mr. C. Hopper, who Departed This Life on Friday March 5th 1802, in the 80th Year of His Age. Manchester: 1802. V. 73

ALTON, MAILLARD C.
Dreams and Their Meanings and a Compendium of Useful Information. Ashland: 1950. V. 68

ALTROCCHI, JULIA COOLEY
Snow Covered Wagons: a Pioneer Epic: The Donner Party Expedition, 1846-1847. New York: 1936. V. 69; 71

ALTSHELLER, JOSEPH A.
The Horsemen of the Plains: A Story of the Great Cheyenne War. New York: 1910. V. 72

ALTSHULER, CONSTANCE W.
Cavalry Yellow and Infantry Blue - Army Officers in Arizona Between 1851-1886. Tucson: 1991. V. 72
Chain of Command, Arizona and The Army 1856-1875. Tucson: 1991. V. 72

ALUJA, M.
Fruit Flies. Boca Raton: 2000. V. 70

ALVANLEY, RICHARD PEPPER ARDEN, 1ST BARON
Catalogue of the Choice, Valuable and Well Selected Library of the Late Right Hon. Lord Alvanley.... London: 1858. V. 70

ALVANLEY, WILLIAM ARDEN, BARON
The State of Ireland Considered and Measures Proposed for Restoring Tranquility to that Country. London: 1841. V. 71

ALVAREZ, A.
Hers. New York: 1975. V. 72

ALVAREZ, JULIA
Homecoming. New York: 1984. V. 69; 72
How the Garcia Girls Lost Their Accents. Chapel Hill: 1991. V. 68; 69; 71; 72
In the Time of the Butterflies. Chapel Hill: 1994. V. 68; 70
My English. Chapel Hill: 1991. V. 68
The Other Side, El Otro Lado. New York: 1995. V. 73

ALVERDES, PAUL
The Whistlers' Room. London: 1929. V. 72

ALVERSON, MARGARET BLAKE
Sixty Years of California Song. Oakland: 1913. V. 72

ALVORD, BENJAMIN
Head-Quarters, District of Oregon, Fort Vancouver, W.T. March 1, 1865. To the People of Oregon: I Write This to Make an Earnest Appeal to the State, to Raise the Regiment of Cavalry Which the War Department Has Called For. Fort Vancovuer: 1865. V. 68

ALVORD, CLARENCE WALWORTH
The First Explorations of the Trans-Allegheny Region by the Virginians 1650-1674. Cleveland: 1912. V. 73

ALVORD, JOHN W.
The Illinois River and Its Bottom Lands. Springfield: 1919. V. 73

AMADO, JORGE
Tent of Miracles. New York: 1971. V. 69; 71
The Two Deaths of Quincas Wateryell. New York: 1965. V. 69

AMALGAMATED COTTON MILLS TRUST
Concerning Cotton: a Brief Account of the Aims and Achievements of the Amalgamated Cotton Mills Trust Limited and Its Component Companies. 1921. V. 71

AMALGAMATED ENGINEERING UNION
Rules of the Amalgamated Society of Engineers Machinists, Millwrights, Smiths and Pattern Makers.... London: 1874. V. 71

AMARAL, ANTHONY
Comanche. The Horse that Survived the Custer Massacre. 1961. V. 68
Mustang: Life and Legends of Nevada's Wild Horses. Reno: 1977. V. 73
Will James. 1967. V. 68
Will James. Los Angeles: 1967. V. 69
Will James. Reno: 1980. V. 72

THE AMARANTH; *a Gift for All Seasons.* Philadelphia: 1842. V. 71

AMATEUR Work. Ward. V. 72

AMBLER, CHARLES
A Review of the Proceedings and Arguments in a Cause of Chancery, Between James Fox, Esq. and Robert Mackreth, Esq. In which Lord Kenyon, the Master of the Rolls, Pronounced a Decree in Favour of Mr. Fox.... London: 1792. V. 70

AMBLER, ERIC
The Army of the Shadows and Other Stories. Helsinki: 1986. V. 70
Background to Danger. New York: 1937. V. 69; 70; 72
Cause for Alarm. New York: 1939. V. 70
The Dark Frontier. London: 1936. V. 69
Here Lies Eric Ambler. An Autobiography. London: 1985. V. 71; 73
Intrigue. New York: 1943. V. 69
Journey into Fear. New York: 1940. V. 68; 71
Judgment on Deltchev. London: 1951. V. 68
The Light of Day. New York: 1962. V. 70
The Mask of Dimitrios. London: 1939. V. 69
Skytip. London: 1951. V. 68

AMBLER, LOUIS
The Old Halls & Manor Houses of Yorkshire. London: 1913. V. 73

AMBROSE, STEPHEN E.
Crazy Horse and Custer. New York: 1975. V. 72
Duty, Honor, Country: a History of West Point. Baltimore: 1966. V. 72
Undaunted Courage - Meriwether Lewis, Thomas Jefferson, and the Opening of the American West. New York: 1996. V. 70; 71

AMBROSIUS, SAINT
Saint Ambrose His Christian Offices...Whereunto Is Added His Conviction of Symmacvs the Gentile. London: 1637. V. 69; 73

AMELIARANNE and the Green Umbrella. London: 1936. V. 72

AMELIARANNE in Town. London: 1930. V. 72

AMER, LAURA ADAMS
Dark Circle of Branches. New York: 1933. V. 73
The Trader's Children. New York: 1937. V. 73
Waterless Mountain. New York: 1931. V. 73

AMERICA A Prophecy. New York: 1973. V. 72

THE AMERCIAN Advertising Directory, for Manufacturers and Dealers in American Goods for the Year 1831. New York: 1831. V. 70

THE AMERICAN Annual Cyclopaedia and Register of Important Events of the Year 1863 and 1864. New York: 1866. V. 68

AMERICAN ANTI-SLAVERY SOCIETY
The Anti-Slavery Record. Volume I for 1835. New York: 1835. V. 70

AMERICAN Antique Cookbooks. Birmingham: 1984-1985. V. 70

AMERICAN Book Prices Current. Washington: 1976-1996. V. 71

AMERICAN COLONIZATION SOCIETY
Report of the Naval Committee to the House of Representatives, August 1850, in Favor of the Establishment of a Line of Mail Steamships to the Western Coast of Africa.... Washington: 1850. V. 71

AMERICAN COMMISSION ON CONDITIONS IN IRELAND
Evidence on Conditions in Ireland: Comprising the Complete Testimony, Affidavits & Exhibits. Washington: 1922. V. 68

AMERICAN CONSTITUTIONAL ASSOCIATION
Life in a West Virginia Coal Field. Charleston: 1923. V. 72

AMERICAN Domestic Cookery, Formed on the Principles of Economy, for the Use of Private Families. New York: 1823. V. 73

AMERICAN ELECTRIC AND ILLUMINATING COMPANY
The American System of Electric Lighting, Progress of Electric Science. Boston: 1884. V. 73

AMERICAN Etchers. New York: 1929-1931. V. 71

AMERICAN ETHNOLOGICAL SOCIETY
Transactions. volume I. New York: 1845. V. 70

AMERICAN FACE BRICK ASSOCIATION
Brickwork in Italy: a Brief Review from Ancient to Modern Times. Chicago: 1925. V. 69; 72

THE AMERICAN Farmer. Baltimore: 1825. V. 70

AMERICAN Film Criticism from the Beginnings to Citizen Kane. New York: 1972. V. 72

AMERICAN Gothic Tales. New York: 1996. V. 72

AMERICAN Guide Series - Montana, A State Guide Book. New York: 1939. V. 72

THE AMERICAN Military Pocket Atlas, Being an Approved Collection of Correct Maps, Both General and Particular, of the British Colonies.... London: 1776. V. 70

THE AMERICAN Musical Miscellany.... Northampton: 1798. V. 68

AMERICAN PHILOSOPHICAL SOCIETY
Catalogue of the Library of the American Philosophical Society, Held at Philadelphia for Promoting Useful Knowledge. Philadelphia: 1824. V. 69

AMERICAN Poets: An Anthology of Contemporary Verse. Munchen: 1923. V. 72

THE AMERICAN Review. Volume I. New York: 1845. V. 68

AMERICAN SOCIETY FOR COLONIZING THE FREE PEOPLE OF COLOUR
The Fourteenth Report. Washington: 1831. V. 71

AMERICAN Southwest. 1984. V. 71

THE AMERICAN Spectator, or Matrimonial Preceptor.... Boston: 1797. V. 73

AMERICAN Stuff. New York: 1937. V. 71

AN AMERICAN Synagogue for Today and Tomorrow; a Guide Book to Synagogue Design and Construction. New York: 1954. V. 72

AMERICAN TRACT SOCIETY
Home Evangelization: a View of the Wants and Prospects of Our Country.... V. 68

AMERICAN UNION OF ASSOCIATIONISTS
Industrial Association. An Address to the People of the United States. Boston?: 1850. V. 71

THE AMERICAN'S Guide. Trenton: 1813. V. 69

AMERY, L. S.
The Problem of the Army. London: 1903. V. 72

AMES, DELANO
Murder Maestro, Please. New York: 1952. V. 71

AMES, ERNEST, MRS.
Little Red Fox. London: 1908. V. 70

AMES, FISHER
Works of Fisher Ames. Boston: 1809. V. 70

AMES, JOSEPH
Typographical Antiquities: or An Historical Account of the Origin and Progress of Printing in Great Britain and Ireland.... London: 1785-1790. V. 71

AMES, NATHANIEL
An Astronomical Diary; or Ames' Almanack 1773. Boston: 1772. V. 70

AMES, O.
Oakes Ames Jottings of a Harvard Botanist 1874-1950. Cambridge: 1979. V. 71
Orchidaceae.... Boston: 1915. V. 70
Orchids of Guatemala. Chicago: 1952-1953. V. 73

AMHERST, JEFFERY
The Journal of Jeffery Amherst. Toronto and Chicago: 1931. V. 73

AMHERST, WILLIAM
The Recapture of St. John's Newfoundland in 1762. 1928. V. 73

AMHERSTBURG REGULAR MISSIONARY BAPTIST ASSOCIATION
A History of the Amherstburg Regular Missionary Baptist Association: Its Auxiliaries and Churches. Amherstburg?: 1940. V. 69

AMHURST, NICHOLAS
Terrae Filius; or, the Secret History of the University of Oxford in Several Essays. London: 1726. V. 68; 69

AMIRTHALINGAM, C.
A Guide to the Common Commercial and Freshwater Fishes in the Sudan. Khartoum: 1965. V. 73

AMIS ET AMILE
Of the Friendship of Amis and Amile. 1894. V. 71

AMIS, KINGSLEY
The Book of Bond or Every Man His Own 007. London: 1965. V. 69; 73
Colonel Sun. London: 1968. V. 68; 71
The Crime of the Century. New York: 1989. V. 71
The Darkwater Hall Mystery. Edinburgh: 1978. V. 72; 73
Difficulties with Girls. London: 1988. V. 72
The Egyptologists. London: 1965. V. 69
Every Day Drinking. London: 1983. V. 69
The Fantasy Poets. Number Twenty-Two. Swinford: 1954. V. 73
A Frame of Mind. Reading: 1953. V. 73
The Green Man. London: 1969. V. 70
The James Bond Dossier. London: 1965. V. 70
The James Bond Dossier. New York: 1965. V. 72
The King's English. New York: 1998. V. 72
A Look Round the Estate - Poems 1957-1967. London: 1967. V. 68
Memoirs. London: 1991. V. 68; 72
New Maps of Hell. London: 1961. V. 71
The Old Devils. London: 1986. V. 70
Stanley and the Women. London: 1984. V. 72
That Uncertain Feeling. London: 1955. V. 70; 71

AMIS, MARTIN
Dead Babies. London: 1975. V. 70; 71; 73
Dead Babies. New York: 1976. V. 68
Einstein's Monsters. London: 1987. V. 72
Experience. London: 2000. V. 68; 70; 73
Heavy Water and Other Stories. London: 1998. V. 70
The Information. London: 1995. V. 68; 70; 72; 73
London Fields. London: 1989. V. 68; 72; 73
London Fields. New York: 1989. V. 68
Money. London: 1984. V. 68; 70; 72; 73
Money. New York: 1984. V. 71
The Moronic Inferno and Other Visits to America. New York: 1987. V. 68
Night Train. London: 1997. V. 68; 72
Other People: a Mystery Story. London: 1981. V. 70
The Rachel Papers. London: 1973. V. 70; 71
The Rachel Papers. New York: 1974. V. 68; 70
Success. London: 1978. V. 71; 73
Success. New York: 1987. V. 68
Time's Arrow or the Nature of the Offence. London: 1991. V. 70; 72; 73
Time's Arrow or the Nature of the Offense. New York: 1991. V. 68
Two Stories: Denton's Death and Let Me Count the Times. London: 1994. V. 68; 70
Visiting Mrs. Nabokov. London: 1993. V. 68
The War Against Cliche. Essays and Reviews 1971-2000. London: 2001. V. 69

AMIS, REESE T.
Knox County in the World War 1917-1919. Knoxville: 1919. V. 68

AMITH, J. L. B.
A Living Coelacanthid Fish from South Africa. Cape Town: 1939. V. 72

AMMEN, DANIEL
U.S.N. The Old Navy and the New. Philadelphia: 1891. V. 69

AMMIANUS, MARCELLINUS
The Roman Historie. London: 1609. V. 69

AMMONS, A. R.
Changing Things. Ithaca: 1981. V. 68
Expressions of Sea Level. Columbus: 1963. V. 71
Selected Poems. Ithaca: 1968. V. 71
Six-Piece Suite: Poems. Ithaca: 1978. V. 68
Sumerian Vistas: Poems. New York: 1987. V. 68

AMOR, ARTHUR J.
An X-Ray Atlas of Silcosis. Bristol: 1943. V. 68

AMORIS Divini Emblemata. Antwerp: 1660. V. 70

AMORY, ROBERT
A Treatise on Electrolysis and Its Applications to Therapeutical and Surgical Treatment in Disease. New York: 1886. V. 72

AMORY, THOMAS
The Life of John Buncle, Esq. London: 1825. V. 70

AMOS, PRESTON. E.
Above and Beyond In the West Black Medal of Honor Winners 1870-1890. Falls Church (VA): 1974. V. 72

AMOUR, J. OGDEN
The Packers, The Private Car Line and The People. Philadelphia: 1906. V. 71

AMPHIAREO, VESPASIANO
Opera di Frate Vespasiano Amphiareo da Ferrara. Venice: 1580. V. 70

AMPHLETT, J.
The Botany of Worcestershire. Birmingham: 1909. V. 69

AMPHORA: A Collection of Prose and Verse.... 1912. V. 71

AMSDEN, CHARLES A.
Navaho Weaving: Its Technic and History. Santa Ana: 1934. V. 68; 69
Navaho Weaving: Its Technic and History. Albuquerque: 1949. V. 70; 72; 73
Navaho Weaving: Its Technic and History. Chicago: 1964. V. 68
Prehistoric Southwesterners from Basketmaker to Pueblo. Los Angeles: 1949. V. 72

AMSINCK, PAUL
Tunbridge Wells and Its Neighbourhood, Illustrated by a Series of Etchings and Historical Descriptions. London: 1810. V. 70

AMUCHASTEGUI, AXEL
Some Birds and Mammals of Africa. 1979. V. 70; 72; 73
Some Birds and Mammals of North America. London: 1971. V. 73
Some Birds and Mammals of South America. London: 1966. V. 73
Studies of Birds and Mammals of South America. 1967. V. 73

THE AMULET; or Christian and Literary Remembrancer. London: 1828. V. 71

AMUNDSEN, ROALD
The South Pole. London and New York: 1913. V. 70

THE AMUSING Companion or, Interesting Story Teller. Binghamton: 1815. V. 73

THE AMUSING Instructor; or, Tales and Fables in Prose and Verse for the Improvement of Youth with Used and Pleasing Remarks on Different Branches of Science. London: 1777. V. 70

AMY Morgan Price and Her Drawings. London: 1929. V. 70

ANACREON
Anacreon Done Into English Out of the Original Greek. Oxford: 1683. V. 69; 73
Anacreon. Done into English out of the original Greek. London: 1923. V. 71
Anakreon. The Extant Fragments. Translated by Guy Davenport. 1991. V. 69; 73
Odaria (in Greek).... Parma: 1785. V. 68; 69; 73
Odaria, ad Textus Barnesiani Fidem Emendata. London: 1802. V. 72
Odes. London: 1800. V. 72
(Odes). London: 1923. V. 71
Poeta Lyricus. Cantabrigiae: 1705. V. 73

ANALYSIS of the Evidence Before the Select Committees Upon the Slave Trade. London: 1850. V. 72

LES ANAMORPHOSES. 1870. V. 72

ANAND, VALERIE
The Norman Pretender. New York: 1979. V. 71

ANAYA, RUDOLFO
Albuquerque. Albuquerque: 1992. V. 69
A Chicano in China. Albuquerque: 1986. V. 69; 71; 73
Zia Summer. New York: 1995. V. 69

ANBUREY, THOMAS
Travels through the Interior Parts of America. London: 1789. V. 68; 69; 73

THE ANCHOR Magazine - the House Organ of Barclay Perkins and Co. Commemorating the 150th Anniversary of the Firm 1781-1931. London: 1931. V. 69

THE ANCIENT History of Whittington and His Cat.... London: 1817. V. 69

AND It Was So. Philadelphia: 1958. V. 73

ANDERSEN, HANS CHRISTIAN
Ardizzone's Hans Andersen - Fourteen Classic Tales. New York: 1979. V. 72
Danish Fairy Tales and Legends. London: 1846. V. 71
The Dream of Little Tuk, and Other Tales. Boston and Cambridge: 1848. V. 68; 70; 73
Eventyr, Fortalte for Børn. (Tales Told for Children). Copenhagen: 1837. V. 72
Eventyr, Fortalte for Børn. (Tales Told for Children). Copenhagen: 1839-1846. V. 72
Andersen's Fairy Tales. London: 1913. V. 68
Fairy Tales. London: 1872. V. 68
Fairy Tales. London: 1900. V. 72
Fairy Tales. London: 1910. V. 68
Fairy Tales. London: 1921. V. 68
Fairy Tales. New York: 1924. V. 72
Fairy Tales. London: 1932. V. 73
Fairy Tales. London: 1936. V. 68
Fairy Tales. New York: 1942. V. 69; 70
Fairy Tales and Stories. London: 1905. V. 70
Fairy Tales from Andersen. Chicago: 1905. V. 71
Fairy Tales from Hans Christian Andersen. London: 1939. V. 71
Fairy Tales, Newly Translated by H. L. Braekstad. London: 1900. V. 70
Hans Andersen's Fairy Tales. London: 1914. V. 71; 73
Hans Andersen's Fairy Tales. London: 1932. V. 69; 70; 73
Hans Andersen's Stories. London: 1932. V. 71
The Ice Maiden. London: 1863. V. 68
Kjaerlighed Paa Nicolai Taarn Eller Hvad Siger Parterret. (Love on St. Nicholas Tower, or What Does the Pit Say?). Copenhagen: 1829. V. 72
Later Tales. London: 1869. V. 72
The Little Tin Soldier. London: 1900. V. 69
Little Totty. New York: 1879. V. 73
Lykkens Blomst. Eventyr-Comedie. (The Flower of Fortune). Copenhagen: 1845. V. 72
The Red Shoes. Bristol: 1928. V. 71
The Sand-Hills of Jutland. Boston: 1860. V. 68
The Sand-Hills of Jutland. London: 1860. V. 70

ANDERSEN, HANS CHRISTIAN continued
Stories for the Household. London: 1866. V. 69
Stories From Hans Andersen. London. V. 70; 72
Stories from Hans Andersen. London: 1912. V. 72
The Story of the Ugly Duckling Retold. London. V. 70
Tales for the Young. 1847. V. 71
Tales of the Sun-Rays. Boston: 1877. V. 70
The Ugly Duckling. Akron: 1931. V. 70; 71

ANDERSON, A. A.
Experiences and Impressions: The Autobiography of...Successful Wyoming Rancher, Artist and Founder of The American Art Association in Paris. New York: 1933. V. 72
Twenty-Five Years in a Waggon. Sport and Travel in South Africa. 1974. V. 69; 70; 72

ANDERSON, ALAN
A Bibliography of the Writings of Frances Cornford. Edinburgh: 1975. V. 72

ANDERSON, ALEX DWIGHT
The Silver Country of the Great Southwest, a Review of the Mineral and Other Wealth.... New York: 1877. V. 68; 70

ANDERSON, ALEXANDER W. S.
Notes on the Sugar Cane, and the Manufacture of Sugar in the West Indies. Trinidad: 1860. V. 70

ANDERSON, ANNE
The Anne Anderson Fairy Tale Book. New York: 1923. V. 69
The Busy-Bunny Book. London. V. 69
The Cuddly Kitty. London: 1920. V. 71
The Cuddly-Kitty Book. London. V. 68
The Funny Gunnby ABC - A Book of Bunnies and Bairnies (children) with Pictures for Painting. London: 1912. V. 72
The Maisie-Daisie Book. London: 1912. V. 73
The Mischievous Mousie Book. London. V. 69
The Sleepy Song Book. 1915. V. 72
The Sleepy Song Book. London. V. 70

ANDERSON, ARCHER
The Campaign and Battle of Chickamauga. Richmond: 1881. V. 69; 70

ANDERSON, C. W.
Deep Through the Heart. New York: 1940. V. 69

ANDERSON, CHARLES C.
Fighting by Southern Federals. New York: 1912. V. 69; 70

ANDERSON, D. M.
Big Middle and Little, the Three Bears. Cumberlege: 1948. V. 69

ANDERSON, EDWARD
Thieves Like Us. 1937. V. 73
Thieves Like Us. New York: 1937. V. 71

ANDERSON, ERNEST
Esquire's Jazz Book. 1947. V. 71

ANDERSON, ERNEST B.
Sailing Ships of Ireland. 1951. V. 69

ANDERSON, F. J.
An Illustrated History of the Herbals. New York: 1977. V. 71

ANDERSON, FREDERICK IRVING
Adventures of the Infallible Godahi. New York: 1914. V. 70
The Book of Murder. New York: 1930. V. 71
The Notorious Sophie Lang. London: 1925. V. 69

ANDERSON, G. F. REYNOLDS
The White Book of the Muses. Edinburgh: 1895. V. 69

ANDERSON, J. CORBET
The Roman City of Uriconium at Wroxeter, Salop; illustrative of the history and social life of our Roman-British forefathers. London: 1867. V. 70

ANDERSON, J. R. L.
High Mountains and Cold Seas. 1980. V. 73
High Mountains and Cold Seas. London: 1980. V. 69

ANDERSON, JAMES
The Constitutions of the Free-Masons Containing the History, Charges, Regulations, etc. of the Most Ancient and Right Worshipful Fraternity. London: 1723. V. 68; 73
Libri de rebus Britannicis, Scilicet, Anglicis, Scoticis et Hibernicis. Edinburgh: 1723. V. 70
Essays Relating to Agriculture and Rural Affairs. Edinburgh: 1775. V. 72

ANDERSON, JESSICA
Tirra Lirra by the River. South Melbourne: 1978. V. 69

ANDERSON, JOHN
The Unknown Turner. Revelations Concerning the Life and Art of J. M. W. Turner.... New York: 1926. V. 70; 72

ANDERSON, JOHN HENRY
The Fasionable Science of Parlor Magic: Being a Series of the Newest Tricks of Deception.... Philadelphia: 1851?. V. 71
The Wizard's Book of Conundrums. New York: 1852. V. 70

ANDERSON, JOHN P.
The Book of British Topography. London: 1881. V. 68; 72

ANDERSON, JOHN Q.
A Texas Surgeon in the C.S.A. Tuscaloosa: 1957. V. 68

ANDERSON, JOHN W.
From the Plains to the Pulpit. Goose Creek TX: 1907. V. 71

ANDERSON, JON
Counting the Days. Lisbon;: 1974. V. 73

ANDERSON, JOSEPH
The Orkneyinga Saga. Edinburgh: 1873. V. 70
Scotland in Early Christian Times. (with) Scotland in Pagan Times. 1879-1880. V. 71

ANDERSON, K.
Tales from the Indian Jungle. 1970. V. 70
The Tiger Roars. 1967. V. 70

ANDERSON, KENT
Night Dogs. New York: 1996. V. 73
Night Dogs. Tucson: 1996. V. 68; 69; 70; 71; 73
Sympathy for the Devil. Garden City: 1987. V. 68; 69; 70; 71; 72; 73

ANDERSON, KEVIN J.
Ruins (The X Files). NY: 1996. V. 73

ANDERSON, LAURIE
United States. New York: 1984. V. 70

ANDERSON, M. D.
Animal Carvings in British Churches. 1938. V. 68

ANDERSON, MABEL WASHBOURNE
The Life of General Stand Watie. Pryor: 1915. V. 69
The Life of General Stand Watie. Prior: 1931. V. 70

ANDERSON, MADGE
The Heroes of the Puppet Stage. London: 1924. V. 70

ANDERSON, MARGARET
The Fiery Fountains. 1953. V. 70

ANDERSON, MARTIN
The Humours of Cynicus. London: 1891. V. 71
The Satires of Cynicus. Cartoons Social and Political. London: 1893. V. 70; 71

ANDERSON, MAXWELL
Both Your Houses. New York: 1933. V. 71; 72
Key Largo. Washington: 1939. V. 71
Knickerbocker Holiday. Washington. V. 68
Mary of Scotland. Washington: 1933. V. 71
The Miracle of the Danube. New York: 1941. V. 71
Night Over Taos. New York: 1932. V. 69; 70
Valley Forge. Washington: 1934. V. 71
Winterset. Washington: 1935. V. 71

ANDERSON, POUL
Brain Wave. London: 1955. V. 70
Murder Bound. New York: 1962. V. 73
Murder in Black Letter. New York: 1960. V. 69; 71; 73
Murder Bound. New York: 1962. V. 69
Operation Chaos. New York: 1971. V. 70
Perish the Sword. New York: 1959. V. 69; 73
Three Bears and Three Lions. New York: 1961. V. 69
Vault of the Ages. Philadelphia: 1952. V. 69

ANDERSON, R.
Ballads in the Cumberland Dialect.... Wigton: 1808. V. 71
Ballads in the Cumberland Dialect.... Wigton: 1815. V. 71
Cumberland Ballads.... Wigton: 1830. V. 71

ANDERSON, R. A.
Fighting the Mill Creeks. Chico: 1909. V. 69

ANDERSON, RASMUS B.
The Norse Discovery of America. London: 1906. V. 73

ANDERSON, RICHARD
Lightning Conductors. Their History, Nature and Mode of Application. London: 1880. V. 73

ANDERSON, ROBERT
I Never Sang for My Father. New York: 1968. V. 72
The Life of Samuel Johnson, LL.D., with Critical Observations on His Works. London: 1795. V. 68; 69
Tea and Sympathy. New York: 1953. V. 71

ANDERSON, SHERWOOD
Beyond Desire. New York: 1932. V. 70
Death in the Woods and Other Stories. New York: 1933. V. 72
Hello Towns!. New York: 1929. V. 68
Horses and Men, Tales, Long and Short, From Our American Life. New York: 1923. V. 70; 71
Kit Brandon. A Portrait. New York: 1936. V. 70
Many Marriages. New York: 1923. V. 69
Marching Men. New York: 1917. V. 71
A New Testament. New York: 1927. V. 69
No Swank. Philadelphia: 1934. V. 72

ANDERSON, SHERWOOD continued
Plays, Winesburg and Others. New York: 1937. V. 69
Poor White. New York: 1920. V. 73
Sherwood Anderson's Notebook. New York: 1926. V. 71; 73
A Story Teller's Story. New York: 1924. V. 71
Tar. 1926. V. 69; 73
Tar. New York: 1926. V. 68
The Triumph of the Egg. New York: 1921. V. 70
Winesburg, Ohio. New York: 1919. V. 71
Winesburg, Ohio. New York: 1921. V. 69

ANDERSON, TEMPEST
Volcanic Studies in Many Lands. London: 1903-1917. V. 70

ANDERSON, W. W.
Fishes of Western North Atlantic. Part 5. New Haven: 1966. V. 69

ANDERSON, WALTER
Birds. Jackson: 1990. V. 70; 72; 73

ANDERSON, WILLIAM
Glimpses of Natural Science, and Art for the Young. London: 1853. V. 68
The Pictorial Arts of Japan. Boston and New York: 1886. V. 71
The Pictorial Arts of Japan. London: 1886. V. 72
The Scottish Nation. Edinburgh: 1860. V. 71
System of Surgical Anatomy. New York: 1822. V. 73

ANDERSON, WILLIAM MARSHALL
The Rocky Mountain Journals of William Marshall Anderson, The West in 1834. San Morino: 1960. V. 71

ANDERSSON, KARL JOHAN
Lake Ngami. London: 1856. V. 69; 72
Lake Ngami. New York: 1856. V. 72; 73

ANDERTON, BASIL
Fragrance Among Old Volumes. Essays and Idylls of a Book Lover. London: 1910. V. 68

ANDRADE, C. S.
Love Life of the Birds. Buenos Aires: 1952. V. 72

ANDRADE, CARLOS DRUMMOND DE
Souvenir of the Ancient World. New York: 1976. V. 69

ANDRADE, EDWARD NEVILLE DA COSTA
The Structure of the Atom. London: 1927. V. 72

ANDRAL, G.
Medical Clinic: Diseases of the Encephalon, with Extracts from Olliver's Work on Diseases of the Spinal Cord and Its Membranes. Philadelphia: 1843. V. 68; 70; 72

ANDRE Kertesz: a Lifetime of Perception. New York: 1982. V. 68

ANDRE, EUGENE
A Naturalist in the Guianas.... London: 1904. V. 72

ANDRE, GEORGE
The Draughtsman's Hand Book of Plan and Map Drawing.... London: 1874. V. 72

ANDRE, JOHN
Andre's Journal, an Authentic Record of the Movements and Engagements of the British Army in America from June 1777 to November 1778. Boston: 1903. V. 73

ANDRE, RICHARD
Up Stream. London: 1883. V. 68

ANDREADES, A.
History of the Bank of England. London: 1909. V. 71

ANDREAE, CHRISTINE
Trail of Murder. New York: 1992. V. 68; 71

ANDREAE, PERCY
Stanhope of Chester. London: 1895. V. 68

ANDREAS, FRED
The Trial of Gregor Kaska. New York: 1932. V. 69

ANDREE, S. A.
The Andree Diaries, Being the Diaries and Records...Written During their Balloon Expedition to the North Pole in 1897 and Discovered on White Island in 1930.... London: 1931. V. 73

ANDREW, GEORGE
The Draughtsman's Hand Book of Plan and Map Drawing.... London: 1874. V. 68

ANDREW Marvell 1621-1678, Tercentenary Tributes. London: 1922. V. 68; 71

ANDREWS, C. E.
The Innocents of Paris. New York: 1928. V. 71

ANDREWS, C. REGINALD
The Story of Wortley Ironworks. Mexborough: 1950. V. 73

ANDREWS, CHARLES M.
The Colonial Period of American History. New Haven: 1947. V. 68

ANDREWS, DONNA
Murder with Peacocks. New York: 1999. V. 69

ANDREWS, FRANCES E.
A Collection of Recollections. Boston: 1900. V. 68

ANDREWS, FRANK A.
Dirigible. New York: 1931. V. 70

ANDREWS, JAMES
American Wildflower Florilegium. Denton: 1992. V. 73
Lessons in Flower Painting. London: 1835. V. 73

ANDREWS, JAMES PETTIT
Anecdotes &c., Ancient and Modern, with Observations. Dublin: 1789. V. 68; 73
Anecdotes, Etc., Antient and Modern, with Observations. London: 1789. V. 69

ANDREWS, JEAN
Peppers: the Domesticated Capsicums. Austin: 1984. V. 72; 73

ANDREWS, JOHN
Remarks on the French and English Ladies, in a Series of Letters.... London: 1783. V. 69; 73

ANDREWS, JOHN H.
A Paper Landscape: the Ordnance Survey in the 19th Century Ireland. 1975. V. 69

ANDREWS, L.
Catalogue of the Flowering Plants and Ferns of Springfield, Massachusetts.... Springfield: 1924. V. 68

ANDREWS, LORRIN
Grammar of the Hawaiian Language. Honolulu: 1854. V. 68; 73

ANDREWS, MATTHEW PAGE
Virginia: the Old Dominion. Garden City: 1937. V. 71

ANDREWS, R. C.
Across Mongolian Plains. 1921. V. 70; 72; 73
This Business of Exploring. New York: 1935. V. 68

ANDREWS, RAYMOND
Appalachee Red. New York: 1978. V. 72
Baby Sweets. New York: 1983. V. 72
Rosiebelle Lee. NY: 1980. V. 72

ANDREWS, RICHARD
Literary Fables, from the Spanish of Yriarte. London: 1835. V. 71

ANDREWS, ROBERT
Windfall: a Novel About Ten Million Dollars. New York: 1931. V. 71

ANDREWS, ROBERT D.
The Stolen Husband. New York: 1931. V. 70

ANDREWS, STEPHEN PEARL
The Complete Phonographic Class-Book. Boston: 1846. V. 73
Love, Marriage and Divorce and the Sovereignty of the Individual. New York: 1853. V. 69
The Phonographic Reader. Boston: 1845. V. 69; 73
The Phonographic Reader. Boston: 1846. V. 73
The Science of Society...No. 1. New York: 1851. V. 69; 73

ANDREWS, T. F.
Debates and Proceedings of the Constitutional Convention for the Territory of Minnesota. St. Paul: 1858. V. 73

ANDREWS, VAL
Sherlock Holmes adn the Eminent Thespian. Romford, Essex: 1989. V. 71

ANDREWS, WAYNE
Who Has Been Tampering with These Pianos?. New York: 1948. V. 72

ANDREWS, WILLIAM
Historic Yorkshire. Reeves and Turners and Leeds: 1883. V. 73

ANDREWS, WILLIAM LORING
Gossip About Book Collecting. New York: 1900. V. 71
Roger Payne and His Art. New York: 1892. V. 71; 73

ANDREYEV, LEONID
The Dark. London: 1922. V. 68

ANDRY, DE BOISREGARD, NICOLAS
De la Generation des vers dans Le Corps de l'Homme. De la Nature & Des Especes de Cette Maladie, de Ses Effets.... Paris: 1700. V. 70

ANDRY DE BOISREGARD, NICOLAS
An Account of the Breeding of Worms in Human Bodies; Their Nature and Several Sorts, Their Effects, Symptoms and Prognostics. London: 1701. V. 71

ANDRZEYEVSKI, GEORGE
The Gates of Paradise. London: 1962. V. 70

ANDY'S Exciting Day. London: 1950. V. 73

ANECDOTE for Great Men. Hartford: 1787. V. 71

ANECDOTES of a Convent. London: 1771. V. 73

ANECDOTES of the Life of the Right Honourable William Pitt, Earl of Chatham; and of the Principal Events of His Time.... London: 1793. V. 69

ANECDOTES of the Life of...William Pitt, (1st) Earl of Chatham 1708- 1778. London: 1794. V. 71

ANGEL, GILDA
Sephardic Holiday Cooking: Recipes and Traditions. Mount Vernon: 1986. V. 72
Sephardic Holiday Cooking Recipes and Traditions. New York: 1986. V. 73

ANGEL, MARIE
Angel's Alphabet. London: 1986. V. 72
The Ark. New York: 1973. V. 72
Catscript. London: 1984. V. 73

ANGELL, HENRY C.
The Sight and How to Preserve It. London: 1878. V. 68

ANGELL, ROGER
A Day in the Life of Roger Angell. 1970. V. 71; 72

ANGELO, HENRY
Reminiscences.... London: 1830. V. 72
The Reminiscences.... London: 1904. V. 68; 72

ANGELOU, MAYA
All God's Children Need Traveling Shoes. Franklin Center, PA: 1986. V. 68; 70; 71
All God's Children Need Traveling Shoes. New York: 1986. V. 72
And Still I Rise. New York: 1978. V. 69
Even the Stars Look Lonesome. NY: 1997. V. 72
Gather Together in My Name. New York: 1974. V. 69
I Know Why the Caged Bird Sings. New York: 1969. V. 70; 71
I Know Why the Caged Bird Sings. New York: 2002. V. 73
Oh Pray My Wings Are Gonna Fit Me Well. New York: 1975. V. 69; 71
On the Pulse of Morning. New York: 1993. V. 71; 73
Singin' and Swingin' and Gettin' Merry Like Christmas. New York: 1976. V. 68; 69; 70; 71
Wouldn't Take Nothing for My Journey Now. New York: 1993. V. 72; 73

ANGELUS DE CLAVASIO
Summa Angelica de Casibus Conscientiae. Strassburg: 1491. V. 69; 73

ANGER, KENNETH
Hollywood Babylon. San Francisco: 1975. V. 69

ANGLERS' CLUB OF NEW YORK
The Anglers' Club Story 1906-1956. New York: 1956. V. 72
The Best of the Anglers' Club Bulletin. New York: 1972. V. 72

ANGLESEY, RICHARD, 6TH EARL OF
The Trial in Ejectment (At Large) Between Campbell Craig, Lessee of James Annesley, Esq. and Others, Plaintiff; and the Right Honourable Richard, Earl of Anglesey, Defendant. London: 1744. V. 70

L'ANGLETERRE en 1800. Cologne: 1801. V. 69; 72

THE ANGLO-SAXON Review. London: 1899-. V. 70; 71

THE ANGORA Twinnies. New York: 1915. V. 70

ANGUS, JAMES STOUT
A Glossary of the Shetland Dialect. Paisley: 1914. V. 71

THE ANIMAL ABC. London: 1930. V. 69

ANIMAL ABC. Chicago: 1935. V. 70

ANIMAL Book. Akron: 1904. V. 72

THE ANIMAL Picture Book for Kind Little People. London. V. 72

ANIMALS Everywhere. New York: 1940. V. 69

THE ANIMAL'S Towering Club. 1913. V. 70

AN ANIMATED Alphabet. Cambridge: 1971. V. 70; 72

ANKENY, NESMITH
The West As I Knew It. Lewiston: 1953. V. 71; 73

ANKER, J.
Bird Books and Bird Art, an Outline of the Literary History and Iconography of Descriptive Ornithology Based Principally on the Collection of Books...in the University Library at Copenhagen.... Copenhagen: 1938. V. 70

ANNALS of Medical History. New York: 1917-1942. V. 68

ANNANDALE, N.
Fauna of the Chilka Lake. Calutta: 1915-1928. V. 69

ANNESLEY, JAMES
The Trial of James Annesley and Joseph Redding, at the Sessions-House in the Old-Bailey, on Thursday the 15th of July, 1742. For the Murder of Thomas Egglestone. London: 1742. V. 69

ANNOTATIONS on a Late Pamphlet Intituled, Considerations on the Proposal for Reducing the Interest of the National Debt. London: 1750. V. 72

AN ANNUAL ABSTRACT of the Sinking Fund for Michaelmas 1718, When It Was First Stated to Parliament, to the 10th of October 1763. London: 1764. V. 72

THE ANNUAL Miscellany; for the Year 1694. London: 1694. V. 68; 70

THE ANNUAL of Book Making. New York: 1938. V. 69

ANNUNZIO, GABRIELE D'
The Victim. London: 1899. V. 72

ANOUILH, JEAN
The Lark. New York: 1956. V. 70

ANSA, TINA MC ELROY
Ugly Ways. New York: 1993. V. 71; 72

ANSCOMBE, FRANCIS C.
I Have Called you Friend, the Story of Quakerism in North Carolina. Boston: 1959. V. 73

ANSELL, GEORGE FREDERICK
The Royal Mint: Its Working, Conduct and Operations, Fully and Practically Explained; with Suggestions for Its Better Scientific and Official Management. London: 1870. V. 72

ANSON, ADRIAN C.
A Ball-Players Career: Being the Personal Experiences and Reminiscences of Adrian C. Anson, Late Captain of the Chicago Baseball Club. Chicago: 1900. V. 70

ANSON, B. J.
Callander's Surgical Anatomy. Philadelphia: 1952. V. 71

ANSON, JAY
The Amityville Horror. Englewood Cliffs: 1977. V. 68; 71

ANSON, WILLIAM R.
Principles of the English Law of Contract and of Agency In Its Relation to Contract. Chicago: 1887. V. 68

ANSTED, D. T.
Geology, Introductory, Descriptive and Practical. London: 1844. V. 68
The Gold-Seeker's Manual. London: 1849. V. 73
The Ionian Islands in the Year 1863. London: 1863. V. 68
Scenery, Science and Art. London: 1854. V. 72
A Short Trip in Hungary and Transylvania in the Spring of 1862. London: 1862. V. 68

ANSTEY, CHRISTOPHER
An Election Ball in Poetical Letters from Mr. Incle, at Bath to His Wife At Glocester; with a Poetical Address to John Miller, Esq. at Batheaston Villa. Bath: 1776. V. 69; 70; 73
The New Bath Guide.... Bath: 1807. V. 68

ANSTEY, F.
Puppets at Large. London: 1897. V. 72

ANSTEY, JOHN
The Pleader's Guide, a Didactic Poem, in Two Parts.... London: 1810. V. 72

AN ANSWER to The Lord Digbies Speech in the House of Commons to the Bill of Attainder of the Earle of Strafford.... London: 1641. V. 73

AN ANSWER to the Severall Petitions of Late Exhibited to the High Court of Parliament and To His Excellency the Lord Generall Cromwell, by the Poor Husband-Men, Farmers and Tenants in Several Counties of England. London: 1652. V. 72

AN ANSWER to Old Doctor Wilde's New Poem, to His Old Friend Upon the New Parliament. 1679. V. 69

ANTHOENSEN, FRED
John Bell Type. Portland: 1929. V. 72
John Bell Type. Portland: 1939. V. 70

ANTHONY, DAVID
Stud Game. London: 1977. V. 73

ANTHONY, EARL
Picking Up the Gun: A Report on the Black Panthers. New York: 1970. V. 72

ANTHONY, EDWARD
The Fairies Up-To-Date. London: 1925. V. 71; 73
The Pussycat Princess. New York: 1922. V. 69

ANTHONY, GORDON
Russian Ballet. 1939. V. 68
The Sleeping Princess: Camera Studies. London: 1940. V. 68
The Vic-Wells Ballet Camera Studies. London: 1938. V. 68

ANTHONY, H. E.
The Indigenous Land Mammals of Porto Rico, Living and Extinct. New York: 1918. V. 70

ANTHONY, KATHERINE
Feminism in Germany and Scandinavia. New York: 1915. V. 72

ANTHONY, MICHAEL
The Games Were Coming. Boston: 1968. V. 72

ANTHONY, WILDER
Men of Mystery. New York: 1926. V. 68

THE ANTI-PHILISTINE. Edinburgh: 1897. V. 73

ANTIQUARIAN BOOKSELLERS' ASSOCIATION
Books and the Man: Antiquarian Booksellers' Association Annual. London: 1953. V. 71

ANTIQUARIAN SOCIETY OF NEWCASTLE UPON TYNE
First Annual Report (being for the year 1813). Newcastle: 1814. V. 73

ANTLER Development in Cervidae. USA: 1983. V. 72

ANTON, FERDINAND
Ancient Mexican Art. New York: 1969. V. 71; 72; 73

ANTON, JOHN
American Precedents of Declarations. Boston: 1802. V. 69

ANTONIN Raymond, Architectural Details 1938. Tokyo: 1938. V. 68

ANTONINUS, BROTHER
The Blowing of the Seed. New Haven: 1966. V. 70; 73
The Engendering Flood: Book One of Dust Shall be the Serpent's Food (Cantos I-V). Santa Rosa: 1990. V. 69; 71

ANTONINUS, BROTHER continued
The High Embrace. 1986. V. 69; 71
In the Fictive Wish. Berkeley: 1967. V. 73
Renegade Christmas. Northridge: 1984. V. 69; 71
The Residual Years. New York: 1948. V. 68
Robinson Jeffers: Fragments of an Older Fury. Berkeley: 1968. V. 68
The Rose of Solitude. Garden City: 1967. V. 68
San Joaquin. Los Angeles: 1939. V. 73
Single Source. The Early Poems 1934-1940. Berkeley: 1966. V. 73
Triptych for the Living. Oakland: 1951. V. 69; 72
Who Is She That Looketh Forth as the Morning. Santa Barbara: 1972. V. 73

ANTONINUS FLORENTINUS
Defecerunt Scrutantes Scrutinio (i.e. Summa Confessionum). Memmingen: 1483. V. 73
Summa Theologia, Pars III. Venice: 1485. V. 73
Summa Theologia, Quarta Pars. Strassburg: 1490. V. 69
Trilogus Super Evangelia (and other works). Venice: 1495. V. 73

ANTONIO, NICHOLAS
Bibliotheca Hispana sive Hispanorum Qui Usquam Unquamue Sive Latina Sive Populari Sive Aliam Quamis Lingua Scripto.... Rome: 1672. V. 70; 73

ANTONY, PAUL
Ian Fleming's Incredible Creation. Chicago: 1965. V. 69

ANTRAM, C. B.
Butterflies of India. Calcutta: 1924. V. 69

ANTRIM, DONALD
Elect Mr. Robinson for a Better World. 1993. V. 72

ANTRIM, DORON K.
Secrets of Dance Band Success. 1936. V. 70; 72

APENSZLAK, JACOB
The Black Book of Polish Jewry. New York: 1943. V. 68

THE APERTURE History of Photography Series. Volumes 1-15. New York: 1976-1979. V. 73

APLIN, O. V.
The Birds of Oxfordshire. 1889. V. 73

THE APOCRYPHA. According to the Authorized Version. 1929. V. 71

APOLLINAIRE, GUILLAUME
Le Bestiaire. 1967. V. 69
Zone. Dublin/London: 1972. V. 70

APOLLODORUS ATHENIENSIS
Grammatici Bibliotheces, Sive de Deorum Origina Libri III. Heidelberg: 1599. V. 73

APOLLONIO, U.
Marino Marini, Sculptor. Milan: 1953. V. 72

APOLLONIUS OF RHODES
(Greek title, then) Apollonii Rhodii Argonauticorum, Carmine Heroico. Basel: 1572. V. 69

APOLLONIUS OF TYRE
Apollonius of Tyre. Waltham St. Lawrence: 1956. V. 71

AN APOLOGY for the Pulpits: Being in Answer to a Late Book, Intituled, Good Advice to the Pulpits. London: 1688. V. 68

APOSTOOL, CORNELIUS
The Beauties of the Dutch School.... London: 1793. V. 72

AN APPEAL to the Common Sense of Scotsmen, Especially Those of the Landed Interest, and More Especially Freeholders, If Their Own Conduct Be Not the Source of Their Misery?. Edinburgh: 1747. V. 69

AN APPEAL to the Landholders Concerning the Reasonableness and General Benefit of an Excise Upon Tobacco and Wine. London: 1733. V. 72

APPEL, BENJAMIN
The Power House. New York: 1939. V. 70

APPERLEY, CHARLES JAMES
The Chace. London: 1837. V. 72
The Chace. 1852. V. 68
The Horse and the Hound. 1843. V. 68
The Life of a Sportsman. London: 1842. V. 69
The Life of Edward Moxon.... London: 1877. V. 70
The Life of John Mytton, Esq. of Halston, Shropshire.... London: 1871?. V. 68
Memoirs of the Life of the Late John Mytton. London: 1837. V. 68
Memoirs of the Life of the Late John Mytton. 1900. V. 68
Nimrod's Hunting Tour in Scotland and the North of England. 1857. V. 68

APPERLEY, NEWTON WYNNE
North Country Hunting Half a Century Ago. Darlington: 1924. V. 73

APPERSON, G. L.
Bygone London Life. Pictures from a Vanished Past. London: 1903. V. 71

APPIANUS
De Civilibus Romanoru Bellis Historiarum Libri Quinque. Paris: 1538. V. 68; 70; 73
The History of Appian of Alexandria, in Two Parts. London: 1679. V. 69; 73
(Greek letters) (...) Rwmaika (...) Rom. Historiarum, Punica, sive Carthaginiensis, Syriaca, Parthica, Mithridatica, Iberica, Annibalica.... Paris: 1592. V. 72

APPLE Pie. (No. 5). Belper: 1830-1846. V. 69

APPLE, MAX
The Oranging of America and Other Stories. New York: 1976. V. 69; 71

APPLEGATE, FRANK G.
Native Tales of New Mexico. Philadelphia: 1932. V. 69

APPLEGATE, JESSE
A Day With the Cow Column in 1843. Chicago: 1934. V. 71
A Day With the Cow Column in 1843. Portland: 1982. V. 71

APPLEGATE, JOHN S.
Early Courts and Lawyers of Monmouth County, Beginning at Its First Settlement and Down to the Last Half Century. Freehold: 1911. V. 69
Reminiscences and Letters of George Arrowsmith of New Jersey, Late Lieutenant-Colonel...New York State Volunteers. Red Bank: 1893. V. 69

APPLER, A. C.
Bank and Train Robbers of the West, Etc. Frank and Jesse James. Chicago: 1882. V. 72

APPLETON, ELIZABETH HAVEN
Insurrection at Magellan. Narrative of the Imprisonment and Escape of Capt. Chas. H. Brown from the Chilian Convicts. Boston: 1854. V. 70

APPLETON, LE ROY H.
Indian Art of the Americas. New York: 1950. V. 70; 71

APPLETON, NATHANIEL
The Crown of Eternal Life, the Sure Reward of the Faithful Exhibited in Two Discourses on June 11, 1769. Boston: 1769. V. 71
A Plain and Faithful Testimony Against that Abominable, but too Fashionable Vice of Profane Swearing. Boston: 1765. V. 71

APPLETON, VICTOR
Tom Swift and His Giant Magnet. New York: 1932. V. 69

APPLETON & COMPANY, D.
Appleton's Hand-Book of American Travel. Northern and Eastern Tour. New York: 1876. V. 72
Appleton's Hand-Book of American Travel. Southern Tour. New York: 1876. V. 72

APPLEWHITE, JAMES
Ode to the Chinaberry Tree and Other Poems. Baton Rouge: 1986. V. 73

APPLIED Art: A Collection of Designs Showing the Tendencies of American Industrial Art. Volume I. New York: 1919. V. 71

APPLIN, ARTHUR
Sweeter than Honey. New York: 1936. V. 70

APPONYI, H., COUNT
My Big Game Hunting Diary. 1937. V. 69

APTHEKER, HERBERT
The Negro in the Civil War. New York: 1938. V. 68

APULEIUS
Cupid and Psyche. London: 1923. V. 70; 71
Cupid and Psyche. Waltham St. Lawrence: 1934. V. 72
De Cupidinis et Psyches Amoribus Fabula Anilis. London: 1901. V. 72
The Golden Ass. London: 1924. V. 69
The Golden Ass. New York: 1932. V. 73
The Golden Asse. 1923. V. 70
The XI Bookes of the Golden Asse. Waltham St. Lawrence: 1923. V. 73
Metamorphoseos, Siue Lusus Asini Libri XI. Venice: 1521. V. 68
Metamorphoseos, Sive de Asino Aureo Libri Vndecim. Parisiis: 1536. V. 73
The Metamorphosis, or Golden Ass and Philosophical Works. London: 1822. V. 70
Opera.... Parissis: 1688. V. 72

ARABIAN NIGHTS
Arabian Nights. London: 1912. V. 72
The Arabian Nights. New York: 1925. V. 69
The Arabian Nights. New York: 1930. V. 69
The Arabian Nights Entertainment. New York: 1955. V. 72
The Arabian Nights' Entertainments; or the Thousand and One Nights. London: 1811. V. 72
The Arabian Nights: Tales from the Thousand and One Nights. London: 1924. V. 70
The Child's Arabian Nights. London: 1903. V. 72
Le Livre des Mille Nuits et Une Nuit. Paris: 1908-1912. V. 71
A Plain and Literal Translation of the Arabian Nights' Entertainments, now Entitled The Book of the Thousand Nights and a Night. (with) Supplemental Nights to the Book of the Thousand Nights and a Night.... London: 1885-1886. V. 73
Sinbad the Sailor and Other Stories from the Arabian Nights. London: 1914. V. 73

ARAGO, FRANCOIS
Biographies of Distinguished Science Men. Boston: 1859. V. 68

ARAGON, LOUIS
Henri Matisse: a Novel. New York: 1971. V. 69; 71; 73
Le Creve-Coeur. London: 1942. V. 71
Paris Peasent. London: 1971. V. 71

ARAGONA, TULLIA D'
Dialogo Dela Infinita di Amore. Vinegia: 1547. V. 69

ARAM, EUGENE
The Genuine Life, Trial and Dying Words of Eugene Aram, Who Was Convicted the 3d of August at York Assizes and Executed the 6th for the Murder of Daniel Clarke, of Knaresborough which he Committed in the Year 1744-5. London: 1759?. V. 72

ARATUS OF SOLI
Ciceronis in Arati Phaenomena Interpretatio. Paris: 1540,. V. 73

ARBER, AGNES
Herbals, Their Origin and Evolution, A Chapter in the History of Botany 1470-1670. Cambridge: 1912. V. 71; 73
Herbals, Their Origin and Evolution, a Chapter in the History of Botany 1470-1670. Cambridge: 1938. V. 70

ARBERRY, A. J.
The Legacy of Persia. Oxford: 1953. V. 72

ARBLAY, FRANCES BURNEY D'
Camilla. London: 1796. V. 73
Camilla. London: 1802. V. 70; 73
Cecilia, or Memoirs of an Heiress. London: 1825. V. 70
Diary and Letters. London: 1842-1846. V. 68
Diary and Letters. London: 1854. V. 69
Diary and Letters. London: 1893. V. 69; 73
Evelina. London: 1783. V. 69
Evelina. London: 1874?. V. 68; 69
Evelina. London: 1893. V. 69
Evelina. London: 1968. V. 72
The Novels. London: 1893-1894. V. 68

ARBOGAST, L. F. A.
Du Calcul des Derivations. Strasbourg: 1800. V. 72

ARBUCKLE, DOREEN MENZIES
The North West Miramichi. 1978. V. 73

ARBUTHNOT, J.
Natural History of Those Fishes That Are Indigenous To, Or Occasionally Frequent The Coasts Of Buchan. Aberdeen: 1815. V. 72

ARBUTHNOT, JOHN
An Essay Concerning the Nature of Ailments, and the Choice of Them.... London: 1732. V. 70
An Essay Concerning the Nature of Aliments.... London: 1735-1736. V. 71
A Sermon Preach'd to the People, at the Mercat-Cross of Edinburgh; on the Subject of the Union. London: 1707. V. 72

ARCANA of Science and Art; or an Annual Register of Useful Inventions and Improvements.... 1834. V. 71

ARCH, JOSEPH
Joseph Arch: the Story of His Life Told by Himself. London: 1898. V. 71

ARCHAEOLOGICAL INSTITUTE OF AMERICA
Papers of the Archaeological Institute of America - American Series IV Final Report of Investigations Among the Indians of the Southwestern United States, Carried On Mainly in the Years 1880 to 1885 Part II. Cambridge: 1892. V. 69

ARCHAEOLOGICAL INSTITUTE OF GREAT BRITAIN AND IRELAND
Memoirs, Chiefly Illustrative of the History and Antiquities of the County and City of Oxford. 1854. V. 72

ARCHBOLD, R.
New Guinea Expedition. Fly River Area 1936-1937. New York: 1940. V. 69

ARCHDALE, JOHN
A New Description of that Fertile and Pleasant Province of Carolina...(with) Notices of the Early History of South Carolina. Charleston: 1822. V. 68

ARCHER, CHRISTON I.
The Army in Bourbon Mexico 1760-1810. Albuquerque: 1977. V. 71

ARCHER, G.
The Birds of British Somaliland and the Gulf of Aden.... London and Edinburgh: 1937-1961. V. 73

ARCHER, JEAN C.
The Adventures of Samuel Selina. London: 1902. V. 72

ARCHER, JEFFREY
Not a Penny More, Not a Penny Less. London: 1976. V. 69; 71

ARCHER, JOHN WYKEHAM
Vestiges of Old London. London: 1851. V. 71

ARCHER, M.
The Kangaroo. McMahons Point: 1985. V. 70
William Hedley, the Inventor of Railway Locomotion on the Present Principle. Newcastle-upon-Tyne: 1882. V. 68

ARCHER, S.
Gerry Anderson: the Authorised Biography. 1996. V. 72

ARCHER, THOMAS
Charles Dickens: a Gossip About His Life, Works and Characters, with Eighteen Full Page Character Sketches.... London: 1894?. V. 70; 73
William Ewart Gladstone and His Contemporaries. London: 1883. V. 71
William Ewart Gladstone and His Contemporaries. London: 1898. V. 70; 71; 72

ARCHER, WILLIAM
The Fashionable Tragedian. London: 1877. V. 71
Henry Irving, Actor and Manager, A Critical Study. London: 1883. V. 72

THE ARCHER'S Complete Guide. New York: 1878. V. 69

ARCHIBALD, E. H. H.
The Wooden Fighting Ship in the Royal Navy, AD 897-1860. London: 1968. V. 70

ARCHIMEDES
Opera. Paris: 1615. V. 73

THE ARCHITECT & Engineer of California, Pacific Coast States. San Francisco: 1911. V. 68

ARCHITECTURAL & ARCHAEOLOGICAL SOCIETY OF DURHAM &...
Transactions. Volume II. 1869-1879. Durham: 1883. V. 71

ARCHITECTURAL LEAGUE OF NEW YORK
Fourteenth Annual Exhibition. New York: 1899. V. 72

ARCHITECTURAL Terra Cotta: Standard Construction. New York: 1914. V. 71

THE ARCHITECTURE and Landscape Gardening of the Exposition; a Pictorial Survey of the Most Beautiful of Architectural Compositions of the Panama Pacific International Exposition...San Francisco. San Francisco: 1915. V. 72

THE ARCHITECTURE and the Gardens of the San Diego Expedition, a Pictorial Survey.... San Francisco: 1916. V. 68

ARCO, GIOVANNI BATTISTA GHERARDO D'
Della Influenza Del Gehtto Nello Stato. Venice: 1782. V. 72

ARCTIC Bilbiography. Washington: 1953-1957. V. 73

ARDENER, EDWIN
Plantation and Village in The Cameroons. London: 1960. V. 72

ARDITO, STEPANO
Peaks of Glory. London: 1993. V. 69

ARDIZZONE, EDWARD
From Edward Ardizzone's Indian Diary. London: 1983. V. 68
Lucy Brown and Mr. Grimes. London: 1970. V. 68
Nicholas and the Fast Moving Diesel. London: 1947. V. 71
Paul the Hero of the Fire. 1948. V. 68
Peter the Wanderer. London: 1963. V. 72
Ship's Cook Ginger. London: 1977. V. 68
Tim and Ginger. New York: 1965. V. 72
Tim and Lucy Go to Sea. London: 1938. V. 70
Tim to the Lighthouse. 1968. V. 73
The Young Ardizzone - an Autobiographical Fragment. New York: 1970. V. 72

ARDLEY, PATRICIA B.
The Adventures of Mr. Horace Hedgehog. London: 1935. V. 70
Mr. and Mrs. Hedgehog. London: 1936. V. 70

ARENA, JAY M.
Davison of Duke, His Reminiscences. Durham: 1986. V. 70

ARENAS, REINALDO
Hallucinations. New York: 1971. V. 68; 71

ARENSBERG, CONRAD M.
Family and Community in Ireland. 1940. V. 71

ARETINO, LEONARDO BRUNI
Libro Della Prima Gverra Delli Carthaginesi Con Li Romani. Firenze: 1526. V. 73

ARGENS, JEAN BAPTISTE DE BOYER, MARQUIS D'
The Jewish Spy.... London: 1766-1765. V. 68
Lettres Chinoises ou Correspondence Philosophique, Historique & Critique.... La Haye: 1766. V. 72
Lettres Juives ou Correspondence Philosophique, Historique & Critique, Entre un Juif Voiageur en Differens Etats de l'Europe.... La Haye: 1738. V. 72
New Memoirs Establishing a True Knolwege of Mankind, by Discovering the Affections of the Heart.... London: 1747. V. 72

ARGENTI, NICHOLAS
The Postage Stamps of New Brunswick and Nova Scotia. London: 1962. V. 73

ARGUS, M. K.
Moscow-on-the-Hudson. New York: 1951. V. 72

ARGYLL, DUKE OF
Scotland As It Was and As It Is. New York: 1887. V. 72

ARIOSTO, LODOVICO
Orlando Furioso. Venice: 1556. V. 72
Orlando Furioso. London: 1785. V. 70
Orlando Furioso. Paris: 1786. V. 73

ARIS, ERNEST
A Bad Little Bear. London: 1910. V. 70; 73
Dollikin Dutch and How She Helped Piet and Nella. London: 1909. V. 68

ARISTOPHANES
The Birds. London: 1824. V. 72
Comedies Grecques d'Aristophane.... Paris: 1692. V. 68
(Greek title) Comoediae Undeci(m). Graece & Latine.... Leyden: 1625. V. 73
The Ecclesiazusae or Female Parliament. Oxford: 1833. V. 69; 73
The Frogs. 1937. V. 73

ARISTOTELES
Aristotelous Peri Psyche (Greek). Aristotle on the Vital Principle. Cambridge: 1855. V. 68
De Arte Rhetorica Libri Tres Graece et Latine.... Helmstadt: 1672. V. 73

ARISTOTELES continued
De Historia Animalium. Libri IX. De Partibus Animalium & Earum Causis. Libri III. De Generatione Animalium, Libri V. De Communi Animalium, Gressu, Liber I. De Communi Animalium Motu, Libri I. Paris: 1553. V. 68
Historia Animalium. Oxford: 1910. V. 68
In Hoc Volumine...De Historia Animalium. Libri IX: De Partibus Animalium & Earum Causis Libri III; De Generatione Animalium, Libri V: De Colmmuni Animalium, Gressu Liber I. De Communi Animalium Motu, Libri I. Paris: 1533. V. 72
Opera Omnia Quae Extant Graece & Latine. Paris: 1619. V. 73
Poetics and Rhetoric in Rhetores in Hoc Volumine Habentur Hi... (Greek). Venice: 1509. V. 73
Politics and Poetics. Lunenberg: 1964. V. 68
La Rhetorique d'Aristote en Francois. Lyon: 1691. V. 69
S. Thomae Aquinatis Praeclarissima Commentari in Libros Aristotelis Peri Hermenias.... Venice: 1562. V. 73
A Treatise on Government. London: 1778. V. 72
(Works in Greek). Volume I. 1495. V. 73

ARISTOTLE, PSEUD.
Aristotle's Complete Master Piece: in Three Parts: Displaying the Secrets of Nature in the Generation of Man.... Worcester: 1795. V. 72
The Works of Aristotle, the Famous Philosopher in Four Parts. New England: 1813. V. 68
The Works of Aristotle, the Famous Philosopher in Four Parts. New England: 1821. V. 68; 69; 71; 73
The Works of Aristotle, the Famous Philosopher. New England: 1831. V. 69

ARIZONA: a State Guide. New York: 1940. V. 69

ARIZONA
Report of the Governor of Arizona...1900. Washington: 1901. V. 71

ARKWRIGHT, RICHARD
The Trial of a Cause Instituted by Richard Peper Arden, Esq. His Majesty's Attorney General, by Writ of Scire Facia, to Repeal a Patent Granted the Sixteenth of December 1775 to Mr. Richard Arkwright for an Invention of Certain Instruments.... London: 1785. V. 70; 73

ARKWRIGHT, WILLIAM
Utinam: a Glimmering of Goddesses. London: 1917. V. 70; 73

ARLDT, C. W.
Ansichten aus dem Park zu Muskau.... Dresden: 1840. V. 70

ARLEN, MICHAEL
The Green Hat. London: 1924. V. 69
Lily Christine: a Romance. Garden City: 1928. V. 71
A Young Man Comes to London. London: 1932. V. 69; 71

ARLINGTON, L. C.
The Chinese Drama from the Earliest Times Until To-Day.... Shanghai: 1930. V. 71

ARLOTT, JOHN
Clausentum. London: 1946. V. 71

ARMAN, MARK
A Diary of Engravings and Linocuts. 1986. V. 71
Fleurons: Their Place in History and Print. 1988. V. 71
Letterpress, Printers' Types and Decorations. Thaxted, Essex: 1993. V. 70

ARMANI, GEORGIO
Marrakech. Milano: 1992. V. 69

ARMBRUSTER, EUGENE L.
The Eastern District of Brooklyn. New York: 1912. V. 68

ARMER, LAURA ADAMS
Dark Circles of Branches. New York: 1933. V. 69
Southwest. New York: 1935. V. 69
The Trader's Children. New York: 1937. V. 69
Waterless Mountain. New York: 1931. V. 69

ARMES, ETHEL
Stratford Hall: the Great House of the Lees. Richmond: 1936. V. 68; 73
Stratford on the Potomac. Greenwich: 1928. V. 72

ARMES, GEORGE
Ups and Downs of An Army Officer. Washington, DC: 1900. V. 72

ARMFIELD, CONSTANCE
Sylvia's Travels. London: 1911. V. 68

ARMITAGE, ETHEL
A Country Garden. London: 1936. V. 70

ARMITAGE, EVELYN N.
The Quaker Poets of Great Britain and Ireland. 1896. V. 69

ARMITAGE, MERLE
Igor Stravinsky. New York: 1949. V. 72
Operations Santa Fe. New York: 1948. V. 73
Pagans Conquistadores Heros and Martyrs. Fresno: 1960. V. 71
Stella Dysart of Ambrosia Lake. New York: 1959. V. 73

ARMITAGE, SIMON
The Walking Horses. Nottingham: 1988. V. 73

ARMITT, MARY L.
Rydal. Kendal: 1916. V. 71

ARMOUR, ALEXANDER WILLIAM
Notables and Autographs. New York: 1939. V. 69

ARMOUR, G. D.
Bridle and Brush. London: 1937. V. 72
Pastime with Good Company. 1914. V. 70

ARMOUR, J. OGDEN
The Packers: the Private Car Lines and the People. Philadelphia: 1906. V. 68

ARMOUR, MARGARET
The Eerie Book. London: 1898. V. 73

ARMSTRONG, A. M.
The Place-Names of Cumberland. Cambridge: 1950-1952. V. 71
The Place-Names of Cumberland. Cambridge: 1971. V. 71

ARMSTRONG, AMZI
A Syllabus of Lectures on the Visions of the Revelation.... Morris Town: 1815. V. 69

ARMSTRONG, ANTHONY
The Secret Trail. 1929. V. 73

ARMSTRONG, CHARLOTTE
The Albatross. New York: 1957. V. 69

ARMSTRONG, EDWARD A.
Birds of the Grey Wind. 1940. V. 69

ARMSTRONG, F. CLAUDIUS
The Queen of the Seas. London: 1878. V. 68

ARMSTRONG, J. B.
Developmental Biology of the Axolotl. New York: 1989. V. 72

ARMSTRONG, J. H.
A Trip To The Land of The Pharaohs. Newcastle-upon-Tyne: 1890. V. 72

ARMSTRONG, JAMES
Carolina Light Infantry's Record in the Great War: the Story of a Gallant Company.... Charleston: 1912. V. 69; 70
Life of a Woman Pioneer, as Illustrated in the Life of Elsie Strawn Armstrong 1789-1871. Chicago: 1931. V. 70

ARMSTRONG, JOHN
Miscellanies. London: 1770. V. 68; 69
Practical Illustrations of the Scarlet Fever, Measles, Pulmonary Consumption and Chronic Diseases, with Remarks on Sulphureous Waters &c. London: 1818. V. 71
Practical Illustrations of Typhus and Other Fevers; of Pulmonary Consumption, Measles.... Boston: 1829. V. 69
The Art of Preserving Health: a Poem. London: 1744. V. 70; 71; 72; 73
Of Benevolence; an Epistle to Eumenes. London: 1751. V. 68
The Poetical Works.... Perth: 1792. V. 73
The Poetical Works.... Edinburgh: 1858. V. 72

ARMSTRONG, LOUIS
Louis Armstrong's Own Original Tunes. Swing Song Folio. New York: 1938. V. 72
Satchmo. My Life in New Orleans. Englewood Cliffs: 1954. V. 68
Satchmo. My Life in New Orleans. Englewood Cliffs: 1955. V. 73
Swing that Music. New York: 1936. V. 69; 71; 72

ARMSTRONG, MARTIN
The Romantic Adventures of Mr. Darby and of His Wife Sarah. London: 1931. V. 71
Saint Christopher's Day. London: 1928. V. 73

ARMSTRONG, MAURICE W.
The Great Awakening in Nova Scotia 1776-1809. Hartford: 1948. V. 72

ARMSTRONG, MOSES K.
The Early Empire Builders of the Great West. St. Paul: 1901. V. 73

ARMSTRONG, N.
After Big Game in the Upper Yukon. 1995. V. 69; 70; 72

ARMSTRONG, NEIL
First on the Moon. Boston: 1970. V. 69

ARMSTRONG, PERRY A.
The Sauks and The Black Hawk War with Biographical Sketches Etc. Slringfield (sic): 1887. V. 70

ARMSTRONG, R.
A Practical Essay on Steam Engine Boilers.... Manchester: 1838. V. 71

ARMSTRONG, W. G.
A Record of the Opera in Philadelphia. Philadelphia: 1884. V. 71
Sir W. G. Armstrong and Co. and Mr. J. Scott Russell. Correspondence and Documents Submitted to, with Minutes of Evidence Taken Before the Council of the Institution of Civil Engineers. London: 1867. V. 73
A Visit to Egypt in 1872. Newcastle: 1874. V. 68

ARMSTRONG, WALTER
Fine Art at the Royal Jubilee Exhibition. Manchester: 1887. V. 71
Sir Henry Raeburn. London: 1901. V. 71; 72

ARMSTRONG, WILLIAM CLINTON
The Axfords of Oxford, New Jersey: a Genealogy Beginning in 1725. Morrison: 1931. V. 69

ARMSTRONG, WILLIAM H.
Sounder. New York: 1969. V. 71

AN ARMY Doctor's Wife On The Frontier Letters From Alaska and The Far West 1874-1876. Pittsburg: 1962. V. 72

ARMYTAGE, EDITH B.
The Parish Register of Hartshead, in the County of York, 1612-1812. London: 1903. V. 73

ARNASON, H. H.
Robert Motherwell. New York: 1982. V. 69; 72

ARNAUD, GEORGES
The Wages of Fear. London: 1952. V. 71

ARNDT, JOHN STOVER
The Story of the Arndts. The Life, Antecedents and Descendants of Bernhard Arndt who Emigrated to Pennsylvania in the Year 1731. Philadelphia: 1922. V. 69

ARNETT, R. H.
American Insects: A Handbook of Insects of America North of Mexico. New York: 1985. V. 69

ARNO, PETER
Peter Arno's Parade. 1929. V. 73

ARNOLD & SONS
A Catalogue of Scientific Instruments. London: 1879. V. 71

ARNOLD, A. C. L.
The Living World.... Boston: 1868. V. 70

ARNOLD, B. W.
Jamaican Fossil Echini.... Cambridge: 1927. V. 68; 71

ARNOLD, E. C.
British Waders. Cambridge: 1924. V. 73

ARNOLD, EDWIN
The Chaurapanchasika, an Indian Love Lament. London: 1896. V. 68
Death - and Afterwards. London: 1887. V. 68
The Feast of Belshazzar. A Prize Poem Recited in the Theatre, Oxford June XXIII. MDCCCLII. Oxford: 1852. V. 73
The Light of Asia. London: 1879. V. 73
The Light of Asia. London: 1926. V. 68
Poems Narrative and Lyrical. Oxford: 1853. V. 73
Seas and Lands. London: 1891. V. 72

ARNOLD, ELLIOTT
Blood Brother. New York: 1947. V. 72

ARNOLD, EVE
In China. New York: 1980. V. 68
Marilyn Monroe, an Appreciation. New York: 1987. V. 73

ARNOLD, F. H.
Flora of Sussex. 1887. V. 69

ARNOLD, H. H.
Global Mission. New York: 1949. V. 70

ARNOLD, HERBERT
The Popular Guide to House Painting, Decoration, Varnishing, WhiteWashing, Colour Mixing.... Manchester & London: 1905. V. 68

ARNOLD, JOHN
What Happened at Andals?. New York: 1930. V. 72

ARNOLD, LLOYD
Hemingway, High on the Wild. Papa's Late Years, Revealed by a Friend. 1977. V. 71

ARNOLD, M. E.
The Painted Window. London: 1856. V. 68; 72

ARNOLD, MARY ELLICOTT
The Story of Tompkinsville. New York: 1940. V. 71

ARNOLD, MATTHEW
Cromwell: a Prize Poem. Oxford: 1843. V. 73
Empedocles on Etna, and Other Poems. 1852. V. 73
The Forsaken Merman. London: 1900. V. 73
A French Eton; or, Middle Class Education and the State. London: 1864. V. 68
A French Eton, or Middle-Class Education and the State. New York: 1892. V. 68
Friendship's Garland; Being the Conversations, Letters and Opinions of the Late Arminius, Baron Von Thunder-Ten-Tronckh. London: 1871. V. 73
Merope. London: 1858. V. 68; 72; 73
New Poems. London: 1867. V. 73
New Poems. London: 1868. V. 73
Poems. London: 1853. V. 73
Poems. London: 1854. V. 73
Poems. London: 1857. V. 73
Poems. London: 1869. V. 73
Poems. London: 1877. V. 73
Poems. London: 1888-1890. V. 73
Poems. Second Series. London: 1855. V. 73
Selected Poems of Matthew Arnold. London: 1902. V. 68
The Strayed Reveller and Other Poems. 1849. V. 72; 73
The Strayed Reveller and Other Poems. London: 1849. V. 68
The Twice-Revised Code. London: 1862. V. 73

ARNOLD, OREN
Hot Irons, Heraldry of the Range. New York: 1940. V. 68; 69; 71

ARNOLD, RICHARD
The Customs of London, Otherwise called Arnold's Chronicle.... London: 1811. V. 68; 71

ARNOLD, ROBERT
The Dismal Swamp and Lake Drummond: Early Recollections. Norfolk: 1888. V. 68

ARNOLD, STEVEN
Epiphanies. Pasadena: 1987. V. 68

ARNOLD, THOMAS JACKSON
Early Life and Letters of Thomas J. Jackson. New York: 1916. V. 69; 70

ARNOLD, THOMAS JAMES
Reynard the Fox. After the German Version of Goethe. London: 1855. V. 71

ARNOLD, THOMAS W.
Painting in Islam. Oxford: 1928. V. 72; 73

ARNOLD, W. E.
Summer in the Winter Time. Savannah: 1891-1892. V. 70

ARNOLD, W. H.
Ventures in Book-Collecting. New York: 1923. V. 68

ARNOLD, WALTER
The Life and Death of the Sublime Society of Beef Steaks. London: 1871. V. 68

ARNOLDI, M. J.
Crowning Achievements. African Arts of Dressing the Head. Los Angeles: 1995. V. 69

ARNOLDUS DE VILLA NOVA
De Somniorum Interpretations and De Mutatione Aeris. Toulouse: 1485. V. 73

ARNOT, ALLEN
The Dempsey Diamonds. London: 1912. V. 70

ARNOT, DAVID
The Land Question of Griqualand West: Into Various Claims to Land in that Territory; Together with a Brief History of the Griqua Nation. Cape Town: 1875. V. 68

ARNOT, FRED S.
Garenganze. London: 1889. V. 72

ARNOT, HUGO
The History of Edinburgh, from the Earliest Accounts to the Present Time. Edinburgh: 1788. V. 69

ARNOULD, JOSEPH
Memoir of Thomas, First Lord Denman Formerly Lord Chief Justice of England. London: 1873. V. 73

ARNOW, HARRIETTE
The Dollmaker. New York: 1954. V. 72
Flowering of the Cumberland. & Seedtime on the Cumberland. New York: 1963-1960. V. 73
Mountain Path. New York: 1936. V. 70

ARP, JEAN
On My Way - Poetry and Essays 1912-1947. New York: 1948. V. 71

ARRIGHI, LUDOVICO DEGLI
The Calligraphic Models of Ludovico Degli Arrighi, Surnamed Vincentino: a Complete Facsimile. Paris: 1926. V. 71

ARRINGTON, LEONARD J.
History of Idaho. 1994. V. 68

ARROW, JOHN
J. C. Squire v. D. H. Lawrence - a Reply to Mr. Squire's article in Thhe Observer of March 9th, 1930. London: 1930. V. 68; 72

ARROW, SIMON
Count Fanny's Nuptials: Being the Story of a Courtship. 1907. V. 73

ARROWSMITH, JAMES
The Paper-Hanger's Companion: a Treatise on Paper Hanging.... Philadelphia: 1852. V. 69

ARSENAULT, BONA
Histoire et Genealogie des Acadiens. Ottawa: 1978. V. 72

ARSENIO, P. F.
Antilogiae Sive Contradictiones Apparenes Sacrae Scripturae.... Montibus: 1744?. V. 69

THE ART Album. London: 1861. V. 71; 72

ART De La Verrerie. Paris: 1752. V. 70

THE ART Journal: The Illustrated Catalogue of the (Paris) Universal Exhibition Published with the Journal. London: 1868. V. 70

THE ART of Drawing and Painting in Water-Colours. London: 1731. V. 69; 72

THE ART of Drawing in Perspective.... 1777. V. 71
THE ART of Drawing in Perspective.... London: 1786. V. 71

THE ART of Drawing in Perspective...(with) The Art of Drawing, and Painting in Water-Colours. London: 1757. V. 71

THE ART of Healing and Health Care in India: Twelve Miniatures. 1980. V. 72

THE ART of Preserving the Feet.... London: 1818. V. 68; 69; 72

THE ART of Puffing, an Inaugural Oration. Edinburgh: 1765. V. 73

L'ART Revue Hebdomadaire Illustree. Premiere Annee. Paris: 1875. V. 68

ART Work of Lake Superior Region of Michigan. Oshkosh: 1898. V. 68

ART WORKERS GUILD
Sketches Made on the Lithography Night 14th April 1905 by Members of the Art Worker's Guild, Clifford's Inn Hall. London: 1905. V. 72

ARTAUD, ANTONIN
The Theater and Its Double. New York: 1958. V. 72

ARTHAUD, C.
Enchanted Visions: Fantastic Houses and Their Treasures. New York: 1972. V. 69
Homes of the Great. Paris: 1967. V. 69

ARTHUR, GEORGE C.
A True History of Bill Wilson, Bushwacker - a Story of Missouri's Most Famous Desperado. Rolla: 1938. V. 69

ARTHUR, JOHN PRESTON
Western North Carolina. Asheville: 1914. V. 71

ARTHUR, RICHARD
Odysseus and Calypso. Paris: 1902. V. 70

ARTHUR, TIMOTHY SHAY
Confessions of a Housekeeper. Philadelphia: 1851. V. 69
Trials and Confessions of a Housekeeper. London: 1875. V. 68

ARTHUR, WILLIAM
Italy in Transition: Public Scenes and Private Opinions in the Spring of 1860.... London: 1860. V. 71

ARTINGSTALL & HIND
Catalogue of an Important Collection of Over 3000 Orchids, Formed by the Late Mr. George Toll. Manchester: 1884. V. 69

THE ARTIST'S Assistant; or, School of Science. London: 1807. V. 71

ARTS, P. L. W.
Japanese Porcelain. Lochem: 1983. V. 72

ARTS Revealed, and Universal Guide.... New York: 1853. V. 73

ART TREASURES EXHIBITION, 1857. MANCHESTER
The Art-Treasures Examiner: a Pictorial, Critical and Historical Record of the Art-Treasures Exhibition at Manchester in 1857. Manchester: 1857. V. 71
A Handbook to the Gallery of British Paintings in the Art Treasures Exhibition. London: 1857. V. 71
Photographs of the Gems of the Art Treasures Exhibiton. Manchester: 1858. V. 71

ARTUS, WILIBALD
Hand-Atlas Sammtlicher Medicinisch-Pharmaceutischer Gewachse oder Naturgetreue Abbildungen.... Jena: 1876. V. 70

ARTZYBASHEFF, BORIS
Poor Shaydullah. New York: 1931. V. 73

ARVADA CENTER FOUNDATION
Black Hills, White Sky - Photographs From Collection of Arvada Center Foundation. New York: 1978. V. 72

ARYTON, MICHAEL
The Minotaur. London: 1970. V. 71

ASAHINA, S.
A List of the Odonata from Thailand. Bangkok: 1993. V. 69

ASAHINA, Y.
Chemistry of Lichen Substances. Tokyo: 1954. V. 72

ASBJORNSEN, PETER CHRISTEN
East of the Sun and West of the Moon. New York. V. 73
East of the Sun and West of the Moon. London: 1914. V. 73
East of the Sun and West of the Moon. 1991. V. 72

ASBURY, S. E.
The Texas Nativist. College Station: 1914-1915. V. 68

ASCH, OSCAR
Chu Chin Chow: a Musical Tale of the East. New York: 1917. V. 71

ASCHAM, ROGER
The Schoolemaster. London: 1570. V. 73
The Schoolemaster. London: 1589. V. 70; 73
The English Works of Roger Ascham.... London: 1767. V. 68

ASCHER, KARL W.
The Aqueous Veins. Biomicroscopic Study of the Aqueous Humor Elimination. Springfield, IL: 1961. V. 72

ASH, CHARLES BOWKER
The Poetical Works. London: 1831. V. 69

ASH, EDWARD C.
Dogs, Their History and Development. 1927. V. 70

ASH, JAMES
The Art of Double Counting on the Lathe.... 1881. V. 71

ASH, JOHN
The New and Complete Dictionary of the English Language. London: 1775. V. 69

ASH, LEE
Serial Publications Containing Medical Classics. New Haven: 1961. V. 71

ASHBEE, CHARLES ROBERT
American Sheaves and English Seed. 1901. V. 70
Conradin: a Philosophical Ballad. 1908. V. 70
From Whitechapel to Camelot. London: 1892. V. 70
The Masque of the Edwards: Being a Coronation Pageant to Celebrate the Crowning of the King. London: 1902. V. 69
Where the Great City Stands; a Study in the New Civics. London: 1917. V. 73

ASHBEE, EDMUND W.
The Interlude of Jacke Jugeler, printed by Wm. Copland. London. V. 71

ASHBEE, HENRY SPENCER
Forbidden Books of the Victorians. London: 1970. V. 70

ASHBERY, JOHN
As We Know - Poems. New York: 1979. V. 72
Coventry. New York: 1993. V. 73
Hotel Lautreamont. New York: 1991. V. 73
A Nest of Ninnies. New York: 1969. V. 69; 72
Novel. New York: 1998. V. 69
Selected Poems. 1985. V. 69
Self-Portrait In A Convex Mirror. New York: 1975. V. 68; 72
Some Trees. New Haven: 1956. V. 72
Three Poems. New York: 1972. V. 72
Turandot And Other Poems. New York: 1953. V. 72
The Vermont Notebook. Los Angeles: 1975. V. 69
Who Knows What Constitutes a Life. Calais: 1999. V. 69; 73

ASHBROOK, H.
The Baby in the Ash Can. New York: 1944. V. 68
The Murder of Steven Kester. New York: 1931. V. 71

ASHBURN, JESSE A.
History of the Fisher's River Primitive Baptist Association from Its Organization in 1832 to 1904. Laurel Fork: 1905. V. 72

ASHBURN, P. M.
A History of the Medical Department of the United States Army. Boston: 1929. V. 72

ASHBURNHAM, JOHN
Narrative by...of His Attendance on King Charles the First...Never Before Printed. London: 1830. V. 69

ASHBY and White; or, the Great Question, Whether an Action Lies at Common Law for an Elector, Who is Deny'd His Vote for Members of Parliament? Debated and Resolv'd.... London: 1705. V. 70; 72

ASHBY, R. C.
Death on Tiptoe. London. V. 73
He Arrived at Dusk. 1933. V. 73
Out Went the Taper. 1934. V. 73

ASHBY, THOMAS A.
Life of Turner Ashby. New York: 1914. V. 69; 70
The Valley Campaigns. New York: 1914. V. 69; 70

ASHE, S. W.
The Trial and Death of Henry Wirz with Other Matters Pertaining Thereto. Raleigh: 1908. V. 69

ASHE, SAXON
I Am Saxon Ashe. New York: 1940. V. 70

ASHE, SHOLEM
Mottke the Thief. New York: 1935. V. 70

ASHE, THOMAS
The Spirit of The Book or, Memoirs of Caroline Princess of Hasburgh, a Political and Amatory Romance. London: 1811. V. 73

ASHENHURST, THOMAS R.
Design in Textile Fabric. London: 1885. V. 71

ASHER & Adams' New Statistical and Topographical Atlas of the United States with Maps Showing the Dominion of Canada, Europe and the World. New York: 1872. V. 70

ASHER, MICHAEL
Theisiger. A Biography. London: 1994. V. 70; 72

ASHFORD, DAISY
Daisy Ashford: Her Book. New York: 1920. V. 69
Love and Marriage. London: 1965. V. 72
The Young Visiters. 1919. V. 69
The Young Visiters. New York: 1919. V. 71

ASHFORD, FAITH
Things Unseen - a Book of Verse. Ditchling, Sussex: 1924. V. 72

ASHLEY, JAMES
The Case and Appeal of James Ashley, of Broad Street, London.... London: 1753. V. 73

ASHLEY, JOHN
The Art of Painting On and Annealing in Glass.... London: 1801. V. 69; 73

ASHLEY, LEONARD R.
George Alfred Henty and the Victorian Mind. Bethesda: 1999. V. 73

ASHLEY-COOPER, JOHN
The Great Salmon Rivers of Scotland. An Angler's Guide to the Rivers Dee, Spey, Tay and Tweed. London: 1980. V. 71
A Salmon Fisher's Odyssey. 1982. V. 73

ASHMEAD, W. H.
Classification of the Chalcid Flies or the Superfamily Chalcidoidea.... Pittsburgh: 1904. V. 70; 72
Harriman Alaska Expedition. Volume 8 Insects. Washington: 1910. V. 69
A Monograph of the North American Proctotrypidae. Washington: 1893. V. 72

ASHMOLE, B.
Architect and Sculptor in Classical Greece. New York: 1972. V. 69; 72

ASHMORE, OWEN
The Industrial Archaeology of Lancashire. Newton Abbot: 1969. V. 73

ASHMUN, JEHUDI
History of the American Colony in Liberia, from December 1821 to 1823. Washington City: 1826. V. 68
The Liberia Farmer; or Colonist's Guide to Independence and Domestic Comfort. Philadelphia: 1835. V. 70

ASHTON, E. H.
Perspectives in Primate Biology.... London: 1981. V. 70

ASHTON, FREDERICK T.
The Theory and Practice of the Art of Designing Fancy Cotton and Woolen Cloths from Sample. Philadelphia: 1874. V. 72

ASHTON, HELEN
Doctor Serocold. London: 1930. V. 69

ASHTON, HERBERT
The Locked Room: a Comedy Mystery in Three Acts. New York: 1934. V. 69

ASHTON, JOHN
A Century of Ballads, Collected, Edited and Illustrated in Facsimile of the Originals. London: 1887. V. 70
Hyde Park from Domesday-Book to Date. London: 1896. V. 71

ASHTON, LEIGH
An Introduction to the Study of Chinese Sculpture. London: 1924. V. 70; 72

ASHTON, R. E.
Rare and Endangered Biota of Florida. Gainesville: 1992. V. 70; 73

ASHTON, THOMAS
Visits to the Museum of the Manchester Natural History Society. Manchester: 1860. V. 69

ASHWORTH, THOMAS
The Salmon Fisheries of England 1868.... London: 1868. V. 68; 72

ASIMOV, ISAAC
Banquets of the Black Widowers. Garden City: 1984. V. 68; 69
Casebook of the Black Widowers. Garden City: 1980. V. 69; 71
The Caves of Steel. New York: 1954. V. 71
The Complete Robot. New York: 1982. V. 69
The Death Dealers. New York: 1958. V. 69
Foundation. 1951. V. 68
Foundation. New York: 1951. V. 70
Foundation and Empire. 1952. V. 68; 69
How Did We Find Out About the Beginning of Life?. New York: 1982. V. 73
The Kingdom of the Sun. New York: 1960. V. 69
More Tales of the Black Widowers. Garden City: 1976. V. 69; 72
Murder at the ABA. New York: 1976. V. 68; 69
Pebble in the Sky. Garden City: 1950. V. 69
Pebble in the Sky. New York: 1990. V. 70
Prelude to Foundation. 1988. V. 70
The Relativity of Wrong. New York: 1988. V. 73
Robots and Empire. 1985. V. 70
Robots and Empire. New York: 1985. V. 69
Robots of Dawn. 1983. V. 70
The Robots of Dawn. New York: 1983. V. 69
Second Foundation. 1953. V. 68
Tales of the Black Widowers. New York: 1974. V. 69
The Union Club Mysteries. New York: 1983. V. 69
A Whiff of Death. New York: 1968. V. 69

ASKEW, ANTHONY
Bibliotheca Askewviana, Sive Catalogus Librorum Rarissimorum Antonii Askew. London: 1773. V. 70; 72

ASKEW, MISS
A Review of the Reigns of George II & II. Berwick: 1792. V. 73

ASKIN, JOHN
The John Askin Papers (1747-1820). Detroit: 1928-1931. V. 69

ASKINS, C.
Asian Jungle African Bush. 1959. V. 70; 72; 73

ASLANAPA, O.
Turkish Art and Architecture. New York: 1971. V. 69; 72

ASMODEUS, DON JUAN, PSEUD.
A Political Lecture on Heads, Alias Blockheads!. London: 1818?. V. 68

ASPIN, J.
Cosmorama: A View of the Costumes and Peculiarities of All Nations. London: 1827. V. 68
Cosmorama: the Manners, Customs and Costumes, of All the Nations of the World.... London: 1834. V. 73

ASQUITH, CYNTHIA
The Flying Carpet. 1925. V. 71

THE ASSASSINATION of Abraham Lincoln...and the Attempted Assassination of William H. Seward.... Washington: 1867. V. 68

ASSAY, KAROL
Gray Head and Long Hair, The Benteen-Custer Relationship. Paris: 1983. V. 72

ASSELINEAU, LEON AUGUSTE
Meubles et Objets Divers du Moyen AGe et de la Renaissance Issues d'Apres Nature et Lithographes par Asselineau. Paris: 1854?. V. 70

THE ASSEMBLY of Birds. Chelmsford: 1815. V. 71

ASSOCIATION FOR THE STUDY OF NEGRO LIFE & HISTORY
Journal of Negro History. Washington: 1916-1929. V. 68

ASTBURY, WILLIAM THOMAS
Fundamentals of Fibre Structure. Oxford: 1933. V. 69

ASTLE, THOMAS
A Catalogue of Manuscripts in the Cottonian Library. London: 1777. V. 69

ASTLEY, JOHN DUGDALE
Fifty Years of My Life. London: 1895. V. 72

ASTLEY, PHILIP
Astley's System of Equestrian Education, Exhibiting the Beauties and Defects of the Horse.... London: 1801. V. 72

ASTLEY, THEA
A Kindness Cup & The Acolyte. New York: 1988. V. 71

ASTRAND, IRMA
Aerobic Work Capacity in Men and Women with Special Reference to Age. Stockholm: 1960. V. 68

ASTRUC, JOHANNES
De Morbis Venereis Libri Novem. Paris: 1740. V. 72

ASTRUP, P.
The History of Blood Gases, Acids and Bases. Munksgaard: 1986. V. 70; 71

ASTURIAS, MIGUEL ANGEL
Mulata de Tal. Buenos Aires: 1963. V. 69
Los Ojos de Los Enterrados. Buenos Aires: 1960. V. 69
Viento Fuerte. Guatemala: 1950. V. 68; 69; 70
Week-End en Guatemala. Buenos Aires: 1956. V. 69

ATALANTA'S Garden: Being the Book of the Edinburgh University Women's Union 1926. Edinburgh: 1926. V. 70

ATCHESON, NATHANIEL
A Letter Addressed to Rowland Burdon, Esq. M.P. on the Present State of the Carrying Part of the Coal Trade. London: 1802. V. 70

ATCHISON, TOPEKA & SANTA FE RAILWAY
The Grand Canyon of Arizona. Santa Fe: 1902. V. 70

ATCHLEY, S. C.
Wild Flowers of Attica. Oxford: 1938. V. 70

ATEN, IRA
Six and One Half Years in the Ranger Service - the Memoirs of... Sergeant, Company D, Texas Rangers. Bankers: 1945. V. 69

ATGET, EUGENE
Atget: Photographs de Paris. New York: 1930. V. 68; 70
A Vision of Paris. New York: 1963. V. 68

ATHEARN, ROBERT
Forts of the Upper Missouri. Englewood Cliffs, NJ: 1967. V. 69; 72
William Tecumseh Sherman and the Settlement of the West. Norman: 1956. V. 68; 72

ATHERTON, FAXON DEAN
The California Diary of...1836-1839. San Francisco: 1964. V. 68

ATHERTON, GERTRUDE
The Conqueror. New York: 1902. V. 69; 72
The Sophisticates. London: 1931. V. 70
What Dreams May Come. Chicago, New York: 1888. V. 70

ATHERTON, NANCY
Aunt Dimity's Death. New York: 1992. V. 68

ATKESON, RAY
The Cascade Range. Portland: 1969. V. 69

ATKEY, BERTRAM
Easy Money. Boston: 1908. V. 69

ATKIN, G. DUCKWORTH
House Scraps.... London: 1887. V. 72

ATKINS, ACE
Crossroad Blues. 1998. V. 70
Crossroad Blues. New York: 1998. V. 73

ATKINS, MARY
The Diary of Mary Atkins. Mills College: 1937. V. 70

ATKINS, SARAH
The India Cabinet Opened; or Natural Curiosities Rendered a Source of Amusement to Young Minds.... London: 1823. V. 68; 70

ATKINSON, BROOKS
This Bright Land. New York: 1972. V. 69

ATKINSON, D. H.
Ralph Thoresby, The Topographer: His Town (Leeds) and Times. Leeds: 1885. V. 72; 73

ATKINSON, F.
Acromegaly. London: 1932. V. 71

ATKINSON, GEORGE
Supplement to the Cabinet-Makers' London Book of Prices, and Designs of Cabinet-Work, Calculated for the Convenience of Cabinet-Makers in General. London: 1805. V. 68
The Worthies Of Westmorland. London: 1849. V. 71; 72

ATKINSON, GEORGE FRANCKLIN
Curry and Rice on Forty Plates. London: 1911. V. 72
Pictures from the North in Pen and Pencil.... London: 1848. V. 73

ATKINSON, J. BEAVINGTON
An Art Tour to Northern Capitals of Europe. London: 1873. V. 68

ATKINSON, J. C.
British Birds' Eggs and Nests. London: 1861. V. 68
Forty Years in a Moorland Parish. London: 1891. V. 69; 73
A Handbook for Ancient Whitby & Its Abbey. 1882. V. 73
Memorials of Old Whitby or Historical Gleanings From Ancient Whitby Records. London: 1894. V. 73
Walks, Talks, Travels and Exploits of Two Schoolboys. London: 1898. V. 73

ATKINSON, KATE
Emotionally Weird. London: 2000. V. 69; 72; 73

ATKINSON, SARAH
St. Fursey's Life and Visions and Other Essays. 1907. V. 69

ATKINSON, SOLOMON
The Effects of the New System of Free Trade Upon Our Shipping, Colonies and Commerce, Exposed in a Letter to the Right Hon. W. Huskisson, President of the Board of Trade. London: 1827. V. 72

ATKINSON, THOMAS WITLAM
Oriental and Western Siberia. London: 1858. V. 72
Oriental and Western Siberia. New York: 1858. V. 69
Travels in the Regions of the Upper and Lower Amoor and Russian Acquisitions on the Confines of India and China. New York: 1860. V. 70; 72

ATKINSON, WILLIAM
Views of Picturesque Cottages with Plans, Selected from a Collection of Drawings Taken in Different Parts of England and Intended as Hints for the Improvement of Village Scenery. London: 1805. V. 68

THE ATLANTIC Souvenir; a Christmas and New Year's Offering...for 1832. Philadelphia: 1832. V. 71

ATLANTIC City and County, New Jersey, Biographically Illustrated. Philadelphia: 1899. V. 69

ATLAS of Bergen County, New Jersey. Reading: 1876. V. 69

ATLAS of Monmouth County, New Jersey.... Lincroft: 1986. V. 71

ATLAY, J. B.
Lord Haliburton. A Memoir of His Public Service. Toronto: 1909. V. 72

ATLEE, BENGE
Black Atlee. New York: 1039. V. 71

ATLEE, YOUNG AND BAINBRIDGE
The Attorney-General Versus Messrs. Atlee, Young and Bainbridge. Proceedings on the Trial of this Information in the Court of Exchequer, by a Special Jury, Before the Right Hon. Lord Abinger, on Saturday and Monday the 16th and 18th of May 1835. Chiswick: 1835. V. 72

ATMORE, CHARLES
A Brief Memoir Of The Life And Death Of Mr. C. Hopper, Who Departed This Life on Friday March 5th 1802, in the 80th Year of His Age. Manchester: 1802. V. 72

ATOMICS for the Millions. New York: 1947. V. 70

ATTAR, FARID AL-DIN
Pendeh-I-Attar. The Counsels of Attar. London: 1809. V. 72

ATTENBOROUGH, DAVID
Journeys to The Past. Guildford: 1981. V. 72

ATTERBURY, FRANCIS
An Account and Defence of the Protestation Made by the Lower House of Convocation, April 30th, 1707. London: 1707. V. 73
The Rights, Powers and Privileges of an English Convocation, Stated and Vindicated. London: 1700. V. 73

ATTERBURY, P.
Art Deco Patterns: a Source Book. New York: 1990. V. 69; 72

ATTHILL, WILLIAM
Documents Relating to the Foundation and Antiquities of the Collegiate Church of Middleham, in the County of York. London: 1847. V. 73

ATTI Della Coronzazione Fatta in Campidoglio Della Insigne Poetessa D.na Maria Maddalena Morelli Fernandez, Pistoiese.... Parma: 1779. V. 70

ATTICUS BOOKS
The Hombre Invisible. Atticus Books Catalogue 8. San Diego: 1981. V. 71

ATTIRET, JEAN DENISE
A Particular Account of the Emperor of China's Gardens Near Pekin.... London: 1752. V. 68

ATTIWILL, KEN
Thirteen Sailed Home. New York: 1935. V. 69

THE ATTORNEY'S Compleat Pocket-Book: Containing Near Three Hundred and Fifty of Such Choice and Approved Precedents in Law, Equity and Conveyancing, as an Attorney May Have Occasion for, When Absent from His Office.... London: 1741. V. 70

ATTWELL, MABEL LUCIE
Lots of Things. England: 1950. V. 73
Lucie Attwell's ABC 123 Pop-up Book. 1979. V. 72
Lucie Attwell's Rocker Book. London: 1950. V. 73
Peeps Into Picture-Land. London: 1910. V. 71
Twice Once are Two. London: 1905-1910. V. 71

ATWATER, CALEB
An Essay on Education. Cincinnati: 1841. V. 71
Remarks Made on a Tour to Prairie Du Chien: Thence to Washington City in 1829. Columbus: 1831. V. 70; 72

ATWATER, RICHARD
Mr. Popper's Penguins. London: 1939. V. 71

ATWOOD, F. T.
An Account of the Endowed Charities and Benefactions of the Parish of Hammersmith, Showing Their Origin, Progress, Present Amount of Funds and Mode of Distribution. Hammersmith: 1856. V. 72

ATWOOD, MARGARET
Alias Grace. London: 1996. V. 68
Alias Grace. Toronto: 1996. V. 69; 70
The Blind Assassin. London: 2000. V. 68; 70
The Blind Assassin. New York: 2000. V. 72
The Blind Assassin. Toronto: 2000. V. 69
Bluebeard's Egg. Toronto;: 1983. V. 69
Dancing Girls & Other Stories. Toronto: 1977. V. 69; 71
The Edible Woman. Boston: 1969. V. 73
The Edible Woman. London: 1969. V. 70
Encounters with the Element Man. Concord: 1982. V. 70
The Handmaid's Tale. Toronto: 1985. V. 70
The Handmaid's Tale. Boston: 1986. V. 69; 72
The Handmaid's Tale. London: 1986. V. 68
Hurricane Hazel and Other Stories. Helsinki: 1987. V. 70
Lady Oracle. New York: 1976. V. 71
Lady Oracle. Toronto: 1976. V. 72
Life Before Man. Toronto: 1979. V. 69
Power Politics. New York: 1971. V. 69
Power Politics. Toronto: 1971. V. 70
Procedures for the Underground. Boston: 1970. V. 69
The Robber Bride. London: 1993. V. 70
Surfacing. New York: 1972. V. 69; 72; 73
Surfacing. Toronto: 1972. V. 70
Two-Headed Poems. New York: 1978. V. 71
Wilderness Tips. London: 1991. V. 68; 71; 72

ATWOOD, WILLIAM
The Superiority and Direct Dominion of the Imperial Crown of England, Over the Crown and Kingdom of Scotland, and the Divine Right of Succession to both Crowns, Asserted, In Answer to Sir Thomas Craigs Treatises of Homage and Succession. London: 1704. V. 70

AUBERT, ROSEMARY
Free Reign. Bridgehampton: 1997. V. 68; 69
Free Reign. New York: 1997. V. 69

AUBIER, DOMINIQUE
Fiesta in Pampona. London: 1956. V. 71

AUBIGNAC, FRANCOIS HEDELIN, ABBE D'
The Whole Art of the Stage. London: 1684. V. 73

AUBIN, J. HARRIS
Register of the Military Order of the Loyal Legion of the United States. Boston: 1906. V. 68

AUBISSON DE VOISINS, JEAN FRANCOIS D'
Traite de Geognosie, ou Expose des Connaissances Actuelles sur la Constitution Physique et Minerale du Globe Terrestre. Strasbourg: 1819. V. 68

AUBOURN, A. D.
The French Convert; Being a True Relation of the Happy Conversion of a Noble French Lady from the Errors and Superstitions of Popery.... Haverill: 1794. V. 69; 73

AUBREY, JOHN
Brief Lives and Other Selected Writings. London: 1949. V. 68
Miscellanies, upon the Following Subjects. Day Fatality. II. Local Fatality. III. Ostenta. IV. Omens. V. Dreams. VI. Apparitions...XXI Second Sighted Persons. London: 1721. V. 73
Miscellanies Upon Various Subjects. London: 1784. V. 69
Monumenta Britannica. Boston: 1981. V. 72
Three Prose Works: Miscellanies, Remains of Gentilisme and Judaisme and Observations. Sussex: 1972. V. 70

AUBYN, ALAN
A Fellowship of Trinity. London: 1891. V. 68

AUCASSIN ET NICOLETE
Aucassin and Nicolete. London: 1887. V. 68; 71
Aucassin and Nicolete. London: 1897. V. 71
Aucassin and Nicolete. London: 1911. V. 71
Aucassin and Nicolete. London: 1925. V. 68
C'est d'Aucassin et de Nicolete. 1903. V. 73
Of Aucassin and Nicolete - a Translation in Prose and Verse from the Old French Together with Anabel and Amoris. London: 1925. V. 71

AUCHINCLOSS, JOHN
The Sophistry of Both the First and Second Part of Mr. Paine's Age of Reason, or a Rational Vindication of the Holy Scriptures as a Positive Revelation from God. Edinburgh: 1796. V. 70

AUCHINCLOSS, LOUIS
Civil Wars: Three Tales of Old New York. New York: 1999. V. 69; 73
Diary of a Yuppie. Franklin Center: 1986. V. 72
Powers of Attorney. Boston: 1963. V. 68

AUCKLAND, WILLIAM EDEN, BARON
Principles of Penal Law. London: 1775. V. 73

AUDELAY, JOHN
The Poems. A Specimen of the Shropshire Dialect in the Fifteenth Century. Edited by James Orchard Halliwell. London: 1844. V. 71

AUDEN, WYSTAN HUGH
Academic Graffiti (clerihews). London: 1971. V. 73
The Age of Anxiety. New York: 1947. V. 69; 70; 72
Another Time: Poems. New York: 1940. V. 69
A Certain World. A Commonplace Book. 1971. V. 70
City Without Walls. London: 1969. V. 68; 70; 71
Collected Longer Poems. New York: 1969. V. 72
The Double Man. New York: 1941. V. 69; 72
Education Today - and Tomorrow. London: 1939. V. 70
An Elizabethan Song Book - Lute Songs, Madrigals and Rounds. London: 1957. V. 68; 72
The Enchafed Flood. New York: 1950. V. 71; 72
For the Time Being. New York: 1944. V. 69
A Gobble Poem Snatched from the Notebooks of W. H. Auden and Now Believed to Be in the Morgan Library. London: 1967. V. 73
Homage to Clio. London: 1960. V. 73
Homage to Clio. New York: 1960. V. 72
Letters from Iceland. London: 1937. V. 69; 71
Louis MacNiece: a Memorial Address. London: 1963. V. 70
Natural Linguistics. 1970. V. 70
Nones. 1952. V. 68
Nones. London: 1952. V. 70; 71; 73
Norse Poems. London: 1981. V. 69
The Old Man's Road. New York: 1956. V. 69
The Platonic Blow. New York: 1965. V. 71
Poems. London: 1930. V. 68; 69; 70; 73
Poems. Cincinnati: 1964. V. 70
Poems 1928. 1973. V. 70
Poems 1928. Ilkley: 1973. V. 71; 73
The Rake's Progress: Opera in Three Acts. London: 1951. V. 71
Selected Poems. 1938. V. 70
The Shield of Achilles. New York: 1955. V. 69; 71
Some Poems. London: 1940. V. 70
Spain. London: 1937. V. 70; 72
Spain. London: 1940. V. 71
The Table Talk of W. H. Auden. New York: 1989. V. 69; 73
Thank You, Fog. London: 1974. V. 70

AUDSLEY, GEORGE ASHDOWN
The Practical Decorater and Ornamentists for the Use of Architects, Practical Painters, Decorators and Designers.... Glasgow: 1892. V. 69

AUDSLEY, W.
Polychromatic Decoration as Applied to Buildings in the Mediaeval Styles. London: 1882. V. 71

AUDUBON, JOHN JAMES
Audubon and His Journals. London: 1898. V. 72
The Audubon Folio. New York: 1964. V. 72
Audubon's America. Boston: 1940. V. 72
Audubon's Quadrupeds of North America. Secaucus: 1989. V. 69
Audubon's Western Journal 1849-1850. Cleveland: 1906. V. 70
Birds of America. New York: 1985. V. 73
Birds of America. 1997. V. 73
Delineations of American Scenery and Character. New York: 1926. V. 69
John James Audubon: The Watercolors for the Birds of America. New York: 1993. V. 73
Journal...Made During His Trip to New Orleans in 1820-1821. Boston: 1929. V. 68; 72
The Original Water-Color Paintings by John James Audubon for the Birds of America. New York: 1966. V. 68; 70; 73
Original Water-Colour Paintings for the Birds of America. London: 1966. V. 68; 69; 72
The Quadrupeds of North America. New York: 1854. V. 73
Selected Birds of America and Selected Quadrupeds of North America. Kent: 1977. V. 70

AUDUBON, MARIA R.
Audubon and His Journals. New York: 1897. V. 69

AUEL, JEAN M.
The Clan of the Cave Bear. New York: 1980. V. 68; 69; 70; 71; 72; 73
The Valley of Horses. New York: 1982. V. 68; 71

AUENBRUGGER, LEOPOLD
Novelle Methode Pour Reconnaitre les Maladies Internes de la Poitrine par la Percussion de Cette. Paris: 1808. V. 68

AUER, ALOIS
Die Entdeckung des Naturselbstdruckes.... Vienna: 1853. V. 70
Die Entdeckung des Naturselbstdruckes.... Vienna: 1854. V. 70; 72

AUER, LEOPOLD
Violin Playing as I Teach It. New York: 1921. V. 73

AUERBACH, ERNA
Paintings And Sculpture At Hatfield House. London: 1971. V. 72

AUEROLI, PETRUS
Compendium Biblie Totius. Strassburg: 1514. V. 69

AUFFENBERG, W.
The Bengal Monitor. Gainesville: 1994. V. 68

AUGUST, J. A.
A Description of the Hot Springs of Virginia. Bath: 1887. V. 71

AUGUST, JOHN
Troubled Star. Boston: 1939. V. 70; 73

AUGUSTINUS, AURELIUS, SAINT, BP. OF HIPPO
The Confessions. London: 1900. V. 71
The Confessions. Philadelphia: 1900. V. 70
De Civitate Dei Libri XXII. Francof. ac. Hamburgi: 1661. V. 72
De Trinitate. Basel: 1489. V. 69
Explanatio Psalmorum. Venice: 1493. V. 69; 73
Libri XII Confessionum. Coloniae Agrippinae: 1649. V. 72
The Meditations, Soliloqvia and Manvall of the Glorious Doctour S. Augustine. Paris: 1655. V. 70; 71
Opuscula. Venice: 1483. V. 69
A Preciovs Booke of Heavenly Meditations. A Right Christian Treatise Entituled S. Avgvstines Prayers. Saint Avgvstines Manvall: Containing Speciall, and Picked Meditations, and Godly Prayers. London: 1629. V. 73

AULD, T. M.
The Book of Thomas Rhymer. London: 1946. V. 71

AULNOY, MARIE CATHERINE LEJUMEL DE BARNEVILLE, COMTESSE D'
D'Aulnoy's Fairy Tales. Philadelphia: 1923. V. 73
Fairy Tales and Novels. London: 1817. V. 72
Fortunia. New York: 1974. V. 71; 72; 73
Memoirs of the Court of France. London: 1692. V. 69; 73
Memoirs of the Court of France, and City of Paris.... London: 1702. V. 69
Relation du Voyage D'Espagne. La Haye: 1692. V. 72
The White Cat and Other Old French Fairy-Tales. New York: 1928. V. 73

AULT & WYBORG COMPANY OF CANADA
Poster Album of Color Combinations. Toronto: 1942. V. 68

AULT, LENA
Sammy and the Snarlywink. London: 1904. V. 69

AULT, NORMAN
The Rhyme Book. London: 1906. V. 69

AULT, T. M.
The Book of Thomas Rhymer. London: 1946. V. 70

AUNGERVILLE, RICHARD
Philobiblon, a Treatise on the Love of Books. London: 1832. V. 70
The Philobiblon of Richard De Bury. New York: 1945. V. 70

AUNT Friendly's Everlasting Nursery Gift Book. London: 1875. V. 71

AUNT Louisa's London Favourite. London: 1870. V. 73

AUNT Louisa's London Gift Book. London. V. 71; 73

AUNT Louisa's Object ABC. London: 1880. V. 73

AUNT Louisa's Sunday Picture Book. London: 1867. V. 69; 73

AUNT LOUISA
Aunt Louisa's Alphabet. London: 1880. V. 72
Coloured Gift Book. London: 1890. V. 69
The Little Folks' Book of Birds. London: 1900. V. 72
Nursery Fairy Tales. London: 1900. V. 72

AURELIANUS, CAELIUS
Caelius Aurelianus. On Acute Diseases and on Chronic Diseases. Chicago: 1950. V. 70

AURELIUS ANTONINUS, MARCUS, EMPEROR OF ROME
The Commentaries.... London: 1747. V. 70
The Emperor Marcus Antoninus His Conversation with Himself. London: 1701. V. 71
The Emperor Marcus Antoninus His Conversation with Himself. London: 1708. V. 68; 72
The Thoughts. 1909. V. 68; 72

AUREOLI, PETRUS
Compendium Biblie Totius. Strassburg: 1514. V. 73

AUROUSSEAU, MARCEL
Beyond the Pyrenees. New York: 1931. V. 73
Highway Into Spain. New York: 1931. V. 73

AUSCHER, E. S.
A History and Description of French Porcelain. London: 1905. V. 72

AUSLANDER, JOSEPH
Hell in Harness. New York: 1929. V. 70; 72

AUSONIUS, DECIMUS MAGNUS
Opera. Geneva: 1608. V. 73

AUSTEN, JANE
Emma. London: 1816. V. 68
Emma. London: 1851. V. 69
Emma. London: 1892. V. 70
Emma. London: 1897. V. 70
Emma. 1901. V. 73
Emma. New York: 1964. V. 68; 69
Emma. London: 1971. V. 71
Five Letters to Her Niece Fanny Knight. Oxford: 1924. V. 68; 70; 73
Frederic and Elfrida. 1987. V. 73
Frederic and Elfrida. London: 1987. V. 68; 70
Jane Austen's Letters To Her Sister Cassandra And Others. London: 1952. V. 72
Jane Austen's Manuscript Letters in Facsimile. Carbondale and Edwardsville: 1990. V. 68; 70; 73
Jane Austen's Works. London: 1900. V. 73
Lady Susan. 1925. V. 73
Lady Susan. Oxford: 1925. V. 70
The Letters of.. London: 1884. V. 70; 73
Letters to Her Sister Cassandra and Others. London: 1932. V. 68
Letters to Her Sister Cassandra and Others. Oxford: 1932. V. 70
Love and Friendship and Other Early Works. London: 1922. V. 68; 69; 70; 73
Love and Friendship and Other Early Works. New York: 1922. V. 68; 70; 73
Mansfield Park. London: 1814. V. 70; 71
Mansfield Park. London: 1833. V. 68; 70
Mansfield Park. London: 1837. V. 70; 73
Mansfield Park. London: 1853. V. 73
Mansfield Park. London: 1875. V. 68; 73
Mansfield Park. London: 1883. V. 70
Mansfield Park. London: 1892. V. 70
Mansfield Park. London: 1897. V. 70
Northanger Abbey. London: 1870. V. 68
Northanger Abbey. London: 1872. V. 68
Northanger Abbey. London: 1907. V. 73
Northanger Abbey and Persuasion. London: 1851. V. 73
Northanger Abbey and Persuasion. London: 1877. V. 70
Northanger Abbey and Persuasion. London: 1883. V. 70
Northanger Abbey and Persuasion. London: 1897. V. 70
The Novels of.... Boston: 1899-1901. V. 69
The Novels of.... New York: 1906. V. 70
The Novels of.... Oxford: 1923. V. 73
The Novels of.... Oxford: 1926. V. 70
The Novels of.... Oxford: 1943. V. 73
The Novels of.... Oxford: 1946. V. 70
The Novels of.... 1947-1948. V. 73
The Novels. (with) Jane Austen's Letters to Her Sister Cassandra and Others. Oxford: 1923-1932. V. 73
Orgueil et Preventions. (Pride and Prejudice). Bruxelles: 1946. V. 69
Persuasion. Philadelphia: 1832. V. 73
Persuasion. 1946. V. 73
Persuasion. 1977. V. 70
Pride and Prejudice. 1817. V. 68
Pride and Prejudice. 1844. V. 73
Pride and Prejudice. London: 1885. V. 69
Pride and Prejudice. London: 1890. V. 73
Pride and Prejudice. 1940. V. 68
Sanditon. 1925. V. 73
Sanditon. Oxford: 1925. V. 69; 70
Sense and Sensibility. London: 1811. V. 70
Sense and Sensibility. London: 1813,. V. 71
Sense and Sensibility. London: 1833. V. 71
Sense and Sensibility. London: 1849. V. 68
Sense and Sensibility. London: 1853. V. 73
Sense and Sensibility. 1890. V. 73
Sense and Sensibility. London: 1893. V. 70
Sense and Sensibility. London: 1898. V. 70
Sense and Sensibility. 1949. V. 73
Sense and Sensibility. 1957. V. 68; 73
Seven Letters to Frank and Charles Austen. 1992. V. 70
Sir Charles Grandison. London: 1980. V. 70
Three Evening Prayers. San Francisco: 1940. V. 68; 73
Two Chapters of Persuasion. 1926. V. 73
Two Chapters of Persuasion. Oxford: 1926. V. 70
Volume the First: Now First Printed from the Manuscript in the Bodleian Library. Oxford: 1933. V. 68; 70; 73
Volume the Second. 1963. V. 73
Volume the Second. Oxford: 1963. V. 70
Volume the Third. Oxford: 1951. V. 68; 73
The Watsons. London: 1923. V. 68; 70
The Watsons. 1927. V. 73
The Watsons. Oxford: 1927. V. 70
The Works. London: 1898-1900. V. 73
Works. 1905-1909. V. 73
The Works. London: 1996. V. 68

AUSTEN, JOHN
Historical Notes On Old Sheffield Druggists. Sheffield: 1961. V. 72

AUSTEN, N. LAURENCE
Natural History Papers and Memoir Of N. Laurence Austen. In Memoriam. London: 1877. V. 72

AUSTEN-LEIGH, EMMA
Jane Austen and Steventon. 1937. V. 73

AUSTEN-LEIGH, J. E.
Jane Austen, A Memoir. London: 1871. V. 68
A Memoir of Jane Austen. London: 1870. V. 68; 70; 71; 73
A Memoir of Jane Austen. London: 1886. V. 70
A Memoir of Jane Austen, to which is Added Lady Susan and Fragments. 1886. V. 73

AUSTEN-LEIGH, R. A.
Jane Austen and Lyme Regis. London: 1946. V. 73

AUSTER, PAUL
The Art of Hunger. London: 1982. V. 71
The Art of Hunger. Los Angeles: 1992. V. 71; 73
Auggie Wren's Christmas Story. Birmingham: 1992. V. 69
Auggie Wren's Christmas Story. New York: 1992. V. 73
Disappearances. Woodstock, NY: 1988. V. 71
Effigies. 1987. V. 72
Facing the Music. Barrytown: 1980. V. 69
Ghosts. Los Angeles: 1986. V. 68; 69
Hand to Mouth. New York: 1997. V. 71; 72
Leviathan. New York: 1992. V. 71
Lulu on the Bridge. New York: 1998. V. 72
Moon Palace. New York: 1989. V. 68; 69
The Music of Chance. New York: 1990. V. 69
The Music of Chance. London: 1991. V. 72
The New York Trilogy. Los Angeles: 1974. V. 69
The New York Trilogy: City of Glass, Ghosts, The Locked Room. New York: 1985-1986. V. 70
Paul Auster's New York. New York: 1997. V. 68
Timbuktu. London: 1999. V. 73
Unearth. Weston: 1974. V. 72; 73
Wall Writing. Berkeley: 1976. V. 68
Why Write?. Providence: 1996. V. 69; 71

AUSTIN, A. R.
An Angler's Anthology. London: 1930. V. 71

AUSTIN, ALFRED
Albert Victor Duke of Clarence and Avondale, born January 8th 1864, died January 14th 1892. London: 1892. V. 73
A Betrothal, May 3rd, 1893. London: 1893. V. 73
Savonarola. London: 1881. V. 68
The Season: a Satire. London: 1861. V. 73

AUSTIN, CYRIL F.
The Adventures of Benjamin and Christabel. London: 1911. V. 70
Edward Buttoneye and His Adventures. London: 1910. V. 69

AUSTIN, F. BRITTEN
The Road to Glory - a Novel. London: 1935. V. 72

AUSTIN Fire Department, Austin, Texas 1858-1976. Austin: 1976?. V. 69

AUSTIN, FREDERIC L.
Henry Irving in England and America 1838-1884. London: 1884. V. 71

AUSTIN, GABRIEL
The Library of Jean Grolier. A Preliminary Catalogue. New York: 1971. V. 70

AUSTIN, HUGH
The Upside Down Murders. New York: 1937. V. 73

AUSTIN, J. P.
The Blue and the Gray. Atlanta: 1899. V. 69; 70

AUSTIN, JOHN
The Christian Moderator, in Two Parts. London: 1652. V. 71

AUSTIN, JOHN OSBURNE
American Authors' Ancestry. Providence: 1915. V. 68

AUSTIN, MARY
The Basket Woman: A Book of Fanciful Tales for Children. Boston: 1904. V. 69
The Flock. Boston/New York: 1906. V. 69; 70; 71; 73
The Land of Journey's Ending. New York: 1924. V. 68; 69
The Land of Little Rain. Boston/New York: 1903. V. 68; 71
The Land of Little Rain. Boston: 1904. V. 69
The Land of Little Rain. Boston: 1950. V. 68; 70
Lost Borders. New York: 1909. V. 73
Mother of Felipe and Other Early Stories. Los Angeles: 1950. V. 73
One Smoke Stories. Boston: 1934. V. 69; 70
Philip Freneau: the Poet of the Revolution. New York: 1901. V. 69
The Trail Book. Boston: 1918. V. 73

AUSTIN, PAUL BRITTEN
The Wonderful Life and Adventures of Tom Thumb. (First and Second Parts). Stockholm: 1954-1955. V. 70; 73

AUSTIN, RICHARD T.
The Acts of Adonis the Great, King of Bull. London: 1820. V. 71

AUSTIN, SAMUEL
The Columbian Preacher; or a Collection of Original Sermons.... Catskill: 1808. V. 68

AUSTIN, SARAH
The Story Without End. London: 1868. V. 68

AUSTIN, THOMAS GEORGE
The Straw Plaiting and Straw Hat and Bonnet Trade, with a Recent Digest of the Recent Census for the Luton District.... Luton: 1871. V. 71

AUSTIN, WILLIAM
Haec Homo. Wherein the Excellency of the Creation of Women Decribed by Way of an Essaie. London: 1638. V. 73

THE AUSTRALIAN Irrigation Colonies on the River Murray in Victoria and South Australia. London: 1888. V. 72

AUSTRALIAN ABORIGINES' PROTECTION SOCIETY
The Colonial Intelligencer; or, Aborigines' Friend. 1852-1854. 1852-1855. V. 69

AN AUTHENTIC Account of the Conversion and Experience of a Negro. Leeds. V. 70; 73

AN AUTHENTIC Detail of Particulars Relative to the Late Duchess of Kingston (Elizabeth Chudleigh). London: 1788. V. 69

AN AUTHENTIC Narrative of Mr. Kemble's Retirement from the Stage; Including Farewell Address, Criticisms, Poems &c. London: 1817. V. 68

AUTHENTIC Papers from America; Submitted to the Dispassionate Consideration of the Public. London: 1775. V. 73

AN AUTHENTIC Record of the Public Banquet Given to Mr. Charles Dickens at the Freemason's Hall, London, on Saturday, November 2, 1867, Prior to His Departure for the United States. London: 1867. V. 69

AUTHENTICUS
Ireland, in Answer to the Charges Against Them, Contained in the Rt. Hon. Henry Grattan's Speeches Relating to Tithes.... Dublin: 1788. V. 71

AUTHORATIVE Tour Book of California. San Francisco: 1916. V. 68

AUTHORS Take Sides on the Spanish War. 1937. V. 68
AUTHORS Take Sides on the Spanish War. London: 1937. V. 72

AUTOGRAPHS for Freedom. Boston: 1853. V. 71
AUTOGRAPHS for Freedom. Auburn & Rochester: 1854. V. 71

AVALLONE, MIKE
The Case of the Bouncing Betty and The Case of the Violent Virgin. London: 1959. V. 70
The Crazy Mixed-Up Corpse. Greenwich: 1957. V. 72
Meanwhile Back At The Morgue. Greenwich: 1960. V. 72
Missing!. New York: 1969. V. 72

AVANTIERE, SYLVESTER
A Rep For Murder. New York: 1991. V. 72

AVARY, MYRTA LOCKETT
Joel Chandler Harris and His Home. Atlanta: 1913. V. 70

AVEDON, RICHARD
An Autobiography - Richard Avedon. New York: 1993. V. 68
Avedon. Photographs 1947-1977. New York: 1978. V. 70
In the American West. New York: 1985. V. 70; 72; 73
Observations. New York: 1959. V. 73
Portraits. New York: 1976. V. 68

AVELING, JAMES HOBSON
English Midwives: Their History and Prospects. London: 1872. V. 68
English Midwives: Their History and Prospects. London: 1967. V. 68

AVELING, STEPHEN T.
Carpentery and Joinery. London: 1878?. V. 68

AVERILL, ESTHER
Daniel Boone. New York: 1945. V. 69

AVERY, GILES B.
A Juvenile Guide, or Manual of Good Manners. Canterbury: 1844. V. 73

AVERY, GILLIAN
The Elephant War. London: 1960. V. 71
In the Window-Seat. London: 1960. V. 68

AVERY, JANE GREENOUGH
The Old Distillery; or, Hope Archer. Boston: 1865. V. 73

AVERY, MILTON
Milton Avery Paintings 1930-1960. New York and London: 1962. V. 73

AVERY, SAMUEL PUTNAM
Catalogue Raisonnee Works on Bookbinding, Practical and Historical, Examples of Bookbindings of the XVIth to XIXth Centuries. New York: 1903. V. 73

AVIRETT, JAMES B.
The Memoirs of General Turner Ashby and His Compeers. Baltimore: 1867. V. 69; 70

AVRIL, LOUIS, ABBE
Temples Anciens et Modernes ou Observations Historiques et Critiques sur les plus Celebres Monumens d'Architecture Grecque et Gothique. Londres: 1774. V. 68; 70

THE AWAKENING of America's Conscience. Boston: 1927. V. 68

AWDRY, W.
Henry the Green Engine. 1951. V. 72

AXELROD, GEORGE
Blackmailer!. New York: 1952. V. 72
The Seven Year Itch. New York: 1952. V. 73

AXELSON, G. W.
Commy: The Life Story of the Grand Old Roman of Baseball Charles A. Comiskey. Chicago: 1919. V. 69

AXON, WILLIAM E. A.
Echoes of Old Lancashire. London: 1899. V. 73

AXTHELM, PETE
The Kid. New York: 1878. V. 70

AXTIUS, JOHANN CONRAD
Tractatus de Arboribus Coniferis et Pice Conficienda. Jena: 1679. V. 72

AXTON, MAE BOREN
Country Singers As I Know Em. Austin: 1973. V. 72

AYCKBOURN, ALAN
Conversations with Alan Ayckbourn. London: 1981. V. 73
Joking Apart, Just Between Ourselves, Ten Times Table. London: 1979. V. 72
Three Plays. Absurd Person Singular; Absent Friends; Bedroom Farce. London: 1977. V. 72

AYENSU, E. S.
Medicinal Plants of the West Indies. Allgonac: 1981. V. 72

AYER, A. J.
Language, Truth and Logic. London: 1936. V. 70

AYER, EMMA BURBANK
A Motor Flight through Algeria and Tunisia. Chicago: 1911. V. 70

AYER'S Almanac for 1881 in English, German, Dutch, Norwegian, Swedish, French, Spanish, Portuguese and Bohemian. Lowell: 1880. V. 73

AYERS, JAMES L.
Gold and Sunshine, Reminiscences of Early California. Boston: 1922. V. 70

AYLOFF, JOSEPH
An Historical Description of an Ancient Picture in Windsor Castle. London: 1773. V. 72

AYME, MARCEL
The Magic Pictures. New York: 1954. V. 73

AYRES, PHILIP
Emblemata Amatoria. London (i.e. Amsterdam): 1683. V. 73
Emblemata Amatoria. London: 1690. V. 68; 69

AYRES, RUBY
Candle Light. New York: 1924. V. 71
Living Apart. Garden City: 1937. V. 70
Look to the Spring. Garden City: 1933. V. 71
The Planter of the Tree. New York: 1927. V. 71
Week-End Woman. New York: 1939. V. 71

AYRES, THOMAS A.
The Mammoth Tree Grove, Calaveras County, California. San Francisco: 1855. V. 68

THE AYRSHIRE Wreath. MDCCCXLV. A Collection of Original Pieces, in Prose and Verse . . . Kilmarnock: 1844. V. 71

AYRTON, MICHAEL
Archilochos. London: 1977. V. 71
Drawings and Sculpture. London: 1962. V. 71
Fabrications. London: 1972. V. 71
Giovanni Pisano Sculptor. New York: 1969. V. 69; 72
Tittivulus or the Verbiage Collector. London: 1953. V. 71

AYSCOUGH, SAMUEL
An Index to the Remarkable Passages and Words Made Use of by Shakespeare; Calculated to Point Out the Different Meanings to Which the Words are Applied. London: 1790. V. 72

THE AYSHIRE Wreath. MDCCCXLV, A Collection of Original Pieces in Prose and Verse, chiefly by Native Authors, On Subjects Relating to Ayshire. Ed. by James McKie. Kilmarnock: 1844. V. 71

AYTOUN, WILLIAM EDMONSTOUNE
The Book of Ballads. 1845. V. 73
Firmilian; or, the Student of Badajoz, a Spasmodic Tragedy. Edinburgh and London: 1854. V. 73
Lays of the Scottish Cavaliers and Other Poems. London: 1881. V. 69; 71

AZEMA, MARC ANTONIN
The Conquest of Fitzroy. London: 1957. V. 69

B

B., H.
Leaf and Flower Pictures and How to Make Them. 1857. V. 68
Leaf and Flower Pictures and How to Make Them. New York: 1857. V. 69

B., W. P.
Messina After the Great Disaster.... 1909. V. 70

BAAS, J. H.
Outlines of the History of Medicine and the Medical Profession. New York: 1889. V. 68

BABBAGE, CHARLES
On the Economy of Machinery and Manufactures. London: 1832. V. 73
On the Economy of Machinery and Manufactures. London: 1835. V. 71

BABBITT, BRUCE E.
Color and Light: The Southwest Canvases of Louis Akin. Flagstaff: 1973. V. 69

BABCOCK, BETTY
The Expandable Pig. New York: 1949. V. 73

BABCOCK, DWIGHT V.
Murder for Hannal. London: 1941. V. 71

BABCOCK, GEORGE
Yezad: a Romance of the Unknown. Bridgeport: 1922. V. 68

BABCOCK, HAVILAH
The Best of Babcock. New York/Chicago/S.F: 1974. V. 69
Tales of Quails 'n Such. New York: 1951. V. 72

BABCOCK, SIDNEY
The Boy's Book of Sports: A Description of the Exercises and Pastimes of Youth. New Haven: 1939. V. 70

BABER, D. F.
The Longest Rope: The Truth About the Johnson County Cattle War. Caxton: 1940. V. 70

THE BABES in the Wood. Dundee: 1907. V. 70

BABINGTON, C. C.
Memorials, Journals and Botanical Correspondence. 1897. V. 72

BABINGTON, CHARLES
Flora of Cambridgeshire, or a Catalogue of Plants Founded in the County of Cambridge.... London: 1860. V. 71

BABINGTON, S. H.
Navajos Gods and Tom-Toms. New York: 1950. V. 69

BABKIN, B. P.
Secretory Mechanism of the Digestive Glands. New York: 1944. V. 71

BABSON, NAOMI LANE
All the Tomorrows. New York: 1939. V. 71

BABY Animals of the Wild. London: 1920. V. 68

BABY Bunting ABC. New York: 1911. V. 72

BABY'S 1, 2, 3 Book. London: 1920. V. 72

BABY'S ABC Book. London: 1900. V. 72
BABY'S ABC Book. Akron: 1904. V. 69; 73

BABY'S Birthday Book. London: 1890. V. 70

BABY'S Diary. London. V. 70

BABY'S Linen Book of Animals with Large Coloured Pictures of Animals and Birds. London: 1900. V. 73

THE BABY'S Opera: A Book of Old Rhymes and New Dresses. New York: 1914. V. 70

BABY'S Picture Book. London: 1915. V. 72

BABY'S Red Letter Days. Syracuse: 1901. V. 69; 70
BABY'S Red Letter Days. Syracuse: 1906. V. 70

BACA, MANUEL C. DE
Vicente Silva and His 40 Bandits. Washington: 1947. V. 69

BACCHETONI, HIERONYMUS LEOPOLD
Anatomia Medicinae Theoreticae et Practicae Minisra, Cautelisque in Praxi Observandis Illustrata. Oeniponti (Innsbruck): 1740. V. 72

BACH, RICHARD
Jonathan Livingston Seagull. New York: 1970. V. 69; 73
Stranger to the Ground. New York: 1963. V. 69

BACHE, ALEXANDER D.
Report on the Organization of a High School for Girls, and Seminary for Female Teachers. Philadelphia?: 1840?. V. 69

BACHELER, CLEMENTINE
The Nun of the Ca'Frollo. The Life and Letters of Henrietta Gardner Macy. New York: 1931. V. 72

BACHELLER, IRVING
Dawn. New York: 1927. V. 70; 71
The Harvesting. New York: 1934. V. 69
The House of the Three Ganders. Indianapolis: 1928. V. 71
The Turning of Griggsby. New York: 1913. V. 70

BACHMAIR, JOHN JAMES
A Complete German Grammar, in Two Parts. Philadelphia: 1772. V. 69

BACHMAN, WALTER
Swiss Gateaux Designs And Decorations.... London: 1950. V. 68

BACK, GEORGE
Narrative of the Arctic Land Expedition to the Mouth of the Great Fish River and Along the Shores of the Arctic Ocean in the years 1833, 1834 and 1835. Philadelphia: 1836. V. 73

BACKBERG, C.
Cactus Lexicon.... 1977. V. 70; 73
Cactus Lexicon.... Poole: 1977. V. 71

BACKHOUSE, JAMES
The Life and Correspondence Of William and Alice Ellis, of Airton. York: 1849. V. 72; 73

BACKHOUSE, JANET
The Illuminated Manuscript. Oxford: 1979. V. 70

BACKUS, ANNA JEAN
Mountain Meadows Whitness - the Life and Times of Bishop Philip Kilingensmith. Spokane: 1995. V. 68

BACKUS, R. H.
Georges Bank. Cambridge: 1987. V. 70

BACKWATERS - Excursions in the Shades. London: 1932. V. 71

BACKWOOD, W.
Atlas of Neuropathology. Baltimore: 1949. V. 72

BACON, CHARLOTTE
A Private State. Amherst: 1998. V. 68; 70; 73

BACON, EDWIN M.
The Connecticut River, and the Valley of the Connecticut: Three Hundred and Fifty Miles from Mountain to Sea. (Historical and Descriptive). New York: 1906. V. 68

BACON, FRANCIS, VISCOUNT ST. ALBANS
Baconiana. Or Certain Genuine Remains of Sr. Francis Bacon. London: 1679. V. 72
Bacon's Essays and Wisdom of the Ancients. Boston: 1917. V. 71
Bacon's Essays; with Annotations by Richard Whateley. London: 1857. V. 72
The Essays. London: 1903. V. 68; 71
Essays and Colours of Good and Evil. London: 1878. V. 70
Essays or Councils, Civil and Moral...With a Table of the Colours of Good and Evil and a Discourse of the Wisdom of the Ancients. London: 1696. V. 70
The Essays or Counsels Civil and Moral and Wisdom of the Ancients of Francis Bacon.... London: 1836. V. 70
Francisci Baconi de Verulamio Scripta in Naturali et Universali Philosophia. Amsterdam: 1653. V. 71
Historia Naturalis and Experimentalis de Ventis. Amstelodami: 1662. V. 70
The Historie of the Raigne of King Henry the Seventh. London: 1622. V. 73
Letters. London: 1702. V. 69
A New Edition of the Works. London: 1825-1834. V. 71
Of the Advancement and Proficiencie of Learning of the Partitions of Sciences. Oxford: 1640. V. 70
(Opera Omnia) Francisci Baconi Baronis de Verulamio, Vicercomitis Sancti Albani, Magni Angliae Cancellearii Opera Omnia, Quator Voluminibus Comprehensa Hacetenus Edita.... Londini: 1730. V. 73
Sylva Sylvarum: or a Natural History... Whereunto Is Newly Added the HIstory Natural and Experimental of Life and Death... Articles of Enquiry Touching Metals and Minerals... the New Atlantis... Epitomy of... Novum Organum. London: 1676. V. 73
Sylva Sylvarum; or a Natural History in Ten Centuries. (with) New Atlantis. London: 1635. V. 72
The Two Bookes of Francis Bacon. Of the Proficience and Advancement of Learning, Divine and Humane. London: 1605. V. 70; 73
The Two Books of Francis Lord Verulam. London: 1825. V. 70

BACON, GEORGE W.
Near the Cross: a Collection of Sacred Songs Both New and Old. Hudson: 1917. V. 71

BACON, J.
The Theory of Colouring.... London: 1866. V. 68

BACON, J. M.
The Dominion of the Air. The Story of Aerial Navigation. London: 1902. V. 73

BACON, JAMES
The Life and Times of Francis the First, King of France. London: 1829. V. 72

BACON, JOHN
Liber Regis et Thesaurus Rerum Ecclesiasticarum. London: 1786. V. 70; 72

BACON, LEONARD
The Legend of Quincibald. New York: 1928. V. 69
A Plea for Africa; Delivered in New Haven July 4th 1825. New Haven: 1825. V. 71

BACON, MARY ANN
Flowers and Their Kindred Thoughts. London: 1848. V. 72
Winged Thoughts. London: 1851. V. 72

BACON, NATHANIEL
The Annals of Ipswche. The Laws, Customes and Government.... London: 1884. V. 68
An Historical and Political Discourse of the Laws of Government of England.... London: 1739. V. 73

BACON, PEGGY
The Ghost of Opalina or Nine Lives. Boston;: 1967. V. 73

BACON, R. H.
The Life of Lord Fisher of Kilverstone, Admiral of the Fleet.... London: 1929. V. 68

BACON, REGINALD
The Dover Patrol 1915-1917. New York: 1919. V. 68

BACON, RICHARD MAC KENZIE
A Memoir of the Life of Edward, Third Baron Suffield. Norwich: 1838. V. 70

BACON, ROGER
Opera Quadem Hactenus Inedita. London: 1859. V. 68
Opus Majus ad Clementem Quartum, Pontificem Romanum. London: 1733. V. 68; 73
The Opus Majus of Roger Bacon. Philadelphia: 1928. V. 68

BACON, STEUBEN T.
The Ballot: Dangers from Its Perversion. Cambridge: 1881. V. 71

BACON, THOMAS
First Impressions and Studies from Nature in Hindostan.... London: 1837. V. 72

BADCOCK, JOHN
Conversations on Conditioning. The Grooms' Oracle and Pocket Stable Directory.... London: 1830. V. 68; 73
Philosophical Recreations, or Winter Amusements.... London: 1820?. V. 72

BADCOCK, WILLIAM
A New Touch-Stone for Gold and Silver Wares. 1970. V. 69
A Touch-Stone for Gold and Silver Wares. London: 1677. V. 71

BADDELEY, ST. CLAIR
Rome And Its Story. London: 1904. V. 72

BADE, W. F.
Life and Letters of John Muir. Boston: 1924. V. 69

BADEAU, ADAM
Conspiracy: a Cuban Romance. London: 1898. V. 68
Military History of U. S. Grant. New York: 1881. V. 71

BADELIER, ADOLPH FRANCIS ALPHONSE
The Gilded Man. New York: 1893. V. 73
Indians of the Rio Grande Valley. Albuquerque: 1937. V. 73

BADEN-POWELL, GEORGE
The Saving of Ireland, Industrial, Financial, Political. 1898. V. 69

BADEN-POWELL, R.
Indian Memories. Recollections of Soldiering and Sport. 1915. V. 69; 70; 72; 73
Pig-Sticking or Hog-Hunting. 1924. V. 72

BADESLADE, THOMAS
Thirty-Six Different Views of Noblemen and Gentlemen's Seats in the County of Kent.... London: 1750. V. 70; 72

BADESSI, LAURENT ELLIE
Skin. Zurich: 2000. V. 68

BADGER, C. M., MRS.
Wild Flowers Drawn and Colored from Nature. New York: 1859. V. 73

BADHAM, C.
A Treatise on the Esculent Funguses of England. London: 1863. V. 69

BADHAM, C. DAVID
Prose Halieutics. 1854. V. 72
Prose Halieutics. London: 1854. V. 68

BADIUS ASCENSIUS, JODOCUS
Nauis Stultifere Collectanea. Paris: 1513. V. 68; 70; 73

BADOVICI, JEAN
Frank Lloyd Wright, Architecte Americain. Paris: 1932. V. 68

BADRICK, FREDERICK C.
The Spanish Galleon: a West Country Romance. London: 1893. V. 68

BAEDEKER, KARL
Belgium and Holland. Leipsic: 1878. V. 72
The Dominion of Canada. Leipsic: 1894. V. 69
The Eastern Alps. Leipsic: 1907. V. 72
Egypt And The Sudan. Leipsic: 1908. V. 72
Greece. Handbook for Travellers. Leipsic: 1894. V. 73
The Rhine From Rotterdam to Constance. Coblenz and Leipsic: 1873. V. 72
The Riviera. Leipzig: 1931. V. 72
Russia...Handbook for Travellers. Leipzig: 1914. V. 70
United States with an Excursion into Mexico. Leipsic: 1899. V. 72

BAER, WILL CHRISTOPHER
Kiss me, Judas. New York: 1998. V. 72

BAERLEIN, HENRY
Mexico, the Land of Unrest. Philadelphia. V. 70

BAERNREITHER, JOSEPH M.
English Associations of Working Men. London: 1893. V. 71

BAGBY, GEORGE WILLIAM
What I Did With My Fifty Millions. Philadelphia: 1874. V. 69

BAGE, ROBERT
Hermsprong; or, Man As He Is Not. London: 1799. V. 69

BAGEHOT, WALTER
Economic Studies. London: 1880. V. 72
The English Constitution. London: 1872. V. 71
The English Constitution. London: 1878. V. 71
The English Constitution. London: 1882. V. 72
Essays on Parliamentary Reform. London: 1883. V. 72
Estimates of Some Englishmen and Scotchmen, a Series of Articles reprinted...from the National Review. London: 1858. V. 71
The History of the Unreformed Parliament and Its Lessons. London: 1860. V. 72
Lombard Street: a Description of the Money Market. London: 1873. V. 68; 71
Lombard Street: a Description of the Money Market. London: 1894. V. 71
Some Articles on the Depreciation of silver and on Topics Connected with It. London: 1872. V. 72
Some Articles on the Depreciaton of Silver and on Topics Connected with It. London: 1877. V. 72

BAGENAL, PHILIP H.
Crime in Ireland. Dublin: 1880. V. 69
Foreign Land Tenures and the Irish Tenant. Dublin: 1880. V. 69

BAGG, A. C.
Birds of the Connecticut Valley in Massachusetts. Northampton: 1937. V. 70; 73

BAGGETT, BONNIE
A History in Flames, The Story of the Volunteer Firemen of the State of Delaware. 1976. V. 69

BAGLOLE, HARRY
Exploring Island History. Belfast: 1977. V. 73

BAGNALL, J. E.
The Flora of Warwickshire. London and Birmingham: 1891. V. 69

BAGNOLD, ENID
Alice and Thomas and Jane. New York: 1931. V. 72
National Velvet. London: 1935. V. 71

BAGOT, RICHARD
Anthony Cuthbert. London: 1908. V. 68

BAGSHAWE, EDWARD
Two Arguments in Parliament, the First Concerning the Cannons, the Second Concerning the Premunire (i.e Praemunire) upon those Cannons. London: 1641. V. 73

BAGWELL, RICHARD
Ireland Under the Tudors. London: 1885-1890. V. 71

BAHR, HOWARD
The Black Flower. Baltimore: 1997. V. 73

BAHR, JEROME
All Good Americans. New York: 1937. V. 70

BAIGENT, FRANCIS JOSEPH
A Practical Manual Of Heraldry, And Of Heraldic Illumination. London: 1864. V. 72

BAIKOFF, N. A.
The Root of Life (Panax Ginseng). Harbin: 1926. V. 72

BAILEY, A. E.
Cottonseed and Cottonseed Products, Their Chemistry and Chemical Technology. New York: 1948. V. 72

BAILEY, A. M.
Birds of Arctic Alaska. Denver: 1948. V. 73
Birds of Colorado. Denver: 1965. V. 69; 70; 73

BAILEY, ALICE COOPER
The Skating Gander. Joliet: 1927. V. 71

BAILEY, BEN P.
Border Lands Sketchbook. Waco: 1976. V. 69

BAILEY, CAROLYN SHERWIN
Miss Hickory. New York: 1946. V. 69

BAILEY, DAVID
Another Image: Papua New Guinea. London: 1975. V. 69
David Bailey's Box of Pin-Ups. London: 1965. V. 70
Trouble and Strife. London: 1980. V. 68

BAILEY, FLORA L.
Some Sex Beliefs and Practices in a Navaho Community. Cambridge: 1950. V. 69

BAILEY, FLORENCE MERRIAM
Birds of New Mexico. 1928. V. 73

BAILEY, G. H.
Watchmakers & Clockmakers of the World. London: 1976. V. 72

BAILEY, H.
Notable Names in Medicine and Surgery. London: 1959. V. 68; 70; 71

BAILEY, H. C.
The Apprehensive Dog. New York: 1941. V. 68
The Bishop's Crime. 1941. V. 68
The Bishop's Crime. New York: 1941. V. 73
Call Mr. Fortune. London: 1920. V. 73
Call Mr. Fortune. New York: 1921. V. 73
Case for Mr. Fortune. London: 1932. V. 73
Case for Mr. Fortune. New York: 1932. V. 73
Dead Man's Effects. London: 1945. V. 69; 72
The Life Sentence. Garden City: 1946. V. 72
Meet Mr. Fortune. Garden City: 1942. V. 71
Mr. Clunk's Text. New York: 1939. V. 70
Mr. Fortune Explains. London: 1930. V. 73
Mr. Fortune Finds a Pig. New York: 1943. V. 71
Mr. Fortune Here. London: 1940. V. 73
Mister Fortune Objects. New York: 1935. V. 73
Mr. Fortune Please. London: 1927. V. 73
Mr. Fortune Please. New York: 1928. V. 73
Mr. Fortune Speaking. London: 1930. V. 68
Mr. Fortune Wonders. London: 1933. V. 73
Mr. Fortune Wonders. New York: 1933. V. 73
Mr. Fortune's Practice. London: 1923. V. 73
The Red Castle. London: 1932. V. 73
Save A Rope. Garden City: 1948. V. 72
Shadow on the Wall. London: 1934. V. 68; 69; 73
Slippery Ann. London: 1944. V. 69; 72
This is Mr. Fortune. London: 1938. V. 73
The Vernon Mystery. London: 1939. V. 69; 73
The Wrong Man. New York: 1945. V. 68; 72

BAILEY, HAROLD H.
The Birds of Florida. Baltimore: 1925. V. 70
The Birds of Virginia. Lynchburg: 1913. V. 69

BAILEY, HILARY
The Cry From Street To Street. London: 1992. V. 72

BAILEY, J. D.
Commanders at Kings Mountain. Gaffney: 1926. V. 71
Some Heroes of the American Revolution. Spartanburg: 1924. V. 71

BAILEY, J. M.
The Book of Ensilage; or the New Dispensation for Farmers, Experience with Ensilage at Winning Farm. Billerica: 1880. V. 72

BAILEY, J. W.
The Mammals of Virginia, an Account of the Furred Animals of Land and Sea.... Richmond: 1946. V. 70

BAILEY, JESSIE BROMILOW
Diego de Vardas and the Reconquers of New Mexico. Albuquerque: 1940. V. 68; 73

BAILEY, JOHN
A General View of the Agriculture of the County of Nothumberland (Cumberland and Westmoreland).... London: 1805. V. 71

BAILEY, JOHN W.
Pacifying the Plains - General Alfred Terry and the Decline of the Sioux 1866-1890. Conn: 1979. V. 72

BAILEY, KENNETH P.
The Ohio Company of Virginia and the Westward Movement 1748-1792.... Glendale: 1939. V. 69; 71

BAILEY, LIBERTY HYDE
The Cultivated Conifers in North America.... New York: 1933. V. 71
Cyclopedia of America Horticulture.... New York: 1909. V. 71
The Gardens of Larkspurs. New York: 1939. V. 71
Hortus Third, A Concise Dictionary of Plants Cultivated in the United States and Canada. New York: 1976. V. 71; 73
The Standard Cyclopedia of Horticulture.... New York: 1928. V. 71; 73

BAILEY, LYNN R.
Bosque Rendondo. 1970. V. 69
Cochise County Stalwarts - A Who's Who of Territorial Years: Volume One A-K. Volume Two L-Z. Tucson: 2000. V. 73
The Long Walk. Los Angeles: 1964. V. 69

BAILEY, N.
The Antiquities of London and Westminster. London: 1722. V. 71

BAILEY, P. R. O.
The Genus Monadenium, with Descriptions of 21 New Species. Berne: 1961. V. 71

BAILEY, PAUL
A Distant Likeness. London: 1973. V. 68
Ghost Dance Messiah. Los Angeles: 1970. V. 71
Jacob Hamblin: Buckskin Apostle. Los Angeles: 1961. V. 69
Wovoka, the Indian Messiah. Los Angeles: 1957. V. 69

BAILEY, PEARL
Pearl's Kitchen - an Extraordinary Cookbook. New York: 1973. V. 68

BAILEY, PHILIP JAMES
Festus, a Poem. London: 1839. V. 73
Festus, a Poem. London: 1848. V. 73

BAILEY, PHILLIP A.
Golden Mirages. Ramona: 1940. V. 69

BAILEY, ROBERT G.
Hell's Canyon: a Story of the Deepest Canyon on the North American Continent.... Lewiston: 1943. V. 69; 70; 71; 73
River of No Return, Historical Stories of Idaho. Lewiston: 1935. V. 73

BAILEY, ROSALIE FELLOWS
Pre-Revolutionary Dutch Houses and Families in Northern New Jersey and Southern New York. New York: 1936. V. 69; 72

BAILEY, RUFUS WILLIAM
The Issue, Presented in a Series of Letters on Slavery. New York: 1837. V. 71

BAILEY, RUTH
A Dialogue on Modern Poetry. London: 1939. V. 69

BAILEY, S. H.
Mr. Roosevelt's Experiments. London: 1935. V. 71

BAILEY, SAMUEL
Essays on the Formation and Publication of Opinions and on Other Subjects. London: 1821. V. 69
Essays on the Pursuit of Truth, on the Progress of Knowledge, and on the Fundamental Principle of all Evidence and Expectation. London: 1829. V. 70

BAILEY, TEMPLE
Fair as the Moon. Philadelphia: 1935. V. 70
I've Been to London. Philadelphia: 1937. V. 71
Wallflowers. Philadelphia: 1927. V. 70

BAILEY, THOMAS
The Carnival of Death. London: 1822. V. 70
What is Life? and Other Poems. London: 1820. V. 70

BAILEY, VERNON HOWE
Empire State, a Pictorial Record of Its Construction. New York: 1931. V. 68; 70; 72

BAILEY, WILLIAM
The Advancement of Arts, Manufactures, and Commerce, or Descriptions of the Useful Machines and Models.... 1776-1779. V. 71
The Angler's Instructor: a Treatise on the Best Modes of Angling... and On the Habits of the Fish. London: 1857. V. 71
One Hundred and Six Copper Plates of Mechanical Machines and Implements of Husbandry Approved and Adopted by the Society for the Encouragement of Arts, Manufactures and Commerce.... 1782. V. 71

BAILEY DENTON, E.
The Water Supply and Sewerage of Country Mansions & Estates. London: 1901. V. 68

BAILIE, DUKE
Through Mighty Waters Saved. Chicago: 1889. V. 71

BAILLIE, G. H.
Britten's Old Clock's and Watches and Their Makers. London: 1956. V. 72

BAILLIE, JOANNA
A Collection of Poems, Chiefly Manuscript, and from Living Authors. London: 1823. V. 70
Dramas. London: 1836. V. 69

BAILLIE, JOHN
Rivers in the Desert; or, Mission Scenes in Burmah. London: 1858. V. 68

BAILLIE, MATTHEW
The Morbid Anatomy of Some of the Most Important Parts of the Human Body. London: 1797. V. 73
A Series of Engravings, Accompanied by Explanations, Which are Intended to Illustrate the Morbid Anatomy of the Most Important Parts of the Human Body. London: 1812. V. 69

BAILLIE, W. W., MRS.
Days and Nights of Shikar. 1921. V. 72; 73

BAILLIE GROHMAN, W. A.
The Master of Game. 1909. V. 68
Sport in the Alps in the Past and Present.... 1896. V. 69; 70

BAILLY, JEAN SYLVAIN
Traite de l'Astronomie Indienne et Orientale, Ouvrage qui Peut Servir de Suite a L'Histoire de l'Astronomie Ancienne. Paris: 1787. V. 73

BAILY, FRANCIS
The Doctrine of Life Annuities and Assurances Analytically Investigated and Explained, Together with Several Useful Tables Connected with the Subject and a Variety of Practical Rules from the Illustration of the Same. London: 1810. V. 72

BAILY, J. T. HERBERT
Emma, Lady Hamilton. London: 1905. V. 70

BAILY, JOHN
A Treatise on the Differential Calculus. Cambridge: 1838. V. 72

BAILY, LESLIE
The Gilbert and Sullivan Book. London: 1952. V. 68

BAILY, W. H.
Figures of Characteristic British Fossils; (Palaeozoic Division). London: 1875. V. 68

BAILY'S Hunting Directory 1913-1914: with Diary. London: 1913. V. 72

BAILY'S Hunting Directory 1916-1917: with Diary. 1916. V. 72

BAIN, ALEXANDER
James Mill: a Biography. London: 1882. V. 71

BAIN, FRANCIS
The Natural History of Prince Edward Island Authorized for the Use of Schools by the Board of Education. Charlottetown: 1890. V. 73

BAIN, FRANCIS J.
A Child of the Carnival. San Fernando: 1974. V. 72

BAIN, IAIN
The Watercolours and Drawings of Thomas Bewick and His Workshop Apprentices. Winchester: 1981. V. 70

BAIN, JOHN WILLIAM
The Pilgrim. Boston: 1879. V. 70

BAINBRIDGE, BERYL
Something Happened Yesterday. London: 1993. V. 69
Sweet William. London: 1975. V. 71
Young Adolf. London: 1978. V. 68
Young Adolf. New York: 1979. V. 72

BAINBRIDGE, GEORGE C.
The Fly Fisher's Guide. Liverpool: 1816. V. 69; 73
The Fly Fisher's Guide. 1992. V. 68

BAINBRIDGE, H. C.
Twice Seven: the Autobiography of H. C. Bainbridge. London: 1933. V. 71

BAINES, EDWARD
A Companion to the Lakes of Cumberland, Westmoreland and Lancashire: in a Descriptive Account of a Family Tour.... London: 1834. V. 71
History, Directory, and Gazetteer, of the County Palatine of Lancaster. Liverpool: 1824-1825. V. 73
History of The Wars of The French Revolution. London: 1817. V. 70; 72
The History of the County Palatine and Duchy of Lancaster. London: 1868-1870. V. 73
The Social, Educational and Religious State of the Manufacturing Districts.... London: 1843. V. 69

BAINES, F. E.
Records of the Manor, Parish and Borough of Hampstead.... London: 1890. V. 71

BAINES, H.
The Flora of Yorkshire: a Supplement to Baines' Flora. London and Halifax: 1850-1854. V. 69

BAINES, T.
Greenhouse and Stove Plants.... London: 1894. V. 71; 73

BAINES, THOMAS
The Gold Regions of South Eastern Africa.... London: 1877. V. 72
History of the Commerce and Town of Liverpool. London: 1852. V. 73
Lancashire and Cheshire Past and Present. London. V. 73
Yorkshire Past and Present. London. V. 73

BAIRD, D. E.
The Biological Report of the Royal Society Expedition to Tristan Da Cunha, 1962. London: 1965. V. 72

BAIRD, DAVID
The Life of General, the Right Honourable.... London: 1832. V. 69

BAIRD, HENRY C.
The Painter, Gilder and Varnisher's Companion.... Philadelphia: 1850. V. 69

BAIRD, HENRY M.
The Huguenots and Henry of Navarre. (with) *The Huguenots & the Revocation of the Edict of Nantes.* New York: 1886-1895. V. 71

BAIRD, JONATHAN
Day Job. Boston: 1998. V. 72

BAIRD, JOSEPH A.
Time's Wondrous Changes: San Francisco Architecture 1776-1915. San Francisco: 1962. V. 69; 72

BAIRD, JOSIE
Tom Bond Bronc-Buster, Cow Poke, Trail Driver. Sweetwater: 1960. V. 73

BAIRD, ROBERT
View of the Valley of the Mississippi, or the Emigrant's and Traveler's Guide to the West. Philadelphia: 1832. V. 68
View of the Valley of the Mississippi, or the Emigrant's and Traveller's Guide to the West. Philadelphia: 1834. V. 68

BAIRD, SPENCER FULLERTON
The Birds of North America.... Philadelphia and Salem: 1860-1870. V. 73
Catalogue of North American Reptiles in the Museum of the Smithsonian Institution. Washington: 1853. V. 72
Directions for Collected, Preserving and Transporting Specimens of Natural History. Washington: 1854. V. 73
History of North American Birds. Boston: 1874-1884. V. 71
A History of North American Birds. Land Birds. Boston: 1875. V. 70; 73
A History of North American Birds. Boston: 1905. V. 73
Report on the Fishes Observed on the Coasts of New Jersey and Long Island During the Summer of 1854. Washington: 1855. V. 73
The Water Birds of North America. Boston: 1884. V. 70

BAIRD, WILLIAM
Annals of Duddingston and Portobello. Edinburgh: 1898. V. 70

BAIRNSFATHER, BRUCE
Fragments from France.... London: 1916. V. 71

BAKELESS, JOHN
Daniel Boone: Master of the Wilderness. New York: 1939. V. 69

BAKER, A. I.
Ruins of Kenilworth Castle. London: 1822. V. 70; 72

BAKER, C. H. C.
Design in Modern Industry The Year Book of Design and Industries Association 1922. 1922. V. 70

BAKER, CARLOTTA
Damaged Wives. New York: 1940. V. 71

BAKER, CHARLES H.
Gentleman's Companion. New York: 1934. V. 69; 73

BAKER, CORNELIA
Coquo and the King's Children. Chicago: 1902. V. 71

BAKER, DAVID ERSKINE
Biographica Dramatica; or, a Companion to the Playhouse. London: 1782. V. 69
The Companion to the Play-House; or an Historical Account of all the Dramatic Writers (and Their Works) That Have Appeared in Great Britain and Ireland.... London: 1764. V. 73

BAKER, DOROTHY
Young Man With a Horn. Boston: 1938. V. 71

BAKER, EDWARD CHARLES STUART
The Game Birds of India, Burma and Ceylon. London: 1921-1930. V. 73
Game Birds of India, Burma and Ceylon. London and Bombay: 1921-1935. V. 73
The Indian Ducks and Their Allies. London: 1908. V. 70; 73
Indian Pigeons and Doves. London: 1913. V. 73
The Nidification of Birds of the Indian Empire. 1932-1935. V. 73

BAKER, EZEKIEL
Remarks on Rifle Guns.... London: 1823. V. 73
Remarks on Rifle Guns.... London: 1829. V. 73

BAKER, F. C.
The Mollusca of the Chicago Area. Part I. The Pelcypoda. Chicago: 1898. V. 68

BAKER, FRANK
The Downs So Free. London: 1948. V. 70

BAKER, FRANKLIN T.
Everyday Classics. Fourth Reader. New York: 1917. V. 68

BAKER, GEORGE
Janus. London: 1935. V. 72

BAKER, H. A.
Ericas in Southern Africa. Cape Town and Johannesburg: 1967. V. 73

BAKER, HENRY
An Attempt Towards a Natural History of the Polype: in a Letter to Martin Folkes, Esq. London: 1743. V. 69; 70; 73
The Microscope Made Easy.... London: 1742. V. 70
The Microscope Made Easy.... London: 1744. V. 73
The Microscope Made Easy.... Lincolnwood: 1987. V. 68; 71

BAKER, HENRY BARTON
Our Old Actors. London: 1878. V. 72

BAKER, HENRY H.
A Reminiscent Story of the Great Civil War. New Orleans: 1911. V. 69

BAKER, HOZIAL H.
Overland Journey to Carson Valley and California. San Francisco: 1973. V. 69

BAKER, J.
The History of the Inquisition, as It Subsits in the Kingdoms of Spain, Portugal &c and in the Indies to this Day. London: 1734. V. 70

BAKER, J. G.
A Flora of the English Lake District. London: 1885. V. 69
A New Flora of Northumberland and Durham. Northumberland and Durham: 1868. V. 69
North Yorkshire; Studies of Botany, Geology, Climate and Physical Geography. London: 1863. V. 73

BAKER, JAMES
Pictures From Bohemia Drawn with Pen and Pencil. London. V. 72

BAKER, JAMES A.
The Politics of Diplomacy. New York: 1995. V. 73

BAKER, JOHN
Death Minus Zero. London: 1996. V. 70

BAKER, JOHN MILNES
The Baker Family and the Edgar Family of Rahway, New Jersey and New York City. Middletown: 1972. V. 69

BAKER, JOHN R.
Abraham Trembley of Geneva, Scientist and Philosopher 1710-1784. London: 1952. V. 68; 72
Man and Animals in the New Hebrides. 1929. V. 69; 70; 72; 73

BAKER, KARLE WILSON
Family Style. New York: 1937. V. 70

BAKER, LEDRU
The Cheaters. New York: 1952. V. 72

BAKER, MARGARET J.
Hannibal and the Bears. London: 1965. V. 71; 72; 73
The Wishing Nut Tree. London. V. 69

BAKER, NICHOLSON
The Mezzanine. New York: 1988. V. 68; 71
The Mezzanine. London: 1989. V. 70
Room Temperature. Cambridge: 1990. V. 71
Room Temperature. New York: 1990. V. 73
Vox. New York: 1992. V. 68; 69; 70; 71; 72; 73

BAKER, PEARL
The Wild Bunch at Robbers Roost. Los Angeles: 1965. V. 69

BAKER, R. T.
A Research on the Pines of Australia. Sydney: 1910. V. 70; 71

BAKER, SAMUEL WHITE
The Albert N'Yanza. 1867. V. 73
The Albert N'Yanza. London: 1870. V. 70
The Albert N'Yanza. London: 1879. V. 72
The Albert N'Yanza Great. London: 1888. V. 73
Cyprus As I Saw It In 1879. London: 1879. V. 72
Eight Years in Ceylon. 1891. V. 70
Eight Years in Ceylon. 1909. V. 72
Ismalia. 1874. V. 72; 73
The Nile Tributaries of Abyssinia and the Sword Hunters of the Hamran Arabs. 1987. V. 69
On the Sources of the Nile. 1866. V. 72
The Rifle and the Hound in Ceylon. London: 1854. V. 70
The Rifle and the Hound in Ceylon. 1874. V. 73

BAKER, T. H.
Notes on St. Martin's Church and Parish. Salisbury: 1906. V. 73

BAKER, W. R.
Medallic Portraits of Washington, with Historical and Critical Notes and a Descriptive Catalogue of the Coins Medals Tokens and Cards. Philadelphia: 1885. V. 69; 72

BAKER, WILLIAM KING
John T. Dorland. London: 1898. V. 71

BAKER, WILLIAM S.
The Engraved Portraits of Washington, with Notices of the Originals and Brief Biographical Sketches of the Painters. Philadelphia: 1880. V. 70
Itinerary of General Washington from..1775 to...1783. Philadelphia: 1892. V. 69

BAKIS, KIRSTEN
Lives of the Monster Dogs. New York: 1997. V. 68

BALABAN, JOHN
After Our War. 1974. V. 69

BALBIRNIE, JOHN
Hydropathic Aphorisms. London: 1859. V. 68; 73

BALCH, EDWIN SWIFT
The North Pole and Bradley Land. Philadlephia: 1913. V. 73

BALCH, THOMAS
The French in America During the War of Independence. Philadelphia: 1891-1895. V. 69

BALD, ROBERT
Report of a Mineral Survey Along the Track of the Propsed North or Level Line of Canal Betwixt Edinburgh and Glasgow, as Projected by John Rennie, Esq. Civil Engineer Anno 1798. (and) Observations Occasioned by the Mineral Survey of Mr. Robert Bald.... Leith: 1814. V. 72

BALDERSTON, ROBERT R.
Ingleton: Bygone and Present. 1888. V. 73

BALDRIDGE, CYRUS LE ROY
I Was There. With the Yanks on the Western Front 1917-1919. New York: 1919. V. 72

BALDRIDGE, M.
A Reminiscence of the Parker H. French Expedition through Texas and Mexico to California in the Spring of 1850. Los Angeles: 1959. V. 68; 73

BALDRY, A. L.
The Life and Work of Marcus Stone, R.A. London: 1896. V. 73
Sir John Everett Millais, His Art And Influence. London: 1899. V. 72

BALDUS, S. A.
The New Capitalism. Chicago: 1923. V. 68

BALDWIN, ALICE B.
Memoirs of Major General Frank D. Baldwin. Los Angeles: 1929. V. 72

BALDWIN, C. E.
The History and Development of the Port of Blyth. Newcastle upon Tyne: 1929. V. 73

BALDWIN, CHARLES N.
A Universal Biographical Dictionary.... New York: 1826. V. 69

BALDWIN, EBENEZER
Annals of Yale College, in New Haven, Connecticut, From Its Foundation to the Year 1831. New Haven: 1831. V. 68

BALDWIN, EDWARD
History of Rome.... London: 1809. V. 73

BALDWIN, FAITH
The Heart Has Wings. New York: 1937. V. 70
The Incredible Year. New York: 1929. V. 70
Three Women. New York: 1926. V. 70
Thresholds. Boston: 1923. V. 71

BALDWIN, GORDON
The Warrior Apache - A Story of The Ciricahua and Winter Apache. Tucson: 1965. V. 72

BALDWIN, H.
The Orchids of New England, A Popular Monograph. New York: 1884. V. 73
The Orchids of New England.... New York: 1894. V. 71

BALDWIN, J. D.
Ancient America. New York: 1871. V. 69

BALDWIN, J. H.
The Large and Small Game of Bengal and the North Western Provinces of India. 1877. V. 72; 73

BALDWIN, JAMES
The Amen Corner. New York: 1968. V. 73
Another Country. London: 1963. V. 70
Blues for Mister Charlie. New York: 1964. V. 73
Blues for Mister Charlie. London: 1965. V. 71
The Devil Finds Work. London: 1976. V. 68
The Devil Finds Work. New York: 1976. V. 70
The Evidence of Things Not Seen. New York: 1985. V. 71; 72
The Fire Next Time. New York: 1963. V. 71
Giovanni's Room. New York: 1956. V. 68; 70
Giovanni's Room. London: 1957. V. 69
Go Tell It on the Mountain. New York: 1953. V. 73
Go Tell It On the Mountain. Franklin Center, PA: 1979. V. 69; 71
Going to Meet the Man. New York: 1965. V. 68; 70; 73
Gypsy and Other Poems. 1989. V. 70; 72
If Beale Street Could Talk. New York: 1974. V. 68; 69; 71; 72
Just Above My Head. New York: 1979. V. 71
The Negro Protest. Boston: 1963. V. 68; 71
No Name in the Street. New York: 1972. V. 72
Nobody Knows My Name. More Notes of a Native Son. New York: 1961. V. 71
Notes of a Native Son. Boston: 1955. V. 68; 71; 73
One Day When I Was Lost. London: 1972. V. 73
A Rap on Race. Philadelphia & New York: 1971. V. 68
Tell Me How Long the Train's Been Gone. New York: 1963. V. 68
Tell Me How Long the Train's Been Gone. New York: 1968. V. 68

BALDWIN, ROBERT
A Kind of Rapture. New York: 1998. V. 72

BALDWIN, SAMUEL
A Survey of the British Customs.... London: 1770. V. 72

BALDWIN, THOMAS
Narrative of the Massacre, by the Savage of the Wife and Children of Thomas Baldwin.... New York: 1835. V. 68; 73
Suggestions on the State of Ireland; Chiefly Given in Evidence. 1883. V. 69

BALDWIN, WILLIAM
A Treatise of Morrall Philosophie; Wherein is Contained the Worthy Sayings of Philosophers, Emperours, Kings and Orators, Their Liues and Answeres.... London: 1620. V. 70

BALE, JOHN
Acta Romanovm Pontificvm, A Dispersione Discipulorum Christi. Francofvrti ad Mionum: 1567. V. 73

BALESTRINI, NANNI
The Unseen. London: 1989. V. 71

BALFOUR, ANDREW
First (Second, Third and Fourth) Report of the Wellcome Tropical Research Laboratories at the Gordon Memorial College Khartoum. Khartoum and London: 1904-1911. V. 71

BALFOUR, FRANCES
Dr. Elsie Inglis. London: 1920. V. 72

BALFOUR, J. H.
The Plants of the Bible. London: 1866. V. 70

BALFOUR BROWNE, V. R.
The Stalking Letters and Sketches of V. R. Balfour-Browne. 1978. V. 70

BALFOUR KINNEAR, G. P. R.
Flying Salmon. 1937. V. 68

BALL, BRIAN
Death of a Low-handicap Man. London: 1974. V. 70

BALL, CHARLES
Slavery in the United States: a Narrative of the Life and Adventures of Charles Ball, a Black Man.... Lewistown: 1836. V. 71

BALL, EUSTACE HALE
The Gaucho. New York: 1923. V. 72
The Legion of the Condemned. New York: 1929. V. 70

BALL, EVA
An Apache Odyssey. Provo: 1980. V. 73
Ma'am Jones of the Pecos. Tucson: 1969. V. 68; 73

BALL, EVE
In the Days of Victorio, Recollections of a Warm Springs Apache. Tucson: 1970. V. 69

BALL, J.
The Alpine Guide: The Western Alps. 1898. V. 70; 73
Notes of a Naturalist in South America. London: 1887. V. 70
Spicilegium Florae Maroccanae. London: 1878. V. 69

BALL, JOHN
The Central Alps. Part II. London: 1911. V. 69
The Cool Cottontail. New York: 1966. V. 68
In the Heat of the Night. New York: 1962. V. 70
In the Heat of the Night. New York: 1965. V. 69; 70; 71; 72; 73
John Ball Member of the Wyeth Expedition to the Pacific Northwest 1832, and Pioneer of the Old Northwest - Autobiography. Glendale: 1925. V. 68; 73
Peaks, Passes and Glaciers. London: 1859. V. 70
Peaks, Passes and Glaciers. London: 1860. V. 69
The Western Alps. London: 1898. V. 69

BALL, LARRY D.
Desert Lawmen - the High Sheriffs of New Mexico and Arizona 1846-1912. Albuquerque: 1992. V. 68; 73
The United States Marshals of New Mexico and Arizona Territories, 1846-1912. Albuquerque: 1978. V. 72

BALL, NICHOLAS
The Pioneers of '49 - a History of the Excursion of the Society of California Pioneers. Boston: 1891. V. 70

BALL, ROBERT
Great Astronomers. London: 1920. V. 68

BALL, T. H.
Encyclopedia of Genealogy and Biography of Lake County Indiana. Evansville: 1974. V. 72

BALL, W. V.
Reminiscences and Letters of Sir Robert Ball. 1915. V. 69

BALLANCE, CHARLES
Some Points in the Surgery of the Brain and Its Membranes. London: 1907. V. 68; 70; 72

BALLANTYNE, J. W.
The Byrth of Mankynde: Its Author, Editions and Contents. London: 1907. V. 68

BALLANTYNE, R. M.
Hudson's Bay: or Every-Day Life in the Wilds.... Edinburgh: 1848. V. 71
Photographs of Edinburgh, with Descriptive Letterpress. Glasgow: 1870. V. 70

BALLANTYNE, ROBERT MICHAEL
The Butterfly's Ball and The Grasshopper's Feast. London: 1874. V. 70
Robber Kitten. New York: 1897. V. 70

BALLANTYNE, ROBERT MONTGOMERY
The World of Ice; or Adventure in the Polar Regions. New York: 1860. V. 73

BALLARD, G. A.
The Black Battlefleet. Lymington: 1980. V. 69

BALLARD, GEORGE
Memoirs of British Ladies Who Have Been Celebrated for Their Writing or Skill in the Learned Languages, Arts and Sciences. London: 1775. V. 70; 73

BALLARD, J. G.
The Atrocity Exhibition. London: 1970. V. 73
Crash. London: 1973. V. 68; 69
Crash. New York: 1973. V. 68; 70
The Crystal World. London: 1966. V. 68; 71
The Day of Creation. New York: 1988. V. 72
The Disaster Area. London: 1967. V. 68; 70; 71
The Drowned World. London: 1962. V. 70; 73
Empire of the Sun. London: 1984. V. 68; 69; 70
Hello America. London: 1981. V. 72
The Kindness of Women. London: 1991. V. 70
Myths of the Near Future. London: 1982. V. 72
News from the Sun. London: 1982. V. 72
Super-Cannes. London: 2000. V. 70; 73
Terminal Beach. New York: 1964. V. 71
The Unlimited Dream Company. New York: 1979. V. 72
A User's Guide to the Millennium: Essays and Reviews. London: 1996. V. 70
War Fever. London: 1990. V. 70
Why I Want to Fuck Ronald Reagan. Brighton: 1968. V. 70

BALLENGER, T. L.
Around Tahequah Council Fires. Muskogee: 1935. V. 68

BALLIETT, WHITNEY
The Sound of Surprise. New York: 1959. V. 69
Super-Drummer a Profile of Buddy Rich. Indianapolis: 1968. V. 69

BALLINGER, BILL S.
The Longest Second. New York: 1957. V. 68

BALLINGER, H. H.
Does It Pay? A Book on the Stock Industry of Southwestern Kansas. Brendam, TX: 1997. V. 71

BALLOU, ADIN
Autobiography. Lowell: 1896. V. 73
Christian Non-Resistance, In All Its Important Bearings. Philadelphia: 1846. V. 68; 73
An Exposition of Views Respecting the Principal Facts, Causes and Peculiarities Involved in Spirit Manifestations.... Boston: 1852. V. 69
History of the Town of Milford, Worcester County, Massachusetts from Its First Settlement in 1881. Boston: 1882. V. 68
The Inestimable Value of Souls. Boston: 1830. V. 68
Memoir of Adin Augutus Ballou. Hopedale: 1853. V. 73
Practical Christian Socialism. New York: 1854. V. 69

BALLOU, ELLIS
The Patent Hat: Designed to Promote the Growth of Certain Undeveloped Bumps and Thereby Increase the Thinking, Reasoning, Acting.... New York: 1855. V. 69

BALLOU, JENNY
Spanish Prelude. Boston: 1937. V. 72

BALLOU, ROBERT
Early Klickitat Valley Days. Goldendale: 1938. V. 70

BALLY, P. R. O.
The Genus Monadenium. Berne: 1961. V. 70

BALMER, EDWIN
Five Fatal Words. New York: 1932. V. 69
The Shield of Silence. New York: 1936. V. 71
Waylaid by Wireless. Boston: 1909. V. 72

BALSAM, L. G.
A. G. Warshawsky, Master Painter and Humanist. 1954. V. 69; 72

BALSTON, THOMAS
The Cambridge University Press Collection of Private Press Types. 1951. V. 71

BALTIMORE, FREDERICK CALVERT, BARON
A Tour to the East in the Years 1763 and 1764. With Remarks on the City of Constantinople and the Turks. 1767. V. 73
The Trial of Frederick Calvert, Esq., Baron of Baltimore in the Kingdom of Ireland, for a Rape on the Body of Sarah Woodcock and of Eliz. Griffinburg, and Anne Harvey, Otherwise Darby.... London: 1768. V. 71

BALTIMORE MUSEUM OF ART
2000 Years of Calligraphy: a Three-Part Exhibition Organized by the Baltimore Museum of Art...June 6-July 18, 1965. London: 1972. V. 72

BALTZER, FRITZ
Theodor Boveri. Life and Work of a Great Biologist 1862-1915. Los Angeles: 1967. V. 68

BALZAC, HONORE DE
The Alkahest or the House of Claes. London: 1887. V. 68
Bureaucracy or a Civil Service Reformer. London: 1891. V. 68
Le Chef-d'Oeuvre Inconnu. Paris: 1931. V. 70
La Comedie Humaine. London: 1897. V. 73
The Comedy of Human Life. Chicago: 1896. V. 68
La Fille aux Yeux d'Or. (The Girl with the Golden Eyes). London: 1896. V. 72
Histoire de la Grandeur et de la Decadence de Cesar Bitotteau.... Paris: 1838. V. 71
John Herring; a West of England Romance. London: 1886. V. 68
John Herring: a West of England Romance. London: 1887. V. 68
Mehalah: a Story of the Salt Marshes. London: 1885. V. 68
Pere Goriot. London: 1888. V. 68
The Physiology of Marriage, or Meditations of an Eclectic Philosopher on Happiness and Unhappiness in Marriage. London: 1925. V. 71
The Physiology of Marriage; or Meditations of an Eclectic Philosopher on Happiness and Unhappiness in Marriage. New York: 1925. V. 72
Richard Cable the Lightshipman. London: 1889. V. 68

BALZAC, HONORE DE continued
Richard Cable the Lightshipman. London: 1898. V. 68
Sons of the Soil. London: 1891. V. 68
A Street of Paris and Its Inhabitants. New York: 1900. V. 70

BALZAC, JEAN LOUIS GUEZ, SIEUR DE
Lettres de Feu Monsieur De Balzac a Monsieur Conrart. Leide: 1659. V. 70
Le Prince. Paris: 1632. V. 68; 72

BAMBARA, TONI CADE
Raymond's Run. Mankato: 1990. V. 70
The Sea Birds are Still Alive: Collected Stories. New York: 1977. V. 72

BAMBERGER, HEINRICH VON
Lehrbuch der Krankhetten des Herzens. Vienna: 1857. V. 72

BAMBERGER, LOUIS
Memoirs of Sixty Years In The Timber And Pianoforte Trades. London. V. 72

BAMFORD, SAMUEL
Passages in the Life of a Radical. London: 1844. V. 71

BAMPFIELD, R. W.
An Essay on the Curvatures and Diseases of the Spine, Including All the Forms of Spinal Distortion to Which the Fothergillian Gold Medal Was Awarded by the Medical Society of London.... London: 1824. V. 68; 71; 72

BAMPFYLDE, JOHN
Poems. Oxford: 1988. V. 68

BANATEANU, T.
Folk Costumes, Woven Textiles and Embroideries of Rumania. Rumania: 1958. V. 69

BANBURY, JEN
Like a Hole in the Head. Boston: 1998. V. 68; 71

BANCROFT, CAROLINE
Gulch of Gold. Denver: 1958. V. 69

BANCROFT, EDWARD
Experimental Researches Concerning the Philosophy of Permanent Colours; and the Best Means of Producing Them by Dyeing, Callico Printing &c. Philadelphia: 1814. V. 70

BANCROFT, FREDERIC
Slave Trading in the Old South. Baltimore: 1931. V. 68

BANCROFT, GEORGE
History of the United States of America. New York: 1885. V. 68
Poems. Cambridge: 1823. V. 68

BANCROFT, HUBERT HOWE
History of Arizona and New Mexico 1530-1888. San Francisco: 1889. V. 69
History of Arizona and New Mexico 1530-1888. Albuquerque: 1962. V. 69
History of Mexico. San Francisco: 1883. V. 71
The History of Oregon. San Francisco: 1886. V. 70
History of the North Mexican States and Texas: 1531-1889. Santa Fe: 1889. V. 70
History of the Pacific States of North America. Volume XII - Arizona and New Mexico 1530-1888. San Francisco: 1888. V. 68; 73
Popular Tribunals. San Francisco: 1871. V. 69
The Works of Hubert Howe Bancroft. San Francisco: 1882-1890. V. 72
The Works of Hubert Howe Bancroft. Volume XXIX. History of Oregon. Volumes I and II. San Francisco: 1886-1888. V. 68
The Works of...History of Central America. Volumes VI, VII & VIII. San Francisco: 1883-1887. V. 68; 73
The Works of...Volume XXXII...British Columbia. San Francisco: 1887. V. 68; 73
The Works of...Volume XXXV. California Inter Pocula. San Francisco: 1888. V. 68; 73
Works. Volume XVIII. San Francisco: 1889. V. 70
The Zamorano Index to History of California. Los Angeles: 1985. V. 68

BANCROFT, JOHN
The Borodin Affair. Crawley, Sussex: 1966. V. 72

BANDELIER, ADOLPH FRANCIS ALPHONSE
The Delight Makers. New York: 1918. V. 69
Hemenway Southwestern Archaeolgoical Expedition. Cambridge: 1890. V. 68; 70
A History of the Southwest. Volume I. and Supplement. Rome: 1969. V. 70
Indians of the Rio Grande Valley. Albuquerque: 1937. V. 70
The Southwest Journals of Adolph F. Bandelier 1880-1882. Santa Fe: 1966. V. 69
The Southwestern Journals of Adolph F. Bandelier. Albuquerque: 1966. V. 68

BANDINI, M.
Tapie un Art Autre: Torino, Parigi, New York Osaka. 1997. V. 72

BANGS, JOHN KENDRICK
Alice in Blunderland - an Iridescent Dream. New York: 1907. V. 70
Bikey the Skicycle and Other Tales of Jimmieboy. New York: 1902. V. 73
The Dreamers: a Club. New York: 1899. V. 70
The Enchanted Type-Writer. New York: 1899. V. 70
A House Boat on the Styx. New York: 1896. V. 70
Mr. Munchausen. Boston: 1901. V. 70
Mr. Munchausen. New York: 1901. V. 71
Molly and the Unwiseman Abroad. Philadelphia: 1910. V. 70
A Quest for Song. Boston: 1915. V. 69
R. Holmes and Co. New York: 1906. V. 70

BANGS, LESTER
Psychotic Reactions and Carburettor Dung. New York: 1987. V. 71

BANHAM, R.
A Concrete Atlantis: U.S. Industrial Building and European Modern Archtiecture. Cambridge: 1986. V. 72
Los Angeles: The Architecture of Four Ecologies. New York: 1971. V. 70; 73

BANISTER, HENRY
Gas Manupulation, with a Description of the Various Instruments and Apparatus in the Analysis of Coal and Coal Gas. London: 1863. V. 69

BANK, MELISSA
The Girls Guide to Hunting and Fishing. New York: 1999. V. 69

BANK OF BOMBAY
Report of the Committee of English Shareholders. London: 1868. V. 72

BANK OF MADRAS
Proceedings of the Annual General Meeting of Proprietors of the Bank of Madras, Held on Monday the 2d of March 1846. Madras: 1846. V. 71

BANKS, CHARLES EDWARD
The Planters of the Commonwealth. Boston: 1930. V. 70

BANKS, ELEANOR
Wandersong. Caldwell: 1950. V. 72

BANKS' *Florilegium.* London: 1988. V. 70

BANKS, IAIN
Complicity. Boston: 1993. V. 68
The Player of Games. London: 1988. V. 70
Walking on Glass. Boston: 1985. V. 71
Walking on Glass. London: 1985. V. 68
The Wasp Factory. Boston: 1984. V. 71

BANKS, JOHN
A Short Critical Review of the Political Life of Oliver Cromwell. London: 1769. V. 72
A Treatise on Mills, in four Parts.... London: 1795. V. 72

BANKS, JOSEPH
The Endeavour Journal of Joseph Banks 1768-1771. Sydney: 1962. V. 73
A Speech Delivered to the Royal Society, on Wednesday November 30, 1780, Being their Anniversary. London: 1780. V. 72

BANKS, LANGLEY
The Joiners' Companion to a New System of Handrailing, Namely the Square Cut. Manchester: 1854. V. 72

BANKS, LOUIS ALBERT
Immortal Songs of Camp and Field. Cleveland: 1899. V. 70

BANKS, LYNNE REID
Dark Quartet, the Story of the Brontes. London: 1976. V. 70
The L-Shaped Room. London: 1960. V. 73

BANKS, MICHAEL EDWARD BORG
Rakaposhi. London: 1959. V. 69

BANKS, RAYMOND
Meet Me In Darkness. New York: 1960. V. 72

BANKS, RUSSELL
Affliction. New York: 1989. V. 72
Family Life. New York: 1985. V. 69
Hamilton Stark. Boston: 1978. V. 70
Rule of the Bone. New York: 1995. V. 70
Searching for Survivors. New York: 1975. V. 68; 71; 73
Trailerpark. Boston: 1981. V. 68; 71; 72

BANKS, WILLIAM MITCHELL
On the Wolffian Bodies of the Foetus and Their Remains in the Adult.... Edinburgh: 1864. V. 72

BANKS, WILLIAM STOTT
List of Provincial Words in Use at Wakefield in Yorkshire; with Explanations, Including a few Descriptions of Buildings and Localities. 1865. V. 73
Walks in Yorkshire: Wakefield and Its Neighbourhood. 1871. V. 73

BANKSON, RUSSELL A.
The Klondike Nugget. Caldwell: 1935. V. 68; 73

BANNATYNE, DUGALD J.
Handbook of Republican Institutions in the United States of America. Edinburgh: 1887. V. 70

BANNERMAN, DAVID ARMITAGE
Birds of the Atlantic Islands. 1963. V. 70
Birds of the Atlantic Islands. Edinburgh and London: 1963-1968. V. 73
The Birds of the British Isles. 1953. V. 69
The Birds of the British Isles. Edinburgh: 1953-1963. V. 73
The Birds of the British Isles. London: 1953-1963. V. 69
The Birds of Tropical West Africa.... London: 1930-1951. V. 73
The Birds of West and Equatorial Africa. 1953. V. 69; 70; 72; 73
The Canary Islands.... 1922. V. 69; 72
Handbook of the Birds of Cyprus. 1971. V. 69
History of the Birds of the Cape Verde Islands. 1968. V. 73

BANNERMAN, HELEN
Little Black Sambo. New York: 1943. V. 69; 71
The Little Black Sambo Story Book. New York: 1926. V. 70

BANNERMAN, HELEN continued
The Story of Little Black Quibba. London. V. 70
The Story of Little Black Sambo. New York: 1900. V. 70
The Story of Little Black Sambo. London: 1911. V. 69
The Story of Little Black Sambo. London: 1924. V. 70
The Story of Little Black Sambo. Racine: 1937. V. 69

BANNET, IVOR
The Amazons. Waltham St. Lawrence: 1948. V. 70; 71

BANNING, MARGARET CULKIN
The Iron Will. New York: 1936. V. 69

BANNING, WILLIAM
Six Horses. New York: 1930. V. 69

BANNISTER, ARTHUR THOMAS
A Descriptive Catalogue of the Manuscripts in the Hereford Cathedral Library. Hereford: 1927. V. 70

BANOGLU, N. A.
Turkey, a Sportsman's Paradise. 1954. V. 70; 72

BANTA, THEODORE M.
A Frisian Family. The Banta Genealogy. Descendants of Epke Jacobse, who Came from Friesland, Netherlands, to New Amsterdam, Feb. 1659. New York: 1893. V. 69

BANTING, WILLIAM
Letter on Corpulence, Addressed to the Public. London: 1864. V. 72

BANTOCK, GAVIN
Eirenikon. A Poem. 1972. V. 68

BANTOCK, NICK
Griffin & Sabine an Extraordinary Correspondence. San Francisco: 1991. V. 68; 70
Griffin & Sabine. (with) *Sabine's Notebook.* (with) *The Golden Mean.* San Francisco: 1991-1993. V. 69

BANVARD, JOHN
Description of Banvard's Panorama of the Mississippi River, Painted on Three Miles of Canvas.... Boston: 1847. V. 68

BANVILLE, JOHN
The Book of Evidence. New York: 1990. V. 68
Eclipse. London: 2000. V. 69
Eclipse. New York: 2001. V. 71
Kepler. London: 1981. V. 69
Long Lankin. London: 1970. V. 72
Mefisto. London: 1986. V. 68
The Newton Letter. Boston: 1987. V. 68
Nightspawn. London: 1971. V. 69; 73
Nightspawn. New York: 1971. V. 68; 71

BAQUET, CAMILLE
History of the First Brigade, New Jersey Volunteers, from 1861 to 1865. Trenton: 1910. V. 69

BARAGA, FREDERIC
A Dictionary of the Otchipwe Language, Explained in English. Cincinnati: 1853. V. 71

BARAKA, IMAMU AMIRI
Blues People. Negro Music in White America. New York: 1963. V. 69; 72

BARBA, ALVARO ALONSO
Arte de Los Metales, en Que se Ensena el Verdadero Beneficio de Los de Oro, y Plata Por Azogue.... Madrid: 1729. V. 68
Arte de los Metales, en Que se Ensena el Verdadero beneficio de los de Oro, y Plata por Azogue.... Madrid: 1770. V. 72
Grundlicher Unterricht vn den Metallen, Darinnen Beschrieben Wird, Wie sie Werden in Der Erden Generitt.... Ephrata: 1763. V. 68

BARBARA Morgan. 1972. V. 68

BARBARITIES of the Enemy, Exposed in a Report. Worcester: 1814. V. 69

BARBARO, FRANCESCO
De Re Uxoria, Libri Duo. Hagenau: 1533. V. 73

BARBATO, BARTOLOMEO
Delle Lettere di Bartolomeo Barbato Padovano Volume Primo. Padova: 1625. V. 70; 73

BARBATO, JOSEPH
Heart of the Land: Essays on Last Great Places. New York: 1994. V. 70
Heart of the Land: Essays on Last Great Places. New York: 1995. V. 69

BARBAULD, ANNA LAETITIA AIKIN
The Force of Example: a Nursery Rhyme from the Celebrated Lessons for Children by.... London: 1822. V. 71
Hymns in Prose for Children. London: 1880. V. 68
Poems. London: 1773. V. 73
Poems. London: 1792. V. 69
Simple Stories And Lessons For Children. London: 1850. V. 72
Tales, Poems and Essays. Boston: 1884. V. 69

BARBAULT, JEAN
Les Plus Beaux Monuments de Rome Ancienne.... Rome: 1761. V. 69; 72

BARBEAU, M.
Haida Myths. 1953. V. 69
Totem Poles. 1950. V. 69
Totem Poles. 1964. V. 69

BARBEAU, MARIUS
Assumption Sash. 1945. V. 68; 73
Indian Days in the Canadian Rockies. Toronto: 1923. V. 68; 73

BARBER, ANTONIA
The Mousehole Cat. New York: 1990. V. 70

BARBER, HENRY
Furness and Cartmel Notes, or Jottings of Topographical, Ecclesiastical and Popular Antiquities.... Ulverston;: 1894. V. 71

BARBER, JAMES
The Court of Directors of the East India Company, Versus Her Majesty's Ministers, the Resolutions of the House of Commons and the Public of India and England.... London: 1839. V. 73
Letter to the Members of the East India and China Association, on the Subject of Steam Communication with India. London: 1839. V. 73
Philojohannes Unmasked, and the Truth Told Relative to the East India Company's Management of Steam Communication with India. London: 1839. V. 73
Steam Communications with India, via the Red Sea, on a Comprehensive Plan. 1840. V. 73

BARBER, JOHN
The Life and Character of John Barber.... London: 1741. V. 72

BARBER, JOHN WARNER
Historical Collections of New Jersey Past and Present.... New Haven: 1868. V. 69
Historical Collections of the State of New Jersey: Containing a General Collection of the Most Interesting Facts, Traditions, Biographical Sketches, Anecdotes, etc. New York: 1844. V. 69
Historical Collections of the State of New York.... New York: 1842. V. 69

BARBER, JONATHAN
A Practical Treatise on Gesture, Chiefly Abstracted from Austin's Chironomia.... Cambridge: 1831. V. 68

BARBER, NOEL
Conversations with Painters. London: 1964. V. 68

BARBER, THOMAS WALTER
The Engineer's Sketch Book of Mechanical Movements. London: 1890. V. 71

BARBER, WILLETTA ANN
Drawn Conclusion. Garden City: 1942. V. 70

BARBETTE, PAUL
Opera Chirurgico Anatomica, ad Circularem Sanguinis Motum, Aliaque Recentiorum Inventa, Accomondate, Accedit De Peste Tractatus Observationibus Illustratus. Lugd Batav: 1672. V. 68; 72
Praxis Barbettiana, cum Notis & Observationibus Frederici Deckers. Amsterdam: 1678. V. 70; 72

BARBEY D'AUREVILLY, JULES
The Anatomy of Dandyism, with Some Observations on Beau Brummel. London: 1928. V. 70
What Never Dies. Paris: 1902. V. 68

BARBIER, ANTOINE ALEXANDRE
Dictionnaire Des Ouvrages Anonymes. Mansfield Centre: 1999. V. 71

BARBIER, MARIE ANNE
Les Tragedies et Autres Poesies de.... Leide: 1723. V. 68

BARBIERE, JOE
Scraps from the Prison Table, at Camp Chase and Johnson's Island. Doylestown: 1868. V. 73

BARBOUR, BARTON H.
Tales of the Mountain Men. Santa Fe: 1984. V. 71

BARBOUR, GABRIEL
Kind, Kind and Gentle is She. New York: 1837-1841. V. 73

BARBOUR, R. H.
Death in the Virgins. New York: 1940. V. 68

BARBOUR, R. W.
Bats of America. Lexington: 1969. V. 70

BARBOUR, T.
Herpetology of Cuba. Cambridge: 1919. V. 69
Sphaerodactylus. Cambridge: 1921. V. 68; 72

BARCIA CARBALLIDO Y ZUNIGA, ANDRES GONZALES DE
Ensayo Cronologico Para la Historia General de la Florida...Desde el Ano de 1512...Hasta el de 1722.... Madrid: 1723. V. 68; 70; 73

BARCLAY, A. E.
The Alimentary Tract; a Radiographic Study. London and Manchester: 1915. V. 71
The Foetal Circulation. Oxford: 1944. V. 71

BARCLAY, EDGAR
Stonehenge and Its Earthworks. 1895. V. 71
Stonehenge and Its Earthworks. London: 1895. V. 73

BARCLAY, JOHN
Argenis. Lugd. Bat: 1630. V. 72
A Description of the Arteries of the Human Body. Edinburgh: 1820. V. 71; 72
The Muscular Motions of the Human Body. Edinburgh: 1808. V. 71; 72
A Series of Engravings of the Bones of the Human Skeleton. Edinburgh: 1819-1820. V. 71

BARCLAY, ROBERT
Apologia de la Verdadera Theologia Christiana: Como Ela es Professada, y Predicada, por el Pueblo, llamado en Menosprecio los Tembladore. Londres: 1710. V. 72
An Apology for the True Christian Divinity. London: 1736. V. 72
An Apology for the True Christian Divinity. Birmingham: 1765. V. 70; 73

BARCROFT, JOSEPH
The Respiratory Function of the Blood. Part II. Haemoglobin. Cambridge: 1928. V. 71

BARD, FLOYD
Horse Wrangler. Sixty Years in the Saddle in Wyoming and Montana. 1960. V. 68

BARD, SAMUEL
A Compendium of the Theory and Practice of Midwifery.... New York: 1807. V. 68; 70; 73
Tentamen Medicum Inaugurale. De Viribus Opii: Quod. Edinburgh: 1765. V. 68; 70

BARDEEN, JOHN
Physical Principles Involved in Transistor Action in Bell System Technical Journal, April 1949. V. 73

BARDELEBEN, K. VON
Atlas of Applied (Topographical) Human Anatomy.... London and New York: 1906. V. 71

BARDESCHI, M. D.
Frank Lloyd Wright. London: 1972. V. 68

BARDIN, JOHN FRANKLIN
The Burning Glass. New York: 1950. V. 73
The Case Against Butterfly by Gregory Tree. New York: 1951. V. 68; 72

BARDOLPH, RICHARD
The Negro Vanguard. New York: 1959. V. 72

BARDWELL, THOMAS
Practical Treatise on Painting in Oil-Colours. London: 1795. V. 73
The Practice of Painting and Perspective made Easy.... London: 1756. V. 71

BAREHAM, T.
A Bibliography of George Crabbe. Folkeston: 1978. V. 72

BARER, BURL
The Saint: A Complete History In Print, Radio, Film And Television. Jefferson: 1993. V. 72

BARHAM, RICHARD HARRIS
The Ingoldsby Legends. London: 1840-1842. V. 71
The Ingoldsby Legends. London: 1840-1847. V. 73
The Ingoldsby Legends. London: 1855. V. 72
The Ingoldsby Legends. London: 1864. V. 71
The Ingoldsby Legends. London: 1866. V. 71
The Ingoldsby Legends. London: 1870. V. 68
The Ingoldsby Legends. London: 1930. V. 68
The Lay of St. Aloys. A Legend of Blois. by Thomas Ingoldsby. London. V. 71

BARHAM, WILLIAM
Descriptions of Niagara. Gravesend. V. 72

BARI, VALESKA
The Course of Empire, First Hand Accounts of California in the Days of the Gold Rush of '49. New York: 1931. V. 69

BARICH, BILL
Hat Creek and the McCloud. Santa Rosa: 1988. V. 72

BARILLET, J.
Les Pensees, Histoire, Culture - Multiplication - Emploi...Ouvrage Orne de Nombreuses Vignettes.... Paris: 1869. V. 71; 73

BARING, FRANCIS
Observations on the Establishment of the Bank of England and on the Paper Circulation of the Country.... London: 1797. V. 72
Observations on the Publications of Walter Boyd, Esq. M.P. London: 1801. V. 68

BARING, MAURICE
A Year in Russia. London: 1907. V. 71

BARING GOULD, SABINE
Amazing Adventures. London: 1903. V. 72
Arminell: a Social Romance. London: 1891. V. 68
The Deserts of Southern France, an Introduction to the Limestone and Chalk Plateaux of Ancient Aquitaine. 1894. V. 70
The Lives of the Saints. 1877. V. 69
The Vicar Of Morwenstow. A Life Of Robert Stephen Hawker. London: 1876. V. 72

BARING GOULD, WILLIAM SABINE
Nero Wolfe of West Thirty-fifth Street. New York: 1969. V. 68
Sherlock Holmes of Baker Street. New York: 1962. V. 68; 69

BARJAUD, J. B.
Description de Londres et de ses Edifices. Paris: 1810. V. 71
Homere, ou L'Origine de l'Iliade et de l'Odyssee, Poeme, Suivi de Fragmens d'Un Poeme Intitule Charlemagne. Paris: 1811. V. 68

BARKDULL, TOM
Lonesome Walks. New York: 1971. V. 69

BARKER, ANSELM HOLCOMB
Anselm Holcomb Barker 1822-1895; Pioneer Builder and Early Settler of Auraria. Denver: 1959. V. 70

BARKER, BENJAMIN
Blackbeard; or, the Pirate of the Roanoke. Boston: 1847. V. 68

BARKER, CHARLES A.
Background of the Revolution in Maryland. New Haven: 1940. V. 73

BARKER, CICELY MARY
Autumn Songs with Music from Flower Fairies of Autumn. London: 1927. V. 69; 72
Fairy Alphabet. London: 1934. V. 72
Flower Fairies of the Autumn. London: 1926. V. 68; 71; 72; 73
Flower Fairies of the Garden. London: 1955. V. 69
Flower Fairies of the Spring. London: 1923. V. 72; 73
Flower Fairies of the Spring. London: 1926. V. 68
Flower Fairies of the Summer. London: 1925. V. 72; 73
A Little Book of Old Rhymes. London: 1936. V. 68
Spring Songs with Music from Flower Fairies of the Spring. London. V. 73

BARKER, CLIVE
The Books of Blood. New York: 1988. V. 68
Books of Blood, Volumes I and II. London: 1984. V. 68; 71
Cabal. London: 1988. V. 70
Coldheart Canyon: A Hollywood Ghost Story. New York: 2001. V. 71
The Damnation Game. London: 1986. V. 73
The Damnation Game. New York: 1987. V. 70; 73
The Great and Secret Show. 1989. V. 68
The Great and Secret Show. London: 1989. V. 71; 73
The Great and Secret Show. New York: 1989. V. 73
In the Flesh. New York: 1986. V. 70; 72
The Inhuman Condition. New York: 1986. V. 69
The Man Who Wasn't There. London: 1989. V. 68
Shadows in Eden. 1991. V. 68
The Thief of Always. New York: 1992. V. 70; 73
Weaveworld. New York: 1987. V. 69
Weaveworld. London: 1987. V. 68

BARKER, E. S.
When the Dogs Bark Treed. 1946. V. 69

BARKER, ELSA
The Redman Cave Murder. New York: 1930. V. 72

BARKER, EUGENE C.
The Life of Stephen F. Austin, Founder of Texas, 1793-1836. Nashville: 1925. V. 68

BARKER, F. C.
Lake and Forest As I Have Known Them. Boston: 1903. V. 73

BARKER, GEORGE
Alanna Autumnal. 1933. V. 70
Thirty Preliminary Poems. 1933. V. 70
Thirty Preliminary Poems. London: 1933. V. 71
The View from a Blind Eye. London: 1962. V. 68

BARKER, H. GRANVILLE
The Marrying of Anne Leete. 1909. V. 70

BARKER, JACOB
An Appeal to Thinking Men. Natchez: 1860. V. 68

BARKER, JOHN THEODORE
The Beauty of Flowers in Field and Wood.... Bath. V. 70

BARKER, K. F.
Champion. 1936. V. 68

BARKER, LEWELLYS
The Nervous System and Its Constituent Neurons. New York: 1899. V. 68; 71; 72
Time and the Physician. The Autobiography of.... New York: 1942. V. 71

BARKER, MATTHEW HENRY
Greenwich Hospital, a Series of Naval Sketches, Descriptive of the Life of a Man-of-War's Man. London: 1826. V. 70
Jem Bunt: A Tale of the Land and the Ocean. London: 1841. V. 71
Walks Round Nottingham. London: 1835. V. 70

BARKER, NICOLAS
Bibliotheca Lindesiana. London: 1978. V. 68
The Printer and the Poet: an Account of the Printing of The Tapestry Based Upon Correspondence Between Stanley Morison and Robert Bridges. 1970. V. 71
Stanley Morison. Cambridge: 1972. V. 68

BARKER, PAT
Another World. London: 1998. V. 71
Blow Your House Down. New York: 1984. V. 71
Border Crossing. London: 2001. V. 68
The Ghost Road. London: 1995. V. 68; 71
The Ghost Road. New York: 1995. V. 68; 71
The Man Who Wasn't There. London: 1989. V. 68
Regeneration. New York: 1992. V. 69

BARKER, S. OMAR
Buckaboo Ballads. Santa Fe: 1928. V. 71; 73

BARKER, THOMAS
Forty Lithographic Impressions from Drawings.... Bath: 1813. V. 73

BARKER, W. G. M. JONES
Historical and Topographical Account of Wensleydale and the Valley of the Yore in the North Riding of Yorkshire. London: 1856. V. 73
The Three Days of Wensleydale: The Valley of the Yore. London: 1854. V. 73

BARKLEY, T. M.
Flora of the Great Plains by the Great Plains Flora Association. Lawrence: 1986. V. 72

BARLAS, JOHN
Selections from the Poems of John E. Barlas. London: 1925. V. 68

BARLER, MILES
Early Days in Llano. 1905. V. 68; 73

BARLETT, LANIER
The Lash. New York: 1930. V. 70

BARLOW, ARTHUR
Kivet of the Bush. Bloemfontein: 1950. V. 71

BARLOW, CLIVE
A Field Guide to Birds of the Gambia and Senegal. East Sussex: 1997. V. 68

BARLOW, EDWARD
Barlow's Journal of His Life at Sea in King's Ships, East & West Indiamen and Other Merchantmen from 1659 to 1703. London: 1934. V. 72

BARLOW, FRANCIS
Barlow's Birds and Beasts, in Sixty-Seven Excellent and Useful Prints, Being a Collection of the Chief Works of the Eminent Master.... 1775. V. 69

BARLOW, JANE
Bog-Land Studies. London: 1892. V. 68
Bog Lane Studies. London: 1893. V. 69
The End of Elfintown. (Poems). London: 1894. V. 70

BARLOW, JOEL
A Letter to the National Convention of France, on the Defects of the Constitution of 1791.... London: 1793. V. 71
An Oration, Delivered at the North Church in Hartford, at the Meeting of the Connecticut Society of the Cincinnati, July 4th, 1787, in Commemoration of the Independence of the United States. Hartford: 1787. V. 71

BARLOW, JOHN
On Man's Power Over Himself to Prevent or Control Insanity. London: 1843. V. 71

BARLOW, P. W.
Observations on the Niagara Railway Suspension Bridge, Made During a Recent Tour in America. London: 1860. V. 69

BARLOW, STEPHEN
The History of Ireland, from the Earliest Period to the Present Time.... London: 1814. V. 70

BARLOW, THOMAS
Brutum Fulman: or the Bull of Pope Pius V. London: 1681. V. 70
The Gunpowder-Treason: with a Discourse of the Manner of Its Discovery.... London: 1679. V. 70; 72

BARMAN, C.
The Bridge. A Chapter in the History of Building. London: 1926. V. 71; 72

BARMBY, CUTHBERT
James Cope. New York: 1899. V. 70

BARNARD, ALFRED
Orchards and Gardens Ancient and Modern. London: 1895. V. 68; 69; 72

BARNARD, CHARLOTTE ALINGTON
Thoughts, Verses and Songs. London: 1877. V. 69

BARNARD, EVAN G.
A Rider of the Cherokee Strip. Boston. V. 71
A Rider of the Cherokee Strip. New York: 1936. V. 71

BARNARD, GEORGE
Drawing from Nature. London: 1865. V. 72
Drawing from Nature. London: 1877. V. 72
Handbook of Foliage and Foreground Drawing. London: 1876. V. 69
The Theory and Practice of Landscape Painting in Water Colours. London: 1855. V. 69

BARNARD, GEORGE PHILIP
The Selenium Cell, Its Properties and Applications.... London: 1930. V. 69

BARNARD, HENRY
School Architecture; or Contributions to the Improvement of School-Houses in the United States. New York: 1849. V. 73

BARNARD, J. G.
Report on the North Sea Canal of Holland; and on the Improvement of Navigation from Rotterdam to the Sea; to the Chief of Engineers, United States Army. Washington: 1872. V. 69

BARNARD, JOHN
Considerations on the Proposal for Reducing the Interest on the National Debt. London: 1750. V. 72
A Defence of Several Proposals for Raising of Three Millions for the Service of the Government for the Year 1746. London: 1746. V. 72
A Present for an Apprentice: a Sure Guide to Gain Both Esteem and Estate. London: 1750. V. 68; 69; 72

BARNARD, K. H.
Contributions to the Knowledge of South African Marine Mollusca. 1958-1964. V. 73

BARNARD, MARJORIE
North of the Yellowstone, South of the Bulls. Billings: 1978. V. 70

BARNARD, ROBERT
Blood Brotherhood. London: 1977. V. 69
A Corpse in a Gilded Cage. London: 1984. V. 69
Death and the Princess. London: 1982. V. 69; 71
Death in a Cold Climate. London: 1980. V. 69
Death in Purple Prose. London: 1987. V. 72
Death of an Old Goat. London: 1974. V. 72; 73
Death of an Old Goat. New York: 1977. V. 71
Death on the High C's. London: 1977. V. 69; 71
The Disposal of the Living. London: 1985. V. 72
A Little Local Murder. London: 1976. V. 69; 71
Little Victims. London: 1983. V. 69
Posthumous Papers. London: 1979. V. 73

BARNBAUM, BRUCE
Visual Symphony: A Photographic Work in Four Movements. New York: 1986. V. 73

BARNEBY, WILLIAM HENRY
Life and Labour in the Far, Far, West.... London New York etc: 1884. V. 71
The New Far West and the Old Far East.... London: 1889. V. 71

BARNES, ALFRED C.
The New York and Brooklyn Bridge. New York: 1883. V. 68

BARNES, ANNIE MARIA
Matoouchon: a Story of Indian Child Life. Philadelphia: 1895. V. 71

BARNES, CHARLES D.
Readings in Neurophysiology. New York: 1968. V. 72

BARNES, DALLAS
See The Woman. London: 1974. V. 72
See the Woman. London: 1977. V. 68
Yesterday is Dead. London: 1977. V. 68; 72

BARNES, DJUNA
The Antiphon: a Play. London: 1958. V. 71
Greenwich Village As It Is. New York: 1978. V. 71
Ladies Almanack. Paris: 1928. V. 73
Nightwood. London: 1936. V. 69; 71; 73
Ryder. New York: 1928. V. 71
To the Dogs. 1982. V. 70; 72
To the Dogs. Rochester: 1982. V. 69; 73
Vagaries Malicieux: Two Stories. New York: 1974. V. 71

BARNES, F. C.
Cartridges of the World. 1965. V. 70; 72; 73

BARNES, JAMES
Naval Actions of the War of 1812. New York: 1896. V. 73

BARNES, JOSEPH K.
Medical and Surgical History of the Rebellion. Washington: 1875-1888. V. 69; 70; 72

BARNES, JULIAN
Before She Met Me. London: 1982. V. 69
Cross Channel. London: 1996. V. 68; 71
Duffy. London: 1980. V. 68; 70; 71
England, England. London: 1998. V. 71; 72
England, England. New York: 1999. V. 72
Fiddle City. London: 1981. V. 69
Flaubert's Parrot. London: 1984. V. 69; 70; 72
Flaubert's Parrot. New York: 1985. V. 68; 69; 71; 73
A History of the World in 10 1/2 Chapters. New York: 1989. V. 69
Love, etc. London: 2000. V. 70
Metroland. London: 1980. V. 70; 71
The Porcupine. London: 1992. V. 71
Putting the Boot In. London: 1985. V. 69; 70
Staring at the Sun. London: 1986. V. 73
Steel Guitar. New York: 1991. V. 68
Talking It Over. London: 1991. V. 68; 69; 70; 73
Talking It Over. New York: 1991. V. 69; 70; 72

BARNES, KIM
In the Wilderness. New York: 1995. V. 69
In the Wilderness. New York: 1996. V. 69

BARNES, LINDA
Bitter Finish. New York: 1983. V. 69
Cities of the Dead. New York: 1986. V. 68; 71
Coyote. New York: 1990. V. 71
Gold Case. New York: 1997. V. 71
The Snake Tattoo. New York: 1989. V. 71
A Trouble of Fools. New York: 1987. V. 68; 69; 70; 71

BARNES, MABEL LOUISA
Happy Memories of Robert Barnes. Oxford: 1875. V. 68

BARNES, MACON
Lion Takes a Trip. Toano: 1960. V. 73

BARNES, MADELINE
Tub-Time Tales. 1920. V. 68
Tub-Time Tales. London: 1920. V. 69

BARNES, MARGARET
Westward Passage. Boston: 1931. V. 71

BARNES, RAYMOND P.
History of Roanoke. Roanoke?: 1968. V. 72

BARNES, RUTH A.
I Hear America Singing. An Anthology of Folk Poetry. Philadelphia: 1937. V. 71

BARNES, W.
Illustrations of the North American Species of the Genus Catocala. New York: 1918. V. 72

BARNES, WARNER
A Bibliography of Elizabeth Barrett Browning. Austin: 1967. V. 72

BARNES, WILL C.
Apaches and Longhorns: The Reminiscences of Will C. Barnes. Los Angeles: 1941. V. 69; 71
Tales From the X Bar Horse Camp, The Blue Outlaw and Other Stories. Chicago: 1920. V. 71
Western Grazing Grounds and Forest Ranges- A History of the Livestock Industry. Chicago: 1913. V. 71

BARNES, WILLIAM
Dorset Poems. London: 1989. V. 73
Early England and the Saxon-english: With Some Notes on the Father- stock of the Saxon- English, the Frisians. London: 1869. V. 71
Hwomely Rhymes. A Second Collection of Poems in the Dorset Dialect. London: 1859. V. 71; 73
Orra: a Lapland Tale. Dorchester: 1822. V. 73
Poems of Rural Life in Common English. London: 1868. V. 71; 73
Poems of Rural Life in the Dorset Dialect. 1844. V. 73
Poems of Rural Life in the Dorset Dialect. 1862. V. 73
Poems of Rural Life in the Dorset Dialect. London: 1888. V. 71
Poems Partly of Rural Life. 1846. V. 73
Select Poems of William Barnes. London: 1908. V. 71

BARNETT, ADA
The Joyous Adventurer. London: 1938. V. 69

BARNETT, ANTHONY
Power and the Throne. The Monarchy Debate. London: 1994. V. 73

BARNETT, HENRIETTA
Canon Barnet: His Life, Work and Friends. London: 1918. V. 72

BARNETT, P. NEVILLE
Armorial Book-Plates, Their Romantic Origin and Artistic Development. Sydney: 1932. V. 70

BARNETT, S. A.
A Century of Darwin. London: 1958. V. 68

BARNEY, JAMES M.
Tales of Apache Warfare. 1933. V. 72

BARNITZ, ALBERT
Life in Custer's Cavalry Diaries & Letters of Albert & Jennie Barnitz 1867-1868. New Haven: 1977. V. 72

BARNS, CASS G.
The Sod House Reminiscent Historical and Biographical Sketches Featuring Nebraska Pioneers. Madison, NE: 1930. V. 71

THE BARNUM & Bailey New and Thrilling Military Spectacular Drama and the Mahdi, or, for the Victoria Cross.... London: 1898. V. 70

BARNUM and Jumbo's ABC. London: 1880. V. 73
BARNUM and Jumbo's ABC. London: 1884. V. 72

BARNUM, PHINEAS TAYLOR
P. T. Barnum's Circus, Museum and Menagerie. New York and London: 1888. V. 72
Struggles and Triumphs. Hartford: 1869. V. 69; 72
Struggles and Triumphs. New York: 1871. V. 68
Struggles and Triumphs. Buffalo: 1878. V. 71; 73
Struggles and Triumphs. Buffalo: 1889. V. 69

BAROJA, PIO
Weeds. New York: 1923. V. 70

BARON, JOHN
The Life of Edward Jenner, M.D. LL.D. F.R.S., Physician Extraordinary to the King &c. 1827. V. 73

BARON, JOHN AUGUSTUS
The Bills of Exchange Act 1890. Toronto: 1890. V. 72

BARON, PETER
The Opium Murders. New York: 1930. V. 68

BARON, STANLEY
All My Enemies. New York: 1952. V. 72

BARONIO, GIUSEPPE
On Grafting in Animals. Boston: 1985. V. 70; 71

BARONIO, JOYCE
42nd Street Studio. New York: 1980. V. 68

BARONTI, PRINCESS GERVEE
The Noble Courtesan. New York: 1930. V. 71

BARR, ALFRED H.
Fantastic Art, Dada, Surrealism. 1946. V. 72
Fantastic Art, Dada, Surrealism. New York: 1946. V. 69
Matisse - His Art and His Public. New York: 1951. V. 72

BARR, JEROME
All Good Americans. New York: 1937. V. 68

BARR, NEVADA
Bittersweet. New York: 1984. V. 69; 70; 73
Ill Wind. New York: 1995. V. 72; 73
A Superior Death. New York: 1994. V. 68; 69; 71; 72
Track of the Cat. New York: 1993. V. 68; 69; 70; 71; 73

BARR, ROBERT
The Triumphs of Eugene Valmont. 1906. V. 71
The Triumphs of Eugene Valmont. New York: 1906. V. 69

BARRATT, THOMAS J.
The Annals of Hampstead. London: 1912. V. 73

BARRE, RICHARD
The Innocents. 1995. V. 70
The Innocents. New York: 1995. V. 68; 69

BARRE, WILLIAM VINCENT
History of the French Consulate Under Napoleon Buonaparte. London: 1804. V. 68

BARRERA, A. DE
Memoirs of Rachel. London: 1858. V. 68

BARRERE, P.
Ornithologicae Specimen Novum, sive Series Avium in Ruscinone, Pyrenaeis Montibus, Atque Gallia Aequinoctiali Observatarum. Perpignan: 1745. V. 73

BARRETT, ALFRED WALTER
Industrial Explorings In and Around London. 1896. V. 71

BARRETT, ANDREA
Dead Dog Blues. New York: 1994. V. 68
The Forms of Water. New York: 1993. V. 68; 69
Lucid Stars. New York: 1988. V. 69; 72
Lucid Stars. London: 1989. V. 68; 71
The Middle Kingdom. New York: 1991. V. 69
Secret Harmonies. New York: 1989. V. 72
Ship Fever and Other Stories. New York and London: 1996. V. 68; 69; 73

BARRETT, C. G.
The Lepidoptera of the British Islands. London: 1892-1907. V. 69

BARRETT, C. J.
Barn Elms and the Kit Kat Club now the Ranelagh Club. An Historical Sketch. London: 1884. V. 72

BARRETT, EATON STANNARD
All the Talents. London: 1807. V. 68; 73
Woman, A Poem: Occasional Poems. London: 1822. V. 71

BARRETT, EDWARD
Gunnery Instructions Simplified for the Volunteer Officers of the U. S. Navy; with Hints to Executive and Other Officers. New York: 1862. V. 70

BARRETT, FRANK
Lieutenant Barnabas. London: 1890. V. 68
The Smuggler's Secret. London: 1893. V. 68

BARRETT, FRANKLIN A.
Caughley and Coalport Porcelain. Leigh-on-Sea: 1951. V. 72
Worcester Porcelain. London: 1966. V. 72

BARRETT, JOHN
An Essay on the Earlier Part of the Life of Swift. 1808. V. 72
An Essay on the Earlier Part of the Life of Swift. London: 1808. V. 68

BARRETT, NEAL
The Hereafter Gang. 1991. V. 70
Pink Vodka Blues. New York: 1992. V. 68; 71

BARRETT, PETER
Great True Hunts. 1967. V. 69; 70; 72; 73

BARRETT, S. A.
Maintonomah and Other Poems. New York: 1849. V. 73

BARRETT, S. M.
Geronimo's Story of His Life. New York: 1906. V. 69

BARRETT, TOM
The Mollies Were Men. New York: 1969. V. 68

BARRETT, W. P.
The Trial of Jenne L'Aire. New York: 1932. V. 68

BARRETT, WILLIAM E.
The Lilies of the Field. Garden City: 1962. V. 69; 71

BARRETT & CO., P.
General and Commercial Directory of Blackburn, Accrington, Darwin, Clitheroe, Great Harwood, Rishton, Church and Oswaldtwistle, ClaytonLeMoors, Whaley and Adjacent Villages and Townships. Preston: 1912. V. 73

BARRETT-LENNARD, C. E.
Travels in British Columbia: with the Narrative of a Yacht Voyage Round Vancouver's Island. London: 1862. V. 71

BARRIE, JAMES MATTHEW
The Admirable Crichton. London. V. 71
The Admirable Crichton. London: 1915. V. 69
Auld Licht Idylls. London: 1888. V. 68
Courage. London: 1922. V. 70
An Edinburgh Eleven. London: 1889. V. 68
Jane Annie; or the Good Conduct Prize. London: 1893. V. 70
A Lady's Shoe. New York: 1898. V. 68
The Little White Bird. New York: 1902. V. 68; 70
The Blampied Edition of Peter Pan. New York: 1940. V. 70
Peter and Wendy. London: 1911. V. 69; 73
Peter Pan. 1909. V. 71; 72
Peter Pan. London: 1928. V. 70
Peter Pan. Norwalk: 1946. V. 69
Peter Pan and Wendy. London: 1921. V. 70
Peter Pan and Wendy. London: 1925. V. 70
Peter Pan and Wendy. 1935. V. 73
Peter Pan and Wendy. New York: 1940. V. 73
Peter Pan and Wendy. London: 1988. V. 73
Peter Pan in Kensington Gardens. London: 1906. V. 70; 72
Peter Pan in Kensington Gardens. London: 1908. V. 68; 70
Peter Pan In Kensington Gardens. London: 1950. V. 73
Peter Pan or the Boy Who Would Not Grow Up. London: 1928. V. 69
The Peter Pan Picture Book. 1925. V. 73
Quality Street. London. V. 71
Quality Street. Edinburgh: 1901. V. 68
Quality Street. London: 1901. V. 73
Quality Street. 1913. V. 70
A Tillyloss Scandal. New York: 1893. V. 70
When a Man's Single. London: 1888. V. 68

BARRIERE, DOMENICO
Villa Aldobrandina Tusculana. Roma: 1647. V. 68

BARRINGER, MARIE
The Four and Lena. New York: 1938. V. 73

BARRINGTON, E.
The Duel of Queens: a Romance of Mary, Queen of Scotland. New York: 1930. V. 71
The Garden of Vision: a Story of Growth. New York: 1929. V. 71
The House of Fulfillment: the Romance of a Soul. New York: 1927. V. 71

BARRINGTON, EMILIE ISABEL
G. F. Watts: Reminiscences. London: 1905. V. 73
The Life, Letters and Work of Frederic Leighton. London: 1906. V. 73

BARRINGTON, F. H.
Kansas Day. Topeka: 1892. V. 72

BARRINGTON, GEORGE
The Frauds and Cheats of London Detected. London: 1802. V. 73

BARRINGTON, SHUTE
The Political Life Of William Wildman Viscount Barrington. London: 1814. V. 72

BARRON, ARCHIBALD F.
Vines and Vine Culture. London: 1892. V. 68

BARRON, S.
The Avant Garde in Russia 1910-1930: New Perspectives. Los Angeles: 1981. V. 72

BARRON, STEPHANIE
Jane and the Unpleasantness at Scargrave Manor. New York: 1996. V. 73

BARROUGH, PHILIP
The Method of Phisick.... London: 1590. V. 69

BARROW, A. S.
More Shires and Provinces by Sabretache. London: 1928. V. 70
Shires and Provinces. 1927. V. 70

BARROW, JOHN
A Chronological History of Voyages Into The Arctic Regions. London: 1818. V. 72
Dictionarium Medicum Universale; or a New Medicinal Dictionary. London: 1749. V. 72
Dictionarium Polygraphicum; or, the Whole Body of Arts Regularly Digested. London: 1735. V. 71
A Family Tour Through South Holland. London: 1839. V. 72
Mountain Ascents in Cumberland and Westmorland. London: 1886. V. 69; 71
Sketches of the Royal Society and Royal Society Club. London: 1971. V. 68
Some Account of the Public Life and a Selection from the Unpublished Writings of the Earl of Macartney.... London: 1807. V. 68
Travels into the Interior of Southern Africa. London: 1806. V. 72
Voyages of Discovery and Research Within the Arctic Regions, from the Year 1818 to the Present Time.... London: 1846. V. 71; 73
Voyages of Discovery and Research Within the Arctic Regions, from the Year 1818 to the Present Time.... New York: 1846. V. 72

BARROW RESEARCH LABORATORY
Permanence/Durability of the Book, a Two Year Research Program. Richmond: 1963-1969. V. 68

BARROW, WILLIAM
Twelve Nights in the Hunters' Camp - A Narrative of Real Life. Boston: 1868. V. 72

BARROWS, ANNA
Eggs: Facts and Fancies about Them. Boston: 1890. V. 69

BARROWS, JOHN R.
Ubet. Caldwell: 1934. V. 69; 71

BARROWS, MARJORIE
The Bright-Eye Book. Chicago: 1941. V. 70; 73
Snuggles. Chicago: 1935. V. 72
Who's Who in the Zoo. Chicago: 1932. V. 71

BARROWS, W. B.
The English Sparrow (Passer Domesticus) in North America.... Washington: 1889. V. 68

BARROWS, WILLIAM
The Indian's Side of the Indian Question. Boston: 1887. V. 69

BARRUS, CLARA
The Life and Letters of John Burroughs. New York: 1968. V. 68

BARRY, CHARLES
The Detective's Holiday. London: 1926. V. 73

BARRY, DAVE
Big Trouble. New York: 1999. V. 68
Dave Barry Does Japan. New York: 1992. V. 71

BARRY, DAVID
David F. Barry's Indian Notes On The Custer Battle. Baltimore: 1949. V. 72
Forty Years in Washington. Boston: 1924. V. 72

BARRY, IRIS
The Last Enemy. Indianapolis: 1929. V. 70

BARRY, JEROME
Murder with Your Malted. New York: 1941. V. 70

BARRY, JOHN BROOKS
The Michaelmas Girls. London: 1975. V. 69

BARRY, LOUISE
The Beginnings of the West, Annals of the Kansas Gateway to the American West 1540-1854. Topeka: 1972. V. 68; 73

BARRY, LYNDA
Cruddy. New York: 1999. V. 71

BARRY, PHILIP
White Wings. New York: 1927. V. 72

BARRY, ROBERT
Untitled (Robert Barry). Amsterdam: 1974. V. 70

BARSTOW, STAN
A Kind of Loving. London: 1960. V. 70; 73

BARTELL, E.
Hints for Picturesque Improvements in Ornamental Cottages, and their Scenery.... London: 1804. V. 68; 70; 72

BARTELS, NICOLAUS ADOLPHUS
Disputatio Medica Inauguralis de Phthisi. Hamburg: 1662. V. 68

BARTER, JOHN
Barter's Guide to Beautiful Writing. London: 1886. V. 68

BARTH, HENRY
Travels and Discoveries in North and Central Africa, from the Journal of an Expedition Undertaken, Under the Auspices of H.B.M.'s Government, in the Years 1849-1855. Philadelphia: 1859. V. 69

BARTH, JOHN
Coming Soon!!!. Boston/New York: 2001. V. 69
Don't Count On It: a Note on the Number of the 1001 Nights. Northridge: 1984. V. 72
The End of the Road. New York: 1958. V. 73
The Floating Opera. New York: 1956. V. 70
The Floating Opera. London: 1968. V. 73
The Friday Book: Essays and Other Nonfiction. New York: 1984. V. 70; 72
Giles Goat-Boy. Garden City: 1966. V. 68; 70
Letters. New York: 1979. V. 70; 72
Lost in the Funhouse. New York: 1968. V. 68; 70; 73
The Sot-Weed Factor. Garden City: 1960. V. 69; 70
Todd Andrews to the Author. Northridge: 1979. V. 70; 71

BARTHELEMY, JEAN JACQUES
The Travels of Anarchasis the Younger, in Greece, During the Middle of the Fourth Century Before the Christian Era. London: 1798. V. 69

BARTHELME, DONALD
Come Back, Dr. Caligari. Boston: 1964. V. 69; 70
The Emerald. Los Angeles: 1980. V. 70
Here in the Village. Northridge: 1978. V. 70; 71; 73
Presents. Dallas: 1980. V. 70
Sadness. New York: 1972. V. 70
Sixty Stories. New York: 1981. V. 68; 70; 73
Snow White. New York: 1967. V. 70; 73
Unspeakable Practices, Unnatural Acts. London: 1969. V. 71

BARTHELME, FREDERICK
Natural Selection. New York: 1990. V. 73
Rangoon. New York: 1970. V. 69
Second Marriage. New York: 1984. V. 73
Two Against One. New York: 1988. V. 73
War and War. Garden City: 1971. V. 69; 73

BARTHES, ROLAND
Le Degre Zero de l'ecriture. Paris: 1953. V. 70
Mythologies. Paris: 1957. V. 71
Mythologies. London: 1972. V. 68

BARTHEZ, PAUL JOSEPH
Traite des Maladies Goutteuses. Paris: 1802. V. 68

BARTHOLOMAEUS, ANGLICUS
De Proprietatibus Rerum. Nurembergi: 1492. V. 68
Opus: De Rerum Proprietatibus. Nuremberg: 1519. V. 69

BARTHOLOMEW, E.
The Biographical Album of Western Gunfighters. Houston: 1958. V. 69; 70
Cullen Baker, Premier Texas Gunfighter. Houston: 1954. V. 68
Jesse Evans: a Texas Hide-Burner. Houston: 1955. V. 69
Wyatt Earp. 1963. V. 69

BARTISCH, GEORG
Augen-Dienst; Oder Kurtz und Deutlich Verfasster Bericht von Allen und Jeden in-und Ausserlichen Mangeln, Schaden, Gebrechen und Zufallen der Augen, wie sie Immer Namen Haben Mogen.... Nuremberg: 1686. V. 69
(Greek text) Das Ist Augendienst.... Colophon Dresden: 1583. V. 73

BARTLETT, ALFRED DURLING
An Historical and Descriptive Account of Cumnor Place, Berks, with Biographical Notices of the Lady Amy Dudley and of Anthony Forster Esq. London: 1850. V. 72
An Historical and Descriptive account of Cumnor Place, Berks, with Biographical Notices of the Lady Amy Dudley and of Anthony Forster, Esq.... Oxford: 1850. V. 72

BARTLETT, D. W.
The Life and Public Services of Hon. Abraham Lincoln. New York: 1860. V. 68; 70
The Life of General Franklin Pierce of New Hampshire. Buffalo: 1852. V. 72

BARTLETT, ELISHA
An Inquiry Into the Degree of Certainty in Medicine; and Into the Nature and Extent of Its Power Over Disease. Philadelphia: 1848. V. 70

BARTLETT, HARRIET T.
The True Idea of Christ. Los Angeles: 1910. V. 72

BARTLETT, JOHN
A Collection of Familiar Quotations, with Complete Indices of Authors and Subjects. Cambridge: 1855. V. 70; 72

BARTLETT, JOHN RUSSELL
Bibliography of Rhode Island. A Catalogue of Books and Other Publications Relating to...Rhode Island. Providence: 1864. V. 73
Bibliotheca Americana: A Catalogue of Books Relating to North and South America. Part III. 1701-1800. New York: 1963. V. 70
Dictionary of American Isms. Boston: 1859. V. 73
Personal Narrative of Explorations and Incidents in Texas, New Mexico, California, Sonora and Chihuahua. New York: 1854. V. 68; 69; 72
Personal Narrative of Explorations and Incidents in Texas, New Mexico, California, Sonora and Chihuahua. 1965. V. 70

BARTLETT, LANIER
On the Old West Coast, Being Further Reminiscences of a Ranger - Major Horace Bell. 1930. V. 68

BARTLETT, N. GRAY, MRS.
Mother Goose of '93. Boston: 1893. V. 73

BARTLETT, NAPIER
Clarimonde: a Tale of New Orleans Life, and of the Present War. Richmond: 1863. V. 69; 70
A Soldier's Story of the War.... New Orleans: 1874. V. 70

BARTLETT, ROBERT A.
The Last Voyage of the Karluk. Boston: 1916. V. 68

BARTLETT, WILLIAM A.
The History and Antiquities of the Parish of Wimbledon, Surrey, with Sketches of the Earlier Inhabitants. 1865. V. 68

BARTLETT, WILLIAM HENRY
Forty Days in The Desert on The Track of The Israelites. London. V. 72
Jerusalem Revisited. London: 1855. V. 73
The Nile Boat; or Glimpses of the Land of Egypt. London: 1849. V. 71
The Pilgrim Fathers; or the Founders of New England in the Reign of James the First. London: 1853. V. 71; 72
Syria and The Holy Land Illustrated. London. V. 72

BARTLEY, JAMES AVIS
Lays of Ancient Virginia and Other Poems. Richmond: 1855. V. 73

BARTLEY, NALBRO
The Devil's Lottery. New York: 1931. V. 71
The Godfather. New York: 1929. V. 71
Her Mother's Daughter. New York: 1926. V. 70
The Immediate Family. New York: 1930. V. 69; 71

BARTOK, BELA
Mikrokosmos. London: 1940. V. 70

BARTOLI, PIETRO SANTI
Colonna Trajana Eretta dal Senato, e Poplo Romano all' Imperatore Trajano Augusto nel Suo Foro in Roma. Rome: 1673. V. 68; 72

BARTOLINI, LUIGI
Bicycle Thieves. New York: 1950. V. 71; 73

BARTOLOZZI, FRANCESCO
Bartolozzi and His Work by Andrew W. Tuer. London: 1885. V. 68

BARTON, A. H.
With a Flag and a Bucket and a Gun. London: 1959. V. 68

BARTON, B. S.
Elements of Botany.... London: 1804. V. 69
Fragments of the Natural History of Pennsylvania. London: 1883. V. 68
A Memoir Concerning the Disease of Goitre, as It Prevails in Different Parts of North America. Philadelphia: 1800. V. 68

BARTON, BERNARD
Poems. London: 1820. V. 68
Selections From the Poems and Letters Edited by His Daughter. London: 1849. V. 70; 71

BARTON, BLANCHE
The Secret Life of a Satanist: The Authorized Biography of Anton La Vey. New York: 1990. V. 71

BARTON, GEORGE
Great Cases of Famous Detectives. Philadelphia: 1913. V. 72
History of New South Wales from the Records Volume I - Governor Phillip.... Sydney: 1889. V. 72
Strange Adventures of Bromley Barnes. Boston: 1918. V. 72

BARTON, HENRY W.
Texas Volunteers in the Mexican War. Wichita Falls: 1970. V. 70

BARTON, L. C.
Topographical and Historical Guide to Corfe Castle in the Isle of Purbeck, Dorset. London: 1885. V. 68

BARTON, PAULE
The Woe Shirt. Lincoln: 1980. V. 69

BARTON, R. S.
Fragments of the Natural History of Pennsylvania. London: 1883. V. 73

BARTON, R. T.
Pleading and Practice in the Courts of Chancery. Richmond: 1893. V. 71
The Practice in the Courts of Law in Civil Cases. Richmond: 1877. V. 72

BARTON, RALPH
God's Country: a Short History. New York: 1929. V. 69

BARTON, RICHARD
Lectures in Natural Philosophy.... Dublin: 1751. V. 68

BARTON, W. P. C.
Compendium Florae Philadelphicae; Containing a Description of the Indigenous and Naturalized Plants Found Within. Philadelphia: 1818. V. 68; 69

BARTON, WILLIAM
A Dissertation on the Freedom of Navigation and Maritime Commerce. Philadelphia: 1802. V. 73
Memoirs of the Late David Rittenhouse. Philadelphia: 1813. V. 73

BARTONS OF CLAPHAM (N. YORKS)
Motorists' Route Guide from Clapham. Clapham. V. 73

BARTRAM, E. B.
Manual of Hawaiian Mosses. Honolulu: 1933. V. 72

BARTRAM, JOHN
Correspondence of John Bartram 1734-1777. Gainesville: 1992. V. 72

BARTRAM, WILLIAM
Botanical and Zoological Drawings 1756-1788.... Philadelphia: 1968. V. 70; 71; 73
The Travels of William Bartram. New York: 1958. V. 70
Travels through North and South Carolina, Georgia, East and West Florida. London: 1792. V. 68; 70
Travels through North and South Carolina, Georgia, East and West Florida. London: 1794. V. 69
Travels through North and South Carolina, Georgia, East and West Florida. Savannah: 1973. V. 70

BARWICK, PETER
The Life Of The Reverend Dr. John Barwick, D.D. London: 1724. V. 72
Vita Johannis Barwick, S. T. P. London: 1721. V. 72

BARWICK, PETRO
Vita Johannis Barwick.... London: 1721. V. 71

BARWIS, JACKSON
Three Dialogues Concerning Liberty. London: 1776. V. 71

BARY, A. DE
Comparative Morphology and Biology of Fungi, Mycetozoa and Bacteria. Oxford: 1887. V. 69; 72

BARZUN, JACQUES
A Catalogue of Crime. New York: 1971. V. 69; 72; 73
A Catalogue of Crime. New York: 1973. V. 70
A Catalogue of Crime. New York: 1989. V. 69; 70; 71

BASBANES, NICHOLAS
A Gentle Madness. New York: 1995. V. 68; 69
Patience and Fortitude: A Roving Chronicle of Book People, Book Places, and Book Culture. New York: 2001. V. 70

BASHAN, RAPHAEL
The Victory. The Six-Day War of 1967. Tel Aviv: 1968. V. 69

BASHFORD, HERBERT
A Man Unafraid - The Story of John Charles Fremont. San Francisco: 1927. V. 69

BASIC Pre-Primer Dick and Jane. Chicago: 1936. V. 72

BASIL, DON
Cat and Feather. London: 1931. V. 73

BASILE, GIOVANNI BATTISTA
The Pentamerone, or the Story of Stories, Fun for the Little Ones. London: 1848. V. 68

BASILICA Carolina Opus Grande...Dedicata di XVIII. Maii anno MDCCLX a Collegio Societatis Jesu.... Mannheim: 1760. V. 70

BASILIUS, SAINT, THE GREAT, ABP. OF CAESAREA
Opera. Rome: 1515. V. 73
Opera. Coloniae: 1531. V. 72

BASKERVILLE, BEATRICE
The Enchanted Garden. New York: 1921. V. 71

BASKERVILLE, W.
Show Collies and Shetland Sheep Dogs. 1910. V. 68

BASKETT, JOHN
The Drawings of Thomas Rowlandson in the Paul Mellon Collection. London: 1977. V. 70

BASKIN, ESTHER
Creatures of Darkness. Boston: 1962. V. 70; 71

BASKIN, HOSEA
A Book of Dragons. New York: 1985. V. 69
Hosie's Alphabet. New York: 1972. V. 69

BASKIN, LEONARD
Jewish Artists of the Early and Late Renaissance. Northampton: 1993. V. 69
To Colour Thought: a Lecture. New Haven: 1967. V. 69; 71

BASLER, ROY
The Muse and the Librarian. Westport: 1974. V. 71

BASOLI, ANTONIO
Raccolta di Prospettive Serie, Rustiche, e di Paesaggio.... Bologna: 1810. V. 72

BASS, ALTHEA
The Arapaho Way: A Memoir of an Indian Boyhood. New York: 1966. V. 69

BASS, EBEN E.
Aldous Huxley: an Annotated Bibliography of Criticism. New York and London: 1981. V. 71

BASS, MICHAEL T.
Street Music in the Metropolis. London: 1864. V. 70

BASS, RICK
The Book of Yaak. New York: 1996. V. 70
Colter. Boston/New York: 2000. V. 72
The Deer Pasture. College Station: 1985. V. 69; 72
In the Loyal Mountains. Boston: 1995. V. 69; 72
New Wolves. New York: 1998. V. 70
The Ninemile Wolves. Livingston: 1992. V. 69
Oil Notes. Boston: 1989. V. 69; 70
Oil Notes. London: 1989. V. 68
Platte River. Boston: 1994. V. 70
The Sky, the Stars, the Wilderness. Boston/New York: 1997. V. 68; 69; 72
The Watch. New York: 1989. V. 70; 72
Where the Sea Used to Be. Boston: 1998. V. 69
Wild to the Heart. Harrisburg: 1987. V. 69; 71; 73
Winter. Boston: 1991. V. 68

BASS, ROBERT D.
Game Cock: the Life and Campaigns of General Thomas Sumter. New York: 1961. V. 72

BASSANI, E.
Jacob Epstein Collector. Milano: 1989. V. 69

BASSANI, GIORGIO
The Garden of the Finzi-Continis. London: 1965. V. 69

BASSERMANN-JORDAN, ERNST
Montres, Horloges et Pendules. Paris: 1964. V. 70

BASSETT, DAVID L.
A Stereoscopic Atlas of the Human Anatomy - The Central Nervous System. Portland: 1952. V. 70; 71

BASSETT, JAMES
Harm's Way. Cleveland & New York: 1962. V. 71; 73

BASSETT, JOHN SPENCER
Slavery in the State of North Carolina. Baltimore: 1899. V. 68

BASSETT, MARNIE
The Hentys. Oxford: 1954. V. 72
The Hentys. London/Melbourne/Wellington: 1955. V. 73

BASSETT-LOWKE, W. J.
Ships and Men. London: 1946. V. 72

BASSO, HAMILTON
Beauregard - the Great Creole. New York: 1933. V. 73
The View from Pompey's Head. Garden City: 1954. V. 68

BASTERFIELD, GEORGE
Crags for Climbing in and Around Great Langdale: Rock Climbing in Buttermere. London: 1925. V. 69
Songs of A Cragsman. London: 1930. V. 69

BASTIAN, HENRY CHARLETON
The Brain as an Organ of Mind. London: 1880. V. 68; 71

BASTIAT, CLAUDE FREDERIC
Economic Sophisms. Edinburgh: 1873. V. 71
Popular Fallacies Regarding General Interests, being a Translation of the Sophismes Economiques. London: 1849. V. 71

BASTIN, BRUCE
Never Sell a Copyright. Chigwell: 1990. V. 68

BATCHELDER, E. A.
Design in Theory and Practice. New York: 1910. V. 69; 72

BATCHELOR, JOHN CALVIN
The Birth of the People's Republic of Antartica. New York: 1983. V. 72

BATE, C. S.
A History of the British Sessile-Eyed Crustacea. 1863-1868. V. 69; 73

BATE, GEORGE
Elenchus Motuum Nuperorum In Anglia. London: 1685. V. 72

BATE, PERCY
The English Pre-Raphaelite Painters. London: 1899. V. 68

BATE, WALTER JACKSON
Storming the Main Gate: The Dictionary.... New York and London: 1975. V. 69

BATEMAN, H. M.
Adventures at Golf. London: 1928. V. 73

BATEMAN, J.
The General Turnpike Road Act, 3 Geo. IV. Cap. 126. With an Appendix of Forms and the Standing Orders of Both Houses of Parliament with Respect to Private Road Bills &c. To Which are Added, an index and notes. (with) A Supplement to the General Turnpike. London: 1822-1823. V. 72

BATEMAN, JAMES
The Orchidaceae of Mexico and Guatemala. New York: 1974. V. 72
A Second Century of Orchidaceous Plants.... London: 1867. V. 73

BATEMAN, JOHN FREDERIC LA TROBE
History and Description of the Manchester Waterworks. 1884. V. 73

BATEMAN, ROBERT
The Art of Robert Bateman. New York: 1981. V. 68
The Art of Robert Bateman. Toronto: 1981. V. 68
The World of Robert Bateman. New York: 1985. V. 68
The World of Robert Bateman. Toronto: 1985. V. 68

BATEMAN, THOMAS
The Royal Ecclesiastical Gazetteer.... Newark: 1791. V. 70
A Treatise on Agistment Tithe, in Which the Nature, Right Objects, Mode of Payment, and Method of Ascertaining the Value of Each Species of It.... London: 1775-1778?. V. 72

BATEN, LEA
The Image And the Motif. Japanese Dolls. Tokyo: 1986. V. 72

BATES, CHARLES F.
Custer's Indian Battles. New York: 1936. V. 72

BATES, CLARA DOTY
Doll Rosy's Days. Boston: 1884. V. 70

BATES, CRAIG D.
Tradition and Innovation, a Basket History of the Indians of the Yosemite Mono Lake Area. Yosemite National Park: 1990. V. 70

BATES, D.
The Passing of the Aborigines. London: 1938. V. 69
The Passing of the Aborigines. Melbourne: 1944. V. 69

BATES, D. B., MRS.
Incidents on Land and Water, or Four Years on the Pacific Coast. Boston: 1857. V. 68

BATES, E. S.
Touring in 1600. A Study in the Development of Travel as a Means of Education. London: 1911. V. 72

BATES, ED F.
History and Reminiscences of Denton Country. Denton: 1989. V. 68; 71

BATES, ELY
Rural Philosophy; or Reflections on Knowledge, Virtue and Happiness.... London: 1803. V. 71

BATES, GEORGE WASHINGTON
Sandwich Island Notes by a Haole. New York: 1854. V. 70

BATES, HERBERT ERNEST
Achilles and Diana. London: 1963. V. 71
Achilles the Donkey. London: 1962. V. 71
An Aspidistra in Babylon: four Novellas. London: 1960. V. 71
Autobiography, Comprising: The Vanished World. The Blossoming World. The World in Ripeness. London: 1969. V. 70
The Autobiography: The Vanished World; The Blossoming World; The World in Ripeness. London: 1969-1972. V. 72
The Beauty of the Dead and Other Stories. London: 1940. V. 68
The Black Boxer - Tales. London: 1932. V. 69; 71; 73
A Breath of Fresh Air. London: 1959. V. 68; 71
Catherine Foster. London: 1929. V. 68; 71
Charlotte's Row. London: 1931. V. 69; 71
Christmas 1930: a Poem. London: 1930. V. 71
Colonel Julian and Other Stories. London: 1951. V. 71
The Country Heart. London: 1949. V. 71
The Country of White Clover. London: 1952. V. 68; 71
A Crown of Wild Myrtle. London: 1962. V. 71
The Cruise of the Breadwinner. London: 1946. V. 68; 71
Cut and Come Again: Fourteen Stories. London: 1935. V. 71
The Daffodil Sky. London: 1955. V. 68; 71
The Day of Glory: a Play in Three Acts. London: 1945. V. 68
The Day of the Tortoise. London: 1961. V. 71
Day's End and Other Stories. London: 1928. V. 69; 71
Dear Life. London: 1950. V. 71
Death of a Huntsman. London: 1957. V. 68; 71
Down the River. London: 1937. V. 69; 71
The Duet. London: 1935. V. 69; 71
The Fabulous Mrs. V. London: 1964. V. 68; 71
The Face of England. London: 1952. V. 71; 72
Fair Stood the Wind for France. Boston: 1944. V. 68
Fair Stood the Wind for France. London: 1944. V. 71
The Fallow Land. London: 1932. V. 71
The Feast of July. London: 1954. V. 71
Flowers and Faces. Waltham St. Lawrence: 1935. V. 68; 71
A German Idyll. Waltham St. Lawrence: 1932. V. 68; 71
The Golden Oriole: Five Novellas. London: 1962. V. 71
The Hessian Prisoner. London: 1930. V. 68; 71
Holly and Sallow. 1931. V. 71
A House of Women. London: 1936. V. 71
How Sleep the Brave and Other Stories. London: 1943. V. 71
In the Heart of the Country. London: 1942. V. 71
The Jacaranda Tree. London: 1949. V. 68; 71
The Larkin Family Quartet. The Darling Buds of May. A Breath of French Air. When the Green Woods Laugh. Oh! To Be in England. London: 1958. V. 70
The Last Bread: a Play in One Act. London: 1926. V. 70; 71
Love for Lydia. London: 1952. V. 68; 71
Mrs. Esmond's Life. London: 1931. V. 71
The Modern Short Story - A Critical Survey. London: 1941. V. 71; 72
My Uncle Silas: Stories. London: 1939. V. 71
The Nature of Love: three Short Novels. London: 1953. V. 71
Now Sleeps the Crimson Petal and Other Stories. London: 1961. V. 71
Oh! To Be in England. London: 1963. V. 71
Pastoral on Paper. New Hythe, Maidstone: 1953. V. 71
The Poacher. London: 1935. V. 71
The Purple Plain. London: 1947. V. 71
Sally Go Round the Moon. London: 1932. V. 71
The Scarlet Sword. London: 1950. V. 71
The Seekers. London: 1926. V. 68; 70; 71
Seven Tales And Alexander. 1929. V. 71
Seven Tales and Alexander. London: 1929. V. 68
The Sleepless Moon. London: 1956. V. 71
Something Short and Sweet: Stories. 1937. V. 69
Song for December: a Poem. London: 1928. V. 71
The Story Without an End and the Country Doctor. London: 1932. V. 71
Sugar for the Horse. London: 1957. V. 71
A Threshing Day. London: 1931. V. 71
Through the Woods. London: 1936. V. 69; 71
The Tinkers of Elstow. London: 1945. V. 71
The Tree: a Story. London: 1930. V. 71
The Two Sisters. London: 1926. V. 68; 71

The Vanished World. An Autobiography. Volume One. London: 1969. V. 68
The Vanished World. The Blossoming World. The World in Ripeness. London: 1969-1972. V. 71
The Watercress Girl and Other Stories. London: 1959. V. 71
When the Green Woods Laugh. London: 1960. V. 71
The Woman Who Had Imagination and Other Stories. London: 1934. V. 71
The Woman Who had Imagination and Other Stories. New York: 1934. 68; 71

BATES, JOSEPH
Atlantic Salmon Flies and Fishing. Harrisburg: 1970. V. 68
The Early Life and Later Experience and Labors of.... Battle Creek: 1877. V. 69

BATES, PAULINA
The Divine Book of Holy and Inspired Wisdom, Revealing the Word of God.... Canterbury: 1849. V. 73

BATES, ROBERT H.
Five Miles High. London: 1940. V. 72

BATES, SYLVIA CHATFIELD
The Long Way Home. New York: 1937. V. 70

BATES, WALTER
Henry Moore Smith. The Mysterious Stranger. St. John: 1910. V. 73

BATES, WILLIAM
Spiritual Perfection, Unfolded and Enforced. London: 1699. V. 72
The Works.... London: 1700. V. 72

BATESON, WILLIAM
Materials for the Study of Variation. London: 1894. V. 69
Mendel's Principles of Heredity. Cambridge: 1909. V. 68; 70; 71
Mendel's Principles of Heredity. Cambridge: 1909-1913. V. 69

BATEY, MAVIS
The Historic Gardens of Oxford and Cambridge. London: 1989. V. 70

BATH, WILLIAM PULTENEY, EARL OF
The Case of the Revival of the Salt Duty, Fully Stated and Considered.... London: 1732. V. 72
An Enquiry into the Conduct of Our Domestick Affairs, from the Year 1721 to Christmas 1733. London: 1734. V. 72
Some Considerations on the National Debts, the Sinking Fund, and the State of Publick Credit; in a Letter to a Friend in the Country. London: 1729. V. 72
A State of the National Debt, As It Stood December the 24th 1716. London: 1727. V. 72

BATHGATE, ALEXANDER
Colonial Experiences; or Sketches of People and Places in the Province of Otego, New Zealand. Glasgow: 1874. V. 73

BATKIN, MAUREEN
Wedgwood Ceramics 1846-1959. A New Appraisal. London: 1982. V. 72

BATSON, HAROLD
A Select Bibliography of Modern Economic Theory 1870-1929. London: 1930. V. 71

BATTENBERG, LOUIS
Men-of-War Names. Their Meaning and Origin. London: 1897. V. 68

BATTERSHALL, FLETCHER
Bookbinding for Bibliophiles. Greenwich: 1905. V. 73

BATTEUX, ABBE CHARLES
Les Beaux Arts Reduits a un Meme Principe. Paris: 1747. V. 71

BATTEY, GEORGE M.
A History of Rome and Floyd County. Atlanta: 1922. V. 72

BATTEY, THOMAS C.
The Life and Adventures of A Quaker Among The Indians. Boston: 1875. V. 72
The Life and Adventures of A Quaker Among the Indians. Boston: 1876. V. 72

BATTIE, DAVID
The Price Guide to 19th and 20th Century British Pottery. London: 1979. V. 72

BATTINE, CECIL
The Crisis of the Confederacy, a History of Gettysburg and the Wilderness. London: 1905. V. 69; 70

THE BATTLE of Fort Sumter and First Victory of the Southern Troops, April 13th 1861. Charleston: 1861. V. 69; 70

BATTLE Of Shiloh. Official Report of the 2nd Brigade 1st Division April 6, 1862. Memphis: 1862. V. 70

THE BATTLE with the London Anarchists, The Only Account of the Houndsditch Tragdies and the Historic Siege of Foreign Anarchists in the East End of London. London: 1911. V. 73

BATTY, ELIZABETH FRANCES
Italian Scenery From Drawings Made in 1817. London: 1820. V. 72

BATTY, JOSEPH
Over the Wilds to California; or Eight Years from Home. Leeds: 1867. V. 69

BAUDELAIRE, CHARLES
Les Fleurs du Mal. Paris: 1928. V. 69
Les Fleurs du Mal. Paris: 1951. V. 73
Intimate Journals. London: 1930. V. 69
The Intimate Journals. Hollywood: 1947. V. 70
Intimate Journals. London: 1949. V. 71; 73

BAUDELAIRE, CHARLES continued
Les Paradis Artificiels. Opium et Haschisch. Paris: 1860. V. 70
Selections from Baudelaire. London: 1943. V. 69

BAUDELOCQUE, JEAN LOUIS
An Abridgment of Mr. Heath's Translation of Baudelcoque's Midwifery. Philadelphia: 1823. V. 70

BAUDER, EMMA POW
Ruth and Marie. Chicago/Philadelphia: 1895. V. 69; 73

BAUDIN, P.
Fetichism and Fetich Worshipers. New York: 1885. V. 70

BAUDOUIN, BENOIT
B. Balduinus de Calceo Antiquo, et Jul Nigronus De Caliga Veterum. Amstelodami: 1667. V. 68

BAUER, LOUIS
Hip Disease. A Clinical Lecture Delivered at the Long Island College Hospital of Brooklyn. Nashville: 1859. V. 71

BAUER, LOUIS AGRICOLA
Land Magnetic Observations 1905-1910. Washington: 1912. V. 69
Terrestrial Magnetism: an International Quarterly Journal. Chicago: 1896-1946. V. 72

BAUER, MAX
Precious Stones. London: 1904. V. 71

BAUER, PAUL
Himalayan Campaign. Oxford: 1937. V. 69
Himalayan Quest. 1938. V. 73
Himalayan Quest. London: 1938. V. 69
The Siege of Nanga Parbat. 1956. V. 73

BAUER, R.
The New Catalogue of Historical Records. 189-1908/9. London: 1970. V. 72

BAUER, R. T.
Crustacean Sexual Biology. New York: 1991. V. 72; 73

BAUERLE, ADOLFE
Wiener Allgemeine Theaterzeitung und Originalblatt fur Kunst, Literatur, Musik, Mode und Geselliges Leben.... Vienna: 1837-1847. V. 70

BAUGHAN, PETER E.
North of Leeds. The Leeds-Settle-Carlisle Line and Its Branches. London: 1966. V. 71; 73

BAUGHMAN, ROBERT W.
Kansas in Maps. Topeka: 1961. V. 71

BAUGHMAN, ROLAND
The Centenary of Arthur Rackham's Birth September 19 1867. New York: 1969. V. 73

BAUGHMAN, THEODORE
The Oklahoma Scout. Chicago. V. 71

BAUHIN, CASPAR
Pinax Theatri Botanici.... Basel: 1623. V. 72

BAUM, FRANK J.
The Laughing Dragon of Oz. Racine: 1935. V. 70; 72
To Please a Child: a Biography of L. Frank Baum, Royal Historian of Oz. Chicago: 1961. V. 71; 73

BAUM, LYMAN FRANK
The Emerald City of Oz. Chicago: 1910. V. 69; 73
The Enchanted Island of Yew. Chicago: 1913. V. 69
The Fate of a Crown. Chicago: 1905. V. 68
Father Goose: His Book. Chicago: 1899. V. 71
Father Goose: His Book. Chicago: 1913. V. 71
Glinda of Oz. Chicago: 1920. V. 68; 69; 70; 73
A Kidnapped Santa Claus. Indianpolis: 1969. V. 70
Little Dorothy and Toto. Chicago: 1913. V. 71
The Lost Princess of Oz. Chicago: 1917. V. 69; 71
The Magic Cloak. Chicago: 1916. V. 69
The Magic of Oz. Chicago: 1919. V. 69; 70
The Marvelous Land of Oz. Chicago: 1904. V. 70; 72
The New Wizard of Oz. Indianapolis: 1925. V. 69
Ozma. Chicago: 1907. V. 69
Ozma of Oz. Chicago: 1961. V. 69
The Patchwork Girl of Oz. Chicago: 1913. V. 69
Rinkitink in Oz. Chicago: 1916. V. 69; 71
The Road to Oz. Chicago: 1909. V. 69
The Scarecrow of Oz. Chicago: 1915. V. 69; 73
Tik-Tok of Oz. Chicago: 1914. V. 69
The Wizard of Oz. Indianapolis: 1939. V. 71
Wizard of Oz. London: 1940. V. 70; 71; 73
The Wizard of Oz Adapted by Allen Chaffee. New York: 1950. V. 69
The Wizard of Oz Picture Book. Racine: 1939. V. 73
The Wonderful Wizard of Oz. Chicago: 1900. V. 70
The Wonderful Wizard of Oz. West Hatfield: 1985. V. 72

BAUM, VICKI
Grand Hotel. London: 1930. V. 71
Martin's Summer. New York: 1931. V. 71

BAUMAN, J. E.
Out of the Valley of the Forgotten, or From Trinil to New York:. Easton: 1923. V. 70

BAUMANN, GUSTAVE
Frijoles Canyon Pictographs Recorded in Woodcuts and Hand printed by Gustave Baumann. Santa Fe: 1939. V. 68; 69; 70

BAUMEL, J. J.
Nomina Anatomica Avium. London: 1979. V. 73

BAUMER, LEWIS
Did You Ever?. London: 1905. V. 68

BAUMGARTNER, L.
A Bibliography of the Poem Syphilis sive Morbus Gallicus by Giroloma Fracastoro of Verona. New Haven: 1935. V. 71

BAUR, J. I. H.
New Art in America: Fifty Painters of the 20th Century. 1957. V. 69
New Art In America: Fifty Painters of the 20th century. Greenwich: 1957. V. 72

BAUSCH, RICHARD
In the Night Season. New York: 1998. V. 72
Rebel Powers. Boston/New York: 1993. V. 68; 72
Violence. Boston: 1992. V. 68; 72

BAUSNER, BARTHOLOMAEUS
De Consenu Partium Humani Corporis. Libri III.... Amsterdam: 1656. V. 72

BAVIN, BILL
Dead Regimental. London: 1968. V. 69

BAWDEN, EDWARD
The Delectable History of Fortnum and Mason. London: 1956. V. 72
Travellers' Verse. 1946. V. 69

BAX, CLIFFORD
Florence Farr, Bernard Shaw and W. B. Yeats. 1941. V. 68
Florence Farr, Bernard Shaw and W. B. Yeats. Dublin: 1941. V. 73
Ideas and People. London: 1936. V. 73
The Venetian. New York: 1931. V. 71

BAX, E. IRONSIDE
Popular Electric Lighting, Being Practical Hints to Present and Intending Users of Electric Energy for Illuminating Purposes, with a Chapter on Electric Motors. London: 1891. V. 69

BAX, ROGER
Death Beneath Jerusalem. London: 1938. V. 73

BAXENDALE, ESTHER M.
Your With All My Heart, Her Own Story.... Boston: 1904. V. 69

BAXTER, ANDREW
Matho; or, the Cosmotheoria Puerilis, a Dialogue. London: 1740. V. 69

BAXTER, CHARLES
First Light. New York: 1987. V. 70; 73
Shadow Play. New York: 1993. V. 68
The South Dakota Guidebook. New York: 1974. V. 70; 73
Through the Safety Net. 1985. V. 71; 72
Through the Safety Net. New York: 1985. V. 70

BAXTER, EVELYN V.
The Birds of Scotland, their History, Distribution and Migration. 1953. V. 73
The Birds of Scotland. Their History, Distribution, and Migration. London: 1953. V. 70; 71

BAXTER, GEORGE OWEN
Call of the Blood. New York: 1934. V. 70

BAXTER, GLEN
Blizzards of Tweed. Bloomsbury: 1999. V. 70
Stories. Kent: 1973. V. 70

BAXTER, JAMES PHINNEY
A Memoir of Jacques Cartier, Sieur de Limoilou. New York: 1906. V. 68

BAXTER, LUCY
The Life Of William Barnes. Poet and Philologist. London: 1887. V. 72

BAXTER, RICHARD
A Call to the Unconverted, to Turn and Live; and Accept of Mercy, While Mercy May Be Had.... New Brunswick: 1797. V. 69
A Call to the Unconverted, to Turn and Live, and Accept of Mercy While Mercy May be Had.... Newark: 1813. V. 69
The Saints Everlasting Rest; or, a Treatise of the Blessed State of the Saints in Their Enjoyment of God in Heaven.... Brunswick: 1801. V. 69

BAXTER, WILLIAM
Glossarium Antiquitatum Britannicarum, sive Syllabus Entymologicus Antiquitatum Veteris Britanniae atque Iberniae Temporibus Romanorum. London: 1719. V. 71

BAY, JENS CHRISTIAN
A Handful of Western Books (-A Second Handful of Western Books - A Third Handful of Western Books). Cedar Rapids: 1935. V. 70
The Koh-I-Noor of Books. Cedar Rapids: 1938. V. 68
The Pickwick Papers: Some Bibliographical Remarks. Chicago: 1938. V. 69

BAYARD, FERDINAND M.
Travels of a Frenchman in Maryland and Virginia with a Description of Philadelphia and Baltimore in 1791 or Travels in the U.S. to Bath, Winchester, in the Valley of the Shenandoah, etc. During the Summer of 1791. Williamsburg: 1950. V. 72

BAYARD, SAMUEL J.
A Sketch of the Life of Com. Robert F. Stockton...His Correspondence with the Navy Department Respecting His Conquest of California.... New York: 1856. V. 69; 72

BAYER, HERBERT
Book of Drawings. Chicago: 1961. V. 70

BAYER, WILLIAM
Peregrine. London: 1981. V. 68
Peregrine. New York: 1981. V. 68; 70; 72
Punish Me with Kisses. New York: 1980. V. 68
Switch. New York: 1984. V. 68
Tangier. New York: 1978. V. 68

BAYFIELD, E. G., MRS.
Fugitive Poems. London: 1805. V. 69

BAYFIELD, HENRY WOLSEY
The St. Lawrence Survey Journals of Captain Henry Wolsey Bayfield 1829-1853. Toronto: 1984-1986. V. 68; 73

BAYLE, A. L. J.
A Manual of General Anatomy, Containing a Concise Description of the Elementary Tissues of the Human Body. Philadelphia: 1828. V. 71
An Variae Organorum Degenerationes ab Una Et Eadem Causa Pendent? Theses...Faculatate Medica Parisiensi...anno 1826. Paris: 1826. V. 72

BAYLEY, FRANK W.
Five Colonial Artists of New England. Boston: 1929. V. 69

BAYLEY, FREDERICK W. N.
Blue Beard. 1842. V. 73
Blue Beard. London: 1842. V. 68

BAYLEY, HAROLD
A New Light on the Renaissance. London: 1909. V. 72

BAYLEY, JOHN
Iris: a Memoir of Iris Murdoch. London: 1998. V. 69

BAYLEY, NICOLA
La Corona and the Tin Frog. London: 1979. V. 73
The Mousehole Cat. 1990. V. 68
One Old Oxford Ox. New York: 1977. V. 70
The Patchwork Cat. New York: 1981. V. 70

BAYLEY, VICTOR
Underground Enemy. London: 1944. V. 72

BAYLIS, TREVOR
Clock This: My Life as an Inventor. London: 1999. V. 70

BAYLISS, F. C.
The Master Salesman: Being a Handbook of Technical information and Instruction.... London: 1915. V. 69

BAYLISS, MARGUERITE F.
Bolinvar. New York: 1937. V. 69

BAYLOR, GEORGE W.
John Robert Baylor, Confederate Governor of Arizona. Tucson: 1966. V. 68; 73

BAYLY, ERIC
The House of Strange Secrets. New York: 1899. V. 68

BAYLY, MARY
Workmen and Their Difficultie. London: 1861. V. 72

BAYLY, THOMAS HAYNES
Musings and Prosings. Boulogne: 1833. V. 68
The Puseyad. A Poem. London: 1850. V. 73
Weeds of Witchery. London: 1837. V. 72

BAYNARD, M.
Weldon's Practical Fancy Dress or Suggestions for Fancy and Calico Balls, also Fancy Bazaars. London: 1887. V. 68

BAYNE, ALEXANDER
Notes for the Use of Students of the Municipal Law in the University of Edinburgh. Edinburgh: 1749. V. 73

BAYNE, PETER
The Life and Letters of Hugh Miller. London: 1871. V. 70; 71; 72
Two Great Englishwomen: Mrs. Browning and Charlotte Bronte. 1881. V. 70

BAYNES CARRIAGE CO. LTD.
Baynes High Grade Vehicles. 1917. (No. 38). Brantford: 1917. V. 73

BAYNES, ROBERT H.
The Illustrated Book of Sacred Poems. London: 1867. V. 73

BAZIN, GILLES AUGUSTINE
The Natural History of Bees. London: 1744. V. 73

BEACH, DAVID NELSON
Beach Family Reminiscences and Annals. Meriden: 1931. V. 69

BEACH, EDWARD L.
Dust on the Sea. New York: 1972. V. 68
Run Silent, Run Deep. London: 1955. V. 68; 69

BEACH, REX
Flowing Gold: a Stirring Story of the Oil Fields. New York: 1922. V. 68
Oh, Shoot!. London: 1921. V. 72
The Spoilers. New York: 1906. V. 69
Valley of Thunder. New York: 1939. V. 69

BEACH, S. A.
The Apples of New York. Albany: 1905. V. 69; 72

BEACH, SYLVIA
Ulysses. New York: 1956. V. 73

BEACH, WOOSTER
The American Practice Condensed or the Family Physician.... New York: 1847. V. 71; 73
A Treatise on Anatomy, Physiology and Health Designed for Students, Schools and Popular Use Illustrated with Numerous Plates. New York: 1847. V. 70

BEACHWOOD Borough Directory, Who's Who and Year Book. New York: 1924. V. 69

THE BEACON; or Warnings to Thoughtless Boys. New York: 1856-1866. V. 70

THE BEACONSFIELD Birthday Book. London: 1884. V. 71

BEADLE, DELOS WHITE
Canadian Fruit, Flower and Kitchen Gardener.... Toronto: 1872. V. 68

BEADLE, J. H.
Life in Utah, or the Mysteries and Crimes of Mormonism. 1870. V. 68
Western Wilds, and the Men Who Redeem Them. Cincinnati: 1879. V. 68

BEADLE, JOHN H.
Das Leben in Utah; Oder, Die Mysterien und Verbrechen des Mormonenthums. Philadelphia: 1870. V. 69; 71

BEADLE, L. C.
The Inland Waters of Tropical Africa. London: 1981. V. 70

BEADLE, N. C. W.
Handbook of the Vascular Plants of the Sydney District and Blue Mountains. Armidale: 1962. V. 72

BEADLE, R.
New Science Out of Old Books. Studies in Manuscripts and Early Printed Books in Honour of A. I. Doyle. Aldershot: 1995. V. 70

BEAGLE, PETER S.
A Fine and Private Place. London: 1960. V. 72
A Fine and Private Place. New York: 1960. V. 69; 70; 71

BEAGLEHOLE, J. C.
The Journals of Captain James Cook on His Voyages of Discovery. Sydney: 2000. V. 70

BEALE, LIONEL
Disease Germs. Their Nature and Origin. London: 1872. V. 72
How to Work with the Microscope. London. V. 73
How to Work with the Microscope. London: 1857. V. 68
How to Work with the Microscope. 1868. V. 73
How to Work with the Microscope. 1880. V. 68
How to Work with the Microscope. London: 1880. V. 71
A Treatise on the Distortions and Deformities of the Human Body Exhibiting a Concise View of the Nature and Treatment of the Principal Malformations and Distortions of the Chest, Spine and Limbs. London: 1833. V. 68; 71; 72

BEALE, R. L. T.
History of the 9th Virginia Cavalry. Petersburg: 1890. V. 69
History of the 9th Virginia Cavalry. Richmond: 1899. V. 70

BEALES, P.
Classic Roses.... New York: 1985. V. 71
Classic Roses.... New York: 1997. V. 71

BEALL, JOHN YATES
Trial of John Y. Beall as a Spy and Guerrillero, by a Military Commission. New York: 1865. V. 70

BEALS, FRANK L.
Buffalo Bill. Chicago: 1943. V. 72

BEALS, RALPH
Archaeological Studies in Northeast Arizona. Berkeley: 1945. V. 72
Indian Land Use and Occupancy in California. New York: 1974. V. 68
Material Culture of the Pima, Papago, and Western Apache. Berkeley: 1934. V. 69
Preliminary Report on the Ethnography of the Southwest. Berkeley: 1935. V. 69

BEAMISH, A. E.
First Steps to Lawn Tennis. Boston: 1922. V. 69

BEAMISH, RICHARD
Memoir of the Life of Sir Marc Isambard Brunel. London: 1862. V. 69
The Psychonomy of the Hand; or the Hand, an Index of Mental Development.... London: 1865. V. 73

BEAMONT, T.
The Complete Cow Doctor; Being a Treatise on the Disorders Incident to Horned Cattle. Leeds: 1812. V. 73

BEAMONT, WILLIAM
Annals of the Lords of Warrington and Bewsey from 1587-1833. Manchester: 1873. V. 73

BEAN, ALAN
Apollo: an Eyewitness Account by Astronaut/Explorer Artist/Moonwalker Alan Bean. Norwalk: 1998. V. 69; 71

BEAN, W. J.
Trees and Shrubs Hardy in the British Isles. London: 1936. V. 71; 73
Wall Shrubs and Hardy Climbers. New York: 1940. V. 72

BEAR, GREG
Darwin's Radio. New York: 1999. V. 73
Eon. 1985. V. 70

BEAR, NICHOLAS
The Resurrection Founded on Justice; or, a Vindication of this Great Standing Reason Assigned by the Ancients and Modern.... London: 1700. V. 68

BEARBLOCK, JAMES
A Treatise Upon Tithes: Containing an Estimate of Every Titheable Article in Common Cultivation.... London: 1818. V. 72
A Treatise Upon Tithes.... 1813. V. 69

BEARCROFT, PHILIP
An Historical Account of Thomas Sutton Esq. and of His Foundation in Charter House. London: 1737. V. 69; 72

BEARD, ALICE
The Magic String Book. New York: 1916. V. 69

BEARD, CHARLES
Whither Mankind: A Panorama of Modern Civilization. New York: 1928. V. 72

BEARD, FRANK
One Hundred Sermon Pictures. Chicago: 1902. V. 69

BEARD, GEORGE MILLER
Sexual Neurasthenia (Nervous Exhaustion). New York: 1891. V. 69
Stimulant's and Narcotics. New York: 1871. V. 69

BEARD, JAMES
New James Beard. New York: 1981. V. 73

BEARD, PATTERN
Marjorie's Literary Dolls. New York: 1916. V. 73

BEARD, PETER
The Adventures and Misadventures of Peter Beard in Africa. Boston: 1993. V. 70
The End of the Game. 1965. V. 69; 70; 72; 73
The End of the Game. 1978. V. 70; 72; 73

BEARDSLEY, AUBREY VINCENT
Last Letters of Aubrey Beardsley. London: 1904. V. 69
Portfolio of Drawings for Salome. London: 1907. V. 73
Uncollected Work of Aubrey Beardsley. London: 1925. V. 71

BEARDSMORE, J. H.
History of Hucknall Torkard. Mansfield: 1909. V. 70

BEARSS, EDWIN C.
Rebel Victory at Vicksburg. Vicksburg?: 1963. V. 72

BEASLEY, DELILAH L.
The Negro Trail Blazers of California. Los Angeles: 1919. V. 70

BEASLEY, GERTRUDE
My First Thirty Years. 1989. V. 70

BEATIE, RUSSEL H.
Saddles. Norman: 1981. V. 70

THE BEATLES *Illustrated Lyrics.* London: 1969. V. 70

BEATON, CECIL
Ballet. London: 1951. V. 70; 72
The Best of Beaton. New York: 1968. V. 68
Cecil Beaton. London: 1994. V. 72
Cecil Beaton. Electa Editrice Portfolios. Milan: 1982. V. 70
Cecil Beaton's Scrapbook. London: 1937. V. 73
The Face of the World. London: 1957. V. 73
The Magic Image: the Genius of Photography from 1839 to the Present Day. Boston: 1975. V. 68
My Royal Past.... London: 1960. V. 68
Time Exposure.... London: 1946. V. 71

BEATON, K.
A Warden's Diary. 1949. V. 70; 72

BEATSON, ROBERT
A Political Index to the Histories of Great Britain and Ireland; or a Complete Register of the Hereditary Honours, Public Offices and Persons in Office.... London: 1788. V. 72

BEATTIE, ANN
Alex Katz. New York: 1987. V. 69; 73
Chilly Scenes of Winter. Garden City: 1976. V. 69; 73
Distortions. Garden City: 1976. V. 70; 73
Falling in Place. New York: 1980. V. 70
Jacklighting. Worcester: 1981. V. 70

Love Always. New York: 1985. V. 69; 72; 73
Park City. New York: 1998. V. 72
Perfect Recall. New York: 2001. V. 69; 72
Secrets and Surprises. Short Stories. New York: 1978. V. 70
Spectacles. NY: 1985. V. 73
What Was Mine and Other Stories. New York: 1991. V. 70

BEATTIE, GEORGE WILLIAM
Heritage of the Valley: San Bernadino's First Century. Pasadena: 1939. V. 70; 73

BEATTIE, JAMES
The Minstrel, in Two Books, with Some other Poems. London: 1779. V. 73
The Minstrel; or the Progress of Genius with some Other Poems. London: 1805-1803. V. 68
The Theory of Language. London: 1788. V. 69

BEATTIE, WILLIAM
Switzerland, Illustrated in a Series of Views Taken Expressly for this Work by W. H. Bartlett. London: 1836. V. 70
Switzerland...Illustrated in a Series of Views.... London: 1838. V. 71

BEATY, JOHN O.
Swords in the Dawn: a Story of the First Englishman. New York: 1937. V. 68

BEAUBOURG, MAURICE
Nouvelles Passionnes. Paris: 1893. V. 71

BEAUCHAMP, WILLIAM M.
Metallic Ornaments of the New York Indians. Albany: 1903. V. 73

BEAUCLERK, HELEN
The Mountain and the Tree. New York: 1936. V. 70

BEAUFORT, DUKE OF
Driving. London: 1890. V. 69
Fox Hunting. 1980. V. 68

BEAUFORT, EMILY ANNE
Egyptian Sepulchres and Syrian Shrines.... London: 1861. V. 72

BEAUFORT, FRANCIS
Karamania, or a Brief Description of the South Coast of Asia-Minor and of the Remains of Antiquity. London: 1817. V. 72

BEAUFOY, MARK
Nautical and Hydraulic Experiments with Numerous Scientific Miscellanies. 1834. V. 72
Nautical and Hydraulic Experiments with Numerous Scientific Miscellanies. London: 1834. V. 69

BEAUGRAND, H.
Six Mois Dans Les Montagnes-Rocheuses Colorado - Utach - Nouveau Mexique. Montreal: 1890. V. 68

BEAUHARNAIS, HORTENSE
Memoirs of Queen Hortense, Mother of Napoleon III. London: 1862. V. 69

BEAUMANN, GUSTAV
Frijoles Canyon Pictographs. Santa Fe: 1939. V. 69

BEAUMONT, C. W.
New Paths. Verse. Prose. Pictures 1917-1918. London: 1918. V. 72

BEAUMONT, CHARLES
Best of Charles Beaumont. New York: 1982. V. 69
The Hunger. New York: 1957. V. 70; 73

BEAUMONT, CYRIL W.
Complete Book of Ballets. 1937. V. 68
Five Centuries of Ballet Design. 1937. V. 68
The History of Harlequin. London: 1926. V. 68
A History of the Ballet in Russia (1613-1881). London: 1930. V. 70
The Romantic Ballet in Lithographs of the Time. London: 1938. V. 68
The Strange Adventures of a Toy Soldier. London: 1926. V. 69
Toys-Rhymes. London: 1930. V. 70

BEAUMONT, FRANCIS
Comedies and Tragedies. London: 1647. V. 72
The Maids Tragedy. London: 1650. V. 70
Salmacis and Hermaphroditus. Waltham St. Lawrence: 1951. V. 71; 73
Works. London: 1711. V. 73

BEAUMONT, GEORGE
The Warrior's Looking-Glass.... Sheffield: 1808. V. 68; 71; 73

BEAUMONT, GUSTAVE
Origin and Outline of the Penitentary System in the United States of North America. London: 1833. V. 72

BEAUMONT, J. G. BARBER
A Brief Account of the Beaumont Trust and Its Founder. 1887. V. 71

BEAUMONT, JOHN
Bosworth-Field. London: 1629. V. 68; 70; 73
Bosworth-Field. London: 1710. V. 70
The Works. Edinburgh: 1812. V. 71

BEAUMONT, ROBERTS
Carpets and Rugs. London: 1924. V. 72

BEAUMONT, W. WORBY
Motor Vehicles and Motors. Their Design, Construction and Working by Steam, Oil and Electricity. Westminster: 1902-1906. V. 72

BEAUMONT, WILLIAM
Experiments and Observations on the Gastric Juice and the Physiology of Digestion. Plattsburgh: 1833. V. 71; 73
Experiments and Observations on the Gastric Juice and the Physiology of Digestion. Boston: 1834. V. 68; 71; 73

BEAUREGARD, G. T.
A Commentary on the Campaign and Battle of Manassas of July 1861. New York: 1891. V. 70

THE BEAUTIES of the British Senate.... London: 1786. V. 72

THE BEAUTIES of the Dutch School; Selected from Interesting Pictures of Admired Landscape Painters. London: 1793. V. 69

BEAUTIFUL Britain, the Scenery and Splendors of the United Kingdom.... Chicago: 1859. V. 71; 73

BEAUVOIR, SIMONE DE
The Blood of Others. New York: 1948. V. 69
Force of Circumstance. New York: 1965. V. 70; 71
L'Invitee. Paris: 1945. V. 69
Les Mandarins. Paris: 1954. V. 69
The Second Sex. Franklin Center: 1979. V. 69
The Woman Destroyed. London: 1969. V. 69

BEAVAN, R.
Handbook of the Freshwater Fishes of India. 1877. V. 69

BEAVEN, PAUL W.
For the Welfare of Children. The Addresses of the First Twenty-Five Presidents of the American Academy of Pediatrics. Springfield: 1955. V. 71

BEAVER, HERBERT
Reports and Letters of Herbert Beaver 1836-1838. Portland: 1959. V. 68

BEAWES, WYNDHAM
Lex Mercatoria Rediviva; or the Merchant's Directory. London: 1761. V. 73

BEAZLEY, C. RAYMOND
John and Sebastian Cabot. The Discovery of North America. London: 1898. V. 73

BECANUS, MARTINUS
Analogia Veteris Ac Novi Testamenti, In Qua Primum Status Veteris, Deinde Consensus, Proportio and Conspiratio Illius Cum Novo Explicatur. Lovanii: 1754. V. 69

BECCARI, ODOARDO
Wanderings in the Great Forests of Borneo Travels and Researches of a Naturalist in Sarawak. London: 1904. V. 72

BECCARIA, CESARE BONESANA, MARCHESE DI
Dei Delitti e delle Pene. Livorno: 1764. V. 68
An Essay on Crimes and Punishments. London: 1767. V. 68

BECCO, HORACIO JORGE
Jorge Luis Borges. Bibliografia Total 1923-1973. Buenos Aires: 1973. V. 71

BECHDOLT, FREDERICK R.
Giants of the Old West. New York: 1930. V. 69
Tales of the Old-Timers. New York: 1924. V. 69

BECHDOLT, FREDERICK R
When the West Was Young. 1922. V. 68

BECHER, JOHN JOACHIM
Magnalia Naturae, or the Philosophers-Stone, Lately Expos'd to Publick Sight and Sale.... London: 1680. V. 69

BECHET, SIDNEY
Treat It Gentle. New York: 1960. V. 72

BECHSTEIN, LUDWIG
The Rabbit Catcher and Other Fairy Tales. New York: 1962. V. 69; 72

BECHTEL, H.
The Manual of Cultivated Orchid Species. Cambridge: 1981. V. 71

BECHTOLD, FRITZ
Nanga Parbat Adventure. London: 1935. V. 69

BECK, BARRY F.
Eighth International Congress of Speleology. Georgia: 1981. V. 72

BECK, CARL
Fractures. Philadelphia: 1900. V. 70

BECK, FRANK VER
Little Black Sambo and the Baby Elephants. Philadelphia: 1925. V. 70

BECK, HENRY CHARLTON
Death by Clue. New York: 1933. V. 69
Murder in the News Room. New York: 1931. V. 69

BECK, JOHANN JODOCUS
Tractatus de eo Quod Justum est Circa Conjugalis Debiti Praestationum. Frankfurt & Leipzig: 1733. V. 71
Tractatus de Juribus Judaeorum von Recht der Juden. Nuremberg: 1731. V. 72

BECK, JOHN B.
Medicine in the American Colonies. Albuquerque: 1966. V. 71

BECK, L. C.
Mineralogy of New York.... Albany: 1842. V. 70; 72

BECK, LUDWIG MARIA
Das Kasperlbuch. Munchen: 1948. V. 71

BECK, MARY ELIZABETH
Birthday, and Other Poems. Ashford: 1890. V. 69

BECK, RICHARD
A Treatise on the Construction, Proper Use and Capabilities of Smith, Beck and Beck's Achromatic Microscopes. London: 1865. V. 73
A Treatise on the Construction, Proper Use and Capabilities of Smith, Beck and Beck's Achromatic Microscopes. Lincolnwood: 1987. V. 68

BECKE, LOUIS
Ridan the Devil and Other Stories. London: 1899. V. 68

BECKEN, A. C., & CO.
Catalog 1912. Chicago: 1912?. V. 72

BECKER, BERNARD H.
Scientific London. London: 1874. V. 71

BECKER, CARL
Kunstwerke und Gerathschaften des Mittelalters und der Renaissance. Frankfurt: 1852-. V. 70

BECKER, ROBERT H.
Designs On the Land: Disenos of California Ranchos And Their Makers. San Francisco: 1969. V. 71
The Plains and the Rockies.... San Francisco: 1982. V. 70
Thomas Christy's Road Across the Plains. Denver: 1969. V. 73

BECKETT, SAMUEL
All that Fall. London: 1957. V. 69
All that Fall. New York: 1957. V. 70
As the Story was Told. Cambridge: 1987. V. 70
Bing. Paris: 1966. V. 69
Collected Poems in English and French. New York: 1977. V. 68
Company. London: 1980. V. 69
Echo's Bones and Other Precipitates. Paris: 1935. V. 73
Eh Joe and Other Writings. London: 1967. V. 71
En Attendant Godot. Paris: 1952. V. 73
En Attendant Godot. London: 1966. V. 72
Endgame. London: 1958. V. 69; 71; 73
Endgame. London: 1992. V. 70
An Exagmination of James Joyce: Analysis of the Work in Progress. Norfolk CT. V. 70
Film. London: 1972. V. 71
Film - Suivi de Souffle. Paris: 1972. V. 69
Fin de Partie. Paris: 1957. V. 70
Fizzles. London and New York: 1975-1976. V. 70
From an Abandoned Work. London: 1958. V. 72
How It Is. London: 1964. V. 71; 72; 73
Ill Seen, Ill Said. Northridge: 1982. V. 73
Imagination Dead Imagine. London: 1965. V. 69; 72
Krapp's Last Tape and Embers. London: 1959. V. 72
The Lost Ones. London: 1972. V. 69; 71
The Lost Ones. New York: 1972. V. 68; 70
Mal Vu Mal Dit. Paris: 1981. V. 69
Molloy. Paris: 1951. V. 73
Molloy. Paris: 1955. V. 69
Molloy, Malone Dies, The Unnamable. Paris: 1959. V. 72
Nohow On. New York: 1989. V. 69
No's Knife. London: 1967. V. 71
Poems in English. London: 1961. V. 69; 73
Proust. London: 1931. V. 72; 73
Soubresauts. Paris: 1989. V. 69
Still. Milano: 1974. V. 72
Waiting for Godot. New York: 1954. V. 73
Waiting for Godot. London: 1955. V. 70
Waiting for Godot. London: 1956. V. 69; 70
Watt. Paris: 1953. V. 69
Whoroscope. Paris: 1930. V. 73
Worstward Ho. London: 1983. V. 69; 72

BECKETT, SYLVESTER BREAKMORE
Guide Book of the Atlantic and St. Lawrence, and St. Lawrence and Atlantic Rail Roads.... Portland: 1853. V. 70

BECKFORD, PETER
Thoughts on Hunting. 1910. V. 68; 70
Thoughts on Hunting in a Series of Familiar Letters to a Friend. 1781. V. 70
Thoughts on Hunting in a Series of Familiar Letters to a Friend. London: 1820. V. 69
Thoughts Upon Hunting. Sarum: 1784. V. 72

BECKFORD, WILLIAM
An Arabian Tale. 1786. V. 73
An Arabian Tale. London: 1786. V. 68
Biographical Memoirs of Extraordinary Painters. London: 1780. V. 70

BECKFORD, WILLIAM continued
Italy; with Sketches of Spain and Portugal. London: 1834. V. 68; 70; 72
The Journal of William Beckford in Portugal and Spain 1787-1788. London: 1954. V. 70
Life at Fonthill 1807-1822 with Interludes in Paris and London: from the Correspondence of William Beckford. London: 1957. V. 70
Recollections of an Excursion to the Monasteries of Alcobaca and Batalha. London: 1835. V. 70; 72; 73
Thoughts on Hunting in a Series of Familiar Letters to a Friend. 1810. V. 70
Vathek. 1816. V. 73
Vathek. London: 1929. V. 68; 70; 71

BECKMAN CO., CLEVELAND
Northern Ohio Woolware 1921-1922. 1921. V. 69

BECKMANN, JOHANN
Beytrage zur Geschichte der Erfindungen. Leipzig: 1786-1805. V. 68

BECKONINGS from Little Hands. Eight Studies in Childlife. Philadelphia: 1893. V. 69

BECKWITH, GEORGE C.
A Sermon on the Mode of Baptism. Andover: 1828. V. 68

BECKWITH, THOMAS
The Indian or Mound Builder. Cap Girardeau: 1911. V. 69

BECKWOURTH, JAMES P.
The Life and Adventures of James P. Beckwourth, Mountaineer Scout, Pioneer and Chief of the Crow Nation of Indians. London: 1892. V. 73

BECLEMICHEFF, CLEO
Beauty: a Legend of Georgia. Paris: 1932. V. 69

BECQUEREL, HENRI
Recherches sur une Propriete Nouvelle de la Matiere. Paris: 1903. V. 71

BEDDARD, F. E.
Animal Coloration, an Account of the Principal Facts and Theories.... London: 1892. V. 68

BEDDING, FRANCIS
The Black Arrows. New York: 1938. V. 72

BEDDOE, JOHN
Memories of Eighty Years. Bristol: 1910. V. 68

BEDDOES, THOMAS
Essay on the Causes, Early Signs and Prevention of Pulmonary Consumtpion for the Use of Parents and Perceptors.... London: 1799. V. 70
Observations on the Nature and Cure of Calculus, Sea Scurvy, Consumption, Catarrh and Fever. Philadelphia: 1797. V. 73

BEDDOES, THOMAS LOVELL
The Bride's Tragedy. London: 1822. V. 73
The Complete Works of Thomas Lovell Beddoes. London: 1928. V. 70
Death's Jest-Book or the Fool's Tragedy. London: 1850. V. 73
The Letters of Thomas Lovell Beddoes. London: 1894. V. 71
The Poems Posthumous and Collected. London: 1851. V. 72
Poems...with a Memoir. London: 1851. V. 73

BEDDOME, R. H.
Handbook to the Ferns of British India, Ceylon and the Malay Peninsula, with Supplement. Calcutta: 1892. V. 70

BEDE
Axiomata Philosophica, Vererabilis Bedae.... London: 1592. V. 69
Historiae Ecclesiasticae Gentis Libri Quinque.... Cambridge: 1722. V. 72
The History of the Primitive Church of England.... 1814. V. 73
Opera Historica, Historiam Ecclesiasticam, Gentis Anglorum.... Oxford: 1896. V. 70
Opera Theologica, Moralia, Historica, Philosophica, Mathematica and Rethorica.... Cologne: 1688. V. 68

BEDE, CUTHBERT
Photographic Pleasures: Popularly Portrayed with Pen and Pencil. London: 1855. V. 68

BEDELL, CLYDE
How to Write Advertising That Sells. New York: 1940. V. 73

BEDELL, G. T.
The Religious Souvenir for 1833. Philadelphia: 1832. V. 71
The Religious Souvenir for 1834. Philadelphia: 1834. V. 71

BEDFORD, EVAN
The Evan Bedford Library of Cardiology. London: 1977. V. 70

BEDFORD, F.
Sketches in York. York: 1841. V. 72

BEDFORD, F. D.
Through Merrie England - the Pageantry and Pasttimes of the Village and the Town. London: 1928. V. 71

BEDFORD, HERBERT
The Heroines of George Meredith. London. V. 71

BEDFORD, JOHN THOMAS
Robert; or Notes from the Diary of a City Waiter. London: 1885. V. 73

BEDFORD Park. London: 1882. V. 72

BEDFORD, SYBILLE
Aldous Huxley - a Biography 1894-1963. London: 1973-1974. V. 71; 72
A Legacy. London: 1956. V. 73
A Legacy. New York: 1957. V. 70

BEDFORD-JONES, H.
The King's Pardon. New York: 1933. V. 71

BEDICHEK, ROY
Adventures with a Texas Naturalist. Garden City: 1947. V. 69

BEDINGER, MARGERY
Indian Silver Navajo and Pueblo Jewelers. Albuquerque: 1973. V. 73
Navajo Indian Silver-Work. Denver: 1936. V. 69

BEDINI, SYLVIO
The Life of Benjamin Banneker. New York: 1972. V. 72

BEEBE, LUCIUS
Mansions on Rails: the Folklore of the Private Railway Car. Berkeley: 1959. V. 71; 73
Mr. Pullman's Elegant Palace Car. New York: 1961. V. 73
Narrow Gauge in the Rockies. Berkeley: 1970. V. 70
Virginia and Truckee: a Story of Virginia City and Comstock Times. Oakland: 1949. V. 69; 71

BEEBE, STUART
The Time and Lunar Register, Referring to the Year, Month, Days of the Month and Week from the Advent of Our Saviour to the Close of the Nineteenth Century. Hartford: 1827. V. 73

BEEBE, WILLIAM
The Arcturus Adventure. London: 1926. V. 68; 72
Galapagos: World's End. New York: 1924. V. 70
A Monograph of the Pheasants. London: 1918-1922. V. 70; 72
A Monograph of the Pheasants. New York: 1990. V. 70
Pheasant Jungles. 1928. V. 70; 72
Pheasants, Their Lives and Homes. Garden City: 1931. V. 73
Tropical Wild Life in British Guiana. Volume I. New York: 1917. V. 73

BEECHAM, AUDREY
The Coast of Barbary. London: 1957. V. 71

THE BEECHER Island Annual. Wray: 1930. V. 72

BEECHER, CATHERINE E.
The American Woman's Home; or, Principles of Domestic Science.... New York: 1869. V. 68; 69
Letters to the People on Health and Happiness. New York: 1855. V. 68; 73
The Moral Instructor; for Schools and Families.... Cincinnati: 1838. V. 71
Physiology and Caliesthenics, for Schools and Familes. (with) Calistentic Exercises for Schools, Families and Health Establishments. New York: 1856. V. 69; 73
Suggestions Respecting Improvements in Education, Presented to the Trustees of the Hartford Female Seminary and Published at their Request. Hartford: 1829. V. 71
Truth Stranger than Fiction.... New York: 1850. V. 68; 69

BEECHER, EDWARD
The Papa Conspiracy Exposed and Protestantism Defended in the Light of Reason, History and Scripture. Bsoton: 1855. V. 68

BEECHER, HENRY WARD
Plain and Pleasant Talk About Fruits, Flowers and Farming. New York: 1859. V. 68

BEECHER, HERBERT W.
First Light Battery, Conn. Vols. 1861-1865 History and Reminiscences. New York: 1901. V. 70

BEECHER, JOHN
John Beecher: Collected Poems, 1924-1974. New York: 1974. V. 71

BEECHER, LYMAN
A Plea for the West. Cincinnati: 1835. V. 69
The Remedy for Duelling. A Sermon, Delivered Before the Presbytery of Long-Island, at the Opening of Their Session, at Aquebogue, April 16, 1806.... New York: 1809. V. 70

BEECHEY, F. W.
A Voyage of Discovery Towards the North Pole, Performed in His Majesty's Ships Dorothea and Trent, Under the Command of Captain David Buchan 1818 to Which is Added, a Summary.... London: 1843. V. 73

BEECHING, HENRY CHARLES
Love in Idleness, a Volume Of Poems. London: 1883. V. 73
Love's Looking Glass: a Volume of Poems. 1891. V. 73
Mensae Secundae, Verses Written in Balliol College. Oxford and London: 1879. V. 73

BEECHY, HENRY WILLIAM
The Literary Works of Sir Joshua Reynolds, First President of the Royal Academy. London: 1886. V. 70

BEEDE, A.
Sitting Bull-Custer. Bismarck: 1913. V. 69

BEEDING, FRANCIS
The Big Fish. London: 1938. V. 73
Death Walks in Eastrepps. 1931. V. 68; 73
Death Walks in Eastrepps. New York: 1931. V. 72
Eleven Were Brave. New York: 1941. V. 68; 70; 71
The Emerald Clasp. Boston: 1933. V. 68
Hell Let Loose. London: 1937. V. 71
House of Dr. Edwardes. Boston: 1928. V. 72
The Ten Holy Horrors. New York: 1939. V. 70; 71
There Are Thirteen. London: 1946. V. 71

BEEDING, FRANCIS continued
There are Thirteen. New York: 1946. V. 68
The Two Undertakers. Boston: 1933. V. 68

BEEDOME, THOMAS
Select Poems Divine and Humane. London: 1928. V. 70; 71; 73

BEEHLER, B. M.
Birds of New Guinea. Princeton: 1986. V. 70; 73

BEEKMAN, GEORGE C.
Early Dutch Settlers of Monmouth County, New Jersey. Freehold: 1915. V. 69

BEELER, JOE
Cowboys and Indians - Characters in Oil and Bronze. Norman: 1960. V. 69
Cowboys and Indians: Characters in Oil and Bronze. Norman: 1967. V. 69
Cowboys and Indians, Characters in Oil and Bronze. Norman: 1975. V. 69
Joe Beeler, In the Cradle of Cattle Kingdom,. San Antonio: 1985. V. 68; 71
The Joe Beeler Sketchbook. Flagstaff: 1974. V. 68

BEER, G. J.
The Art of Preserving the Sight Unimpaired to an Extreme Old Age and of Re-Establishing and Strengthening It When It Becomes Weak.... London: 1815. V. 68; 73

BEER, GEORGE L.
The Old Colonial System 1660-1754. New York: 1913. V. 70

BEERBOHM, MAX
And Even Now. London: 1920. V. 68; 71; 72
Bernard Shaw and Max Beerbohm at Covent Garden. London: 1981. V. 68
A Book of Caricatures. 1907. V. 69
A Christmas Garland. London: 1912. V. 70
A Christmas Garland. London: 1950. V. 68
Fifty Caricatures. London: 1913. V. 70; 73
Fifty Caricatures. New York: 1913. V. 71
Illustrated Zuleika Dobson. New Haven and London: 1985. V. 72; 73
A Luncheon. 1946. V. 73
Max in Verse, Rhymes and Parodies. Brattleboro: 1963. V. 73
Observations. London: 1926. V. 68
The Poets' Corner. London: 1904. V. 73
Rossetti and His Circle. London: 1922. V. 68
A Survey. London: 1921. V. 68
Things New and Old. London: 1923. V. 70
Zuleika Dobson. London: 1911. V. 72
Zuleika Dobson. Oxford: 1975. V. 68; 73

BEERS, F. W.
Atlas of the City of Worcester;. New York: 1870. V. 71

BEESLY, A. H.
Sir John Franklin. New York: 1881. V. 73

BEESON, JOHN
A Plea for the Indians; with Facts and Features of the Late War in Oregon. New York: 1858. V. 69

BEETHAM, BENTLEY
Borrowdale. London: 1953. V. 69
Borrowdale. London: 1960. V. 69
Borrowdale. London: 1966. V. 69

BEETON, ISABELLA
The Book of Garden Management: Comprising Information on Laying-Out and Planting Gardens.... London: 1875. V. 72
The Book of Household Management. 1861. V. 73
The Book of Household Management. London: 1870. V. 71
The Book of Household Management. London: 1907. V. 70
Mrs. Beeton's Cookery Book. London. V. 71

BEETON, SAMUEL O.
Beeton's Dictionary of Industries and Commerce. London: 1888. V. 71

BEFOREST, BARRY
Pushover. New York: 1936. V. 71

BEGBIE, HAROLD
Life of William Booth: the Founder of the Salvation Army. London: 1920. V. 71
Life of William Booth: the Founder of the Salvation Army. London: 1925. V. 71
The Political Struwwelpeter. London: 1899. V. 68; 69

BEGHTOL, CHARLES
The Little Blue Flute. New York: 1930. V. 72

BEGLEY, JOHN
The Diocese of Limerick. 1906-1938. V. 73

BEGLEY, LOUIS
About Schmidt. New York: 1996. V. 68; 71
Wartime Lies. London: 1991. V. 68
Wartime Lies. New York: 1991. V. 68; 69; 71; 73

BEHAN, BRENDAN
Brendan Behan's Island; an Irish Sketch-Book. 1962. V. 70
Confessions of an Irish Rebel. London: 1965. V. 68
The Hostage. 1958. V. 68
The Hostage. London: 1958. V. 72

The Scarperer. London: 1966. V. 73

BEHAN, BRIAN
With Breast Expanded. London: 1964. V. 72

BEHM, MARC
Eye of the Beholder. New York: 1980. V. 72
The Queen of the Night. Boston: 1977. V. 71

BEHN, APHRA
All the Histories and Novels. London: 1718. V. 70
All the Histories and Novels. London: 1735. V. 73
Love Letters Between a Nobleman and His Sister.... London: 1708. V. 68
Love Letters Between a Nobleman and His Sister.... London: 1718. V. 68; 69; 73
Seventeen Histories and Novels.... London: 1718. V. 68; 69
The Works. London: 1992. V. 73

BEHREND, MOSES
Diseases of the Gall Bladder and Allied Structures. Diagnosis and Treatment. Philadelphia: 1947. V. 71

BEHRENS, JACOB
Sir Jacob Behrens 1806-1889. Bradford. V. 73
Sir Jacob Behrens 1806-1889. Bradford: 1925. V. 72

BEHRMAN, S. N.
Brief Moment: a Comedy in Three Acts. New York: 1931. V. 73
Wine of Choice. New York: 1938. V. 71

BEI BIENKO, G. Y.
Keys to the Insects of the European USSR. Jerusalem: 1967. V. 72

BEIER, ULI
Contemporary Art In Africa. New York: 1968. V. 72

BEIGBEDER, FREDERIC
99 Francs. Paris: 2000. V. 73

BEIN, ALBERT
Let Freedom Ring. New York: 1936. V. 70

BEING and Doing. Liverpool: 1901. V. 68; 72

BEINHART, LARRY
No One Rides for Free. New York: 1986. V. 68; 69; 70; 73

BEITH, GILBERT
Edward Carpenter, in Appreciation. London: 1931. V. 71

BEITH, JANET
Sand Castle. New York: 1936. V. 71

BEKASSY, FERENC
Adriatica and Other Poems. London: 1925. V. 71

BEKAY'S Successful Angling Series. 1990. V. 73

BEKE, CHARLES TILSTONE
The British Captives in Abyssinia. London: 1867. V. 68

BEKEN, FRANK
Beauty of Sail. London: 1964. V. 70

BEKESY, GEORG VON
Experiments in Hearing. New York: 1960. V. 71
Sensory Inhibition. Princeton;: 1967. V. 68

BEKHTEREW, VLADIMIR MIKHAILOVICH VON
Die Leitunsbahnen im Gehirn und Ruckenmark. Leipzig: 1894. V. 68; 72

BEL-Air Country Club - a Living Legend. 1993. V. 73

BELASCO, DAVID
The Music Master. New York. V. 70

BELCHER, HENRY
Degrees & Degrees. London: 1872. V. 68

BELCHER'S Farmer's Almanack for the Province of Nova Scotia for the Year of Our Lord 1872. Halifax: 1872. V. 73

BELDEN, JOHN
Life of David Belden. New York: 1891. V. 70

BELEGEN, THEODORE
Sibley, Autobiography and Letters. Minneapolis: 1932. V. 71

BELGRAVE, M.
Children's Stories from the Northern Legends. London: 1915. V. 72

BELHAVEN, JOHN HAMILTON, SECOND BARON
The Lord Belhaven's Speech in Parliament, the 15th day of November 1706, on the Second Article of the Treaty. 1706. V. 73

BELIDOR, BERNARD FOREST DE
Architecture Hydraulique ou l'Art de Conduire d'Elever et de Menager les Eaux Pour les Differens Besoins de la Vie. Paris: 1737-1753. V. 73
Le Bombardier Francois ou Nouvelle Methde de Jetter les Bombes avec Precision. Amsterdam: 1734. V. 69
La Science des Ingenieurs dans la Conduite des Travaux de Fortification et d'Architecture Civile. Paris: 1729. V. 70; 72; 73

BELISARIO, A. M.
A Report of the Trial of Arthur Hodge, Esquire (Late One of the Members of His Majesty's Council for the Virgin Islands) at the Island of Tortola on the 25th April, 1811 and Adjourned to the 29th of the Same Month, for the Murder of His Negro Man Slave. Middletown: 1812. V. 73

BELISLE, DAVID W.
The American Family Robinson; or, the Adventures of a Family Lost in the Great Desert of te West. Philadelphia: 1854. V. 68

BELKNAP, BAKER & CO.
Catalogue for 1895. Grand Rapids: 1895. V. 71

BELKNAP, JEREMY
The Foresters, an American Tale. Boston: 1796. V. 73

BELKNAP, WALDRON PHOENIX
American Colonial Painting: Materials for a History. Cambridge: 1959. V. 71

BELL, A. C.
History of the Manchester Regiment First and Second Battalions 1922- 1948. Altrichan: 1954. V. 73

BELL, A. E.
Christian Huygens and the Development of Science in the Seventeenth Century. London: 1947. V. 68; 72

BELL, ALEXANDER GRAHAM
Establishment for the Study of Vocal Physiology for the Correction of Stammering and Other Defects of Utterance; and for Practical Instruction in Visible Speech. Boston: 1872. V. 71
Lectures Upon the Mechanism of Speech.... New York and London: 1906. V. 69

BELL, ANNE OLIVIA
Editing Virginia Woolf's Diary. Oxford: 1989. V. 71

BELL, ARTHUR
Representative Painters of the XIXth Century. London: 1899. V. 68

BELL, BARBARA
Zuni - the Art and the People. Dallas, Grants: 1975-1977. V. 70

BELL, BENJAMIN
A System of Surgery Extracted from the Works of Benjamin Bell of Edinburgh. Philadelphia: 1791. V. 68; 71
Three Essays on Taxation of Income, with Remarks on the Late Act of Parliament on that Subject. London: 1799. V. 72
A Treatise on Gonorrhea, Virulenta, and Lues Venerea. Philadelphia: 1795. V. 72
A Treatise on Gonorrhoea, Virulenta, and Lues Venera. Edinburgh: 1797. V. 71

BELL, C. W.
Fox Hunting. A Treatise. 1899. V. 68

BELL, CATHERINE D.
Ella and Marian; or, Rest and Unrest. London: 1876. V. 68

BELL, CHARLES
The Anatomy of the Brain Explained in a Series of Engravings. London: 1802. V. 68; 72
Animals Mechanics. Cambridge: 1902. V. 70; 71
Engravings from Specimens of Morbid Parts, Preserved in the Author's Collection, Now in Windmill Street and Selected from the Divisions Inscribed Urethra. London: 1813. V. 68; 72
The Hand, Its Mechanism and Vital Endowments as Evincing Design. 1837. V. 71
The Hand its Mechanism and Vital Endowments as Evincing Design. London: 1837. V. 72
Illustrations of Great Operations in Surgery, Trepan, Hernia, Amputation, Aneurism and Lithotomy. London: 1821. V. 68
Manuscript Drawings of the Arteries. 1971. V. 70
The Nervous System of the Human Body Including the Papers Delivered Before the Royal Society on the Subject of Nerves. Washington: 1833. V. 70
A System of Dissections, Explaining the Anatomy of the Human Body, and the Manner of Displaying Parts, the distinguishing the Nature from the Diseases Appearances.... Baltimore: 1814. V. 71
A System of Operative Surgery. London: 1814. V. 68; 72

BELL, CHARLES FREDERIC MOBERLY
From Pharaoh to Fellah. London: 1885. V. 73

BELL, CHRISTINE
The Perez Family. New York: 1990. V. 72
Saint. Englewood: 1985. V. 68; 71

BELL, CLIVE
The Legend of Monte Della Sibilla.... Richmond: 1923. V. 69

BELL, EDWARD ALLEN
A History of Giggleswick School from Its Foundation 1499 to 1912. Leeds: 1912. V. 73

BELL, EVANS
The Great Parliamentary Bore. London: 1869. V. 71

BELL, GEORGE
A Treatise on the Cow-Pow.... Edinburgh: 1802. V. 68

BELL, GERTRUDE
Arab War. London: 1940. V. 73
The Arab War. Waltham St. Lawrence: 1940. V. 71
Persian Pictures. London: 1937. V. 72

BELL, GRAHAM
The Artist and His Public. London: 1939. V. 69

BELL, H. T. MAC KENZIE
A Forgotten Genius: Charles Whitehead - a Critical Monograph. London: 1884. V. 69

BELL, HENRY NUGENT
The Huntingdon Peerage. London: 1821. V. 72

BELL, HORACE
Reminiscences of a Ranger. Los Angeles: 1881. V. 70
Reminiscences of a Ranger. Santa Barbara: 1927. V. 73
Reminiscences of a Ranger. Los Angeles: 1933. V. 68

BELL, J. H. B.
A Progress in Mountaineering. Scottish Bens to Alpine Peaks. London: 1950. V. 69; 70; 71; 73

BELL, JOHN
The Art Treatment of Granitic Surfaces. 1860. V. 68
Engravings of the Bones, Muscles and Joints. Philadelphia: 1815. V. 73
The Principles of Surgery. New York: 1810. V. 68

BELL, JOHN, & CO.
Rules. To Be Observed at the Establishment of John Bell & Co., 338, Oxford Street. London: 1897. V. 71

BELL, JOHN R.
The Journal of Captain John R. Bell, Official Journalist for Stephen H. Long Expedition to the Rocky Mountains. Glendale: 1957. V. 70

BELL, JOSEPHINE
Death of a Con Man. London: 1968. V. 68
New People at the Hollies. New York: 1961. V. 69
The Seeing Eye. London: 1958. V. 68

BELL, KATHERINE M.
Swinging the Censor - Reminiscences of Old Santa Barbara. Santa Barbara: 1931. V. 70

BELL, LOUISE PRICE
Kitchen Fun-Teaches Children to Cook Successfully. Cleveland: 1932. V. 70

BELL, M. C.
Little Yellow Wang-Lo. London: 1906. V. 69

BELL, MACKENZIE
Christina Rossetti. A Biographical and Critical Study. London: 1898. V. 71; 72

BELL, MADISON SMARTT
All Souls' Rising. New York: 1995. V. 68; 69; 70; 72
Barking Man and Other Stories. New York: 1990. V. 70
Doctor Sleep. New York: 1991. V. 73
Doctor Sleep. San Diego: 1991. V. 70
Soldier's Joy. New York: 1989. V. 69; 70
Straight Cut. New York: 1986. V. 70
Straight Cut. London: 1987. V. 68; 72
Straight Cut. New York: 1989. V. 71
Waiting for the End of the World. New York: 1985. V. 68; 70; 71
The Washington Square Ensemble. New York: 1983. V. 68; 69; 70; 71
The Year of Silence. New York: 1987. V. 69; 70
Zero db and Other Stories. New York: 1987. V. 70

BELL, MAJOR HORACE
Reminiscences of a Ranger of Early Times in Southern California. Santa Barbara: 1927. V. 69

BELL, MALCOLM
Edward Burne-Jones. London: 1892. V. 68

BELL, NANCY
Nuremberg. London: 1905. V. 72

BELL, QUENTIN
Virginia Woolf. A Biography. London: 1972. V. 68; 69; 70; 72

BELL, R. C.
Trademen's Tickets and Private Tokens 1785-1819. Newcastle upon Tyne: 1966. V. 72

BELL, RAMSAY
Dragon Under Ground. London: 1937. V. 68

BELL, T. HEDLEY
The Birds Of Cheshire Together with: A Supplement to the Birds of Cheshire. Altrincham: 1962. V. 73

BELL, THOMAS
The Anatomy, Physiology and Diseases of the Teeth. 1835. V. 72
The Anatomy, Physiology and Diseases of the Teeth. London: 1835. V. 70
A History of British Quadrupeds Including the Cetacea. 1837. V. 73
A History of British Quadrupeds, Including the Cetacea. London: 1837. V. 70; 72
A History of British Reptiles. London: 1849. V. 72

BELL, VANESSA
Notes on Virginia's Childhood: a Memoir. New York: 1974. V. 72
Sketches in Pen and Ink - a Bloomsbury Notebook. London: 1997. V. 68

BELL, W. S.
Old Fort Benton. Helena: 1909. V. 68

BELL, WALTER DALRYMPLE MAITLAND
Bell of Africa. London: 1960. V. 72
The Wanderings of an Elephant Hunter. 1940. V. 70

BELL, WALTER DALRYMPLE MAITLAND continued
The Wanderings of an Elephant Hunter. 1958. V. 72; 73

BELL, WILLIAM
Poetry from Oxford in Wartime. London: 1945. V. 72

BELL, WILLIAM DIXON
The Moon Colony. 1937. V. 73
The Moon Colony. Chicago: 1937. V. 68

BELL, WILLIAM E.
Carpentry Made Easy; or the Science and Art of Framing.... Philadelphia: 1904. V. 73

BELL, WILLIAM GARDNER
Will James; the Life and Works of a Lone Cowboy. Flagstaff: 1987. V. 69

BELL, WINTHROP PICKARD
The Foreign Protestants and the Settlement of Nova Scotia. Toronto: 1961. V. 72
The Foreign Protestants and the Settlement of Nova Scotia. Sackville: 1992. V. 73

BELLAIRS, GEORGE
Bones in the Wilderness. London: 1959. V. 69; 73
The Case of the Demented Spiv. London: 1949. V. 69; 73
Death of a Busybody. New York: 1943. V. 72
Murder Gone Mad. London: 1968. V. 70

BELLAIRS, H. W.
Traditions of Nuneaton and Its Neighbourhood (in verse). Nuneaton: 1860. V. 72

BELLAMANN, HENRY
King's Row. New York: 1940. V. 71; 73

BELLAMY, DANIEL
Ethic Amusements. London: 1768. V. 68
Ethic Amusements. London: 1770. V. 73

BELLAMY, GUY
I Have a Complaint to Make. London: 1979. V. 68
The Secret Lemonade Drinker. London: 1977. V. 68

BELLAMY, H. S.
Moons, Myths and Man: a Reinterpretation. London: 1936. V. 72

BELLAMY, JOSEPH
Four Sermons on the Wisdom of God in the Permission of Sin. Morris town: 1804. V. 69
True Religion Delineated; or, Experimental Religion, as Distinguished from Formality on the One Hand, and Enthusiasm on the Other.... Boston: 1804. V. 69

BELLARD, ALFRED
Gone for a Soldier. The Civil War Memoirs of Private Alfred Bellard. Boston: 1975. V. 69

BELLAY Differentes Pensees d'Ornements Arabesques a Divers Usages... Premiere (-Seconde) Partie. Paris: 1750. V. 68; 70; 72

BELLEW, HENRY WALTER
From the Indus to the Tigris. A Narrative of a Journey through the Countries of Balochistan, Afghanistan, Khorassan and Iran, in 1872. London: 1874. V. 68; 72

BELLIN, JACQUES NICOLAS
Essai Geographique sur les Isles Britanniques. Paris: 1759. V. 72

BELLIN DE LA LIBORLIERE, LOUIS FRANCOIS MARIE
La Nuit Anglaise, ou les Aventures.... 1799. V. 73

BELLINGHAM, O'BRYEN
A Treatise on Diseases of the Heart. Dublin: 1853. V. 70

BELL-IRVING, D. J.
Talley-Ho. Fifty Years Sporting Reminiscences. Dumfries: 1920. V. 71; 72

BELLMER, HANS
Sombre Printemps. Paris: 1970. V. 70

BELLOC, HILAIRE
Advice. 1960. V. 68
Emmanuel Burden Merchant of Thames St., in the City of London, Exporter of Hardware. London: 1904. V. 68
First and Last. London: 1911. V. 73
Four Cautionary Tales and a Moral. London: 1909. V. 73
The Haunted House. New York: 1928. V. 68
Hills and the Sea. London: 1927. V. 71
Lambkin's Remains. Oxford: 1900. V. 70
The Missing Masterpiece. London: 1929. V. 68; 71
The Modern Traveller. London: 1898. V. 73
The Old Road. London: 1910. V. 73
The Path to Rome. London: 1902. V. 68; 73
Richlieu. London: 1930. V. 70
Robespierre; a Study. London: 1901. V. 68
Six British Battles. London: 1931. V. 70
The Verse of Hilaire Belloc. London: 1954. V. 71; 73
Verses. London: 1954. V. 70
Verses and Sonnets. 1896. V. 73
Verses and Sonnets. London: 1896. V. 68

BELLOW, SAUL
The Adventures of Augie March. New York: 1953. V. 68; 69; 70; 71; 73
Dangling Man. New York: 1944. V. 69; 70; 73
Dangling Man. London: 1946. V. 71

The Dean's December. Franklin Center: 1982. V. 73
The Dean's December. New York: 1982. V. 69; 71; 73
Henderson the Rain King. London: 1959. V. 68; 70
Henderson the Rain King. New York: 1959. V. 69; 73
Herzog. New York: 1964. V. 72
Him with His Foot in His Mouth. New York: 1984. V. 69
The Last Analysis. New York: 1965. V. 71; 72
Mr. Sammler's Planet. London: 1970. V. 69; 70
Mr. Sammler's Planet. New York: 1970. V. 68
More Die of Heartbreak. New York: 1987. V. 68; 71; 72
Nobel Lecture. New York: 1979. V. 68; 69; 70
The Noble Savage - Number 3. Cleveland and New York: 1961. V. 71
Ravelstein. New York: 2000. V. 73
Seize the Day. New York: 1956. V. 68; 69; 70; 73
Seize the Day. London: 1957. V. 71
A Silver Dish. New York: 1979. V. 69; 71
The Victim. New York: 1947. V. 68; 69; 72
The Victim. London: 1948. V. 69; 71

BELLOWS, ALBERT J.
Philosophy of Eating. New York: 1867. V. 73

BELLOWS, GEORGE W.
His Lithographs. New York: 1928. V. 69; 72

BELL'S British Theatre. London: 1791-1797. V. 70

BELO, A. H., & CO.
Texas Almanac and State Industrial Guide: 1904. Galveston: 1904. V. 70

BELOE, WILLIAM
Anecdotes of Literature and Scarce Books. London: 1807-1812. V. 71

BELON, P.
La Nature & Diuersite des Poissons, avec Leurs Purtaicts, Representez au Plus Pres du Naturel. Paris: 1555. V. 73

BELOT, JEAN
Les Oeuvres...Contenant la Chiromance, Physionomie, l'Art de Memoire de Raymond Lulle.... Lyon: 1654. V. 68

BELOUS, RUSSELL E.
Will Soule Indian Photographer at Fort Sill, Oklahoma 1869-1874. Los Angeles: 1969. V. 68; 70; 72

BELSHAM, WILLIAM
Essays Philosophical and Moral, Historical and Literary.... London: 1799. V. 69

BELT, THOMAS
The Naturalist in Nicaragua. London: 1888. V. 73

BELTON, FREDERICK
Random Recollections of an Old Actor. London: 1880. V. 69

BELTRAMI, GIACOMO CONSTANTINO
A Pilgrimage in Europe and America, Leading to the Discovery of the Sources of the Mississippi and the Bloody River.... London: 1828. V. 68

BEMBO, PIETRO, CARDINAL
Gli Asolani. Venice: 1540. V. 73
Rerum Venetarum Historiae Libri XII. Paris: 1551. V. 68; 70

BEMELMANS, LUDWIG
Are You Hungry Are You Cold. London: 1961. V. 73
Bemelman's Italian Holiday. Boston: 1961. V. 71
The Donkey Inside. New York: 1941. V. 71
The High World. New York: 1954. V. 72
Holiday In France. Boston: 1957. V. 69
Madeline. New York: 1939. V. 70
Madeline and the Bad Hat. New York: 1957. V. 69; 71
Madeline and the Gypsies. New York: 1959. V. 69; 70
Rosebud. New York: 1942. V. 69
Sunshine. New York: 1950. V. 69; 70
Welcome Home!. New York: 1960. V. 72

BEMIS, GEORGE
Report of the Case of John W. Webster, Master of the Arts and Doctor of Medicine of Harvard University...Indicted for the Murder of George Parkman.. Boston: 1850. V. 71

BEMISS, ELIJAH
The Dyer's Companion. New York: 1815. V. 73

BEMMELEN, J. F. VAN
Guide Through Netherlands, India. London: 1903. V. 72

BEMROSE, WILLIAM
Fret-Cutting and Perforated Carving with Practical Instructions. London and Derby: 1870. V. 68

BENATAR, MOLLY
Alice and the Cheshire Cat. London: 1930. V. 69

BENAVIDES, FRAY ALONSO DE
The Memoirs of.... Los Angeles: 1900-1901. V. 68
The Memorial of Fray Alonso de Benavides 1630. Chicago: 1916. V. 71

BENBOW, H. L.
Report of the Special Joint Committee, in Regard to Certain Public Property on Hand at the Evacuation of Columbia, and the Surrender of Gen. Johnston's Army. Columbia: 1866. V. 70

BENCHLEY, NATHANIEL
The Off-Islanders. New York: 1961. V. 72
Side Street. New York: 1950. V. 70; 71

BENCHLEY, PETER
The Deep. Garden City: 1976. V. 71
Jaws. Garden City: 1974. V. 68; 70; 71; 72
Jaws. London: 1974. V. 68

BENCHLEY, ROBERT
The Reel Benchley: Robert Benchley at His Hilarious Best in Text and Pictures. New York: 1950. V. 69

BENDA, CLEMENS E.
The Child with Mongolism. New York and London: 1960. V. 68

BENDELOWES, PHILIP
An Inquiry into the Cause Which Obstructed the Reformation, and Hath Hitherto Prevented Its Progress.... London: 1768. V. 70

BENDER, AVERAM B.
The March of Empire Frontier Defence of The Southwest 1848-1866. Lawrence, KS: 1952. V. 72

BENDER, TEX
Ten Years A Cowboy. Chicago: 1891. V. 71

BENDIRE, C.
Life Histories of North American Birds.... Washington: 1895. V. 73

BENEDICT, BARRY
Short Turns. New York: 1926. V. 70

BENEDICT, CARL P.
A Tenderfoot Kid On Gyp Water. Austin: 1943. V. 71

BENEDICT, ERASTUS C.
The American Admiralty: Its Jurisdiction and Practice with Practical Forms and Directions. Albany: 1925, V. 73

BENEDICT, FRANK LEE
Her Friend Laurence. New York: 1879. V. 70

BENEDICT, H. T. N.
Murray's English Grammar. Frankfort: 1832. V. 68

BENEDICT, PICKNEY
Town Smokes. Princeton: 1987. V. 73

BENEDICT, WILLIAM
History of the Town of Sutton, Massachusetts from 1704 to 1876. 1966. V. 71

BENEDICT, WILLIAM H.
New Brunswick in History. New Brunswick: 1925. V. 69

BENEDICTUS
Variations. Paris. V. 71

BENEDIKIT, MORIZ
Anatomical Studies Upon Brains of Criminals. New York: 1881. V. 70; 71

BENEFIELD, BARRY
Buggles in the Night. New York: 1927. V. 69
Little Clown Lost. New York: 1928. V. 69
Short Turns. New York: 1926. V. 69

BENET, LAURA
Enchanting Jenny Lind. NY: 1939. V. 72

BENET, STEPHEN VINCENT
The Devil and Daniel Webster. Weston: 1937. V. 71
Heavens and Earth. New York: 1920. V. 71
James Shore's Daughter. Garden City: 1934. V. 68
John Brown's Body. Garden City: 1928. V. 73
Nightmare at Noon. New York: 1940. V. 73

BENET, WILLIAM ROSE
The Dust Which is God. New York: 1942. V. 71
Timothy's Angel's. New York: 1947. V. 72
Wild Goslings: A Selection of Fugitive Pieces. New York: 1927. V. 72

BENEZET, ANTHONY
Some Account of Guinea, Its Situation, Produce and the General Disposition of Its Inhabitants. Philadelphia: 1772. V. 72
Some Historical Account of Guinea, Its Situation, Produce and the General Disposition of Its Inhabitants. Philadelphia: 1771. V. 68; 70; 73

BENEZRA, NEAL
Stephen Balkenhol Sculptures and Drawings. Washington: 1995. V. 68

BENGER, ELIZABETH O.
Memoirs of Mr. John Tobin. London: 1820. V. 71

BENGIS, NATHAN L.
Baker Street Legacy: The Will of Sherlock Holmes. New York: 1951. V. 69

BEN GORION, JOSEPH
A Compendious and Most Mervailous Historie of the Latter Times of the Iews Common Weale. London: 1593. V. 73

BEN-GURION, DAVID
Israel: a Personal History. New York: 1971. V. 68; 70; 72; 73

BENHAM & SONS
Benham & Sons, Manufacturing and Furnishing Ironmongers, Hot Water & Gas Engineers, Stove, Range and Bath Makers. London: 1870. V. 70
Manufacturing and Furnishing Ironmongers, Hot Water and Gas Engineers, Stove, Range and Bath Makers. London: 1870. V. 68

BENHAM, CANON W.
Medieval London. London: 1901. V. 71
Old St. Paul's Cathedral. London: 1902. V. 71
The Tower of London. London: 1906. V. 71

BENHAM, GEORGE CHITTENDEN
A Year of Wreck, a True Story, by a Victim. New York: 1880. V. 71

BENITEZ, SANDRA
A Place Where the Sea Remembers. Minneapolis: 1993. V. 69

BENJAMIN, ASHER
The American Builder's Companion; or, a System of Architecture, Particularly Adapted to the Present Style of Building.... Boston: 1816. V. 68

BENJAMIN Disraeli, Earl of Beaconsfield, K.G. *In Upwards of 100 Cartoons from the Collection of Mr. Punch.* London: 1878. V. 71

BENJAMIN, JUDAH
Treatise on the Law of Sale of Personal Property. Boston and New York: 1892. V. 68

BENJAMIN, S. G. W.
The Cruise of the Alice May in the Gulf of St. Lawrence and Adjacent Waters. New York: 1885. V. 73
The Life and Adventures of a Free Lance. Burlington: 1914. V. 68

BENKARD, ERNST
Undying Faces - a Collection of Death Masks from the 15th Century to the Present Day. London: 1929. V. 72

BENKOVITZ, MIRIAM J.
A Bibliography of Ronald Firbank. London: 1963. V. 69
Supplement to a Bibliography of Ronald Firbank. London: 1980. V. 72

BENN, TONY
Arguments for Socialism. London: 1979. V. 71

BENNET, BENJAMIN
Discourses on the Credibility of the Scriptures. New Brunswick: 1795. V. 69

BENNET, DONALD
The Southern Highlands,. Edinburgh: 1972. V. 69

BENNET, E.
Shots and Snapshots in British East Africa. London: 1914. V. 72

BENNET, ESTELLINE
Old Deadwood Days. New York: 1935. V. 69

BENNET, J. HENRY
Winter and Spring on the Shores of the Mediterranean; or the Riviera, Mentone, Italy, Corsica, Sicily, Algeria, Spain and Biarritz. London: 1870. V. 73

BENNET, THOMAS
Directions for Studying I. A General System or Body of Divinity. II. The Thirty Nine Articles of Religion. London: 1727. V. 70

BENNETT, A. W.
The Flora of the Alps. New York: 1898. V. 71; 73

BENNETT, AGNES MARIA
Anna; or, Memoirs of a Welch Heiress.... London: 1785. V. 73

BENNETT, ALAN
Forty Years On. London: 1969. V. 70

BENNETT, ALFRED W.
The Flora of the Alps.... London: 1896. V. 70; 72

BENNETT, ARNOLD
Accident. London: 1929. V. 69
Anna of the Five Towns. London: 1902. V. 73
The Card. London: 1911. V. 73
The Card. London: 1913. V. 73
The Gates of Wrath. London: 1903. V. 73
The Journals of Arnold Bennett. London: 1932-1933. V. 72
Leonora. London: 1903. V. 73
The Matador of the Five Towns and other stories. London: 1912. V. 72
Mr. Proback. New York: 1922. V. 68
Over There: War Scenes on the Western Front. London: 1915. V. 73
Riceyman Steps. London: 1923. V. 73
Things That Have Interested Me; Third Series. London: 1926. V. 72
Things that Interested Me: Being Leaves from a Journal. Burslem: 1907. V. 73
Things That Interested Me: Being Leaves from a Journal. Third Series. Burslem: 1908. V. 73
Venus Rising from the Sea. London: 1931. V. 69

BENNETT, BOB
Kerr County Texas 1856-1956. San Antonio: 1956. V. 70

BENNETT, CHARLES
The Book of Blockheads. London: 1863. V. 73

BENNETT, CHARLES H.
Shadow and Substance. London: 1860. V. 70

BENNETT, E.
The Three Kittens. Boston: 1890. V. 70

BENNETT, E. H.
The Sectional Anatomy of Congenital Coecal Hernia. London: 1888. V. 71

BENNETT, E. T.
The Gardens and Menagerie of the Zoological Society Delineated. 1830-1831. V. 69; 70; 72; 73
The Tower Menagerie.... London: 1829. V. 72

BENNETT, H.
The Chemical Formulary.... New York: 1933-1951. V. 69

BENNETT, HAL
Seventh Heaven. Garden City: 1976. V. 72

BENNETT, HENRY
Winter and Spring on the Shores of the Mediterranean.... New York: 1870. V. 69

BENNETT, J. H.
Text-Book of Physiology, General, Special and Practical. Edinburgh: 1870-1872. V. 71

BENNETT, JACK
Gallipoli. New York: 1981. V. 71

BENNETT, JIM
A Man for Dalhousie. (Henry Davies Hicks). Halifax: 1980. V. 72

BENNETT, JOAN
Virginia Woolf. Her Art as a Novelist. Cambridge: 1945. V. 69

BENNETT, JOHN
Letters to a Young Lady, on a Variety of Useful and Interesting Subjects. Hartford: 1798. V. 69
Master Skylark. New York: 1922. V. 69
The Pigtail of Ah Lee Ben Loo.... New York: 1928. V. 73

BENNETT, KAY
Kaibah: Recollection of a Navajo Girlhood. Los Angeles: 1964. V. 69
A Navajo Saga. San Antonio: 1969. V. 69

BENNETT, LERONE
Before the Mayflower: A History of Black America. Chicago: 1970. V. 72
Confrontation: Black and White. Chicago: 1965. V. 72
Pioneers in Protest. Chicago: 1968. V. 72

BENNETT, MARGUERITE
My Arnold Bennett. London: 1931. V. 73

BENNETT, NOEL
The Weaver's Pathway: a Clarification of the Spirit Trail in Navajo Weaving. 1974. V. 69

BENNETT, PAUL
The Typophiles. New York: 1966-1968. V. 70

BENNETT, PAUL A.
Postscripts on Dwiggins. New York: 1960. V. 69

BENNETT, RICHARD
The Story of Bovril. 1953. V. 69
The Story of Bovril. Bovril: 1953. V. 73

BENNETT, ROBERT
The Wrath of John Steinbeck of St. John Goes to Church. Los Angeles: 1939. V. 71

BENNETT, W.
The History of Burnley. London: 1946-1951. V. 73

BENNETT, WHITMAN
A Practical Guide to American Book Collection. New York: 1941. V. 71

BENNISON, W.
The Cause of the Present Money Crisis Explained, In Answer to the Pamphlet of Mr. J. Horsley Palmer; and a Remedy Pointed Out. London: 1837. V. 69

BENOIS, ALEXANDRE
The Russian School of Painting. London: 1916. V. 72

BENRAN, MEIJI
Japanese Names and How to Read Them. London: 1923. V. 70

BENSCHOTER, GEORGE E.
Book of Facts Concerning The Early Settlement of Sherman County and .... Loup City, NE: 1890. V. 71

BENSON, A. E.
History of the Massachusetts Horticultural Society. 1929. V. 73

BENSON, ARTHUR CHRISTOPHER
The Book of the Queen's Doll House. London: 1924. V. 68; 70
Le Chaier Jaune. Poems. Eton: 1892. V. 68
Lord Vyet and Other Poems. London: 1897. V. 73
Ode in Memory of the Rt. Honble. William Ewart Gladstone. Eton: 1898. V. 73
Thomas Gray. Eton: 1895. V. 73

BENSON, BEN
The Blonde in Black. New York: 1958. V. 69; 73
The Venus Death. New York: 1953. V. 70

BENSON, C. E.
Crag and Hound in Lakeland. London: 1902. V. 71

BENSON, E. F.
The Angel of Pain. London: 1906. V. 72
The Blotting Book. New York: 1908. V. 68
David Blaize and the Blue Door. London: 1918. V. 71
The House of Defense. London: 1907. V. 72
The Judgement Books. London: 1895. V. 68
The Kaiser and English Relations. London: 1936. V. 71
The Luck of the Vails. London: 1901. V. 72; 73
Reaping. London: 1909. V. 72
The Relentless City. London: 1903. V. 68; 73
Spook Stories. London: 1928. V. 71
Thorley Weir. London: 1913. V. 72
The Worshipful Lucia. New York: 1935. V. 73

BENSON, E. R.
Charlotte Bronte. London: 1932. V. 73

BENSON, EGBERT
Vindication of the Captors of Major Andre. New York: 1817. V. 71; 73

BENSON, ELIZABETH P.
Dumbarton Oaks Conference on the Olmec: October 28th and 29th 1967. Washington: 1968. V. 71

BENSON, GODFREY R.
Tracks in the Snow. London: 1906. V. 72

BENSON, HENRY C.
Life Among the Choctaw Indians and Sketches of the South West. Cincinnati: 1860. V. 70

BENSON, MARGARET
Capital, Labour and Trade and the Outlook. London: 1891. V. 68

BENSON, MARY SUMNER
Women in Eighteenth Century America. New York: 1935. V. 72

BENSON, RAYMOND
Doubleshot. London: 2000. V. 72
The Facts of Death. London: 1998. V. 72
The World is Not Enough 007. London: 1999. V. 68; 70; 71

BENSON, ROBERT HUGH
The Necromancers. St. Louis: 1909. V. 70
The Sentimentalists. London: 1906. V. 71

BENSON, SALLY
Junior Miss. New York: 1941. V. 72
Meet Me in St. Louis. New York: 1941. V. 73
Meet Me in St. Louis. New York: 1942. V. 72

BENSON, STELLA
Pipers and a Dance. London: 1924. V. 69
Worlds Within Worlds. New York: 1929. V. 71

BENSON, THOMAS
Vocabularium Anglo-Saxonicum, Lexico Gul. Somneri Manga Parte Auctius. London: 1701. V. 71; 72

BENT, A. C.
Life Histories of North American Birds of Prey. 1961. V. 68
Life Histories of North American Wild Fowl, Order Anseeres. Washington: 1923-1925. V. 70
Life Histories of North American Woodpeckers. Bloomington: 1992. V. 70

BENT, GEORGE PAYNE
Four Score and More - Bits of Biography and Humorous History. Los Angeles: 1929. V. 68; 73

BENT, SILAS
Justice Wendell Holmes: a Biography. New York: 1932. V. 72

BENT, THEODORE
Southern Arabia. London: 1900. V. 72

BENTEEN, FREDERICK W.
The Benteen Golden Letters on Custer and His Last Battle. New York: 1974. V. 72
Cavalry Scraps- The Writing of Frederick W. Benteen. Athens: 1979. V. 72

BENTHALL, MRS.
When I Was. London: 1911. V. 72

BENTHAM, EDWARD
An Introduction to Moral Philosophy. Oxford: 1745. V. 73
A Letter to a Young Gentleman of Oxford. (with) A Letter to a Fellow of a College. Oxford: 1748. V. 73
Reflexions Upon the Study of Divinity. Oxford: 1771. V. 73

BENTHAM, GEORGE
Genera Plantarum ad Exemplaria Imprimis in Herbariis Kewensibus Servata Definita. London: 1862-1863. V. 72

BENTHAM, GEORGE continued
Handbook of the British Flora. London: 1865. V. 71
Labiatarum, Genera et Species.... London: 1832-1836. V. 72

BENTHAM, JEREMY
Chrestomathia: Being a Collection of Papers, Explanatory of the Design of an Institution, Proposed to be set on Foot... (with) Chrestomathia, Part II. Appendix No V. London: 1816-1817. V. 69
Defence of Usury; Shewing the Impolicy of the Present Legal Restraints on the Terms of Pecuniary Bargains in a Letter to a Friend. London: 1816. V. 71; 72
A Fragment of Government.... London: 1823. V. 72
An Introduction to the Principles of Morals and Legislation. London: 1823. V. 71
Leading Principles of a Constitutional Code, for any State. London: 1823. V. 70
Papers Relative to Codification and Public Instruction: Including Correspondence with the Russian Emperor, and Divers Constituted Authorities in the American United States. London: 1817. V. 73
Theory of Legislation. London: 1882. V. 71

BENTHAM, SAMUEL
Desiderata in a Naval Arsenal, or an Indication as Officially Presented, of the Several Particulars Proper to be Attended to In the Formation or Improvement of Naval Arsenals.... London: 1814. V. 73
Representations on the Causes of Decay in Ships of War, Together with Proposals for Effecting the Due Seasoning of Timber, and the Oeconomical and Expeditious Construction of Ships of War. London: 1814. V. 73

BENTLEY, ARTHUR
The Deer of Australia. 1978. V. 69

BENTLEY, E. C.
Trent's Last Case. London: 1913. V. 68; 69; 70
Trent's Own Case. New York: 1936. V. 68

BENTLEY, ELIZABETH
Miscellaneous Poems: Being the Genuine Compositions of Elizabeth Bentley, of Norwich. Norwich: 1835. V. 69

BENTLEY, JOHN
The Eyes Of Death. Garden City: 1934. V. 72
Mr. Marlow Chooses Wine. Boston: 1941. V. 72
Mr. Marlow Takes To Rye. Boston: 1942. V. 71; 72

BENTLEY, NICOLAS
The Floating Dutchman. London: 1950. V. 72
Inside Information. London: 1974. V. 72
Third Party Risk. London: 1953. V. 72
The Tongue-Tied Canary. London: 1948. V. 72

BENTLEY, R.
Some Stray Notes Upon Slough and Upton Collected from Various Sources. Slough: 1892. V. 71

BENTLEY, RICHARD
The Bentley Ballads. London: 1861. V. 71
A Dissertation Upon the Epistles of Phalaris. London: 1699. V. 72
The Folly and Unreasonableness of Atheism Demonstrated from the Advantage and Pleasure of a Religious Life, the Faculties of Human Souls, the Structure of Animate Bodies.... London: 1692-1693. V. 73
The Folly and Unresaonableness of Atheism Demonstrated from the Advantage and Pleasure of a Religious Life.... London: 1693. V. 68

BENTLEY, WILLIAM
A Funeral Discourse, Delivered in the East Meeting-House, Salem...on the Death of Major General John Fiske. Salem: 1797. V. 71

BENTON, ARTHUR L.
Right-Left Discrimination and Finger Localization. Development and Pathology. New York: 1959. V. 68

BENTON, FRANK
Cowboy Life On the Sidetrack. Denver: 1903. V. 71

BENTON, JESSE JAMES
Cow by the Tail. Boston: 1943. V. 69

BENTON, JOSEPH AUGUSTINE
The California Pilgrim: a Series of Lectures. Sacramento: 1853. V. 70

BENTON, JOSIAH H.
Voting in the Field. Boston: 1915. V. 70

BENTON, THOMAS HART
Historical and Legal Examination of that Part of the...Dred Scott Case, Which Declares the Unconstitutionality of the Missouri Compromise. New York: 1857. V. 69
Thirty Year's View, or a History of the Working of the American Government for Thirty Years from 1820 to 1850. New York: 1854. V. 70

BENUZZI, FELICE
No Picnic on Mount Kenya. London: 1953. V. 69

BENVENISTE, ASA
A Word in Your Season. London. V. 70

BENY, ROLOFF
Persia: Bridge of Turquoise. London: 1975. V. 68; 72

BEOWULF
Beowulf. London: 1999. V. 69; 72
Beowulf. London: 2000. V. 68
Beowulf. New York: 2000. V. 69

BEQUAERT, J.
A Revision of the Vespidae of the Belgian Congo Based on the Collection of the American Museum Congo Expedition.... New York: 1918. V. 72

BERALDI, HENRI
Estampes et Livres 1872-1892. Paris: 1892. V. 73

BERANGER, PIERRE JEAN DE
The Songs of Beranger in English, with a Sketch of the Author's Life. Philadelphia: 1844. V. 70

BERENDT, J. E.
Jazz: a Photo History. New York: 1979. V. 68

BERENDT, JOACHIM
Jazz Life. Offenburg (Baden): 1961. V. 69

BERENDT, JOHN
Midnight in the Garden of Good and Evil. New York: 1994. V. 68; 69; 70; 71; 73
Midnight in the Garden of Good and Evil. London: 1998. V. 68
Midnight in the Garden of Good and Evil. Norwalk: 1998. V. 68

BERENGARIO DA CAPRI, JACOPO
Isagogae Brevis P(er)lucide ac Uberrime in anatomiam Humani Corporis.... Bologna: 1523. V. 68; 72

BERENS, EDWARD
Advice to a Young Man Upon First Going to Oxford, in Ten Letters, from an Uncle to His Nephew. London: 1832. V. 69

BERENSON, BERNARD
Italian Pictures of the Renaissance: the Venetian School. 1957. V. 72
A Sienese Painter of the Franciscan Legend. New York: 1909. V. 68

BERENSTAIN, STANLEY
Berenstain's Baby Book. New York: 1951. V. 68

BERESFORD, J. D.
Love's Illusion. New York: 1930. V. 71
Signs and Wonders: Tales. Waltham St. Lawrence: 1921. V. 71
Taken from Life. London: 1922. V. 72

BERESFORD, JAMES
Bibliosophia; or Book Wisdom. London: 1810. V. 71

BERESFORD, WILLIAM
Reis Naar de Noord-West Kust van Amerika. Gedaan in e Jaren 178, 1786, 1787, en 1788.... Amsterdam: 1795. V. 73

BERESINER, YASHA
A Collector's Guide to Paper Money. NY: 1977. V. 72

BERG, ELIZABETH
Talk Before Sleep. New York: 1994. V. 70

BERG, GUSTAV VON
From Kapuvar to California 1893. Travel Letters of Baron Gustav von Berg. San Francisco: 1979. V. 73

BERG, L. S.
Freshwater Fishes of the USSR and Adjacent Countries. 1962-1965. V. 72; 73

BERG, WALTER G.
Buildings and Structures of American Railroads. New York: 1904. V. 69

BERGEN, TEUNIS G.
Register in Alphabetical Order, of the Early Settlers of Kings County, Long Island, N.Y. from Its First Settlement by Europeans to 1700.... New York: 1881. V. 72

BERGER, ADOLPHE
Histoire de l'Eloquence Latine Depuis l'Origine de Rome Jusqu'a Ciceron. Paris: 1872. V. 73

BERGER, CLEO LUND
Detour: a Novel of Life in a CCC-Camp During the Depression Era. New York: 1959. V. 71

BERGER, FRANCESCO
97. Stories of Dickens, Thackeray, Gilbert, Sullivan.... London: 1931. V. 69

BERGER, JOHN
And Our Faces, My Heart, Brief as Photos. New York: 1984. V. 69; 72
Corker's Freedom. New York: 1993. V. 69; 72
Lilac and Flag. New York: 1990. V. 69; 72
Pig Earth. New York. V. 69; 72
To the Wedding. New York: 1995. V. 69; 72

BERGER, K.
Gericault Drawings and Watercolors. New York: 1946. V. 72
Odilon Redon: Fantasy Colour. London: 1964. V. 72

BERGER, L.
Odilon Redon: Fantasy and Color. London: 1964. V. 69

BERGER, M.
Benny Carter. A Life in American Music. Metuchen: 1982. V. 73

BERGER, SIDNEY E.
Printing and the Mind of Merker: a Bibliographic Study. New York: 1997. V. 73

BERGER, THOMAS
The Feud. New York: 1983. V. 68; 72
Killing Time. New York: 1967. V. 71; 72

BERGER, THOMAS continued
Little Big Man. New York: 1964. V. 68; 69; 70; 71; 72
Little Big Man. London: 1965. V. 69
Little Big Man. New York: 1983. V. 71
Neighbors. New York: 1980. V. 68; 73
Nowhere. New York: 1985. V. 68
Regiment of Women. New York: 1973. V. 69
Reinhart in Love. New York: 1962. V. 69
Reinhart's Women. New York: 1981. V. 68
Robert Crews. New York: 1994. V. 72
Who is Teddy Villanova?. 1977. V. 68

BERGHAUS, HEINRICH
Die Voker der Erdballs. Brussels, Leipzig and Ghent: 1851. V. 70

BERGIUS, PETER JONAS
Descriptiones Plantarum ex Capite Bonae Spei.... Stockholm: 1767. V. 69; 72; 73

BERGMAN, INGMAR
Autumn Sonata. New York: 1979. V. 70

BERGMAN, ROBERT
A Kind of Rapture. New York: 1998. V. 68; 72

BERGMAN, STEN
Sport and Exploration in the Far East. 1933. V. 72

BERGSMA, DANIEL
Birth Defects Compendium. London: 1979. V. 68

BERINGTON, JOSEPH
The History of the Reign of Henry the Second, and of Richard and John, His Sons.... Basil: 1793. V. 69
A Literary History of the Middle Age: Comprehending an Account of the State of Learning. London: 1814. V. 71

BERJEAU, J. P.
The Book-Worm. London: 1866-1869-. V. 69
The Homoeopathic Treatment of Syphilis. Philadelphia: 1870. V. 71

BERKELEY, California: A City of Homes. Berkeley: 1905. V. 68

BERKELEY, ANTHONY
Before the Fact. London: 1932. V. 73
Death in the House. New York: 1939. V. 73
Jugged Journalism. London: 1925. V. 73
The Layton Court Mystery. London: 1925. V. 73
Malice Aforethought. London: 1931. V. 73
Mr. Pidgeon's Island. New York: 1934. V. 73
Murder in the Basement. 1932. V. 73
The Mystery at Lover's Cave. 1927. V. 73
The Mystery of Lover's Cave. New York: 1927. V. 70
Not to be Taken. London: 1938. V. 73
The Piccadilly Murder. New York: 1930. V. 70
The Poisoned Chocolates Case. New York: 1929. V. 73
Roger Sheringham and the Vane Mystery. London: 1928. V. 69
The Roger Sherringham Stories. London: 1994. V. 73
The Silk Stockings Murder. New York: 1928. V. 73
Top Story Murder. New York: 1931. V. 73
Trial and Error. London: 1937. V. 73
Trial and Error. New York: 1937. V. 73

BERKELEY, E.
The Correspndence of John Bartram 1734-1777. Gainesville: 1992. V. 73

BERKELEY, EDMUND CALLIS
Circuit Algebra - Introduction. New York: 1952. V. 71

BERKELEY, GEORGE, BP. OF CLOYNE
Philosophical Reflexions and Inquiries Concerning the Virtues of Tar Water. London: 1744. V. 69
Recherches sur les Vertus de l'Eau de Goudron.... Amsterdam: 1745. V. 73

BERKELEY, M.
A Naval Alphabet. London: 1922. V. 73

BERKELEY, M. F. F.
A Letter Addressed to Sir John Barrow, Bart, on the System of War and Peace. London: 1839. V. 68; 72

BERKELEY, M. J.
Handbook of British Mosses. 1863. V. 73
Outlines of British Fungology. London: 1860. V. 69; 70

BERKENHOUT, J.
Synopsis of the Natural History of Great Britain and Ireland. 1789. V. 72; 73

BERKENHOUT, JOHN
Clavis Anglica Linguae Botanicae, or, a Botanical Lexicon. London: 1764. V. 69
A Volume of Letters from Dr. Berkenhout to His Son at the University. Cambridge: 1790. V. 69

BERKEY, C. P.
Geology of Mongolia, a Reconnaissance Report Based on the Investigations of the Years 1922-1923. New York: 1927. V. 70; 72

BERKLEY, HENRY J.
A Treatise on Mental Diseases. New York: 1900. V. 70; 71

BERKMAN, ALEXANDER
Prison Memoirs of an Anarchist. New York: 1912. V. 68

BERLANT, ANTHONY
Walk in Beauty, the Navajo and Their Blankets. Boston: 1977. V. 69; 70

BERLIN, SVEN
Alfred Wallis: Primitive. London: 1949. V. 72
I Am Lazarus. London: 1961. V. 72

BERMAN, ALEX
Pharmeceutical Historiography. Madison: 1967. V. 72

BERMAN, JEREMIAH J.
Shehitah. New York: 1941. V. 69

BERMEN, ROBERT
The House on the Cove. London: 1987. V. 68

BERNA, PAUL
A Hundred Million Francs. London: 1957. V. 71

BERNAL, IGNACIO
100 Great Masterpieces of the Mexican National Museum of Anthropology. New York: 1969. V. 72

BERNAL, RALPH
Catalogue of the Very Choice, Valuable and Beautiful Library Formed by the Late Ralph Bernal, Esq.... London: 1855. V. 70

BERNANOS, GEORGE
The Diary of a Country Priest. New York: 1986. V. 69

BERNARD, APRIL
Prayers and Sermons for the Stations of the Cross. New York: 1983. V. 73

BERNARD, CLAUDE
Lecons de Physiologie Experimentale Appliquee a La Medecine Faites College France. Paris: 1855-1856. V. 71; 72
Lecons de Physiologie Operatoire. Paris: 1879. V. 72
Lecons sur la Chaleur Animale sur les Effets de la Chaleur et sur la Fievre. Paris: 1876. V. 68; 71
Lecons sur la Physiologie et la Pathologie du Systeme Nerveux.... Paris: 1858. V. 68; 72
Lecons sur Les Proprietes des Tissus Vivants. Paris: 1866. V. 71
Nouvelle Fonction de Foie Considere Comme Organe Producteur de Matiere Sucree Chez l'Homme et les Animaux. Paris: 1853. V. 71

BERNARD, DAVID
Light on Masonry.... Utica: 1829. V. 68

BERNARD, FERNAND
A Travers Sumatra. Paris: 1904. V. 68

BERNARD, GEORGE S.
The Battle of the Crater in Front of Petersburg, July 30, 1864. Petersburg: 1890. V. 69; 70
War Talks of Confederate Veterans. Petersburg: 1892. V. 69; 70

BERNARD, JOHN
Retrospections of the Stage. London: 1830. V. 69

BERNARD, KENNETH
Nullity. Mount Horeb: 2000. V. 71

BERNARD, RICHARD
A Short View of the Prelaticall Church of England. London: 1641. V. 70

BERNARD, ROBERT
Bodies. London: 1986. V. 72

BERNARDI, MARZIANO
Antonello in Sicilia. Torino: 1957. V. 70

BERNARDIS, CALOGERO DE
Insurrection In Sicily, 1820. London: 1820. V. 72

BERNARDO, JOSE RAVL
The Secret of the Bulls. New York: 1996. V. 71

BERNARD OF GORDON
Bern. Gordonii Opvs Lilvm, Medicinae Inscriptum de Morborum Prope Omnium Curatione, Septem Particulis Distributum. Lvgduni: 1559. V. 70

BERNARD OF MORLAIX
The Rhythm of Bernard de Morlaix, Monk of Cluny, on the Celestial Country. London: 1866. V. 68; 72

BERNATZIK, H. A.
South Seas. New York: 1935. V. 69

BERNAYS, ALBERT J.
Manuals of Health. Food. London: 1876. V. 68

BERNAYS, ANNE
Professor Romeo. New York: 1989. V. 68; 71

BERNDT, R. M.
Australian Aboriginal Art. London and Sydney: 1964. V. 69

BERNE, SUZANNE
A Crime in the Neighbourhood. Chapel Hill: 1997. V. 68

BERNEDE, A.
The Mystery of The Louvre. London: 1929. V. 73

BERNEN, ROBERT
The House on the Cove. 1987. V. 71

BERNERS, GERARD HUGH TYRWHITT
The Camel, a Tale. London: 1936. V. 69
Count Omega. London: 1941. V. 69; 70
A Distant Prospect: a Sequel to First Childhood. London: 1945. V. 69
Far From the Madding War. London: 1941. V. 69; 71
The Romance of a Nose. London: 1941. V. 69; 70

BERNERS, JULIANA
An American Edition of the Treatyse of Fysshynge wyth an Angle.... New York: 1875. V. 73
A Treatyse of Fyshing wyth an Angle. 1880. V. 68; 73
A Treatyse of Fysshinge with an Angle. London: 1903. V. 68
A Treatyse of Fysshynge Wyth an Angle. 1903. V. 71

BERNERS, LORD
A Distant Prospect - A Sequel to First Childhood. London: 1945. V. 72

BERNHARD, RUTH
The Eternal Body: a Collection of 50 Nudes. Carmel: 1986. V. 68

BERNHARDT, C.
Indian Raids In Lincoln County, Kansas, 1864 and 1869. Lincoln: 1910. V. 72

BERNHEIMER, CHARLES L.
Rainbow Bridge: Circling Navajo Mountain and Explorations in the Bad Lands of Southern Utah and Northern Arizona. Garden City: 1929. V. 69

BERNI, FRANCESCO
Il Secondo Libro Dell'Opeere Burlesche.... Londra: 1723. V. 68

BERNIER, G.
The Best in 20th Century Architecture. New York: 1964. V. 69

BERNIER, R. L.
Art in California. San Francisco: 1916. V. 69

BERNOULLI, JAKOB
Ars Conjectandi Opus Post-Human. Basel: 1713. V. 68; 70; 73

BERNUTZ, GUSTAVE
Clinical Memoirs on the Diseases of Women. London: 1866-1867. V. 72
Clinique Medicale sur les Maladies des Femmes. Paris: 1860-1862. V. 71

BERQUIN, ARNAUD
The Blossoms of Morality, Intended for the Amusement and Instruction of Young Ladies and Gentlemen. London: 1801. V. 70
The Children's Friend. London: 1793. V. 70
Idylles par M. Berquin. Paris: 1775. V. 69
The Looking Glass for the Mind; or Intellectual Mirror.... London: 1809. V. 70

BERQUIN, JACQUES
Architectura of Wiskunstige Verhandeling om de Voornaamste Eigenschappen der Burgerlyke Bouwkonst.... Amsterdam: 1789-1790. V. 68; 70; 72

BERQUIST, LILLIAN
Your Shot, Darling. New York: 1948. V. 68

BERRA, YOGI
Yogi. It Ain't Over. New York: 1989. V. 68

BERRIAULT, GINA
The Descent. New York: 1960. V. 69
The Lights of Earth. San Francisco: 1984. V. 71; 72

BERRIDGE, ELIZABETH
House of Defence. London: 1945. V. 72

BERRIMAN, ALGERNON
Aviation, An Introduction to the Elements of Flight. 1913. V. 72

BERRIMAN, WILLIAM
An Historical Account of the Controversies that Have been in the Church, Concerning the Doctrine of the Holy and Everblessed Trinity: In Eight Sermons.... London: 1725. V. 73

BERRY, DON
A Majority of Scoundrels - an Informal History of the Rocky Mountain Fur Company. New York: 1961. V. 68; 73

BERRY, E. W.
Revision of the Lower Eocene Wilcoxe Flora of the Southeastern States.... Washington: 1930. V. 72

BERRY, GEOFFREY
Across Northern Hills. Kendal: 1975. V. 71; 73

BERRY, LEONIDES H.
I Wouldn't Take Nothin' For My Journey: Two Centuries of an Afro-American Minister's Family. Chicago: 1981. V. 72

BERRY, MARY
A Comparative View of Social Life in England and France from the Restoration of Charles the Second to the Present Time. London: 1844. V. 71

BERRY, N. H.
Selections. Meridian: 1911. V. 70

BERRY, R. J.
The Natural History of Shetland. London: 1986. V. 71

BERRY, ROTHA MC CLAIN
Swift Deer: the Navajo. San Antonio: 1953. V. 69; 71

BERRY, WENDELL
The Broken Ground. New York: 1964. V. 71; 73
Clearing. New York: 1977. V. 69
The Country of Marriage. New York: 1973. V. 71
The Discovery of Kentucky. Frankfurt: 1991. V. 69
Farming: a Hand Book. New York: 1970. V. 71
Fidelity. New York/San Francisco: 1992. V. 72
The Gift of Good Land. San Francisco: 1981. V. 68; 70
The Hidden Wound. Boston: 1970. V. 71; 72
Home Economics. Berkeley: 1987. V. 69
The Kentucky River: Two Poems. Monterey: 1976. V. 71; 72
Life is a Miracle: an Essay Against Modern Superstition. Washington: 2000. V. 72; 73
The Long-Legged House. New York: 1969. V. 68
The Memory of Old Jack. New York: 1974. V. 71
Nathan Coulter. Boston: 1960. V. 71; 72
Remembering. San Francisco: 1988. V. 70
Sabbaths 1987. Monterey: 1991. V. 70
Sayings and Doings. Lexington: 1975. V. 68; 70
The Unforeseen Wilderness. Lexington: 1971. V. 69; 71; 72
The Unsettling of America: Culture and Agriculture. San Francisco: 1977. V. 68
What Are People For?. Berkeley: 1990. V. 71; 72
The Wild Birds. San Francisco: 1986. V. 69
A World Lost. Washington D.C: 1996. V. 72

BERRY, WILLIAM
County Genealogies. Pedigrees of the Families in the County of Hants. London: 1833. V. 70
Encyclopedia Heraldica, or Complete Dictionary of Heraldry. London: 1828-1830?. V. 70

BERRYMAN, JOHN
Berryman's Sonnets. New York: 1967. V. 68
The Dispossessed. New York: 1948. V. 72
The Dream Songs. New York: 1969. V. 68; 70; 71; 72
Henry's Fate and Other Poems. New York: 1976. V. 68
His Toy, His Dream, His Rest: 308 Dream Songs. New York: 1968. V. 68
Homage to Mistress Bradstreet. New York: 1956. V. 69; 71; 73
Homage to Mistress Bradstreet. London: 1959. V. 68
Homage to Mistress Bradstreet. New York: 1967. V. 72
Love and Fame. New York: 1970. V. 71
Poems. Norfolk: 1942. V. 72; 73
Recovery. New York: 1973. V. 68
77 Dream Songs. New York: 1964. V. 68; 72
Stephen Crane. New York: 1950. V. 72
Two Poems. New York: 1970. V. 69

BERSE Drelincourt Charity School. Wrexham: 1813. V. 72

BERSENBRUGGE, MEI-MEI
Hiddenness. Poem. Richard Tuttle. Illuminations. New York: 1987. V. 69

BERSON, MORTON I.
Atlas of Plastic Surgery. New York: 1948. V. 70; 71

BERTATI, GIOVANNI
Alcina, a New Comic Opera. Dublin: 1781. V. 69

BERTI, DOMENICO
Il Processo Originale di Galileo Galilei Pubblicato per la Prima Volta. Roma: 1876. V. 72

BERTOLONI, ANTONIO
Amoenitates Italicae. (and) Excerpta de re Herbaria. Bononiae: 1819-1820. V. 68

BERTON, FRANCIS
A Voyage on the Colorado. Los Angeles: 1953. V. 68; 73

BERTOTTI SCAMOZZI, OTTAVIO
Il Forestiere Istrutto Della Cose Piu Rare Di...Vicenza, Dialogo. Vicenza: 1761. V. 70; 71; 72; 73

BERTRAM, CHARLES
Isn't It Wonderful?. 1896. V. 70

BERTRAM, JAMES G.
The Harvest of the Sea. London: 1869. V. 68
The Harvest of the Sea Including Sketches of Fisheries and Fisher Folk. London: 1873. V. 68

BERTRAM, JAMES GLASS
The Merry Order of St. Bridget.... York: 1857. V. 69; 73

BERTRAND, LOUIS A.
Memoires d'un Mormon. Paris: 1862. V. 70; 73

BERWICK & KELSO RAILWAY
Calculations of the Probable Benefit to the Neighbouring Country, and to the Proprietors of an Iron Rail Way From Berwick to Kelso.... Kelso: 1809. V. 69

BESANT, ANNIE
The Law of Population. London: 1877?. V. 71
The Law of Population. Bound Brook: 1886. V. 69

BESANT, ANNIE continued
Occult Chemistry: Clairvoyant Observations on the Chemical Elements. London: 1919. V. 71

BESANT, WALTER
All Sorts and Conditions of Men: an Impossible Story. London: 1886. V. 68
Armorel of Lyonesse; a Romance of To-Day. London: 1907. V. 68
Beyond the Dreams of Avarice. London: 1895. V. 70
The Captain's Room, etc. London: 1891. V. 68
Children of Gibeon. London: 1888. V. 68
Dorothy Forster: a Novel. London: 1906. V. 68
For Faith and Freedom. London: 1891. V. 68
Herr Paulus. His Rise, His Greatness and His Fall. London: 1888. V. 68
In Deacon's Orders etc. London: 1898. V. 68
The Rise of the Empire. London: 1897. V. 71
St. Katherine's by the Tower. London: 1891. V. 72
St. Katherine's by the Tower. London: 1893. V. 68
The Seamy Side: a Story. London: 1899. V. 68
'Twas in Trafalgar's Bay and Other Stories. London: 1887. V. 68
With Harp and Crown. London: 1884. V. 68
The World Went Very Well Then. London: 1889. V. 68

BESKOW, ELSA
Sol-Agget. (Sun Egg). Stockhom: 1932. V. 71

BESLER, B.
The Garden at Eichstatt, the Book of Plants. Kohn: 2000. V. 73

BESSE, JOSEPH
Life And Posthumous Work of Joseph Claridge. London: 1726. V. 72

BESSEL, FRIEDRICH WILHELM
Fundamenta Asatronomiae Pro Anno MDCCLV Deducta ex Observationibus Virgi Incomparabilis James Bradley in specula Astronomica.. Regiomonoti;: 1818. V. 72

BESSON, JACQUES
Theatre des Instrvmens Mathematiqves et Mechaniqves. Geneve: 1596. V. 69

BESSON, MAURICE
The Scourge of The Indies. London: 1929. V. 72

THE BEST American Essays. New York: 1989. V. 72

THE BEST American Essays 1988. New York: 1988. V. 72

THE BEST American Mystery Stories 2000. Boston/New York: 2000. V. 72

THE BEST American Short Stories. 1971. London: 1971. V. 68

THE BEST American Short Stories. 1974. Boston: 1974. V. 68

THE BEST American Short Stories. 1980. Boston: 1980. V. 71; 72

THE BEST American Short Stories 1984. Boston: 1984. V. 72

THE BEST American Short Stories 1988. Boston: 1988. V. 68; 72

THE BEST American Short Stories 1989. Boston: 1989. V. 72

THE BEST American Short Stories 1990. Boston: 1990. V. 72

THE BEST American Short Stories 1992. Boston: 1992. V. 72

THE BEST American Short Stories 1995. Boston: 1995. V. 72

THE BEST American Short Stories. 2000. Boston/New York: 2000. V. 69

BEST, HERBERT
The Twenty-Fifth Hour. New York: 1940. V. 70

BEST, J. W.
Forest Life in India. 1935. V. 69
Tiger Days. 1931. V. 72

THE BEST Of The Pips with introduction by Richard Warner Clarke. New York: 1955. V. 72

BEST, R. I.
The Oldest Fragment of the Senchas Mar from Ms. H2.15 in the Library. 1931. V. 71

BEST, THOMAS
A Concise Treatise of Angling, Confirmed by Actual Experience and Minute Observations.... London: 1794. V. 69

BESTER, ALFRED
Tiger! Tiger!. London: 1956. V. 70

BETENSON, LULA PARKER
Butch Cassidy, My Brother. Provo: 1975. V. 70

BETHAM, MATILDA
A Biographical Dictionary of Celebrated Women of Every Age and Country. London: 1804. V. 68; 69

BETHEA, JACK
Cotton. Boston: 1928. V. 71

BETHUNE, GEORGE W.
The British Female Poets: with Biographical and Critical Notices. Philadelphia: 1848. V. 73

BETHUNE, MARY DRINKWATER
The River Mole, or Emlyn Stream. 1839. V. 69; 70

BETHUNE, THOMAS GREENE
The Marvelous Musical Prodigy, Blind Tom, the Negro Boy Pianist... Baltimore: 1876. V. 69
The Marvelous Musical Prodigy, Blind Tom, the Negro Boy Pianist.... Baltimore: 1866. V. 69
The Marvelous Musical Prodigy, Blind Tom, the Negro Boy Pianist.... New York: 1876. V. 71

BETJEMAN, JOHN
Archie and the Strict Baptists. London: 1977. V. 68; 71
Betjeman in Miniature: Selected Poems of Sir John Betjeman. 1976. V. 71
Church Poems. London: 1980. V. 71
Church Poems. London: 1981. V. 71
Collected Poems. London: 1958. V. 71
Collected Poems. Boston: 1971. V. 71
Collins Guide to English Parish Churches Including the Isle of Man. London: 1958. V. 71
Continual Dew; a Little Book of Bourgeois Verse. London: 1937. V. 69
English, Scottish and Welsh Landscape - 1700 - c. 1860. London: 1944. V. 72
A Few Late Chrysanthemums. London: 1954. V. 71
First and Last Loves. London: 1969. V. 73
Ghastly Good Taste; or, A Depressing Story of the Rise and Fall of English Architecture. London: 1933. V. 69; 71
Ghastly Good Taste; or, a Depressing Story of the Rise and Fall of English Architecture. London: 1970. V. 71
High and Low. London: 1966. V. 71
John Betjeman's Collected Poems. London: 1970. V. 72
John Betjeman's Collected Poems. London: 1974. V. 73
Letters. Volume One: 1926 to 1951: Volume Two: 1951 to 1984. London: 1994-1995. V. 71
Murray's Berkshire Architectural Guide. London: 1949. V. 71
Murray's Buckinghamshire Architectural Guide. London: 1948. V. 71
New Bats in Old Belfries. London: 1945. V. 69; 71
A Nip in the Air. 1974. V. 69
A Nip in the Air. London: 1974. V. 70; 71
Old Lights for New Chancels: Verses Topographical and Amatory. London: 1940. V. 71
An Oxford University Chest. London: 1938. V. 70
A Pictorial History of English Architecture. London: 1972. V. 71
Poems in the Porch. London: 1957. V. 69; 71
A Ring of Bells: Poems of John Betjeman. London: 1962. V. 71
Selected Poems. London: 1948. V. 71
Shropshire: a Shell Guide. 1951. V. 71
Summoned by Bells. London: 1960. V. 69; 71
Summoned by Bells. London: 1976. V. 71
Uncollected Poems. London: 1982. V. 71
Victorian and Edwardian Oxford From Photographs. London: 1971. V. 68
Vintage London. London: 1942. V. 71

BETTANY, G. T.
Eminent Doctors, Their Lives and Their Work. 1885. V. 71
Life of Charles Darwin. London: 1887. V. 69

BETTELHEIM, BRUNO
The Children of the Dream. New York: 1969. V. 71
The Empty Fortress. Infant, Autism and The Birth of the Self. New York: 1967. V. 73

BETTERTON, THOMAS
The Life and Times of that Excellent and Renowned Actor Thomas Betterton, of the Duke's and United Companies, at the Theatres in Portugal Street, Dorset Gardens, Drury Lane &c. During the Latter Half of the Seventeenth century. London: 1888. V. 72

BETTMANN, OTTO L.
A Pictorial History of Medicine. Springfield. V. 68; 70; 71

BETTRIDGE, WILLIAM
A Brief History of the Church in Upper Canada.... 1838. V. 71

BETTS, A. D.
Experiences of a Confederate Chaplain. Greenville: 190-?. V. 69; 70

BETTS, DORIS
Heading West. New York: 1981. V. 68
The Scarlet Thread. New York: 1964. V. 68

BETTY Crocker's Picture Cook Book. New York: 1950. V. 73

BETZINEZ, JASON
I Fought with Geronimo. Harrisburg: 1959. V. 69; 72

BEUNAT, JOSEPH
Recueil des Dessins D'Ornements D'Architecture de la Manufacture de Joseph Beunat.... Sarrebourg and Paris: 1813. V. 70

BEUQUE, ETIENNETTE
Rebeles au Martyrs?. 1928. V. 69

BEURDELEY, MICHEL
Chinese Furniture. Tokyo: 1979. V. 73

BEVAN, JOSEPH GURNEY
Extracts From The Letters And Other Writings Of The Late Joseph Gurney Bevan. London: 1821. V. 72
Memoirs of the Life and Travels in the Service of the Gospel, or Sarah Stephenson. London: 1807. V. 72

BEVANS, J.
The Sedgefield Country in the 70's and 80's. 1904. V. 68

BEVERIDGE, ALBERT J.
Abraham Lincoln 1809-1858. Boston: 1928. V. 68

BEVERIDGE, ALBERT J. continued
The Life of John Marshall. Boston and New York: 1916. V. 68

BEVERIDGE, THOMAS J.
English Renaissance Woodwork 1660-1730. London: 1921. V. 68

BEVERIDGE, WILLIAM
Social Insurance and Allied Services. (with) *Social Insurance and Allied Services, Memoranda from Organisations.* London: 1942. V. 69

BEVERLEY, ROBERT
Histoire de la Virginie: Contentant.... Paris: 1707. V. 70
The History and Present State of Virginia in Four Parts.... London: 1705. V. 68
The History of Virginia, in Four Parts.... London: 1722. V. 73

BEVIER, ROBERT S.
History of the First and Second Missouri Confederate Brigades 1861- 1865. St. Louis: 1879. V. 69; 70

BEWICK, ELIZABETH
Comfort Me with Apples and Other Poems. 1987. V. 71

BEWICK, JOSEPH
Geological Treatise on The District of Cleveland. 1861. V. 73

BEWICK, THOMAS
Bewick Memento. London: 1894. V. 68
Figures of British Land Birds Engraved on Wood.... Newcastle-upon-Tyne: 1800. V. 69
A General History of Quadrupeds. Newcastle-upon-Tyne: 1791. V. 71
A General History of Quadrupeds. Newcastle-upon-Tyne: 1792. V. 68
A General History of Quadrupeds. Newcastle-upon-Tyne: 1807. V. 68; 69; 70
A General History of Quadrupeds. 1811. V. 69; 70; 72; 73
A General History of Quadrupeds. Newcastle upon Tyne: 1811. V. 69; 71
A General History of Quadrupeds. 1820. V. 72
A General History of Quadrupeds. Newcastle-upon-Tyne: 1820. V. 69
A General History of Quadrupeds. London: 1824. V. 69
History of British Birds. Newcastle: 1797. V. 73
History of British Birds. Newcastle: 1797-1804. V. 70
A History of British Birds. Newcastle-upon-tyne: 1816. V. 69
History of British Birds. Newcastle-upon-Tyne: 1832. V. 69; 71
A History of British Birds. Newcastle: 1847. V. 69
History of British Birds. (with) *a General History of Quadrupeds.* Newcastle-upon-Tyne: 1797. V. 72
A Memoir of Thomas Bewick. Newcastle-upon-Tyne: 1862. V. 68
Memoir of Thomas Bewick Written by Himself 1822-1828. 1924. V. 73
Memoir of Thomas Bewick Written by Himself 1822-1828. London: 1924. V. 69
Select Fables.... Newcastle-upon-Tyne: 1820. V. 69; 70
A Selection of Stories; Containing the History of the Two Sisters, The Fisherman, The King and Fairy Ring, and Honesty Rewarded. Glasgow: 1814. V. 71
Ten Working Drawing Reproductions Shown with Impressions of the Corresponding Drawings. Chicago: 1972. V. 68; 71
The Watercolours and Drawings of Thomas Bewick and His Workshop Apprentices. Cambridge: 1981. V. 73
The Watercolours and Drawings of Thomas Bewick and His Workshop Apprentices. 1989. V. 69
The Watercolours and Drawings of Thomas Bewick and His Workshop Apprentices, introduced and with editorial notes by Iain Bain. 1981. V. 72

BEY, PILAFF
Venus in the Kitchen; or Love's Cookery Book. London: 1952. V. 70

BEYENS, HUBERT
Germany Before the War. London: 1916. V. 68

BEYER, ADOLPH
Otia Metallica Oder Bergmannische Neben Stunden Darinnen Verschiedene Abhandlungen von Berg-Sachen aus Denen Geschichhten.... Schneeberg: 1748-. V. 68

BEYER, W. F.
Deeds of Valor. Detroit: 1906. V. 71
Deeds of Valor. Detroit: 1907. V. 69

BEZE, THEODORE DE
A Discourse...Containing the Life and Death Of M. John Calvin.... Middleburg: 1587?. V. 73
Tractatio de Repvdiis et Divortiis: in Qva Pieraeqve De Causis Matrimonialibus.... Genevae: 1569. V. 68; 69; 73

BEZZERIDES, A. I.
Long Haul. London: 1938. V. 73
Thieves' Market. New York: 1949. V. 70

BHATTI, H. K.
The Integument and Ermal Skeleton of Siluroidea. London: 1938. V. 72

BIAGI, GUIDO
The Book in Italy During the Fifteenth and Sixteenth Centuries.... New York: 1928. V. 69

BIANCHI BANDINELLI, RANUCCIO
Hellenistic-Byzantine Miniatures of the Iliad. Olten: 1955. V. 68

BIANCO, MARGERY WILLIAMS
Poor Cecco. London: 1925. V. 73
Poor Cecco. New York: 1925. V. 70; 71

BIANCONI, CARLO
Esemplare di Alcuni Ornati per la Gioventus Amante del Disegno.... Bologna: 1770. V. 70; 72

BIANCONI, GIOVANNI LODOVICO
Descrizione dei Circhi Particolarmente di Quello di Caracalla.... Rome: 1789. V. 68

BIBBY, CYRIL
T. H. Huxley. Scientist, Humanist and Educator. London: 1959. V. 68

THE BIBELOT. New York: 1925. V. 71

BIBIENA, BERNARDO DOVIZI DA
Calandra. Fiorenza: 1559. V. 73

BIBIENA, JEAN GALLI
Le Poupee. Londres: 1782. V. 73

BIBLE. ARABIC - 1616
The New Testament. Leidae: 1616. V. 69; 73

BIBLE. DANISH - 1633
Bible in Danish. Copenhagen: 1633-1632. V. 69

BIBLE. DUTCH - 1557
Ghesneden Figvern Vvyten Ouden (Nieuvven) Testamente Naer Tleune met Huerlier Bedietsele. Lyons: 1557. V. 70

BIBLE. DUTCH - 1648
Biestkens Bible. Amsterdam: 1648. V. 69; 73

BIBLE. DUTCH - 1657
(Roman Catholic Bible in Dutch). l'Antwerpen: 1657-1646. V. 69

BIBLE. DUTCH - 1682
(Bible in Dutch). Te Dordrecht: 1682. V. 69

BIBLE. DUTCH - 1702
(Biestkens Bible). Amsterdam: 1702. V. 70

BIBLE. ENGLISH
Bible Stories; with Coloured Pictures, of the Most Remarkable Events Therein Recorded. New Testament Series. London. V. 70

BIBLE. ENGLISH - 1549
(Matthew's Bible). London: 1549. V. 70

BIBLE. ENGLISH - 1551
Matthew's Bible. London: 1551,. V. 73
The Paraphrases of the New Testament. London: 1551-1552. V. 70

BIBLE. ENGLISH - 1568
(The Bishop's Bible). London: 1568. V. 70

BIBLE. ENGLISH - 1569
(The Great Bible). (with) *The Whole Booke of Psalmes, Collected into English Metre.* London: 1569. V. 70

BIBLE. ENGLISH - 1582
(The Rheims New Testament). Rheims: 1582. V. 70

BIBLE. ENGLISH - 1589
The Geneva Bible. London: 1589. V. 73
The Text of the New Testament of Iesus Christ.... London: 1589. V. 68

BIBLE. ENGLISH - 1591
The Bishop's Bible. London: 1591. V. 73

BIBLE. ENGLISH - 1595
The Bible, that is the Holy Scriptures.... Imprinted at London: 1595. V. 70

BIBLE. ENGLISH - 1609
(The Douai-Rheims Bible). Doway: 1609-1610. V. 70

BIBLE. ENGLISH - 1611
The Holy Bible (and Apocrypha) Reprinted According to the Authorised Version 1611. London: 1924-1927. V. 68
The Holy Bible Reprinted According to the Authorised Version 1611. (with) *The Apocrypha.* London: 1925-1927. V. 68

BIBLE. ENGLISH - 1613
The King James Bible. London: 1613. V. 70; 73

BIBLE. ENGLISH - 1615
The Bible. London: 1615. V. 68

BIBLE. ENGLISH - 1616
The King James Bible. London: 1616. V. 70; 73

BIBLE. ENGLISH - 1617
The Text of the New Testament of Iesus Christ.... London: 1617. V. 68

BIBLE. ENGLISH - 1629
The Holy Bible, Conteining the Old Testament and the New. (bound with) *The Whole Booke of Psalmes Collected Into English Meeter by Thomas Sternhold, Iohn Hopkins and Others.* London: 1629. V. 70

BIBLE. ENGLISH - 1632
The Holy Bible.... London: 1633. V. 72

BIBLE. ENGLISH - 1633
The Bible, That is, The Holy Scriptures Conteined in the Old and New Testament. London: 1633. V. 73
The King James Bible. bound after The Book of Common Prayer. bound before The Whole Books of Psalmes Collected into English Meeter. London: 1633,. V. 73

BIBLE. ENGLISH - 1634
The King James Bible. London: 1634. V. 73

BIBLE. ENGLISH - 1640
(The King James Bible). London: 1640. V. 70

BIBLE. ENGLISH - 1653
The Holy Bible Containing the Old and New Testaments, etc. London: 1653. V. 69

BIBLE. ENGLISH - 1679
The Holy Bible Containing the Old Testament and the New Testament.... 1679. V. 68

BIBLE. ENGLISH - 1683
(The King James Bible with Geneva Notes). (with) The Psalms of David in Meeter. Amsterdam: 1683. V. 70

BIBLE. ENGLISH - 1699
(The King James Bible). Oxford: 1699. V. 70

BIBLE. ENGLISH - 1700
The Pslames of David. 1700. V. 69

BIBLE. ENGLISH - 1750
The Holy Bible. Oxford: 1750-1751. V. 72; 73

BIBLE. ENGLISH - 1765
The Whole Book of Psalms, Collected Into English Metre.... Cambridge: 1765. V. 69

BIBLE. ENGLISH - 1769
(Blayney's Standard Bible). Oxford: 1769. V. 70

BIBLE. ENGLISH - 1780
The Bible in Miniuture (sic) or a Concise History of the Old and New Testaments. London: 1780. V. 71

BIBLE. ENGLISH - 1792
A New Version of the Psalms of David.... London: 1792. V. 69
The Self-Interpreting Bible: Containing the Sacred Text of the Old and New Testaments. New York: 1792. V. 68

BIBLE. ENGLISH - 1796
The Holy Bible Translated from the Latin Vulgate. Edinburgh: 1796. V. 69

BIBLE. ENGLISH - 1797
The Bible in Miniature: or a Concise History of the Old and New Testaments. Gainsborough: 1797. V. 68

BIBLE. ENGLISH - 1798
The Holy Bible. Philadelphia: 1798. V. 68; 70

BIBLE. ENGLISH - 1800
(The Holy Bible) Embellished with Engravings from Pictures and Designs by the Most Eminent English Artists. London: 1800. V. 70

BIBLE. ENGLISH - 1811
The Holy Bible. New York: 1811. V. 68

BIBLE. ENGLISH - 1813
The Holy Bible Containing the Old and New Testaments.... London: 1813. V. 68

BIBLE. ENGLISH - 1821
A Miniature History of the Holy Bible, Embellished with nearly 50 Engravings. Hartford: 1821. V. 68

BIBLE. ENGLISH - 1822
The Columbian Family and Pulpit Bible. Boston: 1822. V. 71

BIBLE. ENGLISH - 1823
The Holy Bible, According to the Authorized Version. Prepared and Arranged by the Rev. George D'Oyly. Cambridge: 1823. V. 72

BIBLE. ENGLISH - 1830
The Holy Bible According to the Authorized Bible Version with Explanatory Notes. London: 1830. V. 72

BIBLE. ENGLISH - 1837
The English Version of the Polyglot Bible. Baltimore: 1837. V. 69

BIBLE. ENGLISH - 1845
The Child's Bible. Philadelphia, New York: 1845. V. 68
The Sermon on the Mount. London: 1845. V. 68

BIBLE. ENGLISH - 1846
The Illuminated Bible, Containing the Old and New Testaments.... New York: 1846. V. 68; 69; 71; 73

BIBLE. ENGLISH - 1848
The Holy Bible. London: 1848. V. 72

BIBLE. ENGLISH - 1849
The Song of Songs. London: 1849. V. 68

BIBLE. ENGLISH - 1850
The New Testament of Our Lord and Saviour Jesus Christ. New York: 1850. V. 73

BIBLE. ENGLISH - 1861
The Psalms of David. London: 1861. V. 70; 72

BIBLE. ENGLISH - 1865
The New Testament of Our Lord and Saviour Jesus Christ. London: 1865. V. 73

BIBLE. ENGLISH - 1884
The Coloured Picture Bible for Children in Four Sections. London: 1884. V. 70

BIBLE. ENGLISH - 1896
The Book of Ruth and The Book of Esther. 1896. V. 68

BIBLE. ENGLISH - 1897
The Song of Solomon. London: 1897. V. 71

BIBLE. ENGLISH - 1901
The Revelation of Saint John the Divine. 1901. V. 70
Revelation of St. John the Divine. Detroit: 1901. V. 69

BIBLE. ENGLISH - 1909
The Song of Songs, Which is Solomon's. London: 1909. V. 68; 72

BIBLE. ENGLISH - 1911
The Sermon on the Mount. London: 1911. V. 72

BIBLE. ENGLISH - 1914
The Book of Genesis, now printed in the Authorised Version and illustrated after drawings by F. Cayley Robinson. London: 1914. V. 71

BIBLE. ENGLISH - 1923
The Book of Ruth Translated Out of the Original Tongues: and with the Former Translations Diligently Compared and Revised by His Majesy's Special Command. London: 1923. V. 70; 72

BIBLE. ENGLISH - 1924
The Holy Bible, reprinted according to the Authorised Version 1611. Together with The Apocrypha. London: 1924-1925. V. 71
The Holy Bible (and Apocrypha). London: 1924-1927. V. 71

BIBLE. ENGLISH - 1925
The Holy Bible Reprinted According tot he Authorised Version 1611. (with) Apocrypha. 1925-1927. V. 72
Samson and Delilah, from the Book of Judges According to the Authorised Version. Waltham St. Lawrence: 1925. V. 68; 70; 71
The Song of Songs Called by Many the Canticle of Canticles. Waltham St. Lawrence: 1925. V. 68; 71

BIBLE. ENGLISH - 1927
The Book of Ruth. 1927. V. 72

BIBLE. ENGLISH - 1931
The Revelation of Saint John the Divine. London: 1931. V. 71

BIBLE. ENGLISH - 1932
Ecclesiasticus. The Wisdom of Jesus, The Son of Sirach, Commonly Called Ecclesiasticus. 1932. V. 73
The Revelation of Saint John the Divine. Newtown: 1932. V. 68; 72

BIBLE. ENGLISH - 1933
The Lamentations of Jeremiah. Montgomeryshire: 1933. V. 72

BIBLE. ENGLISH - 1934
The Book of Ruth. 1934. V. 70

BIBLE. ENGLISH - 1935
Samson and Delilah. From the Book of Judges. Waltham St. Lawrence: 1935. V. 68
The Song of Songs Which is Solomon's. New York: 1935. V. 69; 71

BIBLE. ENGLISH - 1937
The Song of Solomon According to the Authorized Version. Cambridge: 1937. V. 71

BIBLE. ENGLISH - 1941
Ecclesiastes reprinted from the Authorised Version. Cambridge: 1941. V. 70

BIBLE. ENGLISH - 1946
The Book of Job. New York: 1946. V. 69; 73

BIBLE. ENGLISH - 1947
The Book of Ruth. New York: 1947. V. 69

BIBLE. ENGLISH - 1949
Bible. Cleveland and New York: 1949. V. 71

BIBLE. ENGLISH - 1955
The Newe Testamente. 1955. V. 68

BIBLE. ENGLISH - 1958
The New Testament of Our Lord and Saviour Jesus Christ. London and New York: 1958. V. 69; 73
The New Testament of Our Lord and Saviour Jeus Christ. Verona: 1958. V. 69

BIBLE. ENGLISH - 1962
The Holy Gospel According to Matthew, Mark, Luke and John. Verona: 1962. V. 73

BIBLE. ENGLISH - 1963
The Holy Bible: the Authorized or King James Version of 1611 Now Reprinted with the Apocrypha. London: 1963. V. 72

BIBLE. ENGLISH - 1965
Ecclesiastes or the Preacher, in the King James Translation of the Bible. New York: 1965. V. 68

BIBLE. ENGLISH - 1967
Ecclesiastes, or, the Preacher. Paris: 1967. V. 68

BIBLE. ENGLISH - 1975
Bible in English. Kent: 1975. V. 71

BIBLE. ENGLISH - 1979
The Book of the Prophet Isaiah in the King James Version. New York: 1979. V. 70
The Book of Jonah. Taken from the Authorised Version of King James I. London: 1979. V. 70

BIBLE. ENGLISH - 1989
The First Book of Moses, Called Genesis. The King James Version. New York: 1989. V. 72

BIBLE. ENGLISH - 1999
The Holy Bible. New York: 1999. V. 69; 72
The Holy Bible Containing All the Books of the Old and New Testaments. North Hatfield: 1999. V. 71

BIBLE. FRENCH - 1531
(The Bible Historiale). Lyon: 1531. V. 70

BIBLE. FRENCH - 1789
La Sainte Bible. Paris: 1789-1804. V. 72

BIBLE. FRENCH - 1810
Le Nouveau Testament de Notre Seigneur Jesus Christ, en Francais sur la Vulgate. Boston: 1810. V. 69

BIBLE. FRENCH - 1931
Cantique des Cantiques de Salomon. Paris: 1931. V. 69

BIBLE. GAELIC - 1848
(Old Testament, New Testament & Psalms) in Gaelic. Edinburgh: 1848. V. 68
(Old Testament, New Testament & Psalms) in Gaelic. Glasgow: 1848. V. 68

BIBLE. GERMAN - 1507
Bible in German. Augsburg: 1507. V. 71

BIBLE. GERMAN - 1550
Bible in German. Nuremberg: 1550. V. 71

BIBLE. GERMAN - 1729
Bible in German. Basel;: 1729. V. 71

BIBLE. GERMAN - 1823
Das Neue Testament Unsers Herrn und Heilandes Jesu Christi.... Baireuth: 1823. V. 73

BIBLE. GREEK - 1545
Bible in Greek. Basileae: 1545. V. 71

BIBLE. GREEK - 1617
'E Kaine Diatheke. Novum Testamentum. Geneva: 1617. V. 70

BIBLE. GREEK - 1685
Novum Testamentum. Amsterdam: 1685. V. 70

BIBLE. GREEK - 1812
Psalterium Graecum e Codice Ms. Alexandrino. Londini: 1812. V. 71

BIBLE. GREEK - 1840
New Testament (in Greek). London: 1840. V. 73

BIBLE. HEBREW - 1815
The Hebrew Bible; from the Edition of Everardo van der Hooght. Nos. 1 and 2. New York: 1815. V. 73

BIBLE. HIEROGLYPHIC - 1794
A New Hieroglyphical Bible, for the Amusement and Instruction of Children. London: 1794. V. 72

BIBLE. HIEROGLYPHIC - 1842
New Hieroglyhic Bible. Boston: 1842-1844. V. 70

BIBLE. ITALIAN - 1641
Bible in Italian. Geneva: 1641. V. 71

BIBLE. LATIN - 1477
(Bible in Latin). Basel: 1477. V. 69

BIBLE. LATIN - 1479
(Bible in Latin). Nuremberg: 1479. V. 69

BIBLE. LATIN - 1482
(Bible in Latin). Basel: 1482. V. 69
(Bible in Latin). Venice: 1482-1483. V. 69

BIBLE. LATIN - 1483
(Bible in Latin). Venice: 1483. V. 69

BIBLE. LATIN - 1484
(Bible in Latin). Venice: 1484. V. 69

BIBLE. LATIN - 1491
(Bible in Latin). Basel: 1491. V. 69

BIBLE. LATIN - 1496
Biblia cum Concordantiis in Margine.... Brescia: 1496. V. 68

BIBLE. LATIN - 1497
(Bible in Latin). Lyon: 1497. V. 69

BIBLE. LATIN - 1498
(Bible in Latin). Basel: 1498. V. 69
(Bible in Latin). Venice: 1498. V. 69

BIBLE. LATIN - 1522
Bible in Latin. Lyon: 1522. V. 71

BIBLE. LATIN - 1527
Biblia Cum Concordantiis Veteris et Nouvi Testamenti et Sacrorum Canonum. Lugduni (Lyons): 1527. V. 71

BIBLE. LATIN - 1528
Bible in Latin. Parisiis: 1528. V. 71

BIBLE. LATIN - 1543
New Testament. Lipsiae: 1543. V. 71

BIBLE. LATIN - 1546
(Bible in Latin). Lvtetiae: 1546. V. 72

BIBLE. LATIN - 1548
Testamenti Nova. Lyons: 1548. V. 72

BIBLE. LATIN - 1554
(Bible in Latin). Basileae: 1554. V. 72

BIBLE. LATIN - 1588
(Bible in Latin). Venice: 1588. V. 72

BIBLE. LATIN - 1590
(Bible in Latin). Genevae: 1590. V. 72

BIBLE. LATIN - 1602
Testamenti Veteris Biblia Sacra, Sive Libri Canonici.... Hanau: 1602. V. 68; 72

BIBLE. LATIN - 1617
Testamenti Veteris Biblia Sacra, Sive Libri Canonici Priscae Judaeorum Ecclesiae.... Geneva: 1617. V. 72

BIBLE. LATIN - 1697
(Bible in Latin). Francofvrti: 1697. V. 72

BIBLE. LATIN - 1740
(Bible in Latin). Lovanii: 1740. V. 72

BIBLE. LATIN - 1926
Passio Domini Nostri Jesu Christi: Being the 26th and 27th Chapters of Saint Matthew's Gospel from the Latin Text. Waltham St. Lawrence: 1926. V. 68

BIBLE. LATIN - 1954
The Holkham Bible Picture Book. London: 1954. V. 71

BIBLE. LATIN - 1961
Bible in Latin. Paterson: 1961. V. 68

BIBLE. LATIN - 1968
The Gutenberg Bible. New York: 1968. V. 71

BIBLE. MICMAC - 1859
AE Buk ov Samz. (Book of Psalms). Bath: 1859. V. 73

BIBLE. MOHAWK - 1804
Nene Karighwiyoston Tsinihorighhoten Ne Saint John. The Gospel According to Saint John. London: 1804. V. 68

BIBLE. MOHAWK - 1839
Ne Kaghyadonghsera Ne Royadadokenghdy Ne Isaiah. New York: 1839. V. 68

BIBLE. PHONETIC - 1848
The New Testament of Our Lord and Saviour Jesus Christ.... Philadelphia: 1848. V. 73

BIBLE. POLYGLOT - 1565
New Testament. Geneva: 1565. V. 71

BIBLE. POLYGLOT - 1570
(title in Greek, then) Novvm Testmentvm Iesv Christi Filii Dei, Ex Versione Erasmi. Basileae: 1570. V. 71

BIBLE. POLYGLOT - 1571
(Old Testament in Hebrew and Latin, New Testament in Greek and Latin). Antverpiae: 1571-1572. V. 72

BIBLE. POLYGLOT - 1582
New Testament. Geneva: 1582. V. 71

BIBLE. POLYGLOT - 1694
Cantique des Cantiques...avec une Explication Tree Des Saints Peres & Des Auteurs Ecclesiastiques. Paris: 1694. V. 71

BIBLE. POLYGLOT - 1901
Da Njoe Testament Vo Wi Masra En Helpiman Jezus Kristus. London: 1901. V. 72

BIBLE. URDU - 1900
(Gospels and Acts). 1900. V. 73

BIBLE Pictures for Our Pets. 1877. V. 71

BIBLIA Pauperum, Conteynynge Thytie and Eyghte Wodecuttes Illustraynge the Lyfe, Parablis, and Miraclis Off Oure Blessid Lorde & Savioure Jhesus Christ.... London: 1884. V. 72

BIBLIA Pauperum: Facsimile edition of the Forty-Leaf Blockbook in the Esztergom Cathedral. 1967. V. 70; 72; 73

BIBLIA PAUPERIUM
A Smaller Biblia Pauperium, Conteynynge Thytie and Eyghte Wodecuttes Illustratynge the Lyfe, Parablis and Miraclis Off Oure Blessid Lorde & Savioure Jhesus Christ.... London: 1884. V. 73

THE BIBLIOGRAPHER. London and New York: 1882-1884. V. 69

BIBLIOGRAPHICAL Essays: a Tribute to Wilberforce Eames. Cambridge: 1924. V. 69

BIBLIOGRAPHICAL SOCIETY
Index to Selected Bibliographical Journals 1933-1970. 1982. V. 72

BIBLIOGRAPHICAL SOCIETY OF AMERICA
The Papers of the Bibliographical Society of America. Volume 62. 1968. Austin: 1968. V. 70

BIBLIOGRAPHY and Index of Geology Exclusive of North America. Washington: 1934-1958. V. 70

BIBLIOGRAPHY Of Household Books Published in Britain. Prospect: 1875-1914. V. 72

A BIBLIOGRAPHY of the Negro in Africa and America. Mansfield: 1998. V. 72

A BIBLIOGRAPHY of the Writings of Harvey Cushing Prepared On the Occasion of His Seventieth Birthday. Park Ridge: 1993. V. 68

BICK, EDGAR M.
Source Book of Orthopaedics. New York: 1968. V. 68

BICKERDYKE, J.
Angling for Coarse Fish. 1922. V. 68
The Book of the All Round Angler. 1888. V. 68; 73

BICKERDYKE, JOHN
The Curiosities of Ale and Beer.... London: 1886. V. 68

BICKERIDGE, ANTHONY
Jennings in Particular. London: 1968. V. 68

BICKERSTAFF, LAURA M.
Pioneer Artists of Taos. Denver: 1955. V. 72
Pioneer Artists of Taos. Denver: 1983. V. 68

BICKERSTETH, HENRY
Medical Hints, Designed for the Use of Clergymen and Others.... London: 1829. V. 68

BICKERTON, THOMAS H.
A Medical History of Liverpool from the Earliest Days to the Year 1920. London: 1936. V. 68

BICKHAM, GEORGE
The British Monarchy; or, a New Chorographical Description of All the Dominions Subject to the King of Great Britain. London: 1748. V. 73
The Musical Entertainer. London: 1737-1739. V. 68

BICKHAM, WARREN STONE
Operative Surgery Covering the Operative Technic Involved in the Operations of General and Special Surgery. Philadelphia: 1930. V. 71

BICKMORE, ALBERT SMITH
Travels in the East Indian Archipelago. London: 1868. V. 68; 72

BICKNELL, AMOS JACKSON
Specimen Book of One Hundred Architectural Designs.... New York: 1880. V. 73

BICKNELL, F.
Twelve Views of Bognor. Bognor: 1869. V. 70

BICKNELL, PETER
The Illustrated Wordsworth's Guide to the Lakes. London: 1984. V. 71
The Picturesque Scenery of the Lake District 1752-1855. Winchester: 1990. V. 70; 71

THE BICYCLE Boy. New York: 1896. V. 70

BIDAL, LILLIAN
The Run of the Elk - a Biography of Angie Lydia Hendrix Cleve. El Paso: 1996. V. 69

BIDART, FRANK
Golden State. New York: 1973. V. 69

BIDDLE, ELLEN M.
Reminiscences of A Soldier's Wife. Philadelphia: 1907. V. 72

BIDDLE, TYRREL E.
Hints to Beginners in Amateur Yacht Designing.... London: 1890. V. 68
A Treatise on the Construction, Rigging and Handling of Model Yachts, Ships and Steamers.... London: 1879. V. 68

BIDDLE, VIOLET PARTON
Small Gardens and How to Make The Most of Them. London: 1901. V. 68

BIDIE, GEORGE
Report on Neilgherry Loranthaceous Parasitical Plants Destructive to Exotic Forest and Fruit Trees. Madras: 1874. V. 69

BIDLAKE, W. H.
Dry Rot in Timber. London: 1889. V. 68

BIDLOO, GOVARD
Anatomia Humani Corporis, Centum & Quinque Tabulis, Per Artificiossis G. De Lairesse Ad Vivum Delineatis.... Amsterdam: 1685. V. 69

BIDPAI
Calila et Dimna, ou Fables de Bidpai, en Arabe.... Paris: 1816. V. 70; 72

BIDWELL, JOHN
A Bibliophile's Los Angeles. Essays for the International Association of Bibliophiles on the Occasion of Its XIVth Congress 30 September - 11 October 1985. Los Angeles: 1985. V. 73
Echoes of the Past. Chico: 1914. V. 70
A Journey to California with Observations about the Country, Climate and the Route to this Country. San Francisco: 1937. V. 68

BIEBUYCK, D. P.
The Arts of Central Africa, an Annotated Bibliography. Boston;: 1987. V. 69
The Power of Headdresses. Brussels: 1984. V. 69
Statuary from the Pre-Bembe Hunters: Issues in the Interpretation of Ancestral Figurines Ascribed to the Basikasingo-Bembe-Boyo. Tervuren: 1982. V. 69

BIEDL, ARTUR
The Internal Secretory Organs: Their Physiology and Pathology. New York: 1913. V. 73

BIELER, LUDWIG
Ireland, Harbinger of the Middle Ages. 1963. V. 69

BIELFELD, JACOB FRIEDRICH, BARON
The Elements of Universal Erudition.... London: 1770. V. 69

BIELSCHOWSKY, A.
Lectures on Motor Anomalies. Hanover: 1940. V. 71

BIEMOND, A.
Recent Neurological Research. Amsterdam: 1959. V. 68

BIERCE, AMBROSE
Black Beetles in Amber. San Francisco/New York: 1892. V. 70
Can Such Things Be?. 1903. V. 71
Collected Works of Ambrose Bierce. New York: 1966. V. 69
The Dance of Death. San Francisco: 1877. V. 73
Fantastic Fables. New York and London: 1899. V. 70
Ten Tales. London: 1925. V. 70

BIERMAN, JOHN
Dark Safari. The Life Behind the Legend of Henry Morton Stanley. 1990. V. 70

BIERMANN, A.
60 Fotos. Berlin: 1930. V. 68; 70

BIERSTADT, EDWARD
Sunlight Pictures, Hartford, Artotypes by E. Bierstadt, N.Y. Hartford: 1892. V. 68

BIERSTADT, EDWARD HALE
Satan Was a Man. Garden City: 1935. V. 68; 69; 73

BIESTA, LABOULAYE & CIE.
Epreuves de Caracteres Biesta, Laboulaye & Cie, successeurs de Firmin Didot, Mole, Lion, Tarbe, Crosnier, Everat, Laboulaye Freres. Paris: 1843. V. 68

THE BIG Book of Fables. New York: 1912. V. 71

BIG Business Girl by One of Them. New York: 1930. V. 69

THE BIG Game of North America. 1890. V. 72

BIGANDET, P.
The Life or Legend of Gaudama, the Budha of the Burmese.... Rangoon: 1866. V. 72

BIGELOW, H. B.
Fishes of the Western North Atlantic. New Haven: 1958. V. 69
Plankton of the Offshore Waters of the Gulf of Maine. Washington: 1926. V. 72
Studies of the Waters of the Continental Shelf Cape Cod to Chesapeake Bay. 1939. V. 68

BIGELOW, HENRY JACOB
Insensibility During Surgical Operations Produced by Inhalation. Boston: 1846. V. 72

BIGELOW, JACOB
Florula Bostoniensis. Boston: 1824. V. 69

BIGELOW, JOHN
The Campaign of Chancellorsville: a Strategic and Tactical Study. New Haven;: 1910. V. 69
On the Bloody Trail of Geronimo. Los Angeles: 1968. V. 69

BIGELOW, JOHN MASON
Death is an Early Riser. New York: 1940. V. 69; 70; 72

BIGGAR, HENRY PERCIVAL
The Percursors of Jacques Cartier 1497-1534. Ottawa: 1911. V. 73
The Voyages of Jacques Cartier. Ottawa: 1924. V. 73

BIGGERS, DON HAMPTON
A Biggers Chronicle. Lubbock: 1961. V. 69; 70
Buffalo Guns and Barbed Wire. 1991. V. 68
Buffalo Guns and Barbed Wire. Lubbock: 1991. V. 70
From Cattle Range to Cotton Patch. Bandera: 1944. V. 71
Shackelford County Sketches. Albany: 1974. V. 71; 73

BIGGERS, EARL DERR
Behind that Curtain. Indianapolis: 1928. V. 71
Behind that Curtain. New York: 1928. V. 68
The Black Camel. New York: 1929. V. 68
Charlie Chan Carries On. Indianapolis: 1930. V. 68; 70; 72
Charlie Chan Carries On. New York: 1930. V. 70; 71
Charlie Chan Carries On. New York: 1943. V. 68; 71
The Chinese Parrot. New York.
The Chinese Parrot. Indianapolis: 1926. V. 70; 72; 73
El Criado Chino. (Keeper of the Keys). Barcelona: 1946. V. 69
Fifty Candles. Indianapolis: 1926. V. 72
The House Without a Key. Indianapolis: 1925. V. 69
The House Without a Key. New York: 1925. V. 69
Love Insurance. Indianapolis: 1914. V. 70
Seven Keys to Baldpate. Indianapolis: 1913. V. 69; 71; 73

BIGGERS, J. R.
Finchley and the Neighbourhood Old and New. London: 1903. V. 71

BIGGS, E. W., & CO.
Fur Goods Made to Your Order. Kansas City: 1900. V. 72

BIGGS-DAVISON, JOHN
The Hand is Red. 1973. V. 70

BIGHAM, CLIVE
A Year in China 1899-1900 with Some Account of Admiral Sir E. Seymour's Expedition. London: 1901. V. 72

BIGLAND, EILEEN
Lord Byron. London: 1956. V. 70

BIGLAND, J.
The History of England. Boston: 1815. V. 68
A Natural History of Birds, Fishes, Reptiles and Insects. Philadelphia: 1831. V. 70
A Selection of Miscellaneous Pieces, in Prose and Verse. Doncaster: 1814. V. 68

BIGLY, CANTELL A.
Aurifodina; or, Adventures in the Gold Region. New York: 1849. V. 70

BIGMORE, E. C.
A Bibliography of Printing with Notes and Illustrations. London: 1969. V. 69

BIHALJI-MERIN, O.
Masters of Naive Art: a History.... New York: 1970. V. 69; 72

BIKALES, VICTOR W.
Freudian Follies of 1952. Topeka: 1952. V. 73

BILHAUD, PAUL
Les Vacances de Bob & Lisette. Paris: 1890. V. 71

BILL, I. E.
Fifty Years with the Baptist Ministers and Churches of the Maritime Provinces of Canada. Saint John: 1880. V. 73

BILLER, SARAH
Halkam, the Scenes of My Childhood and Other Poems. London: 1839. V. 69

BILLINGHAM, MARK
Sleepyhead. London: 2001. V. 70; 73

BILLINGS, ARCHIBALD
Practical Observations on Disease of the Lungs and Heart. London: 1832. V. 68; 70
Practical Observations on Diseases of the Lungs and Heart. London: 1852. V. 71

BILLINGS, JOHN S.
Circular No 4 Report on Barracks and Hospitals with Descriptions of Military Posts. New York: 1974. V. 72
Circular No 8 Report on The Hygiene of The United States with Descriptions of Military Posts and Circular No 9 Report To The Surgeon General on Transportation of Sick and Wounded by Pack Animals. New York: 1974. V. 72

BILLINGS, ROBERT WILLIAM
Architectural Illustrations, History and Description of Carlisle Cathedral. London: 1840. V. 71
The Baronial and Ecclesiastial Antiquities of Scotland. Edinburgh and London: 1852. V. 72
The Baronial and Ecclesiastical Antiquities of Scotland. London: 1845. V. 71
The Baronial and Ecclesiastical Antiquities of Scotland. Edinburgh and London: 1848-1852. V. 70
The Infinity of Geometric Design Exemplified. Edinburgh: 1849. V. 71
The Power of Form Applied to Geometric Tracery. Edinburgh: 1851. V. 71

BILLINGTON, D. P.
Robert Maillart's Bridges: the Art of Engineering. Princeton: 1979. V. 69; 72

BILLINGTON, MONROE L.
New Mexico's Buffalo Soldiers, 1866-1900. Niwot: 1991. V. 72

BILLINGTON, RAY ALLEN
The Genesis of the Frontier Thesis. San Marino: 1971. V. 68

BILLMARK, C. J.
Chateau Royal d'Ulriksdal. Paris: 1871. V. 70; 72

BILLROTH, THEODOR
The Medical Sciences in the German Universities. New York: 1924. V. 68

BILLY Bounce. Chicago: 1912. V. 68

BIMET, CLAUDE
Quatrains Anataomiques des Os et des Muscles du Corps Humain: Ensemble un Discours de la Circulation du Sang. Lyons: 1664. V. 70

BINDER, H. W., & CO.
Southwestern Iowa, the Garden Spot of the Great West. Council Bluffs in Its Metropolis and Distributing Center. 1913. V. 68

BINDING, TIM
In the Kingdom of Air. London: 1993. V. 71
Island Madness. London: 1998. V. 71
A Perfect Execution. London: 1996. V. 71

THE BINDINGS of To-Morrow. A Record of the Work of the Guild of Women-Binders and of the Hampstead Bindery. London: 1902. V. 73

BINDLOSS, HAROLD
The Dark Road. New York: 1927. V. 70

BINET, RENE
Esquisses Decoratives. Preface de Gustave Geffroy. Paris: 1905. V. 68; 70; 72

BINFIELD, CLYDE
The History of The City of Sheffield 1843-1993. London: 1993. V. 73

BING, ALEXANDER
War-Time Strikes And Their Adjustment. New York: 1921. V. 72

BINGHAM, CLIFTON
The Airship in Animal Land. London: 1913. V. 73
Changing Pictures: a Book of Trnasformation Pictures. London: 1893. V. 73
Christmas Morning. London. V. 70
Dissolving Views - a Book of Revolving Pictures. London: 1896. V. 72
Fun at the Zoo. London: 1906. V. 73
Pleasant Surprises. London: 1890. V. 70
Proverbs Old Newly Told. London: 1912. V. 73
Something New for Little Folk. London: 1899. V. 70; 72
Surprise Pictures from Fairy Land. London: 1907. V. 70
Surprising Pictures. London: 1890. V. 68

BINGHAM, HELEN
History of Green County, Wisconsin. Milwaukee: 1877. V. 68
In Tamal Land. San Francisco: 1906. V. 70

BINGHAM, HIRAM
Bingham's Sandwich Islands, a Residence of Twenty-One Years; or the Civil, Religious and Political History of Those Islands. Hartford: 1847. V. 70
A Residence of Twenty-One Years in the Sandwich Islands.... Hartford: 1847. V. 68

BINGHAM, ROBERT
Incendiary Letter & Arson. Report of the Trials of the Rev. Robert Bingham, Curate of Mansfield, Sussex, on Charges of Writing a Threatening Letter and of Setting Fire to His House.... London: 1811. V. 70

BINGHAM, ROGER
The Church at Heversham. Milnthorpe: 1984. V. 71

BINGLEY, W.
Animal Biography, or Popular Zoology.... London: 1813. V. 68; 69
North Wales, Delineated from Two Excursions through all the Interesting Parts of that High Beautiful and Romantic Country.... London: 1814. V. 71; 72

BINION, CHARLES H.
An Introduction to El Paso's Scenic and Historic Landmarks. El Paso: 1970. V. 71

BINNEY, W. G.
A Manual of American Land Shells. Washington: 1885. V. 68

BINNS, RICHARD WILLIAM
Catalogue Of A Collection of Worcester Porcelain In The Museum At The Royal. Worcester: 1882. V. 72
A Century of Potting in the City of Worcester.... London: 1865. V. 71

BINSTOCK, R. C.
The Soldier. New York: 1996. V. 71

BINYON, LAURENCE
The Death of Adam and Other Poems. London: 1904. V. 69; 73
The Drawings and Engravings of William Blake. London: 1922. V. 70; 72
Dream-Come-True. 1905. V. 73
The Engraved Designs of William Blake. London: 1926. V. 70; 72
The Garland of New Poetry by Various Writers. London: 1899. V. 73
Joan of Arc. 1888. V. 73
Lyric Poems. London: 1894. V. 70
Niobe, Milton Prize Poem. Apposition. St. Paul's School, July 20, 1887. 1887. V. 73
Painting in the Far East. London: 1923. V. 70
Persephone. The Newdigate Poem, 1890. Oxford and London: 1890. V. 73
Poems of Nizami. London: 1928. V. 69; 72
Porphyrion and Other Poems. London: 1898. V. 68
Shilling Garland. Numbers I-X. London: 1896-1899. V. 73

BINYON, T. J.
Murder Will Out: The Detective in Fiction. Oxford: 1989. V. 70

BIOGRAPHICAL and Genealogical History of Morris County, New Jersey. New York: 1899. V. 71

BIOGRAPHICAL, Genealogical and Descriptive History of the First Congressional District of New Jersey. New York: 1900. V. 69

BIOGRAPHICAL Memoir of the Life of Admiral Lord Nelson, Duke of Bronti (sic) K. B. &c. Interspersed with Anecdotes.... Hereford: 1805. V. 70

BIOGRAPHICAL Review....Biographical Sketches of the Leading Citizens of Otsego County, New York. Boston: 1893. V. 72

BIOGRAPHICAL Review...Containing...Life Sketches of Leading Citizens of Burlington and Camden Counties, New Jersey. Boston: 1897. V. 69

BIOGRAPHICAL Sketch of Millie Christine, the Carolina Twin. Cincinnati: 1902-1912. V. 71

THE BIOLOGY of the Crustacea. London: 1982-1983. V. 69

BIOY CASARES, ADOLFO
The Invention of Morel and Other Stories. Austin: 1964. V. 69

BIRCH, S.
Fac-similes of the Egyptian Relics, Discovered at Thebes in the Tomb of Queen Aah-Hotep (ca. BC 1800). London: 1863. V. 72

BIRCH, THOMAS
The History of the Royal Society of London.... London: 1756. V. 68; 71
The Life of the Honourable Robert Boyle. London: 1744. V. 72

BIRCH, WALTER DE GRAY
City of Lincoln. Catalogue of the Royal Charters and Other Documents and List of Books Belonging to the Corporation of Lincoln, Now Preserved in the Muniment Room of the Corporation. Lincoln: 1906. V. 70

BIRCH, WILLIAM
Delices de la Grande Bretagne. London: 1791. V. 69; 71

BIRD, A. F. RYDER
Boating in Bavaria, Austria and Bohemia, Down the Danube, Moldau and Elbe. Hull: 1893. V. 72

BIRD, ANNIE LAURIE
My Home Town. Caldwell: 1968. V. 68; 73

BIRD, CHARLES
A Short Sketch of the Geology of Yorkshire. London: 1881. V. 72

BIRD, HARRISON
Navies in the Mountains. The Battles on the Waters of Lake Champlain and Lake George 1609-1814. New York: 1962. V. 73

BIRD, J. M.
Einstein's Theories of Relativity and Gravitation. New York: 1921. V. 68

BIRD, JAMES
Cosmo, Duke of Tuscany; a Tragedy, in Five Acts. London: 1822. V. 69

BIRD, JAMES BARRY
An Assistant to the Practice of Conveyancing; Containing Indexes or References to the Several Deeds, Agreements and Other Assurances.... London: 1796. V. 70
The Laws Respecting Highways and Turnpike Roads. London: 1801. V. 70
The Laws Respecting Highways and Turnpike Roads. London: 1824. V. 68
The Laws Respecting Tithes. London: 1801. V. 72

BIRD, KENNETH
The Mozart Fiddle. London: 1969. V. 69

BIRD, T. H.
A Hundred Grand Nationals. 1937. V. 68

BIRD, WILL R.
Ghosts Have Warm Hands. Toronto and Vancouver: 1968. V. 71
No Retreating Footsteps. The Story of the North Nova Scotia Highlanders. Kentville. V. 72
Off-Trail in Nova Scotia. Toronto: 1956. V. 72
The Two Jacks. The Amazing Adventures of Major Jack M. Veness and Major Jack L. Fairweather. Toronto: 1954. V. 71; 72

BIRDSALL, KATHARINE NEWBOLD
Tiny and Tim. New York: 1904-. V. 72

BIRDWELL, CLEO
Amazons: an Intimate Memoir by the First Woman Ever to Play in the National Hockey League. New York: 1980. V. 70

BIRGE, JOHN KINGSLEY
The Bektashi Order of Dervishes. London: 1937. V. 72

BIRGE, JULIUS C.
The Awakening of the Desert. Boston: 1912. V. 72

BIRINGUCCIO, VANNOCCIO
De La Pirotechnia. Libri X. Venice: 1540. V. 68

BIRK, L. A.
Paphiopedilum Grower's Manual. Santa Barbara: 1983. V. 71

BIRKBECK, JOHN A.
A Selection of Blocks from the Collection of John A. Birkbeck. Edinburgh: 1971. V. 71

BIRKELAND, KNUT B.
The Whalers of Akutan. New Haven: 1926. V. 71

BIRKENHEAD, COUNTY BOROUGH OF
Abstract of the Treasurer's Accounts 1944-1949. London: 1945-1949. V. 73

BIRKENHEAD, F. E. SMITH, EARL OF
Catalogue of the Major Portion of the Birkenhead Library.... London: 1930. V. 68

BIRKERTS, SVEN
The Gutenberg Elegies. The Fate of Reading in an Elecronic Age. Boston/London: 1994. V. 70

BIRKET SMITH, K.
Ethnography of the Egedesminde District, With Aspects of the General Culture of West Greenland. New York: 1976. V. 69

BIRKETT, BILL
Lakeland's Greatest Pioneers. 100 Years of Rock Climbing. London: 1983. V. 69

BIRKIN, ANDREW
J. M. Barrie and the Lost Boys. London: 1979. V. 72

BIRLEY, ERIC
Research of Hadrian's Wall. Kendal: 1961. V. 71; 73

BIRMINGHAM
Report of the Committee Appointed by the Town Council, September 3rd 1839, to Investigate the Causes of the Late Riots. Birmingham: 1840. V. 69

BIRMINGHAM, G. A.
Benedict Kavanagh. London: 1907. V. 68
Irishmen All. 1913. V. 70

BIRMINGHAM Health Lectures. First Series (-Second Series and Third Series). Birmingham: 1883-1884-. V. 72

BIRNBAUM, MARTIN
Jacovleff and Other Artists. New York: 1946. V. 73
Oscar Wilde, Fragments and Memories. New York: 1914. V. 68

BIRNEY, HOFFMAN
Grim Journey. New York: 1934. V. 69
Zealots of Zion. Philadelphia: 1931. V. 68; 73

BIRNEY, JAMES G.
Letter on Colonization. New York: 1834. V. 68

BIRNIE, WILLIAM
The Blame of Kirk-Buriall, Tending to Perswade Cemiteriall Civilitie. London: 1833. V. 68; 72

BIRRELL, AUGUSTINE
Frederick Locker-Lampson, a Character Sketch. London: 1920. V. 68
The Life of Charlotte Bronte. London: 1887. V. 70; 73
Obiter Dicta. London: 1885. V. 68
Res Judicatae. Papers and Essays. London: 1892. V. 73

BIRRELL & GARNETT, LTD.
Catalogue of: I. Typefounder's Specimens. II. Books Printed in Founts of Historic Importance. III. Works on Type. Surrey: 1972. V. 70; 72

THE BIRTHDAY ABC. London. V. 71

THE BIRTHDAY Dinner to Thomas Addis Emmet, M.D., LL.D., Given by His Professional Friends at Delmonico's, New York May 29, 1905. New York: 1905. V. 68

BISBEE, WILLIAM H.
Through Four American Wars, The Impressions and Experiences of Brigadier General William Haymond Bisbee. Boston: 1931. V. 72

BISCHOFF, ERNEST PHILIPP EDUARD
Microscopic Analysis of the Anastomoses Between the Cranial Nerves.... Hanover: 1977. V. 71

BISCHOFF, IGNAZ RUDOLPH
Beobactungen Uber den Typhus und Die Nervenfieber Nebst Ihrer Behandlung aus der Klink. Prague: 1814. V. 72

BISCHOFF, S. J.
Jesuits in Oregon. Caldwell: 1945. V. 68; 73

BISE, GABRIEL
The Illuminated Naples Bible (Old Testament): 14th Century Manuscript. New York: 1979. V. 70

BISHOP, ABRAHAM
An Oration on the Extent and Power of Political Delusion. Delivered in New Haven... September 1800.... Newark: 1800. V. 69
The Triumph of Truth, History and Visions of Clio. Boston: 1791. V. 71

BISHOP, CARTER RICHARD
The Cockade City of the Union. Petersburg: 1907. V. 72

BISHOP, CHARLES
The Red Blood Cell. A Comprehensive Treatise. New York: 1964. V. 68

BISHOP, CLAIRE HUCHET
Martin De Porres, Hero. Boston: 1954. V. 68; 71

BISHOP, ELIZABETH
An Anthology of Twentieth Century Brazilian Poetry. Middletown: 1972. V. 69
The Ballad of the Burglar of Babylon. New York: 1968. V. 69; 72
The Collected Prose. New York: 1984. V. 69; 71; 72
Geography III. New York: 1976. V. 69
North and South. Boston: 1946. V. 69; 72
Poem. New York: 1973. V. 69; 72; 73
Poems. London: 1956. V. 69; 72
Poems. North and South - A Cold Spring. Boston: 1955. V. 69
Poems. North and South - A Cold Spring. Boston: 1956. V. 69; 72
Questions of Travel. New York: 1965. V. 69

BISHOP, FREDERICK
The Illustrated London Cookery Book.... London: 1852. V. 68

BISHOP, GEORGE
Observations, Remarks and Means to Prevent Smuggling, Humbly Submitted to the Consideration of the Rt. Honourable the House of Peers, and the Honourable House of Commons, in Parliament Assembled, by Their Obedient, Humble Servant, George Bishop. Madistone: 1783. V. 69

BISHOP, H. H.
Pictorial Architecture in Greece and Italy. London: 1887. V. 72

BISHOP, ISABELLA LUCY BIRD
The Englishwoman in America. London: 1856. V. 73
The Golden Chersonese and the Way Thither. London: 1883. V. 68; 72
A Lady's Life in the Rocky Mountains. London: 1894. V. 69
Six Months Among the Palm Groves, Coral Reefs, and Volcanoes of the Sandwich Islands. London: 1882. V. 73

BISHOP, J. E.
Limnology of Small Malayan River, Sungai Gombak. The Hague: 1973. V. 70

BISHOP, JAMES
Epitaph for a Desert Anarchist. New York: 1994. V. 72

BISHOP, JOHN GEORGE
A Peep into the Past Brighton in the Olden Time with Glances at the Present. Brighton: 1892. V. 73

BISHOP, MORRIS
The Widening Stain. New York: 1942. V. 72

BISHOP, PAUL
Citadel Run. New York: 1988. V. 68

BISHOP, PHILIP R.
Thomas Bird Mosher, Private Prince of Publishers. New Castle: 1998. V. 68

BISHOP, R. H.
A Manual of Logic. Oxford: 1830. V. 73

BISHOP, ROBERT
American Decorative Arts. New York: 1982. V. 68; 72; 73
American Folk Art: Expressions of a New Spirit. New York: 1982. V. 69
Centuries and Styles of the American Chair, 1640-1970. New York: 1972. V. 68; 73

BISHOP, S. C.
Handbook of Salamanders, the Salamanders of the United States of Canada and of Lower California. New York: 1962. V. 72

BISHOP, WILLIAM HENRY
The Brown Stone Boy and Other Queer People. London: 1888. V. 68

BISHOP, ZEALIA
The Curse of Yig. Sauk City: 1953. V. 69

THE BISHOP'S Advice to Persons Who Have Been Confirmed; to Which are Added Prayers for the Unity Of Peace and Happiness of the Church, from the New Testament and the Book of Common Prayer. Carmarthen: 1811. V. 68

BISLAND, ELIZABETH
A Candle of Understanding. New York: 1903. V. 69

BISNO, BEATRICE
Tomorrow's Bread. Philadelphia: 1938. V. 68

BISSE, THOMAS
The Beauty of Holiness in the Common Prayer.... London: 1718. V. 69

BISSELL, RICHARD
Say, Darling. London: 1957. V. 69

BISSET, JAMES
The Second and Improved Edition of the Descriptive Guide of Leamington Priors.... Coventry: 1816. V. 70
A Poetic Survey Round Birmingham with a Brief Description of the Different Curiosities and Manufactories of the Place, Intended as a Guide to Strangers.... Birmingham. V. 70

BISSET, P.
The Book of Water Gardening. New York: 1907. V. 71

BITTING, KATHERINE
Gastronomic Bibliography. San Francisco: 1939. V. 68; 70
Gastronomic Bibliography. London: 1981. V. 68; 70
Gastronomic Bibliography. Mansfield: 1995. V. 68

BITTON, DAVIS
Guide to Mormon Diaries and Autobiographies. Provo: 1977. V. 71

BIVERO, PEDRO DE
Sacrvm Sanctvarivm Crvcis et Patientiae Crvcifixorvm et Crvciferorvm. Antverpiae: 1634. V. 73

BIVINS, JOHN
The Moravian Potters in North Carolina. Chapel Hill: 1972. V. 71

BIZOT, PIERRE
Histoire Metallique de vla Republicque de Hollande. Amsterdam: 1688-1690. V. 72

BJORKLUND, ANDERS
Beskrifning Ofver Kongl. Lust-Slotten Drottningholm Och China. Stockholm: 1796. V. 68; 70

BJORKMAN, FRANCES
Woman Suffrage, History Arguments and Results. New York: 1917. V. 71

BJORNSTJERNA, COUNT
The British Empire in the East (India). London: 1840. V. 68

BLACHFORD, ROBERT
Dismal England. 1901. V. 71

BLACK, A.
Black's Guide to Dublin and the Wickow Mountains. Edinburgh: 1881. V. 71

BLACK, A. P.
The End of the Long Horn Trail. Selfridge, ND: 1936. V. 71

BLACK Bunnies. London: 1907. V. 68

BLACK, CYRUS
Historical Record of the Posterity of William Black, Who Settled in This Country in the Year Seventeen Hundred and Seventy Five.. Amherst;: 1885. V. 73

BLACK, DAVIDSON
Asia and the Dispersal of Primates. London: 1925. V. 71
On an Adolescent Skull of Sinanthropus Pekinensis in Comparison with an Adult Skull of the Same Species and With Other Hominid Skulls.... Peiping: 1931. V. 68

BLACK, DOROTHY
Corner House. New York: 1937. V. 71; 72
The Magic Egg. London: 1922. V. 70
Wise Folly. Philadelphia: 1933. V. 71

BLACK, ELANDRA
The Gold Rush Song Book - a Compilation of Famous Songs by the Men who Came to California to Mine for Gold in 1849. San Francisco: 1940. V. 69

BLACK, ETHAN
Broken Hearts Club. 1999. V. 68

BLACK, F. MICHAEL
Mirando City. Laredo: 1972. V. 69

BLACK, G. A.
Angel Site, an Archaeological, Historical and Ethnological Study. 1967. V. 69

BLACK, GLENN
Angel Site, an Archeaological, Historical and Ethnological Study. Indianapolis: 1967. V. 68; 73

BLACK, J. D.
A Rhode Island Chaplain in the Revolution Letters of Ebenezer David to Nicholas Brown 1775-1778. Providence: 1949. V. 68

BLACK, JOHN
Poems by the Rev. John Black, Minister of Butley, Suffolk. Ipswich: 1799. V. 72

BLACK, LADBORKE
Mr. Preed Investigates. New York: 1939. V. 72

BLACK List. A List of Those Tories Who Took Part with Great Britain, in the Revolutionary War, and Were Attained of High Treason, Commonly Called the Black List!. Philadelphia: 1802. V. 73

THE BLACK Military Experience in The American West. New York: 1971. V. 72

BLACK, MRS.
Household Cookery and Laundry Work. London: 1875. V. 68

BLACK, PATTI CARR
Eudora. Jackson: 1984. V. 70

BLACK, PETER
Harvey Cushing at the Brigham. Park Ridge: 1993. V. 68
The Surgical Art of Harvey Cushing. Park Ridge: 1992. V. 68

BLACK Politics In Philadelphia. New York: 1973. V. 72

BLACK, R. D. COLLISON
Economic Thought and the Irish Question 1817-1870. 1960. V. 73

BLACK, ROBERT CLIFFORD
The Railroads of the Confederacy. Chapel Hill: 1952. V. 70

BLACK, WILLIAM
The Beautiful Wretch. The Four MacNicols. The Pupil of Aurelius. Three Stories. London: 1881. V. 68
Some Overtures and Cautions in Relation to Trade and Taxes, Humbly Offered to the Parliament. Edinburgh?: 1707. V. 72
The Strange Adventures of A Phaeton. London: 1874. V. 70; 71

BLACK, WILLIAM HENRY
History and Antiquities of the Worshipful Company of Leathersellers. London: 1871. V. 71

BLACKADDER, H. HOME
Observations on Phagedaena Gangraenosa. Edinburgh: 1818. V. 71

BLACKAH, THOMAS
Dialect Poems & Prose. With a Short Biography by Harald John Lexow Bruff. York: 1937. V. 73

BLACKALL, W. E.
How to Know Western Australian Wildflowers.... Nedlands: 1954-1956. V. 72

THE BLACKBERRY Girl. New York: 1851-1865. V. 73

BLACKBRIDGE, JOHN
The Complete Poker Player. New York: 1880. V. 69

BLACKBURN, ALEXANDER
A Sunrise Brighter Still. Athens, OH: 1991. V. 72

BLACKBURN, HENRY
Randolph Caldecott: A Personal Memoir Of His Early Art Career. London: 1886. V. 72
Randolph Caldecott...His Early Career. New York: 1886. V. 69

BLACKBURN, I. W.
Illustrations of the Gross Morbid Anatomy of the Brain in the Insane. Washington: 1908. V. 71
Intracranial Tumors Among the Insane. Washington: 1902. V. 71
Intracranial Tumors Among the Insane: A Study of 29 Intracranial Tumors Found in 1642 Autopsies in Cases of Mental Disease. Washington: 1903. V. 70

BLACKBURN, JANE
Birds from Moidart and Elsewhere. 1895. V. 69

BLACKBURN, PAUL
Gin: Four Journal Pieces. Mt. Horeb: 1970. V. 73

BLACKBURN, PAUL continued
Guillem de Poitou. His Eleven Extant Poems. Mt. Horeb: 1976. V. 73
The Journals: Blue Mounds Entries. Mt. Horeb: 1971. V. 73
The Omitted Journals. Mt. Horeb: 1983. V. 73
The Reardon Poems. Mt. Horeb: 1967. V. 73
The Selection of Heaven. Mt. Horeb: 1980. V. 73
Under Twenty-Five. Duke Narrative and Verse, 1945-1962. Durham: 1963. V. 71

BLACKBURN, THOMAS
The Feast of the Wolf. London: 1971. V. 70

BLACKBURN, WILLIAM
One and Twenty: Duke Narrative and Verse. Durham: 1945. V. 73

BLACKBURNE, FRANCIS
Considerations on the Present State of the Controversy Between the Protestants and Papists of Great Britain and Ireland.... London: 1768. V. 68; 70; 73

BLACKBURNE, JOHN
Register Book of Ingleby Juxta Grenhow. Canterbury: 1889. V. 73

BLACKER, IRWIN R.
Search and Destroy. New York: 1966. V. 68

BLACKER, W.
Blacker's Art of Fly Making. 1994. V. 68; 73

BLACKERBY, SAMUEL
The Justice of Peace, His Companion, or a Summary of all the Act of Parliament, Whereby One, Two or More Justices of the Peace, are Authorized to Act.... London: 1723. V. 69

BLACKFORD, CHARLES M.
Annals of the Lynchburg Home Guard. Lynchburg: 1891. V. 69; 70
Campaign and Battle of Lynchburgh, Virginia. Lynchburg: 1901. V. 69; 70

BLACK HAWK, SAUK CHIEF
Autobiography of Ma-Ka-Tai-Me-She-Kia-Kiak Or Black Hawk. St. Louis: 1882. V. 71

BLACKIE'S Children's Annual. 19th Year. 1922. V. 68; 73

BLACKIE'S Children's Annual. 1923. V. 72

BLACKIE'S Children's Annual. 28th Year. London: 1925. V. 72; 73

BLACKIE'S Children's Annual. 31st Year. London: 1934. V. 69

BLACKIE'S Children's Annual. 34th Year. 1937. V. 70

BLACKIE'S Children's Annual. 36th Year. 1939. V. 70

BLACKMAR, FRANK W.
The Life of Charles Robinson - the First State Governor of Kansas. Topeka: 1902. V. 70
Spanish Institutions of the Southwest. Baltimore: 1891. V. 70

BLACKMORE, RICHARD DODDRIDGE
Alice Lorraine; a Tale of the South Downs. London: 1892. V. 68
Epullia. 1854. V. 73
The Fate of Franklin...in aid of the Spilsby Fund for Erecting a Statue of Franklin in His Native Town. 1860. V. 73
Fringilla or Tales in Verse. Cleveland: 1895. V. 68
Lorna Doone. London: 1891. V. 68
Lorna Doone. Springfield: 1922. V. 70
Poems by Melanter (pseud). London: 1854. V. 73
Tales from the Telling-House. London: 1896. V. 68; 70; 71

BLACKMUR, R. P.
The Double Agent. New York: 1935. V. 69

BLACK'S Guide to Paris International Exhibition of 1878. Edinburgh: 1878. V. 71

BLACK'S Guide to the County of York. Edinburgh: 1884. V. 73

BLACK'S Picturesque Guide to the English Lakes. Edinburgh: 1858. V. 71

BLACK'S Picturesque Guide to the English Lakes Including an Essay on the Geology of the District by John Phillips. Edinburgh: 1861. V. 72

BLACK'S Picturesque Guide to Yorkshire. Edinburgh: 1858. V. 73
BLACK'S Picturesque Guide to Yorkshire. Edinburgh: 1868. V. 73
BLACK'S Picturesque Guide to Yorkshire. Edinburgh: 1871. V. 73

BLACK'S Tourists Guide to Ireland. 1888. V. 73

BLACKSTONE, WILLIAM
The Case of the Late Election for the County of Middlesex, Considered on the Principles of the Constitution, and the Authorities of Law. London: 1769. V. 69
Commentaries on the Laws of England. Oxford: 1768-1769. V. 69
Commentaries on the Laws of England. Oxford: 1774. V. 73
Commentaries on the Laws of England. London: 1787. V. 69
Commentaries on the Laws of England. London: 1793. V. 73
Commentaries on the Laws of England. Philadelphia: 1881. V. 72
Commentaries on the Laws of England. Book the First. Oxford: 1766. V. 73
Commentaries on the Laws of England. Book the First. Oxford: 1768. V. 73
Commentaries on the Laws of England. Book the Fourth. Oxford: 1770. V. 73
Commentaries on the Laws of England in Four Books. Oxford: 1778. V. 73
Reports of Cases Determined in the Several Courts of Westminster Hall, from 1746 to 1799. London: 1781. V. 72

BLACKWELDER, R. E.
Checklist of the Coleopterous Insects of Mexico, Central America and the West Indies and South America. Washington: 1982. V. 68; 72

BLACKWELL, ALICE STONE
Lucy Stone, Pioneer of Woman's Rights. Boston: 1930. V. 72

BLACKWELL, ELISABETH
Herbarivm Blackwell-Lianvm. Norimbergae: 1757. V. 69

BLACKWOOD, ALGERNON
The Human Chord. London: 1916. V. 69
Incredible Adventures. London: 1914. V. 73
John Silence: Physician Extraordinary. New York: 1909. V. 69
The Last Valley. London: 1910. V. 68
A Prisoner in Fairyland. London: 1913. V. 68
Shocks. New York: 1936. V. 70
Tongues of Fire and Other Sketches. London: 1924. V. 70
The Wave: An Egyptian Aftermath. New York: 1916. V. 72

BLACKWOOD, CAROLINE
For All That I Found There. London: 1973. V. 70

BLADES, WILLIAM
The Enemies of Books. London: 1880. V. 71

BLAGROVE, WILLIAM
The Elements of Chess; a Treatise Combining Theory with Practice.... Boston: 1805. V. 68
The Elements of Chess.... Boston: 1805. V. 73

BLAIKIE, FRANCIS
The Farmer's Instructor for the Planting and Management of Forest Trees. 1810. V. 70
A Treatise on Smut in Wheat, with Means of Prevention. Wells: 1821. V. 70

BLAIKIE, THOMAS
Diary of a Scotch Gardener at the French Court at the End of the Eighteenth Century. London: 1931. V. 70

BLAIKIE, WILLIAM G.
Six Lectures Addressed to the Working Classes on the Improvement of Their Temporal Condition. Edinburgh: 1849. V. 71

BLAINE, D. P.
An Encyclopedia of Rural Sports...Complete Account, Historical, practical, and Descriptive of Hunting, Shooting, Fishing, Racing &c. &c. 1852. V. 71

BLAIR, CLAUDE
Arms, Armour and Base-Metal-Work. London: 1974. V. 68

BLAIR, CLAY
Silent Victory. Philadelphia: 1975. V. 71

BLAIR, DAVID
The Universal Preceptor: Being a General Grammar of Arts, Sciences and Useful Knowledge. Philadelphia: 1817. V. 70

BLAIR, EMILY NEWELL
A Woman of Courage. New York: 1931. V. 70

BLAIR, HUGH
Lectures on Rhetoric and Belles Letters. Philadelphia: 1784. V. 68
Sentimental Beauties from the Writings of Dr. Blair. London: 1798. V. 69
Sermons. London. V. 71

BLAIR, JOHN
The Chronology and History of the World, From the Creation to the Year of Christ, 1790. London: 1790. V. 70

BLAIR, ROBERT
The Grave. London: 1808. V. 70
The Grave. New York: 1903. V. 71

BLAIR, W. F.
Evolution in the Genus Bufo. Austin: 1972. V. 72

BLAIR, WALTER
Half Horse Half Alligator: the Growth of the Mike Fink Legend. Chicago: 1956. V. 69

BLAIR, WALTER A.
A Raft Pilot's Log: a History of the Great Rafting Industry on the Upper Mississippi 1840-1915. Cleveland: 1930. V. 69; 71; 73

BLAISDELL, ELINORE
Tales of the Undead. New York: 1947. V. 71

BLAISDELL, MARY FRANCES
Twilight Town. Boston: 1920. V. 72

BLAKE, CHARLES
An Historical Account of the Providence Stage.... Providence: 1868. V. 68

BLAKE, E. R.
Manual of Neotropical Birds. Volume I. Chicago: 1977. V. 73

BLAKE, E. VALE
Arctic Experiences, Containing Capt. George E. Tysons' Wonderful Drift on the Ice-Floe, A History of the Polaris Expedition, the Cruise of the Tigress and Rescue of the Polaris Survivors. New York: 1874. V. 73

BLAKE, ELEANOR
Wherever I Choose. New York: 1938. V. 71

BLAKE, FORRESTER
Riding the Mustang Trail. New York: 1935. V. 71

BLAKE, FRANCIS
A Proposal for the Liquidation of the National Debt; the Abolition of Tithes.... London: 1783. V. 72

BLAKE, G. E.
Blake's New and Complete Perceptor for the Spanish Guitar & Lyre. Philadelphia: 1820. V. 72

BLAKE, J. L.
The Family Encyclopedia of Useful Knowledge and General Literature. New York: 1834. V. 69; 71

BLAKE, JAMES
The Joint. Garden City: 1971. V. 72

BLAKE, JOHN
The Private Instructor and Young Gentleman's Pocket Companion.... Trenton: 1815. V. 69

BLAKE, MRS.
The Realities of Freemasonry. 1879. V. 69; 73

BLAKE, NICHOLAS
The Beast Must Die. London: 1938. V. 73
The Beast Must Die. New York: 1938. V. 70
Head of a Traveler. London: 1949. V. 69; 73
Minute for Murder. London: 1947. V. 73
A Penknife in My Heart. New York: 1958. V. 73
The Private Wound. London: 1968. V. 73
Shell of Death. 1936. V. 73
The Smiler with the Knife. New York: 1939. V. 73
The Whisper in the Gloom. London: 1954. V. 73
The Widow's Cruise. London: 1959. V. 73

BLAKE, PETER
An American Synagogue for Today and Tomorrow: a Guide Book to Synagogue Design and Construction. New York: 1954. V. 69
God's Own Junkyard: the Planned Deterioration of American Landscape. New York: 1964. V. 69; 72
Marcel Breuer: Sun and Shadow: the Philosophy of an Architect. New York: 1953. V. 69
The Master Builders: Le Corbusier, Mies Van Der Rohe, Frank Lloyd Wright. New York: 1960. V. 68

BLAKE, S. F.
Geographical Guide to Floras of the World, an Annotated List with Special Reference to Useful Plants and Common Plant Names. Washington: 1942-1961. V. 69; 71; 73

BLAKE, W. O.
The History of Slavery and the Slave Trade, Ancient and Modern.... Columbus: 1858. V. 69
History of Slavery and the Slave Trade, Ancient and Modern.... Columbus: 1859. V. 68

BLAKE, WILLIAM
All Religions are One. London: 1970. V. 69
All Religions Are One. Paris: 1970. V. 70
Blake's Pencil Drawings: Second Series. London: 1956. V. 71
The Book of Los. 1976. V. 72
The Book of Los. Paris: 1976. V. 70
The Complete Portraiture of William and Catherine Blake. Paris: 1977. V. 70
Europe: a Prophecy. Clairvaux: 1969. V. 68
The Gates of Paradise: For Children - For the Sexes. London: 1968. V. 72
Illustrations from the Book of Job by William Blake.... New York: 1935. V. 72
Illustrations of the Book of Job. London: 1825. V. 72
The Illustrations of William Blake for Thornton's Virgil with the First Eclogue and the Imitation by Ambrose Philips. London: 1937. V. 70
Jerusalem, the Emanation of the Giant Albion. London: 1877. V. 73
The Marriage of Heaven and Hell. Edmonton: 1885. V. 70; 72
The Marriage of Heaven and Hell. London: 1960. V. 71
The Poems of William Blake. London: 1893. V. 71
Poems of William Blake. 1910. V. 70
Poetical Sketches. London: 1868. V. 72
Songs of Innocence and Experience Showing the Two Contrary States of the Human Soul. (with) Sketches.... London: 1868. V. 73
The Tyger. 1996. V. 71
Water-Color Designs for the Poems of Thomas Gray. Paris: 1971. V. 68
The Writings of William Blake. London: 1925. V. 69; 72

BLAKEBOROUGH, JOHN F.
Great Ayton, Stokesley & District, Past and Present; with a Chapter on Bilsdale and Its Hunt. Middlesborough: 1901. V. 73

BLAKEBOROUGH, RICHARD
Wit, Character, Folklore & Customs of the North Riding of Yorkshire. London: 1898. V. 73

BLAKENEY, THOMAS S.
Sherlock Holmes: Fact or Fiction?. London: 1932. V. 69; 70

BLAKER, RICHARD
But Beauty Vanishes. London: 1936. V. 70
The Jefferson Secret. Garden City: 1929. V. 69; 73
Medal Without Bar. London: 1930. V. 69

BLAKERS, M.
The Atlas of Australian Birds. Melbourne: 1984. V. 72

BLAKESTON, OSWELL
The Cat with the Moustache. London: 1935. V. 73
Death on the Swim. London: 1934. V. 73
Few Are Chosen. London: 1931. V. 73
In Reverse. London: 1961. V. 73
Magic Aftermath: a Romantic Study in the Pleating of Time. New Barnet: 1932. V. 73
Murder Among Friends. 1933. V. 73

BLAKISTON, NOEL
The Collected Stories of Noel Blakiston. London: 1977. V. 71
Men of Letters and Other Stories. London: 1955. V. 71
That Thoughtful Boy and Other Stories. London: 1965. V. 71

BLAKSTON, W. A.
The Illustrated Book of Canaries and Cage Birds, British and Foreign. London: 1880. V. 73

BLANC, A., & CO.
Illustrated Catalogue of Rare Cacti. Philadelphia: 1893. V. 70

BLANC, CHARLES
Art in Ornament and Dress. London: 1877. V. 69

BLANC, LOUIS
The History of Ten Years 1830-1840. London: 1844. V. 69

BLANCH, WILLIAM HARNETT
Ye Parish of Camerwell. London: 1875. V. 71

BLANCHAN, N.
The American Flower Garden. New York: 1909. V. 71

BLANCHARD, AMY E.
My Own Dolly. London: 1883. V. 70

BLANCHARD, ELIZABETH AMIS CAMERON
The Life and Times of Sir Archie: the Story of America's Greatest Thoroughbred 1805-1833. Chapel Hill: 1958. V. 71

BLANCHARD, JERROLD
The Best of All Good Company.... London: 1871. V. 69

BLANCHARD, LEOLA HOWARD
Conquest of Southern Kansas Wichita. Wichita: 1931. V. 70
Conquest of Southwest Kansas. Wichita: 1931. V. 69

BLANCO County Heritage Book. 1997. V. 70

BLANCO, FRANCISCO MANUEL
Flora de Filipinas. Segun el Sistema Sexual de Linneo. Manila: 1837. V. 73

BLAND, ALDEN
Behold a Cry. New York: 1947. V. 69

BLAND, CAPTAIN
The Northern Atalantis: or, York Spy. London. V. 70; 71; 72

BLAND COUNTY CENTENNIAL CORPORATION
History of Bland County (Virginia). Radford: 1961. V. 68

BLAND, DAVID
A History of Book Illustration. London: 1958. V. 69; 70
A History of Book Illustration. 1969. V. 68
The Illustration of Books. London: 1951. V. 71

BLAND, E.
Annals of Southport and District. Manchester: 1887. V. 73

BLAND, HUMPHREY
A Treatise of Military Discipline; in Which is Laid Down and Explained the Duty of the Officer and Soldier. London: 1740. V. 69
A Treatise of Military Discipline; in Which is Laid Down and Explained the Duty of the Officer and Soldier. London: 1759. V. 73

BLAND, WILLIAM
Experimental Essays on the Principles of Construction in Arches, Piers, Buttresses &c. London: 1839. V. 69

BLANDY, MARY
The Tryal of...Spinster, for the Murder of Her Father, Francis Blandy, Gent. London: 1752. V. 68; 69; 73

BLANFORD, W.
The Fauna of British India....Mammalia. London: 1888-1891. V. 73
Observations on the Geology and Zoology of Abyssinia. 1870. V. 68

BLANKENHORN, H.
The Strike for Union. New York: 1924. V. 68

BLANKMEYER, HELEN VAN CLEVE
The Three Goats Gruff. 1914. V. 68

BLANSHARD, FRANCES
Portraits of Wordsworth. London: 1959. V. 71

BLANTON, WYNDHAM B.
Medicine in Virginia in the 17th Century. Richmond: 1930. V. 68
Medicine in Virginia in the Nineteenth Century. Richmond: 1933. V. 70

BLASCHE, BERNHARD HEINRICH
Papyro-Plastics, or the Art of Modelling in Paper; Being an Instructive Amusement for Young Persons of Both Sexes. 1825. V. 71

BLASCO IBANEZ, VINCENT
Blood and Sand. London: 1913. V. 71

BLASINGAME, IKE
Dakota Cowboy, My Life in the Old Days. 1958. V. 68
Dakota Cowboy (My Life in the Old Days). New York: 1958. V. 71

BLATCHFORD, ROBERT
The Dolly Ballads. London. V. 72
The Nunquam Papers. London: 1895. V. 68

BLATCHLEY, WILLIS STANLEY
In Days Agone: Notes on the Fauna and Flora of Subtropical Florida in the Days When Most of Its Area was a Primeval Wilderness. Indianapolis: 1932. V. 71

BLATCHLY, JOHN
The Bookplates of Edward Gordon Craig. London and Birmingham: 1997. V. 70

BLATTER, E.
Beautiful Flowers of Kashmir. Westminster: 1928. V. 73

BLATTY, WILLIAM PETER
The Exorcist. New York: 1971. V. 68; 69; 71; 72

BLAUNER, PETER
Slow Motion Riot. New York: 1991. V. 72

BLAYLOCK, JAMES P.
The Last Coin. 1988. V. 70

BLAZEBY, WILLIAM
Rotherham: The Old Meeting-House and its Ministers, with Supplementary Chapters. Rotherham: 1906. V. 73

BLAZE DE BURY, MARIE PAULINE ROSE STEWART, BARONESS
Voyage en Autriche en Hongrie et en Allemagne Pendant Les Evenements de 1848 et 1849. Paris: 1851. V. 71

A BLEAK HOUSE Narrative of Real Life; Being a Faithful Detail of Facts Connected with a Suit in the Irish Court of Chancery, from the Year 1826 to 1851. London: 1856. V. 73

BLEDSOE, ALBERT T.
An Essay on Liberty and Slavery. Philadelphia: 1856. V. 68

BLEECK, OLIVER
The Brass Go-Between. 1969. V. 69

BLEGEN, THEODORE C.
The Crowded Box-Room: Sherlock Holmes as Poet. LaCrosse: 1951. V. 69

BLENKARN, J.
British Timber Trees: Their Rearing and Subsequent Management, in Woods, Groves and Plantations.... London: 1859. V. 71

BLESH, RUDI
They All Played Ragtime. New York: 1950. V. 73

BLESSINGTON, COUNTESS OF
The Lottery of Life. Paris: 1842. V. 70

BLESSINGTON, JOSEPH P.
The Campaigns of Walker's Texas Division. New York: 1875. V. 69; 70

BLEW, WILLIAM C.
A History of Steeple Chasing. London: 1901. V. 73

BLIER, BERTRAND
Going Places. Philadelphia: 1974. V. 72

BLIGH, J.
Essays on Temperature Regulation. Amsterdam: 1972. V. 68

BLIGH, WILLIAM
A Voyage to the South Sea...In His Majesty's Ship the Bounty. London: 1792. V. 69

BLIGHT, J. T.
A Week at Land's End. London: 1861. V. 68

BLINKEY Bill. Racine: 1935. V. 70

BLISH, HELEN
A Pictographic History of Oglala Sioux. Lincoln: 1967. V. 70; 71; 72; 73

BLISH, JAMES
A Case of Conscience. London: 1959. V. 70
Earthman Come Home. New York: 1955. V. 69; 70

BLISS, ADAM
Murder Upstairs. Philadelphia: 1934. V. 70
Murder Upstairs. London: 1935. V. 69; 73

BLISS, B. K., & SONS
Illustrated Hand book for the Farm and Garden and Catalogue of Garden Field and Flower Seeds etc. New York: 1882. V. 69

BLISS, CAREY
A Leaf from the 1583 Rembert Dodoens Herbal Printed by Christopher Plantin. San Francisco: 1977. V. 68

BLISS, D. E.
The Biology of Crustacea. London: 1982-1985. V. 73

BLISS, DOUGLAS PERCY
Border Ballads. London: 1925. V. 73

BLISS, MRS.
Practical Cook Book. Philadelphia: 1856. V. 68; 73

BLISS, PHILIP
Catalogue of...the Extensive, Interesting and Valuable Library, Formed by the Late Rev. Philip Bliss.... London: 1858. V. 70

BLOCH, E. MAURICE
George Caleb Bingham: the Evolution of an Artist (with) George Caleb Bingham: a Catalogue Raisonne. Berkeley: 1967. V. 72; 73

BLOCH, LOUIS
Labor Agreements in Coal Mines. New York: 1931. V. 68

BLOCH, M. E.
Fishes. 1959. V. 73

BLOCH, ROBERT
Blood Runs Cold. New York: 1961. V. 69; 73
Night-World. New York: 1972. V. 73
The Opener of the Way. Sauk City: 1945. V. 69
Pleasant Dreams. Sauk City: 1960. V. 69
Psycho. New York: 1959. V. 70; 71; 72
Psycho II. Binghamton: 1982. V. 68; 72
The Scarf. 1947. V. 69; 70; 73
Screams. San Rafael: 1989. V. 68; 72
The Skull of the Marquis de Sade and Other Stories. London: 1975. V. 73
Spiderweb. New York: 1954. V. 69

BLOCHMAN, LAWRENCE G.
Clues for Dr. Coffee. 1964. V. 68
Clues for Dr. Coffee. Philadelphia: 1964. V. 69; 73
Death Walks in Marble Halls. New York: 1951. V. 69
Diagnosis: Homicide. 1950. V. 68
See You at the Morgue. New York: 1941. V. 69; 72

BLOCK, ANDREW
The Book Collector's Vade Mecum. London: 1932. V. 71

BLOCK, ETTA
One-Act Plays from the Yiddish. Cincinnati: 1923. V. 70

BLOCK, HERBERT
Straight Herblock. New York: 1964. V. 73

BLOCK, LAURIE
An Odd Bestiary.... 1982. V. 71

BLOCK, LAWRENCE
After Hours. Albuquerque: 1995. V. 70; 71; 72
After Hours. Gallup: 1995. V. 71
April North by Sheldon Lord. New York: 1961. V. 71; 72
Ariel. New York: 1980. V. 68; 69; 70; 72; 73
Born To Be Bad, by Sheldon Lord. New York: 1959. V. 71; 72
The Burglar in the Closet. New York: 1978. V. 73
The Burglar in the Library. Harpenden: 1997. V. 69
The Burglar in the Library. London: 1997. V. 69; 71; 72; 73
The Burglar Who Liked to Quote Kipling. New York: 1979. V. 70; 71; 72; 73
The Burglar Who Painted Like Mondrian. New York: 1983. V. 68; 69; 70; 71; 72; 73
The Burglar Who Painted Like Mondrian. London: 1984. V. 72
The Burglar Who Studied Spinoza. New York: 1980. V. 68; 69; 70; 71; 72; 73
Burglar Who Traded Ted Williams. New York: 1994. V. 70
Burglars Can't Be Choosers. New York: 1977. V. 71; 73
The Canceled Czech. New York: 1994. V. 69; 70; 71; 72; 73
The Collected Mystery Stories. London: 1999. V. 71
Community Of Women by Sheldon Lord. New York: 1961. V. 72
A Dance at the Slaughterhouse. New York: 1991. V. 69; 70; 71; 72; 73
Deadly Honeymoon. 1967. V. 68
Death Pulls a Doublecross. Greenwich: 1961. V. 69
Ehrengraf for the Defense. 1994. V. 68
Eight Million Ways to Die. New York: 1982. V. 68; 69; 70; 71; 72; 73
Even the Wicked. London: 1996. V. 68; 69; 71; 72
Everybody Dies. New York: 1998. V. 72
Five Little Rich Girls. London: 1984. V. 69
The Girl with the Long Green Heart. London: 1980. V. 70; 71
Here Comes a Hero. Greenwich: 1968. V. 69
Hit List. London: 2000. V. 71
Hit List. New York: 2000. V. 72
Hope To Die. New York: 2001. V. 72
The House of 7 Sins by Andrew Shaw. New York: 1961. V. 72
In the Midst of Death. Delavan: 1995. V. 69; 70
Me Tanner, You Jane. New York: 1970. V. 71
Mona. Unity, Maine: 1999. V. 69; 70; 72; 73
Not Comin' Home to You. New York: 1974. V. 70; 71
Of Shame and Joy by Sheldon Lord. New York: 1960. V. 71; 72
One Night Stands. Norfolk: 1999. V. 70; 71
Out on the Cutting Edge. New York: 1989. V. 69; 71; 72; 73
Random Walk. New York: 1988. V. 68; 73
Ronald Rabbit is a Dirty Old Man. New York: 1971. V. 69; 73
Ronald Rabbit is a Dirty Old Man. 1995. V. 68
The Scoreless Thai. Burton, Michigan: 2000. V. 69; 70; 71; 72; 73

BLOCK, LAWRENCE continued
The Sins of the Fathers. New York: 1976. V. 71
The Sins of the Fathers. Arlington Heights: 1992. V. 70; 73
Sometimes They Bite. New York: 1983. V. 71
The Specialists. Aliso Viejo, CA: 1996. V. 68; 69; 70; 71; 72; 73
Spider, Spin Me A Web: Lawrence Block On Writing Crime Fiction. Cincinnati: 1988. V. 71; 72
A Stab in the Dark. New York: 1981. V. 71
Such Men are Dangerous. New York: 1969. V. 69; 71
The Thief Who Couldn't Sleep. New York: 1994. V. 69; 70; 71; 72; 73
Threesome. Mission Viejo: 1999. V. 70; 71; 73
A Ticket to the Boneyard. New York: 1990. V. 69; 71; 72; 73
Time To Murder And Create. Arlington Heights: 1993. V. 72; 73
The Topless Tulip Caper. London: 1984. V. 69; 70; 71; 72; 73
The Triumph of Evil. New York: 1971. V. 68; 69; 70; 71; 73
The Trouble with Eden. New York: 1973. V. 72; 73
Two for Tanner. Greenwich: 1968. V. 69
When the Sacred Ginmill Closes. New York: 1986. V. 70; 73
A Woman Must Love by Sheldon Lord. New York: 1960. V. 71; 72
Writing the Novel from Plot to Print. Cincinnati: 1979. V. 71; 72

BLOCKSON, CHARLES L.
Catalog of the Charles L. Blockson Afro-American Collection. Philadelphia: 1990. V. 68

BLODGETT, JEAN
Kenojuak. Toronto: 1985. V. 69

BLODGETT, MABEL FULLER
Peasblossom. The Adventures of the Pine Tree Fairy and Others. New York: 1917. V. 70

BLOIS, JOHN T.
Gazetteer of the State of Michigan.... Detroit: 1838. V. 69; 73

BLOK, ALEKSANDR
Ramzes. Petersburg: 1921. V. 68

BLOMBERG, NANCY J.
Navajo Textiles. The William Randolph Hearst Collection. Tucson: 1988. V. 70

BLOME, RICHARD
Hawking or Faulconry. London: 1929. V. 70

BLOMFIELD, ARTHUR
Lars Porsena. Oxford: 1875. V. 73

BLOMFIELD, R.
The Formal Garden in England. London: 1892. V. 71

BLOMQUIST, H. L.
Ferns of North Carolina. Durham: 1934. V. 68

BLONDEL, JACQUES
Emily Bronte, Experience Spirituelle et Creation Poetique. 1955. V. 73

BLONDEL, JACQUES FRANCOIS
De La Distribution des Maisons de Plaisance. Paris: 1737-1738. V. 72

BLONDELLO, DAVIDE
De Ioanna Papissas ive Famous' Qu'stionis, an Femina ulla Inter Leonem IV and Benedictum III, Romanos Pontifices, Media Sederit, Anakrisis. Amsterdam: 1657. V. 72

BLOOM, AMY
Come to Me. New York: 1993. V. 70; 71; 72
Love Invents Us. New York: 1996. V. 71
Love Invents Us. New York: 1997. V. 72

BLOOM, HAROLD
Ruin the Sacred Truths. Cambridge: 1989. V. 69

BLOOM, J. HARVEY
English Seals. London: 1906. V. 72

BLOOM, URSULA
Better to Marry. New York: 1933. V. 71

BLOOMFIELD, J. A.
Lakes of New York State. New York: 1978. V. 72

BLOOMFIELD, ROBERT
The Banks of Wye. London: 1811. V. 68; 70; 71; 72; 73
The Banks of Wye: a Poem. London: 1813. V. 73
The Farmer's Boy. London: 1800. V. 73
The Farmer's Boy. London: 1827. V. 73
The Farmer's Boy. London: 1857. V. 70; 71
Good Tidings; or, New from the Farm. A Poem. London: 1804. V. 73
Hazelwood Hall: a Village Drama. London: 1823. V. 73
May Day with the Muses. London: 1822. V. 73
The Poems of.... Burlington: 1803. V. 69
Rural Tales, Ballads and Songs. London: 1802. V. 71; 72; 73
Wild Flowers, or, Pastoral and Local Poetry. London: 1806. V. 68; 70; 73

BLORE, EDWARD
The Monumental Remains of Noble and Eminent Persons. 1824-1826. V. 70
The Monumental Remains of Noble and Eminent Persons. 1826. V. 68
The Monumental Remains of Noble And Eminent Persons. London: 1826. V. 70; 72

BLOSS, C. A.
Heroines of the Crusades. Auburn: 1853. V. 73

BLOUNT, CHARLES
Anima Mundi, or an Historical Narration of the Opinions of the Ancients Concerning Man's Soul.... London: 1679,. V. 72

BLOUNT, THOMAS
Boscobel; or the Compleat History of the Most Miraculous Preservation of King Charles II after the Battle of Worcester, September the 3d 1651. London: 1725. V. 73
Fragmenta Antiquitatis. Antient Tenures of Land and Jocular Customs of Some Manors Made Publick for the Diversion of Some and Instruction of Others. London: 1679. V. 70; 72
Glossographia Anglicana Nova; or a Dictionary, Interpreting Such Hard Words of Whatever Language, as Are Present Used in the English Tongue, with their Etymologies.... 1719. V. 73

BLOUNT, THOMAS POPE
De Re Poetica; or, Remarks Upon Poetry. London: 1694. V. 69; 73

BLOWER, ELIZABETH
Features from Life; or, a Summer Visit. Dublin: 1788. V. 73

BLUE Beard. New York: 1882. V. 70

THE BLUE Beard Picture Book. London: 1875. V. 72

BLUE Book of American Shipping. Cleveland: 1896-. V. 71

THE BLUE Review: Literature, Drama, Art, Music. Volume 1 Number 1. London: 1913. V. 73

BLUEBELL, Kingcups and Mignionette: the Bouquet, Culled from Marylebone Gardens. London: 1852. V. 73

BLUETT, EDGAR E.
Chinese Pottery and Porcelain in the Collection of Mr. and Mrs. Alfred Clark. 1934. V. 70

BLUME, CARL LUDWIG
Flora Javae.... Brussels: 1828-1851. V. 70; 73
Flora Javae.... Brussels: 1829-1830. V. 70; 73
Portions of Flora Javae and Rumphia.... Brussels; Leiden: 1847-1848. V. 73

BLUMENBACH, JOHAN FRIEDRICH
Decas Collectionis Suae Craniorum diversaum Gentium Illustrata. Gottingen: 1790-1800. V. 70

BLUMENFIELD, RALPH
Home Town. New York. V. 71

BLUMENSON, MARTIN
The Patton Papers. Boston: 1972-1974. V. 68
Patton: the Man Behind the Legend 1885-1945. New York: 1985. V. 68

BLUMENTHAL, JOSEPH
Art of the Printed Book 1455-1955: Masterpieces of Typography through Five Centuries from the Collections of the Pierpont Morgan Library. New York: 1973. V. 70
The Printed Book in America. London: 1977. V. 69

BLUMGART, HERMAN L.
Congestive Heart Failure and Angina Pectoris. The Therapeutic Effect of Thyroidectomy on Patients Without Clinical or Pathologic Evidence of Thyroid Toxicity. Chicago: 1933. V. 72

BLUNDELL, NICHOLAS
Blundells's Diary. Comprising Selections From The Diary Of Nicholas Blundell, Esq., From 1702 to 1728. Crosby Records Series. Liverpool: 1895. V. 72

BLUNDELL, R. H.
Trial of Buck Ruxton. London: 1937. V. 73

BLUNDEN, EDMUND
The Church of the Holy Trinity Long Melford. Long Melford: 1966. V. 73
Halfway House. London: 1932. V. 68
Near and Far: New Poems. London;: 1929. V. 73
Pastorals: A Book of Verses. London: 1916. V. 71; 73
Poems by E. C. Blunden of Christ's Hospital 1913 and 1914. 1914. V. 73
Poems Translated from the French (July 1913-January 1914). 1914. V. 73
Retreat (New Sonnets and Poems). 1928. V. 73
A Summer's Fancy. London: 1930. V. 73
Undertones of War. 1928. V. 73
Undertones of War. London: 1928. V. 72

BLUNDEN, WILLIAM
William Crowe B.C.L. Beaminster, Dorset: 1963. V. 68

BLUNT, A.
Baroque and Rococo: Architecture and Decoration. London: 1978. V. 69; 72
Isfahan, Pear of Persia. London: 1966. V. 72
Nicolas Poussin. New York: 1967. V. 69; 72

BLUNT, CHARLES
The Beauty of the Heavens: a Pictorial Display of the Astronomical Phenomena of the Universe. London: 1845. V. 71
An Essay on Mechanical Drawing, Comprising an Elementary Course of Practice in the Perspective Delineation of Machinery. London: 1811. V. 71

BLUNT, D. E.
Elephant. 1933. V. 73

BLUNT, JOSEPH
The Merchant's and Shipmaster's Assistant.... New York: 1822. V. 73

BLUNT, JOSEPH continued
The Shipmaster's Assistant and Commercial Digest. New York: 1837. V. 68

BLUNT, REGINALD
The Carlyles' Chelsea Home, Being Some Account of No. 5, Cheyne Row. London: 1895. V. 72
Paradise Row or a Broken Piece of Old Chelsea Being the Curious and Diverting Annals of a Famous Village Street Newly Destroyed Together with Particulars of Sundry Noble and Notable Persons Who in Former Times Dwelt There.... London: 1906. V. 73
Red Anchor Pieces. London: 1928. V. 73

BLUNT, WILFRED
The Ark in the Park. London: 1976. V. 68
The Art of Botanical Illustration. London: 1950. V. 72
The Art of Botanical Illustration. London: 1955. V. 71; 72; 73
The Art of Botanical Illustration. London: 1971. V. 72
The Compleat Naturalist, a Life of Linnaeus. New York: 1971. V. 72
Gerard van Spaendonck: Flowers Drawn from Nature.... Sharpthorne: 1957. V. 71; 73

BLUNT, WILFRID
Cockerell. Sydney Cockerell, Friend of Ruskin and William Morris and Director of the Fitzwilliam Museum, Cambridge. New York: 1965. V. 70
John Christie of Glyndebourne. London: 1968. V. 68

BLUNT, WILFRID SCAWEN
In Vinculis. 1889. V. 71
In Vinculis. London: 1889. V. 73
The Love Lyrics and Songs of Proteus. With the Love Sonnets of Proteus. Hammersmith: 1892. V. 68
The Love Sonnets of Proteus. London: 1881. V. 68; 73
A New Pilgrimage and other Poems. London: 1889. V. 68; 73
Sonnets and Songs. London: 1875. V. 73

BLUNT, WILLIAM O.
A Thousand Years of the Church in Chester-le-Street. London. V. 73

BLY, ROBERT
Iron John. New York: 1990. V. 69
Visiting Emily Dickinson's Grave and Other Poems. Madison: 1979. V. 73

BLYTON, ENID
ABC with Noddy. 1959. V. 72
ABC with Noddy. London: 1959. V. 68
The Adventures of Binkle and Flip. London: 1950. V. 73
The Adventures of Mr. Pink-Whistler. London: 1942. V. 71
The Adventures of Scamp. 1943. V. 72; 73
Adventures of the Wishing Chair. London: 1937. V. 69; 70
Adventures of the Wishing Chair. 1960. V. 72
The Adventures of the Wishing Chair. 1964. V. 73
The Adventures of the Wishing Chair. London: 1968. V. 72
The Adventurous Four. 1950. V. 73
The Adventurous Four Again. 1963. V. 73
Aesop's Fables Reading Practice. 1925. V. 72
Amelia Jane Again. 1946. V. 72
Away Goes Sooty. 1955. V. 72
The Bad Little Monkey, an Enid Blyton Picture Book. 1946. V. 72
The Bad Little Monkey, an Enid Blyton Picture Book. London: 1946. V. 70
Be Brave Little Noddy. 1956. V. 72
Before I Go to Sleep. 1947. V. 72
Benny and the Princess. 1951. V. 68; 71
Benny and the Princess. London: 1951. V. 69
The Big Noddy Book. Number 3. London: 1953. V. 68
Billy-Bob Tales. London: 1943. V. 71
The Bird Book. London: 1926. V. 69
Bom and the Rainbow. 1959. V. 71
Bom Goes to Magic Town. 1960. V. 71; 73
A Book of Little Plays Reading Practice. 1927. V. 73
A Book of Naughty Children. London: 1947. V. 72; 73
The Boy Who Wanted a Dog. 1963. V. 72
Boys' & Girls' Story Book No. 2. 1934. V. 68
Boys' & Girls' Story Book No. 3. 1935. V. 73
Boys' & Girls' Story Book No. 5. 1937. V. 69; 71; 72; 73
Brer Rabbit. 1940. V. 72
The Brown Family. 1945. V. 71; 72
Bumpy and His Bus. London: 1943. V. 68
The Buttercup Farm Family. 1961. V. 73
The Caravan Family. London: 1945. V. 69
The Castle of Adventure. 1905. V. 72
The Castle of Adventure. London: 1946. V. 71
The Castle of Adventure. 1950. V. 68; 71
The Castle of Adventure. London: 1952. V. 70
The Castle of Adventure. 1957. V. 72
The Children of Kidillin. London: 1946. V. 69
The Christmas Book. 1946. V. 73
Circus Days Again. 1952. V. 73
The Circus of Adventure. 1952. V. 72
The Circus of Adventure. London: 1952. V. 70; 71
The Circus of Adventure. 1966. V. 68
Claudine at St. Clare's. London: 1961. V. 72

Come Along Twins. 1952. V. 72; 73
Come Along Twins. Brockhampton: 1952. V. 68
Come Along Twins. London: 1952. V. 70
Down at the Farm with Enid Blyton. London: 1951. V. 72
The Enchanted Wood. London: 1949. V. 68
The Enchanted Wood. London: 1952. V. 69
Enid Blyton Gay Story Book. 1952. V. 72
The Enid Blyton Holiday Book. London: 1958. V. 68
Enid Blyton's Animal Lover's Book. 1952. V. 72
Enid Blyton's BOM Annual. 1958. V. 72
Enid Blyton's Book of the Year. 1959. V. 72; 73
Enid Blyton's Circus Book. 1949. V. 69
Enid Blyton's Eighth Brer Rabbit Book. London: 1958. V. 70
Enid Blyton's Fourth Brer Rabbit Book. 1955. V. 72
Enid Blyton's Jolly Story Book. 1955. V. 68
Enid Blyton's Jolly Story Book. London: 1955. V. 69
Enid Blyton's Jolly Story Book. 1959. V. 72; 73
Enid Blyton's Road Safety Colouring Book. 1948. V. 69
Enid Blyton's Robin Hood Book. 1949. V. 72; 73
Enid Blyton's Robin Hood Book. London: 1949. V. 70
Enid Blyton's Second Brer Rabbit Book. 1954. V. 72
Enid Blyton's Seventh Brer Rabbit Book. London: 1957. V. 70
Enid Blyton's Sunny Story Book. 1945. V. 72
Enid Blyton's Sunny Story Book. 1951. V. 73
Entertaining Stories for Children.... 1929. V. 72
The Family at Red-Roofs. 1959. V. 69
The Famous Big Five Book.... 1964. V. 72
The Famous Five Special. London: 1959. V. 70
The Famous Jimmy. 1936. V. 71
The Famous Jimmy. 1942. V. 68
The Faraway Tree. London: 1964. V. 70
Father Christmas and Belinds. London: 1951. V. 73
The Fifth Holiday Book. London: 1950. V. 70; 72
First Term at Malory Towers. London: 1955. V. 69
Five Are Together Again. 1963. V. 71; 73
Five are Together Again. London: 1963. V. 69
Five Fall into Adventure. 1950. V. 71; 72; 73
Five Fall into Adventure. London: 1950. V. 69; 70
Five Get Into a Fix. 1958. V. 68
Five Get Into a Fix. London: 1958. V. 69; 72
Five Get Into Trouble. 1949. V. 68; 72
Five Get Into Trouble. London: 1949. V. 69; 70; 72
Five Get Into Trouble. 1950. V. 71
Five Go Adventuring Again. 1943. V. 72
Five Go Adventuring Again. London: 1943. V. 70
Five Go Adventuring Again. 1950. V. 73
Five Go Down to the Sea. 1953. V. 68; 71; 72; 73
Five Go Down to the Sea. London: 1953. V. 69; 70
Five Go Off in a Caravan. London: 1948. V. 69
Five Go Off in a Caravan. 1949. V. 73
Five Go Off in a Caravan. London: 1949. V. 71
Five Go Off in a Caravan. London: 1950. V. 72
Five Go Off to Camp. 1948. V. 72
Five Go Off to Camp. 1950. V. 71
Five Go Off to Camp. 1952. V. 68
Five Go to Demon's Rocks. 1961. V. 68; 71
Five Go to Demon's Rocks. London: 1961. V. 69; 70
Five Go to Mystery Moor. 1954. V. 71; 72; 73
Five Go to Mystery Moor. London: 1954. V. 69; 70
Five Go to Smuggler's Top. 1949. V. 68
Five Go to the Billycock Hill. 1957. V. 68
Five Go to the Billycock Hill. London: 1957. V. 69
Five Go to the Smuggler's Top. London: 1949. V. 70
Five Have a Mystery to Solve. 1962. V. 68; 73
Five Have a Mystery to Solve. London: 1962. V. 69; 70
Five Have a Wonderful Time. 1952. V. 68; 71; 72
Five Have a Wonderful Time. London: 1952. V. 69
Five Have Plenty of Fun. London: 1955. V. 69; 70
Five on a Hike Together. 1951. V. 68; 72
Five on a Hike Together. London: 1951. V. 69; 70; 71
Five on a Secret Trail. 1956. V. 68
Five on a Secret Trail. London: 1956. V. 69; 70
Five on a Treasure Island. 1947. V. 68
Five on a Treasure Island. London: 1947. V. 70
Five on a Treasure Island. 1949. V. 73
Five On Finniston Farm. 1960. V. 72
Five on Finniston Farm. Chicago: 1961. V. 72
Five Run Away Together. London: 1950. V. 70
Four in a Family. 1956. V. 72
Fun for the Secret Seven. 1963. V. 73
Fun for the Secret Seven. Brockhampton: 1963. V. 69
Good Old Secret Seven. Brockhampton: 1960. V. 69
The Green Goblin Book. 1935. V. 71; 72; 73
Happy Day Stories. 1960. V. 71; 72

BLYTON, ENID continued
Happy Day Stories. London: 1960. V. 69
Here Comes Noddy Again. 1951. V. 72
How Funny You Are Noddy. London: 1954. V. 68; 70
I'll Tell You Another Story. 1943. V. 71; 72; 73
I'll Tell You Another Story. London: 1943. V. 70
The Island of Adventure. 1949. V. 73
The Island of Adventure. 1956. V. 72
The Island of Adventure. 1994. V. 68
Last Term at Malory Towers. London: 1967. V. 72
Let's Garden. 1948. V. 69; 72
Let's Go to the Circus. 1951. V. 68
Look Out Secret Seven. 1962. V. 71
Look Out Secret Seven. Brockhampton: 1962. V. 68
Look Out Secret Seven. London: 1962. V. 70
Merry Mister Meddle. London: 1966. V. 69
Mr. Galliano's Circus. London: 1939. V. 69; 70
Mr. Meddle's Mischief. London: 1947. V. 72
Mr. Meddle's Mischief. 1960. V. 72
Mr. Pink-Whistle Interferes. 1951. V. 72
Mr. Tumpy and His Caravan. 1949. V. 71
The Mountain of Adventure. 1949. V. 72
The Mountain of Adventure. London: 1949. V. 70; 71
The Mountain of Adventure. 1958. V. 73
My Second Nature Book. The Spell That Went Wrong. London: 1953. V. 68; 69; 71
The Mystery of Banshee Towers. London: 1961. V. 68; 69; 72
The Mystery of Tally-Ho Cottage. 1954. V. 71
The Mystery of Tally-Ho Cottage. London: 1954. V. 72; 73
The Mystery of Tally-Ho Cottage. 1958. V. 72
The Mystery of Tally-Ho Cottage. London: 1960. V. 68
The Mystery of the Burnt Cottage. London: 1943. V. 73
The Mystery of the Disappearing Cat. London: 1944. V. 69
The Mystery of the Disappearing Cat. London: 1949. V. 68
The Mystery of the Hidden House. 1949. V. 71
The Mystery of the Hidden House. London: 1949. V. 69
The Mystery of the Invisible Thief. London: 1950. V. 68
The Mystery of the Invisible Thief. London: 1952. V. 69
The Mystery of the Invisible Thief. 1959. V. 71
The Mystery of the Invisible Thief. London: 1959. V. 73
The Mystery of the Invisible Thief. 1960. V. 72
The Mystery of the Missing Man. London: 1956. V. 69; 72; 73
The Mystery of the Missing Man. 1962. V. 68
The Mystery of the Missing Necklace. London: 1957. V. 70; 72
The Mystery of the Missing Necklace. London: 1961. V. 72
The Mystery of the Pantomime Cat. 1955. V. 68
The Mystery of the Pantomime Cat. London: 1955. V. 72
The Mystery of the Pantomime Cat. 1961. V. 72
The Mystery of the Secret Room. 1961. V. 71
The Mystery of the Spiteful Letters. 1958. V. 68
The Mystery of the Strange Bundle. 1952. V. 71
The Mystery of the Strange Bundle. London: 1952. V. 68
The Mystery of the Strange Messages. London: 1957. V. 69; 71; 72
The Mystery that Never Was. London: 1961. V. 73
The Naughtiest Girl Again. London: 1942. V. 68
The Naughtiest Girl Again. London: 1943. V. 69
The Naughtiest Girl in the School. London: 1942. V. 68
The Naughtiest Girl in the School. London: 1951. V. 72; 73
The Naughtiest Girl in the School. London: 1958. V. 69
The Naughtiest Girl is a Monitor. London: 1945. V. 70
The Naughtiest Girl is a Monitor. London: 1953. V. 69
The Naughtiest Girl is a Monitor. 1956. V. 72
Naughty Amelia Jane. 1942. V. 72; 73
The New Big Noddy Book. Number 4. London: 1954. V. 69
Noddy a Purnell Shape Book. 1973. V. 68
Noddy Album of Chivers Farm Animals. 1955. V. 70
Noddy Album of Chivers Farm Animals. Chivers: 1955. V. 68
Noddy and the Noah's Ark. London: 1967. V. 68
Noddy and the Tootles. London: 1967. V. 70
Noddy Be Careful!. London: 1957. V. 68; 71
Noddy Goes to Toyland. London: 1949. V. 72
Noddy Meets Father Christmas. London: 1955. V. 71
Noddy's ABC Pop-Up Picture Book. 1968. V. 69
Noddy's Book of British Birds. 1955. V. 72
Noddy's Book of British Birds. London: 1955. V. 70
Noddy's Castle of Books. London: 1954. V. 68
Noddy's New Big Book. Number 7. London: 1957. V. 68; 71
Noddy's Toyland Train Picture Book. 1961. V. 68
Old English Stories Read Practice. 1925. V. 72
Omnibus!. London. V. 73
The O'Sullivan Twins. London: 1954. V. 69
A Picnic Party with Enid Blyton. 1951. V. 72
The Plays the Thing!. 1923. V. 68; 73
The Plays the Thing!. 1927. V. 71; 72
The Put-em-Rights. 1946. V. 69; 71

Puzzle for the Secret Seven. 1958. V. 71; 72
Puzzle for the Secret Seven. London: 1958. V. 70
The Rat-a-Tat Mystery. 1956. V. 68; 73
The Rat-a-Tat Mystery. London: 1956. V. 69; 70
Real Fairies. 1923. V. 68; 71; 72; 73
Real Fairies. London: 1923. V. 70
Responsive Singing Games. 1923. V. 71
Ring O'Bells Mystery. 1951. V. 72
Ring O'Bells Mystery. London: 1951. V. 70
The River of Adventure. 1955. V. 72; 73
The River of Adventure. London: 1955. V. 69; 70; 71
The River of Adventure. 1964. V. 68
The Rockingdown Mystery. 1949. V. 72
The Rockingdown Mystery. London: 1949. V. 69; 70
Round the Clock Stories. London: 1945. V. 69
The Rubadub Mystery. 1952. V. 72; 73
The Rubadub Mystery. London: 1952. V. 70
The Saucy Jane Family. 1947. V. 69
The Sea of Adventure. 1948. V. 72
The Sea of Adventure. New York: 1948. V. 69; 71
The Sea of Adventure. 1949. V. 73
The Sea of Adventure. 1958. V. 72
Second Form at Malory Towers. London: 1949. V. 68
Second Form at Malory Towers. London: 1956. V. 73
Second Form at Malory Towers. London: 1959. V. 69
The Second Form at St. Clare's. London: 1959. V. 68
The Secret of Cliff Castle. London: 1955. V. 69
The Secret Seven. 1949. V. 72; 73
The Secret Seven. Brockhampton: 1949. V. 69
The Secret Seven. London: 1949. V. 70
Secret Seven Annual: Secret Seven Adventure. 1981. V. 68
Secret Seven Fireworks. 1959. V. 71; 72; 73
Secret Seven Fireworks. London: 1959. V. 70
Secret Seven Go on the Trail. 1952. V. 72
Secret Seven Mystery. Brockhampton. V. 69
Secret Seven Mystery. 1957. V. 72; 73
Secret Seven on the Trail. London: 1952. V. 70
Shadow, the Sheep Dog. 1943. V. 72
Shadow, the Sheep Dog. London: 1943. V. 73
The Ship of Adventure. London: 1950. V. 68; 69; 70; 72
The Ship of Adventure. 1952. V. 73
The Ship of Adventure. 1955. V. 72
Shock for the Secret Seven. 1961. V. 72
Shock for the Secret Seven. Brockhampton: 1961. V. 69
Silver and Gold. 1925. V. 71
Silver and Gold. London and Edinburgh: 1925. V. 72
Silver and Gold. 1930. V. 72; 73
The Six Bad Boys. 1951. V. 69; 71
Six O'Clock Tales. London: 1945. V. 68
Smuggler Ben. London: 1950. V. 69
Songs for Infants. London: 1949. V. 71
The Story of My Life. 1952. V. 72; 73
A Story Party at Green Hedges. London: 1949. V. 69
The Strange Tale of Mr. Wumble. 1940. V. 72
Summer Term at St. Clare's. London: 1950. V. 68
Summer Term at St. Clare's. London: 1959. V. 72; 73
Tales About Toys. 1950. V. 72
The Talking Teapot. 1940. V. 72
The Third Holiday Book. London: 1948. V. 70
Third Year at Malory Towers. London: 1962. V. 73
The Three Golliwogs. London: 1946. V. 70
The Three Golliwogs. London: 1947. V. 69
The Three Golliwogs. 1952. V. 72
Too Wise The Wonderful Wizard. 1951. V. 71
The Train that Lost Its Way: an Enid Blyton Picture Book. 1944. V. 73
Tricky the Goblin. 1950. V. 73
Twenty Minute Tales. London: 1944. V. 69; 72
Twenty Minute Tales. London: 1947. V. 70
The Twins at St. Clare's. 1943. V. 71
The Twins at St. Clare's. London: 1943. V. 69
The Twins at St. Clare's. London: 1949. V. 72
The Twins at St. Clare's. London: 1953. V. 68; 73
Upper Fourth at Malory Towers. London: 1949. V. 73
The Valley of Adventure. 1957. V. 72; 73
Well Done Noddy!. 1952. V. 72
Well Done, Secret Seven!. 1951. V. 72
Well Done, Secret Seven!. London: 1951. V. 70
What an Adventure. 1950. V. 72
What an Adventure. London: 1950. V. 70
The Wilfred Pickles Gay Street Book. 1949. V. 68
The Wishing Chair Again. 1950. V. 73
The Wishing Chair Again. 1959. V. 72
The Wishing Chair Again. London: 1959. V. 69; 71
The Wishing Chair Again. 1967. V. 72

BLYTON, ENID continued
The Wishing Chair Again. London: 1967. V. 68; 70
The Yellow Fairy Book. 1936. V. 71
You Funny Little Noddy. London: 1955. V. 71

BOADEN, JAMES
An Inquiry into the Authenticity of Various Pictures and Prints, Which, from the Decease of the Poet to Our Own Times.... London: 1824. V. 72
The Life of Mrs. Jordan.... London: 1831. V. 71

BOARDING-OUT Pauper Children: Report of a Public Meeting to Promote the Extension of This System. Birmingham: 1870. V. 68

BOARDMAN, BESS
Sincerely Yours. San Francisco: 1952. V. 73

BOARDMAN, JOHN
The European Community in Later Pre-History: Studies in Honour of C. F. C. Hawkes. 1971. V. 69

BOARDMAN, PETER
Sacred Summits. 1982. V. 70; 73
Sacred Summits. London: 1982. V. 69
The Shining Mountain. 1978. V. 73
The Shining Mountain. London: 1978. V. 69
The Shining Mountain. New York: 1982. V. 69

BOARDMAN, RUBY
Poems. London: 1928. V. 70
Saint Tropez: Poems and a Drawing. London: 1932. V. 70

BOARDMAN, SAMUEL LANE
The Naturalist of the Saint Croix. Bangor: 1903. V. 73

BOAS, FRANZ
Materials for the Study of Inheritance in Man. New York: 1928. V. 68
The Mind of Primitive Man. New York: 1911. V. 71
Native Americans, Kathlamet Texts. Washington;: 1901. V. 68
Primitive Art. Oslo: 1927. V. 69

BOASE, HENRY
Guineas an Unnecessary and Expensive Incumbrance on Commerce.... London: 1802. V. 71

BOATRIGHT, MODY C.
From Hell to Breakfast. Austin/Dallas: 1944. V. 69

BOAZ, H.
The Angler's Progress. 1820. V. 68

BOB Norberry; or Sketches from the Note Book of an Irish Reporter. Dublin: 1844. V. 68

BOBBS, HOWARD
New Mexico Watercolors. Santa Fe: 1980. V. 72

BOBBY Bear's Annual. 1941. V. 71

BOBBY Bear's Annual (1939). V. 71

BOBROW, JILL
Classic Yacht Interiors. London: 1983. V. 72

BOCCACCIO, GIOVANNI
Amorous Fiammetta. London: 1929. V. 73
Contes et Nouvelles. Cologne: 1702. V. 68
The Decameron. London: 1822. V. 71
The Decameron. London: 1903. V. 71
The Decameron. New York: 1925. V. 69
The Decameron. London: 1930. V. 71
The Decameron. New York: 1930. V. 69
The Decameron. New York: 1940. V. 70
The Decameron. Garden City: 1949. V. 72
Il Decamerone. 1702. V. 71
Le Decameron.... Londres (Paris): 1757-1761. V. 69
Il Decamerone. London: 1702. V. 72
Life of Dante. New York: 1900. V. 68
The Nymphs of Fiesole. Verona: 1952. V. 71
Tales From Boccaccio. London: 1899. V. 72

BOCCALINI, TRAJANO
Pietra del Paragone Politico. Cosmpoli: 1671. V. 71

BOCCONE, PAOLO
Icones & Descriptiones Rariorum Plantarum Siciliae, Melitae, Galliae & Italiae. London: 1674. V. 68; 71
Museo di Fisica e di Esperienze Variato e Decorato di Osservazioni Naturali, Note Medicinali, e Ragionamenti Secondo i Principii de'Moderni.... Venice: 1697. V. 68

BOCHART, SAMUEL
Geographia Sacra. Frankfurt: 1681. V. 72

BOCK, J.
Pop Winer, Naive Painter. 1974. V. 68

BOCKLER, GEORG ANDREAS
Theatrum Machinarum Novum, Das Ist: Neuvermehrter Schauplatz der Mechanischen Kunsten. Nuremberg: 1661. V. 69

BODDIE, JOHN BENNETT
Seventeenth Century Isle of Wight County, Virginia. Chicago: 1938. V. 70

BODDIE, WILLIAM WILLIS
History of Williamsburg. Columbia: 1923. V. 68

BODDING, P. O.
Studies in Santal Medicine and Connected Folklore. Calcutta: 1925-1940. V. 71

BODDINGTON, C.
America, The Men and Their Guns That Made Her Great. Los Angeles: 1981. V. 72
Deer Hunting Coast to Coast. 1990. V. 69

BODDY, E. MANCHESTER
Japanese in America. Los Angeles: 1921. V. 68

BODE, WILHELM
Antique Rugs from the Near East. New York: 1922. V. 68

BODE, WINSTON
A Portrait of Pancho. Austin: 1965. V. 69

BODENHEIM, MAXWELL
New York Madness. New York: 1933. V. 71
Replenishing Jessica. New York: 1925. V. 72

BODENS, CHARLES
The Modish Couple. London: 1732. V. 69

BODIN, ED
Scare Me! A Symposium on Ghosts and Black Magic. New York: 1940. V. 69

BODINI, JEAN
Io. Bodoni Andeg. In Parisovm Sentatv Advocati Methodvs, ad Facilem Historiavm Cognitionem. Parisiis: 1572. V. 70

BODKIN, M.
Dora Myrl: the Lady Detective. London: 1900. V. 71; 73

BODKIN, THOMAS
Hugh Lane and His Pictures. 1932. V. 70

BODMER, KARL
People of the First Man: Life Among the Plains Indians in Their Final Days of Glory. New York: 1976. V. 69

BODONI, GIOVANNI BATTISTA
Manuale Tipografico. Parma: 1818. V. 68
Manuale Tipografico 1788. Verona: 1968. V. 70; 71
Le Piu Pitture Parmensi Indicate Agli Amatori delle Belle Arti. Parma: 1809. V. 68

BOEHME, JACOB
The Third Booke of the Author, Being the High and Deepe Searching Out of the Threefold Life of Man through (or According to) the Three Principles. London: 1650. V. 69
The Third Booke of the Authour, Being the High and Deepe Searching Out of the Threefold Life of Man Through (or According to) the Three Principles. London: 1850. V. 73

BOEHME, S. E.
Seth Eastman. A Portfolio of North American Indians. Afton: 1995. V. 69

BOEHN, MAX VON
Dolls and Puppets. London: 1932. V. 72

BOELTER, HOMER R.
Portfolio of Hopi Kachinas. Hollywood: 1969. V. 68

BOER, J. G. W.
The Geonomoid Palms. Amsterdam: 1968. V. 72

BOERHAAVE, HERMANN
Abrege de la Theorie Chymique. Paris: 1741. V. 69
Atrocis, Nec Descripti Prius, Morbi Historia. Secundum Medicae Artis Leges Conscripta ab Hermanno Boerhaave. (with) Atrocis Rarissimique Morbi Historia Altera. Conscripta ab Hermanno Boerhaave. Leyden: 1724. V. 68; 72
De Morbis Oculorum. Gottingae: 1750. V. 72
Historia Plantarum, Quae in Horto Academico Lugduni-Batavorum Crescunt. Rome: 1727. V. 69
A New Method of Chemistry. London: 1753. V. 70
Opusculum Anatomicum de Fabrica Glandularum in Corpore Humano, Continens Binas Epistolas. Leyden: 1722. V. 72
Praelectiones Academicae De Morbis Nervorum Quas ex Auditorum Manuscriptis Collectas Edi Curavit Jacobus van Eems, Medicus Leydensis.... Venetiis: 1762. V. 68
Praxis Medica Boerhaavena. London: 1716. V. 72

BOESEN, GUDMUND
Old Danish Silver. Copenhagen: 1949. V. 72

BOETHIUS
Summum Bonum, or an Explication of the Divine Goodness. Oxford: 1674. V. 69

BOGAN, LOUISE
The Blue Estuaries. Poems 1923-1968. New York: 1968. V. 69; 72
A Final Antidote from the Journals of Louise Bogan. Omaha: 1991. V. 73

BOGAN, P. M.
Yaqui Indian Dances of Tucson, Arizona. Tucson: 1925. V. 69

BOGAN, ZACHARY
(Greek title, then) Compartio Homeri cum Scriptoribus Sacris Quoad Normam Loquendi. Oxoniae: 1658. V. 70

BOGARDE, DIRK
A Particular Friendship. London: 1989. V. 70
A Postillion Struck by Lightning. London: 1977. V. 72

BOGDANOVICH, PETER
Who the Devil Made It. New York: 1997. V. 72

BOGDANOW, FANNI
The Romance of the Grail - a Study of the Structure and Genesis of a Thirteenth Century Arthurian Prose Romance. Manchester: 1966. V. 69

BOGER, A. J.
The Road I Travelled. 1936. V. 73

BOGERT, FRANK M.
Palm Spring First Hundred Years. Palm Springs. V. 73

BOGG, EDMUND
From Edenvale to the Plains of York. London. V. 73
The Golden Vale of Mowbray. London: 1909. V. 73
Lakeland and Ribblesdale. Leeds: 1898. V. 71
Lower Wharfeland: The Old City of York and the Ainsty, the Region of Historic Memories. London: 1904. V. 73
Nidderdale: and the Vale of the Nidd from Nun Monkton to Great Whernside. Leeds. V. 73
The Old Kingdom of Elmet: York and the Ainsty District. London: 1902. V. 73
Richmondshire: An Account of its History and Antiquities, Characters and Customs Legendary Lore and Natural History. Elliot Stock and Leeds: 1908. V. 73
A Thousand Miles in Wharfedale and the Wharfe. London. V. 73
A Thousand Miles of Wandering Along the Roman Wall, the Old Border Region, Lakeland and Ribblesdale. Leeds: 1898. V. 71; 73
Two Thousand Miles in Wharfedale. London: 1904. V. 73
Two Thousand Miles of Wandering in the Border Country, Lakeland and Ribblesdale. Leeds: 1898. V. 71; 73
The Vale of Mowbray. Elliot Stock and Leeds: 1908. V. 73
Wensleydale. Leeds. V. 73

BOGGS, K. D.
Prints and Plants of Old Gardens. Richmond: 1932. V. 71; 73

BOGGS, MAE HELENE BACON
My Playhouse Was a Concord Coach an Anthology of Newspaper Clippings and Documents Relating to Those Who Made California History During the Years 1822-1888. 1942. V. 68

BOGGS, VERNON W.
Salsiology. Afro-Cuban Music and the Evolution of Salsa in New York City. Westport: 1992. V. 72

BOGGS, WILLIAM ROBERTSON
Military Reminiscences of General Wm. R. Boggs, C.S.A. Durham: 1913. V. 69; 70

BOGOSIAN, ERIC
Pounding Nails in the Floor With My Forehead. New York: 1994. V. 70

BOGUE, DAVID
Baths and Bathing. London: 1879. V. 68
Baths and Bathing. London: 1880. V. 68

BOHART, R. M.
Sphecid Wasps of the World: A Generic Revision. Berkeley: 1976. V. 69

BOHLIN, DIANE DE GRAZIA
Prints and Related Drawings by the Carracci Family: a Catalogue Raisonne. Bloomington: 1979. V. 73

BOHLIN, EDWARD H.
Catalog of The World's Finest Riding Equipment Accessories and Silver & Leather Goods. Hollywood: 1941. V. 68

BOHLKE, J. E.
Fishes of the Bahamas and Adjacent Tropical Waters. 1968. V. 69
Fishes of the Bahamas and Adjacent Tropical Waters. Wynnewood: 1968. V. 73

BOHMAN, NILS
Jim, Jock and Jumbo. New York: 1946. V. 72

BOHM-BAWERK, EUGEN V.
Karl Marx and the Close of His System. London: 1898. V. 69

BOHN, HENRY
Bibliotheca Parriana. A Catalogue of the Library of the Late Reverend and Learned Samuel Parr, LL.D. London: 1827. V. 70

BOHN, HENRY G.
The Hand-Book of Games. London: 1850. V. 69; 70

BOHR, NIELS
Atomic Physics and Human Knowledge. New York: 1958. V. 69
On the Constitution of Atoms and Molecules. Parts I-III in The London, Edinburgh and Dublin Philosophical Magazine and Journal of Science, Sixth Series. Number CLI. July 1913. London: 1913. V. 72
Studier Over Metallernes Elektrontheorie. Copenhagen: 1911. V. 68

BOHTE, J.
Catalogue of Books in English Literature Offered at Greatly Reduced Prices, for Ready Money. London: 1822. V. 70

BOHUN, EDMUND
The Justice of Peace His Calling. London: 1684. V. 69

BOIASTUAU, PIERRE
Histoires Prodigieuses. Colophon Paris: 1560. V. 73

BOIES, ANDREW J.
Record of the Thirty-Third Massachusetts Volunteer Infantry from Aug. 1862 to Aug. 1865. Fitchburg: 1880. V. 68

BOILEAU, DANIEL
Counsels at Home; Interspersed with Entertaining Tales and Interesting Anecdotes. London: 1831. V. 68; 72

BOILEAU, ETHEL
A Gay Family. New York: 1936. V. 70

BOILEAU, PIERRE
The Living and the Dead. New York: 1957. V. 71
Spells of Evil. London: 1961. V. 68; 72
The Woman Who Was No More. New York: 1954. V. 68; 71; 73

BOILEAU DESPREAUX, NICOLAS
The Art of Poetry. London: 1683. V. 73
Oeuvres. Paris: 1798. V. 69
Oeuvres Diverses. Amsterdam: 1702. V. 72

BOISGELIN, LOUIS DE
Ancient and Modern Malta. London: 1805. V. 72

BOISGUILLEBERT, PIERRE LE PESANT DE
The Life of Mary Stewart, Queen of Scotland And France. Edinburgh;: 1725. V. 73

BOISSEREE, SULPIZ
Geschichte und Beschreibung des Doms von Koln, Nebst Untersuchungen Uber die Alte Kirchenbau-Kunst.... Stuttgart: 1823-. V. 70; 72

BOIVIN, MARIE ANNE VICTORIE
Memorial de l'Art des Accouchemens, ou Principes Fondes sur La Pratique de l'Hospice de la Maternite De Paris.... Paris: 1824. V. 72

BOJER, JOHAN
The Face of the World. New York: 1919. V. 72

BOLAM, GEORGE
The Birds of Northumberland and the Eastern Borders. 1912. V. 69
Birds of Northumberland and the Eastern Borders. Alnwick: 1912. V. 73

BOLAN, MARC
The Warlock of Love. Plymouth: 1969. V. 73

BOLAND, D. J.
Forest Trees of Australia. East Melbourne: 1984. V. 72

BOLAND, EAVAN
Limitations. New York: 2000. V. 73

BOLAS, BERNARD
A Handbook of Laboratory Glass Blowing. London: 1921. V. 69

BOLDE, SAMUEL
A Plea for Moderation Towards Dissenters: Occasioned by Grand-Juries Presenting the Sermon Against Persecution, at the Last Assizes Holden at Sherburn in Dorset-shire. London: 1682. V. 70

BOLEY, EDWIN J.
The Masked Halters. Seymour: 1977. V. 69

BOLEY, JEAN
The Restless. New York: 1946. V. 72

BOLINGBROKE, HENRY ST. JOHN, 1ST VISCOUNT
A Letter to Sir William Windham. II. Some Reflections on the Present State of the Nation. III. A Letter to Mr. Pope. London: 1753. V. 70; 72
Letters on the Spirit of Patriotism: on the Idea of a Patriot King. London: 1752. V. 69
Letters, on the Spirit of Patriotism; on the Idea of a Patriot King; and on the State of Parties, at the Accession of King George the First. London: 1750. V. 73
Letters on the Spirit of Patriotism: on the Idea of a Patriot King; and on the State of Parties, at the Accession of King George the First. with A Familiar Epistle to the Most Impudent Man Living. London: 1749. V. 68
Letters on the Study and Use of History. London: 1752. V. 73
The Philosophical Works.... London: 1754. V. 73
A Voyage to the Demerary, Containing a Statistical Account of the Settlements There and Of Those on the Essequebo, the Berbice and Other Contiguous Rivers of Guyana. London: 1807. V. 70
The Works. Dublin: 1793. V. 70

BOLIS, LIANA
Comparative Physiology: Locomotion, Respiration, Transport and Blood. Amsterdam: 1973. V. 71

BOLITHO, SYBIL
Call for a Chaperon. New York: 1936. V. 71

BOLITHO, WILLIAM
Murder For Profit. NY: 1926. V. 72; 73

BOLL, HEINRICH
Billards at Half Past Nine. London: 1961. V. 70

BOLLAN, WILLIAM
Coloniae Anglicanae Illustrata; or, the Acquest of Dominion, and the Plantation of Colonies Made by the English in America, with the Rights of the Colonists, Examined, Stated and Illustrated. London: 1762. V. 70

BOLTON, A. M.
The Independency of the Mind Affirmed. Wheeling: 1807. V. 70

BOLTON, CHARLES KNOWLES
The Founders; Portraits of Persons Born Abroad who Came to the Colonies in North America Before the Year 1701. Boston;: 1919-1926. V. 69

BOLTON, HANNAH
Drawing from Objects, Being an Abstract of Lessons on Linear Drawing, Given at the Home and Colonial Training Schools. London: 1850. V. 73

BOLTON, HERBERT EUGENE
Anza's California Expeditions. 1930. V. 71
Athanase De Mezieres and the Louisiana - Texas Frontier 1768-1780. New York: 1970. V. 68; 73
The Colonization of North America 1492-1783. New York: 1920. V. 73
Coronado: Knight of Pueblos and Plains. New York: 1949. V. 69
Coronado On the Turquoise Trail, Knight of Pueblo and Plains. Albuquerque: 1949. V. 68
Cross Swords and Gold Pan, a Group of Notable Full Color Paintings Depicting Outstanding Episodes in the Exploration of the West by Carl Oscar Borg and Millard Sheets.... Los Angeles: 1936. V. 68
Font's Complete Diary - a Chronicle of the Founding of San Francisco. Berkeley: 1931. V. 70
Font's Complete Diary: a Chronicle of the Founding of San Francisco. Berkeley: 1933. V. 68; 73
Fray Juan Crespi. Missionary Explorer on the Pacific Coast 1769-1774. Berkeley: 1927. V. 68
Greater America. Berkeley: 1945. V. 69
Pageant in the Wilderness: the Story of the Escalante Expedition in the Interior Basin, 1776. Salt Lake City: 1950. V. 70; 73
Rim of Christendom: a Biography of Eusebio Francisco Kino Pacific Coast Pioneer. New York: 1936. V. 69; 70
Spanish Exploration in the Southwest 1542-1706. New York: 1916. V. 69
Texas in the Middle Eighteenth Century. New York: 1962. V. 70

BOLTON, JOHN
Geological Fragments Collected Principally from Rambles Among the Rocks of Furness and Cartmel. London: 1869. V. 69
Geological Fragments Collected Principally from Rambles Among the Rocks of Furness and Cartmel. Ulverston: 1869. V. 71

BOLTON, R. P.
The Indian Life of Long Ago in the City of New York. New York: 1934. V. 69

BOLTON, W. F.
The English Language - Essays by English and American Men of Letters. Cambridge: 1966-1969. V. 72

BOLUS, H.
The Orchids of the Cape Peninsula. Capetown: 1888. V. 73

BOMBAL, MARIA LUISA
House of Mist. 1947. V. 70

BOMBERG, DAVID
Russian Ballet. London: 1919. V. 70

BOMER, ANTON
Triumphus Novem Seculorum Imperii Romano-Germanici...Auctus et Recusu a Joanne Andrea Pfeffel. Augsburg: 1725. V. 70; 72

BOMPAS, CHARLOTTE SELINA
A Heroine of the North. Memoirs of.... Toronto: 1929. V. 73

BONAFOUS, MATTHIEU
Traite de L'Education des Vers a Soie et de la Culture Du Murier, Suivi de Divers Memores sur l'Art Sericicole. Paris: 1840. V. 72

BONAPARTE, NAPOLEON
Napoleon's Memoirs. Waltham St. Lawrence: 1945. V. 71

BONAPARTE, ROLAND
Les Habitants de Suriname.... Paris: 1884. V. 69
Notes Pteridologiques. Paris: 1915-1925. V. 72

BONAR, JAMES
Malthus and His Work. London: 1885. V. 71

BONARELLI DELLA ROVERE, GUIDUBALDO, CONTE
Filli Di Sciro, Favola Pastorale. Ferrara: 1607. V. 69; 73

BONATTI, WALTER
On the Heights. London: 1964. V. 69; 73

BONAVIA-HUNT, D. A.
Pemberley Shades. New York: 1949. V. 70

BONCENNE, PIERRE
De la Navigation du Clain, et de Sa Jonction a la Charente et a la Sevre-Niortaise. Poitiers: 1807. V. 71

BOND, J. WESLEY
Minnesota and Its Resources to Which are Appended Camp-Fire Sketches or Notes of a Trip from St. Paul to Pembina and Selkirk Settlement on the Red River of the North. Chicago: 1856. V. 69

BOND, JAMES H.
From Out of the Yukon. 1948. V. 70; 73
From Out of the Yukon. Oregon: 1948. V. 69; 72

BOND, JOHN
A Complete Guide for Justice of the Peace, According to the Best Approved Authors. London: 1687. V. 69

BOND, MICHAEL
Paddington Takes the Air. London: 1970. V. 68
Paddington Takes the Test. London: 1979. V. 68

BOND, T. E. T.
Wild Flowers of the Ceylon Hills.... London: 1953. V. 72

BONDAGE a Moral Institution. Macon: 1837. V. 73

BONE, DAVID W.
Merchantman Rearmed. London: 1949. V. 69

BONER, CHARLES
Chamois Hunting in the Mountains of Bavaria and in the Tyrol. 1860. V. 73
Forest Creatures. 1861. V. 70

BONET, THEOPHILE
Sepulchretun: sive, Anatomica Practica, ex Cadaveribus Morbo Denatis. Lugduni: 1700. V. 68

BONGE, LYLE
The Sleep of Reason: Jargon 77. 1974. V. 68

BONIFACE, ELEANOR
Nellie's Welsh Fairy Tales. Newtown: 1929. V. 73

BONINGTON, CHRIS
Annapurna South Face. London: 1971. V. 69
Everest South West Face. London: 1973. V. 69
The Everest Years. London: 1986. V. 69
Kongur. China's Elusive Summit. London: 1982. V. 69
Mountaineer. Thirty Years of Climbing on the World's Great Peaks. London: 1989. V. 69
Quest for Adventure. London: 1981. V. 69

BONINGTON, R. P.
A Series of Subjects from the Works of the Late R. P. Bonnington, Drawn on Stone by J. P. Harding. London: 1829. V. 69

BONNAC, MARQUIS DE
Catalogue Raisonne d'une Collection Considerable De Coquilles Rares et Choisies.. Paris: 1757. V. 68

BONNEFONS, NICOLAS DE
Le Jardinier Francois, qui Enseigne a Cultiver les Arbres & Herbes.... Paris: 1755. V. 70

BONNEFOY, YVES
On the Motion and Immobility of Douve. Athens: 1968. V. 68
Selected Poems. London: 1968. V. 70

BONNELL, HENRY E.
Charlotte Bronte: George Eliot: Jane Austen. Studies in Their Works. London: 1902. V. 73

BONNER, CINDY
Lily. Chapel Hill: 1992. V. 69; 71

BONNER, HYPATIA BRADLAUGH
Charles Bradlaugh: a Record of His Life and Work.... London: 1894. V. 71

BONNER, M. G.
How To Play Baseball. New York: 1955. V. 71

BONNER, SHERWOOD
Dialect Tales. New York: 1883. V. 71

BONNER, T. D.
The Life and Adventures of James P. Beckwourth. New York: 1856. V. 69
The Life and Adventures of James P. Beckwourth. New York: 1931. V. 68
The Life and Adventures of James P. Beckwourth. 1965. V. 68

BONNET, CHARLES
Recherches sur l'Usage des Feuilles dans les Plantes et sur Quelques Autres Sujets Jelatifs a l'Histoire de la Vegetation. Gottingen: 1754. V. 69; 72; 73

BONNETT, FRANK
Mixed and Rough Shooting. A Book for Men of Moderate Means. 1914. V. 71

BONNEY, CECIL
Looking Over My Shoulder; Seventy-five Years in the Pecos Valley. Roswell, NM: 1971. V. 70; 72

BONNEY, JOSEPH L.
Death by Dynamite. New York: 1940. V. 68

BONNEY, ORRIN
Battle Drums and Geysers: The Life and Journal of Lt. Gustavus Cheney Doane, Soldier and Explorer of The Yellowstone and The Snake River Regions. Chicago: 1970. V. 72

BONNICKSEN, T. M.
America's Ancient Forests.... New York: 2000. V. 68

BONNYCASTLE, JOHN
A Treatise on Plane and Spherical Trigonometry.... London: 1806. V. 69

BONOMI, JOSEPH
Catalogue of a Collection of Egyptian Antiquities, the Property of Henry Abbot, Esq. M.D. Cairo: 1846. V. 70
The Proportions of the Human Figure. London: 1880. V. 68

BONSAL, STEPHEN
Edward Fitzgerald Beale, a Pioneer in the Path of Empire 1822-1903. New York: 1912. V. 73

BONSOR, N. P. R.
North Atlantic Seaway. London: 1975-1980. V. 68

BONTEMPS, ARNA
Cavalcade of the American Negro. Chicago: 1940. V. 72
Chariot in the Sky. Philadelphia: 1951. V. 71
Hold Fast to Dreams: Poems Old and New. Chicago: 1969. V. 72

BONUOMO, MICHELE
Italo Scanga. La Jolla: 1989. V. 69

BONVALOT, GABRIEL
Through the Heart of Asia: Over the Pamir to India. London and New York: 1889. V. 70

BONWICK, JAMES
The Bushrangers: Illustrating the Early Days of Van Diemen's Land. Melbourne: 1856. V. 70
Discovery and Settlement of Port Phillip; Being a History of the Country Now Called Victoria.... Melbourne: 1856. V. 68; 72
French Colonies and Their Resources. London: 1886. V. 71

THE BOO-Boos and Bunty's Baby. Dundee: 1921. V. 72

A BOOK About Theodore Dreiser and His Work. New York: 1925. V. 68

A BOOK for the Children of Maine, for the Use of Families and Schools. Portland: 1831. V. 69

A BOOK for the Sea-Side. London: 1852. V. 68

BOOK of Allegiance; or a Report of the Arguments of Counsel, and Opinions of the Court of Appeals of South Carolina on the Oath of Allegiance. Columbia: 1834. V. 68

THE BOOK of Baby Pets. London: 1910. V. 73

BOOK of Biographies...Biographical Sketches of Leading Citizens of Chenango County, New York. Boston: 1898. V. 70

THE BOOK of Bosh. London: 1889. V. 73

THE BOOK of Days. A Miscellany of Popular Antiquities in Connection with the Calendar . . . London: 1864. V. 71

THE BOOK of Fair Tales. London: 1914. V. 72

THE BOOK of Fate. New York: 1817. V. 68

A BOOK of Favourite Modern Ballads. London: 1860. V. 69

BOOK of Games and Sports. London: 1856. V. 70

BOOK of Greek Myths. Garden City: 1962. V. 70

THE BOOK of Kells. Reproductions from the Manuscript in Trinity College Dublin. London: 1974. V. 70

BOOK of Letters and Pictures. (Number 1). Greenfield: 1848. V. 73

THE BOOK of Little Girls. Birmingham: 1911. V. 72

BOOK OF MORMON
The Book of Mormon. New York: 1830. V. 70
The Book of Mormon. Palmyra: 1830. V. 73
The Book of Mormon. Lamoni: 1874. V. 73
The Book of Mormon. 1920. V. 69
Ka Buke a Moramona. Salt Lake City: 1905. V. 73

A BOOK of Old Ballads. London: 1934. V. 71

THE BOOK of Oz Cooper: an Appreciation of Oswald Bruce Cooper, with Characteristic Examples of His Art in Lettering, Type Designing and Such of His Writings as Reveal the Cooperian Typographic Gospel. Chicago: 1949. V. 69

THE BOOK of Pictures. Albany: 1822. V. 73

THE BOOK of Scottish Pasquils. Edinburgh: 1868. V. 71

THE BOOK of Shells.... London: 1836. V. 68

BOOK of Simples. London: 1908. V. 70

THE BOOK of the Bear Being Twenty-One Tales from the Russian. London: 1926. V. 69; 71; 73

THE BOOK of the Bench. London: 1900. V. 68; 71

THE BOOK of the Household; or Family Dictionary of Everything Connected with Housekeeping and Domestic Medicine.... London: 1862-1864. V. 68

THE BOOK of the Ocean, and Life on the Sea: Containing Thrilling Narratives and Adventures of Ocean Life in All Countries.... New York: 1854. V. 73

THE BOOK of the Poets. Chaucer to Beattie. London: 1848. V. 71

THE BOOK Of the Queen's Dolls' House. London: 1924. V. 72

A BOOK of the Winter. London: 1950. V. 68

THE BOOK of Trade Secrets. London: 1909?. V. 68

THE BOOK of Trades; or, Circle of the Useful Arts. Glasgow: 1841. V. 71

THE BOOK of Wedding Days for Every Day in the Year. London: 1889. V. 68

THE BOOK! Or, the Proceedings and Correspondence Upon the Subject of the Inquiry into the Conduct of Her Royal Highness the Princess of Wales Under a Commission Appointed by the King in the Year 1806.... London: 1813. V. 68; 72

BOOKANO Stories with Fairy Cottage, Tower of London.... London. V. 68

BOOKANO Stories with Pictures that Spring Up in Model Form: No. 1. London: 1934. V. 70

BOOKANO Stories with Pictures that Spring Up in Model Form. No. 11. London: 1944. V. 73

BOOKANO Stories with Pictures That Spring Up in Model Form. London: 1945. V. 70

BOOKANO Stories with Pictures that Spring Up in Model Form. London: 1950. V. 73

BOOKED UP
Catalog 1. Washington: 1971. V. 71

BOOKER, LUKE
A Moral Review of the Conduct and Case of Mary Ashford, in Refutation of the Arguments Adduced in Defence of Her Supposed Violator and Murderer. 1819. V. 69

BOOKER, ROBERT
Political Hints; with a Memoir of the Author. 1851. V. 71

THE BOOKMAN Christmas Number 1914. V. 73

THE BOOKMAN Christmas Number 1920. V. 73

THE BOOKMAN Christmas Number 1932. V. 73

BOOKS and the Public. London: 1927. V. 68

BOOKWATER, THOMAS E.
Honor Tarnished - The Reno Court of Inquiry. Ohio: 1979. V. 72

BOOKWAYS; A Quarterly for the Book Arts. Austin: 1991-1995. V. 72

BOOL, F. H.
M. C. Escher, His Life and Complete Graphic Work, with Fully Illustrated Catalogue. New York: 1982. V. 69; 72

BOOLDS, H. J.
Proposed Cellular Ship of War...Read Before the Scottish Shipbuilders' Association, 6th Feb. 1865. Glasgow: 1865. V. 69

BOOLE, GEORGE
On a General Method in Analysis (extracted from the Philosophical Transactions of the Royal Society of London for MDCCCXLIV, Part I). V. 73
A Treatise on the Calculus of Finite Differences. London: 1880. V. 71

BOON, K. G.
Rembrandt, the Complete Etchings. New York: 1963. V. 69; 70; 72; 73

BOORMAN, J.
The Nigerian Butterflies. Ibadan: 1957-1961. V. 69; 73

THE BOOT And Shoe-Maker's Assistant, Containing a Treatise on Clicking and the Form and Fitting-Up of Lasts Scientifically Considered. Manchester: 1853. V. 72

BOOTH, ABRAHAM
Commerce in the Human Species, and the Enslaving of Innocent Persons, Inimical to the Laws of Moses and the Gospel of Christ. London: 1792. V. 69

BOOTH, BRAMWELL
Echoes and Memories. London: 1925. V. 71

BOOTH, CHARLES
Condition and Occupations of the People of the Tower Hamlets 1886- 1887. 1887. V. 71
Life and Labour of the People in London. London: 1902. V. 71

BOOTH, CHARLES G.
Mr. Angel Comes Aboard. Garden City: 1944. V. 70; 72
Murder at High Tide. 1930. V. 73
Murder at High Tide. New York: 1930. V. 72

BOOTH, CHRISTOPHER B.
Mr. Clackworthy, Con Man. 1927. V. 73

BOOTH, E. E.
By Observations And Experiences In The United States Army. Los Angeles: 1944. V. 72

BOOTH, EDWIN
Edmund Booth (1810-1905) Forty Niner, the Life Story of a Deaf Pioneer. Stockton: 1953. V. 68; 73

BOOTH, EVA SELINA GORE
Poems. London: 1898. V. 69

BOOTH, M. L.
The Marble-Workers' Manual. New York: 1856. V. 70
New and Complete Clock and Watchmakers' Manual. New York: 1863. V. 68

BOOTH, STANLEY
Rythm Oil. A Journey Through the Music of the American South. London: 1991. V. 71
The True Adventures of the Rolling Stones. London: 1985. V. 73

BOOTH, STEPHEN
Blood on the Tongue. London: 2002. V. 73
The Book Called Holinshed's Chronicles. San Francisco: 1968. V. 73

BOOTH, WILLIAM
An Examination of General Booth's Social Scheme. London: 1890. V. 71
In Darkest England and the Way Out. London: 1893?. V. 71
Orders and Regulations for the Salvation Army. London: 1880. V. 68
Twenty-One Years' Salvation Army. Under the Generalship of William Booth. London: 1889. V. 68

BOOTHBY, GUY
Across the World for a Wife. 1898. V. 68
A Bid for Fortune. New York: 1895. V. 68
The Childerbridge Mystery. London: 1902. V. 73
Doctor Nikola. London: 1896. V. 71
Dr. Nikola. New York: 1896. V. 68
Dr. Nikola's Experiment. London: 1899. V. 71
Farewell Nikola. London: 1901. V. 71
The Kidnapped President. London: 1902. V. 70
The Lust of Hate. London: 1898. V. 71
Pharos the Egyptian. London: 1899. V. 71

BOOTH-CLIBBORN, EDWARD
My Father and Edward Ardizzone - a Lasting Friendship. London: 1983. V. 72

BOOTHROYD, B.
The History of the Ancient Borough of Pontefract. Pontefract: 1807. V. 73

BORASSATI, GIUSTINIANO
Il Gimnasta in Practica, Ed in Teorica. Venice: 1753. V. 70

BORCKE, HEROS VON
Memoirs of the Confederate War for Indepdendence. Edinburgh and London: 1866. V. 69; 70

BORDEAUX, WILLIAM
Custer's Conqueror. 1952. V. 68

BORDEN, MARY
The Forbidden Zone. London: 1919. V. 70

BORDER, DANIEL
Polypharmakos ka'i Chymistes (Greek title transliterated) or, The English Unparall'd Physitian and Chyrurgian. London: 1651. V. 72

BORDEUX, WILLIAM J.
Conquering The Mighty Sioux. Sioux Falls: 1929. V. 72

BORDEWICH, FERGUS M.
Killing the White Man's Indian. New York: 1996. V. 72

BOREHAM, F. W.
When the Swans Fly High. New York: 1931. V. 71

BOREIN, EDWARD
Borein's West. Santa Barbara: 1952. V. 68
Etchings of the West. Santa Barbara: 1950. V. 68
Stagecoaches of the Old West. Santa Fe: 1968. V. 69

BORELLA, S. P.
Cake Tops and Sides. Commercial Designs. London and Glasgow: 1935. V. 68

BOREMAN, THOMAS
A Description of More than Three Hundred Animals.... Glasgow: 1801. V. 68
The Gigantick History, Volume the Second, Which Completes the History of the Guildhall, London. London: 1741. V. 68; 71

BORENIUS, TANCRED
Catalogue of a Collection of Pottery Belonging to W. H. Woodward. 1928. V. 72
A Catalogue of the Pictures at Elton Hall in huntingdonshire in the Possession of Colonel Douglas James Proby. London: 1924. V. 69

BORGES, JORGE LUIS
El Aleph. Buenos Aires: 1949. V. 71
The Aleph and Other Stories. London: 1971. V. 72
Antologia Personal. Buenos Aires: 1961. V. 71
The Book of Imaginary Beings. New York: 1969. V. 69; 71
The Book of Imaginary Beings. London: 1970. V. 70
Collected Fictions. 1998. V. 72
The Congress. London: 1974. V. 73
The Craft of Verse. Cambridge: 2000. V. 72
Doctor Brodie's Report. New York: 1972. V. 69
Dreamtigers. Austin: 1964. V. 69
Evaristo Carriego. Buenos Aires: 1930. V. 70; 71
Extraordinary Tales. London: 1973. V. 73
Ficciones. Buenos Aires: 1944. V. 71
Ficciones. London: 1962. V. 72
Ficciones. New York: 1962. V. 71
Ficciones. 1984. V. 70; 72
Ficciones. New York: 1985. V. 69
El Libro de los Seres Imaginarios. Buenos Aires: 1967. V. 68; 70
El Martin Fierro. Buenos Aires: 1953. V. 68; 71
Otras Inquisiciones (1937-1952). Buenos Aires: 1952. V. 68; 70; 71
Poemas (1922-1943). Buenos Aires: 1943. V. 71
Prologos. Buenos Aires: 1975. V. 71
Selected Non-Fictions. 1999. V. 72
Selected Poems 1923-1967. 1972. V. 69
Selected Poems 1923-1967. London: 1972. V. 71

A Universal History of Infamy. London: 1973. V. 73

BORLAND, R.
Border Raids and Reivers. Dalbeattie: 1898. V. 71

BORN, MAX
The Constitution of Matter. Modern Atomic and Electron Theories. London: 1923. V. 69
Problems of Atomic Dynamics. Cambridge: 1926. V. 69

BORNE, ALAIN
Le Facteur Cheval. Les Hautes Plaines de Mane: 1969. V. 71

BORONIA Babies. Sydney: 1917. V. 72

BOROWSKI, TADEUSZ
This Way for the Gas, Ladies and Gentlemen and Other Stories. London: 1967. V. 71

BORRADAILE, L. A.
The Invertebrates. Cambridge: 1959. V. 68

BORRER, W.
The Birds of Sussex. 1891. V. 69; 73

BORROW, GEORGE
The Bible in Spain; Or, the Journey, Adventures, and Imprisonments of and Englishman in an Attempt to Circulate the Scriptures in the Peninsula. London: 1896. V. 71
Celebrated Trials and Remarkable Cases of Criminal Jurisprudence, from the Earliest Records to the Year 1825. London: 1825. V. 68

BORROW, GEORGE HENRY
Lavengro: the Scholar, the Gypsy, the Priest. London: 1936. V. 73
Romantic Ballads. Norwich: 1826. V. 73
The Romany Rye: a Sequel to Lavengro. London: 1857. V. 68
Targum. Or Metrical Translations from Thirty Languages and Dialects. St. Petersburg: 1835. V. 73
The Zincali; or an Account of the Gypsies of Spain. London: 1843. V. 71; 73

BORTON, BENJAMIN
On the Parallels or Chapters of Inner History. Woodstown: 1903. V. 69

THE BORZOI. New York: 1925. V. 72

BOSANQUET, CHARLES
Pratical Observations on the Report of the Bullion-Committee.. London: 1810. V. 73

BOSANQUET, EUSTACE F.
English Printed Almanacks and Prognostications. London: 1917. V. 69

BOSCANA, GERONIMO
Chinigchinich. Santa Ana: 1933. V. 68

BOSNAL, STEPHEN
Edward Fitzgerald Beale a Pioneer in the Path of Empire 1822-1903. New York: 1912. V. 68

BOSSCHERE, JEAN DE
Beasts and Men. Folk Tales Collected in Flanders. London: 1918. V. 69
Weird Islands. New York: 1922. V. 69

BOSSERT, H.
Folk Art of Asia, Africa, Australia and the Americas. London: 1975. V. 69
Folk Art of Europe. London: 1954. V. 72
Folk Art of Primitive Peoples. New York: 1955. V. 69

BOSSU, MR.
Travels through that Part of North America Formerly Called Louisiana. London: 1771. V. 70

BOSSUET, JACQUES
Maxims and Reflexions Upon Plays. London: 1699. V. 68

BOSTOCK, JOHN
An Elementary System of Physiology. Boston: 1825-1828. V. 72

BOSTON
Report on a Thoroughfare Plan for Boston. Prepared by the City Planning Board, Robert Whitten, Consultant. Boston: 1930. V. 71
Report on the Street Traffic Control Problem of the City of Boston. Boston: 1928. V. 68

BOSTON. COMMITTEE OF CORRESPONDENCE
The Votes and Proceedings of the Freeholders and Other Inhabitants of the Town of Boston, in Town Meeting assembled, According to the Law.... Boston: 1772. V. 71

BOSTON ATHENAEUM
Catalogue of Books in the Boston Athenaeum.... Boston;: 1827. V. 69
Catalogue of the Eighth Exhibition of Paintings in the Athenaeum Gallery. Boston: 1834. V. 71

BOSTON FEMALE ANTI-SLAVERY SOCIETY
Report...to the Annual Meeting of 1835. Boston: 1836. V. 68

BOSTON, L. M.
An Enemy at Green Knowe. London: 1964. V. 68

BOSTON TRANSIT COMMISSION
First Annual Report of the Boston Transit Commission, for the Year Ending August 15, 1895. Boston: 1895. V. 70

BOSTON, VIRGINIA
Shockwave. London: 1978. V. 71

BOSWELL, CHARLES
Dancing in the Movies. Iowa City: 1986. V. 68

BOSWELL, JAMES
An Account of Corsica, the Journal of a Tour to that Island and Memoirs of Pascal Paoli.... London: 1768. V. 68
An Account of Corsica, the Journal of a Tour...and Memoirs of Pascal Paoli.... London: 1769. V. 69
Boswell in Holland 1763-1764. London: 1952. V. 68
Boswell On The Grand Tour: Germany And Switzerland 7164. London: 1953. V. 71; 72
Boswell's Life of Johnson: Including Their Tour to the Hebrides. London: 1853. V. 68; 71
Boswell's London Journal 1762-1763. New York: 1950. V. 73
Boswell's London Journal 1762-1763 Together with Journal of My Jaunt Harvest 1762. London: 1951. V. 69
Dorando, a Spanish Tale. London: 1930. V. 68
The Hypochondriack.... Stanford: 1928. V. 68
James Boswell Distilled. New York: 1981. V. 72
The Journal of A Tour To Corsica; & Memoir of Pascal Paoli. Cambridge: 1923. V. 72
A Journal of a Tour to the Hebrides with Samuel Johnson. . . Dublin: 1785. V. 70; 71
The Journal of a Tour to the Hebrides with Samuel Johnson. London: 1785. V. 68; 69
A Journal of a Tour to the Hebrides with Samuel Johnson. London: 1786. V. 69
The Journal of A Tour to the Hebrides, with Samuel Johnson. London: 1807. V. 71; 72
The Journal of a Tour to the Hebrides with Samuel Johnson. London: 1852. V. 71
Letters, Addressed to the Rev. W.J. Temple, now first published from the original MSS. 1857. V. 72
Letters of James Boswell, Addressed to the Rev. W. J. Temple Now First Published from the Original Mss. London: 1857. V. 68
Life and Conversations of Dr. Samuel Johnson.... London: 1874. V. 68
The Life of Samuel Johnson. London: 1791. V. 68; 70; 71
The Life of Samuel Johnson. London: 1791-1793. V. 68; 69
The Life of Samuel Johnson. London: 1792. V. 71
The Life of Samuel Johnson. London: 1793. V. 68; 69; 71
The Life of Samuel Johnson. London: 1799. V. 71
The Life of Samuel Johnson. Boston: 1807. V. 73
The Life of Samuel Johnson. London: 1811. V. 73
The Life of Samuel Johnson. London: 1821. V. 68
The Life of Samuel Johnson. London: 1822. V. 68; 72; 73
The Life of Samuel Johnson. London and Oxford: 1826. V. 70; 71
The Life of Samuel Johnson. London: 1831. V. 68
The Life of Samuel Johnson. London: 1836. V. 73
The Life of Samuel Johnson. London: 1852. V. 68
The Life of Samuel Johnson. London: 1857. V. 73
The Life of Samuel Johnson. London: 1901. V. 68; 70
The Life of Samuel Johnson. London: 1910. V. 68; 72
The Life of Samuel Johnson. Boston: 1925. V. 70
The Life of Samuel Johnson. London: 1925. V. 68
The Life of Samuel Johnson. New York: 1946. V. 68
The Life of Samuel Johnson, LL.D. and the Journal of His Tour to the Hebrides.... London: 1885. V. 70
The Life of Samuel Johnson, LL.D., with marginal comments and markings from two copies annotated by Hester Lynch Thrale Piozzi. New York: 1963. V. 73
London Journal and Journal of My Jaunt. London: 1951. V. 71; 72
Private Papers of James Boswell from Malahide Castle in the Collection of Lt. Col. Ralph Heyward Isham... (and) Boswell's Journal of the Tour to the Hebrides with Samuel Johnson and Index. New York: 1928-1937. V. 70
The Private Papers of James Boswell: Volume One: Correspondence of James Boswell and John Johnston of Grange. London: 1966. V. 68
The Private Papers of James Boswell: Boswell in Search of a Wife 1766-1769. London: 1957. V. 68
The Private Papers of James Boswell: Boswell for the Defence 1769-1774. London: 1960. V. 68
The Private Papers of James Boswell: The Ominous Years 1774-1776. London: 1963. V. 68

BOSWELL, ROBERT
American Owned Love. New York: 1997. V. 72
Crooked Hearts. New York: 1987. V. 68; 72
Living to Be 100. New York: 1994. V. 72
Mystery Ride. New York: 1993. V. 68

BOSWORTH, NEWTON
Hochelaga Depicta: the Early History and Present State of the City and Island of Montreal. Toronto: 1901. V. 73

BOTANISCHES Centralblatt, Referirendes Organ der Association International des Botanistes.... Jena: 1880-1915. V. 72

THE BOTANIST'S Calendar, and Pocket Flora; Arranged According to the Linnaean System. London: 1797. V. 69

BOTKIN, B. A.
Folk Say a Regional Miscellany 1930. Norman: 1930. V. 70

BOTTERWECK, G. JOHANNES
Theological Dictionary of the Old Testament. Grand Rapids: 1977-1980. V. 70

BOTTIGER, C. A.
Sabina, Oder, Morgenszenen in Putzzimer Einer Reichen Roemrin. Leipzig: 1806. V. 69

BOTTO, ANTONIO
The Children's Book. Lisbon: 1935. V. 71

BOTTOME, PHYLLIS
Old Wine. London: 1926. V. 71
Windlestraws. Boston: 1929. V. 71

BOTTOMLEY, GORDON
Chambers of Imagery. Chambers of Imagery (Second Series). London: 1907-1912. V. 73
The Mickle Drede and Other Verses. Kendal: 1896. V. 73
Scenes and Plays. London: 1929. V. 71
A Vision of Giorgione. Three Variations on Venetian Themes. Portland: 1910. V. 73

BOTUME, ELIZABETH HYDE
First Days Among the Contrabands. Boston: 1890. V. 70

BOUCH, C. M. L.
The Lake Counties 1500-1830. Manchester: 1961. V. 71
Prelates and People of the Lake Counties. A History of the Diocese of Carlisle 1133-1933. Kendal: 1948. V. 71

BOUCHER, ANTHONY
The Case of the Baker Street Irregulars. New York: 1940. V. 69
The Case of the Crumpled Knave. 1939. V. 73
The Case of the Seven of Calvary. 1937. V. 73
The Case of the Seven Sneezes. 1942. V. 73
The Case of the Solid Key. 1941. V. 73
The Compleat Werewolf. 1969. V. 70; 73
Ellery Queen: a Double Profile. 1951. V. 69
The Great American Detective Stories. 1945. V. 68
The Marble Forest. New York: 1951. V. 70
Multiplying Villainies, Selected Mystery Criticism 1942-1968. 1973. V. 73
Rocket to the Morgue. New York: 1942. V. 70

BOUCHER, FRANCOIS
Livre de Cartouches Inventes. Paris: 1780. V. 72
Recueil de Fontaines (Second Livre de Fontaines). Paris. V. 70

BOUCHER, JONATHAN
Reminiscences of an American Loyalist 1738-1789. Boston: 1925. V. 73

BOUCHER D'ARGIS, A. G.
Principles sur la Nullite du Mariage Pour Cause d'Impuissance. Londres (Paris): 1756. V. 73

BOUDARD, JEAN BAPTISTE
Iconologie Tiree de Divers Auteurs. Parma: 1759. V. 69

BOUDIER DE VILLEMERT, PIERRE JOSEPH
The Friend of Women. Philadelphia: 1803. V. 69; 73
The Ladies Friend, from the French of Monsieur de Gravines. London: 1766. V. 71

BOUDINOT, ELIAS
Address, of the New Jersey Bible Society to the Publick.... New Brunswick: 1810. V. 69
Life of the Rev. William Tennent, Formerly Pastor of the Presbyterian Church at Freehold, in New Jersey. New York: 1848. V. 69
Memoirs of the Rev. William Tennent, Formerly Pastor of the Presbyterian Church at Freehold, in New Jersey.... Poughkeepsie: 1815. V. 69
A Star in the West; or a Humble Attempt to Discover the Long Lost Ten Tribes of Israel.... Trenton: 1816. V. 68; 69; 73

BOUGAINVILLE, LOUIS ANTOINE DE, COMTE
Voyage Autour du Monde, Par le Fregate du Roi La Boudeuse, et la Flute L'Etoile: en 1766, 1767, 1768 and 1769. Paris: 1772. V. 71

BOUGHTON, ALICE
Photographing the Famous. New York: 1928. V. 68

BOUILLAUD, JEAN BAPTISTE
Recherches Cliniques Propres a Demonter que le Sens Du Langage Articule et le Principe Coordinateur des Mouvements de La Parole Resident dans Les Lobules Anterierus Du Cerveau. Paris: 1848. V. 68

BOUILLON, J. P.
Art Nouveau 1870-1914. New York: 1985. V. 69; 72

BOUILLY, JEAN NICOLAS
Contes a Ma Fille. Londres: 1811. V. 72
Contes a Ma Fille. Paris: 1814. V. 72

BOULAINVILLIERS, HENRI DE, COUNT
The Life of Mahomet. London: 1731. V. 72

BOULE, MARCELLIN
Fossil Men. London: 1957. V. 68

BOULENGER, G. A.
Catalogue of the Fresh-Water Fishes of Africa, in the British Museum. London: 1909-1916. V. 68; 71
Catalogue of the Perciform Fishes in the British Museum. 1895. V. 72
Zoology of Egypt. The Fishes of the Nile. 1907. V. 73

BOULESTIN, X. M.
The New Keepsake for the Year 1921. London and Paris: 1920. V. 69; 72; 73

BOULGER, MEMETRIUS
Chinese Gordon. London: 1884. V. 72

BOULLE, PIERRE
The Bridge on the River Kwai. London: 1954. V. 71
The Bridge Over the River Kwai. New York: 1954. V. 69
Le Pont de la Riviere Kwai. Paris: 1952. V. 73
Monkey Planet. London: 1963. V. 70
Planet of the Apes. New York: 1963. V. 71

BOULNOIS, H. P.
The Construction of Carriageways and Footways. London: 1895. V. 69

BOULTON & WATT
A Catalogue of the Valuable Machinery and Plant of the Soho Mint, Long Celebrated and in High Repute with the Government of Great Britain, as also with Foreign Powers in Euorpe, Asia and America, the East India Company.... London: 1850. V. 73

BOULTON, MATTHEW
Report from the Committee Appointed to Enquire Into the State of the Copper Mines and Copper Trade of This Kingdom. London: 1799. V. 73

BOULTON, WILLIAM C.
The Amusements of Old London Being a Survey of the Sports and Pastimes, Tea Gardens and Parks, Playhouses and Other Diversions of the People of London from the 17th to the Beginning of the 19th Century. London: 1901. V. 72

BOUQUET, MICHEL
The Tourist's Ramble in the Highlands.... London: 1850. V. 70

BOURASSE, ABBE J. J.
The Miracles of Madame Saint Katherine of Fierbois. Chicago: 1897. V. 69; 73

BOURDIER, A.
Fontainebleau. Versailles. V. 72

BOURDILLON, F. W.
Ailes d'Aloeutte. Oxford: 1890. V. 72
Where Lilies Live and Waters Wind Away. London: 1890. V. 70

BOURGARDE, ARMAND
Polichinelle: La Diable Rosse. Paris: 1880. V. 72

BOURGERY, D. M. P.
A Treatise on Lesser Surgery; or, the Minor Surgical Operations... Translated from French, with Notes and Appendix; by William C. Roberts & James B. Kissam. NY: 1834. V. 72

BOURGET, DOM JOHN
The History of the Royal Abbey of Bec, Near Rouen in Normandy. London: 1779. V. 70

BOURGET, PAUL
Pastels. Paris. V. 70
Pastels. Paris: 1895?. V. 71

BOURGUET, LOUIS
Traite des Petrifications. Paris: 1742. V. 68

BOURINOT, GEORGE
A Manual of the Constitutional History of Canada from the Earliest Period to the Year 1888.... Montreal: 1888. V. 73

BOURINOT, JOHN G.
Builders of Nova Scotia. A Historical Review. Toronto: 1900. V. 69; 72

BOURJAILY, VANCE
The End of My Life. New York: 1947. V. 68

BOURKE, JOHN G.
An Apache Campaign In The Sierra Madre- An Account of the Expedition in Pursuit of the Hostile Chiricahua Apaches in Spring of 1883. New York: 1886. V. 69; 72
Mackenzie's Last Fight With The Cheyennes. Bellevue, Nevada: 1970. V. 72
The Medicine Men of the Apache. Pasadena: 1971. V. 69; 70
On The Border With Crook. New York: 1891. V. 72
The Snake Dance of the Moquis of Arizona. Chicago: 1962. V. 69
Urine Dance of the Zuni Indians of New Mexico. Ann Arbor: 1885. V. 68

BOURKE, THOMAS
A Concise History of the Moors in Spain, from their Invasion of that Kingdom to their Final Expulsion of it. London: 1811. V. 72

BOURKE, ULICK J.
The College Irish Grammar. 1856. V. 69; 73

BOURKE-WHITE, MARGARET
Dear Fatherland Rest Quietly. New York: 1946. V. 70
The Photographs of Margaret Bourke-White. New York: 1972. V. 68
Portrait of Myself. New York: 1963. V. 72
Shooting the Russian War. New York: 1942. V. 71
They Called It Purple Heart Valley - a Combat Chronicle of the War in Italy. New York: 1944. V. 71

BOURNE, BENJAMIN FRANKLIN
The Captive in Patagonia or, Life Among the Giants. Boston: 1853. V. 70

BOURNE, GEORGE
Picture of Slavery in the United States of America. Middletown: 1834. V. 71

BOURNE, HERMON
Flores Poetici. The Florist's Manual.... Boston: 1833. V. 68

BOURNE, MICHAEL
Corsage. 1977. V. 68

BOURNE, VINCENT
The Poetical Works. Oxford and London: 1821. V. 68; 70

BOURRIENNE, LOUIS ANTOINE
Memoirs of Napoleon Bonaparte. 1836. V. 72
Memoirs of Napoleon Bonaparte. Glasgow Edinburgh & London: 1855. V. 69

BOUSSARD, J.
Constructions et Decorations pour Jardins. Kiosques - Orangeries Volieres - Arbis Divers. Paris: 1881. V. 68; 70

BOUTCHER, WILLIAM
A Treatise on Forest Trees. Edinburgh: 1778. V. 69

BOUTELL, CHARLES
A Manual of British Archaeology. London: 1858. V. 73

BOUTET, CLAUD
Traite de la Mignature, Pur Apprendre Aisement a Peindre sans Maitre. The Hague: 1688. V. 73

BOUTOURLIN, COMTE DE
Catalogue de la Bibliotheque de feu M. Le Comte D. Boutourlin. Paris: 1839. V. 70

BOUVIER, JACQUELINE
One Special Summer. New York: 1974. V. 72

BOVA, BEN
Mars. New York: 1992. V. 68; 71

BOVALLIUS, CARL
Nicaraguan Antiquities. Stockholm: 1886. V. 72

BOVE, FRANK JAMES
The Story of Ergot: for Physicians, Pharmacists, Nurses, Biochemists, Biologists and Others Interested in the Life Sciences. Basel and New York: 1970. V. 68

BOVERI, THEODOR
The Origin of Malignant Tumors. Baltimore: 1929. V. 73

BOW, ROBERT HENRY
Economics of Construction in Relation to Framed Structures. London: 1873. V. 69
A Treatise on Bracing with Its Application to Bridges and Other Structures of Wood or Iron. New York: 1874. V. 69

BOWDEN, CHARLES
Frog Mountain Blues. Tucson: 1987. V. 71; 72
Killing the Hidden Waters. Austin: 1977. V. 69; 71; 72
Mezcal. Tucson: 1988. V. 69
Red Line. New York: 1989. V. 72
Street Signs Chicago. Chicago: 1981. V. 69

BOWDEN, HANNAH MARSH
Poetical Remains of Hannah Bowden of Croydon.... London: 1861. V. 69

BOWDEN, LEWIS, MRS.
Kenilworth Castle, and Other Poems. Wellington, Salop: 1818. V. 69

BOWDEN, MARK
Black Hawk Down. New York: 1999. V. 71; 72

BOWDEN, PETER
Coyote Wind. New York: 1994. V. 72

BOWDEN, W.
Peculiar Mode of Treatment of the Cucumber During the Winter Seasons. Wallingford (Berkshire): 1820?. V. 70

BOWDITCH, A. J.
Terrestrial Mammals of Martha's Vineyard, Massachusetts, with Special Reference to Peromyscus. Northamptn: 1965. V. 72

BOWDITCH, HENRY INGERSOLL
An Address on the Life and Character of James Deane, M.D. of Greenfield, Mass....August 4, 1858. Greenfield: 1858. V. 68

BOWDITCH, NATHANIEL
Mathematical Papers from the Fourth Volume of the Memoirs of the American Academy of Arts and Sciences. Boston: 1820. V. 68

BOWDITCH, NATHANIEL I.
A History of the Massachusetts General Hospital (to August 5, 1851). Boston: 1872. V. 71; 72
Memoir of Nathaniel Bowditch. Boston: 1840. V. 73
Suffolk Surnames. Boston: 1858. V. 68

BOWDITCH, W. R.
On Coal-Gas; a Discourse Delivered to Some Directors and Managers of Gas-Works June 13, 1860, and Published at Their Request. London: 1860. V. 69

BOWDLER, JANE
Poems and Essays by the Late Miss Bowdler.... New York: 1811. V. 72

BOWDLER, JOHN
Reform or Ruin; Take Your Choice!. London: 1797. V. 73

BOWDOIN, W. G.
The Rise of the Book-Plate. New York: 1901. V. 68

BOWE, NICOLA GORDON
Harry Clarke: His Graphic Art. Los Angeles: 1983. V. 72

BOWEN, C. E.
Frisky the Squirrel. London: 1880. V. 70

BOWEN, DANA THOMAS
Lore of the Lakes. Daytona Beach: 1940. V. 72
Memories of the Lakes. Daytona Beach: 1946. V. 72

BOWEN, ELIZABETH
Afterthought. Pieces about Writing. London: 1962. V. 73
Bowen's Court. London: 1942. V. 73
Collected Impressions. New York: 1950. V. 72
The Collected Stories of Elizabeth Bowen. London: 1980. V. 68
Day in the Dark and Other Stories. London: 1965. V. 73
The Death of the Heart. London: 1938. V. 70
Eva Trout. London: 1969. V. 73
The Shelbourne - A Centre in Dublin Life for More Than a Century. London: 1951. V. 72
A Time in Rome. New York: 1950. V. 73
The Tommy Crans and All's Well. N.P. noted (Chelsea): 1930. V. 70; 73
A World of Love. London: 1955. V. 73

BOWEN, ESSEX
A Statement of Facts, in Answer to Mrs. Gunning's Letter, Addressed to His Grave the Duke of Argyll. London: 1791. V. 73

BOWEN, EUROS
Poems. Llandysul: 1974. V. 71

BOWEN, F. W.
History of Port Elizabeth, Cumberland County, New Jersey, Down to the Present Time. Philadelphia: 1885. V. 69

BOWEN, FRANK C.
The Sea, Its History and Romance. 1925. V. 69
Sea Slang - Dictionary of the Old Timers' Expressions and Epithets. London: 1929. V. 70

BOWEN, GEORGE F.
Thirty Years of Colonial Government...Queensland, New Zealand...Hong Kong. London: 1889. V. 70

BOWEN, LOUISE DE KOVEN
The Girl Employed in Hotels and Restaurants. Chicago: 1912. V. 72
The Straight Girl on the Crooked Path. Chicago: 1915. V. 72

BOWEN, MARJORIE
Black Magic. A Tale of the Rise and Fall of Antichrist. 1909. V. 73

BOWEN, PETER
Coyote Wind. New York: 1994. V. 69; 70; 73
Kelly Blue. New York: 1991. V. 71
Notches. New York: 1997. V. 71
Yellowstone Kelly. Ottawa: 1987. V. 69

THE BOWER Book of Knowledge. London: 1840. V. 73

BOWER, B. M.
The Heritage of the Sioux. Boston: 1916. V. 68

BOWER, F. O.
Ferns (Filicales). New Delhi: 1963. V. 69
Sixty Years of Botany in Britain (1875-1935). Impressions of an Eye-Witness. London: 1938. V. 71; 72

BOWER, GEORGE S.
Doe Crags and Climbs Around Coniston. Barrow-in-Furness: 1922. V. 69

BOWER, JOHN
Description of the Abbeys of Melrose, and Old Melrose, with Their Traditions. Edinburgh: 1822. V. 70; 72
Description of the Abbeys of Melrose, and Old Melrose, with Their Traditions. Edinburgh: 1827. V. 68

BOWER, WARREN
New Directions - Second Series. Philadelphia: 1941. V. 69

BOWERMAN, M. L.
The Flowering Plants and Ferns of Mount Diablo, California. Berkeley: 1944. V. 72

BOWERS, C. G.
Rhododendrons and Azaleas, Their Origins, Cultivation and Development. New York: 1936. V. 71; 73

BOWERS, DOROTHY
The Bells At Old Bailey. London: 1947. V. 72
Fear and Miss Betony. New York: 1942. V. 72

BOWERS, JOHN Z.
Advances in American Medicines: Essays at the Bicentenial. New York: 1976. V. 71

BOWES, JAMES L.
Notes on Shippo. Liverpool: 1895. V. 72

BOWIE, EFFIE G.
Across the Years in Prince George's County: a Genealogical and Biographical History of Some Prince George's County, Maryland and Allied Families. Baltimore: 1975. V. 72

BOWIE, JOHN
The Scots Worthies. Edinburgh: 1870. V. 70

BOWIE, WALTER RUSSELL
The Story of Jesus for Young People. New York: 1937. V. 71
Sunrise in the South. The Life of Mary Cooke Branch Munford. Richmond: 1942. V. 72

BOWKER, RICHARD ROGERS
Copyright: Its History and Its Law. Boston and New York: 1912. V. 73

BOWLBY, WARD H.
A Voyage from Canada to Egypt and a Two Months' Trip on the River Nile in a Houseboat. Toronto: 1902. V. 68

BOWLES, CARRINGTON
Bowles's New Perceptor in Drawing; Consisting of Variety of Classes.... 1764. V. 71; 73

BOWLES, E. A.
My Garden in Spring. My Garden in Summer. My Garden in Autumn and Winter. London: 1914-1915. V. 70
My Garden in Spring, Summer, Autumn and Winter. 1972. V. 73
My Garden in Spring/Summer/Autumn and Winter. 1914. V. 69
My Garden in Summer. 1914. V. 73

BOWLES, JANE
Two Serious Ladies. New York: 1943. V. 70

BOWLES, JOHN
A Protest Against T. Paine's Rights of Man Addressed to the Members of the Book Society of.... London: 1792. V. 68

BOWLES, PAUL
Collected Stories 1939-1976. Santa Barbara: 1979. V. 73
Conversations with Paul Bowles. Jackson: 1993. V. 73
Dear Paul, Dear Ned: the Correspondence of Paul Bowles and Ned Rorem. North Pomfret: 1997. V. 69; 73
The Delicate Prey and Other Stories. New York: 1950. V. 70; 71; 72; 73
Desultory Correspondence. Zurich: 1997. V. 68
The Echo, contained in Prize Stories of 1947. Garden City: 1947. V. 73
Five Eyes: Stories by Abdeslam Boulaich, Mohamed Choukri, Larbi Layachi, Mohammed Mrabet, Ahmed Yacoubi. Santa Barbara: 1979. V. 73
From Notes Taken in Ceylon and The Hours Before Noon contained in Zero Anthology of Literature and Art. New York: 1956. V. 73
The Hours After Noon. London: 1959. V. 68; 70; 71
In Touch: The Letters of Paul Bowles. New York: 1993. V. 73
In Touch: The Letters of Paul Bowles. New York: 1994. V. 73
Journal Tangerois 1987-1989. 1989. V. 73
Let It Come Down. London: 1952. V. 68; 70; 71
Let It Come Down. New York: 1952. V. 73
Let It Come Down. Santa Barbrara: 1980. V. 73
A Little Stone. London: 1950. V. 68; 73
Midnight Mass. Santa Barbara: 1981. V. 73
Next to Nothing: Collected Poems 1926-1977. Santa Barbara: 1981. V. 72; 73
Photographs. New York: 1994. V. 72
Scenes. Los Angeles: 1968. V. 68; 71; 73
She Woke Me Up So I Killed Her. San Francisco: 1985. V. 71; 73
The Sheltering Sky. London: 1949. V. 68; 70; 73
The Sheltering Sky. New York: 1949. V. 73
The Spider's House. New York: 1955. V. 70; 71; 72; 73
The Spider's House. London: 1957. V. 73
The Spider's House. Santa Barbara: 1982. V. 73
Their Heads are Green and Their Hands are Blue. New York: 1963. V. 70; 72
Thicket of Spring: Poems 1926-1969. Los Angeles: 1972. V. 73
Things Gone and Things Still Here. Santa Barbara: 1977. V. 73
A Thousand Days for Mokhtar and Other Stories. London: 1989. V. 73
The Time of Friendship. New York: 1967. V. 71
Up Above the World. New York: 1966. V. 69; 71
Up Above the World. London: 1967. V. 68
Without Stopping: an Autobiography. New York: 1972. V. 68; 72

BOWLES, WILLIAM LISLE
Sonnets and Other Poems...To Which is Added Hope, an Alleogrical Sketch on Recovering Slowly from Sickness. London: 1800. V. 73
A Wiltshire Parson And His Friends. London: 1926. V. 72

BOWLES'S Polite Recreation in Drawing, Containing Picturesque Portraits of Fashionable Faces.... London: 1779. V. 69

BOWLEY, ADA L.
Old Mother Goose. London: 1916. V. 71

BOWLT, JOHN E.
Twentieth Century Russian and East European Painting (in the) Thyssen-Bornemisza Collection. London: 1993. V. 68

BOWMAN, A. K.
The Life and Teaching of Sir William MacEwen. London: 1942. V. 68
The Life and Times of Sir William MacEwen. London: 1942. V. 73

BOWMAN, DAVID
Let the Dog Drive. 1992. V. 70
Let the Dog Drive. New York: 1992. V. 68; 69; 71
Let the Dog Drive. New York: 1993. V. 68

BOWMAN, JOE
Reminiscences of Joe Bowman and the Ullswater Foxhounds. Kendal: 1923. V. 72

BOWMAN, MAY ELLENOR STAFFORD
Descendants of Isaac Van Tuyl, Sr. and Mary McCarter of Bernards Township, Somerset County, New Jersey. Baltimore: 1970. V. 69

BOWMAN, W.
Lectures on the Parts Concerned in the Operations of the Eye. London: 1849. V. 71

BOWNAS, SAMUEL
An Account of the Captivity of Elizabeth Hanson. London: 1787. V. 71
A Description of the Qualifications Necessary to a Gospel Minister.... London: 1750. V. 70
A Description of the Qualifications Necessary to a Gospel Minister.... London: 1767. V. 71

BOWNE, FORD
Outlaw Spy. New York: 1970. V. 73

BOWRING, JOHN
Minor Morals for Young People Illustrated in Tales and Travels. London: 1834-1839. V. 70
Observations on the Oriental Plague and on Quarantines, as a means of Arresting Its Progress, Addressed to the British Associaton of Science, Assembled at Newcastle in August 1838. Edinburgh: 1838. V. 73
Servian Popular Poetry. London: 1827. V. 72
A Visit to the Phillipine Islands. London: 1859. V. 68; 72

BOWYER, VERA
Bears! Three Nursery Bear Stories. London: 1919. V. 73

BOWYER, WILLIAM
The Origin of Printing. London: 1776-1781. V. 69
The Origin of Printing. In Two Essays. I. The Substance of Dr. Middleton's Dissertaton on the Origin of Printing in England. II. Mr. Meerman's Account of the Invention of Art at Harlem, And Its Progress to Mentz. London: 1776. V. 70

BOX, EDGAR
Death in the Fifth Position. New York: 1952. V. 69

BOX, MICHAEL JAMES
Capt. James Box's Adventures and Explorations in New and Old Mexico. New York: 1869. V. 70

BOX, SYDNEY
Alibi in the Rough. London: 1977. V. 73

BOXHORN, MARCUS ZUERIUS
Arcana Imperii Detecta; or, Divers Select Cases in Government; More Particularly, Of the Obeying the Unjust Commands of a Prince. London: 1701. V. 70
Historiae Augustae Scriptorum Latinorum Minorum, Pars Tertia. Lugd. Batavo: 1632. V. 72

THE BOY and His Pony, and Other Stories. New York: 1852. V. 73

BOYAJIAN, ZABELLE C.
Armenian Legends and Poems. London: 1916. V. 68

BOYCE, ANNE OGDEN
Records of a Quaker Family: The Richardsons of Cleveland. London: 1889. V. 73

BOYCE, ROBERT
The Family Surgeon and Physician; or Every Man His Own Doctor.... Hull: 1825. V. 71

BOYCE, W. D.
The Philippine Islands. Chicago and New York: 1914. V. 69

BOYD, ANDREW K. H.
Twenty-five Years of St. Andrews, September 1865-September 1890. London: 1892. V. 71; 72

BOYD, BLANCHE MC CRARY
Mourning the Death of Magic. New York: 1977. V. 68; 71
Nerves. Plainfield: 1973. V. 68; 73
The Redneck Way of Knowledge. New York: 1995. V. 71

BOYD, DONALD
Walking in the Pennines. London: 1937. V. 69

BOYD, E.
Popular Arts of Spanish New Mexico. Santa Fe: 1974. V. 69; 70; 72
Saints and Saint Makers of New Mexico. Santa Fe: 1946. V. 69

BOYD, E. R.
A Yarn of War. Palestine and France 1917-1918. Glasgow: 1919. V. 70

BOYD, ERNEST
Ireland's Literary Renaissance. London: 1923. V. 72

BOYD, EUNICE MAYS
Murder Wears Mukluks. New York: 1945. V. 70

BOYD, J.
The Human Placenta. Cambridge: 1970. V. 71

BOYD, JAMES
Drums. New York: 1928. V. 68
Long Hunt. New York: 1930. V. 68

BOYD, JAMES P.
Recent Indian Wars. 1891. V. 72

BOYD, JULIA
Gleanings: Being Impressions from Copperplates and Wood Block, Engraved in the Bewick Workshop.... 1886. V. 69

BOYD, L. A.
The Coast of Northeast Greenland.... New York: 1948. V. 69

BOYD, MARK
Reminiscences of Fifty Years. London: 1871. V. 71

BOYD, MAURICE
Kiowa Voices, Myths, Legends and Folktales. Fort Worth: 1983. V. 68

BOYD, OPSEMUS
Cavalry Life In Tent And Field. NY: 1894. V. 72

BOYD, ROBERT
The Office, Powers and Jurisdiction of His Majesty's Justices of the Peace, and Commissioners of Supply. Edinburgh: 1787. V. 69

BOYD, W.
Littondale Past and Present. Leeds: 1893. V. 73

BOYD, WALTER
A Letter to the Right Honourable William Pitt, on the Influence of the Stoppage of Issues in Specie at the Bank of England.... London: 1801. V. 69

BOYD, WILLIAM
The Blue Afternoon. London: 1993. V. 70
Brazzaville Beach. London: 1990. V. 70; 72; 73
Brazzaville Beach. New York: 1990. V. 68
Cork. 1994. V. 68
Cork. London: 1994. V. 73
The Destiny of Nathalie and Other Stories. London: 1995. V. 70
A Good Man in Africa. London: 1981. V. 70; 71; 72; 73
A Good Man in Africa. New York: 1982. V. 68; 69
A Good Man in Africa. New York: 1991. V. 73
On the Yankee Station. London: 1981. V. 70
On the Yankee Station. New York: 1984. V. 68
Protobiography. 1998. V. 68; 71
Protobiography. London: 1998. V. 72
Stars and Bars. London: 1984. V. 69; 70
Stars and Bars. New York: 1984. V. 68

BOYD, WILLIAM KENNETH
Some Eighteenth Century Tracts Conerning North Carolina. Raleigh: 1927. V. 73

BOYD, ZACHARY
Four Letters of Comforts for the Deaths of the Earl of Hadingtoun and of the Lord Boyd. Edinburgh: 1878. V. 68

BOYDELL, JOHN
Boydell's Graphic Illustrations of the Dramatic Works of Shakespeare. London: 1791-1803. V. 69
Boydell's Graphic Illustrations of the Dramatic Works of Shakespeare. London: 1803. V. 68
A Collection of Prints from Pictures for the Purpose of Illustrating the Dramatic Works of Shakespeare, by the Artists of Great Britain. London: 1803. V. 70

BOYER, ABEL
The English Theophrastus; or the Manners of the Age.... London: 1702. V. 69

BOYER, CHARLES S.
Early Forges and Furnaces in New Jersey. Philadelphia: 1931. V. 69
Old Inns and Taverns in West Jersey. Camden: 1962. V. 69
Rambles through Old Highways and Byways of Camden, New Jersey. (with) *Indian Trails and Early Paths.* Camden: 1936-1938. V. 69

BOYER, GLENN G.
I Married Wyatt Earp, the Recollections of Josephine Sarah Marcus Earp. Tucson: 1976. V. 73
Illustrated Life of Doc Holliday. 1966. V. 69
An Illustrated Life of Doc Holliday. Glenwood Springs: 1966. V. 73
Suppressed Murder of Wyatt Earp. San Antonio: 1967. V. 69
Wyatt Earp: Facts. Volume V - By Wagon Train from Iowa to California 1864. Rodeo: 1997. V. 68

BOYER, MARIE-FRANCE
Private Paris. The Most Beautiful Apartments. New York: 1988. V. 72

BOYER, RICHARD L.
The Giant Rat of Sumatra. New York: 1976. V. 73
The Giant Rat of Sumatra. London: 1977. V. 69

BOYER, RICK
Billingsgate Shoal. 1982. V. 68
Billingsgate Shoal. Boston: 1982. V. 73

BOYER, WARREN E.
Vanishing Trails of Romance. Denver: 1923. V. 73

BOYERS, BETTINA
The White Mazurka. New York: 1946. V. 68

BOYES, W.
Surgeon's Diary With The Custer Relief Columns. Washington, DC: 1974. V. 72

BOYINGTON, GREGORY
Baa Baa Black Sheep. Fresno: 1958. V. 71; 73

BOYKIN, RICHARD M.
Captain Alexander Hamilton Boykin. New York: 1942. V. 69; 70

BOYLE, ELEANOR VERE
Beauty and the Beast. London: 1875. V. 68; 73
A Midsummer-Night Dream. 1887. V. 68; 73

BOYLE, F.
The Woodlands Orchids.... London: 1901. V. 70

BOYLE, JACK
Boston Blackie. New York: 1919. V. 69; 71; 73

BOYLE, JACK *continued*
Boston Blackie. Boston: 1979. V. 68

BOYLE, KAY
Collected Poems. New York: 1962. V. 71
Death of a Man. New York: 1936. V. 71
Plagued by the Nightingale. London: 1931. V. 71
Wedding Day and Other Stories. London: 1932. V. 71
The White Horses of Vienna. London: 1937. V. 71

BOYLE, MARY LOUISA
The Bridal of Melcha; a Dramatic Sketch. London: 1844. V. 69
The State Prisoner, a Tale of the French Regency. London: 1837. V. 69; 73

BOYLE, ROBERT
Certain Physiological Essays and Other Tracts.... London: 1669. V. 71
Chymista Scepticus.... Geneva: 1680. V. 71
An Essay of the Great Effects of Even Languid and Unheeded Motion. London: 1685. V. 68; 70; 73
The Excellency of Theology, Compar'd with Natural Philosophy...(with) About the Excellency and Grounds of Mechanical Hypothesis. London: 1674. V. 68
Experimentorum Novorum Physico-Mechanicorum Continuatio Secunda. London: 1680. V. 68; 70; 73
The Martyrdom of Theodora and of Didymus. London: 1687. V. 72
Medicinal Experiments: or, a Collection of Choice and Safe Remedies for the Most Part Simple and Easily Prepar'd.... London: 1712. V. 70
Natural and Artificial Methods of Ventilation. London: 1899. V. 68
Occasional Reflections Upon Several Subjects. London: 1665. V. 69
The Philosophical Works of the Honorable Robert Boyle Esq. Abridged, Methodizes and Disposed Under the General Heads of Physics, Statics, Pneumatics, Natural History.... London: 1738. V. 70; 71
Some Motives and Incentives to the Love of God, Pathetically Discours'd of in a Letter to a Friend. London: 1665. V. 70
The Strange Subtilty of Effluviums. 1673. V. 72
Tentame Porologicum Sive ad Porositatem Corporm tum Animalium, tum Solidorum Detegendam. Geneva: 1686. V. 71
Tracts...Containing New Experiments Touching the Relation Betwixt Flame and Air. And About Explosion. London: 1672. V. 69

BOYLE, T. CORAGHESSAN
Budding Prospects. New York: 1984. V. 68; 70; 71; 72
Descent of Man. Boston: 1979. V. 68; 69; 70; 71; 72; 73
Descent of Man. New York: 1980. V. 68
East is East. New York: 1990. V. 68; 70; 71; 73
Greasy Lake and Other Stories. New York: 1985. V. 68; 70; 71
If the River Was Whiskey. New York: 1989. V. 68; 70; 71
Riven Rock. 1998. V. 72
Riven Rock. Franklin Center: 1998. V. 70
Riven Rock. New York: 1998. V. 72
The Road to Wellville. Franklin Center: 1993. V. 68; 70
The Road to Wellville. New York: 1993. V. 69; 70; 71; 72; 73
The Tortilla Curtain. New York: 1995. V. 70; 71
Water Music. Boston: 1981. V. 68; 69; 70; 71; 73
Water Music. London: 1981. V. 68; 72
Water Music. London: 1982. V. 68; 71
World's End. New York: 1987. V. 68; 69; 70; 71

BOYLE'S Fashionable Court and Country Guide, and Town Visiting Directory. London: 1831. V. 71

BOYNS, R. E.
A Grass Widow. San Francisco: 1919. V. 69

BOYNTON, CHARLES B.
History of the Navy During the Rebellion. New York: 1870-1869. V. 69
A Journey Through Kansas; With Sketches of Nebraska: describing the country, climate, soil, mineral, manufacturing, and other resources. Cincinnati: 1855. V. 72

BOYNTON, HENRY V.
Was General Thomas Slow at Nashville?. New York: 1896. V. 69

BOYNTON, SEARLES R.
The Painter Lady; Grace Carpenter Hudson. Eureka, Calif: 1978. V. 72

BOYS' and Girls Fairy Stories. London: 1903. V. 68

THE BOYS and Girls Primer. Philadelphia: 1863-1864. V. 70

BOYS, EDWARD
Boys' Captivity and Adventures. 1831. V. 72
Boy's Captivity and Adventures. London: 1831. V. 68

BOYS' Out-door Sports. Boston: 1860-1872. V. 71

THE BOY'S Own Annual. 1911-1912. V. 68
THE BOY'S Own Annual. 1932-1933. V. 68

THE BOY'S Own Book. London: 1887. V. 71

BOYS, THOMAS SHOTTER
London as It Is. Drawn from Nature Expressly for This Work and Lithographed by Thomas Shotter Boys.... London: 1842. V. 71

THE BOZ Ball. Cedar Rapids: 1908. V. 69

BOZEMAN, JOHN LEEDS
The History of Maryland.... Baltimore: 1837. V. 73

BR Today: A Selection of His Books, with Comments. New York: 1982. V. 72

BRACE, CHARLES L.
The New West or California in 1867-1869. New York: 1869. V. 68

BRACHET, JEAN
The Biological Role of Ribonucleic Acids. Amsterdam: 1960. V. 68

BRACKEN, HENRY
The Traveller's Pocket Farrier, or a Treatise Upon the Distempers and Common Incidents Happening to Horses Upon a Journey. London: 1743. V. 68; 72

BRACKENBURY, RICHARD
Western Sketches and War Poems. La Jolla: 1945. V. 68; 71

BRACKENRIDGE, HENRY MARIE
History of the Western Insurrection in Western Pennsylvania, Commonly called the Whiskey Insurrection. Pittsburgh: 1859. V. 73
Views of Louisiana: Containing Geographical Statistical and Historical Notices of that Vast and Important Portion of America. Baltimore: 1817. V. 73

BRACKENRIDGE, HUGH HENRY
Incidents of the Insurrection in the Western Parts of Pennyslvania, in the Year 1794. Philadelphia: 1795. V. 73

BRACKETT, ANNA CALLENDER
The Education of American Girls, Considered in a Series of Essays. New York: 1874. V. 69
Woman and the Higher Education. New York: 1893. V. 69

BRACKETT, LEIGH
An Eye for an Eye. Garden City: 1957. V. 69; 71; 73
No Good from a Corpse. Tucson: 1999. V. 73
Silent Partner. New York: 1969. V. 68; 69; 71; 73
The Starmen. New York: 1952. V. 69
The Sword of Rhiannon. New York: 1953. V. 71
The Tiger Among Us. New York: 1957. V. 73

BRACKETT, OLIVER
English Furniture Illustrated. London: 1950. V. 72
Thomas Chippendale. Boston: 1935. V. 69

BRADBROOK, WILLIAM
The Register of the Parish of Woughton-on-the-Green in the County of Buckinghamshire 1558 to 1718, and 1718 to 1812. Olney: 1906-1908. V. 71

BRADBURY, EMILIE C.
Hansel and Gretel. Sandusky: 1931-1943. V. 70

BRADBURY, FREDERICK
History of Old Sheffield Plate. London: 1912. V. 71
History of Old Sheffield Plate. Sheffield: 1983. V. 72

BRADBURY, HENRY
Printing: Its Dawn, Day and Destiny. London: 1858. V. 71

BRADBURY, JOHN
Travels in the Interior of America in the Years 1809, 1810 and 1811. Cleveland: 1904. V. 70

BRADBURY, MALCOLM
Eating People is Wrong. London: 1959. V. 73
To the Hermitage. London: 2000. V. 72

BRADBURY, RAY
Dandelion Wine. New York: 1957. V. 70
Dandelion Wine. New York: 1975. V. 68
Dark Carnival. Sauk City: 1947. V. 73
Death is a Lonely Business. New York: 1985. V. 69
Death is a Lonely Business. New York: 1995. V. 68
The Dragon. 1988. V. 73
The Dragon. New York: 1988. V. 69
Fahrenheit 451. New York: 1953. V. 69; 70
Fahrenheit 451. New York: 1982. V. 69; 72
The Golden Apples of the Sun. New York: 1953. V. 70
The Illustrated Man. New York: 1951. V. 71; 73
The Last Circus and the Electrocution. Northridge: 1980. V. 71
Long After Midnight. New York: 1976. V. 69
The Machineries of Joy. New York: 1964. V. 73
The Martian Chronicles. Garden City: 1950. V. 70; 72; 73
Martian Chronicles. Avon: 1974. V. 69; 73
The Mummies of Guanajuato. New York: 1978. V. 70
The Stories of Ray Bradbury. New York: 1980. V. 69
The Toynbee Convector - Stories. New York: 1988. V. 70
When Elephants Last in the Dooryard Bloomed. New York: 1974. V. 68

BRADBY, VIOLET
Matthew and the Miller. London: 1915. V. 69

BRADD, LESTER M.
Sopac Saga. San Francisco: 1946. V. 72

BRADDON, E.
Thirty Years of Shikar. 1895. V. 69

BRADDON, M. E.
Aladdin; or, the Wonderful Lamp, Sinbad the Sailor; or the Old Man of the Sea; Ali Baba; or the Forty Thieves. V. 71

BRADDON, W. & CO.
Patentees and Manufacturers of Every Description of Oil Stoves. Birmingham: 1915. V. 68

BRADFIELD, JOHN EDWIN
Tramways or Railways on Metropolitan Streets Will be Mischievous and Dangerous Obstructions and Nuisances. London: 1867. V. 72

BRADFIELD, SCOTT
The Secret Life of Houses. London: 1988. V. 68

BRADFIELD, W.
Cameron Creek Village. 1931. V. 69

BRADFORD, ALDEN
History of Massachusetts from 1764 (to 1820). Boston: 1822-1829. V. 73

BRADFORD, DUNCAN
The Wonders of the Heavens, Being a Popular View of Astronomy.... Boston: 1837. V. 71

BRADFORD, GAMALIEL
Confederate Portraits. Boston and New York: 1914. V. 69; 70
Darwin. Boston: 1926. V. 71

BRADFORD HISTORICAL & ANTIQUARIAN SOCIETY
Journal of the Bradford Historical & Antiquarian Society. Bradford: 1888. V. 73

BRADFORD, JOHN
John Bradford's Historical &c Notes on Kentucky from the Western Miscellany. San Francisco: 1932. V. 73

BRADFORD, M. F.
Audubon. New Orleans: 1897. V. 72

BRADFORD, PERRY
Born With the Blues. New York: 1965. V. 72

BRADFORD, REUBEN
Opera Once Over Lightly. (with) More Opera Once Over Lightly. Dallas: 1952-1953. V. 72

BRADFORD, ROARK
The Green Roller. New York: 1949. V. 69

BRADFORD TEXTILE SOCIETY
The Journal. Bradford: 1962-1970. V. 72; 73

BRADFORD, WILLIAM
History of Plymouth Plantation, 1620-1647. Boston: 1912. V. 73

BRADFORD OLD BANK, LTD.
Memorandum and Articles of Association. Bradford: 1864. V. 71

BRADLAUGH, CHARLES
John Churchill, Duke of Marlborough. London: 1884. V. 71

BRADLEE, FRANCIS BOARDMAN CROWNINSHIELD
Blockade Running During the Civil War and the Effect of Land and Water Transportation on the Confederacy. Salem: 1925. V. 69; 70
Piracy in the West Indies and Its Suppression. Salem: 1923. V. 70

BRADLEY, A. G.
Highways and Byways in the Lake District. London: 1901. V. 71
Sketches from Old Virginia. London: 1897. V. 71

BRADLEY, BILL
Time Present, Time Past: a Memoir. New York: 1996. V. 69

BRADLEY, CHARLES WILLIAM
Patronomatology: from an Essay on the Philosophy of Surnames.... Baltimore: 1842. V. 71

BRADLEY, DAVID
The Chaneysville Incident. New York: 1981. V. 71; 72
South Street. New York: 1975. V. 71

BRADLEY, EDWARD
The Adventures of Mr. Verdant Green. London. V. 71
The Adventures of Mr. Verdant Green. 1860. V. 73
The Visitor's Handbook to Rosslyn and Hawthornden. Edinburgh: 1864. V. 73

BRADLEY, GEORGE
Midden. New York: 1986. V. 73
Where the Blue Begins. New York: 1985. V. 73

BRADLEY, GLENN D.
Winning The Southwest A Story of Conquest. Chicago: 1912. V. 72

BRADLEY, H. MARTIN
The Library of H. Bradley Martin. Magnificent Color-Plate Ornithology sold June 7 1989. New York: 1989. V. 72

BRADLEY, HELEN
And Miss Carter Wore Pink. London: 1971. V. 71
In the Beginning Said Great-Aunt Jane. London: 1974. V. 71
Miss Carter Came With Us. London: 1973. V. 70; 71

BRADLEY, JAMES H.
The March of the Montana Column. A Prelude to the Custer Disaster. Norman: 1961. V. 72

BRADLEY, JOHN HODGDON
Farewell Thou Busy World. Los Angeles: 1935. V. 70

BRADLEY, MARION ZIMMER
The Mists of Avalon. New York: 1982. V. 68; 69; 71

BRADLEY, MARTHA
The British Housewife; or, the Cook, Housekeeper's and Gardiner's Companion. London: 1760. V. 73

BRADLEY, MARY H.
Murder in Room 700. New York: 1931. V. 69; 73
Trailing the Tiger. 1929. V. 72

BRADLEY, OMAR
A Soldier's Story. New York: 1951. V. 70

BRADLEY, RICHARD
New Improvements of Planting and Gardening.... London: 1717. V. 69
The Virtue and Use of Coffee with Regard to the Plague and Infectious Distempers.... London: 1721. V. 69

BRADLEY, THOMAS
Practical Geometry, Linear Perspective and Projection.... London: 1840. V. 71

BRADLEY, TOM
The Old Coaching Days in Yorkshire. Leeds: 1889. V. 73
The Ouse. Yorkshire Rivers No.5, with Bird's Eye View of the River and Roads Adjoining. Leeds: 1891. V. 73

BRADLEY, VAN ALLEN
The Book Collector's Handbook of Values: Third Edition 1978-1979. New York: 1978. V. 70

BRADLEY, WILL
Peter Poodle. Toy Maker to the King. New York: 1906. V. 73
Wonderbox Stories. New York: 1916. V. 71

BRADLOW, EDNA
Thomas Bowler of the Cape of Good Hope. Cape Town and Amsterdam: 1955. V. 72

BRADSHAW, GEORGE
Bradshaw's Railway Almanack, Directory, Shareholders' Guide and Manual for 1848.... London: 1848. V. 72

BRADSHAW, HERBERT C.
History of Prince Edward County, Virginia. Richmond: 1955. V. 69

BRADSHAW, PETER
18th Century English Porcelain Figures 1745-1795. London: 1981. V. 72

BRADSHAW'S Illustrated Travellers' Hand-Book to France. London: 1878. V. 72

BRADSTREET, ANNE
The Works of.... Charlestown: 1867. V. 68

BRADWAY, CHATTIN
Political Romanism: an Organized Opposition to Progress Destructive of Free Institutions. Washington: 1912. V. 68

BRADWOOD, WAT
The O. V. H. or How Mr. Blake Became an M.F.H. London: 1884. V. 68

BRADY, BUCKSKIN
Stories and Sermons By.... Toronto: 1905. V. 71

BRADY, CYRUS T.
Northwestern Fights and Fighter. New York: 1907. V. 72

BRADY, G. S.
Challenger Voyage. Zoology. Part 23. Copepoda. 1883. V. 73
A Monograph of the Free and Semi-Parasitic Copepoda of the British Islands. London: 1978-1980. V. 73

BRADY, LEO
The Edge of Doom. New York: 1949. V. 69

BRADY, NICHOLAS
Proposals for Publishing a Translation of Virgil's Aeneids in Blank Verse. London: 1713. V. 69

BRADY, ROBERT
A Complete History of England, from the First Entrance of the Romans Under the Conduct of Julius Caesar, Unto the End of the Reign of King Henry III...(with) A Continuation of the Complete History of England; Containing the Lives and Reigns of Edward I,. London: 1685. V. 70

BRAGG, JEFFERSON DAVIS
Louisiana in the Confederacy. Baton Rouge: 1941. V. 69; 70

BRAGG, MELVYN
A Place in England. London: 1970. V. 71

BRAHMS, CARYL
A Bullet in the Ballet. 1941. V. 73
The Moon on My Left. London: 1930. V. 69

BRAID, JAMES
Neurypnology, or the Rationale of Nervous Sleep, Considered in Relation with Animal Magnetism. London: 1843. V. 73

BRAIDLEY, BENJAMIN
Memoir of Benjamin Braidley, Esq. London: 1845. V. 71

BRAIM, THOMAS HENRY
A History of New South Wales, from the Settlement to the Close of the Year 1844. London: 1846. V. 72

BRAINARD, JOE
29 Mini-Essays. Calais: 1978. V. 73

BRAINE, JOHN
Life at the Top. London: 1962. V. 71
Room at the Top. Boston: 1957. V. 70; 71
Room at the Top. London: 1957. V. 69; 71
The Vodi. London: 1959. V. 68

BRAINE, SHEILA E.
Moving Animals: a Novel Book for Children. New York: 1890. V. 70

BRAINERD, C. N.
My Diary: Three Weeks on the Wing - A Peep at the Great West. New York: 1868. V. 68; 73

BRAINERD, E.
Some Natural Violet Hybrids of North America. Burlington: 1924. V. 72

BRAITHWAIT, GEORGE FOSTER
The Salmonidae of Westmorland, Angling Reminscences and Leaves from an Angler's Note Book. Kendal: 1884. V. 71

BRAITHWAITE, E. R.
Paid Servant. London: 1962. V. 72
To Sir, With Love. London: 1959. V. 71; 72

BRAITHWAITE, EDWARD
Islands. London: 1969. V. 72

BRAITHWAITE, G. F.
The Salmonidae of Westmorland. 1884. V. 68

BRAITHWAITE, J. W.
Guide to Kirkby Stephen, Appleby, Brough, Warcop, Ravenstonedale, Mallerstang &c. Kirkby Stephen: 1884. V. 71

BRAITHWAITE, JOSEPH BEVAN
Memoirs of Joseph John Gurney. Norwich: 1854. V. 72

BRAITHWAITE, ROBERT
The British Moss Flora. London: 1887-1905. V. 68; 69; 72
The Sphagnaceae or Peat Mosses of Europe and North America. London: 1878. V. 68; 72

BRAITHWAITE, WILLIAM
Our Lady's Choir: A Contemporary Anthology of Verse by Catholic Sisters. Boston: 1931. V. 72

BRAITHWAITE, WILLIAM STANLEY
The Poetic Year for 1916 a Critical Anthology. Boston: 1917. V. 70
Selected Poems. New York: 1948. V. 70

BRAIVE, M. F.
The Photograph: a Social History. New York: 1966. V. 68

BRALY, JOHN HYDE
Memory Pictures. Los Angeles: 1912. V. 70

BRAMBELL, F. W. ROGERS
The Transmission of Passive Immunity from Mother to Young. Amsterdam: 1970. V. 68

BRAMLETT, JIM
Ride for the High Points - the Real Story of Will James. Missoula: 1987. V. 70

BRAMLEY MOORE, WILLIAM
The Six Sisters of the Valleys; an Historical Romance. London: 1864. V. 72

BRAMMER, WILLIAM
The Gay Place. Boston: 1961. V. 70

BRAMSTON, JAMES
The Art of Politics. London: 1729. V. 70
The Man of Taste, Occasion'd by an Epistole of Mr. Pope's on that Subject. London: 1733. V. 70

BRAMWELL, BYROM
The Diseases of the Spinal Cord. Edinburgh: 1882. V. 71

BRANAGAN, THOMAS
The Excellency of the Female Character Vindicated.... New York: 1807. V. 69
The Flowers of Literature. Trenton: 1806. V. 69

BRANCH, DOUGLAS
The Cowboy And His Interpretors. New York: 1926. V. 71

BRANCH, EDGAR M.
The Literary Apprenticeship of Mark Twain. Urbana: 1950. V. 68

BRANCH, HETTYE WALLACE
The Story of 80 John, a Biography of One of the Most Respected Negro Ranchmen in the Old West. 1960. V. 68
The Story of 80 John, a Biography of One of the Most Respected Negro Ranchmen in the Old West. New York: 1960. V. 69

BRANCH, LOUIS LEON
Los Bilitos: The Story of Billy the Kid and His Gang. New York: 1980. V. 73

BRAND *Book of the State of Kansas.* Topeka: 1943. V. 71

BRAND *Book of Wheatland and Sweet Grass Counties, Montana.* Harlowton, MT: 1928. V. 68; 71

BRAND, CHRISTIANNA
The Brides Of Aberdar. London: 1982. V. 72
Cat and Mouse. New York: 1950. V. 68; 72
Court Of Foxes. London: 1969. V. 72

The Crooked Wreath. New York: 1946. V. 68; 72
The Rose in Darkness. London: 1979. V. 69
Suddenly at His Residence. 1947. V. 72
The Three Cornered Halo. London: 1957. V. 69; 70

BRAND, DONALD D.
So Live the Works of Men: Seventieth Anniversary Volume Honoring Edgar Lee Hewett. Albuquerque: 1939. V. 70

BRAND, JOHN
Bibliotheca Brandiana. London: 1807. V. 70
Observations on Popular Antiquities: Including the Whole of Mr. Bourne's Antiquitates Vulgares . . . Newcastle upon Tyne: 1777. V. 71
Observations on Popular Antiquities Including the Whole of Mr. Bourne's Antiquities Vulgares.... London: 1810. V. 71

BRAND, M.
Fields of Peace; a Pennsylvania German Album. Garden City: 1970. V. 68

BRAND, MAX
The Blue Jay. New York: 1926. V. 71
The Blue Jay. New York: 1927. V. 69; 70
Calling Dr. Kildare. New York: 1940. V. 71
Dan Barry's Daughter. New York: 1959. V. 70
Dr. Kildare Takes Charge. New York: 1941. V. 69; 70; 73
Dr. Kildare's Crisis. New York: 1942. V. 71
The Luck of the Spindrift. New York: 1972. V. 70
The Notebooks and Poems of Max Brand. New York: 1957. V. 70
The Secret of Dr. Kildare. London: 1940. V. 68
Smiling Charlie. New York: 1931. V. 72
Timbal Gulch Trail. New York: 1934. V. 69; 73

BRAND, MILLEN
The Outward Room. New York: 1937. V. 70

BRAND, R. H.
War and National Finance. London: 1921. V. 71

BRANDAU, R. S.
History of Homes and Gardens of Tennessee. Nashville: 1936. V. 71
History of Homes and Gardens of Tennessee. Nashville: 1964. V. 71; 73

BRANDE, W. T.
A Descriptive Catalogue of the British Specimens Deposited in the Geological Collection of the Royal Institution. 1816. V. 68

BRANDEIS, LOUIS
Other People's Money and How the Bankers Use It. New York: 1914. V. 68; 70

BRANDEN, NATHANIEL
Who is Ayn Rand?. New York: 1962. V. 70; 71

BRANDES, RAY
Troopers West: Military and Indian Affairs on the American Frontier. San Diego: 1970. V. 70; 71

BRAND-HOLLIS, THOMAS
The Trials on the Informations which in Pursuance of an Order of the House of Commons Were Filed by His Majesty's Attorney General Against Richard Smith, Esq. and Thomas Brand Hollis, Esq. for Having Been Guilty of Notorious Bribery. . . London: 1776. V. 70

BRANDIS, D.
Report on the Teak Forests of Pegu. London: 1860. V. 69

BRANDRETH, JEREMIAH
A Report of the Whole of the Proceedings, Under the Special Commission, Held in the County Hall, at Derby, in the Month of October, 1817.... Nottingham: 1817. V. 70

BRANDT, BILL
Camera in London. 1948. V. 68; 71; 72
The English at Home. London: 1936. V. 70
Nudes 1945-1980. Boston: 1980. V. 68

BRANDT, GERARD
The History of the Reformation and Other Ecclesiastical Transcations in and About the Low Countries.... London: 1720-1723. V. 72

BRANDT, H.
Arizona in Its Bird Life, A Naturalist's Adventures with Nesting Birds on the Deserts, Grasslands, Foothills and Mountains of Southeastern Arizona. Cleveland: 1951. V. 69; 73

BRANDT, J. F.
Spicilegia Ornitholgica Exotica. St. Petersburg: 1839. V. 70

BRANDT, JOHN C.
The International Halley Watch Atlas of Large Scale Phenomena. Boulder: 1992. V. 69

BRANDT, JOHN D.
Gunnery Catechism, as Applied to the Service of Naval Ordnance. New York: 1864. V. 70

BRANDT, JOHN H.
Asian Hunter. New Mexico: 1989. V. 72

BRANGWYN, FRANK
Windmills. London: 1923. V. 72

BRANIN, M. LELYN
The Early Makers of Handcrafted Earthenware and Stoneware in Central and Southern New Jersey. Rutherford: 1988. V. 69

BRANNER, J. C.
A Bibliography of Clays and the Ceramic Arts. Columbus: 1906. V. 68; 73
The Stone Reefs of Brazil, their Geological and Geographical Relations with a Chapter on Coral Reefs. Cambridge: 1904. V. 70; 73

BRANSON, H. C.
I'll Eat You Last. New York: 1941. V. 68; 71
The Prickling Thumb. New York: 1942. V. 69

BRANSON, L. H.
Indian Conjuring. London and New York: 1922. V. 71

BRANT, IRVING
James Madison. Indianapolis: 1941-1961. V. 71

BRANT, NEIL
Fountain Boy. New York: 1933. V. 71

BRAQUE, GEORGES
Cahier de Georges Braque 1917-1947. Paris: 1948. V. 69
Georges Braque: His Graphic Work. New York: 1961. V. 69

BRASH, J. C.
Cunningham's Text-Book of Anatomy. New York: 1937. V. 71
Neuro-Vascular Hila of Limb Muscles. Edinburgh: 1955. V. 68

BRASHER, R.
Birds and Trees of North America. New York: 1961-1962. V. 70; 72; 73

BRASK, OLE
Jazz People. New York: 1976. V. 71

BRASSEY, ANNIE ALLNUTT, BARONESS
The Flight of the Meteor 1869-1871. London: 1872. V. 72
Sunshine & Storm In The East. London. V. 72
A Voyage in the Sunbeam. London: 1881. V. 72

BRASSEY, EARL
The Sunbeam. R.Y.S. Voyages and Experineces in Many Waters. London: 1917. V. 68

BRASSEY, THOMAS
The British Navy. London: 1882-1883. V. 71

BRASSEY, THOMAS ALLNUTT
Sixteen Months' Travel 1886-1887. London: 1888. V. 69

BRASSINGTON, W. SALT
Historic Bindings in the Bodleian Library, Oxford. London: 1891. V. 70

BRATBY, M.
Notes on Some British and Foreign Wildfowl. 1951. V. 71

BRATHWAITE, RICHARD
Drunken Barnaby's Four Journeys to the North of England. London: 1716. V. 69
Drunken Barnaby's Four Journeys To The North of England. London: 1723. V. 72; 73
Drunken Barnaby's Four Journeys to the North of England. London: 1822. V. 71; 73
The English Gentlewoman, Drawne Out to the Full Body.... London: 1631. V. 69; 73

BRATT, JOHN
Trails of Yesterday. Chicago: 1921. V. 71

BRAUDEL, FERNAND
The Mediterranean and the Mediterranean World in the Age of Philip II. 1972-1973. V. 73

BRAUN, ALEXANDER
The Glacial Epoch of Our Globe. Boston: 1870. V. 68

BRAUN, ALOLPHE ARMAND
Hieroglyphic or Greek Method of Life Drawing, with contributions by Dorothy Lees, H.R. Miller, W. Champneys, Bernard Foster Stokes etc. 1919. V. 72

BRAUN, E. L.
The Woody Plants of Ohio, Trees, Shrubs and Woody Climbers, Native, Naturalized and Escaped. Columbus: 1961. V. 68

BRAUN, HUGH
An Introduction to English Mediaeval Architecture. London: 1961. V. 70

BRAUN, LILIAN JACKSON
The Cat Who Could Read Backwards. London: 1966. V. 73
The Cat Who Could Read Backwards. New York: 1966. V. 68; 69; 70; 71

BRAUND, J.
Illustrations of Furniture, Candelabra, Musical Instruments from the Great Exhibitions of London and Paris, with Examples of Similar Articles from Royal Palaces and Noble Mansions. London: 1858. V. 68

BRAUTIGAN, RICHARD
The Abortion: an Historical Romance 1966. New York: 1971. V. 68
A Confederate General from Big Sur. New York: 1964. V. 68; 73
Dreaming of Babylon. New York: 1977. V. 68
The Edna Webster Collection of Undiscovered Writings. Berkeley & Forest Knolls: 1999. V. 68; 70; 73
Four New Poets. San Francisco: 1957. V. 70
The Galilee Hitch-Hiker. San Francisco: 1958. V. 68; 71
The Galilee Hitch-Hiker. San Francisco: 1966. V. 68; 70
The Hawkline Monster. New York: 1974. V. 68; 71; 72; 73
I Watched the World Glide Effortlessly Bye and Other Pieces. 1996. V. 71; 73
In Watermelon Sugar. San Francisco: 1968. V. 68
Loading Mercury with a Pitchfork. New York: 1976. V. 71; 73
The Octopus Frontier. San Francisco: 1960. V. 68; 69; 71
The Pill Versus the Springhill Mine Disaster. San Francisco: 1968. V. 68; 70
Revenge of the Lawn: Stories 1962-1970. London: 1971. V. 70
Rommel Drives on Deep Into Egypt. New York: 1970. V. 68; 71
So the Wind Won't Blow It All Away. London: 1983. V. 73
Sombrero Fallout. New York: 1976. V. 68; 69; 71; 73
The Tokyo-Montana Express. New York: 1979. V. 68; 71; 72
The Tokyo-Montana Express. New York: 1980. V. 68; 70; 72; 73
Trout Fishing in America. London: 1970. V. 71
Trout Fishing in America, The Pill Versus the Springhill Mine Disaser, and In Watermelon Sugar. New York: 1969. V. 69; 73
An Unfortunate Woman and You Can't Catch Death. New York: 2000. V. 72
Willard and His Bowling Trophies. New York: 1975. V. 68; 69; 72

BRAVERMAN, KATE
Dropping In: Putting It All Back Together. Los Angeles: 1973. V. 70
Lithium for Medea. New York: 1978. V. 73
Palm Latitudes. New York: 1988. V. 70

BRAVO DE SOBEMONTE RAMIREZ, GASPAR
Resolutionum Et Consvltationvm medicarvm Editio Post Tres Gallicas Quarta in Germania Tribvs Tomis Distincta.... Cologne: 1674. V. 72

BRAWLEY, BENJAMIN
The Negro Genius. New York: 1937. V. 68; 70

BRAY, WILLIAM
Sketch of a Tour into Derbyshire and Yorkshire.... 1778. V. 71
Sketch of A Tour into Derbyshire and Yorkshire.... London: 1783. V. 69

BRAYER, HERBERT
American Cattle Trails 1590-1900. Bayside, NY: 1952. V. 71
The Cattle Barons Rebellion Against Law and Order - First Eyewitness Accounts of the Johnson County War in Wyoming 1892. Evanston: 1955. V. 68; 71
Stock Raising in the Northwest. Evanston: 1951. V. 69; 71
To Form a More Perfect Union- The Lives of Charles Frances and Mary Clarke From Their Letters 1847-1871. Albuquerque: 1941. V. 72; 73
William Blackmore: The Spanish Mexican Land Grants of New Mexico and Colorado. Denver: 1949. V. 71

BRAYER, HERBERT OLIVER
William Blackmore: the Spanish Mexican Land Grants of New Mexico and Colorado. Denver: 1948. V. 73

BRAYLEY, EDWARD WEDLAKE
The Beauties of England and Wales. London: 1801-1815. V. 70
Views in Suffolk, Norfolk and Northamptonshire. 1806. V. 73

BRAYNARD, FRANK O.
Fifty Famous Liners. Cambridge: 1982-1987. V. 68

BRAYSHAW, THOMAS
A History of the Ancient Parish of Giggleswick. London: 1932. V. 73
Hurtley's Poems on the Natural Curiosities of Malham, in Craven, Yorkshire. Settle: 1917. V. 73

BRAZER, ESTHER S.
Early American Decoration. Springfield, Mass: 1940. V. 72

BRAZIER, MARION HOWARD
The Professional Women's Club, 1907-1927. Massachusetts: 1927. V. 69

BRAZIER, MARY A. B.
The Central Nervous System and Behaviour. Washington: 1959. V. 68

BRAZIL, ANGELA
The New Girl at St. Chad's. London: 1912. V. 68

BREAKENRIDGE, WILLIAM M.
Helidorado Brining, the Law to the Mesquite. Boston: 1928. V. 73

THE BREAKFAST Book: a Cookery-Book for the Morning Meal, or Breakfast Table.... London: 1865. V. 68

BREAKING Into Print. New York: 1937. V. 68

BREAKWELL, IAN
Six Phototext Sequences. 1973. V. 70

BREAR, HOLLY BEACHLEY
Mexican Side of the Texan Revolution 1836. Dallas: 1956. V. 70

BREASTED, JAMES H.
Ancient Records of Egypt: Historical Documents from the Earliest Times to the Persian Conquest. Chicago: 1906. V. 68; 73
The Edwin Smith Surgical Papyrus.... Chicago: 1930. V. 69
A History of Egypt From the Earliest Times to the Persian Conquest. London: 1912. V. 72

BREATHNACH, SARAH BAN
Mrs. Sharpe's Traditions. New York: 1990. V. 69

BREAZEALE, J. F.
The Pima and His Basket. Tucson: 1923. V. 70

BREBEUF, JEAN DE
The Travels & Sufferings of Father Jean de Brebeuf Among the Hurons of Canada as Described by Himself and Edited & Translated from the French and Latin. London: 1938. V. 71

BREBEUF, JEAN DE *continued*
The Travels and Sufferings of Father Jean De Brebeuf Among the Hurons of Canada. Waltham St. Lawrence: 1938. V. 70; 71; 72

BREBNER, JOHN BARTLET
The Neutral Yankees of Nova Scotia. New York: 1937. V. 72

BREBNER, PERCY JAMES
Christopher Quarles College Professor and Master Detective. 1914. V. 73
Christopher Quarles: College Professor and Master Detective. New York: 1914. V. 69; 71

BRECHT, BERTOLT
The Threepenny Opera. New York: 1982. V. 68

BRECK, J.
New Book of Flowers. New York: 1866. V. 71; 73

BRECKENRIDGE, GERALD
Brief Kingdom. New York: 1936. V. 71

BRECKINRIDGE, SOPHONISBA P.
Marriage and the Civic Rights of Women. Chicago: 1931. V. 72

BRECKINRIDGE, W. C. P.
The Celebrated Trial: Madeline Pollard Vs. (Col. W. C. P.) Breckinridge, The Most Noted Breach of Promise Suit in the History of Court Records. 1894. V. 73

BREDALBANE, MARCHIONESS
The High Tops of Blackmount. 1935. V. 70; 73

BREE, C. R.
A History of the Birds of Europe, Not Observed in the British Isles. London: 1859-1863. V. 70; 73
A History of the Birds of Europe, Not Observed in the British Isles. London: 1875-1876. V. 71

BREESKIN, ADELYN D.
Romaine Brooks Thief of Souls. Washington: 1971. V. 68; 69

BREHM, A. E.
From North Pole to Equator. 1896. V. 72

BRELIN, JOHANNES
Anmarkningar wid Byggnings-Konsten. Stockholm: 1763. V. 68

BREMER, FREDRIKA
Brothers and Sisters, a Tale of Domestic Life. London: 1848. V. 68; 69
The President's Daughters: Including Nina. London: 1843. V. 68; 69

BREMSER, BONNIE
Troia: Mexican Memoirs. New York: 1969. V. 70

BRENAN, GERALD
The Lighthouse Always Says Yes. London: 1966. V. 72

BREND, WILLIAM ALFRED
An Inquiry into the Statistics of Deaths from Violence and Unnatural Causes in the United Kingdom.... London: 1915. V. 69

BRENDEL, JOHANN PHILIPP
Consilia Medica Celeberrimorum Quorundam Germaniae Medicorum. Frankfurt am Main: 1615. V. 70; 72

BRENNAN, JOSEPH PAYNE
The Casebook of Lucius Leffing. New Haven: 1973. V. 69; 72

BRENNER, ANITA
The Boy Who Could Do Anything and Other Mexican Folk Tales. New York: 1952. V. 68
Idols Behind Altars. New York: 1929. V. 71
The Wind that Swept Mexico: the History of the Mexican Revolution 1910-1912. New York: 1943. V. 71

BRENT, LYNTON WRIGHT
The Bird Cage: A Theatrical Novel of Old Tombestone. Philadelphia: 1945. V. 69

BRENTANO, CLEMENS
The Tale of Gockel, Hinkel and Gaceliah. New York: 1961. V. 72

BRENT DYER, ELINOR M.
Adrienne and the Chalet School. 1965. V. 69
The Chalet Girls in Camp. London: 1934. V. 68
The Chalet School Goes To It. 1941. V. 71
The Feud in the Chalet School. 1962. V. 71
Gay from China at the Chalet School. 1950. V. 73
Jane and the Chalet School. London: 1964. V. 69
Jo to the Rescue. London: 1946. V. 68
The Maids of La Rochelle. 1952. V. 71
Redheads at the Chalet School. London: 1964. V. 69
The Rivals of the Chalet School. London: 1929. V. 68
Trials for the Chalet School. London: 1959. V. 72

BRENTON, EDWARD P.
Naval History of Great Britain...1783-1836. London: 1837. V. 69

BRERETON, AUSTIN
The Lyceum and Henry Irving. London: 1903. V. 71

BRERETON, F. S.
The Great Aeroplane. New York: 1911. V. 69
Rough-Riders of the Pampas. 1909. V. 71

BRESLAUER, BERNARD H.
Count Heinrich IV zu Castell. A German Renaissance Book Collector.... Austin: 1987. V. 73

BRESSON, ROBERT
Notes on Cinematography. New York: 1975. V. 73
Notes sur la Cinematographie. Paris: 1975. V. 73

BRETANO, PETER
Translations from the Old Testament (Dividing of Time) Explaining the Causes of Solidity and Perpetual Motion. Bideford: 1827. V. 68

BRETEZ, LOUIS
La Perspective Practique de l'Architecture.... Paris: 1706. V. 72

BRETON, ANDRE
The Magnetic Fields. London: 1985. V. 70
Nadja. Paris: 1928. V. 69

BRETON, NICHOLAS
A Mad World My Masters and other prose works. London: 1929. V. 71
The Twelve Monehts. Waltham St. Lawrence: 1927. V. 68; 71

BRETON, WILLIAM HENRY
Scandanavian Sketches or a Tour in Norway. London: 1835. V. 68

BRETT, BRETT
Hints on Bivouac and Camp Life!. Halifax: 1855. V. 72

BRETT, DAVID
10 Little Niggers. London: 1910. V. 69

BRETT, DOROTHY
Lawrence and Brett. A Friendship. Philadelphia: 1933. V. 72

BRETT, JOHN WATKINS
The Illustrated Catalogue of the Valuable Collection of Pictures and Other Works of Art of the Egyptian...of the eminent Connoisseur John Watkins Brett.... London: 1864. V. 72

BREUIL, H.
Four Hundred Centuries of Cave Art. Dordogne: 1952. V. 69

BREVAL, JOHN DURANT
Remarks on Several Parts of Europe. London: 1726. V. 69

BREVANNES, ROLAND
Seduction. Jeunes Amours au Chateau, a la Pension. Paris: 1919. V. 70

BREVE *Narratione Della Vita Della Beata Giovanna Principessa di Portogallo dell' Ordine di San Domenico.* Roma: 1693. V. 73

BREWER, A. T.
History Sixty-First Regiment Pennsylvania Volunteers 1861-1865. Pittsburgh: 1911. V. 72

BREWER, GIL
The Angry Dream. New York: 1957. V. 71
The Three-Way Split. Greenwich: 1960. V. 72

BREWER, J. MASON
Aunt Dicy Tales. Snuff Dipping Tales of the Texas Negro. 1956. V. 70
Dog Ghosts and Other Texas Negro Folk Tales. Austin: 1958. V. 70

BREWER, J. S.
An Elementary Atlas of History and Geography. London: 1855. V. 72
Monumenta Franciscana; Scilicet, I. Thomas de Eccleston de adventu fratrum minorum in Angliam. II. Adae de Marisco epistolae. III Registrum fratrum minorum Londoniae. Chronicles and Memorials of Great Britain and Ireland During the Middle Ages serie. London: 1858. V. 72

BREWER, JAMES F.
An Historian Looks at Custer In 1966 Denver Westerners' Brand Book Vol 22. Denver: 1967. V. 72

BREWER, JAMES NORRIS
Histrionic Topography: or The Birthplaces, Residences, and Funeral Monuments of the Most Distinguished Actors. London: 1818. V. 72

BREWER, L. A.
My Leigh Hunt Library: the First Editions. Cedar Rapids: 1938. V. 70

BREWER, LUTHER
Leigh Hunt and Charles Dickens. Cedar Rapids: 1930. V. 69

BREWER, THOMAS
The Life and Death of the Merry Deuill of Edmonton. 1819. V. 71

BREWERTON, GEORGE DOUGLAS
In the Buffalo Country. 1970. V. 68
Overland with Kit Carson: a Narrative of the Old Spanish Trail in '48. New York: 1930. V. 69; 71; 73

BREWSTER, DAVID
Letters on Natural Magic. London: 1832. V. 69
Letters on Natural Magic. London: 1833. V. 72
Letters on Natural Magic. London: 1842. V. 69
The Life of Sir Isaac Newton. London: 1821. V. 69
The Life of Sir Isaac Newton. London: 1831. V. 71; 73
The Martyrs of Science, or the Lives of Galileo, Tycho Brahe and Kepler. London: 1841. V. 68
Memoirs of the Life, Writings and Discoveries of Sir Isaac Newton. Edinburgh: 1860. V. 71

BREWSTER, EARL
D. H. Lawrence. Reminiscences and Correspondence. London: 1934. V. 72

BREWTON, JOHN E.
Gaily We Parade. New York: 1940. V. 71; 73
Under the Tent of the Sky-a Collection of Poems About Animals Large and Small. New York: 1937. V. 71

BREX, J. TWELLS
The Civil War of 1915. London: 1912. V. 70

BREYFOGLE, J. D.
Diary of J. D. Breyfogle Sr. 1950. V. 68

BRICE, MITFORD
The King's Dogs. 1935. V. 70

BRICE, SEWARD W.
The Coal-Field of North Somersetshire. London: 1867. V. 70

THE BRICK Reader. Toronto: 1991. V. 71

BRICKDALE, ELEANOR FORTESCUE
Golden Book of Famous Women. London: 1923. V. 69

BRICKELL, CHRISTOPHER
An English Florilegium. London: 1987. V. 72

BRICKELL, JOHN
The Natural History of North-Carolina. Dublin: 1737. V. 68

BRICKER, HERSCHEL
Our Theatre Today. New York: 1936. V. 71

BRICKNER, SAMUEL MAX
The Medical Pickwick. New York: 1915-1916. V. 69

BRICUSSE, LESLIE
Christmas 1993 or Santa's Last Ride. London: 1987. V. 70; 72

BRIDGE, JAMES HOWARD
The Inside History of the Carnegie Steel. New York: 1903. V. 68

BRIDGEMAN, T.
The Florist's Guide.... New York: 1840. V. 71

BRIDGENS, RICHARD
Furniture with Candelabra and Interior Decoration. London: 1838. V. 68; 70

BRIDGES, A.
Alphonse Mucha: The Complete Graphic Works. New York: 1980. V. 72

BRIDGES, GEORGE
Plain Dealing; or the Whole Method of Wool Smuggling Clearly Discover'd and the Weakness of the Laws in Force.... London: 1744. V. 70; 71

BRIDGES, JOHN HENRY
The Life and Work of Roger Bacon. London: 1914. V. 68

BRIDGES, ROBERT
Achilles in Scyros. London: 1892. V. 73
Demeter: a Mask. Oxford: 1905. V. 73
Eros and Psyche. London: 1885. V. 68
Eros and Psyche. London: 1894. V. 73
Eros and Psyche. Newtown: 1935. V. 68; 70; 73
The Growth of Love. London: 1876. V. 73
The Growth of Love. Oxford: 1889. V. 73
The Humours of the Court, a Comedy, and Other Poems. 1893. V. 68
The Humours of the Court, a Comedy, and Other Poems. London: 1893. V. 73
Ibant Obscuri; an Experiment in the Classical Hexameter. Oxford: 1917. V. 73
New Verse Written in 1921. Oxford: 1925. V. 73
New Verse Written in 1921. Oxford: 1926. V. 68
October and Other Poems with Occasional verses on the War. London: 1920. V. 73
Ode for the Bicentenary Commemoration of Henry Purcell, with Other Poems. London: 1896. V. 68
On Hearing the Death of Theodore Watts-Dunton: a Parody. Winchester: 1940. V. 73
Poems. 1873. V. 73
Poems. London: 1879. V. 73
Poems. Oxford: 1884. V. 70
Poems Written in the Year MCMXIII. 1914. V. 71
Poems...First Series. London: 1880. V. 73
The Poetical Works of Robert Bridges. London: 1898-1905. V. 68
The Poetical Works of Robert Bridges, Excluding the Eight Dramas. London: 1912. V. 73
Prometheus the Firegiver. London: 1884. V. 68
The Shorter Poems of Robert Bridges. London: 1890. V. 68; 73
The Tapestry Poems. 1925. V. 73
The Testament of Beauty. Oxford: 1927-1929. V. 73
The Testament of Beauty. Oxford: 1929. V. 70; 73
Verses Written for Mrs. Daniel. Oxford: 1932. V. 73

BRIDGES, VICTOR
The Happy Murderers. London: 1932. V. 70
I Did Not Kill Osborne. Philadelphia: 1934. V. 72
The Secret of the Creek. Boston: 1930. V. 69

THE BRIDGEWATER Treatises n the Power Wisdom and Goodness of God as Manifested in the Creation. No.s I-VIII (in 12 volumes). London: 1834-1840. V. 72

BRIDGING Normandy To Berlin. London: 1945. V. 72

BRIDGMAN, ELIJAH COLEMAN
Description of the City of Canton; with an Appendix.... Canton: 1834. V. 69

BRIDGMAN, FREDERICK ARTHUR
Winters in Algeria. New York: 1890. V. 70; 72

BRIDSON, G.
Plant, Animal and Antomical Illustration in Art and Science. Winchester: 1990. V. 70

A BRIEF Account of the New York Hospital. New York: 1804. V. 71

A BRIEF Account of the Proceedings of the Committee, Appointed by the Yearly Meeting of Friends, Held in Baltimore, for Promoting the Improvement and Civilization of the Indian Natives. London: 1806. V. 68

A BRIEF Account of the Proceedings of the Committee Appointed in the Year 1795 by the Yearly Meeting of Friends of Pennsylvania, New Jersey, etc.... Philadelphia: 1806. V. 69

A BRIEF History of Seventh Engineers, 5th Division. 1919. V. 73

BRIEF Memories of Niagara. Its Rapids, Falls and Whirlpool. London: 1900?. V. 73

BRIERLEY, BEN
Ab-O'Th-Yate Sketches and Other Short Stories. Oldham: 1896. V. 71; 73

BRIERLEY, HENRY
The Registers of Barton, Baptisms and Marriages 1666-1812, Burials 1666-1830. Kendal: 1917. V. 71
The Registers of Bolton-Le-Sands 1655-1736 and Over Kellet 1652-1812. Kendal: 1911. V. 73
The Registers of Brough Under Stainmore 1556-1812. Kendal: 1923-1924. V. 71
The Registers of Crosthwaite. Volume II. 1600-1670. Penrith: 1930. V. 73
The Registers of Crosthwaite. Volume IV. Penrith: 1931. V. 71
The Registers of Kendal. Westmorland 1558-1687. Kendal: 1921. V. 71
The Registers of Milburn, Westmorland 1679-1812. Kendal: 1913. V. 71
The Registers of St. Michael's on Wyre 1659-1707 and Woodplumpton 1604-1659. Cambridge: 1906. V. 73
The Registers of the Parish Church of Cartmel in the County of Lancaster.... Rochdale: 1907. V. 71
The Registers of the Parish Church of Dacre, Cumberland 1559-1716. Kendal: 1912. V. 71
The Registers of the Parish Church of Skelton, Cumberland, 1580-1812. Kendal: 1921-1973. V. 71
The Registers of the Parish Church of Skelton, Cumberland 1805-1812. Kendal: 1918. V. 71

BRIERRE DE BOISMONT, A.
A History of Dreams, Visions, Apparitions, Ecstasy, Magnetism and Somnambulism. Philadelphia: 1855. V. 69

BRIGG, JOHN J.
The King's Highway in Craven. Cross Hills: 1927. V. 73

BRIGGS, ASA
Essays in the History of Publishing in Celebration of the 250th Anniversary of the House of Longman 1724-1974. London: 1974. V. 71

BRIGGS, C. L.
The Wood Carvers of Cordova, New Mexico. Knoxville: 1980. V. 69

BRIGGS, CHARLES F.
Homes of American Authors; Comprising Anecdotical, Personal and Descriptive Sketches by Various Writers. New York: 1857. V. 71

BRIGGS, D. E.
Malting and Brewing Science. London: 1981-1982. V. 73

BRIGGS, ELLIS O.
Shots Heard Round the World. New York: 1957. V. 72

BRIGGS, HAROLD
Frontiers of the Northwest. New York: 1940. V. 71

BRIGGS, J.
The Lonsdale Magazine, or, Provincial Repository.... Kendal: 1829-1822. V. 71

BRIGGS, LLOYD VERNON
Arizona and New Mexico 1882; California 1886; Mexico 1891. Boston: 1932. V. 71; 73
California and the West 1881 and Later. Boston: 1931. V. 69

BRIGGS, RAYMOND
Father Christmas Goes on Holiday. London: 1975. V. 69

BRIGGS, WALTER
Without Noise of Arms. Flagstaff: 1976. V. 70; 73

BRIGHAM, AMARIAH
Remarks on the Influence of Mental Cultivation and Mental Excitement Upon Health. Glasgow: 1836. V. 68

BRIGHAM, CLARENCE S.
Bibliography of American Editions of Robinson Crusoe to 1830. Worcester: 1958. V. 70
History and Bibliography of American Newspapers 1960-1820. Worcester: 1947. V. 69

BRIGHAM, S. J.
Under Blue Skies. New York: 1886. V. 70

BRIGHAM, WILLIAM T.
The Volcanoes of Kilauea and Mauna Loa in the Island of Hawaii. Honolulu: 1909. V. 70

BRIGHOUSE, HAROLD
Six Fantasies. New York: 1931. V. 70

BRIGHT & SON
ABC Descriptive Priced Catalogue of the World's Postage Stamps.... Bournemouth: 1896. V. 68

BRIGHT, CHARLES
The Life Story of Charles Tilston Bright by his Brother Edward Brailsford and his Son Charles Bright. London: 1899. V. 71
The Life Story of Sir Charles Tilston Bright.... London: 1908. V. 68
Submarine Telegraphs their History, Construction and Working. London: 1898. V. 69

BRIGHT, J. S.
Dorking: a History of the Town.... Dorking: 1876. V. 70

BRIGHT, JOHN
The Public Letters.... London: 1885. V. 71
Speeches on Parliamentary Reform, &c. by John Bright, Esq. M.P., Delivered During the Autumn of 1866 to the People of England, Scotland and Ireland at Birmingham, Manchester Lees, Glasgow, Dublin and London. London: 1866. V. 72

BRIGHT, R.
Original Papers...on Renal Disease. London: 1937. V. 71

BRIGHT, RICHARD
Travels from Vienna through Lower Hungary; With Some Remarks on the State of Vienna During the Congress, in the Year 1814. Edinburgh: 1818. V. 72

BRIGHT, ROBERT
Me and the Bears. 1951. V. 72; 73

BRIGHTLY, WILLIAM
Lilliput Lyrics. London: 1899. V. 70

BRIGHTMAN, CAROL
Writing Dangerously. NY: 1992. V. 72

BRIGHTON, J. G.
Admiral of the Fleet, Sir Provo W.P. Wallis, G.C.B. Etc. A Memoir. London: 1892. V. 72

BRIGHTWELL, C. L.
Romantic Incidents in the Lives of Naturalists and Celebrated Travellers. London: 1863. V. 68; 70; 72

BRIKBECK, MORRIS
Notes on a Journey in America from the Coast of Virginia to the Territory of Illinois...(with) Letters from Illinois. Dublin: 1818,. V. 73

BRILIOTH, BORJE
A Grammar of the Dialect of Lorton (Cumberland). 1913. V. 71

BRILL, CHARLES J.
Conquest Of The Southern Plains-Uncensored Narrative Of The Battle Of The Washita And Custer's Southern Campaign. Oklahoma City: 1938. V. 72

BRILL, GEORGE REITER
Rhymes of Golden Age. Philadelphia: 1908. V. 71

BRILLAT SAVARIN, JEAN ANTHELME
Physiology of Taste. New York: 1971. V. 68

BRIMLOW, GEORGE FRANCIS
Cavalryman Out of the West: Life of General William Carey Brown. Caldwell: 1944. V. 72

BRIN, DAVID
The Postman. New York: 1985. V. 72

BRINCKERHOFF, SIDNEY B.
Lancers for the King. Phoenix: 1965. V. 69; 71; 73
Spanish Military Weapons in Colonial America 1700-1821. 1972. V. 69

BRINCKMANN, JOHN
The Tuckerton Railroad. Edison: 1973. V. 69

BRINDLEY, JAMES
The History of Inland Navigations, Particularly that of the Duke of Bridgwater. London: 1766. V. 69

BRINE, MARY DOW
From Gold to Grey. New York/London/Paris: 1886. V. 69
Little Lad Jamie. New York: 1895. V. 70

BRINGER, RUDOLPHE
Trente ans D'Humour. Paris: 1924. V. 68

BRININSTOOL, E. A.
The Custer Fight, Captain Benteen's Story of The Little Big Horn June 25-26 1876. Hollywood: 1933. V. 72
Fighting Indian Warriors. 1953. V. 68
Fighting Indian Warriors. Harrisburg: 1953. V. 72
A Trooper with Custer - And Other Historic Incidents of the Battle of The Little Big Horn. Columbus: 1925. V. 72
Troopers with Custer: Historic Incidents of the Battle of the Little Big Horn. Harrisburg: 1952. V. 69; 71; 73

BRINK, ANDRE P.
The Ambassador. Johannesburg: 1964. V. 70

BRINNIN, JOHN MALCOLM
Grand Luxe. The Transatlantic Style. London: 1988. V. 68

BRINTON, DANIEL G.
Rig Veda Americanus - Sacred Songs of the Ancient Mexicans. Philadelphia: 1890. V. 70

BRIQUET, C. M.
Les Filigranes. Dictionnaire Historique des Marques du Papier, des leur Apparition vers 1282 jusqu'en 1600. Paris: 1907. V. 70

BRISBIN, JAMES S.
The Beef Bonanza; Or How to Get Rich On the Plains. Philadelphia: 1881. V. 71

BRISCOE, JOHN
A Discourse on the Late Funds of the Million-Act, Lottery Act and Bank of England. London: 1696. V. 72
Mr. John Asgill His Plagiarism Detected; and His Several Assertions.... London: 1696. V. 69

BRISDON, GAVIN
Printmaking and Picture Printing: a Bibliographical Guide to Artistic and Industrial Techniques in Britain 1750-1900. Oxford and Williamsburg: 1984. V. 71

BRISEUX, CHARLES ETIENNE
Architecture Moderne ou l'Art de Bien Batir Pour Toutes Sortes de Personnes.... Paris: 1728-1729. V. 68; 70; 72
Traite du Beau Essentiel dans les Arts, Applique Particulierement a l'Architecture.... Paris: 1752. V. 68; 70; 72

BRISSENDEN, PAUL FREDERICK
The I. W. W. A Study of American Syndicalism. New York: 1919. V. 68; 69
The Launching of the Industrial Workers of the World. New York: 1971. V. 68

BRISSON, BARNABE
De Ritu Nuptarum Liber singularis. Paris: 1564. V. 68; 73

BRISTED, JOHN
The Resources of the United States of America. New York: 1818. V. 72

BRISTOL, GEORGE DIGBY, EARL OF
Letters Between the Lord George Digby and Sir Kenelm Digby Concerning Religion. London: 1651. V. 73

BRISTOL, JOHN DIGBY, EARL OF
The Speeches of the Lord Digby in the High Court of Parliament, Concerning Grievances and the Triennial Parliament. London: 1641. V. 73

BRISTOW, D.
Soweto: Portrait of a City. London: 1990. V. 68

BRISTOW, GWEN
The Gutenberg Murders. New York: 1931. V. 69
The Invisible Host. 1930. V. 73
The Mardi Gras Murders. New York: 1932. V. 68
Two and Two Make Twenty-Two. 1932. V. 73

BRITAINE, WILLIAM LE
Human Prudence; or the Art by Which a Man May Raise Himself and His Fortune to Grandeur. London: 1739. V. 69; 73

BRITE, POPPY Z.
Are You Loathsome Tonight?. Springfield: 1998. V. 68
Lost Souls. New York: 1992. V. 68

BRITISH & AMERICAN JOINT COMMISSION FOR THE FINAL SETTLEMENT
Volume 5. In the Matter of the Claim of the Hudson's Bay Company, Closing Argument of the Claimants in Reply to the Responsive Argument of the United States. Montreal: 1869. V. 71
Volume 6. Memorial and Argument on the Part of the Puget's Sound Agricultural Company. Montreal: 1868. V. 71
Volume 8. Evidence for the United States in the Matter of the Claim of the Hudson's Bay Company. First Part. Washington: 1867. V. 71
Volume 9. Evidence for the United States in the Matter of the Claim of the Hudson's Bay Company. Second Part. Washington: 1867. V. 71
Volume 10. Evidence for the United States in the Matter of the Claim of the Puget's Sound Agricultural Company. Washington: 1867. V. 71
Volume 11. Evidence for the United States in the Matter of the Claims of the Hudson's Bay and Pueget's Sound Agricultural Companies. Miscellaneous. Washington: 1867. V. 71

BRITISH & FOREIGN ANTI-SLAVERY SOCIETY
General Gordon and the...on the Suakin-Berber Railway. London?: 1882,. V. 73
Scandals at Cairo in Connection with Slavery. Cairo: 1885. V. 73

BRITISH Antarctic Expedition 1910-1913. Calcutta: 1919. V. 70

BRITISH ASSOCIATION FOR THE ADVANCEMENT OF SCIENCE
Handbook for New South Wales. Sydney: 1914. V. 72
Report of the 48th Meeting Held at Dublin in August 1878. 1879. V. 69

THE BRITISH Champion; or Honour Rewarded. York: 1800?. V. 69

THE BRITISH Chronologist; Comprehending Every Material Occurrence, Ecclesiastical, Civil, or Military.... London: 1789. V. 68

BRITISH Columbia Horse and Cattle Brands. 1944. Victoria: 1945. V. 70

BRITISH COLUMBIA. LEGISLATURE - 1872
Journals of the Legislative Assembly of the Province of British Columbia...Being the First Session of the First Parliament of British Columbia. Victoria: 1872. V. 71

BRITISH COLUMBIA. SUPREME COURT - 1880
In the Supreme Court of British Columbia. The Queen vs. Allan McLean, Archibald McLean, Charles McLean and Alexander Hare, Indicted, Found Guilty and Sentenced to Death for the Murder of John Ussher, Judgement of the Court.... Victoria: 1880. V. 71

BRITISH LIBRARY
Short Title Catalogue of Hungarian Books Printed Before 1851 in the British Library. London: 1995. V. 70

THE BRITISH Martial; or an Anthology of English Epigrams.. London: 1806. V. 72

BRITISH MUSEUM
Catalogue of Books Printed in the XVth Century Now in the British Museum. London: 1908-1963. V. 72
Catalogue of Books Printed in the XVth Century Now in the British Museum. London: 1963. V. 70
Catalogue of Manuscripts in the British Museum. New Series. Volume I. Part I: Arundel Manuscripts. Part II: Burney Manuscripts. Part III: Index to the Arundel & Burney Manscripts. Part I. London: 1834-1840. V. 70
Catalogue of the Birds in the British Museum. London: 1874-1898. V. 73
Catalogue of the Books, Manuscripts, Maps and Drawings in the British Museum. London: 1903-1940. V. 70
Catalogue of the Books, Manuscripts, Maps and Drawings in the British Museum (Natural History). New York: 1992. V. 72
History of the Collections. Volume I. Libraries, Botany, Geology and Minerals. Volume II. Zoology. Volume II. Appendix General History of Dept. of Zoology from 1856-1895. London: 1904-1912. V. 70

THE BRITISH Musical Miscellany, or, the Delightful Grove.... London: 1734-1737. V. 68

THE BRITISH Novelists, with an Essay.... London: 1810. V. 68

BRITISH Numismatic Journal, and Proceedings of the British Numismatic Society. London: 1905-1912. V. 72

THE BRITISH Poets. London: 1855. V. 73

BRITISH Quadrupeds. London. V. 70

BRITISH Volunteers. London: 1866. V. 70

BRITISH Yachting. Edinburgh: 1897. V. 70

BRITTAIN, VERA
Honourable Estate - A Novel of Transition. London: 1936. V. 72
Poems of the War and After. New York: 1934. V. 72
Testament of Experience - An Autobiographical Story of the Years 1925-1950. London: 1957. V. 72
Testament of Youth. London: 1935. V. 70
The Women of Oxford - A Fragment of History. London: 1960. V. 72

BRITTEN, F. J.
Old Clocks and Watches & Their Makers. Woodbridge: 1977. V. 72
Old Clocks and Watches & Their Makers. London: 1986. V. 72

BRITTIAN, PHIL
Texan on the Halfshell. Garden City: 1982. V. 72

BRITTON, JOHN
The Autobiogrpahy of John Britton. London: 1850. V. 73
The Beauties of England and Wales. London: 1801. V. 73
The Beauties of England and Wales. London: 1802. V. 73
Biographical Sketch of the Life and Writings of John Britton. 1828. V. 73
A Brief Memoir of the Life and Writings of John Britton. London: 1825. V. 73
An Historical Account of Corsham House, in Wiltshire; the Seat of Paul Cobb Methuen, Esq. with a Catalogue of His Celebrated Collection of Pictures.... London: 1806. V. 68
The History and Description...of Cassiobury Park, Hertfordshire, the Seat of the Earl of Essex.... London: 1837. V. 68
Illustrations of the Early Domestic Architecture of England. London: 1846. V. 70; 72

BRITTON, N. L.
Botany of Porto Rico and the Virgin Islands.... New York: 1922-1930. V. 71
Botany of Porto Rico and the Virgin Islands.... New York: 1923-1930. V. 68
The Cactaceae: Descriptions and Illustrations of Plants of the Cactus Family. Pasadena: 1937. V. 73
The Cactaceae, Descriptions and Illustrations of Plants of the Cactus Family. Washington: 1937. V. 71; 73
The Cactaceae, Descriptions and Illustrations of Plants of the Cactus Family. New York: 1963. V. 71; 73
Catalogue of Plants Found in New Jersey. Trenton: 1889. V. 70
An Illustrated Flora of the Northern United States, Canada and the British Possessions. New York: 1913. V. 70
An Illustrated Flora of the Northern United States, Canada and the British Possessions. New York: 1936. V. 70
Illustrated Flora of the Northern United States, Canada and the British Possessions. New York: 1947. V. 69

BRITTON, WILEY
The (Five Civilized Indian Nations) Union Indian Brigade in the Civil War. Kansas City: 1922. V. 69; 70
The Union Indian Brigade in the Civil War. Kansas City: 1922. V. 73

BRITWELL COURT LIBRARY
The Britwell Handlist or Short-Title Catalogue of the Principal Volumes from the Time of Caxton to the Year 1800, Formerly in the Library of Britwell Court, Buckinghamshire. London: 1933. V. 70

BRIZGUZ Y BRU, ATANASIO GENARO
Escuela de Arquitectura Civil.... Valencia: 1804. V. 68; 70; 72

BROADBENT, ARTHUR T.
The Minor Domestic Architecture of Gloucesterhire. London: 1931. V. 68

BROADBENT, ELLINOR LUCY
Alpine Valleys of Italy from San Remo to Lake Orta. London: 1928. V. 69

BROADBENT, WILLIAM HENRY
The Pulse. Philadelphia;: 1890. V. 69

BROADCAST MUSIC, INC.
Meet the Artists. New York: 1952. V. 73

BROADLEY, A. M.
Dr. Johnson and Mrs. Thrale. London and New York: 1910. V. 72

BROADLEY, JOHN
Memoirs of the Life of Master John Shawe, Sometime Vicar Rotherham. Hull: 1824. V. 69

BROADUS, EDMUND KEMPER
Saturday and Sunday. Toronto: 1935. V. 73

BROCH, HERMANN
The Unknown Quantity. New York. V. 70; 71

BROCK, ALAN ST. H.
A History of Fireworks. London: 1949. V. 72

BROCK, C. E.
Atlas of Human Anatomy. New York: 1881. V. 71

BROCK, H. M.
Jack and the Beanstalk. London: 1930. V. 73
Valentine and Orson. The Old Fairy Tales. London: 1914. V. 73

BROCK, HENRY IRVING
Colonial Churches in Virginia. Richmond: 1930. V. 72

BROCK, J. ELMER
Power River Country, The Papers of J. Elmer Brock. Cheyenne: 1989. V. 72

BROCK, R. A.
Virginia and Virginians. Richmond and Toledo: 1888. V. 71

BROCK, SAMUEL
Injuries of the Brain and Spinal Cord and Their Coverings. Baltimore: 1949. V. 72

BROCKBANK, EDWARD MANSFIELD
Sketches of the Lives and Work of the Honorary Medical Staff of the Manchester Infirmary from Its Foundation in 1752 to 1830.... Manchester: 1894. V. 68

BROCKBANK, ELISABETH
Richard Hubberthorne of Yealand, Yeoman, Soldier, Quaker 1628-1682. London: 1929. V. 71; 72

BROCKBANK, WILLIAM
Portrait of a Hospital 1752-1948 to Commemorate the Bi-Centenary of the Royal Infirmary, Manchester. Toronto: 1952. V. 68

BROCKEDON, WILLIAM
Finden's Illustrations of the Life and Works of Lord Byron. London: 1833-1834. V. 71
Italy, Classical, Historical, and Picturesque. London: 1842-1843. V. 72
Journals of Excursions in the Alps: The Pennine. London: 1833. V. 68

BROCKETT, JOHN TROTTER
A Glossary of North Country Words, in Use. Newcastle-upon-Tyne: 1825. V. 71; 73
A Glossary of North Country Words, in Use. Newcastle upon Tyne: 1846. V. 73

BROCKETT, LINUS PIERPONT
Our Western Empire or the New West Beyond the Mississippi. Philadelphia: 1881. V. 68
The Silk Industry in America. 1876. V. 69
Woman: Her Rights, Wrongs, Privileges and Responsibilities. Hartford: 1870. V. 69

BROCKETT, PAUL
Bibliography of Aeronautics. Washington: 1910. V. 70

BROCKLEHURST, H. C.
Game Animals of the Sudan. 1931. V. 73

BROCKMAN, W.
Portrait of a Hospital 1752-1948...the Royal Infirmary, Manchester. London: 1952. V. 71

BRODAL, ALF
The Reticular Formation of the Brain Stem. Edinburgh: 1957. V. 68

BRODER, PATRICIA JANIS
American Indian Painting and Sculpture. New York: 1981. V. 69; 70; 72
Bronzes of the American West. New York: 1973. V. 70; 71; 72
Hopi Painting - The World of the Hopis. New York: 1978. V. 69; 70; 72
Hopi Painting: The World of the Hopis. New York: 1979. V. 69
Taos: a Painter's Dream. Boston: 1980. V. 73

BRODIE, BENJAMIN COLLINS
Pathological and Surgical Observations on Diseases of the Joints. London: 1834. V. 72
The Works of Sir Benjamin Collins Brodie.... London: 1863. V. 68; 72

BRODKEY, HAROLD
A Poem About Testimony and Argument. New York: 1986. V. 73
The Runaway Soul. London: 1991. V. 70

BRODMAN, ESTELLE
The Development of Medical Bibliography. 1954. V. 71

BRODRICK, GEORGE C.
English Land and English Landlords. London: 1881. V. 71

BRODSKY, JOSEPH
Elegy to John Donne and Other Poems. London: 1967. V. 72
To Urania. New York: 1988. V. 69; 73

BRODY, CATHARINE
Cash Item. New York: 1933. V. 69; 70

BRODY, J. J.
The Anaszi. New York: 1990. V. 69
Indian Painters and White Patrons. Albuquerque: 1971. V. 71

BROGAN, HUGH
The Life of Arthur Ransome. London: 1984. V. 70

BROGGER, SUZANNE
Deliver Us from Love. 1976. V. 68

BROGGER, W. C.
Fridtjof Nansen 1861-1893. London: 1896. V. 68

BROGGIA, CARLO ANTONIO
Trattato de Tributi, Dele Monete, a Del Governo Politico Della Sanita.... Naples: 1743. V. 72

BROGLIE, LOUIS CESAR VICTOR MAURICE DE
Ondes et quanta (with) Quanta de Lumiere, Diffraction et Interferences (with) Les Quanta, la Theorie Cinetique des Gaz et le Principe de Fermat. In: Comptes Rendus des Seances de l'Academie des Sciences, Tome 1777, Juillet - Decembre 1923. Paris: 1923. V. 72

BROKAW, TOM
The Greatest Generation Speaks. New York: 1999. V. 68

BROKE, GEORGE
With Sack and Stock in Alaska. London: 1891. V. 70

BROMELL, HENRY
The Slightest Distance. Boston: 1974. V. 69

BROMFIELD, LOUIS
Night in Bombay. New York: 1940. V. 71
The Rains Came. New York: 1937. V. 72
The Wild Country. New York: 1948. V. 69

BROMLEY, GEORGE T.
The Long Ago and the Later On - or Recollections of Eighty Years. San Francisco: 1904. V. 70

BROMLEY, THOMAS
The Way to the Sabbath of Rest. Germantown: 1759. V. 71

BROMLEY, WILLIAM
Several Years Travels through Portugal, Spain, Italy, Germany, Prussia, Sweden, Denmark and the United Provinces. London: 1702. V. 72

BRONAUGH, W. C.
Youngers' Fight for Freedom: a Southern Soldier's Twenty Years Campaign to Open Northern Prison Doors - with Anecdotes of War Days. Columbia: 1906. V. 70

BRONDSTED, P. O.
Voyages et Cecherches dans la Grece.... Paris: 1826-1830. V. 72

BRONK, WILLIAM
Five Cummington Poems 1939. Cummington: 1939. V. 72
Life Supports. New Rochelle: 1981. V. 72
Light and Dark. Ashland: 1956. V. 73
That Tantalus. New Rochelle: 1971. V. 71

BRONOWSKI, JACOB
The Ascent of Man. Boston: 1973. V. 69
The Identity of Man. Garden City: 1965. V. 70

BRONSON, EDGAR BEECHER
Cowboy Life On the Western Plains, Reminiscences of A Ranchman. New York: 1910. V. 71
In Closed Territory. Chicago: 1910. V. 69
Reminiscences of a Ranchman. New York: 1908. V. 69; 71; 73

BRONSON, F. W.
The Bulldog Has the Key. New York: 1949. V. 69

BRONSON, J.
The Domestic Manufacturer's Assistant and Family Directory, in the Arts of Weaving and Dyeing.... Utica: 1817. V. 70

BRONSON, WILFRED S.
Fingerfins. New York: 1930. V. 69

BRONTE, ANNE
Agnes Grey. Oxford: 1988. V. 70
The Complete Poems. London: 1920. V. 68; 70; 71
The Complete Poems. New York: 1920. V. 70; 73
Dreams and Other Poems. 1917. V. 73
The Tenant of Wildfell Hall. 1854. V. 73
The Tenant of Wildfell Hall. London: 1873. V. 70

BRONTE, CHARLOTTE
The Adventures of Ernest Alembert, a Fairy Tale. 1896. V. 68; 73
The Adventures of Ernest Alembert, a Fairy Tale. London: 1896. V. 70
The Complete Poems of.... London: 1923. V. 70; 73
Darius Codomannus: a Poem. 1920. V. 73
Five Novelettes: Passing Event, Julia, Mina Laury, Captain Henry Hastings, Caroline Vernon. 1971. V. 73
Jane Eyre. 1847. V. 73
Jane Eyre. London: 1847. V. 72
Jane Eyre. Boston: 1848. V. 68; 70; 73
Jane Eyre. Leipzig: 1850. V. 73
Jane Eyre. London: 1857. V. 70
Jane Eyre. London: 1911. V. 70
Jane Eyre. Franklin Center: 1981. V. 73
Kitty Bell, the Orphan. 1914. V. 73
Legends of Angria. New Haven: 1933. V. 70
Letters Recounting the Deaths of Emily, Anne and Branwell Bronte. To Which are Added Letters signed "Currer Bell" and "C. B. Nicholls". London: 1913. V. 73
The Poems of.... New York: 1883. V. 70
The Poems of.... 1984. V. 73
The Professor. London: 1857. V. 68; 70; 73
The Professor. New York: 1857. V. 70; 73
The Professor. London: 1860. V. 68; 73
The Professor. London: 1922. V. 70; 73
The Red Cross Knight and Other Poems. 1917. V. 73
Richard Coeur de Lion & Blondel, a Poem. 1912. V. 73
Saul and Other Poems. 1913. V. 73
Saul and Other Poems. London: 1913. V. 68; 70
Self Communion - a Poem. 1900. V. 73
Shirley. London: 1849. V. 73
Shirley. New York: 1850. V. 70
Shirley. London: 1857. V. 73
Shirley. London: 1866. V. 73
Shirley. London: 1922. V. 70
Shirley. Paris: 1933. V. 70; 73
Le Sortilege. (The Spell). Paris: 1946. V. 73
The Spell, an Extravaganza. 1931. V. 73
The Twelve Adventurers and Other Stories. London: 1925. V. 68; 70; 73
Two Tales: The Secret Hart & Lily Hart. 1978. V. 73
Villette. London: 1853. V. 68
Villette. London: 1855. V. 70; 73
Villette. London: 1873. V. 70
The Works. London. V. 71

BRONTE, EMILY
Un Amant. Paris: 1892. V. 73
The Complete Poems of.... London: 1923. V. 70
Gondal Poems. Oxford: 1938. V. 70; 73
Gondal's Queen. Austin: 1955. V. 73
Les Hauts de Hurle-Vent. (Wuthering Heights). Paris: 1925. V. 70; 73
Poems. London: 1923. V. 70; 73
Poems. London: 1963. V. 70
Selected Poems. 1944. V. 70
Selected Poems of Emily Bronte. London: 1952. V. 69
Wuthering Heights. New York: 1848. V. 73
Wuthering Heights. New York: 1855. V. 68
Wuthering Heights. New York: 1862. V. 70; 73
Wuthering Heights. London: 1931. V. 68; 70
Wuthering Heights. New York: 1931. V. 70
Wuthering Heights. New York: 1940. V. 73
Wuthering Heights. Franklin Center: 1978. V. 70
Wuthering Heights. 1980. V. 73

BRONTE, PATRICK
And the Weary Are at Rest. Leeds: 1924. V. 73
And the Weary Are At Rest. London: 1924. V. 68; 70
Bronteana: His Collected Works and Life. 1898. V. 70
The Cottage in the Woods. 1818. V. 70
The Cottage in the Woods. Bradford: 1818. V. 68
Cottage Poems. Halifax: 1811. V. 73
The Rev. Patrick Bronte. His Collected Works and Life. 1898. V. 73
The Rev. Patrick Bronte. His Collected Works and Life. New York: 1978. V. 73
The Rural Minstrel: a Miscellany of Descriptive Poems. Halifax: 1813. V. 73

BRONTE SOCIETY
Bronte Society Transactions, Vols. 1-6. 1898-1925. V. 73
Catalogue of the Bonnell Collection in the Bronte Parsonage Museum. Haworth: 1932. V. 73

BRONTE, THE SISTERS
Jane Eyre (and) Wuthering Heights. New York: 1943. V. 68; 70
Novels. Edinburgh: 1905. V. 73
The Novels. London: 1905-1909. V. 70; 73
The Novels. Edinburgh: 1924. V. 70; 73
The Novels. 1931-1933. V. 70; 73
The Novels. London: 1964-1970. V. 73
The Novels. London: 1991. V. 68; 70
Poems. London: 1846. V. 68
Poems. London: 1846-1848. V. 70; 73
Poems. 1915. V. 73
Poems. London: 1915. V. 70
Poems by Currer, Ellis and Acton Bell. London: 1846. V. 73

BRONTE, THE SISTERS continued
Wuthering Heights and Agnes Grey. London: 1851. V. 70
Wuthering Heights and Jane Eyre. New York: 1943. V. 70; 73
Wuthering Heights, together with Agnes Grey (by Anne Bronte). London: 1850. V. 71

THE BRONTES, Their Lives, Friendships and Correspondence. 1932. V. 70; 73

THE BRONTOS and the Tootle Bird. Edinburgh & London: 1905. V. 69

BRONX MUSEUM OF ARTS
Latin American Spirit: Art and Artists in the U.S. 1920-1970. 1988. V. 72

BROOK, A. W.
Witch's Hollow or the New Babes in the Wood. New York: 1921. V. 72

BROOK, G.
Catalogue of the Madreprorarian Corals in the British Museum. 1893-1928. V. 69

BROOK, PETER
The Empty Space. New York: 1968. V. 72

BROOK, R.
The Cyclopaeda of Botany.... 1854. V. 69

BROOKE, BRIAN
The Poems of Brian Brooke (Korongo). London: 1917. V. 70

BROOKE, FULKE GREVILLE, 1ST BARON
Caelica. Newtown: 1937. V. 68; 72
Certaine Learned and Elegant Workes. 1633. V. 72
Certaine Learned and Elegant Workes. London: 1633. V. 68
The Life of the Renowned Sir Philip Sidney. London: 1652. V. 71

BROOKE, HENRY
Annals of the Revolution; or, a History of the Doans. Philadelphia: 1843. V. 68
The Fool of Quality; or, the History of Henry Earl of Moreland. London: 1767-1770. V. 73
The History of Henry Earl of Moreland. London: 1793. V. 69

BROOKE, J.
The Wild Orchids of Britain. London: 1950. V. 71; 73

BROOKE, JOCELYN
The Crisis in Bulgaria - or Ibsen to the Rescue!. London: 1956. V. 72
The Elements of Death and Other Poems. Aldington, Kent: 1952. V. 71
The Goose Cathedral. London: 1950. V. 68; 73
Private View - Four Portraits. London: 1954. V. 72

BROOKE, JOHN HEDLEY
Thinking About Matter. Studies in the History of Chemical Philosophy. Aldershot, Hampshire: 1995. V. 71

BROOKE, LAURENCE
Three Fair Daughters. London: 1883. V. 68

BROOKE, LEONARD LESLIE
Johnny Crow's New Garden. London: 1935. V. 71
The Story of the Three Bears. London. V. 72

BROOKE, RALPHE
A Discoverie of Certaine Errours Published in Print in the Much Commended Britannia, 1594 . . . London: 1723. V. 71
A Discoverie Of Certaine Errours Published in Print In The Much Commended Britannia, 1594. London: 1723-1724. V. 72

BROOKE, RUPERT
Amphora: A Collection of Prose and Verse Chosen by the Editor of the Bibelot. Portland: 1912. V. 68
Collected Poems. New York: 1915. V. 73
The Collected Poems. London: 1919. V. 68; 69; 73
Democracy and the Arts. London: 1946. V. 68
Democracy and the Arts. London: 1947. V. 68
John Webster and Elizabethan Drama. London: 1916. V. 73
Letters. London: 1968. V. 73
Letters from America. 1916. V. 73
Letters from Rupert Brooke to His Publisher 1911-1914. New York: 1975. V. 68
1914 and Other Poems. London: 1915. V. 70; 72; 73
1914 and Other Poems. New York: 1915. V. 70
The Old Vicarage Grantchester. London: 1916. V. 68; 70; 73
Poems. London: 1911. V. 73

BROOKE-LITTLE, J. P.
Beasts in Heraldry. Brattleboro: 1974. V. 72

BROOKER, W. D.
A Century of Scottish Mountaineering. 1988. V. 70; 73

BROOKES, RICHARD
The Art of Angling, Rock and Sea-Fishing: with the Natural History of River, Pond and Sea-Fish. London: 1740. V. 69
The General Dispensatory.... 1753. V. 72
The General Gazetteer; and Geographical Dictionary. London: 1876. V. 72
The General Gazetteer; or Compendious Geographical Dictionary. London: 1820. V. 72
The General Practice of Physic. London: 1754. V. 72
The General Practice of Physic. London: 1763. V. 71
A New and Accurate System of Natural History. London: 1771-1772. V. 69

BROOKES, S.
An Introduction to the Study of Conchology. 1815. V. 69

BROOKFIELD, ARTHUR M.
Autobiography of Thomas Allen. Edinburgh: 1882. V. 71

THE BROOKLYN Waterworks and Sewers. A Descriptive Memoir. New York: 1867. V. 72

BROOKNER, ANITA
The Bay of Angels. London: 2001. V. 70
Brief Lives. London: 1990. V. 68
Family and Friends. London: 1985. V. 70; 73
The Genius of the Future - Studies in French Art Criticism. London: 1971. V. 69
Greuze; the Rise and Fall of an Eighteenth-Century Phenomenon. 1972. V. 70
Hotel du Lac. London: 1984. V. 69; 71
Incidents in the Rue Laugier. London: 1995. V. 70
Jacques-Louis David. London: 1980. V. 70
Latecomers. London: 1988. V. 68; 70; 71
A Private View. London: 1994. V. 70
Providence. London: 1982. V. 70
A Start in Life. London: 1981. V. 68; 70; 71; 72; 73
Undue Influence. London: 1999. V. 70

BROOKS, BRYANT B.
Memoirs Of...Cowboy, Trapper, Lumberman, Stockman, Oilman, Banker and Governor of Wyoming. Glendale: 1939. V. 71

BROOKS, CHANDLER
The Historical Development of Physiological Thought. New York: 1999. V. 69

BROOKS, CLEANTH
An Affair of Honor: Larry Brown's Joe. An Essay. Chapel Hill: 1991. V. 68
An Anthology of Stories from the Southern Review. 1953. V. 70
Modern Poetry and the Tradition. Chapel Hill: 1939. V. 71

BROOKS, DAVID
Story of Richmond in Yorkshire. London: 1924. V. 73
The Story Of Richmond In Yorkshire. London: 1946. V. 73

BROOKS, DR.
The Physician's Assistant, Consisting of a Short and Comprehensive Materia Medica.... 1833. V. 73

BROOKS, ELISHA
A Pioneer Mother of California. San Francisco: 1922. V. 70

BROOKS, GWENDOLYN
Annie Allen. New York: 1949. V. 71
The Bean Eaters. New York: 1960. V. 71
Bronzeville Boys and Girls. New York: 1963. V. 73
Jump Bad: A New Chicago Anthology. Detroit: 1971. V. 72
Selected Poems. New York: 1963. V. 71
A Street In Bronzeville. New York: 1945. V. 71
We Asked Gwendolyn Brooks.... 1967?. V. 71

BROOKS, H. ALLEN
Prairie School Architecture: Studies from the Western Architect. Toronto: 1975. V. 68; 69; 72

BROOKS, JAMES J.
Whiskey Drips. Philadelphia: 1873. V. 69

BROOKS, JAMES L.
Broadcast News. New York: 1988. V. 72

BROOKS, JOHN D. F.
Hand Shadow Stories. Boston: 1863. V. 68

BROOKS, JUANITA
Dudley Leavitt - Pioneer to Southern Utah. 1942. V. 73
John Doyle Lee - Zealot, Pioneer, Builder, Scapegoat. Glendale: 1962. V. 68; 73
John Doyle Lee: Zealot - Pioneer Builder - Scapegoat. Glendale: 1964. V. 69
The Mountain Meadows Massacre. Stanford: 1950. V. 70
The Mountain Meadows Massacre. Norman: 1962. V. 69

BROOKS, NOAH
The Boys of Fairport. New York: 1919. V. 72
First Across the Continent - the Story of the Lewis and Clark Expedition in 1803-1805. New York: 1901. V. 69; 70
Our Baseball Club and How It Won the Championship. New York: 1884. V. 70

BROOKS, RICHARD
The Brick Foxhole. New York: 1945. V. 71

BROOKS, S. H.
Rudimentary Treatise on the Erection of Dwelling Houses; or, the Builder's Comprehensive Director.... London: 1860. V. 68

BROOKS, ULYSSES R.
Butler and His Cavalry in the War of Secession 1861-1865. Columbia: 1909. V. 69; 70
Stories of the Confederacy. Columbia: 1912. V. 69; 70

BROOKS, VAN WYCK
The Ordeal of Mark Twain. New York: 1920. V. 72

BROOKS, W. K.
The Foundations of Zoology. New York: 1899. V. 68

BROOKS, WALTER R.
Freddy and Simon the Dictator. New York: 1956. V. 71; 73
Freddy and the Baseball Team from Mars. New York: 1955. V. 71
Freddy and the Dragon. New York: 1958. V. 69; 71
Freddy and the Flying Saucer Plans. New York: 1957. V. 69
Freddy and the Men from Mars. New York: 1954. V. 69; 73
Freddy and the Perilous Adventure. New York: 1942. V. 71
Freddy the Pilot. New York: 1952. V. 73
To and Again. New York: 1927. V. 71

BROOKS BOAT MANUFACTURING CO., BAY CITY, MICHIGAN
Originators of the Printed Pattern System of Boat Building. 1906. V. 68

BROOKSHAW, GEORGE
Six Birds Drawn and Coloured After Nature with Full Instructions for the Young Artist.... London: 1817. V. 73
Supplement to the Treatise on Flower Painting, Consisting of Eight Plates of Flowers.... 1817. V. 73

BROOKSIDE Primer. Randolph: 1830. V. 73

BROOKS MANUFACTURING CO., SAGINAW, MICHIGAN
Brooks Boats, 1917. Catalogue No. 32. V. 69

BROOM Hill, Broughton-in-Furness. The Residence of the Late Mrs. Bridson...Including Antique Carved Oak and Chippendale Furniture, Oil Paintings, Water Colour Drawings, Etchings, Engravings and Coloured Prints.... Kendal: 1903. V. 71

BROOM, R.
The South African Fossil Ape-Men - the Australopithecinae. New York: 1978. V. 68

BROOME, WILLIAM
The Poetical Works of Dr. Will Broome. Edinburgh: 1781. V. 69

BROOMHEAD, FRANK
The Zaehnsdorfs (1842-1947) Craft Bookbinders. 1986. V. 71

BROONZY, BILL
Big Bill Blues. London: 1955. V. 69

BROSE, DAVID S.
Ancient Art of the American Woodland Indians. New York: 1985. V. 71

BROSNAN, C. J.
History of the State of Idaho. New York: 1918. V. 73

BROSNAN, CORNELIUS
Jason Lee Prophet Of the New Oregon. New York: 1932. V. 71

BROSNAN, JIM
The Long Season. New York: 1960. V. 69

BROSSA, JOAN
Novel-la. Barcelona: 1965. V. 70

BROSSARD, CHANDLER
The Bold Saboteurs. New York: 1953. V. 71
The Spanish Scene. New York: 1968. V. 73
Who Walk in Darkness. New York: 1952. V. 73

BROSTER, D. K.
Couching at the Door. London: 1942. V. 73

BROSTER, JOHN
A Walk Round the Walks and City of Chester. Chester: 1821. V. 68

BROTHERS, MARY HUDSON
Billy the Kid. Farmington, NM: 1949. V. 72
A Pecos Pioneer. Albuquerque: 1943. V. 71; 72

BROTHWELL, D. R.
Dental Anthropology. Oxford: 1963. V. 68

BROUADEL, PAUL CAMILLE HIPPOLYTE
Les Asphyxies par les Gaz les Vapeures et les Anesthetiques. Paris: 1896. V. 71

BROUCHAC, JOSEPH
The Waters Between. Hanover: 1998. V. 72

BROUGH, JOHN CARGILL
The Fairy Tales of Science. London: 1866. V. 68; 70

BROUGH, ROBERT
The Wonderful Drama of Punch and Judy. London: 1890. V. 69

BROUGH, ROBERT B.
A Cracker Bon-Bon for Christmas Parties. 1861. V. 71

BROUGHAM, JOHN
Dombey and Son. Dramatized from Dickens' Novel. New York: 1875. V. 70

BROUGHAM AND VAUX, HENRY PETER BROUGHAM, 1ST BARON
Historical Sketches of Statesmen, Who Flourished in the Time of George III. London: 1845. V. 71
Installation Address (as Chancellor of the University of Edinburgh) Delivered the 18th of May. Edinburgh: 1860. V. 71
Speeches...Upon Questions Relating to Public Rights, Duties and Interests.... Edinburgh: 1838. V. 71

BROUGHTON, CHARLES
Memoir Respecting a New Theory of Numbers. Edinburgh: 1814. V. 69

BROUGHTON, JAMES
High Kukus. New York: 1968. V. 68
A Long Undressing. Collected Poems 1949-1969. New York: 1971. V. 73
The Playground. San Francisco: 1949. V. 68
75 Life Lines. Highlands: 1988. V. 73

BROUGHTON, JOHN
Pyschologia; or, an Account of te Nature of the Rational Soul. London: 1703. V. 70

BROUGHTON, RHODA
A Waif's Progress. London: 1905. V. 73

BROUMAS, OLGA
Soie Sauvage. Port Townsend: 1979. V. 73

BROUN, HEYWOOD
Seeing Things at Night. New York: 1921. V. 70

BROUSSAIS, F. J. V.
History of Chronic Phlegmasiae, or Inflammations, Founded on Clinical Experience and Pathological Anatomy Exhibiting a View of the Different Varieties and Complications of these Diseases with their Various Methods of Treatment.... Philadelphia: 1831. V. 70

BROUSSEAU, KATE
Mongolism. London: 1928. V. 68

BROVEN, JOHN
Rhythm and Blues in New Orleans. Gretna: 1978. V. 73

BROWER, DAVID
Wildlands in Our Civilization. San Francisco: 1964. V. 71

BROWER, J. H.
The Mills of Mammon. Joliet: 1909. V. 71

BROWER, JACOB V.
The Mississippi River and Its Source, a Narrative and Critical History of the Discovery of the River and Its Headwaters. Minneapolis: 1893. V. 72; 73

BROWN & JACKSON
The British Calculator, Consisting of Tables for the Use of the Gentleman, Farmer, Land Steward and Man of Business in Scotland, England and Ireland.... Cupar: 1814. V. 71

BROWN, A.
Indian Relics and Their Values. Chicago: 1942. V. 69

BROWN, A. GORDON
South and East African Year Book & Guide. London: 1942. V. 72

BROWN, ABBIE FARWELL
The Lonesomest Doll. New York: 1928. V. 72

BROWN, ALAN
Audrey Hepburn's Neck. New York: 1996. V. 72

BROWN, ALEXANDER
The Cabells and their Kin: a Memorial Volume of History, Biography and Genealogy. Richmond: 1895. V. 69

BROWN, ALICE
The Story of Thyrza. Boston and New York: 1909. V. 73

BROWN, ANDREW
The Philosophy of Physics, or Process of Creative Development.... New York: 1854. V. 71

BROWN, ARNESBY
The Work of Arnesby Brown, R. A., Modern Painting III. London: 1921. V. 70

BROWN, BARROW
Comanche The Sole Survivor of All The Forces in Custer's Last Stand, The Battle of The Little Big Horn. Kansas City: 1935. V. 72

BROWN, BEN
Theatre At The Left. Stagecraft In Soviet Russia. 1938. V. 72

BROWN, BENJAMIN
Testimonies for the Truth; a Record of Manifestations of the Power of God, Miraculous and Providential, Witnessed in the Travels and Experience of Benjamin Brown, High Priest in the Church of Jesus Christ of Latter-Day Saints. Liverpool: 1853. V. 68; 71

BROWN, BETH
Applause. New York: 1928. V. 70
Wedding Ring. Garden City: 1930. V. 71

BROWN, BOB
Let There Be Beer. New York: 1932. V. 69

BROWN, C. W.
Salt Dishes. Leion, Iowa: 1968. V. 72

BROWN, CAMPBELL
The First Manassas: Correspondence Between Generals R.S. Ewell and G. T. Beauregard, To Which are Added Extracts from a Letter of Gen. Fitz Lee. Nashville: 1885. V. 69; 70

BROWN, CECIL
The Life & Loves of Mr. Jiveass Nigger. NY: 1969. V. 72

BROWN, CHARLES BROCKDEN
Alcuin: a Dialogue. New Haven: 1935. V. 73
Wieland; or the Transformation. New York: 1798. V. 68

BROWN, CHARLES EDWARD
Old Stormalong Yarns. 1933. V. 69

BROWN, CHARLES EDWARD continued
Paul Bunyan Natural History. 1935. V. 69

BROWN, CORNELIUS
The Annals of Newark-upon-Trent Comprising the History, Curiosities and Antiquities. London: 1879. V. 70; 71

BROWN, CURTIS
Ingrid Bergman. A Star Book. London. V. 73

BROWN, D. WOLFE
The New Northwest: an Address by Hon. William D. Kelley, on the Northern Pacific Railway. Philadelphia: 1871. V. 73

BROWN, DALE
Flight of the Old Dog. New York: 1987. V. 73

BROWN, DEE
Bury My Heart at Wouned Knee. New York: 1970. V. 69; 72
Fort Phil Kearny: An American Saga. New York: 1962. V. 72
The Galvanized Yankees. Urbana: 1913. V. 72
Trail Driving Days. New York: 1952. V. 68; 69; 71; 72; 73

BROWN, DENISE
Sarah Vaughan. A Discography. Westport: 1991. V. 72

BROWN, DOUGLAS S.
Sketches of Greensville County, Virginia 1650-1967. Emporia: 1968. V. 70

BROWN, E.
Rimfire Rifleman. 1951. V. 72

BROWN, EDWARD
A Brief Account of Some Travels in Divers Parts of Europe, viz. Hungaria, Servia, Bulgaria, Macedonia, Thessaly, Austria.... London: 1685. V. 72
Poultry Breeding and Production. New York: 1929. V. 71

BROWN, ELEANOR
Dr. Eleanor Singer...a Memoir. 1998. V. 71

BROWN, F. M.
Jamaica and Its Butterflies. London: 1972. V. 70

BROWN, FORD K.
The Life of William Godwin. London: 1926. V. 72

BROWN, FRANK LONDON
The Myth Maker. Chicago: 1969. V. 72
Trumbull Park. Chicago: 1959. V. 68

BROWN, FRED R.
History Of The Ninth U.S. Infantry 1799-1909. Chicago: 1909. V. 72

BROWN, FREDDIE
Cricket Musketeer. London: 1954. V. 73

BROWN, FREDRIC
And the Gods Laughed. West Bloomfield: 1987. V. 71
Angels and Spaceships. New York: 1954. V. 69; 70
Before She Kills. San Diego: 1984. V. 72
Brother Monster. Miami Beach: 1987. V. 72
The Case of the Dancing Sandwiches. New York: 1951. V. 68; 69; 70; 72; 73
The Case of the Dancing Sandwiches. Volcano, Hawaii: 1985. V. 69; 71; 72; 73
The Dead Ringer. New York: 1948. V. 69
Death Has Many Doors. New York: 1951. V. 70
The Fabulous Clipjoint. New York: 1947. V. 70
The Far Cry. New York: 1951. V. 68
The Five Day Nightmare. New York: 1962. V. 68
4 Novels. London: 1983. V. 73
The Freak Show Murders. Belen: 1985. V. 72
The Gibbering Night. Hilo: 1991. V. 72
Happy Ending. Missoula: 1990. V. 69; 71; 72; 73
Here Comes a Candle. New York: 1950. V. 69
His Name Was Death. New York: 1954. V. 69; 70; 72
Homicide Sanitarium. San Antonio: 1984. V. 72
A Key To Fredric Brown's Wonderland: A Study And An Annotated Bibliographical Checklist By Newton Baird. Georgetown: 1981. V. 72
Knock Three-One-Two. New York: 1959. V. 68; 70; 72
The Late Lamented. New York: 1959. V. 68; 69
The Lenient Beast. New York: 1956. V. 68; 70; 72
The Lights in the Sky are Stars. New York: 1953. V. 68
Mad Man's Holiday. Volcano: 1985. V. 72
Madball. NY: 1953. V. 72
Martians, Go Home. New York: 1955. V. 68; 70; 73
Mrs. Murphy's Underpants. New York: 1963. V. 70
Murder Can Be Fun. New York: 1948. V. 68
The Murderers. New York: 1961. V. 69; 72
Night of the Jabberwock. New York: 1950. V. 69
Nightmare in Darkness. Miami Beach: 1987. V. 72
The Office. New York: 1958. V. 70; 71; 72
The Office. Miami Beach: 1987. V. 71
The Office. Miami Beach: 1995. V. 70
One for the Road. New York: 1958. V. 68; 70; 72
Pardon My Ghoulish Laughter. 1986. V. 69; 71; 72; 73
The Pickled Punks. Hilo: 1991. V. 69; 71; 72; 73
Red is the Hue of Hell. Miami Beach: 1986. V. 72
The Screaming Mimi. New York: 1949. V. 68; 72
Selling Death Short. Missoula: 1988. V. 72
Sex Life on the Planet Mars. Miami Beach: 1986. V. 70; 72
The Shaggy Dog and Other Murders. New York: 1963. V. 69
The Shaggy Dog and Other Murders. London: 1964. V. 69
Space On My Hands. 1951. V. 69; 71; 73
Space on My Hands. Chicago: 1951. V. 68; 70; 71; 72
Thirty Corpses Every Thursday. Belen: 1986. V. 72
Three-Corpse Parlay. Missoula: 1988. V. 69; 72
The Water-Walker. Missoula: 1990. V. 69; 71; 72; 73
We All Killed Grandma. New York: 1952. V. 68
The Wench is Dead. New York: 1955. V. 69
What Made Universe. New York: 1949. V. 69
What Made Universe. San Francisco: 1978. V. 69
Whispering Death. Missoula: 1989. V. 72
Who Was That Blonde I Saw You Kill Last Night?. Miami Beach: 1988. V. 72

BROWN, G.
European and Japanese Gardens.... Philadelphia: 1902. V. 71
Melanesians and Polynesians. Their Life and Histories Described and Compared. London: 1910. V. 69

BROWN, G. BALDWIN
The Arts in Early England. The life of Saxon England in its relation to the arts; ecclesiastical architecture in England from the conversion of the Saxons to the Norman conquest. London: 1903. V. 70; 72

BROWN, GEORGE
The New and Complete English Letter-writer.; or, whole art of general correspondence. . . . London: 1798. V. 70; 71
South Durham and Lancashire Union, and Eden Valley Railway Companies. 1863. V. 69

BROWN, GEORGE H.
On Foot Round Settle. Settle: 1888. V. 73
On Foot Round Settle. Settle: 1896. V. 73

BROWN, GEORGE MAC KAY
Fishermen with Ploughs: a Poem Cycle. London: 1969. V. 70
Foresterhill. Babel: 1992. V. 68
Greenvoe: a Novel. London: 1972. V. 70
Magnus: a Novel. London: 1973. V. 70
Orkney: Pictures and Poems by George Mackay Brown and Gunnie Moberg. Grantown-on-Spey: 1996. V. 70
Stone. Foss: 1987. V. 70
A Time to Keep and Other Stories. London: 1969. V. 70; 71
Winter Tales. London: 1995. V. 70; 72
The Year of the Whale. London: 1965. V. 70

BROWN, GEORGE R.
Washington: A Not too Serious History. Baltimore: 1930. V. 73

BROWN, GEORGE S.
Yarmouth, Nova Scotia: a Sequel to Campbell's History. Boston: 1888. V. 72

BROWN, GEORGE W.
Dictionary of Canadian Biography. Volume I 1000-1700. Toronto: 1979. V. 72

BROWN, GLENN
1860-1930 Memories: a Winning Crusade to Revive George Washington's Vision of a Capital City. Washington: 1931. V. 70

BROWN, H. Y. L.
Record of the Mines of South Australia; the Wadnaminga Goldfield, with Report and Plans. Adelaide: 1898. V. 71

BROWN, HAMISH
Hamish's Mountain Walk. London: 1978. V. 69
The Island of Rhum. Manchester: 1972. V. 69

BROWN, HARRY
A Sound of Hunting. New York: 1946. V. 69
The Stars in Their Courses. New York: 1960. V. 71
A Walk in the Sun. New York: 1944. V. 71

BROWN, HELEN
Jane Austen, a Play. London: 1939. V. 68; 70

BROWN, HENRY
A Narrative of the Anti-Masonick Excitement, in the Western Part of the State of New York, During the Years 1826, '7, '8 and a Part of 1829. Batavia: 1829. V. 73

BROWN, HORATIO F.
John Addington Symonds. A Biography Compiled From His Papers and Correspondence. London: 1895. V. 72
The Venetian Printing Press. New York and London: 1891. V. 69

BROWN, HYPKIN
Farmer Bibbins. Boston: 1914. V. 70

BROWN, INA CORINNE
The Story of the American Negro. New York: 1936. V. 70

BROWN, ISAAC V.
Memoirs of the Rev. Robert Finley, D.D. Late Pastor of the Presbyterian Congregation at Basking Ridge, New Jersey and President of Franklin College.... New Brunswick: 1819. V. 69

BROWN, J. CAMPBELL
Catalogue of Trotting and Pacing Bred Stock. Property of Campbell Brown.... Nashville: 1886. V. 70

BROWN, J. H.
Spectropia: or Surprising Spectral Illusions, SHowing Ghosts Everywhere, and of Any Colour. London: 1864. V. 70
Toxicology and Pharmacology of Venoms from Poisonous Snakes. Springfield: 1973. V. 68

BROWN, J. MAC MILLAN
The Dutch East. London: 1914. V. 68; 72

BROWN, J. P. S.
Jim Kane. New York: 1970. V. 71

BROWN, JAMES B.
Journal of a Journey Across the Plains in 1859. San Francisco: 1970. V. 68; 73

BROWN, JAMES WALTER
Round Carlisle Cross. Carlisle: 1921-1929. V. 71

BROWN, JENNIE B.
Fort Hall On The Oregon Trail, A Historical Study. Caldwell: 1932. V. 72

BROWN, JESSE
The Black Hills Trails - A History Of The Struggles Of The Pioneers In The Winning Of The Black Hills. Rapid City: 1924. V. 72

BROWN, JOE
The Hard Years. 1967. V. 70; 73
The Hard Years. London: 1967. V. 69
The Hard Years. 1972. V. 73
The Hard Years. 1974. V. 73
The Hard Years. London: 1974. V. 69

BROWN, JOHN
Horae Subsecivae. Locke and Sydneham with other Occasional Papers. Edinburgh: 1858. V. 71
Occasional Suggestions Relative to Ireland and the Church of Ireland from 1818. Aberdeen: 1838. V. 69
A Particular Plain and Brief Memorative Account of the Reverend Mr. Thomas Symmes. Boston: 1726. V. 71; 72

BROWN, JOHN GREGORY
Decorations in a Ruined Cemetery. New York: 1994. V. 70; 72

BROWN, JOHN H.
Indian Wars And Pioneers Of Texas. Austin: 1896. V. 72
Indian Wars And Pioneers Of Texas. Austin: 1988. V. 72

BROWN, JOHN P.
Old Frontiers. The Story of the Cherokee Indians from the Earliest Times to the Date of their Removal to the West, 1838. Kingsport: 1938. V. 69; 70; 71; 73

BROWN, JOHN S.
Routes to the Desert Watering Places in the Salton Sea Region, California. Washington: 1920. V. 70

BROWN, JOHN WALKER
Constance or the Merchant's Daughter, a Tale of Our Times. New York: 1841. V. 73

BROWN, JONATHAN
Velazquez: Painter and Courtier. New Haven: 1986. V. 70; 72; 73

BROWN, JOSEPH EPES
The Sacred Pipe; Black Elk's Account of the Seven Rites of the Oglala Sioux. Norman;: 1953. V. 73

BROWN, L.
The Birds of Africa. London: 1982-1988. V. 73

BROWN, LARRY
Big Bad Love. Chapel Hill: 1989. V. 73
Big Bad Love. Chapel Hill: 1990. V. 68
Dirty Work. Chapel Hill: 1989. V. 69
Facing the Music. Chapel Hill: 1988. V. 69; 70
Father & Son. Chapel Hill: 1996. V. 73
Joe. Chapel Hill: 1991. V. 72
A Late Start. Chapel Hill: 1989. V. 68; 71
On Fire. Chapel Hill: 1994. V. 72

BROWN, LARRY K.
You Are Respectfully Invited to Attend My Execution - Untold Stories of men Legally Executed in Wyoming Territory. 1997. V. 73
You are Respectfully Invited to Attend My Execution - Untold Stories of Men Legally Executed in Wyoming Territory. Glendo: 1997. V. 68

BROWN, LESLIE
Eagles, Hawks and Falcons of the World. Feltham: 1968. V. 70
Eagles, Hawks and Falcons of the World. New York: 1968. V. 69; 73
Eagles, Hawks and Falcons of the World. 1989. V. 70

BROWN, LINDA BEATRICE
Crossing Over Jordan. New York: 1995. V. 71

BROWN, MARCIA
Dick Whittington and His Cat. New York: 1950. V. 72

BROWN, MARGARET WISE
A Child's Good Morning. New York: 1952. V. 69
Christmas in the Barn. New York: 1952. V. 69
Country Noisy Book. New York: 1940. V. 71
Little Fur Family. New York: 1946. V. 73
The Noisy Book. New York: 1939. V. 69

BROWN, MARIE A.
The Icelandic Discoverers of America; or, Honour to Whom Honour is Due. London: 1887. V. 73

BROWN, MARION
Recollections. Frankfort: 1984. V. 69; 71

BROWN, MARK H.
Before Barbed Wire. New York: 1956. V. 68; 69
The Flight Of The Nez Perce. New York: 1967. V. 72
The Frontier Years: L. A. Huffman, Photographer of the Plains. New York: 1955. V. 69
The Plainsmen Of The Yellowstone, A History Of The Yellowstone Basin. New York: 1961. V. 72

BROWN, MONTY
Where Giants Trod. 1989. V. 69; 70; 72

BROWN, NORMAN
Journey to Pleasant Hill - The Civil War Letters of Captain Elijah P. Petty - Walker's Texas Division, C.S.A. San Antonio: 1982. V. 68; 73
Life Against Death. Middletown: 1959. V. 73

BROWN, P.
New Illustrations of Zoology, Containing...Non-Descript Birds with a Few Quadrupeds, Reptiles and Insects. 1776. V. 73

BROWN, P. HUME
George Buchan, Humanist and Reformer. Edinburgh: 1962. V. 71

BROWN, PHILIP A. H.
London and Publishers and Printers, 1800-1870. London: 1961. V. 68

BROWN, PHILIP FRANCIS
Reminiscences of the War of 1861-1865. Roanoke: 1912. V. 69; 70

BROWN, R.
Miscellaneous Botanical Works. London: 1866-1868. V. 69

BROWN, R. LUNDIN
Klatasassan and Other Reminiscences of Missionary Life in British Columbia. London: 1873. V. 68

BROWN, R. N. RUDMOSE
Spitsbergen. London: 1920. V. 72

BROWN, R. P.
Edward Wilson Of Nether Levens And His Kin. 1930. V. 72

BROWN, RICHARD
The Coal Field and Coal Trade of the Island of Cape Breton. London: 1871. V. 69
A History of the Island of Cape Breton with Some Account of the Discovery and Settlement of Canada, Nova Scotia and Newfoundland. London: 1869. V. 69; 72
Sacred Architecture, Its Rise, Progress and Present State, Embracing the Babylonian Indian Egyptian, Greek and Roman Temples.... 1845. V. 71

BROWN, RICHARD BLAKE
Yellow Brimstone. London: 1931. V. 73

BROWN, RITA MAE
In Her Day. Plainfield: 1976. V. 68
A Plain Brown Rapper. Oakland: 1976. V. 69; 71
Rubyfruit Jungle. New York: 1988. V. 73
Venus Envy. New York: 1983. V. 73

BROWN, ROBERT
The Miscellaneous Botanical Works of Robert Brown.... London: 1866-. V. 70
Our Earth and Its Story. London. V. 72
Pterocymbium, with Observation on Sterculieae...from Dr. Horsfshield's Plantae Javanicae Rariores. London: 1844. V. 69
Strictures and Remarks on the Earl of Selkirk's Observations on the Present State of the Highlands of Scotland, with a View of the Causes and Probable Consequences of Emigration. Edinburgh: 1806. V. 70

BROWN, ROBERT L.
An Empire of Silver - a History of the San Juan Silver Rush. Caldwell: 1965. V. 68; 73

BROWN, ROSELLEN
The Autobiography of My Mother. Garden City: 1976. V. 72
Civil Wars. New York: 1984. V. 72
Some Deaths in the Delta. 1970. V. 68; 71
Street Games. Garden City: 1974. V. 73
Tender Mercies. New York: 1978. V. 71; 72

BROWN, STANLEY MC KEOWN
With the Royal Canadians. Toronto: 1900. V. 73

BROWN, STERLING
The Collected Poems of Sterling A. Brown. New York: 1980. V. 72

BROWN, STEWARDSON
Alpine Flora of the Canadian Rocky Mountains. New York and London: 1907. V. 70; 72; 73

BROWN, T. N.
The Life and Times of Hugh Miller. New York: 1859. V. 70; 72

BROWN, THOMAS
An Account of the People Called Shakers; Their Faith, Doctrines and Practice, Exemplified in the Life.... Troy: 1812. V. 71; 73
Amusements Serious and Comical, Calculated for the Meridian of London. London: 1700. V. 73
The Conchologist's Text-Book. London: 1835. V. 70
The Elements of Conchology. London: 1816. V. 68; 70
Lectures on the Philosophy of the Human Mind. Edinburgh: 1820. V. 71
Letters from the Dead to the Living. London: 1702. V. 73
Observations on the Zoonomia of Eramus Darwin, M.D. Edinburgh: 1798. V. 70
Reasons of Mr. Bays Changing His Religion. London: 1688. V. 73
A Treatise on the Philosophy of the Human Mind, Being the Lectures of the Late Thomas Brown, M.D. Cambridge: 1827. V. 70
The Works of Mr. Thomas Brown, Serious and Comical, In Prose and Verse, With his Remains. London: 1760. V. 69

BROWN, THOMAS EDWARD
Betsy Lee, a Fo'c's'le Yarn. London: 1873. V. 73
Captain Tom and Captain Hugh: a Manx Story in Verse. Douglas: 1877. V. 73
Christmas Rose. Cockermouth: 1873. V. 73
The Doctor. 1876. V. 73
The Doctor. London: 1887. V. 73
Fo'c's'le Yarns Including Betsy Lee and Other Poems. London: 1881. V. 73
Fo'c's'le Yarns Including Betty Lee and Other Poems. London and New York: 1889. V. 73
The Manx Witch and Other Poems. London and New York: 1889. V. 73
Old John. Douglas: 1881?. V. 73
Poems of T. E. Brown. London: 1908. V. 73

BROWN, VARINA DAVIS
A Colonel at Gettysburg and Spotsylvania. Columbia: 1931. V. 69

BROWN, W. NORMAN
The Story of Kalaka. (with) Descriptive Catalogue of Miniature Paintings of the Jaina Kalpastura. Washington: 1933-1934. V. 71

BROWN, W. SORLEY
The Life and Genius of T.W.H. Crosland. London: 1928. V. 70

BROWN, WALTER C.
Laughing Death. Philadelphia: 1932. V. 73

BROWN, WESLEY
Tragic Magic. New York: 1978. V. 71; 73

BROWN, WILL C.
The Border Jumpers. New York: 1955. V. 71

BROWN, WILLIAM
Documents And Proceedings Connected with the Donation of a Free Public Library And Museum to the Town of Liverpool. Liverpool: 1858. V. 73
The Labour Question. Philadelphia: 1872. V. 69
Look Before Ye Loup; or, a Healin'sa' for the Crackit Crowns of Country Politicians. Edinburgh: 1793. V. 71

BROWN, WILLIAM C.
The Indian Side Of The Story. Spokane: 1961. V. 72

BROWN, WILLIAM H.
Portrait Gallery of Distinguished American Citizens, with Biographical Sketches and facsimiles of Original Letters. New York: 1931. V. 71

BROWN, WILLIAM LAWRENCE
An Essay on the Natural Equality of Men.... London: 1794. V. 69

BROWN, WILLIAM NORMAN
Workshop Wrinkles for Decorators, Painters, Paperhangers and Others. London: 1907. V. 69

BROWN, WILLIAM ROBINSON
Horse of the Desert. New York: 1929. V. 72

BROWN, WILLIAM WELLS
The Black Man: His Antecedents, His Genius and His Achievements. New York: 1863. V. 68
A Lecture Delivered Before the Female Anti-Slavery Society of Salem, at Lyceum Hall, Nov. 14, 1847. Boston: 1847. V. 71
The Rising Son; or, the Antecedents and Advancement of the Colored Race. New York: 1874. V. 71

BROWNBILL, JOHN
A Calendar of That Part of the Collection of Deeds and Papers of the Moore Family of Bankhall, Co.Lanc now in the Liverpool Public Library. London: 1913. V. 73

BROWNE, ALEXANDER
Ars Pictoria, or an Academy Treating of Drawing, Limning, and Etching. London: 1669. V. 69; 71

BROWNE, B.
The Conquest of Mount McKinley. 1913. V. 68; 73
The Conquest of Mount McKinley. 1956. V. 68; 70

BROWNE, CHARLES
The Gun Club Cook Book. New York: 1930. V. 72
The Gun Club Drink Book. New York: 1939. V. 72

BROWNE, CHARLES FARRER
Artemus Ward's Lecture (As Delivered at the Egyptian Hall, London). New York: 1869. V. 71

BROWNE, EDGAR
Phiz and Dickens as They Appeared to Edgar Browne. London: 1913. V. 70

BROWNE, EDWARD G.
Arabian Medicine Being the Fitzpatrick Lectures Delivered at the Royal College of Physicians in November 1919 and November 1920. Cambridge: 1921. V. 68

BROWNE, EUGENE
Industrial and Picturesque Rockford. Rockford: 1891. V. 68

BROWNE, FELICIA DOROTHEA
England and Spain; or, Valour and Patriotism. London: 1808. V. 69

BROWNE, FRANCES
Granny's Wonderful Chair. London: 1963. V. 68

BROWNE, G. F.
The Ancient Cross Shafts at Bewcastle and Ruthwell. Enlarged from the Rede Lecture Delivered Before the University of Cambridge on 20 May 1916. Cambridge: 1916. V. 71

BROWNE, G. WALDO
A Daughter of Maryland. New York: 1895. V. 73

BROWNE, GERALD A.
Slide. New York: 1976. V. 68

BROWNE, HABLOT K.
The Chronicles of Crime or The New Newgate Calendar. London: 1841. V. 72
Dombey and Son. The Four Portraits of Edith, Florence, Alice and Little Paul. London: 1848. V. 69
Sketches of the Seaside and the Country. 1869. V. 73

BROWNE, HAROLD
Halo for Satan. 1948. V. 69
Incredible Ink. Tucson: 1997. V. 69; 70; 72; 73
Thin Air. New York: 1954. V. 69; 70

BROWNE, IRVING
Humorous Phases of the Law. San Francisco: 1876. V. 73

BROWNE, ISAAC HAWKINS
De Animi Immortalitate. Londini: 1754. V. 70
Poems Upon Various Subjects, Latin and English. London: 1768. V. 72

BROWNE, JAMES
A History of the Highlands and of the Highland Clans. Glasgow: 1838. V. 73

BROWNE, JOHN
The History of the Metropolitan Church of St. Peter, York.... London: 1838-1847. V. 69

BROWNE, JOHN A.
A Dissertatio Chirurgica Inauguralis de Morbo Coxae. Edinburgi: 1813. V. 72

BROWNE, JOHN ROSS
Adventures in Apache Country. New York: 1874. V. 69
Adventures in the Apache Country. New York: 1869. V. 73
The Indians of California. San Francisco: 1944. V. 69
Report of the Debates in the Convention of California On the Formation of the State Constitution in September and October 1849. Washington: 1850. V. 68

BROWNE, JOSEPH
Institutions in Physick, Collected from the Writings of the Most Eminent Physicians.... London: 1714. V. 70; 71

BROWNE, L. B.
Experimental Analysis of Insect Behaviour. Berlin: 1974. V. 72

BROWNE, LEWIS
All Things are Possible. New York: 1935. V. 69

BROWNE, M. H.
The Dolls' Villa. London: 1890. V. 73

BROWNE, MAURICE
Recollections of Rupert Brooke. Chicago: 1927. V. 68

BROWNE, MOSES
Angling Sports: in Nine Piscatory Eclogues...with an Essay in Defence of This Undertaking. London: 1773. V. 70; 73

BROWNE, O'DONEL T. D.
The Rotunda Hospital 1745-1945. Baltimore: 1947. V. 68
The Rotunda Hospital 1745-1945. Edinburgh: 1947. V. 68

BROWNE, P. W.
Where the Fishers Go: the Story of Labrador. New York and Halifax: 1909. V. 72

BROWNE, PETER
The Procedure, Extent and Limits of Human Understanding. London: 1737. V. 73
Things Divine and Supernatural Conceived by Analogy. 1733. V. 69

BROWNE, R.
The Conquest of Mount McKinley. 1913. V. 70

BROWNE, THOMAS
Certain Miscellany Tracts. London: 1684. V. 68
The English Replicas Thomas Browne Hydriotaphia. London: 1927. V. 70

BROWNE, THOMAS continued
A Letter to a Friend Upon the Occasion of the Death of an Intimate Friend Together with Christian Morals. Waltham St. Lawrence: 1923. V. 70
Of Unicornes Hornes. 1984. V. 71
Pseudodoxia Epidemica. London: 1646. V. 68; 69
Pseudodoxia Epidemica. London: 1650. V. 70
Pseudodoxia Epidemica. London: 1658. V. 70; 73
Pseudodoxia Epidemica. London: 1669. V. 68
Pseudodoxia Epidemica. Easthampton: 1984. V. 72
Sir Thomas Browne's Pseudodoxia Epidemica. Oxford: 1981. V. 70
Religio Medici. London: 1678. V. 68; 70
Religio Medici. London: 1883. V. 70
Religio Medici Argentorai. 1665. V. 70
Religio Medici. Its Sequel Christian Morals. London: 1844. V. 70
Religio Medici, Letter to a Friend, And Christian Morals. London: 1926. V. 70
Sir Thomas Browne's Works. London: 1835-1836. V. 70; 72
The Works. London: 1686. V. 68; 72
Works, Including His Life and Correspondence. London: 1836. V. 72
The Works of Sir Thomas Browne. London: 1880. V. 70
The Works of Sir Thomas Browne. London: 1928. V. 72
The Works of Sir Thomas Browne. London: 1964. V. 68

BROWNE, THOMAS GUNTER
Hermes Unmaksed; or, the Art of Speech Founded on the Association of Words and Ideas. London: 1795. V. 71

BROWNELL, CHARLES DE WOLF
Indian Races of North and South America. New York: 1856. V. 73

BROWNING, ELIZABETH BARRETT
Aurora Leigh. London: 1857. V. 73
Casa Guidi Windows. A Poem. London: 1851. V. 73
A Drama of Exile: and Other Poems. New York: 1845. V. 70
An Essay on Mind with Other Poems. 1826. V. 73
Last Poems. London: 1862. V. 71; 72
Last Poems. New York: 1862. V. 71
The Letters of Elizabeth Barrett Browning. London: 1897. V. 71
Poems. London: 1844. V. 73
Poems Before Congress. London: 1860. V. 70
Poetical Works. London: 1873. V. 71
Prometheus Bound and Other Poems. New York: 1851. V. 71
The Seraphim and Other Poems. London: 1838. V. 73
Sonnets from the Portuguese. New Rochelle: 1901. V. 68
Sonnets from the Portuguese. 1914. V. 73
Sonnets from the Portuguese. New York: 1948. V. 68; 69
Twenty-Two Unpublished Letters of Elizabeth Barrett Browning and Robert Browning addressed to Henrietta and Arabella Moulton-Barrett. New York: 1935. V. 72
Two Poems. London: 1854. V. 73

BROWNING, R. W. BARRETT
Catalogue of Pictures, Drawings and Engravings, Autograph Letters and Manuscripts, Books and Works of Art, the Property of.... London: 1913. V. 70

BROWNING, ROBERT
Browning's Essay on Chatterton. Cambridge: 1948. V. 70
Christmas Eve and Easter Day. London: 1850. V. 73
Dramatic Idylls. London: 1879. V. 73
Dramatic Idylls. Second Series. London: 1880. V. 73
Dramatis Personae. London: 1864. V. 71; 73
Dramatis Personae. 1910. V. 70
Jocoseria. London: 1877. V. 73
La Saisiaz: the Two Poets of Croisic. London: 1878. V. 71; 73
Love Among the Ruins. New York: 1922. V. 71
Men and Women. London: 1855. V. 73
Men and Women. Hammersmith: 1908. V. 71
Paracelsus. London: 1835. V. 73
Parleyings with Certain People of Importance in Their Day. London: 1887. V. 68; 70
Pictor Ignotus, Fra Lippo Lippi, Andrea del Sarto. Waltham St. Lawrence: 1925. V. 68; 71
The Pied Piper of Hamelin. New York: 1880. V. 72
The Pied Piper of Hamelin. London: 1898. V. 71
The Pied Piper of Hamelin. New York: 1905-1910. V. 70
The Pied Piper of Hamelin. London: 1934. V. 70; 73
The Pied Piper of Hamelin. London: 1939. V. 69; 71
The Pied Piper of Hamelin. 1940. V. 72
Poems. London: 1849. V. 73
The Poetical Works of Robert Browning. (with) New Poems By Robert Browning and Elizabeth Barrett Browning. London: 1889-1914. V. 73
The Ring and the Book. London: 1868-1869. V. 68; 73
The Ring and the Book. London: 1872. V. 68
A Selection from the Works. London: 1865. V. 73
Some Poems by Robert Browning. 1904. V. 70
Sordello. London: 1840. V. 73
Strafford: An Historical Tragedy. London: 1837. V. 71; 72; 73

BROWNLEE, CLAUDIA J.
Colonel Joe, The Last Of The Rough Raiders. New York: 1978. V. 72

BROWNLOW, JOHN
Memoranda: or Chronicles of the Foundling Hospital, Including Memoirs of Captain Coram. London: 1847. V. 68; 71

BROWNLOW, RICHARD
Declarations and Pleadings in English; Being the Most Authentique Forme of Proceeding in Courts of Law.... London: 1652. V. 68

BROWNLOW, WILLIAM CANNAWAY
Sketches of the Rise, Progress and Decline of Secession: with a Narrative of Personal Adventure Among the Rebels. Philadelphia: 1862. V. 70; 71

BROWNRIGG, GAWEN
Star Against Star. New York: 1936. V. 72

BROWN-SEQUARD, CHARLES E.
Course of Lectures of the Physiology and Pathology of the Central Nervous System. Delivered at the Royal College of Surgeons of England in May 1858. Philadelphia: 1860. V. 68; 70
Experimental and Clinical Researches on the Physiology and Pathology of the Spinal Cord, and Some Other Parts of the Nervous Centres. (and) Experimental Researches Applied to Physiology and Pathology. Richmond: 1855. V. 68; 72
Journal De La Physiologie De L'Homme et des Animaux. Paris: 1858-1862. V. 71
Lectures on the Diagnosis and Treatment of Functional Nervous Affections. Philadelphia: 1868. V. 68; 70

BROWNSMITH, JOHN
The Contrast; or, New Mode of Management. Salisbury: 1776. V. 71

BROWNSON, JOHN W.
The Vermont Disciplinarian; Containing a System of Instructions in the Rudiments of Military Science. Bennington: 1805. V. 73

BROWSE, LILLIAN
Degas Dancers. London: 1949. V. 72; 73

BROXBOURNE LIBRARY
Catalogue of Valuable Printed Books from the Broxbourne Library Illustrating the Spread of Printing (The Property of John Ehrman, Esq.). London: 1977. V. 70

BRUCCOLI, MATTHEW J.
Chandler Before Marlowe. 1973. V. 73
F Scott Fitzgerald. A Descriptive Bibliography. Pittsburgh: 1987. V. 68
Kenneth Millar/Ross Macdonald. A Checklist. Detroit: 1971. V. 71; 73
Raymond Chandler, a Descriptive Bibliography. 1979. V. 70
Raymond Chandler: a Descriptive Bibliography. Pittsburgh: 1979. V. 68; 72; 73
Ross MacDonald: a Checklist. Detroit: 1971. V. 69; 70
Ross Macdonald/Kenneth Millar. A Descriptive Bibliography. Pittsburgh: 1983. V. 72; 73

BRUCE, ALEXANDER
An Index, or Abridgment of Such Acts of the British Parliament, as Either Equally Concern the Whole Kingdom, or Particularly Relate to Scotland.... Edinburgh: 1726. V. 69

BRUCE, C. G.
Himalayan Wanderer. 1934. V. 68; 70; 73

BRUCE, D. F.
Nancy at St. Bride's. 1946. V. 72

BRUCE, DAVID
Poems Chiefly in the Scottish Dialect, Originally Written Under the signature of the Scots-Irishman, by a Native of Scotland. Washington: 1801. V. 71

BRUCE, DONALD
Radical Dr. Smollett. Boston: 1965. V. 69; 72

BRUCE, EDWARD
Art in Federal Buildings. Volume I Mural Designs. Washington, DC: 1936. V. 70; 71

BRUCE, ELI
Argument of A. G. Riddle, Esq., of Cleveland Delivered at the Court House in Jefferson, Ohio, on the 26th and 27th of November, 1858, in the Case of the State of Ohio Vs. Hiram Cole, Tried for Poisoning His Wife on the 9th of Sept. 1857... Cleveland: 1859. V. 68

BRUCE, GEORGE
The Land Birds in and Around St. Andrews, Including a Condensed History of the British Land Birds, with Extracts from the Poets... Dundee: 1895. V. 71

BRUCE, J. COLLINGWOOD
The Hand Book to the Roman Wall. London: 1885. V. 71

BRUCE, JAMES
Travels to Discover the Source of the Nile. Edinburgh and London: 1790. V. 70
Travels to Discover the Source of the Nile. Edinburgh: 1813. V. 68; 72

BRUCE, JANE
Poems on Sacred Subjects Written by the author.... London: 1854. V. 69

BRUCE, JEAN
Shock Tactics. 1965. V. 73

BRUCE, JOHN C.
The Bayeau Tapestry Elucidated. London: 1856. V. 69
The Roman Wall. 1851. V. 73

BRUCE, LYDIA BERESFORD
Sketches of Ceylon. London: 1914. V. 72

BRUCE, MICHAEL
Lochleven, and Other Poems. Edinburgh: 1837. V. 68
Poems on Several Occasions. Edinburgh: 1782. V. 69

BRUCE, MINER
Alaska: Its History and Resources, Gold, Fields, Routes and Scenery. Seattle: 1895. V. 70

BRUCE, PHILIP ALEXANDER
The Virginia Plutarch. Chapel Hill: 1929. V. 71

BRUCE, THOMAS
Heritage of the Trans-Alleghany Pioneers, or Resources of Central West Virginia. Baltimore: 1894. V. 73

BRUCE, WILLIAM CABELL
John Randolph of Roanoke 1733-1833. New York: 1922. V. 71

BRUCHAC, JOSEPH
The Arrow Over the Door. New York: 1998. V. 68
Bowman's Store. A Journey to Myself. New York: 1997. V. 68
Entering Onondaga. Austin: 1978. V. 68
The Girl Who Married the Moon. 1994. V. 72
The Ice-Hearts. Austin: 1979. V. 68
Indian Mountain and Other Poems. Ithaca: 1971. V. 68
The Road to Black Mountain. Berkeley: 1976. V. 71
Thirteen Moons on Turtle's Back. New York: 1992. V. 68
Translator's Son. Merrick: 1980. V. 68
Turtle Meat and Other Stories. Duluth: 1992. V. 68
Walking With My Sons. Madison: 1986. V. 68

BRUCKNER, D. J. R.
Frederic Goudy. New York: 1990. V. 70

BRUECK, ERIC T.
Doris Lessing: a Bibliography. London: 1984. V. 73

BRUEGMANN, ROBERT
Holabird & Roche, Holabird & Root. An Illustrated Catalog of Works, 1880-1940. NY & London: 1991. V. 72

BRUEHL, ANTON
Tropic Patterns. Hollywood: 1970. V. 68

BRUFF, HARALD JOHN LEXOW
T'ill An' T'Oade Uns Upuv Greenho'. An Account of the Traditions, Life & Work of the Old Led Miners of Greenhow Hill in Yorkshire. York: 1920. V. 73
T'miners. York. V. 73

BRUFF, J. GOLDSBOROUGH
Gold Rush - the Journals, Drawings and Other Papers of J. Goldsborough Bruff. New York: 1944. V. 70; 73

BRUGIS, THOMAS
Vade Museum: or, a Companion for a Chirurgion, Fitted for Times of Peace or War. London: 1670. V. 72

BRUGUIERE, FRANCIS
San Francisco. San Francisco: 1918. V. 68

BRUHNS, KARL
Life of Alexander Von Humboldt. London: 1873. V. 70

BRUMBAUGH, GAIUS M.
Maryland Records: Colonial Revolutionary, County and Church. Baltimore: 1975. V. 72

BRUNEFILLE, G. E.
Topo, a Tale About English Children. London: 1878. V. 69; 70
Topo. A Tale About English Children in Italy. London: 1880. V. 68; 72

BRUNEL, I. K.
An Address from the Directors of the Cheltenham and Great Western Union Railway Company to the Shareholders. (with) Cheltenham and Great Western Union Railway. Schedule of Claim to be filled in by occupiers. Cirencester: 1836. V. 72
Hungerford and Lambeth Suspension Foot Bridge Over the Thames. Prospectus. London: 1840. V. 69

BRUNEL, M. J.
A New Plan of Tunnelling, Calculated for Opening a Roadway Under the Thames. London: 1823. V. 72

BRUNHOFF, JEAN DE
ABC of Babar. New York: 1936. V. 69; 73
Babar and Father Christmas. London: 1940. V. 71
Babar and Father Christmas. New York: 1940. V. 73
Babar at Home. London: 1942. V. 68
Babar the King. New York: 1935. V. 73
Babar the King. London: 1936. V. 69
Babar the King. London: 1937. V. 68
Babar's Anniversary Album. New York: 1981. V. 70
Babar's Friend Zephir. London: 1937. V. 68
Babar's Travels. London: 1935. V. 68
Babar's Travels. London: 1936. V. 68
Histoire de Babar la Petit Elephant. Paris: 1950. V. 71
The Story of Babar. New York: 1935. V. 69
The Travels of Barbar. New York: 1934. V. 73
Zephir's Holidays. New York: 1937. V. 73

BRUNHOFF, LAURENT DE
Bonhomme and the Huge Beast. New York: 1974. V. 73

BRUNN, H. O.
The Story of the Original Dixieland Jazz Band. Baton Rouge: 1960. V. 73

BRUNNICH, M. T.
Dyrenes Historie og Dyre-Samlingen Udi Universitetets Natur-Theater. Forste Bind. Copenhagen: 1782. V. 73

BRUNO, JOSEPH
Baseball's Golden Dozen. Hicksville NY: 1976. V. 72

BRUNSKILL, R. W.
Vernacular Architecture of the Lake Counties. London: 1978. V. 70

BRUNT, SAMUEL, PSEUD.
A Voyage to Cackogallinia; with a Description of the Religion, Policy, Customs and Manner of that Country. London: 1727. V. 70

BRUNTON, MARY
Discipline. Edinburgh: 1814. V. 68; 72
Self-Control. London: 1832. V. 69

BRUNTON, THOMAS LAUDER
Modern Developments of Harvey's Works. The Harveian Oration 1894 Delivered Before the Royal College of Physicians October 18th, 1894. London. V. 70
On the Science of Easy Charis...On Posture and Its Indications. London: 1892. V. 69
Therapeutics of the Circulation. Eight Lectures Delivered in the Spring of 1905 in the Physiological Laboratory of the University of London. Philadelphia: 1908. V. 70; 71

BRUSCABILE, JEAN DESALAURIERS
Les Oeuvres de Bruscambile. Rouen: 1626. V. 70

BRUSH, GEROME
Boston Symphony Orchestra. Boston: 1936. V. 73

BRUSH, KATHARINE
Young Man of Manhattan. New York: 1930. V. 70

BRUYN, CORNEILLE DE
Voyages De Corneille Le Brun Par la Moscovie, en Perse, et Aux Indes Orientales. Amsterdam: 1718. V. 71

BRYAN, B.
Archaelogical Explorations on San Nicolas Island. 1970. V. 69

BRYAN, DANIEL
The Mountain Muse: Comprising the Adventures of Daniel Boone. Harrisonburg: 1813. V. 71

BRYAN, FRANCIS T.
Report Concerning the Operations of a Party Assigned to Explore the Route from Fort Riley to Bridger's Pass. Washington: 1857. V. 69

BRYAN, WILLIAM S.
Our Islands and Their People as Seen with Camera and Pencil. St. Louis: 1899. V. 69

BRYANT, A. T.
The Zulu People. As They Were Before the White Man Came. Pitermaritzburg: 1940. V. 69

BRYANT, CHARLES
Flora Diaetetica; or, History of Esculent Plants. London: 1783. V. 70

BRYANT, EDWIN
What I Saw in California: Being the Journal of a Tour by the Emigrant Route and South Pass of the Rocky Mountains, Across the Continent of North America.... Santa Ana: 1936. V. 73

BRYANT, PETER
Red Alert. New York: 1958. V. 71

BRYANT, SARA C.
Epaminondas and His Auntie. Boston and New York: 1938. V. 70

BRYANT, WILBUR F.
The Blood of Abel. Hastings: 1885. V. 72

BRYANT, WILLIAM BAILEY
Nineteenth Century Handbook on the Manufacture of Liquors, Wines and Cordials. Chicago: 1899. V. 69

BRYANT, WILLIAM CULLEN
Letters of a Traveller. New York: 1850. V. 68; 70
Picturesque America. New York: 1872. V. 71
Picturesque America. New York: 1872-1874. V. 68
Picturesque America. New York: 1974. V. 73
Poems. Cambridge: 1821. V. 69; 71; 73
Poems. London: 1858. V. 71
Thirty Poems. New York: 1864. V. 68; 72

BRYCE, GEORGE
Sketch of the Life and Discoveries of Robert Campbell. Winnipeg: 1898. V. 73

BRYCE, IVAR
You Only Live Once: Memories of Ian Fleming. London: 1975. V. 72

BRYCE, JAMES
The American Commonwealth. London: 1889. V. 71
The American Commonwealth. New York: 1910. V. 68
Geology of Arran and Clydesdale with an Account of the Flora and Marina Fauna of Arran.... Glasgow: 1865. V. 68; 70; 71

BRYCE, W.
Panorama of Canadian Scenery. London. V. 68

BRYDGES, SAMUEL EGERTON
Five Sonnets, Addressed to Woottoon the Spot of the Author's Nativity. Kent: 1819. V. 72
Sonnets and Other Poems. London: 1789. V. 73

BRYDGES, THOMAS
A Burlesque Translation of Homer. London: 1797. V. 72

BRYDONE, PATRICK
A Tour through Sicily and Malta. London: 1773. V. 72
A Tour Through Sicily and Malta. London: 1775. V. 69; 72

BRYDSON, A. P.
The Early Registers of Blawith. Ulverston: 1913. V. 71
Sidelights on Mediaeval Windermer. Kendal: 1911. V. 71
Some Records of Two Lakeland Townships (Blawith and Nibthwaite).... London. V. 71

BRYERS, DUANE
The Bunkhouse Boys from the Lazy Daisy Ranch. Flagstaff: 1974. V. 68

BRYHER, W.
Development. 1920. V. 73

BRYNER, EDNA
Andy Brandt's Ark. New York: 1927. V. 71

BRYOM, JOHN
Miscellaneous Poems.... Manchester: 1773. V. 69

BRYSON, BILL
Notes from a Small Island. London: 1995. V. 71; 72
A Walk in the Woods. London: 1987. V. 68

BRYSON, H. COURTNEY
Rock Climbs Round London, Being a Guide. Brentford: 1936. V. 69

BUBBLES Annual. 1930. V. 68
BUBBLES Annual. 1936. V. 68

BUCHAN, JAMES
A Parish of Rich Women. London: 1984. V. 68

BUCHAN, JOHN
Andrew Jamieson, Lord Ardwell. 1913. V. 69
Augustus. 1937. V. 69
The Battle of Jutland. 1916. V. 68
The Battle of Somme. New York: 1917. V. 70
The Blanket of the Dark. 1931. V. 69
A Book of Escapes and Hurried Journeys. 1922. V. 69
Book of Escapes and Hurried Journeys. London: 1922. V. 73
Canadian Occasions. 1940. V. 69
Castle Gay. 1930. V. 69
Castle Gay. Boston: 1930. V. 68; 70; 71
The Courts of the Morning. London: 1929. V. 69; 70; 73
Episodes of the Great War. 1936. V. 69
Francis and Riverdale Grenfell. 1920. V. 69
Francis and Riverdale Grenfell. London: 1920. V. 70
The Free Fishers. 1934. V. 69
The Gap in the Curtain. 1932. V. 68; 69
Gordon of Khartoum. 1934. V. 69
Greenmantle. 1916. V. 69
Greenmantle. London: 1916. V. 70
Grey Weather. 1899. V. 69
A History of the Great War. Boston, New York, and London: 1922. V. 69; 73
The History of the Royal Scots Fusilers. 1925. V. 69
The History of the South African Forces in France. 1920. V. 69
Homilies and Recreations. 1926. V. 69
Homilies and Recreations. London: 1926. V. 72
The House of the Four Winds. 1935. V. 69
Huntingtower. London: 1922. V. 70
The Interpreter's House. 1938. V. 69
The Interpreter's House. London: 1938. V. 72
The Island of Sheep. 1919. V. 69
The Island of Sheep. London: 1936. V. 69; 73
The King's Grace. 1935. V. 69
The King's Grace. London: 1935. V. 68; 73
The Last Secrets. London: 1923. V. 72
The Long Traverse. London: 1941. V. 69; 72
The Magic Walking Stick. London: 1932. V. 71
The Massacre of Glencoe. 1933. V. 69
Memorial Showing the Advantages the Kingdom of Scotland May Have by the Undertaking, and Improvement of Fishings for Export, Whether by Societies, of Singular Persons, Mostly Taken from the Pens and Mouths of Men of the Greatest Knowledge... London: 1700. V. 68
Memory Hold the Door. 1940. V. 69
Naval Episodes of the Great War. 1938. V. 69
Oliver Cromwell. 1934. V. 69
The Path of the King. Boston: 1931. V. 70
The Power House. Edinburgh and London: 1916. V. 68; 70
Prester John. London: 1910. V. 69
Prester John. 1919. V. 69
A Prince of Captivity. 1933. V. 69
Salute to Adventurers. 1915. V. 69
Sick Heart River. London: 1941. V. 69; 73
Sir Quixote of the Moors. 1895. V. 69
Sir Quixote of the Moors. London: 1895. V. 71
Sir Quixote of the Moors. London: 1924. V. 69
Sir Walter Raleigh. 1911. V. 69
Some Eighteenth Century Byways and Other Essays. 1908. V. 69
The Thirty-Nine Steps. 1915. V. 69
The Thirty-Nine Steps. Edinburgh and London: 1915. V. 70; 71; 73
The Thirty-Nine Steps. Boston: 1928. V. 70
Two Ordeals of Democracy. 1925. V. 69
Witch Wood. 1927. V. 69
Witch Wood. London: 1927. V. 71

BUCHAN, WILLIAM
Advice to Mothers on the Subject of Their Own Health; and on the Means of Promoting the Health, Strength and Beauty of Their Offspring. Philadelphia: 1804. V. 72
Domestic Medicine. Philadelphia: 1784. V. 72
Domestic Medicine. Philadelphia: 1797. V. 68
Domestic Medicine. Edinburgh: 1802. V. 69
Domestic Medicine. Halifax: 1864. V. 69
Every Man His Own Doctor, or a Treatise on the Prevention and Cure of Disease, by Regimen and Simple Medicines. New Haven: 1816. V. 70

BUCHANAN, A. W. PATRICK
The Buchanan Book - the Life of Alexander Buchanan of Montreal.... Montreal: 1911. V. 73

BUCHANAN, DAVID
The Treasure of Auchlinleck, the Story of the Boswell Papers and Their Discovery. London: 1975. V. 69

BUCHANAN, EDNA
Nobody Lives Forever. New York: 1990. V. 71

BUCHANAN, GEORGE
The Franciscan Friar, a Satire; and the Marriage Ode of Francis of Valois and Mary, Sovereigns of France and Scotland. Glasgow;: 1809. V. 72
Poemata Quae Extant. Amsterdam: 1676. V. 72
Rerum Scoticarum Historia. Edimbvrgi: 1582. V. 69
Rerum Scoticarum Historia. Edinburgi: 1700. V. 71; 72; 73

BUCHANAN, J.
The Indigenous Grasses of New Zealand. Wellington: 1880. V. 69

BUCHANAN, JAMES
Cases Decided in the Supreme Court of the Cape of Good Hope During the Year 1868.... Cape Town: 1869. V. 68; 72

BUCHANAN, JOSEPH R.
Outlines of Lectures on the Neurological System of Anthropology, as Discovered, Demonstrated and Taught in 1841 and 1842. Cincinnati: 1854. V. 71

BUCHANAN, R.
The Life and Adventures of John James Audubon.... London: 1869. V. 73

BUCHANAN, ROBERT
The Charlatan. Chicago: 1895. V. 69; 73
The Heir of Lime. London: 1892. V. 68
Wayside Poets: Original Poems of the Country Life. London: 1867. V. 68

BUCHANAN, THOMAS G.
Who Killed Kennedy?. London: 1964. V. 69

BUCHANAN, W.
Memoirs of Painting with a Chronological History of the Importation of Pictures of the Great Masters Into England Since the French Revolution. London: 1824. V. 70; 72

BUCHANNAN, JOHN
Albert: a Poem in Two Cantos. Hilda and Other Poems. London: 1831. V. 69

BUCHARD, JAMES
Correspondence Relative to the Condition of Affairs in Utah Territory -36th Congress, 1st Session, House of Representatives.. Washington: 1800. V. 70

BUCHHEIM, LOTHAR GUNTHER
The Boat. New York: 1975. V. 68

BUCK, CHARLES NEVILLE
Alias Red Ryan. New York: 1923. V. 69

BUCK, DANIEL
Indian Outbreaks. Mankato, MN: 1904. V. 72

BUCK, FRANK
Animals Like That. 1939. V. 69
On Jungle Trails. Yonkers-on-Hudson: 1936. V. 70

BUCK, IRVING ASHBY
Cleburne and His Command. New York and Washington: 1908. V. 69; 70

BUCK, LILLIE WEST BROWN
Amy Leslie at the Fair. Chicago: 1893. V. 71

BUCK, PEARL S.
The Good Earth. New York: 1931. V. 70; 71
Is There a Case for Foreign Missions?. New York: 1932. V. 69
Stories for Little Children. New York: 1940. V. 68
The Water-Buffalo Children. New York: 1943. V. 69
Yu Lan: Flying Boy of China. New York: 1945. V. 69

BUCK, SAMUEL
The Castles, Abbeys and Priories of the County of Cumberland. Carlisle: 1877. V. 71

BUCKBEE, EDNA B.
Pioneer Days at Angels Camp, California. Calaveras: 1932. V. 68; 73
The Saga of Old Tuolumne. New York: 1935. V. 70; 73

BUCKE, R. M.
Cosmic Consciousness: a Study in the Evolution of the Human Mind. Philadelphia: 1901. V. 68

BUCKE, RICHARD M.
Walt Whitman. Philadelphia: 1883. V. 69; 71

BUCKERIDGE, A.
Jennings Abounding. 1967. V. 72
Jennings Again. 1991. V. 72
Jennings Again. London: 1991. V. 69
Jennings in Particular. 1968. V. 72
Speaking of Jennings. 1973. V. 71
Take Jennings for Instance. 1958. V. 68

BUCKINGHAM, GEORGE VILLIERS, 2ND DUKE OF
The Rehearsal, as It Is Now Acted at the Theatre Royal. London: 1675. V. 73

BUCKINGHAM, JAMES SILK
America, Historical, Statistic and Descriptive. London: 1841. V. 72
America, Historical, Statistic and Descriptive. New York: 1841. V. 73
Canada, Nova Scotia, New Brunswick, and the Other British Provinces in North America, with a Plan of National Colonization. London: 1843. V. 73

BUCKINGHAM, JOHN SHEFFIELD, 1ST DUKE OF
An Essay Upon Poetry. London: 1682. V. 68; 70
The Works.... London: 1729. V. 71

BUCKINGHAM, NASH
Blood Lines: Tales of Shooting and Fishing. New York: 1938. V. 70; 72
De Shootinest Gentleman and Other Tales. New York: 1934. V. 70
Mark Right!: Tales of Shooting and Fishing. New York: 1936. V. 70; 72
Ole Miss'. New York: 1936. V. 70
Ole Miss'. New York: 1937. V. 72

BUCKINGHAM, WILLIS J.
Emily Dickinson's Reception in the 1890's. Pittsburg: 1989. V. 70

BUCKLAND, FRANK
Curiosities of Natural History. London: 1893. V. 68; 70
Familiar History of British Fishes. London: 1873. V. 68
Fish Hatching. London: 1863. V. 68
Log-Book of a Fisherman and Zoologist. London: 1891. V. 68
Natural History of British Fishes. London: 1891. V. 68
Natural History Papers and Memoir of N. Laurence Austen. London: 1877. V. 70
Notes and Jottings from Animal Life. London: 1886. V. 68

BUCKLAND, WILLIAM
Reliquiae Diluvianae; or Observations on the Organic Remains Contained in Caves, Fissures, and Diluvial Gravel.. London: 1824. V. 68; 70

BUCKLAND WRIGHT, JOHN
Cockerel Calvacade. London: 1988. V. 71

BUCKLE, JOHN STANLEY
The Manufacturer's Compendium.... London & Manchester: 1864. V. 68

BUCKLER, BENJAMIN
A Complete Vindication of the Mallard of All Souls College, Against the Injurious Suggestions of the Rev. Mr. (John) Pointer. London: 1751. V. 68; 69

BUCKLEY, E. E.
Venoms. Washington: 1956. V. 73

BUCKLEY, GAIL LUMET
The Hornes: An American Family. New York: 1986. V. 72

BUCKLEY, H.
The Airedale Terrier. 1900. V. 68

BUCKLEY, MICHAEL J.
Day at the Farm: a Poem. San Francisco: 1937. V. 71

BUCKLEY, PETER
Ernest. New York: 1978. V. 69

BUCKMAN, S. S.
Arcadian Life. London: 1891. V. 71
A Monograph of the Ammonites of the Inferior Oolite Series. 1887-1908. V. 69

BUCKMASTER, JOHN CHARLES
Buckmaster's Cookery.... London: 1874. V. 68

BUCKNILL, J. A.
The Birds of Surrey. 1900. V. 69

BUCKROSE, J. E.
Rambles in the North Yorkshire Dales. London: 1913. V. 73
The Round-About. New York: 1916. V. 71
Young Hearts. New York: 1920. V. 71

BUCKTON, CATHERINE M.
Health in the House. London: 1876. V. 68

BUCKTON, G. B.
Monograph of the British Aphides. London: 1876-. V. 71
Monograph of the British Aphides. 1876-1883. V. 73
Monograph of the British Aphides. London: 1876-1883. V. 69

BUCQUOY, E.
Les Mollusques Marins du Roussillon. Paris: 1882-1898. V. 73

BUDD, GEORGE
On Diseases of the Liver. London: 1852. V. 69

BUDDEN, MARIA ELIZABETH
Always Happy!!!. London: 1815. V. 71

BUDGE, ERNEST ALFRED WALLIS THOMPSON
Amulets and Superstitions. London: 1930. V. 72
British Museum. A Guide to the Egyptian Galleries (Sculpture). London: 1909. V. 68; 72
Cook's Handbook for Egypt And The Sudan. London: 1906. V. 72
From Fetish To God In Ancient Egypt. Oxford: 1934. V. 72
The Nile. London: 1901. V. 72
Syrian Anatomy Pathology And Therapeutics or "The Book of Medicines". London: 1913. V. 68; 70; 72

BUDGEL, EUSTACE
Memoirs of the Life and Character of the Late Earl of Orrery, and of the Family of Boyles. London: 1732. V. 72

A BUDGET of Cornish Poems, by Various Authors. Devonport: 1869. V. 71

BUDLONG, CAROLINE GALE
Memories, Pioneer Days in Oregon and Washington Territory. Eugene: 1949. V. 70

BUECHNER, FREDERICK
Treasure Hunt. New York: 1977. V. 72
The Wizard's Tide. San Francisco: 1990. V. 72

BUECHNER, THOMAS S.
Norman Rockwell. Artist and Illustrator. New York: 1970. V. 71

BUEL, J. W.
The Border Outlaws. St. Louis: 1881. V. 69
Glimpses of America. Boston: 1894. V. 68
Life and Marvelous Adventure of Wild Bill, The Scout - Being a True and Exact History of all the Sanguinary Combats and Hair Breadth Escapes of the Most Famous Scout and Spy America Ever Produced. Chicago: 1880. V. 69
The Younger Brothers, The Notorious Border Outlaws. Baltimore. V. 73

BUELL, MARJORIE HENDERSON
Little Lulu and the Organ Grinder Man. Springfield: 1946. V. 70
Little Lulu at Grandma's Farm. Springfield: 1946. V. 70
Little Lulu at the Circus. Springfield: 1946. V. 70; 73
Little Lulu at the Seashore. Springfield: 1946. V. 70
Little Lulu-Her Train Ride to Grandma's. Springfield: 1946. V. 70
Little Lulu Plays Pirate. Springfield: 1946. V. 70

BUETTNER-JANUSCH, J.
Evolutionary and Genetic Biology of Primates. New York: 1963-1964. V. 68; 72

BUFF, MARY
Dancing Cloud the Navajo Boy. New York: 1957. V. 72

BUFFALO BILL HISTORICAL CENTER
The West of Buffalo Bill: Frontier Art, Indian Crafts, Memorabilia From The Buffalo Bill Historical Center. New York: 1974. V. 72

BUFFALO Bill's Wild West. Hartford: 1887. V. 71

BUFFALO Fire Department (1880-1980). Buffalo: 1980?. V. 69

BUFFET, EDWARD P.
The Layman Revato: a Story of a Restless Mind in Buddhist India at the Time of Greek Influence. New York: 1914. V. 70

BUFFETT, F. M.
The Story of the Church in Newfoundland. Toronto: 1939?. V. 72

BUFFON, GEORGES LOUIS LECLERC DE
Buffon's Natural History. (with) Natural History of Birds, Fish, Insects and Reptiles.... London: 1797-1807. V. 70

BUFFON, JEAN LOUIS LECLERC, COUNT DE
A Natural History of Water Birds. Alnwick: 1809. V. 72

BUFFUM, GEORGE T.
Smith of Bear City and Other Frontier Sketches. New York: 1906. V. 71; 73

BUHL, H.
Nanga Parbat Pilgrimage. 1956. V. 68; 70; 73

THE BUILDER'S Dictionary; or Gentleman's and Architect's Companion.... London: 1734. V. 71

THE BUILDING Chronicle. Volume II. Edinburgh: 1856. V. 71

BUIST, K. A.
Birds, their Cages and Their Keep, Being a Practical manual of BirdKeeping and Bird-Rearing. London: 1874. V. 73

BUIST, R.
The Rose Manual.... Philadelphia: 1847. V. 71; 73

BUIST, ROBERT
The Stormontfield Piscicultural Experiments 1853-1866. Edinburgh: 1866. V. 68

BUITENHUIS, PETER
Five American Moderns. Toronto: 1968. V. 72

BUKOWSKI, CHARLES
At Terror Street and Agony Way. Los Angeles: 1968. V. 68; 69; 73
Burning In Water, Drowning in Flame. Los Angeles: 1974. V. 69; 71; 73
Burning in Water, Drowning in Flame. Santa Barbara: 1974. V. 68
Cornered. Santa Barbara: 1985. V. 68
Crucifix in a Deathhand. New York: 1965. V. 68; 71
Dangling in the Tournefortia. Santa Barbara: 1981. V. 69
The Day It Snowed in L.A. Santa Barbara: 1986. V. 69; 71; 73
Erections, Ejaculations, Exhibitions and General Tales of Ordinary Madness. San Francisco: 1972. V. 71
Factotum. Santa Barbara: 1975. V. 69; 71
Factotum. London: 1981. V. 70
Gold in Your Eye. Santa Barbara: 1986. V. 71
Ham on Rye. Santa Barbara: 1982. V. 68; 69; 70; 71; 73
Heat Wave. Santa Rosa: 1995. V. 68
Hot Water Music. Santa Barbara: 1983. V. 69; 73
If You Let Them Kill You, They Will. Santa Rosa: 1989. V. 71
In the Shadow of the Rose. Santa Rosa: 1991. V. 71
It Catches My Heart in Its Hands: New and Selected Poems 1955-1963. New Orleans: 1963. V. 73
The Last Night of the Earth Poems. Santa Rosa: 1992. V. 71
Love is a Dog From Hell: Poems 1974-1977. Santa Barbara: 1977. V. 69
Luck. Santa Rosa: 1987. V. 71
Mockingbird Wish Me Luck. Los Angeles: 1972. V. 69; 71
The Movie Critics. Santa Rosa: 1988. V. 71
The Night Torn Mad with Footsteps. Santa Rosa: 2001. V. 73
Poems 1981-1984. Santa Barbara: 1984. V. 68
Post Office. Los Angeles: 1971. V. 70
Run With the Hunted. Chicago: 1962. V. 73
Run with the Hunted: a Charles Bukowski Reader. New York: 1993. V. 69; 71; 73
Septuagenarian Stew. Santa Roa: 1990. V. 73
There's No Business. Santa Barbara: 1984. V. 69
2 by Bukowski. Los Angeles: 1967. V. 68
War All the Time: Poems 1981-1984. Santa Barbara: 1984. V. 69; 71; 73
We Ain't Got No Money Honey, But We Got Rain. Santa Rosa: 1990. V. 71
You Get So Alone at Times It Just Makes Sense. Santa Rosa: 1986. V. 69; 71; 73

BULFINCH, THOMAS
The Age of Fable. Boston: 1855. V. 71

BULL, A.
Noel Streatfeild: a Biography. 1984. V. 72

BULL, BARTLE
Safari. A Chronicle of Adventure. 1988. V. 70

BULL, J.
Birds of New York State. Garden City: 1974. V. 73

BULL, JOHN
Sermons on the Fifty First Psalm, with Others on Doctrinal and Practical Subjects.... London: 1824. V. 68

BULL, JOSEPH WHITE, CHIEF
Warrior Who Killed Custer. Lincoln: 1969. V. 72

BULL, MARCUS
Experiments to Determine the Comparative Value of the Principal Varieties of Fuel Used in the United States.... Philadelphia: 1827. V. 68; 73

BULL, WILLIAM PERKINS
From Medicine Man to Medical Man. Toronto: 1934. V. 70
From Oxford to Ontario. Toronto: 1941. V. 73

BULLARD, MARION
The Somersaulting Rabbit. New York: 1927. V. 70

BULLEID, H. A. V.
Special Effects in Cinematography. London: 1954. V. 69

BULLEIN, WILLIAM
Bulleins Bulwarke of Defence Againste All Sicknes, Sornes and Worundes that dooe Daily Assaulte Mankinde. London: 1562. V. 68

BULLEN, A. H.
England's Helicon. London: 1887. V. 70
England's Helicon. London: 1899. V. 71
Lyrics from the Dramatists of the Elizabethan Age. London: 1889. V. 70
Musa Proterva; Love Poems of the Restoration. London: 1889. V. 68

BULLEN, FRANK T.
The Cruise of the Cachalot Round The World After Sperm Whales. London: 1901. V. 72
Deep-Sea Plunderings; a Collection of Stories of the Sea. London: 1901. V. 68
The Log of a Sea Waif. London: 1899. V. 68
A Sack of Shakings. London: 1901. V. 68
The Way They Have in the Navy: Being a Day-to-Day Record of a Cruise in H.M. Battleship Mars during the Naval Manoeuvres of 1899. London: 1899. V. 68

BULLEN, GEORGE
Caxton Celebration. Catalogue of the Loan Collection of Antiquities, Curiosities and Appliances Connected with the Art of Printing. South Kensington: 1877. V. 71

BULLEN, KEITH
Salamander. Cairo: 1942-. V. 71
Salamander. London: 1947. V. 68

BULLER, A.
Researches on Fungi. London and Toronto: 1909-1950. V. 71

BULLER, A. H. REGINALD
Researches on Fungi. London and Toronto: 1909-1950. V. 68

BULLER, FRED
The Domesday Book of Mammoth Pike. 1979. V. 73
Pike and the Pike Angler. 1981. V. 73

BULLER, WALTER L.
Buller's Birds of New Zealand. Honolulu: 1967. V. 73
Buller's Birds of New Zealand. London: 1967. V. 72
A History of the Birds of New Zealand. 1967. V. 69
Manual of the Birds of New Zealand. 1882. V. 69

BULLET, JEAN BAPTISTE
Recherches Historiques sur Les Cartes a Jouer.... Lyons: 1757. V. 72

BULLFINCH, THOMAS
Legends of Charlemagne. New York: 1924. V. 70; 71; 73

BULLIARD, JEAN BAPTISTE FRANCOIS
Herbier de la France ou Collection Complete des Plantes Indigenes de ce Royaume... (with) Histoire des Plantes Veneuses et Suspects de la France. (with) Dictionnaire Elementaire de Botanique. Paris: 1780-1798. V. 68; 71

BULLINGBROOKE, EDWARD
The Duty and Authority of Justices of the Peace and Parish Officers for Ireland.... Dublin: 1788. V. 69

BULLINS, ED
The Duplex: A Black Fable in Four Movements. New York: 1971. V. 72
Five Plays. Indianapolis/NY: 1969:. V. 72
How Do You Do. New York: 1965:. V. 72
The New Lafayette Theater Presents Plays with Aesthetic Comments by Six Black Playwrights. New York: 1973. V. 72

BULLOCH, JAMES D.
The Secret Service of the Confederate States in Europe. London: 1883. V. 70; 71
The Secret Service of the Confederate States in Europe. New York: 1884. V. 69; 70
The Secret Service of the Confederate States in Europe. New York: 1959. V. 71

BULLOCH, W.
The History of Bacteriology. London: 1938. V. 71

BULLOCK, HELEN
The Williamsburg Art of Cookery or, Accomplish'd Gentlewoman's Companion. Williamsburg: 1955. V. 71

BULLOCK, WYNN
Photography: a Way of Life. Dobbs Ferry: 1973. V. 68

BULLOCK WEBSTER, H.
Memories of Sport and Travel Fifty Years Ago. 1938. V. 68

BULLOUGH, D. T. C.
A Fishing Holiday. The Song of the Salmon. the Tale of a Trout. 1903. V. 70

BULMER, GEORGE BERTRAM
Architectural Studies in Yorkshire. London: 1887. V. 73

BULMER, T., & CO.
History, Topography and Directory of Cumberland.... Preston: 1901. V. 71
History, Topography and Directory of Cumberland...Volume II. Preston: 1901. V. 71
History Topography and Directory of East Cumberland.... Manchester: 1884. V. 71
History, Topography and Directory of Furness & Cartmel.... Preston. V. 71
History, Topography and Directory of West Cumberland.... Preston: 1883. V. 71
History, Topography and Directory of Westmoreland.... Manchester: 1885. V. 71
History, Topography and Directory of Westmoreland.... Preston: 1906. V. 71

BULOW, ERNIE
Navajo Taboos. Gallup: 1991. V. 69

BULPIN, T. V.
The Ivory Trail. 1954. V. 70; 72

BULWER, HENRY LYTTON
Historical Characters: Talleyrand - Cobbett - Mackintosh - Canning.... London: 1868. V. 71
The Monarchy of the Middle Classes, or France, Social, Literary, Political. Second Series. Paris: 1836. V. 71

BULWER, JOHN
Chirologia; or the Natural Language of the Hand....(with) Chironomia; or, the Art of Manuall Rhetorique.... London: 1648-1644. V. 73

BUMP, G.
The Ruffed Grouse, Life History, Propagation, Management. Albany: 1947. V. 73

BUMP, ORLANDO F.
The Title Judiciary in the Revised Statutes of the United States and the Rules Promulgated by the Supreme Court, & Forms.... Baltimore: 1881. V. 68

BUMPUS, J. & E.
Catalogue of an Exhibition Arranged to Illustrated New Paths in Book Collecting. London: 1934. V. 69

BUNBURY, E. H.
A History of Ancient Geography Among the Greeks and Romans. London: 1883. V. 70

BUNBURY, HENRY W.
An Academy for Grown Horsemen, Containing the Completest Instructions for Walking, Trotting, Cantering, Galloping, Stumbling and Tumbling. London: 1808. V. 69; 73

BUNBURY, S.
The Star Of The Court, or The Maid of Honour and Queen of England, Anne Boleyn. London: 1844. V. 71; 72

BUNDY, G.
Birds of the Eastern Province of Saudi Arabia. London: 1989. V. 73

BUNDY, J. M.
The Life of Gen. James A. Garfield. New York: 1880. V. 70

BUNGENER, L. F.
History of the Council of Trent. London/Edinburgh: 1852. V. 70

BUNIN, I. A.
The Gentleman from San Francisco and Other Stories. Richmond: 1922. V. 69; 72
The Gentleman from San Francisco and Other Stories. New York: 1923. V. 72

BUNKER, EDWARD
The Animal Factory. New York: 1977. V. 72
Mr. Blue: Memoirs of a Renegade. New York: 1999. V. 70
No Beast so Fierce. New York: 1973. V. 71

BUNN, ALFRED
Old England and New England in a Series of Views Taken on the Spot. London: 1853. V. 69
Old England and New England, in a Series of Views Taken on the Spot. Philadelphia: 1853. V. 70

BUNNELL, LAFAYETTE H.
Discovery of the Yosemite and the Indian War of 1851 Which Led to that Event. Los Angeles: 1911. V. 70

BUNNELL, P. C.
The Eye That Shapes. Princeton: 1991. V. 68

BUNNER, HENRY CUYLER
The Seven Old Ladies of Lavender Town. New York: 1910. V. 70
A Woman of Honor. Boston: 1883. V. 70

BUNNY the Bold. London: 1917. V. 70

BUNSEN, CHRISTIAN J.
Egypts in Place in Universal History. London: 1848. V. 71

BUNSEN, FRANCES, BARONESS
Memoir of Baron Bunsen, Late Minister...of His Majesty Frederic William IV. London: 1868. V. 69

BUNTING, BAINBRIDGE
Early Architecture in New Mexico. Albuquerque: 1976. V. 70

BUNTING, BASIL
Briggflatts. London: 1966. V. 69; 72
Collected Poems. 1968. V. 70
Collected Poems. 1970. V. 73
Loquitur. 1965. V. 70
Loquitur. London: 1965. V. 69; 71; 73
The Spoils. Newcastle upon Tyne: 1965. V. 71
What the Chairman Told Tom. 1967. V. 70
What the Chairman Told Tom. Cambridge: 1967. V. 73

BUNTING, WILLIAM FRANKLIN
History of St. John's Lodge, F. & A. M. of Saint John, New Brunswick. Together with Sketches of All Masonic Bodies in New Brunswick, from A.D. 1784 to A.D. 1894. St. John: 1895. V. 73

BUNTLINE, NED
Buffalo Bill and His Adventures in the West. New York: 1886. V. 73

BUNTON, MARY T.
A Bride On the Old Chisholm Trail in 1866. San Antonio: 1939. V. 71

BUNTS, FRANK EMORY
Letters from the Asiatic Station 1881-1883. Cleveland: 1938. V. 71

BUNYAN, JOHN
The Holy War, Made by Shadai Upon Diabolus, for the Regainning of the Metropolis of the World.... Edinburgh: 1784. V. 69
The Land of Beulah: Being an Extract from the Pilgrim's Progress. London: 1974. V. 68
The Life and Death of Mr. Badman Presented to the World in a Familiar Dialogue Between Mr. Wiseman and Mr. Attentive. New York: 1900. V. 69
Pilgrim's Progress. Burlington: 1805. V. 69
The Pilgrim's Progress. Newark: 1819?. V. 69
Pilgrim's Progress. London: 1860. V. 70
The Pilgrim's Progress. London: 1901. V. 68; 69
The Pilgrim's Progress. London: 1906. V. 70
The Pilgrim's Progress. New York: 1938. V. 68
Pilgrim's Progress. New York: 1939. V. 71; 73
The Pilgrim's Progress and The Life and Death of Mr. Badman. London: 1928. V. 70; 71

A True Relation of the Holy War Made by King Shaddai Upon Diabolus. London: 1860. V. 69
Works. Glasgow: 1858. V. 71
The Works. Glasgow: 1861. V. 73

BUNZEL, R.
The Pueblo Potter. New York: 1929. V. 69

BUONAMICI, CASTRUCCIO, CONTE
Commentaries of the Late War In Italy. London: 1753. V. 69

BUONANNI, FILIPPO
Gabinetto Armonico Pieno D'Istromenti Sonori.... Rome: 1722. V. 73
Observationes circa Viventia, Quae in Rebus Non Viventibus Repriuntur. Rome: 1691. V. 68

BURBANK, E. A.
Burbank Among the Indians. Caldwell: 1944. V. 73
Burbank Among The Indians. Caldwell: 1946. V. 72

BURBANK, LUTHER
How Plants are Trained to Work for Man. New York: 1921. V. 71; 73
Luther Burbank, His Methods and Discoveries and Their Practical Application, Prepared from His Original Field Notes Covering More than 100, 000 Experiments. New York: 1914-1915. V. 70

BURBIDGE, F. W.
The Chrysanthemum, Its History, Culture, Classification and Nomenclature. London: 1885. V. 71
Domestic Floriculture. London: 1874. V. 69
Domestic Floriculture, Window Gardening and Floral Decorations. 1875. V. 72
Domestic Floriculture, Window Gardening and Floral Decorations. Edinburgh and London: 1875. V. 71; 73
The Gardens of the Sun.... London: 1880. V. 70

BURBIDGE, THOMAS
Ambarvalia. Poems. London: 1849. V. 72; 73
Poems Longer and Shorter. London: 1838. V. 73

BURBIDGE, W. F.
The Mysterious A.C.2. - a Biographical. Bognor: 1943. V. 68

BURCHILL, JULIE
The Boy Looked at Johnny. The Obituary of Rock and Roll. London: 1978. V. 71

BURCKHARDT, CHARLES
The Art of I. Compton-Burnett - a Collection of Critical Essays. London: 1972. V. 68

BURDEKIN, KATHERINE
The Rebel Passion. London: 1929. V. 71

BURDELL, HARVEY
Observations on the Structure, Physiology, Anatomy and Diseases of the Teeth. New York: 1838. V. 68; 72

BURDEN, DOUGLAS
Look to the Wilderness. 1961. V. 72

BURDER, SAMUEL
Memoirs of Eminently Pious Women of the British Empire. London: 1815. V. 68; 69; 73

BURDETT, CHARLES
Kit Carson - the Life and Adventures of Christopher Carson. Philadelphia: 1860. V. 68; 73

BURDETT, HENRY C.
Cottage Hospitals, General Fever and Convalescent.... London: 1880. V. 69

BURDETT, JOHN S.
Evidence Take Before the Senate Sitting Upon the Trial of John S. Burdett, Treasurer of the State of West Virginia, Upon Articles of Impeachment Exhibited Against Him by the House of Delegates. Wheeling: 1875. V. 68

BURDETT, OSBERT
A Little Book of Cheese. London: 1935. V. 72
Songs of Exuberance, Together with the Trenches. London: 1915. V. 73

BURDETT COUTTS, ANGELA, BARONESS
Catalogue of the Collection of Ancient and Modern Pictures.... London: 1922. V. 68

BURDICK, USHER L.
David F. Barry's Indian Notes on The Custer Battle. 1849. V. 68
The Last Battle of The Sioux nation. Fargo: 1929. V. 72
Life and Exploits of John Goodall. Watford City: 1931. V. 71
Some Of the Old-Time Cattlemen of the Great West. Baltimore: 1957. V. 71

BURDICK, WILLIAM
An Oration on the Nature and Effects of the Art of Printing. Boston: 1802. V. 68

BURDON, ERIC
I Used to Be an Animal, But I'm All Right Now. Boston and London: 1986. V. 70

BURDON-SANDERSON, GHETAL
Sir John Burdon Sanderson, a Memoir.... Oxford: 1911. V. 71

BURDSALL, R.
Men Against the Clouds. 1935. V. 68

BUREAU OF AMERICAN ETHNOLOGY
21st Annual report of the Bureau of American Ethnology. Washington: 1903. V. 72
23rd Annual Report of the Bureau of American Ethnology. Washington: 1904. V. 72

BURGE, WILLIAM
Commentaries on the Colonial and Foreign Laws Generally, and in Their Conflict, with Each Other and with the Law of England. London: 1838. V. 70

BURGER, GOTTFRIED AUGUSTUS
The Chase and William and Helen: Two Ballads from the German. Edinburgh: 1796. V. 72
Leonora. London: 1796. V. 68; 72

BURGER, J.
Shorebirds, Breeding Behavior and Populations. New York: 1984. V. 73

BURGESS, ANTHONY
Abba Abba. London: 1977. V. 68
Any Old Iron. London: 1989. V. 71
A Clockwork Orange. London: 1962. V. 68; 70; 71; 72
A Clockwork Orange. New York: 1963. V. 73
A Clockwork Orange. New York: 1965. V. 71
Devil of a State. London: 1961. V. 70
Enderby Outside. London: 1968. V. 72; 73
The Enemy in the Blanket. London: 1958. V. 72
Ernest Hemingway and His World. New York: 1978. V. 68; 69
Flame Into Being - The Life and Work of D. H. Lawrence. London: 1985. V. 71
Joysprick. London: 1973. V. 68; 72
The Kingdom of the Wicked. London: 1985. V. 72
The Long Day Wanes. New York: 1964. V. 71
A Long Trip to Teatime. 1976. V. 71
1985. London: 1978. V. 69
The Right to an Answer. London: 1960. V. 70; 71
The Right to an Answer. New York: 1961. V. 71
Time for a Tiger. London: 1956. V. 72
Tremor of Intent. London: 1966. V. 69; 73
Urgent Copy - Literary Studies. London: 1968. V. 69
A Vision of Battlements. London: 1965. V. 70
The Wanting Seed. London: 1962. V. 69
The Worm and the Ring. London: 1961. V. 70; 71; 73
You've Had Your Time. London: 1990. V. 68

BURGESS, FREDERICK W.
The Practical Retail Draper.... London: 1912-1914. V. 71

BURGESS, GELETT
Blue Goops and Red. New York: 1909. V. 69
The Goop Song Book. Cincinnati: 1941. V. 69
Ladies in Boxes. New York: 1942. V. 70
The Lark. San Francisco: 1859-. V. 68
The Lively City o' Ligg. London: 1900. V. 71
The Master of Mysteries. Indianapolis: 1912. V. 68; 69; 71
The Picardoons. London: 1904. V. 71
Why Men Hate Women. New York: 1927. V. 73

BURGESS, H. W.
Studies of Trees. London: 1837. V. 71
Studies of Trees. London: 1873. V. 70

BURGESS, J. H. M.
The Chronicles of Clapham (Clapham Common). London: 1929. V. 71

BURGESS, JOHN CART
An Easy Introduction to Perspective. 1828. V. 71
An Easy Introduction to Perspective. London: 1840. V. 69; 72

BURGESS, KENNETH FARWELL
Colonists of New England and Nova Scotia, Burgess and Heckman Families. 1956. V. 73

BURGESS, MELVIN
Junk. London: 1996. V. 73

BURGESS, THORNTON W.
The Adventures of Bob White. Boston: 1919. V. 71; 72
The Adventures of Buster Bear. Boston: 1916. V. 69; 73
The Adventures of Chatterer The Red Squirrel. Boston: 1915. V. 69
The Adventures of Danny Meadow Mouse. Boston;: 1915. V. 69
The Adventures of Grandfather Frog. Boston: 1944. V. 70
The Adventures of Jerry Muskrat. Boston: 1914. V. 69
The Adventures of Mr. Mocker. Boston: 1914. V. 69; 73
The Adventures of Ol' Mistah Buzzard. Boston: 1919. V. 71
The Adventures of Poor Mrs. Quack. Boston: 1917. V. 69
The Adventures of Prickly Porky. Boston: 1916. V. 72
The Adventures of Sammy Jay. Boston: 1915. V. 69
Bowser the Hound Meets His Match. New York: 1928. V. 69
Buster Bear Invites Old Mr. Toad to Dine. New York: 1928. V. 71
The Dear Old Briar-Patch. Boston: 1947. V. 70
Digger the Badger Decides to Stay. New York: 1928. V. 69
The Discontent of Peter Rabbit. New York: 1922. V. 69
Grandfather Frog Fools Farmer Brown's Boy. New York: 1928. V. 69
A Great Joke on Jimmy Skunk. New York: 1928. V. 69
Happy Jack. Boston: 1918. V. 73
Happy Jack Squirrel Helps Unc' Billy. New York: 1928. V. 69
Happy Jack Squirrel's Bright Idea. New York: 1928. V. 69
Jumper the Hare Cannot Sleep. New York: 1928. V. 71
Lightfoot the Deer. Boston: 1921. V. 73

BURGESS, W.
Fishes of Sri Lanka (Ceylon) the Maldive Islands and Mobasa. Neptune City: 1973. V. 72

BURGESS, W. E.
Pacific Marine Fishes. 1971-1976. V. 69; 73

BURGGREN, W. W.
Biology of the Land Crabs. New York: 1988. V. 72

BURGH, JAMES
Political Disquisitions; or an Enquiry into Public Errors, Defects and Abuses. London: 1774-1775. V. 69
Thoughts on Education, Tending Chiefly to Recommend to the Attention of the Public, Some Particulars Relating to that Subject. Boston: 1749. V. 73

BURGIN, RICHARD
Conversations with Jorge Luis Borges. New York: 1969. V. 69

BURGON, JOHN WILLIAM
Petra. A Prize Poem, Recited in the Theatre Oxford June IV, MDCCCXLV. Oxford: 1845. V. 73

BURGOYNE, ARTHUR G.
Homstead. Pittsburgh: 1893. V. 68

BURGOYNE, JOHN
Rudimentary Treatise on the Blasting and Quarrying of Stone for Building and Other Purposes. London: 1849. V. 69; 71
A State of the Expedition from Canada, as Laid Before the House of Commons...and Verified by Evidence, with a Collection of Authentic Documents. London: 1780. V. 68; 73

BURGUM, JASAMINE S.
Zezula Or Pioneer Days In The Smoky Water Country. Valley City: 1937. V. 72

BURK, JOHN N.
The Life Works of Beethoven. New York: 1943. V. 73

BURK, MARGARET TANTE
Are The Stars Out Tonight? The Story of the Ambassador and Cocoanut Grove. Los Angeles: 1980. V. 68

BURKART, A.
Flora Illustrada de Entre Rios (Aragentian). Parts 2, 3, 5 and 6. Buenos Aires: 1969-1987. V. 73

BURKE, A. L.
The Mayberry Murder Mstery of Bonito City. Alamogordo. V. 70

BURKE, BERNARD
A Genealogical and Heraldic Dictionary of the Landed Gentry of Great Britain and Ireland. London: 1862. V. 72
The Rise Of Great Families, Other Essays, and Stories. London: 1873. V. 70; 72

BURKE, CLIFFORD
Printing Poetry: a Workbook in Typographic Reification. San Francisco: 1980. V. 70; 72

BURKE, EDMUND
A General Reply to the Several Answerers, &c. of a Letter Written to a Noble Lord, by the Right Honourable Edmund Burke. London: 1796. V. 71
Lessons to a Young Prince, by an Old Statesman, on the Present Disposition in Europe to a General Revolution. London: 1791. V. 70
A Letter from Edmund Burke, Esq....to John Farr and John Harrs, Esqrs...on the Affairs of America. London: 1777. V. 69
Mr. Burke's Speech, on the 1st December 1783, Upon the Question for the Speaker's Leaving the Chair, in Order for the House to Resolve Itself Into a Committee on Mr. Fox's East India Bill. London: 1784. V. 69
Mr. Edmund Burke's Speeches at the Arrival at Bristol, and at the Conclusion of the Poll. London: 1775. V. 69
Observations on a Late State of the Nation. London: 1782. V. 69
A Philosophical Enquiry into the Origin of Our Ideas of the Sublime and Beautiful. London: 1764. V. 69
A Philosophical Enquiry into the Origin of Our Ideas of the Sublime and Beautiful. London: 1770. V. 73
A Philosophical Enquiry Into the Origin of Our Ideas of the Sublime and Beautiful. London: 1773. V. 69
A Philosophical Enquiry into the Origin of Our Ideas of the Sublime and Beautiful. Basil: 1792. V. 69
A Philosophical Enquiry into the Origin of Our Ideas of the Sublime and Beautiful. London: 1793. V. 69
A Philosophical Inquiry Into the Origin of Our Ideas of the Sublime and Beautiful. Philadelphia: 1806. V. 68; 71
Reflections on the Revolution in France, and on Proceeding in Certain Societies in London Relative to that Event. London: 1790. V. 68; 73
Speech of Edmund Burke, Esq. on American Taxation April 19, 1774. London: 1775. V. 69
Speech of Edmund Burke, Esq. at the Guildhall in Bristol, Previous to the Late Election in that City, Upon Certain Points Relative to His Parliamentary Conduct. London: 1782. V. 69
Speech of Edmund Burke, Esq. on American Taxations. London: 1775. V. 69
Speech of Edmund Burke, Esq. on Moving His Resolutions for Conciliation with the Colonies March 22, 1775. London: 1778. V. 69
Speech of Edmund Burke, Esq...On Presenting to the House of Commons (on the 11th of February 1780).... London: 1780. V. 69
Thoughts on the Cause of the Present Discontents. London: 1770. V. 72
Thoughts on the Cause of the Present Discontents. London: 1784. V. 69
A Treatise on the First Principles of Christiniaity, in which all Difficulties Stated by Ancient and Modern Skeptics.... Halifax: 1808. V. 72
Two Letters Addressed to a Member of the Present Parliament, on the Proposals for Peace with the Regicide Directory of France. London: 1796. V. 70; 72; 73

BURKE, EDMUND continued
Two Letters from Mr. Burke to the City of Bristol, on the Bills Depending in Parliament, Relative to the Trade of Ireland. London: 1778. V. 69
The Works. Dublin: 1792. V. 72
Works. London: 1823. V. 71
The Works. London: 1854. V. 71
The Works. London: 1899. V. 73

BURKE, J. BERNARD
Anecdotes of the Aristocracy, and Episodes in Ancestral Story. London: 1850. V. 73

BURKE, JAMES LEE
Bitterroot. New Orleans: 2001. V. 69; 72
Bitterroot. New York: 2001. V. 69
Black Cherry Blues. Boston: 1989. V. 68; 69; 70; 71; 72; 73
Black Cherry Blues. London: 1989. V. 72; 73
Black Cherry Blues. London: 1990. V. 69
Burning Angel. New Orleans: 1995. V. 68; 69; 70; 72; 73
Burning Angel. New York: 1995. V. 72
Cadillac Jukebox. New Orleans: 1996. V. 68; 69; 70; 72; 73
Cadillac Jukebox. New York: 1996. V. 69
Cimarron Rose. London: 1997. V. 68; 69; 70; 71; 72; 73
Cimarron Rose. New Orleans: 1997. V. 68; 69; 70; 72; 73
Cimarron Rose. New York: 1997. V. 72
The Convict. Baton Rouge: 1985. V. 68; 69; 70; 72
The Convict. London: 1995. V. 69; 70; 73
Dixie City Jam. New York: 1994. V. 68; 69; 70; 71; 72
Half of Paradise. Boston: 1965. V. 68; 69; 70; 71; 72
Heartwood. New Orleans: 1999. V. 68; 69; 70; 71; 72; 73
Heaven's Prisoners. New York: 1987. V. 68
Heaven's Prisoners. 1988. V. 70; 71
Heaven's Prisoners. New York: 1988. V. 68; 69; 70; 71; 72; 73
Heaven's Prisoners. Boston: 1989. V. 70
Heaven's Prisoners. London: 1990. V. 69
In the Electric Mist with Confederate Dead. New York: 1993. V. 68; 70; 72
Jolie Blon's Bounce. New Orleans: 2002. V. 72; 73
The Last Words of Dutch Schultz. New York: 1975. V. 68
Lay Down My Sword and Shield. New York: 1971. V. 68; 69; 70; 71; 72
The Lost Get-Back Boogie. Baton Rouge: 1986. V. 68; 69; 71; 72
The Lost Get-Back Boogie. New York: 1986. V. 72
A Morning for Flamingos. Boston: 1990. V. 68; 69; 73
A Morning for Flamingos. New York: 1990. V. 69
The Neon Rain. 1987. V. 71
The Neon Rain. New York: 1987. V. 68; 69; 70
The Neon Rain. London: 1989. V. 69
Purple Cane Road. London: 2000. V. 68; 70
Purple Cane Road. New Orleans: 2000. V. 68; 70; 71; 72; 73
Purple Cane Road. New York: 2000. V. 70; 72
A Stained White Radiance. New York: 1992. V. 68; 69; 71; 72
Sunset Limited. Blakeney: 1998. V. 68; 69; 70; 72; 73
Sunset Limited. New York: 1998. V. 70; 72
Texas City 1947. 1992. V. 69
Texas City, 1947. Northridge: 1992. V. 68; 70
To the Bright and Shining Sun. New York: 1970. V. 68; 69
To the Bright and Shining Sun. 1992. V. 69; 70
To the Bright and Shining Sun. Huntington: 1992. V. 72
Two for Texas. New York: 1982. V. 68; 69; 71; 73
Two for Texas. Huntington Beach: 1992. V. 69; 70; 72; 73
Winter Light. Huntington Beach: 1992. V. 68; 70; 71; 72; 73

BURKE, JOHN
Dreams and Derisions. New York: 1927. V. 72

BURKE, JOHN BERNARD
Romantic Records of Distinguished Families. London: 1850. V. 70

BURKE, RICHARD
The Dead Take No Bows. Boston: 1941. V. 71
Here Lies the Body. New York: 1942. V. 71

BURKE, THOMAS
East of the Mansion House. New York: 1926. V. 71
Murder at Elstree or Mr. Thurtell and His Gig. London: 1936. V. 68; 73
Twinkle Toes. New York: 1924. V. 71
Whispering Windows. 1921. V. 73
The Wind in the Rain. 1924. V. 73

BURKE, WILLIAM
The Letters of Valens. London: 1777. V. 70
The Mineral Springs of Virginia. Richmond: 1851. V. 71
The Mineral Springs of Virginia. Richmond: 1853. V. 71
West Port Murders; or an Authentic Account of the Atrocious Murders Committed by Burke and His Associates. Edinburgh: 1829. V. 73

BURKHARDT, F.
A Calendar of the Correspondence of Charles Darwin 1821-1882 with Supplement. Cambridge: 1994. V. 72

BURKHOLDER, JOSEPH L.
State of New Mexico; Middle Rio Grande Conservancy District; Report of the Chief Engineer. Albuquerque: 1928. V. 72

BURKHOLDER, PETER
The Confession of Faith, of the Christians Known by the Name of Mennonites. Winchester: 1837. V. 68

BURKLEY, FRANK J.
The Faded Frontier. Omaha: 1935. V. 70

BURKS, MARTIN P.
Common Law and Statutory Pleading and Practice. Charlottesville: 1952. V. 68

BURLAMAQUI, JEAN JACQUES
The Principles of Politic Law: Being a Sequel to the Principles of Natural Law. London: 1752,. V. 68

BURLAND, C. A.
Magic Books from Mexico. London: 1953. V. 72

BURLAND, REBECCA
A True Picture of Emigration. 1848. V. 68

BURLEND, REBECCA
A True Picture of Emigration. London: 1848. V. 69; 73

BURLESON, GEORGIA J.
The Life and Writings of Rufus C. Burleson. 1901. V. 68

BURLEY, W. J.
Death in Willow Pattern. London: 1969. V. 69
Wycliffe and the Dead Flautist. London: 1991. V. 72
Wycliffe and the Dunes Mystery. London: 1993. V. 72
Wycliffe and the House of Fear. London: 1995. V. 72

BURLINGAME, ROGER
High Thursday. New York: 1928. V. 71

BURLINGHAM, FREDERICK
How to Become an Alpinist. London: 1914. V. 69

BURLINGTON
Charter and Ordinances of the City of Burlington. Burlington: 1895. V. 69
Charter of the City of Burlington, with the Ordinances. Burlington: 1851. V. 69

BURLINGTON, CHARLES
The Modern Universal British Traveller. London: 1779. V. 70

BURMAN, BEN LUCIEN
Steamboat Round the Bend. New York: 1933. V. 71

BURMANNUS, PETRUS
Poetae Latini Minores sive Gratii Falisci Cynegeticon. . . Leyden: 1731. V. 71

BURMEISTER, HERMAN
The Black Man. New York: 1853. V. 68

BURN, JOHN SOUTHERDEN
The History of the French, Walloon, Dutch and Other Foreign Protestant Refugees Settled in England from the Reign of Henry VIII to the Revolution of the Edict of Nantes.... London: 1846. V. 71

BURN, RICHARD
The Justice of the Peace, and Parish Officer. London: 1756. V. 69

BURN, ROBERT SCOTT
The Colonist's and Emigrant's Handbook of the Mechanical Arts. Edinburgh: 1854. V. 68
The Illustrated Architectural, Engineering and Mechanical Drawing-Book. London. V. 69
The Illustrated Architectural, Engineering and Mechanical Drawing-Book. London: 1856. V. 72
The Illustrated London Architectural, Engineering and Mechanical Drawing Book. London: 1853. V. 68
Mechanics and Mechanism.... London: 1854. V. 71
The New Guide to Carpentry, General Framing and Joinery, Theoretical and Practical. Edinburgh & London: 1868-1872. V. 71
The Practical Directory for the Improvement of Landed Property, Rural and Suburban and the Economic Cultivation of Its Farms. Edinburgh: 1882. V. 68
Practical Ventilation as Applied to Public, Domestic and Agricultural Structures. Edinburgh and London: 1850. V. 69
Working Drawings and Designs in Mechanical Engineering & Machine Making; with Essays on Various Subjects. Edinburgh & London: 1864-1868. V. 71
Year-Book of Agricultural Facts for 1859. 1860. V. 72

BURN, THOMAS
An Essay on the Abolition of Slavery Throughout the British Dominions, Without Injury to the Master of His Property.... Frome: 1833. V. 69

BURNABY, ANDREW
Travels through the Middle Settlements in North America. London: 1775. V. 68; 73

BURNABY, ANTHONY
Two Proposals Humbly Offer'd to the Honourable House of Commons, Now Assembled in Parliament. I. That a duty be laid on malt, in the stead of the present duty on beer and ale...II. That a duty be laid on malt and the present duty on beer and ale be.... London: 1696. V. 71

BURNAND, FRANCIS
Humbug Rhymes. London: 1908. V. 71

BURNAND, FRANCIS COWLEY
Happy Thought Hall. London: 1872. V. 68

BURNAND, T.
Toute La Camargue. Paris: 1938. V. 72

BURNAP, GEORGE W.
The Sphere and Duties of Woman. Baltimore: 1848. V. 69

BURNAP, WILLARD A.
One Man's Lifetime 1840-1920, a Review of Some Great and Near Great and Little Events. Fergus Falls: 1929. V. 70

BURNE, J. B.
Parson and Peasant. Some chapters of Their Natural History. London: 1891. V. 73

BURNE-JONES, EDWARD
The Beginning of the World - Twenty-Five Pictures. London: 1902. V. 68; 71
The Flower Book. 1905. V. 68
Letters to Katie. London: 1925. V. 69

BURNELL, GEORGE ROWDON
The Rudiments of Hydraulic Engineering. London: 1868. V. 71

BURNET, FRANK MAC FARLANE
Virus an Organism. Cambridge: 1945. V. 72

BURNET, GILBERT, BP. OF SALISBURY
Bishop Burnet's History of His Own Time. London: 1724. V. 69
Bishop Burnet's History of His Own Time. Oxford: 1823. V. 68; 72; 73
The Bishop of Salisbury, His Speech in the House of Lords, on the First Article of the Impeachment of Dr. Henry Sachevrell,. London: 1710;. V. 73
A Discourse of the Pastoral Care. London: 1692. V. 71
An Essay on the Memory of the Late Queen.... London: 1695. V. 73
The Last Confession, Prayers and Meditations of Lieutenant John Stern, Delivered by Him on the Cart Immediately Before His Execution, to Dr. Burnet. London: 1682. V. 70
The Lives of Matthew Hale...Wilmot, Earl of Rochester and Queen Mary. London: 1774. V. 73
The Memoires of the Lives and Actions of James and William Dukes of Hamilton and Casateleherald &c. London: 1677. V. 72
Some Letters. Amsterdam: 1686. V. 69
Some Letters. Rotterdam: 1686. V. 69; 72; 73

BURNET, JOHN
Practical Essays on Various Branches of the Fine Arts. London: 1848. V. 71
Practical Hints on Colour in Painting. London: 1830. V. 72
Practical Hints on Composition in Painting. London: 1845. V. 72
Practical Hints on Light and Shade in Painting. London: 1849. V. 72
A Practical Treatise on Painting in Three Parts. London: 1830. V. 68

BURNET, THOMAS
Archaeologiae Philosophicae; sive Doctrina Antiqua de Rerum Originibus. Libri Duo. Londini: 1692. V. 70
De Fide and Officiis Christianorum. 1728. V. 72
The Sacred Theory of the Earth.... London: 1734. V. 70
Telluris Theoria Sacra; Orbis Nostri Originem & Mutationes Generales, Quas aut jam Subilt aut olim Subiturus est, Complectens...(Part II). London: 1681-1689. V. 68
The Theory of the Earth Containing an Account of the Original of the Earth, and of All the General Changes Which It Hath Already Undergone, Or Is To undergo Till the Consummation of All Things. London: 1697. V. 73
The Theory of the Earth...(Part II). London: 1684. V. 68

BURNETT, FRANCES HODGSON
Editha'a Burglar. Boston: 1925. V. 69
His Grace of Osmond. New York: 1897. V. 70
Little Lord Fauntleroy. London. V. 69
Little Lord Fauntleroy. London: 1886. V. 71
Little Lord Fauntleroy. New York: 1886. V. 70
The Little Princess. New York: 1911. V. 69
Louisiana and that Lass o' Lowrie's: two Stories. London: 1889. V. 68
The Making of a Marchioness. New York: 1901. V. 70
The Secret Garden. New York: 1911. V. 69
The Shuttle. London: 1907. V. 72
That Lass O'Lowries. New York: 1877. V. 70
Through One Administration. London: 1885?. V. 68
The Troubles of Queen Silver-Bell. New York: 1906. V. 73
Vagabondia. New York: 1889. V. 69
The White People. New York and London: 1917. V. 71

BURNETT, HALLIE SOUTHGATE
A Woman in Possession. New York: 1951. V. 72

BURNETT, J. H.
The Vegetation of Scotland. Edinburgh: 1964. V. 72

BURNETT, SWAN M.
A Theoretical and Practical Treatise on Atigmatism. St. Louis: 1887. V. 73

BURNETT, W. H.
Blackburn Parish Church. Blackburn: 1906. V. 73
Holiday Rambles by Road and Field Path. 1889. V. 73

BURNETT, W. R.
Adobe Walls. New York: 1953. V. 71
Adobe Walls. London: 1954. V. 71
The Asphalt Jungle. New York: 1949. V. 68
The Asphalt Jungle. London: 1950. V. 73
The Dark Command. New York: 1938. V. 71
4 Novels. Little Caesar. The Asphalt Jungle. High Sierra. Vanity Row. London: 1984. V. 70
The Giant Swing. New York: 1932. V. 69
High Sierra. New York: 1940. V. 71; 73
Iron Man. New York: 1930. V. 68; 71
It's Always Four O'Clock. New York: 1956. V. 69
Little Caesar. 1929. V. 68
Little Caesar. New York: 1929. V. 69
Little Men, Big World. New York: 1951. V. 69
Nobody Lives Forever. New York: 1945. V. 71
Round the Clock at Volari's. Greenwich: 1961. V. 71
Underdog. New York: 1957. V. 71
Vanity Row. New York: 1952. V. 68

BURNETT, WHIT
The Maker of Signs. New York: 1934. V. 68

BURNEY, CHARLES
A General History of Music, from the Earliest Ages to the Present Period. London: 1776-1789. V. 70

BURNEY, F. H.
The Musical Bijou, an Album of Music Poetry for MCCCCXLII. 1842. V. 71

BURNEY, SARAH HARRIET
Tales of Fancy. London: 1816-1820. V. 73

BURNFORD, SHEILA
The Incredible Journey. London: 1961. V. 71

BURNHAM, DANIEL H.
Plan of Chicago. New York: 1970. V. 68; 69; 72

BURNHAM, HAROLD B.
Keep Me Warm One Night: Early Handweaving in Eastern Canada. Toronto: 1986. V. 69

BURNHAM, JOHN B.
The Rim of Mystery. 1929. V. 69; 70; 72; 73

BURNINGHAM, JOHN
Would You Rather.... London: 1978. V. 71

BURNLEY, JAMES
Two Sides of the Atlantic. London: 1880. V. 71; 73

BURNOUF, E.
L'Inde Francaise. Paris: 1827. V. 68

BURNS, JAMES DAWSON
Three Years Among the Working-Classes in the United States During the War. London: 1865. V. 71

BURNS, JAMES R.
Battle of Williamsburgh, with Reminiscences of the Campaign. New York: 1865. V. 71

BURNS, JOHN
The Principles of Midwifery; Including the Diseases of Women and Children. New York: 1837. V. 68; 71

BURNS, JOHN H.
Memoirs of A Cow Pony, As Told By Himself. Boston: 1906. V. 71

BURNS, OLIVE ANN
Cold Sassy Tree. New York: 1984. V. 71

BURNS, ROBERT
Auld Lang Syne. London: 1859. V. 71; 72
The Complete Poetical Works of Robert Burns. Boston/NY: 1897. V. 72
The Complete Writings. Boston: 1926. V. 69
The Complete Writings. London: 1927. V. 70
The Cotter's Saturday Night. Hampstead: 1908. V. 73
Poems, Chiefly in the Scottish Dialect. London: 1787. V. 73
Poetical Works. London: 1839. V. 72
The Poetical Works with Memoir, Critical Dissertation and Explanatory Notes.... Edinburgh: 1856. V. 71
The Poetry. 1896. V. 68
The Poetry. Edinburgh: 1896. V. 71
The Soldier's Return. London: 1857. V. 71
Songs. Waltham St. Lawrence: 1925. V. 70; 71
Songs and Ballads. London. V. 71
The Works. 1887. V. 71
The Works. London: 1887. V. 70
The Works of Robert Burns; With an Account of His Life, and a Criticism on His Writings. London: 1801. V. 70

BURNS, ROBERT E.
I Am a Fugitive from a Georgia Chain Gang!. New York: 1932. V. 71

BURNS, ROBERT IGNATIUS
The Jesuits and the Indian Wars of the Northwest. New Haven: 1966. V. 71

BURNS, WALTER NOBEL
Tombstone. New York: 1929. V. 69

BURNS, WILLIAM J.
The Crevice. New York: 1915. V. 71

BURNS-BEGG, ROBERT
The Lochleven Angler. Kinross: 1874. V. 68; 71; 73

BURNSIDE, A. E.
First Report of the Society of the Burnside Expedition and of the Ninth Army Corps. At the Meeting in New York Feb. 8th 1869. New York: 1869. V. 70

BURNSIDE, H. M.
The Childrens (sic) Wonderland. London. V. 73
Doggie's Note Book. London: 1890. V. 70
Wonderland Pictures. London. V. 73

BURPEE, LAWRENCE J.
Among The Canadian Alps. London: 1915. V. 72
The Search for the Western Sea: The Story of the Exploration of North Western America. Toronto: 1935. V. 69; 71

BURR, NELSON R.
Education in New Jersey, 1630-1871. Princeton: 1942. V. 69

BURRAGE, HENRY S.
Maine at Louisburg in 1745. Augusta: 1910. V. 73

BURRARD, GERALD
Big Game Hunting in the Himalayas and Tibet. 1925. V. 69; 70; 72; 73
Big Game Hunting in the Himalayas and Tibet. London: 1925. V. 72
Notes on Sporting Rifles. 1953. V. 72

BURRARD, SIDNEY GERALD
A Sketch of the Geography and Geology of the Himalaya Mountains and Tibet. Calcutta: 1907-1908. V. 68; 72

BURRELL, JAMES
History of Clear Creek and Boulder Valleys, Colorado.... Chicago: 1880. V. 71; 73

BURRELL, SOPHIA
Poems. London: 1793. V. 69

BURRISH, ONSLOW
Batavia Illustrata; or, a View of the Policy and Commerce of the United Provinces: Particularly of Holland. London: 1731. V. 72

BURROUGHES, JEREMIAH
A Sermon Preached Before the Honorable House of Commons Assembled in Parliament, at Their Late Solemn Fast, August 26, 1646, etc. London: 1646. V. 73

BURROUGHS, CHARLES GORDON
Home. Chicago: 1987?. V. 68

BURROUGHS, DOROTHY
The Magic Herb. London. V. 72

BURROUGHS, EDEN
A Faithful Narrative of the Wonderful Dealings of God, Towards Polly Davis of New Gratham, in the State of New Hampshire. Worcester: 1793. V. 71

BURROUGHS, EDGAR RICE
Carson of Venus. Tarzana: 1939. V. 71; 73
Carson of Venus. Tarzana: 1946. V. 69
The Chessmen of Mars. Chicago: 1922. V. 68
The Chessmen of Mars. 1930. V. 68
The Deputy Sheriff of Comanche County. 1940. V. 69
Escape on Venus. Tarzana: 1946. V. 71; 73
The Girl from Hollywood. 1923. V. 70
The Gods of Mars. London: 1935. V. 68; 72
The Illustrated Tarzan Book No. 1. 1929. V. 68; 69
Jungle Girl. London: 1933. V. 68
Jungle Girl. 1934. V. 68
Jungle Tales of Tarzan. 1919. V. 73
Jungle Tales of Tarzan. 1930. V. 68
The Lad and the Lion. 1938. V. 69
The Land that Time Forgot. 1924. V. 68
Llana of Gathol. Tarzana: 1948. V. 72
The New Adventures of Tarzan. Chicago: 1935. V. 73
Official Guide of the Tarzan Clans of America. Tarzana: 1939. V. 73
Pellucidar. 1923. V. 73
Pirates of Venus. Tarzana: 1934. V. 69
Swords of Mars. Tarzana: 1936. V. 72
Tanar of Pellucidar. New York: 1930. V. 68
Tarzan and the Golden Lion. 1923. V. 73
Tarzan and the Golden Lion. New York: 1924. V. 68
Tarzan and the Leopard Man. Tarzana: 1935. V. 71
Tarzan and the Lost Empire. 1929. V. 69
Tarzan, Lord of the Jungle. Chicago: 1928. V. 70
Tarzan, Lord of the Jungle. London: 1928. V. 68
Tarzan: the Lost Adventure. Milwaukie, Oregon: 1995. V. 70
Tarzan the Untamed. 1920. V. 73
Tarzan Triumphant. 1932. V. 69
The Tarzan Twins. 1927. V. 68

BURROUGHS, EDWARD
Essays on Husbandry and Rural Economy. Dublin: 1827. V. 69

BURROUGHS, FRANKLIN
Compression Wood. Haverford: 1999. V. 70; 72; 73
Horry and the Waccamaw. New York: 1992. V. 70; 72
Passion or Conquest. Haverford: 2001. V. 70; 72

BURROUGHS, JOHN
Birds and Poets with Other Papers. Boston: 1895. V. 69; 71
Camping and Tramping with Roosevelt. Boston: 1907. V. 73
Notes on Walt Whitman, as Poet and Person. New York: 1867. V. 69; 71
Under the Maples. Boston: 1921. V. 71
Wake-Robin. New York: 1871. V. 70

BURROUGHS, JOHN ROLFE
Where the Old West Stayed Young. New York: 1962. V. 69

BURROUGHS, WILLIAM S.
The Adding Machine. London: 1985. V. 71
Ah Pook is Here and Other Texts. London and New York: 1979. V. 71; 73
Ali's Smile. Brighton: 1971. V. 69; 71; 73
Ali's Smile. Gottingen: 1973. V. 72
APO-33. San Francisco: 1968. V. 71
Blade Runner. Berkeley: 1979. V. 69
The Book of Breathing. Berkeley: 1980. V. 69; 71
Cities of the Red Night. New York: 1981. V. 70; 71
Cobble Stone Gardens. Cherry Valley: 1976. V. 68
Dead Fingers Talk. London: 1966. V. 71
The Dead Star. San Francisco: 1969. V. 69; 70
Doctor Benway. Santa Barbara: 1979. V. 69; 71
Early Routines. Santa Barbara: 1981. V. 69; 71
Electronic Revolution 1970-1971. Cambridge: 1971. V. 68
The Exterminator. San Francisco: 1960. V. 70; 73
Exterminator!. New York: 1973. V. 68; 71; 72
The Final Academy. London: 1982. V. 72
Ghost of Chance. New York: 1991. V. 69; 73
Ghost of Chance. London: 1995. V. 70
The Hombre Invisible. 1981. V. 73
Interzone. London: 1989. V. 73
The Job. London: 1984. V. 71
Junkie. Confessions of an Unredeemed Drug Addict. New York: 1953. V. 69; 70; 73
Junkie. Confessions of an Unredeemed Drug Addict. London: 1973. V. 73
Last Words. New York: 2000. V. 71; 72
The Last Words of Dutch Schultz. London: 1970. V. 69; 70; 71; 73
The Last Words of Dutch Schultz. New York: 1975. V. 73
The Letters of William S. Burroughs. 1993. V. 71; 72
Letters to Allen Ginsberg 1953-1957. Geneva: 1978. V. 71
Letters to Allen Ginsberg 1953-1957. New York: 1982. V. 70; 73
Naked Lunch. New York: 1959. V. 69; 70
The Naked Lunch. Paris: 1959. V. 68; 70; 73
Naked Lunch. New York: 1962. V. 68; 70; 71; 72; 73
The Naked Lunch. London: 1986. V. 71
Nova Express. New York: 1964. V. 73
Nova Express. London: 1966. V. 72
Port of Saints. Berkeley: 1980. V. 71
Roosevelt After Inauguration. New York: 1964. V. 71
The Seven Deadly Sins. New York: 1991. V. 72
The Soft Machine. Paris: 1961. V. 69; 70; 71
The Soft Machine. 1968. V. 73
The Soft Machine. London: 1968. V. 70
The Streets of Chance. New York: 1981. V. 71; 73
The Ticket that Exploded. Paris: 1962. V. 69; 70; 71; 73
Time. New York: 1965. V. 72
Tornado Alley. Ann Arbor: 1989. V. 73
The Western Lands. New York: 1987. V. 68; 71; 72
White Subway. London: 1973. V. 69; 71

BURROW, E. I.
Elements of Conchology. London: 1815. V. 69
Elements of Conchology. 1818. V. 68
Elements of Conchology. London: 1818. V. 70
Elements of Conchology. London: 1894. V. 71

BURROW, E. J.
Elements of Conchology. 1844. V. 69; 73

BURROWAY, JANET
Opening Nights. New York: 1985. V. 68; 71

BURROWS, GEORGE
On Disorders of the Cerebral and Circulation and on the Connection Between Affections of the Brain and Diseases of the Heart. Philadelhia: 1848. V. 68; 72

BURROWS, LARRY
Larry Burrows: Compassionate Photographer. 1972. V. 73

BURROWS, MONTAGU
Imperial England. London: 1880. V. 71

BURRUS, ERNEST J.
Kino and the Cartography of Northwestern New Spain. Tucson: 1965. V. 68; 70; 71; 73
Kino Reports to Headquaters: Correspondence of Eusebio F. Kino From New Spain With Rome. Rome: 1954. V. 68
Kino Escribe a la Duquesa; Correspondencia del P. Eusebio Francisco Kingo con la Duquesa de Aveiro y Otros Documentos. Madrid: 1964. V. 70
Kino's Plan for the Development of Pimneria Alta, Arizona and Upper California. Tucson: 1961. V. 71

BURSILL, HENRY
Hand Shadows to be Thrown Upon the Wall: a Series of Novel and Amusing Figures Formed by the Hand. London: 1860. V. 71

BURT, E. A.
The Thelephoraceae of North America. St. Louis: 1914-1926. V. 70

BURT, S. W.
The Rocky Mountain Gold Regions. Denver: 1962. V. 70

BURT, STRUTHERS
The Delectable Mountains. New York: 1927. V. 71

BURTIN, M. FRANCOIS-XAVIER DE
Treatise on the Knowledge Necessary to Amateurs in Pictures. London: 1845. V. 68

BURTON, ALFRED
The Adventures of Johnny Newcome in the Navy. London: 1818. V. 68

BURTON, BEATRICE
Easy. New York: 1930. V. 70

BURTON, DECIMUS
A Description of the Royal Colosseum, Re-Opened in MDCCCXLV...ReEmbellished in 1848. (with) Description of the Royal Cyclorama, or Music Hall. London: 1848-1849. V. 70

BURTON, E. F.
The Electron Microscope. New York: 1942. V. 68
Reminiscences of Sport in India. 1885. V. 69; 70; 72; 73

BURTON, E. MILBY
Charleston Furniture 1700-1825. Charleston: 1955. V. 71

BURTON, EDWARD
A Description of the Antiquities and Other Curiosities of Rome, from Personal Observation During a Visit to Italy in the Years 1818-1819. London: 1828. V. 73

BURTON, GEORGE F.
Cake Making. Blackpool: 1920. V. 68
The New Era Chocolate Book. 1924. V. 68

BURTON, JOHN
An Essay Towards a Complete New System of Midwifery, Theoretical and Practical. 1751. V. 70
An Essay Towards a Complete New System of Midwifery, Theoretical and Practical.... London: 1751. V. 68
A Genuine and True Journal of the Most Miraculous Escape of the Young Chevalier.... London: 1749. V. 68
Lectures on Female Education and Manners. Elizabeth-town: 1799. V. 69; 73
The Parish Priest: a Poem. London: 1800. V. 68

BURTON, JOHN HILL
The Book-Hunter. Edinburgh and London: 1882. V. 71
The History of Scotland; from Agricola's Invasion to the Extinction of the Last Jacobite Resurrection. Edinburgh and London: 1897. V. 73
Political and Social Economy; its Practical Applications. Edinburgh: 1849. V. 71

BURTON, MARY E.
The Letters of Mary Wordsworth 1800-1855. Oxford: 1958. V. 70

BURTON, MILES
Death in a Duffle Coat. London: 1956. V. 70; 71
Death Paints a Picture. London: 1960. V. 71
The Moth Watch Murder. London: 1957. V. 71
The Secret of High Eldersham. London: 1930. V. 73
Situation Vacant. London: 1946. V. 69

BURTON, R. G.
A Book of Man-Eaters. 1931. V. 69
A Book of Man-Eaters. 1946. V. 72; 73
The Book of the Tiger. 1933. V. 73
Sport and Wild Life in the Deccan. 1928. V. 72; 73
The Tiger Hunters. 1936. V. 72

BURTON, RICHARD FRANCIS
Abeokuta and the Cameroons Mountains: an Exploration. London: 1863. V. 70
The Book of the Sword. London: 1884. V. 68; 70; 72
The City of the Saints and Across the Rocky Mountains to California. New York: 1862. V. 68; 70
Etruscan Bologna: a Study. London: 1876. V. 70
Explorations of the Highlands of the Brazil. London: 1869. V. 70
First Footsteps in East Africa; or an Exploration of Harar. London: 1856. V. 68; 72
First Footsteps in East Africa or Exploration of Harar. 1982. V. 73
The Gold Mines of Midian and the Ruined Midianite Cities. London: 1878. V. 68; 70; 72
The Gold Mines of Midian and the Ruined Midianite Cities. London: 1878-1879. V. 71
The Highlands of Brazil. London: 1869. V. 68; 72
The Kasidah of Haji Abdu El-Yezdi. London: 1900. V. 69
The Kasidah of Haji Abdu El-Yezdi. Portland: 1905. V. 68
The Kasidah of Haji Abdu El-Yezdi. Portland: 1915. V. 69
The Kasidah of Haji Abdu El-Yezdi. Philadelphia: 1931. V. 72
The Lake Regions of Central Africa.... New York: 1961. V. 71
The Land of Midian (Revisited). London: 1879. V. 72
Letters from the Battlefields of Paraguay. London: 1870. V. 70
A Mission to Gelele, King of Dahome. London: 1864. V. 68; 72
A Mission to Gelele, King of Dahome. London: 1893. V. 70
Personal Narrative of a Pilgrimage to El Medinah and Meccah. London: 1857. V. 68; 72
Selected Papers on Anthropology, Travel and Exploration. London: 1924. V. 70
The Source of the Nile. The Lake Regions of Central Africa. London: 1993. V. 68
Two Trips to Gorilla Land and the Cataracts of the Congo. London: 1876. V. 70
Ultima Thule; or a Summer in Iceland. London and Edinburgh: 1875. V. 70
Wanderings in West Africa. London: 1863. V. 68

BURTON, ROBERT
The Anatomy of Melancholy. Oxford: 1621. V. 69
The Anatomy of Melancholy. Oxford: 1624. V. 73
The Anatomy of Melancholy. Oxford: 1660. V. 68; 72
The Anatomy of Melancholy. London: 1827. V. 69
The Anatomy of Melancholy. London: 1840. V. 69
The Anatomy of Melancholy. New York: 1885. V. 70; 71

BURTON, THOMAS
The History and Antiquities of the Parish of Hemingbrough in the County of York. York: 1888. V. 73

BURTON, TIM
The Melancholy Death of Oyster Boy and Other Stories. London: 1998. V. 70

BURTON, VIRGINIA LEE
Katy and the Big Snow. Boston: 1943. V. 69
Mike Mulligan and His Steam Shovel. Boston: 1939. V. 69

BURTON, WILLIAM
A History and Description of English Earthenware and Stoneware (to the beginning of the 19th Century). London: 1904. V. 72

BURTON, WILLIAM E.
Bibliotheca Dramatica. Catalogue of the Theatrical and Miscellaneous Library of the Late William E. Burton, the Distinguished Comedian.... New York: 1860. V. 68

BURY, ADRIAN
John Varley of the Old Society. Leigh-on-Sea: 1946. V. 72
Shadow of Eros: a Bibliographical and Critical Study of the Life and Works of Sir Alfred Gilbert. 1952. V. 71

BURY, J. B.
The Life of St. Patrick and His Place in History. 1905. V. 69

BURY, P. S.
Polycistins, Figures of Remarkable Forms &c., in the Barbados Chalk Deposit.... London: 1868. V. 70

BURY, THOMAS TALBOT
Coloured Views of the Liverpool and Manchester Railway. London: 1834. V. 69; 72
Coloured Views on the Liverpool and Manchester Railway. Oldham: 1976. V. 73
Rudimentary Architecture: for the Use of Beginners. London: 1857. V. 68

BUSBEQUIUS, A. GISLENIUS
Omnia Quae Extant. Leyden: 1633. V. 71

BUSCAGLIA, LEO F.
The Way of the Bull. 1973. V. 70; 72

BUSCH, FREDERICK
Breathing Trouble and Other Stories. London: 1973. V. 72
Domestic Particulars. New York: 1976. V. 72
I Wanted a Year Without Fall. London: 1971. V. 72
The Night Inspector. New York: 1999. V. 68

BUSCH, NIVEN
Day of the Conquerors. New York: 1946. V. 69
Duel in the Sun. NY: 1944. V. 72
The Furies. New York: 1948. V. 71
They Dream of Home. New York: 1944. V. 71

BUSCH, W. D. N.
The Development of an Aquatic Habitat Classification System for Lakes. Boca Raton: 1992. V. 71

BUSH, CHRISTOPHER
The Case of the Benevolent Bookie, A Ludvic Travers Mystery Novel. 1955. V. 72
The Case of the Fourth Detective. 1951. V. 72
The Case Of The Grand Alliance. London: 1964. V. 72
The Perfect Murder Case. London: 1929. V. 73
The Perfect Murder Case. New York: 1929. V. 68; 72; 73

BUSH, GEORGE
All the Best, George Bush. My Life in Letters and Other Writings. New York: 1999. V. 69
Looking Forward. New York: 1987. V. 71

BUSH, I. J.
Gringo Doctor. Caldwell: 1939. V. 73

BUSH, JAMES
The Choice; or Lines on the Beatitudes. London: 1841. V. 71

BUSHELL, STEPHEN W.
Catalogue of the Morgan Collection of Chinese Porcelains. NY: 1910. V. 72

BUSH-FEKETE, L.
Embezzled Heaven. New York: 1945. V. 69

BUSHNELL, CANDACE
Sex and the City. New York: 1996. V. 70

BUSHNELL, G. H. S.
Ancient American Pottery. London: 1955. V. 68

BUSINESS Directory of Sheffield, Rotherham, Masbro' and Attercliffe. 1862. 1862. V. 71

A BUSINESS Directory of the Subscribers to the New Map of Maine. Portland: 1862. V. 68

BUSINESS Life: the Experinces of a London Tradesman with Practical Advice and Directions for Avoiding Many of the Evils Connected with Our Present Commerical System and State of Society. London: 1861. V. 71

BUSINESS MEN'S CLUB OF SAN ANTONIO
Beautiful San Antonio, the Commercial and Industrial Center of the Southwest. The Great Health Resort of America. 1904. V. 70

BUSK, DOUGLAS
The Delectable Mountains. London: 1946. V. 69
The Delectable Mountains. London: 1947. V. 69

BUSK, G.
Challenger Voyage. Zoology. Parts 30, 50 and 79 Polyzoa. 1884-1889. V. 73

BUSK, HANS
The Rifle and How to Use It. 1858. V. 70; 73
The Rifle and How to Use It. 1859. V. 70; 72; 73
Rifle Volunteers. 1859. V. 70; 72; 73

BUSS, HENRY
Eighty Years Experience of Life. London: 1893. V. 71

BUSY Bears. New York: 1907. V. 69

BUTCHER, C. J. F.
Theory of Electric Polarisation. Amsterdam: 1952. V. 69

BUTCHER, CLYDE
Portfolio I. Florida Landscapes. Fort Myers: 1994. V. 68

BUTCHER, DAVID
The Stanbrook Abbey Press 1956-1990. Lower Marston;: 1992. V. 72
The Whittington Press: a Bibliography 1971-1981. Andoversford: 1982. V. 72

BUTCHER, MARGARET J.
The Negro in American Culture. New York: 1956. V. 72

BUTEN, DAVID
18th Century Wedgwood. New York: 1980. V. 72

BUTLER, ARTHUR GARDINER
British Birds with Their Nests and Eggs. London. V. 70
Foreign Finches in Captivity. London: 1894-1896. V. 72; 73
Foreign Finches in Captivity. Hull and London: 1899. V. 70
Illustrations of Typical Specimens of Lepidotera Heterocera in the Collection of the British Musuem. London: 1877-1893. V. 73
Lepidoptera Exotica or Descripiton and Illustrations of Exotic Lepidoptera. London: 1874. V. 73

BUTLER, BENJAMIN F.
Private and Official Correspondence. 1917. V. 71

BUTLER, CHARLES
The Feminine Monarchie; or the Historie of Bees. London: 1623. V. 68; 70

BUTLER, ELIZABETH
Letters From The Holy Land. London: 1912. V. 72

BUTLER, ELLIS PARKER
Philo Gubb - Correspondence School Detective. Boston: 1918. V. 69; 70; 71; 73

BUTLER, EWAN
Barry's Flying Column. 1971. V. 73

BUTLER, FRANCES ANNE KEMBLE
Journal. Philadelphia: 1835. V. 73

BUTLER, H. J.
The Black Book of Edgeworthstown and Other Edgeworth Memories 1858-1817. 1927. V. 69; 73

BUTLER, HENRY
South African Sketches. London: 1841. V. 72

BUTLER, J. R.
Floralia, Garden Paths and by Paths of Eighteenth Century. Chapel Hill: 1938. V. 71; 73

BUTLER, JOSEPH
The Analogy of Religion, Natural and Revealed, to the Constitution and Course of Nature. London: 1736. V. 68

BUTLER, NEVILLE R.
Perinatal Mortality. Edinburgh: 1963. V. 68

BUTLER, ROBERT OLEN
The Alleys of Eden. New York: 1981. V. 68; 69; 70; 71; 73
Countrymen of Bones. New York: 1983. V. 68; 69; 71; 72
A Good Scent from a Strange Mountain. New York: 1992. V. 68; 69; 71
Mr. Spaceman. New York: 2000. V. 69
On Distant Ground. New York: 1985. V. 68; 72; 73
Sun Dogs. New York: 1982. V. 68; 69; 70; 71; 72
Tabloid Dreams. New York: 1996. V. 68; 71

They Whisper. Huntington: 1994. V. 72
They Whisper. New York: 1994. V. 72
Wabash. New York: 1987. V. 68; 69

BUTLER, SAMUEL
An Atlas of Ancient Geography. London: 1829. V. 72
Butleriana. London: 1932. V. 71
Erewhon. New York: 1934. V. 68; 69
Erewhon. Newtown: 1992. V. 70
Hudibras. London: 1689. V. 70; 73
Hudibras. London: 1704. V. 72
Hudibras. London: 1716. V. 69
Hudibras. London: 1720. V. 69
Hudibras. London: 1732. V. 71
Hudibras. London: 1739. V. 73
Hudibras. London: 1764. V. 69
Hudibras. Glasgow: 1769. V. 73
Hudibras. London: 1775. V. 71
Hudibras. London: 1799. V. 70; 72; 73
Hudibras. London: 1801. V. 71
Hudibras. London: 1811. V. 71
Hudibras. London: 1819. V. 68; 70; 72
Hudibras. London: 1835. V. 71
Life and Habit. London: 1878. V. 68
Luck, or Cunning, as the Means of Organic Modification?. London: 1887. V. 68
The Note-Books of Samuel Butler. London: 1912. V. 69
Poetical Works. London: 1835. V. 72
The Posthumous Works of Samuel Butler.... London: 1754. V. 69
Unconscious Memory: a Comparison Between the Theory of Dr Ewald Hering, Professor of Physiology at the University of Prague, and the Philosophy of the Unconscious by Dr. Edward Von Hartmann.... London: 1880. V. 69

BUTLER, SAMUEL, BP. OF LICHFIELD & COVENTRY
Catalogue of the Library of the Late Rev. Samuel Butler, D.D., Lord Bishop of Lichfield. Part III: Early Printed Books and Manuscripts. London: 1841. V. 70

BUTLER, W. C.
Butler's Modern Practical Confectioner. Manchester: 1898. V. 68

BUTLER, W. F.
Akim-Foo: the History of a Failure. London: 1875. V. 72
The Great Lone Land. London: 1872. V. 73
The Great Lone Land. London: 1874. V. 73
The Wild North Land. London: 1874. V. 72
The Wild North Land: Being the Story of a Winter Journey, with Dogs Across North America. Montreal: 1874. V. 73

BUTLER, WILLIAM
The Land of the Veda. New York: 1895. V. 72
The Land of The Veda. New York: 1906. V. 72

BUTLER, WILLIAM VIVIAN
Clampdown. London: 1971. V. 72

BUTOR, M.
Ethnic Jewelry. New York: 1994. V. 69

BUTOR, MICHEL
Second Thoughts. London: 1958. V. 72

BUTSCHER, EDWARD
Conrad Aiken: Poet of White Horse Vale. Athens: 1988. V. 68

BUTT, ISAAC
The Irish People and the Irish Land. Dublin: 1876. V. 68

BUTT, KHAN S. J.
Shikar. 1963. V. 72

BUTTER, WILLIAM
An Account of Puerperal Fevers, as They Appear in Derbyshire and Some of the Counties Adjacent. London: 1775. V. 69

BUTTERFIELD, CONSUL WILSHIRE
Brule's Discoveries and Explorations 1610-1628. Cleveland: 1898. V. 71
History of the Girtys. Cincinnati: 1890. V. 73

BUTTERFIELD, GEORGE E.
Bay County: Past and Present. Bay City: 1918. V. 73

BUTTERFIELD, IRVINE
The High Mountains of Britian and Ireland. London: 1986. V. 69

BUTTERFIELD, LINDSAY P.
Flora Forms in Historic Design. London. V. 72

BUTTERWORTH, BENJAMIN
The Growth of Industrial Art. Washington: 1892. V. 71

BUTTERWORTH, HEZEKIAH
Zig Zag Journeys in Acadia and New France: A Summer Journey.... Boston: 1884. V. 71
Zig Zag Journeys in Acadia and New France: A Summer Journey.... Boston: 1886. V. 71
Zigzag Journeys in Australia: or, a Visit to the Ocean World. Boston: 1891. V. 72

BUTTERWORTH, JOHN
A New Concordance and Dictionary to the Holy Scriptures. New York: 1811. V. 70

BUTTRE, J. C.
Catalogue of Engravings by J. C. Buttre, Publisher, Engraver and Plate Printer. New York: 1870. V. 73

BUTTRICK, DANIEL SABIN
Antiquities of the Cherokee Indians. Vinita: 1884. V. 71

BUTTS, MARY
Ashe of Rings. London: 1933. V. 71
Scenes from the Life of Cleopatra. London: 1935. V. 72

BUXBAUM, ANDREAS
Disputatio Inauguralis medica de Ventriculi Inflatione Quam deo Duce and Authoritate.... Erfurti: 1686. V. 72

BUXTON, BERTHA HENRY
Great Grenfell Gardens: a Novel. London: 1883. V. 68

BUXTON, E. N.
Short Stalks. 1892. V. 70; 73
Short Stalks. 1893. V. 70; 72; 73

BUXTON, JOHN
Atropos and Other Poems. London: 1946. V. 73
Judas: a Play in Four Acts. Oxford: 1938. V. 73

BUXTON, R.
A Botanical Guide to the Flowering Plants, Ferns, Mosses and Algae Found Indigenous Within Sixteen Miles of Manchester.... London and Manchester: 1849. V. 69; 73

BUXTON, THOMAS FOLWELL
Memoirs.... London: 1860. V. 71

BUXTON FORMAN, MAURICE
A Bibliography of the Writings in Prose and Verse of George Meredith, togheter with Meredithiana Being a Supplement.... Edinburgh: 1922-1924. V. 72
John Keats and His Family. A Series of Portraits. Edinburgh: 1933. V. 72

BUXTORF, JOHANN
Lexicon Chaldaicum, Talmudicum et Rabbinicum. Basle: 1640. V. 72
Synagoga Judaica Noviter Restaurata; Das Ist.... Frankfurt: 1728. V. 72

BUZZATI, DINO
Restless Nights. Berkeley: 1983. V. 72

BY the Light of the Nursery Lamp. 1885. V. 71

BYATT, A. S.
Angels and Insects. London: 1992. V. 68; 70; 71; 73
Angels and Insects. Franklin Center: 1993. V. 70
Babel Tower. Franklin Center: 1996. V. 70
Babel Tower. London: 1996. V. 70
The Biographer's Tale. London: 2000. V. 70; 72
The Djinn in the Nightingale's Eye. London: 1994. V. 68
Elementals. London: 1991. V. 73
Heavenly Bodies. Atlanta: 1999. V. 70
Possession. New York: 1990. V. 70
Still Life. London: 1985. V. 73
The Virgin in the Garden. 1978. V. 73
Wordsworth and Coleridge in Their Time. London: 1970. V. 72

BYE-Bye Rhymes. London. V. 68

BYERS, S. H. M.
The Knights of the Frozen Sea, a Narrative of Arctic Discovery and Adventure. New York: 1867. V. 70
With Fire and Sword. New York: 1911. V. 70

BYFIELD, NATHANAEL
An Account of the Late Revolution in New England. Together with the Declaration of the Gentlemen, Merchants and Inhabitants of Boston and the Country Adjacent. London: 1689. V. 68

BYI, CHARLOT
Christmas on Stage. 1950. V. 69

BYLES, C. E.
The Life and Letters of Robert Stephen Hawker. London: 1905. V. 72
Life and Letters of Robert Stephen Hawker. London: 1906. V. 68

BYLES, JOHN BARNARD
Observations on the Usury Laws, and on the Effect of the Recent Alterations.... London: 1845. V. 70
Sophisms of Free-Trade and Popular Political Economy Examined. London: 1850. V. 71

BYNE, ARTHUR
Decorated Wooden Ceilings in Spain: a Collection of Photographs and Measured Drawings with Descriptive Text. New York and London: 1920. V. 71
Spanish Architecture of the Sixteenth Century: General View of the Plateresque and Herrera Styles. New York: 1917. V. 69; 72
Spanish Irownwork. 1915. V. 72

BYNG, DOUGLAS
More Byng Ballads. London: 1935. V. 69

BYNG, JOHN
An Exact Copy of a Remarkable Letter from Admiral Byng to the Right Hon. W. P. Esq, dated March 12, 1757, two days before his execution. London: 1757. V. 73
The Trial of the Honourable Admiral John Byng, at a Court Martial, as Taken by Mr. Charles Fearne, Judge-Advocate of His Majesty's Fleet.... London: 1757. V. 70

BYNNER, WITTER
Against the Cold. New York: 1940. V. 68
Photographs of D. H. Lawrence. Santa Fe: 1981. V. 72
Tiger. New York: 1913. V. 88

BYRD, RICHARD EVELYN
Little America. New York: 1930. V. 68
Little America. London: 1931. V. 72

BYRD, WILLIAM
Description of the Dismal Swamp and a Proposal to Drain the Swamp. Metuchen: 1922. V. 71
The Westover Manuscripts.... Petersburg: 1841. V. 68

BYRGE, DUANE
The Screwball Comedy Films. A History and Filmography 1934-1942. Jefferson: 1991. V. 68

BYRNE, ALEXANDER S.
Observations on the Uses and Advantages of Compressed Peat. New York: 1841. V. 68

BYRNE, DAVID
The New Sins. New York: 2001. V. 71
Strange Ritual. San Francisco: 1995. V. 72

BYRNE, JULIA CLARA BUSK
Realities of Paris Life. London: 1859. V. 68; 72

BYRNE, P. E.
Soldiers Of The Plains. New York: 1926. V. 72

BYROM, JOHN
Careless Content. Chichester: 1932. V. 71
Miscellaneous Poems. Leeds: 1814. V. 70

BYRON, GEORGE GORDON NOEL, 6TH BARON
Beauties of English Poets. Venice: 1852. V. 73
Beppo, a Venetian Story. London: 1818. V. 73
The Bride of Abydos. London: 1813. V. 72
Catalogue of the Library of the Late Lord Byron, to Which is Added the Library of a Gentleman, Deceased. London: 1827. V. 69
Childe Harold's Pilgrimage. London: 1812. V. 73
Childe' Harold's Pilgrimage. Paris and London: 1931. V. 69; 73
Childe Harold's Pilgrimage. Paris/New York: 1931. V. 72
Childe Harold's Pilgrimage. Canto the Fourth. London: 1818. V. 73
Childe Harold's Pilgrimage. Canto the third. London: 1816. V. 73
The Corsair, a Tale. London: 1814. V. 73
Don Juan. 1820-1823. V. 73
Don Juan (Cantos I and II). London: 1819-1824. V. 73
Don Juan. (Cantos I-V). London. V. 68
Don Leon: a Poem by the Late Lord Byron.... 1866. V. 73
English Bards and Scotch Reviewers. 1809. V. 73
English Bards and Scotch Reviewers. London: 1809. V. 68
English Bards and Scotch Reviewers. 1810. V. 73
English Bards and Scotch Reviewers. London: 1810. V. 68
English Bards and Scotch Reviewers. London: 1811. V. 68
The Genuine Rejected Addresses, Presented to the Committee of Management for Drury Lane Theatre.... 1812. V. 73
The Giaour, a Fragment of a Turkish Tale. London: 1813. V. 73
Hebrew Melodies. London: 1815. V. 73
Hours of Idleness. Newark: 1807. V. 73
Hours of Idleness. London: 1820. V. 68
The Lament of Tasso. London: 1817. V. 73
Lara, A Tale. London: 1814. V. 73
Lara, a Tale. Jacqueline, a Tale. London: 1814. V. 73
Letters and Journals. London: 1830. V. 71; 72
Letters and Journals. 1973-1980. V. 73
Manfred. London: 1817. V. 70; 73
Manfred. London: 1929. V. 71
Marino Faliero, Doge of Venice. London: 1821. V. 70; 71; 72; 73
Mazeppa, A Poem. London: 1819. V. 71; 73
Ode to Napoleon Buonaparte. London: 1814. V. 73
Poems. Newark: 1808. V. 71
Poems. London: 1814. V. 70
Poems. London: 1816. V. 73
Poems on Various Occasions. Newark: 1807. V. 73
Poems Original and Translated. Newark: 1808. V. 73
The Prisoner of Chillon. London: 1816. V. 70
The Prisoner of Chillon. London: 1836. V. 73
The Prisoner of Chillon. London: 1865. V. 68; 73
Sardanapalus, a Tragedy. The Foscari, a Tragedy. London: 1821. V. 71; 73
Selections From Poetry, Letters & Journals. London: 1949. V. 72
The Siege of Corinth. A Poem. London: 1816. V. 73
Waltz: an Apostrophic Hymn. 1813. V. 73
Werner, a Tragedy. London: 1823. V. 68; 72; 73
Works. London: 1816. V. 68
The Works. Philadelphia: 1825. V. 70
The Works. London: 1833. V. 70; 71; 72
The Works. Leipzig: 1842. V. 73
The Works. London: 1898-1901. V. 73

BYRON, HENRY J.
Paid in Full. London: 1881. V. 68

BYRON, MAY
A Day with Omar Khayyam. London: 1914. V. 69
Friday and Saturday. The Adventures of Two Little Pickles. London. V. 73
Jack and Jill. London: 1914. V. 71
The Little Wee Bear and Goldenhair. London: 1910. V. 70; 73
The Little Yellow Duckling. New York: 1922. V. 70

BYRON, ROBERT
The Birth of Western Painting - a History of Colour, Form and Iconography.... London: 1930. V. 71
An Essay on India. London: 1931. V. 70
First Russia Then Tibet. London: 1933. V. 72
The Road to Oxiana. London: 1937. V. 69
The Station. Athos: Treasures and Men. London: 1928. V. 69; 72
The Station. Athos: Treasures and Men. New York: 1928. V. 70

BYSSHE, EDWARD
The Art of English Poetry. London: 1710. V. 73
The Art of English Poetry. London: 1718. V. 71

BYTHNER, VICTORINUS
Lyra Prophetica Davidii Regis. London: 1650. V. 72

BZOVIUS, ABRAHAM
Romanus Pontifex. Coloniae Agrippinae: 1619. V. 73

C

C., I. E. B.
The Country House: a Collection of Useful Information & Recipes.... London: 1883. V. 68

CABALA: sive Scrinia Sacra. Mysteries of State and Government in Letters of Illustrious Persons...in the Reigns of King Henry the Eighth; Q. Elizabeth; K. James and K. Charles. London: 1663. V. 72

CABALA, sive Scrinia Sacra; Mysteries of State and Government, in Letters of Illustrious Persons and Great Ministers of State.... London: 1691. V. 69

CABANNE, P.
The Brothers Duchamp: Jacques Villon, Raymond Duchamp-Villon, Marcel Duchamp. Boston: 1976. V. 69; 72

CABELL, J. L.
An Account of the Hot Springs, Bath County, Virginia.... Richmond: 1875. V. 71

CABELL, JAMES BRANCH
The Certain Hour. London: 1931. V. 70
Domnei. A Comedy of Woman-Worship. New York: 1920. V. 68
The Eagle's Shadow. New York: 1923. V. 68
Gallantry. New York: 1922. V. 72
Jurgen. New York: 1919. V. 72
Jurgen. Waltham St. Lawrence: 1949. V. 71; 72
The Line of Love. New York: 1905. V. 71
The Majors and Their Marriages. Richmond: 1915. V. 70
The Nightmare has Triplets: an Author's Note on Smire. 1937. V. 69
Something About Eve. New York: 1927. V. 68; 69
Something About Eve. New York: 1929. V. 69
These Restless Heads. New York: 1932. V. 68
The Way of Ecben. New York: 1929. V. 69

CABELL, JULIA MAYO
An Odd Volume of Facts and Fictions. Richmond: 1852. V. 69

CABELL, MARGARET C.
Sketches and Recollections of Lynchburg. Richmond: 1858. V. 68; 70

THE CABINET-Makers Assistant, a Series of Original Designs for Modern Furniture, With Descriptions and Details of Construction. Glasgow: 1853. V. 69

CABINET Maker's Album of Furniture.... Philadelphia: 1868. V. 68; 71

CABLE, BOYD
A Hundred Year History of the P & O 1837-1937. London: 1937. V. 69

CABLE, GEORGE WASHINGTON
Bonaventure. New York: 1899. V. 69
The Cavalier. New York: 1901. V. 69
Dr. Sevier. New York: 1899. V. 69
The Grandissimes. New York: 1880. V. 71
The Grandissimes. New York: 1898. V. 69
The Grandissimes. New York: 1899. V. 69
John March, Southerner. New York: 1900. V. 69
Old Creole Days. New York: 1879. V. 69; 71; 73
Old Creole Days. New York: 1891. V. 69
The Southern Struggle for Pure Government. Boston: 1890. V. 68
Strong Hearts. New York: 1899. V. 69

CACUT, L.
Fisherman's Handbook. 1977-1979. V. 68; 73

CADBURY, EDWARD
Sweating. London: 1907. V. 71

CADBURY, GEORGE
Town Planning with Special Reference to the Birmingham Schemes. London: 1915. V. 71

CADBURY, R.
Cocoa: All About It. London: 1896. V. 70

CADDY, FLORENCE
Through the Fields with Linnaeus; a Chapter in Swedish History. London: 1887. V. 69

CADELL, ELIZABETH
Money to Burn. New York: 1955. V. 69

CADMAN, A.
Tales of a Wildflower. 1957. V. 71

CADMAN, SAMUEL PARKES
The Parables of Jesus. Philadelphia: 1931. V. 71

CADOGAN, MARY
Chin Up Chest Out Jemima! A Celebration of the School Girls' Story. London: 1989. V. 70
Frank Richards the Chap Behind the Chums. 1988. V. 70
Frank Richards the Chap behind the Chums. New York: 1988. V. 72; 73
The Lady Investigates Women Detectives and Spies in Fiction. 1981. V. 72
The William Companion. 1990. V. 72

CADOGAN, WILLIAM
A Dissertation on the Gout, and All Chronic Diseases, Jointly Considered, as Proceeding from the Same Causes. London: 1771. V. 72
A Dissertaton on the Gout, an All Chronic Diseases, Jointly Considered.... New York: 1772. V. 71

CADWELL, SARAH
The Shortest Way to Hades. London: 1984. V. 71

CADY, HARRISON
A Harrison Cady Picture Book. Racine: 1928. V. 69; 73

CADY, JOHN H.
Arizona's Yesterday, Being The Narrative Of John H. Cady, Pioneer. Patagonia: 1916. V. 72

CADZOW, D. A.
Archaeological Studies of the Susquehanock Indians of Pennsylvania. 1936. V. 69

CAEMMERER, H. PAUL
The Life of Pierre Charles L'Enfant, Planner of the City Beautiful: the City of Washington. Washington: 1950. V. 68

CAESAR, GAIUS JULIUS
De Bellis Gallico et Civili Pompeiano. Leyden: 1737. V. 70
(Omnia Opera) Quae Exstant.... Edinbrugii: 1806. V. 72
(Opera). Cambridge: 1706. V. 72
(Opera). Glasgow: 1750. V. 72; 73

CAFFEY, THOMAS E.
Battle-Fields of the South, from Bull Run to Fredericksburg.... London: 1863. V. 70

CAFKY, MORRIS
Colorado Midland. Denver: 1965. V. 69

CAGE, JOHN
Silence. Connecticut: 1961. V. 70

CAGNEY, PETER
No Diamonds for a Doll. London: 1960. V. 70

CAHALAN, JAMES M.
Edward Abbey. Tucson: 2001. V. 71; 73

CAHILL, HOLGER
Max Weber. New York: 1930. V. 68

CAHN, PHYLLIS
Lateral Line Detectors. Bloomington: 1967. V. 68

CAHOONE, SARAH S.
Visit to Grand-papa; or, a Week at Newport. New York: 1840. V. 68

CAIDIN, MARTIN
Cyborg. New York: 1972. V. 69

CAIL, ROBERT E.
Land, Man and the Law. The Disposal of Crown Lands in British Columbia 1871-1913. Vancouver: 1974. V. 68

CAILLARD, EMMA MARIE
Charlotte Corday and other Poems. London: 1884. V. 69

CAILLARD, VINCENT H. P.
Imperial Fiscal Reform. London: 1903. V. 71

CAILLE, JEAN DE
Histoire de l'Imprimerie et de la Libraire, Ou l'on voit son Origine & Son Progres, Jusqu'en 1689. Paris: 1689. V. 72

CAILLER, P.
Catalogue Raisonne De L'Oeuvre Lithographie et Grave.... Geneve: 1969. V. 72

CAIN, GEORGES
Nooks and Corners of Old Paris. London: 1907. V. 73

CAIN, JAMES M.
The Butterfly. New York: 1947. V. 73
Cain X 3. New York: 1969. V. 73
Cloud Nine. New York: 1984. V. 72
Jealous Woman. London: 1955. V. 68; 70; 72; 73
Love's Lovely Counterfeit. New York: 1942. V. 72; 73
The Magician's Wife. New York: 1965. V. 69; 73
Mignon. London: 1963. V. 69; 73
Mildred Pierce. New York: 1941. V. 69
The Moth. New York: 1948. V. 69; 73
Our Government. New York: 1930. V. 69
The Postman Always Rings Twice. London: 1934. V. 68; 69; 70; 72; 73
The Postman Always Rings Twice. New York: 1934. V. 73
Rainbow's End. New York: 1975. V. 68; 73
Serenade. Boston: 1937. V. 73
Sinful Woman. New York: 1947. V. 73
Sinful Woman. Cleveland & New York: 1948. V. 69; 70; 73
Three of a Kind. New York: 1943. V. 71
Three of a Kind. New York: 1944. V. 73
Three of a Kind. London: 1945. V. 69; 70

CAIN, JULIEN
Humanisme Actif: Melanges D'Art et de Litterature. Paris: 1968. V. 72
The Lithographs of Chagall 1962-1968. Boston: 1969. V. 73
The Lithographs of Chagall. Volume I. New York: 1960. V. 73

CAIN, PAUL
Fast One. New York: 1933. V. 70; 73
Fast One. Carbondale: 1978. V. 70

CAIN, S. A.
Foundations of Plant Geoegraphy. New York: 1944. V. 72

CAINE, CAESAR
Cleator and Clator Moor: Past and Present. Kendal: 1916. V. 71
The Martial Annals of the City of York. London: 1893. V. 73

CAINE, HALL
The Deemster. London: 1889. V. 68
The Deemster. London: 1893. V. 68
The Deemster. London: 1896. V. 68
Recollections of Dante Gabriel Rossetti. London: 1882. V. 68
The Shadow of a Crime. London: 1898. V. 68
The Woman of Knockaloe: A Parable. New York: 1923. V. 70

CAINE, N.
History of the Royal Rock Beagle Hunt. Liverpool: 1895. V. 68; 70

CAINE, W. RALPH HALL
The Cruise of The Port Kingston. London: 1908. V. 72
Lancashire. Biographies, Rolls of Honour. London: 1917. V. 72; 73

CAIRD, MONA
Romantic Cities of Provence. London: 1906. V. 72

CAIRNES, JOHN ELLIOT
Essays in Politcal Economy. Theoretical and Applied. London: 1873. V. 71; 72
Political Essays. London: 1873. V. 72
The Slave Power: Its Character, Career and Probable Designs. New York: 1862. V. 68

CAIRNS, MARY L.
The Olden Days. Denver: 1954. V. 69

CALAMY, EDWARD
Satan Deluding by Feigned Miracles. Discovered by the Notorious Falsehood and Dissimulation of Nicholas Ware and Matthew Hall.... London: 1655. V. 71

CALCOTT, GEORGE SYMES
A Descriptive Account of a Descent Made Into Penpark-Hole, in the Parish of Westbury.... Bristol: 1792. V. 68

CALCOTT, WELLINS
A Candid Disquisition of the Principles and Practices of the... Masons; Together with Some Strictures on the Origin, Nature and Design of that Institution. Boston: 1772. V. 71

CALDECOTT, RANDOLPH
The Babes in the Wood. London: 1880. V. 72; 73
Gleanings From The Graphic. London: 1889. V. 72
Last Graphic Pictures. London: 1888. V. 72
More Graphic Pictures. London: 1887. V. 72
Picture Book (No. 1) Containing the Diverting History of John Gilpin, The House that Jack Built, an Elegy on the Death of a Mad Dog, The Babes in the Wood. London: 1906. V. 72; 73
R. Caldecott's First Collection of Pictures and Songs. London: 1919. V. 68
R. Caldecott's Second Collection of Pictures and Songs. London: V. 72
Randolph Caldecott's Graphic Pictures. London: 1889. V. 72
A Sketch-Book. London: 1883. V. 68

CALDER, ALEXANDER
Three Young Rats and Other Rhymes. New York: 1944. V. 68

CALDER, F. W. GRANT
Practical Hints on the Cure of Squinting by Operation. London: 1841. V. 72

CALDER-MARSHALL, ARTHUR
At Sea - a Novel. London: 1934. V. 68
A Crime Against Cania. London: 1934. V. 71

CALDER MARSHALL, ARTHUR
A Crime Against Cania. Waltham St. Lawrence: 1934. V. 68; 69; 70; 71

CALDERON, V. G.
The Lottery Ticket. Waltham St. Lawrence: 1945. V. 71
The White Llama. Waltham St. Lawrence: 1938. V. 71

CALDERON, W. F.
The Painting and Anatomy of Animals. London: 1936. V. 69; 72

CALDERON DE LA BACA, MME.
Life in Mexico During a Residence of Two Years in that Country. London: 1852. V. 71

CALDERONE, JOHN A.
Wheels of the Bravest, A History of FDNY Fire Apparatus 1865-1982. Howard Beach: 1984. V. 69

CALDERWOOD, W. L.
The Life of the Salmon. 1907. V. 68
Salmon. Experiences and Reflections. 1938. V. 68
The Salmon Rivers and Lochs of Scotland. 1909. V. 73
The Salmon Rivers and Lochs of Scotland. 1921. V. 73

CALDWELL, CHARLES
An Elegiac Poem on the Death of General Washington. Philadelphia: 1800. V. 70
Medical and Physical Memoirs, Containing Among other Subjects, a Particular Enquiry into the Origin and Nature of the Late Pestilential Epidemics of the United States. Philadelphia: 1801. V. 68

CALDWELL, ERSKINE PRESTON
Afternoons in Mid-America. New York: 1976. V. 73
American Earth. New York: 1931. V. 73
Around About America. New York: 1964. V. 70; 73
The Courting of Susie Brown. New York: 1952. V. 73
Episode in Palmetto. New York: 1950. V. 73
Georgia Boy. New York: 1943. V. 73
Gulf Coast Stories. Boston: 1956. V. 73
Jenny by Nature. New York: 1961. V. 70
Journeyman. New York: 1935. V. 73
Journeyman. New York: 1938. V. 68
Journeyman. London: 1955. V. 70
Kneel to the Rising Sun and Other Stories. New York: 1935. V. 68; 69; 71; 73
Molly Cottontail. Boston: 1958. V. 73
North of the Danube. New York: 1939. V. 73
Place Called Estherville. New York: 1949. V. 73
The Sacrilege of Alan Kent. Portland: 1936. V. 73
Say, Is This the U.S.A. New York: 1941. V. 69; 70; 73
Some American People. New York: 1935. V. 73
Southways. New York: 1938. V. 73
Tobacco Road. New York: 1932. V. 70; 71
Tobacco Road. Savannah: 1974. V. 71
Tragic Ground. New York: 1944. V. 73
We Are the Living. New York: 1933. V. 68; 73
With All My Might. Atlanta: 1987. V. 73
You Have Seen Their Faces. New York: 1937. V. 68

CALDWELL, JOHN EDWARDS
A Tour through Part of Virginia, in the Summer of 1808. New York: 1809. V. 70; 71

CALHOUN, JAMES C.
The Works. New York: 1888. V. 71

CALHOUN, JAMES S.
The Official Correspondence of James S. Calhoun - While Indian Agent at Santa Fe and Superintendent of Indian Affairs in New Mexico. Washington: 1915. V. 69

CALHOUN, JOHN C.
Exposition and Protest, Reported by Special Committee of the House of Representatives, on the Tariff; Read and Ordered to be Printed Dec. 19th 1828. Columbia: 1829. V. 68

CALHOUN, WILLIAM LOWNDES
History of the 42nd Regiment, Georgia Volunteers. Atlanta: 1900. V. 69; 70

CALICO, CATHERINE, PSEUD.
Fairy Tales, for Youth. London: 1826. V. 68

CALIFORNIA. UNIVERSITY OF
Spain and Spanish America in the Libraries of the University of California. New York: 1969. V. 72

THE CALIFORNIA Brand Book 1919. San Francisco: 1919. V. 70

CALIFORNIA Mines and Minerals. San Francisco: 1899. V. 70

THE CALIFORNIA Star. Yerba Buena and San Francisco. Berkeley: 1965. V. 68

CALKINS, DICK
The Pop-Up Buck Rogers in the Dangerous Mission. New York: 1934. V. 73

CALKINS, EARNEST ELMO
Franklin Booth. New York: 1925. V. 69

CALL, JAN VAN
Admirandorum Quadruplex Spectaculum, Delectum, Pictum et Aeri Incisum. Amsterdam: 1700. V. 68

CALL, WILLIAM TIMOTHY
Blackmail. Brooklyn: 1915. V. 69; 73

CALLAGHAN, MORLEY
No Man's Meat. Paris: 1931. V. 72

CALLAHAN, HARRY
Harry Callahan: Color 1941-1980. Providence: 1980. V. 68
Photographs. Harry Callahan. Santa Barbara: 1964. V. 73

CALLAHAN, JAMES M.
Diplomatic History of the Southern Confederacy. Baltimore: 1901. V. 69
History of West Virginia, Old and New. Chicago and New York: 1923. V. 71

CALLAWAY, REV. CANON
Nursery Tales, Traditions and Histories of the Zulus. Natal: 1868. V. 68

CALLCOTT, WILFRID HARDY
Santa Anna. Norman: 1936. V. 70

CALLENDER, JAMES
A History of the United States for 1796.... Philadelphia: 1797. V. 73
Sketches of the History of America. Philadelphia: 1798. V. 68

CALLERY, BERNADETTE G.
The Tradition of Fine Bookbinding in the Twentieth Century. Catalogue of an Exhibition 12 Nov. 1979 to 15 Feb. 1980. Pittsburgh: 1979. V. 70

CALLIACHI, NICOLAI
De Ludis Scenicis Mimorum & Pantomimrum. Padua: 1713. V. 70

CALLIERES, JACQUES DE
Le Courtisan Predestine ou le Duc de Joyeuse Capucin, Divise en Deux Parties. Paris: 1668. V. 73

CALLINGHAM, JAMES
The Painters' and Grainers' Handbook. London: 1885. V. 71
Sign Writing and Glass Embossing; a Complete Illustrated Manual of the Art. London: 1880. V. 69

CALLISHER, HORTENSE
Herself. New York: 1972. V. 72
On Keeping Women. New York: 1977. V. 72
Queenie. New York: 1971. V. 72

CALLISON, BRIAN
Dawn Attack. London: 1972. V. 72
The Flock of Ships. London: 1970. V. 72
A Plaque of Sailors. London: 1971. V. 72
A Thunder of Crude. London: 1986. V. 72
The Trojan Hearse. London: 1990. V. 72
A Web of Salvage. London: 1973. V. 72

CALLISON, JOHN J.
Bill Jones of Paradise Valley Oklahoma. Chicago: 1914. V. 68

CALLOW, WILLIAM
William Callow. R. W. S., F. R. G. S. An Autobiography. London: 1908. V. 68; 72

CALLOWAY, CAB
Of Minnie the Moocher and Me. New York: 1976. V. 70; 72

CALMAN, A. L.
Life And Labours Of John Ashworth. 1876. V. 70; 72; 73

CALMANN, G.
Ehret, Flower Painter Extraordinary. Boston: 1977. V. 73

CALMETTE, A.
Venoms, Venomous Animals and Anti-Venomous Serum Therapeutics. 1908. V. 73
Venoms, Venomous Animals and Antivenomous Serum - Therapeutics. London: 1908. V. 68

CALT, STEPHEN
King of the Delta Blues. The Life and Music of Charlie Patton. Newton: 1988. V. 68

CALTHORPE, SOMERSET JOHN GOUGH
Letters from Head-Quarters; or, the Realities of the War in Crimea. London: 1856. V. 68

CALTHROP, D. C.
The Charm of Gardens. London: 1910. V. 71
The Harlequinade: An Excursion. London: 1918. V. 70

CALTHROP, HENRY
The Liberties, Usages and Customs of the City of London, Confirmed by Especial Acts of Parliament.... London: 1674. V. 73
Reports of Special Cases Touching Severall Customs and Liberties of the City of London. London: 1655. V. 70

CALVERLEY, CHARLES STUART
The Complete Works of C. S. Calverley. London: 1905. V. 68; 70
Fly Leaves. Bristol and London: 1872. V. 73
Verses and Translations. Bristol and London;: 1862. V. 73

CALVERLEY, WILLIAM SLATER
Notes on the Early Sculptured Crosses, Shrines and Monuments in the Present Diocese of Carlisle. Kendal: 1899. V. 71

CALVERT, A. F.
Southern Spain. London: 1908. V. 72

CALVERT, FREDERICK
Picturesque Views by Calvert. 1823. V. 70
Picturesque Views by Calvert. London: 1823. V. 71

CALVERT, ROBERT
Notes on the Geology & Natural History of the County of Durham. Bishop Auckland: 1884. V. 73

CALVERT, W. R.
Wild Life on Moor and Fell. London: 1937. V. 71

CALVERT, WALTER
Sir Henry Irving and Miss Ellen Terry. London and New York: 1897. V. 71
Souvenir of Miss Ellen Terry. London: 1897. V. 71

CALVERTON, V. F.
The Man Inside. New York: 1936. V. 69

CALVESI, MAURIZIO
Treasures of the Vatican, St. Peter's Basilica. The Vatican Museums and Galleries. The Treasure of St. Peter's. The Vatican Grottoes and Necropolis. The Vatican Palaces. 1962. V. 73

CALVIN, H. C.
The Merchant Shipping Industry. New York: 1925. V. 71

CALVIN, JOHN
An Abridgement of the Institution of the Christian Relgion.... Edinburgh: 1587. V. 70
The Institutes of Christian Religion. Edinburgh: 1845. V. 72

CALVIN, ROSS
River of the Sun. Albuquerque: 1946. V. 71
River of the Sun, Stories of the Storied Gila. Albuquerque: 1946. V. 71

CALVINO, ITALO
The Baron in the Trees. London: 1959. V. 69
The Baron in the Trees. New York: 1959. V. 73
The Castle of Crossed Destinies. London: 1977. V. 68; 71
The Castle of Crossed Destinies. New York: 1977. V. 73
Cosmicomics. London: 1969. V. 68; 69; 72
Difficult Loves. London: 1983. V. 68
If On a Winter's Night A Traveller. London: 1981. V. 68; 71
Italian Folk Tales. London: 1975. V. 68; 71
Italian Folk Tales. New York: 1980. V. 68; 71
The Literature Machine. London: 1987. V. 68
Marcovaldo. London: 1983. V. 68
Mr. Palomar. London: 1985. V. 68
Mr. Palomar. San Diego: 1985. V. 69; 72
Numbers in the Dark. New York: 1995. V. 69; 72
The Path to the Nest of Spiders. London: 1998. V. 68
The Silent Mr. Palomar. New York: 1981. V. 72
Six Memos for the Next Millennium. Cambridge: 1988. V. 68; 69; 72; 73
Sotto Il Sole Giaguaro. Milan: 1986. V. 68
The Watcher and Other Stories. New York: 1971. V. 69
Why Read the Classics?. London: 1999. V. 68

CAMAC, CHARLES NICOLL BANCKER
Epoch-Making Contributions to Medicine, Surgery, and the Allied Sciences. Philadelphia: 1909. V. 68

CAMBELL, SYLVIA
The Practical Cook Book.... Cincinnati: 1855. V. 71

CAMBERWICK Green Pop-Up and Playbook. 1968. V. 73

CAMBRENSIS, GIRALDI
Opera. 1861-1891. V. 73

THE CAMBRIAN Directory; or, Cursory Sketches of the Welsh Territories. Salisbury: 1800. V. 73

THE CAMBRIDGE Bibliography of English Literature. 1940-1957. V. 70
THE CAMBRIDGE Bibliography of English Literature. Cambridge: 1940-1957. V. 71

CAMBRIDGE CAMDEN SOCIETY
Churches of Cambridgeshire and the Isle of Ely. Cambridge: 1845. V. 73

THE CAMBRIDGE Guide, Including Historical and Architectural Notices of the Public Buildings, and a Concise Account of the Customs and Ceremonies.... Cambridge: 1837. V. 73

THE CAMBRIDGE History of English Literature. Cambridge: 1908. V. 71

CAMBRIDGE Poetry, 1929. London: 1929. V. 69

CAMBRIDGE, RICHARD OWEN
A Dialogue Between a Member of Parliament and His Servant. London: 1752. V. 69
The Scribleriad; an Heroic Poems. London: 1751. V. 70

CAMBRY, JACQUES DE
Promenades d'Automne en Angleterre. Paris: 1791. V. 70

CAMDEN, WILLIAM
Annales Rervm Anglicarvm, et Hibernicarvm, Regnante Elizabetha. Londini: 1615. V. 73
Britannia; or, a Chorographical Description of the Flourishing Kingdoms of England, Scotland and Ireland.... London: 1789. V. 68
Britannia, Sive Florentiss. Amsterdam: 1639. V. 72
Britannia sive Florentissimorum Regnorum, Angliae Scotiae, Hiberniae.... 1590. V. 72
Britannia; Sive Florentissimorvm Regnorvm, Angliae, Scotiae, Hiberniae, et Insvlarvm Adiacentivm. Francofvurdi: 1590. V. 70
The Historie of the Most Renowned and Victorious Princesse Elizabeth, Late Queene of England.... London: 1630. V. 73
Remaines Concerning Britaine: Their Languages, Names, Surnames, Allusions, Anagrammes, Armories, Monies, Empreses, Apparell, Artillarie, Wise Speeches, Proverbs, and Epitaphes. London: 1637. V. 73

CAMERARIUS, JOACHIM
Symboloru(m) et Emblematum Centuria. Francofurt: 1654. V. 72; 73

CAMERARIUS, PHILLIPUS
The Living Librarie, or Meditations and Observations Historical, Natural, Moral, Political and Poetical, Written in Latin by P. Camerarius and Done into English by John Molle Esquire. London: 1625. V. 70

CAMERON, A. G.
The Wild Red Deer of Scotland. 1923. V. 70; 72; 73

CAMERON, AGNES D.
The New North. London: 1910. V. 72

CAMERON, ALLAN GORDON
The Wild Red Deer of Scotland. London: 1923. V. 71

CAMERON, CAROLINE
Jack's Secret. London: 1893. V. 68
Pure Gold. London: 1885. V. 68

CAMERON, DON
White for a Shroud. New York: 1947. V. 72

CAMERON, IAN
Mountains of the Gods. London: 1984. V. 69

CAMERON, JAMES M.
Industrial History of New Glasgow District. New Glasgow: 1960. V. 72
The Pictonian Colliers. Halifax and Kentville: 1974. V. 72

CAMERON, JOHN
Researches in Craniometry. Halifax: 1928-1931. V. 71

CAMERON, KENNETH NEILL
The Carl H. Pforzhiemer Library: Shelley and His Circle 1773-1822. Cambridge: 1961. V. 72

CAMERON, L. L. B., MRS.
The Nursery and Infants' School Magazine. London: 1830. V. 72

CAMERON, P.
A Monograph of the British Phytophagous Hymenoptera. 1882-1893. V. 73

CAMERON, RODERICK
Pioneer Days in Kansas: a Homesteader's Narrative of Early Settlement and Farm Development on the High Plains Country of Northwest Kansas. Belleville: 1951. V. 69

CAMERON, VERNEY LOVETT
Across Africa. London: 1877. V. 72
Across Africa. 1885. V. 72; 73

CAMESASCA, E.
History of the House. New York: 1971. V. 69; 72

CAMILL, CAMILLO
Imprese Illustri di Diversi, coi Discorsi. Venice: 1586. V. 68; 70; 73

CAMIS, MARIO
The Physiology of the Vestibular Apparatus. Oxford: 1930. V. 68

CAMM, DOM BEDE
Forgotten Shrines, an Account of Some Old Catholic Halls and Familes in England and of Relics and Memorials of the English Martyrs. 1936. V. 73
Forgotten Shrines. An Account of Some Old Catholic Halls and Families In England And Of Relics And Memorials Of The English Martyrs. 1910. V. 72

CAMMACK, JOHN HENRY
Personal Recollections of Private John Henry Cammack, a Soldier of the Confederacy 1861-1865. Huntington: 1920. V. 69

CAMOENS, LUIS DE
The Lusiad; or the Discovery of India, an Epic Poem. Oxford: 1776. V. 69

CAMP, C. L.
Bibliography of Fossil Vertebrates 1949-1953. New York: 1961. V. 72
Bibliography of Fossil Vertebrates 1954-1958. New York: 1964. V. 72

CAMP, CHARLES
George C. Yount and His Chronicles of the West. Denver: 1966. V. 68; 73
James Clyman. Portland: 1960. V. 73
James Clyman. Portland: 1966. V. 70

CAMP, JOHN
The Empress File. New York: 1991. V. 69

CAMP, WALTER
Custer in '76, Walter Camp's Notes on The Custer Fight. Provo: 1976. V. 72

CAMPAN, JEANNE LOUISE HENRIETTE
The Private Journal.... London: 1825. V. 68

CAMPANELLA, TOMMASO
Aplogia pro Galileo, Mathematico Florentino. Frankfurt: 1622. V. 68; 73
De Sensu Rerum et Magia, Libri Quatuor, Pars Mirabilis Occultae Philosohiae, Ubi Demonstratur.... Frankfurt: 1620. V. 68

CAMPBELL, AGNES
Report on Public Baths and Wash-Houses in the United Kingdom. 1918. V. 71

CAMPBELL, ALBERT
Report Upon the Pacific Wagon Roads Constructed Under the Direction of the Hon. Jacob Thompson, Secretary of the Interior, in 1857-1858-1859. Washington: 1859. V. 68

CAMPBELL, ALEXANDER
A Journey From Edinburgh Through Parts of North Britain Containing Remarks on Scotish (sic) Landscape .... London: 1802. V. 71

CAMPBELL, ALICE
With Baited Breath. New York: 1946. V. 68; 71

CAMPBELL, ARCHIBALD
Lexiphanes, a Dialogue. London: 1767. V. 73
A Voyage Around the World, from 1806 to 1812; in Which Japan, Kamschatka, the Aleutian Islands, and the Sandwich Islands were Visited.... Charleston: 1822. V. 71

CAMPBELL, BEBE MOORE
Brothers and Sisters. New York: 1994. V. 70
Your Blues Ain't Like Mine. New York: 1992. V. 70; 71; 73

CAMPBELL, CHARLES A. R.
Bats, Mosquitoes and Dollars. 1925. V. 70

CAMPBELL, DONALD
Arabian Medicine and Its Influence on the Middle Ages. London: 1926. V. 68; 70

CAMPBELL, DUNCAN
Nova Scotia, in Its Historical, Mercantile and Industrial Relations. Montreal: 1873. V. 73

CAMPBELL, GEORGE
The Philosophy of Rhetoric. London: 1776. V. 73

CAMPBELL, GEORGE F.
A Soldier of the Sky. Chicago: 1918. V. 72

CAMPBELL, HARRIETTE
The String Glove Mystery. New York: 1936. V. 68

CAMPBELL, HELEN KNOX
Darkness and Daylight; or, Lights and Shadows of New York Life. Hartford: 1891. V. 69
Darkness and Daylight; or, Lights and Shadows of New York Life. Hartford: 1896. V. 68; 69
Darkness and Daylight; or, Lights and Shadows of New York Life. Hartford: 1900. V. 72
Household Economics. A Course of Lectures in the School of Economics of the University of Wisconsin. New York: 1905. V. 72

CAMPBELL, HUGH
The Wanderer in Ayrshire; a Tour.... Kilmarnock: 1817. V. 68; 72

CAMPBELL, IAIN
Ian Fleming: a Catalogue of a Collection - A Prelimary to a Bibliography. Liverpool: 1978. V. 70

CAMPBELL INVESTMENT CO.
A Book of Opportunity. Chicago: 1896. V. 68

CAMPBELL, J. A.
Biology of the Pitvipers. 1992. V. 69

CAMPBELL, J. F.
Popular Tales of the West Highlands Orally Collected. Edinburgh: 1860-1862. V. 69

CAMPBELL, J. R.
A History of the County of Yarmouth, Nova Scotia. Saint John: 1876. V. 72

CAMPBELL, J. RAMSEY
New Tales of the Cthulhu Mythos. Sauk City: 1980. V. 69

CAMPBELL, JAMES HAVELOCK
McClellan: a Vindication of the Military Career of General George B. McClellan. New York: 1916. V. 69; 70

CAMPBELL, JOHN
An Exact and Authentic Account of the Greatest White-Herring-Fishery in Scotland. Edinburgh: 1885. V. 68
The Lives of the Chief Justices of England. Northport: 1894-1899. V. 71
Maritime Discovery and Christian Missions, Considered in their Mutual Relations. London: 1840. V. 68
Memoirs of the Duke of Ripperda, First Embassador from the States- General to His Most Catholick Majesty, the Duke and Grandee of Spain.... London: 1740. V. 73
The Military History of the Late Prince Eugene of Savoy, and of the Late John Duke of Marlborough, Including a Particular Description of the Several Battles, Sieges, &c. 1736-1737. V. 70
A Political Survey of Britain: Being a Series of Reflections on the Situation, Lands, Inhabitants, Revenues, Colonies and Commerce of this Island.... London: 1774. V. 69; 70
The Present State of Europe. London: 1750. V. 72

CAMPBELL, JOHN MENZIES
A Dental Bibliography. British and American 1682-1880.... London: 1949. V. 69

CAMPBELL, JOHN W.
Collected Editorials from Analog. Garden City: 1966. V. 69

CAMPBELL, JOHN W. continued
Who Goes There?. Chicago: 1948. V. 70

CAMPBELL, JOSEPH
Sermons by the Late Joseph Campbell, D.D. of the Synod of New Jersey. Belvidere: 1842. V. 69

CAMPBELL, LANG
Rig-Ma-Role Picture Land. Newark: 1925. V. 73

CAMPBELL, LEWIS
The Life of James Clerk Maxwell, with a Selection from His Correspondence and Occasional Writings and a Sketch of His Contributions to Science. London: 1882. V. 72

CAMPBELL, MARIE
Folks Do Get Born. New York: 1946. V. 71

CAMPBELL, MARIUS R.
Guidebook of the Western United States: Part 3. The Denver and Rio Grande Western Route. Washington: 1922. V. 68

CAMPBELL, MARJORIE WILKINS
McGillivrary Lord of the Northwest. Toronto: 1962. V. 69
The Northwest Company. Toronto: 1957. V. 69

CAMPBELL, MARY MASON
Betty Crocker's Kitchen Gardens. New York: 1971. V. 71; 73

CAMPBELL, MAURICE
The Hound of the Baskervilles: Dartmoor or Herefordshire?. 1953. V. 69
Sherlock Holmes and Dr. Watson: A Medical Digression. London: 1935. V. 69

CAMPBELL, ORSON
A Treatise on Carriage, Sign and Ornamental Painting.... New York: 1841. V. 68

CAMPBELL, REAU
Campbell's New Revised Complete Guide and Descriptive Book of Mexico. Mexico City: 1899. V. 68
Winter Cities in Summer Lands. Cincinnati: 1885. V. 69

CAMPBELL, ROBERT
A Few Facts, Relating to Lagos, Abbeokuta, and Other Sections of Central Africa. Philadelphia: 1860. V. 71
The Life of the Most Illustrious Prince John, Duke of Argyle and Greenwich. London: 1745. V. 70
Malloy's Subway. New York: 1981. V. 71
The Rocky Mountain Letters of Robert Campbell. 1955. V. 69

CAMPBELL, ROY
Adamastor. 1930. V. 70
Adamastor. New York: 1931. V. 72
Adamastor. Cape Town: 1950. V. 72
Broken Record. 1934. V. 70
Broken Record. London: 1934. V. 69
Choosing a Mast. London: 1931. V. 69
The Collected Poems of Roy Campbell. London: 1949. V. 68; 73
Collected Works. 1985. V. 70
The Flaming Terrapin. London: 1924. V. 73
The Georgiad - a Satirical Fantasy in Verse. London: 1931. V. 69; 73
Mithraic Emblems: Poems. 1936. V. 73
Pomegranates. London: 1932. V. 69
Talking Bronco. London: 1946. V. 69; 73
The Wayzgoose. London: 1928. V. 68

CAMPBELL, RUTH
Small Fry and Winged Horse. Joliet: 1927. V. 70
Turtle Whose Snap Unfastened. Joliet: 1927. V. 70

CAMPBELL, THOMAS
Dr. Campbell's Diary of a Visit to England in 1775. Cambridge: 1947. V. 69
Frederick the Great, His Court and Times. London: 1842. V. 71
Gertrude of Wyoming; a Pennsylvania Tale and Other Poems. London: 1809. V. 68; 70; 72; 73
The Pleasures of Hope. London: 1822. V. 71
Poems. London: 1848. V. 72; 72
The Poetical Works. London: 1840. V. 70; 71
Specimens of the British Poets.... London: 1819. V. 73

CAMPBELL, THOMAS J.
The Upper Tennessee. Chattanooga: 1932. V. 73

CAMPBELL, W.
The Old Forest Ranger. 1845. V. 72

CAMPBELL, WILFRED
Canada. London: 1907. V. 72; 73

CAMPBELL, WILLIAM C.
From the Quarries of Last Chance Gulch, a New History of Helena and Its Masonic Lodges. Helena: 1964-1965. V. 69

CAMPBELL, WILLIAM CAREY
A Colorado Colonel and Other Sketches. Topeka: 1901. V. 70

CAMPBELL, WILLIAM W.
Annals of Tryon County; or, the Border Warfare of New York During the Revolution. Cherry Valley: 1880. V. 71

CAMPBELL, WILSON
Vincente, the Yaqui: a Western Story. New York: 1928. V. 69

CAMPE, JOACHIM H.
The New Robinson Crusoe; an Instructive and Entertaining History. Boston: 1790. V. 69; 71
Polar Scenes, Exhibited in the Voyages of Heemskirk and Barenz to the Northern Regions.... New York: 1823. V. 68

CAMPION, G. B.
W. H. Mason's New Drawing Book of Sketches from Brighton Beach. Brighton: 1840. V. 69

CAMPION, J. S.
On the Frontier. London: 1878. V. 68; 72

CAMPION, SARAH
Dr. Golightly. London: 1946. V. 72

CAMPION, THOMAS
Campion's Works. Oxford: 1909. V. 69
Campion's Works. Oxford: 1934. V. 73
Fifty Songs by Thomas Campion. London: 1896. V. 68
Selected Songs of Thomas Campion. Boston: 1973. V. 68
The Works. London: 1889. V. 71

CAMPOMANES, PEDRO RODRIGUES, CONDE DE
Discurso Sobre El Fomento De La Industria Popular. Madrid: 1774. V. 69

CAMUS, ALBERT
Caligula and Cross Purpose. London: 1947. V. 69
Carnets 1935-1942; 1942-1951. London: 1963-1966. V. 72
Exile and the Kingdom. London: 1958. V. 69
Exile and the Kingdom. New York: 1958. V. 73
The Fall. New York: 1956. V. 70
The Fall. New York: 1957. V. 73
L'Homme Revolte. Paris: 1951. V. 72
The Outsider. London: 1946. V. 69; 70; 73
The Plague. London: 1948. V. 72; 73
Resistance, Rebellion and Death. New York: 1961. V. 73
Speech of Acceptance Upon the Award of the Nobel Prize for Literature. London: 1958. V. 72

CANADA
Report of the Commission Appointed to Enquire into the Condition of Navigable Steams. Ottawa: 1873. V. 73

CANADA. DEPARTMENT OF MINES AND RESOURCES
Investigations in Ore Dressing and Metallurgy 1923-1939. Ottawa: 1925-1941. V. 72

THE CANADIAN Crisis and Lord Durham's Mission to the North American Colonies.... London: 1838. V. 73

THE CANADIAN Girl's Annual. London: 1920. V. 73

CANADIAN NATIONAL RAILWAYS
Fishing in Canada. 1925-1930. V. 73

THE CANADIAN Naturalist. Montreal: 1857-1863. V. 73

CANADIAN PACIFIC RAILWAY
Alaska Puget Sound British Columbia. Summer Trips. Sights Worth Seeing. Rest and Recreation. Montreal: 1907. V. 68
Canadian Pacific Primers - III. Summer Tours. Montreal: 1888. V. 68
The Gold Fields of the Cariboo and the Far Famed Kootenay British Columbia Reached Only by the Canadian Pacific Railway. Montreal: 1896. V. 70
Western Canada Manitoba, Assiniboia, Alberta Saskatchewan and Northern Ontario. 1898. V. 73
Yukon Gold Fields. Handbook of Information Illustrated With Maps and Charts of the Routes. Ottawa: 1879. V. 71

CANALETTO, GIOVANNI ANTONIO DA CANALE
Fifty Drawings by Canaletto from the Royal Library, Windsor Castle. London: 1983. V. 70

CANAVAN, MYRTELLE
Elmer Ernest Southard and His Parents. Cambridge: 1925. V. 71

CANBY, HENRY SEIDEL
The Brandywine. New York: 1941. V. 69; 71

A CANDID Examination of the History of Sir Charles Grandison. London: 1755. V. 69

CANDOLLE, A. P. DE
A Review of the Natural Order Myrsineae. 1833. V. 70

CANE, PERCY S.
Garden Design of To-Day. London: 1934. V. 70

CANESTRELLI, PHILIP
A Kootenai Grammar. Spokane: 1959. V. 70

CANETTI, ELIAS
Crowds and Power. London: 1962. V. 68; 69
The Tower of Babel. New York: 1947. V. 71

CANFIELD, CHAUNCEY L.
The Diary of a Forty Niner. 1947. V. 68

CANFIELD, DOROTHY
Basque People. New York: 1931. V. 72
Bonfire. New York: 1933. V. 71; 72

CANFIELD, FREDERICK A.
A History of Thomas Canfield and of Matthew Camfield.... Dover: 1897. V. 69

CANIN, ETHAN
Blue River. Boston: 1991. V. 72
Carry Me Across the Water. New York: 2001. V. 70
Emperor of the Air. Boston: 1988. V. 68; 69; 73
The Emperor of the Air. New York: 1988. V. 72
For Kings and Planets. New York: 1998. V. 70; 72
The Palace Thief. New York: 1994. V. 72
We Are Nighttime Travelers. Boston: 1987-1988. V. 70

CANNAN, GILBERT
Noel. London: 1922. V. 70

CANNAN, JOANNA
Poisonous Relations. New York: 1950. V. 70; 72

CANNELL, J. C.
100 Mysteries for Armchair Detectives. London: 1932. V. 73

CANNIFF, WILLIAM
The Medical Profession in Upper Canada 1783-1850. Toronto: 1894. V. 68

CANNING, ALBERT S. G.
The Divided Irish: an Historical Sketch. 1894. V. 69
The Philosophy of Dickens. London: 1880. V. 69

CANNON, CORNELIA JAMES
The Fight for the Pueblo: The Story of Onate's Expedition and Founding of Santa Fe 1598-1609. Boston: 1934. V. 69

CANNON, D. F.
Explorer of the Human Brain. The Life of Santiago Ramon Y Cajal. New York: 1949. V. 68; 73

CANNON, H. GRAHAM
A Method of Illustration for Zoological Parts. London: 1936. V. 68

CANNON, MILES
Toward The Setting Sun. Portland: 1953. V. 72
Waiilatpa, its Rise and Fall 1836-1847. Boise: 1915. V. 70

CANNON, RALPH
Grid Star. Chicago: 1933. V. 69

CANNON, WALTER B.
Autonomic Neuro-Effector Systems. New York: 1937. V. 68
Bodily Changes in Pain, Hunger, Fear and Rage, an Account of Recent Researches into the Function of Emotional Excitement. New York: 1915. V. 68
The Supersensitivity of Denervated Structures. New York: 1949. V. 68

CANNON-BROOKES, PETER
Michael Ayrton. London: 1978. V. 72

CANOVA, ANTONIO
Monumentum Aerternae Memoriae Mariae Christinae Archiducis Austriae a Ser. Conjuge Alberto Saxone, Duce Tesch.. Vienna: 1813. V. 70
The Works of Antonio Canova.... London: 1821-1824. V. 72

CANTACUZINO, S.
New Uses for Old Buildings. New York: 1975. V. 69; 72

CANTON, FRANK
Frontier Trails, The Autobiography of Frank Canton. Boston: 1930. V. 71

CANTON, WILLIAM
The True Annals of Fairy-Land: the Reign of King Herla. London: 1900. V. 69

CANTOR, EDDIE
Caught Short! A Saga of Wailing Wall Street. New York: 1929. V. 72

CANTOR, GEORGE
The Tigers of '68. Dallas: 1997. V. 69

CANTU, IGNAZIO
L'Italiano in Viaggio per Londra. Guida Indispendsabie per Compiere Gita Con Minore Spesa e Maggiore Profitto pei Diversi Stradali di Piemonte, Svizzera, Germania, Reno, Belgio e Francia.... Milano: 1851. V. 71

CANTWELL, J. C.
Report of the Operations of the U. S. Revenue Steamer Nunivak on the Yukon River Station, Alaska, 1899-1901. Washington: 1904. V. 70

CANTY, KEVIN
Into the Great Wide Open. New York: 1996. V. 70
A Stranger in This World. New York: 1994. V. 69

CANTY, THOMAS
A Monster at Christmas. West Kingston: 1985. V. 71

CANU, F.
North American Early Tertiary Bryozoa. Washington: 1920. V. 72

CAPA, CORNELL
Farewell to Eden. New York: 1946. V. 68
Robert Capa Photographs. New York: 1985. V. 68

CAPA, ROBERT
Death in the Making. New York: 1938. V. 69
Report on Israel. New York: 1950. V. 68

THE CAPE and Its People. Cape Town: 1869. V. 71

CAPEK, KAREL
How They Do It. London: 1945. V. 70
Krakatit. New York: 1925. V. 70
Letters from Spain. New York: 1932. V. 68
An Ordinary Life. London: 1936. V. 70; 72
War With the Newts. New York: 1937. V. 68; 70

CAPEK, THE BROTHERS
And So Ad Infinitum. (The Life of the Insects). Oxford: 1923. V. 70

CAPERN, EDWARD
Wayside Warbles. London: 1865. V. 68; 73

CAPERS, CHARLOTTE
The Capers Papers. Jackson: 1982. V. 73

CAPERS, G.
Bondage, a Moral Institution, Sanctioned by the Scriptures. Macon: 1837. V. 72

CAPON, PAUL
The World at Bay. Philadelphia: 1954. V. 69

CAPONIGRO, PAUL
The Wise Silence: Photographs. 1983. V. 68
The Wise Silence: Photographs by Paul Caponigro. New York: 1985. V. 68

CAPOTE, TRUMAN
Answered Prayers. The Unfinished Novel. London: 1986. V. 70
Breakfast at Tiffany's. London: 1958. V. 69
Breakfast at Tiffany's. New York: 1958. V. 69; 70; 73
A Christmas Memory. New York: 1966. V. 69
The Dogs Bark. New York: 1973. V. 72
The Grass Harp. New York: 1951. V. 70; 72; 73
The Grass Harp. New York: 1952. V. 69; 70
House of Flowers. New York: 1968. V. 70
In Cold Blood. 1965. V. 73
In Cold Blood. New York: 1965. V. 68; 69; 70; 71; 73
Local Color. New York: 1950. V. 72; 73
The Muses Are Heard. NY: 1956. V. 72
Music for Chameleons. New York: 1980. V. 69; 70; 71; 73
One Christmas. New York: 1983. V. 68; 69; 73
One Christmas. New York: 1985. V. 68
Other Voices, Other Rooms. New York: 1948. V. 69; 70; 71; 72; 73
Other Voices, Other Rooms. Franklin Center: 1979. V. 69
The Thanksgiving Visitor. New York: 1967. V. 71; 73
A Tree of Night and Other Stories. New York: 1949. V. 72

CAPP, AL
The World of Li'l Abner. New York: 1953. V. 69

CAPPON, LESTER J.
The Adams-Jefferson Letters. The Complete Correspondence Between Thomas Jefferson and Abigail and John Adams. Chapel Hill: 1959. V. 73
Atlas of Early American History: the Revolutionary Era 1760-1790. Princeton: 1976. V. 73

CAPPS, EDWARD
The Currency Question in a Nut-Shell. London: 1844. V. 71

CAPRIULO, G. M.
Ecology of Marine Protozoa. New York: 1990. V. 72; 73

CAPTAIN Parolles at M-nden; a Rough Sketch for the Royal Academy... Dedicated to Temple Luttrell.... London: 1778. V. 73

CAPTIVITY Narrative of Hannah Duston Related by Cotton Mather, John Greenleaf Whittier, Nathaniel Hawthorne and Henry David Thoreau, Four Versions of Events in 1697. San Francisco: 1987. V. 70

CAPUTO, PHILIP
Horn of Africa. New York: 1980. V. 68
A Rumor of War. New York: 1977. V. 70; 72

THE CAR of 1911. Bridgeport: 1911. V. 73

CARACCIOUT, LOUIS A. DE
Advice from a Lady of Quality to Her Children, in the Last Stage of a Lingering Illness. Boston: 1796. V. 68; 69; 73

CARADOG OF LLANCARVAN
The Historie of Cambria, Now Called Wales: A Part of the Most Famous Yland of Brytaine , , , Translated Into English by H. Lhoyd (sic). London: 1584. V. 73

CARASI, CARLO
Le Pubbliche Pitture di Piacenza. Piacenza: 1780. V. 69

CARB, DAVID
Sunrise in the West. New York: 1931. V. 70

CARBERRY, ETHNA
Songs from The Four Winds of Eirinn. Dublin: 1906. V. 69

CARBUTT, E. H., MRS.
Five Months' Fine Weather in Canada, Western United States and Mexico. London: 1889. V. 69

CARCATERRA, LORENZO
Sleepers. New York: 1995. V. 72

CARCLOCK, WILLIAM BRYAN
A Compilation of the Historical and Biographical Writings of William B. Carlock. 1923. V. 70

CARCO, FRANCIS
Vertes. New York: 1946. V. 69

CARD, HENRY
An Essay on the Holy Eucharist; or a Refutation of the Hoadlyan Scheme Of It. Worcester: 1814. V. 73

CARD, ORSON SCOTT
Ender's Game. 1985. V. 69
Ender's Game. New York: 1985. V. 70
Hot Sleep. 1979. V. 70
The Memory of Earth. 1992. V. 71
A Planet Called Treason. 1979. V. 70
A Planet Called Treason. New York: 1979. V. 68
The Ships of Earth. 1994. V. 70
Speaker for the Dead. New York: 1986. V. 69; 70
Speaker for the Dead. 1987. V. 71

CARDANO, GIROLAMO
De Subtilitate Libri XXI. Nunc Denum ab Ipso Autore Recogniti, Atque Perfecti. Lyon: 1558. V. 68
Mediolanensis Proxeneta: Seu de Prudentia Civili Liber. Geneva: 1630. V. 69

CARDEN, ALLEN
The Missouri Harmony. Cincinnati: 1835. V. 68
The Missouri Harmony. Cincinnati: 1839. V. 72

CARDENAS, JEFFREY
Marquesa, a Time and Place with Fish. Stone Harbor: 1995. V. 72

CARDEW, CORNELIUS
Schooltime Compositions. London: 1968. V. 70

CARDINELL, CHARLES
Adventures on the Plains. San Francisco: 1922. V. 69

CARDNELL, ERNEST A.
Advanced Piping and Cake Designs. London: 1950. V. 68

CARDOZO, CHRISTOPHER
Sacred Legacy - Edward S. Curtis and the North American Indian. New York/Canada: 2000. V. 68; 73

CARE, HENRY
Draconica; or, an Abstract of All the Penal Laws Touching Matters of Religion; and the Several Oaths and Tests Thereby Enjoyed. London: 1688. V. 72

CAREER Women of America. New York: 1941. V. 71; 72

CARELESS, JOHN, PSEUD.
The Old English Squire. London: 1821. V. 68; 70; 72

CAREW, THOMAS
Poems. London: 1640. V. 70; 73
A Rapture. Waltham St. Lawrence: 1927. V. 72
The Works of Thomas Carew, Sewer in ordinary to Charles the First. Edinburgh: 1824. V. 71

CAREY, CHARLES
The Van Suyden Sapphires. 1905. V. 71

CAREY, DAVE
Jazz Directory 1-6. 1949-1957. V. 70

CAREY, DAVID
Life in Paris: Comprising the Rambles, Sprees and Amours, of Dick Wildfire.... London: 1822. V. 68

CAREY, H. C.
The Slave Trade, Domestic and Foreign: Why It Exists and How It May Be Extinguished. Philadelphia: 1856. V. 70

CAREY, HARRY
Company of Heroes. 1994. V. 68

CAREY, HENRY
Songs and Poems. Waltham St. Lawrence: 1924. V. 71

CAREY, HENRY CHARLES
The Geography, History and Statistics of America and the West Indies.... London: 1823. V. 68

CAREY, MATTHEW
Observations on Dr. Rush's Enquiry into the Origin of the Late Epidemic Fever in Philadelphia. Philadelphia: 1793. V. 70
A Short Account of the Malignant Fever, Lately Prevalent in Philadelphia.... Philadelphia: 1764. V. 70
A Short Account of the Malignant Fever, Lately Prevalent in Philadelphia.... Philadelphia: 1793. V. 70
Twenty-One Golden Rules to Depress Agriculture, Impede the Progress of Manufactures, Paralize Commerce, Impair National Resources, Produce a Constant Fluctation in the Vale of Every Species of Property and Blight and Blast the Bounties of Nature.... Salem: 1824. V. 71

CAREY, PATRICK
Trivial Poems and Triolets. London: 1820. V. 73

CAREY, PETER
The Big Bazoohley. London: 1995. V. 72
Bliss. London: 1981. V. 69
Bliss. St. Lucia: 1981. V. 70
Bliss. Sydney: 1983. V. 70
The Fat Man in History. St. Lucia: 1974. V. 70
The Fat Man in History. New York: 1980. V. 70; 71
The History of the Kelly Gang. New York: 2001. V. 69
Illywhacker. 1985. V. 73
Illywhacker. London: 1985. V. 71
Illywhacker. New York: 1985. V. 69
Jack Maggs. 1997. V. 71
Jack Maggs. London: 1997. V. 72
Jack Maggs. New York: 1998. V. 71; 72
A Letter to Our Son. St. Lucia: 1994. V. 70
Oscar and Lucinda. New York: 1988. V. 69; 70; 73
The Tax Inspector. Franklin Center: 1991. V. 72
The Tax Inspector. London: 1991. V. 72
The Tax Inspector. St. Lucia: 1991. V. 70
30 Days in Sydney. London: 2001. V. 70
True History of the Kelly Gang. London: 2001. V. 71
True History of the Kelly Gang. New York: 2001. V. 71
The Unusual Life of Tristan Smith. London: 1994. V. 70; 71
The Unusual Life of Tristan Smith. St. Lucia: 1994. V. 70
War Crimes. St. Lucia: 1979. V. 70

CAREY, ROSA NOUCHETTE
Heriot's Choice. London: 1879. V. 71
Nellie's Memories. London: 1868. V. 73

CAREY, WILLIAM
The Stranger's Guide through London; or, a View of the British Metropolis. London: 1808. V. 71

CARGILL, LESLIE
Death Goes By Bus. London: 1936. V. 72; 73
The Man From The Rhine. London: 1943. V. 72

CARION, JOHANNES
The Thre Bokes of Cronicles, Whyche John Carion.... 1550. V. 68

CARITON, MAUD
All the Way Round Pictures and Rhymes. London: 1900. V. 70

CARKESSE, CHARLES
The Act on Tonnage and Poundage, and Rates of Merchandize, with the Further Subsidy, the 1/3 and 2/3 Subsidies; the Old Impost; the Additional Impost; and All Other Duties Relating to His Majesty's Customs.... London: 1726. V. 68; 72

CARL, MELVIN JAMES
The Life of Melvin James Carl: An Autobiography. New York: 1970:. V. 72

CARLANDER, K. D.
Handbook of Freshwater Fisher Biology. Ames: 1969-1977. V. 70

CARLEN, EMILIE
Twelve Months of Matrimony. London: 1886. V. 68

CARLETON, GEORGE
Tithes Examined and Proued to be Due to the Clergie by a Diuine Right. London: 1611. V. 73

CARLETON, J. HENRY
The Prairie Logbooks, 1844-1845, Dragoon Campaigns To The Pawnee Villages In 1844 And To The Rocky Mountains In 1845. Chicago: 1943. V. 72

CARLETON, WILLIAM
Tales and Sketches, Illustrating the Character, Usages, Traditions, Sports and Pastimes of the Irish Peasantry. Dublin: 1845-1846. V. 73
Tales of Ireland. 1834. V. 73

CARLEVALE, JOSEPH WILLIAM
Americans of Italian Descent in New Jersey. Clifton: 1950. V. 69

CARLILE, RICHARD
An Exposure of Freemasonry, or, A Mason's Printed Manual.... London: 1831. V. 71
The Report of the Proceedings of the Court of King's Bench..Being the Mock Trials of Richard Carlile, for Alledged Blasphemous Libels, in Publishing Thomas Paine's Theological Works and Elihu Principles of Nature. London: 1826. V. 68; 71

CARLINGFORD, SAMUEL BASIL
Who Wins?. London: 1864. V. 71

CARLISLE, A. D.
Round The World In 1870. London: 1872. V. 72

CARLISLE, ANTHONY
An Essay on the Disorders of Old Age, and on the Means of Prolonging Human Life. London: 1818. V. 73

CARLISLE, BILL
Bill Carlisle, Lone Bandit an Autobiography. Pasadena: 1946. V. 68; 73

CARLISLE, GEORGE WILLIAM FREDERICK HOWARD, 7TH EARL OF
Lines on Yorkshire. London: 1860. V. 72
Lines on Yorkshire. London: 1864. V. 72

CARLISLE, NICHOLAS
An Historical Account of the Origin of the Commission, Appointed to Inquire Concerning Charities in England and Wales.... London: 1828. V. 70

CARLLEW, LORIS
Alice in Plunderland. London: 1910. V. 70

CARLOWITZ, HANS KARL VON
Sylvicultural Oeconomica, oder Hausswirthliche Nachricht und Naturmassige Anweisung zur Wilden baum zucht...(with) Historia Naturalis Arborum et Fruticum Sylvestrium Germaniae.... Leipzig: 1732. V. 72

CARLSON, PAUL H.
Pecos Bill - A Military Biography Of William R. Schafter. College Station: 1989. V. 72

CARLSON, RON
The News of the World. New York: 1987. V. 68

CARLYLE, ALEXANDER
Autobiography of the Rev. Dr. Alexander Carlyle, Minister of Inveresk.... Edinburgh and London: 1860. V. 71

CARLYLE, JANE WELSH
Letters and Memorials of...Prepared for Publication by Thomas Carlyle. London: 1883. V. 69; 73

CARLYLE, THOMAS
Inaugural Address at Edinburgh April 2, 1866...on Being Installed as Rector of the University There. Edinburgh: 1866. V. 70
Montaigne, and Other Essays Chiefly Autobiographical. London: 1897. V. 72
Past and Present. London: 1843. V. 72
Sartor Resartus. London: 1898. V. 73
Sartor Resartus (1831). Lectures on Heroes (1840). London: 1871. V. 71
Sartor Resartus; the Life and Opinions of Herr Teufelsdroeckh. 1907. V. 70
The Works. London: 1865-1869. V. 73
The Works. London: 1896-1899. V. 73
Works. Boston: 1900. V. 68

CARMAN, BLISS
Ballads and Lyrics. London: 1902. V. 68

CARMEL, JOHN PROSPER
Blottentots and How to Make Them. San Francisco: 1907. V. 69

CARMICHAEL, REBEKAH
Poems. Edinburgh: 1790. V. 69

CARMICHAEL, RICHARD
Clinical Lectures on Venereal Diseases. Dublin: 1842. V. 69

CARMICHAEL, SARAH E.
Poems. San Francisco: 1866. V. 73

CARMICHAEL, VIRGINIA
Jackson's Flank Movement and Guiney's Station. Fredericksburg: 1935. V. 70

CARNARVON, GEORGE EDWARD STANHOPE, 5TH EARL OF
Catalogue of Books Selected from the Library of an English Amateur. Part I. London: 1893. V. 70

CARNE, J.
Letters From The East. London: 1830. V. 72
Syria, the Holy Land, Asia Minor &c. London: 1836-1838. V. 72

CARNE, PETER
Deer of Britain and Ireland. 2000. V. 72; 73

CARNEGIE, ANDREW
A Carnegie Anthology. New York: 1915. V. 71
Round the World. New York: 1884. V. 69; 71
Triumphant Democracy. New York: 1886. V. 68; 70; 71; 72

CARNEGIE MUSEUM
Memoirs of the Carnegie Museum 1913-1914. Pittsburgh: 1914. V. 72

CARNEY, A. L.
Diagnosis and Treatment of Brain Ischemia.... New York: 1981. V. 71

CARNOT, LAZARE-NICOLAS-MARGUERITE
Geometrie de Position. Paris: 1803. V. 72

CAROE, W. D.
Sefton. A Descriptive and Historical Account Comprising the Collected notes and researchs of the Late Rev. Englebert Horley. London: 1893. V. 73

CAROLINE *Hargrave, the Merchant's Daughter....* Salem: 1845. V. 71

CAROLINE, QUEEN OF GREAT BRITAIN
The Trial at Large of Her Majesty Caroline Amelia Elizabeth, Queen of Great Britain: in the House of Lords, on Charges of Adulterous Intercourse.... London: 1821. V. 72

CAROLINO, PEDRO, PSEUD.
The New Guide of the Conversation in Portuguese and English.... Boston: 1883. V. 70

CAROVE
The Story Without an End. London: 1868. V. 68

CARPENTER, A.
Nature Notes for Ocean Voyagers. London: 1915. V. 71

CARPENTER, EDWARD
Angels' Wings.... London: 1908. V. 71
British Aristocracy and the House of Lords. London: 1908. V. 72
Chants of Labour. London: 1888. V. 71
Days with Walt Whitman. London: 1906. V. 71
Intermediate Types Among Primitive Folk. London: 1914. V. 71
My Days and Dreams. London: 1916. V. 71
My Days and Dreams. London: 1921. V. 71
Never Again!. London: 1916. V. 72
Sketches from Life in Town and Country. London: 1908. V. 71; 72
Who Shall Command the Heart. London: 1902. V. 71

CARPENTER, G. D. H.
A Naturalist on Lake Victoria.... New York: 1920. V. 72

CARPENTER, GRANT
The Night Tide. NY: 1920. V. 72

CARPENTER, HUMPHREY
The Inklings: C. S. Lewis, J.R.R. Tolkien, Charles Williams and Their Friends. London: 1978. V. 72

CARPENTER, J. ESTLIN
James Martineau, Theologian and Teacher. London: 1905. V. 71

CARPENTER, P. H.
Challenger Voyage. Zoology. Part 32. Crinoidea. The Stalked Crinoids. 1884. V. 73

CARPENTER, PHILIP
Microcosom. A Grand Display of the Wonders of Nature. London: 1827. V. 69

CARPENTER, R. R. M.
Game Trails from Alaska to Africa. New York: 1938. V. 68

CARPENTER, SAMUEL
A Statement of the Evidence and Arguments of Counsel before the Committee of the House of Commons Upon the Controverted Election for Saltash. London: 1809. V. 70

CARPENTER, STEPHEN CULLEN
Memoirs of the Hon. Thomas Jefferson.... New York: 1809. V. 72; 73

CARPENTER, W. B.
The Microscope and Its Revelations. London: 1901. V. 70

CARPENTER, W. M.
Kipling's College. Evanston: 1929. V. 70

CARPENTER, WILLIAM
The Angler's Assistant: Comprising Practical Directions for Bottom Fishing, Trolling...Tackle and Bats.... London: 1848. V. 70
The Israelites Found in the Anglo-Saxons. London: 1872. V. 72
Political Letters and Pamphlets, Published for the Avowed Purpose of Trying with the Government the Question of Law.... London: 1830-1831. V. 73

CARPENTER, WILLIAM B.
The Microscope and Its Revelations. London: 1856. V. 73
The Microscope and Its Revelations. London: 1901. V. 73

CARPENTER, WILLIAM W.
Travels And Adventures In Mexico: In The Course Of Journeys Upward Of 2500 Miles Performed On Foot. New York: 1851. V. 72

CARPENTIER, ALEJO
The Kingdom of this World. New York: 1987. V. 69

CARR, CALEB
The Alienist. New York: 1994. V. 68; 70; 71
America Invulnerable. New York: 1988. V. 70
The Angel of Darkness. Franklin Center: 1997. V. 68
The Angel of Darkness. New York: 1997. V. 70; 72
Casing the Promised Land. New York: 1980. V. 69
The Devil Soldier. New York: 1992. V. 71

CARR, CAMILLUS
A Cavalryman in Indian Country. Ashland: 1974. V. 68

CARR, GLYN
Swing Away, Climber. New York: 1959. V. 68; 70
The Youth Hostel Murders. New York: 1953. V. 69; 73

CARR, HARRY
The West is Still Wild. Boston: 1932. V. 69

CARR, HERBERT
A Climber's Guide to Snowdon and the Beddgellert Region. 1926. V. 69
The Mountains of Snowdonia in History, the Sciences, Literature and Sport. London: 1948. V. 69

CARR, J. L.
How Steeple Sinderby Wanderers Won the F.A. Cup. London: 1975. V. 73
A Month in the Country. 1990. V. 68; 71
A Season in Sinji - a Novel. London: 1967. V. 69

CARR, JOHN
Pioneer Days in California. Fresno. V. 69
Pioneer Days in California. Eureka: 1891. V. 70; 73
The Stranger in France; or a Tour From Devonshire to Paris.... London: 1803. V. 72
A Synopsis of Practical Philosophy, Alphabetically Arranged.... London: 1828. V. 70
A Vulcan Among the Argonauts, Being Vivid Excerpts from those Most Original and Amusing Memories of John Carr, Blacksmith. San Francisco: 1936. V. 68; 73

CARR, JOHN DICKSON
And So to Murder. 1940. V. 73
The Arabian Nights Murder. New York: 1936. V. 70
Behind the Crimson Blind. New York: 1952. V. 70
Below Suspicion. London: 1950. V. 70
The Blind Barber. 1934. V. 71
The Blind Barber. New York: 1934. V. 70
The Bride of Newgate. London: 1950. V. 70
Captain Cut-Throat. London: 1955. V. 70
The Case of the Constant Suicides. New York: 1941. V. 70
The Cavalier's Cup. 1953. V. 73
The Corpse in the Waxworks. New York: 1932. V. 71
Crime On The Coast & No Flowers By Request. London: 1984. V. 72
The Crooked Hinge. New York: 1938. V. 70; 71
The Crooked Hinge With Introduction Notes And Checklist By Robert E. Briney. San Diego: 1976. V. 72
The Curse of the Bronze Lamp. 1945. V. 73
The Dead Man's Knock. London: 1958. V. 71
The Dead Man's Knock. New York: 1958. V. 68
Death Turns the Tables. New York: 1941. V. 71
Death Watch. 1935. V. 71
Death Watch. New York: 1935. V. 70
The Demoniacs. 1962. V. 70
The Demoniacs. New York: 1962. V. 72
Dr. Fell, Detective and Other Stories. New York: 1947. V. 70
A Dr. Fell Omnibus. London: 1959. V. 69
The Door to Doom. New York: 1980. V. 71
The Emperor's Snuff-Box. New York: 1942. V. 69; 70
The Four False Weapons. New York: 1937. V. 70
The Ghosts' High Noon. New York: 1969. V. 71
The Ghosts' High Noon. 1970. V. 70
The Gilded Man. 1942. V. 73
Hag's Nook. New York: 1933. V. 70
He Who Whispers. London: 1946. V. 70
The House At Satan's Elbow. London: 1965. V. 72
In Spite Of Thunder. London: 1960. V. 72
It Walks by Night. New York: 1930. V. 70
The Judas Window. New York: 1938. V. 70; 72
The Life of Sir Arthur Conan Doyle. London: 1949. V. 71
The Lost Gallows. London: 1931. V. 70
The Lost Gallows. New York: 1931. V. 70
The Man Who Could Not Shudder. New York: 1940. V. 70; 71
The Man Who Explained Miracles. London: 1956. V. 70
Merrivale March and Murder. 1991. V. 73
Most Secret. New York: 1964. V. 71
The Murder of Sir Edmund Godfrey. New York: 1936. V. 70
My Late Wives. London: 1947. V. 68
Night at the Mocking Window. 1950. V. 73
Nine and Death Makes Ten. 1940. V. 73
The Nine Wrong Answers. London: 1952. V. 70
The Nine Wrong Answers. New York: 1952. V. 70
Panic in Box C. London: 1966. V. 72
Papa La-Bas. New York: 1968. V. 72; 73
Patrick Butler for the Defence. London: 1956. V. 68; 70
The Problem of the Green Capsule. New York: 1939. V. 70
The Problem of the Wire Cage. New York: 1939. V. 70
The Punch and Judy Murders. 1937. V. 73
Seeing Is Believing. 1941. V. 73
She Died a Lady. 1943. V. 73
She Died a Lady. New York: 1943. V. 70; 72
The Skeleton in the Clock. 1948. V. 73
The Sleeping Sphinx. London: 1947. V. 70
The Sleeping Sphinx. New York: 1947. V. 69
The Third Bullet And Other Stories. London: 1954. V. 72
The Third Bullet and Other Stories. London: 1984. V. 68
The Three Coffins. New York: 1935. V. 70; 72
Till Death Do Us Part. New York: 1946. V. 70
To Wake the Dead. New York: 1938. V. 70; 71
The Witch of the Low-Tide. London: 1961. V. 71

CARR, LUCILE
A Catalogue of the Vanderpoel Dickens Collection at the University of Texas. Austin: 1968. V. 68

CARR, RICHARD
Classical Scholar's Guide. London: 1832. V. 71; 73

CARR, ROBERT
The Literary Pancratium; or a Series of Dissertations on Theological, Literary, Moral and Controversial Subjects. London: 1832. V. 72

CARR, THOMAS
Carr's Patent Disintegrator (With Recent Important Improvements). Bristol: 1871. V. 73

CARR, W.
The Dialect of Craven, in the West-Riding of the Country of York. London: 1828. V. 73

CARR, WILLIAM
A Particular Account of the Last Siege of Mastrict; with the Sundry Remarkable Circumstances Thereto Relating.... London: 1676. V. 71

A CARRIAGE and Pair: A Picture Book for Little Books. London: 1896. V. 70

CARRICK, ALICE VAN LEER
Shades of Our Ancestors: American Profiles and Profilists. Boston: 1928. V. 68

CARRICK, T. W.
The Story of Wigton (Cumberland).... Carlisle: 1949. V. 71

CARRIE, WILLIAM
The Ballantyne Press and Its Founders 1796-1908. Edinburgh: 1909. V. 70

CARRIER, SCOTT
Running After Antelope. Washington: 2001. V. 69; 72

CARRIGAN, MINNIE BOCE
Captured by the Indians - Reminiscences of Pioneer Life in Minnesota. Buffalo Lake: 1912. V. 69

CARRIGHAR, SALLY
One Day on Beetle Rock. New York: 1944. V. 71

CARRIKER, R. C.
An Army Wife On The Frontier - The Memoirs Of Alice Blackwood. Salt Lake City: 1975. V. 72

CARRINGTON, B.
British Hepaticae.... London: 1874. V. 69

CARRINGTON, ELAINE STERNE
The Crimson Goddess. New York: 1936. V. 69

CARRINGTON, HENRY B.
Letter To The Secretary of War...Official Reports. Papers And Facts In Relation To The Causes And Extent Of United States Troops By Indians At Fort Phil Kearney, Washington, DC. Sec. Doc. 15, 1867. V. 72
Some Phases of The Indian Question - An Address. Boston: 1909. V. 72

CARRINGTON, MARGARET
Absaraka. 1950. V. 68
Absaraka Home of The Crows Being The Experiences of An Officer's Wife on The Plains. Philadelphia: 1878. V. 72

CARROLL, B. R.
Historical Collections of South Carolina Embracing Many Rare and Valuable Pamphlets and Other Documents Relating to the History of that State.... New York: 1836. V. 68; 71

CARROLL, CAMPBELL
Three Bar. The Story of Douglas Lake. Vancouver: 1958. V. 72

CARROLL, H. BAILEY
Three New Mexico Chronicles The Exposicion of Don Pedro Bautista Pino 1812; the Ojeada of Lic. Antonio Barreiro 1832; and the additions by Don Jose Agustin de Escudero, 1849. Albuquerque: 1942. V. 72

CARROLL, JIM
The Basketball Diaries. Bolinas: 1978. V. 70; 71; 72
Living at the Movies. New York: 1973. V. 69; 72; 73
poem, interview, photographs. Louisville: 1994. V. 72

CARROLL, JOHN
Donkey Nina and the Giant. New York: 1989. V. 70

CARROLL, JOHN EGGENHOFER
The Pulp Years. Fort Collins: 1975. V. 68

CARROLL, JOHN M.
Bards Of The Little Big Horn. Bryan: 1978. V. 72
Cavalry Bits One of Seven Volumes - The Yellowstone Expedition in The American West. New York: 1986. V. 72
Charley Reynolds - Soldier, Hunter, Scout And Guide. Bryan. V. 72
Custer in Periodicals a Bibliographic Checklist. Ft. Collins: 1975. V. 68
Custer in Texas - An Interrupted Narrative. New York: 1975. V. 72
Custer In The Civil War-His Unfinished Memoir. San Raphael: 1977. V. 72
Cyclorama of General Custer's Last Fight. El Segundo: 1988. V. 72
Eggenhofer: the Pulp Years. 1957. V. 69
General Custer and the Battle of the Washita. The Federal View. 1978. V. 68
General Custer And The Battle Of The Washita: The Federal View. Bryan: 1978. V. 72
The Grand Duke Alexis in The United States of America. New York: 1972. V. 72
I. Varnum, The Autobiograhical Reminscences Of Custer's Chief Of Scouts. Bryan n.d. V. 72
The Medal Of Honor: Its History And Its Recipients For The Indian Wars. Mattituck, Mt. V. 72
The Papers of the Order of Indian Wars. 1975. V. 68
The Papers of the Order of Indian Wars. Fort Collins: 1975. V. 71; 72
Roll Call On The Little Big Horn, June 28, 1876. Bryan. V. 72
Roll Call on The Little Big Horn, June 28, 1876. Fort Collins: 1974. V. 72
Three Hits And A Miss. Bryan: 1981. V. 72
The Two Battles Of The Little Big Horn. NY: 1974. V. 72

CARROLL, JONATHAN
The Land of Laughs. New York: 1980. V. 69; 71; 73

CARROLL, PAUL
Odes. Chicago: 1969. V. 68

CARROLL, PAUL VINCENT
Irish Stories and Plays. New York: 1958. V. 69
Shadow and Substance. 1937. V. 69

CARROLL, PETER OWEN
The Life and Adventures of Detective Peter Owen Caroll. 1924?. V. 72

CARROLL, WALTER
River and Rainbow. London: 1934. V. 73

CARRUTH, HAYDEN
Asphalt Georgics. New York: 1985. V. 69
The Clay Hill Anthology. Iowa City: 1970. V. 73
Collected Longer Poems. Port Townsend: 1993. V. 69
Journey to a Known Place. Norfolk: 1961. V. 69

CARRUTHERS, CLIVE HARCOURT
Alicia in Terra Mirabili. New York: 1964. V. 70

CARRUTHERS, D.
Beyond the Caspian, a Naturalist in Central Asia. London: 1949. V. 69

CARRY and the Candle. New York: 1885. V. 71

CARRYL, CHARLES
Davy and the Goblin, or What Followed Reading Alice's Adventures in Wonderland. Boston: 1886. V. 70

CARSE, ROBERT
Department of the South. Hilton Head Island in the Civil War. Columbia: 1961. V. 69; 70
Siren Song. New York: 1930. V. 72

CARSON, ANNE
Eros the Bittersweet. Princeton: 1988. V. 69
Men in the Off Hours. New York: 2000. V. 69
Plainwater. Essays and Poetry. New York: 1995. V. 69

CARSON, HAMPTON L.
History of the Celebration of the One Hundredth Anniversary of the Promulgation of the Constitution of the U.S. Philadelphia: 1889. V. 72

CARSON, JAMES H.
Recollections of the California Mines - an Account of the Early Discoveries of Gold with Anecdotes and Sketches of California and Miner's Life, and a Description of the Great Tulare Valley. Oakland: 1950. V. 70

CARSON, RACHEL
The Edge of the Sea. Boston: 1955. V. 71; 73
The Sea Around Us. New York: 1951. V. 69; 72; 73
The Sea Around Us. New York: 1961. V. 69
The Sea Around Us. New York: 1980. V. 70; 72
Silent Spring. Boston: 1961. V. 72
Silent Spring. Boston: 1962. V. 69; 70; 71
Under the Sea-Wind. New York: 1941. V. 73

CARSTAIRS, HENRY
Secretary Of State For Death. London: 1946. V. 72

CARSTAIRS, JOHN PADDY
Lollipop Wood. London: 1947. V. 69

CARSTENSEN, A. R.
Two Summers in Greenland. 1890. V. 69
Two Summers in Greenland. London: 1890. V. 70

CARSWELL, CATHERINE
The Savage Pilgrimage - a Narrative of D. H. Lawrence. London: 1932. V. 71; 72; 73

CARSWELL, EDWARD
The Temperance Alphabet. New York: 1866. V. 68

CARSWELL, ROBERT
Pathological Anatomy. London: 1838. V. 70

CARTARI, VINCENZO
Les Images de Dievx Des Anciens. Lyon: 1581. V. 73
Le Imagine con la Spositione de i Dei de Gli Antichi. Venice: 1556. V. 69; 72

CARTER, A. C. R.
The Year's Art 1895. London: 1895. V. 73

CARTER, ANGELA
The Bloody Chamber. London: 1979. V. 73
The Bloody Chamber. New York: 1979. V. 71; 73
Fireworks. New York: 1981. V. 72
Honey Buzzard. New York: 1966. V. 68
The Infernal Desire Machines of Doctor Hoffman. London: 1972. V. 73
Love. London: 1971. V. 73
Moonshadow. London: 1982. V. 72
The Passion of New Eve. London: 1977. V. 72
Shadow Dance. London: 1966. V. 72; 73

CARTER, DENNY
Henry Farny. New York: 1978. V. 69; 70; 71; 72

CARTER, ELIZABETH
Poems on Several Occasions. London: 1776. V. 73

A Series of Letters Between Mrs. Elizabeth Carter and Miss Catherine Talbot, from the Year 1741 to 1770, To Which are Added, Letters from Mrs. Elizabeth Carter to Mrs. Vesey, Between the Years 1763 and 1787. London: 1819. V. 70

CARTER, FORREST
The Education of Little Tree. New York: 1976. V. 70
Gone to Texas. 1976. V. 69
The Rebel Outlaw: Josey Wales. Gantt: 1973. V. 69
The Vengeance of Josey Wales. 1976. V. 72
The Vengeance Trail of Josey Wales. New York: 1976. V. 71; 73

CARTER, FREDERICK
D. H. Lawrence and the Body Mystical. London: 1932. V. 72
Gold Like Glass. London: 1932. V. 72

CARTER, GEORGE R.
The Tendency Towards Industrial Combination. London: 1913. V. 71

CARTER, H. B.
Sir Joseph Banks (1743-1820). Winchester: 1987. V. 71

CARTER, HARVEY LEWIS
Dear Old Kit. The Historical Christopher Carson. Norman: 1968. V. 69; 70; 73

CARTER, HENRY F.
Reports on Malaria and Mosquitoes, Ceylon. Colombo: 1914-1927. V. 72

CARTER, HOWARD
The Tomb of Tut-Ankh-Amen: Discovered by the Late Earl of Carnarvon and Howard Carter. London: 1923. V. 70; 72
The Tomb of Tut-Ankh-Amen: Discovered by the Late Earl of Carnarvon and Howard Carter. London: 1923-1933. V. 73

CARTER, JAMES
Two Lectures on Taste, Read Before the Philosophical Society of Colchester in the Years 1825 and 1827. Colchester: 1834. V. 72

CARTER, JAMES EARL
Always a Reckoning. New York: 1995. V. 68; 71; 73
The Blood of Abraham. Boston: 1985. V. 69; 71
Everything to Gain. New York: 1987. V. 69; 70; 71
Keeping Faith. New York: 1982. V. 71; 73
Keeping Faith. Norwalk: 1982-1986. V. 69
Keeping Faith. Norwalk: 1986. V. 68
The Little Baby Snoogle-Fleejer. New York: 1995. V. 69; 71
Living Faith. New York: 1996. V. 72; 73
The Virtues of Aging. New York: 1998. V. 70

CARTER, JOHN
A. E. Housman: a Bibliography. London: 1982. V. 72
ABC for Book Collectors. London: 1952. V. 68
Binding Variants in English Publishing 1820-1900. London: 1931. V. 71
Collecting Detective Fiction. London: 1934. V. 73
An Enquiry into the Nature of Certain Nineteenth Century Pamphlets. London: 1983. V. 70
Government by Contempt. London: 1968. V. 71
More Binding Variants. London: 1938. V. 71
New Paths in Book Collecting. London: 1934. V. 70; 73
New Paths in Book Collecting. New York: 1934. V. 73
Old Things and New Things, in Scraps and Fragments or Things New and Old, in Prose and Verse. Sleaford: 1831. V. 73
Printing and the Mind of Man. London: 1963. V. 71
Taste and Technique in Book Collecting. 1949. V. 71
Taste and Technique in Book Collecting. 1970. V. 71

CARTER, KEITH
Holding Venus. Santa Fe: 2000. V. 68

CARTER, MATHEW
Honor Redivivus; or the Analysis of Honor and Armory.... London: 1673. V. 68

CARTER, NICK
The Katmandu Contract. London: 1978. V. 69; 73
Sign of the Cobra. London: 1977. V. 69; 73

CARTER, RAY
An Exhibition of Works by Sir John Betjeman from the Collection of Ray Carter in the Art Gallery of St. Paul's School February-March MCLXXIII. London: 1983. V. 71

CARTER, ROBERT G.
The Old Sergeant's Story - Fighting Indians and Bad Men in Texas From 1870 to 1876. Mattituck, Mt./Bryan, TX: 1982. V. 72
On The Border With Mackenzie or Winning West Texas From The Comanches. New York: 1961. V. 72

CARTER, ROSALYN
First Lady from Plains. Boston: 1984. V. 71; 73

CARTER, RUBIN
The Sixteenth Round: from Number 1 Contender to #45472. New York: 1974. V. 73

CARTER, SAMUEL
Lex Custumaria; or, Treatise of Copy-Hold-Estates, in Repsect of the Lord, Copy Holder.... London: 1696. V. 68

CARTER, SEBSTIAN
Twentieth Century Type Designers. London: 1987. V. 70

CARTER, SUSANNAH
The Frugal Housewife; or, Complete Woman Cook. Philadelphia: 1796. V. 68; 71; 73

CARTER, W. H.
Horses, Saddles and Bridles. Leavenworth, KS: 1906. V. 72
Old Army Sketches. Baltimore: 1906. V. 71

CARTER, W. N.
Harry Tracy - the Desperate Western Outlaw. Chicago: 1902. V. 73
A Tragedy of the Plains (Harry Tracy). Chicago: 1913. V. 69

CARTER, WILLIAM
Preservation Hall. New York: 1991. V. 73

CARTER, WILLIAM H.
McCurtain County and Southeastern Oklahoma. Idabel: 1923. V. 70

CARTERET BOOK CLUB
Catalogue: an Exhibition of the Evolution of the Art of the Book, and in Praise of Printing. Newark: 1920. V. 69

CARTERET, JOHN DUNLOE
A Fortune Hunter of the Old Stone Corral - a Tale of the Santa Fe Trail. Cincinnati: 1888. V. 68; 71; 73

CARTEY, WILFRID
The Africa Reader: Independent Africa. New York: 1970. V. 72

CARTIER-BRESSON, HENRI
About Russia. London: 1974. V. 72
Les Danses A Bali. Paris: 1954. V. 70
The Decisive Moment. New York: 1952. V. 68; 73
The Europeans: Photographs. New York: 1955. V. 68
From One China to the Other. New York: 1956. V. 68
The People of Moscow. New York: 1955. V. 68
The World of Henri Cartier-Bresson. New York: 1968. V. 68

CARTLAND, BARBARA
Husbands and Wives. London: 1961. V. 70; 73
The Passion and the Flower. New York: 1978. V. 68

CARTWRIGHT, A. P.
The Corner House. Cape Town: 1965. V. 72

CARTWRIGHT, EDMUND
The Prince of Peace; and Other Poems. London: 1779. V. 73

CARTWRIGHT, H., MRS.
Letters Moral and Entertaining. London: 1780. V. 69

CARTWRIGHT, JAMES J.
The Memoirs of Sir John Reresby of Thrybergh. London: 1875. V. 73

CARTWRIGHT, WILLIAM
Comedies, Tragi-Comedies with Other Poems. London: 1651. V. 73

CARUS, J. V.
Prodromus Faunae Mediterraneae Sive Descriptio Animalium Maris Mediterranei Incolarum. Stuttgart: 1884-1893. V. 73

CARVER, JONATHAN
Carver's Travels in Wisconsin. New York: 1838. V. 70; 71
Three Years Travels Throughout the Interior Parts of North America for More than Five Thousand Miles. Portsmouth: 1794. V. 70
Travels through the Interior Parts of North America, in the Years 1766, 1767 and 1768. London: 1778. V. 71
Travels through...North America.... London: 1781. V. 69

CARVER, RAYMOND
All of Us. New York: 1998. V. 71; 73
At Night the Salmon Move. Santa Barbara: 1976. V. 68; 69; 71
Call If You Need Me. New York: 2001. V. 68; 69; 72
Carnations: a Play in One Act. Vineburg: 1992. V. 70; 72
Carnations. A Play in One Act. Vineburg, CA: 1993. V. 72
Cathedral. New York: 1983. V. 68; 70; 72; 73
Dostoevsky. A Screenplay. Santa Barbara: 1985. V. 73
Early for the Dance. Concord: 1986. V. 72
Fires. Santa Barbara: 1983. V. 70
Fires. London: 1985. V. 73
If It Please You. Northbridge: 1984. V. 70
In a Marine Light. London: 1987. V. 71
Music. Concord: 1985. V. 71
A New Path to the Waterfall. London: 1989. V. 72
A New Path to the Waterfall. New York: 1989. V. 71; 72; 73
No Heroics, Please. New York: 1992. V. 69; 73
Put Yourself in My Shoes. Santa Barbara: 1974. V. 68; 70; 72
This Water. Concord: 1985. V. 69
Those Days. Elmwood: 1987. V. 69
Two Poems. Salisbury: 1982. V. 70; 73
Two Poems. Concord: 1986. V. 68; 71
Ultramarine. New York: 1986. V. 68; 69; 70; 71; 72
What We Talk About When We Talk About Love. New York: 1981. V. 68; 71; 73
What We Talk About When We Talk About Love. London: 1982. V. 72
Where I'm Calling From. Franklin Center: 1988. V. 68; 70; 71; 72
Where I'm Calling from. New York: 1988. V. 68; 69; 70; 71; 72; 73

Where Water Comes together with Other Water. New York: 1985. V. 70; 71; 72
Will You Please Be Quiet, Please?. New York: 1976. V. 68; 69; 70
Will You Please Be Quiet, Please?. New York: 1978. V. 69

CARVER, ROBIN
Stories About Boston and Its Neighbourhood. Boston: 1833. V. 68

CARWEW, JAN
The Third Gift. Boston: 1974,. V. 72

CARY, ALICE
Pictures of Country Life. New York: 1859. V. 69

CARY, ELISABETH LUTHER
The Works of James MacNeill Whistler. New York: 1907. V. 68

CARY, HENRY
A Practical Treatise on the Law of Partnership, with Precedents of Co-Partnership Deeds. London: 1827. V. 72

CARY, JOHN
Cary's New Itinerary; or an Accurate Delineation of the Great Roads Both Direct and Cross throughout England and Wales.... 1821. V. 73
Traveller's Companion, or a Delineation of the Turnpike Roads of England and Wales. London: 1812. V. 73

CARY, JOYCE
The African Witch. London: 1936. V. 70
Aissa Saved. London: 1932. V. 69
An American Visitor. London: 1933. V. 69; 71
Castle Corner. London: 1938. V. 69
A Fearful Joy. London: 1949. V. 68
The Horse's Mouth. London: 1944. V. 69; 71
The Horse's Mouth. New York: 1944. V. 70; 73
The Horse's Mouth. Rainbird: 1957. V. 73
A House of Children. London: 1951. V. 69
Illustrations by Joyce Cary for the Old Strife at Plant's. Oxford: 1956. V. 71
Mister Johnson. New York: 1951. V. 73
The Old Strife At Plant's. Oxford: 1956. V. 71

CARY, MELBERT
The Woman Without a Country. Boston: 1934. V. 70

CARY, RICHARD MILTON
Skirmishers' Drill and Bayonet Exercise (as Now Used in the French Army) with Suggestions for the Soldier in Actual Conflict. Richmond: 1861. V. 70

CARY, TRISTRAM
Dictionary of Musical Technology. Westport: 1992. V. 73

CARY, VIRGINIA
Letters on Female Character, Address to a Young Lady. Richmond: 1830. V. 69; 70; 73

CARYL, CHARLES
New Era. Presenting the Plans for the New Era Union to Help Develop and Utilize the Best Resources of This Country. Denver: 1897. V. 73

CASANOVA DE SEINGALT, GIROLAMO
Casanova's Escape from Leads - Being His Own Account. London: 1925. V. 68
Casanova's Memoirs. New York: 1946. V. 72
Histoire de Ma Vie. Weisbaden & Paris: 1960-1961. V. 70

CASATI, GAETANO
Ten Years in Equatoria and the Return with Emin Pasha. London and New York: 1891. V. 69
Ten Years in Equatoria and the Return with Emin Pasha. London and New York: 1892. V. 68

CASAUBON, MERIC
De Quatuor Linguis Commentationis pars Prior; quae, de lingua Hebraica; ed de lingua Saxonica. London: 1650. V. 71

CASAUX, CHARLES, MARQUIS DE
Considerations sur Quelques Parties du Mechanisme des Societes. Londres: 1785. V. 71

THE CASE and Appeal of James Ashley, of Bread-Street, in London, Addressed to the Publick in General. In Relation to I. The Apprehending Henry Simons, the Polish Jew, on a Warrant Issued out Against him for Perjury. II. His Trial and Conviction.... London: 1753. V. 70

CASE, E. C.
The Environment of Vertebrate Life in the Late Paleozoic in North America.... Washington: 1919. V. 72
New Reptiles and Stegocephalians from the Upper Triassic of Western Texas. Washington: 1922. V. 70
The Permo-Carboniferous red Beds of North America and the Vertebrate Fauna. Washington: 1915. V. 72

CASE, JOSEPH YOUNG
At Midnight on the 31st of March. Boston: 1938. V. 70

THE CASE of Anthony Earl of Shaftsbury; as It Was Argued Before His Majesties Justices of the King's Bench.... London: 1679. V. 69

THE CASE of the Quo Warranto Against the City of London. Wherein the Judgment in the Case, and the Arguments in Law Touching the Forfeitures and Surrenders of Charters, are Reported. London: 1690. V. 70

CASELA, L.
An Illustrated and Descriptive Catalouge of Surveying, Philosophical, Mathematical, Optical, Photographic and Standard Meteorological Instruments.... 1871. V. 71

CASEMENT, DAN D.
Random Recollections - the Life and Times and Something on the Personal Philosophy of the 20th Century Cowman.. Kansas City: 1955. V. 68; 71; 72

CASES and Resolutions of Cases, Adjudg'd In the Court of King's Bench. Concerning Settlements and Removals, from the First Year of King George I, to the Present Time. London: 1742. V. 69

CASES on Appeals, Concerning the Duties on Houses and Windows, Servants and Inhabited Houses, with the Determinations of the Commissioners and Opinions of all the Judges Thereon. And also an Abstract of the Statutes. London: 1780. V. 70

CASEY, BERNIE
Look at The People. Garden city: 1969. V. 72

CASEY, CLIFFORD
Mirages, Mysteries and Reality: Brewster County Texas, The Big Bend of the Rio Grande. Hereford: 1972. V. 70

CASEY, JOHN
An American Romance. New York: 1977. V. 70; 72
Spartina. New York: 1989. V. 68
Testimony and Demeanor. New York: 1979. V. 71; 72

CASEY, PATRICK
The Strange Story of William Hyde. New York: 1916. V. 71

CASEY, ROBERT J.
The Texas Border and Some Border-Liners: a Chronicle and a Guide. Indianapolis: 1950. V. 71; 73

CASH, M. C.
Origins of New Mexico Families in the Colonial Period. Santa Fe: 1954. V. 69
Our Lady of the Conquest. Santa Fe: 1948. V. 69

CASH, W. J.
The Mind of the South. New York: 1941. V. 70; 71

CASIER, E.
Faune Ichthyologique du London Clay. 1966. V. 72

CASLEY, DAVID
A Catalogue of the Manuscripts of the Kings Library; an Appendix to the Catalogue of the Cottonian Library; Together with an Account of Books Burnt or Damaged by a Late Fire.... London: 1734. V. 70

CASPAR, MAX
Kepler. London and New York: 1959. V. 72

CASPARIAN, HARRY
Instructions: the Law and Approved Forms for Virginia and West Virginia. Charlottesville: 1931. V. 68

CASPER, GERALDINE J.
Glass Paperweight In The Art Institute of Chicago. Chicago: 1991. V. 72

CASPRAY, VERA
Bedelia. London: 1945. V. 69; 70; 73
Bedelia. London: 1946. V. 69
A Chosen Sparrow. New York: 1964. V. 69
Evvie. London: 1960. V. 70
The Husband. New York: 1957. V. 70
Stranger Than Truth. New York: 1946. V. 71
Stranger Than Truth. London: 1947. V. 72

CASS, DONN A.
Negro, Freemasonry and Segregation. Chicago: 1957. V. 72

CASS, LEWIS
A Discourse Delivered at the First Meeting of the Historical Society of Michigan September 18, 1829. Detroit: 1830. V. 70; 72
France and Its King, Court and Government. New York: 1840. V. 73
Substance of a Speech Delivered by Hon. Lewis Cass, of Michigan, in Secret Session of the Senate of the United States, On the Ratification of the Oregon Treaty, with Additions, July 1846. Detroit: 1846. V. 68

CASSADY, NEAL
Drive Five. Pleasant Hill: 1974. V. 69
The First Third. San Francisco: 1971. V. 69; 73

CASSAGNE, ARMAND
Practical Perspective: Applied to Artistic and Industrial Design. 1886. V. 68

CASSAN, SARAH
Poems. London: 1806. V. 69

CASSAVETES, JOHN
Minnie and Moskowitz. Los Angeles: 1973. V. 68; 69; 71

CASSEDY, J. ALBERT
The Firemen's Record, as Gleaned from All Available Sources of the History of the Baltimore City Fire Department.... Baltimore: 1914. V. 69

CASSEL, G.
The Nature and Necessity of Interest. London: 1903. V. 71

CASSELL & CO.
Cassell's Book of In-Door Amusements, Card Games and Fireside Fun. London: 1892. V. 68
Cassell's Household Guide to Every Department of Practical Life.... London: 1884-1885?. V. 68
Great Industries of Great Britain. London: 1878. V. 71

CASSELL, JOHN
Social Science: Being Selections from John Cassell's Prize Essays.... London: 1861. V. 71

CASSELL'S Illustrated History of England. London. V. 70

CASSELS, ROBERT
A Digest of Cases Decided by the Supreme Court of Canada from.... Toronto: 1886. V. 71

CASSELS, WALTER R.
Cotton: an Account of Its Culture in the Bombay Presidency, Prepared from Government Records and Other Authentic Sources in Accordance with a Resolution of the Government of India. Bombay: 1862. V. 71

CASSERLY, GORDON
The Monkey God. New York: c.1929. V. 70

CASSIDY, JOHN
A Station in the Delta. New York: 1979. V. 72

CASSIN, JOHN
Illustrations of the Birds of California, Texas, Oregon, British and Russian America. Philadelphia: 1856. V. 73
Illustrations of the Birds of California, Texas, Oregon, British and Russian America. Austin: 1991. V. 73

CASSIN, RICCARDO
50 Years of Alpinism. London: 1981. V. 69
50 Years of Alpism. 1981. V. 71; 73

CASSINARI, VALENTINO
A Central Pain - a Neurological Survey. Cambridge: 1969. V. 68

CASSIODORUS, FLAVIUS MAGNUS AURELIUS
Variarvm Libri XII. De Anima Liber Vnvs. Augustae Vindelic ex aedibus: 1533. V. 69

CASSIODORUS, MAGNUS ARELIUS
...Psalterii Davidici Expositio: Quoque Plurima Enucleans Que Vel Idioma Aliquod Divino Eloquio Proprium vel Dogma Singularae.... Parisiis: 1519. V. 72

CASSON, EDMUND
Poems. London: 1938. V. 71

CASSON, JOHN
Lewis & Sybil. London: 1972. V. 70

CASSON, STANLEY
Rupert Brooke and Skyros. London: 1921. V. 70

CASTANEDA, CARLOS
Journey to Ixtlan. New York: 1972-1973. V. 73
The Second Ring of Power. New York: 1977. V. 73
A Separate Reality. New York: 1971. V. 73
Tales of Power. New York: 1974. V. 73
The Teachings of Don Juan. Berkeley: 1968. V. 73

CASTELLLANE, BONIFACE LOUIS ANDRE, LE COMPTE DE
The Opinion of Monsieur le Compte de Castellane, on the Declaration of Rights. Delivered on the first of August MDCCLXXXIX, in the French National Assembly. 1789?. V. 73

CASTELLO, IGNAZIO PATERNO
De Vasi Murrini Ragionamento. (with) Ragionamento a Madama N. N. sopra gli Antichi Ornamenti e Trastulli de'Bambini. Florence: 1781. V. 72

CASTERA, J.
History of Catharine II Empress of Russia. London: 1800. V. 73

CASTIER, JULES
Rather Like...Some Endeavors to Assume the Mangles of the Great.... London: 1920. V. 71

CASTIGLIONI, ARTURO
Adventures of the Mind. Philadelphia: 1946. V. 71
A History of Medicine. London: 1947. V. 68
A History of Medicine. New York: 1947. V. 68; 70
A History of Medicine. New York: 1958. V. 70; 72
A History of Medicine. New York: 1971. V. 71

CASTILLO, ANA
The Mixquiahuala Letters. Binghamton: 1986. V. 68; 71

CASTLE, AGNES
Our Sentimental Garden. London: 1914. V. 71; 72

CASTLE, EGERTON
English Book-Plates. London: 1894. V. 72

CASTLE HOWELL SCHOOL
The Castle Howell School Record. Lancaster: 1888. V. 73

CASTLE, R. LEWIS
Packing and Selling Fruit and Vegetables for Cottagers and Small Holders of Land.... London: 1903. V. 68

CASTLE, S.
A Monograph on the Fox Terrier. 1905. V. 68

CASTLE, VERNON, MRS.
My Husband. New York: 1919. V. 69

CASTLEMAN, JOHN B.
Active Service. Louisville: 1917. V. 73

CASTLEMAN, RIVA
American Impressions: Prints Since Pollack. New York: 1985. V. 69
Henri De Toulouse-Lautrec. Images of the 1890's. NY: 1985. V. 72

CASTRO, CASIMIRO
Mexico y Sus Alrededores: Collection de Vistas, Trajes y Monumentos. Mexico: 1972. V. 68

CASWALL, EDWARD
Sketches of Young Ladies.... London: 1838. V. 70

CASWELL, HARRIET S.
Our Life Among the Iroquois Indians. Boston and Chicago: 1892. V. 68

CASWELL, JOHN EDWARDS
Arctic Frontiers - United States Explorations in the Far North. Norman: 1956. V. 69

CATALINA Island California - The Magic Isle. Chicago: 1920. V. 68

CATALOGUE of a Very Extensive and Singularly Curious Collection of Books, Engravings, Drawings and Miniatures Relating to the Two Wards of Farringdon...The Select Topographical and Historical Library of a Gentleman.... London: 1857. V. 70

CATALOGUE of Lubin's Films. Philadelphia: 1899. V. 69

CATALOGUE of the Conjuring Apparatus, Electrical Goods, Steam Boats, Engines &c.... Kensington (London): 1890. V. 72

CATALOGUE of the Exhibition of Objects Ilustrative of the Fine Arts, Natural History, Philosophy, Machinery, Manufactures, Antiquities &c at Ripon for the Benefit of the Mechanics' Institute and the Dispensary. Ripon: 1840. V. 69

CATALOGUE of the Various Agricultural Implements...and Other Articles Exhibited at the Sixty-First Annual Exhibition at York, Saturday June 16th 1900...and Four Following Days. 1900. V. 73

CATALOGUE of the Walter Frank Perkins Agricultural Library. Southampton: 1961. V. 70

CATCOTT, GEORGE SYMES
A Descriptive Account of a Descent Made Into Penpark Hole, in the Parish of Westbury-upon-Trim, in the County of Gloucester, in the Year 1755.... Bristol;: 1792. V. 70

CATE, G. TEN
The Intrinsic Embryonic Development. Amsterdam: 1956. V. 68

CATE, WIRT A.
Two Soldiers; the Campaign Diaries of Thomas J. Key, CSA, Dec. 7, 1863-May 7, 1865 and Robert J. Campbell, USA Jan. 1-July 21, 1864. Chapel Hill: 1938. V. 69

CATESBY, MARK
The Natural History of Carolina, Florida and the Bahama Islands. Savannah: 1974. V. 68; 70

CATHCART, CHARLES W.
Johnston's Students' Atlas of Bones And Ligaments. London: 1885. V. 72

CATHCART, WILLIAM
The Baptist Encyclopaedia. Philadelphia: 1883. V. 68

CATHER, WILLA SIBERT
Alexander's Bridge. Boston & New York: 1912. V. 70; 71
April Twilights. New York: 1923. V. 72
April Twilights. New York: 1933. V. 73
Death Comes for the Archbishop. New York: 1927. V. 68
Death Comes for the Archbishop. New York: 1929. V. 69; 71
Death Comes for the Archbishop. New York: 1937. V. 70
Father Junipero's Holy Family. Lexington: 1955. V. 68
A Lost Lady. New York: 1923. V. 69
Lucy Gayheart. London: 1935. V. 68
Lucy Gayheart. New York: 1935. V. 70; 71; 73
O Pioneers!. Boston/New York: 1913. V. 73
Obscure Destinies. New York: 1932. V. 69
The Old Beauty and Others. New York: 1948. V. 72
On Writing: Critical Studies on Writing as an Art. New York: 1949. V. 72
Sapphira and the Slave Girl. New York: 1940. V. 69; 70; 72; 73
Shadows on the Rock. New York: 1931. V. 68; 70; 71; 73
The Troll Garden. New York: 1905. V. 71; 73

CATHERALL, ARTHUR
Vibrant Brass - a Novel. London: 1954. V. 68

CATHOLIC CHURCH
A Manual of the Ceremonies Used in the Catholic Church. Boston: 1833. V. 71; 73
The Office of the Holy Week, According to the Roman Missal and Breviary. Baltimore: 1810. V. 71
Officium B. Mariae Virginis Nuper Reformatum. Antwerp: 1677. V. 70
Officium in Epiphania Domini, et Per Totam Octavam.... Madrid: 1765. V. 70

CATHOLIC CHURCH. LITURGY & RITUAL. HOURS
Ces Presentes Heures a Lusaige de Romme. Paris. V. 73
Livre De Prieres, Tisse D'Apres les Enluminures des Manuscrits du XIV e au XVIe Siecle. Lyon: 1886. V. 69
Le Livre d'Heures de La Reine Anne De Bretagne. Paris: 1861. V. 69

CATHOLIC CHURCH. LITURY & RITUAL. HOURS
Heures de Nostre Dame a L'Usage de Rome, en Latin et en Francois.... Paris: 1582. V. 70

CATLEY, ANNE
The Life of Miss Anne Catley Celebrated Singing Performer of the Last Century Including an Account of Her Introduction to Public Life.... London: 1888. V. 72

CATLIN, GEORGE
The Boys Catlin, My Life Among the Indians. New York: 1909. V. 68
Catlin's Notes of Eight Year's Travel and Residence in Europe with His North American Indian Collection. New York: 1848. V. 69; 73
Drawings of the North American Indians. Garden City: 1984. V. 71
Episodes from Life Among the Indians and Last Rambles. Norman: 1979. V. 68
Illustrations of the Manners, Customs and Conditions of the North American Indians.... London: 1851. V. 69
Letters and Notes of the Manners, Customs, and Condition of the North American Indians. London: 1841. V. 68; 69; 70; 73
Letters and Notes on the Manners, Customs, and Condition of the North American Indians. London: 1844. V. 72
Letters and Notes on the Manners, Customs and Condition of the North American Indians.... Minneapolis: 1965. V. 68
O-Kee-Pa: a Religious Ceremony and Other Customs of the Mandans. Philadelphia: 1867. V. 69
Shut Your Mouth and Save Your Life. London: 1873. V. 71

CATLOW, AGNES
The Children's Garden and What Made Of It. London: 1865. V. 68
Drops of Water; Their Marvellous and Beautiful Inhabitants Displayed by the Microscope. London: 1851. V. 68; 70

CATON, J. D.
The Antelope and Deer of America.... New York: 1877. V. 72

THE CAT's Party by Tom Mouser, Esq. London: 1860. V. 71

THE CATS' Quadrille. London: 1870. V. 72

CATSIMPOOLAS, NICHOLAS
Methods of Cell Separation. New York: 1977. V. 68

CATTAN, CHRISTOFE DE
La Geomance. Paris: 1571. V. 69; 73

CATTANEO, GIOVANNI, COUNT
The Source, the Strength, and the True Spirit of the Laws. London: 1753. V. 70

CATTELL, J.
American Men of Science. Tempe: 1960-1961. V. 72

CATTERMOLE, E. G.
Famous Frontiermen, Pioneers and Scouts, The Vanguards of American Civilization. Chicago. V. 72

CATULLUS, CAIUS VALERIUS
The Carmina. London: 1894. V. 70; 73
Catulli Veronensis Liber. London: 1896. V. 68
Catulli, Tibulli et Propertii Opera. Birmingham: 1772. V. 69

CAUDWELL, SARAH
The Shortest Way to Hades. London: 1984. V. 69; 70
The Sirens Sang of Murder. London: 1989. V. 69; 70
Thus Was Adonis Murdered. New York: 1981. V. 70; 71

CAUDWELL, VERA
THe Sole Condition. London: 1926. V. 70

CAUFFMAN, STANLEY HART
The Witchfinders. Philadelphia: 1934. V. 69; 70

CAUGHEY, JOHN WALTON
Bernardo De Galvez in Louisiana 1776-1783. Berkeley: 1934. V. 73
Gold is the Cornerstone. Berkeley: 1948. V. 69
Rushing for Gold: Pacific Coast Branch of the American Historical Association. Berkeley: 1949. V. 68

CAULFIELD, JAMES
The Antiquity, Honor and Dignity of Trade, Particularly as Connected with the City of London.... London: 1813. V. 70

CAULFIELD, RICHARD
Journal of the Very Rev. Rowland Davies, LL.D., Dean of Ross. 1847. V. 71

CAULFIELD, S. F. A.
The Dictionary of Needlework. London. V. 72

CAULKING, FRANCES MANWARING
History of New London, Connecticut.... New London: 1852. V. 68

CAULKINS, NEHEMIAH
Narrative of Nehemiah Caulkins, an Extract from "American Slavery, As It Is". New York: 1849. V. 71

CAUNITZ, WILLIAM J.
One Police Plaza. New York: 1984. V. 68

CAUS, ISAAC DE
Hortus Penbrochianus. Le Jardin de Vuilton.... London: 1895. V. 68; 70

CAUSEY, GILBERT
The Cell of Schwann. Edinburgh: 1960. V. 68

CAUSLEY, CHARLES
Farewell, Aggie Weston. Aldington: 1951. V. 70
Underneath the Water. London: 1968. V. 70

CAUSLEY, CHARLES continued
Union Street: Poems. London: 1957. V. 70

CAUSTEN, JAMES H.
View of the Claims of American Citizens, Which Were Reserved Against the French Republic, by the Convention of the 30th of September 1800.... Washington: 1829. V. 73

CAUTLEY, H. MUNRO
Suffolk Churches and Their Treasures. 1954. V. 68

CAUTY, W.
Natura, Philosophia & Ars in Concordia. London: 1772. V. 68; 69
Natura, Philosophia and Ars in Concordia. 1772. V. 71

CAVAFY, C. P.
Collected Poems. London: 1975. V. 69

CAVALCANTI, GUIDO
Sonnets and Ballate of Guido Cavalcanti. London: 1912. V. 73

CAVALLO, A. S.
Tapestries of Europe and of Colonial Peru in the Museum of Fine Arts, Boston. Boston: 1967. V. 69

CAVALLO, TIBERIUS
The Elements or Experimental Philosophy. Philadelphia: 1819. V. 70
An Essay on the Theory and Practice of Medical Electricity. London: 1781. V. 70
The History and Practice of Aerostation. London: 1785. V. 69
A Treatise on the Nature and Properties of Air, and Other Permanently Elastic Fluids, to Which is Prefixed and Introduction to Chymistry. London: 1781. V. 69

CAVANAGH, PROFESSOR
The New Science of the Thumbs and Finger Nails. Toronto: 1916. V. 72

CAVANILLES, ANTONIO JOSE
Icones et Descriptiones Plantarum Quae aut Sponte in Hispania Crescunt. Madrid: 1791. V. 69

CAVAZZA, ELISABETH
Don Finimondone Calabarian Sketches. New York: 1892. V. 68

CAVE, A. J. E.
On the Human Crania from New Guinea. Kingswood: 1937. V. 70; 71
On the Human Crania from New Guinea Collected by Lord Moyne's Expedition. 1937. V. 68

CAVE, C. J. P.
Roof Bosses In Medieval Churches: an Aspect of Gothic Sculpture. Cambridge: 1948. V. 69; 72

CAVE, F. O.
Birds of the Sudan.... Edinburgh: 1955. V. 73

CAVE, HENRY
An Answer to a Paper Importing a Petition of the Archbishop of Canterbury and Six Other Bishops, to His Majesty.... London: 1688. V. 71

CAVE, HENRY W.
Golden Tips. London: 1900. V. 72
Golden Tips. London: 1901. V. 72
Picturesque Ceylon. Colombo and the Kelani Valley. (Volume 3. Nuwara Eliya and Adam's Peak). London: 1893-1895. V. 72

CAVE, HUGH B.
Long Live the Dead. Norfolk: 2000. V. 70

CAVE, JOY B.
What Became of Corporal Pittman?. Portugal Cove: 1976. V. 73

CAVE, RODERICK
The Private Press. London: 1971. V. 70; 71

CAVE, WILLIAM
Scriptorum Ecclesiasticorum: Historia Literaria. London: 1698. V. 70

CAVENDISH, GEORGE
The Life and Death of Cardinal Wolsey. Boston: 1905. V. 68
Life and Death of Thomas Wolsey. London: 1899. V. 73
Life of Cardinal Wolsey...and Metrical Visions.... Chiswick: 1825. V. 70
The Life of Thomas Wolsey, Cardinal, Archbishop of York. 1893. V. 72
The Negotiations of Thomas Woolsey. London: 1641. V. 69; 70

CAVERS, F.
The Inter-Relationships of the Bryophyta. Cambridge: 1911. V. 71

CAWEIN, MADISON
Weeds By The Wall. Louisville: 1901. V. 72

CAWTHORNE, JAMES
Poems, by the Rev. Mr. Cawthorn. London: 1771. V. 73

CAYLEY, CHARLES BAGOT
Poems and Translations. 1880. V. 73
The Psalms in Metre. London: 1860. V. 73
Psyche's Interludes. London: 1857. V. 73

CAYLEY, N.
Australian Parrots. 1938. V. 69; 72
Australian Parrots. Sydney: 1938. V. 69; 70; 73

CAYLUS, COMTE DE
Histoire de Joseph, Accompagnee de Dix Figures Relatives Aux principaux Evenemens de la Vie de Ce Fils du Patriarche Jacob.... Amsterdam: 1757. V. 69

CAZEAUX, P.
A Theoretical and Practical Treatise On Midwifery Including the Attentions Required by the Child from Birth to the Period of Weaning. Philadelphia: 1866. V. 72

CAZELLES, RAYMOND
Illuminations of Heaven and Earth, the Glories of the Tres Riches Heures du Duc de Berry. New York: 1988. V. 70

CAZENAVE, P. L. A.
Lecons sur les Maladies de la Peau. 1856. V. 71
Manual of the Diseases of the Skin. New York: 1846. V. 68

CAZNEAU, WILLIAM L., MRS.
Eagle Pass: or, Life on the Border. New York: 1852. V. 73

CAZOTTE, JACQUES
A Thousand and One Follies and His Most Unlooked-for Lordship. London: 1927. V. 68; 71

CECI, CARLO
Piccoli Bronzi del Real Museo Borbonico.... Naples: 1854. V. 69

CECIL, DAVID
The Cecils of Hatfield House. London: 1973. V. 69
A Portrait of Jane Austen. London: 1978. V. 69

CECIL, HENRY
Brief To Counsel. London: 1958. V. 72
Daughters In Law. London: 1961. V. 71
Independent Witness. London: 1963. V. 71
A Woman Named Anne. London: 1967. V. 71

CECIL, RICHARD
A Friendly Visit to the House of Mourning. New Brunswick: 1801. V. 69

CELAN, PAUL
Selected Poems and Prose of Paul Celan. New York: 2000. V. 72
Wolfsbohne/Wolf's-bean. New York: 1997. V. 73

CELEBRATED Actor-Folks' Cookeries. New York: 1916. V. 69; 73

CELEBRATION of the Seventy-Fifth Anniversary of the Chatham Artillery of Savannah May 1, 1861. Savannah: 1861. V. 69; 70

CELESIA, DOROTHEA
Almida, a Tragedy as It Is Performed at the Theatre Royal in Drury Lane. London: 1771. V. 73

CELINE, LOUIS FERDINAND
Death on the Installment Plan. London: 1966. V. 72
Voyage au Bot de la Nuit. (Journey to the End of Night). Paris: 1932. V. 73

CELIZ, FRANCISCO
Diary of the Alarcon Expedition Into Texas 1718-1719. 1967. V. 70

CELLINI, BENVENUTO
The Autobiography of.... Garden City: 1946. V. 71
Due Trattati uno Intorno alle Otto Principali Arti Dell'Oreficeria. Florence: 1568. V. 72
The Firebrand. New York. V. 70
The Life of Benvenuto Cellini. New York: 1906. V. 68; 71
The Life of Benvenuto Cellini. London: 1927. V. 70
Vita. In Colonia: 1792. V. 72

CELNART, MME.
The Gentleman and Lady's Book of Politeness and Propriety of Deportment, Dedicated to the Youth of Both Sexes. Boston: 1833. V. 69
The Gentleman and Lady's Book of Politeness and Propriety of Deportment, Dedicated to the Youth of Both Sexes. Philadelphia: 1848. V. 73

CELSO DE ROSINIS
Lycevm Lateranense Illvstrivm Scriptorvm Sacri Apostolici Ordinis Clericorum Canonicorum Regularium Salvatoris Lateranensis Elogia. Caesenae: 1970. V. 73

CELSUS, AULUS CORNELIUS
De Medicina Libri Octo, Ex Recognitione Joh. Antonidae Vander Linden. Lugduni Batavorum: 1665. V. 69
Medicinae Libri Octo ex Recensione Leonardi Targa Editio altera accuratior.... Verona: 1810. V. 72

CENDRARS, BLAISE
Panama or The Adventures of My Seven Uncles. New York: 1931. V. 72; 73
La Prose du Transsiberian, et de La Petite Jehanne de France. Paris: 1913. V. 70

CENNINI, CENNINO
A Treatise on Painting. London: 1844. V. 72

CENTENNIAL Celebration of the Ordination and Induction of the Late Rev. Alexander Dick. Presbyterian Minister Maitland, Hants County, Nova Soctia June 21st and 23rd 1903. Truro: 1903. V. 73

CENTRE GEORGES POMPIDOU
Salvador Dali Retrospective 1920-1980. 1980. V. 72

A CENTURY of American Medicine. 1776-1876. Philadelphia: 1876. V. 68
A CENTURY of American Medicine. 1776-1876. Brinklow: 1962. V. 68

CERAMICS of Derbyshire 1750-1975. London: 1978. V. 72

THE CEREMONIES and Religious Customs of the Various Nations of the Known World. London: 1731-1739. V. 69

THE CEREMONIES of a Japanese Marriage. Kobe. V. 69

CERIO, EDWIN
That Capri Air. London: 1929. V. 68; 71; 72

CERMONY, JOHN C.
Life Among The Apaches. San Francisco: 1868. V. 72

CERNOHORSKY, W. O.
Marine Shells of Pacific. 1967-1978. V. 73

CERNY, JAROSLAV
Hieratic Ostraca. Oxford: 1957. V. 70

CERTAIN Sermons or Homilies Appointed to be read in Churches, in the Time of Queen Elizabeth of Famous Memory.... London: 1673. V. 73

CERULLI, DOM
The Jazz World. London: 1962. V. 69; 71

CERVANTES SAAVEDRA, MIGUEL DE
Don Quixote de la Mancha. London: 1842. V. 71
Don Quixote de la Mancha. London: 1930. V. 68; 70; 71
Don Quixote de la Mancha. Madrid: 1966. V. 72
Don Quixote of the Mancha retold by Judge Parry. 1900. V. 73
The First (and Second) Part of the History of the Valorous and Wittie Knight Errant Don Quixote of the Mancha. 1927-1928. V. 71
The History and Adventures of the Renowned Don Quixote. London: 1792. V. 71
The History and Adventures of the Renowned Don Quixote. Dublin: 1796. V. 73
The History of Don Quixote. London: 1880. V. 71
The History of Don Quixote de la Mancha. London: 1922. V. 71
The History of the Renowned Don Quixote de la Mancha. London: 1774. V. 70
The History of the Valorous and Witty Knight-Errant Don Quixote of The Mancha. London: 1901. V. 71
L'Ingenieux Hidalgo Don Quichotte De La manche. Paris: 1869. V. 69
The Much Esteemed History of the Ever Famous Knight, Don Quixote de la Mancha.... London: 1716. V. 69
Two Humorous Novels, viz. A Diverting Dialogue Between Scipio and Bergansa...the Comical History of Rinconete & Cortadillo. London: 1741. V. 72

CERVER, F. A.
Architectural Houses 3: Houses by the Sea. Barcelona: 1991. V. 69; 72

CESARESCO, EVELYN M.
The Fairies' Fountain and Other Stories. London: 1909. V. 71

CESCINSKY, HERBERT
English and American Furniture. New York: 1929. V. 72
English Domestic Clocks. New York: 1968. V. 72
English Furniture of the Eighteenth Century. London: 1909-1911. V. 72
Gentle Art of Faking Furniture. London: 1921. V. 69

CESNOLA, ALEXANDER PALMA DI
Salaminia (Cyprus): the History, Treasures and Antiquities of Salamis in the Island of Cyprus. London: 1882. V. 72
Salaminia (Cyprus): the History, Treasures and Antiquities of Salamis in the Island of Cyprus. London: 1884. V. 71

CESSOLIS, JACOBUS DE
The Game of Chess. London: 1976. V. 70

CHABERT, M. DE
Voyage Fait Pr Ordre du Roi en 1750 et 1751, dans L'Amerique Septentrionale Pour Rectifier les Cartes des Cootes de l'Acadie, de L'Isle Royale & de L'Isle de Terre Neuve.... Paris: 1753. V. 72

CHABON, MICHAEL
The Amazing Adventures of Kavalier and Clay. New York: 2000. V. 68; 70
The Amazing Adventures of Kavalier and Clay. New York: 2001. V. 68
The Mysteries of Pittsburgh. New York: 1988. V. 68; 69; 70; 71; 72; 73
Wonder Boys. New York: 1994. V. 73

CHABOT, FREDERICK C.
The Alamo, Altar of Texas Liberty. San Antonio: 1931. V. 70
The Perote Prisoners. San Antonio: 1934. V. 70
San Antonio and Its Beginnings 1691-1731. San Antonio: 1931. V. 70

CHABOUILLET, A.
Description des Antiquities et Objets d'art Composant le Cabinet de M. Louis Fould. Paris: 1861. V. 69

CHACON, PEDRO
De Triclinio Sive de Modo Convivandi.... Amsterdam: 1689. V. 70

CHADBOURN, JAMES HARMON
Lynching and the Law. Chapel Hill: 1933. V. 71

CHADWICK, E. H., MRS.
In the Footsteps of the Brontes. 1914. V. 70; 73
Mrs. Gaskell. New York: 1911. V. 70
Mrs. Gaskell. 1913. V. 68; 70

CHADWICK, EDWIN
The Health of Nations. London: 1887. V. 71

CHADWICK, HENRY
Sports and Pastimes of American Boys. New York: 1894. V. 72

CHADWICK, JAMES R.
Admission of Women to the Massachusetts Medical Society. Boston: 1882. V. 68

CHADWICK, JOHN READ
The Study and Practice of Medicine by Women.... New York: 1879. V. 69

CHADWICK, W. S.
Life Stories of Big Game. 1930. V. 70

CHADWICK'S 1918 Pocket Guide and City Street Directory with Maps of Los Angeles City and County. Los Angeles: 1917. V. 70

CHAFFERS, WILLIAM
Collector's Handbook of Marks and Monograms on Pottery and Porcelain of the Renaissance and Modern Periods. London: 1877. V. 69; 72
Marks & Monograms on European and Oriental Pottery and Porcelain. London: 1908. V. 72
Marks & Monograms on European and Oriental Pottery and Porcelain. London: 1974. V. 72
Marks and Monograms on Pottery and Porcelain. London: 1866. V. 72
The New Keramic Gallery. London: 1926. V. 72

CHAFFIN, LORAH B.
Sons of the West: Biographical Account of Early Day Wyoming. Caldwell: 1941. V. 69

CHAGALL, BELLA
Burning Lights. New York: 1946. V. 71

CHAGALL, MARC
Chagall Lithographs 1980-1985. New York: 1986. V. 68
Chagall's Posters: a Catalogue Raisonne. New York: 1975. V. 70; 72
Dessins Pour La Bible. Paris: 1960. V. 68
The Jerusalem Windows. New York: 1962. V. 69; 70
The Lithographs of Chagall. Volume I. New York: 1960. V. 69
The Lithographs of Chagall. Volume II. Boston: 1963. V. 69
The Lithographs. Volume II 1957-1962. Monte Carlo: 1963. V. 72
Marc Chagall. New York: 1946. V. 72
Marc Chagall: His Graphic Work. New York: 1957. V. 69

CHAI, C. K.
Taiwan Aboriginals. A Genetic Study of Tribal Variations. Cambridge: 1967. V. 69

CHAILLE, STANFORD
Historical Sketch of the Medical Department of the University of Louisiana: Its Professors and Alumni, from 1835 to 1862. New Orleans: 1861. V. 69; 70

CHAILLOU, JACQUES
Questions de ce temps sur l'Origine et le Mouvement du Sang, Reveues & Augmenteess d'une Explication des Fleveres, Intermittentes. Paris: 1664. V. 71
Recherches de l'Origine et du Mouvement du Sang, du Coeur, et de ses Vaisseaux, du Lait, des Fievres Intermittentes & des Huymeurs. Paris: 1687. V. 70

CHALFANT, W. A.
Outposts of Civilization. Boston: 1928. V. 69
Tales of the Pioneers. Stanford: 1942. V. 69

CHALIAPIN, FEODOR IVANOVICH
Chaliapin - an Autobiography as told to Maxim Gorky. London: 1968. V. 71

CHALK, ELIZA
A Peep into Architecture. London: 1845. V. 68

CHALK, THOMAS
Journals Of The Lives, Travels And Gospel Labours Of Thomas Wilson, And James Dickinson. London: 1847. V. 72

CHALKLEY, THOMAS
A Collection of the Works of that...Servant of Christ...Who Departed This Life in the Island of Tortola, the Fourth Day of the Ninth Month 1741. London: 1791. V. 73

CHALKLIN, CHRISTOPHER WILLIAM
The Provincial Towns of Georgian England: a Study of the Building Process 1740-1820. 1974. V. 72

CHALLENGER Voyage. Physics and Chemistry. 1884-1889. V. 73

CHALMERS, D. G.
Biological Aspects of Occlusive Vascular Disease. Cambridge: 1964. V. 68

CHALMERS, GEORGE
An Apology for the Believers in the Shakespeare-Papers Which were Exhibited in Norfolk Street. London: 1797. V. 70
Considerations on Commerce, Bullion and Coin, Circulation and Exchanges; with a View to Our Present Circumstances. London: 1811. V. 73
An Estimate of the Comparative Strength of Great Britain, During the Present and Four Preceding Reigns; and of the Losses of Her Trade from Every War Since the Revolution. London: 1794. V. 72
Political Annals of the Present United Colines, from their Settlement to the Peace of 1763.... London: 1780. V. 72

CHALMERS, J.
Fighting the Matabele. London/Glasgow/Dublin: 1898. V. 68

CHALMERS, JAMES
The Channel Railway, Connecting England and France. London: 1861. V. 72
Plain Truth: Addressed to the Inhabitants of America. London: 1776. V. 68; 70; 73

CHALMERS, LIONEL
An Account of the Weather and Diseases of South Carolina. London: 1776. V. 73

CHALMERS, P. R.
Birds Ashore and Aforeshore. 1935. V. 71
The Cecil Aldin Book. 1932. V. 68; 70
Deerstalking. 1935. V. 70; 73
Field Sports of Scotland. 1936. V. 69; 71
The History of Hunting. 1936. V. 68
Mine Eyes Unto the Hills. An Anthology of the Highland Forest. London: 1931. V. 71

CHALMERS, PATRICK
The Cricket in the Cage. London: 1933. V. 70; 71

CHALMERS, ROBERT
Ancient Sea-Margins as Memorials of Changes in the Relative Level of Sea and Land. Edinburgh: 1848. V. 70

CHALMERS, THOMAS
The Application of Christianity to the Commercial and Ordinary Affairs of Life, in a Series of Discourses. Glasgow: 1820. V. 72
The Christian and Civic Economy of Large Towns. Glasgow: 1826. V. 69
Observations on a Passage in Mr. Playfair's Letter to the Lord Provost of Edinburgh Relative to the Mathematical Pretensions of the Scottish Clergy. London: 1805. V. 71
On Natural Theology. (with) On the Miraculous and Internal Evidences of the Christian Reveleation.... Glasgow: 1836. V. 71
On the Power Wisdom and Goodness of God as Manifested in the Adaptation of External Nature to the Moral and Intellectual Constitution of Man. London: 1839-1835. V. 69

CHALMERS-HUNT, J. M.
Natural History Auctions 1700-1792.... London: 1976. V. 72

CHALON, JOHN JAMES
Twenty-Four Subjects Exhibiting the Costume of Paris, the Incidents Taken from Nature. London: 1822. V. 69

CHAMBER, JOHN
Beken of Cowes 1897-1914. London: 1966. V. 68

CHAMBER, R.
The Book of Days. London: 1864. V. 70

CHAMBERLAIN, BASIL HALL
A Handbook for Travellers in Japan. London: 1903. V. 72

CHAMBERLAIN, BERNARD P.
A Treatise on the Making of Palatable Table Wines. Charlottesville: 1931. V. 70

CHAMBERLAIN, GEORGE AGNEW
Rackhouse. New York: 1922. V. 70

CHAMBERLAIN, JOSEPH
Mr. Chamberlain's Speeches. London: 1914. V. 71

CHAMBERLAIN, SARAH
The Three Bears. Portland: 1983. V. 73

CHAMBERLAIN, WILT
A View from Above. New York: 1991. V. 71

CHAMBERLAINE, WILLIAM W.
Memoirs of the Civil War Between the Northern and Southern Sections of the United States of America 1861 to 1865. Washington: 1912. V. 69; 70

CHAMBERLAYNE, JOHN
Magnae Britanniae Notitia: or The Present State of Great Britain, with divers Remarks Upon the Antient Statae Thereof. London: 1729. V. 70
Magnae Britanniae Notitia: or, the Present State of Great Britian; with Diverse Remarks Upon the Ancient State Thereof. London: 1737. V. 70

CHAMBERLAYNE, JOHN HAMPDEN
Ham Chamberlayne, Virginian: Letters and Papers of an Artillery Officer in the War for Southern Independence 1861-1865. Richmond: 1932. V. 69; 70

CHAMBERS, A. H.
Observations on the Formation, State and Condition of Turnpike Roads and Other Highways with Suggestions for Their Permanent Improvement on Scientific Principles by means of the Natural Materials of Which they are Composed. London: 1820. V. 72

CHAMBERS, ANDREW J.
Recollections. 1947. V. 70; 71

CHAMBERS, DANA
The Court of Shadows. New York: 1943. V. 68
The Last Secret. New York: 1943. V. 72

CHAMBERS, DAVID
Cock-a-Hoop. Waltham St. Lawrence: 1961. V. 69
Cock-a-Hoop. Pinner, Middlesex: 1976. V. 68; 71
Lucien Pissarro: Notes on a Selection of Woodblocks Held at the Ashmolean Museum. Oxford: 1980. V. 70

CHAMBERS, E.
Cyclopaedia; or, an Universal Dictionary of Arts and Sciences.... London: 1741-1743. V. 70

CHAMBERS, ELEANOR
Blackie's New Systematic English Readers. Second Reader. London: 1913. V. 71

CHAMBERS, ERNEST JOHN
Canada's Fertile Northland. Ottawa: 1907. V. 68

CHAMBERS, H. S.
A Work of Plain Practical Utility. London: 1876. V. 68

CHAMBERS, HOMER F.
The Enduring Rock History of Reminescences of Blackwell, Oklahoma and the Cherokee Strip. Blackwell, OK: 1954. V. 71

CHAMBERS, JESSIE
D. H. Lawrence. A Personal Record. London: 1935. V. 72

CHAMBERS, JOHN
Autobiography of John Chambers. Iowa City: 1908. V. 71
A Pocket Herbal.... Bury St. Edmonds, Gedge: 1800. V. 71

CHAMBERS, JULIUS
On a Margin. New York: 1884. V. 69

CHAMBERS, LENOIR
Stonewall Jackson. New York: 1959. V. 69; 73

CHAMBERS, RICHARD
Catalogue of the Remaining Library of Richard Chambers...also a Selection from a Very Distinguished Library.... London: 1860. V. 70

CHAMBERS, ROBERT
Cyclopaedia of English Literature. London: 1860. V. 71
Explanations: a Sequel to Vestiges of the Natural History of Creation. London: 1845. V. 70
Explorations into the Nature of the Living Cell. Cambridge: 1961. V. 68
Vestiges of the Natural History of Creation. London: 1845. V. 70

CHAMBERS, ROBERT W.
America or The Sacrifice: a Romance of the American Revolution. New York: 1924. V. 71
The Fifth Horseman. New York: 1937. V. 71
In Secret. New York: 1919. V. 69; 70
The Laughing Girl. New York: 1918. V. 71
The Painted Minx. New York: 1930. V. 70
The Slayer of Souls. New York: 1920. V. 70
The Tracer of Lost Persons. New York: 1906. V. 71

CHAMBERS, THEODORE FRELING-HUYSEN
The Early Germans of New Jersey. 1895. V. 69

CHAMBERS, W.
Chambers's Encyclopaedia; a Dictionary of Universal Knowledge. London: 1906. V. 73

CHAMBERS, WHITMAN
Murder for a Wanton. Garden City: 1934. V. 71
Murder for a Wanton. Garden City: 1935. V. 69; 73

CHAMBERS, WILLIAM
The Asiatick Miscellany, Consisting of Translations, Imitations, Fugitive Pieces, Original Productions, etc. Calcutta Printed: 1787. V. 69
Chamber's Miscellany of Useful and Entertaining Tracts. Edinburgh;: 1844-1847. V. 68; 73
Dessins des Edifices, Meubles, Habits, Machines et Ustensiles des Chinois.... London: 1757. V. 68; 70; 72
A Treatise on the Decorative Part of Civil Architecture.... London: 1862. V. 68
Wintering at Mentone. London: 1870. V. 70

CHAMBERS'S *Repository of Instructive and Amusing Tracts.* Edinburgh: 1852-1854. V. 68

CHAMBI, MARTIN
Martin Chambi. Washington: 1993. V. 68

CHAMBLIN, THOMAS S.
Historical Encyclopedia of Texas. 1982. V. 70

CHAMBLISS, J. E.
The Life and Labors of David Livingstone. Philadelphia: 1875. V. 71

CHAMBON DE MONTAUX, NICOLAI
Observationes Clinicae, Curationes Morborum Periculosiorum et Rariorum, aut Phaenomena Ipsorum.... Paris: 1789. V. 73

CHAMFORT, SEBASTIAN ROCH NICHOLAS DE
Maxims and Considerations. Waltham St. Lawrence: 1926. V. 68; 71

CHAMFORT, SEBASTIAN ROCH NICOLAS DE
Maximes et Anecdotes. Monaco: 1944. V. 69

CHAMISSO, ADELBERT VON
Peter Schlemihl. London: 1861. V. 69

CHAMOISEAU, PATRICK
Texaco. Paris: 1992. V. 69

CHAMPION, F. W.
The Jungle in sunlight and Shadow. 1930. V. 72

CHAMPION, SARAH E.
Our Flag: Its History and Changes from 1620-1896. New Haven: 1896. V. 73

CHAMPLAIN, SAMUEL DE
The Voyages and Explorations of Samuel De Champlain (1604-1616). Toronto: 1911. V. 73

CHAMPLIN, JOHN D.
Cyclopedia of Painters and Paintings. New York: 1887. V. 71

CHAMPNEY, LIZZIE W.
In the Sky Garden. Boston: 1877. V. 68
Three Vassar Girls Abroad. Boston: 1883. V. 68

CHANCE, FREDERICK
Some Notable Cumbrians. Carlisle: 1931. V. 72

CHANCE, J.
The Flyfishers' Anthology to Mark the Centenary of the Flyfisher's Club. 1984. V. 68

CHANCE, JAMES FREDERICK
The Pattinsons of Kirklington. London: 1899. V. 72
The Pattinsons of Kirklington. Witherby: 1899. V. 71
Some Notable Cumbrians. Carlisle: 1931. V. 71

CHANCE, JOHN NEWTON
Death Stalks the Cobbled Square. New York: 1946. V. 69

CHANCELLOR, E. BERESFORD
The Annals of Fleet Street. London: 1912. V. 71
Memorials of St. James's Street Together with the Annals of Almack's. London: 1922. V. 71
Original View of London, As It Is, by Thomas Shotter Boys, 1842. London: 1926. V. 71

CHANCELLOR, JOHN
The Dark God. New York: 1928. V. 68; 72

CHANDLER, ERNEST
Awnings and Tents. Construction and Design. New York: 1914. V. 68

CHANDLER, GEORGE
Four Centuries of Banking. As Illustrated by the Bankers, Customers and Staff Associated with the Constituent Banks of Martins Bank Ltd. London: 1963-1968. V. 73
Liverpool Under Charles I. Liverpool: 1965. V. 73

CHANDLER, LLOYD H.
A Summary of the Work of Rudyard Kipling, Including Items Ascribed to Him. New York: 1930. V. 70

CHANDLER, MARY
The Description of Bath. A Poem. London: 1736. V. 69

CHANDLER, MELBOURNE C.
Garryowen In Glory The History of The Seventh United States Regiment of Cavalry. Annandale, VA: 1960. V. 72; 73

CHANDLER, R.
Ionian Antiquities, Published with Permission of the Society of Dilettanti. (with) (The Antiquities) of Ionia, Published by the Society of Dilettanti. Part the Second. London: 1769. V. 68

CHANDLER, RAYMOND
Backfire: Story for the Screen. Santa Barbara: 1984. V. 69; 71; 73
The Ballad of Cat Ballou. Boston: 1956. V. 69
Bang to Rights. London: 1958. V. 71; 73
The Big Sleep. New York: 1939. V. 69; 70; 71
The Big Sleep. Cleveland: 1945. V. 70
Farewell My Lovely. New York: 1940. V. 70
Farewell My Lovely. Cleveland: 1946. V. 70
The Finger Man and Other Stories. New York: 1946. V. 70; 71; 73
Five Sinister Characters. 1945. V. 71
The High Window. New York: 1942. V. 69; 70
The High Window. New York: 1945. V. 72
Killer in the Rain. Boston: 1964. V. 69; 70; 71
Killer in the Rain. London: 1964. V. 72; 73
The Lady in the Lake. New York: 1943. V. 70
The Lady in the Lake. London: 1944. V. 70
Letters: Raymond Chandler and James M. Fox. Santa Barbara: 1978. V. 69; 70; 73
Little Sister. Boston: 1949. V. 71; 72
The Little Sister. London: 1949. V. 69; 70
The Long Good-Bye. London: 1953. V. 71
The Long Goodbye. 1953. V. 68
The Long Goodbye. Boston: 1954. V. 68; 69; 71
The Notebooks of Raymond Chandler and English Summer. New York: 1976. V. 70
Playback. London: 1958. V. 73
The Raymond Chandler Omnibus. London: 1953. V. 71; 72; 73
The Raymond Chandler Papers. New York: 2000. V. 69; 72
Raymond Chandler Speaking. London: 1962. V. 73
Raymond Chandler's Unknown Thriller: The Screenplay of Playback. New York: 1985. V. 69; 70
Red Wind. Cleveland: 1946. V. 70; 73
The Second Chandler Omnibus. London: 1962. V. 73
The Simple Art of Murder. Boston: 1950. V. 69; 71; 72; 73
The Simple Art of Murder. London: 1950. V. 68
The Simple Art of Murder. New York: 1968. V. 71
Spanish Blood: a Collection of Short Stories. Cleveland and New York: 1946. V. 68; 70; 73
Speaking. London: 1962. V. 73
Stories and Early Novels and Later Novels and Other Writings. New York: 1995. V. 69

CHANDLER, RICHARD
Travels in Asia Minor 1764-1765. London: 1971. V. 72

CHANDLER, THOMAS BRADBURY
The Life of Samuel Johnson, D.D. The First President of King's College in New York.... New York: 1805. V. 69

CHANEY, EDWARD
Oxford, China, Italy; Writings in Honour of Sir Harold Action on His Eightieth Birthday. Florence: 1984. V. 70

THE CHANNEL *Islands; or, a Peep At Our Neighbours.* London: 1847. V. 73

CHANNEL TUNNEL CO. LTD.
Notes on the Report of the Economic Advisory Council.... London: 1930. V. 70

CHANNING, WALTER
A Treatise on Etherization in Childbirth. Boston;: 1848. V. 70

CHANNING, WILLIAM ELLERY
Lectures on the Elevation of the Labouring Portion of the Community. London: 1840. V. 71
Poems. Boston: 1843. V. 68; 70; 71; 73
Thoreau: the Poet-Naturalist. Boston: 1902. V. 70

CHANSLOR, ROY
The Ballad of Cat Ballou. Boston: 1956. V. 71
Johnny Guitar. New York: 1953. V. 71; 72

A CHANT, a Myth, a Prayer Pai-Ya-Ti-Ma God of Deward the Drum. San Francisco: 1955. V. 68; 73

CHANTICLEER, Pertelote, Cockalorum, Gock-A-Hoop. Waltham St. Lawrence: 1936-1976. V. 71

CHANTREY, F. L.
Chantrey's Peak Scenery or Views in Derbyshire. Derby: 1886. V. 69

CHANTRY, ART
Instant Litter: Concert Posters from Seattle Punk Culture. Seattle: 1985. V. 70

CHAPELLE, HOWARD I.
Boatbuilding. New York: 1941. V. 70
The History of American Sailing Ships. London: 1935. V. 68
The History of American Sailing Ships. New York: 1935. V. 68; 71; 73

CHAPIN, FREDERIC
Pinkey and the Plumed Knight. Akron: 1909. V. 71

CHAPIN, FREDERICK H.
The Land of the Cliff Dwellers. Boston: 1892. V. 73
Mountaineering in Colorado - The Peaks About Estes Park. Boston: 1889. V. 70; 73

CHAPIN, HARRY
Looking...Seeing: Poems and Song Lyrics by Harry Chapin. Ridgefield: 1975. V. 69

CHAPIN, JAMES P.
The Birds of the Belgian Congo. New York: 1932-1954. V. 70; 73

CHAPIN, OLIVER W.
A History of the First Presbyterian Church of Hanover, 1718-1968. Hanover: 1968. V. 69

CHAPIN, WILLIAM
Wasted. New York: 1972. V. 70

CHAPLIN, CHARLIE
My Trip Abroad. New York: 1922. V. 69; 71

CHAPLIN, PATRICE
By Flower and Dean Street and The Love Apple. London: 1976. V. 69

CHAPLIN, RALPH
Bars and Shadows. New York: 1922. V. 68
Somewhat Barbaric. Seattle: 1944. V. 68
Wobbly. The Rough and Tumble Story of an American Wobbly. Chicago: 1948. V. 68

CHAPLIN, RUTH A.
Types and Bookmaking. Portland: 1943. V. 68

CHAPMAN, A.
The Borders and Beyond - Arctic, Cheviot, Tropic. London: 1924. V. 72
On Safari. 1988. V. 70
Unexplored Spain. 1910. V. 72
Wild Spain. 1893. V. 72

CHAPMAN, A. EDWARDS
The Ready Blade: A Medieval Tapestry. New York: 1934. V. 72

CHAPMAN, ABEL
Bird-Life of the Borders. London: 1889. V. 73
Bird-Life of the Borders on Moorland and Sea, with Faunal Notes Extending over Forty Years. London: 1907. V. 71; 73
Memories of Four Score Years Less Two. 1851-1929. 1930. V. 71; 73
Retrospect. Reminiscences and Impressions of a Hunter- Naturalist in Three Continents 1851-1928. 1928. V. 71
Savage Sudan, It's Wild Tribes, Big Game and Bird Life. 1921. V. 73

CHAPMAN, ARTHUR
The Pony Express. New York: 1932. V. 68; 69; 73

CHAPMAN, B. B.
The Founding of Stillwater - a Case Study in Oklahoma History. Oklahoma City: 1948. V. 68

CHAPMAN BROTHERS
Portrait and Biographical Album of Ingham and Livingston Counties, Michigan. Chicago: 1891. V. 72
Portraits and Biographies of the Governors of Michigan and of the Presidents of the U.S. Chicago: 1885. V. 72

CHAPMAN, CHARLES E.
The Founding of Spanish California: the Northwestward Expansion of New Spain 1687-1783. New York: 1916. V. 68

CHAPMAN, D.
Fallow Deer. 1975. V. 70

CHAPMAN, DENNIS
Biological Membranes. London: 1968-1973. V. 68

CHAPMAN, E.
Memories of Fourscore Years Less Two 1851-1929. 1930. V. 73

CHAPMAN, F. M.
Bird Life, a Guide to the Study of Our Common Birds. 1904. V. 72
The Distribution of Bird-Life in Ecuador. New York: 1926. V. 73
The Warblers of North America. New York: 1923. V. 72

CHAPMAN, FREDERIC
Ancient Royal Palaces in and Near London. London and New York: 1902. V. 68

CHAPMAN, FREDERIK HENRIK
Architectura Navalis Mercatoria. London: 1971. V. 70

CHAPMAN, GUY
A Passionate Prodigality. A Fragment of Autobiography. London: 1965. V. 73

CHAPMAN, JEAN
Do You Remember What Happened. London: 1969. V. 72

CHAPMAN, JOHN JAY
Cupid and Psyche. New York: 1916. V. 68
A Glance Toward Shakespare. Boston: 1922. V. 68
Practical Agitation. New York: 1900. V. 68; 73
The Unity of Human Nature. 1901. V. 68
Victor Chapman's Letters from France. New York: 1917. V. 68; 73
William Lloyd Garrison. New York: 1913. V. 68

CHAPMAN, JOHN RATCLIFFE
Instructions to Young Marksmen.... New York: 1848. V. 69

CHAPMAN, KENNETH M.
The Pottery of San Ildefonso Pueblo. Albuquerque: 1977. V. 71
Pottery of Santo Domingo Pueblo. Santa Fe: 1936. V. 68; 70
Pottery of Santo Domingo Pueblo. Santa Fe: 1936-1938. V. 68
The Pottery of Santo Domingo Pueblo. Santa Fe: 1953. V. 68
Pueblo Indian Pottery of the Post Spanish Period. Santa Fe: 1938. V. 68

CHAPMAN, MARIA WESTON
Right and Wrong in Massachusetts. Boston: 1839. V. 68

CHAPMAN, N.
Discourses on the Elements of Therapeutics and Materia Medica. Philadelphia: 1817. V. 73

CHAPMAN, R. W.
Jane Austen. A Critical Bibliography. Oxford: 1953. V. 70
Jane Austen. Facts and Problems. Oxford: 1948. V. 70

CHAPMAN, WILLIAM
Observations on the Various Systems of Canal Navigation, with Inferences Practical and Mathemataical.... London: 1797. V. 72
Report on the Measures to be Attained to in the Survey of a Line of Navigation, from Newcastle Upon Tyne to the Irish Chancel. Newcastle: 1795-1796. V. 72

CHAPON, FRANCOIS
Rouault Oevre Grave (Graphic Work). Monte Carlo: 1978. V. 70; 72

CHAPONE, HESTER
Letters on the Improvement of the Mind. London: 1815. V. 71
Letters on the Improvement of the Mind. London: 1822. V. 71; 72

CHAPPE D'AUTEROCHE, JEAN
A Voyage to California, to Observe the Transit of Venus.... London: 1778. V. 68; 70; 73

CHAPPELL, EDWARD
Narrative of a Voyage to Hudson's Bay in His Majesty's Ship Rosamond Containing Some Account of the North-Eastern Coast of America and of the Tribes Inhabiting that Remote Region. London: 1817. V. 73

CHAPPELL, FRED
Dagon. New York: 1968. V. 71
The Gaudy Place. New York: 1973. V. 71
The Inkling. New York: 1965. V. 71

CHAPPELL, GEORGE S.
Shoal Water. New York: 1933. V. 71

CHAPPELL, GORDON
Brass Spikes And Horsehair Plumes. Tucson: 1996. V. 72
Search For The Well-Dressed Soldier 1865- 1890. Tucson: 1972. V. 72

CHAPPELL, WALTER
Walter Chappell: Vintage Photographs 1954-1978. New York: 2000. V. 69; 72

CHAPPELL, WILLIAM
Fonteyn: Impressions of a Ballerina. London: 1951. V. 70

CHAPTAL DE CHANTELOUP, JEAN ANTOINE CLAUDE, COMTE
Elements of Chemistry.. 1795. V. 68

CHAPUIS, A.
Automata. A Historical and Technological Study. Neuchatel: 1958. V. 70

CHAPUT, DON
Virgil Earp. Western Peace Officer. 1994. V. 68

CHAR, RENE
A Une Serenite Crispee. Paris: 1951. V. 70

CHARACTERISTIC Sketches of Young Gentlemen. London: 1838. V. 70

CHARAKA CLUB
Proceedings of the Charaka Club. Volumes I-XII. New York: 1902-1985. V. 68
Proceedings of Volume 12. New York: 1985. V. 72
The Proceedings of.... New York: 1910. V. 68
Proceedings of.... New York: 1916. V. 68
Proceedings of.... New York: 1938. V. 68
Proceedings of....Volume 4. New York: 1916. V. 71
Proceedings of...Volume IX. New York: 1938. V. 72

CHARAS, MOYSE
The Royal Pharmacopoea, Galenical and Chymical, According to the Practice of the Most Eminent and Learned Physitians of France. London: 1678. V. 69; 73

CHARCOT, J. M.
Clinical Lectures on Senile and Chronic Diseases. London: 1881. V. 68; 69; 70
Lectures on the Diseases of the Nervous System, Delivered at La Salpetriere...Second Series. London: 1881. V. 69
Lectures on the Localisation of Cerebral and Spinal Diseases. London: 1877-. V. 68

CHARDON, C. E.
The Mycological Explorations of Venezuela. 1934. V. 71

CHARDON, FRANCIS A.
Chardon's Journal at Fort Clark 1834-1839. Pierre: 1932. V. 70; 71; 73
Chardon's Journal at Fort Clark 1834-1839. Pierre: 1937. V. 69

CHARHADI, DRISS BEN HAMED
A Life Full of Holes. New York: 1964. V. 68; 69; 71; 73

CHARKE, CHARLOTTE
A Narrative of the Life of Mrs. Charlotte Charke.... London: 1755. V. 70

CHARLES, BEATRICE ETHEL
Songs in the Night. London: 1894. V. 69

CHARLES ILFELD COMPANY
Wholesale Hard¹vare. 1928. V. 69

CHARLES, ROBERT H.
A Roundabout Turn. London: 1930. V. 71; 73

CHARLES, TOM, MRS.
More Tales of the Tularosa. Alamogordo: 1961. V. 71
Tales of the Tularosa. Alamogordo: 1953. V. 71

CHARLES CAMMELL & CO., LTD.
Views of Works the Property of Charles Cammell and Co. Ltd., Sheffield. Sheffield: 1880?. V. 71

CHARLES D. YOUNG & CO., ENGINEERS, IRON FOUNDERS, CONTRACTOR
Illustrated and Descriptive Catalogue of Machinery, Implements Tools, Manufactured Articles, Raw Materials &c.... London: 1853. V. 71

CHARLES I, KING OF GREAT BRITAIN
His Majesties Answer to a Book entituled, The Declaration of Remonstrance of the Lords and Commons, of the 19th of May, 1642. London: 1642. V. 73
His Majesties Declaration to All His Loving Subjects, Upon Occasion of His Late Message to Both Houses of Parliament, and their refusall to treat with Him for the Peace of the Kingdome. Oxford: 1642. V. 73
His Majesties Declaration to All His Loving Subjects, Occasioned by a False and Scandalous Imputation Laid Upon His Majestie, of an Intention of Raising and Levying War Against Parliament and of Having Raised Force to that End. Cambridge: 1642. V. 73

CHARLES II, KING OF ENGLAND
His Declaration to all His Loving Subjects of the Kingdome of England...Together with his Maiesties Letter of the Same Date; to His Excellence the Ld. Gen. Monck to be Communicated to the L. President of the Council of State. London: 1660. V. 70

CHARLESTON
Annual Report of the City Registrar, Comprising Return of Deaths, with a Classification of the Disease, Age, Sex.... Charleston: 1861. V. 69

CHARLESTON Papers - Sold for the Benefit of the Charleston Trust. London: 1980. V. 71

CHARLESTON, R. J.
Meissen and Other European Porcelain/Oriental Porcelain. National Trust: 1971. V. 72

CHARLETON, RICE
A Treatise on the Bath Waters. Bath: 1754. V. 69

CHARLETON, WALTER
Exercitationes de Differentiis & Nominibus Animalium Quibus Acedunt Mantissa Anatomica, et Quaedam de Variis Fossilium Generibus. Oxford: 1677. V. 72; 73
Exercitationes Physico Anatomicae de Oeconomia Animali, Novis in Medicina Hypothesibus Superstructa, et Mechanice Explicata.... The Hague: 1681. V. 70; 72

CHARLEVOIX, PIERRE FRANCOIS XAVIER DE
History and General Description of New France. Chicago: 1962. V. 73

CHARLOT, JEAN
100 Original Woodcuts by Posada. Mexico: 1947. V. 71

CHARLTON, W. H.
The Life of William Cecil, Lord Burghley...a Description of Burghley House. Stamford: 1847. V. 70; 72

CHARNOCK, JOHN
An History of Marine Architecture Including an Enlarged and Progressive View of the Nautical Regulations and Naval History, Both Civil and Military of All Nations.... London: 1800-1802. V. 70

CHARNOCK, RICHARD STEPHEN
Local Etymology:. London: 1859. V. 72

CHAROSH, PAUL
Berliner Gramophone Records. American Issues, 1892-1900. Westport: 1995. V. 72

CHARRIERE, HENRI
Papillon. London: 1970. V. 70

CHARRON, PIERRE
Of Wisdom. London: 1729. V. 69

CHARTERED GAS LIGHT & COKE CO.
Chartered Gas Company. Description of the Beckton Gas-Works, with Selections from the Working Drawings. London: 1871. V. 69
Considerations on the Nature and Objects of the Intended Light and Heat Company. London: 1808. V. 69
Minutes of Evidence Taken before the Committee to Whom the Bill to Incorporate Certain Persons for Procuring Coke, Oil, Tar, Pitch, Ammoniacal Liquor, Essential Oil and Inflammable Air, from Coal.... London: 1809. V. 69

CHARTERIS, EVAN
The Life and Letters of Sir Edmund Gosse. London: 1931. V. 71

CHARTERIS, LESLIE
The Ace of Knaves. New York: 1937. V. 68
The Ace of Knaves. London: 1938. V. 73
Boodle. London: 1936. V. 73
The Brighter Buccaneer. London: 1933. V. 73
The Brighter Buccaneer. London: 1936. V. 73
Call from the Saint. New York: 1948. V. 70
Daredevil. London: 1929. V. 73
Featuring the Saint. London: 1931. V. 73
Featuring the Saint. London: 1935. V. 73
The First Saint Omnibus. London: 1939. V. 68; 72
The Holy Terror. London: 1936. V. 73
Knight Templar. London: 1937. V. 73
Lady on a Train. 1945. V. 69
Lady on a Train. Hollywood: 1945. V. 71
Lady on a Train. New York: 1945. V. 69
Meet the Tiger!. New York: 1929. V. 69
The Misfortune of Mr. Teal. London: 1935. V. 73
Once More the Saint. London: 1937. V. 73
Prelude for War. London: 1939. V. 73
Saint Around the World. 1957. V. 68
Saint Errant. New York: 1940. V. 69
Saint Errant. London: 1949. V. 68
The Saint Goes On. London: 1936. V. 73
The Saint Goes West. Garden City: 1942. V. 68; 72
The Saint in Miami. London: 1941. V. 70; 71; 73
The Saint in Miami. 1953. V. 73
The Saint in New York. New York: 1935. V. 70
The Saint on Guard. Garden City: 1944. V. 69; 70; 71; 72; 73
Saint Overboard. London: 1973. V. 73
The Saint Steps in. New York: 1943. V. 69; 70; 71
The Saint to the Rescue. New York: 1959. V. 68
Senior Saint. London: 1959. V. 68
Thanks to the Saint. Garden City: 1957. V. 73
Thanks to the Saint. London: 1958. V. 70; 71
Vendetta for the Saint. New York: 1964. V. 68

CHARTERS, ANN
Beats & Company: Portraits of a Literary Generation. 1986. V. 68
Scenes Along the Road. New York: 1970. V. 71

CHARTERS, SAMUEL
Blue Faces: a Portrait of the Blues. Boston: 2000. V. 68
The Country Blues. New York: 1959. V. 68; 73
Jazz. A History of the New York Scene. Garden City: 1962. V. 73
A Sermon, Preached at the Anniversary Meeting of the Society in Scotland for Propagating Christian Knowledge on Thursday June 3, 1779. Edinburgh: 1779. V. 68

CHARTIER, EMILE AUGUSTE
Mars, or the Truth About War. London: 1930. V. 69

CHARYN, JEROME
American Scrapbook. New York: 1969. V. 72
4 Novels. London: 1984. V. 73

CHASE, ALVIN W.
Dr. Chase's Recipes; or Information for Everybody.... Ann Arbor: 1864. V. 69
Dr. Chases's New Receipt Book, or Information for Everybody. Toronto: 1889. V. 73

CHASE, ARTHUR M.
Peril at the Spy Nest. New York: 1943. V. 68

CHASE, BORDEN
Red River. New York: 1948. V. 72

CHASE, CARROLL
The First Hundred Years of United States Territorial Postmarks 1787-1887. Federalsburg: 1950. V. 68; 73

CHASE, CHARLES M.
The Editor's Run in New Mexico and Colorado. Lyndon: 1882. V. 71

CHASE, DORIS HARTER
Crossing the Plains. Sacramento: 1957. V. 68

CHASE, ELIZA B.
Over the Border. Acadia. The Home of "Evangeline". Boston: 1884. V. 72
Transcontinental Sketches. Philadelphia: 1909. V. 70; 72

CHASE, HAROLD W.
Dictionary of American History. New York: 1976. V. 68

CHASE, PHILIP H.
Confederate Treasury Notes. The Paper Money of the Confederate States of America 1861-1865. Philadelphia: 1947. V. 69

CHASE, ROSE MAGILL
Squip, Weep and Pilfrid. London: 1922. V. 69

CHASE, SAMUEL
The Answer and Pleas of Samuel Chase, One of the Associate Justices of the Supreme Court of the United States, to the Articles of Impeachment, Delivered Against Him.... Washington City: 1805. V. 73

CHASE, W. DEMPSTER
History and Reunion of Falley Seminary. Fulton: 1890. V. 73

CHASE-RIBOUD, BARBARA
From Memphis and Penking. New York: 1974. V. 72

CHASTAINE, BEN H.
History Of the 18th U.S. Infantry-First. New York: 1919. V. 72

CHASTELLUX, FRANCOIS JEAN, MARQUIS DE
Travels in North America. Dublin: 1787. V. 69

CHATEAUBRIAND, FRANCOIS AUGUSTE RENE, VICOMTE DE
Recollections of Italy, England and America, with Essays.... Philadelphia: 1818. V. 73
Souvenirs D'Italie, D'angleterre et D'Amerique, Suivis de Morceaux Divers De Morale et de Literature. Londres: 1815. V. 70

CHATELAIN, CLARA DE
The Silver Swan. London: 1847. V. 73

CHATELET, PAUL HAY, MARQUIS DE
Traitte de La Politique De France. (with) Second Partie. Utrecht: 1670. V. 69

CHATHAM, RUSSELL
The Angler's Coast. New York: 1976. V. 69; 73
Silent Seasons. New York: 1978. V. 70

CHATHAM, WILLIAM PITT, EARL OF
Letters Written by the Late Earl of Chatham to His Nephew, Thomas Pitt, Esq. at Cambridge.... London: 1804. V. 68; 72
Letters Written by the Late Earl of Chatham to His Nephew Thomas Pitt.... 1804. V. 73

CHATTAWAY, G. A.
By The Water's Edge. 2000. V. 71

CHATTERTON, EDWARD KEBLE
Old Sea Paintings. 1928. V. 69
Sailing Ships, the Story of Their Development from the Earliest Times to the Present Day. 1909. V. 68

CHATTERTON, FENIMORE C.
Yesterday's Wyoming. Aurora, Colo: 1957. V. 72; 73
Yesterday's Wyoming. Denver: 1957. V. 72

CHATTERTON, FREDERICK
Shop Fronts. 1927. V. 71

CHATTERTON, HENRIETTA GEORGIANA MARCIA, LADY
Leonore, a Tale; and Other Poems. London and Cambridge: 1864. V. 69

CHATTERTON, THOMAS
Poems, Supposed to Have Been Written at Bristol, by Thomas Rowley and Others. 1777. V. 73
Poems, Supposed to Have Been Written at Bristol, by Thomas Rowley and Others. London: 1777. V. 68; 69; 72
Poems Supposed to Have Been Written at Bristol, by Thomas Rowley and Others. Cambridge: 1794. V. 70
Poetical Works. Cambridge: 1842. V. 72
The Rowley Poems. London: 1898. V. 72
Works. (with) His Life, by G. Gregory. London: 1803. V. 69

CHATTO, WILLIAM ANDREW
Scenes and Recollections of Fly-Fishing in Northumberland, Cumberland and Westmoreland. 1834. V. 68; 73

CHATTOCK, R. S.
Wensleydale. London: 1872. V. 73

CHATWIN, BRUCE
Anatomy of Restlessness. 1996. V. 72
In Patagonia. London: 1977. V. 68; 69; 71
In Patagonia. New York: 1977. V. 73

CHATWIN, BRUCE continued
In Patagonia. New York: 1978. V. 68; 71
On the Black Hill. New York: 1943. V. 73
On the Black Hill. London: 1982. V. 69; 70; 71
On the Black Hill. New York: 1982. V. 70
On the Black Hill. New York: 1983. V. 68; 71; 73
Patagonia Revisited. London: 1985. V. 69; 70
Photographs and Notebooks. London: 1993. V. 69; 70; 71
The Songlines. Franklin Center: 1986. V. 68; 71; 72
The Songlines. Franklin Center: 1987. V. 70; 73
The Songlines. London: 1987. V. 69; 71; 72
The Songlines. New York: 1987. V. 70
Utz. London: 1988. V. 68; 71
Utz. New York: 1988. V. 70
The Viceroy of Ouidah. London: 1980. V. 69
The Viceroy of Ouidah. New York: 1980. V. 68; 70; 71
What Am I Doing Here. London: 1989. V. 69; 70

CHAUCER, GEOFFREY
The Canterbury Tales. London: 1934. V. 69
The Complete Works. Oxford: 1894-1900. V. 73
The Merchant's Tale. 1960. V. 71
Poetical Works. London: 1845. V. 72
The Poetical Works. London: 1870. V. 73
The Prioress's Tale and Other Tales by Geoffrey Chaucer. London: 1904. V. 71
The Prologue to the Canterbury Tales of Geoffrey Chaucer. Los Angeles: 1975. V. 73
The Prologue to the Tales of Caunterbeury. 1898. V. 71
The Romaunt of the Rose. 1908. V. 73
The Romaunt of the Rose. 1911. V. 68
Troilus and Criseyde. Waltham St. Lawrence: 1927. V. 68; 72
The Workes of Our Ancient and Learned English Poet, Geffrey Chaucer. London: 1602. V. 68; 69; 70; 72
The Works, a Facsimile of the William Morris Kelmscott Chaucer... Cleveland and New York: 1958. V. 72
The Works of Geoffrey Chaucer. Hammersmith: 1896. V. 68; 70
The Works of Our Antient and Learned English Poet.... London: 1598. V. 70

CHAUDHURI, AMIT
Freedom Song. London: 1998. V. 72
A New World. London: 2000. V. 71; 72

CHAUDON, JEAN BAPTISTE
The Case of Mrs. Mary Catharine Cadiere, Against the Jesuit Father John Baptist Girard. London: 1732. V. 68

CHAUDRON, A. DE V.
Chaudron's Spelling Book. Mobile: 1865. V. 69; 70

CHAUNCEY, CHARLES
A Letter to a Friend, Containing Remarks on Certain Passages in a Sermon Preached by...John Lord Bishop of Landaff.... Boston: 1767. V. 68; 69; 70; 73

CHAUNDLER, CHRISTINE
Arthur and His Knights. London: 1920. V. 72
The Children's Story Hour. London: 1938. V. 73
The Golden Years. 1950. V. 72
Princess Carroty-top and Timothy. London: 1924. V. 69

CHAUVOIS, LOUIS
William Harvey. His Life and Times: His Discoveries; His Methods. London: 1957. V. 68; 72

CHAVEZ, AGUSTIN VELAZQUEZ
Contemporary Mexican Artists. New York: 1937. V. 71

CHAVEZ, FRAY ANGELICO
But Time and Chance. Santa Fe: 1981. V. 73
Clothed With the Sun. Santa Fe: 1939. V. 71
La Conquistadora: the Autobiography of an Ancient Statue. Paterson: 1954. V. 68
Origins of New Mexico Families. Santa Fe: 1954. V. 72
The Oroz Codex. Washington: 1972. V. 71
The Song of Francis. Flagstaff: 1973. V. 68

CHAYTOR, A. H.
Letters to a Salmon Fisher's Sons. 1936. V. 68

THE CHEARFUL Companion, a Collection of Favourite Scots and English Songs, Catches &c. Perth: 1780. V. 73

CHEATHAM, KITTY
A Nursery Garland. New York: 1917. V. 71

A CHECKLIST of the Book Illustrations of John Buckland Wright. Pinner: 1968. V. 73

CHECKLISTS of Twentieth Century Authors. First Series. Milwaukee: 1931. V. 69

CHEDSEY, ZONA
Idaho Country Voices - a People's History from the Pioneers to the Present. Grangeville: 1990. V. 69

CHEEK, JOHN
The Young Angler's Guide...(with) J. Cheek, Fishing Rod and Tackle, Umbrella, Parasol, Walking Stick and Riding Whip Manufacturer (a Trade Catalogue with Prices). London: 1839. V. 70

THE CHEERFUL Warbler, or Juvenile Song Book. 1820. V. 72; 73
THE CHEERFUL Warbler, or Juvenile Song Book. London: 1820. V. 68

CHEESEMAN, BRUCE
The Book of All Christendom: Tom Lea, Carl Hertzog, and the Making of the King Ranch. Kingsville: 1992. V. 70

CHEESMAN, R. E.
Lake Tana and the Blue Nile an Abyssinian Quest. London: 1936. V. 72

CHEETHAM, JAMES
A Narrative of the Suppression by Col. Burr, of the History of the Administration of John Adams, Written by John Wood.... New York: 1802. V. 68

CHEEVER, GEORGE B.
The Dream; or the True History of Deacon Giles's Distillery, and Deacon Jones's Brewery. New York: 1859. V. 68
The Guilt of Slavery and the Crime of Slaveholding. New York: 1860. V. 68
Wanderings of a Pilgrim in the Shadow of Mont Blanc and the Jungfrau Alp. Aberdeen: 1848. V. 69
William Cowper: His Life, Genius and Insanity. London: 1856. V. 68

CHEEVER, HENRY T.
The Whale and His Captors; or, the Whaleman's Adventures and the Whale's Biography, as Gathered on the Homeward Cruise of the "Commodore Preble". London: 1855. V. 68; 70

CHEEVER, JOHN
Atlantic Crossing. Cottondale: 1986. V. 73
The Brigadier and the Golf Widow. New York: 1964. V. 73
The Day the Pig Fell into the Well. Northridge: 1978. V. 68; 71
The Enormous Radio and Other Stories. New York: 1953. V. 68; 73
Expelled. 1987. V. 71
Expelled. Los Angeles: 1987. V. 73
Expelled. Los Angeles: 1988. V. 73
Homage to Shakespeare. Stevenson: 1968. V. 68; 73
The Housebreaker of Shady Hill and Other Stories. New York: 1958. V. 68; 69; 72; 73
The Letters of John Cheever. New York: 1988. V. 72
The National Pastime. Los Angeles: 1982. V. 69
Oh What a Paradise It Seems. New York: 1982. V. 72
Some People, Places and Things That Will Not Appear in My Next Novel. New York: 1961. V. 73
The Stories of John Cheever. New York: 1978. V. 69; 72; 73
The Stories of John Cheever. London: 1979. V. 68
The Wapshot Chronicle. New York: 1957. V. 69
The Wapshot Scandal. New York: 1963. V. 68

CHEEVER, LAWRENCE O.
The House of Morrell. Cedar Rapids: 1948. V. 71

CHEIRO, LOUIS HAMON
Cheiro's Language of the Hand. Chicago and New York: 1894. V. 70

CHEKHOV, ANTON
The Cherry Garden (aka The Cherry Orchard). New Haven: 1908. V. 69
The Horse Stealers and Other Stories. New York: 1921. V. 69
Kashtanka. San Diego: 1995. V. 72
My Life and Other Stories. London: 1920. V. 69
Stories of Russian Life. New York: 1914. V. 68
Three Sisters. Dublin: 1981. V. 70

CHELLEW, T.
West End, City and Provincial Tailoring. 1912. V. 68

CHEMI, JAMES M.
The George L. Leach Correspondence. 1972. V. 70

CHEMIST'S Windows. London: 1915. V. 71

CHENEY, BRAINARD
Lightwood. Boston: 1939. V. 70

CHENEY, EDNAH DOW
Reminiscences. Boston: 1902. V. 69

CHENEY, ROBERT K.
Maritime History of the Merrimac. Shipbuilding. Newburyport: 1964. V. 73

CHENG, S. K.
Shanghai Restaurant Chinese Cookery Book. London: 1936. V. 68

CHENG, T. C.
Aspects of the Biology of Symbiosis. Baltimore: 1971. V. 72

CHENU, J. C.
Manuel de Conchyliologie et de Paleontologie Conchyliologique. Paris: 1859-1962. V. 73

CHER, MARIE
The Door Unlatched. New York: 1928. V. 70

CHEROKEE NATION
Compiled Laws of the Cherokee Nation. Tahlequah: 1881. V. 73

CHERRY, J. L.
Stafford in Olden Times; Being a Reprint of Articles Published in The Staffordshire Advertiser. Stafford: 1890. V. 72

CHESBRO, GEORGE C.
Shadow of a Broken Man. New York: 1977. V. 68; 71; 73

CHESEBROUGH, CAROLINE
Peter Carradine, or the Martindale Pastoral. New York: 1863. V. 71

CHESELDEN, WILLIAM
The Anatomy of the Human Body. London: 1722. V. 73
The Anatomy of the Human Body. London: 1756. V. 68; 72
Oestographia, or the Anatomy of the Bones. London. V. 70; 72

CHESHIRE, F. R.
Bees and Bee Keeping, Scientific and Practical. London: 1886-1888. V. 69

CHESI, G.
The Last Africans. Worgl: 1977. V. 69

CHESLEY, HARRY E.
Adventuring With the Old-Times, Trails Travelled- Tales Told. Midland, TX: 1979. V. 71

CHESNEY, GEORGE T.
The German Conquest of England in 1875 and Battle of Dorking. Philadelphia: 1871. V. 70

CHESNUT, MARY BOYKIN
A Diary from Dixie.... New York: 1905. V. 70

CHESNUTT, CHARLES WADDELL
The Colonel's Dream. New York: 1905. V. 70; 73
The Conjure Woman. Boston and New York: 1899. V. 70; 71; 73
The Marrow of Tradition. Boston: 1901. V. 71
The Short Fiction of Charles W. Chesnutt. Washington, D.C: 1974. V. 72

CHESNUTT, HELEN
Charles Waddell Chesnutt: Pioneer of the Color Line. Chapel Hill: 1952. V. 72

CHESSON, NORA
Old Fairy Legends in New Colours. London: 1903. V. 68
Selected Poems. London: 1906. V. 69
With Louis Wain to Fairyland. London: 1903. V. 70

CHESTER, A. S. M.
Up the Chimney to Ninny Land. London: 1894. V. 68

CHESTER, GEORGE RANDOLPH
Five Thousand an Hour: How Johnny Gamble Won the Heiress. New York: 1912. V. 71
Get Rich Quick Wallingford. London: 1908. V. 71
Wallingford in His Prime. Indianapolis: 1913. V. 68

CHESTER PLAYS
The Chester Play of the Deluge. Waltham St. Lawrence: 1927. V. 68; 72
The Chester Play of the Deluge. London: 1977. V. 70

CHESTER, S. BEACH
The Arsene Lellpline-Herlock Soames Affair. Boulder: 1976. V. 72

CHESTER, WILLIAM REGINALD
Bibliography of Coal Gas; a Subject Index to Interesting Matters Published in Connection with Coal Gas to End of Year 1891. Nottingham: 1892. V. 69

CHESTERFIELD Burlesqued, or, School for Modern Manners. London: 1811. V. 70

CHESTERFIELD, PHILIP DORMER STANHOPE, 4TH EARL OF
Letters...to his Son...Together with Other Pieces.... London: 1774. V. 69; 73
Letters....Written to His Son Philip Stanhope; together with... several other pieces, etc. Dublin: 1776. V. 73
Lord Chesterfield's Advice to His Son on Men and Manners.... London: 1788. V. 73
Miscellaneous Works. London: 1777. V. 69
Miscellaneous Works. London: 1779. V. 70
Practical Morality, or a Guide to Men and Manners.... London: 1813. V. 68

CHESTERFIELD, PHILIP STANHOPE, 2ND EARL OF
Correspondence with Various Ladies.... London: 1930. V. 70

CHESTERMAN, HUGH
The New Decameron. The Fifth Day. Oxford: 1927. V. 70

CHESTERTON, CECIL, MRS.
I Lived in a Slum. London: 1939. V. 71

CHESTERTON, GILBERT KEITH
Appreciations and Criticisms of the Works of Charles Dickens. London: 1911. V. 73
Autobiography. London: 1936. V. 72; 73
The Ball and the Cross. London: 1910. V. 73
Chaucer. London: 1932. V. 72; 73
The Club of Queer Trades. London: 1905. V. 71
The Club of Queer Trades. New York: 1905. V. 73
The Collected Poems. London: 1927. V. 68; 69
The Collected Poems. London: 1954. V. 73
The Coloured Lands. New York: 1938. V. 71
The Defendant. London: 1901. V. 68
The Everlasting Man. London: 1925. V. 73
G. K. Chesterton Explains the English. London: 1935. V. 70
Greybeards at Play, Literature and Art for Old Gentlemen: Rhymes and Sketches. 1900. V. 73
I Say A Democracy Means.... New York: 1941. V. 70
The Incredulity of Father Brown. London: 1926. V. 70; 71; 73
The Innocence of Father Brown. London: 1911. V. 71; 73
The Man Who Knew Too Much. London: 1922. V. 73
The Man Who Knew Too Much. New York: 1922. V. 71
Manalive. 1912. V. 71
Mr. Chesterton Comes to Tea, or; How the King of England Captured Redskin Island. Bedford: 1978. V. 70
The Napoleon of Notting Hill. London: 1904. V. 73
The New Jerusalem. London: 1920. V. 72; 73
Orthodoxy. London: 1909. V. 73
The Outline of Sanity. London: 1926. V. 68
The Paradoxes of Mr. Pond. London: 1936. V. 71
The Poet and the Lunatics. 1929. V. 71
The Poet and the Lunatics. London: 1929. V. 68; 70
The Resurrection of Rome. London: 1930. V. 73
The Resurrection of Rome. London: 1934. V. 72
The Scandal of Father Brown. London: 1935. V. 70; 71; 73
The Secret of Father Brown. London: 1927. V. 71
Tales of the Long Bow. London: 1925. V. 71; 73
What I Saw in America. London: 1922. V. 73
The Wisdom of Father Brown. London: 1914. V. 70; 71

CHESTON, CHARLES
Greece in 1887. London: 1887. V. 71

CHETHAM, JAMES
The Angler's Vade Mecum, or a Compendious Yet Full Discourse of Angling. London: 1700. V. 69

CHETLAIN, AUGUSTUS L.
Recollections of 70 Years. Galena: 1899. V. 70

CHETWODE, ANNA
Blue Stocking Hall. London: 1827. V. 68

CHETWOOD, WILLIAM
The Voyages, Dangerous Adventures and Imminent Escapes of Captain Richard Falconer.... 1764. V. 68

CHETWOOD, WILLIAM RUFUS
A General History of the Stage, from Its Origin in Greece to the Present Time. London: 1749. V. 70; 72
A Tour Through Ireland. In Several Entertaining Letters.... London: 1748. V. 70

CHETWYND, HENRY W.
A March Violet. London: 1883. V. 73

CHEUSE, ALAN
The Bohemians. Cambridge: 1982. V. 71

CHEVALIER, MAURICE
Ma Route et mes Chansons. Paris: 1946. V. 68

CHEVALIER, TRACY
Girl with a Pearl Earring. New York: 2000. V. 68; 72

CHEVES, ELIZABETH WASHINGTON FOOTE
Sketches in Prose and Verse. Baltimore: 1849. V. 73

CHEVEY, PIERRE
Iconographie Ichtyologique de l'Indochine. Saigon: 1932. V. 70; 73

CHEVREUL, M. E.
The Principles of Harmony and Contrast of Colours, and Their Applications to the Arts. London: 1854. V. 69; 71
The Principles of Harmony and Contrast of Colours, and Their Applications to the Arts. London: 1860. V. 70
The Principles of Harmony and Contrast of Colours, and Their Applications to the Arts. London: 1890. V. 73

CHEW, JOEL
The Water-Cure in Pregnancy and Childbirth. New York: 1851-1850. V. 68

CHEYNE, GEORGE
The English Malady; or, a Treatise of Nervous Diseases of All Kinds, as Spleen, Vapours, Lowness of Spirits, Hypochondriacal and Hysterical Distempers &c. in Three Parts. London: 1733. V. 69
The English Malady; or a Treatise of Nervous Diseases of All Kinds, as Spleen, Vapours, Lowness of Spirits, Hypochrondriacal and Hysterical Distempers. London: 1734. V. 72
An Essay on Health and Long Life. London: 1724. V. 70
An Essay on Health and Long Life. London: 1725. V. 70; 72
An Essay on Health and Long Life. London: 1745. V. 70; 72
An Essay on Regimen. Together with Five Discourses, Medical, Moral and Philosophical.... London: 1740. V. 70; 72
Philosophical Principles of Natural Religion.... London: 1705. V. 71
Philosophical Principles of Religion. London: 1724. V. 70
Philosophical Principles of Religion, Natural and Revealed.... London: 1725. V. 70

CHEYNE, T. K.
Encyclopedia Biblica. A Critical Dictinary of the Literary, Political and Religious History.... London: 1903. V. 70

CHEYNE, WILLIAM WATSON
Tuberculous Disease of Bones and Joints: Its Pathology, Symptons and Treatment. Edinburgh and London: 1895. V. 70

CHEYNEY, PETER
Dark Hero. London: 1946. V. 69
The Dark Street. London: 1944. V. 72
Ladies Won't Wait. London: 1951. V. 72
Sinister Errand. London: 1945. V. 72
They Never Say When. London: 1944. V. 69

CHEYNEY, PETER continued
This Man Is Dangerous. London: 1936. V. 70
Try Anything Twice. London: 1948. V. 72

CHEYNEY, RALPH
Touch and Go. New York: 1926. V. 73
Unrest: the Rebel Poets' Anthology for 1929. London: 1930. V. 68

CHIBBETT, DAVID
History of Japanese Printing and Book Illustration. New York: 1977. V. 70

CHICAGO & ALTON RAILROAD
Summer Trips to Chicago and Vactionaland Via.... 1912?. V. 70

CHICAGO & NORTH WESTERN RAILWAY
The Indian, the Northwest 1600-1900. Chicago: 1901. V. 70

CHICAGO ARCHITECTURAL CLUB
13th Annual Exhibiton. Chicago: 1900. V. 68

CHICAGO, BURLINGTON & QUINCY RAILROAD
A Hand Book of Colorado. Chicago: 1902. V. 68
Washington for the Farmer. 1924. V. 72

CHICAGO LITERARY CLUB
The Bryant Celebration by the Chicago Literary Club. Chicago: 1875. V. 68

CHICAGO, MILWAUKEE, ST. PAUL & PACIFIC RAILROAD
South Western North Dakota. 1928. V. 68

CHICHESTER, FRANCIS
The Chichester Star Compass. London: 1945. V. 69

CHICKERING, JESSE
A Statistical View of the Population of Massachusetts from 1765-1840. Boston: 1846. V. 71

CHIFFNEY, SAMUEL
Genius Genuine.... London: 1795. V. 70

CHIHULY, DALE
Chihuly: Color, Glass and Form. Tokyo/New York/S. F: 1986. V. 69

CHIKAMATSU
Masterpieces of Chikamatsu, the Japanese Shakespeare. London: 1926. V. 68

CHIKUSHI, H.
Genes and Genetical Stocks of the Silkworm. Tokyo: 1972. V. 68; 72

CHILD, ANDREW
Overland Route to California. Description of the Route, Via Council Bluffs, Iowa.... Los Angeles: 1946. V. 69; 73

CHILD, HAMILTON
Gazetteer and Business Directory of Wayne county, N.Y., for 1867-8. Syracuse: 1867. V. 72

CHILD, JOSIAH
A New Discourse of Trade.... London: 1694. V. 72
A New Discourse of Trade.... London: 1745?. V. 69; 72

CHILD, LEE
Die Trying. London: 1998. V. 71
Killing Floor. London: 1997. V. 68; 71
Killing Floor. New York: 1997. V. 69; 72
Tripwire. New York: 1999. V. 72

CHILD, LINCOLN
Reliquary. New York: 1997. V. 72

CHILD, LYDIA MARIA
An Appeal in Favor of that Class of Americans Called Africans. Boston: 1833. V. 68; 69
An Appeal in Favor of That Class of Americans Called Africans. New York: 1836. V. 71
The Girl's Own Book. London: 1837. V. 72
Isaac T. Hopper, a True Life. Boston: 1853. V. 68; 69
Letters from New York. (First Series). New York: 1843. V. 73
The Patriarchal Institution as Described by Members of Its Own Family. New York: 1860. V. 73
The Right Way the Safe Way Proved by Emancipation in the British West Indies and Elsewhere. New York: 1860. V. 71

CHILD, MARY S.
The Adventures of Freddie the Frog Combined with the Frog Theatere. New York: 1945. V. 72

CHILDERS, ERSKINE
The Riddle of the Sands. London: 1903. V. 73
The Riddle of The Sands. London: 1927. V. 72

CHILDISH, BILLY
Chatham Town Welcomes Desperate Men. Seattle: 2000. V. 70; 73

THE CHILDREN of Apollo: a Poem. London: 1794?. V. 69

CHILDREN of the Village. London: 1903. V. 69

THE CHILDREN'S Cargo - Lady Cynthia Asquith's Annual. London. V. 72

CHILDREN'S Favourite Tales. London: 1880. V. 69

THE CHILDREN'S Golden Treasure Book for 1937. 1936. V. 71

THE CHILDREN'S Red Books (Volume XI). Chicago: 1908. V. 70

CHILDREN'S Songs with Pictures and Music. 1893. V. 69

CHILDRESS, ALICE
Black Scenes. Garden City: 1971. V. 72
Like One of the Family. Brooklyn: 1956. V. 73
A Short Walk. New York: 1979. V. 73

CHILDRESS, MARK
Crazy in Alabama. New York: 1993. V. 71

THE CHILD'S Easy and Amusing Guide to Reading. Barnstable: 1832-1836. V. 71

CHILD'S First Book. New York: 1858. V. 71

CHILDS, GEORGE
English Landscape Scenery; an Advanced Drawing Book. London: 1860. V. 69

CHILDS, GEORGE BORLASE
On the Improvement and Preservation of the Female Figure.... London: 1840. V. 68

THE CHILD'S Instructor or Picture Alphabet. Glasgow: 1812-1819. V. 70

THE CHILD'S Pictorial Annual 1886. V. 70

CHILTON, JOHN
Who's Who of Jazz. Philadelphia: 1972. V. 71

CHILTON, LANE
New Mexico, a New Guide to the Colorful State. Albuquerque: 1974. V. 70

CHI-LU, CHEN
Material Culture of the Formosan Aborigines. Taipei: 1968. V. 69

CHINA in Miniature.... Boston: 1834. V. 71

CHINARD, GILBERT
The Correspondence of Jefferson and Du Pont de Nemours. Baltimore: 1931. V. 73

CHINESE Bronzes of Yunnan. London: 1983. V. 72

CHINNERY, VICTOR
Oak Furniture, the British Tradition. 1979. V. 69

CHIPMAN, ELIZA ANN
Memoir of Mrs. Eliza Ann Chipman, Wife of the Rev. William Chipman of Pleasant Valley, Cornwallis. Wolfeville: 1855. V. 72

CHIPP, ELINORE
Doubting Castle. New York: 1922. V. 71

CHIPPENDALE, G. M.
Eucalyptus. New York: 1983. V. 71; 73

CHIPPENDALE, JOHN
The Gentleman and Cabinet Makers Director's. London: 1939. V. 72

CHIPPENDALE, THOMAS
Chippendale's One Hundred and Thirty Three Designs of Interior Decorations in the Old French and Antique Styles.... London: 1834. V. 68
Collection of Ornamental Designs, Applicable to Furniture, Frames and the Decoration of Rooms. 1860. V. 68
Gentleman and Cabinet Maker's Director. New York: 1938. V. 71

CHISHOLM, A. H.
The Story of Elizabeth Gould. Melbounre: 1944. V. 72

CHISHOLM, JOE
Brewery Gulch, Frontier Days of Old Arizona- Last Outpost of the Great Southwest. San Antonio: 1949. V. 71

CHISHOLM, L.
The Enchanted Land: Tales Told Again. New York: 1906. V. 69
Nursery Rhymes Told to the Children. London: 1910. V. 69

CHISHULL, EDMUND
Antiquitates Asiaticae Christianam acram Antecedentes.... London: 1728. V. 68; 72

CHISLETT, RALPH
Northward Ho! - For Birds. London: 1933. V. 71
Yorkshire Birds. London: 1953. V. 73

CHISTMAN, HARRY E.
Lost Trails of the Cimarron. Denver: 1961. V. 69

CHITTENDEN, FRED J.
The Royal Horticultural Society Dictionary of Gardening. Oxford: 1976-1977. V. 73

CHITTENDEN, HIRAM MARTIN
The American Fur Trade in the Far West.... New York: 1902. V. 68; 73
H. M. Chittenden; A Western Epic. Tacoma: 1961. V. 72
History Of Early Steamboat navigation On The Missouri River, Life And Adventures of Joseph Labarge, 2 Volumes. New York: 1909. V. 72
A History of the American Fur Trade of the Far West. Stanford: 1954. V. 68
Life, Letters and Travels of Father Pierre Jean De Smet, S. J. 1801- 1873. New York: 1969. V. 69; 73
Thirty Pounds Rails, the Denver and Rio Grandes Narrow Gauge. Palmer Lake. V. 68

CHITTENDEN, NEWTON
Travels in British Columbia. Victoria: 1882. V. 71

CHITTICK, HATTIE
Hantsport. The Smallest Town. Hantsport, Nova Scotia. Hansport: 1940. V. 72

CHITTICK, JAMES
Silk Manufacturing and Its Problems. New York: 1913. V. 69

CHITTICK, V. L. O.
Thomas Chandler Haliburton. A Study in Provincial Toryism. New York: 1924. V. 72

CHITTY, JOSEPH
Supplement to a Treatise on Pleading.... Philadelphia: 1821. V. 73
A Treatise on Pleading and Parties to Actions with Second and Third Volumes. Springfield: 1847. V. 68

CHOCKLETT, GEORGE A.
Tales Told by a Country Parson. Lynchburg: 1930. V. 68

CHODSKO, ALEX
Fairy Tales of the Slav Peasants and Herdsmen-from the French of Alex. Chodsko. London: 1896. V. 70

CHOISEUL MEUSE, FELICITE, COMTESSE DE
Entre Chien et Loup. Londres: 1894. V. 68; 71

CHOISY, FRANCOIS TIMOLEON, ABBE DE
Journal du Voyage de Siam fait en 1685 & 1686. Paris: 1687. V. 68
Journal ou Suite du Voyage du Siam. Amsterdam: 1687. V. 72
Memories Pour Servir a l'Histoire de Louis XIV. Utrecht: 1727. V. 72

CHOLMELEY, ISOBEL CURTIS
The Fountain and Other Poems. London: 1858. V. 69

CHOLMONDELEY PENNELL, H.
The Angler's Naturalist. 1863. V. 68
Bottom or Float-Fishing. London: 1876. V. 68
Fly-Fishing and Worm-Fishing for Salmon, Trout and Grayling. London: 1876. V. 68
The Modern Practical Angler. 1870. V. 68
Puck on Pegasus. London: 1868. V. 71
Trolling for Pike, Salmon and Trout. London: 1876. V. 68

CHOPIN, KATE
The Awakening. Chicago and New York: 1899. V. 73

CHORLEY, HENRY F.
Memorials of Mrs. Hemans, with Illustrations of Her Literary Character From Her Correspondence. New York: 1836. V. 69

CHORLTON, WILLIAM
American Grape Grower's Guide Intended Especially for the American Climate. New York: 1865. V. 68

CHOU, IO
Monographia Rhopalocerorum Sinensium. 1994. V. 72

CHOUKRI, MOHAMED
For Bread Alone. London: 1973. V. 73
Jean Genet in Tangier. New York: 1974. V. 73
Tennessee Williams in Tangier. Santa Barbara: 1979. V. 71; 72; 73

CHOULANT, LUDWIG
History and Bibliography of Anatomic Illustration. Mansfield Centre: 1998. V. 69

CHOYCE Drollery; Songs and Sonnets. Boston, Lincolnshire: 1876. V. 71

CHOYCE, A. NEWBERRY
Crimson Stains Poems of War and Love. London: 1917. V. 70

CHOYSELAT, PRUDENT
The Discours Oeconomique. 1951. V. 69; 73

CHRETIEN, CHARLES PETER
An Essay on Logical Method. Oxford: 1848. V. 72

CHRISMAN, HARRY E.
The Ladder of Rivers- The Story of I. P. Olive. Denver: 1965. V. 71
Lost Trails of the Cimarron. Denver: 1964. V. 71

CHRIST, JAY FINLEY
Flashes by Fanlight. Chicago: 1946. V. 69
Gleanings by Gaslight. Chicago: 1947. V. 69

CHRIST Was Born on Christmas Day. New York: 1864. V. 69

CHRISTENSEN, ERWIN OTTOMER
The Index of American Design. NY and Washington, D.C: 1950. V. 72
Primitive Art. NY: 1955. V. 72

CHRISTIAN Lyrics: Chiefly Selected from Modern Authors. London: 1868. V. 72

CHRISTIAN, CATHERINE M.
Great Stories of All Time. London: 1930. V. 69

CHRISTIAN, EMMA J.
Emma Jane's Cook Book. Willimasburg: 1937. V. 69

THE CHRISTIAN Family Annual. Volume III. New York: 1844. V. 69; 71

CHRISTIAN, GEORGE L.
North Carolina and Virginia in the Civil War. Nashville: 1904. V. 70

CHRISTIAN Lyrics: Chiefly Selected from Modern Authors. London: 1868. V. 68

CHRISTIE, AGATHA
The Adventure of the Christmas Pudding. London: 1960. V. 68; 70; 71
The Agatha Christie Hour. London: 1982. V. 71
And Then There Were None. New York: 1940. V. 71
And Then There Were None. New York: 1945. V. 69
At Bertram's Hotel. London: 1965. V. 68; 70
The Bommerang Clue. New York: 1935. V. 68
Cards at the Table. New York: 1937. V. 73
A Caribbean Mystery. London: 1964. V. 68; 69; 72
A Caribbean Mystery. New York: 1964. V. 69
A Caribbean Mystery. New York: 1965. V. 68
Cat Among the Pigeons. London: 1959. V. 68; 70
The Clocks. New York: 1964. V. 68
The Clocks. New York: 1965. V. 68
Crooked House. London: 1949. V. 73
Crooked House. New York: 1949. V. 69
Curtain. London: 1975. V. 73
A Daughter's a Daughter. London: 1952. V. 71; 72
Dead Man's Folly. London: 1956. V. 70; 73
Dead Man's Folly. New York: 1956. V. 72
Dead Man's Mirror. London: 1937. V. 71
Death Comes as the End. London: 1945. V. 68; 70; 71; 72; 73
Death on the Nile. London: 1937. V. 72
Death on the Nile. 1938. V. 70
Death on the Nile. New York: 1938. V. 68; 69
Destination Unknown. London: 1954. V. 70; 73
Elephants Can Remember. London: 1972. V. 70; 73
The Eleventh Little Nigger. London: 1979. V. 68
Five Little Pigs. London: 1942. V. 72
4:50 from Paddington. London: 1957. V. 68; 69; 70; 71; 73
The Golden Ball and Other Stories. London: 1971. V. 73
Hercule Poirot's Christmas. London: 1939. V. 70
Hickory Dickory Dock. London: 1955. V. 68; 70; 72
The Hollow. London: 1946. V. 72; 73
The Hound of Death and Other Stories. London: 1933. V. 68; 69; 71; 72
The Labours Of Hercules. London: 1947. V. 72; 73
The Man in the Brown Suit. New York: 1924. V. 68; 69; 72
The Mirror Crack'd. London: 1962. V. 70
The Mirror Cracked. New York: 1962. V. 71
Miss Marple's 6 Final Cases. London: 1979. V. 68
Mr. Parker Pyne, Detective. 1934. V. 73
Mr. Parker Pyne Detective. New York: 1934. V. 69; 70
Mrs. McGinty's Dead. London: 1952. V. 73
Mrs. McGinty's Dead. New York: 1952. V. 69
The Mousetrap. 1954. V. 73
The Moving Finger. London: 1943. V. 68; 71
The Moving Finger. London: 1964. V. 68
The Murder at Hazelmoor. New York: 1931. V. 68; 69
Murder at the Vicerage. London: 1930. V. 73
Murder in Mesopotamia. London: 1936. V. 73
Murder in Mesopotomaia. New York: 1936. V. 70
Murder in Retrospect. New York: 1942. V. 69
Murder in the Calais Coach. 1934. V. 69
Murder in the Mews and Other Stories. London: 1937. V. 70; 72; 73
Murder in Three Acts. New York: 1934. V. 68
A Murder Is Announced. London: 1950. V. 71; 73
A Murder is Announced. New York: 1950. V. 70
Murder is Easy. London: 1939. V. 73
The Murder of Roger Ackroyd. 1926. V. 71
The Murder of Roger Ackroyd. New York: 1926. V. 69
The Mysterious Affair At Styles. London: 1921. V. 73
The Mysterious Mr. Quin. London: 1930. V. 73
N Or M?. London: 1941. V. 72
Nemesis. London: 1971. V. 70; 72
Ordeal by Innocence. London: 1958. V. 68; 70; 72; 73
The Pale Horse. London: 1961. V. 73
The Pale Horse. New York: 1962. V. 71
The Pale Horse. New York: 1963. V. 68
Parker Pyne Investigates. London: 1934. V. 73
Peril at End House. 1932. V. 73
A Pocket Full of Rye. London: 1953. V. 73
Postern of Fate. London: 1973. V. 71
The Regatta Mystery. New York: 1964. V. 68
The Rose and the Yew Tree. New York: 1948. V. 72
The Secret Adversary. New York: 1922. V. 70
The Secret of Chimneys. New York: 1925. V. 70
The Seven Dials Mystery. New York: 1929. V. 71
Sleeping Murder: Miss Marple's Last Case. London: 1976. V. 70; 73
Sparkling Cyanide. London: 1945. V. 72
Spider's Web. London: 2000. V. 71
Taken at the Flood. London: 1948. V. 72; 73
Tape-Measure Murder in Fifth Mystery Book. New York: 1944,. V. 71
Ten Little Niggers. London: 1939. V. 73
There is a Tide.... New York: 1948. V. 69; 70
They Came to Baghdad. London: 1951. V. 73
They Came to Baghdad. New York: 1965. V. 68
They Do It With Mirrors. London: 1952. V. 72

CHRISTIE, AGATHA continued
13 for Luck!. London: 1966. V. 68
Towards Zero. London: 1944. V. 72
Towards Zero. London: 1948. V. 70
The Under Dog and Other Stories. 1951. V. 73
Why Didn't They Ask Evans?. London: 1934. V. 73

CHRISTIE, JAMES
A Disquisition Upon Etruscan Vases; Displaying their Probable Connection with the Shows at Eleusis. London: 1806. V. 68; 72
An Essay on the Earliest Species of Idolatry, the Worship of the Elements. Norwich: 1814. V. 73

CHRISTISON, DR.
Manual of Practical Toxicology; Condensed from Dr. Christison's Treatise on Poisons. Baltimore: 1833. V. 71

CHRISTISON, ROBERT
On the Construction of Oil and Coal Gas Burners, and the Circumstances that Influence the Light Emitted by the Gases During Their Combustion.... Edinburgh: 1825. V. 69

CHRIST-JANER, A.
Boardman Robinson.... Chicago: 1946. V. 69; 72

CHRISTMAN, ENOS
One Man's Gold, the Letters and Journals of a Forty-Niner. New York: 1930. V. 73

CHRISTMAS Block Speller. New York: 1895. V. 70

CHRISTMAS Entertainments.... London: 1883. V. 71

CHRISTMAS Eve With the Spirits; or, the Canon's Wanderings through Ways Unknown. 1870. V. 70; 73

THE CHRISTMAS Pantomine. London: 1890. V. 73

CHRISTMAS Roses and New Year's Gift. Boston: 1848. V. 71

CHRISTMAS Roses and New Year's Gift for 1849. Boston: 1849. V. 71

CHRISTMAS Tales of Flanders. London: 1917. V. 73
CHRISTMAS Tales of Flanders. New York: 1917. V. 70

CHRISTMAS with the Poets: a Collection of Songs, Carols and Descriptive Verses, Relating to the Festival of Christmas from the Anglo- Norman Period to the Present Time. London: 1869. V. 68

CHRISTMASTIME in Action. Newton: 1949. V. 70

CHRISTO
Christo: Surrounded Islands, Biscayne Bay, Greater Miami, Florida. New York: 1986. V. 72; 73
Christo: The Pont Neuf, Wrapped, Paris 1975-1985. New York: 1990. V. 72; 73
Over the River (Project for Arkansas River, State of Colorado). (with) The Gates (Project for Central Park, New York City). 1998. V. 73
The Umbrellas, Japan-USA, 1984-1991. Koln: 1998. V. 72; 73
Wrapped Reichstag, Berlin 1971-1996. Koln: 1996. V. 72; 73

CHRISTOPHER, FREDERICK
A Textbook of Surgery by American Authors. Philadelphia: 1942. V. 71

CHRISTY, GEORGE
George Christy's Essence of Old Kentucky. New York: 1862. V. 71

CHRISTY, HOWARD CHANDLER
The American Girl. New York: 1906. V. 69

CHRISTY, MILLER
The Silver Map of the World: A 'Contemporary Medallion Commemorative of Drake's Great Voyage (1577-1580). London: 1900. V. 72

CHRISTY, THOMAS
Thomas Christy's Road Across the Plain. Denver: 1969. V. 70

CHRISTYN, JEAN BAPTISTE
Basilica Bruxelles sive Monumenta Antiqua, Inscriptiones, et Coenotaphia Aedis DD. Michaeli Arachangelo & Gudilae Virgini Sacrae. Amsterdam: 1677. V. 70

CHRONICUM Saxonicum ex MSS. Codicibus Nunc Primum Integrum Edidit.... Oxonii: 1692. V. 69

CHRYSLER, M. A.
The Ferns of New Jersey.... New Brunswick: 1947. V. 68

CHRYSTAL, R. A.
Angling at Lochboisdale. 1939. V. 73

CHUBB, JOHN
The Construction of Locks and Keys. London: 1850. V. 68

CHUBB, RALPH
The Cloud and the Voice. Curridge, Newbury: 1927. V. 73
A Fable of Love and War: a Romantic Poem, Designed and Decorated with Woodcuts by the Author. Curridge, Berkshire: 1925. V. 73
Manhood. Berkshire: 1924. V. 70
Woodcuts. London: 1928. V. 70; 73

CHUINARD, E. G.
Only One Man Died, the Medical Aspects of the Lewis and Clark Expedition. Glendale: 1980. V. 69

CHUKOVSKY, KORNEI
Putanitsa. Leningrad: 1926. V. 70

CH'UN-LIN, C.
A Short History of the Study on Fishes in Huang Po Hai. Shanghai: 1955. V. 73

CHURCH, A. H.
The Chemistry of Paints and Painting. London: 1901. V. 69
Colour. London: 1872. V. 72
Colour. London: 1878. V. 68

CHURCH OF ENGLAND
Articles Whereupon It Was Agreed by the Archbishoppes and Bishoppes of Both Provinces and the Whole Cleargie, in the Convocation Holden at London in the yere...1562.... London: 1571. V. 73
Certaine Sermons or Homilies Appointed to be Read in Chvrches. London: 1623. V. 69; 73
The Orthodox Communicant...According to the Liturgy of the Church of England. London: 1721. V. 70

CHURCH OF ENGLAND. BOOK OF COMMON PRAYER
Book of Common Prayer. Oxford: 1693. V. 72
The Book of Common Prayer. Cambridge: 1761. V. 68
Book of Common Prayer. Cambridge: 1788. V. 73
The Book of Common Prayer. Oxford: 1795. V. 69
The Book of Common Prayer. Oxford: 1798. V. 71
Book of Common Prayer. Cambridge: 1806. V. 72
The Book of Common Prayer. London: 1850. V. 68
The Book of Common Prayer. 1903. V. 71
The Booke of Common Prayer. Edinburgh: 1637. V. 73
The Collects for Sundays and Holydays, Throughout the Year. York: 1799. V. 69

CHURCH OF SCOTLAND
The Confession of Faith, the Larger and Shorter Catechisms.... Philadelphia: 1745. V. 73

CHURCH OF SCOTLAND. BOOK OF COMMON PRAYER
THE Booke of Common Prayer . . . For the Use of the Church of Scotland. Edinburgh: 1637. V. 69; 73

CHURCH, RICHARD
The Food of Life and Other Poems. 1917. V. 70
North of Rome. London: 1960. V. 71
Selected Poems from North of Rome. 1981. V. 68

CHURCH, WILLIAM C.
The Life of John Ericson. New York: 1906. V. 68

CHURCHILL, CHARLES
Gotham, a Poem. London: 1764. V. 70
Memorials of Missionary Life in Nova Scotia. London: 1845. V. 72
Poems. London: 1766. V. 70
Poetical Works. London: 1844. V. 72
The Works. London: 1774. V. 68; 69

CHURCHILL, EDWARD
Wings to the Sun. New York: 1940. V. 69

CHURCHILL, FLEETWOOD
Essays On The Puerperal Fever and Other Diseases Peculiar To Women. London: 1849. V. 72
On the Theory and Practice of Midwifery. London and Dublin: 1842. V. 71

CHURCHILL, RANDOLPH S.
Men, Mines, and Animals in South Africa. London: 1897. V. 72
Winston S. Churchill. London: 1966. V. 70

CHURCHILL, SETON
Betting and Gambling.... London: 1894. V. 71

CHURCHILL, W. A.
Watermarks in Paper in Holland, England, France etc. in the XVII and XVIII Centuries and Their Interconnection. Amsterdam: 1935. V. 70

CHURCHILL, WINSTON
Divi Britannici: Being a Remark Upon the Lives of all the Kings of this Isle, from the Year of the World 2855 unto the Year of grace 1660. London: 1675. V. 69

CHURCHILL, WINSTON LEONARD SPENCER
The Celebrity. New York: 1898. V. 70
Frontiers and Wars. London: 1962. V. 73
Great Contemporaries. London: 1937. V. 68
A History of the English Speaking Peoples. London: 1956. V. 70
A History of the English Speaking Peoples. London: 1956-1958. V. 68; 69
A History of the English Speaking Peoples. New York: 1957-1958. V. 69
Ian Hamilton's March. London: 1900. V. 69; 72
India. Speeches, with an Introduction. 1931. V. 73
London to Ladysmith via Pretoria. London: 1900. V. 69
London to Ladysmith via Pretoria. New York: 1900. V. 70
Lord Randolph Churchill. London: 1906. V. 72; 73
Marlborough. His Life and Times. Volume 1. London: 1936. V. 72
Marlborough. His Life and Times. Volume 2. London: 1936. V. 72
Marlborough. His Life and Times. Volume 3. London: 1936. V. 72
My African Journey. London: 1908. V. 69
Painting as a Pastime. New York: 1950. V. 68
The Second World War. London: 1948-1954. V. 68; 72
The Second World War. London: 1949. V. 70
The Second World War - a History Combining New Selections from the Greatest Chronicler of the War and the Most Memorable Illustrations by the Men Who Took Part In It. New York: 1959. V. 68

CHURCHILL, WINSTON LEONARD SPENCER continued
Step by Step 1936-1939. New York: 1939. V. 70
While England Slept: a Survey of World Affairs 1932-1938. New York: 1938. V. 72

CHURCHMAN, JOHN
An Account of the Gospel Labours, and Christian Experiences of a Faithful Minister of Christ, John Churchman, Late of Nottingham in Pennsylvania, Deceased. Philadelphia: 1779. V. 69
An Account Of The Gospel Labours And Christian Experiences Of A Faithful Minister Of Christ, John Churchman, Late of Nottingham, in Pennsylvania, deceased. London: 1781. V. 72

CHUTE, CAROLYN
The Beans. London: 1985. V. 68
The Beans of Egypt Maine. New York: 1985. V. 68; 73

CHUTE, ROBIN
Shooting Flying. London: 2001. V. 70

CIAMPINI, GIOVANNI
De Sacris Aedificiis a Constantino Magno Constructis Synopsis Historica. Rome: 1693. V. 68; 70; 72

CIARDI, JOHN
An Alpha Bestiary. New York: 1966. V. 73

CIBBER, COLLEY
Another Occasional Letter from Mr. Cibber to Mr. Pope. London: 1744. V. 72
An Apology for the Life of Colley Cibber. London: 1774. V. 73
Apology for the Life of Colley Cibber. 1925. V. 73
An Apology for the Life of Mr. Colley Cibber. London: 1740. V. 68; 71
An Apology for the Life of Mr. Colley Cibber. London: 1822. V. 72
An Apology for the Life of Mr. Colley Cibber. London: 1826. V. 68
An Apology for the Life of Mr. Colley Cibber. London: 1889. V. 71
The Egotist; or Colley Upon Cibber. London: 1743. V. 70
A Letter from Mr. Cibber, to Mr. Pope, Inquiring into the Motive that Might Induce Him in His Satyrical Works, to be so Frequently Fond of Mr. Cibber's Name. London: 1742. V. 73
Love's Last Shift; or, the Fool of Fashion. London: 1696. V. 70

CICERI, PIERRE LUC
Larbouillat. Recueil De Decorations Theatrales et Autres Objets d'Ornement.... Paris: 1830. V. 72

CICERO, MARCUS TULLIUS
Cato Major. London: 1744. V. 69
Cato Major, or His Discourse of Old Age. Philadelphia: 1744. V. 73
Cato; or an Essay on Old Age. London: 1773. V. 72
De Amicitia Dialogus. Lutetiae: 1771. V. 71
De Officiis Libri Tres. cato major, vel de senectute. . . Amsterdam: 1664. V. 71
De Oratore, or, His Three Dialogues Upon the Character and Qualifiations of an Orator. London: 1742. V. 69
De Philosophia. Venetiis: 1523. V. 69
Epistolae Ad Atticum, Ad M. Brutum, Ad Quintum Fratren. Venetiis: 1548. V. 73
Epistolae Familiares. Lvgdvni: 1550. V. 70
Epistolarum. Argentorati: 1581. V. 73
Episttolae Ad Atticum, Ad M. Brutum, Ad Quintum Fratrem: Multorum Locorum Correctione Illustratae.... Venice: 1548. V. 69
The Letters of Marcus Tullius Cicero to Several of His Friends. London: 1799. V. 73
Libri Rhetorici. London: 1830. V. 72
Opera, Quae Supersunt, Omnia, Cum Asconio and Scholiaste Veteri. Amsterdam: 1724. V. 68
Orationes Omnes. Basileae: 1583. V. 73
Orationes Quaedam Selectae. London: 1722. V. 72
Philosophicorvm Volvmen Secundum. Argentorati: 1541. V. 73
Pro A. Clventio M. Tullii Ciceronis Orato. Paris: 1530. V. 73
Rhetoricorum ad C. Herennium Libri III. Incerto Auctore.... Venice: 1559. V. 73
Rhetoricorum ad Herennium Libri Quatuor. Venice: 1550. V. 73
Three Bookes of Dueties to Marcus His Sonne. London: 1558. V. 73
Tully's Three Books of Offices. London: 1699. V. 69; 73
Tvscvlanarvm Qvaestionvm Ciceronis Ad M. Brvtvm Libri F. Venetiis: 1569. V. 73

CIERMANS, JOHANNES
Disciplinae Mathematicae Traditae Anno Institutae Societatis Jesu Seculari. Louvain: 1640. V. 68

CIGARS of the Pharaoh. London: 1971. V. 68

CIKOVSKY, N.
George Inness. New York: 1971. V. 69; 72

CIMENT, MICHAEL
John Boorman. London: 1986. V. 70
Kubrick. New York: 1980. V. 73

CINCINNATI. COMMISSIONERS OF WATERWORKS
A Brief History of the Old Waterworks, Leading Up to and Including the Construction of the New Waterworks.... 1909. V. 70
Report on the Invesitagions Into the Purification of the Ohio River Water for the Improved Water Supply of the City of Cincinnati, Ohio. Cincinnati: 1899. V. 70

CINDERELLA. 1825. V. 71

CINDERELLA.. Philadelphia: 1835. V. 70
CINDERELLA. Albany: 1850. V. 70

CINDERELLA. London: 1852. V. 71
CINDERELLA. London: 1854. V. 71

CINDERELLA.. London: 1904. V. 72; 73
CINDERELLA. New York: 1933. V. 72
CINDERELLA. New York: 1945. V. 70
CINDERELLA. London: 1961. V. 70

CINDERILLA (sic); or the Little Glass Slipper designed for the Entertainment of all Good Little Misses. Albany: 1810. V. 73

THE CINEOGRAPH and Stereopticon Combined, Made Only by S. Lubin, Manufacturer of Life-Motion Picture Machines, Films.... Philadelphia: 1899?. V. 69

CIPRIANI, GIOVANNI BATTISTA
Cipriani's Rudiments of Drawing Engraved by F. Bartolozzi. 1786. V. 71
Monumenti di Fabbriche Antiche Estratti Dai Disegni Dei Piu Celebri Autori. Rome: 1794-1807. V. 68
Su i Dodici Obelischi egizj che Adornano la Citta di Roma. Rome: 1823. V. 70

CIPRIANI, LEONETTO, COUNT
California and Overland Diaries of Count Leonetto Cipriani from 1853- 1871. Portland: 1962. V. 71

CIRANNA, ALFONSO
Giorgio de Chirico: Catalogo Delle Opere Grafiche (Incision e Lithografie) 1921-1969. Milano: 1969. V. 70; 72

CIRCUMNAVIGATION of the Globe. Edinburgh: 1837. V. 68

THE CIRCUS. Philadelphia: 1846?. V. 70

CIRCUS Sights. New York: 1890. V. 70

CIRCUS Tricks. New York: 1890. V. 71

CISNEROS, ANTONIO
Spider Hangs Too Far From the Ground. New York: 1970. V. 73

CISNEROS, JOSE
Jose Cisneros at Paisano. 1969. V. 68
Riders Across the Centuries: Horsemen of the Spanish Borderlands. El Paso: 1988. V. 71

CISNEROS, SANDRA
Bad Boys. San Jose: 1980. V. 68; 73
Woman Hollering Creek. New York: 1991. V. 71

THE CITIZEN'S Pocket Chronicle.... London: 1827. V. 71

THE CITIZEN'S Procession, or, the Smuggler's Success and the Patriots Disappointment. 1733. V. 71

THE CITY of London's Plea to the Quo Warranto (an information) Brought Against Their Charter in Michaelmas Term, 1681. London: 1682. V. 68

THE CITY Of New Brunswick: Its History, Its Homes and Its Industries. New Brunswick: 1908. V. 72

CITY Scenes, or a Peep into London. London: 1828. V. 71

THE CITY Triumphant; or, the Burning of the Excise-Monster. London: 1733. V. 69

CIUBA, GARY M.
Walker Percy: Books of Revelations. Athens: 1991. V. 73

CIVIL War Naval Chronology 1861-1865. Washington: 1961. V. 73

CLAIBORNE, J. F. H.
Life and Correspondence of John A. Quitman. New York: 1860. V. 69
Life and Times of Gen. Sam. Dale, the Mississippi Partisan. New York: 1860. V. 69; 71

THE CLAIMS of the People of England, Essayed. London: 1701. V. 72

CLAIR, COLIN
A History of Printing in Britian. New York: 1966. V. 70

CLAIR, MAXINE
Coping with Gravity. Washington: 1988. V. 68; 73
October Brown. Baltimore: 1992. V. 68
Rattlebone. New York: 1994. V. 68

CLAMPITT, AMY
A Homage to John Keats. New York: 1984. V. 69; 72
Multitudes, Multitudes. New York: 1973. V. 69; 72
What the Light Was Like. New York: 1985. V. 72

CLAMPITT, JOHN W.
Echoes from the Rocky Mountains. Chicago: 1889. V. 69
Echoes from the Rocky Mountains. Chicago: 1890. V. 68

CLAN LAMONT SOCIETY
Clan Lamont Journal of the Clan Lamont Society. Founded 1895. Hereford & Gloucester: 1912-1925. V. 69

CLANCEY, P. A.
A Handlist of the Birds of Southern Mocambique. 1971. V. 69

CLANCY, TOM
The Cardinal of the Kremlin. 1988. V. 70
Debt of Honor. 1994. V. 70
The Hunt for Red October. Annapolis: 1984. V. 68; 69; 70; 71; 72
Patriot Games. New York: 1987. V. 68

CLANCY, TOM continued
Red Storm Rising. New York: 1986. V. 69
Submarine. New York: 1993. V. 70; 71
Without Remorse. 1993. V. 70

CLANDON, HENRIETTA
Inquest. London: 1933. V. 73

CLAPHAM, A. R.
Flora of the British Isles: Illustrations. Cambridge: 1957-1965. V. 73
Upper Teesdale. London: 1978. V. 73

CLAPHAM, RICHARD
The Book of the Otter. Heath Cranton: 1922. V. 71

CLAPP & COMPANY BANKERS
Valuable Information of Leading American Exchanges 1893. New York: 1894. V. 72

CLAPP, HENRY
Husband vs. Wife. New York: 1858. V. 68

CLAPP, SUSANNAH
With Chatwin. New York: 1997. V. 72

CLAPPE, LOUISE AMELIA KNAPP SMITH
California in 1851, The Letters of Dame Shirley, 2 Volumes. San Francisco: 1933. V. 71
The Shirley Letters from California Mines in 1851-1852. San Francisco: 1922. V. 73

CLAPPERTON, HUGH
Journal of A Second Expedition Into the Interior of Africa. London: 1829. V. 72

CLAPPERTON, ROBERT HENDERSON
Modern Paper-Making. Oxford: 1941. V. 72

CLARE, JOHN
Poems by John Clare. Rugby: 1901. V. 73
Poems Chiefly from Manuscript. London: 1920. V. 72
Poems Descriptive of Rural Life and Scenery. London: 1820. V. 73
The Rural Muse, Poems. London: 1835. V. 73
Selected Poems and Prose of John Clare. London: 1967. V. 70
The Shepherd's Calendar; with Village Stories and Other Poems. 1827. V. 71
The Shepherd's Calendar; with Village Stories and Other Poems. London: 1827. V. 73
Sketches in the Life of John Clare by Himself. London: 1931. V. 68
The Village Minstrel and Other Poems. London: 1821. V. 73

CLARE, MARTIN
The Motion of Fluids, Natural and Artificial.... London: 1735. V. 69
The Motion of Fluids, Natural and Artificial.... London: 1747. V. 70

CLAREMON, NEIL
East by Southwest. New York: 1970. V. 73

CLARENDON, EDWARD HYDE, 1ST EARL OF
A Brief View and Survey of the Dangerous and Pernicious Errors to Church and State, in Mr. Hobbes's Book entitled Leviathan. Oxford: 1676. V. 70
History of the Rebellion and Civil Wars in England, Begun In the Year MDCXLI, to The Happy End of the King's Blessed Restoration and Return, 29th May, MDCLX. London. V. 72
History of the Rebellion and Civil Wars of England Begun in the Year 1641.... Oxford: 1705-1706. V. 71
The Life of.... Oxford: 1759. V. 70

CLARIDGE, R. T.
Hydropathy; or the Cold Water Cure, as Practised by Vincent Priessnitz at Graefenberg, Silesia, Austria. London: 1842. V. 71; 72

CLARIDGE, W.
Origin and History of the Bradford Grammar School. Bradford: 1882. V. 73

CLARISSA, PSEUD.
The New Fortune Teller; or the Poetical Fate Book. New York: 1864. V. 68

CLARK, A. H.
The Butterflies of Virginia. Washington: 1951. V. 71; 72
A Monograph of the Exisiting Crinoids. Washington: 1915-1967. V. 69; 72

CLARK, ALAN R.
High Wall. New York: 1936. V. 73

CLARK, ALICE
Working Life of Women in the Seventeenth Century. London: 1919. V. 73

CLARK, ALSON
Wallace Neff: Architect of California's Gold Age. Santa Barbara: 1986. V. 69; 72

CLARK, ANDREW
Practical Directions for Preserving the Teeth.... London: 1825. V. 68; 72
The Shirburn Ballads 1585-1616. Oxford: 1907. V. 72

CLARK, ANN
Little Herder in Spring. Washington: 1941. V. 69

CLARK, ANN NOLAN
Looking-for-Something. New York: 1952. V. 73

CLARK, BARZILLA W.
Bonneville County in the Making. Idaho Falls: 1941. V. 73

CLARK, BETTY
Shall We Join the Ladies? Wood Engravings by Women Artists of the Twentieth Century. Oxford: 1979. V. 70

CLARK, CALVIN PERRY
Two Diaries. Este es: 1962. V. 69

CLARK, CAROL
Thomas Moran - Watercolors of the American West. Austin: 1980. V. 68; 73

CLARK, CAROL HIGGINS
Decked. 1992. V. 70

CLARK, CHARLES
A Summary of Colonial Law, the Practice of the Court of Appeals, from Plantations and of Laws and their Administration in all the Colonies, with Charters of Justice, Orders in Council &c. 1834. V. 70

CLARK, CHARLES E.
Prince and Boatswain: Sea Tales from the Recollection of Rear Admiral Charles E. Clark. Greenfield: 1915. V. 68

CLARK, CHARLES H.
Sedbergh School Classrooms and Cloisters From the Cricket Field. London. V. 73

CLARK, CHARLES HEBER
Elbow Room. London: 1876. V. 68
An Old Fogey. And Other Stories. London: 1891?. V. 68

CLARK, CUMBERLAND
Charles Dickens and Clarson Stanfield. London: 1918. V. 69
Charles Dickens and the Begging Letter Writer. London: 1923. V. 69
Dickens and Democracy. London: 1926. V. 69
Dickens and Talfourd. London: 1919. V. 69
Dickens' London. London: 1923. V. 69
A Study of Mac Beth. 1925. V. 68

CLARK, E.
The Fishes of the Red Sea: Order Plectognathi. Cairo: 1953. V. 71

CLARK, E. KITSON
The History of 100 Years of Life of the Leeds Philosophical and Literary Society. Leeds: 1924. V. 73

CLARK, EDNA MARIA
Ohio Art and Artists. Richmond: 1952. V. 71

CLARK, EDWARD
Description of a Plan for Navigating the Rapids in the Rivers with an Account of Some Experiments, Instituted to Establish Its Practicability. Philadelphia: 1823. V. 68

CLARK, ELLERY H.
Boston Red Sox: 75th Anniversary History 1901-1975. Hicksville: 1975. V. 71
The Strength of the Hills: The Story of Andrew Jackson, and the Pioneers of Tennessee. New York: 1929. V. 69; 72

CLARK, EWAN
Miscellaneous Poems. Whitehaven: 1779. V. 72
The Rustic: a Poem. London: 1805. V. 71

CLARK, G. B.
The Transvaal and Bechuanaland. London: 1882. V. 73

CLARK, GALEN
Early Days in Yosemite Valley. Los Angeles: 1964. V. 70
Indians of the Yosemite. Yosemite Valley: 1904. V. 71
Indians of the Yosemite. Yosemite: 1907. V. 70
Indians of the Yosemite. Yosemite: 1910. V. 68

CLARK, GEORGE ROGERS
Col. George Rogers Clark's Sketch of His Campaign in the Illinois in 1778-9. Cincinnati: 1869. V. 68
The Conquest of the Illinois. 1920. V. 68

CLARK, GEORGIANA C.
Serviettes, Dinner Napkins and How to Fold Them. London: 1875. V. 68

CLARK, H. L.
Cataloque of Recent Ophiurans: Based on the Collection of the Museum of Comparative Zoology. Cambridge: 1915. V. 70

CLARK, HARRY HAYDEN
James Russell Lowell: Representative Selections.... New York: 1947. V. 71

CLARK, HARTLEY
Bokhara, Turkoman and Afghan Rugs. London: 1922. V. 72

CLARK, HARVEY
My Experiences with Burnside's Expediton and 18th Army Corps. Gardner: 1914. V. 70

CLARK, HENRY W.
History of Alaska. New York: 1930. V. 68; 73

CLARK, HUGH
A Short and Easy Introduction to Heraldry in Two Parts. London: 1788. V. 69

CLARK, J. F.
The Society in Search of Truth; or, Stock Gambling in San Francisco. Oakland: 1878. V. 73

CLARK, J. KENT
Goodwin Wharton. London: 1984. V. 70

CLARK, J. L.
Trails of the Hunted. 1928. V. 69

CLARK, J. S.
Life in the Middle West - Reminiscences of J. S. Clark. Chicago. V. 69

CLARK, JAMES
Observations on the Shoeing of Horses; Together with a New Inquiry into the Causes of Diseases in the Feet of Horses. Edinburgh: 1782. V. 73
The Santative Influence of Climate.... London: 1841. V. 68
A Treatise on the Prevention of Diseases Incidental to Horses, from Bad Management in Regard to Stables, Food, Water, Air and Exercise. Philadelphia: 1791. V. 72

CLARK, JAMES A.
Spindletop. New York: 1952. V. 68

CLARK, JAMES MAXWELL
Colonial Days. Denver: 1902. V. 70

CLARK, JEFF
Sun on 6. Illustration by Jasper Johns. Calais: 2000. V. 69; 73

CLARK, JOHN
Elements of Drawing and Painting in Water Colours.... London: 1848. V. 69; 71

CLARK, JOHN WILLIS
The Life and Letters of the Rev. Adam Sedgwick. Cambridge: 1890. V. 68; 69; 71; 72; 73
The Life and Letters of the Reverend Adam Sedgwick. 1970. V. 69

CLARK, JOSHUA J.
Some Fallacies of Seventh Day Adventism. Louisville: 1920. V. 72

CLARK, JUDITH
Arrows of Desire. New York: 1930. V. 72

CLARK, KATE MC COSH
Maori Tales and Legends. London: 1896. V. 68

CLARK, KEITH
Terrible Trail; the Meek Cutoff, 1845. Caldwell: 1966. V. 68; 73

CLARK, KENNETH
Landscape into Art. London: 1949. V. 68; 69; 72
Ruskin Today. London: 1964. V. 68

CLARK, L. J.
Wild Flowers of British Columbia. Sidney: 1973. V. 70; 72; 73

CLARK, LA VERNE HARRELL
The Sang for Horses: the Impact of the Horse on Navajo and Apache Folklore. Tucson: 1966. V. 69

CLARK, LARRY
Kids. New York: 1995. V. 68
Tulsa. New York: 1971. V. 68; 71
Tulsa. New York: 1979. V. 68; 72

CLARK, LATIMER
General Description of the Britannia and Conway Tubular Bridges on the Chester and Holyhead Railway. London: 1850. V. 68

CLARK, LINDSAY
The Chymical Wedding. New York: 1989. V. 71

CLARK, MARY HIGGINS
Aspire to the Heavens: a Portrait of George Washington. New York: 1968. V. 70
Stillwatch. New York: 1984. V. 70
Where Are the Children?. New York: 1975. V. 69

CLARK, MARY SHERRERD
In the Olden Days. Papers Colonial and Revolutionary. Greenwich: 1905. V. 69

CLARK, O. S.
Clay Allison of the Washita. Houston: 1954. V. 69

CLARK, R.
A Picture History of Mountaineering. 1956. V. 68; 71; 73

CLARK, R. INGHAM
A Few Notes on Varnishes and Fossil Resins. London: 1891. V. 68

CLARK, R. S.
Through Shen-Kan. The Account of the Clark Expedition in North China 1908-1909. 1912. V. 73

CLARK, ROBERT A.
The Arthur H. Clark Company. A Bibliography and History 1902-1992. Spokane: 1993. V. 68; 72

CLARK, ROBERT STERLING
Through Shen-kan, the Account of the Clark Expedition in North China 1908-1909. London: 1912. V. 68; 71; 72

CLARK, ROLAND
Roland Clark's Etchings. New York: 1938. V. 68; 70; 73
Stray Shots. New York: 1931. V. 70

CLARK, RONALD W.
The Early Alpine Guides. London: 1949. V. 69
An Eccentric In The Alps. The Story of W. A. B. Coolidge, The Great Victorian Mountaineer. London: 1959. V. 72
Men, Myths and Mountains. London: 1976. V. 69
Mountaineering in Britain. London: 1957. V. 69
The Victorian Mountaineers. London: 1953. V. 69

CLARK, SAMUEL
The Little Mineralogist; or First Book of Mineralogy. London. V. 68; 70

CLARK, SUSIE C.
The Round Trip from the Hub to the Golden Gate. Boston: 1890. V. 69; 71

CLARK, T. & C., CO.
Original Patentees of Enamelled Cast-Iron. London: 1900. V. 68

CLARK, T. B.
Omai: First Polynesian Ambassador to England. San Francisco: 1940. V. 69

CLARK, VAN
Peetie the Pack Rat and Other Desert Stories. 1960. V. 69

CLARK, VICTORIANUS
A Rhyming Geography, or a Poetic Description of the United States of America. &c. Hartford: 1819. V. 68

CLARK, W. E. LE GROS
Early Forerunners of Man. London: 1934. V. 70
Essays on Growth and Form Presented to D'Arcy Wentworth Thompson. Oxford: 1945. V. 70; 71
The Fossil Evidence for Human Evolution. Chicago: 1955. V. 70; 71

CLARK, W. E. LEGROS
The Hypothalamus - Morphological, Functional, Clinical and Surgical Aspects. Edinburgh: 1938. V. 68

CLARK, W. S.
The Circulation of Sap in Plants, a Lecture Delivered Before the Massachusetts State Board of Agriculture, at Fitchburg, December 2, 1873. Boston: 1874. V. 72

CLARK, WALTER
Histories from the Several Regiments and Battalions from North Carolina in the Great War 1861-1865. Goldsboro: 1901. V. 69; 70
Under the Stars and Bars or Memoirs of Four Years Service with the Oglethorpes of Augusta, Georgia. Augusta: 1900. V. 69; 70

CLARK, WALTER TILBURG
The Watchful Gods and Other Stories. New York: 1950. V. 71

CLARK, WILLIAM
Field Notes of Captain William Clark 1803-1805. New Haven: 1964. V. 73

CLARK, WILLIAM BELL
Lambert Wickes, Sea Raider and Diplomat. New Haven: 1932. V. 72

CLARK, WILLIAM L.
Hand-book of the Law of Contracts. St. Paul: 1894. V. 72
Handbook of the Law of Contracts. St. Paul: 1904. V. 72

CLARKE, ADAM
A Bibliographical Dictionary. (with) The Bibliographical Miscellany. Liverpool and London: 1802-1804. V. 69

CLARKE, ARTHUR C.
Childhood's End. London: 1954. V. 70
The Coming of the Space Age. New York: 1967. V. 70; 73
The Deep Range. 1957. V. 69
Islands in the Sky. Philadelphia: 1952. V. 69
The Other Side of the Sky. New York: 1958. V. 70
Rendezvous with Rama. London: 1973. V. 68; 69; 71; 73
Rendezvous with Rama. New York: 1973. V. 68
Sands of Mars. New York: 1952. V. 69
2001 a Space Odyssey. 1968. V. 70; 71
2001 a Space Odyssey. London: 1968. V. 70; 73
2001: a Space Odyssey. New York: 1968. V. 68; 70; 73
2010: Odyssey Two. New York: 1982. V. 72

CLARKE, AUSTIN
The Vengeance of Fionn. Dublin and London: 1917. V. 72

CLARKE, C. B.
Illustrations of Cyperaceae. London: 1909. V. 72
A Review of the Ferns of Northern India. London: 1880. V. 68

CLARKE, C. C.
The Hundred Wonders of The World. London: 1821. V. 72

CLARKE, CHARLES
Architectura Ecclesiastica Londini.... London: 1819. V. 71
Drawing the Corks: Being a Round of Stories for Christmas. London: 1869. V. 69
The Flying Scud, a Sporting Novel. London: 1867. V. 73
Recollections of Writers. London: 1878. V. 70

CLARKE, CHARLES C.
Crumbs from a Sportsman's Table. London: 1879. V. 68

CLARKE, CHARLES COWDEN
The Grasshopper and the Cricket, 30 December 1816. New Rochelle: 1992. V. 73

CLARKE, CHARLES G.
The Men of the Lewis and Clark Expedition - a Biographical Roster of the Fifty-One Members. Spokane: 2001. V. 69

CLARKE, CHARLES HENRY MONTAGUE
Farrago; or Facts, Fun and Fancies. London: 1864. V. 73

CLARKE, CHARLES MANSFIELD
Observations on Those Diseases of Females, Which are Attended by Discharges Illustrated with Copper-Plates of the Diseases &c. London: 1821. V. 70; 71

CLARKE, DONALD HENDERSON
Murderer's Holiday. New York: 1940. V. 71

CLARKE, DWIGHT L.
Stephen Watts Kearny - Soldier of the West. Norman: 1961. V. 70

CLARKE, EDWARD
A Letter to a Friend in Italy (a Poem). And Verses Occasioned on Reading Montfaucon. London: 1755. V. 69

CLARKE, EDWARD DANIEL
Testimonies of Different Authors Respecting the Colossal Statue of Ceres Placed in the Vestibule of the Public Library at Cambridge July the First 1803; with Short Account of Its Removal from Eleusis Nov. 22, 1801. Cambridge: 1803. V. 70
The Tomb of Alexander. Cambridge: 1805. V. 70

CLARKE, EDWARD H.
Sex in Education; or, a Fair Chance for Girls. Boston: 1873. V. 69
Visions: a Study of False Sight (pseudopia). Boston: 1878. V. 71

CLARKE, EDWIN
The Human Brain and Spinal Cord. Berkeley: 1968. V. 68
The Human Brain and Spinal Cord. San Francisco: 1996. V. 68; 70
An Illustrated History of Brain Function. 1972. V. 70
An Illustrated History of Brain Function. San Francisco: 1996. V. 68; 72
Modern Methods in the History of Medicine. London: 1971. V. 71

CLARKE, G. R.
The History and Description of the Town and Borough of Ipswich, Including the Villages and Country Seats in Its Vicinity.... Ipswich: 1830. V. 70; 72

CLARKE, H. C.
Clarke's Confederate Household Almanac for the Year 1863. Vicksburg: 1863. V. 70
Confederate States Almanac and Repository of Useful Knowledge for 1862. Vicksburg: 1862. V. 70
Confederate States Almanac and Repository of Useful Knowledge for the Year 1865. Mobile: 1864. V. 69; 70
Diary of the War for Separation, a Daily Chronicle.... Vicksburg: 1863. V. 70

CLARKE, H. L.
History of Sedbergh School 1525-1925. Sedbergh: 1925. V. 71; 73

CLARKE, H. T.
The Chemistry of Penicillin.... Princeton;: 1949. V. 71

CLARKE, HENRY
A Concise Treatise on the Usury Laws. London: 1824. V. 70

CLARKE, HENRY, & SONS
Wholesale Trade Catalogue of Garden, Agricultural and Flower Seeds. (Season of 1876-1877). 1876. V. 68

CLARKE, HERMANN FREDERICK
John Coney, Silversmith 1655-1722. Boston and New York: 1932. V. 69

CLARKE, ISABEL C.
The Custody of the Children. New York: 1941. V. 71
Decree Nis. New York: 1933. V. 71

CLARKE, J. B. B.
An Account of the Infancy, Religious and Literary Life of the Rev. Adam Clarke. 1833. V. 70

CLARKE, J. JACKSON
Congenital Dislocation of the Hip. London: 1910. V. 71

CLARKE, J. M.
The Eurypterida of New York. Albany: 1913. V. 70; 72

CLARKE, JAMES
History of Cricket in Kendal from 1836 to 1905. Kendal: 1906. V. 71
Practical Directions for Laying Out and Making Roads. Dublin: 1818. V. 72

CLARKE, JOHN
An Essay Upon the Education of Youth in Grammar-Schools. Dublin: 1734. V. 70
Treatise on the Mulberry Tree and Silkworm. Philadelphia: 1839. V. 69

CLARKE, JOHN S.
Satires, Lyrics And Poems. Glasgow: 1919. V. 72; 73

CLARKE, JOSEPH
Schools and School Houses; a Series of Views, Plans and Details for Rural Parishes. 1852. V. 73
Schools and School Houses: a Series of Views, Plans and Details for Rural Parishes. London: 1852. V. 71

CLARKE, LEWIS
Narrative of the Sufferings of Lewis Clarke, During a Captivity of More than Twenty-five Years, Among the Algerines of Kentucky, One of the So Called Christian States of North America. Boston: 1845. V. 69

CLARKE, LINDSAY
The Chymical Wedding - a Romance. London: 1989. V. 69
Sunday Whiteman. London: 1987. V. 68

CLARKE, LOUISA LANE
The Common Seaweeds of the British Coast and Channel Islands.... London: 1865. V. 72
The Common Seaweeds of the British Coast and Channel Islands.... London: 1881. V. 68

CLARKE, M. ST. CLAIR
Cases of Contested Elections, from the Year 1789 to 1834 Inclusive. Washington: 1834. V. 72

CLARKE, MARCUS
Australian Tales of the Bush. Melbourne: 1897. V. 68

CLARKE, MARY ANNE
The Rival Princes. London: 1810. V. 69; 73
The Rival Princes. New York: 1810. V. 69; 73

CLARKE, MARY COWDEN
The Girlhood of Shakespeare's Heroines: a Series of Fifteen Tales. London: 1890. V. 70

CLARKE, MARY WHATLEY
A Century Of Cow Business- The First Years of the Texas and Southwestern Cattle Raisers Association. Fort Worth, TX: 1976. V. 71
David G. Burnet. Austin: 1969. V. 73
The Slaughter Ranches and Their Makers. Austin: 1979. V. 71

CLARKE, MICHAEL
The Arrogant Conoissuer; Richard Payne Knight 1751-1824. Manchester: 1982. V. 73

CLARKE, PETER
Hell and Paradise. The Norfolk - Bounty - Pitcairn Saga. London: 1986. V. 72

CLARKE, S. R.
Hortus Anglicus; or, the Modern English Garden.... London: 1822. V. 69
A Treatise on the Criminal Law as Applicable to the Dominion of Canada. Toronto: 1872. V. 70

CLARKE, SAMUEL
An Item Against Sacriledge; or, Sundry Queries Concerning Tithes. London: 1653. V. 72
The Laws of Chance; or, a Mathematical Investigation of the Probablilities Arising from any Proposed Circumstance of Play. London: 1758. V. 69

CLARKE, SARA KLEIN
The Lord Will Love Thee. Philadelphia: 1959. V. 73

CLARKE, STEPHEN
Clitheroe in Its Old Coaching & Railway Days. Clitheroe: 1929. V. 73
Clitheroe in its Railway Days. Clitheroe: 1900. V. 73

CLARKE, STEPHEN REYNOLDS
The New Lancashire Gazette, or Topographical Dictionary. London: 1830. V. 73

CLARKE, THOMAS BROOKE
An Historical and Political View of the Disorganization of Europe.... London: 1803. V. 72
A Statistical View of Germany, in Respect to the Imperial and Territorial Constitutions, Forms of Government, Legislation, Administration of Justice and Ecclesiastical State.... London: 1790. V. 72

CLARKE, THOMAS C.
The American Railway: Its Construction, Development and Appliances. New York: 1889. V. 70

CLARKE, W. E.
A Handbook of the Vertebrate Fauna of Yorkshire. 1881. V. 73

CLARKE, W. F.
The Canada Farmer: a Fortnightly Journal of Agriculture, Horticulture and Rural Affairs Volume II. January to December 1865. Toronto: 1865. V. 72

CLARKE, WILLIAM
Boy's and Girl's Book of Sports. Providence: 1841. V. 73
Boy's and Girl's Book of Sports. Providence: 1843. V. 73
The Boy's Own Book: A Complete Encyclopedia of All the Diversions, Athletic, Scientific and Recreative of Boyhood and Youth. London: 1848. V. 70
Every Night Book; or, Life After Dark. London: 1827. V. 70
Macy's Book of Sports and Pastimes. New York: 1885. V. 72
Pompeii; Its Past and Present State; Its Public and Private Buildings, etc. London: 1846. V. 73
Three Courses and a Desert. London: 1830. V. 68; 70; 72

CLARKE, WILLIAM EAGLE
Studies in Bird Migration. 1912. V. 69

CLARKE, WILLIAM L.
Hopkins' Selected Cases on the Law of Contracts, Arranged with Reference to Clark's Handbook of Contracts. St. Paul: 1896. V. 71

CLARK-KENNEDY, A. E.
The London 1740-1948. London: 1962. V. 70
Stephen Hales, D.D., F.R.S. Cambridge: 1929. V. 68

CLARKSON, CHRISTOPHER
The History of Richmond, in the County of York;. Richmond: 1814. V. 73

CLARKSON, DAVID
The Case of Protestants in England Under a Popish Prince, If Any Shall Happen to Wear the Imperial Crown. London: 1681. V. 69

CLARKSON, L.
Little Stay-At-Home and Her Friends. Philadelphia: 1879. V. 71; 73

CLARKSON, THOMAS
The History of the Rise, Progress and Accomplishment of the Abolition of the African Slave-Trade by the British Parliament. London: 1808. V. 72
Memoirs of The Public And Private Life Of William Penn. London: 1849. V. 72
Thoughts on the Neccesity of Improving the Condition of the Slaves in the British Colonies.... London: 1823. V. 72

CLASON, CLYDE B.
Blind Drifts. New York: 1937. V. 73
The Death Angel. New York: 1936. V. 73
Dragon's Cave. New York: 1939. V. 71; 73
The Fifth Tumbler. New York: 1936. V. 73
Green Shiver. New York: 1941. V. 73
The Man from Tibet. New York: 1938. V. 73
Murder Gone Minoan. New York: 1939. V. 73
Poison Jasmine. New York: 1940. V. 71; 73
The Purple Parrot. New York: 1937. V. 73
The Whispering Ear. New York: 1938. V. 73

CLASSES of Hazards and Rates of Premiums for Insurance Against Loss or Damage by Fire, in the Cities of New York and Brooklyn. New York: 1846. V. 71

CLATER, FRANCIS
Every Man His Own Cattle Doctor; or a Practical Treatise on the Diseases of Horned Cattle.... Philadelphia: 1815. V. 68

CLAUDE, JEAN
An Historical Defence of the Reformation: in Answer to a Book Intituled, Just Prejudices Against the Calvinists. London: 1683. V. 73

CLAUDIANUS, CLAUDIUS
Opera. Venetiis: 1523. V. 69; 73
Opera. Lvgdvni: 1535. V. 73
Opera Omnia. London: 1821. V. 72
...Quae Exstant. Nic Heinsius Dan. Amsterdam: 1665. V. 72

CLAUDY, CARL H.
The Land of No Shadow. New York: 1933. V. 70

CLAUSEN, R. T.
Sedum of North America North of the Mexican Plateau. Ithaca: 1975. V. 71

CLAVELL, JAMES
The Children's Story. New York: 1981. V. 68; 71
King Rat. Boston and Toronto: 1962. V. 68; 69; 71
Shogun. New York: 1975. V. 68; 69
Shogun. New York: 1983. V. 71
Tai-Pan. New York: 1966. V. 68

CLAVIO, CHRISTOFORO
Arithmetica Prattica.... Rome: 1626. V. 69; 73
Epitome arithmeticae Practicae. Romae: 1585. V. 73

CLAXTON, WILLIAM
Jazz West Coast. Hollywood: 1954. V. 72; 73
Steve McQueen. Santa Fe: 2000. V. 68

CLAY, C. H.
Design of Fishways and Other Fish Facilities. 1961. V. 68

CLAY, CHARLES
Geological Sketches and Observations, on Vegetable Fossil Remains &c.... London: 1839. V. 71

CLAY, ENID
Sonnets and Verses. Waltham St. Lawrence: 1925. V. 68; 70; 72

CLAY, JEHU CURTIS
Annals of the Swedes on the Delaware from Their First Settlement in 1636 to the Present Time. Philadelphia: 1858. V. 69

CLAY, JOHN
My Life On the Range. Chicago: 1924. V. 71
My Recollections of Ontario. Chicago: 1918. V. 68; 71
Old Days Recalled. Chicago: 1915. V. 69; 71

CLAY, R. S.
The History of the Microscope. London: 1975. V. 68

CLAY, ROBERT
Carmen Sheila. Philadelphia: 1929. V. 71

CLAYE, ANDREW MOYNIHAN
The Evolution of Obstetric Analgesia. London: 1939. V. 68

CLAYPOOLE, H. G. C.
The Witchery of Water. 1970. V. 68

CLAYTON, AUGUSTIN S.
The Office and Duty of a Justice of te Peace, and a Guide to Clerks, Constables, Coroners...According to the Laws of the State of Georgia. Milledgeville: 1819. V. 68; 73

CLAYTON, DAVID
A Short but Thorough Search Into What May be the Real Cause of the Present Scarcity of Our Silver Coin. London: 1717. V. 73

CLAYTON, JACQUELINE
The Twirly-Whiry Book. London: 1913. V. 69

CLAYTON, JOHN
The Works of Sir Christopher Wren. London: 1848-1849. V. 70; 72

CLAYTON, MARGARET
Amabel and Crispin: a Fairy Tale. London: 1911. V. 72

CLAYTON, MURIEL
Catalogue of Rubbings of Brasses and Incised Slabs. London: 1929. V. 72

CLAYTON, POWELL
Aftermath of the Civil War in Arkansas. New York: 1915. V. 69; 70

CLAYTON, SYLVIA
Sabbatical. London: 1972. V. 71

CLAYTON, W. F.
A Narrative of the Confederate States Navy. Weldon: 1910. V. 70

CLAYTON, W. WOODFORD
History of Bergen and Passaic Counties, New Jersey, with Biographical Sketches.... Philadelphia: 1882. V. 69

CLEAGE, ALBERT B.
The Black Messiah. New York: 1968. V. 72

CLEARE, JOHN
Sea Cliff Climbing in Britain. London: 1973. V. 69

CLEATON, IRENE
Books and Battles: American Literature, 1920-1930. Boston: 1937. V. 72

CLEAVELAND, GEORGE A.
American Landmarks. Boston: 1893. V. 71

CLEAVELAND, NEHEMIAH
Green-Wood Illustrated in Highly Finished Line Engraving.... New York: 1847. V. 70

CLEAVER, ELDRIDGE
Eldridge Cleaver. Post-Prison Writings and Speeches. New York: 1969. V. 71

CLEAVLAND, AGNES M.
No Life For a Lady. Boston: 1941. V. 71

CLEEVE, BOURCHIER
A Scheme for Preventing a Further Increase of the National Debt and for reducing the Same. London: 1756. V. 72

CLEGG, SAMUEL
Cleggs' Patent Atmospheric Railway. London: 1839. V. 72
A Practical Treatise on the Manufacture and Distribution of Coal-Gas.... London: 1841. V. 69
A Practical Treatise on the Manufacture and Distribution of Coal-Gas.... London: 1866. V. 69

CLEGHORN, HUGH FRANCIS CLARKE
The Forests and Gardens of South India. London: 1861. V. 68

CLEGHORN, THOMAS
The Hydro-Aeronaut, or Naviagtor's Life-Buoy.... London: 1810. V. 70

CLELAND, JAMES
The Rise and Progress of the City of Glasgow, Comprising an Account of Its Public Buildings, Charities and Other Concerns. Glasgow: 1820. V. 69

CLELAND, JOHN
Additional Articles to the Specimen of an Etimological Vocabulary.... London: 1769. V. 69
Memoirs of a Coxcomb. London: 1751. V. 68; 72
Memoirs of a Coxcomb. London: 1926. V. 71; 72
Memoirs of a Woman of Pleasure. Keene: 1814. V. 68; 73

CLELAND, R. E.
Oenothera, Cytogenetics and Evolution. London: 1972. V. 72

CLELAND, ROBERT GLASS
California - the Pathfinders. San Francisco: 1929. V. 68
The Cattle On a Thousand Hills, Southern California, 1850-1870. San Marino: 1941. V. 69; 71
El Molino Viejo. Los Angeles: 1950. V. 68
The Irving Ranch of Orange County 1810-1950. San Marino: 1952. V. 71

CLELAND, THOMAS MAITLAND
The Decorative Work of T. M. Cleland. New York: 1929. V. 70

CLEMENS, CYRIL
Mark Twain Anecdotes. La Jolla: 1929. V. 68; 70

CLEMENS, SAMUEL LANGHORNE
The Adventures of Huckleberry Finn. London: 1884. V. 71; 72
Adventures of Huckleberry Finn. New York: 1885. V. 68; 69; 70; 71; 72; 73
The Adventures of Huckleberry Finn. New York: 1933. V. 68; 73
Adventures of Huckleberry Finn. New York: 1942. V. 69; 73
The Adventures of Huckleberry Finn. London: 1950. V. 72; 73
The Adventures of Huckleberry Finn. (with) The Adventures of Tom Sawyer. New York: 1940-1936. V. 70
The Adventures of Huckleberry Finn. London: 1948. V. 72
The Adventures of Tom Sawyer. Hartford: 1876. V. 68; 70; 71; 72; 73
The Adventures of Tom Sawyer. London: 1876. V. 73
The Adventures of Tom Sawyer. Toronto: 1876. V. 68; 71
The Adventures of Tom Sawyer. London: 1877. V. 73
The Adventures of Tom Sawyer. Toronto: 1878. V. 71; 72

CLEMENS, SAMUEL LANGHORNE continued
The Adventures of Tom Sawyer. New York: 1910. V. 73
The Adventures of Tom Sawyer. New York: 1930. V. 73
The Adventures of Tom Sawyer. Cambridge: 1939. V. 69
The Adventures of Tom Sawyer. London: 1947. V. 72
The American Claimant. New York: 1892. V. 68; 71; 72; 73
The Celebrated Jumping Frog of Calaveras County, and Other Sketches. New York: 1867. V. 68; 69; 73
The Choice Humorous Works of Mark Twain. London: 1873. V. 73
Christian Science. New York: 1907. V. 70
A Connecticut Yankee in King Arthur's Court. New York: 1889. V. 68; 70; 71
A Connecticut Yankee in King Arthur's Court. New York: 1949. V. 69
A Curious Dream: and Other Sketches. London: 1877. V. 68
The Curious Republic of Gondour and Other Whimsical Sketches. New York: 1919. V. 68
Death-Disk. New York: 1913. V. 70
A Double Barrelled Detective Story. New York: 1902. V. 70; 71; 73
Early Tales and Sketches 1851-1865. Berkeley: 1979-1981. V. 72
Editorial Wild Oats. New York: 1905. V. 72
English as She is Taught with Biographical Sketch of Author. Boston: 1900. V. 71; 72
Europe and Elsewhere. New York: 1923. V. 73
Eve's Diary.... New York: 1906. V. 73
Extracts from Adam's Diary. New York: 1904. V. 73
Fireside Conversation in the Time of Queen Elizabeth; or, "1601". 1920. V. 73
Following the Equator. Hartford: 1897. V. 68; 70; 71; 72; 73
The Gilded Age. Hartford: 1873. V. 70
A Horse's Tale. London & New York: 1907. V. 71; 73
A Horse's Tale. New York: 1908. V. 70
How to Tell a Story and Other Essays. New York: 1897. V. 68; 73
The Innocents Abroad. Hartford: 1869. V. 68; 70; 73
Is Shakespeare Dead?. New York: 1909. V. 71; 72; 73
King Leopold's Soliloquy. Boston: 1905. V. 70
Letters From the Sandwich Islands. San Francisco: 1937. V. 73
Library of Humour. London: 1888. V. 73
Life on the Mississippi. Boston: 1883. V. 68; 70; 71; 72; 73
Life on the Mississippi. London: 1883. V. 70; 71; 72; 73
The Life and Adventures of Tom Sawyer. Hartford: 1876. V. 70
The Loves of Alonzo Fitz Clarence and Rosannah Ethelton. New York: 1898. V. 70
The Man that Corrupted Hadleyburg and Other Stories and Essays. New York: 1900. V. 73
Mark Twain: San Francisco Correspondent. San Francisco: 1957. V. 73
Mark Twain's Autobiography. New York: 1924. V. 72
Mark Twain's (Burlesque) Autobiography and First Romance. New York: 1871. V. 68; 70; 72; 73
Mark Twain's Burlesque Autobiography. Larchmont: 1930. V. 73
Mark Twain's Letters. New York: 1917. V. 73
Mark Twain's Letters in the Muscatine Journal. Chicago: 1942. V. 68
Mark Twain's Notebooks and Journals 1855-1883. Berkeley: 1975. V. 72
Mark Twain's Rubaiyat. Austin & Santa Barbara: 1983. V. 68
Mark Twain's Sketches. Hartford: 1875. V. 71; 73
Mark Twain's Speeches. New York: 1910. V. 68; 70; 72; 73
Mark Twain's Strange Dream. Hawaii: 1921-1932. V. 70
More Tramps Abroad. London: 1897. V. 70
The Mysterious Stranger: a Romance. New York: 1916. V. 73
The Niagra Book. Buffalo: 1893. V. 70
The Notorious Jumping Frog and Other Stories. New York: 1970. V. 71
Old Times on the Mississippi. Toronto: 1876. V. 70; 71; 73
The 1,000,000 Pound Bank-Note and Other New Stories. London: 1893. V. 73
The 1,000,000 Pound Bank-Note and Other Stories. New York: 1893. V. 70; 71; 73
Personal Recollections of Joan of Arc. London: 1896. V. 69
Personal Recollections of Joan of Arc. New York: 1896. V. 73
The Prince and the Pauper. Montreal: 1881. V. 70
The Prince and the Pauper. Boston: 1882. V. 68; 70; 71; 72; 73
The Prince and the Pauper. New York: 1917. V. 73
The Prince and the Pauper. Philadelphia: 1937. V. 71
Pudd'nhead Wilson. London: 1894. V. 71; 72
Punch, Brothers, Punch! and Other Sketches. New York: 1878. V. 71; 72
Roughing It. Hartford: 1872. V. 68
Saint Joan of Arc. New York: 1919. V. 70
1601 or Conversation at the Social Fireside As It Was in the Time of the Tudors. New York: 1927. V. 73
The Stolen White Elephant. London: 1882. V. 72
The Stolen White Elephant. London: 1892. V. 71
The $30,000 Bequest and Other Stories. New York: 1906. V. 68
Tom Sawyer Abroad. London: 1894. V. 70; 71; 73
The Tragedy of Pudd'nhead Wilson and the Comedy of Those Extraordinary Twins. Hartford: 1894. V. 68; 69; 70; 71; 73
A Tramp Abroad. London: 1880. V. 70; 71; 73
A True Story and Recent Carnival of Crime. Boston: 1877. V. 70; 73
War Prayer. New York: 1968. V. 72
The Washoe Giant in San Francisco: Being Heretofore Uncollected Sketches by Mark Twain. San Francisco: 1935. V. 73
The Writings of Mark Twain. New York: 1920. V. 69
The Writings of Mark Twain. New York: 1922-1935. V. 69
The Writings of Mark Twain. New York: 1929. V. 69; 71
A Yankee in King Arthur's Court. New York: 1889. V. 71

CLEMENS, WILL M.
Famous Funny Fellows, Brief Biographical Sketches of American Humorists. Cleveland: 1882. V. 68

CLEMENT, ARTHUR W.
Our Pioneer Potters. New York: 1947. V. 69

CLEMENT, E. PIKE
Selections from the Correspondence of Arthur Capel, Earl of Essex 1675-1677. 1913. V. 73

CLEMENT, J.
Noble Deeds of American Women; with Biographical Sketches of Some of the More Prominent. Buffalo: 1851. V. 73

CLEMENT, JOHN
Sketches of the First Emigrant Settlers in Newton Township, Old Gloucester County, West New Jersey. Camden: 1877. V. 69

CLEMENT, LEWIS
Modern Wildfowling. 1880. V. 71
Shooting Adventures, Canine Lore and Sea Fishing Trips. 1879. V. 71
Shooting and Fishing Trips in England, France &c. 1876. V. 70; 71
Shooting, Yachting and Sea Fishing Trips at Home and on the Continent. 1877. V. 71

CLEMENT, MARGUERITE
In France. New York: 1956. V. 73

CLEMENT, OF ALEXANDRIA
Opera. Florence: 1550. V. 73

CLEMENTS, COLIN CAMPBELL
Plays for Pagans. New York: 1924. V. 70
Sea Plays. Boston: 1925. V. 71

CLEMENTS, WILBUR F.
What the Sam Hill. New York: 1911. V. 73

CLEMMONS, PETER
Poor Peter's Call to His Children and to All Others Who Can Hear and Believe. Salisbury: 1812. V. 68; 70

CLEMOW, FRANK G.
The Geography of Disease. Cambridge: 1903. V. 68

CLENCH, W. J.
Johnsonia, Monographs of the Marine Mollusks of the Western Atlantic. Cambridge: 1941-1959-. V. 69
Occasional Papers on Mollusks, published by the Museum of Comparative Zoology, Harvard. Cambridge: 1945-1976. V. 69

CLENDON, JOHN C.
On Some Severe Forms of Disease Arising from the Retention of Decayed Teeth. London: 1858. V. 73

CLEOPATRA'S Needle. 1878. V. 71

THE CLERGYMAN'S Intelligencer; or, a Compleat Alphabetical List of all the Patrons in England And Wales....* London: 1745. V. 72

CLERICUS
Rambles and Recollections of a Fly Fisher. 1854. V. 68

CLERK, JOHN
Unto His Grace John Marquess of Tweeddale, Her Majesties High Commissioner, and the Honourable Estates of Parliament, the Report of the Commissioners Appointed for Stating and Examining Public Accompts. Edinburgh: 1704. V. 72

CLERKE, AGNES M.
Problems in Astrophysics. 1903. V. 69; 73
Problems in Astrophysics. London: 1903. V. 69
The System of the Stars. 1890. V. 71
The System of the Stars. 1905. V. 69; 73

THE CLERK'S Instructor in the Ecclesiastical Courts....* Dublin: 1766. V. 72

CLERY, M.
A Journal of Occurrences At The Temple, during the Confinement of Louis XVI, King of France. Translated From The Original Manuscript by R.SC. Dallas. London: 1798. V. 72

CLEVELAND BOARD OF TRADE
Annual Report of the Cleveland Board of Trade. Cleveland: 1885. V. 68

CLEVELAND, CHARLES B.
The Great Baseball Managers. New York: 1950. V. 71

CLEVELAND, GROVER
Fishing and Shooting Sketches. New York: 1906. V. 71
Public Papers...March 4, 1885 to March 4, 1889. Washington: 1889. V. 68; 72; 73
The Venezuelan Boundary Controversy. Princeton,: 1913. V. 69

CLEVELAND, JOHN
The Character of a Country Committe-Man, with the Eare-Marke of a Sequestrator. London: 1649. V. 68; 69
The Idol of the Clownes, or Insurrection of Wat the Tyler, with His Priests Baal and Straw.... London: 1654. V. 68; 70; 73
Majestas Intemarata. Or, the Immortality of the King. London: 1849. V. 70
Poems, Orations, Epistles and Other of His Genuine Incomparable Pieces with Never Before Published Additions. London: 1660. V. 73

CLEVELAND, NEHEMIAH
Green-Wood Illustrated in Highly finished Line Engraving.... New York: 1847. V. 68; 72

CLEVERDON, DOUGLAS
The Growth of Milk Wood. 1969. V. 68

CLEVERLY, BARBARA
The Last Kashmiri Rose. London: 2001. V. 73

CLEWS, HENRY
Twenty-Eight Years in Wall Street. New York: 1888. V. 70

CLEYRE, VOLTAIRINE DE
Anarchism and American Traditions. Chicago: 1932. V. 68

CLIFFE, CHARLES FREDERICK
The Book of South Wales, the Bristol Channel, Monmouthshire, and the Wye. London: 1847. V. 73

CLIFFORD, ANNE, LADY
The Diary of the Lady Anne Clifford. London: 1923. V. 72

CLIFFORD, C.
How to Lower Ships' Boats. A Treatise on the Dangers of the Present System and Their Remedy.... London: 1859. V. 70

CLIFFORD, D.
A History of Garden Design. New York: 1963. V. 71

CLIFFORD, FREDERICK
The Agricultural Lock-Out of 1874.... Edinburgh: 1875. V. 71

CLIFFORD, ISIDORE E.
Crown, Bar, and Bridge-Work: New Methods of Permanently Adjusting Artificial Teeth Without Plates. London: 1885. V. 72

CLIFFORD, JAMES L.
Samuel Johnson - A Survey and Bibliography of Critical Studies. Minneapolis: 1970. V. 72

CLIFFORD, P. D.
Art of Costa Rica. Pre-Columbian and Sculpted Ceramics from the Arthur M. Sackler Collection. Washington: 1985. V. 69

CLIFT, WILLIAM
Certain Places. Santa Fe: 1987. V. 68
A Hudson Landscape. Photographs by William Clift. Santa Fe: 1993. V. 73

CLIFTON, FRANCIS
Hippocrates Upon Air, Water, and Situation; Upon Epidemical Diseases and Upon Prognosticks, in Acute Cases Especially. London: 1734. V. 69

CLIFTON, H. E.
Mayvale. 1951. V. 68

CLIFTON, LUCILLE
Good Times. Poems. New York: 1969. V. 72
Ten Oxherding Pictures. Santa Cruz: 1988. V. 69; 72

CLIFTON, VIOLET
The Book of Talbot. 1933. V. 69; 70; 72; 73

CLIFTON, WILLIAM
Poems, Chiefly Occasional, by the Late Mr. Clifton. New York: 1800. V. 73

CLIMATES of the States.... Port Washington: 1974. V. 68

CLIMBERS' CLUB
Journal. Old Series. London: 1899-1909. V. 69

CLINCH, GEORGE
English Costume from Prehistoric Times to the End of the Eighteenth Century. London: 1909. V. 72

CLINE, GLORIA GRIFFIN
Peter Skene Ogden and the Hudson's Bay Company. Norman: 1974. V. 71; 73

CLINE, WALTER M.
The Muzzle-Loading Rifle Then and Now. West Virginia: 1942. V. 72

CLINGHAM, GREG
New Light on Boswell. Cambridge: 1933. V. 69

CLINTON, HENRY
Memorandums &c &c. London: 1794. V. 73
Narrative of Lieutenant-General Sir Henry Clinton, K.B. Relative to His Conduct During Part of His Command of the King's Troops in North America. London: 1783. V. 71

CLINTON, HILLARY RODHAM
It Takes A Village and Other Lessons Children Teach Us. New York: 1996. V. 69; 71

CLOAK, EVELYN CAMPBELL
Glass Paperweights. London: 1969. V. 72

CLODD, ALAN
Selected Verse Translations. London: 1970. V. 71

CLODD, EDWARD
Pioneers of Evolution from Thales to Huxley. London: 1897. V. 72
Pioneers of Evolution From Thales To Huxley. London: 1903. V. 72

CLOOTS, JEAN BAPTISTE DU VAL DE GRACE, BARON DE
The Sentiments of a Member of the Jacobins, in France, Upon the Religion of Reason and Nature.... London: 1792. V. 71

CLOPET, LILIANE M.
Once Upon a Time. London: 1945. V. 72

Once Upon a Time. London: 1946. V. 72

CLOSE, FRANCIS
The Testers Tested; or Table Moving, Turning and Talking, Not Diabolical: a Review of the Publications of the Rev. Messrs. Godfrey, Gillson, Vincent and Dibdin. London: 1853. V. 68

CLOUGH, ARTHUR HUGH
The Bothie of Toper-nafuosich. A Long-Vacation Pastoral. Oxford: 1848. V. 73
The Close of the Eighteenth Century. Rugby: 1835. V. 73
Poems. 1850. V. 73
The Poems. Boston: 1862. V. 73
The Poems and Prose Remains.... London: 1869. V. 68
The Poems and Prose Remains.... London: 1969. V. 71
Poems...with a Memoir. Cambridge and London: 1862. V. 73
Poems...with a Memoir. London: 1863. V. 73
The Rugby Magazine. London: 1835-1837. V. 73

CLOUGH, ROBERT T.
The Lead Smelting Mills of the Yorkshire Dales. London: 1962. V. 73
The Lead Smelting Mills of the Yorkshire Dales. London: 1980. V. 73
The Townscape of Keighley, West Yorkshire. Keighley: 1980. V. 73

CLOUSTON, B.
Landscape Design with Plants. New York: 1979. V. 72

CLOUSTON, J. STORER
The Mystery of No. 47. New York: 1912. V. 69
The Prodigal Father. London: 1909. V. 68

CLOUSTON, W. A.
Arabian Poetry for English Readers. Glasgow: 1881. V. 73

CLOUZOT, MARIANNE
Jeunesse. 1945. V. 69

CLOWES, WILLIAM L.
The Royal Navy: a History. Boston and London: 1897-1903. V. 70

CLOWNES, FREDERIC
A Description of the East Window of S. Martin's Windermere.... Kendal: 1874. V. 71

CLUBBE, WILLIAM
The Omnium: Containing the Journal of a Late Three Days Tour into France. Ipswich: 1798. V. 68

CLUM, JOHN P.
It All Happened in Tombstone. Flagstaff: 1965. V. 69

CLUM, WOODWORTH
Apache Agent: The Story of John P. Clum. Boston: 1936. V. 68; 73

CLUNAN, J. M.
Gas Turbines and Jet Propulsion, an Outline of the Principles Involved in the New Thermal Jet System of Aircraft Propulsion. London: 1945. V. 69

CLUNN, HAROLD P.
The Face of London, the Record of a Century's Changes and Development. London: 1935. V. 71

CLUSIUS, C.
Rariorum Aliquot Stirpium per Hispanias Observatrum Historia. Antwerp: 1576. V. 69
Rariorum Aliquot Stirpium per Pannoniam, Austriam & Vincinas Quasdam Prouincias Obseruataum Historia. Antwerp: 1583. V. 69

CLUTTERBUCK, HENRY
Observations on the Prevention and Treatment of the Epidemic Fever, at Present Prevailing in this Metropolis and Most Parts of the United Kingdom. London: 1819. V. 69

CLUTTON, CECIL
Watches. London: 1965. V. 72

CLUTTON, HENRY
Remarks with Illustrations on the Domestic Architecture of France, from Charles VI to Louis XII. London: 1853. V. 71

CLUVER, PHILIP
Introductionis in Universam Geographiam Tam Veterem Quam Novam Libri VI. Tabulis Aeneis. Amsterdam: 1661. V. 68

CLYMAN, JAMES
James Clyman Frontiersman: the Adventures of a Trapper and Covered Wagon Emigrant as Told in His Own Reminiscences and Diaries. Portland: 1960. V. 71
Journal of a Mountain Man. Missoula: 1984. V. 68

CLYNE, GERALDINE
The Jolly Jump-Ups See the Circus. Springfield: 1946. V. 72
Ten Toys. Springfield: 1938. V. 71

COAKLEY, CORNELIUS GODFREY
A Manual of Diseases of the Nose and Throat. Philadelphia: 1899. V. 71

COALBROOKDALE COMPANY LTD.
Illustrated Spring Catalogue, Comprising a Selection of Garden Seats, Chairs, Rolls, Fountains, Edging, Vases and Pedestals, Flower Stands, Park Seats.... 1888. V. 71

COALE, CHARLES B.
Life and Adventures of Wilburn Waters, the Famous Hunter and Trapper of White Top Mountain; Embracing the Early History of Southwestern Virginia. Richmond: 1878. V. 68

COATES, DANDESON
The New Zealand Company and the New Zealand Missionaries. London: 1845. V. 72

COATS, ALICE
The Book of Flowers. London: 1973. V. 72
The Story of Horace. London. V. 72

COATS, ALICE M.
The Book of Flowers, Four Centuries of Flower Illustration. New York: 1973. V. 71; 73

COATS, P.
Great Gardens of the Western World. New York: 1963. V. 71
House and Garden Book of Garden Decoration. New York: 1970. V. 71

COATSWORTH, ELIZABETH
The Golden Horseshore. New York: 1935. V. 71

COBB, B.
Ferns, and Their Related Families of Northeastern and Central North America, with a Section on Species Also Found in the British Isles and Western Europe. Norwalk: 1985. V. 72

COBB, BELTON
Double Detection. London: 1945. V. 71; 73

COBB, ERNEST
Miles Mc Carthy, a Drama in Five Acts. 1928. V. 69

COBB, HUMPHREY
Paths of Glory. New York: 1935. V. 70; 71; 72

COBB, IRVIN S.
Down Yonder with Judge Priest. New York: 1932. V. 73
Faith, Hope and Charity. Indianapolis: 1934. V. 69; 72
From Place to Place. New York: 1920. V. 69
Piano Jim and the Impotent Pumpkin Vine or Charlie Russell's Best Story to My Way of Thinking. Lexington: 1947. V. 68

COBB, MARY
Extracts from the Diary and Letters of Mrs. Mary Cobb. 1805. V. 71

COBB, RUTH
Somewhere Street a Story with Poems. 1933. V. 68

COBB, STANLEY
A Preface to Nervous Disease. Baltimore: 1936. V. 71

COBBAN, J. MACLAREN
Golden Tooth. New York: 1901. V. 72

COBBE, JOHN
Wilson Barrett. Memoranda for Press Use Only. London: 1886?. V. 72

COBBETT, JAMES PAUL
A Grammar of the Italian Language; or, A Plain and Compendious Introduction to the Study of Italian. London: 1834. V. 71

COBBETT, WILLIAM
Advice to Young Men, and (Incidentally) to Young Women, in the Middle and Higher Ranks of Life. 1830. V. 68
Advice to Young Men and (Incidentally) to Young Women, in the Middle and Higher Ranks of Life. London: 1830. V. 72
The American Gardener; or a Treatise on the Situation, Soil, Fencing and Laying-Out of Gardens.... London: 1821. V. 70
A Bone to Gnaw for the Democrats. London: 1797. V. 69
Cobbett's Manchester Lectures, in Support of the Fourteen Reform Propositions . . . London: 1832. V. 71
Cobbett's Paper Against Gold.... London: 1817. V. 71
Cobbett's Tour in Scotland; and in the Four Northern Counties of England: in the Autumn of the Year 1832. London: 1833. V. 71
Cobbett's Two-Penny Trash; or Politics for the Poor. London: 1831-1832. V. 71
Cottage Economy. London: 1838. V. 68
Cottage Economy. London: 1916. V. 68
The English Gardener. London: 1829. V. 71
The English Gardener. London: 1883. V. 69
A Grammar of the English Language, in a Series of Letters.... London: 1826. V. 71
A Grammar of the English Language, in a Series of Letters.... London: 1844. V. 72
A History of the Protestant Reformation in England and Ireland. London. V. 71
A History of the Protestant Reformation in England and Ireland. London: 1824-1826. V. 72
A History of the Protestant Reformation in England and Ireland. 1829. V. 70
Letters on the Late War Between the United States and Great Britain. New York: 1815. V. 70
Le Maitre de'Anglais, ou, Grammaire Raisonne.... Paris: 1815. V. 72
Memoirs of the Late William Cobbett, Esq. London: 1836. V. 71
Paper Against Gold: Containing the History and Mystery of the Bank of England, the Funds, the Debt, the Sinking Fund, the Bank Stoppage.... London: 1817. V. 70
A' Protestans Reformatio' Historiaja Angliaban 's Irlandban. Nagyvaradon: 1834. V. 72
Rural Rides, in the Counties of Surrey, Kent, Sussex...Durham and Northumberland in the Years 1821...1832.... London: 1853. V. 71; 72
The Woodlands; or a Treatise on the Preparing of Ground for Planting.... London: 1825. V. 71

COBBEY, J. E.
A Practical Treatise on the Law of Replevin as Administered by the Courts of the United States. Beatrice: 1890. V. 69

COBBOLD, ELIZABETH KNIPE
Six Narrative Poems; the Vizir. The Village Wake. The Return from the Crusade. Atomboke and Omaza. Humanity. London: 1787. V. 69

COBBOLD, EVELYN
Wayfarers in the Libyan Desert. London: 1912. V. 68; 72

COBBOLD, RALPH P.
Innermost Asia. 1900. V. 69; 70

COBBOLD, RICHARD
The Character of Woman, in a Lecture, Delivered at the Hanover Square Rooms, April 13th 1848, for the Benefit of the Governesses Benevolent Institution. 1848. V. 69; 70

COBBOLD, T. SPENCER
Entozoa: an Introduction to the Study of Helminthology...(with) Entozoa, being a Supplement to the Introduction.... London: 1864-1869. V. 68

COBBOLD, THOMAS SPENCER
Observations on the Canal of Petit. Edinburgh: 1852. V. 71

COBDEN, RICHARD
1793 and 1853 in Three Letters. London: 1853. V. 72
Speeches on Questions of Public Policy by.... London: 1870. V. 72

COBDEN SANDERSON, THOMAS JAMES
The Arts and Crafts Movement. Hammersmith: 1905. V. 70; 73
Catalogue Raisonne of Books Printed and Published at the Doves Press. 1911. V. 71
Catalogue Raisonne of Books Printed and Published at the Doves Press. London: 1911. V. 70
The City Planned: Reprinted from the Westminster Gazette, 27 October 1910. Hmmersmith: 1911. V. 71
Ecce Mundus. 1902. V. 71
Ecce Mundus. Hammersmith: 1902. V. 73
Four Lectures by T. J. Cobden-Sanderson. San Francisco: 1974. V. 73
The Journals...1879-1922. 1926. V. 71
London: a Paper Read at a Meeting of the Art-Workers Guild, March 6, 1891. Hammersmith: 1906. V. 71
The New Science Museum: a Letter with additions Addressed to the Editor of The Times, 16 September 1913. Hammersmith: 1913. V. 71
Note on a Passage in Shelley's Ode to Liberty. Hammersmith: 1914. V. 71

COBEN, HARLAN
Deal Breaker. New York: 1995. V. 72
Miracle Cure. New York: 1991. V. 70
Play Dead. New York: 1990. V. 70

COBEN, LAWRENCE
Japanese Cloisonne. NY and Tokyo: 1982. V. 72

COBIN, A.
Short and Plain Principles of Linear Perpsective, Adapted to Naval Architeture. London: 1794. V. 71

COBLE, GEORGE
The History of the Tulsa Fire Department 1905-1973. 1973?. V. 69

COBLENTZ, STANTON A.
Villains and Vigilantes. New York: 1936. V. 68
When the Birds Fly South. Mill Valley CA/NY: 1945. V. 72

COBURN, ALVIN LANGDON
Alvin Langdon Coburn, Photographer: an Autobiography. London: 1966. V. 72; 73
Moor Park Rickmansworth. London: 1915. V. 72
More Men of Mark. London. V. 70
More Men of Mark. London: 1922. V. 73

COBURN, LOUIS HELEN
Showhegan on the Kennebec. Showhegan: 1941. V. 73

COBURN, WALT
Pioneer Cattlemen in Montana-The Story of the Circle C Ranch. Norman: 1968. V. 71

COCH, JOANNE
Duo Tituli Thalmudici Sanhedrin et Maccoth: Quorum Ille agit de Synedriis, Judicis, Suppliciis Captalibus Ebraeorum.... Amsterdam: 1629. V. 72

COCHIN FILS AND BELLICARD, J. C.
Observations sur les Antiquites de la Ville d'Herculanum.... Paris: 1754. V. 72

COCHRAN, DORIS M.
The Herpetology of Hispaniola. Washington: 1941. V. 72
Poisonous Reptiles of the World: a Wartime Handbook. Washington: 1943. V. 71

COCHRAN, HAMILTON
Captain Ebony. Indianapolis: 1943. V. 69

COCHRAN, JOHN H.
Dallas County - a Record of It's Pioneers and Progress. Dallas: 1928. V. 70

COCHRAN, JOHN S.
Bonnie Belmont, a Historical Romance of the Days of Slavery and the Civil War. Wheeling: 1907. V. 69

COCHRANE, BASIL
An Expose of the Conduct of the Victualling Board to the Honourable Basil Cochrane, as Contractor and Agent Victualler to His Majesty's Ships on the East India Station. London: 1824. V. 68

COCHRANE, CHARLES
Journal of a Tour Made by Senor Juan De Vega, the Spanish Minstrel of 1828-9, Through Great Britain and Ireland.... London: 1830. V. 73

COCHRANE, GEORGE
On The Economy of the Law; Especially in Relation to the Court of Chancery.... London: 1856. V. 73

COCHRANE, J. A.
Dr. Johnson's Printer, the Life of William Strahan. Cambridge: 1964. V. 69

COCHRANE, JOHN DUNDAS
A Pedestrian Journey Through Russia and Siberian Tartary. Edinburgh: 1829. V. 72

COCHRANE, PETER
Tips for Time Travellers. London: 1997. V. 71

COCK Robin. New York: 1872. V. 71

THE COCK Robin Alphabet. London: 1865. V. 69

COCK-A-Doodle-Doo. London. V. 73

COCK-a-Hoop, a Sequel to Chanticleer, Pertelote and Cockalorum. Being a Bibliography of the Golden Cockerel Press. 1949-1961. 1961. V. 73

COCKALORUM.. Waltham St. Lawrence: 1950. V. 68; 70; 71

COCKBURN, W.
An Answer to What Dr. Freind Has Written in His History of Physick. London: 1727. V. 70
Profluvia Ventris; or the Nature and Causes of Looosenesses Plainly Discovered, Their Symptoms and Sorts Evidently Settled.... London: 1701. V. 70; 72

COCKE, SARAH JOHNSON
Bypaths in Dixie: Folk Tales of the South. New York: 1911. V. 71

COCKE, THOMAS
Kitchin-Physick; or, Advice to the Poor, by Way of Dialogue Betwixt Philanthropos, Physician, Eugenius, Apothecary, Lazarus, Patient. London: 1676. V. 69

COCKER, EDWARD
Cocker's Arithmetick. London: 1734. V. 69
Cocker's Arithmetick. London: 1745. V. 70; 73
The Young Clerk's Tutor Enlarged: Being a Most Useful Collection of the Best Presidents of Recognizances...Bills of sale...Together with Directions of Writs of Habeas Corpus.... London: 1693. V. 73

COCKERELL, SIDNEY
A Psalter and Hours, Executed Before 1270 for Isabelle of France... Now in the Collection of Henry Yates Thompson. Described by S. C Cockerell. London: 1905. V. 68

THE COCKOLLY Bird. Droll Doings. London: 1900. V. 72

COCKRELL, W. D.
Industrial Control. A Guide to the Understanding of Electronic Control Circuits for Industrial Use. New York/Toronto/London: 1950. V. 68

COCKROFT, BARRY
The Dale That Died. London: 1975. V. 73

COCKS, ANNA S.
Renaissance Jewels, Gold Boxes and Objects De Vertu. London: 1984. V. 72

COCKS, JAMES
Memorials of Hatherlow and of the Old Chadkirk Chapel. Stockport: 1895. V. 73

COCKTON, HENRY
The Life and Adventures of Valentine Vox the Ventriloquist. London: 1849. V. 71
The Life and Adventures of Valentine Vox the Ventriloquist. London: 1875?. V. 68
The Life and Adventures of Valentine Vox the Ventriloquist. London: 1887. V. 68
The Life and Adventures of Valentine Vox the Ventriloquist. London: 1843. V. 72
Sylvester Sound the Somnambulist. London: 1885. V. 68

COCLES, BARTOLOMEO
Physiognomiae & Chiromantiae Compendium. Argentorati: 1555. V. 69

COCQUIEL, CHARLES, CHEVALIER DE
Industrial Instruction in England, Being a Report Made to the Belgian Government.... London: 1853. V. 73

COCTEAU, JEAN
The Blood of a Poet - a Film. New York: 1949. V. 71
A Call to Order. London: 1926. V. 71; 73
Cock and Harlequin: Notes on Music. London: 1921. V. 73
The Infernal Machine - a Play in Four Acts. London: 1936. V. 70
Le Grand Ecart. Paris: 1923. V. 71
My Journey Around the World. London: 1958. V. 71
Opium. Paris: 1930. V. 70

CODE, C.
Handbook of Physiology...Section 6: Alimentary Canal. Washington: 1967-1968. V. 71

CODE de la Nature, ou le Vertiable Esprit de ses Loix, de Tout Neglige ou Meconnu. Paris or Liege?: 1755. V. 72

CODERE, HELEN
Fighting with Property. A Study of Kwakiutl Potlatching and Warfare 1792-1930. New York: 1950. V. 70

CODMAN, JOHN
The Round Trip by Way of Panama Through California, Oregon, Nevada, Utah, Idaho and Colorado. New York: 1881. V. 69

CODRESCU, ANDREI
A Serious Morning. Santa Barbara: 1973. V. 69; 71; 73

CODRINGTON, ROBERT
The Life and Death of the Illustrious Robert Earle of Essex.... London: 1646. V. 70; 73

CODY CLUB
The Buffalo Bill Country, Cody, Wyoming. The Heart of the Dude Ranch Industry. V. 68

CODY, LIZA
Backhand. London: 1991. V. 73
Bucket Nut. London: 1992. V. 73
Head Case. London: 1985. V. 69; 70; 72
Monkey Wrench. London: 1994. V. 73
Muslebound. London: 1997. V. 73
Stalker. London: 1984. V. 72

THE CODY Road to Yellowstone Park. 1932. V. 68

CODY, WILLIAM F.
Buffalo Bill and His Wild West Companions. Chicago: 1893. V. 73
Buffalo Bill's Own Story of His Life and Deeds. 1917. V. 68
Buffalo Bill's Wild West. Hartford: 1884. V. 72
Life of Buffalo Bill. New York: 1887. V. 71
Story of the Wild West and Camp Fire Chats. Chicago: 1901. V. 73
Story of The Wild West And Campfire Chats. Chicago: 1902. V. 72

COE, CHARLES FRANCIS
Me-Gangster. New York: 1927. V. 69
The River Pirate. New York: 1928. V. 71

COE, CHARLES H.
Juggling a Rope, Lariat Roping and Spinning Knots and Splices Also the Truth About Tom Horn. Pendleton: 1927. V. 68; 71

COE, ELMER
Fort Scott As I Knew It. Fort Scott: 1940. V. 71; 73

COE, GEORGE W.
Frontier Fighter. Boston: 1934. V. 72
Frontier Fighter. Albuquerque: 1951. V. 69

COE, JONATHAN
The House of Sleep. London: 1997. V. 72; 73

COE, MICHAEL
In the Land of the Olmec. Austin: 1980. V. 71; 72
The Jaguar's Children: Pre-Classic Central Mexico. New York: 1965. V. 71

COE, R. T.
Lost and Found Traditions: Native American Art 1965-1985. 1986. V. 69; 72

COE, WILBUR
Ranch On the Ruidoso- The Story of a Pioneer Family in New Mexico, 1871-1968. New York: 1968. V. 71; 72

COEHOORN, BARON VAN
A Catalogue of a Valuable Collection of Prints, Drawings, Books of Prints, &c. London: 1802. V. 72

COEL, MARGARET
The Dream Stalker. Berkely: 1997. V. 70
The Eagle Catcher. Boulder: 1995. V. 68; 69; 70; 71; 72
The Eagle Catcher. Niwot, CO: 1995. V. 69; 71
The Ghost Walker. Berkeley: 1996. V. 68; 70
The Ghost Walker. New York: 1996. V. 71; 72
Hole in the Wall. 1998. V. 68
Hole in the Wall. Royal Oak: 1998. V. 69; 71; 72
Honor. Royal Oak: 1999. V. 71; 72
Stolen Smoke. 2000. V. 68; 70
Stolen Smoke. Royal Oak: 2000. V. 71; 72
The Thunder Keeper. Berkeley: 2001. V. 70
The Woman Who Climbed to the Sky. Clarkston, Michigan: 2001. V. 70; 71; 72

COEN, ETHAN
Gates of Eden. New York: 1998. V. 71

COERS, C.
The Innervation of Muscle. A Biopsy Study. Oxford: 1959. V. 68

COETLOGON, DENIS DE
Natural Sagacity, the Principal Secret, If Not the Whole in Physick.... London: 1742. V. 71

COETZEE, J. M.
Age of Iron. New York: 1990. V. 72
Disgrace. London: 1999. V. 68; 69; 70
Disgrace. New York: 2000. V. 69
Dusklands. Johannesburg: 1974. V. 70; 73
Dusklands. London: 1982. V. 69
Dusklands. New York: 1985. V. 73
From the Heart of the Country. New York: 1976. V. 70
In the Heart of the Country. London: 1977. V. 71
In the Heart of the Country. New York: 1977. V. 69; 73
Life and Times of Michael K. London: 1983. V. 73
The Life and Times of Michael K. New York: 1983. V. 70
Life and Times of Michael K. New York: 1984. V. 69

COETZEE, J. M. *continued*
Waiting for the Barbarians. London: 1980. V. 70
Waiting for the Barbarians. 1982. V. 73

THE COFFEE Publichouse; How to Establish and Manage It. London: 1879. V. 72

COFFEY, AENEAS
Observations on the Rev. Edward Chichester's Pamphlet Entitled Oppressions and Cruelties of Irish Revenue Officers. London: 1818. V. 71

COFFEY, DIARMID
O'Neill and Ormond; a Chapter in Irish History. 1914. V. 70

COFFIN, CHARLES CARLETON
Redeeming The Republic- The Third Period Of The War Of The Rebellion In The Year 1864. New York: 1889. V. 72

COFFIN, GEOFFREY
Murder in the Senate. 1935. V. 73

COFFIN, LEWIS A.
Brick Architecture of the Colonial Period in Maryland and Virginia. New York: 1919. V. 69; 70; 72

COFFIN, MORSE H.
Battle Of Sand Creek. Waco: 1965. V. 72

COFFIN, ROLAND FOLGER
Archibald the Cat and Other Sea Yarns. New York: 1878. V. 70

COFFMAN, EDWARD M.
Old Army, A Portrait Of The American Army In Peacetime 1784-1898. New York: 1986. V. 72

COFFMAN, RAMON
Uncle Ray's Story of the Stone-Age People. Chicago: 1936. V. 69

COFYN, CORNELIUS
The Death Riders. New York: 1936. V. 72

COGGESHALL, GEORGE
History of the American Privateers and Letters of Marque, During Our War With England...1812, 1813 and 184. New York: 1856. V. 69

COGHILL, JAMES
Poems, Songs and Sonnets. Glasgow: 1890. V. 71

COGHLAN, MARGARET MONCRIEFFE
Memoirs of Mrs. Coghlan...Being Interspersed with Anecdotes of the Late American and Present French War, with Remarks, Moral and Political.... New York: 1795. V. 68; 69

COHEN, CHAPMAN
Woman and Christianity. London: 1919. V. 72

COHEN, FELIX S.
Felix S Cohen's Handbook of Federal Indian Law. Albuquerque. V. 72

COHEN, I. BERNARD
Isaac Newton's Papers & Letters on Natural Philosophy. Cambridge: 1958. V. 71

COHEN, JANE R.
Charles Dickens and His Original Illustrators. Columbus: 1980. V. 70

COHEN, LEONARD
Beautiful Losers. New York: 1966. V. 69; 73
Beautiful Losers. London: 1970. V. 68
The Energy of Slaves. London: 1972. V. 70
The Favourite Game. London: 1963. V. 70
Selected Poems 1956-1968. New York: 1968. V. 72
The Spice-Box of Earth. London: 1973. V. 73

COHEN, MENDES
Report on Coke and Coal Used with Passenger Trains on the Baltimore and Ohio Rail Road. Baltimore: 1854. V. 73

COHEN, OCTAVIUS ROY
Black to Nature. Boston: 1935. V. 70
Black to Nature. New York: 1935. V. 70
Cameos. New York: 1931. V. 71
Epic Peters: Pullman Porter. New York: 1930. V. 70
Florian Sappy Goes Abroad. Boston: 1928. V. 70
Florian Slappey. New York: 1938. V. 68
Jim Hanvey Detective. New York: 1923. V. 70; 71
Lilies of the Alley. New York: 1931. V. 71
Polished Ebony. New York: 1919. V. 70
Scrambled Yeggs. 1934. V. 73
Sound of Revelry. 1943. V. 73

COHN, ALBERT
George Cruikshank. A Catalogue Raisonne. London: 1924. V. 71

COHN, LARRY
Nothing but the Blues. New York: 1993. V. 69

COHN, LOUIS HENRY
A Bibliography of the Works of Ernest Hemingway. New York: 1931. V. 69

COHN, WILLIAM
Chinese Painting. London: 1948. V. 73

COHOE
A Cheyenne Sketchbook. Norman: 1964. V. 69

COKE, DESMOND
The Nouveau Poor. 1921. V. 71

COKE, ROGER
Justice Vindicated from the False Fucus Put Upon It, by Thomas White, Gent. Mr. Thoms Hobbs, and Hugo Grotius. London: 1660. V. 70

COKE, VAN DEREN
Photography in New Mexico.... 1979. V. 68
Photography in New Mexico.... Albuquerque: 1979. V. 69
Taos and Santa Fe: the Artist's Environment 1882-1942. Albuquerque: 1963. V. 68

COKER, JAMES LIDE
History of Company G, Ninth S. C. Regiment, Infantry, S.C. Army and of Company E, Sixth S.C. Regiment, Infantry, S.C. Army. Charleston: 1899. V. 69; 70

COKER, W. C.
The Clavarias of the United States and Canada. Chapel Hill: 1923. V. 71

COLBATCH, JOHN
A Dissertation Concerning Mistletoe.... London: 1719. V. 69
A Dissertation Concerning Mistletoe.... London: 1720. V. 69

COLBECK, ALFRED
A Summer's Cruise in the Waters of Greece, Turkey and Russia. London: 1887. V. 68; 72

COLBECK, NORMAN
A Bookman's Catalogue: the Norman Colbeck Collection of Nineteenth Century and Edwardian Poetry and Belles Lettres in the Special Collections of the University of British Columbia. 1987. V. 71

COLBERG, NANCY
A Descriptive Bibliography of Wallace Stegner. Lewiston: 1990. V. 69; 72

COLBURN, FRONCA E.
In Old Vintage Days. San Francisco: 1937. V. 72

COLBY, CHARLES
The Diamond Atlas. New York: 1857. V. 69
The Diamond Atlas...The Western Hemisphere. New York: 1859. V. 69

COLBY, JOHN
The Life, Experience and Travels of John Colby, Preacher of the Gospel... Volume II. Andover: 1819. V. 69

COLBY, T. F.
Ordnance Survey of the County of Londonderry. Dublin: 1837. V. 73

COLCORD, CHARLES F.
The Autobiography of 1859-1934. 1970. V. 71

COLDEN, CADWALLADER DAVID
Memoir, Prepared at the Request of a Committee of the Common Council of the City of New York. New York: 1825. V. 68; 69
Memoir, Prepared at the Request of a Committee of the Common Council of the City of New York. New York: 1826. V. 68

COLDEN, JANE
Botanic Manuscript of Jane Colden 1724-1766. New York: 1963. V. 73

COLDSTREAM, W.
Illustrations of Some of the Grasses of the Southern Punjab.... London: 1889. V. 70

COLE, BENJAMIN THOMAS HALCOTT
The Renegade; and Other Poems. London: 1833. V. 71

COLE, CHRISTIAN
Historical and Political Memoirs, Containing Letters Written by Sovereign Princes, State Ministers, Admirals and General Officers &c.... London: 1735. V. 71

COLE, CORNELIUS
Memoirs of...Ex Senator of the United States from California. New York: 1908. V. 69

COLE, F. C.
Rediscovery Illinois. Chicago: 1937. V. 69

COLE, F. J.
A History of Comparative Anatomy. London: 1944. V. 68

COLE, F. R.
The Flies of Western North America. Berkeley: 1969. V. 68; 72

COLE, FREDERICK WING
Poems by Frederick Wing Cole.... Albany: 1845. V. 73

COLE, G. D. H.
The Blatchington Tangle. New York: 1926. V. 68; 70; 72
The Brooklyn Murders. London: 1923. V. 73
Dr. Tancred Begins. New York: 1935. V. 68
End of an Ancient Mariner. New York: 1934. V. 71
Knife in the Dark. London: 1942. V. 73
The Murder at Crome House. 1927. V. 73
The Murder at the Munition Works. 1940. V. 73
Superintendent Wilson's Holiday. London: 1928. V. 73

COLE, HARRY ELLSWORTH
Stagecoach and Tavern Tales of the Old Northwest. Cleveland: 1930. V. 71

COLE, HEIDI B.
A Wild Cowboy. Cambridge: 1992. V. 71

COLE, HENRY
Dialogues of the Gauges. London: 1846. V. 68
Fallacies of the Broken Gauge. Mr. Lushington's Arguments in Favour of Broad Gauge and Breaks of Gauge Refuted. London: 1846. V. 68
Railway Eccentrics. Inconsistencies of Men of Genius Exemplified in the Practice and Precept of Isambard Kingdom Brunel, Esq.... London: 1846. V. 68
The Veritable History of Whittington and His Cat. London: 1847. V. 68; 72; 73

COLE, JAMESON
A Killing In Quail County. New York: 1996. V. 68; 69; 71

COLE, JOHN
A Bibliographical and Descriptive Tour from Scarborough to the Library of a Philobiblist in It's Neighbourhood. Scarborough: 1824. V. 68
Historical Sketches of Scalby, Burniston, and Cloughton. Scarborough: 1829. V. 73
The History and Antiquities of Filey in The County of York. Scarborough: 1828. V. 73
The Scarborough Collector, and Journal of the Olden Time. Scarborough: 1828. V. 73
Scarborough Guide. Scarborough: 1825. V. 73
Scarborough Tales By a Visitant. Scarborough: 1830. V. 73
Union Harmony; or Music Made Easy; a New and Pleasing Selection of Psalm and Hymn Tunes.... Baltimore: 1829. V. 68

COLE, JOHN N.
Striper. A Story of Fish and Man. Boston: 1978. V. 71

COLE, JULIE KRAMER
Interwoven. Loveland: 1995. V. 70

COLE, PETER
Rift. New York: 1986. V. 73

COLE, PHILIP G.
Montana in Miniature: the Pictorial History of Montana from Early Exploration to Early Statehood. Kalispell: 1966. V. 69; 70; 71; 72

COLE, RICHARD JOHN
Pantomime Budgets and by Special Command a Tete-a-Tete Between Sir John Barleycorn and the Old Lady of Threadneedle Street. London: 1853. V. 71

COLE, S. W.
American Fruit Book: Containing Directions for Raising, Propagating and Managing Fruit Trees, Shrubs and Plants. Boston: 1849. V. 68; 72

COLE, SELINA
First Impressions of Florence. Liverpool: 1906. V. 72; 73

COLEBROOK, LEONARD
Almroth Wright. Provocative Thinker.... London: 1954. V. 68

COLEBY, R. J. W.
Regional Angling Literature. 1979. V. 68

COLEGATE, ISABEL
The Blackmailer. London: 1958. V. 70
Deceits of Time. London: 1988. V. 73
The King Family Trilogy: Orlando King; Orlando at the Brazen Threshold; Agatha. London: 1968-1971. V. 68
The King Family Trilogy: Orlando King; Orlando at the Brazen Threshold; Agatha. London: 1968-1973. V. 73
Orlando at the Brazen Threshold. London: 1971. V. 68; 71

COLEMAN, A. D.
The Grotesque in Photography. New York: 1977. V. 68

COLEMAN, CHAPMAN, MRS.
The Life of John J. Crittenden. New York: 1871. V. 70

COLEMAN, DOROTHY S.
The Collector's Encyclopadeia of Dolls. New York: 1968. V. 72

COLEMAN, GEORGE P., MRS.
Virginia Silhouettes: Contemporary Letters Concerning Negro Slavery in the State of Virginia. Richmond: 1934. V. 70

COLEMAN, J. WALTER
The Molly Maguire Riots. Richmond: 1936. V. 68

COLEMAN, J. WINSTON
Slavery Times in Kentucky. Chapel Hill: 1940. V. 71

COLEMAN, JOHN
The Truth About the Dead Heart. London: 1890. V. 71

COLEMAN, KENNETH
The American Revolution in Georgia 1763-1789. Athens: 1958. V. 71; 73

COLEMAN, MC ALISTER
Eugene V. Debs. A Man Unafraid. New York: 1930. V. 68

COLEMAN, OLIVER
Successful Houses. Chicago/New York: 1898. V. 72

COLEMAN, P.
The Western Pacific: Island Arcs, Marginal Seas, Geochemistry. New York: 1973. V. 68

COLEMAN, W. H.
The Flora of Leicestershire. London and Edinburgh: 1886. V. 69

COLEMAN, W. S.
British Butterflies. London: 1867. V. 71
British Butterflies. London: 1872?. V. 68
British Butterflies. London: 1895. V. 68

COLEMAN, WANDA
Hand Dance. Santa Rosa: 1993. V. 71
Imagoes. Santa Barbara: 1983. V. 72

COLEMAN, WILLIAM
Georges Cuvier, Zoologist. Cambridge: 1954. V. 68
Georges Cuvier, Zoologist. Cambridge: 1964. V. 68

COLERIDGE, ERNEST HARTLEY
Life Of Thomas Coutts, Banker. London: 1920. V. 72

COLERIDGE, HARTLEY
Biographia Borealis; of Lives of Distinguished Northerns. London: 1833. V. 71; 72; 73
Essays and Marginalia. London: 1851. V. 70; 71; 72
Lives of Illustrious Worthies of Yorkshire, & C. Hull: 1835. V. 72; 73
Poems. Leeds: 1833. V. 73
Poems. With a Memoir of His Life by his Brother. London: 1851. V. 70; 71

COLERIDGE, SAMUEL TAYLOR
Aids to Reflection. London: 1861. V. 70
Anima Poetae. London: 1895. V. 73
Biographia Literaria; or Biographical Sketches of My Literary Life and Opinions. London: 1817. V. 68
Christabel; Kubla Khan, a Vision: the Pains of Sleep. London: 1816. V. 73
Christabel, Kubla Khan, Fancy in Nubibus and Song from Zapolya. 1904. V. 73
Confessions of an Inquiring Spirit. London: 1840. V. 68; 72
Essays on His Own Times. London: 1850. V. 70
The Fall of Robespierre. An Historic Drama. London: 1794. V. 73
The Friend. London: 1844. V. 68; 72
The Friend. London: 1850. V. 70
Hints Towards the Formation of a More Comprehensive Theory of Life. 1848. V. 71
Hints Towards the Formation of a More Comprehensive Theory of Life. London: 1848. V. 73
The Letters of Samuel Taylor Coleridge. London: 1950. V. 71
A Moral and Political Lecture, Delivered at Bristol. Bristol: 1795. V. 69
On the Constitution of the Church and State According to the Idea of Each. Lay Sermons. London: 1839. V. 73
Poems. 1803. V. 73
Poems Chosen Out of the Works.... Hammrsmith: 1896. V. 72
Poems on Various Subjects. 1796. V. 73
Poems...to which are now added Poems by Charles Lamb and Charles Lloyd. Bristol and London: 1797. V. 73
Poetical Works.... London: 1828. V. 72
The Poetical Works.... New York: 1857. V. 71
Remorse: a Tragedy, in Five Acts. London: 1813. V. 73
The Rime of the Ancient Mariner. 1899. V. 71
The Rime of the Ancient Mariner. London: 1899. V. 70; 72
The Rime of the Ancient Mariner. London: 1910. V. 72
The Rime of the Ancient Mariner. Bristol, Cleverdon: 1929. V. 68; 71
The Rime of the Ancient Mariner. Oxford: 1930. V. 71
The Rime of the Ancient Mariner. London: 1943. V. 69
The Rime of the Ancient Mariner. London: 1945. V. 69; 73
The Rime of the Ancient Mariner. New York: 1945. V. 69
Specimens of the Table Talk of Coleridge. London: 1836. V. 70
The Statesman's Manual.... Burlington: 1832. V. 68
Sybilline Leaves: a Collection of Poems. 1817. V. 73
Zapolya; a Christmas Tale, in Two Parts: the Prelude Entitled the Usurper's Fortune and The Sequel Entitled The Usurper's Fate. 1817. V. 73

COLERIDGE, SARA
Phantasmion. London: 1837. V. 73

COLES, ABRAHAM
Lectures on the Theory and Practice of Surgery. Dublin: 1850. V. 72

COLES, CHARLES
Game Birds. 1981. V. 70

COLES, ELISHA
An English Dictionary, Explaining the Difficult Terms...Hard Words... Together with the Etymological Derivation of Them.... London: 1732. V. 69

COLES, MANNING
Drink to Yesterday. New York: 1941. V. 69; 73
The Fifth Man. London: 1946. V. 73
Not Negotiable. London: 1949. V. 73
Nothing to Declare. New York: 1960. V. 73
They Tell No Tales. New York: 1942. V. 72
The Three Beans. London: 1957. V. 71
A Toast to Tomorrow. 1941. V. 73
With Intent to Deceive. 1947. V. 73
Without Lawful Authority. New York: 1943. V. 71

COLETTE, SIDONIE GABRIELLE
Break of Day. New York: 1983. V. 70
The Indulgent Husband. New York: 1935. V. 72
The Innocent Wife. New York: 1934. V. 72
Mes Cahiers. Paris: 1941. V. 69

COLETTE, SIDONIE GABRIELLE continued
The Pure and the Impure. New York: 1967. V. 69
Sept Dialogues de Betes. Paris: 1912. V. 69

COLFAX, RICHARD H.
Evidence Against the Views of the Abolitionists, Consisting of Physical and Moral Proofs of the Natural Inferiority of the Negroes. New York: 1833. V. 71

COLFER, EOIN
Artemis Fowl. London: 2001. V. 70
Artemis Fowl. New York: 2001. V. 73
Artemis Fowl. New York: 2002. V. 72

COLGAN, NATHANIEL
Flora of County Dublin. 1904. V. 71

COLGATE, WILLIAM
The Toronto Art Students' League 1886-1904. Toronto: 1954. V. 73

COLIN, GALEN C.
Storm King Rides. New York: 1933. V. 69

COLLADO, LUIS
Pratica Manuale di Arteglieria; Nellaquale si Tratta Della Inventione di Essa, dell'ordine di Conduria & Piantarla Sotto a Qualunque Fortezza, Fabricar Mine da far Volar in Alto le Fortezze.... Venice: 1586. V. 69

COLLAR, N. J.
Threatened Birds of the Americas. Cambridge: 1992. V. 73

COLLARD, ALLAN OVENDEN
The Oyster & Dredgers of Whitstable. London: 1902. V. 68

COLLECT, C. D.
The New Crusade Against Islam Under Pretence of Abolishing Slavery. London: 1888. V. 71

THE COLLECTED Colorado Rail Annual- A Journal of Railroad History in the Rocky Mountains West. Golden: 1974. V. 71

A COLLECTION and Selection of English Prologues and Epilogues. Commencing with Shakespeare, and concluding with Garrick. London: 1779. V. 71

A COLLECTION of All the Letters Which Have Appeared in the Newcastle Papers, with Other Documents, Relating to the Safety Lamps. London: 1817. V. 69

A COLLECTION Of Anthems Used in His Majesty's Chapel Royal and Most Cathedral Churches in England and Ireland. London: 1769. V. 73

A COLLECTION of Articles, Injunctions, Canons, Orders, Ordinances and Constitutions Ecclesiastical, With Other Publick Records of the Church of England, Chiefly in the Times of K. Edward VI, Q. Elizabeth, K. James & K. Charles I. London: 1661. V. 73

A COLLECTION of Birds and Riddles. 1820. V. 72
A COLLECTION of Birds and Riddles. London: 1820. V. 68

A COLLECTION of Birds and Riddles by Miss Polly and Master Tommy. 1820. V. 73

A COLLECTION of Epigrams. London: 1727. V. 69
A COLLECTION of Epigrams. London: 1735. V. 71

A COLLECTION of Fables, for the Instruction and Amusement of Little Misses and Masters. London: 1825. V. 68

COLLECTION of Nebraska Pioneer Reminiscences. Cedar Rapids: 1916. V. 70

A COLLECTION of Old Ballads. London: 1872. V. 68

A COLLECTION of Poems in Six Volumes. By Several Hands. London: 1775. V. 72

A COLLECTION of Publick Acts and Papers Relating to the Principles of Armed Neutrality, Brought Forward in the Years 1780 and 1781. London: 1801. V. 72

A COLLECTION of Right Merrie Garlands for North Country Anglers. Newcastle: 1842. V. 70; 72

THE COLLECTION of the Garden Ltd. Magnificent Books and Manuscripts. New York: 1989. V. 68

A COLLECTION of the Several Addresses in the Late King James's Time: Concerning the Conception and Birth of the Pretended Prince of Wales. London: 1710?. V. 72

A COLLECTION of the Statutes Relating to the Admiralty, Navy, Ships of War, and Incidental Matters, to the Eighth Year of King George the Third. London: 1768. V. 72

COLLECTIONS With Regard to the Case of the American Loyalists. London?: 1783?. V. 70

COLLECTOR, STEPHEN
Law of the Range- Portraits of Old-Time Brand Inspectors. Livington, MT: 1991. V. 71

COLLEGE OF MIDWIFERY OF THE CITY OF NEW YORK
Woman's Work in the Field of Meidicine. New York: 1883. V. 68

COLLER, DUFFIELD WILLIAM
The People's History of Essex.... Chelmsford: 1861. V. 68

COLLES, RAMSAY
The History of Ulster from the Earliest Times to the Present Day. 1919. V. 70

COLLETON, JOHN
A Just Defence of the Slandered Priestes: Wherein the Reasons of Their Bearing Off to Receiue Maister Blackwell to Their Superior Before the Arrivall of His Holines Breve, are Layed Down. London: 1602. V. 68

COLLIBER, SAMUEL
Columna Rostrata; or, a Critical History of the English Sea-Affairs.... London: 1727. V. 73

COLLIE, J. N.
Climbing on the Himalaya and Other Mountain Ranges. 1902. V. 73

COLLIE, MICHAEL
George Meredith: a Bibliography. London: 1974. V. 72

COLLIER, JANE
An Essay on the Art of Ingenious Tormenting, with Proper Rules for the Exercise of that Amusing Study.... London: 1753. V. 68; 69; 70; 73

COLLIER, JEREMY
A Defence of the Short View of the Profaneness and Immorality of the English Stage. London: 1699. V. 73
Essays Upon Several Moral Subjects. In Two Parts. (with) Part III. (with) Part IV. London: 1709. V. 73
A Short View of the Immorality, and Profaneness of the English Stage, Together with the Sense of Antiquity Upon this Argument. London: 1698. V. 70

COLLIER, JOHN
Defy the Foul Fiend, or the Misadventures of a Heart. London: 1934. V. 72
Fancies and Goodnights. New York: 1951. V. 69
His Monkey Wife or Married to a Chimp. New York: 1931. V. 70
The Indians of the Americas. New York: 1947. V. 69
The Miscellaneous Works of Tim Bobbin. London: 1775. V. 70; 71; 72; 73
The Miscellaneous Works of Tim Bobbin. Rochdale: 1819. V. 71
The Miscellaneous Works of Tim Bobbin. Manchester: 1862. V. 71
No Traveller Returns. London: 1931. V. 70; 72
Patterns and Ceremonials of the Indians of the Southwest. New York: 1949. V. 70
Tim Bobbin's Lancashire Dialect; and Poems. London: 1833. V. 73
Tom's A-Cold. London: 1933. V. 73
Tom's A-Cold. London: 1953. V. 68
The Works of Tim Bobbin, Esq. Rochdale: 1819. V. 73
The Works of Tim Bobbin, Esq. Manchester: 1862. V. 72; 73

COLLIER, JOHN PAYNE
Punch and Judy. London: 1881. V. 70
Punch and Judy. New York: 1937. V. 69
The Tragic Comedy or Comical Tragedy of Punch and Judy Set Down in 1828. New York: 1937. V. 70

COLLIGNON, CHARLES
An Enquiry into the Structure of the Human Body, Relative to Its Influence on the Morals of Mankind. Cambridge: 1764. V. 69

COLLINGS, ELLSWORTH
The 101 Ranch. Norman: 1937. V. 69

COLLINGWOOD, STUART DODGSON
The Lewis Carroll Picture Book. London: 1899. V. 70
The Life and Letters Of Charles Lutwidge Dodgson. 1899. V. 68
The Life and Letters of Lewis Caroll. London: 1898. V. 73

COLLINGWOOD, W. G.
Coniston Tales. Ulverston: 1899. V. 71
The Lake Counties. London: 1932. V. 71
The Likeness of King Elfwald. Kendal: 1917. V. 71
The Memoirs of Sir Daniel Fleming. Kendal: 1928. V. 71
Northumbrian Crosses of the Pre-Norman Age. London: 1927. V. 73

COLLINS' Illustrated Guide to London and Neighbourhood.... 1875. V. 71

COLLINS, ANTHONY
A Discourse of Free-thinking, Occasion'd by the Rise and Growth of a Sect Call'd Free Thinkers. London: 1713. V. 72

COLLINS, BILLY
Sailing Alone Around the Room: New and Selected Poems. New York: 2001. V. 71

COLLINS, CHARLES A.
The Bar Sinister. London: 1868. V. 68

COLLINS, CHARLES S.
A Telegraphic Code for Finger-Print Formulae & A System for SubClassification of Single Digital Impressions. London: 1921. V. 69

COLLINS, D.
A Tear for Somalia. 1960. V. 70; 72

COLLINS, DALE
The Haven. New York: 1925. V. 70
The Haven. New York: 1935. V. 70

COLLINS, DENNIS
The Indians Last Fight or the Dull Knife Raid. Girard: 1915. V. 70

COLLINS, EDWARD JAMES MORTIMER
A Fight with Fortune. London: 1907. V. 68

COLLINS, GEORGE K.
149th New York Volunteer Regiment Infantry - an Abbreviated Account of the Certain Men of Onondaga County Who Did Service in the War 1861-1865. Syracuse: 1928. V. 69

COLLINS, GILBERT
Murder at Brambles. New York: 1932. V. 72

COLLINS, HUBERT E.
Warpath and Cattle Trail. New York: 1928. V. 71

COLLINS, JENNIE
Nature's Aristocracy; or, Battles and Wounds in Time of Peace. Boston and New York: 1871. V. 69

COLLINS, JOHN
Voices of the Dumb Creation. Philadelphia: 1893. V. 72

COLLINS, JOHN S.
Across the Plains in '64: Incidents of Early Days West of the Missouri River.... Omaha: 1904. V. 71
Across the Plains in '64: Incidents of Early Days West of the Missouri River.... Omaha: 1911. V. 71

COLLINS, MARY
Death Warmed Over. New York: 1947. V. 69

COLLINS, MAURICE
Raffles. London: 1966. V. 71

COLLINS, MAX ALLAN
The Killer Inside Him. Cedar Rapids, Iowa: 1983. V. 69; 71; 73

COLLINS, MICHAEL
The Meat Eaters. London: 1992. V. 69; 71; 73

COLLINS, REBA
Will Rogers. Courtship and Correspondence of the World's Greatest Catch. Oklahoma City: 1992. V. 72

COLLINS, SAMUEL
The Present State of Russia, in a Letter to a Friend at London.... London: 1671. V. 70

COLLINS, STEPHEN
Miscellanies. Philadelphia: 1842. V. 69

COLLINS, VARNUM LANSING
The Continental Congress at Princeton. Princeton: 1908. V. 69
Early Princeton Printing. Princeton: 1911. V. 69

COLLINS, W. J. TOWNSHEND
Tales from the New Mabinogion, arranged and decorated by Fred Richards. London: 1923. V. 71

COLLINS, WILKIE
After Dark. London: 1863. V. 73
Antonia, or, the Fall of Rome. London: 1875. V. 73
Armdale. London: 1888. V. 68
The Black Robe. London: 1881. V. 73
The Evil Genius. Chicago: 1986. V. 71
The Fallen Leaves. London: 1879. V. 73
The Legacy of Cain. London: 1889. V. 73
Man and Wife. New York: 1870. V. 68; 69; 72
Man and Wife. London: 1875. V. 73
The Moonstone. London: 1868. V. 69
The Moonstone. New York: 1868. V. 68; 70; 72
The Moonstone. London: 1902. V. 72
The Moonstone. London: 1944. V. 69
My Miscellanies. London: 1863. V. 73
The New Magdalen. London: 1877. V. 68
The New Magdalen. London: 1913. V. 68
Poor Miss Finch. London: 1895. V. 68
The Queen of Hearts. New York: 1859. V. 69
The Queen of Hearts. London: 1871. V. 68
The Woman in White. London: 1860. V. 68
The Woman in White. London: 1871. V. 68

COLLINS, WILLIAM
Odes on Several Descriptive and Allegoric Subjects. London: 1747. V. 69
The Poetical Works. London: 1765. V. 70; 73
The Poetical Works. London: 1798. V. 73

COLLINS, WILLIAM EDWARD
Archbishop Laud Commemoration, 1895. Lectures on Archbishop Laud together with a Bibliography of Laudian Literature and the Laudian Exhibition Catalogue. Barking: 1895. V. 70

COLLIS, J.
The Builder's Portfolio of Street Architecture. London: 1837. V. 70; 72

COLLIS, SEPTIMA M.
A Woman's Trips to Alaska: Being an Account of a Voyage through the Inland Seas of the Sitkin Archipelago in 1890. New York: 1890. V. 70

COLLISON, ROBERT L.
Dictionaries of Foreign Languages: a Bibliographical Guide to the General and Technical Dictionaries of the Chief Foreign Languages.... New York: 1955. V. 73

COLLISON, WILLIAM
The Apostle of Free Labour and the Life Story of William Collison Founder and General Secretary of the National Free Labour Association. London: 1913. V. 71

COLLISON, WILSON
Dark Dame. New York: 1935. V. 71
Sexational Eve. New York: 1933. V. 73

COLLOMB, ROBIN G.
Alpine Guide. London: 1969. V. 69
Alpine Points of View. London: 1961. V. 69
Selected Climbs in the Pennine Alps. London: 1968. V. 69

COLLUM, CHARLES
New York Nude. New York: 1981. V. 68

COLLYER, ROBERT
Ilkley: Ancient and Modern. Otley: 1885. V. 73
Lights and Shadows of American Life. Boston c: 1838. V. 73

COLMADA, MIGUEL
The Treasvre of the Soule. London: 1596. V. 73

COLMAN, GEORGE
The Connoisseur. Oxford: 1767. V. 73
The Grand Dramatic Romance of Blue Beard; or Female Curiosity.... London: 1798. V. 70
The Law of Java; or, the Poison Tree. London: 1822. V. 69
Random Records. London: 1830. V. 72
The Rodiad. London: 1927. V. 70
Songs, Choruses &c. in the Battle of Hexham; or days of Old. London: 1789. V. 72

COLNETT, JAMES
Journal...Abroad the Argonaut from April 26, 1789 to Nov. 3, 1791. Toronto: 1940. V. 71

COLOMBO, CRISTOFORO
Lettere Di Cristoforo Colombo: Autografi Conservati Nel Pallazzo Municipale di Genova. Genova: 1912. V. 69

COLOMBO, MATTEO REALDO
De re Anatomicalibri XV. Hisce Iam Aecesserum Joannis Posthii Med. D. Observationes Anatomicae. Frankfurt am Main: 1590. V. 70; 72
De Re Anatomica Libri XV. Frankfurt am Main: 1593. V. 70

COLONNA, FRANCESCO
La Hypnerotomachia di Poliphilo, Cio' Pugna D'Amore in Sogno. Venice: 1545. V. 69

COLORADO. (TERRITORY). LEGISLATIVE ASSEMBLY - 1865
General Laws and Joint Resolutions - Memorials and private Acts Passed at the Fourth Session of the Legislative Assembly of the Territory of Colorado. Denver: 1865. V. 68; 70

COLORADO. (TERRITORY). LEGISLATIVE ASSEMBLY - 1867
Council Journal of the Legislative Assembly of the Territory of Colorado Sixth Session. Central City: 1867. V. 68; 70; 73

COLORED NATIONAL LABOR CONVENTION
Proceedings of the Colored National Labor Convention Held in Washington, D.C. on December 6-10, 1869. Washington: 1870. V. 68; 71

COLOUR Show Pictures of Ten Little Nigger Boys. London: 1950. V. 73

COLQUHOUN, ARCHIBALD
China in Transformation. London: 1898. V. 72
China in Transformation. New York: 1898. V. 70; 72

COLQUHOUN, IAIN
Highland Gatherings. Being Accounts of Braemar, Northern and Luss Meetings. London: 1927. V. 71

COLQUHOUN, JOHN
The Moor and the Loch. 1888. V. 70; 72; 73
Sporting Days. London: 1866. V. 71

COLQUHOUN, PATRICK
A Treatise on Indigence; Exhibiting a General View of the National Resources for Productive Labour.... London: 1806. V. 69
A Treatise on the Commerce and Police of the River Thames.... London: 1800. V. 71; 73
A Treatise on the Police of the Metropolis.... London: 1796. V. 69
A Treatise on the Police of the Metropolis.... London: 1797. V. 70; 73
A Treatise on the Wealth, Power and Resources of the British Empire, In Every Quarter of the World.... London: 1814. V. 72
A Treatise on the Wealth, Power and Resources of the British Empire, in Every Quarter of the World.... London: 1815. V. 70

COLT, J. B.
The First and Second Part of a Work on Government. Hartford: 1870. V. 69

COLT, SAMUEL
Armsmear: the Home, the Arm and the Armory of Samuel Colt. New York: 1866. V. 70

COLTART, J. S.
Scottish Church Architecture. London: 1936. V. 71

COLTER, CYRUS
The Hippodrome. Chicago: 1973. V. 68; 72

COLTON, CALVIN
Four Years in Great Britain 1831-1835. New York: 1826. V. 70

COLTON, GEORGE
A Maryland Editor Abroad. What He Saw and What He Thought of it. Annapolis: 1881. V. 70

COLTON, HAROLD S.
Potsherds. Flagstaff: 1953. V. 73
The Sinagua. Flagstaff, AZ: 1946. V. 72

COLTON, J.
The Parnasse Francois: Titon du Tillet and the Origins of the Monument to Genius. New Haven: 1979. V. 72

COLTON, J. H.
Colton's Traveler and Tourist's Guide-Book through the United States of America and the Canadas. New York: 1850. V. 70
Colton's Traveler and Tourist's Guide-Book Through the Western States and Territories.... 1855. V. 68

COLTON, JOHN
Rain: A Play in Three Acts. New York: 1923. V. 72

COLTON, ROBERT
Pedestrian and Other Reminiscences at Home and Abroad; with Sketches of Country Life. London: 1846. V. 71

COLTON, WALTER
The California Diary. Oakland: 1948. V. 68; 73
Deck and Port: or Incidents of a Cruise in the U.S. Frigate Congress to California...Sketches of Rio Janeiro, Vaparaiso, Lima, Honolulu and San Francisco. New York: 1850. V. 70
Three Years in California. Cincinnati: 1850. V. 73

COLTRANE, JAMES
A Good Day To Die. New York: 1999. V. 72

COLUM, PADRAIC
The Frenzied Prince, Being Heroic Stories of Ancient Ireland. Philadelphia: 1943. V. 69; 72
The King of Ireland's Son. 1920. V. 69
The Six Who Were Left in a Shoe. Chicago: 1923. V. 70
Ten Poems. Dublin: 1957. V. 69
Three Men. London: 1930. V. 73

COLUMBANI, P.
Vases and Tripods on Twelve Plates. London: 1775. V. 68; 70; 72

THE COLUMBIAN Riddler, or Entertaining Puzzle Book. Neark: 1840. V. 70

COLVER, ALICE ROSS
Forever is So Long. Philadelphia: 1942. V. 71
Under the Rainbow. Philadelphia: 1926. V. 71

COLVILE, EDEN
London Correspondence Inward from Eden Colvile, 1849-1852. London: 1956. V. 73

COLVILLE, ALEX
Diary of a War Artist. Halifax: 1981. V. 72

COLWALL, JAMES GILBERT SHELDON
The Coombsberrow Mystery. London: 1891. V. 68

COLYER, VINCENT
Bombardment of Wrangel, Alaska: Report of the Secretary of War, Secretary of the Interior and Letter to the President. Washington: 1870. V. 70
Brief Report of the Services Rendered by the Freed People to the United States Army in North Carolina, in the Spring of 1862, After the Battle of Newbern. New York: 1864. V. 70

COMAN, KATHERINE
Economic Beginnings of the Far West. New York: 1912. V. 73

COMBE, GEORGE
Lectures on Phrenology by George Combe.... New York: 1841. V. 68; 71; 73
Moral Philosophy; or, The Duties of man Considered In His Individual Social and Domestic Capacities. Edinburgh: 1841. V. 71
Remarks on National Education. Edinburgh: 1847. V. 68
A System of Phrenology.... Edinburgh: 1836. V. 72

COMBE, WILLIAM
The Auction: a Town Eclogue. London: 1778. V. 73
Doctor Syntax's Three Tours in Search of the Picturesque, Consolation and a Wife. London. V. 71
The English Dance of Death from the Designs of Thomas Rowlandson. and The Dance of Life. London: 1814-1816. V. 70
The English Dance of Death. (with) The Dance of Life. London: 1815-1817. V. 68
The First of April, or the Triumphs of Folly, a Poem. London: 1777. V. 70
The Grand Master, or Adventures of Qui Hi?. London: 1816. V. 68
The History of Johnny Quae Genus, the Little Foundling of the Late Dr. Syntax: a Poem. London: 1822. V. 68
A History of Madeira. London: 1821. V. 70
The History of the Abbey Church of St. Peter's Westminster, Its Antuqities and Monuments. London: 1812. V. 68
Life of Napoleon, a Hudibrastic Poem. London: 1815. V. 73
The Second Tour of Doctor Syntax: In Search of Consolation, a Poem. London: 1903. V. 70
(The Three Tours of Dr. Syntax). In Search of the Picturesque...In Search of Consolation...in Search of a Wife. London: 1812. V. 72
(The Three Tours of Dr. Syntax) In Search of the Picturesque...In Search of Consolation...In Search of a Wife. London: 1855. V. 70
The Three Tours of Doctor Syntax. London. V. 69
The Wars of Wellington, a Narrative Poem: in Fifteen Cantos. London: 1821. V. 68
A Word in Season, to the Traders and Manufacturers of Great Britain. London: 1792. V. 72

COMBEMERLE, MARY WOOLEY GIBBINGS, VISCOUTNESSE
A Friar's Scourge. London: 1876. V. 73

COMBER, J. B.
Orchids of Java. 1990. V. 70

COMBER, THOMAS
Adultery Analyzed; an Inquiry Into the Causes of the Prevalence of that Vice in These Kingdoms at the Present Day. London: 1810. V. 69
A Companion to the Temple; or a Help to Devotion in the Use of the Common Prayer. London: 1684. V. 70

COMBERMERLE, MARY WOOLEY GIBBINGS
A Friar's Scourge. London: 1876. V. 69

COMBINATION Atlas Map of Salem and Gloucester Counties, New Jersey. Philadelphia: 1876. V. 69

COMBS, TREY
The Steelhead Trout, Life History - Early Angling, Contemporary Steelheading. Portland: 1971. V. 69

COME Lasses and Lads. London: 1884. V. 70

COMENIUS, JOHAN AMOS
Orbis Sensualium Pictus... Visible World; or a Nomenclautre and Pictures of all the Chief Things that are in the World.... 1777. V. 72

COMES, NATALIS
Natalis Comitvm Veneti De Venatione Libri IIII. Venetiis: 1551. V. 69

COMFORT, ARTHUR
Pen and Ink Drawings. Toll Houses and Other Drawings from Carlisle to Melrose. . . Halifax. V. 71

COMFORT, JANE LEVINGTON
From These Beginnings. New York: 1937. V. 69

COMFORT, WILL LEVINGTON
Apache. New York: 1936. V. 69
Trooper Tales-A Series Of Sketches Of the Real American Private Soldier. New York: 1899. V. 72

COMIC Capers Library. New York: 1938. V. 70

COMICAL Pictures. London: 1900. V. 70

COMMELIN, CASPARUS
Beschryvinge Van Amsterdam. Amsterdam: 1726. V. 69

THE COMMERCIAL Room. London: 1847. V. 71

COMMERELL, ABBE DE
An Account of the Culture and Use of the Mangel Wurzel, or Root of Scarcity. London: 1787. V. 70; 72
An Account of the Culture and Use of the Mangel Wurzel, or Root of Scarcity. London: 1788. V. 70

COMMINES, PHILIPPE DE
The Historie. London: 1601. V. 69
The Historie. London: 1614. V. 73
Les Memoires. Paris: 1572. V. 69

COMMISSIONERS FOR ADJUSTING THE BOUNDARIES OF THE BRITISH
The Memorials of the English and French Commissaries Concerning the Limits of Nova Scotia or Acadia. London: 1755. V. 72

COMMONS, JOHN
A Documentary History of American Industrial Society. New York: 1958. V. 71
History of Labour in the United States. New York: 1926-1935. V. 68

A COMPANION to the Magdalen-Chapel. London: 1780?. V. 69

COMPANION to the Medicine Chest, with Plain Rules for Taking the Medicines in the Cure of Diseases, in a Style Adapted to every Capacity. New York: 1832. V. 73

A COMPANION to the Theatre, or the Usefulness of the Stage to Religion, Government and the Conduct of Life. London: 1736. V. 72

A COMPANION to the Weather-Glass; or the Nature, Construction and Use of the Barometer, Thermometer and Hygrometer.... Edinburgh: 1796. V. 69

A COMPENDIOUS History of the Taxes of France, and of the Oppresive Methods of Raising of them. London: 1694. V. 72

COMPENDIUM for Printers and Buyers of Printing.... London: 1937. V. 72

THE COMPLEAT Sheriff: Wherein is Set Forth, His Office and Authority; with Directions, How and In what Manner to Execute the Same.... London: 1727. V. 70

A COMPLETE Collection of the English Poems Which Have Obtained the Chancellor's Gold Medal. London: 1894. V. 70

THE COMPLETE Fortune Teller. Providence: 1811. V. 71

THE COMPLETE Governess: a Course of Mental Instruction for Ladies.... London: 1826. V. 69

THE COMPLETE Grazier; or, Gentleman and Farmer's Directory. London: 1767. V. 73

THE COMPLETE Guide to Fustian Manufacturing, Designed for Manufacturers, Managers and Jobbers.... Bury: 1885. V. 71

A COMPLETE Illustrated History of Animals Contained in the Department of Comparative Zoology with P. T. Barnum's Greatest Show on Earth, and the Great London Circus.... New York: 1887. V. 72

THE COMPLETE Young Man's Companion: or, Self Instructor.... Manchester: 1811. V. 70

THE COMPLETE Young Man's Companion; or Self Instructor.... Manchester: 1801. V. 73

COMPTON, THOMAS
The Northern Cambrian Mountains; or a Tour through the North Wales. London: 1820. V. 70

COMPTON-BURNETT, IVY
Brothers and Sisters. New York: 1929. V. 68
Darkness and Day. London: 1951. V. 68
A God and His Gifts. London: 1963. V. 68
A Heritage and Its History. London: 1959. V. 68
Men and Wives. London: 1931. V. 73
The Mighty and Their Fall. London: 1961. V. 68
Mother and Son. London: 1955. V. 68
Pastors and Masters. Heath Cranton: 1925. V. 70
Pastors and Masters. London: 1925. V. 68; 70
The Present and the Past. London: 1953. V. 68

COMRIE, JOHN D.
History of Scottish Medicine to 1860. 1927. V. 68
History of Scottish Medicine to 1860. Balliere: 1927. V. 71
History of Scottish Medicine to 1860. London: 1927. V. 70

COMROE, JULIUS H.
The Top Ten Clinical Advances in Cardiovascular-Pulmonary Medicine and Surgery 1945-1975. Final Report January 31, 1977. Washington: 1977. V. 72

COMSTOCK, FRANCIS ADAMS
A Gothic Vision: F. L. Griggs and His Work. Oxford: 1966. V. 70; 72; 73

COMSTOCK, J. A.
Butterflies of California. Los Angeles: 1927. V. 69

COMSTOCK, J. H.
The Spider Book. New York: 1948. V. 71

COMSTOCK, J. L.
Elements of Chemistry in Which the Recent Discoveries in the Sciences are Included.... New York: 1838. V. 68
Outlines of Physiology, Both Comparative and Human; Functions to Muscular Exercise.... New York: 1843. V. 68

COMSTOCK, JIM
West Virginia Picture Book. Richwood: 1978. V. 72

COMSTOCK, JOHN L.
History of the Greek Revolution Compiled from Official Documents of the Greek Government. New York: 1828. V. 71

COMSTOCK, W. P.
Butterflies of the American Tropics, the Genus Anaea.... New York: 1961. V. 70; 72
The Housing Book. New York: 1919. V. 68; 69; 72

COMTE, AUGUSTE
The Catechism of Positive Religion. London: 1891. V. 71
The Philosophy of Mathematics.... New York: 1851. V. 71
The Positive Philosophy. London: 1853. V. 71

COMUNALE, ANTHONY R.
Art on the Stone by the American Indians in New Jersey. New York: 1963. V. 69

COMYNS, JOHN
Reports of Cases Argued and Adjudged in the Courts of King's Bench, Common Pleas, and Exchequer. London: 1792. V. 73

CONANT, CHARLES A.
A History of Modern Banks of Issue. New York and London: 1896. V. 71

CONARD, HENRY S.
The Waterlilies. Washington: 1905. V. 69

CONAWAY, JAMES
The Big Easy. Boston: 1970. V. 68

THE CONCEITED Boy. New York. V. 71

CONCERTS of Antient Music, Under the Patronage of Their Majesties; as Performed at the New Rooms, Tottenham-Street. London: 1787-1788-. V. 72

A CONCISE Description of Bury St. Edmunds and Its Environs Within the Distance of ten Miles.... London: 1827. V. 70; 72

A CONCISE History of Birds: Interspersed with a Variety of Anecdotes. Edinburgh: 1850. V. 72

A CONCISE Introduction to the Knowledge of the Most Eminent Painters.... London: 1778. V. 69; 72

CONDE, MARYSE
Tree of Life. New York: 1992. V. 72

CONDER, JOSIAH
Modern Traveller, a Description, Geographical, Historical.... London: 1830. V. 68; 71

CONDILLAC, ETIENNE BONNOT DE
Essai Sur l'Origine des Connoissances Humaines. Amsterdam (i.e. Paris): 1746. V. 68
The Logic of Condillac. Philadelphia: 1809. V. 71
Traite des Sensations a Madame la Comtesse de Vasse. London and Paris: 1754. V. 69; 70; 72

CONDIT, JOTHAM H.
Genealogical Record of the Condit Family. 1916. V. 69

CONDON, EDDIE
Eddie Condon's Treasury of Jazz. New York: 1956. V. 69; 71

CONDON, RICHARD
The Ecstasy Business. London: 1967. V. 68
The Manchurian Candidate. New York: 1959. V. 68; 69
The Manchurian Candidate. London: 1960. V. 69
Mexican Stove. Garden City: 1973. V. 72
Prizzi's Honor. New York: 1982. V. 72

CONDORCET, MARIE JEAN ANTOINE NICOLAS DE CARITAT, MARQUIS DE
Esquisse d'un Tableau Historique des Progres de l'Esprit Humain. Paris: 1795. V. 72

CONERLY, CHARLIE
The Forward Press. New York: 1960. V. 72

CONFEDERATE STATES OF AMERICA
Army Regulations, Adopted for the Use of the Army of the Confederate States. New Orleans: 1861. V. 69
CONFEDERATE States Navy Register for 1862. Richmond: 1862. V. 70
Constitution of the Confederate States of America.... New Orleans: 1861. V. 69; 70
General Orders from the Adjutant and Inspector General's Office Confederate States Army for the Year 1863. Richmond: 1864. V. 69; 70
A Manual of Military Surgery, Prepared for the Use of the Confederate States Army. Richmond: 1863. V. 70
Official Report of the Battle of Chickamauga. Richmond: 1864. V. 69
Ordnance Instructions for the Confederate States Navy Relating to te PReparation of Vessels of War for Battle to the Duties of Officers and Others When at Quarters, to Ordnance and Ordnance Stories and to Gunnery.... London: 1864. V. 69; 70
Regulations for the Government of the Ordnance Department of the Confederate States of America. Richmond: 1862. V. 69; 70
Regulations for the Medical Department of the C.S. Army. Richmond: 1863. V. 69
Rules for the House of Representatives of the Confederate States. Richmond: 1862. V. 69

CONFUCIUS
The Analects. Shanghai: 1933. V. 69
Confucian Analects. New York: 1951. V. 72

CONGER, AMY
Edward Weston in Mexico 1923-1926. Albuquerque: 1983. V. 70; 71

CONGER, EMILY BRONSON
An Ohio Woman in the Philippines. Akron: 1904. V. 70

CONGER, ROGER NORMAN
Highlights of Waco History. Waco: 1945. V. 68

CONGER, SARAH P.
Letters from China with Particular Reference to the Empress Dowager and the Women of China. Chicago: 1910. V. 71

CONGREGATIONAL CHURCH IN MASSACHUSETTS
Proceedings of the Convention of Congregational Ministers in the Commonwealth of Massachusetts; together with a Statement of the Number and Names of the Congregational Associations, Ministers, Candidates, Vacancies &c.... Boston: 1795. V. 68

CONGREVE, RICHARD
International Policy. Essays on the Foreign Relations of England. London: 1866. V. 72

CONGREVE, WILLIAM
The Double Dealer, a Comedy, Acted at the Theatre Royal, by Their Majesties Servants. London: 1694. V. 73
The Dramatick Works. Dublin: 1731. V. 73
The Way of the World and Love for Love. London: 1929. V. 68; 69
The Works of Mr. William Congreve. London: 1730. V. 69

CONKLE, E. P.
200 Were Chosen. New York: 1937. V. 72

CONKLIN, EMMA B.
A Brief History of Logan County, Colorado with Reminiscences by Pioneers. Sterling: 1928. V. 68; 71

CONKLING, MARGARET C.
Memoirs of the Mother and Wife of Washington. Auburn: 1850. V. 68

CONKLING, ROSCOE
The Butterfield Overland Mail 1867-1869.... Glendale: 1947. V. 70

CONLEY, ROBERT J.
Killing Time. New York: 1988. V. 72
Nickajack. New York: 1992. V. 69
The Way of the Priests. New York: 1992. V. 71

THE CONNECTICUT Cookbook Being a Collection of Recipes from Connecticut Kitchens.... Westport: 1943. V. 71
THE CONNECTICUT Cookbook Being a Collection of Recipes from Connecticut Kitchens.... New York: 1944. V. 71

CONNECTICUT WOMAN SUFFRAGE ASSOCIATION
Annual Meeting of the Connecticut Woman Suffrage Association Held at Hartford, Sept. 9, 1870. Report of the Executive Committee.... Hartford: 1871. V. 69

CONNELL, ARTHUR
Analysis of Coprolites and Other Organic Remains.... 1836. V. 68

CONNELL, ED
Hackamore Reinsman. Ciso: 1952. V. 69

CONNELL, EVAN S.
The Anatomy Lesson. New York: 1957. V. 69; 71; 73
The Aztec Treasure House. Washington: 2001. V. 69
The Connoisseur. New York: 1974. V. 68; 72
Mesa Verde. New York: 1993. V. 69; 73
Mrs. Bridge. New York: 1959. V. 68; 69; 70; 71
Son of the Morning Star. San Francisco: 1984. V. 68; 72; 73

CONNELL, P. H.
Native Housing, A Collective Thesis. Johannesburg: 1939. V. 68

CONNELL, RICHARD
Variety. New York: 1925. V. 71

CONNELL, ROBERT
Arkansas. New York: 1947. V. 69

CONNELL, WILL
In Pictures: a Hollywood Satire. New York: 1937. V. 68; 73

CONNELLEY, WILLIAM E.
Doniphan's Expedition and the Conquest of New Mexico and California. Kansas City: 1907. V. 69; 70
Doniphan's Expedition and the Conquest of New Mexico and California. Topeka: 1907. V. 68
Quantrill and the Border Wars. Cedar Rapids: 1910. V. 69; 70
Wild Bill and His Era. New York: 1933. V. 73

CONNELLY, MARC
The Green Pastures. New York: 1929. V. 68

CONNELLY, MICHAEL
Angels Flight. London: 1998. V. 71
The Black Echo. Boston: 1992. V. 68; 69; 70; 71; 72
The Black Ice. Boston: 1993. V. 68; 70; 71; 72
The Black Ice. London: 1993. V. 72
The Black Ice Score. Boston: 1993. V. 70
Blood Work. 1987. V. 68
Blood Work. 1997. V. 69
Blood Work. Boston: 1997. V. 71; 72
Blood Work. Tucson: 1997. V. 69
Chasing the Dime. Tucson: 2002. V. 73
City Of Bones. Boston: 2002. V. 72
City Of Bones. Tucson: 2002. V. 72; 73
The Concrete Blonde. Boston: 1994. V. 68; 70; 72
A Darkness More than Night. 2000. V. 68
A Darkness More than Night. Boston: 2000. V. 72
Darkness More Than Night. London: 2000. V. 71
A Darkness More than Night. New Orleans: 2000. V. 71; 72
A Darkness More than Night. Boston: 2001. V. 70
A Darkness More Than Night. New York: 2001. V. 72
The Last Coyote. Boston: 1995. V. 68; 71; 72
The Poet. Boston: 1996. V. 70
Trunk Music. Boston: 1997. V. 68; 72
Trunk Music. London: 1997. V. 68; 69; 71
Void Moon. Tucson: 1999. V. 68; 69; 70; 71; 72; 73
The Wire in the Blood. Scottsdale: 1998. V. 71

CONNELLY, WILLIAM E.
Life Of Preston B. Plumb 1837-1891. Chicago: 1913. V. 72

CONNER, DANIEL ELLIS
Joseph Reddeford Walker and the Arizona Adventure. Norman: 1956. V. 69

CONNER, REARDEN
Time to Kill. New York: 1936. V. 68; 69

CONNETT, EUGENE
Fishing a Trout Stream. 1934. V. 68
My Friend the Trout. 1961. V. 68
Upland Game Bird Shooting in America. New York: 1930. V. 73

CONNICK, C. J.
Adventures in Light and Color: an Introduction to the Stained Glass Craft. New York: 1937. V. 69; 72

CONNINGTON, J.
Death At Swaything Court. Boston: 1926. V. 70
Jack-in-the Box. Boston: 1944. V. 70

CONNINGTON, J. J.
The Brandon Case. Boston: 1934. V. 73
The Case with Nine Solutions. 1929. V. 73
Jack-in-the-Box. Boston: 1944. V. 68
The Omnibus. London: 1930. V. 73
The Tragedy at Ravensthorpe. Boston: 1928. V. 69
The Two Ticket Puzzle. 1930. V. 73

CONNOLD, E. T.
British Vegetable Galls. London: 1901. V. 69

CONNOLLY, CYRIL
Enemies of Promise. London: 1938. V. 72
Previous Convictions. London: 1963. V. 72; 73
The Rock Pool. Paris: 1936. V. 70
The Unquiet Grave. London: 1944. V. 69
The Unquiet Grave. London: 1945. V. 68

CONNOLLY, JOHN
Dark Hollow. London: 2000. V. 69; 70; 71; 72
Every Dead Thing. London: 1999. V. 69; 70; 71; 72; 73
The Killing Kind. London: 2000. V. 69; 72
The Killing Kind. London: 2001. V. 70; 71
The Killing Kind. London: 2002. V. 73
The White Road. London: 2002. V. 72

CONNOR, D. R.
BG Off the Record. Fairless Hills, PA: 1958. V. 71

CONNOR, LINDA
Solos. Millerton: 1979. V. 68

CONNOR, RALPH
Treading the Winepress. New York: 1925. V. 71

CONNORS, JO
Who's Who in Arizona. Tucson: 1913. V. 70

CONOVER, G. W.
Sixty Years in Southwest Oklahoma, Or the Autobiography of.... Anadarko: 1927. V. 71

CONQUEST, JOAN
Chastity: A Drama of the East. New York: 1929. V. 70
The Desert's Secret. New York: 1933. V. 69
The Hawk of Egypt. New York: 1922. V. 70
Leonie of the Jungle. New York: 1921. V. 71
Zarah the Cruel. New York: 1923. V. 71

CONRAD, EARL
Everything and Nothing: the Dorothy Dandridge Tragedy. New York: 1970. V. 69

CONRAD, HOWARD LOUIS
Uncle Dick Wootton. Chicago: 1890. V. 68; 70
Uncle Dick Wootton. Chicago: 1957. V. 69

CONRAD, JOSEPH
Almayer's Folly: a Story of an Eastern River. London: 1895. V. 73
The Arrow of Gold. London: 1919. V. 68; 69
The Arrow of Gold. New York: 1919. V. 72; 73
Chance. London: 1913. V. 68
Chance. London: 1914. V. 68; 73
Chance. New York: 1914. V. 72; 73
The Children of the Sea. New York: 1898. V. 71
Complete Works. New York: 1924. V. 70
Conrad's Manifesto: Preface to a Career. Philadelphia: 1966. V. 68; 72
The Dover Patrol. Canterbury: 1922. V. 71; 72; 73
Falk. Amy Foster. To-morrow. Three Stories. New York: 1903. V. 69
Heart of Darkness. New York: 1992. V. 69
John Galsworthy: an Appreciation. Canterbury: 1922. V. 69
Joseph Conrad on the Art of Writing. Being a reprinting of the original preface to The Nigger of the Narcissus. Garden City: 1914. V. 72
Laughing Anne. London: 1923. V. 71; 72
Laughing Anne and One Day More: Two Plays. London: 1924. V. 68
The Mirror of the Sea. London: 1906. V. 69; 70; 71; 73
Mirror of the Sea. New York: 1906. V. 71
The Nature of a Crime. London: 1924. V. 69
The Nature of a Crime. New York: 1924. V. 71; 72; 73
The Nigger of the Narcissus. London: 1898. V. 68
Nostromo. London: 1904. V. 68; 71; 72
Nostromo. New York: 1904. V. 73
Nostromo. New York: 1980. V. 70
Notes on Life and Letters. London: 1921. V. 68
Notes on My Books. London: 1921. V. 71
One Day More. Garden City: 1920. V. 68; 71
An Outcast of the Islands. London: 1896. V. 68
An Outcast of the Islands. New York: 1896. V. 69; 70
An Outcast of the Islands. London: 1907. V. 69
An Outcast of the Islands. New York: 1975. V. 73
A Personal Record. New York: 1912. V. 68
A Personal Record. New York: 1919. V. 71
The Point of Honor. New York: 1908. V. 71; 73
The Rescue. London: 1920. V. 68; 69; 73
Romance. New York: 1904. V. 71
The Rover. London: 1923. V. 71; 73
The Rover. New York: 1923. V. 71
The Secret Agent. London: 1907. V. 68
The Secret Agent. New York: 1907. V. 72
The Secret Agent. London: 1923. V. 68; 69; 70; 71; 72; 73
The Secret Sharer. 1985. V. 71
The Secret Sharer. New York: 1985. V. 72
A Set of Six. London: 1908. V. 69; 71; 73
The Shadow-Line. London: 1917. V. 68
The Sisters. New York: 1928. V. 69; 71
The Sisters. Milan: 1968. V. 72

CONRAD, JOSEPH continued
Some Reminiscences. London: 1912. V. 68
Suspense. London: 1925. V. 68; 69; 71
Tales of Unrest. London: 1898. V. 68
Twixt Land and Sea. London: 1912. V. 68; 69; 70
Typhoon. New York: 1902. V. 69; 71
Typhoon. London: 1903. V. 68; 70; 71; 72; 73
Under Western Eyes. London: 1911. V. 73
Victory. London: 1915. V. 68; 73
Within the Tides. London: 1915. V. 68
The Works. Garden City: 1920. V. 71
The Works. London: 1921. V. 73
The Works. London: 1925. V. 73
Youth. London: 1902. V. 68; 71

CONRAD, TIMOTHY ABBOTT
A Geological Vision and Other Poems. Trenton: 1871. V. 69

CONRADS, U.
The Architecture of Fantasy. New York: 1962. V. 68; 69; 72

CONROY, FRANK
Midair. New York: 1985. V. 68; 72
Stop-Time. New York: 1967. V. 68; 73

CONROY, J. W.
The Northern Barrage. Mine Force United States Atlantic Fleet. Annapolis: 1919. V. 68

CONROY, JACK
The Disinherited. New York: 1993. V. 70
Unrest 1931. New York: 1931. V. 68

CONROY, PAT
Beach Music. New York: 1995. V. 68; 69; 72
The Boo. Atlanta: 1988. V. 70; 72
The Great Santini. Boston: 1976. V. 69; 70
The Lords of Discipline. Boston: 1980. V. 68; 69; 71; 73
The Lords of Discipline. New York: 1980. V. 70
The Lords of Discipline. London: 1981. V. 69
The Prince of Tides. Boston: 1986. V. 70
Thomas Wolfe. Atlanta: 2000. V. 70

CONSELMAN, DIERDRE
Keedle. New York: 1940. V. 73

CONSENTINO, F. J.
Boehm's Birds, the Porcelain Art of Edward Marshall Boehm. New York: 1960. V. 72

THE CONSEQUENCES of a Law for Reducing the Dutys Upon French Wines, Brandy, Silks and Linen to Those of Other Nations. London: 1713. V. 70; 72; 73

CONSET, HENRY
The Practice of the Spiritual or Ecclesiatical Courts. London: 1685. V. 73

CONSETT, MATTHEW
A Tour Through Sweden, Swedish-Lapland, Finland and Denmark. Stockton: 1815. V. 72

CONSIDERATIONS On the Present State of Popery in England. London: 1723. V. 69

CONSIDERATIONS on two Papers, Published at Antwerp, Respecting a Loan for 3,600,000 Guilders to be Subscribed at the Houses of Messieurs J. E. Werbrouck and C. J. M. De Wolf, of that City. London: 1791. V. 72

CONSIDERATIONS Touching Trade, with the Advance of the Kings Revenue and Present Reparation. London?: 1641. V. 72

CONSTABLE, JOHN
The Conversation of Gentlemen Considered in Most of the Ways, that Make Their Mutual Company Agreeable, or Disagreeable. London: 1738. V. 69; 73

CONSTABLE, W. G.
Canaletto Giovanni Anmtonio Canala. Oxford: 1976. V. 71
Richard Wilson. London: 1953. V. 72

CONSTANT, BENJAMIN
Adolphe, Illustrations en Couleur par Serge De Solomko. Paris: 1913. V. 70

CONSTANT DE REBECQUE, FRANCOISE MARC SAMUEL
Camille, ou Lettres de Deux Filles de ce Siecle. Londres: 1785. V. 69

CONSTANTIA: or, the Distressed Friend. London: 1770. V. 73

CONSTANTINE, K. C.
The Blank Page. New York: 1974. V. 68
Blood Mud. New York: 1999. V. 70
A Fix Like This. New York: 1975. V. 68; 73
Joey's Case. New York: 1988. V. 71
The Man Who Liked Slow Tomatoes. Boston: 1982. V. 68
The Man Who Liked to Look at Himself. New York: 1973. V. 68; 69
The Rocksburg Railroad Murders. 1972. V. 68

CONSTITUTIO Criminalis Theresiana Oder der Romisch Kaiserl, Zu Hungarn und Boheim a. a. Konigl. Apost. Majestat Maria Theresia.... Vienna: 1769. V. 68

CONSTITUTIONS and Canons Ecclesiastic, all Treated Upon by the Bishop of London.... London: 1678. V. 72

CONTACT Collection of Contemporary Writers. Paris: 1925. V. 70

CONTEMPORARY American Sculpture. New York: 1929. V. 69

CONTEMPORARY Art: Thirty Etchings and Chromolithographs After the Original Pictures by Eminent Artists of the Present Day. London: 1876. V. 69

CONTI, NATALE
Natalis Comitvm Veneti De Venatione, Libri IIII. Venitiis: 1551. V. 73

CONTINENTAL CONGRESS
Journal of the Proceedings of the Congress Held at Philadelphia, May 10, 1775. Philadelphia: 1776. V. 73
Journal of the Proceedings of the Congress, Held at Philadelphia, Sept. 5th, 1774. London: 1775. V. 73

CONTINO, VITTORUGO
Spots and Dots. Ezra Pound in Italy. Venezia: 1970. V. 73

CONTRIBUTIONS to Medical and Biological Research Dedicated to Sir William Osler...in Honor of His Seventieth Birthday July 12, 1919 by His Pupils and Co-workers. New York: 1919. V. 68; 73

A CONVERGENCE of Birds. New York: 2001. V. 69

CONVERSATIONS with Peter Taylor. Jackson: 1987. V. 71

THE CONVERSION of English Timber. 1884. V. 71

CONVERSIONS Remarquables de Quelques Protestans. Paris & Liege: 1790. V. 69

THE CONVEYANCER'S Assistant and Director Being a Treatise Containing Tables to All Sorts of Conveyances; as leases, Grants, Bargains, Sales Mortgages, Lease and Re-lease. London: 1702. V. 72

CONWAY, ANNE
The Principles of the Most Ancient and Modern Philosophy. The Hague: 1982. V. 71

CONWAY, J.
Letters from the Highlands. 1859. V. 73

CONWAY, J. N.
Climbing on the Himalaya and Other Mountain Ranges. 1902. V. 68; 70

CONWAY, MARTIN
Aconcagua and Tierra del Fuego. London: 1902. V. 69
The Alps. London: 1904. V. 69; 72
The Alps from End to End. London: 1895. V. 69; 72
The Alps from End to End. London: 1905. V. 69
The Bolivian Andes. 1901. V. 68; 70; 73
The Bolivian Andes. New York: 1901. V. 72
Catalogue of the Loan Exhibition of Flemish and Belgian Art, Burlington House.... London: 1927. V. 68; 69; 70
Climbing and Exploration in the Karakoram-Himalayas. 1894. V. 68; 70
The First Crossing of Spitsbergen.... London: 1897. V. 70
Mountain Memories. London: 1920. V. 69

CONWAY, MONCURE
Barons of the Potomack and the Rappahannock. New York: 1892. V. 69; 71; 73
A Necklace of Stories. London: 1880. V. 73

CONWAY, R. S.
Melandra Castle. Manchester: 1906. V. 70

CONWELL, RUSSELL H.
History of the Great Fire in Saint John June 20 and 21, 1877. Boston: 1877. V. 73

CONWENTZ, H.
The Care of National Monuments (i.e. Nature Reserves).... Cambridge: 1909. V. 69

CONYBEARE, W. D.
Outlines of the Geology of England and Wales. 1822. V. 68; 69; 73
Outlines of the Geology of England and Wales. Part I. London: 1822. V. 69

COOK, C. D. K.
Aquatic and Wetland Plants of India. Oxford: 1996. V. 72; 73

COOK, C. J. R.
The Quarter Deck. First Series. London: 1844. V. 72

COOK, CAMPBELL
Captain James Cook, R.N., F.R.S. 1936. V. 68

COOK, CYRIL
The Life and Work, Of Robert Hancock. London: 1948. V. 72

COOK, E. T.
The Life of John Ruskin. London: 1911. V. 71; 73
The Life of John Ruskin. London: 1912. V. 73

COOK, EDWARD
The Life of Florence Nightingale. London: 1913. V. 70

COOK, ELIZA
Poems. London: 1860. V. 71

COOK, ELLIOTT WILKINSON
Land Ho! The Diary of a Forty-Niner. Baltimore: 1935. V. 68; 73

COOK, FREDERICK ALBERT
My Attainment of the Pole Being the Record of the Expedition that First Reached the Boreal Center 1907-1909 with the Final Summary of the Polar Controversy. New York: 1911. V. 72
Through the First Antarctic Night 1898-1899. New York: 1909. V. 70

COOK, FREDERICK ALBERT continued
To the Top of the Continent, Discovery, Exploration and Adventure in Sub-Arctic Alaska. London: 1909. V. 68

COOK, G. & D., & CO.
Illustrated Catalogue of Carriages and Special Business Advertiser. New Haven: 1860. V. 68
Illustrated Catalogue of Carriages and Special Business Adviser. New York: 1860. V. 71

COOK, GEORGE H.
Geology of New Jersey. Newark: 1868. V. 69

COOK, HARTLEY
Over the Hills and Far Away - Three Centuries of Holidays. London: 1947. V. 72

COOK, HARVEY TOLIVER
Rambles in the Pee Dee Basin, South Carolina. Volume I. Columbia: 1926. V. 68

COOK, JAMES
Bibliography of the Writings of Charles Dickens, with Many Curious and Interesting Particulars Relating to His Works. London: 1879. V. 68
Complete Set of First Editions of Cook's Voyages. London: 1773. V. 70
A New, Authentic Collection of Captain Cook's Voyages Round the World, Undertaken by Order of His Present Majesty.... Sheffield: 1786. V. 68
A Voyage to the Pacific Ocean: Undertaken by Command of His Majesty, for Making Discoveries in the Northern Hemisphere; Performed Under the Direction of Captain's Cooke, Clerke, and Gore in the Years 1776, 1777, 1778, 1779 and 1780.... London: 1784. V. 68; 73
A Voyage Towards the South Pole, and Round the World. Performed in His Majesty's Ships the Resolution and Adventure, in the Years 1772, 1773, 1774 and 1775.... London: 1777. V. 68; 72

COOK, JAMES K.
Fifty Years On the Old Frontier As Cowboy, Hunter, Guide, Scout, and Ranchman. New Haven: 1923. V. 69; 71; 73

COOK, JOHN
King Charles His Case; or, an Appeal to All Rational Men, Concerning His Tryal, etc. London: 1649. V. 73
Observations on Fox Hunting and the Management of Hounds in the Kennel and the Field. London: 1826. V. 73

COOK, JOHN R.
The Border and the Buffalo, an Untold Story of the Southwest Plains. Topeka: 1907. V. 70

COOK, KARIN
What Girls Learn. New York: 1997. V. 73

COOK, KATHERINE M.
The House of the People: an Account of Mexico's New Schools of Action. Washington: 1932. V. 70

COOK, MARGARET
America's Charitable Cooks. Kent: 1971. V. 68

COOK, MOSES
The Manner of Raising, Ordering and Improving Forest-Trees, with Directions How to Plant, Make and Keep Woods, Walks, Avenues, Lawns, Heges &c. London: 1724. V. 70

THE COOK *Not Mad, or Rational Cookery: Being a Collection of Original and Selected Receipts, Embracing Not Only the Art of Curing Various Kinds of Meats and Vegetables for Future Use, But of Cooking, In Its General Acceptation to the Taste Habits....* Watertown: 1830. V. 69; 72

COOK, O. F.
Shade in Coffee Culture. Washington: 1901. V. 72

COOK, OLIVE
Collector's Items from the Saturday Book. London: 1955. V. 73
Movement in Two Dimensions. London: 1963. V. 72

COOK, PETER
Melting Architecture. 1975. V. 70

COOK, ROBIN
The Legacy of the Stiff Upper Lip, or the Astonishing Social Hinterland of a Lapse. London: 1966. V. 71; 72

COOK, SPRULL
J. Frank Dobie Bibliography. Waco: 1968. V. 73

COOK, T. A.
Twenty-Five Great Houses of France. London. V. 68; 69

COOK, TENNESSEE CELESTE, LADY
Constitutional Equality, a Right of Woman; or a Consideration of the Various Relations Which She Sustains as a Necessary Part of the Body of Society and Humanity.... New York: 1871. V. 68; 73
Essays on Social Topics by Lady Cook, Nee Tennessee Claflin. London: 188-?. V. 73
Talks and Essays. London: 1897. V. 71

COOK, THEODORE A.
Old Provence. London: 1914. V. 72

COOK, THOMAS
Hand-Book of Excursions to Scotland. Leicester: 1849. V. 73

COOK, THOMAS H.
Blood Innocents. New York: 1980. V. 69; 70; 73
The Chatham School Affair. New York: 1996. V. 69; 72
Evidence of Blood. New York: 1991. V. 72
The Interrogation. New York: 2002. V. 72

The Orchids. Boston: 1982. V. 68; 69

COOKE, ALFRED R.
Wellington: the Story of His Life, His Battles and Political Career. London: 1852. V. 68

COOKE, EDWARD
A Voyage to the South Sea, and Round the World, Perform'd in the Years 1708, 1709, 1710 and 1711. London: 1712. V. 73

COOKE, EDWARD WILLIAM
Views of the Old and New London Bridges.... London: 1833. V. 73

COOKE, G. A.
A Topographical and Statistical Description of the County of Lancaster. London. V. 73

COOKE, GILES B.
Just Before and After Lee Surrendered to Grant. Houston: 1922. V. 70

COOKE, JOHN
The Dublin Book of Irish Verse 1728-1909. Dublin: 1909. V. 72
Wakeman's Handbook of Irish Antiquities. 1903. V. 70

COOKE, JOHN ESTEN
A Life of Gen. Robert E. Lee. New York: 1871. V. 69
A Life of Gen. Robert E. Lee. New York: 1873. V. 70
The Life of Stonewall Jackson. Richmond: 1863. V. 70
The Virginia Comedians; or Old Days in the Old Dominion. New York: 1854. V. 71
The Virginia Comedians; or, Old Days in the Old Dominion. New York: 1855. V. 71
Wearing of the Gray. New York: 1867. V. 70

COOKE, M. C.
British Fresh Water Algae. London: 1882-1884. V. 69
Handbook of British Hepaticae.... London: 1894. V. 71
Rust, Smut, Mildew and Mould. 1865. V. 69
Rust, Smut, Mildew and Mould. London: 1878. V. 72
Rust, Smut, Mildew and Mould. 1898. V. 73

COOKE, MORDECAI CUBITT
A Fern Book for Everybody. New York: 1875?. V. 68
One Thousand Objects for the Microscope. London: 1895?. V. 68
Ponds and Ditches. London: 1880. V. 68
Toilers in the Sea. London: 1889. V. 68

COOKE, THOMAS
Tales, Epistles, Odes, Fables &c. London: 1729. V. 73

COOKE, THOMAS FOTHERGILL
Authorship of the Practical Electric Telegraph of Great Britain.... London: 1868. V. 68

COOKE, W. B.
The Fungi of Our Mouldy Earth. Berlin: 1986. V. 71

COOKE, WILLIAM
The Life of Samuel Johnson, LL.D. with Occasional Remarks on His Writings.... Dublin: 1785. V. 68
Memoirs of Samuel Foote, Esq. with a Collection of His Genuine Bon- Mots, Anecdotes, Opinions and Mostly Original. London: 1805. V. 73
A Practical and Pathological Enquiry into the Sources and Effects of Derangements of the Digestive Organs.... London: 1828. V. 68

COOKERY *Made Easy.* London: 1850. V. 70

COOK-LYNN, ELIZABETH
From the River's Edge. New York: 1991. V. 72

COOLEY, G. E.
On the Reserve Cellulose of the Seeds of Lilaceae and of Some Related Orders. Boston: 1895. V. 71

COOLEY, TIMOTHY MATHER
Sketches of the Life and Character of the Rev. Lemuel Haynes, for Many Years Pastor of a Church in Rutland, Vt. and Late in Granville New York. New York: 1838. V. 71

COOLIDGE, CALVIN
The Autobiography of Calvin Coolidge. New York: 1929. V. 70; 71; 72; 73
Have Faith in Massachusetts. Boston: 1919. V. 69; 71
Inaugural Address of the President of the United States March 4, 1925. Washington: 1925. V. 71

COOLIDGE, DANE
Arizona Cowboys. New York: 1938. V. 69
Fighting Men of the West. New York: 1932. V. 69
Gringo Gold. New York: 1939. V. 69
The Navajo Indians. Boston: 1930. V. 69; 72
Old California Cowboys. New York: 1939. V. 71
Texas Cowboys. New York: 1937. V. 69; 71

COOLIDGE, MARY ROBERTS
The Navajo Indians. Boston: 1930. V. 69
The Rain Makers. Boston: 1929. V. 69

COOLIDGE, W. A. B.
Alpine Studies. London: 1912. V. 69
The Alps in Nature and History. 1908. V. 68
The Alps in Nature and History. London: 1908. V. 69
The Central Alps of the Dauphiny. London: 1905. V. 69
An Eccentric in the Alps. London: 1959. V. 69
Guide to Switzerland. London: 1901. V. 69

COOM, CHARLES S.
The Baronet Rag-Picker. Boston: 1905. V. 68

COOMBES, A. E.
Reinventing Africa. New Haven: 1994. V. 69

COOMBS, A. E.
History of the Niagara Peninsula and the New Welland Canal. Toronto: 1930. V. 73

COOMBS, JOHN HARTLEY
Dr. Livingstone's 17 Years' Exploration and Adventures in the Wilds of Africa. Philadelphia: 1857. V. 71

COONEY, ROBERT
A Compendious History of the Northern Part of the Province of New Brunswick, and of the District of Gaspe, in Lower Canada. Chatham: 1896. V. 73

COONTS, STEPHEN
The Flight of the Intruder. Annapolis: 1986. V. 68; 70; 71; 73
The Intruders. New York: 1994. V. 70

COOP, J. O.
The Story of The 55th (West Lancashire) Division. Liverpool: 1919. V. 72; 73

COOPE, R.
The Diagnosis of Pancreatic Disease. London: 1927. V. 71

COOPER, ASTLEY
Lectures on the Principles and Practice of Surgery as Delivered in the Theatre of St. Thomas's Hospital.... London: 1829. V. 71; 72
Oeuvres Chirurgicales Completes.... Paris: 1833. V. 70; 72
A Series of Lectures on the Most Approved Principles and Practice of Modern Surgery...at the United Hospitals of Guy and St. Thomas.... Boston: 1823. V. 71
A Treatise on Dislocations and Fractures of the Joints. Boston: 1832. V. 70
A Treatise on Dislocations and Fractures of the Joints. Philadelphia: 1844. V. 70

COOPER, BERNARD
Maps to Anywhere. Athens: 1990. V. 70

COOPER, BRANSBY B.
Lectures on Osteology, Including the Ligaments which Connected the Bones of the Human Skelton. London: 1844. V. 70
Lectures on the Prinicples and Practice of Surgery. Philadelphia: 1852. V. 71
Surgical Essays: the Result of Clinical Observations Made at Guy's Hospital. London: 1843. V. 72

COOPER, C. S.
The Outdoor Monuments of London. 1928. V. 71
Trees & Shrubs of the British Isles Native and Acclimatised. London: 1909. V. 68

COOPER Camp. New York: 1943. V. 69

COOPER, CHARLES PURTON
Bibliotheca Cooperiana. Catalogue of a Further Portion of the Library of Mr. Purton Cooper, Directed by Him to be Sold in the Spring of 1857. London: 1856. V. 70

COOPER, COURTNEY RYLEY
Circus Day. New York: 1931. V. 70

COOPER, DOUGLAS
Great Family Collections. London: 1965. V. 72

COOPER, DUFF
Translations and Verses. London: 1947. V. 72

COOPER, EDMUND
Muker: The Story of a Yorkshire Parish. London: 1948. V. 73

COOPER, ELIZABETH
The Muses Library; or, a Series of English Poetry.... London: 1741. V. 69

COOPER, FRED G.
Letters and Cartoons from FGC to WDM 1916-1926 and Brief Reference to Caricature in Relation to Nature, Travel, Golf, the Bible and Parochial Life. Boston: 1927. V. 71

COOPER, FREDERICK FOX
The Tale of Two Cities. London: 1862. V. 70
A Tale of Two Cities. London: 1885. V. 70

COOPER, HENRY ST. JOHN
Bulldogs and All About Them. V. 68

COOPER, J. W.
The Experienced Botanist or Indian Physician.... Lancaster: 1840. V. 71

COOPER, JAMES FENIMORE
The American Democrat, or Hints on the Social and Civic Relations of the United States of America. Cooperstown: 1838. V. 69
The American Democrat, or Hints on the Social and Civic Relations of the United States of America. New York: 1838. V. 73
Autobiography Of A Pocket-Handkerchief. Chapel Hill: 1949. V. 72
The Battle of Lake Erie, or Answers to Messrs. Bruges, Duer and MacKenzie. Cooperstown: 1843. V. 70
The Bravo: A Tale. Philadelphia: 1831. V. 72
Captain Spike, or the Islets of the Gulf. London: 1848. V. 73
The Chainbearer; Or, The Littlepage Manuscripts. New York: 1845. V. 72
Cooper's Works. Boston: 1880. V. 73
The Deerslayer Or: The First War-Path. New York: 1961. V. 72
The Headsman; Or, The Abbaye Des Vignerons. Philadelphia: 1833. V. 72; 73
The Heidenmauer; or the Benedictines. Philadelphia: 1832. V. 70; 72; 73
Home As Found. Philadelphia: 1838. V. 72
Jack Tier; Or The Florida Reef. New York: 1848. V. 72
The Last of the Mohicans. London: 1826. V. 69; 71; 72; 73
The Last of the Mohicans. Philadelphia: 1826. V. 69; 70; 72
The Last Of The Mohicans. Philadelphia: 1835. V. 72
The Last of the Mohicans. New York: 1919. V. 70
A Letter to His Countrymen. New York: 1834. V. 68
Lionel Lincoln; Or, The Leaguer Of Boston. New York. V. 72
Lives of Distinguished American Naval Officers. Philadelphia: 1846. V. 70
Mercedes of Castile; or the Voyage to Cathay. Philadelphia: 1840. V. 72; 73
Miles Wallingford; or, Afloat and Ashore. London: 1854. V. 68
The Monikins; Edited By The Author Of the Spy, In Two Volumes. Philadelphia: 1835. V. 72
Oeuvres. Paris: 1842-1828. V. 69
The Pathfinder. Philadelphia: 1840. V. 72
The Pathfinder. Lunenburg, VT: 1965. V. 72
The Pilot. London: 1849. V. 68
The Pilot. Baltimore: 1968. V. 72
The Pioneers. London: 1823. V. 68; 73
The Pioneers. New York: 1823. V. 69
The Prairie. London: 1827. V. 68; 73
The Prairie. London: 1850. V. 68
The Prairie. Menasha: 1940. V. 72
The Red Rover. London: 1827. V. 68; 73
The Redskins; Or, Indian And Injin: Being The Conclusion of The Littlepage Manuscripts. New York: 1846. V. 70; 72
The Sea Lions; Or, The Lost Sealers. New York: 1848. V. 72
Sketches of Switzerland. Philadelphia: 1836. V. 70
The Spy. London: 1852. V. 68
The Two Admirals. Philadelphia: 1842. V. 70
The Water Witch. London: 1830. V. 70; 73
The Water Witch. Philadelphia: 1831. V. 72
The Water Witch. London: 1850. V. 68
The Wept of Wish Ton-Wish: a Tale. Philadelphia: 1829. V. 70; 71

COOPER, JANE
Maps and Windows. New York: 1974. V. 72

COOPER, JOE E.
With or Without Beans. Dallas: 1952. V. 68

COOPER, JOHN
Artists in Crime: an Illustrated Survey of Crime. Aldershot Scolar: 1995. V. 70
Detective Fiction: the Collector's Guide. Somerset: 1988. V. 70
Detective Fiction: The Collector's Guide. Aldershot, Hants: 1994. V. 70; 71
Detective Fiction: The Collector's Guide. London: 1994. V. 71
SEE: JOHN COOPER. V. 73

COOPER, JOSEPH
The Lost Continent; or Slavery and the Slave Trade in Africa, 1875. London: 1875. V. 71
Minox Pocket Companion. New York: 1962. V. 68

COOPER, LANE
Louis Agassiz as a Teacher. London: 1945. V. 68; 72

COOPER, LETTICE
The Ship of Truth. Boston: 1930. V. 72

COOPER, MADISON
Sironia, Texas (the Haunted Hacienda). Boston: 1952-1955. V. 73

COOPER, MERIAN C.
Grass. New York: 1925. V. 69

COOPER, MICHAEL
Blinds and Shutters. London: 1990. V. 73

COOPER, REV.
A New History of England from the Earliest Period to the Present Time, on a Plan Recommended by the Earl of Chesterfield. Dublin: 1817. V. 73

COOPER, ROBERT
The Holy Scriptures Analyzed.... Manchester: 1839. V. 68
The Immortality of the Soul, Religiously and Philosophically Considered: a Series of Lectures. London: 1853. V. 68

COOPER, SAMUEL
A Dictionary of Practical Surgery.... London: 1822. V. 71
The First Lines of the Practice of Surgery.... London: 1807. V. 71
A Treatise on the Diseases of the Joints. Hanover: 1811. V. 73

COOPER, SUSAN
The Grey King. New York: 1975. V. 69; 71

COOPER, SUSAN ROGERS
Houston in the Rearview Mirror. New York: 1990. V. 68; 69; 71
The Man in the Green Chevy. New York: 1989. V. 69

COOPER, SUSIE
Catalogue of Bone China & Earthenware. Burslem. V. 70

COOPER, TERRANCE G.
The Tools of Biochemistry. New York: 1977. V. 68

COOPER, THOMAS
Consolidation. Columbia: 1830. V. 68

COOPER, THOMAS continued
Cooper's Journal; or, Unfettered Thinker and Plain Speaker for Truth, Freedom and Progress. 1850. V. 68
The Introductory Lecture of Thomas Cooper, Esq. Professor of Chemistry at Carlisle College Pennsylvania/. Carlisle: 1812. V. 71
Some Information Concerning Gas Lights. Philadelphia: 1816. V. 69
Thesavrvs Lingvae Romanae & Britannicae . . . Accessit Dictionarivm Historicum & Poeticum. Londini: 1584. V. 73
A Treatise on the Law of Libel and the Liberty of the Press; showing the Origin, Use and Abuse of the Law of Libel.... New York: 1830. V. 69

COOPER, W. HEATON
The Hills of Lakeland. London: 1938. V. 71
The Hills of Lakeland. London: 1946. V. 71
Lakeland Portraits. London: 1954. V. 71
The Lakes. London: 1966. V. 71
The Lakes. London: 1970. V. 71
Mountain Painter. Kendal: 1984. V. 71
The Tarns of Lakeland. London: 1960. V. 71
The Tarns of Lakeland. Kendal: 1983. V. 71
The Tarns of Lakeland. London: 1983. V. 71

COOPER, WILLIAM
The Beauties of Church Music, and the Sure Guide to the Art of Singing. Boston: 1804. V. 68
Yachts and Yachting. New York: 1979. V. 69

COOPER, WILLIAM DURRANT
The History of Winchelsea, One of the Ancient Towns Added to the Cinque Ports. London/Hastings: 1850. V. 70

COOPER, WILLIAM T.
The Birds of Paradise and Bower Birds. Boston: 1979. V. 70; 73

COOPER, WILLIAM WHITE
On Wounds and Injuries of the Eye. London: 1859. V. 72

COOTE, C. H.
Johann Schoner, Professor of Mathematics at Nuremberg. London: 1888. V. 70

COOTE, WALTER
Wanderings, South and East. London: 1882. V. 72

COOVER, ROBERT
Charlie in the House of Rue. Lincoln: 1980. V. 73
Gerald's Party. New York: 1986. V. 72
The Origin of the Brunists. New York: 1966. V. 70; 71; 72; 73
The Origin of the Brunists. London: 1967. V. 73
Pinocchio in Venice. New York: 1991. V. 70
Pricksongs and Descants. New York: 1969. V. 68; 70
The Public Burning. New York: 1977. V. 70
Spanking the Maid. New York: 1982. V. 70
The Stone Wall Book of Short Fictions. Iowa City: 1973. V. 70
A Theological Position - Plays The Kid. Love Scene. Rip Awake. A Theological Position. New York: 1972. V. 69; 70
The Universal Baseball Association, Inc. J. Henry Waugh, Prop. New York: 1968. V. 69; 70; 71; 73

COPE, CHARLES HENRY
Reminiscences of Charles West Cope. London: 1891. V. 73

COPE, DAWN
Postcards from the Nursery, the Illustrators of Children's Books and Postcards 1900-1950. 2000. V. 69

COPE, E. D.
The Crocodilians, Lizards and Snakes of North America. Washington: 1900. V. 69; 73
On Vertebrata from the Tertiary and Cretaceous Rocks of the North West Territory. Montreal: 1891. V. 71
Synopsis of the Fishes of the Peruvian Amazon, Obtained by Professor Orton During his Expedition of 1873 and 1877. Philadelphia: 1878. V. 72
Vertebrata of the Tertiary Formations of the West. Book I. Washington: 1883. V. 71

COPE, JACK
The Golden Oriole. London: 1958. V. 68

COPE TOBACCO CO.
Smoker's Garland. Liverpool;: 1889-1890. V. 70

COPE, WENDY
Is that the New Moon?. London: 1990. V. 70
Making Cocoa for Kingsley Amis: Poems. London: 1986. V. 68
Men and Their Boring Arguments. Winchester: 1988. V. 73
The River Girl. London: 1991. V. 72

COPE, ZACHARY
Sidelights on the History of Medicine. London: 1957. V. 68
William Cheselden 1688-1752. London: 1953. V. 68

COPELAND, R. M.
Country Life: a Handbook of Agriculture, Horticulture and Landscape Gardening. Boston: 1859. V. 71

COPELAND, THOMAS
Observations on the Principal Diseases of the Rectum and Anus; Particularly Stricture of the Rectum and the Haemorrhoidal Excrescence and Fistula in Ano. London: 1814. V. 71; 72

COPELAND, WALTER
Babes and Blossoms. 1908. V. 73

COPEMAN, EDWARD
A Collection of Cases of Apoplexy.... London: 1845. V. 72

COPEMAN, W. S. C.
A Short History of the Gout and the Rheumatic Diseases. Berkeley: 1964. V. 71

COPINGER, WALTER A.
Heraldry Simplified; an Easy Introduction to the Science. 1910. V. 70

COPLESTON, EDWARD
Advice to a Young Reviewer, with a Specimen of the Art. Oxford: 1807. V. 72
A Reply to the Calumnies of the Edinburgh Review (No. 31) Against Oxford. Oxford: 1810. V. 72

COPLEY, JOHN M.
A Sketch of the Battle of Franklin, Tennessee; with Reminiscences of Camp Douglas. Austin: 1893. V. 69; 70

COPLEY, MRS.
Female Excellence; or Hints To Daughters. Designed For Their Use From The Time of Leaving School Till Their Settlement In Life. London. V. 72

COPP, HENRY N.
Public Land Laws Passed by Congress from April 1, 1882 to January 1, 1890. Washington: 1890. V. 69

COPPARD, ALFRED EDGAR
Adam and Eve and Pinch Me. Waltham St. Lawrence: 1921. V. 69
Clorinda Walks in Heaven. London: 1922. V. 71
Clorinda Walks in Heaven. Waltham St. Lawrence: 1922. V. 68
Count Stefan. Waltham St. Lawrence: 1928. V. 68; 71; 72
The Field of Mustard. London: 1926. V. 71
Fishmonger's Fiddle. Tales. London: 1925. V. 71
Hips and Haws. Waltham St. Lawrence: 1922. V. 68; 71
The Hundredth Story. London: 1931. V. 71
The Hundredth Story. Waltham St. Lawrence: 1931. V. 68; 69; 71; 72
Nixey's Harlequin: Tales. London: 1931. V. 69; 70; 71
Pelagea & Other Poems. London: 1926. V. 71
Pelagea and Other Poems. Waltham St. Lawrence: 1926. V. 68; 71; 72
Pink Furniture: a Tale for Lovely Children with Noble Natures. London: 1930. V. 69; 71
Silver Circus. London: 1926. V. 71
Tapster's Tapestry. London: 1938. V. 71
Tapster's Tapestry. Waltham St. Lawrence: 1938. V. 68; 71

COPPARD, LAWRENCE
A Correct Report of the Trial of Lawrence Coppard, Apprentice to John Smith, Carver, Gilder and Picture Dealer.... London: 1828. V. 71

COPPENS, AUGUSTIN
Perspectives des Ruines de la Ville de Bruxelles, Designees au Naturel. Brussels: 1695. V. 68; 70

COPPLESTONE, BENNET
Madame Gilbert's Cannibal. New York: 1920. V. 73

COPPS, DALE
The Sherlock Holmes Puzzle Book. Garden City: 1981. V. 69

COPSEY, TONY
Book Distribution and Printing in Suffolk 1534-1850: Booksellers, Stationers, Binders and Printers. Ipswich: 1994. V. 70

A COPY of the Poll for the Knights of the Shire for the County of Norfolk. Taken at Norwich March 23, 1768. Candidates, Sir Armine Wodehouse, Bart 2680. Thomas de Grey, Esq. 2754. Sir Edward Astley, Bart 2977. Wenman Coke, Esq. 2610. Norwich: 1768. V. 72

CORA, SUE
Maid in Panama. New York: 1938. V. 71

CORBETT, GEORGE, MRS.
Secrets of a Prviate Enquiry Office, Being Tales Weird and Tales Ghostly, Tales Humorous and Tales Pathetic, Tales Exciting and Tales Curious. London: 1890. V. 70

CORBETT, J.
The River Irwell. Manchester: 1907. V. 73

CORBETT, JAMES
The Merrivale Mystery. 1931. V. 73

CORBETT, JIM
The Man Eating Leopard of Rudraprayag. 1948. V. 73

CORBETT, THOMAS B.
Colorado Mining Directory. The Colorado Directory of Mines, Containing a Description of the Mines and Mills, and the Mining and Milling Corporations of Colorado.... Denver: 1879. V. 71

CORBITT, HELEN
Helen Corbitt Cooks for Company. Boston: 1974. V. 73

CORBUSIER, WILLIAM T.
Verde To San Carlos, Recollections Of A Famous Army Surgeon And His Observant Family On The Western Frontier 1869-86. Tucson: 1968. V. 70; 72; 73

CORBY, JANE
As Deadly Does. New York: 1961. V. 71

CORCORAN, TOM
The Mango Opera. New York: 1998. V. 70

CORDASCO, FRANCESCO
A Bibliography of Robert Watt, M.D. Author of the Bibliotheca Britannica. New York: 1950. V. 68

CORDELL, EUGENE FAUNTLEROY
Historical Sketch of the University of Maryland School of Medicine (1807-1890).... Baltimore: 1891. V. 73

CORDER, E. M.
The Deer Hunter. New York: 1979. V. 72

CORDER, PHILIP
A Roman Villa at Langton, Near Malton, E. Yorkshire. Leeds: 1932. V. 73

CORDIER, J.
Histoire de la Navigation Interieure, et Particulierement d Celle d'Angleterre jusqu'en 1803...(and) Histoire de la Navigation Intgerieure, et Particulierement de celle des Etats-Unis d'Amerique.... Paris: 1819-1820. V. 72

CORDINER, CHARLES
Antiquities and Scenery of the North of Scotland in a Series of Letters. London: 1780. V. 68; 70
Remarkable Ruins, and Romantic Prospects, of North Britain. London: 1788. V. 68; 70; 72
Remarkable Ruins, and Romantic Prospects, of North Britain. London: 1795. V. 71

CORDRY, DONALD
Mexican Indian Costumes. Austin: 1968. V. 69; 71

CORE, GEORGE
Southern Excursions. Charlotte: 1997. V. 71; 73

CORELL, PHILIP
History of Union Coast Guard, With N.Y.S. Volunteers. With Reminiscences from June 1st 1862 to June 19th 1863. New York: 1901. V. 70

CORELLI, MARIE
Boy: a Sketch. London: 1900. V. 68
Cameos: Short Stories. London: 1896. V. 68
The Greatest Queen in the World. A Tribute to the Majesty of England 1837-1900. London. V. 73
The Master Christian. London: 1900. V. 68
The Murder of Delicia. Philadelphia: 1896. V. 73
Ziska; the Problem of a Wicked Soul. Bristol: 1897. V. 68

COREY, HERBERT
Crime at Cobb's House. New York: 1934. V. 69

COREY, P. L.
Faces Voices and Dreams. Sitka: 1987. V. 69

CORFIELD, F. D.
The Origins and Growth of Mau Mau - an Historical Survey. Nairobi: 1960. V. 72

CORIDON'S Song and Other Verses from Various Sources. London: 1894. V. 71

CORK, BARRY
Laid Dead. London: 1990. V. 71

CORK AND ORRERY, JOHN BOYLE, 5TH EARL OF
Letters from Italy, in the Years 1754 and 1755. London: 1773. V. 68; 70
Remarks on the Life and Writings of Dr. Jonathan Swift. London: 1752. V. 69; 71

CORKE, HELEN
D. H. Lawrence. The Croydon Years. Austin: 1965. V. 72
D. H. Lawrence's Princess. Surrey: 1951. V. 72
Neutral Ground. London: 1933. V. 72
Songs of Autumn and Other Poems. Austin: 1960. V. 72

CORLE, EDWIN
Billy the Kid. New York and Boston: 1953. V. 69; 71
Burro Alley. New York: 1938. V. 69
Desert Country. New York: 1941. V. 69
Fig Tree John. New York: 1935. V. 69
People on the Earth. New York: 1937. V. 69

CORLETT, W. T.
The Medicine Man of the American Indian and His Cultural Background. Springfield and Baltimore: 1935. V. 69

CORLISS, ALLENE
Smoke in Her Eyes. New York: 1935. V. 71

CORMACK, J. M. R.
Notes on the History of the Inscribed Monuments of Aphrodisias. 1955. V. 69; 73

CORMACK, JOHN ROSE
Natural History, Pathology and Treatment of the Epidemic Fever.... London: 1843. V. 72

CORMAN, AVERY
Kramer Versus Kramer. New York: 1977. V. 70

CORMAN, CID
Clocked Stone. Poems. Kyoto: 1959. V. 69; 73
Cool Gong. Ashland, MA: 1959. V. 71
For Jim. New Rochelle: 1986. V. 73
In No Time. Kyoto: 1963. V. 69
Johnny Cake. New Rochelle: 1998. V. 73
Lines and Smudges. New Rochelle: 2001. V. 73
Origin; Fourth Series. Boston: 1977-1982. V. 69
Origin: Third Series. Kyoto: 1966-1971. V. 69; 71; 73
'S. New Rochelle: 1976. V. 69; 71
Sun Rock Man. Kyoto: 1962. V. 71
Words for Each Other. London: 1967. V. 69

CORMIER, ROBERT
Now and at the Hour. New York: 1960. V. 71

CORN, ALFRED
An Xmas Murder. New York: 1987. V. 68

CORNARO, LUIGI
Discourses on a Sober and Temperate Life. London: 1768. V. 69
The Immortal Mentor, or Man's Unerring Guide to a Healthy, Wealthy and Happy Life. Philadelphia: 1796. V. 71
Sure and Certain Methods of Attaining a Long and Healthy Life, with Means of Correcting a Bad Constitution. London: 1737. V. 70

CORNEILLE, PIERRE
Nicomede. Paris: 1750. V. 70

CORNELIUS, MARY HOOKER
The Young Housekeeper's Friend; or a Guide to Domestic Economy and Comfort. Boston: 1852. V. 68
The Young Housekeeper's Friend; or Guide to Domestic Economy and Comfort. Boston: 1854. V. 73

CORNELL, JOSEPH
Joseph Cornell: Portfolio. New York: 1976. V. 70

CORNELL, STEPHEN
The Traders Ready Reckoner. Hudson: 1819. V. 70

CORNELL UNIVERSITY
The Living Bird, Annals of the Cornell Laboratory of Orinthology. Ithaca: 1962-1981. V. 72

CORNER, BERYL
Prematurity. The Diagnosis, Care and Disorders of the Premature Infant. London: 1960. V. 68

CORNER, BETSY COPPING
William Shippen, Jr., Pioneer in American Medical Education. Philadelphia: 1951. V. 71

CORNER, JULIA
The History of Ireland: From the Earliest Period to the Present Time. London: 1840. V. 70
The History of Spain and Portugal; from the Earliest Periods to the Present Time. London: 1840. V. 68

CORNET, J.
A Survey of Zairian Art: the Bronson Collection. Raleigh: 1978. V. 69

CORNFORD, FRANCES
Autumn Midnight. London: 1923. V. 70
Death and the Princess. 1912. V. 70
Poems. Hampstead: 1901. V. 73

CORNFORD, JOHN
John Cornford: a Memoir. London: 1938. V. 68

THE CORNHILL Gallery. London: 1865. V. 73

THE CORNHILL Magazine. London: 1860. V. 71
THE CORNHILL Magazine. London: 1860-1881. V. 72

CORNISH, CHARLES
Sir William Henry Fowler, K.C.B. a Personal Memoir. 1904. V. 73

CORNISH, CHARLES J.
Sir William Henry Fowler, K.C.B., F.R.S., LL.D., D.C.L., Late Director of the Natural History Museum, and President of the Royal Zoological Society. London: 1904. V. 68

CORNISH, GEOFFREY
The Architects of Golf. NY: 1993. V. 73

CORNMAN, F.
Some Account of a Remarkable Old House Formerly Existing in Chick Lane, Clerkenwell. London: 1900. V. 68

CORNWALL, BRUCE
Life Sketch of Pierre Barlow Cornwall. San Francisco: 1906. V. 69

CORNWALLIS, CAROLINE FRANCES
Christian Sects in the Nineteenth Century in a Series of Letters to a Lady. London: 1846. V. 68
On the Principles of Criminal Law. London: 1846. V. 71

CORNWALLIS, CHARLES, EARL OF
An Answer to that Part of the Narrative of Lieutenant-General, Sir Henry Clinton, K.B. Which Relates to the Conduct of Lieutenant-Genearl Earl Cornwallis, during the Campaign in North America, in the Year 1781. London: 1783. V. 71; 73

CORNWALLIS, KINAHAN
Royalty in the New World, or the Prince of Wales in America. London: 1860. V. 73

CORNWELL, BERNARD
Copperhead. London: 1994. V. 68
Enemy of God. London: 1996. V. 68; 70; 71
Enemy of God. New York: 1997. V. 68
Harlequin, the Grail Quest. London: 2000. V. 69

CORNWELL, BERNARD continued
Rebel. London: 1993. V. 68; 72
Sharpe's Battle. London: 1995. V. 68; 71
Sharpe's Company. London: 1982. V. 70
Sharpe's Eagle. London: 1981. V. 68; 73
Sharpe's Eagle. New York: 1981. V. 68; 69; 70; 71
Sharpe's Enemy. New York: 1984. V. 69
Sharpe's Fortress. London: 1999. V. 68; 70
Sharpe's Gold. London: 1981. V. 68
Sharpe's Siege: Richard Sharpe in the Winter Campaign. London: 1987. V. 68
Sharpe's Skirmish. London: 1999. V. 73
Sharpe's Tiger. Blakeney: 1997. V. 72
Sharpe's Tiger. London: 1997. V. 68; 70
Sharpe's Trafalgar. London: 2000. V. 68
Sharpe's Trafalgar. New York: 2001. V. 69
Sharpe's Triumph. London: 1998. V. 68; 71
Sharpe's Triumph. New York: 1999. V. 72
Stormchild. London: 1991. V. 68

CORNWELL, PATRICIA D.
All that Remains. Boston: 1992. V. 68
All That Remains. London: 1992. V. 68; 69; 70; 71; 73
All that Remains. New York: 1992. V. 68; 69; 70
Black Notice. 1999. V. 68
The Body Farm. New York: 1994. V. 68; 70; 72
Body of Evidence. New York: 1991. V. 68; 69; 71; 72; 73
Cause of Death. 1996. V. 68
Cruel and Unusual. New York: 1993. V. 68; 71
From Potter's Field. 1995. V. 68
Hornet's Nest. New York: 1996. V. 72
Hornet's Nest. 1997. V. 68
The Monkey's Raincoat. New York: 1993. V. 70
Point of Origin. 1998. V. 69
Point of Origin. New York: 1998. V. 70
Postmortem. New York: 1990. V. 68; 69; 71; 72; 73
Southern Cross. New York: 1999. V. 72
Unnatural Exposure. 1997. V. 68

CORONADO, FRANCISCO VAZQUEZ DE
The Journey of.... San Francisco: 1933. V. 71

CORONELLI, VICENZO MARIA
Memoire Istoriografiche delli Regni della Morea e Negroponte e luoghi Adiacenti.... Venice: 1686. V. 70

THE CORPORATION Annual; or, Recollections (Not Random) of the First Reformed Town Council, of the Borough of Newcastle upon Tyne. Newcastle-upon-Tyne: 1836. V. 72

CORPORATION OF THE CITY OF LONDON
Report on the City Day-Census 1881 by the Local Government and Taxation Committee of the Corporation of London. London: 1881. V. 71

THE CORRECT Art of Candy Making. Paris London New York: 1902. V. 68

A CORRECT Narrative of the Distressing Shipwrecks, that Unhappily Took Place in Seaford Bay, on Thursday Morning Dec. the 7th 1809, with Other Interesting Matter Relative Thereto. Brighton: 1810. V. 71

CORRELL, D. S.
Manual of the Vascular Plants of Texas. 1979. V. 72

CORRELL, J. LEE
Through White Men's Eyes: a Contribution to Navajo History. Window Rock: 1979. V. 70

CORRIGAN, DOUGLAS
That's My Story. New York: 1938. V. 69

CORRIN, SARA
The Pied Piper of Hamelin...retold by.... London: 1988. V. 70

CORRY, JOHN
The History of Bristol, Civil and Ecclesiastical.... Bristol: 1816. V. 73
A Satirical View of London. London: 1801. V. 72
A Satirical View of London. 1809. V. 72

CORRY, JOHN PITTS
Indian Affairs in Georgia 1732-1756. Philadelphia: 1936. V. 68

CORSARO, FRANK
The Love for Three Oranges. 1984. V. 68
The Love for Three Oranges. London: 1984. V. 69
The Love for Three Oranges. New York: 1984. V. 73

CORSO, GREGORY
The American Express. Paris: 1961. V. 70
Selected Poems. London: 1962. V. 69

CORTAZAR, JULIO
End of the Game. New York: 1967. V. 71
Hopscotch. New York: 1966. V. 73
Hopscotch. London: 1967. V. 73
A Manual for Manuel. New York: 1978. V. 70
The Winners. New York: 1965. V. 73

CORTELYOU, JOHN VAN ZANDT
The Ancestors of Two Sisters. Lincoln: 1954. V. 69

CORTES, HERNANDO
Five Letters 1519-1526. New York: 1929. V. 68

CORVISART, J. N.
Essai sur les Maladie et les Lesions Organique du Coeur et des Gros Vaisseaux. Paris: 1811. V. 73

CORVISART DES MARETS, JEAN NICOLAS, BARON
Essai sur les Maladie et les Lesions Organique du Coeur et des Gros Vaisseaux.... Paris: 1811. V. 70; 72
An Essay on the Organic Diseases and Lesions of the Heart and Great Vessels from the Clinical Lectures of.... Philadelphia: 1812. V. 70
A Treatise on the Diseases and Organic lesions of the Heart and Great Vessels.... London: 1813. V. 70; 72

CORWIN, EDWARD TANJORE
Historical Discourse on Occasion of the Centennial Anniversary of the Reformed Dutch Church of Millstone, 1866. New York: 1866. V. 69

CORWIN, HUGH
The Kiowa Indians - Their History and Life Stories. Lawton: 1958. V. 69; 70; 72

CORY, CHARLES B.
The Birds of Haiti and San Domingo. Boston: 1885. V. 73
The Birds of Illinois and Wisconsin. Chicago: 1909. V. 73
Birds of the Bahama Islands. Boston: 1880. V. 70; 73

CORY, H.
African Figurines, their Ceremonial Use in Puberty Rites in Tanganyika. London: 1956. V. 69

CORY, WILLIAM
Ionica. London: 1858. V. 73
Ionica. London and Orpington: 1891. V. 73
Ionica II. Cambridge: 1877. V. 73

CORYATE, THOMAS
Coryat's Crudities. London: 1611. V. 68
Coryat's Crudities. Salisbury: 1776. V. 73

COSENTINO, F. J.
Edward Marshal Boehm 1913-1969. Chicago: 1970. V. 73

COSGRAVE, GEORGE
Early California Justice. San Francisco: 1948. V. 68

COSGROVE, RACHEL R.
Hidden Valley of Oz. Chicago: 1951. V. 73

COSINDAS, MARIE
Color Photographs. Boston: 1978. V. 68

COSSE, MADAME DE
Catalogue d'une Belle Collection de Tableaux Originales des Trois Ecoles.... Paris: 1778. V. 69

COSSERAT, JANE G. H.
The Pastor and His Flock. London: 1853. V. 72

COSSERY, ALBERT
If All Men Were Beggars. London: 1957. V. 72

COSSLEY BATT, JILL L.
The Last of the California Rangers. New York and London: 1928. V. 72

COSTA, MARGARET
Margaret Costa's Four Seasons Cookery Book. London: 1970. V. 69

COSTA DU RELS, ADOLFO
Bewitched Lands. New York: 1945. V. 71

COSTAGUTI, GIOVANNI BATTISTA
Architecttura della Basilica di S. Pietro in Vaticano.... Roma: 1684. V. 72

COSTANSO, MIGUEL
The Portola Expedition of 1769-1770: Diary of Miguel Costanso. Berkeley: 1911. V. 70

COSTE, JEAN BAPTISTE
Petites Fabriques Italiennes. Paris: 1809. V. 69

COSTELLO, DUDLEY
Holidays with Hobgoblins: and Talk of Strange Things. London: 1861. V. 71

COSTELLO, JESSIE
Uncensored Testimony of the Cop who Kissed and Told. The Costello Murder Trial. Peabody: 1932. V. 68

COSTELLO, LOUISA STUART
The Rose Garden of Persia. London. V. 71
The Rose Garden of Persia. London: 1888. V. 69

COSTELLOW, THOMAS
A Selection of Psalms and Hymns with Favorite and Approved Tunes for the Use of Bedford Chapel near Bedford Square. London: 1791. V. 73

COSTENOBLE, JOHANN CONRAD
Ueber Altdeutsche ARchitektur und Dere Ursprung. Halle: 1812. V. 70

COSTERMANS, L.
Native Trees and Shrubs of South Eastern Australia. Sydney: 1983. V. 72

THE COSTUME, Manners and Peculiairites of Different Inhabitants of the Globe, Calculated to Instruct and Amuse the Little Folks of all Countries. 1821. V. 73

COSTUMES d'Ivanhoe Au Bal.... Brussels: 1823. V. 70

COSY Corner Stories. Buffalo: 1900. V. 69

COTERILL, R. S.
The Southern Indian - The Story of the Civilized Tribes Before Removal. Norman: 1954. V. 69

COTES, ROGER
Hydrostatical and Pneumatical Lectures.... London: 1775. V. 69; 73

COTT, H. B.
Adaptive Coloration in Animals. London: 1966. V. 68

COTTAGES: How to Arrange and Build Them to Ensure Comfort, Economy and Health, With Hints on Fittings and Furniture. London: 1879. V. 68

COTTEAU, EDMOND
De Paris Au Japon. A Travers La Siberie. Paris: 1883. V. 69

COTTEAU, M. GUSTAVE
Etudes sur les Echinides Fossiles du Dept. de L'yonne. Paris: 1856. V. 68

COTTEN, BRUCE
An Adventure in Alaska During the Gold Excitement of 1897-1898. Baltimore: 1922. V. 68

COTTEN, SALLIE SOUTHALL
Negro Folk Lore Stories. Charlotte: 1923. V. 69

COTTER, JOHN L.
Archaeological Excavations at Jamestown: Colonial National Historical Park and Jamestown National Historic Site.... Washington: 1958. V. 68

COTTIN, MARIE RISTEAU SOPHIE
Elisabeth, Ou Les Exiles de Siberie.... Paris: 1806. V. 73

COTTLE, JAMES
Early Recollections, Chiefly Relating to the Late Samuel Taylor Coleridge During His Long Residence in Bristol. London: 1837. V. 70

COTTLE, JOSEPH
Alfred, an Epic Poem, In Twenty-Four Books. London: 1800. V. 69
Malvern Hills: a Poem. London: 1798. V. 73

COTTON, from the Pod to the Factory: a Popular View of the Natural and Domestic History of the Plant.... London: 1842. V. 71

COTTON, CHARLES
Poems on Several Occasions. London: 1689. V. 69; 71; 72; 73
Scarronnides, or, Virgile Travestie. a Mock-Poem, on the First and Fourth Books of Virgil's Aenaeis in English Burlesque. London: 1709. V. 71

COTTON, ELLA EARLS
A Spark For My People: A Sociological Autobiography of a Negro Teacher. New York: 1954. V. 72

COTTON, JANE BALDWIN
Things is Goin as Usule. Boston;: 1928. V. 73
Wall-Eyed Caesar's Ghost and Other Sketches. Boston: 1925. V. 73

COTTON, JOHN
The Birds of Great Britain.... London: 1835-1836. V. 73

COTTON, NATHANIEL
Visions in Verse, for the Entertainment and Instruction of Young Minds. London: 1767. V. 69
Visions in Verse, for the Entertainment and Instruction of Younger Minds. London: 1771. V. 70
Visions in Verse, for the Entertainment of Younger Minds. London: 1798. V. 73

COTTON, ROBERT
Cottoni Posthuma. Divers Choice Pieces of that Renowned Antiquary Sir Robert Cotton, Knight and Baronet.... London: 1672. V. 70

COTTON, WILLIAM CHARLES
A Short and Simple Letter to Cottagers from a Conservative Bee- Keeper. Oxford: 1838. V. 70

COTTRELL, DOROTHY
The Singing Gold. Boston/ NY: 1929. V. 72

COUCH, BERTHA
Life of Jonathan Couch, F.L.S. Liskeard: 1891. V. 68; 70; 72

COUCH, GRACE
Deep Sea Monkey. London: 1947. V. 68
Scarecrow Sambo. 1947. V. 72

COUCH, J.
A History of the Fishes of the British Islands. 1877-1878. V. 73

COUCH, J. N.
The Genus Coelomomyces. Orlando: 1985. V. 70; 72

COUCH, JONATHAN
Illustrations of Instinct Deduced from the Habits of British Animals. London: 1847. V. 68

COUCH, WILLIAM, JR.
New Black Playwrights: An Anthology. Baton Rouge: 1968. V. 72

COUCHAUD, ANDRE
Choix d'Eglises Bysantines en Grece. Paris: 1841-1842. V. 68

COUDRAY, ANGELIQUE M. LE BOURSIER DU
Abrege de l'Art des Accouchements.... Paris: 1785. V. 73

COUES, ELLIOTT
Birds of the Northwest: a Handbook of Ornithology of the Region Drained by the Missouri River and its Tributaries. Washington: 1874. V. 73
The Expeditions of Zebulon Montgomery Pike, to Headwaters of the Mississippi River, through Louisiana Territory, and in New Spain During the Years 1805-1806-1807. 1895. V. 68
Expeditions of Zebulon Montgomery Pike, to the Headwaters of the Mississippi River, through Louisiana Territory and in New Spain, During the Years 1805-1806-1807. New York: 1895. V. 69; 70; 73
Field Ornithology...and A Check List of North American Birds. Salem: 1874. V. 72
Forty Years a Fur Trader on the Upper Missouri; the Personal Narrative of Charles Larpenteur. New York: 1898. V. 70; 72
History of the Expedition Under the Command of Lewis and Clark to the Sources of the Missouri River.... New York: 1893. V. 73
The History of the Lewis and Clark Expediton to the Sources of the Missouri River.... 1893. V. 68
The Manuscript Journals of Alexander Henry Fur Trader of the Northwest Company and of David Thompson, Official Geographer and Explorer of the Same Company. Minneapolis: 1965. V. 69
Monographs of North American Rodentia. Washington: 1887. V. 69
New Light on the Early History of the Greater Northwest. The Journals of Alexander Henry and David Thompson. New York: 1897. V. 70
On the Trail of a Spanish Pioneer: the Diary and Itinerary of Francisco Garces (Missionary Priest) in His Travels through Sonora, Arizona, and California 1775-1776. New York: 1900. V. 69

COUEY, OWEN
The Story of a Fire Department, the Los Angeles County Fire Department. Los Angeles: 1975. V. 69

COUGHLIN, WILLIAM J.
The Stalking Man. New York: 1979. V. 68; 69; 71

COULING, SAMUEL
History of the Temperance Movement in Great Britain and Ireland. London: 1862. V. 72

COULON, MARCEL
Poet Under Saturn - the Tragedy of Verlaine. London: 1932. V. 68

COULTAS, HARLAND
The Home Naturalist. London: 1877. V. 68

COULTER, E. MERTON
The Civil War and Readjustment in Kentucky. Chapel Hill: 1926. V. 70

COULTER, J. M.
Botany of Western Texas.... Washington: 1891-1894. V. 68

COULTER, JOHN
Adventures on the Western Coast of South America and the Interior of California.... London: 1847. V. 70
Complete Story of the Galveston Horror. Chicago: 1900. V. 70

COULTHARD, H. C.
Blast Engines. London: 1867. V. 69

COULTHURST, S. L.
How to Make Lantern Slides. London: 1910. V. 69; 73

COULTON, G. G.
Friar's Lantern. London: 1906. V. 71
A Victorian Schoolmaster: Henry Hart of Sedbergh. London: 1923. V. 70

COUNCE, S. J.
Developmental Systems: Insects. London: 1972-1973. V. 68

THE COUNCIL of Dogs. Philadelphia: 1809. V. 73

COUNSELL, CHARLES O.
The Stenographer or Self Instructor in the Art of Short-Hand. New York: 1839. V. 68

COUNTER, S. ALLEN
I Sought My Brother: an Afro-American Reunion. London: 1981. V. 72

COUNTRY Fair. The Country Life Annual for 1938. London: 1938. V. 71

THE COUNTRY-MAN'S Garland. Tewkesbury: 1775?. V. 71

THE COUNTRY Gentleman's Vade Mecum; or His Companion for the Town.... London: 1699. V. 69

COUPER, ROBERT
The Tourifications of Malachi Meldrum, Esq. of Meldrum Hall. Aberdeen: 1803. V. 73

COURNOS, JOHN
The Mask. London: 1919. V. 69
The New Candide. New York: 1924. V. 72

COURNOT, ANTOINE AUGUSTIN
Recherches sur les Princpes Mathematiques de la Theorie des Richesses. Paris: 1838. V. 73

COURSEY, O. W.
Wild Bill James Butler Hickok. Mitchell: 1924. V. 72

COURT, PIETER DE LA
The True Interest and Political Maxims of the Republic of Holland and West Friesland. London: 1702. V. 72

COURTEAU, EUGENE G.
The Coins and Tokens of Nova Scotia. St. Jacques: 1910. V. 72

COURTENAY, BOOT
Wildflowers and Weeds. New York: 1972. V. 68

COURTENAY, BRYCE
The Power of One. New York: 1989. V. 71

COURTENAY, J.
A Poetical Review of the Literary and Moral Character of the Late Samuel Johnson, LL.D. London: 1786. V. 71
Verses Addressed to His Royal Highness the Prince Regent. London: 1812. V. 69

COURTHION, PIERRE
Georges Roualt: Including a Catalogue of Works Prepared with the Collaboration of Isabelle Rouault. New York: 1961. V. 70; 72; 73

COURTILZ DE SANDRAS, GATIEN
The Life of the Famous John Baptist Colbert, Late Minister and Secretary of State to Lewis XIV the Present French King. London: 1695. V. 69

COURTNEY, ROGER
Africa Calling. 1935. V. 70

COURTNEY, WILLIAM P.
A Bibliography of Samuel Johnson; with Johnsonian Bibliography.... Oak Knoll: 1984. V. 70

COURTONNE, JEAN
Traite de la Perspective Pratique, Avec des Remarques sur l'Architecture.... Paris: 1725. V. 72

THE COURTSHIP, Marriage and Picnic Dinner of Cock Robin and Jenny Wren. York: 1820. V. 68

THE COURTSHIP, Merry Marriage and Pic-Nic Dinner of Cock Robin and Jenny Wren. To Which is Added The Doleful Death of the Bridegrom. 1845. V. 71

COURVILLE, CYRIL B.
Untoward Effects of Nitrous Oxide Anesthesia. Mountain View: 1939. V. 71

COUSIN, C.
Collections de Charles Cousin. Livres, Manuscrits, Faiences Anciennes, Tableaux, Dessins, Objets D'Art. Paris: 1891. V. 70

COUSIN, VICTOR
Introduction to the History of Philosophy. Boston: 1832. V. 69
Lectures on the True, the Beautiful and the Good. New York: 1857. V. 69
The Philosophy of Kant: Lectures. London: 1854. V. 71

COUSINS, M.
20th Century Glass. Secaucus: 1989. V. 69

COUSINS, SHEILA
To Beg I Am Ashamed. Paris: 1928. V. 69
To Beg I Am Ashamed. Paris: 1938. V. 70

COUSMONT, E. F. TURGOT, MARQUIS DE
Memoire Instructif sur la Maniere de Rassembler, de Preparere, de Conserver, et D'Envoyer les Diverses Curiosites d'Histoire Naturelle.... Paris: 1758. V. 70

COUSTILLAS, PIERRE
Gissing: the Critical Heritage. London: 1972. V. 72

COUSTOS, JOHN
The Sufferings of John Coustos, for Free Masonry, and for His Refusing to Turn Roman Catholic.. London: 1746. V. 68; 73

COUTANT, C. G.
History of Wyoming (the Far West). New York: 1966. V. 73

COUTLER, E. MERTON
Georgia's Disputed Ruins. Chapel Hill: 1937. V. 71

COUTLER, J. M.
Botany of Western Texas, a Manual of the Phanerogams and Pteridophytes of Western Texas. Washington: 1891-1894. V. 71

COUTS, CAVE JOHNSON
Hepah, California! The Journal of Cave Johnson Couts. Tucson: 1961. V. 72

COUTTS, JAMES
A History of the University of Glasgow, from Its Foundation in 1451 to 1909. Glasgow: 1909. V. 68; 71

COUZYN, JENI
Twelve to Twelve. London: 1970. V. 69

COVARRUBIAS, MIGUEL
The Eagle, the Jaguar and the Serpent, Indian Art of the Americas. North America: Alaska, Canada, the United States. New York: 1954. V. 71
Indian Art of Mexico and Central America. New York: 1957. V. 71

COVE, MORGAN
An Inquiry into the Necessity, Justice and Policy of a Commutation of Tithes. Hereford: 1800. V. 72

THE COVENT-Garden Magazine; or Amorous Repository.... London: 1773-1774. V. 72

COVENTRY, FRANCIS
The History of Pompey the Little, or the Life and Adventures of a Lap Dog. Waltham St. Lawrence: 1926. V. 68; 71

COVENTRY, GEORGE
A Critical Inquiry Regarding the Real Authorship of the Letters of Junius.... London: 1825. V. 71

COVILLE, F. V.
Botany of the Death Valley Expedition. Washington: 1893. V. 70

COVINGTON, VICKI
Gathering Home. New York: 1988. V. 71

COWAN, BUD
Range Rider. Garden City: 1930. V. 71

COWAN, CHARLES
Reminiscences. London: 1878. V. 71

COWAN, GEORGE J.
Window Backgrounds. A Collection of Drawings and Descriptions of Store Window Backgrounds. Chicago: 1920. V. 69

COWAN, JOHN F.
The You-Ought-to-Buy-Ography of an Ink-Slinger. Hohala: 1915. V. 70

COWAN, P. J.
The Wellland Ship Canal Between Lake Ontario and Lake Erie 1913-1932. 1935. V. 73

COWAN, ROBERT ERNEST
A Bibliography of the History of California 1510-1930. Los Angeles: 1964. V. 68

COWAN, SAMUEL K.
Play, a Picture Book of Boys Girls and Babies. London: 1884. V. 70

COWARD, NOEL
Bitter Sweet. London: 1929. V. 69
Chelsea Buns. 1924. V. 68
Future Indefinite. London: 1954. V. 70
Home Chat. London: 1927. V. 69; 73
Poems by Hernia Whittlebot with an Appreciation by Noel Coward. 1923. V. 73
Post-Mortem. Garden City: 1931. V. 69; 71
Present Indicative. Garden City;: 1937. V. 72
Spangled Unicorn. 1932. V. 68
Suite in Three Keys. Garden City: 1967. V. 68
The Vortex - a Play in Thre Acts. London: 1925. V. 68

COWARD, T. A.
The Birds of the British Isles and Their Eggs. 1947. V. 70
The Vertebrate Fauna of Cheshire and Liverpool Bay. 1910. V. 73

COWBOY Artists of America Seventeenth Annual Exhibition. Flagtaff: 1982. V. 73

COWBOY Artists of America Twelfth Annual Exhibition. Flagstaff: 1977. V. 73

COWBOY Artists of America Twenty-First Annual Exhibition. Flagstaff: 1986. V. 68; 73

COWBOY Artists of America Twenty-Fourth Annual Exhibition. Flagstaff: 1989. V. 73

COWBOY Artists of America Twenty-Second Annual Exhibition. Flagstaff: 1987. V. 73

COWBOY Artists of America Twenty-Seventh Annual Exhibition. Flagstaff: 1992. V. 73

COWBOY Artists of America Twenty-Sixth Annual Exhibition. Flagstaff: 1991. V. 73

COWBOY Artists of America Twenty-Third Annual Exhibition. Flagstaff: 1988. V. 73

COWBOY Artists of America Eighteenth Exhibition. Flagstaff: 1983. V. 68

COWBOY Artists of America Nineteenth Exhibition. Flagstaff: 1984. V. 68

COWBOY Artists of America Twentieth Exhibition. Flagstaff: 1985. V. 68

COWDEN, JAMES
The Elder Dempster Fleet History 1852-1985. London: 1986. V. 68

COWDRY, RICHARD
A Description of the Pictures, Statues, Busto's, Basso-Relievo's and Other Curiosities at the Earl of Pembroke's House at Wilton. London: 1752. V. 69; 71

COWELL, M. H.
A Floral Guide for East Kent. Faversham: 1839. V. 69

COWELL, WILLIAM
An Oration in Defence of the Theatre Delivered at M'Vicker's Theatre, December 30th 1865. Chicago: 1865. V. 71

COWHAM, HILDA
The Hilda Cowham Post Card Painting Book. London: 1920. V. 73
Mother Goose's Rag Book. New York: 1910. V. 73

COWIE, G.
The Bookbinder's Manual.... London: 1829. V. 70

COWIE, GEORGE
The Bookbinder's Manual.... London: 1832. V. 73
Cowie's Bookbinder's Manual.... London: 1852. V. 73

COWING, FANNY
Harvestings: Sketches in Prose and Verse. Boston: 1855. V. 69

COWLES, JOHN CLIFFORD
The Whispering Buddha. Los Angeles: 1932. V. 71

COWLEY, ABRAHAM
The Mistress with Other Select Poems. London: 1926. V. 70; 71
Poems: viz. I. Miscelanies II. The Mistress, or, Love Verses. III. Pinarique Odes. IV. Davideis, or a Sacred Poem of the Troubles of David. London: 1656. V. 73
Prose Works. London: 1826. V. 70
The Works of Mr. Abraham Cowley. London: 1688. V. 69

COWLEY, HANNAH
The Runaway. London: 1776. V. 68; 70

COWLEY, JOHN J.
The Candidates Guide or the Electors Rights Decided Shewing the Determination of the Rights of Elections, by the Honble. the Commons of Great Britain in Parliament, In All Contraverted Elections for the Counties and Boroughs of South Britain, from the ye. London: 1735. V. 70

COWLEY, JOHN LODGE
An Illustration and Mensuration of Solid Geometry; in Seven Books. 1787. V. 71
The Theory of Perspective Demonstrated; in a Method Entirely New. London: 1766. V. 71

COWLEY, MALCOLM
Exile's Return: a Literary Odyssey of the 1920's. New York: 1981. V. 68; 70; 71; 72

COWLING, ERIC T.
Rombalds Way. A Prehistory of Mid-Wharfedale. Otley: 1946. V. 73

COWPER, FRANCES MARIA
Original Poems on Various Occasions. Newark: 1808. V. 69

COWPER, H. SWAINSON
Hawkshead. London: 1899. V. 71
Through Turkish Arabia. London: 1894. V. 68; 72

COWPER, J. MEDOWS
A Supplicacyon for the Beggars. London: 1871. V. 72

COWPER, MARY, 1ST COUNTESS
Diary of Mary Countess Cowper, Lady of the Bedchamber to the Princess of Wales 1714-1720. London: 1865. V. 71

COWPER, WILLIAM
The Correspondence. Arranged in Chronological Order with Annotations by Thomas Wright. London: 1904. V. 71
Cowper, Illustrated by a Series of Views in, or Near, the Park of Weston-Underwood, Buck. London: 1803. V. 70; 71; 72
Illustrations of the Poems of Cowper from Designs by Craig. London: 1803. V. 70
Johnny Gilpin's Diverting Journey to Ware. 1829. V. 73
Myotomia Reformata; or an Anatomical Treatise on the Muscles of the Human Body. London: 1724. V. 68; 72
Poems. 1782-1785. V. 73
Poems. London: 1788. V. 70; 72
Poems. London: 1793. V. 73
Poems. London: 1794. V. 70; 71
Poems. London: 1794-1795. V. 68
Poems. London: 1800. V. 69
Poems. London: 1803. V. 72
Poems. London: 1841. V. 72
Poems by...of the Inner Temple. London: 1823. V. 72
Poems...with a Biographical and Critical Introduction.... London: 1841. V. 68
Poetical Works. London: 1843. V. 72
The Task, a Poem in Six Books. Philadelphia: 1787. V. 68; 70

COX, ANTHONY BERKELEY
Before the Fact. London: 1932. V. 71
Jugged Journalism. London: 1925. V. 70

COX, ARAS B.
Foot Prints...on the Sands of Time, a History of Southwestern Virginia and North Western North Carolina. Sparta: 1900. V. 71

COX, DAVID
A Series of Progressive Lessons Intended to Elucidate the Art of Landscape Painting in Water Colours.... 1828. V. 70; 71; 73
A Treatise on Landscape Painting and Effect in Water Colours.... London: 1814. V. 70

COX, E. G.
A Reference Guide to the Literature of Travel Including Voyages, Geographical Descriptions, Adventures, Shipwrecks and Expeditions. Seattle: 1935-1938. V. 68

COX, E. H. M.
Farrer's Last Journey, Upper Burma, 1919-1920. London: 1926. V. 69; 70
The Modern English Garden. London: 1927. V. 69
New Flora and Silva. 1929-1940. V. 69
Plant-Hunting In China. London: 1945. V. 72

COX, FRANCIS AUGUSTUS
Memoirs of Miss Ann Tomes, Late of Hackney, Aged 19 by the Rev. F. A. Cox, LL.D. London: 1832. V. 72

COX, GEORGE
Black Gowns and Red Coats, or Oxford in 1834. London: 1834. V. 68

COX, GEORGE H.
Consumption: Its Cause, Prevention and Cure. London: 1912. V. 72

COX, I. E. B.
The Angler's Diary and Tourist Fisherman's Gazetteer. 1907. V. 73
Facts & Useful Hints Relating to Shooting and Fishing. 1874. V. 71

COX, J. C.
The Paris Church of Giggleswick-In-Craven. Leeds: 1920. V. 73

COX, J. H.
Hawaiian Sculpture. Honolulu: 1974. V. 72

COX, J. M.
A Cultural Table of Orchidaceous Plants. Sydney: 1946. V. 71; 73

COX, JAMES
Historical Biographical Record Of the Cattle Industry and the Cattlemen of Texas and Adjacent Territory. New York: 1929. V. 71
The Wanderings of Woe, or Conjugal Affection. London: 1813. V. 69

COX, JOHN E.
Five Years in The United States Army - Reminiscences of An Ex- Regular. Owensville, IN: 1892. V. 72

COX, JOHN H.
Folk-songs of the South: Collected Under the Auspices of the West Virginia Folk-Lore Society. Cambridge: 1925. V. 73

COX, JOSEPH
A Faithful Narrative of the Most Wicked and Inhuman Transactions of that Bloody-Minded Gang of Thief-Takers, Alias Thief Makers, Macdaniel, Berry, Salmon, Eagan, alias Gahagan.... London: 1756. V. 72

COX, JOSEPH MASON ANDREWS
New and Selected Poems 1966-1978. Bronx: 1978. V. 72

COX, MARY L.
Narrative of Dimmock Charlton, a British Subject, Taken from the Brig Peacock by the U.S. Sloop Hornet. Philadelphia?: 1859?. V. 71

COX, MORRIS
14 Triads. 1967. V. 68; 71
The Whirligig and Other Poems. London: 1954. V. 73

COX, NELLIE
Footprints on the Arizona Strip. St. George: 1973. V. 73

COX, NICHOLAS
The Gentleman's Recreation: In Four Parts, Viz, Hunting, Hawking, Fowling, Fishing.... 1721. V. 70; 71

COX, PALMER
Brownie Year Book. New York: 1895. V. 72
Queer Stories about Queer Animals Told in Rhymes and Jingles. Philadelphia: 1905. V. 73

COX, ROSS
The Columbia River. Norman: 1957. V. 68; 73

COX, SAMUEL S.
Search for Winter Sunbeams in the Riviera, Corsica, Algiers and Spain. New York: 1870. V. 69

COX, THOMAS
Yorkshire. West-Riding. London: 1720-1731. V. 73

COX, WILLIAM R.
Luke Short and His Era. Garden City: 1961. V. 69

COXE, DANIEL
A Description of the English Province of Carolana. London: 1722. V. 71
A Description of the English Province of Carolana. London: 1741. V. 71

COXE, GEORGE
Southern Excursions. Charlotte: 1997. V. 70

COXE, GEORGE HARMON
The Camera Club. New York: 1937. V. 73
The Charred Witness. New York: 1942. V. 73
Four Frightened Women. New York: 1939. V. 73
The Jade Venus. New York: 1945. V. 68
Mrs Murdock Takes a Case. New York: 1941. V. 73
No Time To Kill. New York: 1941. V. 73

COXE, RICHARD SMITH
A New Critical Pronouncing Dictionary of the English Language.... Burlington: 1813. V. 69

COXE, WILLIAM
Account of the Russian Discoveries Between Asia and America. London: 1787. V. 68; 72
Account of the Russian Discoveries Between Asia and America. London: 1803. V. 71
Sketches of the Natural, Civil and Political State of Swisserland.... Dublin: 1779. V. 69
A View of the Cultivation of Fruit Trees, and the Management of Orchards and Cider.... Philadelphia: 1817. V. 68; 70; 71

COXHEAD, A. C.
Thomas Sothard: an Illustrated Monograph. London: 1906. V. 73

COY, OWEN C.
Gold Days. San Francisco: 1929. V. 68; 73

COYBEE, EDEN
A Flower Book. London: 1903. V. 72

COYLE, KATHLEEN
The French Husband. New York: 1932. V. 69

COYLER, VINCENT
Peace With The Apaches Of New Mexico And Arizona Report Of Vincent Colyer, Member Of Board Of Indian Commissioners, 1871. Tucson: 1964. V. 72

COYNE, W. P.
Ireland: Industrial and Agricultural. 1901. V. 71
Ireland; Industrial and Agricultural. 1902. V. 69

COZENS, ALEXANDER
Principles of Beauty Relative to the Human Head. 1778. V. 71
Principles of Beauty Relative to the Human Head. London: 1778. V. 69

COZZENS, FREDERIC S.
Acadia; or a Month with the Blue Noses. New York: 1859. V. 72; 73
Father Tom and the Pope. New York: 1867. V. 73

COZZENS, JAMES GOULD
Cock Pit. New York: 1928. V. 70
Michael Scarlett. New York: 1925. V. 69

COZZENS, SAMUEL WOODWORTH
The Marvellous Country. Boston: 1873. V. 70
The Marvelous Country. Amherst: 1874. V. 68

CRABB, ARTHUR
Samuel Lyle Criminologist. New York: 1920. V. 72

CRABBE, GEORGE
The Borough: a Poem in Twenty Four Letters. London: 1810. V. 70; 73
The Library. A Poem. London;: 1781. V. 73
The News-Paper: a Poem. London: 1785. V. 73
Peter Grimes. 1985. V. 71
Poems. London: 1807. V. 73
Poems. London: 1808. V. 71
Poems. London: 1809. V. 73
Poems. London: 1810. V. 73
Tales. London: 1812. V. 73
Tales of the Hall. London: 1819. V. 70; 72; 73
Universal Technological Dictionary.... London: 1823. V. 70
The Village: a Poem in Two Books. London: 1783. V. 73

CRACE, JIM
Continent. London: 1986. V. 70
Continent. New York: 1987. V. 69
The Devil's Larder. London: 2001. V. 71
Quarantine. New York: 1997. V. 73
Quarantine. New York: 1998. V. 69; 72

CRACE, JOHN D.
The Art of Colour Decoration; Being an Explantion of the Purposes to Be Kept in View and the Means of Attaining Them. London: 1912. V. 70

CRADDOCK, CHARLES E.
The Phantoms of the Foot-Bridge and Other Stories. New York: 1895. V. 71

CRADDOCK, HARRY
The Savoy Cocktail Book. London: 1930. V. 73

CRADLE Songs of Many Nations. New York: 1882. V. 70

CRADOCK, H. C., MRS.
Josephine and Her Dolls. London: 1930. V. 71
Josephine, John and the Puppy. London. V. 72
Josephine Keeps House. London. V. 72
Josephine's Birthday. London: 1920. V. 73
Josephine's Christmas Party. London: 1927. V. 72

CRADOCK, JOSEPH
An Account of Some of the Most Romantic Parts of North Wales. London: 1777. V. 69
Some Account of the Most Romantic Parts of North Wales. London: 1777. V. 68

CRADOCKE, FRANCIS
Wealth Discovered; or, an Essay Upon a Late Expedient for Taking Away All Impositions, and Raising a Revenue Without Taxes. London: 1661. V. 72

CRAFTS, WILLIAM
Sullivan's Island, the Raciad and Other Poems. Charleston: 1820. V. 71; 73

CRAGG, JOHN
A Prophecy Concerning the Earle of Essex that Now Is. London: 1641. V. 69

CRAGG, MARY ANNE
Morning Conversations of a Governess and Her Pupils.... London: 1830. V. 69

CRAGG, R. BALDERSTON
Legendary Rambles. London: 1890. V. 71
Legendary Rambles. Ingleton & Lonsdale. London. V. 73

CRAGG'S Guide to Hull. Hull: 1817. V. 69

CRAIG, AUSTIN
...Ourselves: Our Principles; Our Present Controversy; Our Immediate Duties. An Address...in Camptown, N.J....May 18, 1850. Feltville: 1850. V. 69

CRAIG, CLIFFORD
Mr. Punch in Tasmania. Colonial Politics in Cartoons 1866-1879. Hobart: 1980. V. 70

CRAIG, DAVID
A Man and His Mountains. London: 1984. V. 69

CRAIG, E. T.
An Irish Commune, the History of Ralahine. 1921. V. 71

CRAIG, EDWARD GORDON
The Art of the Theatre. London: 1905. V. 70
Books and Theatres. London: 1925. V. 70
Gordon Craig. The Story Of His Life. London: 1968. V. 70; 72
Henry Irving. London: 1930. V. 72
Henry Irving, Ellen Terry. A Book of Portraits. Chicago: 1899. V. 70; 71
Index to the Stor, of My Days. London: 1957. V. 70
A Living Theatre. The Gordon Craig School. The Arena Goldoni. The Mask Setting Forth the Aims and Objects of the Movement.... Florence: 1913. V. 70
On the Art of the Theatre. Chicago: 1911. V. 68
On the Art of the Theatre. London: 1911. V. 70
The Page. Hackbridge: 1899. V. 70; 71
The Page. Vol. 2, No. 3. Hackbridge: 1899. V. 71
The Page, Vol Two, Number 4. Hackbridge: 1200. V. 71
The Theatre Advancing. London: 1921. V. 72; 73
Woodcuts and Some Words. London: 1924. V. 70

CRAIG, G. DUNDAS
The Modernist Trend in Spanish-American Poetry. Berkeley: 1934. V. 73

CRAIG, HUGH
Johnson's Household Book of Nature. New York: 1880. V. 73
Johnson's Household Book of Nature. New York: 1897. V. 69

CRAIG, J. D.
Canada's Arctic Islands. Ottawa: 1923. V. 73

CRAIG, JOHN R.
Ranching with Lords and Commons or Twenty Years on the Range. Toronto: 1903. V. 68

CRAIG, MAURICE
Dublin 1660-1860. 1952. V. 69; 73
Irish Bookbindings 1600-1800. London: 1954. V. 70; 73

CRAIG, PHILIP R.
A Beautiful Place to Die. New York: 1989. V. 69
The Woman Who Walked into the Sea. New York: 1991. V. 68

CRAIG, REGINALD S.
The Fighting Parson. Biography of Col. John M. Chivington. Los Angeles: 1959. V. 68

CRAIG, T. R.
The Adam Smith Club Glasgow 1868-1968. Glasgow: 1969. V. 68

CRAIG, W. H.
Dr. Johnson and the Fair Sex a Study of Contrasts. London: 1895. V. 69

CRAIG, WILLIAM MARSHALL
A Course of Lectures on Drawing Painting and Engraving, Considered as Branches of Elegant Education. London: 1821. V. 69

CRAIGIE, PEARL MARY TERESA RICHARDS
The Ambassador. London: 1898. V. 68
A Bundle of Life. New York: 1894. V. 73
The Dream and the Business. London: 1906. V. 73
The Vineyard. London: 1904. V. 73

CRAIK, DINAH MARIA MULOCK
The Fairy Book. London: 1913. V. 70; 72
John Halifax, Gentleman. London: 1912. V. 72
The Little Lame Prince. Chicago: 1909. V. 73
The Little Lame Prince and His Travelling Cloak. London: 1875. V. 68
Little Lizzie and the Fairies and Sunny Hair's Dream. Boston. V. 70
A Woman's Thoughts About Women. London: 1858. V. 72

CRAIK, GEORGE LILLE
The Pursuit of Knowledge Under Difficulties. London: 1847. V. 69

CRAIK, GEORGE LILLIE
Sketches of Popular Tumults; Illustrative of the Evils of Social Ignorance. London: 1937. V. 71

CRAIK, GEORGIANA M.
Riverston. London: 1882. V. 68

CRAIK, JAMES
An Address Delivered on the Occasion of Laying the Corner-Stone of Christ Church, Lexington, Kentucky. Lexington: 1847. V. 71

CRAIS, ROBERT
Demolition Angel. New York: 2000. V. 72
Free Fall. 1993. V. 68
Free Fall. New York: 1993. V. 69; 70; 71; 72; 73
Hostage. Blakeney: 2001. V. 70; 71; 73
Hostage. New York: 2001. V. 68
Hostage With Appreciation By Michael Connelly. Blakeney: 2001. V. 72
Indigo Slam. New York: 1997. V. 71; 72
L.A. Requiem. New York: 1999. V. 72

CRAIS, ROBERT continued
Lullaby Town. New York: 1992. V. 68; 69; 70; 71; 72; 73
The Monkey's Raincoat. New York: 1987. V. 68; 69; 70; 71; 72; 73
The Monkey's Raincoat. New York: 1993. V. 68; 69; 73
Stalking the Angel. 1989. V. 68
Stalking the Angel. New York: 1989. V. 69; 71; 72; 73
Sunset Express. Aliso Viejo: 1996. V. 71; 72
Sunset Express. New York: 1996. V. 69; 71; 72
Voodoo River. New York: 1995. V. 72

CRAKER, L. E.
Herbs, Spices and Medicinal Plants, Recent Advances in Botany, Horticulture and Pharmacology. New York: 1988-1995. V. 69; 73

CRAMER, JOHN D.
Documentary History of the Construction and Development of the United States Capitol Building and Grounds. Washington: 1904. V. 73

CRAMER, ZADOCK
The Navigator. Pittsburgh: 1811. V. 68; 69

CRAMP, STANLEY
Handbook of the Birds of Europe, the Middle East and North Africa. Oxford: 1977-1993. V. 69; 73
Handbook of the Birds of Europe, the Middle East and North Africa. London: 1983. V. 69

CRANACH, LUCAS
Sammlung von Nachbildungen Seiner Vorzuglichsten Holzschnitte und Seiner Stiche. Berlin: 1895. V. 69

CRANDALL, B. J.
Morphology and Development of Branches in the Leafy Hepaticae. Lehure: 1969. V. 72

CRANDALL, NORMA
Emily Bronte. 1957. V. 70

CRANDALL, REUBEN
The Trial of Reuben Crandall, M.D. Charged with Publishing and Circulating Seditious and Incendiary Papers &c.... Washington City: 1836. V. 68; 73

CRANE, ALBERT L.
Race Offerings in Inhibition. New York: 1923. V. 68

CRANE, E.
Bees and Beekeeping, Science, Practice and World Resources. Ithaca: 1990. V. 70

CRANE, FRANCES
Murder on the Purple Water. New York: 1947. V. 69

CRANE, HART
The Bridge. Paris: 1930. V. 72
The Bridge. New York: 1981. V. 70; 72
The Collected Poems of Hart Crane. New York: 1933. V. 69
The Letters of Hart Crane. New York: 1952. V. 72

CRANE, J.
Fiddler Crabs of the World. Ocypodidae: Genus UCA. Princeton: 1975. V. 73

CRANE, JOAN
Guy Davenport: a Descriptive Bibliography 1947-1995. Haverford: 1996. V. 72

CRANE, LEO
Indians of the Enchanted Desert. Boston: 1929. V. 69

CRANE, P. R.
Evolution, Systematics and Fossil History of the Hamanelidae. Oxford: 1989. V. 69; 72

CRANE, STEPHEN
The Black Riders and Other Lines. Boston: 1895. V. 68; 73
Great Battles of the World. Philadelphia: 1901. V. 71
The Little Regiment and Other Episodes of the American Civil War. New York: 1896. V. 70
The Little Regiment and Other Episodes of the American Civil War. London: 1897. V. 68
Maggie: a Girl of the Streets. Avon: 1974. V. 72
Maggie; Together with George's Mother and the Blue Hotel. New York: 1931. V. 69
The Open Boat. New York: 1898. V. 71
The O'Ruddy. New York: 1903. V. 69; 73
The Red Badge of Courage. New York: 1896. V. 73
The Third Violet. New York: 1897. V. 68
Wounds in the Rain. London: 1900. V. 68

CRANE, THOMAS
Abroad. London. V. 69

CRANE, W. J. E.
Bookbinding for Amateurs: Being Descriptions of the Various Tools and Appliances Required and Minute Instructions for Their Effective Use. London: 1903. V. 70; 72

CRANE, WALTER
The Alphabet of Old Friends. London: 1875. V. 73
Baby's Own Alphabet. London: 1875. V. 71
The Bases of Design. London: 1898. V. 72
The Bases of Design. London: 1902. V. 72
Belle-Etoile. London: 1875. V. 73
The Bluebeard Picture Book. London: 1875. V. 71
Cartoons for the Cause. Designs and Verse for the Socialist and Labour Movement 1886-1896. London: 1976. V. 71
Chattering Jack. London: 1867. V. 73
The Claims of Decorative Art. London: 1892. V. 72
A Floral Fantasy in an Old English Garden. New York: 1899. V. 72
Flora's Feast. A Masque of Flowers. London: 1889. V. 72; 73
The Frog Prince. London: 1870. V. 68
Goody Two Shoes Picture Book. London: 1874. V. 69
Grammar in Rhyme. London: 1868. V. 73
Pan Pipes. A Book of Old Songs. London: 1883. V. 68
Pan-Pipes. A Book of Old Songs, Newly Arranged with Accompaniments by Theo Marzials. London. V. 72
Princess Belle Etoile. London: 1870. V. 68
Queen Summer, or the Tourney of the Lily and the Rose. London: 1891. V. 73
The Work...with Notes by the Artist. London: 1898. V. 72

CRANFIELD, SYDNEY WHITE
Houses for the Working Classes in Urban Districts.... London: 1900. V. 68

CRANFILL, J. B.
Dr. J. B. Cranfill's Chronicle: a Story of Life in Texas. New York: 1916. V. 70

CRANMER, THOMAS
Reformatis Legum Ecclesiasticarum. 1641. V. 72
Reformatis Legum Ecclesiasticarum. London: 1641. V. 70

CRANSTON, CLAUDIA
Murder Maritime. Phila: 1935. V. 72

CRANTZ, DAVID
The History of Greenland: Containing a Description of the Country to Its Inhabitants.... London: 1767. V. 73

CRAPANZANO, VINCENT
The Fifth World of Bennett: Portrait of a Navaho. New York: 1972. V. 69

CRAPSEY, ADELAIDE
Verse. Rochester: 1915. V. 73

CRARY, A. M.
The A. M. Crary Memoirs and Memoranda. Herington: 1915. V. 70

CRARY, MARY
The Daughter of the Stars. London: 1939. V. 71

CRASTER, H. H. E.
The Parish of Corbridge. 1914. V. 73

CRAVEN, C. W.
Poems. Keighley: 1889. V. 73

CRAVEN, FRANK
That's Gratitude!. New York: 1931. V. 71

CRAVEN, JOHN V.
The Leaf is Green. New York: 1931. V. 71

CRAVEN, JOSEPH
A Bronte Moorland Village and its People. London: 1907. V. 73

CRAVEN, TUNIS AUGUSTUS MAC DONOUGH
A Naval Campaign in the Californias - 1846-1849; the Journal of Lieutenant Craven, U.S.N. United States Sloop of War. San Francisco: 1973. V. 73

CRAVEN, WESLEY FRANK
The Army Air Forces in World War II. Volume I. Chicago: 1958. V. 68
The Army Air Forces in World War II. Volume II. Chicago: 1951. V. 68

CRAVENS, R. H.
Brett Weston: Photographs from Five Decades. 1980. V. 68

CRAVER, REBECCA
Tom Lea: an Oral History. El Paso: 1995. V. 69; 71; 73

CRAWFORD, A. L.
Aida, Life and Ceremony of the Gogodala. Bathurst: 1981. V. 69

CRAWFORD, ADAIR
Experiments and Observations on Animal Heat, and the Inflammation of Combustible Bodies.... London: 1788. V. 70; 72

CRAWFORD, ANN FEARS
The Eagle. Austin: 1967. V. 68

CRAWFORD, ARTHUR
Our Troubles in Poona and The Deccan. London: 1897. V. 72

CRAWFORD, BRYCE L.
Cultivating Sherlock Holmes. La Crosse: 1978. V. 69

CRAWFORD, CORA HAYWARD
The Land of the Montezumas. New York: 1889. V. 71

CRAWFORD, DANIEL
Back to The Long Grass. London. V. 72
Back to the Long Grass. London: 1922. V. 68

CRAWFORD, ELIZABETH
The Woman Suffrage Movement: a Reference Guide 1866-1928. London: 1999. V. 72

CRAWFORD, FRANCIS MARION
Ave Roma Immortalis. New York: 1898. V. 70
Gleanings from Venetian History. London: 1905. V. 68; 73
A Lady of Rome. London: 1906. V. 68

CRAWFORD, FRANCIS MARION continued
Paul Patoff. London: 1887. V. 68; 72
Pietro Ghisleri. London: 1893. V. 68; 72
Sant' Ilario. London: 1889. V. 73
Saracinesca. 1887. V. 72
Saracinesca. London: 1887. V. 68
Whosoever Shall Offend.... London: 1904. V. 68
With the Immortals. London: 1888. V. 73

CRAWFORD, J. H.
Wild Flowers of Scotland. London: 1898. V. 71

CRAWFORD, JACK
Lariattes - a Book of Poems and Favorite Recitations. Sigourney: 1904. V. 68
Poet Scout. New York: 1886. V. 72
The Poet Scout. St. Paul: 1891. V. 68

CRAWFORD, JOHN
Chinese Calligraphy and Painting in the Collection of John M. Crawford, Jr. New York: 1962. V. 72; 73
Cursus Medicine or a Complete Theory of Physic in Five Parts.... London: 1724. V. 72

CRAWFORD, LEWIS F.
Badlands and Broncho Trails. Bismark: 1922. V. 69; 71; 73
Ranching Days in Dakota and Custer's Black Hills Expedition of 1874. 1950. V. 68
Rekindling Campfires: The Exploits of Ben Arnold(Connor)(Wa-Si-Cu Tam-A-He-Ca). Bismarck: 1926. V. 72

CRAWFORD, ROBERT
Across the Pampas and the Andes. London: 1884. V. 68

CRAWFORD, STANLEY G.
Gascoyne. London: 1966. V. 69

CRAWFURD, OSWALD
Horses and Riders and Other Essays. London: 1889?. V. 68

CRAWHALL, JOSEPH
Andrew Robinson, Stoney Bowes Esquire. London: 1883. V. 72
Border Notes and Mixty Maxty. 1880. V. 71
A Collection of Right Merrie Garlands for North Country Anglers... Continued to the Present Year. Newcastle-upon-Tyne: 1864. V. 72
Ducks and Green Peas. London: 1883. V. 72
The Gloamin' Buchte. London: 1883. V. 72
Impresses Quaint. Newcastle-upon-Tyne: 1889. V. 68
John Cunningham. London: 1883. V. 72
Olde Tayles Newlye Related. London: 1883. V. 72

CRAWHALL'S Chap-Book Chaplets. London: 1976. V. 72

CRAWLEY, RAWDON, PSEUD.
The Card Players' Manual. London: 1877. V. 68

CRAWSHAW, RICHARD
Poems Selected and Arranged, with Notes by J. R. Tutin. 1887. V. 70; 71
Steps to the Temple, the Delights of the Muses and Carmen Deo Nostro. (with) Poemata et Epigrammata, quae scripsit Latina & Graeca.. London: 1670. V. 68

CRAWSHAW, WILLIAM
Decimarum and Oblationum Tabula. London: 1665. V. 72

CRAWSHAY, GEORGE
Proselytism Destructive of Christianity and Incompatible with Political Dominion. London: 1858. V. 71

CRAWSHAY, RICHARD
The Birds of Tierra del Fuego. London: 1907. V. 68; 73

CRE-FYDD'S Family Fare. The Young Housewife's Daily Assistant. London: 1866. V. 68

CREAGER, LEWIS
An Inaugural Essay on the Dysentery. Philadelphia: 1806. V. 72

CREALOCK, HENRY
Among the Red Deer. 1983. V. 70
Deer-Stalking in the Highlands of Scotland. 1981. V. 73

CREASEY, JOHN
The Baron and the Missing Old Masters. London: 1968. V. 71
Find the Body. New York: 1967. V. 71
The Flying Stowaways. London: 1938. V. 72
Gideon's Lot. London: 1965. V. 71
Good, God and Man - an Outline of Philosophy of Self-ism. London: 1967. V. 71
Leave it to the Toff. London: 1963. V. 68
Murder, London-South Africa. London: 1966. V. 71
Optimists in Africa. Cape Town: 1963. V. 71
Puzzle for Inspector West. London: 1951. V. 73
The Return of Blue Mask. Philadelphia: 1937. V. 68
The Toff and the Teds. London: 1961. V. 72
The Toff in Wax. London: 1966. V. 71
Wicked as the Devil. London: 1966. V. 71

CREASY, EDWARD
The Fifteen Decisive Battles of the World. New York: 1969. V. 70; 72

CREATON AND SON
Improvements at Westminster, Capital Building Materials. A Catalogue of the Very Excellent Materials Contained in Two Substantial First-Rate Dwelling Houses. London: 1810. V. 71

CREDLAND, W. R.
Days Off. Manchester: 1898. V. 73

CREECH, WILLIAM
An Account of the Trial of William Brodie and George Smith, Before the High Court of Justiciary, on the 27th and 28th Days of August 1788.... Edinburgh: 1788. V. 70
Letters Addressed to Sir John Sinclair, Bart. Respecting the Mode of Living Arts, Commerce, Literature, Manners &c. Edinburgh: 1793. V. 72

CREED, R. S.
Reflex Activity of the Spinal Cord. London: 1938. V. 71; 73

CREELEY, ROBERT
Black Mountain Review. 1954. V. 71
The Charm: Early and Uncollected Poems. Mt. Horeb: 1967. V. 73
The Charm: Early and Uncollected Poems. San Francisco: 1969. V. 69
A Day Book. Berlin: 1972. V. 69
Divisions and Other Early Poems. Mt. Horeb: 1968. V. 73
The Gold Diggers. Palma de Mallorca: 1954. V. 72; 73
The Immoral Proposition. Karlsruhe-Durlach/Baden: 1953. V. 69; 73
The Island. New York: 1963. V. 68
Later. New York: 1979. V. 73
Le Fou. Columbus: 1952. V. 69; 73
Loops: Ten Poems. Kripplebush: 1995. V. 73
Mother's Voice. 1981. V. 68
Numbers. West Germany: 1968. V. 69; 73
Pieces. Los Angeles: 1968. V. 73
Thinking. Calais: 2000. V. 69; 73
The Whip. Worcester: 1957. V. 69

CREIGHTON, CHARLES
An Allegory of King Lear. London: 1913. V. 68
Microscopic Researches on the Formative Property of Glycogen. London: 1896-1899. V. 68

CREIGHTON, HELEN
Songs and Ballads from Nova Scotia. Toronto and Vancouver: 1932. V. 72

CREIGHTON, MANDELL
Queen Elizabeth. London: 1896. V. 71
The Story of Some English Shires. London: 1897. V. 73

CRELLIN, J. K.
Medical Ceramics. A Catalogue of the English and Dutch Collections in the Museum of the Wellcome Institute of the History of Science. London: 1969. V. 71

CREMER, JOHN DORLAND
Records of the Dorland Family in America, Embracing the Principal Branches Dorland, Dorlon, Dorlan, Durland, Durling, in the United States and Canada.... Washington: 1898. V. 69

CREMER, ROBERT
Lugosi: The Man Behind the Cape. Chicago: 1976. V. 73

CREMER, W. H.
The Magician's Own Book. London: 1871. V. 70; 71

CREPAZ, ADELE
The Emancipation of Women and Its Probable Consquences. London: 1893. V. 69

CRESCENZI, PIETRO
Tradotto Novamente per M. Francesco Sansovino Ned Quale si Trattano le Cose Della Villa Con le Figure Delle Herbe Poste Nel Fine. Venice: 1564. V. 71; 72; 73

CRESPIGNY, CLAUDE DE
Forty Years of a Sportsman's Life. 1910. V. 70; 72

CRESSALL, HARVEY
Palestine Parodies - Being the Holy Land in Verse and Worse. Tel Aviv: 1938. V. 71

CRESWELL, BEATRICE F.
The Royal Progress of King Pepito. London: 1889. V. 68

CRESWELL, K. A. C.
A Bibliography of the Architecture, Arts and Crafts of Islam to 1st Jan. 1960. 1961. V. 69
A Bibliography of the Architecture, Arts and Crafts of Islam to 1st Jan. 1960. (with) Supplement Jan. 1960-Jan. 1972. 1961-1973. V. 72
The Muslim Architecture of Egypt. New York: 1978. V. 68

CRESY, EDWARD
An Encyclopaedia of Civil Engineering, Historical, Theoretical and Practical. London: 1847. V. 69

CREWDSON, THOMAS
An Inquiry Into the Effect of the Corn Laws on the Prosperity of Great Britain and Ireland. London: 1830. V. 69

CREWE, ROBERT CREW-MILNES, MARQUESS OF
Lord Rosebery. London: 1931. V. 69; 71; 72

CREWS, DONALD
Carousel. New York: 1982. V. 72

CREWS, HARRY
All We Need of Hell. New York: 1987. V. 72

CREWS, HARRY continued
Blood and Grits. New York: 1979. V. 69; 70
Body. New York: 1990. V. 72
Car. New York: 1972. V. 72
Car. London: 1973. V. 72; 73
A Childhood. New York: 1978. V. 68; 69; 71; 72; 73
The Enthusiast. New York: 1918. V. 69
A Feast of Snakes. New York: 1976. V. 68; 70; 72; 73
Florida Frenzy. Gainesville: 1982. V. 72
The Gospel Singer. New York: 1968. V. 68; 69; 72
The Gypsy's Curse. New York: 1974. V. 68; 70; 72
The Hawk is Dying. New York: 1973. V. 68; 72; 73
Karate is a Thing of the Spirit. New York: 1971. V. 68; 69; 71; 72
The Knockout Artist. New York: 1988. V. 72
The Mulching of America. New York: 1995. V. 68; 72
Naked in Garden Hills. New York: 1969. V. 70; 72
Scar Lover. New York: 1992. V. 68; 72
This Thing Don't Lead to Heaven. New York: 1970. V. 71; 72

CREWS, JUDSON
The Southern Temper. Waco: 1946. V. 71

CREYKE, W. R.
Book of Modern Receipts. Hanley: 1883. V. 68

CRIBB, P.
The Genus Paphiopedilum. Kota Kinabalu: 1998. V. 72; 73

CRICHTON, KYLE S.
Law and Order Ltd., the Rousing Life of Elfego Baca of New Mexico. Santa Fe: 1927. V. 70
Law and Order Ltd. The Rousing Life of Elfeso Baca of New Mexico. Santa Fe: 1928. V. 69; 70; 71; 73
The Marx Brothers. London: 1951. V. 69

CRICHTON, MICHAEL
Airframe. New York: 1996. V. 68
The Andromeda Strain. New York: 1969. V. 68; 69; 70; 71
The Andromeda Strain. New York: 1979. V. 68
Binary. London: 1972. V. 72
Binary. New York: 1972. V. 68; 69; 70; 71; 72
A Case of Need. New York: 1968. V. 73
Eaters of the Dead. New York: 1976. V. 68; 69; 73
Electronic Life. New York: 1983. V. 69; 70; 71; 72
Five Patients. New York: 1970. V. 70
Five Patients. London: 1971. V. 69
Jurassic Park. Franklin Center: 1990. V. 69; 71
Jurassic Park. New York: 1990. V. 70; 73
Jurassic Park. New York: 1991. V. 70
Jurassic Park. New York: 1993. V. 68
The Lost World. New York: 1995. V. 72
Odds On. New York: 1966. V. 71
Sphere. New York: 1987. V. 71; 72
The Terminal Man. New York: 1972. V. 69; 70; 73
Timeline. New York: 1995. V. 72
Travels. Franklin Center: 1988. V. 71
Travels. New York: 1988. V. 71

CRICK, THORNE, PSEUD.
Sketches from the Diary of a Commercial Traveller. London: 1847. V. 71

THE CRIES of London for the Information of Little Country Folk.... London: 1825. V. 71

CRIES of the Metropolis or, Humble Life in New York. Rutland: 1858. V. 73

CRIM, MATT
In Beaver Cove and Elsewhere. New York: 1892. V. 72

CRIMINAL Trials Illustrative of the Tale entitled The Hearts of MidLothian Published from the Original Record . . . Edinburgh: 1818. V. 68; 71

CRINITUS, PETRUS
De Honesta Disciplina, Libri XXV; De Poetis Latinis Eiusdem, Libri V; Poemarum Quoque Illius, Libri II. Basileae: 1532. V. 73

CRIPPEN MANUFACTURING CO., MOUNT PLEASANT, MICHIGAN
The Crippen Bean Picker, a Bushel a Minute. Saginaw: 1921. V. 68

CRIPPS, A. S.
Cinderella in the South. London: 1918. V. 68

CRIPPS, F. SOUTHWELL
Gasholder and Tank (of one million cubic feet capacity) at the Sutton Gas-Works. London: 1898. V. 69

CRIPPS, WILFRED J.
Old English Plate. London: 1901. V. 72

THE CRISIS; or, a Letter to the Right Honourable the Chancellor of the Exchequer; stating the True Cause of the Present Alarming State of the Country, with a Remedy.... London: 1816. V. 72

CRISP, FRANK
Medieval Gardens. London: 1924. V. 68; 72

CRISP, QUENTIN
Colour in Display. London: 1938. V. 70

CRISPIN, EDMUND
Beware of the Trains. 1962. V. 73
Beware of the Trains. New York: 1962. V. 72
Holy Disorders. London: 1945. V. 68; 73
Holy Disorders. Philadelphia: 1946. V. 72

CRISSEY, JOHN T.
The Dermatology and Syphilology of the Nineteenth Century. New York: 1981. V. 71

CRISSO, W. D.
From Where the Sun Now Stands: Addresses by a Posse of Western Speakers. Santa Fe: 1963. V. 69

CRISWELL, ELIJAH HARRY
Lewis and Clark: Linguistic Pioneers. Columbia: 1940. V. 73

CRITCHETT, B.
The Post-Office Annual Directory for the Year 1806. London: 1806. V. 71
The Post-Office Directory for 1834. London: 1834. V. 71

CRITCHLEY, MAC DONALD
The Divine Banquet of the Brain and Other Essays. New York: 1979. V. 70
The Parietal Lobes. London: 1953. V. 68; 72

CRITES, ARTHUR S.
Pioneer Days in Kern County. Los Angeles: 1951. V. 70

CRITTENDEN, H.
The Crittenden Memoirs. New York: 1936. V. 73

CROCE, FABIO
Ville di Tivoli Descritte da l'Arciprete Fabio Croce di detta Citta. Roma: 1664. V. 70; 72

CROCE, FLAMINIO DELLA
Theatro Militare...La Seconda Volta Dato all'Impressione con 'Aggiunta di Molte Figure Molti Capitoli Nuovi & Gli Altri Ampliati. Antwerp: 1617. V. 69

CROCKER, CHARLES
The Vale of Obscurity, the Lavant and Other Poems. Chichester: 1830. V. 73

CROCKER, JAMES F.
Prison Reminiscences. Portsmouth: 1906. V. 69; 70

CROCKETT Almanac 1852 Containing Life, Manners and Adventures in the Back Woods, and Rows, Sprees and Scrapes On the Western Waters. Boston: 1851. V. 70

CROCKETT, DAVY
The Adventures of Davy Crockett, told Mostly by Himself. New York: 1935. V. 73
Davy Crockett's 1838 Almanack of Wild Sports in the West.... Nashville: 1837. V. 71

CROCKETT, S. R.
Cleg Kelly: Arab of the City. London: 1896. V. 68
Dulce Cor, Beig the Poems of Ford Bereton. London: 1866. V. 68
Flower-O'-The-Corn. London: 1902. V. 68
Love Idylls. London: 1901. V. 68
The Playactress. London: 1894. V. 68
The Surprising Adventures of Sir Toady Lion, with Those of General Napoleon Smith.... London: 1897. V. 68

CROCKETT, W. S.
Abbotsford. London: 1905. V. 71

CROFT, CYRUS W.
Commerical Panics and Their Causes; with Some Practical Suggestions for the True Basis of National Currency. London: 1868. V. 72

CROFT, HERBERT
Love and Madness. London: 1780. V. 69; 70
Proposals for Publishing, in May Next, Croft's Johnson's Dictionary.... 1792. V. 73

CROFT, P. J.
Autograph Poetry in the English Language. London: 1973. V. 72; 73

CROFT COOKE, RUPERT
Same Way Home. New York: 1940. V. 70

CROFTS, FREEMAN WILLS
Antidote to Venom. London: 1938. V. 73
Anything to Declare?. London: 1957. V. 70; 72
The Cask. London: 1920. V. 73
Circumstantial Evidence. 1941. V. 73
Crime at Guildford. London: 1935. V. 73
Crime on the Solent. 1934. V. 73
Dark Journey. 1951. V. 73
Death of a Train. London: 1946. V. 68; 70; 72; 73
Death of a Train. 1947. V. 73
Death of a Train. New York: 1947. V. 71
Double Tragedy. 1943. V. 69
Enemy Unseen. London: 1945. V. 73
Fatal Venture. London: 1939. V. 73
The Four Gospels in One Story. London: 1949. V. 68; 72
The Futile Alibi. 1938. V. 73
Golden Ashes. 1940. V. 73
Golden Ashes. London: 1940. V. 70

CROFTS, FREEMAN WILLS continued
Inspector French's Greatest Case. 1925. V. 73
The Loss of the Jane Vosper. London: 1936. V. 73
Man Overboard!. London: 1936. V. 73
Many a Slip. London: 1955. V. 73
Murderers Make Mistakes. London: 1947. V. 72; 73
Mystery in the Channel. London: 1931. V. 73
Mystery in the English Channel. New York: 1931. V. 73
The Mystery of the Sleeping Car Express. London: 1956. V. 71; 73
Mystery on Southampton Water. London: 1934. V. 73
The Pit-Prop Syndicate. London: 1922. V. 73
The Pit-Prop Syndicate. 1925. V. 73
The Ponson Case. London: 1921. V. 73
The Sea Mystery. London: 1928. V. 73
Silence for the Murderer. New York: 1948. V. 69
Silence for the Murderer. London: 1949. V. 71; 73
Tragedy in the Hollow. 1939. V. 73
Wilful and Premeditated. 1934. V. 73
Young Robin Brand, Detective.... 1947. V. 68

CROFUTT, GEORGE A.
Crofutt's New Overland Tourist, and Pacific Coast Guide. Omaha: 1880. V. 72

CROIZET, L'ABBE
Panbiogeography, or, an Introductory Synthesis of Zoogeography, Phytogeography and Geology. 1958. V. 73
Recherches sur les Ossemens Fossiles du Department du Puy-de-Dome. Paris: 1828. V. 73

CROKE, ALEXANDER
A Report on the Case of Horner Against Liddiard, Upon the Question of What Consent is Necessary to the Marriage of Illegitimate Minors.... London: 1800. V. 68

CROKER, BITHIA MARY
A Family Likeness: a Sketch in the Himalayas. London: 1894. V. 68
Interference. London: 1894. V. 68
To Let etc. London: 1893. V. 68
Two Masters. London: 1893. V. 68

CROKER, JOHN WILSON
The Croker Papers. London: 1884. V. 71
The Croker Papers. London: 1885. V. 71
Familiar Epistles to Frederick (Jones) on the Present State of the Irish Stage. Dublin: 1804. V. 70

CROKER, THOMAS CROFTON
Killarney Legends. 1879. V. 69; 73
The Popular Songs of Ireland. 1839. V. 70

CROLL, PAULINE
Just for You. Chicago: 1918. V. 73

CROLLY, GEORGE
The Life of the Most Rev Doctor Crolly, Archbishop of Armagh. 1851. V. 69; 73

CROLY, GEORGE
May Fair. London: 1827. V. 68
Tarry though Till I Come; or Salahiel the Wandering Jew. New York: 1901. V. 71

CROLY, JANE CUNNINGHAM
Jennie Juneiana: Talks on Women's Topics. Boston: 1864. V. 70

CROLY, JENNIE JUNE
History of the Woman's Club Movement in America. New York: 1898. V. 70

CROMBIE, A. C.
Augustine to Galileo. London: 1957. V. 68

CROMBIE, BENJAMIN W.
Modern Athenians. Edinburgh: 1882. V. 70

CROMBIE, DEBORAH
A Share in Death. New York: 1993. V. 68

CROMBIE, JOHN
All Manner of Things. 1991. V. 71
Cette Galere. 1991. V. 71
Gloom and Bloom. 1992. V. 71
A Rolling Stone. 1989. V. 71
Rough Passage. 1993. V. 71
Tutti Frutti. 1987. V. 71
Words Words Words. 1993. V. 71

CROME, JOHN
Etchings of Views in Norfolk, but the Late John Crome, Founder of the Norwich Society of Artists, Together with a Biographical Memoir.... Norwich: 1838-1850. V. 69

CROMPTON, HENRY
Industrial Conciliation. London: 1876. V. 72

CROMPTON, RICHMAL
Just - William. London: 1953. V. 68
Just William's Luck. 1948. V. 71; 72
Just William's Luck. London: 1948. V. 69; 70
Just William's Luck. London: 1952. V. 68
More William. 1948. V. 72
More William. London: 1953. V. 68
The Outlaw. London: 1928. V. 69
Still - William. 1940. V. 73
Still - William. London: 1950. V. 68
Sweet William. London: 1936. V. 69
Sweet William. London: 1952. V. 68
William. London: 1954. V. 68
William. London: 1959. V. 72
William Again. London: 1950. V. 68
William and A.R.P. London: 1940. V. 70
William and the Brains Trust. London: 1945. V. 70
William and the Brains Trust. 1952. V. 72; 73
William and the Brains Trust. London: 1952. V. 68
William and the Evacuees. London: 1949. V. 68
William and the Masked Ranger. 1966. V. 72; 73
William and the Masked Ranger. London: 1966. V. 70
William and the Masked Ranger. London: 1968. V. 71
William and the Moon Rocket. 1954. V. 71
William and the Pop Singers. London: 1965. V. 70; 71
William and the Space Animal. 1961. V. 72
William and the Tramp. 1952. V. 71; 72
William and the Tramp. London: 1952. V. 68; 69; 70
William and the Witch. 1964. V. 71; 72
William and the Witch. London: 1964. V. 69; 70
William Carries On. London: 1942. V. 70
William Carries On. London: 1952. V. 68
William Does His Bit. London: 1952. V. 68
William in Trouble. London: 1927. V. 70
William in Trouble. London: 1953. V. 68
William the Bad. London: 1951. V. 68
William the Bad. 1954. V. 72; 73
William the Bold. London: 1950. V. 70
William the Bold. 1952. V. 72
William the Bold. London: 1952. V. 68
William the Conqueror. London: 1926. V. 70
William the Conqueror. London: 1936. V. 69
William the Conqueror. London: 1951. V. 68
William the Detective. London: 1935. V. 69
William the Detective. London: 1952. V. 68
William the Dictator. London: 1952. V. 68
William the Explorer. London: 1960. V. 70; 71
William the Fourth. London: 1924. V. 71
William the Fourth. London: 1950. V. 68
William the Gangster. London: 1951. V. 68
William the Good. London: 1928. V. 70; 71
William the Good. 1953. V. 72
William the Good. London: 1953. V. 68
William the Lawless. 1970. V. 72; 73
William the Lawless. London: 1970. V. 70
William the Outlaw. London: 1927. V. 70
William the Outlaw. London: 1953. V. 68
William the Pirate. London: 1951. V. 68
William the Rebel. London: 1951. V. 68
William the Showman. London: 1937. V. 70
William the Showman. 1939. V. 73
William the Showman. 1949. V. 72
William the Showman. London: 1952. V. 68
William the Superman. 1968. V. 72
William's Crowded Hours. 1937. V. 72
William's Crowded Hours. London: 1942. V. 70
William's Crowded Hours. London: 1951. V. 68
William's Happy Days. London: 1937. V. 69
William's Happy Days. London: 1951. V. 68
William's Television Show. 1958. V. 72
William's Treasure Trove. 1962. V. 71; 72; 73
William's Treasure Trove. London: 1962. V. 69; 70

CROMWELL, OLIVER
A Most Learned, Conscientious and Devout Exercise, Held Forth...at Sir Peter Temples in Lincolnes-Inne-Fields.... London: 1649. V. 69

CROMWELL, THOMAS KITSON
Excursions in the County of Suffolk; Comprising a Brief Historical and Topographicl Delineation of Every Town and Village. London: 1818. V. 70

CRONHOLM, BORJE
Phantom Limbs in Amputees. Stockholm: 1951. V. 68

CRONIN, A. J.
Hatter's Castle. 1931. V. 69
Jupiter Laughs. Boston: 1940. V. 72
The Keys of the Kingdom. Boston: 1941. V. 71; 72
The Stars Look Down. Boston: 1935. V. 70
Three Lives. London: 1932. V. 73

CRONIN, FRANCIS D.
Under the Southern Cross: the Saga of the American Division. Washington: 1951. V. 69

CRONISE, TITUS FEY
The Natural Wealth of California. New York: 1868. V. 70

CRONQUIST, A.
An Integrated System of Classification of Flowering Plants. New York: 1981. V. 69
Vascular Flora of the Southeastern United States. Volume I. Asteraceae. Chapel Hill: 1980. V. 72

CROOK, WILFRID HARRIS
The General Strike. Chapel Hill: 1931. V. 71

CROOKE, W.
The North-Western Provinces of India. London: 1897. V. 72

CROPPER, JAMES
Notes & Memories. Kendal: 1900. V. 70

CROPPER, MARGARET
The End of the Road. London: 1935. V. 71

CROPPER, MICHAEL
Works of Arthur Conan Doyle: The Michael Cropper Collection. San Francisco: 1983. V. 69

CROS, CHARLES
Le Fleuve. Eaux-Fortes d'Edouard Manet. Paris: 1874. V. 70

CROSBIE, EDWARD WILLIAM
An Accurate and Impartial Narrative of the Apprehension, Trial and Execution on the 5th of June, 1798, of Sir Edward William Crosbie, Bart. Bath: 1801. V. 69

CROSBY, B.
Crosby's Merchant's and Tradesman's Pocket Dictionary. 1808. V. 71

CROSBY, CARESSE
The Passionate Years. London: 1955. V. 68

CROSBY, GEORGE
Crosby's General Political Reference Book.... Leeds: 1838. V. 71
Illustrated Guide to Scarborough. Scarborough: 1846. V. 73

CROSBY, HARRY
The Cave Paintings of Baja California: the Great Murals of an Unknown People. 1975. V. 71
Chariot of the Sun. (with) Transit of Venus. (with) Sleeping Together. (and) Torchbearer. Paris: 1931. V. 72
Devour the Fire. Selected Poems. Berkeley: 1983. V. 68; 71
Red Skeletons. Paris: 1927. V. 70; 73
Shadows of the Sun: The Diaries of Harry Crosby. Santa Barbara: 1977. V. 71
Transit of Venus. Poems. Paris: 1929. V. 70; 72; 73

CROSBY, NICHOLS, LEE AND CO.
Catalogue of....Publications. Boston: 1860. V. 68

CROSBY, THELMA
Bob Crosby World Champion Cowboy. Clarendon: 1966. V. 69

CROSFIELD, ARTHUR
Reminiscences of Kenwood and the Northern Heights. London: 1925. V. 71

CROSFIELD, GEORGE
Memoirs Of the Life and Gospel Labours Of Samuel Fothergill, With Selections From His Correspondence. Also An Account of the Life and Travels of His Father, John Fothergill; and Notices of Some Of His Descendants. London: 1857. V. 72; 73

CROSFIELD, HELEN G.
Margaret Fox of Swarthmoor Hall. London: 1913. V. 71

CROSS Child. New York. V. 70

CROSS, AMANDA
The Theban Mysteries. New York: 1971. V. 69

CROSS, ELIZABETH D.
An Old Story and Other Poems. London: 1868. V. 69

CROSS, HELEN REID
Humpty Dumpty's Little Son. London: 1907. V. 71
Simple Simon. London: 1908. V. 69

CROSS, JOE
Cattle Clatter. Kansas City: 1938. V. 71

CROSS, JOHN KEIR
The Other Passenger. London: 1944. V. 69

CROSS, K. W.
Foetal and Neonatal Physiology. Cambridge: 1973. V. 68

CROSS, MARK
The Shadow of the Four. London: 1934. V. 73

CROSS, ODO
The Snail that Climbed the Eiffel Tower and Other Stories. London: 1947. V. 71

CROSS, ROY
The Tall Ship in Art. London: 1998. V. 70

CROSS, W. L.
The Life and Times of Laurence Sterne. New Haven: 1925. V. 68

CROSSE, JOHN GREEN
A Treatise on the Formation, Constituents, and Extraction of the Urinary Calculus; Being the.... London: 1835. V. 71

CROSSKEY, WILLIAM W.
Politics and the Constitution in the History of the United States. Chicago and London: 1953. V. 70

CROSSLEY, FRED H.
English Church Monuments A.D. 1150-1550. London: 1933. V. 69

CROSSLEY, R. S.
Accrington: Chronological Notes and Men of Mark. Accrington: 1924. V. 73

CROSSLEY-HOLLAND, KEVIN
Arthur: At the Crossing Places. London: 2001. V. 71
Eleanor's Advent: a Poem. 1992. V. 71

CROSSTREE, CHRISTOPHER COLUMBUS
The Kaleidoscope, or the Spirit of Periodicals. Philadelphia: 1831-1832. V. 69

CROSTHWAITE, J. FISHER
Brief Memoir Of Major-Gen. Sir John Geo. Woodford. 1883. V. 72
Brief Memoir of Major-Gen. Sir John Geo. Woodford, a Paper Read to the Keswick Lit. and Sci. Soc. March 29th 1880. London: 1883. V. 71
The Last Of The Derwentwaters. A Paper read to the Keswick Literary Society, February 2nd, 1874. Cockermouth: 1874. V. 72

CROSTON, JAMES
A History of the Ancient Hall of Salmesbury in Lancashire. London: 1871. V. 73

CROTCH, W. WALTER
The Pagent of Dickens. London: 1915. V. 69
The Secret of Dickens. London: 1919. V. 69

CROTCH, WILLIAM
Six Etchings...of the Ruins of the Late Fire at Christ Church, Oxford. Oxford: 1809. V. 72
Six Etchings...of the Ruins of the Late Fire at Christ Church, Oxford. Oxford: 1909. V. 70

CROTHERS, RACHEL
As Husbands Go. New York: 1931. V. 70; 71

CROTHERS, SAMUEL MC CHORD
The Children of Dickens. New York: 1928. V. 73
Meditations on Votes for Women, Together with Animadversions on the Closely Related Subject of Votes for Men. Boston and New York: 1914. V. 70

CROUCH, ARCHER PHILIP
Silvertown and Neighbourhood. London: 1900. V. 71

CROUCH, E. A.
An Illustrated Introduction to Lamarck's Conchology. 1827. V. 69

CROUCH, F.
Understanding Barbel. 1990. V. 73

CROUCH, HENRY
A Complete View of the British Customs. London: 1724-1725. V. 72
A Complete View of the British Customs. London: 1731. V. 72

CROUCH, NATHANIEL
A New View and Observations on the Ancient and Present State of London and Westminster.... 1730. V. 71

CROWE, CAMERON
Fast Times at Ridgemont High. New York: 1981. V. 69; 70

CROWE, EARLE
Men of El Tejon: Empire of the Tehachapis. Los Angeles: 1957. V. 68

CROWE, PAT
Spreading Evil - Pat Crowe's Autobiography. New York: 1927. V. 73

CROWE, PHILIP K.
Sport is Where You Find It. New York: 1953. V. 68

CROWE, WILLIAM
Lewesdon Hill, a Poem. Oxford: 1788. V. 73

CROWELL, EDWIN
A History of Barrington Township and Vicinity, Shelburn County, Nova Scotia 1604-1870 with a Biographical and Genealogical Appendix. Yarmouth: 1923. V. 72

CROWELL, JOHN
The Interpreter; or Book Containing the Signification of Words. London: 1658. V. 69

CROWELL, JOSEPH E.
The Young Volunteer. The Everyday Experiences of a Soldier Boy in the Civil War. New York: 1906. V. 69

CROWEN, T. J., MRS.
Every Lady's Cook Book. New York: 1854. V. 69

CROWFOOT, GRACE
Flowering Plants of the Northern and Central Sudan. Leonminster: 1929. V. 69

CROWLEY, ALEISTER
Aceldama, A Place to Bury Strangers In. London: 1898. V. 68
The Book of the Law. London: 1938. V. 73
The Diary of a Drug Fiend. London: 1922. V. 68
The Diary of a Drug Fiend. New York: 1923. V. 71
Moonchild. London: 1929. V. 68
The Stratagem. London: 1929. V. 71
The Stratagem. London: 1930. V. 70

CROWLEY, ELFRIDA MARY
Poems.... Croydon: 1892. V. 69

CROWLEY, JOHN
Aegypt. New York: 1987. V. 68; 73
Antiquities. Seattle: 1993. V. 73
Beasts. Garden City: 1975. V. 72
Beasts. Garden City: 1976. V. 70
Daemonomania. Norwalk: 2000. V. 70; 73
An Earthly Mother Sits and Sings. Minneapolis: 2000. V. 73
Little, Big. London: 1982. V. 68; 69; 70
Little, Big. Norwalk: 1997. V. 73
Novelty. New York: 1989. V. 68; 69; 72; 73

CROWLEY, T. J.
Tectonic Boundary Conditions for Climate Reconstructions. New York: 1998. V. 68

CROWNE, WILLIAM
A True Relation of all the Remarkable Places and Passages Observed in the Travels of the Right Honourable Thomas, Lord Howard, Earle of Arundell and Surrey, Primer Earle, and Earle Marshall of England.... London: 1637. V. 68

THE CROWNING Year and Other Poems. 1937. V. 71

CROWNINSHIELD, B. B.
Fore-and-Afters. Boston: 1940. V. 68; 73

CROWS, MEHITABEL
The Jump-Up Story of Sleeping Beauty. New York: 1933. V. 70

CROWTHER, J. G.
The Cavendish Laboratory 1874-1874. New York: 1974. V. 69

CROWTHER, JOHN
Firebase. New York: 1975. V. 72
Silva Gars (Grass Wood) and Guide to Grassington and Upper Wharfedale. Keighley: 1932. V. 73

CROXALL, SAMUEL
The Fables of Aesop, and Others, with Instructive Applications. London: 1834. V. 71
The Fables of Aesop, and others, with Instructive Applications. Halifax: 1844. V. 71

CROY, HOMER
Fancy Lady. New York: 1927. V. 72
Jesse James Was My Neighbor. New York: 1949. V. 68; 69

CROZIER, BLANCHE
Smiley's Haven. Boston: 1928. V. 69

CROZIER, GLADYS BEATTIE
The Art of Arthur Rackham. The Girl's Realm. Volume II. London: 1908. V. 73

CROZIER, W. P.
Letters of Pontius Pilate. New York: 1928. V. 69

CRUDEN, ALEXANDER
A Complete Concordance to the Holy Scripture of the Old and New Testament: in Two Parts. London: 1738. V. 69
The History of Richard Potter, a Sailor and Prisoner in Newgate, Who Was Tried at the Old Bailey in July 1763 and Received Sentence of Death for Attempting, at the Instigation of Another Sailor.... London: 1763. V. 71; 73

CRUEL Boy and the Magic. New York: 1874. V. 71

CRUIKSHANK, E. A.
The Origin and Official History of the Thirteenth Battalion of Infantry and a Description of the Work of the Early Militia of the Niagara Peninsula in the War of 1812 and the Rebellion of 1837. Hamilton: 1899. V. 73

CRUIKSHANK, GEORGE
The Comic Almanack. London. V. 70
The Comic Almanack. First Series 183-1843 and Second Series 1844- 1853. London: 1871. V. 69
The Comic Almanack for 1838.... London: 1838. V. 69
Cruikshank's Water Colours. London: 1903. V. 70
Gallery of Comicalities.... London: 1891. V. 71
George Cruikshank's Magazine. London: 1854. V. 68
Greenwich Hospital. A Series of Naval Sketches. London: 1826. V. 68; 71
Hop-O'My-Thumb and the Seven League Boots. London: 1860. V. 68
Illustrations of Don Quixote, in a Series of Fifteen Plates. London: 1834. V. 73
Illustrations of Time. 1827. V. 68; 72
Illustrations to Punch and Judy. London: 1828. V. 68
Phrenological Illustrations.... London: 1873. V. 69
Sunday in London. London: 1833. V. 71

CRUIKSHANK, I. R.
The Political Dr. Syntax, a Poem. London: 1820. V. 68

CRUIKSHANK, PERCY
The Enchanted Mice. London: 1860. V. 71
Hints to Emigrants; or, Incidents in the Emigration of John Smith of Smith-Town. London: 1848. V. 68
Percy Cruikshank's Comic Almanack for 1869. London: 1869. V. 73

CRUM, H. A.
Mosses of Eastern North America. New York: 1981. V. 72

CRUM, JOSIE MOORE
Ouray County, Colorado. Durango. V. 69

CRUM, M.
First-Line Index of English Poetry 1500-1800 in Manuscripts of the Bodleian Library, Oxford. New York: 1969. V. 70

CRUMB, ROBERT
The Story O' My Life. Santa Rosa: 1990. V. 70
The Yum Yum Book. San Francisco: 1975. V. 73

CRUMLEY, JAMES
Bordersnakes. New York: 1996. V. 72
Bordersnakes. Tucson: 1996. V. 69; 70; 72; 73
The Collection. London: 1991. V. 73
Dancing Bear. New York: 1983. V. 69; 71; 72; 73
The Final Country. New York: 2001. V. 72
The Final Country. Sun City: 2001. V. 70
The Final Country. Tucson: 2001. V. 70; 71; 72; 73
Introduction to Kent Anderson's Sympathy for the Devil. Tacoma: 1997. V. 71
The Last Good Kiss. New York: 1978. V. 68; 69; 70; 71; 72; 73
The Mexican Pig Bandit. Mission Viejo: 1998. V. 70; 71
The Mexican Tree Duck. New York: 1993. V. 69; 71; 72
The Muddy Fork. Northridge: 1984. V. 71; 72
The Muddy Fork. Livingston: 1991. V. 70
One to Count Cadence. New York: 1969. V. 68; 69; 70; 71; 73
One to Count Cadence. New York: 1976. V. 69
The Pigeon Shoot. Santa Barbara: 1987. V. 70; 71; 72; 73
Whores. Missoula: 1988. V. 69; 70; 71; 72
The Wrong Case. New York: 1975. V. 70; 71; 72

CRUMMELL, ALEX
The Future of Africa: Being Addresses, Sermons, Et., Etc. Delivered in the Republic of Liberia. New York: 1862. V. 68
The Greatness of Christ and Other Sermons. New York: 1882. V. 69

CRUMMER, LE ROY
A Catalogue of Manuscripts and Medical Books printed before 1640 in the Library of Le Roy Crummer, Omaha Nebraska. Omaha: 1927. V. 70

CRUMP, PAUL
Burn, Killer, Burn!. Chicago: 1962. V. 70; 71

CRUMPE, SAMUEL
An Essay on the Best Means of Providing Employment for the People. Dublin: 1793. V. 73

CRUMPTON, M. NATALINE
The Silver Buckle. Philadelphia: 1899. V. 69

CRUNDEN, JOHN
Convenient and Ornamental Architecture, Consisting of Original Designs, for Plans, Elevations and Sections.... London: 1791. V. 68

CRUTCHLEY, BROOKE
Two Men: Walter Lewis and Stanley Morison at Cambridge:. Cambridge: 1968. V. 68; 71

CRUZ, M. DE LA
The Badianus Manuscript. Baltimore: 1940. V. 70

CRUZ, RICARDO CORTEZ
Straight Outta Compton. Normal and Boulder: 1992. V. 68

CSAKY, T.
Pharmacology of Intestinal Permeation. Berlin: 1984. V. 71

CUBBON, WILLIAM
Thomas Edward Brown, the Manx Poet (1830-1897): a Bibliography, Being a Section...from...A Bibliographical Account of Works Relating to the Isle of Man. Douglas: 1934. V. 72

CUBITT, W.
Proposed New Bridge at Londonderry. 1857. V. 69

CUDWORTH, RALPH
Systema Intellectuale Huius Universi.... Jena: 1733. V. 73

CUDWORTH, WARREN H.
History of the First Regiment. Boston: 1856. V. 69

CUDWORTH, WILLIAM
Historical Notes on the Bradford Corporation. Bradford: 1881. V. 73
Life and Correspondence of Abraham Sharp. 1889. V. 72; 73
Old Bradford Views. Bradford: 1897. V. 73

CUENDIAS, MANUEL DE
L'Espagne Pittoresque Artistique et Monumentale. Paris: 1848. V. 70

CUITT, GEORGE
Eight Etchings of Old Buildings, in the City of Chester.... Chester and Oxford: 1809-1814. V. 69; 72
Wanderings and Pencillings Amongst Ruins of the Olden Time.... London: 1855. V. 68

CULBERT, T. PATRICK
The Classic Maya Collapse. Albuquerque: 1973. V. 71

CULIN, STEWART
Korean Games with Notes on the Corresponding Games of China and Japan. Philadelphia: 1895. V. 73

CULLEN, COUNTEE
Caroling Dusk An Anthology of Verse by Negro Poets. New York: 1927. V. 70
Color. New York and London: 1925. V. 69; 72

CULLEN, COUNTEE continued
Copper Sun. New York: 1927. V. 70
The Medea and Some Poems. New York: 1935. V. 70
On These I Stand. New York: 1947. V. 71

CULLEN, JAMES BERNARD
The Story of the Irish in Boston. Boston: 1889. V. 69

CULLEN, WILLIAM
First Lines of the Practice of Physic.... Edinburgh: 1778. V. 72
First Lines of the Practice of Physic.... Edinburgh: 1784. V. 71
A Letter to Lord Cathcart...Concerning the Recovery of Persons Drowned, and Seemingly Dead.... Edinburgh: 1776. V. 72

CULLERIER, M. A.
Atlas of Venereal Diseaes. Philadelphia: 1868. V. 73

CULLEY, JOHN H.
Cattle Horses & Men On the Western Range. Los Angeles: 1940. V. 69; 71

CULLIMORE, CLARENCE
Santa Barbara Adobes. Santa Barbara: 1948. V. 70

CULLINGFORD, GUY
Post Mortem. London: 1953. V. 70; 71

CULLIS, CHARLES
Faith Cures; or, Answers to Prayer in the Healing of the Sick. Boston: 1879. V. 69

CULLUM, RIDGWELL
The Saint of the Speedway. New York: 1924. V. 69; 72
The Tiger of Cloud River. Philadelphia: 1929. V. 69

CULMANN, LEONHART
Sententiae Pueriles Anglo Latinae...Sentences for Children. Boston: 1702. V. 71

CULPEPER, NICHOLAS
The British Herbal and Family Physician. Halifax: 1818?. V. 68; 70
The British Herbal and Family Physician. London and Wakefield: 1870. V. 71
Complete Herbal and English Physician. 1805. V. 69
The English Physician Enlarged. London: 1733. V. 72
The English Physician Enlarged. 1801. V. 71
The English Physician Enlarged. London: 1801. V. 69
The English Physician Enlarged. London: 1814. V. 69
The English Physitian Enlarged. London: 1656. V. 68
Health for the Rich and Poor, by Dyet Without Physick. London: 1656. V. 72
Pharmacopoeia Londiensis.... Boston: 1720. V. 68; 70; 73
A Physical Directory. London: 1651. V. 68; 72

CUMBERLAND & WESTMORLAND ANTIQUARIAN & ARCHAEOLOGICAL ASSOC.
Transactions - Old Series. Volumes 1-16. Kendal: 1874-1899. V. 71
Transactions - Old Series. Volumes 6-14 Inclusive. Kendal: 1883-1897. V. 71
Transactions - Old Series. Volumes 6-16 Inclusive. Kendal: 1881-1899. V. 71

CUMBERLAND, GEORGE
An Essay on the Utility of Collecting the Best Works of the Ancient Engravers of the Italian School. London: 1827. V. 71
Outlines from the Antients, Exhibiting Their Principles of Composition in Figures and Basso-Relievos Taken Chiefly from Inedited Monuments of Greek and Roman Sculpture.... London: 1829. V. 69
Thoughts on Outline, Sculpture, and the System that Guided the Ancient Artists in Composing Their Figures and Groups.... London: 1796. V. 70

CUMBERLAND, MARTEN
The Man Who Covered Mirrors. London: 1951. V. 73
Out of this World. London: 1958. V. 69; 73
Steps in the Dark. New York: 1945. V. 68

CUMBERLAND, RICHARD
Calvary: or, the Death of Christ. Burlington: 1795. V. 69
Calvary; or, the Death of Christ. Morris Town: 1815. V. 69
Henry. London: 1795. V. 69
Memoirs. London: 1806. V. 68; 70
Memoirs. London: 1807. V. 72
The Observer. London: 1790. V. 73

CUMBERLEGE, G. F. J.
Essays Mainly on the Nineteenth Century Presented to Sir Humphrey Milford. London: 1948. V. 69

CUMING, E. D.
Wonders in Monsterland. London: 1901. V. 72

CUMING, FORTESCUE
Sketches of a Tour to the Western Country, through the States of Ohio and Kentucky.... Pittsburgh: 1810. V. 68; 73

CUMINGS, JOHN N.
Cerebral Lipidoses - a Symposium. Oxford: 1957. V. 68
Modern Scientific Aspects of Neurology. London: 1960. V. 68

CUMMING, C. F. GORDON
In the Himalayas and on the Indian Plains. 1882. V. 72; 73

CUMMING, GERSHOM
Views at Dunkeld with Descriptive Illustrations. Dundee: 1839. V. 72

CUMMING, JOHN
The Lives And Lessons Of The Patriarchs. London. V. 72

CUMMING, WILLIAM P.
The Southeast in Early Maps. Chapel Hill: 1999. V. 68

CUMMINGS, A. L.
The Framed Houses of Massachusetts Bay 1625-1725. 1979. V. 72
The Framed Houses of Massachusetts Bay 1625-1725. Cambridge: 1979. V. 69

CUMMINGS, BYRON
First Inhabitants of Arizona and the Southwest. Tucson: 1953. V. 71
Kinishba: a Prehistoric Pueblo of the Great Pueblo Period. Tucson: 1940. V. 70

CUMMINGS, CAREY
The Biorhythmic Holmes a Chronological Perspective: Volume 2. 1980. V. 71

CUMMINGS, D. C.
A Historical Survey of the Boiler Makers' and Iron and Steel Ship Builder's Society from August 1834 to August 1904. Newcastle-on-Tyne: 1905. V. 71

CUMMINGS, EDWARD ESTLIN
Collected Poems. New York: 1938. V. 69
Complete Poems 1904-1962. New York: 1991. V. 73
Complete Poems 1913-1962. London: 1968. V. 68
Complete Poems. Volume One 1913-1935. Volume Two 1936-1962. Great Britain: 1968. V. 69
Eimi. New York: 1933. V. 69; 70; 71; 73
The Enormous Room. New York: 1922. V. 70
The Enormous Room. London: 1928. V. 68; 71
50 Poems. New York: 1940. V. 68; 69; 72
XLI Poems. New York: 1925. V. 68
Him. New York: 1927. V. 71
i; six nonlectures. Cambridge: 1953. V. 68; 70
Is 5. New York: 1926. V. 68; 70; 73
A Miscellany. New York: 1958. V. 69; 71; 72
95 Poems. New York: 1958. V. 68; 70
No Thanks. New York: 1935. V. 69; 72
1 x 1. New York: 1944. V. 69; 71; 72
1 x 1. London: 1947. V. 68; 72
Santa Claus. A Morality. New York: 1946. V. 69
Selected Letters. London: 1972. V. 68
Selected Poems. New York: 1994. V. 71; 72
Selected Poems 1923-1958. London: 1960. V. 73
73 Poems. New York: 1962. V. 73
Xaipe. Seventy-One Poems. New York: 1950. V. 68
Tom. New York: 1935. V. 71
Tulips and Chimneys. New York: 1923. V. 69
(Untitled). New York: 1930. V. 70
W (Viva). New York: 1931. V. 72
Xaipe: Seventy-One Poems. New York: 1950. V. 68; 73

CUMMINGS, JEANE
Look Here, J. B.!. Philadelphia: 1957. V. 69

CUMMINGS, JIM
Jim Cummings' Book, Written by Himself, the Life Story of the James and Younger Gang and their Comrades.... Denver: 1903. V. 73

CUMMINGS, RAY
The Girl in the Golden Atom. London: 1922. V. 71
Tales of the Scientific Crime Club. London: 1979. V. 69

CUMMINGS, THAYER
Seven on Sherlock: Some Trifling Observations on the Greatest of all Private Consulting Detectives. 1968. V. 69

CUMMINS, D. DUANE
William Robinson Leigh: Western Artist. Norman: 1980. V. 69

CUMMINS, GERALDINE
Fires of Beltane. 1936. V. 70

CUMMINS, MARIA S.
Haunted Hearts. Boston: 1864. V. 69

CUMSTON, CHARLES GREENE
An Introduction to the History of Medicine from the Time of the Pharaohs to the End of the XVIIIth Century. London: 1926. V. 68

CUNARD, NANCY
Outlaws. London: 1921. V. 70
Parallax. London: 1925. V. 70
Poems. London: 1930. V. 70
Los Poetas del Mundo Defienden al Pueblo Espanol/Les Poetes du Monde Defendent le Peuple Espagnol/Les Poetes du Monde Defendent le Peuple Espagnol. Chapelle-Ranville: 1937. V. 69

CUNDALL, H. M.
Birket Foster, R. W. S. London: 1906. V. 72

CUNDALL, JOSEPH
Songs Madrigals and Sonnets. London: 1849. V. 73

CUNHA DE AZEREDO COUTINHO, JOSE JOAQUIM DE
A Political Essay on the Commerce of Portugal and Her Colonies, Particularly of Brasil in South America. London: 1801. V. 72

CUNLIFFE, BARRY
Excavations of Fishbourne 1961-1969. Reports of the Research Committee of the Society of Antiquaries of London No. XXVI and No. XXVII. Leeds: 1971. V. 73

CUNNINGHAM, A. B.
Death Rides a Sorrel Horse. New York: 1946. V. 68
Death Visits the Apple Hole. New York: 1945. V. 70
Murder at Deer Lick. New York: 1939. V. 73

CUNNINGHAM, ALLAN
Sir Michael Scott, a Romance. London: 1828. V. 73

CUNNINGHAM, C. D.
The Pioneers of the Alps. London: 1888. V. 69; 70; 72

CUNNINGHAM, D.
Calisthenics and Drilling Simplified for Schools and Families. 1870. V. 72
The Regulation of Human Respiration.... Oxford: 1963. V. 71

CUNNINGHAM, D. J.
The Lumbar Curve in Man and Apes. 1886. V. 69; 73

CUNNINGHAM, D. W.
Report on the Sewerage and Drainage of the City of Stillwater (Minnesota). Stillwater: 1881. V. 72

CUNNINGHAM, E. V.
Alice. New York: 1963. V. 70

CUNNINGHAM, EUGENE
Triggernometry. 1934. V. 68
Triggernometry - A Gallery of Gunfights with Technical Notes of a Leather Slapping as a Fine Art, Gathered from Many a Loose Holstered Expert Over the Years. New York: 1934. V. 69; 70

CUNNINGHAM, FRANK
General Stand Watie's Confederate Indians. San Antonio: 1959. V. 69

CUNNINGHAM, G. H.
The Rust Fungi of New Zealand, Together with the Biology, Cytology and Therapeutics of the Uredinales. Dunedin: 1931. V. 71

CUNNINGHAM, J. V.
Doctor Drink. Poems. Cummington: 1950. V. 68; 73
The Helmsman. San Francisco: 1942. V. 73
Selected Poems. Mt. Horeb: 1971. V. 69; 73
Some Salt. 1967. V. 69
Some Salt. Mt. Horeb: 1967. V. 73
To What Strangers, What Welcome. Denver: 1964. V. 69

CUNNINGHAM, J. W.
The Velvet Cushion. London: 1817. V. 71

CUNNINGHAM, JOHN
Poems, Chiefly Pastoral. London: 1766. V. 68; 72

CUNNINGHAM, KATE RICHARDS
In Prison, Being a Report by...to the President of the United States as to the Conditions Under Which Women Federal Prisoners are Confined in the Missouri State Penitentiary.... St. Louis: 1920. V. 68

CUNNINGHAM, LOUIS ARTHUR
Valley of the Stars. Philadelphia: 1938. V. 71

CUNNINGHAM, MERCE
Dancers on a Plane. New York: 1990. V. 73

CUNNINGHAM, MICHAEL
Golden States. New York: 1984. V. 68; 69; 71
A Home at End of the World. New York: 1990. V. 69
The Hours. New York: 1990. V. 69
The Hours. New York: 1998. V. 69; 71; 72; 73

CUNNINGHAM, PETER
Hand-Book of London Past and Present. London: 1850. V. 71
The Story of Nell Gwyn; and the Sayings of Charles the Second. London: 1852. V. 69; 70; 72

CUNNINGHAM, T. M.
Hugh Wilson, a Pioneer Saint. Dallas: 1938. V. 71

CUNNINGHAM, TIMOTHY
The History of Our Customs, Aids, Subsidies, National Debts and Taxes. London: 1761. V. 72
A New Treatise on the Laws Concering Tithes: Containing all the Statutes, Adjudged Cases, Resolutions and Judgements Relative thereto. London: 1765. V. 72

CUNNINGHAM, WILLIAM
The Growth of English Industry and Commerce. Cambridge: 1910-1912. V. 71
Politics and Economics. London: 1885. V. 71

CUNNINGHAME GRAHAM, G.
Father Archangel of Scotland, and Other Essays. London: 1896. V. 68

CUOMO, MARIO
Diaries of...the Campaign for Governor. New York: 1984. V. 69
More than Words: the Speeches of Mario Cuomo. New York: 1995. V. 71

CUPID'S Horn-Book. Songs and Ballads of Marriage and of Cuckoldry. Mt. Vernon: 1936. V. 71

THE CURATE of Mersden; or, Pastoral Conversations Between a Minister and his Parishioners. London: 1839. V. 71

CUREAU DE LA CHAMBRE, MARIN
Novae Methodi Pro Explicandis Hippocrate & Aristotele Specimen. Paris: 1662. V. 70

THE CURIOUS History of Punch and Judy; with Elegant Engravings. Otley: 1847. V. 71

CURLE, ALEXANDER O.
The Treasure of Traprain. Glasgow: 1923. V. 71

CURLE, RICHARD
Collected American First Editions. Its Pitfalls and Its Pleasures. Indianapolis: 1930. V. 70
Into the East - Notes on Burma and Malaya. London: 1923. V. 72

CURLING, T. B.
A Practical Treatise on the Diseases of the Testis, and of the Spermatic Cord and Scrotum. London: 1843. V. 73
A Practical Treatise on the Diseases of the Testis, and of the Spermatic Cord and Scrotum. Philadelphia: 1856. V. 72

CURLL, EDMUND
Curll Papers. Stray Notes on the Life and Publications of Edmund Curll. London: 1879. V. 71
Faithful Memoirs of the Life, Amours and Performances of Mrs. Anne Oldfield. London: 1731. V. 68
The Life Of The late Honourable Robert Price, Esq. London: 1734. V. 72

CURRAN, J. J.
Mr. Voley of Salmon - a Story of Life in a California Village. San Jose: 1907. V. 69

CURRAN, JOHN P.
The Unparalleled Speech of Mr. Curran, on the Trial of Mr. Peter Finerty (sic) for a Libel on Earl Camden, Lord Lieutenant of Ireland. Dublin: 1798. V. 70

CURRENT, W. R.
Greene and Greene, Architects in the Residential Style. Ft. Worth: 1974. V. 69

CURRER, FRANCES RICHARDSON
Catalogue of the Principal Portion of the Magnificent Library of the Late Miss Richardson Currer, of Eshton Hall, Yorkshire. London: 1862. V. 70

CURREY, LLOYD W.
Bibliography of Yosemite, The Central and Southern High Sierra, and the Big Trees 1839-1900. Los Angeles: 1992. V. 69

CURRIE, BARTON W.
Officer 666. New York: 1912. V. 68; 71

CURRIE, MARY MONTGOMERIE LAMB SINGLETON, BARONESS
Collected Verses. London: 1880. V. 69
Poems. London: 1892. V. 69

CURRIE, P. J.
Encyclopaedia of Dionosaurs. 1997. V. 73

CURRIER, JAY L.
Cargo of Fear. New York: 1947. V. 71; 72

CURRY, J. L. M.
Southern States of the American Union. Atlanta: 1895. V. 71

CURRY, JAMES
Observations from Apparent Death from Drowning, Hanging, Suffocation by Noxious Vapours, Fainting-Fits, Intoxication, Lightning, Exposure to Cold &c &c. London: 1815. V. 72

CURRY, JANE LOUISE
Beneath the Hill. New York: 1967. V. 68

CURRY, JOHN P.
Volunteers' Camp and Field Book. Richmond: 1862. V. 69

CURRY, MANFRED
Wind and Water. London: 1930. V. 68

CURRY, RICHARD
Fatal Light. New York: 1988. V. 72

CURSORY Remarks on the Subject of Reform Addressed to the Members of the Reading Societies, Established by the Radicals and Intended to be Read at Their Meeting. Newcastle: 1819. V. 71

CURTIES, MARIANNE
Classical Pastime, in a Set of Poetcial Enigmas, on the Planets and Zodiacal Signs. Reading: 1813. V. 68; 69

CURTIES, T. J. HORSLEY
Ancient Records, or the Abbey of Saint Oswyth. London: 1801. V. 73

CURTIN, JEREMIAH
Myths and Folk-Tales of the Russians, Western Slavs and Magyars. Boston: 1895. V. 69

CURTIN, L. S. M.
By the Prophet of the Earth. Santa Fe: 1949. V. 69; 70; 72
Healing Herbs of the Upper Rio Grande. Santa Fe: 1947. V. 71

CURTIS, ALICE TURNER
A Frontier Girl of Pennsylvania. Philadelphia: 1937. V. 70

CURTIS, BENJAMIN R.
Memoir of Benjamin Robbins Curtis. Boston: 1879. V. 69

CURTIS, C. H.
Orchids for Everyone. London: 1910. V. 71; 73
Orchids, Their Description and Cultivation. London: 1950. V. 71

CURTIS, CHRISTOPHER PAUL
Bud not Buddy. New York: 1999. V. 73

CURTIS, EDWARD S.
In the Land of the Head Hunters. Yonkers-on-Hudson: 1915. V. 70; 71
Papers Of Edward S. Curtis-Relating To The Curtis Fight. El Segundo: 2000. V. 72
Portraits from North American Indian Life. New York: 1972. V. 69; 71; 73

CURTIS, GEORGE WASHINGTON
Prue and I. New York: 1856. V. 70

CURTIS, GEORGE WILLIAM
Niles Notes of a Howadji. New York: 1851. V. 71

CURTIS, JOHN
British Entomology. London: 1823-1840. V. 73
Farm Insects: Being the Natural History and Economy of the Insects Injurious to the Field Crops of Great Britian and Ireland.... Glasgow and London: 1860. V. 68; 69; 72
The Genera of British Lepidoptera. 1858. V. 69

CURTIS, L. P.
Apes and Angels: the Irishman in Victorian Caricature. 1971. V. 69

CURTIS, NATALIE
The Indian's Book. New York: 1907. V. 70
The Indian's Book. New York: 1923. V. 69
The Indian's Book. New York: 1933. V. 68

CURTIS, PAUL
The Highlander. Boston: 1937. V. 69

CURTIS, S.
The Spirit of Seventy-Six; or the Comming Woman a Prophetic Drama Followed by a Change of Base and Doctor Mondschein. Boston: 1868. V. 69; 73

CURTIS, T. A.
State of the Question of Steam Communication with India Via the Red Sea. London: 1839. V. 73

CURTIS, WARDON
The Strange Adventures fo Mr. Middleton. Chicago: 1903. V. 70
The Strange Adventures of Mr. Middleton. Chicago: 1913. V. 71

CURTIS, WILLIAM
Curtis's Botanical Magazine; or Flower Garden Displayed. London: 1827-1887. V. 72; 73
Lectures on Botany, as Delivered to His Pupils. London: 1803-1804. V. 71; 73

CURTIS, WILLIAM E.
A Summer Scamper Along the Old Santa Fe Trail and through the Gorges of Colorado to Zion. Chicago: 1883. V. 71

CURTISS, URSULA
The Second Sickle. New York: 1950. V. 71

CURTIUS, PSEUD.
Torch Light. An Examination of the Origin, Policy, and Principles of the Opposition to the Administration and an Exposition of the Official Conduct of Thomas H. Benton. St. Louis?: 1826. V. 68

CURTIUS RUFUS, QUINTUS
Historiarum Libri.... Lugd. Batavorum: 1633. V. 68
The Historie of Quintus Curtius, Conveying the Actes of the Great Alexander. London: 1592. V. 70

CURWEN, HAROLD
Processes of Graphic Reproduction in Printing. New York: 1934. V. 73

CURWEN, HENRY
A History of Booksellers, the Old and the New.... London: 1873. V. 72

CURWEN, JOHN CHRISTIAN
Hints on Agricultural Subjects, and on the Best means of Improving the Condition of the Labouring Classes.... London: 1809. V. 73
The Rules and the Proceedings of the Anniversary of the Workington Agricultural Society; and Reports of the Society by the President. Workington: 1810. V. 73

CURWEN, JOHN F.
The Ancient Parish of Heversham with Milnthorpe.... Kendal: 1930. V. 71

CURWOOD, JAMES OLIVER
The Black Hunter. New York: 1926. V. 70
The Country Beyond. New York: 1922. V. 70
A Gentleman of Courage. New York: 1924. V. 69
The Golden Snake. New York: 1921. V. 69

CURZON, GEORGE NATHANIEL, 1ST BARON
British Government In India. The Story of the Viceroys and Government Houses. London: 1925. V. 72

CURZON, WILLIAM D.
The Manufacturing Industries of Worcestershire.... 1883. V. 71

CUSHING, ELIZA L.
Yorktown: an Historical Romance. Boston: 1826. V. 68

CUSHING, F. H.
A Preliminary Report on the Exploration of Ancient Key Dweller Remains of the Gulf Coast of Florida. Philadelphia: 1897. V. 69

CUSHING, FRANK HAMILTON
My Adventures in Zuni. Santa Fe: 1941. V. 69
The Nation of the Willows. 1965. V. 69
Zuni Breadstuff. New York: 1920. V. 68; 70; 72
Zuni Folk Tales. New York: 1901. V. 72
Zuni Folk Tales. New York: 1931. V. 69; 72

CUSHING, HARVEY WILLIAMS
A Bio-Bibliography of Andreas Vesalius. New York: 1943. V. 68; 70; 72
A Classification of the Tumors of the Glioma Group in a Histogenetic Basis with a Correlated Study of Prognosis. Philadelphia: 1926. V. 68; 70; 72
Consecreatio Medici and Other Papers. Boston: 1928. V. 72
From a Surgeon's Journal 1915-1918. Boston: 1936. V. 68; 71
The Harvey Cushing Collection of Books and Manuscripts. New York: 1943. V. 68; 70
Intracranial Tumours. Notes Upon a Series of Two Thousand Verified Cases with Surgical Mortality Percentages Pertaining Thereto. Springfield: 1932. V. 68; 70; 72
The Life of Sir William Osler. London: 1925. V. 68; 73
The Life of Sir William Osler. Oxford: 1925. V. 68; 69; 70; 71
The Life of Sir William Osler. London: 1940. V. 71
The Life of Sir William Osler. Birmingham: 1988. V. 69
Meningiomas. Their Classification, Regional Behaviour, Life History and Surgical End Results. Springfield: 1938. V. 72
Meningiomas. Their Classification, Regional Behaviour, Life History and Surgical End Results. New York: 1969. V. 68; 70
Paper Relating to the Pituitary Body, Hypothalmus and Parasympathetic Nervous System. Springfield: 1932. V. 68; 70
The Pathological Findings in Four Autopsied Cases of Acromegaly with a Discussion of Their Significance. New York: 1927. V. 70
The Pituitary Body and Its Disorders. Philadelphia: 1912. V. 68; 70; 72
Studies in Intracranial Physiology and Surgery. The Third Circulation. The Hypophysis. The Gliomas. The Cameron Prize Lectures. 1926. V. 72
Studies in Intracranial Physiology and Surgery. The Third Circulation. The Hypophysis. The Gliomas. The Cameron Prize Lectures. London: 1926. V. 68; 70
The Surgical Art of Harvey Cushing. Park Ridge: 1992. V. 72
Tumors Arising from the Blood-Vessels of the Brain, Angiomatous Malformations and Hemangioblastomas. Springfield: 1928. V. 68; 70; 72
Tumors of the Nervus Acusticus and the Syndrome of the Cerebellopontine Angle. Philadelphia: 1917. V. 68; 70; 72
A Visit to le Puy-En-Velay. Cleveland: 1986. V. 68; 70; 71; 72

CUSHING, LUTHER S.
Manual of Parliamentary Practice. Boston;: 1845. V. 69

CUSHING, MARSHALL
The Story of Our Post Office. Boston: 1893. V. 68; 73

CUSHING, PAUL, PSEUD.
A Woman with a Secret. London: 1885. V. 73

CUSHING, WILLIAM
Initials and Pseudonyms. New York: 1886-1888. V. 70

CUSHMAN, CLARISSA FAIRCHILD
This Side of Regret. Boston: 1937. V. 69

CUSHMAN, DAN
Stay Away, Joe. New York: 1953. V. 69

CUSHMAN, J. A.
Foraminifera of the Atlantic Ocean. Washington: 1918-1931. V. 72
A Monograph of the Foraminifera of the North Pacific Ocean. Washington: 1910-1917. V. 71

CUSSLER, CLIVE
Cyclops. New York: 1986. V. 73
Deep Six. New York: 1984. V. 68
Inca Gold. New York: 1994. V. 68
Pacific Vortex. Aliso Viejo: 2000. V. 69
Raise the Titanic. New York: 1976. V. 68; 70; 71; 73

CUSSLER, CLIVE.
Valhalla Rising. Aliso Viejo: 2001. V. 73

CUSSLER, CLIVE
Valhalla Rising. New York: 2001. V. 70; 72; 73
Vixen 03. New York: 1978. V. 68

CUST, HENRY
Occasional Poems. Jerusalem: 1918. V. 73

CUST, LADY
The Invalid's Own Book. London: 1853. V. 68

THE CUSTER Semi-Centennial Commemoration 1876-1926. Casper: 1926. V. 72

CUSTER, BRICE C.
Sacrificial Lion: George Armstrong Custer. 1999. V. 68

CUSTER, ELIZABETH B.
Boots and Saddles or Life in Dakota with General Custer. New York: 1885. V. 68; 70; 72
Following The Guidon. New York: 1890. V. 72
Tenting On The Plains Or General Custer In Kansas And Texas. New York: 1889. V. 72; 73

CUSTER, GEORGE A.
My Life On The Plains. New York: 1874. V. 68; 72
My Life on the Plains. 1952. V. 68

CUSTOMS and Privileges of the Manors of Stepney and Hackney in the County of Middlesex. London: 1736. V. 70

CUTBUSH, JAMES
The American Artist's Manual, or Dictionary of Practical Knowledge in the Application of Philosophy to the Arts and Manufacturers. Philadelphia: 1814. V. 68; 73
A System of Pyrotechny, Comprehending the Theory and Practice, with the Application of Chemistry.... Philadelphia: 1825. V. 68

CUTCLIFFE, H. C.
The Art of Trout Fishing on Rapid Streams. 1863. V. 68; 73

CUTHBERTSON, BENNETT
Cuthbertson's System for the Complete Interior Management and Oeconomy of a Battalion of Infantry. Bristol: 1776. V. 73

CUTHBERTSON, DAVID
Rosslyn Lyrics. Edinburgh: 1878. V. 68

CUTLER, BENJAMIN C.
Twelve House On The Wreck; or, The Stranding of The Sheffield. New York: 1844. V. 72

CUTLER, CARL C.
Greyhounds of the Sea. New York: 1930. V. 71

CUTLER, JERVIS
A Topographical Description of the State of Ohio, Indiana Territory, and Louisiana. Boston: 1812. V. 68; 72

CUTLER, MARVIN
Homosexuals Today: A Handbook of Organizations & Publications. Los Angeles: 1956. V. 72

CUTLER, THOMAS
The Surgeon's Practical Guide in Dressing, and in the Methodic Application of Bandages. London: 1836. V. 68

CUTLER, W. P.
Life, Journals and Correspondence of Rev. Manasseh Cutler.... Cincinnati: 1888. V. 69

CUTRIGHT, PAUL RUSSELL
Elliott Coues, Naturalist and Frontier Historian. 1981. V. 68
A History of the Lewis and Clark Journals. Mansfield Centre: 2000. V. 70
Lewis and Clark: Pioneering Naturalists. 1969. V. 68

CUTTER, CHARLES
Cutter's Official Guide to Mount Clemens, Michigan, and Its World Famous Mineral Baths. 1916. V. 73

CUTTER, GEORGE W.
The Mafia and Foreign Immigration. Newport: 1891. V. 73

CUTTER, IRVING S.
A Short History of Midwifery. Philadelphia and London: 1964. V. 68; 71

CUTTER, ROBERT A.
Sherlockian Studies: Seven Pieces of Sherlockiana. Jackson Heights: 1947. V. 69

CUTTS, EDWARD L.
An Essay on the Christmas Decoration of Churches.... London: 1866. V. 73

CUTTS, JAMES M.
The Conquest of California and New Mexico.... Philadelphia: 1847. V. 68

CUTTS, JOHN P.
Seventeenth Century Songs Now First Printed from a Bodleian Manuscript. 1956. V. 73

CUTTS, MRS.
Almeria; or, Parental Advice: a Didactic Poem. London: 1775. V. 73

CUVIER and Zoology. A Popular Biography, With An Historical Introduction And Sequel. London: 1844. V. 68; 72

CUVIER, GEORGES, BARON
The Animal Kingdom. 1827. V. 73
The Animal Kingdom. London: 1859. V. 70
Animal Kingdom. Insects. London: 1832. V. 69
The Illustrated Natural History. London: 1834. V. 72
Recherches sur les Ossemens Fossiles.... Paris and Amsterdam: 1821-1824. V. 68
Recherches sur les Ossemens Fossiles.... 1821-1825. V. 68

CYGELMAN, ADELE
Palm Springs Modern. New York: 1999. V. 68

CYRANO DE BERGERAC, SAVINIEN
The Comical History of the States and Empires of the Worlds of the Moon and Sun. London: 1687. V. 68

CZARNECKI, LOUISA AGNES
The Hero of Italy and Other Poems. Edinburgh: 1861. V. 69

CZERNIN, OTTOKAR
In the World War. London: 1919. V. 69

CZERNY, CHARLES
Letters to a Young Lady, on the Art of Playing the Pianoforte, from the Earliest Rudiments to the Highest Stage of Cultivation. 1842. V. 71

CZESTOCHOWSKI, JOSEPH
Arthur B. Davies: a Catalogue Raisonne of the Prints. Newark: 1987. V. 72; 73

CZWIKLITZER, C.
Picasso's Posters. New York: 1970-1971. V. 72

D

DABBS, GEORGE H. R.
The Child-Healer. Shanklin, Isle of Wight: 1910. V. 73

DABNEY, OWEN P.
The Lost Shackle; Seven Years with the Indians. Salem, OR: 1897. V. 72

DABNEY, R. L.
Life and Campaigns of Lieut. Gen. Thomas J. Jackson (Stonewall Jackson). New York: 1866. V. 70; 73
Life of Lieut. Gen. Thomas J. Jackson (Stonewall Jackson). London: 1864-1866. V. 69; 70

D'ABRERA, B.
Butterflies of the Afrotropical Region. East Melbourne: 1980. V. 69
Butterflies of the Australian Region. London: 1971. V. 69; 73
Butterflies of the Oriental Region. Part 3 - Lycaenidae and Riodinidae. East Melbourne: 1986. V. 69

DABROWSKI, MAGDALENA
Contrasts of Form. Geometric Abstract Art 1910-1980. New York: 1985. V. 68

DA CAMARA, KATHLEEN
Laredo on the Rio Grande. San Antonio: 1949. V. 70

DACRE, CHARLOTTE
Hours of Solitude. London: 1805. V. 69
Zofloya or the Moor. London: 1928. V. 71; 73

DACUS, J. A.
Annals of the Great Strikes in the United States. Chicago: 1877. V. 68
Illustrated Lives and Adventures of Frank and Jesse James and the Younger Brothers, The Noted Western Outlaws. St. Louis: 1880. V. 71
A Tour of St. Louis; or, the Inside Life of a Great City. St. Louis: 1878. V. 68

DAFFRONE, JAMES
The Albert Memorial, Hyde Park: Its History and Description. London: 1877. V. 71

DAGGETT, DAVID
Count the Cost. Hartford: 1804. V. 68
Steady Habits Vindicated; or a Remonstrance to the People of Connecticut.... Hartford: 1805. V. 68

D'AGINCOURT, SEROUX
History of Art by Its Monuments from..the Fourth Century to...the 16th. London: 1847. V. 71

DAGLEY, RICHARD
Death's Doings...Illustrations in Prose and Verse.... London: 1827. V. 70

DAGLIESH, ALICE
The Davenports and Cherry Pie. New York: 1949. V. 73
The Land of Nursery Rhyme. London: 1932. V. 72

DAGLISH, ERIC FITCH
Animals in Black and White. London: 1928-1929. V. 72

DAGUERRE, LOUIS JACQUES MANDE
The Hand-Book of Heliography: or, the Art of Writing or Drawing by the Effect of Sun-Light. London: 1840. V. 72

D'AGUIAR, FRED
Dear Future. London: 1996. V. 68

DAHL, ROALD
The Best of Roald Dahl. London: 1983. V. 73
Boy. London: 1984. V. 68
The Boy. New York: 1984. V. 73
Charlie and the Great Glass Elevator. New York: 1972. V. 68; 70
Danny, the Champion of the World. London: 1975. V. 73
The Enormous Crocodile. London: 1978. V. 71
Esio Trot. 1990. V. 72; 73
The Giraffe and the Pelly and Me. London: 1985. V. 73
Going Solo. London: 1986. V. 70; 73
James and the Giant Peach. New York: 1961. V. 72
Kiss Kiss. London: 1960. V. 73
Kiss Kiss. New York: 1960. V. 70; 73
The Magic Finger. London: 1968. V. 73
Matilda. 1988. V. 73
Matilda. London: 1988. V. 72
More Tales of the Unexpected. London: 1980. V. 70; 73
My Uncle Oswald. London: 1979. V. 68; 70; 73
My Year. 1989. V. 71
Over to You. 1946. V. 73

DAHL, ROALD continued
Over to You. London: 1946. V. 72
Rhyme Stew. 1989. V. 73
Rhyme Stew. London: 1989. V. 71
Some Time Never - a Fable for Supermen. New York: 1948. V. 70
Someone Like You. New York: 1953. V. 73
Sometime Never. 1949. V. 73
Switch Bitch: Stories. London: 1974. V. 70
Twenty-Nine Kisses. 1969. V. 70
The Twits. 1980. V. 72
Two Fables. London: 1986. V. 72
Two Fables (The Princess and the Poacher, Princess Mammalia). New York: 1986. V. 73
The Vicar of Nibbleswicke. London: 1991. V. 68
The Witches. 1983. V. 70

DAHLBERG, EDWARD
Bottom Dogs. London: 1929. V. 72
The Flea of Sodom. London: 1950. V. 71
From Flushing to Calvary. London: 1933. V. 71
The Olive of Minerva or the Comedy of a Cuckold. New York: 1976. V. 72
The Sorrows of Priapus. Norfolk: 1957. V. 69
The Sorrows of Priapus. New York: 1957. V. 68
Those Who Perish. New York: 1934. V. 69

DAHLGREN, B. E.
Index of American Palms.... Chicago: 1936. V. 69; 72

DAICHES, DAVID
D. H. Lawrence. 1963. V. 72

DAILEY, M. D.
Ecology of the Southern California Blight, a Synthesis and Interpretation. Berkeley: 1993. V. 72

DAILEY, W. N. P.
History of the Old Fort Herimer Church, German Flatts Reformed Church 1723. St. Johnsville: 1928. V. 72

DAINELLI, GIOTTO
Buddhists and Glaciers of Western Tibet.... London: 1933. V. 72

DAISY Dell Farm ABC. 1905. V. 68

DAIX, P.
Picasso, the Blue and Rose Periods: a Catalogue Raisonne of the Paintings 1900-1906. 1967. V. 69; 72

DAKIN, D. MARTIN
A Sherlock Holmes Commentary. Newton Abbott: 1972. V. 72

DAKIN, SUSANNA BRYANT
A Scotch Paisano: Hugo Reid's Life in California. 1832-1852: Derived from His Correspondence. Berkeley: 1939. V. 68

DAKOTA TERRITORY
Resources of Dakota 1887 - an Official Publication Compiled by the Commissioner of Immigration. Sioux Falls: 1887. V. 70

DAKOTA TERRITORY. LAWS, STATUTES, ETC. - 1862
General Laws and Memorials of the Territory of Dakota Passed at the First Session of the Legislative Assembly.... Yankton: 1862. V. 70

DAKOTA TERRITORY. LAWS, STATUTES, ETC. - 1879
Laws Passed at the the Thirteenth Session of the Legislative Assembly of the Territory of Dakota. Yankton: 1879. V. 70

DAKOTA TERRITORY. LAWS, STATUTES, ETC. - 1887
Laws Passed at the Seventeenth Session of the Legislative Assembly of the Territory of Dakota. Bismarck: 1887. V. 70

DAKOTA TERRITORY. LAWS, STATUTES, ETC. - 1887
General and Special Laws Passed at the Sixteenth Session of the Legislative Assembly of the Territory of Dakota. Sioux Falls: 1887. V. 70

DALE, BRYAN
The Good Lord Wharton. London: 1906. V. 70
The Good Lord Wharton: His Family, Life and Bible Charity. London: 1906. V. 71; 72

DALE, EDWARD EVERETT
Cow Country. Norman: 1942. V. 69
The Indians of the Southwest: A Century of Development Under the United States. Norman: 1949. V. 69
Lafayette Letters. Oklahoma City: 1925. V. 69
The Range Cattle Industry. Norman: 1930. V. 68

DALE, HARRISON CLIFFORD
The Ashley-Smith Exploration and the Discovery of a Central Route to the Pacific 1822-1829. Cleveland: 1918. V. 69

DALE, HENRY HALLETT
Adventures in Physiology with Excursions in Autopharmacology. London: 1965. V. 71

DALE, J.
Angling Days. 1895. V. 68

DALE, NELLIE
Steps to Reading. London: 1902. V. 70

DALE, SAMUEL
Quakers and Cock Robins; or Hypocrisy Unmasked. London: 1828. V. 72

DALE, THOMAS
The Widow of the City of Nain; and Other Poems. London: 1821. V. 71

DALECHAMP, JACQUES
Histoire Generale des Plantes. Lyon: 1653. V. 73

DAL FABBRO, MARIO
How to Build Modern Furniture. New York: 1951-1952. V. 69; 72

DALHOUSIE, GEORGE RAMSAY, 9TH EARL OF
The Dalhousie Journals. Ottawa: 1978-1982. V. 72
The Dalhousie Journals. Toronto: 1982. V. 71

DALI, SALVADOR
Les Diners de Gala. Felicie, New York: 1973. V. 72
Hidden Faces. London and Brussels: 1947. V. 70
Metamorphosis of Narcissus. New York: 1937. V. 69
The Secret Life of Salvador Dali. Translated by Haakon M. Chevalier. London: 1949. V. 71; 72

DALL, CAROLINE HEALY
Barbara Fritchie, a Study. Boston: 1892. V. 69; 73
The Life of Dr. Anandabi Joshee, a Kinswoman of the Pundita Ramabal. Boston: 1888. V. 69
A Practical Illustration of Woman's Right to Labor, or, a Letter fro m Marie E. Boston: 1860. V. 68; 69

DALL, WILLIAM HEALEY
A Preliminary Catalogue of the Shell-Bearing Marine Mollusks and Brachiopods of the Southeastern Coast of the United States. Washington: 1889. V. 68; 71
Spencer Fullerton Baird. 1915. V. 68
Spencer Fullerton Baird. London: 1915. V. 72

DALLAS, FRANCIS GREGORY
The Papers of...., United States Navy. Correspondence and Journal, 1837-1859. New York: 1917. V. 73

DALLAS, SANDRA
No More Than Five in a Bed: Colorado Hotels in the Old Days. Norman: 1967. V. 69

DALLOWAY, JAMES
Anecdotes of the Arts in England; or Comparative Remarks on Architecture, Sculpture and Painting. London: 1800. V. 68; 70; 73

DALLY, JOSEPH W.
Woodbridge and Vicinity. New Brunswick: 1873. V. 69

D'ALMEDIA, WILLIAM B.
Life in Java. London: 1864. V. 70

D'ALMEIDA, ANNA
A Lady's Visit to Manilla and Japan. London: 1863. V. 68; 72

DALRYMPLE, CAMPBELL
Extracts from a Military Essay, Containing Reflections on the Raising, Arming, Clothing and Discipline of the British Infantry and Cavalry. Philadelphia: 1776. V. 71; 73

DALRYMPLE, DAVID
The Opinions of Sarah Duchess-Dowager of Marlborough. 1788. V. 73

DALRYMPLE, JOHN
Memoirs of Great Britain and Ireland. From the Dissolution of the Last Parliament of Charles II, Until the Sea-Battle of La Hogue. Edinburgh: 1771-1773. V. 73

DALRYMPLE, LEONA
Kenny. Chicago: 1917. V. 71

DALRYMPLE, WILLIAM
From the Holy Mountain - a Journey in the Shadow of Byzantium. London: 1997. V. 71

DALSEY, JULES
Human Forces, a New System of Human Philosophy. Chicago: 1924. V. 72

THE DALTON Brothers and Their Astounding Career of Crime by an Eyewitness. Chicago: 1892. V. 73

THE DALTON Brothers. New York: 1954. V. 69

DALTON, DAVID
Janis. New York: 1971. V. 70

DALTON, EDWARD TUITE
Descriptive Ethnology of Bengal. Calcutta;: 1872. V. 72

DALTON, EMMETT
When the Daltons Rode. New York: 1931. V. 71

DALTON, JOHN
Experiments and Observations on the Heat and Cold Produced by the Mechanical Condensation and Rarefaction of Air. Manchester: 1801. V. 68
Experiments and Observations on the Power of Fluids to Conduct Heat; with Reference to Count Rumford's Seventh Essay. Manchester: 1799. V. 68
History of the County of Dublin. 1838. V. 71

D'ALTON, JOHN
Illustrations, Historical and Genealogical of King James's Irish Army List 1689. 1861. V. 69; 73
The Memoirs of the Archbishops of Dublin. 1838. V. 73
The Memoirs of the Archbishops of Dublin. Dublin: 1838. V. 69

DALTON, JOHN
Meteorological Observations and Essays. London: 1793. V. 72

DALTON, JOHN C.
Topographical Anatomy of the Brain. Philadelphia: 1885. V. 68

DALTON, KIT
Under the Black Flag. Memphis: 1914. V. 69

DALTON, MICHAEL
The Country Justice; containing the Practice of the Justices of the Peace Out of Their Sessions. London: 1690. V. 72

DALTON, MORAY
The Night of Fear. 1931. V. 73
One by One they Disappeared. 1929. V. 73

DALTON, W.
The White Elephant; or the Hunters of Ava and the King of the Golden Foot. New York: 1881. V. 72

DALTON, WILLIAM
Will Adams, the First Engishman in Japan. London: 1890. V. 68

DALY, AUGUSTIN
Woffington. A Tribute to the Actress and the Woman. Philadelphia: 1888. V. 72; 73

DALY, CAROLL JOHN
Emperor of Evil. 1937. V. 73
Mr. Strang. 1936. V. 73
The Snarl of the Beast. 1927. V. 73

DALY, CARROLL JOHN
The Third Murderer. New York: 1931. V. 68; 70
The White Circle. New York: 1926. V. 68; 70
The White Circle. London: 1927. V. 73

DALY, ELIZABETH
Arrow Pointing Nowhere. New York: 1944. V. 72
The Book of the Lion. New York: 1948. V. 72
Deadly Nightshade. New York: 1940. V. 72
Death And Letters. New York: 1950. V. 72
Murders in Volume Two. New York: 1941. V. 72
Somewhere In The House. New York: 1946. V. 72

DALY, LOUISE HASKELL
Alexander Cheves Haskell: the Portrait of a Man. Norwood: 1934. V. 69; 70

DALYELL, JOHN GRAHAM
Musical Memoirs of Scotland. London: 1849. V. 71

DALZIEL, GEORGE
Mattie Grey and Other Poems. 1873. V. 71
Unconsidered Trifles. London: 1898. V. 70

DALZIEL, HUGH
The Collie. 1904. V. 68

D'AMBROSIO, JOE
Daisies Never Tell. Sherman Oaks: 1982. V. 70
Oaxaca and the Saguaro Cactus. Phoenix: 1996. V. 70

DAME Trot and Her Comical Cat. New York: 1903. V. 69

DAME Hubbard and Her Dog. London: 1920. V. 71

DAME Trot and Her Cat. New York: 1875. V. 71

DAME Wiggins of Lee and Her Seven Wonderful Cats. London: 1885. V. 70

DAMON, C. A.
Art of Shooting. Fenton: 1892. V. 68

DAMON, ROBERT
Handbook to the Geology of Weymouth and the Island of Portland. London: 1860. V. 70

DAMON, S. FOSTER
Eight More Harvard Poets. New York: 1923. V. 71

DAMON, WILLIAM E.
Ocean Wonders; a Companion for the Seaside. New York: 1879. V. 68

DAMPIER, WILLIAM
Dampier's Voyages; Consisting of a New Voyage Round the World, a Supplement to the Voyage Round the World, Two Voyages to Campeachy, a Discourse of Winds, a Voyage to New Holland.... London: 1906. V. 70

DAMS, JEANNE M.
The Body in the Transept. New York: 1995. V. 72

DANE Dare Annual 1974. 2 Action Packed Adventures of Fiction's Greatest Hero. 1973. V. 72

DAN Rice's Old Time Circus Songster. New York: 1882. V. 71

DANA, C. L.
Contributions to Medical and Biological Research Dedicated to Sir William Osler, in Honour of His Seventieth Birthday July 12, 1919, by His Pupils and Co-Workers. New York: 1919. V. 71

DANA, CHARLES A.
Lincoln and His Cabinet. A Lecture Delivered Tuesday, March 10, 1896 Before the New Haven Colony Historical Society. New York: 1896. V. 70

DANA, DANIEL
Memoirs of Eminently Pious Women, Who Were Ornaments to Their Sex.... Newburyport: 1803. V. 69; 73

DANA, JAMES D.
Characteristics of Volcanoes, with Contributions of Facts and Principles from the Hawaiian Islands.... London: 1891. V. 70
Corals and Coral Islands. London: 1872. V. 70
Manual of Geology: Treating of the Principes of the Science with Special Reference to American Geological History.... Philadelphia: 1863. V. 69
Manual of Mineralogy and Lithology.... London: 1882. V. 68
Manual of Mineralogy, Including Observations on Mines, Rocks, Reduction of Ores and the Applications of the Science to the Arts. New Haven: 1848. V. 68
A System of Mineralogy: Descriptive Mineralogy, Comprising the Most Recent Discoveries. New York: 1880. V. 71

DANA, KATHERINE FLOYD
Our Phil and Other Stories. Boston: 1889. V. 73

DANA, RICHARD HENRY
Journal. Cambridge: 1968. V. 68
Poems and Prose Writings. New York: 1850. V. 73
Two Years Before the Mast. New York: 1840. V. 68; 70
Two Years Before the Mast. London: 1904. V. 73
Two Years Before the Mast. Boston: 1912. V. 69
Two Years Before the Mast. New York: 1936. V. 73
Two Years Before the Mast. Los Angeles: 1964. V. 71; 72; 73

DANA, ROBERT
Blood Harvest. Iowa City: 1987. V. 73

DANBY, FRANCIS
Three Views, Illustrative of the Scenery of Bristol and Its Vicinity. London: 1823. V. 69

DANCE, S. P.
The Art of Natural History. New York: 1978. V. 72
The Art of Natural History. New York: 1990. V. 72

THE DANCING Dolls. London: 1910. V. 73

DANCKERS, ULRICH
A Compendium of the Early History of Chicago. River Forest: 2000. V. 73

DANDRIDGE, RAYMOND GARFIELD
The Poet and Other Poems. Cincinnati: 1920. V. 68; 72

THE DANDY Book. 1953. V. 72

DANDY, WALTER
Benign, Encapsulated Tumors in the Lateral Ventricles of the Brain. Baltimore: 1934. V. 68
Benign, Encapsulated Tumors in the Third Ventricle of the Brain; Diagnosis and Treatment. London: 1934. V. 70
Benign Tumors in the Third Ventricle of the Brain, Diagnosis and Treatment. London: 1933. V. 70
Benign Tumors in the Third Ventricle of the Brain; Diagnosis and Treatment. Springfield: 1933. V. 68
Intracranial Arterial Aneurysms. Ithaca: 1945. V. 68; 70
Orbital Tumors Results Following the Transcranial Operative Attack. New York: 1941. V. 68; 70
Selected Writings of Walter E. Dandy. Springfield: 1957. V. 68

DANE, CLEMENCE
Enter Sir John. New York: 1928. V. 71
First the Blade. New York: 1918. V. 69

DANE, R.
Sport in Asia and Africa. 1921. V. 70; 72; 73

DANEAU, LAMBERT
Traite des Danses, Auquel est Amplement Resolue la Question, a Savoir s'il est Permis aux Chrestiens de Danser. Geneva: 1579. V. 68; 73

DANET, PIERRE
Dictionarium Antiquitatum Romanarum Et Graecarum. Lutetiae Parisiorum: 1698. V. 73

DANFRIE, PHILIPPE
Declaration de L'Vsage du Graphometre. Paris: 1597. V. 70

DANGEL, EDWARD M.
The Laws of Labor Unions. Boston: 1941. V. 71

THE DANGER of Improving Physick; with a Brief Account of the Present Epidemick Fever. London: 1730. V. 70; 71

DANGERFIELD, THOMAS
The Information of (T.D.) Delivered at the Bar of the House of Commons, Tuesday the Twentieth Day of October in the Year of Our Lord 1680. London: 1680. V. 70; 72

DANICAN, FRANCOIS ANDRE
Analysis of the Game of Chess. London: 1790. V. 72

DANIE, GLYN
Some Small Harvest. London: 1986. V. 70

DANIEL, DAVID
The Heaven Stone. New York: 1994. V. 69

DANIEL, GABRIEL
A Voyage to the World of Cartesius. London: 1694. V. 69; 72

DANIEL, GEORGE
Merrie England in Olden Time. London: 1842. V. 71
The R...L First-Born; or, the Baby Out of His Leading-Strings.... London: 1812. V. 68

DANIEL, J. F.
The Elasmobranch Fishes. Berkeley, Calif: 1922. V. 72

DANIEL, JOHN HENRY
A Companion for the Cornish Talia, Being Original Humorous Pieces (in verse) in the Cornish and Devonshire Dialects.... Devonport: 1865. V. 71
A Great Mine Conference. The Gwennap Bal Boys. The Prechen Cappen. The Fox Outwitted by a Cock. A Legend of St. Germans. Dialogue About India, China, Railways and Unions. The Poor Man and His Paris Church. Devonport: 1869. V. 71
Humorous Cornish Legends. Devonport: 1869. V. 71

DANIEL, JOHN W.
The Law and Practice of Attachment, Under the Code of Virginia and of Bail and Injunction. Lynchburg: 1869. V. 71

DANIEL, ROBERT MAC KENZIE, MRS.
The Student's Wife. London: 1865. V. 68

DANIEL, ROLAND
Wu Fang an Adventure of the Secret Service. London. V. 73

DANIEL, W.
A Familiar Treatise on Perspective, Designed for Ladies.... London: 1807. V. 71
A Familiar Treatise on Perspective, Designed for Ladies.... London: 1810. V. 73

DANIEL, W. HARRISON
Bedford Co., Virginia 1840-1860. The History of an Upper Piedmont County in the Late Antebellum Era. Bedford: 1985. V. 72

DANIEL, WILLIAM
Catalogue of a Collection of Original Finished Drawings and Sketches. London: 1831. V. 69
Catalogue of a Collection of Original Finished Drawings and Sketches. London: 1833. V. 69

DANIELEWSKI, MARK Z.
House of Leaves. London: 2000. V. 68; 71
House of Leaves. New York: 2000. V. 70; 72

DANIELL, L. E.
Types of Successful Men of Texas. Austin: 1890. V. 70

DANIELL, ROSEMARY
The Hurricane Season. New York: 1992. V. 68; 71

DANIELL, WILLIAM
Views Illustrative of Animated Nature. London: 1809. V. 68; 70

DANIELS, CORA LINN
The Bronze Buddha. Boston: 1899. V. 69; 71; 73

DANIELS, JONATHAN
The Man of Independence. Philadelphia and New York: 1950. V. 68
Mosby: Gray Ghost of the Confederacy. Philadelphia & Lippincott: 1959. V. 70
Thomas Wolfe: October Recollections. Columbia: 1961. V. 70; 71

DANIELS, KATE
The White Wave. Pittsburgh: 1984. V. 68; 69

DANKS, DENISE
Torso. London: 1999. V. 68

DANNENBERG, ERICH CHRISTIAN HEINRICH
Der Harz, ein Gedicht in Sieben Gesangen. Gottingen: 1781. V. 68

DANSEREAU, P.
Biogeography, an Ecological Perspective. New York: 1957. V. 68

DANSON, JOHN TOWNE
Observations on the Speech of Sir William Molesworth in the House of Commons on Tuesday 25th July 1848, on Colonial Expenditure and Government. London: 1848. V. 71

DANTE ALIGHIERI
Dante's Inferno. New York: 1875. V. 71
Dante's Inferno. London: 1985. V. 70
Dante's Inferno. New York: 1985. V. 73
Dante's Inferno. Hopewell: 1993. V. 69; 72; 73
Divina Commedia. Venice: 1491. V. 68
La Divina Commedia. Venice: 1757-1758. V. 69
La Divina Commedia. Florence: 1821. V. 68
La Divina Commedia. Berlin: 1925. V. 68; 72
La Divina Commedia or the Divine Vision. London: 1928. V. 68; 70; 71
The Divine Comedy. New York: 1932. V. 69
Die Gottliche Komodie. Vienna: 1921. V. 71
The New Life. London: 1899. V. 68
The New Life. London: 1900. V. 69
The New Life. London: 1916. V. 69
The Nonesuch Press Divine Comedy. London: 1928. V. 71
Seventeen Cantos of the Inferno.... Boston: 1865. V. 68; 71
The Stone Beloved: Six Poems. Austin: 1986. V. 71
Le Terze Rime. (The Divine Comedy). Venetiis: 1502. V. 69
The Vision of Hell. London. V. 71
The Vision of Hell. (with) The Vision of Purgatory and Paradise. London: 1903. V. 68

DANTICAT, EDWIDGE
Breath, Eyes, Memory. New York: 1994. V. 69; 71; 72; 73
Krik? Krak!. New York: 1995. V. 69; 72

DANTO, ARTHUR C.
Mapplethorpe. New York: 1992. V. 73

D'ANVILLE, JEAN BAPTISTE BOURGUIGNON
Lettre de Monsieur D'Anville.... 1737. V. 70

DANZ, E.
Architecture of Skidmore, Owings and Merrill 1950-1962. London: 1963. V. 72

DANZ, LOUIS
Dynamic Dissonance in Nature and the Arts. New York: 1952. V. 68

DAPPER, OLFERT
Description Exacte des Isles de l'Archipel et de Quelques Autres Adjacentes.... Amsterdam: 1703. V. 68

DARBY, KEN
The Brownstone House of Nero Wolfe. Boston: 1983. V. 68

DARBY, RUTH
If This Be Murder. New York: 1941. V. 71

DARBY, STEPHEN
Chapters in the History of Cookham, Berkshire. Edinburgh: 1909. V. 71

DARBY, WENDY
Scorpio. 1980. V. 72

DARIUS'S *Feast; or, the Force of Truth.* London: 1734. V. 69

DARK, S.
Sir William Orpen: Artist and Man. 1932. V. 70

THE DARK *Side of the Moon.* London: 1946. V. 69

THE DARKIES' *Show.* 1900. V. 69

DARLEY, FELIX OCTAVIUS CARR
Illustrations of Rip Van Winkle, Designed and Etched by Felix O. C. Darley. New York: 1848. V. 68
Sketches Abroad with Pen and Pencil. New York: 1868. V. 70; 71

DARLEY, GEORGE
The Labours of Idleness; or, Seven Nights' Entertainments. 1826. V. 73
Nepenthe: a Poem in Two Cantos. London: 1897. V. 73
Poems. 1889. V. 73
Sylvia; or, the May Queen. 1827. V. 73
Thomas A Beckett: a Dramatic Chronicle in Five Acts; Bound together with Ethelstan; or, the Battle of Brunanburh, a Dramatic Chronicle. London: 1840-1841. V. 73

DARLING, F. FRASER
The Highlands & Islands. London: 1964. V. 71
Natural History in the Highlands & Islands. London: 1947. V. 71

DARLING, ROGER
Benteen's - Scout-To-The-Left - The Route From the Divide to The Morass (June 25, 1876). Spokane: 2000. V. 72
Custer's Seventh Cavalry Comes to Dakota. El Segundo: 1989. V. 72
A Sad and Terrible Blunder, Generals Terry and Custer at The Little Big Horn: New Discoveries. Vienna: 1992. V. 72

DARLING, S.
Chicago Furniture: Art, Craft and Industry 1833-1983. New York and London: 1984. V. 69; 72

DARLINGTON, C. D.
Chromosome Atlas of Flowering Plants. New York: 1956. V. 72

DARLINGTON, E. M.
The Radcliffes of Leigh, Lancashire. Lutterworth: 1918. V. 70; 72; 73

DARLINGTON, IDA
Printed Maps of London, circa 1553-1850. London: 1964. V. 70

DARLINGTON, P. J.
Zoogeography: the Geographical Distribution of Animals. New York: 1957. V. 68; 71

DARLOW, T. H.
Historical Catalogue of the Printed Editions of Holy Scripture in the Library of the British and Foreign Bible Society. New York: 1963. V. 71

DARRAH, H. Z.
Sport in the Highlands of Kashmir. 1898. V. 69; 70; 72; 73

DARRELL, WILLIAM
The Case Review'd or, an Answer to the Case Stated.... London?: 1715. V. 73

DARROW, CLARENCE
Crime: Its Cause and Treatment. New York: 1922. V. 70; 72
Farmington. New York: 1925. V. 69; 72
Farmington. New York: 1928. V. 68; 71
A Persian Pearl. East Aurora: 1899. V. 73
A Persian Pearl. Chicago: 1902. V. 71
The Plea of Clarence Darrow August 22nd, 23rd and 25th. MCMXXIII in Defense of Richard Loeb and Nathan Leopold, Jr. on Trial for Murder. Chicago: 1924. V. 73
The Prohibition Mania. New York: 1927. V. 70
The Story of My Life. New York: 1932. V. 71

DARTON, F. J. HARVEY
Dickens: Positively the First Appearance. London: 1933. V. 68

DARTON, F. J. HARVEY continued
The Good Fairy; or, the Adventures of Sir Richard Whittington.... London: 1922. V. 71
The London Review: a Moral Pantomime.... London: 1923. V. 70

DARTON, N. H.
Guidebook of the Western United States. Part F. The Southern Pacific Lines New Orleans to Los Angeles. Washington: 1933. V. 68
Preliminary Report on the Geology and Underground Water Resources of the Central Great Plains. Washington: 1905. V. 70

DARTON, W.
South America From the Latest Authorities. London: 1807. V. 72

DARTON, WILLIAM
Little Jack of all Trades; or Mechanical Arts Described in Prose and Verse.... London: 1823. V. 73
A Present for a Little Boy. London: 1800. V. 68
A Present for a Little Girl. London: 1797. V. 72

DARTT, ROBERT L.
George Alfred Henry, a Bibliography. Altrincham: 1971. V. 73

DARWIN, BERNARD
A History of Golf in Britain. London: 1952. V. 73
Pack Clouds Away. London: 1941. V. 72
The Tale of Mr. Tottleoo. (with) Tootleoo Two. London: 1925. V. 70; 71

DARWIN, CHARLES ROBERT
Charles Darwin's Notebooks 1836-1844. Ithaca: 1987. V. 69; 72
Correspondence of Charles Darwin. Volumes 1-8, 1821-1860. 1985-1993. V. 69
The Descent of Man. 1875. V. 72
The Descent of Man. London: 1879. V. 69
The Descent of Man. 1888. V. 73
The Descent of Man and Selection in Relation to Sex. 1871. V. 69
The Descent of Man and Selection in Relation to Sex. London: 1871. V. 73
The Descent of Man and Selection in Relation to Sex. New York: 1871. V. 73
The Descent of Man and Selection in Relation to Sex. London: 1875. V. 69
The Descent Of Man and Selection in Relation to Sex. London: 1879. V. 68
The Descent of Man and Selection in Relation to Sex. London: 1881. V. 70; 72
The Descent of Man and Selection in Relation to Sex. London: 1885. V. 73
The Descent of Man and Selection in Relation to Sex. New York: 1887. V. 72
The Descent of Man and Selection in Relation to Sex. London: 1888. V. 70
The Descent of Man and Selection in Relation to Sex. Adelaide: 1971. V. 68; 70; 72
The Different Forms of Flowers on Plants of the Same Species. London: 1877. V. 69; 73
The Effects of Cross and Self Fertilisation in the Vegetable Kingdom. London: 1876. V. 73
The Effects of Cross and Self Fertilisation in the Vegetable Kingdom. London: 1878. V. 69
The Expression of the Emotions in Man and Animals. London: 1872. V. 68; 71; 73
The Formation of Vegetable Mould through the Action of Worms. London: 1881. V. 69; 72; 73
The Formation of Vegetable Mould through the Action of Worms. New York: 1882. V. 69
The Formation of Vegetable Mould through the Action of Worms. New York: 1890. V. 72
The Formation of Vegetable Mould through the Action of Worms. 1897. V. 73
Geological Observations on Coral Reefs, Volcanic Islands, and on South America.... London: 1851. V. 73
Geological Observations on South America...Being the Third Part of the Geology of the Voyage of the Beagle. London: 1846. V. 73
Geological Observations on the Volcanic Islands and Parts of South America Visited During the Voyage of H.M.S. Beagle.... London: 1876. V. 68
Geological Observations on the Volcanic Islands Visited During the Voyage of HMS Beagle...Being the Second Part of the Geology of the Voyage of the Beagle. London: 1844. V. 73
Insectivorous Plants. London: 1875. V. 73
Insectivorous Plants. New York: 1875. V. 70; 72
Journal of Researches into the Geology and Natural History of the Various Countries Visited by H.M.S. Beagle, under the Command of Captain Fitzroy. London: 1839. V. 73
Journal of Researches Into the Natural History and Geology of the Countries Visited During the Voyage of H.M.S. Beagle.... London: 1845. V. 73
The Life and Letters of Charles Darwin. London: 1887. V. 73
The Life and Letters of Charles Darwin. New York: 1888. V. 69
The Life and Letters of Charles Darwin. New York: 1893. V. 72
The Life and Letters of Charles Darwin. New York: 1896. V. 72
A Monograph on the Fossil Lepadidae (Balanidae and Verrucidae). London: 1851-1861. V. 73
A Monograph on the Sub-Class Cirripedia with Figures of all the Species. London: 1851-1854. V. 73
More Letters.... London: 1903. V. 73
The Movements and Habits of Climbing Plants. London: 1875. V. 73
The Movements and Habits of Climbing Plants. London: 1891. V. 69
Narrative of the Surveying Voyages of His Majesty's Ships Adventure and Beagle.... London: 1839. V. 73
Natur Wissenschaftliche Reisen. (Journal of Researches). Braunschweig: 1844. V. 72
On the Origin of Species by Means of Natural Selection. London: 1859. V. 68; 73
On the Origin of Species by Means of Natural Selection. London: 1860. V. 72; 73
On the Origin of Species by Means of Natural Selection. New York: 1860. V. 73
On the Origin of Species by Means of Natural Selection. London: 1866. V. 70; 72; 73
On the Origin of Species by Means of Natural Selection. New York: 1871. V. 70
On the Origin of Species by Means of Natural Selection. Adelaide: 1963. V. 69; 70; 71; 72
On the Structure and Distribution of Coral Reefs.... London: 1900. V. 70
On the Various Contrivances by Which British and Foreign Orchids are Fertilised by Insects.... London: 1862. V. 68; 69; 73
The Origin of Species by Means of Natural Selection. London: 1872. V. 69; 73
The Origin of Species by Means of Natural Selection. London: 1885. V. 70; 72
The Origin of Species by Means of Natural Selection. London: 1886. V. 73
The Origin of Species by Means of Natural Selection. London: 1888. V. 70; 73
The Origin of Species by Means of Natural Selection. London: 1897. V. 73
The Origin of the Species by Means of Natural Selection. 1899. V. 68
The Power of Movement in Plants. London: 1880. V. 72; 73
The Power of Movement in Plants. New York: 1897. V. 71
The Structure and Distribution of Coral Reefs...Being the First Part of the Geology of the Voyage of the Beagle. London: 1842. V. 73
Uber die Entstehung der Arten im Thier-und Pflanzen-Reich durch Naturliche Zuchtung, oder Erhaltung der Vervollkommneten Rassen im Kampfe um's Daseyn... (On the Origin of Species). Stuttgart: 1860. V. 73
The Variation of Animals and Plants Under Domestication. London: 1868. V. 69; 72; 73
The Variation of Animals and Plants Under Domestication. London: 1875. V. 69; 73
The Variation of Animals and Plants Under Domestication. New York: 1876. V. 70
The Variation of Animals and Plants Under Domestication. New York: 1884. V. 72
The Variation of Animals and Plants Under Domestication. London: 1905. V. 68; 70
The Zoology of the Voyage of H.M.S. Beagle During the Years 1832- 1836 Under the Command of Captain Fitzroy. London: 1838-1843. V. 73
The Zoology of the Voyage of H.M.S. Beagle; Part II Mammalia. London: 1839. V. 73

DARWIN, ERASMUS
The Botanic Garden. London: 1791. V. 73
The Botanic Garden. 1791-1789. V. 73
Phytologia; or the Philosophy of Agriculture and Gardening. London: 1800. V. 71
A Plan for the Conduct of Female Education, in Boarding Schools. Derby;: 1797. V. 73
The Poetical Works. London: 1806. V. 70; 71; 73
Zoonomia; or the Laws of Organic Life. London: 1796. V. 70

DARWIN, M. F.
One Moral Standard for All. New York: 191-. V. 68

THE DARWINIAN Theory Examined. London: 1878. V. 73

DARY, DAVID
Comanche. Lawrence: 1976. V. 68

DASENT, G.
The Story of Burnt Njal or Life in Iceland At the End of The Tenth Century. Edinburgh: 1861. V. 72

DASENT, G. W.
Norse Fairy Tales. London: 1910. V. 68

DASSANAYAKE, M. D.
A Revised Handbook of the Flora of Ceylon. Volume IX. New Delhi: 1995. V. 72
A Revised Handbook to the Flora of Ceylon. Rotterdam & New Delhi: 1980-1994. V. 69

D'ASTE, IPPOLITO
Modello di Calligrafia. Fenoa: 1840. V. 70

THE DATE Book for Lincoln and Neighbourhood, from the Earliest Time to the Present. Lincoln: 1866. V. 73

DAUBENMIRE, R.
Plant Geography with Special Reference ot North America. New York: 1978. V. 72

DAUDET, ALPHONSE
One of the Forty. London: 1888. V. 68

DAUGHTERTY, JAMES
Poor Richard. New York: 1941. V. 73

DAUGHTERY, JAMES
Their Weight in Wildcats: Tales of the Frontier. Boston: 1936. V. 69

D'AULAIRE, INGRI
Children of the Northlights. New York: 1935. V. 73
Nils. Garden City: 1948. V. 69
Trolls. Garden City: 1972. V. 72

DAUMAS, MAURICE
Scientific Instruments of the Seventeenth and Eighteenth Centuries and Their Makers. London: 1972. V. 70

DAUMIER
L'Art de Notre Temps. Daumier. 48 Planches hors-texte. Paris. V. 68

DAUNT, ACHILLES
Crag, Glacier and Avalanche. London: 1894. V. 69

DAUZET, MARCELINE
One Happy Day: A Picture-Story Book. Akron: 1939. V. 70

DAVAINE, CASIMIR JOSEPH
L'Oeuvre. Paris: 1889. V. 69

DAVE, RODERICK
The Private Press. London: 1971. V. 72

DAVENANT, CHARLES
A Discourse Upon Grants and Resumptions. London: 1700. V. 72
A Discourse Upon Grants and Resumptions. London: 1704. V. 70
Discourses on the Publick Revenues and on the Trade of England. In Two Parts. London: 1698. V. 72; 73
An Essay Upon Ways and Means of Supplying the War. London: 1695. V. 72

D'AVENANT, WILLIAM
Gondibert: an Heroick Poem. London: 1651. V. 72

D'AVENANT, WILLIAM continued
The Works of.... London: 1673. V. 68; 70; 72; 73

DAVENPORT, BISHOP
Pocket Gazetteer, or Traveller's Guide through North America and the West Indies. Trenton and Baltimore: 1834. V. 69

DAVENPORT, CYRIL
English Embroidered Bookbindings. London: 1899. V. 70
Roger Payne English Bookbinder of the Eighteenth Century. Chicago: 1929. V. 73
Royal English Bookbindings. London: 1896. V. 68; 70; 73
Samuel Mearne. Chicago;: 1906. V. 73
Thomas Berthelet, Royal Printer and Bookbinder to Henry VIII, with Special Reference to His Bookbindings. Chicago: 1901. V. 70; 73

DAVENPORT, GUY
August. Tuscaloosa: 1986. V. 69; 72
The Bicycle Rider. New York: 1985. V. 73
The Bowmen of Shu. New York: 1983. V. 69; 72; 73
Da Vinci's Bicycle. Ten Stories. Baltimore and London: 1979. V. 69; 72
50 Drawings. New York: 1996. V. 73
Flowers and Leaves: Poema Vel Sonata Carmina Autumni Primaeque Veris Transformations. Highlands: 1966. V. 69; 71; 73
Goldfinch Thistle Star. New York: 1983. V. 73
The Hunter Gracchus. Washington: 1996. V. 72
Jonah. New York: 1986. V. 73
The Resurrection in Cookham Churchyard. New York: 1982. V. 69
Tatlin!. New York: 1974. V. 69; 71

DAVENPORT, JOHN
Aphrodisiacs and Anti-Aphrodisiacs: Three Essays on the Powers of Reproduction; With Some Account of the Judicial Congress as Practised in France During the Seventeenth Century. London: 1869. V. 72
Rocks and Thorns. Cambridge: 1929. V. 70

DAVEY, F. H.
Flora of Cornwall. Penryn: 1909. V. 69

DAVEY, RICHARD
Furs and Fur Garments. London: 1895. V. 71

DAVEY, SYDNEY
The Law Relating to Pauper Lunatics. London: 1903. V. 69

DAVID, ROBERT BEEBE
Finn Burnett, Frontierman - The Life and Adventures of An Indian Fighter, Mall Coach Driver, Pioneer, Cattleman, Participant in The Power River Expedition, Survivor of The Hay Field Fight, Associate of Jim Bridger and Chief Washakie. Glendale: 1937. V. 72
Malcolm Campbell, Sheriff. Casper: 1932. V. 69

DAVID, VILLIERS
The Guardsman and Cupid's Daughter and Other Poems. London: 1930. V. 71
A Winter Firework. Waltham St. Lawrence: 1937. V. 71

DAVIDIAN, H. H.
The Rhododendron Species. London: 1992. V. 68

DAVIDOFF, LEO
The Abnormal Pneumoencephalogram. Philadelphia: 1950. V. 70; 71
The Normal Encephalogram. Philadelpphia: 1951. V. 70

DAVIDSON, BRUCE
Bruce Davidson Photographs. New York: 1978. V. 68
East 100th Street. Cambridge: 1970. V. 68; 70
Photographs. New York: 1978. V. 73

DAVIDSON, DIANE MOTT
Catering to Nobody. New York: 1990. V. 68; 72
Dying for Chocolate. New York: 1991. V. 72
The Last Suppers. New York: 1994. V. 71

DAVIDSON, DONALD
Lee in the Mountains and Other Poems. New York: 1938. V. 71
An Outland Piper. Boston and New York: 1924. V. 70
The Tennessee. New York: 1948. V. 73

DAVIDSON, EDGAR
The Edgar and Dorothy Davidson Collection of Canadiana at Mount Allison University. Sackville: 1991. V. 73

DAVIDSON, ELLIS A.
A Practical Manual of House Painting, Granining, Marbling and Sign Writing.... London: 1884. V. 68
A Practical Manual of House-Painting, Graining, Marbling and Sign- Writing. 1896. V. 71
A Pratical Manual of House-Painting, Graining, Marbling and Sign Writing.... London: 1896. V. 68

DAVIDSON, GEORGE
Legend of St. Swithin, a Rhyme for Rainy Weather. London: 1861. V. 69

DAVIDSON, GLADYS
Lancelot and Guenevere. London. V. 72

DAVIDSON, HAROLD G.
Edward Borein Cowboy Artist: the Life and Works of John Edward Borein 1872-1945. Garden City: 1974. V. 69; 70; 72
The Last Works of Edward Borein. Santa Barbara: 1978. V. 70

DAVIDSON, HOMER K.
Black Jack Davidson, A Cavalry Commander on The Western Frontier. The Life of General John W. Davidson. Glendale: 1974. V. 72

DAVIDSON, J.
Spanish Portraits. New York: 1939. V. 72

DAVIDSON, JAMES
The History of Newenham Abbey in the County of Devon. London: 1843. V. 69

DAVIDSON, JOHN
The Ballad of a Nun. 1905. V. 68
Baptist Lake. London: 1894. V. 68
Bruce: a Drama in Five Acts. Glasgow and London: 1886. V. 68
A Full and True Account of the Wonderful Mission of Earl Lavender, Which Lasted One Night and One Day. 1895. V. 68
The Great Men and a Practical Novelist. London: 1891. V. 68
Holiday and Other Poems. London: 1906. V. 68
The Knight of the Maypole.... London: 1903. V. 68
The Last Ballad and Other Poems. London: 1899. V. 68
Mammon and His Message - Being the Second Part of God and Mammon - a Trilogy. London: 1908. V. 71
New Ballads. London and New York: 1897. V. 68
Plays. 1889. V. 68
A Queen's Romance: a Version of Ruy Blas. 1904. V. 68
A Rosary. 1903. V. 68
Self's the Man. London: 1901. V. 68
Smith - A Tragedy. Glasgow: 1888. V. 68

DAVIDSON, L. MARION
Gates of The Dolomites. London: 1914. V. 72

DAVIDSON, LIONEL
The Chelsea Murders. London: 1978. V. 70
Kolymsky Heights. London: 1994. V. 70
A Long Way to Shiloh. London: 1966. V. 70
Making Good Again. London: 1968. V. 68; 70; 72
The Rose of Tibet. London: 1962. V. 70

DAVIDSON, MARSHALL B.
Life in America. Boston: 1951. V. 71

DAVIDSON, RAFFLES
A Record of His Life and Work from 1870-1926. London: 1927. V. 68

DAVIE, DONALD
Brides of Reason. A Selection of Poems. Swinford: 1955. V. 68; 71
Collected Poems - 1950-1970. London: 1972. V. 72
The Poems of Doctor Zhivago. Manchester: 1965. V. 71

DAVIE, O.
Methods in the Art of Taxidermy. Philadelphia: 1900. V. 72
Nest and Eggs of North American Birds. Columbus: 1889. V. 73

DAVIES, CHARLES MAURICE
Unorthodox London; or Phases of Religious Life in the Metropolis. London: 1876. V. 71; 73

DAVIES, DENTNER
Jean Harlow - Hollywood Comet. London: 1937. V. 72

DAVIES, EDWARD
The Life of Bartoleme E. Murillo. London: 1819. V. 69; 72
A Succinct Description of that Elaborate Pile of Art, Call'd the Microcosm. London: 1760. V. 69

DAVIES, HUNTER
Here We Go Round the Mulberry Bush. London: 1965. V. 70
Wainwright. London: 1995. V. 70

DAVIES, J.
The Innkeeper and Butler's Guide, or a Directory in the Making and Managing of British Wines.... Leeds: 1808. V. 68

DAVIES, J. J.
History and Business Directory of Madison County, Iowa. Des Moines: 1869. V. 70

DAVIES, K. G.
Letters from Hudson Bay 1703-1740. London: 1965. V. 70

DAVIES, LINDA
Wilderness of Mirrors. London: 1996. V. 68; 70

DAVIES, MARGARET SIDNEY
The Miss Margaret Sidney Davies Complete Collection of Special Gregynog Bindings. Antwerp: 1995. V. 72

DAVIES, MAURICE
Fun, Ancient and Modern. London: 1878. V. 71

DAVIES, NINA M.
Egyptian Paintings. Harmondsworth: 1954. V. 69
Egyptian Paintings. London: 1954. V. 72

DAVIES, RANDALL
Thomas Girtin's Water-Colours. London: 1924. V. 70; 72

DAVIES, RHYS
Boy With a Trumpet. London: 1949. V. 69

DAVIES, RHYS continued
Rings on Her Fingers. London: 1930. V. 69; 71

DAVIES, RICHARD
An Account of the Convincement, Exercises, Services and Travels of.... Philadelphia: 1770. V. 69

DAVIES, ROBERT
Historical Notices of the King's Manor, York, formerly a Palace of the Abbot of St. Mary's and of the Stuart Kings. York: 1883. V. 73
The Histories of the King's Manour House at York.... York: 1883. V. 70
A Memoir of the York Press, With Notices of Authors, Printers and Stationers, in the Sixteenth, Seventeenth and Eighteenth Centuries. London: 1868. V. 69

DAVIES, ROBERTSON
The Cunning Man. New York: 1995. V. 72
The Deptford Trilogy. Toronto: 1987. V. 73
Fifth Business. Toronto: 1970. V. 73
The Manticore. New York: 1972. V. 73
The Manticore. Toronto: 1972. V. 73
A Masque of Mr. Punch. Toronto: 1963. V. 71
The Papers of Samuel Marchbanks. New York: 1986. V. 73
Tempest-Tost. NY: 1952. V. 72
World of Wonders. New York: 1976. V. 73
World of Wonders. London: 1977. V. 73

DAVIES, SAMUEL
The Vessels of Mercy, and the Vessels of Wrath, Delineated, in a New Uncontroverted, and Practical Light. London: 1758. V. 73

DAVIES, THEODORE
Losing to Win. New York: 1874. V. 69

DAVIES, THOMAS
Dramatic Miscellanies. London: 1784. V. 71
Memoirs of the Life of David Garrick. London: 1780. V. 69
Memoirs of the Life of David Garrick. London: 1808. V. 68

DAVIES, VALENTINE
It Happens Every Spring. New York: 1949. V. 72
Miracle on 34th Street. New York: 1947. V. 71

DAVIES, W. E.
Caverns of West Virginia. Morgantown: 1949. V. 71

DAVIES, WILLIAM
Plays Written for a Private Theatre. London: 1786. V. 71

DAVIES, WILLIAM HENRY
Collected Poems. 1916. V. 73
The Lover's Song-Book. Newtown, Powys: 1933. V. 70; 71
Nature Poems and Others. London: 1908. V. 73
Raptures: a Book of Poems. London: 1918. V. 69
Secrets. London: 1924. V. 70; 71
Selected Poems. Newtown: 1928. V. 69
Shorter Lyrics of the Twentieth Century 1900-1922. London: 1922. V. 71

DAVIESS, MARIA THOMPSON
Andrew the Glad. Indianapolis: 1913. V. 71

DAVILA, H. C.
The Historie of the Civill Warres of France.... London: 1647. V. 68

DAVILLIER, JEAN CHARLES, BARON
Spain. London: 1876. V. 68

D'AVILLIER, JEAN CHARLES, BARON
Spain. London: 1881. V. 70

DAVIS, A. B.
The Finest Instruments Ever Made. A Bibliography of Medical, Dental, Optical and Pharmaceutical Company Trade Literature 1700-1939. Arlington: 1986. V. 70

DAVIS, ALEC
Eric Fraser. 1974. V. 70

DAVIS, ANDREW JACKSON
The Philosophy of Spiritual Intercourse, Being an Explanation of Modern Mysteries. New York: 1851. V. 69

DAVIS, ANGELA
If They Come in the Morning. New York: 1971. V. 71
Women, Race and Class. New York: 1981. V. 69; 71

DAVIS, ASHEL
Antiquities of Central America, and the Discovery of New England by the Northmen, Five Hundred Years Before Columbus. Boston: 1842. V. 73

DAVIS, AUDREY W.
Dr. Kelly of Hopkins. Baltimore: 1959. V. 68

DAVIS, BRITTON
The Truth About Geronimo. New Haven: 1929. V. 72
The Truth About Geronimo. 1951. V. 68

DAVIS, BURKE
The Summer Land. New York: 1965. V. 71

DAVIS, D. D.
The Giant Panda. Chicago: 1964. V. 69

DAVIS, DAVID D.
Elements of Operative Midwifery.... London: 1825. V. 70

DAVIS, E. O.
The First Five Years of the Railroad Era in Colorado. 1948. V. 70
The First Five Years of the Railroad Era in Colorado. Golden: 1948. V. 73

DAVIS, EDWARD HILL
Historical Sketches of Franklin County. Raleigh: 1948. V. 71

DAVIS, EDWARD P.
Operative Obstetrics Including the Surgery of the Newborn. Philadelphia: 1842. V. 73
Operative Obstetrics Including the Surgery of the Newborn. Philadelphia: 1911. V. 70; 71

DAVIS, ELLIS
Davis' Commercial Encyclopedia of the Pacific Southwest. Oakland: 1915. V. 72
The Encyclopedia of Texas. Dallas: 1923. V. 73
The New Encyclopedia of Texas. 1927. V. 70

DAVIS, FREDERICK C.
The Graveyard Never Closes. New York: 1940. V. 73
He Wouldn't Stay Dead. New York: 1939. V. 71
Night Drop. Garden City: 1955. V. 72

DAVIS, GEORGE
Black Life in Corporate America: Swimming in the Mainstream. Garden City: 1982. V. 72
Love, Black Love: Love Stories Adapted from Interviews. Garden City: 1978. V. 68; 72

DAVIS, GEORGE E.
Practical Microscopy. London: 1889. V. 73

DAVIS, GEORGE T. B.
Metlakahtla. A True Narrative of the Red Man. Chicago: 1904. V. 70

DAVIS, GEORGE W.
The Posthumous Papers of the Pickwick Club: Some New Bibliographic Discoveries. London: 1928. V. 68

DAVIS, H. B.
Life and Work of Cyrus Guernsey Pringle. Burlington: 1936-1937. V. 70

DAVIS, HARRY, PSEUD.
My Brother's Wife. New York: 1956. V. 71

DAVIS, HENRY T.
Solitary Places Made Glad, Being Observations and Experience for Thirty-Two Years in Nebraska, with Sketches and Incidents.... Cincinnati: 1890. V. 68; 73

DAVIS, HEWITT
The Resources Farmers Possess for Meeting the Reduced Prices of Their Produce. London: 1844. V. 68

DAVIS, INNIS C.
A Bibliography of West Virginia. Charleston: 1939. V. 72

DAVIS, J. SCARLETT
Fourteen Views in Lithography, of Bolton Abbey, Wharfedale, Yorskhire, from Drawings of this Beautiful Ruin, and the Adjoining Scenery. 1829. V. 71

DAVIS, JAMES LUCIUS
The Trooper's Manual: or, Tactics for Light Dragoons and Mounted Rifleman. Richmond: 1861. V. 70
The Troopers Manual: or, Tactics for Light Dragoons and Mounted Riflemen. Richmond: 1862. V. 69; 70

DAVIS, JAMES W.
On the Fossil Fishes of the Carboniferous Limestone Series of Great Britain. Dublin: 1883. V. 68
West Yorkshire: An Account of its Geology, Physical Geography, Climatology, and Botany. London: 1880. V. 73

DAVIS, JEAN
Shallow Diggin's. Caldwell: 1962. V. 69

DAVIS, JEFFERSON
The Rise and Fall of the Confederate Government. London: 1871. V. 69; 70
The Rise and Fall of the Confederate Government. New York: 1881. V. 68; 69; 70

DAVIS, JOHN
Antique Garden Ornament. Woodbridge: 1991. V. 72
The First Settlers of Virginia, an Historical Novel.... New York: 1806. V. 73
Travels of Four Years and a Half in the United States of America During 1798, 1799, 1800, 1801, and 1802. London: 1803. V. 73

DAVIS, JOHN, MRS.
Lucy Webb Hayes, a Memorial Sketch.... Cincinnati: 1890. V. 68

DAVIS, KATHRYN
The Girl Who Trod on a Loaf. New York: 1993. V. 68; 71

DAVIS, LINDSEY
The Course of Honour. London: 1997. V. 68
A Dying Light in Corduba. Bristol: 1996. V. 72; 73
A Dying Light in Corduba. London: 1996. V. 68; 69; 71
The Iron Hand of Mars. London: 1992. V. 71
Last Act in Palmyra. London: 1994. V. 68; 69; 71
One Virgin Too Many. London: 1999. V. 72

DAVIS, LINDSEY continued
Shadows in Bronze. London: 1990. V. 69; 70; 71; 73
The Silver Pigs. London: 1989. V. 70
Silver Pigs. New York: 1989. V. 68; 71
Three Hands in the Fountain. London: 1997. V. 68; 71
Time to Depart. London: 1995. V. 68; 69; 70; 71
Two for the Lions. London: 1998. V. 68; 69; 72
Venus in Copper. London: 1991. V. 69; 71; 73
Venus in Copper. New York: 1991. V. 68

DAVIS, LUTE L.
Blankets on the Sand. Wichita Falls: 1948. V. 71

DAVIS, LYDIA
Samuel Johnson is Indignant. New York: 2001. V. 71

DAVIS, M. E. M.
A Bunch of Roses, and Other Parlor Plays. Boston: 1903. V. 68
In War Times at La Rose Blanche. Boston: 1888. V. 68
Jaconetta, Her Loves. Boston and New York: 1901. V. 68
The Price of Silence. Boston: 1907. V. 71

DAVIS, MIKE
City of Quartz. London and New York: 1990. V. 68

DAVIS, N.
Ruined Cities Within Numidian And Carthaginian Territories. London: 1862. V. 72

DAVIS, NATALIE ZEMON
The Return of Martin Guerre. Cambridge: 1983. V. 72

DAVIS, NATHAN
Carthage and Her Remains: Being an Account of the Excavations and Researches. London: 1861. V. 70
Ruined Cities Within Numidian and Carthaginian Territories. London: 1862. V. 70

DAVIS, NATHAN SMITH
History of Medicine with the Code of Medical Ethics. Chicago: 1903. V. 68; 70; 71; 72

DAVIS, NICHOLAS A.
The Campaign From Texas to Maryland with The Battle of Fredericksburg. Austin: 1961. V. 72

DAVIS, NORBERT
The Mouse in the Mountain. 1943. V. 73
The Mouse in the Mountain. New York: 1943. V. 70
Sally's in the Alley. 1943. V. 73

DAVIS, OLIVE
The Slow, Tired and Easy Railroad. Fresno: 1976. V. 71

DAVIS, P. H.
Flora of Turkey and the East Aegean Islands. Edinburgh: 1965-1985. V. 71

DAVIS, PAUL
Faces. New York: 1985. V. 71

DAVIS, R. C.
Encyclopedia of American Forest and Conservation History. New York: 1983. V. 70; 71

DAVIS, R. I.
Men's Garments 1830-1900: a Guide to Pattern Cutting. London: 1989. V. 68

DAVIS, R. T.
Native Arts of the Pacific Northwest, from the Rasmusse Collection of the Portland Art Museum. Stanford: 1964. V. 69

DAVIS, REBECCA HARDING
Doctor Warrick's Daughters. New York: 1896. V. 73

DAVIS, RICHARD HARDING
About Paris. New York: 1895. V. 71
Cinderella and Other Stories. New York: 1896. V. 68
The Great Streets of the World. 1892. V. 71
In the Fog. New York: 1901. V. 70
Ransom's Folly. New York: 1902. V. 72

DAVIS, ROBERT H.
Efficiency. New York: 1917. V. 70
Man Makes His Own Mask. New York: 1932. V. 72

DAVIS, RUTH RUSSELL
Auction in Manassas. New York: 1953. V. 69

DAVIS, SAM P.
The History of Nevada. Las Vegas. V. 70

DAVIS, SAMMY
Hollywood in a Suitcase. London: 1980. V. 72

DAVIS, SAMUEL B.
Escape of a Confederate Officer from Prison. Norfolk: 1892. V. 69

DAVIS, STEPHEN
The Law of Radio Communication. New York and London: 1927. V. 72

DAVIS, SUSAN LAWRENCE
Authentic Hisory: Ku Klux Klan 1865-1877. New York: 1924. V. 69

DAVIS, T.
The Architecture of John Nash. London: 1960. V. 69; 72

DAVIS, VARINA H.
Jefferson Davis, Ex-President of the Confederate States of America, a Memoir. New York: 1890. V. 70

DAVIS, W. JEFFERSON
Japan, the Air Menace of the Pacific. Boston: 1928. V. 70

DAVIS, WILLIAM
A Journey Round the Library of a Bibliomaniac; or, Cento of Notes and Reminiscences Concerning Rare, Curious and Valuable Books. London: 1821. V. 70
Nimrod of the Sea. Boston: 1926. V. 69
An Olio of Bibliographical and Literary Anecdotes and Memoranda.... London: 1814. V. 69

DAVIS, WILLIAM HEATH
Seventy-five Years in California. San Francisco: 1929. V. 68; 73
Seventy-Five Years in California. San Francisco: 1987. V. 72
Sixty Years in California - a History of Events and Life in California.... San Francisco: 1889. V. 68; 73

DAVIS, WILLIAM WATTS HART
El Gringo: Or New Mexico and Her People. New York: 1857. V. 68; 69; 73

DAVISON, A. N.
Applied Neurochemistry. Oxford: 1968. V. 68

DAVISON, JOE
The Art of the Cigar Label. New Jersey: 1989. V. 72

DAVISON, LAWRENCE H.
Assorted Articles. New York: 1930. V. 70
Movements in European History. London: 1921. V. 70

DAVY, HUMPHRY
The Bakerian Lecture. An Account of Some New Analytical Researches on the Nature of Certain bodies, Particularly the Alkalies, Phosophorous, Sulphur, Carbonaceous Matter... in Philosohical Transactions of the Royal Society of London for the Year MDCCCIX. London: 1809. V. 72
The Bakerian Lecture for 1809. On Some New Electrochemical Researches on Various Objects, Particulary the Metallic Bodies, from the Alkalies, and Earths, and on Some Combinations of Hydrogene. London: 1810. V. 72
Consolations in Travel, or the Last Days of a Philosopher. Philadelphia: 1830. V. 68
Elements of Agricultural Chemistry, in a Course of Lectures for the Board of Agriculture. London: 1813. V. 73
Elements of Agricultural Chemistry, in a Course of Lectures for the Board of Agriculture.... Philadelphia and Baltimore: 1821. V. 68
Elements of Chemical Philosophy. Philadelphia: 1812. V. 68
New Analytical Researches on the Nature of Certain Bodies, Being an Appendix to the Bakerian Lecture for 1808. In Philosophical Transactions of the Royal Society of London for the Year MDCCCIX Part II. London: 1809. V. 72
On a New Detonating Compound In Philosophical Transactions of the Royal Society of London for the Year MDCCCXIII. Part 1. London: 1813. V. 72
The Papers of Sir H. Davy, Communicated to the Royal Society on the Fire-Damp of Coal Mines, and On Methods of Lighting the Mines So as to Prevent Its Explosion.... Newcastle: 1817. V. 69
Researches on the Oxymuriatic Acid, Its Nature and Combinations and on the Elements of the Muriatic Acid... In Philosophical Transactions of the Royal Society of London for the Year MDCCCX, Part II. London: 1810. V. 72
Salmonia; or Days of Fly Fishing. London: 1828. V. 69
Salmonia; or Days of Fly Fishing. London: 1829. V. 69
Salmonia or Days of Fly Fishing. 1851. V. 68; 73
Some further observations on a new detonating substance (with) Some experiments and observations on the substances produced in different chemical processes on fluor spar. London: 1813. V. 72
Some New Researches on Flame. London: 1817. V. 68

DAVY, J.
The Angler and His Friend. 1853. V. 73
The Angler and His Friend. 1855. V. 68; 73

DAVY, JOHN
The Angler in the Lake District.... London: 1857. V. 71
The Angler in the Lake District.... 1857. V. 68

DAWE, GEORGE
The Life of George Morland with Remarks on His Work. London: 1807. V. 72; 73

DAWES, C. J.
Marine Botany. New York: 1981. V. 72

DAWES, CHARLES G.
Ships of the Past. Salem: 1929. V. 68

DAWES, MATTHEW
Letter to Lord Chatham, Concerning the Present War of Great Britain Against America.... London: 1776. V. 68

DAWKINS, R. M.
Forty-Five Stories from the Dodekanese. Cambridge: 1950. V. 70

DAWKINS, W. BOYD
Cave Hunting: Researches on the Evidence of Caves Respecting the Early Inhabitants of Europe. London: 1874. V. 72

DAWSON, CHARLES
Pioneer Tales of the Oregon Trail of Jefferson County. Topeka: 1912. V. 70

DAWSON, CONIGSBY
Old Youth. New York: 1925. V. 71

DAWSON, E. C.
James Hannington, First Bishop of Eastern Equatorial Africa. London: 1896. V. 72

DAWSON, J. INGRAM
Reminiscences of a Rascally Lawyer. Kendal: 1949. V. 73

DAWSON, J. W.
Acadian Geology. 1855. V. 73
Acadian Geology. Edinburgh: 1855. V. 68
Contributions Toward the Improvements of Agriculture in Nova Scotia; with Practical Hints on the Management and Improvement of Live Stock.... Halifax: 1856. V. 72

DAWSON, JENNIFER
The Ha-Ha. London: 1961. V. 72

DAWSON, K.
Marsh and Mudflat. 1931. V. 71

DAWSON, NELSON
Goldsmiths' and Silversmith's Work. London: 1907. V. 72

DAWSON, NICHOLAS
Narrative of Nicholas Cheyenne Dawson, Overland to California in '41 and '49 and Texas in '51. San Francisco: 1933. V. 71

DAWSON, S. J.
Report on the Exploration of the Country Between Lake Superior and the Red River Settlement. 1968. V. 70

DAWSON, SAMUEL EDWARD
The Saint Lawrence Basin and Its Border-Lands. London: 1905. V. 73
The Voyages of the Cabots. Ottawa: 1897. V. 73

DAWSON, THOMAS F.
Senator Teller - a Brief Account of His Fifth Election to the United States Senate Together with a Sketch of the Proceeding Political Events in the Contest for Bimetalism in the National Campaign of 1896. Washington: 1898. V. 73

DAWSON, W. L.
The Birds of California. San Diego: 1923. V. 70
The Birds of Ohio, A Complete, Scientific and Popular Description. Columbus: 1903. V. 70

DAWSON, WARREN R.
A Leechbook or Collection of Medical Recipes of the Fifteenth Century. London: 1934. V. 70
Memoir of Thomas Joseph Pettigrew...1791-1865. New York: 1831. V. 71
Sir Grafton Elliot Smith. London: 1938. V. 68

DAWSON, WILLIAM, & SONS
Medicine and Science: a Bibliographical Catalogue of Historical and Rare Books from the 15th to the 20th Century. London. V. 68

DAWSON, WILLIAM HARBUTT
History of Independency in Skipton, from 1770 to 1890. 1891. V. 73
History of Skipton (W. R. Yorks). London: 1882. V. 73
History of Skipton (W. R. Yorks). Manchester: 1972. V. 73
Loose Leaves of Craven History. Skipton: 1906. V. 73

DAWSON, WILLIAM LEON
The Birds of California. San Diego: 1923. V. 73
The Birds of Washington.... Seattle: 1909. V. 73

DAY, A. GROVE
Coronado's Quest and the Discovery of the Southern States. Berkeley: 1940. V. 69; 73

DAY, CHARLES H.
The Animal Kingdom Illustrated and Sketches Descriptive of the Wild Beasts Contained in Forepaugh's Menagerie. Philadelphia: 1880. V. 68

DAY, DIANNE
The Strange Files of Fremont Jones. New York: 1995. V. 70; 71

DAY *Dreams Picture Book.* London. V. 71

DAY, FRANCIS
British and Irish Salmonidae. 1887. V. 72; 73
The Fauna of British India, Including Ceylon and Burma. Volume I. Fishes. London: 1889. V. 73
The Fishes of Great Britain and Ireland. 1880-1884. V. 72; 73
The Fishes of India.... London: 1878-1888. V. 72
Yarkand Mission (second) Scientific Results: Ichthyology. Calcutta: 1878. V. 72

DAY, GEORGE
Naturalists and Their Investigations. London. V. 68

DAY, HOLMAN
The Rider of the King Log. New York: 1919. V. 70

DAY, J. W.
Farming Adventure. 1949. V. 71

DAY, JAMES M.
Captain Clint Peoples' Texas Ranger - Fifty Years a Lawman. Waco: 1980. V. 69
Rangers of Texas. Waco: 1969. V. 70

DAY, JAMES W.
King George V as a Sportsman. 1935. V. 69

DAY, JEFFERY
Poems and Rhymes. London: 1919. V. 72

DAY, KENNETH
The Typography of Press Advertisement. London: 1956. V. 72

DAY, L.
The Tragedy of the Klondite - This Book of Travel Gives the true Facts of What Took Place in the Gold Fields Under the British Rule. New York: 1906. V. 70

DAY, L. W.
Story of the One Hundred and First Ohio Infantry. Cleveland: 1894. V. 69

DAY, LEWIS F.
The Nodding Mandarin. London: 1883. V. 72
Text Book of Ornamental Design. London: 1887. V. 68

DAY, SAMUEL PHILLIPS
Down South; or, an Englishman's Experience at the Seat of the American War. London: 1862. V. 68

DAY, ST. JOHN
On Some Points in Certain Theories Concerning the Purpose and Primal Condition of the Great Pyramid of Jeezeh.... Glasgow: 1868. V. 70

DAYES, EDWARD
A Picturesque Tour in Yorkshire and Derbyshire. London: 1825. V. 73
The Works of the Late Edward Dayes. 1805. V. 71
The Works of the Late Edward Dayes. London: 1805. V. 72; 73

DAY-LEWIS, CECIL
The Beast Must Die. New York: 1938. V. 73
Beech Vigil and Other Poems. London: 1925. V. 70
Country Comets. 1928. V. 73
Country Comets. London: 1928. V. 72
The Minds in Chains-Socialism and the Cultural Revolution. London: 1937. V. 72
The Poet. Cambridge: 1956. V. 70
Posthumous Poems. Andoversford: 1979. V. 68; 71
Revolution in Writing. London: 1935. V. 70
Ten Singers: an Anthology. 1924. V. 73
Ten Singers: an Anthology. London: 1924. V. 68
We're Not Going To Do Nothing. London: 1936. V. 70

DAYLIGHT by Night, a Record of Some of the Modern Installations of Gas Lighting in Important Thoroughfares in Great Britain. London: 1931. V. 73

DAY PARSONS, BRIAN
Selected Poems. England: 1964. V. 70

DAYRELL, VIVIENNE
The New Decameron. The Sixth Day. Oxford: 1929. V. 70

DAYS of the Dandies. London: 1900. V. 68

THE DAYS of the Rose and Other Tales. London: 1893. V. 69

THE DAYS When We Had Tails On Us. 1849. V. 71

DAYTON, E.
Dakota Days. May 1886-August 1898. 1937. V. 68
Dakota Days May 1886-August 1898. Clifton Springs, NJ: 1937. V. 71

DAYTON, W. T.
Catalogue of the Scientific Serial Literature in the Following Libraries in Sydney, N.S.W. Sydney: 1889. V. 68

DEACHMAN, WILSON
Auto Bio Chemic (A.B.C.) Treatment, with Introductory Remarks on Patient Himself and Physician Himself. Chicago: 1922. V. 72

DEACOCK, ANTONIA
No Purdah in Padam. London: 1960. V. 69

DEACON, C. W.
Deacon's Map of Yorkshire, with a History of the County, and Geological Notes. London. V. 73

DEACON, WILLIAM ARTHUR
Peter McArthur. Toronto: 1923. V. 73

THE DEAD Sea Scrolls. New York: 1966. V. 69

DEAKIN, JOHN
Rome Alive. A Notebook. London: 1951. V. 70
Today. London: 1949. V. 70

DEAKIN, R.
The Tour of the Prince of Wales to Africa and South America. 1926. V. 70; 72; 73

DEAKIN, RICHARD
The Botanist's Manual.... Sheffield: 1836. V. 73
Florigraphia Britannica; or Engravings and Descriptions of the Flowering Plants and Ferns of Britian. 1857. V. 69

DEAN, AMBER
Dead Man's Float. New York: 1944. V. 68
Wrap It Up. New York: 1946. V. 68

DEAN, AMOS
Lectures on Phrenology. Albany: 1834. V. 68

DEAN, FRANK E.
The Complete Book of Trick and Fancy Riding. Caldwell: 1975. V. 68; 73

DEAN, HENRY
Dean's Analytical Guide to the Art of Penmanship, Containing a Variety of Plates.... New York: 1808. V. 73

DEAN, JOHN
The Rule of Practice Methodized and Improved. London: 1756. V. 70

DEAN, JULIA
The Wonderful Narrative of Miss Julian Dean, the Only Survivor of the Steamship City of Boston Lost at Sea in 1870. Philadelphia: 1881. V. 73

DEAN, PHILLIP HAYES
The Sty of the Blind Pig and Other Plays. Indianapolis/NY: 1973. V. 72

DEAN, ROY
Before the Hand of Man. Los Angeles: 1972. V. 68

DEAN, WILLIAM
An Historical and Descriptive Account of Croome D'Abitot, the Seat of the Rt. Hon. the Earl of Coventry.... Worcester: 1824. V. 68; 70

DE ANDRADE, CARLOS DRUMMOND
Souvenir of the Ancient World. New York: 1976. V. 73

DEANE, EDMUND
Spadacrene Anglica; or, The English Spaw. Leeds: 1736. V. 73
Spadacrene Anglica; or The English Spaw. Bristol: 1922. V. 73

DEANE, ELIZABETH
Easily Persuaded. New York: 1929. V. 71

DEANE, SEAMUS
Reading in the Dark. New York: 1997. V. 69
Rumours. Dublin: 1977. V. 70
Selected Poems. Oldcastle: 1988. V. 72

DE ANGELI, ARTHUR C.
The Empty Barn. Philadelphia: 1966. V. 72

DE ANGELI, MARGUERITE
Ted and Nina Go to the Grocery Store. New York: 1938. V. 71
Ted and Nina Have a Happy Rainy Day. Garden City: 1936. V. 69
Up the Hill. Garden City: 1942. V. 71
Yonie Wondernose. Garden City: 1944. V. 69

DEAN'S Gift Book of Nursery Rhymes. London: 1965. V. 70

DEARBORN, ELWYN
The Down East Printmaker. Carroll Thayer Berry. Camden: 1983. V. 70

DEARBORN, NATHANIEL
Boston Notions: Being an Authentic and Concise Account of "That Village" from 1630 to 1847. Boston: 1848. V. 70

DEARN, T. D. W.
Designs for Lodges and Entrances to Parks, Paddocks and Pleasure Grounds, in the Gothic, Cottage and Fancy Styles.... London: 1823. V. 68

THE DEATH and Burial of Cock Robin. London: 1830. V. 70; 73

THE DEATH and Burial of Cock Robin; as Taken from the Original Manuscript.... Lichfield: 1780. V. 68

THE DEATH and Burial of Cock Robin: to which is Added, Pizarro and Alonzo, or, Industry Better than Gold. York: 1820. V. 73

DEATH, JAMES
The Death of Jim Loney. New York: 1979. V. 70

DEATH of Cock Robin. New York: 1870. V. 71

DEATHERAGE, CHARLES P.
Early History of Greater Kansas City. The Prophetic City at the Mouth of the Kaw. Volume 1 (all published). Kansas City: 1927. V. 69

DEAVER, JEFFERY
Death of a Blue Movie Star. London: 2001. V. 69
Hard News. London: 2001. V. 69
A Maiden's Grave. New York: 1995. V. 70
Manhattan Is My Beat. London: 2000. V. 70
Manhattan is My Beat. London: 2001. V. 69; 73
Praying for Sleep. New York: 1994. V. 69; 70; 73

DE BACA, MANUEL C.
Vicente Silva and His 40 Bandits. Washington: 1947. V. 69

DEBACH, P.
Biological Control by Natural Enemies. London: 1974. V. 68

DEBAIGTS, JACQUES
Swimming Pools. Vermont: 1973. V. 68

DE BARTHE, JOE
The Life and Adventures of Frank Grouard. Norman: 1958. V. 72

DE BARTHE, PENN
The Story of Betty and Teddy. New York: 1916. V. 70

DE BAUSSET, ARTHUR
Aerial Navigation on the Vacuum Principle. Lowell: 1889. V. 68

DE BAUSSET, M. L. F.
The Life of Fenelon, Archbishop of Cambrai. London: 1810. V. 69

DE BEER, G. R.
Alps and Men: Pages from Forgotten Diaries of Travellers and Tourists in Switzerland. 1932. V. 71
Family Travellers in the Alps. 1930. V. 68
Speaking of Switzerland. London: 1952. V. 69

DE BERNIERES, LOUIS
Captain Corelli's Mandolin. London: 1994. V. 68; 69; 70; 71; 72; 73
Corelli's Mandolin. New York: 1994. V. 69; 70; 72
A Day Out for Mehmet Erbil. London: 1998. V. 68
A Day Out for Mehmet Erbil. London: 1999. V. 68; 71
Labels. London: 1993. V. 68; 71
The Latin American Trilogy: The War of Don Emmanuel's Nether Parts. Senor Vivo and the Coca Lord; The Troublesome Offspring of Cardinal Guzman. London: 1990-1992. V. 70; 73
Red Dog. London: 2001. V. 72
Senor Vivo (and) The Coca Lord. London: 1991. V. 69
Senor Vivo and the Coca Lord. New York: 1991. V. 69; 71
The War of Don Emmanuel's Nether Parts. London: 1990. V. 70; 73
The War of Don Emmanuel's Nether Parts. New York: 1990. V. 69
The War of Don Emmanuel's Nether Parts. New York: 1991. V. 70; 72
The War of Don Emmanuel's Nether Parts. (with) Senor Vivo & The Coca Lord. (with) The Troublesome Offspring of Cardinal Guzman. London: 1990. V. 70

DEBO, ANGIE
And Still Waters Run, The Betrayal of the Five Civilized Tribes. Princeton: 1940. V. 70
The Cowman's Southwest.... Glendale: 1953. V. 69; 71
Geronimo: the Man, His Time, His Place. Norman: 1976. V. 71; 72
The Road to Disappearance. Norman: 1941. V. 70
Tulsa, from Creek Town to Oil Capital. Norman: 1942. V. 68; 73
Tulsa, from Creek Town to Oil Capital. Norman: 1943. V. 70

DE BOIS, JOHN VAN DEUSEN
Journals and Letters of Colonel John Van Deusen Du Bois. Tucson: 1949. V. 70

DE BOIS, WILLIAM PENE
The 21 Balloons. New York: 1947. V. 71

DE BORN, EDITH
The Imperfect Marriage. London: 1954. V. 70

DE BOSIS, LAURO
Icaro. New York: 1933. V. 68
The Story of My Death. London: 1933. V. 71

DE BOTTON, ALAIN
How Proust Can Change Your Life. London: 1997. V. 70; 73
The Romantic Movement - Sex, Shopping and the Novel. London: 1994. V. 71

DE BOUFFLERS, STANISLAS JEAN
The Queen of Golconda and Other Tales. London: 1926. V. 69

DE BOVET, MARIE ANNE
Three Months Tour in Ireland. London: 1891. V. 69

DE BOW, JAMES D. B.
The Interest in Slavery of the Southern Non-Slaveholder. Charleston: 1860. V. 68; 71

DE BOZE, CLAUDE GROS
Catalogue des Livres du Cabinet de M. De Zoe. Paris: 1753. V. 70

DEBRETT'S BARONETAGE, Knightage and Companionage. London: 1935. V. 70; 72

DE BRUNHOFF, LAURENT
Babar et ce Coquin D'Arthur. Paris: 1946. V. 72

DEBS, EUGENE V.
Debs and the War. His Canton Speech and His Trial In the Federal Court. Chicago. V. 73
Debs: His Life, Writings and Speeches. St. Louis: 1908. V. 70; 72
Walls and Bars. Chicago: 1927. V. 68

DE CALONNE, ALEXANDER
A Catalogue of All that Noble and Superlatively Capital Assemblage of Valuable Pictures, Drawings, Miniatures and Prints.... London: 1795. V. 68

DE CAMP, L. SPRAGUE
Demons and Dinosaurs. Sauk City: 1970. V. 69
A Gun for Dinosaur and Other Imaginative Tales. New York: 1963. V. 72
The Incomplete Enchanter. New York: 1941. V. 71
Land of Unreason. New York: 1942. V. 71
The Wheels Of If and Other Science-Fiction. Chicago: 1948. V. 71

DE CARAVA, ROY
Photographs. Carmel;: 1981. V. 68

DE CHAIR, SOMERSET
Bring Back the Gods - the Epic Career of Emperor Julian, the Great. London: 1962. V. 71
The Golden Carpet. Waltham St. Lawrence: 1943. V. 71
The Silver Crescent. Waltham St. Lawrence: 1943. V. 71

DE CHAMBRUN, CLARA LONGWORTH
Two Loves Have I: The Romance of William Shakespeare. Philadelphia: 1934. V. 72

DE CHIRICO, GIORGIO
Hebdomeros. London: 1964. V. 68

DECKER, MATTHEW
An Essay on the Causes of the Decline of the Foreign Trade, Consequently of the Value of the Lands of Brtain, and on the Means to Restore Both. London: 1750. V. 70

DECKER, PAUL
Ausfuhrliche Anleitung zur Civilbau-Kunst. Nuremberg: 1710. V. 68

DECKER, THOMAS
The Gull's Hornbook. Bristol: 1812. V. 72

THE DECLARATION of Rights of the People of England; Made by the Lords Spiritual and Temporal and the Commons, Assembled at Westminster, Asserted to and Confirmed by William, Prince of Orange, and the Princess Mary.... 1790. V. 71

DE CLIFFORD, LADY
A Short Journal of A Tour Made through Part of France, Switzerland and the Banks of the Rhine, to Spa, Antwerp, Ghent, &c...in the Months of May, June, July and August in 1817. 1837. V. 69

DE COCK, LILIANE
James Van Der Zee. Dobbs Ferry: 1973. V. 70

DECORATIONS for Parks and Gardens. London: 1810. V. 72

DECORATIVE Art In Modern Interiors. New York: 1972. V. 72

DECORATIVE Garden Statuary.... New York: 1991-2001. V. 71

THE DECORATOR'S Assistant: a Modern Guide for Decorative Artists and Amateurs.... London: 1880. V. 68

THE DECORATOR'S Assitant; a Modern Guide for Decorative Artists and Amateurs.... London: 1920. V. 68

DECOURCEY, R.
Man Displayed in Four Parts. Hamilton: 1857. V. 71

DECTER, JACQUELINE
Nicholas Roerich: The Life and Art of a Russian Master. Rochester: 1989. V. 72; 73

DE DAMPIERRE, F.
The Best of Painted Furniture. London: 1987. V. 72

DEDERA, DON
A Little War Of Our Own - the Pleasant Valley Feud Revisited. Flagstaff: 1988. V. 69

DEDICATION of the New Building for the Free Public Library of Concord, Massachusetts. Concord: 1873. V. 68

DE DIENES, ANDRE
Nude Pattern. London: 1958. V. 68

DEE, JONATHAN
The Liberty Campaign. New York: 1993. V. 72

DEELEY, J. C.
Studies of Trees. London: 1830. V. 71

DEEMS, CHARLES F.
Annals of Southern Methodism for 1855. New York: 1856. V. 72

DEEPING, WARWICK
Folly Island. New York: 1939. V. 70
The House of Spies. New York: 1938. V. 70
Joan of the Tower. New York. V. 70
Marriage by Conquest. New York. V. 71
Martin Valliant. New York: 1930. V. 70

DEER Stories: Life-Like Pictures. Chicago: 1936. V. 70

DEERFORTH, DANIEL
Knock Wood! Superstition through the Ages. New York: 1928. V. 70

DEERING, CHARLES
Catalogus Stirpium &c, or a Catalogue of Plants Naturally Growing and Commonly Cultivated in Divers Parts of England.... Nottingham: 1738. V. 70
Nottinghamia Vetus et Nova. Nottingham: 1751. V. 73

DE FALLOUX, COUNT
Life and Letters of Madame Swetchine. Boston: 1867. V. 73

A DEFENCE Against Conspiracy and Perjury. London: 1813. V. 73

DEFENCE of the Realm Act in Ireland. Dublin: 1915. V. 72

A DEFENCE of the Scots Settlement at Darien. Edinburgh: 1699. V. 71

DEFOE, DANIEL
A Brief Case of the Distillers, and of the Distilling Trade in England, Shewing How Far It Is the Interest of England to Encourage the Said Trade, As It Is So Considerable an Advantage to the Landed Interest.... London: 1726. V. 69
The Complete English Tradesman, in Familiar Letters.... Dublin: 1726. V. 71
The Consolidator; or, Memoirs of Sundry Transactions from the World in the Moon. London: 1705. V. 69
An Essay Upon Loans; or, an Argument Proving that Substantial Funds Settled by Parliament. London: 1710. V. 72
Essays Upon Several Projects; or, Effectual Ways for Advancing the Interest of the Nation. London: 1702. V. 71
The Fortunes and Misfortunes of the Famous Moll Flanders. New York: 1923. V. 70
The History of The Devil, Ancient and Modern. In Two Parts. London: 1793. V. 72
The History of the Great Plague in London in the Year 1665. London: 1754. V. 69
A Journal of the Plague Year, etc. 1665. Bloomfield: 1968. V. 70
Jure Divino. London: 1706. V. 70
A Letter to a Merry Young Gentleman, Intitled Tho. Burnet, Esq. In Answer to One Writ by Him to the Right Honourable the Earl of Halifax, by Which it Plainly Appears, the Said Squire Was Not Awake When He Write the Said Letter. London: 1715. V. 70
The Life and Adventures of Robinson Crusoe. York: 1820?. V. 73
The Life and Adventures of Robinson Crusoe. London: 1888. V. 71
The Life and Most Surprising Adventures of Robinson Crusoe of York, Mariner. Edinburgh: 1769. V. 70
The Life and Most Surprizing Adventures of Robinson Crusoe of York, Mariner. London: 1779. V. 73
The Life and Strange, Surprizing Adventures of Robinson Crusoe... (and) The Farther Adventures of Robinson Crusoe.... London: 1719. V. 72
The Life and Surprising Adventures of Robinson Crusoe. London: 1747. V. 73
The Little Robinson Crusoe. London: 1880. V. 68; 72
A Tour through the Whole Island of Great Britain. London: Tour. V. 69
Memoirs of a Cavalier; or a Military Journal of the Wars in Germany, and...in England from the Year 1632 to...1638. Leeds: 1750?. V. 69
The Novels. Edinburgh: 1810. V. 73
The Novels and Miscellaneous Works. Oxford: 1840. V. 73
The Quarrel of the School-Boys at Athens, as Lately Acted at a School Near Westminster. London: 1717. V. 69
The Re-Representation; or a Modest Search after the Great Plunderers of the Nation.... London: 1711. V. 70
Robinson Crusoe. London: 1831. V. 68
Robinson Crusoe. London: 1910. V. 68
Robinson Crusoe. New York: 1920. V. 71; 73
Robinson Crusoe. Garden City: 1945. V. 69
Serious Reflections During the Life and Surprising Adventures of Robinson Crusoe; with His Vision of the Angelick World. London: 1720. V. 73
A Treatise Concerning the Use and Abuse of the Marriage Bed.... London: 1727. V. 72
The Wonderful Life and Most Surprsing Adventures of Robinson Crusoe of York, Mariner. London: 1755. V. 70
Die Wunderbare Lebensbeschreibung und Erstaunliche Begebenheiten des Beruhmten Helden Robinson Crusoe. Philadelphia: 1809. V. 73

DEFOER, H.
The Golden Age of Dutch Manuscript Painting. New York: 1990. V. 70

DE FONTAINE, FELIX GREGORY
A Cyclopedia of the Best Thoughts of Charles Dickens. New York: 1873. V. 69
The Fireside Dickens. A Cyclopedia of the Best Thoughts. New York: 1883. V. 69
Marginalia; or, Gleanings from an Army Note-Book. Columbia: 1864. V. 69; 70

DE FONTENELLE, BERNARD
A Plurality of Worlds. London: 1929. V. 70

DE FORD, MIRIAM ALLEN
The Theme is Murder. 1967. V. 73
The Theme Is Murder. New York: 1967. V. 68

DE FOREST, EFFINGHAM
Moore and Allied Families. The Ancestry of William Henry Moore. New York: 1938. V. 69

DE FOREST, JOHN WILLIAM
History of the Indians of Connecticut from the Earliest Known Period to 1850. Hartford: 1851. V. 69; 73

DE FOREST, LOUIS EFFINGHAM
Louisbourg Journals 1745. New York: 1932. V. 72

DE FRANCE, A.
The Prisoners of Abd-el-Kader; or, Five Months' Captivity Among the Arabs in the Autumn of 1836. London: 1838. V. 70

DE GALVEZ, BERNARDO
Instructions for Governing the Interior Provinces of New Spain. Berkeley: 1951. V. 68

DEGENHARDT, RICHARD K.
Belleek. The Complete Collector's Guide And Illustrated Reference. Huntington: 1978. V. 72

DEGGE, SIMON
The Parson's Counsellor, with the Law of Tythes or Tything. London: 1685. V. 73

DE GIOVANNI, ACHILLE
Clinical Commentaries Deduced from the Morphology of the Human Body. London: 1909. V. 68

DE GIVRY, GRILLOT
Witchcraft, Magic & Alchemy. London: 1931. V. 70

DE GOLYER, E.
Across Aboriginal America. The Journey of Three Englishmen Across Texas in 1568. El Paso: 1947. V. 68; 70

DE GOUY, LOUIS P.
Derrydale Cook Book of Fish and Game. Lyon: 1937. V. 72; 73

DE GRAFFENRIED, THOMAS P.
History of the De Graffenried Family from 1191 A.D. to 1925. New York: 1925. V. 71

DE GRAZIA, TED
De Grazia Paints Cabeza De Vaca: the First Non-Indian in Texas, New Mexico and Arizona 1527-1536. Tucson: 1973. V. 69
Padre Kino: Memorable Events in the Life and Times of the Immortal Priest-Colonizer of the Southwest Depicted in Drawings by De Grazia. Los Angeles: 1962. V. 69; 71; 73

DE GROOT, IRENE
Maritime Prints by the Dutch Masters. 1980. V. 72
Maritime Prints by the Dutch Masters. London: 1980. V. 70

DE GRUNNE, B.
The Birth of Art in Black Africa. Paris: 1998. V. 69

DE HAMEL, CHRISTOPHER
A History of Illuminated Manuscripts. Boston: 1986. V. 70; 72
A History of Illuminated Manuscripts. London: 1994. V. 70

DE HASS, WILLS
History of the Early Settlement and Indian Wars of Western Virginia. Wheeling: 1851. V. 71; 73

DE HAVEN, TOM
Freaks' Armour. New York: 1979. V. 72

DE HERIZ, PATRICK
La Belle O'Morphi - a Brief Biography. Waltham St. Lawrence: 1947. V. 69; 71

DEHN, PAUL
Quake, Quake, Quake - a London Treasury of English Verse. London: 1961. V. 68

DE HORTHY, EUGENE
The Sport of a Lifetime. 1939. V. 70; 72

DEIGHTON, LEN
Action Cook Book. London: 1963. V. 70
Action Cook Book. London: 1965. V. 68
The Assassination of President Kennedy. London: 1967. V. 71
Battle of Britain. London: 1980. V. 72
Billion Dollar Brain. London: 1966. V. 68; 70
Close-Up. London: 1972. V. 68; 72
Declarations of War. London: 1971. V. 68; 69
An Expensive Place to Die. London: 1967. V. 68; 70
An Expensive Place to Die. New York: 1967. V. 68
Funeral in Berlin. London: 1964. V. 68; 69; 71
Funeral in Berlin. London: 1965. V. 68
Horse Under Water. London: 1963. V. 69; 70
Horse Under Water. London: 1966. V. 68
The Ipcress File. London: 1962. V. 68; 69; 70; 71; 73
The Ipcress File. New York: 1963. V. 69
Len Deighton's Continental Dossier. London: 1968. V. 68; 70
Len Deighton's London Dossier. London: 1967. V. 68; 69
Only When I Larf. London: 1968. V. 68
The Orient Flight LZ 127-Graf Zeppelin: a Philatelic Handbook. 1980. V. 69
The Orient Flight L.Z. 127-Graf Zeppelin: a Philatelic Handbook. Westminster: 1980. V. 70
Ou est le garlic: Len Deighton's French Cook Book. London: 1967. V. 68
Pests - a Play in Three Acts. 1994. V. 73
Spy Story. London: 1974. V. 72
Spy Story. New York: 1974. V. 72
Twinkle, Twinkle, Little Spy. London: 1976. V. 72
Winter. London: 1987. V. 72
Yesterday's Spy. London: 1975. V. 72

DEIHL, EDNA GROFF
Huffy Wants to Be a Pet. New York: 1929. V. 70
The Little Kitten That Would Not Wash Its Face. New York: 1922. V. 72
The Little Kitten that Would Not Wash Its Face. New York: 1941. V. 70
My Twin Kitties. New York: 1924. V. 71
The Teddy Bear that Prowled at Night. New York: 1924. V. 69

DE JONG, MEINDERT
The Little Cow and the Turtle. London: 1961. V. 72
The Singing Hill. New York and Evanston: 1962. V. 70; 73
The Singing Hill. 1963. V. 73

DE JONGH, JAMES
City Cool. New York: 1978. V. 72

DE JUBAINVILLE, H. D'A.
The Irish Mythological Cycle. 1903. V. 69

DE KAY, JAMES E.
Natural History of New York. Part I. Zoology. Volumes 3 and 4 Reptiles, Amphibians and Fishes. Albany: 1842. V. 72; 73
Zoology of New York, or the New York Fauna.... Albany: 1844. V. 70; 73

DE KAY, JOHN
Women and the New Social State. Basel: 1918. V. 72

DE KETHAM, JOHANNES
The Fasciculus Medicinae. Birmingham: 1988. V. 70; 72

DEKOBRA, MAURICE
The Cloven-Footed Angel. New York: 1932. V. 68
The Madonna of the Sleeping Cars. London: 1927. V. 73
Serenade to the Hangman. New York: 1929. V. 70
The 13th Lover. New York: 1928. V. 69; 73

DE KOONING, WILLEM
Drawings. New York: 1967. V. 69

DE KROYFT, S. H.
A Place in they Memory. New York: 1850. V. 73

DE LA BAUME, G.
Les Malheurs de Berlicoquet. Paris: 1928. V. 68

DE LA BEDOLLIERE, EMILE
Le Bois de Vincennes. Paris: 1867. V. 70; 73

DE LA COUCHERE, DOR
Picasso in Antibes. New York: 1960. V. 70

DELACOUR, JEAN
The Living Air. The Memoirs Of An Ornithologist. London: 1966. V. 72
The Pheasants of the World. London: 1951. V. 69; 73
The Pheasants of the World. 1965. V. 69; 73
The Pheasants of the World. London: 1965. V. 70
The Waterfowl of the World. London: 1954-1964. V. 69; 72; 73
Waterfowl of the World. Volume I only. 1954. V. 71

DE LA CROIX DU MAINE, FRANCOIS GRUDE
Premier Volume De La Bibliotheque Du Sieur De la Croix Du Maine. Paris: 1584. V. 70

DE LA DURANTAYE, MOREL
Review of the People of Evangeline with Historical Sketches of the Present and Future. Detroit: 1892. V. 72
A Visit to the Home of Evangeline. 1898. V. 72

DE LA FAILLE, J. B.
Vincent Van Gogh. London. V. 72

DELAFIELD, E. M.
The Brontes: their Lives Recorded by Their Contemporaries. 1935. V. 73
Faster! Faster! - a Novel. London: 1936. V. 73

DELAFIELD, JOSEPH
The Unfortified Boundary: a Diary of the First Survey of the Canadian Boundary Line by Major Joseph Delafield. New York: 1943. V. 73

DELAFIELD, R.
Report on the War in Europe in 1854, 1855 and 1856.... Washington: 1861. V. 69

DE LA FONTINELLE, JEAN
Alphabet. Paris: 1949. V. 73

DELAFOSSE, PETER H.
Trailing the Pioneers, a Guide to Utah's Emigrant Trails 1829-1869. With West From Fort Bridger: the Pioneering of the Emigrant Trails Across Utah 1846-1850. Logan: 1994. V. 70

DE LA HARPE, M.
Three Gifts. An Arab Love Story. London: 1928. V. 71

DE LA HURST, VICTOR
Alice in Durban. Durban: 1948. V. 71; 72

DE LA MARE, COLIN
They Walk Again. London: 1931. V. 73

DE LA MARE, WALTER
Alone. London: 1927. V. 72
Animal Stories. London: 1939. V. 69
Behold This Dreamer of Reverie, Night Sleep, Dream, Love-Dreams, Nightmare, Death, the Unconscious, the Imagination, Divination, the Artist and Kindred Subjects. London: 1939. V. 68
Bells & Grass. A Book of Rhymes. London: 1941. V. 68
The Complete Poems of Walter De La Mare. London: 1969. V. 73
The Connoisseur and Other Stories. London: 1926. V. 71
Crossings - a Fairy Play. London: 1923. V. 71
Down-Adown-Derry - a Book of Fairy Poems. London: 1922. V. 73
The Dutch Cheese. New York: 1931. V. 72
Flora. (Poems). Philadelphia: 1919. V. 73
Henry Brocken. His Travels and Adventures in the Rich, Strange, Scarce-Imaginable Regions of Romance. London: 1904. V. 73
Henry Brocken: His Travels and Adventures in the Rich, Strange, Scarce-Imaginable Regions of Romance. London: 1922. V. 71
The Listeners and Other Poems. London: 1912. V. 73
Memoirs of a Midget. London: 1921. V. 69
Mr. Bumps and His Monkey. Philadelphia: 1942. V. 70
O Lovely England and Other Poems. London: 1953. V. 72
Peacock Pie. London: 1913. V. 73
Peacock Pie. London: 1916. V. 69
Peacock Pie. London: 1924. V. 70; 73
Peacock Pie. New York: 1924. V. 71
Poems. London: 1906. V. 71
Poems for Children. London: 1930. V. 70
The Printing of Poetry. Cambridge: 1931. V. 68
The Return. London: 1910. V. 73
Self to Self: a Poem. London: 1928. V. 71
Seven Short Stories.... London: 1931. V. 71
Songs of Childhood. London New York and Bombay: 1902. V. 73
Songs of Childhood. London: 1923. V. 72; 73
Stories from the Bible. London: 1929. V. 69
This Year; Next Year. London: 1937. V. 71
The Three Mulla-Mulgars. London: 1910. V. 69; 70

DE LA MARE, WALTER continued
Thus Her Tale; a Poem. Edinburgh: 1923. V. 73
To Lucy. London: 1931. V. 72
The Winnowing Dream. London: 1954. V. 70; 71

DELAMAYNE, THOMAS HALLIE
The Senators; or a Candid Examination into the Merits of the Principal Performers of St. Stephen's Chapel. London: 1772. V. 70

DE LA MAZA, FRANCISCO
Enrico Martinez: Cosmografo e Impresor de Nueva Espana. Mexico: 1943. V. 68

DE LA MOTTE, COLONEL
The Principal, Historical, and Allusive, Arms, borne by Families of the United Kingdom of Great Britain and Ireland. 1803. V. 72

DE LA MOTTE, FREEMAN GAGE
Primer of Illumination for the Use of Beginners. London: 1863. V. 71
A Primer of the Art of Illumination for the Use of Beginners. London: 1874. V. 68; 72
A Primer on the Art of Illumination for the Use of Beginners. London: 1912. V. 69

DELAMOTTE, PHILIP H.
The Art of Sketching From Nature. London: 1871. V. 72
Choice Examples of Art Workmanship Selected for the Exhibition of Ancient and Mediaeval Art at the Society of Arts. London: 1851. V. 68
The Practice of Photography. London: 1853. V. 68

DELAND, CHARLES E.
Aborigines of South Dakota in South Dakota Historical Collections, Vol III & IV. Aberdeen/Sioux Falls: 1906. V. 72

DELAND, MARGARET
Dr. Lavendar's People. New York and London: 1903. V. 69
The Kays. New York: 1926. V. 73
Old Chester Tales. New York: 1899. V. 68
Partners. New York & London: 1908. V. 71

DELANNOY, H. BURFORD
Between the Lines: a Detective Story. London: 1901. V. 68

DELANO, ALONZO
Across the Plains and Among the Diggings. New York: 1936. V. 70
Alonzo Delano's California Correspondence. Sacramento: 1952. V. 73
The Miner's Progress; or, Scenes in the Life of a California Miner. Sacramento: 1853. V. 69
Pen-Knife Sketches Or Chips of The Old Block. San Francisco: 1934. V. 71
A Sojourn With Royalty and Other Sketches by Old Block. San Francisco: 1936. V. 71

DELANO, AMASA
Narratives of Voyages and Travels in the Northern And Southern Hemispheres: Comprising Three Voyages Round the World Together with a Voyage of Survey and Discovery in the Pacific Ocean and Oriental Islands. Boston: 1817. V. 72

DELANY, PATRICK
Reflections Upon Polygamy, and the Encouragement Given to that Practice in the Scriptures of the Old Testament. London: 1737. V. 68
Revelation Examined with Candour. London: 1745-1763. V. 72

DELANY, SAMUEL R.
The Bridge of Lost Desire. New York: 1987. V. 72
Empire Star. New York: 1966. V. 72
The Jewels of Aptor. New York: 1962. V. 72
The Jewels of Aptor. London: 1968. V. 73
The Motion of Light in Water. 1988. V. 69
The Motion of Light in Water. New York: 1988. V. 70
Nova. Garden City: 1968. V. 73

DELAPLAINE, JOSEPH
The Author Turned Critic; or the Reviewer Reviewed.... 1816. V. 72
Delaplaine's Repository of the Lives and Portraits of Distinguished Americans. Volume I. Part I. Philadelphia: 1816. V. 69

DE LA PORTE, M.
La Science Des Negocians et Tueneurs de Livres. A Paris: 1748. V. 69

DE LA RAMEE, LOUISE
Ariadne. London: 1877. V. 70
Cecil Castlemaine's Gage and Other Novelettes. London: 1906. V. 68
Cecil Castlemaine's Gage and Other Novelettes. London: 1913. V. 68
Chandos: a Novel. London: 1895. V. 68
Frescoes etc; Dramatic Sketches. London: 1890. V. 68
Held in Bondage, or Granville de Vigne; a Tale of the Day. London: 1898. V. 68
Idalia: a Romance. London: 1909. V. 68
In a Winter City. London: 1882. V. 68
In a Winter City. London: 1890. V. 68
In a Winter City. London: 1906. V. 68
In Maremma: a Story. London: 1913. V. 68
Moufflou. London: 1915. V. 68
Pascarel; only a Story. London: 1900. V. 68
Pipistrello and Other Stories. London: 1881. V. 68
Pipistrello and Other Stories. London: 1882. V. 68
Princess Napraxine. London: 1900. V. 68
Princess Napraxine. London: 1907. V. 68
Puck: His Vicissitudes, Adventures, Observations, Conclusions, Friendships and Philosophies.... London: 1901. V. 68
Signa; a Novel. London: 1907. V. 68
Signa; a Novel. London: 1915. V. 68
Strathmore, or Wrought by His Own Hand: a Life Romance. London: 1879. V. 68
Strathmore, or Wrought by His Own Hand, a Life Romance. London: 1891. V. 68
Tricotrin: the Story of a Waif and Stray. London: 1881. V. 68
Two Little Wooden Shoes. London: 1886. V. 72
Two Little Wooden Shoes. London: 1913. V. 68
Under Two Flags: a Novel. London: 1894. V. 68
Under Two Flags: a Novel. London: 1912. V. 68
Village Commune. London: 1903. V. 68
Wanda. London: 1885. V. 68
Wanda. London: 1893. V. 68

DE LA RIVE, A.
Recherches sur la Cause de l'Electricite Voltaique.... Geneva: 1836. V. 68

DELARUE-MARDRUS, LUCIE
Les Amours d'Oscar Wilde. Paris: 1929. V. 70
Le Far West D'Aujourd'hui. Paris: 1932. V. 69

DELASSAUX, VICTOR
Street Architecture, a Series of Shop Front and Facades, Characteristic of and Adapted to Different Branches of Commerce. 1855. V. 71

DE LA TORRE, LILLIAN
The Detections of Dr. Sam. Johnson. Garden City: 1960. V. 69; 72
Dr. Sam: Johnson, Detector. New York: 1946. V. 68; 69; 72

DELAUNAY, CHARLES
Hot Discography. New York: 1940. V. 68
New Hot Discography. New York: 1948. V. 72

DELAUNAY, SONIA
Alphabet. New York: 1972. V. 73

DELAUNE, THOMAS
Angliae Metropolis; or the Present State of London.... London: 1690. V. 71
The Present State of London; or Memorials Comprehending a Full and Succinct Account of the Ancient and Modern State Thereof. London: 1681. V. 71

DELAVAN, DAVID BRYSON
Early Days of the Presbyterian Hospital in the City of New York. New York: 1926. V. 70

DELAVENAY, EMILE
D. H. Lawrence. L'Homme et la Genese de Son Oeuvre (1885-1919). Paris: 1969. V. 72

DELAWARE
Report of the Committee...Together with the Journal of the Committee...in Regard to the Interference by U.S. Troops with General Election...November 1862. Dover: 1863. V. 68

DELAWARE & HUDSON CANAL CO.
The D&H, A Souvenir. Albany. V. 70

DELAWARE & RARITAN CANAL CO.
First Annual Report of the Delaware and Raritan Canal Co. May 10, 1831. Princeton: 1831. V. 69

DELBREL, E.
Traite et Modeles d'Escaliers d'Art. Paris: 1890. V. 68

DE LEON, DANIEL
A Debate on the Tactics of the Socialist Trade and Labor Alliance, Toward Trade Unions. 1900. V. 71

DE LEON, SOLON
The American Labor Who's Who. New York: 1925. V. 68

DE LEON, THOMAS COOPER
Belles Beaux and Brains of the 60's. New York: 1909. V. 69; 70
Four Years in Rebel Capitals; an Inside View. Mobile: 1890. V. 69
John Holden, Unionist. St. Paul: 1893. V. 70
John Holden, Unionist. New York: 1910. V. 70
South Songs: from the Lays of Later Days. New York: 1866. V. 70

DELILLE, JACQUES M.
The Gardens, a Poem. London: 1805. V. 69
Les Jardins...Poeme. Pari: 1791. V. 68
The Rural Philosopher; or French Georgics. Newbern: 1804. V. 68; 73

DELILLE, JOHN DOUGLAS
Canon Lucifer: a Novel of an English Social Aspect. London: 1887?. V. 68

DELILLO, DON
Amazons: an Intimate Memoir by the First Woman Ever to Play in the National Hockey League. New York: 1980. V. 69; 72; 73
Americana. Boston: 1971. V. 69; 70; 72; 73
The Body Artist. London: 2001. V. 69; 70; 72
The Body Artist. New York: 2001. V. 68; 69; 70; 72
The Day Room. New York: 1987. V. 69; 70; 72
The Day Room. New York: 1988. V. 72
End Zone. Boston: 1972. V. 68; 69; 70; 71; 72; 73
End Zone. London: 1973. V. 70
Great Jones Street. Boston: 1973. V. 68; 70; 71; 72; 73
Great Jones Street. London: 1974. V. 69; 73
Libra. 1988. V. 70; 72
Libra. New York: 1988. V. 70; 71
Mao II. New York: 1991. V. 70; 71
The Names. New York: 1982. V. 68; 69; 71; 72; 73

DELILLO, DON continued
The Names. Sussex: 1983. V. 69
Players. New York: 1967. V. 73
Players. New York: 1977. V. 70; 72
Ratner's Star. New York: 1976. V. 68; 69; 70; 71; 72
Running Dog. New York: 1978. V. 69; 70; 71; 72
Underworld. New York: 1997. V. 68; 69; 70; 71; 72
Underworld. 1998. V. 69; 72
White Noise. London: 1985. V. 71
White Noise. New York: 1985. V. 69; 72

DELINT, CHARLES
Jack the Giant Killer. New York: 1987. V. 70

DELITTLE 1888-1988: the First Years in a Century of a Wood Letter Manufacture 1888-1895. Oxford: 1988. V. 70

DELL, ANTHONY
Llama Land: East and West of the Andes in Peru. New York: 1927. V. 69; 72

DELL, ETHEL M.
The Electric Torch. New York: 1934. V. 69
Live Bait: Shorter Romances. New York: 1932. V. 71
The Silver Bride. New York: 1932. V. 71

DELL, FLOYD
The Ballad of Christopher Streeet. New York: 1933. V. 71
Women as World Builders, Studies in Modern Feminism. Chicago: 1913. V. 72

DELL, JEFFREY
Payment Deferred: A Play in a Prologue, Three Acts and an Epilogue. London: 1934. V. 72

DELLA BELLA, STEFANO
Arts Pictoriae Aestmatori Pertissim ac Obsequii Monumentum. (with) Divers Embarquements. 1790?. V. 72
Recueil de Douze Cartouches.... Paris: 1643. V. 70

DELLA CASA, GIOVANNI
Rime et prose.... Florence: 1572. V. 73
Rime et Prose.... Florence: 1598. V. 73

DELLENBAUGH, FREDERICK S.
Breaking the Wilderness. New York: 1905. V. 68; 73
George Armstrong Custer. New York: 1919. V. 72

DELMAR, VINA
Loose Ladies. New York: 1929. V. 70

DELMONT, JOSEPH
The Submarine City. London. V. 70

DE LOLME, JOHN LOUIS
The Constitution of England, or an Account of the English Government; in Which it is Compared with the Republican Form of Government, and Occasionally with other Monarchies in Europe. London: 1775. V. 73

DELONEY, THOMAS
The History of Thomas of Reading or Six Worthy Yeomen of the West. London: 1827. V. 73

DE LONG, D. G.
Bruce Goff: Toward Absolute Architecture. New York: 1988. V. 72

DE LONG, GEORGE W.
Our Lost Explorers: the Narrative of the Jeannette Arctic Expedition, as Related by the Survivors and in the Records and Last Journals of.... Hartford: 1882. V. 73
Voyage of the Jeannette. Boston: 1888. V. 70

DELORIA, VINE
Custer Died for Your Sins. London: 1969. V. 70
Custer Died for Your Sins. New York: 1969. V. 68
We Talk, you Listen: New Tribes, New Turf. New York: 1970. V. 73

DEL REY, LESTER
... And Some Were Human. Philadelphia: 1949. V. 69
Attack from Atlantis. 1953. V. 70

DE LUC, JEAN ANDRE
Letters on the Physical History of the Earth, Addressed to Professor Blumenbach.... London: 1831. V. 69
Lettres Physiques et Morales, sur les Montagnes et sur l'Histoire de la Terre et de l'Homme: Addressees a la Reine de la grande Bretagne. The Hague: 1778. V. 73

DELVAUX, PAUL
Paul Delvaux. Rotterdam: 1973. V. 70

DEL VECCHIO, JOHN M.
The 13th Valley. New York: 1982. V. 68; 72

DELVING, MICHAEL
The Devil Finds Work. New York: 1969. V. 68

DE LYON NICHOLLS, C. W.
The 469 Ultra-Fashionables of America. New York: 1912. V. 69

DE MAISSE, ANDRE HURAULT
A Journal of All That was Accomplished by Monsieur de Maisse, Ambassador in England From King Henri IV to Queen Elizabeth Anno Domini 1597. Translated from the French and edited with an introduction by G. B. Harrison and R. A. Jones. London: 1931. V. 71

DEMAREST, MARY A.
The Demarest Family: David des Marest of the French Patent on the Hackensack and His Descendants. New Brunswick: 1938. V. 69

DE MARINIS, RICK
Scimitar. New York: 1977. V. 68

DEMBY, WILLIAM
Beetlecreek. New York: 1950. V. 68

DE MILLE, AGNES
Portrait Gallery. Boston: 1990. V. 69

DE MILLE, JAMES
The Cryptogram. New York: 1871. V. 72
A Strange Manuscript Found in a Copper Cylinder with Illustrations by Gilbert Gaul. New York: 1888. V. 72; 73

DE MILLE, NELSON
By the Rivers of Babylon. New York: 1978. V. 68; 70; 72
Cathedral. New York: 1981. V. 68; 69; 71
The Charm School. New York: 1988. V. 68; 73
The Lion's Game. New York: 2000. V. 72
Mayday. V. 72
Talbot Odyssey. New York: 1995. V. 70

DEMING, ROBERT H.
James Joyce: the Critical Heritage. London: 1970. V. 72

DEMING, THERESE O.
Red Folk and Wild Folk with Indian Folk-Lore Stories for Children. New York: 1902. V. 70

THE DEMOCRATIC Book. 1936. V. 69; 71; 72

DE MOIVRE, ABRAHAM
The Doctrine of Chances; or a Method of Calculating the Probability of Events in Play. London: 1718. V. 70

DE MORGAN, AUGUSTUS
A Budget of Paradoxes. Chicago and London: 1915. V. 72
An Essay on Probabilities, and on Their Application to Life Contingencies and Insurance Offices. London: 1838. V. 71

DE MORGAN, MARY
The Necklace of Princess Fiorimonde. London: 1880. V. 72
On a Pincushion and Other Fairy Tales. London: 1877. V. 68

DE MORGAN, WILLIAM
An Affair of Dishonour. London: 1910. V. 68
It Never Can Happen Again. London: 1909. V. 68
A Likely Story. London: 1911. V. 68

DEMOSTHENES
Super Corona Oratio. The Oration of Demosthenes on the Crown. London: 1873. V. 72
The Three Orations of Demosthenes Chiefe Orator Among the Grecians, in Favour of the Olynthians, a People in Thracia, Now Called Romania.... London: 1570. V. 68; 73

DEMOURS, ANTOINE PIERRE
Traite des Maladies des Yeux.... Paris: 1818. V. 72

DEMPSEY, G. DRYSDALE
Rudimentary Treatise on the Drainage of Districts and Lands. London: 1859. V. 71
Tubular and Other Iron Girder Bridges; Particularly Describing the Britannia and Conway Tubular Bridges; with a Sketch of Iron Bridges.... London: 1850. V. 71

DEMPSEY, HUGH A.
History in Their Blood: the Indian Portraits of Nicholas de Grandmaison. New York: 1982. V. 71

DEMPSEY, J. M.
Our Ocean Highways 1871-1872: A Condensed Universal Hand Gazetter. London: 1870. V. 68

DEMPSTER, C.
The Maritime Alps and Their Seaboard. London: 1885. V. 72

DEMPSTER, CHARLOTTE
Iseulte. London: 1877. V. 68

DENCH, EDWARD BRADFORD
Diseases of the Ear. New York: 1896. V. 71

DENHAM, CANON W.
Old St. Paul's Cathedral. London: 1902. V. 68

DENHAM, J. V.
Views Exhibiting the Exterior and Interior and Principal Monuments of the Very Ancient and Remarkable Church of St. Dunstan in the West in the City of London. London: 1831. V. 70

DENHAM, JOHN
Coopers Hill. London: 1655. V. 68
Poems and Translations with the Sophy. London: 1668. V. 68; 70; 72; 73
Poems and Translations; with the Sophy. Glasgow: 1770. V. 73

DENHARDT, ROBERT MOORMAN
The Horse of the Americans. 1947. V. 68
The Horse of Two Centuries. Norman: 1947. V. 71
The King Ranch Quarter Horses. 1970. V. 68
The King Ranch Quarter Horses. Norman: 1972. V. 71
Quarter Horses - a Story of Two Centuries. Norman: 1967. V. 69

DENHART, JEFFREY
Just Bones. Aurora: 1996. V. 68

DENHOLM YOUNG, N.
The Liber Epistolaris of Richard de Bury. Oxford: 1950. V. 69

DENIS, JEAN BAPTISTE
Receuil des memoires et Conferences sur les Arts and Les Sciences presentee a Monseigneur le Dauphin Pendant l'Annee. Amsterdam: 1682. V. 70; 72

DENISON, EDMUND BECKETT
Lectures on Church Building: With Some Practical Remarks on Bells and Clocks. London: 1856. V. 73
A Rudimentary Treatise on Clocks and Watches. London: 1860. V. 68

DENISON, GEORGE T.
Soldiering in Canada. Toronto: 1900. V. 73
The Struggle of Imperial Unity: Recollections and Experiences. London: 1909. V. 71

DENMAN, LESLIE VAN NESS
The Corn Maidens' Dance and Its Greek Analogies. Pai Ya Tu Ma, God of All Dance and His Customs of the Flute, Zuni Pueblo 1932. San Francisco: 1955. V. 70
The Flute Ceremonial - Hotevila and Snake Antelope Ceremonial of the Hopi Mesas. San Francisco: 1956. V. 68

DENMAN, THOMAS
An Introduction to the Practice of Midwifery. London: 1801. V. 72
An Introduction to the Practice of Midwifery. New York: 1821. V. 68

DENMAN, WILLIAM
Greetings from William and Leslie Denman - The Hopi Ladder Dance. San Francisco: 1958. V. 68

DENNE, SAMUEL
The History and Antiquities of Rochester and its Environs.... Rochester: 1772. V. 70

DENNETT, R. E.
Nigerian Studies or the Religious and Political System of the Yoruba. London: 1910. V. 69

DENNIE, CHARLES CLAYTON
A History of Syphilis. Springfield: 1962. V. 68

DENNIS, JOHN
The Advancement and Reformation of Modern Poetry. London: 1701. V. 73
The Comical Gallant; or the Amours of Sir John Falstaffe. London: 1702. V. 68

DENNIS, JONAS
The Landscape Gardener, Comprising the History and Principles of Tasteful Horticulture. London: 1835. V. 68; 70; 71

DENNIS, NIGEL
Cards of Identity. London: 1955. V. 71

DENNIS, WAYNE
The Hopi Child. New York: 1940. V. 68; 73
Readings in the History of Psychology.... New York: 1948. V. 71

DENNISON MANUFACTURING CO.
Art and Decoration in Dennison's Crepe and Tissue Paper. Boston and New York: 1913. V. 68

DENNY, EBENEZER
Military Journal of Major Ebenezer Denny, an Officer in the Revolutionary and Indian Wars. Philadelphia: 1859. V. 70

DENNY, H.
Monographia Anoplurorum Britanniae. 1842. V. 73
Monographia Anoplurorum Britanniae. London: 1842. V. 69
Monographia Pselaphidarum et Scydmaenidarum Britanniae. Norwich: 1825. V. 69

DENNY, M. W.
Biology and the Mechanics of the Wave-Swept Environment. Princeton: 1988. V. 72

DENNY-BROWN, D.
Selected Writings of Sir Charles Sherrington. A Testimonial Presented by the Neurologists Forming the Guarantors of the Journal Brain. London: 1939. V. 70

DENNYS, JOHN
The Secrets of Angling. 1883. V. 73

DE NON, DOMINIQUE VIVANT, BARON
Travels through Sicily and Malta.... Perth: 1790. V. 73

DENON, DOMINIQUE VIVANT, BARON
Voyage en Sicile. A Paris: 1788. V. 69

DENSLOW, W. W.
Barn-Yard Circus. New York: 1904. V. 73
Billy Bounce. New York: 1906. V. 71; 73
Denslow's Animal Fair. New York: 1904. V. 72
Denslow's Humpty Dumpty. New York: 1903. V. 71
Denslow's Jack and the Beanstalk. New York: 1903. V. 71
Denslow's Mother Goose. London: 1902. V. 71
Denslow's Scarecrow and The Tin Man. New York: 1904. V. 72
Denslow's Scarecrow and the Tin-Man and Other Stories. Chicago: 1913. V. 71; 73
Denslow's Three Little Kittens. New York: 1904. V. 72
Johnnie Johnston's Air Ship. New York: 1909. V. 71
Pictures from the Wonderful Wizard of Oz. Chicago: 1903. V. 69
When I Grow Up. New York: 1909. V. 69

DENSON, CLAUDE BAKER
An Address Delivered in Raleigh, N.C. on Memorial Day (May 10), 1895. Raleigh: 1895. V. 69; 70

DENT, C. T.
Mountaineering. London: 1892. V. 69

DENT, JOHN
Catalogue of the Splendid, Curious and Extensive Library of the Late.... London: 1827. V. 70; 72

DENT, LESTER
The Man of Bronze. NY: 1933. V. 72

DENTON, KIT
The Breaker. New York: 1981. V. 73

DENTON, S.
Incidents of a Collector's Rambles in Australia, Nw Zealand and New Guinea. Boston: 1889. V. 69
Pages from a Naturalist's Diary. Boston: 1949. V. 73
Pages from a Naturalist's Diary. Wellesley: 1949. V. 69

DENTON, SHERMAN F.
As Nature Shows Them: Moths and Butterflies of the United States East of the Rocky Mountains. Boston: 1897-1900. V. 70
Moths and Butterflies of the United States, East of the Rocky Mountains. Boston. V. 70

DENTON, WILLIAM
The Soul of Things; or, Psychometric Researches and Discoveries. Boston: 1866. V. 71

D'ENTREMONT, H. LEANDER
The Baronnie de Pombcoup and the Acadians. Yarmouth: 1931. V. 72

DENVER & RIO GRANDE RAILROAD
The Fertile Lands of Colorado. 1904. V. 69
Slopes of the Sangre de Crist. Denver: 1896. V. 68
Tourist's Hand Book Descriptive of Colorado, New Mexico and Utah. New York: 1886. V. 71
Tourist's Hand Book Descriptive of Colorado, New Mexico and Utah. New York: 1887. V. 71

DENVER & RIO GRANDE SYSTEM
Tourists' Handbook Descriptive of Colorado, New Mexico and Utah. 1907. V. 68

DENVER and Vicinity. Colorado. Genealogy and Biography. 1898. V. 68

DENWOOD, J. M.
Cumbrian Nights. Red Ike's Poaching Life. 1932. V. 71

DEORANI, S. C.
Orchids of Nagaland. Dehra Dun: 1995. V. 73

DE PAOLO, PETER
Wall Smacker. 1935. V. 73

DE PEYSTER, JOHN WATTS
Personal and Military History of Phillip Kearny Major General United States Volunteers. NY: 1869. V. 72

DE POLNAY, PETER
Angry Man's Tale. New York: 1939. V. 70

DEPONS, F.
Travels in Parts of South America, During the Years 1801, 1802, 1803, & 1804. London: 1806. V. 72

DE PRADT, D. D.
Du Congres De Vienne.... Paris: 1815. V. 70; 72

DE PUY, E. SPENCE
The Long Knife. New York: 1936. V. 68

DE QUEIRZ, RACHEL
The Three Marias. Austin: 1963. V. 69

DE QUINCEY, THOMAS
The Caesars. Boston: 1851. V. 72
The Collected Writings. London: 1896-1897. V. 68
The Collected Writings. New and enlarged edition by David Masson. Edinburgh: 1899. V. 70; 71
Confessions of an English Opium Eater. London: 1822. V. 70; 72; 73
Confessions of an English Opium Eater. 1823. V. 70
Confessions of an English Opium Eater. Philadelphia: 1823. V. 69
Confessions of an English Opium Eater. New York: 1930. V. 68; 71
The Works. Edinburgh: 1862-1863. V. 70
The Works. Edinburgh: 1862-1874. V. 70

DERANIYAGALA, P. E. P.
A Coloured Atlas of Some Vertebrates From Ceylon, Vol. 1, Fishes. Colombo: 1952. V. 72

DERBY, EDWARD HENRY SMITH STANLEY, EARL OF
Memorandum on Suggested Improvements in the Patent Laws of 1852, 1853. London: 1856. V. 73

DERBY, GEORGE HORATIO
Phoenixiana. Chicago: 1897. V. 68

DERBY, J. C.
Fifty Years Among Authors, Books and Publishers. New York: 1884. V. 73

DE REGNIERS, BEATRICE SCHENK
What Can You Do With a Shoe?. New York: 1997. V. 73

DERHAM, WILLIAM
Astro-Theology or a Demonostration of the Being and Attributes of God, from a Survey of the Heavens. London: 1715. V. 70; 73
Astro-Theology or a Demonstration of the Being & Attributes of God, from a Survey of the Heavens. 1743. V. 68; 70
Physico-Theology: or, A Demonstration of the Being and Attributes of God, From His Works of Creation. London: 1713. V. 69; 72
Physico-Theology...From the Works of Creation.... London: 1714. V. 68; 70

DERLETH, AUGUST WILLIAM
The Adventures of the Orient Express. 1965. V. 71
And You, Thoreau!. Norfolk: 1944. V. 68; 71
Any Day Now. Chicago: 1939. V. 69
Arkham House - The First 20 Years 1939-1959. Sauk City: 1959. V. 70
Beachheads in Space. New York: 1952. V. 69
The Casebook of Solar Pons. Sauk City: 1965. V. 69; 70; 73
The Chronicles of Solar Pons. Sauk City: 1973. V. 70
Consider Your Verdict. New York: 1937. V. 70
Countryman's Journal. New York: 1963. V. 73
Dark of the Moon: Poems of Fantasy and the Macabre. Sauk City: 1947. V. 73
Here on a Darkling Plain. 1940. V. 69
In Re: Shelock Holmes. Sauk City: 1945. V. 69; 70; 71; 73
The Memoirs of Solar Pons. Sauk City: 1951. V. 68; 69; 71
The Milwaukee Road: Its First Hundred Years. New York: 1948. V. 68
Mischief in the Lane. New York: 1944. V. 68; 71; 73
Mr. Fairlie's Final Journey. Sauk City: 1968. V. 70
The Narracong Riddle. New York: 1940. V. 71
No Future for Luana. New York: 1945. V. 68
Not Long for This World. Sauk City: 1948. V. 68; 71
A Praed Street Dossier. Sauk City: 1968. V. 70
Praed Street Papers. 1965. V. 71
The Reminiscences of Solar Pons. 1961. V. 71
The Reminiscences of Solar Pons. Sauk City: 1961. V. 70; 73
The Return of Solar Pons. 1958. V. 71
The Return of Solar Pons. Sauk City: 1958. V. 69; 70; 73
Sentence Deferred. New York: 1939. V. 71; 73
The Seven Who Waited. New York: 1943. V. 71
The Solar Pons Omnibus. Sauk City: 1982. V. 69
Three Problems for Solar Pons. Mycroft: 1952. V. 71
Who Knocks?. New York: 1946. V. 68
Wind Over Wisconsin. New York: 1938. V. 71

DE ROME, F. J.
Notes on the Harbour of Hong Kong. London: 1927. V. 68
Notes on the New Territories of Hong Kong. 1929. V. 68

DE ROS, JOHN FREDERICK FITZGERALD
Personal Narrative of Travels in the United States and Canada in 1826. London: 1827. V. 68; 70; 73

DE ROSSAN, ANNE ELIZABETH
Recit de La Morte Tragique De Madame la Marquise de Castellane.... Paris: 1668. V. 69

DEROSSI, ONORATO
Nuova Guida per la Citta di Torino. Turin: 1781. V. 70

DERRDYDALE PRESS
A Decade of American Sporting Books & Prints by the Derrydale Press 1927-1937. New York: 1937. V. 72

DERRICK, THOMAS
Everyman. London: 1930. V. 69

DERRY, JOSEPH T.
Story of the Confederate States; or, History of the War for Southern Independence.... Richmond: 1895. V. 69; 70

DERWENT, GEORGE HARCOURT JOHNSTONE
Fifty Poems. London: 1931. V. 69

DESAGULIERS, JOHN THEOPHILUS
Optical experiments made in the beginning of August 1728 before the President and several members of the Royal Society and other gentlemen of several nations, upon occasion of Signior Rizzetti's Opticks.... London: 1729. V. 72
A System of Experimental Philosophy.... London: 1719. V. 69; 70

DE SAHAGUN, B.
A History of Ancient Mexico. 1932. V. 69

DESAI, ANITA
Fasting, Feasting. London: 1999. V. 70
The Village by the Sea: an Indian Family Story. New Dehli: 1985. V. 69
Voices in the City. London: 1865. V. 72

DESAI, KIRAN
Hullabaloo in the Guava Orchard. London: 1998. V. 70

DE SAINT-FOND, B. FAUJAS
A Journey through England and Scotland to the Hebrides in 1784. Glasgow: 1907. V. 69

DE SALVO, LOUISE A.
Melymbrosia - an Early Version of The Voyage Out. New York: 1982. V. 70
Virginia Woolf - The Impact of Childhood Sexual Abuse on Her Life and Work. Boston: 1989. V. 70
Virginia Woolf's First Voyage - a Novel in the Making. Totowa: 1980. V. 70

DESAULT, PIERRE JOSEPH
Oeuvres Chirurgicales.... Paris: 1813. V. 72

DE SAUSSURE, WILMOT G.
Names as Far As Can Be Ascertained of the Officers Who Served in the South Carolina Regiments.... Columbia: 1886. V. 68

DESCARTES, RENE
A Discourse of a Method for the Well Guiding of Reason and the Discovery of Truth in the Sciences. London: 1649. V. 73
Oeuvres de Descartes. Paris: 1897-1913. V. 70; 73
Tractatus de Homine et de Romatione Foetus Quorum Prior Notis Perpetuis Ludovici de la Forge, M.D. Amsterdam: 1677. V. 70

DE SCHWEINITZ, G. E.
Diseases of the Eye. Philadelphia: 1896. V. 71; 73

DESCRIPTION des Travaux Entrepris Dans la Construction de la Tonnelle ou Passage sous la Tamise, Entre Rotherhithe et Wapping.... London: 1851. V. 68

A DESCRIPTION of East-Bourne and Its Environs: in the County of Sussex. Eastbourne: 1819. V. 70; 72

A DESCRIPTION of the Basking Shark, Caught at Abbotsbury, in the County of Dorset on Monday May 4, 1801. Bristol: 1801. V. 68

A DESCRIPTION of the Colosseum as Re-opened in MDCCCXLV.... 1845. V. 71

A DESCRIPTION of the Grand Musical Festival, Held in the City of York, September the 23rd (26th) 1823. York: 1823. V. 69

A DESCRIPTIVE Account of the Devil's Bridge, Hafod, Strata Florida Abbey and Other Scenery in that District of Cardiganshire. Hereford: 1796. V. 70

THE DESCRIPTIVE Album of London: a Pictorial Guide Book. 1896. V. 71

A DESCRIPTIVE Guide to Bournemouth, Christchurch, Wimborne and Corfe Castle and Their Interesting Features. Bournemouth: 1878. V. 73

DE SCUDERY, M.
Clelia. 1655. V. 71

DESEINE, FRANCOIS JACQUES
Nouveau Voyage d'Italie Contenant une Description Exacte de Toutes ses Provinces, Villes & Lieux Considerables et des Isles qui en Dependent. Lyon: 1699. V. 72

DE SERVIEZ, JACQUES ROERGAS
The Lives and Amours of the Empresses, Consorts to the First 12 Caesars of Rome.... London: 1723. V. 68; 69; 73

DE SHIELDS, JAMES
Border Wars of Texas. Toga, TX: 1912. V. 68; 69; 72
Cynthia Ann Parker, The Story of Her Capture. St. Louis: 1886. V. 72
Tall Men with Long Rifles.... San Antonio: 1971. V. 70

DESIO, A.
Ascent of K2. 1955. V. 71

DESIRABLE and Practicable, Being an Address to the Inhabitants of Sheffield, with Religious and Political Remarks on the Subjects Discussed at the Public Meeting, Held in Paradise Square, on Wednesday, June 7th 1810. London: 1810. V. 68

DESJARDINS, MARIE CATHERINE HORTENSE
The Loves of Sundry Philosophers and Other Great Men. London: 1673. V. 73

DESMOND, HUGH
Death in the Shingle. London: 1948. V. 72

DESMOND, R.
Bibliography of British Gardens. Winchester: 1988. V. 73

DESNOS, ROBERT
Contree/Country. Twenty-Five Poems. Iowa City: 1994. V. 73

DE SOTO, HERNANDO
Letter of Hernando De Soto and Memoir of Hernando De Escalante Fontaneda. Washington: 1854. V. 72

DE TABLEY, JOHN BYRNE LEICESTER WARREN, 3RD BARON
Ballads and Metrical Sketches: Together with The Threshold of Atrides; and Glimpses of Antiquity; Being a Collection of Metrical Sketches in the Form of Ballads, Lyrics &c.... London: 1860-1861-. V. 72
The Collected Poems. London: 1903. V. 68
Eclogues and Monodramas; or a Collection of Verses. London: 1864. V. 72
Orpheus in Thrace and Other Poems. London: 1901. V. 68
Poems Dramatic and Lyrical. Second Series. London and New York: 1895. V. 72
Poems Dramtic and Lyrical. London and New York: 1893. V. 70; 72
Praeterita. London: 1863. V. 72
Rehearsals: a Book of Verses. London: 1870. V. 72

THE DETECTION CLUB. *The Floating Admiral.* New York: 1932. V. 73

THE DETECTOR Detected; or the Danger To which Our Constitution Now Lies Exposed, Set in a True and Manifest Light. London: 1743. V. 71

DE TERAN, LISA ST. AUBIN
Keepers of the House. London: 1982. V. 72
The Palace. London: 1997. V. 70

DETMOLD, E. J.
The Book of Baby Birds. New York: 1912. V. 69

DETMOLD, MAURICE
Pictures from Birdland. London: 1899. V. 72

DE TROBRIAND, PHILPPE R.
Military Life in Dakota: The Journal of Phillppe Regis De Trobriand. St. Paul: 1951. V. 72

DETROIT DECORATIVE SUPPLY CO.
Architectural and Decorative Plaster Ornaments. Detroit: 1929. V. 68

DETROIT HEATING & LIGHTING CO.
Light for Evening Hours. Detroit: 1909. V. 69

DEULIN, CHARLES
Johnny Nut and the Golden Goose. London: 1887. V. 70

DEUSING, ANTON
Sylva-Caedua Jacens: Seu Disquisitiones Anti-Sylvianae Ulteriores. Groningen: 1665. V. 70; 71

DEUTSCHER, ISAAC
The Prophet Armed; the Prophet Unarmed; the Prophet Outcast. New York: 1963-. V. 68

DEVAL, JACQUES
Tovarich. New York: 1937. V. 71

DEVENS, R. M.
Our First Century: Being a Popular Descriptive Portraiture.... Springfield: 1878. V. 73

DEVENTER, HENRY
Observations Importantes sur le manuel des Accouchemens. Paris: 1734. V. 70
Operationum Chirurgicarum Novum Lumen Exhibentium Obstetricantibus. Lugduni Batavorum: 1733. V. 72

DE VERE, AUBREY
Poems. 1855. V. 73

DE VERE, WILLIAM
Tramp Poems of the West.... Tacoma: 1891. V. 68; 71

THE DEVIL in Dixie: a Tale of the Times. New York: 1865. V. 70

DE VILLAGRA, GASPAR PEREZ
A History of New Mexico. Los Angeles: 1933. V. 68

DEVILLE, E.
Photographic Surveying Including the Elements of Descriptive Geometry and Perspective. Ottawa: 1895. V. 71

DEVILLE, NICOLAS
Histoire des Plantes de l'Europe.... Lyon: 1753. V. 72; 73

DEVINE, DOMINIC
Three Green Bottles. London: 1972. V. 72

DEVINE, S. J.
Across Widest America - New Foundland to Alaska. Montreal: 1905. V. 73

DEVLIN, ALBERT J.
Conversations with Tennessee Williams. Jackson: 1986. V. 73

DEVLIN, DEAN
Independence Day. 1996. V. 71
Independence Day. New York: 1996. V. 73

DEVLIN, JAMES
The Shoemaker. Part I - The Pratical Workman. Part II - The Duties of the Shop. 1850. V. 71

DEVLIN, POLLY
Vogue Book of Fashion Photography. New York: 1979. V. 68

DEVLIN, THOMAS F.
Days of Discord: a Brief Chronology of the Mexican Revolution 1910- 1920. El Paso: 1974. V. 71

DEVOL, GEORGE H.
Forty Years a Gambler on the Mississippi. Austin: 1967. V. 68

DEVONSHIRE, DEBORAH MITFORD, DUCHESS OF
The House. A Portrait of Chatsworth. London: 1982. V. 73

DE VOTO, BERNARD
Across the Wide Missouri; With an Account of the Discovery of the Miller Collection by Mae Reed Porter. Boston: 1947. V. 69; 72

DEVOY, JOHN
Recollections of an Irish Rebel: The Fenian Movement. 1929. V. 68

DE VRIES, LEONARD
Flowers of Delight Culled...from the Osborne Collection of Early Children's Books. London: 1965. V. 70

DE VRIES, P. J.
Butterflies of Costa Rica and Their Natural History. Princeton: 1987. V. 69

DE VRIES, PETER
But Who Wakes the Bugler?. Boston: 1940. V. 69
No But I Saw the Movie. Boston: 1952. V. 69

DE VRIES, THEUN
En God in Haar School: Scene from a Broadcast Play. 1987. V. 71

DE WAAL, L. C.
Ecology and Management of Invasive Riverside Plants. Chichester: 1994. V. 70

DE WAAL, PHILIP
The Mystery of the Green Garnet Murder. London: 1932. V. 73

DE WAAL, RONALD BURT
The World Bibliogrpahy of Sherlock Holmes and Dr. Watson. Boston: 1974. V. 69; 70

DE WALT, A. FOLUMBO I.
Folumbo: a Native African's Own Life Story. Washington: 1923. V. 71

DEWAR, D.
Game Birds. 1928. V. 71

DEWAR, G. A. B.
The Book of the Dry Fly. 1910. V. 68

DEWAR, HUGO
Within the Thunder. Poems of Conscript. London: 1946. V. 68

DEWEES, WILLIAM P.
A Treatise on Physical and Medical Treatment of Children. Philadelphia: 1826. V. 71

DEWEY, D. M.
The Specimen Book of Fruits, Flowers and Ornamental Trees. Rochester: 1880. V. 69

DEWEY, THOMAS
Hue and Cry. New York: 1944. V. 69; 73

DEWEY, THOMAS E.
The Case Against the New Deal. New York: 1940. V. 70

DEWHIRST, IAN
A History of Keighley. London: 1974. V. 73

DEWHURST, KENNETH
Dr. Thomas Sydenham (1624-1689) His Life and Original Writings. London: 1966. V. 73

DE WITT, JACK
Murder on Shark Island. New York: 1940. V. 71

DE WITT, WARD G.
Prairie Schooner Lady - the Journal of Harriet Sherrill Ward 1853. Los Angeles: 1959. V. 68

DE WITT, WILLIAM RADCLIFFE
Woman Her Excellence and Usefulness. Her Price Above Rubies. Harrisburg: 1841. V. 68

DE WITT TALMAGE, T.
The Earth Girdled. Philadelphia: 1896. V. 69

DE WOLF, THOMAS R.
Nova Scotia Registry of Shipping; with Standard Rules for Construction and Classification. Halifax: 1866. V. 72

DE WOLFE, ELSIE
After All. New York and London: 1935. V. 71
The House in Good Taste. New York: 1913. V. 72

DE WOLFF, J. H.
Pawnee Bill, Hs Experience and Adventures on The Western Plains. NP: 1901. V. 72

DEXTER, COLIN
As Good As Gold. London: 1994. V. 72
The Daughters of Cain. London: 1994. V. 68; 70; 71
The Dead of Jericho. London: 1981. V. 69; 72; 73
The Dead of Jericho. New York: 1981. V. 70
Death is Now My Neighbour. London: 1996. V. 68; 69; 70
The Jewel that Was Ours. Bristol: 1991. V. 68; 69; 70; 71; 72; 73
The Jewel That Was Ours. London: 1991. V. 70; 71; 72; 73
Last Bus to Woodstock. London: 1975. V. 70; 73
Last Seen Wearing. London: 1976. V. 68; 73
Last Seen Wearing. New York: 1976. V. 70; 71; 72
Morse's Greatest Mystery and Other Stories. London: 1993. V. 70; 72
The Remorseful Day. London: 1999. V. 70; 71; 72; 73
The Remorseful Day. New York: 1999. V. 72
The Riddle of the Third Mile. London: 1983. V. 68; 69; 70; 71; 72; 73
The Riddle of the Third Mile. New York: 1984. V. 72
The Riddle of the Third Mile. 1999. V. 71
The Secret of Annexe 3. London: 1986. V. 68; 69; 70; 71; 72; 73
The Secret of Annexe 3. New York: 1986. V. 69
Service of All the Dead. London: 1979. V. 70
Service of All the Dead. New York: 1979. V. 69; 72
Service of All the Dead. New York: 1980. V. 68
The Silent World of Nicholas Quinn. New York: 1976. V. 72
The Silent World of Nicholas Quinn. 1977. V. 71
The Silent World of Nicholas Quinn. London: 1977. V. 70; 72
The Way through the Woods. Bristol: 1992. V. 68; 69; 70; 71; 73
The Wench is Dead. London: 1989. V. 68; 69; 73

DEXTER, FRANKLIN
The Anatomy of the Peritoneum. New York: 1892. V. 71

DEXTER, JACQUELINE
Nicholas Roerich: the Life and Art of a Russian Master. Rochester: 1989. V. 70

DEXTER, PETE
Brotherly Love. Franklin Center: 1991. V. 70
Brotherly Love. New York: 1991. V. 70
Deadwood. New York: 1986. V. 70

DEXTER, PETE continued
God's Pocket. New York: 1983. V. 68; 69; 70
Paris Trout. New York: 1988. V. 68; 69; 70; 72

DEXTER, WALTER
The Kent of Dickens. London: 1924. V. 69
Some Rogues and Vagabonds of Dickens. London: 1927. V. 69

DEYEUX, THEOPHILE
Le Vieux Chasseur. Paris: 1835. V. 69

DEZALLIER D'ARGENVILLE, ANTOINE NICOLAS
The Theory and Practice of Gardening.... London: 1712. V. 71
Voyage Pittoresque de Paris, ou Description de Tout Qu'il y a de Plus Beau dans Cette Grande Ville, en Peinture, Sculpture & Architecture. Paris: 1770. V. 69
Voyage Pittoresque de Paris, ou Indiation de Tout qu'il y a de Plus Beau Dans Cette Grande Ville, en Peinture, Sculpture, & Architecture. Paris: 1765. V. 69

DE ZAVALA, ADINA
History and Legends of the Alamo and Other Missions In and Around San Antonio. San Antonio: 1917. V. 70

D'HARCOURT, R.
Ancient Peruvian Textiles. Paris & New York: 1924. V. 69
Textiles of Ancient Peru and Their Techniques. Seattle: 1962. V. 69

D'HERICOURT, MADAME
A Woman's Philosophy of Woman; or Woman Affranchised. New York: 1864. V. 69

DIAL, HARRY
All This Jazz About Jazz. Chigwell: 1984. V. 68

A DIALOGUE Between a Country Gentleman and a Lawyer, upon the Doctrine of Distress for Rent, Shewing What Things May and May Not be Taken at Common Law.... London: 1776. V. 73

A DIALOGUE Betwixt Sam, the Ferryman of Dochet, Will, a Waterman of London and Tom, a Bargeman of Oxford. 1681. V. 70

DIALOGUES, Poems, Songs and Ballads, by Various Writers, in the Westmoreland and Cumberland Dialects.... London: 1839. V. 71

DIAMOND, SARAH
Cold Town. London: 2001. V. 71

DIAMOND, SEYMOUR
The Practicing Physician's Approach to Headache. Baltimore: 1979. V. 71

DIAMONDS And Toads. New York: 1875-1880. V. 73

DIARY of An Excursion to the Ruins of Abo, Quarra and Gran Quivira in New Mexico.... Santa Fe: 1965. V. 71

DIAZ, ABBY MORTON
The Schoolmaster's Trunk Containing Papers on Home-Life in Tweenit. Boston: 1874. V. 69

DIAZ, JUNOT
Drown. New York: 1996. V. 71

DIAZ DEL CASTILLO, BERNAL
Discovery and Conquest of Mexico 1517-1521. Mexico City: 1941-1942. V. 69
The Discovery and Conquest of Mexico 1517-1521. Mexico: 1942. V. 70; 71
The True History of the Conquest of Mexico. London: 1800. V. 69

DIBBLEE, GEORGE
The Psychological Theory of Value. London: 1924. V. 73

DIBDIN, CHARLES
Songs, Naval and National of the Late Charles Dibdin; with a Characteristic Sketch by George Cruikshank. London: 1841. V. 68; 69

DIBDIN, MICHAEL
Dark Spectre. London: 1995. V. 70; 71
Dirty Tricks. London: 1991. V. 71
The Dying of the Light. London: 1993. V. 70; 71
The Last Sherlock Holmes Story. New York: 1978. V. 68; 72
A Long Finish. London: 1998. V. 71
Ratking. London: 1988. V. 70; 72; 73
A Rich Full Death. London: 1986. V. 68; 70; 71

DIBDIN, THOMAS FROGNALL
A Bibliographical Antiquarian and Picturesque Tour in France and Germany. London: 1821. V. 70; 71
A Bibliographical, Antiquarian and Picturesque Tour in France and Germany. London: 1829. V. 71
A Bibliographical Antiquarian and Picturesque Tour in the Northern Counties of England and Scotland. London: 1838. V. 68; 71; 73
The Bibliographical Decameron; or, Ten Days Pleasant Discourse Upon Illuminated Manuscripts and Subjects Connected with Early Enagraving, Typography and Bibliography. London: 1817. V. 71
The Bibliomania; or Book-Madness. London: 1809. V. 72
Bibliomania; or Book-Madness. London: 1811. V. 70
Bibliomania; or, Book-Madness. London: 1842. V. 71
Bibliomania; or Book-Madness. London: 1876. V. 70
The Bibliomania or Book-Madness. Boston: 1903. V. 71
Bibliophobia. London: 1832. V. 71
An Introduction to the Knowledge of Rare and Valuable Editions of the Greek and Latin Classics.... London: 1804. V. 68; 70; 73
The Library Companion; or, the Young Man's Guide and Comfort, in the Choice of a Library. London: 1824. V. 70
The Library Companion; or the Young Man's Guide and the Old Man's Comfort, in the Choice of a Library. London: 1825. V. 71; 72
Reminiscences of a Literary Life. London: 1836. V. 70; 71
The Reminiscences of Thomas Dibdin, of the Theatres Royal Covent Garden, Drury Lane, Haymarket &c.... London: 1827. V. 71
The Vicar of Wakefield: A Melo-Dramatic Burletta.... London: 1817. V. 71

DIBNER, BERN
Heralds of Science as Represented by Two Hundred Epochal Books and Pamphlets Selected from the Burndy Library. Norwalk: 1955. V. 72

DICEY, EDWARD
The Peasant State. London: 1894. V. 71; 73

DICK, PHILIP K.
Confessions of a Crap Artist. London: 1979. V. 68
Do Androids Dream of Electric Sheep?. Garden City: 1968. V. 70; 72
Flow My Tears, the Policeman Said. Garden City: 1974. V. 68; 69; 73
The Golden Man. New York: 1980. V. 68; 71; 72
A Handful of Darkness. London: 1955. V. 68; 70
The Man Who Japed. London: 1978. V. 69
Mary and the Giant. New York: 1987. V. 72
A Maze of Death. London: 1972. V. 73
A Maze of Death. 1977. V. 68
Now Wait for Last Year. Garden City: 1966. V. 69
The Preserving Machine and Other Stories. London: 1969. V. 73
Radio Free Albemuth. New York: 1985. V. 68
Solar Lottery. New York: 1955. V. 68; 73
The Transmigration of Timothy Archer. New York: 1982. V. 72
Ubik. London: 1970. V. 71
Valis. New York: 1981. V. 68
The Variable Man and Other Stories. New York: 1957. V. 72
The World Jones Made. New York: 1956. V. 68
The World Jones Made. London: 1968. V. 70

DICK, STEWART
The Cottage Homes of England. London: 1909. V. 73

DICK, THOMAS
On the Mental Illumination and Moral Improvement of Mankind. Glasgow: 1844. V. 71

DICK Whittington. Dundee: 1907. V. 70

DICK Whittington and His Cat. New York: 1881. V. 71

THE DICKENS Birthday Book. New York: 1882. V. 69

DICKENS, CHARLES
Address Delivered at the Birmingham and Midland Insitute, on the 27th September, 1869. Birmingham: 1869. V. 70
The Adventures of Oliver Twist. London: 1846. V. 73
American Notes. London: 1850. V. 68
American Notes. Avon: 1975. V. 72
American Notes for General Circulation. London: 1842. V. 68; 70
American Notes for General Circulation. New York: 1842. V. 68; 70
American Notes for General Circulation. London: 1843. V. 71
Barnaby Rudge. London: 1841. V. 70
Barnaby Rudge. Philadelphia: 1842. V. 70
Barnaby Rudge. London: 1845?. V. 70
Barnaby Rudge. London: 1870?. V. 70
The Battle of Life. London: 1846. V. 68; 70; 71; 72; 73
The Battle of Life. Leipzig: 1847. V. 68
Bentley's Miscellany. London: 1837. V. 68
Bleak House. London: 1853. V. 70; 72; 73
Bleak House. London: 1880?. V. 70
Bleak House. London: 1890?. V. 70
Captain Boldheart. London: 1948. V. 73
Charles Dickens and Maria Beadnell: Private Correspondence. Boston: 1908. V. 70
Charles Dickens and Maria Beadnell Private Correspondence. Cambridge: 1908. V. 69
Child-Pictures from Dickens. Boston: 1868. V. 69
Child-Pictures From Dickens. London: 1885. V. 72
The Child-Wife from the David Copperfield of Charles Dickens. New York: 1855. V. 68
Children's Stories from Dickens; retold by his Grand-daughter Mary Angela Dickens and Others. London: 1911. V. 73
A Child's Dream of a Star. London: 1899. V. 70
A Child's History of England. London: 1852-. V. 70
A Child's History of England. London: 1852-1854. V. 68
A Child's History of England. London: 1853-. V. 70
A Child's History of England. Leipzig: 1853-1854. V. 69; 70; 71
The Chimes. London: 1845. V. 70; 73
The Chimes. New York: 1911. V. 68
The Chimes. London: 1913. V. 70; 73
The Chimes. London: 1931. V. 69; 70; 72
The Chimes. New York: 1931. V. 70; 72
Christmas Books. 1843-1848. V. 73
The Christmas Books. London: 1843-1848. V. 70
Christmas Books. London: 1852. V. 70; 73
The Christmas Books. London: 1866. V. 68
Christmas Books. London: 1878. V. 70

DICKENS, CHARLES continued
Christmas Books and Uncommerical Traveller. Boston: 1844. V. 73
A Christmas Carol. Philadelphia. V. 70
A Christmas Carol. Leipzig: 1843. V. 70
A Christmas Carol. London: 1843. V. 68; 70; 72; 73
A Christmas Carol. Philadelphia: 1844. V. 71
A Christmas Carol. London: 1858. V. 68; 70
A Christmas Carol. Boston: 1869. V. 69
A Christmas Carol. London: 1911. V. 71
A Christmas Carol. London: 1915. V. 70; 72
A Christmas Carol. London: 1922. V. 70
A Christmas Carol. Boston: 1934. V. 69; 73
A Christmas Carol. New York: 1967. V. 68
A Christmas Carol. New York: 1971. V. 70
A Christmas Carol in Prose; The Chimes; The Cricket on the Hearth. Leipzig: 1846. V. 70
Tre Julhistorier. (A Christmas Carol). Stockholm. V. 68
Christmas Numbers 1858-1865. London: 1858-1865. V. 68
Christmas Stories from Household Words and All the Year Round. London: 1876. V. 70
Christmas Stories from Household Words and All the Year Round. London: 1880. V. 70
Christmas Stories from Household Words and all the Year Round 1852-1867. London: 1852-1867. V. 73
The Complete Works. London: 1901-1907. V. 70
Count Ludwig and other Romances. New York: 1845. V. 68
The Cricket on the Hearth. London. V. 68
The Cricket on the Hearth. London: 1845. V. 70
The Cricket on the Hearth. Boston: 1846. V. 68
The Cricket on the Hearth. London: 1846. V. 70; 71
The Cricket on the Hearth. New York: 1846. V. 68
The Cricket on the Hearth. New York: 1927. V. 70
The Cricket on the Hearth. Waltham St. Lawrence: 1933. V. 73
A Curious Dance Round a Curious Tree. London: 1860. V. 70
Dealings with The Firm of Dombey and Son. London: 1848. V. 73
The Dickens - Kolle Letters. Cambridge: 1910. V. 69
Dickens to His Oldest Friend. The Letters of a Lifetime from Charles Dickens to Thomas Beard. London and New York: 1932. V. 69
Dickens' Working Notes for His Novels. Chicago: 1987. V. 70
Doctor Marigold's Prescriptions. London: 1865. V. 68
Dombey and Son. Leipzig: 1847-1848. V. 70
Dombey and Son. London: 1848. V. 68; 70; 71; 72
Dombey and Son. London: 1858. V. 70
Dombey and Son. London: 1859. V. 70
Dombey and Son. London: 1865. V. 70
Dombey and Son. London: 1870. V. 70
Dombey and Son. London: 1880. V. 70
Dombey and Son. (with) Barnaby Rudge. Philadelphia: 1848-1850. V. 70
Drawn from Life. Sketches of Young Ladies, Young Gentlemen and Young Couples. New York: 1875. V. 70
The Earliest Letters of Charles Dickens (Written to His Friend Henry Kolle). Cambridge: 1910. V. 70
Edwin Drood. London: 1870. V. 70
Edwin Drood. London: 1872. V. 70
Edwin Drood. Brattleboro: 1873. V. 70
Edwin Drood. London: 1873?. V. 70
Epilogue. Philadelphia: 1934. V. 71
The Fireside Dickens. (Works). London: 1903-1907. V. 70
Florence Dombey from the Dombey and Son of Charles Dickens. New York: 1855. V. 71
Gone Astray. London: 1912. V. 68
Great Expectations. Leipzig: 1861. V. 70
Great Expectations. London: 1861. V. 68; 70; 73
Great Expectations. Boston: 1862. V. 68
Great Expectations. London: 1862. V. 70; 73
Great Expectations. London: 1864. V. 70
Great Expectations. London: 1866. V. 70
Great Expectations. London: 1876. V. 70
Great Expectations. New York: 1876. V. 70
Great Expectations. London: 1885. V. 70
Great Expectations. Oxford: 1993. V. 70
Hard Times. New York: 1854. V. 68
Hard Times for These Times. London: 1854. V. 70; 72
The Haunted Man and the Ghost's Bargain. London: 1848. V. 70; 71; 73
The Haunted Man. (with) The Ghost's Bargain. New York: 1849. V. 68
The Holly Tree. East Aurora: 1903. V. 69
The Holly-Tree Inn. London: 1855. V. 68
Home and Social Philosophy; or, Chapters on Every-Day Topics. New York: 1852. V. 69; 73
The Household Narrative of Current Events 1850. London: 1850. V. 68
The Household Narrative of Current Events 1854. London: 1854. V. 68
Household Words. London: 1850-1859. V. 68; 71
(Household Words) Charles Dickens' Uncollected Writings from Household Words 1850-1859. Bloomington: 1968. V. 70
(Household Words) The Uncollected Writings of Charles Dickens: Household Words 1850-1859. London: 1969. V. 70
Hunted Down: A Story. Leipzig: 1860. V. 72
Hunted Down; A Story. London: 1871. V. 70
Immortelles from Charles Dickens. London: 1856. V. 70
Journalism. London: 1994-2000. V. 70

The Lamplighter. London: 1879. V. 70
The Lamplighter's Story; Hunted Down; The Detective Police; and Other Nouvellettes. Philadelphia: 1861. V. 68
The Lazy Tour of Two Idle Apprentices. No Thoroughfare. The Perils of Certain English Prisoners. London: 1890. V. 70
The Letters of Charles Dickens. Oxford. V. 70
The Letters of Charles Dickens. London: 1880-1882. V. 70
Letters of Charles Dickens to Wilkie Collins 1851-1870. London: 1892. V. 69
The Life and Adventures of Martin Chuzzlewit. London: 1843-1844. V. 70
The Life and Adventures of Martin Chuzzlewit. Leipzig: 1844. V. 70
The Life and Adventures of Martin Chuzzlewit. London: 1844. V. 68; 70; 71
The Life and Adventures of Martin Chuzzlewit. Paris: 1844. V. 70
The Life and Adventures of Martin Chuzzlewit. Philadelphia: 1844. V. 70
The Life and Adventures of Martin Chuzzlewit. London: 1857. V. 70
The Life and Adventures of Martin Chuzzlewit. London: 1863. V. 70
The Life and Adventures of Martin Chuzzlewit. London: 1870. V. 70
The Life and Adventures of Martin Chuzzlewit. London: 1891. V. 70
The Life and Adventures of Martin Chuzzlewit. London: 1912. V. 70
The Life and Adventures of Martin Chuzzlewit. Oxford: 1982. V. 70
The Life and Adventures Of Nicholas Nickleby. London: 1838-1839. V. 70
The Life and Adventures Of Nicholas Nickleby. London: 1839. V. 68; 70; 72; 73
The Life and Adventures of Nicholas Nickleby. Paris: 1839. V. 70
The Life and Adventures of Nicholas Nickleby. Philadelphia: 1839. V. 68
The Life and Adventures Of Nicholas Nickleby. Leipzig: 1839-1840. V. 70
The Life and Adventures Of Nicholas Nickleby. London: 1848. V. 70
The Life and Adventures Of Nicholas Nickleby. London: 1850. V. 70
The Life and Adventures Of Nicholas Nickleby. London: 1854. V. 70
The Life and Adventures Of Nicholas Nickleby. London: 1863. V. 70
The Life and Adventures Of Nicholas Nickleby. London: 1875. V. 70
The Life and Adventures Of Nicholas Nickleby. London: 1880. V. 70
The Life Of Our Lord. London: 1897. V. 72
The Life of Our Lord. London: 1934. V. 68; 70; 71; 72; 73
The Life of Our Lord. New York: 1934. V. 68
Little Dorrit. London: 1855-1857. V. 68; 70
Little Dorrit. London: 1857. V. 68; 70; 73
Little Dorrit. London: 1863. V. 70
Little Dorrit. London: 1865. V. 70
Little Dorrit. London: 1870. V. 70
Little Dorrit. London: 1880. V. 70
Little Dorrit. Bloomsbury: 1937. V. 70
Little Dorrit. Oxford: 1979. V. 70
Little Nell, from the Old Curiosity Shop. New York: 1855. V. 68
The Love Romance of Charles Dickens. Told in His Letters to Maria Beadnell (Mrs. Winter). London: 1936. V. 69
The Loving Ballad of Lord Bateman. London: 1839. V. 70
The Loving Ballad of Lord Bateman. New York: 1839. V. 70
The Loving Ballad of Lord Bateman. London: 1851. V. 70
Master Humphrey's Clock. London: 1840-1841. V. 68; 70; 72; 73
Master Humphrey's Clock. Calcutta: 1841-1842. V. 70
A Message from the Sea. London: 1860. V. 68
Mr. and Mrs. Charles Dickens. His Letters to Her. London: 1935. V. 69
Mr. Nightingale's Diary. Boston: 1877. V. 68; 70
Mr. Pickwick. London. V. 71
Mr. Pickwick. London: 1911. V. 68
Mrs. Lirriper's Legacy. London: 1864. V. 68
Mrs. Lirriper's Lodgings. London: 1863. V. 68
The Mudfog Papers. London: 1880. V. 70
Mugby Junction. London: 1866. V. 68; 70
The Mystery of Edwin Drood. London: 1870. V. 69; 73
The Mystery of Edwin Drood. Brattleboro: 1873. V. 68
No Thoroughfare. London: 1867. V. 70
The Nonesuch Dickens. 1937-1938. V. 73
The Nonesuch Dickens. Bloomsbury: 1937-1938. V. 69; 70; 72
The Old Curiosity Shop. London. V. 71
The Old Curiosity Shop. Philadelphia: 1841. V. 68
The Old Curiosity Shop. London: 1848. V. 68
The Old Curiosity Shop. Philadelphia: 1853. V. 70
The Old Curiosity Shop. London: 1870?. V. 70
The Old Curiosity Shop. Oxford: 1997. V. 70
Oliver and the Jew Fagin. New York: 1855. V. 68
Oliver Twist. London: 1838. V. 68; 70; 71; 73
Oliver Twist. London: 1838-1839. V. 72
Oliver Twist. London: 1839. V. 70
Oliver Twist. Paris: 1839. V. 70
Oliver Twist. London: 1841. V. 70
Oliver Twist. New York: 1842. V. 70
Oliver Twist. London: 1846. V. 68; 70; 71
Oliver Twist. London: 1877. V. 70
Oliver Twist. London: 1890?. V. 70
Oliver Twist. Oxford: 1966. V. 70
Oliver Twist. (with) Edwin Drood. London: 1870. V. 70
Our Mutual Friend. London: 1864. V. 68
Our Mutual Friend. London: 1864-1865. V. 70
Our Mutual Friend. London: 1865. V. 70
Our Mutual Friend. New York: 1865. V. 70

DICKENS, CHARLES continued
Our Mutual Friend. Philadelphia: 1865. V. 68
Our Mutual Friend. London: 1870. V. 70
Our Mutual Friend. Bloomsbury: 1938. V. 70
Pearl Fishing: Second Series. Auburn and Buffalo: 1854. V. 71
Pearl Fishing: Second Series. Auburn and Rochester: 1854. V. 71
The Personal History of David Copperfield. London: 1849. V. 68
The Personal History of David Copperfield. Leipzig: 1849-1850. V. 70
The Personal History of David Copperfield. London: 1850. V. 68; 70; 71; 73
The Personal History of David Copperfield. London: 1859. V. 70; 73
The Personal History of David Copperfield. London: 1912. V. 68
The Personal History of David Copperfield. London: 1921. V. 70
La Petite Dorrit. Paris: 1858. V. 70
The Pic-Nic Papers. London: 1841. V. 68; 70
The Pic-Nic Papers. Philadelphia: 1841. V. 68
The Pic-Nic Papers. London: 1870?. V. 70
Pickwick Papers. London: 1837. V. 71; 73
Pictures from Italy. Leipzig: 1846. V. 70
Pictures from Italy. London: 1846. V. 68; 70; 71; 72
Pictures from Italy. Paris: 1846. V. 70
The Plays and Poems. London: 1882. V. 68
The Plays and Poems. London: 1885. V. 70
The Poems and Verses of Charles Dickens. London: 1903. V. 73
The Poor Traveller; Boots At the Holly Tree Inn; and Mrs. Gamp. London: 1858. V. 68; 70
The Posthumous Papers of the Pickwick Club. London: 1836-1837. V. 70
The Posthumous Papers of the Pickwick Club. London: 1837. V. 68; 70; 73
Posthumous Papers of the Pickwick Club. Philadelphia: 1837. V. 68; 70
The Posthumous Papers of the Pickwick Club. London: 1837-1870. V. 70
Posthumous Papers of the Pickwick Club. New York/London: 1838. V. 68; 70
The Posthumous Papers of the Pickwick Club. Philadelphia: 1838. V. 70
The Posthumous Papers of the Pickwick Club. London: 1842. V. 70
The Posthumous Papers of the Pickwick Club. New York: 1842. V. 70
The Posthumous Papers of the Pickwick Club. Philadelphia: 1846. V. 70
The Posthumous Papers of the Pickwick Club. London: 1856. V. 70
The Posthumous Papers of the Pickwick Club. London: 1866. V. 70
The Posthumous Papers of the Pickwick Club. London: 1870. V. 70
The Posthumous Papers of the Pickwick Club. London: 1875. V. 70
The Posthumous Papers of the Pickwick Club. London: 1883?. V. 70
The Posthumous Papers of the Pickwick Club. London: 1887. V. 68
The Posthumous Papers of the Pickwick Club. London: 1910. V. 68; 70; 71; 73
Posthumous Papers of the Pickwick Club. London: 1932. V. 68; 70
Selections from Household Worlds, a Weekly Journal. New York: 1859-1864. V. 68
The Short Stories of Charles Dickens. New York: 1971. V. 68
Sikes and Nancy. A Reading. London: 1921. V. 69
Sketches by Boz. London: 1836. V. 68; 70
Sketches by Boz. London: 1837. V. 70
Sketches by Boz. Paris: 1839. V. 70
Sketches by Boz. Philadelphia: 1839. V. 68
Sketches by Boz. London: 1850. V. 68
Sketches by Boz. London: 1863. V. 70
Sketches by Boz. London: 1867. V. 70
Sketches by Boz. London: 1874. V. 70
Sketches by Boz. London: 1936. V. 68
Sketches by Boz and Early Minor Works. Bloomsbury: 1938. V. 70
(Sketches by Boz). The Tuggs's at Ramsgate, and Other Sketches Illustrative of Every Day Life...To Which is added the Pantomime of Life. Philadelphia: 1837. V. 70
Sketches of Young Couples. London: 1840. V. 68; 70
Sketches of Young Couples, Young Ladies, Young Gentlemen. London: 1869. V. 70
Sketches of Young Gentlemen. London: 1838. V. 70
Speech of Charles Dickens, Esq. As Chairman at the Dinner on Behalf of the Hospital for Sick Children, February 9th, 1858. London: 1874. V. 69
Speech of Charles Dickens, Esq. Delivered at the Meeting of the Administrative Reform Association, at the Theatre Royal, Drury Lane, Wednesday June 27, 1855. London: 1855. V. 70
Speeches Literary and Social. London: 1870. V. 70
Speeches Literary and Social. London: 1871. V. 70
Speeches Literary and Social. London: 1874. V. 70
The Speeches of Charles Dickens. Oxford: 1960. V. 69; 70
The Speeches of Charles Dickens (1841-1870). London: 1884. V. 69
The Story of Little Dombey. London: 1858. V. 70
The Strange Gentleman. London: 1837. V. 70
The Strange Gentleman. London: 1871. V. 70
The Strange Gentleman. 1928. V. 68
Sunday Under Three Heads. London. V. 73
Sunday Under Three Heads. London: 1836. V. 70
Sunday Under Three Heads. London: 1884. V. 70
A Tale of Two Cities. London: 1859. V. 68; 70; 73
A Tale of Two Cities. Philadelphia: 1859. V. 68
A Tale of Two Cities. London: 1860. V. 70
A Tale of Two Cities. London: 1866. V. 70
A Tale of Two Cities. London: 1880. V. 70
To Be Read At Dusk. And Other Stories, Sketches and Essays. Now First Collected. London: 1898. V. 68
The Uncommercial Traveller. London: 1861. V. 70
The Uncommercial Traveller. London: 1880?. V. 70
The Unpublished Letters of Charles Dickens to Mark Lemon. London: 1927. V. 69; 72
The Village Coquettes. London: 1836. V. 68; 70
The Village Coquettes. London: 1878. V. 70
The Village Coquettes. London: 1883?. V. 70
Der Weihnachtsabend. (A Christmas Carol). Zurich: 1918. V. 71
Works. Philadelphia: 1846. V. 69
Works. London: 1858-1859. V. 70
The Works. New York: 1872-1877. V. 70
Works. London: 1874-1876. V. 69; 70; 73
Works. New York: 1879. V. 70
Works. Chicago and New York: 1880. V. 69
Works. London: 1885?. V. 70
Works. London: 1890-1891. V. 70
Works. London: 1899. V. 68; 70
The Works. London: 1899-1901. V. 70
Works. London: 1900. V. 70
The Works. London: 1905?. V. 70
The Works. London: 1906-1908. V. 70
Works. 1930. V. 70
The World Here and There; or Notes of Traveller. New York: 1852. V. 68
The Wreck of the Golden Mary. London: 1856. V. 68

A DICKENS Library: the Sawyer Collection. Letchworth: 1936. V. 68

DICKENS, MARY ANGELA
Children's Stories from Dickens: re-told by His Grand-Daughter. London: 1911. V. 70

DICKENSHEET, DEAN
An Undiscerning Critic Discerned. San Francisco: 1968. V. 69

DICKENSON, J.
The Flora of Liverpool. London: 1851. V. 69

DICKENSON, JONATHAN
God's Protecting Providence, Man's Surest Help and Defence in Times of Greatest Difficulty.... London: 1787. V. 73

DICKENSON, MRS.
Historical Pictures of Pagan and Christian Rome. Addressed to Strangers. Rome: 1855. V. 69

DICKERSON, EDWARD N.
The Steam Engine: Its Principles: Its Development; Its Present Condition; and Its Future Perfection. New York: 1889. V. 70

DICKERSON, PHILIP
History of the Osage Nation, Its People, Resources and Prospects. 1906. V. 70

DICKERSON, R. E.
Fauna of the Martinez Eocene of California. Berkeley: 1914. V. 68

DICKES, WILLIAM
The Babes in the Wood. London: 1863. V. 69

DICKEY, D. R.
The Birds of El Salvador. Chicago: 1938. V. 70

DICKEY, JAMES
Babel to Byzantium: Poets and Poetry Now. New York: 1968. V. 68
Deliverance. Boston: 1970. V. 68; 69; 70; 71
The Eye-Beaters, Blood, Victory, Madness, Buckhead and Mercy. Garden City: 1970. V. 73
Helmets. Middletown: 1964. V. 71
The Owl King. New York: 1977. V. 72
Poems 1957-1967. Middletown: 1967. V. 70
Tucky the Hunter. New York: 1978. V. 68
The Zodiac. New York: 1976. V. 70

DICKEY, ROLAND F.
New Mexico Village Arts. Albuquerque: 1949. V. 69; 72

DICKEY, WILLIAM
Rivers of the Pacific Northwest. San Francisco: 1969. V. 71

THE DICKIE Birdie Book. London: 1916. V. 69

DICKIE, J. F.
Germany. London: 1912. V. 72

DICKINS, RICHARD
Forty Years of Shakespeare on the English Stage, August 1867 to August 1907. 1907. V. 71

DICKINSON, ANNA ELIZABETH
What Answer?. Boston: 1868. V. 73

DICKINSON, C. H.
Biology of Plant Litter Decompositions. London: 1974. V. 72

DICKINSON, CHARLES
Waltz in Marathon. New York: 1983. V. 72

DICKINSON, EMILY ELIZABETH
Bolts of Melody - New Poems. New York and London: 1945. V. 71
Further Poems. London: 1929. V. 71
Further Poems of Emily Dickinson with-held from publication by her sister Lavinia. Boston: 1929. V. 71; 72; 73
Letters of Emily Dickinson. Boston: 1894. V. 68; 71
Poems. Boston: 1891. V. 71

DICKINSON, EMILY ELIZABETH continued
Poems. Boston: 1895. V. 68
Poems. (and) Poems Second Series. (and) Poems Third Series. Boston: 1890-1896. V. 73
Poems. Second Series. Boston: 1891. V. 72
Poems: Second Series. Boston: 1892. V. 71
Two Poems by Emily Dickinson. New York: 1968. V. 72

DICKINSON, I. W.
Yorkshire Life and Character. Hull: 1894. V. 73

DICKINSON, JOHN
Letters from a Farmer in Pennsylvania. Boston: 1768. V. 72
Letters from a Farmer in Pennsylvania. Philadelphia: 1768. V. 70
A New Essay (by the Pennsylvania Farmer) on the Constitutional Power of Great Britain Over the Colonies in America. Philadelphia: 1774. V. 73

DICKINSON, JONATHAN
Familiar Letters to a Gentleman, Upon a Variety of Seasonable and Important Subjects in Religion. Newark: 1797. V. 69

DICKINSON, PATRIC
Soldier's Verse. London: 1945. V. 72

DICKINSON, PETER
A Pride of Heroes. 1969. V. 70

DICKINSON, ROBERT LATOU
A Topographical Hand Atlas - Human Sex Anatomy. Baltimore: 1949. V. 68

DICKINSON, WILLIAM
Cumbriana or Fragments of Cumbrian Life. London: 1875. V. 71
Cumbriana or Fragments of Cumbrian Life. London: 1876. V. 71
Uncollected Literary Remains of William Dickinson.... Carlisle: 1888. V. 71

DICKSEE, J. R.
The School Perspective: Being a Progressive Course of Instruction in Linear Perspective Both Theoretical and Practical. London: 1859. V. 71

DICKSON, ALBERT JEROME
Covered Wagon Days: a Journey Across the Plains in the Sixties, and Pioneer Days in the Northwest, from the Private Journals of Albert Jerome Dickson. Cleveland: 1929. V. 71

DICKSON, CARTER
And So to Murder. New York: 1940. V. 70; 71
Behind the Crimson Blind. New York: 1952. V. 70
Behind the Crimson Curtain. London: 1952. V. 71
The Cavalier's Cup. New York: 1953. V. 70
The Cavalier's Cup. London: 1954. V. 70
The Curse of the Bronze Lamp. New York: 1945. V. 70
Death in Five Boxes. New York: 1938. V. 70
The Department of Queer Complaints. New York: 1940. V. 70
Fatal Descent. New York: 1939. V. 70
Fear Is The Same. 1956. V. 70
The Gilded Man. New York: 1942. V. 70; 71; 73
A Graveyard to Let. London: 1950. V. 71
He Wouldn't Kill Patience. New York: 1944. V. 70
The Judas Window. New York: 1938. V. 70
Lord of the Sorcerers. London: 1946. V. 71
My Late Wives. New York: 1946. V. 70
My Late Wives. London: 1947. V. 69; 71; 73
Night at the Mocking Widow. New York: 1950. V. 70
Nine and Death Makes Ten. New York: 1940. V. 69; 70
The Peacock Feather Murders. New York: 1937. V. 70
The Plague Court Murders. New York: 1934. V. 70; 71
The Reader is Warned. New York: 1939. V. 70
Seeing is Believing. New York: 1941. V. 70
She Died a Lady. New York: 1943. V. 70
The Skeleton in the Clock. New York: 1948. V. 70; 73
The Unicorn Murders. New York: 1935. V. 70
The White Priory Murders. New York: 1944. V. 71

DICKSON, F. A.
Plantation Sermons, or Plain and Familiar Discourses for the Instruction of the Unlearned. Philadelphia: 1856. V. 71

DICKSON, ROBERT
Introduction of the Art of Printing into Scotland. Aberdeen: 1885. V. 70; 71

DICKSON, W. E. CARNEGIE
The Bone-Marrow - A Cytological Study Forming an Introduction to the Normal Histology of the Tissue, More Especially with Regard to Blood Formation, Blood Destruction, etc. London: 1908. V. 68

THE DICTES and Sayings of the Philosophers. 1901. V. 70

DICTIONARY of National Biography. London: 1885-1912. V. 72

A DICTIONARY Of Painters, Sculptors, Architects and Engravers, Containing Biographical Sketches of the Most Celebrated Artists.... 1810. V. 73

DICTIONARY of the Chinook Jargon, or Indian Trade Language of the North Pacific Coast. Victoria: 1887. V. 68

A DICTIONARY of the Holy Bible.... London: 1759. V. 72

THE DICTIONARY of Trade, Commerce and Navigation.... London: 1844. V. 71

DICTIONNAIRE Militaire Encyclopedie des Sciences Militaires... Supplement General. Paris: 1911. V. 72

DICTYS CRETENSIS
De Bello Troiano Historia. Lyon: 1552. V. 73

DIDAY, P.
A Treatise on Syphillis on New-Born Children and Infants at the Breast. London: 1859. V. 71

DIDEROT, DENIS
Les Bijous Indiscrets. Paris: 1748?. V. 69

DIDION, JOAN
After Henry. New York: 1992. V. 72
A Book of Common Prayer. New York: 1977. V. 72
A Book of Common Prayer. Franklin Center: 1981. V. 70; 72
Democracy. New York: 1984. V. 72
Essays and Conversations. Princeton: 1984. V. 69
The Last Thing He Wanted. New York: 1996. V. 70; 72
Play It As It Lays. New York: 1970. V. 68; 69; 73
Run River. New York: 1963. V. 69; 70
Salvador. New York: 1982. V. 71
Salvador. New York: 1983. V. 68; 72
Slouching Towards Bethlehem. New York: 1968. V. 70; 71; 73
Some Women. Boston: 1989. V. 70
Telling Stories. Berkeley: 1978. V. 69
The White Album. New York: 1979. V. 72

DIEBERT, RALPH C.
A History of The Third United States Cavalry 1846-1937. Harrisburg. V. 72

DIEHL, EDITH
Bookbinding: Its Background and Technique. New York and Toronto: 1946. V. 68; 70; 72; 73

DIEHL, WILLIAM
Sharkey's Machine. New York: 1978. V. 68; 69; 70; 71; 73

DIEMBERGER, KURT
Summits and Secrets. 1971. V. 71; 73
Summits and Secrets. London: 1971. V. 69

DIENES, ANDRE DE
The Nude. New York: 1956. V. 68

DIES, MARTIN
The Trojan Horse in America. A Report to the Nation. New York: 1940. V. 68

DIETRICH, LUC
Terre. 1936. V. 70

DIETRICK, ELLEN BATTELLE
Women in the Early Christian Ministry, a Reply to Bishop Doane and Others. Philadelphia: 1897. V. 73

DIETTERLIN, WENDEL
Architectura von Austheilung. Symmetria and Proportion der Funff seulen. Nuremberg: 1655. V. 69

DIETZ, AUGUST
The Postal Service of the Confederate States of America. Richmond: 1929. V. 69

DIFFICULTIES On Southwestern Frontier, 36th Congress, 1st Session. Washington: 1860. V. 70

DIGBY, BASSETT
The Mammoth and Mammoth Hunting in North East Siberia. London: 1926. V. 68; 72
Tigers, Gold and Witch-Doctors. 1928. V. 69; 70; 72

DIGBY, GEORGE
Baseball for Boys. Chicago: 1960. V. 71

DIGBY, KENELM
The Closet of the Eminently Learned Sir Keneleme Digby Kt. Opened Whereby Is Discovered Several Ways for Making of Metheglin, Sider, Cherry Wine &c. Together With Excellent Directions for Cookery.... London: 1671. V. 69
Of Bodies and of Mans Soul. To Discover the Immortality of Reasonable Souls. With Two Discourses of the Powder of Sympathy and Of the Vegetation of Plants. LondonLondon: 1669. V. 71
Two Treatises: In the One of Which, The Nature of Bodies, in the Other, the Nature of Man's Soule is Looked Into.... Paris: 1644. V. 68; 72

DIGBY, KENELM HENRY
The Broad Stone Of Honour. London: 1923. V. 72

DIGGES, DUDLEY
The Compleat Ambassador; or Two Treaties of the Intended Marriage of Qu. Elizabeth...Comprised in Letters of Negociation of Sir Francis Walsingham...Together with the Answers of Lord Burleigh, the Earl of Leicester, Sir Tho. Smith and others.... London: 1655. V. 70; 72
The Unlawfulness of Subjects Taking Up Arms Against Their Soveraigne, in What Case Soever. London: 1679. V. 71
The Unlawfulnesse of Subjects Taking Up Armes Against Their Soveraigne in What Case Soever.... London: 1647. V. 70

DIGHTON, CONWAY
The Dightons Of Clifford Chambers And Their Descendants. London: 1902. V. 72

DIGNAM, C. B.
Black Velvet. London. V. 73

DILKE, CHARLES WENTWORTH
The Fall of Prince Florestan of Monaco, by Himself. London: 1874. V. 70
Problems of Greater Britain. London: 1890. V. 70; 71; 72

DILKE, EMILIA
French Engravers and Draughtsmen of the XVIIIth Century. London: 1902. V. 68

DILL, CLARENCE C.
Radio Law: Practice and Procedure. Washington: 1938. V. 70

DILL, DAVID BRUCE
Life, Heat and Altitude. Physiological Effects of Hot Climates and Great Heights. Cambridge: 1938. V. 68

DILL, R. G.
The Political Campaigns of Colorado, with Complete Tabulated Statements of the Official Vote. Denver: 1895. V. 70

DILL, SAMUEL
Roman Society in the Last Century of the Western Empire. London: 1898. V. 70

DILLARD, ANNIE
An American Childhood. New York: 1987. V. 69
Encounters With Chinese Writers. Middletown: 1984. V. 72
Holy the Firm. New York: 1977. V. 68; 70
Holy the Firm. New York: 1997. V. 73
Living by Fiction. New York: 1982. V. 72
Pilgrim at Tinker Creek. New York: 1974. V. 68; 70
Teaching a Stone to Talk. New York: 1982. V. 68
Tickets for a Prayer Wheel. Columbia: 1974. V. 69; 70; 71
The Writing Life. New York: 1989. V. 68

DILLARD, RICHARD
The Civil War in Chowan County, North Carolina. 1916. V. 69; 70

DILLEN, FREDERICK
Hero. South Royalton: 1994. V. 68

DILLEY, A. U.
Oriental Rugs and Carpets: a Comprehensive Study. New York and London: 1931. V. 69; 72

DILLON, EDWARD
Porcelain. London: 1904. V. 73

DILLON, JOHN B.
Notes on the Historical Evidence in Reference to Adverse Theories of the Origin and Nature of the Government of the USA. New York: 1871. V. 70

DILLON, JOHN JOSEPH
The Question, as to the Admission of Catholics to Parliament, Considered Upon the Principles of Existing Laws. London: 1801. V. 69

DILLON, JOHN TALBOT
Historical and Critical Memoirs of the General Revolution in France, in the Year 1789.... London: 1790. V. 73

DILLON, MYLES
The Celtic Realms. 1967. V. 69

DILLON, RICHARD
California Trail Herd. The 1850 Missouri to California. Journal of Cyrus C. Loveland. Los Gatos: 1961. V. 68
Images of Chinatown. San Francisco: 1976. V. 73
Maynard Dixon or from Coronado to Carion de Chelly, Artist-Illustrato r Maynard Dixon. San Francisco: 1976. V. 73
Texas Argonauts: Isaac H. Duval and the California Gold Rush. 1987. V. 70

DILLWYN, GEORGE
Gathered Fragments: Briefly Illustrative of the Life of George Dillwyn of Burlington, West New Jersey, North America. London: 1858. V. 69
Occasional Reflections, Offered Principally for the Use of Schools. Burlington: 1815. V. 69

DILNOT, GEORGE
The Black Ace. Boston: 1929. V. 71

DILWORTH, THOMAS
The Schoolmasters Assistant. London: 1787. V. 69
The Schoolmaster's Assistant. Philadelphia: 1805. V. 69
The Young Bookkepper's Assistant.... 1815. V. 71

DILWORTH, W. H.
The Life and Heroick Actions of Frederick III, King of Prussia. London: 1758. V. 73

DIMITRY, ADELAIDE STUART
War-Time Sketches, Historical and Otherwise. New Orleans: 1913. V. 69; 70

DIMOCK, A. W.
Florida Enchantments. London: 1909. V. 72

DIMOCK, J. F.
Illustrations of the Collegiate Church of Southwell (Notts) in a Series of Ten Views in Tinted Lithography from Drawings by E. H. Buckler, with an Architectural Description. London: 1854. V. 70; 72

DIMSDALE, JOHN
Sketches at the Colonial and Indian Exhibition. Middlesborough: 1886. V. 71

DIMSDALE, THOMAS
The Present Method of Inoculating for the Small Pox. London: 1767. V. 68

DINE, JIM
Nancy Outside in July: Etchings. West Islip: 1983. V. 69; 72

DINESEN, ISAK
Anecdotes of Destiny. New York: 1958. V. 69; 73
The Angelic Avengers. London: 1946. V. 70
Last Tales. New York: 1957. V. 68; 73
Last Tales. London: 1967. V. 70
Out of Africa. New York: 1938. V. 69; 70; 71; 72
Seven Gothic Tales. New York: 1934. V. 72; 73
Shadows on the Grass. New York: 1960. V. 73
Winter's Tale. New York: 1942. V. 70; 73

DING, S.
Art of Folk Carving. Taipei: 1993. V. 69

DINGMAN, LARRY
Booksellers Marks: an Illustrated Book. Minneapolis: 1986. V. 68

DINGWALL, ERIC JOHN
The Girdle of Chastity; a Medico-Historical Study. London: 1931. V. 68

DINNING, HECTOR
Nile to Aleppo with the Light Horse in the Middle East. London: 1920. V. 70

DINSDALE, ALFRED
First Principles of Television. London: 1932. V. 72

DINSDALE, FREDERICK P.
A Glossary of Provincial Words Used in Teesdale in the County of Durham. 1849. V. 73

DINSDALE, JANET M.
History of the Church and Parish of Saint Andres, Gargrave. London: 1966. V. 73

DINWIDDIE County: *The Country of the Apamatica.* Richmond: 1942. V. 68

DINWOODIE, HEPBURN
Storms on the Labrador. London: 1938. V. 72

DIODORUS SICULUS
Bibliothecae Historicae Libri XVII. Lyon: 1552. V. 73
Delle Antiche Historie Favolose. Venice: 1547. V. 73
Opera. Basileae: 1531. V. 73

DIONIS, PIERRE
Cours D'Operations de Chirurgie. De Montre-es au jardin Royal. Paris: 1740. V. 68; 72

DIONIS DE SEJOUR, MLLE.
Origine des Graces Par.... Paris: 1777. V. 73

DI PESO, CHARLES C.
Casas Grandes - a Fallen Trading Center of the Grand Chicimeca. Flagstaff: 1974. V. 70
The Reeve Ruin of Southeastern Arizona - a Study of a Prehistoric Western Pueblo Migration into Middle San Pedro Valley. Dragoon: 1958. V. 68; 69; 73

DIPLOCK, BRAMAH JOSEPH
A New System of Heavy Goods Transport on Common Roads. London: 1902. V. 72

DIPPIE, BRIAN W.
Remington and Russell. The Sid Richardson Collection. Austin: 1982. V. 69

DIPROSE, JOHN
Diprose's Book of the Stage and the Players. London: 1877. V. 70

DIRAC, PAUL ADRIAN MAURICE
The physical interpretation of the quatum dynamics In Proceedings of the Royal Society, Series A, Volume 11, No. A 765, January I, 1927. London: 1927. V. 72
The quantum theory of dispersion. London: 1927. V. 72
The quantum theory of the electron. In Proceedings of the Royal Society, Series A, Volume 117, No. A 778, February 1, 1928. London: 1928. V. 72

DIRCKS, HENRY
Contribution Towards a History of Electro-Metallurgy, Establishing the Origin of the Art. London: 1863. V. 69
The Life, Times and Scientific Labours of the Second Marquis of Worcester. London: 1865. V. 70; 72

DIRCKS, RUDOLF
Sir Christopher Wren A.D. 1632-1723. London: 1923. V. 72

DIRECTORY of Carroll County Iowa. Minneapolis: 1884. V. 69

DIRECTORY of New Brunswick, also Milltown, South River, Sayreville, South Amboy, Piscataway, Bonhamtown, Metuchen, Raritan River Road, Bound Brook. 1901-1902. New Brunswick: 1901. V. 72

DIRECTORY of Newark for 1835-1836. Newark: 1835. V. 72

DIRECTORY of the City of Newark for 1838-1839. Newark: 1838. V. 72

DIRECTORY of the City of Newark for 1840-1841. Newark: 1840. V. 72

DIRECTORY of the City of Newark for 1841-1842, with a Historical Sketch. Newark: 1841. V. 72

DIRECTORY of the City of Newark for 1844-1845. Newark: 1844. V. 72

DIRECTORY of the City of Newark for 1849-1850. Newark: 1849. V. 72

DIRECTORY of the City of Newark, for 1853-1854. Newark: 1853. V. 72

DIRECTORY of the City of Newark, for 1857-1858. Newark: 1857. V. 72

DIRECTORY of the City of Newark, for 1858-1859. Newark: 1858. V. 72

DIRECTORY of Tobacco Men in the United States. New York: 1867. V. 73

DIROM, ALEXANDER
An Inquiry Into the Corn Laws and Corn Trade of Great Britain and Their Influence on the Prosperity of the Kingdom. Edinburgh: 1796. V. 73

DISBOROUGH, HENRY
An Inaugural Dissertation on Cholera Infantum. Philadelphia: 1798. V. 68

DISBROW, EDWARD D.
The Man Without a Gun- The Stories of Life In the Dakotas in the Early Nineties. Boston: 1936. V. 71

DISCH, THOMAS
Black Alice. Garden City: 1968. V. 71
Black Alice. London: 1969. V. 69
Camp Concentration. London: 1968. V. 71
The Prisoner. London: 1979. V. 71; 73
The Sub. New York: 1999. V. 72

DISCOURS d'une Femme De La Capital, Presente Au Roi. Paris: 1789. V. 73

THE DISCUSSION; or the Character, Education, Prerogatives and Moral Influence of Woman. Boston: 1837. V. 73

DISDIER, FRANCOIS MICHEL
Histoire Exacte Des Os, ou Description Complette De L'Osteologie. Paris: 1745. V. 71; 72

DISFARMER, MIKE
Disfarmer: The Heber Springs Portraits 1939-1946. Danbury: 1976. V. 73

DISHER, M. WILLSON
Clowns and Pantomimes. London: 1925. V. 70

DISMON, BINGA
We Who Would Die and Other Poems. New York: 1943. V. 70

DISNEY, JOHN
Memoirs of Thomas Brand-Hollis, Esq. London: 1808. V. 70
A Practical Abridgment of Election Law, from the Issuing of the Writ to the Return. London: 1812. V. 71

DISNEY, WALT
A B C de Mickey. Paris: 1936. V. 72
Alice and the Mad Hatter's Tea Party. 1969. V. 71; 72
Animals from Snow White and the Seven Dwarfs. Racine: 1938. V. 73
Ave Maria. New York: 1940. V. 70
The Cinderella Magic Wand Book. London: 1950. V. 70; 72
The Cold Blooded Penguin. New York: 1944. V. 70
Contes L'Oncle Remus Extraits de Melodie du Sud. Paris: 1948. V. 72
Dance of the Hours from Walt Disney's Fantasia. New York: 1940. V. 69
Disney's Sleeping Beauty. New York: 1957. V. 70
Don Mickey. London: 1937. V. 73
Donald and Pluto. 1939. V. 72
Donald Duck. 50 Years of Happy Frustration. 1984. V. 72
Donald's Ostrich. London: 1938. V. 69; 73
Dopey, He Don't Talk None. Racine: 1938. V. 69; 73
Ferdinand d'apres. Paris: 1939. V. 72
Ferdinand the Bull Paint Book. New York: 1938. V. 69
Honest John and Giddy. New York: 1940. V. 70
Jiminy Cricket. New York: 1940. V. 70
The Life of Donald Duck. New York: 1941. V. 69
Lullaby Land. London: 1934. V. 69
Mickey Mouse. Racine: 1932-1933. V. 71
Mickey Mouse and His Friends. Racine: 1936. V. 73
Mickey Mouse and Mother Goose. Racine: 1937. V. 72
Mickey Mouse and Pluto. London: 1936. V. 70
Mickey Mouse and Pluto. Racine: 1936. V. 72
Mickey Mouse Annual 1945. 1945. V. 68
Mickey Mouse Crusoe. London: 1935. V. 73
Mickey Mouse Fire Brigade. London: 1936. V. 73
Mickey Mouse Has a Busy Day. Racine: 1937. V. 73
Mickey Mouse Has a Party: a School Reader. Racine: 1938. V. 70
Mickey Mouse on Tour. London: 1935. V. 69
Mickey Mouse Presents Father Noah's Ark a Silly Symphony. London: 1934. V. 71
The Mickey Mouse Safety First Book. London: 1938. V. 69; 73
Mickey Mouse Sky High. London: 1937. V. 73
Mickey Mouse Stories. Book 2. Philadelphia: 1934. V. 68
Mickey Mouse the Boat-Builder. New York: 1938. V. 73
Mickey Mouse's Secret Room. 1947. V. 72
Mickey's Clock. London: 1938. V. 69
Mickey's Magic Hat Cookie Carnival. Racine: 1937. V. 70
More Adventures of Mickey Mouse. London: 1932. V. 70
The Nutcracker Suite. Boston: 1940. V. 70
Pastoral from Walt Disney's Fantasia. New York: 1940. V. 73
Pedro. New York: 1943. V. 70
The Pied Piper. London: 1934. V. 69
Pinocchio's Christmas Party (Kresge Department Store Wishes Every Little Boy and Girl the Happiest Christmas Ever). 1939. V. 69
The Pop-up Minnie Mouse. New York: 1933. V. 70
Santa's Workshop from the Walt Disney Silly Symphony. London: 1934. V. 70
Sketch Book of Snow White and the Seven Dwarfs. London: 1939. V. 71

Snow White and the Seven Dwarfs. New York: 1937. V. 70
Snow White and the Seven Dwarfs. Philadelphia: 1937. V. 70
Snow White and the Seven Dwarfs. Racine: 1938. V. 70; 73
Snow White Magic Mirror Book and The Story of Snow White and the Seven Dwarfs. London: 1939. V. 70
Three Little Pigs. New York: 1933. V. 72
The Three Orphan Kittens. Racine: 1935. V. 69; 72
A Trip with Mickey Mouse. London: 1935. V. 71
Les Trois Petits Cochons. (The Three Little Pigs.). Paris: 1949. V. 70
The Ugly Duckling Adapted from Hans Christian Andersen. Philadelphia: 1939. V. 73
The Walt Disney Annual. Racine: 1937. V. 72
Walt Disney's Bambi. New York: 1941. V. 70
Walt Disney's Donald Duck in the High Andes. NY: 1943. V. 72
Walt Disney's Famous Seven Dwarfs. Racine: 1938. V. 71
Walt Disney's Fiagro and Cleo - a Story Paint Book from the Walt Disney Motion Picture Pinocchio. Racine: 1940. V. 72
Walt Disney's Paintless Paint Book. Racine: 1939. V. 69
Walt Disney's Silly Symphony Annual. London: 1937. V. 70; 71
Walt Disney's Story of Minnie Mouse. Racine: 1938. V. 70
Walt Disney's The Ugly Duckling. Philadelphia: 1939. V. 71
Walt Disney's Version of Pinocchio. New York: 1939. V. 70
The Water Babies. London: 1936. V. 69
The Wonderful Tar Baby. New York: 1946. V. 73

DISORDERLY Girl. New York: 1867. V. 71

A DISPASSIONATE Remonstrance of the Nature and Tendency of the Laws Now in Force for the Reduction of Interest; and the Consequences that Must Inevitably Flow from Them.... London: 1751. V. 70; 72

D'ISRAEL, L. S.
Talmudic Maxims. Boston: 1848. V. 69

DISRAELI, BENJAMIN
Alroy. Ixion in Heaven. The Infernal Marriage. Popanilla. London: 1878. V. 68
Coningsby or the New Generation. London: 1881. V. 68
Contarini Fleming. Leipzig: 1846. V. 73
Contarini Fleming. London: 1878. V. 68
Endymion. London: 1880. V. 68; 70; 72; 73
Endymion. London: 1881. V. 68
England and Denmark. Speech of Mr. Disraeli in the House of Commons, the 19th April 1848 on the Danish Question. London: 1848. V. 71
Henrietta Temple. London: 1878. V. 68
The Infernal Marriage. London: 1929. V. 71
Key to Vivian Grey. London: 1827. V. 73
The Letters of Runnymede. London: 1836. V. 71
Lord George Bentinck: a Political Biography. London: 1852. V. 71
Lothair. London. V. 71
Lothair. London: 1881. V. 68
Novels and Tales. London: 1900. V. 72
The Novels and Tales. London: 1926-1927. V. 73
The Revolutionary Epick (Book I, II, III). London: 1834. V. 73
Sybil or The Two Nations. London: 1878. V. 68
The Tragedy of Count Alarcos. London: 1839. V. 73
Vivian Grey. London: 1826-1827. V. 73
Vivian Grey. London: 1878. V. 68
Vivian Grey. London: 1882?. V. 68
The Voyage of Captain Popanilla. Philadelphia: 1828. V. 68; 73
The Voyage of Captain Popanilla. London: 1829. V. 73
Whigs and Whiggism: Political Writings. London: 1913. V. 71
The Young Duke. London: 1831. V. 73
The Young Duke. London: 1878. V. 68

D'ISRAELI, ISAAC
Curiosities of Literature. London: 1838. V. 69
Curiosities of Literature. Boston: 1858. V. 72
Curiosities of Literature. (with) Curiosities of Literature. Volume the Second. London: 1793. V. 73
The Literary Character; or the History of Men of Genius, Drawn from their own Feelings and Confessions. London: 1828. V. 69
Romances. London: 1799. V. 69
The Works. London: 1881. V. 73

THE DISTILLER Of London. London: 1698. V. 73

DITTON, HUMPHREY
A Treatise of Perspective Demonstrative and Practical. 1712. V. 71

DIVER, MAUD
The Dream Prevails. Boston: 1938. V. 70

DIX, BELAH MARIE
A Legend of Saint Nicholas and Other Plays. New York: 1927. V. 71

DIX, DOROTHEA
Conversations on Common Things; or Guide to Knowledge. Boston: 1828. V. 68
Memorial of D. L. Dix, Praying Grant of Land for the Relief and Support of the Indigent Curable and Incurable Insane in the United States. Washington: 1848. V. 72
A Paraphrase on the Lord's Prayer With an Introduction on the Nature of the Prayer. Raleigh: 1852. V. 68

DIX, JOHN
The Life of Thomas Chatterton, Including His Unpublished Poems and Correspondence. London: 1837. V. 70

DIX, JOHN A.
A Winter in Madeira and a Summer in Spain and Florence. New York: 1850. V. 68

DIX, JOHN ROSS
Local Loiterings and Visits in the Vicinity of Boston. Boston: 1845. V. 68

DIX, MORGAN
Memoirs of John Adams Dix. New York: 1883. V. 69

DIXIE, FLORENCE
In the Land of Misfortune. London: 1882. V. 68; 69; 73

DIXIE, RAYMOND
The Boy Magician: A large number of the latest and best tricks carefully selected for the rising generation of conjurers. Boston: 1922. V. 72

DIXON, CHARLES
The Game Birds and Wild Fowl of the British Islands. Sheffield: 1900. V. 70; 73
The Migration of Birds. 1897. V. 69

DIXON, CLIVE M.
The Leaguer of Ladysmith. London: 1900. V. 70

DIXON, DAVID
Hero of Beecher's Island The Life and Career of George A. Forsyth. Lincoln: 1994. V. 72

DIXON, E.
More Fairy Tales from the Arabian Nights. London: 1895. V. 69

DIXON, F.
The Geology and Fossils of Sussex. London: 1850. V. 68
The Geology and Fossils of Sussex. Brighton: 1878. V. 68
The Geology and Fossils of the Tertiary and Cretaceous Formations of Sussex. London: 1850. V. 70

DIXON, HENRY HALL
The Post and the Paddock. London: 1871. V. 68
Saddle and Sirloin. London: 1870. V. 73
Scott and Sebright. London: 1885. V. 68

DIXON, J. H.
Chronicles and Stories Of The Craven Dales. 1881. V. 72; 73

DIXON, JAMES
Methodism in America; with the Personal Narrative of the Author.... London: 1849. V. 69
The Songs of the Bells and Other Poems. London: 1852. V. 71

DIXON, JAMES D.
History of Charles Dixon, One of the Early English Settlers of Sackville, N.B. Sackville: 1891. V. 73

DIXON, JOSEPH K.
The Vanishing Race. The Last Great Indian Council. Garden City: 1913. V. 73

DIXON, JOSHUA
The Literary Life Of William Brownrigg, D.D., F.R.S. To Which are Added An Account Of The Coal Mines Near Whitehaven; and Observations On The Means Of Preventing Epidemic Fevers. 1801. V. 72
The Literary Life of William Brownrigg, M.D. F.R.S. to which are Added An Account of the Coal Mines Near Whitehaven.... London: 1801. V. 71

DIXON, MAYNARD
Images of the Native American. San Francisco: 1981. V. 70; 73

DIXON, OLIVE K.
Life of Billy Dixon, Scout and Pioneer. Dallas: 1927. V. 73

DIXON, R. W.
The New Flora Britannica. London: 1812. V. 69

DIXON, RICHARD WATSON
Christ's Company and Other Poems. London: 1861. V. 73
Historical Odes and Other Poems. London: 1864. V. 73
Mano. London: 1883. V. 73
Mano. London: 1891. V. 73
The Prize Poem on a Sacred Subject for 1863. S. John in Patmos. Oxford: 1863. V. 73
Songs and Odes. London: 1896. V. 73

DIXON, ROBERT
Blues & Gospel Records, 1902-1942. Harrow: 1963. V. 72; 73
Blues & Gospel Records, 1902-1942. Hatch End, Middlesex: 1963. V. 69
Blues & Gospel Records, 1902-1943. Chigwell: 1982. V. 73
Recording the Blues. New York: 1970. V. 73

DIXON, SAM H.
The Poets and Poetry of Texas. Austin: 1885. V. 68
Romance and Tragedy of Texas History. Houston: 1924. V. 69

DIXON, THOMAS
The Clansman. New York: 1905. V. 69
Companions. New York: 1931. V. 71
The Leopard's Spots. New York: 1902. V. 71
The Way of a Man. New York: 1919. V. 68; 70

DIXON, WILLIAM HEPWORTH
New America. London: 1867. V. 68
William Penn. An Historical Biography. With An Extra Chapter on The Macaulay Charges. London: 1851. V. 72

DIXON, WILLIAM SCARTH
Hunting the Olden Days. 1912. V. 68

DOANE, AUGUSTUS SIDNEY
Surgery Illustrated. New York: 1836. V. 70

DOANE, MICHAEL
The Surprise of Burning. New York: 1988. V. 72

DOBBERT, E.
Was Braven Kindern Gefallt: ein Bilderbuch fur Knaben und Madchen. Munchen: 1895. V. 71

DOBBS, MICHAEL
The Buddha Of Brewer Street. London: 1998. V. 72
Goodfellowe MP. London: 1997. V. 72
House of Cards. London: 1989. V. 72
The Touch of Innocents. London: 1994. V. 70; 72

DOBEGINI, S.
The Singers Vade Mecum, or Complete Vocal Instructor On the Principles of the Most Celebrated Schools in Italy. London: 1800?. V. 68

DOBELL, CECIL CLIFFORD
Antony van Leeuwenhoek and His Little Animals. London: 1932. V. 68; 70
Antony van Leeuwenhoek and His Little Animals. New York: 1932. V. 72

DOBELL, JOHN
A New Selection of Seven Hundred Evangelical Hymns, for Private, Family and Public Worship.... Morris Town: 1810. V. 69
A New Selection of Seven Hundred Evangelical Hymns, for Private Family, and Public Worship.... Morristown: 1815. V. 69

DOBELL, SDYNEY
Balder. London: 1854. V. 73

DOBELL, SYDNEY
England in Time of War. London: 1856. V. 73
The Roman. London: 1850. V. 73
The Roman. London: 1852. V. 73

DOBIE, DUDLEY R.
Adventures in the Canyon, Mountain and Desert Country of the Big Bend of Texas and New Mexico. San Marcos: 1952. V. 70

DOBIE, JAMES FRANK
Apache Gold and Yaqui Silver. Boston: 1939. V. 68; 69
Bob More, Man and Bird Man. Austin: 1965. V. 70
Carl Sandburg and Saint Peter at the Gate. Austin: 1966. V. 70
Coronado's Children. Garden City: 1930. V. 69
Cow People. Boston: 1964. V. 69; 72
The First Cattle in Texas And.... 1939. V. 71
The Flavor of Texas. Dallas: 1936. V. 70
Guide to Life and Literature of the Southwest with a Few Observations. Austin: 1943. V. 69
I'll Tell You a Tale. Boston: 1960. V. 71
John C. Duval - First Texas Man of Letters. Dallas: 1939. V. 70
The Longhorns. Boston: 1941. V. 68; 72
The Longhorns. New York: 1941. V. 71
The Mustangs. Boston: 1952. V. 69; 71
Mustangs and Cow Horses. Austin: 1940. V. 68; 69; 71
On the Open Range. Dallas: 1931. V. 68; 71
Rattlesnakes. Boston: 1965. V. 73
A Schoolteacher in Alpine. Austin: 1962. V. 71
The Seven Mustangs. Austin: 1948. V. 68; 73
Southwestern Lore. Dallas: 1931. V. 69
Tales of Old-Time Texas. Boston: 1955. V. 69; 72
Tales of the Mustang. Dallas: 1936. V. 71
A Texan in England. Boston: 1945. V. 72
Texas and Southwestern Lore. Austin: 1927. V. 69
Tongues of the Monte. Boston: 1936. V. 69
A Vaquero of the Brush Country. New York: 1929. V. 69
The Voice of the Coyote. Boston: 1949. V. 68; 71

DOBIE, JOHN
John Dobie's Journal and Letters from the Mines. Mokelumne Hill, Jackson, Volcano and San Francisco 1851-1865. Denver: 1962. V. 68

DOBROVSKY, JOSEF
Dobrowsky's Slavin. Prague: 1834. V. 69

DOBSON, AUSTIN
The Ballad of Beau Brocade, and Other Poems of the XVIIIth Century. London: 1892. V. 70
Eighteenth Century Vignettes. London: 1892. V. 71; 72
Proverbs in Porcelain to which is added "Au Revoir" a dramatic vignette. London: 1893. V. 71
Thomas Bewick and His Pupils. London: 1889. V. 73

DOBSON, EDWARD
A Rudimentary Treatise on Masonry and Stonecutting. London: 1865?. V. 68
Rudiments of the Art of Building. London: 1854. V. 68
Rudiments of the Art of Building. London: 1871. V. 68

DOBSON, JESSIE
Anatomical Eponyms: Being a Biographical Dictionary of Those Anatomists Whose Names Have Become Incorporated Into Anatomical Nomenclature.... Edinburgh and London: 1962. V. 68
Anatomical Eponyms Being a Dictionary of Those Anatomists Whose Names Have Become Incorporated Into Anatomical Nomenclature.... London: 1946. V. 68

DOBSON, JOHN
Chronological Annals of the War, from Its Beginning to the Present Time. Oxford: 1763. V. 72

DOBSON, SUSANNAH DAWSON
Petrarch's View of Human Life. London: 1791. V. 68; 69; 73

DOBSON, THOMAS
Index to the Bible, in Which the Various Subjects which Occur in the Scriptures are Alphabetically Arranged with accurate References to all the Books of the Old Testaments. Philadelphia: 1804. V. 73

DOBSON, WILLIAM T.
A Narrative of the Peninsular Campaign 1807-1814, Its Battles and Sieges.... 1919. V. 70

DOBYNS, STEPHEN
The Church of Dead Girls. New York: 1997. V. 72
Concurring Beasts. New York: 1972. V. 71
Heat Death. New York: 1980. V. 68
Saratoga Longshot. New York: 1976. V. 68
Saratoga Swimmer. New York: 1981. V. 70

DOCKER, ALFRED
The Colour Prints of William Dickes. London. V. 72

DOCKSTADER, FREDERICK J.
Indian Art in America. Greenwich: 1961. V. 71
Indian Art in Middle America. Greenwich: 1964. V. 70

DR. Goldsmith's Celebrated Elegy on the Glory of Her Sex - Mrs. Mary Blaize. London: 1808. V. 71

DOCTOROW, E. L.
American Anthem. New York: 1982. V. 70
Billy Bathgate. Franklin Center: 1989. V. 70
Billy Bathgate. New York: 1989. V. 72
The Book of Daniel. New York: 1971. V. 68; 69; 70; 72
City of God. Franklin Center: 2000. V. 70
City of God. New York: 2000. V. 68
Drinks Before Dinner. New York: 1978. V. 72
Drinks Before Dinner. New York: 1979. V. 71; 72
Jack London, Hemingway and the Constitutiion. New York: 1993. V. 72
The Lives of the Poets. New York: 1984. V. 68; 72
Loon Lake. New York: 1980. V. 71; 73
The People's Text: A Citizen Reads the Constitution. Jackson: 1992. V. 71; 72
Ragtime. New York: 1974. V. 68
Ragtime. New York: 1975. V. 70; 73
The Waterworks. Franklin Center: 1994. V. 71
The Waterworks. London: 1994. V. 71
World's Fair. New York: 1985. V. 69

DOCUMENTS Relative to the Colonial History of the State of New York: Procured in Holland, England and France. Albany: 1856. V. 71

DODD, BETHUEL L.
Genealogies of the Male Descendants of Daniel Dod, of Branford, Conn., a Native of England 1646 to 1863. Newark: 1864. V. 69

DODD, DAVID O.
Letters of David O. Dodd. 1917. V. 70

DODD, E.
Polynesian Art, the Ring of Fire. Volume I. New York: 1967. V. 69

DODD, EPHRAIM SHELBY
Diary of Ephraim Shelby Dodd. Austin: 1914. V. 69; 70

DODD, GEORGE
Dictionary of Manufactures, Mining, Machinery and the Industrial Arts. New York: 1869. V. 71
Where Do We Get It, and How Is It Made?. London: 1862. V. 68

DODD, JAMES SOLAS
A Satyrical Lecture on Hearts; to which is added, A Critical Dissertation on Noses. London: 1767. V. 73

DODD, STEPHEN
An Historical and Topographical Account Of The Town of Woburn, Its Abbey, and Vicinity. Woburn: 1818. V. 70; 72; 73

DODD, WILLIAM
An Account of the Rise, Progress and Present State of the Magdalen Hospital for the Reception of Penitent Prostitutes. London: 1776. V. 69
The Beauties of Shakespeare. London: 1752. V. 72
A Genuine and Authentic Account of the Life, Trial, Behaviour and Dying Words of William Dodd, LL.D. who Was Executed at Tyburn for Forgery on Friday June 27, 1777. London: 1777. V. 69
An Oration Delivered at the Dedication of Free Masons' Hall, Great Queen-Street, Lincoln's Inn Fields, on Thursday May 23, 1776. London: 1776. V. 70; 72
Thoughts in Prison. London: 1777. V. 68
Thoughts in Prison. London: 1793. V. 68
Thoughts in Prison. London: 1815. V. 71
Thoughts in Prison. 1826. V. 72
Thoughts in Prison. London: 1826. V. 68

DODDRIDGE, JOSEPH
Notes, on the Settlement and Indian Wars of the Western Parts of Virginia and Pennsylvania, from the Year 1763 Until the Year 1783 Inclusive.... Wellsburgh: 1824. V. 68

DODDRIDGE, PHILIP
A Course of Lectures on the Principal Subjects in Pneumatology, Ethics and Divinity.. London: 1763. V. 73
Some Remarkable Passages In the Life Of The Honourable Col. James Gardiner. London: 1748. V. 71; 72

DODERER, HEIMITO VON
Every Man a Murder. New York: 1964. V. 69

DODGE, DAVID
To Catch a Thief. New York: 1952. V. 70; 71

DODGE, E. S.
The Hervey Islands Adzes in the Peabody Museum of Salem. Salem: 1937. V. 69
The Marquesas Islands Collection in the Peabody Museum of Salem. Salem: 1939. V. 69

DODGE, GRENVILLE M.
The Battle of Atlanta and Other Campaign Addresses, Etc. Council Bluff, LA: 1911:. V. 72
Indian Campaigns of The Winter of 1864-1865. Denver: 1907. V. 72

DODGE, H.
A Historical Review of the Mollusks of Linnaeus. New York: 1952-1959. V. 70

DODGE, ORVIL
Pioneer History of Coos and Curry Counties. Salem, OR: 1898. V. 71

DODGE, RICHARD I.
Our Wild Indians: Thirty-Three Years Personal Experience Among The Red Men of The Great West. Hartford: 1886. V. 72

DODGE, THEODORE A.
The Campaign of Chancellorsville. Boston: 1881. V. 69
Riders of Many Lands. New York: 1894. V. 71

DODGE'S Red Picture-Book. Fairy Tales for Little Folk. New York: 1913. V. 73

DODGSON, CAMPBELL
The Etchings of James McNeill Whistler. London: 1922. V. 72
An Iconography of the Engravings of Stephen Gooden. 1944. V. 71
The Woodcuts of the Fifteenth Century in the John Rylands Library, Manchester. Manchester: 1915. V. 72

DODGSON, CHARLES LUTWIDGE
Adventures in Wonderland. London: 1907. V. 70
Ala w Krainie Czarow. (Alice in wonderland). Warsa: 1932. V. 69
Alice au Pays des Merveilles. Paris: 1932. V. 68
Alice au Pays des Merveilles. Paris: 1939. V. 69
Alice au Pays des Merveilles. Paris: 1949. V. 68
Alice au Pays des Merveilles. Lausanne: 1951. V. 68
Alice au Pays des Merveilles & De l'Autre Cote du Miroir. Paris: 1935. V. 71
Alice im Wunderland. Germany: 1922. V. 72
Alice in het Land der Droomen. Amsterdam: 1890. V. 71
Alice in Pictures. 1960. V. 69
Alice in Wonderland. Lower Chelston, Devon. V. 69
Alice in Wonderland. London: 1909. V. 69
Alice in Wonderland. London: 1910. V. 70
Alice in Wonderland. London: 1912. V. 68
Alice in Wonderland. London: 1913. V. 70
Alice in Wonderland. London: 1922. V. 71; 72; 73
Alice in Wonderland. London: 1922. V. 70
Alice in Wonderland. London: 1923. V. 72
Alice in Wonderland. London: 1929. V. 72
Alice in Wonderland. 1943. V. 68
Alice in Wonderland. London: 1945. V. 69; 70
Alice in Wonderland. London: 1947. V. 70
Alice in Wonderland. Amsterdam: 1950. V. 68; 71
Alice in Wonderland. Amsterdam: 1960. V. 71
Alice in Wonderland. London: 1967. V. 70; 72
Alice in Wonderland. Retie, Netherlands: 1970. V. 68
Alice in Wonderland. 1980. V. 71
Alice in Wonderland and Through the Looking Glass. New York: 1926. V. 71
Alice in Wonderland. (and) Through the Looking Glass, and What Alice Found There. London: 1866. V. 68
Alice in Wonderland. (and) Through the Looking Glass and What Alice Found There. London: 1866-1872. V. 69
Alice in Wonderland Painting Book. London: 1925. V. 69
Alice in Wonderland. (with) Through the Looking-Glass and What Alice Found There. London. V. 70
Alice nel Paese delle Meraviglie. Milan. V. 71
Alice Nel Paese Delle Meraviglie. Florence: 1931. V. 68
Alice nel Paese delle Meraviglie. Milan: 1950. V. 68
Alice nel Paese delle Meraviglie. Milan: 1953. V. 71
Alice nel Paese delle Meraviglie. Florence: 1955. V. 68; 71
Alice's Adventures in Wonderland. London. V. 69; 70; 71
Alice's Adventures in Wonderland. Philadelphia. V. 70

DODGSON, CHARLES LUTWIDGE *continued*
Alice's Adventures in Wonderland. London: 1866. V. 70; 72
Alice's Adventures in Wonderland. New York: 1866. V. 69
Alice's Adventures in Wonderland. Boston: 1870. V. 73
Alice's Adventures in Wonderland. New York: 1900. V. 73
Alice's Adventures in Wonderland. New York: 1901. V. 71; 73
Alice's Adventures in Wonderland. London and New York: 1907. V. 69; 70; 72; 73
Alice's Adventures in Wonderland. London: 1908. V. 69; 70; 72
Alice's Adventures in Wonderland. London and Felling-on-Tyne: 1910. V. 68
Alice's Adventures in Wonderland. New York: 1911. V. 72
Alice's Adventures in Wonderland. London: 1912. V. 69
Alice's Adventures in Wonderland. London: 1914. V. 70
Alice's Adventures in Wonderland. New York: 1922. V. 70; 73
Alice's Adventures in Wonderland. London: 1925. V. 73
Alice's Adventures in Wonderland. New York: 1929. V. 72
Alice's Adventures in Wonderland. London: 1930. V. 68
Alice's Adventures in Wonderland. New York: 1932. V. 72
Alice's Adventures in Wonderland. London: 1940. V. 71
Alice's Adventures in Wonderland. London and Leicester: 1944. V. 71
Alice's Adventures in Wonderland. London: 1945. V. 69
Alice's Adventures in Wonderland. Racine: 1955. V. 69
Alice's Adventures in Wonderland. New York: 1969. V. 68; 70
Alice's Adventures in Wonderland. Salt Lake City: 1972. V. 71
Alice's Adventures in Wonderland. 1975. V. 71
Alice's Adventures in Wonderland. New York: 1986. V. 69
Alice's Adventures in Wonderland and Through the Looking Glass. London: 1928. V. 68
Alice's Adventures in Wonderland and Through the Looking Glass. Racine: 1945. V. 71
Alice's Adventures in Wonderland and Through the Looking Glass. London: 1946. V. 70
Alice's Adventures in Wonderland and Through the Looking Glass. New York: 1946. V. 70
Alice's Adventures in Wonderland and through the Looking Glass. Racine: 1955. V. 68; 71
Alice's Adventures in Wonderland. and Through the Looking Glass and What Alice Found There. London: 1927. V. 70
Alice's Adventures in Wonderland. and Through the Looking Glass and What Alice Saw There. Paris: 1950. V. 70; 73
Alice's Adventures in Wonderland and Through the Looking-Glass. New York: 1934. V. 73
Alice's Adventures in Wonderland Retold. London: 1920. V. 72
Alice's Adventures in Wonderland. (with) *Through the Looking Glass and What Alice Found There.* London: 1866-1872. V. 68
Alice's Adventures in Wonerland. (and) *Through the Looking Glass.* New York: 1893. V. 70
Alice's Adventures Under Ground. New York. V. 70
Alice's Adventures Under Ground. London: 1886. V. 69
Alice's Adventures Under Ground. New York: 1954?. V. 70
Alice's Adventures Under Ground, being a facsimile of the original ms. book.... London: 1886. V. 72
Alice's Adventuren Underground. London: 1886. V. 68
Alice's Advonturen in het Wonderland. Amsterdam: 1920. V. 68; 71
Alicia al pais de les Meravelles. Barcelona: 1966. V. 71
Alicia en el Pais de la Maravillas. Barcelona: 1956. V. 71
Alicia en el Pais de la Maravillas. Barcelona: 1958. V. 71
Alicia en el Pais de la Maravillas. Madrid: 1968. V. 71
Alicia en el Pais de la Maravillas. Barcelona: 1972. V. 71
Alicia en el Pais de la Maravillas. Barcelona: 1980. V. 71
Alicia en el Pais de la Maravillas. Barcelona: 1989. V. 71
Alicia en el Pais de las Maravaillas and Other Stories. Barcelona: 1964. V. 71
Alicia en el Pais de Las Maravilillas & Alicia en el Pais de Espejo. Barcelona: 1959. V. 71
Alicia en El Pais de las Maravillas. Barcelona: 1931. V. 68; 71
Alicia in Terra Mirabili.... London: 1964. V. 72; 73
Aliciae per Speculum Transitus. London: 1966. V. 71
Alicie en el Pais de la Maravillas. Barcelona: 1960. V. 71
Alicie en Terra de Meravelles. Barcelona: 1930. V. 71
Aliciae per Speculum Transitus. (Through the Looking Glass). London: 1966. V. 73
La Chasse Au Snark. Paris: 1950. V. 70
Doublets: a Word-Puzzle. London: 1879. V. 72
An Easter Greeting to Every Child Who Loves "Alice". London: 1876. V. 68
Eight or Nine Wise Words About Letter Writing. Oxford: 1908. V. 68
Feeding the Mind. London: 1907. V. 68
The Hunting of the Snark. London: 1876. V. 69; 71; 73
The Hunting of the Snark. London: 1898. V. 68
The Hunting of the Snark. New York: 1903. V. 73
The Hunting of the Snark. Los Altos: 1918. V. 70
The Hunting of the Snark. 1974. V. 68
The Hunting of the Snark. Andoversford: 1975. V. 68; 72
The Hunting of the Snark. Los Altos: 1981. V. 73
The Lewis Carroll Picture Book. London: 1899. V. 71
Logique Sans Peine. Paris: 1966. V. 69
The New Belfry of Christ Chruch, Oxford. Oxford: 1872. V. 68; 70; 71
Nonsense Songs in Wonderland. London: 1908. V. 72
The Nursery Alice. London: 1890. V. 71; 73
Phantasmagoria and Other Poems. London: 1869. V. 73
The Pig-Tale. Boston: 1975. V. 70
The Rectory Umbrella and Misch Masch.... London: 1932. V. 68
Rhyme? and Reason?. 1883. V. 69
Rhyme? and Reason?. London: 1883. V. 71; 72
Songs from Alice in Wonderland and Through the Looking Glass. London: 1921. V. 69
Sylvie and Bruno. London: 1889. V. 71
Sylvie and Bruno Concluded. London: 1893. V. 71; 73
Sylvie and Bruno. (with) Sylvie and Bruno Concluded. London: 1889-1893. V. 72
A Tangled Tale. London: 1885. V. 71; 73
Three Sunsets and Other Poems.... London: 1898. V. 70
Through the Looking Glass. Boston and New York: 1872. V. 73
Through the Looking Glass. New York: 1935. V. 69
Through the Looking Glass and What Alice Found There. London: 1871. V. 70
Through the Looking Glass and What Alice Found There. New York and London: 1872. V. 69; 71
Through the Looking Glass and What Alice Found There. New York: 1902. V. 71
Through the Looking Glass and What Alice Found There. New York: 1931. V. 72
Through the Looking Glass and What Alice Found There. New York: 1935. V. 69; 71; 73
Through the Looking Glass and What Alice Found There. New York: 1973. V. 72
The Visions of the Three T's. A Threnody. Oxford: 1873. V. 73

DODGSON, J.
The Place-Names of Cheshire. London: 1970-1972. V. 73

DODINGTON, GEORGE BUBB
The Diary ...from March 8, 1748-1749 to February 6, 1761.... Salisbury: 1784. V. 69

DODSLEY, ROBERT
A Collection of Poems. London: 1748-1758. V. 70
A Collection of Poems by Several Hands. London: 1775. V. 68; 70
A Collection of Poems by Several Hands. London: 1782. V. 70
The Economy of Human Life. London: 1795. V. 73
The Economy of Human Life. London: 1796?. V. 73
The Economy of Human Life. Manchester: 1797. V. 68
The Economy of Human Life. Kelso: 1802. V. 72
Fugitive Pieces on Various Subjects. London: 1761. V. 70
The King and the Miller of Mansfield. London: 1738. V. 71
The Oeconomy of Human Life. Birmingham: 1790. V. 71
The Oeconomy of Human Life. Berwick: 1793. V. 71
The Preceptor: Containing a General Course of Education. London: 1775. V. 69
Select Fables of Aesop and Other Fabulists. London: 1761. V. 71
Select Fables of Aesop and Other Fabulists. London: 1790. V. 71
Trifles: viz, the Toy-Shop; the Chronicle of Kings of England.... London: 1745. V. 68

DODSON, C. H.
Flora of the Rio Palenque Science Center, Los Rios Province, Ecuador. Sarasota: 1978. V. 72

DODSON, JAMES
The Calculator; Being Correct and Necessary Tables for Computation, Adapted to Science, Business and Pleasure. London: 1747. V. 73
The Mathematical Repository, Containing Analytical Solutions of Near Five Hundred Questions.... London: 1775-. V. 71

DODSON, KENNETH
Away All Boats. Boston: 1954. V. 71

DODWELL, HENRY
A Treatise Concerning the Lawfulness of Instrumental Musick in Holy Offices.... London: 1700. V. 73

DOE, JANET
A Bibliography of the Works of Ambroise Pare: Premier Chirurgien & Conseiller du Roy. Chicago: 1937. V. 68; 70; 73

DOERR, ANTHONY
The Shell Collector. NY: 2002. V. 72

DOERR, HARRIET
Consider This, Senora. New York: 1993. V. 70
Stones for Ibarra. New York: 1984. V. 68

THE DOG and His Shadow and Other Fables. London: 1880. V. 70

DOGEN, MATTHIAS
Architectura Militaris Moderna. Amstelodami: 1647. V. 69; 73

DOGGIE Pranks. New York: 1894. V. 71

A DOG'S Nose: Basil Bunting 1900-1985. Leicester: 1986. V. 70

DOHENY, ESTELLE
The Estelle Doheny Collection. New York: 1987-1989. V. 70

DOHERTY, HUGH
False Association and its Remedy; or, a Critical Introduction to the Late Charles Fourier's Theory of Attractive Industry, and the Moral Harmony of the Passions. London: 1841. V. 70

DOHERTY, P. C.
The Love Knot. 1999. V. 68

DOHERTY, P. C
Love Knot. London: 1999. V. 72

DOHERTY, P. C.
The Masked Man. 1991. V. 68
Murder Wears a Cowl. 1992. V. 68

DOI, ISAMI
Random Vintage. Honolulu: 1941. V. 72; 73

DOIG, IVAN
Bucking the Sun. New York: 1996. V. 68; 69

DOIG, IVAN *continued*
Dancing at the Rascal Fair. New York: 1987. V. 71; 72
Early Forestry Research. 1977. V. 69
English Creek. New York: 1984. V. 68; 70; 71
News: A Consumer's Guide. Englewood Cliffs: 1972. V. 72
News: a Consumer's Guide. New York: 1972. V. 70
The Sea Runners. New York: 1982. V. 70; 72
This House of Sky. New York and London: 1978. V. 68; 69; 71; 73
Winter Brothers. New York: 1980. V. 68; 69; 72

DOISNEAU, ROBERT
Three Seconds from Eternity: Photographs by Robert Doisneau. Boston: 1979. V. 70

DOKE, CLEMENT M.
The Lambas of Northern Rhodesia. London: 1931. V. 72

DOLBEN, DIGBY MACKWORTH
The Poems of.... 1911. V. 73

DOLBY, J.
Six Views of Eton College. Eton: 1838. V. 70

DOLBY, THOMAS
The Shakespearian Dictionary; forming a General Index to all the popular expressions and the most striking passages in the works of Shakespeare . . London: 1832. V. 71

DOLLIE'S ABC. London: 1900. V. 73

DOLLY DEAR. London: 1890. V. 69

DOLLY Pie. London: 1909. V. 68

DOLLY'S Home. London: 1880. V. 73

DOLLY'S New House. London: 1890. V. 72; 73

DOLMAN, FREDERICK
Municipalities at Work. London: 1895. V. 73

DOLMETSCH, H.
Ornamental Treasures. London: 1900. V. 68

THE DOLPHIN. New York: 1933-1941. V. 70
THE DOLPHIN. New York: 1940-1941. V. 70; 72

THE DOME. London: 1897-1900. V. 68

DOMENECH, E. M.
Seven Years' Residence in the Great Deserts of North America. London: 1860. V. 70

DOMETSCH, H.
Der Ornamentenschatz, ein Musterbuch Stilvoller Ornamente aus Allen Kunstepochen.... Stuttgart: 1889. V. 70

DOMINGUEZ, FRANCISCO ATANASIO
The Missions of New Mexico 1776.... Albuquerque: 1975. V. 69; 71; 73

THE DOMINION Arsenal at Quebec 1880-1945. Quebec: 1947. V. 71

DOMINIS, MARCO ANTONIO DE
A Manifestation of the Motives, Whereupon the Most Reuerend Father, Marcvs Antonivs de Dominis, Archbishopof Spalato . . . Vndertooke His Departure Thence. London: 1616. V. 73

DOMON, KEN
The Muro-Ji: An Eighth Century Japanese Temple, Its Art and History. Tokyo: 1954. V. 70

DOMVILLE FIFE, C. W.
Square-Rigger Days. Autobiographies of Sail. London: 1938. V. 69

DON Juan; or, the Battle of Tolosa; a Poem. London: 1816. V. 69

DON Leon. A Poem...forming Part of the Private Journal of His Lordship, Supposed to Have Been Entirely Destroyed by Thos. Moore...to Which is added Leon to Annabella, an Epistle from Lord Byron to Lady Byron. London: 1933. V. 70

DON, R. S.
Wine List Decorations 1961-1963. Bristol: 1963. V. 72

DON Sebastian King of Portugal. London: 1683. V. 73

DONAGHY, LYLE
Into the Light, and Other Poems. Dublin: 1934. V. 71

DONAHEY, MARY DICKERSON
The Adventures of Happy Dolly. New York: 1914. V. 73

DONAHEY, WILLIAM
Adventures of the Teenie Weenies. Chicago: 1920. V. 70; 73
Adventures of the Tennie Weenies. Chicago: 1940. V. 70
Down the River with the Teenie Weenies. Chicago: 1921. V. 71
Down the River with the Teenie Weenies. Chicago: 1940. V. 70
Teenie Weenie Town. New York: 1942. V. 69
Teenie Weenie Neighbors. New York: 1945. V. 70
The Tennie Weenies Under the Rose Bush. Chicago: 1922. V. 70

DONAHO, M. H.
Circle Dot- A True Story of Cowboy Life Forty Years Ago. Topeka: 1907. V. 71

DONALD, DAVID HERBERT
Lincoln at Home: Two Glimpses of Abraham Lincoln's Domestic Life. New York: 1999. V. 73

DONALD, DIANA
Human Passions Delineated: an Exploration of the Work of Tim Bobbin. 1990. V. 71

DONALD, JAY
Outlaws of the Border: A Complete and Authentic.... Cincinnati: 1882. V. 71

DONALDSON, D. J.
Cajun Nights. New York: 1988. V. 68; 70

DONALDSON, H. J.
H. J. Donaldson, Direct Importer from Japan. London: 1911. V. 68
H. J. Donaldson, Direct Importer from Japan. London: 1912. V. 68

DONALDSON, M. E. M.
Wanderings in the Western Highlands and Islands. . . Paisley: 1923. V. 71

DONALDSON, NORMAN
In Search of Dr. Thorndyke. Bowling Green: 1971. V. 71

DONALDSON, P. E. K.
Electronic Apparatus for Biological Research. London: 1958. V. 68

DONALDSON, SCOTT
Hemingway Vs. Fitzgerald. Woodstock: 1999. V. 72

DONALDSON, STEPHEN
Forbidden Knowledge. New York: 1991. V. 70

DONALDSON, STEPHEN R.
The Illearth War. 1977. V. 68
Lord Foul's Bane. 1977. V. 68
The Power that Preserves. 1977. V. 68

DONALDSON, THOMAS
The Public Domain: Its History with Statistics.... Washington: 1884. V. 68

DONALDSON, WALTER ALEXANDER
Fity Years of Green-Room Gossip; or, Recollections of an Actor. London: 1881. V. 68
Theatrical Portraits; or, the Days of Shakespeare, Betterton, Garrick and Kemble. London: 1870. V. 72

DONCASTER, PATRICK
The Long Week. London: 1951. V. 72
A Sign for a Drumbeat. New York: 1948. V. 69

DONISTHORPE, G. SHEILA
Loveliest of Friends!. New York: 1952. V. 72

DONLEAVY, J. P.
The Ginger Man. London: 1958. V. 70
The Ginger Man. Paris: 1958. V. 69
The Ginger Man. New York: 1980. V. 73
Schultz. New York: 1979. V. 68
A Singular Man. Boston: 1963. V. 73

DONLEVY, ANDREW
An Teagasg Criosduidhe de reir Ceasada 7 Freagartha. 1848. V. 69

DONLEY, J. F.
The Orchids of Nova Scotia a Provisional List and Identification Key. Mill Village: 1963. V. 68

DONLEY, ROBERT T.
The Law of Coal, Oil and Gas in West Virginia and Virginia. Charlottesville: 1951. V. 70

DONN, BERTRAM
Atlas of Comet Halley 1910. Washington: 1986. V. 69

DONN, J.
Hortus Cantabrigiensis. Cambridge: 1811. V. 69
Hortus Cantabrigiensis. 1826. V. 72

DONNE, JOHN
The Courtier's Library or Catalogus Librorum Aulciorum Incomparabilium.... London: 1930. V. 70; 71
Death's Duell. A Sermon Delivered Before King Charles I.... Boston: 1973. V. 70
Devotions Upon Emergent Occasions and Several Steps in My Sickness. London: 1624. V. 69
Donne's Sermon of Valediction at His Going Into Germany Preached at Lincoln's Inn April 18, 1619. London: 1932. V. 69
LXXX Sermons Preached by....John Donne. (with) Fifty Sermons...the Second Volume. London: 1640. V. 73
Letters to Several Persons of Honour. London: 1651. V. 70; 73
Mud Walls. Excerpts from the Sermons. Wakefield: 1986. V. 68; 71
Poems. London: 1633. V. 72
Poems by J.D. London: 1639. V. 69
The Poems of John Donne from the Text of the Edition of 1633. New York: 1895. V. 70
A Prayer. New York: 1947. V. 73
Selected Prose. Oxford: 1967. V. 71; 73
Sermon of Valediction at His Going Into Germany, Preached at Lincoln's Inn April 18, 1619. London: 1932. V. 70
X Sermons. London: 1923. V. 68; 70; 71

DONNE, T. E.
Red Deer Stalking in New Zealand. 1924. V. 72
Rod Fishing in New Zealand Waters. 1927. V. 68

DONNELLAN, JOHN
The Proceedings at Large on the Trial of John Donnellan, Esq. for the Wilful Murder (by Poison) of Sir Edward Allesley Boughton, Bart. Late of Lawford-Hall, in the County of Warwick. Tried before Mr. Justice Buller, at the Assizes at Warwick.... London: 1781. V. 72; 73

DONNELLY, ELEANOR C.
Girlhood's Hand-Book of Woman.... St. Louis: 1898. V. 69

DONNELLY, IGNATIUS
The Cipher in the Plays and on the Tombstone. Minneapolis: 1899. V. 69; 71

DONNET, ALEXIS
Architectonographie des Theatres de Paris mis en Parallele entr'eux. Paris: 1821-1824. V. 72

DONOHO, MILFORD H.
Circle Dot, a True Story of Cowboy Life Forty Years Ago. Topeka: 1907. V. 70

DONOSO, JOSE
The Garden Next Door. New York: 1992. V. 72
The Obscene Bird of Night. New York: 1973. V. 72

DONOUGHMORE, EARL OF
Speech...in the House of Lords...January 6th, 1881. 1881. V. 69

DONOVAN, CHARLES HENRY WYNNE
With Wilson in Matabeleland or Sport and War in Zambesia. London: 1894. V. 68

DONOVAN, DANIEL
Sketches in Carbery, County Cork. 1876. V. 70

DONOVAN, DICK
The Chronicles of Michael Danevitch of the Russian Secret Service. London: 1897. V. 69; 73
From Clue to Capture. London: 1893. V. 69
Suspicion Aroused/In the Grip of the Law. London: 1892-1893. V. 69

DONOVAN, E.
The Natural History of British Shells. London: 1799-1803. V. 69

DONOVAN, EDWARD
An Epitome of the Natural History of the Insects of India and the Islands in the Indian Seas. London: 1800-1804. V. 73

DONOVAN, MICHAEL
A Treatise on Chemistry. London: 1832. V. 68

DONWORTH, GRACE
The Letters of Jennie Allen to Her Friend Mis Musgrove. Boston: 1908. V. 68

DOOIJES, D.
A History of the Dutch Poster 1890-1960. Amsterdam: 1968. V. 69

DOOLING, RICHARD
White Man's Grave. New York: 1994. V. 68

DOOLITTLE, BEV
The Art of Bev Doolittle. New York: 1990. V. 70

DOOLITTLE, HILDA
By Avon River. New York: 1949. V. 70; 71
The Hedgehog. 1936. V. 72
Hedylus. Stratford-upon-Avon. 1928. V. 73
Heliodora and Other Poems. 1924. V. 70
Hymen. 1921. V. 70
Kora and Ka. Dijon: 1930. V. 69; 72
Nights. Dijon: 1935. V. 69; 72
Palimpsest. New York: 1926. V. 73
Sea Garden. 1916. V. 70
The Usual Star. London: 1928. V. 69
What Do I Love?. London: 1950. V. 69; 72
Within the Walls. Iowa City: 1993. V. 69; 73

DOOLITTLE, JUSTUS
Social Life of the Chinese. New York: 1865. V. 70; 71
Social Life of the Chinese. London: 1868. V. 73
Social Life of the Chinese. New York: 1876. V. 68

DOPPLER, JOHANN CHRISTAN
Bemerkungen zu meiner theorie des farbigen lichtes der doppelsterne etc. mit vorzuglicher ruschsicht auf die von Herrn Dr. Ballot zu Utrecht dagegen erhobenen Bedenken in Annalen der Physik und Chemie, Band LXVIII no. 5, 1846. Leipzig: 1846. V. 72

DORAN, DR.
Monarchs Retired From Business. London: 1857. V. 72

DORAN, JAMES M.
Erroll Garner. The Most Happy Piano. Metuchen: 1985. V. 73

DORAN, JOHN
Their Majesties Servants, Annals of the English Stage, from Thomas Betterton to Edmund Kean, Actors - Authors - Audiences. London: 1864. V. 70; 72

DORBIN, SANFORD
A Bibliography of Charles Bukowski. Los Angeles: 1969. V. 69

DORE, BENJAMIN
Journal of Benjamin Dore 1849-1850. Berkeley: 1923. V. 69

DORE, GUSTAVE
Londres. Paris: 1876. V. 69

DORE, J. R.
Old Bibles: an Account of the Early Versions of the English Bible. 1888. V. 73

DORFMAN, ARIEL
My House is on Fire. London: 1992. V. 71; 73

DORMAN, RUSHTON M.
The Origin of Primitive Superstitions. Philadelphia: 1881. V. 69

DORMON, C.
Wild Flowers of Louisiana, Including Most of the Herbaceous Wild Flowers of the Gulf States.... Garden City: 1934. V. 71

DORMOY, MARIE
Exposition des Arts Decoratifs, Paris 1925. Paris: 1926. V. 71

DORN, EDWARD
Captain Jack's Chaps or Houston/MLA. Madison: 1983. V. 69
From Gloucester Out. London: 1964. V. 72
Hello, La Jolla. Berkeley: 1978. V. 68
Songs Set Two: a Short Count. 1970. V. 68; 71

DORNBUSCH, C. E.
Regimental Publications and Personal Narratives of The Civil War - A Checklist - 7 Volumes. NY: 1961. V. 72

DORR, NELL
In a Blue Moon. New York: 1939. V. 68
Mother and Child. New York: 1954. V. 72

DORRANCE, ETHEL SMITH
Damned: the Intimate Story of a Girl. New York: 1923. V. 73
Touching Cloud. New York: 1926. V. 69; 70

DORRANCE, JAMES FRENCH
The Golden Alaskan. New York: 1931. V. 70

DORRIS, MICHAEL
The Benchmark. New York: 1993. V. 69
The Broken Cord. New York: 1989. V. 69; 72
Cloud Chamber. New York: 1997. V. 69; 72
The Crown of Columbus. New York: 1991. V. 71
Louise. The Crown of Columbus. New York: 1991. V. 72
Morning Girl. New York: 1992. V. 71
Native Americans: 500 Years After. New York: 1975. V. 69
Working Men. New York: 1993. V. 72
Working Men. London: 1994. V. 72
A Yellow Raft in Blue Water. New York: 1987. V. 68; 69; 70; 73

D'ORSAY, ALFRED
Etiquette; or a Guide to the Usages of Society. New York: 1843. V. 71

DORSET NATURAL HISTORY & ANTIQUARIAN FIELD CLUB
Proceedings. Dorchester: 1877-1879. V. 69

D'ORSEY, ALEX J. D.
English Grammar and Composition. Part I. Edinburgh: 1842. V. 73

DORSEY, GEORGE A.
The Arapaho Sun Dance; the Ceremony of the Offerings Lodge. 1903. V. 69
The Arapaho Sun Dance; the Ceremony of the Offerings Lodge. Millwood: 1973. V. 69
The Cheyenne - Social Organization. New York: 1905. V. 68; 73
The Mishongnovi Ceremonies of the Snake and Antelope Fraternities. Chicago: 1902. V. 69
The Mythology of the Wichita. Washington: 1904. V. 70
Traditions of the Arapaho, Collected Under the Auspices of the Field Colombian Museum and the American Museum of Natural History. 1903. V. 69
Traditions of the Skidi Pawnee. Boston: 1904. V. 68

DORSEY, JOHN SYNG
Elements of Surgery. Philadelphia: 1813. V. 72

DORSEY, LEO M.
Stair Building: Poems. Canada: 1943. V. 72

DORSEY, SARAH A.
Panola. A Tale of Louisiana. Philadelphia: 1877. V. 73
Recollections of Henry Watkins Allen. New York: 1866. V. 69; 70

DORSEY, THOMAS A.
Dorsey's Songs With a Message. Chicago: 1951. V. 72

DORSEY, TIM
Florida Roadkill. New York: 1999. V. 70

DORVAL, MARCELLE
The Heart on the Sleeve. New York: 1943. V. 71

D'ORVILLE, JACQUES PHILIPPE
Sicula, Quibus Siciliae Veteris Rudera, Additis Antiquitatum Tabulis.... Amsterdam: 1764. V. 69

DOS PASSOS, JOHN RODERIGO
The Big Money. New York: 1936. V. 69
The 42nd Parallel. (with) 1919. (with) The Big Money. New York and London: 1930. V. 68
The Fourteenth Chronicle. 1973. V. 73

DOS PASSOS, JOHN RODERIGO continued
Manhattan Transfer. New York: 1925. V. 73
1919. New York: 1932. V. 72
Number One. Boston: 1943. V. 69; 71
Number One. London: 1944. V. 71
State of the Nation. Boston: 1944. V. 71
Three Soldiers. New York: 1921. V. 71
The U.S.A. Trilogy. New York: 1930-1936. V. 70
U.S.A. London: 1938. V. 72

DOSS, JAMES D.
The Shaman Sings. New York: 1994. V. 69; 71

DOSTOEVSKII, FYODOR MIKHAILOVICH
The Brothers Karamazov. New York: 1949. V. 68; 69; 70; 72
The Brothers Karamazov (in Russian). St. Petersburg: 1881. V. 72
Crime and Punishment. New York: 1948. V. 70; 72
The Gambler and Notes from the Underground. New York: 1967. V. 70; 72
The Grand Inquisitor. London: 1930. V. 71
The House of the Dead. New York: 1982. V. 70; 72
The Idiot. New York: 1956. V. 70; 72
The Letters of Dostoyevsky to His Wife. London: 1930. V. 71
The Possessed. New York: 1959. V. 70; 72
A Raw Youth. Verona: 1974. V. 69; 70; 72

DOTEN, ALFRED
The Journals of Alfred Doten. Reno: 1973. V. 68

DOTTIN, PAUL
The Life and Strange Surprising Adventures of Daniel De Foe. New York: 1929. V. 70

DOTY, MARK
Farvile. New York: 1997. V. 73

THE DOUBLE Suicide. New York: 1855. V. 68

DOUBLEDAY, ROMAN
The Hemlock Avenue Mystery. Boston: 1908. V. 69; 71

DOUBLEDAY, THOMAS
The True Law of Population Shewn to be Connected with the Food of the People. London: 1846. V. 70

DOUBTS About Darwinism. London, New York, and Bombay: 1903. V. 69

DOUCE, FRANCIS
Illustrations of Shakespeare and of Ancient Manners; With Dissertations on the Clowns and Fools of Shakespeare on the Collection of Popular Tales Entitled Gesta Romanorum; and on the English Morris Dance. London: 1807. V. 70

DOUGALL, JOHN
Angling Songs and Poems, With Miscellaneous Pieces. Glasgow: 1901. V. 71
The Self Instructor; or Young Man's Companion. Halifax: 1850. V. 72

DOUGHARTY, JOHN
Mathematical Digests, Containing the Elements and Application of Geometry, and Plane Trigonometry, Whether by Instrumental Construction or by Calculation to the Measuring of Heights and Distances, &c. London: 1747?. V. 73

DOUGHITT, KATHERINE CHRISTIAN
Romance and Dim Trails A History of Clay County. Dallas: 1938. V. 71

DOUGHTY, CHARLES MONTAGU
Mansoul (or, the Riddle of the World). London: 1920. V. 70; 72; 73
Travels in Arabia Deserta. New York and London: 1923. V. 70
Travels in Arabia Deserta. London: 1924. V. 68; 72
Travels in Arabia Deserta, with an Introduction by T.E. Lawrence. 1943. V. 72
Wanderings In Arabia. London: 1908. V. 72

DOUGHTY, F. H.
H. G. Wells: Educationist. New York: 1927. V. 71

DOUGHTY, J.
Cabinet of Natural History and American Rural Sports with Illustrations. Philadelphia: 1830-1832. V. 71

DOUGHTY, J. H.
Hill Writings. Manchester: 1937. V. 69; 71

DOUGHTY, JOHN
The Cabinet of Natural History and American Rural Sports. Philadelphia: 1830-1832. V. 68

DOUGLAS, A. E.
The Etiquette of Fashionable Life.... London: 1849. V. 71

DOUGLAS, ALFRED
The City of the Soul. London: 1899. V. 73
The City of the Soul. Girard: 1925. V. 71
The Collected Satires. London: 1926. V. 68
Lyrics. 1935. V. 70
Lyrics. London: 1935. V. 68
New Preface to the Life and Confessions of Oscar Wilde. London: 1925. V. 68
The Pongo Papers and The Duke of Berwick. London: 1907. V. 68
Sonnets. London: 1909. V. 68
Sonnets. 1935. V. 70
Sonnets. London: 1935. V. 68
Sonnets. London: 1943. V. 73

DOUGLAS, AMANDA M.
In Trust; or Dr. Bertrand's Household. Boston: 1866. V. 69

DOUGLAS, C. L.
Cattle Kings of Texas. Dallas: 1939. V. 71
The Gentleman in the White Hats, Dramatic Episodes in the History of the Texas Rangers. Dallas: 1934. V. 69
James Bowie: the Life of a Bravo. Dallas: 1944. V. 69

DOUGLAS, CLARENCE B.
The History of Tulsa Oklahoma. A City with a Personality. Chicago: 1921. V. 70

DOUGLAS, DAVID C.
The Domesday Monachorum of Christ Church Canterbury. London: 1944. V. 70

DOUGLAS, ELLEN
The Rock Cried Out. New York: 1979. V. 68

DOUGLAS, GEORGE
A Cadger's Creel. Edinburgh: 1925. V. 71

DOUGLAS, HOWARD
An Essay on the Principles and Construction of Military Bridges and Passage of Rivers in Military Operations. London: 1816. V. 73
An Essay on the Principles and Construction of Military Bridges, and the Passage of Rivers in Military Operations. London: 1832. V. 73
An Essay on the Principles and Construction of Military Bridges and the Passage of Rivers in Military Operations. London: 1853. V. 73

DOUGLAS, JAMES
Bibliographiae Anatomicae Specimen: sive Catalogus Omnium Pene Auctorum qui ae Hippocrate ad Harveum Rem Anatomicam.... Leinden: 1734. V. 68; 72
Nenia Britannica; or a Sepulchral History of Great Britain.... London: 1793. V. 68; 72

DOUGLAS, JOHN
The Cornutor of Seventy-Five. London: 1748?. V. 73
A Letter Addressed to Two Great men, on the Prospect of Peace. London: 1760. V. 68; 72

DOUGLAS, JONATHAN PERCY
Miscellaneous Poems. Maryport: 1836. V. 69

DOUGLAS, KEITH
Alamein to Zem Zem. London: 1946. V. 68
Collected Poems. London: 1951. V. 73
Middle East Anthology. London: 1946. V. 71
Selected Poems. London: 1964. V. 71

DOUGLAS, LLOYD C.
The Big Fisherman. Boston: 1948. V. 73
The Robe. Boston: 1942. V. 70; 71; 73

DOUGLAS, MARJORY STONEMAN
The Everglades: River of Grass. New York: 1947. V. 69; 71
Florida: The Long Frontier. New York: 1967. V. 70; 73
Freedom River. Miami: 1994. V. 70
Voice of the River: an Autobiography. Englewood: 1987. V. 69

DOUGLAS, NORMAN
An Almanac. Lisbon: 1941. V. 73
An Almanac. London: 1945. V. 72; 73
Alone. London: 1921. V. 73
Birds and Beasts of the Greek Anthology. Florence: 1927. V. 72; 73
Birds and Beasts of the Greek Anthology. London: 1927. V. 73
Capri. 1930. V. 73
Contributions to an Avifauna of Baden. 1894. V. 72
D. H. Lawrence and Maurice Magnus. A Plea for Better Manners. Florence: 1924. V. 68; 71; 72; 73
Fountains in the Sand. London: 1912. V. 68
Fountains in the Sand. 1928. V. 73
In the Beginning. Florence: 1927. V. 73
In the Beginning. London: 1928. V. 68; 71
Late Harvest. London: 1947. V. 72
London Street Games. 1916. V. 73
Looking Back, an Autobiographical Excursion. London: 1933. V. 68; 71; 73
Nerinda. Florence: 1929. V. 73
Paneros. Florence: 1930. V. 68; 70; 73
Paneros, Some Words on Aphrodisiacs and the Like. Orioli: 1930. V. 71
Paneros, Some Words on Aphrodisiacs and the Like. London: 1931. V. 71
Report on the Pumice Stone Industry of the Lipari Islands. La Chapelle-Reanville: 1928. V. 72
Some Antiquarian Notes. Napoli: 1907. V. 72
Some Limericks. Boston: 1942. V. 69
South Wind. London: 1917. V. 73
South Wind. London: 1922. V. 68
South Wind. New York: 1928. V. 68
South Wind. Chicago: 1929. V. 71
South Wind. New York: 1932. V. 68; 71
Summer Islands. London: 1942. V. 72
They Went. London: 1920. V. 73
Unprofessional Tales. London: 1901. V. 72

DOUGLAS, O.
The Day of Small Things. Garden City: 1930. V. 71

DOUGLAS, RONALD
The Irish Book; a Miscellany. 1936. V. 69

DOUGLAS, WALTER
Manuel Lisa. New York: 1964. V. 69; 72

DOUGLAS, WILLIAM
Journal. Volume IX. London: 1906-1907. V. 69

DOUGLAS, WILLIAM, & SONS
Douglas's Encyclopaedia. London: 1924. V. 68

DOUGLAS, WILLIAM SCOTT
Modern Athenians. Edinburgh: 1882. V. 70

DOUGLAS & CLYDESDALE, MARQUESS OF
The Pilot's Book of Everest. London: 1936. V. 69

DOUGLASS & Aikman's Almanack and Register for the Island of Jamaica.... Kingston: 1781. V. 71

DOUGLASS, FREDERICK
Life and Times of.... Hartford: 1881. V. 71
Life and Times of.... Hartford: 1882. V. 70; 71
My Bondage and My Freedom. New York/Auburn: 1855. V. 70; 71; 72
Narrative of the Life of Frederick Douglass, an American Slave. Boston: 1847. V. 73
Narrative of the Life Of....Written by Himself. London: 1847. V. 72

DOUGLASS, GEORGE
The Art of Drawing in Perspective from Mathematical Principles.... Edinburgh: 1805. V. 71

DOULTON & CO.
Terra Cotta Chimney Tops, International Exhibition 1862. London: 1862. V. 68; 70

DOUSA, GEORGE
De Itinere Suo Constinapolitano Epistola. Leyden: 1599. V. 68

DOUTHIT, MARY OSBORN
Souvenir of Western Women. Portland: 1905. V. 70

DOVE, RITA
The Darker Face of Earth. Brownsville, OR: 1994. V. 71
Grace Notes. New York: 1989. V. 68; 72
Lady Freedom Among Us. West Burke: 1994. V. 72
Selected Poems. New York: 1993. V. 68
Thomas and Beulah. Pittsburgh: 1986. V. 69; 72
Through the Ivory Gate. New York: 1992. V. 70; 72

DOVER, C.
American Negro Art. New York: 1967. V. 69; 72

DOVER, LORD
Life of Frederic the Second, King of Prussia. London: 1832. V. 69

DOVES PRESS
Catalogue Raisonne Books Printed and Published at the Doves Press. Hammersmith: 1908. V. 71
Catalogue Raisonne of Books Printed and Published at the Doves Press 1900-1911. (No. 2). Hammersmith: 1911. V. 71

DOW, CHARLES MASON
Anthology and Bibliography of Niagara Falls. Albany: 1921. V. 73

DOW, G. F.
American Vessels Captured by the British During the Revolution and War of 1812. Salem: 1911. V. 73
Whale Ships and Whaling, a Pictorial History of Whaling During Three Centuries, With an Account of the Whale Fishery in Colonial New England. Salem: 1925. V. 70

DOW, LORENZO
The Opinion of Dow, or, Lorenzo's Thoughts on Different Religious Subjects, in an Address to the People of New England. Windham: 1804. V. 69
Quintessence of Lorenzo's Works. Philadelphia: 1816. V. 73

DOW, R. S.
The Physiology and Pathology of the Crebellum. Minneapolis: 1958. V. 71

DOWBEN, ROBERT M.
Cell and Muscle Mobility. New York: 1981-1985. V. 68

DOWELL, COLEMAN
The Grass Dies. London: 1968. V. 72
Island People. New York: 1976. V. 72

DOWELL, STEPHEN
The History and Explanation of the Stamp Duties and the Stamp Laws at Present in Force in the United Kingdom.... London: 1873. V. 71

DOWLING, PHIL
The Mountaineers. Famous Climbers In Canada. Edmonton: 1979. V. 72

DOWLING, RICHARD
The Duke's Sweetheart. London: 1887. V. 68
An Isle of Surrey. London: 1891. V. 68

DOWN by the Sea. London: 1900. V. 70

DOWN, ELIZA
Kenwith Castle and Other Poems. London: 1878. V. 69

DOWNAME, JOHN
A Defence and Vindication of the Right of Tithes, Against Sundry Late Scandalous Pamphlets.... London: 1646. V. 72

DOWNES, WILLIAM HOWE
John S. Sargent: His Life and Work. Boston: 1925. V. 69
John S. Sargent, His Life and Work. London: 1926. V. 72

DOWNEY, FAIRFAX
Indian Fighting Army. New York: 1941. V. 69; 72
Indian Wars of The U.S. Army (1776-1865). New York: 1963. V. 72

DOWNEY, HAL
Handbook of Haematology. New York: 1965. V. 68

DOWNEY, WILLIAM SCOTT
Proverbs. Boston: 1853. V. 72

DOWNING, ANDREW JACKSON
The Horticulturist and Journal of Rural Art and Rural Taste.... Albany: 1847-1848. V. 71; 73
Rural Essays.... New York: 1869. V. 72; 73
Rural Essays.... New York: 1890. V. 71
A Treatise on the Theory and Practice of Landscape Gardening. New York: 1856. V. 69

DOWNING, ANTOINETTE FORRESTER
Early Homes of Rhode Island. Richmond, VA: 1937. V. 72

DOWNING, FANNY MURDAUGH
Nameless. Raleigh: 1865. V. 70

DOWNING, HARRIET
Remembrances of a Monthly Nurse. London: 1852. V. 68

DOWNING, TODD
The Case of the Unconquered Sisters. New York: 1936. V. 70
The Cat Screams. Garden City: 1934. V. 73
The Lazy Lawrence Murders. New York: 1941. V. 71
Murder on the Tropic. Garden City: 1935. V. 73
Vultures in the Sky. 1935. V. 73
Vultures in the Sky. Garden City: 1935. V. 70

DOWNS, NORTON
Essays in Honor of Conyers Read. Chicago: 1953. V. 69

DOWSING, WILLIAM
The Timber Merchant's and Builder's Companion. Hull: 1858. V. 69

DOWSON, ERNEST
Decorations: in Verse and Prose. London: 1899. V. 73
The Letters of Ernest Dowson. London: 1967. V. 68
New Letters from Ernest Dowson. Andoversford: 1984. V. 68
The Poems of Ernest Dowson. London: 1905. V. 68
The Poems; with a Memoir by Arthur Symons. 1905. V. 69
Verses. London: 1896. V. 73

DOYLE, ADRIAN CONAN
The Exploits of Sherlock Holmes. London: 1954. V. 68; 69
The Exploits of Sherlock Holmes. New York: 1954. V. 70; 71
Heaven Has Claws. 1952. V. 68
Sir Arthur Conan Doyle Centenary 1859-1959. Garden City: 1959. V. 69

DOYLE, ARTHUR CONAN
The Adventure of the Blue Carbuncle. New York: 1948. V. 69
The Adventure of the Orient Express. New York: 1965. V. 72
Adventures of Gerard. London: 1903. V. 68
Adventures of Sherlock Holmes. New York: 1892. V. 69; 71
The Adventures of Sherlock Holmes. New York: 1971. V. 70
The Case-Book of Sherlock Holmes. London: 1974. V. 72
The Casebook of Solar Pons. Sauk City: 1965. V. 71; 72
The Coming of the Fairies. New York: 1922. V. 69; 73
The Croxley Master. New York: 1925. V. 69
The Doings of Raffles Haw. London Paris & Melbourne: 1892. V. 69
The Exploits of Sherlock Holmes. New York: 1954. V. 71
The Great Boer War. London: 1900. V. 72
Great Stories. London: 1959. V. 68; 73
His Last Bow. Some Later Reminiscences of Sherlock Holmes. New York: 1917. V. 68; 70; 71
His Last Bow: Some Reminiscences of Sherlock Holmes. London: 1917. V. 69
The Hound of the Baskervilles. 1902. V. 69
The Hound of the Baskervilles. New York: 1902. V. 72
In Re: Sherlock Holmes. Sauk City: 1945. V. 71; 72
An Irregular Guide to Sherlock Holmes. New York: 1947. V. 69
The Land of Mist. New York: 1926. V. 70
The Last Galley. Garden City: 1911. V. 70
The Lost World. London: 1912. V. 73
The Maracot Deep. New York: 1929. V. 70
The Memoirs of Sherlock Holmes. London: 1894. V. 68; 72
Memoirs of Sherlock Holmes. New York: 1894. V. 68; 69; 70; 73
The Memoirs of Sherlock Holmes. London: 1908. V. 70
Memoirs Of Sherlock Holmes. New York: 1984. V. 72
Memoirs of Solar Pons. Sauk City: 1951. V. 69; 72
The Misadventure of Sherlock Holmes. Boston: 1944. V. 69
The Mystery of Cloomber. London: 1895. V. 71; 72

DOYLE, ARTHUR CONAN *continued*
The New Adventures Of Sherlock Holmes. New York: 1987. V. 72
The New Revelation. London: 1918. V. 68
The Notched Hairpin. New York: 1949. V. 69
The Parasite: a Story. New York: 1895. V. 68
Part One. Athens (GA): 1947. V. 72
A Praed Street Dossier. Sauk City: 1968. V. 72
The Private Life of Sherlock Holmes. NY: 1933. V. 72
Profile By Gaslight. New York: 1944. V. 71
The Reminiscences of Solar Pons. Sauk City: 1961. V. 71; 72
The Return of Sherlock Holmes. 1905. V. 68
The Return of Sherlock Holmes. London: 1905. V. 69
The Return of Sherlock Holmes. London: 1913. V. 70
The Return of Solar Pons. Sauk City: 1958. V. 71; 72
Round the Fire Stories. New York: 1908. V. 68
Round the Red Lamp, Being Facts and Fancies of Medical Life. London: 1894. V. 69
Sherlock Holmes. New York: 1935. V. 70
Sherlock Holmes Complete Stories With Introduction By Peter Cushing. London: 1993. V. 68; 72
The Sign of the Four. New York. V. 70
The Sign of the Four. New York: 1899. V. 72
The Sign of the Four. New York: 1900. V. 72
Sir Arthur Conan Doyle's Strange Studies from Life. New York: 1963. V. 69
Songs of Action. London: 1898. V. 71
The Stark Munro Letters. London: 1895. V. 69; 71; 73
A Study in Pictures. Philadelphia: 1954. V. 69
A Study in Scarlet. Chicago: 1900. V. 69
A Study in Scarlet. London: 1993. V. 70
Three of Them. London: 1923. V. 70
Through the Magic Door. London: 1907. V. 72
The Tragedy Of The Korosko. London: 1898. V. 68; 72
221B: Studies in Sherlock Holmes. New York: 1940. V. 71
An Undiscerning Critic Discerned. San Francisco: 1968. V. 71
The Unknown Conan Doyle: Uncollected Stories. London: 1982. V. 70
The Valley of Fear. New York: 1914. V. 70; 71
The Valley of Fear. London: 1915. V. 70
The War in South Africa Its Cause and Conduct. London: 1902. V. 72
The White Company. London: 1891. V. 70
The White Company. New York: 1922. V. 70

DOYLE, C. W.
The Shadow of Quong Lung. Philadelphia: 1900. V. 70; 71

DOYLE, CHARLES
The Tragic and Yet Strictly Moral Story of How Three Little Pigs Went to Market. London and Edinburgh: 1878. V. 71
Wallace Stevens: the Critical Heritage. London: 1985. V. 71

DOYLE, J. A.
English Colonies in America. New York: 1889. V. 71

DOYLE, J. E. P.
Plymouth Church and Its Pastor, Henry Ward Beecher and His Accusers. Hartford: 1874. V. 69

DOYLE, JAMES E.
A Chronicle of England B.C. 55-A.D. 1485. London: 1864. V. 70; 73

DOYLE, JOHN
The Marmosite's Miscellany. London: 1925. V. 72

DOYLE, RICHARD
The American Tour of Messrs. Brown, Jones and Robinson. (with) The Foreign Tour of Messrs. Brown, Jones and Robinson. New York: 1872-1877. V. 70
The Foreign Tour of Messrs Brown, Jones and Robinson. London: 1855. V. 68
In Fairyland, a Series of Pictures from the Elf-World. London: 1870. V. 70
Jack the Giant Killer. London: 1888. V. 69
Richard Doyle's Pictures of Extra Articles and Visitors to the Exhibition. London: 1851. V. 71

DOYLE, RODDY
The Commitments. New York: 1987. V. 71
The Commitments. London: 1988. V. 73
The Commitments. New York: 1989. V. 68
The Giggler Treatment. London: 2000. V. 68; 71
Not Just for Christmas. Dublin: 1999. V. 73
Paddy Clarke Ha Ha Ha. London: 1993. V. 68
Paddy Clarke Ha Ha Ha. New York: 1993. V. 71; 72
Paddy Clarke Ha Ha Ha. New York: 1994. V. 68
The Snapper. New York: 1992. V. 68
A Star Called Henry. London: 1999. V. 68; 70
A Star Called Henry. New York: 1999. V. 72
The Van. New York: 1992. V. 69; 71
The Woman Who Walked Into Doors. 1996. V. 72
The Woman Who Walked into Doors. London: 1996. V. 68

D'OYLY, CHARLES
The European In India. London: 1813. V. 72

A DOZEN Pair of Wedding Gloves. London: 1855. V. 70

DRABBLE, MARGARET
The Garrick Year. New York: 1965. V. 69
Jerusalem the Golden. London: 1967. V. 73
A Natural Curiosity. London: 1989. V. 73
A Summer Bird-Cage. New York: 1964. V. 69
The Waterfall. London: 1969. V. 73
The Witch of Exmoor. London: 1996. V. 73

DRAGO, HARRY SINCLAIR
Great American Cattle Trails. New York: 1965. V. 68
Guardians of the Sage. New York: 1932. V. 72
Rio Rita. New York: 1929. V. 71

DRAKE, BENJAMIN
Cincinnati in 1826. Cincinnati: 1827. V. 71
Life of Tecumseh, and Of His Brother the Prophet; with a Historical Sketch of the Shawanoe Indians. Cincinnati: 1850. V. 73

DRAKE, DANIEL
Discourses Delivered by Appointment, Before the Cincinnati Medical Library Association Jan. 9th and 10th 1852. Cincinnati: 1852. V. 71
An Inaugural Discourse on Medical Education Delivered at the Opening of the Medical College of Ohio in Cincinnati 11 November 1820. New York: 1951. V. 71
Pioneer Life in Kentucky. Cincinnati: 1870. V. 68; 71
A Systematic Treatise, Historical, Etiological and Practical, on the Principal Diseases of the Interior Valley of North America. Cincinnati: 1850. V. 70

DRAKE, H. B.
The Children Reap. New York: 1929. V. 70
Cursed Be the Treausre. New York: 1928. V. 70

DRAKE, JAMES
Drake's Road Book of the London and Birmingham and Grand Junction Railways, Being a Complete Guide to the Entire Line of Railway from London to Liverpool and Manchester.... London: 1840. V. 72

DRAKE, JAMES MADISON
Historical Sketches of the Revolutionary and Civil Wars. New York: 1908. V. 69
The History of the Ninth New Jersey Veteran Volunteers: a Record of Its Service from September 13th, 1861 to July 12th 1865. Elizabeth: 1889. V. 69

DRAKE, JOSEPH RODMAN
The Culprit Fay. A Poem. New York: 1867. V. 68

DRAKE, JUDITH
An Essay in Defence of the Female Sex. London: 1696. V. 69; 73
An Essay in Defence of the Female Sex. London: 1697. V. 73

DRAKE, SAMUEL ADAMS
The Taking of Louisbourg. Decisive Events in American History (Series). Boston: 1891. V. 72

DRAKE, SAMUEL G.
The Old Indian Chronicle Being a Collection of Exceedingly Rare Tracts.... Boston: 1867. V. 72; 73

DRAKE, STILLMAN
Mechanics in Sixteenth Century Italy: Selections from Tartaglia, Benedetti, Guido Ubaldo and Galileo. Madison, Milwaukee & London: 1969. V. 69

DRANE, R. B.
Sketch of St. James's Parish Wilmington, N.C. New York: 1874. V. 68

DRAPER, BOURNE HALL
The Art of Being Happy.... London: 1845. V. 73
The Juvenile Naturalist; or, Walks in the Country, in Spring, Summer, Autumn and Winter. London: 1845. V. 68
Sketches from the Volume of Creation, as Displayed in the Seasons of the Year.... London: 1830. V. 71

DRAPER, DOROTHY
Entertaining Is Fun: How To Be a Popular Hostess. Garden City: 1945. V. 72

DRAPER, GEORGE
Human Constitution. Philadelphia: 1924. V. 68

DRAPER, J.
Thomas Hardy's England. London: 1984. V. 70

DRAPER, JOHN WILLIAM
History of the American Civil War. New York: 1867-. V. 71
History of the American Civil War. New York: 1867-1868. V. 71

DRAPER, LYMAN
King's Mountain and Its Heroes: History of the Battle, Oct. 7th, 1780. Cincinnati: 1881. V. 68; 69

DRAPER, WILLIAM H.
Adel and Its Norman Church. Leeds: 1909. V. 73

DRAPERS' COMPANY
Two Reports of a Deputation Who in Pursuance of the Resolutions of the Court of Assistants of the Drapers' Company of the 23rd January 1817, and 3rd August 1818, Visited the Estates of the Company in the County of Londonderry in Ireland. London: 1818-1821. V. 71

DRAR, M.
Enumeration of the Plants Collected at Gebel Elba During Two Expeditions. Cairo: 1936. V. 68

DRATLER, JAY
The Pitfall. New York: 1947. V. 68; 69

DRAUD, GEORG
Bibliotheca Librorum Germanicorum Classica...(with) Bibliotheca Exotica, sive Catalogus Officinalis Librorum.... Frankfurt: 1611-1610. V. 68; 73

THE DRAWING-Room Album, and Companion for the Boudoir, an Elegant Literary Miscellany. London. V. 70

DRAWING-Room Portrait -Gallery. The Annual Gift-Book. London: 1859. V. 71; 72

DRAYTON, DANIEL
Personal Memoir of...For Four Years and Four Months a Prisoner (for Charity's Sake) in Washington Jail. New York: 1853. V. 69

DRAYTON, GRACE
Dolly Dimples and Bobby Bounce. New York: 1930. V. 71
Kiddie-Land. 1930. V. 71

DRAYTON, JOHN
Letters Written During a Tour through the Northern and Eastern States of America. Charleston: 1794. V. 71
A View of South-Carolina, as Respects Her Natural and Civil Concerns. Charleston: 1802. V. 70

A DREAM of the Past. Toronto: 2000. V. 68

DREAMS that Money Can Buy - Program Book for the Surrealist Film. New York: 1947. V. 73

DREANY, E. JOSEPH
Cowboys in Pop-Up Action Pictures. London: 1951. V. 72

DREIER, MARY E.
Margaret Dreier Robins. Her Life, Letters and Work. New York: 1950. V. 72

DREISER, THEODORE
An American Tragedy. New York: 1925. V. 73
An American Tragedy. Toronto: 1925. V. 69
Chains: Lesser Novels and Stories. New York: 1927. V. 69; 70
Dawn. London: 1931. V. 69
A Gallery of Women. New York: 1929. V. 68; 73
The Hand of the Potter. New York: 1918. V. 72
Jennie Gerhardt. New York and London: 1911. V. 69
Sister Carrie. New York: 1939. V. 70; 73
Tragic America. London: 1932. V. 73
Twelve Men. New York: 1919. V. 70

DRELINCOURT, CHARLES
The Christian's Defence Against the Fears of Death.... Trenton: 1808. V. 69
Opuscula Medica, Quae Reperiri Potuere Omnia.... The Hague: 1727. V. 71

DRENNAN, WILLIAM
Fugitive Pieces in Verse and Prose. Belfast: 1815. V. 73

DRENTTEL, WILLIAM
Paul Auster: a Comprehensive Bibliographical Checklist of Published Works 1968-1994. New York: 1994. V. 73

THE DRESDEN Gallery. 1878. V. 71

DRESSER, CHRISTOPHER
Principles of Decorative Design. London: 1880. V. 73
Studies in Design. London: 1874-1876. V. 68

DRESSER, HENRY EELES
Eggs of the Birds of Europe Including All the Species Inhabiting the Western Palearctic Area. 1905-1910. V. 69; 73
A History of the Birds of Europe. London: 1871-1881. V. 70; 73

DRESSER, PAUL
The Songs of Paul Dresser. New York: 1927. V. 68

DREW, FREDERIC
The Northern Barrier of India. London: 1877. V. 72

DREW, GEORGE A.
Canada's Fighting Airmen. Toronto: 1931. V. 73

DREW, S. C.
Communication from C. S. Drew, Late Adjutant of the Second Regiment of Oregon Mounted Volunteers Giving an Account of the Origin and Early Prosecution of the Indian War in Oregon. Washington: 1860. V. 68

DREW, WILLIAM A.
Glimpses and Gatherings During a Voyage and Visit to London and the Great Exhibition.... Augusta: 1852. V. 71

DREXEL, JEREMIAS
De Aeternitate. Coloniae Agrippinae: 1634. V. 73
Gymnasium Patientiae. Dvaci: 1634. V. 73
Heliotropivm Seu Conformatio Humanae Voluntatis Cum Divina. Dvaci: 1628. V. 73
Noe Architectus Arcae in Diluvio Navarchus Descriptus. Antverpiae: 1652. V. 73
Opera. Monachii: 1628. V. 73
Recta Intentio Omnium Humanarum Actionum Amvssis. Col: 1634. V. 73

DREXLER, A.
The Drawings of Frank Lloyd Wright. New York: 1962. V. 68

DREYFUS, ALFRED
Five Years of My Life. London: 1901. V. 69

DREYFUS, JOHN
Aspects of French Eighteenth Century Typography: a Study of Type Specimens in the Broxbourne Collection at Cambridge University Library. Cambridge: 1982. V. 69
Bruce Rogers and American Typography. 1959. V. 70
Bruce Rogers and American Typography. Cambridge: 1959. V. 71
Four Lectures By T. J. Cobden-Sanderson: Edited, with an Introductory Essay on Cobden'Sanderson's Life and Ideals, with Details of His American Pupils, and His Lectures in the United States in 1907. San Francisco: 1974. V. 70; 72
A History of the Nonesuch Press. London: 1981. V. 68; 71
Italic Quartet. 1966. V. 71
Italic Quartet. Cambridge: 1966. V. 68
Italic Quartet. London: 1966. V. 69
Marienbader Elegie. Montagnola: 1923. V. 71
The Survival of Baskerville's Punches. 1949. V. 71
A Typographical Masterpiece.... 1991. V. 71
William Caxton and His Quincentenary. San Francisco: 1976. V. 70; 72

DREYFUSS, H.
Designing for People. New York: 1955. V. 69

DRIBERG, TOM
Colonnade 1937-1947. London: 1949. V. 68

DRIGGS, B. W.
History of the Teton Valley Idaho. Caldwell: 1926. V. 68

DRIGGS, FRANK
Black Beauty, White Heat. New York: 1982. V. 69; 71; 72

DRIGGS, HOWARD R.
Westward America. New York: 1942. V. 68; 69; 72; 73

DRILL of the Howitzer Company of the First Regiment of Virginia. Richmond: 1860. V. 70

DRING, THOMAS
A Catalogue of the Lords, Knights and Gentlemen that Have Compounded for Their Estates. London: 1655. V. 68

DRINKWATER, JOHN
American Vignettes 1860-1865. Boston: 1931. V. 69
A Book for Bookmen: Being Edited Manuscripts and Marginalia With Essays on Several Occasions. London: 1926. V. 71
Cotswold Characters. New Haven and London: 1921. V. 69
Cromwell and Other Poems. London: 1913. V. 72
Preludes 1921-1922. 1922. V. 70

DRISCOLL, CLARA
In the Shadow of the Alamo. New York: 1906. V. 73

DRISKELL, DAVID
Harlem Renaissance: Art of Black America. New York: 1987. V. 69; 72
Two Centuries of Black American Art. New York: 1976. V. 68

DRIVER, ELIZABETH
Bibliography of Cookery Books Published in Britain 1875-1914. Devon. V. 68
A Bibliography of Cookery Books Published in Britain 1875-1914. London: 1989. V. 70

DROST, WILLIAM E.
Clocks and Watches of New Jersey. Elizabeth: 1966. V. 69

DRUCE, G.
The Flora of Buckinghamshire. 1926. V. 69
The Flora of Oxfordshire. Oxford & London: 1886. V. 69

DRUCKER, P.
The Northern and Central Nootkan Tribes. Washington: 1951. V. 68

DRUITT, ROBERT
The Principles and Practice of Modern Surgery.... Philadelphia: 1844. V. 69

DRUMHELLER, DAN
Uncle Dan Tells Thrills of Western Tales in 1854. Spokane: 1925. V. 73

DRUMMOND, HENRY
The Monkey that Would Not Kill. London: 1898. V. 68; 71

DRUMMOND, JAMES L.
Letters to a Young Naturalist on the Study of Nature and Natural Theology. London: 1831. V. 68; 70

DRUMMOND, MALDWIN
Tall Ships. 1976. V. 72

DRUMMOND, WILLIAM
A Cypress Grove. London: 1919. V. 72
The Poems of William Drummond, of Hawthornden. London: 1833. V. 71

DRUMMOND, WILLIAM HAMILTON
The Battle of Trafalgar, an Heroic Poem. Charleston: 1807. V. 70; 73

DRUMMOND, WILLIAM HENRY
The Habitant, and Other French-Canadian Poems. New York and London: 1897. V. 68

DRUMMOND DE ANDRADE, CARLOS
Souvenir of the Ancient World. New York: 1976. V. 73

DRURY, ALLEN
Advise and Consent. Garden City: 1959. V. 71

DRURY, ANNA HARRIET
Annesley and Other Poems. London: 1847. V. 69
The First of May; a New Version of a Celebrated Ballad. London: 1851. V. 69
Light and Shade, or the Young Artist a Tale. London: 1853. V. 73

DRURY, CLIFFORD M.
Marcus and Narcissa Whitman and the Opening of Old Oregon. Glendale: 1973. V. 70

DRURY, TOM
The Black Brook. Boston/New York: 1998. V. 72
The End of Vandalism. Boston/New York: 1994. V. 68; 72

DRUSIUS, JOHANNES
Lectiones in Prophetas nahum, Hababbuc, Sophoniam, Iolem, Ionam Abdiam. (with) In Prophetam Ionam Lectiones. Leiden: 1595. V. 72

DRY, FLORENCE
The Sources of Jane Eyre. 1940. V. 70
The Sources of Wuthering Heights. 1937. V. 70; 73

THE DRYAD'S Child. Birmingham: 1936. V. 73

DRYANDER, JOHANNES
Anatomiae, hoc est, Corporis Humani Dissectionis.... Marburg: 1537. V. 69

DRYDEN, BRIDGET
Whither I Must. New York: 1932. V. 70

DRYDEN, JOHN
All for Love, or the World Well Lost. 1932. V. 72
Annus Mirabilis: The Year of Wonders, 1666. London: 1667. V. 69; 73
Aureng-Zebe; a Tragedy. London: 1676. V. 69
The Dramatic Work...Chronology of Dramatick Poesie - The Wild Gallant The Rival Ladies - The Indian Queen - The Indian Emperours - Notes. London: 1932. V. 70
Fables Ancient and Modern. London: 1721. V. 73
Fables Ancient and Modern. Glasgow: 1771. V. 73
The First Part of Miscellany Poems. London: 1727. V. 68
The Hind and the Panther. London: 1687. V. 68; 70; 73
Of Dramatick Poesie - an Essay 1668. London: 1928. V. 69; 73
Original Poems. Glasgow: 1770. V. 73
The Poetical Works. London: 1832. V. 71
The Poetical Works. London: 1832-1833. V. 72
The Poetical Works. London: 1843-1844. V. 68; 72
Poetical Works. London: 1852. V. 72
Songs and Poems. Waltham St. Lawrence: 1957. V. 68
The Works. Edinburgh: 1821. V. 73

DRYSDALE, GEORGE
The Elements of Social Science, or, Physical, Sexual and Natural Religion. London: 1869. V. 71

DUANE, DIANE
So You Want to Be A Wizard?. New York: 1983. V. 68

DUANE, WILLIAM
The Law of Nations, Investigated in a Popular Manner. Philadelphia: 1809. V. 69
Report of a Debate, in the Senate of the United States, on a Resolution for Recommending to the Legislatures (sic).... Philadelphia: 1804. V. 68; 72

DUBAR, J.
Osteographie de la Baleine Echouee a L'Est du Port D'Ostende, le 4 Novembre 1827.... Brussels: 1828. V. 72

DU BARTAS, GUILLAUME DE SALUSTE, SEIGNEUR DE
Bartas His Deuine Weekes & Workes. (with) The Historie of Judith. London: 1608. V. 70
Les Oevvres. Paris: 1583. V. 70

DU BELLET, LOUISE P.
Some Prominent Virginia Families. Lynchburg: 1907. V. 69

DUBEUIL, JEAN
The Practice of Perspective; or an easy Method of Representing Natural Objects According to the Rules of Art. London: 1743. V. 73

DUBIE, NORMAN
The Funeral. Calais: 1998. V. 73
The Prayers of the North American Martyrs. Lisbon: 1975. V. 70; 72; 73
Radio Sky. New York: 1991. V. 68; 71
The Springhouse. New York: 1986. V. 68

DUBLIN, Cork and South of Ireland: a Literary, Commercial and Social Review Past and Present.... 1892. V. 71

DUBLIN Delineated in 26 Views of the Principal Public Buildings. 1831. V. 70

DUBOFSKY, MELVYN
Shall We Be All. A History of the Industrial Workers of the World. Chicago: 1969. V. 68

DU BOIS, CHARLES G.
Kick the Dead Lion. Billings: 1954. V. 68

DU BOIS, HENRI PENE
Four Private Libraries of New York, a Contribution to the Study of Bibliophilism in America. New York: 1892. V. 71

DUBOIS, JEAN
The Secret Habits of the Female Sex; Letters Addressed to a Mother on the Evils of Solitude, and Its Seductive Temptations to Young Girls. Philadelphia: 1842. V. 69

DU BOIS, JOHN VAN DEUSEN
Campaigns in the West. Tucson: 1949. V. 68; 70; 72

DU BOIS, JUNE
W. R. Leigh - The Definitive Illustrated Biography. Kansas City: 1977. V. 69; 70

DUBOIS, THEODORA
Death Comes to Tea. Boston: 1940. V. 70
Death Dines Out. Boston: 1939. V. 70
Death Is Late to Lunch. Boston: 1914. V. 70
The Traveling Toys. Philadelphia: 1934. V. 70

DUBOIS, WILLIAM
The Case of the Frightened Fish. Boston: 1940. V. 69
The Island in the Square. New York: 1947. V. 72

DU BOIS, WILLIAM EDWARD BURGHARDT
The African Roots of War. 1915. V. 68
Autobiography of W. E. B. Dubois.... New York: 1968. V. 70
Black Reconstruction. New York: 1935. V. 70
Darkwater: Voices From Within The Veil. New York. 1920. V. 70
The Gift of Black Folks. Boston: 1924. V. 68; 69; 71
In Battle for Peace. The Story of My 83rd Birthday. New York: 1952. V. 71
John Brown. Philadelphia: 1909. V. 68; 70
Mansart Builds a School. NY: 1959. V. 72
The Negro. London: 1915. V. 68; 70
The Negro Artisan. Atlanta: 1902. V. 70
The Philadelphia Negro A Social Study. Philadelphia: 1899. V. 68
The Quest of the Silver Fleece. Chicago: 1911. V. 70
The Souls of Black Folk. Chicago: 1903. V. 71

DUBOIS, WILLIAM EDWARD BURGHARDT
The Souls of Black Folk. Chicago: 1920. V. 68

DU BOIS, WILLIAM EDWARD BURGHARDT
The Souls of Black Folk. New York: 1953. V. 71
The Suppression of the African Slave-Trade to the United States of America 1638-1870. New York: 1896. V. 70
W.E.B. Du Bois in Battle for Peace. The Story of My 83rd Birthday. New York: 1952. V. 71
The World and Africa. New York: 1947. V. 68; 70
Worlds of Color. New York: 1961. V. 70

DU BOIS, WILLIAM PENE
Call me Bandicoot. New York: 1970. V. 73
The Three Policemen or Young Bottsford of Fabre Island. New York: 1938. V. 70; 73

DU BOSE, HENRY KERSHAW
History of Company B, Twenty-First Regiment (Infantry) South Carolina Volunteers, Confederate States Provisional Army. Columbia: 1909. V. 69

DU BOSE, JOHN WITHERSPOON
General Joseph Wheeler and the Army of Tennessee. New York: 1912. V. 70

DU BOUCHET, ANDRE
The Uninhabited: Selected Poems of Andre Du Bouchet. New York: 1976. V. 69; 72

DUBOURG, MATTHEW
Views of the Remains of Ancient Buildings in Rome and Its Vicinity. London: 1820. V. 72
Views of the Remains of Ancient Buildings of Rome, and Its Vicinity. London: 1844. V. 69

DU BREUIL, A.
Vineyard Culture: Improved and Cheapened. Cincinnati: 1867. V. 70

DUBREUIL, JEAN
L'Art Universal des Fortifications, Francoises, Hollandoises, Espagnoles, Italiennes, et Compose'es. Paris: 1665. V. 69
Perspective Practical; or a Plain and Easie Method of True and Lively Representing all Things to the Eye at a Distance by the Exact Rules of Art. London: 1672. V. 69; 72
La Perspective Practique, Necessaire a Tous Peintres, Graveurs, Sculpteurs, Architectes, Orfeures, Brodeurs, Tapissiers & Autres se Seruans du Dessein. Paris: 1642. V. 71
Practical Perspective; or, an Easy Method of Representing Natural Objects According to the Rules of Art. London: 1795?. V. 68

DU BROCA, LOUIS
Interesting Anecdotes of the Heroic Conduct of Women.... Baltimore: 1804. V. 68

DUBUFFET, JEAN
Jean Dubuffet: Towards an Alternative Reality. New York: 1987. V. 70; 72; 73

DUBUISSON, E.
Sketches of Character. London: 1830. V. 69

DUBUS, ANDRE
Adultery and Other Choices. Boston: 1977. V. 69; 70; 71; 72
Blessings. Elmwood: 1987. V. 69
Bluesman. Boston: 1993. V. 70; 72
Broken Vessels. Boston: 1991. V. 72; 73
The Cage Keeper. New York: 1989. V. 71; 72
Dancing After Hours. New York: 1996. V. 70; 71; 72
Dancing After Hours. New York: 1998. V. 72
Finding a Girl in America. Boston: 1980. V. 68
Finding a Girl in America. Boston: 1984. V. 70

DUBUS, ANDRE continued
House of Sand and Fog. New York: 1998. V. 72
House of Sand and Fog. 2000. V. 68
Land Where My Fathers Died. 1984. V. 71; 72
Leslie in California. Otisville: 1989. V. 73
The Lieutenant. New York: 1967. V. 68; 69; 70; 73
Meditations from a Movable Chair. New York: 1998. V. 69; 71; 72; 73
Selected Stories. Boston: 1988. V. 70; 72
Separate Flights. Boston: 1975. V. 72; 73
The Times Are Never So Bad. Boston: 1983. V. 72; 73
Voices From the Moon. Boston: 1984. V. 72
Voices from the Moon. New York: 1984. V. 69
We Don't Live Here Anymore. New York: 1984. V. 68; 72

DUBUT, LOUIS AMBROISE
Architecture Civile. Maisons de Ville et de Campagne de Toutes Formes et de Tous Genres.... Paris: 1802-1803. V. 70; 72

DUBY, GEORGE
A History of Women. Cambridge: 1992-1994. V. 72

DU CANE, ELLA
The Flowers and Gardens of Japan. London: 1908. V. 71
The Flowers and Gardens of Madeira. London: 1909. V. 71

DU CANE, FLORENCE
The Canary Islands. London: 1911. V. 72
The Flowers and Gardens of Madeira. London: 1909. V. 72; 73

DU CANGE, CHARLES DU FRESNE, SIEUR
Glossarium ad Scriptores Mediae et Infimae Latinitatis.... Paris: 1733-1736. V. 73

DUCAREL, ANDREW COLTEE
Anglo-Norman Antiquities Considered in a Tour through Part of Normandy. London: 1767. V. 68; 70; 72

DU CHAILLU, PAUL B.
The Country of the Dwarfs. New York: 1872. V. 72
Land of the Midnight Sun. London: 1881. V. 70
The Land of the Midnight Sun. New York: 1882. V. 70; 72

DUCHENNE DE BOULOGNE, GUILLAUME
Physiology of Motion Demonstrated by Means of Electrical Stimulation and Clinical Observations and Applied to the Study of Paralysis and Deformities.... Philadelphia: 1949. V. 69

DUCHESNE, JOSEPH DE
Tetrade des Plvs Grieves Maladies de Tovt Le Cerveau. Paris: 1625. V. 68

DUCKWORTH, S. G.
Ship Joinery. London: 1923. V. 70

DUCKWORTH, W.
Morphology and Anthropology.... Cambridge: 1915. V. 71

DUCKWORTH, W. L. H.
Galen On Anatomical Procedures - The Later Books. Cambridge: 1962. V. 68

DUCLOS, CHARLES PINOT
The History of Lewis XI. King of France. London: 1746. V. 69

DU CREST, GEORGETTE
Memoirs of the Empress Josephine.... 1829. V. 70

DUDIN, M.
The Art of the Bookbinder and Gilder by M. Dudin 1772. Leeds: 1977. V. 70

DUDLEY, ALBERTUS T.
Making the Nine. Boston: 1904. V. 68

DUDLEY, CARRIE
The Peek-A-Boo Show Book. Minneapolis: 1928. V. 72

DUDLEY, JOHN WILLIAM WARD, 1ST EARL OF
Letters of the Earl of Dudley to the Bishop of Llandaff. London: 1840. V. 71

DUDLEY, THOMAS BRISCOE
From Chaos to the Charter: a Complete History of Royal Leamington Spa.... London: 1901. V. 72

DUELLMAN, W. E.
A Monographic Study of the Colubrid Snake Genus Leptodeira. New York: 1958. V. 72

DUER, JOHN
An Examination of the Controversy Between the Greek Deputies and Two Mercantile Houses of New York.... New York: 1826. V. 70

DUER, WILLIAM ALEXANDER
The Life of William Alexander, Earl of Stirling; Major General in the Army of the United States, During the Revolution.... New York: 1847. V. 69

DUERER, ALBRECHT
Della Simmetria de i Corpi Humani, Libri Quattro. Venice: 1591. V. 68; 70
The Little Passion. Verona: 1971. V. 71
Of the Just Shaping of Letters from the Applied Geometry of.... New York: 1917. V. 70

DU FAUR, FREDA
The Conquest of Mount Cook and Other Climbs. 1915. V. 72
The Conquest of Mount Cook and Other Climbs. London: 1915. V. 69

DUFF, ADRIAN GRANT, MRS.
The Life Work of Lord Avebury (Sir John Lubbock) 1834-1913. London: 1924. V. 68

DUFF, ANDREW HALLIDAY
Comical Fellows; or the History and Mystery of the Pantomime.... London: 1863. V. 68; 72

DUFF, CHARLES
A Handbook on Hanging, Being a Short Introduction to the Fine Art of Execution.... Boston: 1929. V. 69

DUFF, E. GORDON
Catalogue of a Highly Important Collection of Books Printed Entirely Upon Vellum. London. V. 68

DUFF, JAMES GRANT
History of the Mahrattas. Bombay: 1878. V. 73

DUFF, JOHN J.
A Lincoln Prairie Lawyer. 1960. V. 68

DUFFERIN & CLANDEBOYE, HELEN SALINA SHERIDAN BLACKWOOD
Songs, Poems and Verses. London: 1894. V. 69

DUFFEY, J. W.
Mc Neill's Last Charge. Winchester: 1912. V. 69; 70

DUFFY, CAROL ANN
Selling Manhattan. London: 1987. V. 69

DUFFY, CHARLES G.
Four Years of Irish History 1845 to 1849. 1883. V. 69
My Life in Two Hemispheres. New York: 1898. V. 68

DUFIEF, N. G.
The Logic of Facts; or the Conduct of Wm. Rawle.... Philadelphia: 1806. V. 71
Nature Displayed in Her Mode of Teaching Language to Man.... Philadelphia: 1806. V. 73
Nature Displayed in Her Mode of Teaching Language to Man.... Philadelphia: 1821. V. 73
Nature Displayed in Her Mode of Teaching Language to Man.... London: 1822. V. 73
Nature Displayed in Her Mode of Teaching Language to Man.... New York: 1825. V. 73

DUFORT, CLAIRE DE
Ourika. Austin: 1977. V. 70

DUFOUR, JOHN JAMES
The American Vine-Dresser's Guide, Being a Treatise on the Cultivation of the Vine, and the Process of Wine Making, Adpated to the Soil and Climate of the United States. Cincinnati: 1826. V. 70

DUFOUR, PIERRE
Histoire de la Prostitution.... Paris: 1851. V. 70

DUFRAN, DORA
Low Down on Calamity Jane by D. Dee. Rapid City: 1932. V. 69

DUFRESNE, JOHN
Lethe, Cupid, Time and Love. Candia: 1994. V. 70
Louisiana Power and Light. New York and London: 1994. V. 69; 69; 71; 72
The Way That Water Enters Stone. New York: 1991. V. 68; 71; 72
Well Enough Alone: Two Stories and Thirteen Poems. Candia: 1996. V. 68; 71; 72

DU FRESNOY, CHARLES ALPHONSE
The Art of Painting. London: 1750. V. 69
The Art of Painting. York: 1783. V. 69

DUFRESNY, CHARLES RIVIERE
Amusements Serious and Comical; or a New Collection of Bons-mots, Keen Jests, Ingenious Thoughts, Pleasant Tales and Comical Adventures. London: 1719. V. 70

DUFTY, WILLIAM
Sugar Blues. Radnor: 1975. V. 69

DUFY, RAOUL
Selection Chronique de la Vie Artistique I: Raoul Dufy. Anvers: 1928. V. 69

DUGAN, ALAN
Poems 2. New Haven: 1963. V. 69
Sequence. Cambridge: 1976. V. 72

DUGANNE, AUGUSTINE J. H.
Bianca. New York: 1854?. V. 68; 73

DUGDALE, WILLIAM
The Antiquities of Warwickshire Illustrated. London: 1656. V. 68
Monasticon Anglicanum: A History of the Abbies and Other Monasteries, Hospitals, Frieries, and Cathedral and Collegiate Churches, With Their Dependencies, in England and Wales. London: 1817-1830. V. 72
The Restoration of the Beauchamp Chapel at St. Mary's Collegiate Church Warwick 1674-1742. Oxford: 1956. V. 69
A Short History of the Late Troubles in England.... Oxford: 1681. V. 72

DUGGAN, ALFRED
Elephants and Castles. London: 1963. V. 72

DUGGER, SHEPHERD M.
The War Trails of the Blue Ridge. Banner Elk: 1932. V. 73

DUGMORE, ARTHUR RADCLYFFE
Camera Adventures in the African Wilds.... London: 1910. V. 68; 72
In the Heart of the Northern Forests. 1930. V. 69; 72
In The Heart of The Northern Forests. London: 1930. V. 72
The Romance of the Newfoundland Caribou. 1913. V. 69; 70; 72; 73

DUGMORE, ARTHUR RADCLYFFE continued
The Romance of the Newfoundland Caribou. Philadelphia: 1913. V. 72
The Vast Sudan. 1924. V. 73
The Wonderland of Big Game. London: 1925. V. 72

DUGUID, J.
Tiger-Man. 1933. V. 72

DU HALDE, JEAN BAPTISTE
Description Geographique, Historique, Chronologique, Politique et Physique de l'Empire de la Chine. Paris: 1735. V. 73

DUHASSET, MADAME
The Private Memoirs of.... New York: 1827. V. 68; 69; 73

DUHEM, PIERRE MAURICE MARIE
Traite Elementaire de mecanique Chimique Fondee sur la Thermodynamique. Paris: 1897-1899. V. 72

DUJARDIN, EDOUARD
Les Lauriers Sont Coupes. Paris: 1888. V. 70

DUJARDIN, FRANCOIS
Histoire de Chirurgie depuis son Origine Jusqu' a nos Jours. Paris: 1774. V. 72

DUKE, BASIL W.
History of Morgan's Cavalry. Cincinnati: 1867. V. 70; 73
Morgan's Cavalry. New York and Washington: 1906. V. 69; 70
Reminiscences of General Basil W. Duke, C.S.A. Garden City: 1911. V. 69; 70

DUKE, J. A.
Handbook of Legumes of World Economic Importance. New York: 1981. V. 68
Medicinal Plants of China. Algonac: 1985. V. 72

DUKE, JOHN A.
The Columban Church. 1932. V. 70

DUKE Of Cleveland's Fox Hounds. Operations of the Baby Pack, in the Season 1838-1839. Richmond: 1839. V. 70

DUKE, THOMAS S.
Celebrated Criminal Cases of America. San Francisco: 1910. V. 73

DULAC, EDMUND
Address Book. 1983. V. 72
Birthday Book. 1981. V. 72
Edmund Dulac's Fairy-Book; Fairy Tales of the Allied Nations. London: 1927. V. 70; 73
Edmund Dulac Picture Book. London: 1919. V. 73
Fairy Tales of the Allied Nations. London: 1917. V. 68
Fairy-Book. Fairy Tales of the Allied Nations. New York: 1924. V. 71
Lyrics Pathetic and Humorous from A to Z. London: 1908. V. 72; 73

DULANEY, DANIEL
Considerations on the Propriety of Imposing Taxes in the British Colonies, for the Purpose of Raising a Revenue, by Act of Parliament. London: 1766. V. 72

DULUTH & IRON RANGE RAILROAD
The Trout Streams of Northern Minnesota on the Vermilion Route. Duluth. V. 68

DUMAS, ALEXANDRE
Camille. London: 1937. V. 73
Chateau Rouge; or, the Reign of Terror. London: 1859. V. 68
The Corsican Brothers. London: 1880. V. 68
The Count of Monte Cristo. London: 1846. V. 71
The Count of Monte Cristo. New York: 1941. V. 68; 69
Doctor Basilius. London: 1860. V. 68
The Lady with the Camelias. London: 1876. V. 68; 73
The Man in the Iron Mask. New York: 1965. V. 69
The Three Musketeers. New York: 1953. V. 69
Works. New York: 1900. V. 68; 70

DUMAS, F. G.
The Franco-British Exhibition Illustrated Review. London: 1908. V. 71

DUMAS, HENRY
Jonah and the Green Stone. NY: 1976. V. 72

DU MAURIER, DAPHNE
The Apple Tree. London: 1952. V. 71
My Cousin Rachel. Garden City: 1952. V. 71
Rebecca. London: 1938. V. 71

DU MAURIER, GEORGE
The Martian. 1898. V. 70; 71
The Martian. London: 1898. V. 71; 73
Social Pictorial Satire. London: 1898. V. 71
Trilby. London: 1895. V. 71

DUMOLINET, CLAUDE
Le Cabinet de la Bibliotheque de Sainte Genevieve. Paris: 1692. V. 69

DU MONT, JOHN S.
Custer Battle Guns. Cannan: 1988. V. 72

DUN, T. I.
From Cairo to Siwa Across the Libyan Desert with Armoured Cars. 1933. V. 68; 72

DUNBAR, ALICE
The Goodness of St. Rocque and Other Stories. New York: 1899. V. 70

DUNBAR, EDWARD E.
The Romance of the Age, or the Discovery of Gold in California. New York: 1867. V. 70

DUNBAR, H. M.
Catalouge of a Loan Exhibition of Twentieth Century Prints from Several Important American Collections. Chicago: 1933. V. 69

DUNBAR, JENNIE
Young Hopeful. London: 1932. V. 70

DUNBAR, LADY
The Chow Chow. 1914. V. 68

DUNBAR, PAUL LAURENCE
The Best Stories of Paul Laurence Dunbar. New York: 1938. V. 70
The Fanatics. New York: 1901. V. 73
The Heart of Happy Hollow. New York: 1904. V. 70
In Old Plantation Days. New York: 1903. V. 73
Li'l'Gal. New York: 1904. V. 70; 71; 73
The Love of Laundry. New York: 1900. V. 70
Lyrics of Lowly Life. New York: 1896. V. 68; 70
Lyrics of the Hearthside. New York: 1899. V. 70
Majors and Minors: Poems by.... Toledo: 1895. V. 70
Oak and Ivy. Dayton: 1893. V. 73
Oak and Ivy. Dayton: 1895. V. 70
The Paul Laurence Dunbar Reader. New York: 1975. V. 70
Poems of Cabin and Field. New York: 1899. V. 70
Speakin' o' Christmas. New York: 1914. V. 70; 73
The Uncalled. New York: 1898. V. 69; 70; 73
When Malindy Sings. New York: 1903. V. 70

DUNBAR, SEYMOUR
A History of Travel in America. Indianapolis: 1915. V. 71; 72

DUNBAR, SOPHIE
Behind Eclaire's Doors. New York: 1993. V. 68

DUNBAR, WILLIAM
Poems...Now First Collected. Edinburgh: 1834. V. 72

DUNBAR BRANDER, A. A.
Wild Animals in Central India. 1923. V. 69; 70; 72; 73

DUNBAR-NELSON, ALICE
The Dunbar Speaker and Entertainer. Naperville: 1920. V. 72

DUNCAN, A.
American Art Deco. New York: 1986. V. 69; 72
Art Nouveau and Art Deco Book-Binding: French Masterpieces 1880-1940. New York: 1989. V. 69; 72

DUNCAN, ANDREW
Medical Cases, Selected from the Records of the Public Dispensary at Edinburgh.... Edinburgh: 1790. V. 70; 72

DUNCAN, DAVID
Occam's Razor. London: 1958. V. 73

DUNCAN, DAVID JAMES
The River Why. 1983. V. 71
The River Why. San Francisco: 1983. V. 69; 70; 72

DUNCAN, F.
Canada in 1871 or Our Empire in the West. London: 1872. V. 70

DUNCAN, HARRY
Doors of Perception: Essays in Book Typography. Austin: 1983. V. 71; 73

DUNCAN, ISADORA
My Life. New York: 1927. V. 70; 72

DUNCAN, J.
British Butterflies. Edinburgh: 1835. V. 69
Exotic Moths. Edinburgh: 1481. V. 69
Foreign Butterlfies. Edinburgh: 1837. V. 69
Introduction to Entomology. Edinburgh: 1840. V. 69

DUNCAN, J. P.
Sculptured Surfaces in Engineering and Medicine. Cambridge: 1983. V. 68

DUNCAN, JONATHAN
History of Russia from the Foundation of the Empire by Rourick to the Close of the Hungarian War. London: 1854. V. 73

DUNCAN, K.
Supply of Sherman's Army During the Atlanta Campaign. Fort Leavenworth: 1911. V. 72

DUNCAN, KUNIGUNDE
Blue Star - as Told from the Life of Cora Belle Fellows. Caldwell: 1938. V. 68

DUNCAN, MARY GREY LUNDIE
America as I Found It. New York: 1852. V. 68; 69; 73

DUNCAN, NORMAN
Christmas Eve at Topmast Tickle. New York: 1910. V. 68

DUNCAN, P. MARTIN
The Sea-Shore. London: 1880. V. 68

DUNCAN, ROBERT
Caesar's Gate. Poems 1949-1950. Palma de Mallorca: 1955. V. 72; 73
Derivations. Selected Poems 1950-1956. London: 1968. V. 70
The First Decade - Selected Poems 1940-1950. London: 1968. V. 70
From the Mabinogion. Quarterly Review of Literature. 1959. V. 73
Heavenly City Earthly City. Berkeley: 1947. V. 70
Letters. Highlands: 1958. V. 73
Of the War. Passages 22-27. Berkeley: 1996. V. 73
A Paris Visit. Five Poems. New York: 1985. V. 73
Selected Poems 1940-1950. London: 1968. V. 71
Six Prose Pieces. Rochester: 1966. V. 69; 72
The Truth and Life of Myth. New York: 1968. V. 71

DUNCAN, W.
Webs in the Wind, the Habit of Web-Weaving Spiders. New York: 1949. V. 69; 72

DUNCAN, WINTHROP H.
A Narrative of the Captivity of Isaac Webster. Metuchen: 1927. V. 69

DUNCANSON, JOHN VICTOR
Newport - Nova Scotia - A Rhode Island Township. Belleville: 1985. V. 72

DUNCKER, ALEXANDER
Die Landlichen Wohnsitze, Schlosser und Residenzen der Ritterschaftlichen Grundbesitzer in der Preussischen Monarchie.... Berlin: 1857-1883. V. 68; 70; 72

DUNCOMBE, THOMAS
The Life and Correspondence of Thomas Slingsby Duncombe. London: 1868. V. 72

DUNDAS, JOHN
A Summary View of the Feudal Law, with the Differences of the Scots Law.... Edinburgh: 1710. V. 72

DUNDONALD, ARCHIBALD COCHRANE, 9TH EARL OF
The Present State of the Manufacture of Salt Explained; and a New Mode Suggested of Refining British Salt.... London: 1785. V. 73

DUNDONALD, THOMAS COCHRANE, 10TH EARL OF
Brief Extracts from the Memoranda of the Earl of Dundonald, on the Use, Properties and Products of the Bitumen and Petroleum of Trinidad. London: 1857. V. 69

DUNHAM, EDITH
The Diary of a Mouse. New York: 1907. V. 73

DUNHAM, K. C.
Geology of the Northern Pennine Orefield. London: 1967. V. 73

DUNHAM, KATHERINE
Island Possessed. Garden City: 1969. V. 72

DUNIWAY, ABIGAIL SCOTT
David and Anna Matson. New York: 1876. V. 68

DUNKIN, JOHN
The History and Antiquities of Bicester.... London: 1816. V. 68; 72

DUNKIN, ROBERT
In The Land Of The Bora Or Camp Life And Sport In Dalmatia And The Hergezovina 1894-1895-1896. London: 1897. V. 72
The Roedeer. Southampton: 1987. V. 70

DUNKLE, JOHN J.
Prison Life During the Rebellion. Singer's Glen: 1869. V. 69

DUNLAP, SUSAN
The Celestial Buffet and Other Morsels of Murder. Norfolk: 2001. V. 70

DUNLAP, WILLIAM
Peter the Great; or, the Russian Mother. New York: 1814. V. 73
Thirty Years Ago, or the Memoirs of a Water Drinker. New York: 1836. V. 71; 73
A Trip to Niagara; or Travellers in America.... New York: 1830. V. 70
The Wife of Two Husbands: a Drama. New York: 1811. V. 68

DUNLOP, JOHN
The History of Fiction; Being a Critical Account of the Most Celebrated Prose Works of Fiction from the Earliest Greek Romances to the Novels of the Present Age. Edinburgh: 1816. V. 69

DUNLOP, WILLIAM S.
S. Lee's Sharpshooters; or the Forefront of Battle. Little Rock: 1899. V. 70

DUNMORE, HELEN
Burning Bright. London: 1994. V. 72
A Spell of Winter. London: 1995. V. 72
Talking to the Dead. London: 1996. V. 72

DUNN, DOROTHY
American Indian Painting of the Southwest and Plains Areas. Albuquerque: 1958. V. 69
American Indian Painting of the Southwest and Plains Areas. Albuquerque: 1968. V. 69

DUNN, DOUGLAS
Elegies. London: 1985. V. 72
A Rumoured City - New Poets from Hull. Newcastle-upon-tyne: 1982. V. 71
Terry Street. London: 1969. V. 70

DUNN, J. B.
Perilous Trails of Texas. Dallas: 1932. V. 71

DUNN, J. P.
Massacre of The Mountains, A History of The Indian Wars of The Far West. New York: 1886. V. 72

DUNN, JAMES
Modern London: Its Sins and Woes and the Sovereign Remedy. London: 1906. V. 71

DUNN, KATHERINE
Attic. New York: 1970. V. 69; 71
Geek Love. London: 1989. V. 70; 72
Geek Love. New York: 1989. V. 68; 69; 70; 71; 72; 73
Truck. New York: 1971. V. 68; 69; 71

DUNN, NELL
Living Like I Do. London: 1977. V. 71

DUNN, S. T.
Flora of Kwangtung and Hongkong (China). London: 1912. V. 70
Flora of South-West Surrey. London: 1893. V. 69

DUNN, THOMAS
Terry Street. London: 1969. V. 72

DUNNACK, HENRY E.
Maine Forts. Augusta: 1924. V. 73

DUNNE, EDWARD F.
Illinois, the Heart of the Nation. Chicago & NY: 1933. V. 72

DUNNE, J. W.
An Experiment with Time. London: 1927. V. 71

DUNNE, JOHN GREGORY
The Studio. London: 1970. V. 72
True Confessions. New York: 1977. V. 71
Vegas: A Memoir of a Dark Season. New York: 1974. V. 72

DUNNE, PETER FINLEY
Observations by Mr. Dooley. New York: 1902. V. 72

DUNNE, PHILIP
How Green Was My Valley: The Screenplay for the John Ford Directed Film. Santa Barbara: 1990. V. 72

DUNNE, S. J. PETER MASTEN
Black Robes in Lower California. Berkeley: 1952. V. 68

DUNNETT, DOROTHY
Match for a Murderer. 1971. V. 71

DUNNIGAN, BRIAN LEIGH
Frontier Metropolis, Picturing Early Detroit 1701-1838. Detroit: 2001. V. 69

DUNNING, HAROLD MARION
Over Hill and Vale - in the Evening Shadows of Colorado's Long Peak. Boulder: 1956. V. 68

DUNNING, JOHN
Booked to Die. New York: 1992. V. 68; 69; 70; 71; 72; 73
Booked to Die. London: 1993. V. 68; 73
The Bookman's Wake. New York: 1994. V. 73
The Bookman's Wake. New York: 1995. V. 68; 69; 70; 71; 72; 73
Bookscout. Minneapolis: 1998. V. 70; 71; 72; 73
Bookscout - Complete Set. 1999. V. 73
Deadline. Aliso Viejo: 1995. V. 69; 71
Deadline. Huntington Beach: 1995. V. 69; 70; 71; 72; 73
Denver. New York: 1980. V. 73
Dreamer. Huntington Beach: 1995. V. 71
The Holland Suggestions. Indianapolis: 1975. V. 73
Looking for Ginger North. New York: 1980. V. 69
On the Air. New York: 1998. V. 71; 72; 73
The Torch Passes. Hollywood?: 1995. V. 71
The Torch Passes. Huntington Beach: 1995. V. 69
Tune In Yesterday. Englewood Cliffs: 1976. V. 68; 69; 72
Tune in Yesterday. New York: 1976. V. 69; 73
Two O'Clock Eastern Wartime. New York: 2000. V. 71
Two O'Clock Eastern Wartime. New York: 2001. V. 69; 70; 71; 73
Two O'Clock Eastern Wartime. Santa Barbara: 2001. V. 68; 69; 70; 72; 73

DUNRAVEN, CAROLINE, COUNTESS OF
Scenes in Bethany, A Course of Lectures on the Eleventh Chapter of the Gospel According to St John. Limerick: 1837. V. 68

DUNSANY, EDWARD JOHN MORETON DRAX PLUNKETT
Alexander and Three Small Plays. 1925. V. 68
Alexander and Three Small Plays. New York: 1926. V. 70
The Compromise of the King of Golden Isles. New York: 1924. V. 68; 69
The Donnellan Lectures 1943. London: 1945. V. 70
A Dreamer's Tale. London: 1910. V. 68
Five Plays. 1914. V. 68
The Gods of Pegana. 1905. V. 68
His Fellow Men: a Novel. London: 1952. V. 72
If. New York: 1922. V. 70
If I Were Dictator; the Pronouncements of the Grand Macaroni. London: 1934. V. 72
Lord Adrian. Waltham St. Lawrence: 1933. V. 68
My Ireland. London: 1937. V. 72

DUNSANY, EDWARD JOHN MORETON DRAX PLUNKETT continued
A Night at an Inn. 1916. V. 68
The Old Folk of the Centuries. 1930. V. 68
Plays for Earth and Air. 1937. V. 68
Plays of Gods and Men. 1917. V. 68; 69
Selections from the Writings. Churchtown, Dundrum: 1912. V. 71
The Strange Journeys of Colonel Polders. London: 1950. V. 70
The Travel Tales of Mr. Joseph Jorkens. London: 1931. V. 72

DUNSHEATH, J.
Mountains and Memsahibs. London: 1958. V. 69

DUNSTER, HENRY P.
How to Make the Land Pay, or Profitable Industries Connected with the Land and Suitable Industries Connected with the Land and Suitable to All Occupations.... London: 1885. V. 71

DUNSTERVILLE, G. C. K.
Venezuelan Orchids Illustrated. London: 1959-1976. V. 69; 70

DUNTHORNE, GORDON
Flower and Fruit Prints of the 18th and Early 19th Centuries. Washington: 1938. V. 69; 71; 73

DUNTON, JAMES G.
A Maid and a Million Men. New York: 1928. V. 70

DUNTON, JOHN
Athenian Sport, or, Two Thousand Paradoxes, Merrily Argued.... London: 1707. V. 72

DUPARACH, STEFANO PARIGINO
Le Cospicve e Meravigliose Fabriche Degli Antichi Romani Hoggi Ridotte in Rovine Disegnate.... Roma: 1709. V. 68

DUPASQUIER, LOUIS
Monographie de Notre-Dame de Brou.... Paris: 1850. V. 70; 72

DUPATY, ABBE
Lettres sur l'Italie en 1785. Lausanne: 1790. V. 69
Travels through Italy, in a Series of Letters Written in the Year 1785. Dublin: 1789. V. 69; 72

DUPIN, CHARLES
Voyages dans la Grande-Bretagne Entrepris Relativement aux Services Publics de la Guerre, de la Marine, et des Ponts et Chaussees au Commerce et a l'Industrie Depuis 1816. Brussels: 1826. V. 69

DUPIN, JACQUES
Joan Miro: Life and Work. New York: 1962. V. 70; 73

DUPIN, LE MARQUISE DE LA TOUR
Recollections of the Revolution and the Empire. New York: 1920. V. 72

DU PLAIX, GEORGES
Animal Stories. New York: 1944. V. 70; 73

DU PONCEAU, PETER S.
A Discourse on the Early History of Pennsylvania.... Philadelphia: 1821. V. 70

DUPPA, R.
The Life and Literary Works of Michel Angelo Buonarroti. London: 1806. V. 70; 71

DUPPA, RICHARD
The Life of Michel Angelo Buonarroti. London: 1807. V. 73
The Life of Michel Angelo Buonarroti. London: 1816. V. 71

DUPRE DE SAINT MAUR, NICOLAS FRANCOIS
The State of Innocence, and the Fall of man, Described in Milton's Paradise Lost. Trenton: 1813. V. 69

DUPREE, A. HUNTER
Asa Gray, 1810-1888. Cambridge: 1959. V. 68; 72

DUPREE, MARGUERITE
Family Structure in the Staffordshire Potteries 1840-1880. Oxford: 1995. V. 72

DUQUET, ALFRED
Ireland and France. 1916. V. 69

DURAND, E. R.
An Autumn Tour in Western Persia. Westminster: 1902. V. 72

DURANTI, JEAN ETIENNE
De Ritibus Ecclesiae Cathoicae Libri Tres. Paris: 1624. V. 70

DURAS, CLAIRE DE DURFORT, DUCHESSE DE
Ourika. Austin: 1977. V. 71; 72

DURAS, MARGUERITE
Abahn Sabana David. Paris: 1970. V. 71

D'URBAN, W. S. M.
The Birds of Devon. 1892. V. 73
The Birds of Devon. London: 1892. V. 69
The Birds of Devon. 1895. V. 73

DURBRIDGE, FRANCIS
The World of Tim Frazer. London: 1962. V. 68

DURDEN, CHARLES
No Bugles, No Drums. New York: 1976. V. 69

DU REFUGE, EUSTACHE
Arcana Aulica; or Walsingham's Manual of Prudential Maxims for the States-Man and Courtier. London: 1694. V. 72; 73
The Art of Complaisance or the Means to Oblige in Conversation. London: 1677. V. 69

DURET, H.
Etude Generale de la Localisation dans les Centres Nerveux (Memoire presente a l'Academie des Sciences...en 1878). Paris: 1880. V. 72

D'URFEY, THOMAS
Stories, Moral and Comical Viz. The Banquet of the Gods. Titus and Gissipus; or the Power of Friendship. The Prudent Husband.... London: 1707. V. 72

DURHAM
The Poll, at the Election of One Citizen, to Serve in Parliament, for the City of Durham, Taken Before Thomas Dunn, Esquire, Mayor the 1st, 2d, 3d, 4th, 6th, 7th, 8th, 9th and 10th Days of December 1813.... Durham: 1813. V. 71
Proceedings and Poll at the Durham City Election, on the 26th, 27th, and 28th days of July 1837; with the Speeches, on the Day of Nomination, and at the Close of Election. Durham: 1837. V. 71

DURHAM, EDNA REYNOLDS
Samuel Neal - California Pioneer - a Brief History of the Durham Family. 1949. V. 69

DURHAM, GEORGE
Taming the Neuces Strip. Austin: 1962. V. 70

DURHAM, JAMES
The Collection of Pictures at Raynham Hall.... 1926. V. 69; 72

DURHAM, JOHN GEORGE LAMBTON, 1ST EARL OF
The Report of the Earl of Durham, Her Majesty's High Commissioner and Governor-General of British North America. London: 1902. V. 71

DURHAM, M. EDITH
High Albania. London: 1909. V. 70
The Serajevo Crime. London: 1925. V. 70

DURHAM, MARILYN
The Man Who Loved Cat Dancing. New York: 1972. V. 70

DURHAM, PHILIP
Down These Mean Streets a Man Must Go. 1963. V. 70
Down these Mean Streets a Man Must Go. Chapel Hill: 1963. V. 68; 69; 73

DURHAM, WILLIAM
Chronological Notes on the History of the Town of Blackburn: From A. D. 317 TO A.D. 1861; with the Census of 1851 and 1861. Blackburn: 1866. V. 73

DURLACHER, LEWIS
A Concise Treatise on Corns, Bunions and the Disorders of Nails, with Advice for the General Management of the Feet. London: 1858. V. 72

DURLING, RICHARD
A Catalogue of Sixteenth Century Printed Books in the National Library of Medicine. Bethesda: 1967. V. 72

DURNRIDGE, FRANCIS
The Scarf. London: 1960. V. 69

DURRANT, THEO
The Marble Forest. New York: 1951. V. 73

DURRELL, GERALD
Birds, Beasts and Relatives. London: 1969. V. 72
The Donkey Rustlers. New York: 1968. V. 72
The Overloaded Ark. 1953. V. 72
The Stationary Ark. 1976. V. 72

DURRELL, LAWRENCE GEORGE
Alexandria Quartet. London: 1957-1960. V. 71
Alexandria Quartet. New York: 1961. V. 69
The Alexandria Quartet. London: 1962. V. 71; 72
The Alexandria Quartet. New York: 1962. V. 68; 69
Cefalu: a Novel. London: 1947. V. 70
Cities, Plains and People - Poems. London: 1946. V. 68
Clea. London: 1959. V. 71; 72
Collected Poems 1931-1974. London: 1980. V. 68; 69
Deus Loci. Ischia: 1950. V. 69
Down the Styx. Santa Barbara: 1971. V. 71
In Arcadia. 1968. V. 68
Justine. London: 1957. V. 71
Livia. London: 1978. V. 68
Monsieur, or, the Prince of Darkness. London: 1974. V. 68
Mountolive. London: 1958. V. 70; 73
Mountolive. New York: 1959. V. 68
Nothing Is Lost, Sweet Self. 1967. V. 68; 71
Nunquam. London: 1970. V. 68
On Seeming to Presume. London: 1948. V. 71

DURRELL, LAWRENCE, GEORGE
On the Suchness of the Old Boy. 1972. V. 73

DURRELL, LAWRENCE GEORGE
The Plant Magic Man. Santa Barbara: 1973. V. 71
A Private Country. London: 1943. V. 68; 71
The Red Limbo Lingo: a Poetry Notebook. London: 1971. V. 68; 70

DUSARD, JAY
The North American Cowboy. Prescott: 1983. V. 69; 70; 72

DUSEJOUR, DIONIS
The Origin of the Graces. London: 1895. V. 71

DUSSAUNCE, H.
General Treatise on the Manufacture of Vinegar. Philadelphia: 1871. V. 70

DUSTIN, FRED
The Custer Fight. Hollywood: 1936. V. 72
The Custer Tragedy - Events Leading Up to and Following The Little Big Horn Campaign of 1876. El Segundo: 1987. V. 72
Echoes From The Little Big Horn Fight, Reno's Positions in The Valley. Saginaw, MI: 1953. V. 72

THE DUTIFUL Daughter, or, the Tragical History of the Misfortunes and Sufferings of Rt. Hon. Lady Eliza Courtnay V*rn*n (Only Daughter of Colonel V*rn*n), from the Age of Fourteen to Her Unfortunate Death Intersperc'd With the Memoirs of Sir Charles T***. London: 1775?. V. 69

DUTT, W. A.
A Guide to the Norfolk Broads.... 1923. V. 68

DUTTON, BERTHA P.
Sun Father's Way, the Kiva Murals of Kuaua, a Pueblo Ruin, Coronado State Monument, New Mexico. Albuquerque: 1963. V. 70; 71

DUTTON, CHARLES J.
The Shadow of Evil. New York: 1930. V. 68; 71

DUTTON, CLARENCE E.
The Chemistry of the Bessemer Process. Read Before the American Association for the Advancement of Science at Troy, New York, August 20, 1870. Troy?: 1870. V. 71
Tertiary History of the Grand Canyon District, with Atlas. Santa Barbara: 1977. V. 70

DUTTON, E. A. T.
Kenya Mountain. 1929. V. 68; 70; 73
Kenya Mountain. 1930. V. 68; 70; 73
Kenya Mountain. London: 1930. V. 69; 72

DUVAL, ISAAC H.
Texas Argonauts: Isaac Duval and the California Gold Rush. San Francisco: 1988. V. 69

DUVAL, JOHN
Early Times in Texas. Austin: 1892. V. 68; 73

DUVAL, JOHN C.
The Adventures of Big Foot Wallace: The Texas Ranger and Hunter. Macon: 1870. V. 69
The Adventures of Big Foot Wallace: The Texas Ranger and Hunter. Austin: 1935. V. 69

DUVAN, P.
The Tangled Garden: te Art of J. E. H. Mac Donald. Ontario: 1978. V. 72

DUVEEN, DENIS I.
A Bibliography of the Works of Antoine Laurent Lavoisier 1743-1794. London: 1954. V. 72

DUVEEN, EDWARD J.
Colour in the Home. London: 1912. V. 68

DUVERNEY, JOSEPH GUICHARD
Traite de l'Organe de L'ouie. Contenant La Structure, Les Usages and Les Maladies de Toutes Les Parties del'Oreille. Paris: 1683. V. 68

DUVOISIN, ROGER
Santa's Circus. 1948. V. 69

DUYCKINCK, EVERT A.
National Portrait Gallery of Eminent Americans.... New York: 1861. V. 69
Portrait Gallery of Eiminent Men and Women of Europe and America. New York: 1872-1874. V. 70

DUYCKINCK, WHITEHEAD CORNELL
The Duyckinck and Allied Families. New York: 1908. V. 69

DWARRIS, FORTUNATUS
A Letter Addressed to the Lord High Chancellor of England, on His Proposed Scheme for the Consolidation of the Statute Law.... London: 1853. V. 73

DWIGGINS, W. A.
MSS. by WAD - Being a Collection of the Writings of Dwiggins on Various Subjects, Some Critical, Some Philosophical, Some Whimsical. New York: 1947. V. 69

DWIGHT, J.
The Sequence of Plumages and Moults of the Passerine Birds of New York. New York: 1900. V. 73

DWIGHT, NATHANIEL
A Short But Comprehensive System of the Geography of the World.... New York: 1808. V. 69

DWIGHT, THEODORE
History of the Hartford Convention with a Review of the Policy of the United States Government Which Led to the War of 1812. New York and Boston: 1833. V. 69; 73
The Northern Traveller.... New York: 1825. V. 69; 73
The Northern Traveller.... New York: 1830. V. 73

DWIGHT, TIMOTHY
The Conquest of Canaan; a Poem in Eleven Books. Hartford: 1785. V. 72; 73
Travels: in New England and New York. New Haven: 1821-1822. V. 68; 71

DWORKIN, ANDREA
Child. Iraklion, Crete: 1966. V. 70

DWYER, JAMES A.
The Dominicans of Cork City and County. 1896. V. 69; 73

DYBEK, STUART
Childhood and Other Neighborhoods. New York: 1980. V. 68

DYCK, PAUL
Brule, The Sioux People of The Rosebud. Flagstaff: 1971. V. 72
Brule The Sioux People of the Rosebud. Northland: 1985. V. 70

DYDE, W.
The History and Antiquities of Tewkesbury. Tewkesbury: 1798. V. 72

DYE, JOHN
Recollections of a Pioneer 1830-1852. Rocky Mountains, New Mexico.... Los Angeles: 1951. V. 68

DYER, D. B., MRS.
Fort Reno or Picturesque - Cheyenne and Arapahoe Army Life. New York: 1896. V. 72

DYER, GEORGE
The Catalyst Club. New York: 1936. V. 69
The Long Death. New York: 1937. V. 72; 73
The Most General School Assistant. Exeter: 1770. V. 69
Poems. 1792. V. 73
Poems. 1801. V. 73
Poetics; or, a Series of Poems, and Disquisitions on Poetry. 1812. V. 73
The Poet's Fate: a Poetical Dialogue. London: 1797. V. 73

DYER, GILBERT
A Restoration of the Modes of Bestowing Names of the Rivers, Hills, Vallies, Plains and the Settlement of Britain.... Exeter: 1805. V. 71

DYER, JOHN
Poems. London: 1770. V. 73

DYER, JOHN W.
Reminiscences of Four Years in the Confederate Army. Evansville: 1898. V. 70

DYER, PSEUD.
Intensity Coils: How Made, and How Used. London: 1880. V. 68

DYER, ROBERT
Nine Years of an Actor's Life. London: 1833. V. 72

DYER, T. F. THISELTON
Folk-Lore of Women Illustrated by Legendary and Traditional Tales, Folk-Rhymes, Proverbial Sayings, Superstitions, etc. Chicago: 1906. V. 72

DYER, THOMAS H.
Pompeii Photographed. The Ruins of Pompeii...with an Account of the Destruction of the City.... London: 1867. V. 68; 70; 72

DYHRENFURTH, G. O.
To the Third Pole. London: 1955. V. 69

THE DYING Speeches of Several Excellent Persons, Who Suffered for Their Zeal Against Popery, and Arbitrary Government.... London: 1689. V. 71

DYJA, TOM
Play for a Kingdom. New York: 1997. V. 71

DYK, WALTER
Son of Old Man Hat: a Navaho Autobiography. New York: 1938. V. 69

DYKE, T. WEBB
Verses and Impromtus on Various and Occasional Subjects. London: 1811. V. 72

DYKES, JEFF
Billy the Kid - the Biography of a Legend. Albuquerque: 1952. V. 70; 72
Fifty Great Western Illustrators. 1975. V. 70
Fifty Great Western Illustrators. Flagstaff: 1975. V. 69; 71
Russell Roundup 1 - Catalog 18 Winter 1972. College Park: 1972. V. 69
Western High Spots. Flagstaff: 1977. V. 69

DYKES, OSWALD
The Royal Marriage. King Lemuel's Lesson of I. Chastity. 2. Temperance. 3. Charity. 4. Justice. 5. Education. 6. Industry. 7. Frugality. 8. Religion. 9. Marriage.... London: 1722. V. 69; 73

DYKES, THOMAS
Memoir of the Rev. Thomas Dykes, L.L.B. London: 1849. V. 70

DYKES, W. R.
Dykes on Irises. Tunbridge Wells: 1930. V. 71; 73

DYKSTRA, ROBERT R.
The Cattle Towns. New York: 1968. V. 71

DYMENT, CLIFFORD
The Axe in the Wood. London: 1944. V. 70

DYMOND, HENRY
Observations on the Parables of Our Saviour. London: 1825. V. 68

DYRENFORTH, JAMES
Adolf in Blunderland. London: 1939. V. 70

DYSON, DAVID
The Land and Fresh Water Shells of the District Around Manchester: with Their Particular Localities. Manchester: 1850. V. 68

E

E. *Elephant, Esq. Showman.* New York: 1894. V. 73

E., E. P.
Poetry, &c. for Private Circulation. Brighton: 1867. V. 71

EAGER, ALAN R.
A Guide to Irish Bibliographical Material. 1964. V. 69

EAGER, SAMUEL W.
A Outline History of Orange County...Together with Local Traditions and Short Biographical Sketches of Early Settlers.... Newburgh: 1846-1847. V. 72

EAGLE RANGE & FOUNDRY CO.
The Eagle Range. 23 First Prize Medals. 1886. V. 68

EAGLETON, WELLS P.
Brain Abscess, Its Surgical Pathology and Operative Technic. New York: 1922. V. 71

EAKIN, RICHARD M.
History of Zoology at the University of California, Berkeley. 1956. V. 68
The Third Eye. Berkeley: 1973. V. 72

EALES, NELLIE B.
The Cole Library of Early Medicine and Zoology. London: 1969. V. 68; 70
The Littoral Fauna of Great Britain. Cambridge: 1950. V. 68

EAMES, BLANCHE
Principles of Eugenics a Practical Treatise. New York: 1914. V. 72

EARDLEY-WILMOT, S.
Forest Life and Sport in India. 1910. V. 69; 70; 72; 73
The Life of a Tiger. 1911. V. 69; 70; 72

EARHART, AMELIA
The Fun Of It. Random Records of My Own Flying and of Women in Aviation. New York: 1932. V. 69; 71; 72
20 Hours 40 Minutes. New York: 1928. V. 70

EARHART, JOHN F.
The Color Printer. A Treatise on the Use of Colors in Typographic Printing. Cincinnati: 1892. V. 68

EARLE, A. SCOTT
Surgery in America; from the Colonial Era to the Twentieth Century. Philadelphia & London: 1965. V. 68

EARLE, EDWIN
Hopi Kachinas. New York: 1938. V. 69; 73

EARLE, JOHN
A Handbook to the Land Charters and Other Saxonic Documents. Oxford: 1888. V. 71
Micro-Cosmographie or a Piece of the World Discovered in Essayes and Characters. Waltham St. Lawrence: 1928. V. 71
Microcosmography; or, a Piece of the World Discover'd. London: 1732. V. 69

EARLE, MISS
Corinth, and Other Poems. London: 1821. V. 69

EARLEY, TOM
Somehow Form a Family. Chapel Hill: 2001. V. 69

EARLEY, TONY
Here We Are In Paradise. Boston: 1994. V. 71
Jim the Boy. Boston: 2000. V. 69; 70

EARLY *Children's Books and Their Illustrators.* New York: 1975. V. 68; 70

EARLY *History of Atlantic County, New Jersey.* Kutztown: 1915. V. 69

EARLY, JUBAL ANDERSON
Jackson's Campaign Against Pope in August 1862. Baltimore: 1883. V. 69
Lieutenant General Jubal Anderson Early, C.S.A. Autobiogrpahical Sketch and Narrative of the War Between the States. Philadelphia and London: 1912. V. 69; 70
A Memoir of the Last Year of the War for Independence, in the Confederate States of America.... Toronto: 1866. V. 70
A Memoir of the Last Year of the War for Independence, in the Confederate States of America.... Lynchburg: 1867. V. 69; 70

AN EARNEST *Persuasive and Exhortation to the Jews, Occasioned by the Late Act of Parliament in Their Favour.* London: 1753. V. 69

EARP, G. B.
The Gold Colonies of Australia.... London: 1852. V. 69
What We Did in Australia.... London: 1853. V. 69

EARWAKER, J. P.
Local Gleanings Relating to Lancashire and Cheshire. Vol. II January 1877- December 1878. Manchester: 1879. V. 73

THE EASBY *Abbey Breeding Stud.* 1860. V. 68; 70

EASDALE, JOAN ADENEY
Clemence and Clare. London: 1932. V. 69
A Collection of Poems. London: 1931. V. 69

EAST, BEN
Bears. 1977. V. 69; 72

EAST INDIA AND CHINA ASSOCIATION
Proceedings of a Meeting of the East India and China Association, on the Subject of Steam Communication with India. London: 1839. V. 73
Report of the Committee of the London East India and China Association, Presented to the General Meeting, Held at the Jerusalem Coffee- House January 1, 1839. London: 1839. V. 73

EAST INDIA COMPANY
A List of the Company's Civil Servants, at Their Settlements in the East-Indies the Island St. Helena and China. 1790. V. 73
Rules and Regulations for the Benefit and Management of a Fund to Be Provided for the Benefit of the Commodores, Writers and Laborers, in the Service of the United Company of Merchants of England Trading to the East Indies. London: 1790. V. 69

EAST-Bourn, *Being a Descriptive Account of that Village in the County of Sussex, and Its Environs.* 1799. V. 72

EAST-BOURN, *Being a Descriptive Account of that Village, in the County of Sussex, and Its Environs.* London: 1799. V. 70

THE EASTER *Offering; or the History of Master Charles and Miss Kitty Courtley.* York: 1801. V. 72

THE EASTERN *Townships Gazetteer and General Business Directory.* St. Johns: 1867. V. 73

EASTERN TOWNSHIPS BANK
Eastern Townships Bank. Fiftieth Annual Report 1909. Sherbrooke: 1909. V. 73

EASTLAKE, CHARLES LOCK
Contributions to the Literature of the Fine Arts. London: 1848. V. 73
Contributions to the Literature of the Fine Arts. London: 1870. V. 73
Materials for a History of Oil Painting. London: 1847. V. 69; 71

EASTLAKE, ELIZABETH
The Life of John Gibson, R.A. Sculptor. London: 1870. V. 70

EASTLAKE, WILLIAM
Castle Keep. New York: 1965. V. 68; 71
Dancers in the Scalp House. New York: 1975. V. 70; 72
Go in Beauty. New York: 1956. V. 70; 71; 72; 73
Portrait of an Artist with 26 Horses. New York: 1963. V. 71

EASTMAN, C. G.
Sermons, Addresses, and Exhortations by Jedediah Burchard.... Burlington: 1836. V. 71

EASTMAN, C. R.
Catalog of the Fossil Fishes in the Carnegie Museum. 1911-1914. V. 72; 73
Sharks' Teeth and Cetacean Bones from the Red Clay of the Tropical Pacific. Cambridge: 1903. V. 73

EASTMAN, CHARLES
Indian Boyhood. New York: 1902. V. 69
Indian Heroes and Great Chieftains. Boston: 1924. V. 72

EASTMAN, EDWIN
Seven and Nine Years Among the Camanches and Apaches. Jersey City. V. 68; 73
Seven and Nine Years Among the Camanches and Apaches. Jersey City: 1873. V. 69

EASTMAN, GEORGE
Chronicles of an African Trip. 1927. V. 73

EASTMAN, MARY
Dahcotah: Life and Legends of the Sioux. Minneapolis: 1962. V. 69

EASTMAN, MAX
Artists in Uniform. New York: 1934. V. 68

EASTMAN, W. R.
The Parrots of Australia, A Guide to Field Identification and Habits. Sydney: 1966. V. 73

EASTON, ALEXANDER
A Practical Treatise on Street or Horse-Power Railways; Their Location, Construction and Management.... Philadelphia: 1859. V. 73

EASTON, JOHN
An Unfrequented Highway Through Sikkim and Tibet to Chumolaori. London: 1928. V. 72

EASTON, ROBERT
Max Brand, The Big Westerner. Norman: 1970. V. 70

EASTWOOD, B.
A Complete Manual for the Cultivation of the Cranberry.... New York: 1856. V. 70

EASTWOOD, DOROTHEA
River Diary. 1950. V. 68

AN EASY *Introduction to Geography, with a Brief View of the Solar System.* Charleston: 1803. V. 69; 71

AN EASY *Introduction to the Game of Chess....* Philadelphia: 1817. V. 68; 71

EASY *Lessons; or, Leading Strings to Knowledge in Three Parts.* 1838. V. 71

EATES, MARGOT
Paul Nash 1889-1946. London: 1973. V. 72

EATON, A.
Manual of Botany for North America... (with) Eaton's Botanical Grammar and Dictionary. Albany: 1836. V. 72

EATON, A. H.
Handicrafts of New England. New York: 1949. V. 72

EATON, AMOS
North American Botany; Comprising the Native and Common Cultivated Plants, North of Mexico.... Troy: 1840. V. 68

EATON, ARTHUR WENTWORTH HAMILTON
The Famous Mather Blyes, the Noted Boston Tory Preacher, Poet and Wit 1707-1788. Boston: 1914. V. 73
The History of Kings County Nova Scotia.... Belleville: 1972. V. 71

EATON, CHARLES EDWARD
The Shadow of the Swimmer. New York: 1951. V. 71
Write Me from Rio. Winston-Salem: 1959. V. 71

EATON, CHARLOTTE
Rome in the Nineteenth Century: Containing a Complete Account of the Ruins of the Ancient City, the Remains of the Middle Ages and the Monuments of Modern Times. Edinburgh: 1820. V. 70; 72

EATON, DAN C.
Beautiful Ferns. Boston: 1881. V. 68
Ferns of North America. Salem and Boston: 1879-1880. V. 70

EATON, E. H.
Birds of New York. Albany: 1910-1914. V. 70; 73

EATON, FRANK
Pistol Pete, Veteran of the Old West. New York: 1953. V. 72

EATON, HENRY BLACKBURN
Descendants of the Jersey Settlers. Wood River: 1950. V. 71

EATON, J. C.
70 Years Observations of a Trout Fisherman. Richmond, Surrey: 1937. V. 68

EATON, L. K.
Landscape Artist in America: The Life and Work.... Chicago: 1964. V. 68; 69

EATON, SEYMOUR
More About Teddy B. and Teddy G. The Roosevelt Bears. Philadelphia: 1907. V. 70; 73
The Roosevelt Bears Abroad. New York: 1908. V. 69
Roosevelt Bears: Their Travels and Adventures. Philadelphia: 1906. V. 69; 73
The Roosevelt Bears Abroad. Philadelphia: 1908. V. 69
Teddy B. and Teddy G: the Bear Detectives. Philadelphia: 1909. V. 69

EAUCLAIRE, SALLY
The New Color Photography. New York: 1981. V. 68

EBBUTT, PERCY G.
Emigrant Life in Kansas. London: 1886. V. 69

EBELING, KLAUS
Ragamala Painting. London: 1973. V. 72

EBERHARDT, WALTER
A Dagger in the Dark. New York: 1932. V. 71
The Jig-Saw Puzzle Murder. New York: 1933. V. 71

EBERHART, MIGNON G.
Deadly is the Diamond and Three Other Novelettes of Murder: Bermuda Grapevine, The Crimson Paw, Murder in Waltz Time. New York: 1958. V. 71
The Hangman's Whip. New York: 1940. V. 68
Hasty Wedding. New York: 1938. V. 70
The Mystery of Hunting's End. New York: 1930. V. 71
While the Patient Slept. New York: 1930. V. 69
With this Ring. New York: 1941. V. 70

EBERHART, PERRY
Ghosts of Colorado Plains. 1986. V. 69
Guide to the Colorado Ghost Towns and Mining Camps. Denver: 1959. V. 69

EBERHART, RICHARD
The Arts Anthology. Dartmouth Verse 1925. With An Introduction By Robert Frost. Portland: 1925. V. 72
A Bravery of Earth. London: 1930. V. 69
Brotherhood of Man. Pawlet: 1949. V. 68; 73
Chocorua. New York: 1981. V. 73
Poems, New and Selected. Norfolk: 1944. V. 68
Thirty One Sonnets. New York: 1967. V. 68; 70
Ways of Light. New York: 1980. V. 68

EBERLE, JOHN
Notes of Lectures on the Theory and Practice of Medicine Delivered in the Jefferson Medical College at Philadelphia. Philadelphia: 1844. V. 73

EBERLEIN, HAROLD DONALDSON
English Inn Past and Present. New York: 1926. V. 69
Historic Houses of the Hudson Valley. New York: 1942. V. 70
Manor Houses and Historic Homes of Long Island and Staten Island. Philadelphia: 1928. V. 71

The Manors and Historic Homes of the Hudson Valley. Philadelphia and London: 1924. V. 71
The Practical Book of Chinaware. Philadelphia & London: 1925. V. 69

EBERS, G.
Egypt: Descriptive, Historical and Picturesque. London. V. 71; 72

EBERS, VON GEORG
Aegypten in Bild und Wort, Etc. Stuttgart & Leipzig: 1879-1880. V. 68

EBERSTADT, EDWARD
The Annotated Eberstadt Catalogs of Americana in Four Volumes. New York: 1965. V. 68; 70; 72

EBERSTADT, EDWARD & SONS
Texas. New York: 1963. V. 69

EBSWORTH, J. B.
Choyce Drollery; Songs and Sonnets, Being a Collection of Divers Excellent Pieces of Poetry, of Several Eminent Authors..to Which are Added the Extra Songs of Merry Drollery..and an Antidote Against Melancholy.... Boston, Lincolnshire: 1876. V. 68

EBY, CECIL
The Siege of the Alcazar. London: 1966. V. 69

ECCLES, JOHN CAREW
The Cerebellum as a Neuronal Machine. New York: 1967. V. 71
The Human Mystery. 1979. V. 71
The Physiology of Synapses. Berlin: 1964. V. 71

ECCLESTON, ROBERT
Overland to California on the Southwestern Trail, 1849, Diary of.... Berkeley: 1950. V. 68; 73

ECHALAZ, LT. COL.
Complete History of the Echalaz Collection. 1907. V. 69

ECHARD, LAURENCE
The Gazetteer's; or Newsman's Interpreter. London: 1704. V. 69

ECHOES of the Aesthetic Society of Jersey City. New York: 1882. V. 71

THE ECHOES of the Lakes and Mountains, or Wonderful Things in the Lake District.... London: 1880. V. 71

ECILAW, ARY
The Romance of German Court. London: 1886. V. 68

ECK, C.
Traite de Construction en Poteries et Fer a L'Usage des Batimens Civils, Industriels et Militaires. Paris: 1836. V. 73

ECKEL, JOHN C.
The First Editions of Charles Dickens. London: 1913. V. 68
The First Editions of Charles Dickens. London: 1932. V. 68
Prime Pickwick in Parts: Census with Complete Comparison and Comment. New York: 1928. V. 70

ECKENRODE, H. J.
James Longstreet. Lee's War Horse. 1936. V. 68
James Longstreet: Lee's War Horse. Chapel Hill: 1936. V. 69

ECKENSTEIN, OSCAR
The Karakorams and Kashmir. London: 1896. V. 72

ECKER, ALEXANDER
Lorenz Oken. London: 1883. V. 68
On the Convolutions of the Human Brain. London: 1873. V. 68

ECKER, ARTHUR
The Normal Cerebral Angiogram. Springfield: 1951. V. 68

ECKERMANN, JOHANN PETER
Conversations with Goethe in the Last Years of Life. Boston: 1839. V. 68

ECKERT, A. W.
The Owls of North America (North of Mexico), All Species and Sub- species Illustrated.... Garden City: 1974. V. 73
Wilderness Empire. Boston: 1969. V. 73

ECKHARDT, GEORGE H.
Pennsylvania Clocks and Clockmakers. London: 1955. V. 72
Pennsylvania Clocks and Clockmakers. New York: 1955. V. 68; 73

THE ECLECTIC Repertory and Analytical Review, Medical and Philosophical. Philadelphia: 1813. V. 71

ECO, UMBERTO
The Bomb and the General. London: 1989. V. 71; 73
Foucault's Pendulum. San Diego: 1989. V. 68
The Island of the Day Before. New York: 1995. V. 68; 70
The Three Astronauts. London: 1989. V. 71

ECTON, JOHN
Liber Valorum and Decimarum: Being an Account of the Valuations and Yearly Tenths of all Such Ecclesiastical Benefices in England and Wales, as Now Stand Chargeable with the Payment of First-Fruits and Tenths. London: 1711. V. 72
Thesaurus Rerum Ecclesiasticarum. London: 1754. V. 69

EDDA
Edda; or, the Tales of a Grandmother. London: 1875. V. 73
Icelandic Poetry, or The Edda of Saemund Translated into English Verse. Bristol: 1797. V. 73

EDDINS, ROY
History of Falls Church, Texas. Falls Church: 1947. V. 69; 71

EDDISON, E. R.
Mistress of Mistresses. London: 1935. V. 70
Mistress of Mistresses. New York: 1935. V. 69

EDDY, A.
A Handbook of Malesian Mosses. London: 1988-1996. V. 70

EDDY, A. D.
Addresses on the Duties, Dangers and Securities of Youth.... New York and Boston: 1836. V. 69

EDDY, A. J.
Cubists and Post-Impressionism. Chicago: 1914. V. 69; 72

EDDY, CLYDE
Down the World's Most Dangerous River. New York: 1937. V. 73

EDDY, MARY BAKER
Poems. Boston: 1910. V. 70

EDE, H. S.
Savage Messiah. London: 1931. V. 73

EDE, HENRY W.
Modern Railway Administration. London: 1925. V. 70

EDELSTEIN, J. M.
Wallace Stevens: a Descriptive Bibliography. Pittsburgh: 1973. V. 68

EDEN, ANTHONY
Foreign Affairs. London: 1939. V. 69
Toward Peace in Indochina. Boston: 1966. V. 68

EDEN, CHARLES
China, Historical and Descriptive. London: 1877. V. 73

EDEN, FREDERICK MORTON
An Estimate of the Number of Inhabitants in Great Britain and Ireland. London: 1800. V. 70
On the Maritime Rights of Great Britain. London: 1807. V. 69
The State of the Poor. London: 1797. V. 69
The State of the Poor. London: 1928. V. 72

EDEN, ROB
Honeymoon Delayed. New York: 1937. V. 71
Love or Money. New York: 1936. V. 69

EDEN Versus Whistler, the Baronet and the Butterfly: a Valentine with a Verdict. Paris: 1899. V. 69

EDGAR, BOB
Brand of a Legend. 1978. V. 68

EDGAR, HERMAN LE ROY
Early American Editions of the Works of Charles Dickens. (with) *Charles Dickens: His Life as Traced by His Works.* New York: 1929. V. 68

EDGAR, JAMES
James Boys and Their Daring Deeds. Baltimore: 1911. V. 73

EDGAR, M. G.
A Treasury for Little Children. London: 1908. V. 72

EDGAR, WILLIAM
Vectigalium Systema; or a Complete View of that Part of Revenue of Great Britain, Commonly Called Customs.... London: 1714. V. 72

EDGE, FREDERICK MILNES
The Alabama and the Kearsarge. Boston: 1868. V. 69

EDGELL, G. H.
The American Architecture of Today. New York: 1928. V. 72

EDGER, BOB
Brand of Legend. Cody: 1978. V. 73
Lady of a Legend. Cody: 1979. V. 73

EDGERTON, CLYDE
Cold Black Peas. Chapel Hill: 1990. V. 68
The Floatplane Notebooks. Chapel Hill: 1988. V. 68
Raney. Chapel Hill: 1985. V. 69; 70; 71; 73
Walking Across Egypt. Chapel Hill: 1986. V. 71
Walking Across Egypt. Chapel Hill: 1987. V. 73

EDGERTON, SAMUEL Y.
Theaters of Conversion. Albuquerque: 2001. V. 71

EDGEWORTH, F. Y.
Papers Relating to Political Economy. London: 1925. V. 71

EDGEWORTH, MARIA
The Absentee. London: 1856. V. 68; 73
Castle Rackrent: an Hiberian Tale. 1801. V. 73
Ennui, and Emilie de Coulanges.... London: 1856. V. 68
Harrington, a Tale; Ormond, a Tale. London: 1817. V. 73
Harry and Lucy Concluded. London: 1825. V. 68; 71; 73
Helen, a Tale. London: 1834. V. 71; 73
Letters of Maria Edgeworth and Anna Letitia Barbauld. Waltham St. Lawrence: 1953. V. 71

Letters Selected from the Lushington Papers. Waltham St. Lawrence: 1953. V. 71
The Modern Griselda. London: 1819. V. 71
Ormond. London: 1895. V. 69
Patronage. 1893. V. 70
Practical Education. Providence and Boston: 1815. V. 68; 71; 73
Tales and Novels. London: 1848. V. 73
Tales from.... 1903. V. 69
Tales of Fashionable Life. London: 1824. V. 73

EDGEWORTH, RICHARD LOVELL
An Essay on the Construction of Roads and Carriages. London: 1817. V. 72
Essays on Professional Education. London: 1809. V. 73
Memoirs of Richard Lovell Edgeworth.... London: 1821. V. 73
Practical Education. London: 1801. V. 73

EDGINTON, MAY
The Adventures of Napoleon Prince. New York: 1912. V. 68
Dance of Youth. New York: 1932. V. 71
Tropic Flower. New York: 1933. V. 69

EDGLEY, LESLIE
False Face. New York: 1947. V. 68

EDINBURGH Almanack and Imperial Register for 1816. Edinburgh: 1815. V. 70

THE EDINBURGH Almanack, or Universal Scots and Imperial Register for 1818. Edinburgh: 1817. V. 70; 71

THE EDINBURGH Medical and Physical Dictionary, Containing an Explanation of the Terms of Art in Anatomy, Pharmacy, Physiology, Materia Medica.... Edinburgh: 1807. V. 70; 72

EDINGER, LUDWIG
Twelve Lectures on the Structure of the Central Nervous System for Physicians and Students. Philadelphia: 1891. V. 71

EDIS, ROBERT W.
Decoration and Furniture of Town Houses. 1881. V. 73
Decoration and Furniture of Town Houses. London: 1881. V. 68; 69

EDITH'S Alphabet. London: 1865. V. 72

EDKINS, J.
Chinese Currency. Shanghai: 1901. V. 72

EDKINS, JOSHUA
A Collection of Poems, Mostly Original, by Several Hands. (with) *A Collection of Poems Mostly Original by Several Hands....* Dublin: 1789-1790. V. 69

EDMESTON, JAMES
Sacred Lyrics. 1823. V. 73

EDMOND, J. P.
The Aberdeen Printers, Edward Raban to James Nicol 1620-1736. Aberdeen: 1886. V. 70

EDMONDS, JOHN W.
Spiritualism. New York: 1866. V. 71

EDMONDS, S. EMMA E.
Nurse and Spy in the Union Army: the Adventures and Experiences of a Woman in Hospitals, Camps and Battle-Fields. Hartford: 1864. V. 69; 73

EDMONDS, WALTER D.
Chad Hanna. Boston: 1940. V. 71; 72
Drums Along the Mohawk. Boston: 1936. V. 71; 72; 73
Rome Haul. Boston: 1929. V. 71

EDMONDSON, JOSEPH
An Historical and Genealogical Account of the Noble Family of Greville...and some Account of Warwick Castle. London: 1766. V. 68
Precedency. London. V. 72

EDMONDSTON, A.
Observations on the Nature and Extent of the Cod Fishery, Carried On Off the Coasts of Zeland and Orkney Islands. Edinburgh: 1820. V. 68

EDMONSON, J. M.
American Armamentarium Chirurgicum George Tiemann & Co. 1889. The Centennial Edition. San Francisco;: 1989. V. 70

EDMUNDS, LOWELL
Silver Bullet: the Martini in American Civilization. Westport: 1981. V. 70

EDMUNDS, MURRELL
Time's Laughter in Their Ears. New York: 1946. V. 69

EDMUNDS, WILL H.
Pointers and Clues to the Subjects of Chinese and Japanese Art. London. V. 73

EDNA Jane, the Careless Child. Troy: 1852-1857?. V. 70

EDREHI, M.
An Historical Account of the Ten Tribes, Settled Beyond the River Sambayton in the East. London: 1836. V. 69

EDSON, RUSSELL
The Wounded Breakfast. Ten Poems. Madison: 1978. V. 73
Wuck Wuck Wuck!. New York: 1984. V. 73

EDWARD, DAVID B.
The History of Texas, or the Emigrant's, Farmer's and Politician's Guide to the Character, Climate, Soil and.... 1836. V. 68

EDWARD, R. D.
The Great Famine, Studies in Irish History 1845-1852. 1956. V. 70

EDWARDES, DAVID
Introduction to Anatomy - 1532. London: 1961. V. 68

EDWARDES, HERBERT BENJAMIN
Life of Sir Henry Lawrence. London: 1872. V. 73

EDWARDS, A.
Ordinances of the City Council of Charleston: in the State of South Carolina, Passed Since the Incorporation of the City. Charleston: 1802-1807. V. 71

EDWARDS, AMELIA ANN BLANDFORD
Ballads. London: 1865. V. 69

EDWARDS, AMELIA B.
A Midsummer Ramble In The Dolomites. London: 1889. V. 72
Pharaohs, Fellahs and Explorers. New York: 1892. V. 70
A Thousand Miles Up The Nile. London: 1888. V. 72
Untrodden Peaks and Unfrequented Valleys. London: 1873. V. 70
Untrodden Peaks and Unfrequented Valleys. London: 1893. V. 72

EDWARDS, ARTHUR M.
Life Beneath the Waters; or, the Aquarium in America. New York: 1858. V. 68; 69; 70

EDWARDS, CLAYTON
The Story of Evangeline Adapted From Longfellow.... New York: 1913. V. 71

EDWARDS, E. I.
Desert Harvest. Los Angeles: 1962. V. 69; 73
Desert Voices: a Descriptive Bibliography. Los Angeles: 1958. V. 71
Lost Oases Along the Carrizo. Los Angeles: 1961. V. 69
The Valley Whose Name is Death. Pasadena: 1940. V. 73

EDWARDS, F. W.
British Blood-Sucking Flies. London: 1939. V. 73

EDWARDS, FREDERICK
Our Domestic Fire-Places. London: 1870. V. 68

EDWARDS, GEORGE W. WARTON
The Forest of Arden. London: 1914. V. 72

EDWARDS, H. M.
A Monograph of the British Fossil Corals. 1866-1872. V. 69

EDWARDS, HARRY
The Struggle That Must Be. New York: 1980. V. 72

EDWARDS, HARRY STILLWELL
His Defense and Other Stories. New York: 1899. V. 73

EDWARDS, HUGH
All Night at Mr. Stanyhurst's. London: 1963. V. 72

EDWARDS, J. B.
Early Days in Abilene. 1938. V. 68
Early Days in Abilene. Abilene: 1938. V. 73

EDWARDS, J. HUGH
David Lloyd George, the Man an the Statesman. New York: 1929. V. 73

EDWARDS, JENNIE
John N. Edwards. Biography, Memoirs, Reminiscences and Recollection. Kansas City: 1889. V. 70

EDWARDS, JESSE E.
An Atlas of Congenital Anomalies of the Heart and Great Vessels. Springfield: 1954. V. 68

EDWARDS, JIM
The Vanished Splendor III. Oklahoma City: 1985. V. 68

EDWARDS, JOAN
Crewel Embroidery in England. London: 1975. V. 69

EDWARDS, JOHN FRANK
Army Life of Frank Edwards, Confederate Veteran, Army of Northern Virginia 1861-1865. La Grange: 1911. V. 69; 70

EDWARDS, JOHN N.
Shelby's Expedition to Mexico, an Unwritten, Leaf of the War. 1964. V. 68
Shelby's Expedition to Mexico, an Unwritten Leaf of the War. Austin: 1964. V. 69

EDWARDS, JONATHAN
An Account of the Life of the Late Reverend Mr. David Brainerd, Minister of the Gospel, Missionary to the Indians...and Pastor of a Church of Christian Indians in New Jersey. Boston: 1749. V. 70; 73
An Account of the Life of the Rev. David Brainerd...Missionary to the Indians.... Newark: 1811. V. 69
A Faithful Narrative of the Surprising Work of God in the Conversion of Many Hundred Souls in Northampton.... Elizabeth-Town: 1790. V. 69
The History of the Work of Redemption. New York: 1786. V. 69
The Life of Rev. David Brainerd, Chiefly Extracted from His Diary.... New York: 1833. V. 69
Memoirs of the Rev. David Brainerd; Missionary to the Indians on the Borders of New York, New Jersey and Pennsylvania.... New Haven: 1822. V. 69
A Treatise Concerning Religious Affections. Elizabeth-Town: 1787. V. 69

EDWARDS, K. C.
The Peak District.... 1962. V. 68

EDWARDS, KENNETH
We Dive at Dawn. Chicago: 1941. V. 68

EDWARDS, LIONEL
Beasts of the Chase. 1950. V. 68
The Fox. 1949. V. 68
Hunting and Stalking the Deer. 1927. V. 70
Hunting and Stalking the Deer. London: 1927. V. 69
The Huntsmen Past and Present. 1929. V. 68; 70
Reminiscences of a Sporting Artist. 1947. V. 68
Scarlet and Corduroy. 1941. V. 68
Sketches in Stable and Kennel. 1933. V. 68

EDWARDS, MATILDA B.
Lisabee's Love Story. London: 1876. V. 68
Poems. London: 1884. V. 69

EDWARDS, MONICA
The Summer of the Great Secret. 1948. V. 72

EDWARDS, MORTON
A Guide to Modelling in Clay and Wax and for Terra Cotta, Bronze and Silver Chasing.... 1891. V. 68

EDWARDS, OWEN
Clych Atgof. Penodau yn Hanes fy Addsyg. Newtown: 1933. V. 71

EDWARDS, P. L.
Sketch of the Oregon Territory of Emigrant's Guide. Kansas City: 1951. V. 69

EDWARDS, PHILIP L.
California in 1837- Diary of Colonel Philip L. Edwards, Contains.... Sacramento: 1890. V. 71

EDWARDS, RALPH
Connoisseur's Period Guides to the Houses, Decorations, Furnishing and Chattels of the Classic Periods. London: 1956-1958. V. 72
The Dictionary Of English Furniture. Woodbridge: 1986. V. 72
Dictionary of English Furniture from the Middle Ages to the Late Georgian Period. London: 1954. V. 72
Georgian Cabinet Makers c. 1700-1800. London: 1955. V. 68

EDWARDS, RICHARD
Edwards' Great West and Her Commercial Metropolis, Embracing a General View of the West.... New York: 1860. V. 68; 73
Tao-Chi Landscape Album from the Poem of Tu-Pu. Tokyo: 1968. V. 70

EDWARDS, RICHARD KEMBLE
The Mystery of the Miniature. Boston: 1908. V. 69; 73

EDWARDS, ROBERT D.
The Great Famine. Studies in Irish History 1845-1852. 1956. V. 69; 73

EDWARDS, RUTH DUDLEY
Murder in a Cathedral. London: 1996. V. 68

EDWARDS, SYDENHAM TEAK
The New Botanic Garden Illustrated with One Hundred and Thirty-Three Plants.... London: 1812. V. 70

EDWARDS, THOMAS
Reports of the Leading Decisions in the High Court of Admiralty, in Cases of Vessels Sailing Under British Licences. London: 1812. V. 70

EDWARDS, WELDON NATHANIEL
Memoir of Nathaniel Macon, of North Carolina. Raleigh: 1862. V. 68; 69

EDWARDS, WILLIAM
The Early History of the North Riding. London: 1924. V. 73

EDWARDS, WILLIAM H.
Butterflies of North America. First and Second Series. Philadelphia: 1868-1872. V. 70
Football Days. New York: 1916. V. 69

EDWIN *Booth in Twelve Dramatic Characters.* Boston: 1872. V. 68

EDWORDS, CLARENCE E.
Bohemian San Francisco. San Francisco: 1914. V. 70
Camp-Fires of A Naturalist. London: 1893. V. 72

EELLS, MYRON
Hymns in the Shonnok Jargon Language. Portland: 1889. V. 68

EGAN, BERESFORD PATRICK
De Sade. Being a Series of Wounds, Inflicted with Brush and Pen, Upon Sadistic Wolves Garbed in Masochist's Wool. 1929. V. 73
Pollen - a Novel in Black and White. London: 1933. V. 69
The Sink of Solitude. London: 1928. V. 73

EGAN, CHARLES
The Status of the Jews in England, from the Time of the Normans to the Reign of Her Majesty Queen Victoria.... Dublin: 1848. V. 71

EGAN, HOWARD R.
Pioneering the West 1846 to 1878. Richmond: 1917. V. 70

EGAN, JENNIFER
The Invisible Circus. New York: 1995. V. 72

EGAN, JOSEPH B.
The Civil War. Its Photographic History. The War in the East. (also) The War in the West and South and on the Water. Wellesley Hills: 1941. V. 73

EGAN, P. K.
The Parish of Ballinasloe: Its History from...Earliest Times. 1960. V. 70

EGAN, PIERCE
Diorama Anglais ou Promenades Pittoresques a Londres. Paris: 1823. V. 69; 71
The Life of an Actor. London: 1825. V. 69; 70; 71; 73
The Life of an Actor. London: 1892. V. 70
Pierce Egan's Account of the Trial of John Thurtell and Joseph Hunt. London: 1824. V. 72
Real Life in Ireland.... London: 1920. V. 70

EGAN, THOMAS J.
History of the Halifax Volunteer Battalion and Volunteer Companies 1859-1887. Halifax: 1888. V. 72; 73

EGAN, WILLIAM M.
Pioneering the West 1846 to 1878. Major Eagan's Diary.... Salt Lake City: 1917. V. 70

EGBERT, DONALD DREW
Princeton Portraits. Princeton: 1947. V. 69
The Tickhill Psalter and Related Manuscripts: a School of Manuscript Illumination in England During the Early Fourteenth Century. New York: 1940. V. 72; 73

EGE, RALPH
Pioneers of Old Hopewell with Sketches of Her Revolutionary Heroes. Hopewell: 1908. V. 69

EGE, V.
Chauliodus Schn., Bathypelagic Genus of Fishes.... Copenhagen: 1948. V. 72

EGELER, C. G.
The Untrodden Andes. 1955. V. 71

EGERTON, GEORGE
Keynotes. London: 1893. V. 73

EGERTON, THOMAS
The Speech of the Lord Chancellor of England, in the Exchequer Chamber, Touching the Post-nati. London: 1609. V. 70

EGGAN, FRED
Social Organization of the Western Pueblos. Chicago: 1950. V. 69

EGGELING, W. J.
The Indigenous Trees of the Uganda Protectorate. Entebbe: 1940. V. 70; 72

EGGENHOFER, NICK
Horses, Horses, Always Horses - The Life and Art of Nick Eggenhofer. Cody: 1981. V. 69; 70
Wagons, Mules and Men. New York: 1961. V. 69; 71; 73

EGGERLING, W. J.
The Indigenous Trees of the Uganda Protectorate. Entebbe: 1951. V. 68

EGGERS, DAVE
A Heartbreaking Work of Staggering Genius. New York: 2000. V. 68; 69; 71; 72

EGGLER, ALBERT
The Everest-Lhotse Adventure. London: 1957. V. 69

EGGLESTON, GEORGE C.
A Rebel's Recollections. New York: 1875. V. 73

EGGLESTON, GEORGE CARY
The History of the Confederate War. Its Causes and Conduct. New York: 1910. V. 69
Southern Soldier Stories. New York: 1898. V. 70

EGGLESTON, W. M.
Picturesque Weardale. Darlington: 1916. V. 73

EGGLESTON, WILLIAM
Election Eve. Washington: 1977. V. 73
William Eggleston's Guide. New York: 1976. V. 73

EGLINTON, JOHN
Two Essays on the Remnant. 1894. V. 69; 73

EGOLF, TRISTAN
Lord of the Barnyard. London: 1998. V. 71; 72

EGOROV, I. A.
The Architectural Planning of St. Petersburg: Its Development in the 18th and 19th Centuries. 1969. V. 72

EGOROVA, T. V.
The Sedges (Carex L.) of Russia and Adjacent States. St. Petersburg and St. Louis: 1999. V. 72

EHLE, JOHN
Move Over, Mountain. New York: 1957. V. 70

EHRENBURG, ILJA
Moi Parizh. Moscow: 1933. V. 70

EHRENPREIS, IRVIN
Swift, the Man, His Works and the Age. 1946-1983. V. 69

EHRENSTEIN, ALBERT
Tabutsch. New York: 1946. V. 71

EHRHARDT, ALFRED
Das Watt. Hamburg: 1937. V. 70

EHRLICH, BETTINA
Cocolo. London: 1945. V. 68; 72

EHRLICH, GRETEL
Geode/Rock Body. Santa Barbara: 1970. V. 68; 71
Heart Mountain. New York: 1988. V. 71; 72
A Match to the Heart. New York: 1994. V. 68; 70
The Solace of Open Spaces. New York: 1985. V. 69; 71; 72; 73
Words from the Land. Salt Lake City: 1988. V. 68
Wyoming Stories. Santa Barbara: 1986. V. 70

EHRLICH, P.
Histology of the Blood Normal and Pathological. Cambridge: 1900. V. 68

EICHLER, JOSEPH L.
Eichler Homes Designed for Better Living. Palo Alto: 1950. V. 72

EICKEMEYER, CARL
Among the Pueblo Indians. New York: 1895. V. 71
Over the Great Navajo Trail. New York: 1900. V. 68; 71

EICKEMEYER, RUDOLF
Down South. New York: 1900. V. 73

EIDLITZ, WALTHER
Zodiak. New York: 1931. V. 70

EIGENMANN, C. H.
American Characidae. Parts 1-4. Cambridge: 1917-1927. V. 69
Fishes of Western South America. Part I. Pittsburgh: 1922. V. 69

EIGHT *Harvard Poets.* New York: 1917. V. 70; 71

EIGNER, LARRY
Some Token Or. New Rochelle: 1985. V. 73

EIKER, MATHILDE
Over the Boat-Side. Garden City: 1928. V. 71

EILAND, MURRAY L.
Oriental Rugs: a Comprehensive Guide. 1976. V. 69; 72

EINSTEIN, ALBERT
Ather und Relativitatstheorie. Berlin: 1920. V. 68
Die Grundlage der Allgemeinen Relativitats-Theorie. Leipzig: 1916. V. 69; 72; 73
Out of My Later Years. New York: 1950. V. 68; 70
Zur Elektrodynamik Bewegter Korper in Annalen der Physik. 1905. V. 73

EINSTEIN, CHARLES
The Bloody Spur. New York: 1953. V. 70
The Fireside of Baseball, The Second Fireside Book of Baseball, The Third Fireside Book of Baseball. New York: 1956. V. 69

EISELE, FANNIE L.
A History of Covington, Garfield County, Oklahoma and Surrounding Territory. 1952. V. 69

EISELE, WICHERT
The Real Wild Bill Hickock. Denver: 1931. V. 68; 73

EISELEY, LOREN
The Brown Wasps. Mount Horeb: 1969. V. 71
Darwin's Century, Evolution and the Men Who Discovered It. Garden City: 1958. V. 70; 72
The Firmament of Time. London: 1960. V. 71
The Immense Journey. New York: 1957. V. 71
The Invisible Pyramid. New York: 1970. V. 73

EISELIN, MAX
The Ascent of Dhaulagiri. London: 1961. V. 73

EISENBERG, BARON VON
La Perfezione e i Difetti del Cavallo. Florence: 1753. V. 68

EISENHOWER, DWIGHT DAVID
Crusade in Europe. Garden City: 1948. V. 68; 69; 71
The Wartime Papers of.... Baltimore: 1970. V. 73
The White House Years: Mandate for Change 1953-1956. Garden City: 1963. V. 72; 73

EISENSOHN, SISTER M. ALFREDA
Pioneer Days in Idaho Country, 2 Volumes. Caldwell: 1951. V. 71

EISENSTAEDT, ALFRED
Witness to Our Time. New York: 1966. V. 68

EISENSTEIN, SERGEI
Notes of a Film Director. London: 1959. V. 72

EKEMAN, LORENZ
Zeichnungs-Buch zum Selbst-Unterricht im Baum-und Landschafts- Zeichnen.... Munich: 1819. V. 72

ELDER, ELEANOR
Travelling Players. London: 1939. V. 70

ELDER, JANE LENZ
Trading in Sante Fe - John M. Kingsbury's Correspondence with James Josiah Webb 1853-1861. Dallas: 1996. V. 68; 73

ELDERFIELD, JOHN
Frankenthaler. New York: 1989. V. 73

ELDERSHAW, FLORA S.
The Peaceful Army. Sydney: 1938. V. 69

ELDERTON, W. PALIN
Frequency-Curves and Correlation. London: 1906. V. 69

ELDON, M.
Bumble. London: 1950. V. 68

ELDREDGE, ZOETH S.
The Beginnings of San Francisco. San Francisco: 1912. V. 70

ELDRIDGE, ELLEANOR
Elleanor's Second Book. Providence: 1842. V. 73
Memoirs of Elleanor Eldridge. (with) *Elleanor's Second Book.* Providence: 1841. V. 68

ELDRIDGE, LEMUEL B.
The Torrent; or an Account of a Deluge Occasioned by an Unparalleled Rise of the New Haven River.... Middlebury: 1831. V. 71; 73

THE ELECTION. A Quite New Song. London: 1796. V. 68

AN ELECTION Ball. In Poetical Letters, from Mr. Inkle at Bath to His Wife at Gloucester: with a Poetical Address to John Miller, Esq. at Batheaston Villa. Bath: 1776. V. 71

ELEGANT Extracts: Being a Copious Selection...from the Most Eminent British Poets. Volume I. London: 1830. V. 68

AN ELEGY ON the Death and Burial of Cock Robin. 1820. V. 72

AN ELEGY On the Death and Burial of Cock Robin. London: 1820. V. 68

AN ELEGY on the Death of Martin Drayson: Who Departed This Life, September 12, 1773, aged 21 Years. Sevenoaks: 1774. V. 69

AN ELEGY on the Glory of Her Sex: Mrs. Mary Blaize. London: 1885. V. 70

ELEMENTS of Chess. Boston: 1805. V. 69

ELEMENTS of Geography. London: 1820. V. 73

ELFER, MAURICE
Madam Candelaria, Unsung Heroine of the Alamo. Houston: 1933. V. 70

ELFORD, WILLIAM
A Short Essay on the Propagation and Dispersion of Animals and Vegetables, Being Chiefly Intended as an Anwer to a Letter Lately Published.... London: 1786. V. 70; 73

ELGEE, FRANK
Early Man in North-East Yorkshire. Glouchester: 1930. V. 73
The Moorlands of North-Eastern Yorkshire. London: 1912. V. 73

ELGOOD, GEORGE S.
Italian Gardens after Drawings by George S. Elgood, R.I. London: 1907. V. 73
Some English Gardens. London: 1904. V. 71; 73
Some English Gardens. 1933. V. 69; 73

ELIA, IRENE
The Female Animal. Oxford: 1985. V. 71

ELIAS, EDITH L.
The Story of Hiawatha. London: 1914. V. 70

ELIAS, SOL P.
Stories of Stanislaus, a Collection of Stories on the History and Achievements of Stanislaus County. Modesto: 1924. V. 68; 70; 71

ELIASON, ELDRIDGE L.
Practical Bandaging Including Adhesive and Plaster-of-Paris Dressings. Philadelphia: 1914. V. 68

ELIASOPH, PHILIP
Paul Cadmus. Yesterday and Today. Oxford: 1981. V. 70

ELIE DE BEAUMONT, ANNE LOUISE MORIN DUMESNIL
Lettres du Marquis de Roselle. 1765. V. 73

ELIOT, ANDREW
A Discourse on Natural Religion Delivered in the Chapel of Harvard College in Cambraidge, New England May 8, 1771, at the Lecture Founded by the Hon. Paul Dudley. Boston: 1771. V. 68

ELIOT, CHARLES
Charles Eliot, Landscape Grower. Boston: 1902. V. 69

ELIOT, CHARLES W.
The Working of the American Democracy. Cambridge: 1888. V. 68

ELIOT, ELLSWORTH
West Point in the Confederacy. New York: 1941. V. 69; 70

ELIOT, GEORGE, PSEUD.
Adam Bede. London. V. 71
Adam Bede. Edinburgh and London: 1859. V. 69
Daniel Deronda. 1876. V. 73
Daniel Deronda. Edinburgh and London: 1876. V. 68; 70; 72
Daniel Deronda. London: 1877. V. 71
Early Essays. London: 1919. V. 73
Essays and Leaves from a Note-Book. 1884. V. 71
Felix Holt the Radical. Edinburgh and London: 1866. V. 70; 73
Felix Holt the Radical. New York: 1866. V. 68
How Lisa Loved the King. Boston: 1869. V. 68
Impressions of Theophrastus Such. New York: 1879. V. 69; 73
The Legend of Jubal and Other Poems. Edinburgh and London: 1874. V. 70; 73
The Lifted Veil and Brother Jacob. Leipzig: 1878. V. 71; 72
Middlemarch. Berlin: 1872. V. 70
The Mill on the Floss. Edinburgh and London: 1860. V. 73
Romola. Edinburgh. V. 73
Romola. London: 1863. V. 73
Scenes of Clerical Life. Edinburgh and London: 1859. V. 68
Scenes of Clerical Life. London: 1906. V. 68
Silas Marner. Edinburgh & London: 1861. V. 73
Silas Marner. New York: 1861. V. 71; 73
Silas Marner. New York: 1953. V. 68; 71
The Spanish Gypsy: a Poem. Edinburgh and London: 1868. V. 70; 73
The Works. Edinburgh: 1885?. V. 73
The Works. Holly Lodge Edition. Boston: 1898. V. 72

ELIOT, PHILIP
Serpent on the Hill. Dallas: 1982. V. 68

ELIOT, THOMAS STEARNS
After Strange Gods - A Primer of Modern Heresy: The Page-Barbour Lectures at the University of Virginia. London: 1934. V. 68
After Strange Gods: a Primer of Modern Heresy. London: 1935. V. 69
Animula. London: 1929. V. 68; 69; 73
Ara Vus (Vos) Prec. 1920. V. 73
Ash Wednesday. New York/London: 1930. V. 68; 72; 73
A Choice of Kipling's Verse. London: 1941. V. 72
The Classics and the Man of Letters: the Presidential Address to the Classical Association on 15 April 1942. London: 1942. V. 73
The Cocktail Party. London: 1950. V. 69; 70; 71; 72
The Cocktail Party. New York: 1950. V. 69
Collected Poems 1909-1935. London: 1936. V. 68; 69; 71; 72
Collected Poems 1909-1935. New York: 1936. V. 72
Collected Poems 1909-1962. New York: 1963. V. 71
The Confidential Clerk. London: 1954. V. 69; 71; 72
The Confidential Clerk. London: 1982. V. 69
The Cultivation of Christmas Trees. London. V. 69
Dante. London: 1929. V. 69; 72; 73
The Dry Salvages. London: 1941. V. 68
Eeldrop and Appleplex. Turnbridge Wells: 1992. V. 72
The Elder Statesman. London: 1959. V. 69; 70; 73
The Elder Statesman. New York: 1959. V. 71
Ezra Pound: His Metric and Poetry. New York: 1917. V. 69; 72
The Family Reunion. London: 1939. V. 68; 69; 71
For Lancelot Andrewes - Essays on Style and Order. London: 1928. V. 68; 72
Four Quartets. London: 1940-1942. V. 69; 72; 73
Four Quartets. New York: 1943. V. 70
Four Quartets. London: 1944. V. 69; 72; 73
Four Quartets. London: 1960. V. 69; 72
Gamle Possum's Bog om Praktiske Katte. Copenhagen: 1958. V. 70
Homage to John Dryden. London: 1924. V. 69; 70
The Idea of a Christian Society. London: 1939. V. 68; 69
John Dryden - The Poet - The Dramatist - The Critic. Three Essays. New York: 1932. V. 71
The Letters of T. S. Eliot. Volume I 1898-1922. 1988. V. 70
Letters of T. S. Eliot. Volume I 1898-1922. New York: 1989. V. 68
The Literature of Politics. 1955. V. 68
The Literature of Politics. London: 1955. V. 69
Little Gidding. London: 1942. V. 68
Meurtre Dans La Cathedrale. Paris: 1947. V. 72
Murder in the Cathedral. Canterbury: 1935. V. 73
Murder in the Cathedral. London: 1935. V. 69; 72
Murder in the Cathedral. London: 1936. V. 71; 73
Murder in the Cathedral. London: 1952. V. 72
Odemarken og Andre Digte. (The Wasteland). Copenhagen: 1948. V. 68
Old Possum's Book of Practical Cats. London: 1939. V. 73
Old Possum's Book of Practical Cats. New York: 1939. V. 69; 70; 72; 73
Old Possum's Book of Practical Cats. London: 1953. V. 69; 71
On Poetry and Poets. London: 1957. V. 72
Poems. Richmond: 1919. V. 73
Poems. New York: 1920. V. 69; 72; 73
Poems 1909-1925. London: 1925. V. 68; 72
Poems 1909-1925. London: 1926. V. 73
Poems 1909-1925. New York: 1932. V. 69
Poems Written in Early Youth. London: 1967. V. 68; 69; 73
Poetry and Drama: The Theodore Spencer Memorial Lecture, Harvard University, November 21, 1950. London: 1951. V. 69
A Presidential Address to the Members of the London Library. London: 1952. V. 73
Prufrock and Other Observations. London: 1917. V. 70; 72; 73
Religious Drama: Mediaeval and Modern. New York: 1954. V. 69; 70; 71; 72
Reunion by Destruction. Reflections on a Scheme for Church Union in South India. 1943. V. 68
Reunion by Destruction, Reflections on a Scheme for Church Union in South India. London: 1943. V. 71
The Rock. 1934. V. 70; 71
The Rock. London: 1934. V. 69; 70; 72; 73
Selected Essays - 1917-1932. London: 1932. V. 69

ELIOT, THOMAS STEARNS continued
Selected Poems. London: 1954. V. 69
A Song For Simeon. London: 1928. V. 72
A Song for Simeon. London: 1929. V. 69
Sweeney Agonistes. London: 1932. V. 69; 72; 73
T. S. Eliot; the Critical Heritage. London: 1982. V. 71
The Three Voices of Poetry. London: 1953. V. 69
To Criticize the Critic and Other Writings. London: 1965. V. 71
To Criticize the Critic and Other writings. New York: 1965. V. 72
The Undergraduate Poems of T. S. Eliot.... Cambridge: 1949. V. 72
The Value and Use of Cathedrals in England To-Day. 1954. V. 73
The Waste Land. New York: 1922. V. 73
The Waste Land. Richmond: 1923. V. 73
The Waste Land. London: 1945. V. 70
The Waste Land. London: 1961. V. 69; 72
The Waste Land. London: 1962. V. 69; 71
The Waste Land. 1971. V. 70
The Waste Land. London: 1971. V. 69; 72; 73

ELIZABETH, CHARLOTTE
Chapters on Flowers. London: 1853. V. 71
Chapters on Flowers. London: 1866. V. 72

THE ELIZABETHAN Zoo. London: 1926. V. 71

ELIZABETH I, QUEEN
A Most Excellent and Remarkable Speech Delivered by the Mirrour and Miracle of Princes, Queen Elizabeth.... London: 1643. V. 68

ELKHART CARRIAGE & HARNESS MANUFACTURING CO.
Catalogue No. 36. 1897. V. 69

ELKIN, R. H.
The Children's Corner. London: 1914. V. 73
Little People Rhymes. London. V. 72

ELKIN, STANLEY
A Bad Man. New York: 1967. V. 68; 71
Boswell. New York: 1964. V. 68; 71
The Dick Gibson Show. New York: 1971. V. 68
The Franchiser. New York: 1976. V. 72
The Magic Kingdom. New York: 1985. V. 72
The Making of Ashenden. 1972. V. 68
The Making of Ashenden. London: 1972. V. 69
Mrs. Ted Bliss. New York: 1995. V. 73
The Rabbi of Lud. New York: 1987. V. 72
Searches and Seizures. New York: 1973. V. 68

ELKINS, AARON
Curses. New York: 1989. V. 68
The Dark Place. 1983. V. 69
The Dark Place. New York: 1983. V. 70
The Dark Place. New York: 1985. V. 69
A Deceptive Clarity. New York: 1987. V. 68; 69; 73
Murder in the Queen's Armes. New York: 1985. V. 68; 69; 70; 71; 72
Skeleton Dance. New York: 2000. V. 72

ELKINTON, J.
Doukhobors, Their History in Russia, Their Migration to Canada. Philadelphia: 1903. V. 70

ELKUS, RICHARD J.
Alamos: a Philosophy in Living. San Francisco: 1965. V. 70; 71

ELLACOMBE, H. N.
The Plant-Lore and Garden Craft of Shakespeare. 1896. V. 69

ELLENBECKER, JOHN G.
The Jayhawkers of Death Valley. Marysville: 1938. V. 70

ELLENBOROUGH, EDWARD LAW, EARL OF
India and Lord Ellenborough. London: 1844. V. 73

ELLERMAN, J. R.
The Fauna of India, Including Pakistan, Burma and Ceylon. Mamalia, Volume 3. Rodentia. Calcutta: 1961. V. 72

ELLESMERE, HARRIET CATHERINE EGERTON, COUNTESS OF
Journal of a Tour in the Holy Land in May and June 1840. London: 1841. V. 68; 72

ELLESMERE, THOMAS EGERTON, BARON
Certaine Observations Concerning the Office of the Lord Chancellor. London: 1651. V. 72

ELLET, C.
Report on a Suspension Bridge Across the Potomac, for Rail Road and Common Travel; Addressed to the Mayor and City Council of Georgetown. Philadelphia: 1852. V. 73

ELLET, ELIZABETH F.
Domestic History of the American Revolution. New York: 1850. V. 73
The Women of the American Revolution. New York: 1853-1854. V. 71

ELLICE, EDWARD C.
Place-Names in Glengarry and Glenquoich and Their Origin. London: 1898. V. 71
Place-Names in Glengarry and Glenquoich and Their Origin. London: 1931. V. 71

ELLICE, ROBERT
Songs for the Nursery: a Collection of Children's Poems, Old and New. London: 1887. V. 69

ELLICOTT, ANDREW
The Journal of Andrew Ellicott...for Determining the Boundary Between the United States and the Posessions of His Catholic Majesty in America.... Philadelphia: 1803. V. 69

ELLIN, STANLEY
Mirror, Mirror on the Wall. New York: 1972. V. 68
The Specialty of the House & Other Stories. New York: 1979. V. 71

ELLINGER, ESTHER PARKER
The Southern War Poetry of the Civil War. Philadelphia: 1918. V. 69

ELLIOT, DANIEL GIRAUD
The Gallinaceous Game Birds of North America.... New York: 1897. V. 70; 73
Life and Habits of Wild Animals. London: 1874. V. 72
The New and Heretofore Unfigured Species of the Birds of North America. New York: 1866-1869. V. 73
North American Shore Birds, a History of the Snipes, Sandpipers, Plovers and their Allies. New York: 1895. V. 70; 73
A Review of the Primates. New York: 1912-1913. V. 69

ELLIOT, HUGH S. R.
The Letters of John Stuart Mill.... London: 1910. V. 68

ELLIOT, PAUL
Hugger-Mugger In The Louvre. New York: 1940. V. 72

ELLIOT, RICHARD S.
Notes Taken in Sixty Years. St. Louis: 1893. V. 70

ELLIOT, T. S.
Knowledge And Experience In the Philosophy of F. H. Bradley. New York: 1964. V. 72

ELLIOT, W. J.
The Spurs. Spur, TX: 1939. V. 71

ELLIOT, WALLACE W.
History of San Bernardino and San Diego Counties, California. Riverside: 1965. V. 68; 70

ELLIOTSON, JOHN
Numerous Cases of Surgical Operations Without Pain in the Mesmeric State. London: 1843. V. 71

ELLIOTT, BENJAMIN
The Militia System of South Carolina.... Charleston: 1835. V. 68

ELLIOTT, CHARLES
The Bible and Slavery: in Which the Abrahamic and Mosaic Discipline Considered in Connection with the Most Ancient Forms of Slavery. 1857. V. 70

ELLIOTT, CHARLOTTE
Selections from Poems of.... London: 1873. V. 69

ELLIOTT, EBENEZER
(Poems). 1834-1835. V. 73

ELLIOTT, EMILY STEELE
Chimes of Consecration and their Echoes. London: 1875. V. 69

ELLIOTT, ERIC
Anatomy of Motion Picture Art. Territet: 1928. V. 68

ELLIOTT, F. R.
Popular Deciduous and Evergreen Trees and Shrubs.... New York: 1868. V. 72

ELLIOTT, ISAAC
Record of the Services of Illinois Soldiers in the Black Hawk War 1831-1832 and in the Mexican War 1846-1848. Springfield: 1882. V. 72

ELLIOTT, K. A. C.
Neurochemistry. The Chemistry of Brain and Nerve. Springfield: 1962. V. 68

ELLIOTT, LYDIA S.
Kangaroo Coolaroo. London: 1950. V. 69

ELLIOTT, MARY
The Rose, Containing Original Poems for Young People. London: 1824. V. 68; 72

ELLIOTT, MAUD HOWE
Art and Handicraft in the Woman's Building of the Columbian Exposition Chicago, 1893. Paris and New York: 1893. V. 71

ELLIOTT, ROBERT
Views in India, China and on the Shores of the Red Sea.... London: 1835. V. 70

ELLIOTT, ROBERT W.
Lefever: Guns of Lasting Fame. 1986. V. 72

ELLIOTT, RUSSELL R.
Nevada's 20th Century Mining Boom. Reno: 1966. V. 69

ELLIOTT, STEPHEN
Funeral Services at the Burial of the Righ Rev. Leonidas Polk, D.D. Columbia: 1864. V. 70

ELLIOTT, T. C.
Coming of the White Woman 1836 as Told in Letters and Journals of Narcissa Prentiss Whitman. Portland: 1937. V. 70
Peter Sene Ogden: Fur Trader. Portland: 1910. V. 71

ELLIOTT, WILLIAM
Carolina Sports, by Land and Water.... Charleston: 1846. V. 71
Carolina Sports by Land and Water.... New York: 1859. V. 68

ELLIOTT'S Tales for Boys. London: 1829?. V. 69

ELLIS, ALICE THOMAS
The Birds of the Air. London: 1980. V. 70
The Fly in the Ointment. London: 1989. V. 70
The Sin Eater. London: 1977. V. 70
The 27th Kingdom. London: 1982. V. 70

ELLIS, B. TRAPP
India and Other Poems. London: 1877. V. 73

ELLIS, BENJAMIN
The Medical Formulary.... Philadelphia: 1831. V. 69

ELLIS, BRET EASTON
American Psycho. New York: 1991. V. 72
American Psycho. London: 1998. V. 70; 72; 73
The Informers. New York: 1994. V. 72
Less than Zero. New York: 1985. V. 70; 73

ELLIS, DANIEL
An Inquiry into the Changes Induced on Atmospheric Air by the Germination of Seeds, the Vegetation of Plants and the Respiration of Animals. (with) Farther Inquires.... Edinburgh: 1807-1811. V. 69
Memoir of the Life and Writings of John Gordon, M.D. Edinburgh: 1823. V. 72

ELLIS, E. H.
International Boundary Lines Across Colorado and Wyoming. Boulder: 1966. V. 69; 71

ELLIS, E. S.
Ancient Anodynes - Primitive Anaesthesia and Allied Conditions. London: 1948. V. 68

ELLIS, EARL H.
International Boundary Lines Across Colorado and Wyoming.. Boulder: 1966. V. 68; 73

ELLIS, GEORGE
Bell Ranch As I Knew It. Kansas City: 1973. V. 71

ELLIS, GEORGE E.
Extracts from a History of the Massachusetts General Hospital 1810-1851. with Continuation 1851-1872. Boston: 1899. V. 70; 73

ELLIS, GEORGE F.
Bell Ranch As I Knew It. Kansas City: 1973. V. 68

ELLIS, HAROLD
Surgical Case-Histories from the Past. London and New York: 1994. V. 68

ELLIS, HAVELOCK
Analysis of the Sexual Impulse. 1904. V. 73
Chapman. Cambridge: 1934. V. 71
Chapman. London: 1934. V. 70
Concerning Jude the Obscure. London: 1931. V. 72
The Criminal. London: 1890. V. 68; 71
Kanga Creek. . An Australian Idyll. London: 1922. V. 71
Kanga Creek: an Australian Idyll. Waltham St. Lawrence: 1922. V. 71
Sonnets, with Folk Songs from the Spanish. 1925. Waltham St. Lawrence: 1925. V. 68; 71

ELLIS, HENRY
Journal of the Proceedings of the Late Embassy to China Comprising a Correct Narrative of the Public Translations of the Embassy of the Voyage to and From China, and the of the Journey from the Mouth of the Pei-Ho to the return of Canton.... London: 1817. V. 72
Original Letters Illustrative of English History: Including Numerous Royal Letters from Autographs in the British Museum. With 2nd Series. London: 1824-1827. V. 71
Original Letters, Illustrative of English History... Third Series. London: 1846. V. 71
Voyage de la Baye de Hudson, Fiat en 1746 & 1747.... Paris: 1749. V. 73

ELLIS, J.
The Natural History of Many Curious and Uncommon Zoophytes. London: 1786. V. 73

ELLIS, JAMES J.
George Muller of the Ashley Down Orphan Homes, Bristol, Who Received 1,500,000 in Answer to Prayer and Faith Alone. London: 1923. V. 68

ELLIS, JOHN
An Essay Towards a Natural History of the Corallines, and Other Marine Productions of the Like Kind, Commonly Found on the Coasts of Great Britain and Ireland. London: 1755. V. 70
Instructions for Collectors of Excise, in Prosecutions Before Justices of the Peace, for Forfeitures Incurred, or Offences Committed Against the Laws Relating to the Duties of Excise and other Duties Under the Management of the Commissioners of Excise. London: 1735. V. 72

ELLIS, KENNETH
Dolores Divine: Guilty or Innocent. New York: 1931. V. 72

ELLIS, MARTHA D.
Bell Ranch Recollections. Clarendon: 1965. V. 68

ELLIS, MIRIAM ANNE
The Human Ear. London: 1900. V. 68

ELLIS, PETER BERESFORD
Biggles! The Life Story of Captain W. E. Johns. Creator of Biggles, Worrals, Gimlet and Steely. 1993. V. 72

ELLIS, ROWLAND C.
Colonial Dutch Houses in New Jersey. Newark: 1933. V. 69

ELLIS, SALONE
The Last Wilderness. Boston: 1925. V. 72

ELLIS, SARAH
Family Secrets of Hints to Those Who Would Make Home Happy. London: 1841. V. 68; 71
The Women of England, their Social Duties and Domestic Habits. London: 1839?. V. 73

ELLIS, T. MULLET
The Earl's Nose. London: 1900. V. 69

ELLIS, V. B.
Golden Notes. Cleveland: 1953. V. 68

ELLIS, WILLIAM
Polynesian Researches. London: 1829. V. 72
Polynesian Researches. New York: 1833. V. 70; 72
Three Visits to Madagascar During the Years 1853-1854-1856. London: 1858. V. 72
Three Visits to Madagascar During the Years 1853-1854-1856. New York: 1859. V. 71

ELLIS, WILLIAM SMITH
The Parks and Forests of Sussex, Ancient and Modern. Lewis: 1885. V. 70

ELLISON, BERNARD C.
The Prince of Wales's Sport in India. 1925. V. 69; 70; 72; 73

ELLISON, EDITH NICHOLL
The Desert and the Rose. Boston: 1921. V. 73

ELLISON, GLENN R.
Cowboys Under the Mogollon Rim. Tucson: 1970. V. 69

ELLISON, HARLAN
Angry Candy. Boston: 1988. V. 71
Approaching Oblivion. New York: 1974. V. 68; 73
Deathbird Stories. 1990. V. 70
The Essential Ellison. Beverely Hills: 1991. V. 70
Medea: Harlan's World. 1985. V. 71
Partners in Wonder. New York: 1971. V. 71
Shatterday. Boston: 1980. V. 68
Spider Kiss. New York: 1991. V. 70
Strange Wine. New York: 1974. V. 69
Strange Wine. New York: 1977. V. 71
Strange Wine. New York: 1978. V. 71
Watching. Los Angeles: 1989. V. 68; 72

ELLISON, JOSEPH
California and the Nation 1850-1869: a Study of the Relations of a Frontier Community with the Federal Government. Berkeley: 1927. V. 69; 71; 73

ELLISON, RALPH
Going to the Territory. New York: 1986. V. 71
Invisible Man. New York: 1952. V. 71; 72; 73
Invisible Man. Franklin Center: 1980. V. 71
Living with Music. New York: 2001. V. 69; 72
Shadow and Act. New York: 1964. V. 70

ELLISON, ROBERT S.
Fort Bridger, Wyoming - A Brief History. Sheridan: 1938. V. 69; 72

ELLISON, WILL
The Life and Adventures of George Nidever (1802-1883). Berkeley: 1937. V. 68; 73

ELLMANN, RICHARD
Henry James Among the Aesthetes. London: 1983. V. 71
James Joyce. New York: 1959. V. 73
Oscar Wilde. London: 1987. V. 69

ELLROY, JAMES
American Tabloid. London: 1995. V. 69; 70; 72
The Big Nowhere. New York: 1988. V. 68; 69; 70; 71; 73
The Black Dahlia. London: 1987. V. 69
The Black Dahlia. New York: 1987. V. 70; 71
The Black Dahlia. London: 1988. V. 73
Blood on the Moon. New York: 1984. V. 68; 69; 70; 71; 72; 73
Brown's Requiem. London: 1981. V. 70
Brown's Requiem. New York: 1981. V. 69; 70; 73
Brown's Requiem. London: 1984. V. 70
Brown's Requiem. New York: 1994. V. 69; 70; 71
Clandestine. New York: 1982. V. 73
Clandestine. London: 1984. V. 69; 73
The Cold Six Thousand. New York: 2001. V. 69
Crime Wave. New York: 1999. V. 72
Hollywood Nocturnes. New York: 1994. V. 71; 72
L. A. Confidential. New York: 1988. V. 70
L. A. Confidential. New York: 1990. V. 68; 69; 71; 73
My Dark Places. London: 1996. V. 72
My Dark Places. New York: 1996. V. 72
Silent Terror. 1987. V. 69
White Jaxx. New York: 1992. V. 72

ELLS, B. F.
A History of the Romish Inquisition. Hanover: 1835. V. 68

ELLSON, HAL
The Golden Spike. New York: 1952. V. 69

ELLWANGER, GEORGE H.
Pleasures of the Table. New York: 1902. V. 69

ELLWOOD, T.
The Book of the Settlement of Iceland. Kendal: 1898. V. 71; 72
The Landama Book of Iceland.... Kendal: 1894. V. 71

ELLWOOD, THOMAS
Sacred History: or, the Historical Part of the Holy Scriptures.... Burlington: 1804. V. 69

ELMAN, RICHARD M.
An Education in Blood. New York: 1971. V. 72
The Reckoning. New York: 1969. V. 72
Uptight with the Stones. New York: 1973. V. 72

ELMER, LUCIUS Q. C.
The Constitution and Government of the Province and State of New Jersey, with Biographical Sketches of the Governors from 1776 to 1845, and Reminiscences of the Bench and Bar During More than Half a Century. Newark: 1872. V. 69
A Digest of the Laws of New Jersey. Bridgeton: 1838. V. 69

ELMES, JAMES
A General and Bibliographical Dictionary of the Fine Arts, Containing Explanations of the Principal Terms...., London: 1826. V. 69; 72
Memoirs of the Life and Works of Sir Christopher Wren.... London: 1823. V. 68; 71; 73
A Scientific, Historical and Commercial Survey of the Harbour and Port of London. London: 1838. V. 71

ELMORE, ERNEST
The Tail of the Snuffly Snorty Dog. London: 1946. V. 72

ELMSLIE, KENWARD
Album. New York: 1969. V. 71
Motor Disturbance. New York: 1971. V. 69
The Orchid Stories. Garden City: 1973. V. 72

ELPHINSTONE, MOUNTSTUART
Afghanistan. An Account of the Kingdom of Caubul, and Its Dependencies in Persia, Tartary and India. London: 1815. V. 70

ELSAM, RICHARD
Hints for Improving the Condition of the Peasantry...Interspersed with Plans, Elevations and Descriptive Views of Characteristic Designs for Cottages.... London: 1816. V. 68

ELSBERG, CHARLES A.
Surgical Diseases of the Spinal Cord, Membranes, and Nerve Roots, Symptoms, Diagnosis and Treatment. New York: 1941. V. 68

ELSEN, ALBERT
Paul Jenkins. New York: 1973. V. 68

ELSHOLTZ, JOHANN SIGISMUND
Vom Garten-Baw: Oder Unterricht von der Gartnerey auff das Clima der Chur-Marck Brandenburg, wie auch der Benachbarten Teutschen Lander Gerichtet, und in VI. Berlin: 1684. V. 69

ELSON, W. H.
Little Friends Cutout Characters for Your Classroom from the Elson Basic Readers. Chicago. V. 73

ELSTOBB, W.
An Historical Account of the Great Level of the Fens, Called Bedford Level and Other Fens, Marshes and Low Lands in this Kingdom and Other Places. Lynn: 1793. V. 71

ELSYNGE, HENRY
The Ancient Method and Manner of Holding of Parliaments in England. London: 1660. V. 72
The Manner of Holding Parliaments in England. London: 1768. V. 70

ELTON, BEN
Popcorn. London: 1996. V. 68; 69; 72; 73

ELTON, ELMER
The Art of James Bama. New York: 1993. V. 69

ELTON, GODFREY
Against the Sun. Boston: 1928. V. 70

ELTON, JAMES FREDERIC
Travels and Researches Among the Lakes and Mountains of Eastern and Central Africa. London: 1879. V. 72

ELUARD, PAUL
Le Dur Desir De Durer. London: 1950. V. 69
The Mirror of Baudelaire. Norfolk: 1942. V. 71

ELVIN, CHARLES
Records of Walmer together with The Three Castles that Keep the Downs. 1890. V. 72

ELWES, H.
The Trees of Great Britain and Ireland. Edinburgh: 1906-1913. V. 69

ELWES, ROBERT
A Sketcher's Tour Round the World. London: 1854. V. 73

ELWOOD, ANNE KATHARINE
Memoirs of the Literary Ladies of England, from the Commencement of the Last Century. London: 1843. V. 73

ELY, TANKARD
History of the Ely Reunion. New York: 1879. V. 68

EMANUEL, HARRY
Diamonds and Precious Stones.... London: 1867. V. 68

EMANUEL, HYWEL D.
The Latin Texts of the Welsh Laws. Cardiff: 1967. V. 70

EMANUEL, WALTER
A Dog Day. London: 1904. V. 70
The Dog Who Wasn't What He Taught He Was. London: 1914. V. 71

EMBODEN, WILLIAM A.
Leonardo Da Vinci on Plants and Gardens. Portland: 1987. V. 72

EMBREY, ALVIN T.
Waters of the State. Richmond: 1931. V. 71

EMBRY, CARLOS B.
America's Concentration Camps: the Facts About One Indian Reservation Today. New York: 1956. V. 69

EMBURY, A. H.
The Dutch Colonial House.... New York: 1913. V. 69; 72

EMECHETA, BUCHI
Destination Biafra. London: 1982. V. 73
In the Ditch. London: 1972. V. 69
Second-Class Citizen. New York: 1975. V. 69

EMERSON, EARL W.
Black Hearts and Slow Dancing. New York: 1988. V. 69; 71; 72

EMERSON, EDWARD WALDO
Henry Thoreau as Remembered by a Young Friend. Boston: 1917. V. 68

EMERSON, G.
A Report on the Trees and Shrubs Growing Naturally in the Forests of Massachusetts. Boston: 1846. V. 69

EMERSON, GEORGE ROSE
London: How the Great City Grew. London: 1862. V. 71
William Ewart Gladstone, Prime Minister of England. London: 1882. V. 68

EMERSON, JOHN
How to Write Photo Plays. New York: 1920. V. 73

EMERSON, RALPH WALDO
Compensation. East Aurora: 1904. V. 69
The Complete Works of Ralph Waldo Emerson. Boston and New York: 1903. V. 69
The Complete Works.... Cambridge: 1903-1904. V. 68
English Traits. Boston: 1856. V. 68
Essays. London: 1844. V. 71
Essays. 1906. V. 70
Essays. London: 1910. V. 71
Essays and Essays Second Series. Boston: 1841-1844. V. 68
Essays: First Series. Boston: 1850. V. 71
Letters and Social Aims. Boston: 1876. V. 69
May-Day and Other Pieces. Boston: 1869. V. 71
Nature. Boston: 1836. V. 68
Nature: Addresses and Lectures. Boston and Cambridge: 1849. V. 70
An Oration Delivered Before the Literary Societies of Dartmouth College, July 24, 1838. Boston: 1838. V. 68
Poems. Boston: 1847. V. 68; 71; 72
Success. Boston and New York: 1912. V. 71
The Works. London: 1883. V. 71
The Works. London: 1884-1888. V. 73

EMERSON, SARAH HOOPER
Life of Abby Hopper Gibbons. New York: 1897. V. 73

EMERSON, THOMAS
A Concise Treatise on the Courts of Law of the City of London. London: 1794. V. 71

EMERSON, WILLIAM
The Laws of Centripetal and Centrifugal Force. 1769. V. 72
The Mathematical Principles of Geography. (with) *Dialling or the Art of Drawing Dials, on All Sorts of Planes Whatsoever.* London: 1770. V. 70
Mechanics; or the Doctrine of Motion. London: 1769. V. 72
The Projection of a Sphere, Orthographic, Stereographic, and Gnomonical. London: 1769. V. 72

EMERY, GILBERT
Tarnish: a Play in Three Acts. New York: 1924. V. 73

EMERY, M.
Furniture by Architects: 500 International Masterpieces of 20th Century Design and Where to Buy Them. New York: 1983. V. 68; 69; 72

EMERY, SARAH E. V.
Seven Financial Conspiracies Which Have Enslaved the American People. Lansing: 1887. V. 73

EMLYN, THOMAS
The Works. London: 1746. V. 70

EMMART, E. W.
Badianus Manuscript. An Aztec Herbal of 1552. Baltimore: 1940. V. 69

EMMEL, T. C.
Butterflies, Their World Their Life Cycle, Life Behavior. New York: 1975. V. 72

EMMERICH, ANDRE
Sweat of the Sun and Tears of the Moon: Gold and Silver in Pre-Columbian Art. Seattle: 1965. V. 69; 71

EMMERSON, JOAN S.
Catalogue of Pybus Collection of Medical Books, Letters and Engravings 15th-20th Centuries Held in the University Library Newcastle Upon Tyne. Manchester: 1981. V. 68; 70; 71
Catalogue of the Pybus Collection of Medical Books, Letters and Engravings, 15th-20th Centuries, Held in the University Library. Newcastle-upon-Tyne: 1981. V. 72

EMMERTON, ISAAC
A Plain and Practical Treatise on the Culture & Management of the Auricula, Polyanthus, Carnation.... London: 1819. V. 70

EMMET, THOMAS ADDIS
Incidents of My Life. New York & London: 1911. V. 68
The Principles and Practice of Gynecology. London: 1880. V. 71

EMMETT, CHRIS
For Union and the Winning of the Southwest. Norman: 1965. V. 69

EMMITT, CHRIS
Shanghai Pierce, A Fair Likeness. Norman: 1953. V. 68; 71

EMMITT, ROBERT
The Last War Trail: the Utes and the Settlement of Colorado. Norman: 1954. V. 69

EMMONDS, H.
Elementary Botany for South Africa, Theoretical and Practical. London/New York/Bombay: 1897. V. 72

EMMONS, E.
Insects of New York. Albany: 1854. V. 70

EMMONS, RICHARD
The Fredoniad, or Independence Preserved. Boston: 1827. V. 73

EMMONS, WILLIAM HARVEY
The Enrichment of Ore Deposits. Washington: 1917. V. 68

EMORY, WILLIAM CLOSSON
Love in Detroit. Detroit: 1934. V. 69

EMORY, WILLIAM HEMSLEY
Notes of a Military Reconnaissance from Fort Leavenworth in Missouri to San Diego in California, Thirteenth Congress, 1st Session. Washington: 1848. V. 69; 70; 73
Report on the United States and Mexican Boundary Survey. Washington: 1859. V. 70
Report on the United States and Mexican Boundary Survey. Volume I, Volume II Part I and Part II (1857-1859). Austin: 1987. V. 73

EMPSON, P.
The Wood Engravings of Robert Gibbings with Some Recollections by the Artist. London: 1959. V. 70

EMPSON, WILLIAM
Collected Poems. New York: 1949. V. 71
Letter IV: Songs for Sixpence. No. 1. Cambridge: 1929. V. 70; 73
Poems. London: 1935. V. 73

EMRICH, DUNCAN
The Cowboy's Own Brand Book. New York: 1954. V. 69

EMRIK & Binger: *The Merry Ballads of the Olden Time.* London. V. 68

EMY, A. R.
Traite de l'Art de la Charpenterie. Paris: 1837-1841. V. 69

THE ENCHANTED Capital of Scotland. Edinburgh: 1945. V. 73

ENDE, MICHAEL
The Neverending Story. 1983. V. 72
The Neverending Story. Garden City: 1983. V. 68; 69; 71; 73

ENDELL, FRITZ
Old Tavern Signs. Boston: 1916. V. 72

ENDGRAIN. Contemporary Wood Engraving in North America. Mission: 1994. V. 70

ENDICOTT, W.
The Saga of the Tented Cities. 1952. V. 69; 70; 72; 73

ENDLESS Amusement: a Collection of Nearly 400 Entertaining Experiments in Various Branches of Science Including Acoustics, Arithmetic, Chemistry.... London: 1820. V. 71

ENDORE, GUY
Babouk. New York: 1934. V. 70

ENEROTH, OLOF
Herregarder Uti Sodermanland.... Stockholm: 1869. V. 70; 72

ENFIELD, WILLIAM
Prayers for the Use of Families. London: 1770. V. 69
The Speaker; or Miscellaneous Pieces, Selected from the Best English Writers.... London: 1779. V. 71

ENGEL, CLAIRE ELAINE
Mont Blanc. An Anthology. London: 1965. V. 69
Mountaineering in the Alps. London: 1971. V. 69
They Came to the Hills. London: 1952. V. 69

ENGEL, D. H.
Japanese Gardens for Today. Rutland/Tokyo: 1959. V. 69; 72

ENGEL, MARIAN
Bear. Toronto: 1976. V. 72

ENGELBRECHT Different Vuews Dessinees d'Apres Nature sur le Chateau si Renomme de Konigstein. Augsburg: 1735. V. 72

ENGELHARDT, ZEPHYRIN
The Franciscans in Arizona. Harbor Springs: 1899. V. 73
San Buenaventura, the Mission by the Sea. Santa Barbara: 1930. V. 68
San Gabriel Mission and the Beginnings of Los Angeles. San Gabriel: 1927. V. 68; 70
San Juan Capistrano Mission. Santa Barbara: 1922. V. 68
Santa Barbara Mission. San Francisco: 1923. V. 70

ENGELMANN, R.
Pictorial Atlas to Homer's Iliad and Odyssey. New York: 1892. V. 71

ENGELS, FRIEDRICH
The Condition of the Working Classes in England in 1844.... New York: 1888. V. 71
Socialism, Utopian and Scientific. London and New York: 1892. V. 68; 70

ENGER, LEIF
Peace Like A River. London: 2001. V. 72
Peace Like a River. New York: 2001. V. 71; 73

ENGINEERING & ALLIED EMPLOYERS NATIONAL FEDERATION
Wage Movements 1897-1925. London: 1926. V. 70

ENGINEERING. The Cunard Royal Mail Twin-Screw Steamers Campania and Lucania. Sparkford: 1993. V. 68

ENGINEERING. The Cunard Turbine-Driven Quadruple-Screw Atlantic Liner Lusitania. Wellingborough: 1986. V. 68

ENGINEERING. The Cunard Turbine-Driven Quadruple-Screw Atlantic Liner Mauretania. Wellingborough: 1987. V. 68

ENGINEERING. The Quadruple-Screw Turbine-Driven Cunard Liner Aquitania. Wellingborough: 1988. V. 68

ENGLANDER, NATHAN
For the Relief of Unbearable Urges. New York: 1999. V. 69

ENGLAND'S Vanity; or the Voice of God Against the Monstrous Sin of Pride, in Dress and Apparel.... London: 1683. V. 68

ENGLEFIELD, J.
Dry-Fly Fishing for Trout and Grayling. 1908. V. 68

ENGLISH, A. L.
History of Atlantic City, New Jersey. Philadelphia: 1884. V. 69

ENGLISH ARBORICULTURAL SOCIETY
Transactions. Volumes 1-3. London/Carlisle: 1883. V. 70

THE ENGLISH Lady's Catechism. Shewing the Pride and Vanity of the English Quality, in Relieving Foreigners Before Their Own Country Folks. London?: 1776?. V. 73

ENGLISH Lyrics from Spenser to Milton. London: 1898. V. 72

ENGLISH, MARY KATHERINE J.
Prairie Sketches or Fugitive Recollections of An Army Girl of 1899. NP: 1899. V. 72

ENGLISH Poets - British Academy Chatterton Lectures. Oxford: 1988. V. 71

ENGLISH Rustic Pictures. London: 1882. V. 68

ENGLISH, WILLIAM HAYDEN
Conquest of the Country Northwest of the River Ohio 1778-1783 and Life of General George Rogers Clark.... 1896. V. 68

ENGRAMELLE, MARIE DOMINI JOSEPH
Papillons d'Europe. 1788. V. 69

ENGSTRAND, SOPHIA BELZER
Julie Morrow. New York: 1942. V. 71

ENNION, ERIC
Birds and Seasons. 1994. V. 69

ENOCK, C. REGINALD
Mexico: Its Ancient and Modern Civilisation, History and Political Condition, Topography and Natural Resources, Industries and General Development. London: 1909. V. 73

ENRIGHT, D. J.
The Year of the Monkey. Kobe: 1956. V. 73

ENSCHEDE, CHARLES
Typefoundries in the Netherlands from the Fifteenth to the Nineteenth Century. Haarlem: 1974. V. 70
Typefoundries in the Netherlands from the Fifteenth to the Nineteenth Century.... Haarlem: 1978. V. 73

ENSOR, GEORGE
An Inquiry Concerning the Population of Nations; Containing a Refutation of Mr. Malthus's Essay on Population. London: 1818. V. 71

THE ENTERTAINING Story of Little Red Riding Hood. York: 1820. V. 71; 73

L'ENTREE du Roy et De La Royne Dans sa Ville De Lyon....(with) Reception du Tres-Chrestien, Tres-Juste, et Tres-Victorieux Monarque Louis XIII...et de...Anne D'Autriche. Lyons: 1624. V. 70

ENTWISTLE, WILLIAM JAMES
The Spanish Language together with Portuguese, Catalan and Basque. London: 1936. V. 72

ENYEART, JAMES
Bruguiere, His Photographs and His Life...1879-1945. New York: 1977. V. 68
Edward Weston's California Landscape. Boston: 1984. V. 72
Heinecken. 1980. V. 68; 70

EPHRON, NORA
Crazy Salad. New York: 1975. V. 69
Wallflower at the Orgy. New York: 1970. V. 68

EPICTETUS
All the Works of Epictetus.... London: 1758. V. 68; 72
Enchiridionmade English, in a Poetical Paraphrase. London: 1695. V. 72
Epicteti Enchiridion Versibus Adumbratum. Oxford: 1715. V. 68
The Golden Sayings of Epictetus. London: 1920. V. 68
The Golding Sayings of Epictetus with the Hymn of Cleanthes. London: 1903. V. 68
His Morals, with Simpicius His Comment. London: 1694. V. 70

EPICURUS
Epicurus: The Extant Remains of the Greek Text. 1947. V. 68; 72
Epicurus's Morals. London: 1712. V. 71

AN EPISTLE from Joseph Surface, Esq. to Richard Brinsley Sheridan, Esq. of Great Queen Street, Chairman of the Sub-Committee for Westminster (in Verse). London: 1780. V. 69

THE EPITOMIST, a Literary Miscellany and Record of Progress. London: 1854. V. 69

EPITRE a L'Hymen. Paris: 1765. V. 68

EPLING, C.
A Revision of Salvia, Subgenus Calosphace. Berkeley: 1940. V. 72

EPPERSON, HARRY A.
Colorado As I Saw It. Kaysville, UT: 1944. V. 71

EPPS, JOHN
The Life of John Walker, M.D. London: 1832. V. 71

THE EQUESTRIAN: a Handbook of Horsemanship.... London: 1840. V. 72

EQUIANO, OLAUDAH
Intersting Narrative of the Life of Olaudah Equiano or Gustavus Vassa the African Written by Himself. London: 1793. V. 68

ERASMUS, DESIDERIUS
Colloquia Nunc Emendatiora. Lugd. Batavorum: 1636. V. 70
The Complaint of Peace; to Which is Added, Antipolemus; or the Plea of Reasons, Religion and Humanity, Against War.... Boston: 1813. V. 69
Enchiridion Militis Christiani, Saluberrimis Praecepts Refertum. Cambridge: 1685. V. 68; 72; 73
Opus de Conscribedis Epistolis. (with) *Familiariam Colloquibrum Formulae.* Strassburg: 1522. V. 70
Twenty Select Colloquies.... London: 1680. V. 68
Twenty-Two Select Colloquies Out of Erasmus of Roterodamus.... London: 1680. V. 72
Witt Against Wisdom; or, a Panegyrick Upon Folly. Oxford: 1683. V. 70

ERCILLA Y ZUNIGA, ALONSO DE
Primera y Segunda Parte de la Araucana. Madrid: 1578. V. 70

ERCKER, LAZARUS
Aula Subterranea Domina Dominatium Subdita Subditorum. Sas is: Untererdisce Hoffhaltung Ohne Welche Weder die Heren.... Frankfurt: 1736. V. 68

ERCOLANI, GIUSEPPE MARIA
I Tre Ordini d'Architettura Dorico, Ionico e Corintio Presi Dalla Fabbriche piu Celebri dell' Antica.... Rome: 1744. V. 68; 70; 72

ERDRICH, LOUISE
The Antelope Wife. New York: 1998. V. 72
Baptism of Desire. New York: 1989. V. 70
The Beet Queen. New York: 1986. V. 69; 71; 72; 73
The Bingo Palace. New York: 1994. V. 71; 72
The Blue Jay's Dance. New York: 1995. V. 72
Jacklight. New York: 1984. V. 71; 72; 73
The Last Report on the Miracles at Little No Horse. New York: 2001. V. 70
Love Medicine. New York: 1984. V. 68; 69; 71; 72; 73
Love Medicine. London: 1985. V. 70
Love Medicine. New York: 1993. V. 72
Snares. Middlebury: 1987. V. 70
Tales of Burning Love. New York: 1996. V. 72
Tracks. New York: 1988. V. 68; 71; 72; 73

ERFURT, JULIUS
The Dyeing of Paper Pulp. 1901. V. 71

ERGENNES, CHARLES GRAVIER, COMTE DE
Memoire Historique et Politique sur la Louisiane. Paris: 1802. V. 70

ERICHSEN, JOHN ERIC
On Concussion of the Spine, Nervous Shock, and Other Obscure Injuries of the Nervous System in Their Clinical and Medico-Legal Aspects. New York: 1875. V. 70
On Railway and Other Injuries of the Nervous System. Philadelphia: 1867. V. 69

ERICKSON, ARTHUR
The Architecture. New York: 1988. V. 68; 69; 72

ERICKSON, E. H.
A Scanning Electron Microscope Atlas of the Honeybee. 1986. V. 68

ERICKSON, STEVE
Days Between Stations. New York: 1985. V. 70
The Sea Came in at Midnight. New York: 1999. V. 72
Tours of the Black Clock. New York: 1989. V. 68; 72

ERIKSEN, SVEND
Sevres Porcelain. Office du Livre: 1968. V. 72

ERLHOFF, MICHAEL
Designed in Germany Since 1949. Munich: 1990. V. 68

ERMAN, ADOLPH GEORG
Travels in Siberia: Including Excursions Northwards, down the Obi to the Polar Circle, and Southwards, to the Chinese Frontier. London: 1848. V. 72

ERMATINGER, C. O.
The Talbot Regime, or the First Half Century of the Talbot Settlement. St. Thomas, Canada: 1904. V. 73

ERNI, HANS
Esuisses Africains. Zurich: 1966. V. 72

ERNST, F. G.
Orthopaedic Apparatus. London: 1883. V. 71

ERNUL, J. B.
Life of a Confederate Soldier in a Federal Prison. Vanceboro: 1910. V. 69; 70

ERRA Pater. London: 1710?. V. 73
ERRA Pater. Glasgow: 1726. V. 69

ERSKINE, JOHN
Cinderellas Daughter and Other Sequels and Consequences. Indianapolis: 1930. V. 70

ERSKINE, LAURIE Y.
The River Trail. New York: 1923. V. 70

ERSKINE, MICHAEL
The Diary of Michael Erskine.... Midland: 1979. V. 71

ERTE
Things I Remember. An Autobigoraphy. London: 1975. V. 70

ERTZ, SUSAN
Black, White and Caroline. London: 1938. V. 68

ERVINE, ST. JOHN
The First Mrs. Fraser. New York: 1931. V. 70

ERWIN, ALLEN A.
The Southwest of John Horton Slaughter, 1841-1922, Pioneer, Cattleman, and.... Glendale, CA: 1965. V. 69; 70; 71

ERWIN, RICHARD E.
The Truth About Wyatt Earp. Carpinteria: 1992. V. 69

ESAU, K.
Anatomy of Seed Plants. New York: 1977. V. 72
Plant Anatomy. New York: 1953. V. 72

ESCANDON, MARIA AMPARO
Esperanza's Box of Saints. New York: 1999. V. 72

ESCHHENBACH, WOLFRAM VON
The Romance of Parzival and the Holy Grail. Newtown: 1990. V. 70; 71

ESCHMEYER, W. N.
Catalog of Fishes. 1998. V. 72; 73

ESCOFFIER, AUGUSTE
Guide Culinaire. New York: 1982. V. 69

ESCOFFIER, G. A.
A Guide to Modern Cookery. London: 1959. V. 70

ESCOTT, M.
I Told My Love. New York: 1936. V. 70

ESHLEMAN, CLAYTON
Bearings. Santa Barbara: 1971. V. 69; 71; 73
Caterpillar (1-20). New York: 1967-1973. V. 73
Our Lady of the Three-Pronged Devil. New York: 1981. V. 73

ESKES, T. K. A. B.
Classics in Obstetrics and Gynecology; Innovative Papers that Have Contributed to Current Clinical Practice. Carnforth: 1994. V. 68

ESMERALDA, AURORA
Life and Letters of a Forty-Niner's Daughter. San Francisco: 1929. V. 69

ESMONDE, THOMAS
More Hunting Memories. 1930. V. 68; 73

ESPINASSE, FRANCIS
Lancashire Worthies. London: 1874. V. 72; 73

ESPINASSE, ISAAC
A Digest of the Law of Actions at Nisi Prius. Dublin: 1790. V. 71

ESPINASSE, MARGARET
Robert Hooke. London: 1956. V. 68

ESPINOSA, CARMEN
Shawls, Crinolines, Filigree. El Passo: 1970. V. 68

ESPINOSA, J. MANUEL
First Expedition of Vargas into New Mexico 1692. Albuquerque: 1940. V. 68; 73

ESPINOSA, JOSE E.
Saints in the Valleys, Christian Sacred Images in the History, Life and Folk Art of Spanish. Albuquerque: 1960. V. 68; 73

ESPINOSA Y TELLO, J.
A Spanish Voyage to Vancouver and the North West Coast of America, Being the Narrative of the Voyage Made in the Year 1792.... London: 1930. V. 70

ESPY, JAMES
The Philosophy of Storms. Boston: 1841. V. 69

ESQUIRE'S Jazz Book 1947. 1947. V. 72

ESQUIVEL, LAURA
The Law of Love. New York: 1996. V. 72; 73
Like Water for Chocolate. New York: 1992. V. 68; 69; 71; 72; 73

AN ESSAY in Favour of Such Public Remedies, as Are Usually Distinguished by the Name of Quack Medicines; Wherein the Objections Hitherto Made Against Them are Fully Answered.... London: 1773?. V. 71

AN ESSAY, Occasioned by Distemper of the Cattle. London: 1750. V. 69

ESSAY on Quackery, and the Dreadful Consequences Arising from Taking Advertised Medicines.... Kingston-upon-Hull: 1805. V. 69

AN ESSAY on the Present State of Our Publick Roads; Shewing the Absolute Necessity of a Total Prohibiton of the Use of Narrow Wheels, On All Carriages Drawn by More than One Horse Lengthways. London: 1756. V. 72

AN ESSAY Upon the Present State of the Theatre in France, England and Italy. London: 1760. V. 71

AN ESSAY Upon the Principles of Political Economy.... New York: 1837. V. 69

ESSAYS in Biology. In Honor of Herbert M. Evans. Written by his Friends. Berkely and Los Angeles: 1943. V. 72

ESSAYS on the Population of Ireland, and the Characters of the Irish, By a Member of the Last Irish Parliament. London: 1803. V. 73

ESSAYS on the Spirit of Legislation, in the Encouragement of Agriculture, Population, Manufactures and Commerce. Newark: 1800. V. 69; 73

ESSER, K.
Genetics of Fungi. New York: 1967. V. 72

ESSEX, ARTHUR CAPEL, EARL OF
Selections from the Correspondence of...1675-1677. 1913. V. 69

ESSEX, JOHN
The Young Ladies Conduct; or, Rules of Education, Under Several Heads.... London: 1722. V. 68

ESSIG, E. O.
Injurious Beneficial Insects of California. Sacramento: 1915. V. 72

ESSLEMONT, DAVID
The Printer's Flowers. Montgomery: 1999. V. 68

ESSWEIN, HERMANN
Aubrey Beardsley. Munchen: 1912. V. 71

ESTEN, JOHN
Man Ray Bazaar Years. NY: 1988. V. 72

ESTERGREEN, M. MORGAN
Kit Carson: a Portrait in Courage. Norman: 1962. V. 68; 69; 71; 73

ESTEVEN, JOHN
The Door Of Death. New York: 1928. V. 72

ESTIENNE, CHARLES
L'Agriculture, et Maison Rustique. Lyon: 1578. V. 71
De Dissectione Partium Corporis Humani Libri Tres. Paris: 1545. V. 69
De Latinis et Graecis Nominibus Arborum, Fruticum, Herbaru, Piscium & Auium Liber.... Paris: 1544. V. 72
De Re Hortensi Libellus. (and) Seminarivm, et Plantarivm Fructiferarum. (and) Sylua, Frutetum Collis. (and) Arbustum, Fonticvlvs, Spinetvm. (and) Pratum, Lacvs, Arundinetum. Paris: 1539. V. 70
Dictionarium Latino-Grecum.... Paris: 1554. V. 72
Praedium Rusticum.... Paris: 1554. V. 70; 72; 73
Pratum, Lacvs, Arundinetum. Paris: 1543. V. 70
Seminarium et Plantarium Fructiferarum. Paris: 1540. V. 68

ESTIENNE, ROBERT
Ambrosii Calepini Dictionarium.... Geneva: 1554. V. 72

ESTIMATING for Printers. London: 1916. V. 72

ESTIUS, GUILELMUS
Absolutissima in Omnes. Beati Paul et Septem Catholicas Apostolorum Commentaria Tribus Tomus Distincta.... Paris: 1679. V. 72

ESTLEMAN, LOREN D.
Angel Eyes. Boston: 1981. V. 68; 72
Eight Mile and Dequindre. Eugene: 1991. V. 68
General Murders. 1988. V. 68
The Glass Highway. Boston: 1983. V. 68; 70; 72
Dr. Jekyll And Mr. Holmes. Garden City: 1979. V. 72
Lady Yesterday. Boston: 1987. V. 71
The Midnight Man. 1982. V. 70
The Midnight Man. Boston: 1982. V. 72
Mister St. John. Garden City: 1983. V. 69; 71
Motor City Blue. 1980. V. 70
Motor City Blue. Boston: 1980. V. 68; 69; 71; 72
Motor City Blue. London: 1982. V. 68; 69
Murdock's Law. London: 1983. V. 68
Sherlock Holmes vs. Dracula. Garden City: 1978. V. 72
Silent Thunder. Boston: 1989. V. 71

ESTRADES, GODEFROI, COMTE D'
Zeedige Beproeving van de Voorgestalde Karakters, van den RaadPensionaris Johan de Wit.... The Hague: 1757. V. 68

ESTVAN, B.
War Pictures from the South. New York: 1863. V. 70

ETCHECOPAR, R. D.
The Birds of North Africa. 1967. V. 69; 70

ETCHISON, DENNIS
Lord John Ten, A Celebration. Northbridge: 1988. V. 69

ETHEREDGE, GEORGE
The Man of Mode, or Sir Fopling Flatter. London: 1676. V. 72
The Works. Plays and Poems edited, with Critical Notes and Introduction by A. Wilson Verity. London: 1888. V. 72

ETMULLER, MICHAEL
Etmullerus Abridg'd: or, A Complete System of the Theory and Practice of Physic. London: 1703. V. 69

ETON COLLEGE
Loan Collection of Portraits, Views and Other Objects of Interest, Connected With the History of Eton, Made On the Occasion of the 450th Anniversary of the Foundation of the College. Eton: 1891. V. 72

ETON, WILLIAM
A Survey of the Turkish Empire. London: 1798. V. 70; 73

ETROG, SOREL
Etrog. London: 1970. V. 71

ETTER, CARL
Ainu Folklore. Chicago: 1949. V. 70

ETZLER, JOHN ADOLPHUS
Emigration to the Tropical World for the Melioration of all Classes of People of All Nations. Ham Common, Surrey: 1844. V. 73

EUBANK, JOHN L.
An Account of the Medicinal Properties of the Healing Springs, Bath Co.... Richmond: 1869. V. 71

EUCLIDES
Elementorum Libri XV Breviter Demonstrati, Opera Is. Barrow.... Londini: 1659. V. 69
The Elements Explain'd, in a New, But Most Easie Method.... Oxford: 1700. V. 69
The English Euclide, Being the First Six Elements of Geometry, Translated.... Oxford: 1705. V. 71
Euclide's Elements. London: 1732. V. 68; 71
Euclid's Elements of Geometry. To which is added, a Treatise of the Nature of Arithmetick of Logarithms.... 1728. V. 71

EUDORA Welty: a Tribute, 13 April 1984. Winston Salem: 1984. V. 70

EUGENIDES, JEFFREY
The Virgin Suicides. New York: 1993. V. 71; 73

EUGENIUS PHILALETHES, PSEUD.
The Fame and Confession of the Fraternity of R. C. Commonly of the Rosie Cross. London: 1652. V. 71

EULER, LEONHARD
Letters of Euler to a German Princess, on Different Subjects in Physics and Philosophy. London: 1795. V. 70; 73
Theoria Motuum Planetarum et Comentarum.... Berlin: 1744. V. 69

EURIPIDES
The Bacchae: Dionysus, the God. Kentfield: 1972. V. 72
The Tragedie of Euripides. London: 1781-1783. V. 73
Tragoediae Superstites Et Deperditarum Fragmenta Ex Recensione G. Dindorfii. Oxonii: 1832. V. 72

EUROPEAN Liberty: Four Essays on the Occasion of the 25th Anniversary of the Erasmus Prize Foundation. The Hague: 1983. V. 71

EUSTACE, JOHN
A Classical Tour through Italy. London: 1821. V. 73

EUSTACE, JOHN CHETWODE
A Tour through Italy Exhibiting a View of Its Scenery, Its Antiquities, and Its Monuments.... London: 1813. V. 70; 72

EUSTACHIUS, BARTOLOMEO
Tabulae anatomocarum Clarissimi Viri Bartholomaei Eustachei Quas e Tenebris Tandem Vindicatas et Clementis Papae XI. Rome: 1728. V. 68

EUSTIS, HELEN
Horizontal Man. NY: 1946. V. 72

EUTHANASIA, or Turf, Tent and Tomb. London: 1893. V. 68

EUTROPIUS
Breviarium Historiae Romanae. Lutetiae Parisiorum: 1745. V. 70
Historiae Romanae Brevarium Ab Urbe Condita Usque Ad Valentinianum Et Valentem Augustos, Notis Et Emendationibus.... Parissis: 1683. V. 72

EVAN, EVANS
Some Specimens of the Poetry of the Antient Welsh Bards. London: 1764. V. 70; 73

EVANOVICH, JANET
High Five. New York: 1999. V. 71; 72
Hot Six. New York: 2000. V. 72
One for the Money. New York: 1994. V. 68; 69; 70; 73
Seven Up. New York: 2001. V. 72
Three to Get Deadly. New York: 1997. V. 71; 72; 73
Two for the Dough. New York: 1995. V. 69; 73
Two for the Dough. London: 1996. V. 68
Two for the Dough. New York: 1996. V. 69; 71; 72; 73

EVANS, A.
The Peat Garden and Its Plants. London: 1974. V. 72

EVANS, A. H.
Turner on Birds.... Cambridge: 1903. V. 68

EVANS, ABEL
Vertumnus. An Epistle (in verse) to Mr. Jacob Bobart, Botany Professor to the University of Oxford and Keeper of the Physick Garden. Oxford: 1713. V. 72

EVANS, ALBERT S.
Our Sister Republic; a Gala Trip through Tropical Mexico in 1869- 1870. Hartford: 1870. V. 71

EVANS, ARTHUR
The Palace of Minos...at Knossos. London: 1921. V. 69

EVANS, ARTHUR BENONI
The Phylactery. A Poem. London: 1836. V. 70

EVANS, BESSIE
American Indian Dance Steps. New York: 1931. V. 69; 70

EVANS, C. L.
Recent Advances in Physiology. A Collection of the First-Fifth and Seventh Edition. London: 1925-1949. V. 71

EVANS, C. R.
Attention in Neurophysiology. London: 1969. V. 68

EVANS, C. S.
Cinderella. London: 1919. V. 69; 71
The Sleeping Beauty. London and Philadelphia: 1920. V. 68; 69; 70; 71; 73

EVANS, D.
Mather Brown, Early American Artist in England. Wesleyan: 1982. V. 69

EVANS, D. A.
Handbook of Plant Cell Culture. New York: 1983-1984. V. 69

EVANS, DAVID
Big Road Blues. Tradition and Creativity in the Folk Blues. Berkeley: 1982. V. 73

EVANS, DAVID C.
Custer's Last Fight - The Story of the Battle of the Little Big Horn Volume 1. El Segundo: 1999. V. 69; 72

EVANS, DAVID MORIER
City Men and City Manners. London: 1852. V. 69

EVANS, DONALD
Sonnets from the Patagonian: The Secret of Little Hotels. New York: 1914. V. 70

EVANS, E. G. V.
Medical Mycology; a Practical Approach. Oxford: 1989. V. 72

EVANS, EDWARD R. G. R.
South with Scott. 1922. V. 71

EVANS, ELIZABETH
Anne Tyler. New York: 1993. V. 68; 69; 70

EVANS, F. W.
A Short Treatise on the Second Appearing of Christ, in and Through the Order of the Female. Boston: 1853. V. 69; 73

EVANS, FRANCIS
Furness and Furness Abbey.... Ulverston: 1842. V. 71

EVANS, G. H.
Elephants and Their Diseases. 1961. V. 72; 73

EVANS, G. N. D.
Uncommon Obdurate: The Several Public Careers of J. F. W. DesBarres. Salem and Toronto: 1969. V. 71

EVANS, G. P.
Big Game Shooting in Upper Burma. 1912. V. 69; 70; 72

EVANS, GEORGE BIRD
From My Covers, Twenty-Two Selections from the Old Hemlock Collection of Sporting Books and Mystery Novels. Bruceton Mills: 1995. V. 72
Grouse and Woodcock in the Blackwater/Canaan. Bruceton Mills: 1997. V. 72

EVANS, GEORGE H.
The Manifest of Reason. New York: 1828. V. 71

EVANS, GEORGE W. B.
Mexican Gold Trail: the Journal of a Forty-Niner. San Marin: 1945. V. 68; 73

EVANS, GROSE
Benjamin West and the Taste of His Times. Carbondale: 1959. V. 71

EVANS, H.
Falconry. 1973. V. 68

EVANS, HENRY
Some Account of Jura Red Deer. London: 1993. V. 71

EVANS, HENRY RIDGELY
The Spirit World Unmasked. Chicago: 1902. V. 72

EVANS, JAMES W.
Autobiography of Samuel S. Hildebrand.... Jefferson City: 1870. V. 73

EVANS, JOAN
The Conway. London: 1966. V. 69
A History of Jewellry 1100-1870. London: 1953. V. 72
Time and Chance. London: 1943. V. 68

EVANS, JOHN
An Excursion to Windsor in July 1810, through Battersea, Putney, Kew, Richmond, Twickenham, Strawberry Hill and Hampton Court. London: 1817. V. 72
Halo in Brass. 1949. V. 70
Richmond and Its Vicinity, with a Glance at Twickenham, Strawberry Hill and Hampton Court. Richmond: 1824. V. 70

EVANS, JOHN W.
Powerful Rocky - the Blue Mountains and the Oregon Trail 1811-1883. La Grande: 1990. V. 70

EVANS, LAWTON B.
With Whip and Spur Twelve Famous Rides in American History. Springfield, MA: 1928. V. 72

EVANS, LIZ
Who Killed Mailyn Monroe?. London: 1997. V. 69; 73

EVANS, MAX
The Hi Lo Country. New York: 1961. V. 71
The Rounders. New York: 1960. V. 71

EVANS, NATHANIEL
Poems on Several Occasions with Some Other Compositions. Philadelphia: 1772. V. 68; 69; 70; 73

EVANS, NICHOLAS
The Horse Whisperer. London: 1995. V. 68; 69; 73
The Horse Whisperer. New York: 1995. V. 68; 69; 71; 72; 73

EVANS, RICHARD PAUL
The Christmas Box. New York: 1993. V. 68

EVANS, ROBLEY D.
A Sailor's Log. Recollections of Forty Years of Naval Life. New York: 1901. V. 72

EVANS, ROY
Mimbres Indian Treasure in the Land of Baca. Kansas City: 1985. V. 70

EVANS, THOMAS
An Address of the People of Virginia, Respecting the Alien and Sedition Laws. Richmond: 1798. V. 69

EVANS, W. F.
History of Berkeley County, West Virginia. 1928. V. 73

EVANS, WALKER
First and Last. New York: 1978. V. 68; 73
Lost Works. Santa Fe: 2000. V. 68
Message from the Interior. New York: 1966. V. 71; 73

EVANS, WALLACE
Wallace Evans Illustrated Catalogue of Pheasants, Wild Ducks, Wild Geese, Quail, Etc. Oak Park: 1907. V. 68

EVANS, WALTER NORTON
Mount Royal. 1893. V. 73

EVANS, WILL F.
Border Skylines, Fifty Years of Tallying Out on the Bloys Roundup Ground - a History of the Bloys Cowboy Camp Meeting. Dallas: 1940. V. 68; 73

EVANS, WILLIAM
The Mammalian Fauna of the Edinburgh District, with Records of Occurrences of the Rarer Species Throughout the South-East of Scotland Generally. 1892. V. 69

EVANS PRITCHARD, E. E.
The Nuer. A Description of the Modes of Livelihood and Political Institutions of a Nilotic People. Oxford: 1940. V. 69

EVAN THOMAS, OWEN
Domestic Utensils of Wood XVIth to XIXth Century. London: 1932. V. 68

EVARIST, BERNARDINE
Lara. Tunbridge Wells: 1997. V. 72

EVARTS, R. C.
Alice's Adventures in Cambridge. Cambridge: 1913. V. 70

EVELEIGH, JOSEPH
An Account of Reasons why Many Citizens of Exon Have Withdrawn from the Ministry of Mr. Jos. Hallet and Mr. James Pierce, Being an Answer to Mr. Pierce's STate of the Case. Exon: 1719. V. 70

EVELYN, JOHN
Acetaria, a Discourse of Sallets. 1937. V. 71
Diary. London: 1879. V. 73
The Diary. New York: 1901. V. 71
Diary and Correspondence of John Evelyn. London: 1854. V. 72
Directions for the Gardiner at Says Court, but Which May be of Use for Other Gardens. London: 1932. V. 70; 71
Memoirs Illustrative of the Life and Writings.... London: 1818. V. 70
Memoirs of John Evelyn.... London: 1827. V. 68; 69; 70; 73
Memories for My Grand-son. London: 1926. V. 68; 71
Memories for my Grandson. Oxford: 1926. V. 73
Sculptura; or the History and Art of Chalcography, and Engraving in Copper. London: 1755. V. 68
Silva. London: 1729. V. 69; 71
Silva. York: 1776. V. 71; 73
Sylva. London: 1664. V. 68; 70; 72

EVENSON, BRIAN
Altmann's Tongue. New York: 1994. V. 68

EVENTS in the Life of Miss Dollkins. London: 1869. V. 73

EVERARD, EDWARD
A Bristol Printing House. London: 1890?. V. 71

EVERARD, JOHN
Artist's Model. London: 1954. V. 68
Second Sitting: Another Artist's Model. London: 1945. V. 68

EVERARD, ROBERT
A Relation of Three Years Suffering...Upon the Coast of Affada Near Madagascar, in a Voyage to India, in the Year 1686. London. V. 73

EVERARD, THOMAS
Stereometry, or the Art of Gauging Made Easie, by the Help of a Sliding-Rule. London: 1705. V. 70

EVEREST, CHARLES WILLIAM
Babylon: a Poem. Hartford: 1838. V. 73

EVEREST, MARY
The Mathematical Psychology of Gratry and Boole. London: 1897. V. 69

EVERETT, EDWARD
Address of His Excellency Edward Everett, to the Two Branches of the Legislature, on the Organization of the Government, for the Political Year Commencing January 2, 1839. Boston: 1839. V. 68; 72

EVERETT, GEORGE C.
Cattle Cavalcade in Central Colorado from 1866 to 1966. Denver: 1966. V. 68; 71

EVERETT, JAMES
The Wall's End Miner. London: 1838. V. 70

EVERETT, MARSHALL
The Book of the Fair. Philadelphia: 1904. V. 68

EVERETT, PERCIVAL
Suder. New York: 1983. V. 68

EVERETT, T. H.
New Illustrated Encyclopedia of Gardening. New York: 1960-1963. V. 71; 73

EVERMANN, B. W.
Fishes of Porto Rico. Washington: 1900. V. 69

EVERS, JOHN J.
Touching Second: The Science of Baseball. Chicago: 1910. V. 72

EVERWINE, PETER
Keeping the Night. Lisbon: 1977. V. 71; 73

EVERY Man a Good Card Player. London: 1785. V. 73

EVERY Man His Own Printer, or, Lithography Made Easy; Being an Essay Upon Lithography in All Its Branches, showing More Particularly the Advantages of the Patent Autographic Press. 1859. V. 71

EVERY Youth's Drawing Book: Containing the Whole Art of Drawing, the Principles of Perspective.... London: 1828. V. 69

EVERYMAN.. London: 1911. V. 70; 72
EVERYMAN. London: 1925. V. 70
EVERYMAN. London: 1930. V. 73

EWALD, ALEXANDER CHARLES
Leaders of the Senate, a Biographical History of the Rise and Development of the British Constitution. London: 1885. V. 71
The Right Hon. Benjamin Disraeli, Earl of Beaconfield and His Times. London: 1881-1882. V. 71
The Right Hon. Benjamin Disraeli, Early Of Beaconsfield, K. G., And His Times. London: 1882. V. 72

EWAN, J.
John Banister and His Natural History of Virginia 1678-1692. Urbana: 1970. V. 72

EWAN, JAMES
The Geography of the Australian Colonies. Sydney: 1851. V. 70

EWAN, REBECCA FISH
A Land Between Owens Valley, California. Baltimore: 2000. V. 68

EWART, GAVIN
The Balls of the Beaver. Leamington Spa: 1984. V. 70
The Gavin Ewart Show. Poems. 1971. V. 68
Throwaway Lines. London: 1964. V. 71
Twelve Apostles. Belfast: 1970. V. 71

EWBANK, INGA-STINA
Their Proper Sphere. A Study of the Bronte Sisters as Early Victorian Female Novelists. Cambridge: 1966. V. 73

EWELL, THOMAS
Plain Discourses on the Laws or Properties of Matter: Containing the Elements or Principles of Modern Chemistry.... New York: 1806. V. 73
Statement of Improvements in the Theory and Practice of the Science of Medicine. Philadelphia: 1819. V. 73

EWERS, JOHN C.
Adventures of Zenas Leonard Fur Trader. Norman: 1959. V. 73
The Horse in Blackfoot Indian Culture. Washington: 1955. V. 68
Indian Life on the Upper Missouri. Norman: 1968. V. 68; 71
Plains Indian Painting. Stanford: 1939. V. 69

EWERT, THEODORE
Private Theodore Ewerts's Diary Of The Black Hill Expedition Of 1874. Piscataway, NJ: 1986. V. 72

EWING, CHARLES
(Welsh Title) The Farm and Cottage Gardener; or Practical Instructions How and When to Make and Cultivate a Small Garden.... Carnarvon: 1860. V. 68

EWING, D. C.
Pleasing the Spirits, a Catalogue of a Collection of American Indian Art. New York: 1982. V. 69

EWING, HARRIET
Dunrie: a Poem. London: 1819. V. 69

EWING, JAMES
A Treatise on the Office and Duty of a Justice of the Peace, Sheriff, Coroner, Constable...the rules for Conducting an Action in the Court for the Trial of Small Causes. Trenton: 1805. V. 69
A Treatise on the Office and Duty of a Justice of the Peace, Sheriff, Coroner, Constable...The Rules for Conducting an Action in the Court for the Trial of Small Causes. Trenton: 1832. V. 69
A Treatise on the Office and Duty of a Justice of the Peace, Sheriff, Coroner, Constable...the Rules for Conducting an Action in the Court for the Trial of Small Causes. Trenton: 1839. V. 69
A Treatise on the Office and Duty of a Justice of the Peace, Sheriff, Coroner, Constable...the Rules for Conducting an Action in the Court for the Trial of Small Causes. New York: 1848. V. 69

EWING, JULIANA HORATIA
The Brownies. London: 1870. V. 70
The Doll's Wash. London. V. 70
Jackanapes. New York: 1948. V. 73
Lob Lie-by-the-Fire. London: 1909. V. 68
Robin! Robin. Edinburgh & London: 1883. V. 69
A Week Spent in a Glass Pond by the Great Water Beetle. New York: 1883. V. 70

EWING, W. A.
Flora Photographica.... London: 1991. V. 72

EX-JUDGE.. New York: 1930. V. 69

EX-LOVER.. New York: 1930. V. 70; 71

AN EXACT Journal of the Victorious Expedition of the Confederate Fleet, the Last Year, Under the Command of the Right Honourable Admiral Russel.... London: 1695. V. 69

AN EXACT List of the Lords Spiritual and Temporal; Distinguished by the Following Marks. The Knights of the Garter...Those Under Age Who Don't Sit in the House; # Lords of the Treasury.... London: 1734. V. 72

THE EXCHANGE. A Home and Colonial Review of Commerce, Manufactures, and General Politics. London: 1862-1863. V. 71

EXECUTIONS At Nottingham, During the Last Century, with a Short Biographical Sketch of Each Culprit; to Which is Added, an Interesting Account of Two Characters, Who Suffered at Nottingham in 1685 and 1701. Nottingham: 1827. V. 69

EXERCISES, Instructive and Entertaining, in False English.... Leeds: 1788. V. 69

EXHIBITION of the Female Flagellants. London: 1872. V. 68

AN EXHORTATION to the Belief and Practice of Real Religion; with Cautions Against Some Mistakes About It. London: 1729. V. 70

EXLEY, FREDERICK
A Fan's Notes. New York: 1968. V. 68; 71; 72; 73
Last Notes from Home. New York: 1988. V. 72

EXNER, JOHN E.
The Rorschach: A Comprehensive System. New York: 1982. V. 69

AN EXPEDIENT for Peace: Perswading an Agreement Amongst Christians. London: 1688. V. 72

THE EXPERIENCED American Housekeeper, or Domestic Cookery.... New York: 1838. V. 73

EXPERIMENTS on Rail Roads, in England, Illustrative of the Safety, Economy and Speed of Transportation, Which this System, as Now Improved is Capable of Affording. Baltimore: 1829. V. 73

THE EXPLANATION of the Scheme. 1721. V. 70

EXPLICATION des Ouvrages de Peinture, Sculpture, Architecture et Gravure, des Artistes Vivans, Exposes au Musee Royal des Arts le 24 Avril 1817. Paris. V. 73

L'EXPOSITION de Paris (1900). Paris: 1900. V. 68; 70; 72

EXPOSITION of the Property and Prospects of the Bear Creek Consolidated Gold Mining Company Near Turnagain Arm, on Kenai Peninsula, Alaska. New Jersey: 1901. V. 70

EXQUEMELING, ALEXANDRE OLIVIER
The Buccaneers of America. London: 1911. V. 72

THE EXQUISITE. London: 1840. V. 69

AN EXTRACT of the Journals of Mr. Commissary Von Reck, Who Conducted the First Transport of Saltzburgers to Georgia.... London: 1734. V. 73

EXTRACTS from Italian Prose Writers. London: 1828. V. 70

THE EXTRAORDINARY Black Book; an Exposition of the United Church of England and Ireland.... London: 1831. V. 71

THE EXTRAORDINARY Red Book.... London: 1817. V. 71

EYCLESHYMER, ALBERT CHAUNCEY
Anatomical Names: Especially the Basle Nomina Anatomica. New York: 1917. V. 68
A Cross-Section Anatomy. New York and London: 1911. V. 72
A Cross-Section Anatomy. New York: 1930. V. 68
The Gastrulation and Embryo Formation in Amia Calva. Baltimore: 1906. V. 68

AN EYE Salve for the City of London: Discovering Unto Them the Great Engagement that Lyes Upon Them, etc. 1648. V. 73

EYRE-TODD, GEORGE
Byways of the Scottish Border: A Pedestrian Pilgrimage. Selkirk. V. 71
The Princess Louise Scottish Hospital for Limbless Sailors and Soldiers at Erskine House. Glasgow: 1917. V. 71

EYSTON, GEORGE
Speed on Salt. A History of the Bonneville Salt Flats. London: 1936. V. 70

EYTON, R. W.
Court, Household and Itinerary of King Henry II. 1878. V. 73

EZRA Pound: Written on Behalf of the Committee Formed to Obtain His Release. 1956. V. 68

F

F., C.
A Ramble on Rumbald's Moor, Among the Dwellings, Cairns & Circles of the Ancient Britons, in the Summer of 1867. Wakefield: 1868-1869. V. 73

FABER, FREDERICK WILLIAM
The Cherwell Water-Lily, and Other Poems. London and Oxford: 1840. V. 73
The Knights of St. John: a Prize Poem, Recited in the Theatre, Oxford, June 15, 1836. Oxford: 1836. V. 73
The Styrian Lake and Other Poems. London and Oxford: 1842. V. 73

FABER, G. L.
The Fisheries of the Adriatic and the Fish Thereof. London: 1883. V. 69; 72

FABER, T.
Arne Jacobsen. London: 1964. V. 68; 69; 72

FABER, WALTER
Wit and Wisdom of the Shires. Leicester: 1932. V. 68; 72

FABES, GILBERT H.
D. H. Lawrence, His First Editions Points and Values. London: 1933. V. 72

FABIAN, R.
Masters of the Early Travel Photography. New York: 1983. V. 70

FABIAN, WARNER
Sailors' Wives. New York: 1924. V. 71
Summer Bachelors. New York: 1926. V. 70

FABLES Calculated for the Amusement and Instruction of Youth.... Taunton: 1789. V. 69

FABRE, JEAN HENRI
Fabre's Book of Insects. New York: 1935. V. 68
Fabre's Book of Insects. New York: 1936. V. 72

FABRICIUS, GEORGIUS
Roma, Liber ad Opt. Autorum Lectionem Apprime Utilis ac Necessarius.... Basel: 1551. V. 68; 70

FABRICIUS, HIERONYMUS
The Embryological Treatises of Hieronymus Fabricius of Aquapendente. Ithaca: 1967. V. 68
The Embryological Treatises of.... Ithaca: 1942. V. 68; 71
Opera Chirugica. Frankfurt: 1620-1619. V. 71
Opera Chirurgica. Padua: 1647. V. 68

FABRICUS, M. THEODOSIUS
Loci Communes D. Martini Lutheri Viri Dei et Prophetae Germanici, . Magdeburg: 1594. V. 71

FACT Little Known. Southwest Louisiana. 1892. V. 68

FADIMAN, ANNE
Ex Libris. New York: 1998. V. 72

FAENSEN, HUBERT
Early Russian Architecture. New York: 1975. V. 70

FAGAN, MYRON C.
Documentations of the Reds and Fellow Travellers in Hollywood and TV. Hollywood: 1961. V. 68

FAGAN, ROBERTA
Custer And His Times - Book Three. Arkansas: 1987. V. 72

FAGES, PEDRO
A Historical, Political and Natural Description of California. Berkeley: 1937. V. 71

FAGG, W.
African Tribal Images, The Katherine White Reswick Collection. Cleveland: 1968. V. 69
Afro-Portuguese Ivories. London: 1959. V. 69
Nigerian Images. London: 1963-1990. V. 69
Yoruba: Sculpture of West Africa. New York: 1982. V. 69

FAGNANI, JOSEPH
American Beauty Personified as the Nine Muses. 1870?. V. 69

FAHEY, DAVID
Masters of Starlight - Photographers in Hollywood. London: 1988. V. 68

FAHEY, HERBERT
Early Printing in California from Its Beginning in the Mexican Territory to Statehood, September 9 1850. San Francisco: 1956. V. 73

FAHY, E.
Child of the Tides. 1985. V. 68

FAILLE, J. B. DE LA
L'Oeuvre de Vincent Van Gogh Catalogue Raisonne. Prais & Bruxeles: 1928. V. 70
L'Oeuvre de Vincent Van Gogh Catalogue Raisonne. (with) Les Faux Van Gogh. Paris and Bruxelles: 1928-1930. V. 72

FAINLIGHT, HARRY
Selected Poems. London: 1986. V. 69

FAIR, A. A.
Fools Die on Friday. New York: 1947. V. 69

FAIR One With Golden Hair. New York: 1854-1863. V. 71

A FAIR Representation of His Majesty's Right to Nova-Scotia or Acadie. London: 1756. V. 72

FAIRBAIRN, KENNEDY & NAYLOR, WILLINGTON FOUNDRY, LEEDS
List of Engineering and General Workshop Tools. Leeds: 1872. V. 71

FAIRBAIRN, THOMAS
Relics of Ancient Architecture and Other Picturesque Scenes in Glasgow. Glasgow: 1849. V. 73

FAIRBAIRN, WILLIAM
Remarks on the Canal Navigation, Illustrative of the Advantages of the Use of Steam.... London: 1831. V. 69
Useful Information for Engineers. Third Series. London: 1866. V. 71

FAIRBAIRN'S Book of Crests of the Families of Great Britain and Ireland.... 1905. V. 70

FAIRBANKS, DOUGLAS
The Fairbanks Album, Drawn from the Family Archives.... 1975. V. 71
Laugh and Live. New York: 1917. V. 70

FAIRBANKS, LORENZO S.
Genealogy of the Fairbanks Family in America 1633-1897. Boston: 1897. V. 73

FAIRBRIDGE, KINGSLEY
The Emigration of Poor Children to the Colonies. Oxford: 1909. V. 68

FAIRBRIDGE, KINGSLEY continued
The Society for the Furtherance of Child Emigration to the Colonies. Oxford: 1910. V. 68

FAIRBROTHER, NAN
Men and Gardens. London: 1956. V. 70

FAIRBURN, JAMES
The Visitor's Gude to Ripon, Harrogate, and Adjoining Country. Ripon. V. 73

FAIRCHILD, D.
Book of Monsters. Washington: 1914. V. 68; 70
Exploring for Plants.... New York: 1930. V. 70

FAIRCHILD, THOMAS
The London Gardener. London: 1760. V. 68; 69

FAIRCLOUGH, HENRY RUSHTON
Some Aspects of Horace. San Francisco: 1935. V. 68; 72

FAIRFAX, THOMAS
A Declaration of His Excellency Sir Thomas Fairfax.... London: 1647. V. 70
Short Memorials of Thomas Lord Fairfax. London: 1699. V. 69

FAIRFAX MURRAY, C.
Catalogue of a Magnificent Collection of Rare Early Printed German Books, Collected Chiefly for their Illustrations and Mostly in Fine Bindings, Including Five Block Books, forming the First Portion of the Library of C. Fairfax Murray, Esq. London: 1917. V. 70

FAIRHOLT, FREDERICK WILLIAM
A Dictionary of Terms in Art. London: 1854. V. 68
Gog and Magog. The Giants in Guildhall. London: 1859. V. 71
Rambles of an Archaeolgoist Among Old Books and in Old Places.... London: 1871. V. 68

FAIRLESS, MICHAEL
The Gathering of Brother Hilarious. London: 1913. V. 68

FAIRLIE, GERARD
Bulldog Drummond Attacks. London: 1939. V. 69; 73
Bulldog Drummond Attacks. 1940. V. 68

FAIRLIE, ROBERT F.
Railways or No Railways. London: 1872. V. 68

FAIRY ABC. New York: 1875. V. 71

A FAIRY Garland. London: 1928. V. 71

A FAIRY Garland, Being Fairy Tales from the Old French. New York: 1929. V. 72

FAIRY Tales Picture Book. Racine: 1940. V. 73

FAIRYLAND Stories from Grimm and Andersen and Others. London: 1920. V. 68

A FAITHFUL Journal of the Late Expedition to Egypt. London: 1802?. V. 70

FAITHORNE, WILLIAM
The Art of Graveing and Etching.... London: 1662. V. 69; 72

FALCONER, J. D.
On Horseback through Nigeria, or Life and Travel through Central Sudan. 1911. V. 69; 70

FALCONER, THOMAS
Letters and Notes on the Texas Santa Fe Expedition 1841-1842. New York: 1930. V. 70
Texan Santa Fe Expedition. New York: 1930. V. 68

FALCONER, WILLIAM
A Dissertation on the Influence of the Passions Upon Disorders of the Body.... London: 1796. V. 72
Observations Respecting the Pulse: Intended to Point Out with Greater Certainty the Indications Which it Signifies, Especially in Feverish Complaints. London: 1796. V. 70; 71
Remarks on the Influence of Climate, Situation, Nature of Country, Population, Nature of Food and Way of Life.... 1781. V. 71
The Shipwreck. London: 1811. V. 71

FALK, ORSON
Thunder Birds. New York: 1942. V. 69

FALKENER, EDWARD
Ephesus, and the Temple of Diana. London: 1862. V. 68; 72

FALKINER, FREDERICK B.
The Foundation of the Hospital and Free School of King Charles II. 1906. V. 70

FALKUS, HUGH
Freshwater Fishing. 1975. V. 68
Salmon Fishing. 1984. V. 73
Salmon Fishing. 1991. V. 68
Sea Trout Fishing. 1978. V. 68

FALLACI, ORIANA
The Useless Sex. London: 1964. V. 68; 71; 72

FALLADA, HANS
Wolf Among Wolves. New York: 1938. V. 69

FALLOT, ARTHUR
Essai sur le Pneumothorax. Montpellier: 1876. V. 70

A FAMILIAR History of the British Fishes. London: 1859. V. 68

THE FAMILY Receipt Book Containing Eight Hundred Valuable Receipts in Various Branches of Domestic Economy.... Pittsburgh: 1819. V. 70

FAMOUS American Race Horses Being Full Page Portraits. (bound with, as issued) Famous American Trotting Horses. Philadelphia: 1877. V. 70

FANE, JULIAN
Ad Matrem. 1849-1857. 1857. V. 73
Memoir in the Middle of the Journey. London: 1971. V. 71
Poems. London: 1852. V. 73
Tannhauser; or the Battle of the Bards. London: 1861. V. 73
Tannhauser; or the Battle of the Bards. Mobile: 1863. V. 69; 70

FANE, ROBERT GEORGE CECIL
Ministry of Justice: Its Necessity as an Instrument of Law Reform. London: 1848. V. 73

FANI
(Persian) The Dabistan-e-Mazahib, or School of Manners. Calcutta: 1809. V. 71

FANNING, DAVID
Col. David Fanning's Narrative of His Exploits and Adventures as a Loyalist of North Carolina in the American Revolution.... Toronto: 1808. V. 73

FANON, FRANTZ
The Wretched of the Earth. London: 1965. V. 70

FANTE, JOHN
Ask the Dust. Santa Barbara: 1980. V. 68; 69
The Brotherhood of the Grape. Boston: 1977. V. 70

FARADAY, PHILIP MICHAEL
Amasis, an Egyptian Princess. London: 1906. V. 69

FARAH, CYNTHIA
Literature and Landscape. El Paso: 1988. V. 71; 72

FARAMUS, ANTHONY CHARLES
The Faramus Story - Being the Experiences of Anthony Charles Faramus presented by Frank Owen. London: 1954. V. 72

FARBER, ROBERT
The Fashion Photographer. 1981. V. 68

FARGNOLI, A. NICHOLAS
James Joyce A to Z. London: 1995. V. 72

FARINA, RICHARD
Been Down So Long It Looks Like Up to Me. New York: 1966. V. 68; 69
Been Down So Long It Looks Like Up to Me. New York: 1996. V. 69

FARINGTON, JOSEPH
Views of the Lakes, &c. in Cumberland and Westmorland. London: 1789. V. 69

FARIS, J. T.
Old Gardens in and About Philadelphia and Those Who Made Them. Indianapolis: 1932. V. 71

FARISH, THOMAS EDWIN
History of Arizona. Phoenix: 1915. V. 70
History of Arizona. Phoenix: 1915-1918. V. 70

FARJEON, BENJAMIN LEOPOLD
Grif: a Story of Australian Life. London: 1893. V. 68
The House of White Shadows. London: 1886?. V. 68
The House of White Shadows. London: 1887?. V. 68
Samuel Boyd of Catchpole Square. London: 1899. V. 71
Toilers of Babylon. London: 1890. V. 68

FARJEON, ELEANOR
An Alphabet of Magic. London: 1928. V. 68
Cherrystones. 1942. V. 71
The Country Child's Alphabet. London: 1924. V. 69
Dreamsongs for the Beloved. London: 1911. V. 68; 70; 73
Kaleidoscope. London: 1962. V. 69
Katy Kruse at the Seaside or the Deserted Islanders. Philadelphia: 1932. V. 71
One Foot in Fairyland. New York: 1938. V. 71; 73
Pan-Worship and Other Poems. London: 1908. V. 73
Panworship and Other Poems. London. V. 70
The Perfect Zoo. Philadelphia: 1929. V. 73
The Silver Curlew. London: 1953. V. 68

FARJEON, J. JEFFERSON
The 5.18 Mystery. New York: 1936. V. 70
Friday the Thirteenth. Indianapolis: 1940. V. 68; 71
The Oval Table. London: 1946. V. 69; 71; 73
Peril in the Pyrenees. London: 1946. V. 70; 71
Prelude to Crime. London: 1948. V. 69; 71; 73

FARLEIGH, JOHN
Graven Image: an Autobiographical Textbook. London: 1940. V. 68

FARLEY, JOHN
The London Art of Cookery, and Housekeeper's Complete Assistant. 1796. V. 72

FARLEY, RALPH MILNE
The Radio Man. 1948. V. 68

FARLEY, WALTER
The Black Stallion's Sulky Colt. New York: 1954. V. 71

FARLOW, WILLIAM GILSON
Icones Farlowianae: Illustrations of the Larger Fungi of Eastern North America. Cambridge: 1929. V. 70; 72

THE FARM Book. Bob and Betty Visit Uncle John. Boston and New York: 1910. V. 68

FARMER & Mechanic's Pocket Assistant, in Two Parts. Easton: 1819. V. 69

FARMER, BERNARD J.
Death of a Bookseller. London: 1956. V. 69

FARMER, CECILY
Dragons and a Bell. London: 1931. V. 69

FARMER, FANNIE MERRITT
New Book of Cookery. Boston: 1912. V. 70

FARMER, JAMES
Lay Bare the Heart: An Autobiography of the Civil Rights Movement. New York: 1985. V. 72
Practical Observations on Certain Affections of the Head, Commonly called Head-achs.... 1822. V. 72

FARMER, JOHN STEPHEN
Twixt Two Worlds: a Narrative of the Life and Works of William Eglinton.... London: 1886. V. 70

FARMER, PHILIP JOSE
The Adventure of the Peerless Peer. Boulder: 1974. V. 73
A Feast Unknown. 1975. V. 71
Gods of Riverworld. 1983. V. 71
The Green Odyssey. New York: 1957. V. 71
The Image of the Beast. Los Angeles: 1968. V. 70

THE FARMER'S and Mechanic's Guide.... Newark: 1829. V. 69

THE FARMER'S Boy. London: 1881. V. 70

FARMILOE, EDITH
Piccallill. London: 1900. V. 68
Piccallill. 1908. V. 71

FARNAM, G. B.
Description of Farnam's Patent Hydraulic Apparatus for Raising Water.... New York: 1851. V. 68; 70

FARNAM, HENRY W.
Chapters in the History of Social Legislation in the United States to 1860. Washington: 1938. V. 72

FARNAM QUALITY HOME BUILDERS
Designer's Plan Book. Minneapolis: 1910. V. 70

FARNER, D. S.
Avian Biology. 1971-1975. V. 73
Avian Biology. London: 1971-1975. V. 69
Avian Biology. New York: 1971-1985. V. 68
Avian Biology. New York: 1972. V. 70

FARNHAM, ELIZA
California, In-Doors and Out.... New York: 1856. V. 68; 69; 73
Life in Prairie Land. New York: 1847. V. 73

FARNHAM, J. E. C.
Providence to Dallas. A Brief Trip to the Southwest. Providence: 1897. V. 73

FARNHAM, MATEEL HOWE
Marsh-Fire. New York: 1928. V. 69

FARNHAM, T. J.
Life Adventures and Travels in California, Conquest of California, Travels in Oregon and History of the Gold Region. New York: 1850. V. 69

FARNOL, JEFFERY
The Amateur Gentleman. London. V. 71
Another Day. Boston: 1929. V. 69
The Crooked Furrow. Garden City: 1938. V. 69
Peregrine's Progress. Boston: 1922. V. 69

FARQUHAR, DAVID
The Torch of Time; or, The Temporal Advantages Considered in Relation to the Working Classes. London: 1849. V. 71

FARQUHAR, FERDINAND
The Relicks of a Saint. London: 1816. V. 69; 70

FARQUHAR, FRANCIS P.
History of the Sierra Nevada. Berkeley, Los Angeles: 1965. V. 70
A List of Publications Relating to the Mountains of Alaska. New York: 1934. V. 73
Yosemite, the Big Trees and High Sierra.... Berkeley: 1948. V. 70

FARQUHAR, GEORGE
The Works. London: 1772. V. 73

FARQUHAR, WILLIAM H.
Annals of Sandy Spring, or Twenty Years History of Rural Community in Maryland. Baltimore: 1884-1902. V. 70

FARR, D. F.
Fungi on Plant Products in the United States. St. Paul: 1989. V. 72

FARR, M. L.
An Annotated List of Spegazzini's Fungus Taxa. Lehre: 1973. V. 72

FARR, WILLIAM
A Treatise on the Nature of the Scrofula, in which, an Attempt is Made to Account for the Origin of that Disease.... London: 1820. V. 71

FARRAGUT, DAVID GLASGOW
Reports of Naval Engagements on the Mississippi River, Resulting in the Capture of Forts Jackson and St. Philip and the City of New Orleans, and the Destruction of the Rebel Naval Flotilla. Washington: 1862. V. 70

FARRAND, MAX
Records of the Federal Convention of 1787. New Haven: 1966. V. 73

FARRAR, CHARLES A. J.
Up the North Branch, or a Summer's Outing. Boston: 1889. V. 69

FARRAR, EMMIE F.
Old Virginia Houses: the Mountain Empire. Charlotte: 1978. V. 68
Old Virginia Houses the Piedmont. Charlotte: 1975. V. 72

FARRAR, RICHARD
An Expedient for the King; or King Charles His Peac-Offering, Sacrificed at the Altar of Peace.... London: 1648. V. 69

FARRE, HENRY
Sky Fighters of France. Aerial Warfare 1914-1918. Boston and New York: 1919. V. 69

FARRELL, D.
The Stinehour Press: a Bibliographical Checklist of the First Thirty Years. Vermont: 1988. V. 70

FARRELL, HENRY
Whatever Happened to Baby Jane?. New York: 1960. V. 71; 72

FARRELL, J. G.
Girl in the Head. London: 1967. V. 72; 73
The Lung. London: 1965. V. 70
A Man from Elsewhere. London: 1959. V. 72
The Siege of Krishnapur. London: 1973. V. 70; 71; 73

FARRELL, JAMES T.
Ellen Rogers. New York: 1941. V. 72
Father and Son. New York: 1940. V. 73
Father and Son. London: 1943. V. 73
The League of Frightened Philistines. New York: 1945. V. 73
No Star is Lost. New York: 1938. V. 68; 73
The Road Between. London: 1949. V. 69
Young Lonigan. New York: 1932. V. 73

FARREN, GEORGE
Observations on the Importance in Purchase of Land, and in Mercantile Adventures, of Ascertaining the Rates of Laws of Mortality Among Europeans, by Chronic Diseases and Hot Climates.... London: 1826. V. 71

FARRER, MR.
Sentiments of a Corn-Factor on the Present Stipulation of the Corn Trade. London: 1758. V. 73

FARRER, REGINALD
Among the Hills. 1911. V. 73
Among the Hills. London: 1911. V. 69
Among The Hills. London: 1927. V. 72
The Dolomites: King Laurin's Garden. London: 1913. V. 69; 72
The English Rock Garden. 1919. V. 69
The English Rock Garden. London: 1925. V. 71; 73
The English Rock Garden. London: 1955. V. 69; 71
In a Yorkshire Garden. 1909. V. 73
In Old Ceylon. London: 1908. V. 69
On the Eaves of the World. 1917. V. 73
On the Eaves of the World. London: 1917. V. 69
The Plant Introductions of Reginald Farrer. 1930. V. 69
The Rainbow Bridge. London: 1921. V. 69; 72
The Rainbow Bridge. London: 1922. V. 72
The Sundered Streams. The History of a Memory that Had No Full Stops. London: 1907. V. 70

FARRER, RICHARD RIDLEY
A Tour in Greece 1880. Edinburgh & London: 1882. V. 73

FARRER, WILLIAM
Victoria History of the County of Lancaster. London: 1966. V. 73

FARRIER, GEORGE H.
Memorial of the Centennial Celebration of the Battle of Paulus Hook.... Jersey City: 1879. V. 69

FARRINGTON, JOSEPH
The Diary of Joseph Farington. London: 1978-1998. V. 72

FARRINGTON, S. KIP
Atlantic Game Fishing. New York: 1937. V. 71

FARRIS, JACK
A Man to Ride With. Philadelphia: 1957. V. 68
Ramey. Philadelphia: 1953. V. 68

FARRIS, JOHN
Harrison High. 1959. V. 73
King Windom. New York: 1967. V. 73
Sharp Practice. New York: 1974. V. 71
When Michael Calls. 1967. V. 73

FARROW, EDWARD
Camping On The Trail Or Some Of My Experiences In The Indian Country. Philadelphia: 1902. V. 72
Mountain Scouting A Handbook For Officers And Soldiers On The Frontier. New York: 1881. V. 72

FARROW, G. E.
The Adventures of Dodo. London: 1907. V. 72
The Escape of the Mullingong. London: 1907. V. 72
In Search of the Wallypug. 1903. V. 71
The Missing Prince. London: 1897. V. 68
The Wallypug Birthday Book. London: 1904. V. 71
The Wallypug in Fog-Land. 1904. V. 71

FARROW, JOHN PENDLETON
The Romantic Story of David Robertson, Among the Islands and on the Coast of Maine. Belfast: 1898. V. 73

FARSON, DANIEL
Sacred Monsters. Bloomsbury: 1988. V. 70

THE FASHIONABLE American Letter Writer.... Totten: 1828. V. 69
THE FASHIONABLE American Letter Writer.... Newark: 1839. V. 69

FASS, EKBERT
Ted Hughes: The Unaccomodated Universe. Santa Barbara: 1980. V. 71

FASSAM, THOMAS
An Herbarium for the Fair - Being a Book of Common Herbs. London: 1949. V. 70; 73

FASSBENDER, ADOLF
Pictorial Artistry: the Dramatization of the Beautiful in Photography. New York: 1937. V. 70

FASSITT, MARGARET
A Port of Call. Springfield: 1945. V. 73

FAST, HOWARD
The American. New York: 1947. V. 68
The Immigrant's Daughter. Boston: 1985. V. 72
The Picture-Book History of the Jews. New York: 1942. V. 70
Spartacus. New York: 1951. V. 71

FASTOVSKY, D. E.
The Evolution and Extinction of the Dinosaurs. Cambridge: 1996. V. 68

THE FAT Boy from Dickens Pickwick. New York: 1882. V. 73

THE FATAL Choice. London: 1796. V. 68

FATHER Christmas. New York: 1911. V. 73

FATHER Christmas's Book - Tea. London: 1901. V. 73

FATHER Tuck's Annual. London: 1927. V. 71

FATHER Tuck's My Doll's House ABC. London: 1905-1907. V. 69

FAUGERES, MARGARETTA V.
Belisarius: a Tragedy. New York: 1795. V. 70

FAULDING, GERTRUDE M.
The Buttercup Book: a Flower Book for Little Folks. London: 1927. V. 70
The Little Book of Wild Flowers - a Flower Book for Little Folks. London: 1927. V. 72
Summer Flowers - a Flower Book for Little Folks. London: 1927. V. 72
The Sunflower Book: A Flower Book for Little Folks. London: 1927. V. 70

FAULK, ODIE B.
The Geronimo Campaign. New York: 1969. V. 69
The Last Years of Spanish Texas: 1778-1821. The Hague: 1964. V. 70
Tombstone Myth and Reality. New York: 1972. V. 69

FAULKNER, ARTHUR BROOKE
A Treatise on the Plague, Designed to Prove It Contagious, From Facts Collected During the Author's Residence in Malta. London: 1820. V. 68; 73

FAULKNER, WILLIAM HARRISON
Absalom, Absalom!. New York: 1936. V. 68; 69; 70; 72
Absalon! Absalon!. Paris: 1953. V. 69
An Address by William Faulkner Delta Council Annual Meeting. Cleveland MS: 1952. V. 70
Afternoon of a Cow. Iowa City: 1991. V. 68
As I Lay Dying. New York: 1930. V. 73
Big Woods. New York: 1955. V. 69; 70; 73
Collected Stories of William Faulkner. New York: 1950. V. 68; 69; 70; 72
Descends, Moise. (Go Down, Moses). Paris: 1955. V. 69
Doctor Martino and Other Stories. New York: 1934. V. 68; 69; 70; 71; 73
Early Prose and Poetry. Boston: 1962. V. 73
A Fable. New York: 1954. V. 68; 69; 70; 71; 72; 73
Father Abraham. New York: 1983. V. 68; 69; 73
Father Abraham. New York: 1984. V. 73
Faulkner's County - Tales of Yoknapatawpha County. London: 1955. V. 69
Flags in the Dust. New York: 1973. V. 68; 70; 71; 73
Go Down, Moses and Other Stories. New York: 1942. V. 68; 69; 70; 71; 73
The Hamlet. New York: 1940. V. 68; 69; 70
Histoires Diverses. Paris: 1967. V. 69
Hunting Stories. 1988. V. 73
Hunting Stories. New York: 1988. V. 69
I Decline to Accept the End of Man. Rochester NY: 1950. V. 72
Intruder in the Dust. New York: 1948. V. 68; 69; 70; 71; 72; 73
Jealousy and Episode. Minneapolis: 1955. V. 68
Knight's Gambit. New York: 1949. V. 69; 70; 71; 72; 73
L'Arbre Aux Souhaits. (The Wishing Tree). Paris: 1969. V. 69
Light in August. New York: 1932. V. 71; 72; 73
The Mansion. New York: 1959. V. 68; 69; 71; 72; 73
Mayday. New York: 1978. V. 72
Miss Zilphia Gant. Dallas: 1932. V. 69
Mississippi Poems. Oxford: 1979. V. 68
Mosquitoes. New York: 1927. V. 68; 69; 70; 73
Mosquitoes. Garden City: 1937. V. 70
Mosquitoes. London: 1964. V. 69
New Orleans Sketches. Tokyo: 1955. V. 72
New Orleans Sketches. New Brunswick: 1958. V. 73
Notes on a Horsethief. Greenville, MS: 1950. V. 71
The Old Man. New York: 1948. V. 68; 69
The Portable Faulkner. New York: 1967. V. 73
Pylon. New York: 1935. V. 68; 69; 70; 71; 73
The Reivers. London: 1962. V. 69; 72; 73
The Reivers. New York: 1962. V. 68; 70; 71; 72; 73
Requiem for a Nun. New York: 1951. V. 68; 69; 70; 71; 72; 73
Requiem for a Nun. New York: 1959. V. 68
Salmagundi. Milwaukee: 1932. V. 70; 73
Sanctuary. London: 1931. V. 68
Sanctuary. New York: 1931. V. 68; 70
Soldier's Pay. 1926. V. 70
Soldier's Pay. New York: 1926. V. 71; 73
Soldiers' Pay. London: 1930. V. 71
A Sorority Pledge. Northport: 1983. V. 69
The Sound and the Fury. New York: 1929. V. 68
The Sound and the Fury. New York: 1984. V. 73
Southern Reposure. 1956. V. 71
Spotted Horses. Columbia: 1989. V. 71
These 13. New York: 1931. V. 68; 69; 70; 71; 73
This Earth. New York: 1932. V. 69; 72; 73
The Town. New York: 1957. V. 68; 69; 70; 71; 72; 73
The Uncollected Stories of William Faulkner. New York: 1979. V. 73
The Unvanquished. New York: 1936. V. 70
The Unvanquished. New York: 1938. V. 68; 69; 70; 71; 73
The Wild Palms. New York: 1939. V. 68; 69; 71; 73
The Wishing Tree. New York: 1964. V. 68; 69
The Wishing Tree. London: 1967. V. 72

FAULKNER WEST, HERBERT
The Impecunious Amateur Looks Back. Hanover: 1966. V. 70

FAULKS, SEBASTIAN
Birdsong. London: 1993. V. 70
Charlotte Gray. London: 1998. V. 73
Charlotte Gray. New York: 1999. V. 72
The Fatal Englishman, Three Short Lives. London: 1996. V. 71; 72
The Girl at the Lion D'or. London: 1989. V. 73
On Green Dolphin Street. London: 2001. V. 72
On Green Dolphin Street. New York: 2002. V. 71

THE FAUNA of British India, Including Ceylon and Burma. Fishes. Volume 1. London: 1889. V. 72

FAURE-BIGUET, GENERAL
Le Fusil De Chasse, Ses Munitions Et Son Tir. 1891. V. 71

FAUSET, ARTHUR HUFF
Black Gods of the Metropolis. Philadelphia: 1944. V. 70
Folklore from Nova Scotia. New York: 1931. V. 72; 73
For Freedom. Philadelphia: 1927. V. 68

FAUSET, JESSIE REDMON
There is Confusion. New York: 1924. V. 70

FAUSSETT, BRYAN
Inventorium Sepulchrale: an Account of Some Antiquities Dug Up at Gilton, Kingston, Sibertswold, Barfriston.... London: 1856. V. 68

FAUST, FREDERICK
Cross Over Nine. New York: 1935. V. 70
Dr. Kildare's Search and Dr. Kildare's Hardest Case. New York: 1943. V. 70
Ronicky Doone's Treasure. New York: 1926. V. 71

FAUTEUX, AEGIDUS
The Introductin of Printing into Canada a Brief History. Montreal: 1930. V. 72

FAVORITE Authors, a Companion Book of Prose and Poetry. Boston: 1861. V. 71

FAVORITES from Storyland. 1937. V. 69

FAVOURITE Fables and Stories About Animals. London: 1901. V. 68

FAVOURITE Poems by Gifted Bards. London: 1865. V. 73

FAVRE, EDOUARD
Francois Coillard. Paris: 1910. V. 68

FAVYN, ANDRE
The Theater of Honour and Knight-Hood. London: 1623. V. 72

FAWCETT, E. DOUGLAS
Hartmann The Anarchist; or, The Doom of the Great City. London: 1893. V. 70

FAWCETT, HENRY
Essays and Lectures on Social and Political Subjects. London: 1872. V. 71; 73
Free Trade and Protection. London: 1878. V. 68

FAWCETT, JOHN
An Essay on the Propagation of the Christian Religion.... Cambridge: 1791. V. 68
An Essay on the Propagation of the Christian Religion.... Cambridge: 1878. V. 68

FAWCETT, JOHN SAVILL
The Secret Mine: an Equestrian Melo-drama...as Performed at the New York Theatre. New York: 1823. V. 70

FAWCETT, MILLICENT GARRETT
Josephine Butler. Her Work and Principles and Their Meaning for the Twentieth Century. London: 1927. V. 72
Political Economy for Beginners. London: 1974. V. 72
Tales of Political Economy. London: 1874. V. 69; 71; 73

FAWCETT, W.
Thoroughbred and Hunter. 1934. V. 68

FAY, CHARLES EDEY
Mary Celeste. The Odyssey of an Abandoned Ship. Salem: 1942. V. 68

FAY, EDWARD FRANCIS
Unsentimental Journeys. London. V. 68

FAY, JOHN B.
Capture of Generals Crook and Kelley by the McNeil (sic) Rangers, Feb. 21, 1865. Cumberland: 1899. V. 70

FAY, SAM
A Royal Read: Being the History of the London and South Western Railway, from 1825 to the Present Time. Kingston-on Thames: 1883. V. 71

FAY, THEODORE S.
Sydney Clifton; or, Vicissitudes in Both Hemispheres. New York: 1839. V. 70
Views in New York and Its Environs from Accurate, Characteristic and Picturesque Drawings.... New York: 1831-1834. V. 68; 71

FAYRER, J.
The Natural History and Epidemiology of Cholera. London: 1888. V. 68

FEARING, KENNETH
The Big Clock. New York: 1946. V. 69
Clark Gifford's Body. New York: 1942. V. 69
Dead Reckoning. New York: 1938. V. 69
The Generous Heart. New York: 1954. V. 70; 72
The Loneliest Girl in the World. London: 1952. V. 71
Poems. New York: 1935. V. 72

FEARNSIDE, WILLIAM
The History of London: Illustrated by Views in London and Westminster. London: 1845. V. 71
Holmes's Great Metropolis; or, Views and History of London in the Nineteenth Century.... 1851. V. 71

FEATHER, LEONARD
The Encyclopedia Yearbook of Jazz. New York: 1956. V. 69; 71

FEATHERSTONE, DAVID
The Diana Show: Pictures Through a Plastic Lens. Carmel: 1980. V. 68; 70

FEATHERSTONHAUGH, G. W.
Excursion through the Slave States, from Washington on the Potomac to the Frontier With Mexico. London: 1844. V. 68; 73

FEATON, E. H.
The Art Album of New Zealand Flora. Wellington: 1889. V. 69

FEDDEN, ROBIN
Alpine Ski Tour. London: 1956. V. 69
The Enchanted Mountains. London: 1962. V. 69

FEDDEN, ROMILLY
The Basque Country. London: 1921. V. 72

FEDER, NORMAN
American Indian Art. New York: 1965. V. 68; 69
American Indian Art. New York: 1969. V. 69; 71; 72
American Indian Art. New York: 1971. V. 69

THE FEDERALIST.... New York: 1788. V. 72
THE FEDERALIST.... New York: 1802. V. 69
THE FEDERALIST.... Washington: 1818. V. 69; 73

FEDINI, DOMENICO
La Vita Di S. Bibiana. Roma: 1630. V. 73

FEHRENBACH, T. R.
Comanches - The Destruction Of A People. NY: 1974. V. 72

FEICHTMAYER, JOSEPH ANTON
Simetria Deren 5 Saulen-Ordnungen in Alteren Vorgestellt, Sambt Dessen Leichtester Auftheilung und ring Ergreiffenden.... Augsburg: 1760. V. 70

FEIFFER, JULES
Carnal Knowledge. New York: 1971. V. 70; 72
Little Murders. New York: 1968. V. 71

FEIN, HARRY H.
The Flying Chinaman. New York: 1938. V. 71

FEINER, RUTH
The Sunset at Noon. Philadelphia: 1937. V. 70

FEINSTEIN, HAROLD
One Hundred Flowers. New York: 2000. V. 68

FEINSTEIN, ISIDOR
The Court Disposes. New York: 1937. V. 72

FELD, CHARLES
Picasso: His Recent Drawings 1966-1968. New York: 1977. V. 70; 72; 73

FELDMAN, DAVID
Irish Postal History. 1975. V. 70

FELDMAN, F.
Andy Warhol Prints: Catalogue Raisonne. New York: 1985. V. 72

FELDMAN, PAUL H.
Jack The Ripper: The Final Chapter. London: 1997. V. 72

FELIBIEN, ANDRE
Entretiens sur les Vies et les Ouvrages des Plus Excellens Peintures, Anciens et Modernes. Paris: 1685-1688. V. 71
Tapisseries du Roy ou Sont Representez les Quatre Elemens et Les Quatre Saisons Avec Les Devises qui les Accompagnent et leur Explication. Augsburg: 1687. V. 70
Tapisseries Du Roy, Ou Sont Representez les Quatre Elemens et Les Quatre Saisons. (bound with) *Relation De La Feste de Versailles.* Paris: 1679. V. 70

FELIBIEN, JEAN FRANCOIS
Les Plans et les Descriptions de Deux des Plus Belles Maisons de Campagne de Pline le Consul.... Paris: 1699. V. 68

FELICIANO, FELICE
Epistole e Versi Agli Amici Artisti. Verona: 1988. V. 71

THE FELIX Annual: Picture Stories of the Famous Film Cat. London: 1926. V. 72

FELIX, M. L.
Maniema an Essay on the Distribution of the Symbols and Myths as Depicted in the Masks of Great Maniema. Munich: 1989. V. 69

FELKER, CLAY
Casey Stengel's Secret. NY: 1961. V. 72

FELL, ALFRED
The Early Iron Industry of Furness and District.... Ulverston: 1908. V. 71
A Furness Military Chronicle. Ulverston: 1937. V. 71

FELL, JOHN
Daemoniacs. An Enquiry into the Heathen and the Scripture Doctrine of Daemons. London: 1789. V. 71
Specimens of Books Printed at Oxford with the Types Given to the University by John Fell. Oxford: 1925. V. 70

FELLIG, ARTHUR
Naked City. Cincinnati: 1945. V. 68
Naked City. New York: 1945. V. 68; 70; 72
Naked Hollywood. New York: 1953. V. 68
Weegee's Creative Camera. Garden City: 1959. V. 68
Weegee's Creative Photography. London and Melbourne: 1964. V. 70
Weegee's People. New York: 1946. V. 70

FELLOWES, EDMUND H.
The Tenbury Letters. Waltham St. Lawrence: 1942. V. 69; 70; 71

FELLOWES, P.
First Over Everest. 1933. V. 68

FELLOWES, W. D.
A Visit To The Monastery Of La Trappe In 1817. London: 1818. V. 72
A Visit to the Monastery of La Trappe in 1817; with Notes Taken During a Tour through Le Perche, Normandy, Bretagne, Poitou, Anjou, Le Bocage, Touraine, Orleanois and the Environs of Paris. London: 1820. V. 72

FELLOWS, WILLIAM DORSET
A Narrative of the Loss of His Majesty's Packet the Lady Hobart, on an Island of Ice in the Atlantic Ocean, 28th of June 1803. London: 1803. V. 73

FELMINGHAM, M.
The Illustrated Gift Book 1880-1930 with Checklist of 2500 Titles. Aldershot: 1988. V. 70

FELT, E. P.
Insects Affecting Park and Woodland Trees. Albany: 1905-1906. V. 70; 72

FELT, JOSEPH B.
Memorials of William Smith Shaw. Boston: 1852. V. 70

FELTHAM, JOHN
A Tour through the Island of Mann, in 1797 and 1798. Bath: 1798. V. 69

FELTON, HAROLD W.
Legends of Paul Bunyan. New York: 1947. V. 69

FELTON, REBECCA LATIMER
Country Life in Georgia in the Days of My Youth. Atlanta: 1919. V. 68; 72; 73
Life in America. Hull: 1838. V. 68

FELTON, WILLIAM
A Treatise on Carriages. Comprehending Coaches, Chariots, Pahetons, Curricles, Whiskeys &c. London: 1794. V. 71

FEMALE Excellence; Or, Hints to Daughters. London. V. 71

FEMALE Friendship; or the Innocent Sufferer. Dublin: 1770. V. 69

FEMALE Mentor; or, Select Conversations. London: 1798. V. 73

THE FEMALE Mentor; or, Select Conversations. Philadelphia: 1802. V. 68

THE FEMALE Revolutionary Plutarch, Containing Biographical, Historical and Revolutionary Sketches, Characters, and Anecdotes. London: 1806. V. 73

FENELON, FRANCOIS SALIGNAC DE LA MOTHE, ABP.
The Adventures of Telemachus, the Son of Ulysses. Iena: 1749. V. 69
The Adventures of Telemachus the Son of Ulysses. London: 1776. V. 71
The Adventures of Telemachus, the Son of Ulysses. London: 1795. V. 71
Les Aventures de Telemaque. Paris: 1781. V. 70
Les Aventures de Telemaque. Paris: 1824. V. 70
Aventures de Telemaque, fils d'Ulysse.... The Hague: 1726. V. 72
De l'Education des Filles. Amsterdam: 1708. V. 73
Fenelon's Treatise on the Education of Daughters. Albany: 1806. V. 68; 71
Instructions for the Education of a Daughter. London: 1707. V. 73

FENISONG, RUTH
The Butler Died in Brooklyn. Garden City: 1943. V. 68

FENLEY, FLORENCE
Old Times - Their Own Stories. 1939. V. 68
Old Timers- Their Own Stories. Texas: 1939. V. 71
Old Timers of Southwest Texas. Uvalde: 1957. V. 71

FENN, ELEANOR
Cobwebs to Catch Flies; or, Dialogues in Short Sentences Adapted to Children From the Ages of Three to Eight Years. London: 1825. V. 72
Cobwebs to Catch Flies; or, Dialogues in Short Sentences.... London: 1822. V. 73
The Rational Dame; or, Hints Towards Supplying Prattle for Children. Dublin: 1795. V. 73
Rational Sports. London: 1785?. V. 70

FENN, FORREST
The Beat of the Drum and the Whoop of the Dance: a Story of the Life and Work of Joseph Henry Sharp. Santa Fe: 1983. V. 69

FENN, GEORGE MANVILLE
Commodore Junk. London: 1891. V. 68
Diamond Dyke, or the Lone Farm on the Veldt; a Story of South African Adventure. London and Edinburgh: 1895. V. 68
One Maid's Mischief. London: 1882. V. 68
The Rajah of Dah. London and Edinburgh: 1891. V. 68
The Story of an Active Life. 1907. V. 73
The Story of Antony Grace; or Some Stained Pages. London: 1889. V. 68
Witness to the Deed. London: 1895. V. 68

FENN, JOHN
The School-Master's Legacy and Family Monitor; Adapted to every Age and Station in Life, Inculcating the Practice of Religion and Morality.... Woodbridge: 1843. V. 73

FENN, JOSEPH
First (and) Second Volume of the Instructions Given in the Drawing School Established by the Dublin Society, Pursuant to Their Resolution of the Fourth of February 1768. Dublin: 1769-1772. V. 71; 73

FENNELL, C. A. M.
The Opium-Woman and Datchery in the Mystery of Edwin Drood. Cambridge: 1913. V. 69

FENNELL, IRENE
Ghost Light. New York: 1940. V. 71

FENNEMAN, N. M.
Physiography of Western United States. New York: 1931. V. 70

FENNO, JOHN WARD
Desultory Reflections on the New Political Aspects of Public Affairs in the United States. New York: 1800. V. 71

FENOLLOSA, ERNEST
Certain Noble Plays of Japan.... Dundrum: 1916. V. 69
Epochs of Chinese and Japanese Art - an Outline History of East Asiatic Design. New York: 1913. V. 71

FENOLLOSA, MARY
Blossoms from a Japanese Garden. A Book of child-verses. London: 1913. V. 70; 71

FENTON, GEOFFREY
Golden Epistles, Contayning Varietie of Discourse, Both Morall, Philosophical and Divine.... London: 1582. V. 68

FENTON, JAMES
Children in Exile. Edinburgh: 1983. V. 71
Manila Envelope. Philippines: 1989. V. 70
The Memory of War - Poems 1968-1982. Edinburgh: 1982. V. 71
Tom Ross: Outlaw and Stockman. El Paso: 1979. V. 69
A Vacant Possession. London: 1978. V. 71

FENTON, L. L.
The Rifle in India. 1922. V. 72
The Rifle in India. 1923. V. 73

FENTON, WILLIAM N.
The Roll Call of the Iroquois Chiefs. Washington: 1950. V. 73

FENWICK, GEORGE EDGEWORTH
Excision of the Knee-Joint with Report of Twenty-Eight Cases.... Montreal: 1883. V. 73

FENWICK, GEORGE LEE
A History of the Ancient City of Chester From the Earliest Times. Chester: 1896. V. 73

FENWICK, GILLIAN
George Orwell. A Bibliography. Winchester: 1998. V. 70

FENWICK, R. O.
The Goblin Groom: a Tale of Dunse. Edinburgh: 1809. V. 70; 72

FERBER, EDNA
American Beauty. New York: 1931. V. 71
Cimarron. Garden City: 1930. V. 69; 70; 71; 73
Emma McChesney & Co. New York: 1915. V. 69; 70
Giant. New York: 1952. V. 70
Great Son. New York: 1945. V. 70
Half Portions. New York: 1920. V. 73
Saratoga Trunk. New York: 1941. V. 70; 71; 73
Show Boat. Garden City: 1926. V. 71

FERENTILLI, AGOSTINO
Discorso Universale Nel Quale, Discorrendosi Per La Sei Eta, et Le Quattro Monarchie. Venice: 1572. V. 70

FERGUS, HENRY
Class Book of Natural Theology; or the Testimony of Nature to the Being, Perfections and Government of God. Boston: 1837. V. 69
The Testimony of Nature and Revelation to the Being, Perfections and Government of God. Edinburgh: 1833. V. 68; 72

FERGUSON, ADAM
An Essay on the History of Civil Society. Boston: 1809. V. 68

FERGUSON, CHARLES D.
The Experiences of a '49er During the 34 Years Residence in California and Australia. Cleveland: 1888. V. 68; 73

FERGUSON, D.
The Natural History of Redcar and Its Neighbourhood. London: 1860. V. 68; 69

FERGUSON, ERNA
Murder & Mystery in New Mexico. Santa Fe: 1991. V. 72

FERGUSON, JAMES
Astronomy Explained Upon Sir Isaac Newton's Principles. London: 1757. V. 73
Astronomy Explained Upon Sir Isaac Newton's Principles. London: 1790. V. 73
Ferguson's Lectures on Select Subjects, in Mechanics, Hydrostatics, Hydraulis, Pneumatics, Optics, Geography, Astronomy and Dialling, with Notes and an Appendix. Edinburgh: 1806. V. 73
Lectures on Select Subjects in Mechanics, Hydrostatics, Pneumatics and Optics. London: 1770. V. 69

FERGUSON, JOHN
Bibliographical Notes on Histories of Inventions and Books of Secrets. London: 1959. V. 72
Bibliotheca Chemica. Glasgow: 1906. V. 68; 70
Bibliotheca Chemica. 1954. V. 73
Bibliotheca Chemica. London: 1954. V. 69; 72
Ecclesia Antiqua or, The History of an Ancient Church (St. Michael's, Linlithgow)... London: 1905. V. 71

FERGUSON, LADY
Sir Samuel Ferguson in the Ireland of His Day. 1896. V. 70

FERGUSON, M.
The Printed Books in the Library of the Hunterian Museum in the University of Glasgow. Glasgow: 1930. V. 70

FERGUSON, RACHEL
Charlotte Bronte. London: 1933. V. 70

FERGUSON, RICHARD S.
The Boke of Recorde or Register (of Kirkbie Kendall). Kendal: 1892. V. 71
Cumberland and Westmorland M.P.'s (sic) from the Restoration to the Reform Bill of 1867 (1660-1867). London: 1871. V. 71; 72
A Guide to Carlisle and Chief Places of Interest in the Neighbourhood. Carlisle: 1895. V. 71
A History of Cumberland. London: 1890. V. 71
A History of Westmorland. London: 1894. V. 71
A Short Historical and Architectural Account of Lanercost, a Priory of Black Canons, Eight Miles from Carlisle, Upon the North Side of the River Irthing, Close to the Picts Wall. London: V. 71

FERGUSON, ROBERT
Swiss Men and Swiss Mountains. London: 1854. V. 69

FERGUSON, SAMUEL
Lays of the Western Gael and Other Poems. 1865. V. 69

FERGUSON, W.
The Twelve Sketches of Scenery & Antiquities on the Line of the Great North of Scotland Railway. Edinburgh: 1883. V. 71

FERGUSON, W. B. M.
The Pilditch Puzzle. New York: 1932. V. 69; 73

FERGUSSON, C. BRUCE
Uniacke's Sketches of Cape Breton and Other Papers Relating to Cape Breton Island. Halifax: 1958. V. 72

FERGUSSON, ERNA
Dancing Gods. New York: 1931. V. 73
Dancing Gods. New York: 1934. V. 69
Mexican Cookbook. Santa Fe: 1934. V. 71; 72
New Mexico. New York: 1951. V. 69
Our Southwest. New York: 1940. V. 69

FERGUSSON, GORDON
Hounds are Home. 1979. V. 68; 70

FERGUSSON, HARVEY
Rio Grande. New York: 1933. V. 69

FERGUSSON, JAMES
The Curragh Incident. 1964. V. 70
An Historical Inquiry into the True Principles of Beauty in Art.... London: 1849. V. 68
The Illustrated Handbook of Architecture. London: 1859. V. 68

FERGUSSON, T. M.
Border Sport and Sportsmen. Memories of the Merry Past. Hexham: 1932. V. 73

FERLET, RENE
Aconcagua: South Face. London: 1956. V. 69

FERLINGHETTI, LAWRENCE
A Coney Island of the Mind. London: 1959. V. 72; 73
A Coney Island of the Mind. New York: 1968. V. 73
Literary San Francisco. San Francisco: 1980. V. 73
The Sea and Ourselves at Cape Ann. Madison: 1979. V. 73
The Street's Kiss. Boise: 1998. V. 69
These Are My Rivers: New and Selected Poems. 1955-1993. New York: 1993. V. 69

FERMOR, PATRICK LEIGH
Between the Woods and the Water.... London: 1986. V. 70; 72; 73
Roumeli - Travels in Northern Greece. London: 1966. V. 68; 72
A Time to Keep Silence. London: 1957. V. 73

FERNANDEZ, JUSTINO
Danzas de los Concheros en San Miguel de Allende. Mexico: 1941. V. 68

FERNANDO, DOROTHY
Wild Flowers of Ceylon. 1954. V. 68

FERNE, W. T.
Precious Stones. London: 1907. V. 70

FERNEL, JEAN FRANCOIS
Ambiani Vniversa Medicina...(with) Consiliorum Medicinalivm Liber.... Frankfurt: 1602. V. 71
Therapeutices Vniversalis Sev Medendi Rationalis Libris Septem. Opus ad Praxim Perutile.... Lyon?: 1569. V. 68; 72

FERNETT, GENE
Swing Out. Great Negro Dance Bands. Midland: 1970. V. 72

FERRAR, JOHN
A View of Ancient and Modern Dublin. (with) A Tour from Dublin to London in 1795. Dublin: 1796. V. 71

FERRARI, ENRIQUE LAFUENTE
Goya: The Frescos in San Antonio De La Florida in Madrid. New York: 1955. V. 70

FERRARI, GIOVANNI BATTISTA
De Florum Cultura Libri IV. Rome: 1633. V. 72; 73

FERRARIO, GIULIO
Monumenti Sacri e Profani dell' Imperiale e Reale Basilica di SantAmbrogio in Milano.... Milan: 1824. V. 68; 70; 72

FERRARS, E. X.
The Shape of a Stain. 1942. V. 73

FERRARS, ELIZABETH
The Sleeping Dogs. London: 1960. V. 73

FERRARS, MAX HENRY
Burma. London: 1900. V. 68

FERRE, EMMANUEL
L'Irlande: La Crise Agraire et Politique, Ses Causes - Ses Dangers - Sa Solution. Paris: 1887. V. 69

FERRER, LEONARDO
Astronomica Curiosa, y Descripcion del Mundo Superior, y Inferior. Valencia: 1677. V. 68

FERRERIO, PIETRO
Palazzi di Roma de Piu Celebri Architetti...Libro Primo (and) Nuovi Disegni dell'Architecture, e Piante de'Palazzi di Roma de'piu Celebri Architetti...Libro Secondo.... Rome: 1655. V. 70

FERRERIUS, ZACHARIAS
Zacharias Ferrerius. In Die Festo Natalais et Circuncisionis Christi, Sapphicum Alphabeticum. Verona: 1968. V. 73

FERREY, BENJAMIN
The Antiquities of the Priory of Christ Church, Hants. London: 1834. V. 68; 70
A Series of Ornamental Timber Gables, from Exisiting Examples in England and France of the Sixteenth Century. London: 1839. V. 70; 72

FERRIAR, JOHN
An Essay Towards a Theory of Apparitions. London: 1813. V. 69
Illustrations of Sterne; with Other Essays and Verses. London: 1798. V. 70; 73
Medical Histories and Reflections. London: 1810. V. 70
Medical Histories and Reflections. Philadelphia: 1816. V. 70; 71; 72

FERRIER, SUSAN EDMONDSTONE
The Inheritance. Edinburgh: 1824. V. 69
The Inheritance. London: 1824. V. 73
Inheritance. London: 1856?. V. 68
Marriage, a Novel. Edinburgh: 1818. V. 68; 71
Miss Ferrier's Novels. London: 1881-1882. V. 73

FERRIER, WILLIAM WARREN
Origin and Development of the University of California. Berkeley: 1930. V. 68

FERRIGNO, ROBERT
The Cheshire Moon. New York: 1993. V. 72

FERRINI, VINCENT
I Have the World. London: 1967. V. 71

FERRIS & CO.
Ferris & Co.'s Automatic Gas Apparatus. Wilmington: 1864. V. 69

FERRIS, BENJAMIN
A History of the Original Settlements on the Delaware, from Its Discovery by Hudson to the Colonization Under William Penn. Wilmington: 1846. V. 69

FERRIS, WARREN ANGUS
Life in the Rocky Mountains. Denver: 1940. V. 70
Life in the Rocky Mountains. Denver: 1983. V. 68; 73

FERRISS, HUGH
The Metropolis of Tomorrow. New York: 1929. V. 72

FERRO, ANTONIO
Apparato Delle Statue, Nuovamente Trovate Nella Distrutta Cuma.... Naples: 1606. V. 69

FERSEN, EUGENE
Science of Life. New York: 1923. V. 71

FESSENDEN, THOMAS G.
An Essay on the Law of Patents for New Inventions. Boston: 1810. V. 73
The Ladies Monitor, a Poem. Bellow Falls: 1818. V. 68
The Register of Arts; or a Compendious View of Some of the Most Useful Modern Discoveries and Inventions. Philadelphia: 1808. V. 71
Terrible Tractoration, and Other Poems. Boston: 1837. V. 69

THE FESTIVAL of Wit, Being a Collection of Bon-Mots, Anecdotes, Etc. of the Most Exalted Characters. Dresden: 1795. V. 69

FETHERSTON, JOHN
The Visitation of the County of Cumberland in the Year 1615. 1872. V. 71

FETHERSTONHAUGH, T.
Our Cumberland and Village. Carlisle: 1925. V. 71

FETIS, F. J.
Notice of Anthony Stradivari, the Celebrated Violin Maker, Known by the Name of Stradivarius. London: 1864. V. 72

FETTE, W. ELIOT
Dialogues from Dickens. For School and Home Amusement. Boston: 1870. V. 69

FETTER, VERA
British Prosobranch Molluscs. London: 1962. V. 71

FEUCHTWANGER, LION
Jew Suss: a Historical Romance. London: 1926. V. 70
Raquel the Jewess of Toledo. New York: 1954-1956. V. 73

FEUERSICHERE Joly-Treppen Mit Holzbelag Oder Marmorbelag in Schmiedeeisen-Konstruction.... Wittenberg: 1910. V. 68

FEUSS, CLAUDE M.
The Life of Caleb Cushing. New York: 1923. V. 70

A FEW Facts About Twin Falls County, Idaho. 1909. V. 68

A FEW General Observations on the Principal Railways Executed in Progress and Projected in the Midland Counties and North of England, with the Author's Opinion, Upon Them as Investments. London: 1838. V. 68

A FEW Particulars Concerning Chang-Eng, The United Siamese Brothers. New York: 1836. V. 68

A FEW Words Upon the Examiner's Scandalous Peace. London: 1711. V. 73

FEWKES, JESSE WALTER
Dolls of the Tusayan Indians. Leiden: 1894. V. 68
The Snake Ceremonials at Walpi. Boston: 1894. V. 70

FEYENS, THOMAS
De Viribus Imaginationis Tractatus.... Leyden: 1635. V. 72

FFINCH, MICHAEL
Donald Maxwell 1877-1936. Kendal: 1995. V. 70; 72

FFIRTH, JOHN
Truth Vindicated; or, a Scriptural Essay, Wherein the Vulgar and Frivolous Cavils, Commonly Urged Against the Methodist Episcopal Church.... New York: 1810. V. 69

FFOLLIOT & GALLINA
Deer Biology, Habitat Requirements and Management in Western North America. 1981. V. 72

FFOLLIOTT, WILLIAM
Cartmel Parish and Parish Church: and Sermons Preached Therein. London: 1854. V. 71

FFORDE, JASPER
The Eyre Affair. London: 2001. V. 69; 70; 72; 73
The Eyre Affair. London: 2002. V. 72
The Eyre Affair. New York: 2002. V. 72; 73
Lost in a Good Book. London: 2002. V. 73

FICARRA, BERNARD J.
Essays on Historical Medicine. New York: 1948. V. 71

FICHTE, JOHANN GOTTLIEB
Uber den Begriff der Wissenschaftslehre Oder der Sogenannten Philosophie. (with) *Gundlage der Gesammten Wissenschaftslehre, Als Handschrift fur Seine Zuhorer.* (with) *Grundriss des Eigenthumlichen der Wissenschaftslehre in Rucksicht auf Das Theoretische V.* Weimar: 1794. V. 72

FICKLING, G. G.
Honey West: Girl on the Prowl. New York: 1959. V. 71

FIDO, MARTIN
The Crimes, Detection & Death Of Jack The Ripper. London: 1987. V. 72

FIEDLER, JOHN
Colorado: Images of the Alpine Landscape. Englewood: 1985. V. 68

FIEDLER, MILDRED
Wild Bill and Deadwood. Seattle: 1965. V. 69

FIELD, A. E.
Peaks, Passes and Glaciers by Members of the Alpine Club. (Third Series). London: 1932. V. 69

FIELD, D. J.
The Human House. Boston: 1939. V. 68; 72

FIELD, DAVID DUDLEY
Speeches, Arguments and Miscellaneous Papers. New York: 1884. V. 71

FIELD, EUGENE
Child Verses. Akron: 1931. V. 71
Clippings from Denver Tribune. New York: 1909. V. 71; 73
Little Willie. Washington: 1901. V. 73
My Book. St. Louis: 1905. V. 71; 73
Papillot, Clignot et Dodo. (Wynken, Blynken and Nod). London: 1965. V. 72
Poems of Childhood. New York: 1904. V. 70; 73
Sharps and Flats. New York: 1901. V. 68
The Sugar-Plum Tree and Other Verses. Akron: 1930. V. 71
With Trumpet and Drum. New York: 1892. V. 72

FIELD, GEORGE
Chromatics, or an Essay on the Analogy and Harmony of Colours. London: 1817. V. 71
Chromatics; or, the Analogy, Harmony, and Philosophy of Colours. 1845. V. 72
A Grammar of Colouring Applicable to House Painting, Decorative Architecture and the Arts. London: 1867. V. 69

FIELD, HENRY M.
Bright Skies and Dark Shadows. New York: 1890. V. 69; 70
The Irish Confederates and the Rebellion of 179. New York: 1851. V. 71
The Story of the Atlantic Telegraph. New York: 1893. V. 68

FIELD, J. W.
The Microscopic Diagnosis of Human Malaria. Kuala Lumpur: 1948-1956. V. 70; 73

FIELD, JOANNA
A Life of One's Own. London: 1934. V. 73

FIELD, KATE
Pen Photographs of Charles Dickens' Readings. Boston: 1868. V. 69
Pen Photographs of Charles Dickens' Readings. Boston: 1871. V. 69; 70

FIELD, M.
City Architectre or Designs for Dwelling-Houses, Stores, Hotels, etc. New York: 1853. V. 68; 70; 72

FIELD, MATTHEW C.
Prairie and Mountain Sketches. Norman: 1957. V. 69; 71

FIELD, MICHAEL, PSEUD.
Bellerophon. London: 1881. V. 73
Long Ago. London: 1889. V. 73

FIELD, RACHEL
All This and Heaven Too. New York: 1938. V. 70; 71
All This and Heaven Too. New York: 1940. V. 70
Christmas in London. 1946. V. 70
Christmas in London. 1971. V. 70
Hitty Her First Hundred Years. New York: 1929. V. 70; 71
Prayers for a Child. New York: 1944. V. 70
Time Out of Mind. New York: 1935. V. 69

FIELD, RICHARD
Of the Church, Five Bookes. London: 1606. V. 70

FIELD, ROBERT D.
The Art of Walt Disney. London: 1947. V. 70

FIELD, ROSWELL MARTIN
In Sunflower Land. Chicago: 1892. V. 72

FIELD, SAUL
Bloomsday. An Interpretation of James Joyce's Ulysses. Greenwich: 1972. V. 72

FIELD, STEPHEN J.
Personal Reminiscences of Early Days in California with Other Sketches. San Francisco: 1880. V. 72
Personal Reminiscences of Early Days in California with Other Sketches. Washington: 1893. V. 73

FIELD, THOMAS W.
Field Indian Bibliography. Columbus: 1951. V. 73
A Manual for the Propagations, Planing, Cultivation and Management of the Pear Tree. New York: 1859. V. 72

FIELD, WILLIAM B. OSGOOD
Edward Lear On My Shelves. Munich: 1933. V. 72

FIELDING, A.
The Eames-Erskine Case. New York: 1925. V. 69

FIELDING, CHARLES JOHN
The Brothers, an Eclogue. London: 1781. V. 73

FIELDING, HELEN
Bridget Jones. 2000. V. 72
Bridget Jones's Diary. New York: 1996. V. 69
Cause Celeb. London: 1994. V. 69; 72

FIELDING, HENRY
Amelia. London: 1752. V. 70; 71; 72
Amelia. London: 1771. V. 69
Amelie, a Roman. Paris: 1764. V. 73
An Apology for the Life of Mrs. Shamela Andrews. London: 1925. V. 71
An Apology for the Life of Mrs. Shamela Andrews. Waltham St. Lawrence: 1925. V. 68
A Charge Delivered to the Grand Jury, at the Sessions of the Peace, Held for the City and Liberty of Westminster &c. on Thursday the 29th June 1749. London: 1749. V. 73
An Enquiry Into the Causes of the Late Increase of Robbers, &c. London: 1751. V. 69
Histoire de Tom Jones, ou L'Enfant Trouve.... Amsterdam: 1750. V. 69
The History of the Adventures of Joseph Andrews and His Friend Mr. Ab raham Adams. London: 1781. V. 69; 70
The History of the Adventures of Joseph Andrews and His Friend Mr. Ab raham Adams. Dresden: 1783. V. 69
The History of the Adventures of Joseph Andrews and His Friend Mr. Abraham Adams. Edinburgh: 1770. V. 69
The History of Tom Jones. London: 1749. V. 68; 71; 73
The History of Tom Jones. London: 1750. V. 69
The History of Tom Jones. London: 1792. V. 70
The History of Tom Jones. London: 1819. V. 71
The History of Tom Jones. London: 1886. V. 68
The History of Tom Jones. London: 1934. V. 71
An Inquiry Into the Cause of the Late Increase of Robbers &c.... London: 1751. V. 68; 72
The Journal of a Voyage to Lisbon. London: 1755. V. 70
A Journey From This World to the Next. London: 1930. V. 71
A Journey from this World to the Next. Waltham St. Lawrence: 1930. V. 68; 71; 72
The Life of Mr. Jonathan Wild the Great. Waltham St. Lawrence: 1932. V. 69
The Works. London: 1902-1903. V. 73
The Works. (with) *Miscellanies and Poems.* London: 1871-1872. V. 68; 72

FIELDING, LORAINE HORNADAY
French Heels to Spurs. New York: 1930. V. 71

FIELDING, SARAH
The Governess. London: 1789. V. 73
The Governess. Dublin: 1804. V. 72
The Governess. London: 1968. V. 71
The Lives of Cleopatra and Octavia. London: 1757. V. 69
The Lives of Cleopatra and Octavia. London: 1758. V. 73

FIELDING, T. H.
Cumberland, Westmorland and Lancashire Illustrated in a Series of Forty-Four Engravings, Exhibiting Scenery of the Lakes, Antiquities and Other Picturesque Objects. London: 1822. V. 70
The Knowledge and Restoration of Old Paintings, the Modes of Judging Between Copies and Originals and a Brief Life of the Principal Masters in the Different Schools of Painting. London: 1847. V. 69; 73
A Picturesque Description of the River Wye, from the Source to Its Junction with the Severn. London: 1841. V. 71

FIELDING DICKENS, HENRY
The Recollections of Sir Henry Dickens. London: 1934. V. 68

FIELDING HALL, H.
Margaret's Book. London: 1913. V. 71

FIELDS, ANNIE
Life and Letters of Harriet Beecher Stowe. Boston and New York: 1897. V. 70

FIELDS, JAMES T.
Yesterdays with Authors. Boston and New York: 1901. V. 68; 70

FIELDS, JOSEPH
The Ponder Heart: a New Comedy. New York: 1956. V. 73

FIENNES, NATHANIEL
A Most True and Exact Relation of Both the Battels Fought by His Excellency and His Forces Against the Bloudy Cavelliers. London: 1642. V. 70

FIERA, BATTISTA
De Iusticia Pingenda. 1957. V. 71
De Iusticia Pingenda - on the Painting of Justice a Dialogue Between Montegna and Momus. London: 1957. V. 69

FIERSTEIN, HARVEY
Safe Sex. New York: 1987. V. 69

FIFE, AUSTIN
Saints of Sage and Saddle: Folklore Among the Mormons. Bloomington: 1956. V. 69

FIFE, JOHN
Manual of the Turkish Bath. London: 1865. V. 68

FIFE-COOKSON, J. C.
Tiger Shooting in the Doon and Ulwar. 1887. V. 73

FIFOOT, RICHARD
A Bibliography of Edith, Osbert and Sacheverell Sitwell. London: 1971. V. 72

FIFTY Years: a Farrar Straus Giroux Reader. New York: 1996. V. 70

FIFTY Years of Bauhaus.... Toronto: 1969-1970. V. 72

FIFTY Years of Schwinn-Built Bicycles. Chicago: 1945. V. 69

FIGG, ROYAL W.
Where Men Only Dare to Go!. Richmond: 1885. V. 69

FIGGIS, DARRELL
The Paintings of William Blake. 1925. V. 69
The Paintings of William Blake. London: 1925. V. 72

THE FIGHTING Norths And Pawnee Scouts - Narratives And Reminiscences Of Military Service On The Old Frontier. New York: 1932. V. 72

FIGUIER, LOUIS
Le Merveilles de la Science ou Description Populaire des Inventions Modernes. Paris: 1868. V. 70
The Ocean World.... London: 1872. V. 68

FILHOL, ANTOINE MICHEL
Galerie Du Musee de France. Paris: 1814-1815. V. 71
Galerie Du Musee Napoleon. Paris: 1804-1815. V. 71

FILIPPI, F. DE
The Ascent of Mount St. Elias (Alaska) by H.R.H. Prince Luigi Amedeo Di Savoia Duke of the Abruzzi. 1900. V. 68; 70; 73
Il Ruwenzori. Milan: 1908. V. 69
The Italian Expedition to the Himalaya, Karakoram and Eastern Turkestan (1913-1914). London: 1932. V. 72
Karakoram and the Western Himalaya. 1912. V. 68; 70; 73

FILIPPINI, ALESSANDRO
The Table: How to Buy Food, How to Cook It, and How to Serve It. New York: 1889. V. 68

FILISOLA, VICENTE
The History of the War in Texas. Austin: 1987. V. 70

FILLEY, WILLIAM
Life and Adventures of...Who Was Stolen from His Home in Jackson, Michigan by the Indians August 3d, 1837 and His Safe Return from Captivity, October 19, 1866. Chicago: 1867. V. 68; 69

FILLMORE, A. D.
Temperance Musician: a Choice Collection of Original and Select Temperance Music. Cincinnati: 1854. V. 70

FILMER, HENRY
Escape to Cairo. Indianapolis: 1938. V. 69

FILSON, JOHN
Histoire De Kentucke, Nouvelle Colonie a l'Ouest de la Virginie.... Paris: 1785. V. 68; 73

FINAUGHTY, WILLIAM
Recollections of William Finaughty, Elephant Hunter 1864-1875. 1957. V. 70
Recollections of William Finaughty, Elephant Hunter, 1864-1875. South Africa: 1957. V. 72

FINBERG, ALEX J.
The Life of J. M. W. Turner, R. A. Oxford: 1961. V. 70; 72
Turner's Watercolours at Farnley Hall. London. V. 72; 73

FINCASTLE, VISCOUNT
A Frontier Campaign. London: 1898. V. 70

FINCH, CHARLOTTE
Gamut and Time-Table in Verse. London: 1820. V. 71; 73

FINCH, CHRISTOPHER
The Art of Walt Disney. New York: 1973. V. 69; 71

FINCH, GEORGE INGLE
The Making of a Mountaineer. London: 1924. V. 68; 69
The Making of a Mountaineer. London: 1927. V. 69

FINCH, JOHN
To South Africa and Back. 1890. V. 72

FINCH, MARIANNE
An Englishwoman's Experience in America. London: 1853. V. 68

FINCH, ROBERT
Outlands. Boston: 1986. V. 72
The Primal Place. New York: 1983. V. 69

FINCHAM, H. W.
The Order of the Hospital of St. John of Jerusalem and Its Grand Priory of England. Collingridge: 1915. V. 73

FINCK, HENRY T.
Food and Flavor: a Gastronomic Guide to Health and Good Living. New York: 1913. V. 69

FINDLAY, W. P. K.
Wayside and Woodland Fungi. London: 1967. V. 69; 70

FINDLEY, PALMER
The Story of Childbirth. Garden City: 1933. V. 68

FINDLEY, TIMOTHY
The Butterfly Plague. New York: 1969. V. 69; 72

FINDLEY, WILLIAM
History of the Insurrection in the Western Counties of Pennsylvania in the Year 1794. Philadelphia: 1796. V. 68; 69

THE FINE Gentleman's Etiquette; or, Lord Chesterfield's Advice to His Son, Versified. London: 1776. V. 69

FINE, ORONCE
Liber de Geometria Pratica. Argentori: 1544. V. 73

FINEMAN, IRVING
This Pure Young Man. New York: 1930. V. 69

FINER, HERMAN
The Theory and Practice of Modern Government. London: 1932. V. 70

FINERTY, JOHN F.
War Path & Bivouac, or the Conquest of the Sioux. Chicago: 1890. V. 69; 72

FINGER, CHARLES J.
The Affair At the Inn. Camden NJ: 1937. V. 72

FINGER, F. L.
Catalogue of the Incunabula in the Elmer Belt Library of Vinciana. Los Angeles: 1971. V. 72

FINK, B.
The Lichens of Minnesota. Washington: 1910. V. 68; 71

FINK, LARRY
Social Graces. Rochester: 1984. V. 73

FINLAY, G.
History of Greece. B.C. 146 to A.D. 1864. Oxford: 1877. V. 71

FINLAY, IAN HAMILTON
The Dancers Inherit the Party. London: 1969. V. 72
Ian Hamilton Finlay - A visual primer. London: 1992. V. 72

FINLAYSON, CHARLES P.
Clement Litill and His Library. The Origins of Edinburgh University Library. Edinburgh: 1980. V. 70

FINLINSON, HAROLD
With Pen and Ink in Iraq.... Bangalore: 1918. V. 72

FINN, FRANK
Indian Sporting Birds. Calcutta: 1915. V. 73

FINNERTY, PETER
Case of Peter Finnerty, Including a Full Report of All the Proceedings Which Took Place in the Court of King's Bench Upon the Subject.... London: 1811. V. 70

FINNEY, CHARLES G.
The Circus of Doctor Lao. New York: 1935. V. 69; 71
The Circus of Dr. Lao. 1982. V. 71
The Circus of Dr. Lao. Newark: 1984. V. 72; 73
Past the End of the Pavement. New York: 1939. V. 68

FINNEY, JACK
Assault On a Queen. New York: 1959. V. 69
5 Against the House. Garden City: 1954. V. 71
Good Neighbor Sam. London: 1963. V. 69
Marion's Wall. New York: 1973. V. 71
The Night People. Garden City: 1977. V. 71; 73
Time and Again. New York: 1970. V. 68; 69; 71
Time and Again. London: 1980. V. 68; 71

FINNEY, PATRICIA
Unicorn's Blood. London: 1998. V. 72

FINOT, JEAN
Race Prejudice. London: 1906. V. 71

FINOTTI, JOSEPH
The Mystery of the Wizard Clip. (Smithfield, W.Va.). Batlimore: 1879. V. 73

FINSCH, O.
Beitrag zur Fauna Centralpolynesiens, Ornithologie des Viti-Samoa- und Tonga-Inseln. Halle: 1867. V. 73

FIOCCO, ANDREA DOMENICO LUCIUS
Fenestellae de Magistratibus Sacerdotiisq; Romanoru Libellus, iam Primum Nitori Restituts. (with) *Pomponii Laetide Romanorum Legibus, Libellus.* Augsburg: 1533. V. 68

FIOROVANTI, LEONARDO
De Capricci Medicinali Dell' Eccellente Medico & Cirugico Messer Leonardo Fioruanti Bolognese. Venetia: 1629. V. 71

FIRBANK, RONALD
The Artificial Princess. London: 1934. V. 69; 72
Caprice. London: 1917. V. 69
Concerning the Eccentricities of Cardinal Pirelli. 1926. V. 68; 69
Five Novels - Valmouth; The Flower Beneath the Foot; Prancing Nigger; Concerning the Eccentricities of Cardinal Pirelli; The Artificial Princess. London: 1949. V. 68
The Flower Beneath the Foot. 1923. V. 68
The Flower Beneath the Foot. London: 1923. V. 69
The Flower Beneath the Foot. New York: 1924. V. 68; 71; 72
Inclinations. London: 1916. V. 69
Letters to His Mother 1920-1924. Verona: 2001. V. 73
Odette, a Fairy Tale for Weary People. 1916. V. 68; 71
Odette: a Fairy Tale for Weary People. London: 1916. V. 68; 69; 70
Prancing Nigger. New York: 1924. V. 69
The Princess Zoubaroff; a Comedy. London: 1920. V. 69
Santal. London: 1921. V. 69; 70
Sorrow in Sunlight. London: 1924. V. 69
Three Novels - Vainglory, Inclinations (and) Caprice. London: 1950. V. 68
Two Early Stories. New York: 1971. V. 69
Valmouth. 1919. V. 68
Valmouth. London: 1919. V. 72
When Widows Love and A Tragedy in Green: Two Stories. London: 1980. V. 69

FIRDUSI
The Epic of Kings: Stories Retold from Firdusi by Helen Zimmern. London: 1882. V. 68
Roostum Zaboolee and Soohrab, from the History of Persia, Entitled Shah Namuh; or, Book of Kings.... Calcutta: 1829. V. 68

FIREFIGHTING in Johnson County, Kansas. 1978. V. 69

FIREMAN, JANET R.
The Spanish Royal Corps of Engineers in the Western Borderlands. Glendale: 1977. V. 69

FIRISHTAH, MUHAMMAD KASIM IBN HINDU SHAH, ASTARABADI
The History of Hindostan: from the Earliest Account of Time to the Death of Akbar. London: 1768. V. 70

FIRMINGER, T. A. C.
A Manual of Gardening for Bengal and Upper India. London: 1864. V. 71

FIRPO, LUIGI
Medicina Medievale. Torino: 1971. V. 72

FIRSOFF, V. A.
The Cairngorms on Foot and Ski. London: 1949. V. 69

THE FIRST Blossoms of Learning.... Philadelphia: 1835. V. 71

THE FIRST Crusade: the Deeds of the Franks and Other Jerusalemites. Waltham St. Lawrence: 1945. V. 71

FIRST Lady. A Portrait of Nancy Reagan. New York: 1986. V. 69; 71

FIRST Over Everest. London: 1933. V. 69

FIRST Over Everest. London: 1934. V. 69

THE FIRST Spanish Entry Into San Francisco Bay, 1775. San Francisco: 1971. V. 72

FIRST Steps of Our Little Ones Up the Ladder of Learning. London: 1900. V. 72

FIRST EDITION CLUB, LONDON
Bibliographical Catalogue of First Editions, Proof Copies and Manuscripts of Books by Lord Byron Exhibited at the Fourth Exhibition Held by the First Edition Club, January 1925. London: 1935. V. 71

FIRTH, F.
Art and Life in New Guinea. London: 1936. V. 69

FISCHER, BRUNO
Murder In The Raw. Greenwich: 1957. V. 72

FISCHER, CHARLES
Trips. 1994. V. 73

FISCHER, EDGAR H.
A Selection from the Collection of Animals and Birds to H. M. the King. London: 1920. V. 73

FISCHER, JOHANNES KARL
Dispuratio Inauguralis de Natura, Constitutione et Usu Logarithmorum. Jena: 1788. V. 71

FISCHER, JOSEPH
The Discoveries of the Norsemen in America with Special Relation to their Early Cartographical Representation. London: 1903. V. 73

FISCHER, TIBOR
The Collector Collector. London: 1997. V. 68

FISCHER, W.
Bau, Raum, Gerat. Munchen: 1957. V. 72

FISCHER VON ERLACH, JOHANN BERNHARD
Entwurff Einer Historischen Architektur, in Abbildung Unterschiedener Beruhmten Gebaude.... Leipzig: 1725. V. 68; 70; 72

FISH, ROBERT
Mute Witness. Garden City: 1963. V. 71

FISH, ROBERT L.
The Incredible Schlock Holmes With Introduction By Anthony Boucher. New York: 1966. V. 68; 69; 71; 72
The Memoirs of Schlock Homes. Indianapolis: 1974. V. 73

FISH, SIMON
A Supplicacyon for the Beggars. London: 1845. V. 72

FISH, WILLIAM A.
A Memoir of Butler Wilmarth, M.D. One of the Victims of the Late Terrible Railroad Catastrophe at Norwalk Bridge, Ct. Boston: 1854. V. 69

FISHBEIN, MORRIS
Doctors at War. New York: 1943. V. 68

FISHER, AILEEN
My Cat Has Eyes of Sapphire Blue. New York: 1973. V. 73

FISHER, ALEXANDER
The Art of Enamelling Upon Metal with a Short Appendix.... London: 1905. V. 69
A Journal of a Voyage of Discovery, in the Arctic Regions in His Majesty's Ships Hecla dn Griper, in the Years 1819 and 1820. London: 1821. V. 68

FISHER, ARISTA EDWARD
To The Sun. New York: 1929. V. 72

FISHER, F. H.
Reginald Farrer, Author, Traveller, Botanist and Flower Painter. With Additional Notes by E.H.M. Cox and W. E. Th. Ingwersen. London: 1932. V. 72

FISHER, GEORGE
The Instructor, or, Young Man's Best Companion. London: 1750. V. 69

FISHER, GEORGE ADAMS
Yankee Conscript: or Eighteen Months in Dixie. Philadelphia: 1864. V. 70

FISHER, HARRISON
Fair Americans. New York: 1911. V. 69

FISHER, HENRY W.
Abroad with Mark Twain and Eugene Field. New York: 1922. V. 73

FISHER, J.
The Fulmar. London: 1952. V. 73

FISHER, J. HERBERT
Ophthalmological Anatomy with Some Illustrative Causes. London: 1904. V. 71

FISHER, JAMES
Poems on Various Subjects, by James Fisher. Dumfries: 1790. V. 69

FISHER, MARGERY
Shackleton. London: 1957. V. 72

FISHER, MARY
Tales, Local and Legendary; with Miscellaneous Poems. Carlisle: 1860. V. 71

FISHER, MARY FRANCES KENNEDY
The Art of Eating. New York: 1979. V. 71
A Considerable Town. New York: 1978. V. 71
The Gastronomical Me. New York: 1943. V. 72
Here Let Us Feast. Berkeley: 1986. V. 72
How to Cook a Wolf. New York: 1942. V. 70
Spirits of the Valley. New York: 1985. V. 73
With Bold Knife & Fork. New York: 1969. V. 73

FISHER, O. C.
The Speaker of Nubbin Ridge. San Angelo: 1985. V. 70
Texas Emigrant Guides: 1840-1841. Waco: 1964. V. 70
The Texas Heritage of the Fishers and Clarks. Salano: 1963. V. 68; 70; 73

FISHER, P.
The Angler's Souvenir. 1890. V. 68; 73

FISHER, PETER
The History of New Brunswick. St. John: 1921. V. 73

FISHER, REGINALD
The Way of the Cross: a New Mexico Version. Santa Fe: 1958. V. 69; 70

FISHER, RICHARD
Catalogue of a Collection of Engravings, Etchings, and Woodcuts. London: 1879. V. 70

FISHER, RONALD AYLMER
The Genetical Theory of Natural Selection. Oxford: 1930. V. 69

FISHER, RONALD AYLMER continued
The Theory of Inbreeding. London and Edinburgh: 1949. V. 69

FISHER, ROY
The Ship's Orchestra. London: 1966. V. 72

FISHER, RUTH
Stalin and German Communism. A Study in the Origins of the State Party. Cambridge: 1948. V. 68

FISHER SCIENTIFIC COMPANY
Modern Laboratory Appliances for Chemical, Biological, Metallurgical Laboratories. Pittsburgh and Montreal. V. 69

FISHER, STANLEY
Beat Coast: an Anthology of Rebellion. New York: 1960. V. 71

FISHER, STANLEY A.
In the Beginning a Navaho Creation Myth. 1953. V. 69

FISHER, STANLEY W.
English Blue and White Porcelain of the 18th Century. London: 1947. V. 72

FISHER, STEVE
Destination Tokyo. New York: 1943. V. 71; 73
Giveaway. New York: 1954. V. 71
I Wake Up Screaming. New York: 1941. V. 70
No House Limit: a Novel of Las Vegas. New York: 1958. V. 69; 70; 71
Winter Kill. New York: 1946. V. 69; 71

FISHER, T. E.
Picturesque Colorado. 1910. V. 68

FISHER, VARDIS
Children of God. New York: 1939. V. 68
City of Illusion. New York: 1941. V. 69
Gold Rushes and Mining Camps of the Early American West. Caldwell: 1968. V. 69

FISHER, W. K.
Starfishes of the Philippine Seas and Adjacent Waters. Washington: 1919. V. 69; 73

THE FISHERMAN'S Bedside Book. 1945. V. 70

FISHING MASTERS' ASSOCIATION
Fishermen of the Atlantic. A Manual of Information, Issued Annually.... Boston: 1913. V. 69

FISHWICK, HENRY
A History of Lancashire. Popular County Histories. London: 1894. V. 73
The History of the Parish of Bispham in the County of Lancaster. London: 1887. V. 73
The History of the Parish of Kirkham in the County of Lancaster. London: 1874. V. 73
The History of the Parish of Poulton-Le-Fylde, in the County of Lancaster. London: 1885. V. 73
The History of the Parish of Preston in Amounderness in the County of Lancaster. 1900. V. 73
Lancashire & Cheshire Church Surveys. 1649-1655. London: 1879. V. 73
Pleadings and Depositions in the Duchy Court of Lancaster Time of Henry VII and Henry VIII. London: 1896. V. 73
A Record of Fifty Years Municipal Work, 1856 to 1906. Manchester: 1906. V. 73

FISK, CLINTON B.
Plain Counsels for Freedmen: in Sixteen Brief Lectures. Boston: 1866. V. 70

FISK, FRED
The History of Tottenham. Tottenham: 1913. V. 70

FISKE, DWIGHT
Why Should Penguins Fly?. New York: 1936. V. 70
Without Music. New York: 1933. V. 73

FISKE, J. W.
Illustrated Catalogue and Price List of Ornamental Iron and Zinc Vases, Manufactured by J. W. Fiske Iron Works..39 and 41 Park Place, Near Church Street, New York. New York: 1890-1900. V. 68; 70

FISKE, JOHN
Darwinism and Other Essays. London: 1879. V. 69

FITCH, A. J. H., MRS.
Memoir of Lieut. Edward Lewis Mitchell, Who Fell at the Battle of Shiloh, Aged Twenty-Two Years. New York: 1864. V. 69; 70

FITCH, JANET
White Oleander. 1999. V. 72
White Oleander. Boston: 1999. V. 68

FITCH, MICHAEL HENDRICK
Ranch Life and Other Sketches. 1914. V. 68

FITCH, SAMUEL S.
Six Discourses On The functions Of The Lungs. London: 1852. V. 72
A Treatise of the Causes and Curability of the Heart, Stomach, Liver, Bowels, Kidneys &c.... London: 1861. V. 68

FITE, EMERSON D.
A Book of Old Maps Delineating American History from the Earliest Days Down to the Close of the Revolutionary War. Cambridge: 1926. V. 71

FITHIAN, PHILIP VICKERS
Philip Vickers Fithian Journal and Letters 1767-1774. Princeton: 1900. V. 69

FITT, J. N.
Covert-Side Sketches or Thoughts on Hunting Suggested by Many Days in Many Countries with Fox, Deer and Hare. 1879. V. 68

FITZBALL, EDWARD
Joan of Arc, or, the Maid of Orleans. London: 1823. V. 70

FITZ-BARNARD, C. L.
Fighting Sports - Cock Fighting, Dog Fighting, Bull Fighting, ManFighting etc. 1920. V. 73

FITZELL, LINCOLN
In Plato's Garden. Poems 1928-1939. Albuquerque: 1940. V. 68

FITZGERALD, E. A.
Climbs in the New Zealand Alps: Being an Account of Travel and Discovery By.... 1896. V. 68; 70; 73
The Highest Andes. 1899. V. 68; 70; 73
The Highest Andes. London: 1899. V. 69; 72

FITZGERALD, EDWARD
A Fitzgerald Friendship - Being Hietherto Unpublished Letters from Edward Fitzgerald to William Bodham Donne. London: 1932. V. 69
Letters and Literary Remains. London: 1902-1903. V. 73
Polonius: a Collection of Wise Saws and Modern Instances. London: 1852. V. 72
Polonius: A Collection of Wise Saws and Modern Instances. Portland, Maine: 1901. V. 71

FITZGERALD, FRANCES
Fire in the Lake. The Vietnamese and the Americans in Vietnam. Boston: 1972. V. 69; 72

FITZGERALD, FRANCIS SCOTT KEY
Afternoon of an Author: a Selection of Uncollected Stories and Essays. Princeton: 1957. V. 69
All the Sad Young Men. New York: 1926. V. 72
The Basil and Josephine Stories. New York: 1973. V. 68; 72
The Beautiful and the Damned. New York: 1922. V. 68; 69; 72; 73
Bits of Paradise. New York: 1973. V. 72
Borrowed Time: Short Stories Selected by Alan and Jenifer Ross. London: 1951. V. 72
Dear Scott/Dear Max. New York: 1971. V. 72
F. Scott Fitzgerald. A Life in Letters. New York: 1994. V. 72
F. Scott Fitzgerald's Preface to This Side of Paradise. Iowa City: 1975. V. 73
The Great Gatsby. New York: 1925. V. 69; 70; 71; 73
The Great Gatsby. New York: 1980. V. 72
The Letters of F. Scott Fitzgerald. London: 1964. V. 72
Letters to His Daughter. New York: 1965. V. 69
The Short Stories of F. Scott Fitzgerald. New York: 1989. V. 72
The Stories of F. Scott Fitzgerald. New York: 1951. V. 73
Tales of the Jazz Age. New York: 1922. V. 68
Tender is the Night. New York: 1934. V. 69; 70
Tender is the Night. New York: 1982. V. 71; 72
This Side of Paradise. New York: 1920. V. 70; 71
This Side of Paradise. London: 1921. V. 73
This Side of Paradise. New York: 1931. V. 69; 70; 72
The Vegetable or from President to Postman. New York: 1923. V. 73

FITZGERALD, NIGEL
The Student Body. London: 1958. V. 69

FITZGERALD, PENELOPE
Edward Burne-Jones - a Biography. London: 1975. V. 69; 72

FITZGERALD, PERCY
Bardell and Pickwick. London: 1902. V. 69
The Book Fancier. Philadelphia. V. 68
The Book Fancier or the Romance of Book Collecting. London: 1886. V. 69; 71
Bozland: Dickens' Places and People. London: 1895. V. 69
A Critical Examination of Dr. G. Birkbeck Hill's Johnsonian Editions. London: 1898. V. 71
Henry Irving. London: 1893. V. 72
The History of Pickwick. London: 1891. V. 69
The Life of Charles Dickens. London: 1905. V. 68
The Life of James Boswell (of Auchinleck) with an Account of His Sayings, Doings and Writings. London: 1891. V. 68
The Life of Mrs. Catherine Clive with an Account of Her Adventures on and Off the Stage a Round of her Characters Together with Her Correspondence. London: 1888. V. 72
Memories of Charles Dickens. London: 1913. V. 68
Pickwickian Manners and Customs. London: 1897. V. 69
Pickwickian Studies. London: 1899. V. 69
Recreations of a Literary Man, or, Doest Writing Pay?. London: 1882. V. 69
The Second Mrs. Tillotson. London: 1906. V. 68

FITZGERALD, RUTH C.
A Black History of Fredericksburg, Stafford and Spotsylvania, Virginia. 1979. V. 71

FITZ-GERALD, S. J. ADAIR
Dickens and the Drama. London: 1910. V. 68

FITZGERALD, WILLIAM
Gentlemen All. New York: 1930. V. 71

FITZGIBBON, GERALD
Ireland in 1868, the Battle-Field for English Party Strife.... London: 1868. V. 71

FITZ HERBERT, ANTHONY
New Natura Brevium of the Most Reverend Judge, Mr. Anthony Fitz- Herbert.... London: 1687. V. 69

FITZHERBERT, ANTHONY
The New Natura Brevium.... London: 1677. V. 73
L'Office & Auctority de Iustices de Peace. London: 1593. V. 70; 72

FITZHUGH, BESSIE LEE
Bells Over Texas. El Paso: 1955. V. 69

FITZHUGH, GEORGE
Cannibals All!. Richmond: 1857. V. 71

FITZMAURICE, GEORGE
The Plays of George Fitzmaurice. 1967-1970. V. 69

FITZPATRICK, GEORGE
Pictorial New Mexico. Santa Fe: 1949. V. 69

FITZPATRICK, T. J.
Rafinesque a Sketch of His Life with Bibliography. Des Moines: 1911. V. 70

FITZPATRICK, WILLIAM JOHN
Lady Morgan: Her Career Literary and Personal. London: 1860. V. 69

FITZROY, ROBERT
The Weather Book; a Manual of Practical Meteorology. London: 1863. V. 73

FITZSIMMONS, CORTLAND
Death Rings a Bell. Philadelphia: 1942. V. 68
The Evil Men Do. New York: 1941. V. 71
Sudden Silence. New York: 1938. V. 69

FITZSIMONS, F. W.
The Monkey Folk of South Africa. London: 1911. V. 69

FITZSIMONS, V. F. M.
Snakes of Southern Africa. Cape Town: 1962. V. 69
Snakes of Southern Africa. London: 1962. V. 69

FITZ-STEPHEN, WILLIAM
Fitz-Stephen's Description of the City of London, newly translated. London: 1772. V. 71

FIVE Cummington Poems 1939. Cummington;: 1939. V. 73

FIVE Hundred Sketches and Skeletons of Sermons, Suited for All Occasions.... New York: 1856. V. 69

FLACK, PETER
Heart of An African Hunter. 2000. V. 70; 72; 73

FLAGG, FANNIE
Coming Attractions. New York: 1981. V. 69; 70
Fried Green Tomatoes at the Whistle Stop Cafe. New York: 1987. V. 69; 70

FLAGG, OSCAR H.
A Review of the Cattle Business in Johnson County, Wyoming.... Cheyenne: 1967. V. 71

FLAGG, WILLIAM J.
Three Seasons in European Vineyards. New York: 1869. V. 68

FLAHERTY, FRANCES
Sabu the Elephant Boy. New York: 1937. V. 72

FLAHERTY, ROBERT
The Captain's Chair - a Story of the North. London: 1938. V. 68

FLAMEN, ALBERT
Poissons Diverses Especies de Poissons de Mer (...de Poissons d'eau Douce) Designes et Graves Apres le Naturel. Paris: 1664. V. 68; 69

FLANAGAN, JAMES L.
Speech Synthesis and Perception. Berlin: 1972. V. 68

FLANDERS, HELEN HARTNESS
Fifteen Songs from Looking Out of Jimmie. New York: 1929. V. 70

FLANDERS, RALPH BETTS
Plantation Slavery in Georgia. Chapel Hill: 1933. V. 68

FLANIGAN, J. H.
Mormonism Triumphant! Truth Vindicated, Lies refuted, the Devil Mad and Priest Craft in Danger!!!. Liverpool: 1849. V. 68

FLANIGAN, JAMES C.
History of Gwinnett County, Georgia. Hapeville: 1943-1959. V. 72

FLANNEL Flowers and Other Bush Babies. Sydney: 1917. V. 72

FLANNER, HILDEGARDE
Young Girl and Other Poems. San Francisco: 1920. V. 69

FLANNER, JANET
London Was Yesterday: 1934-1939. New York: 1975. V. 71
Men and Monuments. New York: 1957. V. 69; 72; 73
Paris Was Yesterday. New York: 1972. V. 71; 72
What's Wrong with France?. New York: 1945. V. 71

FLANNERY, I. G.
John Hunton's Diary 1876-1877 Vol II. Linske, WY: 1959. V. 72

FLATHER, JOHN J.
Dynamometers and the Measurement of Power: a Treatise on the Construction and Application of Dynamometers. New York: 1892. V. 68

FLAUBERT, GUSTAVE
Bouvard and Pechuchet. London: 1936. V. 72
Madame Bovary. Paris: 1857. V. 68
Madame Bovary. London: 1886. V. 72
Madame Bovary. New York: 1950. V. 69; 72
Salambo. London: 1886. V. 68
Salambo. New York: 1930. V. 72
Salambo. Waltham St. Lawrence: 1931. V. 68; 70; 71
Salambo. 1960. V. 71

FLAVEL, JOHN
Husbandry Spiritualized; or, the Heavenly Use of Earthly Things. Elizabeth Town: 1794. V. 69
Husbandry Spiritualized; or, the Heavenly Use of Earthly Things. Elizabethtown: 1795. V. 69
Navigation Spiritualized; or a New Compass for Seamen. London: 1825. V. 68

FLAXMAN, JOHN
Anatomical Studies of the Bones and Muscles for the Use of Artists from Drawings.... London: 1833. V. 69
Lectures on Sculpture. London: 1829. V. 69; 70; 72; 73

FLAXMAN, WILLIAM
Catalogue of the Valuable Collection of Books, Chiefly Historical and Topographical, The Property of William Flaxman, Esq. of Norfolk...Which Will Be Sold by Auction by Mr. Dodd at His Room No. 101, St. Martin's Lane.... London: 1809. V. 70

FLECKER, JAMES ELROY
The Bridge of Fire. London: 1907. V. 73
Don Juan: a Play in Three Acts. London: 1926. V. 73
Forty-Two Poems. 1911. V. 70
Forty-Two Poems. London: 1911. V. 72; 73
The Golden Journey to Samarkand. 1913. V. 73
The Golden Journey to Samarkand. London: 1913. V. 68
Hassan: The Story of Hassan of Bagdad. London: 1923. V. 68
Hassan. The Story of Hassan of Bagdad. London: 1924. V. 69
The Old Ships. 1915. V. 73
Thirty Six (sic) Poems. 1910. V. 73

FLEET, CHARLES
Glimpses of Our Sussex Ancestors, First and Second and Series. Lewes: 1882-1883. V. 70

FLEETWOOD, W.
A Sermon Preach'd at St. Paul's Cathedral, January 30, 1698/99. 1698-1699. V. 73

FLEG, EDMOND
The Boy Prophet. New York: 1929. V. 71; 72

FLEISCHMAN, A. S.
Yellow Leg. Greenwich, CT: 1960. V. 71

FLEMING, A. B., & CO., LTD.
Specimens of High-Class Chromo-Litho and Poster Printing Inks. Edinburgh and London. V. 70; 72

FLEMING, ALEXANDER
Penicillin. Its Practical Application. London: 1946. V. 69; 70; 72

FLEMING, AMBROSE
Memories of A Scientific Life. London: 1934. V. 72

FLEMING, ARCHIBALD LANG
A Book of Remembrance or The History of St. John's Church, Saint John New Brunswick. Saint John: 1925. V. 73

FLEMING, C. A.
George Edward Lodge, the Unpublished New Zealand Bird Paintings. 1982. V. 69
George Edward Lodge, Unpublished Bird Paintings. 1983. V. 70

FLEMING, DANIEL
The Memoirs of Sir Daniel Fleming. CWAAS Tract Series, No. XI. Kendal: 1928. V. 72

FLEMING, DAVID HAY
St. Andrews Cathedral Museum. London: 1931. V. 71

FLEMING, ELVIS E.
Roundup On the Pecos. Roswell, NM: 1978. V. 68; 71

FLEMING, FRANCIS PHILLIP
Memoir of Capt. C. Seton Fleming, of the Second Florida Infantry, C.S.A. Jacksonville: 1884. V. 69

FLEMING, IAN LANCASTER
Address Given at the Memorial Service for Ian Fleming. 1964. V. 73
Casino Royale. London: 1953. V. 73
Casino Royale. Live and Let Die. Moonraker. Diamonds are Forever. From Russia with Love. Dr. Goldfinger. For Your Eyes Only. Thunderball. The Spy Who loved Me. On Her Majesty's Secret Service. You Only Live Twice. The Man with the Golden Gun. Octopussy. London: 1953-1956. V. 70
Chitty Chitty Bang Bang. London: 1964. V. 70
Chitty Chitty Bang Bang. New York: 1964. V. 69
Diamonds are Forever. London: 1956. V. 70
Dr. No. 1958. V. 72
For Your Eyes Only. London: 1960. V. 69; 70; 71; 72; 73
For Your Eyes Only. New York: 1960. V. 69
From Russia, with Love. New York: 1957. V. 69
Goldfinger. London: 1959. V. 69; 70; 72; 73

FLEMING, IAN LANCASTER continued
Goldfinger. New York: 1959. V. 71
Ian Fleming Introduces Jamaica. London: 1965. V. 69; 70; 72; 73
James Bond For Your 007 Eyes Only. London: 1981. V. 72
Live and Let Die. London: 1954. V. 70; 71
The Man with the Golden Gun. London: 1965. V. 68; 69; 70; 71; 72; 73
The Man with the Golden Gun. New York: 1965. V. 68; 70; 73
Moonraker. London: 1955. V. 69
Octopussy and the Living Daylights. London: 1966. V. 69; 70; 72
On Her Majesty's Secret Service. London: 1963. V. 70; 72; 73
The Property of a Lady. New York: 1964. V. 71
The Spy Who Loved Me. London: 1962. V. 70; 71; 72; 73
Thrilling Cities. London: 1963. V. 70; 71; 72; 73
Thunderball. London: 1961. V. 68; 69; 70; 72; 73
Thunderball. New York: 1961. V. 69
Thunderball. London: 1965. V. 73
You Only Live Twice. London: 1964. V. 68; 69; 70; 72; 73
You Only Live Twice. New York: 1964. V. 73

FLEMING, JOAN
In the Red. London: 1961. V. 73

FLEMING, JOHN
A History of British Animals, Exhibiting the Descriptive Characters and Systematical Arrangement of the Genera and Species of Quadrupeds, Birds, Reptiles, Fishes, Mollusca and Radiata of the United Kingdom.... Edinburgh: 1828. V. 68; 70
The Lithology of Edinburgh. Edinburgh: 1859. V. 68; 70; 71
The Manual of the Kitchen, Fruit and Flower Garden.... Glasgow: 1854. V. 71

FLEMING, LINDSAY
History of Pagham in Sussex. 1949. V. 68

FLEMING, P. L.
Atlantic Canadian Imprints. A Bibliography 1801-1820. Toronto: 1991. V. 72
Upper Canadian Imprints 1801-1841: a Bibliography. Toronto: 1988. V. 70

FLEMING, PETER
The Flying Visit. London: 1940. V. 72; 73
The Sixth Column - a Singular Tale of Our Times. London: 1951. V. 73

FLEMING, R. L.
Birds of Nepal with Reference to Kashmir and Sikkim. Kathmandu: 1984. V. 70

FLEMING, SANDFORD
Report and Documents in Reference to the Canadian Pacific Railway 1880. Ottawa: 1880. V. 73
Report in Reference to the Canadian Pacific Railway. Ottawa: 1879. V. 71
Report of Progress on the Explorations and Surveys Up to January 1874. Ottawa: 1874. V. 71
Reports and Documents in Reference to the Location of the Line and a Western Terminal Harbour. 1878. Ottawa: 1878. V. 71

FLEMING, WALTER
Documentary History of Reconstruction. Cleveland: 1906. V. 69; 70
General W. T. Sherman as College President. Cleveland: 1912. V. 69; 70

FLEMMING, ERNST
Encyclopaedia of Textiles. London: 1958. V. 72

FLENLEY, RALPH
Samuel de Champlain, Founder of New France. Toronto: 1924. V. 73

FLEROV, K. K.
Fauna of the U.S.S.R. Musk Deer and Deer. 1960. V. 69; 70

FLETCHER, A.
Indian Story and Song from North America. Boston: 1907. V. 69

FLETCHER, ARTHUR L.
Ashe County a History. Jefferson: 1963. V. 71

FLETCHER, BANISTER
A History of Architecture on the Comparative Method. London: 1944. V. 70

FLETCHER, C. R. L.
Historical Portraits 1400-1850. With An Introduction on the History of Portraiture in England. Oxford: 1909-1919. V. 72

FLETCHER, CALEB
David, King of Israel: a Sacred Poem, in Twelve Books. York: 1826. V. 69

FLETCHER, DANIEL C.
Reminiscences of California and the Civil War. Ayer: 1894. V. 69

FLETCHER, ELLEN GORDON
A Bride on The Bozeman Trail - The Letters and Diary of Ellen Gordon Fletcher - 1866. Medford, OR: 1970. V. 72

FLETCHER, F. W. F.
Sport on the Nilgiris and Wynaad. 1911. V. 72; 73

FLETCHER, GEORGE U.
The Well of the Unicorn. New York: 1948. V. 71

FLETCHER, H. R.
The Royal Botanic Garden Edinburgh 1670-1970. Edinburgh: 1970. V. 71; 73
The Story of the Royal Horticultural Society 1804-1968. London: 1969. V. 71; 73

FLETCHER, HENRY
The Perfect Politician; or a Full View of the Life and Actions (Military and Civil) of O. Cromwell. London: 1680. V. 69

FLETCHER, HERBERT
The Quest of the Earth's Fullness: the Saga of James Walker Cain. Salado: 1960. V. 68

FLETCHER, IAN
Motets. 1962. V. 69

FLETCHER, INGLIS
Pay, Pack, and Follow: The Story of My Life. New York: 1958. V. 71

FLETCHER, J. J.
The Macleay Memorial Volume. Sydney: 1893. V. 68

FLETCHER, J. S.
Behind the Monocle. 1930. V. 73
Behind the Monocle. Garden City: 1930. V. 68; 71
A Book About Yorkshire. London: 1908. V. 73
The Burma Ruby. London: 1932. V. 69; 73
The Eleventh Hour. New York: 1935. V. 70
Exterior to the Evidence. New York: 1923. V. 68; 69
The Heaven Kissed Hill. New York: 1924. V. 70
The Heaven-Sent Witness. Garden City: 1930. V. 68; 71
The History of the St. Leger Stakes 1776-1901. London: 1902. V. 73
The Investigators. 1930. V. 68
The Making of Matthias. London and New York: 1898. V. 68; 69
Memorial of a Yorkshire Parish. An Historical Sketch of the Parish of Darington. London: 1917. V. 73
The Murder at Wrides Park. New York: 1931. V. 69
Murder in Four Degrees. New York: 1931. V. 68
The Orange-Yellow Diamond. Toronto: 1921. V. 70
Paul Campenhaye. 1918. V. 68
Picturesque History of Yorkshire. London. V. 73

FLETCHER, JOHN
The Difficulties of Protestantism. London: 1829. V. 73
Studies on Slavery.... Natchez: 1852. V. 69

FLETCHER, JOHN GOULD
The Black Rock: Poems. London: 1928. V. 68
Branches of Adam. London: 1926. V. 70; 71
Japanese Prints. Boston: 1918. V. 72

FLETCHER, PHINEAS
Piscatory Eclogues, with Other Poetical Miscellanies. Edinburgh: 1771. V. 71
The Purple Island, or the Isle of Man.... Cambridge: 1633. V. 72

FLETCHER, ROBERT H.
Free Grass to Fences- The Montana Cattle Range Story. New York: 1960. V. 71; 72

FLETCHER, SYDNEY E.
The Cowboy and His Horse. New York: 1951. V. 69

FLETCHER, THOMAS
Coal Gas as a Fuel: A Concise Guide to Fitters and Users. Warrington: 1890. V. 71
Domestic Heating and Cooking Apparatus. Warrington: 1881. V. 69

FLETCHER, WILLIAM ANDREW
Rebel Private Front and Rear. Beaumont: 1908. V. 69; 70
Rebel Private Front and Rear. Austin: 1954. V. 70

FLETCHER, WILLIAM YOUNGER
Bookbinding in France. London: 1894. V. 68; 70
Some Minor Arts as Practised in England. London: 1894. V. 70

FLETT, J. F.
Traditional Dancing in Scotland. London: 1964. V. 72

THE FLEURON. London: 1923. V. 72

FLEURY, CLAUDE
A Short History of the Ancient Israelites with an Account of Their Manners, Customs, Laws.... Burlington: 1813. V. 69

FLEXNER, J. T.
Nineteenth Century American Painting. New York: 1970. V. 69; 72

FLICKINGER, ROBERT E.
The Choctaw Freedman and the Story of Oak Hill Industrial Academy. Pittsburg: 1914. V. 70

FLIET, RUSS
Manual of Woodslore Survival as Developed at Philmont. Cimmaron. V. 69

FLIGHTS of Fancie. London: 1823. V. 68

FLINDERS, MATTHEW
Matthew Flinders' Narrative of His Voyage in the Schooner Francis 1798. Waltham St. Lawrence: 1946. V. 71

FLINT, ABEL
A System of Geometry and Trigonometry: with a Treatise on Surveying. Hartford: 1835. V. 70
A System of Geometry and Trigonometry: with a Treatise on Surveying. Hartford: 1838. V. 70

FLINT, AUSTIN
The Physiology of Man; Designed to Represent the Existing State of Physiological Science as Applied to the Functions of the Human Body. New York: 1870-1874. V. 71

FLINT, CATHERINE SETON
Imps. London. V. 68

FLINT, CHARLES L.
Practical Treatise on Grasses and Forage Plants. New York: 1857. V. 68

FLINT, HELEN
The Angora Twinnies. Rochester: 1915. V. 69
The Betty Fairy Book. New York: 1915. V. 70

FLINT, HENRY M.
Mexico Under Maximilian. Philadelphia: 1867. V. 73

FLINT, JANET A.
The Prints of Louis Lozowick: a Catalogue Raisonne. New York: 1982. V. 73

FLINT, TIMOTHY
Biographical Memoir of Daniel Boone, the First Settler of Kentucky. Cincinnati: 1833. V. 68

FLINT, WILLIAM RUSSELL
The Lisping Goddess. A Figurehead Fantasy. Worcester: 1968. V. 71
Minxes Admonished, or Beauty Reproved. Waltham St. Lawrence: 1955. V. 71
Shadows in Arcady: the Angelus: the Brass Plate: An Alley in Languedoc; The Devil at La Charite. London: 1965. V. 70

FLIPPER, HENRY O.
The Colored Cadet at West Point. New York: 1878. V. 69

THE FLOATING Admiral by Captain Members of the Detective Club. London: 1931. V. 71

FLOIRE ET JEANNE
The Tale of King Florus and the Fair Jehane. 1893. V. 68; 71; 73

FLOOD, C. B.
Trouble at the Top. New York: 1972. V. 73

FLORA of North America, North of Mexico. Volume I. Introduction. New York: 1993. V. 72

FLORA of North America, North of Mexico. Volume 2. Pteridophytes and Gymnosperms. New York: 1993. V. 72

FLORA of North America, North of Mexico. Volume 3. Magnoliophyta: Magnoliidae and Hamamelidae. New York: 1993. V. 72

FLORA of North America, North of Mexico. Volume 22. Magnoliophyta: Alismatidae, Arecidae, Commelinidae.... New York: 2000. V. 72

FLORENCE, P. SARGANT
Economics of Fatigue and Unrest and Efficiency of Labour in English and American Industry. London: 1924. V. 71

FLORENZ, KARL
Poetical Greetings from the Far East. Tokyo: 1896. V. 69

FLOREY, H. W.
Antibiotics: the Clinical Application of Antibiotics. London: 1949-1961. V. 71
A Preliminary Report to the War Office and Medical Research Council on Investigations Concerning the Use of Penicillin in War Wounds. London: 1943. V. 71

THE FLORIDA Pirate, or, an Account of a Cruise in the Schooner Esparanza(!): With a Sketch of the Life of Her Commander. New York: 1823. V. 71

FLORIN, LAMBERT
Boot Hill: Historic Graves of the Old West. Seattle: 1966. V. 69

FLORIS, JACOB
Compertimenta Pictoriis Flosculis Manubiisque Bellicis Variegata. Paris: 1660. V. 68; 70

THE FLORIST. London: 1848-1854. V. 68

FLORUS, LUCIUS ANNAEUS
Rerum Romanarum Libri IV. Venetiis: 1695. V. 72

FLORY, H. C.
An Essay On the Causes of the Indifference to the Study of Modern Languages and Literature in This Town and Vicinity.... Sheffield: 1834. V. 71

FLORY, S. P.
Fragments of Family History. 1. The Family of Collot D'Escury. 2. The Family of Maret de la Rive. 3. The Family of Wilkinson. London: 1896. V. 72

FLOURENS, PIERRE
Eloge Historique de Francois Magendie.... Paris: 1858. V. 71
Recherches Experimentales sur les Proprietes et les Fonctions du Systeme Nerveux dans les animaux Vertebres. Paris: 1824. V. 70; 72

FLOWER, BENJAMIN
The Arena. Volume IV, V. Boston: 1891-1892. V. 69; 73
The French Constitution; with Remarks on some of the Principal Articles.... London: 1792. V. 69

FLOWER, EDWARD FORDHAM
The Stones of London; or Macadam v. Vestries. London: 1880. V. 72

FLOWER, JOHN
Moonlight Serenade. A Bio-discography of the Glenn Miller Civilian Band. New Rochelle: 1972. V. 71

FLOWER, ROBIN
Loves Bitter Sweet. 1925. V. 70

FLOWER, W. H.
An Introduction to the Study of Mammals Living and Extinct. 1891. V. 73
Recent Memoirs on the Cetacea. London: 1866. V. 68; 69; 70

FLOWERS, CHARLES
It Never Rains In Los Angeles. New York: 1970. V. 72

FLOWERS for the Nursery or a Good Child's Nosegay.... Concord: 1837. V. 73

FLOYD, GRACE C.
Busy Bees. London: 1908. V. 72
Dolly Dear. London: 1895. V. 73

FLOYD, JOHN
The Church Conquerant Over Humane Wit. (with) *The Totall Summe.* St. Omer: 1638-1639. V. 68

FLOYD, WILLIAM
Social Progress. A Handbook of the Liberal Movement. New York: 1925. V. 68

FLOYER, JOHN
Psychroloysia (Greek); or, the History of Cold-Bathing, Both Ancient and Modern.... London: 1722. V. 71

FLUCKIGER, F.
Pharmacographia, a History of the Principal Drugs of Vegetable Origin Met with in Great Britain and British India.... London: 1879. V. 69

FLUDD, ROBERT
Philosophia Moysaica. (with) *Responsum ad Hoplocrisma-Songrum M. Fosteri.* Gouda: 1638. V. 73

FLUEHR-LOBBAN, CAROLYN
Historical Dictionary of the Sudan. Metuchen & London: 1992. V. 70

FLYING Days. London: 1905-1910. V. 70

FLYNN, BRIAN
Tread Softly. New York: 1938. V. 68; 71

FLYNN, ERROL
Showdown. New York: 1946. V. 69; 70

FLYNN, MARY
Cornelius on Holidays. Dublin and Cork: 1945. V. 69; 71

FLYNT, JOSIAH
Powers That Prey. New York: 1900. V. 72
The Rise of Ruderick Clowd. New York: 1903. V. 69

FOA, EDOUARD
After Big Game in Central Africa. London: 1899. V. 68; 72

FOENANDER, E. C.
The Big Game of Malaya. 1952. V. 69

FOERSTE, A. F.
The Silurian, Devonian and Irvine Formations of East Central Kentucky. Lexington: 1906. V. 72

FOGARTY, L.
Father John Kenyon. Patriot Priest of '48. V. 69

FOGELMARK, STAFFAN
Flemish and Related Panel Stamped Bindings, Evidence and Principles. New York: 1990. V. 70

FOGG, W. S. R.
The Art of the Wet Fly. 1979. V. 68

FOIGNY, GABRIEL DE
A New Discovery of Terra Incognita Australis, or the Southern World. Paris: 1693. V. 70

FOLCHI-PI, JORDI
Chemical Pathology of the Nervous System. Oxford: 1961. V. 68

FOLENGO, TEOFILO
Opus Merlini Cocaii Poetae Mantuani Macaronicorum.... Venice: 1572. V. 72

FOLEY, ANNE
The Trial of Lady Anne Foley, Wife of the Hon. Edward Foley Esq. and Daughter of William Earl of Coventry, for Adultery, with the Right Hon. Charles Henry Earl of Peterborough.... Dublin: 1786. V. 71

FOLEY, E. D.
The Cotton Manufacturers' Assistant; or, the Art of Arranging Cotton Machinery to Work the Different Sorts of Cotton.... Manchester: 1870. V. 71

FOLEY, RAE
An Ape in Velvet. New York: 1951. V. 71
Wake the Sleeping Wolf. New York: 1952. V. 69

FOLINSBEE, LAWRENCE J.
Environmental Stress. Individual Human Adaptions. New York: 1978. V. 72

FOLK Songs of Bohemia. New York: 1925. V. 71

FOLKARD, HENRY COLEMAN
The Sailing Boat: a Treatise on English and Foreign Boats. London: 1863. V. 68

FOLKENFLIK, ROBERT
Samuel Johnson, Biographer, a Study with a Useful List of the First Editions of Johnson's Biographies, Related Writings and Studies of Johnson's Biographies. London: 1979. V. 69

FOLLETT, KEN
The Bear Raid. Blandford, Dorset: 1976. V. 69
The Key to Rebecca. London: 1980. V. 70; 72; 73
The Man from St. Petersburg. London: 1982. V. 69
On Wings of Eagles. New York: 1983. V. 70
The Pillars of The Earth. New York: 1989. V. 73
Storm Island. London: 1978. V. 73
Triple. London: 1979. V. 68; 70; 72

FOLLEY, E. W.
Romantic Wycoller. A Haunt of the Brontes. 1949. V. 73
Romantic Wycoller. A Haunt of the Brontes. Lancashire: 1949. V. 70

FOLSOM'S New Pock Almanac 1789. Boston: 1788. V. 70

FONAHN, A.
Arabic and Latin Anatomical Terminology Chiefly from the Middle Ages. Kristiania: 1922. V. 68

FONBLANQUE, ALBANY
England Under Seven Administrations. London: 1837. V. 71
How We Are Governed; or the Crown, the Senate and the Bench. London: 1859. V. 71

FONER, JACK D.
The United States Soldier Between Two Wars Army Life And Reforms 1865-1898. New York: 1970. V. 72

FONER, PHILIP S.
The Case of Joe Hill. New York: 1965. V. 71

FONTAINE, HIPPOLYTE
Electric Lighting. A Practical Treatise. London: 1878. V. 69

FONTAINE, NICOLAS
The History of the Old and New Testament. London: 1699. V. 70

FONTAINE, WILLIAM MORRIS
The Potomac or Younger Mesozoic Flora. Washington: 1889. V. 72

FONTAINES, UNA DES
Wedgewood Fairyland Lustre. The Work Of Daisy Makeig-Jones. New York: 1975. V. 72

FONTANA, BERNARD L.
Tarahumara: Where Night is the Day of the Moon. Flagstaff: 1979. V. 71

FONTANA, DOMENICO
Della Trasportatione dell'Obelisco Vaticano et delle Fabriche di Nostro Signore Papa Sisto V. Roma: 1590. V. 73

FONTANA, FELIX
Traite sur le Venin de la Vipere sur les Poisons Americains sur le Laurier-Cerise et sur Quelques Autres Poisons Vegetaux. Florence: 1781. V. 72

FONTANA, ROBERT S.
Congenital Heart Disease: a Review of 357 Cases Studied Pathologically. Philadelphia: 1962. V. 68

FONTENAI, ABBE DE
Galerie du Palais Royal Gravee d'apres les Tableaux des Differentes Ecoles Qui La Composent.... Paris: 1786-1808. V. 69

FONTENELLE, BERNARD LE BOVIER DE
Dialogues of Fontelle. London: 1917. V. 69; 73
Entretiens sur la Pluralite des Mondes. Imprime a Paris: 1686. V. 68
A Plurality of Worlds. London: 1929. V. 71; 72

FONTON, FRANCIS
Genuine and Impartial Memoirs of Francis Fonton, Late of the Bank of England.... London: 1790. V. 70

FOORD, A. H.
Catalogue of the Fossil Cephalopoda in the British Museum (Natural History). London: 1888-1934. V. 70

FOOT, JEFFERY ROBERT
National Education; a Paper Read Beofre the Ruridecanal Chapter of Tutbury. Burton-on-Trent: 1867. V. 73

FOOT, JESSE
The Lives of Andrew Robinson Bowes Esq. and the Countess of Strathmore.... London: 1810. V. 71

FOOT, JOSEPH I.
An Historical Discourse, Delivered at West Brookfield, Mass., Nov. 27, 1828, on the Day of the Annual Thanksgiving. West Brookfield: 1843. V. 72

FOOT, MICHAEL
The Pen and the Sword. London: 1957. V. 72

FOOT, MIRJAM M.
The Henry Davis Gift: a Collection of Bookbindings.... London: 1978-1982. V. 70
The Henry Davis Gift. A Collection of Bookbindings.... London: 1978-1983. V. 73

FOOTE, HORTON
The Chase. New York and Toronto: 1956. V. 71

FOOTE, J. S.
A Contribution to the Comparative Histology of the Femur. Washington D. C: 1916. V. 68; 72

FOOTE, R. H.
Handbook of the Fruit Flies (Diptera: Tephritidae) of America North of Mexico. Ithaca: 1993. V. 68

FOOTE, SAMUEL
The Dramatic Works. London. V. 71

FOOTE, SHELBY
The Civil War: a Narrative. New York: 1974. V. 71
Jordan County. New York: 1954. V. 71
September, September. New York: 1977. V. 71; 72
Shiloh. New York: 1952. V. 69; 73
A View of History. 1981. V. 70

FOOTE, W. M.
Complete Mineral Catalog. Philadelphia: 1909. V. 68

FOOTE, WILLIAM H.
Sketches of North Carolina: Historical and Biographical. New Bern: 1966. V. 73
Sketches of Virginia: Historical and Biographical. Richmond: 1966. V. 73

FOOTNER, HULBERT
Dead Man's Hat. New York: 1932. V. 68
The Murder of a Bad Man. New York: 1936. V. 68; 71
Orchids to Murder. New York: 1945. V. 68; 71
Scarred Jungle. New York: 1935. V. 70
Thieves' Wit. New York: 1918. V. 70
The Whip-Poor-Will Mystery. New York: 1935. V. 68; 72

FOR *Howlin' Hilarity...Try This for Size.* Chicago: 1944. V. 68

FOR *James Merrill: a Birthday Tribute.* New York: 1986. V. 69; 73

FOR *Reynolds Price.* 1983. V. 70

FOR *Rushdie.* New York: 1994. V. 69

FOR *Somebody's Baby.* London: 1920. V. 73

FOR *the Train.* 1932. V. 70

FORAN, W. R.
A Breath of the Wilds. 1958. V. 69; 70; 72; 73
A Hunter's Saga. 1963. V. 70; 72; 73
Legends of the Field. Early Hunters in Africa. 1997. V. 70; 72

FORBES, ALLAN
Yankee Ship Sailing Cards. Boston: 1948-1952. V. 73

FORBES, ARCHIBALD
The Life Of Gordon. Major-General, R. E., C. B. London: 1897. V. 72

FORBES, BRIAN
Notes for a Life. London: 1974. V. 71

FORBES, D. C.
Successful Roach Fishing. 1973. V. 73

FORBES, DAVID R.
A True Story of the Christiana Riot. Quarryville: 1898. V. 71

FORBES, DUNCAN
Reflexions on the Sources of Incredulity and Regard to Religion. Edinburgh: 1750. V. 68

FORBES, E.
A History of British Mollusca and Their Shells. London: 1853. V. 69; 73
A History of British Starfishes and other Animals of the Class Echinodermata. 1841. V. 69; 73

FORBES, EDWARD
Literary Papers by the Late Professor Edward Forbes Selected from his Writings in the Literary Gazette. London: 1855. V. 68; 70

FORBES, EDWIN
Life Studies of the Great Army. New York: 1876. V. 71; 73

FORBES, ESTHER
A Mirror for Witches. Boston: 1928. V. 71

FORBES, H.
Chinese Export Silver 1785 to 1885. Milton: 1975. V. 73

FORBES, J.
Travels through the Alps. 1900. V. 70; 73

FORBES, JACK D.
Warriors of the Colorado - the Yumas of the Quechan Nation and Their Neighbors. Norman: 1965. V. 68; 73

FORBES, JAMES
Oriental Memoirs: Seleted and Abridged from a Series of Familiar Letters. London: 1813. V. 68
Travels through the Alps. 1900. V. 68
Travels through the Alps of Savoy. Edinburgh: 1843. V. 69
Travels through the Alps of Savoy. Edinburgh: 1900. V. 69

FORBES, JAMES GRANT
Sketches Historical and Topographical of the Floridas, More Particularly of East Florida. New York: 1821. V. 73

FORBES, KATHRYN
Mama's Bank Account. New York: 1943. V. 71

FORBES, LESLIE
Bombay Ice. London: 1998. V. 68; 70; 72

FORBES, PATRICK
A Full View of the Public Transactions in the Reign of Q. Elizabeth.... London: 1740-1741. V. 73

FORBES, R.
The Secret of the Sahara: Kufara. London: 1921. V. 69

FORBES, R. B.
A New Rig for Ships and Other Vessels, Combining Economy, Safety and Convenience. Boston: 1851. V. 73

FORBES, R. J.
Studies in Ancient Technology. Leiden: 1955-1964. V. 72

FORBES, ROBERT B.
Personal Reminiscences. Boston: 1882. V. 70

FORBES, ROBERT H.
The Pennington Pioneers of Early Arizona. Lancaster: 1919. V. 73

FORBES, ROSITA
One Flesh. London: 1930. V. 68; 73

FORBES, S. A.
Fishes of Illinois. Springfield: 1919-1920. V. 69

FORBURY Hill: a Poem Inscribed to the Memory the Late Francis Annesley. London: 1813. V. 69

FORBUSH, EDWARD HOWE
Birds of Massachusetts and Other New England States. Boston: 1925-. V. 69
Birds of Massachusetts and Other New England States. Boston: 1925-1929. V. 69; 73
Game Birds, Wild-Fowl, and Shore Birds of Massachusetts and Adjoining States. Massachusetts: 1916. V. 71
A History of the Game Birds, Wild-Fowl and Shore Birds of Massachusetts and Adjacent States. Boston: 1912. V. 69

FORCHE, CAROLYN
The Country Between Us. Port Townsend: 1981. V. 69; 73
The Country Between Us. New York: 1982. V. 68

FORD, ANNA P.
Daisy's Offering and Other Poems. Binghamton: 1879. V. 73

FORD, C.
An Early Victorian Album: The Photographic Masterpieces (1843-1847). New York: 1976. V. 68

FORD, CHARLES HENRI
The Mirror of Baudelaire. 1942. V. 70
Poems for Painters: Duchamp, Fini, Frances, Tanguy, Tchelithew. New York: 1945. V. 72

FORD, COREY
Minutes of the Lower Forty. New York: 1962. V. 72

FORD, FORD MADOX
Ancient Lights and Certain New Reflections: Being the Memories of a Young Man. London: 1911. V. 71; 73
An English Girl. London: 1907. V. 70
The Good Soldier. London: 1915. V. 69
The Good Soldier. New York: 1927. V. 69; 72
The Good Soldier. New York: 1951. V. 71
The Great Trade Route. New York: 1937. V. 68; 71
Ladies Whose Bright Eyes - a Romance. London: 1911. V. 69
A Little Less than Gods - A Romance. London: 1928. V. 72
A Man Could Stand Up. New York: 1926. V. 69
The March of Literature - from Confucius to Modern Times. London: 1939. V. 71
Mister Bosphorus and the Muses. London: 1923. V. 72
New York Essays. New York: 1927. V. 72
On Heaven and Other Poems Written on Active Service. London and New York: 1918. V. 69; 73
The Rash Act. New York: 1933. V. 69
The Shifting of the Fire. London: 1892. V. 68; 70
The Soul of London, a Survey of a Modern City. London: 1905. V. 71

FORD, FRANK R.
Diseases of the Nervous System in Infancy, Chldhood and Adolescence. Springfield: 1952. V. 68

FORD, G. M.
Who in Hell is Wanda Fuca?. New York: 1995. V. 69; 71

FORD, GEORGE
Dickens and His Readers. Aspects of Novel Criticism Since 1836. Princeton: 1955. V. 69

FORD, GERALD R.
Churchill Lecture. Northridge: 1984. V. 69; 71
Humor and the Presidency. New York: 1987. V. 68; 69
Portrait of the Assassin. New York: 1965. V. 72

A Time to Heal. New York: 1979. V. 68; 71
A Time to Heal. Norwalk: 1987. V. 69; 71
A Vision for America. Northridge: 1980. V. 71
The War Powers Resolution: a Constitutional Crisis?. Oroville: 1992. V. 71

FORD, GUS L.
Texas Cattle Brands. Dallas: 1958. V. 70

FORD, HENRY
My Philosophy of Industry. New York: 1929. V. 69

FORD, HENRY CHAPMAN
An Artist Records the California Missions. 1989. V. 71

FORD, ISABELLA O.
Women's Wages and the Conditions Under Which they are Earned. London: 1893. V. 71

FORD, JESSE HILL
Fishes, Birds and Sons of Men. London: 1968. V. 72

FORD, JOHN
By Direction of....Old Park, Enfield, Catalogue of the Contents of the Mansion Furniture.... 1909. V. 68
The Chronicle History of Perkin Warbeck. London: 1714. V. 68
Images of Brighton. Richmond-upon-Thames: 1981. V. 73

FORD, JOHN SALMON
Rip Ford's Texas. Austin: 1963. V. 70

FORD, JULIA ELLSWORTH
Imagina. New York: 1923. V. 68

FORD, KAREN COWAN
Las Yerbas de la Gente: a Study of Hispano-American Medicinal Plants. Ann Arbor: 1975. V. 68

FORD, LESLIE
Mr. Pinkerton Grows a Beard. New York: 1935. V. 69
Mr. Pinkerton Has the Clue. New York: 1936. V. 68; 71
Murder in the OMP. New York: 1942. V. 69
The Sound of Footsteps. New York: 1931. V. 70
The Town Cried Murder. New York: 1939. V. 72

FORD, MARK
Raymond Roussel and the Republic of Dreams. London: 2000. V. 73

FORD, PAUL LEICESTER
The Great K & A Train Robbery. New York: 1897. V. 68
Love Finds the Way. New York: 1904. V. 73
Mason Locke Weems. His Works and Ways. A Bibliography Left Unfinished.... New York: 1929. V. 71
Washington and the Theatre. New York: 1899. V. 69

FORD, RICHARD
Communist. Derry and Ridgewood: 1987. V. 69; 70; 71; 72
English Magnolias. An Exhibition of Mississippi Fiction Printed in England. University, Mississippi: 1992. V. 70; 72
Gatherings from Spain. London: 1846. V. 68
Good Raymond. London: 1998. V. 70
The Granta Book of the American Short Story. London: 1992. V. 68
The Granta Book of the American Short Story. New York: 1992. V. 68
A Hand-Book for Travellers in Spain...and Readers at Home...with Notices on Spanish History. London: 1845. V. 70; 72
The Handbook for Travellers in Spain. London: 1898. V. 71
Independence Day. London: 1995. V. 68; 69; 71
Independence Day. New Orleans: 1995. V. 69; 72
Independence Day. New York: 1995. V. 68; 69; 70; 71; 72; 73
Independence Day. Toronto: 1995. V. 69
Juke Joint. Jackson: 1990. V. 70
My Mother, In Memory. Elmwood: 1988. V. 69; 70; 71; 72; 73
A Piece of My Heart. New York: 1976. V. 68; 69; 70; 71; 72; 73
Rock Springs. New York: 1987. V. 68; 70; 71
The Sportswriter. London: 1986. V. 68; 70; 71
The Sportswriter. New York: 1986. V. 68; 69; 70; 71; 72; 73
The Ultimate Good Luck. Boston: 1981. V. 68; 69; 70; 71; 73
The Ultimate Good Luck. London: 1989. V. 68; 69
Under the Radar. London: 2001. V. 70
Wildlife. Boston: 1990. V. 70
Wildlife. London: 1990. V. 71
Wildlife. New York: 1990. V. 68; 70; 71; 72; 73
Women with Men. London: 1997. V. 72
Women with Men. New York: 1997. V. 68; 70; 72

FORD, ROBERT
A Blues Bibliography. Bromley: 1999. V. 70; 72

FORD, THOMAS
A History of Illinois, from Its Commencement as a State in 1818 to 1847.... Chicago: 1854. V. 69

FORD, TREVOR D.
White Watson (1763-1835) And His Geological Sections. London: 1960. V. 72

FORD, WHITEY
The Fighting Southpaw. Larchmont NY: 1962. V. 70

FORD, WILLIAM
A Description of Scenery in the Lake District Intended as a Guide to Strangers. Carlisle: 1839. V. 71
A Description of Scenery in the Lake District Intended as a Guide to Strangers. Carlisle: 1840. V. 71
A Description of Scenery in the Lake District Intended as a Guide to Strangers. 1847. V. 71
A Description of Scenery in the Lake District Intended as a Guide to Strangers. London: 1847. V. 72

FORD ABBEY, DORSETSHIRE
Catalogue of the Manificent and Matchless Tapestry, Collection of Paintings, Library of Rare Old Books and Manuscripts &c...the Entire Effects of Ford Abbey.... Dorset: 1846. V. 70

FORDE, C. DARYLL
Ethnography of the Yuma Indians. Berkeley: 1931. V. 72

FORDE, H. A.
The Fruit of the Spirit. 1919. V. 73

FORDRIN, LOUIS
Livre de Serrurerie de Composition Angloise... (with) Nouveau Livre de Serrurerie, Contenant Toutes Sortes de Grilles dun Gout Nouveau. Paris. V. 70; 72

FORDYCE, GEORGE
Five Dissertations on Fever. Boston: 1815. V. 70; 71

FORDYCE, JAMES
Addresses to Young Men. Boston: 1782. V. 68; 69; 73
Sermons to Young Women. London: 1766. V. 68
Sermons to Young Women. London: 1767. V. 69

FORDYCE, W.
A History of Coal, Coke, Coal Fields...Duration of the Great Northern Coal Field.... London: 1860. V. 69

FORDYCE, WILLIAM
Fragmenta Chirurgica and Medica. London: 1784. V. 72
A Review of the Venereal Disease and its Remedies. London: 1785. V. 72

FOREMAN, CAROLYN T.
Oklahoma Imprints 1835-1907 - a History of Printing in Oklahoma Before Statehood. Norman: 1936. V. 70

FOREMAN, GRANT
Advancing the Frontier 1830-1860. Norman: 1933. V. 68
The Biography of an Oklahoma Town - Muskogee. Norman: 1943. V. 70
The Five Civilized Tribes. Norman: 1934. V. 68; 69; 72; 73
A History Of Oklahoma. Norman: 1942. V. 72
Indian Removal - the Emigration of the Five Civilized Tribes of Indians. Norman: 1932. V. 69
Indians and Pioneers - the Story of the American Southwest Before 1830. Norman: 1936. V. 69
Marcy and the Gold Seekers.... Norman: 1939. V. 72
Pioneer Days in the Early Southwest. Cleveland: 1926. V. 70
Sequoyah. Norman: 1938. V. 69

FORES, S. W.
Fores's New Chalk Drawing-Book of Heads and Academy Figures.... 1795-. V. 73
Fores's New Chalk Drawing-Book of the Human Figure.... 1794-. V. 73

FORESTA, M. A.
George Tooker. 1983. V. 69; 72
Perpetual Motif: The Art of Man Ray. New York London Paris: 1988. V. 68

FORESTER, CECIL SCOTT
The Barbary Pirates. London: 1956. V. 72
The Bedchamber Mystery With Which is Included the Story of the Eleven Deckchairs and Modernity and Maternity. Toronto: 1944. V. 68
The Captain from Connecticut. London: 1941. V. 72
Captain Horatio Hornblower. Boston: 1939. V. 71
The Earthly Paradise. London: 1940. V. 72
Hornblower and the Hotspur. Boston: 1962. V. 68; 70
Hornblower and the Hotspur. London: 1962. V. 70
Poo-Poo and the Dragons. Boston: 1942. V. 70; 73
Randall and the River of Time. Boston: 1950. V. 71
Randall and the River of Time. London: 1951. V. 69; 70

FORESTER, CECILS SCOTT
The Naval War of 1812. London: 1957. V. 73

FORESTER, JOHN
Life and Times of Oliver Goldsmith. London: 1854. V. 69

FORESTER, THOMAS
Norway and Its Scenery. London: 1853. V. 72
Rambles in the Islands of Corsica and Sardinia. London: 1861. V. 68; 72

FORESTIER, A.
Belgium. London: 1908. V. 71

THE FORFEITURES of London's Charters, or an Impartial Account of the Several Seisures of the City Charter, Together with the Means and Methods that were Used for the Recovery of the Same, with the Causes by Which it Came Forfeited.... London: 1682. V. 70

FORGET Me Not: a Christmas and New Year's Present for MDCCCXXVII. London: 1827. V. 68

FORMAGGIO, FINO
A Book of Miniatures. New York: 1962. V. 70

FORMAN, CHARLES
Mr. Forman's Letter to the Right Honourable William Pulteney, Esq., Shewing How Pernicious, the Imperial Company of Commerce and Navigation.... London: 1725. V. 71

FORMAN, JAMES
Sammy Yonge, Jr.: The First Black Student To Die In the Black Liberation Movement. New York: 1968. V. 72

FORMAN, M. BUXTON
John Keats and his Family. Edinburgh;: 1933. V. 70

FORMAN, W. B.
Exotic Arts. London: 1957. V. 69

FORMILLI, C. G. T.
The Castles of Italy. 1933. V. 73
The Stones of Italy. London: 1927. V. 73

FORNERON, H.
Louise De Kerovalle, Duchess of Portsmouth 1649-1734 or How the Duke of Richmond Gained His Pension. London: 1887. V. 69; 73

THE FORREST Divorce Case, Catherine N. Forrest Against Edwin Forrest. New York: 1852. V. 71

THE FORREST Divorce Suit. Report of the Trial of Catherine N. Forrest vs. Edwin Forrest for Divorce held in the Superior Court of New York, Dec. 1851. New York: 1851. V. 73

FORREST, EARLE R.
Arizona's Dark and Bloody Ground. Caldwell: 1936. V. 68; 71
Lone War Trail of Apache Kid. Pasadena: 1947. V. 69; 70
Missions and Pueblos of the Old Southwest. Their Myths, Legends, Fiestas, and Ceremonies with Some Accounts of the Indian Tribes and Their Dances and of the Penitentes. Cleveland: 1929. V. 69
The Snake Dance of the Hopi Indians. Los Angeles: 1961. V. 69; 71
With a Camera in Old Navaholand. Norman: 1970. V. 69

FORREST, R. E.
Eight Days. London: 1892. V. 68

FORREST, WILLIAM S.
Historical and Descriptive Sketches of Norfolk and Vicinity.... Philadelphia: 1853. V. 71

FORRESTER, ALFRED HENRY
The Boys and the Giant. London: 1878. V. 71
Comic History of the Kings and Queens of England, from William the Conqueror to the Present Time. London: 1860. V. 69
How He Reigned and How He Mizzled. A Railway Raillery. London: 1849. V. 73
The Tutor's Assistant, or Comic Figures of Arithmetic.... 1843. V. 71

FORRESTER, JAMES
Collection of Some of the Finest Prospects in Italy, with Short Remarks on Them, by Abbate R. Venuti, Antiquarian to the Pope and Fellow of the Royal Society of London. London: 1762. V. 69

FORRESTER, MRS.
Fair Women. London: 1876. V. 68

FORRESTER-BROWN, M. F.
Diagnosis and Treatment of Deformities in Infancy and Early Childhood. London: 1929. V. 68

FORSHAW, JOSEPH M.
Australian Parrots. Wynnewood: 1969. V. 69; 73
Kingfishers and Related Birds. Sydney: 1983-1985. V. 70; 73
Kingfishers and Related Birds. Sydney: 1987-1993. V. 70; 73
Parrots of the World. Garden City: 1973. V. 70; 73
Parrots of the World. Melbourne: 1978. V. 73

FORSTER, CHARLES THORNTON
The Life and Letters of Ogier Ghiselin de Busbecq, Seigneur of Bousbeque, Knight, Imperial Ambassador. London: 1881. V. 73

FORSTER, EDWARD MORGAN
Abinger Harvest. London: 1936. V. 72
Alexandria; a History and a Guide. Alexandria: 1922. V. 73
Aspects of the Novel. London: 1927. V. 73
Collected Short Stories of E. M. Forster. London: 1947. V. 69
The Collected Tales of E. M. Forster. New York: 1947. V. 68
The Development of English Prose Between 1918 and 1939. Glasgow: 1945. V. 71
England's Pleasant Land. London: 1940:. V. 72
The Eternal Moment and Other Stories. London: 1928. V. 69; 71; 72; 73
Howards End. London: 1973. V. 72
The Life to Come and Other Stories. London: 1972. V. 70
The Longest Journey. Edinburgh and London: 1907. V. 69
The Longest Journey. New York: 1922. V. 69
A Passage to India. London: 1924. V. 69; 71; 73
A Passage to India. New York: 1924. V. 73
Pharos and Pharillon. New York: 1923. V. 73
Pharos and Pharillon. London: 1961. V. 72
The Story of the Siren. Richmond: 1920. V. 73
Two Cheers for Democracy. London: 1951. V. 71
What I Believe. London: 1939. V. 70

FORSTER, JOHANN GEORG ADAM
A Voyage Round the World, in His Britannic Majesty's Ship, Resolution, Commanded by Capt. James Cook, During the Years 1772, 3, 4 and 5. London: 1777. V. 68; 70; 73

FORSTER, JOHANN REINHOLD
Characteres Generum Plantarum Quas in Itinere ad Insulas Maris Australis, Collegerunt, Descripersunt Delinearunt Annis 1772-1775. London: 1776. V. 73

FORSTER, JOHN
The Life of Charles Dickens. London: 1872-1874. V. 70
The Life of Charles Dickens. London: 1873-1874. V. 70
A Narrative of the Late Dispute Between the Rev. Dr. Hughes and Mr. Forster. Dublin: 1739. V. 71
Walter Savage Landor. A Biography. London: 1869. V. 69

FORSTER, JOSEPH
Studies in Black and Red. London: 1896. V. 70

FORSTER, R. R.
New Zealand Spiders: an Introduction. Auckland: 1973. V. 73
Spiders of New Zealand. Dunedin: 1967-1988. V. 73

FORSTER, THOMAS IGNATIUS
(Greek title) Arati Diosemea, Notis et Collatione Scriptorum Illustravit. London: 1815. V. 72
A Synoptical Catalogue of British Birds.... London: 1817. V. 70

FORSTER, W.
A Treatise on a Section of the Strata from Newcastle-upon-Tyne to the Mountain of Cross Fell in Cumberland.... Newcastle: 1883. V. 69; 73

FORSYTH, EVELYN
Ye Gestes of Ye Ladye Anne. London. V. 70

FORSYTH, FREDERICK
The Day of the Jackal. London: 1971. V. 68; 69; 72; 73
The Day of the Jackal. New York: 1971. V. 68; 72
The Dogs of War. London: 1974. V. 73
The Fourth Protocol. London: 1984. V. 70; 72
The Fourth Protocol. San Francisco: 1984. V. 69
The Negotiator. London: 1989. V. 69; 70; 72; 73
No Comebacks - Collected Short Stories. London: 1982. V. 72
No Comebacks and Other Stories. Helsinki: 1986. V. 69; 70; 72
The Odessa File. London: 1972. V. 69; 70; 72

FORSYTH, GEORGE A.
The Story of the Soldier. NY: 1900. V. 72

FORSYTH, J. S.
The Mother's Medical Pocket-Book.... London: 1824. V. 69

FORSYTH, ROBIN
Murder at Marston Manor. New York: 1935. V. 68

FORSYTH, WILLIAM
Observations on the Diseases, Defects and Injuries In All Kinds of Fruit and Forest Trees. London: 1791. V. 69; 70; 71; 73
A Treatise on the Culture and Management of Fruit Trees. 1802. V. 69
A Treatise on the Culture and Management of Fruit Trees. London: 1802. V. 68; 72
A Treatise on the Culture and Management of Fruit Trees. Albany: 1803. V. 73
A Treatise on the Culture and Management of Fruit Trees. London: 1806. V. 69; 72
A Treatise on the Culture and Management of Fruit Trees. London: 1810. V. 72
A Treatise on the Culture and Management of Fruit Trees. London: 1824. V. 70

FORT, CHARLES
The Book of the Damned. 1920. V. 73

FORT, GEORGE F.
Medical Economy During the Middle Ages.... New York: 1883. V. 68

FORTESCUE, J. W.
The Drummer's Coat. London: 1900. V. 73
The Story of a Red Deer. Newtown, Powys: 1935. V. 70; 71

FORTH, W.
Pharmacology of Intestinal Absorption; Gastrionestinal Absorption of Drugs. Oxford: 1975. V. 71

FORTITUDO Leonina in Utraque Fortuna Maximiliani Emmanuelis, V.B. ac Sup. Palat. Ducis.... Munich: 1715. V. 68; 70

FORTOUL, HIPPOLYTE
La Danse Des Morts Dessinee Par Hans Holbein.... Paris: 1842. V. 70

THE FORTUNE Anthology. London: 1942. V. 68

FORTUNE, ROBERT
Two Visits to the Tea Countries of China and the British Tea Plantations in the Himalaya.... London: 1853. V. 72

FORTY, JEAN FRANCOIS
Oeuvres de Sculptures en Bronze Contenant Girandoles, Flambeau, Feux de Cheminees, Pendules, Bras, Cartels, Barometres et Lustres.... Paris: 1780. V. 69; 72

THE FORTY Thieves. Dundee, London, & Montreal: 1907. V. 69

FORWOOD, W. S.
An Historical and Descriptive Narrative of the Mammoth Cave of Kentucky.... Philadelphia: 1870. V. 70

FOSBROKE, T. D.
The Wye Tour, or Gilpin on The Wye with Picturesque Additions and Archaeological Illustrations. 1838. V. 72

FOSBROOKE, THOMAS DUDLEY
The Economy of Monastic Life (as It Exisited in England), a Poem.... Gloucester: 1795. V. 69

FOSHAY, E. M.
Reflections of Nature, Flowers in American Art. New York: 1984. V. 71

FOSS, SAM WALTER
Dreams in Homespun. Boston: 1897. V. 73

FOSTER, ALAN DEAN
Star Wars.... New York: 1976. V. 71
Star Wars.... New York: 1977. V. 71

FOSTER, BIRKET
Brittany. A Series of Thirty-Five Sketches. London: 1878. V. 68
Pictures of English Landscape. London: 1881. V. 68
Some Places of Note in England. 1888. V. 68

FOSTER, C. W.
The Parrish Register of Brocklesby in the County of Lincoln 1538- 1837. 1912. V. 70

FOSTER, CLEMENT
The Investigation of Mine Air. London: 1905. V. 71

FOSTER, D.
The Scientific Angler. 1880. V. 68
The Scientific Angler. 1882. V. 73

FOSTER, ED
Cummington Poems. Cummington: 1982. V. 73

FOSTER, EDWY WELLS
Man, The Story of His Advent Life and Development. Boston: 1900. V. 71

FOSTER, ELIZABETH
Motolina's History of the Indians of New Spain. Berkeley: 1950. V. 69

FOSTER, FRANK R.
Cricketing Memories. London: 1930. V. 72

FOSTER, HANNAH WEBSTER
The Coquette; or the History of Eliza Wharton. Newburyport: 1811. V. 69; 73

FOSTER, J. J.
French Art from Watteau to Prud'hon Together with an Introduction and Some Studies in the Social History of the Period by Various Authors. 1905. V. 70; 72

FOSTER, J. W.
Pre-Historic Races of the United States of America. Chicago: 1873. V. 71

FOSTER, JAMES
Discourses on All the Principal Branches of Natural Religon and Social Virtue. London: 1749-1752. V. 73

FOSTER, JESSIE
Essays in a Series of Letters, on the following subjects: I. On a man's writing memoirs of himself. II. On Decision of Character. III. On the application of the epithet romantic. IV. On some of the causes by which evangelical religion has been render. London: 1813. V. 71

FOSTER, JOHN
Essays In A Series Of Letters. London: 1813. V. 72

FOSTER, JOHN Y.
New Jersey and the Rebellion: a History of ther Services of the Troops and People of New Jersey in Aid of the Union Cause. Newark: 1868. V. 69

FOSTER, JONATHAN
Domestic Animal's Friend, or the Complete Virginia and Maryland Farrier. Winchester: 1818. V. 72

FOSTER, JOSEPH
The Dictionary of Heraldry. London: 1989. V. 72
The Pedigree of Wilson of High Wray & Kendal and the Families Connected With Them. 1871. V. 70

FOSTER, JOSEPH O'KANE
The Great Montezuma. Ranchos de Taos: 1940. V. 68

FOSTER, MAXIMILIAN
Bubbles. Philadelphia: 1929. V. 71

FOSTER, MICHAEL
Claud Bernard. London: 1899. V. 68; 72
A Report of Some Proceedings on the Commission for the Trial of the Rebels in the Year 1745, in the County of Surrey and Other Crown Cases.... 1792. V. 73

FOSTER, MURIEL
Muriel Foster's Fishing Diary. London: 1980. V. 70; 72

FOSTER, SANDYS B.
The Pedigrees of Crewdson of Crook, Whitwell of Kendal, Pease of Hutton and Low Cross. London: 1890. V. 71

FOSTER, STEPHEN C.
Biography, Songs and Musical Compositions of Stephen C. Foster. Pittsburgh;: 1896. V. 68

FOSTER, STEPHEN S.
The Brotherhood of Thieves, or a True Picture of the American Church and Clergy. New London: 1843. V. 68

FOSTER, W. E.
The Rt. Hon. Lord Boston's Muniments at Hedsor Relating to South Lincolnshire. Horncastle: 1914. V. 70

FOSTER, WILLIAM DEWEY
The Tuileries Brochures. New York: 1929-1932. V. 69

FOSTER, WILLIAM EDWARD
The Royal Descents of the Fosters of Moulton and the Mathesons of Shinness & Lochalsh. London: 1912. V. 71; 72

FOSTER, WILLIAM HARNDEN
New England Grouse Shooting. New York: 1942. V. 68

FOSTER, WILLIAM Z.
Pages from a Worker's Life. New York: 1939. V. 68

FOTHERGILL, ANTHONY
A New Experimental Enquiry into the Nature and Qualities of the Cheltenham Water.... Bath: 1785. V. 69

FOTHERGILL, GEORGE
A North Country Album containing Brief Notes of the signs & Signboards & Sundials in N. Yorkshire & Durham. Darlington: 1901. V. 73
Sermons on Several Subjects and Occasions.... Oxford: 1761. V. 73

FOTHERGILL, JOHN
An Account of The Life And Travels In The Work Of the Ministry, Of John Fothergill. London: 1753. V. 72
An Account of the Life and Travels, in the Work of the Ministry, of John Fothergill to Which are Added Divers Epistles to Friends in Great Britain and America, on Various Occasions. Philadelphia: 1754. V. 70
An Account of the Sore Throat Attended with Ulcers; a Disease Which Hath of Late Years Appeared in This City, and In Several Parts of the Nation. London: 1748. V. 69
An Account of the Sore Throat Attended with Ulcers. London: 1754. V. 70
A Complete Collection of His Medical and Philosophical Works...with an Account of His Life and Occasional Notes by John Elliot, M.D. London: 1781. V. 69; 70
An Innkeeper's Diary; Confessions of an Innkeeper; Cookery Book; My Three Inns. London: 1931-1949. V. 71

FOTHERGILL, JOHN MILNER
Digitalis: Its Mode of Action and Its Use. London: 1871. V. 71

FOTHERINGHAM, PETER MOIR
Blind Hate. London: 1992. V. 72

FOUCAULT, MICHEL
Madness and Civilization - a History of Insanity in the Age of Reason. London: 1967. V. 71

FOUCQUET, JEHAN DE
Oeuvre. Paris: 1866-1867. V. 70

FOUGERA, KATHERINE G.
With Custer's Cavalry From The Memoirs of The Late Katherine Gibson, Widow of Captain Francis Gibson, of The 7th Cavalry. Caldwell: 1942. V. 72

FOULKE, WILLIAM D.
Life of Oliver P. Morton, Including His Important Speeches. Indianapolis/Kansas City: 1899. V. 69

THE FOUNDLING; or, the History of Lucius Stanhope. York. V. 68

FOUNTAIN, PAUL
The Eleven Eaglets of the West. Cleveland: 1906. V. 71; 73

FOUNTAINE, ANDREW
Catalogue of the Celebrated Fountaine Collection of Majolica, Henri II. Ware, Palissy Ware, Evers Ware, Limoges Enamels, Carvings in Ivory, Hone Stone and Rock Crystal, Greek and Roman Coins.... 1884. V. 72
Fountaine Collection Catalogue of the Celebrated Fountaine Collection of Majolica, Henri II.... 1884. V. 69

FOUNTAYNE, JOHN
A Sermon Preached in the Cathedral Church of York, on Friday the 6th of February, 1756.... York: 1756. V. 69

FOUQUIER, MARCEL
Paris Au XVIIIe. Siecle Ses Folies. (With) Paris Aux XVIIIe. Siecle ses Divertis-Sements-Ses Moeurs. Directoire et Consulat. Paris: 1910. V. 70

FOUR Fictions. Kentfield: 1973. V. 72

FOUR New Poets. San Francisco: 1957. V. 68

FOUR Sonnets by Four Friends. New Rochelle: 1986. V. 73

FOUR Visions of America. Santa Barbara: 1977. V. 72

FOUR Years in the Underbrush: Adventures as a Working Woman in New York. New York: 1921. V. 69

FOURCROY, A.
Systeme des Connaissances Chimiques et de Leurs Applications aux Phenomenes de l'Art. 1801-1802. V. 68

FOURIER, FRANCOIS CHARLES MARIE
Political Economy Made Easy. London: 1828. V. 71

FOURIER, JEAN BAPTISTE JOSEPH
The Analytical Theory of Heat. Cambridge: 1878. V. 72
Theorie Analytique de la Chaleur, Par M. Fourier. Paris: 1822. V. 73

FOURNIER, ALAIN
Big Meaulnes. Paris: 1932. V. 71
The Wanderer. Boston and New York: 1928. V. 70; 72

FOURNIER, DANIEL
A Treatise on the Theory and Practice of Perspective. London: 1761. V. 72

FOURNIER, PIERRE SIMON
Manuel Typographique, Utile aux Gens de Lettres.... Paris: 1764-1766. V. 73

THE FOURTH Mystery Book. New York: 1941. V. 72
THE FOURTH Mystery Book. New York: 1942. V. 68

FOWELLS, H. A.
Silvics of Forest Trees of the United States. Washington: 1965. V. 72

FOWKE, EDITH
Lumbering Songs from the Northern Woods. Toronto: 1985. V. 73
Songs of Work and Freedom. Chicago: 1960. V. 69

FOWKE, G.
Archaeological History of Ohio. The Mound Builder and Later Indians. Columbus: 1902. V. 69

FOWLER, ALEX D.
Splinters from the Past: Discovering History in Old Houses. Morristown: 1984. V. 69

FOWLER, EDWARD
A Sermon Preached Before the Judges &c in Time of the Assizes in the Cathedral Church of Gloucester, on Sunday Aug. 7, 1681. London: 1681. V. 70

FOWLER, GENE
Schnozzola: the Story of Jimmy Durante. New York: 1951. V. 71

FOWLER, GEORGE
How to Bottle Fruit, Vegetables, Game, Poultry, Milk, Tomatoes &c. Reading: 1920. V. 68

FOWLER, GUY
The Dawn Patrol. New York: 1930. V. 70
Lilac Time. New York: 1928. V. 69
Sky Hawk. New York: 1929. V. 70

FOWLER, H. W.
A Catalog of World Fishes. Parts I-XXIV. Taipei: 1964-1976. V. 73
A Dictionary of Modern English Usage. Oxford & London: 1926. V. 69
The Fishes of New Jersey. 1905. V. 69; 72; 73
The Fishes of Oceania and Supplement 3. Honolulu: 1928-1949. V. 69; 72
The Fishes of the Families Pseudochromidae, Lobotidae, Pempheridae, Priacanthidae, Lutjanidae, Pomadasyidae and Teraponidae.... Washington: 1931. V. 72
The Marine Fishes of West Africa. New York: 1936. V. 69; 71; 72
A Synopsis of the Fishes of China. Hong Kong and Taipei: 1930-1962. V. 73
A Synopsis of the Fishes of China. The Gobioid Fishes. Taipei: 1960-1962. V. 73

FOWLER, HENRY WATSON
A Dictionary of Modern English Usage. Oxford. V. 70

FOWLER, J.
English Decoration In The 18th Century. Princeton: 1974. V. 72

FOWLER, JACOB
The Journal of Jacob Fowler - Adventure from Arkansas through Indian Territory, Oklahoma, Kansas, Colorado, New Mexico 1821-1822. New York: 1898. V. 69

FOWLER, JAMES
On Mediaeval Representations of the Months and Seasons. London: 1873. V. 72

FOWLER, JOHN
Journal of a Tour in the State of New York in the Year 1830; with Remarks on Agriculture, in those Parts Most Eligible for Settlers. London: 1831. V. 68

FOWLER, O. S.
Fowler's Practical Phrenology.... Philadelphia: 1840. V. 73

FOWLER, ORSON SQUIRE
A Home for All; or a New, Cheap, Convenient and Superior Mode of Building. New York: 1854. V. 69
A Home for All or the Gravel Wall and Octagon Mode of Building New, Cheap, Convenient, Superior and Adapted to Rich and Poor. New York: 1854. V. 70

FOWLER, WILLIAM W.
Woman of the American Frontier. San Francisco: 1884. V. 69

FOWLES, JOHN
The Aristos: a Self Portrait in Ideas. Boston and Toronto: 1964. V. 70; 72
Behind the Magus. London: 1994. V. 70
A Brief History of Lyme. Lyme Regis: 1981. V. 70
Cinderella. London: 1974. V. 72; 73
The Collector. Boston and Toronto: 1963. V. 70; 71; 73
The Collector. London: 1963. V. 68; 70; 71; 72; 73
The Collector. Franklin Center: 1982. V. 70
Daniel Martin. Boston: 1977. V. 70
Daniel Martin. London: 1977. V. 68; 70
The Ebony Tower. Boston: 1974. V. 70; 71
The Ebony Tower. London: 1974. V. 70; 72; 73
The Enigma. Helsinki: 1987. V. 70; 72
The French Lieutenant's Woman. Boston: 1969. V. 70; 71
The French Lieutenant's Woman. London: 1969. V. 70; 71; 72

FOWLES, JOHN continued
The French Lieutenant's Woman. Franklin Center: 1979. V. 70
Introduction: Remembering Cruikshank. Princeton: 1964,. V. 72
Islands. London: 1978. V. 71; 72
Lyme Worthies. 2000. V. 70
A Maggot. Boston: 1985. V. 70; 71; 73
A Maggot. London: 1985. V. 68; 70; 73
The Magus. Boston and Tornto: 1965. V. 68; 71; 72
The Magus. London: 1966. V. 69; 70; 71
Mantissa. Boston and Toronto: 1982. V. 68; 70
Mantissa. London: 1982. V. 68; 70
The Nature of Nature: an Essay. Covelo: 1995. V. 70
Of Memoirs and Magpies. Austin: 1983. V. 69; 70; 73
Poems. New York: 1973. V. 70
Poor Koko. Helsinki: 1987. V. 70; 72
Wormholes. London: 1998. V. 70
Wormholes. New York: 1998. V. 70; 72

FOX, CHARLES JAMES
An Entire New Work. Fox's Martyrs; or a New Book of the Sufferings of the Faithful. London: 1784. V. 70

FOX, CHARLES K.
Rising Trout. 1967. V. 68

FOX, CLIFTON A.
Happy Tho- Broke. Chicago: 1904. V. 73

FOX, CYRIL
Pattern and Purpose. Cardiff: 1958. V. 72

FOX, FRANCES MARGARET
Nannette. Joliet: 1929. V. 70

FOX, FRANK
Switzerland. London: 1914. V. 72
Switzerland. London: 1917. V. 72
Switzerland. London: 1930. V. 72

FOX, GEORGE
An Epistle to Be Read in All Assemblies of the Righteous From G.F. London: 1666. V. 71
The History of Pontefract, in Yorkshire. Pontefract;: 1827. V. 73
A Journal or Historical Account of the Life, Travels, Sufferings. London: 1765. V. 70
A Journal or Historical Account of the Life, Travels, Sufferings, Christian Experiences and Labour of Love in the Work of the Ministry. Leeds: 1836. V. 71

FOX, GEORGE HENRY
Photographic Illustrations of Skin Diseases. New York: 1885. V. 72

FOX, HILDERBRAND LANE
Chronicles of a Wharefedale Parish. Fort-Augustus: 1909. V. 73

FOX, JAMES M.
The Scarlet Slippers. Boston: 1952. V. 69
A Shroud for Mr. Bundy. Boston;: 1952. V. 71

FOX, JOHN
Erskine Dale Pioneer. New York: 1920. V. 71
(Foxe's Book of Martyrs) Acts and Monuments of Matters Most Special...Happening in the Church. London: 1632-1631. V. 71
The Kentuckians, a Novel. London: 1898. V. 72
Little Shepherd of Kingdom Come. New York: 1931. V. 71

FOX, JOHN D.
Life and Poems of John D. Fox,. Bingley: 1914. V. 73

FOX, L. WEBSTER
Diseases of the Eye. New York: 1904. V. 71

FOX, MINNIE C.
The Blue Grass Cook Book. New York: 1904. V. 69

FOX, PAULA
How Many Miles to Babylon?. New York: 1967. V. 68

FOX, R. HINGSTON
Dr. John Fothergill And His Friends. London: 1919. V. 68; 72
William Hunter, Anatomist, Physician, Obstetrician (1718-1783).... London: 1901. V. 70; 72

FOX, RICHARD ALLAN
Archaeology, History and Custer's Last Battle. Norman: 1993. V. 68; 72

FOX, S. MIDDLETON
Verses for Grannie, Suggested by the Children. London: 1899. V. 69

FOX, SARAH PRIDEAUX
Kingsbridge and Its Surroundings. Plymouth: 1874. V. 72
Kingsbridge Estuary; with Rambles in the Neighbourhood. Kingsbridge: 1864. V. 72

FOX, UFFA
Racing, Cruising and Design. London: 1951. V. 68

FOX, WILLIAM
A Discourse of National Fasts, Particularly in Reference to that of April 19, 1793, on Occasion of the War with France. London: 1793. V. 69

FOX, WILLIAM PRICE
Doctor Golf. Philadelphia: 1963. V. 69

FOXALL, P. A.
Sequel To Yesterday's Crime. London: 1979. V. 72

FOX-DAVIES, A. C.
The Mauleverer Murders. London: 1907. V. 70

FOXE, JOHN
A Continuation of the Histories of Forreine Martyrs. 1641. V. 70; 71; 72
A Continuation of the Histories of Forreine Martyrs. London: 1641. V. 69

FOXON, D. F.
English Verse 1701-1750. Cambridge: 1975. V. 70

FOX TALBOT, WILLIAM HENRY
Fox Talbot: Electa Editrice Porftolios. Milan: 1982. V. 73

FOY, DANIEL
Clowning through Life. New York: 1928. V. 69

FRACASTORO, GIROLAMO
Opera Omnia. Venice: 1584. V. 71; 73

FRACE, CHARLES
The Art of Charles Frace. Houston: 1982. V. 68
Nature's Window. 1992. V. 68

FRAGONARD, ALEXANDRE
Recueil de Divers Sujets dans le Style Grec, Composes Dessines et Graves.... Paris: 1815. V. 68; 70

FRAME, JANET
Autobiography. 1983-1985. V. 72

FRAMJEE, DOSABHOY
Travels in Great Britain. Bombay: 1851. V. 70
Travels in Great Britain. Bombay: 1861. V. 71

LA FRANCE en Miniature. Paris: 1825. V. 73

FRANCE
Constitution de la Republique Francaise, Proposee au Peuple Francais par la Convention Nationale. Paris and London: 1795. V. 71

FRANCE. NATIONAL SYNOD OF THE REFORMED CHURCHES
An Extract of the Acts...Assembled by the Kings Permission at Charatoun, Ann. 1644. 26 Decem. and Dayes following: Touching Independencie. Sent from Paris the 17 of January 1645. London: 1645. V. 70

FRANCE, ANATOLE
L'Affaire Crainquebille. Stamford: 1937. V. 72
Bee the Princess of the Dwarfs. London: 1912. V. 70; 71; 73
Clio. Paris: 1900. V. 73
Crainquebille, Putois, Riquet, and Other Profitable Tales. London and New York: 1915. V. 68
Filles et Garcons. Scenes de la Ville et des Champs. Paris. V. 71
The Gods Are Athirst. London: 1927. V. 71
Mother of Pearl. London and New York: 1922. V. 68
Penguin Island. New York: 1929. V. 69
The Revolt of the Angels. New York: 1928. V. 69
Thais. London: 1924. V. 68
La Vie en Fleur. Paris: 1922. V. 70

FRANCE, Her Governmental, Administrative, and Social Organisation, Exposed &c.... London: 1844. V. 71

FRANCE, L. B.
Mountain Trails and Parks in Colorado. Denver: 1888. V. 68

FRANCESCO D'ASSISI
Laudes Creaturarum. Hammersmith: 1910. V. 72

FRANCHERE, GABRIEL
Narrative of a Voyage to the Northwest Coast of America in the Years 1811, 1812, 1813 and 1814 or the First Settlement on the Pacific. New York: 1854. V. 68; 70

FRANCHETTE and Jeannot - a Little Story with Pictures. New York: 1937. V. 70

FRANCIA, FRANCOIS L. T.
Progressive Lessons Tending to Elucidate the Character of Trees.... London: 1813. V. 68

FRANCINI, GIROLAMO
Le Cose Meravigliose Dell'Alma Citta Di Roma...di Nuovo Corrette, Ampliate & Ornate di Bellissime Figure. Rome: 1672. V. 70
Les Mervellies de La Ville de Rome.... Rome: 1690. V. 70

FRANCIS, A. M.
The Catskill Rivers. 1983. V. 68

FRANCIS, DICK
Banker. London: 1982. V. 68; 70; 73
Best Racing and Chasing Stories Edited And With Introduction By Francis & Welcome. London: 1966. V. 72; 73
Blood Sport. London: 1967. V. 70
Blood Sport. New York: 1968. V. 70
Bolt. London: 1986. V. 68; 69; 70; 71; 72; 73
Bolt. New York: 1986. V. 68
Bonecrack. London: 1971. V. 68; 70
Break In. London: 1985. V. 69; 70; 72; 73
Comeback. London: 1991. V. 68
The Danger. London: 1983. V. 68; 69; 70; 71; 72; 73

FRANCIS, DICK continued
Dead Cert. New York: 1962. V. 70
Driving Force. London: 1992. V. 72
The Edge. London: 1988. V. 68; 70
Enquiry. London: 1969. V. 69; 70; 72
Field of 13. London: 1998. V. 68; 69; 70; 71; 72; 73
Flying Finish. London: 1966. V. 68; 69; 70; 71
Flying Finish. New York: 1966. V. 68; 70; 71; 73
For Kicks. 1965. V. 69; 71
For Kicks. London: 1965. V. 68; 70
For Kicks. New York: 1965. V. 70
Forfeit. London: 1968. V. 73
Forfeit. New York: 1969. V. 69; 70; 73
In the Frame. London: 1976. V. 71
High Stakes. London: 1975. V. 68; 70; 73
High Stakes. New York: 1975. V. 71
Hot Money. London: 1987. V. 72
In the Frame. London: 1976. V. 68; 69; 70; 72; 73
In the Frame. New York: 1976. V. 69
Knock Down. London: 1974. V. 68; 69; 70; 71; 72
Lester: The Official Biography. London: 1986. V. 73
The Midwinter Gold Cup. London: 1969. V. 73
Nerve. London: 1964. V. 72
Nerve. New York: 1964. V. 70; 72
Odds Against. London: 1965. V. 70; 71; 72
Odds Against. New York: 1965. V. 69; 70; 71; 73
Proof. London: 1984. V. 68; 69; 70; 71; 73
Rat Race. London: 1971. V. 70; 72
Rat Race. New York: 1971. V. 68
Reflex. London: 1980. V. 68; 72; 73
Risk. London: 1977. V. 68; 69; 70; 71; 72; 73
Second Wind. Blakeney: 1999. V. 68; 69; 70; 71; 72; 73
Second Wind. London: 1999. V. 68; 73
Second Wind. New York: 1999. V. 72
Shattered. London: 2000. V. 68; 69; 70; 71; 72; 73
Slay Ride. London: 1973. V. 68; 71; 73
Smokescreen. London: 1972. V. 68; 70; 73
The Sport of Queens. London: 1957. V. 70; 71
The Sport of Queens. New York: 1969. V. 68; 70
Spring Fever in Classic Lines: More Great Racing Stories. London: 1991. V. 73
Straight. London: 1988. V. 71
Straight. London: 1989. V. 72
10-LB Penalty. London: 1997. V. 68; 73
To the Hilt. Blakeney: 1996. V. 68; 69; 70; 71; 72
To the Hilt. London: 1996. V. 71; 72
To The Hilt. New York: 1996. V. 72
Trial Run. London: 1978. V. 68; 70; 73
Twice Shy. London: 1981. V. 68; 69; 70; 71; 72; 73
Whip Hand. London: 1979. V. 68; 70; 72; 73
Wild Horses. London: 1994. V. 68; 72
Wild Horses. New York: 1994. V. 71

FRANCIS, FRANCIS
A Book of Angling. 1867. V. 69
A Book on Angling. 1885. V. 68; 73

FRANCIS, G.
The Dictionary of the Arts, Sciences and Manufactures.... London: 1842. V. 68

FRANCIS, G. W.
The Little English Flora or a Botanical and Popular Account of All Our Common Field Flowers.... London: 1839. V. 72

FRANCIS, GEORGE WILLIAM
The Dictionary of Practical Receipts; Containing the Arcana of Trade and Manufacture; Domestic Economy; Artistical, Ornamental and Scientific Processes; Pharmaceutical and Chemical Preparations &c. &c. London: 1848. V. 73

FRANCIS, GLORIA A.
Whitman at Auction 1899-1972. Detroit: 1978. V. 69

FRANCIS, GRANT
The Smelting of Copper in the Swansea District, from the Time of Elizabeth to the Present Day. Swansea: 1867. V. 68

FRANCIS, J. G.
Beach Rambles In Search of Sea-Side Pebbles and Crytals. London: 1861. V. 68; 70

FRANCIS, JAMES B.
Lowell Hydraulic Experiments. New York: 1868. V. 68; 71
On the Strength of Cast-Iron Pillars, with Tables for the Use of Engineers, Architects and Builders. New York: 1865. V. 68

FRANCIS, JOHN
Annals, Anecdotes and Legends: a Chronicle of Life Assurance. London: 1853. V. 71
Chronicles and Characters of Stock Exchange. London: 1850. V. 71
History of the Bank of England, Its Times and Traditions, from 1694 to 1844. New York: 1862. V. 71

FRANCIS, JOHN W.
Anniversary Discourse Before the New York Academy of Medicine. New York: 1847. V. 73

FRANCIS, ROBERT
The Trouble with God. 1984. V. 68; 72

FRANCIS, SAM
The Monotypes of Sam Francis. Stuttgart: 1994. V. 70; 72; 73

FRANCIS LEWIS, C.
The Art and Craft of Leatherwork.... Philadelphia: 1928. V. 69

FRANCK, CASPAR
Passional, Inn Welchen Mit Sonderm Fleiss in Schone Figuren. Munich: 1572. V. 70

FRANCK, FREDERICK
African Sketchbook. London: 1962. V. 69

FRANCK, HARRY A.
Tramping through Mexico, Guatemala and Honduras. New York: 1916. V. 69

FRANCK VON FRANCKENAU, GEORG
Flora Francica, H. E. Lexicon Plantarum Hactenus Usalium Ubi Earum Nomen cum Synonymis Latinis, Graecis, Germanicis.... Argentorati: 1685. V. 72; 73

FRANCO, J.
At Grips with Jannu. 1967. V. 73

FRANCOIS-FRANK, CHARLES
Lecons sur les Fonctions Motrices du Cerveau Reactions Volontaires et Oraniques et sur L'Epilepsie Cerebrale. Paris: 1887. V. 71; 72

FRANE, JEFF
A Fantasy Reader, the Seventh World Fantasy Convention. 1981. V. 69

FRANE, PATRICIA
Soft Answer. New York: 1936. V. 71

FRANK, ANNE
The Works of Anne Frank. Garden City: 1959. V. 70

FRANK, BRUNO
The Days of the King. New York: 1927. V. 69

FRANK, GEORGE
Ryedale and North Yorkshire Antiquities. Elliot Stock and York: 1888. V. 73

FRANK, LARRY
Historic Pottery of the Pueblo Indians 1600-1800. Boston: 1974. V. 69
Historic Pottery of the Pueblo Indians 1600-1880. Boston: 1975. V. 69
Indian Silver Jewelry of the Southwest, 1868-1930. Boston: 1978. V. 69
New Kingdom of the Saints. Santa Fe: 1992. V. 69

FRANK, LEONHARD
Clamoring Self. New York: 1930. V. 71

FRANK, PAT
Alas, Babylon. Philadelphia: 1959. V. 68; 71

FRANK, ROBERT
Les Americains. Paris: 1958. V. 70
The Lines of My Hand. 1972. V. 73
The Lines of My Hand. Tokyo: 1972. V. 72
The Lines of My Hand. New York: 1989. V. 73
New York to Nova Scotia. Houston: 1986. V. 68; 70
Pull My Daisy. New York/London: 1961. V. 68; 70

FRANK, WALDO
Salvos: An Informal Book About Books and Plays. New York: 1924. V. 72

FRANKAU, GILBERT
One of Us. London: 1917. V. 72
The Seeds of Enchantment. Garden City: 1921. V. 68

FRANKE, AUGUSTUS HERMANN
Nicodemus; or, a Treatise on the Fear of Man. London: 1740. V. 70

FRANKEN, ROSE
Claudia. New York: 1941. V. 70

FRANKENSTEIN, ALFRED
William Sidney Mount. New York: 1975. V. 72

FRANKFORT, H.
The Art and Architecture of the Ancient Orient. London: 1954. V. 72

FRANKFURTER, FELIX
The Case of Sacco and Vanzetti. Boston: 1927. V. 68
The Labor Injunction. New York: 1930. V. 71
The Public and Its Government. New Haven: 1930. V. 72

FRANKL, PAUL
Principles of Architectural History: the Four Phases of Architectural Style, 1420-1900. 1968. V. 69; 73

FRANKLIN, BENJAMIN
Autobiography of Benjamin Franklin. Philadelphia: 1868. V. 73
Autobiography of Benjamin Franklin.... San Francisco: 1931. V. 68; 73
Experiments and Observations on Electricity, Made at Philadelphia in America.... London: 1774. V. 73
The Life and Works of Dr. Benjamin Franklin. Bungay (Suffolk): 1807. V. 68
Memoires de la Vie Privee. Paris: 1791. V. 69; 70; 73

FRANKLIN, BENJAMIN continued
Observations on Smoky Chimneys, their Causes and Cure; with Considerations on Fuel and Stoves. London: 1793. V. 68; 70; 73
Oeuvres.... Paris: 1773. V. 72
Political, Miscellaneous and Philosophical Pieces. London: 1779. V. 70; 73
Poor Richard's Almanacks for the Years 1733-1758. Philadelphia: 1964. V. 69
Works. Dublin: 1793. V. 73
The Works. London: 1793. V. 72
The Works. Chicago: 1882. V. 71

FRANKLIN, CLAY
These Mortals Among Us. New York: 1935. V. 71

FRANKLIN, COLIN
Bookselling. A Memoir. Cleveland: 1999. V. 72
Emery Walker. Some Light on His Theories of Printing and On His Relations with William Morris and Cobden Sanderson. Cambridge: 1973. V. 68; 71
Themes in Aquatint. San Francisco: 1978. V. 73
The Triple Crown: Kelmscott, Doves and Ashendene. Dallas: 1977. V. 72

FRANKLIN, J. F.
Natural Vegetation of Oregon and Washington. Portland: 1973. V. 72

FRANKLIN, JOHN
Journey to the Shores of the Polar Sea in 1819-1820-1821-1822; with a Brief Account of the Second Journey in 1825-1826-1827. London: 1829. V. 73
Narrative of a Journey to the Shores of the Polar Sea in the Years 1819-1820-1821-1822. London: 1824. V. 72
Sir John Franklin's Journals and Corespondence: The First Arctic Land Expedition 1919-1822. Toronto and Ottawa: 1995. V. 71

FRANKLIN, JOHN H.
The Militant South, 1800-1861. Cambridge: 1956. V. 72
A Southern Odyssey: Travellers in the Antebellum North. Baton Rouge: 1976. V. 73

FRANKLIN, JOHN HOPE
The Free Negro in North Carolina 1790-1860. Chapel Hill: 1943. V. 68

FRANKLIN, KENNETH J.
Joseph Barcroft 1872-1947. Oxford: 1953. V. 68
A Monograph on Veins. Springfield: 1937. V. 68
William Harvey, Englishman 1578-1657. London: 1951. V. 68

FRANKLIN, MARTYN
Sam Langford. The Nova Scotian Tar Baby. Montreal: 1948. V. 72

FRANKLYN, IRWIN R.
Flight. New York: 1929. V. 69

FRANKS, J. M.
Seventy Years in Texas. Gatesville: 1924. V. 71

FRANZEN, JONATHAN
The Corrections. New York: 2001. V. 70; 71
The Corrections. London: 2002. V. 70; 72
My Father's Brain. 2002. V. 73
My Father's Brain. London: 2002. V. 72
Strong Motion. New York: 1992. V. 70; 72; 73
The Twenty-Seventh City. New York: 1988. V. 70; 73

FRAPRIE, FRANK R.
Photographic Amusements including Tricks and Unusual or Novel Effects Obtainable with the Camera. London: 1931. V. 68

FRASCONI, ANTONIO
To Walt Whitman. Purchase: 1981. V. 69
A Whitman Portrait. New York: 1960. V. 72
Woodcuts by Antonio Frasconi. New York: 1957. V. 71

FRASER, ALEC
A Guide to Operations on the Brain. London: 1890. V. 68

FRASER, ALEXANDER
United Empire Loyalists: Enquiry Into their Losses and Services in Consequence of their Loyalty. 1905. V. 73

FRASER, ALEXANDER, MRS.
Daughters of Belgravia: a Novel. London: 1891. V. 68

FRASER, CLAUD LOVAT
Characters from Dickens. London: 1924. V. 73
Sixty-Three Unpublished Designs. London: 1924. V. 71

FRASER, FITZROY
Wounds in the Flesh. London: 1962. V. 69

FRASER, GEORGE MAC DONALD
The Candlemass Road. London: 1993. V. 70
Flash for Freedom. London: 1971. V. 70; 71; 73
Flash for Freedom!. New York: 1972. V. 70
Flashman. 1969. V. 68; 71
Flashman. London: 1969. V. 70; 73
Flashman. New York: 1969. V. 70; 73
Flashman and the Angel of the Lord. London: 1994. V. 68; 69; 73
Flashman and the Dragon. London: 1985. V. 68
Flashman and the Mountain of Light. London: 1990. V. 68
Flashman and the Redskins. London: 1982. V. 68; 70

Flashman and the Tiger. New York: 2000. V. 72
Flashman at the Charge. London: 1973. V. 69; 70; 72; 73
Flashman at the Charge. New York: 1973. V. 70
Flashman in the Great Game. London: 1975. V. 69; 71
Flashman in the Great Game. New York: 1975. V. 70
Flashman's Lady. London: 1977. V. 69; 73
Flashman's Lady. New York: 1978. V. 70
The General Danced at Dawn and Other Stories. New York: 1973. V. 70
The Hollywood History of the World. New York: 1988. V. 70
McAuslan in the Rough. London: 1974. V. 69; 71; 72
McAuslan in the Rough. New York: 1974. V. 70
Royal Flash. London: 1970. V. 70
Royal Flash. New York: 1970. V. 70
The Steel Bonnets. London: 1971. V. 72; 73
The Steel Bonnets. London: 1986. V. 70; 71; 73

FRASER, HUGH
Amid the High Hills. 1923. V. 70; 72; 73
Amid the High Hills. London: 1923. V. 71
Amid the High Hills. 1934. V. 69

FRASER, JAMES BAILLIE
The Persian Adventurer. London: 1830. V. 73

FRASER, JOHN FOSTER
Panama and What It Means. London: 1913. V. 69

FRASER, KATHLEEN
Wing. Mill Valley: 1995. V. 69; 71

FRASER, P. P.
Notes of a Tour Round the world. Melbourne: 1885. V. 68

FRASER, PADDY
G. S. Fraser: a Memoir. London. V. 70

FRASER, ROBERT W.
Ebb and Flow. London: 1860. V. 68
Seaside Divinity. London: 1861. V. 68
The Seaside Naturalist. London: 1868. V. 68

FRASER, RONALD
Flower Phantoms. London: 1926. V. 70

FRAUNCE, ABRAHAM
The Lawiers Logike, Exemplifying the Praecepts of Logike by the Practise of the Common Lawe. London: 1588. V. 70; 73

FRAXI, PISNAUS
Bibliography of Prohibted Books. Bio-Biblio-Iconographical and Critical Notes on Curious Uncommon and Erotic Books. New York: 1962. V. 70

FRAYN, MICHAEL
Constructions. London: 1974. V. 71
Headlong. London: 1999. V. 68
The Tin Men. London: 1965. V. 70

FRAZER, G.
The Native Races of Africa and Madagascar. London: 1938. V. 69

FRAZER, JAMES GEORGE
Anthologia Anthropologica. London: 1938-1939. V. 72
The Belief in Immortality and the Worship of the Dead. Volume I. London: 1913. V. 69
The Golden Bough. New York: 1935. V. 69
The Golden Bough: a Study in Magic and Religion. London: 1930-1936. V. 73
The Growth of Plato's Ideal Theory - an Essay. London: 1930. V. 69

FRAZER, MARIE M.
On the Old Trails in Wyoming - A History of Wyoming for the Elementary Schools Grades 3-8. Laramie: 1928. V. 73

FRAZER, R. W.
Silent Gods and Sun-Steeped Lands. 1894. V. 69

FRAZIER, CHARLES
Cold Mountain. New York: 1971. V. 71
Cold Mountain. London: 1997. V. 68
Cold Mountain. New York: 1997. V. 68; 69; 70; 71; 72; 73

FRAZIER, CHARLES H.
Surgery of the Spine and Spinal Cord. New York: 1918. V. 68; 72

FRAZIER, E. FRANKLIN
The Negro in the United States. New York: 1949. V. 72

FRAZIER, IAN
Dating Your Mom. New York: 1986. V. 73

FRAZIER, MARIE M.
On the Old Trails in Wyoming - a History of Wyoming for the Elementary Schools Grades 3-8. Laramie: 1928. V. 68

FRAZIER, WILLIAM
Analysis of the Rockbridge Alum Springs, in Virginia.... Richmond: 1857. V. 71

FREAKS and Frolics of Little Boys. New York: 1887. V. 71

FREAKS and Frolics of Little Girls. New York: 1887. V. 70; 73

FREART, ROLAND
A Parallel of the Antient Architecture with the Modern, in a Collection of Ten Principles Authors.... London: 1664. V. 70

FREAS, FRANK KELLY
Frank Kelly Freas As He Sees It. 2000. V. 73

FREDDY *Frizzylocks.* London: 1914. V. 73

FREDEMAN, WILLIAM E.
Pre-Raphaelitism. 1965. V. 68
Pre-Raphaelitism. Cambridge: 1965. V. 72

FREDERIC, HAROLD
The Copperhead. New York: 1893. V. 71
The Damnation of Thereon Ware. Chicago: 1896. V. 72

FREDERICA SOPHIA WILHELMINA, PRINCESS ROYAL OF PRUSSIA
Memoirs of Frederica Sophia Wilhelmina, Princess Royal of Prussia, Margarvine of Bareith, Sister of Frederick the Great. London: 1812. V. 70

FREDERICK, CHRISTINE
Scientific Management in the Home. London: 1922. V. 68

FREDERICK, J. L.
Ben Holliday - the Stagecoach King. A Chapter in the Development of Transcontinental Transportation. Glendale: 1940. V. 70

FREDERICKS, ARNOLD
One Million Francs. New York: 1912. V. 71

FREDERICKSON, A. D.
AD Orientem. London: 1889. V. 72

FREDERICS, DIANA
Diana - a Strange Autobiography. New York: 1939. V. 68

FREE and Impartial Remarks Upon the Letters Written by the Late Right Honourable Philip Dormer Stanhope, Earl of Chesterfield, to His Son.... London: 1774. V. 68

FREE LIBRARY OF PHILADELPHIA
Charles Dickens. (Exhibition Catalogue). Philadelphia: 1946. V. 68

FREECE, HANS P.
The Letters of an Apostate Mormon to His Son. New York: 1908. V. 70

FREED, LEONARD
Made in Germany. NY: 1970. V. 72

FREEDMAN, J. F.
Against the Wind. New York: 1991. V. 70

FREEDMAN, RUSSELL
Wendell Berry, a Bibliography. Lexington: 1998. V. 69

FREEHLING, JOAN
Noteworthy. Highland Park: 1991. V. 73

FREELAND, ROBERT
The Soap Maker's Private Manual. Philadelphia: 1876. V. 68; 72

FREELING, NICOLAS
Cook Book. London: 1972. V. 72
The King of the Rainy Country. New York: 1966. V. 70
Love in Amsterdam. New York: 1962. V. 72

FREEMAN, BUD
You Don't Look Like a Musician. Detroit: 1974. V. 68; 70; 72

FREEMAN, DANNY
World's Oldest Rodeo- 100 Year History 1888-1988. Prescott: 1988. V. 71

FREEMAN, DEVERY
Father Sky. New York: 1979. V. 72

FREEMAN, DON
The Chalk Box Story. Philadelphia: 1976. V. 71
Space Witch. New York: 1959. V. 70

FREEMAN, DOUGLAS SOUTHALL
George Washington: a Biography. New York: 1948. V. 68; 73
The Last Parade. Richmond: 1932. V. 68; 70
Lee's Lieutenants. New York: 1942. V. 69; 73
Lee's Lieutenants, a Study in Command. New York: 1942-1944. V. 69; 70
R. E. Lee: a Biography. New York: 1934. V. 69
R. E. Lee. A Biography. New York: 1934-1935. V. 72
R. E. Lee: a Biography. New York: 1935. V. 73
R. E. Lee. A Biography. New York: 1936. V. 70

FREEMAN, EDWARD
A History of Sicily, from the Earliest Times. Oxford: 1891-1894. V. 71

FREEMAN, G. D.
Midnight and Noonday or the Incidental History of Southern Kansas and the Indian Territory. Caldwell: 1892. V. 68; 71

FREEMAN, GILLIAN
The School Girl Ethic. The Life and Work of Angela Brazil. London: 1976. V. 73

FREEMAN, HARRY C.
A Brief History of Butte, Montana. The World's Greatest Mining Camp. Chicago: 1900. V. 70

FREEMAN, IRA S.
A History of Montezuma County, Colorado Land of Fulfillment. Boulder: 1968. V. 68; 71

FREEMAN, JAMES W.
Prose and Poetry of the Livestock Industry of the United States. New York: 1959. V. 69; 71

FREEMAN, JOHN
Fifty Poems. 1911. V. 73
Life of the Ref. William Kirby, M.A., Rector of Barham. London: 1852. V. 68; 70; 71
Presage of Victory and Other Poems of Time. London: 1916. V. 73
Stone Trees and Other Poems. London: 1916. V. 73
Twenty Poems. 1909. V. 73

FREEMAN, JOHN R.
On the Proposed Use of a Portion of the Hetch Hetchy, Eleanor and Cherry Valleys Within and Near to the Boundaries of the Stanislaus U.S. National Forest Reserve and the Yosemite National Park.... San Francisco: 1912. V. 73

FREEMAN, JOSEPH JOHN
A Tour in South Africa. London: 1851. V. 68

FREEMAN, LEILA CROCHERON
Nip and Tuck. New York: 1926. V. 72

FREEMAN, R.
Kentish Poets. A Series of Writers in English Poetry, natives of or residents in the County of Kent . . . Canterbury: 1821. V. 71
The Works of Charles Darwin. London: 1977. V. 73

FREEMAN, R. AUSTIN
The Adventures of Romney Pringle. Philadelphia: 1968. V. 68; 72
As a Thief in the Night. New York: 1928. V. 68; 71
The Blue Scarab. New York: 1924. V. 68
A Certain Dr. Thorndyke. London: 1927. V. 71
A Certain Dr. Thorndyke. New York: 1928. V. 68
The D'Arblay Mystery. London: 1926. V. 68; 71
The D'Arblay Mystery. New York: 1926. V. 71
Dr. Thorndyke Intervenes. London: 1933. V. 71
Dr. Thorndyke Intervenes. New York: 1933. V. 70
Dr. Thorndyke's Case-Book. London: 1923. V. 71
Dr. Thorndyke's Cases. New York: 1931. V. 68; 71
The Exploits of Danby Croker. London: 1924. V. 71
The Eye of Osiris. London: 1911. V. 71
Felo de Se?. London: 1937. V. 71
Flighty Phillis. London: 1928. V. 68
For the Defence: Dr. Thorndyke. London: 1934. V. 71
The Further Adventures of Romney Pringle. Philadelphia: 1969. V. 68; 72
The Golden Pool. London: 1937. V. 71
The Great Portrait Mystery. London: 1918. V. 69; 71
John Thorndyke's Cases. London: 1909. V. 69; 73
Mr. Polton Explains. London: 1940. V. 71
Mr. Polton Explains. New York: 1940. V. 68; 71
Mr. Pottermack's Oversight. New York: 1930. V. 68
The Mystery of 31, New Inn. Philadelphia: 1913. V. 71
The Mystery of Angelina Frood. New York: 1928. V. 69; 73
The Penrose Mystery. New York: 1936. V. 71
The Penrose Mystery. London: 1944. V. 71
Pontifex, Son and Thorndyke. London: 1931. V. 71
Pontifex, Son and Thorndyke. New York: 1931. V. 68
The Puzzle Lock. London: 1925. V. 71
The Queen's Treasure. Philadelphia: 1975. V. 68
The Red Thumb Mark. London: 1907. V. 69
The Red Thumb Mark. 1911. V. 69; 71
The Red Thumb Mark. London: 1911. V. 68; 71
A Savant's Vendetta. London. V. 71
A Savant's Vendetta. London: 1920. V. 70
The Shadow of the Wolf. London: 1925. V. 71
The Singing Bone. London: 1912. V. 71
The Singing Bone. London: 1923?. V. 71
Social Decay and Regeneration. London: 1851. V. 71
The Stoneware Monkey. London: 1938. V. 68; 71
The Stoneware Monkey. New York: 1939. V. 68; 71
The Surprising Experiences of Mr. Shuttlebury Cobb. London: 1927. V. 71
The Surprising Experiences of Mr. Shuttlebury Cobb. London: 1928. V. 68
Thorndyke File. Frederick: 1976-1977. V. 72
Travels and Life in Ashanti & Jaman. London: 1898. V. 70; 71
The Uttermost Farthing. Philadelphia: 1914. V. 68; 71
The Vanishing Man. New York: 1912. V. 68

FREEMAN, R. B.
British Natural History Books 1495-1900. London: 1980. V. 70
The Works of Charles Darwin: an Annotated Bibliographical Handlist. Folkstone, Kent: 1977. V. 72

FREEMAN, STEPHEN
The Ladies Friend or Complete Physical Library, for the Benefit and Particular Use of the Ladies of Great Britain and Ireland.... London: 1785?. V. 73

FREEMAN, STRICKLAND
The Art of Horsemanship.... London: 1806. V. 69

FREEMANTLE, W. T.
A Bibliography of Sheffield and Vicinty. Sheffield: 1911. V. 73

FREEMASONS
Proceedings of the Grand Lodge of Free and Accepted Masons of the Grand Lodge of Free and Accepted Masons of North Carolina. Raleigh: 1865. V. 71

FREIBURG IM BREISGAU
Nuwe Stattrechten und Statuten der Statt Fryburg im Pryszgow Gelegen. Basle: 1520. V. 68; 70; 73

FREIND, JOHN
Emmenologia. London: 1729. V. 68; 70
The History of Physick; from the Time of Galen to the Beginning of the Sixteenth Century, Chiefly with Regard to Practice. London: 1725-1726. V. 70; 72
A Letter to the Learned Dr. Woodward. London: 1719. V. 70

FREITAS, BERNARDINO JOSE DE SENNA
Uma Viagem ao Valle das Furnas na Ilha de S. Miguel em Junho de 1840. Lisboa: 1845. V. 70

FREMONT, JOHN CHARLES
Geographical Memoir Upon Upper California in Illustraton of His Map of Oregon and California. San Francisco: 1964. V. 68
Life Explorations and Public Services of John Charles Fremont. Boston: 1856. V. 71
Memories of My Life.... New York: 1887. V. 70
Report of the Exploring Expedition to the Rocky Mountains and to Oregon and Northern California.... Washington: 1845. V. 68; 70; 73

FRENCH, ALBERT
Billy. New York: 1993. V. 69

FRENCH, ALICE
The Lion's Share. Indianapolis: 1907. V. 69; 72
The Missionary Sheriff. New York: 1897. V. 69

THE FRENCH Anas. London: 1805. V. 68; 71

FRENCH, ARTHUR W.
Stereotomy. New York: 1902. V. 70

FRENCH, B. F.
History of the Rise and Progress of the Iron Trade of the United States from 1621 to 1857. New York: 1858. V. 69

FRENCH, FRANCES J.
The Abbey Theatre Series of Plays: a Bibliography. 1969. V. 69; 73

FRENCH, GEORGE
Printing in Relation to Graphic Art. Cleveland: 1903. V. 70

FRENCH, JAMES
Wild Jim, Captain W. J. French, Texas Ranger, the Texas Cowboy and Saddle King. Chicago. V. 69

FRENCH, JAMES WEIR
Modern Power Generators: Steam Electric and Internal Combustion and Their Application to Present-Day Requirements.... 1907. V. 71

FRENCH, LARRY L.
Notes for the Curious: a John Dickson Carr Memorial Journal. Carrian: 1978. V. 71

FRENCH, NICCI
Beneath the Skin. London: 2000. V. 68
Killing Me Softly. London: 1999. V. 72
The Memory Game. London: 1972. V. 72

THE FRENCH Polisher's Handbook with a Section on Gilding and Bronzing. London: 1921. V. 68

FRENCH, R. N.
Verses by.... Derby: 1808. V. 71

FRENCH, SAMUEL G.
Two Wars: an Autobiograhy. Nashville: 1901. V. 69

FRENCH, WILLIAM
Further Recollections of A Western Ranchman, New Mexico 1883-1899. New York: 1965. V. 71
Some Recollections of a Western Ranchman, New Mexico. 1883-1889. 1928. V. 68
Some Recollections of A Western Ranchman- New Mexico 1883-1899. New York: 1928. V. 71
Some Recollections of Western Ranchman (New Mexico 1883-1899) with Further Recollections of Western Ranchman. New York: 1965. V. 69; 70; 73

FRENEAU, PHILIP
The Poems of Philip Freneau: Poet of the American Revolution. Princeton: 1902-1907. V. 71
Poems Written and Published During the American Revolutionary War.... Philadelphia: 1809. V. 68; 69; 70; 73
Poems Written Between the Years 1768 and 1794. Monmouth: 1795. V. 73

FRERE, SHEPPARD
Verulamium Excavations. Oxford: 1972. V. 73

FRESENBORG, BERNARD
Thirty Years in Hell, or From Darkness to Light. St. Louis: 1904. V. 71

FRESHFIELD, D. W.
Below the Snowline. 1923. V. 68
The Exploration of the Caucasus. 1896. V. 68; 70; 73

FRESHFIELD, DOUGLAS
Below the Snow Line. London: 1923. V. 69
Italian Alps. London: 1875. V. 69; 72
Italian Alps. Oxford: 1937. V. 69
Travels in the Central Caucasus and Bashan.... London: 1869. V. 69

FRETTER, VERA
British Prosobranch Molluscs. London: 1962. V. 68
British Prosobranch Molluscs. London: 1994. V. 73

FREUCHEN, PETER
Arctic Adventure. My Life In The Frozen North. London: 1936. V. 72
It's All Adventure. London: 1938. V. 72
Ivalu, the Eskimo Wife. New York: 1935. V. 70

FREUD, ESTHER
Peerless Flats. London: 1993. V. 73

FREUD, LUCIAN
Lucian Freud. London: 1982. V. 70

FREUD, SIGMUND
Collected Papers. London: 1950. V. 71
Group Psychology and the Analysis of the Ego. New York: 1925. V. 72
Introductory Lectures on Psycho-Analysis. London: 1922. V. 71
The Problem of Lay-Analyses. New York: 1927. V. 71
Selbstdarstellung (Autobiography). Vienna: 1936. V. 72
Studien Uber Hysterie. Leipzig and Vienna: 1895. V. 69
Three Contributions to the Sexual Theory. New York: 1910. V. 70
Die Traumdeutung. (The Interpretation of Dreams.). Leipzig & Vienna;: 1900. V. 73
Uber Den Traum. (On Dreams). Wiesbaden: 1901. V. 70
Das Unbehagen in Der Kultur. (Civilization and Its Discontents). Vienna: 1930. V. 72; 73
Die Zukunst Einer Illusion. Leipzig: 1928. V. 69; 71

FREUND, GISELE
The World in My Camera. New York: 1974. V. 72

FREWEN, MORETON
The Economic Crisis. London: 1888. V. 71
Melton Mowbray and Other Memories. London: 1924. V. 71

FREY, ADOLF
Blumen Ritornelle. Zurich: 1920. V. 70

FREYTAG, ETHEL
A History of Morgan County, Tennessee. 1971. V. 68

FREYTAS, NICHOLAS DE
The Expedition of Don Diego Dionisio de Panalosa, Governor of New Mexico, from Santa Fe to the river Mischipi and Quivira in 1662. NY: 1882. V. 72

FREY-WYSSLING, A.
Sub-Microscopic Morphology of Protoplasm and Its Derivatives. New York: 1948. V. 68

FRIBOURG, RENE
Catalogue of the Collection of the Late Rene Fribourg of 11 East 84th Street, New York City. 1963. V. 70

FRICK, GEORGE
A Treatise on the Diseases of the Eye. Baltimore: 1823. V. 72
A Treatise on the Diseases of the Eye. 1826. V. 73
A Treatise on the Diseases of the Eye. London: 1826. V. 72

FRIDGE, IKE
History of the Chisum War of Life Of Ike Fridge Stirring Events of Cowboy Life On the Frontier. ..... Electra, TX: 1927. V. 71

FRIEDAN, BETTY
The Feminine Mystique. New York: 1963. V. 72

FRIEDERICHS, HULDA
In the Evening of His Days. London: 1896. V. 72

FRIEDLANDER, LEE
The American Monument. New York: 1976. V. 68; 70
Bellocq: Photos from Storyville. New York: 1996. V. 68
Lee Friedlander Portraits. Boston: 1985. V. 70

FRIEDMAN, BRUCE JAY
The Lonely Guy's Book of Life. New York: 1978. V. 72
Steambath. New York: 1971. V. 72

FRIEDMAN, KINKY
Elvis, Jesus and Coca Cola. New York: 1993. V. 73
Frequent Flier. New York: 1989. V. 70; 73
God Bless John Wayne. New York: 1995. V. 71
Greenwich Killing Time. New York: 1986. V. 68; 69; 70; 73
Musical Chairs. New York: 1991. V. 68; 71
When the Cat's Away. New York: 1988. V. 69; 71; 73

FRIEDMAN, MICHAEL
Cowboy Culture- The Last Frontier of American Antiques. West Chester, PA: 1992. V. 71

FRIEDMANN, H.
The Cowbirds, A Study in the Biology of Social Pagination. Springfield: 1929. V. 70; 73

FRIEDRICH II, EMPEROR OF GERMANY
The Art of Falconry. Stanford: 1943. V. 73

FRIEDRICH II, EMPEROR OF GERMANY continued
The Art of Falconry. Stanford: 1961. V. 69
The Art of Falconry. 1969. V. 68; 69

FRIEL, BRIAN
The Loves of Cass McGuire. 1967. V. 70

THE FRIEND, Etc. A Series of Essays to Aid in Formation of Fixed Principles in Politics, Morals and Religon with Literary Amusements Interspersed. Vermont: 1831. V. 70

FRIENDLY Animals. London. V. 71
FRIENDLY Animals. London: 1920. V. 68

FRIENDLY Society Sermons; to Which are Added Some Few for Charitable Societies; All Written with the Same Object of Setting Forth the Causes of Distress Among the Poor.... London: 1831. V. 73

FRIES, B.
A History of Scandinavian Fishes. Stockholm: 1892-1895. V. 72

FRIESEL, UWE
Vladimir Nabokov 1899-1977. Hamburg: 1977. V. 70

FRIESNER, ISIDORE
Cerebellar abscess, Its Etiology, Pathology, Diagnosis and Treatment Including Anatomy and Physiology of the Cerebellum. London: 1916. V. 68

FRINK, ELISABETH
Elisabeth Frink, Sculpture and Drawings 1952-1984. London: 1985. V. 73

FRINK, MAURICE
When Grass Was King- Contributions to the Western Range Cattle Industry Study. Boulder: 1956. V. 71; 73

FRISBIE, W. A.
ABC Mother Goose. Chicago: 1905. V. 71; 73

FRISHIE, CHARLOTTE J.
Kindalda - a Study of the Navajo Girls Puberty Ceremony. Middleston: 1967. V. 68; 73

FRISON-ROCHE, R.
The Lost Trail of the Sahara. New York: 1952. V. 69; 71; 73
Mont Blanc and the Seven Valleys. London: 1961. V. 69
Les Montagnes de La Terre. 1964. V. 71

FRISSELL, TONI
The King Ranch 1939-1944. Ft. Worth: 1975. V. 70

FRISWOLD, CARROLL
The Killing of Chief Crazy Horse. Glendale: 1976. V. 72

FRITH, C. B.
The Birds of Paradise. Oxford: 1998. V. 72

FRITH, FRANCIS
Canterbury Cathedral. Canterbery: 1879. V. 68

FRITH, WALTER
The Sack of Monte Carlo. Bristol: 1897. V. 69; 73

FRITH, WILLIAM POWELL
John Leech. His Life and Work. London: 1891. V. 72
My Autobiography and Reminiscences. London: 1887. V. 73

FRITZ, JEAN
Homesick: My Own Story. New York: 1982. V. 70

FROBISHER, MARTIN
The Three Voyages of Martin Frobisher. London: 1938. V. 73

FRODERSTROM, H.
The Genus Sedum, L. 1936. V. 72

FROG Frolics. New York: 1894. V. 71

FROGER, FRANCOIS
Relation d'un Voyage fait un 1695, 1696 and 1697. Amsterdam: 1699. V. 68

THE FROG'S Wooing. London: 1890. V. 71

FROHAWK, F. W.
Natural History of British Butterflies. London: 1914. V. 70

FROISETH, JENNIE ANDERSON
The Women of Mormonism: or the Story of Polygamy as Told by the Victims Themselves. Detroit: 1887. V. 69

FROISSART, JOHN
Chronicles of England France, Spain and the Adjoining Countries, Etc. London: 1868. V. 68
Cronycles. 1927-1928. V. 70
Cronycles. Oxford: 1927-1928. V. 71
Sir John Froissart's Chronicles of England, France, Spain. London: 1808. V. 71

FROM Fairyland. A Book of Fairy Stories. London: 1915. V. 68

FROM The Nile To The Jordan. Monuments Of The Exodus Of The Israelites. London: 1873. V. 72

FROM Village to Town: a Series of Random Reminiscences of Batley During the Last 30 Years. Batley: 1882. V. 72

FROM Where the Sun Now Stands. Santa Fe: 1963. V. 72

FROM White-Caps to Contrails. A History of Modern Air Formation. 1981. V. 73

FROME, DAVID
The Black Envelope. New York: 1937. V. 69
The Hammersmith Murders. New York: 1930. V. 73

FROST & WINFIELD
Frost and Winfield's Pattern Book of Register Stoves, Tiled Grates and Kerbs for Tiled Hearths.... Derby: 1870?. V. 68

FROST, CHARLES
An Address, Delivered to the Literary and Philosophical Society, at Kingston-upon-Hull; at the Opening of the Seventh Session on Friday, November 5, 1830. Hull: 1831. V. 71
Notices Relative to the Early History of the Town and Port of Hull. London: 1827. V. 69

FROST, DONALD MC KAY
Notes on General Ashley, the Overland Trail and South Pass. 1945. V. 68
Notes on General Ashley, the Overland Trail and South Pass. Worcester: 1945. V. 73

FROST, LAWRENCE A.
The Court Martial of George Armstrong Custer. Norman: 1968. V. 72
The Custer Album - A Pictorial Biography of General George A. Custer. Seattle: 1964. V. 69; 72
Custer Legends. Bowling Green, OH: 1981. V. 72
Custer's 7th Cavalry and The Campaign of 1873. El Segundo: 1986. V. 72
General Custer's Libbie. Seattle: 1976. V. 72
With Custer in '74. Provo: 1979. V. 72

FROST, QUINTIN
The Harper and Other Poems. London: 1806. V. 69

FROST, RICHARD K.
Trial of Dr. Frost, Before the Court Sessions for the City and County of New York.... Philadelphia: 1838. V. 68

FROST, ROBERT LEE
Aforesaid. New York: 1954. V. 70; 72; 73
Away!. New York: 1958. V. 72
A Boy's Will. London: 1913. V. 72
A Boy's Will. New York: 1915. V. 68; 69; 70; 71; 72
A Boy's Will. New York: 1934. V. 71
A Cabin in the Clearing. NY: 1951. V. 72
A Chronological Survey. Middletown: 1936. V. 72
Closed For Good. New York: 1948. V. 72
Collected Poems. London: 1930. V. 72; 73
Collected Poems. New York: 1930. V. 70; 72
Collected Poems. New York: 1939. V. 69; 70; 71; 72; 73
Collected Poems. New York: 1940. V. 72
Complete Poems. New York: 1949. V. 69; 72
Complete Poems. New York: 1950. V. 69; 72
Complete Poems. London: 1956. V. 72
Complete Poems. London: 1961. V. 72
Does No One But Me At All Ever Feel This Way In The Least. New York: 1952. V. 72
Doom to Bloom. New York: 1950. V. 70; 73
From Snow to Snow. New York: 1936. V. 68; 70
A Further Range. New York: 1936. V. 68; 70; 73
The Gift Outright. New York: 1961. V. 71
Hard Not to be King. New York: 1951. V. 70; 71; 72; 73
In the Clearing. 1962. V. 72
In the Clearing. New York: 1962. V. 70; 71; 73
Kitty Hawk 1894. New York: 1956. V. 72
The Lone Striker. New York: 1933. V. 72
A Masque of Mercy. New York: 1947. V. 69; 70; 71
A Masque of Reason. New York: 1945. V. 70; 72
Mountain Interval. New York: 1916. V. 69; 72; 73
My Objection To Being Stepped On. New York: 1957. V. 72
New Hampshire. New York: 1923. V. 69; 72
North of Boston. 1914. V. 70
North of Boston. London: 1914. V. 73
North of Boston. New York: 1915. V. 69; 71; 72
On A Tree Fallen Across The Road (To Hear Us Talk). New York: 1949. V. 72
One Favored Acorn. New York: 1969. V. 69
One Favored Acorn. Ripton: 1969. V. 68
One More Brevity. New York: 1953. V. 72
The Pilgrim Spirit. Boston: 1921. V. 72
The Poems of Robert Frost. New York: 1946. V. 72
The Poetry Of Robert Frost. Barre: 1971. V. 72
Selected Letters Of Robert Frost. New York: 1964. V. 72
Selected Poems. New York: 1923. V. 72
Selected Poems. New York: 1926. V. 69; 71
Selected Poems. New York: 1928. V. 69; 71; 72
Selected Poems. New York: 1929. V. 72
Selected Poems. New York: 1934. V. 72
Selected Poems. New York: 1937. V. 72
Selected Poems. New York: 1938. V. 72
Snow To Snow. New York: 1936. V. 72
Some Science Fiction. New York: 1955. V. 72
Steeple Bush. New York: 1947. V. 68; 70; 72
An Unstamped Letter In Our Rural Letter Box. New York: 1944. V. 69
West-Running Brook. New York: 1928. V. 68; 72; 73
A Wishing Well. New York: 1959. V. 68

FROST, ROBERT LEE continued
A Witness Tree. New York: 1942. V. 68; 70; 72; 73
A Witness Tree. London: 1943. V. 73
You Come Too. New York: 1959. V. 68
A Young Birch. New York: 1946. V. 72

FROST, THOMAS
In Kent with Charles Dickens. London: 1880. V. 69

FROTHINGHAM, RICHARD
Life and Times of Joseph Warren. Boston: 1865. V. 69

FROUDE, JAMES ANTHONY
The English in the West Indies, or the Bow of Ulysses. London: 1888. V. 68
The English in the West Indies, or the Bow of Ulysses. London: 1899. V. 68
History of England from the Fall of Wolsey to the Defeat of the Spanish Armada. London: 1872. V. 73
Oceana, or England and her Colonies. London: 1894. V. 68

FRUCHTER, NORMAN
Coat Upon a Stick. New York: 1963. V. 69

FRY, C. B.
The Book of Cricket. A Gallery of Famous Players. 1899. V. 69

FRY, C. H.
The Birds of Africa. London: 2000. V. 69

FRY, CAROLINE
The Listener. London: 1831. V. 69; 73
A Word to Women, the Love of the World and Other Gatherings.... Philadelphia: 1840. V. 69; 73

FRY, CHRISTOPHER
The Dark is Light Enough. London: 1954. V. 69

FRY, EDMUND
Pantographia; Containing Accurate Copies of All the Known Alphabets in the World.... London: 1799. V. 68; 73

FRY, ELIZABETH
Memoir Of The Life Of Elizabeth Fry. London: 1847. V. 72

FRY, KATHARINE
History of the Parishes of East and West Ham.... 1888. V. 71

FRY, M.
Tropical Architecture in the Humid Zone. London: 1964. V. 69; 72

FRY, ROGER
Architectural Heresies of a Painter - a Lecture Delivered at the Royal Institute of British Architectus May 20th 1921. London: 1921. V. 70
Giovanni Bellini. London: 1899. V. 69

FRY, STEPHEN
The Hippopotamus. London: 1994. V. 70; 73
Making History. London: 1996. V. 73
The Star's Tennis Balls. London: 2000. V. 70

FRYE, F. L.
Biomedical and Surgical Aspects of Captive Reptile Husbandry. Malabar: 1991. V. 70

FRYE, PERCIVAL
A Letter to a Friend, Containing Some Matters Relating to the Church. 1857. V. 73

FRYER, ALFRED C.
Aidan, Apostle of England. 1902. V. 69

FRYER, DONALD S.
Songs and Sonnets Atlantean. Sauk City: 1971. V. 68

FRYER, JANE EAYRE
The Mary Frances First Aid Book. Philadelphia: 1916. V. 68
The Mary Frances Housekeeper or Adventures Among the Doll People. Philadelphia: 1916. V. 71
Mary Frances Knitting and Crocheting Book. Philadelphia: 1918. V. 70; 73
The Mary Frances Sewing Book or Adventures Among the Thimble People. Philadelphia: 1913. V. 70; 72

FRYER, JOHN
A New Account of East-India and Persia, in Eight Letters.... London: 1698. V. 68; 72

FRYER, MICHAEL
The Trial and Life of Eugene Aram, Several of His Letters and Poems; and His Plan and Specimens of an Anglo-Celtic Lexicon.... Richmond: 1832. V. 71

FRYKE, CHRISTOPHER
A Relation of Two Several Voyages Made into the East-Indies.... London: 1700. V. 68

FRYMIR, ALICE W.
Basket Ball for Women. New York: 1928. V. 68

FUCHS, ERNEST
Text-Book of Ophthalmology. New York: 1893. V. 71
Text-Book of Ophthalmology. New York: 1896. V. 73

FUCHS, LEONHART
De Sanadis Totius Humani Corporis Malis Libri Quinque. Ad Quinque Priores Suos Libros. Lugduni: 1547. V. 72
Tabula Oculorum Morbos Comprehendos 1538. A Facsimile. Palo Alto: 1949. V. 68

FUENTES, CARLOS
Burnt Water. New York: 1980. V. 68
The Campaign. New York: 1991. V. 73
Terra Nostra. New York: 1976. V. 68; 69

FUENTES, NORBERTO
Ernest Hemingway Rediscovered. New York: 1998. V. 73

FUERTES, L. A.
Abyssinian Birds and Mammals. Chicago: 1930. V. 73
Birds of New York. Albany: 1916. V. 72

FUESS, CLAUDE MOORE
Daniel Webster. Boston: 1930. V. 73

FUGITIVE Pieces on Various Subjects. London: 1765. V. 73

FUHRMAN, CHRIS
The Dangerous Lives of Altar Boys. Athens and London: 1994. V. 68; 69; 71; 72

FUJITA, J.
Tanka: Poems in Exile. Chicago: 1923. V. 71

FUJIWARA, KANESUKE
The Lady Who Loved Insects. London: 1929. V. 70

FULD, JAMES J.
A Pictorial Bibliography of the First Editions of Stephen C. Foster. Philadelphia: 1957. V. 68; 73

FULFORD, M. H.
Manual of the Leafy Hepaticae of Latin America. New York: 1963-1968. V. 72

FULKE, WILLIAM
A Defense of the Sincere and True Translations of the Holie Scriptures into the English Tong, Against the Manifolde Cauils, Friuolous Quarels and Impudent Slaunders of Gregorie Martin.... London: 1583. V. 70

A FULL and Particular Account of All the Circumstances Attending the Loss of the Steamboat Lexington, in Long Island Sound, on the Night of January 13, 1840. Providence: 1840. V. 71

FULLAM, GEORGE TOWNLEY
Journal of George Townley Fullam, Boarding Officer of the Confederate Sea Raider Alabama. Mobile: 1973. V. 69; 70

FULLER, A. S.
The Nut Culturist, a Treatise on the Propagation, Planting and Cultivation of Nut Bearing Trees and Shrubs.... New York: 1896. V. 72

FULLER, CLAUD E.
Springfield Muzzle-Loading Shoulder Arms. New York: 1930. V. 72

FULLER, E.
The Great Auk. New York: 1999. V. 72

FULLER, FRANCIS
Medicina Gymnastica; or, Every Man His Own Physician. 1771. V. 72
Medicina Gymnastica; or, Every Man His Own Physician. London: 1771. V. 68
Peace in War by Christ, the Prince of Peace. London: 1696. V. 68; 72

FULLER, HENRY B.
The Chevalier of Pensieri-Vani Together with Frequent References to the Prorege of Arcopia. Boston: 1890. V. 68

FULLER, HENRY C.
A Texas Sheriff a Vivid and Accurate Account of Some of the Most Notorious Murder Cases and Feuds. Nacogdoches: 1931. V. 69

FULLER, HENRY WILLIAM
On Diseases of the Lungs and Air-Passages; Their Pathology, Physical Diagnosis, Symptoms and Treatment. Philadelphia: 1867. V. 71

FULLER, J. F. C.
The Second World War 1939-1945: A Strategical and Tactical History. London: 1948. V. 72
The Star in the West. A Critical Essay Upon the Works of Aleister Crowley. New York: 1907. V. 70

FULLER, JOHN
Fairground Music. London: 1961. V. 70

FULLER, MARGARET
The Love Letters of Margaret Fuller 1845-1846. New York: 1903. V. 73

FULLER, R. BUCKMINSTER
Education Automation. Freeing the Scholar to Return to His Studies. Carbondale: 1962. V. 70
No More Secondhand God. Carbondale: 1963. V. 70
No More Secondhand God. Carbondale: 1969. V. 68
Synergetics. New York: 1975. V. 68; 70
Synergetics 2. New York: 1979. V. 68
Untitled Epic Poem on the History of Industrialization. Highlands: 1962. V. 70

FULLER, ROY
Brutus's Orchard - Poems. London: 1957. V. 71
Buff. London: 1965. V. 71
The Carnal Island. London: 1970. V. 71
Consolations. London: 1987. V. 71
From the Joke Shop. London: 1975. V. 71
Home and Dry - Memoirs III. London: 1984. V. 71
Iron Aspidistra. Oxford: 1985. V. 68

FULLER, ROY continued
Lessons of the Summer. Edinburgh: 1987. V. 71
More About Tompkins. 1981. V. 70
New and Collected Poems 1934-1984. London: 1985. V. 71
New Poems. London: 1968. V. 71
Off Course - Poems. London: 1969. V. 71
An Old War. Edinburgh: 1974. V. 69
Outside the Canon. Edinburgh: 1986. V. 71
The Reign of Sparrows. London: 1980. V. 71
Souvenirs. London: 1980. V. 71
Spanner and Pen - Post War Memoirs. London: 1991. V. 71
Stares. London: 1990. V. 71
The Strange and the Good - Collected Memoirs. London: 1989. V. 71
Subsequent to Summer. Edinburgh: 1985. V. 71
Tiny Tears. London: 1973. V. 71
Vamp Till Ready - Further Memoirs. London: 1982. V. 71

FULLER, SAMUEL
144 Piccadilly. New York: 1971. V. 68

FULLER, SARITA
Their Own Desire. New York: 1929. V. 70

FULLER, THOMAS
Good Thoughts in Bad Times, Good Thoughts in Worse Times, Mixt Contemplations in Better Times. (with) The Holy State and the Profane State. (with) The History of the War. London: 1840-1841. V. 73
The History of the Holy War. London: 1840. V. 68; 72

FULLER, TIMOTHY
Harvard Has a Homicide. Boston: 1936. V. 73
Reunion with Murder. Boston: 1941. V. 68; 72; 73
Three Thirds of a Ghost. London: 1947. V. 70

FULLERTON, ANNA M.
A Handbook of Obstetric Nursing for Nurses, Students and Mothers. Philadelphia: 1890. V. 68; 69

FULLERTON, GEORGIANA
Ellen Middleton. Paris: 1845. V. 69

FULLING, E. H.
A Guide to the Pinetum. Bronx: 1929. V. 72

FULOP-MILLER, RENE
The Mind and Face of Bolshevism - An Examination of Cultural Life in Soviet Russia. London: 1927. V. 72

FULTON, ARABELLA
Tales of the Trail. Montreal: 1965. V. 71

FULTON, FRANCES I. SIMS
To and through Nebraska by a Pennsylvania Girl. Lincoln: 1884. V. 69; 70; 73

FULTON, JOHN FARQUHAR
A Bibliography of the Honourable Robert Boyle. Oxford: 1932. V. 70; 72
A Bibliography of Two Oxford Physiologists Richard Lower (1631-1679) John Mayow (1643-1679). Oxford: 1935. V. 71; 72
The Centennial of Surgical Anesthesia; an Annotated Catalogue of Books and Pamphlets Bearing on the Early History of Surgical Anesthesia. Mansfield Centre: 1998. V. 69
The Great Medical Biographers. A Study in Humanism. Philadelphia: 1951. V. 68; 72
Harvey Cushing. A Biography. Springfield: 1946. V. 68; 70
Harvey Cushing. A Biography. Springfield: 1947. V. 68; 70; 71; 72
Michael Servetus Humanist and Martyr. New York: 1953. V. 68; 71
Physiology of the Nervous System. London and New York: 1938. V. 71
Selected Readings in the History of Physiology. Springfield: 1930. V. 68; 72
The Sign of Babinski. Springfield: 1932. V. 68; 71; 72

FULTON, MAURICE G.
Diaries and Letters of Josiah Gregg. Norman: 1941-1944. V. 73
History of the Lincoln County War. Tucson: 1968. V. 70; 71
New Mexico's Own Chronicle. Dallas: 1937. V. 68; 69

FULTON, R.
The Illustrated Book of Pigeons.... London: 1874-1876. V. 73

FULTON, W. S.
An Archaeological Site Near Gleeson, Arizona. 1940. V. 69

FULTZ, FRANCIS M.
The Elfin Forest. Los Angeles: 1927. V. 68

FUMAGALLI, PAOLO
Pompeia, Trattato Pittorico, Storico, e Geometrico. Florence: 1835. V. 70; 72

FUNDABURK, E. L.
Sun Circles and Human Hands. 1957. V. 69

FUNKE, OTTO
Atlas of Physiological Chemistry. London: 1853. V. 70; 72

FUNNY Farm Friends. London: 1900. V. 72

FUNNY Jungleland Moving Pictures. 1909. V. 68

FUNNY Picture Stories in the Struwwelpeter Manner. London: 1874-1876?. V. 73

THE FUNNY Story Book - New Series. London: 1857. V. 73

FURLIMBUNNIE, JERRY
A Great Adventure. London: 1920. V. 73

FURLONG, CHARLES WELLINGTON
Let 'Er Buck: a Story of the Passing of the Old West. New York: 1921. V. 71; 73

FURLONG, LAWRENCE
The American Coast Pilot.... Newburyport: 1798. V. 68

FURMAN, A. L.
Consulting Specialist. New York: 1937. V. 71
Private Practice. New York: 1933. V. 69
Third Mystery Companion. New York: 1945. V. 69

FURMAN, JAMES C.
Sermon on the Death of Rev. James. M. Chiles, Preached at Horeb Church, Abbeville District, S.C. On Sunday, 29th of March, 1863. Greenville: 1863. V. 69; 70

FURMAN, MOORE
The Letters of Moore Furman, Deputy Quarter-Master General of New Jersey in the Revolution. New York: 1912. V. 69

FURMAN, RICHARD
Humble Submission to Divine Sovereignty the Duty of a Bereaved Nation: A Sermon, Occasioned by the Death of His Excellency General George Washington. Charleston: 1800. V. 70

FURNAS, MARTHEDITH
The Far Country. New York and London: 1947. V. 71

FURNAS, ROBERT W.
Nebraska Her Resources - Adventures, Advancement and Promises. New Orleans: 1885. V. 68; 73

FURNESS Year Book. Fifth Annual. Ulverston: 1898. V. 71

FURNESS Year Book. Sixth Annual. Ulverston: 1899. V. 71

FURNESS Year Book. Eighth Annual. Ulverston: 1901. V. 71

FURNESS Year Book. Ninth Annual. Ulverston: 1902. V. 71

FURNESS Year Book. 10th Annual. Ulverston: 1903. V. 71

FURNESS Year Book. 11th Annual. Ulverston: 1904. V. 71

FURNESS Year Book. 14th Annual. Ulverston: 1907. V. 71

FURNESS Year Book. 15th Annual. Ulverston: 1908. V. 71

FURNESS, WILLIAM
History of Penrith, from the Earliest Record to the Present Time. Penrith: 1894. V. 71

FURNISS, HARRY
Flying Visits. Bristol: 1892. V. 68
Lika Joko. London: 1895. V. 72

FURNIVAL, WILLIAM J.
Researches on Leadless Glazes. London: 1898. V. 69

FURST-BISCHOFLICHE Olmucische Residentz-Stadt Crembsier Sambt Denen Nechst Darbey Neuenhobt, und von Grund Zugericht und Erbauten Lust-Blum- und Thier-Garten. Crembsier (i.e. Kromeriz): 1691. V. 68

FURST, ALAN
The Caribbean Account. New York: 1981. V. 71
The Caribbean Account. London: 1983. V. 69; 70; 71
Dark Star. Boston: 1991. V. 69; 71; 72
Dark Star. London: 1991. V. 70; 71; 73
Kingdom of Shadows. London: 2000. V. 70; 71; 72; 73
Kingdom of Shadows. New York: 2001. V. 71; 72
The Paris Drop. Garden City: 1980. V. 68; 69
The Paris Drop. London: 1982. V. 68; 71
The Polish Officer. London: 1995. V. 70; 71; 73
Red Gold. London: 1999. V. 70; 71; 73
Red Gold. New York: 1999. V. 71; 72; 73
Shadow Trade. Garden City: 1983. V. 69
Shadow Trade. London: 1983. V. 69
Shadow Trade. London: 1984. V. 71
The World at Night. London: 1996. V. 71
The World at Night. New York: 1996. V. 69; 71
The World at Night. London: 1997. V. 70
Your Day in the Barrel. New York: 1976. V. 69; 70

FURST, HERBERT
The Modern Woodcut. London: 1924. V. 72; 73

FURST, JILL LESLIE
Pre-Columbian Art of Mexico. New York: 1980. V. 71

FURST, PETER T.
American Indian Art and Paintings by Taos Artists: The David and Peggy Rockefeller Collection. New York: 1988. V. 70
North American Indian Art. New York: 1982. V. 71

FURTH, RALP VAN
Mononuclear Phagocytes. Oxford: 1970. V. 68

FURTTENBACH, JOSEPH
Architectura Recreationis.... Augsburg: 1640. V. 72
Architectura Univeralis. Ulm: 1635. V. 68; 70; 72

FURTTENBACH, JOSEPH continued
Mannhaffter Kunst-Spiegel, Oder Continuatio, und Fortsetzung Allerhand Mathematisch.... Augsburg: 1663. V. 72

FURTWANGLER, ADOLF
Masterpieces of Greek Sculpture. New York: 1895. V. 69

FURUTANI, DALE
Death in Little Tokyo. New York: 1996. V. 70

FUSELI, HENRY
Reflections on the Painting and Sculpture of Greeks.... London: 1765. V. 69

FUTRELLE, JACQUES
The Chase of the Golden Plate. 1906. V. 71
The Diamond Master. 1909. V. 71
My Lady's Garter. 1912. V. 71
The Thinking Machine. New York: 1907. V. 69

FYFIELD, FRANCES
A Question of Guilt. London: 1988. V. 71
Shadows on the Mirror. London: 1989. V. 71

FYLEMAN, ROSE
The Adventure Club,. London: 1925. V. 69
Fairies and Chimneys - Twenty Five Poems. London: 1918. V. 68
The Katy Kruse Dolly Book. London: 1928. V. 70
The Rose Fyleman Fairy Book. London: 1923. V. 72

G

G P H: An Informal Record of George P. Hammond and His Era in the Bancroft Library. Berkeley: 1965. V. 72

G. & D. COOK & CO.
Illustrated Catalogue of Carriages and Special Business Advertiser. New Haven: 1860. V. 69

G. & S. LTD.
Cords, Moles, Cantoons etc. for Breeches and Trousers Always in Stock. 1930?. V. 71

G., A.
Willie and Lucy at the Sea-Side. London: 1868. V. 68; 70

G., C.
An Elegie Upon the Most Lamented Death of the Right Honourable and Truly Valiant, Robert Earle of Essex, etc. 1646. V. 69
A Fortnight's Tour Amongst the Arabs on Mount Lebanon, Including a Visit to Damascus.... London: 1876. V. 69

G., W. E.
Odds and Ends from the Portfolio of an Amateur. London: 1820. V. 69

G., W. O.
An Historical Account of the Farthingale and Hoop-Petticoat. London: 1863. V. 71

GABO, NAUM
Of Divers Arts. London: 1962. V. 69; 72

GABRIEL, GILBERT W.
Brownstone Front. New York: 1924. V. 71

GABRIELSON, I. N.
The Birds of Alaska. Harrisburg: 1959. V. 68; 70
Western American Alpines. New York: 1932. V. 71

GADDIS, PEGGY
Dark Passion. New York: 1950. V. 73

GADDIS, THOMAS E.
Birdman of Alcatraz: the Story of Robert Stroud. New York: 1955. V. 70

GADDIS, WILLIAM
Carpenter's Gothic. New York: 1985. V. 68; 71; 72
A Frolic of His Own. New York: 1994. V. 70
JR. New York: 1975. V. 68; 70; 73
The Recognitions. New York: 1955. V. 70; 71; 72; 73

GADOW, HANS
Jorullo. The History of the Volcano of Jorullo and the Reclamation of the Devasted District by Animals and Plants. Cambridge: 1930. V. 70

THE GAELIC Choir. A Choisir-Chiuil. The St. Columba Collection of Gaelic Songs, Arranged for Part-Singing. Paisley. V. 71

GAERTNER, J.
De Fructibus et Seminibus Plantarum, Accedunt Seminum Centuriae Quinque Priores cum Tabulis Aeneis. Stuttgart: 1788. V. 72

GAETLEIN, FRANK
Harry Jackson. New York: 1969. V. 72

GAG, WANDA
The ABC Bunny. New York: 1933. V. 71
Gone is Gone or the Story of a Man Who Wanted to Do Housework. New York: 1935. V. 72
Millions of Cats. New York: 1928. V. 70

GAGARIN, Y.
Road to the Stars. Moscow: 1962. V. 72

GAGE, JACK
The Johnson County War Ain't A Pack of Lies/Back to Back with Is a Pack of Lies. Cheyenne: 1967. V. 68

GAGE, MATILDA JOSLYN
Woman, Church and State: an Historical Account of the Status of Woman through the Christian Ages.... New York: 1893. V. 73

GAIMAN, NEIL
Angels and Visitations: a Miscellany. Minneapolis: 1993. V. 68; 71

GAINES, CHARLES
Pumping Iron. New York: 1974. V. 72

GAINES, CHARLES KELSEY
Echoes of Many Moods. Mt. Vernon: 1926. V. 73

GAINES, ERNEST J.
The Autobiography of Miss Jane Pitman. New York: 1971. V. 70; 72
Bloodline. New York: 1968. V. 70; 72
Catherine Carmier. New York: 1964. V. 70
A Gathering of Old Men. New York: 1983. V. 70; 71; 72
In My Father's House. New York: 1978. V. 69; 70
A Lesson Before Dying. New York: 1993. V. 68; 69; 70; 71; 72; 73
Obsession. 1994. V. 71
The Turtles. San Francisco: 1956. V. 70

GAINSFORD, SARAH
The Whole Proceedings in a Dispute Between Henry Lys, the Elder, Esquire and Sarah Gainsford, Widow. Gosport: 1789. V. 69

GAIRDNER, WILLIAM TENNANT
Public Health in Relation to Air and Water. Edinburgh: 1862. V. 69

THE GALATHEA Deep Sea Expedition 1950-1952. London: 1956. V. 68

GALATOPOULOS, STELLOS
Callas Prima Donna Assoluta. London: 1976. V. 68

GALBRAITH, DOUGLAS
The Rising Sun. 2000. V. 68

GALE, ETHEL C.
Hints on Dress; or, What to Wear, When to Wear It, and How to Buy It. New York: 1872. V. 69

GALE, NORMAN
Pleasures in Pussytown. London: 1912. V. 70
Songs for Little People. London: 1896. V. 70
Songs for Little People. Westminster: 1896. V. 72

GALE, ROGER
Registrum Honoris de Richmond: Exhibens Terrarum & Villarum Quae Quondam Fuerunt Edwini Comitis Infra Richmundshire Descritionem.... London: 1722. V. 72; 73

GALE, T.
Electricity, or Ethereal Fire, Considered.... Troy: 1802. V. 70

GALE, THOMAS
Opuscula Mythologica, Ethica et Physica Graece & Latine. Cambridge: 1671. V. 73
Opuscula Mythologica, Ethica et Physica Graece & Latine. Amstelaedami: 1688. V. 73

GALE, THOMAS A.
The Wonder of the Nineteenth Century. Rock Oil in Pennsylvania and Elsewhere. 1935. V. 71

GALELLA, RON
Jacqueline. New York: 1974. V. 68

GALENA Illinois City of Galena. 1937. V. 73

GALENA Illinois City of Galena. Illinois: 1937. V. 72

GALENSON, WALTER
The CIO Challenge to the AFL. Cambridge: 1960. V. 71

GALENUS
Epitome Galeni Pergame ni Opervma In Qvatvor Partes Digest, Pvlcherrima Mthodo Vniversam.... Basilaea: 1551. V. 68; 72
Galen on the Usefulness of the Parts of the Body. Ithaca: 1968. V. 68; 71; 72
In Hippocratis Librum de Humoribus, Commentarii Tres.... Venetiis: 1562. V. 68; 70
Introductio in Pulsus ad Teuthram Martino Gregorio Interprete Eiusdem de Pulsuum Usu Thoma Lincaro Interprete. Lyons. V. 70

GALEOTTI, M.
Elements of Conversation, Italian and English. London: 1828. V. 70

GALERIE du Musee Napoleon. Paris: 1804-1815;. V. 72

GALERIE Theatrale, ou Collection des Portraits en Pied, des Principaux Acteurs des Trois Premiers Theatres de la Capitale. Paris: 1812-1834. V. 70

GALILEI, GALILEO
Dialogues Concerning Two New Sciences.... Evanston: 1939. V. 73

GALILEI, GALILEO continued
Discorsi e Dimostrazioni Matematiche, Intorno a Due Nuove Scienze Attenenti Alla Mecanica & i Movimenti Locali.... Leiden: 1638. V. 69

GALL, F. J.
Recherches sur le Systeme Nerveux en General et Sur Celui Du Cerveau En Particulier.... Paris: 1809. V. 68; 72

GALL, WILLIAM
The Solar System Paraphrased, Our Range of Space As It Was and Is.... Aberdeen: 1853. V. 71

GALLAEI, SERVATIUS
Dissertationes de Sibyllis, Earumque Oraculis Cum Figurios Aeneis. Amstelodami: 1688. V. 68; 73

GALLAEUS, SERVATIUS
Sibyllina Oracula. Hoc Est, ex Veteribus Codicibus Emendata.... Amstelodami: 1689. V. 73

GALLAGHER, FRANK
The Indivisible Island: History of the Partition of Ireland. 1957. V. 71

GALLAGHER, STEPHEN
Chimera. New York: 1982. V. 68
Valley of Lights. 1987. V. 68

GALLAGHER, TESS
Moon Crossing Bridge. St. Paul: 1992. V. 68
Stepping Outside. Lisbon, Iowa: 1974. V. 72; 73

GALLAHER, RUTH A.
Legal and Political Status of Women in Iowa an Historical Account of the Rights of Women in Iowa from 1838 to 1918. Iowa City: 1918. V. 72

GALLAND, PIERRE
De Agrorvm Conditionibus & Constitutionibus Limitum...Omnia Figuris Illustrata. Paris: 1554. V. 70

GALLANT, MAVIS
Home Truths. Toronto: 1981. V. 72
In Transit. Markahm: 1988. V. 72
The Other Paris. London: 1957. V. 72
Overhead in a Balloon. Toronto: 1985. V. 72

GALLATIN, A. E.
American Walter Colourists. New York: 1922. V. 69; 72
Notes on Some Rare Portraits of Whistler - With Six Examples Hietherto Unpubished. New York and London: 1916. V. 71
Portraits of Whistler. A Critical Study of Iconography. New York: 1918. V. 71
Sir Max Beerbohm, Bibliographical Notes. Cambridge: 1944. V. 70

GALLAUDET, THOMAS H.
The Child's Book on the Soul. Hartford: 1832. V. 69

GALLAWAY, B. P.
Dark Corner of the Confederacy. Accounts of Civil War Texas as Told by Contemporaries. 1968. V. 70

GALLE, F. C.
Azaleas. Portland: 1987. V. 73

GALLENGA, GUY HARDWIN
Gun, Rifle and Hound, in East and West. 1894. V. 69; 70; 72; 73
The Image of War. 1914. V. 72; 73

THE GALLERY of Modern British Artists; consisting of a Series of Engravings from works of the most eminent artists of the day . . . London: 1835. V. 71

THE GALLERY Of Portraits. With Memoirs. London: 1833-1834. V. 72

GALLETTI, GIORGIO
Giardini Medicei: Giardini de Palazzo e Di Villa Nella Firenze Del Quattro-Cento. Milano: 1996. V. 70

GALLI BIBIENA, FERNANDO
Direzioni a'Giovani Studenti nel Disegno dell'Architettura Civile.... Bologna: 1777-1753. V. 72

GALLICHAN, W.
Fishing and Travel in Spain. 1904. V. 68

GALLICK Reports; or, an Historical Collection of Criminal Cases, Adjudged in the Supeme Courts of Judicature in France. London: 1737. V. 71

GALLICO, PAUL
The Poseidon Adventure. London: 1969. V. 72

GALLO, AGOSTINO
Le Vinte Giorni Sull'Agricoltura et De' Piaceri Della Villa. In Venetia: 1596. V. 68; 70
Le Vinti Giornate Dell'Agricoltura et De'Piaceri Della Villa. In Venetia: 1622. V. 70

GALLON, M.
Arte de Convertir el Cobre en Laton por Medio de la Piedra Calamina. Madrid: 1779. V. 68; 70; 73

GALLOWAY, ELIJAH
History and Progress of the Steam Engine.... 1830. V. 71

GALLUP, DONALD
A Catalogue of the English and American First Editions of Writings by T. S. Eliot. New Haven: 1937. V. 71
Ezra Pound: a Bibliography. Charlottesville: 1983. V. 68

T. S. Eliot: a Bibliography. London: 1952. V. 69
T. S. Eliot: a Bibliography. London: 1969. V. 72

GALLUP, JOSEPH
Sketches of Epidemic Diseases in the State of Vermont, from Its First Settlement to the Year 1815.... Boston: 1815. V. 72

GALLWEY, THOMAS
Lays of Killarney Lakes Descriptive Sonnets and Occasional Poems. 1871. V. 69; 73

GALOPIN, R.
Microscopic Study of Opaque Minerals. Cambridge: 1972. V. 68

GALPIN, JOSEPH
The Joiner's Instructor. London: 1856-1857. V. 68
The Joiner's Instructor. London: 1860?. V. 68

GALSWORTHY, JOHN
A Bit o' Love. London: 1915. V. 68
Caravan. The Assembled Tales. London: 1925. V. 73
Flowering Wilderness. London: 1932. V. 68
The Forsyte Saga. London: 1922. V. 70
Forsytes, Pendyces and Others. London: 1935. V. 70
Four Forsyte Stories. New York: 1929. V. 70
From the Four Winds. London: 1897. V. 68; 70; 73
Jocelyn. London: 1898. V. 73
The Man of Property. New York: 1964. V. 69
A Modern Comedy. London: 1929. V. 68
The Novels, Tales and Plays. New York: 1926. V. 68
On Forstye 'Change. London: 1930. V. 68
The Plays of John Galsworthy. London: 1929. V. 70
Swan Song. London: 1928. V. 68; 70
Verses New and Old. London: 1926. V. 73

GALT, JOHN
The Last of the Lairds; or the Life and Opinions of Malachi Mailings, Esq. of Auldbiggins. Edinburgh: 1826. V. 72
The Life and Studies of Benjamin West, Esq. Philadelphia: 1816. V. 70; 72; 73
The Works. Edinburgh: 1936. V. 73

GALTON, FRANCIS
Hereditary Genius. London: 1869. V. 72
Hereditary Genius. London: 1889. V. 69
Hereditary Genius. London: 1892. V. 71
Memories of My Life. London: 1908. V. 71
Vacation Tourists and Notes of Travel in 1860 (1861-1862-1863). London: 1861-1864. V. 69
Vacation Tourists and Notes of Travel in 1860 (and) 1861. London: 1861-1862. V. 72

GALTREY, S.
The Horse and the War. 1918. V. 68

GALTSOFF, P. S.
Gulf of Mexico: Its Origin, Waters and Marine Life. Washington: 1954. V. 72

GALVAYNE, SYDNEY
The Horse. Glasgow: 1888. V. 68

GALVIN, JOHN
The Comanche Indians: in the Fall of the Year 1845. San Francisco: 1970. V. 69
The Etchings of Edward Borein: a Catalogue of His Works. San Francisco: 1971. V. 68; 69; 70; 72
A Record of Travels in Arizona and California 1775-1776 Fr. Francisco Garces. San Francisco: 1965. V. 71; 72
Throughout the Country of the Comanche Indians in the Fall of the Year 1845. 1970. V. 68

GALWAN, RASSUL
Servant of Sahibs. 1924. V. 70; 72

GAMBOA, FERNANDO
Posada: Printmaker to the Mexican People. Chicago: 1944. V. 71

THE GAMESTER. London: 1796. V. 68

GAMGEE, JOSEPH SAMPSON
Medical Reform a Social Question, Comprehensively Studied.... London: 1857. V. 71

GAMMOND, PETER
A Bibliographical Companion to Betjeman. London: 1997. V. 71
Duke Ellington, His Life and Music. London: 1958. V. 73

GAMOW, G.
Mr. Tompkins in Wonderland. Or Stories of C. G. and H. New York: 1947. V. 69

GANDY, HENRY
Old England; or, the Government of England Prov'd to be Monarchical and Hereditary, by the Fundamental Laws of England, and by the Authorities of Lawyers, Historians and Divines, and Allegiance Due to the King.... London: 1705. V. 70

GANDY, JOSEPH
The Rural Architect... (bound with) Designs for Cottages, Cottage Farms and Other Rural Buildings Including Entrance Gates and Lodges.... London: 1805. V. 70
The Rural Architect... (with) Designs for Cottages, Cottage Farms and Other Rural Buildings, Including Entrance Gates and Lodges. London: 1805-1806. V. 68

GANILH, CHARLES
An Inquiry Into the Various Systems of Political Economy.... London: 1812. V. 70; 71

GANN, ERNEST K.
Island in the Sky. New York: 1944. V. 69; 71

GANNERON, E.
L'Irlande: Depuis son Origine Jusqu'aux Temps Presents. Paris: 1889. V. 69

GANNETT, HENRY
A Gazetteer of Kansas. Washington: 1898. V. 70

GANNON, FRANCIS X.
Biographical Dictionary of the Left. Belmont: 1969-1973. V. 71

GANONG, SUSAN B.
A Sketch of Life at Netherwood the Rothesay School for Girls September 1903-June 1944. Saint John: 1952. V. 72

GANONG, W. F.
Crucial Maps in the Early Cartography and Place-Nomenclature of the Atlantic Coast of Canada. Toronto: 1964. V. 73

GANPAT
The Speakers in Silence. London. V. 70

GANT, RICHARD
Ian Fleming: The Fantastic 007 Man. New York: 1966. V. 72

GANTILLON, SIMON
Maya. New York: 1928. V. 70
Maya. London: 1930. V. 71
Maya. Waltham St. Lawrence: 1930. V. 71

GANTT, W. HORSLEY
A Medical Review of Soviet Russia. London: 1928. V. 71

GANZ, PAUL
The Paintings of Hans Holbein. New York: 1950. V. 73

GANZHORN, JACK
I've Killed Men: an Epic of Early Arizona. New York: 1959. V. 69

GARAT, DOMINIQUE JOSEPH
Memoirs of the Revolution; or, an Apology for My Conduct in the Public Employments Which I Have Held.... Edinburgh;: 1797. V. 70

GARBETT, H.
The History of Harthill-w-Woodall. Ilfracombe: 1950. V. 73

GARCIA, ANDREW
Tough Trip Through Paradise 1878-1879. Boston: 1967. V. 72

GARCIA, CHRISTINA
Dreaming in Cuban. New York: 1992. V. 68; 69; 71; 72; 73

GARCIA LORCA, FEDERICO
Federico. Five Plays. London: 1965. V. 72
Selected Poems of Federico Garcia Lorca. London: 1943. V. 72
Three Tragedies. New York: 1947. V. 69
Three Tragedies. London: 1959. V. 72

GARCIA MARQUEZ, GABRIEL
El Amor en los Tiempos de Colera. Bogota: 1985. V. 69; 73
El Amour en Los Tiempos Del Colera. Mexico: 1985. V. 69
The Autumn of the Patriarch. London: 1977. V. 68; 72
La Aventura de Miguel Littin Clandestino en Chile. Bogota: 1986. V. 68
Chronicle of a Death Foretold. London: 1982. V. 73
Chronicle of a Death Foretold. New York: 1983. V. 73
Cien Anos de Soledad. Barcelona: 1969. V. 70
El Coronel No Tiene Quien Le Escriba. Medellin: 1961. V. 69; 70; 71
Cronica de Una Muerte Anunciada. Bogota: 1981. V. 69
For the Sake of a Country Within Reach of the Children. Bogota: 1996. V. 73
Los Funerales de la Mama Grande. Xalapa: 1962. V. 69; 70
El General en su Laberinto. Mexico City: 1989. V. 69
El General en su Laberinto. Mexico: 1990. V. 69; 72
The General in His Labyrinth. New York: 1990. V. 69; 71; 72
The General in His Labyrinth. London: 1991. V. 68
The General in His Labyrinth. New York: 1993. V. 69
La Hojarasca (Leaf Storm). Bogota: 1955. V. 69; 70
If I Had a Piece of Life. Dundas: 2001. V. 73
In Evil Hour. New York: 1979. V. 69
Innocent Erendira and Other Stories. New York: 1978. V. 68; 69; 71
Leaf Storm and Other Stories. London: 1972. V. 73
Leaf Storm and Other Stories. New York: 1972. V. 69
Love in the Time of Cholera. New York: 1988. V. 68; 69; 72; 73
La Mala Hora. (In Evil Hour). Madrid: 1962. V. 69; 70
News of a Kidnapping. London: 1997. V. 70
No One Writes to the Colonel. New York: 1968. V. 69
No One Writes to the Colonel. London: 1971. V. 69; 70
Of Love and Other Demons. London: 1995. V. 70
Of Love and Other Demons. New York: 1995. V. 69
One Hundred Years of Solitude. London: 1970. V. 68; 69
One Hundred Years of Solitude. New York: 1970. V. 69; 70; 72; 73
El Otono del Patriaraca. (Autumn of the Patriarch). Barcelona: 1975. V. 69; 70; 72; 73

GARD, WAYNE
Along the Early Trails of the Southwest. Austin: 1969. V. 69; 71
The Chisholm Trail. Norman: 1954. V. 70
Frontier Justice. Norman: 1949. V. 71; 73
Sam Bass. Boston: 1936. V. 70

GARDEN, ALEXANDER
Anecdotes of the Revolutionary War in America.... Charleston: 1822. V. 68

THE GARDEN of Caresses. Waltham St. Lawrence: 1934. V. 71

THE GARDEN of Paradise and Other Stories. New York: 1923. V. 68

GARDENER, HELEN
An Unofficial Patriot. New York: 1894. V. 73

GARDENIER, ANDERSON A.
The Successful Stockman and Manual of Husbandry. Canada: 1899. V. 71

GARDENSHIRE, SAMUEL M.
The Long Arm. New York: 1906. V. 69; 71; 73

GARDENSTONE, FRANCIS GARDEN, LORD
Travelling Memorandums, Made in a Tour Upon the Continent of Europe, in the Years 1786, 1787 & 1788. Edinburgh: 1791. V. 70; 72

GARDINER, ALAN H.
The Library of A. Chester Beaty: Description of a Hieratic Papyrus with Mythological Story, Love Songs and Other Miscellaneous Texts. (with) *Hieratic Papyri in the British Museum: Third Series: Chester Beaty Gift.* London: 1931. V. 70

GARDINER, ALFRED GEORGE
John Benn and the Progressive Movement. London: 1925. V. 71
Life of George Cadbury. London: 1923. V. 71

GARDINER, DOROTHY
West of the River. New York: 1941. V. 68; 73

GARDINER, RICHARD
A Letter to Thomas William Coke, Esq. of Holkham. London: 1778. V. 71

GARDINER, ROLF
The Second Coming. Vienna: 1921. V. 73

GARDINER, SAM R.
History of the Commonwealth and Protectorate 1649-1660. London: 1901. V. 71

GARDINER, W.
Twenty Lessons on British Mosses.... London: 1852-1849. V. 69

GARDINER, WREY
Thirteen Stories. 1944. V. 70

GARDNER, A.
The Art and Sport of Alpine Photography. 1927. V. 68; 70; 73

GARDNER, ARTHUR
The Peaks, Lochs and Coasts of the Western Highlands. Edinburgh: 1924. V. 69; 71

GARDNER, C. A.
The Toxic Plants of Western Australia. Perth: 1956. V. 72

GARDNER, CHARLES K.
Court Martial Proceedings of a General Court Martial, Held at Fort Independence (Boston Harbour), for the Trial of Major Charles K. Gardner, at the Third Regiment Infantry, Upon Charges of Misbehaviour, Cowardice in the Face of the Enemy.... Boston: 1816. V. 68

GARDNER, DAVID E.
Genealogical Research In England And Wales. Utah: 1964. V. 72

GARDNER, EDMUND G.
The Story of Siena and San Gimignano. London: 1902. V. 72

GARDNER, ERLE STANLEY
Bedrooms Have Windows. New York: 1949. V. 68
The Bigger They Come. 1939. V. 73
The Case of the Amorous Aunt. New York: 1963. V. 73
The Case of the Angry Mourner. New York: 1951. V. 69; 70; 71
The Case of the Backward Mule. New York: 1946. V. 68; 69; 70; 71; 73
The Case of the Baited Hook. New York: 1940. V. 69; 70
The Case Of The Beautiful Beggar. New York: 1965. V. 72
The Case of the Blonde Bonanza. New York: 1962. V. 68; 71
The Case of the Borrowed Brunette. New York: 1946. V. 69; 70
The Case of the Careless Cupid. New York: 1968. V. 69; 71
The Case of the Careless Kitten. New York: 1942. V. 70
The Case of the Caretaker's Cat. New York: 1935. V. 70
The Case of the Cautious Coquette. New York: 1949. V. 68; 73
The Case of the Counterfeit Eye. 1935. V. 71
The Case of the Crooked Candle. New York: 1944. V. 69
The Case Of The Crying Swallow. New York: 1971. V. 72
The Case of the Daring Decoy. 1957. V. 73
The Case of the Daring Divorcee. New York: 1964. V. 68
The Case of the Demure Defendant. New York: 1956. V. 68
The Case of the Dubious Bridegroom. New York: 1949. V. 68
The Case of the Duplicate Daughter. New York: 1960. V. 70; 71; 73
The Case of the Fan Dancer's Horse. 1947. V. 73
The Case of the Fan Dancer's Horse. New York: 1947. V. 69
The Case Of The Fenced-In Woman. New York: 1972. V. 72
The Case of the Fiery Fingers. New York: 1951. V. 69
The Case of the Foot Loose Doll. New York: 1958. V. 68

GARDNER, ERLE STANLEY continued
The Case of the Fugitive Nurse. New York: 1954. V. 68; 73
The Case of the Golddigger's Purse. New York: 1945. V. 69; 72
The Case of the Green-Eyed Sister. New York: 1953. V. 73
The Case of the Grinning Gorilla. New York: 1942. V. 68
The Case of the Grinning Gorilla. New York: 1952. V. 68; 69; 73
The Case of the Half Wakened Wife. New York: 1945. V. 68
The Case of the Ice-Cold Hands. NY: 1962. V. 72
The Case Of The Irate Witness. New York: 1972. V. 72
The Case of the Lonely Heiress. New York: 1948. V. 68
The Case of the Mischievous Doll. New York: 1963. V. 68; 71
The Case of the Moth-Eaten Mink. New York: 1952. V. 68
The Case of the Negligent Nymph. New York: 1950. V. 69
The Case of the One-Eyed Witness. New York: 1950. V. 68; 69; 71
The Case Of The Phantom Fortune. New York: 1964. V. 72
The Case of the Reluctant Model. New York: 1961. V. 68; 70; 71
The Case of the Restless Redhead. New York: 1954. V. 73
The Case of the Rolling Bones. New York: 1939. V. 71
The Case of the Runaway Corpse. New York: 1954. V. 68; 71; 73
The Case of the Screaming Woman. New York: 1957. V. 68
The Case of the Singing Skirt. New York: 1959. V. 68
The Case of the Sleepwalker's Niece. New York: 1936. V. 68
The Case of the Smoking Chimney. NY: 1943. V. 72
The Case of the Spurious Spinster. New York: 1961. V. 68; 70; 73
The Case of the Stuttering Bishop. New York: 1936. V. 69; 71
The Case of the Sulky Girl. New York: 1933. V. 69
The Case Of The Troubled Trustee. New York: 1965. V. 72
The Case of the Vagabond Virgin. New York: 1948. V. 69; 71
The Case of the Waylaid Wolf. New York: 1959. V. 71
Cats Prowl at Night. New York: 1943. V. 69
The Clew of the Forgotten Murder. 1935. V. 73
The Clew of the Forgotten Murder. New York: 1935. V. 70
Crows Can't Count. New York: 1946. V. 72
The D. A. Breaks an Egg. 1949. V. 73
The D. A. Breaks an Egg. New York: 1949. V. 68; 69
The D. A. Breaks a Seal. New York: 1946. V. 69
The D. A. Calls It Murder. 1937. V. 73
The D. A. Cooks a Goose. New York: 1942. V. 68
The D. A. Draws a Circle. New York: 1939. V. 70
The D. A. Goes to Trial. New York: 1940. V. 71
The D. A. Holds a Candle. 1938. V. 73
The D. A. Takes a Chance. New York: 1948. V. 68; 71
The Desert Is Yours. New York: 1963. V. 71
Erle Stanley Gardner's The Amazing Adventures of Lester Leith. New York: 1980. V. 68
The Hidden Heart of Baja. New York: 1962. V. 71
Hunting the Desert Whale. New York: 1960. V. 71
The Land of Shorter Shadows. New York: 1948. V. 71
Neighborhood Frontiers. 1954. V. 69
Neighborhood Frontiers. New York: 1954. V. 72
Top of the Heap. New York: 1952. V. 69; 70
Two Clues. New York: 1947. V. 70

GARDNER, F. B.
Everybody's Paint Book. New York: 1888. V. 68

GARDNER, J.
The Molluscan Fauna of the Alum Bluff Group of Florida. Washington: 1926-1950. V. 72

GARDNER, JOHN
The Art of Fiction. New York: 1984. V. 68; 71; 72
A Child's Bestiary. New York: 1977. V. 72; 73
Lies! Lies! Lies!: a College Journal of John Gardner. Rochester: 1999. V. 72
The Complete Works of the Gawain-Poet. Carbondale: 1970. V. 72
The Construction of the Wakefield Cycle. Carbondale: 1974. V. 72
The Corner Men. London: 1974. V. 72
Dragon, Dragon. 1965. V. 70
Dragon, Dragon. New York: 1975. V. 72
Every Night's A Bullfight. London: 1971. V. 72
For Special Services. London: 1982. V. 71
Frankenstein. Dallas: 1979. V. 73
Freddy's Book. New York: 1980. V. 73
The Garden Of Weapons. London: 1980. V. 72
Goldeneye. London: 1995. V. 72; 73
Grendel. New York: 1971. V. 70; 73
Grendel. London: 1972. V. 71; 73
Gudgekin the Thistle Girl. New York: 1976. V. 72; 73
In the Suicide Mountains. New York: 1977. V. 69; 73
Jason and Medeia. New York: 1973. V. 72; 73
Licence Renewed. London: 1981. V. 68; 69; 70; 71
The Liquidator. New York: 1964. V. 71
The Miller's Mule. 1965. V. 70
Le Morte D'Arthur. Lincon: 1967. V. 69
Nickel Mountain. New York: 1973. V. 68
The Nostradamus Traitor. London: 1979. V. 72
On Moral Fiction. New York: 1978. V. 70; 73
On Writers and Writing. Reading: 1994. V. 68; 73

The Poetry of Chaucer. Carbondale: 1978. V. 72
The Resurrection. New York: 1966. V. 69; 70; 73
The Revenge Of Moriarty. London: 1975. V. 72
Rumpelstiltskin. Dallas: 1978. V. 69
Rumpelstiltskin. Dallas: 1979. V. 73
Sir Gawain and the Green Knight. London: 1967. V. 73
Stillness and Shadows. London: 1987. V. 72
The Sunlight Dialogues. New York: 1972. V. 68
The Sunlight Dialogues. London: 1973. V. 71
Vlemk the Box-Painter. Northridge: 1979. V. 73
William Wilson. Dallas: 1979. V. 73
The Wreckage of Agathon. New York: 1970. V. 73

GARDNER, JOHN DUNN
Catalogue of the Principal Portion of the Valuable Library of John Dunn Gardner, Esq. of Chatteris, Cambridgeshire, Removed from His Late Residence, Bottisham Hall, Near Newmarket. London: 1854. V. 70

GARDNER, K. B.
Descriptive Catalogue of Japanese Books in the British Library, Printed Before 1700. London: 1993. V. 70

GARDNER, KEITH S.
Sir William Russell Flint 1880-1969. Bristol: 1986. V. 70; 72

GARDNER, LEONARD
Fat City. New York: 1969. V. 69; 70; 71; 73

GARDNER, RAYMOND HATFIELD
The Old Wild West: Adventures of Arizona Bill. San Antonio: 1944. V. 69

GARDNER, ROY
Hellcatraz. The Rock of Despair. 1939. V. 69

GARDNER, W. H.
Gerard Manley Hopkins (1844-1889). London: 1948. V. 70

GARDNER, WILLIAM
Chemical Synonyms and Trade Names. London: 1937. V. 68

GARDNER, WILLIAM H.
Merry Songs for Little Folks. Philadelphia: 1904. V. 70

GARDNER THORPE, CHRISTOPHER
James Parkinson 1755-1824.... Exeter: 1987. V. 68

GARDUNO, FLOR
Witnesses of Time. New York: 2000. V. 73

GARFIELD, BRIAN
Hopscotch. New York: 1975. V. 69; 70; 71; 72; 73

GARFIELD, LEON
Jack Holborn. London: 1964. V. 72; 73

GARGA, D. P.
From My Big Game Diaries. 1944. V. 72
From My Big Game Diaries. Calcutta: 1944. V. 70

GARIBALDI, G.
Autobiography. London: 1889. V. 71

GARIS, HOWARD R.
The Adventures of Uncle Wiggily. Newark: 1924. V. 70
The Second Adventures of Uncle Wiggily: the Bunny Rabbit Gentleman and His Muskrat Lady Housekeeper. Newark: 1925. V. 70
Uncle Wiggily and His Muskrat Lady Housekeeper. Racine: 1937. V. 70; 73

GARIS DAVIES, N. DE
A Corpus of Inscribed Egyptian Funerary Cones. Part I: Plates. Oxford: 1957. V. 70

GARLAND, ALEX
The Beach. London: 1996. V. 69; 70
The Beach. New York: 1997. V. 70
The Tesseract. London: 1998. V. 70; 72
The Tesseract. New York: 1999. V. 70

GARLAND, HAMLIN
The Book of the American Indian. New York: 1923. V. 69; 72
The Shadow World. New York: 1908. V. 71

GARLAND, HUGH
Scientific Aspects of Neurology. Edinburgh and London: 1961. V. 72

GARLAND, JOSEPH E.
Eastern Point. A Nautical, Rustical and Social Chronicle of Gloucester's Outer Shield and Inner Sanctum. Peterborough: 1971. V. 68

A GARLAND of New Songs. The Country Club: the Chandler's Shop: Paddy M'Shane's Seven Ages. London: 1800. V. 68

A GARLAND of Poetry; by Various Authors. Saltaire: 1873. V. 71

GARLAND, RICHARD
A Tour in Teesdale: Including Rokeby, and its Environs. York: 1813. V. 73
A Tour in Teesdale: including Rokeby, and its Environs. London: 1848. V. 73

GARMAN, H.
A Preliminary Report on the Animals of the Waters of the Mississippi Bottoms, Near Quincy, Ill. in August 1888. Springfield: 1889. V. 68; 71; 73

GARMAN, K. E.
The Four Little Piggies. Chicago: 1913. V. 73

GARMAN, S.
Plagiostomia. Cambridge: 1913. V. 69
Reports on Exploration Off the West Coasts of Mexico, Central and South America, and Off the Galapagos Islands.... Cambridge: 1899. V. 72; 73

GARNEAU, FRANCOIS XAVIER
History of Canada, from the Time of Its Discovery.... Montreal: 1860. V. 68
History of Canada, From the Time of Its Discovery.... Montreal: 1862. V. 71

GARNER, ALAN
The Aimer Gate. London: 1978. V. 70
The Guizer - A Book of Fools. London: 1975. V. 68
The Owl Service. 1967. V. 73
The Owl Service. London: 1967. V. 68
Red Shift. London: 1973. V. 73

GARNER, D. P.
The Farmer's Dictionary. New York: 1846. V. 72

GARNER, ELVIRA
Way Down in Tennessee. New York: 1941. V. 70

GARNER, HARRY
Chinese and Japanese Cloisonne Enamels. London: 1970. V. 72
Chinese Lacquer. London: 1979. V. 72

GARNER, R.
The Natural History of the County of Stafford. London: 1844. V. 69

GARNER, ROBERT
Holiday Excursions of a Naturalist Forming a Guide-Book to the Natural History of the Inland and Littoral. London: 1867. V. 68

GARNETT, DAVID
Go She Must!. London: 1927. V. 69
Pocahontas; or, the Nonpareil of Virginia. London: 1933. V. 69
The Sons of the Falcon. London: 1972. V. 71

GARNETT, EDWARD
An Imaged World - Poems in Prose. London: 1894. V. 68

GARNETT, FRANK W.
Westmorland Agriculture 1800-1900. Kendal: 1912. V. 69; 71

GARNETT, J.
Lake Scenery. Windermere. V. 71
Pen and Pencil Sketches of the Lakes. Windermere: 1870. V. 72

GARNETT, JAMES M.
Seven Lectures on Female Education. Richmond: 1824. V. 71

GARNETT, JOHN
Tables Requisite to Be Used with the Nautical Ephemeris for Finding the Latitude and Longitude at Sea.... New Brunswick: 1806. V. 73

GARNETT, LOUISE AYRES
Creature Songs. Boston: 1912. V. 71
The Muffin Shop. Chicago: 1908. V. 70

GARNETT, LUCY MARY JANE
Ottoman Wonder Tales. London: 1915. V. 72
The Women of Turkey and Their Folklore. London: 1890-1891. V. 73

GARNETT, P.
Stately Homes of California. Boston: 1915. V. 69; 72

GARNETT, RICHARD
English Literature. An illustrated record. London: 1903. V. 70; 71
Poems from the German. London: 1862. V. 71
William Shakespeare, Pedagogue and Poacher. London and New York: 1905. V. 73

GARNETT, TAY
Man Laughs Back. New York: 1935. V. 71

GARNETT, THOMAS
Essays on Natural History and Agriculture. 1883. V. 68

GARNIER, CHARLES
Observatoire de Nice. Coupole du Grand Equatorial. Application du Flotteur Annulaire. Paris: 1885. V. 73

GARRARD CLOCKS LTD.
The Garrard 14 Day Striking Clock. 1935?. V. 68

GARRARD, LEWIS H.
Wah-to-Yah and the Taos Trail. 1930. V. 69
Wah-to-Yah and The Taos Trail. San Francisco: 1933. V. 71
Wah-To-Yah and the Taos Trail. San Francisco: 1936. V. 69
Wah-To-Yah and the Taos Trail. Glendale: 1938. V. 70

GARRETT, EDMUND
Elizabethan Songs in Honour of Love and Beautie. Boston: 1895. V. 71

GARRETT, GEORGE
An Evening Performance. Garden City: 1985. V. 68
King of the Mountain. New York: 1957. V. 68
The Succession. Garden City: 1983. V. 72

To Recollect a Cloud of Ghosts. 1979. V. 68

GARRETT, PAT F.
The Authentic Life of Billy the Kid. New York: 1927. V. 69

GARRETT, WILLIAM
From Dusk Till Dawn. New York: 1929. V. 70; 72
The Professional Guest. New York: 1928. V. 69; 70
Treasure Royal. New York: 1926. V. 70

GARRICK, DAVID
Cymbeline. A Tragedy. Altered from Shakespeare by David Garrick. London: 1784. V. 68
The Diary of David Garrick. New York: 1928. V. 72
Memoirs of the Life of David Garrick, Esq. London: 1808. V. 71

GARRISON, F. G.
An Introduction to the History of Medicine, with Medical Chronology, Suggestions for Study and Bibliographic Data. Philadelphia: 1929. V. 70

GARRISON, FIELDING H.
An Introduction to the History of Medicine. Philadelphia: 1922. V. 71
An Introduction to the History of Medicine. Philadelphia: 1929. V. 68; 71; 72
An Introduction to the History of Medicine. Philadelphia: 1966. V. 72
A Medical Bibliography. London: 1943. V. 71
The Principles of Anatomic Illustration Before Vesalius, an Inquiry into the Rationale of Artistic Anatomy. New York: 1926. V. 69

GARRISON, G. R.
Mexican Houses: a Book of Photographs and Measured Drawings. New York: 1930. V. 68; 69; 72

GARRISON, THEODOSIA
The Earth Cry and Other Poems. New York: 1910. V. 68

GARRISON, WILLIAM LLOYD
The Letters of William Lloyd Garrison. Cambridge: 1971-1981. V. 68
Sonnets and Other Poems. Boston: 1843. V. 71
Thoughts on African Colonization; or an Impartial Exhibition of the Doctrines, Principles and Purposes of the American Colonization Society. Boston: 1832. V. 68

GARROD, A. E.
Inborn Errors of Metabolism.... London: 1923. V. 71

GARROD, ARCHIBALD
Garrod's Inborn Errors of Metabolism. London: 1963. V. 68

GARROTT, HAL
Snythergen. New York: 1923. V. 70
Squiffer. New York: 1924. V. 70

GARROW, D. W.
The History and Antiquities of Croydon, with a Variety of Other Interesting Matter.... Croydon: 1818. V. 71

GARSTIN, JOHN
A Treatise on Rivers and Torrents; with the Method of Regulating Their Course and Channels. London: 1818. V. 72

GARTH, DAVID
Angels and Cowards. New York: 1934. V. 71

GARTH, SAMUEL
The Dispensary. London: 1706. V. 70; 71

GARTON, RAY
Crucifax. London: 1989. V. 70
Live Girls. Baltimore: 1997. V. 69
The New Neighbour. 1991. V. 70
Pieces of Hate. Baltimore: 1996. V. 69

GARVAN, BEATRICE B.
The Pennsylvania German Collections. Philadelphia: 1982. V. 70

GARVE, ANDREW
The Shivering Mountain. London: 1959. V. 68

GARVEY, ELEANOR
The Arts of the French Book 1900-1965. Illustrated Books of the School of Paris. Dallas: 1967. V. 70

GARVEY, ROBERT
Good Shabbos. New York: 1951. V. 70

GARY, MADELEINE SOPHIE
Vignettes of the Beam in a Nigger's Eye. NY: 1970. V. 72

GARZONI, TOMMASO
L'Hospidale De' Pazzi Incvrabill. (bound after) Il Theatro De VAri, e Diversi Cervelli Mondani. In Venetia: 1589-1588. V. 70

GASCOIGNE, BAMBER
Image of Twickenham. Richmond-upon-Thames: 1981. V. 73

GASCOYNE, DAVID
April - a Novella. London: 2000. V. 70
Five Early Uncollected Pomes. 1984. V. 70
Journal 1936-1937. 1980. V. 70
Journal 1936-1937. London: 1980. V. 72
Man's Life Is This Meat. London: 1936. V. 71
Poems 1937-1942. London: 1943. V. 68; 69; 72

GASCOYNE, DAVID continued
Roman Balcony and Other Poems. London: 1932. V. 72
A Short Survey of Surrealism. 1935. V. 69; 72
A Short Survey of Surrealism. London: 2000. V. 70

GASH, JONATHAN
Firefly Gadroon. London: 1982. V. 69; 72
The Grace in Older Women. London: 1995. V. 73
The Grail Tree. London: 1979. V. 69
Jade Woman. London: 1988. V. 72
The Judas Pair. London: 1977. V. 70; 71
The Judas Pair. New York: 1977. V. 68; 71
The Lies Of Fair Ladies With Appreciation By H. R. F. Keating. Bristol: 1991. V. 72
Moonspender. London: 1986. V. 69; 72
Pearlhanger. London: 1985. V. 72
A Rag, a Bone and a Hank of Hair. London: 1999. V. 69
The Sleepers of Erin. London: 1983. V. 69
Spend Game. London: 1980. V. 69
Spend Game. New Haven: 1981. V. 68
The Vatican Rip. New Haven: 1982. V. 68
The Very Last Gambado. London: 1989. V. 69; 72

GASK, ARTHUR
The Judgment of Larose. New York: 1935. V. 68

GASK, LILIAN
Dinky's Circus. London: 1918. V. 73
The Fairies and The Christmas Child. London: 1912. V. 72
Folk Tales from Many Lands. London: 1910. V. 68

GASKEIN, TARELLA QUIN
Chimney Town. London: 1934. V. 70

GASKELL, ELIZABETH CLEGHORN
Cranford. London: 1891. V. 70
Cranford. 1896. V. 70
Cranford. London: 1904. V. 70
The Letters of.... Cambridge: 1966. V. 70
Life of Charlotte Bronte. London: 1857. V. 68; 70; 73
The Life of Charlotte Bronte. London: 1858. V. 68; 70
Life of Charlotte Bronte. Leipzig: 1859. V. 73
Mary Barton: a Tale of Manchester Life. London: 1856. V. 68
The Moorland Cottage. New York: 1851. V. 68; 70
My Diary. London: 1923. V. 68
Right at Last and Other Tales. London: 1860. V. 73
Ruth. London: 1853. V. 70
Wives and Daughters. New York: 1866. V. 68; 70
The Works. London: 1906. V. 73

GASKELL, ERNEST
Westmorland And Cumberland Leaders. London. V. 72
Westmorland and Cumberland Leaders. 1910. V. 71

GASKELL, P.
The Manufacturing Population of England, Its Moral, Social and Physical Conditions.... London: 1833. V. 71

GASKIN, L. J. P.
A Bibliography of African Art.... London: 1965. V. 69

GASPARIN, ADRIEN ETIENNE PIERRE DE, COMTE
Des Maladies Contagieuses des Betes a Laine. Paris: 1821. V. 72

GASPER, HOWLAND
The Complete Sportsman. New York: 1893. V. 72

GASPERETTI, J.
The Snakes of Arabia. Basel: 1988. V. 69

GASPEY, W.
Tallis's Illustrated London: in Commemoration of the Great Exhibition of all Nations in 1851. London: 1851-1852. V. 68

GASPEY, WILLIAM
Tallis's Illustrated London: in Commemoration of the Great Exhibition of All Nations in 1851. London: 1851-1852. V. 71

GASS, PATRICK
Gass's Journal of the Lewis and Clark Expedition.... Chicago: 1904. V. 73

GASS, WILLIAM H.
Cartesian Sonata and Other Novellas. New York: 1998. V. 72
Culp. New York: 1985. V. 72; 73
Fiction and the Figures of Life. New York: 1970. V. 72; 73
The First Winter of My Married Life. Northridge: 1979. V. 69
Habitations of the Word. New York: 1985. V. 68; 70
In the Heart of the Heart of the Country. New York: 1968. V. 68; 71
Omensetter's Luck. New York: 1966. V. 68; 69; 72; 73
Reading Rilke. New York: 1999. V. 71; 72
The Tunnel. New York: 1995. V. 69
The World Within the Word. New York: 1978. V. 68

GASSBENDER, ADOLF
Pictorial Aristry: the Dramatization of the Beautiful in Photography.... New York: 1937. V. 68

GASTER, M.
Children's Stories from Rumanian Legends and Fairy Tales. London: 1923. V. 69
The Tittled Bible. London: 1929. V. 70

GASTINEAU, EDWARD T.
A Hobble through the Channel Islands in 1858; or the Seeings, Doings and Musings of One Tom Hobbler.... London: 1860. V. 71

GASTON, A. J.
The Auks, Alcidae. Oxford: 1998. V. 73

GASTON, MARY FRANK
Haviland, Collectables & Objects Of Art. Paducah: 1984. V. 72

GAT, DIMITRI
Nevsky's Demon. New York: 1983. V. 72

GATCHET, ALBERT S.
The Karankawa Indians, the Coast People of Texas. Cambridge: 1891. V. 73

GATES, H. L.
The Devil's Lady. New York: 1933. V. 69; 71
The Laughing Peril. New York: 1933. V. 68

GATES, MAC BURNEY
The Black Pirate. New York: 1926. V. 70; 71

GATES, S. YOUNG
History of the Young Ladies' Mutual Improvement Associaton of the Church of Jesus Christ of Latter-Day Saints from November 1869 to June 1910. Salt Lake City: 1911. V. 72
The Life Story of Brigham Young. London: 1930. V. 69

GATES, THEOPHILUS R.
The Trials, Experience, Exercises of Mind and First Travels of.... Poughkeepsie: 1810. V. 69

GATES, WILLIAM G.
City of Portsmouth Records of the Corporation 1835-1927. Portsmouth: 1928. V. 70
Illustrated History of Portsmouth Lampshire Telegraph Centenary Edition. Portsmouth: 1900. V. 70

GATEWOOD, CHARLES
Badlands. Photographs. Frankfurt: 1999. V. 73

GATEWOOD, WILLARD B.
Smoked Yankees and the Struggle for Empire: Letters from Negro Soldiers. Urbana: 1970. V. 72

GATHORNE-HARDY, A. E.
Autumns in Argylshire with Rod & Gun. London: 1900. V. 71
My Happy Hunting Grounds. 1914. V. 71; 73

GATHORNE-HARDY, ROBERT
The Native Garden. London: 1961. V. 69; 70

GATKE, H.
Heligoland as an Ornithological Observatory. 1895. V. 69

GATLIFF, JAMES
A Firm Attempt at Investigation; or the Twinkling Effort of a Falling Star, to Relieve the Cheshire Full Moon from Those Clouds, Obesities and Excrescencies.... Manchester: 1820. V. 68

GATSCHET, ALBERT S.
The Karankawa Indians, the Coast People of Texas. Cambridge: 1891. V. 70

GATTI, A.
Great Mother Forest. 1936. V. 70; 72; 73

GATTINGER, A.
The Medicinal Plants of Tennessee.... Nashville: 1894. V. 69

GATTY, ALFRED
Sheffield: Past and Present: Being a Biography of the town During Eight Hundred Years. Sheffield: 1873. V. 73

GATTY, MARGARET SCOTT
The Book of Sun-Dials. London: 1872. V. 69
British Sea-Weeds. 1872. V. 69
British Sea-Weeds. London: 1872. V. 71
The Fairy Godmothers and Other Tales. London: 1851. V. 71
Parables from Nature. London: 1884-1885. V. 68
Parables from Nature. London: 1896. V. 68
Waifs and Strays of Natural History. London: 1871. V. 68

GAUDET, MARCIA
Porch Talk with Ernest Gaines. Baton Rouge: 1990. V. 70

GAUER, ALBERTINE
Catalogue of Malayalam Books in the British Library. London: 1971. V. 70

GAUGER, NICHOLAS
Fires Improv'd: Being a New Method of Building Chimneys, so as to Prevent Their Smoking.... London: 1715. V. 68
Fires Improved; or a New Method of Building Chimnies, So as to Prevent Their Smoking. London: 1736. V. 72

GAULD, H. DRUMMOND
Ghost Tales and Legends. London and Edinburgh: 1929. V. 70

GAULT, WILLIAM CAMPBELL
County Kill. New York: 1962. V. 71

GAULT, WILLIAM CAMPBELL continued
Day of the Ram. New York: 1956. V. 70; 71
Dead Hero. New York: 1963. V. 69
Death Out of Focus. New York: 1959. V. 71
Gallant Colt. New York: 1954. V. 70

GAULTIER, BON
The Book of Ballads. London: 1857. V. 71

GAUNT, WILLIAM
Marine Painting An Historical Survey. London: 1975. V. 69

GAUSE, ISAAC
Four Years with Five Armies. New York: 1908. V. 69; 70

GAUTIER, E. F.
Sahara, the Great Desert. New York: 1935. V. 72

GAUTIER, H.
Traite des Ponts, ou Il Est Parle de Ceux des Romains, & de Ceux des Modernes; de leur Construction.... Paris: 1765. V. 73

GAUTIER, THEOPHILE
The Beautiful Vampire. New York: 1927. V. 70
Emaux et Camees. Paris: 1929. V. 69
Jean and Jeanette. Paris: 1895. V. 71
King Candaules. Paris: 1895. V. 71
Mademoiselle de Maupin. London: 1938. V. 71
Mademoiselle de Maupin. Waltham St. Lawrence: 1938. V. 71
A Night of Cleopatra. Paris: 1895. V. 70; 71
Le Roi Candaule. Paris: 1893. V. 68; 72
The Romantic Ballet. London: 1932. V. 68
Wanderings in Spain. London: 1853. V. 73

GAUTREAUX, TIM
Same Place, Same Things. New York: 1996. V. 73

GAVIN, ANTONIO
A Master-Key to Popery, in five Parts. Hagerstown: 1822. V. 68
Observations on a Journy (sic) to Naples, Wherein the Frauds of Romish Monks and Priests are Farther Discover'd. London: 1691. V. 68

GAVIN, HECTOR
The Habitations of the Industrial Classes.... London: 1851. V. 69

GAWAIN AND THE GREEN KNIGHT
Sir Gawain and the Green Knight. London: 1912. V. 68
Sir Gawain and The Green Knight. London: 1930. V. 71; 73
Sir Gawain and the Green Knight. Oxford: 1930. V. 73
Sir Gawain and the Green Knight. Waltham St. Lawrence: 1952. V. 68; 71; 72

GAWSWORTH, JOHN
Crimes Creeps and Thrills. Forty-Five New Stories of Detection, Horror and Adventure. London: 1935. V. 73
E. H. Visiak. London: 1936. V. 71
Known Signatures - New Poems. London: 1932. V. 71
Mishka and Madeleine. A Poem Sequence for Marcia. 1932. V. 73
Poems. London: 1933. V. 72
Poems. London: 1938. V. 71

GAY, C.
Mezcala. Ancient Stone Sculptures from Guerrero Mexico. Geneva: 1992. V. 69

GAY, J. DREW
The Mystery of the Shroud. A Tale of Socialism. Bristol: 1887. V. 70

GAY, JOHN
Achilles. London: 1733. V. 73
The Beggar's Opera. London: 1761. V. 73
The Beggar's Opera. London: 1921. V. 69
The Beggar's Opera. London: 1922. V. 71
Fables. London: 1754. V. 69
Fables. 1757. V. 72; 73
Fables. London: 1757. V. 70
Fables. London: 1788. V. 72
Fables. London: 1793. V. 71; 72; 73
Fables. London: 1808. V. 70; 71
Plays. London: 1772. V. 71
Poems on Several Occasions. Glasgow: 1770. V. 73
Poems on Several Occasions. Edinburgh: 1773. V. 70
Polly. London: 1729. V. 68; 71; 73
Polly. London: 1923. V. 68
The Shepherd's Week in Six Pastorals. London: 1714. V. 70

GAY, PETER
Historians at Work. New York: 1972. V. 68

GAY, THERESSA
James W. Marshall - the Discoverer of California Gold. Georgetown: 1967. V. 68; 73

GAY, WILLIAM
The Long Home. Denver: 1999. V. 69; 71
The Long Home. 2000. V. 70

GAY, ZHENYA
Town Cats. A Book of Drawings. New York: 1932. V. 68

GAYA, LOUIS DE
Marriage Ceremonies; as Now Used in All Parts of the World. London: 1704. V. 70

GAYARRE, CHARLES
Fernando de Lemos: Truth and Fiction. New York: 1872. V. 70

GAYTHORPE, HARPER
Furness Lore.... Kendal: 1900. V. 71

GAZE, HAROLD
The Merry Piper or the Magic Trip in the Sugar Bowl Ship. London: 1925. V. 71

GAZIUS, ANTONIUS
Florida Corona Qua as Sanitatis Hominum Conservationem. Lyon: 1541. V. 68; 73

GAZZARO, ANTONIO
Eden Anto. San Francisco: 1930. V. 69

GEAKE, CHARLES
John Bull's Adventures in the Fiscal Wonderland. London: 1904. V. 70

GEARE, R. I.
A List of the Publications of the United States National Museum (1875-1900). Washington: 1902. V. 68

GEARINO, G. D.
Counting Coup. New York: 1997. V. 70; 73
What the Deaf Mute Heard. New York: 1996. V. 69

GEARY, C.
Things of the Palace, a Catalogue of the Bamum Palace Museum in Foumban (Cameroon). Weisbaden: 1983. V. 69

GEBAUER, P.
The Art of Cameroon. Portland: 1979. V. 69

GEBHARD, DAVID
Romanza: the California Architecture of Frank Lloyd Wright. San Francisco: 1988. V. 68
Tulsa Art Deco: an Architectural Era 1925-1942. Tulsa: 1980. V. 70
200 Years of American Architectural Drawing from the Early Bulfinch to the Late Venturi. New York: 1977. V. 68; 69; 72

GEBLER, KARL VON
Galileo Galilei and the Roman Curia. London: 1879. V. 72

GEDDA, LUIGI
Twins in History and Science. Springfield: 1961. V. 68

GEDDES, ALEXANDER
A Norfolk Tale; or, a Journal from London to Norwich.... London: 1792. V. 70

GEDDES, ELISABETH
Animal Antics. Waltham St. Lawrence: 1937. V. 68

GEDDES, JAMES
An Essay on the Composition and Manner of Writing of the Antients.... Glasgow: 1748. V. 73

GEDDES, MICHAEL
Miscellaneous Tracts. London: 1702. V. 70

GEDDES, PATRICK
Every Man His Own Art Critic at the Manchester Exhibition. London and Manchester: 1887. V. 68

GEDDES, R. STANLEY
Burlington Blue-Grey, a History of the Slate Quarries, Kirkby-in-Furness. Kikby-in-Furness: 1975. V. 71

GEDDES, VIRGIL
The Earth Between and Behind the Night. New York: 1930. V. 71
The Frog: a Play in Five Scenes. Paris: 1926. V. 68

GEDGE, ADAM
On the Abuses of Civil Incorporations; in a Letter to Hudson Gurney, Esq. M.P. London: 1830. V. 71

GEDGE, PAULINE
The Eagle and the Raven. New York: 1978. V. 71

GEE, ERNEST R.
The American Shooter's Manual. By A Gentleman of Philadelphia County. New York: 1928. V. 70; 71

GEELHAAR, C.
Paul Klee and the Bauhaus. 1973. V. 69; 72

GEERLINGS, G. K.
Metal Crafts in Architecture. New York: 1929. V. 69

GEERTSEN, I.
Greenlandic Masks. Copenhagen: 1988. V. 69

GEHEEB, A.
Neue Beitrage zur Moosflora von Neu Guinea. 1889. V. 70

GEHMAN, RICHARD
A Murder in Paradise. New York: 1954. V. 70

GEIGER, MAYNARD
The Life and Times of Fray Juniper Serra of the Man who Never Turned back. Washington: 1959. V. 70
As the Padres Saw Them: California Indian Life in Customs as Reported by the Franciscan Missionaries 1813-1815. Santa Barbara: 1976. V. 70

GEIGER, VINCENT
Trail to California. The Overland Journey Of.... New Haven: 1945. V. 69

GEIKIE, ARCHIBALD
Annals of the Royal Society Club. The Record of a London Dining-Club in the Eighteenth and Nineteenth Centuries. London: 1917. V. 72
Charles Darwin as Geologist. Cambridge: 1909. V. 68
The Founders of Geology. London: 1905. V. 68
Life of Sir Roderick I. Murchison. London: 1875. V. 68
Text-Book of Geology. London: 1862. V. 69
Text-Book of Geology. London: 1903. V. 72

GEIKIE, JAMES
The Great Ice Age and its Relation to the Antiquity of Man. London: 1877. V. 70
Prehistoric Europe, a Geological Sketch. London: 1881. V. 69

GEIL, WILLIAM EDGAR
The Sacred 5 of China is the 5th Book on China. London: 1926. V. 69; 72

GEISEL, THEODOR SEUSS
The Butter Battle Book. New York: 1984. V. 71; 72; 73
The Cat in the Hat. New York: 1985. V. 72
The Cat in the Hat Comes Back. New York: 1958. V. 68
The Cat in the Hat Song Book. New York: 1967. V. 72
The Charity Ball 1966. San Diego: 1966. V. 72
Dr. Seuss's ABC. New York: 1963. V. 70; 72
Dr. Seuss's Sleep Book. New York: 1962. V. 70; 71; 72
The Eye Book. New York: 1968. V. 73
The 500 Hundred Hats of Bartholomew Cubbins. New York: 1938. V. 68; 72
Fox in Socks. New York: 1965. V. 72
Hop on Pop. New York: 1963. V. 72
Horton Hears a Who!. New York: 1954. V. 72
How the Grinch Stole Christmas. New York: 1957. V. 69; 70; 72; 73
Hunches in Bunches. New York: 1982. V. 72
I Am Not Going to Get Up Today!. New York: 1987. V. 70
I Can Read With My Eyes Shut!. New York: 1978. V. 72
I Had Trouble in Getting to Solla Sollew. New York: 1965. V. 72
If I Ran the Circus. New York: 1956. V. 72
If I Ran the Zoo. New York: 1950. V. 72
Marvin K. Mooney Will You Please Go Now. New York: 1972. V. 72
Oh, the Places You'll Go. New York: 1990. V. 72
On Beyond Zebra!. New York: 1955. V. 71; 72; 73
One Fish, Two Fish, Red Fish, Blue Fish. London: 1960. V. 73
The Seven Lady Godivas. New York: 1939. V. 72
The Seven Lady Godivas. New York: 1967. V. 72
Sneetches and Other Stories. New York: 1961. V. 72
Thidwick the Big Hearted Moose. New York: 1948. V. 73
This is Ann-She's Dying to Meet You. Washington: 1944. V. 70
You're Only Old Once. New York: 1986. V. 69; 71; 72; 73

GEISSLER, RUDOLF
Little Max. London: 1869. V. 70

GELBER, JACK
Sleep. New York: 1972. V. 69; 72

GELDART, MARTHA
A Son of Belial. London: 1882. V. 73

GELL, WILLIAM
The Geography and Antiquities of Ithaca. London: 1807. V. 70
Pompeiana: the Topography, Edifices and Monuments of Pompei, the Result of Excavations Since 1819. London: 1832. V. 70
Pompeiana: the Topography, Edifices and Ornaments of Pomepii, the Result of Excavations Since 1819. 1835. V. 72; 73
Pompeiana: the Topography, Edifices and Ornaments of Pompeii, The Result of Excavations Since 1819. London: 1837. V. 68
The Topography of Troy and Its Vicinity. London: 1804. V. 68; 70

GELLERT, CHRISTLIEB EHREGOTT
Metallurgic Chymistry. London: 1776. V. 70

GELLERT, LEON
Songs of a Campaign. Sydney: 1917. V. 68; 72

GELLHORN, MARTHA
Liana. London: 1944. V. 72

GELLI, GIOVANNI BATTISTA
La Circe. Florence: 1550. V. 73

GELLIUS, AULUS
Noctes Atticae. Lugduni: 1555. V. 72
Noctes Atticae. Paris: 1564. V. 73

GENARD, FRANCOIS
The School of Man. London: 1753. V. 69

GENAUER, E.
Chagall at the Met. New York: 1971. V. 69; 72

A GENERAL Account of the Calamities Occasioned by the Late Tremendous Hurricanes and Earthquakes in the West India Islands.... London: 1781. V. 73

GENERAL Observations Upon the Profitable Effects of Any Measures Which Have for Their Object the Increase of the Regular Army.... Edinburgh: 1807. V. 71

GENERAL Order No. 8. Rules and Regulations for the Enrollment of the Militia and the Government of the Organzied Militia. Montpelier: 1865. V. 70

GENEST, JOHN
Some Account of the English Stage, From Restoration in 1660 to 1830. Bath: 1832. V. 71

GENET, EDMOND CHARLES
Memorial on the Upward Forces of Fluids, and Their Applicability to Several Arts, Sciences and Public Improvements. Albany: 1825. V. 68

GENET, JEAN
Journal du Voleur. 1949. V. 70
Our Lady of the Flowers. Pari: 1949. V. 70
The Maids. (and) Deathwatch. New York: 1954. V. 69; 73
Our Lady of the Flowers. New York: 1963. V. 68
The Thief's Journal. Paris: 1954. V. 70

GENGA, BERNARDINO
Anatomia Chirurgica Cioe Istoria Anatomica Dell'Ossa, E. Mvscoli Del Corpo Vmano.. Bologna: 1686. V. 70

GENGENBACH, ERNEST DE
Judas ou Le Vampire Surrealiste. Paris: 1949. V. 71

GENIN, THOMAS H.
The Napolead, in Twelve Books. St. Clairsville: 1833. V. 72

GENLIS, STEPHANIE FELICITE DUCREST DE ST. AUBIN, COMTESSE DE
The Knights of the Swan, or, the Court of Charlemagne.... Edinburgh: 1796. V. 73
Lessons of a Governess to Her Pupils; or, Journal of the Method Adopted by.... Dublin: 1793. V. 69
Madame de Maintenon. Paris: 1806. V. 68
Manuel de Voyageur, or the Traveller's Pocket Companion.... London: 1819. V. 73
Memoirs of the Countess de Genlis Illustrative of the History of the Eighteenth and Nineteenth Centuries. London: 1825-1826. V. 73
Sainclair, or the Victim to the Arts and Sciences, and Hortense, or the Victim to Novels and Travel. Georgetown: 1813. V. 73
Theatre of Education. Dublin: 1783. V. 68; 69
Les Veillees du Chageau, ou Cours de Morale a l'Usage des Enfans.... Geneva: 1784. V. 70; 72

GENSCHOW, ADOLF
Unter Chinesen und Tibetanern.... Rostock: 1905. V. 72

GENT, THOMAS
Annales Regioduni Hullini: Or, The History of the Royal and Beautiful Town of Kingston-upon- Hull. York Ward and Chandler Hull: 1735. V. 73
The Antient and Modern History of the Famous City of York. London: 1730. V. 73
The Antient and Modern History of the Loyal Town of Rippon. 1733. V. 71
The Antient and Modern History of the Loyal Town of Rippon. York: 1733. V. 70; 72
The Life of Thomas Gent, Printer of York, Written by Himself. London: 1832. V. 68; 70
Poems. London: 1828. V. 68

GENTHE, ARNOLD
As I Remember. New York: 1936. V. 68
The Book of the Dance. New York: 1916. V. 68; 70
Impressions of Old New Orleans. New York: 1926. V. 71
Isadora Duncan - Twenty-Four Studies. New York and London: 1929. V. 68; 71
Old Chinatown. New York: 1913. V. 68; 71
Pictures of Old Chinatown. New York: 1908. V. 68
Pictures of Old Chinatown. New York: 1909. V. 68

GENTIL, FRANCOIS
Dissertation sur le Caffe, et sur les Moyens Propres a Prevenir les Effets qui Resultent de sa Preparation Communement.... Paris: 1787. V. 72

GENTILI, SCIPIONE
De Jurisdictione Libri III...(with) De Alimentis Liber Singularis.... Frankfurt: 1601. V. 70

THE GENTLEMAN Angler.... 1786. V. 73

GENTLEMAN, DAVID
The Wood Engravings of.... Montgomery: 2000. V. 68

GENTLEMAN, FRANCIS
The Dramatic Censor; or, Critical Companion. London and York: 1770. V. 70

GENTLEMAN OF THE BAR
The New American Clerk's Magazine and Complete Practical Conveyancer. Hagerstown: 1806. V. 72

THE GENTLEMAN'S Diary, or the Mathematica Repository.. London: 1789. V. 69

GENTLEMAN'S Magazine for June 1774. V. 68

GENTLEMAN'S Pocket Companion for Travelling into Foreign Parts. London: 1722-1723. V. 73

GENTRY, CURT
Frame-Up. New York: 1967. V. 68

GENTRY, THOMAS
Nest and Eggs of Birds of the United States. Philadelphia: 1882. V. 68; 69

THE GENUINE Account of the Trial of Eugene Aram, for the Murder of Daniel Clark, Late of Knaresborough, in the County of York.... Leeds: 1809. V. 69

A GENUINE Narrative of the Conspiracy by Kather, Kane, Alexander, Nickson &c. Against the Hon. Edward Walpole, Esq.... London: 1751. V. 70

GEOGHEGAN, LAURENCE
The Subterranean Club. London: 1932. V. 73

GEOLOGICAL SOCIETY OF LONDON
Geological Literature Added to the Geological Society's Library 18491900, 1901-1906. London: 1895-1907. V. 72

GEOLOGICAL SURVEY OF ENGLAND AND WALES
Memoirs. 1846-1848. V. 68

GEOLOGY of New York. Parts 1-4. Albany: 1842-1843. V. 68; 73

GEOLOGY of the County of Cape May, State of New Jersey. Trenton: 1857. V. 69

GEORGE, ANDREW L.
A Texas Prisoner - Sketches at the Penitentiary, Convict Farms and Railroads etc. 1895. V. 68; 73

GEORGE Bell, the Farmer's Boy. Troy: 1847-1858?. V. 70

GEORGE, ELIZABETH
The Evidence Exposed. 1999. V. 68
The Evidence Exposed. London: 1999. V. 69
A Great Deliverance. New York: 1988. V. 68; 69; 71; 72
Payment in Blood. New York: 1989. V. 68; 71
Remember, I'll Always Love You. 2001. V. 70

GEORGE, G. M.
Prudent Paulina. London: 1905. V. 72

GEORGE, H. B.
The Oberland and Its Glaciers: Explored and Illustrated with Ice-Axe and Camera. 1866. V. 68; 70

GEORGE, HENRY
A Perplexed Philosopher, Being an Examination of Mr. Herbert Spencer's Various Utterances on the Land Question.... London: 1893. V. 71
Progress and Poverty. New York: 1879. V. 69
Progress and Poverty. New York: 1880. V. 68
Progress and Poverty. London: 1884. V. 71
Protection of Free Trade. New York: 1886. V. 72
The Science of Political Economy. London: 1898. V. 71
The Science of Political Economy. Toronto: 1898. V. 71
Social Problems. London: 1884. V. 71

GEORGE, HEREFORD B.
Genealogical Tables illustrative Of Modern History. Oxford: 1875. V. 72

GEORGE, J. N.
English Guns and Rifles. Harrisburg: 1947. V. 72
English Guns and Rifles. Plantersville: 1947. V. 72

GEORGE, JEAN CRAIGHEAD
Julie of the Wolves. New York: 1972. V. 70

GEORGE, M. DOROTHY
Hogarth to Cruikshank: Social Change in Graphic Satire. New York: 1967. V. 71

GEORGE, MARY CAROLYN HOLLERS
Mary Bonner: Impressions of a Printmaker. San Antonio: 1982. V. 68

GEORGE, TODD M.
The Conversion of Cole Younger, the Early Day Bandit Becomes a Christian Citizen. Kansas City: 1963. V. 68; 73

GEORGE, WILLIAM
Some Account of the Oldest Plans of Bristol, and an Enquiry Into the Date of the First Authentic One.... Bristol: 1881. V. 68; 72

GEORGE, WILMA
Biologist Philosopher. A Study Of The Life and Writings Of Alfred Russell. London: 1964. V. 68; 72

GEORGI, JOHANNES
Mid Ice. The Story of the Wegener Expedition to Greenland. London: 1934. V. 73

GEORGIA, A. E.
A Manual of Weeds with Descriptions of All the Most Pernicius and Troublesome Plants in the U.S. and Canada.... New York: 1914. V. 72

GEORGIA. LAWS, STATUTES, ETC. - 1835
Rules of Practice in the Law and in Equity Established by the Judges of the Superior Courts of the State of Georgia June 11, 1835. Milledgeville: 1835. V. 71

GEORGIAN Stories 1926. London: 1926. V. 69

GERARD, ALEXANDER
Account of an Attempt to Penetrate by Bekhur to Gaboo and the Lake Manasarowara: with a letter from the Late J.G. Gerard Detailing a Visit to the Shatool and Boorendo Passes. London: 1840. V. 69
An Essay on Taste. With Three Dissertations on the Same Subject. London: 1759. V. 70; 71

GERARD, FRANCES
Picturesque Dublin, Old and New. 1898. V. 69; 73

GERARD, FRANCIS
Golden Guilt. New York: 1940. V. 70

GERARD, JOHN
The Herball or Generall Historie of Plantes. London: 1633. V. 68; 69; 71; 73

GERARD, JULES
Le Tueur des Lions. The Life and Adventures of Jules Gerard, the Lion-Killer.... London: 1856. V. 68

GERARD, LOUISE
The Flower of the Flame. New York: 1925. V. 70
Jungle Love. New York: 1924. V. 70
Love's Magic. New York: 1928. V. 71
A Son of the Sahara. New York: 1922. V. 70; 71
Winds of Desire. New York: 1929. V. 71

GERARD, M.
Dali. New York: 1968. V. 69; 72

GERBRANDS, ADRIAN
The Asmat of New Guinea.... New York: 1967. V. 73

GERDTS, WILLIAM H.
American Impressionism. Seattle: 1980. V. 72
American Still-Life Painting. New York: 1971. V. 69; 72

GERE, CHARLOTTE
Nineteenth-Century Decoration. The Art Of The Interior. New York: 1989. V. 72

GEREE, JOHN
(Ippos Gurros - Greek title). The Red Horse; or the Bloodlines of War, Represented in a Sermon.... London: 1648. V. 70

GERHARD, JOHANN
Meditationes Sacrae. London: 1657. V. 72

GERHARDI, WILLIAM
The Casanova Fable: a Satirical Revaluation. London: 1934. V. 70
Jazz and Jasper - The Story of Adams and Eva. London: 1928. V. 70; 72
Pending Heaven. London: 1930. V. 72
Pending Heaven. New York: 1930. V. 71

GERICAULT, THEODORE
Etudes de Chevaux. Paris: 1822. V. 69

GERIN, WINIFRED
Anne Bronte. London: 1959. V. 73
Anne Bronte. London: 1976. V. 70
Branwell Bronte. 1961. V. 70
Branwell Bronte. London: 1961. V. 73
Charlotte Bronte. London: 1967. V. 70; 73
Charlotte Bronte. Oxford: 1967. V. 70
Emily Bronte. 1971. V. 73
Emily Bronte. Oxford: 1971. V. 70

GERITS, ANTON
For Bob de Graaf, Antiquarian Bookseller, Publisher, Bibliographer. Festschrift on the Occasion of his 65th Birthday. Amsterdam: 1992. V. 70

THE GERM: Being Thoughts Towards Nature Conducted Principally by Artists. 1850. V. 68

GERMAIN, SOPHIE
Considerations Generales sur l'Etat des Sciences et des Lettres Aux Differentes Epoques de leur Culture. Paris: 1833. V. 73

GERMAN REED, T.
Bibliographical Notes on T. E. Lawrence's Seven Pillars of Wisdom and Revolt in the Desert. London: 1928. V. 68

GERMANY During the Insurrections of 1848. London: 1855. V. 73

GERNER, KEN
The Red Dreams. Port Townsend: 1978. V. 68

GERNING, J. I.
Reise Durch Oestreich Und Italien. Frankfurt: 1802. V. 69

GERNING, J. J. VON, BARON
A Picturesque Tour Along the Rhine, From Mentz to Cologne. London: 1820. V. 68; 72

GERNSHEIM, HELMUT
Alvin Langdon Coburn, Photographer - an Autobiography. London: 1966. V. 68
The History of Photography. London: 1955. V. 68
The History of Photography. New York: 1969. V. 69
Lewis Carroll Photographer. London: 1949. V. 68; 73

GERONIMO - The Apaches Chief. Tucson: 1986. V. 72

GEROW, JOSHUA R.
Alder Lake. A Symposium of Nostalgic and Natural Observation, Written for Our Guests at Alder Lake at the Request of Mr. Charles M. Francisco.... Liberty: 1953. V. 69

GERRALD, JOSEPH
The Trial of Joseph Gerrald, Delegate from the London Corresponding Society, to the British Covnention. Edinburgh: 1794. V. 71

GERRING, CHARLES
A History of the Parish of Gedling, in the County of Nottingham. Nottingham: 1908. V. 70
Notes on Book Binding. Nottingham: 1899. V. 70

GERRISH, THEODORE
Life in The World's Wonderland. Biddeford. V. 72

GERRITSEN, TESS
Harvest. 1996. V. 68; 70
Life Support. 1997. V. 70

GERRITSZ, HESSEL
The Arctic North-East and West Passage. Amsterdam: 1878. V. 71

GERRY, VANCE
L. A. Type: A Concise History of Los Angeles. Pasadena: 2000. V. 68
Some Letters Concerning D. H. Lawrence. From Mabel Dodge Luhan, Dorothy Brett and Frieda Lawrence to Eliot Fay. Fallbrook: 1978. V. 72

GERSDORFF, HANS VON
Feldbuch der Wuntartzney.... 1970. V. 68

GERSH, LEONARD
Butterflies. New York: 1970. V. 71

GERSHWIN, GEORGE
George Gershwin's Song Book. New York: 1932. V. 68

GERSON, VIRGINIA
Rose-Buds. New York: 1885. V. 70

GERSTAECKER, FRIEDRICH WILHELM CHRISTIAN
Bill Johnson, or the Outlaws of Arkansas. New York: 1857. V. 71
Die Regulatoren in Arkansas. Aus dem Waldeben Americas. Philadelphia: 1860. V. 73
Scenes of Life in California. San Francisco: 1942. V. 68
The Two Convicts. London: 1864. V. 68

GERSTER, ARPAD G.
The Rules of Aseptic and Antiseptic Surgery: a Practical Treatise for the Use of Students and the General Practitioner. New York: 1890. V. 70

GERTRUDE, SAINT
Les Insinvations de la Divine Piete de Ste Stertrvde Vierge Abbesse de l'Ordre de S. Benoist avec l'Abbrege de sa vie. Paris: 1671. V. 73

GERTZMAN, JAY A.
A Descriptive Bibliography of Lady Chatterley's Lover, With Essays Towards a Publishing History of the Novel. New York: 1989. V. 72

GERVASI, NICOLA
Raccolta di Tutte le Vedute che Esistevano nel Gabinetto del Duca della Torre Rappresentanti l'Eruzioni del Monte Vesuvio. Naples: 1805. V. 73

GERVASUTTI, GIUSTO
Gervasutti's Climbs. 1957. V. 71; 73
Gervasutti's Climbs. London: 1957. V. 69

GESCHWIND, NORMAN
Selected Papers on Language and the Brain. Boston: 1976. V. 68; 71

GESENIUS, WILLIAM
A Hebrew and English Lexicon of the Old Testament Including the Biblical Chaldee. Boston: 1836. V. 69
A Hebrew and English Lexicon of the Old Testament Including the Biblical Chaldee. Boston: 1844. V. 69

GESNER, ABRAHAM
The Industrial Resources of Nova Scotia. Halifax: 1849. V. 73
A Practical Treatise on Coal, Petroleum and Other Distilled Oils. New York: 1865. V. 68
Remarks on the Geology and Mineralogy of Nova Scotia. Halifax: 1836. V. 68; 72; 73

GESNER, CLARK
You're a Good Man, Charlie Brown. New York: 1968. V. 71

GESNER, KONRAD
Compendivm ex Actvarii Zachariae Libris De Differentijs Urinarum, Iudicijs & Praeuidentijs. Tiguri: 1541. V. 70
De Omni Rarum fossilium Genere, Gemmis, Lapidibus, Metallis, et Huismodi, Libri Aliquot. Tiguri: 1565. V. 72
Epitome Bibiothecae, Conscripta Primum a Conrado Lycosthene...Nune Denueo Recognita.... Zurich: 1555. V. 72

GESSNER, SALOMON
Mort D'Abel. A Paris: 1793. V. 70

GETCHELL, FRANCIS HORACE
An Illustrated Encyclopedia of the Science and Practice of Obstetrics. Philadelphia: 1885. V. 69
An Illustrated Encyclopedia of the Science and Practice of Obstetrics. Philadelphia: 1890. V. 70

GETTY, JOHN PAUL
The Joys of Collecting. London: 1966. V. 70

GEYER, ANDREA
Grundlicher Abriss der Jenigen Zimmer in Welchen bey Noch Furwahrendem Reiches-Tag der en 1663.... Regensburg: 1722. V. 68; 70

GHOSE, SUDHIN N.
Folk Tales and Fairy Stories from India. Waltham St. Lawrence: 1961. V. 71

GHOST *Towns of the Colorado.* New York: 1947. V. 69

GIAFFERRI, PAUL LOUIS DE
The History of French Masculine Costume. New York. V. 71

GIANT Talk. New York: 1975. V. 72

GIARRE, GAETANO
Alfabeto di Lettere Iniziali Adorno di Animali e Proseguito da Vaga Serie di Caratteri. Firenze: 1797. V. 70

GIBB, ROBERT SHIRRA
A Farmer's Fifty Years in Lauderdale. London: 1927. V. 71

GIBB, WILLIAM
The Royal House of Stuart. London and New York: 1890. V. 71

GIBBES, EMILY OLIVER
Gleanings; a Gift to the Women of the World by a Woman. New York: 1892. V. 69

GIBBES, PHOEBE
Hartly House, Calcutta. London: 1789. V. 73
The History of Lady Louisa Stroud, and the Honourable Miss Caroline Stretton. London: 1764. V. 69

GIBBES, R. W.
Documentary History of the American Revolution.... New York: 1855. V. 68; 73

GIBBINGS, ROBERT
Beasts and Saints. London: 1934. V. 69
Blue Angels and Whales: a Record of Personal Experiences Below and Above Water. 1946. V. 69
Coming Down the Seine. 1948. V. 70
Coming Down the Seine. 1953. V. 70; 73
Iorana!. Boston: 1932. V. 71
Lovely is the Life. 1945. V. 73
Over the Reefs. 1948. V. 70
A True Tale of Love in Tonga. 1935. V. 73

GIBBINS, HENRY DE BELTGENS
Industry in England: Historical Outlines. London: 1896. V. 71

GIBBON, ALEXANDER
The Theory of Money.... London: 1844. V. 69

GIBBON, CHARLES
The Dead Heart: a Tale of the Bastille. London: 1881. V. 68
A Princess of Jutedom. London: 1887. V. 68

GIBBON, EDWARD
An Essay on the Study of Literature. London: 1764. V. 70
The History of the Decline and Fall of the Roman Empire. London and Oxford. V. 70
The History of the Decline and Fall of the Roman Empire. London: 1777-1788. V. 69
History of the Decline and Fall of the Roman Empire. London: 1807. V. 71
The History of the Decline and Fall of the Roman Empire. London: 1813. V. 68; 73
The History of the Decline and Fall of the Roman Empire. Oxford and London: 1827. V. 68; 72
The History of the Decline and Fall of the Roman Empire. London: 1862-1872. V. 72
The History of the Decline and Fall of the Roman Empire. London: 1896. V. 70
The History of the Decline and Fall of the Roman Empire. New York: 1946. V. 68
Miscellaneous Works...with Memoirs of His Life...by Himself.... London: 1796. V. 69; 71

GIBBON, MONK
For Daws to Peck At. London: 1929. V. 72

GIBBONS, ALFRED RINGOLD
Recollections of an Old Confederate Soldier. Shelbyville: 1930. V. 69; 70

GIBBONS BROTHERS
A Description of the Gibbons Generator and Regenerator Gas Furnaces Constructed with Gibbons' and Masters' Patent Tiles. 1904. V. 69

GIBBONS, FLOYD
The Red Napoleon. New York: 1929. V. 72

GIBBONS, J. J.
In the San Juan, Colorado, Sketches. 1898. V. 70

GIBBONS, J. S.
The Banks of New York, Their Dealers, the Clearing House and the Panic of 1857. New York: 1859. V. 68

GIBBONS, JAMES
Illustrated Catalogue of Metal Casements and Accessories. 1900?. V. 68

GIBBONS, KAYE
Charms for the Easy Life. New York: 1993. V. 73
A Cure for Dreams. Chapel Hill: 1991. V. 68; 71
Ellen Foster. Chapel Hill: 1987. V. 68; 69; 70; 71; 73
Ellen Foster. London: 1987. V. 68
How I Became a Writer. Chapel Hill: 1988. V. 71
A Virtuous Woman. Chapel Hill: 1989. V. 71; 73

GIBBS, A. HAMILTON
Bluebottles. Boston: 1928. V. 70

GIBBS, CHARLES
Confession of Charles Gibbs the Pirate. To be Executed the 22nd of April, 1831. New York: 1831. V. 68

GIBBS, GEORGE
The Triangle Man. New York: 1939. V. 69; 73

GIBBS, JAMES
A Book of Architecture. London: 1728. V. 68
Rules for Drawing the Several Parts of Architecture, in a More Exact and Easy Manner than Has Been Heretofore Practised, by Which all Fractions, in Dividing the Principal Members and their Parts, are Avoided. London: 1732. V. 68; 70; 73

GIBBS, JOSEPH
Report of Mr. Gibbs, Civil Engineer, Upon the Several Proposed Lines for a Brighton Railway. London: 1836. V. 68

GIBBS, JOSIAH F.
The Mountain Meadows Massacre. Salt Lake City: 1910. V. 69

GIBBS, JOSIAH WILLARD
On the equilibrium of heterogeneous substances. In Transactions of the Connecticut Academy of Arts and Sciences, Volume III. New Haven: 1874-1878. V. 72

GIBBS, MAY
Gum Blossom Babies. Sydney: 1917. V. 71
Gumnut Babies. Sydney: 1917. V. 71

GIBBS, PHILIP
The Middle of the Road. New York: 1923. V. 71
The Wings of Adventure. New York: 1930. V. 69

GIBBS, ROBERT
Worthies of Buckinghamshire and Men of Note of that County. Aylesbury: 1888. V. 71

GIBNEY, VIRGIL PENDLETON
The Hip an Its Diseases. New York and London: 1884. V. 70

GIBRALTAR
and Its Sieges. London: 1884. V. 68; 72

GIBRAN, KAHLIL
Sand and Foam. New York: 1926. V. 68

GIBSON, A. G.
The Nervous Affections of the Heart.... Edinburgh: 1905. V. 71

GIBSON, A. L.
Another Alice Book, Please!. London: 1924. V. 68; 72

GIBSON, A. M.
The Chickasaws. Norman: 1971. V. 71
The Life and Death of Colonel Albert Jennings Fountain. Norman: 1965. V. 68; 73

GIBSON, C. B.
The History of the County and City of Cork. 1861. V. 71

GIBSON, CHARLES DANA
The Education of Dr. Pipp. New York: 1900. V. 71
London as Seen By.... London: 1898. V. 69
The Social Ladder. New York: 1902. V. 71

GIBSON, EDMUND
Codex Juris Ecclesiastici Anglicani; or, the Statutes, Constitutions, Canons, Rubricks and Articles of the Church of England. London: 1713. V. 70; 72
The Right of the Archbishop to Continue or Prorogue the Whole Convocation: Asserted in a Second Letter, by a Reply to a Pamphlet, Entitled the Power of the Lower House of Convocation to Adjourn It Self &c.... London: 1701. V. 73

GIBSON, FLORENCE E.
The Attitude of the New York Irish Toward State and National Affairs 1848-1892. 1951. V. 69; 73

GIBSON, FRANCIS
The Poetical Remains, With Other Detached Pieces. Whitby: 1807. V. 68; 72
Whitby Tracts: Streanshall Abbey. London. V. 73

GIBSON, FRANK
Charles Conder, His Life and Work. London: 1914. V. 73

GIBSON, GEORGE R.
Journal of A Soldier Under Kearny And Doniphan 1846-1847 By George Ruthledge Gibson. Glendale: 1935. V. 72

GIBSON, GREGORY
Demon of the Waters. Boston: 2002. V. 72

GIBSON, J. M.
Wild Flowers of Natal (Coastal Region). Durban: 1975. V. 69

GIBSON, JOE
Old Angelo. San Angelo: 1971. V. 70

GIBSON, JOHN
The Fruit-Gardener. 1768. V. 70
The History of Glasgow, from the Earliest Accounts to the Present Time.... Glasgow: 1777. V. 70
My Evening with Sherlock Holmes. London: 1981. V. 69

GIBSON, JOHN MASON
A Condensation of Matter Upon Anatomy, Surgical Operations and Treatment of Diseases of the Eye, Together with Remarks. Baltimore: 1832. V. 68

GIBSON, RALPH
Days at Sea. 1974. V. 68
Infanta. Brussels: 1991. V. 68

GIBSON, ROBERT
A Treatise of Practical Surveying. Philadelphia: 1796. V. 73

GIBSON, T. ELLISON
Blundell's Diary. Liverpool: 1895. V. 73

GIBSON, THOMAS
Legends and Historical Notes On Places in the East and West Wards. Manchester: 1877. V. 71
Legends and Historical Notes on Places of North Westmoreland. London: 1887. V. 71

GIBSON, W. HAMILTON
Our Edible Toadstools and Mushrooms and How to Distinguish Them. New York: 1895. V. 71

GIBSON, WALTER B.
A Blond for Murder. New York: 1948. V. 68
Eyes of the Shadow. New York: 1931. V. 71
The Shadow and the Golden Master. New York: 1984. V. 68
The Shadow Laughs. New York: 1931. V. 71

GIBSON, WILFRID WILSON
Daily Bread. Books 1, 2 and 3. London: 1910. V. 68
The Early Whistler. London: 1927. V. 72
The Early Whistler. New York: 1927. V. 70
Fires. Books 1-3. 1912. V. 70
Fires. Books I, II and III. London: 1912. V. 68
The Golden Helm and Other Verse. London: 1903. V. 68
The Web of Life. 1908. V. 70

GIBSON, WILLIAM
All Tomorrow's Parties. London: 1999. V. 73
Burning Chrome. London: 1986. V. 72
The Cobweb. New York: 1954. V. 71
Count Zero. London: 1986. V. 70
Count Zero. New York: 1986. V. 69; 70
The Difference Engine. London: 1990. V. 68
Mona Lisa Overdrive. London: 1988. V. 70; 73
Neuromancer. London: 1984. V. 70
Virtual Light. London: 1993. V. 73
Virtual Light. New York: 1993. V. 68

GIBSON, WILLIAM SIDNEY
The History of the Monastery Founded at Tynemouth. London: 1846. V. 72; 73

GIBSON, WILLIAM SYDNEY
Dilston Hall; or the Memoirs of the Right Hon. James Radcliffe, Earl of Derwentwater.... London: 1850. V. 68

GIDDINGS, FRANKLIN H.
Sociology (and Sociology Outline Topics and Readings). New York: 1911-1914. V. 68

GIDDINGS, J. R.
The Exiles of Florida; or the Crimes Committed by Our Government Against the Maroons, Who Fled from South Carolina.... Columbus: 1858. V. 73
Pacificus: The Rights and Privileges of the Several States in Regard to Slavery.... Warren: 1843?. V. 68

GIDE, ANDRE
Amyntas. London: 1958. V. 70
Les Faux Monnayeurs. (The Counterfeiters). Paris: 1925. V. 69
Montaigne. New York: 1929. V. 70
Oscar Wilde. A Study. London: 1905. V. 68
La Tenative Amoureuse ou Le Traite du Vain Desir. Paris: 1921. V. 72

GIDUMAL, DAYARAM
Behramji M. Malabari. London: 1892. V. 69

GIEDION, SIGFRIED
Space, Time and Architecture. Cambridge: 1956. V. 72
Walter Gropius, Work and Teamwork. New York: 1954. V. 69

GIELGUD, JOHN
An Actor And His Time. London: 1979. V. 70; 72

GIELGUD, VAL
Imperial Treasure. Boston: 1931. V. 70

GIENANDT, FRITZ L.
Twentieth Century Book for the Progressive Baker, Confectioner, Ornamenter and Ice Cream Maker. Boston: 1912. V. 68

GIERACH, JOHN
Dances With Trout. New York: 1994. V. 71; 73
Good Flies. New York: 2000. V. 73
Standing in a River Waving a Stick. New York: 1999. V. 73
Where Trout Are As Long as Your Leg. New York: 1991. V. 70; 73

GIESKE, HERMAN EVERETT
Utopia, Inc. New York: 1940. V. 70

GIFFARD, WILLIAM
Cases in Midwifry.... London: 1734. V. 72

GIFFEN, FANNIE REED
Oo-Mah-Ha Ta-Wa-Tha (Omaha City). Lincoln: 1898. V. 72

GIFFORD, BARRY
Jack's Book: an Oral Biography of Jack Kerouac. New York: 1978. V. 72
Wild at Heart: The Story of Sailor & Lula. NY: 1990. V. 72

GIFFORD, DENIS
The British Comic Catalogue 1874-1974. 1975. V. 72
The International Book of Comics. 1900. V. 73
The International Book of Comics. 1984. V. 72

GIFFORD, E. W.
California Indian Nights Entertainments. Glendale: 1930. V. 69
The Cocopa. Berkeley: 1933. V. 72

GIFFORD, JOHN
The Complete English Lawyer: or, Every Man His Own Lawyer.... London: 1824. V. 72
A History of the Political Life of the Right Honourable William Pitt. London: 1809. V. 70; 72
Sketches of Two Eminent Men. Sketches of The right Honourable William Pitt, and Right Honourable Charles James Fox. London: 1807. V. 72

GIFFORD, LEWIS
The Selected Letters of Somerville and Ross. 1989. V. 69

GIFFORD, THOMAS
The Wind Chill Factor. New York: 1975. V. 68; 69; 71

GIFFORD, WILLIAM
The Baviad, a Paraphrastic Imitation of the First Satire of Perseus. London: 1791. V. 70

THE GIFT. 1843. Philadelphia: 1843. V. 68; 69; 71

THE GIFT. 1845. 1844. V. 68

THE GIFT: a Christmas and New Year's Present for 1843. Philadelphia: 1842. V. 68; 70

THE GIFT... for 1837. Philadelphia: 1836. V. 71

THE GIFT...for 1840. Philadelphia: 1839. V. 70

GILB, DAGOBERTO
The Magic of Blood. Albuquerque: 1993. V. 71; 73
Winners on the Pass Line, and Other Stories. El Paso: 1985. V. 69; 73

GILBART, JAMES WILLIAM
The History and Principles of Banking. London: 1834. V. 73
A Practical Treatise on Banking. New York: 1851. V. 72
A Practical Treatise on Banking. London: 1856. V. 71

GILBART, JOHN WILLIAM
A System of Banking Book-Keeping. London: 1849. V. 68

GILBERT, ANTHONY
The Murder Of Mrs. Davenport. New York: 1928. V. 72
No Dust in the Attic. London: 1962. V. 71
30 Days to Live. 1944. V. 68

GILBERT, C.
The Life and Work of Thomas Chippendale. London: 1978. V. 70

GILBERT, COLLEEN
A Bibliography of the Works of Dorothy L. Sayers. 1978. V. 73

GILBERT, FRANK T.
History of San Joaquin County, California. Berkeley: 1968. V. 71

GILBERT, G. K.
Report on the Geology of the Henry Mountains. Washington: 1877. V. 71

GILBERT, GEOFFREY
The Law of Uses and Trusts: Collected and Digested in a Proper Order, from the Reports of Adjudg'd Cases, in the Courts of Law and Equity.... London: 1741. V. 69

GILBERT, H. A.
The Tale of a Wye Fisherman. 1929. V. 68

GILBERT, J. WARREN
The Blue and the Gray. Gettysburg: 1922. V. 69; 70

GILBERT, JACK
The Great Fires. Poems 1982-1992. New York: 1994. V. 72

GILBERT, JEAN EMMANUEL
Histoire des Plantes d'Europe, ou Elemens de Botanique Pratique.... Lyon: 1798. V. 72

GILBERT, JOHN M.
Hunting and Hunting Reserves in Medieval Scotland. Edinburgh: 1979. V. 70
Hunting And Hunting Reserves In Medieval Scotland. London: 1979. V. 72

GILBERT, JOHN T.
Chartularies of St. Mary's Abbey, Dublin, with Register of Its House at Dunbrody and Annals of Ireland. 1884. V. 69; 73
Historic and Municipal Documents of Ireland 1172-1320.... 1870. V. 71; 73
Manuscripts and Correspodnence of James, 1st Earl of Charlemont 1745- 1799. 1891-1894. V. 70
Register of the Abbey of St. Thomas Dublin. 1889. V. 69; 71; 73

GILBERT, JOSIAH
Autobiography and Other Memorials of Mrs. Gilbert (formerly Ann Taylor). London: 1874. V. 73
Cadore or Titian's Country. London: 1869. V. 72
The Dolomite Mountains. 1864. V. 72

The Dolomite Mountains. London: 1864. V. 69

GILBERT, JUDSON BENNETT
Disease and Destiny, a Bibliography of Medical References to the Famous. London: 1962. V. 68; 71

GILBERT, LINNEY
The Beauties and Wonders of Nature and Science.... 1862. V. 71
India Illustrated; An Historical & Descriptive Account of That Important and Interesting Country.... London. V. 72
Russia Illustrated; An Historical & Descriptive Account of That Immense Empire, Particularly as Regards St. Petersburgh and Moscow. London. V. 72

GILBERT, MICHAEL
The Crack in the Teacup. London: 1966. V. 71
The Dust and the Heat. London: 1967. V. 71
The Empty House. London: 1978. V. 71
Fear to Tread. London: 1953. V. 69
The Final Throw. London: 1982. V. 71
Game Without Rules. New York: 1967. V. 71; 72
Paint, Gold And Blood. London: 1989. V. 72
Petrella at Q. London: 1992. V. 69
Trouble. London: 1987. V. 71
Young Petrella. London: 1988. V. 71

GILBERT, OLIVE
Narrative of Sojourner Truth a Northern Slave. Boston: 1850. V. 68

GILBERT, SAMUEL
The Complete Florist; or, the Lady and Gentleman's Recreation in the Flower Garden.... London: 1785?. V. 73
The Florist's Vade Mecum. London: 1702. V. 73

GILBERT, STEPHEN
Ratman's Notebook. New York: 1969. V. 68; 71

GILBERT, VIVIAN
The Way of Romance. New York: 1927. V. 71

GILBERT, WILLIAM
The City. An Inquiry, Into the Corporation, Its Livery Companies and the Administration of Their Charities and Endownments. 1877. V. 71

GILBERT, WILLIAM SCHWENK
The Bab Ballads. London: 1926. V. 68
The Bab Ballads. London: 1960. V. 71
Foggerty's Fairy and Other Tales. London: 1890. V. 71
Her Majesty's Ship Pinafore or the Lass that Loved a Sailor. Boston: 1878. V. 72; 73
The Savoy Operas. London: 1927. V. 68

GILBEY, WALTER
George Morland. His Life and Works. London: 1907. V. 72

GILCHRIST, ALEXANDER
The Life of William Blake. London: 1880. V. 72
Life of William Etty. London: 1855. V. 73

GILCHRIST, D.
Journal of a High Country Hunter. 1992. V. 69; 70; 72; 73

GILCHRIST, ELLEN
The Annunciation. Boston: 1983. V. 68; 71
The Cabal and Other Stories. Boston/New York: 2000. V. 72
Drunk with Love. Boston: 1986. V. 68
In the Land of Dreamy Dreams. Fayetteville: 1981. V. 68; 73
Sarah Conley. Boston: 1997. V. 68
Victory Over Japan. Boston: 1984. V. 69

THE GILCREASE-HARGRETT Catalogue of Imprints. Norman: 1972. V. 72

GILCRHIST, A.
Life of William Blake.... London: 1880. V. 68

GILDEN, K. B.
Hurry Sundown. Garden City: 1964. V. 71

GILDER, RICHARD WATSON
The Poet and His Master and Other Poems. New York: 1878. V. 68

GILDER, WILLIAM H.
Ice-Pack and Tundra. London: 1883. V. 72

GILDON, CHARLES
The Life of Mr. Thomas Betterton, the Late Eminent Tragedian. London: 1710. V. 72; 73

GILES, JOHN
The Tryal of John Giles at the Sessions House in Old Bayly, Held by Adjournment from the 7th Day of July 1680 Until the 14th Day of the Same Month.... London: 1681. V. 70

GILES, LEONIDAS BLANTON
Terry's Texas Rangers. Austin: 1911. V. 69; 70

GILES, WILLIAM BRANCH
The Speeches of Mr. Giles and Mr. Bayard, in the House of Representatives of the United States February 1802, on the Bill Received from the Senate entitled "An Act to Repeal Certain Acts Repecting the Organization of the Courts of the United States". Boston: 1802. V. 73

GILFILLAN, ARCHER B.
Sheep. Boston: 1929. V. 71

GILHAM, WILLIAM
Manual of Instruction for the Volunteers and Militia of the Confederate States. Richmond: 1861. V. 69

GILIGAN, EDMUND
The Gaunt Woman. New York: 1943. V. 69

GILKYSON, WALTER
The Lost Adventurer. New York: 1927. V. 72

GILL, BARTHOLOMEW
McGarr and the Politician's Wife. New York: 1977. V. 68; 71

GILL, BRENDAN
Here at the New Yorker. New York: 1975. V. 69

GILL, ELIZABETH
Strange Holiday. London: 1931. V. 70

GILL, ERIC
Art and Love. Bristol: 1927. V. 69
Art Nonsense and Other Essays. London: 1929. V. 73
Canticum Canticorum Salomonis. 1931. V. 70
Clothes, an Essay Upon Nature and Significance of the Natural and Artificial Integuments Worn by Men and Women. London: 1931. V. 69; 71; 72
Clothing without Cloth: an Essay on the Nude. Waltham St. Lawrence: 1931. V. 71
An Essay on Typography. London: 1931. V. 68
Essays. London: 1947. V. 72
First Nudes. 1954. V. 68
First Nudes. London: 1954. V. 71
Letters of Eric Gill. London: 1947. V. 72
The Lord's Song. Waltham St. Lawrence: 1934. V. 70; 72
Songs Without Clothes.... Ditchling, Sussex: 1921. V. 68; 71
Unholy Trinity. London: 1938. V. 68

GILL, EVAN
Eric Gill. A Bibliography. Winchester. V. 70

GILL, RONALD
Club Route in Europe. Hanover: 1946. V. 70

GILL, T.
Synopsis of the Fresh Water Fishes of the Western Portion of the Island of Trinidad, W. I. New York: 1858. V. 73

GILL, THOMAS
Vallis Eboracensis: Comprising the History of Antiquities of Easingwold and Its Neighborhood. 1852. V. 73

GILL, TOM
Death Rides the Mesa. New York: 1934. V. 69
No Place for Women. New York: 1946. V. 71

GILL, WILLIAM WYATT
Myths and Songs from the South Pacific. London: 1876. V. 73

GILLER, J. U.
The Rhymes of Boyhood. Philadelphia: 1836. V. 71

GILLES, MORA
Walker Evans: The Hungry Eye. New York: 1993. V. 68

GILLES, PIERRE
De Topographia Constantinopoleos, et de Illius Antiquitatibus Libri Quatuor. (with) De Bosporo Thracio Libri III. Lyon: 1561. V. 68

GILLESPIE, DIZZY
To Be or Not to Bop. Garden City: 1979. V. 71; 72

GILLESPIE, W. M.
A Manual of the Principles and Practice of Road-Making Comprising the Location, Construction and Improvement of Roads.... New York: 1847. V. 68

GILLETT, JAMES B.
Six Years with the Texas Rangers 1875 to 1881. Austin: 1921. V. 68; 73; 73

GILLIAM, ALBERT M.
Travels Over the Table Lands and Cordilleras of Mexico. Philadelphia: 1847. V. 71

GILLIAM, TERRY
Brazil. The Evolution of the 54th Best British Film Ever Made. London: 2001. V. 70

GILLIES, JOHN W.
Principles of Pictorial Photography. New York: 1923. V. 68

GILLIES, ROBERT PEARSE
Childe Alariqu, a Poet's Reveries. Edinburgh: 1814. V. 69

GILLILAND, MAUDET T.
Horse Backers of the Brush Country - a Story of the Texas Rangers and Mexican Liquor Smugglers. 1968. V. 69
Wilson County Texas Rangers 1837-1977. 1977. V. 69

GILLILAND, MAURE T.
Rinco'n (Remote Dwelling Place). Brownsville: 1964. V. 71

GILLILAND, THOMAS
The Dramatic Mirror: Containing the History of the Stage, from the Earliest Period to the Present Time.... London: 1808. V. 69
Jack in Office: Containing Remarks on Mr. Braham's Address to the Public.... London: 1805. V. 72

GILLINGHAM, ROBERT C.
The Rancho San Pedro, The Story of a Famous Rancho in Los Angeles County and of Its Owner, The Daminguez Family. Los Angeles: 1961. V. 68; 71

GILLISPIE, CHARLES COULSTON
Lazare Carnot Savant. Princeton: 1971. V. 71

GILLMAN, JAMES
The Life of Samuel Taylor Coleridge. London: 1838. V. 71; 72

GILLMAN, P.
Eiger Direct. 1966. V. 71; 73

GILLMOR, FRANCES
Traders of the Navajos, the Story of the Wethrills of Kayenta. Boston and New York: 1934. V. 69

GILLMORE, PARKER
Encounters with Wild Beasts. 1905. V. 69
Leaves from a Sportsman's Diary. 1896. V. 69; 70; 72; 73
Travels, War and Shipwreck. New York: 1883. V. 70

GILLULY, J.
Tectonic and Igneous Geology of the Northern Shoshone Range, Nevada. Washington: 1965. V. 72

GILLY, WILLIAM STEPHEN
A Memoir of Felix Neff, Pastor of the High Alps; and of His Labours Among the French Protestants of Dauphine.... London: 1832. V. 73
Narrative of an Excursion to the Mountains of Piemont, in the Year MDCCCXXIII. London: 1828. V. 73
Waldemsiam Hesearches During a Second Visit to the Vaoulois of Piement.... 1833. V. 70

GILMAN, CAROLINE
Letters of Eliza Wilkinson, During the Invasion and Possession of Charlestown, S.C. by the British in the Revolutionary War. New York: 1839. V. 68

GILMAN, CHARLOTTE PERKINS
The Crux, a Novel. New York: 1911. V. 71
The Man-Made World or, Our Androcentric Culture. New York: 1911. V. 68
Women and Economics. London: 1899. V. 73
Women and Economics. Boston: 1900. V. 73

GILMAN, PETER
Eiger Direct. London: 1966. V. 69

GILMAN, RICHARD
Decadence. New York: 1979. V. 72

GILMER, GEORGE R.
Sketches of Some of the First Settlers of Upper Georgia, of the Cherokees and the Author. Americus: 1926. V. 68

GILMER, JOHN H.
Letter Addressed to Hon. Wm. C. Rives. Richmond: 1864. V. 69; 70

GILMOR, HARRY
Four Years in the Saddle. New York: 1866. V. 70; 73
Four Years in the Saddle. New York: 1886. V. 69

GILMORE, C. W.
Fossil Lizards of North America. Washington: 1928. V. 69
The Fossil Turtles of the Uinata Formation. Pittsburgh: 1916. V. 68; 71

GILMORE, JAMES ROBERTS
My Southern Friends. New York: 1863. V. 71

GILMOUR, D. E.
An Historical and Descriptive Guide to the Antiquities of Winchester.... Winchester: 1825. V. 70; 72

GILMOUR, MARGARET
Ameliaranne at the Circus. Philadelphia: 1931. V. 70
Ameliaranne at the Seaside. London: 1935. V. 73
Ameliaranne Gives a Concert. London: 1944. V. 71

GILOT, FRANCOISE
Life With Picasso. Middlesex: 1965. V. 73

GILPATRIC, GUY
The Best of Glencannon. New York: 1968. V. 73

GILPATRICK, NOREEN
The Piano Man. New York: 1991. V. 68; 69; 70; 71

GILPIN, J. BERNARD
Sable Island: Its Past History, Present Appearance, Natural History &c. Halifax: 1858. V. 72

GILPIN, LAURA
The Enduring Navaho. Austin and London: 1968. V. 68; 69; 70; 71
The Enduring Navaho. Santa Fe: 1968. V. 70
The Pueblos: a Camera Chronicle. New York: 1941. V. 68; 70
The Rio Grande - River of Destiny. New York: 1949. V. 68; 69; 70; 73
Temples in Yucatan: a Camera Chronicle of Chichen Itza. New York: 1948. V. 68

GILPIN, SIDNEY
Sam Bough, R. S. A. Some Account of His Life and Works. London: 1905. V. 70; 71; 72

GILPIN, THOMAS
On the Representation of Minorities of Electors to Act with the Majority, in Elected Assemblies. Philadelphia: 1844. V. 71

GILPIN, WILLIAM
An Essay on Prints. London: 1781. V. 68
The Life of Bernard Gilpin.... London: 1752. V. 70
The Life of Hugh Latimer, Bishop of Worcester. London: 1755. V. 69
Observations on the Coasts of Hampshire, Sussex and Kent, Relative Chiefly to Picturesque Beauty, Made in Summer of the Year 1774. London: 1804. V. 69
Observations on the River Wye, and Several Parts of South Wales &c.. London: 1782. V. 72
Observations on the Western Parts of England, Relative Chiefly to Picturesque Beauty.... London: 1808. V. 72
Observations on the Western Parts of England. To Which are added, A Few Remarks on the Picturesque Beauties of the Isle of Wight. 1798. V. 71
Observations Relative Chiefly to Picturesque Beauty, Made in the Year 1772, on Several Parts of England.... London: 1792. V. 69; 72
Remarks on Forest Scenery and Other Woodland Views. London: 1794. V. 69; 71; 73
Remarks on Forest Scenery and Other Woodland Views. 1808. V. 71
Remarks on Forest Scenery and Other Woodland Views. Edinburgh: 1834. V. 69; 70
Three Essays: on Picturesque Beauty; on Picturesque Travel; and on Sketching Landscape; to which is added a Poem on Landscape Painting. London: 1808. V. 72
Voyage en Differentes Parties de l'Angleterre et Particulierement dans les Motagnes & sur les Lacs du Cumberland & du Westmoreland. Paris...a Londres: 1789. V. 72

GILRUTH, SUSAN
The Snake Is Living Yet. London: 1963. V. 70

GILSAN, RODNEY
Journal of Army Life. San Francisco: 1874. V. 72

GILSON, DAVID
A Bibliography of Jane Austen. Winchester and New Castle: 1997. V. 70

THE GIMCRACK Jingle Alphabet. London: 1900. V. 69

GIMSON, ERNEST
Ernest Gimson: His Life and Work. Stratford-upon-Avon: 1924. V. 73

GINGLE, JACOB, PSEUD.
The Oxford Sermon Versified. 1729. V. 73

GINSBERG, ALLEN
Ankor Wat. London: 1968. V. 68
Careless Love. Madison: 1978. V. 73
Collected Poems 1947-1980. London: 1985. V. 69; 73
Family Business. New York: 2001. V. 69; 72
First Blues. Rags, Ballads and Harmonium Songs 1971-1974. New York: 1975. V. 71
Howl. San Francisco: 1956. V. 68; 70
Howl. New York: 1986. V. 68; 69
Illuminated Poems. New York: 1996. V. 70; 73
Kaddish and Other Poems 1958-1960. San Francisco: 1961. V. 71
Photographs. Altadena: 1990. V. 72
Planet News. San Francisco: 1968. V. 68
Siesta in Xhalba and Return to the States. Icy Cape: 1956. V. 69
T. V. Baby Poems. London: 1967. V. 72
T. V. Baby Poems. New York: 1968. V. 68
To Eberhart from Ginsberg. A Letter About Howl. Lincoln: 1976. V. 70; 71
Wales - a Visitation July 29th 1967. London: 1968. V. 68
White Shroud. New York: 1986. V. 72
The Yage Letters. San Francisco: 1966. V. 68

GIOIA, DANA
Journeys in Sunlight. Cottondale: 1987. V. 69
Planting A Sequoia. West Chester: 1991. V. 73

GIONO, JEAN
Blue Boy. New York: 1946. V. 68

GIORDANI, GIUSEPPE TOMMASO
The Celebrated Death Song of the Cherokee Indian and Ten Other Songs. London: 1785. V. 73

GIOSTRA Corsa in Torino... Nel Passaggio di Sua Altezza Imperiale e Reale Alessandro, Gran-Duca Principe Imperiale Ereditario di Russia. Turin: 1839. V. 70

GIOVANNI, NIKKI
Black Judgement. Detroit: 1968. V. 69
Shimmy Shimmy Shimmy Like My Sister Kate. New York: 1996. V. 68

GIPSON, FRED
The Cow Killers with the Aftosa Commission in Mexico. Austin: 1956. V. 71
Hound-Dog Man. New York: 1949. V. 70

GIRAFFI, ALEXANDER
An Exact Historie of the Late Revolutions in Naples. London: 1650. V. 70

GIRALDUS CAMBRENSIS
Opera. 1861-1891. V. 69

GIRALDUS DE BARRI
The Itinerary of Archbishop Baldwin through Wales. 1806. V. 72
The Itinerary of Archbishop Baldwin through Wales. London: 1806. V. 68

GIRARD, C.
Contributions to the Fauna of Chile. Washington: 1855. V. 71
United States Explorations and Surveys for a Railroad Route from the Mississippi River to Pacific Ocean: Fishes. Washington: 1857-1860?. V. 73

GIRARD, L. D.
Hydraulique Applique. Nouveau Systeme de Locomotion sur les Chemis de fer. Paris: 1852. V. 72

GIRARDI, ROBERT
Madeline's Ghost. New York: 1995. V. 68; 73

GIRAUD, S. LOUIS
Bookano Stories with Pictures that Spring Up in Model Form. No. 17. London: 1950. V. 72

GIRAUDOUX, J.
La Grande Bourgeoisie ou Toute Femme a la Vocation. Paris: 1928. V. 71
Lying Woman. New York: 1972. V. 71

THE GIRL'S Own Annual. 1884-1885. V. 68

GIRL'S Picture Book. Concord: 1840. V. 70

THE GIRL'S Picture Book. Concord: 1843. V. 69

GIROGI, FELICE
Descrizione Istorica del Teatro di Tor di Nona. Rome: 1795. V. 68

GIRON, AIME
Trois Heros. Paris: 1894. V. 71

GIROUARD, MARK
Alfred Waterhouse and His Natural History Museum. London: 1981. V. 70
Alfred Waterhouse and His Natural History Museum. New Haven: 1981. V. 68
Life in the English Country House, a Social and Architectural History. New Haven: 1978. V. 68
The Victorian Country House. London: 1979. V. 72

GIRSBERGER, H.
Alvar Aalto. New York: 1963. V. 72

GIRSBRGER, H.
Alvar Aalto. New York: 1971. V. 69

GIRTIN, THOMAS
Liber Naturae or a Collection of Prints from the Drawings of Thomas Girtin.... London: 1883. V. 69

GIRTY, G. H
The Guadalupian Fauna. Washington: 1908. V. 70

GIRVIN, BRENDA
Alice and the White Rabbit - Their Trips Round About London. London: 1910. V. 70
The Red Dragon and Other Stories of South Wales. London: 1913. V. 69
Round Fairyland with Alice. Redhill, Surrey: 1948. V. 70

GISBORNE, T.
On the Present Crisis! An Address to the Electors of North Derbyshire. London: 1834. V. 71

GISBORNE, THOMAS
An Enquiry into the Duties of the Female Sex. London: 1797. V. 69
An Enquiry into the Duties of the Female Sex. London: 1798. V. 69; 73

GISSING, GEORGE
Charles Dickens: a Critical Study. London: 1898. V. 69
Critical Studies of the Works of Charles Dickens. New York: 1924. V. 69; 70
New Grub Street. London: 1892. V. 68
Selections Autobiographical from the Works of George Gissing. London: 1929. V. 70
Veranilda; a Romance. London: 1904. V. 68

GISSING, T. W.
The Ferns and Fern Allies of Wakefield and Its Neighbourhood. 1862. V. 69
Materials for a Flora of Wakefield and Its Neighbourhood. Huddersfield: 1867. V. 72

GITTINGER, ROY
The Formation of the State of Oklahoma 1803-1906. Norman: 1939. V. 73

GITTINGS, JOHN G.
Personal Recollections of Stonewall Jackson, also Sketches and Stories. Cincinnati: 1899. V. 69; 70

GLADDEN, WASHINGTON
The Forks of the Road. New York: 1916. V. 69

GLADSTONE, HUGH S.
The History of the Dumfriesshire and Galloway Natural History and Antiquarian Society. Dumfries: 1913. V. 71
Record Bags and Shooting Records. 1930. V. 71
Shooting With Surtees... Shooting Exploits of John Jorrocks.... 1927. V. 71

GLADSTONE, JOHN
Mercator's Reply to Mr. Booth's Pamphlet on Free Trade, as Published in the Liverpool Standard. Liverpool: 1833. V. 71

GLADSTONE, L.
Neil MacLeod: a tale of Literary Life in London. London: 1898. V. 68

GLADSTONE, WILLIAM EWART
Correspondence on Church and Religion. London: 1910. V. 71
The Irish Question: I: History of an Idea. II: Lessons of the Election. 1886. V. 69
The Ministerial Crisis. Speeches of W. E. Gladstone and B. Disraeli. Westminster: 1873. V. 71
Speeches on the Irish Question in 1886.... Edinburgh: 1886. V. 71

GLADSTONES, J. S.
Lupins as Crop Plants, Biology, Production and Utilization. Wallingford: 1998. V. 72

GLADWIN, HAROLD STERLING
Excavations at Snaketown, Material Culture. Tucson: 1965. V. 73
A History of the Ancient Southwest. Portland: 1957. V. 69; 70; 72

GLAESER, ERNST
Class of 1902. New York: 1929. V. 69

GLANCY, DIANE
Monkey Secret. Evanston: 1995. V. 72
Pushing the Bear. New York: 1996. V. 72

GLANCY, RUTH F.
A Tale of Two Cities - an Annotated Bibliography. New York: 1993. V. 68

GLANVILL, JOSEPH
Scepsis Scientifica; or, Confest Ignorance, the Way to Science; in an Essay of the Vanity of Dogmatizing and Confident Opinion. London: 1665. V. 71; 73
The Zealous and Impartial Protestant, Shewing Some Great But Less Heeded Dangers of Popery. London: 1681. V. 70

GLANVILLE, ERNEST
A Fair Colonist. London: 1895. V. 68

GLANVILLE, PHILLIPA
London in Maps. London: 1972. V. 73

GLANVILLE'S GUIDE TO SOUTH AFRICA. London: 1890. V. 72

GLASER, MILTON
Art Is Work. Woodstock: 2000. V. 69

GLASFURD, A. I. R.
Musings of an Old Shikari. 1928. V. 72
Rifle and Romance in the Indian Jungle. 1905. V. 69; 70; 72; 73

GLASGOW
Minutes of Evidence Taken Before Glasgow Municipal Commission on the Housing of the Poor. Glasgow: 1902-1903. V. 69

GLASGOW and Its Environs: a Literary, Commercial and Social Review Past and Present.... 1891. V. 71

GLASGOW, ELLEN
Barren Ground. Garden City: 1925. V. 68; 70
The Battle Ground. New York: 1902. V. 68; 73
The Builders. Garden City: 1919. V. 69
In This Our Life. New York: 1941. V. 71
The Romantic Comedians. Garden City: 1926. V. 71
The Wheel of Life. New York: 1906. V. 71

GLASHEEN, ADALINE
A Census of Finnegans Wake - an Index of the Characters and Their Roles. London: 1957. V. 72

GLASIER, J. BRUCE
Socialism in Song. Manchester. V. 68

GLASPELL, SUSAN
The Comic Artist: A Play in Three Acts. New York: 1927. V. 72
A Jury of Her Peers. London: 1927. V. 68; 69; 70; 71

GLASS. History, Manufacture and Its Universal Application. Pittsburgh: 1923. V. 71

GLASS, DUDLEY
The Songs of Peter Rabbit. London: 1951. V. 69

GLASS, JOSEPH
Eyes. 1997. V. 68

GLASS, ROBERT C.
Virginia Democracy: a History of Achievements of the Party and Its Leaders in the Mother of Commonwealths, the Old Domnion. 1937. V. 69

GLASS, THOMAS
Commentarii Duodecim De Febribus ad Hippocfatis Disciplinam Accomondati.... Lausannae: 1799. V. 71

GLASSBY, WILLIAM J.
Memorials of Old Mexboro. Sheffield: 1893. V. 73

GLASSE, HANNAH
The Art of Cookery. London: 1778. V. 69
Art of Cookery Made Plain and Easy. London: 1755. V. 72
The Art of Cookery Made Plain and Easy. London: 1760. V. 71; 72
The Art of Cookery Made Plain and Easy. London: 1784. V. 68
The Art of Cookery Made Plain and Easy. Alexandria: 1805. V. 71; 73

GLASSE, SAMUEL
Advice from a Lady of Quality to Her Children in the Last Stage of a Lingering Illness.... London: 1778. V. 70

GLASSIUS, SOLOMON
Opuscula. Leiden: 1700. V. 69
Philologia Sacra...Libris Quinique.... Lipsiae: 1743. V. 71

GLASSPOOLE, RICHARD
Mr. Glasspoole and the Chinese Pirates. Waltham St. Lawrence: 1935. V. 71

GLASSTONE, SAMUEL
Principles of Nuclear Reactor Engineering.... Toronto: 1955. V. 72

GLAUBER, JOHN RUDOLPH
The Works of the Highly Experienced and Famous Chymist.... London: 1689. V. 70

GLAZEBROOK, G. P. DE T.
A History of Transportation in Canada. Ryerson: 1938. V. 72

GLAZIER, WILLARD
Three Years with the Federal Cavalry. New York: 1873. V. 69; 72

GLEASON, DUNCAN
Islands of California. Los Angeles: 1950. V. 70

GLEASON, H. A.
The New Britton and Brown Illustrated Flora of the Northeastern United States and Adjacent Canada. New York: 1952. V. 71

GLEASON, JANE
The Young and Happy Rooster. Chicago: 1934. V. 69

GLEDART, HANNAH RANSOM
Memorials of Samuel Gurney. London: 1857. V. 71

GLEDHILL, ALAN
The Republic of India: the Development of Its Laws and Constitution. London: 1951. V. 72

GLEDITSCH, JOHANN GOTTLIEB
Methodus Fungorum Exhibens Genera, Species et Varietates cum Charactere.... Berlin: 1753. V. 68; 71

GLEED, CHARLES E.
From River to Sea. A Tourist's and Miner's Guide from the Missouri River to the Pacific Ocean. Chicago: 1882. V. 68; 73

GLEGG, W. E.
A History of the Birds of Essex. 1929. V. 69; 73
A History of the Birds of Middlesex. 1935. V. 69

GLEICHEN RUSSWORM, WILHELM FRIEDRICH, FREIHERR VON
Histoire de la Mouce Commune de nos Appartemens. Nuremberg: 1766. V. 73

GLEICK, JAMES
Nature's Chaos. New York: 1990. V. 69

GLEIG, GEORGE ROBERT
A Narrative of the Campaigns of the British Army at Washington and New Orleans, Under Generals Ross, Pakenham and Lambert in the Years 1814 and 1815.... London: 1826. V. 73

GLEITER, JAN
Lie Down with Dogs. New York: 1996. V. 69

GLENCONNER, PAMELA
The Sayings of the Children. Oxford: 1918. V. 70; 73
The Significance of the Spiritual World as Revealed to the Mind of Man in Symbols. London: 1918. V. 68

GLENDENNING, VICTORIA
A Suppressed Cry - Life and Death of a Quaker Daughter. London: 1969. V. 71

GLENELG, CHARLES GRANT, 1ST BARON
Lord Glenelg's Despatches to Sir F. B. Head, Bart. During His Administration of the Government of Upper Canada. London: 1839. V. 68

GLENFIELD COMPANY LTD., KILMARNOCK
Illustrated, Descriptive and Priced Catalogue. 1882. V. 71

GLENFIN, PSEUD.
The Fishing-Rod; and How to Use It.... London: 1861. V. 72

GLENN, A. R.
Under the Pole Star. The Oxford University Arctic Expedition 1935- 1936. 1937. V. 70
Under the Pole Star. The Oxford University Arctic Expedition 1935- 1936. London: 1937. V. 73

GLENN, C. W.
Jim Dine Drawings. New York: 1985. V. 69; 72

GLENNIE, JOHN S. STUART
Greek Folk-Songs from the Turkish Provinces of Greece.... London: 1885. V. 68

GLENNY, GEORGE
Glenny's Hand-Book to the Flower Garden. London: 1855. V. 69
Glenny's Hand-Book to the Flower Garden & Greenhouse. London: 1871. V. 69
The Internation Exhibition Remembrancer and Illustrated Forget-Me- Not. London: 1863. V. 71

GLIBOTA, ANTE
Chicago. 150 Years Of Architecture. Paris: 1985. V. 72

GLICKSBERG, CHARLES I.
The Literature of Nihilism. Lewisburg: 1975. V. 73

GLISSANT, EDOUARD
The Ripening. New York: 1959. V. 69

GLOAG, JOHN
The Englishman's Chair. London: 1964. V. 72

GLOTZER, DAVID
Occasions of Grace: Poems. 1979. V. 71

GLOVER, ALAN
Gloriana's Glass. London. V. 71

GLOVER, BONNIE
Diary of a Schoolmarm, Osakis, Minnesota, Who Travels to Osceola, Nebraska 1877-1879. Osakis: 1877. V. 71

GLOVER, RICHARD
Leonidas. London: 1737. V. 69; 71
Leonidas. London: 1739. V. 73

GLOZER, LISELOTTE F.
California in the Kitchen. 1960. V. 68

GLUBB, JOHN BAGOT
Britain and the Arabs, a Study of Fifty Years 1908-1958. 1959. V. 68

GLUCQ, M.
L'Album de l'Exposition 1889. Paris: 1889. V. 72

GLUE and Lacquer: Four Cautionary Tales. Waltham St. Lawrence: 1941. V. 70; 71

GLUT, DONALD F.
Dinosaurs the Encyclopedia. Jefferson: 1997-1996. V. 70

GLYN, ELINOR
Guinevere's Lover. New York: 1913. V. 71
Reflections of Ambrosine. London: 1902. V. 68
This Passion Called Love. New York: 1925. V. 71
Three Weeks. New York: 1907. V. 71

GLYNN, JOSEPH
Rudimentary Treatise on the Construction of Cranes, and Machinery for Raising Heavy Bodies, for the Erection of Buildings and for Hoisting Goods. London: 1849. V. 73

GOAD, JOHN
Astro-Meteogrologia Sana. London: 1690. V. 72

GOADBY, PETER
Big Fish and Blue Water. 1970. V. 68

GOADBY, ROBERT
The Life Voyages and Adventures of Bampfylde-Moore Carew.... London: 1785?. V. 73

GOCAR, JOSEF
Josef Gocar. Geneva: 1930. V. 68

GOD: Stories. Boston/New York: 1998. V. 72

GODBEY, J. E.
Lights and Shadows of Seventy Years. St. Louis: 1913. V. 70

GODCHARLES, FREDERIC A.
Pennsylvania: Political, Governmental, Military & Civil. New York: 1933. V. 72

GODDARD, ARTHUR
Players of the Period. London: 1891. V. 72

GODDARD, JOHN
Trout Flies of Stillwater. 1969. V. 68; 73

GODDARD, PAUL E.
The Anatomy, Physiology and Pathology of Human Teeth.... Philadelphia: 1844. V. 70; 71

GODDARD, PLINY EARLE
Myths and Tales from the San Carlos Apache. New York: 1918. V. 69
Myths and Tales from the White Mountain Apache. New York: 1919. V. 69
Navajo Texts. New York: 1933. V. 69
San Carlos Apache Texts. New York: 1919. V. 73

GODDARD, ROBERT
Set in Stone. London: 1999. V. 68

GODDARD, ROBERT H.
Liquid-Propellant Rocket Development. Washington: 1936. V. 70

GODDARD, WILLIAM G.
An Address to the People of Rhode Island, Delivered at Newport...on the Occasion of the Change in Civil Government.... Providence: 1843. V. 71

GODDEN, GEOFFREY A.
Coalport And Coalbrookdale Porcelains. Woodbridge: 1981. V. 72; 73
The Illustrated Guide to Lowestoft Porcelain. London: 1969. V. 72
Lowestoft Porcelains. Woodbridge: 1989. V. 72
Minton Pottery & Porcelain Of The First Period 1793-1850. London: 1978. V. 72

GODDEN, RUMER
The Tale of the Tales. London: 1971. V. 71

GODFREY, CARLOS E.
The Commander-in-Chief's Guard. Revolutionary War. Washington;: 1904. V. 69

GODFREY, E. L. B.
History of the Medical Profession of Camden County, N.J. Philadelphia: 1896. V. 69; 70

GODFREY, EDWARD SETTLE
An Account of Custer's Last Campaign and The Battle of The Little Big Horn. Palo Alto: 1968. V. 72
The Field Diary of Lt. Edward Settle Godfrey, Commanding Co. K. 7th Cavalry Regiment Under Lt. Colonel George Armstrong Custer in the Sioux Encounter at the Battle of Little Big Horn. Portland: 1957. V. 69; 72

GODFREY, JOHN THOMAS
The History of the Parish and Priory of Lenton, in the County of Nottingham. London: 1884. V. 70

GODFREY, R. K.
Aquatic and Wetland Plants of Southeastern United States. Athens: 1979. V. 72

GODFREY, THOMAS
The Prince of Parthia, a Tragedy. Boston: 1917. V. 73

GODFREY, WALTER H.
Gardens in the Making. London: 1914. V. 70
Swakeleys, Ickenham. 1933. V. 71

GODKIN, JAMES
The Land War in Ireland: a History for the Times. London: 1870. V. 68

GODLEE, R. J.
Lord Lister. Oxford: 1924. V. 68

GODMAN, ERNEST
The Old Palace of Bromley-By-Bow. London: 1902. V. 71

GODMAN, J. D.
Addresses Delivered on Various Public Occasions.... Philadelphia: 1829. V. 71
American Natural History. Part 1. Mastology. Philadelphia: 1831. V. 69; 73

GODON, JULIEN
Painted Tapestry and Its Application to Interior Decoration. London: 1879. V. 72

GODSCHALK, JEAN
Latini Sermons Observationes. Venice: 1536. V. 70

GODSPEED, T. HARPER
Plant Hunters in The Andes. London: 1941. V. 72

GODWIN, BENJAMIN
The Substance of a Course of Lectures on British Colonial Slavery Delivered at Bradford, York and Scarborough. London: 1830. V. 72

GODWIN, GAIL
Dream Children. New York: 1976. V. 73
The Perfectionists. New York: 1970. V. 69; 71; 73

GODWIN, GEORGE
Building & Monuments Modern and Mediaeval.... London: 1850. V. 68
History in Ruins: A Series of Letters to a Lady, Embodying a Popular Sketch of the History of Architecture.... London: 1853. V. 73

GODWIN, THOMAS
Moses and Aaron. (with) *Romanae Historiae.* London: 1655. V. 68

GODWIN, WILLIAM
An Enquiry Concerning Political Justice and Its Influence on General Virtue and Happiness. Dublin: 1793. V. 71
Enquiry Concerning Political Justice and Its Influence on General Virtue and Happiness. London: 1793. V. 73
Enquiry Concerning Political Justice, and Its Influence on Morals and Happiness. London: 1796. V. 69; 70
An Essay on Sepulchres. London: 1809. V. 68; 70; 72
History of the Commonwealth of England. London: 1824-. V. 71
Of Population. An Enquiry Concerning the Power of Increase in the Numbers of Mankind, Being an Answer to Mr. Malthus's Essay on that Subject. London: 1820. V. 68; 71; 72
Things as They Are; or the Adventures of Caleb Williams. London: 1816. V. 73

GOEBEL, JULIUS
Law Enforcement in Colonial New York: a Study in Criminal Procedure 1964-1776. New York: 1944. V. 70

GOEDAERDT, JOHANNES
De Insectis, in Methodum Redactus; cum Notularum Additione. Londini: 1685. V. 72

GOEDDAEUS, CONRADUS
Laus Ululae Ad Conscriptos Ululantium Patres & Patrones. Claucopoli: 1642. V. 70

GOELICKE, ANDREAE OTTOMAR
Historia Chirurgiae Antiqua, Seu Conspectus Plerorumque.... Halle: 1713. V. 72

GOESSLING, ADELINE
Orange Judd Cook Book. Chicago: 1914. V. 68

GOETHE, JOHANN WOLFGANG VON
The Auto-Biography of Goethe. Truth and Poetry...From My Life. Part First-(Second-Third-Fourth). New York: 1846-1847. V. 73
Faust. Boston: 1908. V. 70
Faust. London: 1908. V. 68; 70; 71
Faust. Paris: 1938. V. 72
The Faust of Goethe Attempted in English Rhyme. London: 1835. V. 70
Faustus. London: 1821. V. 68
Goethe's Faust: An American Translation. Norfolk CT: 1941. V. 72
Goethe's Faust. Parts I and II. London: 1951. V. 70
Goethe's Theory of Colours. London: 1840. V. 68; 72
Italian Journey: 1786-1788. London: 1962. V. 73
Italian Journey (1786-1788). Verona: 1962. V. 71
Letters From Goethe. Edinburgh: 1957. V. 72
The Practical Wisdom of Goethe. London: 1933. V. 70
Schriften. Leipzig: 1790. V. 68
The Sorrows of Werter. London: 1784. V. 73

GOETHE, JOHANN WOLFGANG VON *continued*
Les Souffrances du Jeune Werther. Paris: 1809. V. 71

GOETZ, G. F.
Naturgeschichte Einiger Vogel. Hanau: 1782. V. 73

GOETZMANN, WILLIAM H.
Explorations and Empire, The Explorer and The Scientist in Winning of The American West. New York: 1966. V. 72
Karl Bodmer's America. Japan: 1984. V. 69

GOFF, BRUCE
Architecture: Thirty Plates. Billings: 1978. V. 69; 72

GOFF, CLARISSA
Florence & Some Tuscan Cities. London: 1905. V. 72

GOFF, FREDERICK R.
Incunabula in American Libraries. A Third Census. New York: 1964. V. 72

GOFF, RICHARD
Century in the Saddle. Boulder: 1967. V. 71

GOGARTY, OLIVER ST. JOHN
It Isn't This Time of Year at All. 1954. V. 69
An Offering of Swans. London. V. 73
Others to Adorn. 1938. V. 69
Perennial. Baltimore: 1944. V. 68; 71

GOGOL, NIKOLAI
Evening on a Farm Near Dikanka. New York: 1928. V. 70

GOHS, CARL
Ed Quigley - Western Artist. Portland: 1971. V. 69

GOING Ta-Ta. London: 1920. V. 69

GOLD, CHARLES
Oriental Drawings, Sketched Between the Years 1791 and 1798. London: 1806. V. 68

GOLD, GLEN DAVID
Carter Beats The Devil. London: 2001. V. 72

GOLD, HERBERT
The Prospect Before Us. Cleveland and New York: 1954. V. 69

GOLD, IVAN
Sams in a Dry Season. Boston: 1990. V. 68

GOLD, THOMAS D.
History of Clarke County, Virginia and Its Connection with the War Between the States. Berryville: 1914. V. 69; 70

GOLDBARTH, ALBERT
Jan. 31. Garden City: 1974. V. 71

GOLDBERG, ISAAC
The Man Mencken: a Biographical and Critical Survey. Illustrated and Documented. New York: 1925. V. 73

GOLDBERGER, PAUL
The Houses of the Hamptons. New York: 1986. V. 71

GOLDBLATT, BURT
Burt Goldblatt's Jazz Gallery 1. New York: 1982. V. 69

GOLDBORNE, JAMES
The Report of James Goldborne, of the City of Ely, Engineer, in Pursuance of Several Resolutions Passed at a Meeting of the Committee.... Lynn: 1791. V. 71

GOLDEMBERG, ISAAC
The Fragmented Life of Don Jacobo Lerner. New York: 1976. V. 69

GOLDEN Book of Famous Women. London. V. 71

GOLDEN, ARTHUR
Memoirs of a Geisha. New York: 1987. V. 71
Memoirs of a Geisha. New York: 1997. V. 68; 69; 71; 72; 73

GOLDEN Book of Songs & Ballads. London. V. 71

THE GOLDEN Cabinet; Being the Laboratory, or Handmaid to the Arts. Philadelphia: 1793. V. 68

THE GOLDEN Calendar. London: 1865. V. 69

GOLDEN, GEORGE FULLER
My Lady Vaudeville and Her White Rats. New York: 1909. V. 70

GOLDEN Guide to London and Book of Commercial Information. 1884. V. 71

GOLDEN, HARRY
Unseen Acres. New York: 1921. V. 70

GOLDEN, I. J.
Precedent. New York: 1931. V. 69; 70

GOLDEN, MARITA
Long Distance Live. New York: 1989. V. 72

GOLDEN, R.
Sir William Osler. An Annotated Bibliography with Illustrations. San Francisco: 1988. V. 70

GOLDFINCH, RICHARD
Memoirs of a Goldfinch. A Poem. London: 1819. V. 73

GOLDILOCKS.. London: 1915. V. 69

GOLDILOCKS and the Three Bears. London: 1952. V. 69

GOLDING, HARRY
Fairy Tales. London: 1915. V. 70
The Toy Soldiers. London. V. 69

GOLDING, LOUIS
Adventures in Architecture. 1936. V. 71
The Dance Goes On. 1937. V. 71
Give Up Your Lovers. New York: 1930. V. 71
Mario on the Beach and Other Tales. London: 1956. V. 71
Shepherd Singing Ragtime, and Other Poems. London: 1921. V. 70
The Song of Songs. 1937. V. 71; 72
Sorrow of War: Poems. London: 1919. V. 71; 72

GOLDING, WILLIAM
The Brass Butterfly. London: 1958. V. 70
The Brass Butterfly. London: 1963. V. 70
Chute Libre (Free Fall). Paris: 1961. V. 72
Close Quarters. London: 1987. V. 70
Conversations with William Golding. New York: 1970. V. 69
Darkness Visible. London and Boston: 1979. V. 70; 72; 73
The Double Tongue. London: 1995. V. 70
An Egyptian Journal. London: 1985. V. 70
Fire Down Below. London: 1989. V. 70; 72
Free Fall. London: 1959. V. 69; 70; 71; 72
Free Fall. New York: 1960. V. 73
The Hot Gates and Other Occasional Pieces. London: 1965. V. 70
Hot Gates and Other Occasional Pieces. New York: 1966. V. 71
The Inheritors. London: 1955. V. 68; 71; 72
The Inheritors. London: 1959. V. 70
The Inheritors. New York: 1962. V. 73
The Lord of the Flies. London: 1954. V. 71
Lord of the Flies. New York: 1955. V. 69; 70; 71
A Moving Target. London: 1982. V. 70
Nobel Lecture - 7 December 1983. Leamington Spa: 1984. V. 70
The Paper Men. London: 1984. V. 70
Pincher Martin. London: 1956. V. 73
Pincher Martin. London: 1961. V. 71
Poems. London: 1934. V. 70
The Pyramid. London: 1967. V. 68; 70; 71; 73
(I) Rites of Passage. (II) Close Quarters. (III) Fire Down Below. New York: 1980-1989. V. 70
The Scorpion God - Three Short Novels. London: 1971. V. 72
The Scorpion God: Three Short Novels. New York: 1972. V. 71
The Spire. London: 1964. V. 70; 71; 73
To the Ends of the Earth - a Sea Trilogy Comprising Rites of Passage, Close Quarters and Fire Down Below. London: 1991. V. 70; 73

GOLDMAN, EMMA
Anarchism and Other Essays. New York: 1910. V. 68
The Social Significance of the Modern Drama. Boston: 1914. V. 68; 72
Voltairine De Cleyre. Berkeley Heights: 1932. V. 73

GOLDMAN, FRANCISCO
The Long Night of White Chickens. New York: 1992. V. 69

GOLDMAN, LAWRENCE
Fall Guy for Murder. New York: 1943. V. 71

GOLDMAN, R. L.
Out on Bail. New York: 1937. V. 68
The Purple Shells. Chicago: 1947. V. 69

GOLDMAN, SHIFRA M.
Contemporary Mexican Painting in a Time of Change. Austin: 1981. V. 71

GOLDMAN, WILLIAM
Brothers. 1987. V. 68
Butch Cassidy and the Sundance Kid. New York: 1969. V. 69
Magic. New York: 1976. V. 69; 72
Marathon Man. New York: 1974. V. 68; 69; 70; 71
No Way to Treat a Lady. Greenwich: 1964. V. 71
The Princess Bride. Los Angeles: 1979. V. 69
Soldier in the Rain. New York: 1960. V. 71; 73
The Temple of Gold. New York: 1957. V. 68
The Thing of It Is.... New York: 1967. V. 69; 70
Wigger. New York: 1974. V. 69

GOLDONI, CARLO
The Liar - a Comedy in Three Acts. London: 1922. V. 69

GOLDRING, MAUDE
Charlotte Bronte, the Woman. A Study. New York: 1916. V. 70

GOLDSBOROUGH, WILLIAM W.
The Maryland Line in the Confederate Army. 1861-1865. Baltimore: 1900. V. 70

GOLDSCHMIDT, E. P.
Gothic and Renaissance Bookbindings. London: 1928. V. 69
Medieval Texts and Their First Appearance in Print. Meisenheim: 1965. V. 70
The Printed Book of the Renaissance: Three Lectures on Type, Illustration, Ornament. 1950. V. 72

GOLDSCHMIDT, M.
Society of Virtue at Rome. London: 1868. V. 69

GOLDSCHMIDT, RICHARD B.
In and Out of the Ivory Tower. Seattle: 1960. V. 68
Portraits from Memory. Seattle: 1956. V. 68

GOLDSMID, EDMUND
Bibliotheca Curiosa. A Complete Catalogue of all the Publications of the Elzevier Presses at Leyden, Amsterdam, The Hague and Utrecht. Edinburgh: 1886-1888. V. 70

GOLDSMID, FRANCIS HENRY
Memoir. London: 1879. V. 71

GOLDSMID, FREDERIC J.
Telegraph and Travel: a Narrative of the...Development of Telegraphic Communication Between England and India.... London: 1874. V. 70

GOLDSMITH, JOHN
An Almanack for the Year of Our Lord God MDCCXCVII. London: 1797. V. 69
An Almanack for...1789, etc. London: 1789. V. 69

GOLDSMITH, LEWIS
The Secret History of the Cabinet of Bonaparte: Including His Private Life, Character, Domestic Administration.... London: 1810. V. 68

GOLDSMITH, MARTIN
Detour: an Extraordinary Tale. New York: 1939. V. 71
Double Jeopardy. New York: 1938. V. 72

GOLDSMITH, OLIVER
Dalziel's Illustrated Goldsmith; Comprising The Vicar of Wakefield, The Traveller, The Deserted Village, The Haunch of Venison . . . London. V. 71
Dalziel's Illustrated Goldsmith: Comprising the Vicar of Wakefield, The Traveller, The Deserted Village. The Haunch of Venison, the Captivity, an Oratorio, Retaliation, Miscellaneous Poems and The Good Natured Man, She Stoops to Conquer. . . London: 1880. V. 70
The Deserted Village. London: 1770. V. 70
Essays. Dublin: 1767. V. 73
Flavor of the Month. 1993. V. 70
Goldsmith's Natural History, Abridged for the Use of Schools by Mrs. Pilkington. London: 1803. V. 73
Goldsmith's Roman History. Trenton: 1802. V. 69
The History of Greece, From the Earliest Statae to the Death of Alexander the Great. To Which is Added a Summary Account.... London: 1809. V. 70
The History of Little Goody Twoshoes; Otherwise Called Mrs. Margery Twoshoes.... Worcester: 1787. V. 71
An History of the Earth and Animated Nature. London: 1791. V. 72
A History of the Earth and Animated Nature. Glasgow: 1854. V. 71
A History of the Earth and Animated Nature. Edinburgh and London: 1855. V. 71
Lives of Dr. Parnell and Lord Bolingbroke: with the Bee. Belfast: 1818. V. 69
The Mad Dog. London: 1879. V. 70
The Miscellaneous Works. London: 1806. V. 73
The Miscellaneous Works. Glasgow: 1816. V. 73
The Miscellaneous Works of Oliver Goldsmith. London: 1823. V. 69
The Poems of Oliver Goldsmith. London: 1860. V. 72
She Stoops to Conquer or The Mistakes of a Night. London. V. 71
She Stoops to Conquer or the Mistakes of the Night. London: 1912. V. 72
The Traveller. London: 1765. V. 70
The Traveller. London: 1770. V. 71
The Traveller. London: 1856. V. 69
The Vicar of Wakefield. London: 1766. V. 70
The Vicar of Wakefield. Salisbury: 1766. V. 70
The Vicar of Wakefield. Berlin: 1776. V. 69
The Vicar of Wakefield. Paris: 1779. V. 69
The Vicar of Wakefield. Paris: 1784. V. 69
The Vicar of Wakefield. London: 1817. V. 68
The Vicar of Wakefield. London: 1886. V. 71
The Vicar of Wakefield. London: 1890. V. 71; 72
The Vicar of Wakefield. 1903. V. 71
The Vicar of Wakefield. London: 1903. V. 70
The Vicar of Wakefield. London: 1914. V. 71
The Vicar of Wakefield. London and New York: 1926. V. 69
The Vicar of Wakefield. London: 1929. V. 69; 70
The Vicar of Wakefield. Philadelphia: 1929. V. 73
Works. London. V. 70
The Works. New York: 1908. V. 70
Works: Poems, Comedies, Essays, Vicar of Wakefield: with life by Washington Irving. London. V. 71

GOLDSMITH, OLIVIA
The First Wives Club. 1992. V. 70

GOLDSTEIN, ANN
Reconsidering the Object of Art: 1965-1975. Los Angeles: 1995. V. 68

GOLDSTEIN, KURT
Language and Language Disturbances, Aphasic Symptom Complexes and their Significance for Medicine and Theory of Language. New York: 1948. V. 71

GOLDSTON, WILL
Secrets of Scene Painting and Stage Effects. London: 1915. V. 72

GOLDSTONE, ADRIAN H.
The Goldstone Collection of Mystery and Detective Fiction. San Francisco: 1981. V. 73
John Steinbeck: a Bibliographical Catalogue of the Adrian H. Goldstone Collection. Austin: 1974. V. 69

GOLDSWORTHY Lowes Dickinson 6 August 1887-3 August 1932: Fellow of the College 1887-1932. Cambridge: 1932. V. 70

GOLDTHWAITE, EATON K.
You Did It. New York: 1943. V. 69

GOLDWATER, BARRY M.
Delightful Journey Down the Green and Colorado Rivers. Tempe: 1970. V. 68

GOLDWATER, R.
Artists on Art from the XIV to XX Century. New York: 1947. V. 71

GOLDWATER, WALTER
Radical Periodicals in America. New York: 1977. V. 68

GOLL, IVAN
La Chanson De Jean Sans Terre. Poeme en 9 Chants. Paris: 1936. V. 72

GOLLOMB, JOSEPH
The Curtain of Storm. New York: 1933. V. 70
The Portrait Invisible. New York: 1928. V. 68
The Subtle Trail. London: 1930. V. 68

GOLLY Tales Tall Book Series. London: 1950. V. 73

GOLON, SERGEANNE
Angelique in Barbary. Philadelphia: 1961. V. 68; 69

GOLTZIUS, HUBERT
Fastos Magistratvvm et Triumphorvm Romanorvm.... Bruges: 1566. V. 70
Le Vive Imagini di Tutti Quasi Gl'Imperatori da Iulio Caesare, in sino a Carlo V.... Antwerp: 1560. V. 70

GOMES, EDWIN H.
The Sea-Dyaks of Boreno Seventeen Years Missionary in Boreno, with a Chapter on Missionary Work Amongst the Dyaks by the Ven. Westminster Society for the: 1907. V. 72

GOMEZ, ISAAC
Selections of a Father for the Use of His Children. New York: 1820. V. 69

GOMEZ, MANUEL
Poems for Workers. Chicago. V. 69

GOMME, ALICE B.
Children's Singing Games. London: 1894. V. 71

GOMME, G. LAURENCE
The Handbook of Folklore. London: 1890. V. 69
London in the Reign of Victoria (1837-1897). 1898. V. 71

GOMPERS, SAMUEL
Labor in Europe and America. New York: 1910. V. 68

GOMPERTZ, G. ST. G. M.
Chinese Celadon Wares. London: 1980. V. 73
The Gordon Setter. History and Characater. 1976. V. 68

GONCHAROV, IVAN
Oblomov. London: 1929. V. 70
Oblomov. New York: 1929. V. 71

GONCOURT, EDMOND
Renee Mauperin. Paris: 1864. V. 72

GONDI, JEAN FRANCOIS PAUL DE
Memoires du Cardinal de Retz, de Guy Joli, et de la Duchesse de Nemours.... Paris: 1820. V. 72

GONZALES, AMBROSE E.
The Captain. Stories of the Black Border. Columbia: 1924. V. 70; 73
Laguerre: a Gascon of the Black Border. Columbia: 1924. V. 70; 71

GONZALES, BABS
I, Paid My Dues. East Orange: 1967. V. 69

GOOCH, RICHARD
Facetiae Cantabrigienses.... London: 1825. V. 68
Facetiae Cantabrigienses.... London: 1836. V. 71
Nuts to Crack, or Quips, Quirks, Anecdotes and Facetiae of Oxford and Cambridge Scholars. London: 1835. V. 71

GOOCH, ROBERT
Gooch on Some of the Most Important Diseases Peculiar to Women; With Other Papers. Prefactory Essay by Robert Ferguson. London: 1859. V. 72

GOOD, A. I.
The Birds of French Cameroon. 1952-1953. V. 73

THE GOOD Girl. Northampton: 1842. V. 73

GOOD, JOHN MASON
The Study of Medicine.... London: 1829. V. 71

GOOD, PETER P.
The Family Flora and Materia Medica Botanica.... Elizabethtown: 1851?. V. 69

GOOD, R.
The Geography of Flowering Plants. London: 1947. V. 72

GOOD Things Made, Said and Done for Every Home and Household. London: 1880. V. 68

GOODALE, GEORGE L.
Wild Flowers of America. Boston: 1882. V. 69

GOODALL, CHARLES
The Royal College of Physicians of London founded and Established by Law. 1684. V. 72

GOODALL, JANE
The Chimpanzees Of Gombe. Patterns Of Behavior. Cambridge: 1986. V. 72

GOODALL, JOHN S.
The Adventures of Paddy Pork. New York: 1968. V. 70
The Ballooning Adventures of Paddy Pork. New York: 1969. V. 70
Dream Pony. London: 1951. V. 71
Jacko. New York: 1972. V. 70
The Midnight Adventures of Kelly, Dot and Esmeralda. New York. V. 70
Shrewbettina's Birthday. New York: 1971. V. 70
The Story of an English Village. London: 1978. V. 70

GOODALL, WALTER
An Introduction to the History and Anquities of Scotland. Edinburgh: 1773. V. 72

GOODCHILD, GEORGE
Jack O'Lantern. 1930. V. 73
Jack O'Lantern. New York: 1930. V. 68
The Monster of Grammont. 1930. V. 73
The Monster of Grammont. New York: 1930. V. 68; 70
Q33. London: 1933. V. 73
The Rain on the Roof. London: 1928. V. 68
Trooper O'Neill: A Story of the North-West Mounted Police. New York: 1923. V. 72

GOODE, G. B.
Fisheries and Fishery Industries of the United States, Section I, Natural History of Useful Aquatic Animals. Washington: 1884. V. 69; 72; 73
A Memorial Of George Brown Goode Together with A Selection of His Papers on Museums And On The History Of Science In America. Washington: 1901. V. 72
Oceanic Ichthyology, a Treatise on the Deep Sea and Pelagic Fishes of the World. Washington: 1895. V. 69
Virginia Cousins: a Study of the Ancestry and Posterity of John Goode of Whitby: a Virginia Colonist of the 17th Century. Richmond: 1887. V. 69

GOODE, JOHN
Recollections of a Lifetime. New York. V. 73

GOODE, SAMUEL
Some Account of the Medicinal Properties of the Hot Springs, Virginia.... Richmond: 1858. V. 71

GOODE, WILLIAM H.
Outpost of Zion with Limnings of Mission Life. Cincinnati: 1854. V. 73
Outposts of Zion. Cincinnati: 1863. V. 71

GOODEN, STEPHEN
An Iconography of the Engravings of Stephen Gooden. London: 1944. V. 69; 73

GOODIS, DAVID
4 Novels. London: 1983. V. 73
Behold this Woman. New York and London: 1947. V. 69
Black Pudding In Manhunt December 1953. New York: 1953. V. 72
Dark Passage. 1946. V. 69; 70
Dark Passage. New York: 1946. V. 70
4 Novels. London: 1983. V. 69; 70; 72
Night Squad. Greenwich: 1961. V. 69; 72
Nightfall. London: 1948. V. 68
Of Tender Sin. New York: 1952. V. 70

GOODLAKE, THOMAS
The Courser's Manual - or Stud Book. 1828. V. 68

GOODLANDER, C. W.
Early Days of Fort Scott, Memoirs and Recollections of.... Fort Scott: 1900. V. 72
Memoirs and Recollections of...the Early Days of Fort Scott. Fort Scott: 1900. V. 68

GOODMAN, ALLEGRA
Kaaterskill Falls. New York: 1998. V. 69
Total Immersion. New York: 1989. V. 69; 73

GOODMAN, BENNY
The Kingdom of Swing. New York: 1939. V. 73

GOODMAN, DAVID MICHAEL
A Western Panorama 1849-1875: The Travels Writings and Influence of J. Ross Browne on the Pacific Coast and in Texas Nevada, Arizona and Baja California.... Glendale: 1966. V. 71; 73

GOODMAN, JOHN B.
The Key to the Goodman Encyclopedia of the California Gold Rush Fleet. Los Angeles: 1992. V. 68

GOODMAN, PAUL
North Percy. Los Angeles: 1968. V. 70

GOODMAN, RICHARD
Footnote to Lawrence. London: 1932. V. 72

GOODMAN, S. M.
The Birds of Eygpt. Oxford and New York: 1989. V. 70; 73

GOODNIGHT, CHARLES
Pioneer Days in the Southwest From 1850 to1879. Guthrie: 1909. V. 71

GOODNO, WILLIAM C.
The Practice of Medicine with Sections on Diseases of the Nervous System by Clarence Bartlett, M.D. Philadelphia: 1894-1897. V. 70

GOODRICH, ARTHUR
Caponsacchi. New York: 1927. V. 69

GOODRICH, CHARLES A.
The Family Encyclopedia, or Compenium of Useful Knowledge.... New York: 1860. V. 73

GOODRICH, FRANCES
The Diary of Anne Frank. New York: 1956. V. 72

GOODRICH, LLOYD
Edward Hopper. New York: 1970. V. 70
Edward Hopper. New York: 1978. V. 69; 70; 72; 73
Reginald Marsh. New York: 1972. V. 68
Thomas Eakins. Cambridge: 1982. V. 72

GOODRICH, SAMUEL GRISWOLD
Curiosities of Human Nature. Boston: 1855. V. 68
The History of a Little Silver-Fish. Hartford: 1819. V. 71
History of the Indians of North and South America. New York: 1844. V. 73
Johnson's Natural History.... New York: 1872. V. 73
Recollections of a Lifetime. New York and Auburn: 1856. V. 70
Tales About the Sun, Moon and Stars. London: 1837. V. 68
Tales of Humor. Boston: 1840. V. 68
Tales of Love. Volume I-II. (and) Tales of Humor. volume I-II. and Tales of Terror. Volumes I-II. and Moral Tales. Volume I (of two). Boston: 1841-1840. V. 73
The Token. Boston: 1839. V. 71

GOODRICH-FREER, A.
Outer Isles. London: 1902. V. 71

GOODRICKE, H. HENRY
Observations on Dr. Price's Theory and Principles of Civil Liberty and Government, Preceded by a Letter to a Friend, on the Pretensions of the American Colonies, in Respect of Right and Equity. York: 1776. V. 69

GOODRIDGE, RICHARD E. W.
A Year in Manitoba Being the Experience of a Retired Officer in Settling His Sons. London and Edinburgh: 1882. V. 68

GOODSIR, JOHN
The Anatomical Memoirs Of John Goodsir, F. R. S. Edinburgh: 1868. V. 72

GOODSPEED, CHARLES E.
Yankee Bookseller. Being the Reminiscences of Charles E Goodspeed. Boston;: 1937. V. 68

GOODSPEED, EDGAR J.
The Curse in the Colophon. Chicago/NY: 1935. V. 72

GOODSPEED, T. HARPER
Notes on the Californian Species of Trillium I. Berkeley: 1916-1917. V. 72
Plant Hunters in the Andes. New York: 1941. V. 69

GOODWIN, C. C.
The Comstock Club. Salt Lake City: 1891. V. 73

GOODWIN, CARDINAL LEONIDAS
The Trans-Mississippi West (1803-1853). A History of Its Acquisition and Settlement. New York: 1922. V. 68

GOODWIN, ERNEST
Stiletto. Indianapolis: 1924. V. 71

GOODWIN, FRANCIS
Domestic Architecture, Being a Sries of Designs of Mansions, Villas, Rectory Houses, Parsonage Houses, Bailiff's Lodge, Gardener's Lodge, GameKeeper's Lodge, Park Gate Lodges etc.... London: 1850. V. 69; 71

GOODWIN, GEORGE
Trial of Peter Griffiths (The Blackburn Baby Murder). London: 1950. V. 73

GOODWIN, GRENVILLE
Myths and Tales of the White Mountain Apache. New York: 1939. V. 69
The Social Organization of the Western Apache. 1942. V. 68
The Social Organization of the Western Apache. Chicago: 1942. V. 70; 72

GOODWIN, JONATHAN
The Jonathan Goodwin Sale. NY: 1977-1978. V. 73

GOODWIN, JOSEPH
A New System of Shoeing Horses; with an Account of the Various Modes Practicsed by Different Nations.... London: 1820. V. 72

GOODWIN, NAT C.
Nat Goodwin's Book. Boston: 1914. V. 70

GOODWIN, P. D.
The Trans-Mississippi West 1803-1853. New York: 1922. V. 73

GOODWIN, RALPH A.
The Stoenberg Affair. New York: 1913. V. 69; 73

GOODWIN, THOMAS
An Account of the Neutral Saline Waters Recently Discovered at Hampstead.... London: 1804. V. 71

GOODWYN, FRANK
The Devil in Texas. Dallas: 1936. V. 70

THE GOODY Two Shoes Story Book. New York. V. 71

GOODYEAR, CHARLES
A Centennial Volume of the Writings of Charles Goodyear and Thomas Hancock.. Boston: 1939. V. 69

GOODYEAR, W. A.
The Coal Mines of the Western Coast of the United States. San Francisco: 1877. V. 68; 73

GORDIMER, NADINE
The Black Interpreters: Notes on African Writing. Johannesburg: 1973. V. 68; 70
Burger's Daughter. New York: 1979. V. 69; 70; 72
The Conservationist. London: 1974. V. 69; 70; 72
The Conservationist. New York: 1975. V. 68
A Correspondence Course and Other Stories. Helsinki: 1986. V. 69; 70
Face to Face: Short Stories. Johannesburg: 1949. V. 70
Friday's Footprint. London: 1960. V. 70
Friday's Footprint. New York: 1960. V. 69
A Guest of Honor. New York: 1970. V. 69; 72
The House Gun. London: 1998. V. 72
The House Gun. New York: 1998. V. 69; 72
Julys Folk. Stockholm: 1982. V. 70
July's People. New York: 1981. V. 69; 72
Jump. Franklin Center: 1991. V. 69
The Late Bourgeois World. London: 1966. V. 70
Living in Hope and History. New York: 1999. V. 69; 72
Livingstone's Companions. London: 1971. V. 68
Livingstone's Companions. London: 1972. V. 70
The Lying Days. London: 1953. V. 70
My Son's Story. Capetown: 1990. V. 70
None to Accompany Me. New York: 1994. V. 69; 72
Not for Publication. London: 1965. V. 70
Not for Publication. New York: 1965. V. 73
Occasion for Loving. London: 1963. V. 70
Occasion for Loving. New York: 1963. V. 69
Selected Stories. London: 1974. V. 70
Six Feet of the Country. London: 1956. V. 70
Six Feet of the Country. New York: 1956. V. 69; 71; 72; 73
The Soft Voice of the Serpent. New York: 1952. V. 68; 69; 72; 73
The Soft Voice of the Serpent. London: 1953. V. 70
A Soldier's Embrace. London: 1980. V. 69; 72
A Soldier's Embrace. New York: 1980. V. 69; 72
A Sport of Nature. New York: 1987. V. 69; 72
Three in a Bed: Fiction, Morals and Politics. Bennington: 1991. V. 71
Town and Country Lovers. Los Angeles: 1980. V. 69; 70; 72
A World of Strangers. London: 1958. V. 69; 70; 72
A World of Strangers. New York: 1958. V. 69; 72

GORDON, ADAM LINDSAY
Ashtaroth: a Dramatic Lyric. Melbourne: 1867. V. 73
Poems. Sea Spray and Smoke Drift. Bush Ballads and Galloping Rhymes. Miscellaneous Poems. . . London: 1905. V. 71
Sea Spray and Smoke Drift. Melbourne: 1867. V. 73

GORDON, ALEXANDER
The Fitness of Turnpike Roads and Highways for the Most Expeditious, Safe, Convenient and Economical Internal Communication. London: 1835. V. 72

GORDON, ALEXANDER HAMILTON
Remarks on National Defence, Volunteers, and Rifles; with a Report on Experiments with Small Arms, Carried on at the Royal Manufactory at Enfield in 1852. London: 1853. V. 73

GORDON, ALISON
Night Game. Toronto: 1992. V. 71
Striking Out. Toronto: 1995. V. 71

GORDON, ARMISTEAD C.
Memoirs and Memorials of William Gordon McCabe. Richmond: 1925. V. 69; 70

GORDON, CAROLINE
Aleck Maury, Sportsman. New York: 1934. V. 70
The Forest of the South. New York: 1945. V. 69; 71; 72; 73
The Glory of Hera. Garden City: 1972. V. 68
Penhally. New York: 1931. V. 69; 70; 71; 72

The Strange Children. New York: 1951. V. 70; 73

GORDON, D. E.
Ernest Ludwig Kirchner. Cambridge: 1968. V. 72

GORDON, DANIEL M.
Mountain and Prairie: a Journey from Victoria to Winnipeg, Via Peace River Pass. Montreal: 1880. V. 73

GORDON, ELIZABETH
Bird Children. Chicago: 1912. V. 70
Bird Children. Joliet: 1912. V. 73
Flower Children. Joliet: 1910. V. 70

GORDON, G.
Sporting Reminiscences. 1902. V. 72; 73

GORDON, GAVIN C.
Congenital Deformities. Edinburgh: 1961. V. 68

GORDON, GEORGE
The History of Our National Debts and Taxes, from the Year MDCLXXXVIII to the Present Year MDCCLI. London: 1751-1753. V. 72
The Trial of George Gordon, Esquire, Commonly Called Lord George Gordon, for High Treason, at the Bar of the Court of King's Bench, on Monday, February 5th, 1781. (and the Second Part). London: 1781. V. 70

GORDON, GILES
Beyond the Words - Eleven Writers in Search of a New Fiction. London: 1975. V. 70

GORDON, H. LAING
Sir James Young and Chloroform (1811-1870). London: 1897. V. 68; 71; 72

GORDON, J. E. H.
A Physical Treatise on Electricity and Magnetism. New York: 1880. V. 69

GORDON, JAMES
An Introductory Lecture to a Course of Lectures on Clinical Medicine, Delivered in the Theatre of the London Hospital. 1829. V. 71

GORDON, JAN
Two Vagabonds in Albania. London: 1927. V. 70

GORDON, JOHN
Louise Nevelson. New York: 1967. V. 68
Outlines of Lectures on Human Physiology. Edinburgh: 1817. V. 71
Winged Sentries/Sentinelles de l'Air. 1963. V. 73

GORDON, JOHN BROWN
Reminiscences of the Civil War. New York: 1903. V. 69; 70; 73
Reminiscences of the Civil War. New York: 1904. V. 69

GORDON, JULIEN
A Diplomat's Diary. Philadelphia: 1890. V. 72

GORDON, MARY
Final Payments. New York: 1978. V. 72

GORDON, MAURICE BEAR
Aesculapius Comes to the Colonies. 1949. V. 71
Aesculapius Comes to the Colonies. Ventnor: 1949. V. 69

GORDON, MAX
Live at the Village Vanguard. New York: 1980. V. 73

GORDON, MILDRED
The Little Man Who Wasn't There. New York: 1946. V. 68

GORDON, NEIL
The Silent Murders. 1930. V. 73

GORDON, RICHARD
Jack The Ripper. New York: 1980. V. 72

GORDON, ROBERT
Monet. New York: 1989. V. 72

GORDON, SAMUEL
Recollections of Old Milestown. Miles City: 1918. V. 72

GORDON, SETON
The Charm of Skye. London: 1931. V. 71
The Charm of Skye. London: 1934. V. 71
Hebridean Memories. 1923. V. 69; 73
The Immortal Isles. London: 1936. V. 71
The Land of the Hills and the Glens. London: 1920. V. 71
Wanderings of a Naturalist. London: 1921. V. 71

GORDON, SOLON A.
Gravity and the Organism. Chicago: 1971. V. 68

GORDON, SUZANNE
Black Mesa: the Angel of Death. New York: 1973. V. 69

GORDON, THOMAS F.
The History of New Jersey, from Its Discovery by Europeans, to the Adoption of the Federal Constitution. (with) A Gazetteer of the State of New Jersey.... Trenton: 1834. V. 69

GORDON, W. J.
Our Country's Flowers and How to Know Them. 1900. V. 68
Our Country's Shells and How to Know Them. London. V. 68

GORDON, W. J. continued
Round About the North Pole. London: 1907. V. 73

GORDON, WELCHE
Jesse James and His Band of Notorious Outlaws. Chicago: 1891. V. 72

GORDON, WILLIAM
The Separation of the Jewish Tribes after the Death of Solomon, Accounted for, and Applied to the Present Day in a Sermon Preached Before the General Court on Friday, July 4th 1777.... Boston: 1777. V. 68

GORDON, WILLIAM J.
The Captain General. London: 1891. V. 68

GORDON CUMMING, CONSTANCE FREDERICA
Fire Fountains. The Kingdom of Hawaii, Its Volcanoes and the History of Its Missions. Edinburgh and London: 1883. V. 70
In the Hebrides. London: 1883. V. 71
In the Himalayas and on the Indian Plains. 1882. V. 70
The Inventor of the Numeral-Type for China by the Use of Which Illiterate Chinese Both Blind and Sighted Can Very Quickly be Taught to Read and Write Fluently. London: 1898. V. 70

GORDONE, CHARLES
No Place To Be Somebody: A Black Comedy. Indianapolis: 1969. V. 72

GORE, CATHERINE GRACE FRANCES
Hungarian Tales. London: 1829. V. 69
The Opera: a Novel. London: 1832. V. 69
The Tuileries. London: 1831. V. 69

GORE, JOHN
Arithmetic Fairly Laid Open; or, the Trader's Sure Guide. Liverpool: 1769. V. 73

GORE, MRS.
The Rose Fancier's Manual. London: 1838. V. 71

GORE BOOTH, EVA
Poems of Eva Gore Booth. 1929. V. 70

GORER, GEOFFREY
Africa Dances - A Book About West African Negroes. London: 1949. V. 71

GORES, JOE
Dead Skip. New York: 1972. V. 71
Final Notice. New York: 1973. V. 68; 71
Gone, No Forwarding. New York: 1978. V. 71
Interface. New York: 1974. V. 69; 71
Kojak: Case without a File. 1977. V. 72
Stakeout on Page Street and other DKA Files. Norfolk: 2001. V. 70
A Time of Predators. New York: 1969. V. 69

GOREY, EDWARD
Amnphigorey, Too. New York: 1975. V. 68
The Doubtful Guest. 1958. V. 73
The Fantod Pack. New York: 1995. V. 71
The Fatal Lozenge: an Alphabet. New York: 1960. V. 68
The Retrieved Locket. New York: 1994. V. 71
The Salt Herring. New York: 1971. V. 70
The Twelve Terrors of Christmas. New York: 1994. V. 71
The Water Flowers. New York: 1982. V. 73

GORGAS, JOSIAH
The Civil War Diary of General Josiah Gorgas. Tuscaloosa: 1947. V. 70

GORHAM, B. W.
Camp Meeting Manual, a Practical Book for the Camp Ground, in Two Parts. Boston: 1854. V. 68

GORHAM, GEORGE C.
Personal Reminiscences of Early Days in California with Other Sketches by Stephen J. Field. 1893. V. 73

GORHAM MANUFACTURING CO.
The Soul of Alaska: a Comment and a Description to Which is Added a Catalogue Raisonne of a Series of Bronze Statuettes Illustrative of Alaskan Indian Characteristics and Social Habitats, Modelled by Louis Potter & Cast Into Bronze by the Gorham Co. New York: 1905. V. 71

GORIN, GEORGE
History of Ophthalmology. Wilmington: 1982. V. 73

GORING, C. R.
Micrographia.... London: 1837. V. 68

GORING, JOHN P.
The Right to be Wrong. New York: 1941. V. 71

GORKI, MAXIM
Autobiography - My Childhood; In the World; My Universities. London: 1953. V. 72
A Book of Short Stories. London: 1939. V. 71
The Orloff Couple and Malva. London: 1901. V. 72
Reminisceces of Tolstoy, Chekov and Andreev. London: 1934. V. 71
The Specter. New York: 1938. V. 70

GORMAN, ED
The Autumn Dead. Baltimore: 1996. V. 69
The Poker Club. Baltimore: 1999. V. 68
The Poker Club. Edgbaston: 1999. V. 68

GORRELL, LORD
Unheard Melodies. London: 1934. V. 73

GORRINGE, HENRY H.
Egyptian Obelisks. New York: 1882. V. 69; 70

GORSCH, R. V.
Proctolobic Anatomy. Baltimore: 1953. V. 71

GORTON, JOHN
A General Biographical Dictionary. London: 1841. V. 72

GORTON, SAMUEL
Simplicities Defence Against Seven-Headed Policy. London: 1646. V. 71

GOS, CHARLES
Alpine Tragedy. London: 1948. V. 69

GOSHEN BUGGY TOP CO.
Catalog of Buggy Tops. Goshen: 1893. V. 71

GOSHEN HARDWARE CO.
Catalog of Buggy Tops. Goshen: 1896. V. 71

GOSLING, PAULA
Fair Game. New York: 1978. V. 68; 71
The Zero Trap. New York: 1980. V. 70

GOSLING, RAY
Personal Copy - a Memoir of the Sixties. London: 1980. V. 68

GOSNELL, H. T.
The Science of Birdnesting. 1947. V. 69

GOSS, HELEN ROCCA
The California White Cap Murders. Santa Barbara: 1969. V. 70
The Life and Death of a Quicksilver Mine. Los Angeles: 1958. V. 68; 73

GOSS-CUSTARD, J. D.
The Oystercatcher, from Individuals to Populations. Oxford: 1996. V. 72; 73

GOSSE, PHILIP HENRY
Assyria; Her Manners and Customs, Arts and Arms; Restored from Her Monuments. London: 1852. V. 69
The Birds of Jamaica. London: 1847. V. 69
Evenings at the Microscope. London: 1859. V. 68
Evenings at the Microscope. New York: 1860. V. 70; 72
Evenings at the Microscope. London: 1877. V. 69
Evenings at the Microscope. New York: 1896. V. 72
A Manual of Marine Zoology for the British Isles. 1855-1856. V. 69
A Manual of Marine Zoology for the British Isles. London: 1855-1856. V. 68; 71
The Monuments of Ancient Eygpt, and Their Relation to the Word of God. London: 1855. V. 69
Natural History. Fishes. 1851. V. 72
Natural History: Mollusca. London: 1854. V. 69
A Naturalist's Rambles on the Devonshire Coast. London: 1853. V. 71; 73
The Ocean. London: 1854. V. 68
Omphalos: an Attempt to Untie the Geological Knot. London: 1857. V. 69
Tenby: a Sea Side Holiday. London: 1856. V. 68
Wanderings through the Conservatories at Kew. London: 1856. V. 69
A Year at the Shore. London: 1865. V. 68
A Year at the Shore. London: 1877. V. 69

GOSSEL, P.
Architecture in the 20th Century. 1991. V. 72

GOTCH, PHYLLIS M.
The Romance of a Boo-Bird Chick. London: 1903. V. 70
Tuffy and the Merboo. London: 1904. V. 70

GOTHAM BOOK MART
Catalogue 36. New York: 1936. V. 72
We Moderns. 1920-1940. V. 72

GOTHER, JOHN
Prayers for Sundays and Holy Days and Other Festivals from the First Sunday of Advent to Whitsuntide. London: 1718. V. 69

GOTTLIEB, GERALD
Early Children's Books and Their Illustration. 1975. V. 70
Early Children's Books and Their Illustration. New York: 1975. V. 68

GOTTLIEB, SAMUEL H.
Overbooked in Arizona. Scottsdale: 1994. V. 69

GOTTSCHALK, C. W.
Renal Physiology: People and Ideas. Bethesda: 1987. V. 71

GOUDGE, ELIZABETH
The Blue Hills. New York: 1942. V. 69
Green Dolphin Street. New York: 1944. V. 71
Henrietta's House. London: 1942. V. 69

GOUDY, FREDERIC W.
The Alphabet. New York: 1918. V. 69
Typologia. Studies in Type Design and Type Making, with Comments on the Invention of Typography.... Berkeley and Los Angeles: 1940. V. 72

GOUGE, THOMAS
The Principles of Christian Religion Explained to the Capacity of the Meanest. London: 1679. V. 69

GOUGE, WILLIAM
The Whole Armor of God; or a Christians Spiritual Furniture, to Keep Him Safe from all the Assaults of Satan. London: 1619. V. 68

GOUGE, WILLIAM M.
A Short History of Paper Money and Banking in the United States...to Which is Prefixed an Inquiry into the Principles of the System, with Considerations of Its Effects on Morals and Happiness. Philadelphia: 1833. V. 68

GOUGH, JOHN
A Discourse Concerning the Resurrection Bodies; Tending to Shew, From the Writings of Heathens, Jews and Christians.... London: 1788. V. 69
A Treatise of Arithmetic, in Theory and Practice.... Philadelphia: 1796. V. 69

GOUGH, JOHN B.
Sunlight and Shadow, or Gleanings from My Life-Work. London: 1881. V. 71

GOULARD, THOMAS
A Treatise on the Effects and Various Preparations of Lead, Particularly of the Extract of Saturn, for Different Chirurgical Disorders. London: 1773. V. 69

GOULART, RON
Adam and Eve on a Raft. Norfolk: 2001. V. 71

GOULD, A. A.
Report on the Invertebrata of Massachusetts. Boston: 1870. V. 69; 73

GOULD, CECIL
The Paintings of Correggio. Ithaca: 1976. V. 68

GOULD, CHESTER
Dick Tracy Ace Detective. 1943. V. 70
Dick Tracy: the Capture of Boris Arson. Chicago: 1935. V. 72

GOULD, E.
My Book of the Farm. 1940. V. 73

GOULD, FRANCIS CARRUTHERS
Ah-Chin-Chin. His Voyage and Adventures. London: 1890. V. 68
Who Killed Cock Robin? and Other Stories for Children Young and Old. London: 1896. V. 68

GOULD, G. GLEN
Period Lighting Fixtures. New York: 1928. V. 72

GOULD, G. M.
Anomalies and Curiosities of Medicine, Being an Encyclopedic Collection of Rare and Extraordinary Cases.... Philadelphia: 1901. V. 70; 71
Anomalies and Curiosities of Medicine Being an Encyclopedic Collection of Rare and Extraordinary Cases.... London: 1958. V. 71

GOULD, HANNAH F.
New Poems. Boston: 1850. V. 73

GOULD, JOHN
Birds of Australia. 1967. V. 69
The Birds of Australia and the Adjacent Islands. Melbourne: 1979. V. 73
Birds of Europe. 1966. V. 69
Birds of New Guinea. 1970. V. 69
An Introduction to the Birds of Great Britain. London: 1873. V. 73
A Monograph of the Trogonidae, or Family of Trogons. London: 1835-1838. V. 70; 72; 73

GOULD, NAT
The Double Event: a Tale of the Melbourne Cup. London: 1891. V. 68
Golden Ruin. London: 1898. V. 68
The Magpie Jacket: a Tale of the Turf. London: 1896. V. 68
Raymond's Bride. London: 1903. V. 68
Running It Off or Hard Hit. London: 1892. V. 68
Seeing Him Through: a Racing Story. London: 1900?. V. 68
Stuck Up. London: 1894. V. 68
Thrown Away, or Basil Ray's Mistake. London: 1894?. V. 68
Town and Bush: Stray Notes on Australia. London: 1896. V. 68

GOULD, NATHANIEL
A Defence of an Essay on the Public Debts of the Kingdom &c. in Answer to a Pamphlet Entitled, a State of the National Debt. London: 1727. V. 72
An Essay on the Publick Debts of This Kigndom. London: 1726. V. 72

GOULD, R. W.
The Glorious Story of the Fighting 26th.... Montreal: 1918?. V. 71

GOULD, ROBERT
Poems Chiefly Consisting of Satyrs and Satyrical Epistles. London: 1689. V. 68; 72

GOULD, THOMAS R.
The Tragedian; an Essay on the Histrionic Genius of Junius Brutus Booth. New York: 1868. V. 70

GOULD, W.
An Account of English Ants.... London: 1747. V. 69

GOULDER, W. A.
Reminiscences of a Pioneer, Incidents in the Life of a Pioneer in Oregon and Idaho. Boise: 1909. V. 69

GOULDSBURY, C. E.
Tiger Slayer by Order. 1915. V. 69; 70; 72; 73

GOULIMIS, CONSTANTINE N.
Wild Flowers of Greece. Kifissia: 1968. V. 70
Wild Flowers of Greece. London: 1968. V. 69

GOURARD, CHARLES
Socialism Unmasked: a Plain Lecture, from the French. London: 1850. V. 71

GOURAY, JULIE
Memoires d'une Poupee. London: 1840. V. 68

GOURBILLON, JOSEPH ANTOINE DE
Stellino, ou le Nouveau Werther. Paris: 1791. V. 69

GOURLAY, J. L.
History of the Ottawa Valley. Ottawa: 1896. V. 73

GOURMONT, REMY DE
A Virgin Heart. London: 1926. V. 71

GOVE, JESSE
The Utah Expedition 1857-1858. Letters of Captain Jesse Gove. Concord: 1928. V. 69

GOVENAR, ALAN
Meeting The Blues. Dallas: 1988. V. 72

GOVER, ROBERT
One Hundred Dollar Misunderstanding. New York: 1962. V. 68; 72

GOVERNMENTAL Model Farming: Its History, Its Cost and Its Results. 1858. V. 70

THE GOVERNOR'S Visit to the Shell-Mound at Warramuri. February 1866. Demerara: 1866. V. 72

GOVEY, LILIAN A.
Three Little Geese. London: 1915. V. 69

GOWANLOCK, THERESA
Two Months in the Camp of Big Bear. The Life and Adventures of Theresa Gowanlock and Theresa Delaney. Parkdale: 1885. V. 68

GOWANS, FRED R.
Rocky Mountain Rendezvous. Provo: 1975. V. 68

GOWER, B.
The Green Elfin Story Book. London and Birmingham: 1922. V. 68

GOWER, FRANCIS LEVESON
Bygone Years: Recollections. London: 1905. V. 71

GOWER, RONALD
The Great Historic Galleries of England. New York and London: 1882. V. 70
My Reminiscences. London: 1883. V. 70

GOWERS, W. R.
Diagnosis of Diseases of the Brain and of the Spinal Cord. New York: 1885. V. 69
The Diagnosis of Diseases of the Spinal Cord. London: 1881. V. 68
Epilepsy and Other Chronic Convulsive Disorders. New York: 1885. V. 71

GOWING, LAWRENCE
Lawrence Gowing. London: 1983. V. 70

GOYEN, WILLIAM
Arcadio. New York: 1983. V. 72
A Book of Jesus. Garden City: 1973. V. 68
The Fair Sister. Garden City: 1963. V. 68; 71
Ghost and Flesh. New York: 1952. V. 68; 71
Had I A Hundred Mouths. New York: 1984. V. 72
The House of Breath. New York: 1950. V. 68

GOZZI, CARLO
The Memoirs of Count Gozzi. London: 1890. V. 68

GRABAU, AMADEUS W.
The Permian of Mongolia. New York: 1931. V. 68; 69; 71

GRABBE, CHRISTIAN DIETRICH
Comedy, Satire, Irony and Deeper Meaning. London: 1955. V. 73

GRABE, JOHN ERNEST
Septuaginta Interpretum...Quem ex Antiquissimo MS. Codice Alexandrino Accurate Descriptum.... Oxford: 1707-1720. V. 70; 73

GRABER, HENRY WILLIAM
Life Record of H. W. Graber, a Terry Texas Ranger 1861-1865. Dallas?: 1916. V. 69; 70

GRABHAM, OXLEY
Yorkshire Potteries, Pots and Potters. London: 1971. V. 72; 73

GRACE, SHEFIELD
Memoirs of the Family of Grace. (Ireland). 1823. V. 69

GRACE, TOM
Spyder Web. Dexter: 1997. V. 68; 69; 71

GRADUS ad Cantabrigiam; or, New University Guide to the Academical Customs, and Colloquial or Cant Terms Peculiar to the University of Cambridge.... London: 1828. V. 68

GRADY, JAMES
Shadow of the Condor. New York: 1975. V. 69; 70; 73
Six Days of the Condor. London: 1974. V. 68
Six Days of the Condor. New York: 1974. V. 68; 69; 70; 71; 73

GRAEME, BRUCE
Blackshirt. London: 1925. V. 73
Blackshirt the Adventurer. London: 1936. V. 70
Epilogue. London: 1933. V. 73
The Imperfect Crime. Philadelphia: 1933. V. 68
Monsieur Blackshirt. Philadelphia: 1933. V. 69
A Murder of Some Importance. Philadelphia: 1931. V. 68; 71
Not Proven. London: 1935. V. 70
Passion, Murder and Mystery. Garden City: 1928. V. 71
Through the Eyes of the Judge. Philadelphia: 1930. V. 70
Unsolved. Philadelphia: 1932. V. 68; 71

GRAF, A. B.
Exotica. Series 3. 1978. V. 73

GRAFF, JOHN FRANKLIN
Graybeard's Colorado, or, Notes on the Centennial State. Philadelphia: 1882. V. 70

GRAFFENFIED, ADOLF
Architecture Suisse, ou Choix de Maisons Rustiques des Alpes du Canton de Berne.... Berne: 1844. V. 68; 70

GRAFTON, C. W.
The Rat Begins to Gnaw the Rope. 1943. V. 73
The Rope Began to Hang the Butcher. 1944. V. 73

GRAFTON, SUE
A is for Alibi. London: 1982. V. 72; 73
A is for Alibi. New York: 1982. V. 70
A is for Alibi. London: 1986. V. 70; 71; 72
B is for Burglar. New York: 1985. V. 68; 69; 70; 72
C is for Corpse. New York: 1986. V. 68; 69; 70; 72
D Is For Deadbeat. London: 1987. V. 72
D is for Deadbeat. New York: 1987. V. 68; 69; 70; 71; 72
E is for Evidence. New York: 1988. V. 69; 70; 72
F is for Fugitive. New York: 1989. V. 68; 69; 70; 72; 73
G is for Gumshoe. New York: 1990. V. 68; 69; 70; 73
Keziah Dane. New York: 1967. V. 68; 69; 71
M is for Malice. 1996. V. 73
M Is For Malice. New York: 1996. V. 71
N is for Noose. New York: 1998. V. 72
O Is for Outlaw. London: 1999. V. 72
P is for Peril. London: 2001. V. 69; 72

GRAGLIA, G. A.
A Collection of Italian Letters, Moral, Historical &c.... London: 1808. V. 68

GRAHAM, A.
Kate Furbish and the Flora of Maine. Gardiner: 1995. V. 68

GRAHAM, ALISTAIR
Eyelids of Morning- The Mingled Destinies of Crocodiles and Men. Greenwich: 1973. V. 72

GRAHAM, ARCHIBALD
The Industrial Improvement by European Settlers of the Resources of India. London: 1868. V. 71

GRAHAM, C.
Fleshpots of Malibu. New York/Chicago: 1945. V. 70

GRAHAM, CAROLINE
Death In Disguise. London: 1992. V. 72
Death of a Hollow Man. London: 1989. V. 73
The Envy of the Stranger. London: 1984. V. 69; 73
Fire Dance. London: 1995. V. 72
Fire Dance. Sutton: 1995. V. 73
Murder At Madingley Grange. London: 1990. V. 72; 73

GRAHAM, DUFF
How Peter Rabbit Went to Sea. Philadelphia: 1917. V. 69

GRAHAM, EDITH
Nursery Rhyme Animals. London: 1880. V. 69

GRAHAM, FRANK
The Brooklyn Dodgers: an Informal History. New York: 1945. V. 71
The New York Yankees. New York: 1943. V. 71

GRAHAM, GLADYS R.
Tropical Cooking in Panama. Dothan(AL): 1983. V. 72

GRAHAM, HARRY
More Misrepresentative Men. New York: 1905. V. 70

GRAHAM, HARVEY
Eternal Eve. Altrincham: 1950. V. 68
Eternal Eve. Garden City: 1951. V. 68

GRAHAM, JAMES
A Game for Heroes. London: 1970. V. 69
The Khufra Run. New York: 1973. V. 68
The Run to Morning. 1974. V. 71

GRAHAM, JOHN L.
Good Merchant. London: 1934. V. 70

GRAHAM, JORIE
All Things. Iowa City: 2002. V. 73
The Dream of the Unified Field. Hopewell: 1995. V. 69; 72
The Dream of the Unified Field. New York: 1995. V. 69
The End of Beauty. New York: 1987. V. 69
The Turning. Atlanta: 1994. V. 72

GRAHAM, JOSEPH A.
The Sporting Dog. New York: 1904. V. 69

GRAHAM, LEWIS
The Great I Am. New York: 1933. V. 70
The Guinea Pig Turns. New York: 1934. V. 70

GRAHAM, M.
Richard Bowman Brockbank. A Memoir. London: 1912. V. 71; 72

GRAHAM, P.
Sketches of Perthshire. Edinburgh: 1812. V. 68

GRAHAM, REGINALD
Poems of the Chase. 1912. V. 68

GRAHAM, RIGBY
Kippers and Sawdust. 1992. V. 71

GRAHAM, ROBERT BONTINE CUNNINGHAME
Aurora la Cujini; a Realistic Sketch in Seville. London: 1898. V. 68
Bibi. London: 1929. V. 71; 72
Doughty Deeds. London: 1925. V. 72
The Dream of the Magi. 1923. V. 68
The Ipane. London: 1899. V. 72
Jose Antonio Paez. London: 1929. V. 69
Mogreb-El-Acksa. London: 1898. V. 72
Notes on the District of Menteith, for Tourists and Others. London: 1895. V. 68

GRAHAM, ROBRT BONTINE CUNNINGHAME
The Horses of the Conquest. London: 1930. V. 72

GRAHAM, STEPHEN
Tramping with a Poet in the Rockies. London: 1922. V. 69

GRAHAM, T.
Experiments on the Absorption of Vapours by Liquids. Edinburgh: 1828. V. 68
On the Influence of the Air in Determining the Crystallization of Saline Solutions.... Edinburgh: 1828. V. 68

GRAHAM, T. H. B.
The Barony of Gilsland. Kendal: 1934. V. 71

GRAHAM, THOMAS
Chemical Reports and Memoirs on Atomic Volume.... London: 1848. V. 69

GRAHAM, THOMAS J.
Modern Domestic Medicine.... 1853. V. 71
On the Diseases of Females; a Treatise.... 1845. V. 72
Sure Methods of Improving Health, and Prolonging Life.... London: 1831. V. 71

GRAHAM, W. A.
Abstract of The Official of Proceeding of The Reno Court of Inquiry. Harrisburg: 1954. V. 72
The Custer Myth - A Source Book of Custeriana. New York: 1953. V. 72
The Custer Myth: A Source Book of Custeriana. 1953. V. 69
Siam. London: 1924. V. 73
The Story of the Little Big Horn. New York: 1926. V. 73
The Story of The Little Big Horn. New York: 1941. V. 72
The Story of the Little Big Horn. Harrisburg: 1959. V. 69

GRAHAM, W. S.
Letters and Heads: Poems. 1993. V. 71
The Nightfishing. London: 1955. V. 71; 72

GRAHAM, WILLIAM
An Attempt to Prove that Every Species of Patronage is Foreign to the Nature of the Church.... Edinburgh: 1768. V. 73
The One Pound Note in the Rise and Progress of Banking in Scotland and Its Adaptability to England. Edinburgh: 1886. V. 71

GRAHAM, WINIFRED
All Fires Go Out. London: 1939. V. 70
A Spider Never Falls. London: 1944. V. 70

GRAHAM, WINSTON
The House with the Stained Glass Windows. London: 1934. V. 70
Marnie. London: 1961. V. 69; 70; 73
The Riddle of the John Rowe. London: 1935. V. 70

GRAHAM-DIXON, ANDREW
Howard Hodgkin. London: 1994. V. 72
Howard Hodgkin. New York: 1994. V. 73

GRAHAME, JAMES
British Georgics. Edinburgh: 1809. V. 69

GRAHAME, JAMES continued
Poem On The Abolition Of The Slave Trade; Embellished With Engraving From Picture Painted By R. Smirke, Esq., R. A. London: 1809. V. 72

GRAHAME, KENNETH
Christmas Trees. North Newbald, York: 1998. V. 68
Dream Days. New York: 1902. V. 73
Dream Days. 1930. V. 71
Dream Days. London: 1930. V. 69
First Whisper of Wind in the Willows, or, and A River Went Out from Eden. London: 1944. V. 72; 73
The Golden Age. London and New York: 1904. V. 73
The Golden Age. London: 1915. V. 68; 71
The Golden Age. London: 1921. V. 72; 73
Sweet Home. London: 1946. V. 72
Toad Goes Caravanning. London: 1947. V. 72
The Wind in the Willows. Kestrel: 1893. V. 72
The Wind in the Willows. London: 1908. V. 72
The Wind in the Willows. New York: 1908. V. 71
The Wind in the Willows. New York: 1924. V. 70
The Wind in the Willows. London: 1927. V. 72
The Wind in the Willows. London: 1932. V. 69
The Wind in the Willows. New York: 1940. V. 68; 69; 70; 71; 72
The Wind in the Willows. London: 1951. V. 71
The Wind in the Willows. London: 1959. V. 70
The Wind in the Willows. Cleveland: 1966. V. 71; 73
The Wind in the Willows. London: 1983. V. 69

GRAHAME, THOMAS
Essays and Letters on Subjects Conductive to the Improvement and Extension of Inland Communication and Transport. Westminster: 1835. V. 70
A Letter, Addressed to the Proprietors and Managers of Canals and Navigable Rivers, On a New Method for Tracking and Drawing Vessels by a Locomotive Engine Boat.... London: 1825. V. 72

GRAHAME WHITE, CLAUDE
The Story of the Aeroplane. Boston: 1911. V. 68

GRAINGE, WILLIAM
The Battles and Battle Fields of Yorkshire. York: 1854. V. 73
History and Topography of Harrogate... 1871. V. 73
The History and Topography of Harrogate... Leeds: 1988. V. 73
The History and Topography of Harrogate.... London: 1882. V. 68
Memoir of the Life of Sir William Slingsby. Harrogate: 1862. V. 70; 72
Nidderdale. Pateley Bridge: 1863. V. 73
Yorkshire Longevity. Pateley Bridge: 1864. V. 73

GRAINGER, FRANCIS
The Register and Records of Holm Cultram. Kendal: 1929. V. 71

GRAINGER, M. ALLDERDALE
Woodsmen of the West. Toronto: 1908. V. 68

GRAM, JOHAN
Erelman's Album. Leiden. V. 70

GRAMATKY, HARDIE
Little Toot on the Mississippi. New York: 1973. V. 70

GRAMONDO, G. B.
Historiarvm Galliae ab Excessv Henrici IV libri XVIII.... Amsterdam: 1653. V. 70

GRANADA, LUIS DE
A Memorial of a Christian Life, Compendiously Containing All that a Soul, Newly Converted to God, Ought to Do.... London: 1688. V. 69

GRANCSAY, STEPHEN
The Bashford Dean Collection of Arms and Armor in the Metropolitan Museum of Art. Portland: 1933. V. 69

GRAND CANAL OF IRELAND
Estimates and Contracts Delivered and Entered into by Mr. John Trail, for Executing the Masonry, Banking and Sinking of the Grand Canal, Between the City Bason and Sallins Bridge.... Dublin: 1777. V. 72
Grand Canal. Defence of the Court of Directors; Including a Statement of the True Situation of the Company's Affairs; Made by the Hon. Sir William Cusack Smith, Bart, at a General Meeting of the Company, Held at the Mansion House on the 25th Day of Novem. Dublin: 1815. V. 72

THE GRAND
Case of England, So Fiercely Now Disputed by Fire and Sword Epitomized. London: 1643. V. 71

GRAND, GORDON
Redmond C. Stewart: Foxhunter and Gentleman of Maryland. New York: 1938. V. 72

THE GRAND MYSTERY,
or Art of Meditating Over an House of Office, Restor'd and Unveil'd; After the Manner of the Ingenious Dr. S--ft.... London: 1726. V. 69

GRAND, SARAH
The Beth Book. New York: 1897. V. 69
Our Manifold Nature. London: 1894. V. 68

GRAND TRUNK RAILWAY
Playgrounds, a Booklet of Information Regarding the Canadian Tourist, Fishing and Hunting Resorts. 1920. V. 70

GRAND TRUNK RAILWAY SYSTEM
The Lake of Bays, Highlands of Ontario. Montreal: 1911. V. 68

GRAND, W. JOSEPH
Illustrated History of the Union Stockyards. Chicago: 1901. V. 68

GRANDE, JULIAN
The Bernese Oberland in Summer and Winter. London: 1911. V. 69

GRANDJEAN, SERGE
Gold Boxes and Miniatures of the Eighteenth Century. London: 1975. V. 72

GRANDMAMMA
Easy's *New Story About the Queen of Hearts and the Stolen Tarts.* 1845. V. 68

GRANDMAMMA
Easy's *Wonders of a Toy-Shop.* 1850. V. 73

GRANDMAMMA'S
Tales for the Nursery. Williams Tour With His Papa. Holloway (London): 1844-1847. V. 71

GRANDVILLE, JEAN IGNACE ISIDORE GERARD
The Flowers Personified. New York: 1847. V. 73
The Flowers Personified. New York: 1849. V. 69
Les Metamorphoses du Jour. Bruxelles: 1836?. V. 69
Les Metamorphoses du Jour. Paris: 1854. V. 69
Les Metamorphoses du Jour. Paris: 1869. V. 68

GRANELL, E. F.
Isla Cofre Mitico. Puerto Rico: 1951. V. 69

GRANGE, JEAN
Flight of the Storks. 2000. V. 68

GRANGER, BENJAMIN
Address to the Public, Relative to Some Supposed Failures of the Cow Pow, at Repton.... Burton-upon-Trent: 1821. V. 69

GRANGER, K. R. G.
Ten Against Caesar. Boston: 1952. V. 71

GRANIE, PIERRE
Histoire de l'Assembleé Constituante de France. Paris: 1797. V. 68

GRANIT, R.
Sensory Mechanisms of the Retina. London: 1947. V. 71

GRANT, ANNE MAC VICAR
Letters from the Mountains.... London: 1809. V. 68
Memoirs of An American Lady. London: 1808. V. 69; 71; 72
Memoirs of an American Lady.... New York: 1901. V. 72
Poems on Various Subjects. Edinburgh: 1803. V. 69; 73

GRANT, BLANCHE C.
Dona Lona; a Story of Taos and Santa Fe. New York: 1941. V. 70
Kit Carson's Own Story of His Life. Taos: 1926. V. 68; 71; 73
One Hundred Years Ago in Old Taos. Taos: 1925. V. 68
Taos Indians. Taos: 1925. V. 68; 69; 73
When Old Trails Were New, the Story of Taos. New York: 1934. V. 68; 69; 73

GRANT, BREWIN
Christianity and Secularism. London: 1853. V. 71

GRANT, CHRISTINA PHELPS
The Syrian Desert. London: 1937. V. 72

GRANT, DANIEL
Home Politics, or the Growth of Trade Considered in Its Relation to Labour, Pauperism and Emigration. London: 1870. V. 70

GRANT, DUNCAN
Duncan Grant. Richmond: 1923. V. 69

GRANT, FRANCIS
A Letter to a Member of Parliament, Concerning the Free British Fisheries. London: 1750. V. 68; 71

GRANT, GEORGE
An Essay on the Science of Acting. London: 1828. V. 72

GRANT, GEORGE MONRO
The Easternmost Ridge of the Continent, Historical and Descriptive Sketches of the Scenery and Life in New Brunswick, Nova Scotia, Prince Edward Island, and Along the Lower St. Lawrence.... Chicago: 1899. V. 69
Picturesque Canada: the Country As It Was and Is. Toronto. V. 72

GRANT, HENRY
Mariquita, a Collection of Poetry. London: 1863. V. 68; 69

GRANT, J. C. BOILEAU
A Method of Anatomy Descriptive and Deductive. Baltimore: 1938. V. 71

GRANT, JAMES
Bothwell or the Days of Mary Queen of Scots. London: 1870?. V. 68
British Battles On Land And Sea. London. V. 70; 72
British Battles on Land and Sea. London: 1875. V. 71
Cassell's Illustrated History Of India. London. V. 72
Cassell's Old and New Edinburgh.... New York: 1880. V. 71
Dick Rodney, or the Adventures of an Eton Boy. London: 1869?. V. 68
The Duke of Albany's Own Highlanders. London: 1885. V. 68
Dulcie Carlyon: a Novel. London: 1886. V. 68
Fairer a Fairy: a Novel. London: 1886. V. 68
First Love and Last Love: a Tale of the Human Mutiny. London: 1884. V. 68
Harry Ogilvie; or the Black Dragoons. London: 1893. V. 68

GRANT, JAMES continued
Jack Chaloner or the Fighting Forty-Third. London: 1893. V. 68
Jane Seton; or, The King's Advocate. London: 1865. V. 68
The King's Own Borderers: a Military Romance. London: 1865. V. 68
The King's Own Borderers; a Military Romance. London: 1892. V. 68
Mary of Lorraine. London: 1865. V. 68
Memorials of the Castle of Edinburgh. Edinburgh and London: 1850. V. 73
One of The Six Hundred: a Novel. London: 1890?. V. 68
Sketches in London.... London: 1840. V. 71
The Yellow Frigate or, The Three Sisters. London: 1887?. V. 68

GRANT, JOAN
Winged Pharaoh. London: 1937. V. 70

GRANT, KENNETH
Images and Oracles of Austin Osman Spare. London: 1975. V. 70; 73

GRANT, MADISON
The Passing of the Great Race or the Racial Basis of European History. New York: 1916. V. 71

GRANT, MAXWELL
Norgil: More Tales of Prestigitection. 1979. V. 68
Norgil: More Tales of Prestigitection. New York: 1979. V. 71
Norgil the Magician. 1977. V. 68
Norgil the Magician. New York: 1977. V. 71
The Shadow Laughs. 1931. V. 73

GRANT, PHILIP
The Ten Hours' Bill. Manchester: 1866. V. 69

GRANT, R. G.
M15/M16 Britain's Security and Secret Intelligence Services. New York: 1989. V. 70; 71

GRANT, R. H.
Annapurna II. London: 1961. V. 69

GRANT, ROBERT
Shorn!. New York: 1928. V. 69

GRANT, U. S.
Catalogue of the Marine Pliocene and Pleistocene Mollusca of California, and the Adjacent Regions. San Diego: 1931. V. 69

GRANT, ULYSSES S.
Personal Memoirs. New York: 1885. V. 70; 72
Personal Memoirs. New York: 1885-1886. V. 71; 72; 73
Ulysses S. Grant: Memoirs and Selected Letters, Parts One and Two. New York: 1990. V. 71

GRANT, V.
Genetics of Flowering Plants. New York: 1975. V. 70
Plant Speciation. New York: 1971. V. 72

GRANT, WILLIAM LAWSON
George Monro Grant. Edinburgh and Toronto: 1905. V. 72

GRANTA 16. London: 1985. V. 68

GRANTA 21. London: 1987. V. 68

GRANTA 29. London: 1989. V. 68

GRANTA 54. London: 1996. V. 68

GRANTHAM, GEORGE
A Fardel of Fancies, or, the Muse in a Fidget.... London: 1824. V. 72

GRANTHAM, THOMAS
A Marriage Sermon, Called a Wife Mistaken, or a Wife and No Wife; or Leah Instead of Rachel. London: 1710. V. 69; 73

GRANVILLE, A. B.
St. Petersburgh a Journal of Travels to and From that Capital, through Flanders, the Rhenish Provinces, Prussia, Russia, Poland, Silesia, Saxony, the Federated States of Germany and France. London: 1828. V. 71
Spas of England, and Principal Sea-Bathing Places. Bath: 1971. V. 72
The Spas Of Germany. London: 1838. V. 72

GRANVILLE-BARKER, HARLEY
The Eighteen-Seventies - Essays by the Royal Society of Literature. Cambridge: 1929. V. 72

GRAPALDUS, FRANCISCUS MARIUS
De Partibus Aedium. Parma: 1516. V. 68; 70; 72

GRAPHIC PUBLISHING CO.
Klondyke Mining Laws. The Canadian Gold Fields How to Get There. Where to Purchase Supplies. Victoria: 1897. V. 71

GRASS of Parnassus from the Bent O'Buchan. Peterhead: 1997. V. 71

GRASS, GUNTER
Der Butt. (The Flounder). Luchterhand, Darmstadt: 1978. V. 70
Cat and Mouse - A Novel. London: 1963. V. 72
My Century. New York: 1999. V. 69; 70
The Tin Drum. London: 1962. V. 72
The Tin Drum. New York: 1962. V. 72

GRASSET DE SAINT SAUVEUR, JACQUES
L'Antique Rome ou Description Historique et Pittoresque de Tout ce Qui Concerne Le Peuple Romain.... Paris: 1796. V. 69

GRASSI, BENVENTUO
De Oculis Eorumque Egritudinibus et Curis. Stanford: 1929. V. 68

GRATACAP, L. P.
The Evacuation of England: The Twist in the Gulf Stream. New York: 1908. V. 70
The New Northland. New York: 1915. V. 70

GRATIUS, FALISCUS
Cynegeticon. or, a Poem of Hunting. London: 1654. V. 70

GRATTAN, HENRY
An Answer, to a Pamphlet Entitled, the Speech of the Earl of Clare, on the Subject of a Legislative Union, Between Great Britain and Ireland. Dublin: 1800. V. 69
Mr. Grattan's Address to His Fellow-Citizens. Dublin: 1797. V. 69
Observations on the Mutiny Bill; with some Strictures on Lord Buckinghamshire's Administration in Ireland. Dublin: 1781. V. 69
The Select Speeches of...Henry Grattan. Dublin: 1845. V. 69
The Speeches of the Rt. Hon. Henry Grattan in the Irish and Imperial Parliament. 1822. V. 70

GRATTAN, THOMAS COLLEY
Civilized America. London: 1859. V. 71
The Curse of the Black Lady, and Other Tales. London: 1857. V. 68
Legends of the Rhine and of the Low Countries. London: 1832. V. 71

GRAU, SHIRLEY ANN
The Condor Passes. New York: 1971. V. 72
The Keepers of the House. New York: 1964. V. 69
The Wind Shifting West. New York: 1973. V. 72

GRAUMAN, SID
A Shrine to Art: Official Souvenir Autograph Book of Grauman's Chinese Theatre. Los Angeles: 1938. V. 72

GRAUMONT, R.
Encyclopaedia of Knots and Fancy Rope Work. New York: 1977. V. 69

GRAVE, HENRI
Travaux en Fer Forge, Album Grave. Paris: 1873. V. 72

GRAVER, LAWRENCE
Samuel Beckett: the Critical Heritage. London: 1979. V. 71

GRAVES, ALFRED P.
A Celtic Psaltery - from Irish and Welsh Poetry. New York: 1917. V. 69
Father O'Flynn and Other Irish Lyrics. 1889. V. 69
Irish Doric in Song and Story. 1926. V. 69
Irish Literary and Musical Studies. 1913. V. 69
Songs of Irish Wit and Humour. 1884. V. 69

GRAVES, ALGERNON
A Dictionary of Artists Who Have Exhibited Works in the Principal London Exhibitions from 1760 to 1893. London: 1895. V. 72

GRAVES, CHARLES
The Bad Old Days. London: 1951. V. 69
Mr. Punch's History of Modern England. London: 1921-1922. V. 69

GRAVES, ERNEST
The Line Man's Bible: a Foot-Ball text Book of Detailed Instruction. 1921. V. 71

GRAVES, FREDRICK
A Book of Hill School Verse 1920-1926. New York: 1927. V. 70

GRAVES, HENRY
Designs for Sculptered Compartments of a Font in the Paris Church of Binstead, in the Isle of Wight. 1844. V. 71

GRAVES, IDA
Epithalamion. Higham, Colchester: 1934. V. 68

GRAVES, J. A.
Out of Doors California and Oregon. Los Angeles: 1912. V. 71

GRAVES, J. M.
Phrenology or the Doctrine of the Mental Phenomena, Explained.... Norwich: 1838. V. 68; 71; 73

GRAVES, JOHN
Goodbye to a River. New York: 1960. V. 72
Goodbye to a River. 1989. V. 69
Goodbye to a River. Austin: 1989. V. 68

GRAVES, KERSEY
The World's Sixteen Crucified Saviors of Christianity Before Christ. New York. V. 68

GRAVES, R.
A Conspectus of the London, Edinburgh and Dublin Pharmacopoeias.... London: 1824. V. 71

GRAVES, RICHARD
Euphrosyne; or, Amusements on the Road of Life. London: 1776-1780. V. 70
The Festoon: a Collection of Epigrams, Ancient and Modern, Panegyrical, Satryical, Amorous, Moral, Humorous, Monumental. Bath: 1766. V. 70
The Heir Apparent; or the Life of Commodus; the Son and Successor of the Good M. Aurelius Antoninus, Emperor of Rome. London: 1789. V. 72

GRAVES, RICHARD continued
Lubrications: Consisting of Essays, Reveries &c. in Prose and Verse. London: 1786. V. 70
The Spiritual Quixote; or the Summer's Ramble of Mr. Geoffrey Wildgoose. London: 1783. V. 71; 73

GRAVES, ROBERT
Adam's Rib. London: 1955. V. 70
Adam's Rib. 1958. V. 69; 71; 73
An Ancient Castle. New York: 1981. V. 68
Antigua, Penny, Puce. Deya, Majorca: 1936. V. 71
The Antigua Stamp. New York: 1937. V. 69
At the Gate. Poems. 1974. V. 73
At the Gate: Poems. London: 1974. V. 69; 71; 72
Beyond Giving: Poems. London: 1969. V. 71; 72
Claudius, the God and His Wife Messalina. 1934. V. 68
Collected Poems. New York: 1938. V. 72
Collected Poems 1914-1917. 1948. V. 68
Collected Poems 1959. London: 1959. V. 72
Colophon to Love Respelt: Poems. London: 1967. V. 71
Count Belisarius. New York: 1938. V. 68
Country Sentiment. London: 1920. V. 69; 73
The Crowning Privilege, the Clark Lectures 1954-1955. London: 1955. V. 68
On English Poetry. London: 1922. V. 70
Fairies and Fusiliers. London: 1917. V. 72; 73
The Feather Bed. Richmond: 1923. V. 68
Food for Centaurs: Stories, Talks, Critical Studies, Poems. Garden City: 1960. V. 68; 69
Goliath and David. 1916. V. 73
Goliath and David. London: 1916. V. 69; 72
Goodbye to All That. London: 1929. V. 70
Goodbye To All That. New York: 1930. V. 68
Greek Gods and Heroes. Garden City: 1960. V. 72
The Green-Sailed Vessel: Poems. London: 1971. V. 72
Impenetrability or the Proper Habit of the English. London: 1926. V. 70
John Kemp's Wager: A Ballad Opera. Oxford: 1925. V. 72; 73
King Jesus. New York: 1946. V. 68
Lars Porsena or the Future of Swearing and Improper Language. London: 1927. V. 68
Lawrence and the Arabs. London: 1927. V. 70
Life of the Poet Gnaeus Robertulus Graveus. Mallorca: 1990. V. 72
Love Respelt Again. New York: 1969. V. 70; 71
Man Does, Woman Is. London: 1964. V. 68
The Marmosite's Miscellany. London: 1925. V. 73
Mrs. Fisher. London: 1928. V. 70
Mock Beggar Hall. London: 1924. V. 68; 73
The More Deserving Cases: Eighteen Old Poems for Reconsideration. 1962. V. 68; 73
My Head! My Head!. London: 1925. V. 73
New Poems. Garden City: 1963. V. 71
No More Ghosts. London: 1940. V. 68
Occupation: Writer. London: 1951. V. 68; 71
On English Poetry.... 1922. V. 70
On English Poetry.... London: 1922. V. 71
Over the Brazier. London: 1916. V. 73
Over the Brazier. London: 1920. V. 73
A Pamphlet Against Anthologies. Garden City: 1928. V. 71
The Penny Fiddle - Poems for Children. Garden City: 1960. V. 72
Poems. New York: 1980. V. 70; 72
Poems (1914-1927). London: 1927. V. 69; 72; 73
Poems 1926-1930. London: 1931. V. 68
Poems 1929. London: 1929. V. 70; 71; 73
Poems 1930-1933. 1933. V. 70
Poems 1938-1945. London: 1946. V. 72
Poems 1953. London: 1953. V. 72; 73
Poems About War. London: 1988. V. 73
The Real David Copperfield. London: 1933. V. 69; 72
Sergeant Lamb's America. New York: 1940. V. 68
Seventeen Poems Missing from Love Respelt. London: 1966. V. 69; 71; 72
The Shout. London: 1929. V. 68
Ten Poems More. Paris: 1930. V. 71; 73
Timeless Meeting: Poems. London: 1973. V. 69; 71; 72
To Whom Else?. Deya, Majorca: 1931. V. 73
Treasure Box. London: 1919. V. 73
Watch the North Wind Rise. 1949. V. 69
Welchman's Hose. London: 1925. V. 69; 73
Whipperginny. London: 1923. V. 68
The White Goddess. London: 1948. V. 68
The White Goddess. New York: 1948. V. 69; 73

GRAVES, ROSS
William Schurman Loyalist of Bedeque, Prince Edward Island and His Descendants. Summerside: 1973. V. 73

GRAVESANDE, WILLEM JAKOB STORM VAN S'
An Essay on Perspective. London: 1724. V. 71

GRAVINA, VINCENZO
Della Ragion Poetica Libri Due. Roma: 1718. V. 72

GRAY, A. W.
Bino. New York: 1988. V. 68

GRAY, ALASDAIR
Lanark. Edinburgh: 1981. V. 70; 72
Lanark. Edinburgh: 1985. V. 70
Lanark. New York: 1985. V. 69

GRAY, ALEXANDER
Four and Forty - a Selection of Danish Ballads Presented in Scots. Edinburgh: 1954. V. 70

GRAY, ALEXANDER HILL
Sixty Years Ago. Wanderings of a Stonyhurst Boy in Many Lands. London: 1925. V. 72; 73

GRAY, ASA
Contributions to American Botany. Boston: 1886. V. 70
Manual of the Botany of the Northern United States.... New York: 1856. V. 72
Plantae Wrightianae Texano-Neo-Mexicanae.... Washington: 1852-1853. V. 73
Scientific Papers.... London: 1889. V. 69
Synoptical Flora of North America. Washington and New York: 1886-1888. V. 71
Synoptical Flora of North America. New York: 1895-1897. V. 71
Text-book of Western Botany.... New York: 1885-1887. V. 72

GRAY, BARRY
Ale: in Prose and Verse. New York: 1866. V. 68

GRAY, C.
The Great Experiment: Russian Art 1863-1922. New York: 1962. V. 69; 72
Hans Richter. London: 1971. V. 69

GRAY, C. W.
Revival Sermons. Mt. Pleasant. V. 68

GRAY, CARL
A Play Thing of the Gods - a Tale of Old California. Boston: 1912. V. 68; 73

GRAY, CURME
Murder in Millennium VI. Chicago: 1951. V. 71

GRAY, D.
Rope Boy. 1970. V. 71; 73

GRAY, EDWARD
Life and Death of Oregon Cattle King Peter French 1849-1897. Eugene: 1995. V. 72
William Bill W. Brown 1855-1941 Legend of Oregon's High Desert. Eugene: 1993. V. 72

GRAY, ELIZABETH JANET
Adam of the Road. New York: 1942. V. 71

GRAY, ERNEST
Man Midwife. London: 1946. V. 71

GRAY, FRANK S.
The Little Blind God on Rails: a Romant of the Gold Northwest. Chicago: 1888. V. 72

GRAY, HAROLD
Little Orphan Annie and Jumbo, the Circus Elephant. Chicago: 1935. V. 73

GRAY, HENRY
Anatomy, Descriptive and Surgical by Henry Gray. Philadelphia: 1887. V. 71

GRAY, HUGH
Letters from Canada, Written During a Residence There in the Years 1806, 1807 and 1808; Shewing the Present State of Canada, Its Productions.... London: 1809. V. 73

GRAY, ISSAC MCKINLEY
My Observations of Europe and the Middle East. Baltimore: 1953. V. 72

GRAY, JAMES
How Animals Move - the Royal Institution Christmas Lectures 1951. Cambridge: 1953. V. 72

GRAY, JOHN
St. Peter's, Edinburgh. A Brief Description of the Church and Its Contents. Oxford: 1925. V. 70
Silverpoints. London: 1893. V. 70; 73

GRAY, JOHN HENRY
China a History of the Laws, Manners and Customs of the People. London: 1878. V. 72

GRAY, JOHN M.
David Scott, R.S.A. and His Works. Edinburgh and London: 1884. V. 69; 72

GRAY, JOHN S.
Cavalry and Coaches: the Story of Camp and Fort Collins. Fort Collins: 1978. V. 69
Centennial Campaign, The Sioux War of 1876. Fort Collins: 1976. V. 72
Custer's Last Campaign, Mich Boyer and The Little Big Horn Reconstructed. Lincoln: 1991. V. 72

GRAY, JONATHAN
The Owl. Philadelphia: 1937. V. 73

GRAY, L. R. N.
Torridge Fishery. 1957. V. 73

GRAY, MARIA EMMA
Figures of Molluscous Animals, Selected from Various Authors. London: 1874. V. 69; 73

GRAY, NICOLETE
The Painted Inscriptions of David Jones. London: 1981. V. 68

GRAY, P. N.
Records of North American Big Game. 1990. V. 69; 70; 72; 73

GRAY, PETER
The Encyclopedia of the Biological Sciences. New York: 1961. V. 68

GRAY, R.
The Birds of the West of Scotland Including the Outer Hebrides. Glasgow: 1871. V. 69; 71; 73

GRAY, SIMON
Little Portia. London: 1967. V. 72

GRAY, SPALDING
Impossible Vacation. New York: 1992. V. 72

GRAY, THOMAS
An Elegy Written in a Country Church-Yard. London: 1788. V. 73
An Elegy Written in a Country Church-Yard. London: 1868. V. 69
Elegy Written in a Country Church-Yard. London: 1869. V. 71; 72
Elegy Written in a Country Church-Yard. London: 1938. V. 69
Elegy Written in a Country Church-Yard. Waltham St. Lawrence: 1946. V. 71
Gray's Elegy. London: 1846. V. 71; 72
Observations on a General Iron Rail-Way, or Land Steam-Conveyance; to Supersede the Necessity of Horses in all Public Vehicles.... London: 1825. V. 72
Odes. Strawberry Hill: 1757. V. 70; 71; 73
Poems. London: 1768. V. 68
Poems. London: 1778. V. 72
Poems and Letters. London: 1863. V. 71
The Poems of Mr. Gray. London: 1775. V. 69
The Poetical Works of Thomas Gray, with some account of his Life and Writings. London: 1800. V. 71

GRAY, W. H.
A History of Oregon 1792-1849, Drawn from Personal Observations and Authentic Information. 1870. V. 68
A History of Oregon 1792-1849, Drawn from Personal Observations and Authentic Information. San Francisco: 1870. V. 70

GRAY, WESTMORELAND
Manhunt Trail. Philadelphia: 1934. V. 69

GRAY, WILLIAM S.
Before We Read: Developmental Activites for the Pre-Reading Period. Chicago: 1940. V. 70
Fun with Dick and Jane. Chicago: 1940. V. 69
The New Before We Read. Chicago: 1956. V. 71
The New We Work and Play. Chicago: 1956. V. 69
Think-and-Do Book to Accompany Fun with Dick and Jane. The Basic Readers. Chicago: 1941. V. 70
Think and Do Book to Accompany Guess Who. Chicago: 1951. V. 71
Think and Do Book: to Accompany Our New Friends. Chicago: 1940. V. 70
Think and Do Book to Accompany The New We Look and See, We Work and Play, We Come and Go. Chicago: 1956. V. 71
Think and Do Book to Accompany We Look And See, We Work and Play, We Come and Go: Pre Primer Program. Chicago: 1940. V. 70
We Look and See. Chicago: 1940. V. 70

GRAYBILL, FLORENCE CURTIS
Edward Sheriff Curtis: Visions of a Vanishing Race. New York: 1976. V. 71

GRAYL, DRUID, PSEUD.
Pillow Dust Ditties. Oxford: 1917. V. 69

GRAYSON, WILLIAM JOHN
The Hireling and the Slave, Chicora and Other Poems. Charleston: 1856. V. 73

GRAZEBROOK, O. F.
Studies in Sherlock Holmes. New York: 1981. V. 69
Studies in Sherlock Holmes. II. Politics and Premiers. London: 1951. V. 68

GRAZIANO, ROCKY
Somebody Up There Likes Me: The Story of My Life Until Today. New York: 1955. V. 72

GRAZZINI, ANTONIO FRANCESCO, CALLED IL LASCA
The Story of Doctor Manente being the Tenth and Last Story from the Suppers of A. F. Grazzini called Il Lasca. Florence: 1929. V. 71; 72

THE GREAT Book for Girls. London: 1930. V. 68

GREAT BRITAIN. ADMIRALTY - 1828
A List of the Flag Officers and Other Commissioned Officers of His Majesty's Fleet; with the Dates of Their Respective Commissions. London: 1828. V. 68

GREAT BRITAIN. ARMY - 1781
A List of all the Officers of the Army...with an Alphabetical Index of the Whole. 1781. V. 72

GREAT BRITAIN. BOARD OF AGRICULTURE - 1796
List of Members of the Board of Agriculture. London: 1796. V. 73

GREAT BRITAIN. BOARD OF AGRICULTURE - 1800
List of Members of the Board of Agriculture. London: 1800. V. 73

GREAT BRITAIN. COMMISSIONERS OF LONGITUDE - 1776
The Nautical Almanac and Astronomical Ephemeris for the Year 1778. London: 1776. V. 69

GREAT BRITAIN. GAUGE COMMISSION - 1846
Report of the Gauge Commissioners. (and) Gauge Commissioners' Report. Minutes of Evidence Taken Before the Commissioners. London: 1846. V. 68

GREAT BRITAIN. HISTORICAL MANUSCRIPTS COMMISSION - 1897
Report on the Manuscripts of...Buccleuch & Queensberry...at Drumlanrig Castle. 1897-1908. V. 70

GREAT BRITAIN. HISTORICAL MANUSCRIPTS COMMISSION - 1899
Report of the Manuscripts of the Duke of Buccleuch & Queensberry, at Montagu House, Whitehall. 1899-1926. V. 70

GREAT BRITAIN. HISTORICAL MANUSCRIPTS COMMISSION - 1904
Report...Marquis of Bath, Longleat. 1904-1908. V. 70

GREAT BRITAIN. LAWS, STATUTES, ETC. - 1647
An Ordinance of the Lords and Commons Assembled in Parliament, for the Raising of Monies by be Imployed Towards the Maintenance of Forces Within this Kingdom.... London: 1647. V. 69

GREAT BRITAIN. LAWS, STATUTES, ETC. - 1648
An Ordinance...for the True Payment of Tythes. London: 1648. V. 70

GREAT BRITAIN. LAWS, STATUTES, ETC. - 1657
An Act for Continuing and Establishing the Subsidie of Tunnage and Poundage, and for Reviving an Act for the Better Packing of Butter and Redress of Abuses Therein. London: 1657. V. 72

GREAT BRITAIN. LAWS, STATUTES, ETC. - 1704
Act of Parliament: Act of Queen Anne's Bounty. London: 1704. V. 72

GREAT BRITAIN. LAWS, STATUTES, ETC. - 1733
The Statutes at Large Concerning the Provision for the Poor, Being a Compleat Collection of the Acts of Parliament Relating Thereo. London: 1733. V. 69

GREAT BRITAIN. LAWS, STATUTES, ETC. - 1765
An Act for Granting and Applying Certain Stamp Duties and Other Duties in the British Colonies and Plantations in America, Towards Further Defraying the Expences of Defending, Protecting and Securing the Same.... London: 1765. V. 72
An Act for More Effectually Securing and Encouraging the Trade of His Majesty's American Dominions; for Repealing the Indland Duty on Coffeee...For Granting an Inland Duty on All Coffee Imported except Coffe of the Growth of the British Dominions.... London: 1765. V. 72
An Act to Amend and Render More Effectual in His Majesty's Dominions in America...an Act for Punishing Mutiny and Desertion, and for the Better Payment of the Army and Their Quarters. London: 1765. V. 72

GREAT BRITAIN. LAWS, STATUTES, ETC. - 1767
An Act for Granting Certain Duties in the British Colonies and Planations in America; for Allowing a Drawback of the Duties of Customs Upon the Exportation for this Kingdom, of Coffee and Cocoa Nuts of the Produce of the Said Colonies or Plantation.... London: 1767. V. 72

GREAT BRITAIN. LAWS, STATUTES, ETC. - 1774
An Act to Discontinue in Such Manner, and for Such Time as are Therein mentioned, the Landing and Discharging, Lading or Shipping of Goods, Wares, and Merchandise at the Town and Within the Harbour, of Boston, in the Province of Massachuset's Bay.... London: 1774. V. 72

GREAT BRITAIN. LAWS, STATUTES, ETC. - 1794
An Act for Improving the Outfall of the River Welland, in the County of Lincoln, and for the Better Drainage of the Fen Lands, Low Grounds and Marshes, Discharging Their Waters through the Same Sea.... London: 1794. V. 70

GREAT BRITAIN. LAWS, STATUTES, ETC. - 1806
An Act to Prevent the Importation of Slaves by any of His Majesty's Subjects, into any Islands, Colonies, Plantations, or Territories, Belonging to any Foreign Sovereign, State, or Power.... London: 1806. V. 72

GREAT BRITAIN. LAWS, STATUTES, ETC. - 1816
Magna Carta Regis Johannis XV Die Junii Ann Regni XVII A.D. MCCXV. London: 1816. V. 68; 73

GREAT BRITAIN. LAWS, STATUTES, ETC. - 1838
An Act to Amend the Act for the Abolition of Slavery in the British Colonies. 11th April 1838. London: 1838. V. 72

GREAT BRITAIN. LAWS, STATUTES, ETC. - 1868
Hudson's Bay Company. A Bill Intituled an Act for Enabling Her Majesty to Accept a Surrender Upon Terms of the Lands, Privileges and Right of the Governor and Company of Adventurers of England Trading into Hudson's Bay.... London: 1868. V. 68

GREAT BRITAIN. MINISTRY OF MUNITIONS. LABOUR SUPPLY DEPT.
Catalogue. Exhibition of Samples of Women's Work and Official Photographs illustrating the Various Types of Work Upon Which Women are Employed in Engineering and Other Industries of Munitions of War. 1918. V. 71

GREAT BRITAIN. OFFICE OF THE COMMISSIONERS OF PATENTS
Bricks and Tiles. (with) Bridges, Viaducts and Aquaducts. 1750-1866. London: 1862-1868. V. 71
Hydraulics. 1617-1865. London: 1868. V. 71
Lace and Other Looped and Netted Fabrics: Including Those Relating to Braiding and Plaiting, Fringe, Chenille and Other Ornamental Fabrics 16751864. London: 1866. V. 71
Preparation & Use of Tobacco. 1721-1866. (with) Artists' Instruments and Materials. 1618-1866. (with) Plating or Coating Metals with Metals. 1862. London: 1862-1872. V. 71
Skins, Hides and Leather. 1627-1866. 1872. (with) Sewing and Embroidering 1755-1866. London: 1871-1872. V. 71
Spinning: Incuding Those Relating to the Preparation of Fibrous Materials and the Doubling of Yarns and Threads. London: 1866. V. 71
Ventilation. 1632-1866. (with) Air, Gas, and Other Motive Power Engines 1635-1866. London: 1872-1873. V. 71

GREAT BRITAIN. PARLIAMENT - 1642
Propositions Made by Both House of Parliament, to the Kings Majesty, for the Reconciliation of the Differences Between His Majesty, and the..Said Houses. London: 1642. V. 73

GREAT BRITAIN. PARLIAMENT - 1646
The Propositions of the Lords and Commons Assembled in Parliament. London: 1646. V. 72

GREAT BRITAIN. PARLIAMENT - 1648
An Ordinance...for the True Payment of Tythes and Other Duties...27 Oct. 1648. London: 1648. V. 72

GREAT BRITAIN. PARLIAMENT - 1742
A Further Report from the Committee of Secrecy...Appointed to Enquire into the Conduct of Robert, Earl of Orford, During the Last Ten Years of His Being First Commissioner of the Treasury.... London: 1742. V. 68

GREAT BRITAIN. PARLIAMENT - 1789
An Impartial Report of all the Proceedings in Parliament on the Late Important Subject of a Regency.... London: 1789. V. 70

GREAT BRITAIN. PARLIAMENT - 1883
Report from the Joint Select Committee of the House of Lords and House of Commons on the Channel Tunnel; Together with the Proceedings of the Committe, Minutes of evidence, and Appendix. London: 1883. V. 72

GREAT BRITAIN. PARLIAMENT - 1892
Report from the Joint Select Committee of the House of Lords and House of Commons, on the Electric and Cable Railways (Metropolis); Together with the Proceedings of the Committee, Minutes of Evidence.... London: 1892. V. 72

GREAT BRITAIN. PARLIAMENT - 1901
London Underground Railways. Report from the Joint Select Committee of the House of Lords and House of Commons on London Underground Railways. London: 1901. V. 68

GREAT BRITAIN. PARLIAMENT. HOUSE OF COMMONS - 1667
The Proceedings in the House of Commons Touching the Impeachment of Edward Late Earl of Clarendon, Lord High Chancellour of England, Anno 1667. London: 1700. V. 68

GREAT BRITAIN. PARLIAMENT. HOUSE OF COMMONS - 1681
An Exact Collection of the Most Considerable Debates in the Honourable House of Commons at the Parliament Held at Westminster the One and Twentieth of October 1681. London: 1681. V. 72

GREAT BRITAIN. PARLIAMENT. HOUSE OF COMMONS - 1734
Orders and Resolutions of the Honourable House of Commons, on Controverted Elections and Returns, Determining the Qualifications of Candidates and Voters, the Rights of Election for the Several Cities and Boroughs, the Nature of Evidence Proper.... London: 1734. V. 70

GREAT BRITAIN. PARLIAMENT. HOUSE OF COMMONS - 1784
The Resolutions of the House of Commons on the Great and Constitutional Questions Between the privileges of the House of Commons and Prerogative of the Crown, from the 17th of Decemeber 1783 to the 10th of March 1784. London: 1784. V. 72

GREAT BRITAIN. PARLIAMENT. HOUSE OF COMMONS - 1819
Committee on the State of the Police of the Metropolis. Report...with the Minutes of Evidence Taken Before the Committee.... 1819. V. 71

GREAT BRITAIN. PARLIAMENT. HOUSE OF COMMONS - 1828
Second Report from the Select Committee on the State of Smithfield Market. London: 1828. V. 68

GREAT BRITAIN. PARLIAMENT. HOUSE OF COMMONS - 1831
Report from the Select Committee on Steam Carriages, with Minutes of Evidence and Appendix. London: 1831. V. 68

GREAT BRITAIN. PARLIAMENT. HOUSE OF COMMONS - 1832
Report from the Select Committee on Secondary Punishments; Together with the Minutes of Evidence, an Appendix and Index. London: 1832. V. 73

GREAT BRITAIN. PARLIAMENT. HOUSE OF COMMONS - 1835
Report from the Select Committee on Secondary Punishments, Together with the Minutes of Evidence, an Appendix of Papers, and an Index. London: 1835. V. 73

GREAT BRITAIN. PARLIAMENT. HOUSE OF COMMONS - 1836
Report from the Select Committee on Leith Harbour, with the Minutes of Evidence and an Appendix. 4th July 1836. London: 1836. V. 70

GREAT BRITAIN. PARLIAMENT. HOUSE OF COMMONS - 1839
Palace of Westminster - Report from the Select Committee on Lighting the House, Together with the Minutes of Evidence, Appendix and Index. London: 1839. V. 69

GREAT BRITAIN. PARLIAMENT. HOUSE OF COMMONS - 1873
Report from the Select Committee on Locomotives on Roads, Together with Proceedings of the Committee, Minutes of Evidence and Appendix. London: 1873. V. 72
Select Committee on Noxious Businesses. Report...Together with the Proceedings of the Committee, Minutes of Evidence and Appendix. 1873. V. 71

GREAT BRITAIN. PARLIAMENT. HOUSE OF COMMONS - 1879
Report from the Select Committee of the House of Lords on Tramways; Together with Proceedings of the Committee, Minutes of Evidence, and Appendix. London: 1879. V. 72

GREAT BRITAIN. PARLIAMENT. HOUSE OF COMMONS - 1880
Report from the Select Committee on the North British Railway (Tay Bridge) Bill; Together with the Proceedings of the Committee, and Minutes of Evidence. (and) Index to the Report from the Select Committee on the North British Railway (Tay Bridge) Bill. London: 1880. V. 73

GREAT BRITAIN. PARLIAMENT. HOUSE OF COMMONS - 1885
Report from the Select Committee on the Corporation of London Tower Bridge Bill, Together with the Proceedings of the Committee, Minutes of Evidence and Appendix. London: 1885. V. 73

GREAT BRITAIN. POOR LAW COMMISSION - 1835
First Annual Report of the Poor Law Commissioners for England and Wales. London: 1835. V. 72

GREAT BRITAIN. POOR LAW COMMISSION - 1843
Report on the Sanitary Condition of the Labouring Population of Great Britain; a Supplementary Report on the Results of a Special Inquiry Into the Practice of Interment in Towns. London: 1843. V. 72

GREAT BRITAIN. PRIVY COUNCIL - 1831
Papers Relating to the Disease Called Cholera Spasmodica in India Now Prevailing in the North of Europe.... Winchester and Varnham: 1831. V. 72

GREAT BRITAIN. ROYAL COMM. ON DIVORCE AND MATRIMONIAL...
Report of the Royal Commission on Divorce and Matrimonial Causes... Presented to Parliament by Command of His Majesty. London: 1912. V. 68

GREAT BRITAIN. ROYAL COMM. ON HISTORICAL MONUMENTS - 1936
An Inventory of the Historical Monuments in Westmorland. London: 1936. V. 71

GREAT BRITAIN. ROYAL COMMISSION ON LONDON TRAFFIC - 1905
Report of the Royal Commission Appointed to Inquire into and Report Upon the Means of Locomotion and Transport in London. London: 1905-1906. V. 68

GREAT BRITAIN. SOVEREIGNS, ETC. (CHARLES II) - 1666
His Majesties's Declaration to His City of London, Upon Occasion of the Late Calamity by the Lamentable Fire. London: 1666. V. 69

GREAT BRITAIN. TREATIES, ETC. - 1864
Treaty Between Her Majesty and the United States of America, for the Settlement of the Hudson's Bay and Puget's Sound Agricultural Companies. London: 1864. V. 68

GREAT Domesday Book. The County Edition. Buckinghamshire. 1987-1988. V. 70

GREAT EXHIBITION OF THE WORKS OF INDUSTRY OF ALL NATIONS
The Art Journal Illustrated Catalogue. The Industry of All Nations, 1851. London: 1851. V. 71
The Crystal Palace, and Its Contents: Being an Illustrated Cyclopaedia of the Great Exhibition of the Industry of All Nations 1851. London: 1851. V. 71
The Crystal Palace and Its Contents; Being an Illustrated Cyclopaedia of the Great Exhibition of the Industry of All Nations, 1851. London: 1852. V. 71
Exhibition of the Works of Industry of All Nations 1851. Report by the Juries on the Subjects in the Thirty Classes into Which the Exhibition was Divided. London: 1852. V. 69
4th Report of the Commissioners for the Exhibition of 1851.... London: 1861. V. 71
Great Exhibition of the Works of Industry of All Nations 1851. Official, Descriptive and illustrated Catalogue.... London: 1851-1852. V. 71
London as It Is To-Day; Where to Go, and What to See, During the Great Exhibition. London: 1852. V. 71
The London Conductor: Being a Guide for Visitors to the Great Industrial Exhibition.... London: 1851. V. 71
Official Catalogue of the Great Exhibition of the Works of Industry of All Nations, 1851. London: 1851. V. 71
Official Descriptive and Illustrated Catalogue of the Great Exhibition of 1851. London: 1851. V. 71
Reports by the Juries on the Subjects in the Thirty Classes into which the Exhibition Was Divided. London: 1851. V. 71
The World's Fair; or, Children's Prize Gift Book of the Great Exhibition of 1851.... London: 1851. V. 71

GREAT Fiction from the New Esquire Fortnightly. 1979. V. 70

GREAT Irish Stories of Childhood. New York: 1997. V. 68

THE GREAT Masters in the Louvre Gallery. London and Paris: 1899-1900. V. 72

GREAT NORTHERN RAILWAY
List of Towns and Places to and From which the Great Northern Railway Company Convey Mercandise to or from Batley, Bradford, Dewsbury, Halifax, Keighley, Leeds, Shipley & Wakefield. London: 1890. V. 73

GREAT NORTHERN RAILWAY & NORTHERN RAILWAY CO.
The Great Northern Country.... New York: 1894. V. 68

THE GREAT Stir, and Nothing In't. London: 1707. V. 68

GREAT Western Indian Fights. NY: 1886. V. 72

GREAT WESTERN RAILWAY
An Account of the Proceedings of the Great Western Railway Company, with Extracts from the Evidence Given in Support of the Bill, Before the Committee of the House of Commons in the Session of 1834. London: 1834. V. 68
A Letter to the Shareholders of the Great Western Railway. London: 1838. V. 68
The Narrow and Wide Gauges Considered; also Effects of Competition and Government Supervision. London: 1846. V. 68

GREATRAKE, LAWRENCE
The Parallel and Pioneer; or a Pocket Mirror for Protestant Christendom. New Lisbon: 1830. V. 71

GREATREX, CHARLES BUTLER
Jail-birds, or the Secrets of the Cells. London: 1881. V. 71

GREAVES, JOHN PIERREPONT
A Brief Account of the First Concordium, or Harmonious Industrial College, a Home for the Affectionate Skilful, and Industrious Uncontaminated by False Sympathy, Avaricious Cunning, or Excessive Labour. Ham Common, Surrey: 1843. V. 73

GREEGE, THOMAS
The True and Perfecte Newes of the Worthy and Vailaunt Employtes Performed and Done by that Valiant Knight Syr Francis Drake etc. Hartford: 1955. V. 70

GREELEY, A. W.
Earthquake in California - April 18, 1906. Washington: 1906. V. 71

GREELEY, HORACE
The Tribune Almanac 1858-1869. New York. V. 69

GREELY, A. W.
Report on the Climatology of the Arid Regions of the United States with Reference to Irrigation. Washington: 1891. V. 68

GREEN, A. H.
Geology, Part I: Physical Geology. London: 1882. V. 71

GREEN, ANNA KATHARINE
Agatha Webb. New York: 1899. V. 68
Behind Closed Door. London: 1888. V. 68
A Difficult Problem. New York: 1900. V. 69; 73
The Doctor, His Wife, and the Clock. New York: 1895. V. 70
Marked Personal. New York London: 1893. V. 68
A Matter of Millions. New York: 1890. V. 68
One of My Sons. New York: 1901. V. 71
The Sword of Damocles. New York: 1881. V. 68; 71
That Affair Next Door. New York: 1897. V. 68
Three Thousand Dollars. Boston: 1910. V. 68

GREEN, ARCHIE
Only a Miner. Studies in Recorded Coalmining Songs. Urbana: 1972. V. 71

GREEN, B. W.
Word Book of Virginia Folk-Speech. Richmond: 1899. V. 68

GREEN, BEN K.
Ben Green Tales. Flagstaff: 1974. V. 71
The Color of Horses. Flagstaff: 1974. V. 73
The Color of Horses. Northland: 1974. V. 70
Horse Tradin'. New York: 1967. V. 72
The Last Trail Drive through Downtown Dallas. Flagstaff: 1971. V. 69; 70; 71
Some More Horse Tradin'. New York: 1972. V. 70
A Thousand Miles of Mustangin'. Flagstaff: 1972. V. 68; 70; 71
The Village Horse Doctor West of the Pecos. New York: 1971. V. 70; 71
Wild Cow Tales. New York: 1969. V. 69; 71; 72

GREEN, BENJAMIN RICHARD
Illustrations of Perspective, Being a Popular Explanation of the Science and Its Application to Design Generally. London: 1840. V. 69

GREEN, BERIAH
Things for Northern Men to Do; a Discourse...July 17, 1836. New York: 1836. V. 68

GREEN, C. R.
Tales and Traditions of the Marias Des Cygnes Valley. Olathe: 1914. V. 71

GREEN, C. THEODORE
The Flora of the Liverpool District. Arbroath: 1933. V. 73

GREEN, CHARLES FREDERICK
Shakespeare's Crab Tree, with Its Legend and a Descriptive Account.... London: 1862. V. 68

GREEN, CHRISTOPHER
The European Avant-Gardes. Zwemmer: 1995. V. 68

GREEN, DAVID
Grinling Gibbons. London: 1964. V. 72

GREEN, DAVID E.
Mechanisms of Biological Oxidations. Cambridge: 1940. V. 73

GREEN, E. E. R.
Essays in Scotch Irish History. 1969. V. 69

GREEN, EDWIN L.
A History of Richland County. Columbia: 1932. V. 71

GREEN, F. L.
The Magician. New York: 1951. V. 71
Odd Man Out. London: 1945. V. 69; 71

GREEN, GEORGE DAWES
The Caveman. London: 1994. V. 69
The Caveman's Valentine. New York: 1994. V. 68; 69; 70; 71; 72; 73

GREEN, HANNAH
I Never Promised You a Rose Garden. New York: 1964. V. 68; 70

GREEN, HARRY CLINTON
The Pioneer Mothers of America. New York: 1925. V. 72

GREEN, HENRY
Blindness. London: 1926. V. 73
Concluding. London: 1948. V. 70
Doting. London: 1952. V. 71
Loving. New York: 1949. V. 73
Loving/Living/Party Going. New York: 1978. V. 73
Party Going. London: 1939. V. 69

GREEN, J.
Camerawork: a Critical Anthology. 1973. V. 68

GREEN, J. H.
The Dissector's Manual. London: 1820. V. 71

GREEN, J. R.
A Short History of the English People. London: 1902. V. 70

GREEN, JACOB
Astronomical Recreations; Or Sketches of the Relative Position and Mythological History of the Constellations. Philadelphia: 1824. V. 71

GREEN, JOHN
Tales and Ballads of Wearside. Leeds: 1897,. V. 73

GREEN, JOHN LITTLE
English Country Cottages: Their Condition, Cost and Requirements. London: 1899. V. 71

GREEN, JONATHAN
Journal of a Tour on the North West Coast of America in the Year 1829. New York: 1915. V. 68

GREEN, JULIAN
The Pilgrim on the Earth. 1929. V. 73

GREEN, JULIEN
Moira - Roman. Paris: 1950. V. 72

GREEN, LEONARD
Dream Comrades and Other Prose Sketches. Oxford: 1916. V. 73

GREEN, MATTHEW
The Spleen. London: 1737. V. 73
The Spleen and Other Poems. London: 1796. V. 69

GREEN, N. W.
Mormonism: Its Rise, Progress and Present Condition. Hartford: 1870. V. 68

GREEN, NATHAN
The Story of the Galveston Flood. 1900. V. 70

GREEN, PAUL
The Hawthorn Tree. Chapel Hill: 1943. V. 70; 71
Song in the Wilderness. Chapel Hill: 1947. V. 68
This Body the Earth. New York: 1935. V. 71

GREEN, RALPH
Works of Ralph Green: the Iron Hand Press in America.... Cincinnati: 1981. V. 72

GREEN, RENA M.
Mavericks Authentic Account of the Term. San Antonio: 1937. V. 71

GREEN, RICHARD LANCELYN
A Bibliography of A. Conan Doyle. Oxford: 1983. V. 69

GREEN, ROBERT M.
History of the Hundred and Twenty-Fourth Regiment Pennsylvania Voluntters in the War of the Rebellion 1862-1863. Philadelphia: 1907. V. 70

GREEN, ROGER LANCELYN
Into Other Worlds: Space Flight in Fiction from Lucian to Lewis. London and New York: 1957. V. 72

GREEN, S. G.
In Memoriam John Rylands. Manchester: 1899. V. 72; 73

GREEN, SAMUEL G.
French Pictures. Drawn with Pen and Pencil. London. V. 72
Pictures From The German Fatherland. London. V. 72
Swiss Pictures Drawn With Pen And Pencil. London: 1891. V. 72

GREEN, T. H.
An Introduction to Pathology and Morbid Anatomy. London: 1871. V. 71

GREEN, THOMAS
The Universal Herbal; or, Botanical, Medical and Agricultural Dictionary. Liverpool: 1816-1820. V. 70; 72
The Universal Herbal, or Botanical, Medical and Agricultural Dictionary. Liverpool: 1816-1824?. V. 73

GREEN, THOMAS MARSHALL
The Spanish Conspiracy: a Review of Early Spanish Movements. Cincinnati: 1891. V. 69; 73

GREEN, VALENTINE
The History and Antiquities of the City and Suburbs of Worcester. London: 1796. V. 70

GREEN, W. C.
W. C. Green and Co.'s Epitome of Southern Resources and Especially of the Marvelous City of Chattanooga, Tennessee and Vicinity. Chattanooga: 1889. V. 68

GREEN, WARD
Ride the Nightmare. New York: 1930. V. 72

GREEN, WHARTON J.
Address by Col. Wharton J. Green Before the Fayetteville Independent Light Infantry Co. On the Occasion of their Eighty-Eighth Anniversay. Fayetteville: 1881. V. 70

GREEN, WILLIAM
A Collection of 35 Soft Ground Etchings.... Ambleside: 1814. V. 71
A Description of a Series of Sixty Small Prints, Etched by William Green, of Ambleside, from Drawings Made by Himself. 1814. V. 72
A Description of a Series of Sixty Small Prints, Etched by William Green of Ambleside, from Drawings Made by Himself. Ambleside: 1814. V. 71
A Description of Sixty Studies from Nature.... London: 1810. V. 71
The Tourist's New Guide, Containing a Description of the Lakes, Mountains, and Scenery in Cumberland.... Kendal: 1819. V. 69; 71

GREEN, WILLIAM S.
Among the Selkirk Glaciers: Being a Account of a Rough Survey in the Rocky Mountain Regions of British Columbia. London: 1890. V. 70
The High Alps of New Zealand. Christchurch: 1976. V. 69

GREEN Willow and Other Japanese Fairy Tales. London: 1910. V. 68; 70

GREENAWAY, KATE
Almanack for 1883. London: 1883. V. 69; 70; 71
Almanack for 1884. London. V. 71
Almanack for 1885. London: 1885. V. 69; 71
Almanack for 1886. London. V. 71
Kate Greenaway's Almanack for 1888. London: 1888. V. 71
Almanack for 1890. London: 1890. V. 71
Kate Greenaway's Almanack for 1891. 1892. V. 71
Kate Greenaway's Almanack for 1893. 1892. V. 71
Almanack for 1894. London. V. 71
Almanack for 1924. London: 1924. V. 69
Almanack for 1925. London: 1924. V. 71
Alphabet. Paris: 1883?. V. 69
A Apple Pie. London: 1886. V. 69
A Apple Pie. London: 1935. V. 68
A Apple Pie. London: 1940. V. 68
The April Baby's Book of Tunes with the Story of How They Came to Be Written. London: 1900. V. 72
Book of Games. London: 1889. V. 73
A Day in a Child's Life. London: 1881. V. 69; 73
Kate Greenaway. 1910. V. 72
Kate Greenaway Pictures from Original Presented by Her to John Ruskin and Other Personal Friends. London: 1921. V. 73
Kate Greenaway's Alphabet. London: 1885. V. 68; 71; 73
The Margiold Painting Book. London: 1900. V. 72
Marigold Garden. London. V. 73
Marigold Garden. London: 1885. V. 69
The Marigold Painting Book. London: 1900. V. 68
A Painting Book with Outlines of Her Various Works for Girls and Boys to Paint. London: 1884. V. 70
Pictures, from originals presented by her to John Ruskin and other personal friends with appreciation by H.M. Cundall. 1921. V. 72
Three Little Songs. Philadelphia: 1910. V. 68; 72
Under the Window. London. V. 70; 72; 73
Under the Window. London: 1878. V. 68; 69
The Window. London: 1878. V. 70

GREENBERG, DAVID B.
Furrow's End. New York: 1946. V. 69

GREENBERG, G.
Comparative Psychology of Invertebrates.... New York: 1997. V. 72

GREENBERG, MARTIN
The Tony Hillerman Companion. New York: 1994. V. 68

GREENBLATT, S. H.
A History of Neurosurgery in Its Scientific and Professional Contexts. Park Ridge: 1997. V. 68

GREENBURG, MARTIN H.
Weird Tales. 1988. V. 68

GREENE, A. C.
The Last Captive. Austin: 1972. V. 69

GREENE, ABRAHAM
Another Mexico. New York: 1939. V. 71

GREENE, ASA
Travels in America. New York: 1833. V. 68

GREENE, BARBARA
Too Late to Turn Back - Barbara and Graham Greene in Liberia. London: 1981. V. 69

GREENE, E. L.
Landmarks of Botanical History. Stanford: 1983. V. 72

GREENE, EDWARD BURNABY
Whispers of the Ear of the Author of Thelyphthora, in Favor of Reason and Religion, Aspersed through that Work. London: 1781. V. 68

GREENE, FRANCIS V.
The Revolutionary War and the Military Policy of the United States. New York: 1911. V. 73

GREENE, FREDERICK STUART
The Grim Thirteen. Short Stories by Thirteen Authors of Standing. New York: 1917. V. 70

GREENE, GRAHAM
L'Agent Secret. Paris: 1948. V. 70
Babbling April. Oxford: 1925. V. 70
The Basement Room and Other Stories. London: 1935. V. 70; 71
The Bear Fell Free. London: 1935. V. 70
Brighton Rock. London: 1938. V. 69; 71; 73
Brighton Rock. New York: 1938. V. 70
Brighton Rock. Sydney: 1939. V. 73
Brighton Rock. Sydney: 1944. V. 68
British Dramatists. London: 1942. V. 70
A Burnt-Out Case. London: 1961. V. 68; 70; 71; 73
A Burnt-Out Case. New York: 1961. V. 70
The Captain and the Enemy. 1988. V. 71; 72
The Captain and the Enemy. 1998. V. 72
Carving a Statue. London: 1964. V. 70
Collected Essays. London: 1969. V. 70
Collected Stories: Including May We Borrow Your Husband?. New York: 1973. V. 70
The Comedians. London: 1966. V. 68; 70; 71; 73
The Comedians. New York: 1966. V. 68; 70
The Complaisant Lover. London: 1959. V. 70
The Complaisant Lover. New York: 1961. V. 69; 70
The Complete Entertainments. London: 1996. V. 70
The Confidential Agent. London: 1939. V. 70; 73
The Confidential Agent. New York: 1939. V. 70
Dear David, Dear Graham: a Bibliophile Correspondence. Oxford: 1989. V. 70; 71
Doctor Fischer of Geneva; or, The Bomb Party. New York: 1980. V. 70
The End of the Affair. London: 1951. V. 70
The End of the Affair. New York: 1951. V. 69; 70; 71
England Made Me. London: 1935. V. 70
England Made Me. New York: 1935. V. 70
Essais Catholiques. Paris: 1953. V. 69; 73
Garbo and the Night Watchmen-A Selection from the Writings of British and American Film Critics. London: 1937. V. 72
Getting to Know the General. London: 1984. V. 68
The Graham Greene Film Reader. New York: 1994. V. 72
The Great Jowett. London: 1981. V. 70; 73
A Gun for Sale. London: 1936. V. 70; 71; 73
The Heart of the Matter. London: 1948. V. 70
The Heart of the Matter. New York: 1948. V. 70; 73
How Father Quixote Became a Monsignor. Los Angeles: 1980. V. 68; 70
The Human Factor. London: 1978. V. 68; 70; 71; 72
In Search of a Character: Two African Journals. London: 1961. V. 70
In Search of a Character: Two African Journals. New York: 1961. V. 70
Introductions to Three Novels. London: 1962. V. 70
Introductions to Three Novels. Stockholm: 1962. V. 70; 71
It's a Battlefield. Garden City: 1934. V. 70; 71
It's a Battlefield. London: 1934. V. 70; 71
Journey Without Maps. New York: 1936. V. 70
The Labyrinthine Ways. New York: 1940. V. 70; 73
The Lawless Roads. London: 1939. V. 70
The Little Fire Engine. London: 1950. V. 71; 72
The Little Fire Engine. London: 1973. V. 73
The Little Horse Bus. London: 1974. V. 70; 72
The Little Steamroller. Garden City: 1974. V. 72
The Little Steamroller. London: 1974. V. 72
The Little Train. London: 1973. V. 69
The Living Room. London: 1953. V. 70
Loser Takes All. 1955. V. 70
Loser Takes All. London: 1955. V. 68; 71
The Lost Childhood and Other Essays. London: 1951. V. 70
The Man Within. London: 1929. V. 71
The Man Within. New York: 1948. V. 68
May We Borrow Your Husband?. London: 1967. V. 68; 70
May We Borrow Your Husband?. London: 1968. V. 71
The Ministry of Fear. London: 1943. V. 70
Mr. Visconti: an Extract from Travels with My Aunt. London: 1969. V. 68; 70; 73
Monsignor Quixote. London: 1982. V. 68
Monsignor Quixote. New York: 1982. V. 68; 70
Monsignor Quixote. Toronto: 1982. V. 70
The Monster of Capri. Helsinki: 1985. V. 70
The Name of Action. London: 1930. V. 68; 70; 71; 73
The Name of Action. New York: 1931. V. 69; 70
The New House. Helsinki: 1988. V. 70
Nineteen Stories. London: 1947. V. 69; 70; 72
Nineteen Stories. New York: 1949. V. 69; 70
The Old School. Essays by Divers Hands. London: 1934. V. 68; 70; 71
Our Exploits at West Play. London: 1952. V. 69
Our Man in Havana: An Entertainment. London: 1958. V. 70; 71; 72
The Potting Shed. New York: 1957. V. 70
The Potting Shed. London: 1958. V. 70
The Power and the Glory. London: 1940. V. 70
A Quick Look Behind: Footnotes to an Autobiography. Los Angeles: 1983. V. 70
The Quiet American. London: 1955. V. 69; 70; 71; 73
Quiet American. New York: 1956. V. 70; 72; 73
Reflections on Travels with My Aunt. New York: 1989. V. 70
The Return of A. J. Raffles. London: 1975. V. 70; 73
The Revenge. 1963. V. 70; 73
The Revenge. London: 1963. V. 68; 70
Rumour at Nightfall. London: 1931. V. 70
Rumour at Nightfall. New York: 1932. V. 70
A Sense of Reality. London: 1963. V. 68; 70; 72
A Sense of Reality. New York: 1963. V. 70; 72
The Shipwrecked. New York: 1953. V. 70
A Sort of Life. London: 1971. V. 68

GREENE, GRAHAM continued
The Spy's Bedside Book - an Anthology. London: 1957. V. 69; 70
Stamboul Train. London: 1932. V. 68; 70; 71; 73
The Tenth Man. London: 1985. V. 68; 70
The 3rd Man: The Story for the Motion Picture. New York: 1950. V. 69
The Third Man. Helsinki: 1987. V. 70
The Third Man. Helsinki: 1988. V. 73
The Third Man and The Fallen Idol. London: 1950. V. 70; 72
This Gun for Hire. Garden City: 1936. V. 70
To Beg I Am Ashamed. London: 1938. V. 70
Travels with My Aunt. London: 1969. V. 68; 70; 71
Travels with My Aunt. New York: 1970. V. 70
Twenty-One Stories. London: 1954. V. 70
The Virtue of Disloyalty. London: 1972. V. 68; 70; 73
A Visit to Morin. London: 1959. V. 68; 70
Ways of Escape. London: 1980. V. 68
Ways to Escape. Toronto: 1980. V. 70
A Wedding Among the Owls. London: 1977,. V. 70; 73
A Weed Among the Flowers. Los Angeles: 1990. V. 70
Why Do I Write?. London: 1948. V. 70
Why the Epigraph?. London: 1989. V. 68; 70
Winter Words: Poems. London: 1928. V. 69
Yes and No: A Play in One Act. Helsinki: 1983. V. 73
Yes and No: A Play in One Act. Helsinki: 1984. V. 70
Yes and No and For Whom the Bell Chimes. London: 1983. V. 68; 70; 73

GREENE, JEROME A.
Evidence and The Custer Enigma - A Reconstruction of Indian-Military History. Kansas City: 1973. V. 72

GREENE, LAURENCE
O'Mara. Indianapolis: 1938. V. 70

GREENE, LORENZO J.
The Negro Wage Earner. Washington: 1930. V. 68

GREENE, T. FAIRWAY
Mystery of June Twenty-Seventh. Findlay: 1934. V. 70

GREENE, VIVIEN
English Doll's Houses of the Eighteenth and Nineteenth Centuries. London: 1955. V. 68

GREENE, WARD
Cora Potts: a Pilgrim's Progress. New York: 1929. V. 71

GREENE, WILLIAM HOWE
The Wooden Walls Among the Ice Floes Telling the Romance of the Newfoundland Seal Fishery. London: 1933. V. 68; 72

GREENER, W. W.
The Breech Loader and How to Use It. 1892. V. 70
The Gun and Its Development. 1884. V. 71
The Gun and Its Development. London: 1899. V. 72

GREENEWALT, CRAWFORD H.
Hummingbirds. 1960. V. 68
Hummingbirds. New York: 1960. V. 70

GREENFELD, JOSH
Harry and Tonto. New York: 1974. V. 70; 71

GREENFIELD, J. G.
Neuropathology. London: 1958. V. 68

GREENHALGH, THOMAS
The Vicissitudes of Commerce. A Tale of the Cotton Trade. London: 1852. V. 71; 73

GREENHALGH, V. MEGAW
Art in Society. New York: 1978. V. 69

GREENHILL, ELIZABETH
Elizabeth Greenhill, Bookbinder, a Catalogue Raisonne. Frenich, Foss: 1986. V. 70

GREENHOUS, BRERETON
Dragoon The Centennial History of the Royal Canadian Dragoons 1883- 1983. Ottawa: 1983. V. 68

GREENHOW, EDWARD H.
On Diptheria. London: 1860. V. 69

GREENHOW, ROBERT
Memoir, Historical and Political on the North West Coast of North America, and the Adjacent Territories. Washington: 1840. V. 71

GREENHOW, ROSE O'NEAL
My Imprisonment and the First Year of Abolition Rule at Washington. London: 1863. V. 72

GREENLEAF, LAWRENCE N.
King Sham. New York: 1868. V. 70

GREENLEAF, SIMON
Discourse Commemorative of the Life and Character of the Hon. Joseph Story, LL.D., an Associate Justice of the Supreme Court of the United States.... Boston: 1845. V. 70

GREENLEAF, STEPHEN
Death Bed. New York: 1980. V. 71
The Ditto List. New York: 1985. V. 70

Fatal Obsession. New York: 1983. V. 71
Grave Error. New York: 1979. V. 71
State's Evidence. New York: 1982. V. 71

GREENLY, HENRY
Models, Railways and Locomotive. Volume VI. 1914. V. 68

GREENOUGH, GRAFTON
To Boulder and Back. Trip of Samuel M. Vauclain and Party through the Middle West May 21-30, 1923. Philadelphia: 1923. V. 68

GREENOUGH, SARAH
On the Art of Fixing a Shadow: One Hundred and Fifty Years of Photography. 1989. V. 70; 72

GREEN'S *Nursery Annual.* London: 1848. V. 71

GREENSTREET, W. J.
Isaac Newton 1642-1727. A memorial volume edited for the Mathematical Association. London: 1927. V. 72

GREENWAY, J. D.
Wanderings In Corsica. London: 1885. V. 72

GREENWELL, DORA
Poems. London: 1848. V. 73
Poems. Edinburgh: 1861. V. 69

GREENWELL, G. C.
A Practical Treatise on Mine Engineering.... Newcastle: 1892. V. 68

GREENWELL, WILLIAM
British Barrows. Oxford: 1877. V. 71; 73

GREENWOOD, EDWIN
The Deadly Dowager. New York: 1935. V. 68

GREENWOOD, GEORGE
The Tree-Lifter; or, a New Method of Transplanting Forest Trees. London: 1844. V. 70
The Tree-Lifter; or, a New Method of Transplanting Forest Trees. London: 1853. V. 69

GREENWOOD, GRACE
The Little Pilgrim. Philadelphia: 1858. V. 69

GREENWOOD, ISAAC
Arithmetick Vulgar and Decimal; with the Application Thereof, to a Variety of Cases in Trade and Commerce. Boston: 1729. V. 71

GREENWOOD, J.
Narrative of the Late Victorious Campaign In Afghanistan, Under General Pollock.... London: 1844. V. 73
Wild Sports of the World. 1870. V. 69; 70; 72; 73

GREENWOOD, JAMES
Curiosities of Savage Life. London: 1863. V. 68; 72
Dining with Duke Humphrey; or, Curiosities of Life. London. V. 70
The Hatchet Throwers. London: 1866. V. 71; 72
Legends of a Savage Life. London: 1869. V. 68; 72
The London Vocabulary, English and Latin.... London: 1782. V. 71
The Philadelphia Vocabulary, English and Latin.... Philadelphia: 1787. V. 69

GREENWOOD, JOHN
Greenwood's Picture of Hull. Hull: 1835. V. 70

GREENWOOD, JOHN BESWICKE
The Early Ecclesiastical History of Dewsbury. 1859. V. 73

GREENWOOD, M.
Medical Statistics from Grant to Farr...Fitzpatrick Lectures. Cambridge: 1948. V. 71

GREENWOOD, MARTIN
The Designs of William De Morgan. Ilminster: 1989. V. 72

GREENWOOD, P. H.
A Revision of the Lake Victoria Haplochromis Species (Pisces, Cichlidae). London: 1956-1969. V. 73

GREENWOOD, ROBERT
The California Outlaw Tiburcio Vasquez. Los Gatos: 1960. V. 69; 71; 73

GREENWOOD, T.
Nearer Than the Sky. New York: 2000. V. 72

GREENWOOD, THOMAS
Eminent Naturalists. London: 1886. V. 68; 70; 72

GREER, BLANCHE
Thunder's Tail. New York: 1944. V. 73

GREER, GERMAINE
The Female Eunuch. London: 1970. V. 68; 70
The Obstacle Race - The Fortunes of Women Painters and Their Work. London: 1979. V. 72

GREER, JAMES
Bois D'Arc to Barbed Wire, Ken Cary Southwestern Pioneer 1850-1896. Dallas: 1936. V. 71
Buck Barry Texas Ranger. Dallas: 1932. V. 70
Colonel Jack Hays, Texas Frontier Leader and California Builder. New York: 1952. V. 70
Early in the Saddle. Dallas: 1936. V. 71

GREER, ROBERT
The Devil's Hatband. New York: 1996. V. 71

GREESON, P. E.
Wetland Functions and Values; the State of Our Understanding. Minneapolis: 1979. V. 73

GREEVER, GARLAND
A Wiltshire Parson and His Friends; the Correspondence of William Lisle Bowles.... Boston & New York: 1926. V. 70

GREG, PERCY
History of the U.S. from the Foundation of Virginia to the Reconstruction of the Union. Richmond: 1892. V. 68

GREG, R. P.
Manual of the Mineralogy of Great Britian and Ireland. London: 1858. V. 68

GREG, WILLIAM RATHBONE
Enigmas of Life. London: 1873. V. 71
Essays on Political and Social Science, Contributed Chiefly to the Edinburgh Review. London: 1853. V. 71
Political Problems for Our Age and Country. London: 1870. V. 71

GREGER, DEBORA
Black Country. 1985. V. 71
Cartography. Lisbon: 1980. V. 69; 73

GREGG, CECIL FREEMAN
The Murder of Estelle Cantor. New York: 1936. V. 70

GREGG, JACOB RAY
Pioneer Days in Malheur County. Los Angeles: 1950. V. 70

GREGG, JOSIAH
Diaries and Letters of Josiah Gregg. Volume I. Southwest Enterprises 1840-1847. Volume II. Excursions in Mexico and California, 1847-1850. Norman: 1941-1944. V. 68
Diary and Letters of Josiah Gregg. Norman: 1941-1958. V. 70

GREGG, LINDA
Too Bright to See. Port Townsend: 1981. V. 73

GREGG, RICHARD B.
Training for Peace. London: 1936. V. 71

GREGO, JOSEPH
Pictorial Pickwiciana: Charles Dickens and His Illustrators. London: 1899. V. 70

GREGOR, FRANCIS
The Works of Francis Gregor, of Trewarthenick. Exeter: 1816. V. 68

GREGORIUS I, POPE
Moralia, Sive Expositio in Job. Rome: 1475. V. 69

GREGORSON, EDITH RAY
Lemuel. London: 1947. V. 71

GREGORY, ALYSE
Hester Craddock. London: 1931. V. 71

GREGORY, ANNIE R.
Woman's Favorite Cook Book. Nashville: 1907. V. 68

GREGORY, BP. OF TOURS
Opera Omnia. 1699. V. 73

GREGORY, CARL LOUIS
Motion Picture Photography. New York: 1927. V. 68

GREGORY, DICK
Dick Gregory's Political Primer. New York: 1972. V. 68; 72
The Shadow That Scares Me. Garden City: 1968. V. 72
Up From Nigger. New York: 1976. V. 72

GREGORY, GEORGE
Elements of the Theory and Practice of Physic. Philadelphia: 1829. V. 68

GREGORY, HERBERT E.
The Navajo Country. Washington: 1916. V. 68

GREGORY, HORACE
Pilgrim of Apocalypse. New York: 1957. V. 72

GREGORY, ISABELLA AUGUSTA PERSE
Collected Plays. 1970-1971. V. 70
The Golden Apple: a Play for Kiltartan Children. London: 1916. V. 68
Irish Folk History, Plays, First and Second Series. New York: 1912. V. 72
The Kiltartan Poetry Book. New York and London: 1919. V. 70; 71

GREGORY, ISBAELLA AUGUSTA PERSE
My First Play. London: 1930. V. 71

GREGORY, JACK
Choctaw Spirit. Muskogee: 1972. V. 69
Creek Seminole Spirit Tales: Tribal Folklore, Legend and Myth. Pensacola: 1971. V. 72; 73

GREGORY, JACKSON
The Emerald Murder Trap. New York: 1934. V. 71
The House of the Opal. New York: 1975. V. 73

GREGORY, JAMES
Conspectus Medicinae Theoreticae ad Usum Academicum. Edinburgh: 1813. V. 70; 72
Conspectus Medicinae Theoreticae; or a View of the theory of Medicine. Edinburgh: 1833. V. 70
Memorial to the Managers of the Royal Infirmary. Edinburgh: 1800-1803. V. 70; 72

GREGORY, JOHN
A Comparative View of the State and Faculties of Man with Those of the Animal World. London: 1798. V. 73
Observations on the Duties and Offices of a Physician.... London: 1770. V. 69

GREGORY, JOSEPH W.
Gregory's Guide for California Travellers Via the Isthmus of Panama. San Francisco: 1949. V. 69

GREGORY, PADRAIC
Ulster Songs and Ballads. 1920. V. 69

GREGORY, W. K.
Fish Skulls. 1959. V. 72

GREGORY, WILLIAM K.
In Quest of Gorillas. New Bedford: 1937. V. 71

GREGSON, MATTHEW
History of Lancashire. Liverpool: 1817. V. 73
History of Lancashire. Liverpool: 1817-1824. V. 73
Portfolio of Fragments Relative to the History and Antiquities, Topography and Genealogies of the county Palatine and Duchy of Lancaster. London: 1869. V. 73

GREIG, DAVID M.
Clinical Observations on the Surgical Pathology of Home. Edinburgh: 1931. V. 71

GREIG, MAYSIE
Sweet Danger. New York: 1935. V. 71
This Fearful Paradise. New York: 1953. V. 71
Whispers in the Sun. New York: 1949. V. 71

GRELLET, STEPHEN
Memoirs Of The Life And Gospel Labours Of Stephen Grellet. London: 1861. V. 72

GRELLMANN, HENRICH MORITZ GOTTLIEB
Dissertation on the Gipsies, Being an Historical Enquiry, Concerning the Manner of Life, Oeconomy, Customs and Conditions of These People in Europe and Their Origin. London: 1787. V. 70

GRELOT, GUILLAUME JOSEPH
A Late Voyage to Constantinople.... London: 1683. V. 69

GRENFELL, HENRY RIVERSDALE
Love and Law. London: 1851. V. 71

GRENFELL, WILFRED T.
Labrador: The Country and the People. New York: 1922. V. 71
A Man's Faith. Boston and Chicago: 1926. V. 68
The Story of a Labrador Doctor. London: 193-?. V. 73

GRENVILLE, GEORGE
The Speech of a Right Honourable Gentleman on the Motion for Expelling Mr. Wilkes, Friday Feb. 3, 1769. London: 1769. V. 71

GRENVILLE, WILLIAM WYNDHAM
Substance of the Speech of the Right Hon. Lord Grenville, in the House of the Lords, Nove. 30, 1819. London: 1820. V. 69

GRESHAM, WILLIAM LINDSAY
Limbo Tower. New York and Toronto: 1949. V. 69; 71
Nightmare Alley. New York: 1946. V. 68; 71

GRESLEY, WILLIAM
Charles Lever; or the Man of the Nineteenth Century. London: 1841. V. 68

GRESSITT, J. L.
Entomology of Antarctica. Washington: 1967. V. 68
Subantarctic Entomology, Particularlty of South Georgia and Heard Island. Honolulu: 1970. V. 72

GRESSLEY, GENE
Old Travois Trails, Vol 1, no. 1 to Vol 3, no. 3. New York: 1974. V. 72

GRESSON, R. A. R.
Essentials of General Cytology. Edinburgh: 1848. V. 69

GRESTY, JOHN
Gresty's Illustrated Chester, Consisting of Eight Large Chromo Lithographic Views from Photographs.... Chester: 1862. V. 70

GRESWELL, WILLIAM PARR
Annals of Parisian Typography. London: 1818. V. 69

GRETTON, A. L. V.
The Vicissitudes of Italy, Since the Congress of Vienna. London: 1859. V. 68

GREUB, S.
Art of the Northwest New Guinea. New York: 1992. V. 69

GREULICH, WILLIAM WALTER
Radiographic Atlas of Skeletal Development of the Hand and Wrist. Stanford: 1950. V. 68
Radiographic Atlas of Skeletal Development of the Hand and Wrist. Stanford: 1959. V. 68

GREVILLE, CHARLES CAVENDISH FULKE
The Greville Memoirs. London: 1874-1875. V. 71
The Greville Memoirs. London: 1874-1887. V. 71
A Journal of the Reign of Queen Victoria. New York: 1885-1887. V. 73

GREVILLE, CHARLES CAVENDISH FULKE continued
A Journal of the Reign of Queen Victoria from 1837 to 1852. London: 1885. V. 69
Sir Robert Peel and the Corn Law Crisis. London: 1846. V. 71

GREVILLE, ROBERT KAYE
Scottish Cryptogamic Flora.... Edinburgh: 1823-1828. V. 68; 71

GREW, J. C.
Sport and Travel in the Far East. 1910. V. 69; 70; 72

GREW, NEHEMIAH
Anatomie des Plantes Qui Contient Une Description Exacte de Leurs Parties & de Leurs Usages & Qui Fait Voir Comment Elles se Forment.... Paris: 1675. V. 70
The Anatomy of Plants.... London: 1682. V. 70
Cosmologia Sacra; or a Discourse of the Universe. London: 1701. V. 69
An Idea of Phytological History Propounded. Together with a Continuation of the Anatomy of Vegetables, Particularly prosecuted Upon Roots. London: 1673. V. 72
Musaeum Regalis Societatis. 1681. V. 72
Musaeum Regalis Societatis. London: 1681. V. 70

GREY, C. H.
Hardy Bulbs. 1937-1938. V. 69; 72
Hardy Bulbs. London: 1937-1938. V. 69; 71; 73
Hardy Bulbs. Volume 2. 1938. V. 73

GREY, CHARLES
The Early Years of the Prince Consort, Compiled Under the Direction of Her Majesty the Queen. London: 1869. V. 71
Parliamentary Government Considered With Reference to Reform.. London: 1864. V. 71

GREY, EDWARD GREY, 1ST VISCOUNT
Fly Fishing. 1899. V. 68
Fly Fishing. 1947. V. 70
Fly Fishing. 1992. V. 68

GREY, GEORGE
Journals of Two Expeditions of Discovery in Northwest and Western Australia, During the Years 1837, 1838 and 1839. London: 1841. V. 68

GREY, H.
The Victorians by the Sea. London: 1973. V. 68

GREY, HENRY GEORGE GREY, 3RD EARL OF
Parliamentary Government Considered with Reference to a Reform of Parliament. London: 1858. V. 71

GREY, HERBERT
The Voyage of the Lady. London: 1860. V. 68

GREY, KATHARINE
A Little Leaven. Philadelphia: 1922. V. 70; 71

GREY, LOREN
Zane Grey's Odyssey. 1991. V. 68

GREY, MARIA G.
Thoughts on Self-Culture, Addressed to Women. London: 1854. V. 68

GREY, ROMER
The Cruise of the Fisherman, Adventures in Southern Seas. New York: 1929. V. 69

GREY, VIVIAN
Auctioned Off: A Love Story. New York: 1930. V. 70; 71

GREY, WILLIAM
A Picture of Pioneer Times in California. San Francisco: 1881. V. 70

GREY, ZANE
Adventures of a Deep Sea Angler. 1991. V. 68
An American Angler in Australia. 1991. V. 68
The Arizona Clan. 1958. V. 68
The Arizona Clan. New York: 1958. V. 70
Betty Zane. New York: 1933. V. 69
Blue Feather and Other Stories. New York: 1961. V. 69
Desert Gold. New York: 1913. V. 71
Fighting Caravans. New York: 1931. V. 69
Forlorn River. New York: 1927. V. 70
The Fugitive Trail. New York: 1957. V. 68; 70
The Heritage of the Desert. New York: 1932. V. 69
Horse Heaven Hill. New York: 1959. V. 68; 70
The Light of Western Stars. New York: 1914. V. 69
The Lost Wagon Train. New York: 1936. V. 70; 73
Raiders of Spanish Peaks. New York: 1938. V. 70
The Rainbow Trail. New York: 1915. V. 71
Riders of the Purple Sage. New York: 1912. V. 70
The Spirit of the Border. New York: 1930. V. 71
Tales of an Angler's Eldorado - New Zealand. 1991. V. 68
Tales of Fishes. 1991. V. 68
Tales of Fishing Virgin Seas. 1990. V. 68
Tales of Fresh-Water Fishing. New York: 1928. V. 71
Tales of Lonely Trails. New York: 1922. V. 69
Tales of Southern Rivers. 1991. V. 68
Tales of Swordfish and Tuna. 1927. V. 68
Tales of Swordfish and Tuna. London: 1927. V. 73
Tales of Swordfish and Tuna. New York: 1927. V. 70; 73

30,000 on the Hoof. New York: 1940. V. 71
Thunder Mountain. New York: 1935. V. 69
To the Last Man. New York: 1922. V. 69
Under the Tonto Rim. New York: 1926. V. 69; 70
The Vanishing American. New York: 1925. V. 72
Wanderer of the Wasteland. New York: 1923. V. 69
West of the Pecos. London: 1937. V. 72
Western Union. New York: 1939. V. 71
Wild Horse Mesa. New York: 1928. V. 69; 70
Wildfire. New York: 1917. V. 69
The Young Lion Hunter. London: 1919. V. 72

GREYFRIARS *Holiday Annual 1926.* V. 68

GREY OWL
Pilgrims of the Wild. London: 1935. V. 73
Tales of an Empty Cabin. London: 1936. V. 73

GRIAULE, MARCEL
Burners of Men: Modern Ethiopia. Philadelphia: 1935. V. 72

GRIBBIN, JILL
Japanese Antique Dolls. New York: 1984. V. 72

GRIBBLE, FRANCIS
The Early Mountaineers. London: 1899. V. 69; 70; 72
George Sand and Her Lovers. London: 1907. V. 70
The Story of Alpine Climbing. London: 1912. V. 69

GRIBBLE, LEONARD
The Case of the Marsden Rubies. New York: 1930. V. 68; 71
The Secret of Tangles. Philadelphia: 1934. V. 68

GRIBBON, WILLIAM LANCASTER
C.I.D. New York: 1932. V. 69

GRIEN on Rougemont: *The Story of a Modern Robinson Crusoe.* London: 1898. V. 68

GRIER, WILLIAM
The Mechanic's Calculator; Comprehending Principles, Rules and Tables in the Various Departments of Mathemataics and Mechanic's...(with) The Mechanic's Pocket Dictionary.... 1845-1846. V. 71

GRIERSON, H. J. C.
William Blake's Designs for Gray's Poems Reproduced Full-Size in Monochrome or Colour from the Unique Copy Belonging to His Grace the Duke of Hamilton. London: 1922. V. 69

GRIESBACH, A. H. R.
Flora of the British West Indian Islands. Weinheim: 1963. V. 69

GRIESHEIM, LUDWIG WILHELM VON
Versuch Einer Neuen Bruckenbauart. Altenburg: 1773. V. 68

GRIESINGER, W.
Mental Pathology and Therapeutics. London: 1867. V. 68

GRIEVE, CHRISTOPHER MURRAY
Albyn or Scotland and the Future. 1927. V. 68
Collected Poems of Hugh Mac Diarmid. 1962. V. 68
Cunninghame Graham - a Centenary Study. Glasgow: 1952. V. 72
Direadh I, II and III. Foss: 1974. V. 70
A Drunk Man Looks at the Thistle. Edinburgh: 1962. V. 72
First Hymn to Lenin and other poems. London: 1931. V. 72
The Kind of Poetry I Want. Edinburgh: 1961. V. 70
A Kist of Whistles. 1947. V. 68
Penny Wheep. 1926. V. 68
Sangschaw. 1925. V. 68
Sangschaw. Edinburgh and London: 1925. V. 72
Second Hymn to Lenin and Other Poems. 1935. V. 68
To Circumjack Cencrastus. 1930. V. 68

GRIEVE, MAUD
A Modern Herbal.... New York: 1931. V. 70; 71; 73

GRIFFIN, APPLETON P. C.
A Catalogue of the Washington Collection in the Boston Athenaeum. Boston: 1897. V. 73

GRIFFIN, CLARENCE W.
History of Old Tryon and Rutherford Counties North Carolina 1730- 1936. Asheville: 1937. V. 71

GRIFFIN, GERALD
The Collegians. London: 1892. V. 68
The Collegians. Dublin and Cork: 1918. V. 72

GRIFFIN, HARRY
Adventuring in Lakeland. London: 1980. V. 69

GRIFFIN, J. B.
Archaeology of Eastern United States. Chicago: 1952. V. 69

GRIFFIN, JOHN
Memoirs of Captain James Wilson, Containing and Account of His Enterprises and Sufferings in India.... London: 1815. V. 71

GRIFFIN, JOHN H.
The Devil Rides Outside. Fort Worth: 1952. V. 70

GRIFFIN, SUSAN
Dear Sky. Berekeley: 1971. V. 69

GRIFFIN, THOMAS
Minutes of the Proceedings at the Trial of Vice-Admiral Griffin. At a Court-Martial, Held on Board His Majesty's Ship Somerset at Chatham on Monday, December 3, 1750, for an Enquiry into His Conduct.... London: 1751. V. 70
(Mr. Gr)iffin's (App)eal to the Right Hon. th(e) Lords Commissioners (of th)e Admiralty. In a Letter to Their Secretary Against the Sentence Passed on Him at a Court Martial, Held on Board His Majesty's Ship Somerset at Chatham Dec. 3, 1750. London: 1751. V. 70

GRIFFIS, JOSEPH K.
Taken Out of Savagery into Civilization - an Autobiography. New York: 1915. V. 69

GRIFFITH, ELIZABETH
The Morality of Shakespeare's Drama Illustrated. Dublin: 1777. V. 68

GRIFFITH, ERNEST S.
The Modern Development of City Government in the United Kingdom and the United States. London: 1927. V. 71

GRIFFITH, G. W. E.
My 96 Years in the Great West: Indiana, Kansas and California. Los Angeles: 1929. V. 68

GRIFFITH, GEORGE
Going to Markets and Grammar Schools. London: 1870. V. 71; 72
History of the Free-Schools, Colleges, Hospitals and Asylums of Birmingham.... 1861. V. 72
A Mayfair Magician. London: 1905. V. 68

GRIFFITH, HARRISON PATILLO
Variosa: a Collection of Sketches, Essays and Verses. Gaffney: 1911. V. 69

GRIFFITH, J. E.
The Flora of Anglesey & Carnarvonshire. Bangor: 1895. V. 69

GRIFFITH, J. K.
A General Cheltenham Guide Upon an Entirely New Plan. Cheltenham: 1815. V. 71

GRIFFITH, J. W.
The Micrographic Dictionary. London: 1856-1875. V. 68
The Micrographic Dictionary. London: 1860. V. 73
The Micrographic Dictionary. 1883. V. 69
The Micrographic Dictionary. London: 1883. V. 68; 70

GRIFFITH, JOHN
A Journal of the Life, Travels and Labours in the Work of the Ministry, of John Griffith. London: 1779. V. 69

GRIFFITH, JULIA
Autographs For Freedom. New York: 1845. V. 72

GRIFFITH, L. W.
Spring of Young. London: 1935. V. 69

GRIFFITH, MATHEW
Bethel or a Forme for Families, in Which All Sorts, of both Sexes, are So Squared and framed by the Word of God, as They May Best Serve in their Severall Places.... London: 1633. V. 70

GRIFFITH, MOSES
Practical Observations on the Cure of Hectic and Slow Fevers and the Pulmonary Consumption.... London: 1776. V. 69

GRIFFITH, R. H.
A Descriptive Catalogue of an Exhibition of Manuscripts and First Editions of Lord Byron Held in the Library of the University of Texas from April 19 to May 3, 1924, to Commemorate the One Hundredth Anniversary to His Death. Austin: 1924. V. 72

GRIFFITH, RICHARD
Geological and Mining Surveys fo the Coal Districts of the Countess of Tyrone and Antrim, in Ireland. Dublin: 1829. V. 71

GRIFFITH, T. A.
Hunting Songs. 1876. V. 68

GRIFFITH, WILLIAM
An Oration, Delivered to the Citizens of Burlington the 22d of 1800, in Commemoration of Gen. George Washington, Who Died at Mount Vernon, Dec. 14, 1799.... Trenton: 1800. V. 70
Posthumous Papers Bequeathed to the Honourable the East India Company. Calcutta: 1847-1854. V. 69
Posthumous Papers Bequeathed to the Honourable the East India Company. Calcutta: 1849. V. 69
The Scrivener's Guide.... Burlington: 1813. V. 69
A Treatise on the Jurisdiction and Proceedings of the Justices of the Peace in Civil Suits.... Burlington: 1796. V. 69
A Treatise on the Jurisdiction and Proceedings of the Justices of the Peace, in Civil Suits.... Newark: 1797. V. 69
A Treatise on the Jurisidicton and Proceedings of the Justices of the Peace, in Civil Suits in New Jersey.... Burlington: 1813. V. 69

GRIFFITHS, ARTHUR
The Brand of the Broad Arrow. London: 1900. V. 73
Clubs and Clubmen. London: 1907. V. 68
Lola: a Tale of the Rock. London: 1888. V. 68
Secrets of the Prison House or Gaol Studies and Sketches. London: 1894. V. 71

GRIFFITHS, ARTHUR GEORGE FREDERICK
A Wayward Woman. London: 1879. V. 73

GRIFFITHS, CHARLOTTE MARY
Gone with the Storm and Minor Poems. London: 187?. V. 69

GRIFFITHS, ELIZABETH
Delicate Distress. London: 1788. V. 73

GRIFFITHS, JEREMY
Speculum Peccatorum. The Mirror of Sinners Printed in London by Wynkun De Worde c. 1509-10. Cambridge: 1992. V. 70

GRIFFITHS, JULIA
Autographs for Freedom. New York: 1854. V. 68; 69

GRIFFITHS, JULIUS
Travels in Europe, Asia Minor and Arabia. London: 1805. V. 68

GRIFFITHS, PHILIP J.
Vietnam Inc. New York: 1971. V. 72

GRIFFITHS, THOMAS
The Writing Desk and Its Contents.... London: 1844. V. 68

GRIFFITHS, WILLIAM H.
The Story of the American Bank Note Company. New York: 1959. V. 73

GRIGGS, NATHAN K.
Lyrics of the Lariat. Chicago: 1893. V. 71

GRIGGS, ROBERT F.
The Valley Of Ten Thousand Smokes. London: 1922. V. 72
The Valley of Ten Thousand Smokes. Washington: 1922. V. 70

GRIGSBY, HUGH BLAIR
Letters by a South Carolinian. Norfolk: 1827. V. 68

GRIGSON, GEOFFREY
The Englishman's Flora. London: 1955. V. 68

GRILLION'S CLUB
Portraits of Members...from 1813 to 1863. (Semi-Centenary). 1864. V. 70

GRIMALDI, JOSEPH
Memoirs. Edited by Boz. With Notes and Additions, Revised by Charles Whitehead. London: 1853. V. 72
Memoirs of Joseph Grimaldi. London: 1838. V. 68; 70
Memoirs of Joseph Grimaldi. Philadelphia: 1838. V. 70
Memoirs of Joseph Grimaldi. London: 1846. V. 70

GRIMALDI, STACEY
A Suit of Armour for Youth. London: 1824. V. 68; 70

GRIMALKIN
Cats. London: 1901. V. 70

GRIMBLE, A.
The Deer Forests of Scotland. 1896. V. 70
Deer Stalking and the Deer Forests of Scotland. 1901. V. 70
Highland Sport. 1894. V. 70
The Salmon Rivers of England and Wales. 1913. V. 73
The Salmon Rivers of Ireland. 1913. V. 73
The Salmon Rivers of Scotland. 1913. V. 73

GRIMES, ABSALOM
Absalom Grimes, Confederate Mail Runner. New Haven: 1926. V. 69

GRIMES, MARTHA
The Deer Leap. Boston: 1985. V. 69
The Dirty Duck. Boston and Toronto: 1984. V. 71
Help the Poor Struggler. Boston: 1985. V. 69
The Man with a Load of Mischief. Boston: 1981. V. 71
The Man with a Load of Mischief. Boston: 1991. V. 70
The Old Fox Deceiv'd. Boston: 1982. V. 70

GRIMES, RAY
300 Years in Victoris County. Victoria: 1968. V. 68; 70

GRIMKE, ANGELINA EMILY
Letters to Catherine E. Beecher in Reply to an Essay on Slavery and Abolitionism Addressed to A. E. Grimke. Boston: 1838. V. 73

GRIMKE, SARAH MOORE
Letters on the Equality of the Sexes and the Condition of Women. Boston: 1838. V. 69

GRIMKE, THOMAS
A Letter to the People of South Carolina. Charleston: 1832. V. 71

GRIMM, CLAUS
Frans Hals: the Complete Work. New York: 1990. V. 68

GRIMM, JACOB
Teutonic Mythology. London: 1882-1888. V. 70

GRIMM, THE BROTHERS
Grimm's Fairy Tales. London. V. 69
Grimm's Fairy Tales. London: 1909. V. 73
Grimm's Fairy Tales. Offenbach: 1931. V. 69
Grimm's Fairy Tales. London: 1933. V. 70; 73
Grimm's Fairy Tales. London: 1948. V. 71
Fairybus. London. V. 69

GRIMM, THE BROTHERS continued
Faithfull John. Llandogo: 1998. V. 71
Gammer Grethel; or German Fairy Tales. London: 1839. V. 69
Grimm Marchenschass Kinder- und hausmarchen. Berlin-Grunewald: 1923. V. 70
Grimm's Fairy Tales. London: 1902. V. 69
Grimms' Fairy Tales. New York: 1914. V. 73
Grimm's Household Tales. London: 1901. V. 70
Grimm's Tales for Children. London: 1910. V. 68
Hansel and Gretel and Other Stories. New York: 1925. V. 70
Household Stories from the Collection of the Brothers Grimm. London: 1882. V. 70
The Juniper Tree and Other Tales from Grimm. London: 1974. V. 72
Little Brother and Little Sister and Other Tales by the Brothers Grimm. London: 1917. V. 68
Marchenschatz. Berlin-Gruneald: 1927. V. 71
Three Gay Tales. New York: 1943. V. 72

GRIMM, WILHELM
Dear Mili. London: 1988. V. 72
Dear Mili. New York: 1988. V. 72

GRIMMELSHAUSEN, HANS JACOB CHRISTOFFEL VON
Simplicius Simplicissimus. London: 1964. V. 71

GRIMOARD, PHILIPPI HENRI, COMTE DE
Tableau Historique De La Guerre de la Revolution de France, Depuis son Commencement en 1792.... Paris: 1808. V. 72

GRIMSEHL, E.
A Textbook of Physics. London: 1932. V. 73

GRIMSHAW, ANNE
The Horse. 1982. V. 68

GRIMSHAW, BEATRICE
Vaiti of the Islands. New York: 1908. V. 70

GRIMSHAW, JAMES
Robert Penn Warren - a Descriptive Bibliography. Charlottesville: 1981. V. 68

GRIMSHAW, JOHN
A Report on the Repairs Given to Wearmouth Bridge, in the Year 1805. Sunderland: 1818. V. 68
Specification of a Patent Granted to John Grimshaw of Bishopwearmouth, in the County of Durham, Rope-Maker for an Improved Method of Making Flat Ropes by Machinery.... Bishopwearmouth: 1822. V. 69

GRIMWADE, A. G.
The Queen's Silver. London: 1953. V. 72

GRIMWOOD, ELISE
Replay. New York: 1986. V. 68

GRIMWOOD, KEN
Breakthrough. Garden City: 1976. V. 68; 71
Elise. Garden City: 1979. V. 68; 71

GRINDON, LEO HARTLEY
Country Rambles, and Manchester Walks and Wild Flowers. Manchester: 1882. V. 73
Lancashire. London: 1892. V. 73
Manchester Banks and Bankers: Historical, Biographical and Anecdotal. Manchester: 1878. V. 71
The Manchester Flora: A Descriptive List of the Plants Growing Wild Within Eighteen Miles of Manchester, with Notices of the Plants Commonly Cultivated in Gardens Preceded by an Introduction to Botany. London: 1859. V. 73
Summer Rambles in Cheshire, Derbyshire, Lancashire, and Yorkshire. Manchester: 1866. V. 73

GRINNELL, GEORGE BIRD
American Game-Bird Shooting. New York: 1910. V. 73
Beyond the Old Frontier. New York: 1913. V. 73
The Cheyenne Indians. New Haven: 1923. V. 69
The Cheyenne Indians. New Haven: 1924. V. 69
The Cheyenne Indians: Their History and Ways of Life. New York: 1962. V. 72
The Fighting Cheyenne. Norman: 1915. V. 72
The Fighting Cheyennes. New York: 1915. V. 69
Hunting and Conservation. The Book of the Boone and Crockett Club. 1925. V. 69; 70; 73
The North American Indians of Today. London: 1900. V. 68
The Passing of the Great West, Selected Papers of George B. Grinnell. New York: 1972. V. 72
The Story of The Indian. New York: 1895. V. 72
Two Great Scouts and Their Pawnee Battalion. Cleveland: 1928. V. 71; 73
When Buffalo Ran. Hew Haven: 1923. V. 70
When Buffalo Ran. New Haven: 1932. V. 69

GRINNELL, J.
Animal Life in the Yoesmite, an Account of the Mammals, Birds, Reptiles and Amphibians in a Cross Section of the Sierra Nevada. Berkeley: 1924. V. 72
A Distributional Summation of the Ornithology of Lower California. Berkeley: 1928. V. 73
The Game Birds of California. Berkeley: 1918. V. 69

GRISCOM, JOHN
A Year in Europe. Comprising a Journal of Observations in England, Scotland, Ireland, France, Switzerland, the North of Italy and Holland in 1818 and 1819. New York: 1823. V. 72

GRISCOM, L.
The Warblers of America. New York: 1957. V. 72

GRISHAM, JOHN
The Chamber. New York: 1994. V. 68; 71
The Firm. New York: 1991. V. 68; 69; 70; 71; 73
A Painted House. New York: 2001. V. 70
The Pelican Brief. New York: 1992. V. 68
A Time to Kill. New York: 1993. V. 68; 71

GRISSO, W. D.
From Where the Sun Now Stands. Santa Fe: 1963. V. 68

GRISWOLD, DON L.
The Carbonate Camp Called Leadville. Denver: 1951. V. 73

GRISWOLD, FRANCIS
The Tides of Malvern. New York: 1930. V. 69

GRISWOLD, RUFUS WILMOT
The Female Poets of America. Philadelphia: 1854. V. 69; 73

GRITSCH, CONRAD
Quadragesimale. Nuremberg: 1479. V. 69

GROBELI, RENE
Magie Der Schiene. Zurich: 1949. V. 68

GROBER, KARL
Children's Toys of Bygone Days. London: 1928. V. 70; 72

GROCE, GEORGE
The New York Historical Society's Dictionary of Artists in America 1564-1860. New Haven;: 1957. V. 70

GRODDECK, GEORG
The Book Of The It. Psychoanalytic Letters To A Friend. London: 1935. V. 72

GROENEWOUD, C.
Bivariate Normal Offset Circle Probabilty Tables with Offset Ellipse Transformations. New York: 1967. V. 70

GROENING, MATT
Life in Hell. Los Angeles: 1983. V. 72

GROENVELT, JOHN
The Rudiments of Physick Clearly and Accurately Describ'd and Explain'd, in the Most Easy and Familiar Manner.... 1753. V. 73

GROGAN, EMMETT
Ringolevio - a Life Played for Keeps. Boston: 1972. V. 71

GROHMANN, WILL
Wassily Kandinsky. Leipzig: 1924. V. 69

GROLIER, JEAN
The Library of Jean Grolier. New York: 1971. V. 73

GROLIER CLUB, NEW YORK
Books and Prints, Past and Future. New York: 1984. V. 68
BR Today: A Selection of His Books with Comments. New York: 1982. V. 68
Catalogue of an Exhibition of Illuminated and Painted Manuscripts, together with a few Early Printed Books with Illuminations.... New York: 1892. V. 70
Catalogue of An Exhibition of the Works of Charles Dickens. New York: 1913. V. 68
Catalogue of the Works of Rudyard Kipling Exhibited at the Grolier Club. New York: 1930. V. 70
Effigies of the Most Famous English Writers from Chaucer to Johnson. New York: 1891. V. 70
Grolier 75. A Biographical Retrospective to Celebrate the Seventy- Fifth Anniversary of the Grolier Club in New York. New York: 1959. V. 69; 71
The Grolier Club 1884-1984. New York: 1984. V. 68

GROMAIRE, MARCEL
Gromaire Exhibition of Paintings. New York: 1949. V. 69

GRONOVIUS, JOHANN FRIEDRICH
Flora Orientalis sive Recensio Plantarum, Quas Botanicorum Coryphaeus Leonhardus Rauwolffus.... Leiden: 1755. V. 72
Flora Virginia Exhibens Plantas Quas V. C. Johannes Clayton in Virginia Observait Atque Collegit. Leiden: 1743. V. 68

GRONOW, REES HOWELL
Recollections and Ancecdotes of the Camp, the Court and the Clubs. London: 1870. V. 68

GRONTVED, J.
The Pteriodophyta and Spermatophyta of Iceland. Copenhagen and London: 1942. V. 72

GROOM, ARTHUR
Gran'Pop's Annual. London: 1950. V. 72

GROOM, G. LAURENCE
The Singing Sword: A Poem. New York: 1929. V. 72

GROOM, RICHARD
A Defence of Our Laws Against Usury, by an Inquiry into the Causes and Consequences of the Several Reductions in the Rate of Interest in England.... London: 1826. V. 70

GROOM, WINSTON
Better Times than These. New York: 1978. V. 70; 72
Forrest Gump. Garden City: 1986. V. 68; 69; 70; 71; 72

GROSBOIS, CHARLES
Shunga: Images of Spring, Essay on Erotic Elements in Japanese Art. Geneva: 1964. V. 70; 72; 73

GROSE, DONALD
The Flora of Wiltshire... (with) supplement. Devizes: 1957-1975. V. 73

GROSE, FRANCIS
The Account of Pythagoras's School in Cambridge.... Cambridge: 1783?. V. 70
The Antiquarian Repertory. London: 1775. V. 71; 72
A Classical Dictionary of the Vulgar Tongue. London: 1885. V. 71
Military Antiquities Respecting a History of the English Army. (with) A Treatise on Ancient Armour and Weapons. London: 1801. V. 68
A Provincial Glossary.... London: 1811. V. 71
Rules for Drawing Caricaturas.... London: 1791. V. 73
Rules for Drawing Caricaturas.... London: 1800. V. 69

GROSECLOSE, DAVID A.
James Michener. A Bibliography. Austin: 1996. V. 71; 73

GROSLEY, M.
A Tour to London; or, New Observations on England and Its Inhabitants. London: 1772. V. 69

GROSLEY, PIERRE JEAN
Londres. a Lausanne, but Paris: 1770. V. 71; 72
Observations sur l'Italie et sur les Italiens. (with) Les Italiens, Ouvrage Traduit de l'Anglois: Pour servir de Supplement aux Observations sur l'Italie & sur les Italiens. Amsterdam and Paris: 1774. V. 72

GROSS, ALEXANDER, MRS.
Happy Billy Bunny. London: 1919. V. 69

GROSS, ANTHONY
The Very Rich Hours of Le Boulve. Cambridge: 1980. V. 73

GROSS, H. S.
Climbs on Great Gable: Rock Climbing in Borrowdale. London: 1925. V. 69

GROSS, ROBERT E.
The Surgery of Infancy and Childhood. Philadelphia: 1953. V. 71
Surgical Treatment for Abnormalities of the Heart and Great Vessels. Springfield: 1947. V. 68

GROSS, SAMUEL DAVID
Autobiography of.... Philadelphia: 1887. V. 70
A Practical Treatise on Foreign Bodies in the Air Passages. Philadelphia: 1854. V. 70; 71

GROSSE, KARL, MARQUIS OF
The Horrid Mysteries. London: 1927. V. 70

GROSSMAN, MARY LOUISE
Birds of Prey of the World. New York: 1964. V. 69

GROSSMITH, GEORGE
The Diary of a Nobody. Bristol and London: 1892. V. 70; 73

GROSVENOR, CAROLINE
The Thornton Device. London: 1907. V. 68

GROSVENOR, RICHARD
Extracts from the Journal.... Chester: 1830. V. 72

GROTE, GEORGE
Aristotle. London: 1872. V. 72
Speech of George Grote, Esq. M.P. Delivered April 24th, 1833, in the House of Commons, on Moving for the Introduction of the Vote by Ballot at Elections. London: 1833. V. 71
Speech...Delivered April 25th 1833 in the House of Commons, on Moving for the Introduction of the Vote by Ballot at Elections. London: 1833. V. 71

GROTE, JOHN
An Examination of the Utilitarian Philosophy.... Cambridge: 1870. V. 71

GROTIUS, HUGO
Dissertationes de Studiis Instituendis. Amsterdam apud Ludovicum: 1645. V. 71
Of the Law of Warre and Peace. London: 1654. V. 68
Poemata Collecta Olim a fratre ejus Giul. Grotio.... London: 1639. V. 72
The Truth of the Christian Religion.... Oxford: 1818. V. 70

GROTIUS, WILLIAM
De Principis Juris Naturalis Enchiridion. Hagae-Comitis: 1667. V. 68; 70; 73

GROTTA, DANIEL
Architect of the Middle Earth. 1992. V. 72

GROUNDS, JOHN CURETON
Trail Dust of the Southwest. Maryvale: 1977. V. 73

GROUT, A. J.
Moss Flora of North America North of Mexico. Newfane & Staten Island: 1936-1934. V. 69
Mosses with Hand-Lens and Microscope.... New York: 1903. V. 71

GROUT, LEWIS
Zulu-Land; or Life Among the Zulu-Kafirs of Natal and Zulu-Land, South Africa. Philadelphia: 1864. V. 68

GROVE, GEORGE
Grove's Dictionary of Music and Musicians. New York: 1960. V. 69

GROVE, JOHN
Clash of Arms, Stories of Chivalry by Famous Writers. New York: 1931. V. 71

GROVER, EULALIE OSGOOD
Mother Goose. Chicago: 1915. V. 71
The Overall Boys. Chicago: 1930. V. 70

The Sunbonnet Babies' Book. Chicago: 1902. V. 70

GROVER, RAY
English Cameo Glass. NY: 1980. V. 72

GROVES, ERNEST R.
Sex in Marriage. New York: 1938. V. 69

GRUBB, DAVIS
The Night of the Hunter. New York: 1953. V. 71

GRUBB, E. H.
The Potato, A Compilation of Information from Every Available Source. Garden City: 1912. V. 72

GRUBB, MARY B.
Our Alphabet of Toys. Cleveland: 1932. V. 71

GRUBB, SARAH
Some Account of the Life and Religious Labours of Sarah Grubb. Trenton: 1795. V. 69; 70; 73
Some Account Of The Life and Religious Labours of Sarah Grubb. London: 1796. V. 72

GRUBB, W. BARBROOKE
A Church in the Wilds. London: 1914. V. 71

GRUBER, FRANK
The Buffalo Box. New York: 1942. V. 70
The Hungry Dog. New York: 1941. V. 72
The Lock and the Key. New York: 1948. V. 69
Simon Lash, Private Detective. New York: 1941. V. 69; 71
The Talking Clock. New York: 1946. V. 71

GRUDIN, LOUIS
Mr. Eliot Among the Nightingales. Paris: 1932. V. 72

GRUELLE, JOHNNY
All About Cinderella. New York: 1916. V. 70
All About Little Red Riding Hood. New York: 1916. V. 70
Ann's Magical Wishes. Joliet: 1928. V. 72
Beloved Belindy. Chicago: 1926. V. 70; 73
Eddie Elephant. Joliet: 1921. V. 70
Friendly Fairies. Chicago: 1919. V. 70; 72
Johnny Gruelle's Golden Book. Chicago: 1929. V. 70
The Little Brown Bear. Chicago: 1920. V. 70
Little Sunny Stories. Joliet: 1919. V. 70
The Magical Land of Noom with Sundry and Mondry. Chicago: 1922. V. 70; 73
Marcella: a Raggedy Ann Story. Chicago: 1929. V. 70
My Very Own Fairy Stories. Chicago: 1917. V. 70
Orphan Annie Story Book. Indianapolis: 1921. V. 70; 73
The Paper Dragon. Joliet: 1926. V. 70
Raggedy Ann and Andy and the Camel with the Wrinkled Knees. Chicago: 1924. V. 70
Raggedy Ann and Andy and the Camel with the Wrinkled Knees. Joliet: 1924. V. 72
Raggedy Ann and the Golden Ring. Indianapolis: 1961. V. 70
Raggedy Ann and the Happy Toad and Raggedy Ann in the Garden. Sandusky: 1944. V. 70
Raggedy Ann and the Laughing Brook. Springfield: 1943. V. 70
Raggedy Ann and the Laughing Brook and Raggedy Ann Helps Grandpa Hoppergrass. Sandusky: 1944. V. 70
Raggedy Ann and the Slippery Slide. Akron: 1947. V. 70
Raggedy Ann at the End of the Rainbow. Akron: 1947. V. 70
Raggedy Ann Goes Sailing. Springfield: 1941. V. 70
Raggedy Ann Helps Grandpa Hoppergrass. Springfield: 1940. V. 70
Raggedy Ann in the Deep, Deep Woods. Joliet: 1930. V. 70
Raggedy Ann in the Garden. New York: 1946. V. 70
Raggedy Ann in the Magic Book. New York. V. 70
Raggedy Ann Stories. Joliet: 1918. V. 70
Raggedy Ann's Fairy Stories. Chicago: 1928. V. 70
Raggedy Ann's Magical Wishes. Chicago: 1928. V. 70
Raggedy Ann's Sunny Songs. Chicago: 1929. V. 70
Raggedy Ann's Sunny Songs. New York: 1930. V. 71; 73
Wooden Willie. Joliet: 1927. V. 70; 73

GRUFFYDD, W. J.
Caniadau. Montgomery shire: 1932. V. 72

GRUMBACH, DORIS
Chamber Music. New York: 1979. V. 72
The Spoil of the Flowers. Garden City: 1962. V. 70; 71

GRUND, JOHANN GOTTFRIED
Afbildning af Nordmands-Dalen, i den Kongelige Lyst Hauge ved Fredensborg. Copenhagen: 1773. V. 68; 70; 72

GRUNDY, C. R.
Catalogue of the Pictures and Drawings in the Collection of Frederick John Nettlefold. London: 1933-1938. V. 69; 72

GRUNDY, ISOBEL
Samuel Johnson and the Scale of Greatness. 1986. V. 69

GRUNDY, JOHN
The Report of Mess. John Grundy, Langley Edwards and John Smeaton, Engineers, Concerning the Present Ruinous State and Condition of the River Witham.... Lincoln: 1761. V. 71

GRUNDY, JOHN continued
A Scheme for Restoring and Making Perfect the Navigation of the River Witham from Boston to Lincoln and Also for Draining the Low-Lands and Fenns Contiguous Thereto. Stanford?: 1744. V. 71

GRUNER, LOUIS
Decorations de Palais et d'Eglises en Italie Peintes a Fresque ou Executes en Stuc, Dans le Cours du XVeme et du XVI eme Siecle.... Paris: 1854. V. 70; 72

GRUNER, LUDWIG
I Mosaici Della Cupola Nella Cappella Chigiana S. Maria del Popolo in Roma Inventati da Rafaelle.... Rome: 1839. V. 70

GRUNSKY, CARL E.
Stockton Boyhood, Being The Reminiscences Carl Ewald Grunsky, Which Covers the Years From 1855 to 1877. 1959. V. 71

GRUPEN, CHRISTIAN ULRICH
Tractatio de Uxore Romana cum Ea Quae in Manum Convenit, Farre, Coemtione et Usu, tum, Illa, Quae Uxor Tantummodo Habetaur. Hanover: 1727. V. 73

THE GUARDIAN. London: 1756. V. 73

GUARE, JOHN
Cop-Out, Muzeeka, Home Fires: Three Plays by John Guare. New York: 1969. V. 71
Six Degrees of Separation. New York: 1990. V. 68; 70; 72

GUARESCHI, GIOVANNI
The Little World of Don Camillo. London: 1951. V. 72

GUARINI, BATTISTA
Il Pastor Fido. Londra: 1718. V. 72

GUBA, E. F.
Monograph of Monochaetia and Pestolotia. Cambridge: 1961. V. 71

GUBB, A. S.
The Flora of Algeria. London: 1909. V. 72

GUDGER, E. W.
The Breeding Habits, Reproductive Organs and External Embryonic Development of Chlamydoselachus.... New York: 1940. V. 73

GUENEBAULT, J. H.
Natural History of the Negro Race. Charleston: 1837. V. 71

GUENTHER, CONRAD
Darwinism and the Problems of a Life. London: 1906. V. 69

GUERNSEY, CHARLES A.
Wyoming Cowboy Days. New York: 1936. V. 69; 71

GUERNSEY, SAMUEL JAMES
Explorations in Northeastern Arizona. Cambridge, MA: 1931. V. 72

GUERNSEY, WILLIAM JEFFERSON
The Homoeopathic Therapeutics of Haemorrhoids. Philadelphia: 1892. V. 71

GUERRA, FRANCISCO
American Medical Bibliography 1639-1783. A Chronological Catalogue and Critical and Bibliographical Study of Books...printed in the Present Territory of the United States of America During British Dominion and the Revolutionary War. New York: 1962. V. 72

GUERSANT, PAUL LOUIS BENOIT
Surgical Diseases of Infants and Children. Philadelphia: 1873. V. 68; 69; 71

GUEST, BARBARA
Musicality. June Felter, Drawings. 1988. V. 73
Outside of This. Calais: 1999. V. 73

GUEST, EDWIN
A History of English Rhythms. London: 1838. V. 72

GUETTARD, J. E.
Observations sur les Plantes. 1747. V. 69

GUEULLETTE, THOMAS SIMON
Mogul Tales, or the Dreams of Men Awake.... London: 1743. V. 73

GUEVARA, ANTONIO DE
Libro Llamado Menosprecio de Corte y Alabanca de Aldea.... Lyons: 1591. V. 69
The Praise and Happiness of the Countrie-Life. Newtown: 1938. V. 71

GUGGENHEIM, PEGGY
Out of This Century. New York: 1946. V. 69; 72

GUGGISBERG, C. A. W.
Simba; The Life of the Lion. 1963. V. 70; 72

GUGLIELMINI, DOMENICO
Opera Omnia Mathematica Hydraulica, Medica, et Physica Assessit vita Autoris. Geneva: 1719. V. 68

GUICCIARDINI, FRANCESCO
Guicciardini's Account of the Ancient Flemish School of Painting. Bloomsbury: 1795. V. 68

GUICHES, GUSTAVE
La Pudeur de Sodome. Paris: 1888. V. 69

GUIDE a la Tour de Londres; son Histoire et des Objects de Curisoties et des Armures. Londres. V. 68

GUIDE Book to N.W. North Carolina. Salem: 1878. V. 73

THE GUIDE Gift Book. 1950. V. 72

A GUIDE Through the Royal Porcelain Works Worcester.... Worcester: 1875. V. 71

GUIDE To Killarney and Glengariff. 1835. V. 73

GUIDE to Killarney and Glengariff. 1935. V. 69

GUIDE to the City of New-York.... New York: 1840. V. 68

A GUIDE to the English Lake District, Intended principally for the Use of Pedestrians. London: 1865. V. 71

A GUIDE to the Unprotected in Every-Day Matters Relating to Property and Income. London: 1864. V. 71

THE GUIDE to Trade. The Plumber, Painter and Glazier. London: 1845. V. 68

GUIDI, GUIDO
Chirurgia e Graeco in Latinum Conversa Vivo Vidio Florentino Interprete. Paris: 1544. V. 70

GUIDO DE MONTE ROCHERII
Manipulus Curatorum. Venice: 1507. V. 73

GUIDOTT, THOMAS
Anglo-Britanni, De Thermis Britannicis Tractatus. Londini: 1691. V. 70
A Collection of Treatises Relating to the City and Waters of Bath. 1725. V. 71

GUIGET, JEAN
Virginia Woolf and Her Works. London: 1965. V. 70

GUILBERT, ALINE
Prieres. Fac-simile du gau 15 Siecle. Paris: 1838. V. 69

GUILD, GEORGE B.
A Brief Narrative of the Fourth Tennessee Cavalry Regiment. Wheeler's Corps, Army of Tennessee. Nashville: 1913. V. 69; 70

GUILD, THELMA S.
Kit Carson, a Pattern for Heroes. Lincoln: 1984. V. 73

GUILELMUS, ARCHBISHOP OF TYRE
The History of Godefrey of Boloyne and of the Conquest of Iherusalem. 1893. V. 72

GUILFORD, HOWARD A.
High Jinks in Jingle Land. Minneapolis: 1922. V. 72

GUILLAIN, GEORGES
J. M. Charcot 1825-1893. His Life and Work. London: 1959. V. 68

GUILLEMARD, FRANCIS HENRY HILL
The Cruise of the Marchesa to Kamschatka and New Guinea. London: 1886. V. 68; 70; 71
The Cruise of the Marchesa to Kamschatka and New Guinea. London: 1889. V. 68
Cruise of the Marchesa to Kamschatka and New Guinea. New York: 1889. V. 70

GUILLEMIN, J. B. A.
Icones Lithographicae Plantarum Australasiae Rariorum. Paris: 1827. V. 69

GUILLEN, NICOLAS
Selected Poems. Cuba: 1972. V. 70
Tengo. Detroit: 1974. V. 73

GUILLERMUS, EPISCOPUS PARISIENSIS
De Sacramentis. Cur Deus Homo. De Poenitentia. Nuremberg: 1497. V. 69

GUILLET, EDWIN C.
Early Life in Upper Canada. Toronto: 1933. V. 73

GUILLIAM, JOHN
The Bower of Bliss; with Other Amatory Poems.... London: 1814. V. 69

GUILLIAUD, CLAUDE
In Canonicas Apostolorvm Septem Epistolas. Paris: 1548. V. 70

GUINEY, LOUISE IMOGEN
Goose-Quill Papers. Boston: 1885. V. 73
A Roadside Harp. New York: 1893. V. 73

GUINN, J. M.
A History of California and an Extended History of Its Southern Coast. Los Angeles: 1907. V. 70
A History of California and Extended History of Los Angeles and Environs. Los Angeles: 1915. V. 73

GUINNESS, ALEC
My Name Escapes Me - The Diary of a Retiring Actor. London: 1996. V. 70
A Positively Final Appearance - a Journal 1996-1998. London: 1999. V. 70

GUINNESS, BRYAN
A Fugue of Cinderellas. 1956. V. 69
The Story of Priscilla and the Prawn. London: 1960. V. 70

GUINNESS, DESMOND
Irish Houses and Castles. 1971. V. 69; 70

GUINNESS, GERALDINE
In the Far East: Letters from Geraldine Guinness in China. London: 1889. V. 72

GUINNESS LTD.
Alice Versary. The Guinness Birthday Book. London: 1959. V. 71
Can This Be Beeton? A Guinness Gallimaufry. London: 1956. V. 71
My Goodness! My Gilbert and Sullivan!. London: 1961. V. 71
Untopical Songs. Accompanied by Guinness. London: 1959. V. 71
What Will They Think of Next? A Guinness Inventory. London: 1960. V. 71

GUIZOT, FRANCOIS PIERRE GUILLAUME
De la Democratie en France. (Janvier 1849). Paris: 1849. V. 71
The History of France, from the Earliest Times to the Year 1789 (continued to 1848). London: 1883-1882-. V. 71

GULF COAST RESEARCH LABORATORY
Gulf Research Reports. Ocean Springs: 1961-1997. V. 72

GULICK, BILL
Bend of the Snake. Boston: 1950. V. 71

GULICK, PAUL
Strings of Steel. New York: 1926. V. 70

GULL, C. RANGER
A Butterfly on the Wheel. New York: 1912. V. 70
The Woman in the Case. London: 1909. V. 69; 73

GULLAND, W. G.
Chinese Porcelain. London: 1911. V. 73

GULLIVER, LEMUEL, PSEUD.
The Eo-Nauts, or The Spirit of Delusion, a Serio, Comico, Logical, Eulogical, Lyrical, Satirical Poem.... London: 1813. V. 71

GULLY, JOHN
New Zealand Scenery Chromolithographed after Original Water-Color Drawings by John Gully. London: 1877. V. 73

GULSTON, JOSEPHA HEATH
The Goblin's Moonlight Walk. London: 1844. V. 73

GUM-Blossom Babies. Sydney: 1916. V. 72

GUMMER, ELLIS
Dickens' Works in Germany 1837-1937. Oxford: 1940. V. 70

GUMUCHIAN, Les Livres de l'Enfance: a Catalogue of 15th to 19th Century Nursery Books. London: 1985. V. 72

GUNCKEL, J. E.
Studies of Development in Long Shoots and Short Shoots of Ginko Biloba. 1946-1949. V. 72

GUNN, EDWIN
The Great House, Leyton. 1903. V. 71

GUNN, HUGH
Empire Big Game. 1925. V. 70; 72; 73

GUNN, JAMES E.
This Fortress World. New York: 1955. V. 71

GUNN, JOHN M.
Schat-Chen: History Traditions and Narratives of the Queres Indians of Laguna and Acoma. Albuquerque: 1916. V. 73

GUNN, THOM
Collected Poems. London: 1993. V. 72; 73
Death's Door. 1989. V. 69; 73
A Geography. Iowa City: 1966. V. 73
The Hurtless Trees. New York: 1986. V. 73
Mandrakes. 1973. V. 68
Mandrakes. London: 1973. V. 69
The Missed Beat. Newark: 1976. V. 73
Moly. London: 1971. V. 69; 70
Old Stories. New York: 1992. V. 73
Sidewalks. New York: 1985. V. 73
Songbook. New York: 1973. V. 71
Sunlight. New York: 1969. V. 73
Touch. London: 1967. V. 69

GUNN, W.
Cartonensia: or, an Historical and Critical Account of the Tapestries, in the Palace of the Vatican.... London: 1832. V. 72

GUNNISON, J. W.
The Mormons or Latter Day Saints in the Valley of the Great Salt Lake. London: 1852. V. 68; 73

GUNTER, ARCHIBALD CLAVERING
Baron Montez of Panama and Paris: a Novel. London: 1893. V. 68
Baron Montez of Panama and Paris: a Novel. London: 1894. V. 68
Don Balasco of Key West. London: 1900?. V. 68
The First of the English. London: 1895. V. 68
The King's Stockbroker.... London: 1894. V. 68
Miss Dividends: a Novel. London: 1892. V. 68
Mr. Potter of Texas. London: 1888. V. 68
That Frenchman!. London: 1889. V. 68

GUNTHER, A.
Catalogue of the Fishes in the Collection of the British Museum. 1937. V. 69
Catalogue of the Fishes of the British Museum. London: 1964. V. 69

GUNTHER, A. C. L. G.
The Gigantic Land-Tortoises (Living and Extinct) In the Collection of the British Museum. London: 1877. V. 73

GUNTHER, R. T.
Early Science in Oxford. Volume III. Oxford: 1925. V. 68
Early Science in Oxford. Volume XI - Oxford Colleges and Their Men of Science. Oxford: 1937. V. 68

GUNTON, SYMON
The History of the Church of Peterburgh: Wherein the Most Remarkable Things Concerning the Place, from the First Foundation Thereof. 1686. V. 70

GUPPY, H. B.
Observations of a Naturalist in the Pacific Between 1896 and 1899. Volume I. Vanua Levu, Fiji. 1903. V. 73
The Solomon Islands And Their Natives. London: 1887. V. 72

GUPTILL, A. B.
Haynes' Guide to Yellowstone Park. St. Paul: 1896. V. 72

GUPTILL, ARTHUR L.
Sketching and Rendering in Pencil. New York: 1922. V. 68

GURALNICK, PETER
Careless Love: the Unmaking of Elvis Presley. Boston: 1999. V. 70
The Listener's Guide To The Blues. 1982. V. 72
Searching for Robert Johnson. New York: 1989. V. 68; 72

GURGANUS, ALLAN
Oldest Living Confederate Widow Tells All. New York: 1989. V. 68; 71; 72; 73
Plays Well With Others. New York: 1997. V. 68
The Practical Heart. Rocky Mount: 1993. V. 68
White People. New York: 1990. V. 73
White People. New York: 1991. V. 69

GURILEV, A.
(Title in Russian): Izbrannye Pesni, II Sbornik. Muzgiz: 1936. V. 68

GURLT, ERNEST
Geschichte der Chirurgie und Ihrer Ausubung Volkschirurgie - Alterthum Mittelalter- Renaissance. Berlin: 1898. V. 70

GURNEY, J. H.
The Gannet. 1913. V. 69
Rambles of a Naturalist in Egypt and Other Countries. 1876. V. 72
Rambles of a Naturalist in Eygpt and Other Countries. London: 1876. V. 68; 73

GURNEY, JOSEPH JOHN
Memoirs Of Joseph John Gurney. Norwich: 1855. V. 72
Memoirs...with Selections from His Journal and Correspondence. Norwich: 1854. V. 68; 72

GURNEY, PRISCILLA
Hymns Selected from Various Authors, for the Use of Young Persons. Philadelphia: 1826. V. 69

GURNEY, R.
The British Freshwater Copepoda. London: 1931-1933. V. 73

GURNEY, THOMAS
Brachygraphy: or Short-Writing.... London: 1752. V. 70
The Trichologists' Pharmacopoeia. London: 1889. V. 71

GUSTAFSON, RALPH
The Golden Chalice. London: 1935. V. 73

GUTCH, JOHN MATHEW
A Lytell Geste of Robyn Hode and His Meiny.... San Francisco: 1932. V. 70

GUTERSON, DAVID
The Country Ahead of Us, the Country Behind. New York: 1989. V. 68; 69; 70; 71; 73
The Country Ahead of Us, the Country Behind. London: 1996. V. 68; 72
East of the Mountains. New York: 1999. V. 70; 72
Snow Falling On Cedars. New York, San Diego & London: 1994. V. 68; 69; 70; 71; 72; 73
Snow Falling on Cedars. London: 1995. V. 68

GUTHE, C. E.
Pueblo Pottery Making, a Study at the Village of San Ildefonso. Andover: 1925. V. 69
Pueblo Pottery Making, a Study at the Village of San Ildefonso. Mansfield Centre: 2000. V. 69

GUTHEIM, F.
On Architecture; Selected Writings 1894-1940. New York: 1941. V. 68

GUTHRIE, A. B.
The Big Sky. New York: 1947. V. 71
Fair Land, Fair Land. Boston: 1982. V. 71
The Genuine Article. Boston: 1977. V. 71
Playing Catch-Up. Boston: 1985. V. 71
The Way West. New York: 1949. V. 71
Wild Pitch. Boston: 1973. V. 71

GUTHRIE, DOUGLAS
A History of Medicine. London: 1945. V. 70; 71
A Short History of the Royal Society Club of Edinburgh. Edinburgh: 1962. V. 68

GUTHRIE, JAMES
Divine Discontent. 1913. V. 68
His Book of Bookplates, Consisting of 24 Original Designs. Edinburgh: 1907. V. 69

GUTHRIE, MARIA
A Tour Performed in the Years 1795-1796, through the Taurida, or Crimea, the Ancient Kingdom of Bosphorous, the Once Powerful Republic of Tauric Cherson.... London: 1802. V. 70; 72

GUTHRIE, THOMAS ANSTEY
Mr. Punch's Pocket Ibsen. London: 1893. V. 68

GUTHRIE, TYRONE
A New Theatre. New York: 1964. V. 69
Squirrel's Cage, and Two Other Microphone Plays. London: 1931. V. 70

GUTHRIE, W. K. C.
A History of Greek Philosophy. Cambridge: 1962-1965. V. 68

GUTMAN, RICHARD J. S.
American Diner. New York: 1979. V. 68

GUTTERY, D. R.
From Broad-Glass to Cut Crystal. London: 1956. V. 72

GUTZLAFF, CHARLES
Journal of Three Voyages Along the Coast of China in 1831, 1832 and 1833. 1834. V. 72

GUY, JOSEPH
Birmingham and Its Vicinity. Birmingham: 1821. V. 69

GUY, ROSA
Bird at My Window. Philadelphia & New York: 1966. V. 68
Children of Longing. New York: 1970. V. 72

GUY DE CHAULIAC
Chirurgia, Nunc Iterum Non Mediocri Studio Atque Diligentia a Pluribus mendis Purgata.... Lugduni: 1559. V. 72

GUYOMAR, PIERRE MARIE AUGUSTIN
Le Partisan de l'Egalite Politique Entre Les Individus, ou Probeleme Tres Important de l'Egalite en Fait. Paris: 1793. V. 73

GUYON, CLAUDE MARIE
Histoire des Amazones Anciennes et Modernes, Enriche de Medailles. Paris: 1740. V. 73

GUYONNEAU DE PAMBOUR, FRANCOIS MARIE, COMTE
A Practical Treatise on Locomotive Engines.... London: 1836. V. 68
Practical Treatise on Locomotive Engines.... Philadelphia: 1836. V. 73
A Practical Treatise on Locomotive Engines.... London: 1840. V. 68

GUYOT, EDME
Nouveau sisteme du Microsome, ou Traite de la Nature de l'Homme. The Hague: 1727. V. 73
Nouvelles Recreations Physiques et Mathematiques. Paris: 1856. V. 68

GUY'S Porridge Pot: a Poem, in Twenty Four Books. Oxford: 1808. V. 73

GUY'S Porridge Pot; with the Dun Cow Roasted Whole; an Epic Poem in Twenty-Five Books. Part I. Oxford: 1809. V. 73

GWALTNEY, FRANCIS IRBY
The Day the Century Ended. New York: 1955. V. 71

GWILT, JOSEPH
An Encyclopaedia of Architecture. London: 1859. V. 71

GWILYM, DAFYDD
Houses of Leaves: Poems. 1993. V. 71

GWYNN, DENIS
The Struggle for Catholic Emancipation 1750-1829. 1928. V. 69

GWYNN, FREDERICK L.
Sturge Moore and the Life of Art. London: 1952. V. 71

GWYNN, JOHN
London and Westminster Improved. London: 1766. V. 72

GWYNN, STEPHEN
The Anvil of War - Letters Between F. S. Oliver and His Brother, 1914-1918. London: 1936. V. 69
The Famous Cities of Ireland. Dublin & London: 1915. V. 73

GWYNN, TONY
The Art of Hitting. New York: 1998. V. 70

GWYNN BROWNE, A.
F.S.P. - An N.C.O.'s Description of His and Others' First Six Months of War. London: 1942. V. 69

GYLLENSVARD, BO
The World's Great Collections-Oriental Ceramics: Volume i. Museum of Far Eastern Antiquities. Tokyo: 1982. V. 73

GYNGELL, DUDLEY S. HAWTREY
Armourers Marks. London: 1959. V. 68

GYSIN, BRION
The Process. Garden City: 1969. V. 71

H

H., C.
Abbrege de l'Histoire Francoyse, avec les Effigies des Roys, Tirees des plus Rares & Excellentz Cabinetz de la France. Paris: 1585. V. 70

H., M. B.
Home Truths for Home Peace, or Muddle Defeated. London: 1852. V. 68

H., M. C.
Reform. Letter the First; and Possibly the Last. Dublin: 1831. V. 71

HAAB, O.
Atlas and Epitome of Ophthalmoscopy and Ophthalmoscopic Diagnosis. Philadelphia and London: 1901. V. 72
Atlas of the External Diseases of the Eye. Philadelphia and London: 1902. V. 72

HAAS, ERNST
In Germany. New York: 1977. V. 68

HABBERTON, JOHN
Helen's Babies with Some Account of Their Ways.... London: 1877. V. 68; 71

HABEGGER, JERRYLL
Sourcebook of Modern Furniture. New York: 1989. V. 72

HABELER, P.
Everest. Impossible Victory. 1979. V. 71; 73

HABERER & CO.
Cino Motor Cars. Cincinnati: 1911. V. 69

HABERLIN, H. K.
Coiled Basketry in British Columbia and Surrounding Region. Washington: 1928. V. 70

HABERLY, LOYD
Anne Boleyn and Other Poems. Newtown: 1934. V. 68; 70; 71
The Crowning Year and Other Poems. Dorset: 1937. V. 68

HABERMAN, JOHN
The Christian's Companion.... Harrisburg: 1846. V. 71

HABERSHAM, ANNA WYLLY
Journal of Anna Wylly Habersham. Darien: 1964. V. 70

HABERSHON, MATTHEW HENRY
Chapeltown Researches, Archaeological and Historical;. 1893. V. 73

HACHISJUKA, M. U.
A Handbook of the Birds of Iceland. London: 1927. V. 73

HACK, MARIA
Stories of Animals Intended for Childen Between Five and Seven Years Old. 1837. V. 72

HACKETT, CECIL J.
Boomerang Leg and Yaws in Australian Aborigines. London: 1936. V. 68

HACKETT, CHARLES WILSON
New Spain and the Anglo-American West. Lanchester: 1932. V. 69
Revolt of the Pueblo Indians of New Mexico and Otermin's Attempted Reconquest 1680-1682. Albuquerque: 1942. V. 68

HACKETT, JOHN
Select and Remarkable Epitaphs on Illustrious and Other Persons in Several Parts of Europe. 1757. V. 73

HACKETT, R. G.
South African War Books. 1994. V. 72
South African War Books. London: 1994. V. 68

HACKLE, PALMER, PSEUD.
Hints on Angling, With Suggestions for Angling Excursions in France and Belgium.... London: 1846. V. 69

HACKNEY, LOUISE W.
Wing of Fame: A Novel Based on the Life of James Smithson. New York: 1934. V. 71

HACKWORTH, GREEN H.
Digest of International Law. Washington: 1940-1944. V. 68

HADDAN, ARTHUR W.
Councils and Ecclesiastical Documents Relating to Great Britain and Ireland. 1869. V. 69

HADDON, A. C.
Reports of the Cambridge Anthropological Expedition to Torres Straits. Volume V. Sociology, Magic and Religion of the Western Islanders. Cambridge: 1904. V. 69

HADDOX, JOHN
Los Chicanos, An Awakening People. El Paso: 1970. V. 68

HADER, BERTA
Berta and Elmer Hader's Picture Book of Mother Goose. New York: 1930. V. 71

HADES! The Ladies! Being Extracts from the Diary of a Draper Charles Cavers, Esq.... London: 1933. V. 70

HADFIELD, E.
Poetical Weeds. London: 1850?. V. 69

HADFIELD, JOHN
Elizabethan Love Songs. Suffolk: 1955. V. 72
Georgian Love Songs. Preston: 1949. V. 72
Georgian Love Songs. Suffolk: 1949. V. 73
Love on a Branch Line. Boston: 1959. V. 72
Restoration Love Songs. 1950. V. 70
Restoration Love Songs. Preston: 1950. V. 72

HADFIELD, KATHLEEN H.
Historical Notes on Amelia County, Virginia. Amelia: 1982. V. 70; 72

HADFIELD, ROBERT A.
The Work and Postiion of the Metallurgical Chemist. London: 1922. V. 73

HADLEY, D.
Stories Told in Winter. Forest Grove: 1976. V. 69

HADRIAN
Translations, Literal and Free, of the Dying Hadrian's Address to His Soul. Bath: 1876. V. 71

HAEBURLIN, H. K.
The Idea of Fertilization in the Culture of the Pueblo Indians. Lanchester: 1916. V. 68; 73

HAECKEL, E.
Arabische Korallen. Ein Ausflug nach den Korallenbanken des Rothen Meers und eine Blick in das Leben der Korallenthiere. Berlin: 1876. V. 73

HAESER, HENRICUS
Bibliotheca Epidemiographica sive Cataogus Librorum De Historia Morborum Epidemicorum Tam Generali Quam Speciali Conscriptorum. Jenae: 1843. V. 68; 72

HAFEN, LEROY
Broken Hand: the Life Story of Thomas Fitzpatrick, Chief of the Mountain Men. Denver: 1931. V. 70
Broken Hand, the Story of Thomas Fitzpatrick. Denver: 1973. V. 68; 70
The Far West and Rockies - General Analytical Index to the Fifteen Volume Series and Supplement to the Journals of Forty-Niners Salt Lake City to Los Angeles. Glendale: 1961. V. 70
Fremont's Fourth Expedition - a Documentary Account of the Disasters of 1848-1849. Glendale: 1960. V. 68; 70
The Mountain Men and the Fur Trade. Glendale: 1965-1972. V. 68; 73
The Overland Mail 1849-1869: Promoter of Settlement, Percursor of Railroads. Cleveland: 1926. V. 70
Overland Routes to the Gold Fields, 1859, from Contemporary Diaries. Glendale: 1942. V. 70; 73
Pike's Peak Gold Rush Guide Books. Glendale: 1931. V. 70
Reports from Colorado - The Wildman Letters 1859-1865 with Other Related Letters and Newspaper Reports 1859. Glendale: 1961. V. 70
Western America The Exploration, Settlement and Development of the Region Beyond The Mississippi. NY: 1943. V. 72

HAFFENDEN, JOHN
The Critical Hertiage. London: 1938. V. 71

THE HAFFENREFFER Collection of Cigar Store Indians and Other American Trade Signs. 2 Parts. New York: 1956. V. 69

HAFTMANN, W.
Painting in the 20th Century. New York: 1946. V. 72
Painting in the 20th Century. New York: 1960. V. 69

HAGAN, C. S. C.
Exactly in the Right Place - A History of Fort C. F. Smith - Montana Territory 1866-1868. El Segundo: 1999. V. 72

HAGEDORN, HERMANN
Leonard Wood, A Biography, 2 Vols. New York: 1931. V. 72
Roosevelt in the Bad Lands. Boston: 1921. V. 68; 69; 71

HAGEMAN, J. S.
Ohio Furniture Makers, 1790-1845. Volume II: 1790-1860. 1984. V. 69

HAGEMAN, JOHN F.
History of Princeton and Its Institutions. Philadelphia: 1879. V. 69

HAGEMEIJER, WARD J. M.
The EBCC Atlas of European Breeding Birds, Their Distribution and Abundance.... 1997. V. 70

HAGEN, OSKAR
The Birth of the American Tradition in Art. New York and London: 1940. V. 69; 72

HAGENEY, WOLFGANG
Costumes, French Female 1037-1870. Rome: 1981. V. 72

HAGER, ANNA MARIE
Winged Mail: from Avalon to Bunker Hill (1894-1898). Los Angeles: 1985. V. 73

HAGER, J. M.
The Great Rebellion. Buffalo: 1865. V. 70

HAGER, JEAN
The Grandfather Medicine. New York: 1989. V. 69; 70
Ravenmocker. New York: 1992. V. 70
The Redbird's Cry. New York: 1994. V. 72
Seven Black Stones. New York: 1994. V. 72
Seven Black Stones. New York: 1995. V. 70

HAGERTY, DONALD
Leading the West - One Hundred Contemporary Painters and Sculptors. Flagstaff: 1997. V. 69

HAGERTY, HARRY J.
The Jasmine Trail. New York: 1936. V. 70

HAGGADAH
The Haggadah. London: 1940. V. 73
The Haggadah. Jerusalem: 1965?. V. 69

HAGGARD, HENRY RIDER
Allan Quartermain.... London: 1887. V. 73
Ayesha; the Return of She. London: 1911. V. 73
Benita - an African Romance. London: 1906. V. 71
Black Heart and White Heart and Other Stories. London/New York/Bombay: 1900. V. 68; 73
Cleopatra. London: 1889. V. 71; 73
Colonel Quaritch, V.C.: A Tale of Country Life. London: 1888. V. 73
Colonel Quaritch, V.C.: A Tale of Country Life. London: 1889. V. 71
Heart of the World. London: 1896. V. 73
Joan Haste. London: 1895. V. 68; 73
King Solomon's Mines. London: 1886. V. 73
The Last Boer War. London: 1899. V. 68; 71
Maiwa's Revenge; Or, The War of the Little Hand. London: 1888. V. 68; 70; 71; 72
Montezuma's Daughter. London: 1893. V. 71; 72
Moon of Israel. London: 1918. V. 73
Pearl Maiden. London: 1919. V. 68; 69; 71
The People of the Mist. London: 1894. V. 73
Queen of the Dawn: a Love Tale of Old Egypt. London: 1925. V. 73
Queen Sheba's Ring. London: 1910. V. 73
Regeneration - Being an Account of the Social Work of The Salvation Army in Great Britain. London: 1910. V. 72
Rural England: Being an Account of Agricultural and Social Researches Carried Out in the Years 1901 and 1902. London: 1902. V. 70; 72
She. London: 1887. V. 69
She and Allan. London: 1921. V. 68
Stella Fregelius - a Tale of Three Destinies. Londcn: 1904. V. 71
Swallow: a Tale of the Great Trek. London: 1899. V. 68; 73
When the World Shook. New York: 1919. V. 68; 69
The Witch's Head. London: 1885. V. 73
The Wizard. Bristol;: 1896. V. 68

HAGOOD, JOHNSON
Memoirs of the War of Secession. Columbia: 1910. V. 69; 70

HAHN, GEORGE H.
The Catawba Soldier of the Civil War. Hickory: 1911. V. 69; 70

HAHN, OTTO
Otto Hahn: My Life, the Autobiography of a Scientist. New York: 1970. V. 72

HAIDINGER, WILHELM KARL
Anfangsgrunde de Mineralogie. Leipzig: 1829. V. 68

HAIG, BRUCE
A Look At Peter Fidler's Journal. Elthridge: 1993. V. 73

HAIG-BROWN, R.
The Western Angler. 1947. V. 68; 73

HAIGH, JAMES
The Dier's Assistant in the Art of Dying Wool and Woolen Goods. Philadelphia: 1810. V. 69
The Dier's Assistant in the Art of Dying Wool and Woolen Goods. Poughkeepsie: 1813. V. 73
The Dyer's Assistant in the Art of Dying Wool and Woolen Goods. York: 1787. V. 71

HAIGHT, ANNE LYON
Banned Books: Informal Notes on Some Books Banned for Various Reasons at Various Times and in Various Places. London: 1955. V. 68

HAIKO, P.
Joseph Maria Olrich: Architecture. New York: 1988. V. 72

HAILE, BERARD
A Catechism and Guide: Navajo-English. St. Michaels: 1937. V. 70
An Ethnological Dictionary of the Navaho Language. Leipzig: 1929. V. 70; 73
Head and Face Masks in Navaho Ceremonialism. St. Michaels: 1947. V. 69
Learning Navaho. Arizona: 1941-. V. 70
The Navaho Fire Dance. 1946. V. 69
The Navaho Fire Dance. St. Michaels: 1946. V. 70
The Navaho War Dance. 1945. V. 69
Origin Legend of the Navaho Enemy Way. New Haven: 1938. V. 69
Origin Legend of the Navaho Flintway. Chicago: 1943. V. 69
Prayer Stick Cutting in a Five Navaho Ceremonial of the Male Branch of Shootingway. Chicago: 1947. V. 72
Starlore Among the Navaho. 1947. V. 69
Starlore Among the Navaho. Santa Fe: 1947. V. 70

HAILE, ELLEN
Three Brown Boys and Other Happy Children. New York: 1879. V. 70
Two Grey Girls and Their Neighbors. New York: 1881. V. 70

HAILEY, HARRY H.
When New Mexico Was Young. Las Cruces: 1948. V. 68

HAILEY, J. P.
The Naked Typist. New York: 1990. V. 71

HAILEY, JOHN
History of Idaho. Boise: 1910. V. 70

HAILEY, LORD
An African Survey. London: 1945. V. 72

HAILSHAM, LORD
The Dilemma of Democracy - Diagnosis and Prescription. London: 1978. V. 72

HAIN, H. H.
History of Perry County, Pennsylvania Including Descriptions of Indian and Pioneer Life from the Time of the Earliest Settlement. Harrisburg: 1922. V. 71

HAINES, DONAL HAMILTON
Blaine of the Backfield. New York: 1937. V. 69

HAINES, FRANCIS
Appaloosa: the Spotted Horse in Art and History. Fort Worth: 1963. V. 68; 72; 73
Red Eagles of the Northwest. The Story of Chief Joseph and His People. Portland: 1939. V. 69

HAINES, JENNIE DAY
Sovereign Woman Verses Mere Man.... San Francisco: 1905. V. 72

HAINES, JOHN
In a Dusty Light. Port Townsend: 1977. V. 69
Leaves and Ashes. Santa Cruz: 1974. V. 69

HAINES, WILLIAM WISTER
Command Decision. Boston: 1947. V. 71
Slim. Boston: 1934. V. 70

HAINING, PETER
Movable Books. 1979. V. 72
Movable Books. London: 1979. V. 70

HAINSWORTH, D. R.
Stewards, Lords and People. The Estate Steward and His World in Later Stuart England. Cambridge: 1992. V. 73

HAIR, T. H.
Sketches of the Coal Mines in Northumberland and Durham. London: 1969. V. 73

HAJDU, DAVID
Positively 4th Street. New York: 2001. V. 69

HAJEK, LUBOR
Miniatures from the East. London: 1960. V. 70

HAKEWILL, JAMES
An Attempt to Determine the Exact Character of Elizabethan Architecture.... London: 1835. V. 68
Twilight of the Grand Tour. A Catalogue of the Drawings by James Hakewill in the British Shcool at Rome Library.... Rome: 1992. V. 68

HAKLUYT, RICHARD
Collection of the Early Voyages, Travels and Discoveries of the English Nation. London: 1809-1812. V. 72
The Principal Navigations, Voyages, Traffiques, and Discoveries of the English Nation 1589-1600.... London: 1910. V. 73
The Principall Navigationes, Voyages and Discoveries of the English Nation, Made by Sea or Ouer Land.... London: 1589. V. 73
The Voyages of the English Nation to America Before the Year 1600. Edinburgh: 1889-1890. V. 70

HALBERSTAM, DAVID
The Noblest Roman. Boston: 1961. V. 70

HALDANE, CHARLOTTE
Russian Newsreel. An Eye-Witness Account of the Soviet Union at War. London: 1942. V. 73

HALDANE, ELIZABETH
Mrs. Gaskell and Her Friends. New York: 1931. V. 70

HALDANE, J. S.
Organism and Environment as Illustrated by the Physiology of Breathing. New Haven: 1917. V. 71

HALDENMAN-JULIUS, MARCET
Violence. New York: 1929. V. 73

HALE, AGNES BURKE
So Wise So Young. New York: 1935. V. 71

HALE, CHARLES
An American Visits Haworth. 1989. V. 73

HALE, CHRISTOPHER
Hangman's Tie. Garden City: 1943. V. 72

HALE, EDWARD EVERETT
Kanzas and Nebraska the History, Georgraphical and Physical Characteristics, and Political Position of those Territories; an Account of the Emigrant Aid Companies, and Directions to Emigrants. Boston/New York: 1854. V. 68; 69; 72
The Man Without a Country. Boston: 1865. V. 68
The Man Without a Country. London: 1902. V. 71

HALE, GEORGIE
A Deadly Brew. 1998. V. 68
Tread Softly. 2000. V. 68

HALE, J. H.
How to Tie Salmon Flies. 1992. V. 68

HALE, JAMES
Historical Account of the Siamese Twin Brothers from Actual Observations. New York: 1832. V. 68

HALE, JANET CAMPBELL
The Jailing of Cecilia Capture. New York: 1985. V. 72

HALE, JOHN
California as It Is. San Francisco: 1954. V. 69

HALE, JOHN P.
Daniel Boone. Wheeling: 1880. V. 71
Trans-Allegheny Pioneers: Historical Sketches of the First White Settlers West of the Alleghenies 1748 and After. Charleston: 1931. V. 73

HALE, KATHERINE
Canadian Cities of Romance. Toronto: 1933. V. 72

HALE, KATHLEEN
Orlando (The Marmalade Cat) Buys a Cottage. London: 1963. V. 70
Orlando (the Marmalade Cat) Keeps a Dog. London: 1949. V. 72

HALE, LAURA VIRGINIA
History of the Forth-Ninth Virginia Infantry CSA. 1981. V. 70

HALE, MATTHEW
The Primitive Origination of Mankind, Considered and Examined According to the Light of Nature. London: 1677. V. 70; 72
Several Tracts Written by Sr Matthew Hale, Kt. Sometime Lord Chief Justice of England.... London: 1684. V. 68

HALE, N. C.
Embrace of Life: the Sculpture of Gustav Vigeland. New York: 1968. V. 68; 69; 72

HALE, NATHANIEL C.
Pelts and Palisades: the Story of Fur and the Rivalry for Pelts in Early America. Richmond: 1959. V. 69; 71; 73

HALE, SARAH JANE
The Happy Changes. New York: 1860. V. 71

HALE, SARAH JOSEPHA
The Good Little Girl's Book. New York: 1845. V. 70
Mrs. Hale's New Cook Book. Phila: 1857. V. 72
Woman's Record; or Sketches of All Distinguished Women, from "The Beginning" Till A.D. 1850.... New York: 1853. V. 73

HALE, THOMAS
A Compleat Body of Husbandry. London: 1756. V. 71
Social Harmony Consisting of a Collection of Songs and Catches in Two, Three, Four and Five Parts, from the Works of the Most Eminent Masters to Which are Added Several Choice Songs of Masonry. London: 1763. V. 68; 72

HALES, JOHN
Golden Remains, of the Ever Memorable, Mr. John Hales, of Eton Colledge &c. London: 1673. V. 72

HALES, PETER B.
William Henry Jackson and the Transformation of the American Landscape. Philadelphia: 1988. V. 68

HALES, STEPHEN
A Friendly Admonition to the Drinkers of Brandy, and Other Distilled Spirituous Liquors. London: 1733. V. 69
Statical Essays: Containing Haemostatics. New York: 1964. V. 68

HALES, WILLIAM
Irish Pursuits of Literature in A.D. 1798 and 1799.... Dublin: 1799. V. 73

HALEY, ALEX
The Autobiography of Malcolm X. New York: 1965. V. 71
Roots. Garden City: 1976. V. 68; 69; 70; 71

HALEY, JAMES EVETTS
The Alamo Mission Bell. Midland: 1974. V. 71
Charles Goodnight, Cowman and Plainsman. Boston: 1936. V. 71
A Day with Dan Casement. Kansas City: 1949. V. 69; 71
Erie P. Halliburton Genius with Cement. Duncan: 1959. V. 68
F. Reaugh Man and Artist. El Paso: 1960. V. 68
Fort Concho and the Texas Frontier. San Angelo: 1952. V. 68; 73
George W. Littlefield - Texan. Norman: 1943. V. 68
The Heraldry of the Range, Some Southwestern Brands. Canyon: 1949. V. 71
Jeff Milton: a Good Man with a Gun. Norman: 1948. V. 70; 71
Life on the Texas Range. Austin: 1952. V. 69; 70
Robbing Banks Was My Business - the Story of John Harvey Bailey. Canyon: 1973. V. 69
Rough Times-Tough Fiber: a Fragmentary Family Chronicle. Canyon: 1976. V. 69; 71; 73
Some Southwestern Trails. San Angelo: 1948. V. 68; 71
The XIT Ranch of Texas and the Early Days of the Llano Estacado. Norman: 1967. V. 68
The XIT Ranch of Texas and the Early Days of the Llano Estacado. Chicago: 1929. V. 69

HALEY, THOMAS J.
Response of the Nervous System to Longizing Radiation. New York: 1962. V. 68

HALEY, WILLIAM D.
Words for the Workers. Boston: 1855. V. 68

HALF Hours Underground. Volcanoes, Mines and Caves. London: 1888. V. 68; 72

HALFORD, F. M.
Dry-Fly Fishing, Theory and Practice. 1902. V. 73
Dry-Fly Fishing Theory and Practice. 1973. V. 73
Floating Flies and How to Dress Them. 1974. V. 68
Floating Flies and How to Dress Them. 1993. V. 68
Making a Fishery. 1895. V. 73
Making a Fishery. 1902. V. 68; 73
Modern Development of the Dry Fly. 1910. V. 68; 73

HALFORD, HENRY
An Account of What Appeared on Opening the Coffin of King Charles the First, in the Vault of King Henry the Eighth. London: 1813. V. 70; 71; 72
Essays and Orations Read And Delivered at the Royal College of Physicians to Which has added An Account of the Opening of the Tomb of King Charles I. London: 1831. V. 70; 71
Essays and Orations, Read and Delivered at the Royal College of Physicians to Which is Added, an Account of the Opening of the Tomb of King Charles I. London: 1833. V. 72

HALFPENNY, JOSEPH
Fragmenta Vetusta or the Remains of Ancient Buildings in York. York: 1807. V. 72
Gothic Ornaments in the Cathedral Church of York. York: 1795-1800. V. 69; 71

HALFPENNY, WILLIAM
The Art of Sound Building; Demonstrated in Geometrical Problems, Shewing Geometrical Lines for All Kinds of Arches, Nichs, Groins and Twisted Rails.... London: 1725. V. 68
Practical Architecture, or a Sure Guide to the True Working According to the Rules of that Science.... London: 1736. V. 69

HALHEAD, NATHANIEL BRASSEY
Testimony of the Authenticity of the Prophecies of Richard Brothers and of His Mission to Recall the Jews. London: 1795. V. 73

HALIBURTON. A Centenary Chaplet. Toronto: 1897. V. 72

HALIBURTON, THOMAS CHANDLER
The Bubbles of Canada. London: 1839. V. 70
The Clockmaker; or the Sayings and Doings of Samuel Slick.... London: 1843. V. 68
The English in America. London: 1851. V. 69
An Historical and Statistical Account of Nova Scotia. Halifax: 1829. V. 72
An Historical and Statistical Account of Nova Scotia. Belleville: 1973. V. 71

HALICARNASSENSIS, DIONYSIUS
The Roman Antiquities of Dionysius Halicarnassensis. London: 1758. V. 69

HALIFAX, CHARLES LINDLEY
Lord Halifax's Ghost Book. A Collection of Stories of Haunted Houses. Apparitions and Supernatural Occurrences. London: 1936. V. 71

HALIFAX, GEORGE SAVILE, 1ST MARQUIS OF
A Character of King Charles the Second and Political, Moral and Miscellaneous Thoughts and Reflections. London: 1750. V. 69
The Lady's New-Years Gift; or, Advice to a Daughter, Under these Following Heads.... London: 1688. V. 73
Miscellanies. London: 1704. V. 73
Miscellanies.... London: 1717. V. 69; 73

HALKETT, JOHN
Statement Respecting the Earl of Selkirk's Settlement of Kildonan. London: 1817. V. 70

HALKETT, SAMUEL
Dictionary of Anonymous and Pseudonymous English Literature. Edinburgh & London: 1926-1962. V. 68; 70

HALL, A. D.
The Genus Tulipa. 1940. V. 73

HALL, A. M.
Ireland Picturesque. Boston. V. 70
Marian; or a Young Maid's Fortunes. New York: 1840. V. 70

HALL, ADAM
The Pekin Target. London: 1981. V. 69
Quiller Meridian. London: 1993. V. 72
Quiller Salamander. London: 1994. V. 69
The Striker Portfolio. London: 1969. V. 72
The Tango Briefing. London: 1973. V. 72
The Volcanoes of San Domingo. London: 1963. V. 68
The Warsaw Document. London: 1971. V. 69

HALL, ANNA
Uncle Horace. London: 1858. V. 68

HALL, B. P.
Birds of the Harold Hall Australian Expedition 1962-1970. London: 1974. V. 68

HALL, BASIL
Account of a Voyage of Discovery to the West Coast of Corea and the Grea Loo-Cho Island...with an appendix. London: 1818. V. 70
Extracts from a Journal Written on the Coasts of Chili, Peru and Mexico in the Years 1820, 1821, 1822. Edinburgh: 1824. V. 72
Fragments Of Voyages And Travels. Edinburgh: 1831-1832. V. 72
Schloss Hainfield. Paris: 1836. V. 72

HALL, BERT
Round-Up Years, Old Muddy to the Black Hills. Winner, SD: 2000. V. 71

HALL, BERTHA PARKER
Ducky Daddles and the Three Bears. New York: 1921. V. 69
Ducky Daddles' Party. New York: 1918. V. 69

HALL, BRIAN
The Saskiad. New York/Boston: 1997. V. 72

HALL, C. A.
Plant Life. London: 1915. V. 68; 71

HALL, CARROLL
Heraldry of New Helvetia- With Thirty-Two Cattle Brands and Ear Marks. San Francisco: 1945. V. 71
The Terry Broderick Duel. San Francisco: 1939. V. 68; 73

HALL, CHARLES
Negroes in the United States 1920-1932. Washington: 1935. V. 72

HALL, CHARLES FRANCIS
Arctic Researches and Life Among the Esquimaux: Being the Narrative of an Expedition in Search of Sir John Franklin, in the Years 1860, 1861 and 1862. New York: 1865. V. 73
Narrative Of The Second Artic Expedition Made By Charles Hall. Washington: 1879. V. 72

HALL, CLAUDE V.
The Early History of Floyd County. Canyon: 1947. V. 68

HALL, CLAYTON COLEMAN
Narratives of Early Maryland 1633-1684. New York: 1910. V. 73

HALL, COVINGTON
Battle Hymns of Toil. Oklahoma City. V. 73
Battle Hymns of Toil. Oklahoma City: 1946. V. 68; 69

HALL, DAVID
An Essay on Intemperance, Particularly Hard-Drinking.... 1742. V. 72

HALL, DONALD
Carol. Concord: 1988. V. 68
The Dark House. New York: 1958. V. 71; 73
The Ideal Bakery. San Francisco: 1987. V. 68
1 2 3 4 Stories. Sweden, Maine: 1989. V. 70
Remembering Poets. Reminiscences and Opinions: Dylan Thomas, Robert Frost, T. S. Eliot, Ezra Pond. New York: 1978. V. 69
Ric's Progress. Easthampton, MA: 1996. V. 71
The Town of Hill. Boston: 1975. V. 71

HALL, DOUGLAS
The Brittle Thread. Grand Rapids: 1968. V. 71

HALL, E. R.
The Mammals of North America. New York: 1959. V. 70

HALL, EDITH KING
Adventures in Toyland. London: 1897. V. 69

HALL, ELLYN
Miss Browne: the Story of a Superior Mouse. London: 1899. V. 70; 73

HALL, F. G.
The Bank of Ireland, 1783-1946. 1949. V. 69; 71

HALL, FREDERIC
The History of San Jose and Surroundings with Biographical Sketches of Early Settlers. San Francisco: 1871. V. 69; 71; 73

HALL, FREDERIC T.
The Pedigree of the Devil. London: 1883. V. 70

HALL, HERBERT BYNG
The Adventures of a Bric-a-Brac Hunter. London: 1868. V. 69
The Oyster; Where, How and When to Find, Breed, Cook and Eat It. London: 1861. V. 68
The Oyster: Where, How and When to Find, Breed, Cook and Eat It. London: 1863. V. 68; 70
The Sportsman and His Dog; or Hints on Sporting. London: 1850. V. 73

HALL, HOLWORTHY
Rope. New York: 1923. V. 71

HALL, J. J.
The Crystal Bowl-Australian Nature Stories. Melbourne: 1921. V. 71

HALL, J. L.
Around the Horn in '49 - the Journal of the Hartford Union Mining and Trading Company - December 1848 to September 1849. San Francisco: 1928. V. 68; 73

HALL, JAMES
Report on the Geological Survey of the State of Iowa...1855-1857. Albany: 1858. V. 71

HALL, JAMES BAKER
Music for a Broken Piano. New York: 1982. V. 68; 71

HALL, JAMES W.
Bones of Coral. New York: 1991. V. 72
False Statements. Pittsburgh: 1986. V. 70
The Mating Reflex. Pittsburgh: 1980. V. 70
Paper Products. New York: 1990. V. 72
Tropical Freeze. New York: 1989. V. 68; 70

HALL, JAMES W. continued
Under Cover of Daylight. New York: 1987. V. 68; 72

HALL, JIM
Tales of Pioneer Practice- Being Reminiscences of the Ways and By- Ways of the Early- Day Medical Fraternity in Colorado, USA. Denver: 1937. V. 71

HALL, JOHN
The Great Strike on the Q. Chicago: 1889. V. 71

HALL, JOHN E.
The Philadelphia Souvenir.... Philadelphia: 1826. V. 71

HALL, JOHN F.
The Daily Union History of Atlantic City and County. Atlantic City: 1900. V. 69

HALL, LELAND
Salah and His Americans. New York: 1935. V. 69

HALL, LOWIE
Fifty-Six Waterloo Cups. 1922. V. 68

HALL, MARSHALL
A Critical and Experimental Essay on the Circulation of the Blood.... London: 1837?. V. 70
A Descriptive, Diagnostic and Practical Essay on Disorders of the Digestive Organs and General Health, and Particularly.... Keene, NH: 1823. V. 71

HALL, MARTHA H.
The Confederate Army of New Mexico. Austin: 1978. V. 72

HALL, MARTIN J.
Through My Spectacles In Uganda. London: 1898. V. 72

HALL, OAKLEY
The Downhill Racers. New York: 1963. V. 69
A Review of the Webster Case. New York: 1850. V. 71
Warlock. New York: 1958. V. 71

HALL, PARNELL
Detective. New York: 1987. V. 69
Murder. New York: 1987. V. 68; 70

HALL, RADCLYFFE
The Master of the House. London: 1932. V. 68; 72
Songs of Three Counties. 1913. V. 68
The Unit Lamp. Leipzig: 1931. V. 72
Well of Loneliness. New York: 1928. V. 72
The Well of Loneliness. Paris: 1928. V. 70; 71

HALL, RICHARD W.
The Art of Mountain Tramping. London: 1932. V. 69
On Cumberland Fells. Whitehaven: 1927. V. 69

HALL, ROBERT PLEASANTS
Poems, by a South Carolinian. Charleston: 1848. V. 71

HALL, SAMUEL CARTER
The Baronial Halls and Ancient Picturesque Edifices of England.... 1881. V. 70
A Book of Memories of Great Men and Women of the Age, from Personal Acquaintance. London: 1876. V. 73
The Book of the Thames, from Its Rise to Its Fall. 1859. V. 73
Ireland: Its Scenery, Character, &c. London: 1850. V. 68; 72
Ireland: Its Scenery, Character, Etc. London: 1841-1843. V. 73

HALL, SAMUEL R.
Lectures on School-Keeping. Boston: 1829. V. 69

HALL, T. B.
A Flora of Liverpool. 1839. V. 69

HALL, TED B.
Oklahoma Indian Territory. Ft. Worth: 1971. V. 71

HALL, THOMAS S.
A Source Book in Animal Biology. 1951. V. 68

HALL, TOM S.
Tramping in Arran. Glasgow: 1928. V. 69

HALL, TREVOR H.
A Bibliography of Books on Conjuring in English from 1580 to 1850. Minneapolis: 1957. V. 71
Sherlock Holmes and His Creator. London: 1978. V. 71
Sherlock Holmes: Ten Literary Studies. London: 1969. V. 71

HALL, WILLIAM
A Biography of David Cox: with Remarks on His Works and Genius. London: 1881. V. 72
Christmas Pony. New York: 1948. V. 70

HALL, WILLIAM HUTCHESON
Narrative of the Voyages and Services of the Nemesis, from 1840 to 1843, and of the Combined and Military Operations in China.... London: 1844. V. 68

HALL, WILLIAM M.
The Apiarian, or a Practical Treatise on the Management of Bees; with the Best Method of Preventing the Depredations of the Bee Moth. New Haven: 1841. V. 73

HALLAHAN, WILLIAM H.
The Dead of Winter. Indianapolis: 1972. V. 68

HALLAM, ARTHUR HENRY
(Poems). 1830. V. 73
The Poems of Arthur Henry Hallan, Together With His Essay on the Lyrical Poems of Alfred Tennyson. London: 1893. V. 68
Remains, in Verse and Prose. 1834. V. 73
Timbuctoo. 1829. V. 73

HALLAM, HENRY
Introduction to the Literature of Europe, in the Fifteenth, Sixteenth and Seventeenth Centuries. London: 1843. V. 69

HALLAM HIPWELL, HERMIONE
Argentine Interlude. Philadelphia: 1936. V. 71

HALL DUNCAN, N.
History of Fashion Photography. New York: 1979. V. 68

HALLECK, FITZ-GREENE
Alnwick Castle, with Other Poems. New York: 1836. V. 73

HALLENBECK, CLEVE
Land of the Conquistadors. Caldwell: 1950. V. 73
Legends of the Spanish Southwest. Glendale: 1938. V. 73
Spanish Missions of the Old Southwest. Garden City: 1926. V. 70; 72; 73

HALLER, ALBRECHT VON
Bibliotheca Chirurgica, qua Scripta ad Artem Chirurgicam Facientia a Rerum Initiis Recensentur. Bernae paud: 1774-1775. V. 70
Deux Memoires sur le Mouvement du Sang, et sur les Effects d Is Saignee.... Lausanne: 1756. V. 72
Elementa Physiologiae Corporis Humani. Lausanne: 1757-1763. V. 72
First Lines of Physiology. Troy: 1803. V. 68; 72
Oppuscula Sua Anatomica de Respiratione, de Monstris, Aliaque Minora. Gottingen: 1751. V. 68; 72
The Poems. London: 1794. V. 73
Usong. An Eastern Narrative. London: 1772. V. 73

HALLEY, ROBERT
Lancashire: Its Puritanism and Nonconformity. Manchester: 1872. V. 73

HALLIBERG, WILLIAM
The Rub of the Green. New York: 1988. V. 69

HALLIDAY, BRETT
Marked for Murder. New York: 1945. V. 69
Michael Shayne's Long Chance. 1944. V. 68

HALLINAN, TIMOTHY
The Four Last Things. 1989. V. 68

HALLIWELL-PHILLIPPS, JAMES ORCHARD
Dictionary of Archaic and Provincial Words. London: 1881. V. 70
The Literature of the Sixteenth and Seventeenth Centuries. London: 1851. V. 71
The Manuscript Rarities of the University of Cambridge. London: 1841. V. 70
Nugae Poeticae. London: 1844. V. 69
Palatine Anthology: A Collection of Ancient Poems and Ballads, Relating to Lancashire and Cheshire. 1850. V. 71
Palatine Anthology; A Collection of Ancient Poems and Ballards. London: 1850. V. 73
Rara Mathematica; or a Collection of Treatises on the Mathematics and Subjects Connected with Them from Ancient Inedited Manuscripts. London: 1841. V. 69
Tarlton's Jests, and News Out of Purgatory, With Some Account of the Life of Tarlton. London: 1844. V. 72

HALL STEVENSON, JOHN
Makarony Fables: Fables for Grown Gentlemen: Lyrick Epistles; and Several Other Poems; by the Author of Crazy Tales. Dublin: 1772. V. 68

HALLSTROM, G.
Monumental Art of Northern Europe from the Stone Age. I. The Norwegian Localities. Stockholm: 1938. V. 69

HALOUZE, E.
Costumes of South America. New York: 1940-1950. V. 69
Costumes of South America. New York: 1941. V. 69

HALPENNY, FRANCESS G.
Dictionary of Canadian Biography. Volume III. 1741 to 1770. Toronto: 1974. V. 72
Dictionary of Canadian Biography. Volume IV. 1771 to 1800. Toronto: 1979. V. 72
Dictionary of Canadian Biography. Volume IX 1861-1870. Toronto: 1976. V. 72
Dictionary of Canadian Biography Volume X. 1871 to 1880. Toronto: 1972. V. 72

HALPER, ALBERT
Union Square. New York: 1933. V. 69

HALPERN, DANIEL
Songs of Mririda. Greensboro: 1974. V. 72

HALPERT, SAMUEL
...When We Talk About Raymond Carver. Layton: 1991. V. 71

HALPIN, NICHOLAS JOHN
An University Prize Poem on His Majesty King George III. Dublin: 1811. V. 73

HALPIN, THOMAS
Uncle Tom's Adventure in a Hollow Log. Poughkeepsie: 1881. V. 69

HALPIN, WILLIAM
The Cheltenham Mail Bag; or Letters from Gloucestershire. London: 1820. V. 68; 72

HALSE, GEORGE F.
Sir Guy de Guy: A Stirring Romaunt, Showing how a Briton drilled for his Fatherland; won a Heiress; got a Pedigree; and caught the Rheumatism. by Rattlebrain. London: 1864. V. 71

HALSELL, H. H.
Cowboys And Cattleland. Nashville: 1944. V. 71

HALSEY, ALAN
Auto Dada Cafe: Poems. 1987. V. 71
The Text of Shelley's Death. Stoke Prior, Herefordshire: 1995. V. 68

HALSEY, DON P.
A Sketch of the Life of Captain Don P. Halsey of the Confederate States Army. Richmond: 1904. V. 69; 70

HALSEY, FRANCIS W.
The Literary Digest History of the World War. New York: 1920. V. 73
The Pioneers of Unadilla Village 1784-1840 and Reminiscences of Village Life and of Panama and California from 1849-1850. Unadila: 1902. V. 70

HALSEY, FRANK D.
The Last Mile. Garden City: 1922. V. 72

HALSEY, HARLAN PAGE
Macon Moore, the Southern Detective. New York: 1881. V. 68; 69
Phil Scott, the Indian Detective: a Tale of Startling Mysteries. New York: 1882. V. 69; 71

HALSEY, JACOB LAFAYETTE
Thomas Halsey of Hertfordshire, England and Southampton, Long Island, 1591-1679.... Morristown: 1895. V. 69

HALSTEAD, B. W.
Poisonous and Venomous Marine Animals of the World. Washington: 1965-. V. 69
Poisonous and Venomous Marine Animals of the World. Washington: 1965-1967. V. 72

HALSTED, WILLIAM STEWART
The Employment of Fine Silk in Preference to Catgut, the Advantages of Transfixing Tissues and Vessels in Controlling Haemorrhage. Boston: 1939. V. 69
Surgical Papers of William Stewart Halsted. Baltimore: 1924. V. 70; 71; 72

HALTER, ERNEST J.
Collecting First Editions of Franklin Roosevelt. Chicago: 1949. V. 70

HAMADY, MARY LAIRD
Selected Poems 1973-1980. Springfield: 1982. V. 73

HAMADY, WALTER
In Sight of Blue Mounds. Mt. Horeb: 1972. V. 73
Journal Liftings. Madixon: 1987. V. 73
Neopostmodernism, or, Gabberjab Number 6. Mt. Horeb: 1988. V. 69; 73
Seeds and Chairs. Mt. Horeb: 1979. V. 73
Travelling. Mount Horeb: 1996. V. 71
Two Decades of Hamady and the Perishable Press Limited. St. Louis: 1984. V. 73

HAMAYA, HIROSHI
Landscapes of Japan. Tokyo: 1964. V. 68

HAMBIDGE, J.
Dynamic Symmetry: the Greek Vase. New Haven: 1931. V. 69; 72

HAMBLETT, CHARLES
The Crazy Kill. London: 1956. V. 71

HAMBLIN, ROBERT W.
Selections from the William Faulkner Collection of Louis Daniel Brodsky. Charlottesville: 1979. V. 69

HAMBLY, WALLACE B.
The Case Reports and Autopsy Records of Ambroise Pare. Springfield: 1960. V. 68

HAMBLY, WILFRID DYSON
Jamba. Chicago: 1947. V. 69

HAMBOURG, MARIA MORRIS
Walker Evans. New York: 2000. V. 68

HAMBURGER, PHILIP
Our Man Stanley. Indianapolis/NY: 1963. V. 70

HAMEL, GUSTAV
Flying, Some Practical Experiences. 1914. V. 72

HAMER, S. H.
The Story of The Ring. London: 1907. V. 69

HAMERTON, PHILIP GILBERT
An Autobiography 1834-1858. London: 1897. V. 73
Drawing & Engraving. London: 1892. V. 72
Etching and Etchers. London: 1876. V. 71
Landscape. 1885. V. 73
Wenderholm. A Story of Lancashire and Yorkshire. London: 1869. V. 71; 73

HAMILL, PETE
A Drinking Life. Boston: 1994. V. 72; 73
Flesh & Blood. New York: 1977. V. 72
A Killing for Christ. New York: 1968. V. 69

HAMILTON, ALEXANDER
Colonel Hamilton's Second Letter from Phocion to the Considerate Citizens of New York, on the Politics of the Times.... Philadelphia: 1784. V. 73
The Family Female Physician; or a Treatise on the Management of Female Complaints and of Children in Early Infancy. Worcester: 1793. V. 71
Letter from Alexander Hamilton Concerning the Public Conduct and Character of John Adams, Esq., President of the United States. New York: 1800. V. 73
A New Account of the East Indies. London: 1930. V. 69
Observations on Certain Documents Contained in No. V and VI of The History of the United States for the Year 1796 in Which the Charge of Speculation Against Alexander Hamilton, Late Secretary of the Treasury, Is Fully Refuted. Philadelphia: 1797. V. 73
Outlines of the Theory and Practice Midwifery. (with) An Abridgement of the Practice of Midwifery and a Set of Anatomical Tables with Explanations. Philadelphia: 1790-1791. V. 73
Outlines of the Theory and Practice of Midwifery. Northampton: 1797. V. 70
The Works. New York: 1810. V. 71

HAMILTON, ANGUS
In Abor Jungles. 1912. V. 69; 70; 72; 73

HAMILTON, ANN MARY
A Winter at St. James's; or, Modern Manners. London: 1811. V. 73

HAMILTON, ANTHONY
Memoires du Comte de Grammont. London: 1793. V. 72
Memoirs of Count Grammont. London. V. 72
Memoirs of Count Grammont. London: 1811. V. 70
Memoirs of Count Grammont. London: 1885. V. 73

HAMILTON, BRUCE
Too Much of Water. London: 1958. V. 69; 73

HAMILTON, CHARLES
American Autographs. Norman: 1983. V. 68
Collecting Autographs and Manuscripts. Norman: 1961. V. 71
Lincoln in Photographs. Norman: 1963. V. 71

HAMILTON, CICELY
Modern Ireland: as Seen by an Englishwoman. New York: 1936. V. 68

HAMILTON, COSMO
Fulfillment. New York: 1935. V. 71

HAMILTON, DAVID
The Best of David Hamilton. Paris: 1976. V. 68
Dreams of a Young Girl. New York: 1971. V. 68
Sisters. New York: 1973. V. 68

HAMILTON, ELIZABETH
The Cottagers of Glenburnie: a Tale for the Farmer's Inglenook. Edinburgh: 1808. V. 69
Letters, Addressed to the Daughter of a Nobleman.... London: 1806. V. 69
Memoirs of Modern Philosophers. Dublin: 1801. V. 68; 69; 73
Memoirs of the Life of Agrippina, the Wife of Germanicus. Bath: 1804. V. 68; 72
Translation of the Letters of a Hindoo Rajah.... London: 1796. V. 68; 69; 72

HAMILTON, ERNEST
The Outlaws of the Marches. London: 1897. V. 70; 71

HAMILTON, ESME
Rainbow and Speedy. 1952. V. 69

HAMILTON, F. BUCHANAN
An Account of the Fishes Found in the River Ganges and Its Branches. Edinburgh: 1822. V. 69

HAMILTON, FRANK HASTINGS
A Practical Treatise on Fractures and Dislocations. Philadelphia: 1891. V. 70

HAMILTON, FREDERIC
The Holiday Adventures of Mr. P. J. Davenant. London: 1915. V. 71

HAMILTON, GEORGE
Experiences of a Colonist Forty Years Ago: a Journey from Port Phillip to South Australia in 1839 and a Voyage from Port Phillip to Adelaide in 1846. Adelaide: 1880. V. 72

HAMILTON, GEORGE ROSTREVOR
The Greek Portrait. An Anthology of English Verse Translations from the Greek Poets. London: 1934. V. 70; 71
The Latin Portrait, an Anthology.... London: 1929. V. 70; 71

HAMILTON, GERALD
Jacaranda. London: 1961. V. 71

HAMILTON, GUSTAVUS
Elements of Gymnastics, for Boys and of Calisthenics, for Young Ladies. London: 1827. V. 68

HAMILTON, HARRY
All Their Children Were Acrobats. Indianapolis: 1936. V. 70

HAMILTON, HENRY A.
Reminiscences of a Veteran. Concord: 1897. V. 70

HAMILTON, HENRY W.
The Sioux of The Rosebud, A History In Pictures. Norman: 1971. V. 72

HAMILTON, HOLMAN
Zachary Taylor. New York: 1951. V. 71

HAMILTON, IAIN
Embarkation for Cythera. London: 1974. V. 72

HAMILTON, IAN
J. D. Salinger: a Writing Life. New York: 1986. V. 70

HAMILTON, J. G. DE ROULHAC
Reconstruction in North Carolina. New York: 1914. V. 69; 70

HAMILTON, J. P.
Reminiscences of an Old Sportsman. 1860. V. 70; 71
Travels through the Interior Provinces of Columbia. London: 1827. V. 70

HAMILTON, JAMES
Observations on the Utility and Adminstration of Purgative Medicines in Several Diseases. Edinburgh: 1806. V. 73

HAMILTON, JAMES HAMILTON, 1ST DUKE OF
The Several Speeches of Duke Hamilton, Earl of Cambridge, Henry Earl of Holland and Arthur Lord Capel, Upon the Scaffold, etc. London: 1649. V. 73

HAMILTON, JANE
The Book of Ruth. New York: 1988. V. 69; 70; 72; 73
A Map of the World. New York: 1994. V. 71; 72; 73
The Short History of a Prince. New York: 1998. V. 68; 72

HAMILTON, JOHN
Stereography, or, a Compleat Body of Perspective, In All Its Branches. 1738. V. 73
Stereography, or, a Compleat Body of Perspective, In All Its Branches. London: 1738. V. 71

HAMILTON, JOHN R.
New Brunswick and Its Scenery. New Brunswick: 1874. V. 68

HAMILTON, LEONIDAS
Border States of Mexico. San Francisco: 1881. V. 69

HAMILTON, MYRA
Kingdoms Curious. London: 1905. V. 73

HAMILTON, PATRICK
Craven House. London: 1926. V. 70
The Duke In Darkness. London: 1943. V. 70
Gas Light. London: 1939. V. 70
Gas Light. New York: 1939. V. 73
Hangover Square. London: 1941. V. 70
Hangover Square. New York: 1942. V. 70; 73
Impromptu in Moribundia. London: 1939. V. 70
The Man Upstairs. London: 1954. V. 70
The Midnight Bell. London: 1929. V. 70
The Midnight Bell. London: 1936. V. 70
Mr. Stimpson and Mr. Gorse. London: 1952. V. 70
Monday Morning. London: 1925. V. 70
Money with Menaces to the Public Danger. London: 1939. V. 70
The Plains of Cement. London: 1934. V. 70
The Plains of Cement. Boston: 1935. V. 70
The Resources of Arizona. San Francisco: 1884. V. 70
Rope. London: 1929. V. 70; 71
The Siege of Pleasure. London: 1932. V. 70
The Slaves of Solitude. London: 1947. V. 70
Souvenir of Rope for Reginald Denham's Production at Ambassadors Theatre. London: 1929. V. 73
20,000 Streets Under the Sky: a London Trilogy. London: 1935. V. 70
Twopence Coloured. London: 1928. V. 70
Unknown Assailant. London: 1955. V. 70
The West Pier. London: 1951. V. 70

HAMILTON, R.
British Fishes. Volume I. Edinburgh: 1843. V. 69

HAMILTON, RICHARD WINTER
An Essay on Craniology, Being the Substance of a Paper Submitted to the Philosophical and Literary Society, Leeds, December 2, 1825. London: 1826. V. 71

HAMILTON, ROBERT
An Inquiry Concerning the Rise and Progress, the Redemption and Present State, and the Management of the National Debt of Great Britain. Edinburgh: 1814. V. 72

HAMILTON, STEVE
A Cold Day in Paradise. New York: 1998. V. 69; 71

HAMILTON, SYLVIAN
The Bone Pedlar. London: 2000. V. 70

HAMILTON, THOMAS
Men and Manners in America. Edinburgh and London: 1833. V. 70; 72
Men and Manners in America. Edinburgh: 1843. V. 71
A Treatise on the Manner of Raising Forest Trees.... Edinburgh: 1761. V. 70; 71

HAMILTON, VIRGINIA
Paul Robeson: the Life and Times of a Free Black Man. New York: 1974. V. 72
W.E.B. DuBois: A Biography. New York: 1972. V. 72

HAMILTON, W. T.
My Sixty Years on The Plains, Trapping, Trading, Indians. New York: 1975. V. 72

HAMILTON, WILLIAM
Discussions on Philosophy and Literature, Education and University Reform. Edinburgh and London: 1866. V. 70; 71
Observations on Mount Vesuvius, Mount Etna, and Other Volcanoes.... London: 1773. V. 70
Observations on Mount Vesuvius, Mount Etna, and Other Volcanoes.... London: 1774. V. 69
Outlines from the Figures and Compositions Upon the Greek, Roman and Estruscan Vases of the Late Sir William Hamilton.... London: 1814. V. 71

HAMILTON-PATERSON, JAMES
The Bell Boy. London: 1990. V. 68
Gerontius - A Novel. London: 1989. V. 72

HAMLETT, W. C.
Reproductive Biology of South American Vertebrates. New York: 1992. V. 72
Sharks, Skates and Rays. Baltimore: 1999. V. 69

HAMLIN, PERCY GATLING
Old Bald Head. Strasburg: 1940. V. 69; 70

HAMLIN, WILLIAM LEE
The True Story of Billy the Kid. Caldwell, ID: 1959. V. 72; 73

HAMMER, ARMAND
The Armand Hammer Collection; a Loan Exhibition for the Benefit of the Smithsonian Institution.... Washington: 1970. V. 72

HAMMER, KEN
Biographies of the 7th Cavalry June 25, 1876. Ft. Collins: 1972. V. 68
Men With Custer. Fort Collins: 1972. V. 72
Men With Custer. Hardin: 1996. V. 72

HAMMER, LAURA V.
Light 'n Hitch. 1958. V. 68

HAMMER, MINA FISHER
History of the Kodak and Its Continuations: the First Folding and Panromanic Cameras: Magic Lantern - Kodak - Movie Closeup of the Inventor and Kodak State. New York: 1940. V. 70

HAMMERTON, J. A.
Wonders of the Past. The Romance of Antiquity and Its Splendors. New York and London: 1923-1924. V. 69
Wonders of the Past: The Romance of Antiquity and Its Splendours. New York: 1933. V. 71

HAMMERTON, PHILIP GILBERT
The Graphic Arts: a Treatise on the Varieties of Drawing, Painting and Engraving. New York: 1882. V. 71

HAMMETT, DASHIELL
The Adventures of Sam Spade. London: 1944. V. 70
The Adventures of Sam Spade. New York: 1944. V. 68; 69; 72
The Battle of the Aleutians. 1944. V. 69
The Big Knockover. New York: 1966. V. 70; 71; 73
The Complete Dashiell Hammett. New York: 1942. V. 70
The Continental Op. New York: 1945. V. 68; 70; 71
The Creeping Siamese. New York: 1950. V. 68; 70; 73
Creeps by Night. New York: 1932. V. 68
The Dain Curse. New York: 1929. V. 68; 69
The Dashiell Hammett Omnibus: Red Harvest, the Dain Curse, The Maltese Falcon. New York: 1935. V. 68; 70
The Dashiell Hammett Story Omnibus. London: 1966. V. 71; 73
Dead Yellow Women. New York: 1947. V. 70
The Glass Key. London and New York: 1931. V. 69; 70; 73
Hammett Homicides. New York: 1945. V. 71
Hammett Homicides. New York: 1946. V. 68; 70
The Maltese Falcon. New York and London: 1930. V. 69; 70; 71
Maltese Falcon. New York: 1993. V. 72
A Man Named Thin and Other Stories. New York: 1962. V. 70
Modern Tales of Horror. London: 1932. V. 68; 70; 72
Nightmare Town. New York: 1948. V. 69
$106,000 Blood Money. New York: 1943. V. 72
The Return of the Continental Op. New York: 1945. V. 70; 71
Secret Agent X-9. Philadelphia: 1934. V. 70
Secret Agent X-9. New York: 1976. V. 73
Secret Agent X9, Book 2. New York: 1934. V. 70
The Thin Man. New York: 1934. V. 68; 71
Woman in the Dark. 1951. V. 71
Woman In The Dark With Introduction By Robert B. Parker. New York: 1988. V. 72

HAMMOND, CHARLES THOMAS
Modelling in Cardboard. Paper and Leatherette. London: 1911. V. 68

HAMMOND, ERICSSON, MRS.
Swedish French American Cook Book. NY: 1918. V. 72

HAMMOND, GEORGE P.
The Adventures of Alexander Barclay, Mountain Man. Denver: 1976. V. 68
Captain Charles M. Weber - Pioneer of the San Joaquin and Founder of Stockton, California. Berkeley: 1966. V. 69
Coronado Cuarto Centennial Publications 1540-1940. Volume II Narratives at the Coronado Expedition. Albuquerque: 1940. V. 69
The Discovery of New Mexico 1580-1954. Coronado Cuarto Centennial Publications, 1540-1940. Albuquerque: 1966. V. 70
Don Juan De Onate: Colonizer of New Mexico 1595-1628. 1953. V. 69; 71; 73
Don Juan de Onate: Colonizer of New Mexico 1595-1628. Albuquerque: 1953. V. 73
The Duchow Journal - a Voyage from Boston to California in 1852. San Francisco: 1959. V. 69

HAMMOND, GEORGE P. continued
New Mexico in 1602 Juan de Montoya's Relation of the Discovery of New mexico. Alburquerque: 1938. V. 69
New Spain and the Anglo-American West. Los Angeles: 1932. V. 70
Onate - Colonizer of New Mexico 1595-1628. Albuquerque: 1953. V. 68; 73

HAMMOND, HENRY
Of the Power of the Keyes; or, of Binding and Loosing. London: 1647. V. 72

HAMMOND, JOHN LAWRENCE
The Skilled Labourer 1760-1832. London: 1919. V. 71

HAMMOND, MRS.
The Widow's Plea; a Collection of Poetical Pieces, Chiefly Written During By-Gone Years of Peace and Prosperity.... Stourbridge: 1837. V. 69

HAMMOND, R. A.
The Life and Writings of Charles Dickens: a Memorial Volume. Toronto: 1871. V. 68; 70

HAMMOND, ROBERT
The Electric Light in Our Homes. London: 1884. V. 69

HAMMOND, WILLIAM
Military Medical and Surgical Essays. Philadelphia: 1864. V. 68
On Certain Conditions of Nervous Derangement. New York: 1881. V. 72
Sexual Impotence in the Male. New York: 1883. V. 71
A Treatise on Insanity. New York: 1883. V. 70
A Treatise on the Diseases of the Nervous System. New York: 1876. V. 70; 71

HAMNER, EARL
Spencer's Mountain. New York: 1961. V. 69; 71

HAMNER, LAURA V.
Light n'Hitch, A Collection of Historical Writing Depicting Life On the High Plains. Dallas: 1958. V. 68; 71
The No-Gun Man of Texas. Amarillo: 1935. V. 71
Short Grass and Long Horns. Norman: 1943. V. 69; 71

HAMPL, PATRICIA
Resort. A Poem. St. Paul: 1982. V. 72

THE HAMPSHIRE Tragedy: showing How a Servant Maid First Robbed Her Master, and Afterwards Struck Dead for Telling a Lie. 1795. V. 68

HAMPSON, JOHN
A Bag of Stones - a Novel. London: 1952. V. 69
O Providence. London: 1932. V. 71
Saturday Night at the Greyhound. London: 1931. V. 68; 69
Two Stories - The Mare's Nest; The Long Shadow. London: 1931. V. 72

HAMPSON, JOSEPH N.
Origin, History and Achievements of the Besses 'O'Th'Barn Band. Northampton: circa 1893. V. 73

HAMPSON, WALTER
A Wheel in Whareland. London: 1918. V. 73

HAMPTON & SONS
Illustrated Designs of Cabinet Furniture. 1862. V. 68

HAMPTON, CHRISTOPHER
Poems of Shakespeare. London: 1972. V. 69

HAMPTON, J. F.
Modern Angling Bibliography 1881 to 1945. 1947. V. 73

HAMPTON, O. P.
Wounds of the Extremities in Military Surgery. St. Louis: 1951. V. 71

HAMRICK, ALMA WARD
The Call of the San Saba: a History of San Saba County. San Antonio: 1941. V. 71

HAMSUN, KNUT
August. London: 1932. V. 69; 72
On Overgrown Paths. London: 1968. V. 70

HANAFORD, PHEBE A.
The Life and Writings of Dickens: a Woman's Memorial Volume. Boston: 1871. V. 68

HANAWAY, JONAS
An Historical Account of the British Trade Over the Caspian Sea.... London: 1753. V. 72

HANBURY, DAVID
Sport and Life in the Northland of Canada. London: 1904. V. 71

HANBURY, F.
An Illustrated Monograph of the British Hieracia. London: 1889-1899. V. 69

HANCARVILLE, PIERRE FRANCOIS HUGUES D'
Antiquites Etrusques Grecques et romaines, Ou les Beaux Vases Etrusques, Grecs et Romains, et les Peintures Rendues avec les Couleurs qui Leur sont Propres.... Paris: 1785-1788. V. 69

HANCHETT, LELAND J.
The Crooked Trail to Holbrook. Phoenix: 1993. V. 68

HANCOCK, FRANCIS DEAN
The Flowering Vine. New York: 1964. V. 71

HANCOCK, GEORGE
The Pew Question. London: 1853. V. 68

HANCOCK, H. IRVING
Japanese Physical Training. New York & London: 1904. V. 70

HANCOCK, J.
A Catalogue of the Birds of Northumberland and Durham. London: 1874. V. 69
The Herons of the World. New York: 1978. V. 73

HANCOCK, LEVI WARD
The Saving Sacrifice of the Mormon Battalion from the Journals of.... 2000. V. 68; 73

HANCOCK, SAMUEL
The Narrative of Samuel Hancock of His Overland Journey to Oregon in 1845. New York: 1927. V. 73

HANCOCK, TONY
Hancock's Half Hour. London: 1974. V. 72

HANCOCK, WALTER
Narrative of Twelve Years' Experiments, (1824-1836) Demonstrative of the Practicability and Advantage of Employing Steam-Carriages on Common Roads.... London: 1838. V. 72

HAND and Brain: A Symposium of Essays on Socialism. East Aurora: 1898. V. 69

HAND Book of Colorado. Denver: 1872. V. 69

HAND in Hand. London: 1902. V. 70

HAND, RICHARD A.
A Bookman's Guide to the Indians of the Americas. Metuchen: 1989. V. 68

A HAND-BOOK for Oxford; or an Historical and Topographical Guide to the University, City and Environs. Oxford: 1841. V. 73

THE HAND-BOOK of Heliography.... London: 1840. V. 68

HAND-BOOK of Pencil Drawing. London: 1844. V. 71

THE HAND-BOOK of the Toilette. London: 1841. V. 68

THE HAND-BOOK of Useful and Ornamental Amusements and Accomplishments, Including Artificial Flower Making, Engraving, Etching, Painting.... London: 1845. V. 69

HANDASYDE
The Four Gardens. Philadelphia: 1912. V. 73

HANDBOOK of Painting. London: 1879. V. 73

HANDBOOK of the Old Leeds Exhibition Held in the City Art Gallery July 8th-23rd, 1926. Leeds: 1926. V. 73

THE HANDBOOK of Turning: Containing Instructions in Concentric, Elliptic & Eccentric Turning.... London: 1846. V. 71

HANDLER, H.
The Spanish Riding School in Vienna and the Training of the Lipizzaner Horse. 1972. V. 68

HANDS Off Love. Paris: 1927. V. 71

HANDY, W. C.
Blues. An Anthology. New York: 1926. V. 72
Father of the Blues. New York: 1947. V. 72
Father of the Blues. London: 1957. V. 72

HANDYSIDE, P. D.
A Probationary Essay on Osteo-Aneurism, or Aneurism of the Arterial Capillaries of Bone.... Edinburgh: 1833. V. 70

HANES, BAILEY C.
Bill Pickett, Bulldogger. 1977. V. 69

HANEY, J. L.
A Bibliography of Samuel Taylor Coleridge. Philadelphia: 1903. V. 70

HANFF, HELENE
Apple of My Eye. A Personal Tour of New York. Garden City: 1978. V. 68
The Duchess of Bloomsbury Street. Philadelphia/NY: 1973. V. 72
84 Charing Cross Road. New York: 1970. V. 73
Underfoot in Show Business. Boston: 1980. V. 70

HANGER, GEORGE
The Life, Adventures and Opinions of George Hanger. London: 1801. V. 70
Military Reflections on the Attack and Defence of the City of London.... London: 1795. V. 69

HANKE, KEN
Charlie Chan At The Movies: History, Filmography and Criticism. Jefferson: 1989. V. 72

HANKIN, CHRISTIANA C.
Life of Mary Anne Schimmelpenninck Author Of "Select Memoirs of Port Royal". London: 1858. V. 73

HANKINSON, ALAN
Camera on the Crags. London: 1975. V. 71
A Century of the Crags. London: 1988. V. 69

HANKINSON, THOMAS E.
The Ministry of Angels. A Seatonian Poem. 1840. V. 73

HANKS, N. C.
Up the Hills. Chicago: 1921. V. 69

HANLEY, JAMES
Broken Water. London: 1937. V. 73

HANLEY, JAMES continued
Ebb and Flood - a Novel. London: 1932. V. 69
The Face of Winter. Loughton: 1969. V. 71
The Last Voyage. London: 1931. V. 72
Men in Darkness. London: 1931. V. 69; 73
Men in Darkness. New York: 1932. V. 69
Stoker Haslett. A Tale. Chipping Camden: 1932. V. 71

HANLEY, PATRICK
Tiger Trails in Assam. 1961. V. 69; 70; 72; 73

HANLEY, PETER
Random Recollections of the Stage. London: 1884. V. 72

HANLEY, SYLVANUS
The Young Conchologist's Book of Species. Univalves. London: 1840. V. 68; 70

HANLY, J. FRANK
A Day in the Siskiyous - an Oregon Extravaganza. Indianapolis: 1916. V. 68; 73

HANN, JAMES
Mechanics for Practical Men: Containing Explanations of the Principles of Mechanics, the Steam Engine.... Newcastle-upon-Tyne: 1833. V. 70

HANNA, HILTON E.
Picket and the Pen. The Pat Gorman Story. Yonkers: 1960. V. 71

HANNA, PAUL R.
Frank Lloyd Wright's Hanna House: the Clients' Report. New York: 1981. V. 68

HANNA, PHIL TOWNSEND
Libros Californianos or Five Feet of California Books. Los Angeles: 1931. V. 72
Mexico in the Machine Age: a Plea for Industrial Freedom. Los Angeles: 1932. V. 73

HANNAFORD, D. R.
Spanish Colonial or Adobe Architecture of California 1800-1850. New York: 1931. V. 68; 69; 72

HANNAH, BARRY
Airships. New York: 1978. V. 68; 69; 70; 72
Boomerang. Boston: 1989. V. 68
Captain Maximus. New York: 1985. V. 72
Geronimo Rex. New York: 1972. V. 68; 69
Hey Jack!. New York: 1987. V. 68
Never Die. Boston: 1991. V. 68; 72
Nightwatchmen. New York: 1973. V. 68; 69; 71
Ray. New York: 1980. V. 69
The Tennis Handsome. New York: 1983. V. 72

HANNAS, LINDA
The English Jigsaw Puzzle 1760 to 1890. London: 1972. V. 72

HANNAWAY, PATTI
Winslow Homer in the Tropics. Richmond. V. 73

HANNAY, HOWARD
Roger Fry and Other Essays. London: 1937. V. 70

HANNAY, JAMES
The History of Acadia, from Its Discovery to Its Surrender to England by the Treaty of Paris. St. John: 1879. V. 72
History of New Brunswick. St. John: 1909. V. 73
History of the War of 1812. Between Great Britain and the United States of America. Toronto: 1905. V. 73
The Life and Times of Sir Leonard Tilley, Being a Political History of New Brunswick for the Past Seventy Years. St. John: 1897. V. 73

HANNEMAN, AUDRE
Ernest Hemingway: a Comprehensive Bibliography and Supplement. Princeton: 1967-1975. V. 69

HANNETT, JOHN
Bibliopegia; or Bookbinding in Two Parts. London: 1865. V. 73
Bibliopegia; or the Art of Bookbinding. London: 1835. V. 73
Bibliopegia; or the Art of Bookbinding in All Its Branches. London: 1836. V. 73
Bibliopegia; or the Art of Bookbinding, in All Its Branches. Derby: 1848. V. 73
An Inquiry into the Nature and Form of the Books of the Ancients.... London: 1837. V. 72; 73

HANNUM, ALBERTA
Paint the Wind. New York: 1958. V. 69; 71
Spin a Silver Dollar. New York: 1945. V. 69

HANOTAUX, GABRIEL
Jean d'Arc. 1911. V. 72

THE HANS Andersen ABC. London. V. 69

HANS, FRED
The Great Sioux Nation. Chicago: 1907. V. 72

HANSARD, GEORGE AGAR
Trout and Salmon Fishing in Wales. London: 1834. V. 72

HANSARD, LUKE
The Auto-biography Written in 1817. Wakefield: 1991. V. 68; 71

HANSBERRY, LORRAINE
Les Blancs and the Last Plays of Lorraine Hansberry. New York: 1972. V. 71; 72

HANSBROUGH, VIVIAN
History of Greene County, Arkansas. Little Rock: 1946. V. 73

HANSEL and Gretel. Rochester: 1916. V. 73

HANSEL and Grethel. Philadelphia: 1900. V. 70

HANSEN, H. J.
European Folk Art in Europe and the Americas. New York: 1968. V. 69

HANSEN, HARVEY
Wild Oats in Eden - Sonoma County in the 19th Century. Santa Rosa: 1962. V. 68

HANSEN, JOSEPH
Fadeout. New York: 1970. V. 68; 69; 71

HANSEN, NEIL
Prescences of Nature. Words and Images of the Lake District. Carlisle: 1982. V. 69

HANSEN, RON
The Assassination of Jesse James by the Coward Robert Ford. New York: 1983. V. 68
Atticus. New York: 1996. V. 72
Desperadoes. New York: 1979. V. 68; 71; 72
Mariette in Ecstasy. New York: 1991. V. 70; 73
Nebraska. New York: 1989. V. 68; 70; 73

HANSEN, WOODROW JAMES
The Search for Authority in California. Oakland: 1960. V. 68

HANSON, A.
Art and Identity in Oceania. Honolulu: 1990. V. 69

HANSON, J. A.
Little Chief's Gatherings. Crawford: 1996. V. 69

HANSON, JOHN W.
Historical Sketch of the Old Sixth Regiment of Massachusetts Volunteers. Boston: 1866. V. 70

HANSON, JOSEPH M.
The Conquest of The Missouri Being The Story of The Life and Exploits of Captain Grant Marsh. Chicago: 1909. V. 72

HANSON, L. W.
Contemporary Printed Sources for British and Irish Economic History 1701-1750. Cambridge: 1963. V. 70

HANSON, MARGERY FRANCES DAY
Day unto Day. 1978. V. 69

HANTSKE, MADELINE HORRES
The Song of the Cotton Picker. Clinton: 1942. V. 73

HANWAY, J. EDWIN
The Memoirs of J. Edwin Hanway. Douglas: 1942. V. 71

HANWAY, JONAS
Advice from Farmer Trueman to His Daughter Mary, Upon Her Going into Service.... London: 1800. V. 69
The Commemorative Sacrifice of Our Lord's Supper Considered as a Preservative Against Superstitious Fears and Immoral Practices. London: 1777. V. 70
An Historical Account of the British Trade Over the Caspian Sea.... London: 1753. V. 68
Solitude in Imprisonment, with Proper Profitable Labour and a Spare Diet.... London: 1776. V. 73

HAPPY Family. New York: 1880. V. 70

HAPPY Home. Philadelphia: 1850?. V. 71

HARA, H.
The Flora of Eastern Himalaya.... Japan: 1966. V. 71
Origin and Evolution of Diversity in Plants and Plant Communities. Tokyo: 1985. V. 72

HARASZTHY, ARPAD
Wine Making in California.... San Francisco: 1978. V. 68

HARBEN, WILL N.
The Divine Event. New York: 1920. V. 70

HARBESON, JOHN F.
The Study of Architectural Design. New York: 1927. V. 71

HARBIN, GEORGE
The Hereditary Right of the Crown of England Asserted; the History of the Succession since the Conquest Clear'd; and the True English Constitution Vindicated from the Misrepresentations of Dr. Higden's View and Defence. London: 1713. V. 70

HARBISON, MASSY
A Narrative of Sufferings of Massy Harbison, from Indian Barbarity, Giving an Account of Her Captivity.... Pittsburgh: 1828. V. 68; 71; 73

HARBORD, JAMES G.
The American Expeditionary Forces: Its Organization and Accomplishments. Evanston: 1929. V. 72

HARBOTLE, GEORGE
The Northumberland Gold club Story. London: 1978. V. 73

HARBOTTLE, JOHN
A Fisher's Garland. Leeds: 1904. V. 73

HARBOUR, HENRY
Where Flies the Flag. London: 1904. V. 73

HARBRON, DUDLEY
The Conscious Stone. London: 1949. V. 70

HARBURG, E. Y.
Rhymes for the Irreverent. New York: 1965. V. 71

HARCOURT, E. S.
Two Treatises on Falconry. London: 1968. V. 69

HARDAKER, JOSEPH
The Bridal of Tomar; and other poems. London: 1831. V. 71; 72; 73

HARDCASTLE, GEORGE
Wandersing in Wensleydale, Yorkshire. London: 1864. V. 73

HARDEE, WILLIAM J.
Rifle and Light Infantry Tactics; for the Exercise and Manoeuvers of Troops when Acting as Light Infantry or Riflemen. Memphis: 1861. V. 70
Rifle and Light Infantry Tactics, for the Exercise and Manoeuvres of Troops When Acting as Light Infantry or Rifleman. New Orleans: 1861. V. 69; 70

HARDESTY, HENRY
Historical Encyclopedia: Local History Excerpts and Family. Richmond: 1973. V. 72

HARDIE, JAMES
An Account of the Yellow Fever, Which Occurred in the City of New York in the Year 1822, to Which is Prefixed a Brief Sketch of the Different Pestilential Diseases with Which ths City was afflicted in the Years 1798, 1799, 1803 and 1805. New York: 1822. V. 72
The History of the Tread-Mill, Containing an Account of Its Origin, Construction, Operation, Effects As It Respects the Health and Morals of the Convicts.... New York: 1824. V. 71

HARDIE, MARTIN
John Pettie. London: 1908. V. 70; 72
Water-Colour Painting. 1967-1968. V. 69

HARDIN, FLOYD
Campfires and Cowchips. Great Falls: 1972. V. 71

HARDIN, JOHN WESLEY
The Life of John Wesley Hardin. Sequin: 1896. V. 73

HARDING, A. R.
Fur Buyer's Guide. Columbus: 1915. V. 69

HARDING, ALFRED
Tropical Fruit. New York: 1928. V. 71

HARDING, ANNE
Bibliography of Articles and Papers on North American Indian Art. Washington: 1940. V. 72
Bibliography of Articles and Papers on North American Indian Art. Washington: 1969. V. 72

HARDING, BERTITA
Phantom Crown: the Story of Maximilian And Carlota of Mexico. Indianapolis: 1934. V. 71
Royal Purple, the Story of Alexander and Draga of Serbia. Indianapolis: 1935. V. 70

HARDING, E. W.
The Flyfisher and The Trout's Point of View, New Light on Flyfishing Theory and Practice. 1931. V. 73

HARDING, GEORGE L.
Don Agustin V. Zamorano. Statesman, Soldier, Craftsman, and California's First Printer. Los Angeles: 1934. V. 73

HARDING, GEORGE R.
The Acts and Orders Relating to Joint Stock Companies. Brisbane: 1887. V. 70

HARDING, J. D.
Elementary Art, or the Use of the Chalk and Lead Pencil Advocated and Explained. London: 1846. V. 69; 71
Elementary Art; or the Use of the Lead Pencil Advocated and Explained. London: 1838. V. 71
Lessons on Trees. 1880. V. 68
The Principles and Practice of Art. London: 1845. V. 69

HARDING, JOHN W.
The Time, the Place and the Girl. New York: 1908. V. 71

HARDING, SAMUEL BANNISTER
Life of George R. Smith- Founder of Sedalia, MO. Sedalia: 1904. V. 70; 71

HARDWICK, CHARLES
History of the Borough of Preston. 1857. V. 73
Traditions, Superstitions, and Folklore. Manchester: 1872. V. 73

HARDWICK, ELIZABETH
The Simple Truth. New York: 1955. V. 72
A View of My Own. New York: 1962. V. 72

HARDWICK, MICHAEL
Four Sherlock Holmes Plays. London: 1964. V. 69
The Sherlock Holmes Companion. London: 1962. V. 68

HARDWICKE, PHILIP YORKE, 2ND EARL OF
Athenian Letters; or, Epistolary Correspondence of a Agent of the King of Persia, Residing at Athens During the Pelepponnesian War. London: 1798. V. 72
Miscellaneous State Papers from 1501 to 1726. London. V. 73

HARDWICKE, W. W.
Sunday the People's Holiday. London: 1898. V. 68

HARDY, ARTHUR SHERBURNE
Diane and Her Friends. Boston: 1914. V. 69

HARDY, BARBARA
A Reading of Jane Austen. 1975. V. 73
A Reading of Jane Austen. London: 1975. V. 70

HARDY, CAMPBELL
Forest Life in Acadie. Sketches of Sport and Natural History in the Lower Provinces of the Canadian Dominion. London: 1869. V. 73

HARDY, CHARLES E.
John Bowes and the Bowes Museum. Newcastle upon Tyne: 1970. V. 70; 72; 73

HARDY, CHARLES FREDERICK
The Hardys of Barbon and Some Other Westmorland Statesman: Their Kith, Kin and Childer. London: 1913. V. 71; 72

HARDY, D.
Through Cities and Prairie Land Sketches of an American Tour. New York: 1881. V. 69

HARDY, EDWARD JOHN
How to Be Happy though Married Being a Handbook to Marriage by a Graduate in the University of Matrimony. London: 1886. V. 70

HARDY, ERIC
The Birds of the Liverpool Area. Arbroath: 1941. V. 73

HARDY, EVELYN
The Conjured Spirit. 1949. V. 69

HARDY, FRANCIS
Memoirs of the Political and Private Life of James Caulfield, Earl of Charmont. London: 1810. V. 70; 72

HARDY, FREDERICK
The Bijou Book of In-Door Amusements. London: 1868. V. 69

HARDY, J. J.
Salmon Fishing. 1907. V. 73

HARDY, JAMES L.
The House the Hardy Brothers Built. 1998. V. 68; 73

HARDY, R. SPENCE
William Grimshaw, Incumbent of Haworth, 1742-1763. London: 1861,. V. 70; 72; 73

HARDY, THOMAS
A Changed Man, The Waiting Supper and Other Tales. London: 1913. 68; 72
A Changed Man, The Waiting Supper and Other Tales. New York: 1913. V. 71; 72; 73
The Dynasts. 1904-1908. V. 71
The Dynasts. London: 1904-1908. V. 68
The Dynasts. London: 1927. V. 68; 70; 72; 73
The Famous Tragedy of the Queen of Cornwall at Tintagel in Lyonnesse. 1923. V. 70
Human Shows, Far Phantasies: Songs and Trifles. London: 1925. V. 68; 69; 70; 72; 73
Human Shows, Far Phantasies, Songs and Trifles. New York: 1925. V. 71
Jude the Obscure. 1896. V. 68
Jude the Obscure. London: 1896. V. 69; 70
Jude the Obscure. New York: 1896. V. 71
A Laodicean; or the Castle of the De Stancys. London: 1881. V. 73
A Laodicean; or, the Castle of the De Stancy's. London: 1890. V. 68
Late Lyrics and Earlier. 1922. V. 70
Late Lyrics and Earlier, With Many Other Verses. London: 1922. V. 72; 73
Life's Little Ironies; a Set of Tales.... London: 1894. V. 73
Lyrics and Earlier, with Many More Verses. London: 1922. V. 69
A Pair of Blue Eyes. New York: 1873. V. 71
A Pair of Blue Eyes. London: 1877. V. 71
The Patriot. Edinburgh: 1793. V. 69; 71
Poems of the Past and Present. London and New York: 1901. V. 73
Poems of the Past and the Present. London and New York: 1902. V. 69
The Return of the Native. London: 1878. V. 68
The Return of the Native. New York: 1878. V. 71
The Return of the Native. London: 1890. V. 68
The Return of the Native. New York: 1942. V. 71
Satires of Circumstance. 1914. V. 70
Selected Poems. . London: 1916. V. 73
Seld Poems of Thomas Hardy. London: 1940. V. 72
Tess of the D'Urbervilles. New York: 1892. V. 68; 71
Tess of the D'urbervilles. New York: 1924. V. 70
The Three Wayfarers: a Play in One Act. New York: 1930. V. 70
Time's Laughing Stock. London: 1909. V. 68
Time's Laughing Stocks. 1909. V. 70; 73
To Shakespeare After Three Hundred Years. London: 1916. V. 72
The Trial of Thomas Hardy for High Treason at the Sessions House in the Old Bailey, on Tuesday the 28th, Wednesday the 29th, Thursday the 30th, Friday the 31st October, and on Saturday the 1st, Monday the 3rd, Tuesday the 4th and Wednesday the 5th Novemb. London: 1794-1795. V. 70
The Trumpet Major. New York: 1880. V. 69
The Trumpet-Major John Loveday: a Soldier in the War with Buonaparte and Robert His Brother, First Mate in the Merchant Service. London: 1896. V. 69
Two on a Tower. London: 1882. V. 72
Two on a Tower. London: 1890. V. 68
Under the Greenwood Tree. London: 1878. V. 73
Under the Greenwood Tree. London: 1903. V. 70
Under the Greenwood Tree. London: 1913. V. 72; 73
The Well Beloved: a Sketch of a Temperament. London: 1897. V. 68

HARDY, THOMAS continued
The Wessex Novels. London: 1923-1926. V. 73
Wessex Poems and Other Verses. London and New York: 1898. V. 70; 73
Wessex Poems and Other Verses. New York and London: 1899. V. 69
Wessex Tales.... London: 1888. V. 73
Winter Words. 1928. V. 70
Winter Words. London: 1928. V. 68; 71; 72; 73
The Woodlanders. London: 1887. V. 68
The Woodlanders. London: 1906. V. 70
The Works of Thomas Hardy. London: 1919. V. 71
The Works of Thomas Hardy. London: 1919-1920. V. 68
The Writings of Thomas Hardy. New York and London: 1915. V. 69; 71

HARDY, W. G.
Alberta, a Natural History. Alberta: 1967. V. 71

HARDY'S
Angler's Guide. 1937. V. 70

HARE, AUGUSTUS J. C.
The Life and Letters of Maria Edgeworth. London: 1894. V. 73
Paris. London: 1900. V. 72
The Story Of Two Noble Lives. Being Memorial of Charlotte, Countess Canning And Louisa, Marchioness of Waterford. London: 1893. V. 72

HARE, CYRIL
Best Detective Stories Of Cyril Hare. London: 1959. V. 72; 73
An English Murder. London: 1951. V. 68; 70; 73
He Should Have Died Hereafter. London: 1958. V. 68; 72
That Yew Tree's Shade. London: 1954. V. 73
Tragedy at Law. New York: 1943. V. 70
With a Bare Bodkin. London: 1946. V. 68; 72

HARE, J. I.
American Leading Cases; Being Select Decisions of American Courts. Philadelphia: 1871. V. 71

HARE, JAMES R.
Hiking the Appalachian Trail. Emmanus: 1975. V. 71

HARE, R.
Experimental Observations and Improvements in Apparatus and Manipulation.... Philadelphia: 1836. V. 68

HARE, THOMAS
Physiological Views of the Structure, Functions and Disorders of the Stomach and Alimentary Organs of the Human Body. London: 1824. V. 71

HARFORD, JOHN S.
The Life of Michael Angelo Buonarroti. London: 1858. V. 71

HARFORD BATTERSBY, CHARLES FORBES
Pilkington of Uganda. London: 1900. V. 69

HARGRAVE, JAMES
The Hargrave Correspondence 1821-1843. Toronto: 1938. V. 71

HARGRAVE, JOHN
Harbottle. Philadelphia: 1924. V. 69

HARGREAVE, CHARLES JAMES
An Essay on the Resolution of Algebraic Equations. Dublin: 1866. V. 72

HARGROVE, E.
The History of the Castle, Town, and Forest of Knaresborough, with Harrogate. York: 1775. V. 73
History of the Castle, Town, and Forest of Knaresborough, with Harrogate. Knaresboroguh: 1789. V. 73
The History of the Castle, Town, and Forest of Knaresborough, with Harrogate. York: 1798. V. 73
The History of the Castle, Town, and Forest of Knaresborough with Harrogate. Knaresborough: 1809. V. 73
The Yorkshire Gazetteer, or, A Dictionary of the Towns, Villages, and Hamlets: Monasteries and Castles; Principal Mountains, Rivers & C.; in the County of York, and Ainsty, or County of the City, of York. Knarelsborough: 1812. V. 73

HARING, J. VREELAND
The Hand of Hauptmann. The Handwriting Expert Tells the Story of the Lindbergh Case. Plainfield: 1937. V. 69

HARINGTON, EDWARD
A Schizzo on the Genius of Man.... Bath: 1793. V. 69

HARJO, JOY
The Woman Who Fell From the Sky. New York: 1994. V. 72

HARKER, BAILEY J.
Rambles in Upper Wharfedale; Including the Historical and Traditional Lore of the District. Skipton: 1869. V. 73

HARKER, W.
A Practical Grammar of Music.. London: 1830. V. 69

HARKEY, DEE
Mean as Hell. Albuquerque: 1948. V. 69; 71

HARKNESS, HENRY
A Description of a Singular Aboriginal Race Inhabiting the Summit of the Heilgherry Hills, or Blue Mountains.... London: 1832. V. 68

HARLAN, COBEN
Fade Away. New York: 1996. V. 72

HARLAN, JACOB W.
California 46 to 48. San Francisco: 1888. V. 69

HARLAN, ROBERT D.
Chapter Nine: the Vulgate Bible and Other Unfinished Projects of John Henry Nash. San Francisco: 1982. V. 70
The Two Hundredth Book; A Bibliography of the Books Published by the Book Club of California, 1958-1993. San Francisco: 1993. V. 72

HARLAND, HENRY
The Cardinal's Snuff Box. London and New York: 1903. V. 68
My Friend Prospero. London and New York: 1904. V. 68
The Royal End: a Romance. London: 1909. V. 68

HARLAND, J.
Historical Account of the Cistercian Abbey of Salley in Craven, Yorkshire, founded AD 1147. 1853. V. 73
The House and Farm Accounts of the Shuttleworths of Gawthorpe Hall. London: 1856-1858. V. 73
Lancashire Folk-Lore. London: 1867. V. 73
Lancashire Folk-Lore. Manchester: 1867. V. 73
Lancashire Legends, Traditions, Pageants, Sports, & C.,. London: 1882. V. 73
Mamecestre. Manchester: 1851-1862. V. 73

HARLAND, MARION
Charlotte Bronte at Home. New York: 1899. V. 73
Common Sense in the Household. New York: 1885. V. 73
Dinner Year-Book. New York: 1878. V. 68; 73
Some Colonial Homesteads. (with) More Colonial Homesteads. New York and London: 1899. V. 72

HARLAND, WILLIAM, & SON
Monograms and Heraldic Designs from William Harland and Son, Merton Surrey. 1890. V. 71
Monograms and Heraldic Designs from William Harland and Son, Merton Surrey. London: 1890. V. 70

HARLEY, JOHN
William Byrd. Gentleman of the Chapel Royal. London: 1997. V. 73

HARLEY, TIMOTHY
Southward Ho! Notes of a Tour Through the State of Georgia in the Winter of 1885-1886. London: 1886. V. 71

HARLOW, ALVIN F.
Brass-Pounders: Young Telegraphers of the Civil War. Denver: 1962. V. 68
Old Waybills, the Romance of the Express Companies. New York: 1934. V. 69; 70

HARLOW, FRANCIS H.
Matte-Paint Pottery of the Tewa, Keres and Zuni Pueblos. Santa Fe: 1973. V. 70

HARLOW, NEAL
Maps and Surveys of the Pueblo Lands of Los Angeles. Los Angeles: 1976. V. 68; 70; 73

HARLOW, S.
W. H. Davies. A Bibliography. Winchester: 1993. V. 70

HARMAN, APPLETON MILO
The Journal of.... Glendale: 1946. V. 69

HARMAN, FRED
Cowboy Lingo. New York: 1938. V. 69
Great West in Paintings. Chicago: 1969. V. 70

HARMAN, LESLIE
The Parish of S. Giles-in-Reading. Reading: 1946. V. 72

HARMAN, MOSES
The Persecution and the Appreciation. Chicago: 1907. V. 68

HARMER, JOHN
Murder of Mr. Steele. Documents and Observations, Tending to Show a Probability of the Innocence of John Holloway and Owen Haggerty.... London: 1807. V. 70

HARMON, DANIEL WILLIAMS
Harmon's Journal. Toronto: 1904. V. 71

HARMON, J. C.
Crazy - the Kid of the Cowboy Scout. Sioux City: 1921. V. 68

HARMON, R. W.
Bibliography of Animal Venoms. Gainesville: 1948. V. 69; 73

HARMSEN, DOROTHY
American Western Art. Denver: 1977. V. 69
Harmsen's Western Americana. Denver: 1978. V. 69

HARNED, J. E.
Wild Flowers of the Alleghanies, Being a Description of Their Character, Habits, Flowering Season and Location.... Oakland: 1931. V. 70; 72

HARPER, CHARLES G.
The Downs and the Sea, Wild Life and Scenery in Surrey, Sussex and Kent. 1923. V. 70
Mr. Pickwick's Second Time On Earth. London: 1927. V. 69

HARPER, FRANCES E.
Iola Leroy, or Shadows Uplifted. Boston: 1895. V. 70

HARPER, GEORGE WASHINGTON FINLEY
In Memoriam: E.L.R. Lenoir: 1908. V. 70
Reminiscences of Caldwell County, N.C. in the Great War of 1861-'1865. Lenoir: 1913. V. 70

HARPER, IDA HUSTED
The History of Woman Suffrage. New York: 1922. V. 73

HARPER, J. RUSSELL
Paul Kane's Frontier Including Wanderings of an Artist Among the Indians of North America by Paul Kane. 1971. V. 71

HARPER, J. WILSON
Money and Social Problems. Edinburgh and London: 1896. V. 70

HARPER, JOHN
Glimpses of Ocean Life, or Rock, Rock-Pools and the Lessons they Teach. London: 1860. V. 68

HARPER, MALCOLM M'L
Rambles in Galloway. London: 1896. V. 71

HARPER, MICHAEL
Debridement. Garden City: 1973. V. 72
Song: I Want a Witness. Pittsburgh: 1972. V. 72

HARPER, ROBERT GOODLOE
Observations on the Dispute Between the United States and France. London: 1798. V. 73

HARPER, THEODORE ACLAND
His Excellency and Peter. Garden City: 1930. V. 69
Seventeen Chimneys. New York: 1938. V. 71

HARPER, WILHELMINA
The Gunniwolf and Other Merry Tales. Philadelphia: 1936. V. 73

HARPER, WILLIAM
The Remedy by State Interposition or Nullification; Explained and Advocated. Charleston: 1832. V. 68

HARPER'S Household Handbook. New York: 1913. V. 73

HARPER'S Weekly. New York: 1861-1865. V. 70

HARPSFIELD, NICHOLAS
Historia Anglicana Ecclesiastica a Primis gentis Suscepta Fidei Incunabulis ad Nostra Fere Tempora Deducta.... Duaci: 1622. V. 72

HARR, JONATHAN
A Civil Action. New York: 1995. V. 68; 69; 72

HARRADEN, BEATRICE
The Fowler. Edinburgh and London: 1899. V. 68
Ships that Pass in the Night. New York: 1900. V. 73

HARRALL, THOMAS
Picturesque Views of the Severn; with Historical and Topographical Illustrations by.... 1824. V. 72

HARRAP, GEORGE
Love Lyrics from Five Centuries. New York: 1930. V. 68

HARRAR, JAMES A.
The Story of the Lying-in-Hospital of the City of New York. New York: 1938. V. 68

HARRER, HEINRICH
Seven Years in Tibet. New York: 1993. V. 69; 71
The White Spider. London: 1960. V. 69
The White Spider. London: 1968. V. 69

HARRINGTON, ALAN
The Immortalist. New York: 1969. V. 71; 72
The Revelations of Dr. Modesto. New York: 1955. V. 68

HARRINGTON, CHARLES
Summering in Colorado. Denver: 1874. V. 69

HARRINGTON, CONYERS
An Impartial History of the Life and Reign of Her Late Majesty Queen Anne of Immortal Memory. Cambridge: 1744. V. 68

HARRINGTON, EDWARD
A Schizzo on the Genius of Man. Bath: 1793. V. 71

HARRINGTON, ELIZABETH STILL, COUNTESS OF
Ballads and Poems. 1855?. V. 68; 70
Poems by.... London: 1874. V. 68
The Storks. The False Prince. London: 1875. V. 68

HARRINGTON, HARRY
Hanging Judge. Caldwell: 1951. V. 69

HARRINGTON, JAMES
The Censure of the Rota Upon Mr. Miltons Book Entitled, the Ready and Easie Way to Establish a Free Comon-Wealth. London: 1660. V. 70; 73

HARRINGTON, KARL POMEROY
Walks and Climbs in the White Mountains. New Haven: 1926. V. 72

HARRINGTON, KENT
Dia De Los Muertos. Tucson: 1997. V. 70; 71

HARRINGTON, M. R.
Gypsum Cave, Nevada. Report of the Second Sessions Expedition. 1933. V. 69

HARRINGTON, SAMUEL M.
Reports of Cases Argued and Adjudged in the Suerpior Court and Court of Errors and Appeals of the State of Delaware. Dover: 1832-1855. V. 70

HARRINGTON, W. P.
History of Gove County, Kansas. Gove City: 1930. V. 68

HARRIOTT, JOHN
Struggles through Life, Exemplified in the Various Travels and Adventures... London: 1807. V. 73
Struggles through Life, Exemplified in the Various Travels and Adventures... London: 1808. V. 73

HARRIS, ALBERT W.
The Cruise of a Schooner. Chicago: 1911. V. 69
The Cruise of a Schooner. 1958. V. 69; 72; 73

HARRIS, ALEX
A Biographical History of Lancaster County: Being a History of Early Settlers and Eminent Men of the County. Lancaster: 1872. V. 69

HARRIS, BURTON
John Colter, His Years in the Rockies. New York: 1952. V. 68; 69; 73

HARRIS, C.
The Heart and the Vascular System in Ancient Greek Medicine. Oxford: 1973. V. 71

HARRIS, D. T.
The Technique of Ultraviolet Radiology. London and Glasgow: 1932. V. 68

HARRIS, DEAN
By Path and Trail. Chicago: 1908. V. 68
By Path and Trail. Chicago: 1909. V. 69
The Catholic Church in the Utah 1776-1909. Salt Lake City: 1909. V. 69

HARRIS, EILEEN
British Architectural Books and Writers 1556-1785. 1990. V. 68

HARRIS, EMILY CUMMING
New Zealand Berries. Nelson: 1890. V. 69
New Zealand Flowers. Nelson: 1890. V. 69

HARRIS, FRANK
Montes the Matador and Other Stories. New York: 1910. V. 68
My Life and Loves. Fifth Volume. Paris: 1954. V. 70
New Preface to The Life and Confessions of Oscar Wilde. London: 1925. V. 68
Undream'd of Shores. London: 1924. V. 70
The Yellow Ticket and Other Stories. London: 1914. V. 69; 71

HARRIS, GEORGE W.
Sut Lovingood. Yarns Spun by.... New York: 1867. V. 71

HARRIS, GERTRUDE
A Tale of Men Who Knew Not Fear - Sibley's Campaign of 1862. San Antonio: 1935. V. 69; 72

HARRIS, H. A.
The Horse Thief, or the Maidens and Negro. Boston: 1845. V. 71

HARRIS, H. G.
All About Genoese Glaces, Petits Fours and Bon Bons. London: 1910. V. 68

HARRIS, ISAAC
Harris's Pittsburgh Business Directory for the Year 1837.... Pittsburgh: 1837. V. 68

HARRIS, J. R.
An Angler's Entomology. 1952. V. 68; 73

HARRIS, JAMES
Hermes or a Philosophical Enquiry Concerning Universal Grammar. London: 1771. V. 69
Philosophical Arrangements. London: 1775. V. 70
Three Treatises. The First Concerning Art. The Second Concerning Music, Painting and Poetry. The Third Concerning Happiness. London: 1744. V. 70; 72

HARRIS, JOANNE
Blackberry Wine. London: 2000. V. 70
Chocolat. New York: 1999. V. 69; 73

HARRIS, JOEL CHANDLER
The Chronicles of Aunt Minervy Ann. New York: 1899. V. 73
Gabriel Tolliver. New York: 1902. V. 73
Nights with Uncle Remus. Boston: 1883. V. 70
Nights with Uncle Remus. London: 1884. V. 68; 70; 71; 72
Stories from Uncle Remus. London. V. 69
Tales of the Home Folks in Peace and War. Boston and New York: 1898. V. 70; 73
The Tar-Baby and Other Rhymes of Uncle Remus. New York: 1904. V. 69; 72; 73
Uncle Remus. London: 1920. V. 69
Uncle Remus and His Friends. Boston and New York: 1892. V. 71; 73
Uncle Remus and His Legends of the Old Plantation. London: 1881. V. 70; 71; 72
Uncle Remus: His Songs and His Sayings. New York: 1881. V. 69; 71; 72; 73
Uncle Remus: His Songs and His Sayings. New York: 1934. V. 71
Uncle Remus: His Songs and His Sayings. New York: 1957. V. 71
Uncle Remus. His Songs and Sayings. New York: 1895. V. 68
Uncle Remus Stories. Akron: 1934. V. 70
Wally Wanderoon and His Story-Telling Machine. New York: 1903. V. 73

HARRIS, JOEL CHANDLER continued
Wally Wanderoon and His Story-Telling Machine. London: 1904. V. 68; 71

HARRIS, JOHN
Lexicon Technicum; or, an Universal English Dictionary of Arts and Sciences.... London: 1736. V. 70
Sir William Chambers. Knight of the Polar Star. 1970. V. 73

HARRIS, JOHN ETCHER
Illustrations Of The History Of France. London. V. 72

HARRIS, LARRY A.
Pancho Villa and the Columbus Raid. El Paso: 1949. V. 71

HARRIS, LAURA
The Happy Little Choo-Choo. New York: 1944. V. 72

HARRIS, MALCOLM
Old New Kent County: Some Account of the Planters Plantations and Places in New Kent County. West Point: 1977. V. 70

HARRIS, MALCOLM H.
History of Louisa County, Virginia. Richmond: 1936. V. 72

HARRIS, MARK
City of Discontent. Indianapolis: 1952. V. 71
Friedman and Son. New York: 1963. V. 71
The Goy. New York: 1970. V. 71; 72
Lying in Bed. New York: 1984. V. 72
Something About a Soldier. New York: 1957. V. 71
The Southpaw. Indianapolis/New York: 1953. V. 69
Trumpet to the World. New York: 1946. V. 71; 73
Wake Up, Stupid. London: 1960. V. 71

HARRIS, MAX
The Vegetative Eye. Melbourne: 1943. V. 68

HARRIS, MELVIN
The True Face of Jack the Ripper. London: 1994. V. 71

HARRIS, N. DWIGHT
Negro Servitude in Illinois. Chicago: 1904. V. 73

HARRIS, R. COLE
Historical Atlas of Canada. Volume I. From Beginning to 1900. Toronto: 1987. V. 71; 73

HARRIS, ROBERT
Archangel. New York: 1999. V. 72
Enigma. London: 1992. V. 71
Enigma. London: 1995. V. 68; 73
Fatherland. London: 1992. V. 68; 70; 71; 73

HARRIS, ROSEMARY
The Enchanted Horse Set in India.... 1981. V. 71
A Wicked Pack Of Cards. London: 1969. V. 72

HARRIS, SHELDON
Blues Who's Who. New Rochelle: 1979. V. 70; 72

HARRIS, T. M.
The Assassination of Lincoln. Boston: 1892. V. 69

HARRIS, T. W.
A Treatise on Some of the Insects Injurious to Vegetation. New York: 1862. V. 71
A Treatise on Some of the Insects of New England Which are Injurious to Vegetation. Boston: 1852. V. 71

HARRIS, THADDEUS M.
Biographical Memoirs of James Oglethorpe, Founder of Georgia. Boston: 1841. V. 70

HARRIS, THOMAS
Black Sunday. New York: 1975. V. 68; 71; 73
Hannibal. London: 1999. V. 70
Red Dragon. New York: 1981. V. 68; 70; 71
The Silence of the Lambs. New York: 1988. V. 68; 69; 70; 71; 73

HARRIS, THOMAS L.
God's Breath in Man and in Humane Society. Fountaingrove: 1891. V. 69
The New Republic. A Discourse of the Prospects, Dangers, Duties and Safeties of the Times. Fountaingrove: 1891. V. 69

HARRIS, TIMOTHY
Good Night and Good-Bye. New York: 1979. V. 72
Kronski/McSmash. Garden City: 1970. V. 69; 73
Kyd For Hire. London: 1977. V. 72

HARRIS, TINDALL
Here and There. An Angler's Memories. 1924. V. 73

HARRIS, WALTER
De Morbis Acutis Infantum. London: 1689. V. 72

HARRIS, WILFRED
The Facil Neuralgias. Oxford: 1937. V. 68
The Morphology of the Brachial Plexus. London: 1939. V. 68

HARRIS, WILLIAM
Elements of the Chaldee Language, Intended as a Supplement to the Hebrew Grammars, and as a General Introduction to the Aramean Dialects. New York: 1823. V. 71
An Historical and Critical Account of the Life and Writings of Charles I King of Great Britain. London: 1758. V. 73

HARRIS, WILLIAM J.
The History of the Radical Party in Parliament. London: 1885. V. 71

HARRIS, WILLIAM R.
The Catholic Church in Utah. Salt Lake City: 1909. V. 72

HARRIS, WILLIAM SNOW
Rudimentary Electricity: Being a Concise Exposition of the General Principles of Electrical Science. London: 1854. V. 71

HARRIS, WILSON
Da Silva da Silva's Cultivated Wilderness and Genesis of the Clowns. London: 1977. V. 69
The Eye of the Scarecrow. London: 1965. V. 70

HARRISON, CONSTANCE CARY
A Bachelor Maid. New York: 1894. V. 69

HARRISON, D. L.
The Mammals of Arabia. 1964. V. 69
The Mammals of Arabia. 1964-1972. V. 73

HARRISON, E.
Guns and Shooting. 1908. V. 71

HARRISON, E. E.
Kittens. Wickham Market: 1900. V. 69

HARRISON, E. S.
Central California, Santa Clara Valley. San Jose: 1887. V. 73

HARRISON, EDWARD
An Address Delivered to the Lincolnshire Benevolent Medical Society at their Anniversary Meeting in 1809. London: 1810. V. 69

HARRISON, FAIRFAX
The John's Island Stud (South Carolina) 1750-1788. Richmond: 1931. V. 71
Landmarks of Old Prince William: a Study of Origins in Northern Virginia. Berryville: 1964. V. 71
Landmarks of Old Prince William: a Study of Origins in Northern Virginia. Baltimore: 1987. V. 71

HARRISON, FREDERIC
Autobiographical Memoirs. London: 1911. V. 71
My Alpine Jubilee. 1851-1907. London: 1908. V. 69
William The Silent. London: 1898. V. 72

HARRISON, H. S.
A Handbook to the Weapons of War and the Chase. London. V. 69

HARRISON, HARRY
Bill the Galactic Hero. Garden City: 1965. V. 69; 71

HARRISON, HENRY
The Place-Names of the Liverpool District. London: 1898. V. 73
The Sacco-Vanzetti Anthology. New York: 1927. V. 68

HARRISON, HENRY SYDNOR
Angela's Business. Boston: 1915. V. 71
V. V.'s Eyes. Boston: 1913. V. 71

HARRISON, J.
A Field Guide to the Birds of Sri Lanka. Oxford: 1999. V. 68

HARRISON, J. C.
Bird Portraits. 1949. V. 71

HARRISON, J. E.
Greek Vase Painting. London: 1894. V. 71; 72

HARRISON, JAMES M.
The Birds of Kent. 1953. V. 69
Bristow and the Hastings Rarities Affair. 1968. V. 69
A Handlist of the Birds of the Sevenoaks or Western District of Kent. 1942. V. 69

HARRISON, JAMIE
The Edge of the Crazies. 1995. V. 68
The Edge of the Crazies. New York: 1995. V. 71; 72

HARRISON, JIM
After Ikkyu and Other Poems. Boston: 1996. V. 70; 71; 72
The Beast God Forgot to Invent. New York: 2000. V. 68; 72
The Boy Who Ran to the Woods. New York: 2000. V. 70; 73
Dalva. London: 1988. V. 72
Dalva. New York: 1988. V. 68; 69; 72
Farmer. New York: 1976. V. 69; 71; 72; 73
Five Blind Men. Fremont: 1969. V. 68; 72
From Geo-Bestiary. 1998. V. 71
A Good Day to Die. New York: 1973. V. 69; 70; 71; 72; 73
Julip. Boston/New York: 1994. V. 71; 72
Just Before Dark. Livingston: 1991. V. 69; 70; 71; 72; 73
Legends of the Fall. New York: 1979. V. 68; 69
Legends of the Fall. London: 1980. V. 68; 70; 72
Legends of the Fall. New York: 1994. V. 68
Legends of the Fall: (I). Revenge. (II) The Man Who Gave Up His Name. (III) Legends of the Fall. New York: 1978-1979. V. 69; 70; 72

HARRISON, JIM *continued*
Legends of the Fall, Revenge and the Man Who Gave Up His Name. New York: 1978. V. 69
Legends of the Fall, Revenge, The Man Who Gave Up His Name. New York: 1979. V. 69; 71; 72; 73
Letters to Yesenin. Fremont: 1973. V. 73
Locations. New York: 1968. V. 70; 71; 72; 73
Outlyer and Ghazals. New York: 1971. V. 69; 70; 72; 73
Plain Song. New York: 1965. V. 71; 72; 73
Returning to Earth. Berkeley: 1977. V. 68; 72
The Road Home. New York: 1998. V. 68; 69; 72
Selected and New Poems. New York: 1982. V. 69; 70; 72; 73
The Shape of the Journey. Port Townsend: 1998. V. 71
Sundog. New York: 1984. V. 68; 71; 72; 73
The Theory and Practice of Rivers. Seattle: 1986. V. 69; 71; 72; 73
The Theory and Practice of Rivers. Livingston: 1989. V. 70
Warlock. New York: 1981. V. 68; 70; 71; 72; 73
Wolf. New York: 1971. V. 70; 71; 72; 73
The Woman Lit by Fireflies. Boston: 1990. V. 68; 70; 71; 72; 73
The Woman Lit by Fireflies. New York: 1990. V. 69

HARRISON, JOHN
Our Tunis College. Sketches of the History of the Old College of Edinburgh. London: 1884. V. 68

HARRISON, JOSEPH
The Locomotive Engine and Philadelphia's Share in Its Early Improvements. Philadelphia: 1872. V. 71
The Locomotive Engine and Philadelphia's Share in Its Early Improvements. Philadelphia: 1972. V. 73

HARRISON, JOSEPH T.
The Story of The Dining Fork. Cincinnati: 1927. V. 72

HARRISON, KATHRYN
The Kiss. New York: 1997. V. 72

HARRISON, MARTIN
Brian Clark. London: 1981. V. 72

HARRISON, MICHAEL
The Exploits of the Chevalier Dupin. Sauk City: 1968. V. 69; 71; 72
In the Footsteps of Sherlock Holmes. London: 1958. V. 71
Theatrical Mr. Holmes. London: 1974. V. 70
The World Of Sherlock Holmes. New York: 1975. V. 72

HARRISON, SHIRLEY
The Diary Of Jack The Ripper. New York: 1933. V. 72

HARRISON, SUSANNAH
Songs in the Night. Ispwich: 1788. V. 73

HARRISON, T., & SON
A Catalogue of Cheap Books, sold by T. Harrison & Son, Booksellers, Stationers, Printers &c. Airedale Courant Office, York Place, Bingley. Bingley: 1870. V. 70

HARRISON, T. W.
Wills and Administration. Charlottesville: 1927. V. 68

HARRISON, TOM
Living among Cannibals. London: 1943. V. 72
War Begins at Home. London: 1940. V. 71

HARRISON, TONY
Dramatic Verse 1973-1985. Newcastle: 1985. V. 72
Earthworks. Leeds: 1964. V. 68; 71
The Gaze of the Gorgon. Newcastle upon Tyne: 1992. V. 70
A Kumquat for John Keats: a Poem. Newcastle-upon-Tyne: 1981. V. 73

HARRISON, W.
Ripon Millenary. A Record of the Festival Also a History of the City...from the Year 1400.... Ripon: 1892. V. 70

HARRISON, W. H.
The Humourist, a Companion for the Christmas Fireside. London: 1800. V. 69

HARRISON, WILLIAM
Roller Ball Murder. New York: 1974. V. 69; 71
The Substance of the Speech of William Harrison, Esq. Before the Select Committee of the House of Commons, on East India-Built Shipping on Monday April 18, 1814. (bound with) The Substance of the Reply of William Harrison, Esq.... London: 1814. V. 71

HARRISSE, HENRY
Decouverte et Evolution Cartographique de Terre Neuve et des Pays Circonvoisins. Ridgewood: 1968. V. 70

HARRODS LTD. ALLSOP & CO.
Catalogue of Prehistoric and Ethnological Specimens, Savage Implements and Weapons. London: 1939. V. 71

HARROGATE, W. E. A.
History of Harrogate & Knaresborgh. Huddersfield: 1970. V. 73

HARROP, DOROTHY
A History of the Gregynog Press. Middlesex: 1980. V. 70

HARROP, MR.
The History of the Irish Rebellion in the Year 1798. Philadelphia: 1815. V. 70

HARROW, L. W.
Oriental Rugs in Private Collections. 1982. V. 73

HARRY Weinberger: Paintings and Drawings. Coventry: 1983. V. 70

HARSANYI, ZSOLT
Immortal Franz. The Life and Loves of a Genius. New York: 1937. V. 71

HARSHBERGER, J. W.
The Vegetation of the New Jersey Pine Barrens, an Ecologic Investigation. Philadelphia: 1916. V. 69; 71; 73

HART, ALBERT BUSHNELL
The Varick Court of Inquiry: to Investigate the Implication of Colonel Varick.... Boston: 1907. V. 68; 73

HART, CAROLYN
A Settling of Accounts. New York: 1976. V. 70

HART, CHARLES HENRY
Browere's Life Masks of Great Americans. New York: 1899. V. 68

HART, ELIZABETH ANN
Child-Nature. London: 1880. V. 69

HART, FRANCES NOYES
Hide in the Dark. New York: 1929. V. 69

HART, H. C.
Report on the Botany of Sinai and South Palestine. 1885. V. 69
Some Account of the Fauna and Flora of Sinai, Petra and Wady 'Arabah. London: 1891. V. 69

HART, H. MARTYN
The World of the Sea. London: 1873. V. 68

HART, HANK
Here Goes the Circus. Kenosha: 1941. V. 69

HART, HELEN
Little Silver-Tail. Racine: 1916. V. 72

HART, I. R. G.
Torture Island. New York: 1928. V. 68; 71

HART, MARGERY
Furry Folk and Fairies. 1931. V. 72

HART, MARY KERR
Heath Blossoms; or, Poems Written in Obscurity and Seclusion. Ballingdon: 1830?. V. 69

HART, MARY L.
The Blues. A Bibliographical Guide. New York: 1989. V. 70; 72

HART, W. O.
A Boy's Recollection of the War. Oxford: 1912. V. 70

HART, WILLIAM
A Few Remarks, Upon the Ordination of the Rev'd. Mr. James Dana and the Doings of the Consociation, Respecting the Same.... New Haven: 1759. V. 68
Remarks on a Late Pamphlet, Wrote by Mr. Hobart, Entitled, The Principles of Congregational Churches, Relating to the Consitution and Authority of Ecclesiastical Councils.... New Haven: 1760. V. 68
A Scriptural Answer to This Question viz. What are the Necessary Qualifications for a Lawful and Approved Attendance on the Sacraments of the New Convenant?. New London: 1772. V. 68

HART, WILLIAM S.
Told Under a White Oak Tree by Bill Hart's Pinto Pony. Boston: 1922. V. 70

HART-DAVIS, RUPERT
Edmund Blunden 1896-1974: an Address by Rupert Hart-Davis, St. Bride's Church, Fleet Street, 7 March 1974. Oxford: 1974. V. 73

HARTE, BRET
The Argonauts of North Liberty. Toronto: 1888. V. 72
The Bell Ringer of Angel's Etc. London: 1894. V. 69
Clarence. London: 1895. V. 72
Condensed Novels: Second Series. New Burlesques. Boston and New York: 1902. V. 70
Cressy. London: 1889. V. 72
Excelsior Presented by Enoch Morgan's Sons So., New York. New York: 1877. V. 70
The Fool of Five Forks. London: 1875. V. 68
Gabriel Conroy: a Novel. London: 1911. V. 68
The Heritage of Dedlow Marsh and Other Tales. London: 1889. V. 68; 72
The Luck of Roaring Camp and Other Sketches. Boston: 1870. V. 68; 69
Mr. Jack Hamlin's Mediation and Other Stories. London: 1889. V. 72
Outcroppings: Selections of California Verse. San Francisco/New York: 1866. V. 69; 70
The Pliocene Skull. Washington, DC: 1871. V. 71
Poems. Boston: 1871. V. 68; 69
A Protegee of Jack Hamlin's and Other Stories. Boston: 1894. V. 68
The Queen of the Pirate Isle. London: 1886. V. 68; 69; 72
The Queen of the Pirate Isle. Boston: 1887. V. 70
Sketches of the Sixties: Being Forgotten Material Now Collected for the First Time from the Californian 1864-1867. San Francisco: 1926. V. 73
Sketches of the Sixties: Being Forgtten Material Now Collected for the First Time from the Californian 1864-1867. San Francisco: 1927. V. 68
Snow-bound at Eagle's. London: 1886. V. 68
Susy: a Story of the Plains. Boston: 1893. V. 71
Trent's Trust and Other Stories. Boston/New York: 1903. V. 72; 73

HARTE, BRET continued
The Writings of Bret Harte. Boston and New York. V. 71

HARTE, GLENN BOYD
Temples of Power. 1979. V. 71

HARTE, WALTER
Essays on Husbandry. London: 1764. V. 68
Essays on Husbandry. 1770. V. 71
Essays on Husbandry. London: 1770. V. 70

HARTE, WILLIAM
An Essay On Reason. 1735. V. 68; 71
An Essay on Reason. London: 1735. V. 71

HARTFORD, Connecticut, as a Manufacturing, Business and Commercial Center. Hartford: 1889. V. 68

HARTING, J. E.
The Birds of Middlesex. London: 1866. V. 69
Essays on Sport and Natural History. 1883. V. 71
Hints on the Management of Hawks, to Which is Added Practical Falconry. 1898. V. 68; 73
Rambles in Search of Shells, Land and Freshwater. London: 1875. V. 68; 70
Recreations of a Naturalist. Lonton: 1906. V. 70

HARTJE, ROBERT G.
Van Dorn. The Life and Times of a Confederate General. Nashville: 1967. V. 69; 73

HARTLAND, MICHAEL
Frontier of Fear. London: 1988. V. 73
The Third Betrayal. London: 1986. V. 73
The Year of the Scorpion. Bristol: 1991. V. 69

HARTLEY, C. GASQUOINE
The Age of Mother Power, the Position of Woman in Primitive Society. New York: 1914. V. 72

HARTLEY, DAVID
An Account of the Method of Securing Buildings (and Ships) Against Fire. London: 1774. V. 68
An Address to the Committee of the County of York, on the State of the Public Affairs. London: 1781. V. 70
Considerations on the Proposed Renewal of the Bank Charter. London: 1781. V. 69

HARTLEY, DICK
All About Peter Rabbit. New York: 1914. V. 70

HARTLEY, DOROTHY
Water In England. London: 1964. V. 72

HARTLEY, FLORENCE
Ladies' Book of Etiquette and Manual of Politeness. Phila: 1860. V. 72

HARTLEY, G.
Wild Sport and Some Stories. 1912. V. 73
Wild Sport with Gun, Rifle and Salmon-Rod. 1903. V. 72; 73

HARTLEY, HAROLD
The Royal Society Its Origins and Founders. London: 1960. V. 71; 73

HARTLEY, JOHN
Grimes's Trip to America. Bradford: 1920?. V. 68
Grimes's Visit to th' Queen: a Royal Time Among Royalties. London: 1892?. V. 68
Grimes's Visit to th' Queen: A Royal Time Among Royalties. London: 1920?. V. 68; 73
Seets i' Blackpool, Fleetwood, Lytham and Southport, as Seen bi Sammywell Grimes an' his wife Mally.... London: 1916?. V. 68; 73
Yorkshire Lyrics. London: 1898. V. 73

HARTLEY, JOSEPH
The Wholesale and Retail Wine and Spirit Merchant's Companion.... London: 1835. V. 68

HARTLEY, L. P.
The Go-Between. London: 1953. V. 68; 71; 73
The Love Adept - a Variation on a Theme. London: 1969. V. 70
The Sixth Heaven. London: 1946. V. 70
The Travelling Grave and Other Stories. Sauk City: 1948. V. 70
The Travelling Grave and Other Stories. London: 1951. V. 68; 72
The White Wand and Other Stories. London: 1954. V. 70

HARTLEY, LEONARD LAWRIE
Catalogue of the Library of the Late Leonard Lawrie Hartley.... London: 1885-1887. V. 73

HARTLEY, MARIE
The Charm of Yorkshire Churches. Leeds: no date. V. 73
Life in the Moorlands of North-East Yorkshire. London: 1972. V. 73
The Old Hand-Knitters of the Dales. London: 1951. V. 72; 73

HARTLEY, W. G.
The Light Microscope. Its Use and Development. Oxford: 1993. V. 68; 71

HARTMAN, DAVID W.
Biographical Rosters of Florida's Confederate and Union Soliders 1861-1865. Wilmington: 1995. V. 69

HARTMANN, FRANZ
The Life of Paracelsus and His Teachings. London: 1896. V. 68; 70

HARTMANN, G. H. C.
Etude Sure Les Armes De Chasse. Paris: 1897. V. 71

HARTMANN, L.
The Story of Champ D'Asile as told by Two of the Colonists. Dallas: 1937. V. 72

HARTNACK, H.
Unbidden House Guests. Tacoma: 1943. V. 68

HARTNOLL, PHYLLIS
The Grecian Enchanted. Waltham St. Lawrence: 1952. V. 70; 71; 73

HARTSHORNE, ALBERT
Old English Glasses. London: 1897. V. 68

HARTSHORNE, C. H.
The Book Rarities in the University of Cambridge. London: 1829. V. 70

HARTSTONE, ELEANOR
Rice Grain Porcelain. Hartstone: 1978. V. 71

HARTWIG, G.
Denizens of the Deep. London: 1887. V. 68
The Polar and Tropical Worlds. 1871. V. 69
The Sea and Its Living Wonders. London: 1861. V. 68

HARUF, KENT
Plainsong. New York: 1999. V. 70; 71; 72; 73
The Tie that Binds. New York: 1984. V. 70
Where You Once Belonged. New York: 1990. V. 69

HARVARD COLLEGE
Laws of Harvard College. Cambridge: 1820. V. 71

HARVARD COLLEGE LIBRARY
Department of Printing and Graphic Arts Catalogue of Books and Manuscripts. Part I: French 16th Century Books. Cambridge: 1964. V. 70

HARVARD UNIVERSITY
Catalogue of Books and Manuscripts: Italian 16th Century Books. Cambridge: 1974. V. 72; 73
The Houghton Library 1942-1967, a Selection of Books and Manscripts in Harvard Collections. Cambridge: 1967. V. 68

HARVEY, CHARLES
Jazz Parody. London. V. 69

HARVEY Cushing's Seventieth Birthday Party, April 8, 1939. Speeches, Letters and Tributes. Springfield: 1939. V. 68; 70

HARVEY, DANIEL WHITTLE
Inns of Court. The Speech and Reply of D. W. Harvey, Esq. M.P. on the 14th of June 1832, in the House of Commons on Moving for Leave to Bring In a Bill to Empower the Court of King's Bench to Regulate the Admission of Students an Barristers.... London: 1832. V. 70

HARVEY, E. NEWTON
A History of Luminescence from the Earliest Times Until 1900. 1957. V. 68
A History of Luminescence From the Earliest Times until 1900. London: 1957. V. 70

HARVEY, FRED
First Families of the Southwest. Kansas City: 1908. V. 71

HARVEY, G.
Taking Stock. Houston: 1986. V. 73

HARVEY, J.
The Gothic World 1100-1600 - a Survey of Architecture and Art. London: 1959. V. 69

HARVEY, JAMES NEAL
By Reason of Insanity. New York: 1990. V. 68

HARVEY, JOHN
Cold Light. London: 1994. V. 68
Cutting Edge. London: 1991. V. 69; 71; 72
Easy Meat. New York: 1996. V. 70
English Mediaeval Architects. A Biographical Dictionary down to 1550. London: 1954. V. 72
The Gothic World 1100-1600: a Survey of Architecture and Art. London: 1950. V. 72
Lonely Hearts. London: 1989. V. 69
Lonely Hearts. New York: 1989. V. 69
Off Minor. 1992. V. 68
Rough Treatment. London: 1990. V. 69; 72
Wasted Years. London: 1992. V. 69

HARVEY, MARY
Child of Conrad. 1946. V. 71
Child of Coran, a Fairy Story. 1946. V. 68; 73

HARVEY, THOMAS
Jamaica in 1866. A Narrative of a Tour.... London: 1867. V. 71

HARVEY, W. H.
Nereis Boreali-Americana; or, Contributions to the History of the Marine Algae of North America. Washington: 1851-1857. V. 69
Phycologia Britannica, or a History of British Sea Weeds. London: 1846-1851. V. 69
The Sea-Side Book.... London: 1849. V. 68

HARVEY, WILLIAM
An Anatomical Disquisition on the Motion of the Heart and Blood in Animals. London. V. 68
The Anatomical Exercises of Dr. William Harvey. London: 1653. V. 68
The Anatomical Exercises of Dr. William Harvey. London: 1673. V. 70
The Anatomical Exercises of Dr. William Harvey. London: 1928. V. 71; 72

HARVEY, WILLIAM continued
Anatomical Exercitations.... London: 1653. V. 68; 72
The Circulation of the Blood. Two Anatomical Essays.... Oxford: 1958. V. 68
De Motu Locali Animalium 1627. Cambridge: 1959. V. 71
Exercitationes de Generatione Animalium. Amstelodami: 1651. V. 68; 70; 72
Exercitationes de Generatione Animalium. London: 1651. V. 68; 73
London Scenes and London People; Anecdotes, Reminiscences and Sketches of Places, Personages, Events, Customs and Curiosities of London, City, Past and Present. London: 1863. V. 71
Opera Omnia: a Collegio Medicorum Londinensi edita. London: 1766. V. 71
Prelectiones Anatomiae Universlis. London: 1886. V. 70; 72
The Works of William Harvey, M.D. London: 1847. V. 68
The Works of William Harvey.... London. V. 71

HARVEY, WILLIAM F.
The Arm of Mrs. Egan. New York: 1952. V. 68; 70
The Misadventures of Athelstan Digby. 1920. V. 73

HARVEY, WILLIAM HENRY
Phycologia Britannica; or a History of British Sea Weeds. 1871. V. 73

HARVIE BROWN, J. A.
A Fauna of the Moray Basin. Edinburgh: 1895. V. 69
A Vertebrate Fauna of the Hebrides. 1888. V. 69

HARVINS, T. R.
Beyond The Cimarron: Major Earl Van Dorn in Comanche Land. Brownwood: 1968. V. 72
Camp Colorado: A Decade of Frontier Defense. Brownwood, TX: 1964. V. 72

HARWELL, RICHARD B.
Confederate Hundred. Urbana: 1964. V. 69; 70
Confederate Music. Chapel Hill: 1950. V. 69; 70
In Tall Cotton. Austin: 1978. V. 69
Three Months in the Confederate Army. 1952. V. 68; 73

HARWOOD, EDWARD
Biographia Classica; the Lives and Characters of the Greek and Roman Classics. London: 1778. V. 69
A View of the Various Editions of the Greek and Roman Classics. London: 1778. V. 69

HARWOOD, J.
Illustratios of the Lakes. London: 1852. V. 71

HARWOOD, T. EUSTACE
Windsor Old and New. London: 1929. V. 71

HARWOOD, THOMAS
History of New Mexico Spanish and English Missions. Albuquerque: 1908-1910. V. 68

HASBRICK, PETER H.
Frederic Remington, Paintings, Drawings and Sculpture in the Amon Carter Museum and the Sid W. Richardson Foundation Collections. New York: 1973. V. 70

HASFORD, GUSTAV
The Phantom Blooper. New York: 1990. V. 71; 72
The Short-Timers. New York: 1979. V. 70; 72

HASKELL, B.
Charles Demuth. 1987. V. 72

HASKELL, FRANK ARETAS
The Battle of Gettysburg. Portage?: 1879. V. 69

HASKELL, HENRY C.
City of the Future: a Narrative History of Kansas City 1850-1950 and Annals of the City of Kansas. Kansas City: 1950. V. 68

HASKELL, MOLLY
From Reverence to Rape. New York: 1974. V. 72

HASKELL, THOMAS NELSON
The Indian Question - Young Konkaput, The King of Utes and Shawsheen His Maiden Queen.... Denver: 1889. V. 68; 69; 72; 73

HASKETT SMITH, W. P.
Climbing in the British Isles. 1. England. London: 1894. V. 69

HASKINS, CHARLES H.
The Normans in European History. Boston: 1915. V. 69

HASKINS, JAMES
Black Theater In America. New York: 1982. V. 72
Pinckney Benton Stewart Pinchback. New York: 1973. V. 72

HASKINS, JIM
James Van Derzee. The Picture-Takin' Man. New York: 1979. V. 68; 70

HASKINS, R. W.
New England and the West. Buffalo: 1843. V. 71

HASKINS, SAM
Photo Graphics. Geneve: 1980. V. 68

HASLAM, JOHN
Sound Mind; or, Contributions to the Natural History and Physiology of the Human Intellect. London: 1819. V. 73

HASLEM, JOHN
The Old Derby China Factory. London: 1876. V. 72

HASLER, H. G.
Harbours and Anchorages of The North Coast of Brittany. London: 1952. V. 72

HASLETT, G. WYNDHAM
Corunna Road. London: 1926. V. 70

HASLEWOOD, JOSEPH
The Secret History of the Green Room. London: 1792. V. 68; 70

HASLUCK, PAUL N.
Cassell's Cyclopaedia of Mechanics.... London: 1908. V. 71
House Decoration Comprising Whitewashing, Paperhanging, Painting &c. London: 1897. V. 68
House Decoration Comprising Whitewashing, Paperhanging, Painting, &c. London: 1901. V. 68
Portfolio Containing Twenty-Four Plates to Accompany Volume on Cabinet Work and Joinery. London: 1894. V. 68
Practical Graining and Marbling. London: 1910. V. 68
Wood Finishing. London: 1907. V. 68
The Wood Turner's Handy Book. London: 1904. V. 68

HASS, ROBERT
Field Guide. New Haven and London: 1973. V. 69

HASSALL, JOAN
Dearest Sydney: Joan Hassall's Letters to Sydney Cockerell from Italy and France, April-May 1950. 1991. V. 71

HASSANEIN, A. M.
The Lost Oases. New York: 1925. V. 72

HASSARD, JOHN R. G.
A Pickwickian Pilgrimage. Boston: 1881. V. 69

HASSELL, J.
Excursions of Pleasure and Sports on the Thames.... London: 1823. V. 72
Memoirs of the Life of the Late George Morland.... 1806. V. 73
Picturesque Rides and Walks, With Excursions by Water, Thirty Miles Round the British Metropolis.... London: 1817-1818. V. 70
A Series of Original Specimens, Exhibiting the Works of the Most Approved Water Colour Draftsmen. London: 1824. V. 69

HASSELL, JOHN
Tour of the Isle of Wight. London: 1790. V. 71
The Young Artist's Assistant; or a Familiar Introduction to the Art of Drawing with Directions for Colouring &c. London: 1810. V. 68

HASSELT, ANDRE VAN
Ceremonies et Fetes a l'Occasion du XXVe Anniversaire de L'Inauguration de Sa Majeste le Roi Leopold Ier. Brussels: 1856. V. 70

HASSLER, WILLIAM WOODS
A. P. Hill. Lee's Forgotten General. Richmond: 1957. V. 70

HASSRICK, PETER H.
Frederic Remington: Paintings, Drawings and Sculpture in the Amon Carter Museum. New York: 1973. V. 69; 73
Frederic Remington. A Catalogue Raisonne. Seattle: 1996. V. 69
Frederick Remington. A Catalogue Raisonne. Providence: 1864. V. 68
The Way West: Art of Frontier America. New York: 1977. V. 71

HASSRICK, ROYAL B.
The George Catlin Book of American Indians. New York: 1977. V. 69
The Sioux Life and Customs of a Warrior Society. Norman: 1964. V. 69
Western Painting Today. New York: 1975. V. 69

HASTINGS, FRANCIS RAWDON, 1ST MARQUIS OF
Substance of Observations on the State of the Public Finances of Great Britain, by Lord Rawdon, in a Speech on the Third Reading of the Bank Loan Bill in the House of Lords on Thursday, June 9, 1791. London: 1791. V. 71

HASTINGS, FRANK
A Ranchman's Recollections, An Autobiography. Chicago: 1921. V. 68; 71

HASTINGS, J. E.
Hints on the Management of Hawks, to Which is added Practical Falconry. 1898. V. 70

HASTINGS, LANSFORD
The Emigrants' Guide to Oregon and California. Princeton: 1932. V. 73

HASTINGS, SUSANNA WILLARD JOHNSON
Narrative of the Captivity of Mrs. Johnson. Windsor: 1814. V. 68

HASTON, D.
The Eiger. 1974. V. 68
In High Places. 1972. V. 73
In High Places. London: 1972. V. 69

HATA, IKUHIKO
Japanese Naval Aces and Fighter Units in World War II. London: 1990. V. 68

HATCH, BENTON L.
A Chechlist of the Publications of Thomas Bird Mosher of Portland Maine. Amherst: 1966. V. 71

HATCH, EDWIN
Towards Fields of Light. Sacred Poems. London: 1890. V. 73

HATCH, ERIC
Five Days. Boston: 1933. V. 73

HATCH, ERIC continued
My Man Godfrey. Boston: 1935. V. 70
Romance Prescribed. New York: 1930. V. 71

HATCH, RICHARD W.
The Curious Lobster's Island. New York: 1939. V. 69

HATCH, THORN
Custer and The Battle of The Little Bighorn - An Encyclopedia. Jefferson: 1997. V. 72

HATCHER, J. B.
The Ceratopsia. Washington: 1907. V. 69

HATCHER, J. S.
Textbook of Pistols and Revolvers. 1935. V. 69; 70; 71; 72; 73

HATFIELD, C. W.
Catalogue of the Bonnell Collection in the Bronte Parsonage Museum. 1932. V. 68; 70; 73

HATHAWAY, ELLA C.
The Battle of the Big Hole in August 1877. 1919. V. 70

HATHCOCK, R.
Ancient Indian Pottery of the Mississippi River Valley. Camden: 1976. V. 69
The Quapaw and Their Pottery. Camden: 1938. V. 69

HATJE, GERD
New Furniture. London: 1962. V. 72

HATSELL, JOHN
A Collection of Cases of Privilege of Parliament, from the Earliest Records to the Year 1628. London: 1776. V. 70

HATT, ELLA
Our National Heritage: Gardens. London: 1962. V. 72

HATTIE, ROBERT MC CONNELL
Hattie Family Memoirs. An Account of the Families Descended from Alexander Hattie, Emigre of 1786 with Sketches of the Family Pioneers and Related Material. Halifax: 1936. V. 72

HATTON, JOSEPH
Newfoundland the Oldest British Colony Its History, Its Present Condition, and Its Prospects in the Future. London: 1883. V. 72

HATTON, RICHARD G.
Design. London: 1914. V. 72

HATTON, THOMAS
A Bibliography of the Periodical Works of Charles Dickens. London: 1933. V. 68; 70

HAUCK, LOUISE PLATT
If With All Your Hearts. Philadelphia: 1935. V. 71

HAUFF, WILHELM
Dwarf Long-Nose. London: 1979. V. 72

HAUGHTON, H. L.
Sport and Folklore in the Himalaya. 1913. V. 69; 70; 72

HAUGHTON, SAMUEL
Manual of Tides and Tidal Currents. London: 1870. V. 68

HAUPT, LEWIS M.
The Topographer, His Instruments and Methods. New York: 1883. V. 70

HAUPTMAN, TERRY
Rattle. Tulsa: 1982. V. 68

HAURY, E. W.
The Hohokam - Desert Farmers and Craftsman - Excavations at Snaketown 1964-1965. Tucson: 1976. V. 72; 73
Painted Cave Northeastern Arizona. 1945. V. 69

HAUSE, D. J.
Electrical Engineer and Contractor. Cincinnati: 1893. V. 68

HAUSER, A.
The Social History of Art. London: 1951. V. 69; 72

HAUSER, GUNTER
White Mountain and Tawny Plain. London: 1961. V. 69

HAUSMAN, GERALD
The Gift of the Gila Monster. New York: 1993. V. 70

HAUSSEZ, CHARLES LEMERCHER DE LONGPRE, BARON D'
Great Britain in 1833. Philadelphia: 1833. V. 71

HAUTMAN, PETE
Drawing Dead. New York: 1993. V. 68; 69; 71; 72
Mrs. Million. New York: 1999. V. 72
Rag Man. New York: 2001. V. 69; 72

HAUY, RENE JUST
Traite des Caracteres Physiques des Pierres Precieuses, Pour Servir a Leur Determination.... Paris: 1817. V. 73

HAVEN, ALICE NEAL
All's Not Gold That Glitters; or the Young Californian. New York: 1853. V. 71

HAVEN, CHARLES
Thirty Days in New Jersey Ninety Years Ago.... Trenton: 1867. V. 69

HAVERFIELD, F.
Catalogue of the Roman Inscribed and Sculptured Stones in the Grosvenor Museum, Chester. London: 1900. V. 73

HAVERGAL, CECILIA
Child-Sunshine. New York: 1890. V. 70; 73

HAVERSCHMIDT, F.
Birds of Surinam. Edinburgh: 1968. V. 73

HAVILAND, M. D.
A Summer on the Yenesei (1914). London: 1915. V. 69

HAW, GEORGE
No Room to Live. 1900. V. 71

HAWAIIAN Celebrities Cookbook. Kaneohe: 1974. V. 73

HAWARDEN, EDWARD
An Answer to Dr. Clark and Mr. Whiston, Concerning the Divinity of the Son and of the Holy Spirit. London: 1729. V. 72
Charity and Truth; or, Catholicks not Uncharitable in Saying, That None are Sav'd Out of the Catholick Communion. London: 1728. V. 70

HAWEIS, H. R.
Mark Twain and Bret Harte. New York: 1900. V. 70

HAWES, BARBARA
Tales of the North American Indians, and Adventures of the Early Settlers in America. London: 1845?. V. 73

HAWES, CHARLES H.
In The Uttermost East. London: 1904. V. 72

HAWK, JOHN
The House of Sudden Sleep. 1930. V. 73
The House of Sudden Sleep. New York: 1930. V. 71

HAWKE, JESSICA
Follow My Dust. A Biography of Arthur Upfield. London: 1957. V. 70; 73

HAWKER, PETER
The Diary of Colonel Peter Hawker. Two Volumes. 1970. V. 71
The Diary of Colonel Peter Hawker, Volume I only. 1893. V. 71
Instructions to Young Sportsmen in All That Relates to Guns and Shooting. 1844. V. 69; 71

HAWKER, R. S.
The Cornish Balads and Other Poems. London: 1869. V. 71; 72
Cornish Ballads and Other Poems. 1904. V. 70
Ecclesia; a Volume of Poems. Oxford: 1840. V. 68; 72
Footprints of Former Men in Cornwall. London: 1908. V. 71
The Poetical Works. London: 1879. V. 68; 72
Pompeii, a Prize Poem; recited in the Theatre, Oxford, June the Twenty-Seventh MDCCCXXVII. Oxford: 1827. V. 73
The Quest of Sangraal. Chant the First. Exeter: 1864. V. 73
Records of the Western Shore. 1832. V. 73
Tendrils. London: 1821. V. 73

HAWKES, J.
Manufacturers of Every Description of Looking Glasses and Furniture by Steam Power, Wholesale & for Exportation. Birmingham: 1860. V. 68

HAWKES, JACQUETTA
Dragon's Mouth - a Dramatic Quartet in Two Parts. London: 1952. V. 69

HAWKES, JOHN
The Beetle Log. 1951. V. 71
Innocence in Extremis. New York: 1985. V. 73
An Irish Eye. 1997. V. 72
Island. Providence: 1988. V. 68
The Passion Artist. New York: 1979. V. 72
Second Skin. New York: 1964. V. 73
Second Skin. Norfolk CT: 1964. V. 72

HAWKES, NATHAN MORTIMER
Hearths and Homes of Old Lynn. Lynn: 1907. V. 71

HAWKESWORTH, JOHN
Almoran and Hamet; an Oriental Tale. London: 1761. V. 70

HAWKEYE, HARRY
Cowboys of the Wild West. Baltimore: 1908. V. 71
The Dalton Brothers. Baltimore: 1908. V. 69
Tracy the Outlaw. Baltimore: 1908. V. 69

HAWKING, STEPHEN
A Brief History of Time. London: 1988. V. 72
A Brief History of Time. New York: 1988. V. 72; 73

HAWKINS, ANTHONY HOPE
The Dolly Dialogues. London: 1894. V. 73
The Heart of Princess Osra. London: 1896. V. 69
The Prisoner of Zenda. Bristol: 1894. V. 69
The Prisoner of Zenda. London: 1894. V. 69
Rupert of Hentzau. Bristol: 1898. V. 69
Tristram of Blent: an Episode in the Story of an Ancient House. London: 1901. V. 69

HAWKINS, BISSET
Germany: the Spirit of Her History, Literature, Social Condition and National Economy.... London: 1838. V. 71

HAWKINS, DEAN
Skull Mountain. Garden City: 1941. V. 71; 73

HAWKINS, F. W.
The Life of Edmund Kean. London: 1869. V. 72

HAWKINS, FRANCIS BISSET
Elements of Medical Statistics, Containing the Substance of the Gulstonian Lectures Delivered at the Royal College of Physicians.... London: 1829. V. 72

HAWKINS, JOHN
The Life of Samuel Johnson, LL.D. London: 1787. V. 68; 71

HAWKINS, LAETITIA MATILDA
Gossip about Dr. Johnson and Others.... London: 1926. V. 68

HAWKINS, LEW
Minstrel Jokes. New York: 1905. V. 70

HAWKINS, RICHARD
The Observations of Sir Richard Hawkins. London: 1933. V. 70

HAWKINS, THOMAS
A View of the Real Power of The Pope, and of the Power of the Priesthood Over the Laity. London: 1733. V. 73

HAWKINS, WILLARD E.
The Cowled Menace. 1930. V. 73

HAWKINS, WILLIAM
A Treatise of the Pleas of the Crown; or a System of the Principal Matters Relating to that Subject, Digested Under their Proper Heads. In the Savoy: 1724-1721. V. 68

HAWKS, E.
Pioneers of Plant Study. London: 1928. V. 71; 72

HAWKS, FRANCIS L.
A Relation of Maryland. New York: 1865. V. 71
Uncle Philip's Conversations with the Young People About the Whale Fishery and Polar Regions. London: 1837. V. 68

HAWKSLEY, ENID DICKENS
Charles Dickens Brithday Book. London: 1948. V. 68

HAWKSMOOR, NICHOLAS
A Short Historical Account of London Bridge.... London: 1736. V. 71

HAWLEY, JAMES H.
History of the Idaho, the Gem of the Mountains. 1920. V. 68

HAWLEY, W. A.
Oriental Rugs, Antique and Modern. New York: 1925. V. 69; 72
Oriental Rugs: Antique and Modern. New York: 1937. V. 73

HAWORTH, SAMUEL
(Greek text) Or, a Philosophic Discourse Concerning Man, Being the Anatomy Both of His Soul and Body Wherein the Nature, Origin, Union, Immateriality, Immortality, Extension and Faculties of the One, and the Parts.... London: 1680. V. 70; 71

HAWORTH, WALTER NORMAN
The Constitution of Sugars. London: 1929. V. 69

HAWORTH-BOOTH, DIGBY
Kleinias. Poems. Manaton: 1932. V. 71

HAWTHORN, AUDREY
Art of the Kwakiutl and Other Northwest Cost Tribes. Vancouver: 1967. V. 70

HAWTHORN, H. B.
A Survey of the Contemporary Indians of Canada. Ottawa: 1966. V. 73

HAWTHORNE, H.
The Lure of the Garden. New York: 1911. V. 71; 73

HAWTHORNE, HILDEGARDE
The Secret of Rancho Del Sol. New York: 1931. V. 70

HAWTHORNE, JULIAN
A Fool of Nature. New York: 1896. V. 70

HAWTHORNE, LAWRENCE
Happy All the Day. Minneapolis: 1927. V. 70

HAWTHORNE, NATHANIEL
The Blithedale Romance. Boston: 1852. V. 70; 71
Complete Literary Prose. Boston: 1865-1866. V. 69
The Complete Works.... Boston and New York: 1886-1887. V. 73
Dr. Grimshawe's Secret. London: 1883. V. 70
Fanshawe and Other Pieces. Boston: 1876. V. 68; 69; 73
The Gentle Boy; a Thrice Told Tale. Boston: 1839. V. 71
The Golden Touch. 1927. V. 72
The House of the Seven Gables. Boston: 1841. V. 68
The House of the Seven Gables. Boston: 1851. V. 68; 70
The House of the Seven Gables. London: 1851. V. 73
The House of the Seven Gables. Boston: 1851. V. 73
Legends of the Province House. Boston: 1877. V. 68
The Marble Faun; or, the Romance of Monte Beni. Boston: 1860. V. 69; 71; 73
Mosses from an Old Manse. New York: 1846. V. 68
Passages from the French and Italian Note-Books. Boston: 1872. V. 68; 71
The Scarlet Letter. Boston: 1850. V. 68; 70; 72
The Scarlet Letter. London: 1859. V. 73
The Scarlet Letter. Boston: 1860. V. 69
The Scarlet Letter. Toronto: 1879. V. 70
The Scarlet Letter. New York: 1904. V. 68
The Scarlet Letter. London: 1920. V. 71
Septimius: a Romance. London: 1872. V. 73
Septimius Felton. Boston: 1872. V. 68; 69
Sights from a Steeple. New York: 1988. V. 72
The Snow-Image and Other Tales. London: 1851. V. 70
Tanglewood Tales. Boston: 1853. V. 71
Tanglewood Tales. London: 1938. V. 69
Tanglewood Tales for Boys and Girls. Boston: 1853. V. 69; 71; 72
Twice-Told Tales. Boston: 1837. V. 68
Wonder Book. Garden City: 1928. V. 70; 73
A Wonder Book. London: 1957. V. 71
A Wonder Book for Girls and Boys. Boston: 1852. V. 70

HAWTREE, CHRISTOPHER
Night and Day. London: 1985. V. 70

HAXTHAUSEN, AUGUST VON
Trancaucasia. Sketches of the Nations and Races Between the Black Sea and the Caspian. London: 1854. V. 68; 72

HAY, ALEXANDER
The History of Chichester: Interspersed with Various Notes and Observations on the Early and Present State of the City. Chichester: 1804. V. 70

HAY, DAVID RAMSAY
The Laws of Harmonious Colouring.... Edinburgh: 1836. V. 68
A Nomenclature of Colours Applicable to the Arts and Natural Sciences to Manufactures.... Edinburgh and London: 1846. V. 68; 69; 71
A Nomenclature of Colours, Hues, Tints and Shades, Applicable to the Arts and Natural Sciences.... London: 1845. V. 68
The Principles of Beauty in Colouring Systemized. London: 1845. V. 68

HAY, EDWARD
History of the Insurrection of the County Wexford 1798. Dublin: 1898. V. 70

HAY, GEORGE
History of Arbroa.h to the Present Time. Arbroath: 1876. V. 73
A Treatise on Expatriation. Washington: 1814. V. 73

HAY, HELEN
The Little Boy Book. New York: 1900. V. 70

HAY, IAN
The First Hundred Thousand. Boston: 1916. V. 69
Half a Sovereign. Boston: 1926. V. 70
The Midshipmaid: the Tale of a Naval Manoeuvre. London: 1933. V. 73
The Poor Gentleman. Boston: 1928. V. 71

HAY, JOHN
Nicholson's New Carpenter's Guide. London. V. 72
The Pike County Ballads. Boston: 1912. V. 71; 73

HAY, L. F.
It Wasn't a Nightmare. New York: 1937. V. 69

HAY, MARY CECIL
Old Myddelton's Money. London: 1883?. V. 68

HAY, T. DE
A Letter from Paris, Giving an Account. 1680?. V. 73

HAY, THOMAS ROBSON
Hood's Tennessee Campaign. New York: 1929. V. 69; 70

HAYDER, MO
Birdman. London: 2000. V. 72

HAYDN, F. STANSBURY
Aeronautics in the Union and Confederate Armies. Baltimore: 1941. V. 69

HAYDN, JOSEPH
Dictionary of Dates, and Universal Reference, Relating to All Ages and Nations.... London: 1841. V. 73

HAYDON, A. L.
The Riders of The Plains. Chicago: 1910. V. 72

HAYDON, ANDREW
Pioneer Sketches in the District of Bathurst. Toronto: 1925. V. 73

HAYDON, B. R.
Painting, and the Fine Arts: Being the Articles Under Those Heads Contributed to the Seventh Edition of the Encyclopaedia Britannica. Edinburgh: 1838. V. 68

HAYDON, BENJAMIN ROBERT
The Diary of of Benjamin Robert Haydon. Cambridge: 1960. V. 69

HAYDON, F. STANSBURY
Aeronautics in the Union and Confederate Armies. Baltimore: 1941. V. 70

HAYEK, FRIEDRICH AUGUST VON
The Constitution of Liberty. London: 1960. V. 69
The Pure Theory of Capital. London: 1941. V. 69

HAYES, A. A.
New Colorado and the Santa Fe Trail. New York: 1880. V. 70
New Colorado, and the Sante Fe Trail. London: 1881. V. 69

HAYES, BENJAMIN
Pioneer Notes from the Diaries of Judge Benjmain Hayes 1849-1875. 1929. V. 71
Pioneer Notes from the Diary of Judge...1849-1875. Los Angeles: 1925. V. 68; 73

HAYES, BILLY
Midnight Express. New York: 1977. V. 68; 71

HAYES, CHARLES
A Treatise of Fluxions; or, an Introduction to Mathematical Philosophy. London: 1704. V. 68; 70; 73

HAYES, CHARLES W.
A Long Journey. The Story of Daniel Hayes. Portland: 1876. V. 68

HAYES, FLORENCE
Hosh-Ki: The Navajo. New York: 1943. V. 69

HAYES, HELEN
Twice Over Lightly: New York Then and Now. New York: 1972. V. 71

HAYES, ISAAC
The Open Polar Sea: Narrative of a Voyage of Discovery Towards the North Pole in the Schooner United States. New York: 1867. V. 71; 73

HAYES, J. GORDON
The Conquest of the North Pole. The Conquest of the South Pole. 1932-1934. V. 71

HAYES, JESS G.
Apache Vengeance, True Story of Apache Kid. Albuquerque: 1954. V. 69; 71

HAYES, JOSEPH
The Desperate Hours. New York: 1954. V. 72
The Eighty Fifth in France and Flanders. Halifax: 1920. V. 72

HAYES, MILTON
Bad Men Make Good Wives. New York: 1930. V. 70

HAYES, NELSON
Dildo Cay. Boston: 1940. V. 69

HAYES, RICHARD
The Last Invasion of Ireland When Connacht Rose. Dublin: 1937. V. 68
The Negociator's Magazine; or, the Exchanges Anatomiz'd. London: 1726. V. 69
Old Links With France: Some Echoes of Exiled Ireland. 1940. V. 71

HAYES, RUTHERFORD B.
In Memoriam. James M. Comly. 1887. V. 72

HAYES, WILLIAM
Portraits of Rare and Curious Birds with Their Descriptions from the Menagery of Osterly Park.... London: 1794-1799. V. 72; 73

HAYHOE, F. G. J.
Lectures on Haematology. Cambridge: 1960. V. 68

HAYLEY, WILLIAM
An Essay on Sculpture, in a Series of Epistles to John Flaxman with Notes. London: 1800. V. 69; 72
The Life and Posthumous Writings of William Cowper. Chichester: 1803-1804. V. 68
The Life of George Romney. Chichester: 1809. V. 72
The Life of John Milton, with Conjectures on the Origin of Paradise Lost. Basil: 1799. V. 69
Occasional Stanzas, Written at the Request of the Revolution Society; and Recited on their Anniversary, November 4, 1788. London: 1788. V. 73
A Philosophical, Historical and Moral Essay on Old Maids. London: 1785. V. 68; 69; 71; 73
A Philosophical, Historical and Moral Essay on Old Maids, by a Friend to the Sisterhood.... London: 1793. V. 73
The Triumphs of Temper. London: 1781. V. 68; 72
The Triumphs of Temper. London: 1801. V. 68; 72
The Triumphs of Temper. Chichester: 1803. V. 70
The Triumphs of Temper. Chichester: 1817. V. 72

HAYM, NICOLA FRANCESCO
Biblioteca Italiana, o Sia Notizia de'Libri Rari Nella Lingua Italiana. Venice: 1728. V. 70

HAYMAKER, WEBB
The Founders of Neurology. Springfield: 1953. V. 68; 70

HAYMAN, RONALD
John Gielgud. London: 1971. V. 70; 72

HAYMON, S. T.
Death and the Pregnant Virgin. London: 1980. V. 70
Death and the Pregnant Virgin. New York: 1980. V. 69

HAYMOND, CREED
The Central Pacific Railroad: its Relation with the Government, It Has Performed All Its Obligations. 1888. V. 72

HAYNE, COE
Red Men on The Big Horn. Philadelphia: 1929. V. 72
They Came Seeking. 1935. V. 69

HAYNE, DAVID M.
Dictionary of Canadian Biography. Volume II 1701-1740. Toronto: 1969. V. 72

HAYNE, JOHANN
Trifolium Medicum, oder Drey Hochst Nutzliche Tractatlein, deren Erstes von Asatralischen Kranckheiten.... Frankfurt am Main: 1683. V. 68; 70; 73

HAYNES, A.
A B C of Aeroplane Spotting. London: 1944. V. 72

HAYNES, C. VANCE
General Custer and His Sporting Rifles. 1995. V. 68

HAYNES, DRAUGHTON STITH
The Field Diary of a Confederate Soldier. Darien: 1963. V. 69; 70

HAYNES, MARTIN A.
Muster Out Roll of the Second New Hampshire Regiment of the War of the Rebllion. Lakeport: 1917. V. 69

HAYNES, SAMUEL
A Collection of State Papers Relating to Affairs in the Reigns of King Henry VIII, King Edward VI, Queen Mary and Queen Elizabeth from the year 1542 to 1570. London: 1740-1749. V. 73

HAYS, ISAAC
Select Medico-Chirurgical Transactions. Philadelphia: 1831. V. 71

HAYS, MARGARET
Kiddie Land. Philadelphia: 1910. V. 72
Little Pets Book. New York: 1914. V. 71

HAYS, MARY
Female Biography. London: 1803. V. 69
Female Biography. Philadelphia: 1807. V. 68; 69
The Victim of Prejudice. London: 1799. V. 69

HAYTER, GEORGE
A Descriptive Catalogue of the Great Historical Picture, Painted by Mr. George Hayter.... London: 1823. V. 70; 72

HAYTER, S. W.
About Prints. 1962. V. 71

HAYTER, SPARKLE
Nice Girls Finish Last. New York: 1996. V. 68
What's A Girl Gotta Do?. 1994. V. 69
What's a Girl Gotta Do?. New York: 1994. V. 68

HAYTER, THOMAS
An Essay on the Liberty of the Press: Chiefly as it Respects Personal Slander. Dublin: 1755. V. 72; 73

HAYWARD, A.
Dr. Johnson's Mrs. Thrale, Autobiography, Letters and Literary Remains of Mrs. Piozzi. London: 1910. V. 69

HAYWARD, ABRAHAM
The Art of Dining; or, Gastronomy and Gastronomers. London: 1853. V. 68
A Selection from the Correspondence...from 1834 to 1884.... London: 1886. V. 71

HAYWARD, CHARLES H.
English Rooms and Their Decorations at a Glance. London: 1925. V. 68

HAYWARD, HENRY
How the Poor May Be Taught Without Compromise of Principles or Opinions. London: 1855. V. 71

HAYWARD, J. F.
The Art of the Gunmaker. London: 1965. V. 72

HAYWARD, JOHN
A Catalogue of First and Early Editions of the Works of the English Poets from Chaucer to the Present Day Exhibited by the National Book League at 7 Albemarle Street, 1947. Cambridge: 1947. V. 72
A Gazeteer of New Hampshire.... Boston: 1849. V. 71

HAYWARD, P. J.
Handbook of the Marine Fauna of North-West Europe. New York: 1995. V. 72

HAYWARD, RICHARD
Munster and the City of Cork. 1964. V. 70

HAYWARD, WILLIAM
James Hall, of Tynemouth. London: 1896. V. 71

HAYWARD, WILLIAM STEPHENS
Formosa: the Life of a Beautiful Woman. London: 1884?. V. 68
The Rebel Privateer; or the Last Cruise of the Black Angel. London: 1881?. V. 68
The Star of the South. London: 1864. V. 68

HAYWOOD, ANNIE WINDSOR
Shepherd's Tartan and Other Poems. Cupar Fife: 1895. V. 69

HAYWOOD, ELIZA
Memoirs of a Certain Island Adjacent to the Kingdom of Utopia. London: 1726. V. 73
The Wife. London: 1756. V. 68
The Wife. London: 1773. V. 70

HAYWOOD, GAR ANTHONY
Fear of the Dark. 1988. V. 69
Fear of the Dark. New York: 1988. V. 71; 73

HAYWOOD, GAR ANTHONY continued
Not Long for This World. 1990. V. 69
You Can Die Trying. New York: 1990. V. 73
You Can Die Trying. New York: 1993. V. 72

HAYWOOD, HARRY
Black Bolshevik: Autobiography of an Afro-American Communist. Chicago: 1978. V. 72

HAYWOOD, HELEN
The Helen Haywood Christmas Book. London: 1952. V. 73

HAYWOOD, JOHN
Civil and Political History of the State of Tenneessee, from Its Earliest Settlement Up to the Year 1796; Including the Boundaries of the State. Knoxville: 1823. V. 71

HAZARD, JOSEPH
Poems, on Various Subjects. Brooklyn: 1814. V. 73

HAZARD, THOMAS R.
The Jonny-Cake Letters I-XII. Providence: 1880. V. 70

HAZELTON, JOHN M.
History and Hand Book of Herford Cattle and Herford Bull Index. Kansas City: 1925. V. 72

HAZEN, A. T.
A Bibliography of Horace Walpole. New Haven: 1948. V. 71
A Bibliography of Horace Walpole. Folkestone: 1973. V. 70
A Bibliography of the Strawberry Hill Press, with a Record of the Prices at Which Copies Have Been Sold.... New York and Folkestone: 1973. V. 70

HAZEN, R. W.
History of the Pawnee Indians. Fremont, NE: 1893. V. 71

HAZLITT, WILLIAM
Characteristics in the Manner of Rochefoucault's Maxims. London: 1837. V. 72
Characters of Shakspear's Plays. London: 1818. V. 72
The Complete Works. London: 1930. V. 73
Criticisms on Art. London: 1844. V. 68
The Eloquence of the British Senate. London: 1808. V. 68; 72
Essays on the Principles of Human Action; on the Systems of Hartley and Helvetius; and on Abstract Ideas. 1836. V. 72
The Israel of The Alps; A History of The Persecutions Of The Waldenses. London: 1852. V. 72
Notes of a Journey through France and Italy. London: 1826. V. 70
On the Living Poets. New Rochelle: 1986. V. 73
Painting and the Fine Arts. Edinburgh: 1838. V. 69
The Plain Speaker: Opinions on Books, Men and Things. London: 1826. V. 71
Select Poets of Great Britain. London: 1825. V. 72
Selected Essays of William Hazlitt 1778-1830. London: 1930. V. 69
Sketches and Essays. 1839. V. 72
Sketches of the Principal Picture Galleries of England.... London: 1824. V. 69
A View of the English Stage.... London: 1818. V. 68; 72; 73

HAZLITT, WILLIAM CAREW
The Book Collector: a General Survey of the Pursuit and of Those who Have Engaged in It at Home and Abroad from the Earliest Period to the Present Time. London: 1904. V. 71
British Columbia and Vancouver Island.... London: 1858. V. 70
The Confessions of a Collector. London: 1897. V. 71
Hand-book to the Popular, Poetical and Dramatic Literature of Great Britain, from the Invention of Printing to the Restoration. London: 1867. V. 73
Old Cookery Books and Anicent Cuisine. Detroit: 1902. V. 68
A Roll of Honour: a Calendar of the Names of Over 17,000 Men and Women Who Throughout the British Isles and In Our Early Colonies Have Collected Mss. and Printed Books from the XIVth to the XIXth Century.... London: 1908. V. 71

HAZO, SAMUEL
Blood Rights. 1968. V. 68; 71
Stills. New York: 1989. V. 68

HAZZARD, SHIRLEY
Cliffs of Fall. New York: 1963. V. 72
The Evening of the Holiday. New York: 1966. V. 68; 72

HEACOCK, ROLAND T.
Understanding the Negro Protest. New York: 1965. V. 72

HEAD, EDWARD FRANCIS
Poltroonius; a Tragic Farce. Boston: 1856. V. 71; 73

HEAD, FRANCIS BOND
Bubbles from the Brunnens of Nassau. Paris: 1834. V. 68
Descriptive Essays: Contributed to the Quarterly Review. London: 1857. V. 71
The Emigrant. London: 1862. V. 68
A Faggot of French Sticks.... London: 1855. V. 73
A Narrative. London: 1839. V. 71
Rough Notes Taken During Some Rapid Journeys Across the Pampas and Among the Andes. London: 1826. V. 72; 73

HEAD, HENRY
Aphasia and Kindred Disorders of Speech. Cambridge: 1926. V. 68
Studies in Neurology. Oxford: 1920. V. 68; 71; 72

HEAD, HENRY ERSKINE
Observations on Early Rising and on Early Prayer, as a Means of Happiness, and as an Incentive to Devotion. London: 1828. V. 73

HEAD, LOIS
Brief Introduction to Psycho-analysis for Beginners. Atlanta: 1936. V. 72

HEADLAM, CUTHBERT
The Three Northern Counties of England. Gateshead: 1939. V. 71; 73

HEADLEY, J. T.
The Achievements of Stanley and Other African Explorers. Philadelphia: 1878. V. 71
The Second War with England. New York: 1853. V. 73

HEADLEY, JOHN W.
Confederate Operations in Canada and New York. New York: 1906. V. 70

HEAL, AMBROSE
London Tradesmen's Cards of the XVIIth Century. London: 1925. V. 72
The Old Farm House in Tottenham Court Road. 1913. V. 71

HEALD, W. M.
Moscow: an Ode: According to the Arrangement of the Ancient Greek. London: 1813. V. 73

HEALE, THEOPHILUS
New Zealand and the New Zealand Company. London: 1842. V. 68; 72

HEALEY, GEORGE HARRIS
The Cornell Wordsworth Collection. A Catalogue of Books and Manuscripts.... Ithaca: 1957. V. 72

HEALTHFUL Exercises for Girls. London: 1886. V. 69

HEALY, JEREMIAH
Blunt Darts. London: 1984. V. 70
Blunt Darts. New York: 1984. V. 69; 70; 72
The Concise Cuddy. Norfolk: 1998. V. 70

HEALY, JOHN
Maynooth College, Its Centenary History. 1895. V. 69; 71

HEALY, T. M.
Why There is an Irish Land Question and an Irish Land League. 1881. V. 69

HEANEY, SEAMUS
After Summer. Old Deerfield: 1978. V. 69
Among Schoolchildren. Belfast: 1983. V. 69
Audenesque. Paris: 1998. V. 69; 72; 73
Commencement Address. The University of North Carolina at Chapel Hill. Chapel Hill: 1996. V. 72
Crediting Poetry. London: 1995. V. 68
Death of a Naturalist. London: 1966. V. 70
Door into the Dark. London: 1969. V. 70; 72; 73
Door Into the Dark. New York: 1969. V. 69; 71; 73
Electric Light. London: 2001. V. 69; 71; 72
Extending the Alphabet: On Christopher Marlowe's Hero and Leander. 1994. V. 68
Field Work. London: 1979. V. 69
Field Work. New York: 1979. V. 69; 71
Finders Keepers, Selected Prose 1971-2001. London: 2002. V. 72
From the Republic of Conscience. Dublin: 1985. V. 70; 71
Gravities: a Collection of Poems. Newcastle-upon-Tyne: 1979. V. 69
The Haw Lantern: Poems. New York: 1987. V. 69
Hedge School. Sonnets. Salem: 1979. V. 68
An Invocation: a Poem. London: 1992. V. 69
Keeping Going. Concord: 1993. V. 69; 72
A Lough Neagh Sequence. Didsbury: 1969. V. 68
The Makings of a Music: Reflections on the Poetry of Wadsworth and Yeats. 1978. V. 69
The Makings of a Music; Reflections on the Poetry of Wordsworth and Yeats. Liverpool: 1978. V. 69; 70
Night Drive. Gilbertson, Bow Crediton: 1970. V. 71
North. London: 1975. V. 68; 70
North. New York: 1976. V. 69
An Open Letter: a Poem. Derry: 1983. V. 69
Opened Ground - Poems. 1966-1969. London: 1998. V. 69; 70; 73
Place and Displacement. 1984. V. 69
Place and Displacement: Recent Poetry of Northern Ireland. Grasmere: 1984. V. 70
The Place of Writing. Atlanta: 1989. V. 72
Poems 1965-1975: Death of a Naturalist, Door Into the Dark, Wintering Out, North. New York: 1980. V. 69
Poems and a Memoir. New York: 1982. V. 68; 69; 72
The Redress of Poetry. New York: 1995. V. 71
Seeing Things: Poems. London: 1991. V. 69
Selected Poems 1965-1975. London: 1980. V. 69
Selected Poems 1966-1987. New York: 1990. V. 69
The Sounds of Rain. 1988. V. 68
The Sounds of Rain. Atlanta: 1988. V. 72
The Spirit Level. London: 1996. V. 68; 69; 70; 72; 73
Station Island. London: 1984. V. 69; 72
Station Island. New York: 1986. V. 70
Stations. Belfast: 1975. V. 69
Sweeney Astray. Derry: 1983. V. 70
Sweeney Astray. London: 1984. V. 68
Sweeney Astray. New York: 1984. V. 68; 69; 72
The Tree Clock. Belfast: 1990. V. 68
Verses for a Fordham Commencement. New York: 1984. V. 72; 73
Wintering Out. London: 1972. V. 69; 72

HEANEY, SEAMUS continued
Wintering Out. New York: 1973. V. 69; 72

HEAP, GWINN HARRIS
Central Route to the Pacific: With Related Material on Railroad Explorations and Indian Affairs. Glendale: 1957. V. 69; 72; 73

HEAPHY, THOMAS
A Wonderful Ghost Story, Being Mr. H.'s Own Narrative, Reprinted from All the Year Round.... London: 1882. V. 70

HEARD, GERALD
The Notched Hairpin. London: 1951. V. 69; 73

HEARD, H. F.
The Amazing Mycroft Mysteries. 1980. V. 68
The Great Fog and Other Weird Tales. 1944. V. 73
The Great Fog and Other Weird Tales. New York: 1946. V. 71
Murder by Reflection. 1942. V. 73
Murder by Reflection. New York: 1942. V. 71

HEARD, ISAAC V. D.
History of the Sioux War and Massacres of 1862 and 1863. New York: 1863. V. 70

HEARD, JAMES
A Practical Grammar of the Russian Language. St. Petersburg: 1827. V. 68

HEARD MUSEUM
Fred Harvey Fine Arts Collection. Phoenix: 1976. V. 70

HEARN, LAFCADIO
An American Miscellany. London: 1925. V. 71
The Buddhist Writings of.... Santa Barbara: 1977. V. 69
Chita: a Memory of the Last Island. New York: 1889. V. 68
Gombo Zhebes. Little Dictionary of Creole Proverbs. New York: 1885. V. 73
Historical Sketch Book and Guide to New Orleans and Environs. New York: 1885. V. 70
Japan, an Interpretation. New York: 1904. V. 73
Japanese Fairy Tales. Tokyo: 1899-1904. V. 72
Japanese Fairy Tales. Tokyo: 1905. V. 68
Kimiko and Other Japanese Sketches. Boston and New York: 1923. V. 73
Kokoro: Hints and Echoes of Japanese Inner Life. Boston: 1896. V. 73
Kotto. New York and London: 1902. V. 69; 70; 71; 73
Pre-Raphaelite and Other Poets. London: 1923. V. 72; 73
The Romance of the Milky Way. Boston: 1905. V. 70
Shadowings. Boston: 1900. V. 70
Stray Leaves from Strange Literature. Boston: 1884. V. 70
Youma. London: 1890. V. 72

HEARNE, SAMUEL
A Journey from Prince of Wales's Fort in Hudson's Bay to the Northern Ocean in the Years, 1769, 1770, 1771 and 1772. Toronto: 1911. V. 71

HEARNE, T.
Bibliotheca Hearneiana. London: 1848. V. 70

HEARNE, THOMAS
A Collection of Curious Discourses, Written by Eminent Antiquaries.... Oxford: 1720. V. 68

HEARON, SHELBY
Hannah's House. Garden City: 1975. V. 72
Now and Another Time. New York: 1976. V. 72
A Prince of a Fellow. Garden City: 1978. V. 72
The Second Dune. New York: 1973. V. 69; 72

HEARTMAN, CHARLES
The Blue Book. 1936. V. 73

HEARTSEASE and Honesty Being the Pastimes of Sieur de Grammont Steward to the Duc de Richelieu in Touraine Taken from His Notebooks Written in French Never Before Printed and Here Made English by Helen Simpson. Waltham St. Lawrence: 1935. V. 69

HEARTSILL, W. W.
Fourteen Hundred and 91 Days in the Confederate Army. Jackson: 1954. V. 69

HEATH, AMBROSE
Good Potato Dishes. London: 1935. V. 69
Madame Prunier's Fish Cookery Book. London: 1938. V. 73

HEATH, BENJAMIN
A Catalogue of Books, in the Various Branches of Literature, Which Lately Formed the Library of a Distinguished Collector and were Sold by Auction by Mr. Jeffery of Pall Mall, with Their Prices and Purchashers' Names. London: 1810. V. 70

HEATH, CHARLES
Descriptive Accounts of Persfield and Chepstow Including Caerwent and the Passages.... Monmouth: 1793. V. 70
Monmouthshire. Descriptive Accounts of Persfield and Chepstow, Including Caerwent and the Passages. Monmouth Heath: 1793. V. 68; 72

HEATH, CHRISTOPHER
Injuries and Diseases of the Jaws. London: 1868. V. 71

HEATH, DESMOND
The Victorian Poet, Roden Noel. A Wide Angle. London: 1998. V. 70

HEATH, DONALD
Man at High Altitude. Edinburgh: 1981. V. 68

HEATH, FRANCES M.
Sault Ste. Marie. City by the Rapids. Burlington: 1988. V. 73

HEATH, FRANCIS GEORGE
Our Woodland Trees. London: 1878. V. 70

HEATH, LABAN
Heath's Greatly Improved and Enlarged Infallible Government Counterfeit Detector.... Boston and Washington: 1867. V. 69
Heath's Infallible Government Counterfeit Detector. Boston and Washington;: 1877. V. 70

HEATH, ROY
The Murderer. New York: 1978. V. 72

HEATH, W. L.
Violent Saturday. New York: 1955. V. 69; 71; 72

HEATH, WILLIAM
Parish Characters in Ten Plates by Paul Pry Esquire. London: 1829. V. 69

HEATHCOTE, RALPH
The Irenarch; or Justice of the Peace's Manual. London: 1774. V. 69

HEATH'S Infallible Counterfeit Detector at Sight. Boston: 1864. V. 69

HEATH-STUBBS, JOHN
Artorius. London: 1973. V. 72
The Divided Ways. London: 1946. V. 68
Wounded Thammuz. London: 1942. V. 68; 71

HEATLEY, GEORGE S.
The Stock Owners' Guide. London: 1883. V. 72

HEATLEY, JAMES
A Visit To The West Indies. Alnwick: 1891. V. 72

HEAT MOON, WILLIAM LEAST
Blue Highways: a Journey into America. Boston: 1982. V. 70
Prairy Erth. Boston: 1991. V. 70; 72

HEATON, CHARLES, MRS.
Masterpieces of Flemish Art. London: 1869. V. 69

HEATON, J. H.
Australian Dictionary of Dates and Men of the Time Containing the History of Australasia from 1542 to May 1879. Sydney: 1879. V. 68

HEATON COOPER, W.
The Hills of Lakeland. Auction: 1938. V. 68; 71

HEAVENHILL, WILLIAM S.
Siege of the Alamo. San Antonio: 1888. V. 70

HEAVISIDES, EDWARD MARSH
The Poetical and Prose Remains. London: 1850. V. 70

HEBARD, GRACE RAYMOND
The Bozeman Trail. Cleveland: 1922. V. 72; 73
The Bozeman Trail. Glendale: 1960. V. 72
The Pathbreakers From Ocean to Ocean - The Story of The Great West From the Time of Coronado to the Present. Chicago: 1917. V. 72
Sacajawea. 1933. V. 68
Sacajawea. Glendale: 1957. V. 72; 73
Sacajawea. 1967. V. 68
Sacajawea. Glendale: 1967. V. 72
Washakie. Cleveland: 1930. V. 72

HEBENSTREIT, JOHANN ERNST
De Medici Cadavera Secantis Religione Disserens...Panegyrin Medicam Indicit. 1741. V. 71

HEBER, REGINALD
A Ballad. Chester: 1830. V. 73
Europe: Lines on the Present War. London: 1809. V. 73
Hymns written and adapted to the weekly church service of the year. London: 1827. V. 73
Narrative Of A Journey Through The Upper Provinces Of India From Calcutta to Bombay 1824-1825. London: 1828. V. 72
Narrative Of A Journey Through The Upper Provinces Of India, From Calcutta to Bombay 1824-1825. London: 1844. V. 72
Palestine. Oxford: 1803. V. 73
Palestine. London: 1809. V. 73
Poems and Translations. London: 1812. V. 73

HEBERDEN, WILLIAM
Commentaries on the History and Cure of Diseases. Boston: 1818. V. 72
An Epitome of Infantile Diseases, with Their Causes, Symptoms and Method of Cure.... Uttoxeter: 1805. V. 69

HEBRARD, P.
Caminologie, ou Traite des Cheminees, Contenant des Observations sur les Differentes Causes qui Font Fumer les Cheminees.... Dijon: 1756. V. 73

HECHT, ABSALOM
Instructions for Weaving, In All of Its Various Branches. Baltimore: 1849. V. 69

HECHT, ANTHONY
Aesopic. Twenty Four Couplets to Accompany the Thomas Bewick Wood Engravings for Select Fables. Northampton: 1967. V. 72; 73
Flight Among the Tombs. New York: 1996. V. 71
The Venetian Vespers. Boston: 1979. V. 69; 72; 73

HECHT, BEN
The Front Page. New York: 1928. V. 71

HECKETHORN, CHARLES WILLIAM
Lincoln's Inn Fields and the Localities Adjacent; Their Historical and Topographical Associations. London: 1896. V. 71

HECKEWELDER, J.
History, Manners and Customs of the Indian Nations who Once Inhabited Pennsylvania and the Neighbouring States. Philadelphia: 1876. V. 69

HECKSTALL SMITH, B.
A Book of Designs of Deep Sea Racing Craft. London: 1933. V. 69

HECO, JOSEPH
The Narrative of a Japanese. San Francisco. V. 70
The Narrative of a Japanese. San Francisco: 1950. V. 68; 73

HECTOR, WILLIAM
Selections from the Judicial Records of Renfrewshire, Illustrative of the Administration of the Laws of the County . . . Paisley: 1876. V. 71

HEDDLE, ETHEL F.
An Original Girl. New York. V. 72

HEDERICH, BENJAMIN
Graecum, Lexicon Manual. London: 1739. V. 73
Progymnasmata Architectonica, Oder Vor-Ubungen in Beyderley Bau-Kunst und zwar in der Civili.... Leipzig: 1730. V. 70

HEDERMAN, M. P.
The Crane Bag Book of Irish Studies. 1982. V. 69

HEDEVIND, BERTIL
The Dialect of Dentdale in the West Riding of Yorkshire. London: 1967. V. 73

HEDGE, LEVI
Elements of Logick; or a Summary of General Principles and Different Modes of Reasoning. Cambridge: 1816. V. 71

HEDGECOE, JOHN
Henry Moore. New York: 1968. V. 70; 72; 73
Nude Photography. New York: 1984. V. 68

HEDGES, F. A. MITCHELL
Battles with Giant Fish. 1923. V. 68

HEDGES, PETER
An Ocean in Iowa. New York: 1998. V. 72
What's Eating Gilbert Grape. New York: 1991. V. 72

HEDGPETH, DON
Bettina Portraying Life in Art. Flagstaff: 1978. V. 68; 73
From Broncs to Bronzes- The Life and Work of Grant Speed. Flagstaff: 1979. V. 71
Spurs Were a Jinglin' - a Brief Look of the Wyoming Range Country. Flagstaff: 1975. V. 69; 71

HEDIN, SVEN
Jehol, City of Emperors. London: 1932. V. 72
The Silk Road. New York: 1938. V. 69
Trans-Himalaya. Discoveries and Adventures in Tibet. 1909-1913. V. 70

HEDLEY, JOHN
A Practical Treatise on the Working and Ventilation of Coal Mines.... 1851. V. 71

HEDLEY, OSWALD DODD
Who Invented the Locomotive Engine?. London: 1858. V. 68

HEDREN, PAUL L.
The Great Sioux War of 1876. Helena: 1991. V. 72

HEDRICK, ULYSSES P.
The Cherries of New York. Albany: 1915. V. 72
A History of Horticulture in America to 1860. New York: 1950. V. 71
The Peaches of New York. Albany: 1917. V. 72; 73
The Plums of New York. Albany: 1911. V. 72
The Small Fruits of New York. Albany: 1925. V. 70
Sturtevant's Notes on Edible Plants. Albany: 1919. V. 69; 71; 73

HEEREN, A. H. L.
Historical Researches into the Politics, Intercourse and Trade of the Carthaginians, Ethiopians, Egyptians. Oxford: 1838. V. 70
Historical Researches into the Principal Nations of Antiquity. Oxford: 1833. V. 71

HEFFLEY, MIKE
The Music of Anthony Braxton. Westport: 1996. V. 72

HEGEMANN, ELIZABETH COMPTON
Navaho Trading Days. Albuquerque: 1963. V. 69

HEGEMANN, WERNER
The American Vitruvius: an Architect's Handbook of Civic Art. New York: 1922. V. 68
City Planning Housing. Volume III. A Graphic Review of City Art 1922- 1937. New York: 1938. V. 69; 72

HEGENETIUS, GOTTFRIED
Itinerarium Frisio-Hollandicum Et Itinerarium Gallo-Brabanticum. Leyden: 1630,. V. 72

HEGGEN, THOMAS
Mister Roberts. London: 1948. V. 71
Mister Roberts. New York: 1948. V. 68

HEGI, URSULA
Floating in My Mother's Palm. New York: 1990. V. 69; 71
Hotel of the Saints. New York: 2001. V. 69; 72
Intrusions. New York: 1981. V. 70
Salt Dancers. New York: 1995. V. 70
Stones from the River. New York: 1994. V. 73
Unearned Pleasures and Other Stories. Moscow: 1988. V. 69; 71

HEGLAN, JEAN
Into the Forest. Corvallis: 1996. V. 71; 72

HEGNER, ROBERT W.
The Germ-Cell Cycle in Animals. New York: 1914. V. 68

HEIDELOFF, CHARLES
Collection of Architectural Ornaments of the Middle Ages in the Byznatine and Gothic Style. Nuremberg: 1847. V. 70

HEIDEN, JAN VANDER
Beschryving der Nieuwlyks Uitgevonden en Geoctrojeerde Slang-BrandSpuiten en Haare Wyze van Brand-Blussen, Tegenwoordig Binnen Amsterdam.... Amsterdam: 1735. V. 68; 70

HEIKEN, G.
Volcanic Ash. Berkeley: 1985. V. 72

HEILBRUN, CAROLYN G.
The Garnett Family. London: 1961. V. 69

HEILNER, V. C.
Duck Shooting. 1951. V. 71

HEILPRIN, ANGELO
Mont Pelee and the Tragedy of Martinique. Philadelphia and London: 1903. V. 70

HEIM, A.
The Throne of the Gods. 1939. V. 68; 71; 73
Untersuchungen uber den Mehanismus der Gebirgsbildung im Anschluss an die geologische.... Basel: 1878. V. 68

HEIMSATH, CLOVIS
Pioneer Texas Buildings, a Geometry Lesson. 1968. V. 70

HEIN, O. L.
Memoirs of Long Ago...Before and After the Civil War 1855-1865... Western Frontier, In Early Seventies and Eighties. New York: 1925. V. 72

HEINE, HEINRICH
Buch der Lieder. Hamburg: 1827. V. 72
Florentine Nights. London: 1927. V. 71
Poems of Heinrich Heine. New York: 1917. V. 68

HEINE, JOHANN AUGUST
Traite des Batiments Propres a Loger les Animaux Qui sont Necessaires a l'Economie Rurale.... Leipzig: 1802. V. 68

HEINEKEN, PAUL
Lucidum Prospectivae Speculum.... Augsburg: 1727. V. 72

HEINEMANN, LARRY
Close Quarters. New York: 1977. V. 69; 71; 72

HEINLEIN, ROBERT ANSON
Assignment in Eternity. Reading: 1953. V. 72
Between Plants. New York: 1951. V. 70
Beyond this Horizon. Reading: 1948. V. 68; 71; 72
Citizen of the Galaxy. New York: 1957. V. 69
Farmer in the Sky. New York: 1950. V. 69
Farnham's Freehold. 1964. V. 69
Farnham's Freehold. London: 1965. V. 68
Green Hills of Earth. Chicago: 1951. V. 70
Have Space Suit Will Travel. New York: 1958. V. 69; 71
Job: a Comedy of Justice. New York: 1984. V. 71
The Man Who Sold the Moon. 1950. V. 70
Methuselah's Children. 1958. V. 69
The Moon is a Harsh Mistress. 1966. V. 71
The Moon is a Harsh Mistress. London: 1967. V. 68
The Number of the Beast. London: 1980. V. 69
Orphans of the Sky. London: 1963. V. 69; 70
Revolt in 2100. 1953. V. 70
Rocket Ship Galileo. New York: 1947. V. 71
Sixth Column. 1949. V. 69
The Sixth Column. New York: 1949. V. 71
The Star Beast. New York: 1954. V. 69
Starman Jones. New York: 1953. V. 69
Stranger in a Strange Land. New York: 1961. V. 69; 70
Time Enough for Love. New York: 1973. V. 71; 73
Time for the Stars. New York: 1956. V. 69
A Tunnel in the Sky. New York: 1955. V. 69
Waldo and Magic, Inc. Garden City: 1950. V. 71

HEINRICH, BERND
Ravens in Winter. A Zoological Detective Storyl. New York: 1989. V. 72

HEINZ, W. C.
The Professional. New York: 1958. V. 69; 70

HEINZEN, KARL
The Rights of Women and the Sexual Relations. Boston: 1891. V. 69

HEIRS of Hippocrates. The Development of Medicine in a Catalogue of Historic Books.... Iowa: 1990. V. 70; 72

HEISTER, LORENZ
Medical, Chirurgical and Anatomical Cases and Observations.... 1755. V. 68
Medical, Chirurgical and Anatomical Cases and Observations.... London: 1755. V. 72

HEITMAN, FRANCIS B.
Historical Register and Dictionary of The U.S. Army, 1789-1903. Urbana: 1965. V. 72
Historical Register and Dictionary of The U.S. Army, 1789-1903. 1988. V. 72
Historical Register of Officers of the Continental Army During the War of the Revolution April 1775 to December 1783. Washington: 1893. V. 73

HEITZMANN, C.
Anatomy: Descriptive and Topographical.... New York: 1887. V. 71

HEIZER, ROBERT F.
The Indians of Los Angeles County: Hugo Reid's Letters of 1852. Los Angeles: 1968. V. 68

HEJINIAN, LYN
Two Stein Talks. Santa Fe: 1995. V. 73

HELCK, PETER
The Great Auto Races. New York: 1975. V. 70

HELD, G. J.
The Papuans of Waropen. The Hague: 1957. V. 69

HELD, JOHN
The Gods Were Promiscuous. New York: 1937. V. 70

HELLE, ANDRE
L'Arche de Noe. Paris: 1925. V. 69
La Belle Historie Que Voila.... Nancy: 1925. V. 70

HELLENBECK, CLEVE
Legends of the Spanish Southwest. Glendale: 1938. V. 70

HELLER, A.
Tibetan Art. Woodbridge: 1999. V. 69

HELLER, A. A.
Botanical Explorations in Southern Texas During the Season of 1894. Lancaster: 1895. V. 70

HELLER, ELINOR RAAS
A Bibliography of the Grabhorn Press 1915-1940. San Francisco: 1940. V. 73

HELLER, FRANK
The Strange Adventures of Mr. Collin. 1926. V. 73
The Strange Adventures of Mr. Collin. New York: 1926. V. 68; 69

HELLER, JANE
The Club. New York: 1995. V. 71

HELLER, JOSEPH
Catch-22. New York: 1961. V. 68; 69; 70; 71; 72; 73
Catch-22. London: 1962. V. 70; 73
Catch-22. New York: 1973. V. 69
Catch-22. Franklin Center: 1978. V. 71; 73
Catch-22. New York: 1994. V. 68
Closing Time. Franklin Center: 1994. V. 70
Closing Time. New York: 1994. V. 68; 69; 71; 72; 73
God Knows. New York: 1984. V. 70; 72
Good as Gold. New York: 1979. V. 70; 73
Now and Then: From Coney Island to Here. New York: 1998. V. 70; 72
Picture This. New York: 1988. V. 70; 71
Something Happened. New York: 1974. V. 68; 70; 71; 72
We Bombed in New Haven. A Play. New York: 1968. V. 68; 70

HELLER, JULES
Papermaking: the White Art. Scottsdale: 1980. V. 70; 72

HELLER, LORENZ
Murder in Make-up. 1937. V. 68

HELLER, MICHAEL
Accidental Center. Fremont: 1972. V. 68; 71

HELLMAN, LILLIAN
Candide: A Comic Operetta Based on Voltaire's Satire. New York: 1957. V. 72
The Collected Plays. Boston: 1972. V. 72
My Mother, My Father and Me. New York: 1963. V. 71
An Unfinished Woman - a Memoir. Boston: 1969. V. 68

HELLMANN, ELLEN
Problems of Urban Bantu Youth. Johannesburg: 1940:. V. 72

HELLWIG, CHRISTOPH VON
Nosce te Ipsum vel Anatomicum Vivum: Oder, Kurtz Gefasstes Doch Richtig Gestelltes Anatomisches Werck. Erfurt: 1716. V. 68; 72

HELLYER, SAMUEL STEVENS
Lectures on the Science and Art of Sanitary Plumbing. London: 1883. V. 68

HELMAN, ISIDORE STANISLAS
Faits Memorables des Empereurs de la Chine, Tires des Annales Chinoises.... Paris: 1788. V. 68

HELME, ELIZABETH
Instructive Rambles in London and the Adjacent Villages. London: 1798. V. 71

HELMHOLTZ, HERMANN
On the Sensations of Tone, as a Physiological Basis for the Theory of Music. London: 1885. V. 72
On the Sensations of Tone as a Physiological Basis for the Theory of Music. London: 1895. V. 68

HELMONT, FRANCISCUS MERCURIUS VAN
Alphabeti vere Naturalis Hebraici Brevissima Delineatio.... Sulzbach: 1667. V. 68; 70; 73

HELMORE, THOMAS
Affair at Quala - a Novel. London: 1965. V. 70

HELMS, CYNTHIA NEWMAN
Diego Rivera. New York: 1986. V. 70

HELMUT, JEAN BAPTISTE VAN
Ortus Medicinae. Venice: 1651. V. 68

HELMUTH, J. HENRY
A Short Account of the Yellow Fever in Philadelphia for the Reflecting Christian. Philadelphia: 1794. V. 71; 73

HELPER, HINTON ROWAN
The Land of Gold: Reality Versus Fiction. Baltimore: 1855. V. 69; 73

HELPRIN, MARK
A City in Winter. New York: 1996. V. 70
A Dove of the East. New York: 1975. V. 71; 72
Ellis Island and Other Stories. New York: 1981. V. 68
Memoir from Antproof Case. New York: 1995. V. 72
Refiner's Fire. New York: 1977. V. 68; 71
Refiner's Fire. London: 1978. V. 68
The Veil of Snows. New York: 1997. V. 70

HELPS, ARTHUR
The Claims of Labour; an Essay on the Duties of Employers to Be Employed. London: 1845. V. 71
The Conquerors of the New World and Their Bondsmen. London: 1848. V. 72
Correspondence. London: 1917. V. 71
Friends in Council. London: 1861. V. 71
Friends in Council. London: 1877. V. 71
Fruits of Leisure: Essays Written in the Intervals of Business. New York: 1852. V. 73
Ivan de Biron, or, The Russian Court in the Middle of Last Century. Boston: 1874. V. 71
Life and Labours of Mr. Brassey 1805-1870. London: 1872. V. 68; 72
The Life Of Hernando Cortes. London: 1871. V. 72
Oulita the Serf. A Tragedy. London: 1858. V. 71
Social Pressure. London: 1875. V. 71
The Spanish Conquest in America and Its Relation to the History of Slavery and to the Government of Colonies. London: 1855-1861. V. 68
Thoughts Upon Government. London: 1872. V. 71

HELPS, RACEY
Mr. Roley to the Rescue. Philadelphia: 1966. V. 70

HELU, ANTONIO
La Obligacion de Asesinar. (The Compulsion to Murder). Mexico City: 1946. V. 70; 71

HELVETIUS, CLAUDE ADRIEN
De l'Espirt. Paris: 1758. V. 69

HELVICK, JAMES
Beat the Devil. Philadelphia/New York: 1951. V. 71

HEMANS, FELICIA DOROTHEA BROWNE
Poems. Edinburgh: 1854. V. 68; 72; 73
Poems. Edinburgh: 1854-1859. V. 73
The Works. London: 1839. V. 71; 72
The Works. Edinburgh and London: 1841-1846. V. 73

HEMENWAY, A.
Geography and History of Great Britain. Bangkok: 1843. V. 70

HEMINGWAY, ERNEST MILLAR
Across the River and into the Trees. London: 1950. V. 69; 70; 72; 73
Across the River and Into the Trees. New York: 1950. V. 68; 72; 73
Big Two-Hearted River. Portland: 2002. V. 72
By-Line. New York: 1967. V. 68; 69; 71
The Dangerous Summer. New York: 1985. V. 72; 73
Dateline: Toronto. New York: 1985. V. 68; 69
Death in the Afternoon. New York: 1932. V. 70; 71; 73
A Divine Gesture. New York: 1974. V. 71
88 Poems. New York: 1979. V. 71
Ernest Hemingway, Selected Letters 1917-1961. New York: 1981. V. 69
A Farewell to Arms. London: 1929. V. 70
A Farewell to Arms. New York: 1929. V. 68; 69; 70; 71; 72; 73
The Fifth Column and Four Stories of the Spanish Civil War. New York: 1969. V. 69
The Fifth Column and The First Forty-Nine Stories. New York: 1938. V. 69; 70; 71; 73
The Fifth Column and the First Forty-Nine Stories. London: 1939. V. 70

HEMINGWAY, ERNEST MILLAR continued
For Whom the Bell Tolls. New York: 1940. V. 68; 69; 71; 72; 73
For Whom the Bell Tolls. London: 1941. V. 73
The Garden of Eden. New York: 1986. V. 68; 69; 71
The Garden of Eden. London: 1987. V. 73
God Rest You Merry Gentlemen. New York: 1933. V. 68; 72
Green Hills of Africa. New York: 1935. V. 68; 70; 73
Hemingway on Fishing. New York: 2000. V. 69; 72
The Hemingway Reader. New York: 1953. V. 69
Hokum. Wellesley Hills: 1978. V. 69; 71; 73
In Our Time. Paris: 1924. V. 73
In Our Time. New York: 1925. V. 71; 72
In Our Time. New York: 1938. V. 68; 72
Islands in the Stream. London: 1970. V. 68
Islands in the Stream. New York: 1970. V. 68; 70; 73
Men Without Women. New York: 1927. V. 68; 71
A Moveable Feast. New York: 1954. V. 70
A Moveable Feast. London: 1964. V. 68; 69
A Moveable Feast. New York: 1964. V. 69; 70; 71; 73
The Nick Adams Stories. New York: 1972. V. 69; 71; 73
The Old Man and the Sea. London: 1952. V. 69; 70
The Old Man and the Sea. New York: 1952. V. 68; 69; 70; 71; 72; 73
The Old Man and the Sea. London: 1953. V. 72
The Old Man and the Sea. New York: 1990. V. 69; 72
Quintanilla. New York: 1934. V. 69
The Sound of the Trumpet. New York: 1953. V. 68
The Spanish Earth. Cleveland: 1938. V. 71; 72
To Have and Have Not. New York: 1937. V. 70; 71; 72; 73
Today is Friday. Englewood NJ: 1926. V. 72
The Torrents of Spring. New York: 1926. V. 72
The Torrents of Spring. Paris: 1932. V. 71
Two Christmas Tales. Berkeley: 1959. V. 71
The Wild Years. New York: 1962. V. 69
Winner Take Nothing. New York: 1933. V. 68; 69; 70; 71; 72; 73

HEMINGWAY, HILARY
Hunting with Hemingway. New York: 2000. V. 72

HEMINGWAY, PATRICIA S.
The Hemingways, Past and Present and Allied Families. Baltimore: 1988. V. 69

HEMLOW, JOYCE
The History of Fanny Burney. Oxford: 1958. V. 68

HEMON, ALEKSANDAR
The Question of Bruno. London: 2000. V. 70; 71; 72

HEMPEL, AMY
Reasons to Live. New York: 1985. V. 68; 72

HEMPEL, ROSE
The Heian civilization of Japan. London: 1983. V. 72

HEMPHILL, ELVA MURRELL
Early Days in Dallas County. 1954. V. 68

HEMPHILL, PAUL
The Nashville Sound: Bright Lights and Country Music. New York: 1972. V. 71

HEMSTERIUS, SIBBOLDUS
Messis Aurea Exhibens: Anatomica Novissima et Utilissima Experimenta.... Heidelberg: 1659. V. 70

HENDERSON, A.
Field Guide to the Palms of the Americas. Princeton: 1995. V. 73

HENDERSON, ALICE CORBIN
Brothers of Light: the Penitentes of the Southwest. New York: 1937. V. 69; 70
Brothers of Light, the Penitentes of the Southwest. Chicago: 1962. V. 69

HENDERSON, ARCHIBALD
The Conquest of the Old Southwest: The Romantic Story of the Early Pioneers into Virginia, the Carolinas, Tennessee and Kentucky 1740-1790. New York: 1920. V. 73
George Bernard Shaw: Man of the Century. New York: 1956. V. 71
Washington's Southern Tour 1791. Boston: 1923. V. 73

HENDERSON, DAVID
De Mayor of Harlem. New York: 1970. V. 72

HENDERSON, ELLIOTT BLAINE
The Soliloquy of Satan and Other Poems. Springfield: 1907. V. 71

HENDERSON, GEORGE
Ollie Miss. New York: 1935. V. 72
Stonewall Jackson and the American Civil War. London/New York/Bombay: 1898. V. 69

HENDERSON, H. J.
The Cruising Association Library Catalogue. A Collection of Books for Seamen and Students.... London: 1931. V. 68; 73

HENDERSON, HALTON
Artistry in Single Action. Dallas: 1989. V. 71

HENDERSON, JAMES
Memorials of James Henderson, M.D. Medical Missionary to China. London: 1868. V. 72

HENDERSON, JEFF
100 Years in Montague County, Texas. Saint Jo: 1958. V. 73

HENDERSON, JULIAN
Colorado: Short Studies of Its Past and Present. Boulder: 1927. V. 69

HENDERSON, L. J.
Blood: a Study in General Physiology. New Haven: 1928. V. 71

HENDERSON, LAUREN
Chained. 2000. V. 68
The Strawberry Tattoo. London: 1999. V. 70
Too Many Blondes. London: 1996. V. 70

HENDERSON, LESLEY
Twentieth Century Crime & Mystery Writers. Chicago: 1991. V. 71

HENDERSON, M. R.
Malayan Orchid Hybrids. Singapore: 1956-1961. V. 68; 73

HENDERSON, MARY FOOTE
The Aristocracy of Health. Washington: 1904. V. 68

HENDERSON, PAUL
Landmarks on the Oregon Trail. New York: 1953. V. 68; 69; 72; 73

HENDERSON, RANDALL
On Desert Trails: Today and Yesterday. Los Angeles: 1961. V. 69

HENDERSON, WILLIAM
Homoeopathy Fairly Represented in Reply to Dr. Simpson's Homoeopathy Misrepresented. Edinburgh: 1853. V. 69
Trial of William Gardiner (The Peasenhall Case). London: 1934. V. 69

HENDERSON, WILLIAM AUGUSTUS
The Housekeeper's Instructor or Universal Family Cook. 1793. V. 68

HENDERSON, ZENNA
The Anything Box. London: 1966. V. 73
Pilgrimage: the Book of the People. New York: 1961. V. 68

HENDRICKS, GORDON
Albert Bierstadt: Painter of the American West. New York: 1954. V. 69

HENDRIE, DON
Blount's Anvil. Amherst: 1980. V. 72

HENDRIX, JOHN
If I Can Do It On Horseback. Austin: 1964. V. 68

HENDRON, J. W.
Frijoles: a Hidden Valley in the New World. Santa Fe: 1946. V. 68

HENDRY, HAMISH
Holidays & Happy Days. London: 1901. V. 69
Just Forty Winks.... 1897. V. 68

HENDRY, WILLIAM
The Method of Calculating the Values of Life Annuities, Assurances.... Hull: 1820. V. 69

HENDY, JOHN G.
The History of the Postmarks of the British Isles from 1840 to 1876.... London: 1909. V. 68

HENLEY, BETH
Crimes of the Heart. New York: 1982. V. 69; 72

HENLEY, WILLIAM ERNEST
A Book of English Prose - Character and Incident - 1387-1649. London: 1894. V. 68
A Book of Verses. London: 1888. V. 73
A Book of Verses. London: 1889. V. 73
London Types. London: 1898. V. 69; 71
London Types. New York: 1898. V. 69; 72
Lyrica Heroica a book of verse for boys. London: 1892. V. 73
The Plays of W. E. Henley and R. L. Stevenson. London: 1896. V. 71
The Song of the Sword, and Other Verses. London: 1892. V. 69

HENN, T. R.
The Lonely Tower: Studies in the Poetry of W. B. Yeats. 1950. V. 70

HENNEPIN, LOUIS
A New Discovery of a Vast Country in America. Chicago: 1903. V. 73

HENNESSY, W. B.
History of North Dakota - Embracing a Relation of the History of the State from the Earliest Times Down to the Present Day.... Bismarck: 1910. V. 68; 73

HENNING, WILLIAM E.
The Heller. New York: 1947. V. 71

HENNINGSON, CHARLES FREDERICK
Revelations of Russia; or, the Emperor Nicholas and His Empire in 1844. London: 1844. V. 73

HENREY, BLANCHE
British Botanical and Horticultural Literature Before 1800. London: 1975. V. 69
British Botanical and Horticultural Literature Before 1800.... Oxford: 1975. V. 69
British Botanical and Horticultural Literature Before 1800.... London: 1999. V. 72

HENRY Miller; a Book of Tributes 1931-1994. Orlando: 1994. V. 71

HENRY, ALEXANDER
Travels and Adventures in Canada and the Indian Territories Between the Years 1760-1776.... Boston: 1901. V. 70

HENRY, FRANCOISE
La Sculpture Irlandaise Pendant les Douze Premiers Siecles de l'ere Chretienne. Paris: 1933. V. 69

HENRY, FREDERICK PORTEOUS
Standard History of the Medical Profession of Philadelphia. Chicago: 1897. V. 70

HENRY, GARRIT
Janet Fish. New York and Geneva: 1987. V. 69

HENRY, J. Q. A.
The Deadly Cigarette; or the Perils of Juvenile Smoking. London: 1906. V. 68

HENRY, JAMES P.
Resources of the State of Arkansas with Description of Counties, Railroads, Mines and the City of Little Rock. Little Rock: 1872. V. 68; 73

HENRY, JOSEPH
The Papers of Joseph Henry. Washington: 1972-1981. V. 71

HENRY, MARGUERITE
Benjamin West and His Cat Grimalkin. Indianapolis: 1947. V. 70
Justin Morgan Had a Horse. Chicago: 1945. V. 70
Pictured Geography Brazil in Story and Pictures. Chicago: 1941. V. 72
Pictured Geography Canada in Story and Pictures. Chicago: 1941. V. 72
Pictured Geography West Indies in Story and Pictures. Chicago: 1941. V. 72
Sea Star-Orphan of Chincoteague. Chicago: 1949. V. 70

HENRY, ROBERT SELPH
First with the Most Forrest. Indianapolis: 1944. V. 70

HENRY, S. M.
Symbiosis. New York: 1966-1967. V. 72

HENRY, SOPHIA WILLIAMS
A Texas Pilgrimage. Cleveland: 1905. V. 68

HENRY, STUART
Conquering Our Great American Plains. New York: 1930. V. 71

HENRY, SUE
Murder on the Iditarod Trail. New York: 1991. V. 68; 69; 71

HENRY, T. J.
Catalog of the Heteroptera or True Bugs of Canada and the Continental United States. 1988. V. 68

HENRY, THOMAS
Experiments and Observations on the Following Subjects... (with) An Appendix. London: 1773. V. 69

HENRY, THOMAS J.
The Awful and Ethical Allegory of Deuteronomy Smith. Edinburgh: 1892. V. 69

HENRY, WALTER
Events of a Military Life.. London: 1843. V. 68
Trifles from My Port-Folio, or Recollections of Scenes and Small Adventures During Twenty-Nine Years of Military Service, in the...Upper and Lower Canada, by a Staff Surgeon. Quebec: 1839. V. 68; 72

HENRY, WILL
Alias Butch Cassidy. New York: 1967. V. 69
Death of a Legend. New York: 1954. V. 73
I, Tom Horn. Philadelphia: 1975. V. 69
To Follow a Flag. New York: 1953. V. 69

HENRY, WILLIAM CHARLES
Memoirs of the Life and Scientific Researches of John Dalton. London: 1854. V. 68

HENRY, WILLIAM WIRT
Patrick Henry: Life, Correspondence and Speeches. New York: 1891. V. 71

HENRY BANNERMAN & SONS, LTD.
Treatises, etc., Reprinted from Our Diary and Buyers' Guide for 1887, 1888, 1889, 1890, 1891. Manchester: 1892. V. 71

HENSEL, W. U.
The Christiana Riot and the Treason Trials of 1851 an Historical Sketch of These Events, September 9, 1911. Lancaster: 1911. V. 68

HENSHALL, JAMES A.
Bass, Pike, Perch and Others. New York: 1903. V. 69

HENSHAW, J. W.
Mountain Wild Flowers of America. Boston: 1906. V. 73
Mountain Wild Flowers of Canada. Toronto: 1906. V. 73

HENSHAW, ROBERT
The Whole Proceedings of an Information Exhibited at the Instance of the Honourable the East India Company, Against Robert Henshaw, Esq. Custom Master of Bombay for the Corruption in Office, and Receiving Presents in Violation of the Act 33 Geo. 111... Edinburgh: 1807. V. 70

HENSLOW, T. GEOFFREY W.
Ye Sundial Booke. 1914. V. 70

HENSON, EITHNE
The Fictions of Romaticke Chivalry: Samuel Johnson and Romance. London and Toronto: 1992. V. 71

HENSON, GRAVENOR
Henson's History of the Framework Knitters. 1970. V. 72

HENSON, JOSIAH
An Autobiography Of The Rev. Josiah Henson. Boston: 1879. V. 72
An Autobiography of the Rev. Josiah Henson. London: 1882. V. 68
Uncle Tom's Story of His Own Life. London: 1877. V. 68

HENTY, GEORGE ALFRED
Among Malay Pirates in Boy's Own Annual, Volume 20. 1898. V. 73
At Aboukir and Acre. 1899. V. 72
At Agincourt. 1897. V. 72
At Agincourt. London: 1897. V. 68; 71
Beeton's Boys Own Magazine. London. V. 73
Beric the Briton. London: 1893. V. 72
Bonnie Prince Charlie. 1888. V. 72
A Book of Famous Travels. Boston: 1902. V. 73
Both Sides the Border. 1899. V. 72
Both Sides the Border. London: 1899. V. 68
The Brahmin's Treasure, or Colonel Thorndyke's Secret. Philadelphia: 1900. V. 72
Brains and Bravery. 1903. V. 73
The Bravest of the Brave; or with Peterborough in Spain. 1887. V. 71; 72
The Bravest of the Brave, or with Peterborough in Spain. London: 1887. V. 68
Burton and Son in Boy's Own Annual Volume 21. 1899. V. 73
By Conduct and Courage. 1905. V. 72
By England's Aid, or, the Freeing of the Netherlands. London: 1893. V. 71
By Pike and Dyke. 1890. V. 72
By Right of Conquest. 1891. V. 72
By Sheer Pluck. 1884. V. 72
Captain Bayley's Heir. 1889. V. 72
The Cat of Bubastes. 1889. V. 71; 72
The Cat of Bubastes. London: 1889. V. 68
A Chapter of Adventures. 1891. V. 72
A Coaching Adventure in Our Annual. 1883. V. 73
Condemned as a Nihilist. 1893. V. 72
Cornet of Horse. 1881. V. 72
Courage and Conflict. 1901. V. 73
Cuthbert Hartington. London. V. 72; 73
The Dash for Khartoum. 1892. V. 72
A Desperate Gang, in Boys Illustrated Annual, Volume 2. London: 1892-1893. V. 73
A Desperate Gang, in Boy's Illustrated Annual, Volume 2. London: 1893-1894. V. 73
Dorothy's Double. Chicago. V. 72
A Dozen All Told. 1894. V. 72
The Dragon and Raven. 1886. V. 72
The Dragon and the Raven. Chicago. V. 73
Facts, Fiction, History and Adventure. 1892. V. 73
The Fall of Sebastopol. Boston. V. 72
A Fetish Hole. in Boy's Own Annual, Volume 19. 1897. V. 73
For Name and Fame. 1886. V. 72
For Name and Fame. in Every Boy's Annual. London: 1886. V. 73
For the Temple. 1888. V. 72
Friends though Divided. 1883. V. 72
A Girl of the Commune. New York. V. 72; 73
The Golden Canon in Boys Illustrated Annual, Volume I. London: 1892-1893. V. 73
Grit and Go. 1902. V. 73
Hazard and Heroism. 1904. V. 73
In Battle and Breeze. London. V. 72
In Freedom's Cause. 1885. V. 72
In the Grip of the Press Gang In Young England Volume 13. 1892. V. 73
In the Hands of the Cave Dwellers. 1900. V. 73
In the Hands of the Cave Dwellers. New York: 1900. V. 72
In the Hands of the Malays. 1905. V. 72
In the Heart of the Rockies. New York: 1894. V. 73
In the Heart of the Rockies. 1895. V. 72
In the Irish Brigade. 1901. V. 72
In the Reign of Terror. New York. V. 73
In the Reign of Terror. 1888. V. 72
In the Reign of Terror. London: 1888. V. 68
Jack Archer in The Union Jack, volume 4. 1883. V. 73
Jack Archer. Boston. V. 73
A Jacobite Exile. 1893. V. 72
A Jacobite Exile. 1894. V. 72
A Jacobite Exile. London: 1894. V. 69
Joe Polwreath the Hunchback, a Story of the Cornish Coast in Young England, Volume 10. 1889. V. 73
A Knight of the White Cross. London: 1896. V. 69
A Knight of the White Cross. 1897. V. 72
Life of a Special Correspondent in Boy's Own Annual Volume 18. 1896. V. 73
The Lion of St. Mark. 1889. V. 72
Little Mistress Valentia in Nister's Holiday Annual for 1905. London: 1905. V. 73
The Lost Heir. New York. V. 72
Maori and Settler. 1891. V. 72

HENTY, GEORGE ALFRED continued
A March on London: Being a Story of Wat Tyler's Insurrection. London: 1898. V. 72
The March to Coomassie. London: 1874. V. 72
The March to Magdala. London: 1868. V. 72
No Surrender. 1900. V. 72
On the Irrawaddy. 1896. V. 72
On the Irrawaddy. 1897. V. 72; 73
On the Spanish Main. in Young England, Volume 17. 1896. V. 73
Orange and Green. 1888. V. 72
Our Soldiers. 1910. V. 73
Out of the Pampas. 1871. V. 72
Out with Garibaldi. 1901. V. 72
Out With Garibaldi. London: 1901. V. 69
Peril and Prowess. 1899. V. 73
Queen Victoria, Scenes from Her Life and Reign. 1901. V. 73
The Queen's Cup. London: 1897. V. 72
The Queen's Cup. 1898. V. 72
The Ranche in the Valley. London. V. 73
Redskin and Cow-boy. 1892. V. 72
Redskins and Colonists. New York. V. 73
A Roving Commission. 1900. V. 72
Rujub, the Juggler. London: 1893. V. 72
St. Bartholomew's Eve. 1893. V. 72
St. Bartholomew's Eve. 1894. V. 72
The Savage Club Papers. London: 1897. V. 73
Search for a Secret. London: 1911. V. 72
Seth Harper's Story in The Union Jack, Volume I. 1880. V. 73
A Soldier's Daughter. 1906. V. 72
Stirring Adventures Afloat and Ashore. London. V. 73
Stories of Sea and Land. London. V. 73
A Tale of Waterloo. New York. V. 72; 73
Those Other Animals. London. V. 72
Through Fire and Storm. London: 1898. V. 72
Through Russian Snows. 1895. V. 72
Through the Enemy Lines in Stirring Tales. London. V. 73
Through the Sikh War. 1894. V. 72
The Tiger of Mysore. 1896. V. 72
To Herat and Cabul. 1901. V. 72
To Herat and Cabul. 1902. V. 72; 73
Trapped, a Tale of the Mexican War, in The Red Book for Boys.'. London. V. 73
The Treasure of the Incas. 1903. V. 72
True to the Old Flag. 1885. V. 72
Two Sieges. London. V. 73
Under Drake's Flag. 1883. V. 72
Under Wellington's Command. 1899. V. 72
Venture and Valour. 1900. V. 73
When London Burned. 1895. V. 72
Winning His Spurs. 1891. V. 72
Winning His Spurs. 1895. V. 72
With Buller in Natal. 1901. V. 72
With Clive in India. 1884. V. 72
With Cochrane the Dauntless. 1897. V. 72
With Frederick the Great. 1897. V. 72
With Frederick the Great. 1898. V. 72
With Kitchener in the Soudan. 1903. V. 72
With Lee in Virginia. 1890. V. 72
With Moore at Corunna. 1898. V. 72; 73
With Roberts to Pretoria. 1902. V. 72
With the Allies to Pekin. 1903. V. 72
With the Allies to Pekin. 1904. V. 72
With the British Legion. 1903. V. 72
With Wolfe in Canada. 1887. V. 72
A Woman of the Commune. London: 1895. V. 73
Won by the Sword. 1900. V. 72
Wulf the Saxon. 1895. V. 72
The Young Buglers. Boston. V. 73
The Young Carthaginian. 1887. V. 72
The Young Colonists. London: 1885. V. 72
The Young Franc-Tireurs. 1872. V. 72
The Young Franc-Tireurs and their Adventures in the Franco-Prussian War. London: 1872. V. 68
Yule Logs. London: 1898. V. 73
Yule Logs. New York: 1898. V. 72
Yule Logs. London: 1901. V. 73
Yule Tide Yarns. 1901. V. 73

HENTZ, CAROLINE LEE
Courtship and Marriage; or, the Joys and Sorrows of American Life. Philadelphia: 1856. V. 69
Eoline or Magnolia Vale. Philadelphia: 1852. V. 69
Helen and Arthur; or Miss Thusa's Spinning Wheel. Philadelphia: 1853. V. 69
Love After Marriage and Other Stories of the Heart. Philadelphia: 1857. V. 69
Marcus Warland; or the Long Moss Spring. Philadelphia: 1852. V. 69
The Planter's Northern Bride. Philadelphia: 1854. V. 69
Rena; or the Snow Bird. Philadelphia: 1851. V. 69
Robert Graham. Philadelphia: 1855. V. 73

HENTZNER, PAUL
A Journey into England. Strawberry Hill: 1757. V. 72

HENZE, ANTON
Contemporary Church Art. NY: 1956. V. 72

HEPBURN, A. BARTON
The Story of an Outing. New York: 1913. V. 69

HEPBURN, KATHARINE
The Making of the African Queen. New York: 1987. V. 72

HEPPENSTALL, RAYNER
General William Booth Enters Into Heaven and Other Poems. New York: 1924. V. 72

HEPWORTH, BARBARA
Pictorial Autobiography. London: 1970. V. 69

HEPWORTH, GEORGE H.
Starboard and Port: The Nettie Along Shore. New York: 1876. V. 73

HEPWORTH, JIM
Resist Much, Obey Little - Some Notes on Edward Abbey. San Francisco: 1996. V. 69

HERALDIC Journal: Recording the Armorial Bearings and Genealogies of American Families. Boston: 1865-1868. V. 72

HERALDIC Visitation of Westmoreland, Made in the Year 1615, by Sir Richard St. George, Knt., Norroy King at Arms. Early 20th C. London: 1753. V. 72

HERALDIC Visitation of Westmoreland, Made in the Year 1615, by Sir Richard St. George Knt., Norroy King at Arms. London: 1853. V. 71

HERBERT, A. P.
The Bomber Gipsy and other poems. London: 1918. V. 71
Holy Deadlock. London: 1934. V. 72
The Water Gipsies. London: 1930. V. 70

HERBERT, ADAMS
Roger Bennion's Double. London: 1941. V. 72

HERBERT, AGNES
Casuals in the Caucasus, the Diary of a Sporting Holiday. London: 1912. V. 72
Two Dianas in Somaliland. London: 1908. V. 68

HERBERT, ARTHUR R. K.
Culinary Jottings. Calcutta: 1891. V. 68

HERBERT, AUBREY
Ben Kendim. A Record of Eastern Travel. London: 1925. V. 70

HERBERT, B. B.
The First Decennium of the National Editorial Association. Chicago: 1896. V. 68

HERBERT, EDWARD HERBERT
The Autobiography of Edward Lord Herbert of Cherbury. Newtown: 1928. V. 68
The Life. Written by Himself; and Continued to His Death. With Letters Written During His Residence at The French Court & C. London: 1826. V. 72

HERBERT, FRANK
Chapterhouse Dune. New York: 1985. V. 73
The Dragon in the Sea. New York: 1956. V. 69
Dune. Philadelphia and New York: 1965. V. 68; 71; 73
Dune. London: 1978. V. 70
Dune Messiah. New York: 1969. V. 69
40 Years Prospecting and Mining in the Black Hills of South Dakota. Rapid City: 1921. V. 70
God Emperor of Dune. 1981. V. 71
God Emperor of Dune. New York: 1981. V. 73
Heretics of Dune. New York: 1984. V. 73

HERBERT, GEORGE
Poems. Newtown: 1923. V. 70; 71; 72
The Remains. London: 1848. V. 68
The Temple. Sacred Poems and Private Ejaculations. London: 1927. V. 68; 70
The Works. London: 1835. V. 72

HERBERT, H.
Antiquities of the Inns of Court and Chancery. London: 1804. V. 70

HERBERT, HENRY
A Complete Guide to the Places of Amusement, Objects of Interest, Parks, Clubs, Markets, Docks, Principal Railway Routes...Leading Hotels. London: 1876. V. 71

HERBERT, HENRY W.
The Magnolia. 1836. New York: 1835. V. 72

HERBERT, HENRY WILLIAM
The Dog. New York: 1857. V. 71
Frank Forester's Field Sports of the United States and British Provinces, of North America. New York: 1849. V. 68; 69
Frank Forester's Fugitive Sporting Sketches, Being the Miscellaneous Articles Upon Sport and Sporting.... Westfield: 1879. V. 70

HERBERT, J. A.
Illuminated Manuscripts. 1911. V. 70

HERBERT, LAKE
The Engineer's and Mechanic's Encylopaedia.... London: 1839-1836. V. 69

HERBERT, MARY ELIZABETH
Holy Land. Cradle Lands. London: 1857. V. 68

HERBERT, PAUL D.
The Sincerest Form of Flattery: An Historical Survey of Parodies, Pastiches and Other Imitative Writings of Sherlock Holmes 1891-1980. Bloomington: 1983. V. 69

HERBERT Strang's Annual 1909. London: 1909. V. 70

HERBERT, W.
Amaryllidaceae...Followed by a Treatise on Cross-Bred Vegetables. London: 1837. V. 73

HERBERT, WILLIAM
The History of the Twelve Great Livery Companies of London.... London: 1836-1837. V. 73
The History of the Twelve Great Livery Companies of London.... London: 1837. V. 71

HERBERTSON, AGNES GROZIER
Gulliver's Travels. London: 1908. V. 72

HERBST, JOSEPHINE
New Green World. John Bartram And The Early Naturalists. New York: 1954. V. 72
Rope of Gold. New York: 1939. V. 68

HERBST, W.
Fungal Flora of the Lehigh Valley, Pa. Allentown: 1899. V. 70

HERCIK, E.
Folk Toys/Les Jouets Populaires. Prague: 1951. V. 72

HERD, DAVID
Ancient and Modern Scottish Songs, Heroic Ballads, etc. . . . Glasgow: 1869. V. 71

HERD, RICHARD
Songs of Poetry. Kirby Lonsdale: 1837. V. 71

HERDEG, WALTER
Art in the Watermark. Zurich;: 1952. V. 73

HERDMAN, JOHN
An Essay on the Causes and Phenomena of Animal Life. London: 1795. V. 71

HERDMAN, W. A.
Challenger Voyage. Zoology. Parts 17, 38 and 76 Tunicata. 1882-1888. V. 73
Fishes and Fisheries of the Irish Sea and Especially of the Lancashire and Western Sea-Fisheries District. LondonGeorge Philip and Son: 1901. V. 68
Four Addresses Delivered at the Anniversary Meetings of the Linnean Society of London in May 1905, 1906, 1907 and 1908. London: 1905-1908. V. 68

HERDMAN, W. G.
Pictorial Relics of Ancient Liverpool. Liverpool: 1878. V. 73
Thoughts on Speculative Cosmology and the Principles of Art. Liverpool: 1869. V. 72

HERE, A. W. C. T.
Notes on Fishes in the Zoological Museum of Stanford University. Kentfield: 1934. V. 73

HERFORD, BEATRICE
Monologues. New York: 1908. V. 73

HERFORD, OLIVER
An Alphabet of Celebrities. Boston: 1899. V. 73
Excuse It Please. Philadelphia: 1929. V. 70
Happy Days. New York: 1917. V. 68
The Kitten's Garden of Verses. New York: 1911. V. 70
The Rubaiyat of a Persian Kitten. New York: 1904. V. 70

HERGE
The Adventures of Tintin: The Black Island. London: 1966. V. 70
The Adventures of Tintin: the Calculus Affair. London: 1960. V. 73
The Adventures of Tintin: The Castafiore Emerald. London: 1963. V. 70

HERGESHEIMER, JOSEPH
From an Old House. New York: 1925. V. 68
The Limestone Tree. New York: 1931. V. 71
The Party Dress. New York: 1930. V. 71
Quiet Cities. London: 1928. V. 68
Quiet Cities. New York: 1928. V. 71

HERING, GEORGE EDWARDS
Sketches on the Danube, in Hungary and Transylvania. London: 1838. V. 68; 70

HERING, HENRY A.
The Burglars' Club. 1906. V. 71

HERING, KARL HEINZ
Ernst Ludwig Kirchner. Dusseldorf: 1960. V. 72

HERISSE, EMILE
The Art of Pastry Making, According to the French and English Methods.... London: 1895. V. 68

HERITSCH, FRANZ
The Nappe Theory in the Alps. London: 1929. V. 70

HERIZ, PATRICK DE
La Belle O'Morhi, a Brief Biography. Waltham St. Lawrence: 1947. V. 68

HERKLOTS, G. A. C.
Vegetables in South-East Asia. New York: 1972. V. 70

HERLEY, RICHARD
The Penal Colony. New York: 1988. V. 68

HERLIHY, JAMES LEO
Blue Denim. New York: 1958. V. 69
Midnight Cowboy. New York: 1965. V. 68; 69; 70; 72; 73

HERMAN, FRED
Dynamite Cargo. Convoy to Russia. New York: 1943. V. 69

HERMAN, PAUL
Florae Lugduono-Bataae Flores, Sive Enumeratio Stirpium Horti Lugduno-Batavi.... Leiden: 1690. V. 70

HERMANN, BINGER
The Louisiana Purchase and Our Title West of the Rocky Mountains.... Washington: 1898. V. 69; 72; 73

HERMANN, F. J.
Manual of the Carices of the Rocky Mountains and Colorado Basin. Washington: 1970. V. 72

HERMANT, ABEL
Les Confidences d'une Aieule (1788-1863). Paris: 1900. V. 72

HERMES, WILLIAM
A Collection of 30 Lithograph Plates of Cottage and Landscape Scenery. Berlin & London?: 1845. V. 69

THE HERMIT of the Forest and Wandering Infants. Cooperstown: 1819. V. 70

THE HERMIT of the Grove; or, the Fatal Effects of Gaming. 1804. V. 72

THE HERMIT of the Grove; or the Final Effects of Gaming. London: 1804. V. 68

HERNANDEZ, JAIME
Love & Rockets. London: 1987. V. 71

HERNDON, W. L.
Explorations of the Valley of the Amazon, Made Under Direction of the Navy Deparment. Washington: 1853-1854. V. 69

HERNDON, WILLIAM HENRY
Herndon's Lincoln: The True Story of a Great Life. Chicago, New York, S.F: 1889. V. 73
Lincoln and Ann Rutledge and the Pioneers of New Salem. Herrin: 1945. V. 70

HERNDON, WILLIAM LEWIS
Exploration of the Valley of the Amazon, Made Under the Direction of the Navy Department. Washington: 1854. V. 70; 71

HERNE, B.
Uganda Safaris. 1979. V. 70; 72; 73

HERNE, PEREGRINE
Perils and Pleasures of a Hunter's Life; or the Romance of Hunting. Philadelphia: 1855. V. 68

HERNER, CHARLES
The Arizona Rough Riders. Tucson: 1970. V. 69

HERNU, SANDY
Q: The Biography of Desmond Llewelyn. Seaford: 1999. V. 70; 72

HERODIAN
(Greek title, then): Histor(iarum) Lib(ri) VIII. Lvgduni: 1611. V. 70
Herodian's History of His Own Times, or of the Roman Empire After Marcus. London: 1749. V. 70
Historion Biblia H. (Greek Text) Herodiani Histor. Lib VIII. Geneva: 1581. V. 72

HERODOTUS
The History of Herodotus. London: 1935. V. 70; 71

AN HEROIC Congratulation Addressed to the Honourable Augustus Keppel, Admiral of the Blue.... London: 1779. V. 73

THE HEROIC Life and Exploits of Siegfried the Dragon Slayer, and Old German Story. London: 1848. V. 71

HEROLD, J. M.
Entwicklungsgeschichte der Schmetterlinge, Anatomisch und Physiologische Bearbeitet. Cassel & Marburg: 1815. V. 73

HERON, ROBERT
Notes. Grantham: 1852. V. 70

HERON DE VILLEFOSSE, A. M.
Atlas de la Richesse Minerale.... 1838. V. 68

HERR, JOHN K.
The Story of the U.S. Cavalry 1775-1942. Boston: 1953. V. 72; 73

HERR, MICHAEL
Dispatches. New York: 1977. V. 69; 70; 71

HERRICK, CHRISTINE TERHUNE
Consolidated Library of Modern Cooking and Household Recipes. New York: 1905. V. 70; 73

HERRICK, FRANCIS HOBART
Audubon the Naturalist. 1938. V. 68
Audubon The Naturalist. A History of His Life And Time. London: 1938. V. 72

HERRICK, JAMES BRYAN
Peculiar Elongated and Sickle Shaped Red Blood Corpuscles in a Case of Severe Anemia: in - Transactions of the Association of American Physicians Volume 25 pp. (553)-561. Philadelphia: 1910. V. 73

HERRICK, ROBERT
Herrick's Content-His Grange and His Book of Littles. London: 1884. V. 70
One Hundred and Eleven Poems. London: 1955. V. 70; 72
Poems Chose Out of the Works. 1896. V. 73
The Poems of.... 1965. V. 68
The Poetical Works. London: 1921. V. 68; 70
The Works. Edinburgh: 1823. V. 72

HERRIES, J. W.
Adventures in a Coracle. London: 1923. V. 71

HERRIES, JOHN CHARLES
A Reply to Some Financial Mistatements In and Out of Parliament. London: 1803. V. 71

HERRIMAN, GEORGE
Krazy Kat. New York: 1946. V. 69; 71

HERRING, PAUL
Bold Bendigo. Philadelphia: 1927. V. 70

HERRING, R.
Paper and Paper Making, Ancient and Modern. London: 1863. V. 70

HERRING, W. R.
The Grant Works of the Edinburgh and Leith Corporations' Gas Commissioners. London: 1907. V. 69

HERRIOT, EDOUARD
Madame Recamier. London: 1906. V. 72

HERRIOT, JAMES
All Creatures Great and Small. New York: 1972. V. 70
James Herriot's Yorkshire. London: 1979. V. 68
Let Sleeping Vets Lie. London: 1973. V. 70
Vet in a Spin. London: 1977. V. 68

HERRLIGKOFFER, KARL M.
Nanga Parbat. London: 1954. V. 69

HERRLINGER, ROBERT
History of Medical Illustration from Antiquity to 1600. 1970. V. 71

HERROD HEMPSALL, W.
Bee-Keeping New and Old Described with Pen and Camera. London: 1930-1937. V. 69

HERRON, VENNETTE
Peacocks and Other Stories of Java. Garden City: 1927. V. 70

HERSCHDOERFER, S. M.
Quality Control in the Food Industry. London: 1984-1986. V. 68

HERSCHEL, JOHN FREDERICK WILLIAM
Preliminary Discourse on the Study of Natural Philosophy. London: 1830. V. 68; 72

HERSEY, JOHN
Antonietta. New York: 1991. V. 72
A Bell for Adano. New York: 1944. V. 71; 73
Hiroshima. New York: 1946. V. 70; 71; 72
Hiroshima. New York: 1983. V. 69; 71; 72
Into the Valley. New York: 1943. V. 70; 71; 72
Life Sketches. New York: 1989. V. 72
A Single Pebble. New York: 1956. V. 71
The Wall. New York: 1950. V. 72

HERSH, SEYMOUR M.
The Price of Power. Kissinger in the Nixon White House. New York: 1983. V. 70

HERSHKOVITZ, P.
Living New World Monkeys (Platyrrhini) with an Introduction to Primates. Chicago: 1977. V. 69; 73

HERSHOLT, JEAN
The Evergreen Tales, or Tales for the Ageless. New York: 1949-1952. V. 69

HERTER, G. L.
Professional Fly-Tying and Tackle Making Manual and Manufacturer's Guide. 1950. V. 68; 73

HERTRICH, W.
Camellias in the Huntington Gardens. Marino: 1954-1959. V. 73
The Huntington Botanical Gardens 1905-1949. San Marino: 1949. V. 71

HERTWIG, OSCAR
Text-Book of the Embryology of Man and Mammals. London: 1899. V. 68

HERTZ, EMANUEL
The Hidden Lincoln. New York: 1938. V. 70

HERTZKA, THEODOR
Freeland. A Social Anticipation. London: 1891. V. 71

HERVEIANA; Graphic and Literary Sketches, Illusrative of the Life and Writing of Rev. James Hervey.... Scarborough: 1823. V. 69

HERVEY, A. B.
Wayside Flowers and Ferns. Boston: 1899. V. 73

HERVEY, ELIZABETH
The History of Ned Evans. London: 1797. V. 68

HERVEY, JAMES
Eleven Letters from the Late Rev. Mr. Hervey to the Rev. Mr. John Wesley.... London: 1790. V. 72
Meditations and Contemplations. 1748. V. 71
Meditations and Contemplations. London: 1748. V. 72
Meditations and Contemplations. London: 1767. V. 73
Theron and Aspasio; or a Series of Dialogues and Letters Upon the Most Important and Interesting Subjects. London: 1755. V. 73
The Time of Danger, the Means of Safety, and the Way of Holiness.... London: 1790?. V. 69

HERVEY, JOHN HERVEY, BARON
Miscellaneous Thoughts on the Present Posture Both of Our Foreign and Domestic Affairs. London: 1742. V. 73
Some Materials Towards Memoirs of the Reign of King George I. London: 1931. V. 73

HERVEY, THOMAS
A Complaint on the Part of the Hon. Thomas Hervey, Concerning an Undue Proceeding Against Him at Court. London: 1767. V. 73
A Letter from the Hon. Thomas Hervey, to Sir Thomas Hanmer, Bart. London: 1741. V. 73

HERVEY, THOMAS K.
Australia; with Other Poems. London: 1824. V. 69
The Book of Christmas.... 1837. V. 71

HERZENS Opfer Eine Sammlung Geistreicher Lieder.. Lancaster: 1816. V. 68

HERZL, THEODOR
Der Judenstaat. Leipzig & Vienna: 1896. V. 72

HERZOG, T.
Pneumatic Structures: a Handbook of Inflatable Architecture. New York: 1976. V. 68; 69; 72

HESIOD
(Greek title then) *Opera et Dies. Theogonia. Scvtvm Hercvlis.* Venice: 1537. V. 70
Hesiodi Ascrei Opera, Qvae Avidem Extant. Basileae: 1550. V. 70
The Works. London: 1728. V. 70

HESITATION; or, to Marry, Or Not to Marry?. New York: 1819. V. 70

HESKI, THOMAS M.
Icastinyanka Cikala Hanzi - The Little Shadow Catcher. Seattle: 1978. V. 71; 72
Icastinyanka Cikala Hanzi, the Little Shadow Catcher. 1978. V. 68

HESS, ALAN
The Architecture of John Lautner. New York: 1999. V. 68

HESS, ALFRED E.
Rickets Including Osteomalacia and Tetany. Philadelphia: 1929. V. 71

HESS, JOAN
Murder at the Mimosa Inn. New York: 1986. V. 70; 71
Strangled Prose. New York: 1986. V. 71

HESS, JOSEPH
Out of Darkness Into Light - an Autobiography of Joseph F. Hess. Toronto: 1890. V. 69

HESS, W. R.
Hypothalamus and Thalamus. Experimental Documentation. Stuttgart: 1969. V. 68

HESSE, HERMANN
Autobiographical Writings. London: 1973. V. 68
Demian. New York: 1948. V. 73
Demian. London: 1958. V. 73
Gertrude. London: 1955. V. 68
Gertrude. New York: 1969. V. 73
Das Glasperlenspiel. Zurich: 1943. V. 70; 72
The Glass Bead Game. (Magister Ludi). New York: 1969. V. 73
If the War Goes On.... London: 1972. V. 68
In Sight of Chaos. Zurich: 1923. V. 70
Klingsor's Last Summer. London: 1971. V. 69
Knulp. London: 1972. V. 69
Knulps. Berlin: 1915. V. 69; 71
Narcissus and Goldmund. Berlin: 1930. V. 69; 70
Peter Camenzind. London: 1961. V. 72; 73
Rosshalde. London: 1971. V. 69
Steppenwolf. London: 1929. V. 69
Steppenwolf. New York: 1929. V. 69; 73
Steppenwolf. Westport: 1977. V. 68; 69; 70; 72
Eine Stunde Hinter Mitternacht. Leipzig: 1899. V. 69; 71

HESSELBO, A.
The Bryophyta of Iceland. Copenhagen and London: 1918. V. 68

HESSELGRAVED, RUTH AVELINE
Lady Miller and the Batheaston Literary Circle. New Haven: 1927. V. 72

HESSEMER, FRIEDRICH M.
Arabische und Alt-Italienische Bau-Verzierungen.... Berlin: 1852-1853. V. 68; 70; 72

HESSE-WARTEGG, ERNST VON
Korea Eine sommerreise nach dem Lande der Morgenruhe 1894. Dresden und Leipzig: 1895. V. 72

HESTER, GEORGE M.
Woman/Man. 1975. V. 68

HESTON, ALFRED M.
Abesegami: Annals of Eyren Haven and Atlantic City, 1609-1904. Atlantic City: 1904. V. 69
...Heston's Hand-book. Atlantic City: 1900. V. 69
Jersey Waggon Jaunts: New Stories of New Jersey. 1926. V. 69
South Jersey. A History 1664-1924. New York: 1924. V. 69

HETH, EDWARD HARRIS
Some We Loves. Boston: 1935. V. 70

HETH, HENRY
The Memoirs of Henry Heth. Westport: 1974. V. 70

HETHERINGTON, A.
A Practical Guide for Tourists, Miners and Investors, and All Persons Interested...Gold Fields of Nova Scotia. Montreal: 1868. V. 73

HETHERINGTON, A. L.
The Early Ceramics Wares of China. London: 1924. V. 73

HETHERINGTON, WILLIAM
Branthwaite Hall, Canto III. And Other Poems. Cockemouth: 1850. V. 71

HETLEY, CHARLES, MRS.
The Native Flowers of New Zealand. 1888. V. 69

HETTRICK MANUFACTURING COMPANY
America's Largest Manufactuer of Canvas Products Catalog 58. Toledo: 1934. V. 72

HEUSSER, ALBERT H.
The History of the Silk Dyeing Industry in the United States. Paterson: 1927. V. 69

HEUSTIS, JABEZ W.
Physical Observations, and Medical Tracts and Researches of the Topography and Diseases of Louisiana. New York: 1817. V. 71

HEVELIUS, JOHANNES
Prodromus Astronomiae cum Catalogo Fixarum & Firmamentum sobiescianum (sive Uranographia). Danzig: 1690. V. 68

HEWARD, CONSTANCE
Ameliaranne and the Green Umbrella. London: 1920. V. 68
Ameliaranne and the Green Umbrella. London: 1936. V. 68
Ameliaranne Cinema Star. London: 1929. V. 70
Ameliaranne Cinema Star. London: 1934. V. 68; 69
Ameliaranne Keeps School. London: 1940. V. 69
Ameliaranne Keeps Shop. London: 1928. V. 70
Chappie and the Others. London. V. 69
Grandpa and Tiger. Philadelphia: 1924. V. 73
Mr. Pickles at the Party. London: 1926. V. 69

HEWAT, ALEXANDER
Historical Account of the Rise and Progress of the Colonies of South Carolina and Georgia. London: 1779. V. 68

HEWETSON, W. B.
History of Napoleon Bonaparte and the Wars of Europe.... 1842. V. 70

HEWETT, EDGAR L.
Ancient Andean Life. Indianapolis: 1939. V. 69
Ancient Life in Mexico and Central America. Indianapolis: 1936. V. 69
Ancient Life in the American Southwest. Indianapolis: 1930. V. 69
The Chaco Canyon and Its Monuments. Albuquerque: 1936. V. 69
Les Communautes Anciennes dans le Desert Americain. Geneva: 1908. V. 68
Handbooks of Archaeological History. Albuquerque: 1945. V. 69
Indians of the Rio Grande Valley. Albuquerque: 1937. V. 68; 73
Mission Monuments of New Mexico. Albuquerque: 1943. V. 68; 69; 73
The Pueblo Indian World. Albuqerque: 1945. V. 68; 69; 73

HEWETT, JANE B.
The Roster of Union Soldiers 1861-1865 United States Colored Troops. Wilmington: 1997. V. 69

HEWETT, M. C.
Catalogue of the Library of the Massachusetts Horticultral Society. Mansfield. V. 70

HEWICKER, F.
Oceanic Art. London: 1954. V. 72

HEWISON, JAMES KING
The Runic Roods of Ruthwell and Bewcastle with a Short History of the Cross and Crucifix in Scotland. Glasgow: 1914. V. 71

HEWISON, ROBERT
Monty Python: The Case Against. London: 1981. V. 72

HEWITT, ALEXANDER
An Historical Account of the Rise and Progress of the Colonies of South Carolina and Georgia. London: 1779. V. 69

HEWITT, E. R.
Telling on the Trout. 1926. V. 68

HEWITT, GRAILY
Lettering for Students and Craftsmen. London: 1930. V. 70; 71

HEWITT, RANDALL H.
Across the Plains. New York: 1906. V. 68; 73

HEWITT, W.
An Essay on the Encroachment of the German Ocean Along the Norfolk Coast, with a Design to Arrest Its Further. Norwich: 1844. V. 69

HEWLETT, MAURICE
A Masque of Dead Florentines. London: 1895. V. 70
Mrs. Lancelot: a Comedy of Assumptions. London: 1912. V. 69
Quattrocentisteria: How Sandro Botticelli Saw Simonetta in the Spring. New York: 1921. V. 71
The Road in Tuscany. London: 1904. V. 72
Singsongs of the War. London: 1914. V. 70

HEWSON, ISABEL MANNING
The Land of the Lost, a Wonderful Kingdom Where Toys and Other Lost Things Live. London: 1947. V. 68

HEWSON, W.
The Works.... London: 1846. V. 71

HEWTISON, W. C.
Coloured Illustrations of the Eggs of British Birds. 1846. V. 73

HEXT, JULIA A.
Smiles and Tears: Fugitive Pieces. Charleston: 1853. V. 73

HEYEN, WILLIAM
The Bees. Syracuse: 1981. V. 68; 71
Brockport's Poems. Brockport: 1978. V. 68; 71
Noise in the Trees. New York: 1974. V. 73
The Swastika Poems. New York: 1977. V. 71

HEYER, GEORGETTE
Behold, Here's Poison. London: 1936. V. 72; 73
Detection Unlimited. London: 1953. V. 70
Penhallow. Garden City: 1943. V. 71
They Found Him Dead. New York: 1937. V. 72

HEYERDAHL, THOR
American Indians in the Pacific, the Theory Behind the Kon-Tiki Expedition. London: 1952. V. 69
Archaeology of Easter Island. Santa Fe: 1961. V. 68
Great Norwegian Expeditions. Oslo: 1955. V. 73

HEYLYN, PETER
A Help to English History, Containing a Succession of all the Kings of England.... London: 1680. V. 69

HEYMAN, KEN
They Became What They Beheld. New York: 1970. V. 68

HEYMAN, MAX L.
Prudent Soldier - A Biography of Major General E.A. Canby 1817-1875. Glendale: 1959. V. 70; 72

HEYMANS, C.
Reflexogenic Areas of the Cardiovascular System. London: 1958. V. 68

HEYRICK, THOMAS
Miscellany Poems. Cambridge: 1691. V. 70; 73

HEYSINGER, ISAAC W.
Antietam and the Maryland and Virginia Campaigns of 1862. New York: 1912. V. 69; 70

HEYWARD, DU BOSE
Angel. New York: 1926. V. 71
Carolina Chansons, Legends of the Low Country. New York: 1922. V. 71; 73
Lost Morning. New York: 1936. V. 70
Mamba's Daughters. London: 1929. V. 71
Peter Ashley. New York: 1932. V. 69
Porgy. New York: 1925. V. 73
Skylines and Horizons. New York: 1924. V. 68
Star Spangled Virgin. New York and Toronto: 1939. V. 73

HEYWARD, DUNCAN CLINCH
Seed from Madagascar. Chapel Hill: 1937. V. 71

HEYWOOD, ROBERT
A Journey to America in 1834. London: 1919. V. 72; 73
Observations and Instructions Divine and Morall, in Verse. London: 1869. V. 71; 73

HEYWOOD, THOMAS
The Dramatic Works.... London: 1874. V. 72
A Marriage Triumphe Solemnized in An Epithalamium. Bristol: 1936. V. 72
The Moore Rental. London: 1847. V. 73

HEYWOOD, V. H.
Flowering Plants of the World. New York: 1978. V. 73
Taxonomy and Ecology. London: 1973. V. 70

HIAASEN, CARL
Basket Case. New York: 2002. V. 72
A Death in China. New York: 1984. V. 69; 70; 71; 73
Double Whammy. New York: 1983. V. 72
Double Whammy. New York: 1987. V. 68; 69; 71; 72; 73
Double Whammy. New York: 1989. V. 69
Finally...I'm a Doctor. New York: 1976. V. 69
Lucky You. New Orleans: 1997. V. 68; 69; 70; 71; 72; 73

HIAASEN, CARL continued
Lucky You. New York: 1997. V. 70; 72; 73
Native Tongue. New York: 1991. V. 68; 69; 70; 71; 72
Native Tongue. London: 1992. V. 71
Paradise Screwed. New York: 2001. V. 73
Powder Burn. New York: 1981. V. 68; 69; 70; 71; 72; 73
Sick Puppy. New York: 2000. V. 72
Skin Tight. New York: 1989. V. 68; 70; 71; 73
Skin Tight. London: 1990. V. 70
Stormy Weather. Blakeney: 1995. V. 70; 71; 72
Stormy Weather. London: 1995. V. 71
Stormy Weather. New York: 1995. V. 70; 72
Strip Tease. New York: 1993. V. 68; 71; 72; 73
Team Rodent. New York: 1998. V. 69; 70; 71; 73
Tourist Season. New York: 1986. V. 68; 69; 71
Trap Line. New York: 1982. V. 68; 69
Trap Line. London: 1993. V. 68; 71
The Velvet Touch. Norfolk: 2000. V. 70
What? Dead Again?. Baton Rouge: 1979. V. 69; 70; 71

HIATT, CHARLES
Henry Irving. A Record and Review. London: 1899. V. 71

HIBBARD, CHARLES G.
Fort Douglas, Utah - a Frontier Fort 1862-1991. Fort Collins: 1999. V. 68

HIBBARD, HOWARD
Masterpieces of Western Sculpture From Medieval to Modern. London: 1977. V. 72
The Metropolitan Museum of Art New York. London: 1980. V. 73

HIBBEN, SALLY
The New Official James Bond Movie Book. New York: 1989. V. 71
The Official James Bond 007 Movie Poster Book. London: 1987. V. 69; 73

HIBBERD, SHIRLEY
The Amateur's Flower Garden. London: 1884. V. 70
The Book of the Marine Aquarium.... London: 1860. V. 68
The Fern Garden. London: 1879. V. 72
The Fern Garden. London: 1888. V. 70
Profitable Gardening: a Practical Guide to the Culture of Vegetables, Fruits, and Other Useful Out-Door Garden Products. London: 1863. V. 68

HIBBERT, SAMUEL
History of the Extinct Volcanos of the Basin of Neuwied on the Lower Rhine. Edinburgh: 1832. V. 68
Sketches of the Philosophy of Apparitions; or, An attempt to Trace Such Illusions to Their Physical Causes. Edinburgh: 1824. V. 68; 73

HICHENS, ROBERT
The God Within Him. London: 1926. V. 68
The Green Carnation. London: 1894. V. 69
A Spirit in Prison. New York: 1908. V. 69; 71

HICK, JOHN
A List of New Wheel Patterns, Made on a Correct Principle and with Perfect Mechanical Accuracy, Belonging to John Hick and William Hargreaves. Bolton: 1862. V. 68

HICKERSON, THOMAS FELIX
Happy Valley History and Genealogy. Chapel Hill: 1940. V. 71

HICKES, GEORGE
An Apologetical Vindication of the Church of England; in Answer to Her Adversaries Who Reproach Her With the English Heresies and Schisms. London: 1706. V. 73

HICKEY, MICHAEL
The Death of Warren Baxter Earp- A Closer Look. Honolulu: 2000. V. 71
John Ringo - the Final Hours - a Tale of the Old West. Honolulu: 1995. V. 73

HICKEY, WILLIAM
Memoirs 1749 to 1809. 1928-1948. V. 68
Memoirs, edited by Alfred Spencer. 1948. V. 72
The Works of Martin Doyle. Dublin: 1831. V. 70

HICKIN, N. E.
Caddis Larvae. 1967. V. 68

HICKMAN, WARREN EDWIN
An Echo from the Past - a First Hand Narrative of Events into Early History of the Arkansas Valley of Colorado. Denver: 1914. V. 69

HICKOX, GEORGE A.
Legal Disabilities of Married Women in Connecticut. Litchfield: 1870. V. 69

HICKS, EDMUND WARNE
History of Kendall County, Illinois, from the Earliest Discoveries to the Present Time. Aurora: 1877. V. 68

HICKS, F. C.
Forty Years Among the Wild Animals of India.... Allahabad: 1910. V. 72
Forty Years among the Wild Animals of India.... 1911. V. 72
Forty Years among the Wild Animals of India.... Madras: 1911. V. 73

HICKS, FREDERICK C.
High Finance in the Sixties. New Haven: 1929. V. 71

HIEB, LOUIS A.
A Bibliogrpahy of Charles Bowden. Santa Fe: 1994. V. 69
Collecting Tony Hillerman. Santa Fe: 1992. V. 72
Tony Hillerman: A Bibliography. Tuscon: 1990. V. 68; 69; 70; 72; 73
Tony Hillerman: a Bibliography. Gallup: 1991. V. 70
Tony Hillerman Abroad. Santa Fe: 1993. V. 70

HIER und da und Dort in Bild un Wort. Stuttgart. V. 71

HIERON, SAMUEL
An Answere to a Popish Ryme, Lately Scattered Abroad in the West Parts, and Much Relyed Upon by Some Simply-Seduced. London: 1608. V. 70

HIERONYMUS, SAINT
Catalogus Scriptorum Ecclesiasticorum seu de Viris Illustribus Liber Cum Notis.... Francofurti & Lipsiae: 1722. V. 70
Vitas Patrum. Strassburg: 1483. V. 69

HIGDEN, RANULPHUS
Polycronycon. Southwark: 1527. V. 70; 73

HIGGINS & SEITER
Fireplace Fixtures in Iron and Brass. Catalog H. New York: 1909. V. 73

HIGGINS, AIDAN
Images of Africa. London: 1971. V. 72
Langrishe, Go Down. London: 1966. V. 72

HIGGINS, AILEEN CLEVELAND
Dream Blocks. New York: 1908. V. 71

HIGGINS, BRIAN
The Northern Fiddler. London: 1966. V. 73

HIGGINS, BRYAN
Experiments and Observations Made with a View of Improving the Art of Composing and Applying Calcaereous Cements and of Preparing Quick-Lime.... London: 1780. V. 71

HIGGINS, CHARLES A.
New Guide to the Pacific Coast, Santa Fe Route. Chicago and New York: 1894. V. 70

HIGGINS, COLIN
Harold and Maude. Philadelphia/New York: 1971. V. 71

HIGGINS, F. R.
The Gap of Brightness - Lyrical Poems. London: 1940. V. 71

HIGGINS, GEORGE V.
A City on a Hill. New York: 1975. V. 72
The Digger's Game. New York: 1973. V. 68
The Friends of Eddie Coyle. New York: 1972. V. 68; 69; 70
The Judgement of Deke Hunter. Boston: 1976. V. 72

HIGGINS, JACK
Day of Judgment. London: 1978. V. 69; 71; 73
East of Desolation. New York: 1969. V. 69
Exocet. London: 1983. V. 70
A Game For Heroes. London: 1970. V. 72; 73
A Game for Heroes. New York: 1970. V. 71; 73
The Khufra Run. London: 1972. V. 72; 73
The Last Place God Made. New York: 1972. V. 69
A Prayer for the Dying. 1974. V. 73
The President's Daughter. London: 1997. V. 71
The Run to Morning. New York: 1974. V. 71; 73
The Savage Day. London: 1972. V. 72; 73
Storm Warning. London: 1976. V. 72
Touch of the Devil. London: 1982. V. 71
Touch the Devil. London: 1992. V. 69
The Valhalla Exchange. London: 1977. V. 72

HIGGINS, JESSE
Sampson Against the Philistines, or the Reformation of Lawsuits; and Justice Made Cheap, Speedy and Brought Home to Every Man's Door.... Washington: 1805. V. 71

HIGGINS, JOANNA
A Soldier's Book. Sag Harbour: 1998. V. 70

HIGGINS, VIOLET MOORE
The Jump-Up Story of the three Bears. New York: 1933. V. 70

HIGGINS, WILLIAM MULLINGAR
The House Painter; or Decorator's Companion. London: 1841. V. 68; 72

HIGGINSON, A. H.
As Hounds Ran. 1930. V. 68
British and American Sporting Authors, Their Writings and Biographies. Berryville: 1949. V. 72
Try Back. A Huntsman's Reminiscences. New York: 1931. V. 72

HIGGINSON, T. W.
Short Studies of American Authors. New York: 1880. V. 68

HIGGINSON, THOMAS W.
Tales of the Enchanted Islands of the Atlantic. New York: 1898. V. 72

HIGGINSON, THOMAS WENTWORTH
Women and the Alphabet. Boston and New York: 1900. V. 73

HIGHAM, CHARLES FREDERICK
True Story of Jacob Walzer and His Famous Hidden Gold Mine. Phoenix and El Paso: 1940. V. 68

HIGHMORE, NATHANIEL
Case of a Foetus Found in the Abdomen of a Young Man at Sherborne, in Dorsetshire. London: 1815. V. 73

The History of Generation. London: 1651. V. 68

A Letter to a Noble Lord, Touching Some Points in the Constitution of the High Court of Admiralty, with an Occasional Remark on the Late Orders of Council. London: 1808. V. 73

HIGHSMITH, G.
The Fluted Axe. Milwaukee: 1985. V. 69

HIGHSMITH, PATRICIA
The Animal Lover's Book of Beastley Murder. London: 1974. V. 69
The Blunderer. New York: 1954. V. 70
The Boy Who Followed Ripley. London: 1980. V. 70; 71; 72
The Cry of the Owl. New York: 1962. V. 69; 71
A Dog's Ransom. London: 1972. V. 69; 71
A Dog's Ransom. New York: 1972. V. 73
The Glass Cell. New York: 1964. V. 69
Little Tales of Misogyny. New York: 1986. V. 71
Mermaids on the Golf Course. London: 1972. V. 69
Mermaids on the Golf Course. London: 1985. V. 71
Ripley Under Water. London: 1991. V. 68; 70; 71; 72
Ripley's Game. New York: 1974. V. 71
Slowly, Slowly in the Wind. New York: 1985. V. 68; 71
The Snail Watcher and Other Stories. Garden City: 1970. V. 69; 70
The Story-Teller. New York: 1965. V. 71
A Suspension of Mercy. London: 1965. V. 73
The Talented Mr. Ripley. New York: 1955. V. 71
Those Who Walk Away. London: 1967. V. 73
The Tremor of Forgery. London: 1969. V. 69; 70; 73
The Two Faces of January. New York: 1964. V. 69
Where the Action Is and Other Stories. Helsinki: 1989. V. 68; 70; 72

HIGHTOWER, LYNN S.
Satan's Lambs. New York: 1993. V. 68

HIGHWATER, JAMAKE
Anpao, an American Odyssey. Philadelphia: 1977. V. 68; 72; 73
The Ceremony of Innocence. New York: 1985. V. 72
Fodor's Indian America. New York: 1975. V. 69
Kill Hole. New York: 1992. V. 72
Kiowa Indian Art. Santa Fe: 1979. V. 73
The Language of Vision. New York: 1995. V. 72
Legend Days. New York: 1984. V. 72
The Primal Mind. New York: 1981. V. 72
Pueblo Indian Painting. Santa Fe: 1973. V. 70; 72; 73
Song from the Earth: American Indian Painting. Boston: 1976. V. 69; 73
Song from the Earth; American Indian Painting. New York: 1976. V. 72
The Sweet Grass Lives on; fifty Contemporary North American Artists. NY: 1980. V. 72

HIJUELOS, OSCAR
Empress of the Splendid Season. New York: 1999. V. 72
The Mambo Kings Play Songs of Love. New York: 1989. V. 68; 69; 71; 72; 73
Mr. Ives' Christmas. New York: 1995. V. 72
A Simple Havana Melody. New York: 2002. V. 72

HILBERSEIMER, L.
Mies Van Der Rohe. Chicago: 1956. V. 73

HILDEBRAND, E. T.
First Lessons in Singing: a Condensed Primary Vocal Grade for Short Courses in Singing. Basic: 1909. V. 71

HILDER, ROWLAND
Rowland Hilder's England. London: 1992. V. 70; 72

HILDESLEY, P. T.
English Furniture Designs. London: 1923. V. 68

HILDREDTH, A. G.
The Lengthening Shadow of Dr. Andrew Taylor Still. Macon: 1938. V. 68; 71

HILDRETH, RICHARD
Despotism in America; or an Inquiry into the Nature and Results of the Slave-Holding System in the United States. Boston: 1840. V. 68; 72
The Slave; or Memoirs of Archy Moore. Boston: 1840. V. 68
The Slave; or Memoirs of Archy Moore. Boston: 1848. V. 68
The White Slave; or, Memoirs of a Fugitive. London: 1852. V. 68; 71

HILDROP, JOHN
Free Thoughts Upon the Brute Creation; or an Examination of Father Bougeant's Philosophical Amusement. London: 1742. V. 68

HILER, H.
From Nudity to Raiment, an Introduction to the Study of Costume. London: 1929. V. 69
From Nudity to Raiment, an Introduction to the Study of Costume. New York: 1930. V. 69

HILGARTNER, BETH
A Murder for Her Majesty. Boston: 1986. V. 68

HILL, A. V.
Muscular Activity. Baltimore: 1926. V. 71
Muscular Movement in Man. New York: 1927. V. 71
Trails and Trials in Physiology: a Bibliography 1909-1964.... London: 1965. V. 71

HILL, ALAN G.
The Letters of William and Dorothy Wordsworth III, The Later Years - part 1, 1821-1828. London: 1978. V. 70

HILL, ALEX S.
From Home to Home, Autumn Wanderings in the Northwest in the Years 1881, 1882, 1883, 1884. New York: 1966. V. 71

HILL, ALICE POLK
Colorado Pioneers in Picture and Story. Denver: 1915. V. 71
Tales of the Colorado Pioneers. Denver: 1884. V. 68; 69; 70

HILL, ANTHONY
DATA - Directions in At, Theory and Aesthetics. London: 1968. V. 72

HILL, ARCHIBALD VIVIAN
Muscular Activity. Baltimore: 1926. V. 68

HILL, ART
Don't Let Baseball Die: I Came to Watch. Au Train, MI: 1978. V. 72

HILL, BENSON E.
The Epicure's Almanac; or Diary of Good Living.... London: 1841. V. 68

HILL, C.
Subsistence USA. New York: 1973. V. 68

HILL, CONSTANCE
Jane Austen: Her Home and Her Friends. London: 1902. V. 68; 70

HILL, DANIEL HARVEY
Bethel to Sharpsburg. Raleigh: 1926. V. 69; 70
Bethel to Sharpsburg. Wilmington: 1992. V. 69

HILL, EDWIN
Principles of Currency. Means of Ensuring Uniformity of Value and Adequacy of Supply. London: 1856. V. 70

HILL, EDWIN C.
The Human Side of the News. New York: 1934. V. 69
The Iron Horse. New York: 1923. V. 69; 70
The Iron Horse. New York: 1924. V. 71

HILL, FREDERIC
National Force. Economical Defence fo the Country from Internal Tumult and Foreign Aggression. London: 1848. V. 71

HILL, FREDERICK TREVOR
Washington - The Man of Action. New York: 1914. V. 71

HILL, G. F.
The Truth About Old King Cole. London: 1910. V. 72

HILL, G. W.
Memoir of Sir Brenton Halliburton, Late Chief Justice of the Province of Nova Scotia. Halifax: 1864. V. 72
Memorials of Stepney Parish, That Is to Say the Vestry Minutes from 1579 to 1632. Guildford: 1890. V. 71

HILL, GEOFFREY
Fantasy Poets Number Eleven: Poems. Swinford: 1952. V. 68; 71
Mexican Hymns. London: 1971. V. 72
The Mystery of the Charity of Charles Peguy. London: 1983. V. 73
Preghiere. 1964. V. 72

HILL, GEORGE BIRKBECK
Dr. Johnson and His Friends and Critics. London: 1878. V. 69
Footsteps of Dr. Johnson (Scotland). London: 1890. V. 69
Johnsonian Miscellanies. New York: 1897. V. 69
Johnsonian Miscellanies. Oxford: 1897. V. 69
Johnsonian Miscellanies, arranged and edited. 1966. V. 72

HILL, GEORGE FRANCIS
The Development of Arabic Numerals in Europe. Oxford: 1915. V. 72

HILL, GRACE LIVINGSTON
Matched Pearls. Philadelphia: 1933. V. 70
Pansies for Thoughts: from the Writings of Pansy, Mrs. G. R. Alden. Boston: 1893. V. 72
The Strange Proposal. Philadelphia: 1935. V. 70

HILL, H.
A Manual of Boot and Shoe Manufacture. 1900. V. 70

HILL, HEADON
The Cottage in the Chine. London: 1913. V. 73

HILL, HENRY
George Chinnery, 1774-1852. England: 1963. V. 72

HILL, IRA
Antiquities of America Explained. Hagers-town: 1831. V. 69

HILL, JASON
The Contemplative Gardener. London: 1940. V. 70
The Curious Gardener. London: 1932. V. 70

HILL, JASPER S.
The Letters of a Young Miner: Covering the Adventures of Jasper S. Hill During the California Gold Rush 1849-1852. San Francisco: 1964. V. 68

HILL, JOE LOUIS
Negro, National Assett or Liability?. New York: 1930. V. 72

HILL, JOHN
The Actor. London: 1750. V. 73
The Adventures of Mr. George Edwards, a Creole. London: 1751. V. 69
Essays in Natural History and Philosophy. London: 1752. V. 70
Family Herbal, or an Account of All Those English Plants, Which are Remarkable for their Virtues. Bungay: 1808. V. 69
Lucina Sine Concubitu. London: 1750. V. 69; 70
Lucina Sine Concubitu. Waltham St. Lawrence: 1930. V. 70; 71
Ninety-Eight a Story of the Irish Rebellion. London: 1898. V. 68
On the Management and Education of Children, a Series of Letters Written to a Niece.... London: 1754. V. 70
A Review of the Works of the Royal Society of London.... London: 1751. V. 70; 73
A Series of Progressive Lessons, Intended to Elucidate the Art of Flower Painting in Water Colours. Philadelphia: 1818. V. 68
A Series of Progressive Lessons, Intended to Elucidate the Art of Flower Painting in Water Colours. Philadelphia: 1836. V. 71; 73

HILL, JOHN A.
Stories of the Railroad. New York: 1900. V. 71

HILL, JOSEPH
History of Warner Ranch and Its Environs. Los Angeles: 1927. V. 68; 71

HILL, M. N.
The Sea. New York: 1962-1963. V. 70; 72

HILL, MATTHEW DAVENPORT
Suggestions for the Repression of Crime, Contained in Charges Delivered to Grand Juries of Birmingham.... London: 1857. V. 70

HILL, OCTAVIA
Our Common Land (and Other Short Essays). London: 1877. V. 73

HILL, OLIVER
English Country Houses Caroline 1625-1685. London: 1966. V. 72

HILL, PATI
The Snow Rabbit. Boston: 1962. V. 71; 73

HILL, PERCY A.
Romance and Adventure in Old Manila. Manila: 1928. V. 69; 72

HILL, REGINALD
Another Death in Venice. London: 1976. V. 70; 71; 73
Another Death in Venice. London: 1979. V. 69
Captain Fantom. London: 1978. V. 69; 70; 73
The Castle of the Demon. New York: 1971. V. 73
Child's Play. London: 1987. V. 72
Dialogues of the Dead. London: 2001. V. 68
Dream of Darkness. London: 1989. V. 70
Exit Lines. London: 1984. V. 72
A Fairly Dangerous Thing. London: 1972. V. 72; 73
Fell of Dark. London: 1971. V. 69; 73
Killing The Lawyers. London: 1997. V. 72
The Only Game. London: 1991. V. 69; 72
Pictures of Perfection. London: 1994. V. 68
A Pinch of Snuff. New York: 1978. V. 68
Singing The Sadness. London: 1999. V. 72
The Spy's Wife. London: 1980. V. 72
There Are No Ghosts in the Soviet Union. London: 1987. V. 69; 70; 71; 73
Under World. London: 1988. V. 69; 70; 71; 73
Who Guard's A Prince. London: 1982. V. 72
The Wood Beyond. Blakeney, Gloucestershire: 1996. V. 72; 73
The Wood Beyond. London: 1996. V. 72

HILL, RICHARD
The Blessings of Polygamy Displayed, in an Affectionate Address to the Rev. Mr. Madan, Occasioned by His Late Work. London: 1781. V. 68; 69; 73

HILL, RICHMOND C.
A Great White Chief. 1912. V. 72

HILL, ROWLAND
The Life of Sir Rowland Hill...and the Penny Postage. London: 1880. V. 71

HILL, ROY L.
Corrie J. Carroll and Other Poems. Philadelphia: 1962. V. 72
Rhetoric of Racial Hope. Buffalo: 1976. V. 72

HILL, SAMUEL
Bygone Stalybridge, Traditional - Historical - Biographical. Stalybridge: 1907. V. 71

HILL, SUSAN
A Bit of Singing and Dancing. London: 1973. V. 71
Stories from Codling Village. London: 1990. V. 68

HILL, W. A.
Historic Hays. Hays, KS: 1938. V. 72

HILL, W. C. OSMAN
Comparative Anatomy and Taxonomy Primates. Edinburgh: 1953-1960. V. 72
Primates, Comparative Anatomy and Taxonomy. VII. Cynopithecinae.... Edinburgh: 1974. V. 70

HILL, W. F.
Landscape Handbook for the Tropics. Woodbridge: 1995. V. 68

HILL, W. W.
An Ethnography of Santa Clara Pueblo, New Mexico. Albuquerque: 1982. V. 72
The University of New Mexico Bulletin: Navajo Pottery Manufacture. 1937. V. 69

HILL, WILLIAM
Col. William Hill's Memoirs of the Revolution. Columbia: 1921. V. 68

HILLARD, GEORGE STILLMAN
Six Months in Italy. London: 1853. V. 68; 70

HILLARY, WILLIAM
An Appeal to the British Nation, on the Humanity and Policy of forming a National Institution for the Preservation of Lives and Property from Shipwreck. London: 1823. V. 69
Observations on the Changes in the Air, and the Concomitant Epidemical Diseases in the Island of Barbadoes.... Philadelphia: 1811. V. 72; 73

HILLEBRAND, W.
Flora of the Hawaiian Islands.... New York and Heidelberg: 1888. V. 68; 70

HILLER, LAJAREN
Surgery Through the Ages, A Pictorial Chronical by.... New York: 1944. V. 70; 71

HILLER, O. PRESCOTT
American National Lyrics and Sonnets. Boston: 1860. V. 71

HILLERMAN, TONY
The Best of the West. New York: 1991. V. 69; 73
The Blessing Way. London: 1970. V. 68; 70; 72; 73
The Blessing Way. New York: 1970. V. 68; 69; 70
The Blessing Way. New York: 1989. V. 69; 73
The Boy Who Made Dragon Fly. New York: 1972. V. 72; 73
Buster Mesquite's Cowboy Band. Gallup: 2001. V. 70; 72
Canyon de Chelly. Aliso Viejo: 1998. V. 69; 71
Coyote Waits. New York: 1990. V. 68; 69; 70; 72
Dance Hall of the Dead. New York: 1973. V. 68; 69
Dance Hall of the Dead. London: 1985. V. 69
Dance Hall of the Dead. New York: 1991. V. 73
The Dark Wind. New York: 1982. V. 68; 69
The Dark Wind. London: 1983. V. 69
The Fallen Man. New York: 1996. V. 68; 69
Finding Moon. New York: 1995. V. 68; 69; 73
Finding Moon. London: 1996. V. 69
The First Eagle. New York: 1998. V. 68; 69; 73
The First Eagle. London: 1999. V. 72
The Fly on the Wall. New York: 1971. V. 68; 70; 71
Fly on the Wall. New York: 1972. V. 69; 70
The Ghostway. San Diego: 1984. V. 68
The Ghostway. London: 1985. V. 68; 69; 70; 73
The Ghostway. New York: 1985. V. 68; 69; 70; 71; 72; 73
The Great Taos Bank Robbery. Albuquerque: 1973. V. 68; 69; 73
Hillerman Country. New York: 1991. V. 68
Hunting Badger. New York: 1999. V. 68; 69; 70
Indian Country: America's Sacred Land. Flagstaff: 1987. V. 73
The Jim Chee Mysteries. New York: 1989. V. 71
The Jim Chee Mysteries. New York: 1990. V. 69; 73
The Joe Leaphorn Mysteries. New York: 1989. V. 69; 70; 72; 73
Leaphorn and Chee. New York: 1992. V. 68; 69; 73
Listening Woman. New York: 1978. V. 68; 69; 71; 72; 73
Listening Woman. London: 1979. V. 68; 69; 70
New Mexico. Portland: 1974. V. 69
People of Darkness. New York: 1980. V. 69; 71; 73
People of Darkness. London: 1982. V. 69
People of Darkness. London: 1988. V. 68; 73
Rio Grande. Portland: 1975. V. 68; 69; 70; 71; 72
Sacred Clowns. New York: 1993. V. 68; 69; 70; 72; 73
Sacred Land. Buffalo: 2000. V. 68
Seldom Disappointed. New York: 2001. V. 72
Skinwalkers. New York: 1986. V. 68; 69; 70; 71; 73
Skinwalkers. London: 1988. V. 69
The Spell of New Mexico. Albuquerque: 1976. V. 68; 69; 70; 71; 72; 73
Talking God. New York: 1989. V. 68; 69; 70; 72; 73
Talking Mysteries. Albuquerque: 1991. V. 69; 71; 72; 73
A Thief of Time. New York: 1988. V. 68; 69; 70; 71; 73
A Thief of Time. London: 1989. V. 69
The Wailing Wind. New York: 2002. V. 72
Words, Weather and Wolfmen. Gallup: 1989. V. 68; 69; 70; 71; 72
Words, Weather, and Wolfmen. New York: 1989. V. 70

HILLES, F. W.
The Age of Johnson, Essays Presented to Chauncey Brewster Tinker on his Retirement from Teaching. New Haven: 1949. V. 69

HILLGARTH, ALAN
The Black Mountain. New York: 1934. V. 70

HILLIARD, JOHN NORTHERN
The Greater Magic Library. New York: 1956. V. 69

HILLIARD, O. M.
The Manuleae, a Tribe of Scrophulariaceae. Edinburgh: 1994. V. 72

HILLIER, BEVIS
Punorama. Andoversford: 1974. V. 68

HILLIER, JACK
The Art of Hokusai in Book Illustration. 1980. V. 69

HILLMAN, H. W.
Looking Forward: the Phenomenal Progress of Electricity in 1912. Northampton: 1906. V. 68

HILLMAN, WILLIAM
Mr. President. New York: 1952. V. 71

HILLS, A. M.
Life and Labors of Mrs. Mary A. Woodbridge. Ravenna: 1895. V. 73

HILLS, EMILY M.
The Pictures Rocks of Lake Superior and Other Poems. Rome: 1904. V. 68

HILLS, GEORGE MORGAN
History of the Church in Burlington, New Jersey.... Trenton: 1876. V. 69

HILLS, J. W.
A History of Fly Fishing for Trout. 1921. V. 73
A History of Fly Fishing for Trout. 1973. V. 68
River Keeper. The Life of William James Lunn. 1934. V. 68

HILLYARD, M. B.
The New South. Baltimore: 1887. V. 68

HILTON, JAMES
Goodbye, Mr. Chips. London: 1934. V. 69; 71; 72; 73
Goodbye, Mr. Chips. Boston: 1935. V. 68; 71
Goodbye, Mr. Chips. New York: 1935. V. 70
Knight Without Armor. London: 1933. V. 70
Lady Sings the Blues. Garden City: 1956. V. 69
Random Harvest. London: 1941. V. 71; 73
The Story of Dr. Wassell. New York: 1943. V. 73
The Story of Dr. Wassell. London: 1944. V. 68

HILTON, JOHN
Notes on Some of the Developmental and Functional Relations of Certain Portions of the Cranium.... London: 1855. V. 68; 72
Rest and Pain. London: 1877. V. 71

HILTON-SIMPSON, M. W.
Among The Hill-Folk Of Algeria. London: 1921. V. 72
Land and Peoples of the Kasai. London: 1911. V. 73

HIME, REBECCA HELENA
Brian Boru and the Battle of Clontarf: a Ballad. London: 1889. V. 69

HIMES, CHESTER
Une Affaire de Viol. Paris: 1963. V. 72
Black on Black. Garden City: 1973. V. 73
Blind Man with a Pistol. New York: 1969. V. 68; 69; 72
A Case of Rape. New York: 1980. V. 69
A Case of Rape. Washington: 1984. V. 71
Cast the First Stone. New York: 1952. V. 69
Cotton Comes to Harlem. London: 1965. V. 70
Cotton Comes to Harlem. New York: 1965. V. 68; 69
Cotton Comes to Harlem. London: 1966. V. 71
For Love of Imabelle. Greenwich: 1957. V. 68; 69; 71; 72
The Heat's On. New York: 1966. V. 69
If He Hollers Let Him Go. Garden City: 1945. V. 69; 70; 71; 73
If He Hollers Let Him Go. London: 1947. V. 68; 69; 71; 73
Imbroglio Negro. Paris: 1960. V. 68
Lonely Crusade. New York: 1947. V. 69; 73
My Life of Absurdity. Garden City: 1976. V. 72
Pinktoes. New York: 1965. V. 69
Plan B. Jackson: 1983. V. 72
Plan B. Jackson: 1993. V. 69; 70; 71
The Primitive. New York: 1956. V. 69; 71; 73
The Quality of Hurt: the Autobiography of Chester Himes. Volume I. Garden City: 1972. V. 69
Rage in Harlem. London: 1985. V. 72
The Real Cool Killers. London: 1985. V. 71; 73
Run Man Run. New York: 1966. V. 68
Run Man Run. London: 1967. V. 71
The Third Generation. 1954. V. 70
The Third Generation. Cleveland: 1954. V. 69
The Third Generation. New York: 1954. V. 69
Yesterday Will Make You Cry. New York: 1998. V. 72

HIMES, NORMAN EDWIN
Medical History of Contraception. New York: 1963. V. 68

HIMMEL, RICHARD
I'll Find You. New York: 1950. V. 72
The Twenty-Third Web. New York: 1977. V. 72

HINCHCLIFF, THOMAS WOODBINE
Over the Sea and Far Away. London: 1876. V. 68

HINCHCLIFFE, ISAAC
A Backwater in Lakeland (Mardale). Manchester: 1928. V. 71

HINCHCLIFFE, JOHN
Sermons. London: 1796. V. 68

HINCHLIFFE, HENRY JOHN
Thoughts on the Repeal of the Usury Laws, Enclosed in a Letter to a Friend. London: 1828. V. 70

HINCKLEY, F. LEWIS
A Directory of Antique Furniture. NY: 1953. V. 72

HINCKS, T.
A History of the British Marine Polyzoa. 1880. V. 73

HINCKS, THOMAS DIX
Letters Originally Addressed to the Inhabitants of Cork, in Defence of Revealed Religion.... Cork: 1796. V. 73

HINCKS, W. D.
A Systematic Monograph of the Dermaptera of the World.... London: 1955-1959. V. 71

HIND, ARTHUR M.
An Introduction to A History of Woodcut. NY: 1963. V. 72
Wenceslaus Hollar and His Views of London and Windsor in the Seventeenth Century. London: 1922. V. 73

HIND, HENRY YOULE
Eighty Years' Progress of British North America.... Toronto: 1863. V. 72

HINDERWELL, THOMAS
The History and Antiquities of Scarborough, and the Vicinity. York: 1811. V. 73

HINDLEY, CHARLES
Curiosities of Street Literature. London: 1966. V. 70
The History of the Catnach Press at Berwick-upon-Tweed, Alnwick and Northumberland and Seven Dials. London: 1886. V. 70
A History of the Cries of London Ancient and Modern. London: 1885. V. 71
The Life and Times of James Catnatch (Late of Seven Dials), Ballad Monger. London: 1878. V. 71

HINDMAN, SANDRA
The Early Illustrated Book, Essays in Honor of Lessing J. Rosenwald. Washington: 1982. V. 68

HINDS, JAMES PITCAIRN
Bibliotheca Jacksoniana. Kendal: 1909. V. 70; 71

HINDS, ROY W.
The Treasure of Caricar. Philadelphia: 1927. V. 69

HINDS, WILLIAM A.
American Communities: Brief Sketches of Economy, Zoar, Bethel, Aurora, Amana, Icaria the Shakers, Onedia, Wallingford and the Brotherhood of the New Life. Onedia: 1878. V. 73

HINES, DAVID THEO
The Life, Adventures and Opinions of David Tho. Hines, of South Carolina.... New York: 1840. V. 71

HINES, GUSTAVUS
Life of the Plains of the Pacific. Buffalo: 1851. V. 68; 71

HINGSTON, R. W. G.
A Naturalist in Himalaya. Boston: 1920. V. 69; 73
A Naturalist in Himalaya. London: 1920. V. 68
A Naturalist in Hindustan. London: 1923. V. 68
Nature at the Desert's Edge.... Boston: 1925. V. 72
Nature at the Desert's Edge.... London: 1925. V. 68; 71

HINKLE, JAMES F.
Early Days of a Cowboy on the Pecos. Santa Fe: 1965. V. 70; 71

HINKSON, H. A.
Dublin Verses by Members of Trinity College. 1894. V. 69

HINNANT, CHARLES
Samuel Johnson, an Analysis of Johnson's Major Texts.... London: 1988. V. 69

HINSDALE, LAURA F.
Legends and Lyrics of the Gulf Coast. Biloxi: 1896. V. 72

HINSHAW, GLENNIS
A Bibliography of the Writings and Illustrations by Tom Lea. El Paso: 1972. V. 72

HINTON, EDWARD M.
Ireland through Tudor Eyes. Philadelphia: 1935. V. 70

HINTON, HARWOOD P.
History of Cattlemen of Texas. Austin: 1991. V. 71

HINTON, MILT
Bass Line. The Stories and Photographs of Milt Hinton. Philadelphia: 1988. V. 73

HINTON, PERCIVAL
Eden Phillpotts. A Bibliography of First Editions. Birmingham: 1931. V. 71

HINTON, S. E.
The Outsiders. New York: 1967. V. 69

HINTON, TED
Ambush. The Real Story of Bonnie and Clyde. 1979. V. 68

HIORT, JOHN WILLIAM
A Practical Treatise on the Construction of Chimneys...(bound with) Supplement to Mr. Hiort's Treatise on the Architectural Construction of Chimneys...(bound with) Note for the Information of the Public... London: 1826. V. 68; 70

HIPKINS, A. J.
Musical Instruments. London: 1921. V. 72

HIPPISLEY, JOHN COX
Prison Labour, etc. London: 1823. V. 73
Substance of the Speech on Seconding the Motion of Henry Grattan to Refer the Petition of the Roman Catholics of Ireland to the Committee of the House of Commons: 18th May, 1810. 1810. V. 73

HIPPLE, WALTER JOHN
The Beautiful, the Sublime and the Picturesque. 1957. V. 73

HIPPOCRATES
The Genuine Works. London: 1845. V. 71
The History of Epidemics.... London: 1780. V. 70; 72
(Greek, then) Magni Hippocratis Medicorum Opera Omnia Quae Extant.... Geneva: 1657-1662. V. 72
Magni Hippocratis Medicorvm Opera Omnia Quae Extant.... Geneva: 1656-1662. V. 68
The Prognostics and Prorrhetics. Translated From The Original Greek. London: 1788. V. 72

HIRD, FRANK
Lancashire Stories. London: no date. V. 73

HIRD, WILLIAM
An Affectionate Tribute to the Memory of the Late Dr. John Fothergill. London: 1786. V. 70

HIRES, C. S.
Spores - Ferns, Microscopic Illustrations Analyzed. Millburn: 1965-1978. V. 72

HIRSCH, ARTHUR HENRY
The Huguenots of Colonial South Carolina. Durham: 1928. V. 71

HIRSCHBERG, JULIUS
The History of Ophthalmology. Bonn: 1982-1994. V. 71; 72
The Treatment of Shortsight.... New York: 1912. V. 71

HIRSCHFELD, LUDOVIC
Traite et Iconographie du Systeme Nerveux et Des Organes des Sens De l'Homme.... Paris: 1866. V. 71

HIRSCHMAN, JACK
Interchange: for John Cage. Los Angeles: 1964. V. 70

HIRSHORN, PAUL
White Towers. Cambridge: 1979. V. 68

HIRST, BARTON COOKE
Human Monstrosities Illustrated with Photographic Reproductions and Wood Engravings. Edinburgh: 1892-1893. V. 68; 72

HIRTE, TOBIAS
Der Freund in Der Noth, Oder Zwenter Theil, des Neun Auserlesenen Gemeinnutzigen Hand Buchleins.... Germantown: 1793. V. 68

HISLOP, HERBERT R.
An Englishman's Arizona: the Ranching Letters of.... Tucson: 1965. V. 70; 71

HISTOIRE de L'Isle Espagnole ou De S. Domingue. Paris: 1730-1731. V. 68

HISTOIRE de Marie Stuart, reine d'Ecosse et de France, avec les Pieces Justificatives & des Remarques. Londres: 1742. V. 73

HISTOIRE Secrette de la Duchesse de Portsmouth ou l'on Verra Une Relation ses Intrigues de da (sic) cour du R. Ch. II. Durant le Ministere de Cette Duchesse & une Relation Aussi de la Mort de ce Prince. Londres: 1690. V. 73

HISTORIC Interiors in Colour. London: 1929. V. 72

HISTORIC New York Being the Second Series of the Half Moon Papers. New York: 1899. V. 71

HISTORICAL and Biographical Atlas of the New Jersey Coast. Philadelphia: 1878. V. 69

HISTORICAL and Descriptive Account of the Palace and Chapel-Royal of Holyroodhouse. Edinburgh: 1826. V. 71

AN HISTORICAL and Descriptive Account of Ripon Minster...to Which is added An Account of Studley Park, Fountains Abbey, and a Brief Account of the Town of Ripon. Ripon: 1827. V. 69

AN HISTORICAL and Descriptive Account of Old and New Sarum or Salisbury. Salisbury: 1834. V. 71; 72

AN HISTORICAL and Pictorial Record of the 87th Infantry Division in World War II. V. 73

AN HISTORICAL, Genealogical and Poetical Dictionary.... London: 1703. V. 71

AN HISTORICAL Guide to the Town and Castle of Hay and the Neighbourhood. Hay: 1877. V. 72

HISTORICAL RECORDS SURVEY PROJECT
Index of the Official Register of the Officers and Men of New Jersey in the Revolutionary War. Newark: 1941. V. 71
Index of the Official Register of the Officers and Men of New Jersey in the Revolutionary War. Baltimore: 1965. V. 71

HISTORICAL Remarques Upon the Late Revolutions in the United Provinces; Drawn from Ther Own Papers.... London: 1673. V. 70

HISTORICAL Sketch of the County of Carleton. Belleville: 1971,. V. 73

HISTORICAL Sketch of the State Norman School at San Jose. Sacramento: 1889. V. 68

HISTORICAL SOCIETY OF MONTANA
Collections of The Historical Society of Montana - 10 Vols. Boston: 1966. V. 72
Conributions to the Historical Society of Montana - with Its Transactions, Officers and Members. Helena: 1907. V. 70

HISTORICAL SOCIETY OF WISCONSIN
Collection of the State Historical Society of Wisconsin Volume XI. Madison: 1888. V. 71

A HISTORY and Defence of Magna Charta. Dublin: 1769. V. 73
A HISTORY and Defence of Magna Charta. London: 1769. V. 70

HISTORY and Description of the New England Hospital for Women and Children, Codman Avenue, Boston Highlands. Boston: 1876. V. 68

THE HISTORY And Philosophy of Marriage; or, Polygamy and Monogamy Compared. Boston: 1869. V. 73

THE HISTORY of a Little Boy Found Under a Haycock.... 1825. V. 73

THE HISTORY of Aladdin or the Wonderful Lamp. New York: 1858-1862. V. 70

HISTORY of Arizona Territory, Showing and Advantages, Etc. Flagstaff: 1964. V. 69

HISTORY of Beasts and Birds. Cooperstown: 1842. V. 69

HISTORY of Callaway County, Missouri. St. Louis: 1884. V. 70

HISTORY Of Clear Creek and Boulder Valleys Co. Containing a Brief History of the State of Colorado from Its Earliest Settlement to the Present Time.... 1880. V. 68

HISTORY of Clear Creek & Boulder Valleys, Colorado, 1880. Evansville, IN: 1971. V. 71

HISTORY of Contra Costa County California with Biographical Sketches. Los Angeles: 1926. V. 68; 73

THE HISTORY of Curious and Wonderful Insects and Reptiles. New York: 1825-1833. V. 69

THE HISTORY of Dame Crump. London: 1840. V. 73

THE HISTORY of Eliza. London: 1767. V. 69

A HISTORY of Fishes. Dayton: 1830. V. 69

THE HISTORY of Giles Gingerbread. 1820. V. 72; 73
THE HISTORY of Giles Gingerbread. York: 1820. V. 73
THE HISTORY of Giles Gingerbread. London: 1820. V. 68

THE HISTORY of Goody Two Shoes. New York: 1842-1851. V. 71

HISTORY of Howard and Cooper Counties, Missouri Written and Compiled from the Authentic Official and Private Sources, Including a History of Its Townships, Towns and Villages. St. Louis: 1889. V. 69

HISTORY of Indian Depredations in Utah. Salt Lake City: 1919. V. 72

THE HISTORY of Jackey Jungle and Sukey Single. New York: 1863-1867. V. 70

HISTORY Of Jackson County, Michigan. Chicago: 1881. V. 71

HISTORY of Joseph And His Brethern. London. V. 72

THE HISTORY Of Little Fanny. 1810. V. 73

THE HISTORY of Little Goody Two-shoes: Otherwise Called Mrs. Margery Two-shoes. London: 1780. V. 70

THE HISTORY of Little Goody Two-Shoes, Otherwise Called Mrs. Margery Two-shoes. London: 1796. V. 73

THE HISTORY of Little King Pippin, with an Account of the Melancholy Death of Four Naughty Boys Who Were Devoured by Wild Beasts.... Baltimore: 1801. V. 72

THE HISTORY of Little Tom Tucker. 1820. V. 72; 73
THE HISTORY of Little Tom Tucker. London: 1820. V. 68

HISTORY of Los Angeles County California with Illustrations Descriptive of Its Scenery, Residences, Fine Blocks and Manufactories. Oakland: 1880. V. 73

THE HISTORY of Martin. London: 1744. V. 69

THE HISTORY of Miss Delia Stanhope. London: 1767. V. 73

HISTORY Of Monmouth County, New Jersey 1664-1920. New York: 1922. V. 71

HISTORY of Morris County, New Jersey, With Illustrations and Biographical Sketches of Prominent Citizens and Pioneers. New York: 1882. V. 71

HISTORY of Morris County, New Jersey, with Illustrations and Biographical Sketches of Prominent Citizens and Pioneers. Morristown: 1967. V. 71

THE HISTORY of Oliver and Arthur. Cambridge: 1903. V. 69

HISTORY of Peter Brown. Yorkshire: 1840. V. 73

THE HISTORY of Preston in Lancashire. London: 1822. V. 73

THE HISTORY of Prince Lee Boo, a Native of the Pelew Islands. London: 1822. V. 68; 72

HISTORY of Queens County New York. New York: 1882. V. 70

THE HISTORY Of Sam, the Sportman, and His Gun, and Also, of His Wife Joan. 1825. V. 73

HISTORY OF SCIENCE SOCIETY
Johann Kepler 1571-1630. Baltimore: 1931. V. 70

THE HISTORY of Simple Simon. 1820. V. 73

HISTORY of Southwestern Dakota, Its Settlement and Growth. Sioux City: 1881. V. 68; 73

A HISTORY of Spartanburg County. Spartanburg: 1940. V. 71

HISTORY of the Baldwin Locomotive Work 1832-1913. 1913. V. 68

HISTORY of the Campaign of the Sutlej, and the War in the Punjaub, from the Most Authentic Sources, Including Copious Original Information, Memoirs of Many Distinguished Officers, English and Foreign.... London: 1846. V. 70

THE HISTORY of the Children in the Wood. Derby;: 1830. V. 70

THE HISTORY of the Church of Crosthwaite. London: 1853. V. 71

HISTORY of the City of Chester. Chester: 1815. V. 73

HISTORY of the City of Denver, Arapahoe County, and Colorado Containing a History of the State of Colorado.... Chicago: 1880. V. 69; 72; 73

HISTORY of the Design of the Present Flag of the United States. Washington?: 1854. V. 68

HISTORY of the English Bible, as Shown in Facsimile Pages from 1525 to 1611. New York: 1925. V. 71

HISTORY of the First Division During the World War 1917-1919. Philadelphia: 1922. V. 70

THE HISTORY of the Franco Prussian War.... London: 1875?. V. 70

THE HISTORY of the Holy Jesus.... Leonminster: 1813. V. 68

THE HISTORY of the House that Jack Built. London: 1828. V. 73

THE HISTORY of the Inhuman and Unparalleled Murders of Mr. William Galley, a Custom House Officer and Mr. Daniel Chater, a Shoemaker, by Fourteen Notorious Smugglers. Portsea: 1820. V. 70

THE HISTORY of the Little Boy Who Cheated Himself: an Old Story by a Very Old Friend. London: 1847. V. 70

THE HISTORY of the Mitre (Francis Atterbury, Bishop of Rochester) and Purse (Simon Harcourt, Lord Chancellor), in which the First and Second Parts o the Secret History of the White Staff are fully Considered, and the Hypocrisy and Villanies of the Staff. London: 1714. V. 72

THE HISTORY of the Monument of London. London: 1850?. V. 71

THE HISTORY Of the Old and New Testament, Interspersed with Moral and Instructive Reflections, Chiefly Taken from the Holy Fathers. Philadelphia: 1784. V. 73

HISTORY of the Pilgrims; or, a Grandfather Story of the First Settlers of New England. Boston: 1839. V. 68

HISTORY of the Thirty-fifth Regiment Massachusetts Volunteers 1862- 1865. Boston: 1884. V. 72

THE HISTORY of the Times. I. The Thunderer in the Making 1785-1841. II. The Tradition Established 1841-1884. III. The Twentieth Century Text 1884-1912. IV & V. The 150th Anniversary & Beyond 1912-1948. Parts I & II. London: 1935-1952. V. 70

HISTORY of the U.S.S. Leviathan. Brooklyn: 1919. V. 68

THE HISTORY of the Voyages of Christopher Columbus in Order to Discover America and the West Indies. London: 1772. V. 73

THE HISTORY of Tom Thumb. Derby: 1830. V. 68

THE HISTORY of Tommy and Harry. York: 1820. V. 73
THE HISTORY of Tommy and Harry. 1830. V. 72
THE HISTORY of Tommy and Harry. London: 1830. V. 68

THE HISTORY of U.S. Army Base Hospital No. 6 And in Part in the American Expeditionary Forces 1917-1918. Boston: 1924. V. 71

HISTORY of United Mine Workers of America from the Year 1860 to 1890. N.P. V. 69

THE HISTORY Of Whittington and His Cat. 1820. V. 71; 73

THE HISTORY of Whittington and His Cat. York: 1820. V. 68; 73
THE HISTORY of Whittington and His Cat. Derby: 1830. V. 69
THE HISTORY of Whittington and His Cat. London: 1881. V. 71

A HISTORY of Will County. Illinois: 1973. V. 72

THE HISTORY of Woman Suffrage. Volumes I-VII. Rochester: 1889. V. 72

A HISTORY of Wonderful Animals.... London: 1818. V. 69; 73

THE HISTORY of Young Edwin and Little Jessy, Together with an Account of the Pleasant Walk Which William and Winnifred Took with Margery.... 1799. V. 71

THE HISTORY of Young Edwin and Little Jessy; Together with an Account of the Pleasant Walk Which William and Winnifred Took with Margery.... London: 1799. V. 72

HISTORY, Topography and Directory of Buckinghamshire, Cambridgeshire and Hertfordshire, to Which is Prefixed an Abridgment of the Early History of England.... London: 1865. V. 71

HITCHCOCK, C. H.
Hawaii and Its Volcanoes. Honolulu: 1911. V. 73

HITCHCOCK, C. L.
Vascular Plants of the Pacific Northwest. Seattle: 1990-. V. 69

HITCHCOCK, CHARLES H.
Hawaii and Its Volcanoes. Honolulu: 1909. V. 70

HITCHCOCK, DAVID K.
Vindication of Russia and the Emperor Nicholas. Boston: 1844. V. 71

HITCHCOCK, E.
The Religion of Geology. London: 185-. V. 73

HITCHCOCK, E. A.
Remarks Upon Alchemy and the Alchemists, Indicating a Method of Discoverying the True Nature of Hermetic Philosophy. Boston: 1857. V. 69

HITCHCOCK, ENOS
The Farmer's Friend, or the History of Charles Worthy. Boston: 1793. V. 68; 69

HITCHCOCK, FRANK
Thrilling Chase and Capture of Frank Rande. Peoria: 1897. V. 69

HITCHCOCK, FREDERICK H.
The Handbook of Amherst Massachusetts. Amherst: 1891. V. 68

HITCHCOCK, H. R.
Built in USA: Post War Architecture. New York: 1952. V. 68
In the Nature of Materials: the Buildings of Frank Lloyd Wright 1887- 1941. New York: 1942. V. 68
The International Style: Architecture Since 1922. New York: 1932. V. 69; 72

HITCHENER, ELIZABETH
The Fire-Side Bagatelle: Containing Enigmas on the Chief Towns of England and Wales. 1818. V. 73
The Weald of Sussex: a Poem. 1822. V. 73

HITCHENS, ROBERT
Mortimer Brice a Bit of His Life. Garden City: 1932. V. 70

HITCHMAN, FRANCIS
The Life of the Earl of Beaconsfield. London: 1879. V. 71

HITLER, ADOLF
Mein Kampf. London: 1938. V. 70
The New Germany Desires Work and Peace - Speeches by Reich Chancellor Adolf Hitler the Leader of the New Germany. Berlin: 1933. V. 72

HITT, THOMAS
A Treatise of Fruit Trees. 1757. V. 70

HITTELL, JOHN S.
Bancroft's Pacific Coast Guide Book. San Francisco: 1882. V. 71; 73
The Discovery of Gold in California. Palto Alto: 1968. V. 68
A History of the City of San Francisco. San Francisco: 1878. V. 68
The Resources of California: Comprising Agriculture, Mining, Geography, Climate, Commerce, Etc. and the Past and Future Development of the State. San Francisco: 1874. V. 68; 73

HITTELL, THEODORE H.
The Adventures of James Capen Adams, Mountaineer and Grizzly Bear Hunter of California. Boston: 1862. V. 71

HITTORF, JACQUES IGNACE
Architecture Moderne de la Sicile, ou Recueil des Plus Beaux Monumen, Religieux et des Edifices Publics et Particuliers.... Paris: 1835. V. 68; 70
Description de la Rotonde des Panoramas, Elevee dans les Champs Elysees.... Paris: 1842. V. 70

THE HIVE and Its Wonders. Edinburgh: 1852. V. 71

HIX, CHARLES
Looking Good: A Guide for Men. New York: 1977. V. 68

HIYAKU-KEI, FUGAKU
One Hundred Views of Fuji by Hokusai. New York: 1960. V. 70; 72; 73

HJORTSBERG, WILLIAM
Alp. London: 1970. V. 72
Gray Matters. New York: 1971. V. 71

HOADLY, BENJAMIN
A Letter from the Lord Bishop of Winchester, to Clement Chevallier, Esq. Occasioned by Fournier's New Attack, Since the Legal Condemnation of His Note Over the Bishop's Name.... London: 1757. V. 70
The Original and Institution of Civil Government, Viz. I. An Examination of the Patriarchal Scheme of Government. II. A Defense of Mr. Hooker's Judgment &c. Against the Objections of Several Late Writers. London: 1710. V. 70
Several Discourses Concerning the Terms of Acceptance with God. London: 1711. V. 69
Several Tracts Formerly Published: Now Collected into One Volume. London: 1715. V. 70

HOAG, J. D.
Islamic Architecture. New York: 1976. V. 69; 72

HOAGLAND, EDWARD
Cat Man. Boston: 1956. V. 69; 72

HOAGLAND, EDWARD continued
The Circle Home. New York: 1960. V. 68
The Courage of Turtles. New York: 1970. V. 71; 72
Heart's Desire. New York: 1988. V. 72
The Moose on the Wall. London: 1974. V. 71
Notes from the Century Before. New York: 1969. V. 68; 71; 72
The Peacock's Tail. New York: 1965. V. 68
Red Wolves and Black Bears. New York: 1976. V. 71; 72
Seven Rivers West. New York: 1986. V. 71
Tigers & Ice. New York: 1999. V. 72
The Tugman's Passage. New York: 1982. V. 72
Walking the Dead Diamond River. New York: 1973. V. 71

HOAR, W. S.
Fish Physiology. New York: 1969-1970. V. 72

HOARD, SAM
Gods Love to Man-Kinde Manifested by Dis-roving His Absolute Decree for Their Damnation...(with) The Soules Misery and Recovery; or the Grieving of the Spirit, How It is Causes and How Redressed. London: 1658. V. 70

HOARE, CLEMENT
Practical Treatise on the Cultivation of the Grape Vine on Open Walls. London: 1837. V. 70
Practical Treatise on the Cultivation of the Grape Vine on Open Walls. London: 1841. V. 70
Practical Treatise on the Cultivation of the Grape Vine on Open Walls. Boston: 1847. V. 70

HOARE, LOUISE
The Mother's Manual, or Hints for the Improvement of Early Education and Nursery Discipline. Syracuse: 1834. V. 69

HOARE, RICHARD COLT
The Ancient History of Wiltshire. 1975. V. 71
A Classical Tour through Italy and Sicily: Tending to Illustrate Some Districts.... London: 1819. V. 70
A Collection of Forty-Eight Views...in North and South Wales. London: 1806. V. 70

HOARE, SARAH
Poems on Conchology and Botany. London: 1831. V. 68

HOBAN, RUSSELL
Kleinzeit. London: 1974. V. 72
The Lion of Boaz-Jachin and Jachin-Boaz. London: 1973. V. 72
The Lion of Boaz-Jachin and Jachin-Boaz. New York: 1973. V. 70; 72
The Lion of Boaz-Jachin and Jachin-Boaz. London: 1974. V. 72

HOBART, ALICE TISDALE
River Supreme. Indianapolis: 1934. V. 70

HOBART, D. D.
Recollections of My Life - Fifty Years of Itinerancy in the Northwest. Redwing: 1885. V. 68; 73

HOBART, DONALD BAYNE
The Clue of the Leather Noose. Racine: 1929. V. 69; 71
Homicide Honeymoon. New York: 1959. V. 72
Hunchback House. Racine: 1929. V. 71

HOBART, HENRY
The Reports of the Reverend and Learned Judge...Lord Chief Justice of His Majesties Court of Common Pleas. London: 1678. V. 70

HOBART, NOAH
An Attempt to Illustrate and Confirm the Ecclesiastical Constitution of the Consociated Churches in the Colony of Connecticut. New Haven: 1765. V. 71

HOBART HAMPDEN, AUGUSTUS C.
Never Caught. London: 1867. V. 69; 70
Never Caught. New York: 1908. V. 69; 70
Sketches from My Life, by the Late Admiral Hobart Pasha. London: 1886. V. 70

HOBBES, JAMES R.
The Picture Collector's Manual, Being a Dictionary of Painters, Together with an Alphabetical Arrangement of the Scholars, Imitators and Copyists.... London: 1849. V. 69; 72

HOBBES, THOMAS
Leviathan, or the Matter Forme, and Power of A Common-Wealth Ecclesiastical and Civill. London: 1651. V. 68; 73

HOBBS, J. B.
The Fight for Ashes. London: 1923. V. 70

HOBBS, JAMES W.
Wild Life in Far West...Hunting and Trapping Adventures Wtih Kit Carson, Etc. Hartford: 1875. V. 71

HOBBS, ROBERT
Edward Hopper. New York: 1987. V. 69; 72

HOBBS, W. H.
Characteristics of Exisiting Glaciers. New York: 1911. V. 70

HOBBY *Horse.* London: 1889-1890. V. 68

HOBHOUSE, JOHN CAMDEN
Imitations and Translations from Ancient and Modern Classics, Together with Original Poems Never Before Published. London: 1809. V. 73
A Journey through Albania, and Other Provinces of Turkey in Europe and Asia in Constantinople During the Years 1809 and 1810. London: 1813. V. 70
The Wonders of a Week at Bath: in a Doggerel Address to the Hon. T. S. from F. T..., Esq. of that City. 1811. V. 73

HOBHOUSE, P.
Painted Gardens, English Watercolours 1850-1914. New York: 1988. V. 68; 71
Private Gardens of England. New York: 1987. V. 68; 71

HOBSON, ANTHONY
Renaissance Book Collecting. Jean Grolier and Diego Hurtado de Mendoza, Their Books and Bindings. Cambridge: 1999. V. 70

HOBSON, GEOFFREY
English Binding Before 1500. Cambridge: 1929. V. 70
Maioli, Canevari and Others. Boston: 1926. V. 70
Thirty Bindings. London: 1926. V. 70

HOBSON, H. S.
The Famous Cruise of the Kearsarge. Bonds Village: 1894. V. 73

HOBSON, J. A.
A Modern Outlook. Studies of English and American Tendencies. London: 1910. V. 69

HOBSON, LINDA
Gentleman's Agreement. New York: 1947. V. 70

HOBSON, RICHARD
Charles Waterton, His Home, Habits, and Handiwork. London: 1867. V. 68

HOBSON, RICHMOND P.
Grass Beyond the Mountains. Philadelphia/New York: 1951. V. 72

HOBSON, WILDER
American Jazz Music. New York: 1939. V. 70; 72

HOCH, EDWARD D.
Leopold's Way. Carbondale: 1985. V. 68
The Ripper of Storyville and Other Ben Snow Tales. Norfolk: 1997. V. 69; 70; 73
The Thefts of Nick Velvet. New York: 1978. V. 70
The Transvection Machine. New York: 1971. V. 69; 70; 73

HOCHSTETTER, FERDINAND VON
New Zealand. Its Physical Geography, Geology and Natural History with Special Reference.... Stuttgart: 1867. V. 68

HOCKEN, EDWARD OCTAVIUS
A Treatise on Amaurosis and Amaurotic Affections. Philadelphia: 1842. V. 71

HOCKEY, P.
Waders of Southern Africa. Cape Town: 1995. V. 73

HOCKNEY, DAVID
Hockney's Alphabet. London: 1991. V. 70; 71
72 Drawings by David Hockney. New York: 1972. V. 68

HODAPP, WILLIAM
The Pleasure of the Jazz Age. New York: 1948. V. 71

HODDER, GEORGE
Sketches of Life and Character: Taken at the Police Court, Bow Street. London: 1845. V. 68; 70

HODDER, JAMES
Hodder's Arithmetick; or that Necessary Art Made Most Easy. London: 1714. V. 73

HODEL, D. R.
The Palms and Cycads of Thailand. Nong Nooch: 1998. V. 68; 73
The Palms of New Caledonia/Les Plamiers de Nouvelle Caledonie. 1998. V. 73
The Palms of New Caledonia/Les Palmiers de Nouvelle Caledonie. Nong Nooch: 1998. V. 68

HODES, ART
Hot Man. Urbana: 1992. V. 68

HODGE, ARTHUR
The Trial of Arthur Hodge, Esq. (Late One of the Members of His Majstys Council for the Virgin Islands) at the Island of Tortola, on the 25th April, 1811, and Adjourned to the 29th of the Same Month, for the Murder of a Negro Man Slave, Named Prosper. London: 1811. V. 70

HODGE, CHARLES
Systemataic Theology. New York: 1883. V. 71

HODGE, FREDERICK WEBB
Fray Alonso de Benavides, Revised Memorial of 1634. Albuquerque: 1945. V. 68
Hawikuh Bonework. New York: 1920. V. 73
History of Hawikuh New Mexico, One of the So-Called Cities of Cibola. 1937. V. 69
New Mexico, Otherwise the Voiage of Anthony of Espeio...in the Yeare 1583.... Lancaster: 1928. V. 73
Spanish Explorers in the Southern United States 1528-1543. New York: 1907. V. 68; 69; 70; 73
Turquoise Work of Hawikuh New Mexico. New York: 1922. V. 70

HODGE, GEORGE MEANY
The Kachinas are Coming - Pueblo Indian Kachina Dolls with Related Folktales. Flagstaff: 1967. V. 69

HODGE, HIRAM C.
Arizona as It Is: or the Coming Country.... New York: 1877. V. 69

HODGE, JOHN
Trainspotting. The Screenplay. New York: 1996. V. 72

HODGES, JOHN F.
Chemico-Agricultural Society of Ulster. The Raw Material of the Linen Trade: Flax. Belfast: 1865. V. 73

HODGES, PHELPS
Britmis. A Great Adventure of the War Being an Account of Allied Intervention in Siberia and of an Escape Across the Gobi to Peking. London: 1931. V. 70

HODGES, WALTER
The Christian Plan. London: 1755. V. 70

HODGINS, NORRIS
Why Don't You Get Married. New York: 1923. V. 69

HODGKIN, HOWARD
Howard Hodgkin. London: 1994. V. 70

HODGKIN, R. H.
A History of the Anglo-Saxons. London: 1939. V. 70

HODGKINSON, F.
Sepik Diary. Northbridge: 1984. V. 69

HODGSON, ADAM
A Letter to the Right Honorable Sir Robert Peel, Bart. on the Currency. London: 1848. V. 72
Letters from North America Written During a Tour in the United States and Canada. London: 1824. V. 68; 72

HODGSON, C. PEMBERTON
A Residence at Nagaskai and Hakodate in 1859-1860 with an Account of Japan Generally. London: 1861. V. 68

HODGSON, CHRISTOPHER
Practical Directions and Suggestions Concerning Voluntary Commutation of tithes: with the Act of Parliament (6 and 7 Wil Iv. c. 71). London: 1836. V. 72

HODGSON, HENRY W.
A Bibliography of the History and Topography of Cumberland & Westmorland. Carlisle: 1968. V. 70; 71

HODGSON, JOHN
History of Northumberland. London: 1974. V. 73
Textile Manufacture and Other Industries, In Keighley. Keighley: 1879. V. 73

HODGSON, RALPH
The Last Blackbird and Other Lines. London: 1907. V. 72
Poems. London: 1917. V. 70; 72
The Song of Honour. London: 1913. V. 70

HODGSON, REV.
A Topographical and Historical Description of the County of Westmoreland. London: 1813. V. 71
A Topographical and Historical Description of the County of Westmoreland. London: 1820. V. 71

HODGSON, SHADWORTH H.
The Philosophy of Reflection. London: 1878. V. 71
Time and Space. London: 1865. V. 71

HODGSON, W. E.
Trout Fishing. 1904. V. 68

HODGSON, WILLIAM
Flora of Cumberland. Carlisle: 1898. V. 70; 71

HODGSON, WILLIAM HOPE
Carnacki the Ghost Finder. 1947. V. 71
Carnacki the Ghost Finder. Sauk City: 1947. V. 72
Deep Waters. Sauk City: 1967. V. 68; 71
The House on the Borderland. Sauk City: 1946. V. 71

HODGSON, WILLOUGHBY
How to Identify Old Chinese Porcelain. Chicago: 1907. V. 73

HODGSON'S Life and Death of Miss Deborah Diddle of Daisy Mead Green and Sir Gilbert Go-Softly of Gooseberry Hall. Tondon (sic, i.e. London): 1825. V. 71

HODSKINSON, JOSEPH
The Report of Joseph Hodskinson, Engineer, on the Probable Effect Which a New Cut Now in Contemplation from Eau-Brink to a Little Above Lynn.... London: 1793. V. 71

HODSON, A. W.
Trekking the Great Thirst. 1913. V. 69; 70; 72; 73

HODSON, T. C.
The Meithis. London: 1908. V. 72

HODY, HUMPHRY
A History of English Councils and Convocations. London: 1701. V. 73

HOE, RICHARD M.
Catalogue of Brightside Herd of Pure Bred Swine, Berkshires and Small Yorkshires. New York: 1877. V. 73

HOEG, PETER
Smilla's Sense of Snow. New York: 1993. V. 69; 71

HOEVEN, EMMANUEL V. D.
Memoires de Jean De Wit, Grand Pensionnaire de Hollande. Regensburg: 1709. V. 70

HOEYE, MICHAEL
Time Stops for No Mouse. New York: 2002. V. 73

HOFER, P.
Baroque Book Illustration. A Short Survey from the Collection of the Department of Graphic Arts, Harvard College Library. Cambridge: 1951. V. 70

HOFF, E. C.
A Bibliography of Aviation Medicine. Springfield: 1942. V. 68; 70; 71

HOFF, J. WALLACE
Seven Strange Stories. A Little Life, a Little Metaphysics, a Little Love. Trenton: 1894. V. 69

HOFFER, RAIMUND
A Practical Treatise on Caoutchouc and Gutta Percha, Comprising the Properties of the Raw Materials and the Manner of Mixing and Working Them.... Philadelphia: 1883. V. 71

HOFFMAN, ABBIE
Soon to be a Major Motion Picture. New York: 1980. V. 71

HOFFMAN, ALICE
Angel Landing. New York: 1980. V. 71
Angel Landing. London: 1982. V. 69
Fortune's Daughter. New York: 1985. V. 70
Here on Earth. New York: 1997. V. 72
Illumination Night. New York: 1987. V. 69
Illumination Night. London: 1988. V. 68
Property Of. London: 1978. V. 71
The River King. New York: 2000. V. 72
Seventh Heaven. Franklin Center: 1990. V. 69
White Horses. New York: 1982. V. 73

HOFFMAN, BARRY
Gauntlet 2. 1991. V. 73

HOFFMAN, BERNARD G.
Cabot to Cartier. Toronto: 1961. V. 73

HOFFMAN, CHARLES F.
A Winter in the Far West. London: 1835. V. 71
A Winter in the West. New York: 1835. V. 70

HOFFMAN, FREDERICK
William Faulkner: Two Decades of Criticism. East Lansing: 1951. V. 69

HOFFMAN, IRWIN D.
Irwin D. Hoffman. New York: 1936. V. 70; 72; 73

HOFFMAN, LOUIS
Puzzles Old and New. London: 1893. V. 69

HOFFMAN, RICHARD
Don't Nobody Care About Zeds. Van Nuys: 1987. V. 73

HOFFMANN, ALICE SPENCER
The Children's Shakespeare.... London: 1911. V. 72

HOFFMANN, ERNST THEODOR AMADEUS
Nutcracker. New York: 1984. V. 69; 70; 72

HOFFMANN, G.
Dekorative Turen: Einzelanfertigungen und Sonderkonstruktionen in Metall, Glas & Holz. Stuttgart: 1977. V. 72

HOFFMANN, H.
Modern Interiors in Europe and America. New York and London: 1930. V. 69

HOFFMANN, HEINRICH
King Nut-Cracker of the Dream of Poor Reinhold. London: 1853. V. 73

HOFFMANN, R.
A Guide to the Birds of New England. Boston and New York: 1904. V. 70

HOFFMANN-DONNER, HEINRICH
The English Struwwelpeter. London: 1885. V. 70
The English Struwwelpeter. London: 1890. V. 68
Piet de Smeeerpoets. Netherlands: 1900. V. 68
Slovenly Peter. New York: 1935. V. 69; 71
Der Struwwelper in Seiner Ersten Gestalt. Leipzig: 1933. V. 70

HOFMANN, HANS
Hans Hofmann... and Five Essays by Hans Hofmann. New York: 1963. V. 72

HOFMANN, WERNER
Gustav Klimt. Greenwich: 1971. V. 70

HOFMANNSTHAL, HUGO VAN
The Selected Prose of.... London: 1952. V. 70

HOFSTATTER, H. H.
Jugendstil: Graphik und Druck-Kunst. Baden-Baden: 1985. V. 72

HOGABOAM, JAMES J.
The Bean Creek Valley. Incidents of Its Early Settlement. Hudson: 1876. V. 68

HOGAN, DENIS
A Short English Answer to a Long Irish Story; or, a Key to the Mystery of the Barouche and Bank Notes, Proving Brevet Major Hogan's Accusations Against His Royal Highness the Duke of York.... London: 1808. V. 70

HOGAN, DESMOND
Children of Lir - Stories from Ireland. New York: 1981. V. 72; 73

HOGAN, INEZ
Giraffe Twins. New York: 1948. V. 72
Nicodemus and His Little Sister. New York: 1932. V. 73
Nicodemus and His New Shoes. New York: 1937. V. 73
Nicodemus and the Gang. New York: 1939. V. 71
Nicodemus and the Little Black Pig. New York: 1934. V. 73
Nicodemus Laughs. New York: 1941. V. 73

HOGAN, JAMES F.
The Irish in Australia. 1887. V. 73

HOGAN, LINDA
Mean Spirit. New York: 1990. V. 73
Red Clay. Greenfield Center: 1991. V. 72

HOGAN, MARTIN J.
The Shamrock Battalion of the Rainbow. New York: 1919. V. 71

HOGARTH, D. G.
The Life of Charles M. Doughty. London: 1928. V. 70

HOGARTH, WILLIAM
An Account of What Seemed the Most Remarkable in the Five Days Peregrination of the Five Following Persons.... 1782. V. 73
The Analysis of Beauty. London: 1772. V. 73
Complete Works of William Hogarth. London: 1865?. V. 69
(Twelve Illustrations to Samuel Butler's Hudibras.). 1725. V. 73
Works, in a Series of One Hundred and Fifty Steel Engravings, by the First Artists.... London. V. 73
The Works of William Hogarth. London. V. 71

HOGE, A. H., MRS.
The Boys in Blue; or Heroes of the Rank and File. New York;: 1867. V. 73

HOGG, GARRY
Blind Jack Of Knaresborough. Road-builder Extraordinary. London: 1967. V. 72

HOGG, JABEZ
The Microscope: Its History, Construction and Application. London: 1856. V. 73
The Microscope: Its History, Construction and Application. London: 1857. V. 73
The Microscope: Its History, Construction and Application. London: 1867. V. 73
The Microscope: Its History, Construction and Application. London: 1887. V. 73

HOGG, JAMES
Fortunes Made in Business: a Series of Original Sketches.... London: 1891. V. 72
Kilmeny. London and Edinburgh: 1911. V. 69; 72
Tales and Sketches by the Ettrick Shepherd. Glasgow: 1837. V. 73
The Tales of James Hogg, The Ettrick Shepherd. London: 1880. V. 71
The Works of the Ettrick Shepherd. London. V. 70

HOGG, R.
A Selection of the Eatable Funguses of Great Britian. London: 1866. V. 70; 72

HOGG, THOMAS
A Concise and Practical Treatise on the Growth and Culture of the Carnation, Pink, Auricula.... London: 1823. V. 71
A Concise and Practical Treatise on the Growth and Culture of the Carnation, Pink, Auricula.... London: 1824. V. 70

HOGNER, DOROTHY CHILDS
Navajo Winter Nights. New York: 1938. V. 69

HOGROGIAN, NONNY
One Fine Day. New York: 1971. V. 71

HOHLE, PER
Shooting and Fishing in Norway. Oslo. V. 68

HOIG, STAN
The Humor of the American Cowboy. Caldwell: 1958. V. 69
Sand Creek Massacre. Norman: 1961. V. 72
Western Odyssey Of John Simpson Smith, Frontieman, Trapper, Trader And Interpreter. Glendale: 1974. V. 72

HOLBACH, PAUL HEINRICH DIETRICH, BARON D'
Systeme de La Nature. Londres: 1770. V. 69

HOLBEIN, HANS
The Dances of Death, through Various Stages of Human Life. London: 1803. V. 70
Drawings by Holbein from the Royal Library Windsor Castle. London and New York: 1983. V. 73
Icones Mortis. Lugduni: 1547. V. 70
Der Todten-Tanz...La Danse des Morts. Basel: 1843. V. 70

HOLBERG, LUDVIG, BARON
An Introduction to Universal History. London: 1758. V. 69
A Journey to the World Under-Ground. London: 1742. V. 69
Nicolai Klimii iter Subterraneum. Copenhagen & Leipzig: 1741. V. 70

HOLBROOK, J.
Ten Years Among the Mail Bags; or, Notes from the Diary of a Special Agent of the Post-Office Department. Philadelphia: 1874. V. 73

HOLBROOK, JACKSON
All Manner of Folk: Interpretations and Studies. 1912. V. 69

HOLBROOK, L. R.
Mess Officer's Assistant. 1909. V. 72; 73

HOLBROOK'S
Newark City and Business Directory for the Year Ending May 1, 1888. Newark: 1887. V. 72
Newark City and Business Directory for the Year Ending May 1, 1889. Newark: 1888. V. 72
Newark City and Business Directory...for the Year Ending May 1, 1891. Newark: 1890. V. 72

HOLCOMB, RICHMOND C.
A Century with Norfolk Naval Hospital 1830-1930. Portsmouth: 1930. V. 72

HOLCOMBE, HENRY
Sermon, Occasioned by the Death of Lieutenant-General George Washington, Late President of the United States of America.... Savannah: 1800. V. 73

HOLCOMBE, JAMES P.
An Introduction to Equity Jurisprudence, on the Basis of Story's Commentaries. Cincinnati: 1846. V. 71

HOLDEN, CRAIG
The River Sorrow. New York: 1994. V. 68

HOLDEN, E. GOODMAN
A Famous Victory. Chicago: 1880. V. 70

HOLDEN, HORACE
A Narrative of the Shipwreck, Captivity and Sufferings of Horace Holden and Benj. H. Nute, Who Were Cast Away in the American Ship Mentor, on the Pelew Islands, in the Year 1832.... Boston: 1836. V. 68

HOLDEN, WILLIAM CURRY
Alkali Trails or Social and Economic Movements of the Texas Frontier 1846-1900. Dallas: 1930. V. 69; 71
The Espuela Land and Cattle Company. A Study of A Foreign-Owned Ranch in Texas. Dallas: 1970. V. 71
Hill of the Rooster. New York: 1946. V. 68
Hill of the Rooster. New York: 1956. V. 73
A Ranching Saga, the Lives of William Electious Halsell and Ewing Halsell. San Antonio: 1976. V. 73
Rollie Burns Or An Account of the Ranching Industry On the South Plains. Dallas: 1932. V. 71
The Spur Ranch - a Study of the Inclosed Ranch Phase of the Cattle Industry in Texas. Boston: 1934. V. 68; 71

HOLDER, CHARLES FREDERICK
Big Game at Sea. 1908. V. 68; 73
Life in the Open. Sport with Rod, Gun, Horse and Hound in Southern California. New York: 1906. V. 73
Louis Agassiz. His Life and Work. London: 1893. V. 68; 72

HOLDING, ELISABETH SANXAY
Angelica. New York: 1921. V. 70
The Old Battle Ax. New York: 1943. V. 68
The Virgin Huntress. New York: 1951. V. 71

HOLDING, ELIZABETH SANXAY
The Blank Wall. New York: 1947. V. 73
The Death Wish. New York: 1934. V. 71
The Silk Purse. New York: 1928. V. 71

HOLDING, THOMAS HIRAM
Cost Cutting. London: 1902. V. 71
Trousers, Vest, Breeches and Gaiter Cutting. London: 1899. V. 71

HOLDSTOCK, ROBERT
Earthwind. London: 1977. V. 71
In the Valley of Statues. London: 1982. V. 71

HOLDSWORTH, EDWARD
Remarks and Dissertations on Virgil; with some Other Classical Observations. London: 1768. V. 73

HOLDSWORTH, WILLIAM
History of English Law. London: 1938. V. 69
Natural Short-Hand Wherein the Nature of Speech and the Manner of Pronunciation are Briefly Explained.... London: 1770?. V. 70

HOLDSWORTH, WILLIAM A.
The Ballot Act, 1872, for Parliamentary and Municipal Elections. London: 1880. V. 68

HOLE, SAMUEL R.
A Little Tour in Ireland: Being a Visit to Dublin, Galway, Connamara, Kilarney, etc. London: 1870. V. 68

HOLE, WILLIAM
The Ornaments of Churches Considered, with a Particular View to the Late Decoration of the Parish Church of St. Margaret Westminster. Oxford: 1761. V. 68
Quasi Cursores. Portraits of The High Officers and Professors Of the University of Edinburgh At Its Tercentenary Festival. Edinburgh: 1884. V. 71; 72

HOLFORD, MARGARET
Warbeck of Wolfstein. London: 1820. V. 69

HOLGATE, DAVID
New Hall. London: 1987. V. 72

THE HOLIDAY ABC. London. V. 69

HOLIDAY Rambles on the Yorkshire Moors. York: 1875. V. 73

HOLIDAY, BILLIE
Lady Sings the Blues. Garden City: 1956. V. 70; 71

HOLIDAY, F. W.
River Fishing for Sea Trout. 1960. V. 68

HOLIDAY Fun. London: 1875. V. 71

THE HOLIDAYS at Llandudno. London: 1868. V. 68

HOLINSHED, RAPHAEL
Holinshed's Chronicles of England, Scotland and Ireland. London: 1807-1808. V. 72

HOLLAND, ANNE
Dawn Run. 1986. V. 68

HOLLAND, C. F.
Climbs on the Scawfell Group. London: 1924. V. 69

HOLLAND, CHARLES
Crispin Anecdotes: Comprising Interesting Notices of Shoemakers Who Have Been Distinguished for Genius, Enterprise, or Eccentricity. Sheffield and London: 1827. V. 72

HOLLAND, ELIZABETH
The Journal of Elizabeth Lady Holland 1791-1811. London: 1908. V. 70

HOLLAND, HENRY
Resolutions of the Associated Architects; with the Report of a Committee by Them Appointed to Consider the Causes of the Frequent Fires, and the Best Means of Preventing the Like in Future. London: 1793. V. 68

HOLLAND, HENRY SCOTT
Memoir of Madame Jenny Lind-Goldschmidt her Early Art-Life and Dramatic Career 1820-1851. London and New York: 1891. V. 73

HOLLAND, JOHN
A Beach Vision. 1962. V. 69
A Treatise on the Progressive Improvement and Present State of the Manufactures in Metal. London: 1831-1834. V. 69
A Treatise on the Progressive Improvement and Present State of the Manufactures in Metal. London: 1853. V. 69

HOLLAND, JOSEPH F.
The Landing of Two Slaves Named John & Addis in America. New York: 1991. V. 72

HOLLAND, MARGARET
My Winter of Discontent Under Indian Skies. Belfast: 1926. V. 70

HOLLAND, MARY
The Complete Economical Cook.... London: 1848. V. 70

HOLLAND, PATRIC
A Plan for Manning the Navy, Without Impressing, or Expence to Government. London: 1809. V. 69

HOLLAND, RAY
Shotgunning in the Lowlands. New York: 1945. V. 69

HOLLAND, W.
History of West Cork and the Diocese of Ross. 1949. V. 70

HOLLAND, WILLIAM E.
Let a Soldier Die. New York: 1984. V. 68

HOLLANDER, BERNARD
The Revival of Phrenology. The Mental Functions of the Brain. An Investigation into Their Localisation and Their Manifestation in Health and Disease. London: 1901. V. 69

HOLLANDER, JOHN
In Place. Omaha: 1978. V. 72; 73
Kinneret. New Haven: 1986. V. 73
Looking East in Winter. New York: 1990. V. 73
Some Fugitives Take Cover. New York: 1986. V. 73

HOLLES, DENZIL
The Case Stated of the Jurisidiction of the House of Lords in the Point of Impositions. London: 1676. V. 72
A True Relation of the Unjust Accusation of Certain French Gentlemen (Charged with a Robbery, of Which they Were Most Innocent) and the Proceedings Upon It, with their Tryal and Acquittall in the Court of Kings Bench, in Easter Last. London: 1671. V. 73

HOLLEY, ALEX L.
Treatise On Ordnance and Armour...Material Fabrication...Rifling, Projectiles and Breech Loading. New York and London: 1865. V. 70

HOLLEY, FRANCES C.
Once Their Home. Chicago: 1892. V. 72

HOLLEY, GEORGE W.
Niagara. New York City: 1872. V. 72

HOLLEY, MINNIE C.
Glimpses of Tazewell through Holley Heritage. Radford: 1977. V. 71

HOLLICK, A.
The Cretaceous Flora of Southern New York and New England. Washington: 1906. V. 72

HOLLICK, FREDERICK
The Diseases of Woman, Their Causes, and Cure Familiarly Explained. New York: 1850. V. 69

HOLLIDAY, JOHN
The Life of William Late Earl of Mansfield. London: 1797. V. 68; 70; 73

HOLLING, HOLLING CLANCY
The Book of Indians. New York: 1935. V. 70
Claws of the Thunderbird: a Tale of Three Lost Indians. Joliet: 1928. V. 70
Seabird. Boston: 1948. V. 68; 73

HOLLINGHURST, ALAN
The Swimming Pool Library. London: 1988. V. 68; 70; 71; 72

HOLLINGSHEAD, JOHN
Ragged London in 1861. London: 1861. V. 73
The Story of Leicester Square. London: 1892. V. 71
Underground. London: 1862. V. 71

HOLLINGSWORTH, JOHN MC HENRY
The Journal of...of the First New York Volunteers (Stevenson's Regiment) September 1846-August 1849.... San Francisco: 1923. V. 73

HOLLINGSWORTH, MARY H.
How Long the Heart Remembers. Boston: 1977. V. 71

HOLLINGSWORTH, S.
The Present State of Nova Scotia; With a Brief Account of Canada and the British Island on the Coast of North America. Edinburgh: 1787. V. 72

HOLLINGTON, MICHAEL
Charles Dickens: Critical Assessments. London: 1995. V. 70

HOLLINS, WILLIAM
Railroads in the United States of America; or, Protest and Argument Against a Subscription on the Part of the State of Maryland, to the Baltimore and Ohio Railroad Company. Baltimore: 1827. V. 73

HOLLIS, THOMAS
The True Sentiments of America.... London: 1768. V. 73

HOLLISS, RICHARD
The Official 007 File James Bond. London: 1989. V. 72

HOLLISTER, ALONZO
Heaven Anointed Woman. Mt. Lebanon: 1887. V. 73

HOLLISTER, OVANDO J.
Boldly They Rode. Lakewood, CO: 1949. V. 72
The Mines of Colorado. Springfield: 1867. V. 70
The Resources and Attractions of the Territory of Utah - 1879. Omaha: 1879. V. 69

HOLLISTER, P. M.
Famous Colonial Houses. Philadelphia: 1921. V. 69; 72

HOLLOWAY, J. N.
History of Kansas: from the First Exploration of the Mississippi Valley to Its Admission into the Union. Lafayette: 1868. V. 69

HOLLOWAY, JAMES
The Free and Voluntary Confession and Narrative of James Holloway.... London: 1684. V. 69

HOLLOWAY, JANE
Moses P. Pickles and Others. Philadelphia: 1910. V. 73

HOLLOWAY, LAURA C.
An Hour With Charlotte Bronte or Flowers from a Yorkshire Moor. Philadelphia: 1882. V. 73
An Hour With Charlotte Bronte; or, Flowers from a Yorkshire Moor. New York: 1883. V. 70

HOLLOWELL, J. M.
War-Time Reminiscences and Other Selections. Goldsboro: 1939. V. 69; 70

HOLLS, CHRISTOPHER
Evelyn Waugh. London: 1954. V. 69

HOLLY, M.
Die Aquarienfishce in Wort und Bild. Stuttgart: 1934-. V. 73

HOLM, B.
Indian Art of the Northwest Coast. Houston & Seattle: 1976. V. 72
Spirit and Ancestor. Seattle: 1987. V. 69

HOLMAN, ALBERT
Pioneering In The Northwest-Niobrara-Virginia City Wagon Road. Sioux City: 1924. V. 68; 72

HOLMAN, DAVID
Buckskin and Homespun. Austin: 1979. V. 68

HOLMAN, FREDERICK V.
Dr. John McLoughlin, The Father of Oregon. Cleveland: 1907. V. 71

HOLMAN, HUGH
Trout in the Milk. New York: 1945. V. 71

HOLMAN, JAMES
The Narrative of a Journey, Undertaken in the Years 1819, 1820 and 1821, through France, Italy, Savoy, Switzerland, Parts of Germany.... London: 1822. V. 68; 72

HOLMAN, JOHN P.
Sheep and Bear Trails. 1933. V. 70; 72; 73

HOLMAN, JOSEPH GEORGE
A Statement of the Differences Subsisting Between the Proprietors and Performers of the Theatre Royal Covent Garden. London: 1800. V. 71

HOLMAN, RUSSELL
The Freshman. New York: 1925. V. 69

HOLMAN, RUSSELL continued
Speedy. New York: 1928. V. 71; 72

HOLMAN, SHERI
A Stolen Tongue. New York: 1997. V. 71

HOLMAN, WILLIAM R.
Library Publications. San Francisco: 1965. V. 69

HOLMAN HUNT, DIANA
Latin Among Lions: Alvaro Guevara. London: 1974. V. 71

HOLMBOE, J.
Studies of the Vegetation of Cyprus.... Bergen: 1914. V. 72

HOLME, C. G.
Children's Toys of Yesterday. New York and London: 1932. V. 69
Glimpses of Old Japan from Japanese Colour Prints: Birds and Flowers. London: 1930. V. 70

HOLME, CHARLES
Colour Photography and Other Recent Developments of the Art of the Camera. London: 1908. V. 69
Daumier and Gavarni. London: 1914. V. 72
English Water-Colour With Reproductions of Drawings by Eminent Painters. London: 1902. V. 72
Modern British Domestic Architecture and Decoration. London: 1901. V. 68
Pen, Pencil and Chalk. London: 1911. V. 73

HOLME, CONSTANCE
Crump Folk Going Home. London: 1913. V. 71
He-Who-Came?. London: 1930. V. 71
The Things Which Belong. London: 1925. V. 71
The Trumpet in the Dust. London: 1921. V. 72

HOLMES, ABIEL
American Annals; or a Chronological History of America from Its Discovery in MCCCCXCII to MDCCCIV. Cambridge: 1805. V. 68

HOLMES, ARNOLD J.
A Slum Santa Claus, or Tom Nicholas, a Hero of the Slums. Goole: 1909. V. 73

HOLMES, BAYARD
The Surgery of the Head. New York: 1903. V. 71

HOLMES, C. J.
Constable and His Influence on Landscape Painting. London: 1902. V. 72

HOLMES, CHARLES
Old English Country Cottages. London: 1906. V. 73

HOLMES, EFNER TUDOR
Amy's Goose. New York: 1977. V. 73
Carrie's Gift. New York: 1978. V. 70
The Christmas Cat. New York: 1976. V. 70

HOLMES, FRANCIS S.
The Southern Farmer and Market Gardener. Charleston: 1842. V. 71; 73

HOLMES, GEORGE C. V.
Ancient and Modern Ships. London: 1906. V. 69

HOLMES, H. H.
Nine Times Nine. 1940. V. 73
Rocket to the Morgue. 1942. V. 73

HOLMES, JOHN
Catalogue of Ashburnham Mansucripts. The Barrois Manuscripts. London: 1851. V. 70
A New Grammar of the Latin Tongue. London: 1782. V. 69

HOLMES, JOHN CLELLON
The Horn. New York: 1958. V. 72; 73
Nothing More To Declare. New York: 1967. V. 72

HOLMES, JULIA ARCHIBALD
A Bloomer Girl on Pike's Peak. Denver: 1949. V. 72; 73

HOLMES, KENNETH L.
Covered Wagon Women. Diaries and Letters from the Western Trails 18401890. Glendale & Spokane: 1983-1993. V. 69; 72

HOLMES, LOUIS A.
Fort McPherson, Nebraska-Fort Cottonwood, N.T. Guaridan Of The Tracks And Trails. Lincoln: 1963. V. 72

HOLMES, MARY J.
The Cromptons. New York: 1902. V. 71

HOLMES, MAURICE
Captain James Cook: a Bibliographical Excursion. New York: 1968. V. 70

HOLMES, OLIVER WENDELL
An Address Delivered at the Annual Meeting of the Boston Microscopical Society. Cambridge: 1877. V. 70
Astraea. Boston: 1850. V. 68; 69; 71; 73
Autocrat of the Breakfast Table. Boston: 1855. V. 71
The Autocrat of the Breakfast Table. Boston: 1858. V. 68; 72
The Autocrat of the Breakfast Table. Boston: 1859. V. 70; 71
The Autocrat of the Breakfast Table. New York: 1955. V. 70
The Common Law. Boston: 1881. V. 73
Dorothy Q Together with a Ballad of the Boston Tea Party and Grandmother's Story of Bunker Hill Battle. London: 1892. V. 69
Elsie Veneer. Boston: 1861. V. 71
The Guardian Angel. Boston: 1867. V. 68
In Memory of Fitz-Greene Halleck. Boston: 1869. V. 68
The Last Leaf. Cambridge: 1886. V. 68; 72
Oration Delivered Before the City Authorities of Boston, on the Fourth of July 1862. Boston: 1863. V. 70
Our Hundred Days in Europe. Boston: 1887. V. 68
Over the Teacups. Boston and New York: 1891. V. 70
Poem for the Dedication of the Fountain at Stratford-on-Avon Presented by George W. Childs, Esquire of Philadelphia, U.S.A. Boston: 1887. V. 68
Poems. London: 1846. V. 69
The Poetical Works. Boston: 1884. V. 68; 70
The Professor at the Breakfast Table. Boston: 1860. V. 68; 71; 72
Puerperal Fever as a Private Pestilence. Boston: 1855. V. 72
Songs of Many Seasons 1862-1874. Boston: 1875. V. 68
Soundings from the Atlantic. Boston: 1864. V. 69
T. Brigham Bishop's Last and Best Song. The Dear Old Times. Words by Oliver Wendell Holmes, Music by T. Brigham Bishop. San Francisco: 1879. V. 70
Urania: a Rhymed Lesson. Boston: 1846. V. 73

HOLMES, PRESCOTT
The Story of Exploration and Adventure in the Frozen Seas. Philadelphia. V. 73

HOLMES, RICHARD R.
Naval & Military Trophies. London: 1896. V. 72

HOLMES, T.
Introductory Address Delivered at St. George's Hospital, Octobert 2, 1893, on the Centenary of John Hunter's Death. London: 1893. V. 68

HOLMES, THOMAS JAMES
Increase Mather, a Bibliography of His Works.... Cleveland: 1931. V. 70; 73
The Mather Literature. Cleveland: 1927. V. 70; 72

HOLMES, W. D.
Report on Steam Communication with India, via the Red Sea.... London: 1838. V. 73
Safari R.S.V.P. 1960. V. 73

HOLMES, W. KERSLEY
On Scottish Hills. London: 1962. V. 69

HOLMS, FLORENCE
Fun and Frolic. London: 1911. V. 72

HOLROYD, ABRAHAM
Collectanea Bradfordiana: A Collection of Papers on the History of Bradford, and the Neighborhood. Saltaire: 1873. V. 73
A Garland of Poetry; by Various Authors. Saltaire: 1873. V. 70; 73

HOLROYD, JAMES
Seventeen Steps to 221b: a Collection of Sherlockian Pieces by English Writers. London: 1967. V. 69

HOLST, A. ROLAND
Tusschen Vuur en Maan. Maastricht: 1932. V. 70

HOLSTEIN, ANTHONY FREDERIC
Isadora of Milan. London: 1811. V. 69

HOLSTEIN, H. L. V.
Memoirs of Simon Bolivar. Boston: 1829. V. 69

HOLSTON, LEW
Other Gods. Hollywood: 1939. V. 69

HOLT, ADONIRAM J.
Pioneering In The Southwest. Nashville: 1923. V. 72

HOLT, ARDEN
Fancy Dresses Described or What to Wear at Fancy Balls. London: 1887. V. 73

HOLT, DAVID
Incidents in the Life of David Holt, Including a Sketch of Some of the Philanthropic Institutions of Manchester During a Period of Forty Years. Manchester: 1843. V. 71

HOLT, E. EMMETT
The Diseases of Infancy and Childhood. New York: 1899. V. 70; 71

HOLT, EMILY SARAH
Memoirs Of Royal Ladies. London: 1861. V. 72

HOLT, GAVIN
Green Talons. 1931. V. 73
Ivory Ladies. London: 1937. V. 71

HOLT, J. ROBERT
Heavenly Chimes: new Soul Stirring Gospel songs for the Sabbath School Singing Schools Revivials. Greensboro: 1907. V. 72

HOLT, JOHN
General View of the Agriculture of the County of Lancaster. London: 1795. V. 69; 73

HOLT, JOSEPH
The Evil and the Remedy for the Privy System of New Orleans. New Orleans: 1879. V. 72

HOLT, P. C.
The Distributional History of the Biota of the Southern Appalachians. Blacksburg: 1969-1971. V. 68

HOLT, ROSA BELLE
Rugs. Chicago: 1901. V. 72

HOLTBY, WINIFRED
Anderby Wold. London: 1923. V. 73
Virginia Woolf. London: 1932. V. 70

HOLTHAUS, P. D.
Wanderings of a Journeyman Tailor through Europe and the East During the Years 1824 to 1840. London: 1844. V. 71

HOLTON, EDITH AUSTIN
Stormy Weather. Philadelphia: 1936. V. 71

HOLTON, ISAAC F.
New Granada. 1857. V. 69; 70; 72; 73

HOLTTUM, R. E.
A Revised Flora of Malaya. Volume II. Ferns of Malaya. Singapore: 1954. V. 72

HOLT-WHITE, RASHLEIGH
The Life And Letters of Gilbert White of Selborne. London: 1901. V. 72

HOLTZAPFFEL, CHARLES
Descriptive Catalogue of the Woods Commonly Employed in This County For the Mechanical and Ornamental Arts. London: 1843. V. 72

HOLTZAPFFEL, JOHN JACOB
Turning and Mechanical Manipulation, Intended as a Work of General Reference and Practical Instruction.... London: 1846-. V. 69

HOLTZCLAW, WILLIAM
The Black Man's Burden. New York: 1915. V. 68

HOLTZENDORFF VIETMANSDORF, FRANZ VON
An English Country Squire as Sketched at Hardwicke Court, Gloucestershire. Gloucester: 1878. V. 68

HOLWAY, JOHN
Blackball Stars: Negro League Pioneers. Westport CT: 1988:. V. 72

HOLYOAKE, GEORGE JACOB
Bygones Worth Remembering. London: 1905. V. 71
Sixty Years of an Agitator's Life. London: 1893. V. 71

HOLYROYD, ABRAHAM
A Garland of Poetry: by Yorkshire Authors, or Relating to Yorkshire. 1873. V. 73

HOLYROYD, MICHAEL
Bernard Shaw. 1988-1992. V. 69
Lytton Strachey - a Critical Biography. London: 1967-1968. V. 69

HOLZWORTH, JOHN M.
The Wild Grizzlies of Alaska. New York and London: 1930. V. 70; 72; 73

HOMAGE to George Barker on His Sixtieth Birthday. 1973. V. 70

HOMAGE to Marc Chagall. New York: 1969. V. 69

THE HOME Affections of the Poets.... London: 1858. V. 68

HOME and Country Pets. London: 1890. V. 73

HOME, ANDREA
Six Months in the Fourth. London: 1895. V. 68

THE HOME Cook Book. Toronto: 1877. V. 68

HOME, FRANCIS
Essai sur le Blanchiment des Toiles. Paris: 1762. V. 69

HOME, GORDON
Old London Bridge. London: 1931. V. 69; 70
Yorkshire Coast and Moorland Painted and Described. London: 1904. V. 73
Yorkshire Dales and Fells. London: 1906. V. 73
Yorkshire Painted and Described. London: 1908. V. 73

HOME, HENRY
Elements of Criticism. Edinburgh;: 1774. V. 72

HOME, JOHN
Douglas: a Tragedy. London: 1757. V. 70

HOME, ROBERT
Select Views in Mysore, the Country of Tippoo Sultan; from Drawings Taken on the Spot.... London: 1794. V. 69

HOME Thoughts and Home Scenes. London: 1865. V. 68

HOMER, HENRY SACHEVERELL
An Enquiry into the Means of Preserving and Improving the Publick Roads of this Kingdom. Oxford: 1767. V. 70
An Essay on the Nature and Method of Ascertaining the Specifick Shares of Proprietors Upon the Inclosure of Common Fields.... London: 1753. V. 70

HOMERUS
Carmina Homerica, Ilias et Odyssa. (Works). Londini: 1820. V. 68
Homeri et Homeridarum Opera et Reliquiae. (Works in Greek). Lipsiae: 1804-1807. V. 68; 72
The Homeric Hymn to Aphrodite. Waltham St. Lawrence: 1948. V. 71
Hymnus in Cererem (in Greek). Lugduni Batavorum: 1808. V. 68; 72
The Iliad. London: 1715-1720. V. 71
The Iliad and Odyssey. London: 1802. V. 71
The Iliad of Homer. London: 1715-1720. V. 72
The Iliad of Homer. Glasgow: 1771. V. 73
The Iliad of Homer Rendered Into English Blank Verse. London: 1864. V. 70
The Iliad of Homer. The Odyssey of Homer. Haarlem: 1931. V. 69
The Iliads of Homer Prince of Poets. London: 1611?. V. 70
Ilias. Parisiis: 1538. V. 70
Ilias. Oxford: 1695. V. 68
Ilias and Odysseae. Cantabrigiae: 1711. V. 70
Ilias et Odyssea. London: 1831. V. 72
Ilias Garece et Latine. Londini: 1754. V. 72
Nausikaa. Paris: 1899. V. 73
Odyssea. (Odyssey in Greek). Oxonii: 1827. V. 68; 72
L'Odyssee (and) L'Iliade...Traduite en Francois, avec des Remarques par Madame Dacier. Paris: 1716-1719. V. 70
L'Odyssee d'Homere, Traduite en Vers Avec Des Remarques....Par M. De Rochefort. Paris: 1777. V. 70
The Odyssey. Glasgow: 1768. V. 73
The Odyssey. Francfort: 1776. V. 69
The Odyssey. Oxford: 1800. V. 68
The Odyssey. London: 1887. V. 68
The Odyssey. Boston: 1929. V. 69
The Odyssey. New York: 1932. V. 68; 69; 70
The Odyssey. 1981. V. 70
The Odyssey. New York: 1981. V. 70
The Odyssey of Homer Translated from the Greek by T.E. Shaw (Lawrence of Arabia). New York: 1940. V. 72
Les Oeuvres d'Homere Traduites du grec Par Mad. Dacier. Leiden: 1766. V. 70
Pages from the Iliad. Iowa City: 1976. V. 73
Il Primo Canto Del L'Iliade d'Omero. (The First Two Books of the Iliad in Italian). Londra: 1736. V. 69
The Works of Homer. London: 1794. V. 69

HOMES, A. M.
The End of Alice. New York: 1996. V. 68
In a Country of Mothers. New York: 1993. V. 72
The Safety of Objects. New York: 1990. V. 70; 72

HOMES for Millions in Western Canada's Vast Agricultural Domain. 1904. V. 71

HOMES, GEOFFREY
Build My Gallows High. New York: 1946. V. 71
Forty Whacks. New York: 1941. V. 69
Then There Were Three. 1938. V. 73

HOMES of American Authors.... New York: 1855. V. 69

HOMMAGE a Natalia Sedova-Trotsky 1882-1962. Paris: 1962. V. 68

HOMMAGE aux Plus Jolies et Vertueuses Femmes de Paris ou Nomenclature de la Classe la Moins Nombreuse. 1790. V. 73

HONE, E.
The Present State of the Muskox in Arctic North America and Greenland. 1934. V. 73

HONE, J. M.
Bishop Berkeley, His Life, Writings and Philosophy. 1931. V. 69; 73

HONE, JOSEPH
The Private Sector. London: 1971. V. 72

HONE, WILLIAM
Ancient Mysteries Described, Especially the English Miracles Plays.... London: 1823. V. 69
The Every Day-Book; or the Guide to the Year. London: 1826. V. 72
The First Trial of William Hone...(with) The Second Trial of William Hone... (and) The Third Trial.... London: 1818. V. 73
The Three Trials of William Hone.... London: 1818. V. 72
The Yearbook of Daily Recreation and Information, Concerning the Remarkable Men and Manners...(with) The Every-Day Book, or Everlasting Calendar.... London: 1826-1833. V. 73

HONEY, WILLIAM BOWYER
European Ceramic Art From The End Of The Middle Ages To About 1815. London: 1952. V. 72

HONEYMAN, A. VAN DOREN
Northwestern New Jersey. A History of Somerset, Morris, Hunterdon, Warren and Sussex Counties. New York: 1927. V. 69

HONIG, P.
Science and Scientists in the Netherlands Indies. New York: 1945. V. 71; 73

THE HONOR of Parliament and the Justice of the Nation Vindicated. In Reply to Dr. Price's Observations on the Nature of Civil Liberty. London: 1776. V. 69

HONOUR, HUGH
Chinoiserie. London: 1951. V. 72

HOOD, J. DENNIS
Waterspouts on the Yorkshire Wolds. Catacysm at Langtoft and Driffield. Driffield: 1892. V. 73

HOOD, JENNINGS
American Orders and Societies and Their Decorations. Philadelphia: 1917. V. 72

HOOD, JOHN BELL
Advance and Retreat. New Orleans: 1880. V. 69; 70; 73

HOOD, THOMAS
Memorials of.... Boston: 1860. V. 69
Odes and Addresses to Great People. London: 1825. V. 73
The Plea of Midsummer Fairies, Hero and Leander, Lycus and Centaur, and Other Poems. London: 1827. V. 71; 73
Poems. London: 1846. V. 73
Poems. London: 1871. V. 72
The Schoolmaster's Motto. London: 1870. V. 72
Up the Rhine. 1840. V. 72
Up the Rhine. London: 1840. V. 68
Whims and Oddities, in Prose and Verse; With Forty Original Designs. London: 1826. V. 68; 73
Whims and Oddities, in Prose and Verse; with Forty Original Designs. Second Series. London: 1827. V. 73
The Works. London: 1862-1863. V. 73

HOOD, W. H.
The Blight of Insubordination. London: 1903. V. 73

HOOGSTRAAL, H.
Bibliography of Ticks and Tickborne Diseases from Homer. Cairo: 1970-1982. V. 70
Bibliography of Ticks and Tickborne Diseases from Homer (about 800 B. C.) to 31 December 1984. Cairo: 1970-1988. V. 72

HOOIJER, D. A.
Prehistoric and Fossil Rhinoceroses from Malay Archipelago and India. Leiden: 1946. V. 73

HOOK, PHILIP
An Innocent Eye. London: 1994. V. 71
The Innocent Eye. London: 2000. V. 70
The Stonebreakers. London: 1994. V. 69; 70; 71

HOOK, THEODORE
The French Stage and French People, as Illustrated in the Memoirs of M. A. Fleury. London: 1841. V. 69

HOOKE, N.
The Roman History, from the Building of Rome to the Ruin of the Commonwealth. London: 1806. V. 69; 72

HOOKE, N. WARNER
Close of Play. New York: 1936. V. 71

HOOKE, NATHANIEL MARLBOROUGH
An Account of the Conduct of the Dowager Duchess of Marlborough, from Her First Coming to Court to the Year 1710. London: 1742. V. 69; 73

HOOKE, ROBERT
The Diary of Robert Hooke 1672-1680. London: 1968. V. 72
Micrographia. London: 1665. V. 68; 69
Micrographia (1665). Lincolnwood: 1987. V. 68; 71; 73

HOOKER, JOHN
Defence of Mrs. Virginia T. Smith, Hartford City, Missionary Against the Charge of Baby Farming. Hartford: 1892. V. 73

HOOKER, JOSEPH DALTON
The Botany of the Antarctic Voyage...II. Flora Novae-Zelandiae. Part I (only) Flowering Plants. London: 1853. V. 73
Flora of British India. 1875-1897. V. 69
Himalayan Journals.... London: 1854. V. 70
Himalayan Journals.... London: 1855. V. 70; 73
On the Flora of Australia, Its Origin, Affinities and Distribution.... London: 1859. V. 69

HOOKER, RICHARD
Of the Lawes of Ecclesiastical Politie. London: 1676. V. 70

HOOKER, WILLIAM JACKSON
British Jungermanniae. 1818. V. 69
A Century of Ferns, Being Figures with Brief Descriptions of One Hundred New, or Rare, or Imperfectly Known Species of Ferns.... 1854. V. 72
A Century of Ferns... (with) A Second Century of Ferns. London: 1854-1861. V. 70; 71
Exotic Flora, Containing Figures and Descriptions of New, Rare and Otherwise Interesting Exotic Plants.... Edinburgh: 1823-1827. V. 72
Filices Exoticae. London: 1859. V. 68; 70; 73
Flora Scotica. London: 1821. V. 69
Garden Ferns; or, Coloured Figures and Descriptions.... London: 1862. V. 72
Journal of a Tour in Iceland, in the Summer of 1809. London: 1913. V. 70
Journal of a Tour in Iceland.... 1813. V. 69
Muscologia Britannica; Containing the Mosses of Great Britain and Ireland.... London: 1818. V. 71
Muscologia Britannica: Containing the Mosses of Great Britain and Ireland.... London: 1827. V. 69
Niger Flora...Plants of Western Tropical Africa.... London: 1849. V. 73
Synopsis Folium: or a Synopsis of all Known Ferns. 1868. V. 72

HOOKER, WORTHINGTON
Lessons from the History of Medical Delusions. New York: 1850. V. 71

HOOKHAM, RUTH
Neena. New York: 1956. V. 69

HOOLE, BARBARA
A Season at Harrogate. Knarlesborough: 1812. V. 73

HOOLE, CHARLES
Terminationes et Exempla Declinationum & Conjugationum.... London: 1792. V. 69

HOOLE, HENRY E., & CO. LTD.
Trade Catalogue of Fireplaces and Lanterns. Sheffield: 1910. V. 68; 70; 72

HOOPER, BENJAMIN
The Cruise of the Nelly. Manchester: 1870. V. 68

HOOPER, E. J.
Hooper's Western Fruit Book: a Compendious Collection of Facts, from the Notes and Experience of Successful Fruit Culturists Arranged for Practical Use in the Orchard and Garden. Cincinnati: 1857. V. 71

HOOPER, G.
Metabolism of Amines in the Brain. London: 1969. V. 68

HOOPER, J.
Introduction to Algology, with a Catalogue of American Algae or Sea Weeds.... Brooklyn: 1850. V. 71; 73

HOOPER, J. T.
The Art of Primitive Peoples. London: 1953. V. 69

HOOPER, W. EDEN
The Stage in the Year 1900. London: 1901. V. 71

HOOPER, WILLIAM
Rational Recreations, in Which the Principles of Numbers and Natural Philosophy are Clearly and Copiously Elucidated.... London: 1774. V. 70
Rational Recreations; In Which the Principles of Numbers and Natural Philosophy are Clearly and Copiously Elucidated.... 1782-1783. V. 71

HOOPES, D. F.
The American Impressionists. New York: 1972. V. 72
American Watercolor Painting. New York: 1977. V. 72

HOOPINGTON, AMBROSE
A Letter to a Young Lady on the Occasion of Her Approaching Marriage. London: 1934. V. 70

HOOTOON, E. A.
The Indians of Pecos, a Study of Their Skeletal Remains. 1930. V. 69

HOOVER, F. LOUIS
Young Printers II. Worcester: 1968. V. 71

HOOVER, H. A.
Early Days in the Mogollons. El Paso: 1958. V. 73

HOOVER, HERBERT
An American Epic. Chicago: 1960. V. 68
American Individualism. Garden City: 1922. V. 72
Georgius Agricola: De Re Metallica. New York: 1950. V. 70
Memoirs: 1929-1941 the Great Depression. New York: 1952. V. 68
The Memoirs of Herbert Hoover. New York: 1952. V. 70; 71
The New Day. Campaign Speeches of Herbert Hoover 1928. Stanford: 1929. V. 71
On Growing Up: His Letters From and To American Children. New York: 1962. V. 68
The Ordeal of Woodrow Wilson. New York: 1958. V. 71

HOOVER, J. EDGAR
Persons in Hiding. Boston: 1938. V. 69

HOPALONG Cassidy and Lucky at Copper Gulch.
Garden City: 1950. V. 70

HOPE, ALEXANDER JAMES BERESFORD
Poems.... London: 1841. V. 70

HOPE, ANNE
Tommy, Tinker and Tip-Toes: a Tale of Three Little Kittens. Seven Oaks. V. 72

HOPE, ASCOTT R.
Round the World. London: 1905. V. 71
Tales for Toby. London: 1900. V. 72

HOPE, CAMILLA
Long Shadows. Cleveland: 1929. V. 70

HOPE, J. F.
A History of Hunting in Hampshire. 1950. V. 68

HOPE, JAMES
A Treatise of the Diseases of the Heart and Great Vessels, Comprising a New View of the Physiology of the Heart's Action. London: 1832. V. 71
A Treatise on the Diseases of the Heart and Great Vessels, and on the Affections Which May Be Mistaken for Them.... Philadelphia: 1842. V. 70; 72

HOPE, LAURENCE
The Garden of Kama and Other Love Lyrics from India. London: 1914. V. 69; 71

HOPE, ROBERT CHARLES
A Glossary of Dialectal Place Nomenclature to Which is Applied a List of Family Surnames.... London: 1883. V. 73

HOPE, THOMAS
Costume of the Ancients. London: 1809. V. 73
Household Furniture and Interior Decoration.... London: 1807. V. 68; 70; 72

HOPE, W. H. ST. JOHN
The Abbey of St. Mary in Furness, Lancashire. Kendal: 1902. V. 71
Architectural Description of Kirkstall Abbey. Leeds;: 1907. V. 73

HOPKINS, A. B.
Elizabeth Gaskell, Her Life and Work. 1952. V. 70

HOPKINS, A. B. continued
The Father of the Brontes. Baltimore: 1958. V. 70

HOPKINS, ALBERT A.
The Lure of the Lock. New York: 1928. V. 72
Magic Stage Illusions and Scientific Diversions. London: 1897. V. 71
The Scientific Cyclopedia of Receipts, Notes and Queries. New York: 1892. V. 71

HOPKINS, EVAN
On the Connexion of Geology with Terrestrial Magnetism.... London: 1851. V. 69

HOPKINS, FREDERICK GOWLAND
Chemistry and Life. London: 1933. V. 71

HOPKINS, GARLAND EVANS
The First Battle of Modern Naval History. Richmond: 1943. V. 69; 70

HOPKINS, GERARD MANLEY
Poems of Gerard Manley Hopkins. London: 1918. V. 72; 73
Poems of Gerard Manley Hopkins. London: 1930. V. 72
Selected Poems. London: 1954. V. 68

HOPKINS, HENRY CLAYTON
The Moon Boat and Other Verse. Philadelphia: 1918. V. 69

HOPKINS, KENNETH
Foundlings and Fugitives. Austin: 1961. V. 68
The Girl Who Died. London: 1955. V. 72
Six Sonnets. 1938. V. 72

HOPKINS, LUTHER W.
From Bull Run to Appomattox, a Boy's View. Baltimore: 1911. V. 69; 70

HOPKINS, NEVIL MONROE
The Strange Cases of Mason Brant. Philadelphia: 1916. V. 68

HOPKINS, PAULINE E.
Contending Forces a Romance Illustrative of Negro Life North and South. Boston: 1900. V. 70

HOPKINS, SARAH WINNEMUCCA
Life Among the Piutes: their Wrongs and Claims. Boston: 1883. V. 72; 73

HOPKINS, THOMAS SMITH
Colonial Furniture of West New Jersey. Haddonfield: 1936. V. 69

HOPKINSON, FRANCIS
The Miscellaneous Essays and Occasional Writings of Francis Hopkinson. Philadelphia: 1792. V. 68

HOPKINSON, JOSEPH
The Working Engineer's Practical Guide to the Management of the Steam Engine & Boiler.... London: 1866. V. 71

HOPKINSON, TOM
Down the Long Slide. New York: 1950. V. 69
The Transitory Venus - Nine Stories. London: 1948. V. 71

HOPLEY, C. C.
Snakes. London: 1882. V. 73

HOPPE, A. E.
Picturesque Great Britain. London: 1927. V. 68

HOPPER, DENNIS
Out of the Sixties. Pasadena: 1986. V. 68; 72

HOPPER, NORA
Ballads in Prose. London: 1894. V. 68
Under Quicken Boughs. London: 1896. V. 68

HOPPIN, JAMES M.
Life of Andrew Hull Foote, Rear Admiral, U.S. Navy. New York: 1874. V. 69

HOPPING, FRED
Western Canada: Manitoba, Alberta, Saskatchewan and New Ontario. 1906. V. 73

HOPPUS, E.
Hoppus's Tables for Measuring, or Practical Measuring Made Easy.... London: 1837. V. 71

HOPWOOD, AUBREY
Bluebell and the Sleepy King. London: 1906. V. 69

HORACE CLUB
The Book of the Horace Club 1898-1901. Oxford: 1901. V. 73

HORAE Sarisburienses. Salisbury: 1829. V. 71

HORAN, J. W.
West, Nor' West. A History of Alberta. Edmonton: 1945. V. 73

HORAN, JAMES D.
The Authentic Wild West: The Lawmen. New York: 1980. V. 69
The Great American West: A Pictorial History from Coronado to the Last Frontier. New York: 1959. V. 69
The Life and Art of Charles Schreyvogel. New York: 1969. V. 69; 71
The McKenney-Hall Portrait Gallery of American Indians. New York: 1972. V. 69; 71
Timothy O'Sullivan, America's Forgotten Photographer. New York: 1966. V. 71

HORATIUS FLACCUS, QUINTUS
Carmina Alcaica. 1903. V. 71
Carmina Sapphica. 1903. V. 71
Horati Carminum Libri IV. London: 1926. V. 70
In Q. Horatii Flacci Venusini Librum de Arte Poetica Aldi Manutii Paulli F. Aldi N. Commentarius Ad Bartholomaeum Capram.... Venetiis: 1576. V. 72
Lyric Works of Horace.. Philadelphia: 1786. V. 73
The Odes. London: 1737. V. 72
The Odes. 1923. V. 68
Odes. 1990. V. 72
Opera. Londini: 1733-1737. V. 70; 72
Opera. Birmingham: 1777. V. 72
Opera. Londini: 1824. V. 68; 72
(Opera) ad lectiones.... Glasguae: 1756. V. 72
Opera Cum Quibusdam Annotationibus. Strassburg: 1498. V. 69
Opera, cum variis Lectionibus, notis variorum.... Londini: 1792-1793. V. 72
A Poetical Translation of the Works of Horace.... London: 1753. V. 72
(...) in Q. Horatium Flaccum (...) Commentarii Copiosissimmi & ab Auctore plus Tertia Parte Post Primam Editionem Amplificati. Francofurti ad Moenum: 1577. V. 72
Q. Horatii Flacci, Quae Supersunt Recensuit et Notulis Instruxit Gilbertus Wakefield. London: 1794. V. 70
Quintus Horatius Flaccus Ad Lectiones Probatiores Diligenter Emendatus.... Glasgow: 1744. V. 70; 72
La Satire. 1992. V. 71
Select Satires of Horace, Translated Into English Verse.... London: 1779. V. 69

HORBLIT, HARRISON D.
The Celebrated Library of Harrison D. Horblit.... London: 1974. V. 70
One Hundred Books Famous in Science. New York: 1964. V. 71; 72

HORE, J. P.
The History of the Royal Buckhounds. 1895. V. 68
Sporting and Rural Records of the Cheveley Estate. 1899. V. 68; 70

HORGAN, PAUL
A Gallery of Clerihews with The Annotated Clerihew. Middletown, CT: 1984. V. 72
Great River: the Rio Grande in North American History. New York: 1954. V. 71
The Habit of Empire. Santa Fe: 1939. V. 68
Lamy of Santa Fe. New York: 1975. V. 69; 70
Mexico Bay. New York: 1982. V. 70
Peter Hurd - a Portrait Sketch from Life. Fort Worth: 1964. V. 68; 73
Peter Hurd: a Portrait Sketch from Life. Austin: 1965. V. 68
Peter Hurd. A Portrait Sketch from Life. 1966. V. 68
The Return of the Weed. Flagstaff: 1980. V. 68
Under the Sangre de Cristo. Santa Fe: 1985. V. 70

HORLER, SIDNEY
The False Purple. 1932. V. 73

HORLER, SYDNEY
High Stakes. Boston: 1935. V. 71
Peril!. New York: 1930. V. 70

HORN, CALVIN
Confederate Victories in the Southwest with: Union Army Operations in the Southwest. Albuquerque: 1961. V. 71

HORN, HOLLOWAY
The Purple Cow. London: 1935. V. 70

HORN, HOSEA B.
Horn's Overland Guide to California. New York: 1852. V. 70

HORN, J.
A History or Description, General and Circumstantial of Burghley House. Shrewsbury: 1797. V. 70; 72

HORN, STANLEY F.
Tennessee's War 1861-1865. Nashville: 1965. V. 69; 70

HORN, W. DONALD
Witnesses For The Defense Of General George Armstrong Custer. Short Hills, NJ: 1981. V. 72

HORNADAY, WILLIAM
Camp Fires on Desert and Lava. New York: 1909. V. 68; 73
Camp-fires in the Canadian Rockies. New York: 1906. V. 70; 73
The Extermination of the American Bison. Washington: 1889. V. 69
Two Years in the Jungle. 1885. V. 73

HORNBEIN, THOMAS F.
Everest: The West Ridge. New York: 1968. V. 69
Everest: The West Ridge. London: 1971. V. 69

HORNBY, NICK
About a Boy. London: 1998. V. 68; 69; 71; 72
Fever Pitch. London: 1992. V. 68; 72; 73
Fever Pitch. London: 1997. V. 68
High Fidelity. London: 1995. V. 71; 72
High Fidelity. New York: 1995. V. 68; 73
How To Be Good. London: 2001. V. 72

HORNE, HERBERT PERCY
Diversi Colores. London: 1891. V. 70

HORNE, R. H.
A New Spirit of the Age. London: 1844. V. 69

HORNE, R. H. continued
Orion: an Epic Poem in Three Books. 1843. V. 73

HORNE, THOMAS H.
An Introduction to the Critical Study and Knowledge of the Holy Scripture. Philadelphia: 1827. V. 72

HORNE, THOMAS HARTWELL
Clarke's Bibliotheca Legum; or Complete Catalogue of the Common and Statute Law Books of the United Kingdom, with an Account of Their Dates and Prices. London: 1810. V. 70
An Introduction to the Study of Bibliography. London: 1814. V. 68
The Lakes of Lancashire, Westmorland and Cumberland. London: 1816. V. 71

HORNE, W. O.
Work and Sport in the Old I.C.S. 1928. V. 70; 72

HORNER, GEORGE R. B.
Medical Topography of Brazil and Uruguay.... Philadelphia: 1845. V. 70; 71

HORNER, R. A.
Sea Ice Biota. Boca Raton: 1985. V. 72

HORNOT, ANTOINE
Anecdotes Americaines, ou Histoire Abrege des Principaux Evenments Arrives dans le Nouveau Monde.... Paris: 1776. V. 73

HORNSBY, WENDY
Half a Mind. 1990. V. 70

HORNUNG, CLARENCE P.
Treasury of American Design. New York: 1976. V. 73

HORNUNG, E. W.
The Crime Doctor. London: 1914. V. 70
Dead Men Tell No Tales. New York: 1899. V. 69
Mr. Justice Raffles. London: 1909. V. 70
Mrs. Raffles. New York: 1905. V. 69
Raffles. New York: 1901. V. 68

HORODISCH, ABRAHAM
Pablo Picasso als Buchkunstle. Frankfurt am Main: 1957. V. 69

HOROVITZ, FRANCES
Water Over Stone. 1980. V. 70

HORRAX, GILBERT
Neurosurgery - an Historical Sketch. Springfield: 1952. V. 68; 70; 72

HORREBOW, NIELS
The Natural History of Iceland. London: 1758. V. 71

HORROCKS, S. H.
Reading Public Libraries. Local Collection Catalogue of Books and Maps Relating to Berkshire. Reading: 1958. V. 71

HORSBURGH, BOYD
The Game Birds and Water Fowl of South Africa. 1912. V. 72
The Game Birds and Water Fowl of South Africa. London: 1912. V. 70

THE HORSE *and How to Manage Him: an Indispensable Guide to Breeding, Rearing, Training, Grooming, Harness....* London: 1892?. V. 68

HORSEMAN, GILBERT
Notes and Observations on the Fundamental Laws of England: with Some Account of their Origin and Present Establishment. London: 1753. V. 70

HORSFALL, THOMAS
Notes on the Manor of Well and Snape in the North Riding of the County of York. Leeds: 1912. V. 73

HORSLEY, J. S.
Surgery of the Stomach and Small Intestines. New York: 1926. V. 71

HORSLEY, VICTOR
The Cerebellum: Its Relation to Spatial Orientation and to Locomotion. London: 1905. V. 68
The Function of the so-Called Motor Area of the Brain - the Linacre Lecture 1909. London: 1909. V. 70

HORSLEY, WILLIAM
A Treatise on Maritime Affairs or a Comparison Between the Commerce Naval Power of England and France. London: 1744. V. 69

HORSMANDEN, DANIEL
The New York Conspiracy, or a History of the Negro Plot, with the Journal of the Proceedings Against the Conspirators at New York in the Years 1741-1742. New York: 1810. V. 70; 72

HORST
Salute to the Thirties. New York: 1971. V. 71

HORSTI, GREGOR
Centvria Problematuvm Medicorvm (Greek text). Norigergae: 1636. V. 71

HORTICULTURAL Colour Chart. London: 1949. V. 69

HORTON, ROBERT JOHN WILMOT
Protestant Securities Suggested, in an Appeal to the Clerical Members of the University of Oxford. London: 1828. V. 73
The West India Question Practically Considered. London: 1826. V. 70

HORVATH, STEVEN M.
Environmental Physiology: Aging Heat and Altitude. New York: 1981. V. 68

HORWICH, BERNARD
My First Eighty Years. Chicago: 1939. V. 68

HORWITZ, E. L.
Contemporary American Folk Artists. Philadelphia/New York: 1975. V. 69; 72

HORWOOD, E.
Original Poetry for Little People. 1850. V. 73

HOSACK, DAVID
Hortus Elginensis; or a Catalogue of Plants, Indigenous and Exotic, Cultivated in the Elgin Botanic Garden.... New York: 1811. V. 68
An Inaugural Discourse Delivered at the Opening of Rutgers Medical College in the City of New York on Monday, the 6th Day of November 1826. New York: 1826. V. 70
Lectures on the Theory and Practice of Physic...Delivered in the College of Physicians and Surgeons of the University of the State of New York. Philadelphia: 1838. V. 70; 72
Syllabus of the Course of Lectures, on Botany, Delivered in Columbia College. New York: 1795. V. 71

HOSACK, JOHN
Mary Queen of Scots and Her Accusers Embracing a Narrative of Events from the Death of James V in 1542 until the Death of the Regent Murray in 1570. Edinburgh: 1869. V. 73
The Rise and Growth of the Law of Nations.... London: 1882. V. 71

HOSCH, PAUL
D'r Luschdig Zipiti und sini Scbezel. (The Funny Zipiti and His Companions.). Basel: 1915,. V. 73

HOSE, C.
The Field Book of a Jungle Wallah. 1929. V. 69; 70; 72; 73

HOSEA, LEWIS M.
The Campaign of Selma. Cincinnati: 1883. V. 69; 70

HOSHOUR, SAMUEL KLINEFELTER
Letters to Squire Pedant in the East, by Lorenzo Altisonant.... Indianapolis: 1870. V. 71

HOSKEN, J. D.
Verses, by the Way. London: 1893. V. 69

HOSKIN, MICHAEL A.
William Herschel and the Construction of the Heavens. London: 1963. V. 69

HOSKING, WILLIAM
Some Observations Upon the Recent Addition of a Reading Room to the British Museum.... London: 1858. V. 73
Treatises on Architecture, Building, Masonry, Joinery and Carpentery. Edinburgh: 1846. V. 73

HOSKINS, HALFORD LANCASTER
British Routes to India. New York: 1928. V. 73

HOSKOLD, H. D.
A Practical Treatise on Mining, Land, And Railway Surveying, Engineering &c. London: 1863. V. 71

HOSKYNS, CHANDOS WREN
Agricultural Statistics: a Reprint. London: 1857. V. 70
Talpa; or the Chronicles of a Clay Farm. London: 1857. V. 68

HOSMER, JAMES K.
The Colour Guard. Boston: 1864. V. 70
History of The Expedition of Captains Lewis and Clark. Chicago: 1904. V. 73

HOSPITAL, JANETTE TURNER
The Ivory Swing. Toronto: 1982. V. 69; 72
The Ivory Swing. New York: 1983. V. 68
The Tiger in the Tigerpit. New York: 1983. V. 68

HOSTE, PAUL
Soe-Evolutioner Eller en Orlogsflodes Ordener Og Bevaegelser... Uddragne Af P. Paul Hostes Verk L'Art des Armees Navales.... Copenhagen: 1743. V. 70

HOTCHKIN, S. F.
Anicent and Modern Germantown, Mount Airy and Chestnut Hill. Philadelphia: 1889. V. 69

HOTCHKISS, C. C.
The Red Paper. New York: 1912. V. 68

HOTCHNER, A. E.
Sophia - Living and Loving: Her Own Story. London: 1979. V. 68; 73

HOTMAN, FRANCOIS
Franco-Gallia; or, an Account of the Ancient Free State of France, and Most Other Parts of Europe.... London: 1711. V. 73

HOTSON, LESLIE
Shakespeare Versus Shallow. London: 1931. V. 72

HOTZE, HENRY
Three Months in the Confederate Army.... 1952. V. 69

HOUCK, LOUIS
A History of Missouri - from the Earliest Explorations and Settlements Until the Admission of the State into the Union. Chicago: 1908. V. 70

HOUDIN, MICHAEL GABRIEL
My Last Respects and Farewell, to the Late and Great Hero Geo. Washington.... Albany: 1800. V. 70

HOUDIN, ROBERT
Memoirs of Robert-Houdin, Ambassador, Author and Conjuror. Philadelphia: 1859. V. 73

HOUDIN, ROBERT *continued*
The Sharper Detected and Exposed. London: 1863. V. 69

HOUDINI, HARRY
The Right Way to Do Wrong. New York: 1906. V. 68
The Unmasking of Robert Houdin. New York: 1908. V. 72
The Unmasking of Robert Houdin. London: 1909. V. 70

HOUELLEBECQ, MICHEL
Atomised. London: 2000. V. 70; 71
Whatever. London: 1999. V. 71

HOUFE, SIMON
The Dictionary of British Book Illustrators and Caricaturists 1800- 1914. Woodbridge: 1981. V. 70

HOUGARDY, BEULAH C.
Horizons O'er the Musselshell. 1974. V. 71

HOUGH, EMERSON
North of 36. New York: 1923. V. 70
The Story of Cowboy. New York: 1897. V. 71

HOUGH, JOSEPH H.
Origin of Masonry in the State of New Jersey, and the Entire Proceedings of the Grand Lodge, from Its First Organization. Trenton: 1870. V. 69

HOUGH, S. B.
Sweet Sister Seduced. London: 1968. V. 71

HOUGH, WALTER
Archaeological Field Work in Northeastern Arizona. The Museum Gates Expedition of 1901. V. 73
Archaeological Field Work in Northeastern Arizona. The Museum-Gates Expedetion of 1901. Washington: 1903. V. 70
Cotton Fabrics: a Book of Reference for Those Who Are Engaged in the Cotton Industry.... 1922. V. 71
The Moki Snake Dance. Santa Fe: 1898. V. 69

HOUGHTON, CLAUDE
The Beast. Belfast: 1936. V. 73
A Hair Divides. London: 1930. V. 72
This Was Ivor Trent. London: 1935. V. 72
Three Fantastic Tales. London: 1934. V. 71; 72

HOUGHTON, ELIZA P. DONNER
The Expedition of the Donner Party and Its Tragic Fate. Chicago: 1911. V. 71; 73

HOUGHTON, FREDERICK W.
The Story of the Settle-Carlisle Line. Bradford: 1948. V. 71; 73
The Story of the Settle-Carlisle Line. Huddersfield: 1965. V. 73

HOUGHTON, GEORGE L.
Appealed Cases - a History of Certain Court Corruptions in the U.S. and State Courts of Dakota. Vermillion: 1895. V. 68; 73

HOUGHTON, RICHARD MONCKTON MILNES, 1ST BARON
Memorials of a Tour in Some Parts of Greece.... London: 1834. V. 72
Palm Leaves. London: 1844. V. 70; 72
The Poems of Richard Monckton Milnes. London: 1848. V. 72
Selections from the Poetical Works of.... London: 1863. V. 70

HOUGHTON, SAMUEL
A Trace of Desert Waters: The Great Basin Story. Glendale: 1976. V. 68

HOUGHTON, STANLEY
The Works. London: 1914. V. 71; 73

HOUGHTON, THOMAS
Rara Avis in Terris; or the Compleat Miner in Two Books. (bound with) *The Ancient Laws, Customs and Orders of the Miners in the King's Forrest of Mendipp in the County of Somerset....* London: 1681. V. 73
Royal Institutions: Being Proposals for Articles to Establish and Confirm Laws, Liberties and Customs of Silver and Gold Mines, to all the King's Subjects.... London: 1694. V. 73

HOUGHTON, W.
Country Walks of a Naturalist With His Children. London: 1869. V. 68; 70
Country Walks of a Naturalist with His Children. London: 1870. V. 68; 72
Sea-Side Walks of a Naturalist with His Children. London: 1870. V. 68; 70

HOUGHTON, WILLIAM ROBERT
Two Boys in the Civil War and After. Montgomery: 1912. V. 69; 70

HOUGLAN, WILLARD
Santos - a Primitive American Art. New York: 1946. V. 68

HOULDING, HENRY
Rhymes and Dreams, Legends of Pendle forest and Other Poems. Burnley: 1895. V. 72

HOULGATE, DEKE
Frans Nelson- A Biography. Los Angeles: 1940. V. 72

HOUSE Beautiful. 1963. V. 68

HOUSE, H. D.
Wild Flowers of New York:. Albany: 1918. V. 68

HOUSE, HOMER
Wild Flowers of New York. Albany: 1918. V. 73
Wild Flowers of New York. 1921. V. 69

THE HOUSE in the Wood and Other Old Fairy Stories. London: 1909. V. 72

THE HOUSE of Warne - One Hundred Years of Publishing. 1965. V. 71; 72

THE HOUSE That Jack Built. 1815. V. 73

THE HOUSE that Jack Built. London: 1869. V. 69

THE HOUSE That Jack Built. New York: 1880. V. 73
THE HOUSE That Jack Built. New York: 1891. V. 71

THE HOUSE that Jack Built. London: 1900. V. 70
THE HOUSE that Jack Built. Edinburgh: 1937. V. 69

THE HOUSE: the Journal of Home Arts and Crafts. London: 1902. V. 68

THE HOUSEHOLD Book of Irish Eloquence.... New York: 1870. V. 70

HOUSEHOLD, GEOFFREY
The Brides of Solomon. London: 1958. V. 70; 72
Fellow Passenger. London: 1955. V. 73
Rogue Male. London: 1939. V. 73
A Rough Shoot. London: 1951. V. 73
The Salvation of Pisco Gabar and Other Stories. London: 1938. V. 71; 72
The Salvation of Pisco Gabar and Other Stories. Boston: 1940. V. 70
The Third Hour. London: 1937. V. 73
A Time To Kill. London: 1952. V. 72

HOUSEHOLD Management. London: 1877. V. 68

THE HOUSEHOLD of Bouverie; or the Elixir of Gold. New York: 1860. V. 71

HOUSEHOLDER, R.
Grand Slam of American Wild Sheep. 1974. V. 72

THE HOUSEKEEPER'S Guide to Preserved Meats, Fruits, Vegetables &c. London: 1900. V. 68

HOUSEMAN, CLARENCE
The Were-Wolf. London: 1896. V. 72

HOUSEWRIGHT, DAVID
Penance. Woodstock: 1995. V. 68; 69; 70

HOUSHOLDER, R.
Grand Slam of American Wild Sheep. 1974. V. 69; 70; 73

HOUSMAN, ALFRED EDWARD
The Collected Poems of A. E. Housman. London: 1939. V. 73
The Confines of Criticism. The Cambridge Inaugural 1911. Cambridge: 1969. V. 68
Last Poems. London: 1922. V. 68; 69
The Name and Nature of Poetry. New York: 1933. V. 69
A Shropshire Lad. London: 1896. V. 69; 72; 73
A Shropshire Lad. London: 1908. V. 69
A Shropshire Lad. London: 1940. V. 73

HOUSMAN, CLEMENCE
The Were-Wolf. London: 1896. V. 71

HOUSMAN, JOHN
A Descriptive Tour and Guide to the Lakes, Caves, Mountains and Other Natural Curiosities in Cumberland, Westmoreland, Lancashire.... Carlisle: 1800. V. 71
A Descriptive Tour and Guide to the Lakes, Caves, Mountains and Other Natural Curiosities in Cumberland, Westmoreland, Lancashire.... Carlisle: 1802. V. 71
A Descriptive Tour and Guide to the Lakes, Caves, Mountains and Other Natural Curiosities in Cumberland, Westmoreland, Lancashire.... Carlisle: 1808. V. 71
A Descriptive Tour and Guide to the Lakes, Caves, Mountains and Other Natural Curiosities in Cumberland, Westmoreland, Lancashire.... Carlisle: 1812. V. 71

HOUSMAN, LAURENCE
A.E.H. Some Poems, Some Letters and a Personal Memoir by His Brother. London: 1937. V. 68
All Fellows. Seven Legends of Lower Redemption, with Insets in Verse. London: 1896. V. 68; 70; 71
Arthur Boyd Houghton. London: 1896. V. 70; 71
The Blue Moon. London: 1904. V. 69; 71
Cornered Poets. New York: 1929. V. 70
Cynthia. London: 1947. V. 68
A Farm In Fairyland. London: 1894. V. 70; 71
The Field of Clover. London: 1898. V. 70; 71
Green Arras. London: 1896. V. 69; 70
The House of Joy. London: 1895. V. 70; 71
The Little Land. With Songs from Its Four Rivers. London: 1899. V. 71
Princess Baboura, a Tale from the Arabian Nights. 1925. V. 68
The Seven Goslings. London: 1915. V. 71
Spikenard. A Book of Devotional Love Poems. London: 1898. V. 70
Stories from the Arabian Nights. London: 1907. V. 71
Stories from the Arabian Nights. New York: 1924. V. 73

HOUSTON, A. ROSS
War Paper- Read Before The Commandery Of The State Of Wisconsin, Military Order Of The Loyal Legion Of The United States-Vol I. Milwaukee: 1891. V. 72

HOUSTON, ANDREW JACKSON
Texas Independence. Houston: 1938. V. 69

HOUSTON, ARTHUR
The Matinee Murder, or Who Killed Harrison Henley?. 1933. V. 73

HOUSTON, CHARLES
The Savage Mountain. London: 1955. V. 69

HOUSTON, GEORGE
Israel Vindicated: Being a Refutation of the Calumnies Propagated Respecting the Jewish Nation.... New York: 1820. V. 71

HOUSTON, JAMES
The White Dawn. New York: 1971. V. 68

HOUSTON, MATILDA
Texas and the Gulf of Mexico; or, Yachting in the New World. Philadelphia: 1845. V. 68; 71; 73

HOUSTON, PAM
Cowboys are My Weakness. New York: 1992. V. 68; 69; 70; 71; 72; 73
Cowboys are My Weakness. London: 1993. V. 68; 73
Waltzing the Cat. New York: 1998. V. 72

HOUSTON, SAM
Ever Thine Truly. Austin: 1975. V. 73

HOUTCHENS, CAROLYN WASHBURN
The English Romantic Poets and Essayists - A Review of Research and Criticism. New York: 1957. V. 72

HOUTEN, HENDRIK VAN
Verhandelinge van de Grontregelen der Doorzigkunde of Tekenkonst.... Amsterdam: 1705. V. 69

HOUZE, HERBERT G.
Winchester Repeating Arms Company, Its History and Development from 1865 to 1981. 1994. V. 68

HOVEY, HORACE CARTER
Celebrated American Caverns Especially Mammoth, Wyandot and Luray.... Cincinnati: 1882. V. 70
Mammoth Cave of Kentucky an Illustrated Manual. Louisville: 1904. V. 73

HOW, HENRY
The Mineralogy of Nova Scotia. A Report to the Provincial Government. Halifax: 1869. V. 68

HOW, LOUIS
The Penitentes of San Rafael: a Tale of the San Luis Valley. Indianapolis: 1900. V. 71

HOW to Abolish Slavery in America, and to Prevent a Cottom Famine in England.... London: 1858. V. 71

HOW to Amuse an Evening Party. New York: 1869. V. 71

HOW to Make Dolls' Furniture and Furnish a Doll House. London: 1870. V. 70

HOW to Read Character: a New Illustrated-Hand Book on Phrenology and Physiognomy, for...Examiners with a Descriptive Chart. New York: 1871. V. 68; 71

HOWARD, ARTHUR DAVID
History of the Grand Canyon of the Yellowstone. Baltimore: 1937. V. 73

HOWARD, BLANCHE WILLIS
Aulnay Tower. London: 1887?. V. 68

HOWARD, CLARK
The Arm. Los Angeles: 1967. V. 68

HOWARD, D. J.
Endless Forms, Species and Speciation. New York: 1998. V. 69

HOWARD, ELIZABETH JANE
Something in Disguise. London: 1969. V. 73

HOWARD, F.
Imitative Art, or the Means of Representing the Pictorial Appearances of Objects, as Governed by Aerial and Linear Perspective.... London: 1842. V. 71
The Sketcher's Manual; or the Whole Art of Picture Making Reduced to the Simplest Principles. London: 1841. V. 73

HOWARD, F. E.
English Church Woodwork. London: 1917. V. 69
English Church Woodwork. London: 1927. V. 68

HOWARD, FRED K.
History of the Sun-Maid Raisin Growers. Fresno: 1922. V. 73

HOWARD, GEORGE BRONSON
God's Man. Indianapolis: 1915. V. 70

HOWARD, GEORGE W.
The Monumental City, Its Past History and Present Resources. Baltimore: 1873. V. 73

HOWARD, H. ELIOT
The British Warblers, a History with Problems of Their Lives. London: 1907-1915. V. 70; 73

HOWARD, H. H.
A History of New England, Containing Historical and Descriptive Sketches of the Counties, Citites and Principal Towns of the Six England States.... Boston: 1880. V. 70

HOWARD, HAROLD P.
Sacajaewa. Norman: 1971. V. 68

HOWARD, HARTLEY
The Other Side of the Door. London: 1953. V. 73

HOWARD, HELEN A.
Northwest Trail Blazers. Caldwell: 1963. V. 71

HOWARD, HELEN ADDISON
War Chief Joseph. 1958. V. 69

HOWARD, HENRY
The Original Poems of Henry Howard. London: 1929. V. 70; 72

HOWARD, HORTON
A Treatise on the Complaints Peculiar to Females: Embracing a System of Midwifery: the Whole in Conformity with the Improved System of Botanic Medicine. Columbus: 1832. V. 72

HOWARD, IAN P.
Human Visual Orientation. Chichester: 1982. V. 68

HOWARD, JAMES H. W.
Bond and Free; a True Tale of Slave Times. Harrisburg: 1886. V. 69

HOWARD, JAMES K.
Ten Years with the Cowboy Artists of America. Flagstaff: 1976. V. 69; 73

HOWARD, JOHN
An Account of the Principal Lazarettos in Europe.... Warrington: 1789. V. 72
An Account of the Principal Lazarettos in Europe.... London: 1791. V. 68

HOWARD, LAWRENCE C.
Log of Edward Sewall, 1911-1912. Salem: 1958. V. 69

HOWARD, MARIA B.
Hints on the Improvement of Day-Schools. Addressed to School Mistresses and the Friends of General Education. London: 1827. V. 73

HOWARD, MARY M.
Wild Flowers and Their Teachings.... Bath: 1848. V. 69

HOWARD, OLIVER OTIS
Autobiography of...Major Gen. U.S. Army. New York: 1907. V. 69
Famous Indian Chiefs I Have Known. New York: 1908. V. 72
My Life And Experiences Among Our Hostile Indians. Hartford, Conn: 1907. V. 72
Nez Perce Joseph: an Account of His Ancestors...His War, His Pursuit and Capture. Boston;: 1881. V. 69

HOWARD, R. A.
Flora of the Lesser Antilles, Leeward and Windward Islands. Volume III. Monocotyledoneae. Jamaica Plain: 1979. V. 69

HOWARD, RICHARD
Family Values. Poems. New York: 1998. V. 73
Hellenistics. New York: 1984. V. 73
Try These On for Size. East Hampton: 1997. V. 73
Two Poems: Wildflowers, Infirmities. New York: 2001. V. 72

HOWARD, ROBERT
Four New Plays, viz: The Surprisal, The Committee (Comedies), The Indian-Queen, The Vestal-Virgin (Tragedies), as they were Acted by His Majesties Servants at the Theatre-Royal. London: 1665. V. 71
The History of Religion. London: 1695. V. 70

HOWARD, ROBERT E.
The Coming of Conan. New York: 1953. V. 71
Conan the Barbarian. New York: 1954. V. 68; 71; 73
Conan the Conqueror. New York: 1953. V. 71
Singers in the Shadows. 1977. V. 68
Skull-Face Omnibus. London: 1974. V. 68

HOWARD, ROBERT MILTON
Reminiscences. Columbus: 1912. V. 69

HOWARD, SARAH
Pen Pictures of the Plains. Denver: 1902. V. 68; 73

HOWARD, SIDNEY
The Ghost of Yankee Doodle. New York: 1938. V. 70
Paths of Glory. New York: 1935. V. 70

HOWARD, THOMAS
On the Loss of Teeth and Loose Teeth and on the Best Means of Restoring Them. London: 1858. V. 72
On The Loss Of Teeth; And On The Best Means Of Restoring Them. London: 1857. V. 72

HOWARD-BURY, C. K.
Mount Everest. The Reconnaissance, 1921. London: 1922. V. 69; 72

HOWAT, J. H.
The Hudson River and Its Painters. New York: 1972. V. 72

HOWAY, FREDERIC W.
Voyages of the Columbia to the Northwest Coast 1787-1790 and 1790- 1793. Portland: 1990. V. 69

HOWBERT, IRVING
Memories Of A Lifetime In The Pike's Peak Region. New York: 1925. V. 72

HOWBERT, R. A.
Reminiscences of the War. Springfield: 1888. V. 69

HOWDEN, in the Month of April, 1644. Howden: 1834. V. 69

HOWE, BEA
Lady with the Green Fingers - the Life of Jane Loudon. London: 1961. V. 70

HOWE, DONALD W.
Quabbin the Lost Valley. Ware: 1951. V. 71

HOWE, E. W.
Plain People. NY: 1929. V. 72

HOWE, FREDERIC C.
Privilege and Democracy in America. New York: 1910. V. 68

HOWE, HENRY
The Great West. New York & Cincinnati: 1857. V. 68
The Travels and Adventures of Celebrated Travelers in the Principal Countries of the Globe. Cincinnati: 1861. V. 73

HOWE, JOHN
The Christian's Pocket Companion. Enfield: 1826. V. 68

HOWE, JOSEPH
The Heart of Howe. Selections from the Letters and Speeches of Joseph Howe. Toronto: 1939. V. 72

HOWE, JULIA WARD
Later Lyrics. Boston: 1866. V. 68
Masterpieces of Eloquence. New York: 1900. V. 68
Passion-Flowers. Boston: 1854. V. 69
Reminiscences 1819-1899. Boston: 1899. V. 69; 71

HOWE, NELLE ACUFF
My Favorite Recipes. 1951. V. 72; 73

HOWE, OCTAVIUS T.
American Clipper Ships 1833-1858. Salem: 1926-1927. V. 73
Argonauts of '49, History and Adventures of Emigrant Companies from Massachusetts 1849-1850. Cambridge: 1923. V. 68; 73

HOWE, PAUL STRUTEVANT
Mayflower Pilgrim Descendanats in Cape May County, New Jersey...16201920.... Cape May: 1921. V. 69

HOWE, R. H.
The Birds of Rhode Island. 1899. V. 73

HOWE, R. S.
The Great Northern Country: being the Chronicles of the Happy Travellers Club in Their Pilgrimage Across the American Continent as Traversed by the Great Northern Railway Line and Northern Steamship Co. from Buffalo to the Pacific Coast. Buffalo: 1895. V. 69

HOWE, S. FERDINAND
The Commerce of Kansas City in 1886.... Kansas City: 1886. V. 70

HOWE, S. G.
The Reader or Extracts in Prose and Verse from English and American Authors...Part 2. Boston: 1839. V. 73

HOWE, SAMUEL
The Practice and Civil Actions and Proceedings at Law, In Massachusetts. Boston: 1834. V. 69

HOWE, SUSAN
Incloser. An Essay. Santa Fe: 1992. V. 69; 73
The Nonconformist's Memorial. New York: 1992. V. 69; 73

HOWE, W. W.
Kinston, Whitehall and Goldsboro (North Carolina) Expedition December 1862. New York: 1890. V. 69; 70

HOWE, WILLIAM
Narrative of Lieut. Gen. sir William Howe, in a Committee of the House of Commons on the 29th of April, 1779.... London: 1780. V. 71

HOWEGEGO, JAMES
Printed Maps of London, ca. 1553-1850. 1978. V. 73

HOWELL, A. H.
Florida Bird Life. Tallahassee: 1932. V. 68; 73

HOWELL, AGNES ROUS
Fifty Years After: a Tale in Verse. Norwich: 1880. V. 69

HOWELL, ARTHUR R.
Frances Hodgkins - Four Vital Years. London: 1951. V. 69

HOWELL, FRANK
Gifts of the Crow Messengers. Denver: 1984. V. 70; 72; 73

HOWELL, GEORGE
The Conflicts of Capital and Labour Historically and Economically Considered.... London: 1878. V. 71
The Conflicts of Capital and Labour Historically and Economically Considered.... London: 1890. V. 71

HOWELL, GEORGIANA
In Vogue: Sixty Years of International Celebrities and Fashion from British Vogue. New York: 1976. V. 68; 69; 72

HOWELL, JAMES
Cottoni Posthuma: Divers Choice Pieces of that Renowned Antiquary Sir Robert Cotton, Knight and Baronet, Preserved from the Injury of Time. London: 1672. V. 69
(Greek title) a Discourse Concerning the Precedency of Kings: Wherein the Reasons and Arguments of the Three Greatest Monarks of Christendom.... London: 1664. V. 70; 72
Dodona's Grove, or the Vocall Forrest. London: 1640. V. 68; 70; 73
Epistolae Ho-Elianae. London: 1892. V. 68; 70; 71; 72
Epistolae Ho-Elianae or the Familiar Letters. Boston: 1907. V. 71
Instructions and Directions for Forren Travell. 1650. V. 70
A Survay of the Signorie of Venice, Of Her Admired Policy, and Method of Government &c.... London: 1651. V. 70; 72

HOWELL, JOHN W.
Stories for My Children. Washington: 1930. V. 69

HOWELL, WILLIAM
Some Interesting Particulars of the Second Voyage made by the Missionary Ship, the Duff.... Knaresborough: 1809. V. 72

HOWELLS, GEORGE
The Story of Serampore and Its College. Serampore: 1918. V. 68

HOWELLS, MILDRED
A Little Girl Among the Old Masters. Boston: 1884. V. 71

HOWELLS, WILLIAM DEAN
My Mark Twain: Reminiscences and Criticisms. New York: 1910. V. 73
Venetian Life. London: 1891. V. 69

HOWE-NURSE, W.
Berkshire Vale. 1927. V. 69; 70

HOWES, ROYCE
Murder At Maneuvers. Garden City: 1938. V. 72

HOWES, W. J.
The Sporting Chub. 1960. V. 73

HOWGILL, FRANCIS
The Dawnings of the Gospel-Day, and Its Light and Glory Discovered.... London: 1676. V. 68

HOWIE, JOHN
The Scots Worthies. Edinburgh: 1870. V. 71; 72

HOWISON, JOHN
Sketches of Upper Canada, Domestic, Local and Characteristic.... Edinburgh: 1821. V. 72

HOWITT, ANNA MARY
An Art-Student in Munich. London: 1853. V. 73

HOWITT, MARGARET
Twelve Months with Frederika Bremer in Sweden. London: 1866. V. 73

HOWITT, MARY
Birds and Flowers. London: 1871. V. 70
The Cost of Caergwyn. London: 1864. V. 72
The Heir of Wast-Wayland. London: 1860?. V. 68
Hope on, Hope Ever! or, the Boyhood of Felix Law. 1910. V. 73
Hope On, Hope Ever! or, the Boyhood of Felix Law. London: 1910. V. 71
Hope on Hope Ever! or, The Boyhood of Felix Law. Dent: 1988. V. 73
Mary Howitt - an Autobiography; edited by her daughter. London: 1889. V. 71; 72
Pictorial Calendar of the Season exhibiting the pleasures, pursuits, and characteristics of country life for every month in the year. London: 1854. V. 71

HOWITT, SAMUEL
A New Work of Animals. London: 1811. V. 68

HOWITT, WILLIAM
The Rural Life of England. 1838. V. 69
The Rural Life of England. London: 1840. V. 71; 72
Stories of English and Foreign Life. London: 1853. V. 70; 71
Visits to Remarkable Places: Old Halls, Battle Fields and Scenes Illustrative of Striking Passages in English History and Poetry. London: 1840. V. 73
Visits to Remarkable Places: Old Halls, Battle Fields, and scenes illustrative of striking passages in history and poetry . . . London: 1882. V. 71; 73

HOWLAND, ESTHER ALLEN
New England Economical Housekeeper and Family Receipt Book. Montpelier: 1845. V. 70; 73
The New England Economical Housekeeper and Family Receipt Book. New London: 1848. V. 68; 69; 73

HOWLETT, JOHN
An Examination of Dr. Price's Essay on the Population of England and Wales; and the Doctrine of an Increased Population in This Kingdom, Established by Facts. Maidstone: 1781. V. 69

HOWLETT, W. J.
Life of the Right Reverend Joseph P. Machebeuf, D.D. Pueblo: 1908. V. 68

HOWORTH, G.
On the Restoration of Oil Paintings, with a Few Practical Hints to the Owners of Pictures. Boston: 1864. V. 69

HOWORTH, HENRY H.
History of the Mongols, from the 9th to the 19th Century. London: 1876-1880. V. 71

HOWSHIP, JOHN
Practical Observations on the Symptoms, Discrimination and Treatment of Some of the More Important Diseases of the Lower Intestine and Anus.... London: 1821. V. 70; 72

HOWSON, WILLIAM
An Illustrated Guide to the Curiosities of Craven. London: 1850. V. 73

HOYEM, ANDREW
Picture/Poems: an Illustrated Catalogue of Drawings and Related Writings 1961-1974. San Francisco: 1975. V. 70; 72

HOYLE, E.
The History of Barnsley Old Church; its Organ and Bells. Barnsley: 1891. V. 73

HOYLE, EDMOND
The Accurate Gamester's Companion.... London: 1748. V. 69
Hoyle's Games: Containing Laws on Chess, Draughts, Backgammon, Billiards, Cricket, and Games of Cards. London: 1820. V. 73
Hoyle's Games Improved. London: 1775. V. 73
Hoyle's Improved Edition of the Rules for Playing Fashionable Games. Philadelphia: 1838. V. 68

HOYLE, FRED
Ossian's Ride. London: 1959. V. 72

HOYLE, JOHN T.
A Roycroft Anthology. East Aurora: 1917. V. 69

HOYT, EDWIN P.
Paul Robeson: the American Othello. Cleveland and New York: 1967. V. 70

HOYT, HENRY
A Frontier Doctor. Boston;: 1929. V. 69

HOYT, J. K.
Pen and Pencil Pictures on the Delaware, Lackawanna and Western Railroad. New York: 1874. V. 70

HOZIER, H. M.
The Franco-Prussian War: Its Causes, Incidents and Consquences. London: 1871-1872. V. 68

HRDLICKA, ALES
Early Man in South America. Washington: 1912. V. 71
Melanesians and Australians and the Peopling of America. Washington: 1933. V. 71
Physical Anthropology, Its Scope and Aims.... Philadelphia: 1919. V. 68
Physiological and Medical Observations Among the Indians of Southwestern United States and Northern Mexico. Washington: 1908. V. 68; 71
The Skeletal Remains of Early Man. Washington: 1930. V. 68
Tuberculosis Among Certain Tribes of the United States. Washington: 1909. V. 71

HSU, K. J.
The Geology of Switzerland. Princeton: 1995. V. 68

HUARD, C. L.
Livre d'Or de l'Exposition. Paris: 1889. V. 68; 70

HUARTE NAVARRO, JUAN DE DIOS
Examen de Ingenios. The Examination of Mens Wits. London: 1616. V. 70

HUBBARD, ELBERT
The Complete Writings of Elbert Hubbard. East Aurora: 1908. V. 70
The Fra: a Journal of Affirmation. New York: 1908-1915. V. 73
John B. Stetson. East Aurora: 1911. V. 68
The Journal of Koheleth Being a Reprint of Ecclesiastes, with an Essay by Elbert Hubbard. 1896. V. 69
Justinian and Theodora. East Aurora: 1906. V. 73
Little Journeys to the Homes of Eminent Artists. East Aurora: 1902. V. 71
Little Journeys to the Homes of English Authors...Robert Southey. East Aurora: 1900. V. 69
Little Journeys to the Homes of Great Lovers. East Aurora, New York: 1906. V. 71
Little Journeys to the Homes of Great Musicians. New York: 1901. V. 71
The Man of Sorrows. East Aurora: 1906. V. 73
Old John Burroughs. East Aurora: 1901. V. 73
So Here Then are the Preachments Entitled the City of Tagaste and a Dream and a Prophecy. East Aurora: 1900. V. 68
The Titanic. East Aurora: 1923. V. 69

HUBBARD, GURDON SALTONSTALL
Incidents and Events in the Life of Gurdon Saltonstall Hubbard. Chicago: 1888. V. 68

HUBBARD, JEREMIAH
Forty Years Among the Indians. Miami: 1913. V. 68; 73

HUBBARD, JOHN
The Rudiments of Geography.... Barnard: 1814. V. 69; 73

HUBBARD, L. RON
Death's Deputy. Los Angeles: 1948. V. 69; 71; 73
Dianetics. 1950. V. 69
Final Blackout. 1948. V. 69
Final Blackout. Providence: 1948. V. 68; 71
Self Analysis. 1951. V. 69
Self-Analysis in Dianetics. London: 1952. V. 69
Slaves of Sleep. Chicago: 1948. V. 69

HUBBARD, LEONIDAS, MRS.
A Woman's Way Through Unknown Labrador. An Account of .... London: 1908. V. 71

HUBBARD, P. M.
A Thirsty Evil. London: 1974. V. 68

HUBBARD, T.
Tomorrow is a New Day - a Fantasy. London: 1934. V. 69

HUBBLE, EDWIN P.
Photographic Investigations of Faint Nebulae. Chicago: 1920. V. 69

HUBER, PIERRE
The Natural History of Ants. London: 1820. V. 71

HUBER, V. A.
The English Universities from the German...an abridged translation. London: 1843. V. 72

HUBIN, ALLEN J.
The Bibliography of Crime Fiction 1749-1975. San Diego: 1979. V. 70
Crime Fiction 1749-1780: a Comprehensive Bibliography. New York: 1984. V. 70; 72
Crime Fiction 1749-1980: a Comprehensive Bibliography. New York: 1984-1988. V. 70
Crime Fiction II: A Comprehensive Bibliography 1749-1990. New York: 1994. V. 73

HUBL, ARTHUR FREIHERRN VON
Three-Colour Photography. London: 1904. V. 70

HUC, EVARISTE REGIS
Christianity in China, Tartary and Thibet. London: 1857-1858. V. 69
Recollections of a Journey through Tartary, Thibet and China, During the Years 1844, 1845 and 1846. London: 1852. V. 69
Travels in Tartary, Thibet and China During the Years 1844-5-6. London: 1851. V. 73

HUCH, RICARDA
The Deruga Trial. New York: 1929. V. 70

HUCHARD, HENRI
Maladies du Coeur et des Vasseaux. Paris: 1899. V. 72

HUCKABAY, IDA
Ninety-Four Years in Jack County 1854-1948. Austin: 1949. V. 70

HUDDART, JOSEPH
Memoir of the Late Captain Joseph Huddart, F.R.S. London: 1821. V. 68; 71; 72
The Oriental Navigator; or, New Directions for Sailing to and from the East Indies.... Philadelphia: 1801. V. 71; 73

HUDDESFORD, GEORGE
A Proper Reply to a Pamphlet, Entitled, a Defence of the Rector and Fellows of Exeter College &c. Oxford: 1755. V. 68; 72
Salmagundi: a Miscellaneous Combination of Original Poetry.... London: 1791. V. 71
The Wiccamical Chaplet, a Selection of Original Poetry. London: 1804. V. 70

HUDDLE, DAVID
A Dream with No Stamp Roots In It. 1975. V. 70

HUDDLESTON, SISLEY
Back to Montparnasse: Glimpses in Bohemia. Philadelphia: 1931. V. 72

HUDLESTON, C. ROY
An Armorial For Westmorland and Lonsdale. with a Foreword by Roger Fulford. Kendal: 1975. V. 71; 72
Cumberland Families and Heraldry, with a Supplement of an Armorial for Westmorland and Lonsdale. Kendal: 1978. V. 71; 72

HUDSON, CHRISTOPHER
The Killing Fields. London: 1984. V. 69

HUDSON, DAVID
Memoir of Jemima Wilkinson, a Preacheress of the Eighteenth Century.... Bath: 1844. V. 73

HUDSON INDEPENDENT
Reminiscences of Hudson, Ohio for One Hundred Years. Hudson: 1899. V. 73

HUDSON, JOHN
A Complete Guide to the English Lakes. London: 1842. V. 71

HUDSON, NICHOLAS
Samuel Johnson and Eighteenth Century Thought.. Oxford: 1988. V. 69

HUDSON, ROGER
Nelson and Emma. London: 1994. V. 71

HUDSON, S.
Celeste, and Other Sketches. London: 1930. V. 73

HUDSON, WILLIAM
Flora Anglica. 1778. V. 72
Flora Anglica. London: 1778. V. 69
Flora Anglica. 1798. V. 69

HUDSON, WILLIAM HENRY
Adventures Among Birds. London: 1913. V. 68
Birds and Man. London: 1901. V. 69; 72
Birds in London. London: 1898. V. 68
Birds of La Plata. London and Toronto: 1920. V. 70; 73
British Birds.. London: 1895. V. 73
The Collected Works. London: 1923. V. 73
A Crystal Age. London: 1887. V. 68; 71
Dead Man's Plack and an Old Thorn. New York: 1920. V. 72
Famous Missions of California. New York: 1901. V. 71
Far Away and Long Ago. London: 1918. V. 70
Green Mansions. London: 1904. V. 68; 72
Green Mansions. London: 1926. V. 70
Idle Days in Patagonia. London: 1893. V. 69
A Little Boy Lost. London: 1905. V. 69
The Naturalist In La Plata. London: 1892. V. 72; 73

HUDSON, WILLIAM HENRY continued
Nature in Downland. London: 1900. V. 70
El Ombu. London: 1902. V. 69
153 Letters from W. H. Hudson. London: 1923. V. 69; 71
The Purple Land: Being the Narrative of one Richard Lamb's Adventures in the Banda Oriental, in South America, as told by Himself. London: 1904. V. 71
A Shepherd's Life, Impressions of the South Wiltshire Downs. New York: 1910. V. 70

HUDSON'S BAY COMPANY
Andrew Graham's Observations on Hudson's Bay 1767-1791. London: 1969. V. 70
Hudson's Bay Company 1670-1870. Volume I-II. Toronto: 1960. V. 70
The Hudson's Bay Company's First Fur Brigade to Sacramento Valley: Alexander McLeod's 1829 Hunt. Sacramento: 1968. V. 68
Hudson's Bay Miscellany 1670-1870. Winnipeg: 1975. V. 70
Moose Fort Journals 1783-1785. London: 1954. V. 70; 72
The Publications of the Hudson's Bay Record Society Mc Loughlin's Fort Vancouver Letters. Third Series 1844-1846. 1944. V. 68

HUESTON, ETHEL
Ginger and Speed. Indianapolis: 1929. V. 69
Merry O. Indianapolis: 1923. V. 69

HUET, PIERRE
A Philosophical Treatise Concerning Human Understanding. London: 1729. V. 73

HUETSON, ETHEL
Star of the West: the Romance of the Lewis and Clark Expedition. Indianapolis/New York: 1935. V. 73

HUFELAND, GUILLAUME
L'Art de Prolonger la Vie Humaine. Lausanne, Hignou, and Paris: 1799. V. 71

HUFFARD, GRACE THOMPSON
My Poetry Book an Anthology of Modern Verse for Boys and Girls. Philadelphia: 1934. V. 73

HUFFMAN, JAMES
Ups and Downs of a Confederate Soldier. New York: 1940. V. 69; 70

HUGGINS, WILLIAM
The Royal Society or, Science in the State and in the Schools. New York: 1906. V. 71

HUGHEL, AVON CHEW
The Chew Bunch in Browns Park. 1970. V. 68
The Chew Bunch in Browns Park. San Francisco: 1970. V. 73

HUGHES, A. DANIEL
Tombstone Story - the Biography of an Arizona Pioneer. Hicksville: 1979. V. 68; 73

HUGHES, ALTON
Pecos - a History of the Pioneer West. Seagraves: 1978. V. 73

HUGHES, BABETTE
Murder In Church. New York: 1934. V. 72

HUGHES, DICKIE
Pudgy. London: 1909. V. 70

HUGHES, DOROTHY
The Fallen Sparrow. New York: 1942. V. 72
Ride the Pink Horse. New York: 1946. V. 71; 73

HUGHES, EDWARD
North Country Life in the Eighteenth Century. Oxford: 1952. V. 73

HUGHES, G. BERNARD
English, Scottish and Irish Table Glass from the Sixteenth century to 1820. London: 1956. V. 72

HUGHES, J. TREVOR
Pathology of the Spinal Cord. London: 1966. V. 68

HUGHES, JOHN
Itinerary of Provence and the Rhone, Made During the Year 1819. London: 1819. V. 73
Liverpool Banks and Bankers 1760-1837. Liverpool: 1906. V. 71

HUGHES, JOHN ARTHUR
Garden Architecture and Landscape Gardening. London: 1866. V. 70; 72

HUGHES, JOHN T.
Doniphan's Expedition.... Cincinnati: 1848. V. 68; 69
Doniphan's Expedition.... Washington: 1914. V. 71

HUGHES, KATHLEEN
The Church in Early Irish Society. 1966. V. 69

HUGHES, LANGSTON
Ask Your Mama. 12 Moods for Jazz. New York: 1961. V. 69; 71
The Big Sea. New York: 1940. V. 71
The Book of Negro Folklore. New York: 1958. V. 68
Don't You Turn Back. New York: 1969. V. 69
The Dream Keeper and Other Poems. New York: 1937. V. 68
Famous Negro Music Makers. New York: 1955. V. 69; 71
Fields of Wonder. New York: 1947. V. 68; 69; 73
Fine Clothes to the Jew. New York: 1927. V. 71
The First Book of Jazz. Toronto: 1955. V. 68
The Langston Hughes Reader. New York: 1958. V. 68; 69; 73
Mary Had a Little Baby. New York: 1962. V. 70
Montage of a Dream Deferred. New York: 1951. V. 68

A Pictorial History of the Negro in America. New York: 1956. V. 72
Sad Song in de Air. New York: 1934. V. 69
Scottsboro Limited. Four Poems and a Play in Verse. New York: 1932. V. 68
Simple Speaks His Mind. New York: 1950. V. 70; 71
Simple Takes a Wife. New York: 1953. V. 68; 69; 72
The Sweet Flypaper of Life. New York: 1955. V. 70; 71
Tambourines to Glory. New York: 1958. V. 70; 71
The Ways of White Folks. New York: 1934. V. 70

HUGHES, RICHARD
The Fox in the Attic - The Human Predicament - Volume One. London: 1961. V. 71
Gipsy Night and Other Poems. Waltham St. Lawrence: 1922. V. 69; 71
A High Wind in Jamaica. London: 1929. V. 68; 69; 70; 71; 72
Pioneer Years in the Black Hills. Glendale: 1957. V. 69
The Spider's Palace and Other Stories. London: 1931. V. 68; 71; 72
The Wooden Shepherdess. London: 1973. V. 72

HUGHES, ROBERT
Frank Auerbach. London: 1990. V. 70

HUGHES, ROBERT EDGAR
Two Summer Cruises with the Baltic Fleet in 1854-55, Being the Log of the Pet Yacht. London: 1855. V. 72

HUGHES, ROBERT W.
Sound Money: Bimetalism a Necessity of the World. Richmond: 1895. V. 70

HUGHES, RUPERT
Destiny. New York: 1925. V. 70
Fairy Detective. New York: 1919. V. 72
The Golden Ladder. New York: 1924. V. 70
The Last Rose of Summer. New York: 1914. V. 72
Miss 318. New York: 1911. V. 70; 71
The Patent Leather Kid. New York: 1927. V. 70

HUGHES, STELLA
Hashknife Cowboy. Recollections of Mack Hughes. Tucson: 1984. V. 72

HUGHES, SUKEY
Washi: the World of Japanese Paper. Tokyo, New York, & S.F: 1978. V. 70

HUGHES, TED
Animal Poems. Bow, Crediton, Devon: 1967. V. 72
Birthday Letters. London: 1998. V. 68; 69; 71; 72
Cave Birds. London: 1975. V. 69; 72; 73
Cave Birds. London: 1978. V. 71
Chiasmadon. Baltimore: 1977. V. 69; 72; 73
Collected Animal Poems. London: 1995. V. 71
The Coming of the Kings and Other Plays. London: 1970. V. 71
Crow. London: 1970. V. 69; 72
Crow. New York: 1971. V. 71
Crow. London: 1972. V. 71
Crow. London: 1973. V. 69
Earth Dances: Poems. 1994. V. 71
Earth-Moon: Poems. London: 1976. V. 69; 71
The Earth-Owl and Other Moon-People. London: 1963. V. 71; 73
Eclipse: a Poem. Knotting: 1976. V. 71
Ffangs the Vampire Bat and Kiss of Truth. London: 1986. V. 70
Five Autumn Songs for Children's Voices. Crediton, Devon: 1968. V. 70; 71
Fly Inspects. Devon: 1983. V. 69; 72
Four Tales Told by an Idiot. Knotting: 1979. V. 70
Gaudete: Poem. London: 1977. V. 71
Groom's Dream. Northampton: 1957. V. 69; 72
The Hawk in the Rain: Poems. New York: 1957. V. 71
Howls and Whispers. Hadley: 1998. V. 69
The Iron Woman: a Sequel to The Iron Man. London: 1993. V. 70
Meet My Folks. London: 1961. V. 73
Meet My Folks. Indianapolis and New York: 1973. V. 70
Mice Are Funny Little Creatures. Devon: 1983. V. 69; 72
Moortown. London: 1979. V. 68; 70
Moortown. New York: 1980. V. 71
Moortown Elegies. London: 1978. V. 69
New Selected Poems 1957-1994. London: 1995. V. 72
Orts. London: 1978. V. 73
A Primer of Birds. Lurley in Devon: 1981. V. 69; 72
Prometheus On His Crag. 21 Poems. London: 1973. V. 69; 73
Rain-Charm for the Duchy and Other Laureate Poems/The Unicorn. London: 1992. V. 70
Remains of Elmet. London: 1979. V. 72
River. London: 1984. V. 70
River. New York: 1984. V. 71
Roosting Hawk. Northampton: 1959. V. 69; 72
Scapegoats and Rabies - a Poem in Five Parts. London: 1967. V. 68
Seasons Songs: Poems. New York: 1975. V. 71
Selected Poems 1957-1967. New York: 1973. V. 71
Shakespeare's Ovid. London: 1995. V. 69
Shakespeare's Poems. London: 1971. V. 70
A Solstice. Knotting, Bedfordshire: 1978. V. 73
T. S. Eliot: a Tribute. London: 1987. V. 70
Tales from Ovid.... London: 1988. V. 73

HUGHES, TED continued
Under the North Star. New York: 1981. V. 72
Weasels at Work. Devon: 1983. V. 69; 72
What is the Truth?. London: 1984. V. 70; 73
Wodwo. London: 1967. V. 70; 71
Wodwo. New York: 1967. V. 71

HUGHES, THOMAS
David Livingstone - Charles George Gordon. London: 1893. V. 72
G.T.T. Gone to Texas - Letters from Our Boys. London: 1884. V. 72; 73
Memoir of a Brother. London: 1873. V. 68; 72
The Old Church; What Shall We Do with It!. London: 1878. V. 68
Old Traverse des Sioux. 1929. V. 68
The Scouring of the White Horse; of, the Long Vacation Ramble of a London Clerk. London: 1859. V. 71
Tom Brown's School Days. London and Glasgow. V. 69

HUGHES, W. E.
The Journal of a Grandfather. St. Louis: 1912. V. 69

HUGHES, W. J.
Rebellious Ranger. Rip Ford and the Old Southwest. Norman: 1964. V. 70

HUGHES, WILLIAM
The American Physitian; or a Treatise of the Roots, Shrubs, Plants, Fruit, Trees, Herbs &c.... London: 1672. V. 69; 73
A Week's Tramp in Dickens-land. London: 1891. V. 69; 70

HUGHES, WILLIAM EDGAR
The Journal of A Grandfather By H. E. H. Gramp. St. Louis: 1912. V. 71

HUGHES-STANTON, BLAIR
The Wood Engravings of Blair Hughes-Stanton. Pinner: 1991. V. 70

HUGILL, ROBERT
Castles and Peles of Cumberland and Westmorland. Newcastle upon Tyne: 1977. V. 71

HUGMAN, JOHN
Original Poems in the Moral, Heroic, Pathetic and Other Styles. Halesworth: 1835. V. 72

HUGO, HERMANNUS
Pia Desideria Emblematis, Elegiis & Affectibus.... Antwerp: 1628. V. 70

HUGO, RICHARD
Death and the Good Life. New York: 1981. V. 71; 72
What Thou Lovest Well Remains American. New York: 1975. V. 69

HUGO, VICTOR
L'Archipel de La Manche. Paris: 1883. V. 72
The Hunchback of Notre Dame. New York: 1923. V. 69; 70
Les Miserables. Bruxelles: 1862. V. 70
Les Miserables. London: 1884. V. 68
Les Miserables. New York: 1938. V. 68; 69
Notre-Dame de Paris. Paris: 1831. V. 70
Notre-Dame de Paris. Paris: 1930. V. 71
The Novels. Edinburgh: 1903. V. 72
Toilers of the Sea. London: 1877. V. 68
Works. Boston: 1892. V. 68

HUIDEKOPER, A. C.
My Experiences and Investments in the Bad Lands of Dakota and Some of the People I Have Met There. Baltimore: 1947. V. 73

HUIE, WILLIAM BRADFORD
The Execution of Private Slovik. New York and Boston: 1954. V. 71
The Klansman. New York: 1967. V. 68; 71

HUISH, MARCUS B.
British Water-Colour Art in the First Year of the Reign of King Edward the Seventh.... London: 1904. V. 70
The Life and Work of Birket Foster. 1890. V. 73
Samplers and Tapestry Embroideries. London: 1913. V. 68

HUISH, R.
A Treatise on the Nature, Economy and Practical Management of Bees. 1817. V. 69; 73
A Treatise on the Nature, Economy and Practical Management of Bees. London: 1817. V. 68

HUISH, ROBERT
Memoirs of Her Late Majesty Caroline, Queen of Great Britain.... London: 1821. V. 69; 72

HULBERT, ARCHER B.
The Call of the Columbia - Iron Men and Saints Take the Oregon Trail. Denver: 1934. V. 69
Future of Road Making. 1905. V. 68
Marcus Whitman - Crusader. Denver: 1936-1938-. V. 69
The Oregon Crusade - Across a Land to Oregon. Denver: 1935. V. 69
Southwest on the Turquoise Trail - the First Diaries on the Road to Santa Fe. Denver: 1933. V. 68; 73
Where Rolls the Oregon- Prophet and Pessimist Look Northwest. Denver: 1933. V. 71

HULBERT, FOOTNER
Dead Man's Hat. New York: 1932. V. 72

HULBERT, HOMER BEZALEEL
The Passing of Korea. London: 1906. V. 72

HULL, AUGUSTUS LONGSTREET
The Campaigns of the Confederate Army. Atlanta: 1901. V. 69; 70

HULL, E. M.
The Lion Tamer. New York: 1928. V. 71
The Sons of the Sheik. New York: 1925. V. 69; 70

HULL, EDWARD
Deacon's Synchronological Chart Pictorial and Descriptive of Universal History with Maps of the World's Greatest Empires, and a Complete Geological Diagram of the Earth. London: 1900. V. 73

HULL, F. M.
Robber Flies of the World, the Genera of the Family Asilidae. Washington: 1962. V. 72

HULL, HELEN
The Asking Price. New York: 1930. V. 72

HULL, ISAAC
Commodore Hull - Papers of Isaac Hull Commodore United States Navy. Boston: 1929. V. 68

HULL, ROBERT H.
Contemporary Music. London: 1927. V. 69

HULL, SUSAN R.
Boy Soldiers of the Confederacy. New York: 1905. V. 69; 70

HULL, WILLIAM I.
William Penn. NY: 1937. V. 72

HULME, F. EDWARD
Butterflies and Moths of the Country Side. London: 1900. V. 73
Familiar Wild Flowers. London: 1877-1885. V. 73
Familiar Wild Flowers. (Series 1-5). London. V. 68
The Flags of the World: Their History, Blazonry and Associations. London and New York. V. 73

HULME, J. R.
The Scarborough Algae. Scarborough: 1842. V. 69

HULME, KERI
The Bone People. Baton Rouge: 1985. V. 68; 69; 71

HULSE, MICHAEL
The New Poetry. Newcastle upon Tyne: 1993. V. 70

HULSKER, J.
The Complete Van Gogh: Painting, Drawings, Sketches. New York: 1980. V. 69; 72

HULTEN, E.
Flora of Alaska and Yukon. Lund and Leipzig: 1941-1950. V. 71

HULTEN, K. G. PONTUS
The Machine as Seen as the End of the Mechanical Age. New York: 1968. V. 69; 70

HULTON, P.
Luigi Balugani's Drawings of African Plants.... New Haven: 1991. V. 70; 73

THE HUMAN Experience. New York: 1989. V. 68

HUMBER, R. D.
Game Cock and Countryman. 1966. V. 68

HUMBER, WILLIAM
A Comprehensive Treatise on the Water Supply of Cities and Towns. London: 1876. V. 69
A Practical Treatise on Cast and Wrought Iron Bridges and Girders as Applied to Railway Structures and to Buildings Generally.... London: 1857. V. 71
A Record of the Progress of Modern Engineering. London: 1863. V. 68
A Record of the Progress of Modern Engineering. London: 1865. V. 68

HUMBLE, B. H.
The Cuillin of Skye. London: 1952. V. 69; 71
On Scottish Hills. London: 1946. V. 69; 71
Rock Climbs at Arrochar. Edinburgh: 1954. V. 69
Tramping in Skye. Edinburgh: 1933. V. 69; 71
Tramping in Skye. Glasgow: 1947. V. 69

HUMBOLDT, FRIEDRICH HEINRICH ALEXANDER, BARON VON
Cosmos: a Sketch of a Physical Descripton of the Universe.... New York. V. 68
Personal Narrative of Travels to the Equinoctial Regions of America, During the Years 1799-1804. London: 1889-. V. 70
Personal Narrative of Travels to the Equinoctial Regions of the New Continent During the Years 1799-1804. London: 1818-1829. V. 70
Reasearches Concerning the Institutions and Monuments of the Ancient Inhabitants of America.... London: 1814. V. 68; 72
Vues des Cordilleres, et Monumens Des Pueples Indigenes De L'Amerique. Paris: 1810. V. 73

HUME, A.
Some Notices of Metallic Ornaments and Attachments to Leather. Liverpool: 1863. V. 68

HUME, CYRIL
My Sister My Bride. New York: 1932. V. 70

HUME, DAVID
An Abstract of a Treatise on Human Nature 1740 - a Pamphlet Hitherto Unknown. Cambridge: 1938. V. 70
Below the Clock. New York: 1936. V. 71
Bring 'em Back Dead. 1936. V. 73

HUME, DAVID continued
Bring 'Em Back Dead. New York: 1936. V. 71; 72
Dangerous Mr. Dell. 1935. V. 73
Dangerous Mr. Dell. New York: 1935. V. 69
Dialogues Concerning Natural Religion. 1779. V. 72; 73
An Enquiry Concerning the Principles of Morals. London: 1751. V. 70; 72
Essays and Treatises on Several Subjects. London: 1760. V. 73
Essays and Treatises on Several Subjects. Edinburgh: 1817. V. 70
Essays, Moral, Political and Literary. London: 1889. V. 71
Expose Succinct de la Contestation qui s'est Elevee Entre M. Hume et M. Rousseau, avec les Pieces Justificatives. Londres: 1766. V. 70
Four Dissertations. I. The Natural History of Religion. II. Of the Passions. III. Of Tragedy. IV. Of the Standard of Taste. London: 1757. V. 70
The History of England. London: 1754. V. 71
The History of England. London: 1770. V. 68
History of England: The History of England from the Invasion of Julius Caesar to the Abdication of James the Second 1688. Philadelphia: 1865. V. 68
The History of the House and Race of Douglas and Angus. Edinburgh: 1748. V. 73
The History of the Houses of Douglas and Angus. Edinburgh: 1643-1644. V. 71
The Jail Gates Are Open. 1935. V. 73
The Philosophical Works. Boston: 1854. V. 71

HUME, EDGAR ERKSINE
Colonel Theodore O'Hara, Author of te Bivouac of the Dead. Charlottesville: 1936. V. 69; 70

HUME, EVERARD
On the Coagulation by Heat of the Fluid Blood in an Aneurismal Tumor. London: 1826. V. 70; 72

HUME, FERGUS
A Coin of Edward VII. New York: 1903,. V. 69
The Man With a Secret: a Novel. London: 1891. V. 73
Miss Mephistopheles. London: 1891. V. 68
The Mystery of a Hansom Cab. New York: 1889. V. 72
The Sealed Message. New York: 1907. V. 69

HUME, GLADYS GOOCH
Brands of the Southwest- Symbols of Helping Hands At The West Texas Rehabilitation Center A Historical Review. Abilene: 1988. V. 71

HUME, GUSTAVUS
Observations on the Angina Pectoris, Gout and Cow Pox. Dublin: 1804. V. 69

HUME, H. H.
Hollies. New York: 1953. V. 71

HUME, SOPHIA
An Exhortation to the Inhabitants of the Province of South Carolina, to Bring Their Deeds to the Light of Christ.... Philadelphia: 1748?. V. 68; 70; 73

HUMES, THOMAS WILLIAM
The Loyal Mountaineers of Tennessee. Knoxville: 1888. V. 69

THE HUMOUROUS *Adventures of Jump Jim Crow.* Glasgow: 1836. V. 70

THE HUMOURIST: *A Collection of Entertaining Tales....* London: 1819-1820. V. 68

HUMPHREY, E. J., MRS.
Six Years in India; or, Sketches of India and Its People as Seen by a Lady Missionary. New York: 1866. V. 71

HUMPHREY, H. B.
Makers of North American Botany. New York: 1961. V. 72

HUMPHREY, LILLIE M.
Aggie. New York: 1955. V. 72

HUMPHREY, MABEL
The Book of the Child. New York: 1903. V. 71; 72
Children of the Revolution. New York: 1900. V. 73

HUMPHREY, MAUD
Little Grown-Ups. New York: 1897. V. 72
Make Believe Men and Women. New York: 1897. V. 71; 73

HUMPHREY, SETH K.
Following The Prairie Frontier. Minnesota: 1931. V. 72

HUMPHREYS, DAVID
A Poem on Industry, Addressed to the Citizens of the United States of America. Philadelphia: 1794. V. 73
Poems by Colonel David Humphreys, Late Aid-de-Camp to His Excellency General Washington. Philadelphia: 1789. V. 70

HUMPHREYS, HENRY NOEL
Ancient Coins and Medals.... London: 1850. V. 72
British Butterflies and Their Transformation. (with) British Moths and Their Transformations. London: 1841-1857. V. 73
The Butterfly Vivarium; or, Insect Home; Being an Account of a New Method of Observing the Curious Metamorphoses of Some of the Most Beautiful of Our Native Insects. London: 1858. V. 70
The Illuminated Books of the Middle Ages. London: 1989. V. 72
Illuminated Illustrations of Froissart. 1844-1845. V. 71
The Miracles of Our Lord. London: 1848. V. 68
The Origin and Progress of the Art of Writing.... London: 1855. V. 68
Parables of Our Lord. 1847. V. 72
A Record of the Black Prince.... London: 1849. V. 68

River Gardens; Being an Account of the Best Methods of Cultivating Fresh-Water Plants in Aquaria.... London: 1857. V. 68
Ten Centuries of Art. London: 1852. V. 71

HUMPHREYS, JANE
Sleeping Partner. London: 2000. V. 70

HUMPHREYS, JOSEPHINE
Dreams of Sleep. New York: 1984. V. 68; 70
Rich in Love. New York: 1987. V. 68

HUMPHREYS, MILTON W.
A History of the Lynchburg Campaign by Milton W. Humphreys, Member of the King's Artillery, C.S.A. Charlottesville: 1924. V. 69; 70

HUMPHREYS, P. W.
The Practical Book of Garden Architecture. Philadelphia: 1914. V. 71; 73

HUMPHRIES, SYDNEY
Oriental Carpets, Runners and Rugs and some Jacquard Reproductions. London: 1910. V. 72

HUMPTY *Dumpty's Golden ABC.* London: 1850. V. 69

HUNDLEY, NORRIS
Water and the West: The Colorado River Compact and the Politics of Water in the American West. Berkeley Los Angeles London: 1975. V. 68

HUNECK, S.
Identification of Lichen Substances. Berlin: 1996. V. 68

HUNER, J. V.
Crustacean and Mollusk Aquaculture in the United States. New York: 1985. V. 68

HUNGERFORD, EDWARD
The Story of the Baltimore and Ohio Railroad 1827-1927. New York: 1928. V. 69; 73

HUNGERFORD, JOHN B.
Hawaiian Railroads. Reseda: 1963. V. 68

HUNGERFORD, MARGARET WOLFE
Beauty's Daughters. London: 1886. V. 68
Faith and Unfaith. London: 1887. V. 68
Green Pleasure and Grey Grief. London: 1886. V. 68
Lady Branksmere. London: 1887. V. 68
A Lonely Girl. London: 1896?. V. 68
Loys, Lord Berresford and Other Tales. London: 1888. V. 68
A Modern Circe. London: 1892. V. 68
Molly Bawn. London: 1890. V. 68
Portia or By Passions Rocked. London: 1886. V. 68
A Tug of War. London: 1897. V. 68
Under-Currents. London: 1889. V. 68

HUNKINS, RALPH V.
Sod-House Days, Tales Of The Prairies. New York: 1945. V. 72

HUNT *& Co.s Directory & Topography of the Towns of Axbridge, Burnham, Bruton....* 1850. V. 71

HUNT, ALBERT B.
Houseboats and Houseboating. New York: 1905. V. 69

HUNT, ARNOLD
The Book Trade and Its Customers: 1450-1900. Newcastle: 1997. V. 70
The Book Trade and Its Customers 1450-1900. Winchester: 1997. V. 70

HUNT, AURORA
Army Of The Pacific 1860-1866. Glendale: 1951. V. 72
Kirby Benedict, Frontier Federal Judge. 1961. V. 68
Kirby Benedict: Frontier Federal Judge. Glendale: 1961. V. 71
Major General James Henry Carleton, 1814-1873; Western Frontier Dragoon. Glendale, CA: 1958. V. 72

HUNT, BARNARD & CO., LTD.
The Type Book of Hunt, Barnard & Co. Ltd. London: 1950. V. 70

HUNT, BLANCHE SEALE
Stories of Little Brown Koko. Chicago and New York: 1940. V. 69

HUNT, E. HOWARD
Bimini Run. New York: 1949. V. 73

HUNT, ELMER M.
The Gold Rush Diary of Moses Pearson Cooswell of New Hampshire. Concord: 1949. V. 69

HUNT, ELVID
History of Fort Leavenworth 1827-1927. Ft. Leavenworth: 1926. V. 68
History of Fort Leavenworth 1827-1927. Fort Leavenworth: 1937. V. 72

HUNT, F. KNIGHT
The Book of Art: Cartoons, Frescoes, Sculpture and Decorative Art.... London: 1846. V. 69

HUNT, FRAZIER
Cap Mossman: Last of the Great Cowmen. New York: 1951. V. 71; 72; 73
Custer, The Last Of The Cavaliers. New York: 1928. V. 72
I Fought With Custer, The Story Of Sergeant Windolph. New York: 1947. V. 72
The Tragic Days of Billy the Kid. New York: 1956. V. 69; 72; 73

HUNT, G. H.
Outram and Havelock's Persian Campaign.... London: 1858. V. 68; 72

HUNT, HOWARD
East of Farewell. New York: 1942. V. 73
Limit of Darkness. New York: 1944. V. 73

HUNT, JOHN
The Ascent of Everest. London: 1953. V. 70; 72; 73
Irish Medieval Figure Sculpture 1200-1600. 1974. V. 70
The Liberal Verse and Prose from the South. London: 1822-1823. V. 70
Life is Meeting. London: 1978. V. 69
Our Everest Adventure. Leicester: 1954. V. 69
Report of the Proceedings on an Information Filed ex Officio, by His Majesty's Attorney General, Against John Hunt and Leigh Hunt, Proprietors of the Examiner, for Publishing an Article on Military Punishment.... Stamford: 1811. V. 70

HUNT, LEIGH
Captain Sword and Captain Pen: a Poem.... 1835. V. 73
A Copy of Verses Written for the Bellmen. Oxford: 1970. V. 73
The Descent of Liberty, a Mask. 1815. V. 73
The Descent of Liberty, a Mask. 1816. V. 73
The Feast of the Poets, with Note, and Other Pieces in Verse. 1814. V. 73
The Feast of the Poets: with Notes, and Other Pieces in Verse. 1815. V. 73
Foliage; or Poems Original and Translated. 1818. V. 73
Hero and Leander, and Bacchus and Ariadne. 1819. V. 73
Imagination and Fancy; or Selections from the English Poets. New York: 1845. V. 69
Juvenilia; or, a Collection of Poems Written Between the Ages of Twelve and Sixteen. 1801. V. 73
Juvenilia; or a Collection of Poems, Written Between the Ages of Twelve and Sixteen. London: 1802. V. 73
The Liberal. Verse and Prose from the South. 1822-1823. V. 73
Men, Women and Books. London: 1847. V. 71; 72
The Poetical Works. London: 1832. V. 70; 71; 72; 73
Stories from the Italian Poets with Lives of the Writers. London: 1846. V. 70
The Story of Rimini, a Poem. London: 1816. V. 72; 73
The Town: Its Memorable Characters and Events. London: 1848. V. 71; 72

HUNT, LENOIR
Blue Bonnets and Blood- The Romance of Tejas. Houston: 1938. V. 71

HUNT, LILLIAN B.
The Jaunts of Junior. New York: 1911. V. 71

HUNT, M. S.
Nova Scotia's Part in the Great War. Halifax: 1920. V. 72

HUNT, MARY E. QUARRYVILLE
Ct. Diary and Memorandum Book for 1864. Boston: 1864. V. 73

HUNT, P.
Marshall Cavendish Encylopaedia of Gardening. London: 1968-1970. V. 69

HUNT, P. F.
The Country Life Book of Orchids. London: 1978. V. 68; 70; 71; 73

HUNT, ROBERT
Companion to the Official Catalogue. Synopsis of the Contents of the Great Exhibition of 1851. London: 1851. V. 71

HUNT, ROY
The Something Hunt: a Sherlockian Portfolio of 10 Prints. 1967. V. 69

HUNT, T. F.
Designs for Parsonage Houses, Alms Houses, etc., etc.... London: 1841. V. 69; 71

HUNT, THOMAS
The Postscript to Mr. Hunt's Argument, for the Bishop's Right of Judging in Capital Causes in Parliament, Which He Calls, a Letter to a Friend for Vindicating the Clergy and Rectifying Some Mistakes.... London: 1682. V. 70

HUNT, W. H.
Pre-Raphaelitism and the Pre-Raphaelite Brotherhood. New York: 1905. V. 68

HUNT, WILLIAM
Comic Sketches, Drawn on Stone by Thomas Fairland from Original Drawings Exhibitd in the Watercolour Gallery. London: 1844. V. 70

HUNT, WILSON PRICE
The Overland Diary of Wilson Price Hunt. Ashland: 1973. V. 68; 69; 72; 73

HUNTER, ADAM
An Essay on Two Mineral Springs, Recently Discovered at Harrogate, and on the Springs of Thorp-Arch and Ilkley.... Leeds: 1819. V. 71
A Treatise on the Mineral Waters of Harrogate and Its Vicinity. Edinburgh: 1830. V. 73
A Treatise on the Mineral Waters of Harrogate and Its Vicinity. London: 1838. V. 73

HUNTER, ALAN
Fields Of Heather. London: 1981. V. 72
Gabrielle's Way. London: 1981. V. 72

HUNTER, ALEXANDER
Culina Famulatrix Medicinae; or Receipts in Cookery.... York: 1804. V. 72
Johnny Reb and Billy Yank. New York and Washington: 1905. V. 69; 70; 71

HUNTER, ANNE HOME
Poems. London: 1802. V. 69

HUNTER, CYRUS L.
Sketches of Western North Carolina, Historical and Biographical. Raleigh: 1877. V. 73

HUNTER, DARD
Papermaking by Hand in America. Chillicothe: 1950. V. 68; 70; 73
Papermaking by Hand in India. New York: 1939. V. 72
Paper-making in the Classroom. Peoria: 1931. V. 73
Papermaking in Pioneer America. Philadelphia: 1952. V. 70
Papermaking in Southern Siam. Chillicothe: 1936. V. 68
A Papermaking Pilgrimage to Japan, Korea and China. New York: 1936. V. 68; 73
Papermaking: the History and Technique of an Ancient Craft. London: 1947. V. 68; 72
Papermaking through Eighteen Centuries. New York: 1930. V. 69

HUNTER, EVAN
The Blackboard Jungle. New York: 1954. V. 68
Last Summer. Garden City: 1968. V. 68
Lizzie. New York: 1984. V. 72

HUNTER, GEORGE
Reminiscences of an Old Timer. Battle Creek: 1889. V. 71

HUNTER, J. A.
Hunter's Tracks. 1957. V. 70

HUNTER, JOHN
Essays and Observations on Natural History, Anatomy, Physiology, Psychology and Geology.... 1861. V. 69
Observations on Certain Parts of the Animal Oeconomy. London: 1786. V. 69
A Treatise of the Blood Inflamation, and Gun-Shot Wounds. Philadelphia: 1817. V. 68; 72
A Treatise on the Venereal Disease. London: 1788. V. 73

HUNTER, JOHN MARVIN
The Album of Gunfighters. Bandera: 1955. V. 73
The Album of Gunfighters. 1973. V. 70
Pioneer History of Bandera County. Bandera: 1922. V. 70
Trail Drivers of Texas. San Antonio: 1920-1924. V. 72
The Trail Drivers of Texas. Nashville: 1925. V. 68
The Trail Drivers of Texas, 3 Vols. San Antonio: 1924. V. 71

HUNTER, JOSEPH
Hallamshire. The History and Topography of the Parish of Sheffield in the County of York.... London: 1819. V. 71

HUNTER, KRISTIN
Lou in Limelight. New York: 1981. V. 73

HUNTER, LOUIS C.
Steamboats on the Western Rivers - an Economic and Technological History. Cambridge: 1949. V. 73

HUNTER, RICHARD
Silver Bubbles. London: 1908. V. 71

HUNTER, ROBERT
A Texan in the Gold Rush. Bryan: 1982. V. 68

HUNTER, ROBERT E.
Shakespeare and Stratford-upon-Avon, A Chronicle of the Time.... 1864. V. 72

HUNTER, ROBERT HANCOCK
The Narrative of Robert Hancock Hunter.... Austin: 1966. V. 73

HUNTER, STEPHEN
The Day Before Midnight. New York: 1989. V. 68; 71; 72
Dirty White Boys. New York: 1994. V. 70; 72
Hot Springs. New York: 2000. V. 72
The Master Sniper. New York: 1980. V. 68; 69; 70; 71; 72; 73
Point of Impact. New York: 1993. V. 68; 69; 71
The Second Saladin. New York: 1982. V. 68; 69; 71
The Second Saladin. New York: 1997. V. 70
The Spanish Gambit. New York: 1985. V. 68; 69; 71
Time to Hunt. New York: 1998. V. 71

HUNTER, WILLIAM
Anatomia Uteri Humani Gravidi Tabulis Illustrata.... London: 1815. V. 68
Forts on the Pennsylvania Frontier 1753-1758. Harrisburg: 1960. V. 73
Hunter's Lectures of Anatomy. Amsterdam: 1972. V. 68
Scrutiny of Cinema. London: 1932. V. 72

HUNTER, WILLIAM S.
Hunter's Eastern Townships Scenery, Canada East. Montreal: 1860. V. 68

HUNTER, WILLIAM WILSON
The Thackerays in India; and Some Calcutta Graves. London: 1897. V. 73

HUNTERIAN MUSEUM
Descriptive Catalogue of the Pathological Series in the Hunterian Museum.... Edinburgh and London: 1966. V. 68
Descriptive Catalogue of the Pathological Series in the Hunterian Museum.... Edinburgh and London: 1966-1972. V. 68
Descriptive Catalogue of the Physiological Series in the Hunterian Museum of the Royal College of Surgeons of England.... Edinburgh and London: 1970-1971. V. 68
Descriptive Catalogue of the Physiological Series in the Hunterian Museum....Part II. Edinburgh & London: 1971. V. 68

HUNTINGTON, BILL
Both Feet in the Stirrups. Billings: 1959. V. 69
Goodmen and Salty Cusses. Billings: 1952. V. 69

HUNTINGTON, J. C.
The Phur-Pa Tibetan Ritual Daggers. Ascona: 1975. V. 69

HUNTINGTON, WILLIAM
A Valuable and Rare Book Entitled William Huntington Upon Universal Charity. Macon: 1841. V. 68

HUNTLEY, JAMES GORDON
A Summary of Controversies. St. Omer: 1618. V. 68

HUNTON, JOHN
John Hunton's Diary. Volume I-III. Lingle: 1956-1958-. V. 69

HURCOMB, W. E.
Wetherfield Collection of 222 Clocks sold on 1st May, 1928. London: 1929. V. 72

HURD, PETER
The Lithographs. Lubbock: 1968. V. 71
Peter Hurd Sketchbook. Chicago: 1971. V. 71
A Portfolio of Landscapes and Portraits. Albuquerque: 1950. V. 71

HURD, PHILIP
Report of the Case of Adams and Others v. Malkain and Another. Being an Issue Out of Chancery, to try If a London Attorney-at-Law was Liable to the Bankrupt Laws as a Money-Scrivener. London: 1814. V. 70

HURD, RICHARD
Dialogues on the Uses of Foreign Travel.... London: 1764. V. 69
Moral and Political Dialogues; with Letters on Chivalry and Romance. London: 1771. V. 69

HURDIS, JAMES
Adriano; or the First of June, a Poem. 1792. V. 73
The Favorite (sic) Village: a Poem. Bishopstone, Sussex: 1800. V. 73
Poems. 1790. V. 73
Poems. Oxford: 1808. V. 68; 73
Tears of Affliction, a Poem Occasioned by the Death of a Sister Tenderly Beloved. 1794. V. 73
The Village Curate, a Poem. 1788. V. 73
The Village Curate, a Poem. Dublin: 1790. V. 73
The Village Curate, a Poem. Bishopstone, Sussex: 1797. V. 73
The Village Curate, and Other Poems. 1810. V. 73

HURLBUT, ELISHA P.
Essays on Human Rights and Their Political Guaranties. New York: 1845. V. 69

HURLBUTT, FRANK
Bow Porcelain. 1926. V. 73
Bristol Porcelain. London: 1928. V. 72

HURLEY, MICHAEL
Irish Anglicanism 1869-1969. 1970. V. 69

HURLIMAN, BETTINA
Three Centuries of Children's Books in Europe. London: 1967. V. 68

HURRAH for the Bonnet of Blue. Pray Good. Donald of Dundee. The Cypress Wreath. I'd be a Butterfly. Oh Say Not Women's Love is Bought. He's o'er the Hills that I Lo'e Weel. The Captive Manac. London: 1829. V. 68

HURRELL, GEORGE
The Hurrell Style: 50 Years of Photographing Hollywood. New York: 1976. V. 68

HURST & SON
Trade Catalogue of Flower Seeds and Sundries. (1876-7). 1876. V. 68

HURST, ALEX A.
Thomas Somerscales, marine Artist. His Life and Work. Brighton: 1988. V. 72

HURST, CHARLES CHAMBERLAIN
Experiments in Genetics. Cambridge: 1925. V. 69; 72

HURST, FANNIE
Back Street. New York: 1931. V. 71
Humoresque. New York: 1919. V. 70; 71

HURST, JOHN THOMAS
A Hand-Book of Formulae, Tables and Memoranda for Architectural Surveyors and Others Engaged in Building. London: 1871. V. 68

HURSTON, ZORA NEALE
Dust Tracks On a Road. Philadelphia: 1942. V. 70
Go Gator and Muddy the Waters. New York: 1999. V. 72
I Love Myself When I Am Laughing. Old Westbury: 1979. V. 73
Jonah's Gourd Vine. Philadelphia: 1934. V. 70
Moses, Man of the Mountain. Philadelphia: 1939. V. 70; 71
Mules and Men. Philadelphia: 1935. V. 70; 71
Tell My Horse. Philadelphia: 1938. V. 70

HURT, HENRY
Shadrin. New York: 1981. V. 71

HURT, WESLEY R.
Frontier Photographer Stanley J. Marrow's Dakota Years. Vermilion: 1956. V. 72

HURTADO, ALBERTO
Aspectos Fisiologicos y Patologicos de la Vida en la Altura. Lima: 1937. V. 68

HURTLEY, THOMAS
A Concise Account of Some Natural Curiosities, in the Environs of Malham, in Craven, Yorkshire. London: 1786. V. 73

HUSBAND Hunting; or, the Mother and Daughters. London: 1825. V. 69

HUSBAND, JOSEPH
The Story of the Pullman Car. Chicago: 1917. V. 68

HUSEMAN, BEN W.
Wild River, Timeless Canyons. Tucson: 1996. V. 70

HUSENBETH, FREDERICK CHARLES
The History of Sedgley Park School, Staffordshire. London: 1856. V. 70

HUSKISSON, WILLIAM
The Question Concerning the Depreciation of Our Currency Stated and Examined. London: 1810. V. 70; 73
Substance of the Speech of W. Huskisson, Esq. in the House of Commons, in a Committee of the Whole House, Upon the Resolutions Proposed by the Chancellor of the Exchequer Respecting the State of the Finances and the Sinking Fund of Great Britain.... London: 1813. V. 70

HUSON, THOMAS
Round About Helvellyn. London: 1895. V. 71

HUSSEY, A. M.
Illustrations of British Mycology.... London: 1847. V. 68; 71

HUSSEY, CHRISTOPHER
Clarence House. London: 1949. V. 72
English Gardens and Landscapes 1700-1750. New York: 1967. V. 68; 71
The Life of Sir Edwin Lutyens. London: 1953. V. 73
The Picturesque. Studies in a Point of View. 1967. V. 73

HUSSEY, JOHN A.
Champoeg: Place of Transition. Portland: 1967. V. 72; 73
The History of Fort Vancouver and Its Physical Structure. Portland: 1957. V. 68; 73

HUSTON, JOHN
Humphrey Bogart. Los Angeles: 1957. V. 70

HUSTON, MC CREADY
The King of Spain's Daughter. Indianapolis: 1930. V. 71

HUTCHINGS, J. M.
In the Heart of the Sierras. The Yosemite Valley. Oakland: 1886. V. 70

HUTCHINGS, MARGARET
Toys from the Tales of Beatrix Potter. London: 1973. V. 71

HUTCHINS, B. LEIGH
A History of Factory Legislation. 1903. V. 72

HUTCHINSON, A. S. M.
If Winter Comes. New York: 1923. V. 69
This Freedom. Boston: 1922. V. 69
This Freedom. London: 1922. V. 70
The Uncertain Trumpet. Toronto: 1929. V. 69

HUTCHINSON, BENJAMIN
Cases of Tic Douloureux Successfully Treated. London: 1820. V. 72

HUTCHINSON, EDWARD
Girder-Making and the Practice of Bridge Building in Wrought Iron. London: 1879. V. 73

HUTCHINSON, F. E.
Henry Vaughan - a Life and Interpretation. London: 1947. V. 68

HUTCHINSON, GEORGE THOMAS
From the Cape to the Zambesi. London: 1905. V. 68

HUTCHINSON, H. G.
Big Game Shooting. 1905. V. 69; 70; 72; 73
Fishing. 1904. V. 68; 73
Golf. 1892. V. 71
Peter Steele the Cricketer. Bristol: 1895. V. 68
Shooting. Two Volumes. 1903. V. 71

HUTCHINSON, H. N.
Marriage Customs In Many Lands. London: 1897. V. 72

HUTCHINSON, J.
British Wild Flowers. Rutherford: 1972. V. 68
The Families of Flowering Plants.... London: 1926-1934. V. 69
The Families of Flowering Plants.... London: 1934. V. 72
Flora of West Tropical Africa, the British West African Territories, Liberia, the French and Portuguese Territories South of Latitude 18 Degrees No. to Lake Chad...(with) Supplement. London: 1954-. V. 70
The Useful Plants of West Tropical Africa.... London: 1937. V. 70

HUTCHINSON, JOHN A.
Land Titles in Virginia and West Virginia. Cincinnati: 1887. V. 68

HUTCHINSON, JOHN HELY
The Commercial Restraints of Ireland Considered in a Series of Letters to a Noble Lord. Dublin: 1779. V. 73

HUTCHINSON, JONATHAN
The Pedigree of Disease: Being Six Lectures on Temperament, Idiosyncrasy and Diathesis, Delivered in the Theatre of the Royal College of Surgeons in the Session of 1881. London: 1884. V. 72

HUTCHINSON, JULIUS
Memoirs of The Life Of Colonel Hutchinson, Governor of Nottingham Castle and Town, Representative of The Count of Nottingham In The long Parliament, and Of The Town of Nottingham in The First Parliament of Charles II, etc. London: 1808. V. 72

HUTCHINSON, LUCY
Memoirs of the Life of Colonel Hutchinson Governor of Nottingham by His Widow Lucy. London: 1885. V. 68; 72

HUTCHINSON, R. C.
Elephant and Castle. London: 1949. V. 73
The Unforgotten Prisoner. London: 1933. V. 68

HUTCHINSON, ROBERT
A Treatise on the Law of Carriers as Administered in the Courts of the U.S. and England. Chicago: 1891. V. 72

HUTCHINSON, ROD
Carp Now and Then. 1988. V. 73

HUTCHINSON, THOMAS
A Collection of Original Papers Relative to the History of the Colony of Massachusetts Bay. Boston: 1769. V. 73
History of the Colony and Province of Massachusetts Bay. Cambridge: 1936. V. 71

HUTCHINSON, VERONICA
Fireside Poems. New York: 1930. V. 73

HUTCHINSON, W. H.
Another Verdict for Oliver Lee. Clarendon: 1965. V. 68; 73
A Bar Cross Liar. Stillwater: 1959. V. 68
A Bar Cross Man: The Life and Personal Writing of Eugene Manlove Rhodes. Norman: 1956. V. 69; 72; 73
A Note Book Of The Old West. Chicago: 1947. V. 72
Oil, Land and Politics: The California Career of Thomas Robert Bard. Norman: 1965. V. 68
Whiskey Jim and a Kid Named Billie. Clarenden: 1967. V. 68; 72
The World, The Work and the West of W. H. D. Koerner. Norman: 1978. V. 69

HUTCHINSON, W. N.
Dog Breaking. 1865. V. 70; 71

HUTCHINSON, WILLIAM
An Excursion to the Lakes in Westmoreland and Cumberland; with a Tour through Part of the Northern Counties in the Years 1773 and 1774. London: 1776. V. 71

HUTCHISON, JOSEPH CHRISMAN
Contributions to Orthopedic Surgery; Including Observations in the Treatment of Chronic Inflammation of the Hip, Knee and Ankle Joints.... New York: 1880. V. 70

HUTCHISON, W. R.
Tyrone Preceit: a History of the Plantation Settlement of Dungannon and Mountjoint to Modern Times. 1951. V. 70

HUTH, ANGELA
Nowhere Girl. London: 1970. V. 68

HUTH, HENRY
Catalogue of the Famous Library of Printed Books, Illuminated Manuscripts, Autograph Letters and Engravings. London: 1911. V. 70
Catalogue of the Famous Library of Printed Books, Illustrated Manuscripts, Autograph Letters and Engravings.... London: 1911-1922. V. 72; 73

HUTH, JOHANN CHRISTOPH
Kurzer und Deutlicher Unterricht zu Zeichnung und Anglegung der Wohn- und Landwirthschaftsgebaude. Halle: 1787. V. 70

HUTNIK, JOSEPH J.
We Ripened Fast: the Unofficial History of the Seventy-Sixth Infantry Division. Frankfurt: 1948. V. 72

HUTTON, CHARLES
A Complete Treatise on Practical Arithmetic; and Book-Keeping, both by Single and Double Entry. London: 1792. V. 73
A Mathematical and Philosophical Dictionary. 1796-1795. V. 73
A Mathematical and Philosophical Dictionary. London: 1815. V. 68
Miscellanea Mathematica: Consisting of a Large Collection of Curious Mathematical Problems, and Their Solutions. London: 1775. V. 69; 72; 73
Tracts on Mathematical and Philosophical Subjects.... London: 1812. V. 68
A Treatise on Mensuration, Both in Theory and Practice. Newcastle upon Tyne: 1770. V. 70

HUTTON, EDWARD
The Cosmati. London: 1950. V. 72
The Pageant of Venice. London: 1921. V. 72; 73

HUTTON, J. A.
The Life History of the Salmon. Aberdeen: 1924. V. 68
Rod Fishing for Salmon on the Wye. 1920. V. 68; 73
Wye Salmon and Other Fish. 1949. V. 68

HUTTON, JAMES
Dissertations on Different Subjects in Natural Philosophy. Edinburgh: 1792. V. 69
James Hutton in the Field and in the Study. Delmar: 1997. V. 71

HUTTON, JOHN
A Tour to the Caves, in the Environs of Ingleborough and Settle, in the West Riding of Yorkshire. London: 1781. V. 73
A Tour to the Caves, in the Environs of Ingleborough and Settle, in the West Riding of Yorkshire.... London: 1782. V. 69

HUTTON, LLEWELLYN
The Life of William Hutton and the History of the Hutton Family. London: 1875. V. 71

HUTTON, RICHARD
The Arguments of Sir Richard Hutton Knight, One of the Judges of the Common Pleas; and Sir George Croke Knight, One of the Judges of the Kings Bench.... London: 1641. V. 70

HUTTON, S. K.
Among the Eskimos of Labrador. London: 1912. V. 72

HUTTON, STANLEY
Bristol and Its Famous Associations. Bristol: 1907. V. 70

HUTTON, W.
A Trip to Coatham, a Watering Place in the North Extremity of Yorkshire. London: 1810. V. 73

HUTTON, W. R.
Glances At California 1847-1853- Diaries and Letters of William Rich Hutton, Surveyor. Los Angeles: 1942. V. 71

HUTTON, WILLIAM
The Beetham Repository. Kendal: 1906. V. 71
A Brief History of Birmingham. Birmingham: 1805. V. 72
A Description of Blackpool, in Lancashire, Frequented for Sea- Bathing. 1817. V. 71
An History of Birmingham to the End of the Year 1780. Birmingham: 1781. V. 70
The Life of William Hutton...written by himself.... London: 1817. V. 71

HUXHAM, JOHN
An Essay on Fevers.... London: 1750. V. 72
Medical and Chemical Observations Upon Antimony. London: 1756. V. 69

HUXLEY, ALDOUS LEONARD
Adonis and the Alphabet and Other Essays. London: 1956. V. 71
After Many a Summer Dies the Swann. New York & London: 1939. V. 69; 70
Along the Road: Notes and Essays of a Tourist. London: 1925. V. 68; 69
Along the Road: Notes and Essays of a Tourist. New York: 1925. V. 71
Antic Hay. London: 1923. V. 73
Ape and Essence: a Novel. London: 1949. V. 69
Apennine. Gaylordsville: 1930. V. 71
Arabia Felix. 1929. V. 69
Arabia Infelix. New York: 1929. V. 71
Beyond the Mexique Bay. London: 1934. V. 71
Brave New World. Garden City: 1932. V. 70; 71; 72
Brave New World. London: 1932. V. 69; 71
Brave New World Revisited. New York: 1958. V. 70
Brave New World Revisited. London: 1959. V. 69; 73
Brief Candles. London: 1930. V. 69
Brief Candles. New York: 1930. V. 70; 71
The Burning Wheel. Oxford: 1916. V. 70; 73
Chrome Yellow. London: 1921. V. 71
The Cicadas. London: 1931. V. 68; 70
Complete Essays. Chicago: 2000. V. 69
The Crows of Pearlblossom. London: 1967. V. 70
The Defeat of Youth. Oxford: 1918. V. 68; 70; 71
The Devils of Loudon. London: 1952. V. 69
Do What You Will: Essays. London: 1929. V. 68; 69; 70; 71
The Doors of Perception. London: 1954. V. 68; 69
The Doors of Preception. New York: 1954. V. 73
An Encyclopaedia of Pacifism. London: 1937. V. 69
Ends and Means: an Enquiry into the Nature of Ideals and Into the Methods Employed for Their Realization. London: 1937. V. 71
Essays New and Old. London: 1926. V. 71
Essays New and Old. New York: 1927. V. 71
Eyeless in Gaza. London: 1936. V. 69; 70; 71; 72
The Genius and the Goddess. London: 1955. V. 69
Holy Face and Other Essays. London: 1929. V. 68; 69
Island. London: 1962. V. 70; 72
Jesting Pilate: the Diary of a Journey. London: 1926. V. 72
Leda. London: 1920. V. 71
Leda. Garden City: 1929. V. 71
Little Mexican and Other Stories. London: 1924. V. 68; 70; 73
Mortal Coils. London: 1922. V. 69; 71
Music at Night and Other Essays. London: 1931. V. 69; 71; 72; 73
Music at Night and Other Essays. New York: 1931. V. 68; 71
1936...Peace?. 1936. V. 71
The Olive Tree and Other Essays. London: 1936. V. 69
On the Margin. London: 1923. V. 68; 69
100,000 Say No! Aldous Huxley and Dick Sheppard Talk About Pacifisim. 1936. V. 71
Point Counter Point. London: 1928. V. 69; 72; 73
Prisons. 1949. V. 71
Proper Studies. London: 1927. V. 69; 70; 71
Science, Liberty and Peace. London: 1947. V. 69
Selected Poems. Oxford: 1925. V. 68; 70; 71
T. H. Huxley as a Man of Letters. 1932. V. 71
Text and Pretexts. London: 1932. V. 71
Those Barren Leaves. London: 1925. V. 69; 71; 73
Those Barren Leaves. New York: 1925. V. 71
Two or Three Graces and Other Stories. London: 1926. V. 69; 70
Vulgarity in Literature: Digressions from a Theme. London: 1930. V. 68; 69; 70; 71

HUXLEY, ALDOUS LEONARD continued
Words and Their Meanings. Los Angeles: 1940. V. 68; 71
The World of Light. London: 1931. V. 68; 71; 73

HUXLEY, ELSPETH
English Women. London: 1942. V. 72
The Mottled Lizard. London: 1962. V. 69

HUXLEY, JULIAN
A Factor Overlooked by the Philosophes: The Population Explosion. Geneve: 1963. V. 72

HUXLEY, LEONARD
Life and Letters of Sir Joseph Dalton Hooker. London: 1918. V. 69
Life and Letters of Thomas Henry Huxley. London: 1900. V. 69
Life and Letters of Thomas Henry Huxley. New York: 1901. V. 72

HUXLEY, THOMAS HENRY
American Addresses: with a Lecture on the Study of Biology. London: 1877. V. 72
American Addresses, with a Lecture on the Study of Biology. New York: 1877. V. 72
Charles Darwin. Memorial Notices Reprinted from "Nature". London: 1882. V. 73
Darwiniana. New York: 1897. V. 72
Evidence As to Man's Place in Nature. New York: 1863. V. 68
Life and Letters of Thomas Henry Huxley. New York: 1901. V. 73
On a Collection of Fossil Vertebrata from the Jarrow Colliery, County of Kilkenny. Dublin: 1867. V. 68
On Our Knowledge of the Causes of the Phenomena of Organic Nature.... London: 1863. V. 69
Science and Culture and Other Essays. 1881. V. 71
Social Diseases and Worse Remedies. London: 1891. V. 69

HUXLEY, THOMAS LEONARD
Huxley as a Man Of Letters. London: 1932. V. 70

HUYGENS, CHRISTIAN
The Celestial Worlds Discover'd; or, Conjectures Concerning the Inhabitants, Plants and Productions of the Worlds in the Planets.... London: 1698. V. 68
(Cosmotheoros in Greek Text).... Hagae-Comitum: 1698. V. 68; 71

HUYSMANS, JORRIS KARL
Down There (La-Bas). London: 1930. V. 70

HYAMS, E.
Great Botanical Gardens of the World. London: 1969. V. 68
A History of Gardens and Gardening. London: 1971. V. 68; 71
Irish Gardens. New York: 1967. V. 68
Ornamental Shrubs for Temperate Zone Gardens. South Brunswick: 1965. V. 68; 71; 73

HYATT, A.
Genesis of the Arietidae. Cambridge: 1889. V. 68; 71
Genesis of the Arietidae. Washington: 1889. V. 69
The Triassic Cephalopod Genera of America. Washington: 1905. V. 70

HYATT, MARJORIE
Fuel for a Feud. Smiley: 1988. V. 68

HYDE, CHARLES H.
Pioneer Days. The Story of An Adventure and Active Life. New York: 1939. V. 71

HYDE, CHARLES M.
Historical Celebration of the Town of Brimfield, Hampden County, Mass....October 11, 1876. Springfield: 1879. V. 71

HYDE, GEORGE E.
Indians of the Woodlands from Prehistoric Times to 1725. Norman: 1962. V. 71
Life Of George Bent- Written From His Letters. Norman: 1967. V. 72
Rangers and Regulars. Columbus: 1952. V. 68; 72
Red Cloud's Folk. Norman: 1937. V. 72
Red Cloud's Folk. Norman: 1957. V. 69
A Sioux Chronicle. Norman: 1956. V. 69; 71
Spotted Tail's Folk: a History of the Brule Sioux. Norman: 1961. V. 69; 72

HYDE, H. MONTGOMERY
Cases that Changed the Law. 1951. V. 69

HYDE, MARY
The Impossible Friendship, Boswell and Mrs. Thrale.... Cambridge: 1972. V. 69
The Thrales of Streatham Park, Journal of an Eighteenth Century Family. Cambridge: 1978. V. 69

HYDE, PHILIP
Navajo Wildlands As Long as the River Shall Run. San Francisco: 1963. V. 69

HYDE, RALPH
Gilded Scenes and Shining Prospects. Panoramic Views of British Towns 1575-1900. New Haven: 1985. V. 68; 70
Printed Maps of Victorian London, 1851-1900. 1975. V. 73
A Prospect of Britain, the Town Panoramas of Samuel and Nathaniel Buck. 1994. V. 70
Prospect of Britain, the Town Panoramas of Samuel and Nathaniel Buck. London: 1994. V. 68

HYER, HELEN VON KOLNITZ
Santee Songs. Columbia: 1923. V. 68

HYLEN, ARNOLD
Bunker Hill. A Los Angeles Landmark. Los Angeles: 1976. V. 73

HYLL, THOMAS
First Garden Book. Herrin: 1938. V. 69

HYMAN, COLEMAN P.
An Account of the Coins, Coinages, and Currency of Australasia. Sydney: 1893. V. 70

HYMAN, DAVID M.
The Romance of a Mining Venture. Cincinnati: 1981. V. 73

HYMAN, TRINA SHART
Self Portrait: Trina Schart Hyman. Reading: 1981. V. 70

HYMNS for the Camp. Raleigh: 1862. V. 70

HYNDERICK DE THEULEGOET, G.
L'Espece Chevaline a Travers le Monde. Anvers: 1907. V. 73

HYNDMAN, HENRY MAYERS
The Record of an Adventurous Life. London: 1911. V. 71

HYNE, CUTCLIFFE
The Adventures of Captain Kettle. London: 1898. V. 70

I

I Riti Nuziali Degli Antichi romani per le Nozze di S. E. Don Giovanni Lambertini con S.E. Donna Lucrezia Savorgnan. Bologna: 1762. V. 68

I TELL You Now. Lincoln: 1989. V. 72

I W W Songs to Fan the Flames of Discontent. Chicago: 1919. V. 71

IAMS, JACK
Girl Meets Body. New York: 1947. V. 68; 71

IBACH, EARL W.
The Hub of the Tulpehocken. Womelsdorf: 1977. V. 72

IBSEN, HENRIK
Brand: a Dramatic Poem. London: 1894. V. 73
Bygmester Solness. (Master Builder). Copenhagen: 1892. V. 68; 72; 73
The Doll's House. New York: 1889. V. 72
Hedda Gabler. Copenhagen: 1890. V. 68; 70; 72
Hedda Gabler. London: 1891. V. 73
Ibsen's Prose Dramas. London: 1907. V. 73
John Gabriel Borkman. Copenhagen: 1896. V. 68; 72
John Gabriel Borkman. London: 1987. V. 72
The Lady of the Sea. London: 1890. V. 73
Little Eyolf: a Play in Three Acts. London: 1895. V. 72
The Master Builder. London: 1893. V. 73
The Master Builder. Minneapolis: 1893. V. 68
The Master Builder. London: 1903. V. 70
Peer Gynt. Garden City: 1929. V. 73
Three Plays - An Enemy of the People, the Wild Duck and Hedda Gabler. New York: 1964. V. 72
When We Dead Awaken - A Dramatic Epilogue in three acts. London: 1900. V. 72

ICKES, ANNA WILMARTH
Mesa Land. Boston: 1933. V. 69

ICKIS, ALONZO FERDINAND
Bloody Trails Along the Rio Grande: a Day-By-Day Diary of Alonzo Ferdinand Ickis (1836-1917). Denver: 1958. V. 70

ICONES Roxburghianae or Drawings of Indian Plants. Calcutta: 1968-1976. V. 68

IDDESLEIGH, EARL OF
Charms - or An Old World Sensation. London: 1905. V. 72

IDE, JOHN JAY
The Portraits of John Jay (1745-1829). New York: 1938. V. 72

IDE, SIMEON
A Biographical Sketch of the Life of William B. Ide.... Claremont: 1880. V. 70

IDEAS and Beliefs of the Victorians - an Historic Revaluation of the Victorian Age. London: 1949. V. 68

IFETAYO, FEMI FUNMI
We The Black Woman. Detroit: 1971. V. 72

IGNATOW, DAVID
The Gentle Weight Lifter. New York: 1955. V. 70
New and Collected Poems 1970-1985. Middletown: 1986. V. 68

IGNOTUS
The Last Thirty Years in a Mining District or Scotching and the Candle Versus Lamp and Trades-Unions. London: 1867. V. 70

IJZERMAN, R.
Outline of the Geology and Petrology of Surinam (Dutch Guiana). Utrecht. V. 73

IKIKOWITZ, K. G.
Musical and Other Sound Instruments of the South American Indians. Goteborg: 1935. V. 69

ILES, FRANCIS
As for the Woman. New York: 1939. V. 71
Before the Fact. London: 1932. V. 71

I'LL Take My Stand. The South and the Agrarian Traditon. New York and London: 1930. V. 70

ILLINGWORTH, CAYLEY
A Topographical Account of the Parish of Scampton in the County of Lincoln, and of the Roman Antiquities Lately Discovered There; Together with Anecdotes of the Family of Bolles. 1808. V. 70

ILLINGWORTH, JOHN H.
Offshore Ocean Racing, Fast Cruising, Modern Yacht Handling Equipment. Southampton: 1963. V. 69

ILLUSTRATED Doniphan County 1837-1916. Troy: 1916. V. 73

THE ILLUSTRATED Book of Natural History.... Glasgow: 1845. V. 70

ILLUSTRATED Boston, the Metropolis of New England. 1889. New York: 1889. V. 68

ILLUSTRATED Catalogue of The Heraldic Exhibition Burlington House. London: 1896. V. 72

ILLUSTRATED Cincinnati 1909-1910.... Cincinnati: 1910. V. 70

ILLUSTRATED Doniphan County 1837-1916. Troy: 1916. V. 68

THE ILLUSTRATED Engraved Keepsake. London: 1850. V. 70

ILLUSTRATED Exhibitor. London: 1851. V. 72

AN ILLUSTRATED History of New Mexico. Chicago: 1895. V. 69; 70

THE ILLUSTRATED Juvenile Keepsake. London: 1850. V. 72

THE ILLUSTRATED London Spelling Book. London: 1849. V. 72

THE ILLUSTRATED Pear Culturist.... New York and New London: 1857. V. 71

ILLUSTRATED Souvenir Book Showing a Few Pasadena Homes, Schools, Churches etc. with Short Descriptive Data. Pasadena: 1903. V. 68

AN ILLUSTRATED Treatise on the Art of Displaying Pharmaceutical and Allied Goods in Chemist's Shop Windows. London and Melbourne: 1915. V. 70

ILLUSTRATIONS of Northern Antiquities, from the Earlier Teutonic and Scandinavian Romances.... London: 1814. V. 71

ILLUSTRATIONS to the Blue Beryl Treatise of Sangye Gyamtso (1653- 1705).... New York: 1992. V. 70

ILLY, FRANCESO
Book of Coffee. Abbeville: 1989. V. 68

ILTIS, HUGO
Life of Mendel. London: 1932. V. 68

IMAGE DU MONDE
The Mirrour of the World. Kentfield: 1964. V. 72

IMAGES from the Great West. La Canada: 1990. V. 69

IMAGIST Anthology 1930. New York: 1930. V. 68; 71

IMBERT, JEAN
La Practiqve Ivdiciare, Tant Civile Que Criminelle.... Geneva: 1625. V. 72

IMES, BIRNEY
Juke Joint. Jackson: 1990. V. 71; 72

IMISON, JOHN
Elements of Science and Art. London: 1808. V. 70

IMITATIO CHRISTI
De Imitatione Christi. Lugduni: 1658. V. 70
Of the Imitation of Christ. London: 1908. V. 70

IMLACH, JAMES
History of Banff and Familiar Account of Its Inhabitants and Belongings, to Which are Added, Chronicles of the Old Churchyard of Banff. Banff: 1868. V. 70

IMLAY, GILBERT
A Topographical Description of the Western Territory of North America.... London: 1792. V. 68; 69; 73
A Topographical Description of the Western Territory of North America.... London: 1797. V. 68; 73

IMLAY, RICHARD
Imlay's Patent for Improvement in the Mode of Supporting the Bodies of Railroad Cars and Carriages. Philadelphia: 1852. V. 73

IMMELMAN, W. F. E.
Our Green Heritage.... Cape Town: 1973. V. 68

AN IMMORAL Anthology. Mt. Vernon: 1933. V. 68

THE IMMORTAL Mentor; or Man's Unerring Guide to a Healthy, Wealthy and Happy Life. Mill Hill, near Trenton: 1810. V. 71

IMMORTELLES from Charles Dickens. London: 1856. V. 69
IMMORTELLES from Charles Dickens. London: 1858. V. 68

THE IMPRACTICABILITY of a North-west Passsge for Ships, Impartially Considered. London: 1824. V. 68

IMPROVED ORDER OF RED MEN. MANHATTAN TRIBE, NO. 29.
Constitution and By-Laws of.... Frenchtown: 1872. V. 71

IN Acadia. The Acadians in Story and Song. New Orleans: 1893. V. 73

IN Doors and Out. A Book of Pictures and Stories for Little Folk. 1899. V. 69

IN Memoriam: Edward Thomas. London: 1919. V. 70

IN Memoriam: Edwin Grabhorn 1889-1968. San Francisco: 1969. V. 68

IN Memoriam Edwin R. Purple. New York: 1881. V. 69

IN Memoriam Frederick Douglass. Philadelphia: 1897. V. 70; 71

IN Memoriam: Vladimir Nabokov 1899-1977. New York: 1977. V. 70

IN Praise of Wisdom. 1902. V. 73

IN Principio. Hammersmith: 1911. V. 70

IN the Shadow of the Twin Sisters. Lewistown: 1973. V. 68

INAYAT ALLAH
Tales, translated from the Persian of Inatulla of Delhi. London: 1768. V. 73

INCHBALD, MRS.
The British Theatre; or a Collection of Plays Which are Acted at the Theatres Royal Drury Lane, Covent Garden and Haymarket. London: 1808. V. 69

INDAGINE, JOHANNES ROSENBACH
The Book of Palmestry and Physiognomy. London: 1651. V. 69
Chiromantia. 1. Physionomia, ex Aspectu Membrorum Hominis. 2. Periaxiomata de Faciebus Signorum. 3. Canones Astrologici, de Iudiciis Aegritudinum. 4. Astrologia Naturalis. 5. Complexionum Notitia, Iuxta Dominium Planetarum. Paris: 1546. V. 68; 71; 72

INDEPENDENT MAN, PSEUD.
Occasional Letters Upon Taxation: Upon the Means of Raising the Supplies With the Year, to Answer the Expences of a Necessary War.... London: 1780. V. 70

INDESTRUCTIBLE Pleasure Books. With Coloured Pictures. Jenny Wren. Boston. V. 68

INDESTRUCTIBLE Pleasure Books. With Coloured Pictures. The Old Woman and Her Pig. New York. V. 68

INDEX Expurgatorius Librorum Qui Hc Saeculo Prodierunt vel Doctrinae non Sane Erroribus Inspersis.... Strassburg: 1599. V. 72

INDEX Librorum Prohibitorum. Rome: 1758. V. 69; 72

INDEX Librorum Prohibitorum Innocenti XI Pontificio Maximi Jussu Editus. Rome: 1681. V. 68; 73

INDIAN Art in Middle America. Pre-Columbian and Contemporary Arts and Crafts of Mexico, Central America and the Caribbean. Greenwich: 1964. V. 71

INDIAN Art in South America. Greenwich: 1967. V. 71

THE INDIAN As A Soldier At Fort Custer, Montana. El Segundo: 1983. V. 72

INDIAN Hostilities in Oregon and Washington Territories, 34th Congress, 1st Session, Ex Doc 118. Washington, DC: 1856. V. 72

INDIAN Massacre and Tales of The Red Skins. Augusta, ME: 1890. V. 72

INDIANA. LAWS, STATUTES, ETC. - 1828
Laws of the State of Indiana, Passed and Published at the Twelfth Session of the General Assembly. Indianapolis: 1828. V. 73

INDIANA. LAWS, STATUTES, ETC. - 1829
Laws of the State of Indiana, Passed and Published at the Thirteenth Session of the General Assembly. Indianapolis: 1829. V. 73

THE INDICTMENT, Arraignment, Tryal and Judgment at Large of Twenty- Nine Regicides, the Murtherers of His Most Sacred Majesty King Charles the Fifth. London: 1730. V. 70

THE INDUSTRIAL Directory of New Jersey...1915. Camden: 1915. V. 71

INDUSTRIAL Great Britian: a Commercial Review of Leading Firms Selected from Important Towns of England. London: 1890. V. 71

INDUSTRIAL Rivers of the United Kingdom; Namely the Thames, Mersey, Tyne, Tawe, Clyde, Wear, Taff, Avon.... London: 1888. V. 71

INDUSTRIAL WORKERS OF THE WORLD
Proceedings of the First Convention of the Industrial Workers of the World. New York: 1905. V. 71; 72

INDUSTRIES of New Jersey. Part II. Cumberland, Salem, Glouester, Atlantic, Camden and Cape May Counties. New York: 1882. V. 71

INDUSTRIES of New Jersey. Part IV. Middlesex, Somerset and Union Counties. New York: 1882. V. 71

INDUSTRIOUS Boy. New York: 1859-1866. V. 72

INDUSTRY of the Eastern Counties Business Review. London: 1885. V. 71

INFANTE, G. CABRERA
Infante's Inferno. London: 1979. V. 68
Three Trapped Tigers. New York: 1971. V. 69

ING, J.
Johann Gutenberg and His Bible. A Historical Study. New York: 1988. V. 70

INGALLS, RACHEL
Binstead's Safari. London: 1983. V. 71
Theft and the Man who Was Left Behind. Boston: 1970. V. 69; 71

INGE, WILLIAM
Bus Stop. New York: 1955. V. 69; 70
Come Back, Little Sheba. New York: 1950. V. 71
The Dark at the Top of the Stairs. New York: 1958. V. 71
A Loss of Roses. New York: 1960. V. 69
Picnic: A Summer Romance. New York: 1953. V. 70
Summer Brave and Eleven Short Plays. New York: 1962. V. 68; 69; 71

INGERSOLL, CHARLES J.
A Communication on the Improvement of Government. Philadelphia: 1824. V. 68
Inchiquin, the Jesuit's Letters, During a Late Residence in the United States of America.... New York: 1810. V. 71

INGERSOLL, CHESTER
Overland to California in 1847 - Letters Written en Route to California, West from Independence, Missouri to the Editor of the Juliet Signal. Chicago: 1937. V. 70

INGERSOLL, ERNEST
The Canadian Guide-Book. Part II. Western Canada. New York: 1892. V. 73

INGERSOLL, JOSEPH R.
Argument of Joseph R. Ingersoll, Esq. Before the General Assembly of New Jersey, on the Memorial of the Trenton and New Brunswick Turnpike Company, for the Amendment of their Charter, Feburary 19, 1834. Philadelphia: 1834. V. 71

INGERSOLL, LOUISE
Lanier: a Genealogy of the Family Who Game to Virginia and Their French Ancestors in London. Washington: 1970. V. 72

INGERSOLL, LURION DUNHAM
A History of the War Department of the United States. Washington: 1879. V. 70

INGERSOLL, ROBERT G.
Crimes Agains Criminals. East Aurora: 1906. V. 73

INGHAM, ALFRED
Cheshire, Its Traditions & History. Edinburgh: 1920. V. 73

INGHAM, THOMAS G.
Digging Gold Among the Rockies Or Exciting Adventures of Wild Camp Life.... 1882. V. 71

INGLE, DAVID
Analysis of Visual Behaviour. Cambridge: 1982. V. 68

INGLEBY, HELEN
Comparative Anatomy, Pathology and Roentgenology of the Breast. Philadelphia: 1960. V. 68

INGLIS, BRIAN
A History of Medicine. Cleveland: 1965. V. 71

INGLIS, HENRY D.
The Channel Islands: Jersey, Guernsey, Alderney, &c. London: 1834. V. 68; 70
A Journey throughout Ireland, During the Spring, Summer and Autumn of 1834. London: 1834-1835. V. 73
A Personal Narrative of a Journey through Norway, Part of Swden and the Islands and States of Denmark. London: 1873. V. 73
Rambles in the Footsteps of Don Quixote. London: 1837. V. 73
Solitary Walks through many Lands. London: 1828. V. 73
Switzerland, the South of France and the Pyrenees. London: 1837. V. 73
Tales of Ardennes. London: 1825. V. 73

INGLIS, JAMES
Sport and Work on the Nepaul Frontier. 1878. V. 69; 70; 72; 73
Tent Life in Tigerland. 1888. V. 72; 73

INGLIS, RICHMOND, MRS.
Anna and Edgar: or, Love and Ambition. Edinburgh: 1781. V. 69

INGPEN, ABEL
Instructions for Collecting, Rearing, and Preserving British Insects.... London: 1827. V. 68; 70

INGRAHAM, EDWARD D.
A Sketch of Events Which Preceded the Capture of Washington by the British on the Twenty-Fourth of August 1814. Philadelphia: 1849. V. 70

INGRAHAM, FRANC D.
Spina Bifida and Craniu Bifidum. Boston: 1944. V. 68; 71

INGRAHAM, JOSEPH
Joseph Ingraham's Journal of the Brigantine Hope on a Voyage to the Northwest Coast of North America 1790-1792. Barre: 1971. V. 70; 71

INGRAHAM, JOSEPH H.
The South-West. New York: 1835. V. 68; 73

INGRAM, ALLAN
Boswell's Creative Gloom - a Study of Imagery and Melancholy in the Writings of James Boswell. London: 1982. V. 69

INGRAM, JAMES
Memorials of Oxford. Oxford: 1837. V. 73

INGRAM, JOHN H.
Elizabeth Barrett Browning. London: 1888. V. 69

INGRAM, MAURICE
Drop Me a Line, Being Letters Exchanged on Trout and Coarse Fishing. 1964. V. 73

INGRAM, REX
Mars in the House of Death. New York: 1939. V. 71; 73

INGRATITUDE: A Poem. London: 1764. V. 73

INGSTAD, ANNE STINE
The Discovery of a Norse Settlement in America. Oslo: 1977. V. 73

INJURED Innocence; or, Virtue in Distress. London: 1783. V. 69

INMAN, COLIN
The A & C Black Colour Books; A Collector's Guide and Bibliography 1900-1930. London: 1990. V. 70

INMAN, HENRY
The Great Salt Lake Trail. New York: 1898. V. 69

INMAN, WILL
Lament and Psalm. Crescent City, FL: 1960. V. 71
108 Tales of a Po' Buckra form the Lower Cape Fear. New York: 1965. V. 71

INN, H.
Chinese Houses and Gardens. Honolulu: 1940. V. 68; 71; 73
Chinese Houses and Gardens. New York: 1950. V. 68; 71

INNES, J. R. M.
Comparative Neuropathology. New York: 1962. V. 68

INNES, MICHAEL
Appleby Plays Chicken. London: 1956. V. 73
Appleby Talking, Twenty-three Detective Stories. 1954. V. 72
Dead Man's Shoes. New York: 1954. V. 72
Hamlet, Revenge!. New York: 1937. V. 73
The Long Farewell - a detective story. London: 1958. V. 72
Money from Holme. 1964. V. 70
Seven Suspects. New York: 1937. V. 68
The Weight of the Evidence. New York: 1943. V. 71

INNES, THOMAS
The Civil and Ecclesiastical History of Scotland A.D. LXXX-DCCCXVIII. 1853. V. 69

INNIS, BEN
Bloody Knife! Custer's Favorite Scout. Fort Collins: 1972. V. 72

INNIS, HAROLD A.
The Cod Fisheries. New Haven: 1940. V. 68
The Cod Fisheries. Toronto: 1954. V. 73
The Fur Trade of Canada. Toronto: 1928. V. 69
Select Documents in Canadian Economic History 1497-1783 and 1783- 1885. Toronto: 1929-1933. V. 69

THE INNOCENT Epicure, or the Art of Angling. London: 1713. V. 70

INOUE SHINKODO
Hogei Zushiki. 1889. V. 70; 72

AN INQUIRY into the Doctrine of the Presbyterian Church, in the United States of America, Relative to the Proper Subjects of Infant Baptism. Morris Town: 1824. V. 71

THE INSECTS of Australia, a Textbook for Students and Research Workers. 1991. V. 72

INSTRUCTION for Surgeons Under the Commissioners for Conducting His Majesty's Transport Service, for Taking Care of Sick and Wounded Seamen, and for the Care and Custody of Prisoners of War.... London: 1809. V. 71

INSTRUCTIONS for the Use and Management of the New Family Sewing Machine, Which Also Applies to the Medium, Cylinder Arm and Hand Machines. Frankfurt on Main: 1880?. V. 68

INSTRUCTIONS In Household Matters; or the Young Girl's Guide to Domestic Service. London: 1844. V. 73

THE INSTRUCTIVE Alphabet. New York: 1822. V. 71

THE INTELLECTUAL Observer. Review of Natural History, Microscopical Research and Recreative Science. London: 1862-1865. V. 73

INTELLIGENCE Tours through Utah's Geological Wonders. Salt Lake City: 1927. V. 68

INTERCEPTED Correspondence from India: Containing Dispatches from Marquis Wellesley and from the Governor General in Council, to the Secret Committee of the Court of Directors to Majr. Gen. Wellesley &c. London: 1805. V. 70

INTERCONTINENTAL RAILWAY COMMISSION
Report of Surveys and Explorations Made by Corps #1...1891-1893. Washington: 1898. V. 71
Report of the Transactions of the Commission and of the Surveys and Explorations...1891-1898. Washington: 1898. V. 71

INTERNATIONAL BOUNDARY COMMISSION
Joint Report Upon the Survey and Demarcation of the Boundary Between the U.S. and Canada. Washington: 1934. V. 72

INTERNATIONAL BUSINESS MACHINES CORPORATION APPLIED SCIENCE
Proceedings of the Computation Seminar December 1949. New York: 1951. V. 69

THE INTERNATIONAL Competition for a New Administration Building for the Chicago Tribune. 1923. V. 68; 69; 72

INTERNATIONAL CONFERENCE ON PLASMA PHYSICS
Plasma Physics and Controlled Nuclear Fusion Research, Proceedings of the Third Conference. Vienna: 1969. V. 68

INTERNATIONAL EXHIBITION, 1862. LONDON
The Record of the International Exhibition. Glasgow, Edinburgh, & London: 1862. V. 71; 72

INTERNATIONAL HORTICULTURAL CONGRESS
Report of the Thirteenth International Horticultural Congress 1952, London. London: 1953. V. 68

INTERNATIONAL Library of Negro Life and History. New York: 1967. V. 71

INTERNATIONAL NETSUKE COLLECTORS SOCIETY
Journal of... Volume I #1 - Volume 2 #4. V. 73

INTERNATIONAL SOCIETY OF SCULPTORS, PAINTERS AND GRAVERS
Memorial Exhibition of the Works of the Late J. MacNeill Whistler.... London: 1905. V. 69

INTERNATIONAL STEAMSHIP COMPANY
The Sea Coast Resorts of Eastern Maine, New Brunswick, Nova Scotia, Prince Edward Island and Cape Breton. Boston Portland: 1892. V. 73

INTERNATIONAL UNION OF PURE AND APPLIED PHYSICS
Proceedings of the International Conference of Theoretical Physcis, Kyoto and Tokyo, September 1953. Tokyo: 1954. V. 72

LES INTRIGUES Politiques de la France. Cologne: 1688. V. 68

INWOOD, HENRY WILLIAM
The Erechtheion at Athens, Fragments of Athenian Architecture and a Few Remains in Attica, Megara and Epirus.... London: 1827. V. 68; 70; 72

IONESCO, EUGENE
Journeys Among the Dead. New York: 1987. V. 69

IRBY, L. H.
The Ornithology of the Straits of Gibraltar.... 1895. V. 73

IRBY, RICHARD
Historical Sketch of the Nottoway Grays, Afterwards Company G, Eighteenth Virginia Regiment, Army of Northern Virginia. Richmond: 1878. V. 69; 70

IRCASTRENSIS, PSEUD.
Love and Horror: an Imitation of the Present and a Model for All Future Romances. London: 1815. V. 73

IREDALE, TOM
Birds of New Guinea. Melbourne: 1956. V. 70; 73
Birds of Paradise and Bower Birds. 1950. V. 72
Birds of Paradise and Bower Birds. Melbourne: 1950. V. 69; 70; 73

IRELAND, JOHN
Vindiciae Regiae; or a Defence of the Kingly Office. London: 1797. V. 70

IRELAND, M. W.
The Medical Department of the United States Army in the World War. Washington: 1921-1929. V. 72

IRELAND, R. R.
Moss Flora of the Maritime Provinces. Ottawa: 1982. V. 72

IRELAND, SAMUEL
Picturesque Views of the Severn. London: 1824. V. 71
Picturesque Views on the River Medway, from the Nore to the Vicinity of Its Source in Sussex.... London: 1793. V. 70; 72

IRELAND, TOM
Child Labor as a Relic of the Dark Ages. New York: 1928. V. 69; 71

IRELAND, WILLIAM HENRY
Chalcographimania; or, The Portrait-Collector and Printsellers Chronicle with Infatuations of Every Description. London: 1814. V. 71; 72; 73
The Confessions.... London: 1805. V. 70
The Confessions.... London: 1875. V. 70; 72
The Fisher Boy. London: 1808. V. 68; 71
Scribbleomania, or the Printer's Devil's Polychromicon a Sublime Poem. London: 1815. V. 71

IRELAND, WILLIAM W.
The Blot Upon the Brain: Studies in History and Psychology. Edinburgh: 1893. V. 68; 71

IRENAEUS, SAINT
Sancti Irenaei, Episcopi Lugdunensis Libros Quinque Adversus Haereses.... Cambridge: 1857. V. 70

IRISH, WILLIAM
Strangler's Serenade. 1951. V. 69

IRONS, JAMES CAMPBELL
Autobiographical Sketch of James Croll. London: 1896. V. 68; 70

IRONSIDE, H. A.
Commentaries on the Bible. Neptune: 1985. V. 71

IRONSIDE, R.
Pre-Raphaelite Painters. London: 1948. V. 69; 72

IRVIN, ALBERT
Albert Irvin. London: 1994. V. 70

IRVIN Cobb His Book. Friendly Tributes Upon the Occasion of a Dinner Tendered to Irvin Shrewsbury Cobb at the Waldorf Astoria Hotel. New York: 1915. V. 68

IRVINE, A. BARRINGTON
Atlantic City. Its Early and Modern History. Philadelphia: 1868. V. 71

IRVINE, ALEXANDER
The Illustrated Handbook of the British Plants. London: 1858. V. 68
The Man from World's End and Other Stories of Lovers and Fighting Men. London: 1926. V. 71

IRVINE, CHRISTOPHER
Historiae Scoticae Nomenclatura Latino-Vernacula: Multis Flosculis, ex Antiquis Albionorum Monumentis & Lingua Galeciorum Prisca Decerptis.... Edinbruchii: 1682. V. 70

IRVINE, HELEN DOUGLAS
Mirror or a Dead Lady. London: 1940. V. 71

IRVINE, JOHN
Green Altars, Poems. 1951. V. 69

IRVINE, KEITH
The Rise of the Colored Races. New York: 1970. V. 72

IRVINE, WILLIAM FERGUSSON
A Short History of the Township of Rivington in the Country of Lancaster. Edinburgh: 1904. V. 73

IRVING, CHRISTOPHER
A Catechism of Jewish Antiquities.... New York: 1824. V. 69

IRVING, CONSTANCE
A Child's Book Of Hours. London. V. 72

IRVING, HENRY
The Drama. London: 1892. V. 68
The Drama. New York: 1893. V. 70
Mr. Henry Irving and Miss Ellen Terry in America. Chicago: 1884. V. 72
Twelfth Night; or What You Will...as Arranged for the Stage by Henry Irving and Presented at the Lyceum Theatre.... London: 1884. V. 72

IRVING, JOHN
The Cider House Rules. Franklin Center: 1985. V. 68; 69
The Cider House Rules. London: 1985. V. 72
The Cider House Rules. New York: 1985. V. 70; 72
The Fourth Hand. New York: 2001. V. 72; 73
The Hotel New Hampshire. London: 1981. V. 68; 71; 73
The Hotel New Hampshire. New York: 1981. V. 68; 69; 70; 72; 73
The Imaginary Girlfriend. Toronto: 1996. V. 72
My Movie Business. New York: 1999. V. 71
My Movie Business. Toronto: 1999. V. 73
The 158-Pound Marriage. New York: 1974. V. 69; 70; 71; 72; 73
A Prayer for Owen Meany. Franklin Center: 1989. V. 68; 69; 70; 71
A Prayer for Owen Meany. New York: 1989. V. 68; 70; 71; 72
Setting Free the Bears. New York: 1968. V. 69; 70; 72; 73
A Son of the Circus. Franklin Center: 1994. V. 70; 72
A Son of the Circus. New York: 1994. V. 68; 69; 72; 73
Three by Irving. New York: 1980. V. 72
Trying to Save Piggy Sneed. Toronto: 1993. V. 71; 73
Trying to Save Piggy Sneed. New York: 1995. V. 69; 72; 73
Trying to Save Piggy Sneed. New York: 1996. V. 71; 72
The Water-Method Man. New York: 1972. V. 68; 70; 71; 72; 73
A Widow for One Year. London: 1998. V. 68; 72; 73
A Widow for One Year. Media: 1998. V. 69
A Widow for One Year. New York: 1998. V. 70; 71; 72; 73
The World According to Garp. London: 1978. V. 73
The World According to Garp. New York: 1978. V. 68; 69; 70; 71; 72; 73
The World According to Garp. New York: 1983. V. 68

IRVING, JOSEPH
The Book of Dumbartonshire: a History of the County, Brughs, Parishes, and Lands, Memoirs of Familes and Notices of Industries Carried On in the Lennox District. Edinburgh and London: 1879. V. 69

IRVING, PIERRE M.
The Life and Letters of Washington Irving. New York: 1862. V. 72
The Life and Letters of Washington Irving. New York: 1864. V. 73

IRVING, R. L. G.
The Mountain Way. London: 1938. V. 69
The Romance of Mountaineering. London: 1935. V. 69

IRVING, W.
Saxifrages or Rockfoils. London: 1914. V. 68; 71

IRVING, WASHINGTON
An Account of the Funeral Honours Bestowed on the Remains of Capt. Lawrence and Lieut. Ludlow, with the Eulogy Pronounced at Salem, on the Occasion, by Hon. Joseph Story. Boston: 1813. V. 70
The Alhambra. Philadelphia: 1832. V. 68
Astoria; or, Enterprise Beyond the Rocky Mountains. London: 1836. V. 68; 72
A Chronicle of the Conquest of Granada. London: 1855. V. 68
The Crayon Miscellany: a Tour on the Prairies. (and) Abbotsford and Newstead Abbey. (and) Legends of the Conquest of Spain. Philadelphia: 1835. V. 68; 72
A History of New York. London: 1821. V. 70
A History of New York. New York: 1903. V. 71
History of the Conquest of Granada. London: 1850. V. 68

IRVING, WASHINGTON continued
A History of the Life and Voyages of Christopher Columbus,. London: 1828. V. 68
The Journals.... Boston: 1919. V. 71
The Legend of Sleepy Hollow. New York: 1849. V. 71
The Legend of Sleepy Hollow. London: 1928. V. 73
The Legend of Sleepy Hollow. New York: 1931. V. 70
Life of George Washington. New York: 1855-1859. V. 68
Old Christmas. New York: 1908. V. 73
Old Christmas and Bracebridge Hall. London: 1886. V. 73
Old Christmas Sketch Book of.... London: 1876. V. 70
Oliver Goldsmith: a Biography. London: 1865. V. 68
Rip Van Winkle. New York: 1869. V. 73
Rip Van Winkle. East Aurora: 1905. V. 73
Rip Van Winkle. London: 1905. V. 71; 73
Rip Van Winkle. Philadelphia: 1921. V. 68; 70; 71; 72; 73
The Rocky Mountains or Scenes, Incidents and Adventures in the Far West. Philadelphia: 1837. V. 68
Salmagundi. New York: 1835. V. 68
The Sketch Book. London: 1821. V. 70; 71
The Sketch Book. London: 1902. V. 71
The Sketch Book of Geoffrey Crayon. New York: 1819-1820. V. 68
Tales of a Traveller. By Geoffrey Crayon. London: 1829. V. 71
A Tour on the Prairies. Paris: 1835. V. 68
A Tour on the Prairies. Philadelphia: 1835. V. 68
Voyages and Discoveries of the Companions of Columbus. London: 1831. V. 72
Wolpert's Roost and Other Papers. New York: 1855. V. 71
The Works. London: 1866. V. 73
Works. New York: 1895. V. 70

IRWIN, TERESA WILLIAMS
Let the Tail Go with the Hide. El Paso: 1984. V. 69

IRWIN, WALLACE
The Love Sonnets of a Hoodlum. San Francisco: 1902. V. 72

ISAAC, BERT
The Landscape Within. 1992. V. 71

ISAAC, PETER
William Bulmer: the Fine Printer in Context 1757-1830. 1995. V. 71
William Bulmer, the Fine Printer in Context 1757-1850. London: 1993. V. 70

ISAACS, EDITH
Architecture for the New Theatre. New York: 1935. V. 70

ISAACS, JORGE
Maria: a South American Romance. New York: 1890. V. 69

ISABEY, JEAN BAPTISTE
Voyage en Italie en 1822. Paris. V. 69

ISBISTER, ALEXANDER KENNEDY
A Proposal for a New Penal Settlement, in Connexion with the Colonization of the Uninhabited Districts of British North America. London: 1850. V. 70

ISEMONGER, R. M.
Snakes and Snake Catching in Southern Africa. Cape Town: 1955. V. 69

ISHAM, FREDERIC S.
The Strollers. Indianapolis: 1902. V. 69

ISHAM, NORMAN
A History of the Fabric. The Meeting House of the First Baptist Church in Providence. Providence: 1925. V. 68
In Praise of Antiquaries. Boston: 1931. V. 68

ISHERWOOD, CHRISTOPHER
All the Conspirators. London: 1928. V. 68
All the Conspirators. New York: 1958. V. 72
The Berlin Stories. New York: 1945. V. 68; 69; 73
The Berlin Stories. New York: 1954. V. 68
Christopher and His Kind 1929-1939. New York. V. 70
Christopher and His Kind 1929-1939. New York: 1976. V. 69; 73
Exhumations: Stories, Articles, Verses. London: 1966. V. 70
Goodbye to Berlin. London: 1939. V. 73
Goodbye to Berlin. New York: 1939. V. 71
Lions and Shadows. London: 1938. V. 68; 69; 70; 71
Lions and Shadows. Norfolk: 1947. V. 72
A Meeting by the River. New York: 1967. V. 70
The Memorial: Portrait of a Family. London: 1932. V. 70; 72
The Mortmere Stories. London: 1994. V. 70
My Guru and His Disciple. New York: 1980. V. 71
Prison Etiquette. The Convict's Compendium of Useful Information. Bearsville: 1950. V. 68
The Repton Letters. Settrington: 1997. V. 68
A Single Man. London: 1980. V. 70
The World in the Evening. London: 1954. V. 72
The World in the Evening. New York: 1954. V. 70

ISHIGURO, KAZUO
An Artist of the Floating World. London: 1986. V. 68; 69; 70; 71; 72; 73
An Artist of the Floating World. New York: 1986. V. 69
Early Japanese Stories. London: 2000. V. 68
A Pale View of the Hills. London: 1982. V. 68; 70; 73
A Pale View of the Hills. New York: 1982. V. 71; 73
The Remains of the Day. London: 1989. V. 68; 70; 71; 73
The Remains of the Day. New York: 1989. V. 69
The Unconsoled. London: 1995. V. 68; 70; 72; 73
The Unconsoled. New York: 1995. V. 69; 73
The Unconsoled. New York: 1996. V. 70
When We Were Orphans. London: 2000. V. 68; 70

ISHIMOTO, YASUKIRO
Chicago, Chicago. Japan: 1983. V. 68

ISLAND Boy. New York: 1988. V. 69

ISLAND CURIO COMPANY
Aloha from Honolulu. Honolulu: 1910-1915. V. 68

ISSLER, ANNE R.
Stevenson at Silverado. Caldwell: 1939. V. 73

ISTRATI, PANAIT
The Bandits. New York: 1929. V. 69; 71

ISTVANFFI DE CSIK MADEFALVA, GYULA
A Clusius-Codex Mykologiai Meltatasa Adatokkal Clusius.... Budapest: 1900. V. 72

ISUMBRAS
Syr Ysambrace. 1897. V. 73
Syr Ysambrace. Hammersmith: 1897. V. 68

ITHURIEL, PSEUD.
The Trojan Horse; Scottish Versus Classic Music, the Ethical and Aesthetical Aspect of the Question. Edinburgh: 1877. V. 70

ITOH, T.
The Gardens of Japan. Tokyo: 1984. V. 68; 71; 73
Imperial Gardens of Japan. New York and Tokyo: 1970. V. 68; 71; 73

ITTEN, J.
Design and Form: the Basic Course at the Bauhaus. New York: 1964. V. 72

IVANOVA, L. A.
Ethnography and the Art of Oceania. Moscow: 1989. V. 69

IVENS, W. G.
Melanesians of the South East Solomon Islands. London: 1927. V. 69

IVERNOIS, FRANCIS D'
A Cursory View of the Assignats; and Remaining Resources of French Finance (September 6, 1795). London: 1795. V. 70
Effects of the Continental Blockade Upon the Commerce, Finances, Credit and Prosperity of the British Islands.... London: 1810. V. 70

IVES, BURL
Wayfaring Stranger. London: 1952. V. 71

IVES, ELAM
A Manual of Instruction in the Art of Singing. Philadelphia: 1831. V. 70

IVES, JOHN
New England Book of Fruits. Salem: 1847. V. 70
Remarks Upon Garianonum of the Romans: The Site and Remains Fixed and Described. Yarmouth: 1803. V. 70

IVES, SIDNEY
The Parkman Dexter Howe Library. Gainesville: 1983-1995. V. 71
The Trial of Mrs. Leigh Perrot, Wife of James Leigh Perrot, Esq.... 1980. V. 70
The Trial of Mrs. Leigh Perrot, Wife of James Leigh Perrot, Esq.... London: 1980. V. 68

IVY, ROBERT A.
Fay Jones. Washington: 1992. V. 72

IWAMIYA, TAKEJI
Design and Craftsmanship of Japan Stone, Metal, Fibers, and Fabrics. Bamboo. Tokyo: 1963. V. 69
Katachi Japanese Pattern and Design in Wood, Paper and Clay. Tokyo: 1963. V. 69

IZARN, JOSEPH
Manuel du Galvanisme, ou Description et Usage des Divers Appareils Galvaiques Employes Jusqu'a ce Jour, Tant Pour les Recherches Physiques et Chimiques, Que Pour les Applications medicales. Paris: 1804. V. 72

IZLAR, WILLIAM VALMORE
A Sketch of the War Record of the Edisto Rifles 1861-1865. Columbia: 1914. V. 69; 70

IZONS & COMPANY, GENERAL IRON FOUNDERS, BIRMINGHAM
Original Patentees and Manufacturers of the Improved Fine Cast Kitchen and Furniture.... 1810?. V. 71

IZQUIERDO, J. JOAQUIN
Desde un Alto en el Camino. Vision Y Examen Retrospetivos. Mexico City: 1966. V. 68

IZZARD, SEBASTIAN
One Hundred Masterpieces from the Collection of Dr. Walter A. Compton. London: 1992. V. 72

IZZI, EUGENE
Bad Guys. New York: 1988. V. 68; 73
The Booster. New York: 1989. V. 68
Invasions. New York: 1990. V. 73
The Take. New York: 1987. V. 73

IZZO, A.
Frank Lloyd Wright: Three Quarters of a Century of Drawings. London: 1977. V. 68

J

J. BEVAN Braithwaite. A Friend of the Nineteenth Century. London: 1909. V. 71

J., S.
The Shepherd's Kalendar; or, the Citizen's and Country Man's Daily Companion; Treating of Many Things that are Useful and Profitable to Man-Kind. London: 1725?. V. 69

JAASTAD, BEN
Man of the West: Reminiscences of George Washington Oaks 1840-1917. Tucson: 1956. V. 68

JABLONSKI, STANLEY
Illustrated Dictionary of Eponymic Syndromes and Diseases and their Synonyms. Philadelphia: 1969. V. 68

JABOTINSKY, V.
The Jewish War Front. London: 1940. V. 70

JACK and Jill. New York: 1879. V. 71
JACK and Jill and Other Nursery Rhymes. 1900. V. 72
JACK and Jill, and the Old Dame Gill. 1820. V. 68
JACK and the Bean-Stalk. 1920. V. 72
JACK and the Beanstalk. Chicago: 1908. V. 70
JACK and the Beanstalk. London: 1960. V. 73
JACK Dandy's Delight; or the History of Birds and Beasts; in Prose and Verse. 1820. V. 68; 73
JACK Dandy's Delight; or the History of Birds and Beasts, in Prose and Verse. London: 1820. V. 72
JACK Dandy's Delight, or, the History of the Birds and Beasts. York: 1820. V. 71

JACK, DAVID RUSSELL
History of Saint Andrew's Church, Saint John, N.B. St. John: 1913. V. 73

JACK, ELLEN E.
The Fate of a Fairy. Chicago: 1910. V. 72

JACK, FLORENCE B.
The Art of Laundry Work. Edinburgh: 1896. V. 68

JACK Hasty. Greenfield: 1845. V. 73
JACK Jingle, and Sucky Shingle. 1820. V. 73
JACK Jingle and Sucky Shingle. 1825. V. 68; 73
JACK Jingle and Sucky Shingle. 1830. V. 72
JACK Sprat. New York: 1860. V. 73
JACK the Giant Killer. London. V. 73
JACK the Giant Killer. New York: 1916. V. 72

JACK HINTON, COLIN
The Search for the Islands of Solomon 1567-1838. Oxford: 1969. V. 73

THE JACKIE-Jackdaw Book. New York: 1914. V. 71

JACKMAN, JOHN S.
Diary of a Confederate Soldier: John S. Jackman of the Orphan Bridge. Columbia: 1990. V. 69

JACKMAN, JOSEPH
The Sham-Robbery, Committed by Elijah Putnam Goodridge, on His Own Person, in Newbury, Near Essex Bridge, Dec. 19, 1816.... Concord: 1819. V. 68; 71

JACKMAN, W. J.
Flying Machines: Construction and Operation. Chicago: 1910. V. 73

JACKSON, ALFRED
Tints from an Amateur's Palette; or, a Few Stray Lines of Thought. London: 1849. V. 70

JACKSON, ANDREW
The Freedom's Songster.... Syracuse: 1847. V. 69

JACKSON, B. D.
Guide to the Literature of Botany. New York: 1964. V. 68; 71

JACKSON, BASIL
Rage Under the Arctic. New York: 1974. V. 69

JACKSON, CHARLES
The Lost Weekend. New York: 1944. V. 71

JACKSON, CHARLES JAMES
English Goldsmiths and Their Marks. 1921. V. 70
English Goldsmiths and Their Marks. London: 1921. V. 72
An Illustrated History of English Plate, Ecclesiastical and Secular. London: 1911. V. 72
Jackson's Silver & Gold Marks of England, Scotland & Ireland. London: 1989. V. 72

JACKSON, CHARLES ROSS
Quintus Oakes. New York: 1904. V. 71

JACKSON, CHARLES T.
Remarks on the Mineralogy and Geology of Nova Scotia. Cambridge: 1833. V. 72
Report of the Geological and Agricultural Survey of the State of Rhode Island. Providence: 1840. V. 71

JACKSON, CHARLES TENNEY
The Day of Souls. Indianapolis: 1910. V. 71
My Brother's Keeper. Indianapolis: 1910. V. 68

JACKSON, DAVID
David Jackson Scenes from His Life. New York: 1994. V. 73

JACKSON, DONALD
The Expeditions of John Charles Fremont. Urbana: 1970-1984. V. 68
Letters of the Lewis and Clark Expedition with Related Documents 1783-1854. Urbana: 1978. V. 69; 73

JACKSON, EDGAR
Three Rebels Write Home, Including the Letters of Edgar Allan Jackson, James Fenton Bryant, Irvin Cross Wills and Miscellaneous Items. Franklin: 1955. V. 70

JACKSON, ELIZABETH
The Practical Companion to the Work-Table. York: 1845. V. 71

JACKSON, FRED
The Diamond Necklace. New York: 1929. V. 68
The Third Act. New York: 1913. V. 69

JACKSON, FREDERICK GEORGE
The Great Frozen Land. London: 1895. V. 73
A Thousand Days in the Arctic. New York and London: 1899. V. 70; 72; 73

JACKSON, FREDERICK JOHN
The Birds of Kenya Colony and the Uganda Protectorate.... London: 1938. V. 73

JACKSON, GEORGE
Broughton Roundabout. London. V. 73
The Diaries and Letters from the Peace of Amiens to the Battle of Talavera. (with) The Bath Archives. A Further Selection from the Diaries and Letters...from 1809-1816. London: 1872-1873. V. 72

JACKSON, GEORGE A.
Jackson's Diary of '59. Idaho Springs: 1929. V. 70

JACKSON, HARRY
Lost Wax Bronze Casting. Flagstaff: 1972. V. 68

JACKSON, HELEN HUNT
Bits of Talk About Home Matters. Boston: 1873. V. 73
Glimpses of Three Coasts. Boston: 1886. V. 73
The Helen Jackson Year Book. Boston: 1895. V. 73
Ramona. Boston: 1884. V. 70
Ramona. Los Angeles: 1959. V. 70

JACKSON, HENRY
About Edwin Drood. Cambridge: 1911. V. 70

JACKSON, HENRY R.
Tallulah and Other Poems. Savannah: 1850. V. 69; 71

JACKSON, HOLBROOK
All Manner of Folk: Interpretations and Studies. 1912. V. 73
The Anatomy of Bibliomania. 1930. V. 71
The Fear of Books. London and New York: 1932. V. 71
The Printing of Books. 1938. V. 71
The Printing of Books. London: 1947. V. 71
The Story of Don Vincente. 1939. V. 71

JACKSON, HUMPHREY
An Essay on Bread; Wherein the Bakers and Millers are Vindicated from the Aspersions Contained in Two Pamphlets, one intitled Poison Detected; and the other, The Nature of Bread Honestly and Dishonestly Made. London: 1758. V. 69

JACKSON, JACK
Imaginary Kingdom. Texas as Seen by the Rivera and Rubi Military Expedition, 1727 and 1767. Austin: 1995. V. 69
Los Mestenos Spanish. Ranching in Texas, 1721-1821. college Station: 1986. V. 72

JACKSON, JEAN JONES
To Remember J. J. J. 1985. V. 73

JACKSON, JESSE
The Fourteenth Cadillac. Garden City: 1972. V. 72

JACKSON, JOHN
Ambidexterity or Two-Handedness and Two Brainedness. London: 1905. V. 68

JACKSON, JOHN BAPTIST
An Essay on the Invention of Engraving and Printing in Chiaro Oscuro.... London: 1754. V. 68; 72
A Treatise on Wood Engraving, Historical and Practical. London: 1839. V. 72

JACKSON, JOHN H.
Cases of Disease of the Nervous System in Patients the Subjects of Inherited Syphilis. London: 1868. V. 72

JACKSON, JOHN HUGHLINGS
Selected Writings of.... New York: 1958. V. 70

JACKSON, JOHN N.
Welland and the Welland Canal. The Canal By-Pass Project. Belleville: 1975. V. 73

JACKSON, JON A.
The Blind Pig. New York: 1978. V. 69; 70; 71; 72; 73
The Blind Pig. New York: 1979. V. 68
Dead Folk. Tucson: 1995. V. 69; 70; 72
The Diehard. New York: 1977. V. 69; 71; 72
Grootka. Woodstock: 1990. V. 68; 69; 70
Hit on the House. New York: 1993. V. 69
Ridin' with Ray. Santa Barbara: 1995. V. 69; 70; 71; 72; 73

JACKSON, JOSEPH HENRY
Bad Company. New York: 1949. V. 69
Gold Rush Album. New York: 1949. V. 69; 72; 73

JACKSON Landmarks. Jackson: 1982. V. 70

JACKSON, MARGARET WEYMOUTH
Sarah Thornton. Indianapolis: 1933. V. 71

JACKSON, MARY E.
The Life of Nellie C. Bailey or a Romance of the West. Chicago: 1887. V. 69
Topeka Pen and Camera Sketches. Topeka: 1890. V. 68

JACKSON, MONICA
Tents in the Clouds. London: 1956. V. 69

JACKSON, PERCIVAL E.
The Law of Cadavers and of Burial and Burial Places. New York: 1937. V. 70

JACKSON, R.
The Concise Dictionary of Artists' Signatures. London: 1980. V. 69

JACKSON, R. C.
East Tennessee and Georgia Railroad Time-Tables. Athens: 1863. V. 70

JACKSON, R. M. S.
The Mountain. Philadelphia: 1860. V. 70

JACKSON, R. T.
Localized Stages in Development in Plants and Animals. Boston: 1899. V. 68
Phylogeny of the Echini.... Boston: 1912. V. 73
Studies of Arbacia Punctulata and Allies, and of Nonpentamerous Echini. Boston: 1927. V. 68

JACKSON, RICHARD
Yorkshire Castles. Leeds. V. 73

JACKSON, ROWLAND
A Physical Dissertaton on Drowning; in Which Submersion, Commonly Call'd Drowning, to be a Long Time Consistent with the Continuence of Life.... London: 1746. V. 72

JACKSON, SHELDON
Fifteenth Annual Report on Introduction of Domestic Reindeer into Alaska. Washington: 1906. V. 72
The Presbyterian Church in Alaska. Washington: 1886. V. 69

JACKSON, SHIRLEY
The Bird's Nest. New York: 1954. V. 69; 71
Hangsaman. London: 1951. V. 70
The Haunting of Hill House. New York: 1959. V. 70; 71; 72
The Haunting of Hill House. London: 1960. V. 69
Just An Ordinary Day. New York: 1997. V. 72
Life Among the Savages. New York: 1953. V. 73
The Road Through The Wall. New York: 1948. V. 72
The Sundial. London: 1958. V. 69
We Have Always Lived in the Castle. London: 1963. V. 69

JACKSON, THOMAS
Byzantine and Romanesque Architecture. Cambridge: 1920. V. 70
Gothic Architecture in France, England and Italy. Cambridge: 1915. V. 70
Waterloo: a Poem. London: 1832. V. 69

JACKSON, THOMAS GRAHAM
Dalmatia and the Quarnro and Istria.... Oxford: 1887. V. 72

JACKSON, W.
A Letter to the Honourable Commissioners of Rye-Harbour; Humbly Submitting to Their Consideration, a few Suggestions Respecting the Improvement of the Harbour, and the Drainage of the Level.... London: 1797. V. 68

JACKSON, W. P. U.
Wild Flowers of the Fairest Cape. Cape Town: 1980. V. 72; 73

JACKSON, W. TURRENTINE
Wagon Roads West. A Study of Federal Road Surveys And Construction in the Trans Mississipi West 1846-1869. Berkeley: 1952. V. 68; 73

JACKSON, WILFRID SCARBOROUGH
Nine Points of the Law. London: 1903. V. 69; 73

JACKSON, WILLIAM
Book-Keeping, in the True Italian Form of Debtor and Creditor, by Way of Double Entry. New York: 1811. V. 68; 70; 73
The Four Ages: Together with Essays on Various Subjects. London: 1795. V. 69

The Four Ages: Together with Essays on Various Subjects. London: 1798. V. 69
Papers and Pedigrees Mainly Relating To Cumberland and Westmorland. CWAAS Extra Series, Volumes V and VI. London: 1892. V. 69
Thirty Letters on Various Subjects. London: 1783. V. 70

JACKSON, WILLIAM A.
An Annotated List of the Publications of the Reverend Thomas Frognall Dibdin, D.D.... Cambridge: 1965. V. 71
Records of a Bibliographer. 1967. V. 71
Records of a Bibliographer. Cambridge: 1967. V. 68
Records of the Court of the Stationers' Company 1602-1640. London: 1957. V. 70

JACKSON, WILLIAM HENRY
The Diaries of William Henry Jackson Frontier Photographer. Glendale: 1956. V. 68
Picture Maker of the Old West. New York: 1947. V. 69
Time Exposure: the Autobiography of William Henry Jackson. New York and London: 1940. V. 70
William Henry Jackson's Rocky Mountain Railroad Album: Steam and Steel Across the Great Divide. Silverton: 1976. V. 72

JACKSONVILLE, ILLINOIS, CHAMBER OF COMMERCE
Jacksonville, Illinois. 1917. V. 69

JACOB, EDITH S.
Crump and Smiles - the Story of Two Bears. London: 1886. V. 71; 72

JACOB, FRED
Day Before Yesterday. Toronto: 1925. V. 71

JACOB, G. A.
A Concordance to the Principal Upanishads and Bhagavadgita. Bombay: 1891. V. 69

JACOB, GERTRUDE L.
The Raja of Sarawak: an Account of Sir James Brooke. London: 1876. V. 69

JACOB, GILES
The Compleat Parish-Officer, Containing I. The Authority and Proceedings of High Constables. IV. of Surveyors of the Highways. Together with the Statues Relating to Hackney Coaches. London: 1744. V. 69
A Law Grammar; or Rudiments of the Law.... London;: 1744. V. 73
A New Law Dictionary.... London: 1744. V. 72

JACOB, JOHN J.
A Biographical Sketch of the Life of the Late Capt. Michael Cresap. Cumberland: 1881. V. 71

JACOB, PAUL L.
Catalogue des Livres et des Manuscrits, la Plupart Relatifs a l'Histoire de France.... Paris: 1839. V. 70

JACOB, ROSAMUND
The Rise of the United Irishmen 1791-1794. 1937. V. 69; 73

JACOB, VIOLET
Verses. London: 1905. V. 69

JACOB, WILLIAM
An Historical Inquiry into the Production and Consumption of the Precious Metals. 1831. V. 68
An Historical Inquiry Into the Production and Consumption of the Precious Metals. London: 1831. V. 73
A View of the Agriculture, Manufactures, Statistics and State of Society, of Germany and Parts of Holland and France. London: 1820. V. 68

JACOBACCI, VINCENZO
A Giambatista Bodoni, che gli fe 'don dell "Orazio Stampato Co" Suoi Caratteri. Parma: 1791. V. 68

JACOBI, CARL
Revelations in Black. Sauk City: 1947. V. 69

JACOBI, EDUARD
Portfolio of Dermachromes. London: 1904. V. 70
Portfolio Of Dermachromes. London: 1904-1906. V. 72

JACOBS, FRANK
Alvin Steadfast on Vernacular Island. New York: 1965. V. 70

JACOBS, JOSEPH
The Book of Wonder Voyages. London: 1896. V. 68; 72
The Book of Wonder Voyages. New York: 1896. V. 70
The Buried Moon. Englewood Cliffs: 1969. V. 70
Celtic Fairy Tales. (with) More Celtic Fairy Tales. London: 1892-1894. V. 72
Celtic Family Tales. London: 1892. V. 69
More Celtic Fairy Tales. London: 1894. V. 71

JACOBS, M.
The Art of Colour. Garden City: 1926. V. 69; 72

JACOBS, MICHAEL
Notes on the Rebel Invasion of Maryland and Pennsylvania and the Battle of Gettysburg. Philadelphia: 1864. V. 69

JACOBS, NED
The National Cowboy Hall of Fame and Western Heritage Center, March 4 May 14, 1972. Santa Fe: 1972. V. 70; 72; 73

JACOBS, T. C. H.
Sinister Quest. New York: 1934. V. 69

JACOBS, WILLIAM WYMARK
Many Cargoes. London: 1896. V. 69
Odd Craft. London: 1903. V. 69
Sailor's Knots. London: 1909. V. 69
Sea Whispers. New York: 1926. V. 69; 70
Sea Whispers. New York: 1934. V. 73

JACOBSEN, CHARLES W.
Oriental Rugs. Tokyo & Rutland: 1962. V. 70

JACOBSEN, H.
Handbook of Succulent Plants. 1960. V. 69; 72; 73
A Handbook of Succulent Plants. Poole: 1960. V. 68
Handbook of Succulent Plants. 1978. V. 69; 73
Lexicon of Succulent Plants. London: 1974. V. 68; 71; 73
Succulent Plants, Description, Cultivation and Uses of Succulent Plants.... Pasadena: 1946. V. 68

JACOBSON, E.
Seven Designers Look at Trade-Mark Design. Chicago: 1952. V. 69

JACOBSON, HOWARD
Coming from Behind. London: 1983. V. 72

JACOBSON, J. Z.
Art of Today: Chicago 1933. Chicago: 1932. V. 69; 72
Scott of Northwestern. The Life Story of a Pioneer in Psychology and Education. Chicago: 1951. V. 73
Thirty-Five Saints and Emil Armin. Chicago: 1929. V. 69; 72

JACOBSON, ROBERT
Magnificence on Stage at the Met. New York: 1985. V. 68

JACOBSON, SHERWOOD A.
The Post Traumatic Syndrome Following Head Injury Mechanism and Treatment. Springfield: 1963. V. 71

JACOBUS DE VARAGINE
The Golden Legend. 1892. V. 73
The Golden Legend, or Lives of the Saints. New York: 1973. V. 70

JACQUES, BRIAN
Castaways of the Flying Dutchman. London: 2001. V. 69
The Legend of Luke. London: 1999. V. 68; 72
The Long Patrol. London: 1997. V. 68; 73
Lord Brocktree. London: 2000. V. 68; 72
Marlfox. London: 1998. V. 69
Redwall. London: 1986. V. 68; 71

JACQUIN, NICOLAI JOSEPH VON
Miscellanea Austriaca ad Botanicum Chemiam et Historian Naturalem.... Vindobonae: 1778-1781. V. 68; 70; 72; 73

JAEGER, GUSTAV
Selections from Essays on Health Culture and the Sanitary Woollen System. 1886. V. 71

JAFFE, BERNARD
Crucibles. London: 1931. V. 68

JAFFE, MICHAEL
The Devonshire Collection of Italian Drawings. Bolognese and Emilian Schools, Roman and Neapolitan Schools, Tuscan and Umbrian Schools, Venetian and North Italian Schools. London: 1994. V. 69

JAGERSKIOLD, AXEL LEONARD KRISTER EDVARD
Results of the Swedish Zoological Expedition to Egypt and the White Nile 1901.... Uppsala: 1904-1928. V. 68; 72

JAGO, RICHARD
Edge-Hill, or the Rural Prospect Delineated and Moralized. London: 1767. V. 68; 72

JAHN, OTTO
Life of Mozart. London: 1882. V. 71

JAHN, WOLF
The Art of Gilbert and George or An Aesthetic of Existence. London: 1989. V. 72

JAHNS, PAT
The Frontier World of Doc Holliday, Faro Dealer from Dallas to Deadwood. 1957. V. 68

JAHNS, R. H.
Mica Deposits of the Southeastern Piedmont. Washington: 1952-1953. V. 72

JAHODA, GLORIA
Annie. Boston: 1960. V. 68

JAHR, G. H. G.
G. H. G. Jahr's Manual of Homoeopathic Medicine. Allentown: 1836. V. 69; 71
General and Special Therapeutics of Mental Diseases and Physical Disorders.... Manchester: 1857. V. 73

JAIPAL, LT. COL.
Great Hunt. New York: 1981. V. 69

JAKE, JOHN
North and South. New York: 1982. V. 68

JAMBLICHUS, OF CHALCIS
Iamblichus de Mysteriis Aegyptiorum, Chaldaeorum, Assyriorum. Leiden: 1607. V. 69

JAMBON, JEAN
Our Trip to Blunderland. London: 1877. V. 70

JAMES, AHLEE
Tewa Firelight Tales. New York: 1927. V. 70

JAMES, BILL C.
Jim Miller. The Untold Story of a Texas Badman. Wolfe City: 1989. V. 72

JAMES, C. L. R.
A History of Negro Revolt. 1938. V. 68
Mariners, Renegades and Castaways. The Story of Herman Melville and the World We Live In. New York: 1953. V. 68

JAMES, CAROLINE
Nez Perce Women in Transition 1877-1990. Moscow: 1996. V. 68; 73

JAMES, CARY
The Imperial Hotel: Frank Lloyd Wright and the Architecture of Unity. Rutland: 1968. V. 68

JAMES, D. GERAINT
Circulation of the Blood. Tunbridge Wells: 1978. V. 68

JAMES, ED
Hanging and Rattling - Autobiography of W. E. Ed James. Caldwell: 1979. V. 68

JAMES, EDGAR
The Allen Outlaws: a Complete History of Their Lives and Exploits, Concluding with Hillsville Courthouse Tragedy. Baltimore: 1912. V. 73

JAMES, EDWARD
The Gardener Who Saw God. London: 1937. V. 72

JAMES, EDWIN
Account of the Expedition from Pittsburgh to the Rocky Mountains Under the Command of Major Stephen H. Long, from the Notes of Major Long, Mr. T. Say and Other Gentlemen of the Exploring Party.... Barre: 1972. V. 69
A Narrative of the Captivity and Adventures of John Tanner (U.S. Interpreter at the Saut de Ste. Marie) During the Thirty Years Residence Among the Indians in the Interior of North America. Minneapolis: 1956. V. 72

JAMES FORD BELL LIBRARY
An Annotated Catalog of Original Source Materials Relating to the History of European Expansion 1400-1800. 1994. V. 70

JAMES, GEORGE PAYNE RAINSFORD
The Fight of the Fiddlers: a Serio-Comic Verity. London: 1849. V. 68
Heidelberg. A Romance. London: 1846. V. 68
The King's Highway. London: 1840. V. 68
Mary of Burgundy or the Revolt of Ghent. London: 1864?. V. 68
Russell: a Tale of the Reign of Charles III. London: 1847. V. 68
The Works. (with) A History of the Life of Richard Coeur-de-Lion, King of England. London: 1841-1849. V. 73

JAMES, GEORGE WHARTON
Arizona the Wonderland. Boston: 1917. V. 73
Indian Basketry. Pasadena: 1901. V. 70
Indian Basketry. Chicago and New York: 1902. V. 69
Indian Basketry and How to Make Baskets. New York: 1909. V. 70
Indian Blankets and Their Makers. Chicago: 1914. V. 72
Indian Blankets and Their Makers. New York: 1937. V. 70
Indian Blankets and Their Makers. Glorieta: 1970. V. 71
Indians of the Painted Desert Region. Boston: 1903. V. 70
Indians of the Painted Desert Region. Boston: 1903-1907. V. 69
The Indians of the Painted Desert Region. Boston: 1904. V. 69
The Indians' Secrets of Health or What the White Race May learn from the Indian. Pasadena: 1917. V. 71
Living the Radiant Life. Pasadena: 1916. V. 68
Rose Hartwick Thorpe and the Story of Curfew Must Not Ring To'Night. Pasadena: 1916. V. 68
Through Ramona's Country. Boston: 1913. V. 73
Traveler's Handbook to Southern California. Pasadena: 1904. V. 70
Utah - the Land of the Blossorning Valleys. Boston: 1922. V. 68; 73
What the White Race May Learn from the Indian. Chicago: 1908. V. 70
The Wonders of the Colorado Desert (Southern California). Boston: 1906. V. 73

JAMES, GRACE
Green Willow and Other Japanese Fairy Tales. London: 1910. V. 69; 70

JAMES, H. E. M.
Extracts from the Pedigrees of James of Barrock. No. 2. Exeter: 1913. V. 71

JAMES, H. L.
Acoma: the People of the White Crack. 1970. V. 69

JAMES, HARRY C.
The Hopi Indians. Caldwell: 1956. V. 69

JAMES, HENRY
The Ambassadors. New York and London: 1903. V. 69; 72
The American. Boston: 1877. V. 70; 71
The Art of Fiction. Boston: 1885. V. 68; 71
The Aspern Papers Louisa Pallant. The Modern Warning. London: 1888. V. 68
The Awkward Age. New York: 1899. V. 69
The Bodley Head Henry James. London: 1967-1974. V. 69
A Bundle of Letters. Boston: 1880. V. 68
Confidence. Boston: 1880. V. 71

JAMES, HENRY *continued*
Daisy Miller. London: 1883. V. 71
Daisy Miller. New York: 1904. V. 73
Dans La Cage. Paris. V. 70
Embarrassments. New York: 1896. V. 71
English Hours. Boston: 1905. V. 72
The Europeans. Boston: 1879. V. 71
The Finer Grain. New York: 1910. V. 68; 71
The Golden Bowl. New York: 1904. V. 68; 70; 72
Hawthorne. London: 1879. V. 71
Hawthorne. New York: 1880. V. 71
In the Cage. London: 1898. V. 73
An International Episode. New York: 1879. V. 71
Italian Hours. London: 1909. V. 68
The Lesson of the Master. New York: 1892. V. 71
A Little Tour in France. Boston: 1885. V. 68; 71
A Little Tour in France. Boston and New York: 1900. V. 68
A London Life. London and New York: 1889. V. 71
Master Eustace. New York: 1920. V. 71; 73
Notes of a Son and Brother. London: 1914. V. 73
Novels and Tales. New York: 1907-1917. V. 70
The Outcry. New York: 1911. V. 68; 70; 71; 73
A Passionate Pilgrim. Boston: 1875. V. 71; 73
Picture and Text. New York: 1893. V. 68; 69
Pictures and Other Passages from Henry James. London: 1916. V. 71
The Portrait of a Lady. London: 1881. V. 73
Portrait of a Lady. Boston: 1882. V. 68; 71
The Princess Casamassima; a Novel. London: 1889. V. 68
The Question of Our Speech, the Lesson of Balzac. Boston and New York: 1905. V. 68; 71
The Real Thing. London: 1893. V. 71
The Real Thing. New York: 1893. V. 69
Representative Selections, with Introduction, Bibliography and Notes. New York: 1941. V. 69
Roderick Hudson. Boston: 1876. V. 68; 71; 73
The Sacred Fount. London: 1901. V. 69; 70; 73
The Scenic Art - Notes on Acting and the Drama 1872-1901. London: 1949. V. 70
The Sense of the Past. New York: 1917. V. 70; 71
The Siege of London, the Pension Beaurepas, and the Point of View. Boston: 1883. V. 71; 73
Siena. New York: 2000. V. 72
A Small Boy and Others. London: 1913. V. 71; 72
The Soft Side. New York: 1900. V. 68
The Tales of Henry James - Volume One 1864-1869. London: 1973. V. 70
Terminations. New York: 1897. V. 68
Theatricals. Second Series. London: 1895. V. 71
The Tragic Muse. Boston: 1890. V. 72
The Tragic Muse. New York: 1890. V. 68
Transatlantic Sketches. Boston: 1875. V. 71
The Turn of the Screw. 1940. V. 68
Washington Square. London: 1881. V. 73
Washington Square. New York: 1881. V. 71
Watch and Ward. Boston: 1878. V. 71
What Maisie Knew. London: 1898. V. 73
William Wetmore Story and His Friends. Boston: 1903. V. 69
The Wings of the Dove. New York: 1902. V. 70
Within the Rim and Other Essays. London: 1918. V. 68

JAMES, J.
Essay on the Philosophical Construction of Celtic Nomenclature. Bristol: 1869. V. 72

JAMES, JASON W.
Memories and Viewpoints. Rowell: 1928. V. 73

JAMES, JOHN
My Experiences with Indians. Austin: 1925. V. 69

JAMES, JOSEPH
A System of Exchange with Almost All Parts of the World. New York: 1800. V. 71; 73

JAMES, KATY
The Enchanted Waterfall. Tokyo: 1910. V. 72

JAMES, LEWIS
Manufacturers Practical Recipes. London: 1943. V. 68

JAMES, M. R.
The Five Jars. London: 1922. V. 70; 71; 73
Ghost Stories of an Antiquary. London: 1904. V. 72

JAMES, MARK M.
Alameda County, California Center of Western Industry. Oakland?: 1915. V. 68

JAMES, MARQUIS
The Raven. The Life Story of Sam Houston. Indianapolis: 1929. V. 68

JAMES, MERVYN
Mountains. Wymondham: 1972. V. 68; 71; 73

JAMES, NICHOLAS
Poems on Several Occasions. Truro: 1742. V. 69

JAMES, NORAH C.
As High as the Sky. New York: 1938. V. 69; 70

JAMES, P. D.
The Black Tower. London: 1975. V. 69; 70; 71; 72; 73
The Black Tower. New York: 1975. V. 68; 69; 71
A Certain Justice. London: 1997. V. 70
Death in Holy Orders. London: 2001. V. 70
Death of an Expert Witness. London: 1977. V. 71
Devices and Desires. London and Boston: 1989. V. 69
The Girl Who Loved Graveyards. London: 1996. V. 72
Innocent Blood. London: 1980. V. 68; 69; 70; 71; 73
A Mind to Murder. London: 1963. V. 71
Murder in Triplicate. 2001. V. 71; 73
Original Sin. London: 1994. V. 68; 72; 73
Original Sin. Franklin Center: 1995. V. 70
P. D. James Omnibus. London: 1982. V. 73
Shroud for a Nightingale. London: 1971. V. 71
The Skull Beneath the Skin. London: 1982. V. 70; 71; 72
The Skull Beneath the Skin. New York: 1982. V. 68; 70
A Taste for Death. London: 1986. V. 68; 72
Time To Be In Earnest. London: 1999. V. 68
Unnatural Causes. New York: 1967. V. 68; 69; 71
An Unsuitable Job for a Woman. London: 1972. V. 68

JAMES, PHILIP
Children's Books of Yesterday. 1933. V. 68
Early Keyboard Instruments. London: 1930. V. 72

JAMES, R. RUTSON
Studies in the History of Opthalmology in England Prior to the Yar 1800. Cambridge: 1933. V. 73

JAMES, RIAN
Hat-Check Girl. New York: 1932. V. 70

JAMES, RICHARD
Iter Lancastrense: a Poem written A.D. 1636. 1845. V. 73

JAMES Sprunt: a Tribute from the City of Wilmington. Raleigh: 1925. V. 69

JAMES Stirling: Buildings and Projects 1950-1974. New York: 1975. V. 69

JAMES, T.
Notes on Cottage-Building, Read Before the General Committee of the Northampton Architectural Society. Northampton: 1861. V. 71

JAMES, THOMAS
Three Years Among the Mexicans and Indians. St. Louis: 1916. V. 68; 73

JAMES, W. E.
Treasured Reminiscences. Columbia: 1911. V. 69

JAMES, WILL
All in the Day's Riding. New York: 1933. V. 68; 73
The American Cowboy. New York: 1942. V. 69
Big Enough. New York: 1931. V. 72
Cow Country. New York: 1927. V. 71
Cowboy in the Making. New York: 1937. V. 69
Cowboy Life in Texas...Or..27 Years a Maverick. Chicago: 1893. V. 71
Cowboys North and South. New York: 1924. V. 68
Cowboys North and South. New York: 1925. V. 68
Cowboys North and South. New York: 1931. V. 71
The Dark Horse. New York: 1939. V. 70
The Drifting Cowboy. New York: 1925. V. 70
Horses I've Known. New York: 1940. V. 69; 72
Lone Cowboy: My Life Story. New York: 1930. V. 69
Lone Cowboy: My Life Story. New York: 1945. V. 68
Smokey the Cowhorse. New York: 1926. V. 72
Sun Up: Tales of the Cow Camps. New York: 1931. V. 68; 72
The Three Mustangeers. New York: 1933. V. 68

JAMES, WILLIAM
Naval History of Great Britian, From the Declaration of War...in 1793 to...George IV. London: 1860. V. 71
Human Immortality. London: 1898. V. 68; 72
Talks to Teachers on Psychology: and to Students on Some of Life's Ideals. New York: 1904. V. 69

JAMES, WILLIAM DOBEIN
A Sketch of the Life of Brig. General Francis Marion, and a History of His Brigade, from Its Rise in June, 1780 Until Disbanded in December 1782.... Charleston: 1821. V. 73

JAMES I, KING OF ENGLAND
The Works of James the First. Glasgow: 1825. V. 68; 72

JAMES I, KING OF SCOTLAND
The King's Quair. Air: 1815. V. 73
The King's Quair. London: 1903. V. 72

JAMESON, ANNA BROWNELL MURPHY
Characteristics of Women, Moral, Poetical and Historical. Philadelphia: 1833. V. 69
Characteristics of Women, Moral, Poetical and Historical. London: 1836. V. 73
Legends of the Madonna as represented in the Fine Arts. London: 1864. V. 72
Letters of Anna Jameson to Ottilie Von Goethe. London: 1939. V. 69

JAMESON, ANNA BROWNELL MURPHY continued
Memoirs of the Beauties of the Court of Charles II. London: 1838. V. 68
Memoirs of the Beauties of the Court of Charles II. London: 1851. V. 69
Memoirs of the Early Italian Painters, and the Progress of Painting In Italy. London: 1845. V. 72
Sketches in Canada and Rambles Among the Red Men. London: 1852. V. 72

JAMESON, JAMES S.
Story Of The Rear Column Of The Emin Pasha Relief Expedition. London: 1890. V. 72
Story of the Rear Column of the Emin Pasha Relief Expedition. New York: 1890. V. 70

JAMESON, ROBERT
Manual of Mineralogy.... Edinburgh: 1821. V. 68

JAMESON, STROM
The End of This War. London: 1941. V. 73
The Voyage Home. New York: 1930. V. 70

JAMIESON, JOHN
An Etymological Dictionary of the Scottish Language: Illustrating the Words in Their Different Significations . . . Edinburgh: 1808. V. 70; 71
Supplement to the Etymological Dictionary of the Scottish Language. Edinburgh: 1825. V. 73

JAMISON, DAVID F.
The Life and Times of Bertrand Du Guesclin: a History of the Fourteenth Century. Charleston: 1864. V. 70

JAMSHEED, RASHID
Memories of a Sheep Hunter. 1996. V. 69; 70; 72; 73

JAN Saudek: Life, Love, Death and Other Such Trifles. Amsterdam: 1991. V. 68

JANE, FRED T.
Blake of the Rattlesnake or the Man Who Saved England. London: 1895. V. 68

JANE'S Fighting Ships 1919. London: 1919. V. 68

JANE'S Fighting Ships 1939. London: 1939. V. 71

JANES, J. ROBERT
Mannequin. London: 1994. V. 70

JANIN, M. JULES
The American in Paris; or Heath's Picturesque Annual for 1843/1844. 1843-1844. V. 71

JANIS, SIDNEY
Abstract and Surrealist Art in America. New York: 1944. V. 72

JAN KLEYKAMP GALLERIES, NEW YORK
The Jan Kleykamp Collection, Chinese and Japanese Paintings. New York: 1925. V. 69

JANOUCH, GUSTAV
Conversations with Kafka - Notes and Reminiscences. London: 1953. V. 71

JANSEN, MURK
Achondroplasia Its Nature and Its Cause. London: 1912. V. 68

JANSEN, WERNER
The Light of Egypt. New York: 1928. V. 70

JANZEN, D. H.
Costa Rican Natural History. Chicago: 1983. V. 72

A JAPANESE Fairy Tale: the Magic Kite. 1908. V. 73

JAPHET and Happy's Annual 1937. V. 69

JAPRISOT, SEBASTIEN
Goodbye, Friend. New York: 1969. V. 71; 72

JAQUES, FLORENCE PAGE
Francis Lee Jaques: Artist of the Wilderness World. New York: 1973. V. 70

JARAMILLO, CLEOFAS
Shadows of the Past - Sombras Del Pasado. Santa Fe: 1941. V. 70

JARCHO, JULIUS
Postures and Practices During Labor Among the Primitive Peoples. New York: 1934. V. 68

JARDIN des Plantes. Le Menagerie et la Vallee Suisse en estampes. Paris: 1857. V. 73

JARDINE, DOUGLAS
The Mad Mullah of Somaliland.... London: 1923. V. 72

JARDINE, QUINTIN
Skinner's Round. London: 1995. V. 71

JARDINE, WILLIAM
Birds of Great Britain and Ireland - Rasores and Grallatores. 1842. V. 69
Birds of Great Britain and Irleand. Volume III. Gallinaceous Birds. 1843. V. 69
Contributions to Ornithology for 1848-1852. Edinburgh: 1848-1852. V. 73
Lives of Eminent Naturalists. Edinburgh: 1841. V. 68; 70
The Naturalist's Library. Entomology. British Moths, Sphinxes, etc. Edinburgh and London: 1860. V. 72
The Naturalist's Library. Ichthyology. Edinburgh: 1835-1843. V. 70; 73

JARDINS D'Acclimation. Paris: 1860. V. 68

JARMAN, DEREK
At Your Own Risk - a Saint's Testament. London: 1992. V. 71; 73
Modern Nature - the Journals of Derek Jarman. London: 1991. V. 71; 73

JARMAN, THOMAS
A Treatise on Wills. London: 1930. V. 70

JARRELL, RANDALL
The Animal. New York: 1965. V. 72
The Animal Family. London: 1967. V. 72
The Bat Poet. New York: 1964. V. 68
Blood for a Stranger. New York: 1942. V. 69; 70; 72
The Complete Poems. New York: 1969. V. 69
The Death of the Ball Turret Gunner. New York: 1969. V. 72; 73
The Gingerbread Rabbit. New York: 1964. V. 68
Losses. New York: 1948. V. 71
The Lost World. New York: 1965. V. 71
Pictures From an Institution. New York: 1955. V. 72
A Sad Heart at the Supermarket. New York: 1962. V. 69
Selected Poems. New York: 1955. V. 68; 69; 72
Selected Poems. London: 1956. V. 71
The Seven-League Crutches. New York: 1951. V. 71
The Third Book of Criticism. New York: 1969. V. 68
The Woman at the Washington Zoo. Poems and Translations. New York: 1960. V. 68; 69; 72

JARRIN, G. A.
The Italian Confectioner; or Complete Economy of Deserts, According to the Most Modern and Approved Practice. 1829. V. 71

JARRY, ALFRED
Selected Works of Alfred Jarry. London: 1965. V. 68
The Supermale. London: 1968. V. 73
Ubu Roi. 1966. V. 70

JARRY ALFRED
Ubu Roi. London: 1976. V. 73

JARVES, JAMES J.
History of the Hawaiian Islands.... Honolulu: 1847. V. 69

JARVIS, RUPERT C.
The Jacobite Risings of 1715 and 1745. Carlisle: 1954. V. 70; 71
The Jacobite Risings Of 1715 And 1745. London: 1954. V. 72

JASUD, LAWRENCE
Words Sounds and Power. Minneapolis: 1991. V. 68

JAVELLE, EMILE
Alpine Memories. London: 1899. V. 69

JAY, CHARLOTTE
Beat Not the Bones. New York: 1953. V. 69

JAY, J. C.
A Catalogue of the Shells...in the Collection of.... New York: 1839. V. 69

JAY, LEONARD
Four Parables from the Holy Bible. Birmingham: 1927. V. 71
Of Making Many Books There Is No End. Birmingham: 1931. V. 68; 71
The Torch. No. 1. 1933. V. 70

JAY, MAE FOSTER
Green Needles. Boston: 1932. V. 71

JAY, WILLIAM
A Review of the Causes and Consequences of the Mexican War. Boston: 1849. V. 70

JAYBERT, B.
Les Apres-Soupers par L'Auteur de Trois Dizains de Contes Gaulois. Paris: 1883. V. 68
Trois Dizains de Contes Gaulois. Paris: 1882. V. 68

JAYNE, JAMES A.
Tax Income. Cortland: 1927. V. 70

JAYNE, S.
Library Catalogues of the English Renaissance. Berkeley: 1956. V. 70

JAYNE, WALTER ADDISON
The Healing Gods of Ancient Civilizations. New York: 1962. V. 68

JEAFFERSON, J. CORDY
Novels and Novelists, from Elizabeth to Victoria. London: 1858. V. 73

JEALOUS, GEORGE S.
How I Found a Five-Pound Note and What Came Of It. London: 1881. V. 68

JEAN, MARCEL
The History of Surrealist Painting. New York: 1960. V. 69

JEAN AUBRY, G.
Joseph Conrad in the Congo. Boston: 1926. V. 71

JEANNERET-GRIS, CHARLES EDOUARD
Sketchbooks. London: 1981-1982. V. 69
Sketchbooks. 1982. V. 72
Towards a New Architecture. London: 1962. V. 68
Urbanisme. Paris: 1925. V. 68
Vers une Architecture. Paris: 1924. V. 72

JEANNOT Lapin. Amsterdam: 1930. V. 72

JEANS, H. W. S.
Rules for Finding the Names and Positions of All the Stars. Portsea: 1844. V. 70

JEANS, J. S.
Jubilee Memorial of the Railway System. A History of the Stockton and Darlington Railway and a Record of Its Results. London: 1875. V. 72

JEANS, RONALD
Lean Harvest. New York: 1931. V. 70

JEANS, THOMAS
The Tommiebeg Shootings or A Moor in Scotland. 1867. V. 71

JEANSON, MARCEL
The Library of Marcel Jeanson - Hunting. 1987. V. 68

JEAURAT, EDME SEBASTIEN
Traite de Perspective a l'Usage des Artistes. Paris: 1750. V. 69; 71

JEAYS, JOSHUA
The Orthogonal System of Hand-Railing with Practical Illustrations of the Construction of Stairs. London: 1850. V. 68

JEBB, JOSHUA
A Practical Treatise on Strengthening and Defending Outposts, Villages, Houses, Bridges, &c in Reference to the Duties of Officers in Command of Picquets, as Laid Down in the Field Exercise and Evolutions of the Army.... Chatham: 1837. V. 70
Report of the Surveyor General of Prisons on the Construction, Ventilation and Details of Pentonville Prison, 1844. London: 1844. V. 73

JEBB, SAMUEL
The Life of Robert, Earl of Leicester, the Favourite of Queen Elizabeth. London: 1727. V. 72

JECKS, MICHAEL
Traitor of St. Giles. 2000. V. 68

JEFFARES, A. NORMAN
The Critical Heritage. London: 1977. V. 72
W. B. Yeats, the Critical Heritage. 1977. V. 69

JEFFCOCK, JOHN THOMAS
Parkin Jeffcock, Civil and Mining Engineer. London: 1867. V. 73

JEFFERIES, RICHARD
After London, or, Wild England. London: 1885. V. 68
Amaryllis at the Fair. London: 1887. V. 70; 71; 72
The Amateur Poacher. 1879. V. 71
The Amateur Poacher. London: 1879. V. 73
Beauty is Immortal (Felise of The Dewy Morn). Sussex: 1948. V. 72
Field and Hedgerow.... London: 1889. V. 73
Field and Hedgerow.... London: 1897. V. 72
Field and Hedgerow.... London: 1948. V. 72; 73
The Gamekeeper at Home, Sketches of Natural History and Rural Life. London: 1880. V. 70
Hodge and His Masters. London: 1880. V. 73
An Illustrated Anthology, Eye of the Beholder. Southampton: 1897. V. 70
Jefferies' Land. London: 1896. V. 70
The Life of the Fields. London: 1884. V. 68; 73
The Life of the Fields. London: 1947. V. 72
Nature Near London. London: 1883. V. 68; 71; 73
The Old House at Coate and Other Hitherto Unpublished Essays. London: 1948. V. 72
The Open Air. London: 1948. V. 72
Red Deer. London: 1884. V. 68; 73
Round About a Great Estate. London: 1880. V. 71; 73
The Scarlet Shawl. London: 1874. V. 73
Thoughts From the Writings of Richard Jefferies. London: 1895. V. 71
The Toilers of the Field. London: 1892. V. 70; 71
The Toilers of The Field. London: 1898. V. 72
Wild Life in a Southern Country. London: 1879. V. 70; 71
Wood Magic. London: 1881. V. 70; 71; 72

JEFFERS, ROBINSON
The Alpine Christ and Other Poems. 1973. V. 73
Be Angry at the Sun. New York: 1941. V. 69; 71; 72; 73
Cawdor. New York: 1928. V. 69
Cawdor. London: 1929. V. 70
Cawdor. 1983. V. 70
Dear Judas and Other Poems. New York: 1929. V. 68; 69; 73
Descent to the Dead. New York: 1931. V. 70; 71; 73
Flagons and Apples. Los Angeles: 1912. V. 68
Give Your Heart to the Hawks and Other Poems. New York: 1933. V. 72
Roan Stallion. Tamar. New York: 1925. V. 71
Roan Stallion. Tamar. London: 1928. V. 70
Solstice and Other Poems. New York: 1935. V. 72
Songs and Heroes: Previously Unpublished Poems. Los Angeles: 1988. V. 71
Such Counsels You Gave to Me and Other Poems. New York: 1931. V. 73
Such Counsels You Gave to Me and Other Poems. New York: 1937. V. 71
Tragedy Has Obligations. Santa Cruz: 1973. V. 70; 72
The Women at Point Sur. New York: 1927. V. 68; 69

JEFFERSON COUNTY HISTORICAL SOCIETY
With Pride in Heritage: History of Jefferson County. Portland: 1966. V. 69; 72; 73

JEFFERSON, GEOFFREY
The Invasive Adenomas of the Anterior Pituitary. Springfield: 1972. V. 68
Selected Papers. London: 1960. V. 68; 70; 72

JEFFERSON, JOHN C.
A Book of Recollections. London: 1894. V. 71

JEFFERSON, ROBERT L.
Roughing It In Siberia. London: 1897. V. 68

JEFFERSON, SAMUEL
The History and Antiquities of Allerdale Ward, Above Derwent in the County of Cumberland.... Carlisle: 1842. V. 71
The History and Antiquities of Carlisle.... Carlisle: 1838. V. 71
The History and Antiquities of Leath Ward, in the County of Cumberland.... Carlisle: 1840. V. 71

JEFFERSON, T. H.
Accompaniment to the Map of the Emigrant Road From Independence, Missouri, to San Francisco, California. San Francisco: 1945. V. 68

JEFFERSON, THOMAS
Jefferson's Notes on the State of Virginia. Baltimore: 1800. V. 73
A Manual of Parliamentary Practice for the Use of the Senate of the United States. Washington: 1801. V. 68; 71
Memoir, Correspondence and Miscellanies from the Papers of Thomas Jefferson. Charlottesville: 1829. V. 68
Notes on the State of Virginia. London: 1787. V. 73
Notes on the State of Virginia. Philadelphia: 1794. V. 68; 72
Notes on the State of Virginia. Trenton: 1803. V. 71
Thomas Jefferson's Farm Book. Philadelphia: 1953. V. 72
Thomas Jefferson's Garden Book 1766-1824. Philadelphia: 1944. V. 68; 71; 73
The Writings. Washington: 1853. V. 68
Writings. New York: 1857. V. 73
The Writings. Philadelphia: 1871. V. 71
The Writings. 1967. V. 70; 72

JEFFERYS, C. W.
The Picture Gallery of Canadian History. Toronto: 1942-1950. V. 73

JEFFERYS, THOMAS
The Conduct of the French, with Regard to Nova Scotia; from its First Settlement to the Present Time. London: 1754. V. 72

JEFFREY, WILLIAM H.
Richmond Prisons 1861-1862. St. Johnsbury: 1893. V. 68

JEFFREYS, J. G.
British Conchology.... London: 1862-1869. V. 69

JEFFRIES, DAVID
A Treatise on Diamonds and Pearls. London: 1751. V. 68; 70; 73
A Treatise on Diamonds and Pearls. London: 1850. V. 68

JEFFRIES, GRAHAM MONTAGUE
Ten Trails to Tyburn. London: 1944. V. 69

JEFFRIES, JOHN
Narrative of the Two Aerial Voyages...from London Into Kent...From England into France. 1941. V. 70

JEFFRIES, JOY
Color-Blindness: It's Dangers and Its Detection. Boston: 1879. V. 71

JEHN, JANET
Acadian Descendants. Covington: 1975-1978. V. 72

JEKYLL, GERTRUDE
Colour in the Flower Garden. London: 1908. V. 69; 70
Colour Scheme in the Flower Garden. London: 1911. V. 73
Colour Schemes for the Flower Garden. London: 1930. V. 68; 71; 73
A Gardener's Testament - a Selection of Articles and Notes. London: 1937. V. 70
Gardens for Small Country Homes. London: 1912. V. 68
Gardens for Small Country Houses. 1912. V. 69
Gardens for Small Country Houses. London: 1927. V. 69
Gertrude Jekyll, a Memoir. London: 1934. V. 68; 73
Home and Garden.... London: 1910. V. 73
Home and Gardens.... London: 1900. V. 70
Lilies for English Gardens, a Guide for Amateurs. London: 1901. V. 68; 71
Old English Household Life: Some Account of Cottage Objects and Country Folk. London: 1925. V. 70
Old West Surrey - Some Notes and Memories. London: 1904. V. 70
Roses for English Gardens. 1902. V. 69
Roses for English Gardens. London: 1902. V. 70
Some English Gardens. London: 1920. V. 69
Wall and Water Gardens. London: 1901. V. 68; 70; 71; 73
Wall, Water and Woodland Gardens, Including the Rock Garden and the Heath Garden. London: 1933. V. 70
Wood and Garden. London: 1899. V. 68; 71; 73

JELIFFE, S. E.
The Flora of Long Island. 1899. V. 72

JELLETT, E. C.
Germantown, Old and New, Its Rare and Notable Plants. Germantwon: 1904. V. 68; 71

JELLICOE, G.
Baroque Gardens of Austria. London: 1932. V. 69
The Studies of a Landscape Designer Over 80 Years. Woodbridge: 1993-. V. 68; 71

JELLICOE, J.
The Studies of a Landscape Designer Over 80 Years. Woodbridge: 1993-1996. V. 73

JEMMY String. New York: 1867. V. 71; 72

JEN, GISH
Typical American. Boston: 1991. V. 71

JENCKS, CHARLES
Late-Modern Architecture and Other Essays. New York: 1980. V. 68
Towards a Symbolic Architecture: the Thematic House. 1985. V. 69
Towards a Symbolic Architecture: the Thematic House. New York: 1985. V. 68

JENKINS, A. O.
Olive's Last Round-up. Loup City. V. 73

JENKINS, BURRIS
Torrent. Indianapolis: 1932. V. 71

JENKINS, C. E.
Evenings at Haddon Hall. A Series of Romantic Tales of the Olden Time. With illustrations from designs by George Cattermole. London: 1848. V. 71

JENKINS, DAVID
Jenkinsius Redivivus; or the Works.... London: 1681. V. 70; 72
Lex Terrae, or, a Brief Discourse of Law, Whereby It Is Proved that the Supreme Power in this Kingdome is in the King Only and Not in Two Houses of Parliament. London: 1648. V. 70
Pacis Consultum. 1657. V. 72
Pacis Consultum. London: 1657. V. 70
Works.... 1648. V. 72
The Works.... London: 1648. V. 70

JENKINS, DILYS
Llanelly Pottery. Swansea: 1968. V. 72

JENKINS, E. VAUGHAN
Water Divining. London: 1902. V. 70

JENKINS, ELIZABETH
Jane Austen, a Biography. London: 1938. V. 70

JENKINS, ELLA
This is Rhythm. New York: 1962. V. 69; 71

JENKINS, GERAINT
Studies in Folk Life: Essays in Honour of Iorwerth C. Peake. 1969. V. 70

JENKINS, HAROLD
Edward Benlowes - a Biography of a Minor Poet. London: 1952. V. 71

JENKINS, JAMES
The Martial Achievements of Great Britain and Her Allies; from 1799 to 1815. London: 1815. V. 70

JENKINS, JOHN
A Selection of Architectural and Other Ornament, Greek, Roman and Italian, Drawn from the Originals in Various Museums and Buildings in Italy. London: 1827. V. 70; 72

JENKINS, JOHN H.
Audubon and Other Capers: Confessions of a Texas Bookmaker. Austin: 1976. V. 68; 69
Basic Texas Books. Austin: 1983. V. 70
Cracker Barrel Chronicles: a Bibliography of Texas Town and County Histories. Austin: 1965. V. 72
A Full Howes. Austin: 1981. V. 72
I'm Frank Hamer the True Story of Clyde Barrow and Bonnie Parker. 1968. V. 68
The Most Remarkable Texas Book: an Essay on W. W. Heartsill's "Fourteen Hundred and 91 Days in the Confederate Army". Austin: 1980. V. 70
The Papers of the Texas Revolution 1835-1836. Austin: 1973. V. 69

JENKINS, JOHN S.
Voyage Of The U. S. Exploring Squadron Commanded by Captain Charles. Auburn & Roch: 1857:. V. 72

JENKINS, LADY
Sport and Travel in Both Tibets. 1910. V. 70

JENKINS, MINNIE BRAITHWAITE
Girl from Williamsburg. Richmond: 1951. V. 73

JENKINS, SIMON
Images of Hampstead. Richmond-Upon-Thames: 1982. V. 71

JENKINSON, HENRY IRWIN
Practical Guide to the English Lake District. London: 1875. V. 71
Practical Guide to the English Lake District. London: 1876. V. 71

JENKINSON, HILARY
Mediaeval Tallies, Public And Private. London: 1924. V. 72

JENKINSON, MICHAEL
Ghost Towns of New Mexico. 1967. V. 69

JENKS, TOM
Soldiers and Civilians. New York: 1986. V. 70

JENNESS, DIAMOND
The Life of the Copper Eskimos. Report of the Canadian Arctic Expedition 1913-1918. Volume XII. Ottawa: 1922. V. 73

JENNESS, HERBERT T.
Bucket Brigade to Flying Squadron, Fire Fighting Past and Present. Boston: 1909. V. 69

JENNEWEIN, J. LEONARD
Black Hills Booktrails. Mitchell: 1962. V. 69; 72; 73

JENNEY, WALTER P.
Report on the Mineral Wealth, Climate and Rain Fall and Natural Resources of the Black Hills of Dakota. Washington: 1876. V. 70

JENNINGS, AL
Number 30664 by Number 31539 - A Sketch in the Lives of William Sidney Porter and Al Jennings. Hollywood: 1941. V. 69

JENNINGS, ARTHUR SEYMOUR
The Decoration and Renovation of the Home.... London: 1923. V. 68
Paint and Colour Mixing. 1921. V. 68

JENNINGS, BRENDAN
Michael O'Cleirigh, Chief of the Four Masters and His Associates. 1936. V. 70

JENNINGS, ELIZABETH
In Shakespeare's Company. Shipston-on-Stour: 1985. V. 72
Songs for a Birth or a Death and other poems. London: 1961. V. 72

JENNINGS, H. J.
Our Homes and How to Beautify Them. London: 1902. V. 68

JENNINGS, HARGRAVES
The Marine Memorandum Book. London: 1845. V. 70
My Marine Memorandum Book. 1845. V. 72

JENNINGS, J. ELLIS
Color-Vision and Color-Blindness. Philadelphia: 1896. V. 71

JENNINGS, JAMES
A Practical Treatise on the History, Medical Properties and Cultivation of Tobacco. 1830. V. 72

JENNINGS, KENNETH QUAD
Political and Social Force of the New Jersey Press Associaton 1857- 1939. 1941. V. 71

JENNINGS, MAUREEN
Except the Dying. New York: 1997. V. 68

JENNINGS, N. A.
A Texas Ranger. Dallas: 1930. V. 69

JENNINGS, O. E.
A Manual of the Mosses of Western Pennsylvania and Adjacent Regions. Notre Dame: 1951. V. 71
Wild Flowers of Western Pennsylvania and the Upper Ohio Basin. Pittsburgh: 1953. V. 68; 70; 72; 73

JENSEN, ALBRECHT
Massage & Exercise Combined: A Permanent Physical Culture Course for Men, Women and Children.... NY: 1920. V. 72

JENSEN, ANN
Texas Ranger's Diary and Scrapbook. Dallas: 1936. V. 69

JENSEN, J. MARINUS
History of Provo, Utah. Provo: 1924. V. 69

JENSON, NICOLAS
The Last Will and Testament of the Late Nicolas Jenson, Printer, Who Departed this Life at the City of Venice in the Month of December. Chicago: 1928. V. 70

JENYNS, LEONARD
Observations in Natural History. London: 1846. V. 68; 70

JENYNS, SOAME
Later Chinese Porcelain. The Ch'ing Dynasty (1644-1912). London: 1951. V. 73
Ming Pottery And Porcelain. London: 1988. V. 72
Miscellaneous Pieces, in Verse and Prose. London: 1770. V. 70
Thoughts on the Causes and Consequences of the Present High Price of Provisions. London: 1767. V. 73

JEPHSON, HENRY
The Platform, its Rise and Progress. London: 1892. V. 71

JEPHSON, J. M.
Narrative of a Walking Tour in Britanny. London: 1859. V. 68
Shakespere: His Birthplace, Home and Grave. 1864. V. 72

JEPHSON, ROBERT
The Confessions of James Baptiste Couteau, Citizen of France.... London: 1794. V. 73
Roman Portraits. 1794. V. 71
Roman Portraits. London: 1794. V. 72

JEPSON, EDGAR
Arsene Lupin. New York: 1909. V. 69
Memories of an Edwardian and Neo Georgian. London: 1937. V. 70

JEPSON, S.
Big Game Encounters. 1937. V. 72; 73

JEPSON, W. L.
A Manual of the Flowering Plants of California. Berkeley: 1923-1925. V. 72

JERDAN, WILLIAM
National Portrait Gallery of Illustrious and Eminent Personages of the Nineteenth Century. London: 1830. V. 70; 72

JERDON, T. C.
The Mammals of India. Roorkee: 1867. V. 73
The Mammals of India. London: 1874. V. 69

JERMYN, LOUISA EMILY
Poetry for Youth, Original and Selected.... London: 1851. V. 69

JERNINGHAM, EDWARD
The Nunnery. An Elegy. London: 1762?. V. 70
The Nunnery: an Elegy. London: 1764. V. 70
Poems. 1779. V. 72
Poems. London: 1779. V. 71

JERNINGHAM, HUBERT E.
Life in a French Chateau. London: 1867. V. 68; 72
Norham Castle. Edinburgh: 1883. V. 73

JEROME, JEROME K.
The Celebrity - a Play in Three Acts. London: 1926. V. 68
John Ingerfield and Other Stories. London: 1894. V. 69
Three Men in a Boat. Bristol: 1889. V. 73

JERROLD, BLANCHARD
A Brage-Breaker with the Swedes; or Notes from the North in 1852. London: 1854. V. 73
The Life and Remains of Douglas Jerrold. By His Son. London: 1859. V. 70
The Life of George Cruikshank. London: 1882. V. 69; 70

JERROLD, DOUGLAS
Fireside Saints. London: 1904. V. 70
A Man Made of Money. London: 1849. V. 73
Mrs. Caudle In Crinoline. London: 1858. V. 71; 72

JERROLD, DOUGLAS WILLIAM
Quex. New York: 1928. V. 71
The Works. London: 1851. V. 71

JERROLD, THOMAS S.
The Garden that Paid the Rent. London: 1860. V. 68

JERROLD, WALTER
The Big Book of Fables. New York: 1912. V. 73
The Big Book of Fairy Tales. London. V. 72
The Big Book of Fairy Tales. New York: 1911. V. 70; 72; 73
The Big Nursery Rhymes. London. V. 72
Douglas Jerrold. Dramatist and Wit. London: 1914. V. 70

JERSEY. LAWS, STATUTES, ETC. - 1771
A Code of Laws for the Island of Jersey. St. Helier: 1771. V. 68

THE JERSEYMAN. Flemington: 1891-. V. 71

JERSEY'S Heresy Case. Col. Bob Ingersoll Makes a Sober And Very Impressive Speech.... Chicago: 1887. V. 72

THE JERUSALEM Prize for the Freedom of the Individual in Society. Jerusalem: 1999. V. 68; 71

JERVEY, THEODORE D.
Robert Y. Hayne and His Times. New York: 1909. V. 70

JERVICE, SOPHIA
Ines and Other Poems. London: 1816. V. 69

JERVOISE, E.
The Ancient Bridges of the North of England. London: 1931. V. 71; 73
The Ancient Bridges of the South of England- The Ancient Bridges of the North of England- The Ancient Bridges of Mid and Eastern England - The Ancient Bridges of Wales & Western England. 1932. V. 72

JESS, ZACHARIAH
A Compendious System of Practical Surveying, and Dividing of Land... (with) Tables of Difference of Latitude and Departure. Philadelphia: 1799. V. 71

JESSE, EDWARD
Anecdotes of Dogs. London: 1858. V. 70
An Angler's Rambles. 1836. V. 68; 73
An Angler's Rambles. London: 1836. V. 72

JESSE, F. TENNYSON
The Solange Stories. London: 1931. V. 73
Solange Stories. New York: 1931. V. 71

JESSE, J. HENEAGE
Literary and Historical Memorials of London. London: 1847. V. 68

JESSOP, WILLIAM
A Report on the Present State of the Piers of Sunderland Harbour, and the Means Recommended for Their Improvement. Sunderland: 1808. V. 73

JESSUP, RICHARD
The Cincinnati Kid. Boston and Toronto: 1963. V. 69; 70
Wolf Cop. Greenwich: 1961. V. 72

JESTER Annual 1939. V. 69

JETT, STEPHEN C.
House of Three Turkeys: Anasazi Redoubt. Santa Barbara: 1977. V. 73

JETZLEBENDES Italia, das ist Kurtze Doch Grundliche Beschreibung des Welschlands, Wie es Jetziger Zeit Beschaffen.... Lindau: 1681. V. 70

JEUNE, MARGARET S.
School Days in Paris.. New York: 1871. V. 70

JEVONS, WILLIAM STANLEY
Investigations in Currency and Finance. London: 1884. V. 72
Methods of Social Reform and Other Papers. London: 1883. V. 71; 72
Money and the Mechanism of Exchange. New York: 1900. V. 69
The Principles of Economics. London: 1905. V. 68; 72
Studies in Deductive Logic. London: 1880. V. 69

JEWETT, CHARLES
Speeches, Poems and Miscellaneous Writings on Subjects Connected with Temperance and the Liquor Traffic. Boston: 1849. V. 70

JEWETT, JOHN HOWARD
Baby Finger Play and Stories. London: 1906. V. 68
The Little Toy Bearkins. London: 1910. V. 68
The Stories the Baby Bears Told. London: 1910. V. 70
The Toy Bearkins' Christmas Tree. London: 1910. V. 70

JEWETT, S. G.
Birds of Washington State. Seattle: 1953. V. 68

JEWETT, SARAH ORNE
The Country of the Pointed Firs. Boston & New York: 1896. V. 68
The Life of Nancy. Boston & New York: 1895. V. 68
A White Heron. Boston: 1886. V. 68

JEWISH American Literature. New York: 2001. V. 68

JEWITT, JOHN
A Narrative of the Adventures and Sufferings of John Jewitt: only Survivor of the Crew of the Ship of Boston.... Middletown: 1815. V. 70

JEWITT, LLEWELLYN
Handbook of English Coins, Giving a Concise Description of the Various Denominations of Coin. London: 1870. V. 68
History of Ceramic Art in Great Britain. New York: 1878. V. 69

JEWKES, JOHN
An Industrial Survey of Cumberland and Furness. Manchester: 1933. V. 71

JEX BLAKE, SOPHIA
Medical Women. A Thesis and a History. Edinburgh: 1886. V. 69

JEYES, SAMUEL HENRY
The Life and Times of the Marquis of Salisbury.... London: 1895-1896. V. 71
Mr. Chamberlain: His Life and Public Career. London: 1903. V. 71

JHABVALA, RUTH PRAWER
A Backward Place. New York: 1965. V. 68
Esmond in India. New York: 1958. V. 68
Get Ready for Battle. London: 1962. V. 71
Get Ready for Battle. New York: 1963. V. 68
Heat and Dust. London: 1975. V. 68
In Search of Love and Beauty. New York: 1983. V. 68
Like Birds, Like Fishes. London: 1972. V. 72
The Nature of Passion. London: 1956. V. 68; 69; 71
Out of India. New York: 1986. V. 68; 72

JILLSON, WILLARD ROUSE
Early Kentucky Distillers 1783-1800. Louisville: 1940. V. 68

JIMENEZ, JUAN RAMON
Poesias Escojidas 1899-1917. New York: 1917. V. 71

JIN, HA
The Bridegroom. New York: 2000. V. 72; 73
In the Pond. Cambridge: 1998. V. 69
Under the Red Flag. Athens: 1997. V. 69; 71
Waiting. New York: 1999. V. 69; 70; 72
Waiting. London: 2000. V. 70
Wreckage. Brooklyn: 2001. V. 70

JINARAJADASA, C.
The Faith That is the Life. London: 1920. V. 72

JISL, LUMIR
Tibetan Art. London: 1956. V. 72

JOAN, NATALIE
Ameliaranne in Town. London: 1930. V. 68; 72
The Darling Book. 1922. V. 70
In the Garden. London: 1923. V. 69
Pam's Secret House. London: 1927. V. 70
Tales for Teeny Wee. Racine: 1935. V. 73

JOAN the Maid of Orleans Being that Portion of the Chronicles of Saint Denis.... San Francisco: 1938. V. 69

JOANS, TED
Afrodisia. New York: 1970. V. 71
A Black Manifesto in Jazz Poetry and Prose. London: 1971. V. 69

JOBARD, JEAN BAPTISTE AMBROISE MARCELLIN
Nouvelle Economie Sociale, ou Monautopole Industriel, Artistique, Commercial et Litteraire: Fonde sur la Perennite des Brevets d'Invention, Dessins, Modeles et Mrques de Fabrique. Paris: 1844. V. 70

JOBLOT, LOUIS
Descriptions et Usages de Plusieurs Nouveau Microscopes, Tant Simples Que Composez.... Paris: 1718. V. 70
Observations d'Histoire Naturelle, Faits avec le Miscroscope, sur un Grand Nombre d'Insectes & sur les Animalcules Qui se Trouvent dans les Liqueurs.... Paris: 1754-1755. V. 70

JOCELYN, ADA M.
Drawn Blank: a Novel. London: 1895. V. 68

JOCELYN, STEPHEN P.
Mostly Alkali. Caldwell: 1953. V. 72

JOCKO, the Brazilian Ape. London: 1848. V. 70

JOCOSERIUS, WAHRMUND, PSEUD.
Wol-Geschliffener Narren-spiegel, Worinnen Hundert und Vierzehn Arten Allerley Narren Ihr Eben-Bild und Ungestaltes Wesen Ersehen.... ?Nuremberg: 1730. V. 69

JOEL, DAVID
Charles Brooking 1723-1759, and the 18th Century British Marine Painters. London: 2000. V. 70

JOERG, W. L. G.
Problems of Polar Research. New York: 1928. V. 72

JOERSSON, S. A.
Adam Smith Auteur des Recherches sur La Richesse des Nations & Thomas Payne Auteur de La Decadence & De La Ruine Prochaine Des Finances de L'angleterre. Germanie: 1796. V. 70

JOHANNSEN, ALBERT
The House of Beadle and Adams and Its Dime and Nickle Novels. Norman: 1950. V. 69; 72

JOHANSEN, HJALMAR
With Nansen In The North. London: 1899. V. 72

JOHANSEN, J. P.
The Maori and His Religion, In Its Non-Ritualistic Aspects. Copenhagen: 1954. V. 69

JOHN Buchan 1847-1911. 1912. V. 69

JOHN, ANTHONY
The Early Challenges of the America's Cup (1851-1937). London: 1986. V. 69

JOHN, AUGUSTUS
Chiaroscuro. Fragments of Autobiography; First Series. London: 1952. V. 72
Fifty-Two Drawings. London: 1957. V. 68

JOHN Bull's Alphabet. London: 1880. V. 73

JOHN Bull's Neighbour in Her True Light.... London: 1884. V. 71

JOHN, EDMUND
The Flute of Sardonyx. 1991. V. 71

JOHN, ELIZABETH A. H.
Storms Brewed in Other Men's Worlds: the Confrontation of Indians, Spanish and French in the Southwest, 1540-1795. College Station: 1975. V. 71; 72; 73

JOHN, HENRY J.
Jan Evangelista Purkyne. Czech Scientist and Patriot. Philadelphia: 1959. V. 71

JOHN, ROMILLY
The Seventh Child-A Retrospect. London: 1975. V. 72

JOHN Updike. An Exhibition. 1985. V. 71

JOHN, W. D.
English Decorated Trays (1550-1850). Newport: 1964. V. 72

JOHN COOPER
Artists in Crime: An Illustrated Survey of Crime Fiction First Edition Dust Wrappers. Aldershot: 1920-1970. V. 73

JOHNNY Sliderlegs. New York: 1885. V. 71

JOHN OF ARDERNE
Treatises of Fistula in Ano: Hemorrhoids, and Clysters...from an Early Fifteenth-Century Manuscript Translation. London: 1910. V. 73

JOHN OF THE CROSS, SAINT
The Poems of St. John of the Cross. 1951. V. 70
The Song of the Soul. By Saint John-of-the-Cross, Barefooted Carmelite; Doctor of the Church. London: 1927. V. 71

JOHNS, C. A.
Gardening for Children. London: 1848. V. 68
Sea Weeds. London: 1860. V. 68
A Week at the Lizard. London: 1848. V. 68

JOHNS, J.
A Memoir of the Life of the Right Rev. William Meade. Baltimore: 1867. V. 68

JOHNS, JASPER
Seventeen Monotypes. West Islip: 1982. V. 72

JOHNS, VERONICA PARKER
Hush, Gabriel!. New York: 1940. V. 72

JOHNS, W. E.
Adventure Unlimited. 1957. V. 73
The Biggles Adventure Omnibus. 1965. V. 72
Biggles and the Plane that Disappeared. 1963. V. 73
Biggles and the Poor Rich Boy. Leicester: 1961. V. 69
Biggles Annual. Biggles Flies Again - In His First Ever Annual!. 1980. V. 73
Biggles Breaks the Silence. London: 1949. V. 69
Biggles' Chinese Puzzle. 1955. V. 73
Biggles Defies the Swastika. 1945. V. 72
Biggles Follows On. London: 1952. V. 72
Biggles Gets His Men. London: 1950. V. 68; 69
Biggles Goes Home. 1960. V. 73
Biggles Looks Back. 1965. V. 73
Biggles of the Interpol. 1957. V. 68
Biggles on the Home Front. 1957. V. 73
Biggles Takes a Holiday. 1949. V. 73
Biggles Takes the Case. 1952. V. 73
Biggles Works It Out. London: 1951. V. 68
The Cockpit - Flying Adventures for Young Pilots. 1934. V. 73
The Cockpit - Flying Adventures for Young Pilots. London: 1934. V. 69; 71
Comrades in Arms. 1947. V. 71
Gimlet Bores In. 1950. V. 72
Gimlet Off the Map. 1951. V. 72
Mossyface. A Romance of the Air. 1994. V. 72
Orchids for Biggles. Leicester: 1962. V. 69
The Rustlers of Rattlesnake Valley. 1948. V. 72
The Rustlers of Rattlesnake Valley. London: 1948. V. 69
Worrals Investigates. 1950. V. 71
Worrals of the WAAFS in Girl's Own Annual. volume 62. 1941. V. 73

JOHNSON, A. E.
The Russian Ballet. 1913. V. 68
W. Heath Robinson. Containing Many Examples of the Artist's Work in Brush, Pen and Pencil. London: 1913. V. 68

JOHNSON, A. F.
One Hundred Title Pages 1500-1800. London: 1928. V. 69

JOHNSON, A. M.
Genealogy of a Branch of the Johnson Family and Connections, Incidents and Legends. Chattanooga: 1893. V. 72

JOHNSON, ALEXANDER
A Collection of Authentic Cases, Proving the Practicability of Recovering Persons Visibly Dead by Drowning, Suffocation, Stifling, Swooning, Convulsions and Other Accidents. 1775. V. 72

JOHNSON, ALEXANDER BRYAN
A Treatise on Language, or the Relation Which Words Bear to Things in Four Parts. New York: 1836. V. 68; 73

JOHNSON, ALFRED
ABC Land. London: 1901. V. 72

JOHNSON, AMANDUS
The Swedes on the Delaware. 1638-1664. Philadelphia: 1927. V. 71
The Swedish Settlements on the Delaware: Their History and Relation to the Indians, Dutch and English 1638-1664. Philadelphia: 1911. V. 71

JOHNSON, ANDREW
Trial of Andrew Johnson, President of the United States Before the Senate of the U.S. on Impeachment by the House of Representatives for High Crimes and Misdeamnors. Washington: 1869. V. 72

JOHNSON, AUDREY
Furnishing Dolls' Houses. London: 1972. V. 72

JOHNSON, B. S.
All Bull: the National Servicemen. London: 1973. V. 68
Christy Malry's Own Double-Entry. London: 1973. V. 68; 72; 73
House Mother Normal - a Geriatric Comedy. London: 1971. V. 69; 72
Statement Against Corpses. London: 1964. V. 70
Travelling People. London: 1963. V. 70; 73
Trawl. London: 1966. V. 73
The Unfortunates. 1969. V. 71
You Always Remember the First Time. London: 1975. V. 72

JOHNSON, BARRY C.
Case of Marcus A. Reno. London: 1969. V. 69
Flipper's Dismissal. London: 1980. V. 70

JOHNSON, BILL
Moon Over Purgatory. New York: 1995. V. 69

JOHNSON, Boswell and Their Circle. Essays Presented to Lawrence Fitzroy Powell. Oxford: 1965. V. 69

JOHNSON, CHARLES
Being and Race: Black Writing Since 1970. Bloomington: 1988. V. 72
Middle Passage. London: 1990. V. 68
Middle Passage. New York: 1990. V. 71; 73
Middle Passage. London: 1991. V. 69

JOHNSON, CHARLES continued
Sorcerer's Apprentice. New York: 1986. V. 68; 70; 71; 73
The Wife's Relief; or, The Husband's Cure. London: 1712. V. 71

JOHNSON, CHARLES PLUMPTRE
Hints to Collectors of Original Editions of the Works of Charles Dickens. London: 1885. V. 68

JOHNSON, CHARLES, PSEUD.
History of the Pirates, Containing the Lives of Those Noted Pirate Captains, Misson, Bowen, Kidd, Tew, Halsey.... London: 1814. V. 70

JOHNSON, CHARLES R.
Black Humor. Chicago: 1970. V. 73

JOHNSON, CHARLES S.
The Economic Status of Negroes. np: 1933. V. 71

JOHNSON, CLARENCE W.
The History of the 321st Infantry. Columbia: 1919. V. 68

JOHNSON, CLIFTON
Highways and Byways. New York: 1906. V. 68

JOHNSON, CROCKETT
The Emperor's Gifts. New York: 1965. V. 73

JOHNSON, D. L.
The Architecture of Walter Burley Griffin. Adelaide: 1977. V. 69; 72

JOHNSON, DENIS
Already Dead. New York: 1997. V. 72
Angels. New York: 1983. V. 69; 70
Fiskadoro. New York: 1985. V. 70
Resuscitation of a Hanged Man. New York: 1991. V. 68; 70
The Stars at Noon. New York: 1986. V. 70
The Veil. Poems. New York: 1987. V. 70

JOHNSON, DIANA L.
Fantastic Illustration and Design in Britain 1850-1930. Rhode Island School of Desig: 1979. V. 70

JOHNSON, DIANE
Le Divorce. New York: 1997. V. 73

JOHNSON, DOROTHY M.
The Hanging Tree. New York: 1957. V. 70; 71
Indian Country. New York: 1953. V. 71

JOHNSON, FRIDOL
Rockwell Kent: An Anthology of His Works. New York: 1982. V. 72; 73

JOHNSON, G. A. L.
The Geology of Moor House, a National Nature Reserve in North-East Westmorland. London: 1963. V. 71; 73

JOHNSON, GEORGE
The All Red Line. The Annals and Aims of the Pacific Cable Project. Ottawa: 1903. V. 73

JOHNSON, GUY
John Henry. Tracking Down a Negro Legend. Chapel Hill: 1929. V. 72
Standing at the Scratch Line. New York: 1998. V. 72

JOHNSON, GUY B.
John Henry. Tracking Down a Negro Legend. Chapel Hill: 1929. V. 70

JOHNSON, HAROLD
Who's Who in Major League Baseball. Chicago: 1933. V. 68; 72

JOHNSON, HARRY
A History of Anderson County, Kansas. Garnett: 1936. V. 68

JOHNSON, HENRY LEWIS
Gutenberg and the Book of Books with Bibliographical Notes.... New York: 1932. V. 73

JOHNSON, HENRY T.
The Ape Man. London. V. 71

JOHNSON, HONOR
Herbal: Poems. Woodside: 1980. V. 71

JOHNSON, J. C. F.
Getting Gold: a Practical Treatise for Prospectors, Miners and Students. London: 1898. V. 71

JOHNSON, J. R.
The Parachute and Other Bad Shots. London: 1891. V. 72

JOHNSON, JAMES WELDON
The Autobiography of an Ex-Colored Man. Boston: 1912. V. 70; 71
The Book of American Negro Poetry. New York: 1922. V. 73
The Book of American Negro Spirituals. London. V. 69
The Book of American Negro Spirituals. New York: 1925. V. 68
Fifty Years and Other Poems. Boston: 1917. V. 70; 71
God's Trombones. New York: 1927. V. 68; 73
Negro Americans, What Now?. New York: 1934. V. 70
Saint Peter Relates an Incident. New York: 1935. V. 70
The Second Book of Negro Spirituals. New York: 1926. V. 69

JOHNSON, JESSE J.
Ebony Brass. New York: 1967. V. 72

JOHNSON, JOHN
Typographia, or the Printer's Instructor. London: 1824. V. 68; 73
The Unbloody Sacrifice, and Altar, Unvail'd and Supported. London: 1714. V. 70
The Way to Get Married: and the Advantages and Disadvantages of the Marriage State. Philadelphia: 1810. V. 69; 73

JOHNSON, JOHN LIPSCOMB
Autobiographical Notes. Boulder: 1958. V. 70

JOHNSON, JOSEPH
Traditions and Reminiscences Chiefly of the American Revolution in the South.... Charleston: 1851. V. 68

JOHNSON, JOSEPHINE
Winter Orchard. New York: 1935. V. 71

JOHNSON, JOYCE
Bad Connections. New York: 1978. V. 72
Minor Characters. London: 1983. V. 69

JOHNSON, KENNETH M.
Aerial California: an Account of Early Flight in Northern and Southern California 1849 to World War One. Los Angeles: 1961. V. 68
The Fremont Court Martial. Los Angeles: 1968. V. 68; 73
K-344 or the Indians of California vs. the United States. Los Angeles: 1966. V. 68
San Francisco, As It Is, Being Gleanings from the Picayune, 1850-1852. Georgetown: 1964. V. 68; 73

JOHNSON, L. C.
Thoreau's Complex Weave.... Charlottesville: 1986. V. 68

JOHNSON, LAURA WINTHROP
Eight Hundred Miles in an Ambulance. Philadelphia: 1889. V. 70; 72

JOHNSON, LIONEL
Ireland with Other Poems. London: 1897. V. 73
Poems. London: 1895. V. 72; 73
Post Liminium: Essays and Critical Papers. London: 1911. V. 69
Reviews and Critical Papers. London: 1921. V. 71
Some Poems of Lionel Johnson. London: 1912. V. 69; 70

JOHNSON, LYNDON BAINES
The Road to Justice. Three Major Statements on Civil Rights. 1965. V. 71
This America. New York: 1966. V. 69; 71
The Vantage Point: Perspectives of the Presidency 1963-1969. New York: 1971. V. 71

JOHNSON, M. J.
Catalogue of the Small but Extremely Choice Collection of Printed Books and Illuminated Manuscripts Formed by the Late M. J. Johnson, Esq, Radcliffe Observer. London: 1862. V. 70

JOHNSON, M. L.
Intensely Little Volume of True History of The Struggles with Hostile Indians on the Frontier of Texas. Dallas: 1923. V. 72

JOHNSON, MAGGIE P.
Fallen Blossoms. Parkersburg: 1951. V. 68

JOHNSON, MERLE
American First Editions. New York: 1929. V. 73
American First Editions. New York: 1932. V. 69
American First Editions. New York: 1936. V. 73
Hightspots of American Literature. New York: 1929. V. 73

JOHNSON, NEIL R.
The Chaickasaw Rancher. Stillwater: 1961. V. 71; 72

JOHNSON, OLGA
The Story of the Tobacco Plains Country. The Autobiography of a Community. 1950. V. 68

JOHNSON, OWEN
Murder in Any Degree. New York: 1913. V. 69
The Woman Gives. Boston: 1916. V. 70; 71

JOHNSON, P. DEMAREST
Claudius, the Cowboy of Rampao Valley. Middletown: 1894. V. 71

JOHNSON, PAMELA HANSFORD
The Unspeakable Skipton. New York: 1959. V. 68

JOHNSON, PHIL
Life on the Plains. Chicago: 1888. V. 71

JOHNSON, R. BRIMLEY
Famous Reviews Selected and Edited with Introductory Notes. London: 1914. V. 69
Jane Austen, a Biography. London: 1930. V. 70
Jane Austen Her Life, Her Work, Her Family and Her Critics. 1930. V. 73

JOHNSON, R. M.
Systematic Account of the Geology of Tasmania. Hobart: 1888. V. 69

JOHNSON, REBEKAH B.
A Family Album. New York: 1965. V. 71

JOHNSON, RICHARD
A New History of the Grecian States; from their Earliest Period to their Extinction by the Ottomans. Lansingburgh: 1794. V. 68; 70; 73

JOHNSON, RICHARD continued
A New Theatrical Dictionary. London: 1792. V. 73

JOHNSON, ROBERT G.
An Historical Account of the First Settlement of Salem, in West Jersey, by John Fenwick, Esq....with Many of the Important Events that Have Occurred, Down to the Present Generation. Philadelphia: 1839. V. 71

JOHNSON, ROBERT U.
Battles and Leaders of the Civil War. New York: 1884-1887. V. 70
Battles and Leaders of the Civil War. South Brunswick: 1956. V. 70

JOHNSON, ROBERT UNDERWOOD
The Winter Hour, and Other Poems. New York: 1892. V. 69

JOHNSON, RONALD
Ark. The Foundations: 1-33. San Francisco: 1980. V. 72
Assorted Jungles: Rousseau. San Francisco: 1966. V. 72
Gorse, Goose, Rose and Other Poems. Indiana: 1966. V. 72
A Line of Poetry, A Row of Trees. Highlands: 1964. V. 72; 73
Radios OI-OIV. Berkeley: 1977. V. 73
The Spirit Walks, the Rocks Will Talk.... New York and Penland: 1969. V. 73
Sports and Divertissements. Urbana: 1969. V. 72; 73

JOHNSON, SAMUEL
The Adventurer. 1756. V. 72
The Beauties of Samuel Johnson.... London: 1792. V. 68
The Critical Opinions of Samuel Johnson. Princeton: 1926. V. 69
A Diary of a Journey into North Wales in the Year 1774.... London: 1816. V. 68
A Dictionary of the English Language. London: 1755. V. 68; 73
A Dictionary of the English Language. London: 1756. V. 68; 69
A Dictionary of the English Language. London: 1760. V. 69
A Dictionary of the English Language. London: 1765. V. 73
A Dictionary of the English Language. London: 1773. V. 68
A Dictionary of the English Language. London: 1785. V. 71
A Dictionary of the English Language. London: 1786. V. 72
Dictionary of the English Language. London: 1805. V. 73
A Dictionary of the English Language. Philadelphia: 1805. V. 69; 73
A Dictionary of the English Language. Philadelphia: 1813. V. 69
A Dictionary of the English Language. London: 1814. V. 73
A Dictionary of the English Language. London: 1822. V. 68; 71
A Dictionary of the English Language. London: 1990. V. 68
Dictionary of the English Language in Miniature. London: 1812. V. 70
The Pocket Dictionary of the English Language. 1835. V. 68
Doctor Johnson's Prayers.... 1947. V. 68
Doctor Johnson's Table-Talk: containing Aphorisms on Literature, Life and Manners; with Anecdotes of Distinquished Persons, selected and arranged for Mr. Boswells Life of Johnson. 1798. V. 72
Dr. Johnson's Table-Talk.... London: 1798. V. 73
An Essay on Woman, a Poem. London: 1772. V. 69
Facsimile of the Sale Catalogue of Johnson's Library...Reprinted for the Meeting of the Johnson Club in Oxford, June 11, 1892. London: 1892. V. 68
The Fountains, a Fairy Tale. Brisbane: 1984. V. 68
The Harleian Miscellany. London: 1744. V. 68
The History of Rasselas.... Bridgeport: 1809. V. 73
History of Rasselas.... London: 1910. V. 68
The Idler. London: 1761. V. 68
The Idler. 1808. V. 72
Irene, a Tragedy. London: 1749. V. 68
Johnson and Queeney. Letters from Dr. Johnson to Queeney Thrale.... London: 1932. V. 69
Johnsoniana or Supplement to Boswell, Being Anecdotes and Sayings of Dr. Johnson. London: 1836. V. 68; 72
Johnson's Journey to the Western Islands of Scotland and Boswell's Journal of a Tour to the Hebrides with Samuel Johnson . . . London: 1934. V. 71
A Journey to the Western Islands of Scotland. London: 1775. V. 68; 69
A Journey to the Western Islands of Scotland. London: 1795. V. 72
The Letters...With Mrs. Thrale's Genuine Letters to Him. Oxford: 1952. V. 68
The Letters, Collected by R. W. Chapman 1719-1784. Oxford: 1984. V. 68
The Letters of Samuel Johnson 1731-1784. Oxford: 1994. V. 73
Letters of Samuel Johnson, Carefully Selected and Arranged from Various Publications.... Edinburgh: 1822. V. 68
The Letters of Samuel Johnson, Collected and Edited by George Birkbeck Hill. Oxford: 1892. V. 68
The Letters of Samuel Johnson with Mrs. Thrale's Genuine Letters to Him.... Oxford: 1952. V. 68
Letters to and From Samuel Johnson LL.D., to which are added Some Poems.... London: 1788. V. 68; 70
Lives of the English Poets. Oxford: 1905. V. 68
The Lives of the Most Eminent English Poets. London: 1781. V. 68; 71
The Lives of the Most Eminent English Poets. London: 1794. V. 71
The Lives of the Most Eminent English Poets. London: 1800-1801. V. 71
The Lives of the Most Eminent English Poets. 1815. V. 72
The Lives of the Most Eminent English Poets. London: 1824. V. 71
The Lives of the Most Eminent English Poets. London: 1824. V. 71
Marmor Norfolciense; or an Essay on an Ancient Prophetical Inscription in Monkish Rhyme. London: 1739. V. 68
Memoirs of Charles Frederick, King of Prussia. Liverpool: 1790. V. 70
The New London Letter Writer. Waltham St. Lawrence: 1948. V. 70; 71
The Plan of a Dictionary. London: 1747. V. 68
The Plan of a Dictionary. London: 1755. V. 68

The Poetical Works. London: 1785. V. 68; 71
Poetical Works. London: 1789. V. 69; 70; 72
The Poetical Works. Burlington: 1816. V. 71
Political Tracts. 1776. V. 72
Political Tracts. Dublin: 1777. V. 68
The Prayers. New York: 1902. V. 70
Prayers and Meditations. London: 1796. V. 68
Prayers and Meditations. Lichfield: 1927. V. 68
The Prince of Abissinia. London: 1759. V. 68; 73
The Prince of Abissinia. London: 1786. V. 69
The Prince of Abissinia. 1790. V. 72
The Prince of Abissinia. London: 1798. V. 68
The Rambler. Dublin: 1785. V. 68
The Rambler. London: 1816. V. 68
Rasselas. Hartford: 1803. V. 71
Rasselas. London: 1805. V. 68; 71
Rasselas. London: 1816. V. 70
Rasselas. London: 1819. V. 68; 73
Rasselas. London: 1820. V. 68
(Rasselas) The Prince of Abissinia. London: 1759. V. 72
(Rasselas) The Prince of Abissinia. London: 1798. V. 72
Selected Essays from the Rambler, Adventurer and Idler. New Haven: 1968. V. 69
Sermons on Different Subjects Left for Publication by John Taylor, LL.D.... London: 1788-1789. V. 68
Taxation No Tyranny; an Answer to the Resoultions and Address of the American Congress. London: 1775. V. 72
The Works. Dublin: 1793. V. 71; 73
The Works. London: 1796. V. 68
The Works. Boston: 1809-1812. V. 73
The Works. New York: 1835. V. 71; 73
Works. Troy: 1903. V. 70
The Works of the English Poets. London: 1779-1781. V. 70
The Works of the English Poets, with prefaces, biographical and critical. 1790. V. 72

JOHNSON, SHIRLEY
Blood Platelets. London: 1961. V. 68

JOHNSON, THEODORE
California and Oregon; or Sights in the Gold Region and Scenes by the Way. Philadelphia: 1851. V. 73
Sights in the Gold Region and Scenes by the Way. New York: 1849. V. 68; 73
Sights in the Gold Region and Scenes by the Way. New York: 1850. V. 73

JOHNSON, THOMAS BURGELAND
The Shooter's Companion. 1819. V. 72
The Shooter's Companion. 1830. V. 70; 71
The Shooters Companion. London: 1830. V. 72

JOHNSON, VIRGINIA W.
The Unregimented General - A Biography of Nelson A. Miles. Boston: 1962. V. 72

JOHNSON, VIRGINIA WALES
An English Daisy Miller. Boston: 1882. V. 68

JOHNSON, W.
The Octopus. Omaha: 1940. V. 68

JOHNSON, W. BOLINGBROKE
The Widening Stain. New York: 1942. V. 72; 73

JOHNSON, W. R.
Easter. Philadelphia: 1970. V. 73

JOHNSON, WALTER
Gilbert White. London: 1928. V. 68

JOHNSON, WILLIAM
Sketches of the Life and Correspondence of Nathanael Greene, Major General of the Armies of the United States in the War of the Revolution. Charlestown: 1822. V. 71; 73

JOHNSON, WILLIAM PONSONBY
The History of Banbury and Its Neighbourhood. Banbury: 1865. V. 72

JOHNSON, ZOE
Mourning After. London: 1939. V. 72

JOHNSON'S New Illustrated (Steel Plate) Family Atlas.... Richmond: 1860. V. 70
JOHNSON'S New Illustrated (Steel Plate) Family Atlas.... New York: 1863. V. 72

JOHNSTON, ABRAHAM JAMES
Lettsom His Life, Times, Friends and Descendants. London: 1933. V. 70

JOHNSTON, BASIL H.
The Manitous. New York: 1995. V. 72
Tales of the Elders Told. Ojibway Legends. Toronto: 1981. V. 73

JOHNSTON, C. M.
The Valley of the Six Nations. Toronto: 1964. V. 73

JOHNSTON, C. R.
Provincial Poetry 1789-1839. Otley: 1992. V. 70

JOHNSTON, CLIFTON
An Unredeemed Captive Being the Story of Eunice Williams, Who at the Age of Seven Years, Was Carried Away from Deerfield by the Indians in the Year 1704.... Holyoke: 1897. V. 73

JOHNSTON, D. C.
The Galaxy of Wit; or Laughing Philosopher. Boston: 1827. V. 68
Scraps No. I. 1849. New Series. V. 71

JOHNSTON, DENIS
Collected Plays. 1960. V. 69
The Moon in the Yellow River. 1935. V. 70

JOHNSTON, EDWARD
Manuscript and Inscription Letters for Schools and Classes and for the Use of Craftsmen. 1922. V. 68

JOHNSTON, ELIZA GRIFFIN
Texas Wild Flowers. Austin: 1972. V. 69

JOHNSTON, ELLEN
Autobiography, Poems and Songs. Glasgow: 1869. V. 69

JOHNSTON, FREDERICK
Terracina Cloud: Poems. Verona: 1936. V. 71

JOHNSTON, G.
A Flora of Berwick-upon-Tweed. Edinburgh: 1829-1831. V. 69
A History of British Zoophytes. London: 1847. V. 69
An Introduction to Conchology. 1850. V. 73

JOHNSTON, GEORGE
My Brother Jack. London: 1964. V. 69
Selections from the Correspondence of Dr. George Johnston.... Edinburgh: 1892. V. 68

JOHNSTON, GEORGE P.
Catalogue of the Rare and Most Interesting Books and Manuscripts in the library at Drummond Castle.... Edinburgh: 1910. V. 68; 73

JOHNSTON, H. H.
The River Congo from Its Mouth to Bolobo. 1884. V. 69; 73

JOHNSTON, HARRY
George Grenfell and the Congo. London: 1908. V. 72
The River Congo from it's Mouth to Bolobo. 1884. V. 72
The Uganda Protectorate,. London: 1902. V. 72

JOHNSTON, HARRY V.
My Home on the Range: Frontier Ranching in the Badlands. 1942. V. 69

JOHNSTON, ISABEL M.
The Jeweled Toad. Indianapolis: 1907. V. 69; 71; 73

JOHNSTON, J.
Notes of a Visit to Walt Whitman, Etc. in July, 1890. Boston: 1890. V. 69
A Systematic Treatise on the Theory and Practice of Draining Land According to the Most Approved Methods.... Edinburgh: 1834. V. 69

JOHNSTON, J. B.
The Brain of Acipenser. Jena: 1901. V. 68

JOHNSTON, J. E.
Reports of the Secretary of War, with Reconnaissance of Routes from San Antonio to El Paso. Washington: 1850. V. 72

JOHNSTON, J. F. W.
Notes on North America Agricultural, Economical and Social. Edinburgh: 1851. V. 72
Report on the Agricultural Capabilities of the Province of New Brunswick. Fredericton: 1850. V. 73

JOHNSTON, JENNIFER
The Gates. London: 1973. V. 73

JOHNSTON, JOHN
Diary Notes on a Visit to Walt Whitman and Some of His Friends, in 1890. Manchester: 1898. V. 71
Historiae Naturalis de Insectus...De Serpentibus et Draconibus.... Frankfurt: 1653. V. 69

JOHNSTON, JOSEPH E.
Narrative of Military Operations, Direct During the Late War Between the States. New York: 1874. V. 69; 70

JOHNSTON, MADELEINE
Comets Have Long Tails. New York: 1938. V. 70

JOHNSTON, MARY
Lewis Rand. Boston and New York: 1908. V. 73
Miss Delicia Allen. Boston: 1933. V. 70
Sir Mortimer. New York and London: 1904. V. 70

JOHNSTON, PAUL
Biblio-Typographica. New York: 1930. V. 69
The Blood Tree. 2000. V. 68

JOHNSTON, TERRY
Border-Lords. Ottawa: 1982. V. 73
Carry the Wind. Aurora: 1982. V. 73

JOHNSTON, WAYNE
The Colony of Unrequited Dreams. New York: 1999. V. 72

JOHNSTON, WILLIAM
The Waddington Cipher. New York: 1923. V. 68

JOHNSTON, WILLIAM PRESTON
The Life of Gen. Albert Sydney Johnston. New York: 1878. V. 69

JOHNSTONE, CHARLES
Chrysal or the Adventures of a Guinea.... 1767. V. 73
Chrysal or the Adventures of a Guinea.... 1775. V. 73
Chrysal or the Adventures of a Guinea.... 1822. V. 73
The Reverie; or a Flight to the Paradise of Fools. Dublin: 1762. V. 73

JOHNSTONE, CHRISTINA JANE
The Cook and Housewife's Manual. Edinburgh: 1828. V. 70

JOHNSTONE, CHRISTINIA JANE
The Cook and Housewife's Manual. Edinburgh: 1862. V. 73

JOHNSTONE, G.
Asiatic Magnolias in Cultivation. London: 1955. V. 69

JOHNSTONE, IAIN
The World Is Not Enough: A Companion. London: 1999. V. 71

JOHNSTONE, JAMES
Antiquitates Celto-Normannicae...(with) Antiquitates Celto-Scandicae. Copenhagen: 1786. V. 70

JOHNSTONE, JAMES JOHNSTONE, CHEVALIER DE
Memoirs of the Rebellion in 1745 and 1746... London: 1822. V. 71

JOHNSTONE, JOHN
An Harveian Oration and Other Remains. London: 1838. V. 69
The Mode of Draining Land, According to the System Practised by the Late Mr. Joseph Elkington. 1841. V. 71

JOHNSTONE, R. W.
William Smellie. The Master of British Midwifery. Edinburgh: 1952. V. 68

JOHNSTON-LAVIS, HENRY JAMES
Bibliography of the Geology and Eruptive Phenomena of the More Important Volcanoes of Southern Italy.... London: 1918. V. 70

JOHNSTON'S Detroit City Directory and Advertising Gazetteer of Michigan. Detroit: 1861. V. 69

JOLAS, EUGENE
Transition - Numbers I-XII. Paris: 1927-. V. 69
Transition. The Hague: 1936. V. 71
Transition - No. 25. New York: 1936. V. 71
Transition - No. 26. New York: 1937. V. 71

JOLIMONT, F. G. THEODORE BASSET DE
Les Mausolees Francais.... Paris: 1821-1823. V. 72

JOLINE, ADRIAN HOFFMAN
The Diversions of a Book Lover. New York and London: 1903. V. 69
Edgehill Essays. Boston: 1911. V. 69

JOLLIE'S Cumberland Guide and Directory. Carlisle: 1811. V. 71

JOLLY Bears ABC. New York: 1910. V. 70

JOLLY Jack's Annual 1936. V. 70

JOLLY Jingles. New York: 1907. V. 69

THE JOLLY Jump-Ups: Favorite Nursery Stories. Springfield: 1947. V. 73

JOLLY Transformations. No. 1. New York: 1910. V. 70

JOLLY, CLIFFORD J.
Early Hominids of Africa. London: 1978. V. 68

JOLLY, EMILY
Pearl; a novel. London: 1882. V. 68

JOLY, J.
Reminiscences and Anticipations. 1920. V. 69
The Surface History of the Earth. Oxford: 1925. V. 72

JONAITIS, A.
Art of the Northern Tlingit. Seattle: 1986. V. 69

JONAS BROTHERS
Art in Taxidermy. Denver: 1936. V. 72

JONAS, KLAUS
The Maugham Enigma. New York: 1954. V. 71

JONES, A., MRS.
Poems and Songs, Etc. Preston: 1890. V. 69

JONES, BARBARA
Follies and Grottoes. London: 1953. V. 72; 73

JONES, BOB
Rights and Wrongs of Golf. 1935. V. 72

JONES, C.
The Comparative Endocrinology of Vertebrates. Part I. Cambridge: 1955. V. 72

JONES, C. S., MRS.
Household Elegancies. New York: 1875. V. 70

JONES, CHAPLAIN
A Chaplain's Experience Ashore and Afloat The Texas Under Fire. New York: 1901. V. 68; 73

JONES, CHARLES C.
Catechism of Scripture, Doctrine and Practice.... Savannah: 1837. V. 68
Defence of Battery Wagner, July 18th, 1863. Augusta: 1892. V. 69; 70
The Life and Services of Commodore Josiah Tattnall. Savannah: 1878. V. 70
Military Operations in Georgia During the War Between the States. Augusta: 1893. V. 69
Sergeant William Jasper. Albany: 1876. V. 68
The Siege and Evacuation of Savannah, Georgia in December 1864. Augusta: 1890. V. 69
The Siege of Savannah in December, 1864 and the Confederate Operations in Georgia...During General Sherman's March from Atlanta to the Sea. Albany: 1874. V. 70

JONES, CLEMENT
A Tour in Westmorland. Kendal: 1948. V. 71

JONES, CYRUS E., MRS.
Needlework Guild Cook Book. Jamestown: 1910. V. 68

JONES, D. N.
The Megapodes. Oxford: 1995. V. 72

JONES, DAVID
The Anathemata. London: 1952. V. 68; 72; 73
A Compleat History of the Turks, from Their Origin in the Year 755 to the Year 1701...to Which are Added, Their Maxims of State and Religion.... London: 1701. V. 73
The Fatigue.... Cambridge: 1965. V. 68
In Parenthesis. 1937. V. 70
In Parenthesis. London: 1937. V. 68
In Parenthesis. London: 1961. V. 69; 73
On the Value of Annuities and Reversionary Payments, with Numerous Tables. London: 1844. V. 70
The Tribune's Visitation: a Poem. London: 1969. V. 68

JONES, DAVID W.
Forty Years Among the Indians. Salt Lake City: 1890. V. 71

JONES, DOUGLAS C.
Arrest Sitting Bull. New York: 1977. V. 73
The Treaty of Medicine Lodge. Norman: 1966. V. 68; 71
The Treaty of Medicine Lodge. Norman: 1968. V. 72

JONES, E. ALFRED
The Loyalists of New Jersey. Their Memorials, Petitions, Claims, etc. From English Records. Newark: 1927. V. 71
Old English Gold Plate. London: 1907. V. 72; 73
The Old Silver of American Churches. Letchworth: 1913. V. 68

JONES, EBENEEZER
Studies of Sensation and Event: Poems. 1843. V. 73

JONES, ERNEST
The Life and Work of Sigmund Freud. New York: 1953. V. 69

JONES, FRANKLIN D.
Ingenious Mechanisms for Designers and Inventors. New York: 1948. V. 68

JONES, G. F. TREVALLYN
Saw-Pit Wharton. London: 1967. V. 70; 72
Saw-Pit Wharton. Sydney: 1967. V. 71

JONES, GEORGE
Supreme Bon Ton; and Bon Ton by Profession. London: 1820. V. 73

JONES, GERALD
Taking Stock: Painting and Sculpture by G. Harvey. Houston: 1986. V. 70

JONES, GLYN
The Saga of Llywarch the Old. Waltham St. Lawrence: 1955. V. 71

JONES, GUY
There Was a Little Man. New York: 1948. V. 71

JONES, GWYN
The Green Island. Waltham St. Lawrence: 1946. V. 68; 70; 71
The Vikings. London: 1997. V. 73

JONES, H. J.
The Chrysanthemum Album. Lewisham: 1896. V. 68; 71
Chrysanthemum Guide 1895. 1895. V. 69

JONES, H. L.
Mathews: Masterpieces of the California Decorative Style. Santa Barbara: 1980. V. 72

JONES, HENRY
Card Essays, Clay's Decisions and Card-Table Talk. New York: 1880. V. 70
The Scriptures Searched; or Christ's Second Coming and Kingdom at Hand. New York: 1839. V. 73

JONES, HENRY FESTING
Diary of a Journey through North Italy to Sicily in the Spring of 1903.... Cambridge: 1904. V. 71
Samuel Butler. Author of Erewhon (1835-1902). A Memoir. London: 1919. V. 71; 72

JONES, HENRY M.
Ships of Kingston. Plymouth: 1926. V. 68; 73

JONES, HETTIE
Big Star Fallin' Mama. Five Women in Black Music. New York: 1974. V. 73

JONES, HORACE
The Story of Early Rice County. 1928. V. 68

The Story of Early Rice County. Wichita: 1928. V. 71
Up from the Sod-The Life Story of a Kansas Prairie County. Wichita: 1968. V. 71

JONES, HOWARD M.
The Harp that Once - a Chronicle of the Life of Thomas Moore. New York: 1937. V. 69; 73

JONES, HUGH
The Present State of Virginia. New York: 1865. V. 69

JONES, IDWAL
China Boy. Los Angeles: 1936. V. 68
The Vineyard. New York: 1942. V. 68

JONES, INIGO
The Designs...Consisting of Plans and Elevations for Publick and Private Buildings. 1727. V. 69

JONES, J.
Explorations of the Aboriginal Remains of Tennessee. Washington: 1879. V. 69
A Paper on Poor Law Administration Read by Mr. J. Jones, of the Stepney Union, Reperinted from Knight and Co's Report of the Poor Law Conference for the North Midland District, Held at Lincoln on the 16th November 1876. London: 1876. V. 69

JONES, J. EBERT
A Review of Famous Crimes - Solved by St. Louis Policemen. St. Louis. V. 69

JONES, J. M.
Contributions to a Natural History of the Bermudas. Washington: 1884. V. 68

JONES, J. O.
A Cowman's Memoirs. Fort Worth: 1953. V. 71

JONES, J. ROY
Saddle Bags in Siskiyou. Yreka: 1953. V. 68; 73

JONES, J. W.
The Salmon. 1958. V. 68; 73

JONES, J. WILLIAM
Army of Northern Virginia Memorial Volume. Richmond: 1880. V. 69; 70
Christ in the Camp, or Religion in Lee's Army. Richmond: 1887. V. 70

JONES, JAMES
From Here to Eternity. New York: 1951. V. 69; 71; 73
The Pistol. New York: 1958. V. 71
The Thin Red Line. New York: 1962. V. 69; 70; 71; 73
Whistle. Columbia: 1974. V. 69; 71; 73
WWII. New York: 1975. V. 73

JONES, JAMES ATHEARN
Hardenbrass and Haverill; or, the Secret of the Castle, a Novel, in Four Volumes. London: 1817. V. 69

JONES, JAMES EDMUND
Scenes from Dickens. Trials, Sketches, Plays. Toronto: 1923. V. 68

JONES, JOHN
The History and Antiquities of Harewood. 1859. V. 73
Medical, Philosophical and Vulgar Errors of Various Kinds, considered and Refuted. London: 1797. V. 73
The Reason of Man: Part Second. Canterbury: 1793. V. 69
A Treatise on the Process Employed by Nature in Surpressing the Hemorrhage from Divided and Punctured Arteries; and on the Use of the Ligature.... London: 1810. V. 68
Wonders of the Stereoscope with Viewer and 48 Cards. New York: 1976. V. 68

JONES, JOHN B.
A Rebel War Clerk's Diary at the Confederate States Capital. New York: 1935. V. 69

JONES, JOHN F. D.
A Treatise on the Process Employed by Nature in Suppressing the Hemorrhage from Divided and Punctured Arteries.... London: 1810. V. 72

JONES, JOHN PAUL
Letters of John Paul Jones, Printed from the Unpublished Originals in Mr. W. K. Bixby's Collection. Boston: 1905. V. 72
Life and Correspondence.... New York: 1830. V. 72

JONES, JOSEPH
Explorations of the Aboriginal Remains of Tennessee. Washington: 1876. V. 71

JONES, JOSEPH SEAWELL
Memorials of North Carolina. New York: 1838. V. 68

JONES, JUSTIN
The Nun of St. Ursula, or the Burning of the Covent. Boston: 1845. V. 68
Yankee Jack; or, the Perils of a Privateersman. New York: 1852. V. 71; 73

JONES, KATHARINE
Heroines of Dixie. New York: 1955. V. 69; 70
The Plantation South. Indianapolis: 1957. V. 70

JONES, LEONARD A.
A Treatise on the Law of Easements in Continuation of the Law of Real Property. New York: 1898. V. 71

JONES, LOUISE SEYMOUR
The Human Side of Bookplates. 1951. V. 68

JONES, M.
Dr. Kane the Arctic Hero. London: 1886. V. 68

JONES, M. L.
Hydrothermal Vents of the Eastern Pacific: an Overview. Vienna: 1985. V. 72

JONES, MARY ELIZABETH
The Lake and Other Poems. London: 1844. V. 69

JONES, MERVYN
A Survivor. New York: 1986. V. 68

JONES, MOTHER
The Autobiography of Mother Jones. Chicago: 1925. V. 72

JONES, O.
A Gamekeeper's Note Book. 1910. V. 71

JONES, OWEN
The Grammar of Ornament. London: 1856. V. 68
The Grammar of Ornament. London: 1910. V. 69
The Grammar of Ornament. London: 1928. V. 72; 73
The Song of Songs. London: 1849. V. 72

JONES, OWEN GLYNNE
Rock Climbing in the English Lake District. 1900. V. 68; 70; 73
Rock Climbing in the English Lake District. Keswick: 1900. V. 69; 71
Rock Climbing in the English Lake District. Keswick: 1911. V. 69; 71

JONES, P. MANSELL
Emile Verhaeren - a Study in the Development of His Art and Ideas. Cardiff and London: 1926. V. 68

JONES, RAYMOND F.
Planet of Light. Philadelphia: 1953. V. 69
This Island Earth. New York: 1952. V. 73

JONES, ROBERT
Notes on Military Orthopaedics. London: 1917. V. 70
Orthopedic Surgery. New York: 1923. V. 73

JONES, ROBERT T.
Down the Fairway. London: 1927. V. 69
Down the Fairway. London: 1928. V. 70

JONES, S. S.
Northumberland and Its Neighbour Lands. Hexham: 1871. V. 73

JONES, SAMUEL
The Siege of Charleston, and the Operations on the South Atlantic Coast in the War Between the States. New York: 1911. V. 69; 70

JONES, SAMUEL ARTHUR
Pertaining to Thoreau. Detroit: 1901. V. 71

JONES, STEPHEN
A New Biographical Dictionary.... London: 1822. V. 69

JONES, SUSANNA
The Earthquake Bird. 2001. V. 69

JONES, T. R.
Cassell's Book of Birds. 1880. V. 69

JONES, TERRY
The Goblin Companion. Atlanta: 1996. V. 73
Strange Stains and Mysterious Smells. New York: 1996. V. 73

JONES, THOM
The Pugilist at Rest. New York: 1993. V. 73
The Pugilist at Rest. London: 1994. V. 68

JONES, THOMAS
The Gregynog Press, a Paper read to the Double Crown Club on 7 April 1954. London: 1954. V. 73
The Gregynog Press; a Paper Read to the Double Crown Club on 7 April 1954. Newtown: 1954. V. 71
James Cropper & Co., Limited, and Memories of Burneside 1845-1945. Kendal: 1945. V. 71

JONES, THOMAS CAMBRIA
Morality: a Poem. Sung in Solitude. Chester: 1835. V. 71

JONES, THOMAS GOODE
Last Days of the Army of Northern Virginia. Richmond?: 1893. V. 69

JONES, THOMAS H.
Experience and Personal Narrative of Uncle Tom Jones. . . Boston: 1855?. V. 71
Experience and Personal Narrative of Uncle Tom Jones.... New York: 1854. V. 68

JONES, THOMAS RYMER
The Aquarian Naturalist. London: 1858. V. 68; 70

JONES, TOM
The Fantasticks. New York: 1964. V. 70; 71

JONES, W. F.
The Experiences of a Deputy U.S. Marshall of the Indian Territory. Muskogee: 1976. V. 68; 73

JONES, W. H. S.
The Doctor's Oath. Cambridge: 1924. V. 68

JONES, W. NORTHEY
The History of St. Peter's Church in Perth Amboy...from Its Organization in 1698 to the Year of Our Lord 1923.... Perth Amboy: 1924. V. 71

JONES, WALTER
Heating by Hot Water. London: 1894. V. 68

JONES, WILLIAM
The Broad, Broad Ocean. London. V. 70
The Broad, Broad Ocean and Some of Its Inhabitants. London: 1884. V. 68
The Description and Use of a New Portable Orrery.... London: 1799. V. 73
An Essay on the Law of Bailments. London: 1798. V. 70
The Gardener's Receipt Book.... London: 1845. V. 71
The Moallakat, or Seven Arabian Poems.... London: 1782. V. 70
Poems, Consisting Chiefly of Translations from the Asiatick Languages. London: 1777. V. 68
Poeseos Asiaticae Commentariorum Libri Sex. Londini: 1774. V. 70
A Popular Sketch of the Various Proposed System of Atmospheric Railway, Demonstrating the Applicability of the Mechanical Properties of the Atmosphere.... London: 1845. V. 72
Reflections Upon the Perils and Difficulties of the Winter Navigation of the Delaware. Philadelphia: 1822. V. 69
The Speeches of Isaeus in Causes Concerning the Law of Succession to Porperty at Athens with a Prefatory Discourse, Notes Critical and Historical and a Commentary. London: 1779. V. 70
Twelve Months with Tito's Partisans. Bedford: 1946. V. 73

JONG, ERICA
At the Edge of the Body. New York: 1979. V. 72
Half-Lives. New York: 1973. V. 69; 72
How to Save Your Own Life. New York: 1977. V. 71; 72

JONKER, F. P.
A Monograph of the Burmanniaceae. Utrecht: 1938. V. 72

JONSON, BEN
Ben Jonson His Volpone; or the Foxe. London: 1898. V. 70
The English Grammar Made by Ben Jonson for the Benefit of all Strangers Out of His Observation of the English Language Now Spoken and in Use. London: 1928. V. 71
The Masque of Queenes. London: 1930. V. 72
Notes of Ben Jonson's Conversations with William Drummond of Hawthornden. London: 1842. V. 71
The Poems of Ben Jonson. Oxford: 1936. V. 69
Songs. A Selection from the Plays, Masques and Poems, with the Earliest Known Settings of Certain Numbers. Hammersmith: 1906. V. 70
Volpone or the Fox. Oxford: 1952. V. 70
The Works. London: 1816. V. 72
The Works. London: 1860. V. 70

JOPLING, CHARLES M.
Sketch of Furness and Cartmel, Comprising the Hundred of Lonsdale North of the Sands. London: 1843. V. 71

JOPPIEN, R.
The Art of Captain Cook's Voyages. Volume II. New Haven: 1985. V. 68; 72

JORDAN, DAVID STARR
The Aquatic Resources of the Hawaiian Islands, Part 1, The Shore Fishes. Washington: 1905. V. 72; 73
A Catalog of the Fishes of the Island of Formosa or Taiwan, Based on the Collections of Dr. Hans Sauter. Pittsburgh: 1909. V. 72
A Check-List of the Fishes and Fish-Like Vertebrates of North and Middle America. Washington: 1896. V. 72
The Days of a Man. London: 1922. V. 73
The Days of Man, Being Memories of a Naturalist, Teacher and Minor Prophet of Democracy. Yonkers-on-Hudson: 1922. V. 72
Fishes. New York: 1925. V. 70; 73
The Fishes of North and Middle America. Washington: 1896-. V. 70
The Fishes of North and Middle America. Washington: 1896-1900. V. 72; 73
Synopsis of the Fishes of North America. Washington: 1882. V. 72

JORDAN, ELIZABETH
The Devil and the Deep Sea. New York: 1929. V. 70

JORDAN, J. A.
Mangaso. Man Who Is Always Moving. 1956. V. 73

JORDAN, JUNE
Kimako's Story. Boston: 1981. V. 72

JORDAN, NEIL
The Past. London: 1980. V. 69; 73

JORDAN, ROBERT
The Eye of the World. New York: 1990. V. 68

JORDAN, WILLIAM C.
Some Events and Incidents During the Civil War. Montgomery: 1909. V. 69; 70

JORGENSEN, CHRISTINE
A Love to Die For. 1994. V. 68

JORSTAD, I.
Uredinales of the Canary Islands. Oslo: 1958. V. 72

JOSCELYN, ARCHIE
Sign of the Gun. London: 1945. V. 70

JOSEPH, ALICE
A Story of the Papago Indians, the Desert People. Chicago: 1949. V. 68; 73

JOSEPH N. SMITH & CO.
Catalogue for 1896. Detroit: 1896. V. 71

JOSEPHUS, FLAVIUS
De Bello Judaico. De Antiquitate Judaeorum. Verona: 1480. V. 72; 73
The Genuine Works of Josephus Flavius. Boston: 1825. V. 71
The Jewish History, as Well Ecclesiastical as Civil. London: 1708. V. 73

JOSEPHUS, MICHAEL
Michaelis Josephus Morei Carmina. Rome: 1740. V. 71

JOSEPHY, ALVIN M.
500 Nations- An Illustrated History of North American Indians. New York: 1994. V. 71
The Nez Perce Indians and the Opening of the Northwest. New Haven: 1965. V. 68; 70; 73

JOSIPOVICI, GABRIEL
Four Stories. London: 1977. V. 68; 70; 73

JOSS, MORAG
Fearful Symmetry. London: 1999. V. 69; 70; 72
Funeral Music. London: 1998. V. 70; 72

JOST, A. C.
Guysborough Sketches and Essays. Kentville: 1950. V. 72

JOST, LUDWIG
Lectures on Plant Physiology. Oxford: 1907. V. 69

JOUFFROY, ALAIN
Le Septieme Chant. Paris: 1974. V. 68

JOUGHIN, G. LOUIS
The Legacy of Sacco and Vanzetti. New York: 1948. V. 68

JOURDAIN, MARGARET
Regency Furniture 1795-1820. London: 1948. V. 68; 72

JOURNAL of a Week Passed in the Bottom of a Deserted Coal-Pit in the Neighbourhood of Glasgow. Carlisle: 1837. V. 70

JOURNAL of an African Cruiser. New York and London: 1845. V. 71

JOURNAL of Herpetology. 1977-1998. V. 69

JOURNAL of Sentimental Travels in the Southern Provinces of France, Shortly Before the Revolution. London: 1821. V. 68

JOURNEYS.. Rockville: 1996. V. 68; 71

JOUSEE, MATHURIN
Le Theatre de l'Art de Carpentier. A La Fleche: 1627. V. 73

JOUSSE, J.
The Theory and Practice of the Violin...Art of Bowing. London: 1813. V. 71

JOUTEL, HENRI
Journal of the Last Voyage Perform'd by Monsr. De La Salle to the Gulph of Mexico, to Fine Out the Mouth of the Mississippi. London: 1714. V. 68

JOUVE, PIERRE JEAN
Tombeau de Baudelaire. Neuchatel;: 1942. V. 70

THE JOY Book 1923. V. 73

THE JOY Book 1927. V. 73

JOYCE, GEORGE HENRY
Some Records of Troutbeck. Staveley: 1924. V. 71

JOYCE, JAMES
Anna Livia Plurabelle. New York: 1928. V. 70; 71; 72; 73
Anna Livia Plurabelle. London: 1930. V. 72; 73
Chamber Music. Boston: 1918. V. 68; 73
Chamber Music. London: 1923. V. 69; 70
Collected Poems. New York: 1936. V. 69; 70; 73
The Dead. Foss: 1982. V. 70
The Dead from Dubliners. Pitlochry: 1967. V. 72; 73
Dubliners. London: 1934. V. 73
The Dubliners. New York: 1986. V. 68; 69; 70; 72; 73
Epiphanies. Buffalo: 1956. V. 69
Exiles: a Play in Three Acts. London: 1918. V. 71
Finnegans Wake. London: 1939. V. 68; 72; 73
Finnegans Wake. New York: 1939. V. 69
Finnegans Wake. London: 1964. V. 68
Giacomo Joyce. New York: 1968. V. 69; 70; 71; 73
Haveth Childers Everywhere. Paris: 1930. V. 70; 73
Haveth Childers Everywhere. 1931. V. 69
Haveth Childers Everywhere. London: 1931. V. 72
Ibsen's New Drama. (and) James Clarence Mangan. London: 1930. V. 68; 72
James Joyce and Others. London: 1937. V. 72
Letters of James Joyce. New York: 1957. V. 70; 73
The Mime of Mick, Nick and the Maggies: a Fragment from Work in Progress. The Hague: 1934. V. 70
Pomes Penyeach. Paris: 1927. V. 73
Pomes Penyeach. London: 1933. V. 70; 71

A Portrait of the Artist As a Young Man. London: 1968. V. 71
Stephen Hero. 1944. V. 69
Stephen Hero. London: 1944. V. 68; 73
Stephen Hero. New York: 1944. V. 71
Stephen Hero. New York: 1955. V. 73
Tales Told of Shem and Shaun. Paris: 1929. V. 69; 70
Two Tales of Shem and Shaun. 1932. V. 69
Two Tales of Shem and Shaun. London: 1932. V. 71; 72
Ulise. Bucuresti: 1984. V. 69
Ulysses. Shelton. V. 69
Ulysses. Paris: 1922. V. 70; 71
Ulysses. Paris: 1926. V. 71
Ulysses. London: 1927. V. 72
Ulysses. Paris: 1927. V. 73
Ulysses. Hamburg/Paris/Bologna: 1932. V. 69; 72
Ulysses. New York: 1934. V. 68; 69; 70
Ulysses. Hamburg: 1935. V. 69; 73
Ulysses. New York: 1935. V. 68; 69; 71; 73
Ulysses. London: 1937. V. 71; 73
Verbannte (Exiles): Schauspiel in Drei Akten. Zurich: 1919. V. 70

JOYCE, JOHN A.
A Checkered Life. Chicago: 1883. V. 70
Jewels of Memory. Washington: 1895. V. 70

JOYCE, P. J.
John Healy, Archbishope of Tuam. 1931. V. 69

JOYCE, PATRICK W.
Old Irish Folk Music and Songs.... 1909. V. 71
The Origin and History of Irish Names of Places. London: 1910-13. V. 70

JOYCE, STANISLAUS
The Dublin Diary of.... 1962. V. 69
My Brother's Keeper. London: 1958. V. 69

JOYCE, T. ATHOL
Women of All Nations. London. V. 70
Women of All Nations. London: 1908. V. 72

JOYCE, WILLIAM
Dinosaur Bob and His Adventures with the Family Lazardo. New York: 1995. V. 69; 71; 73
Santa Calls. New York: 1993. V. 73

A JOYFUL Ode; Inscribed to the King, on the Late Victory at Dettingen. London: 1743. V. 69

THE JOYFUL Year - an Anthology from the Garden of English Poetry and Prose. London: 1947. V. 69

JOYNES, LUCY
Original Rhymes, Accompanying an Historical Chart of the Borough of Nottingham. Nottingham: 1844. V. 69

JOYNEVILLE, C.
Life and Times of Alexander I, Emperor of All the Russias. London: 1875. V. 71

JUDD, ALAN
Legacy. London: 2001. V. 71

JUDD, WILLIAM BOTSFORD
A Tale of Three Villages, Bernardsville, Basking Ridge, Mendham. Bernardsville: 1899. V. 71

JUDGE, ARTHUR W.
Engineering Workshop Practice. London: 1948. V. 71

JUDICIS, LOUIS
A Collector's Portrait. New York: 1903. V. 72

JUDOVICH, BERNARD
Pain Syndromes, Diagonsis and Treatment. Philadelphia: 1954. V. 72

JUDSON, ADONIRAM BROWN
The Influence of Growth on Congenital and Acquired Deformities. New York: 1905. V. 70

JUDSON, HARRY P.
A History of the Troy Citizens Corps, Troy, New York. Troy: 1884. V. 68

JUDSON, PHOEBE GOODELL
A Pioneer's Search for an Ideal Home. Tacoma: 1966. V. 68; 73

JUKES, J. BEETE
Popular Physical Geology. London: 1853. V. 70

JULIAN, P.
Dreamers of Decadence: Symbolist Painters of the 1890's. New York: 1971. V. 69
The Symbolists. New York: 1973. V. 69; 72

JULIAN Symons Remembered. Tributes from Friends. Council Bluffs: 1996. V. 68; 71

JULIEN, CARL
Ninety Six. Landmarks of South Carolina's Last Frontier Region. Columbia: 1950. V. 71

JULIEN'S Studies of Heads. Selected from the Paintings of Eminent Artists, or Drawn from Nature. London: 1846. V. 73

JUNCHEN, DAVID L.
Encyclopedia of the American Theatre Organ. Volume I. Pasadena: 1985. V. 71

JUNG, CARL GUSTAV
Die Beziehungen Zwischen dem Ich Und Dem Unbewussten. (The Relation of the Ego to the Unconscious). Darnstardt: 1928. V. 72
Dream Analysis. Zurich: 1938. V. 68
Two Essays on Analytical Psychology. New York: 1928. V. 72

JUNGE, MARK
J. E. Stimson: Photogrpaher of the West. Lincoln/London: 1905. V. 68

JUNGER, SEBASTIAN
Fire. New York: 2001. V. 72
The Perfect Storm. London: 1997. V. 68
The Perfect Storm. New York: 1997. V. 70; 71; 72; 73

JUNIUS, FRANCISCUS
The Painting of the Ancients in Three Bookes.... 1638. V. 70
The Painting of the Ancients, in Three Bookes.... London: 1638. V. 68; 69

JUNIUS, PSEUD.
Junius: Including Letters.... London: 1812. V. 71
The Letters. London: 1770. V. 73
The Letters. 1783. V. 73
The Letters. London: 1789. V. 73
The Letters. London: 1791. V. 73
The Letters. London: 1801. V. 71
Letters. London: 1805. V. 71
The Letters. London: 1806. V. 68
The Letters. London: 1820. V. 69
Stat Nominis Umbra. 1772. V. 72
Stat Nominis Umbra. London: 1772. V. 68; 70
Stat Nominis Umbra. London: 1799. V. 68; 69; 72
Stat Nominis Umbra. London: 1801. V. 68; 72
Stat Nominis Umbra. London: 1812. V. 71

JUNKER, WILHELM
Travels In Africa. London: 1892. V. 72

JUNKINS, DONALD
And Sandpipers She Said. Amherst: 1970. V. 68; 71

JUNN, KEM
Tapping the Source. New York: 1984. V. 69

JUNOD, HENRI A.
The Life Of A South African Tribe. Neuchatel: 1912. V. 72

JUSSERAND, JEAN ADRIEN ANTOINE JULES
The Romance of a King's Life. London: 1896. V. 70

JUSSIEU, ANTOINE LAURENT DE
Genera Plantarum Secundum Ordines Naturales Disposita.... Paris: 1789. V. 72

JUST, WARD
The American Ambassador. Boston: 1987. V. 72
Jack Gance. Boston: 1989. V. 72
Twenty-one. Boston: 1990. V. 72

JUSTICE, DONALD
Departures. Iowa City: 1973. V. 69; 73
From a Notebook. Iowa City: 1972. V. 73
L'Homme Qui Se Ferme. Iowa City: 1973. V. 73
Sixteen Poems. Iowa City: 1970. V. 73

JUSTICE, JEAN
Dictionary Of Marks and Monograms of Delft Pottery. London: 1930. V. 72

THE JUSTICE of Peace's Guide, Being a Collection of Precedents, Relating to the Office of a Justice of Peace. Dublin: 1790. V. 69

JUSTINIAN I, EMPEROR
Institvtiones Ivris Civilis D. Iustiniani Imper.: Accuratius Quam Ememdatae.... Venetiis: 1593. V. 70; 72

JUSTIN MARTYR, SAINT
Apologiae Duae & Dialogus cum Tryphoni Judaeo.... Londini: 1722. V. 72

JUSTINOPOLITANO, MUTIO
Il Gentilhuomo. Venetia: 1571. V. 71

JUSTINUS, MARCUS JUNIANUS
De Historiis Philippicis et Totius Mundi Originibus Interpretatione et Notis.... Paris: 1677. V. 68; 72
History of the World from the Assyrian Monarchy Down to the Time of Augustus Caesar. London: 1719. V. 71
Trogi Pompeii Historiis Extremis.... London: 1710. V. 68

JUVENALIS, DECIMUS JUNIUS
D'Jun. Juvenalis et Auli Persii Flaccii Satyrae cum annotat. Amsterdam: 1650. V. 71
Satirae XVI. Oxonii: 1808. V. 68; 72
Satire Dur Les Femmes. Paris: 1923. V. 71
The Satires. London: 1764. V. 69
The Satires. London: 1802. V. 73

THE JUVENILE Scrap-Book for 1849: a Christmas and New Year's Present for Young People. New York: 1849. V. 70

JUVENILE Stories for the Instruction of Children. Concord: 1837. V. 69

K

K., C.
Arts Master-Piece. London: 1702. V. 69

KABATA, Z.
Parasitic Copepoda or British Fishes. London: 1979. V. 68

KABOTIE, FRED
Fred Kabotie: Hopi Indian Artist. Flagstaff: 1977. V. 69

KABRAJI, FREDOON
The Cold Flame - Poems (1922-1924, 1935-1938, 1946-1953). London: 1956. V. 71

KADISH, ALON
The Corn Laws. The Formation of Popular Economics in Britain. London: 1996. V. 73

KAEFFER & CO.
Chalets, Suisses, Bois Decoupes. Paris: 1867-1884. V. 68; 70

KAEMPFER, ENGELBERT
The History of Japan. London: 1727. V. 72

KAEWERT, JULIE WALLIN
Unsolicited. New York: 1994. V. 70

KAFKA, FRANZ
Amerika. Munich: 1927. V. 72
Amerika. Norfolk: 1940. V. 69
The Great Wall of China. London: 1933. V. 71
The Great Wall of China. London: 1946. V. 71
Ein Landarzt. (The Country Doctor). Munich: 1919. V. 72
Metamorphosis. New York: 1984. V. 69; 72
The Trial. London: 1937. V. 73
The Trial. Avon: 1975. V. 72
Das Urteil. (The Judgment). Leipzig: 1916. V. 72
Wedding Preparations in the Country, and Other Posthumous Prose Writings. London: 1954. V. 72

KAFKA, PAUL
Love, Enter. Boston/New York: 1993. V. 72

KAHLENBERG, M. A.
The Navajo Blanket. Los Angeles/New York: 1972. V. 68; 69; 70

KAHLER, ERICH
Man the Measure. New York: 1943. V. 71

KAHLER, HUGH MAC NAIR
Father Means Well. New York: 1930. V. 71

KAHRL, WILLIAM L.
The California Water Atlas. Sacramento: 1979. V. 68

KAIKO, TAKESHI
Into a Black Sun. Tokyo: 1980. V. 69

KAINS-JACKSON, CHARLES PHILIP
Our Ancient Monuments and the Land Around Them. London: 1880. V. 68

KAKONIS, TOM
Michigan Roll. New York: 1988. V. 68

KALATA, BARBARA
A Hundred Years, a Hundred Miles. New Jersey's Morris Canal. Morristown: 1983. V. 71

KALB, LAURIE B.
Crafting Devotions - Tradition in Contemporary New Mexico Santos. Albuquerque: 1994. V. 69

KALEP, ELVY
Air Babies. Denver: 1936. V. 72

KALER, JAMES OTIS
Jenny Wren's Boarding-House. Boston: 1893. V. 72

KALIDASA
A Circle of the Seasons. Waltham St. Lawrence: 1929. V. 68; 71
Sakoontala; or, the Lost Ring; an Indian Drama. Hertford: 1855. V. 69

KALIMSKY, STUART M.
Never Cross a Vampire. New York: 1980. V. 71

KALISPELL and the Famous Flathead Valley. St. Paul: 1895. V. 68

KALLIR, O.
Grandma Moses. New York: 1973. V. 69; 72

KALM, PETER
Peter Kalm's Travels in North America. New York: 1937. V. 71
Travels into North America.... Warrington and London: 1770-1771. V. 68; 71

KAMAL, HASSAN
A Dictionary of Pharaonic Medicine. Cairo: 1967. V. 68

KAMAU, KWADWO AGYMAH
Flickering Shadows. Minneapolis: 1996. V. 71

KAMES, HENRY HOME, LORD
Elements of Criticism. Edinburgh: 1807. V. 68
Sketches of the History of Man. Edinburgh: 1778. V. 72

KAMINSKI, THOMAS
The Early Career of Samuel Johnson, his Life from 1737 to 1746. London: 1987. V. 69

KAMINSKY, STUART M.
Bullet for a Star. New York: 1977. V. 69
Catch a Falling Clown. New York: 1981. V. 69
A Cold Red Sunrise. New York: 1988. V. 69; 70; 71; 73
Exercise in Terror. New York: 1985. V. 70; 71
A Fine Red Rain. New York: 1987. V. 69; 70; 71; 72
High Midnight. New York: 1981. V. 72
The Howard Hughes Affair. New York: 1979. V. 70
Murder on the Yellow Brick Road. New York: 1977. V. 70; 72
Never Cross a Vampire. New York: 1980. V. 68; 70; 71; 72
Red Chameleon. New York: 1985. V. 70; 71; 72
Smart Moves. New York: 1986. V. 71
You Bet Your Life. New York: 1978. V. 68

KAMON, YASUO
Modern Art of Japan Since 1950: Masterpieces in the Museum. Japan: 1985-1986. V. 70; 72; 73

KANE, ELISHA KENT
Arctic Explorations: the Second Grinnell Expedition in Search of Sir John Franklin 1853, '54, '55. Philadelphia: 1856. V. 69; 70; 72; 73
Arctic Explorations: The Second Grinnell Expedition in Search of Sir John Franklin, 1853, '54, '55. London/Edinburgh/New York: 1861. V. 73
Arctic Explorations In Search Of Sir John Franklin. London: 1892. V. 72
The U.S. Grinnell Expedition in Search of Sir John Franklin, a Personal Narrative. New York: 1854. V. 69
The U.S. Grinnell Expedition in Search of Sir John Franklin, a Personal Narrative. Boston: 1857. V. 69

KANE, PAUL
Paul Kane's Frontier - Including Wanderings of an Artist Among the Indians of North America. Austin: 1971. V. 70
Wanderings of an Artist Among the Indians of North America from Canada to Vancouver's Island and Oregon.... London: 1859. V. 71

KANE, ROBERT
The Industrial Resources of Ireland. 1845. V. 70
The Industrial Resources of Ireland. Dublin: 1845. V. 68; 71

KANE, THOMAS LEIPER
A Friend of the Mormons. The Private Diary of.... San Francisco: 1937. V. 70

KANIN, GARSON
Born Yesterday. New York: 1946. V. 71; 73
The Live Wire. New York: 1951. V. 69

KANON, JOSEPH
Los Alamos. New York: 1997. V. 68; 69

KANSAS CENTRAL RAILWAY
Statement of the Condition and Resources of the Kansas Central Railway (Narrow Gauge) from Leavenworth, Kansas to Denver, Colorado. 1871. V. 68

KANSAS HISTORICAL SOCIETY
Kansas Historical Collection. Vol VIV 1915-1918. Topeka: 1918. V. 72

KANSAS the Bountiful. Chicago: 1907. V. 68

KANT, IMMANUEL
Critick of Pure Reason. London: 1838. V. 72
Critik der Reinen Vernunft. Riga: 1797. V. 72
Critique of Pure Reason. London: 1881. V. 71
The Metaphysics of Ethics. Edinburgh: 1836. V. 72; 73

KANTOR, MACKINLAY
Andersonville. Cleveland: 1955. V. 70
Glory for Me. New York: 1945. V. 71; 72
God and My Country. Cleveland: 1954. V. 71
Signal Thirty-Two. New York: 1950. V. 69; 73

KAPER, J. M.
The Chemical Basis of Virus Structure, Dissociaton and Reassembly. Amsterdam: 1975. V. 68

KAPLAN, JOHANNA
O My America!. New York: 1980. V. 72

KAPLAN, PHILIP
Round the Clock. London: 1993. V. 70

KAPLAN, W.
Charles Rennie Mackintosh. New York: 1996. V. 72

KAPP, EDMOND X.
Reflections - a Second Series of Drawings. London: 1922. V. 68

KAPPEL, A. W.
British and European Butterflies and Moths. 1895. V. 69; 73

KAPPLER, CHARLES J.
Indian Affairs, Laws and Treaties. Washington: 1904-1970. V. 68

KARAKA, DOSABHAI F.
History of the Parsis, Including Their Manners, Customs.... London: 1884. V. 69

KARASIK, CAROL
The Turquoise Trail - Native American Jewelry and Culture of the Southwest. New York: 1993. V. 69

KARIYONE, TATSUO
Atlas of Medicinal Plants. Osaka: 1973. V. 68; 70

KARL, FREDERICK R.
Joseph Conrad: the Three Lives. New York: 1978. V. 69

KARLOFF, BORIS
And the Darkness Falls. Cleveland: 1946. V. 68

KARLSTROM, PAUL J.
Louis Michael Eilshemius. New York: 1978. V. 73

KARNS, HARRY J.
Unknown Arizona and Sonora 1633-1721: From the Francisco Fernandez del Castillo Version of Luz De Tierra Incognita by Captain Juan Mateo Manje. Tucson: 1954. V. 71

KAROLEVITZ, ROBERT F.
Doctors of the Old West. New York: 1967. V. 71

KARPINSKI, LOUIS CHARLES
The History of Arithmetic. Chicago and New York: 1925. V. 69

KARR, ALPHONSE
A Tour Round My Garden. London: 1865. V. 68; 71
Voyage Autur de Mon Jardin. Paris: 1845. V. 68

KARR, MARY
The Devil's Tour. 1993. V. 69
The Devil's Tour. New York: 1993. V. 71

KARSH, YOUSUF
Healers of Our Age. Photography and Commentary. Lucerne: 1975. V. 71
Karsh: a Fifty-Year Retropsective. Boston: 1983. V. 70
Karsh Portraits. 1979. V. 68
Portraits. Boston: 1976. V. 70

KARSTEN, R.
The Head-Hunters of Western Amazonas. Helsingfors: 1935. V. 69

KASCHNITZ, MARIE LUISE
Selected Later Poems of.... Princeton: 1980. V. 70

KASDON, S. CHARLES
Atlas of In Situ Cytology. London: 1962. V. 68

KASSAK SZCZUCKA, ZOFJA
The Troubles of a Gnome. London: 1928. V. 68

KAST, ALFRED
Atlas of Pathological Anatomy. Leipzig: 1909. V. 68

KASTNER, ERICH
The Simpletons. New York: 1957. V. 73

KATA, ELIZABETH
Be Ready with Bells and Drums. London: 1961. V. 72

KATAEV, VALENTINE
The Embezzlers. New York: 1929. V. 70

KATER, HENRY
A Treatise on Mechanics.... London: 1852. V. 72

KATES, GEORGE N.
Chinese Household Furniture. New York: 1948. V. 69; 72

THE KATY Kruse Dolly Book. New York: 1927. V. 73

KATZ, D. MARK
Custer in Photographs. Gettysburg: 1985. V. 72

KATZ, WILLIAM LOREN
The Black West - A Documentary and Pictorial History. New York: 1971. V. 68; 72

KATZENBACH, L.
The Practical Book of American Wallpaper. Philadelphia/New York: 1951. V. 69; 72

KAUFFMAN, REGINALD WRIGHT
The Azure. New York: 1919. V. 72
Beg Pardon, Sir!. Philadelphia: 1929. V. 73
The Chasm. New York: 1903. V. 71
The Free Lovers: a Novel of To-Day. New York: 1925. V. 73
Jarvis of Harvard. Boston: 1901. V. 72
Mark of the Beast. New York: 1916. V. 72
Money to Burn: An Adventure Story. New York: 1924. V. 72
My Heart and Stephanie. Boston: 1910. V. 72
Share and Share Alike: an Adventure Story. New York: 1925. V. 71
Spider's Web. New York: 1913. V. 72

KAUFMAN, BEL
Up the Down Staircase. Englewood Cliffs: 1964. V. 72

KAUFMAN, CHARLES H.
Music in New Jersey 1655-1860. Rutherford: 1981. V. 71

KAUFMAN, GEORGE S.
Dinner at Eight. Garden City: 1932. V. 71
I'd Rather Be Right: a Musical Review. New York: 1937. V. 69
The Royal Family. Garden City: 1928. V. 70

KAUFMAN, S. JAY
Highlowbrow and Other Sketches. New York: 1942. V. 72

KAUFMANN, EDGAR
An American Architecture. New York: 1955. V. 68
Fallingwater: a Frank Lloyd Wright Country House. New York: 1986. V. 68
Taliesin Drawings. Wittenborn: 1952. V. 68

KAUFMANN, WILLIAM W.
The McNamara Strategy. New York: 1964. V. 70; 72

KAUP, J. J.
Catalogue of Apodal Fish, in the Collection of the British Museum. London: 1856. V. 70

KAUTZ, AUGUST V.
Customs of Service for Non-Commissioned Officers and Soldiers. Philadelphia: 1864. V. 70

KAVAN, ANNA
A Bright Green Field. London: 1958. V. 73
Eagle's Nest. London: 1957. V. 73
The House of Sleep. Garden City: 1947. V. 73
Ice. London: 1967. V. 73
Julia and the Bazooka. London: 1970. V. 73
A Scarcity of Love. Southport: 1956. V. 73

KAVANAGH, MARTIN
The Assinibione Basin. Winnipeg: 1946. V. 68; 73

KAVANAGH, MORGAN
Myths Traced to Their Primary Source through Language. London: 1856. V. 73

KAVANAU, J. LEE
Structure and Function in Biological Membranes. San Francisco: 1965. V. 68

KAWABATA, YASUNARI
Snow Country. New York: 1990. V. 69

KAWAKITA, M.
Contemporary Japanese Prints. Tokyo/Palo Alto: 1967. V. 72

KAWAKITA, MICHIAKI
Contemporary Japanese Prints. Tokyo/Palo Alto: 1967. V. 69

KAWAMOTO, TOSHIO
Saikei: Living Landscapes in Miniature. Tokyo: 1967. V. 72

KAY County Oklahoma. Ponca City: 1919. V. 71

KAY, GERTRUDE ALICE
Adventures in Geography. Joliet: 1930. V. 71
The Friends of Jimmy. New York: 1926. V. 70

KAY, HELEN
Snow Birthday. New York: 1955. V. 69

KAY, JOSEPH
The Condition and Education of Poor Children in English and in German Towns. London: 1853. V. 73

KAY, M. A.
Healing with Plants in the American and Mexican West. Tucson: 1996. V. 68

KAY, SUSAN
Legacy. New York: 1985. V. 68

KAY, TERRY
The Year the Lights Came On. Boston: 1976. V. 68

KAYE, BARBARA
The Company We Kept. London: 1986. V. 69
The Company We Kept; with Second Impression, Rural Life with a Rare Bookman. London: 1995-1996. V. 71

KAYE, D'ARCY
Columbus. 1978. V. 71
Columbus. London: 1978. V. 68

KAYE, MOLLIE
Potter Pinner Madow. London: 1937. V. 72

KAYE, NINA
She Married a Hero. New York: 1940. V. 71

KAYE, WALTER J.
Records of Harrogate Including the Register of Christ Church (1748- 1812). Leeds: 1922. V. 73

KAYE-SMITH, SHEILA
Joanna Godden. London: 1921. V. 71
Joanna Godden Married. London: 1926. V. 69

KAY-SHUTTLEWORTH, JAMES
Ribblesdale; or, Lancashire Sixty Years Ago. London: 1874. V. 73
Scarsdale; or Life on the Lancashire and Yorkshire Border, Thirty Years Ago. London: 1860. V. 73

KAZANTIZAKIS, NIKOS
The Odyssey: a Modern Sequel. London: 1959. V. 69

KAZANTZAKIS, NIKOS
Freedom and Death. London: 1956. V. 70
The Greek Passion. New York: 1954. V. 73
Zorba the Greek. New York: 1953. V. 73

KAZIN, ALFRED
A Walker in the City. New York: 1951. V. 68; 71

KEABLE, ROBERT
Numerous Treasure. London: 1925. V. 69

KEACH, BENJAMIN
War with the Devil; or the Young Man's Conflict with the Powers of Darkness. London: 1776. V. 70

KEANE, MARCUS
The Towers and Temples of Ancient Ireland: Their Origin and History Discussed from a New Point of View. Dublin: 1867. V. 71

KEARNEY, BELLE
A Slave Holder's Daughter. New York: 1900. V. 72

KEARNEY, LAWRENCE
Kingdom Come. Middleton: 1980. V. 68; 71

KEARSLEY'S Traveller's Entertaining Guide through Great Britain.... 1803. V. 72

KEARTON, ADA C.
On Safari. 1956. V. 70

KEARY, E.
The Magic Valley or Patient Antoine. London: 1877. V. 73

KEAST, A.
Migrant Birds in the Neotropics.... Washington: 1980. V. 73

KEATE, GEORGE
An Account of the Pelew Islands. London: 1788. V. 68; 70; 73
An Account of the Pelew Islands. Basel: 1789. V. 68; 72
An Account of the Pelew Islands. London: 1789. V. 72
An Account of the Pelew Islands. Boston: 1796. V. 68; 69
An Epistle from Lady Jane Gray to Lord Guildford Dudley. London: 1762. V. 70
Relation des Iles Pelew, Situees dans la Partie Occidentale de l'Ocean Pacifique.... Paris: 1788. V. 70

KEATING, ELIZA H.
Plays for the Parlour: a Collection of Acting Charades. (and Charade Plays for the Parlour. Part the Second). London: 186-?. V. 72

KEATING, GEOFFREY
Tribior-Ghaoithe an Bhais. 1931. V. 69

KEATING, GEORGE
Eochair-Sciath an Aifreann, an Explanatory Defence of the Mass. 1898. V. 69

KEATING, J.
The General History of Ireland. 1841. V. 71

KEATING, WILLIAM H.
Narrative of an Expedition to the Source of St. Peter's River, Lake Winnepeek, Lake of the Woods, &c. Philadelphia: 1824. V. 68; 71
Narrative of an Expedition to the Source of St. Peter's River, Lake Winnepeek, Lake of the Woods, &c. London: 1825. V. 68; 72

KEATS, JOHN
The Complete Poetical Works. Boston: 1899. V. 68; 70
The Complete Poetical Works Of John Keats. Boston & New York: 1990. V. 72
Dear Reynolds, As Last Night I Lay in Bed. New Rochelle: 1991. V. 73
Endymion. London: 1818. V. 68; 70; 72; 73
Endymion. Waltham St. Lawrence: 1947. V. 71; 73
Hyperion. 1945. V. 71; 72
Hyperion. London: 1945. V. 72
Isabella or the Pot of Basil. London: 1897. V. 72
Isabella or the Pot of Basil. Edinburgh and London: 1907. V. 68; 70
John Keats to George Felton Mathew. New Rochelle: 1987. V. 73
Lamia, Isabella, The Eve of St. Agnes and Other Poems. London: 1820. V. 73
The Letters of.... New York: 1935. V. 69
The Letters.... London: 1931. V. 71
Poems. London: 1817. V. 73
Poems. Hammersmith: 1894. V. 72
Poems. London: 1927. V. 72
Ten Sonnets. New Rochelle: 1995. V. 73
This Living Hand, Now Warm and Capable. New Rochelle: 1999. V. 73
To Ailsa Rock. New Rochelle: 1995. V. 73
To Charles Cowden Clarke. New Rochelle: 1989. V. 73
To My Brother George. New Rochelle: 1984. V. 73
Wise and Otherwise. In Dialogue with Samuel Johnson and George Steevens. New Rochelle: 1986. V. 73

KEAY, JOHN
When Men and Mountains Meet. London: 1977. V. 69

KEBBEL, THOMAS EDWARD
A History of Toryism: from the Accession of Mr. Pitt to Power in 1783 to the Death of Lord Beaconsfield in 1881. London: 1886. V. 71
Lord Beaconsfield and Other Tory Memories. London: 1907. V. 71

KEBLE, JOHN
The Christian Year; Thoughts in Verse for the Sundays and Holidays Throughout the Year. Oxford: 1827. V. 73
The Christian Year: thoughts in Verse for the Sundays and Holydays throughout the Year. Oxford: 1865. V. 68
Lyra Innocentium: Thoughts in Verse on Christian Children, Their Ways and Their Privileges. Oxford: 1846. V. 73
Ode for the Encaenia at Oxford, June 11, 1834, in Honor of His Grace, Arthur, Duke of Wellington, Chancellor of the University. Oxford: 1834. V. 73
The Psalter or Psalms of David; in English Verse; by a Member of the University of Oxford. Adapted for the Most Part, to Tunes in Common Use. Oxford: 1839. V. 73

KEBLE, JOSEPH
An Assistance to Justices of the Peace, for Easier Performance of Their Duty. London: 1683. V. 69

KECKLEY, ELIZABETH
Behind the Scenes, or; Thirty Years a Slave and Four Years in the White House. New York: 1868. V. 70

KEEFE, ROBERT
Charlotte Bronte's World of Death. 1979. V. 70; 73

KEELE, KENNETH D.
William Harvey, the Man, the Physician and The Scientist. London: 1965. V. 68

KEELER, CHARLES
The Simple Home. Santa Barbara: 1979. V. 72

KEELER, HARRY STEPHEN
The Amazing Web. New York: 1930. V. 70
Behind that Mask. New York: 1938. V. 70
The Chameleon. New York: 1939. V. 70
Cleopatra's Tears. New York: 1940. V. 70
The Defrauded Yeggman. New York: 1937. V. 70
The Face of the Man from Saturn. New York: 1933. V. 70
Finger, Finger. New York: 1938. V. 70
The Five Silver Buddhas. London. V. 71
The Five Silver Buddhas. New York: 1935. V. 70
The Fourth King. New York: 1930. V. 70; 71; 73
The Green Jade Hand. New York: 1930. V. 70; 71
The Man with the Crimson Box. New York: 1940. V. 70
The Riddle of the Traveling Skull. New York: 1934. V. 68; 69; 73
The Riddle of the Traveling Skull. 1938. V. 70
The Riddle of the Yellow Zuri. New York: 1930. V. 70; 72
The Skull of the Waltzing Clown. 1935. V. 70
The Spectacles of Mr. Cagliostro. New York: 1929. V. 70
10 Hours. New York: 1937. V. 71; 73
The Tiger Snake. London. V. 71
The Two Strange Ladies. London: 1945. V. 73
The Vanishing Gold Truck. New York: 1941. V. 70
The Wonderful Scheme of Mr. Christopher Thorne. New York: 1936. V. 70
X. Jones of Scotland Yard. New York: 1936. V. 70

KEELER, RALPH
Vagabond Adventures. Boston: 1870. V. 71

KEELEY, GERTRUDE
Story of the Birds for Young People with Bird Alphabet. New York: 1914. V. 73

KEELING, RALPH F.
Gruesome Harvest. Chicago: 1947. V. 70

KEEN, GREGORY B.
The Descendants of Joran Kyn of New Sweden. Philadelphia: 1913. V. 71

KEENE, DAY
Dead Dolls Don't Talk. Greenwich: 1959. V. 72
Framed in Guilt. New York: 1949. V. 71
This Is Murder Mr. Herbert And Other Stories. New York: 1948. V. 72
Too Hot To Hold. Greenwich: 1959. V. 72

KEENE, JAMES B.
A Handbook of Practical Gauging, for the Use of Beginners, with Instructions in the Mode of Ascertaining the Strength of Spirits by Means of Sikes's Hydrometer.... Philadelphia: 1868. V. 73

KEENE, TALBOT
Miscellaneous Pieces: Original and Collected.... London: 1787. V. 68; 73

KEENLYSIDE, FRANCIS
Peaks and Pioneers. London: 1975. V. 69

KEEPE, HENRY
Monumenta Westmonasteriensia; or, an Historical Account of the Original, Increase and Present State of St. Peter's, or The Abbey Church of Westminster. London: 1682. V. 69

KEEPNEWS, ORRIN
A Pictorial History of Jazz. New York: 1955. V. 69; 71

THE KEEPSAKE for 1852. London: 1852. V. 68

KEEPSAKE Poems. London: 1972-1979. V. 68

KEES, WELDON
The Fall of the Magicians. New York: 1947. V. 72
The Last Man. San Francisco: 1943. V. 69; 72

KEESHAN, ROBERT
She Loves Me...She Loves Me Not.... New York: 1963. V. 71; 73

KEESON, A.
Monts De Piete and Pawnbroking.... 1854. V. 71

KEGLEY, MAX
Loot of a Desert Rat. Phoenix: 1938. V. 70

KEHOE, WILLIAM
A Sweep of Dusk. New York: 1945. V. 71

KEIFER, SARAH J. HARRIS
Genealogical and Biographical Sketches of the New Jersey Branch of the Harris Family, in the United States. Madison: 1888. V. 71

KEIGHLEY, ALEXANDER
Alex Keighley. Wien: 1936. V. 70

KEIGHLEY, WILLIAM
Keighley, Past and present. Keighley: 1879. V. 73

KEIGHTLEY, THOMAS
Tales and Popular Fictions: Their Resemblance and Transmission from Country to Country. 1834. V. 70

KEILL, JOHN
An Examination of Dr. Burnet's Theory of the Earth; Together with Some Remarks on Mr Whiston's New Theory of the Earth. Oxford: 1698. V. 68
An Examination of Dr. Burnet's Theory of the Earth.... Oxford: 1734. V. 72
An Introduction to Natural Philosophy; or, Philosophical Lectures Read in the University of Oxford. London: 1726. V. 72
An Introduction to True Astronomy; or, Astronomical Lectures, Read in the Astronomical School of the University of Oxford. London: 1721. V. 72

KEIM, DE B. RANDOLPH
Sheridan's Troopers on the Borders: a Winter Campaign on the Plains. Philadelphia: 1885. V. 72; 73

KEIRANS, J. E.
George Henry Nuttall and the Nuttal Tick Catalogue. Washington: 1984. V. 68

KEITH, ELMER
Safari. 1968. V. 69; 70

KEITH, GEORGE
An Exact Narrative of the Proceedings at Turner-Hall, the 11th of the Month Called June, 1696. London: 1696. V. 68
A Sermon Preach'd at Turners-Hall the 5th of May 1700. London: 1700. V. 73

KEITH, MELVILLE C.
What I Know About Human Teeth and How to Preserve Them. Boston: 1885. V. 68

KEITH, THOMAS
The Complete Practical Arithmetician.... London: 1798. V. 73
A New Treatise of the Use of the Globes; or a Philosophical View of the Earth and the Heavens. London: 1824. V. 69

KEITHLEY, RALPH
Buckey O'Neill. Caldwell: 1949. V. 69

KELEHER, JULIA
The Padre of Isleta. Santa Fe: 1940. V. 71

KELEHER, WILLIAM A.
The Fabulous Frontier. Santa Fe: 1945. V. 68; 69; 71; 73
Maxwell Land Grant: a New Mexico Item. Santa Fe: 1942. V. 69; 71; 72; 73
Maxwell Land Grant: a New Mexico Item. New York: 1964. V. 71
Memoirs 1892-1969. Santa Fe: 1969. V. 72; 73
Turmoil in New Mexico 1846-1868. 1952. V. 68
Turmoil in New Mexico 1846-1868. Santa Fe: 1952. V. 72; 73
Violence in Lincoln County 1869-1881. Albuquerque: 1957. V. 68; 69; 71; 72

KELEMEN, PAL
Medieval American Art. New York: 1943. V. 71

KELHAM, ROBERT
Britton. Containing the Antient Pleas of the Crown. London: 1762. V. 70

KELK, JOHN
The Scarborough Spa. London: 1841. V. 69
The Scarborough Spa. 1860. V. 73

KELKER & DE LEUW & CO.
Report and Recommendations on a Comprehensive Rapid Transit Plan for the City and County of Los Angeles. Chicago: 1925. V. 70; 73

KELLAND, CLARENCE BUDINGTON
Scattergood Baines Returns. New York: 1940. V. 69

KELLER, DAVID H.
The Devil and the Doctor. New York: 1940. V. 69

KELLER, FRANCES RICHARDSON
An American Crusade: The Life of Charles Waddell Chesnutt. Provo UT: 1978:. V. 72

KELLER, FRANZ
The Amazon and Madeira Rivers. London: 1874. V. 72

KELLER, GOTTFRIED
Green Henry. London: 1960. V. 72

KELLER, HELEN
Helen Keller's Journal. Garden City: 1936-1937. V. 72
Helen Keller's Journal 1936-1937. Garden City: 1938. V. 69; 71; 72; 73
Midstream. My Later Life. Garden City: 1929. V. 71
The Song of the Stone Wall. New York: 1910. V. 69

KELLER BRASS COMPANY, GRAND RAPIDS
Manufacturing Metal Furniture Trimmings, Automobile Mountings, Trimmings, Automobile Mountings, Refrigerator Hardware. Catalog No. 30. Grand Rapids. V. 68

KELLERMAN, FAYE
The Ritual Bath. New York: 1986. V. 71
Sacred and Profane. New York: 1987. V. 71

KELLERMAN, JONATHAN
Blood Test. New York: 1986. V. 68
The Butcher's Theater. New York: 1988. V. 69
Over the Edge. New York: 1987. V. 72
When the Bough Breaks. New York: 1985. V. 68; 69; 70; 71

KELLEY, EMMA DUNHAM
Megda. Boston: 1891. V. 70
Megda. Boston: 1892. V. 68

KELLEY, JOSEPH BUNKO
Thirteen Years in the Oregon Penitentiary. Portland: 1908. V. 70
Thirteen Years in the Oregon Penitentiary. Portland: 1918. V. 68; 73

KELLEY, ROBERT E.
Samuel Johnson's Early Biographers. 1971. V. 69

KELLEY, WILLIAM D.
The New Northwest: an Address by Hon. William D. Kelley on the Northern Pacific Railway. Philadelphia: 1871. V. 68
Why Colord People in Philadelphia are Excluded from the Street Cars. Philadelphia: 1866. V. 73

KELLEY, WILLIAM MELVIN
Dancers on the Shore. Garden City: 1964. V. 73
Dunfords Travels Everywheres. Garden City: 1970. V. 73

KELLNER, L.
Alexander Von Humboldt. London: 1963. V. 68

KELLOG, MARJORIE
Tell Me That You Love Me, Junie Moon. New York: 1968. V. 69

KELLOGG, EDWARD
Labor and Other Capital: the Rights of Each Secured and the Wrongs of Both Eradicated. New York: 1849. V. 73

KELLOGG, J. H.
Man, the Masterpiece, or, Plain Truths Plainly Told, About Boyhood, Youth and Manhood. Battle Creek: 1901. V. 68

KELLOGG, LOUISE P.
The British Regime in Wisconsin and the Northwest. Madison: 1935. V. 73

KELLOGG, MARJORIE
Tell Me That You Love Me, Junie Moon. New York: 1968. V. 72

KELLOGG, W. N., CO.
Kellogg's Funny Jungele and Moving-Pictures. Battle Creek?: 1909. V. 73

KELLOGG'S Story Book of Games. Battle Creek: 1931. V. 73

KELLY, BERNARD
The Mind and Poetry of Gerard Manley Hopkins. Ditchling, Sussex: 1935. V. 73

KELLY, CHARLES
Holy Murder, the Story of Porter Rockwell. New York: 1934. V. 73
Miles Goodyear, First Citizen of Utah - Trapper, Trader and California Pioneer. Salt Lake City: 1937. V. 68
Old Greenwood - the Story of Caleb Greenwood - Trapper, Pathfinder and Early Pioneer of the West. Salt Lake City: 1936. V. 69
Old Greenwood. The Story of Caleb Greenwood, Trapper, Pathfinder and Early Pioneer. Georgetown: 1965. V. 70

KELLY, EMERSON CROSBY
Encylopedia of Medical Sources. Baltimore: 1948. V. 68

KELLY, F.
The Post-Office Directory 1837 (bound with) A New Guide to Stage Coaches, Waggons, Carts, Vessels &c. for 1837. London: 1837. V. 70

KELLY, FRANCIS M.
A Short History of Costume and Armour 1066-1800. 1931. V. 71

KELLY, FRED C.
One Thing Leads to Another. The Growth of an Industry. Boston: 1936. V. 70

KELLY, GEORGE
Legislative History Arizona 1864-1912. Phoenix: 1926. V. 71
Reflected Glory. New York: 1937. V. 72
The Show-Off: a Transcript of Life in Three Acts. Boston: 1924. V. 71

KELLY, H. M.
Great Gable, Borrowdale, Buttermere. Climbing Guides to the English Lake District. London: 1937. V. 69
Pillar Rock and Neighbouring Climbs. London: 1923. V. 69

KELLY, HOWARD A.
Dictionary of American Medical Biography. New York: 1928. V. 68
Diseases of the Kidneys, Ureters and Bladder with Special Reference to the Diseases of Women. New York and London: 1915. V. 70
Some American Medical Botanists.... Troy: 1914. V. 68; 69
The Vermiform Appendix and Its Diseases. Philadelphia: 1905. V. 70; 71

KELLY, JOHN
Etchings and Drawings of Hawaiians. Honolulu: 1943. V. 72

KELLY, LAWRENCE C.
The Navajo Indians and Federal Indian Policy 1900-1935. Tucson: 1968. V. 69
Navajo Roundup: Selected Correspondence of Kit Carson's Expedition Against the Navajo 1863-1865. Boulder: 1970. V. 70

KELLY, LUTHER S.
Yellowstone Kelly The Memoirs of Luther S. Kelly. New Haven: 1926. V. 72

KELLY, LUTHER V.
The Range Men - The Story of Ranchers and Indians of Alberta. Toronto: 1913. V. 69; 70; 71

KELLY, MARY
A Cold Coming. London: 1956. V. 72

KELLY, PATRICK
The Universal Cambist, and Commercial Instructor; Being a General Treatise on Exchange.... London: 1811. V. 68

KELLY, R. TALBOT
Egypt. London: 1903. V. 72
Egypt. London: 1906. V. 72

KELLY, SUSAN
The Gemini Man. New York: 1985. V. 69

KELLY, THOMAS
Payback. New York: 1997. V. 71

KELLY, WALT
Ten Ever-Lovin' Blue-Eyed Years with Pogo. New York: 1959. V. 69

KELLY, WILLIAM
Life in Victoria or Victoria in 1853, and Victoria in 1858. London: 1859. V. 72

KELLY'S Directory of Berkshire. London: 1928. V. 73
KELLY'S Directory of Cambridgeshire, Norfolk & Suffolk. 1896. V. 68
KELLY'S Directory of Cumberland and Westmorland. London: 1894. V. 71
KELLY'S Directory of Derbyshire. London: 1841. V. 73
KELLY'S Directory of Leicestershire and Rutland. London: 1899. V. 73
KELLY'S Directory of Lincolnshire. London: 1909. V. 73
KELLY'S Directory of Lincolnshire. 1930. V. 72
KELLY'S Directory of Lincolnshire. 1933. V. 72
KELLY'S Directory of Lincolnshire. London: 1933. V. 73
KELLY'S Directory of Norfolk. London: 1937. V. 73
KELLY'S Handbook To The Titled, Landed & Official Classes For 1895. London: 1895. V. 72

KELMAN, JAMES
Greyhounds for Breakfast. London: 1987. V. 68

KELMAN, JANET HARVEY
The Sea-Shore Shown to the Children. London. V. 68

KELOWNA BOARD OF TRADE
Kelowna, British Columbia. The Orchard City of the Okanagan. 1912. V. 71

KELSALL, CHARLES
Classical Excursion from Rome to Arpino. Geneva: 1820. V. 68; 70

KELSALL, J. E.
The Birds of Hampshire and the Isle of Wight. London: 1905. V. 73

KELSON, GEORGE M.
The Salmon Fly. 1995. V. 68

KELTIE, JOHN S.
History of the Scottish Highlands...Clans and Regiments.... Edinburgh and London: 1879. V. 69

KELTON, C. G.
The New England Collection of Hymns and Spiritual Songs.... Montpelier: 1829. V. 69

KELTON, ELMER
Art of Frank C. McCarthy. New York: 1992. V. 70
My Kind of Heroes. Austin: 1995. V. 68

KELVIN, WILLIAM THOMSON, 1ST BARON
Reports Regarding Sir William Thomson's Compass and Sounding Machine. Glasgow: 1877. V. 72

KELWAY, A. CLIFTON
A Franciscan Revival. Plaistow: 1908. V. 70

KEMBLE, EDWARD W.
The Blackberries and Their Adventures. New York: 1897. V. 73
Comical Coons. New York: 1898. V. 73
A Coon Alphabet. New York: 1898. V. 71
Kemble's Sketch Book. New York: 1899. V. 73

KEMBLE, FRANCES ANNE
Journal in Two Volumes. Philadelphia: 1835. V. 69
Journal of a Residence on a Georgian Plantation in 1838-1839. New York: 1863. V. 70; 71; 72
Poems. Boston: 1859. V. 69

KEMBLE, JOHN PHILIP
An Authentic Narrative of Mr. Kemble's Retirement from the Stage; Including Farewell Address, Criticisms, Poems &c.... London: 1817. V. 72

KEMBLE, JOHN PHILLIP
Love in Many Masks.... Dublin: 1790. V. 73

KEMELMAN, HARRY
The Nine Mile Walk. New York: 1967. V. 71

KEMMERER, DONALD L.
Path to Freedom. The Struggle for Self Government in Colonial New Jersey 1703-1776. Princeton: 1940. V. 71

KEMMERER, EDWIN WALTER
New Jersey Banking 1902-1927. Newark: 1928. V. 71

KEMP, A.
The Owls of Southern Africa. Cape Town: 1987. V. 73

KEMP, BEN W.
Cow Dust And Saddle Leather. Norman: 1968. V. 71

KEMP, DIXON
A Manual of Yacht and Boat Sailing. London: 1878. V. 68

KEMP, E. G.
The Face of China, Travels in East, North, Central and Western China.... London: 1909. V. 72
The Face Of Manchuria, Korea, and Russian Turkestan. London: 1910. V. 72

KEMP, FRANKLIN W.
Firefighting by the Seashore, a History of the Atlantic City Fire Department December 3, 1874-March 1, 1972. Atlantic City: 1972. V. 69
A Nest of Rebel Pirates. 1966. V. 71

KEMP, SAM
Black Frontiers. New York: 1931. V. 68

KEMPE, ALFRED J.
Manuscripts and Other Rare Documents, Illustrative of Some of the More Minute Particulars.... London: 1836. V. 70

KEMP'S Nine Daies Wonder: Performed in a Daunce from London to Norwich. London: 1840. V. 71

KEMPSTER, FREDERICK
Flowers of Many Hues. Original Poems by Various Authors. Manchester: 1844. V. 69

KENAN, RANDALL
Let the Dead Bury their Dead. New York: 1992. V. 72
The Visitation of Spirits. New York: 1989. V. 70; 72; 73

KENDALL, FRANCIS
A Descriptive Catalogue of the Minerals and Fossil Organic Remains of Scarborough and the Vicinity.... Scarborough: 1816. V. 71

KENDALL, GEORGE WILKINS
Narrative of the Texas Santa Fe Expedition. New York: 1844. V. 70

KENDALL, HOLLIDAY BICKERSTAFFE
The Origin and History of the Primitive Methodist Church. 1905. V. 72

KENDALL, J. F.
Registered Brands And Marks of Osage County, Okla, June 15th, 1941. Pawhuska, OK: 1941. V. 71

KENDALL, JAMES
A Sermon Delivered at the Ordination of Hersey Bradford Goodwin. Concord: 1830. V. 68

KENDALL, JOHN
American Memories: Recollections of a Hurried Run through the United States During the Spring of 1896. Nottingham: 1896. V. 73

KENDALL, KATHERINE
The Interior Castle. Worcester: 1968. V. 73

KENDALL, PERCY FRY
Geology of Yorkshire. 1924. V. 68; 73
Geology of Yorkshire. Leeds: 1924. V. 73
Geology of Yorkshire. London: 1924. V. 69

KENDALL, W. C.
The Fishes of New England. 1914-1935. V. 73
The Fishes of New England, Part 2 The Salmons. 1935. V. 72

KENDERDINE, THADDEUS
California Revisited 1858-1897. Pennsylvania: 1898. V. 68
A California Tramp and Later Footprints; or Life on the Plains and in the Golden State Thirty Years Ago. Newtown: 1888. V. 73

KENDON, FRANK
Arguments and Emblems. London: 1925. V. 73
Thirty-six Psalms. An English Version. Cambridge: 1963. V. 71

KENDREW, JAMES
The Death and Burial of Cock Robin. York. V. 71
The House that Jack Built. York. V. 71
The Sister's Gift, or the Bad Boy Reformed. York: 1826. V. 71
Tom Thumb's Folio; or a Penny Plaything for Little Giants.... London. V. 71

KENDRICK, A. F.
Hand-Woven Carpets, Oriental & European. London: 1922. V. 72

KENDRICK, ARCHIBALD, & SONS
Short Price List of Locks and Latches. West Bromwich: 1912. V. 68

KENDRICK, BAYNARD
Blind Man's Bluff. Boston: 1943. V. 73
Hot Red Money. New York: 1959. V. 69
Out of Control. New York: 1945. V. 69

KENDRICK, MARY F.
Down the Road to Yesterday. 1941. V. 73

KENEALLY, ARABELLA
The Human Gyroscope. London: 1934. V. 72

KENEALLY, THOMAS
Bring Larks and Heroes. Melbourne: 1967. V. 71; 73
The Chant of Jimmie Blacksmith. New York: 1972. V. 68; 69; 71; 72
Confederates. New York: 1980. V. 68
The Fear. Melbourne Victoria: 1965. V. 69
Flying Hero Class. New York: 1991. V. 68; 71
The Great Shame - a Story of the Irish in the Old World and the New. London: 1998. V. 73
Outback. London: 1983. V. 70
The Place at Whitton. London: 1964. V. 72
The Place at Whitton. New York: 1964. V. 72
The Playmaker. London: 1987. V. 71
Schindler's Ark. London: 1982. V. 68; 69; 70; 71; 72
Schindler's Ark. Sydney: 1982. V. 72
Schindler's Ark. London: 1992. V. 70
Schindler's List. New York: 1982. V. 71

KENEDY, R. C.
Grotesques. London: 1975. V. 72

KENLON, JOHN
Fires and Fire-Fighting, a History of Modern Fire-Fighting. New York: 1913. V. 69

KENNA, GEORGE
Siberia And The Exile System. London: 1891. V. 72

KENNA, MICHAEL
Easter Island. Tucson: 2001. V. 73
Night Work. Tuscon: 2000. V. 68

KENNARD, MARY
Fooled by a Woman. London: 1897. V. 68
The Right Sort. London: 1889. V. 68
The Right Sort. London: 1900. V. 68

KENNAWAY, JAMES
Tunes of Glory - a Novel. London: 1956. V. 70

KENNE, LOUIS
Crumps, the Plain Story of a Canadian Who Went. Boston: 1917. V. 69

KENNEDY, A.
Japanese Costume, History and Tradition. Paris: 1990. V. 69

KENNEDY, ALEXANDER
The Birds of Berkshire and Buckinghamshire: a Contribution to the Natural History of the Two Counties. Eton/London: 1868. V. 68

KENNEDY, CHARLES RANN
The Servant in the House. New York: 1908. V. 70

KENNEDY, E. B.
Thirty Seasons in Scandinavia. London: 1903. V. 68
Thirty Seasons in Scandinavia. 1908. V. 68

KENNEDY, G. W.
The Pionner Campfire in Four Parts. Portland: 1914. V. 70

KENNEDY, GRACE
Anna Ross. Malta: 1829. V. 72
The Decision, or, Religion Must Be All, or Is Nothing. Princeton: 1827. V. 71

KENNEDY, JAMES
A Description of the Antiquities and Curiosities in Wilton House. Salisbury: 1769. V. 70

KENNEDY, JOHN
A Treatise Upon Planting, Gardening an the Management of the Hot- House.... Dublin: 1788. V. 70; 71

KENNEDY, JOHN FITZGERALD
Profiles in Courage. New York: 1956. V. 69; 72

KENNEDY, JOSEPH P.
I'm For Roosevelt. New York: 1936. V. 71

KENNEDY, LIONEL
An Official Report of the Trials of Sundry Negroes, Charged with an Attempt to Raise an Insurrection in the State of South Carolina.... Charleston: 1822. V. 68

KENNEDY, LOUISE VENABLE
The Negro Peasant Turns Cityward. New York: 1930. V. 68

KENNEDY, MARGARET
The Constant Nymph. London: 1924. V. 73

KENNEDY, MICHAEL STEPHEN
The Assiniboines. Norman: 1961. V. 69

KENNEDY, P. G.
An Irish Sanctuary: Birds of the North Bull. 1953. V. 69

KENNEDY, PATRICK
Legendary Fiction of the Irish Celts. 1891. V. 70

KENNEDY, R. C.
Grotesques. London: 1975. V. 70

KENNEDY, R. S.
Bibliography of G. A. Henty & Henyana. London: 1956. V. 70

KENNEDY, RAYMOND
Columbine. New York: 1980. V. 72

KENNEDY, ROBERT
To Seek a Newer World. Garden City: 1967. V. 71

KENNEDY, ROBERT F.
Just Friends and Brave Enemies. New York: 1962. V. 69; 72

KENNEDY, RUTH WEDGWOOD
Four Portrait Busts by Francesco Laurana. Northampton: 1962. V. 70; 72

KENNEDY, VANS
A Useful Collection of Translations viz of the Persian Moonshee, of the New Articles of War and Two Court Martials.... Bombay: 1847. V. 72

KENNEDY, WILLIAM
Billy Phelan's Greatest Game. New York: 1978. V. 69; 70
Billy Phelan's Greatest Game. 1982. V. 72
Charlie Malarky and the Belly-Button Machine. Boston: 1986. V. 68; 73
The Flaming Corsage. 1996. V. 72
The Flaming Corsage. Franklin Center: 1996. V. 70
The Flaming Corsage. New York: 1996. V. 71
The Ink Truck. New York: 1969. V. 70; 71; 72; 73
Ironweed. New York: 1983. V. 69; 70; 71; 72; 73
Legs. New York: 1975. V. 69; 72
O Albany!. New York: 1983. V. 68; 70; 71
Quinn's Book. New York: 1988. V. 72; 73
Riding the Yellow Trolley Car. 1993. V. 72
Very Old Bones. 1992. V. 72; 73

KENNEDY, WILLIAM R.
Sporting Sketches in South America. London: 1892. V. 72

KENNEDY-FRASER, MARJORY
Songs of the Hebrides. London. V. 71

KENNER, CHARLES L.
A History of New Mexican Plains Indians Relations. Norman: 1969. V. 68; 73

KENNER, HUGH
The Poetry of Ezra Pound. London: 1951. V. 68
The Pound Era. Berkeley and Los Angeles: 1971. V. 71

KENNETT, BASIL
Romae Antiquae Notitia; or, the Antiquites of Rome. London: 1717. V. 69; 70
Romae Antiquae Notitia; or, the Antiquities of Rome. London: 1731. V. 73
Romae Antiquae Notitia; or the Antiquities of Rome. London: 1737. V. 73
Romae Antique Notitia; or the Antiquities of Rome. London: 1763. V. 71

KENNGOTT, A.
Naturgeschichte des Mineralreichs fur schule und Haus.... Stuttgart: 1888. V. 68

KENNGOTT, GEORGE F.
The Record of a City. A Social Survey of Lowell, Massachusetts. New York: 1912. V. 70

KENNION, GEORGE
Observations of the Medicinal Springs of Harrogate. London: 1867. V. 73

KENNON, BOB
From the Pecos to the Powder. A Cowboy's Autobiography. Norman: 1965. V. 68; 71

KENRICK, THOMAS
The British Stage and Literary Cabinet. February 1821. London: 1821. V. 71
The British Stage, and Literary Cabinet. Volume III. London: 1819. V. 70

KENRICK, TONY
Two For The Price Of One. London: 1974. V. 72

KENSIT, J. A.
Rome Behind Sinn Fein. 1921. V. 69

KENT, ADOLPHUS H.
A Manual of the Coniferae. London: 1881. V. 70

KENT, ALEXANDER
Command a King's Ship. London: 1973. V. 70
The Flag Captain. London: 1971. V. 70; 73
The Flag Captain. New York: 1971. V. 73
To Glory We Steer. London: 1968. V. 73
Honour This Day. London: 1987. V. 72
In Gallant Company. London: 1977. V. 68; 70
The Inshore Squadron. London: 1978. V. 70
Midshipman Bolitho and the Avenger. New York: 1978. V. 68
Sloop of War. London: 1972. V. 71
Stand Into Danger. London: 1980. V. 68
To Glory We Steer. New York: 1968. V. 70

KENT, CHARLES
The Humour and Pathos of Charles Dickens. London: 1884. V. 69

KENT, CHARLES N.
History of the Seventeenth Regiment, New Hampshire Volunteer Infantry 1862-1863. Los Angeles: 1958. V. 69

KENT, JAMES
Commentaries on American Law. Boston: 1896. V. 69
The Opinions of the Judges of the Supreme Court (of New York) Delivered in the Court of Errors, in the Case of Robert Livingston and Robert Fulton, vs. James Van Ingen and Twenty Others. Albany: 1812. V. 68

KENT, NATHANIEL
Hints to Gentleman of Landed Property, to which are Now First Added, Supplementary Hints. London: 1793. V. 69

KENT, ROCKWELL
N by E. New York: 1930. V. 69; 70; 72
A Northern Christmas. New York: 1941. V. 69
Salamina. London: 1936. V. 73
Voyaging Southward from the Strait of Magellan. New York: 1924. V. 69
Wilderness. New York: 1936. V. 72

KENT, SAMUEL
The Grammar of Heraldry. London: 1716. V. 73

KENT, WILLIAM
The Most Material Parts of Kent's Commentaries, Reduced to Questions and Answers. New York: 1890. V. 69

KENT, WILLIAM SAVILLE
A Manual of the Infusoria; Incuding a Description of all Know Flagellate, Ciliate and Tentaculiferous Protozoa, British and Foreign.... London: 1880-1882. V. 72
The Naturalist in America. London: 1897. V. 73

KENTISH, BASIL LEONARD
The Chronicle Of An Ancient Yorkshire Family. The Ullathornes, Or Ullithornes. London: 1963. V. 72

KENTISH, THOMAS
The Pyrotechnist's Treasury; or Complete Art of Making Fireworks. London: 1878. V. 70; 73

THE KENTUCKY Preceptor, Containing a Number of Useful Lessons for Reading And Speaking. Lexington: 1812. V. 73

KENWARD, JAMES
The Suburban Child. Cambridge: 1955. V. 68

KENYON, MICHAEL
The Shooting of Dan McGrew. London: 1972. V. 70

KEON, ROBERT
A Report of the Whole Proceedings Previous to, with a Note of the Evidence on the Trial of Robert Keon, Gent. for the Murder of George Nugent Reynolds, Esq. and also of the Charges and Judges Thereon. Dublin: 1788. V. 70

KEPHART, HORACE
Captives Among the Indians: First-Hand Narrtives of Indian Wars, Customs, Tortures and Habits of Life in Colonial Times. 1916. V. 69

KEPLER, JOHANNES
The Six-Cornered Snowflake. Oxford: 1966. V. 72

KEPPEL, GEORGE
Narrative of a Journey Across the Balcan, by the Two Passes of Selimno and Pravadi; also of a Visit to Azani and Other Newly Discovered Ruins in Asia Minor in the Years 1829-1830. London: 1831. V. 70
Personal Narrative of a Journey from India to England.... London: 1827. V. 72

THE KEPPELIAD; or Injur'd Virture Triumphant. 1779. V. 73

KEPPLER, VICTOR
Man Camera. A Photographic Autobiography. New York: 1970. V. 72

KER, HENRY
Travels through the Western Interior of the United States from the Year 1808 Up to the Year 1816. Elizabethtown: 1816. V. 71

KERCHEVAL, SAMUEL A.
A History of the Valley of Virginia. Woodstock: 1850. V. 68

KERENYI, C.
Asklepios Archetypal Image of the Physician's Existance. New York: 1959. V. 70; 71

KERFOOT, J. B.
Amrican Pewter. Boston: 1924. V. 73

KERKSIS, SYDNEY C.
Heavy Artillery Projectiles of the Civil War 1861-1865. Atlanta: 1968. V. 73
Heavy Artillery Projectiles of the Civil War 1861-1865. Kennesaw: 1972. V. 73

KERLEY, CHARLES GILMORE
Treatment of the Diseases of the Children. Philadelphia: 1908. V. 71

KERLIN, ROBERT T.
The Voice of the Negro 1919. New York: 1920. V. 68

KERMODE, FRANK
D. H. Lawrence. New York: 1973. V. 72

KERN, JEROME
The Library of Jerome Kern. New York: 1929. V. 71

KERN, ROBERT
Thrilling Locations: A Supplement for the James Bond 007 Game. New York: 1985. V. 71

KERNAHAN, J. G.
Bedtime Stories. 1911. V. 71

KERNAHAN, JOHN COULSON
Captain Shannon. London: 1897. V. 68; 70
Scoundrels and Co. London: 1901. V. 68

KERNAN, ALVIN
Printing Technology, Letters and Samuel Johnson. Princeton;: 1987. V. 69

KEROUAC, JACK
Big Sur. New York: 1962. V. 72
Desolation Angels. New York: 1965. V. 70; 73
The Dharma Bums. New York: 1958. V. 69; 70; 72
Doctor Sax. New York: 1959. V. 68; 70
Doctor Sax. London: 1977. V. 70; 73
Door Wide Open. 2000. V. 72
Door Wide Open. New York: 2000,. V. 70
Excerpts from Visions of Cody. New York: 1959. V. 73
Excerpts from Visions of Cody. New York: 1960. V. 72
Home at Christmas. New York: 1973. V. 72
Lonesome Traveler. New York: 1960. V. 68; 70; 72
Maggie Cassidy. New York: 1959. V. 68
Maggie Cassidy. London: 1974. V. 73
Mexico City Blues. New York: 1959. V. 68; 70
Mexico City Blues. New York: 1969. V. 72; 73
On the Road. New York: 1957. V. 68; 69; 70; 71; 73
On the Road. London: 1958. V. 70; 73
The Portable Jack Kerouac. 1995. V. 72
Pull My Daisy. New York and London: 1961. V. 70
Satori in Paris. New York: 1966. V. 70
The Subterraneans. New York: 1958. V. 68; 70
The Town and the City. New York: 1950. V. 69; 70; 71; 73
Tristessa. New York: 1960. V. 68
Vanity of Duluoz: an Adventurous Education 1935-1946. London: 1968. V. 70
Vanity of Duluoz; an Adventurous Education 1935-1946. New York: 1968. V. 70; 71; 73
Visions of Cody. New York: 1972. V. 68; 73
Visions of Cody. London: 1973. V. 70
Visions of Gerard. New York: 1963. V. 68; 72

KERR, ANDREW WILLIAM
History of Banking in Scotland. London: 1918. V. 71

KERR, CHARLES
Juvenile Performances in Poetry. Edinburgh: 1788. V. 69

KERR, J. G.
A Naturalist in the Gran Chaco. Cambridge: 1950. V. 71

KERR, J. M. MUNRO
Historical Review of British Obstetrics and Gynaecology 1800-1950. Edinburgh & London: 1954. V. 68

KERR, JOHN
The History of Curling and Fifty Years of the Royal Caledonian Curling Club. Edinburgh: 1890. V. 70

KERR, JOHN LEEDS
The Story of a Southern Carrier. New York: 1933. V. 70

KERR, PHILIP
The Berlin Noir Trilogy. London: 1989-1991. V. 68; 69; 73
A German Requiem. London: 1991. V. 70
March Violets. London: 1989. V. 68; 69; 70; 72

The Pale Criminal. London: 1990. V. 70; 72

KERR, ROBERT
The Gentleman's House, or, How to Plan English Residences, from the Parsonage to the Palace. London: 1864. V. 70; 71
Memoirs of the Life and Writings, a Correspondence of William Smellie. Edinburgh: 1811. V. 70; 71

KERSAINT, ARMAND GUY SIMON DE COETNEMPREN, COMTE DE
The Speech of Kersaint to the French National Convention, with the Resolutions of that Body Respecting a War with England. London: 1793. V. 70

KERSH, GERALD
The Best of Gerald Kersh. London/Melbourne/Toronto: 1960. V. 73
Clock Without Hands. London: 1949. V. 71
The Great Wash. London: 1953. V. 68
The Hospitality of Miss Tolliver and Other Stories. London: 1965. V. 73
I Got References. London: 1939. V. 73

KERTESZ, ANDRE
Sixty Years of Photography. 1912-1972. New York: 1972. V. 68; 72; 73

KESEY, KEN
The Day After Superman Died. Northridge: 1980. V. 69; 71; 72
Demon Box. 1987. V. 71; 72; 73
Kesey's Garage Sale. New York: 1973. V. 73
One Flew Over the Cuckoo's Nest. New York: 1962. V. 68; 69; 70; 72; 73
Sailor Song. 1992. V. 71; 72
Sailor Song. New York: 1992. V. 68; 69; 70
The Sea Lion. 1991. V. 72
Sometimes a Great Notion. New York: 1964. V. 68; 69; 72; 73

KESSEL, JOHN L.
Kiva, Cross the Crown. Washington: 1979. V. 69

KESSEL, JOSEPH
Belle de Jour. London: 1962. V. 72
Mary de Cork. Paris: 1929. V. 72
Princes of the Night. New York: 1928. V. 71

KESSELL, JOHN L.
Friars, Soldiers, and Reformers; Hispanic Arizona and the Sonora Mission Frontier 1767-1856. Tucson: 1976. V. 68; 73
Mission of Sorrows: Jesuit Guevavi and the Pimas 1691-1767. Tucson: 1970. V. 68; 70
The Missions of New Mexico Since 1776. Albuquerque: 1980. V. 68; 70

KESSELRING, JOSEPH
Arsenic and Old Lace. 1941. V. 73

KESSLER, LEO
Fire in the West. London: 1986. V. 73
Kill Rommel. London: 1995. V. 71
Operation Long Jump. London: 1993. V. 70
Patton's Wall. London: 1999. V. 71

KESSLER, MILTON
Woodlawn North: a Book of Poems. Boston: 1970. V. 69

KESTNER, CHRISTOPHER W.
Bibliotheca Medica.... Jena: 1746. V. 68

KETCHUM, JACK
The Dust of the Heavens. Aliso Viejo: 1997. V. 71
The Girl Next Door. 1996. V. 71

KETCHUM, RICHARD M.
Saratoga. Turning Point of America's Revolutionary War. 1997. V. 68

KETT, HENRY
Elements of General Knowledge, Introductory to Useful Books (...) of Literature and Science.... London: 1815. V. 73

KETTILBY, MARY
A Collection of Above Three Hundred Receipts in Cookery, Physick and Surgery. London: 1719. V. 68
A Collection of Above Three Hundred Receipts in Cookery, Physick and Surgery. London: 1728. V. 72

KETTLEWELL, J.
Of Christian Prudence, or Religious Wisdom; Not Degenerating into Irreligious Craftiness in Trying Times. London: 1691. V. 68

KETTLEWELL, S.
A Short Account of the Reformation in Ireland and the Subsequent History of Its Church. 1869. V. 70

KETTON CREMER, R. W.
Horace Walpole - a Biography. London: 1946. V. 71
Thomas Gray - a Biography. 1955. V. 71

KEVERNE, R.
Jade. New York: 1991. V. 69

KEVERNE, RICHARD
The Lady in Number 4. London: 1944. V. 73

KEY, ELLEN
The Woman's Movement. New York and London: 1912. V. 69

KEY, FRANCIS SCOTT
The Star Spangled Banner in Analectic Magazine... Philadelphia: 1814. V. 73

KEY, TED
Ted Key's Phyllis. New York: 1957. V. 72

KEYES, DANIEL
Flowers for Algernon. New York: 1966. V. 69

KEYES, E. D.
Fifty Years' Observation of Men and Events, Civil and Miliary. New York: 1884. V. 68

KEYES, E. L.
The Venereal Diseases Including Stricture of the Male Urethra. New York: 1880. V. 71

KEYES, FRANCES PARKINSON
Lady Blanche Farm: a Romance of the Commonplace. New York: 1931. V. 73

KEYES, SIDNEY
The Cruel Solstice. London: 1943. V. 73
The Iron Laurel. London: 1942. V. 73

KEYNES, GEOFFREY
The Apologie and Treatise of Ambroise Pare Containing the Voyages Made into Divers Places with Many of His Writings Upon Surgery. Chicago: 1952. V. 68; 70; 71; 73
A Bibliography of Dr. Robert Hooke. Oxford: 1960. V. 70
A Bibliography of Sir Thomas Browne. Cambridge: 1924. V. 68; 70; 72
A Bibliography of the Works of Rupert Brooke. London: 1964. V. 68
A Bibliography of the Writings of Dr. William Harvey. Cambridge: 1953. V. 68
A Bibliography of the Writings of Dr. William Harvey. Winchester: 1989. V. 70
A Bibliography of the Writings of William Harvey, M.D. Discoverer of the Circulation of the Blood 1628-1928. Cambridge: 1928. V. 73
Bibliotheca Bibliographici. A Catalogue of the Library Formed by Geoffrey Keynes. London: 1964. V. 70; 72
The Gates of Memory. Oxford: 1981. V. 71
Henry James in Cambridge. Cambridge: 1967. V. 70
Jane Austen: a Bibliography. London: 1929. V. 70; 73
The Life of William Harvey. Oxford: 1978. V. 73
The Personality of William Harvey. 1949. V. 69
The Personality of William Harvey. Cambridge: 1949. V. 68
The Portraiture of William Harvey. London: 1949. V. 68
A Study of the Illuminated Books of William Blake. London and Paris: 1964. V. 69

KEYNES, JOHN MAYNARD, 1ST BARON
The End of Laissez-Faire. London: 1926. V. 73
Essays In Biography. London: 1933. V. 72
Essays on John Maynard Keynes. 1975. V. 69
General Theory of Employment, Interest and Money. London: 1936. V. 70
The General Theory of Employment Interest and Money. New York: 1936. V. 68
How to Pay for the War. London: 1940. V. 69
Indian Currency and Finance. London: 1913. V. 70; 72; 73
A Revision of the Treaty. London: 1922. V. 68; 70; 72
A Treatise on Probability. London: 1921. V. 68

KEYNES, R. D.
Beagle Record. Selections from Records and Accounts of the Voyage of H.M.S. 1979. V. 69

KEYS, THOMAS EDWARD
The History of Surgical Anesthesia. New York: 1945. V. 68; 71

KEYSERLING, HERMANN
Activity through Silence. 1937. V. 70

KEYSSLER, JOHANN GEORG
Antiquitates Selectae Septentrionales et Celticae.... Hanover: 1720. V. 68

KHAN-MAGOMEDOV, S. O.
Alexandr Vesnin & Russian Constructivism. New York: 1986. V. 72

KHERDIAN, DAVID
Homage to Adana. Mt. Horeb: 1970. V. 73

KIDD, B. J.
A History of the Church to A.D. 461. Oxford: 1922. V. 70

KIDD, BENJAMIN
Social Evolution. London: 1895. V. 72

KIDD, DUDLEY
The Essential Kafir. London: 1925. V. 72

KIDD, J. H.
Personal Recollections Of A Cavalryman With Custer's Michigan Cavalry Brigade In The Civil War. Grand Rapids: 1969. V. 72

KIDD, JAMES
The Rights and Liberties of the Church: Asserted and Vindicated, Against the Pretended Right & Usurpation of Patronage. Aberdeen: 1834. V. 70

KIDD, JOHN
On the Adaptation of External Nature to the Physical Condition of Man.... London: 1852. V. 71; 73
Outlines of Mineralogy. Oxford: 1809. V. 68

KIDD, WILLIAM
Kidd's Magic Mirror.... London: 1836. V. 68

KIDDER, ALFRED VINCENT
The Artifacts of Pecos. New Haven: 1932. V. 72
An Introduction to the Study of Southwestern Archaeology, with a Preliminary Account of the Excavations at Pecos. New Haven: 1924. V. 68; 69

KIDDER, EDWARD J.
Japanese Temples. Tokyo and Amsterdam: 1964. V. 68

KIDDER, FREDERIC
Military Operations in Eastern Maine and Nova Scotia During the Revolution.... Albany: 1867. V. 73

KIDDER, TRACY
Home Town. New York: 1999. V. 72
The Soul of a New Machine. New York: 1997. V. 72

KIDD'S *Picturesque Pocket Companion to Brighton, Worthing, Bognor, etc.* London. V. 70

KIDS *and Kiddies.* Akron: 1914. V. 69

KIDSON, JOSEPH R.
Historical Notices of the Leeds Old Pottery. London: 1970. V. 73

KIEFER, WARREN
The Lingala Code. New York: 1972. V. 69

KIELY, BENEDICT
The Cards of the Gambler - a Folktale. London: 1953. V. 69

KIELY, EDMOND R.
Surveying Instruments, Their History. Columbus: 1979. V. 71

KIENER, LOUIS CHARLES
Species General et Iconographie des Coquilles Vivantes. Paris: 1834-1860. V. 73

KIEPERT, HENRY
Atlas Antiquus. Berlin: 1886. V. 68
Atlas Antiquus. Berlin: 1893. V. 72

KIER, P. M.
Revision of the Cassiduloid Echinoids. Washington: 1962. V. 71

KIERNAN, T. J.
The Irish Exiles in Australia. 1954. V. 69

KIHARA, H.
Fauna and Flora of Nepal Himalaya. Kyoto: 1955. V. 71

KIJEWSKI, KAREN
Copy Kat. New York: 1992. V. 68
Katapult. New York: 1990. V. 68; 69; 71; 73
Kat's Cradle. New York: 1992. V. 68
Katwalk. New York: 1989. V. 68; 69; 71
Wild Kat. Huntington Beach: 1994. V. 69; 71
Wild Kat. New York: 1994. V. 72

KILBY, T.
Original Designs and Sketches from Life an an Amateur. Southampton: 1838. V. 73

KILGORE, D. E.
A Ranger Legacy, 150 Years of Ranger Service to Texas. Austin: 1973. V. 69

KILHAM, WALTER H.
Mexican Architecture of the Vice-Regal Period. New York: 1927. V. 71
Raymond Hood, Architect: From through Function in the American Skyscraper. New York: 1973. V. 68

KILLBRIDE JONES, H. E.
Celtic Craftsmanship in Bronze. 1980. V. 69

KILLEBREW, J. B.
Grasses and Forage Plants (of the South). Knoxville: 1899. V. 68

KILLENS, JOHN OLIVER
Black Man's Burden. New York: 1965. V. 68
The Cotillion. New York: 1971. V. 70; 72

KILLINGTON, F. J.
A Monograph of the British Neuroptera. London: 1936-1937. V. 73

KILLION, TOM
The Coast of California. Boston: 1988. V. 69; 72
Walls: a Journey Across Three Continents. Santa Cruz: 1990. V. 71; 72

KILMER, JOYCE
The Circus and Other Essays. New York: 1916. V. 69
The Circus and Other Essays and Fugitive Pieces. New York: 1921. V. 70
Trees and Other Poems. New York: 1914. V. 70
The Younger Choir. New York: 1910. V. 71

KILNER, J.
The Account of Pythagoras's School in Cambridge: as in Mr. Grose's Antiquities of England and Wales, and Other Notices. Cambridge: 1783?. V. 68

KILPATRICK, JACK FREDERICK
Sequoyah: of Earth & Intellect. Austin: 1965. V. 69; 70

KILVERT, FRANCIS
Selections from the Diary of...1 January 1870-March 1879. 1960. V. 70

KILWORTH, GARRY
The Songbirds of Pain - Stories from the Inscape. London: 1984. V. 71

KIMBALL, CHARLES P.
The San Francisco City Directory, September 1, 1850. San Francisco: 1850. V. 68

KIMBALL, FRANCIS P.
The Capital Region of New York State. Crossroads of Empire. New York: 1942. V. 73

KIMBALL, MARIA B.
A Soldier - Doctor of Our Army - James P. Kimball. Boston: 1917. V. 72

KIMBALL, RICHARD B.
In the Tropics. New York: 1863. V. 68
Virginia Randall; or, Today in New York. London: 1870. V. 68
Was He Successful?. New York: 1864. V. 68

KIMBER, C. T.
Martinique Revisited, the Changing Plant Geographies of a West Indian Island. College Station: 1988. V. 68

KINCAID, DENNIS
British Social Life in India 1608-1937. London: 1938. V. 71

KINCAID, JAMAICA
Annie, Gwen, Lilly, Pam and Tulip. New York: 1986. V. 73
Annie John. New York: 1985. V. 71; 72
At the Bottom of the River. New York: 1983. V. 68; 71; 73
The Autobiography of My Mother. New York: 1996. V. 72

KINCHEN, OSCAR A.
Daredevils of the Confederate Army. Boston: 1959. V. 69

KINDERSLEY, CHARLES
The Ancient and Present State of the Navigation of the Town of Lyn, Wisbeach, Spalding and Boston, of the Rivers that Pass through those Places and the Countries tht Border Thereupon.... London: 1751. V. 71

KINDIG, R. H.
Pictorial Supplement to Denver South Park and Pacific. Denver: 1959. V. 69

KING, ALAN
Early Pennine Settlement. Clapham: 1970. V. 73

KING *Albert's Book: a Tribute to the Belgian King and People.* London: 1914. V. 68

KING, ALEXANDER
The Dreamer. London: 1754. V. 72

KING, BASIL
Going West. New York: 1919. V. 70
The Happy Isles. New York: 1923. V. 71
Satan as Lightning. New York: 1929. V. 71

KING, C.
Mountaineering in the Sierra Nevada. 1935. V. 68; 71

KING, C. DALY
Arrogant Alibi. 1939. V. 73
Bermuda Burial. 1941. V. 73
The Curious Mr. Tarrant. London: 1935. V. 69
Obelists at Sea. London. V. 70
Obelists at Sea. New York: 1933. V. 68; 70; 73
Obelists Fly High. 1935. V. 73
Obelists Fly High. London: 1935. V. 69
Obelists in Route. London: 1934. V. 73

KING, C. W.
Antique Gems: Their Origin, Uses and Value as Interpreters of Ancient History; and as Illustrative of Ancient Art with Hints to Gem Collectors. London: 1860. V. 70
The Handbook of Engraved Gems. London: 1866. V. 72
Handbook of Engraved Gems. London: 1885. V. 73
The Natural History, Ancient and Modern, of Precious Stones and Gems, and of the Precious Metals. London: 1865. V. 72
The Natural History of Gems or Decorative Stones. London: 1867. V. 72

KING, CHARLES
Campaigning with Crook and Stories of Army Life. New York: 1890. V. 68; 69; 71; 72
Indian Campaigns Sketches of Cavalry Service in Arizona and on The Northern Plains. Fort Collins: 1984. V. 72

KING *Christmas.* New York: 1881. V. 70

KING, CLARENCE
Atlas Accompanying volume II on Mining Industry (by James Duncan Hague). New York: 1870-1880. V. 70
Clarence King Memoirs - the Helmet of Mambrino. New York: 1904. V. 73
Report of the Geological Exploration of the Fortieth Parallel. Volume 5. Botany. Washington: 1871. V. 70
United States Geological Exploration of the Fortieth Parallel. Volume I. Systematic Geology. Washington: 1878. V. 73

KING *Dionysius and Squire Damocles.* London: 1796. V. 68

KING, DOROTHY N.
Santa's Merry Carnival. USA: 1955. V. 70

KING, EDWARD
An Essay on the English Constitution and Government. London: 1767. V. 70

KING, FRANK M.
Mavericks: the Salty Comments of an Old-Time Cowpuncher. Pasadena: 1947. V. 73
Longhorn Trail Drivers. Burbank: 1940. V. 69
Mavericks The Salty Command Of An Old Time Cowpuncher. Pasadena: 1947. V. 71; 72
Pioneer Western Empire Builders- A True Story of The Men And Women of Pioneer Days. Pasadena: 1946. V. 71

KING, G.
The Species of Artocarpus Indigenous to British India; the Indo- Malayan Species of Quercus and Castanposis. Calcutta: 1889. V. 70
The Species of Ficus of the Indo-Malayan and Chinese Countries. Calcutta: 1969. V. 69

KING *Gobbles Feast or the Fatal Effects of Pride.* New York: 1869. V. 71

KING, H.
A Survey of the Manor of Settrington. Y.A.S. Record Series Volume CXXVI for 1960. London: 1960. V. 73

KING, HARRIET ELEANOR HAMILTON
The Disciples. London: 1873. V. 70

KING, HENRY
Poems. London: 1925. V. 70

KING, HENRY C.
The History of the Telescope. London: 1955. V. 72

KING, J.
Letters from France. In the Months of August, September and October, 1802. London: 1803. V. 73

KING, J. C. H.
Artificial Curiosities from the Northwest Coast of America. London: 1981. V. 69

KING, JAMES T.
War Eagle- A Life of General Eugene A. Carr. Lincoln: 1963. V. 72

KING, JEFF
Where the Two Came to Their Father: A Navajo War Ceremonial. New York: 1943. V. 69; 72
Where Two Came To Their Father. Princeton: 1969. V. 69

KING, JESSIE M.
Budding Life, a Book of Flowers. London and Glasgow: 1907. V. 68
Mummy's Bedtime Story Book. London: 1929. V. 73

KING, JOHN
Memoir of The Ref. Thomas Dykes, LL.B., Incumbent of St. John's Church, Hull: With Copious Extracts From His Correspondence. Also Sermons, edited by Rev William Knight. London: 1849. V. 72

KING, JOHN GLEN
The Rites and Ceremonies of the Greek Church in Russia.... London: 1772. V. 72

KING, K. DOUGLAS
The Child Who Will Never Grow Old. London and New York: 1898. V. 69

KING, L. J.
Weeds of the World, Biology and Control. London: 1966. V. 72

KING, LAURIE R.
The Beekeeper's Apprentice. New York: 1994. V. 69; 70; 72
A Grave Talent. New York: 1992. V. 71; 73
A Grave Talent. New York: 1993. V. 68; 69; 71
A Grave Talent. London: 1995. V. 68; 71; 73
A Monstrous Regiment of Women. New York: 1995. V. 69
With Child. New York: 1996. V. 72

KING, LEONARD
From Cattle Rustler to Pulpit. San Antonio: 1943. V. 68; 71; 73

KING, LORD
The Life of John Locke, with Extracts from His Correspondence, Journals and Common Place Books. London: 1830. V. 68

KING, MARTIN LUTHER
Chaos or Community?. London: 1968. V. 68
Strength to Love. New York: 1963. V. 68; 69
Stride Toward Freedom. New York: 1958. V. 69; 71
Where Do We Go From Here: Chaos or Community?. New York: 1967. V. 70; 72

KING, MONIQUE
European Textiles in the Keir Collection 400 BC to 1800 AD. London: 1990. V. 72

KING, MOSES
First Catalogue, Moses King, Cambridge, Publisher and Bookseller. Cambridge: 1881. V. 71
How to See Boston. Boston: 1895. V. 69

KING, PETER
An Enquiry into the Constitution, Discipline, Unity and Worship of the Primitive Church. (bound with) the Second Part.. London: 1712. V. 70
The History of the Apostles Creed, with Critcal Observations on Its Several Articles. London: 1737. V. 69
The History of the Apostles Creed; with Critical Observations on Its Several Articles. Elizabeth Town: 1804. V. 71

KING, PETER JOHN LOCKE
Injustice of the Law of Succession to the Real Property of Intestates.... London: 1855. V. 73

KING, RICHARD ASHE BASIL
A Coquette's Conquest. London: 1887. V. 68

KING, ROSS
Domino. London: 1995. V. 70
Ex-Libris. London: 1998. V. 68; 69; 73

KING, RUFUS
Design in Evil. Garden City: 1942. V. 68; 70
The Lesser Antilles Case. New York: 1934. V. 73
Malice in Wonderland. Garden City: 1958. V. 71; 72
Murder by Latitude. New York: 1930. V. 73
Murder by the Clock. New York: 1929. V. 73
Murder on the Yacht. New York: 1932. V. 73
Museum Piece No. 13. New York: 1946. V. 68

KING, S.
Art of Folk Embroidery. Taipei: 1993. V. 69

KING, STEPHEN
Black House. New York: 2001. V. 69
Carrie. Garden City: 1974. V. 69; 70; 71
Carrie. London: 1974. V. 70; 71
Christine. New York: 1983. V. 68
Cujo. New York: 1981. V. 68
Cycle of the Werewolf. Westland: 1983. V. 73
Danse Macabre. New York: 1981. V. 68; 69; 71; 72
The Dark Half. New York: 1989. V. 69
The Dark Tower I: The Gunslinger. 1982. V. 69
The Dark Tower II: Drawing of the Three. 1987. V. 69
The Dark Tower II: The Drawing of the Three. Hampton Falls: 1987. V. 70
The Dark Tower II: The Drawing of the Three. West Kingston: 1987. V. 69
The Dark Tower III: The Wastelands. 1991. V. 69
The Dead Zone. New York: 1979. V. 68; 69; 71
Different Seasons. New York: 1982. V. 68
Dolores Claiborne. New York: 1992. V. 69
Dreamcatcher. New York: 2001. V. 69
Firestarter. New York: 1980. V. 68; 69; 71
Gerald's Game. New York: 1992. V. 69
Hearts in Atlantis. New York: 1999. V. 72
It. New York: 1916. V. 73
My Pretty Pony. New York: 1988. V. 70
My Pretty Pony. New York: 1989. V. 71
Night Shift. Garden City: 1978. V. 68; 69
Nightmares and Dreamscapes. London: 1993. V. 69
Pet Sematary. London: 1983. V. 69
Rose Madder. 1995. V. 72
Salem's Lot. Garden City: 1975. V. 68; 69; 71
The Shining. Garden City: 1977. V. 68; 69; 71; 73
Skeleton Crew. New York: 1985. V. 68
The Stand. Garden City: 1978. V. 69; 70; 71; 72
Stephen King on Writing. New York: 2000. V. 70
The Talisman. New York: 1984. V. 68
Thinner. 1984. V. 69
Thinner. New York: 1984. V. 71

KING, THOMAS
Green Grass, Running Water. Boston: 1993. V. 72
Truth & Bright Water. New York: 1999. V. 72

KING, W. KENT
Massacre - The Custer Cover-Up - The Original Maps of Custer's Battlefield. El Segundo: 2000. V. 72

KING, W. R.
The Sportsman and Naturalist in Canada.... London: 1866. V. 69; 72

KING, WILLIAM
The Art of Love.... London: 1708. V. 68
Doctor King's Apology; or Vindication of Himself from the Several Matters Charged on Him by the Society of Informers. Oxford: 1755. V. 68; 72
Political and Literary Anecdotes of His Own Times. London: 1818. V. 69; 70; 71
A Translation of the Latin Epistle in the Dreamer. 1754. V. 72

KING & CO., LTD., SOUTH CHURCH SIDE, HULL
Illustrated Price List of Furnishing Ironmongery, Marble Chimney Pieces, Tiled Hearths, Stoves &c. Hull: 1890. V. 71

KINGDOM Come. 1941-. V. 71

KINGDON, JONATHAN
East African Mammals. London: 1971-1982. V. 70

KINGDON WARD, FRANCIS
Assam Adventure. London: 1941. V. 70
Burma's Icy Mountains. London: 1949. V. 70
From China to Khamti Long. London: 1924. V. 70
Pilgrimage for Plants. 1960. V. 72; 73
A Plant Hunter in Tibet. 1934. V. 73
Plant Hunter in Tibet. 1937. V. 69; 72
Plant Hunter's Paradise. London: 1934. V. 69
Plant Hunter's Paradise. 1937. V. 72; 73
Plant Hunter's Paradise. London: 1937. V. 69
Plant Hunter's Paradise. 1938. V. 70

Return to the Crawdad. 1956. V. 72
Return to the Irrawaddy. 1956. V. 69

KING-HALL, EDITH
Adventures in Toyland. London: 1901. V. 73

KING HALL, MAGDALEN
I Think I Remember. New York: 1927. V. 69

KING-HALL, STEPHEN
The China of To-Day. London: 1927. V. 72

KINGLAKE, ALEXANDER WILLIAM
Eothen. London: 1845. V. 68
Eothen. New York: 1845. V. 69
Eothen. London: 1913. V. 72
The Invasion of Crimea. Edinburgh & London: 1877-1883. V. 69
The Invasion of Crimea. New York: 1888. V. 71

KINGSBURY, ALICE
Secrets Told. San Francisco: 1879. V. 69

KINGSBURY, BENJAMIN
A Treatise on Razors. London: 1802. V. 73

KINGSBURY, J. M.
Poisonous Plants of the United States and Canada. Englewood Cliffs: 1964. V. 72

KINGSFORD, WILLIAM
The Canadian Canals; Their History and Cost, with an Inquiry Into the Policy Necessary to Advance the Well-Being of the Province. Toronto: 1865. V. 72
The History of Canada. Toronto: 1887-1898. V. 73

KINGSLEY, CHARLES
Alton Locke, Tailor and Poet. London: 1850. V. 68
Andromeda and Other Poems. London: 1858. V. 73
At Last: a Christmas in the West Indies. London and New York: 1871. V. 68; 69
Glaucus; or the Wonders of the Shore. Cambridge: 1855. V. 68; 69
Glaucus; or the Wonders of the Shore. London: 1855. V. 71
Glaucus; or the Wonders of the Shore. 1858. V. 69; 73
Glaucus; or, the Wonders of the Shore. London: 1890. V. 68
The Life and Works. London: 1901-1903. V. 73
Poems. Boston: 1856. V. 73
The Saint's Tragedy; or the True Story of Elizabeth of Hungary. 1848. V. 73
The Saint's Tragedy; or, the True Story of Elizabeth of Hungary. London: 1848. V. 68; 72
Town Geology. London: 1877. V. 68; 70
The Water Babies. London. V. 68
The Water Babies. London: 1863. V. 72
The Water Babies. Philadelphia: 1915. V. 71
The Water Babies. New York: 1916. V. 73
Westward Ho!. 1855. V. 70
Westward Ho!. Cambridge: 1855. V. 71
Westward Ho!. London: 1896. V. 71
Westward Ho!. New York: 1920. V. 73
Westward Ho!. New York: 1947. V. 69

KINGSLEY, G. H.
Notes on Sport and Travel. 1900. V. 72

KINGSLEY, HENRY
Geoffry Hamlyn. London: 1883. V. 68
Hetty and Other Stories. London: 1885?. V. 68
Leighton Court: a Country House Story. London: 1872. V. 68
Leighton Court: a Country House Story. London: 1877. V. 68
Ravenshoe. London: 1872. V. 68
Ravenshoe. London: 1883. V. 68
Reginald Hetherege. London: 1882?. V. 68
Silcote of Silcotes. London: 1872. V. 68

KINGSLEY, JOHN S.
The Riverside Natural History. Boston: 1888. V. 71

KINGSLEY, ROSE G.
Eversley Gardens and Others. London: 1907. V. 70
South by West; or Winter in the Rocky Mountains and Spring in Mexico. London: 1874. V. 71

KINGSMILL, HUGH
The Sentimental Journey: a Life of Charles Dickesn. Adelphi: 1934. V. 68

KINGSOLVER, BARBARA
Animal Dreams. New York: 1990. V. 68; 69; 72; 73
Another America: Otra America. Seattle: 1992. V. 69; 70; 73
The Bean Trees. New York: 1988. V. 69; 72; 73
The Bean Trees. London: 1989. V. 68; 70
The Bean Trees. New York: 1989. V. 73
High Tide in Tucson. New York: 1995. V. 69; 71; 72; 73
Holding the Line: Women in the Great Arizona Mine Strike of 1983. Cornell: 1989. V. 69; 70; 73
Homeland. New York: 1989. V. 68; 69; 70; 73
Pigs in Heaven. London: 1993. V. 68
The Poisonwood Bible. New York: 1998. V. 69; 72; 73

KINGSON, AL
The Pictorial Word Book In English And French, Containing Engravings Of Common Objects For The Amusement And Instruction Of Children. Paris. V. 70; 72

KINGSTON, MAXINE
Hawaii One Summer. San Francisco: 1987. V. 72

KINGSTON, MAXINE HONG
The Woman Warrior. New York: 1976. V. 73

KINIETZ, W. VERNON
John Mix Stanley and His Indian Paintings. Ann Arbor. V. 73

KINLOCH, A. A. A.
Large Game Shooting in Thibet and the North West. 1869-1876. V. 73
Large Game Shooting in Thibet and The North West. 1876. V. 72
Large Game Shooting in Thibet, the Himalayas, Northern and Central India. 1892. V. 69; 70; 72; 73

KINLOCH, BRUCE
The Shamba Raiders. Memories of a Game Warden. 1972. V. 72

KINNAIRD, LAWRENCE
The Frontier of New Spain - Nicolas De LaFors's Description 1766-1768. Berkeley: 1958. V. 73

KINNE, ASA
The Most Important Parts of Blackstone's Commentaries, Reduced to Qustions and Answers. New York: 1839. V. 69

KINNELL, GALWAY
Black Light. Boston: 1966. V. 68; 71
The Last Hiding Places of Snow. New York: 1980. V. 69; 73
Mortal Acts, Mortal Wounds. Boston: 1980. V. 68; 71
A New Selected Poems. Boston/New York: 2000. V. 72
The Past. Boston: 1985. V. 68; 69
Selected Poems. Boston: 1982. V. 68
There Are Things I Tell to No One. New York: 1979. V. 73
When One Has Lived a Long Time Alone. New York: 1990. V. 68; 71

KINNEY, ARTHUR
The Birds and Beasts of Shakespeare. Easthampton: 1990. V. 72
Rogues, Vagabonds and Sturdy Beggars. Barre: 1973. V. 69; 72

KINNEY, TROY
The Etchings of Troy Kinney. Garden City: 1929. V. 70

KINSELLA, THOMAS
Another September. 1958. V. 69; 73
Another September. Dublin: 1958. V. 73
Downstream. Dublin: 1962. V. 70
The Messenger. Dublin: 1978. V. 69; 71; 73
Notes from the Land of the Dead and Other Poems. New York: 1973. V. 72
Poems and Translations. New York: 1961. V. 69
A Selected Life. Dublin: 1972. V. 71
Song of the Night and Other Poems. Dublin: 1978. V. 69; 71
A Technical Supplement. Dublin: 1976. V. 71; 73
Thomas Kinsella. Cecil King. West Germany: 1981. V. 69
Vertical Man: a Sequel to a Selected Life. Dublin: 1973. V. 71; 73
Wormwood. Dublin: 1966. V. 69

KINSELLA, W. P.
The Alligator Report. Minneapolis: 1985. V. 72
Born Indian. Canada: 1981. V. 69; 70
Dance Me Outside. Boston: 1977. V. 70
Dance Me Outside. Canada: 1977. V. 71
Dance Me Outside. Boston: 1986. V. 72
Five Stories. Vancouver: 1986. V. 72
The Iowa Baseball Confederacy. Boston: 1986. V. 69
The Iowa Baseball Confederacy. Toronto: 1986. V. 68; 71
The Moccasin Telegraph and Other Stories. Boston: 1984. V. 71
Red Wolf, Red Wolf. Toronto: 1987. V. 72
Scars. Canada: 1978. V. 70; 71; 72
Shoeless Joe. Boston: 1982. V. 68; 69; 71; 72; 73

KINSEY, ALFRED C.
Sexual Behavior in the Human Female. Philadelphia and London: 1953. V. 72
Sexual Behavior in the Human Male. Philadelphia and London: 1948. V. 72

KINSEY, CHARLES
Abridgment of Decisions, of the Supreme Court of New Jersey, on Certiorari to Courts for the Trial of Small Causes. From May Term 1806 to February Term 1813, Inclusive. Burlington: 1815. V. 71

KINSEY, WILLIAM MORGAN
Portugal Illustrated: in a Series of Letters.... London: 1829. V. 70

KINSLEY, H. M.
One Hundred Recipes for the Chafing Dish. New York: 1894. V. 68

KIOWA Indian Art. Santa Fe: 1979. V. 68

KIP, LAWRENCE
Army Life on The Pacific: A Journal of The Expedition Against The Northern Indians, The Tribes of The Coeur D'Alenes, Spokans And Pelouzes in The Summer of 1858. Redfield: 1859. V. 72

KIPLING, ALICE M.
A Pinchbeck Goddess. London: 1897. V. 73

KIPLING, RUDYARD
Abaft the Funnel. New York: 1909. V. 68; 69
The Absent Minded Beggar. 1899. V. 70
Actions and Reactions. London: 1909. V. 73
All Mowgli Stories. London: 1933. V. 70
Barrack-Room Ballads and Other Verses. London: 1892. V. 69; 70; 71; 72; 73
Captains Courageous. London: 1897. V. 69; 72; 73
Captains Courageous. New York: 1897. V. 68; 70; 73
The City of Dreadful Night and Other Places. Allahabad: 1891. V. 69; 73
The Collah-Wallah (sic) and the Poison Stick. New York: 1925. V. 72
The Complete Stalky & Co. London: 1929. V. 70
The Covenanter. London: 1914. V. 73
The Day's Work. London: 1898. V. 69; 71; 73
The Dead King. London: 1910. V. 70
Debits and Credits. 1926. V. 70
Debits and Credits. London: 1926. V. 69; 73
Departmental Ditties and Other Verses. Lahore: 1886. V. 73
Departmental Ditties and Other Verses. Calcutta: 1895. V. 73
The Feet of the Young Men. Garden City: 1920. V. 70; 71
The Five Nations. London: 1903. V. 69; 73
A Fleet in Being: Notes of Two Trips with the Channel Squadron. London: 1898. V. 69
Four Famous Just So Stories. Garden City: 1942. V. 70
France at War. London: 1915. V. 70
From Sea to Sea, Letters of Travel. New York: 1899. V. 73
L'Habitation Forcee. Paris: 1921. V. 70
Humorous Tales from Rudyard Kipling. London: 1931. V. 70; 71; 73
In Black and White. Allahabad & London. V. 73
The Jungle Book. London: 1908. V. 69
The Jungle Book & The Second Jungle Book. London: 1894-1895. V. 72; 73
Just So Stories for Little Children. London: 1902. V. 71; 72; 73
Kim. London: 1901. V. 70; 72; 73
Land and Sea Tales: for Scouts and Guides. London: 1923. V. 73
Letters of Travel (1892-1913). London: 1920. V. 69; 72
Life's Handicap: Being Stories fo Mine Own People. London: 1892. V. 73
The Light that Failed. London: 1891. V. 69
Limits and Renewals. London: 1932. V. 68; 73
Limits and Renewals. New York: 1932. V. 70
Many Inventions. London: 1893. V. 69; 73
The Naulahka: a Story of the West. London: 1892. V. 69
The Phantom Rickshaw and Other Eerie Tales. London: 1890. V. 71
The Phantom Rickshaw, and Other Tales. Allahabad: 1890. V. 69
Plain Tales from the Hills. Calcutta: 1888. V. 70
Plain Tales from the Hills. London: 1896. V. 73
Puck of Pook's Hill. London: 1906. V. 73
Puck of Pook's Hill. New York: 1906. V. 70; 71; 73
Quartette, the Christmas Annual of the Civil and Military Gazette. Lahore: 1885. V. 70
Rewards and Fairies. Garden City: 1910. V. 69; 71
Rewards and Fairies. London: 1910. V. 73
Rudyard Kipling's Verse. Inclusive Edition 1885-1918. London: 1919. V. 70; 71
The Second Jungle Book. London: 1895. V. 68; 71
The Seven Seas. London: 1896. V. 69; 73
Soldier Tales. London: 1896. V. 73
Something of Myself: for My Friends Known and Unknown. London: 1937. V. 73
A Song of the English. London. V. 71; 73
A Song of the English. London: 1909. V. 70
Songs from Books. Garden City: 1912. V. 70
Songs of the Sea. London: 1927. V. 71
Stalky and Co. London: 1899. V. 73
The Story of the Gadsbys: a Tale Without a Plot. Allahabad: 1890. V. 69; 73
Toomai of the Elephants. London: 1937. V. 73
Traffics and Discoveries. London: 1904. V. 71; 73
The Two Jungle Books. London: 1924. V. 72
Under the Deodars. Allahabad and London. V. 73
Under the Deodars. Allahabad: 1890. V. 69; 73
Wee Willie Winkie and Other Stories. Allahabad: 1890. V. 69; 73
Wee Willie Winkie and Other Stories. London: 1895. V. 73
Wee Willie Winkie, Under the Deodars, The Phantom Rickshaw; and Other Stories. London: 1892. V. 69; 72
The White Man's Burden. London: 1899. V. 72
With the Night Mail. New York: 1909. V. 70; 73
The Works. London: 1913-1938. V. 68; 70
The Years Between. London: 1919. V. 68; 73
The Years Between. New York: 1919. V. 68

KIPPIS, ANDREW
A Narrative of the Voyages Around the World, Performed by Captain James Cook with an Account of His Life.... London: 1889. V. 72
A Narrative of the Voyages Round the World Performed by Captain James Cook.... 1893. V. 68
A Sermon Preached at the Old Jewry on the Fourth of November 1788, Before the Society for Commemorating the Glorious Revolution.... London: 1788. V. 73

KIRA, ALEXANDER
The Bathroom. New York: 1976. V. 69; 73

KIRA, T.
Shells of the Western Pacific in Color. Osaka: 1965-1968. V. 68; 71; 73

KIRALIS, KARL
The Theme and Structure of William Blake's Jerusalem. Canton: 1956. V. 71

KIRBY, EDWARD M.
The Saga of Butch Cassidy and the Wild Bunch. 1977. V. 69

KIRBY, F. VAUGHAN
Sport in East Central Africa Being an Account of Hunting Trips in Portugese and Other Districts of East Central Africa. London: 1899. V. 72

KIRBY, JAMES
The Lower Canada Law Journal. Montreal: 1865-1868. V. 72

KIRBY, JOSHUA
The Perspective of Architecture, in Two Parts. 1761. V. 71; 73

KIRBY, M.
Stories About Birds of Land and Water. Hartford: 1875. V. 68

KIRBY, MARY
The Sea and Its Wonders. London: 1871. V. 68
The World at Home: Pictures and Scenes.... London: 1876. V. 68

KIRBY, R. G.
Mexican Landscape Architecture: from the Street and From Within. 1972. V. 69

KIRBY, WILLIAM
The Golden Dog. Toronto. V. 70
On the Power Wisdom and Goodness of God as Manifested in the Creation of Animals and in Their History Habits and Instincts. London: 1835. V. 72

KIRBY, WILLIAM F.
European Butterflies and Moths. 1882. V. 69
A Handbook to the Order Lepidoptera. 1896-1897. V. 69
An Introduction to Entomology; or Elements of the Natural History of Insects. London: 1822-1826. V. 73
Introduction to Entomology.... London: 1828. V. 69

KIRCHENHOFFER, HERMAN
The Book of Fate, formerly in the possession of Napoleon . . . London: 1824. V. 71
The Book of Fate, Formerly in the Possession of Napoleon.... London: 1823. V. 70

KIRCHER, ATHANASIUS
Itinerarium Exstataicum Quo Mundi Opificium id est Coelestis Expansi Siderumque Tam Erratium, Quam Sixorum Natura... (with) Iter Extacium II. Qui & Mundi Subterranei Prodromus Dicitur....(with) In III. Dialogos Distinctum. Rome: 1657. V. 68
Magnes sive de Arte Magnetica Opus Tripartitum.... Rome: 1641. V. 73
Magnes sive de Arte Magnetica Opus Tripartitum.... Rome: 1654. V. 69
Mundus Subterraneus. Amstelodami: 1668. V. 68; 73

KIRK, DOROTHY
Woman's Home Companion Cook Book. Garden City: 1951. V. 73

KIRK, JOHN F.
History of Charles the Bold, Duke of Burgundy. Philadelphia: 1864. V. 71

KIRK, LAURENCE
Whispering Tongues. New York: 1934. V. 69

KIRK, T.
The Forest Flora of New Zealand. Wellington: 1889. V. 69; 70

KIRKALDY, WILLIAM G.
Illustrations of David Kirkaldy's System of Mechanical Testing as Originated and Carried on by Him During a Quarter Century. London: 1891. V. 68

KIRKBRIDE, JOHN
The Northern Angler, or Fly-Fisher's Companion. 1840. V. 68; 73

KIRKBY, B.
Lakeland Words. Kendal: 1898. V. 71

KIRKBY, JOHN
The Capacity and Extent of Human Understanding; Exemplified in the Extraordinary Case of Automathes.... London: 1745. V. 73

KIRKBY, WILLIAM
The Evolution of Artificial Mineral Waters. Manchester: 1902. V. 68

KIRKE, HENRY
The First English Conquest of Canada: with Some Account of the Earliest Settlements in Nova Scotia and Newfoundland. London: 1871. V. 73

KIRKEBY, ED
Ain't Misbehavin'. The Story of Fats Waller. New York: 1966. V. 69; 71

KIRKER, H.
California's Architectural Frontier: Style and Tradition in the Late 19th Century. San Marino: 1960. V. 69; 72

KIRKLAND, J.
Herbal and Magical Medicine, Traditional Healing Today. Durham: 1992. V. 68

KIRKLAND, JOHN
The Modern Baker, Confectioner and Caterer. London: 1924. V. 68
Modern Baker, Confectioner and Caterer. London: 1931. V. 72

KIRKLAND, THOMAS J.
Historic Camden. Part One: Colonial and Revolutionary. Columbia: 1905. V. 71

KIRKMAN, F. B.
The British Bird Book. London: 1911. V. 70
The British Bird Book. 1911-1913. V. 69

KIRKMAN, JAMES THOMAS
Memoirs of the Life of Charles Macklin, Esq. London: 1799. V. 71

KIRKPATRICK, B. J.
A Bibliography of Virginia Woolf. London: 1957. V. 69; 70
A Bibliography of Virginia Woolf. Oxford: 1980. V. 70
A Bibliography of Edmund Blunden. Oxford: 1979. V. 72

KIRKPATRICK, D.
Eduardo Paolozzi. Greenwich: 1971. V. 72

KIRKPATRICK, E. E.
Crimes' Paradise. The Authentic Inside Story of the Ursche Kidnapping. San Antonio: 1934. V. 69

KIRKPATRICK, JAMES
The Sea-piece. London: 1750. V. 73

KIRKPATRICK, JOHN
Timothy Flint: Pioneer, Missionary, Author, Editor 1780-1840. Cleveland: 1911. V. 69; 70; 72; 73

KIRKPATRICK, THOMAS J.
The Kirkpatrick Story, The Day By Day Report of the Trek Across the Plains by the Kirkpatrick Family in 1854. Orland: 1959. V. 68

KIRKPATRICK, W. T.
Alpine Days and Nights. 1932. V. 70

KIRKSTALL ABBEY
An Historical, Antiquarian, and Picturesque Account of Kirkstall Abbey. 1827. V. 73
History of Kirkstall Abbey. Leeds: 1828. V. 73
History of Kirkstall Abbey. Leeds: 1839. V. 73
History of Kirkstall Abbey. Leeds: 1845. V. 73

KIRKWOOD, EDITH BROWN
Animal Children. Chicago: 1913. V. 70

KIRLICKS, JOHN A.
Sense and Nonsense in Rhyme. Houston: 1913. V. 70

KIRST, HANS HELLMUT
Forward, Gunner Asch!. Boston: 1956. V. 73
The Return of Gunner Asch. London: 1957. V. 70
The Revolt of Gunner Asch. Boston: 1955. V. 68

KIRSTEIN, LINCOLN
Elie Nadelman. New York: 1973. V. 72

KIRSTEN, L.
Tchelitchev. 1994. V. 69; 72

KIRTON, J.
The British Falling Block Breechloading Rifle from 1865. 1997. V. 69; 70; 72; 73

KIRWAN, RICHARD
An Estimate of the Temperature of Different Latitudes. London: 1787. V. 69

KIRWAN, THOMAS
A Report on the Proceedings in the Cases of Thomas Kirwan, Merchant and Edward Sheridan, M.D. for Misdemeanors Charged to be Committed in Violation of the Convention Act. Dublin: 1811. V. 70

KIRWIN, WILLIAM J.
Reminiscences of James P. Howley: Selected Years. Toronto: 1997. V. 68

KISSELL, MARY LOIS
Basketry of the Papago and Pima. New York: 1916. V. 69

KISSEN, DAVID M.
Emotional Factors in Pulmonary Tuberculosis. New York: 1958. V. 71

THE KIT Book for Soldiers, Sailors and Marines. Chicago: 1943. V. 69

KITAY, JULIAN I.
The Pineal Gland. A Review of the Physiologic Literature. Cambridge;: 1954. V. 68

KITCHIN, C. H. B.
Death of My Aunt. London: 1929. V. 73
Streamers Waving. London: 1925. V. 72; 73

KITCHIN, THOMAS
The Traveller's Guide through England and Wales.... London: 1783. V. 69

KITCHINER, WILLIAM
Cook's Oracle. London: 1821. V. 72
Cook's Oracle. Boston: 1822. V. 72
Cook's Oracle. London: 1831. V. 72
The Economy of the Eyes - Part I. Of Spectacles, Opera-Glasses and Theatres.... 1826. V. 73
The Housekeeper's Oracle, or the Art of Domestic Management.... London: 1829. V. 71

KITE, OLIVER
A Fisherman's Diary. 1969. V. 68; 73
A Fisherman's Diary. 1977. V. 73
Nymph Fishing in Practice. 1977. V. 68; 73

KITTO, F. H.
Report of a Preliminary Investigation of the Natural Resources of the Mac Kenzie District and Their Economic Development Made During the Summer of 1920. Ottawa: 1920. V. 68

KITTON, FREDERIC GEORGE
Charles Dickens by Pen and Pencil, including Anecdotes and Reminiscences Collected from His Friends and Contemporaries.... London: 1890. V. 70
Charles Dickens by Pen and Pencil. (with) A Supplement to Charles Dickens by Pen and Pencil: (with) Additional Illustrations. London: 1890-1891. V. 70
Charles Dickens. His Life, Writings and Personality. London. V. 68
Dickens and His Illustrators: Cruikshank, Seymour Buss, "Phiz", Cattermole, Leech, Doyle, Stanfield, Maclise, Tenniel, Frank Stone, Landseer, Palmer, Topham, Marcus Stone and Lake Fildes. London: 1899. V. 69; 70
The Dickens Country. London: 1911. V. 69
Dickensiana: a Bibliography of the Literature. London: 1886. V. 68
John Leech - Artist and Humourist. London: 1884. V. 69
John Leech, Artist and Humourist: a Biographical Sketch. London: 1883. V. 70; 72
The Minor Writings of Charles Dickens. London: 1900. V. 68
Old Lamps for New Ones. New York: 1897. V. 68

KITTREDGE, WILLIAM
Hole in the Sky. New York: 1992. V. 69; 72
The Last Best Place. A Montana Anthology. Helena: 1989. V. 70
Lost Cowboys (but Not Forgotten). New York: 1992. V. 68; 72
Owning It All. St. Paul: 1987. V. 71; 72
Phantom Silver. 1987:. V. 72
The Van Gogh Field and Other Stories. Columbia: 1978. V. 72

KITTRELL, NORMAN G.
Texas Illustrated; or the Romance, the History and Resources of a Great State. Houston: 1911. V. 70

KITZINGER, E.
Byzantine Art in the Making: Main Lines of Stylistic Development in Mediterranean Art 3rd-7th Century. New Haven: 1977. V. 72

KITZMILLER, J. B.
Anopheline Names: Their Derivations and Histories. 1982. V. 73

KIZER, CAROLYN
Knock Upon Silence - Poems by Carolyn Kizer. New York: 1965. V. 72
Mermaids in the Basement. Port Townsend: 1984. V. 71; 72
Midnight Was My Cry. Garden City: 1971. V. 69
The Ungrateful Garden. Bloomington: 1961. V. 68; 71

KLAH, HADTEEN
Navajo Creation Myth, the Story of the Emergence. Santa Fe: 1942. V. 73

KLAPP, H. MINOR
Krider's Sporting Anecdotes, Illustrative of the Habits of Certain Varieties of American Game. Philadelphia: 1853. V. 68; 69

KLAPROTH, H. J.
Chrestomathie Mandchou, ou Recueil de Textes Mandchou, Destine aux Personnes Qui Veulent s'Occuper de l'Etude de Cette Langue. Paris: 1828. V. 69

KLASNER, LILY
My Girlhood Among Outlaws. Tucson: 1972. V. 68

KLAUBER, L. M.
Rattlesnakes, Their Habits, Life Histories and Influence on Mankind. Berkeley: 1972. V. 70; 72
A Statistical Study of the Rattlesnakes. San Diego: 1936-1940. V. 72

KLAVEN, ANDREW
Face of the Earth. New York: 1980. V. 68; 71
The Scarred Man. New York: 1990. V. 71

KLEE, PAUL
The Diaries of...1898-1918. London: 1965. V. 72
The Diaries of...1899-1918. 1965. V. 68
The Inward Vision: Watercolors, Drawings, Writings. New York: 1959. V. 69; 72
Notebooks. Volume I: The Thinking Eye. London: 1973. V. 69

KLEIN, D.
In the Deco Style. New York: 1986. V. 69; 72

KLEIN, E.
Atlas of Histology. London: 1880. V. 68

KLEIN, HERB
Lucky Bwana. The Adventures of a Big Game Hunter in East Africa. 1953. V. 70

KLEIN, JACOB THEODOR
Stemmata Avivm. Lipsiae: 1759. V. 70

KLEIN, JOE
Primary Colors. New York: 1996. V. 70
Woody Guthrie. Boston: 1980. V. 71
Woody Guthrie. New York: 1980. V. 72

KLEIN, WILLIAM
Mister Freedom. Paris: 1970. V. 68
Moscow. New York: 1964. V. 68
New York: Life Is Good and Good For You In New York. Paris: 1956. V. 68
New York: Life is Good and Good For You in New York!. New York: 1995. V. 69

KLEINBERG, SAMUEL
Scoliosis: Rotary Lateral Curvature of the Spine. New York: 1926. V. 69

KLEINER, SALOMON
Representation Naturelle et Exacte de la Favorite de Son Altesse Electorale de Mayence.... Augsburg: 1726. V. 70

KLEIST, FRANZ ALEXANDER VON
Sappho Ein Dramatisches Gedicht. Berlin: 1793. V. 69

KLEMPNER, JOHN
Letter to Five Wives. New York: 1946. V. 71

KLETTE, ERNEST
The Crimson Trail of Joaquin Murieta. Los Angeles: 1928. V. 68; 73

KLINEFELTER, WALTER
Ex Libris A. Conan Doyle, Sherlock Holmes. Chicago: 1938. V. 68; 70; 71; 72
More Christmas Books. Portland: 1938. V. 73
Sherlock Holmes in Portrait & Profile With Introduction By Vincent Starrett. Syracuse: 1963. V. 72

KLINGBERG, MARCUS A.
Drugs and Fetal Development. New York: 1972. V. 68

KLINGMAN, LAWRENCE
His Majesty O'Keefe. New York: 1950. V. 71

KLOCKER, A.
Fermentation Organisms. London: 1903. V. 68

KLOOT, T.
Birds of Australian Gardens. Adelaide: 1980. V. 73

KLOS, H. G.
Handbook of Zoo Medicine. 1982. V. 73

KLOSOVSKII, B. N.
Blood Circulation in the Brain. Jerusalem: 1963. V. 71
Blood Circulation in the Brain. London: 1963. V. 68
The Development of the Brain and Its Disturbance by Harmful Factors. Oxford: 1963. V. 68

KLOSS, C. B.
In the Adamans and Nicobars. London: 1903. V. 69

KLUCKER, CHRISTIAN
Adventures of an Alpine Guide. London: 1932. V. 69

KLUCKHOHN, CLYDE
An Introduction to Navaho Chant Practice. Menasha: 1940. V. 73
The Navaho. Cambridge: 1946. V. 69
Navajo Material Culture. Cambridge: 1971. V. 69

KLUGE, P. F.
Eddie and the Cruisers. New York: 1980. V. 70; 72

KLUTE, JEANETTE
Woodland Portraits. Boston: 1954. V. 68

KLUVER, HEINRICH
Visual Mechanisms. Lancaster: 1942. V. 68

KLYCE, SCUDDER
Universe. Winchester: 1921. V. 72

KNAP, OSWALD G.
An Artist's Love Story. Told in the Letters of Sir Thomas Lawrence, Mrs. Siddons and Her Daughters. London: 1904. V. 72

KNAPP, ANDREW
The Newgate Calendar Improved.... London. V. 70

KNAPP, CHARLES MERRIAM
New Jersey Politics During the Period of the Civil War and Reconstruction. Geneva: 1924. V. 71

KNAPP, J. L.
Gramina Britannica; or, Representations of the British Brasses.... London: 1842. V. 69

KNAPP, JOHN LEONARD
The Journal of a Naturalist. London: 1829. V. 73

KNAPP, MOSES L.
Lectures on the Science of Life Insurance, Addressed to Families, Socieities, Trades, Professions.... Philadelphia: 1853. V. 71

KNAPP, SAMUEL L.
Biographical Sketches of Eminent Lawyers, Statemen, and Men of Letters. Boston: 1821. V. 73
Letters of Shahcoolen, a Hindu Philosopher, Residing in Philadelphia.. Boston: 1802. V. 73

KNATCHBULL HUGESSEN, E. H.
Higgledy Piggledy or Stories for Everybody and Everybody's Children. London: 1875. V. 69
Higgledy-Piggledy, or, Stories for Everybody and Everybody's Children. London: 1877. V. 70

KNATCHBULL HUGESSON, HUGHE
Kentish Family. London: 1960. V. 70; 73

KNEALE, MATTHEW
English Passengers. London: 2000. V. 68

KNEBEL, FLETCHER
Seven Days in May. New York: 1962. V. 71; 72

KNEE, ERNEST
Santa Fe. New York: 1942. V. 69

KNEEDLER, H. S.
Through Storyland to Sunset Seas. Chicago: 1895. V. 70

KNEELAND, ABNER
The Antitheistical Catechism, Being a Complete Refutation of Both Ancient and Modern Theology. Boston: 1831. V. 71
Minutes of a Discussion on the Question Is the Punishment of the Wicked Absolutely Eternal? or is It Only a Temporal Punishment in this World, for Their Good.... Philadelphia: 1824. V. 71

KNEELAND, SAMUEL
The Wonders of the Yosemite Valley and of California. Boston: 1872. V. 68; 70; 73

KNIEF, CHARLES
Diamond Head. New York: 1996. V. 70

KNIGHT, CHARLES
Knight's Cyclopaedia of London. 1851. London: 1851. V. 71
Knight's Cyclopedia of the Industry of All Nations. London: 1851. V. 68
Knight's Dictionary of Arts, Commerce and Manufactures. London: 1851. V. 71
London. London: 1841-1844. V. 71
Old England; a Pictorial Museum of Regal, Ecclesiastical, Municipal, Baronial and Popular Antiquities. London: 1854. V. 72
Passages of A Working Life During Half A Century. London: 1864. V. 71; 72
The Struggles of a Book Against Excessive Taxation. London: 1850. V. 69
The Working-Man's Companion. New York: 1831. V. 71

KNIGHT, CLIFFORD
The Affair Of The Golden Buzzard. Philadelphia: 1946. V. 72
The Affair of the Heavenly Voice. 1937. V. 73
The Affair of the Heavenly Voice. New York: 1937. V. 69
The Affair of the Limping Sailor. 1942. V. 73
The Affair of the Scarlet Crab. 1937. V. 73
Dark Abyss. New York: 1949. V. 73

KNIGHT, CORNELIA
A Description of Latium or la Campagna di Roma. London: 1805. V. 70

KNIGHT, DAVID M.
Natural Science Books in English 1600-1900. London: 1989. V. 68

KNIGHT, E. F.
The Falcon on the Baltic. London: 1889. V. 72

KNIGHT, ELLIS CORNELIA
Dinarbas. London: 1790. V. 69
Dinarbas. London: 1792. V. 69

KNIGHT, F.
Vases and Ornaments. London. V. 72

KNIGHT, HENRY
Ilderi; a Syrian Tale. London: 1816. V. 69

KNIGHT, JAMES
The Founding of Churchill. Being the Journal of Captain James Knight, Governor-in-Chief in Hudson Bay, from the 14th of July to the 13th of September 1717. Toronto/London/Vancouver: 1932. V. 73
Orthopaedia or a Practical Treatise on the Aberrations of the Human Form. New York: 1884. V. 69

KNIGHT, JOHN
Narratives of the Perils and Sufferings of Dr. Knight and John Slover, Among the Indians, During the Revolutionary War.... Cincinnati: 1867. V. 71

KNIGHT, KATHLEEN MOORE
Bells for the Dead. New York: 1942. V. 71
Death Came Dancing. Garden City: 1940. V. 71
Exit a Star. Garden City: 1941. V. 71
The Tainted Token. New York: 1938. V. 71

KNIGHT, LUCIAN LAMAR
Memorials of the Dixie-Land Orations, Essays, Sketches and Poems on Topics Historical, Commemorative, Literary and Patriotic. Atlanta: 1919. V. 69

KNIGHT, M. FORSTER
Uncle Blunder's Studio. London: 1943. V. 69

KNIGHT, MONTAGU GEORGE
Chawton Manor and Its Owners, a Family History. London: 1911. V. 73

KNIGHT, O. W.
The Birds of Maine.... Bangor: 1908. V. 70; 73
A List of the Birds of Maine.... Augusta: 1897. V. 72

KNIGHT, OLIVER
Following The Indian Wars, The Story of The Newspaper Correspondents Among The Indian Campaigners. Norman: 1960. V. 72
Life and Manners in The Frontier Army. Norman: 1978. V. 72

KNIGHT, R. P.
The Landscape: a Didactic Poem in Three Books. London: 1794. V. 73

KNIGHT, RICHARD PAYNE
An Analytical Enquiry into the Principles of Taste. London: 1805. V. 72

KNIGHT, S.
Forms of Prayer, for the Use of Christian Families. York: 1814. V. 69
Forms of Prayer, for the Use of Christian Families. York: 1816. V. 69

KNIGHT, SARAH K.
The Journals of Madam Knight and Rev. Mr. Buckingham. New York: 1825. V. 69

KNIGHT, THOMAS ANDREW
On the Origin and Office of the Alburnum of Trees (and) On the Inconvertibility of Bark into Alburnum. London: 1808. V. 70
Pomona Herefordiensis. London: 1811. V. 68; 72
A Treatise on the Culture of the Apple and Pear, and on the Manufacture of Cider and Perry. London: 1813. V. 68

KNIGHT, THOMAS F.
Nova Scotia and Her Resources. Prize Essay. Halifax: 1862. V. 73

KNIGHT, WILLIAM
Through the Wordsworth Country. London: 1887. V. 71
Through the Wordsworth Country. London: 1906. V. 71
Wordsworthiana - A Selection from Papers Read to the Wordsworth Society. London: 1889. V. 73

KNIGHTS of the Ku Klux Klan. Atlanta: 1919. V. 68

KNITTLE, JOHN
Midnight People. New York: 1931. V. 71

KNOLL, ROBERT E.
Robert McAlmon - Expatriate Publisher and Writer. Lincoln: 1959. V. 71

KNOLLES, RICHARD
The Turkish History, Comprehending the Origin of that Nation, and the Growth of the Othoman Empire, with the Lives and Conquests of Their Several Kings and Emperors. London: 1701. V. 68

KNOOP, JOHANN HERMANN
Beschouwende en Werkdadige Hovenier-Konst of Inteiding tot de Waare Oeffening der Planten.... Leeuwarden: 1753. V. 68

KNOTT, ROBERT ROW
The New Aid to Memory. London: 1839. V. 69

KNOW, KATHLEEN
Fairy Gifts; or, a Wallet of Wonders. London: 1882. V. 69; 70

KNOWER, DANIEL
The Adventures of a Forty-Niner. Albany. V. 73
The Adventures of a Forty-Niner. Albany: 1894. V. 68; 71

KNOWLES, E. H.
The Castle of Kenilworth. Warwick: 1872. V. 68; 71

KNOWLES, GEORGE H.
In the Grip of the Jungles. 1932. V. 70
In the Grip of the Jungles. 1933. V. 73

KNOWLES, HORACE
Countryside Treasures. 1946. V. 72
Countryside Treasures. London: 1946. V. 69
Legends from Fairyland. London: 1908. V. 69

KNOWLES, HORACE J.
Countryside Treasures. London: 1946. V. 71

KNOWLES, JAMES D.
Memoirs of Mrs. Ann H. Judson, Wife of the Rev. Adoniram Judson, Missionary to Burmah. London: 1829. V. 72

KNOWLES, JOHN
Indian Summer. New York: 1966. V. 69
Morning in Antibes. New York: 1962. V. 68
A Separate Peace. London: 1959. V. 70
A Separate Peace. New York: 1960. V. 70
A Separate Peace. New York: 1974. V. 72
Spreading Fires. New York: 1974. V. 68

KNOWLES, JOHN A.
Essays in the History of the York School of Glass-Painting. London: 1936. V. 72; 73

KNOWLES, R. B. SHERIDAN
Glencoonoge. 1891. V. 69

KNOWLSON, JAMES
Samuel Beckett: an Exhibition Held at Reading University Library May to July 1971. London: 1971. V. 69; 72

KNOWLTON, CHARLES
Elements of Modern Materialism. Adams: 1829. V. 73
Fruits of Philosophy. Sheffield: 1878. V. 71

KNOWLTON, ELIZABETH
The Naked Mountain. London: 1933. V. 69

KNOX, A. E.
Autumns of the Spey. 1872. V. 68
Game Birds and Wild Fowl. 1850. V. 70

KNOX, A. E. continued
Ornithological Rambles in Sussex; with a Systematic Catalogue of the Birds of that County, and Remarks on Their Local Distribution. 1855. V. 73

KNOX, E. V.
Blue Feathers. London: 1929. V. 70

KNOX, GEORGE
Catalogue of the Tiepolo Drawings in the Victoria and Albert Museum. London: 1960. V. 68

KNOX, HUBERT T.
The History of the County of Mayo to the Close of the Sixteenth Century. 1908. V. 69

KNOX, JOHN
Historical Journal of the Campaigns in North America for the years 1757, 1758, 1759, and 1760. London: 1769. V. 73
An Historical Journal of the Campaigns In North America for the Years 1757, 1758, 1759, and 1760. Toronto: 1914. V. 71

KNOX, R. A.
Enthusiasm - a Chapter in the History of Religion, with Special Reference to the XVII and XVIII Centuries. Oxford: 1950. V. 68

KNOX, ROBERT
Descriptions, Geological, Topographical and Antiquarian in Eastern Yorkshire, Between the Rivers Humber and Trees. London: 1855. V. 69
An Historical Relation of the Island Ceylon, in the East Indies.... London: 1681. V. 70
A Manual of Artistic Anatomy for the Use of Sculptors and Amateurs. London: 1832. V. 72

KNOX, RONALD
The Footsteps at the Lock. London: 1928. V. 73
Other Eyes than Ours. London: 1926. V. 68
A Selection from the Occasional Sermons of the Right Reverend Monsignor Knox. London: 1949. V. 69
Still Dead. London: 1934. V. 73
Still Dead. New York: 1934. V. 73
The Three Taps. London: 1927. V. 73
The Three Taps. New York: 1927. V. 69
The Viaduct Murder. 1926. V. 68
The Viaduct Murder. New York: 1926. V. 69

KNOX, SAMUEL
An Essay on the Best System of Liberal Education, Adapted to the Genius of the Government of the United States. Baltimore: 1799. V. 68

KNOX, THOMAS W.
The Boy Travellers in Great Britain and Ireland. New York: 1891. V. 70
The Voyage of the Vivian to the North Pole and Beyond. New York: 1885. V. 70

KNOX, VICESIMUS
The Spirit of Despotism. Morris-Town: 1799. V. 71
The Spirit of Despotism. Trenton: 1802. V. 71
Winter Evenings; or Lucubrations on Life and Letters. London: 1790. V. 72

KNOX, WILLIAM
An Appendix to the Present State of the Nation. London: 1769. V. 72
The Present State of the Nation; Particularly with respect to Its Trade, Finances &c. London: 1768. V. 72

KNUTH, PAUL ERICH OTTO WILHELM
Handbook of Flower Pollination Based Upon Herman Muller's Work "The Fertilization of Flowers by Insects". Oxford: 1906-1909. V. 72

KOBAL, JOHN
The Art of the Great Hollywood Portrait Photographers. New York: 1980. V. 68

KOBAYSHI, T.
Geology and Palaeontology of Southeast Asia. Tokyo: 1964-1970. V. 70

KOBBE, GUSTAV
The Complete Opera Book. London: 1922. V. 68
The New Jersey Coast and Pines. Short Hills: 1889. V. 71

KOBEL, JACOB
Wapen. Des Heyligen Romischen Reichs Tetscher Nation. Frankfurt am Main: 1545. V. 68; 69

KOBLER, JOHN
Capone: The Life and World of Al Capone. New York: 1971. V. 71

KOCH, CARL
At Home with Tomorrow. New York: 1958. V. 72

KOCH, CHARLES W.
The Crimea: From Kertch to Perekop. London: 1855. V. 72

KOCH, KENNETH
The Duplications. New York: 1977. V. 71; 72

KOCH, MICHAEL
The Shay Locomotive, Titan of the Timber. Denver: 1971. V. 69
Steam and Thunder in the Timber, Saga of the Forest Railroads. Denver: 1979. V. 69

KOCH, ROBERT A.
Joachim Patinir. Princeton: 1968. V. 70; 72; 73

KOCH, RUDOLF
The Typefoundry in Silhouette: How Printing Type is Developed at Klingspor Bros. in Offenbach on the River Main. San Francisco: 1982. V. 70

KOCH, STEPHEN
Andy Warhol Photographs. New York. V. 68; 69

KOCH, THEO F., & CO.
Hampshire and Winnie, in South East Part of the Texas Gulf Coast. Chicago: 1914. V. 70

KOCHER, PAUL H.
Science and Religion in Elizabethan England. San Marino: 1953. V. 72

KOEBEL, W. H.
In the Maoriland Bush. London: 1911. V. 69

KOEHLER, FRANCIS C.
Hilda. A Romance of the Revolution. Hackensack: 1932. V. 71

KOEHLER, OTTO
Ku-Winda (To Hunt). San Antonio: 1956. V. 69

KOEHLER, ROBERT P.
Sing a Song of Murder. New York: 1941. V. 69

KOENIG, ALEXANDER
Avifauna Spitzbergensis.... Bonn: 1911. V. 70; 73

KOESTLER, ARTHUR
The Age of Longing. London: 1951. V. 71
Darkness at Noon. London: 1940. V. 72
The Gladiators. London: 1939. V. 71; 73
Thieves in the Night. London: 1946. V. 71

KOGAN, GEORGES
The Ascent of Alpamayo. London: 1954. V. 69

KOHL, J. G.
A History of the Discovery of the East Coast of North America. Portland: 1869. V. 71
Kitchi-Gami - Wanderings Round Lake Superior. London: 1860. V. 68; 70; 73

KOHLER, ALBAN
Borderlands of the Normal and Early Pathologic in Skeletal Roentgenology. New York: 1956. V. 68

KOHLER, ARTHUR
Stilkunde: Kurzer Abriss Der Stilkunde, mit Besonderer Berucksichtigung. Bern/Basel: 1942. V. 72

KOHN, D.
Darwinian Heritage. Princeton;: 1982. V. 69

KOHNSTAM, G. L. S.
The Radiological Examination of the Male Urethra. London: 1925. V. 68

KOIZUMI, GUNJI
Lacquer Work. London: 1925. V. 71

KOLARZ, WALTER
Books on Communism, A Bibliography. New York: 1967. V. 70

KOLB, KEN
Getting Straight. Philadelphia: 1967. V. 70

KOLIADES, CONSTANTIN, PSEUD.
Ulysse-Homere, Ou du Veritable Auteur de L'Iliade et de L'Odyssee. Paris: 1829. V. 72

KOLLIKER, A.
A Manual of Human Microscopic Anatomy. 1860. V. 73

KOLLIST, E. J.
French Pastry, Confectionary and Sweets. London: 1929. V. 68

KOLLMAN, P.
The Victoria Nyanza. London: 1899. V. 69

KOLLMYER, A. H.
Chemia Coartata; or, the Key to Modern Chemistry. Philadelphia: 1875. V. 68

KOLLOCK, HENRY
Christ Must Increase. A Sermon, Preached before the General Assembly of the Presbyterian Church in the United States of America...May 23, 1803.... Philadelphia: 1803. V. 71
Sermons on Various Subjects...with a Memoir of the Life of the Author. Savannah: 1822. V. 71

KOLMOGOROV, A. N.
Foundations of the Theory of Probability. New York: 1956. V. 73

KOLODIN, IRVING
The Metropolitan Opera 1883-1935. New York: 1935. V. 68

KOMARA, EDWARD M.
The Dial Recordings of Charlie Parker. Westport: 1998. V. 72

KOMUNYAKAA, YUSEF
Dedications and Other Darkhorses. Laramie: 1977. V. 72

KONIG, PAUL
Voyage of the Deutschland, the First Merchant Submarine. New York: 1916. V. 71

KONIGSBURG, E. L.
The View from Saturday. New York: 1996. V. 73

KONIGSTEIN - Engelbrecht *Different Vue Dessinees d'Apres Nature sur le Chateau si Renomme de Konigstein.* Augsburg: 1735. V. 70

KONIKOW, ANTOINETTE F.
Physcicians' Manual of Birth Control. New York: 1931. V. 72

KONINGS, A.
Konings's Book of Cichlids and all the Other Fishes of Lake Malawi. Neptune City: 1990. V. 72

KONKLE, BURTON A.
Life and Speeches of Thomas Williams 1806-1872. Philadelphia: 1905. V. 69

KONODY, P. G.
Sir William Orpen, Artist & Man. London: 1934. V. 70

KONORSKI, JERZY
The Integrative Action of the Brain. Chicago: 1967. V. 68

KONSTNARSODE, ETT
Carl Oscar Borg. Stockholm: 1953. V. 69

KONVITZ, JEFFREY
The Sentinel. New York: 1974. V. 71

KOONTZ, DEAN R.
After the Last Race. 1974. V. 68
Anti-Man. New York: 1970. V. 69
Chase. New York: 1972. V. 71
Cold Fire. New York: 1991. V. 68; 69; 70
Dark Rivers of the Heart. New York: 1994. V. 72
The Door to December. London: 1987. V. 73
Dragonfly. New York: 1975. V. 68; 70; 72
The Eyes of Darkness. London: 1981. V. 68; 71
Eyes of Darkness. 1989. V. 69
The Face of Fear. Indianapolis: 1977. V. 68; 69; 70; 71
False Memory. London: 1999. V. 68
Fear Nothing. New York: 1998. V. 71
Hanging On. New York: 1973. V. 71
Hanging On. London: 1974. V. 72
The Mask. London: 1989. V. 73
Mr. Murder. London: 1993. V. 69
Nightmare Journey. 1975. V. 69
Oddkins, a Fable for all Ages. New York: 1988. V. 69
Prison of Ice. Philadelphia: 1976. V. 69; 71
Sole Survivor. New York: 1997. V. 72
Strangers. New York: 1986. V. 68
Strike Deep. New York: 1974. V. 71
Ticktock. London: 1996. V. 68; 69; 73
The Vision. 1977. V. 70
Watchers. New York: 1987. V. 71

KOOP, W. E.
Billy the Kid. The Trail of a Kansas Legend. 1965. V. 68

KOOPS, MATTHIAS
Historical Account of the Substances Which Have Been Used to Described Events and to Convey Ideas from the Earliest Date to the Invention of Paper. London: 1800. V. 69

KOPELENT, F. J.
A Description of the Emperor of Austria's Salt Mine, at Wieliczka, in Galicia.... London. V. 69

KOPP, HERMANN
Einleitung in Die Krystallographie und in die Krystallographische.... Bruanschweig: 1849. V. 68

KOPPITZ, RUDOLPH
Rudolph Koppitz. Wien: 1937. V. 68; 70

KORAN
The Alcoran of Mahomet. London: 1688. V. 73
The Koran, Commonly Called the Alcoran of Mahomet. Springfield: 1806. V. 68
The Koran: Commonly called the Alcoran of Mohammed. London: 1850. V. 72
The Koran: Selected Suras. New York: 1958. V. 69

KOREN, NATHAN
Jewish Physicians. Jerusalem: 1973. V. 68; 71

KORNBLUTH, C. M.
Christmas Eve. London: 1956. V. 69
Not This August. New York: 1955. V. 70
The Syndic. Garden City: 1953. V. 73
Takeoff. Garden City: 1952. V. 69

KORNS, J. RODERIC
West from Fort Bridger, the Pioneering of the Immigrant Trails Across Utah 1846-1850. Salt Lake City: 1951. V. 68

KORSCHELT, E.
Text-Book of Embryology of Invertebrates. London: 1895-1900. V. 68

KORSHAK, STEPHEN D.
A Hannes Bok Showcase. 1995. V. 70
A Hannes Bok Treasury. 1993. V. 70

KORSHIN, PAUL J.
Johnson After Two Hundred Years.... 1986. V. 69

KORTHALS, P.
Verhandelingen over de Natuurlijke Gescheidenis der Nederlanddsche Overseesche Bezittingen.... Leiden: 1839-1842. V. 73

KORTRIGHT, F. H.
The Ducks, Geese and Swans of North America.... Washington: 1942. V. 69; 72

KOSINSKI, JERZY
Being There. New York: 1970. V. 69; 70; 71
Blind Date. Boston: 1977. V. 69; 71; 72
Notes of the Author on the Painted Birds. New York: 1967. V. 71
Painted Bird. Boston: 1965. V. 72; 73
Passion Play. New York: 1979. V. 71
Pinball. New York: 1982. V. 72
Steps. New York: 1968. V. 69; 72

KOSSAK SZCZUCKA, Z.
The Troubles of a Gnome. London: 1928. V. 69

KOSUTH, JOSEPH
Two Oxford Reading Rooms. London: 1994. V. 69

KOTTELAT, M.
Freshwater Fishes of Western Indonesia and Sulawesi. Indonesia: 1993. V. 69

KOTZEBUE, OTTO VON
Entdeckungs-Reise in Die Sud-See Und Nach der Berings-Strasse Zur Erforschung Einer Nordostlichen Durchfahrt. Unternommen in Den Jahren 1815, 1816, 1817 und 1818. Weimar: 1821. V. 70
A New Voyage Round theWorld in the Years 1823, 1824, 1825 and 1826. London: 1830. V. 73
Voyage of Discovery in the South Sea and to Behring's Straits in Sach of a North East Passage, Undertaken in the Years 1815, 1816, 1817 and 1818 in the Ship Rurick. London: 1821. V. 68; 70

KOTZWINKLE, WILLIAM
The Bear Went Over the Mountain. New York: 1996. V. 71
Dr. Rat. New York: 1976. V. 68
E. T. The Extra Terrestrial. New York: 1982. V. 71
Elephant Bangs Train. New York: 1971. V. 71; 73
The Exile. New York: 1987. V. 71
Fata Morgana. New York: 1977. V. 71
Herr Nightingale and the Satin Woman. New York: 1978. V. 71
The Hot Jazz Trio. Boston: 1989. V. 72
Jewel of the Moon. New York: 1985. V. 68
Queen of Swords. New York: 1984. V. 68
Return of Crazy Horse. New York: 1971. V. 69
Trouble in Bugland. Boston: 1983. V. 70

KOURY, MICHAEL J.
Custer Centennial Observances 1876. Fort Collins: 1928. V. 72
Diaries of The Little Big Horn. Papillon, NE: 1968. V. 72

KOVEL, R.
American Country Furniture 1780-1875. New York: 1965. V. 69; 72

KOVIC, RON
Around the World in Eight Days. San Francisco: 1984. V. 68; 69; 71
Born on the Fourth of July. New York: 1976. V. 68; 72

KOWALSKY, L.
Battle of Bunker Hill. Boston: 1888. V. 73

KOZISEK, JOSEF
A Forest Story. New York: 1929. V. 73

KOZOL, JONATHAN
The Fume of Poppies. Boston: 1958. V. 73

KRAFT, LOUIS
Custer and the Cheyenne, George Armstrong Custer's Winter Campaign on the Southern Plains. El Segundo: 1995. V. 73
Gatewood & Geronimo. Albuquerque: 2000. V. 72

KRAG, MARTHA ANN
Martha Jane: Nursery Nonsense. Indianapolis: 1897. V. 72

KRAKAUER, JON
Into the Wild. New York: 1966. V. 71; 72
Into Thin Air. New York: 1997. V. 68; 69; 70; 72

KRAKEL, DEAN
James Boren: a Study in Discipline. Flagstaff: 1968. V. 68; 69
The Saga of Tom Horn, The Story of a Cattleman's War With Personal Narratives, Newspaper.... Laramie: 1954. V. 68; 69; 71
Seasons of the Elk. Kansas City: 1976. V. 69
South Platte Country, A History of the Old Welch County, 1739-1900. Laramie: 1954. V. 71; 73
Tom Ryan: a Painter in Four Sixes Country. Flagstaff: 1971. V. 69; 73
Tom Ryan- A Painter in Four Sixes Country. Northland: 1971. V. 71

KRAMER, HAROLD MORTON
The Castle of Dawn. Boston: 1908. V. 70

KRAMER, HILTON
Milton Avery: Paintings 1930-1960. New York: 1962. V. 71
Richard Lindner. Boston: 1975. V. 72

KRAMER, SIDNEY
A History of Stone and Kimball and Herbert S. Stone and Co., with a Bibliography of their Publications 1893-1905. Chicago: 1940. V. 69

KRAMER, W.
Aural Surgery of the Present Day. London: 1863. V. 68

KRANZ, J.
Experimental Techniques in Plant Disease Epidemiology. New York: 1988. V. 72

KRASNA, NORMAN
Dear Ruth. New York: 1945. V. 71

KRASSNOFF, PETER N.
The Black Mass. 1931. V. 70; 72

KRAUS, BERTRAM S.
The Human Dentition Before Birth. London: 1965. V. 68

KRAUS, H. P.
A Rare Book Saga. London: 1979. V. 71

KRAUSE, E.
Erasmus Darwin.... London: 1879. V. 73

KRAUSE, HERBERT
Custer's Prelude to Glory, a Newspaper's Account of Custer's 1874 Expedition to the Black Hills. Sioux Falls: 1974. V. 72

KRAUSE, MARTIN
Gustave Baumann: Nearer to Art. Santa Fe: 1993. V. 72; 73

KRAUSS, JOHANN
Oeconomisches Haus-Und Kunst-Buch...Zum Nutzen Und Gebrauch fur... Handwerker, Kunstler, Und Kunst-Liebhaber.... Allentown: 1819. V. 70

KRAUSS, RUTH
Charlotte and the White Horse. London: 1977. V. 72
Open House for Butterflies. New York: 1960. V. 70; 71
A Very Specal House. New York: 1953. V. 71

KREBS, ROLAND
Making Friends Is Our Business - 100 Years of Anheuser-Busch. NP: 1953. V. 72

KRECIC, P.
Plecnik: the Complete Works. 1993. V. 68; 69; 72

KREFFT, GERARD
The Snakes of Australia; an Illustrated and Descriptive Catalogue of All Known Species. Sydney: 1869. V. 73

KREHBIEL, H. E.
Afro-American Folksongs: A Study in Racial and National Music. NY: 1914. V. 72

KREIDOLF, ERNST
Das Hundefest. (The Dog's Party). Zurich: 1928. V. 70

KREMENTZ, JILL
Happy Birthday, Kurt Vonnegut. New York: 1982. V. 71

KRESSING, HARRY
Cook. New York: 1965. V. 73

KRETSCHMER, A.
Costumes of All Nations, from the Earliest Times. London: 1882. V. 69

KREY, LAURA
On the Long Tide. Boston: 1940. V. 70

KRIDER, J.
Krider's Sporting Anecdotes.... Philadelphia: 1853. V. 70

KRIEG, W. J. S.
Connections of the Frontal Cortex of the Monkey. Springfield: 1954. V. 72

KRIEGER, A. E.
Culture Complexes and Chronology in Northern Texas, with Extension of Puebloan Datings to the Mississippi Valley. 1946. V. 69

KRIGE, E. J.
The Social System of the Zulus. London: 1936. V. 69

KRISHNA, K.
Biology of Termites. Volume II. New York: 1970. V. 72

KRIVATSY, PETER
A Catalogue of Seventeenth Century Printed Books in the National Library of Medicine. Mansfield Centre: 1999. V. 69

KROEKER, MARVIN
Great Plains Command - William B. Hazen In the Frontier West. Norman: 1976. V. 72

KROG, HELGE
Three Plays - the Conch, Triad, The Copy. London: 1934. V. 71

KROGER, L.
My Last Kambaku. 1996. V. 69; 70; 72; 73

KROLL, ERIC
Sex Objects. New York: 1977. V. 70

KRONFELD, PETER C.
The Human Eye in Anatomical Transparencies. New York: 1944. V. 71
The Human Eye in Anatomical Transparencies. New York: 1945. V. 70; 71

KRONHEIM, J. M.
A Description of the Colosseum as Re-opened in MDCCCXLV.... London: 1845. V. 72

KROPOTKIN, PETER
Memoirs of a Revolutionist. Boston: 1899. V. 70

KROUT, MARY H.
Hawaii and a Revolution. New York: 1898. V. 69

KRUSSMANN, G.
Manual of Cultivated Broad-Leaved Trees and Shrubs. Beaverton: 1984-1986. V. 69

KRUTCH, J. W.
Herbal. New York: 1965. V. 68

KRYLOV, IVAN
Krylov's Fables. London: 1926. V. 72

KUBASTA, VOITECH
Gulliver in Bobdingnag. London. V. 70
Moko and Koko in the Jungle. London: 1962. V. 73
Noah's Ark. London: 1960. V. 72
Puss in Boots. London: 1961. V. 72; 73
The Six Singers. London: 1964. V. 70
Snow White. London: 1961. V. 72
Tip-Top Go Camping. London: 1962. V. 70
Up in the Air. Prague: 1986. V. 72

KUBIENA, W. L.
The Soils of Europe. Madrid and London: 1953. V. 68; 71

KUBLER, GEORGE
The Art and Architectre of Ancient America: the Mexican/Maya/ and Andean Peoples. Baltimore: 1962. V. 70; 71
The Religious Architecture of New Mexico in the Colonial Period and Since the American Occupation. 1940. V. 69

KUCK, L. E.
The Art of Japanese Gardens. New York: 1940. V. 68

KUGLER, FRANZ THEODOR
The Schools of Painting In Italy. London: 1851. V. 68

KUGY, JULIUS
Alpine Pilgrimage. London: 1934. V. 69

KUHLMAN, CHARLES
Custer and The Gall Saga. Billings: 1940. V. 72
Legend into History: the Custer Myth, an Analytical Study of the Battle of Little Big Horn. Harrisburg: 1952. V. 69; 72

KUHNELT-LEDDIHN, ERIK MARIA, VON
Night Over the East. London: 1936. V. 72

KULL, IRVING S.
New Jersey. A History. New York: 1930. V. 71
New Jersey. A History. New York: 1932. V. 71

KUMAR, A.
The Family Rosaceae in India. Dehra Dun: 1995. V. 68

KUMAR, NARINDER
Kanchenjunga. London: 1978. V. 69

KUMIN, MAXINE
House, Bridge, Fountain, Gate. New York: 1975. V. 68
The Nightmare Factory. New York: 1970. V. 68
The Privilege. New York: 1965. V. 68
Up Country. New York: 1972. V. 73

KUMM, H. KARL W.
From Hausaland To Egypt, Through The Sudan. London: 1910. V. 72

KUMMER, FREDERIC ARNOLD
The Green God. New York: 1911. V. 72

KUN, BELA
Revolutionary Essays. London. V. 68; 70

KUNCKEL, JOHANN
Ars Vitraria Experimentalis, Oder Volkommene Glasmacher-Kunst, Lehrende.... Frankfurt and Leipzig: 1679. V. 68; 70; 73

KUNDERA, MILAN
Identity. New York: 1998. V. 69; 71; 72; 73
The Joke. London: 1969. V. 69
The Joke. New York: 1969. V. 68; 69
The Joke. New York: 1982. V. 71
Life is Elsewhere. New York: 1974. V. 69
The Unbearable Lightness of Being. New York: 1984. V. 68; 71; 73

KUNIKE, FRIEDRICH ADOLF
Die Bader Bohmens und Deren Umgebungen. Karlsbad, Toplitz, Franzensbrunn, Marienbad u Bilin. Vienna: 1830. V. 70

KUNITZ, STANLEY
The Collected Poems. New York: 2000. V. 72
Selected Poems 1928-1958. Boston: 1958. V. 69

KUNOS, IGNACZ
Forty-Four Turkish Fairy Tales. London: 1913. V. 70

KUNTZ, ALBERT
The Autonomic Nervous System. London: 1929. V. 68

KUNZ, GEORGE FREDERICK
The Curious Lore of Precious Stones.... Philadelphia and London: 1913. V. 70
The Magic of Jewels and Charms. London: 1915. V. 70; 72

KUOMEI, F.
Rare and Precious Wild Flowers of China. Beijing: 1996. V. 68

KUPRIN, ALEXANDRE
Yama (The Pit). New York: 1929. V. 69

KUREISHI, HANIF
The Black Album. London: 1995. V. 68; 73

KURNITZ, HARRY
Fast Company. New York: 1938. V. 70

KURODA, NAGAMICHI
Birds in Life Colours. Tokyo: 1935-1939. V. 73
Birds of the Island of Java. Tokyo: 1933. V. 70
Birds of the Island of Java. Tokyo: 1933-1936. V. 73
Geese and Ducks of the World (Kari to Kamo). Tokyo: 1939. V. 73

KURONUMA, K.
Fishes of Kuwait. Kuwait: 1972. V. 72

KUROSAWA, AKIRA
Something Like an Autobiography. New York: 1982. V. 72

KURTZ, O. L.
Micro-Analytical Entomology for Food Sanitation Control. Washington. V. 73

KURTZWEIL, TOVE
Moment. Copenhagen: 1998. V. 68

KURUTZ, GARY F.
Benjamin C. Truman: California Booster and Bon Vivant. San Francisco: 1984. V. 73

KURZ, PAUL KONRAD
On Modern German Literature. 1970-1977. V. 68

KURZ, RUDOLPH FRIEDRICH
Journal of Rudolph Friedrich Kurz. An Account of His Experiences Among Fur Traders and American Indians on the Mississippi and the Upper Missouri Rivers During the Years 1846 to 1852. Washington: 1937. V. 68; 70

KURZBECK, JOSEPH NOBEL DE
Nouveau Guide par Vienne Pour les Etrangers et les Nationales de l'An 1792. Vienna: 1792. V. 68; 70

KURZWEIL, ALLEN
A Case of Curiosities. Franklin Center: 1992. V. 69
A Case of Curiosities. New York: 1992. V. 69; 70

KUYKENDALL, IVAN LEE
Ghost Riders of the Mogollon. 1954. V. 68

KYD, THOMAS
Blood on the Bosom Devine. Phila: 1948. V. 72
The Tragedie of Solimon and Perseda. London: 1800. V. 69

KYNE, PETER B.
Cappy Ricks Retires. New York: 1922. V. 71
Never the Twain Shall Meet. New York: 1923. V. 69; 71
The Three Godfathers. New York: 1913. V. 71

KYNER, JAMES H.
End of Track. Caldwell: 1937. V. 69

KYOVA HISTORICAL SOCIETY
Heritage of Cabell County (WV). Huntington: 1996. V. 73

KYPER, ALBERT
Anthropoligia, Corporis Humani, Contentorum et Animae Naturam & Virtutes Secundum Circularum Sanguinis Motu Explicans. Leiden: 1660. V. 70

KYRIAZI, GARY
The Great American Amusement Parks. Secaucus: 1976. V. 73

L

L., H.
The Booklover's Litany by H.L. Pasadena: 1930. V. 73

LA SCALA, Milan - 3 August 1778 to 11 May 1946. Milan: 1947. V. 68

LAAR, G. VAN
Magazign van Tuin-Sieraden; of Verzameling van Modellen van Aanleg en Sieraad, voor Groote en Kleine Lust-Hoven.... Zalt-Bommel: 1819. V. 68; 70; 72

LABARTE, M. JULES
Handbook of the Arts of the Middle Ages and Renaissance. London: 1855. V. 72

LABAW, GEORGE WARNE
Preakness and the Preakness Reformed Church, Passaic County, New Jersey. A History 1695-1902. New York: 1902. V. 71

LABBE, LOUISE
The Debate Between Folly and Cupid.... London: 1925. V. 71

LABBE, PHILIPPE
Eruditae Pronuntiationis Catholici Indices...Opera & Studio.... Londini: 1751. V. 70

LABELYE, CHARLES
The Result of a View of the Great Level of the Fens, Taken at the Desire of His Grace the Duke of Bedford &c. London: 1745. V. 71
A Short Account of the Methods Made Use of In Laying the Foundation of the Piers of Westminster Bridge. London: 1739. V. 73

LABERN, JOHN
Original Comic Songs, as Sung at the London and Provincial Theatres, Concerts, Festivals, Parties, etc. London: 1844. V. 69

LABILLARDIERE, JACQUES JULIEN HOUTON DE
Voyage in Search of La Perouse Performed by Order of the Constituent Assembly, During the Years 1791, 1792, 1793 and 1794. London: 1800. V. 70

LA BLACHE, FANNY
Starlight Stories Told to Bright Eyes and Listening Ears. London: 1877. V. 70
Starlight Stories Told to Bright Eyes and Listening Ears. London: 1886. V. 69

LABORDE, J. V.
Le Ramollissement et La Congestion Du Cerveau Principalement Consideres Chez Le Vieillard. Paris: 1866. V. 72

LABORDE, LEON DE
Journey Through Arabia Petrae to Mount Sinai. London: 1836. V. 72
Journey through Arabia Petrae to Mount Sinai. 1838. V. 70

LABROT, SYL
Pleasure Beach. New York: 1976. V. 70

LACEPEDE, BERNARD GERMAIN ETIENNE DE LA VILLE
Oeuvres Comprenant l'Histoire Naturelle des Quadrupedes, Ovipares, des Serpents, des Poissons et des Cetaces. Paris: 1826-1833. V. 69
Oeuvres du Comte de Lacepede.... Paris: 1828-1833. V. 73

LACERDA, K.
Brazilian Orchids. Tokyo: 1995. V. 68

LACK, DAVID
Darwin's Finches. 1947. V. 69
Darwin's Finches. Cambridge: 1947. V. 68; 72
Island Biology. Berkeley: 1976. V. 68

LACKINGTON, JAMES
The Confessions of J. Lackington, Late Bookseller.... New York: 1808. V. 68
Memoirs of James Lackington, Who from the Humble Station of a Journeyman Shoemaker by Great Industry, Amassed at Large Fortune. Newburgh: 1796. V. 73
Memoirs of the Forty-five First Years of the Life of James Lackington.... 1791. V. 72

LACKINGTON, JOHN
The Confessions of...Late Bookseller at the Temple of the Muses.... London: 1804. V. 69

LA CONDAMINE, CHARLES MARIE DE
Journal of a Tour to Italy. Dublin: 1763. V. 70

LA COUR, TAGE
Ex Bibliotheca Holmesiana: the First Editions of the Writings of Sherlock Holmes. Copenhagen: 1951. V. 69

LA CROIX, ARDA
Billy the Kid. New York: 1907. V. 68; 73

LACROIX, PAUL
The Arts in the Middle Ages, and at the Period of the Renaissance. London: 1870. V. 68; 72
The Eighteenth Century. London: 1876. V. 68
The Eighteenth Century. New York: 1876. V. 68
Manners, Customs and Dress During the Middle Ages and During the Renaissance Period. London: 1876. V. 68; 72
Military and Religious Life in the Middle Ages and at the Period of the Renaissance. London: 1874. V. 68
Science and Literature in the Middle Ages, and at the Period of the Renaissance. London: 1878. V. 68

LA CROIX-LAVAL, FERDINAND ANTOINE
Collection De La Croix-Laval: Album De Soixante-et-Onze Reproductions De Reliures d'Art Executees sur Des Editions De Grande Luxe Par Les Meilleurs Maitres Contemporains. Paris: 1902. V. 72

LACTANTIUS, LUCIUS CAECILIUS FIRMIANUS
Opera. Paris: 1513. V. 70
A Relation of the Death of the Primitive Persecutors. Amsterdam: 1687. V. 68; 70; 73

LACY, ED
Harlem Underground. New York: 1965. V. 71
In Black & Whitey. New York: 1967. V. 71
The Sex Castle. New York: 1963. V. 71
South Pacific Affair. New York: 1961. V. 71

LACY, GEORGE
Pictures of Travel, Sport and Adventure. 1899. V. 69; 72; 73

LADA-MOCARSKI, VALERIAN
Bibliography of Books on Alaska Published Before 1868. New Haven: 1969. V. 73

LADD, B. F.
History of Vineland. Its Soil, Products, Industries and Commercial Interests. Vineland: 1881. V. 71

LADD, JOHN
The Structure of a Moral Code; a Philosophical Analysis of Ethical Discourse Applied to the Ethics of the Navaho Indiands. Cambridge: 1957. V. 70; 72; 73

LADIES AID SOCIETY OF WEST WARD PRESBYTERIAN CHURCH
Radford Cook Book. Radford: 1893. V. 72

THE LADIES' Diary; or Woman's Almanack, for...1789. London: 1789. V. 69

LADIES' Indispensable Assistant, Being a Companion for the Sister, Mother and Wife. New York: 1853. V. 73

LADIES LIBRARY ASSOCIATION
Sandusy House-Keeper. Sandusky: 1888. V. 70

LADIES OF SAN RAFAEL
San Rafael Cook Book 1906. San Rafael: 1906. V. 68

LADIES OF STATE STREET PARISH
Fish, Flesh and Fowl A Book of Recipes for Cooking Fish Flesh and Fowl.... Portland: 1877. V. 68

LADIES OF THE MISSION
The Old Brewery, and the New Mission House at the Five Points. New York: 1854. V. 68

LADNER, MILDRED D.
O. C. Seltzer: Painter of the Old West. 1979. V. 69
O. C. Seltzer: Painter of the Old West. Norman: 1979. V. 70
William De La Montagne Cary: Artist on the Missouri River. Norman: 1984. V. 69

LADOFF, ISADOR
The Passing of Capitalism. Terre Haute: 1901. V. 68

THE LADY'S Drawing Room. London: 1748. V. 69

LAENNEC, RENE THEOPHILE HYACINTHE
De L'Ausculation Mediate ou Traite du Diagnostic des maladies des Poumons et du Coeur, Fonde Principallement sur ce Nouveau Moyen d'Exploration. Paris: 1819. V. 68
De l'Auscultation Mediate; our Traite du Diagnostic des Maladies des Poumouns et du Coeur. Brussels: 1837. V. 72
Propositions sur la Doctrine D'Hippocrate.... Paris: 1923. V. 72
A Treatise on the Disease of the Chest, in Which They are Described According to Their Anatomical Characters.... London: 1827. V. 70; 72
A Treatise on the Diseases of the Chest, and on Mediate Auscultation.... New York: 1830. V. 72
A Treatise on the Diseases of the Chest, in Which They are Described According to their Anatomical Characters and their Diagnosis Established on a New Principle by Means of Acoustick Instruments.... London: 1834. V. 69; 70

LAENNEC, RENE THEOPHILE HYACYNTHE
Propositions sur al Doctrine d'Hippocrate.... Denver: 1981. V. 68

LAET, JOANNES DE
Portugallia Sive de Regis Portugalliae et Opibus Commentarius. Leiden: 1641. V. 69

LA FARGE, CHRISTOPHER
Mesa Verde. New York: 1945. V. 69

LA FARGE, HENRY
Lost Treasurers of Europe. New York: 1946. V. 72

LA FARGE, JOHN
Catalogue of Works of John La Farge From January Twenty-Fourth to the February Twenty-Third MCMI. New York: 1901. V. 73

LA FARGE, OLIVER
As Long as the Grass Shall Grow: Indians Today. New York: 1940. V. 69
The Changing Indian. Norman: 1942. V. 69
The Enemey Gods. Boston: 1937. V. 69
Laughing Boy. Boston: 1929. V. 69
Santa Fe: The Autobiography of a Southwestern Town. Norman: 1959. V. 73

LA FAYE, GEORGES DE
Principles de Chirurgie. Paris: 1797. V. 72

LAFAYETTE, MARIE MADELEINE PLOCHE DE LA VERGNE, COMTESSE DE
Oeuvres. Amsterdam, Paris: 1786. V. 69
The Princess of Cleves. London: 1679. V. 70

LAFFERTY, R. A.
The Fall of Rome. New York: 1971. V. 70

LAFITAU, JOSEPH FRANCOIS
Customs of the American Indians Compared with the Customs of Primitive Times. Toronto: 1974-1977. V. 68
Moeurs des Sauvages Ameriquains, Comparees aux Moeurs des Premiers Temps.... Paris: 1724. V. 68

LAFITTE, or the Baratarian Chief: an American Tale. Wells River: 1834. V. 71

LAFONTAINE, GARY
The Dry Fly, New Angles. Helena: 1990. V. 72

LA FONTAINE, JEAN DE
Contes et Nouvelles en Vers. Amsterdam: 1699. V. 73
Contes et Nouvelles en Vers. Amsterdam: 1764. V. 69
Excerpta ou Fables Choisies. De La Fontaine, avec des Notes Nouvelles.... New York: 1810. V. 73
Fables. Paris: 1789. V. 70
The Fables. London: 1870. V. 73
The Fables. New York: 1930. V. 69
Fables. London: 1931. V. 68; 71; 72
The Fables. London: 1933. V. 69
The Fables. New York: 1954. V. 71; 73
Fables and Tales from La Fontaine. London: 1734. V. 70
Fables Choisies, Mises en Vers. Paris: 1715. V. 69
Fables Choisies, Mises en Vers. Paris: 1765-1775. V. 70
La Fontaine's Fables. London: 1905. V. 69
Selected Fables. New York: 1948. V. 68

LAFORGUE, JULES
Quelques Poemes. London: 1973. V. 68

LA GARDE, LOUIS A.
Gunshot Injuries. London: 1917. V. 68; 71; 72

LAGDEN, GODFREY
The Basutos, the Moutaineers and Their Country. 1909. V. 69

LAGERCRANTZ, S.
African Methods of Fire-Making. Upsuliensia: 1954. V. 69

LAGERKVIST, PAR
Evening Land. Detroit: 1975. V. 69
The Sibyl. London: 1958. V. 73
The Sibyl. New York: 1958. V. 69

LA GUMA, ALEX
A Walk in the Night. Ibadan: 1962. V. 72

LAHAM, HIRAM
Trans-Missouri Stock Raising: The Pasture Lands of North America, Winter Grazing. Denver: 1962. V. 69

LAHIRI, JHUMPA
Interpreter of Maladies. Boston/New York: 1999. V. 68; 69; 72
Interpreter of Maladies. London: 1999. V. 68

LAHR, JOHN
Notes on a Cowardly Lion: The Biography of Burt Lahr. New York: 1969. V. 72

LAINE, FRANKIE
That Lucky Old Son. The Autobiography of Frankie Laine. Ventura: 1993. V. 68

LAIN ENTRALGO, PEDRO
Historia Universal de la Medicina. Barceona: 1972-1976. V. 72

LAINEZ, MANUAL MUJICA
Cantata di Bomarzo. Verona: 1981. V. 71

LAING, ALEXANDER
The Motives of Nicholas Holtz. New York: 1936. V. 69

LAING ART GALLERY
Water Colours in the Laing Art Gallery, Newcastle upon Tyne. Newcastle upon Tyne: 1942. V. 72

LAING, D.
Hints for Dwellings: Consisting of Original Designs for Cottages, Farm-Houses, Villas &c Plain and Ornamental.... London: 1823. V. 70

LAING, DAVID
Catalogue of the First Portion of the Extensive and Valuable Library of the Late David Laing, Comprising an Extraordinary Collection of Works by Scottish Writers or Relating to Scotland. London: 1879. V. 70

LAING, JANET
Villa Jane. New York: 1929. V. 72

LAING, MALCOLM
The History of Scotland, from the Union of the Crowns...to the Union of Kingdoms.... London: 1819. V. 71

LAING, SAMUEL
Notes of a Traveller, On the Social and Political State of France, Prussia, Switzerland, Italy...During the Present Century. London: 1842. V. 68
Observations on the Social and Political State of Denmark and the Duchies of Sleswick and Holstein in 1851. London: 1852. V. 73
Pre-Historic Remains of Caithness. London and Edinburgh: 1866. V. 68; 72

LAIRE, FRANCIS XAVIER
Index Librorum ab Inventa Typographia ad Annum 1500.... Sens: 1791. V. 70

LAIRESSE, GERARD DE
Les Tableaux qui se Trouvent a la Haye, Gravez par d'Habiles Maitres d'Apres les Desseins de Nicolas Verkolje. Amsterdam: 1737. V. 72

LAIT, JACK
Gangster Girl. New York: 1930. V. 70

LAJTHA, ABEL
Handbook of Neurochemistry. New York: 1969. V. 68

LAKE, AUGUSTUS
The Island of Grenada. London: 1884. V. 68

LAKE, CARLTON
Baudelaire to Beckett, a Century of French Art and Literature. Austin: 1976. V. 68

LAKE, DEVEREUX
A Personal Narrative of Some Branches of the Lake Family in America, with Particular Reference to the Antecedents and Descendents of Richard Lake, Georgia Pioneer. 1937. V. 71

LAKE, STUART N.
Wyatt Earp: Frontier Marshall. Boston: 1931. V. 69

LAKEMAN, STEPHEN
What I Saw in Kaffir-Land. Edinburgh: 1880. V. 68; 72

LAKES, ARTHUR
Prospecting for Gold and Silver. Scranton: 1895. V. 68

LAKTIONOV, A. F.
Recent Soviet Scientific Investigations in the North Polar Regions. 1956. V. 72

LALA, RAMON REYES
The Philippine Islands.... New York: 1899. V. 72

LA LANDE, JOSEPH DE
Plates from Art Du Faire le Papier, Marbreur de Papier and Art du Faire le Parchemin. 1772. V. 70

LAL BEHARI DAY
Folk-Tales of Bengal. London: 1912. V. 70

LALLEMAND, CHARLES
Costumes of the Nineteenth Century, the Black Forest. Reading: 1864. V. 73

LALOR, JOHN J.
Cyclopaedia of Political Science, Political Economy, and of the Political History of the United States. Chicago: 1881. V. 72

LAMANTIA, PHILIP
I Demand Extincton of Laws Prohibiting Narcotic Drugs!. San Francisco: 1959. V. 72

LAMAR, E.
The Clothing Workers in Philadelphia. Philadelphia: 1940. V. 68

LAMAR, HOWARD L.
The Reader's Encyclopedia of the American West. New York: 1977. V. 72

LAMARCK, JEAN BAPTISTE DE
Flore Francoise ou Description Succincte de Toutes les Plantes Qui Croissent Naturellement en France.... Paris: 1778. V. 72
Recherches sur les Causes des Principaux Faits Physiques, et Particulierement, Sur Celles de la Combustion, de l'Elevation de l'Eau Dans l'Etat de Vapeurs.... Paris: 1794. V. 70
Systeme des Animaux san Vertebres.... Paris: 1801. V. 70; 72
Zoological Philosophy. London: 1914. V. 72

LAMARTINE, ALPHONSE MARIE LOUIS DE PRAT
Graziella. London: 1929. V. 69; 71
History of the Girondists; or, Personal Memoirs of the Patriots of the French Revolution from Unpublished Sources. New York: 1859. V. 71

LA MARTINIERE, PIERRE MARTIN DE
A New Voyage to the North.... London: 1706. V. 69

LAMB, ARTHUR H.
Tragedies of the Osage Hills as Told by the Sage of Osage. Pawhuska: 1935. V. 68; 69; 72; 73

LAMB, CAROLINE
Glenarvon. London: 1816. V. 68; 69

LAMB, CHARLES
Album Verses, with a Few Others. London: 1830. V. 69; 73
Beauty and the Beast. London: 1887. V. 71
A Dissertation Upon Roast Pig. London. V. 72
Elia and the Last Essays of Elia. Newtown: 1929-1930,. V. 68
Elia. Essays Which Have Appeared Under that Signature in the London Magazine. Philadelphia: 1828. V. 71
Essays of Elia. (&) The Last Essays of Elia. Edinburgh: 1885. V. 72; 73
The Essays of Elia and the Last Essays of Elia. London: 1902. V. 70
John Woodvil: a Tragedy. London: 1802. V. 73
The Life, Letters and Writings. London: 1876. V. 71; 73
A Masque of Days. From the Last Essays of Elia: Newly Dressed and Decorated. London: 1901. V. 72
Mrs. Leicester's School; or the History of Several Young Ladies, Related by Themselves. London: 1827. V. 73
The Poetical Works of Charles Lamb. London: 1836. V. 68; 72
Poetry for Children. 1872. V. 72
Prince Dorus. 1889. V. 73
Prince Dorus. London: 1889. V. 68; 71; 72
Prose Works. London: 1838. V. 68
Stories of Old Daniel, or Tales of Wonder and Delight. London: 1820. V. 69; 73
Tales from Shakespeare. London: 1901. V. 70
Tales from Shakespeare. London: 1909. V. 71
Tales from Shakespeare. London: 1923. V. 72
Tales from Shakespeare Designed for the Use of Young Persons. London: 1816. V. 68
The Works.... London: 1818. V. 73
The Works.... London: 1903. V. 69
The Works.... London: 1908. V. 71

LAMB, DANA S.
Green Highlanders and Pink Ladies. Barre: 1971. V. 70
Some Silent Places Still. Barre: 1969. V. 70; 72

LAMB, E.
The Illustrated Reference on Cacti and Other Succulents. London: 1969-. V. 68

LAMB, E. J.
Memories of the Past and Thoughts of the Future. South Bend: 1906. V. 68

LAMB, GENE
Rodeo Cowboy. 1959. V. 68

LAMB, LAWRENCE
Symposium on Cardiology in Aviation. In: The American Journal of Cardiology, Volume VI No. 1, pages 1-232, July 1960. V. 73

LAMB, MARTHA J.
History of the City of New York: Its Origin, Rise and Progress. New York: 1877-1880. V. 68

LAMB, PATRICK
Royal Cookery; or the Complete Court-Cook.... 1710. V. 70

LAMB, WALLY
I Know This Much Is True. New York: 1998. V. 70; 72; 73
She's Come Undone. New York: 1992. V. 69; 70; 72

LAMBARADE, WILLIAM
A Perambulation of Kent.... London: 1596. V. 73

LAMBDIN, DEWEY
The French Admiral. New York: 1990. V. 69

LAMBERT, ADELMA
Guide for Nut Cookery. Battle Creek: 1899. V. 69; 72

LAMBERT, CATHOLINA
Catalogue of the Valuable Paintings and Sculptures by the Old and Modern Masters Forming the Famous Catholina Lambert Collection.... New York: 1916. V. 71

LAMBERT, CHARLES
The Voyage of the Wanderer from the Journals and Letters.... London: 1883. V. 68; 72

LAMBERT, FRED
Bygone Days of the Old West. Kansas City: 1948. V. 68; 73
Bygone Days of the Old West. Fort Worth: 1970. V. 73

LAMBERT, GAVIN
The Slide Area: Scenes of Hollywood Life. London: 1955. V. 73

LAMBERT, H. P.
Infectious Diseases Illustrated. An Integrated Text and Colour Atlas. Oxford: 1982. V. 73

LAMBERT, IRA C.
Roger Lambert and His Descendants. Toms River: 1933. V. 71

LAMBERT, JOHN
Travels through Canada and the United States of North America in the Years 1806, 1807 and 1808. London: 1816. V. 68

LAMBERT, M. LEON
Catalogue of the Collection of Books on Cookery and Gastronomy the Proeprty of M. Leon LAmbert. London: 1966. V. 73

LAMBERT, ROSA
The Mystery of the Golden Wings. New York: 1936. V. 70; 72

LAMBERT, SAMUEL W.
When Mr. Pickwick Went Fishing. New York: 1924. V. 69

LAMBERT, WILLIAM
Abstracts of Calculations to Ascertain the Longitude of the Capitol in the City of Washington, from Greenwich Observatory, in England. Washington City: 1817. V. 70

LAMBERTVILLE
Charter, Supplements and Ordinances. Lambertville: 1885. V. 71

LAMBETH, JOSEPH A.
Lambeth Method of Cake Decoration and Practical Pastries. London: 1936. V. 68
Lambeth Method of Cake Decoration and Practical Pastries. London: 1937. V. 68

LAMBOURNE, L.
Utopian Craftsmen: the Arts and Crafts Movement from the Cotswolds to Chicago. Salt Lake City: 1980. V. 69; 72

LAMBTON TALLY HO! CLUB
Rules of the Lambton Tally Ho! Club. Sunderland: 1805. V. 72

LAMI, EUGENE
Les Agrements de la Vie de Chateau. Paris: 1828-1833. V. 70
Souvenirs du Camp de Luneville. Paris: 1829. V. 69; 70

LAMMING, GEORGE
Of Age and Innocence. London: 1958. V. 69

LAMOND, H.
Lock Lomond. A Study of Angling Conditions. 1931. V. 73
The Sea Trout. 1916. V. 68; 72; 73
The Sea Trout. London: 1916. V. 69; 70

LAMONT, JAMES
Yachting in The Arctic Seas. London: 1876. V. 72

LA MONT, VIOLET
Ballet in Pop-Up Action. New York: 1953. V. 70

LAMOTT, ANNE
Hard Laughter. New York: 1980. V. 69
Hard Laughter. London: 1989. V. 68
Joe Jones. San Francisco: 1985. V. 71; 73

LA MOTTA, JAKE
Raging Bull. Englewood Cliffs: 1970. V. 71; 72; 73

LA MOTTE, GUILLAME MAUQUET DE
Traite Complet Des Accouchemens Naturels, non Naturels et Contre Nature. Paris: 1765. V. 72

LA MOTTE FOUQUE, FRIEDRICH HEINRICH KARL, FREIHERR DE
Peter Schlemihl: from the German of La Motte Fouque. London: 1824. V. 69
Undine. London: 1909. V. 70; 71; 72; 73
Undine. New York: 1930. V. 69

L'AMOUR, LOUIS
Bendigo Shafter. New York: 1979. V. 68; 71
The Californios. New York: 1974. V. 68; 71
Catlow. New York: 1963. V. 72
Dark Canyon. New York: 1963. V. 72
Fair Blows the Wind. New York: 1978. V. 70
Frontier. Toronto: 1984. V. 73
Hondo. New York: 1983. V. 71
Hopalong Cassidy and the Trail to Seven Pines. London: 1952. V. 69
How the West Was Won. New York: 1963. V. 72
Jubal Sackett. New York: 1985. V. 68; 69
Over on the Dry Side. New York: 1975. V. 71
Rivers West. New York: 1975. V. 68; 71
Sitka. New York: 1957. V. 70
Smoke from the Altar. 1939. V. 70
To the Far Blue Mountains. New York: 1976. V. 68; 71

LAMPLOUGH, EDWARD
Yorkshire Battles. Hull: 1891. V. 73

LAMPMAN, B. H.
The Coming of the Pond Fishes, an Account of the Introduction of Certain Spiney-Rayed Fishes and Other Exotic Species into the Waters of the Lower Columbia River Region and the Pacific Coast States. Portland: 1946. V. 72; 73

LAMPS and Mineral Oil for the Army. Philadelphia: 1881. V. 71

LAMPUGNANI, V. M.
Architecture of the 20th Century in Drawings: Utopia and Reality. London: 1982. V. 69
Architecture of the 20th Century in Drawings: Utopia and Reality. New York: 1982. V. 68; 72

LAMSON, MARY SWIFT
Life and Education of Laura Dewey Bridgman, the Deaf, Dumb and Blind Girl. Boston: 1879. V. 69

LA MURE, PIERRE
Moulin Rouge. New York: 1950. V. 71

LAMY, BERNARD
A Treatise of Perspective. London: 1702. V. 69; 71
A Treatise of Perspective. 1710. V. 71

THE LANCASHIRE Dialect; or the Whimsical Adventures and Misfortunes of a Lancashire Clown. Halifax: 1820. V. 72

LANCASHIRE Leaders. Social and Political. Price Three Guineas. Exeter: 1895. V. 72; 73

LANCASTER & CARLISLE RAILWAY
Historical and Descriptive Account of the Lancaster and Carlisle Railway. 1846?. V. 68

LANCASTER, H. BOSWELL
Liverpool and Her Potters. Liverpool: 1936. V. 72

LANCASTER, I.
The Soaring Birds. Chicago: 1900. V. 73

LANCASTER, JOHN
The Debt to Pleasure. London: 1996. V. 70
The Debt to Pleasure. New York: 1996. V. 72

LANCASTER, JOSEPH
The Lancasterian System of Education, with Improvements. Baltimore: 1821. V. 73

LANCASTER, OSBERT
All Done From Memory. London: 1953. V. 71
All Done From Memory. London: 1963. V. 71
Sailing to Byzantium - an Architectural Companion. London: 1969. V. 69
With an Eye to the Future. London: 1967. V. 71

LANCASTER, ROBERT A.
Historic Virginia Homes and Churches. Philadelphia: 1915. V. 71

LANCELOTT, F.
Australia As It Is: Its Settlements, Farms and Gold Fields. London: 1853. V. 72

LANDACRE, PAUL
California Hills and Other Wood Engravings. Los Angeles: 1931. V. 70

LANDAU, EDMUND
Differential and Integral Calculus. New York: 1965. V. 73

LANDAUER, BELLA C.
Printers' Mottoes. New York: 1926. V. 73

LANDBERG, L. C. W.
The Chumash Indians of Southern California. 1965. V. 69

LANDE, ALFRED
Quantum mecahnics and thermodynamic continuity (II) In American Journal of Physics, Volume XX, XXII, 1952, 1954. V. 72

LANDE, LAWRENCE
Adventures in Collecting Books and Blake and Buber. Montreal: 1975. V. 68

LANDE, LOUIS
Essai sur l'Aplasie Lamineuse Progressive (Atrophie du Tissu Connectif) celle de la Face en Particular (trophenevrose de Romberg). Paris: 1860. V. 72

LANDELLS, EBENEZER
The Boy's Own Toy-Maker: a Practical Illustrated Guide to the Useful Employment of Leisure Hours. New York: 1860. V. 69

LANDER, FREDERICK W.
Maps and Reports of the Fort Kearney, South Pass and Honey Like Wagon Road - 36th Congress, 2nd Session, House of Representatives. Washington. V. 70

LANDER, GEORGE
An Answer to the Pamphlet of Matthew Robinson Boulton, Esq. of Soho, Relative to His Father's Funeral. Birmingham: 1811. V. 73

LANDER, RICHARD
Records of Captain Clapperton's Last Expedition to Africa. London: 1830. V. 72

LANDER, S.
Our Own Primary Arithmetic. Greensboro: 1863. V. 71

LANDERS, JOSEPH
Who's Who in the Rockies. Denver: 1923. V. 72

LANDERY, CHARLES
Mr. Smith Goes to Washington - a novel adapted from Frank Capra's Columbia Picture. London: 1940. V. 72

LANDESMAN, PETER
The Raven. Dallas: 1995. V. 69

LANDIS, C. S.
Twenty-Two Calibre Varmint Rifles. 1947. V. 70; 72

LANDIS, CHARLES K.
The Founder's Own Story of the Founding of Vineland, New Jerse. Vineland: 1903. V. 71

LANDIS, ROBERT W.
Bethlehem Church and Its Pastor; or a Narrative of the Injurious Proceedings of the Rev. Messrs. Albert Barnes and H. W. Hunt, Senr., in Relation to the Pastor of the Presbyterian Church, Bethlehem, N.J. 1851. V. 71

THE LANDLORDS Law; or, the Law Concerning Landlords, Tenants and Farmers.... London: 1739. V. 68

LANDO, ORTENSIO
Semoni Funebri de Vari Authori Nella Morte de Diversi Animali. Venice: 1548. V. 73
Sette Libri de Cathaloghi a Varie Cose Aparetenenti Non Solo Antiche, Ma Anche Moderne, Opera Utile Molto all Historia et da Cui Prender si Po Materia di Favellare. Venice: 1553. V. 70

LANDOLT, E.
A Manual of Examination of the Eyes. Philadelphia: 1879. V. 71

LANDON, LETITIA
Duty and Inclination. London: 1838. V. 69

LANDOR, ARNOLD HENRY SAVAGE
Across Unknown South America. London: 1913. V. 72
In The Forbidden Land. London: 1899. V. 72

LANDOR, WALTER SAVAGE
Andrea of Hungary, and Giovanna of Naples. London: 1839. V. 68
Citation and Examination of William Shakespeare...Before the Worshipful Sir Thomas Lucy...Touching Deer Stealing. London: 1834. V. 68; 70
Count Julian: a Tragedy. London: 1812. V. 73
Dry Sticks, Fagoted. Edinburgh: 1858. V. 73
The Dun Cow: an Hyper-Satirical Dialogue in Verse. London: 1808. V. 73
Gebir; a Poem in Seven Books. 1798. V. 73
Gebir; a Poem: in Seven Books. 1803. V. 73
Gebir, Count Julian and Other Poems. London: 1831. V. 73
Gebirus, Poema. Oxford: 1803. V. 73
The Hellenics of Walter Savage Landor. London: 1847. V. 73
The Hellenics of Walter Savage Landor. Edinburgh: 1859. V. 73
Imaginary Conversations. 1936. V. 73
Imaginary Conversations. New York: 1936. V. 69
Imaginary Conversations. Verona: 1936. V. 70
The Last Fruit Off an Old Tree. London: 1853. V. 72; 73
Pericles and Aspasia. London: 1836. V. 68; 73
Poems from the Arabic and Persian: with Notes. Warwick: 1803. V. 73

LANDOR, WALTER SAVAGE continued
The Poems of Walter Savage Landor, Continued as Moral Epistle.... London: 1795. V. 73
Poetry. London: 1802. V. 73
Simonidea. Bath: 1806. V. 73

LANDRETH, MARSHA
Holiday Murders. 1992. V. 69

LANDRUM, J. B. O.
History of Spartanburg County. Atlanta: 1900. V. 71

LANDSBOROUGH, D.
Arran: Its Topography, Natural History and Antiquities. Ardrossan: 1875. V. 68
Excursions to Arran, Ailsa Craig and the Two Cumbraes.... Edinburgh: 1851. V. 68
Popular History of British Seaweeds.... London: 1857. V. 68
Popular History of British Zoophytes, or Corallines. London: 1852. V. 68; 70

LANDSDELL, SARAH
The Tower; or the Romance of Ruthyne. London: 1798. V. 69

LANDSDOWNE, HENRY WILLIAM PETTY FITZMAURICE, 6TH MARQUIS OF
The Queeney Letters, Being Addressed to Hester Maria Thrale by Doctor Johnson, Fanny Burney and Mrs. Thrale-Piozzi. London: 1934. V. 69

LANDSEER, JOHN
Lectures on the Art of Engraving, Delivered at the Royal Institution of Great Britain. London: 1807. V. 69; 71

LANE, ALLEN STANLEY
Emperor Norton, the Mad Monarch of America. Caldwell: 1939. V. 70

LANE, EDWARD WILLIAM
An Account of the Manners and Customs of the Modern Egyptians, Written in Egypt During the Years 1833-1835. London: 1842. V. 68
An Account of the Manners and Customs of the Modern Egyptians, Written in Egypt During the Years 1833-1835. London: 1895. V. 73

LANE, JACK C.
Chasing Geronimo - the Journal of Leonard Wood May-September 1886. 1970. V. 69

LANE, LEVI COOPER
The Surgery of the Head and Neck. Philadelphia: 1898. V. 68

LANE, LYDIA S.
I Married a Soldier or Old Days in the Old Army. Albuquerque: 1964. V. 72

LANE, MILLS
The Rambler in Georgia.... Savannah: 1973. V. 71
War is Hell. Savannah: 1974. V. 70

LANE, RICHARD
Studies of Figures by Gainsborough Executed in Exact Imitation of the Originals by Richard Lane. London: 1825. V. 69

LANE, ROSE WILDER
The Discovery of Freedom. New York: 1943. V. 68
Gordon Blake. London: 1925. V. 68; 70

LANE, W.
Sherlock Holmes And The Wood Green Empire Mystery. New York: 1985. V. 72

LANE, WALTER
The Adventures and Recollections of General Walter P. Lane, A San Jacinto Veteran. Marshall TX: 1928. V. 72

LANE, WALTER P.
Adventures and Recollections of General Walter P. Lane, A San Jacinto Veteran. Marshall, TX: 1887. V. 70

LANE, WHEATON J.
From Indian Trail to Iron Horse. Travel and Transportation in New Jersey 1620-1860. Princeton: 1939. V. 71

LANE, YOTI
African Folk Tales. London: 1946. V. 69

LANES, SELMA G.
The Art of Maurice Sendak. London: 1980. V. 72
The Art of Maurice Sendak. London: 1981. V. 72

LANG, ANDREW
Angling Sketches. London: 1891. V. 69
The Arabian Nights Entertainments. London: 1898. V. 68; 70
Ballades and Verses Vain. New York: 1884. V. 72
Ban and Arriere Ban: a Rally of Fugitive Rhymes. London: 1894. V. 69
The Blue Poetry Book. London: 1891. V. 70; 73
The Book of Princes and Princesses. 1908. V. 68
The Brown Fairy Book. London: 1904. V. 68; 71; 72
Custom and Myth. London: 1884. V. 73
The Gold of Fairnilee. Bristol: 1888. V. 68; 71
The Green Fairy Book. Philadelphia: 1925. V. 68
History of Scotland from the Roman Occupation. New York, Edinburgh, London: 1903-1907. V. 71
Homer and the Epic. London and New York: 1893. V. 68
Homes and Haunts of Famous Authors. London: 1906. V. 69
John Jasper's Secret.... London: 1871-1872. V. 70
Johnny Nut And The Golden Goose. London: 1887. V. 72
The Library. London: 1881. V. 70

The Library with a Chapter on Modern English Illustrated Books by Austin Dobson. London: 1892. V. 72
The Lilac Fairy Book. London: 1910. V. 71
The Mark of Cain. Bristol: 1886. V. 73
New Collected Rhymes. London: 1905. V. 69
Old Friends: Essays in Epistolary Parody. London: 1890. V. 72
The Orange Fairy Book. London: 1906. V. 70
Pictures at Play, or Dialogues of the Galleries, by Two Art Critics. London: 1888. V. 69
Prince Charles Edward. Paris: 1900. V. 68
Prince Prigio. Bristol: 1889. V. 68; 69; 72
Prince Ricardo of Pantouflia. Bristol: 1893. V. 68; 72
The Princess Nobody. London: 1884. V. 68; 72
The Puzzle of Dickens's Last Plot. London: 1905. V. 68
The Red Book of Animal Stories. London: 1899. V. 71
The Red Book of Heroes. London: 1909. V. 69
The Red Romance Book. London: 1905. V. 71
The Red Book of Romance. 1905. V. 68
The Red True Story Book. 1895. V. 68
Tales of a Fairy Court. London: 1907. V. 71
The True Story Book. 1893. V. 68
The World of Homer. London: 1910. V. 72
The Yellow Fairy Book. London: 1894. V. 68
The Yellow Fairy Book. London: 1906. V. 70

LANG, CHARLES H.
Cochiti- A New Mexico Pueblo, Past and Present. Austin: 1959. V. 71

LANG, HARRY
The Corpse On The Hearth. Philadelphia: 1946. V. 72

LANG, K.
Alpine Flowering Plants in China. Beijing: 1997. V. 68; 73

LANG, LEONORA BLANCHE
The Book of Saints and Heroes. London: 1912. V. 72
Princes and Princesses. London: 1908. V. 71

LANG, W. B.
The First Overland Mail: Butterfield Trail. St. Louis to San Francisco 1858-1861. 1940. V. 71

LANGBAINE, GERARD
The Answer of the Chancellor, Masters and Scholars of the University of Oxford to the Petition, Articles of Grievance, and Reasons of the City of Oxon. Oxford: 1678. V. 72

LANGBRIDGE, ROSAMOND
Charlotte Bronte. A Psychologial Study. London: 1929. V. 70; 73

LANGDON, EMMA F.
The Cripple Creek Strike. A History of Industrial Wars in Colorado. 1903-1904-1905. Denver: 1904-1905. V. 68; 71

LANGDON, WILLIAM B.
A Descriptive Catalogue of the Chinese Collection Now Exhibiting at St. George's Place, Hyde Park Corner. London: 1843. V. 70; 72

LANGE, CHARLES H.
Cochiti. Austin: 1959. V. 72
The Southwestern Journals of Adolph F. Bandelier. Albuquerque: 1984. V. 72

LANGE, DOROTHEA
An American Exodus: a Record of Human Erosion in the Thirties. New York: 1939. V. 68; 70; 73
To a Cabin. New York: 1973. V. 68

LANGE, JAKOB E.
Flora Agaricina Danica. Copenhagen: 1935-1940. V. 68; 71

LANGE, JOHANNES
Crime as Destiny. A Study of Criminal Twins. London: 1931. V. 68

LANGE, JOHN P.
A Commentary on the Holy Scriptures and the Acts of the Apostles. New York: 1866. V. 70

LANGELLIER, JOHN P.
Myles Keogh, The Life and Legend of An Irish Dragoon In The Seventh Cavalry. El Segundo: 1999. V. 72

LANGER, FRANTISEK
The Camel through the Needle's Eye. New York: 1929. V. 69

LANGEWIS, L.
Decorative Art in Indoensian Textiles. Amsterdam: 1964. V. 69

LANGFELD, WILLIAM R.
Washington Irving. A bibliography. New York: 1933. V. 72

LANGFORD, NATHANIEL PITT
Diary of the Washburn Expedition to the Yellowstone and Firehole Rivers in the Year 1870. 1905. V. 68
Diary of the Washburn Expedition to the Yellowstone and Firehole Rivers in the Year 1870. St. Paul: 1905. V. 70; 73
The Discovery of Yellowstone Park, 1870. The Complete Story of the Washburn Expedition to the Headquarters of the Yellowstone and Fireholes Rivers in 1870. St. Paul: 1923. V. 68; 73
Vigilante Days and Ways - the Pioneers of the Rockies - the Makers and Making of Montana, Idaho, Oregon, Washington and Wyoming. Boston;: 1890. V. 70

LANGFORD, R.
An Introduction to Trade and Business, Published by R. Langford, Haydon-Square, Minories, London. London;: 1819. V. 73

LANGFORD, SONDRA GORDON
Red Bird of Ireland. New York: 1983. V. 68

LANGHAM, JAMES R.
Sing a Song of Homicide. New York: 1940. V. 68; 69; 71

LANGHOFF, D. B.
Tom Horn and the Langhoff Gang of Wyoming. Albuquerque: 1994. V. 68

LANGHORNE, JOHN
Frederic and Pharamond, or the Consolations of Human Life. London: 1769. V. 72

LANGLAND, WILLIAM
Pierce the Ploughman's Crede. London: 1814. V. 68; 72
The Vision of Pierce Plowman.... London: 1561. V. 70
The Vision of William Concerning Piers the Plowman. Oxford: 1924. V. 70

LANGLE, JOSEPH ADOLPHE FERDINAND
Les Contes Du Gay Scavoir. Paris: 1828. V. 70

LANGLEY, ADRIA LOCKE
A Lion is in the Streets. New York: 1945. V. 72

LANGLEY, BATTY
Ancient Architecture Restored and Improved, by a Great Variety of Grand and Useful Designs.... London: 1741-1742. V. 70; 72
The Builder's Director, or Bench-Mate: Being a Pocket-Treasury of the Grecian, Roman and Gothic Orders of Architecture.... London: 1751. V. 69
The Builder's Jewel; or, the Youth's Instructor.... London: 1763. V. 73
The Builder's Jewel; or, The Youth's Instructor.... London: 1797. V. 73
Gothic Architecture, Improved by Rules and Proportions in Many Grand Designs.... London: 1747. V. 68; 70
Gothic Architecture, Improved by Rules and Proportions in Many Grand Designs.... London: 1774. V. 72
Practical Geometry Applied to the Useful Arts of Building, Surveying, Gardening and Mensuration.... 1726. V. 73
Practical Geometry Applied to the Useful Arts of Building, Surveying, Gardening and Mensuration.... London: 1726. V. 71

LANGLEY, NOEL
Somebody's Rocking My Dreamboat. London: 1949. V. 70

LANGLEY, S. P.
The Temperature of the Moon. (in) Memoirs of the National Academy of Scienes Volume IV Part 2. Washington: 1889. V. 73

LANGLEY, SAM
Langley Memoir on Mechanical Flight...1887 to 1903. Washington: 1911. V. 71

LANGLOIS DE FANCON, FRANCOIS
The Favourites Chronicle. 1621. V. 68; 72

LANGMAN, I. K.
A Selected Guide to the Literature on the Flowering Plants of Mexico. Philadelphia: 1964. V. 68; 71

LANGSNER, J.
Man Ray: an Exhibition.... Los Angeles: 1966. V. 72

LANGSTAFF, JOHN
Over in the Meadow. New York: 1957. V. 70

LANGSTAFF, JOHN BRETT
David Copperfield's Library. London: 1924. V. 69

LANGSTON, MRS. GEORGE
History of Eastland County, Texas. Dallas: 1904. V. 71

LANGTOFT, PETER
Peter Langtoft's Chronicle from the Death of Cadwalader to the end of K. Edward the First's Reign. Oxford: 1725. V. 73

LANGTON, DAVID HERBERT
A History of the Parish of Flixton (Lancashire), Comprising the Townships of Flixton and Urmston.... Manchester: 1898. V. 71

LANGTON, JANE
The Swing in the Summerhouse. New York: 1967. V. 71
The Transcendental Murder. New York: 1964. V. 68; 69; 72

THE LANGUAGE of Flowers Including Floral Poetry. London. V. 71; 73

LANGUET, THOMAS
Copper's Chronicle Contenynge the Whole Discourse of the Histories as Well of Thys Relame as All Other Countrees.... London: 1565. V. 68

LANIER, SIDNEY
The Boy's King Arthur. New York: 1926. V. 69
The Boy's Mabinogion, Being the Earliest Welsh Tales of King Arthur in the Famous Red Book of Hergest. New York: 1881. V. 69

LANIER, VIRGINIA
Death in Bloodhound Red. 1995. V. 68; 69
Death in Bloodhound Red. Sarasota: 1995. V. 69
House on Bloodhound Lane. New York: 1996. V. 68; 69

LANKESTER, EDWIN
Cholera: What Is It? and How to Prevent It. London: 1866. V. 68
Half Hours with the Microscope.... London: 1874. V. 68
Memorials of John Ray, Consisting of His Life by Dr. Derham.... London: 1846. V. 68
On Food. (with) The Use of Animals in Relation to the Industry of Man.... London: 1862. V. 68
Vegetable Substances Used for the Food of Man. London: 1846. V. 72

LANKESTER, MRS.
Wild Flowers Worth Notice. 1861. V. 68

LANMAN, CHARLES
Adventures in the Wilds of North America. London: 1854. V. 72
Adventures of an Angler in Canada, Nova Scotia and the United States. London: 1848. V. 72
Letters from the Alleghany Mountains. New York: 1849. V. 68

LANSDALE, JOE R.
Act of Love. New York: 1981. V. 72
Act Of Love. London: 1989. V. 72; 73
Act of Love. Baltimore: 1992. V. 68; 69
Batman In Terror On The High Skies. Boston: 1992. V. 72
The Board. Burton: 1998. V. 70
The Bottoms. New York: 2000. V. 69
By Bizarre Hands. Shingletown: 1989. V. 70; 73
Cold In July. Shingletown: 1990. V. 72
Dead in the West. London: 1990. V. 70; 72; 73
The Drive In. London: 1989. V. 72; 73
The Drive in 2. London: 1990. V. 73
A Fist Full of Stories (and Articles). Baltimore: 1996. V. 70
Freezer Burn. Holyoke: 1999. V. 69; 73
The Good, the Bad and the Indifferent. Burton: 1997. V. 70
The Long Ones. Orlando: 1999. V. 70
The Magic Wagon. Garden City: 1986. V. 68; 70
Mister Weed-Eater. Huntington Beach: 1993. V. 68; 69; 72
Mucho Mojo. Baltimore: 1994. V. 69; 70; 73
My Dead Dog, Bobby. Sacramento: 1995. V. 72
The Nightrunners. Arlington Heights: 1987. V. 69; 70
Rumble Tumble. Burton: 1998. V. 69; 73
Savage Season. Shingletown: 1990. V. 73
The Two Bear Mambo. New York: 1995. V. 70; 72
Writer of the Purple Rage. Baltimore: 1994. V. 70

LANSDOWNE, J. F.
Birds of the Eastern Forest. Boston: 1968-1970. V. 73
Birds of the Eastern Forest, 1 and 2. Boston: 1970. V. 73
Birds of the West Coast. Boston: 1980. V. 73
Birds of the West Coast. Volume I. Boston: 1976. V. 73

LANSDOWNE, WILLIAM, MARQUIS OF
Bibliotheca Lansdowniana. A Catalogue of the Entire Library of the Late Most Noble William Marquis of Lansdowne. (with) Bibliotheca Manuscripta Lansdowniana. A Catalogue of the Entire Collection of Manuscripts, on Paper and Vellum.... London: 1806. V. 70

LANUZA, JOSE LUIS
The Gaucho. London: 1968. V. 72

LANZI, ABATE LUIGI
The History of Painting in Italy. London: 1847. V. 72

LANZI, LUIGI
The History of Painting in Italy. 1828. V. 70
The History of Painting in Italy. London: 1828. V. 71

LA PAGE, JOHN
The Story of Baildon. Bradford: 1951. V. 73

LAPHAM, I. A.
Report of the Diastrous Effects of the Destruction of Forest Trees, Now Going On so Rapidly.... Madison: 1867. V. 71

LAPINER, A.
Pre-Columbian Art of South America. New York: 1976. V. 69

LA PLACE, PIERRE ANTOINE DE
Tom Jones ou L'Enfant Trouve. Imitation de L'Anglois de M. H. Fielding. Londres: 1767. V. 70

LA PLACE, PIERRE SIMON, MARQUIS DE
Mecanique Celeste. Boston: 1829-. V. 69
Politiqve Discourses, Treating of the Differences and Inequalities of Vocations.... London: 1578. V. 68; 69; 73
The System of the World. London: 1809. V. 72
Traite de Mecanique Celeste. Paris: 1799-1825. V. 73
Traite de Mecanique Celeste. Paris: 1829-. V. 69
A Treatise Upon Analytical Mechanics. Nottingham: 1814. V. 72

LAPORTE, JOHN
The Progress of a Water-Coloured Drawing. London: 1802. V. 69; 72

LAPP, RUDOLPH M.
Archy Lee: a California Fugitive Slave Case. San Francisco: 1969. V. 73

LA PRADE, ERNEST
Alice in Orchestralia. Garden City: 1925. V. 70

LAQUIER, LEO
Clarisse, or the Old Cook. London: 1926. V. 68

LA QUINTINIE, JEAN DE
The Compleat Gard'ner; or Directions for Cultivating and Right Ordering of Fruit-Gardens and Kitchen-Gardens. London: 1699. V. 69; 71

LARA, BENJAMIN
Dictionary of Surgery; or the Young Surgeon's Pocket Assistant. London: 1796. V. 68; 71

LARBAUD, VALERY
Samuel Butler - Conference Faite le 3 Novembre 1920 a la Maison des Amis des Livres. Paris: 1920. V. 69

LARCOM, HENRY
Distressing Narrative of the Loss of the Ship Margaret of Salem. 1810. V. 71

LARDEN, WALTER
Argentine Plains and Andine Glaciers. London: 1911. V. 69; 72
Recollections of an Old Mountaineer. 1910. V. 68; 70; 73
Recollections of an Old Mountaineer. London: 1910. V. 69; 72

LARDNER, DIONYSIUS
The Museum of Science and Art. Volume II. London: 1855. V. 68
A Rudimentary Treatise on the Steam Engine, for the Use of Beginners. London: 1859. V. 71
The Steam Engine Explained and Illustrated.... London: 1840. V. 68

LARDNER, RING
Bib Ballads. Chicago: 1915. V. 73
Bib Ballads. New York: 1915. V. 69
My Four Weeks in France. Indianapolis: 1918. V. 73
Round Up. New York: 1929. V. 68; 73
Say It With Oil. A Few Remarks About Wives. New York: 1923. V. 70
Treat 'Em Rough. Indianapolis: 1918. V. 73
What Of It!. New York: 1925. V. 68
You Know Me Al: A Busher's letters. New York: 1916. V. 70

LARG, DAVID
Giuseppe Garibaldi - a Biography. London: 1934. V. 72

LARIMER, SARAH L.
The Capture and Escape; or, Life Among the Sioux. Philadelphia: 1870. V. 71

LARIMER, WILLIAM H. H.
Reminiscences of General William Larimer and Of His Son William H. H. Larimer - Two of the Founders of Denver. Lancaster: 1918. V. 70

LARISON, CORNELIUS W.
The Clas Abrod. A Descripshun ov the Tenting Tur mad bi the Techerz and students ov the Academi ov Siens; and Art at Ringus. Ringoes: 1888. V. 71
Elements of Orthoepy: Consisting of the Most Essential Facts and Principles.... Ringoes: 1881. V. 71
Geografy: a Text Buk in Fonic Orthografy. Ringoes: 1885. V. 71
Iz the Sol a Substans?. Ringoes: 1904. V. 71
The Larisun Famili: a Biografic Scetch ov the Desendants ov Jon Larisun, the Dan, thru hiz Sun Jamz Larisun.... Ringoes: 1888. V. 71
Reminissensez ov a Techer. (volume I). Ringoes: 1898. V. 71
Reminissensez ov Scul Lif. Ringoes: 1896. V. 71
A Skech of the Agin Family of Old Amwell Township in Hunterdon County, New Jersey. Ringoes: 1889. V. 71
The Sol: Hwens?-Hwither?. Ringoes: 1908. V. 71
Solomon'z Song.... Ringoes: 1888. V. 71
Spelin-Reform Jemz. Ringoes: 1887. V. 71
The Tenting School.... Ringoes: 1883. V. 71

LA RIVE, ARTHUR AUGUSTE DE
A Treatise on Electricity in Theory and Practice. London: 1853-1858. V. 72

LARIVE DUPAS, MADAME DE
Essai sur l'Education de l'Enfance. Geneve: 1837. V. 73

LARKIN, PHILIP
All What Jazz. London: 1970. V. 70; 71
All What Jazz. London: 1985. V. 72
Aubade. Salem: 1980. V. 69; 73
Collected Poems. London: 1988. V. 68; 70; 73
Femmes Damnees. Oxford: 1978. V. 71
High Windows. London: 1974. V. 70
Jill. London: 1946. V. 69; 70; 73
Jill. London: 1964. V. 71
Jill. Woodstock: 1976. V. 72
The Less Deceived. Hessle: 1955. V. 69; 73
The North Ship. London: 1966. V. 72
Required Writing - Miscellaneous Pieces 1955-1982. London: 1984. V. 72; 73
Selected Poems. Kyoto: 1994. V. 72
The Whitsun Weddings. London: 1964. V. 68; 73

LARKING, CUTHBERT
Bandobast and Khabar. 1888. V. 69; 70; 72; 73

LARNED, WILLIAM TROWBRIDGE
Fairy Tales from France. New York: 1920. V. 70

LA ROCHE, R.
Pneumonia Its Supposed Connection, Pathological and Etiological with Autumnal Fevers.... Philadelphia: 1854. V. 68; 71; 72

LA ROCHEFOUCAULD, FRANCOIS, DUC DE
Maximes et Reflections Morales. Paris: 1827. V. 68
Maxims and Moral Relfections. Edinburgh: 1783. V. 69
Moral Maxims. Dublin: 1751. V. 69
Moral Maxims and Reflections. London: 1706. V. 69

LA ROCHEFOUCAULD-LIANCOURT, FRANCOIS ALEXANDRE FREDERIC
Travels in Canada 1795. Toronto: 1917. V. 73
Voyages Dans Les Etats-Unis d'Amerqiue Fait en 1795, 1796, et 1797. Paris: 1799. V. 72

LA ROCQUE, A.
Pleistocene Mollusca of Ohio. Columbus: 1964-1970. V. 68

LA ROQUE, JEAN DE
Voyage de L'Arabie Heureuse.... Amsterdam: 1716. V. 70
A Voyage to Arabia Faelix, through the Eastern Ocean and the Sreights of the Red-Sea.... London: 1732. V. 69

LA ROQUE, JOSEPH DE
Tour of Inspection Made by Sieur de La Roque. Census. 1752. Ottawa: 1906. V. 73

LARPENT, GEORGE GERAD DE HOCHEPIED
A Letter to the Members of the East India and China Association on the Subject of Steam Communication with India. London: 1839. V. 73

LARRABEE, E.
Knoll Design. New York: 1990. V. 72

LARRIMORE, LIDA
Stars Still Shine. Philadelphia: 1940. V. 71

LARSEN, CARL
The Naked and the Dead and the Pride and the Passion (etc.) and Other Poems. Torrance: 1963. V. 71
Notes form Machine Shop. Alondro: 1956. V. 71

LARSEN, ELLOUISE BAKER
American Historical Views on Straffordshire China. New York: 1939. V. 73

LARSEN, LYLE
Dr. Johnson's Household, an Account of Francis Barber, Anna Williams, Robert Levett, Elizabeth Desmoulins and Poll Carmichael.... 1985. V. 69

LARTER, C. ETHELINDA
Notes on the Botany of North Devon. Ilfracombe: 1898. V. 69

LARTIGUE, JACQUES-HENRI
Boyhood Photos.... 1966. V. 68
Diary of a Century. New York: 1978. V. 73

LARWOOD, JACOB
The History of Signboards. London: 1884. V. 69
The Story of the London Parks. London. V. 68

LASATER, LAWRENCE
The Lastest Philosophy of Cattle Raising. El Paso: 1972. V. 71

LASCARAIS, CONSTANTINUS
De Octo Partibus Orationis. Venitiis: 1512. V. 73

LASCARIS, EVADNE
The Golden Bed of Kydno. London: 1935. V. 71

LAS CASES, EMMANUEL, COMTE DE
Memorial de Sainte Helene...Journal of the Private Life and Conversations of the Emperor Napoleon at Saint Helene.... 1823. V. 70

LASCELLES, MARY
The Adversaries and other poems. Cambridge: 1971. V. 71

LASCHE'S Magazine for the Practical Distiller. Milwaukee. V. 72

LASDUN, JAMES
The Silver Age. London: 1985. V. 71

LASH, JOSEPH
Eleanor and Franklin. Franklin Center: 1981. V. 69

LASINIO, CARLO
Serie di 12 Ritratti di Persone Facete, che Servono a Divertire il Pubblico Fiorentino.... Florence: 1800. V. 69

LASKEY, J.
A Description of the Series of Medals Struck at the national Medal Mint by Order of Napoleon Bonaparte. London: 1818. V. 72
A General Account of the Hunterian Museum, Glasgow. Glasgow: 1813. V. 72; 73

LASSAIGNE, JACQUES
Marc Chagall. The Ceiling of the Paris Opera. New York: 1966. V. 69
Marc Chagall. Drawings and Water Colors for the Ballet. New York: 1969. V. 69

LASSELS, RICHARD
The Voyage of Italy; or, a Compleat Journey through Italy. London: 1686. V. 73

THE LAST Blow; or an Unanswerable Vindication of the Society of Exter College. London: 1755. V. 68

LASTEYRIE DU SAILLANT, CHARLES PHILIBERT, COMTE DE
Lettres Autographes et Inedites de Henri IV. Paris: 1815. V. 68

LASTINGER, L. E.
The Confederate War. Berrien County: 1928. V. 70

LASTRES, JUAN B.
Historia De La Medicina Penuana. Lima: 1951. V. 72

THE LATE King James's Manifesto Answer'd Paragraph by Paragraph. London: 1697. V. 73

LATEEF, YUSEF
A Night in the Garden of Love. New York: 1988. V. 69

THE LASTEST Views of Los Angeles. Portland: 1910. V. 68

LATHAM, H.
Trans-Missouri Stock Raising: The Pasture Lands of North America; Winter Grazing.... Denver: 1962. V. 71; 72

LATHAM, JOHN
A General Synopsis of Birds. Supplement to the General Synopsis of Birds. Part I (of II). Index Ornithologicus Sive Systema Ornithologiae.... London: 1781-1785. V. 70

LATHAM, P. M.
The Collected Works of Dr. P. M. Latham. London: 1878. V. 71

LATHAM, PHILIP
Missing Men of Saturn. Philadelphia: 1953. V. 69

LATHAM, R. G.
The Native Races of the Russian Empire. London: 1854. V. 72
The Natural History Department of the Crystal Palace Described. London: 1854. V. 68; 70

LATHAM, SYMON
Falconry; or the Falcons Lure and Cure, In Two Bookes. New and Second Booke of Falconry.... London: 1618. V. 70
Falconry; or the Falcons Lure and Cure, In Two Bookes. New and Second Booke of Falconry.... London: 1615-1618. V. 72

LATHEM, EDWARD CONNERY
Robert Frost 100. Boston: 1974. V. 72

LATHEN, EMMA
Banking on Death. 1961. V. 70
Banking on Death. New York: 1961. V. 69
Murder Against the Grain. 1967. V. 70
A Place for Murder. New York: 1963. V. 69

LATHRAP, MARY T.
The Poems and Written Addresses of Mary T. Lathrap, President of the Michigan Woman's Christian Temperance Union for Fourteen Years.... Michigan: 1895. V. 72

LATHROP, DOROTHY P.
Hide and Go Seek. New York: 1938. V. 71; 73
Let Them Live. New York: 1951. V. 71
The Little White Goose. New York: 1933. V. 72
Presents for Lupe. New York: 1940. V. 70; 73

LATHROP, ELISE
Historic Houses of Early America Illustrated. New York: 1927. V. 70

LATHROP, GEORGE
Memoirs of a...Pioneer Being the Autobiography of.... Lusk: 1917. V. 73
Some Pioneer Recollections Being the Autobiography of George Lathrop. Philadelphia: 1927. V. 68

LATHROP, GILBERT A.
Little Engines and Big Men. Caldwell: 1955. V. 68

LATHROP, LORIN
Lal. Bristol: 1890. V. 68

LATHROP, S. K.
Treasures of Ancient America. Cleveland: 1964. V. 71

LATHY, THOMAS PIKE
The Angler: a Poem in Ten Cantos.... London: 1819. V. 72

LATIMER, HUGH
Frvtefvll Sermons Preached by the Right Reuerend Father and Constant Martyr of Iesus Christ M. Hugh Latymer. London: 1575?-1571. V. 70

LATIMER, JONATHAN
Black is the Fashion for Dying. 1959. V. 73
The Dead Don't Care. New York: 1938. V. 73
The Lady in the Morgue. New York: 1936. V. 73
The Mink-Lined Coffin. London: 1960. V. 69; 73
Red Gardenias. New York: 1939. V. 73
Sinners and Shrouds. 1955. V. 73
Sinners and Shrouds. London: 1956. V. 70
Solomon's Vineyard. Santa Barbara: 1982. V. 69; 70; 73
The Westland Case. Garden City: 1937. V. 69; 73

LATIMER, ROBERT SLOAN
Under Three Tsars: Liberty of Conscience in Russia 1856-1909. London: 1909. V. 73

LA TOUCHE, FRANCIS
Sonnets Paiens. London: 1909. V. 70

LATROBE, BENJAMIN HENRY
Description of a New Form of Edge Rail, to be Called the Z Rail, with Its Supports, Fastenings, &c.... Baltimore: 1840. V. 68
The Journal of Latrobe: Being the Notes and Sketches of an Architect, Naturalist and Traveler in the United States from 1796 to 1820. New York: 1905. V. 71
The Papers of Benjamin Henry Latrobe. New Haven and London: 1977. V. 68

LATROBE, CHARLES JOSEPH
The Rambler in Mexico. London: 1836. V. 69

LATSIS, MARIANNA
After Byzantium: the Survival of Byzantine Sacred Art. London: 1996. V. 73

LATT, MIMI
Powers of Attorney. New York: 1993. V. 70

LATTA, FRANK F.
California Indian Folklore. Shafer: 1936. V. 70; 73
Handbook of Yokuts Indians. Oildale: 1949. V. 69
Tailholt Tales. Santa Cruz: 1976. V. 69

LATTA, ROBERT R.
Reminiscences of Pioneer Life. Kansas City: 1912. V. 70

LAUBIN, REGINALD
Indian Dances of North America, Their Importance to Indian Life. Norman: 1977. V. 71

LAUBREAUX, ALIN
Happy Glutton; or How to Eat & How to Cook. London: 1931. V. 72

LAUDERDALE, JAMES MAITLAND, 8TH EARL OF
The Depreciation of the Paper Currency of Great Britian Proved. London: 1812. V. 69
An Inquiry Into the Nature and Origin of Public Wealth and Into the Means and Causes of Its Increase. Edinburgh: 1804. V. 70
Substance Of the Earl of Lauderdale's Speech in the House of Lords on Thursday, the 2nd November 1820, on the Second Reading of the Bill, Entitled an Act to Deprive Her Majesty, Caroline Amelia Elizaeth, of the Titles, Prerogatives.... Edinburgh: 1820. V. 69

LAUDERDALE, R. J.
Life on the Range and on the Trail. San Antonio: 1936. V. 73

LAUFER, BERTHOLD
Archaic Chinese Jades Collected in China by A. W. Bahr. New York: 1927. V. 72
Chinese Baskets. Chicago: 1925. V. 69

LAUFERTY, LILIAN
The Hungry House. New York: 1943. V. 72

THE LAUGHING Philosopher; or Repository of Wit.... 1800. V. 70

LAUGHLIN, JAMES
Angelica. New York: 1993. V. 73
Gists & Piths. A Memoir of Ezra Pound. Iowa City: 1982. V. 69; 73
The House of Light: Poems. 1986. V. 71
The Pig. Mt. Horeb: 1970. V. 73

LAUGHTON, JAMES W.
The General Receipt-Book, Containing an Extensive Collection of Valuable Receipts.... London: 1838. V. 68

LAUGHTON, L. G. CARR
Old Ship Figure-Heads & Sterns. London: 1925. V. 72

LAUMER, KEITH
Galactic Diplomat. New York: 1965. V. 68
Reteif and the Warlords. 1968. V. 70
Retief and the Warlords. New York: 1968. V. 68

LAUREMBERG, PETER
Horticultura, Libris II. Comprehensa...(bound together with) Apparatus Plantarius: Tributis in Duos Libros.... Frankfurt: 1654. V. 70

LAURENCE Duggan 1905-1948: in Memoriam. 1949. V. 71

LAURENCE, DAN H.
Bernard Shaw: Collected Letters 1874-1910. 1965-1972. V. 70

LAURENCE, EDWARD
The Young Surveyor's Guide.... London: 1716. V. 71

LAURENCE, JANET
A Deepe Coffyn. London: 1989. V. 69
A Tasty Way to Die. London: 1990. V. 69

LAURENCE, JOHN
The Linkram Jewels. London: 1924. V. 72

LAURENCE, MARGARET
A Jest of God. Toronto: 1966. V. 71

LAURENTS, ARTHUR
Home of the Brave. New York: 1946. V. 69; 71
West Side Story. New York: 1958. V. 69

LAURIE, JOSEPH
The Homoeopathic Domestic Medicine. London: 1857. V. 72

LAURITZEN, HENRY
Sherlock Holmes Klubben 1950-1975. Aalborg: 1975. V. 69
Sherlock Holmes Loser Edwin Drood Gaaden (Sherlock Holmes Solves the Edwin Drood Riddle). Aalborg: 1964. V. 71

LAURITZEN, J.
Arrows into the Sun. New York: 1943. V. 69

LAUT, AGNES C.
The Blazed Trail of the Old Frontier. New York: 1926. V. 70

LAUTERBACH, ANN
Book One. New York: 1975. V. 69; 72
Closing Hours. New York: 1983. V. 69
A Clown, Some Colors, A Doll, Her Stories, A Song, A Moonlit Cove. New York: 1995. V. 69; 73
Later that Evening. New York: 1981. V. 73
Many Times, But Then. Austin and London: 1979. V. 69
Sacred Weather. New York: 1984. V. 73
Thripsis. Calais: 1998. V. 73

LAUTREAMONT, COMTE DE
Maldoror. 1943. V. 72
Oeuvres Completes. Paris: 1938. V. 71

LA VALLIERE, LOUISE FRANCOISE LA BAUME LE BLANC DE, DUCHESSE
The Penitent Lady; or Reflections on the Mercy of God.... London: 1722. V. 73

LAVATER, JOHANN CASPAR
An Die Fraulein Margrieth von Haeften zu Wadenoyen auf Ihren Hochzeittag eine Bruderliche Zeile, von Johann Casper Lavater. Zurich: 1774. V. 70
Aphorisms of Man. London: 1794. V. 69; 73
Essays in Physignomy. London: 1804. V. 69

LAVELLE, PATRICK
The Irish Landlord Since the Revolution. 1870. V. 69

LAVELLI, JACAPO
De Publius ad Tyrones, Liber et Commentarii in Primum Librum Prognosticorum Hippocrates. Venice: 1602. V. 70; 72

LAVENDER, DAVID
The Fist in the Wilderness: a Narrative History of the American Fur Trade. New York: 1964. V. 69; 72; 73

LAVER, HENRY
The Colchester Oyster Fishery.... Colchester: 1916. V. 68; 71

LAVER, JAMES
Ladies' Mistakes. London: 1933. V. 68; 71
A Stitch in Time; or Pride Prevents A Fall. London: 1927. V. 71

LAVERS, G. R.
Anglo-Italian Maritime Equivalents BR 100/37. London: 1937. V. 69

LAVERY, BRIAN
The Ship of the Line. Volume I: Development of the Battlefleet 1650- 1850. Volume II: Design Construction and Fittings. London: 1983-1984. V. 68
The Ships, Men and Organisation 1793-1815. New York: 1989. V. 69

LAVERY, EMMET
American Portrait. New York: 1959. V. 69
The First Legion. New York: 1937. V. 71

LAVERY, FELIX
Irish Heroes in the War. 1917. V. 70

LAVIN, MARY
The Becker Wives and Other Stories. London: 1946. V. 69; 73
Happiness and Other Stories. London: 1969. V. 68
The House in Clewe Street. Boston: 1945. V. 72
A Likely Story. Dublin: 1967. V. 72
The Second Best Children in the World.... 1972. V. 71
The Stories of Mary Lavin. 1970-1985. V. 70
Tales from Bective Bridge. Boston: 1942. V. 69

LAVINGTON, MARGARET
The Noah's Ark Book. London: 1919. V. 72

LAVOSINE
A Complete Genealogical, Historical, Chronological Atlas. Philadelphia: 1821. V. 70

LAW, ALICE
Patrick Branwell Bronte. (with) Emily Jane Bronte. 1923. V. 70

THE LAW and Modern Practice of Ejectments with the Latest Determinations Both in K.B. and C. B. Selecte Precedents; and Three Distinct Tables to the Whole. London: 1779. V. 71

A LAW Grammar; or, an Introduction to the Theory and Practice of English Jurisprudence.... Dublin: 1791. V. 69

LAW, HENRY
The Construction of Roads and Streets. London: 1877. V. 72
The Rudiments of Civil Engineering, for the Use of Beginners. Part I (and) Part II. London: 1848-1849. V. 68

LAW, JOHN
Address Delivered Before the Vincennes (Ind.). Louisville: 1839. V. 71
Het Groote Tafereel Der Dwaasheid, Vertoonende de Opkomst Voortgang en Ondergang der Actie, Bubbel en Windnegotie in Vrankryk.... Amsterdam: 1720. V. 69

THE LAW of Actions: Being an Exact, Brief and Methodical Collection of All Adjudg'd Cases Out of All the Reports of the Law to His Day, and Likewise from Roll's Abridgment.... London: 1710. V. 70

THE LAW of Parliament in the Present Situation of Great Britain Considered. London: 1788. V. 73

LAW, WILLIAM
A Practical Treatise Upon Christian Perfection. London: 1738. V. 70
Remarks on the Fable of the Bees.... Cambridge: 1844. V. 70
A Serious Call to a Devout and Holy Life. London: 1729. V. 73

LAW, WILLIAM JOHN
Comments on the New Scheme of Insolvency, with Some Remarks on the Change in the Law of Certifcate in Bankruptcy. London: 1843. V. 71

LAWFORD, G. L.
The Telcon Story. 1850-1950. London: 1950. V. 73

LAWKERRY, NEHEMIAH
A Motion Propounded to the Committee of Parliament for Redresse of the Publique Grievances of the Kingdome, etc. London: 1648. V. 73

LAWLER, DENNIS
Lines on Catholic Emancipation.. London: 1808. V. 73

LAWLESS, EMILY
The Point of View. 1909. V. 69

LAWLOR, HENRY CAIRNES
Ulster and Its Archaeology and Antiquities. 1928. V. 70

LAWLOR, HUGH J.
The Fasti of St. Patrick's, Dublin. 1930. V. 73

LAWRENCE, ADA
Young Lorenzo. Early Life of D. H. Lawrence Containing Hithterto Unpublished Letters, Articles and Reproductions of Pictures. Florence: 1931. V. 72

LAWRENCE, ALEXANDER A.
Johnny Leber and the Confederate Major: a Tale of the Last Months of the Confederacy. Darien: 1962. V. 70

LAWRENCE Block Bibliography 1958-1993. Royal Oak: 1993. V. 69

LAWRENCE COUNTY HISTORICAL SOCIETY
Atlas of Lawrence County, Ohio. Hardesty 1882. Lake 1887. Ironton: 1985. V. 73

LAWRENCE, DAVID HERBERT
Aaron's Rod. London: 1922. V. 71
Aaron's Rod. New York: 1922. V. 71
L'Amazone Fugitive. (A Woman Who Rode Away). Paris: 1936. V. 72
Amores. London: 1916. V. 71
Amores. New York: 1916. V. 71
Apocalypse. Florence: 1931. V. 72
Apocalypse. New York: 1932. V. 72
Apropos of Lady Chatterley's Love. London: 1930. V. 71
Assorted Articles. London: 1930. V. 71
Assorted Articles. New York: 1930. V. 69; 71
Autumn in New Mexico. 1971. V. 72
Bay. Westminster: 1919. V. 71
Birds, Beasts and Flowers. London: 1923. V. 71
Birds, Beasts and Flowers. New York: 1923. V. 71
Birds, Beasts and Flowers. London: 1930. V. 71; 72
A Book of Poems. Westminster: 1919. V. 71
The Boy in the Bush. London: 1924. V. 71
The Boy in the Bush. New York: 1924. V. 71
The Captain's Doll. New York: 1923. V. 71
The Centaur Letters. 1970. V. 72
The Collected Poems. London: 1928. V. 71
The Collected Poems. New York: 1929. V. 72
The Collected Poems. London: 1932. V. 68; 71
The Complete Poems. New York: 1964. V. 72
Consciousness. N.P. but Santa Barbara?. V. 72
David. London: 1926. V. 68; 71
David. New York: 1926. V. 71
England, My England. New York: 1922. V. 71
England, My England. London: 1924. V. 71
The Escaped Cock. Paris: 1929. V. 71
Etruscan Places. London: 1932. V. 71
Etruscan Places. New York: 1932. V. 72
Etudes sur la Litterature Classique Americaine. (Studies in Classic American Literature). Paris: 1948. V. 72
Fantasia of the Unconscious. New York: 1922. V. 71
Fantasia of the Unconscious. London: 1923. V. 71
Femmes Amoureuses. (Women in Love). Paris: 1932. V. 72
Les Filles du Pasteur. Paris: 1933. V. 72
Fire and Other Poems. San Francisco: 1940. V. 70; 72
Foreword to Pansies. Wiltshire: 1988. V. 72
Glad Ghosts. London: 1926. V. 71
Ile, mon Ile. (England, My England). Paris: 1930. V. 72
John Thomas and Lady Jane (the second version of Lady Chatterley's Lover). London and New York: 1972. V. 71
Kangaroo. 1923. V. 70
Kangaroo. London: 1923. V. 71
Kangaroo. New York: 1923. V. 69; 71
Lady Chatterley's Lover. Florence: 1928. V. 70; 71; 73
Lady Chatterley's Lover. Paris?: 1928. V. 71
Lady Chatterley's Lover. Paris: 1929. V. 70; 71
Lady Chatterley's Lover. London: 1932. V. 71
Lady Chatterley's Lover. 1935. V. 71

LAWRENCE, DAVID HERBERT continued
Lady Chatterley's Lover. Stockholm: 1950. V. 70
Lady Chatterley's Lover. Harmondsworth, Middlesex: 1960. V. 69; 71
The Ladybird. London: 1923. V. 71
L'Amant de Lady Chatterley. Paris: 1932. V. 72
L'Amante di Lady Chatterley. Milan and Verona: 1946. V. 72
Last Poems. Florence: 1932. V. 72; 73
Last Poems. London: 1933. V. 72
Last Poems. New York: 1933. V. 72
Letters from D. H. Lawrence to Martin Secker 1911-1930. London: 1970. V. 68
The Letters of D. H. Lawrence. London and New York: 1932. V. 72
The Letters of D. H. Lawrence and Amy Lowell 1914-1925. Santa Barbara: 1985. V. 72
Letters to Bertrand Russell. New York: 1948. V. 71
Letters to Thomas and Adele Seltzer. Santa Barbara: 1976. V. 72
The Life of J. Middleton Murry. 1930. V. 71
Look! We Have Come Through!. London: 1917. V. 71
The Lost Girl. London: 1920. V. 71
The Lost Girl. New York: 1921. V. 71
Love Among the Haystacks and Other Pieces. London: 1930. V. 68; 69; 71; 72; 73
Love Poems and Others. London: 1913. V. 71
The Lovely Lady. London: 1932. V. 72
The Lovely Lady. New York: 1933. V. 72
The Man Who Died. London: 1931. V. 68; 71; 72; 73
The Man Who Died. New York: 1931. V. 71
The Man Who Died. London: 1935. V. 68; 69; 73
The Man Who Died. Covelo: 1992. V. 71
Mananas En Mexico. (Mornings in Mexico). Mexico: 1942. V. 72
Memoir of Maurice Magnus. Santa Rosa: 1987. V. 72
A Modern Lover. London: 1934. V. 72
Mornings in Mexico. London: 1927. V. 71
Mornings in Mexico. New York: 1927. V. 69; 71
Mornings in Mexico. Detroit: 1945. V. 72
Movements in European History. Edinburgh: 1921. V. 71
Movements in European History. 1925. V. 71
My Skirmish with Jolly Roger. New York: 1929. V. 69; 71
Nettles. London: 1930. V. 71; 72
New Poems. London: 1918. V. 71; 73
New Poems. New York: 1920. V. 71
An Original Poem. London: 1934. V. 72
The Paintings of D. H Lawrence. London: 1929. V. 71
Pansies. London: 1929. V. 71
Pansies. New York: 1954. V. 71
Phoenix. The Posthumous Papers.... London: 1936. V. 72
The Plays. London: 1933. V. 72
The Plumed Serpent. 1926. V. 69
The Plumed Serpent. London: 1926. V. 71
The Plumed Serpent. New York: 1926. V. 71
Poems. London: 1929. V. 71
Poems. Florence: 1932. V. 69
Pornography and Obscenity. London: 1929. V. 71; 72
Pornography and So On. London: 1936. V. 72
A Prelude. Surrey: 1949. V. 72
Psychoanalysis and the Unconscious. New York: 1921. V. 68; 71
Psychoanalysis and the Unconscious. London: 1923. V. 71
The Rainbow. London: 1915. V. 71
The Rainbow. New York: 1916. V. 70; 71
Rawdon's Roof. London: 1929. V. 71
Reflections on the Death of a Porcupine. Philadelphia: 1925. V. 68; 71
St. Mawr Together with the Princess. London: 1925. V. 71; 73
Sea and Sardinia. New York: 1921. V. 71
Selected Poems. London: 1934. V. 72
Sex Locked Out. London: 1928. V. 71
The Ship of Death and Other Poems. London: 1933. V. 72
Snake. Edinburgh: 1984. V. 72
Sons and Lovers. London: 1913. V. 71
Sons and Lovers. New York: 1913. V. 71
Sons and Lovers. Avon: 1975. V. 69
Studies in Classic American Literature. New York: 1923. V. 71
Sun. London: 1926. V. 68; 71
Sun. Paris: 1928. V. 71
Sun. 1929. V. 71
The Symbolic Meaning. Fontwell, Arundel: 1962. V. 71
The Tales. London: 1934. V. 72
Tortoises. New York: 1921. V. 71
Touch and Go. London: 1920. V. 71; 73
Touch and Go. New York: 1920. V. 68; 71
The Trespasser. London: 1912. V. 71
The Trespasser. New York: 1912. V. 71
The Triumph of the Machine. London: 1930. V. 70; 72
Twilight in Italy. London: 1916. V. 71
The Universe and Me. New York: 1935. V. 72
Unpublished Foreword to Women in Love 1919. San Francisco: 1936. V. 71
The Virgin and the Gipsy. Florence: 1930. V. 72
The Virgin and the Gipsy. New York: 1930. V. 72; 73
We Need One Another. New York: 1933. V. 72
The White Peacock. New York: 1910. V. 71
The White Peacock. London: 1911. V. 71; 73
The White Peacock. New York: 1911. V. 71
The Widowing of Mrs. Holroyd. London: 1914. V. 71; 73
The Widowing of Mrs. Holroyd. New York: 1914. V. 71
The Woman Who Rode Away. London: 1928. V. 71; 73
The Woman Who Rode Away. New York: 1928. V. 71
Women in Love. New York: 1920. V. 71
Women in Love. London: 1921. V. 71
The Women Know Best. Santa Rosa: 1994. V. 72

LAWRENCE, ELIZABETH A.
His Very Silence Speaks - Comanche, The Horse Who Survived Custer's Last Stand. Detroit: 1989. V. 72

LAWRENCE, FRIEDA
Not I, But the Wind.... Santa Fe: 1934. V. 72
Not I, But the Wind.... London: 1935. V. 72

LAWRENCE, GEORGE A.
Silverland. London: 1873. V. 71

LAWRENCE, GERARD
The Automobile, Its Construction and Management.... London: 1902. V. 69

LAWRENCE, GRACE L.
Nettleton Cook Book. Kansas City: 1909. V. 68

LAWRENCE, HEATHER
Yorkshire Pots and Potteries. London: 1974. V. 72; 73

LAWRENCE, HILDA
The Pavilion. New York: 1946. V. 72

LAWRENCE, J. W.
Foot-Prints; or, Incidents in Early History of New Brunswick. Saint John: 1883. V. 73

LAWRENCE, JANET
Deepe Coffyn. New York: 1990. V. 73

LAWRENCE, JEROME
Inherit the Wind. NY: 1955. V. 73

LAWRENCE, JOHN
The New Farmer's Calendar. 1801. V. 71
The New Farmer's Calendar. London: 1802. V. 70

LAWRENCE, JOSEPHINE
Kiddie Wonder Box. New York: 1926. V. 72
Man in the Moon Stories Told Over the Radio-Phone. New York: 1922. V. 70

LAWRENCE, MARGARET
Hearts and Bones. New York: 1996. V. 72

LAWRENCE, MARGERY
Number Seven Queer Street. Sauk City: 1969. V. 72

LAWRENCE, MARTHA
Murder in Scorpio. New York: 1995. V. 69

LAWRENCE, RICHARD
Elgin Marbles, from the Parthenon at Athens:. London: 1818. V. 72

LAWRENCE, THOMAS
Franci Nicholsii, M.D. Georgii Secundi Magnae Britanniae regis medici Ordinarii, Vita.... Londini: 1780. V. 72

LAWRENCE, THOMAS EDWARD
Correspondence with Bernard and Charlotte Shaw. 1922-1926. Fordingbridge: 2000. V. 68; 71; 73
Correspondence with Henry Williamson. Fordingbridge: 2000. V. 68; 71
Crusader Castles. I. The Thesis. London: 1936. V. 71; 72
Diary of T. E. Lawrence MCMXI. 1937. V. 71
An Essay on Flecker. Garden City: 1937. V. 70
The Letters of T. E. Lawrence. London: 1938. V. 68; 69; 72
Letters to T. E. Lawrence. London: 1962. V. 68
Lettres de T. E. Lawrence. Paris: 1948. V. 68
Men in Print: Essays in Literary Criticism. London: 1940. V. 70
Men in Print: Essays in Literary Criticism. Waltham St. Lawrence: 1940. V. 71
The Mint. London: 1955. V. 69; 70; 71; 73
Oriental Assembly. London: 1939. V. 68; 70; 71
Revolt in the Desert. London: 1927. V. 68
Revolt in the Desert. New York: 1927. V. 70; 71
Secret Despatches from Arabia. London: 1939. V. 69; 70
Secret Despatches from Arabia. Waltham St. Lawrence: 1939. V. 71
Seven Pillars of Wisdom. Garden City: 1935. V. 68; 70; 73
Seven Pillars of Wisdom. London: 1935. V. 68; 70; 71; 72; 73
Seven Pillars of Wisdom. London: 1939. V. 71
Seven Pillars of Wisdom. Fordingbridge, Hampshire: 1997. V. 68
Shaw-Ede: T. E. Lawrence's Letters to H. S. Ede 1927-1935. Waltham St. Lawrence: 1942. V. 71
Shaw-Ede: T.E. Lawrence's Letters to H. S. Ede. London: 1942. V. 73
T. E. Lawrence: Letters to E. T. Leeds. Andoversford: 1988. V. 72
T. E. Lawrence to His Biographer, Robert Graves. (with) T. E. Lawrence to His Biographer, Liddell Hart. New York: 1938. V. 69; 70; 71; 73

LAWRENCE, WILLIAM
A Treatise on the Diseases of the Eye. London: 1833. V. 72

LAWRENCE, WILLIAM BEACH
Visitation and Search; or, an Historical Sketch of the British Claim to Exercise a Maritime Police Over the Vessels of All Nations, in Peace, as Well as War.... Boston: 1858. V. 73

LAWRIE, W. H.
International Trout Flies. 1969. V. 68; 73
A Reference Book of English Trout Flies. 1967. V. 73

LAWS and Ordinances of the Baltimore and Ohio Rail Road Company. Baltimore: 1850. V. 73

LAWSON, ELIZABETH
Scottsboro's Martyr. New York: 1932-1933. V. 72

LAWSON, J. MURRAY
Yarmouth Past and Present. A Book of Reminiscences. Yarmouth: 1902. V. 73

LAWSON, JAMES
Giordano. New York: 1832. V. 71

LAWSON, JOAN
Dressing for the Ballet. 1958. V. 68

LAWSON, JOHN
The History of Carolina, Containing the Exact Description and Natural History of that Country. Raleigh: 1860. V. 68

LAWSON, JOHN PARKER
The Book of Perth: An Illustration of the Moral and Ecclesiastical State of Scotland Before and After the Reformation . . . Edinburgh: 1847. V. 71

LAWSON, JOSEPH
Letters to the Young on Progress in Pudsey During the Last Sixty Years. Stannington: 1887. V. 73

LAWSON, JUDITH A.
Geology Explained Around Glasgow and South West Scotland, Including Arran. London: 1976. V. 70

LAWSON, LIZZIE
Under the Mistletoe. New York: 1886. V. 70

LAWSON, MARIE
Dragon John. New York: 1943. V. 70

LAWSON, RICHARD
History of Flixton, Urmston and Davyhulme. Manchester: 1898. V. 73

LAWSON, ROBERT
Captain Kidd's Cat. Boston: 1956. V. 72
Captain Kidd's Cat. Chronicle of Wm. Kidd...of New York. London: 1956. V. 71
Dick Whittington and His Cat. New York: 1949. V. 71
Edward, Hoppy and Joe. New York: 1952. V. 71
The Fabulous Flight. Boston: 1949. V. 70
Mr. Revere and I. A Chronicle of Stirring Events in the Career of One Paul Revere. Boston: 1953. V. 71; 73
The Tough Winter. New York: 1954. V. 73

LAWSON, WILLIAM
New Orchard & Garden. London: 1927. V. 72

LAWSON, WILLIAM D.
Lawson's Tyneside Celebrities. Newcastle-upon-Tyne: 1873. V. 73

LAWSON, WILLIAM JOHN
A Handy Book of the Law of Banking: Its Principles, Customs, and Practice in England, Scotland and Ireland. London: 1859. V. 71

LAWTON, CHARLES
Jungle Menace Starring Frank Buck. NY: 1937. V. 72

LAWTON, E.
Moss Flora of the Pacific Northwest. Nichinan: 1971. V. 72

LAWTON, GEORGE
A Brief Treatise of Bona Notabilia; Together with an Account of the Archiepiscopal Courts of Probate; within the Province of York. London: 1825. V. 69

LAWTON, HARRY
Willie Boy: A Desert Manhunt. Balboa Island (CA): 1960. V. 71; 72

LAWTON, JOHN
Black Out. New York: 1995. V. 71
Old Flames. London: 1996. V. 70; 73

LAWYER, SARAH R.
The Jonathan and Hannah Steelman Family. Elkton: 1952. V. 71

LAX, ERIC
Woody Allen. New York: 1991. V. 72

LAX, JOSHUA
Historical and Descriptive Poems. Durham: 1884. V. 70; 73

LAX, ROGER
The Great Song Thesaurus. NY: 1984. V. 73

LAXTON, WILLIAM
Laxton's Builder's Price Book for 1862.... London: 1862. V. 68

LAY, H. NELSON
Memoirs of a Mariner. Stittsville: 1982. V. 73

LAYARD, AUSTEN HENRY
The Buried City of the East, Ninevah.... London: 1851. V. 73
The Monuments of Nineveh. (with) a Second Series of the Monuments. London: 1853. V. 71
Nineveh and Its Remains. (with) Discoveries in the Ruins of Nineveh and Babylon. London: 1849-1853. V. 69; 72
Nineveh and Its Remains.... New York: 1850. V. 69
Paper on Mosaic Decoration, a Read at a Meeting of the Royal Institute of British Architects. London: 1869. V. 68; 69

LAYARD, GEORGE SOMES
The Life and Letters of Charles Samuel Keene. London: 1892. V. 73
The Life and Letters of Charles Samuel Keene. London: 1893. V. 73

LAYARD, NINA FRANCES
Poems. London: 1890. V. 69

LAYCOCK, JOHN
Some Shorter Climbs (in Derbyshire and Elsewhere). Manchester: 1913. V. 69

LAYCOCK, SAMUEL
Warblin's Fro' an Own Songster. 1893. V. 73

LAYCOCK, THOMAS
The Antagonism of Law and Medicine in Insanity, and Its Consequences. Edinburgh: 1862. V. 73
On the Naming and Classification of Mental Diseases. London: 1863. V. 73
On the Principles and Method of a Practical Science of Mind. A Reply to a Criticism. London: 1862. V. 73
Practical Notes on Diagnosis, Prognosis and Treatment in Cases of Delirium Tremens. Edinburgh: 1862. V. 73
The Scientific Place and Principles of Medical Psychology; an Introductory Address. Edinburgh: 1861. V. 73

LAYMAN, RICHARD
Dashiell Hammett: A Descriptive Bibliography. Pittsburgh: 1979. V. 72; 73

LAYNE, J. GREGG
Books of the Los Angeles Disctrict. Los Angeles: 1950. V. 68
Western Wayfaring Routes of Exploration and Trade in the American Southwest. Los Angeles: 1954. V. 68

LAYS of the Holy Land from Anicent and Modern Poets. London: 1858. V. 68

LAZAR, HANK
On Equal Terms. Charles Bernstein, David Ignatow, Denise Levertov, Louis Simpson, Gerald Stern. 1984. V. 73

LAZAREV, VIKTOR
Old Russian Murals and Mosaics from the XI to the XVI Century. London: 1966. V. 69; 70; 72; 73

LAZARUS, EMMA
Songs of a Semite: the Dance to Death and Other Poems. New York: 1882. V. 68; 71

LAZARUS, HENRY
The English Revolution of the Twentieth Century.... London: 1897. V. 71

LAZY Lucy. New York. V. 71

LEA, ARNOLD W. W.
Puerperal Infection. London: 1910. V. 68

LEA, FANNY HEASLIP
Doree. New York: 1934. V. 71

LEA, ISAAC
Contributions to Geology. Philadelphia: 1833. V. 68; 73
A Synopsis of the Family of Naiads. Philadelphia: 1836. V. 69; 73

LEA, JOHN
Cruisers in the Clouds. Wells Gardner: 1910. V. 70
Cruisers in the Clouds, illustrated by H.J. Rhodes. 1911. V. 72

LEA, T. G.
Catalogue of the Plants, Native and Naturalized, Collected in the Vicinity of Cincinnati, Ohio, During the Years 1834-1844. Philadelphia: 1849. V. 72

LEA, TOM
In the Crucible of the Sun. Kingsville, TX: 1974. V. 72
The King Ranch. Boston: 1957. V. 73
The King Ranch. Kingsville, TX: 1957. V. 69; 70; 71
Peleliu Landing. El Paso: 1945. V. 69; 70
A Picture Gallery. Boston: 1968. V. 69; 70
Western Beef Cattle A Series of Eleven Printings by Tom Lea Depicting.... Austin: 1967. V. 71
Western Beef Cattle, a Series of Painting By.... Dallas: 1967. V. 69

LEACH, A. J.
A History of Antelope County Nebraska, from Its First Settlement in 1868 to the Close of the Year 1883. Chicago. V. 73
A History of Antelope County Nebraska, from Its First Settlement in 1868 to the Close of the Year 1883. Chicago: 1909. V. 68

LEACH, ARTHUR FRANCIS
Early Yokshire Schools. London: 1899-1903. V. 73

LEACH, D. G.
Rhododendrons of the World and How to Grow Them. New York: 1961. V. 68; 71; 73

LEACH, EDMUND
A Treatise of Universal Inland Navigations and the Use of All Sorts of Mines.... London: 1791. V. 72

LEACH, HENRY
The Happy Golfer.... 1914. V. 73

LEACH, JOSIAH GRANVILLE
Genealogical and Biographical Memorials of the Reading, Howell, Yerkes, Watts, Latham and Elkins Families. Philadelphia: 1898. V. 71

LEACOCK, STEPHEN
The Hohenzollerns in America, and Other Impossibilities. London: 1919. V. 73
The Hohenzollerns in America with the Bolsheviks in Berlin and Other Impossibilities. New York: 1919. V. 68
My Discovery of the West - a Discussion of East and West in Canada. Toronto: 1937. V. 72
Short Circuits. New York: 1928. V. 71
Winsome Winne and Other Nonsense Novels. New York: 1920. V. 70

LEADBEATER, J.
The Gentleman and Tradesman's Compleat Assistant; or, the Whole Art of Measuring and Estimating, Made Easy. London: 1770. V. 70

LEADBETTER, CHARLES
Mechanick Dialling; or, the New Art of Shadows.... 1737. V. 72
Mechanick Dialling; or the New Art of Shadows.... London: 1737. V. 68
Mechanick Dialling; or the New Art of Shadows.... London: 1750. V. 73

LEADBITTER, MIKE
Blues Records 1943-1965. New York: 1968. V. 73
Blues Records 1943-1966. London: 1968. V. 72

LEADER, JOHN DANIEL
The Records of the Burgery of Sheffield. London: 1897. V. 73

LEADMAN, ALEX D. H.
Proelia Eboracensia-Battles Fought in Yorkshire. London: 1891. V. 73

LEAF, MUNRO
Being an American Can Be Fun. Philadelphia: 1964. V. 73
Fair Play. New York: 1939. V. 73
Ferdinandus Taurus. New York: 1962. V. 70
The Story of Ferdinand. New York: 1936. V. 71; 73
The Story of Ferdinand. London: 1942. V. 73
The Story of Simpson and Sampson. New York: 1941. V. 71
Wee Gillis. New York: 1938. V. 73

LEAGUE OF AMERICAN WHEELMEN. NEW JERSEY DIVISION
Road Book of New Jersey. Edition 1897. 1897. V. 71

LEAHY, EDMUND
A Practical Treatise on Making and Repairing Roads. London: 1844. V. 72

LEAHY, JOHN
The Art of Swimming in the Eton Style.... London: 1875. V. 68

LEAHY, W. A.
The Incendiary. Chicago: 1897. V. 71

LEAKE, CHAUNCEY D.
Some Founders of Physiology. Washington: 1956. V. 71

LEAKE, JOHN
Dissertation on the Properties and Efficacy of Lisbon Diet-Drink, and Its Extract, in the Cure of Venereal Disease and Scurvy. London: 1783. V. 69
A Lecture Introductory to the Theory and Practice of Midwifery.... London: 1773. V. 69

LEAKE, STEPHEN MARTIN
Heraldo Memoriale; or, Memoirs of the College of Arms from 1727 to 1744. 1981. V. 69

LEAKEY, L. S. B.
White African, an Early Autobiography. Cambridge: 1966. V. 69

LEAKY, JOHN
The West That Was, from Texas to Montana. Dallas: 1958. V. 68; 73

LEAR, EDWARD
The Edward Lear Alphabet Book.... Chicago: 1915. V. 72
Edward Lear's Nonsense Alphabet. London: 1949. V. 70
Illustrations of the Family of Psittacidae, or Parrots.... London: 1978. V. 70
Journals of a Landscape Painter in Albania.... London: 1851. V. 69
Journals of a Landscape Painter in Southern Calabria. London: 1842. V. 69

LEAR , EDWARD
Journals of a Landscape Painter in Southern Calabria. London: 1852. V. 73

LEAR, EDWARD
The Jumblies. London: 1935. V. 72
The Jumblies. New York: 1968. V. 68; 70
More Nonsense. London: 1888. V. 70
Nonsense Drolleries. The Owl and the Pussy-Cat - The Duck and the Kangaroo. London: 1889. V. 72
Nonsense Songs. London. V. 68
Nonsense Songs and Stories. London: 1920. V. 70
Nonsense Songs and Stories. With additional songs and an introduction by Sir E. Strachey. London: 1901. V. 71
Nonsense Songs, Stories, Botany and Alphabets. 1872. V. 72
The Story of the Four Little Children Who Went Round the World and the History of the Seven Families of the Late Pipple-Popple: Nonsense Stories. 1990. V. 71
Two Nonsense Stories: the Story of the Four Little Children Who Went Round the World and The History of the Seven Families of the Late Pipple- Popple. 1989. V. 71

LEAR, JOHN
Kepler's Dream, with the Full Text and Notes of Somnium, Sive Astronomia Lunaris, Ioannis Kepleri. Berkeley and Los Angeles: 1965. V. 72

LEAR, MOYA OLSEN
An Unforgettable Flight. Reno: 1996. V. 69; 71

LEAR, P. G.
The Strange and Striking Adventures of Four Authors in Search of a Character. London: 1926. V. 70

LEARNING to Count; or One, Two, Buckle My Shoe. New York: 1861. V. 73

LEARY, TIMOTHY
Confessions of a Hope Fiend. New York: 1973. V. 72
High Priest. New York: 1968. V. 73
Psychedelic Prayers. Kerhonkson: 1966. V. 68; 70; 73

LEASOR, JAMES
A Week Of Love. London: 1969. V. 72

LEAST HEAT MOON, WILLIAM
Blue Highways. Boston: 1982. V. 68

LEATHER, STEPHEN
The Birthday Girl. London: 1995. V. 70
The Bombmaker. London: 1999. V. 70; 71
The Chinaman. London: 1992. V. 71
The Double Tap. London: 1996. V. 70; 71
The Stretch. London: 2000. V. 72
The Vets. London: 1993. V. 72
The Vets. New York: 1993. V. 71

LEAVEN for Doughfaces: or Threescore and Ten Parables Touching Slavery. Cincinnati: 1856. V. 69

LEAVES of Grass Imprints. American and European Criticisms of "Leaves of Grass". Boston: 1860. V. 68

LEAVIS, F. R.
D. H. Lawrence. Cambridge: 1930. V. 68
Gerard Manley Hopkins: Reflections After Fifty Years. London: 1971. V. 70
Revaluation - Tradition and Development in English Poetry. London: 1936. V. 71

LEAVITT, DAVID
Family Dancing. New York: 1984. V. 68; 72
While England Sleeps. 1993. V. 71; 72
While England Sleeps. New York: 1993. V. 69

LEAVITT, JONATHAN
A Summary of the Laws of Massachusetts, Relative to the Settlement, Support, Employment and Removal of Paupers. Greenfield: 1810. V. 68; 73

LEAVITT, RICHARD
The World of Tenneessee Williams. New York: 1978. V. 71

LEBAR, F. M.
Ethnic Groups of Insular Southeast Asia. Volume I: Indonesia, Andaman Islands and Madagascar. New Haven: 1972. V. 69
Ethnic Groups of Insular Southeast Asia. Volume II. Phillippines and Formosa. New Haven: 1975. V. 69

LE BARON, FRANCIS
The Poet and His Song. Charleston: 1848. V. 73

LEBEL, R.
Marcel Duchamp. New York: 1959. V. 69; 72

LEBLANC, MAURICE
Arsene Lupin. London: 1909. V. 68; 71
Arsene Lupin, Gentleman Burglar. New York: 1910. V. 69
Arsene Lupin Intervenes. New York: 1929. V. 70
Arsene Lupin Versus Herlock Sholmes. Chicago: 1910. V. 70
The Blonde Lady. New York: 1910. V. 71
The Confessions of Arsene Lupin. London: 1912. V. 71
The Confessions of Arsene Lupin. Garden City: 1913. V. 70; 71
The Eight Strokes of the Clock. New York: 1922. V. 68; 70
The Eight Strokes of the Clock. New York: 1992. V. 69
The Golden Triangle: The Return of Arsene Lupin. New York: 1917. V. 69; 71; 73
The Hollow Needle. New York: 1910. V. 68
The Teeth of the Tiger. Garden City: 1914. V. 71
The Teeth of the Tiger. London: 1915. V. 71
The Tremendous Event. New York: 1922. V. 71
Wanton Venus. New York: 1935. V. 72

LE BLANC, V.
The Engineer and Machinist's Drawing-Book.... 1878. V. 71
The Engineer and Machinist's Drawing-Books.... Glasgow &c: 1862. V. 71

LE BLOND, E. A. F.
Adventures on the Roof of the World for Non-Climbers Young and Old. London: 1907. V. 69
The High Alps in Winter.... London: 1883. V. 69
Mountaineering in the Land of the Midnight Sun. London: 1908. V. 69

LE BLOND, E. A. F. continued
True Tales of Mountain Adventure for Non-Climbers Young and Old. London: 1906. V. 69

LE BON, GUSTAVE
La Civilisation des Araes.... Paris: 1884. V. 72

LE BOURDAIS, D. M.
Northward on the New Frontier. Ottawa: 1931. V. 73

LE BOURSIER DU COUDRAY, ANGELIQUE MARGUERITE
Abbrege De L'Art des Accouchemens. A Saintes: 1769. V. 71

LE BOUTILLIER, CORNELIA
The Bright Thread. Garden City: 1929. V. 71

LE BRUYN, M. CORNEILLE
Voyage to the Levant; or Travels in the Principal Parts of Asia Minor...(with) Travels into Muscovy, Persia and Part of the East Indies.... London: 1702-1737. V. 71

LE CAIN, ERROL
King Arthur's Sword. London: 1968. V. 70

LE CARRE, JOHN
Call for the Dead. London: 1961. V. 68
Call for the Dead. New York: 1962. V. 68; 70
The Clandestine Muse. The G. Harry Pouder Memorial Lecture Delivered at Johns Hopkins University. Newark: 1986. V. 69; 73
The Constant Gardener. London: 2001. V. 68; 69; 70
The Constant Gardener. New York: 2001. V. 69
George Smiley Goes Home, In The Bell House Book. London: 1979. V. 71; 72
The Honourable Schoolboy. Franklin Center: 1977. V. 68
Le Carre Omnibus. London: 1962. V. 73
Le Carre Omnibus. London: 1964. V. 70
Le Carre Omnibus. London: 1965. V. 69
The Little Drummer Girl. New York: 1983. V. 68; 71
The Little Drummer Girl. London: 1984. V. 72
The Looking-Glass War. London: 1965. V. 68; 69; 70; 71
A Murder of Quality. London: 1962. V. 68; 71
A Murder of Quality. New York: 1963. V. 71; 72
A Murder of Quality. London: 1991. V. 70
The Naive and Sentimental Lover. London: 1971. V. 68; 70; 71; 72
The Naive and Sentimental Lover. London: 1974. V. 68
Nervous Time. London: 1998. V. 68; 70; 73
The Night Manager. London: 1993. V. 69; 70; 71; 73
The Night Manager. New York: 1993. V. 71
Our Game. London: 1995. V. 68; 69; 70; 72
Our Game. New York: 1995. V. 69
A Perfect Spy. London: 1986. V. 69
A Perfect Spy. New York: 1986. V. 69; 71
The Russia House. London: 1989. V. 68; 69; 70; 71; 72; 73
The Russia House. New York: 1989. V. 69
Sarratt and the Draper of Watford. 1999. V. 71
Sarratt and the Draper of Watford. Watford: 1999. V. 69; 70; 72
The Secret Pilgrim. London: 1991. V. 68; 70; 72
The Secret Pilgrim. New York: 1991. V. 72
Single and Single. Franklin Center: 1999. V. 71; 72
Single and Single. London: 1999. V. 68; 70; 71; 72; 73
A Small Town in Germany. London: 1968. V. 68; 73
A Small Town in Germany. New York: 1968. V. 69; 70; 72; 73
Smiley's People. London: 1979. V. 68; 69; 71; 72
Smiley's People. London: 1980. V. 70; 71
The Spy Who Came In from the Cold. London: 1963. V. 70; 71
The Spy Who Came in from the Cold. New York: 1964. V. 71
The Spy who Came In from the Cold. London: 1968. V. 70
The Tailor of Panama. London: 1993. V. 71
The Tailor of Panama. London: 1996. V. 68; 69; 70; 72
The Tailor of Panama. New York: 1996. V. 72
Tinker, Tailor, Soldier, Spy. London: 1974. V. 68
Tinker, Tailor, Soldier, Spy. New York: 1974. V. 71

LE CERT, LOUIS
Le Papier. Recherches et Notes Pour Servir a l'Histoire du Papier, Principalement a Troyes et Aux Environs Depuis le Quatorzieme Siecle. Paris: 1926. V. 70

LE CHATELIER, HENRI LOUIS
Recherches Experimentales et Theoriques sur les Equilibres Chimiques. Paris: 1888. V. 72

LE CHAU, GERAUD DE
Dissertation sur les Attributs de Venus qui a Obtenu l'Accessit au Jugement de l'Academie Royale des Inscriptions et Belles Lettres.... Paris: 1776. V. 70

LECHEVALIER, JEAN BAPTISTE
Ulysse-Homere, Ou du Veritable Auteur de l'Iliade et de L'Odyssee. Paris: 1829. V. 68

LECKENBY, CHARLES H.
The Tread of Pioneers. Steamboat Springs: 1945. V. 69; 71

LECKIE, ROBERT
The Buffalo Soldiers - A Narrative of The Negro Calvary In The West. Norman: 1967. V. 72

LECKIE, WILLIAM H.
The Military Conquest of The Southern Plains. Norman: 1963. V. 72
Unlikely Warriors - General Benjamin Grierson and His Family. Norman: 1984. V. 72

LECKY, W. E. H.
A History of England in the Eighteenth Century. London: 1919. V. 70
History of the Rise and Influence of Rationalism in Europe. London: 1866. V. 71

LE CLERC, DANIEL
Bibliotheca Anatomica. Geneva: 1699. V. 73
Histoire de la Medecine.... The Hague: 1729. V. 71

LE CLERC, SEBASTIAN
The Art of Drawing, without a Master, from Mons. Le Clerc. 1786. V. 73

LE CLERCQ, CHRISTIEN
New Relation of Gaspesia with the Customs and Religion of the Gaspesian Indians. Toronto: 1910. V. 73

LE COMTE, LOUIS DANIEL
Nouveaux Memoires sur l'Etat Present de la Chine. Amsterdam: 1698. V. 72

LE CONTE, EMMA
When the World Ended. New York: 1957. V. 69

LE CONTE, J. L.
Classification of Coleoptera of North America. Washington: 1883. V. 69

LE COUVREUR, FRANK
From East Prussia to the Golden Gate. New York: 1906. V. 68; 73

LEDDEROSE, LOTHAR
Ten Thousand Things: Module and Mass Production in Chinese Art. Princeton: 2000. V. 69

LEDERER, JOHN
The Discoveries of John Lederer, in There Several Marches from Virginia to the West of Carolina.... Rochester: 1902. V. 68

LEDERER, WILLIAM J.
Timothy's Song. New York: 1965. V. 71
The Ugly American. New York: 1958. V. 71

LEDFORD, PRESTON LAFAYETTE
Reminiscences of the Civil War 1861-1865. Thomasville: 1909. V. 69; 70

LE DRAN, HENRI FRANCOIS
Observations de Chirurgie.... Paris: 1731. V. 72

LEDWIDGE, FRANCIS
Songs of the Fields. London: 1916. V. 70

LEE, AMY FREEMAN
Hobby Horses. New York: 1940. V. 70; 72

LEE, ARTHUR
A Speech, Intended to Have Been Delivered in the House of Commons, in Support of the Petition from the General Congress at Philadelphia. London: 1775. V. 73

LEE, AUDREY
The Clarion People. New York: 1968. V. 72

LEE, AUSTIN
Miss Hogg and the Bronte Murders. 1957. V. 70

LEE, BABS
Measured Murder. New York: 1944. V. 72
A Model is Murdered. New York: 1942. V. 71

LEE, BRIAN
Bookplates by Simon Brett. Wakefield: 1989. V. 68; 71

LEE, C. Y.
The Flower Drum Song. New York: 1957. V. 71

LEE, CHANG-RAE
Native Speaker. New York: 1995. V. 69; 70; 72

LEE, CHARLES
Memoirs of the Life of the Late Charles Lee, Esq.... London: 1792. V. 73

LEE, CHARLES H.
The Judge Advocate's Vade Mecum; Embracing a General View of Military Law, and the Practice Before Courts Martial.... Richmond: 1863. V. 70

LEE, CHAUNCEY
The Trial of Virtue, a Scared Poem.... Hartford: 1806. V. 68

LEE, CHRISTOPHER
The Bright Cloud. Cambridge: 1961. V. 70
Poems. London: 1937. V. 69
World War One. Under the Sun - Poems. London: 1948. V. 72

LEE, D. N.
Art on the Rocks of Southern Africa. London: 1974. V. 69

LEE, DAVID
Wayburn Pig. Waldron Island: 1997. V. 69; 71

LEE, ELEANOR
History of the School of Nursery of the Presbyterian Hosptial, New York, 1892-1942. New York: 1942. V. 68

LEE, FITZHUGH
General (Robert E.) Lee. New York: 1894. V. 69

LEE, FRANCIS BAZLEY
Genealogical and Memorial History of the State of New Jersey. New York: 1910. V. 71

LEE, FRANCIS BAZLEY continued
Genealogical and Personal Memorial of Mercer County, New Jersey. New York: 1907. V. 71
History of Trenton, New Jersey. Trenton: 1895. V. 71
History of Trenton, New Jersey. Trenton: 1898. V. 71
New Jersey as a Colony and as a State. New York: 1902. V. 71

LEE, G. HERBERT
An Historical Sketch of the First Fifty Years of the Church of England in the Province of New Brunswick (1783-1833). St. John: 1880. V. 73

LEE, GEORGE W.
River George. New York: 1937. V. 69; 73

LEE, GUS
China Boy. New York: 1991. V. 68

LEE, GYPSY ROSE
The Strip-Tease Murders. London: 1942. V. 70

LEE, HANNAH FARNHAM
Familiar Sketches of Sculpture and Sculptors. Boston: 1854. V. 68; 69; 73

LEE, HARPER
Romance and High Adventure. Birmingham: 1993. V. 70
To Kill a Mockingbird. London: 1960. V. 68; 69; 70; 71; 72; 73
To Kill a Mockingbird. Philadelphia: 1960. V. 68; 69; 70; 72
To Kill a Mockingbird. New York: 1995. V. 68
To Kill a Mockingbird. New York: 1999. V. 68; 69

LEE, HARRIET
The New Peerage; or, Our Eyes May Deceive Us. Dublin: 1788. V. 69

LEE, HENRY
Memoirs of the War in the Southern Department of the United States. Philadelphia: 1812. V. 68
Memoirs of the War in the Southern Department of the United States. Washington: 1827. V. 68
Observations Upon the Writings of Thomas Jefferson with Particular Reference to the Attack they Contain on the Memory of the Late Gen. Henry Lee.... New York: 1832. V. 68; 72
Plain Truth Addressed to the People of Virginia. Richmond?: 1799. V. 69

LEE, HOLME
Legends from Fairyland, Narrating the History of Prince Glee and Princess Trill. London: 1907. V. 71

LEE, J. K.
The Volunteer's Hand Book. Richmond: 1861. V. 69; 70

LEE, JACK H.
Power River, Let'er Buck. Boston: 1930. V. 68; 73
West of Powder River: Tales of the Far West Told in Narrative Verse. New York: 1933. V. 72; 73

LEE, JAMES
An Introduction to Botany. Edinburgh: 1806. V. 72

LEE, JOHN D.
A Mormon Chronicle: The Diaries of John D. Lee 1848-1876. San Marino: 1955. V. 73

LEE, JOHN EDWARD
Delineations of Roman Antiquities Found at Caer Leon (the Ancient Isca Silurum) and the Neighbourhood. London: 1845. V. 68

LEE, JOSEPH
Ballads of Battle. London: 1916. V. 70

LEE, K. F.
Big Game Hunting and Marksmanship. 1941. V. 69; 72

LEE, L. P.
History of the Spirit Lake Massacre!. New Britain: 1857. V. 73

LEE, LAURIE
As I Walked Out One Midsummer Morning. London: 1969. V. 70
The Bloom of Candles. London: 1947. V. 70
I Can't Stay Long. London: 1975. V. 68
Land at War, the Official Story of British Farming 1939-1944. London: 1945. V. 70
The Sun My Monument. London: 1944. V. 70

LEE, LORENZO PORTER
History of The Spirit Lake Massacre! 8th March, 1857 and Miss Abigail Gardiner's Three Months Captivity Among The Indians. New Britain, CT: 1857. V. 72

LEE, LUTHER
Universalism Examined and Refuted, and the Doctrine of the Endless Punishment...Established. Watertown: 1836. V. 73

LEE, M.
Erte at 95: the Complete New Graphics. New York: 1987. V. 69; 72

LEE, MARGUERITE D.
Virginia Ghosts and Others. Richmond: 1932. V. 68

LEE, MARSHALL
The Trial of 6 Designers. Lock Haven: 1968. V. 69

LEE, NATHANIEL
The Tragedy of Nero, Emperour of Rome. London: 1675. V. 68

LEE, NELSON
The Life of a Fairy. London: 1850. V. 71
The Royal Acting Punch and Judy, As Played Before the Queen. London: 1880. V. 70

LEE, R. W.
Antique Fakes and Reproductions. 1938. V. 72
Antique Fakes and Reproductions. Framingham Centre: 1938. V. 69

LEE, RAWDON B.
History and Description of the Modern Dogs of Great Britain and Ireland. 1904. V. 68
A History and Description of the Modern Dogs of Great Britain and Ireland. 1906. V. 68; 70

LEE, ROBERT E.
Address to the Veterans. Richmond: 1907. V. 71
Recollections and Letters of General Robert E. Lee. New York: 1904. V. 70
The Wartime Papers of R. E. Lee. Boston: 1961. V. 69

LEE, ROBERT M.
China Safari. 1988. V. 69; 70; 72; 73

LEE, RONALD CURRIE
Gallant Dust. Philadelphia: 1936. V. 71

LEE, SARAH WALLIS BOWDICH
Memoirs of Baron Cuvier. London: 1833. V. 68
Trees, Plants and Flowers; their Beauties, Uses and Influences. 1854. V. 69

LEE, SHERMAN E.
History of Far Eastern Art. London: 1964. V. 72

LEE, SOPHIA
A Hermit's Tale. London: 1787. V. 70
The Recess; or a Tale of Other Time. Dublin: 1791. V. 68; 69; 73

LEE, STEPHEN DILL
Campaign of General Grant and Sherman Against Vicksburg in December 1862...Known as the Chicksaw Bayou Campaign. 1901. V. 70

LEE, TANITH
The Castle of Dark. London: 1978. V. 70
East of Midnight. London: 1977. V. 70
Madame Two Swords. 1988. V. 70
The Winter Players. London: 1976. V. 70

LEE, THORNE
The Monster Of Lazy Hook. New York: 1949. V. 72

LEE, TSUNG DAO
Selected Papers.... Boston: 1986. V. 72

LEE, VISCOUNT
A Catalogue of the Principal Works of Art at Chequers. London: 1923. V. 70

LEE, WESTON
Torrent in the Desert. Flagstaff: 1962. V. 69

LEE, WILLIAM MACK
History of the Life of Rev. Wm. Mack Lee. Newport News: 1918. V. 69; 70

LEECH, JOHN
Pictures of Life and Character. London: 1870. V. 69

LEECH, MARGARET
The Feathered Nest. New York: 1928. V. 71
Poems on Various Subjects. London: 1816. V. 69

LEECH, WILLIAM
The Obliviad: a Satire. New York: 1879. V. 71

LEEDS, E. T.
Celtic Ornament in the British Isles Down to AD 700. Oxford: 1933. V. 69; 73

LEEDS, LEWIS W.
Lectures on Ventilation: being a Course Delivered in the Franklin Institute of Philadelphia During the Winter of 1866-1867. New York: 1868. V. 71; 72

LEEDS, W. H.
Rudimentary Architecture; for th Use of Beginners and Students. London: 1859. V. 68

LEEPER, D. R.
The Argonauts of Forty-Nine - Some Reproductions of the Plains and the Diggings. 1894. V. 70

LEES, FREDERICK ARNOLD
The Flora of West Yorkshire. London: 1888. V. 73

LEES, G. ROBINSON
Life and Adventure Beyond Jordan. London: 1906. V. 72

LEES, GENE
And Sleep Till Noon. New York: 1966. V. 69; 71

LEESER, ISAAC
The Law of God. Philadelphia: 1845. V. 68

LEES-SMITH, HASTINGS BERTRAND
The Encyclopaedia of the Labour Movement. London: 1928. V. 71

LEET, FRANK R.
Purr and Miew. Akron: 1931. V. 70; 71; 73

LEEUWENHOEK, ANTONI VAN
Arcana Naturae Detecta...(with) Continuatio Arcanorum Naturae Detectoru, Qua Continetur Quicquid Hactenus. Delft: 1697. V. 68
Episolae Physioloicae. Delft: 1719. V. 70
On the Circulation of the Blood. Nieuwkoop: 1962. V. 72

LEFANT, JACQUES
Histoire de la Papesse Jeanne Fidelement Tire'e de la Dissertation Latine de Mr. De Spanheim. Cologne: 1694. V. 73

LE FANU, ALICIA
Memoirs of the Life and Writings of Mrs. Frances Sheridan, Mother of the Late Right Hon. Richard Brinsley Sheridan and Author of Sidney Biddulph, Nourjihad, and The Discovery. London: 1825. V. 69; 72

LE FANU, JOSEPH SHERIDAN
The Evil Guest. London: 1895. V. 70
The House by the Churchyard. 1866. V. 71
The House by the Churchyard. London: 1881. V. 68
The House by the Churchyard. London: 1899. V. 71
The Tenants of Malory; a Novel. London: 1867. V. 73
Uncle Silas: a Tale of Bartram Haugh. London: 1883. V. 68
Wylder's Hand. 1865. V. 71

LE FANU, W. R.
A Bio-Bibliogrpahy of Edward Jenner 1749-1823. Philadelphia: 1951. V. 71; 72

LE FANU, WILLIAM
A Catalogue of the Portraits and Other Paintings in the Royal College, of Surgeons of England. Edinburgh and London: 1960. V. 69

LEFEBURE, MOLLY
Scratch & Co. The Great Cat Expedition. London: 1968. V. 72

LEFEVRE, GEORGE SHAW
Agrarian Tenures: a Survey of the Laws and Customs Relating to the Holding of Land In England, Ireland and Scotland.... London: 1893. V. 72

LEFEVRE, L. A.
The Lions' Gate and the Beaver to the Empress. Vancouver: 1903. V. 68

LEFEVRE, RAOUL
Recuyell of the Historyes of Troye. 1892. V. 73

LEFFEL, JAMES
The Construction of Mill Dams: Comprising Also the Building of Race and Reservoir Embankments and Head Gates.... Springfield: 1874. V. 71

LEFFEL, JAMES, & CO.
Standard (and) Special and Samson Water Wheels. Springfield: 1894. V. 73

LEFFINGWELL, WILLIAM BRUCE
Shooting on Upland, Marsh and Stream. Chicago: 1890. V. 73
Wild Fowl Shooting. Chicago: 1890. V. 71

LEFFMANN, HENRY
About Dickens. Being a Few Essays on Themes Suggested by the Novels. Philadelphia: 1908. V. 69

LE FORS, JOE
Wyoming Peace Officer-An Autobiography. Laramie: 1953. V. 71

LEFROY, ANNE
Mary Hamilton. 1927. V. 73

LEFROY, EDWARD C.
Echoes from Theocritus: a Cycle of Sonnets. Blackheath: 1883. V. 73

LEFROY, W. CHAMBERS
The Ruined Abbeys of Yorkshire. London: 1883. V. 73

LE GAL, EUGENE
The School of the Guides or the Practical Soldier.... New Orlenas: 1861. V. 70

LE GALLIENNE, EVA
Flossie and Bossie. New York: 1949. V. 70

LE GALLIENNE, RICHARD
The Book-Bills of Narcissus: an Account Rendered by RLG. London: 1895. V. 69
English Poems. London and New York: 1892. V. 73
The Lonely Dancer and Other Poems. London: 1914. V. 69
My Ladies' Sonnets.... Liverpool: 1887. V. 73
Omar Repentant. London: 1908. V. 71
The Quest of the Golden Girl. London and New York: 1896. V. 69; 73
The Religion of a Literary Man. London: 1893. V. 69
Retrospective Reviews: a Literary Log. Volume I 1891-1893. (and) Volume II 1893-1895. London: 1896. V. 69
Robert Louis Stevenson: an Elegy and Other Poems Mainly Personal. London: 1895. V. 69
The Romance of Perfume. New York and Paris: 1928. V. 68; 70
The Romance of Zion Chapel. London and New York: 1898. V. 69
Rudyard Kipling: a Criticism. London: 1900. V. 69
There Was a Ship. Garden City: 1930. V. 70
Volumes in Folio. London: 1889. V. 73

LEGEND of Saint Robert The Hermit Of Knaresborough, The. Knaresborough: 1838. V. 72

LEGENDRE, ADRIEN MARIE
Essai sur la Theorie des Nombres. Paris: 1797. V. 73

LEGENDS Of Lancashire. 1841. V. 73

LEGENDS Of Westmorland and the Lake District. London: 1868. V. 71

LEGER, ALEXIS SAINT-LEGER
Anabasis. London: 1930. V. 69; 71; 73

LEGG, THOMAS
Low Life; or, One Half of the World, Knows Not How the Other Half Lives.... London: 1764. V. 70

LEGGATT, ASHLEY
Stalking Reminiscences 1914-1920. 1922. V. 70; 73

LEGGE, A. H.
Air Pollutants and Their Effects on the Terrestrial Ecosystem. New York: 1986. V. 71

LEGGE, ALFRED O.
Sunny Manitoba: Its People and Its Industries. London: 1893. V. 70

LEGGE, J. G.
The Millenium. Oxford: 1927. V. 70

LEGGETT, BERNARD J.
The Theory and Practice of Radiology. London: 1928. V. 68

THE LEGION Book. London: 1929. V. 71

LEGOUVE, GABRIEL
La Merite des Femmes, et Autres Poesies. Paris: 1809. V. 68; 72

LE GRAND, JULIA
Journal of Julia Le Grand. New Orleans 1862-1863. Richmond: 1911. V. 71

LE GRAND, M.
Fabliaux or Tales.... London: 1815. V. 72

LEGRAS, CHARLES
Terre D'Irlande. Paris: 1898. V. 69

LE GRICE, CHARLES VALENTINE
Analysis of Paley's Principles of Moral and Political Philosophy. Cambridge: 1799. V. 73
A Prize Declamation, Spoken in Trinity College Chapel, May 28, 1794, on the Following Subject: Richard Cromwell, If He Had Possessed His Father's Abilities, Might Have Retained the Protectorate. Cambridge: 1795. V. 73

LE GROS, W. B.
Fables and Tables, Suggested by the Frescoes of Pompeii and Herculaneum. London: 1835. V. 73

LE GUIN, URSULA K.
The Adventure of Cobbler's Rune. New Castle: 1982. V. 73
Always Coming Home. New York: 1985. V. 73
Always Coming Home. London: 1986. V. 73
The Beginning Place. New York: 1980. V. 73
The Compass Rose. Portland: 1982. V. 73
The Dispossessed. London: 1974. V. 73
The Dispossessed. New York: 1974. V. 69
Dreams Must Explain Themselves. New York: 1975. V. 73
The Farthest Shore. New York: 1972. V. 68; 71; 73
The Farthest Shore. London: 1973. V. 69; 71
From Elfland to Poughkeepsie. Portland: 1973. V. 73
Gwilan's Harp. Northridge: 1981. V. 73
In the Red Zone. Northridge: 1983. V. 73
The Language of the Night. New York: 1979. V. 73
Leese Webster. New York: 1979. V. 73
The Left Hand of Darkness. London: 1969. V. 73
The Left Hand of Darkness. New York: 1969. V. 70; 73
The Left Hand of Darkness. New York: 1972. V. 73
The Left Hand of Darkness. 1992. V. 71
Malafrena. New York: 1979. V. 73
The Other Wind: A New Earthsea Novel. New York: 2001. V. 71
Solomon Leviathan's Nine Hundred and Thirty-First Trip Around the World. New Castle: 1983. V. 73
The Tombs of Atuan. New York: 1971. V. 68; 71
The Tombs of Atuan. London: 1972. V. 69
The Visionary: the Life Story of Flicker of the Serpentine. Santa Barbara: 1984. V. 68
The Water is Wide. Portland: 1976. V. 73
Wild Angels. Santa Barbara: 1975. V. 73
Wild Oats and Fireweed. New York: 1988. V. 73
The Wind's Twelve Quarters. New York: 1975. V. 73
The Wind's Twelve Quarters. London: 1976. V. 70
A Wizard of Earthsea. 1968. V. 70

LEHANE, DENNIS
Darkness, Take My Hand. New York: 1996. V. 69; 70; 73
A Drink Before the War. New York: 1994. V. 68; 69; 70; 71; 73
Gone Baby Gone. New York: 1998. V. 69; 72
Mystic River. New York: 2001. V. 70
Prayers for Rain. New York: 1999. V. 70; 71
Sacred. New York: 1997. V. 73

LEHMAN, ANTHONY
Paul Landacre: a Life and a Legacy. Los Angeles: 1983. V. 70; 73

LEHMAN, PAUL EVAN
Blood of the West. New York: 1934. V. 72

LEHMAN, V. W.
Forgotten Legions. El Paso: 1969. V. 72

LEHMANN, JOHN
Autobiography. London: 1955-1966. V. 72
Folios of New Writing. London: 1940. V. 72
The Garden Revisited and Other Poems. London: 1931. V. 73
The Noise of History. London: 1934. V. 70
Orpheus. London: 1948-1949. V. 72
Thrown to the Woolfs. London: 1978. V. 70
Virginia Woolf and Her World. London: 1975. V. 70
The Whispering Gallery: Autobiography.... London: 1955-1966. V. 70

LEHMANN, LOTTE
Midway in My Song. Indianapolis: 1938. V. 69

LEHMANN, R. C.
Charles Dickens as Editor. London: 1912. V. 69

LEHMANN, ROSAMOND
Dusty Answer. London: 1927. V. 70
The Echoing Grove. London: 1953. V. 72
A Note in Music. London: 1930. V. 68; 70
The Weather in the Streets. London: 1936. V. 70

LEHMANN, V. W.
Forgotten Legions. El Paso: 1964. V. 71
Forgotten Legions. El Paso: 1969. V. 68

LEHMANN, W.
The Art of Old Peru. New York: 1924. V. 69
The Art of Old Peru. New York: 1974. V. 69

LEHMANN-HAUPT, HELLMUT
Bookbinding in America, Three Essays. New York and London: 1967. V. 70
Two Essays on the Decretum of Gratian...Together with an Original Leaf Printed on Vellum by Peter Schoeffer at Mainz in 1472. Los Angeles: 1971. V. 73

LEHNDORFF, VERA
Veruschka Transfigurations. London: 1986. V. 70

LEIBER, FRITZ
The Green Millennium. New York: 1954. V. 72
The Green Millennium. London: 1977. V. 73
Night's Black Agents. 1947. V. 69
The Wanderer. London: 1967. V. 73

LEIBNIZ, GOTTFRIED WILHELM
Protogaea Sive de Prima Facie Telluris et Antiquissimae Historiae Vestigiis in Ipsis Naturae. Gottingen: 1743. V. 68

LEIBOVITZ, ANNIE
Photographs 1970-1990. New York: 1990. V. 68
Photographs 1970-1990. New York: 1991. V. 68; 73

LEIDING, HARRIETE KERSHAW
Charleston, Historic and Romantic. Philadelphia: 1931. V. 71

LEIGH, CHARLES
The Natural History of Lancashire and the Peak District with an Account of the British, Phoenician, Armenian Greek and Roman Antiquities in Those Parts. Oxford: 1700. V. 73

LEIGH COURT
A Catalogue of the Pictures at Leigh Court, Near Bristol; the Seat of Philip John Miles. London: 1822. V. 71

LEIGH, SAMUEL
Leigh's New Picture of London. London: 1834. V. 71

LEIGH, WILLIAM R.
The Western Pony. New York: 1933. V. 69; 71

LEIGH FERMOR, PATRICK
Between the Woods and the Water. London: 1986. V. 71

LEIGHLY, JOHN
California as an Island: an Illustrated Essay.... San Francisco: 1972. V. 68; 72

LEIGHTON, A.
American Gardens in Eighteenth Century. Boston: 1976. V. 68
Early American Gardens For Meate or Medicine. Boston: 1970. V. 71

LEIGHTON, ALEXANDER H.
Come Near. New York: 1971. V. 73
The Navajo Door. 1944. V. 69

LEIGHTON, CAROLINE C.
Life at Puget Sound, with Sketches of Travel in Washington Territory, British Columbia, Oregon and California 1865-181. Boston and New York: 1884. V. 70

LEIGHTON, CLARE
Four Hedges. A Gardener's Chronicle. London: 1935. V. 70
Sometime Never. London: 1939. V. 69
Woodcuts. London: 1930. V. 69

LEIGHTON, DOROTHEA
Children of the People. Cambridge: 1947. V. 69

LEIGHTON, JOHN
Comic-Art Manufactures. London: 1851. V. 71
London Cries and Public Edifices. London: 1856. V. 71

LEIGHTON, MARIE
Convict 99. London: 1898. V. 68

LEIGHTON, R.
The New Book of the Dog. 1900. V. 68; 70

LEIGHTON, ROBERT
The Whole Works.... London: 1830. V. 70

LEIGHTON, W. A.
A Flora of Shropshire. Shrewsbury: 1841. V. 69
The Lichen-Flora of Great Britain, Ireland, and the Channel Islands. Shrewsbury: 1879. V. 72

LEINSTEIN, MADAME
Punctuation in Verse; or, the Good Child's Book of Stops. Philadelphia: 1835. V. 71

LEIPNIK, F. L.
A History of French Etching from the Sixteenth Century to the Present Day. London: 1924. V. 69; 72

LEIRIS, MICHEL
African Art. New York: 1968. V. 71
Francis Bacon: Full Face and Profile. New York: 1987. V. 72

LEITCH, A.
A Scottish Fly-Fisher. 1911. V. 73

LEITCH, MAURICE
The Liberty Lad. London: 1965. V. 72

LEITH, A. A.
The Birthday Book of Flower and Song.... London and New York: 1877. V. 71

LEITH, MARY CHARLOTTE JULIA
A Martyr Bishop and Other Verses. London: 1878. V. 69

LEITHART, JOHN
Practical Observations on the Mechanical Structure, Mode of Formation, the Repletion of Filling Up and the Intersection and Relative Age of Mineral Veins.... London: 1838. V. 73

LEITH-ROSS, S.
African Women. A Study of the Ibo of Nigeria. London: 1939. V. 69

LEITICH, A. T.
Wiener Biedermeier. Kultur, Kunst & Leben der alten Kaiserstadt vom Wiener Kongress bis zum Sturmjahr 1845. Bielefeld: 1941. V. 72

LEJARD, ANDRE
The Art of the French Book. London. V. 72

LE JEUNE, J. M.
Elements of Shorthand After the Duployan System Arranged for the English Language. Kamloops: 1893. V. 70

LEJEUNE, RITA
The Legend of Roland in the Middle Ages. London: 1971. V. 68

LELAND, CHARLES G.
Algonquin Legends of New England, or Myths and Folk Lore of the Micmac, Passamaquoddy and Penobscot Tribes. London: 1884. V. 73

LELAND, EFFIE WILLIAMS
Crossin' Over. Columbia: 1937. V. 73

LELIEVRE, J. F.
Nouveau Jardinier De La Louisiane.... Nouvelle Oreleans: 1838. V. 68

LELONG, B. M.
Culture of the Citrus in California. Sacramento: 1900. V. 68

LELONG, D. G.
Bruce Goff: Toward Absolute Architecture. New York: 1988. V. 69

LE MAIR, H. WILLEBEEK
Christmas Carols for Young Children. 1976. V. 73

LE MARCHAND, ELIZABETH
Alibi For A Corpse. London: 1969. V. 72
Buried In The Past. London: 1974. V. 72
Change For The Worse. London: 1980. V. 72
Cyanide With Compliments. London: 1972. V. 72
The Glade Manor Murder. London: 1988. V. 72
Unhappy Returns. London: 1977. V. 72

LEMARCHAND, JACQUES
Genevieve. London: 1974. V. 68

LE MAY, ALAN
Empire for a Lady. New York: 1937. V. 71
One of Us Is a Murderer. Garden City: 1930. V. 70
The Searchers. New York: 1954. V. 69; 71
The Unforgiven. New York: 1957. V. 70

LEMERCHER DE LONGPRE, CHARLES
Great Britain in 1833. London: 1833. V. 69
Great Britain in 1833. Philadelphia: 1833. V. 69; 72

LEMERY, LOUIS
A Treatise of all Sorts of Foods, Both Animal and Vegetable, Also of Drinkables. London: 1745. V. 71

LEMERY, NICHOLAS
A Course of Chymistry. London: 1677. V. 72

LEMIRE, RONALD J.
Normal and Abnormal Development of the Human Nervous System. 1975. V. 68

LEMMON, ED
Boss Cowman. The Recollections of Ed Lemmon 1857-1946. Lincoln: 1969. V. 70

LEMNIUS, LE VINUS
Di Miraculis Occultus Naturae, Libri III. 1588. V. 69

LEMOINE, HENRY
Typographical Antiquities. History, Origin and Progress of the Art of Printing from Its First Invention in Germany.... 1797. V. 72

LE MOINE, J. M.
Picturesque Quebec: a Sequel to Quebec Past and Present. Montreal: 1882. V. 73

LEMON, MARK
The Chimes.... London: 1845. V. 70
A Christmas Hamper. London: 1860. V. 68

LE MOYNE, PIERRE
Of the Art Both of Writing and Judging of History with Reflections Upon Ancient as Well As Modern Historians Shewing through What Defects there are so Few Good.... London: 1695. V. 69

LENCKER, HANS
Perspectiva.... Nuremberg: 1571. V. 72

LENCLOS, NINON DE
Memoirs of Ninon de Lenclos. Philadelphia: 1806. V. 69

LENDENFELD, R. VON
A Monograph of the Horny Sponges. 1889. V. 69

LENGEL, FRANCESA
The Carnal Days of Helen Seferis. Paris: 1954. V. 73

L'ENGLE, MADELEINE
Dare to be Creative!. Washington: 1984. V. 73
Many Waters. 1986. V. 71

LENGLET-DUFRESNOY, N.
Le Cabinet Satyrique, ou Recueil de Vers Piquans & Galliards de Ces Temps. Amsterdam?: 1697. V. 69

LENIN, VLADIMIR IL'ICH
Collected Works. Moscow. V. 71

LENNART, ISOBEL
Funny Girl. New York: 1964. V. 71

LENNBERG, ROY
Custer - A Sketchbook of The Seventh Cavalry at The Little Big Horn. Salem, OR: 1989. V. 72

LENNON, JOHN
In His Own Write. London: 1964. V. 68
In His Own Write and a Spaniard in the Works. London: 1981. V. 72
A Spaniard in the Works/En spann jord i maskineriet. Sweden: 1997. V. 72

LENNON, WALTER CAULFIELD
Proposals for Building a Pier or Harbour in Madras Road, as Submitted to the Hon. the President in Council at Fort St. George in July 1798; together with Extracts from the Minutes of that Government Concerning the Same. London: 1801. V. 73

LENNOX, CHARLOTTE
The Female Quixote; or, the Adventures of Arabella. London: 1752. V. 70
Shakespeare Illustrated; (with) Shakespeare Illustrated, the Third and Final Volume. London: 1753-1754. V. 73

LENORMANT, AMELIE
Madame de Stael and the Grand Duchess Louise. London: 1862. V. 69

LENSKI, LOIS
Arabella and Her Aunts. New York: 1932. V. 71
Blueberry Corners. New York: 1940. V. 71
Cowboy Small. New York: 1949. V. 71
Let's Play House. New York: 1944. V. 70
Shoo-Fly Girl. Philadelphia: 1963. V. 73
Spring is Here. New York: 1945. V. 70
Strawberry Girl. Philadelphia: 1945. V. 70; 71
Sugarplum House. New York: 1935. V. 71
We Live in the North. Philadelphia: 1965. V. 73

LENT, JEFFREY
In the Fall. New York: 2000. V. 68; 72

LENZ, G. R.
Opiates. 1986. V. 73

LEON & BROTHER
Catalogue of First Editions of American Authors, Poets, Philosophers, Historians, Statesmen, Essays, Dramatists, Novelists, Travellers, Humorists, etc. New York: 1885. V. 68

LEON, SIMON I.
Encyclopedia of Candy and Ice-Cream Making. New York: 1959. V. 72

LEONARD, DANIEL
Massachusettensis: or a Series of Letters.... Boston: 1776. V. 70

LEONARD, E. C.
The Acanthaceae of Colombia. Washington: 1951-1953. V. 71
The Acanthaceae of Colombia. Washington: 1951-1958. V. 68

LEONARD, ELIZA LUCY
The Ruby Ring; or the Transformations. London: 1816. V. 70; 72

LEONARD, ELMORE
Bandits. New York: 1987. V. 69; 73
The Big Bounce. Greenwich: 1969. V. 69; 73
The Big Bounce. New York: 1969. V. 71
The Big Bounce. New York: 1989. V. 71; 73
The Bounty Hunters. Boston: 1954. V. 71; 73
Cat Chaser. New York: 1982. V. 68; 73
City Primeval. New York: 1980. V. 68; 69; 70
Dutch Treat. 1985. V. 73
Escape from Five Shadows. Boston: 1956. V. 69; 70
Fifty-Two Pickup. London: 1974. V. 73
Forty Lashes Less One. New York: 1972. V. 71; 73
Freaky Deaky. New York: 1988. V. 73
Get Shorty. New York: 1990. V. 72; 73
Glitz. Middlesex: 1985. V. 73
Glitz. New York: 1985. V. 68; 70; 73
Hombre. New York: 1961. V. 69; 70; 72; 73
Hombre. New York: 1989. V. 73
The Hunted. New York: 1977. V. 68; 69; 70; 71; 73
The Hunted. London: 1978. V. 69
Killshot. New York: 1989. V. 73
La Brava. New York: 1983. V. 68; 69; 73
La Brava. Middlesex: 1984. V. 73
Last Stand at Saber River. New York: 1949. V. 73
Last Stand at Saber River. Thorndike, Maine: 1986. V. 71
Maximum Bob. New York: 1991. V. 68; 72; 73
Mr. Majestyk. New York: 1974. V. 69
The Moonshine War. New York: 1969. V. 70
The Moonshine War. Culver City: 1970. V. 71
Notebooks. Northridge: 1990. V. 69; 73
Rum Punch. Hastings-on-Hudson: 1962. V. 70
Rum Punch. Hastings-On-Hudson: 1992. V. 68; 69; 72; 73
Split Images. New York: 1981. V. 68; 70; 71
Stick. New York: 1983. V. 68; 69; 70
Stick. London: 1984. V. 73
Swag. New York: 1976. V. 68; 69; 70; 71; 72; 73
The Switch. New York: 1978. V. 69; 70; 73
The Switch. London: 1979. V. 68; 69; 70; 71
The Tall T. New York: 1957. V. 71
Tishomingo Blues. New York: 2002. V. 72
Touch. New York: 1987. V. 73
Unknown Man No. 89. London: 1977. V. 70; 71; 72
Unknown Man No. 89. New York: 1977. V. 68; 73

LEONARD, IRVING A.
The Mercurio Volante of Don Carlos De Siquenza Y Gongora - an Account of the First Expedition of Don Diego De Vargas into New Mexico in 1692. Los Angeles: 1932. V. 68; 73

LEONARD, SETH
The Book of Light for All Nations of the Earth. 1838. V. 68

LEONARD, THOMAS H.
From Indian Trail to Electric Rail. History of the Atlantic Highlands, Sandy Hook and Original Portland Point.... Atlantic Highlands: 1923. V. 71

LEONARD, WILLIAM ELLERY
Two Lives: a Poem. New York: 1922. V. 71

LEONARDI, DOMENICO FELICE
La Delizie della Villa di Castellazzo Descritte in Verso. Milan: 1743. V. 70; 72

LEONARDO, RICHARD ANTHONY
History of Gynecology. New York: 1944. V. 68

LEONARDO DA VINCI
Characturas from Drawings by Wenceslaus Hollar Out of the Portland Museum. London: 1786. V. 71
The Notebooks. London: 1938. V. 72
The Notebooks. New York: 1938. V. 68
El Tratado de la Pintura Por Leonardo da Vinci, Y Los Tres Libros Que Sobre el Mismo Arte Escribio Leon Bautista Alberti. Madrid: 1784. V. 68
A Treatise of Painting. 1721. V. 71; 73

LEONI, MICHELE
Prose. Lugano: 1829. V. 68

LEOPOLD, ALDO
Round River: From the Journals of Aldso Leopold. New York: 1953. V. 70

LEOPOLD CASELLA & CO.
The Dyeing of Wool Including Wool Printing with Dyestuffs of Leopold Cassella.... Frankfort: 1905. V. 71

LEPELLETIER, EDMOND
Madame Sans Gene, a Romance.... London: 1897. V. 68

LE PEROUSE, JEAN FRANCOIS GALAUP DE
The Voyage of La Perouse Round the World, in the Years 1785, 1786, 1787 and 1788.... London: 1798. V. 69

LEPINEY, JAQUES
Climbs on Mont Blanc. London: 1930. V. 69

LEPINOIS, ERNEST DE BUCHERE DE
Souvenirs de Couy, Dessins Lithographies.... Coucy: 1834. V. 70

LE PLONGEON, ALICE DIXON
Queen Moo's Talisman. London: 1902. V. 72

LEPREUX, GEORGES
Gallia Typographica ou Repertoire Biographique et Chronologique de Tous Les Imprimeurs de France. Paris: 1909-1914. V. 68

LE PRINCE DE BEAUMONT, JEANNE MARIE
Magasin des Enfans. The Young Ladies Magzine, or Polite Tutoress. Dublin: 1786. V. 70

LEPSIUS, RICHARD
Discoveries in Egypt, Ethiopia, and the Peninsula of Sinai, in the Years 1842-1845. London: 1853. V. 68; 71

LE QUEUX, WILLIAM
Behind the Bronze Door. New York: 1923. V. 72; 73
The Doctor of Pimlico. New York: 1920. V. 70
Guilty Bonds. New York: 1892. V. 71
Her Majesty's Minister. London: 1901. V. 68
Hidden Hands. London: 1926. V. 69
Hushed Up!. London: 1911. V. 68
The Lawless Hand. 1928. V. 68
The Mysterious Mr. Miller. London: 1906. V. 68
Of Royal Blood. London: 1900. V. 72
The Place of Dragons. London: 1919. V. 71
The Power of the Borgias: The Story of the Great Film. London: 1921. V. 69
Rasputinism in London. London: 1919. V. 69
A Secret Service Being Strange Tales of a Nihilist. London: 1896. V. 70
Zoraida. London: 1895. V. 69

LERCHE, WILLIAM
The Esophagus and Pharynx in Action. Springfield: 1950. V. 68

LERICHE, RENE
The Surgery of Pain. London: 1939. V. 68

LERMAN, LEO
The Museum, One Hundred Years and the Metropolitan Museum of Art. New York: 1969. V. 71

LERMAN, RHODA
Eleanor. New York: 1979. V. 72

LERMONTOV, MIKHAIL YUREVICH
A Hero of Our Own Times. London: 1940. V. 71; 73

LERNER, ALAN JAY
Paint Your Wagon. New York: 1952. V. 69; 71

LEROI-GOURHAN, ANDRE
Treasures of Prehistoric Art. New York: 1967. V. 71; 73

LE ROS, CHRISTIAN
Christmas Day and How It Was Spent by Four Persons in the House of Fograss, Fograss, Mowton and Snorton, Bankers. London: 1873. V. 68; 73

LE ROUGE, GEORGE LOUIS
Les Curiositez de Paris, de Versailles, De Marly De Vincennes, De Saint Cloud, et Des Environs. Paris: 1742. V. 70

LEROUX, GASTON
The Bride of the Sun. London: 1916. V. 69
The Double Life. New York: 1909. V. 68
The Man of a Hundred Faces. New York: 1930. V. 73
The Mystery of the Yellow Room. New York: 1908. V. 69; 70
Nomads of the Night. New York: 1925. V. 68
The Phantom Clue. New York: 1926. V. 73
The Phantom of the Opera. New York: 1911. V. 71
The Secret of the Night. New York: 1914. V. 71

LEROUX, HUGHES
Acrobats and Mountebanks. London: 1890. V. 70

LEROY, J. T.
The Heart is Deceitful Above All Things. New York and London: 2001. V. 71; 73

LE ROY, JULIEN DAVID
Les Ruines des Plus Beaux Monuments de la Grece. Paris: 1758. V. 68; 70

LE SAGE, ALAIN RENE
Aventuras de Gil Blas De Santillana Robadas a espana.... Valencia/Benito/Monfort: 1788-1789. V. 71
The Adventures of Gil Blas of Santillane. London: 1785. V. 73
The Adventures of Gil Blas of Santillane. London: 1807. V. 71
The Adventures of Gil Blas of Santillane. London: 1819. V. 71
The Adventures of Gil Blas of Santillane. London: 1881. V. 68; 72
The Devil Upon Two Sticks. London: 1757. V. 70; 71

LESCARBOT, MARC
Nova Francia. A Description of Acadia. 1606. New York & London: 1928. V. 73
The Theatre of Neptune in New France. Boston: 1927. V. 73

LESH, U. S.
A Knight of the Golden Circle. Boston: 1911. V. 70

LESIEUTRE, ALAIN
Spirit and Splendour of Art Deco. New Jersey: 1974. V. 72

LESKOV, NICOLAI S.
Evrei V. Rossii. St. Petersburg: 1884. V. 73

LESKY, ERNA
The Vienna Medical School of the 19th Century. Baltimore and London: 1976. V. 68

LESLEY, CRAIG
River Song. Boston: 1989. V. 70; 73
Winterkill. Boston: 1984. V. 69
Winterkill. Boston: 1989. V. 72

LESLEY, LEWIS BURT
Uncle Sam's Camels. Cambridge: 1928. V. 70
Uncle Sam's Camels. Cambridge: 1929. V. 73

LESLIE, ALFRED
100 Views Along the Road. New York: 1988. V. 68

LESLIE, AMY
Some Players: Personal Sketches. Chicago: 1899. V. 69

LESLIE, C. R.
Hand-Book for Young Painters. London: 1870. V. 68
Life and Letters of John Constable. London: 1896. V. 73

LESLIE, CHARLES
Gallienus Redivivus, or, Murther Will Out &c. Edinburgh: 1695. V. 73

LESLIE, CHARLES ROBERT
Autobiographical Recollections. London: 1860. V. 73

LESLIE, DAVID
Among the Zulus and Amatongas with Sketches of the Natives, Their Language and Customs.... Edinburgh: 1875. V. 71

LESLIE, FRANK
Frank Leslie's Illustrated History of the Civil War. New York: 1895. V. 71

LESLIE, JOHN
De Illustrium Foeminarum in Repub(lica) Administranda.... Reims: 1580. V. 68; 69
The Philosophy of Arithmetic: Exhbiting a Progressive View of the Theory and Practice of Calculation.... Edinburgh: 1820. V. 73

LESLIE, LIONEL A. D.
Wilderness Trails In Three Continents. London: 1931. V. 72

LESLIE, P. DUGUD
A Philosophical Enquiry into the Cause of Animal Heat.... London: 1778. V. 69

LESQUEREUX, L.
Contributions to the Fossil Flora of the Western Territories. Part II. Washington: 1878. V. 68
The Flora of the Dakota Group. Washington: 1891. V. 72

LESSER, ALEXANDER
The Pawnee Ghost Dance Hand Game - A Study of Cultural Change. New York: 1933. V. 69

LESSER, ELLEN
The Other Woman. New York: 1988. V. 68

LESSER, MILTON
Spaceman, Go Home. 1961. V. 70
The Star Seekers. Philadelphia: 1953. V. 69

LESSER, S., & SONS LTD., SHEFFIELD
Catalogue of Sterling Silver Ware. London: 1910?. V. 68

LESSING, DORIS
African Stories. London: 1964. V. 73
African Stories. New York: 1965. V. 73
Briefing for a Descent into Hell. London: 1971. V. 73
Briefing for a Descent into Hell. New York: 1971. V. 73
Canopus in Argos: Archives. London: 1979-1983. V. 73
Children of Violence. Volume III. A Ripple from the Story. Volume Four: Landlocked. New York: 1966. V. 69
The Diary of a Good Neighbor. New York: 1983. V. 72
The Four-Gated City. London: 1969. V. 73

LESSING, DORIS continued
The Four-Gated City. New York: 1969. V. 69
Fourteen Poems. Middlesex: 1959. V. 73
Going Home. London: 1957. V. 73
The Golden Notebook. New York: 1962. V. 73
The Golden Notebook. London: 1972. V. 73
The Good Terrorist. London: 1985. V. 68; 73
The Good Terrorist. New York: 1985. V. 69
The Grass is Singing. London: 1950. V. 73
The Grass is Singing. New York: 1950. V. 73
The Habit of Loving. London: 1957. V. 73
In Pursuit of the English. London: 1960. V. 68
Landlocked. London: 1965. V. 73
Love, Again. New York: 1995. V. 73
A Man and Two Women. London: 1963. V. 73
A Man and Two Women. New York: 1963. V. 73
The Marriages Between Zones Three, Four and Five. New York: 1980. V. 73
Martha Quest. London: 1952. V. 73
The Memoirs of a Survivor. London: 1974. V. 73
The Memoirs of a Survivor. New York: 1975. V. 73
Play with a Tiger. London: 1962. V. 73
Prisons We Choose to Live Inside. London: 1987. V. 73
A Proper Marriage. London: 1954. V. 73
Retreat to Innocence. London: 1956. V. 73
A Ripple from the Storm. London: 1958. V. 73
The Sentimental Agents in the Volyen Empire. New York: 1983. V. 73
Shikasta. New York: 1979. V. 73
The Sirian Experiments - the Report by Ambien II of the Five. London: 1981. V. 70
The Story of a Non-Marrying Man and Other Stories. London: 1972. V. 73
The Summer Before Dark. London: 1973. V. 69; 73
The Summer Before Dark. New York: 1973. V. 72
This Was the Old Chief's Country. New York: 1951. V. 73
This was the Old Chief's Country and the Sun Between their Feet. London: 1972-1973. V. 73
To Room Nineteen and The Temptation of Jack Orkney. London: 1978. V. 73
Walking in the Shade. Volume Two of My Autobiography. 1949-1962. New York: 1997. V. 70

LESSING, GOTTHOLD EPHRAIM
Laokoon: Ober Uber die Grenzen der Mahlerey und Poesie. Berlin: 1766. V. 72

LESS-MILNE, JAMES
Earls of Creation - Five Great Patrons of Eighteenth-Century Art. London: 1962. V. 72

LESSON, RENE PRIMEVERE
Histoire Naturelle des Oiseaux de Paradis et des Epimaques. Paris: 1829-1830. V. 73

LES STYLES, FRANCAIS
Le Mobilier Du Modern Age Au Modern Style 1500-1900. Paris: 1964. V. 72

LESTER, CHARLES EDWARDS
The Glory and the Shame of England. New York: 1841. V. 70
The Glory and the Shame of England. New York: 1866. V. 71
The Light and Dark of the Rebellion. Philadelphia: 1863. V. 73

LESTER, HENRY M.
Leica 1937 Photo Annual. New York: 1936. V. 68

LESTER, JOHN ERASTUS
The Atlantic to the Pacific. London: 1873. V. 68; 72

LESTER, JULIUS
Search for a New Land. New York: 1968. V. 72

LESTER, W. W.
A Digest of the Military and Naval Laws of the Confederate States. Columbia: 1864. V. 70

LESTERMAN, JOHN
The Adventures of a Trafalgar Lad - a Tale of the Sea. London: 1926. V. 69

LESTOCK, RICHARD
Vice-Adm--l L-sto-k's Account of the Late Engagement Near Toulon, Between His Majesty's Fleet and the Fleets of France and Spain.... London: 1745. V. 73

LE SUEUR, MERIDEL
North Star Country. New York: 1945. V. 72
Salute to Spring. New York: 1940. V. 69

LESY, MICHAEL
Wisconsin Death Trip. New York: 1973. V. 68

LETCHER, OWEN
Big Game Hunting in North-Eastern Rhodesia. London: 1911. V. 68

LETHEBY, H.
Report to the Special Gas Committee of the Honourable the Commissioners of Sewers of the City of London, on the Existing Conditions and Circumstances Affecting the Gas Supply in the City of London 10th December 1864. London: 1865. V. 69

LETHEM, JOANTHAN
Gun With Occasional Music. New York: 1994. V. 70

LETHEM, JONATHAN
Amnesia Moon. New York: 1995. V. 68; 72
As She Climbed Across the Table. New York: 1997. V. 70
Gun, with Occasional Music. New York: 1994. V. 68; 69; 71; 72; 73
Motherless Brooklyn. New York: 1999. V. 73

LETI, GREGORIO
The Amours of Messalina Late Queen of Albion.... London: 1689. V. 68; 69; 73

LETOURNEAU, CHARLES
Sociology Based Upon Ethnography. London: 1881. V. 71

LET'S Have a Game. Stories for You and Me. London: 1911. V. 69

LET'S Laugh. London: 1939. V. 70

LETT, WILLIAM PITTMAN
Recollections of Bytown and Its Old Inhabitants. Ottawa: 1874. V. 73

A LETTER Concerning the Consequences of an Incorporating Union, In Relation to Trade. Edinburgh: 1706. V. 73

A LETTER From A Gentleman in Scotland, to His Friend in London, Upon the Highland Insurrection. Edinburgh?: 1745. V. 69

A LETTER from One of the Society of Friends, Relative to the Conscientious Scrupulousness of Its Members to Bear Arms. Philadelphia?: 1795. V. 68

A LETTER to a Freeholder, on the Late Reduction of the Land Tax to One Shilling in the Pound. By a Member of the House of Commons. London: 1732. V. 72

A LETTER To a Member of Congress, on the Subject of a British War. Providence: 1812. V. 73

A LETTER to James Scarlett, Esq., M.. On His Bill Relating to the Poor Laws. London: 1821. V. 71

LETTER to the Founders of the Highland Society of Edinburgh. Edinburgh: 1784. V. 73

A LETTER to the Rev. Mr. Madan, Concerning the Chapter on Polygamy, in His Late Publication Entitled Thelyphthora. London: 1780. V. 68

LETTER to the Rt. Hon. C. P. Thomson, M.P. President of the Board of Trade, &c. in Explanation and Defence of the Principles and Practices of Joint Stock Banking. Manchester: 1834. V. 70

LETTERMAN, JONATHAN
Medical Recollections of the Army of the Potomac. New York: 1866. V. 73

LETTERS and Papers on Agriculture, Planting &c. Selected from the Correspondence of the Bath and West of England Society, for the Encouragement of Agriculture, Arts, Manufactures and Commerce. Bath: 1802. V. 71

LETTERS From the Mountains Being the Real Correspondence of a Lady, Between the Years 1773 and 1807. London: 1813. V. 71

LETTERS of an Irish Catholic Layman: Being an Examination of the Present State of Irish Affairs in Relation to the Irish Church and the Holy See. 1885. V. 70

LETTERS on the Condition of Kentucky in 1825. New York: 1916. V. 71

LETTERS To a Bookstore. New York: 1988. V. 70

LETTERS to Thomas Paine; in Answer to His Late Publication on the Rights of Man.... London: 1791. V. 73

LETTICE, JOHN
A Plan for te Safe Removal of Inhabitants, Not Military, from Towns and Villages on the Coasts of Great Britain and Ireland, in the Case of the Threatened Invasion; with Reflections Calculated to Hasten Preparations for that Measure. London: 1803. V. 69

LETTRES d'un Viellard a un Jeune Homme Qui Entre dans le Monde. Paris: 1788. V. 73

LETTRES Edifiantes et Curieuses, Ecrites des Missions Etrangers par Quelques Missionaires de La Compagnie de Jesus V. Recueil. Paris: 1705. V. 70

LETTS, J. M.
California Illustrated: Including a Description of the Panama and Nicaragua Routes. New York: 1853. V. 69
A Pictorial View of California.... New York: 1853. V. 73

LETTSOM, JOHN COAKLEY
An Appeal Addressed to the Calm Reflection of the Authors of the Critical Review. London: 1803. V. 70
Dissertatio Inauguralis Medica, Sistens Observationes ad Vires Theae Pertinenies.... Ludg. Batavorum: 1765. V. 73
Histoire De L'Origine De La Medicine. London and Paris: 1787. V. 72
Histoire Naturelle Du The Avec Des Observations Sur ses Qualites Medicales. Paris: 1773. V. 72
History of the Origin of Medicine: an Oration, Delivered at the Anniversary Meeting of the Medical Society of London, January 19, 1778. London: 1778. V. 68; 72
The Naturalist's and Traveller's Companion. London: 1772. V. 73
The Naturalist's and Traveller's Companion. London: 1774. V. 70; 72
The Naturalist's and Traveller's Companion. London: 1799. V. 69; 73
Observations on the Cow-Pock. London: 1801. V. 73
Observations Preparatory to the Use of Dr. Myersbach's Medicines.... London: 1776. V. 70
Recollections of Dr. Rush by Dr. Lettsom. London: 1815. V. 70
Selections from the Medical Papers and Correspondence of the Late John Coakley Lettsom.... London: 1871. V. 70

LETTY, C.
Wild Flowers of the Transvaal. Pretoria: 1962. V. 68; 71

LEUPOLD, JACOB
Theatrum Machinarum Molarium, OderSchau-Platz der Muhlen-Bau-Kunst. Leipzig: 1735. V. 71
Theatrum Pontificale, oder Shau-Platz der Brucken und Brucken-aues.... Leipzig: 1726. V. 69

LEUPP, HAROLD L.
Spain and Spanish America in the Libraries of the University of California. New York: 1969. V. 72

LEUSDEN, JOHANNE
Philologus Hebraeus, in quo Pleraeque Quaestiones Generales Philologico-Hebraeum. (with) Philolgus Hebraeomixtus, Una Cuma Spicilegio Philogico... (with) Philologus Hebraeo-Graecus Generalis Continens Quaestiones Hebraeo-Graecas.... Utrecht: 1657. V. 72

LEVACK, DANIEL J. H.
PKD. A Philip K. Dick Bibliography. San Francisco: 1980. V. 68

LEVAILLANT, FRANCOIS
Histoire Naturelle d'une Partie D'Oiseaux Nouveaux et Rares de L'Amerique et des Indes.... Paris: 1801-1802. V. 73

LEVASSEUR, EMILE
Histoire des Classes Ouvrieres de France Depuis la Conquete de Jules Cesar jusqu'a la Revolution. Paris: 1859. V. 73

LE VAYER DE BOUTIGNY, ROLLAND
A Dissertation Shewing the Invalidity of All Proof by Similitude of Hands, in Criminal Cases. London: 1744. V. 70

LEVEILLE, JOSEPH HENRI
Iconographie des Champignons de Paulet.... Paris: 1955. V. 68; 71

LEVENSON, LEW
Butterfly Man. New York: 1932. V. 69

LEVENSON GOWER, FRANCIS
Translations from the German; and Original Poems. London: 1824. V. 73

LEVER, C.
The Naturalized Animals of the British Isles. London: 1977. V. 72

LEVER, CHARLES
Charles O'Malley. 1841-1844. V. 70
The Confessions of Harry Lorrequer. With numerous illustrations by Phiz. Dublin: 1839. V. 71
The Daltons. 1852. V. 69
The Daltons. London: 1852. V. 68
Davenport Dunn, the Man of Our Day. London: 1871. V. 68
A Day's Ride: a Life's Romance. London: 1864. V. 73
A Day's Ride; a Life's Romance. London: 1872. V. 68
The Dodd Family Abroad. London: 1872. V. 68
Gerald Fitzgerald. New York: 1873. V. 68
Harry Lorrequer. London: 1893?. V. 68; 73
The Knight of Gwynne. London: 1847. V. 71
The Knight of Gwynne. London: 1867. V. 68
The Knight of Gwynne. London: 1875. V. 68
Lord Kilgobbin: a Tale of Ireland In Our Own Time. London: 1872. V. 73
Luttrell of Arran. London: 1865. V. 68
Maurice Tiernay, the Soldier of Fortune. London: 1865. V. 68
The Military Novels of Charles Lever. Boston;: 1892. V. 68
Nuts and Nutcrackers. London: 1845. V. 68
The O'Donoghue; a Tale of Ireland Fifty Years Ago. Dublin: 1845. V. 68; 71
One of Them. London: 1861. V. 68
Our Mess (Tom Burke). Dublin: 1843-1844. V. 68
Paul Gosslett's Confessions. London: 1868. V. 68
A Rent in a Cloud. London: 1869. V. 68
A Rent in a Cloud. London: 1877?. V. 68
Roland Cashel. London: 1873. V. 68
Roland Cashel. London: 1875. V. 68
St. Patrick's Eve. London: 1845. V. 68
St. Patrick's Eve. London: 1855. V. 71
Sir Brook Fossbroke. London: 1879. V. 68
Sir Jasper Carew. London: 1855. V. 68
Sir Jasper Carew. London: 1874. V. 68
Tales of the Trains. London: 1845. V. 68; 73
Tony Butler. London: 1885?. V. 68

LEVER, CHARLES JAMES
One of Them. London: 1861. V. 72

LEVER, DARCY
The Young Sea Officer's Sheet Anchor; or a Key to the Leading of Rigging and to Practical Seamanship. London: 1808. V. 68; 70
The Young Sea Officer's Sheet Anchor; or a Key to the Leading of Rigging and to Practical Steamanship. Philadelphia: 1819. V. 68; 72
The Young Sea Officer's Sheet Anchor; or a Key to the Rigging and to Practical Seamanship. London and Leeds: 1835. V. 69

LEVERAGE, HENRY
The Ice Pilot. Garden City: 1921. V. 73

LEVERETT, F.
Glacial Formations and Drainage Features of the Erie and Ohio Basins. Washington: 1902. V. 70

LEVERTOV, DENISE
Batterers. West Burke: 1996. V. 69; 72
Here and Now. San Francisco: 1957. V. 69; 72
In the Night. A Story. New York: 1968. V. 73
Life In The Forest. New York: 1978. V. 72; 73
A Marigold from North Viet Nam. New York: 1968. V. 73
The Menaced World. Concord: 1985. V. 73
Modulations for Solo Voice. San Francisco: 1977. V. 70; 72
A New Year's Garland for My Students/MIT 1969-1970. Mt. Horeb: 1970. V. 73
O Taste and See. Norfolk: 1964. V. 71
Overland to the Islands. Highlands: 1958. V. 69; 73
Pig Dreams: Scenes from the Life of Sylvia. Woodstock: 1981. V. 69; 71; 73
The Sorrow Dance. New York: 1967. V. 69
Summer Poems / 1969. Berkeley: 1970. V. 73
Three Poems. Mt. Horeb: 1968. V. 73
Wanderer's Daysong. Port Townsend: 1980. V. 69

LEVESQUE DE POUILLY, LOUIS JEAN
The Theory of Agreeable Sensations. Edinburgh: 1766. V. 73
The Theory of Agreeable Sensations. London: 1774. V. 71

LEVETUS, A. S.
Frank Brangwyn. Der Radierer. Vienna: 1924. V. 72

LEVI, COOPER
The Surgery of the Head and Neck. Philadelphia: 1898. V. 72

LEVI, LEONE
The History of British Commerce and of the Economic Progress of the British Nation 1763-1878. London: 1880. V. 68; 72

LEVI, PETER
The Greek World. New York: 1980. V. 68

LEVI, PRIMO
If Not Now, When?. London: 1986. V. 72
The Truce - a Survivor's Journey Home from Auschwitz. London: 1965. V. 73

LEVI, W. M.
The Pigeon. Columbia: 1945. V. 73
The Pigeon. 1963. V. 70

LEVIN, HARRY
James Joyce - a Critical Introduction. Norfolk: 1941. V. 72

LEVIN, IRA
The Boys from Brazil. New York: 1976. V. 71
Deathtrap. New York: 1979. V. 69
A Kiss Before Dying. New York: 1953. V. 68; 71; 72
No Time for Sergeants. New York: 1956. V. 69
Rosemary's Baby. New York: 1967. V. 68; 69; 71; 72
The Spell of Time: a Tale of Love in Jerusalem. New York: 1974. V. 68
The Stepford Wives. New York: 1972. V. 68; 71; 72

LEVIN, JENNIFER
Water Dancing. New York: 1982. V. 72

LEVIN, MEYER
Citizens. New York: 1940. V. 68

LEVINE, PAUL
To Speak for the Dead. New York: 1990. V. 71

LEVINE, PHILIP
Ashes. Poems New and Old. Port Townsend: 1979. V. 72; 73
The Bread of Time: Toward an Autobiography. New York: 1994. V. 72
The Names of the Lost. Poems. Iowa City: 1976. V. 69; 72; 73
New Season. Port Townsend: 1975. V. 68; 72
1933. New York: 1974. V. 68; 71
Not This Pig. Middletown: 1968. V. 72
On the Edge. Iowa City: 1963. V. 69; 72; 73
One for the Rose. New York: 1981. V. 72
Pili's Wall. Santa Barbara: 1971. V. 73
The Poem of Chalk. Huntington Woods: 1995. V. 72; 73
Selected Poems. New York: 1984. V. 72
Smoke. Toledo: 1997. V. 72; 73
What Work Is. New York: 1991. V. 68

LEVINE, RHODA
He Was There from the Day We Moved In. New York: 1968. V. 68

LEVINGE, R. G. A.
Echoes from the Backwoods; or, Sketches of Transatlantic Life. London: 1846. V. 73

LEVINGER, ELMA
Bread for Beauty. London: 1935. V. 71

LEVINREW, WILL
Death Points a Finger. New York: 1933. V. 70

LEVINSOHN, JOHN L.
Frank Morrison Pixley of the Argonaut. San Francisco;: 1989. V. 73

LEVINTON, J. S.
Marine Biology, Function, Biodiversity, Ecology. New York: 1995. V. 73

LEVIS, H. C.
Notes on the Early British Engraved Portraits Issued in Various Series from 1521 to the End of the 18th Century. 1917. V. 71

LEVIS, LARRY
The Afterlife. Iowa City: 1977. V. 72; 73
Elegy With a Thimbleful of Water in the Cage. Richmond: 1994. V. 69; 73

LEVISON, ERIC
The Eye Witness. Indianapolis: 1921. V. 69

LEVITAS, MICHAEL
America in Crisis. New York: 1969. V. 72

LEVITT, DOROTHY
The Woman and the Car. London: 1909. V. 69

LEVRET, ANDRE
L'Art des Accouchemens Demontre Par Des Principes de Physique et de Mechanique.... Paris: 1766. V. 72
Observations Les Causes et Les Accidens De Plusieurs Accouchemens Labroieux, Avec Des Remarques sur ce Qui a et e Propose ou Mis en Usage Pour Lesterminer.... Paris: 1770. V. 72

LEVY, BENN W.
This Woman Business. Boston: 1927. V. 70; 71

LEVY, D. A.
North American Book of the Dead. Cleveland: 1965. V. 68
Private No Parking. Madison: 1972. V. 69

LEWENHAUPT, C., COUNT
Sport Across the World. 1933. V. 69; 70

LEWES, GEORGE HENRY
Aristotle: A Chapter from the History of Science, Including Analyses of Aristotle's Scientific Writings. London: 1864. V. 68; 70; 71
Comte's Philosophy of the Sciences: Being an Exposition of the Principles of the Cours de Philosophie Positive of Auguste Comte. London: 1853. V. 71
Sea-Side Studies at Ilfracombe, Tenby, the Scilly Isle and Jersey. London: 1860. V. 68; 70
Studies in Animal Life. London: 1862. V. 68; 70

LEWES, VIVIAN B.
Cantor Lectures on the Use of Gas for Domestic Lighting. London: 1897. V. 69

LEWIN, MICHAEL Z.
Ask the Right Question. New York: 1971. V. 68; 72
Ask the Right Question. London: 1972. V. 70

LEWIN, THOMAS
Life and Epistles of St. Paul. London: 1878. V. 69

LEWIN, WILLIAM
The Birds of Great Britain. London: 1795-1796. V. 70; 73

LEWINE, J.
Bibliography of Eighteenth Century Art and Illustrated Books. London: 1898. V. 73

LEWIS, ALBERT WALTER
Rock Island, County Sea, Rock Island County, Illinois. Rock Island: 1915. V. 68

LEWIS, ALFRED HENRY
Confessions of a Detective. New York: 1906. V. 69
Wolfville. New York: 1897. V. 70
Wolfville Nights. New York: 1902. V. 68; 73

LEWIS, ALUN
Inwards Where the Battle Is. Newtown, Powys: 1997. V. 73
The Last Inspection. London: 1942. V. 68

LEWIS, CAROLINE
Clara in Blunderland. London: 1902. V. 69; 70
Lost in Blunderland. London: 1903. V. 70

LEWIS, CECIL
Pathfinders - A Novel. London: 1943. V. 72

LEWIS, CLIVE STAPLES
The Art of Wyndham Lewis. London: 1951. V. 70
Beyond Personality - the Christian Idea of God. London: 1944. V. 70
Boxen - the Imaginary World of the Young. London: 1985. V. 72
The Discarded Image - an Introduction to Medieval and Renaissance Literature. Cambridge: 1964. V. 70; 73
Dymer. London: 1926. V. 71
English Literature in the Sixteenth Century Excluding Drama. London: 1954. V. 72
An Experiment in Criticism. Cambridge: 1961. V. 69
The Great Divorce - a Dream. London: 1945. V. 71
A Grief Observed. London: 1961. V. 69; 70
The Hideous Strength. London: 1945. V. 71; 73
The Horse and His Boy. New York: 1954. V. 70
The Last Battle. London: 1956. V. 70; 72
Letters of C. S. Lewis. London: 1966. V. 71
The Lion, The Witch and The Wardrobe. New York: 1950. V. 70
The Lion, The Witch and the Wardrobe. 1958. V. 71
The Magician's Nephew. London: 1955. V. 70; 71
A Note on Jane Austen. Oxford: 1954. V. 71
Out of the Silent Planet. London: 1938. V. 70
Out of the Silent Planet. New York: 1943. V. 72
Perelandra, a Novel. London: 1943. V. 71
Prince Caspian - the Return to Narnia. 1951. V. 72
Prince Caspian - the Return to Narnia. 1969. V. 71
The Problem of Pain. 1940. V. 70
Reflections on the Psalms. London: 1958. V. 72
Rehabilitations and Other Essays. London: 1939. V. 70
The Screwtape Letters and Screwtape Proposes a Toast. London: 1961. V. 71
The Silver Chair. New York: 1953. V. 70; 73
They Stand Together - the Letters of C. S. Lewis to Arthur Greeves (1914-1963). London: 1979. V. 69
Till We Have Faces - a Myth Retold. London: 1956. V. 71; 72; 73
Undeceptions - Essays on Theology and Ethics. London: 1971. V. 72
Vivisection. London: 1947. V. 68
The Voyage of the Dawn Trader. 1952. V. 72
The Voyage of the Dawn Trader. New York: 1952. V. 70

LEWIS, DAVID
Miscellaneous Poems by Several Hands. 1726. V. 72

LEWIS, DIO
The New Gymnastics for Men, Women and Children. Boston: 1862. V. 71

LEWIS, EDWARD
Edward Carpenter. An Exposition and an Appreciation. London: 1915. V. 71

LEWIS, F. C.
Scenery of the River Dart, Being a Series of Thirty-Five Views. London: 1821. V. 72

LEWIS, G. GRIFFIN
The Practical Book of Oriental Rugs. Philadelphia & New York: 1945. V. 69

LEWIS, GEORGE
A Series of Groups, Illustrating the Physiognomy, Manners and Character of the People of France and Germany. London: 1823. V. 71

LEWIS, GEORGE CORNEWALL
An Essay on the Government of Dependencies. London: 1841. V. 71

LEWIS, GEORGE E.
The Indiana Company 1763-1798: a Study in Eighteenth Century Frontier Land Speculation and Business Venture. Glendale: 1941. V. 69

LEWIS, GRACEANNA
The Development of the Animal Kingdom: a Paper Read at the Fourth Meeting of the Association for the Advancement of Woman. Nantucket: 1877. V. 70

LEWIS, H. H.
Thinking of Russia. Holt: 1932. V. 68

LEWIS, HENRY
The Valley of the Mississippi Illustrated. St. Paul: 1967. V. 70

LEWIS, HENRY C.
Papers and Notes on the Glacial Geology of Great Britain and Ireland. 1894. V. 69; 73

LEWIS, IRA MAE
The Tock Book: Poetry for the Last Days. NY: 1985. V. 72

LEWIS, J. VOLNEY
The Geology of New Jersey. Trenton: 1940. V. 71

LEWIS, JAMES
Digest of the English Census of 1871. London: 1873. V. 71; 73

LEWIS, JANET
The Wheel in Midsummer. Lynn: 1927. V. 71

LEWIS, JEFFERSON
Something Hidden. A Biography of Wilder Penfield. Toronto: 1981. V. 73

LEWIS, JOHN
A Complete History of the Several Translations of the Holy Bible and New Testament into English, Both in Ms. and In Print. London: 1739. V. 71
Pratt Ware. London: 1984. V. 72

LEWIS, JOHN FREDERICK
Lewis's Sketches and Drawings of the Alhambra. London: 1835. V. 68; 70

LEWIS, JOHN L.
The Miners' Fight for American Standards. Indianapolis: 1925. V. 68

LEWIS, JOHN W.
The Life, Labors and Travels of Elder Charles Bowles of the Free Will Baptist Denomination, Together with an Essay on the Character and Condition of the African Race by the Same; also an Essay on the Fugitive Law.... Watertown: 1852. V. 69; 71

LEWIS, JOSEPH
Thomas Paine; Author of the Declaration of Independence. New York: 1947. V. 70

LEWIS, M. B.
Tales of Wonder. Dublin: 1801. V. 70

LEWIS, MARX
Max Zaritsky at Fifty. The Story of an Aggressive Labor Leadership. New York: 1935. V. 71

LEWIS, MATTHEW GREGORY
Feudal Tyrants; or, the Counts of Carlsheim and Sargans. London: 1806. V. 71
The Monk. New York: 1952. V. 69
Romantic Tales.. London: 1808. V. 73

LEWIS, MATTHEW GREGORY continued
Tales of Wonder. London: 1801. V. 68; 73

LEWIS, MERIWETHER
History of the Expedition Under the Command of Captains Lewis and Clark, to the Sources of the Missouri.... Philadelphia: 1814. V. 68; 72; 73
History of the Expedition Under the Command of Lewis and Clark, to the Sources of the Missouri River.... New York: 1903. V. 73
The Journal of Lewis and Clarke, to the Mouth of the Columbia River Beyond the Rocky Mountains in the Years 1804-1805-1806. 1840. V. 68
The Journals of the Expedition Under the Command of Capt. Lewis and Clark to the Sources of the Missouri, Thence Across the Rocky Mountains, and Down the River Columbia to the Pacific Ocean.... New York: 1962. V. 68; 69; 70; 73
The Journals of the Lewis and Clark Expedition. Lincoln: 1986-2000. V. 68; 73
Original Journals of the Lewis and Clark Expedition 1804-1806. New York: 1904. V. 68
The Travels of Captains Lewis and Clarke.... London: 1809. V. 73
Travels to the Source of the Missouri River and Across the American Continent to the Pacific Ocean. London: 1814. V. 71; 73
Travels to the Source of the Missouri River and Across the the American Continent to the Pacific Ocean. London: 1815. V. 73

LEWIS, N. LAWSON
The Sculpture of Max Kalish. Cleveland: 1933. V. 69

LEWIS, NELSON P.
The Planning of the Modern City: a Review of the Principles Governing City Planning. New York: 1923. V. 72

LEWIS, NORMAN
Sand and Sea in Arabia. London: 1938. V. 72

LEWIS, OSCAR
Lola Montez. San Francisco: 1938. V. 70
Second Reading. Selections from the Quarterly News Letter 1933-1963. San Francisco: 1965. V. 73

LEWIS, RICHARD
The Candid Philosopher, or, Free Thoughts on Men, Morals and Manners. London: 1778. V. 68

LEWIS, SARAH
Woman's Mission. Boston: 1840. V. 69

LEWIS, SINCLAIR
Ann Vickers. Garden City: 1933. V. 73
Bethel Merriday. New York: 1940. V. 69
Cass Timberlane. New York: 1945. V. 70; 71; 73
Dodsworth. New York: 1929. V. 70; 71; 72
Elmer Gantry. New York: 1927. V. 70; 73
Hike and the Aeroplane. New York: 1912. V. 72
In the Panorama of Modern Literature. Garden City: 1934. V. 70
It Can't Happen Here. Garden City: 1935. V. 69
The Job. New York: 1917. V. 71
Main Street. New York: 1920. V. 73
Main Street. Chicago: 1937. V. 69; 71; 73
Mantrap. New York: 1926. V. 70; 71; 72
Martin Arrowsmith. London: 1925. V. 69
Our Mr. Wrenn. New York: 1914. V. 69
The Prodigal Parents. Garden City: 1938. V. 73
The Trail of the Hawk. New York: 1915. V. 71

LEWIS, SYDNEY J.
Old Glass and How to Collect It. London: 1928. V. 68

LEWIS, T. R.
A Report of Microscopical and Physiological Researches into the Nature of the Agent or Agents Producing Cholera. Calcutta: 1872. V. 73

LEWIS, THOMAS
The Blood Vessels of the Human Skin and Their Responses. London: 1927. V. 68
Clinical Disorders of the Heart Beat. London: 1912. V. 68
Vascular Disorders of the Limbs. London: 1936. V. 68
Vascular Disorders of the Limbs. New York: 1936. V. 71

LEWIS, TRACY HAMMOND
Along the Rio Grande. New York: 1916. V. 69

LEWIS, W.
New Traveller's Guide or a Pocket Edition The English Counties. London: 1819. V. 73

LEWIS, W. M.
Eutrophication and Land Use, Lake Dillon, Colorado. New York: 1984. V. 72

LEWIS, WELLS
They Still Say No. New York: 1939. V. 70

LEWIS, WILLIAM C.
A System of Physical Chemistry. London: 1916. V. 71

LEWIS, WILLIAM S.
Ranald MacDonald. The Narrative Of His Early Life On The Columbia Under The Hudson's Bay Company's Regime; Of His Experiences In The Pacific Whale Fishery. Spokane: 1923. V. 72

LEWIS, WILLIE N.
Between Sun and Sod. Clarendon: 1939. V. 71

LEWIS, WILMARTH SHELDON
Horace Walpole's Library. 1958. V. 71

LEWIS, WYNDHAM
The Apes of God. London. V. 73
The Apes of God. 1930. V. 68; 71
Apes of God. London: 1930. V. 69
The Caliph's Design: Architects! Where is Your Vortex?. London: 1919. V. 70
The Childermass: Section I. London: 1928. V. 71
Creatures of Habit and Creatures of Change: Essays 1914-1956. Santa Rosa: 1989. V. 73
The Demon of Progress in the Arts. London: 1954. V. 70
The Diabolical Principle and the Dithyrambic Spectator. London: 1931. V. 71
Doom of Youth. London: 1932. V. 68; 71
The Human Age. London: 1955-1956. V. 68
The Jews: Are They Human?. London: 1939. V. 70
The Mysterious Mr. Bull. London: 1938. V. 71
One-Way Song. London: 1933. V. 69; 73
One-Way Song. London: 1960. V. 68
The Red Priest. London: 1956. V. 68
The Revenge for Love. London: 1952. V. 68
The Roaring Queen. London: 1973. V. 71
Rude Assignment: a Narrative of My Career Up-to-Date. London: 1950. V. 69
Satire and Fiction. Preceded by the History of a Rejected Review by Roy Campbell. London: 1930. V. 70
Tarr. London: 1918. V. 71; 73
Thirty Personalities and a Self Portrait. 1932. V. 68
Time and Western Man. London: 1927. V. 71
Timon of Athens. London: 1913. V. 70
The Wild Body - a Soldier of Humour and Other Stories. London: 1927. V. 71
Wyndham Lewis the Artist - from "Blast" to Burlington House. London: 1939. V. 68

LE WITT, JAN
The Vegetabull. New York: 1956. V. 73

LEWITT, SOL
Irish. Edinburgh: 1977. V. 69

LEWKENOR, LEWIS
The Estate of English Fugitives Under the King of Spaine and His Ministry. London: 1595. V. 68; 72

LEWTHWAITE, JOHN W.
Ballads of a Coach Driver. 1927. V. 71

LEY, BEATRICE
Fiesole. London: 1886. V. 70
A Golden May-Bud. London: 1883. V. 70

LEYBOURN, WILLIAM
Arithmetick: Vulgar, Decimal, Instrumental, Algebraical, in Four Parts. London: 1684. V. 71
The Line of Proportion or Numbers Commonly Called Gunter's Line, Made Easie. London: 1726. V. 71
Panarithmologia; or, the Trader's Sure Guide. London: 1780. V. 71

LEYCESTER'S Common-Wealth: Conceived, Spoken and Published with Most Earnest Protestation of all Dutifull Good Will and Affection Towards This Realm.... 1641. V. 70

LEYDET, FRANCOIS
Time and the River Flowing: Grand Canyon. San Francisco: 1964. V. 69

LEYLAND, FRANCIS
The Bronte Family, with Special Reference to Patrick Branwell Bronte. London: 1886. V. 73

LEYLAND, JOHN
Views of Ancient Buildings Illustrative of the Domestic Architecture of the Parish of Halifax. Halifax: 1879. V. 73
The Yorkshire Coast and the Cleveland Hills and Dales. London: 1892. V. 73

LIANG-YU, LIU
Sung Wares: a Survey of Chinese Ceramics. Taipei: 1991. V. 73
Sung Wares: a Survey of Chinese Ceramics 2. Taipei: 1991. V. 72

LIBBY, O. G.
The Arikara Narrative of the Campaign Against the Hostile Dakotas June 1876. 1920. V. 68
The Arikara Narrative of The Campaign Against The Hostile Dakotas, June 1876. Bismarck: 1920. V. 72

LIBERMAN, ALEXANDER
The Art and Technique of Color Photography. New York: 1951. V. 68

LIBERTY & CO.
Additions to the Curio Stock for the Month of November. Series LXXXII. 1906. 1906. V. 68
A Collection of Eastern and Other Curios, Antiques, &c. Exhibited at Chesham House, Regent St. 1893. V. 73

THE LIBERTY Bell. Boston: 1848. V. 73

THE LIBERTY Bell by Friends of Freedom. Boston: 1851. V. 69

LIBRARY COMANY OF PHILADELPHIA
Supplement to the Catalogue of Books, Belonging to,... Philadelphia: 1838. V. 68; 71

LIBRARY OF CONGRESS
American and English Genealogies in the Library of Congress. Washington: 1919. V. 71
Boxes for the Protection of Rare Books, Their Design and Construction. Washington: 1982. V. 68

THE LIBRARY of Fiction, or Family Story-Teller.... London: 1836-1837. V. 70

THE LIBRARY of Fiction, or Family Story-Teller: Consisting of Original Tales, Essays and Sketches of Character. London: 1837. V. 68

THE LIBRARY of Fiction, or Family Story-Teller.... London: 1837. V. 70

THE LIBRARY of Romance, A Collection of Tales and Romances. London: 1845. V. 70

LIBRARY of the Fine Arts, or, Repertory of Painting, Sculpture, Architecture and Engraving. Volume I. London: 1831. V. 68

LIBRI, G.
Catalogue de la Bibliotheque. Paris: 1847. V. 68
A Catalogue of the Choicer Portion of the Magnificent Library formed by.... London: 1859. V. 68; 70; 73

LICETUS, FORTUNIUS
De Lucernis Antiquorum Reconditis.... Udine: 1652. V. 69
De Monstris. Ex Recensione Geradi Blasii M.D. & P.P. Amsterdam: 1665. V. 69
De Monstrorum Caussi, Natura, et Differentiis, Libri Duo. Patavia: 1634. V. 68
De Spontaneo Viventium Ortu.... Vicetiae: 1618. V. 68

LICHTENBERG, GEORG CHRISTOPH
Aphorisms and Letters. London: 1969. V. 70

LICHTENBERGER, HENRI
The Gospel of Superman, the Philosophy of Friedrich Nietzsche. Edinburgh and London: 1910. V. 68

LICK, ROSEMARY
The Generous Miser: the Story of James Lick of California. 1967. V. 72

LIDA
Fluff - the Little Wild Rabbit. New York: 1937. V. 70
Spiky the Hedgehog. New York: 1938. V. 70

LIDDELL, DONALD M.
Chessmen. London: 1938. V. 72

LIDDELL, HENRY GEORGE
A Greek-English Lexicon. Oxford: 1863. V. 70

LIDDELL, ROBERT
Lay of the Last Angler in Five Cantos, also Jack's Dangers and Deliverances. Keslo: 1888. V. 72

LIDDIC, BRUCE R.
Camp On Custer - Transcribing The Custer Myth. Spokane: 1995. V. 72
I Buried Custer, The Diary of Pvt Thomas W. Coleman, 7th U. S. Cavalry. College Station: 1979. V. 72

LIDDY, G. GORDON
Out of Control. New York: 1979. V. 71

LIEB, FREDERICK G.
Connie Mack: Grand Old Man of Baseball. New York: 1945. V. 71
The Detroit Tigers. New York: 1946. V. 68; 71

LIEBAERS, HERMAN
Flemish Art From The Beginning Till Now. Antwerp: 1985. V. 72

LIEBER, FRANCIS
What is Our Constitution, -- League, Pact, or Government?. New York: 1861. V. 73

LIEBERMAN, ARCHIE
The Israelis. Chicago: 1965. V. 73

LIEBIG, JUSTUS
Animal Chemistry, or Organic Chemistry in Its Application to Physiology and Pathology. London: 1842. V. 69
Die Organichen Chemie in Ihrer Anwendung auf Agricultur und Physiologie. Braunscheig: 1840. V. 73
Researches on the Motion of the Juices in the Animal Body. 1848. V. 72

LIEBLING, A. J.
The Most of A. J Liebling. New York: 1963. V. 73
Normandy Revisited. New York: 1958. V. 73

LIEBMANN, FREDERIK MICHAEL
Chenes de L'Amerique Tropicale, Iconographie des Especes Novelles ou Peu Connues. Leipzig: 1869. V. 70

LIEBOVITZ, DAVID
Chroncile of an Infamous Woman. New York: 1933. V. 71

LIEFERANT, HENRY
Doctors' Wives. Boston: 1930. V. 70

LIENHARD, HEINRICH
A Pioneer at Sutter's Fort. 1846-1850. The Adventures of .... Los Angeles: 1941. V. 73

LIERE, EDWARD J. VAN
A Doctor Enjoys Sherlock Holmes. New York: 1959. V. 71

LIETZE, ERNST
Modern Hiegoraphic Processes. A Manual of Instruction in the Art of Reproducing Drawings, Engravings.... New York: 1888. V. 68

THE LIFE and Adventures of Mrs. Christian Davies, Commonly Call'd Mother Ross; Who, in Several Campaigns Under King William and the Late Duke of Marlborough, in the Quality of a Foot Solider and Dargoon.... London: 1740. V. 70

LIFE and Adventures of Robert the Hermit of Massachusetts, Who Has Lived 14 Years in a Cave, Secluded from Human Society.... Providence: 1829. V. 71

THE LIFE and Adventures of that Most Eccentric Character James Hirst. Knottingley: 1840. V. 70

LIFE and Death of Cock Robin. New York: 1864. V. 71

THE LIFE and Death of Jenny Wren. 1820. V. 68; 73

THE LIFE and Death of Little Jenny Wren. London: 1840. V. 73

THE LIFE and Memoirs of Mr. Ephraim Tristram Bates, Commonly Called Corporal Bates, a Broken Hearted Solider.... London: 1756. V. 73

LIFE, Confession, and Letters of Courtship of Rev. Jacob S. Harden, of te M.E. Church, Mount Lebanon, Hunterdon Co., N.J. Hackettstown: 1860. V. 68

THE LIFE of a Sponge. London: 1824. V. 68

THE LIFE of Bartolome E. Murillo.... London: 1819. V. 69; 71

THE LIFE of Jack Sprat, His Wife and His Cat. 1820. V. 68

THE LIFE of John Metcalf Commonly Called Blind Jack of Knaresbrough.... Knaresborough: 1812. V. 72

THE LIFE of Little Jack Sprat. London: 1840. V. 73

THE LIFE of Mahomet; or the History of that Imposture Which was Begun, Carried On and Finally Established by Him in Arabia.... Worcester: 1802. V. 73

THE LIFE of Miss Fanny Bell, and the Female Hermit. Part II. The Indian Girl, or the Father's Revenge. Boston: 1849. V. 68

THE LIFE of Mr. James Quin, Comedian.... London: 1887. V. 69

THE LIFE of the Right Honourable Sir Robert Peel, Bart.... London: 1850. V. 68; 71

THE LIFE of the Right Honourable W. E. Gladstone: a Popular Biography. London: 1889. V. 68

THE LIFE, Persecutions, and Sufferings of Sophia Dorothea, Princess of Zell, Wife of George I, King of England, who was Imprisoned Thirty-Six Years in the Castle of Ahlen in the Electorate of Brunswick, on a Charge of Supposed Incontinency. London: 1820?. V. 73

LIGENFELTER, RICHARD E.
Steamboats on the Colorado River 1852-1916. Tucson: 1978. V. 73

LIGGETT, WALTER
The River Riders. New York: 1928. V. 70

LIGHT Blue, Dark Blue - an Anthology of Recent Writing from Oxford and Cambridge Universities. London: 1960. V. 71

LIGHTING FIXTURE DEALERS SOCIETY OF CLEVELAND
A Guide to the Fixture Dealer. Cleveland: 1926. V. 68

LIGHTMAN, ALAN
Einstein's Dreams. New York: 1993. V. 68; 71
Time Travel and Papa Joe's Pipe. New York: 1984. V. 71

LIGNE, PRINCE CHARLES DE
Catalogue Raisonne des Desseins Originaux du Cabinet de Feu.... Vienna: 1794. V. 69
Coup d'Oeil sur Beloeil. Beloeil: 1781. V. 68; 70; 72

LIKENS, G. E.
An Ecosystem Approach to Aquatic Ecology, Mirror Lake and Its Environment. New York: 1985. V. 71

LIKINS, J. W., MRS.
Six Years Experience as a Book Agent in California. 1992. V. 71

LILBURNE, JOHN
Iuglers Discoverd, in Two Letters Writ by Col. John Lilburne, Prerogative Prisoner in the Tower of London, the 28 September 1647 to His Excellency, Sir Thomas Fairfax. n.p: 1647. V. 73

LILE, WILLIAM MINOR
An Outline of the Equity Pleading and Practice with Forms and the Federal Equity Rules. University of Virginia: 1922. V. 73

LILFORD, THOMAS LITTLETON POWYS, 4TH BARON
Coloured Figures of the Birds of the British Islands. 1891-1897. V. 69
Coloured Figures of the Birds of the British Islands. London: 1891-1897. V. 73

LILLIE, GORDON W.
Life Story of Pawnee Bill. 1916. V. 70

LILLY, ELI
Prehistoric Antiquities of Indiana. Indianapolis: 1937. V. 70

LILLY, JOHN CUNNINGHAM
The Mind of the Dolphin: a Non-human Intelligence. Garden City: 1967. V. 71

LILLY, WILLIAM SAMUEL
A Century of Revolution. London: 1890. V. 71

LILY, WILLIAM
A Short Introduction of Grammar Compiled and Set Forth for the Bringing Up Of All that Intended to Attain to the Knowledge of the Latin Tongue. (bound with) *Lily's Rules Construed..* London: 1776-1778. V. 71

A Short Introduction of Grammar, Generally to Be Used...(with) Propria Quae Maribus Quae Genus.... London: 1784-1786. V. 73

LIMA, P. ALMEIDA
Cerebral Angiography. 1950. V. 72
Cerebral Angiography. London: 1950. V. 68

LIMA DE FARIA, A.
Handbook of Molecular Cytology. Amsterdam: 1969. V. 68

LIMBECK, R. R. V.
The Clinical Pathology of the Blood. London: 1901. V. 68

LIMBORCH, PHILIP
The History of the Inquisition, as It Has Subsisted in France, Italy, Spain.... London: 1816. V. 68

LIMEBEER, ENA
To a Proud Phantom. Richmond: 1923. V. 72

LIMITED EDITIONS CLUB
Quarto-Millenary. New York: 1954. V. 69

LIMITED EDITONS CLUB
Quarto-Millenary. An Illustrated Survey...of the First 250 Publications of the Limited Editions Club. New York: 1959. V. 72

LIMPUS, LOWELL M.
History of the New York Fire Department. New York: 1940. V. 69

LIN, W. H.
Phalaenopsis Kingdom from Formosa. Taipei: 1987. V. 68

LINCOLN, Grimsby and District Trade Directory. Accompanied with a Gazetteer of England. Edinburgh: 1919. V. 72

LINCOLN, ABRAHAM
Abraham Lincoln Letters. Boston: 1913. V. 69
Collected Works. Princeton: 1953. V. 68
Political Debates Between Hon. Abraham Lincoln and Hon. Stephen A. Douglas in the Celebrated Campaign of 1858, in Illinois. Columbus: 1860. V. 68

THE LINCOLN Album...Containing the Largest Collection of Lincoln Portraits that Has Ever Been Assembled in a Single Work.... St. Louis: 1907. V. 69

LINCOLN, CHARLES H.
Naval Records of the American Revolution 1775-1788. Washington: 1906. V. 71

LINCOLN, FREEMAN
Nod. New York: 1933. V. 71

LINCOLN, JOSEPH C.
Extricating Obadiah. New York: 1917. V. 69
Out of the Fog. New York: 1940. V. 69
The Ownley Inn. New York: 1939. V. 68; 70

LINCOLN, MARY JOHNSON BAILEY
Carving and Serving. Boston: 1887. V. 73
Mrs. Lincoln's Boston Cook Book. Boston: 1884. V. 72; 73
Mrs. Lincoln's Boston Cook Book. Boston: 1889. V. 73
Mrs. Lincoln's Boston Cook Book. Boston: 1891. V. 68

LINCOLN, NATALIE SUMNER
Marked Cancelled. New York: 1930. V. 68
P.P.C. New York: 1927. V. 70
The Red Seal. New York: 1920. V. 68

LINCOLN, VICTORIA
The Swan Island Murders. New York: 1930. V. 69

LIND, J.
Danish Fungi as Represented in the Herbarium of E. Rostrup. Copenhagen: 1913. V. 70

LIND, JOHN
Remarks on the Principal Acts of the Thirteenth Parliament of Great Britain.... London: 1775. V. 68
Three Letters to Dr. Price, Containing Remarks on His Observations on the Nature of Civil Liberty, the Principles of Government, and the Justice and Policy of the War With America. London: 1776. V. 69

LIND, L. R.
Studies in Pre-Vesalian Anatomy, Biography, Translations, Documents. Philadelphia: 1975. V. 72

LIND, MICHAEL
The Alamo. Boston: 1997. V. 71

LINDBERGH, CHARLES A.
Of Flight and Life. New York: 1948. V. 70; 73
The Spirit of St. Louis. New York: 1953. V. 73
We. New York: 1927. V. 69; 70; 71; 72; 73

LINDBERGH, REEVE
John's Apples. Mt. Horeb: 1995. V. 69

LINDBLOM, G.
The Akamba in British East Africa. Uppsala: 1920. V. 69

LINDBLOM, K. G.
Fighting Bracelets and Kindred Weapons in Africa. Stockholm: 1927. V. 69

LINDEN, DIEDERICK WESSEL
Three Lectures on Mining and Smelting, in Which a Method is Laid Down, Whereby These Useful Sciences May be Greatly Improved. London: 1750. V. 73

LINDEN, JAMES
Printers to the Club. A Portfolio. San Francisco: 1986. V. 73

LINDEN, JOHANNES ANTOINE VAN DER
De Scriptis Medicis Libri Dvo. Amsterdam: 1662. V. 68; 72
Lindenius Renovatus: sive Johannis Antonidae van der Linden De Scriptis Medicis Libri Du.... Nuremberg: 1686. V. 70

LINDER, LESLIE
A History of the Writings of Beatrix Potter. 1971. V. 68
A History of the Writings of Beatrix Potter. London: 1971. V. 69; 71; 73

LINDER, USHER F.
Reminiscences of the Early Bench and Bar of Illinois. Chicago: 1879. V. 71

LINDERMAN, FRANK B.
American - The Life Story of A Great Indian Plenty-Coups, Chief of The Crows. New York: 1930. V. 72
Blackfeet Indians. St. Paul: 1935. V. 69; 70
Bunch Grass and Blue Joint. New York: 1921. V. 69; 71; 73
Indian Old-Man Stories. New York: 1920. V. 68
Lige Mounts - Free Trapper. New York: 1922. V. 68
Recollections of Charley Russell. Norman: 1980. V. 69

LINDLEY, ERNEST
Franklin D. Roosevelt: a Career in Progressive Democracy. Indianapolis: 1931. V. 70; 71

LINDLEY, JOHN
The Fossil Flora of Great Britain. London: 1831-1837. V. 69
Ladies Botany; or a Familiar Introduction to the Study of the Natural System of Botany. 1834. V. 69
Rosarum Monographia; or a Botanical History of Roses. 1820. V. 69
Rosarum Monographia; or, a Botanical History of Roses. London: 1820. V. 68; 72
Sertum Orchidacenum; a Wreath of the Most Beautiful Orchidaceous Flowers. New York and Amsterdam: 1974. V. 68; 71
The Theory of Horticulture; or an Attempt to Explain the Principal Operations of Gardening Upon Physiological Principle. New York: 1841. V. 71; 73

LINDLEY, L.
History of Sutton in Ashfield; or, Past Links with the Present. Sutton-in-Ashfield: 1907. V. 70

THE LINDLEY Library, Catalogue of Books, Pamphlets, Manuscripts and Drawings. London: 1927. V. 68

LINDMAN, MAJ
Flicka, Ricka, Dicka and The Strawberries. Chicago: 1945. V. 70; 73
Flicka, Ricka, Dicka Bake a Cake. Chicago: 1955. V. 71
Snipp, Snapp, Snurr and the Red Shoes. Chicago: 1944. V. 70

LINDNER, ROBERT M.
Rebel Without a Cause: The Hypnoanalysis of a Criminal Psychopath. New York: 1944. V. 70; 71

LINDO, A. A.
A Retrospect of the Past As Connected with the Preparatory to a Faithful Exposition Intended to be Given of the Divine Will and Dispensation Disclosed in the Sacred Books Received as Authority by the Jews. Cincinnati: 1848. V. 71

LINDOP, AUDREY ERSKINE
Tall Headlines. New York: 1950. V. 72

LINDSAY, HOWARD
The Prescott Proposals. New York: 1954. V. 73

LINDSAY, IAN G.
Inverary and the Dukes of Argyll. Edinburgh: 1973. V. 71

LINDSAY, JACK
The Barriers are Down - a Tale of the Collapse of a Civilisation. London: 1945. V. 71
The London Aphrodite. London: 1928-1929. V. 73
Men of Forty-Eight. London: 1948. V. 71
William Blake: Creative Will and the Poetic Image. 1927. V. 71
William Blake: Creative Will and the Poetic Image. London: 1927. V. 70
William Blake: Creative Will and The Poetic Image. London: 1929. V. 72

LINDSAY, JOAN
Picnic at Hanging Rock. Melbourne: 1967. V. 70

LINDSAY, NICHOLAS VACHEL
Adventures While Preaching the Gospel of Beauty. New York: 1914. V. 71
The Candle in the Cabin. New York: 1926. V. 68
Collected Poems. New York: 1923. V. 70
Collected Poems. New York: 1925. V. 68
The Congo and Other Poems. New York: 1914. V. 71
Every Soul is a Circus. New York: 1929. V. 69
General William Booth Enters Into Heaven and Other Poems. New York: 1921. V. 68
The Golden Book of Springfield. New York: 1920. V. 70
The Golden Whales of California and Other Rhymes in the North American Language. New York: 1920. V. 70; 72
Rhymes to Be Traded for Bread. Springfield: 1912. V. 69
The Tree of Laughing Bells. New York: 1905. V. 69

LINDSAY, NORMAN
Every Mother's Son. New York: 1930. V. 71
Hyperborea. 1928. V. 68
Hyperborea. London: 1928. V. 71
The Magic Pudding. Sydney: 1918. V. 71
Norman Lindsay's Pen Drawings. Sydney: 1931. V. 71

LINDSAY, PAUL
Code Name: Gentkill. New York: 1995. V. 71

LINDSEY, DAVID L.
A Cold Mind. New York: 1983. V. 68

LINDSEY, JOHN
The Lady and the Mute. New York: 1931. V. 72

LINDSLEY, JOHN BERRIEN
The Military Annals of Tennessee. Confederate. Wilmington: 1995. V. 69

LINDSLY, PHILIP
A Plea for the Theological Seminary at Princeton, N.J. Trenton: 1821. V. 71

LINDUSKA, J. P.
Waterfowl Tomorrow. USA: 1964. V. 71

LINEN, JAMES
The Golden Gate. San Francisco: 1869. V. 73

LINES, KATHLEEN
Lavender's Blue. London: 1954. V. 69

LING, W. N.
The Northern Highlands. Edinburgh: 1936. V. 69

LINGENFELTER, RICHARD E.
The Rush of '89; The Baja California Gold Fever and Captain James Edward Friend's Letters from the Santa Clara Mines. Los Angeles: 1967. V. 71
Steamboats on the Colorado River 1852-1916. Tucson: 1978. V. 68

LINGS, MARTIN
The Quaranic Art of Calligraphy and Illumination. London: 1976. V. 72

LINGSTONE, ROWE
John Chinaman. London: 1891. V. 70

LINK, MARGARET SCHEVILL
The Pollen Path: a Collection of Navajo Myths. Stanford: 1956. V. 69

LINK, O. WINSTON
Night Trick: Photographs of the Norfolk and Western Railway.1950-1960. London: 1983. V. 73

LINKLATER, ERIC
Juan in America. London: 1931. V. 71
Judas. New York: 1939. V. 70
Position at Noon. 1958. V. 68
The Sailor's Holiday. London: 1937. V. 70
The Secret Larder. London: 1969. V. 68
A Sociable Plover. London: 1957. V. 73
To the Prime Minister. 1964. V. 68
The Wind on the Moon. 1944. V. 68
A Year of Space. 1953. V. 68

LINN, JOHN J.
Reminiscences of Fifty Years in Texas. Austin: 1986. V. 68; 69

LINNE, CARL VON
Entomologia, Fauna Suecicae Descriptionibus Aucta.... Lugduni: 1789. V. 70; 72
Flora Anglica. Uppsala: 1754. V. 69
Flora Lapponica. Amsterdam: 1737. V. 69
Flora Suecica. Stockholm: 1745. V. 69
Genera Plantarum. Leiden: 1742. V. 69
A Genera Plantarum. Halle: 1752. V. 72
Genera Plantarum. Stockholm: 1754. V. 69
A General System of Nature, through the Three Grand Kingdoms of Animals, Vegetables and Minerals.... London: 1806. V. 72
A Generic and Specific Description of British Plants. 1775. V. 68
A Generic and Specific Description of British Plants. Kendal: 1775. V. 72
Hortus Cliffortianus Plantas Exhibens in Hortis tam vivis Quam Siccis, Hartecampi in Hollandia, Coluit.... Amsterdam: 1737. V. 68; 69
Lachesis Lapponica, or a Tour in Lapland. London: 1811. V. 71
Philosophiae Botanica. Stockholm and Amsterdam: 1751. V. 73
Vernatio Arborum...Haraldus Barck. Upsala: 1753. V. 69

LINNECAR, RICHARD
The Miscellaneous Works of Richard Linnecar, of Wakefield. Leeds: 1789. V. 69

LINNINGTON, ELIZABETH
Crime by Chance. Philadelphia: 1973. V. 68
Double Bluff. New York: 1963. V. 68

LINPERGH, PIETER
Architectura Mechanica...Moole Boek, of Eenige Opstalle van Moolens Nessen Shaare Gronden.... Amsterdam: 1685. V. 70

LINSDAY, JOHN
Notices of Remarkable Greek, Roman and Anglo-Saxon and Other Medieval Coins in the Cabinet of the Author. 1860. V. 70

LINSENMAIER, W.
Insects of the World. New York: 1972. V. 69; 72

LINSTRUM, DEREK
Historic Architecture of Leeds. Newcastle upon Tyne: 1969. V. 73

LINTHICUM, RICHARD
A Book of Rocky Mountain Tales. Denver: 1892. V. 68; 73

LINTON, E. LYNN
Ione. London: 1885. V. 68
The Lake Country. London: 1864. V. 71

LINTON, M. B.
The Tragic Race. 1926. V. 68
The Tragic Race. Aberdeen: 1926. V. 70

LINTON, R.
The Tanala, a Hill Tribe of Madagascar. 1933. V. 69

LINTON, W. J.
The Ferns of the English Lake Country. Windermere: 1878. V. 70
Poetry of America. London: 1878. V. 70; 71

THE LION'S Den. New York: 1886. V. 72

LIPHANT, M.
Jerusalem its History and Hope. London: 1891. V. 70

LIPMAN, A.
Divinely Elegant: the Work of Ernest Dryden. London: 1989. V. 69; 72

LIPMAN, JEAN
American Folk Art in Wood, Metal and Stone. New York: 1948. V. 72
Primitive Painters in America 1750-1950: an Anthology. New York: 1950. V. 72

LIPPARD, L. R.
Eva Hesse. New York: 1976. V. 72

LIPPINCOTT, HORACE MATHER
Early Philadelphia. Its People, Life and Progress. Philadelphia: 1917. V. 71

LIPPINCOTT, J. G.
Design for Business. Chicago: 1947. V. 72

LIPPMANN, WALTER
H. L. Mencken. New York: 1926. V. 69
Public Opinion. New York: 1922. V. 72

LIPPS, OSCAR
A Little History of the Navajos. Cedar Rapids: 1909. V. 71

LIPSCHUTZ, PEGGY
The World of Peggy Lipschutz. Chicago. V. 68

LIPSEY, JOHN J.
The Lives of James John Hagerman: Builder of the Colorado Midland Railway. Denver: 1968. V. 72; 73

LISFRANC, JACQUES
Memoire sur de Nouvelles Applications de Stethoscope de M. le Professeur Laennec. Paris: 1825. V. 72

LISH, GORDON
Dear Mr. Capote. New York: 1983. V. 68

LISIANSKY, V.
Voyage Round the World in the Years 1803, 1804, 1805 and 1806. Amsterdam and New York: 1968. V. 69

LISLE, EDWARD
Observations in Husbandry. London: 1757. V. 71

LISS, DAVID
A Conspiracy of Paper. New York: 2000. V. 70; 71

A LIST of all the Prisoners in the Upper Bench Prison, Remaining in Custody the Third of May, 1653. Delivered in by Sir John Lenthall to the Committee Appointed to the Councel of State, for Examining of the State of Said Prisons. London: 1653. V. 70

A LIST of References to Literature Relating to the Union Pacific System. Newton: 1975. V. 68

LISTER, FLORENCE C.
Chihuahua: Storehouse of Storms. Albuquerque: 1966. V. 70

LISTER, MARTIN
Conchykiorum Bivalvium Utriusque Aquae Exercitatio Anatomica Tertia. London: 1696. V. 73
Exercitatio Anatomica. London: 1694. V. 68

LISTER, RAYMOND
Hammer and Hand: an Essay on the Ironwork of Cambridge. 1969. V. 71

LISTER, ROBERT H.
The Coombs Site. Salt Lake City: 1959-1961. V. 72

LISTER, T. H.
The Life and Administration of Edward, First Earl of Clarendon (Edward Hyde 1609-1674). London: 1838. V. 71

LISTER, THOMAS
A Mirror for Princes, in a Letter to...The Prince of Wales. London: 1797. V. 73

LISTON, ROBERT
Elements of Surgery. Philadelphia: 1837. V. 68; 71; 72

LITCHFIELD, FREDERICK
Illustrated History of Furniture from the Earliest to the Present Time. London: 1899. V. 69

LITCHFIELD, H.
Emma Darwin, a Century of Family Letters 1792-1896. New York: 1915. V. 69

LITERARY AND PHILOSOPHICAL SOCIETY OF MANCHESTER
Memoirs. Warringotn: 1785. V. 73

THE LITERARY Museum; or, Ancient and Modern Repository. London: 1792. V. 68

LITT, TOBY
Adventures in Capitalism. London: 1996. V. 72

LITTELL, ROBERT
An Agent In Place. New York: 1991. V. 72
The Amateur. New York: 1981. V. 72
The Debriefing. New York: 1979. V. 72
The Defection of A.J. Lewinter. Boston: 1973. V. 71
The Once And Future Spy. New York: 1990. V. 72
The Revolutionist. New York: 1988. V. 72
The Sisters. New York: 1986. V. 72

LITTLE BIG HORN ASSOCIATION
Custer And His Times Book I. El Paso: 1981. V. 72

LITTLE Bo Peep. New York: 1886. V. 73

THE LITTLE Bombardier and Pocket Gunner. 1801. V. 69; 70; 71

A LITTLE Book of Pussy Cats. London: 1908. V. 72

LITTLE Boy Blue. Akron: 1910. V. 69

LITTLE, CONSTANCE
The Black Eye. New York: 1945. V. 69
The Black Goatee. Garden City: 1947,. V. 73

LITTLE, E. L.
Common Trees of Puerto Rico and the Virgin Islands. Washington: 1964-1974. V. 68

LITTLE, EDDIE
Another Day in Paradise. New York: 1997. V. 68

LITTLE Fables for Little Folks. London: 1870. V. 70

LITTLE Folks' ABC Pictures. London: 1900. V. 72

LITTLE Folks at Play. London: 1890. V. 69

LITTLE Folks in Tabbyland. New York: 1910. V. 69

THE LITTLE Folks Painting Book. New York: 1879. V. 70

LITTLE Folk's Peep Show. London: 1898. V. 73

LITTLE Folks 1891. V. 69

LITTLE Folks 1904. Volume 60. V. 70

LITTLE Folks 1912. V. 69

LITTLE Folks 1916. Volume 84. V. 70

LITTLE Folks 1926. Volume 104. V. 70

LITTLE Frank's Almanack to Show Little Boys and Girls Their Play Days. Concord: 1836. V. 69

LITTLE Froggie Green. Akron: 1915. V. 70

LITTLE Frolic (1899). V. 70

LITTLE Goody Two-Shoes. Philadelphia: 1858. V. 71
LITTLE Goody Two-Shoes. New York: 1859-1862. V. 70

LITTLE, JAMES A.
From Kirtland to Salt Lake City. Salt Lake City: 1890. V. 68; 73
Jacob Hamblin. Salt Lake City: 1881. V. 68; 73
Jacob Hamblin. Salt Lake City: 1909. V. 68; 73

LITTLE, JAMES BROOKE
The Law of Allotments for the Poor.... London: 1887. V. 71

LITTLE Jane and Her Brother. London. V. 70

LITTLE Jane and Charles. New York: 1843-1856. V. 71

LITTLE Jane or the Consequences of Playing With Fire. Bath: 1841-1844. V. 71

LITTLE Lasses and Lads. Boston: 1869. V. 71

LITTLE Lays for Little Folks. New York: 1869. V. 71

LITTLE, LEWIS P.
Imprisoned Preachers and Religious Liberty in Virginia. Lynchburg: 1938. V. 69

THE LITTLE London Directory of 1677. London: 1863. V. 71

LITTLE, LOYD
Parthian Shot. New York: 1975. V. 69; 72

LITTLE Ninny Nonny - a Southern Folk Tale. Joliet: 1928. V. 71

THE LITTLE One's Delight. 1903. V. 71; 72

LITTLE One's Toys. Akron: 1909. V. 71

LITTLE Pets. London: 1896. V. 72

LITTLE Pets Linen ABC. New York: 1886?. V. 73

LITTLE Picture Songs. 1918. V. 71

LITTLE Playfellows. Cincinnati: 1884. V. 71

A LITTLE Present for a Good Child. (Number 4). Greenfield: 1848. V. 73

LITTLE Red Riding Hood. New York: 1860. V. 71
LITTLE Red Riding Hood. New York: 1867. V. 71
LITTLE Red Riding Hood. New York: 1888. V. 71
LITTLE Red Riding Hood. Chicago: 1908. V. 70
LITTLE Red Riding Hood. New York: 1911. V. 73
LITTLE Red Riding Hood. New York: 1915. V. 70
LITTLE Red Riding Hood. New York: 1934. V. 70

THE LITTLE Riddler. Worcester: 1842-1853. V. 73

THE LITTLE Sketch-Book; or Useful Objects Illustrated. New York: 1856-1866. V. 71

LITTLE Songs of Long Ago. 1912. V. 70

LITTLE Stories for Little Children. New York: 1825-1833. V. 73

LITTLE Tot's Play-Time Book. London: 1920. V. 73

THE LITTLE Traveller; or, a Sketch of the Various Nations of the World.... London: 1830. V. 73

LITTLE, WEE WILLIE
Tall Base-Ball Stories...Every One a Five-Base Hit!. New York: 1948. V. 71

LITTLE Wide-Awake, 1889. London: 1889. V. 73

LITTLE, WILLIAM
The Easy Instructor; or, a New Method of Teaching Sacred Harmony. Utica: 1818. V. 71

LITTLE, WILLIAM JOHN
Symbolae ad Talipedem Varum Cognoscendum...Dissertatio Inauguralis Medica.... Berlin: 1837. V. 69

LITTLEDALE, HENRY ANTHONY
King Henry's Well and Pudsay's Leap. Ballads Founded on Craven Legends. 1856. V. 71

LITTLEFIELD, S.
Visions of Paradise, Themes and Variations on the Garden. New York: 1985. V. 68

LITTLETON, ADAM
Sixty One Sermons Preached Mostly on Public Occasions. London: 1680. V. 72

LITTLEWOOD, JOAN
Oh What a Lovely War. London: 1965. V. 73

LITTLEWOOD, S. R.
Valentine and Orson. The Twin Knights of France. London: 1919. V. 68; 71

LIVELY, PENELOPE
Astercote. London: 1970. V. 72
The Driftway. London: 1972. V. 69; 72
Moon Tiger. New York: 1988. V. 68

LIVERMORE, MARY A.
My Story of the War: a Woman's Narrative of Four Years Personal Experience as a Nurse in the Union Army.... Hartford: 1889. V. 69

LIVERMORE, THOMAS L.
History of the Eighteenth New Hampshire Volunteers, 1864-1865. Boston: 1904. V. 71

LIVERPOOL A Few Years Since. 1852. V. 73

LIVERPOOL, CHARLES JENKINSON, 1ST EARL OF
A Treatise on the Coins of the Realm; in a Letter to the King. Oxford: 1805. V. 68

THE LIVERPOOL Directory for the Year 1766.... Liverpool: 1860?. V. 71

THE LIVES of the Ancient Philosophers, Containing an Account of Their Several Sects, Doctrines, Actions and Remarkable Sayings. London: 1702. V. 70

LIVES of the Most Remarkable Criminals: Who Have Been Condemned and Executed for Murder, the Highway &c. London: 1927. V. 73

LIVESEY, MARGOT
Homework. 1990. V. 72

LIVINGSTON. The Story of a Community. Livingston: 1939. V. 71

LIVINGSTON, B. E.
The Distribution of Vegetation in the United States, As Related to Climatic Conditions. 1921. V. 73

LIVINGSTON, FLORENCE BINGHAM
Under a Thousand Eyes. New York: 1923. V. 70

LIVINGSTON, J. A.
Birds of the Eastern Forest. Boston: 1968. V. 72
Birds of the Eastern Forest. Boston and Toronto: 1968-1970. V. 71

LIVINGSTON, JOHN H.
A Dissertation on the Marriage of a Man With his Sister-in-Law. New Brunswick: 1816. V. 71
A Funeral Service, or Meditations Adapted to Funeral Addresses. Selected from Sacred Scriptures. New Brunswick: 1812. V. 71
Oratio Inauguralis de Veritate Religionis Christianae. New York: 1785. V. 68; 71

LIVINGSTON, ROBERT R.
Essay on Sheep; Their Varieties...Raising a Flock in the United States.... New York: 1810. V. 71

LIVINGSTON, WALTER
The Mystery of Burnleigh Manor. 1930. V. 73
The Mystery of Villa Sineste. 1931. V. 73

LIVINGSTONE, DAVID
The Last Journals...in Central Africa, from 1865 to His Death. London: 1874. V. 68
Livingstone's Travels and Researches in South Africa.... Philadelphia: 1858. V. 71
Missionary Travels and Researches in South Africa. London: 1857. V. 68; 70; 71
Missionary Travels and Researches in South Africa. New York: 1858. V. 71
A Popular Account Of Missionary Travels And Researches In South Africa. London: 1861. V. 72

LIVINGSTONE-LEARMONTH, DAVID
Horse in Art. London: 1958. V. 72

LIVINSKY, ISIDORE
Reminiscences of Poland, Her Revolutionary and Her Rights. London: 1848. V. 73

LIVRE *des Routes d'Italie a l'Isage des Seigneurs Qui Voyagent par la Poste....* 1780. V. 69

LIVY
Historiarum Ab Urbe Condita. Edinburgi: 1751. V. 71
Historiarum ab Urbe Condita Libri Qui supersunt. Oxford: 1708. V. 68
Historiarum que Supersunt ex Recensione Arn. Drakenborchii. Oxford: 1813. V. 73
The Romanae Historie.... London: 1600. V. 68; 72

LIZARS, JOHN
A System of Anatomical Plates of the Human Body.... Edinburgh: 1823-1827?. V. 73
A System of Anatomical Plates of the Human Body.... Edinburgh: 1856. V. 72

LLEWELLYN, RICHARD
How Green Was My Valley. London: 1939. V. 69; 70; 71; 73
None But the Lonely Heart. 1943. V. 68
None but the Lonely Heart. London: 1943. V. 73

LLEWLLYN, KARL N.
The Cheyenne Way, Conflict and Case Law in Primitive Juries Prudence. Norman: 1941. V. 73

LLOYD, ANGLESEA
Mary Clarkson; Or The Kirkstall Abbey Murder. Leeds. V. 72

LLOYD, B. E.
Lights and Shades in San Francisco. San Francisco: 1876. V. 68

LLOYD BROTHERS & CO.
Recollections of the Great Exhibition 1851. London: 1851. V. 73

LLOYD, CHARLES
The Anatomy of a Late Negociation. London: 1763. V. 73
Blank Verse. 1798. V. 73
Desultory Thoughts in London, Titus and Gisippus, with Other Poems. 1821. V. 73
Nugae Canorae. Poems. 1819. V. 73
Poems. London: 1823. V. 73
Poems on the Death of Priscilla Farmer by Her grandson, Charles Lloyd. Bristol: 1796. V. 73
Poems on Various Subjects. 1795. V. 73

LLOYD, DAVID
The Cell Division Cycle. London: 1982. V. 68

LLOYD, E.
A Visit to the Antipodes: with Some Reminiscences of a Sojourn in Australia. London: 1846. V. 71

LLOYD, EDWARD, LTD.
The Battle with the London Anarchists.... 1910. V. 71

LLOYD, EUSEBIUS ARTHUR
A Treatise on the Nature and Treatment of Scrophula.... 1821. V. 72

LLOYD, FREDERICK
An Impartial Life of Viscount Nelson, Duke of Bronte in Sicily, Knight of the Most Honourable Order of the Bath, Grand Cross of the Orders of St. Ferdinand and of Merit.... Ormskirk: 1806. V. 73

LLOYD, GENERAL
A Political and Military Rhapsody on the Invasion and Defence of Great Britain and Ireland. London: 1795. V. 73

LLOYD, H. ALAN
Some Outstanding Clocks Over Seven Hundred Years 1250-1950. London: 1958. V. 72

LLOYD, JAMES T.
Lloyd's Steamboat Directory and Disasters on the Western Waters.... Cincinnati: 1856. V. 68

LLOYD, JOHN H.
The History, Topography and Antiquities of Highgate. London: 1888. V. 71

LLOYD, L.
Field Sports Of The North Of Europe. London: 1831. V. 72

LLOYD, MARY
Brighton: a Poem. London: 1809. V. 69

LLOYD, NELSON
The Robberies Company, Ltd. New York: 1906. V. 71

LLOYD, T. IVESTER
Hounds. 1934. V. 68

LLOYD, W.
Sketches of Indian Life. London: 1890. V. 72

LLOYD GEORGE, DAVID
War Memoirs. London: 1933-4. V. 70

LLOYDS, F.
Practical Guide to Scene Painting and Painting in Distemper. London: 1860. V. 69; 72
Practical Guide to Scene Painting and Painting in Distemper. London: 1875. V. 69

LOBEL, ANITA
On Market Street. New York: 1981. V. 70

LOBEL, ARNOLD
Bear's Busy Morning, Bear Gets Dressed, Bear Goest Shopping, Bear All Year. Set of Four Guessing Game Stories. 1986. V. 72
Fables. New York: 1980. V. 70; 72
Frog and Toad Together. New York: 1972. V. 70

LOBLEY, J. LOGAN
Mount Vesuvius. London: 1868. V. 70
Mount Vesuvius. London: 1889. V. 70

LOBO, JERONYMO
A Voyage to Abyssinia. London: 1735. V. 68; 70; 72

LOCH, JAMES
An Account of the Improvements on the Estates of the Marquess of Stafford, in the Counties of Stafford and Salop and on the Estate of Sutherland. London: 1820. V. 68; 70

LOCHNELL
Saxon Lyrics & Legends after Aldhelm. London. V. 70; 71

LOCHNER, A.
Vornehme Wohnraume. Germany/Austria: 1910. V. 70

LOCK, JOHN
A Man of Sorrow. The Life, Letters and Times of the Rev. Patrick Bronte 1777-1861. 1965. V. 70; 73

LOCKARD, FRANK M.
Black Kettle. Goodlands, KS: 1924. V. 71

LOCKE, A.
The Tigers of Trengannu. 1954. V. 72

LOCKE, ALAIN
The New Negro. New York: 1925. V. 71
The New Negro. New York: 1927. V. 68
Plays of Negro Life. New York: 1927. V. 70

LOCKE, HAROLD
A Bibliographical Catalogue of the Published Novels and Ballads of William Harrison Ainsworth. London: 1925. V. 73
A Bibliographical Catalogue of the Writings of Sir Arthur Conan Doyle, M.D., LL.D. 1879-1928. New York: 1928. V. 73

LOCKE, JAMES
Tweed and Don; or, Recollection and Reflections of an Angler for the Last Fifty Years. Edinburgh: 1860. V. 71

LOCKE, JOHN
A Collection of Several Pieces.... London: 1720. V. 69
The Conduct of the Understanding...to Which is Added, an Abstract of Mr. Locke's Essay on Human Understanding. Cambridge: 1781. V. 71
An Essay Concerning Human Understanding and Life of the Author. London: 1795. V. 69
An Essay Concerning Humane Understanding. London: 1706. V. 73
Some Thoughts Concerning Education. Edinburgh: 1752. V. 73
Some Thoughts Concerning Education. London: 1800. V. 69
Some Thoughts Concerning Education. London: 1809. V. 71
Two Treatises of Government. London: 1713. V. 69
The Works. London: 1801. V. 73

LOCKE, SAMUEL
A New Abstract of the Excise Statutes; Including the Whole of the Late Regulations, to the End of the Session of the 28th, George III.... Sherborne: 1788. V. 72

LOCKE, WILLIAM E.
Centennial Discourse, Containing a History of the Scotch Plains Baptist Church, New Jersey, During the Fist Century of Its Ecclesiastical Existence. New York: 1847. V. 71

LOCKE, WILLIAM J.
The Coming of Amos. London: 1924. V. 69
Far-Away Stories. New York: 1919. V. 69; 71
The Golden Journal of Mr. Paradyne. London: 1924. V. 70
The House of Baltazar. London: 1920:. V. 72
Morals for the Young. London: 1915. V. 71
Perella. New York: 1926. V. 71

LOCKE, WILLIAM J. continued
The Town of Tombarel. London: 1930. V. 69

LOCKER-LAMPSON, FREDERICK
London Lyrics. London: 1857. V. 73
London Lyrics. London: 1881. V. 68
A Selection from the Works of Frederick Locker. London: 1865. V. 69

LOCKER-LAMPSON, HANNAH JANE
What the Black Bird Said: a Story in Four Chirps. London: 1881. V. 69

LOCKHART, AGNES HELEN
Gems from Scotia's Crown. Boston: 1897. V. 73

LOCKHART, ARTHUR JOHN
The Papers of Pastor Felix. Cincinnati & New York: 1903. V. 68

LOCKHART, J.
Wild America. Nashville: 1979. V. 68

LOCKHART, JOHN GIBSON
Memoirs of Sir Walter Scott. London: 1900. V. 70
Memoirs of the Life of Sir Walter Scott. Edinburgh: 1837-1838. V. 71
Peter's Letters to His Kinsfolk. London: 1819. V. 70; 71
Valerius: a Roman Story. Edinburgh: 1821. V. 68

LOCKINGE, HENRY
Historical Gleanings on the Memorable Field of Naseby. London: 1830. V. 72

LOCKLEY, R. M.
Dream Island. A Record of the Simple Life. London: 1931. V. 71

LOCKMAN, JOHN
A History of the Cruel Sufferings of the Protestants, and Others, by Popish Persecutions.... London: 1760. V. 69

LOCKRIDGE, FRANCES
Death of a Tall Man. Philadelphia: 1946. V. 69; 72
The Norths Meet Murder. 1940. V. 73
Untidy Murder. Philadelphia: 1947. V. 71

LOCKRIDGE, RICHARD
Mr. and Mrs. North. 1936. V. 73
One Lady, Two Cats. Philadelphia: 1967. V. 71

LOCKRIDGE, ROSS
Raintree County. Boston: 1948. V. 70; 71; 72

LOCKWOOD, A. G. B.
Gardens of Colony and State, Gardens and Gardeners of the American Colonies and of the Republic Before 1840. New York: 1931-1934. V. 68; 71; 73

LOCKWOOD, ANTHONY
A Brief Description of Nova Soctia, with Plates of the Principal Harbors.... London: 1818. V. 73

LOCKWOOD, FRANK C.
The Apache Indians. New York: 1938. V. 72
Arizona Characters. Los Angeles: 1928. V. 70
The Frank Lockwood Sketch Book. London: 1898. V. 70; 71; 72
The Law and Lawyers of Pickwick. London: 1896. V. 69
Life in Old Tucson 1854-1864. Los Angeles: 1943. V. 68; 73
The Life of Edward E. Ayer. Chicago: 1929. V. 73
Pioneer Days in Arizona. New York: 1932. V. 68; 69; 70; 72; 73
Tucson - the Old Pueblo. Phoenix. V. 68

LOCKWOOD, JAMES D.
Life and Adventures of A Drummer Boy or Seven Years A Soldier. Albany, NY: 1893. V. 72

LOCKWOOD, JOHN PALMER
Darkey Sermons from Charleston County. Columbia: 1925. V. 71

LOCKWOOD, LUKE VINCENT
Colonial Furniture in America. New York: 1901. V. 72

LOCKYER, A. M.
The Robbers of Squeak. London: 1890. V. 70

LOCKYER, J. NORMAN
The Chemistry of the Sun. London and New York: 1887. V. 69
The Total Solar Eclipse of August 9, 1896. Report on the Expedition to Kio Island. London: 1897. V. 69

LOCY, WILLIAM A.
Contribution to the Structure and Development of the Vertebrate Head. Boston;: 1895. V. 68
The Growth of Biology. London: 1925. V. 68

LODDIGES, CONRAD & SONS
Botanical Cabinet, Consisting of Coloured Delineations of Plants from all Countries. London: 1824. V. 69

LODGE, DAVID
The Art of Fiction. London: 1992. V. 70
The British Museum is Falling Down. 1965. V. 71
Ginger, You're Barmy. London: 1962. V. 70
Graham Greene. New York and London: 1966. V. 70
How Far Can You Go?. London: 1980. V. 70; 73
Language of Fiction - Essays in Criticism and Verbal Analysis of the English Novel. London: 1966. V. 72
The Man Who Wouldn't Get Up and Other Stories. London: 1998. V. 68
The Novelist at the Crossroads and Other Essays on Fiction and Criticism. London: 1971. V. 72
Rolfe's Bestiary. London: 1963. V. 70
Small World: an Academic Romance. London: 1984. V. 69

LODGE, EDMUND
Illustrations of British History, Biography and Manners in the Reigns of Henry VIII, Edward VI, Mary, Elizabeth and James I.... London: 1838. V. 71
Portraits of Illustrious Personages of Great Britain. 1835. V. 71
Portraits of Illustrious Personages of Great Britain. London: 1849-1850. V. 71
Portraits of Illustrious Personages of Great Britain. London and New York: 1860. V. 68; 72

LODGE, GEORGE E.
Memoirs of an Artist Naturalist. 1946. V. 69
Memoirs of an Artist Naturalist. London: 1946. V. 72

LODGE, R. B.
Bird Hunting through Wild Europe. 1908. V. 68
Bird Hunting Through Wild Europe. Montenegro: 1908. V. 72

LOEB, HAROLD A.
Doodab. New York: 1925. V. 69

LOEB, THEOPHILUS
Medical Practice of Curing Fevers: Correspondent to Rational Methods &c. and to Those Curative Indications.... London: 1735. V. 73

LOEHR, CHARLES T.
War History of the Old First Virginia Infantry Regiment, Army of Northern Virginia. Richmond: 1884. V. 69; 70

LOEWER, P.
American Gardens, a Tour of the Nation's Finest Private Gardens. New York: 1988. V. 68

LOEWINSOHN, MICHAEL
My Green Streetcar. 1966. V. 71

LOEWY, RAYMOND
Never Leave Well Enough Alone. New York: 1951. V. 72

LOFFLER, F.
Otto Dix: Life and Work. New York and London: 1982. V. 69; 72

LOFTHOUSE, J.
A Thousand Miles from a Post Office Or, Twenty Years' Life and Travel in the Hudson's Bay Region. London: 1922. V. 73

LOFTIE, ARTHUR G.
Great Salkeld: Its Rectors and History. London: 1900. V. 71
The Rural Deanery of Gosforth, Diocese of Carlisle, Its Churches & Endowments. Kendal: 1889. V. 71

LOFTIE, W. J.
Chapters for Travellers by Sea and Land. London: 1890. V. 69
A History of London. London: 1883. V. 71
The Inns of Court and Chancery. London: 1893. V. 71
Lessons in the Art of Illuminating. London: 1880. V. 72
Lessons in the Art of Illuminating. Glasgow, Edinburgh, Dublin: 1885. V. 68
London City. 1891. V. 71
Views of Wickow and Killarney. 1875. V. 69

LOFTING, HUGH
Doctor Dolittle and the Secret Lake. Philadelphia and New York: 1948. V. 68
Doctor Dolittle and the Secret Lake. London: 1949. V. 71
Doctor Dolittle in the Moon. New York: 1928. V. 70; 72
Doctor Dolittle's Birthday Book. New York: 1935. V. 72
Doctor Dolittle's Caravan. New York: 1926. V. 70; 71; 73
Doctor Dolittle's Garden. New York: 1927. V. 70; 71
Doctor Dolittle's Post Office. New York: 1923. V. 71
Doctor Dolittle's Return. New York: 1933. V. 70; 72
Doctor Dolittle's Zoo. New York: 1925. V. 71
Gub Gub's Book: an Encyclopedia of Food in Twenty Volumes. New York: 1932. V. 70; 72
The Story of Doctor Dolittle. New York: 1920. V. 73
The Story of Zingo: the Commercial Traveler. Jersey City: 1924. V. 70
Tommy Tilly and Mrs. Tubbs. London: 1938. V. 70
The Twilight of Magic. New York: 1930. V. 72
The Voyages of Doctor Dolittle. New York: 1922. V. 72

LOFTS, NORAH
Blossom Like the Rose. New York: 1939. V. 70

LOFTUS, WILLIAM R.
Loftus's New Mixing and Reducing Book. London: 1869. V. 68

LOGAN, JAMES
Experiments at Meletemata de Plantarum Generatione Experiments and considerations on the Generation of Plants. London: 1747. V. 72
The Scottish Gael: or, Celtic Manners, as Preserved Among the Highlanders. Hartford: 1853. V. 72

LOGAN, JOHN
Sermons by the Late Reverend John Logan, F.R.S.... Edinburgh: 1793. V. 70

LOGAN, JOHN A., MRS.
Reminiscences of a Soldier's Wife, an Autobiography. New York: 1913. V. 69; 70

LOGAN, RAYFORD W.
The Negro and the Post War World, a Primer. Washington: 1945. V. 71
Two Bronze Titans: Frederick Douglass and William Edward Burghardt Du Bois. Washington: 1972. V. 72

LOGGAN, DAVID
Oxonia Illustrata, Sive Omnium Celeberrimae Illius Universitatis Collegoorum, Aularum.... Oxford: 1675. V. 70

LOGSDON, GENE
The Man Who Created Paradise. Cleveland: 1998. V. 73

LOGSDON, GUY
The Whorehouse Bells Were Ringing and Other Songs Cowboys Sing. Urbana: 1989. V. 68

LOGUE, CHRISTOPHER
Devil, Maggot and Son. Tunbridge Wells: 1956. V. 68
The Man Who Told His Love: 20 Poems Based on Pablo Neruda's Los Cantos d'Amores. London: 1958. V. 71
Wand and Qaudrant. Paris: 1953. V. 71

LOGUE, ROSCOE
Tumbleweeds and Barb Wire Fences. Amarillo: 1936. V. 71

LOHMEYER, J.
Prince Fridolin's Courtship. 1888. V. 70

THE LOITERER, a Periodical Work.... London: 1789-1790. V. 69

LOMAS, JOHN
In Spain. London: 1908. V. 72

LOMAX, ABRAHAM
Royal Lancastrian Pottery 1900-1938. Bolton: 1957. V. 73

LOMAX, ALAN
Mister Jelly Roll. New York: 1950. V. 68; 72; 73

LOMAX, GEORGE
Mr. Plausible Prate; or the Adventures of an Assurance Agent. London: 1855. V. 71

LOMAX, JAMES
Diary of Otter Hunting. 1892. V. 68; 70
Otter Hunting Diary 1829-1871. 1910. V. 70

LOMAX, JOHN A.
Adventures of a Ballad Hunter. New York: 1947. V. 70
Cow-Camps and Cattle Herd. Austin: 1967. V. 71
Cowboy Songs and Other Frontier Ballads. New York: 1920. V. 69
Songs of the Cattle Trail and Camp. New York: 1939. V. 69
Songs of the Cattle Trail and Cow Camp. New York: 1919. V. 68; 71

LOMAX, JOHN T.
Digest of the Laws Respecting Real Property...in the United States... in Virginia. Richmond: 1885. V. 71
A Treatise on the Laws of Executors and Administrators: Generally in the Use in the U.S.... Philadelphia: 1857. V. 71

LOMAX, THOMAS
Encyclopedia of Architecture: Being a New and Improved Edition of Nicolson's Dictionary of the Ssience and Practice of Architecture, Building, Etc. London: 1852. V. 70

LOMAZZO, GIOVANNI PAOLO
A Tracte Containing the Artes of Curious Paintinge, Carvyinge & Buildinge, Written First in Italian.... Oxford: 1598. V. 69
Trattato dell'Arte de la Pittura. Diviso in Sette Libri. Milan: 1584. V. 69; 71

LOMBARD, NAP
The Grinning Pig. New York: 1943. V. 72

LOMBROSO, CESARE
L'Antisemitismo e le Scienze Mordene. Torino-Roma: 1894. V. 69
Due Tribuni Studiati Da un Alienista. Roma: 1883. V. 72
The Female Offender. London: 1895. V. 72
The Female Offender. New York and London: 1899. V. 69

LOMMEL, A.
Masks, Their Meaning and Function. New York: 1972. V. 69

THE LONDON City Livery Companies' Vindication. London: 1885. V. 73

THE LONDON Gazette For The Year 1950. London: 1950. V. 72

LONDON Sights for Little Folks. London: 1830. V. 68

LONDON
Report. Improvements and Town Planning Committee...on the Preliminary Draft Proposals for Post-War Reconstruction in the City of London 1944. London: 1944. V. 71
The Royal Charter of Confirmation Granted by King Charles II. To the City of London.... London: 1680. V. 71

LONDON. COMMISSIONERS OF SEWERS
London Street Lighting. Report of the Special Committee of the Commissioners of Sewers on Gas. Feb. 28th, 1865. London: 1865. V. 69

LONDON; a Descriptive Poem. New York: 1820. V. 73

LONDON Almanack for the Year of Christ 1761. London: 1871. V. 68

LONDON Almanack for the Year of Christ 1793. London: 1793. V. 68

LONDON Almanack for the Year of Christ 1797. London: 1797. V. 68; 71

LONDON Almanack for the Year of Christ 1798. London: 1797. V. 71

LONDON Almanack for the Year of Christ 1814. London: 1814. V. 68

LONDON Almanack for the Year of Christ 1818. London: 1818. V. 68

LONDON Almanack for the Year of Christ 1822. London: 1822. V. 68

LONDON Almanack for the Year of Christ 1823. London: 1823. V. 68

LONDON Almanack for the Year of Christ 1827. London: 1827. V. 68

LONDON Almanack for the Year of Christ 1830. London: 1830. V. 68

LONDON Almanack for the Year of Christ 1832. London: 1832. V. 68

LONDON Almanack for the Year of Christ 1833. London: 1833. V. 68; 71

LONDON Almanack for the Year of Christ 1835. London: 1835. V. 68

LONDON Almanack for the Year of Christ 1861. London: 1860. V. 68; 71
LONDON Almanack for the Year of Christ 1861. 1861. V. 72

LONDON Almanack(s) printed for the Company of Stationers. London: 1871-. V. 71

LONDON AND BIRMINGHAM RAILWAY
Book of Reference, Containing the Names of Owners, or Reputed Owners, and Occupiers of the Lands in Or Through Which the Said Railway is Intended to Pass. Birmingham: 1833. V. 68

LONDON and Fashionable Resorts.... 1895. V. 71

THE LONDON and Greenwich Railway Guide.... London: 1837. V. 69

LONDON and Its Environs: or, The General Ambulator and Pocket Companion for the Tour of the Metropolis and Its Vicinity.... 1820. V. 71

THE LONDON Chair-Makers' and Carvers' Book of Prices for Workmanship. London: 1829. V. 68

LONDON, CHARMIAN
The New Hawaii. London: 1923. V. 73
A Woman Among the Head Hunters, a Narrative of the Voyage of the Snark in the Years 1908-1909. London: 1915. V. 68

LONDON, CHATHAM & DOVER RAILWAY
Contractor's Jobs. No. I. The East Kent Railway. London: 1860. V. 68

LONDON COUNTY COUNCIL
Indication of Houses of Historical Interest in London. London: 1909-1938. V. 71; 72

LONDON Cries for Children. Philadelphia: 1810. V. 73

LONDON DIALECTICAL SOCIETY
Report on Spiritualism, of the Committee of the London Dialectical Society, Together with the Evidence, Oral and Written and a Selection from the Correspondence. London: 1871. V. 68

THE LONDON Directory of 1677. London: 1878. V. 71

LONDON, H. STANFORD
The Queen's Beasts. London: 1953. V. 71

LONDON, HANNAH R.
Shades of My Forefathers. Springfield: 1941. V. 71

LONDON, HENRY ARMAND
An Address on the Revolutionary History of Chatham County, N.C. Stanford: 1894. V. 71

LONDON, JACK
The Abysmal Brute. New York: 1913. V. 68; 69; 72
Before Adam. London: 1908. V. 73
Burning Daylight. New York: 1910. V. 69
Call of the Wild. New York: 1935. V. 69
The Cruise of the Dazzler. London: 1906. V. 73
The Game. London: 1905. V. 73
The Game. New York: 1905. V. 68; 71
The God of His Fathers and Other Stories. New York: 1901. V. 71; 73
Hearts of Three. New York: 1920. V. 68; 71
The Human Drift. 1919. V. 73
The Iron Heel. Moscow: 1934. V. 72
Island Tales. 1920. V. 73
Jack London: a Sketch of His Life and Work. New York: 1905. V. 71
The Jacket (The Star Rover). London: 1915. V. 72
John Barleycorn. New York: 1913. V. 68; 71
John Barleycorn. London: 1914. V. 72
The Kempton-Wace Letters. New York: 1903. V. 69; 71; 73
The Little Lady of the Big House. New York: 1916. V. 73
Lost Face. New York: 1910. V. 71
Martin Eden. New York: 1909. V. 73
Moon Face. New York: 1906. V. 70
The Mutiny of the Elsinore. 1915. V. 73
The Night Born. New York: 1913. V. 71
The Red One. 1919. V. 73
The Red One. London: 1919. V. 68
Revolution. Chicago: 1909. V. 71
Revolution. New York: 1910. V. 73
The Road. New York: 1907. V. 69; 71
The Sea Wolf. London: 1904. V. 73
The Sea Wolf. New York: 1904. V. 71

LONDON, JACK continued
Smoke Bellew. New York: 1912. V. 70; 73
A Son of the Sun. Garden City: 1912. V. 68
A Son of the Sun. 1913. V. 73
The Son of the Wolf. Boston: 1900. V. 71
The Son of the Wolf. Isbister: 1902. V. 73
Tales of the Fish Patrol. London: 1906. V. 73
War of the Classes. New York: 1905. V. 72; 73
White Fang. Lunenburg: 1973. V. 68

LONDON Jests: or a Collection of the Choicest Joques and Repartees, Out of the Most Celebrated Authors Ancient and Modern. London: 1690. V. 68

LONDON Marriage Licenses 1521-1869. London: 1887. V. 68

LONDON Oddities; or, the Theatrical Cabinet; Being Neat Tit Bits for the Lovers of Humour and Eccentricity.... London: 1822. V. 70

LONDON SURVEY COMMITTEE
Eastbury Manor House, Barking, Being the Eleventh Monograph of the London Survey Committee. 1930. V. 71

LONDON TO Dublin: with a Trip to the Irish Lakes and the Mountains of Connemara. London: 1855?. V. 71

LONDON: What to See and How to See It. London: 1850. V. 71
LONDON: What to See and How to See It. 1851. V. 71

LONG, A. L.
Memoirs of Robert E. Lee. His Military and Personal History. New York: 1887. V. 69; 70

LONG, ALEXANDER
Speech of Honorable Alexander Long, of Ohio, Delivered in the Federal House of Representatives April 8, '64. Shreveport: 1864. V. 70

LONG, BASIL
British Miniaturists 1520-1860. London: 1966. V. 72

LONG, E. A.
Ornamental Gardening for Americans.... New York: 1885. V. 68

LONG, ESMOND R.
The Chemistry and Chemotherapy of Tuberculosis. Baltimore: 1958. V. 71
A History of Pathology. Baltimore: 1928. V. 73

LONG, FRANK BELKNAP
The Hounds of Tindalos. Sauk City: 1946. V. 70

LONG, GEORGE
An Introduction to the Study of Grecian and Roman Geography. Charlottesville: 1829. V. 69

LONG, HANIEL
Pinon Country. New York: 1941. V. 69
Pittsburgh Memoranda. Santa Fe: 1935. V. 68; 70; 72
Poems. New York: 1920. V. 68
Walt Whitman and the Springs of Courage. Santa Fe: 1938. V. 68

LONG, J. A.
The Rise of Fishes. Baltimore: 1995. V. 72; 73

LONG, JAMES
Strike, but Hear!. Calcutta: 1861. V. 71
Trial of Rev. James Long, for the Publication of the "Nil Durpan (or Indigo Planting Mirror)" with Documents Connected with Its Official Circulation, Including Minutes by the Hon. J. P. Grant, Lieut. Governor of Bengal. London: 1861. V. 70

LONG, JOHN
Voyages and Travels of an Indian Interpreter and Trader.... London: 1791. V. 68; 71
Voyages chez Differentes Nations Sauvages de l'Amerique Septentrionale.... Paris: 1794. V. 68; 70; 73

LONG, JOHN DAVIS
Papers of John Davis Long 1897-1904. Boston: 1939. V. 71

LONG, JOHN LUTHER
Billy-Boy: a Study in Responsibilities. New York: 1906. V. 70

LONG, MARGARET
The Oregon Trail. Denver: 1954. V. 70
The Santa Fe Trail - Following the Old Historic Pioneer Trails on the Modern Highways. Denver: 1954. V. 70
The Shadow of the Arrow. Caldwell: 1941. V. 68; 69
The Smoky Hill Trail, Following the Old Historic Pioneer Trails on the Modern Highways. Denver: 1947. V. 68

LONG, MASON
The Life of Mason Long, the Converted Gambler. Chicago: 1878. V. 72

LONG, MAX
Death Goes Native. Philadelphia: 1941. V. 69

LONG, ROBERT CROZIER
The Swedish Woman. London: 1924. V. 69

LONG, S. H.
Narrative of the Proceedings of the Board of Engineers of the Baltimore and Ohio Rail Road Company, From Its Organization to Its Dissolution, Together with an Exposition of Facts.... Baltimore: 1830. V. 73

LONG, WILLIAM HENRY
A Dictionary of the Isle of Wight Dialect, and of Provincialisms Used in the Island.... London: 1886. V. 72

LONGACRE, EDWARD G.
From Union Stars to Top Hat - A Biography of The Extraordinary General James Harrison Wilson. Harrisburg: 1972. V. 72

LONGACRE, JAMES
National Portrait Gallery of Distinguished Americans. Philadelphia: 1837-. V. 71

LONGACRE, JOHN BARTON
National Portrait Gallery of Distinguished Americans. New York: 1970. V. 71

LONGFELLOW, HENRY WADSWORTH
The Birds of Killingworth. New York: 1974. V. 72
The Courtship of Miles Standish. Boston: 1858. V. 71; 72
The Courtship of Miles Standish. Indianapolis: 1903. V. 70
The Courtship of Miles Standish. Boston: 1920. V. 72
The Day is Done. London: 1902. V. 68
The Divine Tragedy. Boston: 1871. V. 71
Evangeline. Boston: 1847. V. 68
Evangeline. Boston: 1850. V. 68; 73
Evangeline. London: 1860. V. 70
Evangeline. Boston: 1897. V. 71
Evangeline. New York: 1900. V. 72
Evangeline. New York: 1903. V. 68
Evangeline. Indianapolis: 1905. V. 71
Evangeline Conte D'Acadie par.... Liege: 1883. V. 71
Excelsior, Illustrated. Springfield: 1873. V. 71
Flower-de-Luce. London: 1867. V. 73
The Golden Legend. London: 1851. V. 71
Hiawatha's Childhood. London: 1984. V. 70
Hyperion: a Romance. Boston: 1839. V. 71
Hyperion, a Romance. New York: 1839. V. 68; 70; 71
Kavanagh. Boston: 1849. V. 73
The New England Tragedies. I. John Endicott. II. Giles Corey of the Salem Farms. Boston: 1868. V. 73
Nuremberg. Philadelphia: 1888. V. 71
Poems. Boston: 1850. V. 68
The Poetical Works. London: 1865. V. 72
The Poetical Works. Boston: 1880. V. 73
The Poetical Works. London: 1890. V. 71
The Poetical Works. London: 1968. V. 72
The Seaside and the Fireside. Boston;: 1850. V. 70
The Song of Hiawatha. Boston: 1855. V. 68; 69; 71; 72; 73
The Song of Hiawatha. London: 1855. V. 70; 72
The Song of Hiawatha. London: 1856. V. 68; 73
The Song of Hiawatha. Boston: 1891. V. 72
The Song of Hiawatha. Chicago: 1911. V. 70
The Spanish Student. Cambridge: 1843. V. 68
Tales of a Wayside Inn. Boston: 1863. V. 69; 71
Tales of a Wayside Inn. Boston: 1864. V. 68
Tales of A Wayside Inn. London: 1864. V. 73
There Was a Little Girl. New York: 1883. V. 70
The Wreck of the Hesperus. Boston: 1845?. V. 73

LONGFIELD, C.
The Dragonflies of the British Isles. London: 1949. V. 68

LONGFORD, ELIZABETH
Images of Chelsea. Richmond-upon-Thames: 1980. V. 73

LONGHI, GIUSEPE
La Calcografia. Milano: 1830. V. 69

LONGHURST, MARGARET
Catalogue of Carvings in Ivory. London: 1927-1929. V. 70
English Ivories. London: 1926. V. 69

LONGHURST, P.
Hibiscus. Melbourne: 1978-1979. V. 70

LONGINUS, DIONYSIUS
A Treatise of the Loftiness or Elegancy of Speech. London: 1680. V. 71

LONGLEY, MICHAEL
Out of the Cold: Drawings and Poems for Christmas. Newry and Belfast: 1999. V. 70

LONGMAN, C. J.
Archery. London: 1901. V. 73

LONGMAN, HURST, REES, ORME AND BROWN
A General Catalogue of Valuable and Rare Old Books, in the Ancient and Modern Languages, and Various Classes of Literature.... London: 1814. V. 70

LONGMORE, THOMAS
A Treatise on Gunshot Wounds. Philadelphia: 1862. V. 68

LONGON, JEAN
The Tres Riches Heures of Jean, Duke of Berry. New York: 1969. V. 70

LONGRIDGE, C. NEPEAN
The Anatomy of Nelson's Ships. London: 1895. V. 68
The Cutty Sark. The Ship and the Model. London: 1975. V. 68

LONGSTAFFE, W. HYTON
Richmondshire, its Ancient Lords and Edifices. 1852. V. 73

LONGSTREET, AUGUSTUS BALDWIN
Georgia Scenes, Characters, Incidents &c. in the First Half Century of the Republic. New York: 1840. V. 68

LONGSTREET, HELEN
Lee and Longstreet at Hightide. Gainesville: 1905. V. 69; 70

LONGSTREET, JAMES
From Manassas to Appomattox. Philadelphia: 1896. V. 68; 69; 70; 71

LONGSTREET, T. MORRIS
Murder at Belly Butte and Other Mysteries from the Records of the Mounted Police. New York: 1931. V. 69; 73

LONGSTRETCH, R.
On the Edge of the World: Four Architects in San Francisco at the Turn of the Century. 1983. V. 68; 69; 72

LONGSWORTH, BASIL N.
Diary of Basil Longsworth, March 15, 1853 to January 22, 1854 Covering His Migration from Ohio to Oregon. Denver: 1927. V. 69

LONGUS
Les Amours Pastorales de Daphnis et de Chloe. A Paris: 1757. V. 71
Daphnis and Chloe. London. V. 71
Daphnis and Chloe. Penzance: 1803. V. 68
Daphnis and Chloe. Waltham St. Lawrence: 1923. V. 70
Daphnis et Chloe. London: 1878. V. 68; 72
The Pastoral Loves of Daphnis and Chloe. London: 1924. V. 71

LONGWORTH, ISRAEL
Life of S. G. W. Archibald. Halifax: 1881. V. 73

LONSDALE, HENRY
George Graham, F. R. S., Abraham Fletcher, William Brownrigg, F. R. S., Edward Troughton, F.R.S., . Rev. W. Pearson, F.R.S.,Rev. Fearon Falows, F.R.S. Robert Rigg, F.R.S., John F. Miller, F. R. S. Sir Joseph Williamson, William Woodville, M.D. London: 1875. V. 72
The Howards, Rev. R. Mathews, John Rooke, Captain Joseph Huddart. The Worthies of Cumberland, Vol 3. London: 1872. V. 72
The Life and Works of Musgrave Lewthwaite Watson, Sculptor. London: 1866. V. 71; 72; 73
Sir J. R. G. Graham Bart of Netherby. Worthies of Cumberland, Vol 2. London: 1868. V. 72
A Sketch of the Life and Writings of Robert Knox, the Anatomist. London: 1870. V. 68; 70; 71; 72

LONSDALE, JOHN, VISCOUNT
Memoir of the Reign of James II. York: 1808. V. 70; 71; 72

LOOK, AL
Harold Bryant - Colorado Maverick with a Paint Brush. Denver: 1962. V. 68; 73

LOOK Here. London: 1920. V. 69

LOOMES, BRIAN
Yorkshire Clockmakers. London: 1972. V. 70; 72; 73

LOOMIS, ALFRED
Lectures on Fevers. New York: 1881. V. 71

LOOMIS, ALFRED F.
Fair Winds in the Baltic. London: 1928. V. 68

LOOMIS, ANDREW
Creative Illustration. New York: 1948. V. 68; 69
Successful Drawings. New York: 1951. V. 69

LOOMIS, AUGUSTUS WARD
English and Chinese Lessons. New York: 1872. V. 69

LOOMIS, LEANDER V.
A Journal of the Birmingham Emigration Company. Salt Lake City: 1928. V. 68; 73

LOOMIS, NOEL M.
Pedro Vial and the Roads to Santa Fe. Norman: 1967. V. 72
The Texan Santa Fe Pioneers. Norman, OK. V. 72
The Texan Santa Fe Pioneers. Norman: 1958. V. 69

LOOMIS, ROGER SHERMAN
The Development of Arthurian Romance. London: 1963. V. 72

LOOS, ANITA
But Gentlemen Marry Brunettes. New York: 1928. V. 70
Gentlemen Prefer Blondes. New York: 1925. V. 71
Gigi. New York: 1952. V. 69

LOOSE Leaves of My Scrap Book. 1833. V. 73

LOPE DEL RODO, JUAN
Idea Sucinta Del Probablismo, Que Contiene la Historia Abreviada de su Origen.... Lima: 1772. V. 69

LOPEZ, BARRY
About This Life: Journeys on the Threshold of Memory. New York: 1998. V. 71; 72
Arctic Dreams. London: 1986. V. 68; 72
Arctic Dreams. New York: 1986. V. 69; 70; 71
Coyote Love. Portland: 1989. V. 73
Crossing Open Ground. New York: 1988. V. 68; 70
Crow and Weasel. San Francisco: 1990. V. 70; 72
Desert Notes. Kansas City: 1976. V. 70
Desert Reservation. 1980. V. 71
Field Notes. New York: 1994. V. 72
Giving Birth to Thunder, Sleeping With His Daughter. Kansas City: 1977. V. 69
Lessons from the Wolverine. Athens: 1997. V. 72
The Letters of Heaven. New York: 2000. V. 69
Light Action in the Caribbean. New York: 2000. V. 69; 72
Looking in a Deeper Lair: a Tribute to Wallace Stegner. Eugene: 1996. V. 68; 70; 71
Of Wolves and Men. New York: 1978. V. 68; 69; 70; 72
River Notes. The Dance of Herons. Kansas City: 1979. V. 68; 70; 72
Winter Count. New York: 1981. V. 71; 72

LOPEZ, INEZ
Whitney and Son. New York: 1941. V. 69

LOPEZ, KEN
Robert Stone. A Bibliography 1960-1992. Hadley: 1992. V. 72

LOQUE, CHRISTOPHER
New Numbers. New York: 1970. V. 68

LORAC, E.
Death Came Softly. New York: 1943. V. 68; 70
Dishonor Among Thieves. London: 1959. V. 68

LORCA, FEDERICO GARCIA
Lament for Ignacio. Paris: 1995. V. 70
Lament for the Death of a Bullfighter and Other Poems. New York: 1937. V. 70

LORD, ALBERT B.
Russian Folk Tales. New York: 1970. V. 70; 72

THE LORD is My Shepherd: The Twenty-Third Psalm. New York: 1980. V. 73

LORD, J. L.
Defence of Dr. Charles T. Jackson's Claims to the Discovery of Etherization. Boston: 1848. V. 68

LORD, JAMES
Alberto Giacometti Drawings. Greenwich: 1971. V. 70; 72; 73

LORD, JOHN
Bygone Bury. Rochdale: 1903. V. 73
Memoir of John Kay of Bury, County of Lancaster. Rochdale: 1903. V. 73
Memoir of John Kay of Bury, County of Lancaster. Rochdale: 1968. V. 72

LORD, JOHN KEAST
At Home in the Wilderness. London: 1876. V. 72
The Naturalist in Vancouver Island and British Columbia. London: 1866. V. 73

LORD John Ten, a Celebration. Northridge: 1988. V. 69; 72

LORD, JOSEPH
The Militiaman's Pocket Companion; with a Method to Form Company.... Hudson: 1822. V. 68

LORD, JOSEPH L.
A Defence of Mr. Charles T. Jackson's Claims to the Discovery of Etherization. Boston: 1848. V. 71

LORD, MYRA B.
History of the New England Woman's Press Association 1885-1931. Newton: 1932. V. 73

LORD, TOM
Clarence Williams. Chigwell: 1976. V. 71

LORD, W. B.
Crab, Shrimp, and Lobster Lore, Gathered Amongst the Rocks at the Sea-Shore.... London: 1867. V. 68

LORD, WALTER
A Night to Remember. New York: 1955. V. 69
A Night to Remember. Norwalk: 1999. V. 68

LORDE, AUDRE
The First Cities. New York: 1968. V. 73

THE LORDS and Commons Reasons for Deprivation and Deposat of James II. From the Imperial Thorne of England. Edinburgh: 1689. V. 72

LORENS, M. K.
Sorrowheart. New York: 1993. V. 71

LORENTO, PROFESSOR
Amatuer Amusements. New York: 1878. V. 73

LORENTZ, H. A.
The Theory of Electrons and Its Applications to the Phenomena of Light and Radiant Heat. Leipzig: 1909. V. 69

LORENZINI, CARLO
The Adventures of Pinocchio. New York: 1929. V. 70; 72
Pinocchio. Philadelphia: 1920. V. 70
Pinocchio. New York: 1937. V. 69

LORENZO, CAROL LEE
Nervous Dancer. Athens: 1995. V. 70

LORIMER, E. O.
Tales from the Arabian Nights. London: 1932. V. 72

LORING, EDWARD G.
The Text-Book of Ophthalmoscopy. New York: 1893-1891. V. 70

LORING, EMILIE
Give me One Summer. Philadelphia: 1936. V. 71
We Ride the Galel. Philadelphia: 1934. V. 71

LORING, J.
Tiffany's 20th Century: a Portrait of American Style. New York: 1997. V. 68; 69; 72

L'ORME, PHILIBERT DE
Le Premier Tome de l'Architecture. Paris: 1568. V. 70; 72

LORTON, WILLIAM B.
Over the Salt Lake Trail in the Fall of '49. Los Angeles: 1957. V. 70

LORWIN, LEWIS L.
Labor Relations Boards. Washington, DC: 1935. V. 71

LORY, GABRIEL
Voyage Pittoresque de Geneve a Milan par le Simplon. Basel: 1819. V. 73

LOS ANGELES
Complete Report on Construction of the Los Angeles Aqueduct. Los Angeles: 1916. V. 70; 73

LOS ANGELES COUNTY PIONEER SOCIETY
The Los Angeles County Pioneer Society Historical Record and Souvenir. Los Angeles: 1923. V. 68

LOS ANGELES MUSEUM OF CONTEMPORARY ART
Ad Reinhardt. 1991-1992. V. 72

LOSCOMBE, C. W.
Catalogue of the Valuable Library and Choice Manuscripts Collected by the Late C. W. Loscombe, Esq. F.S.A. of Clifton. London: 1854. V. 70

LOSSEN, HERMAN FRIEDRICH
Grundriss der Frakturen und Luxationem. Stuttgart: 1897. V. 69

LOSSING, BENSON JOHN
A History of the Civil War 1861-1865 and the Causes that Led Up to the Great Conflict. New York: 1912. V. 73
The Pictorial Field-book of the Revolution; or Illustrations.... New York: 1851. V. 71
Seventeen Hundred and Seventy-Six, or the War of Independence, a History of the Anglo-Americans, from the Period of the Union of the Colonies Against the French.... New York: 1849. V. 73

LOST Classics. New York: 2001. V. 69

LOTHIAN, WILLIAM SCHOMBERG ROBERT KERR, MARQUIS OF
The Confederate Secession. Edinburgh and London: 1864. V. 73

LOTHROP, AMY
Casper. London: 1856. V. 72

LOTHROP, S. K.
Pre-Columbian Art, Robert Woods Bliss Collection. New York: 1957. V. 69
Pre-Columbian Art; Robert Woods Bliss Collection. New York: 1959. V. 71
Treasures of Ancient America: Pre-Columbian Art from Mexico to Peru. Geneva: 1972. V. 71
Treasures of Ancient America: The Arts of the Pre-Columbian Civilizations from Mexico to Peru. 1964. V. 72

LOTI, PIERRE
The Book of Pity and Death. London, Paris, & Melbourne: 1892. V. 69
An Iceland Fisherman. New York: 1931. V. 69
Madame Chrysantheme. Paris: 1888. V. 72
A Phantom from the East. London: 1892. V. 69

LOTT, BRET
The Man Who Owned Vermont. New York: 1987. V. 68; 70

LOTTINI, GIOVANNI FRANCESCO
Avvedimenti Civili...al Serenissimo D. Francesco Medici.... Florence: 1574. V. 68; 70; 73

LOUBAT, J. F.
The Medallic History of the United States of America, 1776-1876. New Milford: 1967. V. 69

LOUDER Than Words. New York: 1989. V. 72

LOUDIN, HENRI
Across Canada. James Bay. The Overflowing of Moose River, Spring 1903. Quebec: 1903. V. 70
Across Canada. Journey on Foot from James Bay to Quebec and Return. Winter 1903. Quebec: 1904. V. 70

LOUDON, JANE WELLS
The Amateur Gardener's Calendar. London: 1875. V. 73
Facts form the World of Nature.... London: 1848. V. 68; 70
Gardening for Ladies and Companion to Flower-Garden. New York: 1843. V. 71
Glimpses of Nature, and Objects of Interest Described.... London: 1848. V. 68
The Ladies' Companion to the Flower-Garden. London: 1858. V. 70
The Ladies' Flower Garden or Ornamental Annuals. London: 1849. V. 68; 71; 73
Lady's Country Companion. London: 1845. V. 73
The Year-Book of Natural History, for Young Persons. London: 1842. V. 70

LOUDON, JOHN CLAUDIUS
Arboretum et Fruticetum Britannicum; or, the Trees and Shrubs of Britain, Native and Foreign, Hardy and Half-Hardy.... London: 1844. V. 68
Cottage, Farm and Villa Architecture and Furniture. London and New York: 1846. V. 70
An Encyclopaedia of Gardening. London: 1834. V. 70
The Green House Companion. 1824. V. 69
The Green House Companion. London: 1832. V. 69
Hortus Britannicus. London: 1832. V. 70
Loudon's Hortus Britannicus. 1830. V. 72
The Suburban Gardener. London: 1838. V. 70

LOUGH, THOMAS
England's Wealth, Ireland's Poverty. 1896. V. 69

LOUGHBOROUGH, MARY ANN
My Cave Life in Vicksburg. New York: 1864. V. 73

LOUGY, ROBERT E.
Martin Chuzzlewit - an Annotated Bibliography. New York: 1990. V. 68

LOUHI, E. ALEXANDER
New York Nights. New York: 1941. V. 71

LOUIS, ANTOINE
Recueil d'Observations d'Anatomie et de Chirurgie. Paris: 1766. V. 68; 70; 72

LOUIS, JOE
My Life Story. New York: 1947. V. 69; 71

LOUIS, P. C. A.
Anatomical, Pathological and Therapeutic Researches on the Yellow Fever of Gibraltar of 1828.... Boston: 1839. V. 73
Recherches Anatomico-Pathologiques sur la Phthisie. Paris: 1825. V. 68

LOUISA; a Narrative of Facts Supposed to Throw Light on the Mysterious History of The Lady of the Hay-Stack. New York: 1801. V. 68

LOUISIANA. LAWS, STATUTES, ETC. - 1825
Code Civil de L'Etat de la Louisiane. Paris: 1825. V. 71

LOUISIANA. LAWS, STATUTES, ETC. - 1864
Acts Passed by the Twenty-Seventh Legislature of the State of Louisiana in Extra Session at Opelousas, December 1862 and December 1863. Natchitoches: 1864. V. 70

LOUISIANA PURCHASE
Documents Relating to the Purchase and Exploration of Louisiana. Boston: 1904. V. 73

LOUNSBERRY, A.
A Guide to the Trees. New York: 1900. V. 68

LOUNSBERRY, CLEMENT A.
North Dakota, A History and People, 3 Vols. Chicago: 1916. V. 72

LOUREIRO, J. DE
Flora Conchinchineses: Sistens Plantas in Regno Conchinchina Nascentes.... Ulyssipone (Lsbon): 1790. V. 72

LOUSON, W. S.
Charlottetown. The Beautiful City of Prince Edward Island. The Capital of the Garden of the Gulf. Grand Rapids: 1910?. V. 73

LOUTHERBOURG, PHILIPPE JACQUES DE
The Romantic and Picturesque Scenery of England and Wales. London: 1805. V. 68; 72

LOUVET DE COUVRAY, JEAN BAPTISTE
The Life and Adventures of the Chevalier de Fabulas.... London: 1793. V. 73
Quelques Notices Pour l'Histoire et le Recit de Mes Perils Depuis le 31 Mai 1793. Paris: 1794?. V. 70

LOUVRE
The Great Masters in the Louvre Gallery. First and Second Volumes. New York and Paris: 1898-1900. V. 71
Guide through the Galleries of Paintings of the Imperial Museum of the Louvre. Paris: 1862. V. 70

LOUYS, PIERRE
Aphrodite: a Novel of Ancient Morals. London: 1928. V. 69
The Songs of Bilitis. New York: 1926. V. 72
The Twilight of the Nymphs. 1928. V. 68
The Twilight of the Nymphs. London: 1928. V. 69; 72

LOVASIK, LAWRENCE
Making Marriage Click. St. Paul: 1947. V. 70

LOVE, J. KERR
The Causes and Prevention of Deafness. London: 1913. V. 69

LOVE, JOHN
Geodaesia; or the Art of Surveying and Measuring Land Made Easy. London: 1768. V. 70; 71

LOVE, NAT
The Life and Adventures of Nat Love. New York: 1968. V. 71

LOVE, ROBERTUS
The Rise and Fall of Jesse James. New York: 1926. V. 68; 73

LOVE, THOMAS
The Art of Cleaning, Dyeing, Scouring and Finishing, on the Most Approved English and French Methods. London: 1854. V. 68; 69

LOVECHILD, ELEANOR FENN
Sketches of Little Girls. London: 1859. V. 71

LOVECRAFT, H. P.
Beyond the Wall of Sleep. 1943. V. 69

LOVECRAFT, H. P. continued
Collected Poems. Sauk City: 1963. V. 72
Marginalia. Sauk City: 1944. V. 73
The Outsider and Others. Sauk City: 1939. V. 69; 70
Selected Letters of H. P. Lovecraft, Volume I: 1911-1924. Sauk City, WI: 1965. V. 71
The Shadow Out of Time and Other Tales of Horror. London: 1968. V. 72
The Shuttered Room and Other Pieces. Sauk City: 1959. V. 68
Something About Cats and Other Pieces. Sauk City: 1949. V. 68

LOVELACE, RICHARD
Lucasta Et Cetera. Mount Vernon: 1948. V. 70; 72
The Poems of Richard Lovelace. Oxford: 1925. V. 68; 72

LOVELL, DEVORA
Edgar Allan Poe Memorial. Muse Anthology of Contemporary Poets. New York: 1938. V. 71

LOVELL, DOROTHY ANN
In the Land of the Thinsies. London: 1944. V. 73

LOVELL, EDITH H.
Captain Bonneville's County. Idaho: 1963. V. 68; 73

LOVELL, JIM
Lost Moon: The Perilous Voyage of Apollo 13. Norwalk: 1994. V. 69; 71

LOVELL, ROBERT
Bristol: a Satire. London: 1794. V. 73

LOVER, SAMUEL
The Lyrics of Ireland, edited and annotated. London: 1858. V. 71
Rory O'More: a National Romance. London: 1892. V. 68

THE LOVER'S Miscellany; or, Poems on Several Occasions, Amorous and Gallant. London: 1719. V. 73

THE LOVES of Camarupa and Camalta, an Ancient Indian Tale. London: 1793. V. 73

LOVESEY, PETER
A Case of Spirits. London: 1975. V. 70
A Case of Spirits. New York: 1975. V. 71
The Detective Wore Silk Drawers. London: 1971. V. 70
The False Inspector Dew. London: 1982. V. 70
Keystone. London: 1983. V. 68
Waxwork. London: 1978. V. 68; 70
Wobble to Death. London: 1970. V. 70

LOVESTONE, JAY
The Government Strikebeaker. New York: 1923. V. 68

LOVETT, H. A.
Canada and the Grand Trunk 1829-1924. The Genesis of Railway Construction in British America and the Story of the Grand Trunk Railway Company of Canada from Its Inception to Its Acquisition by Canada. Montreal: 1924. V. 72

LOVETT, RICHARD
The English Bible in the John Rylands Library. London and Aylesbury: 1899. V. 71
Irish Pictures Drawn with Pen and Pencil. 1888. V. 70

LOVETT, WILLIAM
The Life and Struggles.... London: 1876. V. 71

LOVILL, JUSTIN
Notable. London: 1999. V. 72

LOVING, J. C.
The Loving Brand Book. Austin: 1965. V. 68; 71

LOVISI, GARY
Science Fiction Detective Tales: A Brief Overview of Futuristic Detective Fiction in Paperback. Brooklyn: 1986. V. 71
Sherlock Holmes: The Great Detective in Paperback. Brooklyn: 1990. V. 71

LOW, ALBERT PETER
Report on the Dominion Government Expedition to Hudson Bay and the Arctic Islands on Board the D.G.S. Neptune 1903-1904. Ottwa: 1906. V. 69; 72

LOW, CHARLES RATHBONE
Her Majesty's Navy. 1885. V. 69

LOW, DAVID
On Landed Property and the Economy of Estates.... London: 1844. V. 71
On Landed Property and the Economy of Estates.... London: 1856. V. 71

LOW, FRANCES
Queen Victoria's Dolls. London: 1894. V. 69

LOW, G. C.
The Literature of the Charadrilformes from 1894-1928.... London: 1931. V. 73

LOW, GEORGE
Fauna Orcadensis; or, the Natural History of the Quadrupeds, Birds, Reptiles and Fishes of Orkney and Shetland. Edinburgh: 1813. V. 70; 72

LOWE, ALFRED W.
A Popular Illustrated Handbook to Knaresborough. Knaresborough: 1890. V. 73

LOWE, CHARLES
Four National Exhibitions in London and Their Organiser. London: 1892. V. 71

LOWE, CONSTANCE M.
What a Surprise; a Mechanical Book for Children. London: 1895. V. 70

LOWE, E. J.
Beautiful Leaved Plants. 1891. V. 72
Fern Growing.... New York: 1898. V. 68
Ferns: British and Exotic. London: 1856-1860. V. 73

LOWE, F. A.
The Heron. 1954. V. 69

LOWE, G. S.
Foxhounds. 1907. V. 68

LOWE, JOSEPH
The Present State of England in Regard to Agriculture, Trade and Finance, with a Comparison of the Prospects of England and France. London: 1822. V. 70

LOWE, PERCIVAL G.
Five Years a Dragoon (1949-1954) and Other Adventures On The Great Plains. Kansas City: 1906. V. 72

LOWE, RICHARD THOMAS
A History of the Fishes of Madeira. London: 1843-1860. V. 73

LOWE, ROBSON
The British Postage Stamp. London: 1968. V. 72

LOWE, SAMUEL E.
A Box for Bedtime. The Bunny and the Porcupine; Sunny Bunny Years Good News; Old Roly Bear Visits His Cousin; Peter Fox Finds a New Home. 1926. V. 68

LOWE, WILLOUGHBY P.
The Trail that is Always New. 1932. V. 69; 70; 72; 73

LOWELL, AMY
A Dome of Many Coloured Glass. Boston and New York: 1912. V. 70
John Keats. Boston: 1925. V. 68
Legends. Boston and New York: 1921. V. 70
Men, Women and Ghosts. New York: 1916. V. 71
A Shard of Silence: Selected Poems of Amy Lowell. New York: 1957. V. 69
Six French Poets. New York: 1915. V. 68
Some Imagist Poets. New York: 1915. V. 70

LOWELL, ANNA CABOT JACKSON
Theory of Teaching, with Few Practical Illustrations. Boston: 1841. V. 68

THE LOWELL Directory for the Year 1872. No. XXVI. Lowell: 1872. V. 70

LOWELL, JAMES RUSSELL
The Biglow Papers. Cambridge: 1848. V. 72
The Biglow Papers. London: 1859. V. 73
The Cathedral. Boston: 1870. V. 73
Conversations on Some of the Old Poets. Cambridge: 1845. V. 68
The Courtin'. Boston: 1874. V. 69
Four Poems. The Ballad of the Stranger. King Retro. The Royal Pedigree. A Dream I Had. Hingham: 1906. V. 70
Meliboeus-Hipponax: the Biglow Papers. Cambridge: 1848. V. 71
The Poetical Works of.... Boston: 1869. V. 68
The Present Crisis. Eugene: 1941. V. 68; 72
Under the Willows and Other Poems. Boston: 1869. V. 68; 70
The Writings of James Russell Lowell in Poetry and Prose. Boston/New York: 1899. V. 73

LOWELL, JOHN
Peace Without Dishonour-War Without Hope. Boston: 1807. V. 73
Supplement to the Late Analysis of the Public Correspondence Between Our Cabinet and those of France and Great Britain. Boston?: 1809. V. 69

THE LOWELL Offering: a Repository of Original Articles, Written Exclusviely by Females Actively Employed in the Mills. First Volume. London: 1840. V. 70

LOWELL, PERCIVAL
Mars as the Abode of Life. New York: 1909. V. 71

LOWELL, ROBERT
Day by Day. New York: 1977. V. 71; 72
For the Union Dead. London: 1960. V. 69
For the Union Dead. New York: 1964. V. 71
History. London: 1973. V. 71
Land of Unlikeness. Poems. Cummington: 1944. V. 73
Life Studies. New York: 1959. V. 68; 69; 71
Lord Weary's Castle. New York: 1946. V. 68; 69; 71; 73
Lord Weary's Castle. New York: 1947. V. 73
The Mills of the Kavanaughs. New York: 1951. V. 71; 73
Near the Ocean. New York: 1967. V. 71
Notebook. New York: 1970. V. 71
Notebook 1967-1968. New York: 1969. V. 68; 71
The Oresteia of Aeschylus. New York: 1978. V. 71
Poems 1938-1949. London: 1950. V. 68; 73
Prometheus Bound. New York: 1969. V. 71
The Voyage and Other Versions of Poems by Baudelaire. London: 1961. V. 71
The Voyage and Other Versions of Poems by Baudelaire. London: 1968. V. 68

LOWELL, SUSAN
The Three Little Javelinas. Flagstaff: 1992. V. 73

LOWENFELD, VIKTOR
The Nature of Creative Activity. London: 1959. V. 72

LOWENFELS, WALTER
Apollinaire. Paris: 1930. V. 68

LOWER, MARK ANTHONY
The Worthies of Sussex.... Lewis: 1865. V. 70

LOWER, RICHARD
Tractatus de Corde. Item De Motu & Colore Sanguinis et Chyli in Eum Transitu. Amstelodami: 1669. V. 71
Tractatus de Corde. Item De Motu & Colore Sanguinis et Chyli in Eum Transitu. London: 1669. V. 69

LOWERY, WOODBURY
Descriptive List of Maps of the Spanish Possessions With the Present Limits of the United States, 1502-1820. Washington: 1912. V. 71

LOWIE, ROBERT H.
The Crow Indians. New York: 1935. V. 71

LOWMAN, AL
Printer at the Pass: the Works of Carl Hertzog. San Antonio: 1972. V. 69
Printing Arts in Texas. Austin: 1975. V. 68
Printing Arts in Texas. Austin: 1981. V. 70; 72
Remembering Carl Hertzog; a Texas Printer and His Books. Dallas: 1985. V. 72

LOWMAN, F. G.
Estuarine and Marine Ecology.... Columbus: 1970. V. 72

LOWNDES, BELLOC, MRS.
The Uttermost Farthing. London: 1908. V. 70

LOWNDES, FRANCIS
Observations on Medical Electricity.... London: 1787. V. 69

LOWNDES, MARIE ADELAIDE
Before the Storm. New York: 1941. V. 69
The Heart of Penelope. London: 1904. V. 73
Letty Lynton. London: 1931. V. 69
Motive. London: 1938. V. 73

LOWNDES, MARIE BELLOC
And Call It Accident. New York: 1936. V. 68
Studies in Love and in Terror. London: 1913. V. 71

LOWNDES, THOMAS
The Merchants Guide; Consisting of Tables for the Computation of the Duties, and Directions for Transacting the Business of the Custom House. Liverpool: 1774. V. 72

LOWNDES, WILLIAM THOMAS
The Bibliographer's Manual of English Literature.... London: 1834. V. 70; 71

LOWNE, BENJAMIN THOMPSON
The Anatomy, Physiology, Morphology and Development of the Blow-Fly. London: 1890-. V. 69

LOWRY, H. D.
Make Believe. London: 1896. V. 70

LOWRY, MALCOLM
Ultramarine. London: 1933. V. 71
Ultramarine. Philadelphia and New York: 1962. V. 68; 69
Ultramarine. San Francisco: 1962. V. 71
Under the Volcano. London: 1947. V. 68; 71; 73
Under the Volcano. New York: 1947. V. 68; 70; 71; 72; 73
Under the Volcano. Paris: 1950. V. 68

LOWRY, ROBERT
New York Call Girl. New York: 1958. V. 71

LOWTH, ROBERT
The Life of William of Wykeham, Bishop of Winchester. London: 1759. V. 69
A Short Introduction to English Grammar.... London: 1778. V. 69
A Short Introduction to English Grammar.... London: 1783. V. 69

LOWTHER, ALICE
When It Was June. Richmond: 1923. V. 70

LOWTHER, C.
Our Journall Into Scotland Anno Domini 1629, 5th of November, From Lowther. Edinburgh: 1894. V. 71

LOWTHER, CHARLES C.
Dodge City, Kansas. Philadelphia: 1940. V. 69

LOWTHER, GEORGE
The Adventures of Superman. New York: 1942. V. 69

LOWTHER, H. C.
From Pillar to Post. 1911. V. 69; 70

LOY, MINA
The Last Lunar Baedeker. Highlands: 1982. V. 73
The Lost Lunar Baedeker. New York: 1996. V. 72
Lunar Baedecker. Paris: 1923. V. 73
Lunar Baedeker and Time-Tables. Selected Poems. Highlands: 1958. V. 73

LOYALIST'S Centennial Souvenir: 1783-1883. Saint John: 1887. V. 68; 73

THE LOYALIST'S Daughter, a Novel. London: 1867. V. 69

LOYOLA, IGNACIO DE, SAINT
Epistolae Genuinae...Quae nunc Videntur ex Bibliotheca Florentina. Amstelodami: 1646. V. 72

L'STRANGE, A. G.
The Life of Mary Russell Mitford, authoress of Our Village, etc. related in a selection from her letters to her friends. London: 1870. V. 71

LUARD, HENRY RICHARDS
Lives of Edward the Confessor. London: 1858. V. 73

LUARD, L. D.
Horses and Movement From Paintings and Drawings. London: 1921. V. 70; 72

LUBBOCK, BASIL
American Deep-water Sailing Ships 1869-1929. Glasgow: 1929. V. 73
The Best of Sail. New York: 1975. V. 68
The Blackwall Frigates. Glasgow: 1922. V. 68
The Blackwall Frigates. Glasgow: 1950. V. 73
The Opium Clippers. Glasgow: 1933. V. 68
Sail the Romance of the Clipper Ships. Volume III. London: 1936. V. 69
The Western Ocean Packets. Glasgow: 1956. V. 73

LUBBOCK, J.
A Contribution to Our Knowledge of Seedlings. London: 1896. V. 72

LUBBOCK, J. G.
Aspects of Art and Science. Leicester: 1969. V. 68
Love for the Earth. Cambridge: 1990. V. 68; 72

LUBBOCK, RICHARD
Observations on the Fauna of Norfolk.... Norwich: 1879. V. 70

LUCAS, CLEO
I Jerry Take Thee, Joan. Garden City: 1931. V. 71

LUCAS, CURTIS
Lila. New York: 1955. V. 72

LUCAS, E. V.
Edwin Austin Abbey...His Life and Work. London and New York: 1921. V. 69
Forgotten Tales of Long Ago. New York: 1906. V. 70
Luck of the Year. New York: 1923. V. 70
Old Fashioned Tales. London: 1905?. V. 70
The Open Road. A Little Book for Wayfarers. London: 1923. V. 71
The Original Poems and Others by Ann and Jane Taylor and Adelaide O'Keeffe. New York: 1905. V. 70
Twelve Songs from Playtime and Company. London: 1926. V. 69
The Visit to London. London: 1902. V. 68
The Visit to London. New York: 1902. V. 73

LUCAS, F. L.
Gilgamesh, King of Erech. Waltham St. Lawrence: 1948. V. 69; 71
The Golden Cockerel Greek Anthology. London: 1937. V. 71
The Golden Cockerel Greek Anthology. Waltham St. Lawrence: 1937. V. 70; 71
Time and Memory. London: 1929. V. 69

LUCAS, FRED W.
Appendiculae Historicae; or, Shreds of History Hung on a Horn. London: 1891. V. 70

LUCAS, J.
Hunt and Working Terriers. 1931. V. 68

LUCAS, JOSEPH
Studies in Nidderdale. London. V. 73

LUCAS, KEITH
The Conduction of the Nervous Impulse. London: 1917. V. 70

LUCAS, MATTIE DAVIS
A History of Grayson County, Texas. Sherman: 1936. V. 73

LUCAS, RICHARD
(I) An Inquiry after Happiness...(II) Humae Life, or a Second Part of the Enquiry...(III) Religious Perfection, or a Third Part of the Enquiry. London: 1692-1696-. V. 72
Practical Christianity; or, an Account of the Holiness Which the Gospel Enjoins.... London: 1700. V. 69

LUCAS, W. J.
British Dragonflies. 1900. V. 69; 73

LUCAS, WALTER ARNDT
From the Hills to the Hudson. 1944. V. 71

LUCAS, WILLIAM JOHN
British Dragonflies (Odonata). London: 1899. V. 70; 72

LUCAS, WINIFRED M.
Units. London: 1896. V. 69

LUCE, A. A.
Fishing and Thinking. 1959. V. 68
The Life of George Berkeley, Bishop of Cloyne. 1949. V. 73

LUCE, EDWARD S.
Keogh Comanche and Custer. Ashland: 1974. V. 72

LUCE, ROBERT
Legislative Procedure. Boston: 1922. V. 73

LUCERO-WHITE, AURORA
The Folklore of New Mexico. Santa Fe: 1941. V. 73
Literary Folklore of the Hispanic Southwest. San Antonio: 1953. V. 73

LUCHETTI, CATHY
Women of the West. 1982. V. 68

LUCIAN
Deorum Dialogi Numero.... Augsburg: 1515. V. 73
The Dialogues of Lucian. London: 1930. V. 68; 72
Lucian's Dialogues. Dublin: 1772. V. 68
The True Historie of Lucian the Samosatenian. London: 1927. V. 71
The True Historie of Lucian the Samosatenian. Waltham St. Lawrence: 1927. V. 68; 72
The Works of Lucian of Samosata. Oxford: 1905. V. 73

LUCIAN, PSEUD.
1920: Dips Into the Near Future. London: 1918. V. 68

LUCIE SMITH, EDWARD
Beasts with Bad Morals. London: 1984. V. 68; 70

LUCILE Cook Book. 1892. V. 72; 73

LUCKENBACH, ABRAHAM
Forty-Six Select Scripture Narratives from the Old Testament. New York: 1838. V. 71

LUCKERT, KARL W.
The Navajo Hunter Tradition. Tucson: 1975. V. 69

LUCKOCK, JOSEPH
Essays on the Theory of the Tides, the Figure of the Earth, the Anatomical Philosophy, and the Moon's Orbit. London:: 1817. V. 68; 72

LUCKY, ROCHELLE
Cookery in the Middle Ages. Fallbrook: 1978. V. 72

LUCRETIA; or the Triumph of Virture. New York: 1808. V. 73

LUCRETIUS CARUS, TITUS
De Rerum Natura Libri Sex. Londini: 1717. V. 72
De Rerum Natura Libri Sex. Biminghamae: 1772. V. 70
De Rerum Natura Libri Sex. Birminghamiae: 1773. V. 69
De Rerum Natura. Libri Sex. London: 1824. V. 71
De Rerum Natura Libri Sex. 1913. V. 73
De Rerum Natura Libri Sex. Cambridge: 1920. V. 72
The Epicurean Philosopher, His Six Books De Natura Rerum Done into English Verse with Notes. Oxford: 1683. V. 71
An Essay on the First Book of T. Lucretius Carus. London: 1656. V. 71
The Nature of Things. London: 1813. V. 72
Of the Nature of Things. London: 1715-1714. V. 71

THE LUCUBRATIONS of Isaac Bickerstaff, Esq. London: 1713. V. 73
THE LUCUBRATIONS of Isaac Bickerstaff, Esq. London: 1749. V. 69

LUCY Webb Hayes. A Memorial Sketch by...as Read at the Annual Meeting of the Woman's Home Missionary Society of the Methodist Episcopal Church Held at Indianapolis, Nov. 1889. Cincinnati: 1890. V. 69

LUDLOW, WILLIAM
Report of a Reconnaissance from Carroll, Montana Territory, on the Upper Missouri, to the Yellowstone National Park, and Return, Made in the Summer of 1875. Washington: 1876. V. 70; 73
Report of A Reconnaissance of The Black Hills of Dakota Made in The Summer of 1874 by Captain William Ludlow, Corps of Engineers. Washington, DC: 1875. V. 72

LUDLUM, ROBERT
The Bourne Ultimatum. New York: 1990. V. 68
The Chancellor Manuscript. New York: 1977. V. 68
The Osterman Weekend. New York: 1972. V. 69
The Road to Gandolfo. New York: 1975. V. 68; 69; 71
The Road to Omaha. New York: 1992. V. 70
The Scarlatti Inheritance. Cleveland: 1971. V. 68
The Scarlatti Inheritance. London: 1971. V. 68; 73
The Scarlatti Inheritance. New York: 1971. V. 68; 69; 73
Trevayne. New York: 1973. V. 68

LUDWIG, CHARLES
Playmates of the Towpath, Happy Memories of the Canal Swimmers' Society. Cincinnati: 1929. V. 68

LUDWIG, COY
Maxfield Parrish. New York: 1973. V. 72; 73

LUDWIG, EMIL
Beethoven - Life of a Conqueror. London: 1945. V. 72
On Mediterranean Shores. New York: 1931. V. 70

LUER, C. A.
The Native Orchids of Florida. New York: 1972. V. 71

LUGAR, ROBERT
Plans and View of Buildings Executed in England and Scotland, in the Castellated and Other Styles. London: 1811. V. 69
Villa Architecture: a Collection of Views with Plans, of Buildings Executed in England, Scotland &c. London: 1828. V. 68; 70; 72

LUGS, J.
Firearms Past and Present. 1973. V. 69; 70; 72; 73

LUHAN, MABEL DODGE
Edge of Taos Desert, an Escape to Reality. New York: 1937. V. 70
Lorenzo in Taos. London: 1933. V. 72
Ma Vie Avec Lawrence an Nouveau Mexique. Paris: 1933. V. 72
Taos and Its Artists. New York: 1947. V. 69

LUHRS, VICTOR
The Longbow Murder. New York: 1941. V. 73

LUIS DE GRANADA
A Memorial of a Christian Life, Wherein are Treated All Such Things as Apperteyne Unto a Christian to Doe. Rouen: 1586. V. 72

LUKACH, HARRY CHARLES
The Fringe of the East: a Journey through Past and Present Provinces of Turkey. London: 1913. V. 70; 71

LUKAN, KARL
The Alps and Alpinism. London: 1968. V. 69

LUKAS, JAN
The Prague Ghetto. London: V. 68

LUKASIEWICZ, JAN
Elements of Mathematical Logic. New York: 1963. V. 69

LUKIN, JAMES
Turning Lathes. Colchester: 1894. V. 72

LUKIS, W. C.
An Account of Church Bells; with Some Notices of Wiltshire Bells and Bell-Founders. London and Oxford: 1857. V. 68
A Guide to the Principal CHambered Barrows and Other Pre-Historic Monuments in the Islands of the Morbihan, the COmmunes of Locmariaker, Carnac, Plouharnel, and Erdeven; and the peninsulas of Quiberon and Rhuis, Brittany. Ripon: 1875. V. 70

LULLIUS, RAIMUNDUS
De Secretis Naturae Sive Quinta Essentia Libri Duo. Strasbourg: 1541. V. 68
Libelli Aliquot Chemici.... Basel: 1572. V. 68
The Order of Chivalry. (with) L'Ordene de Chevalerie. 1893. V. 68

LUM, EDWARD H.
Genealogy of the Lum Family. Somerville: 1927. V. 71

LUMHOLTZ, CARL
Among Cannibals. London: 1890. V. 72
New Trails in Mexico. New York: 1912. V. 69; 70

LUMMIS, CHARLES F.
The Awakening of a Nation: Mexico of To-Day. New York: 1898. V. 71
A Bronco Pegasus. Boston: 1928. V. 69
The Enchanted Burrow: Stories of New Mexico and South America. Chicago: 1897. V. 68
General Crook and the Apache Wars. Flagstaff: 1966. V. 69; 71
Land of Poco Tiempo. New York: 1893. V. 68
The Land of Poco Tiempo. New York: 1928. V. 69
The Man Who Married the Moon and Other Pueblo Indian Folk Stories. New York: 1894. V. 71
Mesa, Canon and Pueblo. New York and London: 1925. V. 69; 70
Some Strange Corners of Our Country - the Wonderful of the Southwest. New York: 1898. V. 69

LUMPKIN, GRACE
Some Take a Lover. New York: 1933. V. 69
The Wedding. New York: 1939. V. 69

LUMPKINS, WILLIAM
La Casa Adobe. Santa Fe: 1961. V. 69

LUMSDAINE, J. P.
The Prints of Adolf Dehn: a Catalogue Raisonne. St. Paul: 1987. V. 69

LUNACHARSKY, ANATOLY VASILYEVICH
(Russian title) (Chancellor and Locksmith). Moscow: 1922. V. 69

LUNARDI, VINCENT
An Account of the First Aerial Voyage in England in a Series of Letters to his Guardian, Chevalier Gherardo Campagni, Written under the Impressions of the Various Events that affected the Undertaking. London: 1784. V. 70

LUND, HARALD
Familien Mus. Copenhagen: 1920. V. 73

LUNDELL, C. L.
Flora of Texas. 1944. V. 72
Flora of Texas. Renner: 1967-. V. 68; 72
The Genus Parathesis of the Myrainaceae. Renner: 1966. V. 72

LUNDIN, LEONARD
Cockpit of the Revolution. The War for Independence in New Jersey. Princeton: 1940. V. 71

LUNDY, BENJAMIN
The Origin and True Causes of the Texas Insurrection Commenced in the Year 1835. Philadelphia: 1836. V. 68; 71

LUNN, ARNOLD
Spanish Rehearsal. London: 1938?. V. 73
The Swiss and Their Mountains. London: 1963. V. 69

LUNNEY, D.
Herpetology in Australia, a Diverse Discipline. Mosman: 1993. V. 68

LUNT, DOLLY SUMNER
Woman's War-Time Journal. Macon: 1927. V. 69; 70

LUOMALA, KATHERINE
Navaho Life of Yesterday and Today. Berkeley: 1938. V. 69

LUPTON, WILLIAM
A Discourse of Murther, Preach'd in the Chapel at Lincoln's-Inn, and Publishe'd at the Request of the Worshipful the Masters of the Bench. London: 1725. V. 69

LURAY Caverns Fold Viewbook. New York: 1884. V. 72

LURCAT, ANDRE
Architecture: Illustre de 72 Photographies. Paris: 1929. V. 72

LURIE, ALISON
Foreign Affairs. Franklin Center: 1984. V. 69
Foreign Affairs. New York: 1984. V. 69; 72; 73
Imaginary Friends. London: 1967. V. 72
Love and Friendship. London: 1962. V. 73
Only Children. London: 1979. V. 68; 72
Real People. New York: 1969. V. 68
The War Between the Tates. New York: 1974. V. 68

LURIE, EDWARD
The Founding of the Museum of Comparative Zoology. Cambridge: 1959. V. 68
Louis Agassiz: A Life in Science. Chicago: 1960. V. 68

LUSCINIUS, OTHMAR
Musurgia Seu Praxis Musicae. Strasburg: 1536. V. 69

LUSHINGTON, HENRY
The Broad and the Narrow Gauge; or Remarks on the Report of the Gauge Commissioners. London: 1846. V. 68

LUSSAN, RAVENEAU DE
Raveneau de Lussan, Buccaneer of the Spanish Main and Early French Filibuster of the Pacific. (English translation of his Journal of a Voyage into the South Seas in 1684). Cleveland: 1930. V. 69

LUST, H. C.
The Complete Graphics and Fifteen Drawings. New York: 1970. V. 69; 72

LUSTGARTEN, EDGAR
One More Unfortunate. New York: 1947. V. 71
Turn the Light Out as You Go. London: 1978. V. 71

LUTHER Burbank, His Methods and Discoveries and Their Practical Application. New York: 1914. V. 69

LUTHER, MARTIN
A Commentarie Vpon the XV Psalmes Called Psalmsi Graduum, that is Psalmes of Degrees. (with) A Commentarie...Vpon the Epistle of S. Pavl to the Galathians. London: 1637-1644. V. 71
Contra Henricum Regem Angliae. VVittembergae: 1522. V. 71
Enchiridion; or the Small Catechism of Dr. Martin Luther. New Market: 1888. V. 69
Special and Chosen Sermons of Dr. Martin Luther, Collected Out of His Writings and Preachings for the Necessary Instruction and Edification of Such, as Hunger and Seeke after the Perfect Kowledge and Inestimable Glorie Wich is in Christ Iesu.... London: 1581. V. 70

LUTHER, TAL
Custer High Spots. Fort Collins: 1972. V. 72

LUTHERAN LADIES' AID, WHITE HALL WISCONSIN
Cook Book of Popular Norwegian Recipes. Northfield: 1924. V. 72

LUTTIG, JOHN C.
Journal of a Fur Trading Expedition on the Upper Missouri 1812-1813. St. Louis: 1920. V. 73

LUTTRELL, CLAUDE
The Creation of the First Arthurian Romance: a Quest. London: 1974. V. 69

LUTTRELL, HENRY
Advice to Julia. London: 1820. V. 72

LUTTRELL, NARCISSUS
A Brief Historical Relation of State Affairs from Sept 1678 to April 1714. Oxford: 1857. V. 71

LUTZ, E. G.
Practical Graphic Figures; the Technical Side of Drawing for Cartoons and Fashions. New York: 1925. V. 72

LUX, J. A.
Otto Wagner: Eine Monographie. Munchen: 1914. V. 69; 72

LUX, THOMAS
Memory's Handrenade. Cambridge: 1972. V. 73

LUXAN, DIEGO PEREZ DE
Expedition into New Mexico Made by Antonio de Espejo, 1582-1583.. New York: 1967. V. 68

LUXBOROUGH, HENRIETTA KNIGHT, BARONESS
Letters Written by the Late Right Honourable Lady Luxborough to William Shenstone, Esq. London: 1775. V. 69

LUXEMBURG, ROSA
Briefe an Karl und Luise Kautsky (1896-1918). Berlin: 1923. V. 68

LUYET, B. J.
Life and Death at Low Temperatures. Normandy: 1940. V. 69; 73

LUYKEN, JAN
Het Menselyk Bedryf. Vertoond, in 100. Amsterdam: 1694. V. 70

LUYNES, H.
Metaponte. Paris: 1833. V. 70

LUZERNE, FRANK
The Lost City!. New York. V. 68

LYALL, ALFRED COMYN
The Relation of Witchcraft to Religion. New York: 1876. V. 73

LYCETT, J.
A Monograph of the British Fossil Trigoniae. London: 1872-1879. V. 68

LYDE, SAMUEL
An Appeal for the Ansyreeh of Northern Syria. London: 1853. V. 68

LYDEKKER, RICHARD
Catalogue of Fossil Birds. London: 1891. V. 73
The Game Animals of Africa. 1926. V. 69; 70
A Handbook to the Carnivora. 1896. V. 70; 72
A Handbook to the Carnivora. Part 1 - Cats, Civets and Mungooses. 1896. V. 69; 73
The Royal Natural History. London: 1893-1894. V. 72
Sir William Flower. London: 1906. V. 68

LYDELL, D. D.
Memories of an African Hunter. 1990. V. 69

LYDON, A. F.
English Lake Scenery. London: 1880. V. 71
Scottish Loch Scenery. London: 1882. V. 71

LYELL, CHARLES
Elements of Geology. 1838. V. 73
Elements of Geology. London: 1838. V. 68; 69; 72
The Geological Evidences of the Antiquity of Man. London: 1863. V. 69; 72
The Geological Evidences of the Antiquity of Man. London: 1873. V. 69
Life, Letters and Journals of Charles Lyell, Bart. London: 1881. V. 72
A Manual of Elementary Geology; or the Ancient Changes of the Earth and Its Inhabitants.... London: 1855. V. 72
Principles of Geology. 1834. V. 73
Principles of Geology. London: 1834. V. 69
Principles of Geology. 1853. V. 72; 73
Principles of Geology. London: 1868-1872. V. 69
The Principles of Geology. London: 1875. V. 72
A Second Visit to the United States of North America. New York: 1849. V. 73
A Second Visit to the United States of North America. 1850. V. 73
A Second Visit to the United States of North America. London: 1850. V. 69
The Student's Elements of Geology. London: 1871. V. 72
Travels in North America, with Geological Observations on the United States, Canada and Nova Scotia. London: 1845. V. 70; 72

LYELL, D. D.
Memories of an African Hunter. 1913. V. 73
Memories of an African Hunter. 1990. V. 70; 72; 73

LYLE, DAVID
The Art of Short Hand Improved, Being an Universal Character Adapted to the English Language Where-by Every Kind of Subject May be Expressed or Taken Down in a Very Easy, Compendius and Legible Manner.... London: 1762. V. 70

LYLE, MARIUS
Unhappy in They Daring. New York: 1916. V. 70
The Virgin. A Tale of Woe. Manaton: 1932. V. 71

LYLE, R. C.
Royal Newmarket. 1945. V. 68; 73

LYLE, ROSTER
The Architecture of Historic Lexington. Charlottesville: 1977. V. 70

LYMAN, ALBERT R.
Indians and Outlaws. 1962. V. 69

LYMAN, BENJAMIN SMITH
General Report on the Punjab Oil Lands. Lahore: 1870. V. 73

LYMAN, T.
Challenger Voyage, Zoology. Part 14. Ophiuroidea. 1882. V. 73

LYMAN, THEODORE
Meade's Headquarters 1863-1865. Letters from the Wilderness to Appomattox. Boston: 1922. V. 73
The Spectroscopy of the Extreme Ultra-Violet. London: 1914. V. 72

LYNCH, ANNE C.
The Rhode-Island Book.... Providence: 1841. V. 68

LYNCH, FRANCES
Prehistoric Man in Wales and the West. Bath: 1972. V. 70

LYNCH, JAMES D.
The Bench and Bar of Texas. St. Louis: 1885. V. 71

LYNCH, JAMES J.
Box, Pit and Gallery, Stage and Society in Johnson's London. 1953. V. 69

LYNCH, JEREMIAH
A Senator of the Fifties - David C. Broderick of California. San Francisco: 1911. V. 69

LYNCH, LAWRENCE L.
No Proof. London: 1895. V. 68

LYNCH, PATRICIA
The Turf-cutter's Donkey. 1934. V. 69

LYNCH, VIRGINIA
Washington Irving Footprints. New York: 1922. V. 72

LYNCH, WILLIAM
The Law of Election in the Ancient Cities and Towns of Ireland Traced from Original Records. London: 1831. V. 70

LYNCH ROBINSON, C.
Intelligible Heraldry. 1948. V. 69

LYND, S. W.
Memoir of the Rev. William Staughton, D.D. Boston: 1834. V. 71

LYNDSAY, DAVID
The Poetical Works. Edinburgh: 1871. V. 73

LYNE, MICHAEL
From Litter to Later On. 1973. V. 68; 70
A Parson's Son. 1974. V. 68; 70

LYNEDOCH, THOMAS GRAHAM, BARON
The History of the Campaign of 1796 in Germany and Italy. London: 1797. V. 72

LYNES, GEORGE PLATT
Ballet. Pasadena: 1985. V. 68
George Platt Lynes: Photographs 1931-1955. Pasadena: 1981. V. 68; 70

LYNN, CATHERINE
Wallpaper in America. New York: 1980. V. 68

LYNN, MARGARET
To See a Stranger. New York: 1962. V. 68

LYON, B. B. VINCENT
Non-Surgical Drainage of the Gall Tract. A Treatise Concerned with the Diagnosis and Treatment of Certain Diseases of the Biliary and Allied Systems, in Their Relation to Gastro-Enterology and General Clinical Medicine. Philadelphia: 1923. V. 73

LYON, DANNY
The Bikeriders. New York: 1968. V. 68; 70; 73
Knave of Hearts. Sante Fe: 1999. V. 68
Pictures from the New World. Millerton: 1981. V. 68

LYON, FRANK
The Gladstone Umbrella, or Political Dainties. London: 1885. V. 71

LYON, GEORGE FRANCIS
A Brief Narrative of an Unsuccessful Attempt to Reach Repulse Bay, through Sir Thomas Rowe's Welcome in His Majesty's Ship Griper, in the Year MDCCCXXIV. London: 1825. V. 73
A Narrative of Travels in Northern Africa in the Years 1818, 1819, and 1820.... London: 1821. V. 70
The Private Journal of Captain G. F. Lyon of H.M.S. Hecla, During the Recent Voyage of Discovery Under Captain Parry. London: 1824. V. 70; 73

LYON, IRVING WHITALL
The Colonial Furniture of New England. Boston: 1891. V. 70

LYON, P. H. B.
Songs of Youth and War. London: 1918. V. 70

LYON, SARAH M.
The Musical Geography; a New and Natural Arrangement of the Names of All the Physical Features of the Globe.... Troy: 1848. V. 73

LYONS, A. B.
Manual of Practical Pharmaceutical Assaying Including Details of the Simplest and Best Methods of Determining the Strength of Crude Drugs.... Detroit: 1886. V. 71

LYONS, ARTHUR
All God's Children. New York: 1975. V. 69
The Dead Are Discreet. New York: 1974. V. 69; 72
The Killing Floor. New York: 1976. V. 69
The Second Coming of Satanism in America. New York: 1970. V. 71

LYONS, F. S. L.
Charles Stewart Parnell. 1977. V. 69
John Dillon, a Biography. 1968. V. 69

LYONS, GARY
Desert Gardens. New York: 2000. V. 68

LYONS, HENRY
The Royal Society 1660-1940. Cambridge: 1944. V. 68

LYONS, JOSEPH A.
Silver Jubilee of the University of Notre Dame, June 23, 1869. Chicago: 1869. V. 71

LYONS, LOUIS
The Sewing Machine. London: 1924. V. 68

LYONS, NATHAN
Aaron Siskind, Photographer. Rochester: 1965. V. 68
Under the Sun: the Abstract Art of Camera Vision. New York: 1960. V. 68

LYOTARD, JEAN FRANCOIS
Duchamp's TRANS/formers. Venice: 1990. V. 70
Pacific Wall. Venice: 1990. V. 70

LYRA Eboracensis; or Native Lays; Containing a Brief Historical and Descriptive Sketch of the Ancient City of York.... Hamilton: 1839. V. 69

THE LYRE, a Selection of Popular Psalm and Hymn Tunes. 1820. V. 72
THE LYRE, a Selection of Popular Psalm and Hymn Tunes. London: 1820. V. 70

A LYRIC of the Martyr Age by a Child of the Resurrection. Glagow: 1870. V. 70

LYRICS Pathetic & Humorous from A to Z. London: 1908. V. 71

LYSAGHT, A. M.
The Book of Birds.... London: 1975. V. 73

LYSAGHT, EDWARD
Poems. Dublin: 1811. V. 72

LYSIAK, W.
Frank Lloyd Wright. Berlin: 1983. V. 68

LYSONS, D.
Magna Britannia; Being a Concise Topographical Account of the Several Counties of Great Britain. London: 1816. V. 71

LYSONS, DANIEL
Origin and Progress of the Meeting of the Three Choirs of Gloucester, Worcester and Hereford. London: 1864. V. 68

LYSONS, SAMUEL
A Collection of Gloucester Antiquities. London: 1804. V. 68

LYTE, HENRY FRANCIS
Miscellaneous Poems. London/Oxford/Cambridge: 1868. V. 73
Poems, Chiefly Religious. 1833. V. 73
Remains of the Late Rev. Henry Francis Lyte, M.A., Incumbent of Lower Brixham, Devon. 1850. V. 73
The Spirit of Psalms; or the Psalms of David Adapted to Christian Worship. Brixham: 1834. V. 73
Tales in Verse Illustrative of the Several Petitions of the Lord's Prayer. 1826. V. 73

LYTLE, ANDREW NELSON
Bedford Forest and His Critter Company. New York: 1931. V. 70
Reflections of a Ghost. Dallas: 1980. V. 70

LYTTELTON, GEORGE LYTTELTON, 1ST BARON
Dialogues of the Dead. London: 1760. V. 68; 69; 73
A Gentleman's Tour through Monmouthshire and Wales, in the Months of June and July. London: 1794. V. 68
Observations on the Conversion and Apostleship of St. Paul...In a Letter to Gilbert West, Esq. Burlington: 1805. V. 71
What Will He Do With It?. 1859. V. 73

LYTTELTON, THOMAS LYTTELTON, 2ND BARON
Letters of the Late Lord Lyttelton. London: 1793-1792. V. 73

LYTTON, CONSTANCE
Prisons and Prisoners, Some Personal Experiences. London: 1914. V. 72

LYTTON, EDWARD GEORGE EARLE LYTTON BULWER-LYTTON, 1ST BARON
Athens, Its Rise and Fall. Leipzig: 1843. V. 70; 71
Caxtoniana; a Series of Essays on Life, Literature and Manners. Leipzig: 1864. V. 73
The Caxtons, a Family Picture. London: 1849. V. 68
Eugene Aram. London: 1860. V. 68
The Last Days of Pompeii. Leipzig: 1842. V. 70; 71
The New Timon. London: 1846. V. 71
Night and Morning. Leipzig: 1843. V. 70; 71
Not So Bad As We Seem: or, Many Sides to a Character. London: 1851. V. 68
Novels. Boston: 1895. V. 68
Paul Clifford. London: 1830. V. 72
The Pilgrims of the Rhine. London: 1840. V. 71
The Pilgrims of the Rhine. London: 1854. V. 68

LYTTON, EDWARD ROBERT BULWER-LYTTON, 1ST EARL OF
Poems. Boston: 1881. V. 69

LYTTON, HENRY A.
The Secrets of a Savoyard. London: 1921. V. 72

M

MAAS, PETER
Serpico. New York: 1973. V. 72

MAASKAMP, E.
Vues Remarquables, Edifices. Monuments et Statues dans les Provinces Septentrionales du Royaume des Pays-Bas. Amsterdam: 1816. V. 70

MABBE, JAMES
The Rogue, or, The Life of Guzman de Alfarache written in Spanish by Matheo Aleman... London: 1924. V. 71

MABIE, HAMILTON WRIGHT
The Young Folks' Treasury. New York: 1909. V. 73

MABIE, M. L.
The Saints, the Devil, and the King. Indianapolis: 1930. V. 69; 71

MABIE, PETER
The A to Z Book. Racine: 1929. V. 69; 72

MABINOGION
The Golden Cockerel Mabinogion: a New Translation.... Waltham St. Lawrence: 1948. V. 71
The Mabinogion. Waltham St. Lawrence: 1948. V. 68; 72

MAC KILLS Choice. London: 1953. V. 68

MAC ALISTER, A. W. G.
The Bench and Bar of the Provinces of Quebec, Nova Scotia and New Brunswick. Montreal: 1907. V. 73

MAC ALISTER, ALEXANDER
James Macartney. A Memoir. London: 1900. V. 68

MAC ALISTER, EDITH F. B.
Sir Donald Macalister of Tartbert. London: 1935. V. 68

MAC ANDREW, BARBARA MILLER
Elijah and Other Poems. London: 1880. V. 68

MAC ANDREW, DONALD
The House of Forsaken Hope. 1942. V. 70

MACARDLE, DOROTHY
The Irish Republic: Documented Chronicle of the Anglo-Irish Conflict and Partioning of Ireland.... London: 1937. V. 68

MAC ARTHUR, DOUGLAS
Military Demolitions. Ft. Leavenworth: 1909. V. 73

MAC ARTHUR, IAIN C.
The Caledonian Steam Packet Co. Ltd. Glasgow: 1971. V. 73

MACARTNEY, CLARENCE E.
The Bonpartes in America. Philadelphia: 1939. V. 71

MAC ASKILL, WALLACE R.
Lure of the Sea. Leaves from my Pictorial Log. Halifax: 1951. V. 68; 73
Out of Halifax. A Collection of Sea Pictures. New York: 1937. V. 73

MACAULAY, CATHERINE
(The History of England from the Accession to James I to that of the Brunswick Line). The History of England from the Accession of James I to the Elevation of the House of Hanover. London: 1769-1772. V. 69

MACAULAY, DAVID
Pyramid. Boston: 1975. V. 72

MACAULAY, KENNETH
The History of St. Kilda. London: 1764. V. 70

MACAULAY, ROSE
Catchwords and Claptrap. London: 1926. V. 71
Orphan Island. New York: 1925. V. 71
Potterism. New York: 1920. V. 69
The Two Blind Countries. London: 1914. V. 68
The Writings of E. M. Forster. London: 1938. V. 71

MACAULAY, THOMAS BABINGTON MACAULAY, 1ST BARON
Critical and Historical Essays contributed to the Edinburgh Review. London: 1866. V. 71
Critical and Historical Essays contributed to the Edinburgh Review. London: 1874. V. 71
Critical and Historical Essays contributed to the Edinburgh Review. London: 1890. V. 71
Evening. A Poem.... Cambridge: 1821. V. 73
The History of England from the Accession of James the Second. London: 1850-1861. V. 73
History of England, from the Accession of James the Second. London: 1860-1862. V. 71
Lays of Ancient Rome. London: 1842. V. 73
Lays of Ancient Rome. London: 1848. V. 73
Lays of Ancient Rome and Ivory and the Armada. London: 1867. V. 69
Lays of Ancient Rome, with Ivra and the Armada. London. V. 71
The Works. London: 1879. V. 68
The Works. London: 1898. V. 71

MACAULEY, ELIZABETH WRIGHT
The Wrongs of Her Royal Highness the Princess Olive of Cumberland. London: 1833. V. 71

MAC BEATH, GEORGE
Champlain and the St. John 1604-1954. St. John: 1954. V. 73

MAC BRAYNE, DAVID
Summer Tours in the Western Highlands & Islands of Scotland. The Royal Route, by the Royal Mail Steamers "Columba", "Iona", etc. Glasgow: 1910. V. 68; 71

MAC BRIDE, DAVID
Experimental Essay on Medical and Philosophical Subjects.... London: 1767. 70

MAC BRIDE, MAC KENZIE
Wild Lakeland. London: 1928. V. 71

MAC CAFFREY, JAMES
The Catholic Church from...Renaissance to the French Revolution. 1915. V. 69

MAC CALLUM, ANDREW
A Collection of Photographs from Some of the Works of Andrew Mac Callum. London: 1878. V. 68

MAC CALLUM, D. C.
Addresses. Montreal: 1901. V. 73

MAC CARTHY, DESMOND
Remnants. London: 1918. V. 68

MAC CARTHY, FIONA
Wood Engravings of David Gentleman. Montgomery: 2000. V. 68; 71

MAC CIONNAITH, L.
Focloir Bearla Agus Gaedhilge. 1935. V. 69
Focloir Bearla Agus Gaedhilge: English - Irish Dictionary. 1943. V. 69

MACCLESFIELD List of Prices. Macclesfield: 1873. V. 68

MAC CLURE, RAFAEL ELIZALDE
Los Angeles de Hollywood. Santiago: 1939. V. 70

MAC CLURE, VICTOR
Death on the Set. Philadelphia: 1935. V. 68
The Diva's Emeralds. London: 1937. V. 69

MAC CORKLE, WILLIAM ALEXANDER
White Sulphur Springs. Charleston: 1924. V. 68; 70

MAC CULLAGH, RICHARD JOHN
Viking's Wake Cruising Southern Scandinavian Waters. London: 1958. V. 69

MAC CULLOCH, DONALD B.
The Wondrous Isle of Staffa. Its History, Geology, Features and Associations. Glasgow: 1934. V. 71

MAC CURDY, RAHNO M.
The History of the California Fruit Growers Exchange. Los Angeles: 1925. V. 68

MAC DERMOT, E. T.
The History of the Forest Exmoor. Taunton: 1911. V. 68

MAC DIARMID, HUGH
First Hymn to Lenin and Other Poems. London: 1931. V. 71
The Kind of Poetry I Want: a Long Poem. Edinburgh: 1961. V. 71
Northen Numbers - Being Representative Selections from Certain Living Scottish Poets. London and Edinburgh: 1920. V. 71
Selected Essays of Hugh Mac Diarmid. London: 1969. V. 71

MAC DIARMID, JOHN
Lives of British Statesmen. London: 1807. V. 70

MAC DONAGH, THOMAS
Thomas Campion and the Art of English Poetry. 1913. V. 70

MAC DONALD, A. B.
Hands Up!. New York: 1927. V. 69

MAC DONALD, A. D.
Euphrates Exile. London: 1936. V. 71

MAC DONALD, ARCHIBALD
Peace River. A Canoe Voyage from Hudson's Bay to Pacific, by the Late George Simpson...in 1828. Ottawa: 1872. V. 68

MAC DONALD, B.
Practical Woody Plant Propagation for Nursery Growers. Volume I. Portland: 1986. V. 68

MAC DONALD, BETTY
Mrs. Piggle Wiggle's Farm. New York: 1954. V. 70
Mrs. Piggle Wiggle's Farm. Philadelphia: 1954. V. 73

MAC DONALD, D.
Cape North and Vicinity, Incuding Pioneer Families History.... 1933. V. 73

MAC DONALD, DWIGHT
Discriminations. New York: 1974. V. 72
The Memoirs of a Revolutionist. New York: 1957. V. 72

MAC DONALD, F.
The Sercet of Charlotte Bronte. 1914. V. 73

MAC DONALD, G. F.
Haida Art. 1996. V. 69

MAC DONALD, GEORGE
At the Back of the North Wind. New York: 1871. V. 70

MAC DONALD, GEORGE continued
At the Back of the North Wind. 1900. V. 68
At the Back of the North Wind. Philadelphia: 1910. V. 73
At the Back of the North Wind. London: 1911. V. 69
At the Back of the North Wind. Philadelphia: 1926. V. 73
The Back of the North Wind. Philadelphia: 1919. V. 73
Dealings with the Fairies. London: 1867. V. 68
The Gold Coast Past and Present. London: 1898. V. 71
The Imagination. Boston: 1883. V. 69
The Light Princess. New York: 1969. V. 73
Malcolm. London: 1887?. V. 68
Phantastes: a Faerie Romance for Men and Women. London: 1905. V. 68; 72
Poems. London: 1857. V. 68; 72
The Princess and Curdie. Philadelphia: 1883. V. 69
The Princess and Curdie. London: 1911. V. 69
The Princess and Curdie. 1912. V. 68
The Princess and the Goblin. Philadelphia: 1907. V. 72
The Princess and the Goblin. Philadelphia: 1920. V. 73
A Threefold Cord: Poems by Three Friends. London: 1883. V. 69
The Tragedie of Hamlet, Prince of Denmarke. A Study with the Text of the Folio of 1623. London: 1885. V. 69
The Vicar's Daughter. London: 1881. V. 68
Warlock O'Glenwarlock. A Homely Romance. Boston: 1881. V. 73
Wilfrid Cumbermede, an Autobiographical Story. New York: 1872. V. 70

MAC DONALD, GREVILLE
The Sanity of William Blake. London: 1908. V. 70

MAC DONALD, H. M.
Memorable Years in the History of Antigonish. Antigonish: 1964. V. 73

MAC DONALD, HUGH
Days at the Coast: a Series of Sketches, Descriptive of the Firth of Clyde.... Glasgow: 1878. V. 68
Thomas Hobbes a Bibliography. London: 1952. V. 70; 71

MAC DONALD, J. E. H.
My High Horse. Thornhill: 1934. V. 73

MAC DONALD, J. R. L.
Soldiering & Surveying in British East Africa, 1891-1894. Folkestone & London: 1973. V. 70

MAC DONALD, JAMES
Food from the Far West. London: 1878. V. 71

MAC DONALD, JAMES S.
Annals North British Society of Halifax, Nova Scotia for One Hundred and Twenty-Five Years from Its Foundation, 26th March 1768 to the Festival of St. Andrew 1893. Halifax: 1894. V. 72

MAC DONALD, JOHN A.
Troublous Times in Canada. Toronto: 1910. V. 73

MAC DONALD, JOHN D.
All Those Condemned. New York: 1954. V. 70
All Those Condemned. London: 2001. V. 71; 72
The Annex and Other Stories. Helsinki: 1987. V. 68; 69; 70; 71
Ballroom of the Skies. New York: 1952. V. 69; 72
Border Town Girl. New York: 1954. V. 70
Border Town Girl. New York: 1956. V. 69; 72
Border Town Girl. London: 1970. V. 68; 70; 72
The Brass Cupcake. New York: 1950. V. 68; 69; 72
Bright Orange for the Shroud. Philadelphia: 1972. V. 69
A Bullet for Cinderella. New York: 1955. V. 70
Cancel All Our Vows. New York: 1953. V. 68; 71; 72
Condominium. Philadelphia: 1977. V. 69; 70
Contrary Pleasure. New York: 1954. V. 69; 73
The Crossroads. New York: 1959. V. 70
The Damned. Greenwich: 1952. V. 73
Darker than Amber. Greenwich: 1966. V. 69; 72
Darker than Amber. London: 1966. V. 69; 70
Darker than Amber. London: 1968. V. 70; 73
Darker than Amber. Philadelphia: 1970. V. 69; 70
Dead Low Tide. New York: 1943. V. 69
Dead Low Tide. New York: 1953. V. 72
Dead Low Tide. London: 1976. V. 68; 69; 70; 72; 73
Deadly Shade of Gold. Philadelphia: 1974. V. 73
Deadly Welcome. New York: 1959. V. 72
No Deadly Drug. New York: 1968. V. 69
The Deceivers. New York: 1958. V. 69
The Deceivers. London: 1968. V. 70
The Deep Blue Good-By. Greenwich: 1964. V. 69
The Deep Blue Good-by. Philadelphia: 1964. V. 68
The Deep Blue Good-By. Philadelphia: 1975. V. 68; 69; 71
The Deep Blue Good-by. Philadelphia: 1976. V. 69
The Dreadful Lemon Sky. Philadelphia: 1974. V. 68; 69; 71; 73
Dress Her In Indigo. Greenwich: 1969. V. 72
Dress Her in Indigo. Philadelphia/NY: 1971. V. 69; 72
The Drowner. Greenich: 1963. V. 69; 70
The Empty Copper Sea. Philadelphia: 1972. V. 71
The Empty Copper Sea. Philadelphia: 1978. V. 68
The Empty Copper Sea. London: 1979. V. 68
The Empty Trap. London: 2000. V. 71; 72
The End of the Night. New York: 1960. V. 69; 70; 73
The End of the Night. London: 1964. V. 68; 70; 71; 72
End of the Tiger & Other Stories. Greenwich: 1966. V. 72
The Executioners. 1958. V. 69
The Executioners. New York: 1958. V. 72
A Flash of Green. 1962. V. 71
Free Fall in Crimson. New York: 1981. V. 73
The Girl in the Plain Brown Wrapper. Philadelphia and New York: 1973. V. 69; 71; 73
The Girl, the Gold Watch & Everything. London: 1974. V. 69; 71; 72; 73
The Good Old Stuff. New York: 1982. V. 73
House Guests. New York: 1965. V. 72
Judge Me Not. London: 1999. V. 70; 71; 72
A Key to the Suite. Greenwich: 1962. V. 69; 70
The Lonely Silver Rain. New York: 1985. V. 70
The Long Lavender Look. Greenwich: 1970. V. 70
The Long Lavender Look. Philadelphia: 1970. V. 70
The Long Lavender Look. Philadelphia: 1972. V. 68; 69; 70; 71; 73
A MacDonald Potpourri. Gainesville: 1988. V. 70
Murder for the Bride. New York: 1951. V. 69; 70
Murder for the Bride. London: 1977. V. 69
Nightmare in Pink. Philadelphia and New York: 1976. V. 68; 69; 70; 71; 73
No Deadly Drug. New York: 1968. V. 69; 70
The Official Travis McGee Quiz Book. New York: 1984. V. 71
One Fearful Yellow Eye. Greenwich: 1966. V. 70; 72
One Fearful Yellow Eye. Philadelphia and New York: 1977. V. 69; 70; 71; 73
One Monday We Killed Them All. Greenwich: 1961. V. 70
The Only Girl in the Game. Greenwich: 1960. V. 70
Pale Gray for Guilt. Greenwich: 1968. V. 70
Pale Gray for Guilt. Philadelphia and New York: 1971. V. 69; 70; 71
Please Write for Details. 1959. V. 69
Please Write for Details. New York: 1959. V. 70; 71; 73
The Price Of Murder. New York: 1957. V. 72
A Purple Place for Dying. Philadelphia and New York: 1976. V. 68; 69; 70; 71; 73
The Quick Red Fox. Greenwich: 1964. V. 70
The Quick Red Fox. New York: 1973. V. 72
The Quick Red Fox. Philadelphia: 1974. V. 69
Reading for Survival. Washington: 1987. V. 69; 72
The Scarlet Ruse. London: 1975. V. 69
The Scarlet Ruse. Philadelphia: 1980. V. 69; 70; 72
Seven. Greenwich: 1971. V. 69; 70
Seven. London: 1971. V. 70
Seven. London: 1974. V. 69; 71; 72; 73
Slam the Big Door. Greenwich: 1960. V. 70
A Tan and Sandy Silence. Philadelphia: 1979. V. 68; 69; 70; 73
Three for Mc Gee. Garden City: 1967. V. 69; 73
The Turquoise Lament. Philadelphia and New York: 1973. V. 69
The Way Some People Die. New York: 1951. V. 69
Wine of the Dreamers. New York: 1951. V. 69; 70; 71
You Live Once. London: 1976. V. 69; 72; 73

MAC DONALD, JOHN SANDFIELD
Proceedings at the Unveiling of the Statue of John Sandfield Macdonald First Prime Minister of Ontario in Queen's Park, Toronto November 16th 1909. Toronto: 1909. V. 73

MAC DONALD, MARIANNE
Blood Lies. London: 2001. V. 69; 70
Death's Autograph. London: 1996. V. 70; 71
Death's Autograph. New York: 1997. V. 70
Ghost Walk. New York: 1998. V. 70
Ghost Walk. London: 1997. V. 70
Road Kill. London: 2000. V. 70; 71
Smoke Screen. 1999. V. 68
Smoke Screen. London: 1999. V. 70

MAC DONALD, MAY
Life and Natural History Notes of Ewen Kennedy. Edinburgh: 1913. V. 69

MAC DONALD, PHILIP
The Crime Conductor. New York: 1931. V. 68; 69; 73
Death and Chicanery. Garden City: 1962. V. 69; 73
Death and Chicanery. London: 1963. V. 72
Forbidden Planet. New York: 1956. V. 71
The Link. New York: 1930. V. 73
The List of the Adrian Messenger. Garden City: 1959. V. 69
The Man Out of the Rain. New York: 1955. V. 69; 70; 73
Menace. New York: 1933. V. 73
Patrol. New York: 1928. V. 70
Persons Unknown. New York: 1931. V. 68; 70
Persons Unknown. New York: 1933. V. 73
The Polferry Riddle. New York: 1931. V. 73
Rope to Spare. 1932. V. 73
Rope to Spare. Garden City: 1932. V. 68; 69
The Rynox Murder Mystery. New York: 1931. V. 73
Something to Hide. New York: 1952. V. 73

MAC DONALD, PHILIP continued
Warrant for X. New York: 1938. V. 73
The White Crow. New York: 1928. V. 70

MAC DONALD, ROSS
Archer at Large. New York: 1970. V. 68
Archer in Hollywood. New York: 1967. V. 68
Archer in Jeopardy. New York: 1979. V. 69
The Barbarous Coast. New York: 1956. V. 69; 70
The Barbarous Coast. London: 1957. V. 73
Black Money. New York: 1966. V. 68; 69; 70; 71; 72; 73
Blue City. New York: 1947. V. 68; 69; 70; 71; 72; 73
The Blue Hammer. New York: 1976. V. 69; 73
The Chill. New York: 1963. V. 73
The Chill. London: 1964. V. 73
The Chill. New York: 1964. V. 68; 69; 70
A Collection of Reviews. Northridge: 1979. V. 69; 71
The Doomsters. New York: 1958. V. 69
The Drowning Pool. New York: 1950. V. 69
The Far Side of the Dollar. London: 1965. V. 73
The Far Side of the Dollar. New York: 1965. V. 69
The Ferguson Affair. New York: 1960. V. 70
The Ferguson Affair. London: 1961. V. 73
Find a Victim. New York: 1954. V. 69; 70; 71; 72
Find a Victim. London: 1955. V. 73
Find a Victim. London: 1976. V. 69
The Galton Case. New York: 1959. V. 69; 70
The Galton Case. London: 1960. V. 73
The Goodbye Look. New York: 1969. V. 68; 69; 70
The Instant Enemy. New York: 1968. V. 68; 69; 73
The Ivory Grin. New York: 1952. V. 69; 70; 72
Lew Archer Private Investigator. New York: 1977. V. 69
Meet Me at the Morgue. New York: 1953. V. 68; 69; 71; 72
The Moving Target. New York: 1949. V. 69; 71
The Moving Target. London: 1951. V. 73
The Name is Archer. New York: 1955. V. 70
Self Portrait: Ceaselessly Into the Past. Santa Barbara: 1981. V. 68; 69; 70; 71
Sleeping Beauty. New York: 1973. V. 69
Trouble Follows Me. New York: 1946. V. 69; 70; 71
The Underground Man. New York: 1971. V. 69; 72; 73
The Way Some People Die. New York: 1951. V. 69; 70
The Wycherly Woman. New York: 1961. V. 69
The Zebra Striped Hearse. New York: 1962. V. 69; 71

MAC DONALD, W. J.
A Pioneer 1851. Victoria: 1914?. V. 68

MAC DONALD CLARK, JANET
Legends of King Arthur and His Knights. London: 1914. V. 72

MAC DONELL, ALICE CLARE
Lays of the Heather: Poems. London: 1896. V. 69

MAC DONELL, ANNE
The Italian Fairy Book. London: 1911. V. 72

MAC DONNELL, A. G.
The Crew of the Anaconda. London: 1940. V. 68
England Their England. London: 1942. V. 72
My Scotland. London: 1937. V. 68
The Spanish Pistol and Other Stories. London: 1939. V. 71

MAC DONNELL, ALEXANDER
A Sketch of the Life of the Honourable and Right Reverened Alexander MacDonell, Chaplain of the Glengarry Fencible or British Highland Regiment.... Alexandria: 1890. V. 72

MAC DOUGALL, E. B.
Gardens of Naples. New York: 1995. V. 68

MAC DOUGALL, FRANCES HARRIET WHIPPLE GREEN
Elleanor's Second Book. Providence: 1839. V. 69
Memoirs of Elleanor Eldridge. Providence: 1840. V. 69

MAC DOUGALL, J. L.
History of Inverness County, Nova Scotia. Truro: 1922. V. 73

MAC DOWALL, R. J. S.
The Control of the Circulation of the Blood. London: 1956. V. 68

MAC DOWELL, R. B.
Irish Public Opinion 1750-1800. 1944. V. 69; 73

MAC DUFF, ALISTAIR
Lords of the Stone: an Anthology of Eskimo Sculpture. North Vancovuer: 1982. V. 69

MACER FLORDIUS
De Viribus Herbar(um) Famosissimus Medicus et Medicor(um) Speculum. Geneva: 1496. V. 68; 69

MACERONE, FRANCIS
Expositions and Illustrations, Interesting to All those Concerned in Steam Power, Whether As Applied to Rail-Roads, Common Roads, or to Sea and Inland Navigation. London: 1835. V. 72

A Few Facts Concerning Elementary Locomotion. London: 1833. V. 72

MAC EWEN, W.
Atlas of Head Sections. New York: 1893. V. 68; 73
The Growth and Shedding of the Antler of the Deer. 1920. V. 72
The Growth and Shedding of the Antler of the Deer. Glasgow: 1920. V. 69; 70; 73
Pyogenic Infective Diseases of the Brain and Spinal Cord. Glasgow: 1893. V. 68; 71; 73

MAC FADDEN, BERNARR
Mac Fadden's Encyclopedia of Physical Culture. New York: 1924. V. 68; 72
MacFadden's New Hair Culture, Rational, Natural Methods for Cultivating Strength and Luxuriance of the Hair. New York: 1905. V. 70; 72

MAC FADZEAN, JAMES
The Parallel Roads of Glenroy. Edinburgh/Dumfries: 1882. V. 70; 71

MAC FALL, HALDANE
The Book of Lovat, Claud Fraser. London: 1923. V. 70; 72
The French Pastellists of the Eighteenth Century. London: 1909. V. 72
Sir Henry Irving. Edinburgh and London: 1906. V. 72
The Splendid Wayfaring. London: 1913. V. 69

MAC FARLAND, F. M.
Studies of Opisthobranchiate Mollusks of the Pacific Coast of North America. San Francisco: 1966. V. 69; 73

MAC FARLANE, CHARLES
The Armenians. A Tale of Constantinople. 1830. V. 73
A History of British India. London: 1854. V. 72
A Memoir of the Duke of Wellington. London: 1852. V. 68

MAC FARLANE, J.
The Coal Regions of America.... New York: 1873. V. 70

MAC FARLANE, RODERICK ROSS
Land and Sea Birds in the Lower Mackenzie River District, as Observed by.... Winnipeg: 1890. V. 73

MAC FARLANE, WALTER, & CO.
Examples Book of Macfarlane's Castings. Glasgow. V. 73
Illustrated Catalogue of Macfarlane's Castings. Glasgow. V. 73
Illustrated Catalogue of Macfarlane's Castings. London: 1900. V. 70
Illustrated Catalogue of MacFarlane's Castings. Glasgow: 1906 V. 71

MAC FARLANE, WALTER & CO.
Illustrated Examples of Macfarlane's Architectural Ironwork. Glasgow: 1915. V. 72

MAC FARLANE & ROBINSON, LTD.
Price List of Steel Enamelled Hollow-Ware. Glasgow: 1910. V. 68

MAC FIE, MATTHEW
Vancouver Island and British Columbia. London: 1865. V. 71

MAC GAHAN, J. A.
Campaigning on the Oxus. London: 1874. V. 71

MAC GEORGE, A.
Flags; Some Account Of Their History And Uses. London: 1881. V. 72

MAC GEORGE, ANDREW
William Leighton Leitch, Landscape Painter. London: 1884. V. 73

MAC GILL, PATRICK
Glenmornan. New York: 1918. V. 70
Soldier Songs. London: 1917. V. 70
Songs of a Navvy. Windsor: 1911. V. 73

MAC GILL, THOMAS
An Account of Tunis. Glasgow: 1811. V. 71
An Account of Tunis. London: 1816. V. 73

MAC GILLIVRAY, WILLIAM
The Conchologist's Text-Book. London. V. 68; 70
The Conchologists Text-Book. London: 1853. V. 68
Descriptions of the Rapacious Birds of Great Britain. 1836. V. 69
A History of British Birds, Indigenous and Migratory. 1852. V. 69
Lives of Eminent Zoologists.... Edinburgh: 1834. V. 68; 70; 72
Manual of British Birds. 1846. V. 69
The Travels and Researches of Alexander Von Humboldt.... Edinburgh: 1832. V. 68

MAC GOEGHEGAN, JAMES
The History of Ireland. New York: 1868?. V. 73

MAC GOWAN, JOHN
The Life of Joseph the Son of Israel. Windsor: 1795. V. 71

MAC GRATH, HAROLD
The Blue Rajah Murder. New York: 1930. V. 73
The Carpet from Bagdad. Indianapolis: 1911. V. 71
The Changing Road. New York: 1928. V. 68
Deuces Wild. Indianapolis: 1913. V. 69; 73
The Goose Girl. Indianapolis: 1909. V. 71
The Million Dollar Mystery. New York: 1915. V. 69
The Ragged Edge. Garden City: 1922. V. 72
The Sporting Spinster. Garden City: 1926. V. 71
The Wolves of Chaos. Garden City: 1929. V. 73

MAC GREGOR, BARRINGTON
King Longbeard. Or Annals of the Golden Dreamland. London and New York: 1898. V. 72

MAC GREGOR, BRUCE A.
South Pacific Coast, an Illustrated History of the Narrow Guage South Pacific Coast Railroad. Berkeley: 1968. V. 71

MAC GREGOR, FRANCES COOKE
Twentieth Century Indians. New York: 1941. V. 69

MAC GREGOR, GORDON
Warriors Without Weapons: A Study of the Society and Personality Development of the Pine Ridge Sioux. Chicago: 1946. V. 69
Warriors Without Weapons: A Study of The Society and Personality Development of The Pine Ridge Sioux. Ohio: 1946. V. 72

MAC GREGOR, J.
A Thousand Miles in the Rob Roy Canoe on Rivers and Lakes of Europe. London: 1878. V. 68

MAC GREGOR, JOHN
British America. Edinburgh and London: 1832. V. 73
Through the Buffer State. London: 1896. V. 71

MACHARG, WILLIAM
The Achievements of Luther Trant. Boston: 1910. V. 69

MACHELL, HUGH
John Peel Famous in Sport and Song. London: 1926. V. 71; 72
Some Records of the Annual Grasmere Sports. Carlisle: 1911. V. 71

MACHEN, ARTHUR
The Bowmen and Other Legends of the War. London: 1915. V. 73
Dog and Duck. London: 1924. V. 68
Hieroglyphics,. London: 1902. V. 68
The Hill of Dreams. London: 1922. V. 71
Ornaments in Jade. New York: 1924. V. 69

MACHIAVELLI, NICCOLO
The Art of War, in Seven Books. Albany: 1815. V. 73
Machiavels Discourses. London: 1636. V. 68; 70; 71; 73
Historical, Political and Diplomatic Writings. Boston: 1882. V. 71
Le Prince. Amsterdam: 1686. V. 73
The Prince. New York: 1954. V. 70

MAC ILVANNEY, WILLIAM
Remedy is None. Oxford: 1907. V. 73

MAC ILWAIN, GEORGE
Memoirs of John Abernethy, F.R.S.... New York: 1853. V. 71
Memoirs of John Aberneity, with a View of His Lectures, His Writings and Character, with Additional Extracts from Original Documents.... London: 1856. V. 72

MAC INNES, ALLAN A.
Straight as a Line: an Australian Sporting Story. London: 1895. V. 68

MAC INNES, COLIN
Absolute Beginners. 1959. V. 73
June In Her Spring. London: 1952. V. 70
Mr. Love and Justice. London: 1960. V. 72

MAC INNES, HAMISH
Climb to the Lost World. London: 1974. V. 69
Scottish Climbs. London: 1981. V. 69

MAC INTYRE, D.
Hindu-Koh: Wanderings and Wild Sport On and Beyond the Himalayas. 1891. V. 69; 70; 72; 73
Round the Seasons on a Grouse Moor. 1924. V. 71

MAC ISAAC, FRED
Murder C.O.D. Racine: 1937. V. 70

MAC ISSAC, FRED
M.D. - Doctor of Murder. Racine: 1937. V. 70

MACK, ARTHUR
Shellproof Mack, an American's Fighting Story. Boston: 1918. V. 70

MACK, CHARLES E.
Two Black Crows in the A. E. F. Indianapolis: 1928. V. 70; 71

MACK, EFFIE MONA
Mark Twain in Nevada. New York: 1947. V. 68

MACK, JAMES LOGAN
The Border Line from the Solway Firth to the North Sea, Along the Marches of Scotland and England. London: 1926. V. 71; 73

MACK, LIZZIE
Bo-Peep and Little Boy-Blue. New York: 1894. V. 70; 73

MACK, LOUISE
The World is Round. London: 1896. V. 69

MACK, W. H.
Mr. Birdsall Breezes Through. New York: 1937. V. 73

MAC KAIL, DENIS
Another Part of the Wood. Boston;: 1929. V. 70

MACKAIL, JOHN WILLIAM
Homer: an Address Delivered on Behalf of the Inedpendent Labor Party. London: 1905. V. 68; 72
The Life of William Morris. London: 1899. V. 68
Socialism and Politics: an Address and a Programme. Hammersmith: 1903. V. 69
William Morris, An Address delivered the XIth November MDCCCC at Kelmscott House Hammersmith Before the Hammersmith Socialist Society. 1901. V. 70
William Morris: an Address Delivered the XIth Novembr MDCCCC at Kelmscott House, Hammersmith Before the Hammersmith Socialist Society. Hammersmith: 1901. V. 71; 72

MAC KAREL, PETER
Flights of Fancy. Andoversford: 1976. V. 68; 71

MACKARNESS, MATILDA ANNE
Odd Joliffe; not a Goblin Story. London: 1850. V. 70; 73

MAC KAY, ALEXANDER
The Western World; or Travels in the United States in 1846-1847. London: 1850. V. 70

MAC KAY, CHARLES
A Collection of Song and Ballads Relative to the London Prentices and Trades.... 1941. V. 71
History of the Mormons; or, Latter Day Saints. Auburn: 1853. V. 68
The Life of Charles Bradlaugh, M.P. London: 1888. V. 71
Memoirs of Extraordinary Popular Delusions and Madness of Crowds. London: 1852. V. 73
Memoirs of Extraordinary Popular Delusions and Madness of Crowds. London: 1869. V. 70
The Mormons; or Latter Day Saints. London: 1851. V. 69; 73
The Scenery and Poetry of the English Lakes. London: 1846. V. 71

MAC KAY, DOUGLAS
The Honorable Company. A History of the Hudson's Bay Company. Indianapolis: 1936. V. 69

MAC KAY, MALCOLM S.
Cow Range and Hunting Trail. 1925. V. 68
Cow Range and Hunting Trail. New York: 1925. V. 69; 71; 72; 73

MAC KAY, THOMAS
A Plea for Liberty; an Argument Against Socialism and Soclialistic Legislation.... London: 1891. V. 71

MAC KAYE, KEITH
Honey Holler. New York: 1930. V. 69

MAC KAYE, LORING
The Great Scoop. New York: 1956. V. 72

MAC KAYE, MARION MORSE
Emma. 1941. V. 73
Emma. New York: 1941. V. 68; 70
Pride and Prejudice. 1928. V. 73

MAC KAYE, PERCY
The Far Familiar. London: 1938. V. 71; 73
Jeanne D'Arc. New York: 1911. V. 72

MAC KAYE, STEELE, MRS.
Pride and Prejudice. New York: 1906. V. 68; 72
Pride and Prejudice. New York: 1922. V. 70
Pride and Prejudice. 1928. V. 70

MACKCOULL, JAMES
Memoir of the Life and Trial of James Mackcoull of Moffat, who Died in the County Jail of Edinburgh on the 22d December 1820.... Edinburgh: 1822. V. 73

MAC KELLAR, C. D.
A Pleasure Pilgrim in South America. London: 1908. V. 71
Scented Isles and Coral Gardens. London: 1912. V. 71

MAC KELLAR, SMITHS & JORDAN CO.
Specimens of Printing Types. (Eighteenth Specimen Book). Philadelphia: 1888. V. 69

MACKEN, WALTER
Rain on the Wind. 1950. V. 70

MAC KENNA, F. S.
F. S. Mackenna Collection of English Porcelain. Part I. Leigh-on-Sea: 1972. V. 72
Worcester Porcelain. The Wall Period And Its Antecedents. Leigh-on-Sea: 1950. V. 72

MAC KENZIE, AGNES MURE
Scottish Pageant. London: 1948. V. 71

MAC KENZIE, ALEXANDER
Voyages from Montreal through the Continent of North America to the Frozen and Pacific Oceans in 1789 and 1793.... New York: 1902. V. 69

MAC KENZIE, COLIN
One Thousand Processes in Manufactures and Experiments in Chemistry; Collected from the Best Modern Authorities, British and Foreign with a View to Promote the Successfull Cultivation of all the Useful Arts.... London: 1823. V. 69

MAC KENZIE, COMPTON
The Early Life and Adventures of Sylvia Scarlett. London: 1918. V. 68
Extremes Meet. London: 1928. V. 70
First Athenian Memories. London: 1931. V. 72
Gallipoli Memories. London: 1929. V. 70
Guy and Pauline. 1915. V. 68
Kensington Rhymes. London: 1912. V. 73
Plashers Mead. New York: 1915. V. 70

MAC KENZIE, COMPTON continued
Santa Claus in Summer. London: 1924. V. 70
Sylvia and Michael. New York: 1919. V. 72
The Vanity Girl. London: 1920. V. 70

MAC KENZIE, DONALD A.
Myth and Legend in Literature in Art. London: 1912. V. 73
Wonder Tales of the East. 1923. V. 71
Wonder Tales of the East. London: 1923. V. 68

MAC KENZIE, FREDERICK A.
From Tokyo to Tiflis. London: 1905. V. 71

MAC KENZIE, GEORGE
Catalogus Librorum bibliothecae Juris Utriusque...Cum Historicis Graecis and Latinis, Literatis & Philosophis Plerisque Celebrioribus.... Edinburgh: 1692. V. 70
Essays Upon Several Moral Subjects, viz, The Religious Stoic. London: 1713. V. 72
Memoirs of the Affairs of Scotland From the Restoration of King Charles II A. D. MDCLX. Edinburgh: 1821. V. 71

MAC KENZIE, GEORGE STEUART
Travels in the Island of Iceland During the Summer of the Year MDCCCX. Edinburgh: 1811. V. 71

MAC KENZIE, HENRY
The Anecdotes And Egotisms Of Henry Mackenzie (1745-1831). Oxford: 1927. V. 72
Julia de Roubigne, a Tale. London: 1782-1781. V. 72
The Lounger. London: 1794. V. 69
The Man of Feeling. Loncon: 1778. V. 71
The Man of Feeling. London: 1799. V. 69
The Man of Feeling. Paris: 1807. V. 73
The Man of the World. London: 1787. V. 69
The Mirror. London: 1783. V. 69

MAC KENZIE, J. FORD
The Pleasures of House-Building: a Story of Struggle and Adventure Jerrywise and Otherwise. London: 1877. V. 68

MAC KENZIE, JAMES
Essays: on Retirement from Business: On Old Age; and on the Employment of the Soul After Death. London: 1812. V. 70
The General Grievances and Oppression of the Isles of Orkney and Shetland. Edinburgh: 1836. V. 72
The History of Health and the Art of Preserving It; or, An Account of all That Has Been Recommended by Physicians and Philosophers.... Edinburgh: 1760. V. 73
The Study of the Pulse, Arterial, Venous and Hepatic and of the Movements of the Heart. Edinburgh and London: 1902. V. 68
Symptoms and Their Interpretation. London: 1909. V. 68

MAC KENZIE, JOHN
Austral Africa. London: 1887. V. 71

MAC KENZIE, JOHN GORDON
Dissertatio Medica Inauguralis de Typho.... Glasgow: 1801. V. 68; 72

MAC KENZIE, JOHN WHITEFORD
Catalogue of the....Very Extensive and Valuable Library of Rare and Curious Books of the Late John Whiteford Mackenzie, Esq. Edinburgh: 1886. V. 70

MAC KENZIE, M.
Great Danes Past and Present. 1912. V. 68; 70

MAC KENZIE, PETER
An Exposure of the Spy System Pursued in Glasgow, During the Years 1816-17-18-19 and 20.... Glasgow: 1832. V. 68

MAC KENZIE, R. SHELTON
Life of Charles Dickens. Philadelphia: 1870. V. 68

MAC KENZIE, RANALD S.
Ranald S. MacKenzie's Official Correspondence Relating To Texas 1871- 1873 & 1873-1879. Lubbock: 1968. V. 72

MAC KENZIE, W. M.
Hugh Miller. A Critical Study. London: 1905. V. 68
Pompeii. London: 1910. V. 72

MAC KENZIE, W. ROY
Ballads and Sea Songs from Nova Scotia. Cambridge: 1928. V. 73
Ballads and Sea Songs From Nova Scotia. Hatboro, PA: 1963. V. 71

MAC KENZIE, WILLIAM
The History of Galloway, From the Earliest Period to the Present Time. Kircudbright: 1841. V. 71
A Practical Treatise on the Diseases of the Eye. Boston: 1833. V. 69; 73
A Practical Treatise on the Diseases of the Eye. Philadelphia: 1855. V. 71

MAC KENZIE, WILLIAM L.
The Lives and Opinions of Benj'n Franklin Butler (1795-1858). Boston: 1845. V. 72

MAC KENZIE, WILLIAM M.
Climbing Guide to the Cuillin of Skye. Edinburgh: 1958. V. 69

MAC KEURTAN, GRAHAM
The Cradle Days of Natal 1497-1845. London: 1930. V. 71

MACKIE, PETER J.
The Keeper's Book. A Guide to the Duties of a Gamekeeper. 1929. V. 71

MACKIE, GEORGE
Lynton Lamb Illustrator. A Selection of Work Arranged and Introduced by.... 1978. V. 71

MACKIE, JOHN
The Devil's Playground: a Story of the Wild North West. London: 1894. V. 69

MACKIE, L. W.
Turkmen Tribal Carpets and Traditions. Washington: 1980. V. 69; 72

MAC KINNON, ALAN
The Oxford Amateurs. London: 1910. V. 68; 72

MACKINNON, JOHN
Account of Messingham in the County of Lincoln. Hertford: 1881. V. 73

MAC KINSTRY, ELIZABETH
The Fairy Alphabet as Used by Merlin. New York: 1933. V. 73

MAC KINTOSH, D.
The Scenery of England and Wales.... London: 1869. V. 72

MAC KINTOSH, HAROLD
Early English Figure Pottery. London: 1938. V. 70; 72

MAC KINTOSH, JAMES
Vindiciae Gallicae. Philadelphia: 1792. V. 68

MACKLEY, GEORGE
Engraved in the Wood: a Collection of Wood Engravings by George Mackley. London: 1968. V. 70; 72

MACKLIN, ELIZABETH
You've Just Been Told. New York: 2000. V. 69

MACKLIN, ROBERT J.
The Solar Wind. Proceedings of a Conference Held at the California Institute of Technology...April 1-4, 1964 and sponsored by the Jet Propulsion Laboratory. Pasadena: 1965. V. 69

MAC KNIGHT, THOMAS
Benjamin Disraeli, M.P. A Literary and Political Biography. London: 1854. V. 71

MACKWORTH, DIGBY
Diary of a Tour through Southern India, Egypt and Palestine in the Years 1821 and 1822. London: 1823. V. 70; 72

MACKWORTH PRAED, C.
Birds of Eastern and North Eastern Africa. London: 1952-1960. V. 73
Birds of Eastern and North Eastern Africa. London: 1957-1960. V. 69
Birds of Eastern and North Eastern Africa. London: 1980. V. 69

MACKWORTH PRAED, WINTHROP
Poems. Boston: 1909. V. 69

MAC LAGAN, T. J.
Rheumatism. Its Nature, Its Pathology and Its Succesful Treatment. New York: 1886. V. 71

MAC LAREN, ARCHIBALD
The Fairy Family: a Series of Ballads and Metrical Tales.... London: 1857. V. 68; 72

MAC LAREN, C.
A Sketch of the Geology of Fife and the Lothians. Edinburgh: 1866. V. 69; 73

MAC LAREN, IAN
Afterwards and Other Stories. London: 1898. V. 69
Beside the Bonnie Brier Bush. London: 1894. V. 69

MAC LAREN ROSS, J.
Better than a Kick in the Pants - Short Stories. London: 1945. V. 70
Bitten by the Tarantula. A Story of the South of France. 1945. V. 73
Memoirs of the Forties. London: 1965. V. 69
The Nine Men of Soho. 1946. V. 73
Of Love and Hunger. 1947. V. 73
The Weeping and the Laughter. London: 1953. V. 70

MAC LAUCHLAN, HENRY
The Roman Wall and Illustrations of the Principal Vestiges of Roman Occupation in the North of England (Together with) The Walting Street the Chief Line of Roman Communication Leading Across the Counties of Durham and Northumberland.... 1857. V. 70

MAC LAURIN, COLIN
An Account of Sir Isaac Newton's Philosophical Discoveries, in Four Books. London: 1748. V. 69
An Account of Sir Isaac Newton's Philosophical Discoveries in Four Books.... London: 1750. V. 72
Geometria Organica; sive Descriptio Linearum Curvarum Universalis. London: 1720. V. 72

MAC LAVERTY, BERNARD
A Time to Dance and Other Stories. London: 1982. V. 72

MACLAY, EDGAR S.
A History of American Privateers. New York: 1899. V. 70

MACLAY, WILLIAM
Sketches of Debate in the First Senate of the United States in 17891790-1791. Harrisburg: 1880. V. 73

MAC LEAN, A.
A Compendium of Kafir Laws and Customs. Grahamstown: 1906. V. 71

MACLEAN, ALISTAIR
The Dark Crusader. London: 1961. V. 72; 73
The Guns of Navarone. London: 1957. V. 70; 71; 73
H.M.S. Ulysses. London: 1955. V. 69; 70
Ice Station Zebra. Garden City: 1963. V. 71
Ice Station Zebra. London: 1963. V. 73
Ice Station Zebra. Sydney: 1963. V. 72
Night Without End. London: 1959. V. 72
The Satan Bug. New York: 1962. V. 68
South By Java Head. London: 1958. V. 72

MAC LEAN, FITZROY
Eastern Approaches. London: 1949. V. 72

MAC LEAN, J. ROSS
LSD-25 and Mescaline as Therapeutic Adjuvants: Experience from a Seven Year Study Conducted at Hollywood Hospital, New Westminster, B.C. New Westminster: 1965. V. 70
The Use of LSD-25 in the Treatment of Alcoholism and Other Psychiatric Problems. New Haven: 1961. V. 70

MAC LEAN, JOHN
Historical and Traditional Sketches of Highland Families and of the Highlands. Dingwall: 1848. V. 73
History of the College of New Jersey, from Its Origin in 1746 to the Commencement of 1854. Philadelphia: 1877. V. 71

MACLEAN, JOHN S.
The Newcastle & Carlise Railway 1825-1862. Newcastle upon Tyne: 1948. V. 71; 73

MAC LEAN, MAGNUS
The Literature of the Celts: Its History and Romance. 1926. V. 69

MACLEAN, NORMAN
A River Runs Through It. Chicago: 1976. V. 71; 72; 73
Young Men and Fire. Chicago: 1992. V. 71; 73

MAC LEAN, NORMAN F.
Manual for Instruction in Military Maps and Aerial Photographs. New York: 1943. V. 72

MAC LEAN, VIRGINIA
A Short-Title Catalogue of Household and Cookery Books Published in the English Tongue 1701-1800. London: 1981. V. 70

MACLEHOSE, JAMES
The Glasgow University Press 1638-1931.... Glasgow: 1931. V. 73

MAC LEISH, ARCHIBALD
A Continuing Journey. Boston: 1968. V. 68
An Evening's Journey to Conway Massachusetts; and Outdoor Play. Northampton: 1967. V. 72
Land of the Free. New York: 1938. V. 68; 70
Nobodaddy. Cambridge: 1926. V. 68
The Pot of Earth. Boston: 1925. V. 68
Tower of Ivory. New Haven: 1917. V. 70

MACLELLAN, ANGUS
Stories from South Uist. London: 1961. V. 71

MAC LEOD, ALISTAIR
Island. Toronto: 2000. V. 70

MAC LEOD, CHARLES STUART
Peter Rabbit and the Big Brown Bear. Philadelphia: 1924. V. 69

MACLEOD, CHARLOTTE
Next Door to Danger. New York: 1965. V. 71; 72
Rest You Merry. Garden City: 1978. V. 70

MAC LEOD, DONALD A.
A Treatise on the Second Sight, Dreams and Apparitions.... Glasgow: 1819. V. 70

MAC LEOD, FIONA
The Divine Adventure. 1903. V. 71
The Immortal Hour. Edinburgh and London: 1908. V. 69
The Isle of Dreams. 1905. V. 71

MAC LEOD, GEORGE H. B.
Notes on the Surgery of the War in the Crimea with Remarks on the Treatment of Gunshot Wounds. Richmond: 1862. V. 69; 70

MAC LEOD, JOSEPH GORDON
The Ecliptic. London: 1930. V. 68

MAC LEOD, NORMAN
The Starling. A Scotch Story. London and Glasgow: 1910. V. 68

MACLIAMMOIR, MICHAEL
All for Hecuba. Dublin: 1961. V. 70
An Oscar of No Importance. London: 1968. V. 70

MACLISE, DANIEL
The Maclise Portrait Gallery of "Illustrious Literary Characters".... London: 1883. V. 73

MACLISE, JOSEPH
Surgical Anatomy. London: 1851. V. 68
Surgical Anatomy. London: 1856. V. 68

MACLOW, JACKSON
The Twin Plays: Port-Au-Prince and Adams County Illinois. New York: 1966. V. 71

MACLURE, W.
Observations on the Geology of the United States of America. Philadelphia: 1817. V. 68

MACLURE, WILLIAM
Opinions on Various Subjects, Dedicated to the Industrious Producers. New Harmony: 1831. V. 68; 70; 71; 73
Opinions on Various Subjects, Dedicated to the Industrious Producers. New Harmony: 1831-1838. V. 73

MAC LYSAGHT, EDWARD
Irish Families: Their Names, Arms and Origins. 1957. V. 69
Irish Life in the Seventeenth Century. 1939. V. 69

MAC MAHON, HENRY
The Ten Commandments. New York: 1924. V. 71

MAC MANUS, M. J.
Irish Cavalcade 1550-1850. 1939. V. 69

MAC MARTIN, D. F.
Thirty Years in Hell or The Confession of a Drug Fiend. Topeka KS: 1921. V. 72

MAC MICHAEL, H. A.
The Tribes of Northern and Central Kordofan. Cambridge: 1912. V. 71

MAC MICHAEL, WILLIAM
The Gold-Headed Cane. London: 1827. V. 73
The Gold-Headed Cane. London: 1828. V. 68; 71; 73
The Gold-Headed Cane. New York: 1915. V. 71
The Gold-Headed Cane. New York: 1926. V. 73
The Gold-Headed Cane. New York: 1932. V. 71
The Gold-Headed Cane. London: 1968. V. 72
Lives of British Physicians. London: 1830. V. 68; 71; 73
Medicine and Medical Men. London: 1825. V. 73
Professional Anecdotes, or Annal of Medical Literature. London. V. 68; 73

MAC MILLAN, DONALD B.
Four Years In The White North. London: 1925. V. 72

MAC MILLAN, H. F.
Tropical Planting and Gardening. London: 1943. V. 68; 71

MAC MILLAN, JOHN C.
The Early History of the Catholic Church in Prince Edward Island. 1905. V. 73
The History of the Catholic Church in Prince Edward Island from 1835 till 1891. Quebec: 1913. V. 68

MAC MINN, G. R.
The Theater of the Golden Age in California. Caldwell: 1941. V. 69

MAC NAB, DUNCAN
An Exact Description of the Island and Kingdom of Sicily, Its Provinces, Towns and Remarkable Places.... Falkirk: 1784. V. 68

MAC NAB, JOHN ALLEYNE
Song of the Passaic. New York: 1890. V. 71

MAC NAIR, HENRY
Great Lakes Motor Tours. 1923. V. 68

MAC NAIR, P.
The Geology and Scenery of the Grampians and the Valley of Strathmore. Glasgow: 1908. V. 69

MAC NAMEE, JAMES J.
History of the Diocese of Ardagh. 1954. V. 70

MAC NEICE, LOUIS
Astrology. London: 1964. V. 69
Blind Fireworks. London: 1929. V. 73
Collected Poems of Louis MacNeice. London: 1966. V. 71
Holes in the Sky - Poems 1944-1947. London: 1948. V. 69
The Mad Islands and the Adminsitrator - Two Radio Plays. London: 1964. V. 72
Modern Poetry - A Personal Essay. London: 1938. V. 72
Out of the Picture - a Play in Two Acts. London: 1937. V. 68; 70; 72
Poems. London: 1935. V. 73
Visitations. London: 1957. V. 70
Zoo. 1938. V. 68
Zoo. London: 1938. V. 69

MAC NUTT, FRANCIS
Bartholomew De Las Casas, His Life, Apostolate and Writings. Cleveland: 1909. V. 70

MAC NUTT, W. S.
New Brunswick, A History: 1784-1867. Toronto: 1963. V. 72

MACON, THOMAS J.
Reminiscences of the First Company of Richmond Howitzers. Richmond: 1909. V. 69; 70

MACONCHINE, ALLAN
Directions for the Preparing Manure from Peat. Edinburgh: 1815. V. 70

MAC ORLAN, PIERRE
Aux Lumieres de Paris. Paris: 1925. V. 69; 71

MACOUN, JOHN
Autobiography of John Macoun, Canadian Explorer and Naturalist. Ottawa: 1922. V. 73
Catalogue of Canadian Birds. Ottawa: 1900-1904. V. 73
Catalogue of Canadian Plants. Montreal: 1883-1888. V. 68

MACOUN, JOHN continued
Manitoba and the Great North-West: The Field for Investment. The Home of the Emigrant. London: 1883. V. 69

MAC PHAIL, ANDREW
The Master's Wife. Montreal: 1939. V. 73

MAC PHAIL, I.
The Sterling Morton Library Bibliographies in Botany and Horticulture. Lisle: 1981-1992. V. 68

MAC PHAIL, JAMES
The Gardener's Remembrancer.... London: 1819. V. 69

MAC PHERSON, H. A.
The Birds of Cumberland. Carlisle: 1886. V. 69; 71
A Vertebrata Fauna of Lakeland, Including Cumberland and Westmorland with Lancashire North of the Sands. Edinburgh: 1892. V. 71

MAC PHERSON, J. PENNINGTON
Life of the Right Hon. John A. MacDonald. St. John, NB: 1891. V. 71

MAC PHERSON, JAMES
Fingal, an Ancient Epic Poem, in Six Books. Together With other Poems, Composed by Ossian the Son of Fingal. London: 1762. V. 69; 70
Ossian, fils de Fingal. Paris: 1777. V. 73
The Poems of Ossian. London: 1807. V. 70
The Poems of Ossian. Leipzig: 1847. V. 69
Temora, an Ancient Epic Poem. London: 1763. V. 70

MAC PHERSON, JOHN
Critical Dissertations on the Origin, Antiquities, Language, Government, Manners and Religion of the Ancient Caledonians.... London: 1768. V. 73

MAC PHIE, J. P.
Pictonians at Home and Abroad. Boston: 1914. V. 73

MAC PIKE, EUGENE FAIRFIELD
Dr. Edmond Halley (1656-1742). A Bibliographical Guide to His Life and Work Arranged Chronologically. London: 1939. V. 71

MAC QUEEN, PETER
In Wildest Africa. Boston: 1909. V. 69

MAC QUOID, PERCY
The Dictionary of English Furniture from the Middle Ages to the Late Georgia Period. London and New York: 1924-1927. V. 70
A History of English Furniture. London: 1988. V. 72

MAC QUOID, THOMAS KATHARINE
Pictures and Legends from Normandy and Britanny. London: 1879. V. 73

MAC RAE, A.
Handbook of Deer-Stalking. 1880. V. 70

MACRAE, DAVID
The Americans at Home: Pen and Ink Sketches of America Men, Manners and Institutions. Glasgow: 1885. V. 73

MAC RAY, WILLIAM DUNN
Annals of the Bodleian Library Oxford with a Notice of the Earlier Library at the University. Oxford: 1890. V. 68

MACREADY, CATHERINE F. B.
Cowl and Cap; or the Rival Churches; and Minor Poems. London: 1865. V. 68

MAC RITCHIE, DAVID
Dwarf Types in the Eastern Pyrenees. 1895. V. 68
The Testimony of Tradition. 1890. V. 70

MAC ROBERT, HARRY
Ben Nevis. Edinburgh: 1954. V. 69
The Central Highlands. Edinburgh: 1934. V. 69
The Central Highlands. Edinburgh: 1952. V. 69

MACROBIUS, AVEBROSIUS THEODOSEUS
Opera. Leipzig: 1774. V. 72
Works. Paris: 1845. V. 72

MACROSTY, HENRY W.
The Trust Movement in British Industry. London: 1907. V. 71

MACROW, BRENDA G.
Unto the Hills. London: 1946. V. 69

MAC SWINEY, TERENCE
The Music of Freedom. Cork: 1907. V. 73

MAC VICAR, ANGUS
The Canisbay Conspiracy. London: 1966. V. 70; 73
The Hammers of Fingal. London: 1963. V. 73

MAC VICAR, W. M.
A Short History of Annapolis Royal. The Port Royal of the French from Its Settlement in 1604 to the Withdrawal of the British Troops in 1854. Toronto: 1897. V. 72

MADACH, IMRE
The Tragedy of Man. London: 1933. V. 72

MADAN, FALCONER
The Early Oxford Press: a Bibliography of Printing and Publishing at Oxford 1468-1640. Oxford: 1895. V. 70; 73

MADAN, MARTIN
Five Letters, Addressed to Abraham Rees, D.D..... London: 1783. V. 68
Letters on Thelyphthora; with an Occasional Prologue and Epilogue. London: 1782. V. 68
Thelyphthora. London: 1780. V. 73
Thelyphthora. London: 1781. V. 73
Thelyphthora. London: 1780-1781. V. 68

MADARIAGA, DE SALVADOR
Christopher Columbus. London: 1939. V. 71

MADDEN, DAVID
Remembering James Agee. Baton Rouge: 1974. V. 72

MADDEN, HENRY MILLER
Xantus Hungarian Naturalist in the Pioneer West. Linz: 1949. V. 68

MADDEN, JOE
Set 'Em Up. New York: 1939. V. 71

MADDEN, R. R.
The Connexion Between the Kingdom of Ireland and the Crown of England. Dublin: 1845. V. 70

MADDEN, SAMUEL
Reflections and Resolutions Proper for the Gentlemen of Ireland, as to Their Conduct for the Service of Their Country, as Landlords, As Masters of Families, As Protestants, As Descended from British Ancestors.... Dublin: 1816. V. 73

MADDISON, R. E. W.
The Life of the Honourable Robert Boyle, F.R.S. London: 1969. V. 72
The Portraiture of the Honourable Robert Boyle, Fellow of the Royal Society. London: 1962. V. 72

MADDOCK, J.
The Florist's Directory, or a Treatise on the Culture of Flowers.... London: 1792. V. 69

MADDOCK, STEPHEN
I'll Never Like Friday Again. London: 1945. V. 69

MADDOW, BEN
Let Truth Be the Prejudice: W. Eugene Smith, His Life and Photographs. New York: 1985. V. 73

MADEIRA, PERCY C.
Hunting in British East Africa. Philadelphia and London: 1909. V. 69

MADER, G.
The English Formal Gardens, Five Centuries of Design. New York: 1997. V. 68

MADIGAN, MARY JEAN
Steuben Glass. An American Tradition in Crystal. New York: 1982. V. 72; 73

MADISON; *the Capital of Wisconsin, Its Progress, Capabilities and Destiny.* Madison: 1855. V. 71

MADISON, JAMES
Letters and Other Writings of.... New York: 1884. V. 71
The Papers of James Madison Purchased by Order of Congress, Being His Correspondence and Reports of Debates During the Congress of the Confederation and His Reports of Debates in the Federal Convention.... Washington: 1840. V. 68

MADSEN, BRIGHAM D.
The Bannock of Idaho. Caldwell: 1958. V. 72
The Northern Shoshoni. Caldwell: 1980. V. 68

MAEDER, HERBERT
The Mountains of Switzerland. London: 1968. V. 69

MAETERLINCK, MAURICE
Der Blaue Vogel (The Blue Bird). Berlin: 1920. V. 69
The Blue Bird. London: 1911. V. 70; 71
The Blue Bird. New York: 1911. V. 70
The Blue Bird. London: 1912. V. 71
The Double Garden. London: 1904. V. 68; 69
The Double Garden. London: 1940. V. 71
The Life of the Bee. 1912. V. 69
News of Spring and Other Nature Studies. New York: 1913. V. 73
Pelleas at Melisande. Bruxelles: 1920. V. 68
La Vie Des Fourmis. Paris: 1930. V. 69

MAFFEI, SCIPIONE
Compendio della Verona Illustrata Principalmente ad Uso de'Forestieri, Coll'Aggiunta del Museo Lapidario.... Verona: 1795. V. 70

MAGALOTTI, LORENZO
Travels of Cosmo the Third, Grand Duke of Tuscany, through England, During the Reign of King Charles the Second (1669). London: 1821. V. 70; 71

MAGARET, HELENE
Father De Smet: Pioneer Priest of the Rockies. New York: 1940. V. 69

MAGATI, CESARE
De Rara Medicatione Vulnerum Seu de Vulneribus Raro Tractandis, Libri Duo.... Venice: 1676. V. 70

MAGEE, DAVID
A Course in Correct Cataloguing; or, Notes to the Neophyte. (with) The Second Course in Correct Cataloguing; or Further Notes to the Neophyte. San Francisco: 1958. V. 71
The Hundredth Book; a Bibliography of the Publications of the Book Club of California & A History of the Club. San Francisco: 1958. V. 72

MAGEE, DAVID continued
Infinite Riches, the Adventures of a Rare Book Dealer. New York: 1973. V. 71
Victoria R. I. A Collection of Books, Manuscripts, Autograph Letters, Original Drawings, etc.... San Francisco: 1969-1970. V. 72

MAGEE, DOROTHY
Bibliography of the Grabhorn Press 1940-1946. San Francisco: 1957. V. 73

MAGENDIE, FRANCOIS
An Elementary Treatise on Human Physiology, on the Basis of the Precis Elementaire de Physiologie.... New York: 1844. V. 68
Precis Elementaire de Physiologie. Paris: 1816-1817. V. 68; 73
Recherches Physiologiques et Medicales sur les Causes, les Symptomes et le Traitement de la Gravelle.... Paris: 1828. V. 73

MAGENS, MARGENS DORRIEN
An Inquiry Into the Real Difference Between Actual Money, Consisting of Gold and Silver.... London: 1804. V. 73

MAGGS BROS.
Bibliotheca Incunabulorum. A Collection of Books Printed in the Fifteenth Century from Over 250 Presses in Germany, Italy, Switzerland, France, The Netherlands, Austria, Spain, England, Czecho-Slovakia and Portgual. Catalogue 656. London: 1938. V. 70
Bookbinding in the British Isles. Sixteenth to the Twentieth Century. Catalogue 1075. London: 1987. V. 70
Description of an Original Signed Autograph Manuscript of Lope De Vega. The Spanish Shakespeare. London: 1927. V. 70
The First Guide to Rome and Its Churches A.D. 1475. London: 1931. V. 70
Food and Drink through the Ages. Catalouge 645. London: 1937. V. 70
A Selection of Books, Manuscripts, Engravings and Autograph Letters, Remarkable for their Interest and Rarity Being the Five Hundredth Catalogue Issued by Maggs Bros.... London: 1928. V. 70
Seven American Incunables. Printed Before 1600. London: 1931. V. 70
Shakespeare and Shakespeareana Selected from the Stock of Maggs Bros. London: 1927. V. 70

THE MAGIC Ball. London: 1910. V. 69

MAGIC Fairy Tales: Alice in Wonderland. Springfield: 1943. V. 69

MAGIE, DAVID
Debts; the Substance of Three Sermons, Delivered in the Second Presbyterian Church, Elizabeth-Town. Elizabeth-Town: 1830. V. 71
The Ministry Magnified. Newark: 1837. V. 71

MAGILL, MARCUS
Murder Out of Tune. Philadelphia: 1931. V. 71

MAGINI, GIOVANNI ANTONIO
Novae Coelestium Orbium Theoricae Congruentes cum Observationibus N. Copernici. Venice: 1589. V. 73

MAGIRUS, C. D.
Alle Theile des Feuer - Losch - Wesens. Ulm: 1850. V. 70

MAGIRUS, JOHANNES
Physiologicae Peripateticae Libri Sex cum Commentariis.... Cambridge: 1642. V. 68

MAGNELL, ALFRED E.
Baseball Averages at a Glance. London: 1909. V. 71

MAGNONE, G.
The West Face. 1955. V. 71

MAGNUS, JOANNES, ABP. OF UPSALA
Gothorum Sueonumque Historia, ex Probatis Antiquorum Monumentis Collecta & in xxiii Libris Redacta.... Basileae: 1558. V. 73

MAGNUS, MAURICE
Memoirs of the Foreign Legion. New York: 1925. V. 72

MAGNUSON, RICHARD G.
Coeur D'Alene Dairy. Portland: 1968. V. 68; 73

MAGNUSSON, A. H.
Lichens from Central Asia. Stockholm: 1940-1944. V. 70
Studies in Species of Lecanora.... Stockholm: 1939. V. 68

MAGOFFIN, SUSAN SHELBY
Down the Santa Fe Trail and Into Mexico. New Haven: 1926. V. 69; 70

MAGONIGLE, H. VAN HUREN
Architectural Rendering in Wash. New York: 1921. V. 69

MAGOUN, H. W.
Spasticity. The Stretch-Reflex and Extra-Pyramidal Systems. Springfield: 1947. V. 68

MAGRATH, JOHN RICHARD
The Obituary Book Of Queen's College, Oxford. Oxford: 1910. V. 70; 72

MAGRIEL, PAUL
Pavlova. An Illustrated Monograph. New York: 1947. V. 73

MAGUIRE, JACK
A President's Country: a Guide to the Hill Country of Texas. Austin: 1964. V. 68

MAGUIRE, JAMES G.
Ireland and the Pope: A Brief History of Papal Intrigues Against Irish Liberty from Adrian IV to Leo XIII. San Francisco: 1888. V. 73

MAGUIRE, JOHN
Patty Hearst From Heiress to Revolutionary. North Miami: 1975. V. 70

MAHAFFY, J. P.
A History of Classical Greek Literature. London: 1903-1908. V. 73
Problems in Greek History. London and New York: 1892. V. 69

MAHAN, ALFRED THAYER
The Influence of Sea Power Upon the French Revolution and Empire 1793-1812. Boston: 1902. V. 69
The Life of Nelson. Boston: 1897. V. 69

MAHAN, BRUCE E.
Old Fort Crawford and The Frontier. Iowa City: 1926. V. 72

MAHAN, DENNIS HART
An Elementary Treatise on Advanced Guard, Out-Post, and Detachment Services of Troops and the Manner of Posting and Handling Them in Presence of an Enemy. New Orleans: 1862. V. 69
An Elementary Treatise on Advanced Guard, Out-Post and Handling Them in Presence of an Enemy. New Orleans: 1861. V. 70
A Treatise on Field Fortification.... Richmond: 1862. V. 70

MAHEW, ELISHA
A Journal of the Voige in the Sloop Union. Providence: 1929. V. 73

MAHFOUZ, NAGUIB
Place of Desire. New York: 1991. V. 70

MAHON, DEREK
The Chimeras.... Dublin: 1982. V. 72

MAHONY, FRANCIS SYLVESTER
Facts and Figures from Italy. London: 1847. V. 69; 70

MAHOOD, RUTH I.
Photographer of the Southwest, Adam Clark Vroman 1856-1916. 1961. V. 69
Photographer of the Southwest Adam Clark Vroman, 1856-1916. Los Angeles: 1969. V. 68; 71

MAHR, ADOLPH
Christian Art in Ancient Ireland. 1932-1941. V. 69; 73

MAIDEN, J. H.
The Flowering Plants and Ferns of New South Wales.... Sydney: 1895-1898. V. 70; 72; 73
The Useful Native Plants of Australia (including Tasmania). Sydney and London: 1889. V. 70

MAIDMENT, JAMES
Bibliotheca Curiosa. A North Countrie Garland. Edinburgh: 1884. V. 70; 72
A Book of Scotish Pasquils, 1568-1715. Edinburgh: 1868. V. 71

MAILER, NORMAN
Advertisements for Myself. New York: 1959. V. 68
An American Dream. New York: 1965. V. 68; 72; 73
Ancient Evenings. Boston: 1983. V. 68; 71
Barbary Shore. New York: 1951. V. 68; 71; 72; 73
Barbary Shore. London: 1952. V. 70; 71
Deaths for the Ladies and Other Disasters. New York: 1962. V. 71; 73
The Deer Park. New York: 1955. V. 73
The Executioner's Song. Boston: 1979. V. 70; 72; 73
Existential Errands. Boston: 1972. V. 68
A Fragment from Vietnam. Helsinki: 1985. V. 72
The Gospel According to the Son. New York: 1997. V. 68; 70
Harlot's Ghost. New York: 1991. V. 70; 72
The Long Patrol. New York: 1971. V. 72
The Naked and the Dead. New York and Toronto: 1948. V. 68; 69; 70; 71; 73
The Naked and the Dead. Franklin Center: 1979. V. 68; 69; 71; 73
Of a Fire on the Moon. Boston: 1970. V. 68; 69
Oswald's Tale. New York: 1995. V. 68
Some Honorable Men. Boston: 1976. V. 72
Tough Guys Don't Dance. New York: 1984. V. 70
Why Are We In Vietnam?. New York: 1967. V. 69; 73

MAILING, E.
In-Door Plants and How to Grow Them: for the Drawing Room, Balcony and Greenhouse.... London: 1864. V. 68

MAILLART, ELLA K.
Turkestan Solo. 1934. V. 70
Turkestan Solo. London: 1938. V. 71

MAILS, HAMISH
Fair Perthshire. London: 1930. V. 71

MAILS, THOMAS E.
The Cherokee People. Tulsa: 1992. V. 69
Dog Soldiers, Bear Men and Buffalo Women. Englewood Cliffs: 1973. V. 69; 70; 72
The Mystic Warriors of the Plains. Garden City: 1972. V. 69; 72
The People Called Apache. 1974. V. 69
The People Called Apache. Englewood Cliffs: 1974. V. 68; 72; 73
The Pueblo Children of the Earth Mother. New York: 1983. V. 69; 70
Sundancing At Rosebud and Pine Ridge. Lake Mills: 1978. V. 72
Sundancing at Rosebud and Pine Ridge. Sioux Falls: 1978. V. 69

MAIN, JAMES
The Villa and Cottage Florist's Directory. London: 1830. V. 69

MAINE FEDERATION OF WOMEN'S CLUBS
The Trail of the Maine Pioneer. Lewiston: 1916. V. 72

MAINE, FLOYD S.
Lone Eagle...The White Sioux. Albuquerque: 1956. V. 72

MAINE, HENRY SUMNER
The Early History of the Property of Married Women, as Collected from Roman and Hindoo Law. Manchester: 1873. V. 68

MAINTENON, MADAME DE
Lettres. Dresde: 1753. V. 73
Lettres. London?: 1870. V. 72
Memoirs for the History of Madame de Maintenon and the Last Age. London: 1757. V. 68; 73
The Secret Correspondence of.... London: 1827. V. 70

MAINVILLERS, GENU SOALHAT, CHEVALIER DE
The Beau-Philosopher; or, the History of the Chevalier Mainvillers. London: 1751. V. 69

MAIOLI, SIMON
Dies Caniculares...Hoc est Colloquia Physica.... Mainz: 1625. V. 68; 73

MAIR, CHARLES
Through the Mac Kenzie Basin. Toronto: 1908. V. 71

MAIR, JOHN
Book-Keeping Modernised; or Merchant-Accounts by Double Entry, According to the Italian Form...Reduced to Practice.... Edinburgh: 1786. V. 73
Never Come Back. Boston: 1941. V. 68

MAIRE, N.
Topographie de Paris ou Atlas Topographique et Statistique du Plan Geometral de al Ville de Paris.... Paris: 1813. V. 70

MAIRET, ETHEL M.
Vegetable Dyes. Ditchling, Sussex: 1924. V. 73

MAIRS, NANCY
Plain Text. Tucson: 1986. V. 73

MAIS, CHARLES
Surprising Case of Rachel Baker, Who Prays and Preaches in Her Sleep.... New York: 1814. V. 68

MAISEY, J. G.
Santana Fossils: an Illustrated Atlas. Neptune City: 1991. V. 68; 73

MAISON, K. E.
Honore Daumier: Catalogue Raisonne of the Paintings, Watercolours and Drawings. New York: 1968. V. 72; 73

MAITLAND, BARRY
The Malcontenta. London: 1995. V. 73
The Marx Sisters. London: 1994. V. 70; 73
Silvermeadow. 2000. V. 68

MAITLAND, DEREK
Setting Sails. A Tribute to the Chinese Junk. Hong Kong: 1981. V. 69

MAITLAND, ELLA FULLER
Parva. (Poems). Edinburgh: 1886. V. 69

MAITLAND, FREDERIC
The Life and Letters of Leslie Stephen. New York: 1906. V. 68

MAITLAND, J. RAMSAY GIBSON
The History of Howietoun. Stirling, New Brunswick: 1887. V. 68; 71; 73

MAITLAND, JULIA CHARLOTTE
The Doll and Her Friends; or, Memoirs of the Lady Seraphina. London: 1852. V. 70

MAITLAND, WILLIAM
The History of London, From Its Foundation by the Romans to the Present Time. London: 1739. V. 71
The History of London from Its Foundation to the Present Time. London: 1756. V. 71
The History of London From Its Foundation to the Present Time. London: 1772. V. 73

MAJENDIE, MAJOR
Report on the Explosion of Gunpower in the Regent's Park on the 2nd October 1874. London: 1875. V. 68

MAJOR, CLARENCE
The Dark & Feeling. Reflections on Black American Writers and Their Works. New York: 1974. V. 72

MAJOR, HOWARD
Domestic Architecture of the Early American Republic: the Greek Revival. Philadelphia: 1926. V. 71

MAJOR, RALPH
Classic Descriptions of Disease.... Springfield: 1932. V. 68
Classic Descriptions of Disease.... Springfield: 1939. V. 71
Classic Descriptions of Disease.... Springfield: 1943. V. 68; 70; 71; 73
A History of Medicine. Springfield: 1954. V. 68; 70; 71; 73

MAJOR, RICHARD HENRY
Early Voyages to Terra Australis. London: 1859. V. 71

MAJOR, THOMAS
The Ruins of Paestum, Otherwise Posidonia, in Magna Graecia. London: 1768. V. 68; 70

MAJORS, ALEXANDER
Seventy Years on the Old Frontier, Alexander Majors Memoirs. Chicago: 1893. V. 68; 73

MAKAR, NAGUIB
Urological Aspects of Bilharziasis in Eygpt. Cairo: 1955. V. 71

THE MAKING of Asbestos-Cement Roofing. Trafford Park, Manchester. V. 71

MAKINS, GEORGE HENRY
Surgical Experiences in South Africa 1899-1900.... London: 1913. V. 71

MAKINSON, R. L.
Greene and Greene: Architecture as a Fine Art. Salt Lake City: 1977. V. 68; 69; 72

MAKOS, CHRISTOPHER
White Trash. New York: 1977. V. 70

MAKOWER, FRANCES
The Path to Calvary. 1994. V. 72

MAKOWER, STANLEY V.
Perdita: a Romance in Biography. London: 1908. V. 71

MALAMUD, BERNARD
The Assistant. New York: 1957. V. 68; 69; 70; 71
Dubin's Lives. New York: 1979. V. 68
The Fixer. New York: 1966. V. 70
The Magic Barrel. New York: 1958. V. 70; 73
The Natural. New York: 1952. V. 70; 71
A New Life. New York: 1961. V. 68; 73
Rembrandt's Hat. New York: 1973. V. 70

MALANGA, GERARD
Prelude to International Velvet Debutante. Milwaukee: 1967. V. 70
Resistance to Memory. Santa Fe: 1998. V. 68

MALATESTA, JOE
Incognito in Hollywood: Impressions. Los Angeles: 1935. V. 70

MALBY, R.
With Camera and Rucksack in the Oberland and Valais. 1913. V. 70; 73

MALCOLM, ALEXANDER
Malcolm's Treatise of Music, Speculative, Practical and Historical. London: 1776. V. 70
A Treatise of Musick, Speculative, Practical and Historical. London: 1730. V. 69; 72

MALCOLM, CHARLES A.
The Bank of Scotland 1695-1945. Edinburgh. V. 71

MALCOLM, HOWARD
Travels in South-Eastern Asia, Embracing Hindustan, Malaya, Siam and China.... London: 1839. V. 71

MALCOLM, J. P.
An Historical Sketch of the Art of Caricature (Principally in England).... London: 1813. V. 68; 69; 71; 72

MALCOLM, JOHN
The Godwin Sideboard. London: 1984. V. 73
History of Persia. London: 1829. V. 69

MALCOLM, W.
Gold Fields of Nova Scotia. Ottawa: 1929. V. 68

MALCOLM-SMITH, GEORGE
Professor Peckam's Adventures in a Drop of Water. NY: 1931. V. 72

MALCOLMSON, ANNE
Song of Robin Hood. Boston: 1947. V. 73

MALCOLM X
The Autobiography of Malcolm X. New York: 1964. V. 70
The Autobiography of Malcolm X. New York: 1965. V. 70; 72

MALDEN, HENRY
An Account of King's College Chapel, in Cambridge. Cambridge: 1769. V. 72

MALEBRANCHE, NICOLAS
De La Recherche de la Verite. Ou L'On Traite de la Nature de l'Esprit de l'Homme. & de l'Usage qu'il en Doit.... Glasgow: 1861. V. 73

MALET, GUY
Deutsches Museum, Munich. London. V. 72

MALET, MARIANNE DORA
Violet; or the Danseuse. London: 1859. V. 68

MALFILATRE, JACQUES CHARLES LOUIS DE CLINCHAMP DE
Narcisse Dans L'Isle de Venus. Paris: 1769. V. 71

MALHAM, JOHN
A Dictionary of the Common Prayer, or, the Church of England Man's Companion. London: 1795. V. 68

MALHAM-DEMBLEBY, JOHN
The Key to the Bronte Works. 1911. V. 70; 73
Original Tales and Ballads in the Yorkshire Dialect. London: 1912. V. 73

MALINOWSKI, BRONISLAW
Argonauts of the Western Pacific. London: 1922. V. 69
Argonauts of the Western Pacific. London: 1932. V. 71

MALINOWSKI, BRONISLAW continued
Coral Gardens and Their Magic. London: 1935. V. 69
The Sexual Life of Savages in North Western Melanesia. London: 1929. V. 71

MALINS, E.
Irish Gardens and Demesnes from 1830. New York: 1980. V. 68

MALKIN, BENJAMIN HEATH
A Father's Memoirs of His Child. London: 1806. V. 68
An Introductory Lecture on History Delivered in the University of London, March 11, 1830. London: 1830. V. 68
The Scenery, Antiquities and Biography of South Wales.... London: 1804. V. 68; 72

MALLANDAINE, EDWARD
First Victoria Directory, Fifth Issue and British Columbia Guide.... Victoria: 1874. V. 68
First Victoria Directory, Second Issue and British Columbia Guide.... Victoria: 1868. V. 68
First Victoria Directory, Third Issue, and British Columbia Guide.... Victoria: 1869. V. 68

MALLARME, STEPHANE
L'Apres-Midi D'un Faune. Waltham St. Lawrence: 1956. V. 68; 71
Dice Thrown Will Never Annul Chance. Dublin: 1965. V. 71
Poesies. Edinburgh: 1986. V. 70

MALLEA, EDUARDO
The Bay of Silence. New York: 1944. V. 71

MALLESON, F. A.
Holiday Studies of Wordsworth by Rivers, Woods and Alps. London: 1890. V. 71; 73

MALLET, DAVID
The Life of Francis Bacon, Lord Chancellor of England. London: 1740. V. 72; 73

MALLET, M.
Northern Antiquities; or an Historical Account of the Manners, Customs, Religion and Laws, Maritime Expeditions and Discoveries, Language and Literature of the Ancient Scandinavians. London: 1847. V. 73

MALLET, R.
The Dynamics of Earthquakes. Dublin: 1846. V. 68

MALLETT, D. T.
Mallett's Index of Artists: International - Biographical. New York: 1948. V. 69

MALLOCH, ARCHIBALD
Finch and Baines a Seventeenth Century Friendship. 1917. V. 70
Finch and Baines a Seventeenth Century Friendship. Cambridge: 1917. V. 71
Short Years. The Life and Letters of John Bruce MacCallum M.D. 1876- 1906. Chicago: 1938. V. 73

MALLOCH, P. D.
Life History and Habits of the Salmon, Sea-Trout and Other Fresh-Water Fish. 1912. V. 68
Life History Habits of the Salmon, Sea-Trout and Other Fresh-Water Fish. 1910. V. 73

MALLOCK, WILLIAM H.
In an Enchanted Island. London: 1889. V. 71
Labour and the Popular Welfare. London: 1893. V. 71
The New Republic; or Culture, Faith and Philosophy in an English Country House. London: 1877. V. 68
The New Republic, or Culture, Faith and Philosophy in an English Country House. London: 1889. V. 68

MALLON, THOMAS
Arts and Sciences. New York: 1988. V. 71; 72
Aurora 7. New York: 1991. V. 69; 71; 72

MALLORY, DANIEL
The Life and Speeches of the Hon. Henry Clay. New York: 1844. V. 70

MALLORY, GEORGE
Boswell the Biographer. London: 1912. V. 69

MALLOY, JOHN EDWARD
Potomac Poppies. NY: 1953. V. 72

MALLY, E. LOUISE
The Mocking Bird is Singing. New York: 1944. V. 69

MALMESBURY, JAMES HARRIS, 1ST EARL OF
Diaries and Correspondence.... London: 1844. V. 72

MALO, CHARLES
Panorama D'Angleterre, ou Ephemerides Anglaises, Politiques et Litteraires. Paris: 1817. V. 72

MALONE, DUMAS
The Fry & Jefferson Map of Virginia and Maryland. New Jersey: 1950. V. 70

MALONE, E. J.
Irish Trout and Salmon Flies. 1993. V. 68; 73

MALONE, JAMES H.
The Chicksaw Nation, a Short Sketch of a Noble People. Louisville: 1922. V. 69

MALONE, MICHAEL
Dingley Falls. New York: 1980. V. 68
First Lady. Naperville, IL: 2001. V. 71
Painting the Roses Red. New York: 1974. V. 69
Time's Witness. Boston: 1989. V. 70; 71; 73

MALONE, R. EDWARD
Three Years' Cruise in the Australian Colonies. London: 1854. V. 71

MALONEY, T. J.
U. S. Camera 1935. New York: 1935. V. 68
U. S. Camera 1958. New York: 1957. V. 68

MALORTIE, BARON DE
Egypt. London: 1882. V. 71

MALORY, THOMAS
The Birth, Life and Acts of King Arthur, of His Noble Knights of the Round Table, their Marvellous Enquests and the Adventures, the Achieving of the San Greal.... London: 1893-1894. V. 70
La Mort D'Arthur. London: 1816. V. 70
Le Morte d'Arthur. London: 1893-1894. V. 73
Le Morte d'Arthur. London: 1923. V. 68
Le Morte D'Arthur. London: 1927. V. 70
The Works.... Oxford: 1948. V. 68

MALOT, HECTOR
Nobody's Boy. New York: 1916. V. 70

MALOUF, DAVID
Remembering Babylon. London: 1993. V. 73
Remembering Babylon. New York: 1993. V. 72

MALPIGHI, MARCELLO
Anatome Plantarum. London: 1675-1679. V. 69
Dissertatio Epistolica de Bombyce, Societati Regiae Londini ad Scientiam Naturalem Promovendam Institutae, Dicta. London: 1669. V. 69
Marcello Malpighi and the Evolution of Embryology. Ithaca: 1966. V. 73
Opera Omnia Figuris Elegantissimis in aes Incisis Illustrata Tomis Duobus Comprehensa Quorum Catalogum Sequens Pagina Exhibet. London: 1686. V. 70; 73
Opera Posthuma. Quibus Praefationes & Animadversiones.... Venice: 1698. V. 68

MALRAUX, ANDRE
Saturne: Essai Sur Goya. Paris: 1950. V. 73
The Walnut Trees of Altenburg. London: 1952. V. 71

MALTBY, W. J.
Captain Jeff of Frontier Life in Texas with the Texas Rangers. Colorado: 1906. V. 69

MALTHUS, THOMAS ROBERT
Additions to the Fourth and Former Editions of an Essay on the Principal of Population. London: 1817. V. 68; 72
An Essay on the Principle of Population.... London: 1798. V. 68
An Essay on the Principle of Population.... London: 1803. V. 69
An Essay on the Principle of Population.... London: 1806. V. 69; 71
An Essay on the Principle of Population.... London: 1807. V. 68; 69; 70; 71
An Essay on the Principle of Population.... London: 1817. V. 69; 70
An Essay on the Principle of Population.... London: 1826. V. 69; 70; 72
An Essay on the Principle of Population.... London: 1966. V. 72
Principles of Political Economy Considered with a View to Their Application. London: 1820. V. 68; 70; 72
Principles of Political Economy Considered with a View to Their Practical Application. London: 1836. V. 72

MALTON, JAMES
An Essay on British Cottage Architecture.... 1798. V. 71; 73
A Picturesque and Descriptive View of the City of Dublin. 1978. V. 70

MALTON, THOMAS
A Compleat Treatise on Perspective in Theory and Practice; on the True Principles of Dr. Brook Taylor. (with) An Appendix, or Second Part, to the Compleat Treatise.... 1779-1783. V. 71
A Compleat Treatise on Perspective, in Theory and Practice...(with) An Appendix or Second Part.... London: 1779-1783. V. 69
Views of Oxford. London: 1810. V. 70

MALTZ, ALBERT
The Citizen Writer. Hollywood: 1943. V. 69

MALTZAN, HEINRICH, FREIHERR VON
Reise in Den Regentschaften Tunis und Tripolis.... Leipzig: 1870. V. 69

MAMA'S Old Time Jingles. Akron: 1918. V. 69

MAMET, DAVID
American Buffalo. New York: 1976. V. 70
American Buffalo. San Francisco: 1992. V. 72
The Cabin: Reminiscences and Diversions. New York: 1992. V. 70
Glengarry Glen Ross. New York: 1984. V. 70
House of Games. New York: 1985. V. 69
House of Games. New York: 1987. V. 70
Jafsie and John Henry. New York: 1999. V. 72
Lakeboat. New York: 1981. V. 71
A Life in the Theatre. New York: 1977. V. 70
The Old Religion. New York: 1997. V. 72
Reunion. Dark Pony. Two Plays. New York: 1979. V. 70
Some Freaks. New York: 1989. V. 68
Things Change: a Screenplay. New York: 1988. V. 70
True and False. New York: 1997. V. 72
The Village. Boston: 1994. V. 68; 70
The Water Engine and Mr. Happiness. New York: 1978. V. 70; 71

MAMET, DAVID continued
We're No Angels. New York: 1990. V. 70
The Woods. New York: 1979. V. 70; 71

LAS MAMIS. New York: 2000. V. 72

THE MAMMOTH Menagerie. New York. V. 72

MAN, FELIX H.
Artists' Lithographs. A World History from Senefelder to the Present Day. London: 1970. V. 70

A MAN in Arms. New York: 1935. V. 70

MAN on the Moon A Picture Chronology of Man in Space Exploration. Dallas: 1969. V. 68

MAN, THOMAS
Picture of a Factory Village; to Which are Annexed, Remarks on Lotteries. Providence: 1833. V. 70

MANBY, CHARLES W.
Tom Racquet and His Three Maiden Aunts.... 1850. V. 71

MANCHESTER ANGLERS ASSOCIATION
Anglers' Evenings, Papers by Members Read at Their Monthly Meetings.... Manchester: 1880. V. 69

MANCHESTER ART EXHIBITION
Exhibition of Art Treasures of the United Kingdom held at Manchester in 1857. Report of the Executive Committee. Manchester: 1859. V. 68

MANCHESTER ATHENAEUM
Addresses 1835-1885, also Report of the Proceedings of the Meeting of the Members in Celebration of the 50th Anniversary of the Institution October 26th, 1885. Manchester: 1888. V. 70

MANCHESTER CITY ART GALLERY
Catalogue of the Ruskin Exhibition Spring 1904. V. 68

MANCY, A. JARRY DE
Atlas Historique et Chronologique des Litteratures Anciennes et Modernes, des Sciences et des Beaux Arts. Paris: 1831. V. 72

MANDAT GRANCEY, EDMOND, BARON DE
La Breche Aux Buffles Un Ranch Francais Dans Le Dakota. Paris: 1889. V. 70

MANDEL, GEORGE
Flee the Angry Stranger. Indianapolis: 1952. V. 69

MANDELBAUM, DAVID G.
Soldier Groups and Negro Soldiers. Berkeley: 1952. V. 72

MANDEL'SHTAM, OSIP
Selected Poems. Cambridge: 1973. V. 71; 73

MANDER, RAYMOND
A Theatrical Companion to Shaw - A Pictorial record of the First Performances of the Plays of George Bernard Shaw. London: 1954. V. 72

MANDEVILLE, BERNARD DE
The Fable of the Bees. London: 1724. V. 69
The Fable of the Bees. London: 1725. V. 68; 71
The Fable of the Bees. London: 1732-1729. V. 68
The Fables of the Bees. Edinburgh: 1755. V. 69
Private Vices, Publike Benefits?. Solihull: 1997. V. 71
A Treatise of the Hypochrondriack and Hysterick Diseases. London: 1730. V. 68

MANDEVILLE, JOHN
The Marvelous Adventures of Sir John Maundevile Kt. Westminster: 1895. V. 69

MANFRED, FREDERICK
Lord Grizzly. New York: 1954. V. 69
Riders of Judgment. New York: 1957. V. 73
Wanderlust: a Trilogy. Denver: 1962. V. 69

MANGAN, TERRY WILLIAM
Colorado on Glass: Colorado's First Half Century as Seen by the Camera. Denver: 1975. V. 68; 73
Colorado on Glass. Colorado's First Half Century as Seen by the Camera. 1980. V. 68

MANGIN, A.
The Famous Parks and Gardens of the World. London: 1880. V. 69

MANGUM, NEIL C.
Battle of the Rosebud, Prelude to The Little Big Horn. El Segundo: 1987. V. 72

MANHATTAN COMPANY
An Act of Incorporation of the Manhattan Company. New York: 1799. V. 70

MANIFESTO 5/8. London: 1960. V. 69

MANILIUS, MARCUS
Astronomicon. Strasbourg: 1655. V. 73
Astronomicon - Libri I-V. London: 1903-1930. V. 68

MANITOBA: Pictorial and Biographical. De Luxe Supplement. Winnipeg: 1913. V. 71; 73

MANITOU to the Summit of Pike's Peak, Altitude 14,147 Feet. Printed in Germany. V. 71

MANKELL, HENNING
Faceless Killers. New York: 1997. V. 70; 73

MANKIEWICZ, JOSEPH L.
All About Eve. New York: 1951. V. 70

MANKOWITZ, WOLF
A Kid for Two Farthings. London: 1953. V. 70
Make Me an Offer. London: 1952. V. 69
Make Me an Offer. New York: 1953. V. 71
Wedgwood. London: 1966. V. 72

MANLEY, MARY DE LA RIVIERE
Secret Memoirs and Manners of Several Persons of Quality of Both Sexes. London: 1716. V. 69
Secret Memoirs and Manners of Several Persons of Quality of Both Sexes. London: 1720. V. 73
Secret Memoirs of Several Persons of Quality of Both Sexes. London: 1709. V. 71

MANLEY, WILLIAM
A Collection of the Laws of the Customs Now in Force, to Prevent Frauds and Abuses in the Revenue, and the Illegal Importation and Exportation of Prohibited and Uncustomed Goods. London: 1742. V. 72

MANN, ERIC
Comrade George (Jackson) An Investigation into the Official Story. Cambridge: 1966. V. 73

MANN, HORACE
An Oration, Delivered at Dedham, (Mass.) July 4th 1823. Dedham: 1823. V. 71

MANN, J. J.
Round the World in a Motor Car. London: 1914. V. 71

MANN, JACK
Gees' First Case. London: 1936. V. 73
Her Ways are Death. London: 1941. V. 73
Kleinert Case. London: 1938. V. 73

MANN, JAMES
The American Bird-Keeper's Manual; or Directions for the Proper Management of American and Foreign Singing Birds. Boston: 1848. V. 71
Medical Sketches of the Campaigns of 1812, 13, 14. Dedham: 1816. V. 68; 71

MANN, LEONARD
A Murder In Sydney. New York: 1937. V. 73

MANN, MARTY
Marty Mann's New Primer on Alcoholism: How People Drink, How to Recognize Alcoholics and What to Do About Them. New York: 1958. V. 71

MANN, MARY TYLER
Moral Culture of Infancy and Kindergarten Guide with Music for the Plays. New York: 1874. V. 69

MANN, PATRICK
Dog Day Afternoon. New York: 1974. V. 68; 71

MANN, SALLY
Second Sight - the Photographs of Sally Mann. Boston: 1983. V. 70

MANN, THADEUS
The Biochemistry of Semen and of the Male Reproductive Tract. London: 1964. V. 68

MANN, THOMAS
Der Betrogene. (The Black Swan). Berlin: 1953. V. 73
Buddenbrooks. New York: 1938. V. 72
Buddenbrooks. New York: 1940. V. 73
Freud, Goethe, Wagner. New York: 1937. V. 73
Herr und Hund. Berlin: 1919. V. 73
Neue Studien. Stockholm: 1948. V. 69
Nocturnes. New York: 1934. V. 71
Nocturnes. New York: 1941. V. 70
Royal Highness a Novel of German Court Life. New York: 1916. V. 69
The Transposed Heads. London: 1941. V. 68
The Transposed Heads. New York: 1941. V. 68; 69

MANN, WILLIAM
A Description of a New Method of Propelling Locomotive Machines, and of Communicating Power and Motion to all other Kinds of Machinery. London: 1830. V. 72

MANNE, LOUIS FRANCOIS
Observations du Chirurgie au Sujet d'une Playe a la tete avec Fracas, et Une piece d'os Implantee dans le Cerveau Pendant un Mois san Aucun Simptome.... Avignon: 1729. V. 70

MANNERING, E.
Flower Portraits. 1961. V. 69

MANNERING, GEORGE EDWARD
With Axe and Rope in the New Zealand Alps. London: 1891. V. 69; 71; 72

MANNERS, CATHERINE REBECCA
Poems by.... London: 1794. V. 71
Review of Poetry, Ancient and Modern. London: 1799. V. 68; 70; 72

MANNERS, MARY E.
The Bishop and the Catepillar. London: 1895. V. 68

MANNERSHEIM, CARL GUSTAV EMIL VON
Across Asia from West to East in 1906-1908. Oosterhout: 1969. V. 71

MANNERS-SUTTON, D.
Black God. the Story of the Congo. NY: 1934. V. 72

MANNEX, P. J.
History, Gazetteer and Directory of Cumberland.... Beverley: 1847. V. 71
History, Gazetteer and Directory of Cumberland.... Beckermet: 1974. V. 71
History, Topography and Directory of Westmorland and Lonsdale North of the Sands.... London: 1849. V. 71

MANNEX & CO., P.
Topography and Directory of Lancaster and Sixteen Miles Round. Preston: 1881. V. 73
Topography and Directory of North and South Lonsdale. Preston: 1866. V. 73

MANNING, ALFRED
Scenes and Portraits. London: 1930. V. 72

MANNING, CARDINAL
Ireland. Portions of a Letter on the Land Question Addressed to Earl Grey in 1868. London: 1881. V. 69

MANNING, E. F.
The Children's Book of Happy Days. London: 1890. V. 73

MANNING, FREDERIC
Eidola. London: 1917. V. 72
The Middle Parts of Fortune. Somme & Ancre 1916. London: 1929. V. 69; 73
Poems. London: 1910. V. 73
Scenes and Portraits. London: 1909. V. 68
The Vigil of Brunhild: a Narrative Poem. London: 1907. V. 69; 72

MANNING, J. A.
The Alphabet Annotated for Youth and Adults. London: 1853. V. 73

MANNING, OLIVIA
The Danger Tree. The Battle Lost and Won. The Sum of Things. London: 1977-1980. V. 68
The Remarkable Expedition - the Story of Stanley's Rescue of Emin Pasha from Equatorial Africa. London: 1947. V. 68

MANNING, PHYLLIS A.
Spirit Rocks and Silver Magic. 1962. V. 69

MANNING, ROBERT
Book of Fruits.... Salem: 1838. V. 70; 71
England's Conversion and Reformation Compared; or, the Young Gentleman Directed in the Choice of His Religion. Antwerp: 1725. V. 70

MANNING, ROSEMARY
Look, Stranger. London: 1960. V. 68

MANNINGHAM, RICHARD
The Symptoms, Nature, Causes and Cure of the Febricula or Little Fever. London: 1750. V. 72

MANNING SANDERS, RUTH
Children by the Sea. London: 1938. V. 70
Elephant. New York: 1938. V. 70
Luke's Circus. Boston: 1940. V. 71

MANNIX, DANIEL P.
Kiboko. Philadelphia/NY: 1958. V. 72

MANNON, W.
Devotion, the Book of the Film about the Brontes. 1946. V. 70

MANNS, WILLIAM
Painted Ponies: American Carousel Art. New York: 1989. V. 72

MANO, D. KEITH
The Proselytizer. New York: 1972. V. 68
War is Heaven. New York: 1970. V. 68

MAN RAY
Man Ray: The Photographic Image. Woodbury: 1980. V. 68
Photographs by Man Ray, 1920. Paris 1934. Hartford: 1934. V. 68
Self Portrait. Boston: 1963. V. 68

MANRING, B. F.
Conquest of the...Couer D'Alenes Spokanes & ..Palouses.... Spokane: 1912. V. 72

MANRIQUE, JAIME
Colombian Gold. New York: 1983. V. 71

MANRIQUE, MANUEL
Island in Harlem. New York: 1966. V. 68

MANSBRIDGE, ALBERT
The Older Universities of England - Oxford & Cambridge. London: 1923. V. 70

MANSEL, HENRY LONGUEVILLE
Prolegomena Logica. Oxford: 1851. V. 71
Prolegomena Logica. Boston: 1860. V. 73
Scenes from an Unfinished Drama, Entitled Phronisterion, or, Oxford in the 19th Century. Oxford: 1852. V. 68

MANSEL, ROBERT
A Defence of the Drama.... New York: 1826. V. 70

MANSFIELD, CHARLOTTE
Via Rhodesia. London. V. 71

MANSFIELD, JAYNE
Jayne Mansfield's Wild, Wild World. Los Angeles: 1964. V. 72

MANSFIELD, K.
The Art of Angling. 1957. V. 68; 73

MANSFIELD, KATHERINE
The Aloe. London: 1930. V. 70; 71
The Aloe. New York: 1930. V. 70
The Dove's Nest and Other Stories. London: 1923. V. 71
The Garden Party and Other Stories. London: 1922. V. 70
The Garden Party and other stories. London: 1939. V. 72
The Garden Party and Other Stories. London: 1947. V. 73
Letters. London: 1928. V. 68; 71
Poems. 1923. V. 68
Prelude. Richmond: 1918. V. 71
Something Childish and Other Stories. 1924. V. 69
Something Childish and Other Stories. London: 1924. V. 70

MANSFIELD, M. F.
Kiplingiana.... New York: 1899. V. 68

MANSON, ALEXANDER
Medical Researches on the Effects of Iodine, In Bronchocele, Pralusis, Chorea, Scrophula, fistula Lachrymalis, Deafness, Dysphagia, White Swelling and Distortions of the Spine. 1825. V. 73

MANSON, J. B.
The Life and Work of Edward Degas. London: 1927. V. 69

MANSON, R. T.
Zig-Zag Ramblings by a Naturalist. Darlingotn;: 1884. V. 73

MANTELL, GIDEON ALGERNON
Geological Excursions Round the Isle of Wight. London: 1847. V. 69; 73
Geological Excursions Round the Isle of Wight. London: 1851. V. 68; 70
The Invisible World Revealed by the Microscope.... London: 1850. V. 68
The Journal of Gideon Mantell, Surgeon and Geologist. London: 1940. V. 68
The Medals of Creation; or First Lessons in Geology and in the Study of Organic Remains. London: 1844. V. 68
Thoughts on a Pebble. London: 1849. V. 68; 70
Thoughts on Animacules; or a Glimpse of the Invisible World Revealed by the Micrscope. London: 1846. V. 69; 72

MANTLE, MICKEY
The Mick. Garden City: 1985. V. 68; 69
My Favorite Summer. New York: 1991. V. 72

MANTZ, RUTH ELVISH
The Critical Bibliography of Katherine Mansfield. London: 1931. V. 71
The Life of Katherine Mansfield. London: 1933. V. 68

A MANUAL of the Typewriter; a Practical Guide to Commercial Literary, Legal, Dramatic and All Classes of Typewriting Work. London: 1893. V. 71

MANVILL, P. D., MRS.
Lucinda; or the Mountain Mourner. Johnstown: 1807. V. 68; 73
Lucinda; or the Mountain Mourner. Ballston Spa: 1810. V. 71

MANWARING, ELIZABETH WHEELER
Italian Landscape in Eighteenth Century England. London: 1925. V. 73

MANWOOD, THOMAS
A Treatise and Discourse of the Laws of the Forrest.... London: 1598. V. 70

MANZU, GIACOMO
Homage a Manzu. Paris: 1984. V. 73

MAO TSE-TUNG
Quotations from Chairman Mao Tse-Tung. Peking: 1966. V. 72
Red China. London: 1934. V. 72

MAPLE Street Cook Book. Meridien: 1918. V. 68

MAPLE & CO.
Illustrations of Wall Treatments in Panelled Wood and Plaster & of Parquet Floors. London Paris Buenos Aires: 1920?. V. 68

MAPOTHER, EDWARD DILLON
The Body and Its Health: a Book for Primary Schools. Dublin: 1870. V. 68

MAPPLETHORPE, ROBERT
Black Book. New York: 1986. V. 68; 72
Certain People: a Book of Portraits. Pasadena: 1985. V. 68; 70
Early Works. New York: 1991. V. 68
Flowers. Boston: 1990. V. 72
Mapplethorpe. New York: 1992. V. 68; 70; 72

MAPSON, JO-ANN
Fault Line. Irving: 1989. V. 68
Hank and Chloe. New York: 1993. V. 72

MARACLE, LEE
Sundogs. Penticton: 1992. V. 72

MARAINI, F.
Karakoram. 1961. V. 68; 71
Meeting with Japan. 1959. V. 71
Where Four Worlds Meet. 1959. V. 68
Where Four Worlds Meet. 1964. V. 71

MARAINI, FOSCO
Where Four Worlds Meet. New York: 1964. V. 69

MARAN, RENE
Batouala. New York: 1922. V. 69; 71; 73
Batouala. New York: 1932. V. 72

MARASCO, ROBERT
Child's Play. New York: 1970. V. 69

THE MARBLE-WORKERS' Manual. New York: 1856. V. 69

MARCET, JANE
Conversations for Children on Land and War. London: 1843. V. 73
Conversations on Chemistry. New Haven: 1809. V. 73
Conversations on Chymistry, in Which the Elements of that Science are Familiarly Explained and Illustrated by Experiments and Plates.... Philadelphia: 1809. V. 69
Conversations on Political Economy; in Which the Elements of that Science are Familiarly Explained. New York: 1820. V. 68
Willy's Holidays, or, Conversations on Different Kinds of Governments. London: 1836. V. 72

THE MARCH of The Mounted Riflemen. Glendale: 1940. V. 72

MARCH, J.
The Jolly Angler; or Water Side Companion. London: 1833. V. 72
The Jolly Angler; or Water Side Companion. London: 1836. V. 73

MARCHALONIS, JOHN J.
Immunity in Evolution. London: 1977. V. 68

MARCHAND, ANDRE
Pierre a Feu. Cannes - A Paris: 1945. V. 72

MARCHANT, S.
Handbook of Australian, New Zealand and Antarctic Birds. Melbourne: 1990. V. 73

MARCHANT, W. T.
In Praise of Ale, or Songs, Ballads, Epigrams & Anecdotes Relating to Beer, Malt and Hops. London: 1888. V. 70

MARCHESINUS, JOHANNES
Mammotrectus Super Bibliam. Strassburg: 1474. V. 69
Mammotrectus Super Bibliam. Venice: 1479. V. 69

MARCHIAFAVA, E.
Two Monographs on Malaria and Parasites of Malarial Fevers. London: 1894. V. 72

MARCHIO, VINCENZO
Il Forestiere Informato Delle Cose di Lucca. Luca: 1721. V. 68

MARCHMONT, FREDERICK
The Three Cruikshanks. London: 1897. V. 68

MARCOS, SUBCOMANDANTE
The Story of Colors. El Paso: 1999. V. 73

MARCOSSON, ISAAC F.
The Autobiography of a Clown. New York: 1931. V. 69

MARCOU, JULES
Life, Letters and Works of Louis Agassiz. London: 1896. V. 68

MARCUS, L. S.
The American Store Window. New York: 1978. V. 72

MARCUSE, HERBERT
Das Ende der Utopie.... Berlin: 1967. V. 69

MARCY, MARY
Out of the Dump. Chicago: 1909. V. 68

MARCY, RANDOLPH BARNES
Border Reminiscences. New York: 1872. V. 72
Exploration of the Red River of Louisiana in the Year 1852. Washington: 1854. V. 69
The Prairie Traveler: a Hand-Book for Overland Expeditions. New York: 1859. V. 70
The Prairie Traveler, a Hand-Book for Overland Expeditions. London: 1863. V. 68

MARDEN, BRICE
Cold Mountain Studies. Munich: 1991. V. 70

MARDER, ARTHUR J.
From the Dreadnought to Scapa Flow. London: 1961-1970. V. 68

MARDER, WILLIAM
Anthony. The Man, the Company, the Cameras. Amesbury: 1982. V. 72

MARDERSTEIG, GIOVANNI
Felice Feliciano: Alphabetum Romanum. Verona: 1960. V. 70
Giovanni Mardersteig on G. B. Bodoni's Type Faces. Verona: 1968. V. 73
Die Officina Bodoni: Das Werk Einer Handpresse 1923-1977. Verona: 1979. V. 68
The Officina Bodoni: an Account of the Work of a Hand Press. 1923- 1977. (with) Original Leaves from Books of the Officina Bodoni Printed Between 1924 and 1976. Verona: 1980. V. 70

MARES, M. A.
Mammalian Biology in South America, A Symposium held at the Pymatuning Laboratory of Ecology May 10-14, 1981. Linsville: 1982. V. 68

MARETZEK, MAX
Crotchets and Quavers; or, Revelations of an Opera Manager in America. New York: 1855. V. 70

MAREY, E. J.
Animal Mechanism: a Treatise on Terrestrial and Aerial Locomotion. New York: 1874. V. 71
Physiologie Experimentale; Travaux du Laboratoire. Paris: 1876-1880. V. 73

MARFIELD, DWIGHT
The Ghost on the Balcony. New York: 1939. V. 69

THE MARGARET Tarrant Nursery Rhyme Book. London: 1953. V. 70

MARGARY, AUGUSTUS RAYMOND
The Journey of Augustus Raymond Margary, from Shanghae to Bhamo, and Back to Manwyne. London: 1876. V. 71

MARGERISON, SAMUEL
The Registers of the Parish Church of Calverley. Bradford: 1880-1887. V. 73

MARGESSON, D.
The Brontes and Their Stars. 1928. V. 70

MARGOLIN, PHILLIP
Gone, But not Forgotten. New York: 1993. V. 73

MARGOLIN, PHILLIP M.
The Last Innocent Man. Boston: 1981. V. 71

MARGUERITE D'ANGOULEME, QUEEN OF NAVARRE
Memoirs of.... London: 1813. V. 69; 73

MARGUERITE DE VALOIS, QUEEN OF NAVARRE
Memoirs of.... London: 1813. V. 68
Memoirs of.... London: 1895. V. 68

MARIANI, A.
Coca and Its Therapeutic Application. New York: 1892. V. 68

MARIAS, JAVIER
A Heart So White. London: 1995. V. 72

MARIE, F. C. M.
Geometrie Stereographique, ou Reliefs des Polydres Pour Faciliter l'etude des Corps.... Paris: 1835. V. 72

MARIE, J.
Marly. Paris: 1947. V. 71

MARIE, QUEEN OF ROMANIA
The Lost Princess. 1924. V. 71
Ordeal: the Story of My Life. New York: 1935. V. 68

MARIGNY TAITBOUT DE, CHEVALIER
Three Voyages in the Black Sea to the Coast of Circassia. London: 1837. V. 71

MARION, F.
Wonderful Balloon Ascents; or the Conquest of the Skies, A History of Balloons and Balloon Voyages. London: 1875. V. 73

MARION, FRANCES
How to Write and Sell Film Stories. New York: 1937. V. 70

MARIOTTI, JEAN
Tales of Poindi. New York: 1938. V. 70

MARITAIN, RAISSA
Chagall ou l'Orage Enchantee. 1965. V. 69
Patriarch Tree. Thirty Poems. Worcester: 1965. V. 70

MARIUS, RICHARD
The Coming of Rain. New York: 1969. V. 72; 73

MARJORIBANKS, ALEXANDER
Travels in New South Wales. London: 1847. V. 71

MARK, JAN
Fun with Mrs. Thum. 1993. V. 72

MARK, MARY ELLEN
Indian Circus. San Francisco: 1993. V. 73

MARK, VERNON
Violence and the Brain. New York: 1970. V. 71

MARKHAM, ALBERT HASTINGS
The Cruise of the Rosario Amongst the New Hebrides and Santa Cruz Islands, Exposing the Recent Atrocities.... London: 1873. V. 71
Northward Ho!. London: 1879. V. 73

MARKHAM, CHRISTOPHER
Pewter Marks and Old Pewter Ware. London: 1909. V. 72

MARKHAM, CLEMENTS ROBERT
The Arctic Navy List: or, a Century of Arctic and Antarctic Officers 1773-1873.... Bournemount: 1992. V. 73
The Conquest of New Granada. New York: 1912. V. 69
The Fifty Years' Work of the Royal Geographical Society 1881. London: 1881. V. 73
A History of the Abyssinian Expedition. London: 1869. V. 71
History of the Incas. Cambridge: 1907. V. 71
The Incas of Peru. London: 1910. V. 71
A Selection of Papers on Arctic Geography and Ethnology. London: 1975. V. 71
The War of Las Salinas. London: 1923. V. 71

MARKHAM, EDWIN
The Man With the Hoe. San Francisco: 1899. V. 70

MARKHAM, GERVASE
The Citizen and Countryman's Complete Farrier.... Chambersburg: 1839. V. 68
Country Contentments or the Husbandmans Recreations. London: 1668. V. 71
Markham's Farewel to Husbandry; or the Enriching of All Sorts of Barren and Sterile Grounds In Our Nation.... London: 1684. V. 73

MARKHAM, J.
The Citizens and Countryman's Experienced Farrier. Chambersburg: 1839. V. 72
The Citizens and Countryman's Experienced Farrier. Chambersburg: 1840. V. 72
The Citizens and Countryman's Experienced Farrier. Chambersburg: 1841. V. 72

MARKHAM, JOHN
A Naval Career During the Old War.... London: 1883. V. 69

MARKHAM, M. ROLAND
Alcar, the Captive Creole; a Story of the South, in Verse. Homer: 1857. V. 73

MARKHAM, PETER
Poison Detected; or Frightful Truths; and Alarming to the British Metropolis. London: 1757. V. 69

MARKHAM, VIRGIL
The Black Door. New York: 1930. V. 73
Inspector Rusby's Finale. 1933. V. 73

MARKINO, YOSHIO
My Recollections and Reflections. London: 1913. V. 73

MARKLAND, A. B.
Pteryplegia; or, the Art of Shooting Flying. A Poem. 1727. V. 71; 72

MARKLOVE, H.
Views of Berkeley Castle, Taken on the Spot and Drawn on Stone.... London: 1840. V. 70

MARKMAN, EARNEST
10,000 Miles in a Balloon!. Saint Louis: 1873. V. 73

MARKMAN, SIDNEY DAVID
Colonial Architecture of Antigua Guatemala. Philadelphia: 1966. V. 70; 71

MARKS, DAVID
A Treatise on the Faith of the Freewill Baptists.... Dover: 1834. V. 69; 73

MARKS, JEANNETTE
The Sun Chaser. Cincinnati: 1922. V. 69

MARKS, JOHN GEORGE
Life and Letters of Frederick Walker. London: 1896. V. 73

MARKS, PAULA M.
And Die in the West, The Story of the OK Corral Gunfight. New York: 1989. V. 68; 73

MARKSON, DAVID
The Ballad of Dingus Magee. Indianapolis/Kansas City: 1965. V. 71; 72

MARKUS, JULIUS
Uncle. Boston: 1978. V. 69

MARKUS, KURT
Buckaroo, Images from the Sagebrush Basin. Boston;: 1987. V. 68

MARLITT, EUGENIE
The Old Maid's Secret. London: 1874. V. 68

MARLOWE, CHRISTOPHER
Doctor Faustus. London: 1903. V. 70; 71
Edward the Second. 1929. V. 68; 71; 73
The Famous Tragedy of the Rich Jew of Malta. 1933. V. 71
The Famous Tragedy of the Rich Jew of Malta. London: 1933. V. 72
Hero and Leander. London: 1894. V. 73
The Life and Death of Tamburlane the Great.... London: 1930. V. 68
The Tragical History of Doctor Faustus. London: 1903. V. 70
The Tragicall History of Doctor Faustus. 1932. V. 71
The Tragicall History of Doctor Faustus. London: 1932. V. 72

MARLOWE, DAN J.
Doorway to Death. New York: 1959. V. 71
Shake a Crooked Town. New York: 1961. V. 71

MARMELSZADT, WILLARD
Musical Sons of Aesculapius. New York: 1946. V. 69; 72

MARMIER, XAVIER
Voyage Pittoresque en Allemagne, Partie Meridionale. Paris: 1859. V. 72
Voyage Pittoresque en Allemagne. Partie Septentrionale. Paris: 1860. V. 72

MARMONTEL, JEAN FRANCOIS
Belisarius. London: 1767. V. 69
Les Contes Moraux. Paris: 1765. V. 71
Marmontel's Tales. London: 1799. V. 71

MARMORA, ANDREA
Della Historia di Corfu Libri Otto.... Venice: 1672. V. 68; 70

MAROLOIS, SAMUEL
Opera Mathematica, ou Oeuvres Mathematiques Traictans de Geometrie, Perspective, Architecture et Fortification.... Amsterdam: 1662. V. 69
Perspectiva das ist: Die Weitberuhmte Kunst Einer Scheinenden in Oder Durchsehnden Augen Gesichts Punct. Amsterdam: 1628. V. 72

MARON, MARGARET
Bloody Kin. New York: 1985. V. 70
Bootleggers Daughter. 1992. V. 68
Bootlegger's Daughter. New York: 1992. V. 69
Corpus Christmas. New York: 1989. V. 70
Death in Blue Folders. New York: 1985. V. 68
Past Imperfect. New York: 1991. V. 68
Shoveling Smoke. Norfolk: 1997. V. 70; 71
Up Jumps the Devil. New York: 1996. V. 69

MARPERGER, PAUL JACOB
In Natur- und Kunst-Sachen Neueroffnetes Kaufmanns-Magazin zum Unterricht und Dienst aller, der Medicin, Kaufmanns-Magazin zum Unterricht und Dienst aller, der Medicin, Botanic.... Hamburg: 1748. V. 68; 69

MARPLES, THEO
Prize Dogs. 1912. V. 68

MARQUAND, JOHN P.
Last Laugh Mr. Moto. London: 1943. V. 68
Stopover: Tokyo. London: 1957. V. 69

MARQUART, JOHN
Miscellaneous Valuable Receipts. Philadelphia: 1860. V. 68
600 Miscellaneous Valuable Receipts. Philadelphia: 1860. V. 73
Six Hundred Receipts, Worth Their Weight in Gold. Philadelphia: 1867. V. 71

MARQUIS, DON
A Variety of People. Garden City: 1929. V. 70

MARQUIS, DONALD M.
In Search of Buddy Bolden, First Man of Jazz. Baton Rouge: 1978. V. 71

MARQUIS, THOMAS B.
Custer, Cavalry and Crows. The Story of William White. Ft. Collins: 1975. V. 68
Memoirs of a White Crow Indian (Thomas H. Leforge). New York: 1928. V. 71; 72
A Warrior Who Fought Custer. Minnesota: 1931. V. 72

MARR, J. E.
The Geology of the Lake District and the Scenery as Influence by Geological Structure. Cambridge: 1916. V. 71

MARR, SCOUT
Into the Frozen South. London: 1923. V. 71

MARRACCI, LODOVICO
Rimedio per Curare la Vanita Feminile Composto tre Ingresienti. Roma: 1680. V. 73

MARRAT, W.
The History of Lincolnshire, Topographical, Historical and Descriptive. Boston: 1814-1816. V. 70

THE MARRIAGE Register of Stanwix. London. V. 71

MARRINGTON, PAULINE
The October Horse. New York: 1975. V. 68; 71

MARRIOTT, ALICE
Hell On Horses and Women. Norman: 1953. V. 71
Indians of the Four Corners. New York: 1952. V. 69
Maria: the Potter of San Ildefonso. Norman: 1970. V. 68
These Are the People. Santa Fe: 1949. V. 69; 70

MARRIOTT, F.
Artistic Homes of California. Issued with S.F. News Letter 1887-1888. San Francisco: 1888. V. 73

MARRIOTT, JOHN
A Short Account of John Marriott, Including Extracts from some of His Letters.... Doncaster: 1803. V. 73

MARROT, H. V.
A Bibliography of the Works of John Galsworth. 1928. V. 73

MARRYAT, F. S.
Mountains and Molehills or Recollections of a Burn Journal. New York: 1855. V. 70

MARRYAT, FREDERICK
The Children of the New Forest. New York: 1927. V. 68
A Diary in America, With Remarks on Its Institutions. London: 1839. V. 72
A Diary in America, With Remarks on Its Institutions. New York: 1839. V. 68
Japhet in Search of a Father. Trenton: 1835. V. 71
Masterman Ready; or the Wreck of the Pacific. London: 1841-1842. V. 73
The Mission; or Scenes in Africa. London: 1845. V. 68; 69
Mr. Midshipman Easy. London: 1836. V. 73
Narrative of the Travels and Adventures of Monsieur Violet, in California, Sonora and Western Texts. London: 1843. V. 70
The Naval Officer; or, Scenes and Adventures in Life of Frank Mildmay. London: 1829. V. 70
The Pirate, and the Three Cutters. London: 1836. V. 70
The Pirate, and The Three Cutters. London: 1854. V. 71
Poor Jack. London: 1840. V. 73
Poor Jack. London: 1846. V. 71

MARRYAT, JEAN FRANCOIS
Narrative of the Travels and Adventures of Monsieur Violet, in California, Sonora and Western Texas. London: 1843. V. 72

MARRYAT, JOSEPH
Collections Towards a History of Pottery and Porcelain, in the 15th (to) 18th Centuries. London: 1850. V. 72
A Reply to Arguments, Contained in Various Publications, Recommending an Equalization of the Duties on East and West Indian Sugar. London: 1823. V. 70; 72
The Substance of A Speech Delivered...in the House of Commons, on Tuesday the Twentieth February 1810, Upon Mr. Manning's Motion for the Appointment of a Select Committee, to Consider of the Act of the 6th of George the First and Of Our Present Means of. London: 1810. V. 69

MARS, F. ST.
The Prowlers. 1913. V. 69

MARSALIS, WYNTON
Sweet Swing Blues on the Road. New York: 1994. V. 68; 69

MARSDEN, JOSHUA
The Narrative of a Mission to Nova Scotia, New Brunswick and the Somers Island; with a Tour of Lake Ontario. Plymouth Dock: 1816. V. 73

MARSEILLES, Genoa and Pisa. 1998. V. 69

MARSH, ANNE
Mount Sorel; or the Heiress of the De Veres. London: 1882. V. 68

MARSH, BOWER
Alumni Carthusiani. A Record of the Foundation Scholars of Charterhouse, 1614-1872. London: 1913. V. 72

MARSH, C. C.
The Science of Double-Entry Book-Keeping, Simplified. New York: 1859. V. 73

MARSH, CATHERINE
Memorials of Captain Hedley Vicars. Ninety-Seventh Regiment. London: 1856. V. 72

MARSH, CHARLES W.
Recollections 1837-1910. Chicago: 1910. V. 68; 71

MARSH, E. L.
Where The Buffalo Roamed. Toronto: 1980. V. 71

MARSH, EDWARD
Georgian Poetry 1911-1912. London: 1912. V. 68
Georgian Poetry 1911-1912. London: 1923. V. 68; 72
Georgian Poetry 1920-1922. London: 1922. V. 72

MARSH, GWEN
The Land of No Strangers. London: 1951. V. 69

MARSH, HONORIA
Shades from Jane Austen. 1975. V. 73
Shades from Jane Austen. London: 1975. V. 70

MARSH, LEWIS
Old Time Tales (Tales of Many Lands). London: 1917. V. 70

MARSH, MABEL A.
My Very First Book. a Picture Alphabet Book for Little Folks. 1905. V. 71

MARSH, NGAIO
Artists in Crime. London: 1938. V. 73
Black Beech and Honeydew. Boston: 1965. V. 71
Clutch of Constables. London: 1968. V. 73
Colour Scheme. London: 1943. V. 72; 73
Died In The Wool. London: 1945. V. 72; 73
Died in the Wool. London: 1972. V. 70
False Scent. 1960. V. 70
Final Curtain. London: 1947. V. 71; 73
A Man Lay Dead. London: 1934. V. 73
The Nursing Home Murder. London: 1935. V. 73
Off with His Head. London: 1957. V. 73
Opening Hunt. London: 1951. V. 73
Overture to Death. 1939. V. 73
Scales of Justice. London: 1955. V. 71; 73
Singing in the Shrouds. London: 1959. V. 71; 73
Spinsters in Jeopardy. Boston: 1953. V. 70
Spinsters in Jeopardy. Boston: 1954. V. 73
Surfeit of Lampreys. London: 1941. V. 73
Swing Brother, Swing. London: 1949. V. 73
Tied up in Tinsel. London: 1972. V. 73
Vintage Murder. London: 1937. V. 73

MARSH, O. C.
Dinocerata: a Monograph of an Extinct Order of Gigantic Animals. Washington: 1884. V. 68
Odontornithes; a Monograph on the Extinct Toothed Birds of North America.... Washington: 1880. V. 72

MARSH, PETER
The Devil's Daughter. New York: 1942. V. 69

MARSHAK, SONDRA
Star Trek: the New Voyages 2. New York: 1978. V. 71

MARSHAL, ANDREW
The Morbid Anatomy of the Brain in Mania and Hydrophobia; with the Pathology of These Two Diseases as Collected from the Papers of Andrew Marshal, M.D.... London: 1815. V. 68; 73

MARSHALL, A. J.
The Black Musketeers. London: 1937,. V. 71

MARSHALL, A. MILNES
Vertebrate Embryology. London: 1893. V. 68

MARSHALL, AGNES B.
The Book of Ices. London: 1900. V. 68
Mrs. A. B. Marshall's Larger Book of Extra Recipes. London: 1894. V. 72

MARSHALL, ALFRED
Memorials. London: 1925. V. 71
Official Papers. London: 1926. V. 71

MARSHALL, BRUCE
The Fair Bride. London: 1953. V. 68
Girl in May. London: 1956. V. 68
Only Fade Away. London: 1954. V. 68

MARSHALL, C. F.
Lectures on the Darwinian Theory Delivered by the Late Arthur Milnes Marshall. New York: 1894. V. 70

MARSHALL, CATHERINE
Christy. New York: 1967. V. 69

MARSHALL, CHARLES
An Aide-de-Camp of Lee. Boston: 1927. V. 69; 70
An Introduction to the Knowledge and Practice of Gardening.... Boston: 1799. V. 70

MARSHALL, EDISON
The Deadfall. New York: 1927. V. 69
Ocean Gold. New York: 1925. V. 70
The Viking. New York: 1951. V. 69; 71
The Voice of the Pack. Boston: 1920. V. 70

MARSHALL, H. RISSIK
Coloured Worcester Porcelain of the First Period (1751-1783). Newport: 1954. V. 72

MARSHALL, HOWARD
Men Against Everest. London: 1954. V. 69

MARSHALL, J. D.
The Industrial Archaeology of the Lake Counties. London: 1969. V. 71
The Lake Counties from 1830 to the Mid-Twentieth Century. Manchester: 1981. V. 71

MARSHALL, JENNER
Memorials of Westcott Barton, in the County of Oxford. 1870. V. 72

MARSHALL, JOHN
Atlas to the Life of George Washington. Philadelphia: 1832. V. 69
The Life of George Washington. Philadelphia: 1804-1807. V. 68; 73
The Life of George Washington. Philadelphia: 1805-1807. V. 71
Outlines of Physiology Human and Comparative. Philadelphia: 1868. V. 71

MARSHALL, JOHN GEORGE
Confederation Considered On Its Merits.... Halifax: 1867. V. 69
The Justice of the Peace and County and Township Officer, in the Province of Nova Scotia. Halifax: 1837. V. 73
The Justice of the Peace and County and Township Officer, in the Province of Nova Socita. Halifax: 1846. V. 69
A Patriotic Call. To Prepare in a Season of Peace, for One of Political Danger.... Halifax: 1819. V. 73

MARSHALL, N. B.
Aspects of Marine Zoology.... London: 1967. V. 72

MARSHALL, NINA L.
Mushroom Book. New York: 1903. V. 73

MARSHALL, PAULE
The Chosen Place, the Timeless People. New York: 1969. V. 69
Daughters. New York: 1991. V. 72
The Fisher King. New York: 2000. V. 72

MARSHALL, RICHARD
Robert Mapplethorpe. New York: 1988. V. 68

MARSHALL, ROSAMOND
Duchess Hotspur. New York: 1946. V. 72

MARSHALL, THOMAS
Lives of the Most Celebrated Actors and Actresses. London: 1847. V. 70

MARSHALL, THOMAS C.
Into the Streets and Lanes: the Beginnings and Growth of the Social Work of the Episcopal Church 1887-1947. Claremont: 1948. V. 68

MARSHALL, THOMAS M.
Christianity in China: a Fragment. London: 1858. V. 69

MARSHALL, W. T.
Cactaceae. Pasadena: 1941. V. 69; 73

MARSHALL, WILLIAM
Agriculture Pratique des Differentes Parties de l'Angleterre. Paris: 1803. V. 71; 73
On the Management of Landed Estates; a General Work; for the Use of Professional Men. London: 1806. V. 71
Planting and Ornamental Gardening; a Practical Treatise. London: 1785. V. 73

MARSHALL, WILLIAM continued
Planting and Rural Ornament. London: 1796. V. 68; 69
Planting and Rural Ornament. London: 1803. V. 69; 70; 71
The Review and Abstract of the County Reports to the Board of Agriculture, from the Several Agricultrual Departments of England. 1969. V. 72
A Review of the Landscape, a Didactic Poem; also an Essay on the Picturesque Together with Practical Remarks on Rural Ornament. London: 1795. V. 70
The Rural Economy of Yorkshire. London: 1788. V. 70; 72

MARSHMAN, JOHN C.
History of India. London: 1871. V. 71

MARSON, G. F.
Ghost, Ghouls and Gallows. London. V. 69

MARSTEN, RICHARD
Danger: Dinosaurs!. Philadelphia: 1953. V. 69
Rocket to Luna. 1953. V. 73

MARSTON, A. E.
The Lions Of The North. London: 1996. V. 72
The Wolves of Savernake. London: 1993. V. 68; 69

MARSTON, ANNA LEE
Records of a California Family, Journals and Letters of Lewis C. Gunn and Elizabeth Le Breton Gunn. San Diego: 1928. V. 70

MARSTON, EDWARD
The Elephants of Norwich. London: 2000. V. 68
The Queen's Head. London: 1988. V. 71

MARSTON, JOHN
The Metamorphosis of Pigmalion's Image. Waltham St. Lawrence: 1926. V. 68; 71; 72

MARSTON, JOHN WESTLAND
Gerald: a Dramatic Poems and Other Poems. London: 1842. V. 73

MARSTON, R. B.
Walton and Some Earlier Writers on Fish and Fishing. 1903. V. 68

MARSTON, WESTLAND
Our Recent Actors. London: 1888. V. 72

MARTELL, DOMINIC
Gitana. London: 2000. V. 72
Gitana. London: 2001. V. 73

M'ARTHUR, JOHN
The Antiquities of Arran; with a Historical Sketch of the Island, Embracing an Account of the Sudreyjar Under the Norsemen. Glasgow: 1861. V. 73

MARTIALIS, MARCUS VALERIUS
Epigrammata. London: 1823. V. 72
Epigrammata ad Optimas Editiones Collata. Biponti i.e. Zweibrucken: 1784. V. 72
Epigrammatum Libri XIV. London: 1720. V. 72

MARTI-IBANEZ, FELIX
The Crystal Arrow. Essay on Literature, Travel, ARt, Love and the History of Medicine. New York: 1964. V. 68

MARTIN, ANNIE
Home Life On An Ostrich Farm. London: 1890. V. 72

MARTIN, BENJAMIN
Bibliotheca Technolgoica; or a Philological Library of Literary Arts and Sciences. 1737. V. 72
Bibliotheca Technologica; or a Philologica Library of Literary Arts and Sciences. London: 1737. V. 72
The Philosophical Grammar; Being a View of the Present State of Experimental Physiology, or Natural Philosophy. London: 1748. V. 72

MARTIN, BENJAMIN ELLIS
The Stones of Paris in History and Letters. New York: 1899. V. 71

MARTIN, CECIL P.
Prehistoric Man In Ireland. 1935. V. 70

MARTIN, DAVID
The Crying Heart Tattoo. New York: 1982. V. 72

MARTIN, DOUGLAS
Charles Keeping - an Illustrator's Life. London: 1993. V. 73
The Telling Line - Essays on Fifteen Contemporary Book Illustrators. London: 1989. V. 73

MARTIN, E. S.
Martin's System of Practical Penmanship Taught in 24 Lessons at His Writing and Book Keeping Academy. Worcester: 1847. V. 71
Martin's System of Practical Penmanship Taught in 24 Lessons at His Writing and Book Keeping Academy No. 182 Main Street, Worcester, Mass. Worcester: 1848. V. 73

MARTIN, EDWARD A.
Amidst Nature's Realms.... London: 1892. V. 68
Bibliography of Gilbert White. London: 1934. V. 68; 69; 70; 72
A Bibliography of Gilbert White, The naturalist & Antiquarian of Selborne. London: 1970. V. 72

MARTIN, EDWARD LE BRETON
A History of Westbury (Buckinghamshire). London: 1928. V. 71

MARTIN, EMILE
Pont de Cubzac. Dessins et Description des Piliers en Fonte de Fer. Paris: 1841. V. 73

MARTIN, EUSTACE MEREDYTH
A Tour through Indian in Lord Canning's Time. Remington: 1881. V. 68

MARTIN, F.
Martin's Natural History. New York. V. 70

MARTIN, F. X.
Friar Nugent: a Study of Francis Lavalin Nugent 1569-1635. Rome: 1962. V. 69

MARTIN, FRANCIS
Scutum Fidei Contra Haereses Hodiernas: Seu Tillotsonianae Concionis Sub Titulo: Strena Opportuna Contra Papismum Refutatio. Lovanii: 1714. V. 69

MARTIN, FRANK A.
Under the Absolute Amir. London: 1907. V. 71

MARTIN, GEOFFREY
The Modern Soap and Detergent Industry. Edinburgh: 1930. V. 69

MARTIN, GEORGE V.
For Our Vines Have Tender Grapes. 1940. V. 69; 71
For Our Vines Have Tender Grapes. New York: 1940. V. 68

MARTIN, H. BRADLEY
The Library of H. Bradley Martin. New York: 1989-1990. V. 73
The Library of H. Bradley Martin, John James Audubon, Magnificent Books and Manuscripts. New York: 1989. V. 69; 72

MARTIN, HENRI
The Age of Louis XVI. (with) Decline of the French Monarchy. Boston: 1865-1866. V. 71

MARTIN, ISAAC
A Journal of the Life, Travels, Labours and Religious Exercises of Isaac Martin.... Philadelphia: 1834. V. 71

MARTIN, J. W.
The Trent Otter's Little Book of Angling, Being Practical.... London: 1910. V. 69

MARTIN, J. WALLIS
A Likeness in Stone. London: 1997. V. 70

MARTIN, JACK
Border Boss, Captain John R. Hughes - Texas Ranger. San Antonio: 1942. V. 69

MARTIN, JAMES C.
Maps of Texas and the Southwest 1513-1900. Albuquerque: 1984. V. 70

MARTIN, JOHN
An Account of the Natives of the Tonga Islands, in the South Pacific Ocean. London: 1818. V. 70

MARTIN, JOHN PATRICK
The Story of Dartmouth. Dartmouth: 1957. V. 73

MARTIN, JOSEPH
A New and Comprehensive Gazetteer of Virginia and the District of Columbia.... Charlottesville: 1835. V. 71
Select Tales. Charlottesville: 1833. V. 68

MARTIN, KENNETH
Aubade. New York: 1958. V. 69

MARTIN, LOUIS
L'Eschole de Salerne en Svite Le Poeme Marcaroniqve. Paris: 1664. V. 68

MARTIN, NANCY
Legends in Labrador. 1980. V. 68

MARTIN, NED
Bit and Spur Makers in the Texas Tradition: a Historical Perspective. Nicasio: 2000. V. 68; 73

MARTIN, P. S.
Anasazi Painted Pottery in Field Museum of Natural History. Mansfield Centre & Mill Vall: 2000. V. 69

MARTIN, PAUL
Anasazi Painted Pottery in the Field Museum of Natural History. Chicago: 1940. V. 72; 73

MARTIN, PERCY F.
Mexico of the XXth Century. London: 1907. V. 71

MARTIN, R.
Haute Couture. New York: 1995. V. 71
Historical Notes and Personal Recollections of West Hartlepool and Its Founder. West Hartlepool: 1924. V. 73

MARTIN, ROBERT MONTGOMERY
Australia. London. V. 71
The History, Antiquities, Topography and Satistics of Eastern India.... London: 1838. V. 69
History of Nova Scotia, Cape Breton and the Sable Islands, New Brunswick, Prince Edward Island, the Bermudas, Newfoundland &c. London: 1837. V. 73

MARTIN, RUSSELL
Cowboy: the Enduring Myth of the Wild West. New York: 1983. V. 69

MARTIN, SALLIE
Gospel Songbook of the Singing Caravans No. 27. Chicago: 1958. V. 72

MARTIN, SAMUEL
An Essay Upon Plantership, Humbly Inscribed to His Excellency George Thomas, Esq.... Antigua and London: 1765. V. 72
The Useful Arts; Their Birth and Development. London: 1851. V. 71

MARTIN, SARAH CATHERINE
Old Mother Hubbard. London: 1938. V. 70
Old Mother Hubbard and Her Wonderful Dog. Cincinnati: 1877-1889. V. 71; 73

MARTIN, T. MOWER
Canada Painted by T. Mower Martin. London: 1907. V. 68

MARTIN, THOMAS
A Lecture on Education, in Reference, More Especially, to Popular Education: Delivered at the Town Hall, Reigate, to the Members of the Mechanic's Institution on Thursday the 27th September, 1838. Reigate: 1838. V. 70

MARTIN, THOMAS, PSEUD.
The Circle of the Mechanical Arts.... London: 1813. V. 73
The Circle of the Mechanical Arts.... London: 1818. V. 73

MARTIN, THOMAS RICAUD
The Great Parliamentary Battle and Farewell Addresses of the Southern Senators on the Eve of the Civil War. New York and Washington: 1905. V. 69; 70

MARTIN, VALERIE
The Consolation of Nature. Boston: 1988. V. 72

MARTIN, WILLIAM
Petrificata Derbiensia; or, Figures and Descriptions of Petrifactions Collected in Derbyshire. Wigan: 1809. V. 73

MARTINDALE, T.
Sport Indeed. Toronto. V. 71
Sport Indeed. 1901. V. 72
Sport Indeed. Philadelphia: 1901. V. 69

MARTINDELL, E. W.
A Bibliography of the Works of Rudyard Kipling (1881-1923). London: 1922. V. 70
A Bibliogrpahy of the Works of Rudyard Kipling 1881-1923. London: 1923. V. 70

MARTIN DU GARD, ROGER
Summer 1914. New York: 1941. V. 69

MARTINE, GEORGE
Essays Medical and Philosophical. London: 1740. V. 73

MARTINEAU & SMITH
Patent Cocks.... Birmingham. V. 70

MARTINEAU, HARRIET
A Complete Guide to the English Lakes.... Windermere: 1855. V. 71; 73
A Complete Guide to the English Lakes.... Windermere: 1866. V. 71
Deerbrook. London: 1839. V. 69
The English Lakes. Windermere: 1858. V. 71
Feats on the Fjord. London: 1901. V. 68
Guide to Windermere, With Tours to the Neighbouring Lakes and Other Interesting. Windermere: 1854. V. 69
Harriet Martineau's Autobiography. London: 1877. V. 69; 71
History of England During the 30 Year's Peace 1816-1846. London: 1849-1850. V. 69
A History of the American Compromises. London: 1856. V. 71
The Playfellow (General Title): the Settlers at Home. London: 1841. V. 73
Retrospect of Western Travel. London: 1838. V. 69; 73
Retrospect of Western Travel. New York: 1838. V. 72

MARTINEAU, R. A. S.
Rhodesian Wild Flowers. Cape Town: 1953. V. 68

MARTINEAU, VIOLET
John Martineau - the Pupil of Kingsley. London: 1921. V. 71

MARTINENT, JOANNES FLORENTIUS
The Catechism of Nature, for the Use of Children. Trenton: 1812. V. 71

MARTINGALE, PSEUD.
Sporting Scenes and Country Characters. London: 1840. V. 68

MARTINI, JOHAN JACOB
Dissertatio Inauguralis medica de Hydatidibus Quam Favente Numine Consensu et Authoritate.... Heidelberg: 1681. V. 72

MARTINI, MATHAUS
De Morbis Mesenterii Abstrusioribus. In Scholis Medicorum Hactenus Praetermissis.... Leipzig: 1630. V. 73

MARTINUS, EMMANUEL
Epistolarum Libri Duodecim. Amsterdam: 1738. V. 72

MARTIUS, C.
Nova Genera et Species Plantarum Quas in Itinere per Brasiliam annis MCCCXVII-MDCCCXX.... Munich: 1823-1832. V. 69; 73

MARTON, FRANCESCA
Mrs. Betsy or Widowed and Wed. New York: 1955. V. 70

MARTYN, FREDERICK
A Holiday in Gaol. London: 1911. V. 71

MARTYN, THOMAS
Guide du Voyageur en Italie.... Lausanne: 1791. V. 68

MARTYRS Of The Revolution 1649: Prints. King Charles 1 And The Heads Of The Noble Earls, Lords, And Others. London: 1870. V. 72

MARULLI, VINCENZO
L'Arte di Ordinare i Giardini. Naples: 1804. V. 68

MARVELL, ANDREW
A Letter from a Gentleman in Ireland to His Brother in England Relating to the Concerns of Ireland in Matter of Trade. London: 1677. V. 70
Miscellaneous Poems. London: 1923. V. 70
The Rehearsal Transpos'd; or Animadversions Upon a Late Book, Intituled, a Preface Shewing What Grounds There are of Fears and Jealousies of Popery. London: 1672. V. 69
The Rehearsall Transpos'd: the Second Part. London: 1673. V. 69
The Works. London: 1722. V. 69

MARX, GROUCHO
Beds. New York: 1930. V. 70
Many Happy Returns: an Unofficial Guide to Your Income Tax Problems. New York: 1942. V. 73

MARX, KARL
Le Capital. Paris: 1875. V. 72
Capital. Moscow: 1971. V. 73
The Eighteenth Brumaire of Louis Bonaparte. New York: 1898. V. 73
The Eighteenth Brumaire of Louis Bonaparte. London: 1926. V. 68
Theories of Surplus Value. Moscow: 1968-1971. V. 68

MARY and Her Dog Tray. London: 1888. V. 72

MARY, the Maid of the Inn; an Interesting Narrative, Detailing the Singular Way She Discovered Her Lover to be a Robber and Murderer.... Alnwick: 1800. V. 73

MARYE, GEORGE T.
From '49 to '83 in California and Nevada, Chapters from the Life of George Thomas Mayre, a Pioneer of '49. San Francisco: 1923. V. 69

MARYLAND. STATE LIBRARY - 1851
Catalogue of the Maryland State Library. Annapolis: 1851. V. 68

MARYLAND COURT OF APPEALS - 1865
October Term, 1865. The State of Maryland Use of Mary Coughlan, vs. The Baltimore and Ohio Rail Road Co. Patrick Bannon, by his next Friend James Coughlan vs. the Baltimore and Ohio Rail Road Co. 1865. V. 73

MARYLAND. GOVERNOR - 1822
Message of the Governor of Maryland, Communicating the Report of the Commissioners Appointed to Survey the River Potomac. Annapolis: 1822. V. 73

MARYLAND HISTORICAL SOCIETY
Archives of Maryland. Volumes 1-46. Baltimore: 1883-1929. V. 72

MARZIALS, FRANK T.
Life of Charles Dickens. London: 1887. V. 68

MASCALL, LEONARD
A Booke of Fishing with Hooke and Line...Reprinted from the Edition of 1590. London: 1884. V. 72
A Booke of the Arte and Maner How to Plant and Grasse All Sortes of Trees, How to Set Stones and Sowe Pepins.... London: 1582. V. 70; 73

MASCHLER, TOM
Declaration. London: 1957. V. 68

MASCLET, DANIEL
Nus La Beaute de la Femme. Paris: 1933. V. 73

MASEFIELD, JOHN
Captain Margaret. London: 1908. V. 73
Chaucer. New York: 1931. V. 68
Eggs and Baker or the Days of Trial. London: 1936. V. 70; 71
Gallipoli. London: 1916. V. 70; 72
A Generation Risen. 1942. V. 73
Land Workers. London: 1942. V. 73
Live and Kicking Ned. New York: 1939. V. 70
Martin Hyde - the Duke's Messenger. London: 1910. V. 71
The Midnight Folk. London: 1927. V. 73
Midsummer Night and Other Tales in Verse. London: 1928. V. 70; 71; 72
My Faith in Woman Suffrage. London: 1910. V. 72
Reynard the Fox or the Ghost Heath Run. New York: 1920. V. 70
Salt-Water Ballads. London: 1902. V. 73
Sea Life in Nelson's Time. London: 1905. V. 69
Selected Poems. London: 1922. V. 70; 71
The Widow in the Bye Street. London: 1912. V. 73

MASEN, JAKOB
Sarcotis. Carmen. 1757. V. 71

MASINI, L. V.
Art Nouveau. Secaucus: 1984. V. 72

THE MASK. A Journal of the Art of the Theatre. Florence: 1927. V. 72

MASKELL, ALFRED
Ivories. London: 1905. V. 72

MASKELYNE, JOHN NEVIL
Sharps and Flats. London: 1894. V. 70

MASKS and Faces. 1930. V. 71

MASLEN, K.
An Early London Printing House at Work.... New York: 1993. V. 70

MASLEN, T. J.
The Friend of Australia. London: 1836. V. 71

MASON, A. E. W.
The Three Gentlemen. London: 1932. V. 73

MASON, ALFRED BISHOP
A Duchess and Her Daughter. New York: 1929. V. 71

MASON, ALFRED EDWARD WOODLEY
At the Villa Rosa. New York: 1910. V. 70; 71
The Broken Road. New York: 1906. V. 71
Fire Over England. London: 1936. V. 72
The Four Feathers. London: 1902. V. 71
The House in Lordship Lane. London: 1946. V. 68; 72
Konigsmark. London: 1938. V. 69
Lawrence Clavering. London: 1897. V. 69
No Other Tiger. London: 1927. V. 69
Running Water. New York: 1907. V. 69
The Sapphire. London: 1933. V. 68; 69
The Three Gentlemen. Garden City: 1932. V. 68; 72
The Three Gentlemen. London: 1932. V. 68; 72

MASON, ARTHUR
The Roving Lobster. New York: 1931. V. 71
The Wee Men of Bally-Wooden. Garden City: 1930. V. 71

MASON, BOBBIE ANN
Clear Springs. New York: 1999. V. 72
Feather Crowns. New York: 1993. V. 72
In Country. New York: 1985. V. 68; 70; 71
Shiloh and Other Stories. New York: 1982. V. 68; 69; 71
Spence and Lila. New York: 1988. V. 68; 70
Zigzagging Down a Wild Trail. New York: 2001. V. 69

MASON, CAROLINE ATWATER
The Little Green God. New York: 1902. V. 69

MASON, CATHERINE GEORGE WARD
Family Portraits, or Descendants of Trelawney. New York: 1834. V. 70

MASON, EDWARD T.
Samuel Johnson, His Words and His Ways.... New York: 1973. V. 69

MASON, F.
Creation by Evolution.... New York: 1928. V. 68

MASON, FINCH
Sporting Nonsense Rhymes. London: 1906. V. 73

MASON, GEORGE
An Essay on Design in Gardening. London: 1768. V. 68; 70
A Supplement to Johnson's English Dictionary.... London: 1801. V. 73

MASON, GEORGE HENRY
The Costume of China, with Explanations in English and French. London: 1810. V. 71
The Punishments of China, Illustrated by Twenty-Two Engravings.... London: 1801. V. 70

MASON, H.
Where the River runs Dry. 1934. V. 72

MASON, H. T.
Picturesque Grange-Over Sands and District, and the English Lakes. Grange-over-Sands. V. 71

MASON, HENRY J. M.
Essay on the Antiquity and Constitution of the Parliaments in Ireland. 1891. V. 70
Primitive Christianity in Ireland; a Letter to Thomas Moore. 1836. V. 70

MASON, JOHN
More Papers Handmade by John Mason. Leicester: 1960. V. 70
Paper Making as an Artistic Craft. Leicester: 1963. V. 70; 73

MASON, KENNETH
Abode of Snow. 1955. V. 68; 71; 73
Abode of Snow. London: 1955. V. 69
Abode of Snow. London: 1987. V. 69
The Himalayan Journal. Calcutta: 1929. V. 71

MASON, MICHAEL H.
Where the River Runs Dry. 1934. V. 73

MASON, MIRIAM E.
Susannah: The Pioneer Cow. New York: 1941. V. 73

MASON, MONCK
Account of the Late Aeronautical Expedition from London to Weilburg Accomplished by Robert Hollond, Esq., Monck Mason, Esq. and Charles Green. New York: 1837. V. 69

MASON, OTIS T.
Aboriginal American Basketry, Studies in Textile Art Without Machinery. Glorieta: 1970. V. 68

MASON, SARA ELIZABETH
The Crimson Feather. NY: 1945. V. 72

MASON, STUART
Bibliography of Oscar Wilde. London: 1914. V. 68
Bibliography of Oscar Wilde. London: 1967. V. 72
A Bibliography of the Poems of Oscar Wilde. New York: 1908. V. 68

MASON, VAN WYCK
The Branded Spy Murders. New York: 1932. V. 73
The Bucharest Ballerina Murders. 1940. V. 73
The Cairo Garter Murders. Garden City: 1938. V. 72
The Rio Casino Intrigue. New York: 1941. V. 68; 69; 70
Seeds of Murder. 1930. V. 73
The Shanghai Bund Murders. Garden City: 1933. V. 68; 70; 72
The Sulu Sea Murders. Garden City: 1937. V. 68

MASON, WILLIAM
Elfrida; a Dramatic Poem. (with) Caractacus, a Dramatic Poem. London: 1759. V. 73
Essays, Historical and Critical on English Church Music. York: 1795. V. 69
Odes. Cambridge: 1756. V. 68; 72; 73
Poems. York: 1796. V. 70

MASON, WILLIAM P.
Water Supply, Considered Principally from a Sanitary Standpoint. New York: 1896. V. 72

THE MASQUE of Poets: A Collection of New Poems by Contemporary American Poets. New York: 1918. V. 72

MASQUERIER, LEWIS
Sociology; or the Reconstruction of Society, Government and Property. New York: 1877. V. 68

MASSACHUSETTS
Patriotic Proceedings. Boston: 1809. V. 71

MASSACHUSETTS BAY
The Charter Granted by Their Majesties King William and Queen Mary, to the Inhabitants of the Province of Massachusetts Bay in New England. (and) Acts and Laws of His Majesty's Province of the Massachusetts Bay in New England. Boston: 1726. V. 73

MASSACHUSETTS BAY COLONY
An Act, Passed at the Great and General Court or Assembly of the Province of the Massachusetts Bay in New England.... Boston: 1774. V. 68; 70; 73

MASSACHUSETTS HORTICULTURAL SOCIETY
Catalogue of the Library of the Massachusetts Horticultural Society. Mansfield: 1994. V. 71

MASSACHUSETTS MEDICAL SOCIETY
Medical Communications of the Massachusetts Medical Society. Second Series. Volume I. Parts I and II. Boston: 1830-1831. V. 68

MASSAM, J. A.
The Cliff Dwellers of Kenya. London: 1927. V. 71

MASSE, GERTRUDE D. E.
A Bibliography of First Editions of Books Illustrated by Walter Crane. London: 1923. V. 72

MASSEE, G.
British Fungi, with a Chapter of Lichens. London: 1911. V. 72
British Fungus Flora. London: 1892-1895. V. 69; 72

MASSETT, STEPHEN C.
Drifting About or What Jeems Pipes of Pipesville Saw and Did. New York: 1863. V. 70

MASSEY, EDMUND
A Sermon Against the Dangerous and Sinful Practice of Inoculation Preach'd at St. Andrew's Holborn, on Sunday, July the 8th, 1722. London: 1722. V. 69

MASSEY, GERALD
Craigcrook Castle. London: 1856. V. 73

MASSEY, JOHN
Massey and Sons Comprehensive Pudding Book.... London: 1880. V. 68

MASSEY, P. H.
Eastern Mediterranean Lands. London: 1928. V. 71

MASSEY, WILLIAM N.
A History of England During the Reign of George the Third. London: 1855-1863. V. 71

MASSIE, JOSEPH
Observations Relating to the Coin of Great Britain.... London: 1760. V. 69
A Representation Concerning the Knowledge of Commerce As a National Concern: Pointing Out the Proper Means of Promoting Such Knowledge in this Kingdom. London: 1760. V. 68

MASSINGER, PHILIP
The Dramatic Works.... London: 1761. V. 73
The Plays of Philip Massinger. London: 1813. V. 68; 72

MASSINGERD, W. O.
History of the Parish of Ormsby-cum-Ketsby, in the Hundred of Hill and County of Lincoln.... Lincoln: 1898. V. 71

MASSINGHAM, DOROTHY
The Lake. Garden City: 1934. V. 71

MASSINGHAM, H. J.
Country Relics. Cambridge: 1939. V. 72

MASSON, DAVID
The Life of John Milton.... London: 1871-1881. V. 68; 72

MASSON, ELSIE R.
An Untamed Territory. London: 1915. V. 71

MASSON, FLORA
Robert Boyle: a Biography. London: 1914. V. 72

MASSON, FREDERICK
Napoleon et Les Femmes. Paris: 1906. V. 70

MASSON, IRVINE
The Mainz Psalters and Canon Missae 1457-1459. London: 1954. V. 70

MASSON, JOANNIS
C. Plinii Secundi Junioris Vita Ordine Chronologico sic Digesta. Amsterdam: 1709. V. 68

MASSON, L. R.
Les Bourgeois de la Compagnie du Nord-Ouest. NY: 1960. V. 72

MASSON, ROSALINE
Edinburgh. London: 1912. V. 71

MASSON, THOMAS L.
Tom Masson's Annual for 1923: The Humor of the Year. New York: 1923. V. 69

MASSUET, PIERRE
Recherches Interssantes sur l'Origine, la Formation, le Developement, la St ructure, &c.... Amsterdam: 1733. V. 72

MASSY, P. H. H.
Eastern Mediterranean Lands. London: 1928. V. 71

MASTELLONI, ANDREA
La Prima Chiesa Dedicata a S. Maria Maddalena de Pazzi Carmelitone. Naples: 1675. V. 68

MASTER Mousie's Supper Party Showing How When Puss is Away the Mice Will Play. London: 1869. V. 73

MASTERMAN, N.
Chalmers on Charity; a Selection of Passages and Scenes to Illustrate the Social Teaching and Practical Work of Thomas Chalmers, D.D. London: 1900. V. 72

MASTERMAN, WALTER S.
The Curse of the Reckaviles. New York: 1927. V. 70

MASTEROFF, JOE
Cabaret. New York: 1967. V. 71

MASTERPIECES of Dickens. New York: 1892. V. 69

MASTERS, C. O.
Encyclopedia of the Water Lily. Neptune City: 1974. V. 72

MASTERS, EDGAR LEE
A Book of Verses. Chicago: 1898. V. 68
Domesday Book. New York: 1920. V. 68; 72
Kit O'Brien. New York: 1927. V. 68; 69
Mitch Miller. New York: 1920. V. 69
The Serpent in the Wilderness. New York: 1933. V. 73
Skeeters Kirby. New York: 1923. V. 69
Spoon River Anthology. New York: 1915. V. 68; 70
Spoon River Anthology. New York: 1942. V. 69; 71

MASTERS, J.
The Complete Indian Angler. 1938. V. 73

MASTERS, JOHN
Bhowani Junction. London: 1954. V. 71
The Rock. London: 1970. V. 71

MASTERS, JOSEPH G.
Shadows Across The Little Big Horn. Laramie: 1951. V. 72

MASTERS, MARTIN KEDGWIN
Progress of Love. A Poem. Boston: 1808. V. 73

MASTERS, PRISCILLA
Winding Up the Serpent. London: 1995. V. 69; 73
A Wreath for My Sister. London: 1997. V. 73

MASTERS, S. J.
Sketches of Travel. Auburn: 1872. V. 68

MASTERSON, W. B.
Famous Gunfighters of the Western Frontier. Houston: 1957. V. 69

MASTERSON, WHIT
All Through the Night. New York: 1955. V. 71

MASTERSON, WILLIAM
The Authentic Confessions of William Masterson, the Cruel Murderer of His Father and Mother!. Richmond: 1854. V. 71

MASTRIANO, M. M.
Tucson Fire Department 1881-1981. 1981?. V. 69

MASUCCIO
The Novellino of Masuccio. London: 1895. V. 69

MASUR, HAROLD Q.
Bury Me Deep. New York: 1947. V. 72
Suddenly a Corpse. New York: 1949. V. 69

MATE, W., & SONS
The English Lake District. Mournemouth: 1903. V. 71

MATEAUX, C. L.
The Wonderland of Work. London: 1881. V. 71

MATHER
Rambles Round Rossendale. Rawtenstall: 1894. V. 73

MATHER, COTTON
Decus Ac Tutamen: a Brief Essay on the Blessings Enjoyed by a People...Commemoration...Gurdon Saltonstall. New London: 1724. V. 72

MATHER, HELEN
One Summer in Hawaii. New York: 1891. V. 68

MATHER, INCREASE
Brief History of the War with the Indians in New England. From June 24 1675...to August 12, 1676. London: 1676. V. 68

MATHER, SAMUEL
An Apology for the Liberties of the Churches in New England.... Boston: 1738. V. 68
The Life of the Very Reverend and Learned Cotton Mather. Boston: 1729. V. 68; 72

MATHERS, EDWARD POWYS
Love Night: a Laotian Gallantry. Waltham St. Lawrence: 1936. V. 68
Procreant Hymn. Waltham St. Lawrence: 1926. V. 68
Zambesia. London: 1891. V. 71

MATHERS, HELEN
Story of a Sin. London: 1882. V. 68

MATHERS, POWYS
The Book of the Thousand and One Nights. London: 1947. V. 70; 71
The Book of the Thousand Nights and One Night. London: 1980. V. 71

MATHERS, WILLIAM
The Rise, Progress and Downfall of Aristocracy...and the Certain Deliverance of the Family of Man.... Wheeling: 1831. V. 73

MATHES, J. HARVEY
Old Guard in Gray...Sketches of Memphis Veterans Who Upheld Her Standard in the West.... Memphis: 1897. V. 70

MATHES, W. MICHAEL
Los Misiones de Baja California/The Mission of Baja California 1683- 1849. La Paz, Baja: 1977. V. 70
The Pearl Hunters in the Gulf of California 1668. Los Angeles: 1966. V. 71

MATHESON, JOHN
The Needle in the Haystack. New York: 1930. V. 73

MATHESON, RICHARD
Hell House. New York: 1971. V. 69; 70; 71; 72
I Am Legend. New York: 1970. V. 68; 69
Shock! Thirteen Tales to Thrill and Terrify. New York: 1961. V. 69
The Shrinking Man. London: 1956. V. 70
The Shrinking Man. 2001. V. 69; 70

MATHEW, ARNOLD H.
The Life of Sir Tobie Mathew. 1907. V. 70

MATHEWS, ANNE
Anecdotes of Actors; with Other Desultory Recollections, etc. London: 1844. V. 72
Memoirs of Charles Mathews, Comedian. London: 1839. V. 68; 72

MATHEWS, CHARLES
The London Mathews... (bound with) Mr. Mathews' New Entertainment for 1826. London: 1825. V. 70
Proteus the 2nd, Alias Metamorphosis ad Libitum, or, an Old Friend with a New Face. London: 1822. V. 68
Sketches of Mr. Mathews' Invitations.... London: 1826. V. 69

MATHEWS, CHARLES EDWARD
The Annals of Mont Blanc. London: 1898. V. 69

MATHEWS, EDWARD JAMES
Crossing the Plains: Adventures of Edward James Mathews in '59. 1930?. V. 71

MATHEWS, HARRY
The Conversions. New York: 1962. V. 69
Immeasurable. Venice: 1991:. V. 72
A Mid-Season Sky: Poems 1954-1991. Manchester: 1992. V. 69
Oulipo Compendium. London: 1998. V. 68
Selected Declarations of Dependence. Calais: 1977. V. 70
Singular Pleasures. New York: 1988. V. 69; 73
Tlooth. New York: 1966. V. 69; 70
The Way Home. New York: 1988. V. 72; 73
The Way Home. 1989. V. 69

MATHEWS, JOANNA H.
Bessie at School. London: 1869. V. 69

MATHEWS, JOHN JOSEPH
The Osages: Children of the Middle Waters. Norman: 1961. V. 69
Sundown. New York: 1934. V. 68

MATHEWS, LEMUEL
The Argument of Archdeacon Mathews for a Commission of Delegates Upon His Appeals and Querel of Nullities. Dublin: 1704. V. 70

MATHEWS, MITFORD M.
A Dictionary of Americanisms on Historical Principals. Chicago: 1956. V. 72

MATHEWS, SHAILER
The Woman Citizen's Library. Chicago: 1913/. V. 72

MATHEWSON, CHRISTY
Pitching in a Pinch. New York: 1912. V. 69

MATHEWSON, WORTH
Best Birds- Upland and Shore. 2000. V. 71

MATHIAS, THOMAS JAMES
The Pursuits of Literature. London: 1798. V. 69

MATHIS, JYMMY
The Great Dannye Boy! by A Certain Young Man. Brooklyn: 1972. V. 72

MATILAND, FOWLER
Building Estates. A Rudimentary Treatise on the Development, Sale, Purchase and General Management of Building Land.... London: 1883. V. 69

MATIN, HENRI
A Popular History of France from the First Revolution to the Present Time. Boston: 1877. V. 71

MATISSE, Munch, Rouault: Fauvism Expressionism. Geneva: 1950. V. 70

MATISSE, HENRI
Jazz. Paris: 1947. V. 70

MATRIX I-XVI. Gloucestershire: 1981-1996. V. 68

MATSON, DONALD
The Treatment of Acute Compound Injuries of the Spinal Cord Due to Missiles. Springfield: 1948. V. 71

MATTER of Fact for the Multitude. London: 1798. V. 68

MATTERS, LEONARD
Through the Kara Sea. London: 1932. V. 71

MATTES, MERRILL J.
Platte River Road Narratives; a Descriptive Bibliography of Travel Over The Great Central Overland Route to Oregon, California, Utah, Colorado, Montana, and Other Western States and Territories, 1812-1866. V. 72

MATTHAY, F.
The Cure of Disease by Osteopathy, Hydropathy and Hygiene. 1900. V. 73

MATTHEW, SALLIE R.
Interwoven, A Pioneer Chronicle. El Paso: 1958. V. 71

MATTHEWS, ADRIAN
Vienna Blood. London: 1999. V. 69; 73

MATTHEWS, ALFRED HERBERT HENRY
Fifty Years of Agricultural Politics, Being the History of the Central Chamber of Agriculture 1865-1915. 1915. V. 72

MATTHEWS, BRANDER
Actors and Actress of Great Britain and the United States from the Days of David Garrick to the Present Time. New York: 1866. V. 72
Aspects of Fiction and Other Ventures in Criticism. New York: 1896. V. 70
Poems of American Pariotism. New York: 1922. V. 71
Tales of Fantasy and Fact. New York: 1896. V. 68; 72

MATTHEWS, C. C.
Twixt Here and Sun Down. St. Louis: 1957. V. 71

MATTHEWS, ETTA LANE
Over the Blue Wall. Chapel Hill: 1937. V. 68

MATTHEWS, HENRY
The Diary of an Invalid: Being the Journal of a Tour in Pursuit of Health in Portugal, Italy, Switzerland, and France in the Years 1817, 1818 and 1819. London: 1822. V. 72

MATTHEWS, JAMES M.
Digest of the Laws of Virginia, of a Civil Nature and of a Permanent Character and General Operation. Richmond: 1856. V. 73
Digest of the Laws of Virginia of a Criminal Nature. Richmond: 1871. V. 71
A Guide to Commissioners in Chancery, With Practical Forms for the Discharge of Their Duties Adapted to the Statute Law of Virginia. Richmond: 1871. V. 71
The Statutes at Large of the Provisional Government of the Confederate States of America, from the Institution of the Government Feb. 8, 1861.... Richmond: 1864. V. 70

MATTHEWS, JOHN JOSEPH
The Osages; Children of the Middle Waters.The Osages; Children of the Middle Waters. Norman, OK: 1961. V. 72

MATTHEWS, JOSEPH M.
A Treatise on Diseases of the Rectum, Anus and Sigmoid Flexure. New York: 1895. V. 71

MATTHEWS, L. J.
South African Proteaceae in New Zealand. Manakau via Levin: 1983. V. 68

MATTHEWS, RICHARD BORLASE
The Aviation Pocket Book for 1913. London: 1913. V. 70

MATTHEWS, THOMAS
Advice to Whist Players. New York: 1813. V. 73

MATTHEWS, WASHINGTON
Ethnography and Philology of Hidatsa Indians. Washington: 1877. V. 72
The Night Chant, a Navajo Ceremony. New York: 1902. V. 69

MATTHEWS, WILLIAM
A Collection of Affidavits and Certifiates, Relative to the Wonderful Cure of Mrs. Ann Mattingly, Which Took Place in the City of Washington, D.C. on the Tenth of March 1824. City of Washington: 1824. V. 71
A Compendium of Gas-Lighting, Adapted for the Use of Those Who are Unacquainted with Chemistry.... London: 1827. V. 69

MATTHIESSEN, PETER
African Silences. New York: 1991. V. 68
At Play in the Fields of the Lord. New York: 1965. V. 68; 69; 70; 71; 73
The Birds of Heaven. Travels with Cranes. New York: 2001. V. 71; 72
Blue Meridian. New York: 1971. V. 71
Bone by Bone. New York: 1999. V. 68
The Cloud Forest. New York: 1961. V. 68; 71; 72
Far Tortuga. New York: 1975. V. 68; 73
The Great Auk Escape. London: 1972. V. 72
In the Spirit of Crazy Horse. New York: 1980-1983. V. 69
In the Spirit of Crazy Horse. New York: 1983. V. 68; 69; 70; 71; 72; 73
Indian Country. New York: 1984. V. 68; 69; 72; 73
Lost Man's River. New York: 1997. V. 70; 71; 72
Men's Lives. London: 1988. V. 71
Nine-Headed Dragon River. London: 1986. V. 71
On the River Styx. New York: 1986. V. 71
Oomingmak, the Expedition to the Musk Ox Island in the Bering Sea. New York: 1967. V. 68; 70
Partisans. New York: 1955. V. 68; 71
Race Rock. New York: 1954. V. 68; 71
Raditzer. New York: 1961. V. 68; 71; 72
Raditzer. London: 1962. V. 71; 72
Sal Si Puedes. New York: 1969. V. 71
Sand Rivers. New York: 1981. V. 69
The Shorebirds of North America. New York: 1967. V. 68; 69; 71; 73
The Snow Leopard. Franklin Center: 1978. V. 68; 73
The Snow Leopard. New York: 1978. V. 69; 70; 71; 72
Under the Mountain Wall. New York: 1962. V. 68; 70; 72
Wildlife in America. New York: 1959. V. 68; 69; 70; 71
The Wind Birds. New York: 1973. V. 71

MATTIOLI, PIETRO ANDREA
Herbar Aneb Bylinar. Prague: 1596. V. 73

MATURIN, FRED, MRS.
Adventures Beyond the Zambesi of the O'Flaherty; the Insular Miss; the Soldier Man; and the Rebel Woman. 1913. V. 69; 70

MATZ, B. W.
Dickensian. London: 1908. V. 69
The Dickensian. Volume II. London: 1906. V. 69
The Dickensian. Volume III. London: 1907. V. 69
The Dickensian. Volume IV. London: 1908. V. 69
The Inns and Taverns of Pickwick. London: 1921. V. 69

MAUBRAY, JOHN
The Female Physician.... London: 1730. V. 70

MAUDE, AYLMER
A Peculiar People. The Doukhobors. London: 1905. V. 73

MAUDE, THOMAS
A Legend of Ravenswood and Other Poems. London: 1823. V. 68
Viator, a Poem; or, a Journey from London to Scarborough by the Way of York. 1782. V. 73
Wensleydle; or Rural Contemplations: A Poem. Richmond: 1816. V. 71; 73

MAUDE ROXBY, RODERICK
Bulgy in Wombolia. London: 1945. V. 69

MAUDSLAY, ANNE CARY
A Glimpse at Guatemala and Some Notes on the Ancient Monuments of Central America. London: 1899. V. 69; 71

MAUDSLEY, HENRY
The Physiology and Pathology of the Mind. New York: 1867. V. 68; 70; 73

MAUERSBERG, H. R.
Matthews' Textile Fibers. Their Physical, Microscopical and Chemical Properties. New York: 1947. V. 68

MAUGHAM, R. C. F.
Zambesia. London: 1910. V. 71

MAUGHAM, ROBERT
A Treatise on the Principles of the Usury Laws.... London: 1824. V. 70

MAUGHAM, ROBIN
The Servant. London: 1948. V. 70

MAUGHAM, WILLIAM SOMERSET
The Book Bag. Florence: 1932. V. 73
Books and You. London: 1940. V. 73
Cakes and Ale. London: 1930. V. 73
Cakes and Ale. London: 1953. V. 69
Cakes and Ale. London: 1954. V. 70; 71; 73
Catalina. London: 1948. V. 69

MAUGHAM, WILLIAM SOMERSET continued
Christmas Holiday. London: 1939. V. 73
The Circle: A Comedy in Three Acts. New York: 1921. V. 72
The Complete Short Stories of W. Somerset Maugham. London: 1951. V. 69
Creatures of Circumstance. London: 1947. V. 68
Don Fernando. Garden City: 1935. V. 70
Don Fernando. London: 1935. V. 68; 73
East of Suez. New York: 1922. V. 72
The Explorer. New York: 1909. V. 71
The Hour Before the Dawn. Garden City: 1942. V. 71
Liza of Lambeth. London: 1897. V. 69
Liza of Lambeth. London: 1947. V. 70
The Magician. New York: 1909. V. 69
The Making of a Saint. Boston: 1898. V. 70
The Making of a Saint. London: 1898. V. 70
Mr. Ashenden Agent Secret. Paris: 1930. V. 69
The Mixture as Before. London: 1940. V. 68
The Moon and Sixpence. London: 1919. V. 69; 71
Obras Completas (Complete Works). Barcelona: 1950-1952. V. 68
Of Human Bondage. New York: 1915. V. 71
Of Human Bondage. Garden City: 1936. V. 70; 73
Of Human Bondage. New Haven: 1938. V. 69
Points of View. London: 1958. V. 69
Points of View. New York: 1959. V. 70
Princess September and the Nightingale. London: 1939. V. 70
Purely for My Pleasure. London: 1962. V. 69
Rain and Other Stories. New York: 1921. V. 70
The Razor's Edge. Garden City: 1944. V. 68; 69; 70; 71
The Razor's Edge. London: 1944. V. 70; 71
Sheppey: A Play in Three Acts. London: 1933. V. 69; 70
Six Stories Written in the First Person Singular. London: 1931. V. 72
Strictly Personal. New York: 1941. V. 70; 73
The Summing Up. Garden City: 1940. V. 73
The Summing Up. Garden City: 1954. V. 69; 73
Ten Novels and Their Authors. London: 1954. V. 69
The Vagrant Mood: Six Essays. London: 1952. V. 69; 70
A Writer's Notebook. Garden City: 1949. V. 70; 73
A Writer's Notebook. London: 1949. V. 73

MAUGHAN, JANET
The Co-Heiress. London: 1866. V. 73

MAULDIN, BILL
This Damn Tree Leaks. Mediterranean: 1945. V. 72

MAUND, BENJAMIN
The Botanic Garden: Consisting of Highly Finished Representations of Hardy Ornamental Plants. 1850. V. 69

MAUNDER, E. WALTER
Are the Planets Inhabited?. London and New York: 1913. V. 72

MAUNDRELL, HENRY
A Journey from Aleppo to Jerusalem at Easter A.D. 1697. Oxford: 1708. V. 71

MAUNZIO, PAOLO
In Epistolas Ciceronis Ad Atticvm. Venetiis: 1547,. V. 73

MAUPERTUIS, PIERRE LOUIS MOREAU DE
Dissertation Physique a l'Occasion du Negre Blanc. Leyden: 1744. V. 70

MAURER, E. M.
The Native American Heritage. Chicago;: 1977. V. 69

MAURICE, ALFRED
Bouwkundig Teekenen. Gent: 1937. V. 68

MAURICE, FREDERICK
Statesmen and Soldiers of the Civil War. New York: 1926. V. 69

MAURICE, FREDERICK DENISON
Learning and Working. Six Lectures Delivered in Willis's Rooms, London, in June and July 1854. Cambridge: 1855. V. 73
Subscription no bondage, or the practical advantages afforded by the thirty-nine articles as guides in all the branches of academical education.... Oxford: 1835. V. 73

MAURICE, JEAN BAPTISTE
Le Blason des Armoiries de Tous les Chevaliers de l'Ordre de la Toson d'or Depuis la Premiere Institution Jusques a Present. La Haye: 1667. V. 70

MAURICE, THOMAS
Grove-Hill a Descriptive Poem with an Ode to Mithra. London: 1799. V. 70
The History of Hindostan, Its Arts and Its Science, as Connected with the History of the Other Great Empires of Asia.... London: 1820-1819. V. 72
Observations Connected with Astronomy and Ancient History, Sacred and Profane, of the Ruins of Babylon.... London: 1816. V. 70; 73

MAURICEAU, A. M.
The Married Woman's Private Medical Companion. New York: 1847. V. 71; 73
The Married Woman's Private Medical Companion. New York: 1848. V. 69; 73
The Married Woman's Private Medical Companion. New York: 1851. V. 68
The Married Woman's Private Medical Companion. New York: 1855. V. 69

MAURICEAU, FRANCOIS
The Diseases of Women with Child, and in Child-Bed.... London: 1727. V. 73
Traite de Maladies de Femmes Grosses, et de Celles qui Sont Nouvellement Accouchees.... Paris: 1675. V. 72

MAUROIS, ANDRE
Ariel ou La Vie de Shelley. Paris: 1923. V. 71; 72
Chelsea Way. London: 1930. V. 68
A Civil War Album of Paintings by Prince De Joinville. New York: 1964. V. 72
Mape, the World of Illusion. New York: 1926. V. 69; 72

MAURY, DABNEY H.
Recollections of a Virginian in the Mexican, Indian and Civil Wars. New York: 1894. V. 70; 72

MAURY, JEAN SIFFREIN
The Principles of Eloquence.... London: 1793. V. 68

MAURY, MATTHEW FONTAINE
The Physical Geography of the Sea. New York: 1856. V. 69
The Physical Geography of the Sea. London: 1860. V. 70

MAURY, RICHARD L.
The Battle of Williamsburg. Richmond: 1880. V. 70

MAVERICK, SAMUEL
A Briefe Description of New England and the Several Townes Therein. Boston: 1885. V. 70

MAVITY, NANCY BARR
The Tule Marsh Murder. Garden City: 1929. V. 68

MAVOR, HENRY A.
On Public Lighting by Electricity. Glasgow: 1890. V. 69

MAVOR, JAMES
The Scottish Railway Strike 1891. A History and Criticism. Edinburgh: 1891. V. 69

MAVOR, WILLIAM
The Catechism of Health.... New York: 1819. V. 73
The English Spelling Book. London: 1885. V. 69

MAVROGORDATO, J. G.
A Falcon in the Field, a Treatise on the Training and Flying of Falcons. London: 1966. V. 69

MAVROGORDATO, JOHN
And Other Poems. London: 1927. V. 72
The Erotokritos. London: 1929. V. 72

MAW & CO.
Patterns of...Encaustic Tile, Geometrical Mosaic and Plain Title Pavements.... 1848?. V. 68

MAWE, JOHN
Familiar Lessons on Mineralogy and Geology. London: 1819. V. 68; 70
Familiar Lessons on Mineralogy and Geology. 1821. V. 68
A Treatise on Diamonds and Precious Stones, Including Their History Natural and Commercial.... London: 1813. V. 68; 72

MAWE, THOMAS
The Complete Gardener, or Gardener's Calendar.... London: 1836. V. 68
Every Man His Own Gardener. London: 1787. V. 73
Every Man His Own Gardener. London: 1788. V. 73
Every Man His Own Gardener. London: 1791. V. 68; 71
Every Man His Own Gardener. London: 1818. V. 70
Every Man His Own Gardener. London: 1822. V. 68; 71

MAWMAN, JOSEPH
An Excursion to the Highlands of Scotland and the English Lakes, With Recollections, Descriptions, and References to Historical Facts. London: 1805. V. 71
A Picturesque Tour Through France, Switzerland, on the Banks of the Rhine and through Part of the Netherlands in the Year 1816. London: 1817. V. 68; 72; 73

MAWSON, DOUGLAS
The Home of the Blizzard. London: 1930. V. 71

MAWSON, THOMAS H.
Amounderness. London: 1937. V. 73

MAXIM, HUDSON
Real Pen-Work Self-Instructor in Penmanship. Pittsfield: 1884. V. 69
Real Pen-Work Self-Instructor in Penmanship. Pittsfield: 1894. V. 71

MAXIM, JOHN
Abel Baker Charley. Boston: 1983. V. 69

MAXIM, JOHN R.
Platforms. New York: 1980. V. 71

MAXIMOFF, NICHOLAS
Afanassiev is Dead. New York: 1964. V. 70

MAXON, W. R.
Studies of Tropical American Ferns. Washington: 1908-1922. V. 70

MAXSE, F. I.
Seymour Vandeleur. London: 1906. V. 71

MAXWEL Creek Group of Mines. San Francisco: 1879. V. 73

MAXWELL, A.
Partridges and Partridge Manors. 1911. V. 71

MAXWELL, A. continued
Pheasants and Convert Shooting. 1913. V. 71

MAXWELL, A. E.
The Frog and the Scorpion. Garden City: 1986. V. 71

MAXWELL, CONSTANTIA
Country and Town in Ireland Under the Georges. 1949. V. 70

MAXWELL, DONALD
The Book of the Clyde. Being a Connected Series of Drawings and Observations of the River from its Source to the Firth. London: 1927. V. 71
A Dweller In Mesopotamia. London: 1921. V. 72
Excursions in Colour. London: 1927. V. 71; 72

MAXWELL, E. B.
For Better, For Worse. New York: 1920. V. 69

MAXWELL, HENRY
Angius in Herba, or the Fatal Consequences of a Treaty with France. London: 1711. V. 73

MAXWELL, HERBERT
British Fresh Water Fish. 1904. V. 68; 73
Chronicles of the Houghton Fishing Club. 1822-1908. 1908. V. 68; 73
Fishing at Home and Abroad. London: 1913. V. 70
Life and Times of William Henry Smith, M.P. Edinburgh: 1893. V. 71
The Lowland Scots Regiments. Their Origin, Character and Services Previous to the Great War of 1914. Glasgow: 1918. V. 71
Salmon and Sea Trout. 1900. V. 73

MAXWELL, JOHN
The Gold Coast Handbook. London: 1928. V. 71

MAXWELL, LILIAN M. BECKWITH
An Outline of the History of Central New Brunswick to the Time of Confederation. Sackville: 1937. V. 73

MAXWELL, M.
Stalking Big Game with a Camera in Equatorial Africa, with a Monograph on the African Elephant. London: 1925. V. 72

MAXWELL, MARY ELIZABETH BRADDON
All Along the River. London: 1890. V. 68
Aurora Floyd. London: 1895. V. 68
The Captain of the Vulture. London: 1868. V. 72
The Captain of the Vulture. London: 1886. V. 68
Charlotte's Inheritance. London: 1895. V. 68
The Christmas Hirelings. London: 1894. V. 72
The Conflict. London: 1903. V. 68
The Day Will Come. London: 1890. V. 68; 73
Dead Men's Shoes: a Novel. London: 1888?. V. 68
Dead Sea Fruit. London: 1883?. V. 68
Eleanor's Victory. London: 1890. V. 68
Fatalite. Pairs: 1889. V. 73
Fenton's Quest. London: 1880. V. 73
Hostages to Fortune: a Novel. London: 1893. V. 68
The Infidel; a Story of the Great Revival. London: 1900. V. 68
John Marchmont's Legacy. London: 1880. V. 73
Just As I Am: a Novel. London: 1880?. V. 68
Lady Audley's Secret. London: 1893. V. 68
The Lady's Mile: a Novel. London: 1892. V. 68
Like and Unlike. London: 1888. V. 68
The Lovels of Arden. London: 1893. V. 68
Mohawks; a Novel. London: 1887. V. 68; 73
One Thing Needful. London: 1886. V. 68
One Thing Needful. London: 1887?. V. 68
Phantom Fortune: a Novel. London: 1886. V. 68
Phantom Fortune: a Novel. London: 1893?. V. 68
Rupert Godwin. London: 1885. V. 68
Sons of Fire. London: 1896?. V. 68
A Strange World. London: 1890. V. 68
The Trail of the Serpent. London: 1884. V. 68
Under the Red Flag: a Novel. London: 1891. V. 68
The Venetians. London: 1893. V. 68
Vixen. London: 1880. V. 68

MAXWELL, SPENCER
Collecting Abbey. Santa Fe: 1991. V. 72; 73

MAXWELL, W.
Iona and the Ionians. Glasgow: 1857. V. 72

MAXWELL, W. B.
Fernande. London: 1925. V. 69
The Man Who Pretended. Garden City: 1929. V. 71
To What Green Altar?. London: 1930. V. 70

MAXWELL, WILLIAM
All the Days and Nights. New York: 1995. V. 70; 72
Ancestors. New York: 1971. V. 68
The Chateau. New York: 1961. V. 68; 73
The Folded Leaf. New York: 1945. V. 73
The Happiness of Getting It Down Right. New York: 1996. V. 68

The Heavenly Tenants. New York: 1946. V. 70
Over by the River. New York: 1977. V. 73
So Long, See You Tomorrow. New York: 1980. V. 68
They Came Like Swallows. New York: 1937. V. 71
Time Will Darken It. New York: 1948. V. 72
The Writer as Illusionist. New York: 1955. V. 72

MAXWELL, WILLIAM A.
Crossing the Plains. Days of '57 - a Narrative of Early Emigrant Travel to California by the Ox Team Method. San Francisco: 1915. V. 68; 73

MAXWELL, WILLIAM H.
Sports and Adventures in the Highlands and Islands of Scotland.... London: 1853. V. 68
Sports and Adventures in the Highlands and Islands of Scotland.... London: 1872. V. 68

MAXWELL, WILLIAM HAMILTON
History of the Irish Rebellion in 1798: With Memoirs of the Union & Emmett's Insurrection in 1803. New York: 1875. V. 68
History of the Irish Rebellion in 1798; with Memoirs of the Union and Emmetts' Insurrection in 1803. London: 1887. V. 71
Life of Field Marshal His Grace the Duke of Wellington. London: 1839-1841. V. 71

MAY, J. B.
The Hawks of North America, Their Field Indentification and Feeding Habits. New York: 1935. V. 73

MAY, JOHN AMASA
South Carolina Secedes. Columbia: 1960. V. 70

MAY, PHIL
Phil May's ABC: Fifty-Two Original Designs Forming Two Humorous Alphabets.... London: 1897. V. 71
Phil May's Gutter Snipes. London: 1896. V. 68; 71

MAY, ROBERT
Rudolph the Red Nosed Reindeer. 1939. V. 71; 73

MAY, ROSE E.
Merry Moments for Merry Little Folk. London: 1892. V. 72

MAY, THOMAS
The Roman Forts of Templeborough nar Rotherham. Rotherham: 1922. V. 73

MAY, W.
Helwan And The Egyptian Desert. London: 1901. V. 72
The Little Book of British Birds. London: 1840. V. 68; 72

MAY, WILLIAM
Essay on Pulmonary Consumption, Including the Histories of Several Remarkable Instances of Recovery.... Plymouth: 1792. V. 70; 71

MAYBECK, BERNARD R.
Palace of Fine Arts and Lagoon: Pan Pacific International Exposition 1915. San Francisco: 1915. V. 69; 72

MAYDON, H. C.
Big Game of India. 1937. V. 69; 70; 72
Big Game Shooting in Africa. 1951. V. 69

MAYER, BRANTZ
Mexico as It Was and As It Is. New York: 1844. V. 71
Mexico, Aztec, Spanish and Republican.... Hartford: 1852. V. 68

MAYER, HENRY
A Trip to Toyland. London: 1900. V. 73

MAYER, JOHN
The Sportsman's Directory; or Park and Gamekeeper's Companion. London: 1828. V. 72

MAYER, JOSEPH
Catalogue of Mayer Free Library, Bebington. Lending Department. Liverpool: 1876. V. 70

MAYER, L. A.
Islamic Astrolabists. Geneva: 1956. V. 68

MAYER, S. R. TOWNSHEND
Afghanistan, Its Political and Military History, Geography and Ethnography.... London: 1879. V. 69

MAYER, TOM
The Weary Falcon. Boston: 1971. V. 72

MAYES, FRANCES
The Book of Summer. Woodside: 1995. V. 69

MAYFIELD, JOHN S.
Mark Twain Vs. the Street Railway Co. 1926. V. 71

MAYHALL, JOHN
The Annals and History of Leeds. Leeds;: 1860. V. 73
The Annals of Yorkshire. Leeds: 1861. V. 73
The Annals of Yorkshire. Leeds: 1862. V. 73

MAYHALL, MILDRED P.
The Kiowas. Norman, OK: 1962. V. 72

MAYHEW, AUBREY
The World's Tribute to John F. Kennedy in Medalic Art. New York: 1966. V. 68; 73

MAYHEW, HENRY
1851; or, the Adventures of Mr. and Mrs. Sandboys an Family, Who Came to London to...See the Great Exhibition. London: 1851. V. 69; 71
The Greatest Plague of Life, or, The Adventures of a Lady in Search of a Good Servant.... London: 1869?. V. 68
The Greatest Plague of Life, or the Adventures of a Lady In Search of a Good Servant.... London: 1896. V. 68
Labour and the Poor. Report of the Speech of Henry Mayhew, esq. and the Evidence Adduced at a Public Meeting Held at St. Martin's Hall, Long Acre, on Monday Evening Oct. 28, 1850.... London: 1850. V. 71
London Labour and the London Poor. London: 1851-. V. 71
London Labour and the London Poor. London: 1861. V. 71
London Labour and the London Poor. London: 1861-1862. V. 71
London Labour and the London Poor. London: 1861-1865. V. 71
London Labour and the London Poor. London: 1864-1865. V. 71
The Upper Rhine. London: 1858. V. 72
Whom to Marry and How to Get Married!. London: 1896. V. 68

MAYHEW, JONATHAN
Two Discourses Delivered October 9th 1760. Boston: 1760. V. 68; 70; 73

MAYHEW, THE BROTHERS
The Good Genius that Turned Everything into Gold or the Queen Bee and Magic Dress. London: 1847. V. 71
The Good Genius, that Turned everything into Gold, or The Queen Bee and the Magic Dress: a Christmas Fairy Tale. New York: 1850. V. 73

MAYLE, PETER
A Year in Provence. London: 1989. V. 72

MAYLIN, ANNE WALTER
Lays of Many Hours. Philadelphia: 1847. V. 71

MAYNARD, C. J.
The Birds of Eastern North America. Newtonville: 1881. V. 70; 73
The Birds of Eastern North America. Newtonville: 1896. V. 73
A Manual of North American Butterflies. Boston: 1891. V. 69
The Naturalist's Guide in Collecting and Preserving Objects of Natural History.... Boston: 1870. V. 72
Vocal Organs of Talking Birds and Some Other Species. West Newton: 1928. V. 73

MAYNARD, HENRY N.
Handbook to the Crumlin Viaduct, Monmouthshire.... Crumlin: 1862. V. 73

MAYNARD, JOE
William S. Burroughs. A Bibliography 1953-1973. Charlottesville: 1978. V. 71

MAYNARD, MARY
Poems. London: 1851. V. 69

MAYNE, JOHN
The Siller Gun. Glocester (sic): 1808. V. 69

MAYNE, R. G.
An Expository Lexicon of the Terms, Ancient and Modern, in Medical and General Science.... London: 1860. V. 68; 73

MAYNE, WILLIAM
The Blue Boat. London: 1957. V. 69
A Grass Rope. London: 1959. V. 70
The Rolling Season. London: 1960. V. 69
While the Bells Ring. London: 1979. V. 69

MAYNE, ZACHARY
The Dissertations Concerning Sense, and the Imagination. London: 1728. V. 73

MAYNEARD, C. J.
The Naturalist's Guide in Collecting and Preserving Objects of Natural History.... Boston: 1870. V. 71

MAYNWARING, ROBERT
The French King's Promise to the Pretender; Being a Publick Assurance Solemnly Given Both to Him and the Late King James, Just Before the Death of that King. London: 1712. V. 73

MAYO, E. L.
The Diver. Minneapolis: 1947. V. 68

MAYO, EARL OF
The Thames Valley from Cricklade to Staines a Survey of Its Existing State and Some Suggestions for Its Future Preservation. London: 1929. V. 71

MAYO, EILEEN
Nature's ABC. 1944. V. 68

MAYO, ELIZABETH
Lessons on Shells, as Given to Children Between the Ages of Eight and Ten.... London: 1832. V. 68

MAYO, KATHERINE
The Isle of Fear. London: 1925. V. 71

MAYO, ROBERT
Political Sketches of Eight Years in Washington. Baltimore: 1839. V. 70; 73

MAYS, WILLIE
Danger in Center Field. Larchmont: 1963. V. 73

MAZE, PAUL
A Frenchman in Khaki. 1934. V. 73

MAZEAUD, PIERRE
Naked Before the Mountain. 1974. V. 68
Naked Before the Mountain. London: 1974. V. 69

MAZIER DE HEAUME, HIPPOLYTE
Voyage d'uyn Jeune Grec a Paris. Paris: 1824. V. 72

MAZUCHELLI, ELIZABETH SARAH
Magyarland. London: 1881. V. 71

MAZUCHELLI, NINA
The Indian Alps and How We Crossed Them. London: 1876. V. 69; 72

MAZUMDER, S. N.
A.O. Nagas. Calcutta: 1925. V. 71

MAZURSKY, PAUL
Harry and Tonto. New York: 1974. V. 69; 71

MAZYCK, ARTHUR
Guide to Charleston Illustrated. Charleston: 1875. V. 71

MAZZANOVICH, ANTON
Trailing Geronimo. 1926. V. 68
Trailing Geronimo. New York: 1931. V. 69

MAZZINI, JOSEPH
The Duties of Man. London: 1862. V. 68

MAZZULA, FRED
Al Packer- A Colorado Cannibal. Denver: 1968. V. 71

M'BAIN, J.
The Merrick and the Neighbouring Hills. Tramps by Hill, Stream and Loch. Ayr: 1929. V. 71

MC BIRNEY & CO. LTD.
Bedsteads. French and Italian. Birmingham and London: 1910. V. 68; 70

MC MENEMY & MARTIN, INC.
Old Trails and New Trails. Chicago: 1897. V. 68

M'CABE, JOHN COLLINS
Scraps. Richmond: 1835. V. 68

MC ADAM, J. L.
Statement by the Committee Appointed Upon the Line of Road Between Caitha, in the County of Roxburgh by Jedburgh, and the Carter Fell to Newcastle. Jedburgh: 1829. V. 72

M'CALL, H. B.
The Early History of Bedale in the North Riding of Yorkshire. London: 1907. V. 73

MC ALLESTER, DAVID P.
The Myth and Prayers of the Great Star Chant and the Myth of the Coyote Chant. Santa Fe: 1956. V. 69

MC ALLISTER, BRUCE
Dream Baby. New York: 1989. V. 71

MC ALLISTER, ISABEL
Alfred Gilbert. London: 1929. V. 71

MC ALMON, ROBERT
Explorations. 1921. V. 68
Explorations. London: 1921. V. 71
A Hasty Bunch. Paris: 1922. V. 70; 72
Post-Adolescence. Paris: 1923. V. 71

MC ALPINE, WILLIAM HENRY
A Catalogue of the Law Library at Hartwell House, Buckinghamshire. London: 1865. V. 73

MC ARTHUR, JOHN
Financial and Political Facts of the Eighteenth and Present Century; with Comparative Estimates of the Revenue, Expenditure, Debts, Manufactures, and Commerce. London: 1803. V. 72

MC ATEE, JOHN
Brief for the Cherokee Strip Live Stock Association. Bryan, TX: 1999. V. 71

MC BAIN, ED
The April Robin Murders. New York: 1958. V. 69
Ax. New York: 1964. V. 69; 70; 71
The Big Bad City. New York: 1999. V. 72
Blood Relatives. New York: 1975. V. 69
Candyland. New York: 2001. V. 69; 72
Cut Me In. New York: 1954. V. 73
The 87th Precinct. New York: 1949. V. 69
The 87th Precinct. New York: 1959. V. 69; 71; 72; 73
The 87th Precinct. London: 1966. V. 71
Even the Wicked. New York: 1958. V. 71; 72
Give the Boys a Great Big Hand. New York: 1960. V. 69
Goldilocks. 1977. V. 73
Goldilocks. New York: 1977. V. 69; 70; 71
Hail, Hail the Gang's All Here. New York: 1971. V. 69
Hail, Hail, the Gang's All Here!. New York: 1973. V. 72
The Heckler. New York: 1960. V. 69; 70; 71; 73
Jigsaw. Garden City: 1970. V. 69; 70; 71
The Jungle Kids. New York: 1956. V. 70
Killer's Choice. New York: 1957. V. 72

MC BAIN, ED continued
Killer's Choice. New York: 1958. V. 71
Killer's Payoff. New York: 1958. V. 71
Lady Killer. New York: 1958. V. 71; 72
Lady, Lady, I Did It!. New York: 1961. V. 72
The Last Dance. New York: 1999. V. 72
Let's Hear It from the Deaf Man. New York: 1973. V. 69
Money, Money, Money. New York: 2001. V. 69; 72
The Pusher. New York: 1956. V. 69
Runaway Black. New York: 1954. V. 71
See Them Die. New York: 1960. V. 69; 70; 71; 73
The Sentries. New York: 1965. V. 69
Ten Plus One. New York: 1963. V. 69; 70; 71; 72; 73
Vanishing Ladies. New York: 1957. V. 71

MC BARRON, H. CHARLES
The American Soldier. Washington: 1964. V. 68

MC BEAN, ANGUS
Vivien. A Love Affair in Camera. Oxford: 1989. V. 73

MC BETH, KATE C.
The Nez Perce Since Lewis and Clark. New York: 1908. V. 69

MC BRIDE, MARY MARGARET
Paris is a Woman's Town. New York: 1929. V. 71; 73

MC BRIDE, WILL
Show Me! A Picture Book of Sex for Children and Parents. New York: 1974. V. 68

MC BRIDGE, JOSEPH
Searching for John Ford. New York: 2001. V. 69

MC BURNEY, CHARLES
A Contribution to Cerebral Surgery, Diagnosis, Localization and Operation for Removal of Three Tumors of the Brain.... 1893. V. 70; 73

MC BURNIE, DAVID
Mental Exercises of a Working Man. London: 1854. V. 70

MC CABE, ALICE S.
Gwinnett Co., Georiga. Deaths 1818-1989. Lawrenceville: 1991. V. 72

MC CABE, JAMES D.
The Gray Jackets: and How They Lived, Fought and Died for Dixie. Richmond: 1867. V. 69; 70
Life and Campaigns of General Robert E. Lee. Atlanta: 1866. V. 70
Life and Campaigns of General Robert E. Lee. St. Louis: 1866. V. 69

MC CABE, JOSEPH
Life and Letters of George Jacob Holyoake. London: 1908. V. 71

MC CABE, PATRICK
Breakfast on Pluto. London: 1998. V. 72
The Dead School. New York: 1995. V. 71; 72
Mondo Desperado. New York: 1999. V. 72

MC CABE, W. GORDON
Brief Sketch of Andrew Reid, Venable, Jr. Richmond: 1909. V. 69; 70
Major General George Washington Custis Lee. 1914. V. 70

MC CAFFERTY, W. P.
Aquatic Entomology, the Fishermen's and Ecologist's Illustrated Guide to Insects and Their Relatives. Boston: 1981. V. 72

MC CAFFREY, ANNE
Dragon Flight. 1988. V. 71
The Worlds of Anne McCaffrey: Restoree, Decision at Doona, the Ship Who Sang. London: 1981. V. 71

MC CAFFREY, ANNE INEZ
Forty Years of Publishing: an International Bibliography. Seattle: 1992. V. 69

MC CALEB, WALTER F.
The Aaron Burr Conspiracy. New York: 1936. V. 73

MC CALL, GEORGE A.
Colonel McCall's Reports in Relation to New Mexico. Washington: 1851. V. 68; 73
Letters From the Frontier - Written During A Period of Thirty Years Service In The Army of The United States. Phila: 1868. V. 72

MC CALL, H. B.
Richmondshire Churches. London: 1910. V. 73

MC CALLESTER, DAVID
The Myth and Prayers of the Great Star Chant and the Myth of the Coyote Chant. Santa Fe: 1956. V. 68

MC CALLUM, JAMES DOW
The Letters of Eleazar Wheelcock's Indians. Hanover: 1932. V. 72

MC CAMMON, ROBERT R.
Bethany's Sin. 1989. V. 69
Bethany's Sin. London: 1989. V. 68
Blue World. 1989. V. 69
Mystery Walk. 1963. V. 69
Mystery Walk. New York: 1983. V. 68
Night Boat. 1990. V. 69
The Night Boat. London: 1990. V. 68
They Thirst. London: 1990. V. 68
They Thirst. Arlington Heights: 1991. V. 68

MC CANDLISH, W. L.
The Scottish Terrier. 1910. V. 68

MC CANN, COLUM
Everything in This Country Must. London: 2000. V. 68; 70
Fishing in the Sloe-Black River. London: 1994. V. 69; 70
Fishing in the Sloe-Black River. New York: 1996. V. 69; 72
This Side of Brightness. London: 1998. V. 68; 69; 70

MC CANN, IRVING GOFF
With the National Guard on the Border; Our National Military Problem. St. Louis: 1917. V. 72

MC CARDELL, ROY L.
The Book of My Uncle Oswald. NY: 1931. V. 72

MC CARRISON, ROBERT
The Work of Sir Robret McCarrison. London: 1953. V. 73

MC CARRY, CHARLES
The Bride Of The Wilderness. New York: 1988. V. 72
The Last Supper. New York: 1983. V. 72
The Miernik Dossier. New York: 1973. V. 68; 69

MC CARTHY, ALBERT
The PL Yearbook of Jazz 1946. London: 1946. V. 68

MC CARTHY, CARLTON
Detailed Minutiae of Soldier Life in the Army of Northern Virginia. Richmond: 1884. V. 69; 70

MC CARTHY, CORMAC
All the Pretty Horses. London: 1992. V. 68; 71
All the Pretty Horses. New York: 1992. V. 68; 69; 70; 71; 72; 73
Blood Meridian. New York: 1985. V. 69; 70; 71; 73
Blood Meridian. London: 1989. V. 71; 73
Blood Meridian. London: 1990. V. 68; 70; 72
The Border Trilogy. New York: 1999. V. 72
Child of God. New York: 1973. V. 69; 70; 71; 72; 73
Child Of God. London: 1975. V. 72; 73
Cities of the Plain. London: 1998. V. 71; 72
Cities of the Plain. New Orleans: 1998. V. 68; 70; 71; 72; 73
Cities of the Plain. New York: 1998. V. 68; 69; 70; 71; 72; 73
The Crossing. London: 1994. V. 68; 71
The Crossing. New York: 1994. V. 69; 70; 71; 72
The Gardener's Son. Hopewell: 1996. V. 70; 71; 73
The Gardener's Son. New York: 1996. V. 69; 73
The Orchard Keeper. New York: 1965. V. 69; 71; 72; 73
The Orchard Keeper. London: 1966. V. 68; 69; 71; 72
Outer Dark. New York: 1968. V. 69; 71; 72; 73
Outer Dark. London: 1970. V. 68; 70; 71; 72; 73
The Stonemason. Hopewell: 1994. V. 69; 70; 71; 72
Suttree. New York: 1979. V. 69; 71; 72; 73

MC CARTHY, DESMOND
Experience. London: 1935. V. 72

MC CARTHY, FLORENCE LINDNER
The Lindner and Mccarthy Families of Hoboken, Newark and Elizabethport, New Jersey. Baltimore: 1988. V. 71

MC CARTHY, J.
Reports on Trindad Exhibits, Prepared Under Supervision of the Society of Arts. Port-of-Spain: 1888. V. 70

MC CARTHY, JAMES
Surveying and Exploring in Siam. London: 1902. V. 71

MC CARTHY, JOHN G.
A Plea for the Home Government of Ireland. 1871. V. 69

MC CARTHY, JUSTIN
The Daily New Jubilee. London: 1896. V. 69
The Dictator. London: 1895. V. 68
A Fair Saxon. London: 1895. V. 68
A History of Our Own Times, From the Accession of Queen Victoria to the General Election of 1880 (for the Diamond Jubilee). London: 1899-1900. V. 71
A History of Our Own Times, from the Accession of Queen Victoria to the General Election of 1880 (to the Diamond Jubilee). London: 1901-1908. V. 73
Miss Misanthrope. London: 1880. V. 68

MC CARTHY, MARY
A Charmed Life. New York: 1955. V. 73
The Group. New York: 1963. V. 71
Medina. New York: 1972. V. 72
The Oasis. New York: 1949. V. 73
Vietnam. New York: 1967. V. 72

MC CARTHY, SHAUN
Lucky Ham. London: 1977. V. 68

MC CARTNEY, ALLEN P.
Thule Eskimo Prehistory Along Northwestern Hudson Bay. Ottawa: 1977. V. 73

MC CARTNEY, HARRY S.
The Merger Case. Petition for Rehearing (an Appeal from the Younger Generation). Chicago: 1905. V. 73

MC CARTNEY, PAUL
Blackbird Singing. London: 2001. V. 69

MC CARTY, JOHN
Some Experiences of Boss Neff in the Texas and Oklahoma Panhandle. Amarillo: 1968. V. 71

MC CAULEY, JAMES E.
A Stove Up Cowboy's Story. Austin: 1942. V. 71

MC CAULEY, ROBERT H.
Liverpool Transfer designs on Anglo-American Pottery. Portland: 1942. V. 73

MC CAUSLAND, ELIZABETH
Changing New York: Photographs by Berenice Abbott. New York: 1939. V. 69

MC CLANAHAN, ED
A Congress of Wonders. Washington: 1996. V. 71
My Vita, If You Will. Washington, DC: 1998. V. 72
The Natural Man. New York: 1983. V. 71; 72

MC CLAREN, L. L.
High Living. San Francisco: 1904. V. 72; 73

MC CLATCHIE, A. J.
Eucalyptus Cultivated in the United States. Washington: 1902. V. 68

MC CLATCHY, J. D.
An Old Song Ended. New York: 1987. V. 73

MC CLATCHY, JOHN
Kilim. New York: 1987. V. 68

MC CLEARY, DOROTHY
Naked to Laughter. Garden City: 1937. V. 71

MC CLELLAN, GEORGE B.
Mc Clellan's Own Story. The War for the Union. New York: 1887. V. 70

MC CLELLAN, HENRY BRAINARD
Life and Campaigns of Major-General J. E. B. Stuart. Boston, New York, Richmond: 1885. V. 69; 70

MC CLELLAN, R. GUY
The Golden State: a History of the Region West of the Rocky Mountains. Philadelphia: 1872. V. 73

MC CLELLAN, WILLIAM
Call Girl. New York: 1939. V. 71
Never a Bride. New York: 1942. V. 71

MC CLELLAND, GORDON
Rick Griffin. New York: 1980. V. 69

MC CLELLAND, NANCY
Duncan Phyfe and the English Regency 1795-1830. New York: 1939. V. 70
Historic Wall-Papers. New York and London: 1924. V. 68; 69

MC CLENDON, LISE
The Bluejay Shaman. New York: 1994. V. 69

MC CLINTOCK, FRANCIS L.
A Narrative of the Discovery of the Fate of Sir John Franklin and His Companions. London: 1859. V. 73
The Voyage of the Fox in the Arctic Seas. 1859. V. 70

MC CLINTOCK, JAMES H.
Arizona: Prehistoric - Aboriginal - Pioneer - Modern. Chicago: 1916. V. 70
Mormon Settlement in Arizona. A Record of Peaceful Conquest of the Desert. Phoenix: 1921. V. 69

MC CLINTOCK, JOHN S.
Pioneer Days In The Black Hills. Deadwood: 1939. V. 72

MC CLINTOCK, WALTER
Old Indian Trails. Boston: 1923. V. 72
The Old North Trail. London: 1910. V. 70; 71; 72

MC CLOSKEY, ROBERT
Blueberries for Sal. New York: 1948. V. 71
Burt Dow Deep-Water Man - A Tale of the Sea in the Classic Tradition. New York: 1963. V. 73
Lentil. New York: 1940. V. 70

MC CLUNG, JOHN A.
Sketches of Western Adventures. Philadelphia: 1832. V. 68

MC CLURE, A. K.
Three Thousand Miles Through The Rocky Mountains. Philadelphia: 1869. V. 72

MC CLURE, ALEXANDER K.
Lincoln as a Politician. Putnam: 1916. V. 70

MC CLURE, D. F.
1887 Resources of Dakota an Official Publication Compiled by the Commission of Immigration. Sioux Falls: 1887. V. 72

MC CLURE, JAMES
Four and Twenty Virgins. London: 1973. V. 70

MC CLURE, MARJORIE BARKLEY
Many Waters. New York: 1928. V. 71

MC CLURE, MEADE
Major Andrew Drumm. Missouri: 1919. V. 71

MC CLURE, MICHAEL
The Book of Benjamin. Berkeley: 1982. V. 73
Gargoyle Cartoons. New York: 1971. V. 72
Hymns to St. Geryon, and Other Poems. San Francisco: 1959. V. 72
(Mandalas). San Francisco: 1966. V. 73
The Sermons of Jean Harlow and the Curses of Billy the Kid. San Francisco: 1968. V. 73
The Surge. 1969. V. 71

MC CLURE, S. S.
My Autobiography. New York: 1914. V. 71

MC COMAS, E. S.
A Journal of Travel. Champoeg: 1954. V. 71

MC COMBE, LEONARD
Navaho Means People. Cambridge: 1951. V. 69

MC CONATHY, DALE
Hollywood Costume. New York: 1976. V. 70

MC CONAUGHY, J. W.
The Boss. New York: 1911. V. 72
Madam X: A Story of Mother Love. NY: 1910. V. 72

MC CONKEY, HARRIET E.
Dakota War Whoop. St. Paul: 1864. V. 73

MC CONKEY, JAMES
Rowan's Progress. New York: 1992. V. 70
Stories from My Life With Other Animals. Boston: 1993. V. 71

MC CONNAUGHEY, JAMES
Village Chronicle. NY: 1936. V. 72

MC CONNEL, JOSEPH CARROLL
The West Texas Frontier or a Descriptive History of Early Times in Western Texas. 1933. V. 68

MC CONNELL, FRANK
Murder Among Friends. New York: 1983. V. 68

MC CONNELL, H. H.
Five Years a Cavalryman; or, Sketches of Regular Army Life on the Texas Frontier. Jacksboro: 1889. V. 72; 73

MC CONNELL, JOSEPH C.
The West Texas Frontier. Jacksboro: 1933. V. 70

MC CONNELL, NEWTON
Mc Connell's Vanity Fair. Toronto: 1912. V. 73

MC CONNELL, R. G.
Preliminary Report on the Klondike Gold Fields, Yukon District, Canada. Ottawa: 1900. V. 71

MC CONNELL, W. J.
Early History of Idaho. Caldwell: 1913. V. 68; 73

MC CONNOCHIE, A. I.
The Deer and Deer Forests of Scotland. Historical, Descriptive, Sporting. London: 1923. V. 71
The Deer and Deer Forests of Scotland. Historical, Descrptive, Sporting. 1923. V. 70
Deer Forest Life. 1932. V. 73
Deer Stalking in Scotland. 1924. V. 70
The Rivers Oykell and Cassley in Sutherland and Ross. 1924. V. 68

MC COOK, H. C.
American Spiders and Their Spinningwork: a Natural History. London: 1889-1893. V. 71
The Natural History of Agricultural Ants of Texas.... Philadelphia: 1879. V. 69

MC CORD, JOSEPH
Heart's Heritage. Philadelphia: 1935. V. 71
Sweet for a Season. Philadelphia: 1939. V. 73

MC CORKLE, JILL
Carolina Moon. Chapel Hill: 1996. V. 71
The Cheer Leader. Chapel Hill: 1984. V. 68; 69; 73
Crash Diet. Chapel Hill: 1992. V. 68; 72
Ferris Beach. Chapel Hill: 1990. V. 68; 72
Tending to Virginia. Chapel Hill: 1987. V. 68

MC CORKLE, JOHN
Three Years with Quantrell - a True Story Told by His Scout. Armstrong. V. 69

MC CORMICK, ALMA HEFLIN
Merry Makes a Choice. Boston: 1949. V. 71

MC CORMICK, KYLE
The Story of Mercer County. Charleston: 1957. V. 68

MC CORMICK, RICHARD C.
Arizona: Its Resources and Prospects: a Letter to the editor of the New York Tribune. New York: 1865. V. 68; 73

MC COURT, FRANK
Angela's Ashes. London: 1996. V. 70
Angela's Ashes. New York: 1996. V. 68; 69; 70; 71; 73
'Tis. London: 1999. V. 69

MC COURT, PETER
Biographical Sketch of the Honourable Edward Whelan, Together with a Compilation of His Principal Speeches. Charlottetown: 1888. V. 73

MC COWN, LEONARD
Indianola Scrap Book. Austin: 1974. V. 69

MC COY, E.
Five California Architects: Maybeck, Irving Gill, Charles and Henry Greene, R.M. Schindler. New York: 1960. V. 68; 69; 72
The Second Generation. Salt Lake City: 1984. V. 68

MC COY, HORACE
4 Novels. London: 1983. V. 70; 72; 73
I Should Have Stayed Home. New York: 1938. V. 70
Kiss Tomorrow Good-Bye. 1948. V. 73
Scalpel. New York: 1952. V. 69; 70; 72
They Shoot Horses, Don't They?. 1935. V. 73
They Shoot Horses, Don't They?. New York: 1935. V. 70

MC COY, ISAAC
Annual Register of Indian Affairs Within the Indian or (Western) Territory. Shawanoe Baptist Mission: 1836. V. 68

MC COY, JOSEPH G.
Historic Sketches of the Cattle Trade of the West and Southwest. Columbus: 1951. V. 68; 71

MC CRACKEN, ELIZABETH
Desiderata. Cyberspace: 1997. V. 70
The Giant's House. New York: 1996. V. 69; 72
Here's Your Hat What's Your Hurry?. New York: 1992. V. 69
Here's Your Hat What's Your Hurry?. New York: 1993. V. 68; 69; 70; 72; 73

MC CRACKEN, HAROLD
The American Cowboy. Garden City: 1973. V. 68; 69
The Charles M. Russell Book, the Life and Work of the Cowboy Artist. Garden City: 1957. V. 69; 71
The Frank Tenney Johnson Book. Garden City: 1974. V. 69; 71
Frederic Remington: Artist of the Old West. Philadelphia & New York: 1947. V. 69
The Frederic Remington Book. Garden City: 1966. V. 69; 70
George Catlin and the Old Frontier. New York: 1959. V. 69; 70; 71
Nicolai Fechin. New York: 1961. V. 69; 70
Portraits of the Old West With a Bibliographical Check List of Western Artists. New York: 1952. V. 69; 71
Rough-Necks and Gentlemen. 1968. V. 70; 72; 73
The West of Buffalo Bill: Frontier Art, Indian Craft, Memorabilia from the Buffalo Bill Historical Center. New York: 1974. V. 70; 72; 73

MC CRACKEN, JOSEPHINE CLIFFORD
Women Who Lost Him And Tales Of The Army Frontier. Pasedena: 1913. V. 72

MC CRAE, HUGH
Satyrs and Sunlight: Being the Collected Poetry of Hugh McCrae. London: 1928. V. 71

MC CRAE, JOHN
In Flanders Field. London: 1919. V. 72
In Flanders Field. New York: 1919. V. 68
In Flanders Field. Toronto: 1919. V. 73

MC CRARY, JOHN R.
First of the Many. A Journal of Action with the Men of the Eighth Air Force. New York: 1944. V. 68

MC CRAW, ELOISE JARVIS
Merry Go Round in Oz. Chicago: 1963. V. 71

MC CREADY, T. L.
Adventures of a Beagle. New York: 1959. V. 73
Adventures of a Beagle. London: 1961. V. 72
Biggity Bantam. New York: 1954. V. 70
Mr. Stubbs. New York: 1956. V. 73
Pekin White. New York: 1955. V. 73

MC CREIGHT, M. I.
Firewater And Forked Tongues-A Sioux Chief Interprets US History. Pasadena: 1947. V. 72

MC CRIE, THOMAS
The Life of John Knox, the Scottish Reformer. London: 1880. V. 68

MC CRUMB, SHARYN
If I Ever Return, Pretty Peggy-O. New York: 1990. V. 68
If I'd Killed Him When I Met Him. New York: 1995. V. 72
MacPherson's Lament. New York: 1992. V. 71
She Walks These Hills. New York: 1994. V. 70; 72
The Windsor Knot. New York: 1990. V. 70
Zombies of the Gene Pool. New York: 1991. V. 68

MC CULLAGH, WILLIAM TORRENS
Memoirs of Richard Lalor Sheil. London: 1855. V. 71

MC CULLERS, CARSON
The Ballad of the Sad Cafe. Boston: 1951. V. 70; 71; 73
Clock without Hands. Boston: 1961. V. 69; 70
Clock Without Hands. London: 1961. V. 71; 72
Collected Short Stories. (and) The Ballad of the Sad Cafe. Boston: 1955. V. 69
Collected Short Stories and The Ballad of the Sad Cafe. Boston: 1961. V. 70
The Heart is a Lonely Hunter. Boston: 1940. V. 70
Member of the Wedding. Boston: 1946. V. 72; 73
The Member of the Wedding. New York: 1951. V. 68; 71
Reflections in a Golden Eye. Boston: 1941. V. 69
Seven. New York: 1954. V. 71

MC CULLEY, JOHNSTON
The Demon. New York: 1925. V. 69

MC CULLOCH, JOHN RAMSAY
A Descriptive and Statistical Account of the British Empire.... London: 1854. V. 70
A Dictionary; Geographical, Statistical and Historical, of the Various Countries, Places and Principal Natural Objects in the World. London: 1866. V. 72
London in 1850-1851. From the Geographical Dictionary of J. R. McCulloch, Esq. London: 1851. V. 70
The Principles of Political Economy. Edinburgh: 1843. V. 71
The Principles of Political Economy. Edinburgh: 1849. V. 71

MC CULLOGH, DAVID
John Adams. New York: 2001. V. 73

MC CULLOUGH, COLLEEN
Morgan's Run. New York: 2000. V. 72

MC CUNE, EVELYN
The Arts of Korea. Rutland: 1962. V. 70

MC CURRACH, J. C.
Palms of the World. New York: 1960. V. 68; 70; 71
Palms of the World. 1970. V. 72

MC CUTCHEON, GEORGE B.
The Daughter of Anderson Crow. New York: 1907. V. 71
Graustark. Chicago: 1901. V. 69; 71; 73

MC DADE, THOMAS M.
The Annals of Murder: a Bibliography of Books and Pamphlets on American Murders from Colonial Times to 1900. Norman: 1961. V. 72

MC DANIEL, RUEL
Vinegarroon: the Saga of Judge Roy Bean "Law West of the Pecos". Kingsport: 1936. V. 69

MC DERMID, VAL
Booked for Murder. London: 1996. V. 71
Common Murder. Sutton: 1994. V. 73
A Place of Execution. New York: 1999. V. 68
A Place of Execution. New York: 2000. V. 72
The Wire in the Blood. Scottsdale: 1997. V. 68; 69
The Wire In The Blood. Scottsdale: 1998. V. 72
The Writing On the Wall and Other Stories. 1997. V. 68

MC DERMOTT, ALICE
At Weddings and Wakes. New York: 1992. V. 73
The Bigamist's Daughter. New York: 1982. V. 68; 73
Charming Billy. New York: 1998. V. 68; 70
That Night. New York: 1987. V. 68; 71; 73

MC DERMOTT, JOHN FRANCIS
Seth Eastman: Pictorial Historian of the Indian. Norman: 1961. V. 69; 72

MC DERMOTT, MYRA E.
Lariat Letters. 1907. V. 68

MC DERMOTT, P. L.
British East Africa or IBEA. London: 1893. V. 71

MC DIARMID, E. W.
Exploring Sherlock Holmes. La Crosse: 1957. V. 69

MC DONALD, CORNELIA
Diary With Reminiscences of the War and Refugee Life in the Shenandoah Valley. Nashville: 1935. V. 69; 70

MC DONALD, EDWARD D.
A Bibliography of the Writings of D. H. Lawrence. Philadelphia: 1925. V. 70; 72
A Bibliography of the Writings of Norman Douglas. Philadelphia: 1927. V. 68
The Writings of D. H. Lawrence 1925-1930. A Bibliographical Supplement. Philadelphia: 1931. V. 72

MC DONALD, GREGORY
Fletch. 1974. V. 69

MC DONALD, JOHN
Biographical Sketches of General Nathaniel Massie, General Duncan Amarthur, Captain William Wells and General Simon Kenton; who Were Early Setters in the Western Country. 1838. V. 68

MC DONALD, STERLING B.
Color: How to Use It. Chicago: 1940. V. 71

MC DONALD, WILLIAM N.
A History of the Laurel Brigade. Baltimore: 1907. V. 69; 70
A History of The Laurel Brigade - Originally The Ashby Cavalry of The Army of Northern Virginia and Chew's Battery. Baltimore: 1969. V. 72

MC DOUGALL, D.
Goose Fever. The Diaries of an Amateur Wildfowler. 1975. V. 71
Two Royal Domains of France - the Tuileries and Versailles in Garden History, Art and Anecdote. London: 1931. V. 70

MC DOUGALL, HARRIETTE
Letters from Sarawak.... London: 1854. V. 71

MC DOWALL, ARTHUR
Peaks and Frescoes. Oxford: 1928. V. 69; 72

MC DOWALL, J. R.
Charges Preferred Against the New York Female Benevolent Society, and the Auditing Committee in 1835 and 1836.... New York: 1836. V. 73

MC DOWALL, RODDY
Double Exposure. New York: 1989-1993. V. 68

MC DOWALL, STEVEN & CO.
McDowall, Steven & Co.; Architectural Iron Founders and Sanitary Engineers, Milton Iron Works, Glasgow. 1881. V. 71

MC DOWALL, WILLIAM
History of the Burgh of Dumfries, With Notices of Nithsdale, Annandale, and the Western Border. Edinburgh: 1873. V. 71

MC DOWELL, BART
I Was a Career Girl's Consort. Philadelphia/NY: 1960. V. 72

MC DOWELL, ELLIOTT
Photographs. Boston: 1981. V. 68

MC DUFF, J. R.
The Story of a Shell. London: 1882. V. 68

MC ELRATH, CLIFFORD
On Santa Cruz Island. The Ranching Recollections of.... Los Angeles: 1967. V. 73

MC ELREE, R. L.
Home Treatment of Female Diseases. Chattanooga: 1894. V. 72

MC ELROY, C. J.
The SCI Record Book of Trophy Animals. 1982. V. 69; 70; 73

MC ELROY, COLLEEN J.
Music from Home. Carbondale: 1976. V. 73

MC ELROY, JOHN
Andersonville: A Story of Rebel Military Prisons. Toledo: 1879. V. 70

MC ELROY, JOSEPH
Ancient History: a Paraphrase. New York: 1971. V. 72; 73
Hind's Kidnap. New York: 1969. V. 72
Lookout Cartridge. New York: 1974. V. 72
Plus. New York: 1977. V. 72
A Smuggler's Bible. New York: 1966. V. 68; 70; 72; 73
Women and Men. New York: 1987. V. 73

MC ELROY, ROBERT
Grover Cleveland, the Man and the Statesman. New York and London: 1923. V. 70

MC ELROY, ROBERT MC NUTT
The Winning of the Far West. A History of the Regaining of Texas. New York: 1914. V. 69

MC EVOY, J. P.
Potters: An American Comedy. Chicago: 1924. V. 72

MC EWAN, IAN
Amsterdam. London: 1998. V. 68; 69; 72
Amsterdam. New York: 1999. V. 69; 72
Atonement. London: 2001. V. 70; 73
Black Dogs. London: 1992. V. 68; 73
The Cement Garden. London: 1978. V. 68; 70; 73
The Cement Garden. New York: 1978. V. 73
The Child in Time. 1987. V. 68
The Child in Time. Boston: 1987. V. 69; 72
The Child in Time. London: 1987. V. 70; 73
The Comfort of Strangers. London: 1981. V. 71
The Comfort of Strangers. New York: 1981. V. 69; 71
The Daydreamer. London: 1994. V. 70
Enduring Love. London: 1997. V. 70
First Love, Last Rites. London: 1975. V. 69; 70; 71; 72
First Love, Last Rites. New York: 1975. V. 71; 73
In Between the Sheets. London: 1978. V. 68; 70; 71
Or Shall We Die?. London: 1983. V. 70; 71; 72
Soursweet. London: 1988. V. 71

MC FADDEN, HARRY A.
Rambles in the Far West. Hollidayburg: 1906. V. 69

MC FADDEN, JOHN H.
Catalogue of the Collection of Pictures Formed by.... London: 1917. V. 72

MC FALL, FRANCES ELIZABETH CLARK
The Beth Book. New York: 1897. V. 69
The Heavenly Twins. New York: 1893. V. 69; 73

MC FARLAND, DENNIS
The Music Room. Boston: 1990. V. 69; 72

MC FARLAND, W. L.
Salmon of the Atlantic. New York: 1925. V. 70

MC FARLANE, ALEXANDER
The Scriptural Doctrine of Predestination, in Reference to the Present and Eternal Condition of Men, Stated and Vindicated. Bridgeton: 1827. V. 71

MC FARLING, LLOYD
Exploring the Northern Plains. Caldwell, ID: 1955. V. 72

MC FAUL, JAMES A.
The Pastoral Letters, Addresses and Other Writings of the Rt. Rev. James A. McFaul, D.D.... Trenton: 1915. V. 71

MC FEE, WILLIAM
The Beachcomber. Garden City: 1935. V. 70
North of Suez. London: 1930. V. 69

MC GAHERN, JOHN
The Barracks. London: 1963. V. 69
The Dark. London: 1965. V. 72
Pornographer. London: 1979. V. 69

MC GARLING, LLOYD
Exploring the Northern Plains. 1804-1876. 1955. V. 68

MC GARRELL, ANN
Flora: Being a Recollection of Four Friends' Excursion from Umbria.... Mount Horeb: 1990. V. 71

MC GARRITY, MICHAEL
Tularosa. New York: 1996. V. 68; 69

MC GARRY, SHERIDAN L.
Mormon Money. N.P. V. 68; 73

MC GARRY, SUSAH H.
West of Camelot. The Historical Paintings of Kenneth Riley. Tucson: 1993. V. 69

MC GAUGHEY, NEIL
Otherwise Known as Murder. New York: 1994. V. 71

MC GEE, TOM G.
Who Killed Pat Hennessey. Oklahoma: 1941. V. 68; 73

MC GILLYCUDDY, JULIA B.
McGillycuddy Agent. Stanford: 1941. V. 72

MC GINLEY, WILLIAM A.
Greely Relief Expedition. Reception of Lieut. A. W. Greely and His Comrades and of the Arctic Relief Expedition at Portsmouth, N.H. on August 1 and 4, 1884. Washington;: 1884. V. 73

MC GINNIS, JOE
The Miracle of Castel di Sango. Boston: 1999. V. 72

MC GINTY, BILLY
The Old West As Written in the Words of Billy Mcginty. Ripley, Okla: 1937. V. 72

MC GIVERN, WILLIAM
Heaven Ran Last. New York: 1949. V. 69
The Road to the Snail. New York: 1961. V. 70
Seven Lies South. New York: 1960. V. 70

MC GLASHAN, C. F.
History of the Donner Party - a Tragedy of the Sierras. Truckee: 1879. V. 70

MC GLASHAN, NORMAN
Autumn Gold. New York: 1939. V. 71

MC GOVERN, JOHN P.
Humanism in Medicine. Springfield: 1973. V. 71

MC GOVERN, MELVIN P.
Specimen Pages of Korean Moveable Types. Los Angeles: 1966. V. 70

MC GOVERN, WILLIAM MONTGOMERY
To Lhasa in Disguise. New York: 1924. V. 71

MC GOWAN, EDWARD
California Vigilantes. Oakland: 1946. V. 71

MC GRANDLE, LEITH
Europe: the Quest for Unity: Speeches ad Writings. London: 1975. V. 71

MC GRATH, R.
Glass in Architecture and Decoration. London: 1961. V. 69; 72

MC GRAW, ELOISE JARVIS
Merry Go Round in Oz. Chicago: 1963. V. 73

MC GREGOR, ALEXANDER LEE
Surgery of the Sympathetic. Bristol: 1955. V. 68

MC GREGOR, FAY
Alice in Starland or The Land of the Little Star. London: 1952. V. 72

MC GREGOR, JOHN C.
Southwestern Archaeology. New York: 1941. V. 69

MC GREW, R. BROWNELL
R. Brownell McGrew. 1978. V. 68

MC GREW, R. BROWNWELL
R. Brownwell McGrew. Kansas City: 1978. V. 69

MC GROARTY, JOHN STEVEN
Los Angeles from the Mountains to the Sea. Chicago: 1921. V. 73

MC GUANE, THOMAS
The Bushwacked Piano. New York: 1970. V. 69
The Bushwacked Piano. New York: 1971. V. 69; 72
Keep the Change. Boston: 1989. V. 68; 71; 72; 73
Live Water. Far Hills: 1996. V. 72
Live Water. Stone Harbor: 1996. V. 69; 73
Ninety-Two in the Shade. London: 1974. V. 68; 73
Nobody's Angel. New York: 1982. V. 73
Nothing But Blue Skies. Boston: 1992. V. 68
An Outside Chance. New York: 1980. V. 71
Panama. New York: 1978. V. 70; 72; 73
Some Horses. New York: 1999. V. 73
The Sporting Club. New York: 1968. V. 71; 72; 73
The Sporting Club. New York: 1969. V. 72; 73

MC GUIRE, PAUL
The Black & White Books Rose Murder. New York: 1932. V. 73
Enter Three Witches. 1940. V. 73
A Funeral in Eden. 1938. V. 73
A Funeral in Eden. New York: 1938. V. 72
Murder at High Noon. New York: 1935. V. 73
The Spanish Steps. London: 1940. V. 73
Three Men Dead. New York: 1932. V. 73

MC GUIRE, STUART
The Profit and Loss Account of Modern Medicine. Richmond: 1915. V. 72

MC HALE, TOM
Farragan's Retreat. New York: 1971. V. 68

MC HANEY, PEARL AMELIA
Eudora Welty: Writers' Reflections Upon First Reading Welty. Athens: 1999. V. 68; 70
A Writer's Eye: Collected Book Reviews. 1994. V. 70

MC HARG, I. L.
Design with Nature. New York: 1969. V. 68; 69; 72

MC HENRY, LAWRENCE
Garrison's History of Neurology. Springfield: 1969. V. 68; 70; 70; 71; 73

MC HUGH, FRANCES Y.
The Dropped Living Room. New York: 1971. V. 71

MC ILLHANY, EDWARD WASHINGTON
Recollections of a '49er. Kansas City: 1908. V. 72

MC ILVAINE, C.
Toadstools, Mushrooms, Fungi, Edible and Poisonous. One Thousand American Fungi. Indianapolis: 1900. V. 70

MC ILVANNEY, WILLIAM
Laidlaw. New York: 1977. V. 68

MC ILWAINE, RICHARD
Memories of Three Score Years and Ten. New York: 1908. V. 69

MC INERNEY, JAY
Bright Lights, Big City. New York: 1984. V. 72; 73
Bright Lights, Big City. London: 1985. V. 69; 72; 73
Model Behavior. New York: 1998. V. 72
Ransom. New York: 1985. V. 68

MC INERNY, M. H.
A History of the Irish Dominicans from Original Sources and Unpublished Records. Volume I. Irish Dominican Bishops 1224-1307. 1916. V. 69; 73

MC INERNY, RALPH
Lying Three. New York: 1979. V. 71

MC INTOSH, JOHN
The Origin of the North American Indians.... New York: 1843. V. 73

MC INTOSH, WILLIAM
Sermons from a Philistine Pulpit. East Aurora: 1898. V. 69

MC INTYRE, JOHN T.
Death at Dakar. New York: 1942. V. 68
Ninth Floor: Middle City Tower. New York: 1943. V. 68

MC IVOR, W. G.
Hepaticae Britannicae; or, Pocket Herbarium of British Hepaticae. New Brentford: 1847. V. 69

MC KAY, BARRY
Patterns and Pigments in English Marbled Papers: an Account of the Origins, Sources and Documentary Literature to 1811. Kidlington: 1988. V. 71

MC KAY, CLAUDE
Banjo. New York: 1929. V. 72
Harlem: Negro Metropolis. New York: 1940. V. 68; 70

MC KAY, DONALD
Daring Donald McKay; Or the Last War Trail of The Modocs. Erie: 1885. V. 72

MC KAY, HERBERT
The Ark Afloat. London: 1951. V. 72

MC KAY, R. H.
Little Pills, An Army Story. Pittsburgh: 1918. V. 72

MC KAY, SETH
Seven Decades of the Texas Constitution of 1876. Lubbock: 1942. V. 69
W. Lee O'Daniel and Texas Politics: 1938-1942. Lubbock: 1944. V. 69

MC KEAN, EMMA C.
Fairy Tales: Alice in Wonderland. Springfield: 1943. V. 73

MC KEE, E. D.
The Environmental History of the Toroweap and Kaibab Formations of Northern Arizona and Southern Utah. Washington: 1938. V. 70

MC KEE, IRVING
Alonzo Delano's California Correspondence. Sacramento: 1952. V. 68

MC KEE, LOUISE
Dusty Desert Tales. Caldwell: 1941. V. 69

MC KELVEY, S. D.
Botanical Exploration of the Trans-Mississippi West 1790-1850. Jamaica Plain: 1955. V. 73
The Lilac, a Monograph. New York: 1928. V. 68; 69

MC KENDRICK, JOHN GRAY
Hermann Ludwig Ferdinand von Helmholtz. London: 1919. V. 68

MC KENNA, JAMES A.
Black Range Tales, Chronicling Sixty Years of Life And Adventures in the Southwest. New York: 1936. V. 71

MC KENNA, JOHN
Hide and Seek Riddle Book. New York: 1943. V. 72

MC KENNA, MARIAN C.
Tapping Reeve an the Litchfield Law School. New York: 1986. V. 72

MC KENNA, RICHARD
The Sand Pebbles. New York: 1962. V. 71; 72
The Sand Pebbles. New York: 1962-1963. V. 69

MC KENNA, STEPHEN
The Datchley Inheritance. New York: 1930. V. 68

MC KENNEY, THOMAS LORRAINE
History of the Indian Tribes of North America. Philadelphia: 1855. V. 71
History of the Indian Tribes of North America. Kent: 1978. V. 68
Indian Tribes of North America.... Edinburgh: 1933. V. 73
The Indian Tribes of North America.... Edinburgh: 1934. V. 70
Sketches of a Tour to the Lakes, of the Character and Customs of the Chippeway Indians. Baltimore: 1827. V. 70
Sketches of a Tour to the Lakes of the Character and Customs of the Chippeway Indians and of Incidents Connected with the Treaty of Fond du Lac. Barre: 1972. V. 69; 73

MC KENZIE, C. H.
The Religious Sentiments of Charles Dickens. London: 1884. V. 69

MC KENZIE, N. R.
The Gael Fares Forth: the Romantic Study of Waipu and Her Sister Settlements. Wellington: 1942. V. 69

MC KEOWN, TOM
The Cloud Keeper. Dublin: 1972. V. 68

MC KERROW, RONALD BRUNLEES
Printers' and Publishers' Devices in England and Scotland. 1485-1949. London. V. 68

MC KILLIP, PATRICIA
Harpist in the Wind. New York: 1979. V. 73
Heir of Sea and Fire. New York: 1977. V. 73
The Riddle-Master of Hed. New York: 1976. V. 73
The Riddle-Master of Hed. London: 1979. V. 73
The Throme of the Erril of Sherill. New York: 1973. V. 73

MC KIM, RANDOLPH HARRISON
The Gettysburg Campaign. Richmond: 1915. V. 69; 70
The Numerical Strength of the Confederate Army. New York: 1912. V. 69; 70
A Soldier's Recollections. New York: 1911. V. 69; 70
A Soldier's Recollections. London: 1921. V. 69

MC KINLEY, ROBIN
The Hero and the Crown. New York: 1985. V. 72

MC KINLEY, WILLIAM
Speeches and Addresses of William Mckinley from March 1, 1897 to May 30 1900. New York: 1900. V. 73

MC LAIN, JOHN SCUDDER
Alaska and the Klondike. New York: 1905. V. 68

MC LANE, HIRAM H.
The Capture of the Alamo: a Historical Tragedy, in Four Acts with a Prologue. San Antonio: 1886. V. 68

MC LAREN, BARBARA
Women of the War. New York: 1918. V. 70

MC LAREN, JACK
A Diver Went Down. London: 1929. V. 69; 73

MC LAREN, JOHN
Gardening in California, Landscape and Flower. San Francisco: 1909. V. 72

MC LAREN, L. L.
Pan Pacific Cook Book. San Francisco: 1915. V. 73

MC LAUGHLIN, DANIEL
Sketch of a Trip from Omaha to Salmon River. Chicago: 1954. V. 69

MC LAUGHLIN, JAMES
My Friend, The Indian. Boston: 1910. V. 72
My Friend the Indian. Seattle: 1970. V. 69

MC LAUGHLIN, MAY BEATRIX
Cherie at Sacred Heart. New York: 1930. V. 71

MC LAURIN, JOHN J.
Sketches in Crude-Oil: some Accidents and Incidents of the Petroleum Development in All Parts of the Globe. Harrisburg: 1896. V. 70

MC LEAN, ANGUS WILSON
Lumber Rivers Scots and their Descendants: the McLeans, The Purcells, the McIntyres, the Torreys, the Gilchrists. Richmond: 1942. V. 71

MC LEAN, RUARI
Joseph Cundall. A Victorian Publisher. Notes On His Life And A Check-List Of His Books. Pinner: 1976. V. 69; 72
Modern Book Design from William Morris to the Present Day. London: 1958. V. 71
The Reminiscences of Edmund Evans - Wood Engraver and Colour Printer 1826-1905. London: 1967. V. 71
Victorian Book Design and Colour Printing. London: 1963. V. 70; 71
Victorian Book Design and Colour Printing. London: 1972. V. 71
Victorian Publishers' Book Bindings in Cloth and Leather. 1974. V. 69
Victorian Publishers' Book-Bindings in Cloth and Leather. London: 1974. V. 71
Victorian Publishers' Book-Bindings in Paper. London: 1983. V. 71

MC LELLAN, LEIGH
Artist's Proof: Brief History, Type Specimen and Checklist of the Meadow Press,. San Francisco: 1990. V. 72

M'CLELLAND, J.
Indian Cyprinidae. Calcuta: 1839. V. 73

MC LENNAN, J. S.
Louisbourg. From Its Foundation to Its Fall 1713-1758. London: 1918. V. 73

MC LEOD, J.
The Cathedral Libraries Catalogue. London: 1948-1998. V. 70

MC LEOD, M.
The Asante. London: 1981. V. 69

MC LEOD, MALCOLM
The Problem of Canada. Ottawa: 1880. V. 71

MC LUHAN, MARSHALL
Take Today: The Executive as Dropout. Don Mills: 1972. V. 70

MC LUHAN, T. C.
Dream Tracks, the Railroad and the American Indian 1890-1930. New York: 1985. V. 69

MC LUKE, LUKE
The National Smoke. Cincinnati: 1914. V. 68

M'CLURE, ROBERT
The Discovery of the North-West Passage. London: 1856. V. 71
The Discovery of the North-West Passage. London: 1857. V. 73

MC MAHON, JOHN R.
Toilers and Idlers. New York: 1907. V. 73

MC MASTERS, SUSANNE
The Gallant Heart: The Story of a Race Horse. Garden city: 1954. V. 72

MC MECHEN, EDGAR CARLISLE
Life of Governor Evans - Second Territorial Governor of Colorado. Denver: 1924. V. 69
The Moffet Tunnel of Colorado: an Epic of Empire. Denver: 1927. V. 71

MC MILLAN, M.
A Journey to Java. London: 1914. V. 71

MC MILLAN, MARGARET
Labour and Childhood. London: 1907. V. 73

MC MILLAN, TERRY
Disappearing Acts. London: 1990. V. 69
How Stella Got Her Groove Back. New York: 1996. V. 70
Mama. Boston: 1987. V. 69; 70; 73
Waiting to Exhale. 1992. V. 73
Waiting to Exhale. New York: 1992. V. 68; 72

MC MURRAY, WILLIAM J.
History of the Twentieth Tennessee Regiment Volunteer Infantry. Nashville: 1904. V. 69; 70

MC MURRICH, J. PLAYFAIR
The Development of the Human Body. London: 1907. V. 68

MC MURRY, W. H.
History of the Twentieth Tennessee Regiment Volunteer Infantry, C.S. A. 1904. V. 68

MC MURTRIE, DOUGLAS C.
A Bibliograhy of Mississippi Imprints, 1798-1830. Beauvoir Community: 1945. V. 71
A Bibliography of Morristown Imprints 1798-1820. Newark: 1936. V. 71
Early Printing in Tennessee. Chicago: 1933. V. 71
El Payo de Nueno Mejico. Albuquerque: 1933. V. 68
The First Printing in New Mexico with Cuaderno de Ortografia. Chicago: 1929. V. 70; 72
Jean Gutenberg, Inventor of Printing. New York: 1926. V. 70
The Mining Laws of the Third District of Idaho. Evanston: 1944. V. 68
Notes on Early Printing in Utah Outside of Salt Lake City. Los Angeles: 1938. V. 68
Oregon Imprints 1847-1870. Eugene: 1950. V. 70; 72; 73
The Sweetwater Mines - A Pioneer Wyoming Newspaper. Minneapolis: 1935. V. 68

MC MURTRY, LARRY
All My Friends Are Going to Be Strangers. New York: 1972. V. 69; 71
Anything for Billy. New York: 1988. V. 73
Buffalo Girls. New York: 1990. V. 68; 72; 73
Buffalo Girls. London: 1991. V. 72
Cadillac Jack. New York: 1982. V. 70; 72; 73
The Desert Rose. New York: 1983. V. 71; 72; 73
Duane's Depressed. New York: 1989. V. 71
The Evening Star. New York: 1992. V. 73
Film Flam. New York: 1987. V. 71; 72; 73
Horseman, Pass By. New York: 1961. V. 71; 72; 73
In a Narrow Grave. Austin: 1968. V. 68; 69; 70; 71
It's Always We Rambled. An Essay on Rodeo. New York: 1974. V. 69; 70
The Last Picture Show. New York: 1966. V. 69; 70; 73
Leaving Cheyenne. New York: 1963. V. 69; 70; 72
Lonesome Dove. New York: 1985. V. 68; 69; 70; 71; 72; 73
Maurizius Forever. Waco: 1946. V. 71
Moving On. New York: 1970. V. 68; 70; 71
Paradise. New York: 2001. V. 69
Pretty Boy Floyd. New York: 1994. V. 71; 73
Some Can Whistle. New York: 1989. V. 71; 72; 73
Somebody's Darling. New York: 1978. V. 70
Still Wild. New York: 2000. V. 69
Streets of Laredo. New York: 1993. V. 72
Terms of Endearment. New York: 1975. V. 70
Texasville. New York: 1987. V. 72
Zeke and Ned. New York: 1997. V. 72

MC NAIR, ARNOLD
Dr. Johnson and the Law, a Study. Cambridge: 1948. V. 69

MC NAMARA, JOHN
In Perils by Mine Own Countrymen: Three Years on the Kansas Border. New York: 1856. V. 69; 72; 73

MC NAMEE, EOIN
The Last of Deeds. Dublin: 1989. V. 72
Resurrection Man. London: 1994. V. 68; 71

MC NAUGHTON, MARGARET
Overland to Cariboo, an Eventful Journey of Canadian Pioneers to the Gold Fields of British Columbia in 1862. Toronto: 1896. V. 68; 71

MC NEAL, T. A.
When Kansas Was Young. Topeka: 1934. V. 72

MC NEER, MAY
Martin Luther. New York: 1953. V. 70
The Wolf of Lambs Lane. Boston: 1967. V. 70

MC NEIL, MARION L.
Jingleman Jack - Circusman. Akron: 1930. V. 71
Jingleman Jack - Engineer. Akron: 1930. V. 71
Jingleman Jack - Policeman. Akron: 1929. V. 71

MC NEILE, H. C.
Bulldog Drummond Strikes Back. Garden City: 1933. V. 70
The Human Touch. New York: 1918. V. 70
Knock-Out. London: 1933. V. 73
Mufti. New York: 1919. V. 70

MC NEILL, GEORGE E.
The Labor Movement: The Problem of Today. Boston & New York: 1887. V. 71

MC NEILL, MALCOM
In Pursuit of the Mad Mullah. London: 1902. V. 71

MC NICKLE, D'ARCY
The Hawk is Hungry. Tucson: 1992. V. 72
Indian Man. Bloomington: 1971. V. 72

MC NICOLL, DAVID H.
A Handbook for Southport, Medical and General.... London: 1861. V. 68; 73

MC NITT, FRANK
The Indian Traders. 1962. V. 69
Navaho Expedition Journal of a Military Reconnaissance From Santa Fe, New Mexico to the Navaho Country Made in 1849 by Lt. James H. Sampson. Norman: 1964. V. 73
Navajo Wars. 1972. V. 69
Navajo Wars-Military Campaigns Slave Raids and Reprisals. Norman: 1972. V. 71
Richard Wetherhill: Anasazi. Albuquerque: 1957. V. 68; 73

MC PALMER, JOHN
History of The 22nd United States Infantry. 1972. V. 72

MC PHAIL, RODGER
Fishing Seasons. 1990. V. 68

MC PHEE, FAIRBAIRNE
March to the Gods that Heal and Other Stories. London: 1933. V. 70

MC PHEE, JOHN
Annals of the Former World. New York: 1983. V. 69; 71; 73
Annals of the Former World. New York: 1998. V. 73
Coming into the Country. New York: 1977. V. 73
The Crofter and the Laird. New York: 1970. V. 69; 73
The Curve of Binding Engery. New York: 1974. V. 71
The Deltoid Pumpkin Seed. New York: 1973. V. 72
Encounters with the Archdruid. New York: 1971. V. 68
Giving Good Weight. New York: 1979. V. 72; 73
The Headmaster. New York: 1966. V. 68; 69; 71; 73
In Suspect Terrain. New York: 1983. V. 69; 73
In the Highlands and Islands. London: 1986. V. 71; 73
Irons in the Fire. New York: 1997. V. 69
La Place de la Concorde Suisse. New York: 1984. V. 69; 72
Levels of the Game. New York: 1969. V. 69; 73
Oranges. New York: 1967. V. 70; 71; 72
Outcroppings. Salt Lake City: 1988. V. 69
Pieces of the Frame. New York: 1975. V. 69; 71
The Pine Barrens. New York: 1968. V. 69; 71; 73
The Ransom of Russian Art. New York: 1994. V. 71
A Roomful of Hovings and Other Profiles. New York: 1968. V. 69; 73
The Second John McPhee Reader. New York: 1996. V. 70
A Sense of Where You Are. New York: 1965. V. 70; 71
The Survival of the Bark Canoe. New York: 1975. V. 68; 69; 73
The Survival of the Bark Canoe. New York: 1976. V. 70; 71
Table of Contents. New York: 1985. V. 72
Wimbledon, A Celebration. New York: 1972. V. 71; 73

MC PHERREN, IDA
Empire Builders - a History of the Founding of Sheridan. Sheridan: 1942. V. 69
Imprints on Pioneer Trails. Boston: 1950. V. 68
Trails End. Casper: 1938. V. 70

MC PHERSON, AIMEE SEMPLE
The Holy Spirit. Los Angeles: 1931. V. 72
This if That: Personal Experiences, Sermons and Writings. Los Angeles: 1921. V. 72

MC PHERSON, EDWARD
Political History of the U.S....During the Period of Construction. Washington: 1871. V. 71
A Political Manual from 1866 and 1867 of Executive Legislative Judical Politico-Military and General Facts. Washington: 1867. V. 71

MC PHERSON, JAMES ALAN
Elbow Room. Boston: 1977. V. 69; 72
Elbow Room. New York: 1977. V. 69
Hue and Cry. Boston and Toronto: 1969. V. 69; 70; 72; 73
A Region Not Home. New York: 1999. V. 71; 72

MC PHERSON, SANDRA
Radiation. New York: 1973. V. 73

MC QUADE, W.
Architecture in the Real World: the Work of HOK. New York: 1984. V. 68; 72

MC QUEEN, IAN
Sherlock Holmes Detected. Abbot: 1974. V. 72

MC QUHAE, WILLIAM
The Decorators & Artisans Guide Book.... Cockermouth: 1890. V. 68

MC QUILLAN, KARIN
Deadly Safari. New York: 1990. V. 68; 69; 71

MC SHERRY, RICHARD
Essays and Lectures on I. The Early History of Maryland. 2. Mexico and Mexican Affairs. Baltimore: 1869. V. 73

MC SHINE, K.
Joseph Cornell. New York: 1980. V. 69; 72

MC SPARRAN, ARCHIBALD
The Irish Legend of McDonnell, and the Norman de Borgos.... Glasgow: 1877?. V. 68

MC SWAIN, JOHN
Reports of the Visitors of Schools for the Three Counties of Prince Edward Island, for the Year 1874. Charlottetown: 1875. V. 71

M'CULLOCH, THOMAS
Popery Condemned by Scripture and the Fathers.... Edinburgh;: 1808. V. 69

MC VEY, E. E.
The Crow Scout Who Killed Custer. Billings: 1952. V. 72

MC VICKER, JAMES HUBERT
The Theatre: its Early Days in Chicago. Chicago: 1884. V. 70

MC VICKER, MARY LOUISE
The Writings of J. Frank Dobie: a Bibliography. Lawton: 1968. V. 68

MC VOY, J. P.
The Bam-Bam Clock. Chicago: 1920. V. 70

MC WATTERS, GEORGE S.
The Detective of Europe and America, or Life in the Secret Service. Hartford: 1883. V. 73

MC WHORTER, JOHN C.
The Scout of the Buckon-Gehanon: an Historical Romance of the Western Virginia Border. 1764-1782. Boston: 1927. V. 69

MC WHORTER, LUCULLUS VIRGIL
Yellow Wolf: His Own Story. 1940. V. 68
Yellow Wolf: His Own Story. Caldwell: 1948. V. 68; 72

MC WILLIAM, JOHN MORELL
The Birds of the Firth of Clyde, Including Ayrshire, Renfrewshire, Buteshire, Dumbartonshire and South Argyllshire. 1936. V. 73

MC WILLIAMS, JOHN
Recollections of...His Youth Experience in California and the Civil War. Princeton: 1919. V. 69

M'DONALD, JOHN
Letters...Addressed To the Friends of Religion. Albany: 1801. V. 73

M'DOWALL, WILLIAM
Memorials of St. Michael's. The Old Parish Churchyard of Dumfries. Edinburgh: 1876. V. 71

MEACHAM, A. B.
Wigwam and War-Path of the Royal Chief in Chains. Boston: 1875. V. 72

MEACHAM, M. I.
The Kate Greenaway Collection of Miss M. I. Meacham. New York: 1921. V. 70

MEAD, CHARLES
Mississippian Scenery; a Poem. Philadelphia: 1819. V. 73

MEAD, MARGARET
World Enough. Boston: 1975. V. 69

MEAD, P. B.
An Elementary Treatise on American Grape Culture and Wine Making.... New York: 1867. V. 68; 71

MEAD, RICHARD
De Imperio Solis ac Lunae in Corpora Humana, et Morbis Inde Oriundis. Londini: 1704. V. 72
De Variolis et Morbillis Liber.... London: 1747. V. 73
A Discourse on the Plague.... London: 1744. V. 70
A Mechanical Account of Poisons in Several Essays. London: 1702. V. 73
A Mechanical Account of Poisons In Several Essays. London: 1708. V. 72
A Mechanical Account of Poisons, in Several Essays. London: 1745. V. 71
Medical Precepts and Cautions. London: 1755. V. 72
The Medical Works. London: 1762. V. 68; 69; 73
Oratio Anniversaria Harveiana; in Theatro Regii Medicorum Londinensium Collegii Habita. London: 1724. V. 70; 73

MEADE, BISHOP WILLIAM
Old Churches, Ministers and Families of Virginia. Philadelphia: 1910. V. 68

MEADE, GLENN
The Sands of Sakkara. London: 1999. V. 69
Snow Wolf. London: 1995. V. 69; 73

MEADE, L. T.
The Brotherhood of the Seven Kings. London: 1899. V. 70
The Home of Silence. London: 1907. V. 70

MEADE, RICHARD
An Introduction to the History of General Surgery. Philadelphia: 1968. V. 70

MEADE, ROBERT D.
Judah P. Benjamin: Confederate Statesman. New York: 1943. V. 70

MEADOWS, CATHERINE
Friday Market. New York: 1938. V. 70

MEADS, JIM
They Still Meet at Eleven. 1979. V. 68

MEAGHER, NICHOLAS
The Religious Warfare in Nova Scotia 1855-1860. Halifax: 1927?. V. 73

MEAGHER, WILLIAM
Notices of the Life and Character of Most Rev. Daniel Murray, Late Archbishop of Dublin. 1853. V. 69

MEAKIN, BUDGETT
The Moorish Empire. London and New York: 1899. V. 69

MEALS and Memoirs: Recipes and Recollections of African Americans in Tucson. Tucson: 1993. V. 72

MEANS, FLORENCE CRANNELL
The Singing Wood. Boston: 1937. V. 71

MEANS, PHILIP AINSWORTH
History of the Spanish Conquest of Yucatan and of the Itzas. Cambridge: 1917. V. 69
Peruvian Textiles, Examples of the Pre-Incaic Period with a Chronology of Early Peruvian Cultures. New York: 1930. V. 69

MEANY, TOM
Babe Ruth, the Big Moments of the Big Fellow. New York: 1947. V. 69
Baseball's Greatest Pitchers. New York: 1951. V. 71
The Yankee Story. New York: 1960. V. 70

MEARSON, LYON
The Whisper on the Stair. New York: 1924. V. 72

MEASE, JAMES
An Essay on the Disease Produced by the Bite of a Mad Dog, or Other Rabid Animal. Philadelphia: 1793. V. 73
An Inaugural Dissertation on the Disease Produced by the Bite of a Mad Dog, or Other Rabid Animal.... Philadelphia. V. 68; 73

MEASOM, GEORGE
The Official Illustrated Guide to the Great Northern Railway.... 1857. V. 71

MECHI, JOHN JOSEPH
On the Principles which Ensure Success in Trade. London: 1850. V. 68

MECHNIKOV, ILIA IL'CH
Etudes sur la Nature Humaine. Essai de Philosophie Optimiste. Paris: 1903. V. 72

MECKAUER, WALTER
The Books of the Emperor Wu Ti. New York: 1931. V. 69

MECKEL, JOHANN F.
Dissertatio Inauguralis Medica Anatomico, Physiologica de Quinto Pare Nervorom Cerebri.... Tottingae: 1748. V. 70
Manual of General Descriptive and Pathological Anatomy.... Philadelphia: 1832. V. 73

MEDBERY, JAMES K.
Men and Mysteries of Wall Street. Boston: 1870. V. 73

MEDEM, RICARDO
En La Cruz Del Anteojo. Madrid: 1974. V. 69; 70

MEDER, JOHANNES
Quadragesimale de Filio Prodigo. Basel: 1497. V. 69

MEDHURST, G.
Calculations and Remarks, Tending to Prove the Practicability, Effects and Advantages of a Plan for the Rapid Conveyance of Goods and Passengers Upon an Iron Road through a Tube of 30 Feet in Area by the Power and Velocity of Air. London: 1812. V. 68

MEDHURST, W. H.
China. London: 1838. V. 69; 71

MEDICAL Facts and Observations. Volume the Fourth. London: 1793. V. 72

MEDICINAL Plants in Siri Ruckhachati Garden. 1992. V. 68

MEDICINE CROW, JOSEPH
From the Heart of the Crow Country. New York: 1992. V. 72

MEDINA, ANDRES
El Mundo Magico de los Mayas. Mexico: 1964. V. 72

MEDIONI, GILBERT
Art in Ancient Mexico. New York: 1941. V. 73

THE MEDLEY (No. 2). Portland: 1830. V. 73

MEDLEY, JULIUS GEORGE
The Roorkee Treatise on Civil Engineering in India. Roorkee: 1867-1869. V. 71

MEDLEY, SARAH
Original Poems, Sacred and Miscellaneous. Liverpool: 1807. V. 69

MEDVED, MICHAEL
Hollywood vs. America - Popular Culture and the War on Traditional Values. London: 1992. V. 69

MEDWIN, THOMAS
Conversations of Lord Byron, Noted During a Residence with His Lordship at Pisa in the Years 1821 and 1822. London: 1824. V. 68; 70; 72
Journal of the Conversations of Lord Byron. New York: 1824. V. 68; 70

MEE, JOSIAH
Thomas Champness as I Knew Him. London: 1906. V. 68

MEEHAN, THOMAS
The Native Flowers and Ferns of the United States. Boston: 1878. V. 68; 69
Native Flowers and Ferns of the United States. Boston: 1878-1879. V. 69; 73

MEEK, A. S.
A Naturalist in Cannibal Land. London: 1913. V. 71

MEEK, C. K.
The Northern Tribes of Nigeria. London: 1925. V. 72
A Sudanese Kingdom, an Ethnographical Study of the Jukun-Speaking Peoples of Nigeria. London: 1931. V. 69
Tribal Studies in Northern Nigeria. London: 1931. V. 69; 73
Tribal Studies in Northern Nigeria. New York: 1978. V. 69

MEEK, CHARLES
The Will to Function: a Philosophical Study. 1929. V. 71

MEEK, S. E.
The Marine Fishes of Panama. Chicago: 1923-1928. V. 69; 72; 73

MEEK, STEPHEN
The Autobiography of a Mountain Man. 1805-1889. Pasadena: 1948. V. 70

MEEKER, CLAUDE
The Home of the Brontes. 1916. V. 68; 70; 73

MEEKER, ELIZA
Ventures and Adventures of Ezra Meeker or Sixty Years of Frontier Life The Oregon Trail. Seattle: 1908. V. 69

MEEKER, EZRA
The Busy Life of Eighty-Five Years. Seattle: 1916. V. 68; 73
Pioneer Reminiscences of Puget Sound - the Tragedy of Lesch. Seattle: 1905. V. 69

MEEKER, N. C.
Life in the West, or Stories of the Mississippi Valley. New York: 1868. V. 69

MEEKEREN, JOB JANSZOON VAN
Observationes Medico-Chirurgicae, ex Belgico in Latinum.... Amstelodami: 1682. V. 68; 73

MEETWELL, JAMES, PSEUD.
The Autobiography of a Merchant, or the Story of James Meetwell.... London: 1881. V. 68

MEGGENDORFER, LOTHAR
Immer Lustig! (Always Jolly). Munchen: 1886. V. 73
Artistic Pussy and Her Moving Pictures with Other Tales. Chicago: 1910. V. 70
Attention. London: 1900. V. 73
Aus dem Leben. Lustiges Ziehbilderbuch. (Taken from Life). Munchen: 1887. V. 72
The Genius of Lothar Meggendorfer. London: 1985. V. 70
Gute Bekannte. (Very Well Known). Suttgart: 1879. V. 72
Lustige Ziehbilder. Esslingen: 1892. V. 68; 70
Lustiges Automaten-Theater. Esslingen: 1890. V. 70
Martin L'Ours ou La Maison de Sucre. Paris: 1887. V. 70; 73
Nah und Fern. (Far and Wide). Munchen: 1887. V. 72
Pierino Porcospino Vivente. Milano: 1905. V. 68; 73
Verschiedene Leute ein Ziehbilderbuch. (Various People). Esslingen: 1894. V. 72
Voyages et Aventures Extraordinaires de Mr. Raphael de Rubensmouche L'illustre Artiste!. Paris: 1900. V. 68

MEGLINGER, CASPAR
Der Todtentanz, Germalde auf der Muhlenbrucke in Lucern.... Luzern: 1867. V. 69

MEHERIN, ELENORE
Chickie. New York. V. 70
Sandy. New York: 1926. V. 69; 70

MEHEUT, M.
Etude de la Foret.... Paris: 1927. V. 72

MEHTA, SOLI
Exploring the Hidden Himalaya. London: 1990. V. 69

MEIER, AUGUST
Along the Color Line: Explorations in the Black Experience. Urbana: 1976. V. 72

MEIER, LILI
The Auschewitz Album: a Book Based Upon an Album Discovered by a Concentration Camp Survivor. New York: 1981. V. 71

MEIGNAN, VICTOR
From Paris to Pekin. London: 1885. V. 73

MEIGS, CHARLES D.
A Treatise on Acute and Chronic Diseases of the Neck of the Uterus.... Philadelphia: 1854. V. 70

MEIGS, JOHN
The Cowboy in American Prints. Chicago: 1972. V. 69; 70; 72
The Peter Hurd Sketchbook. Chicago: 1971. V. 69
Peter Hurd: the Lithographs. Lubbock: 1969. V. 68

MEIGS, MONTGOMERY CUNNINGHAM
The Three Days' Battle of Chattanooga, 23rd, 24th, 25th November 1864. Washington: 1864. V. 69

MEIK, CHARLES S.
Royal Commission on London Traffice. Proposed London Main Avenues 1903-04. Description and Drawings. London: 1903-1904. V. 72

MEIKLE, DESMOND
Wild Flowers of Cyprus. London and Chichester: 1973. V. 68; 73

MEIN, ROBERT
The City Cleaned and Country Improven. Edinburgh: 1760. V. 70

MEINERTZHAGEN, R.
Birds of Arabia. Edinburgh: 1954. V. 73
Kenya Diary. 1902-1906. London: 1957. V. 70
Middle East Diary. 1960. V. 69; 70; 72
Pirates and Predators, the Piratical and Predatory Habits of Birds. 1959. V. 73

MEINHOLD, WILHELM
The Amber Witch. New York: 1845. V. 69

MEINZER, OSCAR E.
Physics of the Earth: Hydrology. New York: 1949. V. 72

MEISELAS, SUSAN
Carnival Strippers. New York: 1976. V. 70; 72

MEISEN, V.
Prominent Danish Scientists Through the Ages with Facsimiles from their Works. London: 1932. V. 72

MEISNER, LEONHARD FERDINAND
Caffe, Chocolate, Herbae Thee ac Nicotianne Natura, Usa et Abusu.... Nuremberg: 1721. V. 72

MEISSONIER, JEAN
Sailing Ships of the Romantic Era. London: 1968. V. 70

MEISTER, JACQUES HENRI
Souvenirs de mes Voyages en Angleterre. Zurich: 1795. V. 69

MELANCHTHON, PHILIP
Th Loci Communes of Philip Melanchthon. Boston: 1944. V. 72

MELBERG, J. C.
Romare Bearden: 1970-1980. Charlotte: 1980. V. 69; 72

MELEAGER
The Songs of Meleager. London: 1937. V. 70; 71

MELESKI, PATRICIA F.
Echoes of the Past. Albuquerque: 1972. V. 69

MELFORD, LARRY
The Meetings and Other Stories. New York: 1980. V. 72

MELLICK, ANDREW D.
The Story of an Old Farm, or Life in New Jersey in the Eighteenth Century. Somerville: 1889. V. 71

MELLICK, HENRY GEORGE TIMOTHY
Timothy's Boyhood, or Pioneer Country Life on Prince Edward Island by Timothy, a Country Boy. Kentville: 1933. V. 73

MELLINS FOOD CO.
The Care and Feeding of Infants. Boston: 1901. V. 71

MELLISH, ANNIE ELIZABETH
Our Boys Under Fire or New Brunswick and Prince Edward Island Volunteers in South Africa. Charlottetown: 1900. V. 68

MELLISS, CHARLES JOHN
Lion-Hunting in Somali-Land Also an Account of "Pigsticking" the African Wart Hog.... London: 1895. V. 69; 71

MELLO, J. M.
Hand-Book to the Geology of Derbyshire. London and Derby. V. 69; 73

MELLON, ANDREW W.
Taxation: the People's Business. New York: 1924. V. 70; 72

MELLON, J.
African Hunter. New York: 1975. V. 70

MELLON, JAMES
The Face of Lincoln. New York: 1979. V. 68

MELLOS, FRANCISCO MANUEL DE
The Government of a Wife or Wholsom and Pleasant Advice for Married Men, in a Letter to a Friend. London: 1697. V. 68

MELLY, ANDRE
Lettres d'Egypte et de Nubie. September 1850 a Janvier 1851. London: 1852. V. 71

MELMOTH, WILLIAM
The Letters of Sir Thomas Fitzosborne, on Several Subjects. London: 1784. V. 70
The Modern Universal Story-Teller; or, a New Picture of Human Life.... London: 1780?. V. 69

MELNICK, ROBERT
Manhole Covers of Los Angeles. Los Angeles: 1974. V. 73

MELTON, A. B.
Seventy Years in the Saddle. Kansas City: 1948. V. 71

MELTZER, BERNARD
Labor Law. Cases, Materials, and Problems. Boston: 1970. V. 71

MELTZL VON LOMNITZ, KARL HUGO DE
The Black Wodas. Kolozsvar: 1879. V. 70

MELVIL, JAMES
The Memoires of Sir James Melvil of Hal-Hill; Containing an Impartial Account of the Most Remarkable Affairs of State...Under the Reigns of.... London: 1683. V. 70

MELVILLE, GEORGE W.
In The Lena Delta. Boston: 1884. V. 72

MELVILLE, HEBERT S.
Narrow Gauge Speedier than Broad Gauge Railways, as Well as Cheaper. London: 1846. V. 68

MELVILLE, HERMAN
Battle-Pieces and Aspects of the War. New York: 1866. V. 68; 70; 72
Benito Cereno. London: 1926. V. 69; 71; 72
The Confidence Man: His Masquerade. New York: 1857. V. 68; 72
The Encantadas; or, Enchanted Isles. Burlingame: 1940. V. 73
Israel Potter: His Fifty Years of Exile. New York: 1855. V. 68; 70
John Marr and Other Poems. Princeton: 1922. V. 70; 73
Journal of a Visit to London and the Continent. Cambridge: 1948. V. 70
Mardi; and a Voyage Thither. New York: 1849. V. 70
Moby Dick. London: 1851. V. 71; 72; 73
Moby Dick. New York: 1851. V. 68; 70; 71; 72; 73
Moby Dick. Chicago: 1930. V. 68
Moby Dick. New York: 1930. V. 72
Moby Dick. Brattleboro: 1943. V. 69
Moby Dick. Berkeley: 1981. V. 70; 72
Omoo: a Narrative of Adventures in the South Seas. London: 1847. V. 68; 72
Omoo: a Narrative of Adventures in the South Seas. New York: 1847. V. 70; 73
The Piazza Tales. New York: 1856. V. 68; 69; 70
Pierre; or the Ambiguities. New York: 1852. V. 70
Pierre, or the Ambiguities. New York: 1929. V. 68
Redburn: His First Voyage. New York: 1849. V. 69
The Refugee. (Israel Potter). Philadelphia: 1865. V. 71
Selected Poems of Herman Melville. London: 1943. V. 69
Typee. New York: 1846. V. 68; 70; 71; 72
Typee. London: 1850. V. 68; 71
Typee. New York: 1935. V. 69
White Jacket; or, the World in a Man-of-War. London: 1853. V. 68; 71; 72
The Works.... London: 1922-1924. V. 71

MELVILLE, LEWIS
The London Scene. London: 1926. V. 71

MEMOIRS, British And Foreign, Of the Lives And Families Of The Most Illustrious Persons Who Dy'ed In The Year 1711. London: 1712. V. 72

MEMOIRS of a London Doll Written by Herself. Boston: 1852. V. 70

MEMOIRS of a Stomach. London. V. 68

MEMOIRS of an Oxford Scholar. London: 1756. V. 68

MEMOIRS of Count Boruwlaski.... Durham: 1820. V. 71

THE MEMOIRS of the Harcourt Family; a Tale for Young Ladies. London: 1816. V. 70

MEMOIRS of the Lord Viscount Dundee, The Highland Clans, and the Massacre of Glenco . . . London: 1714. V. 71

MEMORABLES of the Montgomeries, a Narrative in Rhyme, Composed Before the Present Century. Glasgow: 1770. V. 69

THE MEMORANDUMS of John Watts. 1950. V. 69

MEMORIAL Cyclopedia of New Jersey. Newark: 1915. V. 71

MEMORIAL Sketch of William Frederick Poole. Chicago: 1895. V. 71

MEMORIAL Tributes to Walker Percy. 1991. V. 71; 73

MEMORIALS and Letters Relating to the History of Britain in the Reign of James the First. Glasgow: 1766. V. 69

MEMORIALS Concerning Several Ministers, And Others Deceased; Of The Religious Society Of Friends; With Some Of Their Last Expressions. New York: 1814. V. 72

MEMORY'S Gift. New York: 1849?. V. 69

MEN of California. San Francisco: 1900-1902. V. 68

MEN of California: Western Personalities and Their Affiliations. San Francisco/Los Angeles: 1925. V. 68

MENABONI, ATHOS
Menaboni's Birds. New York: 1950. V. 70; 72

MENCKEN, ALICE DAVIS
On the Side of Mercy: Problems in Social Readjustment. New York: 1933. V. 68

MENCKEN, HENRY L.
The American Credo. New York: 1920. V. 69
The American Language. New York: 1919. V. 73
Christmas Story. New York: 1946. V. 70; 71
Heathen Days 1890-1936. New York: 1943. V. 68; 70
Heliogabalus: A Buffoonery in Three Acts. New York: 1920. V. 72
A Little Book in C Major. New York: 1916. V. 70
Menckeniana: a Schimpflexikon. New York: 1928. V. 69; 71; 73
Minority Report: H. L. Mencken's Notebooks. New York: 1956. V. 70
Prejudices Second Series. New York: 1920. V. 68
A Second Mencken Chrestomathy. New York: 1995. V. 72
Treatise on Right and Wrong. New York: 1934. V. 69
Ventures Into Verse. Baltimore: 1903. V. 73

MENDELSHON, JANE
I Was Amelia Earhart. New York: 1996. V. 71

MENDELSOHN, HARVEY L.
Bauhaus Photography. Cambridge: 1985. V. 70

MENDELSOHN, JANE
I Was Amelia Earhart. New York: 1996. V. 69; 70; 72; 73
Innocence. New York: 2000. V. 72

MENDELSSOHN, MOSES
Phadon Oder Uber die Unsterblichkeit der Seele. Berlin: 1767. V. 73

MENDES DA COSTA, JACOB
The Proceedings at Large in the Arches Court of Canterbury, Between Mr. Jacob Mendes Da Costa and Mrs. Catharine Da Costa Villa Real, Both of the Jewish Religion and Cousin Germans. 1734. V. 70

MENDHAM, JOSEPH
An Account of the Indexes, Both Prohibitory and Expurgatory, of the Church of Rome. London: 1826. V. 68

MENESTRIER, CLAUDE FRANCOIS
Traite des Tournois, Iovstes, Carrovsels, et Avtres Spectacles Pvlics. Lyon: 1669. V. 72

MENGARINI, GREGORY
Recollections of the Flathead Mission.... Glendale: 1977. V. 72; 73

MENGER, ANTON
Das Burgerliche Recht und die Besitzlosen Volksklassen. Tubingen: 1890. V. 70

MENINSKI, FRANCISZEK
Grammatica Seu Institutio Policae Linguae, in Qua Etymologia, Syntaxis & Reliquae Partes Exacte Tractantur. Dantisci: 1649. V. 69

MENKEN, ADAH ISAACS
Infelicia. London: 1868. V. 70
Infelicia. London/Paris/New York: 1869. V. 70
Infelicia. Philadelphia: 1888. V. 68

MENNIE, DONALD
The Pageant of Peking Comprising Sixty-Six Vandyck Photogravures of Peking and Environs from Photographs.... Shanghai: 1920. V. 69; 71

MENNINGER, E. A.
Color in the Sky, Flowering Trees in Our Landscape. 1975. V. 73
Colors in the Sky. Stuart: 1975. V. 68; 71
Flowering Trees of the World, for Tropics and Warm Climates. New York: 1962. V. 71

MENNINGER, KARL
Sparks. New York: 1973. V. 69

MENOCHIUS, JACOBUS
...De Praesumptionibus, Coniecturis, Signis & Indicis, in Sex Distincta Libros, et recens in Luca Edita: Varia.... Coloniae: 1595. V. 72

MENPES, MORTIMER
China. London: 1909. V. 71
War Impressions. London: 1901. V. 71
Whistler As I Knew Him. London: 1904. V. 71; 72

MENSAERT, G. P.
Le Peintre Amateur et Curieux, ou Description Generale des Tableaux des plus Habiles Maitres qui Font l'Ornement des Eglises, Couvents, Abbayes, Prieures & Cabinets.... London: 1854. V. 69

MENTEATH, A. STUART, MRS.
Lays of the Kirk and Covenant. Edinburgh: 1850. V. 69

MENTEL, JACOBUS
De Vera Typographia Origine Paraenesis.... Paris: 1650. V. 73

MENTRE, MIREILLE
Illuminated Manuscripts of Medieval Spain. New York: 1996. V. 70

MENZEL, WOLFGANG
Europe in MDCCCXL. Edinburgh: 1841. V. 68

MENZIES' Vignette Views of the Lakes of Cumberland and Westmoreland.... Edinburgh: 1860. V. 72

MENZIES, ROBERT
A Dissertation on Respiration. Edinburgh: 1796. V. 69

MENZIES, W.
The Salmon. 1931. V. 68

MERA, H. P.
The Alfred I. Barton Collection of Southwestern Textiles. Santa Fe: 1949. V. 71
Lincoln Black on Red. Santa Fe: 1931. V. 69
Navajo Textile Arts. Santa Fe: 1947. V. 69; 70
Pueblo Indian Embroidery. Santa Fe: 1943. V. 68; 69; 73
The Rainbird - a Study in Pueblo Design. Santa Fe: 1937. V. 69
Reconnaissance and Excavations in Southeastern New Mexico. Menasha: 1938. V. 68; 73
Style Trends of Pueblo Pottery. Santa Fe: 1939. V. 70; 73

MERCATI, MICHELE
De Gli Obelischi Roma. Roma: 1589. V. 68; 70; 72

MERCER, A. S.
The Banditti of the Plains or the Cattlemen's Invasion of Wyoming in 1892. 1894. V. 68
The Banditti of the Plains, or the Cattlemen's Invasion of Wyoming in 1892. San Francisco: 1935. V. 71; 72
Wyoming in 1892 on the Cattleman's Invasion of the Bandit of the Plains. San Francisco: 1936. V. 69; 71

MERCER, CHARLES FENTON
A Discourse on Popular Education: Delivered in the Church at Princeton...September 26, 1826. Princeton: 1826. V. 71

MERCER, H. C.
The Lenape Stone, or the Indians and the Mammoth. New York: 1885. V. 69

MERCHANT, THOMAS, PSEUD.
Peace and Trade; War and Taxes; Or, the Irreparable Damage of Our Trade in Case of War. London: 1729. V. 73

MERCIER, LOUIS SEBASTIEN
Memoirs of the Year Two Thousand Five Hundred. Philadelphia: 1795. V. 68; 70; 73

MERCIER, VIVIAN
1000 Years of Irish Prose. New York: 1953. V. 70

MERCURIALE, GIROLAMO
De Arte Gymnastica Libri Sex. Venice: 1601. V. 71
De Arte Gymnastica Libri Sex. Amsterdam: 1672. V. 68

MEREDITH, GEORGE
Ballads and Poems of Tragic Life. London: 1887. V. 73
Diana of the Crossways. London: 1885. V. 73
The Egoist. London: 1879. V. 73
The Egoist. London: 1880. V. 73
An Essay on Comedy and the Uses of the Comic Spirit. London: 1897. V. 68; 72
The George Meredith Birthday Book. London: 1898. V. 70
Letters of George Meredith. London: 1912. V. 73
The Letters of George Meredith to Alice Meynell with Annotations Thereto 1896-1907. London: 1923. V. 71
Letters to Alice Meynell 1896-1907.... London: 1923. V. 68; 71
Modern Love. Portland: 1891. V. 73
Modern Love and Poems of the English Roadside. London: 1862. V. 68; 71; 73
The Nature Poems. London: 1898. V. 73
One of Our Conquerors. London: 1891. V. 73
Poems. 1851. V. 73
Poems and Lyrics of the Joy of Earth. London: 1883. V. 73
Poems: the Empty Purse with Odes to the Comic Spirit, to Youth in Memory and Verses. London: 1892. V. 73
A Reading of Earth. London and New York: 1888. V. 73
A Reading of Life. London: 1901. V. 73
Selected Poems. Westminster: 1897. V. 72
The Shaving of Shagpat. An Arabian Entertainment. London: 1856. V. 73
The Works of George Meredith. New York: 1909-1912. V. 72

MEREDITH, HUGH
An Account of the Cape Fear Country 1731. Perth Amboy: 1922. V. 71

MEREDITH, JAMES CREED
Proportional Representation in Ireland. 1913. V. 69

MEREDITH, LOUISA ANNE TWAMLEY
My Home in Tasmania, During a Residence of Nine Years. London: 1852. V. 73
Notes and Sketches of New South Wales, During a Residence in that Colony from 1839 to 1844. London: 1844. V. 71
Our Wild Flowers Familiarly Described and Illustrated. London: 1843. V. 68
Some of My Bush Friends in Tasmania. London: 1860. V. 71

MEREDITH, MARGARET
Adventure for Jane. London: 1946. V. 69

MEREDITH, ROY
Mr. Lincoln's Camera Man. New York: 1946. V. 70

MEREDITH, WILLIAM
The Wreck of the Thresher. New York: 1964. V. 68

MERIGOT, JAMES
Promenades ou Itineraire des Jardins de Chantilly.... Paris: 1791. V. 68
A Select Collection of Views and Ruins in Rome and Its Vicinity. London: 1815-1816. V. 69
Select Collections of Views and Ruins in Rome and Its Vicinity. London. V. 71

MERIMEE, PROSPER
Carmen. 1941. V. 69; 72
Carmen. New York: 1941. V. 68

MERINGTON, MARGUERITE
The Custer Story. New York: 1950. V. 68

MERITON, THOMAS
Love and War. London: 1658. V. 72

MERIWETHER, ROBERT L.
The Expansion of South Carolina 1729-1765. Kingsport: 1940. V. 73

MERK, FREDERICK
Fur Trade and Empire, George Simpson's Journal. Cambridge: 1931. V. 70

MERKEL, ANDREW
Schooner Bluenose. Toronto: 1948. V. 68

MERKLEY, CHRISTOPHER
Biography of.... Salt Lake City: 1887. V. 68; 73

MERKIN, R.
Velvet Eden: The Richard Merkin Collection of Erotic Photography. New York: 1979. V. 68

MERLET, JEAN
L'Abrege des Bons Fruits, Avec la Maniere de les Connoitre & de Cultiver les Arbres. Paris: 1690. V. 70

Traite de la Connoissance des Bons Fruits, Avec la Maniere de Cultiver Toutes Sortes d'Arbres Fruitiers, Suivi, d'une Instruction Pour Ceux quie Veulent, conserver des fruits.... Paris: 1782. V. 71

MERREL, CONCORDIA
The Marriage of Anne. New York: 1927. V. 71

MERRETT, HENRY S.
A Practical Treatise on the Science of Land and Engineering Surveying, Levelling, Estimating Quantities &c. London: 1887. V. 71

MERRIAM, C. H.
The Mammals of the Adirondack Region, Northeastern New York.... New York: 1886. V. 72

MERRIAM, C. HART
The Dawn of the World, Myths and Weird Tales.. Cleveland: 1910. V. 68; 73

MERRIAM, GEORGE S.
The Life ad Times of Samuel Bowles. New York: 1885. V. 69

MERRIAM, JOHN C.
The Felidae of Rancho La Brea. Washington: 1932. V. 72

MERRICK, GEORGE BYRON
Old Times on the Upper Mississippi - The Recollections of a Steam Boat Pilot from 1854 to 1863. Cleveland: 1909. V. 70

MERRICK, HUGH
The Alps in Colour. London: 1970. V. 69
Rambles in the Alps. London: 1951. V. 69

MERRICK, RICE
A Book of Glamorganshire's Antiquities. 1825. V. 73
A Book of Glamorganshire's Antiquities. Middle Hill: 1825. V. 68

MERRIFIELD, MARY PHILADELPHIA
Original Treatises, Dating from the Twelfth to the Eighteenth Centuries on the Arts of Painting in Oil, Miniature, Mosaic and On Glass.... London: 1849. V. 69
A Sketch of the Natural History of Brighton and Its Vicinity. Brighton: 1864. V. 68

MERRILD, KNUD
A Poet and Two Painters. London: 1938. V. 72

MERRILL, DANIEL
The Mode and Subjects of Baptism Examined, in Seven Sermons. Burlington: 1805. V. 71

MERRILL, E. D.
A Bibliography of Eastern Asiatic Botany. Jamaica Plain: 1938. V. 68; 72
A Botanical Bibliography of the Islands of the Pacific. Washington: 1947. V. 71
On Miguel's Kwangtung Species as Based on Krone's Collection.... Hong Kong: 1930. V. 70
Polynesian Botanical Bibliography 1773-1935. Honolulu: 1937. V. 71

MERRILL, JAMES
Bronze. New York: 1984. V. 73
The (Diblos) Notebook. New York: 1965. V. 69
The Image Maker: a Play in One Act. 1986. V. 73
Japan: Prose of Departure. New York: 1987. V. 73
Jim's Book: a Collection of Poems and Short Stories. New York: 1942. V. 73
Last Poems. New York: 1998. V. 69; 73
Marbled Paper. Salem: 1982. V. 73
Nine Lives. New York & Kripplebush: 1993. V. 73
Occasions and Inscriptions. New York: 1984. V. 69; 73
Overdue Pilgrimage to Nova Scotia. New York: 1990. V. 73
Short Stories. Pawlet: 1954. V. 69; 73
Souvenirs. New York: 1984. V. 73
The Thousand and Second Night. Athens: 1963. V. 69; 73
Water Street. Poems. New York: 1962. V. 69; 73
Yannina. New York: 1973. V. 73
The Yellow Pages. 59 Poems. Cambridge: 1974. V. 69

MERRILL, LOUIS P.
Aristocrats of the Cow Country. 1973. V. 70

MERRILL, MARION
The Animated Pinocchio. New York: 1945. V. 70

MERRIMAN, N. J.
The Kafir, the Hottentot and the Frontier Farmer. London: 1853. V. 71

MERRIT, PERCIVAL
The True Story of the So-Called Love Letters of Mrs. Piozzi.... Cambridge: 1927. V. 69

MERRITT, A.
The Fox Woman (&) Hannes Bok. The Blue Pagoda. New York: 1946. V. 72
The Moon Pool. New York. V. 68

MERRITT, DORA W.
The Story of Four Little Sabots. London. V. 72

MERRITT, EDWIN A.
Recollections 1828-1911. Albany: 1911. V. 73

MERRITT, H. HOUSTON
The Cerebrospinal Fluid. Philadelphia: 1938. V. 68; 71; 73

MERRITT, HENRY
Dirt and Pictures, Separated in the Works of the Old Masters. London: 1854. V. 68; 72

THE MERRY Alphabet A to Z. New York: 1888. V. 73

MERRY and Bright. Dundee: 1915. V. 71

MERRY Days at Home. London: 1910. V. 70

MERRY Dick. 1890. V. 70

MERRY, ELEANOR C.
The Flaming Door: a Preliminary Study of the Mission of the Celtic Folk-Soul by Means of Legends and Myths. 1936. V. 69; 73

MERRY Times Pleasant Pages for Every One with Illustrations in Color and Photogravure. Boston: 1890. V. 73

MERRYMAN, BRYAN
The Midnight Court - a Rhythmical Bacchanalia from the Irish of.... London and Dublin: 1945. V. 69

MERRYMAN, JOHN
The Merryman Habeas Corpus Case, Baltimore. Jackson: 1861. V. 70

MERRY'S Museum, an Illustrated Magazine for Boys and Girls. Boston: 1868. V. 68
MERRY'S Museum, an Illustrated Magazine for Boys and Girls. Boston: 1869. V. 68

MERSEREAU, JOHN
Murder Loves Company. Philadelphia: 1940. V. 69

MERSHON, GRACE L. O.
My Folks. Story of the Forefathers of Oliver Francis Mershon, M.D. 1946. V. 71

MERSHON, WILLIAM B.
Recollections of My Fifty Years Hunting and Fishing. Boston: 1923. V. 69

MERTON, THOMAS
A Catch of Anti-Letters. Thomas Merton, Robert Lax. Kansas City: 1978. V. 68
The Christmas Sermons of BL. Guerric of Igny. Louisville: 1959. V. 68; 69
The Climate of Monastic Prayer by Thomas Merton. Trappist, Kentucky: 1965. V. 73
Early Poems 1940-1942. Lexington: 1971. V. 69; 73
Events and Pseudo-Events: Letter to a Southern Churchman by Thomas Merton for Katallagete, February 1966. Trappist: 1966. V. 73
A Man in the Divided Sea. New York: 1946. V. 68
The Spiritual Father in the Desert Tradition. Trappist: 1966. V. 73
The Tears of Blind Lions. New York: 1949. V. 70
The Tower of Babel. New York and Hamburg: 1957. V. 68; 69; 71

MERVIN, AUDLEY
A Speech Made by Captaine Audley Mervin to the Upper House of Parliament in Ireland March 4, 1640. Together with Certaine Articles (of High Treason) Against Sir Richard Bolton Lord Chancellor, John Lord Bishop of Derrie, Sir Gerard Lowther.... London: 1641. V. 69

MERWIN, SAMUEL
Knife in My Back. New York: 1945. V. 70
The Trufflers. Indianapolis: 1916. V. 71

MERWIN, W. S.
The Dancing Bears. New Haven: 1954. V. 72
The Folding Cliffs. New York: 1998. V. 72
Fox Sleep. New York: 1996. V. 73
Green With Beasts. London: 1956. V. 72
Houses and Travellers. New York: 1977. V. 72
KOA. New York: 1988. V. 73
A Mask For Janus. New Haven: 1952. V. 72
Signs. Iowa City: 1971. V. 73
Unframed Originals: Recollections. New York: 1982. V. 73

MERY, JEAN
Oeuvres Completes (Anatomie, Physiologie, Chirurgie).... Paris: 1888. V. 73

MERY, JOSEPH
Les Etoiles. Paris: 1849. V. 72

MERYMAN, RICHARD
Andrew Wyeth. Boston: 1968. V. 68; 70; 71
Louis Armstrong--A Self-Portrait. New York: 1971. V. 71

MERYON, EDWARD
On the Functions of the Sympatheti System of Nerves, as a Physiological Basis for a Rational System of Therapeutics. London: 1872. V. 69

MESCHAN, ISADORE
An Altas of Normal Radiographic Anatomy. Philadelphia: 1959. V. 68

MESENS, E. L. T.
Troisieme Front - Poems de Guerre, Suivi de Pieces Detachees. London: 1944. V. 70; 71

MESERVE, FREDERICK HILL
The Photographs of Abraham Lincoln. New York: 1944. V. 73

MESNY, WILLIAM
Tungking. London: 1884. V. 71

MESSALINA.. 1821. V. 73

MESSITER, CHARLES A.
Sport and Adventures Among The North-American Indians. New York: 1965. V. 72

MESSLER, ABRAHAM
Centennial History of Somerset County. Somerville: 1878. V. 71
First Things in Old Somerset. Somerville: 1899. V. 71
Forty Years at Raritan. New York: 1873. V. 71

MESSNER, R.
The Big Walls. 1978. V. 68
Everest. 1979. V. 73
K2: Mountain of Mountains. 1981. V. 73
Mountain and Mountains. 1981. V. 68

MESSNER, REINHOLD
All 14 Eight-Thousanders. 1993. V. 69

MESTROVIC, IVAN
Gospa Od Andela; Zaduzbina Porodice Racic Cavtat. Zagreb: 1937. V. 72

METCALF, PAUL
Firebird. Minneapolis: 1987. V. 73

METCALF, SAMUEL L.
A Collection of Some of the Most Interesting Narratives of Indian Warfare in the West.... Lexington: 1821. V. 68; 73
A New Theory of Terrestrial Magnetism. New York: 1833. V. 73

METCALFE, C. R.
Anatomy of the Monocotyledons. Oxford: 1982. V. 70

METCALFE, JOHN
The Smoking Leg. New York: 1926. V. 69

METCALFE, WALTER C.
The Visitation of Berkshire in 1566, by William Harvey, Clarenceux Rex Armorum. Exeter: 1883-1885. V. 71

METCHKINOFF, OLGA
Life Of Elie Metchnikoff 1845-1916. With a Preface By Sir Ray Lankester. London: 1921. V. 68; 72

METCOFF, JACK
Hereditary, Developmental and Immunologic Aspects of Kidney Disease. 1962. V. 68

METHESIUS, JOHANNES
Bergpostilla, Oder Sarepta, Darinn von Allerley Bergkwerck und Metallen.... Nurnberg: 1578. V. 68

METHLEY, NOEL T.
The Life-Boat and Its Story. Philadelphia: 1912. V. 70

METHODIST EPISCOPAL CHURCH
The Doctrines and Discipline of the Methodist Episcopal Church in America, Revised and Approved at the General Conference Held at Baltimore... in November 1792.... Philadelphia: 1792. V. 68

METHODIST MISSIONARY SOCIETY
Letter from the Methodist Missionary Society to the SuperintendentGeneral of Indian Affairs Respecting British Columbia Troubles, with Affidavits, Declarations, etc. Toronto: 1889. V. 70

METHVEN, ROBERT
The Log of a Merchant Officer. London: 1854. V. 71

METHVIN, J. J.
Andele, or the Mexican Kiowa Captive. Aranarko: 1899. V. 73

METLAKE, GEORGE
The Life and Writings of St. Columban.... Philadelphia: 1914. V. 70

METRAUX, ALFRED
Voodoo in Haiti. London: 1959. V. 69

A METRICAL Description of a Fancy Ball Given at Washington, 9th April 1858. Washington: 1858. V. 69

METRO-VICK SUPPLIES LTD.
Electric Light Fittings. 1928. V. 69

METROPOLIS, N.
A History of Computing in the Twentieth Century: a Collection of Essays. New York: 1980. V. 72

METROPOLITAN MUSEUM OF ART, NEW YORK
The Painterly Print: Monotypes from the 17th to the 20th Century. 1981. V. 69; 72

METTENIUS, C.
Alexander Braun's Leben, Nach Seinem Handshriftlichen Nachlass. Berlin: 1882. V. 70

METTLER, CECILIA C.
History of Medicine. Philadelphia: 1947. V. 70; 71; 73

METTLER, FRED A.
Psychosurgical Problems. The Columbia Greystone Associates Second Group. Philadelphia: 1952. V. 70; 71

METZ, LEON C.
Dallas Stoudenmire - El Paso Marshall. Austin: 1969. V. 73
Fort Bliss; An Illustrated History. El Paso: 1981. V. 72
John Selman - Texas Gunfighter. New York: 1966. V. 68
John Wesley Harden, Dark Angel of Texas. El Paso: 1996. V. 72

METZLER, NORBERT
Illustrated Halifax. Its Civil, Military and Naval History.... Montreal: 1891. V. 73

MEURSIUS, JOHANNES
Historica Danica Pariter & Belgica; uno Tomo Comprehensa.... Amsterdam: 1638. V. 70

MEW, CHARLOTTE
The Farmer's Bride. London: 1916. V. 72

M'EWEN, G.
The Culture of the Peach and Nectarine. Groombridge: 1859. V. 73

MEWSHAW, MICHAEL
Man in Motion. New York: 1970. V. 68; 71

MEXIA, PEDRO
The Historie of all the Romane Emperors.... London: 1604. V. 71

MEYER, ALFRED
Prefontal Leucotomy and Related Operations: Anatomical Aspects of Success and Failure. Edinburgh: 1954. V. 68

MEYER, ARTHUR WILLIAM
An Analysis of the De Generatione Animalium of William Harvey. Stanford: 1936. V. 68

MEYER, CARL
Nach Dem Sacramento. Germany: 1855. V. 68

MEYER, CHARLES
The Shadows of Life. London: 1899?. V. 68

MEYER, CONRAD FERDINAND
The Saint. New York: 1930. V. 69

MEYER, ERNEST H. F.
Geschichte der Botanik. Konigsberg: 1854-1857. V. 72

MEYER, F.
Marc Chagall: His Graphic Work. New York: 1957. V. 72

MEYER, F. J.
Steam Towing on Rivers and Canals by Means of a Submerged Cable. London: 1876. V. 72

MEYER, H. L.
Coloured Illustrations of British Birds. London: 1842-1850. V. 73

MEYER, HANS
Der Kilimandjaro. Reisen und Studien.... Berlin: 1900. V. 71

MEYER, JEROME S.
Advice on the Care of Babies (By a Bachelor Who Can't Bear Them). New York: 1927. V. 72

MEYER, THOMAS
At Dusk Iridescent: a Gathering of Poems 1972-1997. Winston Salem: 1999. V. 73
May. Champaign: 1983. V. 73
Monotypes and Tracings. German Romantics. London: 1994. V. 73
Poikilos. Urbana: 1971. V. 73
Sonnets and Tableaux. London: 1987. V. 73

MEYER, VIRGINIA M.
Adventurers of Purse and Person, Va. 1607-1624/5. 1987. V. 72

MEYER DE SCHAUENSEE, R.
A Guide to the Birds of Venezuela. Princeton: 1978. V. 73
The Species of Birds of South America and their Distribution. Philadelphia: 1966. V. 73

MEYEROWITZ, JOEL
Cape Light: Color Photos. Boston: 1978. V. 68

MEYERS, ALFRED
Murder Ends the Song. New York: 1941. V. 72

MEYERS, JEFFREY
Hemingway: the Critical Heritage. London: 1982. V. 71

MEYERS, WILLIAM H.
Naval Sketches of the War in California. New York: 1939. V. 70

MEYERSTEIN, E. H. W.
Bollond and other stories. London: 1958. V. 72
Terence in Love. London: 1928. V. 71

MEYNELL, ALICE
Mary, the Mother of Jesus: an Essay. London: 1912. V. 70; 71; 72
Poems. London: 1893. V. 72
Preludes. London: 1874. V. 72
Ten Poems 1913-1915. 1915. V. 73

MEYNELL, FRANCIS
Poems and Pieces 1911-1961. London: 1961. V. 69; 71
Typography. The Written Word and Printed Word.... London. V. 70

MEYNELL, LAURENCE W.
The Door in the Wall. New York: 1937. V. 70
The Shadow and the Stone. New York: 1929. V. 72

MEYNELL, VIOLA
The Vest of Friends. London: 1956. V. 72

MEYNELL, WILFRID
The Child Set in the Midst, by Modern Poets. London: 1892. V. 71

MEYRICK, W.
The New Family Herbal or Domestic Physician. Birmingham: 1790. V. 69

MEYRINK, GUSTAV
The Golem. Boston: 1928. V. 71
The Golem. London: 1928. V. 70

MEZZROW, MEZZ
Really the Blues. New York: 1946. V. 69; 73

M'GAVIN, WILLIAM
The Protestant Reformation Vindicated; a Reply to Cobbett's History of the Reformation. Glasgow: 1826. V. 71

M'GOVAN, JAMES
Brought to Bay, or Experience of a City Detective. Edinburgh: 1884. V. 68

M'GREGOR, THE BROTHERS
The Trials of James, Duncan and Robert M'Gregor, Three Sons of the Celebrated Rob Roy, Before the High Court of Justiciary, in the years 1752, 1753, and 1754. Edinburgh: 1818. V. 71

MICHAEL, J. T.
Report of the Trial of Rev. J. T. Michael, a Traveling Elder in the Newark Annual Conference of the Methodist Episcopal Church. Phillipsburg: 1880. V. 71

MICHAELIS, H. VON
Wings of the Wild. Capetown: 1953. V. 68

MICHAELS, ANNE
Fugitive Pieces. Toronto: 1996. V. 69
Fugitive Pieces. New York: 1997. V. 68; 69; 72
Poems. New York: 2000. V. 69

MICHAELS, BARBARA
Ammie, Come Home. New York: 1968. V. 68
The Grey Beginning. New York: 1984. V. 71
The Master of Blacktower. 1966. V. 71
Patriot's Dream. New York: 1976. V. 68

MICHAELS, LEONARD
Going Places. New York: 1969. V. 69
The Men's Club. New York: 1981. V. 72

MICHALS, DUANE
Album - the Portraits of Duane Michals 1958-1988. Pasadena: 1988. V. 68
Changements. Paris: 1981. V. 70
Duane Duck: Photographs/Sequences/Texts 1958-1984. Oxford: 1984. V. 70
Real Dreams: Photo Stories. Danbury: 1976. V. 68

MICHAUD, JOSEPH F.
History of the Crusades. Philadelphia: 1875. V. 71
History of the Crusades. Philadelphia: 1890. V. 70

MICHAUX, A.
Flora Boreali-Americana. Paris and Strasburg: 1803. V. 69

MICHAUX, FRANCOIS ANDRE
The North American Sylva, or a Description of the Forest Trees, of the United States, Canada, and Nova Scotia. Philadelphia: 1817-1819. V. 68
Travels to the Westward of the Allegany Mountains, in the States of Ohio, Kentucky and Tennessee, and Return to Charlestwon, through the Upper Carolinas.... London: 1805. V. 68

MICHAUX, HENRI
Henri Michaux: A Selection. Consigny: 1979. V. 73
The Major Ordeals of the Mind and the Countless Minor Ones. London: 1974. V. 71

MICHEAUX, OSCAR
The Conquest...By a Negro Pioneer. Lincoln, NE: 1913. V. 72
The Wind from Nowhere. New York: 1944. V. 69; 71

MICHEL, M. SCOTT
Dear Dead Harry. New York: 1949. V. 68

MICHELET, JULES
The Mountain. London: 1886. V. 69
The People.... London: 1846. V. 68
The Women of the French Revolution. Philadelphia: 1855. V. 73

MICHELI, MARIO DE
Siqueiros. New York: 1968. V. 71

MICHELI, PIER ANTONIO
Nova Plantarum Genera.... Florence: 1729. V. 68; 70; 72

MICHELL, E. B.
The Art and Practice of Hawking. 1900. V. 68; 70; 73

MICHELL, THOMAS
Russian Pictures Drawn With Pen and Pencil. London: 1889. V. 72

MICHELOTTI, FRANCESCO DOMENICO
Spierimenti Idraulici...a Confermare la Teorica e Facilitare la Pratica del Musurare le Acque Correnti.... Turin: 1767-1771. V. 72

MICHELS, NICHOLAS A.
Blood Supply and Anatomy of the Upper Abdominal Organs with a Descriptive Atlas. Philadelphia: 1955. V. 71

MICHELSON, ALBERT ABRAHAM
On the Application of Interference Methods to Astronomical Measurements. 1920. V. 69

MICHELSON, MIRIAM
Petticoat King. New York: 1929. V. 69

MICHENER, JAMES ALBERT
The Bridge at Andau. New York: 1957. V. 69
The Bridges at Toko-Ri. New York: 1953. V. 68; 70
Caravans. New York: 1963. V. 71
Centennial. New York: 1974. V. 70; 71; 73
Centennial. (with) About Centennial. New York: 1974. V. 69
A Century of Sonnets. Austin: 1997. V. 73
Chesapeake. New York: 1978. V. 70; 71
The Drifters. New York: 1971. V. 69; 72
The Eagle and the Raven. Austin: 1990. V. 71
The Floating World. New York: 1954. V. 70; 72
The Good Mother. New York: 1986. V. 71
Hawaii. New York: 1959. V. 69; 71
The Hokusai Sketchbooks: Selections from Manga. Rutland: 1958. V. 72
Iberia. New York: 1968. V. 70; 72; 73
Japanese Prints from the Early Masters to the Modern. Rutland: 1960. V. 73
Kent State: What Happened and Why. New York: 1971. V. 73
Legacy. New York: 1987. V. 69
Literary Reflections. Austin: 1993. V. 70; 71; 73
Mexico. New York: 1992. V. 68
The Mirror. New York: 1978. V. 72
My Lost Mexico. Austin: 1992. V. 71; 73
Nightmare Country. New York: 1981. V. 72
Rascals in Paradise. New York: 1957. V. 71
Recessional. Franklin Center: 1994. V. 68; 71
Recessional. New York: 1994. V. 69; 72
Report of the County Chairman. New York: 1961. V. 73
Sayonara. New York: 1954. V. 71; 72
The Source. New York: 1965. V. 71
South Pacific. San Diego: 1992. V. 73
Space. London: 1982. V. 68
Spence. New York: 1982. V. 72
Tales of the South Pacific. New York: 1947. V. 68; 70; 71
Tales of the South Pacific. New York: 1950. V. 68; 69; 71
Texas. Austin: 1986. V. 68; 71
The Threshold. New York: 1984. V. 72
Ventures in Editing. Huntington Beach: 1995. V. 71; 73

MICHIE, CHRISTOPHER YOUNG
The Larch. London: 1885. V. 70

MICHIGAN
Report of the State Board of Geological Survey of Michigan for the Year 1905. Lansing: 1906. V. 68

MICHIGAN CENTRAL RAILROAD
Mackinac Island and Michigan Resorts. 1927. V. 68
A Summer Note-Book. 1897. V. 69

MICHIGAN City Illustrated. 1900. V. 69

MICHIGAN STEEL BOAT CO., DETROIT
Steel Motor Boats, Steel Racing Boats, Steel Launches.... 1914. V. 69

MICHLER, N.
Routes from the Western Boundary of Arkansas to Santa Fe and the Valley of the Rio Grande - 31st Congress 1st Session, House of Representatives. Washinbton: 1850. V. 70

MICKEL, SAMUEL L.
The Mickels of South Jersey. Bridgeton: 1955. V. 71

MICKIEWICZ, ADAM
Forefathers Part III. London: 1946. V. 70

MICKLE, ISAAC
Reminiscences of Old Gloucester; or Incidents in the History of the Counties of Gloucester Atlantic and Camden, New Jersey. Philadelphia: 1845. V. 71

MICQUELLUS, JOHANNES LODOICUS
Aureliae Vrbis memorabilis ab Anglis Obsidio, Anno. 1428. Paris: 1560. V. 68; 69; 73

MICROCOSM of Oxford. London: 1840-1850. V. 70

THE MICROCOSM of London, or London in Miniature. London: 1808-1810. V. 68

MIDDENDORP, G. M.
The Hero in the Feminine Novel. Middelburg: 1931. V. 70

MIDDLEMASS, JEAN
Vaia's Lord. London: 1889. V. 68

MIDDLESEX County Directory. 1896. New Brunswick: 1896. V. 72

MIDDLETON, ALICIA HOPTON
Life in Carolina and New England During the Nineteenth Century. Bristol: 1929. V. 71

MIDDLETON, BERNARD C.
A History of English Craft Bookbinding Technique. New York and London: 1963. V. 69
A History of English Craft Bookbinding Technique. London: 1978. V. 69

MIDDLETON, CHARLES
Picturesque and Architectural Views for Cottages, Farm Houses and Country Villas. London: 1795. V. 68; 70

MIDDLETON, CONYERS
The History of the Life of Marcus Tullius Cicero. London: 1741. V. 68; 73
The Origin of Printing: in Two Essays. London: 1774. V. 73

MIDDLETON, DOROTHY
Victorian Lady Travellers. London: 1965. V. 69

MIDDLETON, GEORGE
Hiss! Boom!! Blah!!!. New York: 1933. V. 71; 72

MIDDLETON, J. HENRY
The Engraved Gems of Classical Times. Cambridge: 1891. V. 72

MIDDLETON, RICHARD
The Day Before Yesterday. London: 1912. V. 68
Epigrams and Satyres. London: 1608. V. 73
Epigrams and Satyres. Edinburgh: 1840. V. 71

MIDDLETON, SCUDDER
Streets and Faces. Arlington NJ: 1917. V. 72

MIDDLETON, THOMAS
A Tragi-Comedie Called the Witch. London: 1778. V. 71

MIDDLETON, THOMAS C.
Historical Sketch of the Augustinian Monastery, College and Mission of St. Thomas of Villanova, Delaware Co., Pa. Philadelphia: 1893. V. 68

THE MIDNIGHT Spy; or A View of the Transactions of London and Westminster, from the Hours of Ten in the Evening, Till Five in the Morning.... London: 1766. V. 73

THE MIDSHIPMAN in China or Recollections of The Chinese. London: 1845. V. 72

A MIDSUMMER Night's Dream. London: 1914. V. 70

MIEGE, GUY
The New State of England Under Their Majesties K. William and Q. Mary in Three Parts. London: 1691. V. 68

MIERS, EARL SHENCK
Big Ben. Philadelphia: 1942. V. 72

MIES VAN DER ROHE, LUDWIG
Ludwig Mies Van der Rohe: Drawings in the Collection of the Museum of Modern Art. New York: 1969. V. 69

MIGEOD, FREDERICK W. H.
Across Equatorial Africa. London: 1923. V. 71

MIGHELS, PHILIP VERRILL
Buvver Jim's Baby. New York: 1904. V. 69

MIGNAN, ROBERT
Travels in Chaldaea. London: 1829. V. 71

MIKA, N.
Mosaic of Kingston. Belleville: 1969. V. 73

MIKKELSEN, EJNAR
Conquering the Arctic Ice. London: 1909. V. 71

MILBANK, CAROLINE REYNOLDS
Couture. The Great Designers. NY: 1985. V. 72

MILES, ANNE PETTE
Monmouth Families. 1980-1981. V. 71

MILES, DIONE
Something In Common. An I.W.W. Bibliography. Detroit: 1986. V. 68

MILES, EMMA BELL
Strains from a Dulcimore. Atlanta: 1930. V. 69

MILES, HENRY DOWNES
The Two Circuses and the Two Surrey Theatres. London: 1866. V. 72

MILES, KEITH
Bullet Hole. London: 1986. V. 70; 71
Double Eagle. London: 1987. V. 71

MILES, NELSON A.
Personal Recollections & Observations of...Embracing A Brief View.... Chicago: 1896. V. 69; 72
Personal Recollections of General Nelson A. Miles. Chicago/New York: 1897. V. 70

MILES, W. J.
Modern Practical Farriery. 1880. V. 68

MILES, WILLIAM
Journal of the Sufferings and Hardships of Capt. Parker H. French's Overland Expedition to California. Austin: 1965. V. 68

MILES, WILLIAM AUGUSTUS
A Letter to the Earl of Wycombe, &c, &c. from Mr. Miles on the Present State of Ireland. London: 1804. V. 69

MILHOUS, KATHERINE
The Egg Tree. New York: 1950. V. 72

MILITARY Events in Italy 1848-1849. London: 1851. V. 73

THE MILITIA and Patrol Laws of South Carolina. Columbia: 1842. V. 71

MILL, HUGH ROBERT
The English Lakes.... London: 1895. V. 71
The Life of Sir Ernest Shackleton. London: 1923. V. 69

MILL, JAMES
Analysis of the Phenomena of the Human Mind. London: 1878. V. 71; 73
Elements of Political Economy. London: 1824. V. 68
Elements of Political Economy. London: 1826. V. 68
Elements of Political Economy. London: 1844. V. 71; 73

MILL, JOHN STUART
Auguste Comte and Positivism. London: 1865. V. 71; 73
Autobiography. London: 1873. V. 68; 70; 71; 72
Autobiography. London: 1874. V. 71
Autobiography. New York: 1874?. V. 71
Considerations on Representative Government. London: 1861. V. 71
Dissertations and Discussions: Political, Philosophical and Historical.... London: 1859-1867. V. 71
Essays on some Unsettled Questions of Political Economy. London: 1877. V. 71
An Examination of Sir William Hamilton's Philosophy and of the Principal Philosophical Questions Discussed in His Writings. London: 1865. V. 71
The Letters. London: 1910. V. 68; 71; 73
Nature, The Utility of Religion and Theism. London: 1874. V. 71
Nature, The Utility of Religion and Theism. London: 1885. V. 71
On Liberty. London: 1859. V. 70
Principles of Political Economy. London: 1849. V. 71
Principles of Political Economy. London: 1852. V. 68
Principles of Political Economy. London: 1862. V. 69
Principles of Political Economy. London: 1865. V. 71
The Subjection of Women. London: 1869. V. 68; 69; 70; 71
The Subjection of Women. New York: 1869. V. 73
The Subjection of Women. Philadelphia: 1869. V. 73
The Subjection of Women. London: 1870. V. 71
The Subjection of Women. London: 1878. V. 71
A System of Logic, Ratiocinative and Inductive.... New York: 1848. V. 70
A System of Logic, Ratiocinative and Inductive.... London: 1865. V. 68; 71; 72
A System of Logic Ratiocinative and Inductive.... London: 1868. V. 71
A System of Logic Ratiocinative and Inductive.... London: 1872. V. 72
Thoughts on Parliamentary Reform. London: 1859. V. 71
Utilitarianism. London: 1863. V. 71
Utilitarianism. London: 1864. V. 71
Utilitarianism. London: 1888. V. 71

MILLAIS, JOHN GUILLE
A Breath from the Veldt. 1895. V. 69; 70
A Breath from the Veldt. London: 1899. V. 69
British Deer and Ground Game, Dogs, Guns and Rifles. 1913. V. 70; 73
British Deer and Their Horns. 1982. V. 73
British Diving Ducks. 1913. V. 70; 71
British Diving Ducks. London: 1913. V. 70; 73
Far Away Up the Nile. 1924. V. 70; 72; 73
Far Away Up the Nile. London: 1924. V. 69; 70; 71; 72
Game Birds and Shooting Sketches. 1892. V. 70; 71
Game Birds and Shooting Sketches. London: 1892. V. 70; 73
Game Birds and Shooting Sketches. 1894. V. 71
Life of Frederick Courtenay Selous. 1918. V. 70; 72
The Mammals of Great Britain and Ireland. London: 1904. V. 70; 73
The Mammals of Great Britain and Ireland. 1906. V. 70; 72
The Natural History of British Game Birds. 1909. V. 70; 71
The Natural History of British Game Birds. London: 1909. V. 73
The Natural History of the British Surface-Feeding Ducks. London: 1902. V. 73
Newfoundland and It's Untrodden Ways. 1907. V. 70; 72; 73
Newfoundland and Its Untrodden Ways. London: 1907. V. 71
Rhododendrons in Which Is Set Forth an Account of All Species of the Genus Rhododendron.... London: 1917-1924. V. 68; 70; 73
Wanderings and Memories. 1919. V. 70; 72
Wanderings and Memories. London: 1919. V. 72
The Wildflower in Scotland. 1901. V. 70; 71
The Wildflower in Scotland. 1974. V. 71

MILLAR, E. G.
The Luttrell Psalter. London: 1932. V. 70

MILLAR, JOHN
An Historical View of the English Government from the Settlement of the Saxons in Britain to the Accession, of the House of Stewart.... London: 1790. V. 68

MILLAR, MARGARET
The Iron Gates. New York: 1945. V. 68; 69

MILLAR, OLIVER
Italian Drawings and Paintings in the Queens Collection. 1965. V. 70

MILLAR, RONALD
The Affair, The New Men, The Masters: Three Plays Based on the Novels of C. P. Snow. London: 1964. V. 72
The Case in Question: a Play. London: 1975. V. 72

MILLARD, C.
The Printed Work of Claude Lovat Fraser. 1923. V. 68

MILLARD, RUTH TRACY
Candeflame. Philadelphia: 1938. V. 70

MILLAY, EDNA ST. VINCENT
The Buck in the Snow. London: 1928. V. 68
The Buck in the Snow. New York: 1929. V. 71
Edna St. Vincent Millay's Poems Selected for Young People. New York: 1929. V. 72
Fatal Interview. New York: 1931. V. 73
A Few Figs from Thistles. New York: 1922. V. 68
The King's Henchman. New York: 1927. V. 70
Make Bright the Arrows. New York: 1940. V. 71
Mine the Harvest. New York: 1954. V. 71
The Murder of Lidice. New York: 1942. V. 70; 71
Renascence and Other Poems. New York: 1917. V. 68
Second April. New York: 1921. V. 71
Wine from these Grapes and Epitaph for the Race of Man. New York: 1934. V. 69; 71

MILLBURN, JOHN R.
Adams of Fleet Street, Instrument Makers to King George III. Aldershot: 2000. V. 68

THE MILLENIUM; or, The Thousand Years of Prosperity, Promised to the Church of God...Shortly to Commence, and to be Carried on to Perfection.... Elizabeth Town: 1794. V. 71

MILLER & RICHARDS
Specimens of Book Newspaper Jobbing and Ornamental Types (1873). Lincolnshire: 1974. V. 70

MILLER, ADAM
Life in Other Worlds, Including a Brief Statement of the Origin and Progress of Life in Our World. Chicago: 1878. V. 72

MILLER, AGNES
The Colfax Book-Plate. New York: 1926. V. 69

MILLER, ALFRED JACOB
The West of Alfred Jacob Miller. Norman: 1951. V. 69

MILLER, ALICE DUER
Manslaughter. New York: 1922. V. 70
Women Are People!. New York: 1917. V. 70

MILLER, ANNA RIGGS
Letters from Italy, Describing the Manners, Customs, Antiquities, Paintings &c. of that Country in the Years MDCCLXX and MDCCLXXI, to a Friend Residing in France. Dublin: 1776. V. 73

MILLER, ANNE ARCHBOLD
The Little Old Outlaws. Chicago: 1910. V. 70

MILLER, ARTHUR
Arthur Miller's Collected Plays. New York: 1957. V. 73
Chinese Encounters. New York: 1979. V. 69; 72; 73
Collected Plays. New York: 1957. V. 73
Collected Plays. Franklin Center: 1980. V. 69; 71; 73
The Creation of the World and Other Business. New York: 1973. V. 68
The Crucible. New York: 1953. V. 69; 73
Death of a Salesman. London: 1949. V. 73
Death of a Salesman. New York: 1949. V. 68; 69; 70; 71; 72
Death of a Salesman. London: 1959. V. 71
Death of a Salesman. New York: 1981. V. 69; 73
Death of a Salesman. New York: 1984. V. 69; 71
Death of a Salesman. New York: 1999. V. 68; 69; 70; 73
An Enemy of the People. New York: 1951. V. 70
Focus. New York: 1945. V. 69
Homely Girl. New York: 1992. V. 70; 72
Homely Girl. New York: 1995. V. 71
I Don't Need You Any More. New York: 1967. V. 70
In Country. New York: 1977. V. 69
In Russia. New York: 1969. V. 69
Incident at Vichy. New York: 1965. V. 70
The Misfits. New York: 1961. V. 69; 70
The Misfits: The Story of a Shoot. London: 2000. V. 70
The Portable Arthur Miller. New York: 1971. V. 70
Salesman in Beijing. New York: 1984. V. 68
Situation Normal. New York: 1944. V. 68
Timebends: a Life. New York: 1987. V. 70

MILLER, D. HENRY
The Baptists of Trenton, 1787-1867: an Historical Discourse, Delivered at the First Baptist Church.... Trenton: 1867. V. 71

MILLER, DAVID E.
Hole-in-the-Rock - an Epic in the Colonization of the Great American West. Salt Lake City: 1959. V. 68; 73

MILLER, DAVID H.
Custer's Fall The Indians' Side of The Story. New York: 1957. V. 72
Ghost Dance. New York: 1959. V. 69; 72

MILLER, E. A. HASWELL
Military Drawings and Paintings in the Collection of Her Majesty the Queen. London: 1966-1970. V. 73

MILLER, EDGAR G.
American Antique Furniture. New York: 1937. V. 70

MILLER, EDWARD
The History and Antiquities of Doncaster and its Vicinity. Doncaster: 1804. V. 73

MILLER, ERNEST H.
Miller's Mount Airy, N.C. City Directory 1928-1929. Asheville: 1928. V. 71

MILLER, FRANCIS TREVELYAN
The Photographic History of the Civil War. New York: 1911-1912. V. 70
The World in the Air. New York: 1930. V. 69; 71

MILLER, FRANCIS W.
Cincinnati's Beginnings. Cincinnati: 1880. V. 70

MILLER, G. S.
The Families and Genera of Bats. Washington: 1907. V. 72
The Families and Genera of Bats. Lehre: 1967. V. 72
The North American Species of Nymphaea. Washington: 1912. V. 72

MILLER, GEORGE
The Trial of Frank James for Murder with Confessions of Dick Liddle and Clarence Hite and History of the James Gang. Kansas City: 1898. V. 73

MILLER, GEORGE C.
Blackburn: The Evolution of a Cotton Town. Blackburn: 1951. V. 73
Hoghton Tower in History and Romance. Preston: 1954. V. 73

MILLER, GEORGE J.
David A. Borrenstein: a Biographical and Bibliographical Study. 1936. V. 71

MILLER, HELEN TOPPING
Song After Midnight. New York: 1939. V. 71

MILLER, HENRY
The Air-Conditioned Nightmare. New York: 1945. V. 70
Between Heaven and Hell: A Symposium. Big Sur CA: 1961. V. 72
Big Sur and the Oranges of Hieronymous Bosch. New York: 1957. V. 71
Black Spring. Paris: 1936. V. 70; 73
Black Spring. Paris: 1938. V. 71
The Colossus of Maroussi. San Francisco: 1941. V. 72
The Colossus of Maroussi. Paris: 1958. V. 71
The Cosmological Eye. Norfolk CT: 1939. V. 71; 72
Echolalia: Reproductions of Water Colors. Berkeley: 1945. V. 68
First Impressions of Greece. Santa Barbara: 1973. V. 72
Insomnia or the Devil at Large. Albuquerque: 1970. V. 71
Into the Night Life. Berkeley: 1947. V. 68; 72
Journey to an Antique Land. Big Sur: 1970. V. 71
Letters of Henry Miller and Wallace Fowlie (1943-1972). New York: 1975. V. 71
Love Between the Sexes. New York: 1978. V. 71
Maurizius Forever. Waco: 1946. V. 68
Max and the White Phagocytes. Paris: 1938. V. 68; 70; 71; 73
Max and the White Phagocytes. Paris: 1945. V. 71
The Mezzotints. Ann Arbor: 1993. V. 71
Money and How It Gets that Way. Paris: 1938. V. 72
Murder the Murderer. Big Sur: 1944. V. 71
Murder the Murderer. Fordingbridge Hants: 1946. V. 71
My Bike and Other Friends. Santa Barbara: 1978. V. 71
My Life and Times. New York: 1971. V. 71
The Nightmare Notebook. New York: 1975. V. 68; 71; 72
Notes on Aaron's Rod and Other Notes on Lawrence from the Paris Notebooks. Santa Barbara: 1980. V. 71
Order and Chaos Chez Hans Reichel. Tucson: 1967. V. 70
Patchen. Man of Anger and Light. New York: 1946. V. 71
Plexus. London: 1963. V. 71
Quiet Days in Clichy. Paris: 1956. V. 69
Quiet Days in Clichy. Paris: 1958. V. 69
The Red Notebook. Highlands NC: 1958. V. 72
Remember to Remember. New York: 1947. V. 68
The Rosy Crucifixion: Sexus, Plexus, Nexus. New York: 1965. V. 72
Semblance of a Devoted Past. Berkeley: 1944. V. 72
The Smile at the Foot of the Ladder. New York: 1958. V. 69
Sunday After the War. Norfolk: 1944. V. 72
Sunday After the War. New York: 1961. V. 70
To Paint Is To Love Again. Alhambra: 1960. V. 73
The Tropic of Cancer. Paris: 1934. V. 73
Tropic of Cancer. New York: 1961. V. 69; 73
Tropic of Capricorn. Paris: 1939. V. 72; 73
Tropic of Capricorn. Paris: 1945. V. 73
Tropic of Capricorn. New York: 1962. V. 73
The Waters Reglitterized. 1950. V. 70
What Are You Going to Do About Alf?. Paris: 1935. V. 70
What are You Going to do about Alf?. London: 1971. V. 71; 72
The World of D. H. Lawrence. Santa Barbara: 1980. V. 72

MILLER, HUGH
The Cruise of the Betsey on a Summer Holiday in the Hebrides.... Edinburgh: 1870. V. 68
Edinburgh and Its Neighbourhood Geological and Historical;; with the Geology of the Bass Rock. Edinburgh: 1864. V. 68; 71
First Impressions of England and Its People. London: 1847. V. 68

MILLER, HUGH continued
Footprints of the Creator or the Asterolepis of Stromness. Edinburgh: 1889. V. 68
My Schools and Schoolmasters. Edinburgh: 1857. V. 68
My Schools and Schoolmasters. Edinburgh: 1889. V. 68
The Old Red Sandstone. Edinburgh: 1841. V. 68
The Old Red Sandstone. Edinburgh: 1842. V. 69; 73
The Old Red Sandstone. Edinburgh: 1858. V. 68; 71
My Schools and Schoolmasters. The Story of My Education. Edinburgh: 1857. V. 71
Testimony of the Rocks. Edinburgh: 1857. V. 68
The Testimony of the Rocks. London: 1857. V. 72

MILLER, J. HILLIS
William Carlos Williams. Englewood Cliffs: 1966. V. 73

MILLER, JACOB W.
An Address Delivered Before the New Jersey State Agricultural Society, at Camden, Friday September 21st, 1855...to Which is Appended a List of Premiums Awarded by the Society. Somerville: 1855. V. 71

MILLER, JAMES
The Humours of Oxford. London: 1730. V. 71

MILLER, JASON
That Championship Season. New York: 1972. V. 69

MILLER, JOAQUIN
The Building of the City Beautiful. Cambridge & Chicago: 1893. V. 68
The Danites; and Other Choice Selections. New York: 1878. V. 73
'49 The Gold-Seeker of the Sierras. New York: 1884. V. 73
My Own Story. London: 1891. V. 68

MILLER, JOHN
An Illustration of the Sexual System of Linnaeus. London: 1779-1789. V. 69

MILLER, JOSEPH
Botanicum Officianale; or a Compendious Herbal. London: 1722. V. 70

MILLER, K.
The International Karakoram Project. Cambridge: 1984. V. 71

MILLER, KELLY
Race Adjustment. Essays on the Negro in America. New York and Washington: 1908. V. 68

MILLER, LEWIS B.
A Crooked Trail. Boston: 1911. V. 71
Saddles and Lariats. Boston: 1909. V. 69; 71

MILLER, LIAM
The Dun Emer Pess, Later the Cuala Press. Dublin: 1973. V. 72

MILLER, M. A.
Birds. A Guide to the Literature. New York: 1986. V. 70

MILLER, MAX
I Cover the Waterfront. New York: 1932. V. 71
A Stranger Came to Port. New York: 1938. V. 70

MILLER, NYLE
Why the West Was Wild, A Contemporary Look At Some Highly Publicized Kansas County Personalities. Topeka: 1963. V. 71

MILLER, OLIVE BEAUPRE
My Bookhouse. Chicago: 1925. V. 70
Sunny Rhymes for Happy Children. Chicago: 1917. V. 73

MILLER, PATRICK
Ana the Runner. London: 1937. V. 71
Ana the Runner. Waltham St. Lawrence: 1937. V. 71
The Green Ship. Waltham St. Lawrence: 1936. V. 72
Woman in Detail: a Scientific Survey. Waltham St. Lawrence: 1947. V. 71

MILLER, PAUL EDWARD
Esquire's 1945 Jazz Book. New York: 1945. V. 69; 71

MILLER, PHILIP
The Gardeners Kalendar.... London: 1748. V. 73
The Gardeners Kalendar.... London: 1775. V. 68

MILLER, R. G.
History and Atlas of the Fishes of the Antarctic Ocean. Carson City: 1993. V. 72

MILLER, S. N.
The Roman Fort at Balmuildy (Summerston, near Glasgow) on the Antonine Wall. Being an account of excavations conducted on behalf of the Glasgow Archaeological Society. Glasgow: 1922. V. 70; 71

MILLER, SAMUEL
A Brief Retrospect of the Eighteenth Century.... New York: 1803. V. 71; 73
A Discourse Delivered in the Chapel of Nassau-Hall, Before the Literary and Philosophical Society of New Jersey, at Its First Annual Meeting, September 27, 1825. Princeton: 1825. V. 71
The Importance of the Gospel Ministry; an Introdcutory Lecture, Delivered at...the theological Seminary at Princeton, New Jersey, Nov. 9, 1827. Princeton: 1827. V. 71
A Letter to a Gentleman of Baltimore, in Reference to the Case of the Rev. Mr. Duncan. Princeton: 1826. V. 71
Letters on Clerical Manners and Habits; Addressed to a Student in the Theological Seminary, at Princeton, N.J. New York: 1827. V. 71
Letters on Unitarianism: Addressed to the Members of the First Presbyterian Church, in the City of Baltimore. Trenton: 1821. V. 71
The Literary Foundations Healed: a Sermon Preached in the Chapel of the College of New Jersey, March 9th 1823. Trenton: 1823. V. 71
The Utility and Importance of Creeds and Confessions: an Introductory Lecture, Delivered at...the Theological Seminary of the Presbyterian Church, Princeton, July 2, 1824. Princeton: 1824. V. 71

MILLER, SAMUEL F.
Lectures on the Constitution of the United States. New York and Albany: 1893. V. 69

MILLER, SUE
The Good Mother. New York: 1986. V. 72; 73
Inventing the Abbots and Other Stories. New York: 1987. V. 72
While I Was Gone. New York: 1999. V. 68

MILLER, THOMAS
Historical and Genealogical Record of the First Settlers of Colchester County. Down to the Present Time. Halifax: 1873. V. 73
Picturesque Sketches of London, Past and Present. 1850. V. 69

MILLER, WADE
Calamity Fair. New York: 1950. V. 71

MILLER, WALTER M.
A Canticle for Leibowitz. 1960. V. 69

MILLER, WARREN HASTINGS
Under the Admiral's Stars. New York: 1929. V. 70

MILLER, WILLIAM
Evidence from Scripture (!) and History of the Second Coming of Christ, About the Year 1843, Exhibited in a Course of Lectures. Troy: 1836. V. 68; 71
Evidence from Scripture and History of the Second Coming of Christ, about the Year 1843: Exhibited in a Course of (18) Lectures. New York: 1838. V. 71
A Full and Complete Confession of the Horrid Transactions in the Life of George Hamilton, the Murderer of Mary Bean, the Factory Girl.... 1852. V. 73
Scottish Nursery Songs and Other Poems. Glasgow: 1863. V. 73
Views of the Prophecies...with a Memoir of His Life...(and) Evidence from Scripture and History of the Second coming of Christ, about the Year 1843. Boston: 1841. V. 73
Wintering in the Riviera. London: 1879. V. 73

MILLER'S *Planter's & Merchant's Almanac for the Year of Our Lord 1849....* Charleston: 1848. V. 68

MILLET, F. D.
A Capillary Crime and Other Stories. New York: 1892. V. 68

MILLETT, EDWARD, MRS.
An Australian Parsonage. London: 1872. V. 71

MILLETT, MARCUS W.
Jungle Sport in Ceylon. London: 1914. V. 71

MILLHAUSER, STEVEN
Edwin Mullhouse - the Life and Death of an American Writer 1943-1954. New York: 1972. V. 69; 70; 73
Enchanted Night. New York: 1999. V. 72
From the Realm of Morpheus. New York: 1986. V. 70
In the Penny Arcade. New York: 1986. V. 69; 70; 72
The Knife Thrower. New York: 1998. V. 72
Martin Dressler. New York: 1996. V. 69; 70; 72
Portrait of a Romantic. New York: 1977. V. 69; 70; 72

MILLHOUSE, ROBERT
Vicissitude a Poem in Four Books. Nottingham: 1821. V. 70

MILLICAN, JOHN
Rivers in the Desert. 1982. V. 70
Rivers in the Desert. Esher, Surrey: 1982. V. 71

MILLIGAN, ROBERT H.
The Fetish Folk of West Africa. New York: 1912. V. 68; 72

MILLIGAN, SPIKE
Adolf Hitler: My Part in His Downfall. London: 1971. V. 69

MILLIKEN, E. F.
Catalogue of Mr. E. F. Milliken's Private Collection of Valuable Paintings.... New York: 1902. V. 69; 72

MILLIKIN, ROBERT
Historico-Masonic Tracts, Being a Concise History of Freemasonry. Cork: 1848. V. 70

MILLIN, AUBIN LOUIS
Monumens Francois, Tels Que Tombeaux, Inscriptions, Statues, Vitraux, Mosaiques, Fresques, etc. Tires des Abbayes, Monasteres, Chateaux et Autres Lieux. Paris: 1802. V. 68; 70; 72

MILLIN, GEORGE FRANCIS
Life in Our Villages. London: 1891. V. 71

MILLING, J. C.
The R.I.C. A.B.C. or, Police Duties in Relation to Acts of Parliament in Ireland. Belfast: 1910. V. 71

MILLINGTON DRAKE, TEDDY
Poems. Paris: 1977. V. 70

MILLNER, JOHN
A Compendious Journal of all the Marches, Famous Battles, Sieges and Other...Actions of the Triumphant Armies.... 1733. V. 73

MILLOT, JACQUES ANDRE
L'Art de Procreer les Sexes a Volonte, ou Systeme Complet de Generation.... Paris: 1800. V. 69

MILLS, ALISON
Francisco. Berkeley: 1974. V. 72

MILLS, ANSON
My Story. Washington, DC: 1918. V. 69; 72

MILLS, ARTHUR
Colonial Constitutions: an Outline of the Constitutional History and Existing Government of the British Dependencies.... London: 1856. V. 70; 71

MILLS, C. WRIGHT
The New Men of Power. America's Labor Leaders. New York: 1948. V. 71

MILLS, CHARLES
The History of the Crusades, for the Recovery and Possession of the Holy Land. Philadelphia: 1826. V. 71

MILLS, CHARLES K.
Harvest of Barren Regrets, The Army Career of Frederick William Benteen. Glendale: 1985. V. 72

MILLS, D. A. C.
Geology of the Country Around Barnard Castle. London: 1976. V. 73

MILLS, D. E.
A Collection of Tales from Uji - a Study and Translation of Uji Shui Monogatari. Cambridge: 1970. V. 69

MILLS, DEREK
Salmon and Trout. Edinburgh: 1971. V. 68

MILLS, E. L.
Biological Oceanography, an Early History 1870-1960. Ithaca: 1989. V. 72; 73

MILLS, ENOS
The Rocky Mountain National Park. Garden City: 1924. V. 68

MILLS, G. R.
The Talking Dolls. New York: 1930. V. 70; 73

MILLS, J. P.
The Lhota Nagas. London: 1922. V. 71

MILLS, JOHN
The Flyers of the Hunt. London: 1859. V. 68; 72
The Flyers of the Hunt. London: 1865. V. 68
Our County. London: 1850. V. 71
The Sportsman's Library. 1845. V. 68; 70; 71
A Treatise on Cattle.... London: 1776. V. 71

MILLS, LESTER
A Sagebrush Saga. Springville: 1956. V. 68; 73

MILLS, W. JAY
Historic Houses of New Jersey. Philadelphia: 1903. V. 71

MILLS, W. W.
Forty Years at El Paso, 1858-1898. El Paso: 1962. V. 71

MILLS, WILLIAM
Marrow of Practical Medicine and Family Guide.... St. Clairsville: 1848. V. 70

MILLS, WORD H.
Evolution of Society. From Primitive Savagery to the Industrial Republic. New York: 1927. V. 72; 73

MILMAN, HENRY HART
The History of the Jews. London: 1829. V. 69

MILN, LOUISE JORDAN
By Soochow Waters. New York: 1929. V. 69
Mr. Wu. New York: 1920. V. 70
Ruben and Ivy Sen. New York: 1925. V. 71

MILNE, ALAN ALEXANDER
By Way of Introduction. New York: 1929. V. 69; 73
The Christopher Robin Reader. New York: 1929. V. 70
The Christopher Robin Story Book. London: 1929. V. 70
Four Days Wonder. London: 1933. V. 70
Fourteen Songs from When We Were Very Young. London: 1924. V. 70
A Gallery of Children. 1925. V. 73
A Gallery of Children. London: 1925. V. 68; 70
A Gallery of Children. Philadelphia: 1925. V. 73
The House at Pooh Corner. London: 1928. V. 68; 69; 70; 72; 73
The House at Pooh Corner. New York: 1928. V. 68; 70
The Hums of Pooh. London: 1929. V. 70
The Ivory Door: a Legend in a Prologue and Three Acts. London: 1929. V. 71; 73
The King's Breakfast. London: 1925. V. 71; 73
The King's Breakfast. New York: 1947. V. 70
Michael and Mary: a Play. London: 1930. V. 73
Now We Are Six. London: 1927. V. 68; 70; 71; 72; 73
Now We Are Six. New York: 1927. V. 68; 70; 73
Now We Are Six. London: 1928. V. 69; 70; 71; 73
Now We Are Six. London: 1977. V. 71; 73
Once On a Time. New York: 1922. V. 70
Once On a Time. London: 1925. V. 68
The Princess and the Apple Tree. New York: 1937. V. 70
Pu Der Bar. Berlin. V. 69
The Red House Mystery. London: 1922. V. 71; 73
The Secret and Other Stories. New York: 1929. V. 68
Teddy Bear and Other Songs from When We Were Very Young. New York: 1926. V. 73
Toad of Toad Hall. London: 1929. V. 69; 70; 71; 73
Very Young Verses. London: 1929. V. 70
When I Was Very Young. New York: 1930. V. 70; 71; 73
When We Were Very Young. London: 1924. V. 68; 70; 71
When We Were Very Young. London: 1927. V. 70; 72
Winnie the Pooh. London: 1926. V. 70; 71; 72
Winnie the Pooh. London: 1973. V. 68; 72
A Winnie the Pooh a Reproduction of the Original Manuscript. London: 1971. V. 70
Winnie the Pooh and the House at the Pooh Corner. (In Russian). 1967. V. 72
The World of Christopher Robin. New York: 1958. V. 73
The World of Pooh. New York: 1957. V. 70

MILNE, COLIN
A Botanical Dictionary; or Elements of Systematic Botany. London: 1778. V. 69

MILNE, DAVID
On Circulating Credit; with Hints for Improving the Banking System of Britain and Preliminary Observations on some of the Modern Doctrines of Political Economy. Edinburgh: 1832. V. 73
On the Parallel Roads of Lochaber; with Remarks on the Change of the Relative Levels of Sea and Land in Scotland and on the Detrital Deposits in the Country. Edinburgh: 1847. V. 70

MILNE, JAMES
Travels In Hope A Book of Wayfaring Essays. London: 1932. V. 71; 72

MILNE, JAMES FAIRWEATHER
T. E. Lawrence in Buchan. Peterhead: 1954. V. 73

MILNE, JOHN STEWART
Surgical Instruments in Greek and Roman Times. Oxford: 1907. V. 68

MILNE, KENNETH
A History of the Royal Bank of Ireland Limited. 1964. V. 69

MILNE, MALCOLM
The Book of Modern Mountaineering. London: 1968. V. 69

MILNE EDWARDS, H.
A Monograph of the British Fossil Corals. London: 1850-1891. V. 69

MILNER, C. DOUGLAS
The Dolomites. London: 1952. V. 69
Mont Blanc and the Aiguilles. London: 1955. V. 69

MILNER, DUNCAN C.
Lincoln and Liquor. New York: 1920. V. 70

MILNER, J.
An Inquiry into Certain Vulgar Opinions Concerning the Catholic Inhabitants and Antiquities of Ireland. 1808. V. 69; 73

MILNER, JOE E.
California Joe, Noted Scout & Indian Fighter With An Authentic Account of Custer's Last Fight By Col. W. O. Bowen. Caldwell: 1935. V. 72

MILNER, JOHN
The Cruise of H.M.S. Galatea, Captain H.R.H. The Duke of Edinburgh, K.G. in 1867-1868. London: 1869. V. 71
The History Civil and Ecclesiastical, & Survey of the Antiquities of Winchester. Winchester: 1809. V. 68

MILNER, MARY
The Life of Isaac Milner, D.D., F.R.S. London: 1844. V. 71
The Life of Isaac Milner, D.D., F.R.S. Seeley: 1844. V. 70

MILNER, THOMAS
A Gallery Of Nature. London: 1852. V. 72

MILNER, W. C.
The Basin of Minas and Its Early Settlers. Wolfville: 1919?. V. 73

MILNE THOMSON, L. M.
Theoretical Hydrodynamics. London: 1938. V. 69

MILNOR, WILLIAM
Memoirs of the Gloucester Fox Hunting Club near Philadelphia. New York: 1927. V. 71

MILOSZ, CZESLAW
The Captive Mind. London: 1953. V. 69
The Collected Poems 1931-1987. New York: 1988. V. 69; 73
The Issa Valley. New York: 1981. V. 69
The Land of Ulro. New York: 1984. V. 69; 73
Unattainable Earth. New York: 1986. V. 69
Visions from San Francisco Bay. New York: 1982. V. 69; 72

MILTON, ERNEST
To Kiss the Crocodile. New York: 1928. V. 71

MILTON, JOHN
Areopagitica. Hammersmith: 1908. V. 71

MILTON, JOHN continued
Areopagitica. Cambridge: 1973. V. 68; 70; 71
Comus. London: 1906. V. 73
Comus. New York: 1921. V. 72
Comus. London: 1926. V. 68
Comus. Newtown: 1931. V. 70
A Defence of the People of England...In Answer to Salmasiu's Defence of the King. London: 1692. V. 73
Ioannis Miltoni, Angli, Pro Populo Anglicano, Defensio, Contra Claudii Anonymi, Alias Salmasii, Defensionem Regiam. Amsterdam: 1651. V. 70
John Milton Poems in English with Illustrations by William Blake. Miscellaneous Poems, Paradise Regain'd & Samson Agonistes. London: 1926. V. 73
L'allegro and Il Penseroso. London: 1848. V. 71
The Mask of Comus. London: 1937. V. 72
The Masque of Comus. Cambridge: 1954. V. 70; 72
The Masque of Comus. New York: 1954. V. 73
Milton's Paradise Lost Illustrated with Texts of Scripture by John Gillies. London: 1788. V. 73
Milton's Paradise Lost. (with) The Poetical Works of John Milton. London: 1732. V. 69
Paradise Lost. London: 1749. V. 69
Paradise Lost. London: 1750. V. 71
Paradise Lost. London: 1753. V. 73
Paradise Lost. Washington: 1801. V. 68
Paradise Lost. London: 1802. V. 70; 71
Paradise Lost. London: 1825. V. 68
Paradise Lost. London: 1882. V. 68
Paradise Lost. 1902. V. 70
Paradise Lost. London: 1905. V. 68; 72
Paradise Lost (and) Paradise Regain'd. Birmingham: 1758. V. 69
Paradise Regain'd. London: 1671. V. 72; 73
Paradise Regain'd. Glasgow: 1772. V. 73
Paradise Regain'd. London: 1773. V. 73
Paradise Regain'd. 1905. V. 70
Paradise Regained, Samson Agonistes, Comus, Arcades, Lycidas, etc. Chiswick: 1823. V. 70
Paradise Regained. London: 1795. V. 71
The Poems. New York: 1925. V. 68; 72
The Poetical Works. London: 1822. V. 68
Poetical Works. London: 1835. V. 68; 72
The Poetical Works. London: 1843. V. 69
The Poetical Works. London: 1852. V. 68; 72
The Poetical Works. London: 1860. V. 70
Pro Populo Anglicano Defensio Secunda. 1654. V. 72
Samson Agonistes: a Dramatic Poem. 1931. V. 71
The Works...Historical, Political and Miscellaneous.... London: 1753. V. 68

MILTON, THOMAS
The Chimney-Piece-Maker's Daily Assistant, or a Treasury of New Designs for Chimney-Pieces. 1766. V. 73

MILTON, WILLIAM FITZWILLIAM
A History of the San Juan Water Boundary Queston, as Affecting the Division of Territory Between Great Britain and the United States.... London and New York: 1869. V. 71
The Northwest Passage by Land. London: 1867. V. 68

MILTOUN, FRANCIS
The Spell of Algeria and Tunisia. Boston: 1924. V. 72

M'ILWAINE, W.
Death Conquered: and Other Poems. London: 1842. V. 72

MINARIK, ELSE HOLMELUND
A Kiss for Little Bear. New York: 1968. V. 73

MINASIAN, KHATCHIK
The Simple Songs of.... San Francisco: 1950. V. 69

MINCE Pies For Christmas. London: 1805. V. 70; 72

MINCHIN, H. COTTON
The Legion Book. 1929. V. 71
The Legion Book. London: 1929. V. 68

MINCOFF, ELIZABETH
Pillow Lace. London: 1907. V. 72

MINELLI, A.
The Botanical Garden of Padua 1545-1995. Venice: 1995. V. 68

MINER, DOROTHY
Illuminated Books of the Middle Ages and Renaissance. Baltimore: 1949. V. 70

MINER, FREDERICK R.
The Outdoor Southland of California. Los Angeles: 1923. V. 71

MINER, JOHN
The Cruise of H.M.S. Galatea, Captain H.R.H. The Duke of Edinburgh, K.G. in 1867-1868. London: 1869. V. 69

MINER, N. H.
The Iowa - Little Histories of North American Indians No. 2. Cedar Rapids: 1911. V. 69

MINER, THOMAS
Essays on Fevers and Other Medical Subjects. Middletown: 1823. V. 72

THE MINERS Own Book - Containing Correct Illustrations and Descriptions of the Various Modes of California Mining. San Francisco: 1949. V. 68; 73

THE MINES of New Mexico. Santa Fe: 1896. V. 71

MINGUS, CHARLES
Beneath the Underdog. New York: 1971. V. 73

MINICK, ROGER
Delta West: the Land and People of the Sacramento San Joaquin Delta. 1969. V. 68

MINIFIE, WILLIAM
A Text Book of Geometrical Drawing for the Use of Mechanics & Schools. Baltimore: 1850. V. 70

MINKOWSKI, ALEXANDRE
Regional Development of the Brain in Early Life. Oxford: 1967. V. 68

MINNESOTA
The Geology and General History Survey of Minnesota. Minneapolis: 1884-1900. V. 69; 72

MINNICH, J. W.
Inside of Rock Island Prison, from December 1863 to June 1865. Nashville: 1908. V. 69

MINNIGERODE, MEADE
The Seven Hills. New York: 1923. V. 71

MINOGUE, ANNA C.
Loretto- Annais of the Century. New York: 1912. V. 71

MINOR, JOHN B.
Exposition of the Crimes and Punishments. Richmond: 1894. V. 68

MINOR, RALEIGH C.
Conflict of Laws. Boston: 1901. V. 72

MINOT, GEORGE RICHARDS
History of the Insurrections, in Massachusetts in the Year MDCCLXXXVI and Rebellion Consequent Thereon. Worcester: 1788. V. 73

MINOT, SUSAN
Evening. New York: 1998. V. 68; 72
Monkeys. New York: 1986. V. 68
Rapture. New York: 2002. V. 72

THE MINSTREL Boy, a Collection of the Most Fashionable and Delightful Songs. Philadelphia: 1827. V. 71

MINTO, 4TH EARL OF
Lord Minto's Canadian Papers. A Selection of the Public and Private Papers of the Fourth Earl of Minto 1898-1904. Toronto: 1981-1983. V. 68

MINTORN, J. H., MRS.
The Hand-Book to Paper-Flower Making. London: 1864. V. 68

M'INTOSH, CHARLES
The Greenhouse, Hot House and Stove.... London: 1840. V. 70

M'INTOSH, W. C.
The Marine Invertebrates and Fishes of St. Andrews, Together With: Additions to the Marine Fauna of St. Andrews Since 1874. London: 1875. V. 71
The Marine Invertebrates and Fishes of St. Andrews, together with: Additions to the Marine Fauna of St. Andrews Since 1984. London/Edinburgh: 1927. V. 70
The Marine Invertebrates and Fishes of St. Andrews. (with) Additions to the Marine Fauna of St. Andrews Since 1874. London: 1857. V. 68

MINTURN, ROBERT B.
From New York to Delhi. London: 1858. V. 71

MINUTES of a Conspiracy Against the Liberties of America. Philadelphia: 1865. V. 73

MINUTES of Evidence Taken Before the Committee for Privileges, To whom the Petition of Alan Legge Gardner to His Majesty Claiming the Barony of Gardner, was Referred. London: 1825-1826. V. 70

MIR, TIRICH
The Norwegian Himalaya Expedition. London: 1952. V. 71

MIRABAL, N.
Voyage d'Italie, et de Grece; avec une Dissertation sur La Bizarrerie des Opinions des Hommes. Paris: 1698. V. 72

MIRABEAU, HONORE GABRIEL DE RIQUETTI, COMTE DE
Gallery of Portraits of the National Assembly, Supposed to Have Been Written by Count de Mirabeau. Dublin: 1790. V. 73
Gallery of Portraits of the National Assembly, Supposed to Have Been Written by Count de Mirabeau. London: 1790. V. 73
Letters, During his Residence in England; with anecdotes, maxims &c., now first translated from the original manuscripts . . . London: 1832. V. 71

MIRABEAU, VICTOR RIQUETTE, MARQUIS DE
L'Ami des Hommes, ou Traite de la Population. Avingon: 1756. V. 68

MIRACLES of Perception: the Art of Willa Cather. 1980. V. 70

MIRBEL, CHARLES FRANCOIS BRISSEAU DE
Elemens de Physiologie Vegetale et de Botanique. Paris: 1815. V. 72

MIREHOUSE, JOHN
A Practical Treatise on the Law of Tithes. London: 1818. V. 72
A Practical Treatise on the Law of Tithes. London: 1822. V. 72

MIR HASSAN ALI, B., MRS.
Observations on the Mussulmauns of India; Descriptive of their Manners, Customs, Habits and Religious Opinions Made During a Twelve Years' Residence in their Immediate Society. London: 1832. V. 69; 73

MIRO, JOAN
Cartones 1959-1965. An Exhibition of New Works by Miro at the Pierre Matisse Gallery. New York: 1965. V. 68
Joan Miro. London: 1966. V. 69
Quelques Fleurs Pour des Amis. Paris: 1964. V. 69

MIRROR Grange - The Book of the Daily Mirror's House for Pip, Squeak and Wilfred. London: 1930. V. 69

MIRTLE, JACK
The Music of Billy May. A Discography. Westport: 1998. V. 73

MISCELLANEA. Part I. The Rymour Club. Edinburgh: 1902. V. 68

MISHIMA, YUKIO
Confessions of a Mask. Norfolk: 1958. V. 69
Forbidden Colors. New York: 1968. V. 69
Runaway Horses. New York: 1973. V. 73
The Sailor Who Fell from Grace with the Sea. New York: 1965. V. 69
The Sea of Fertility Tetralogy. Spring Snow. Runaway Horses. The Temple of Dawn. The Decay of the Angel. New York: 1972-1974. V. 69
The Sound of Waves. New York: 1956. V. 68; 69
The Way of the Samurai. New York: 1977. V. 69

MISONE, LEONARD
Leonard Misone. Wien: 1936. V. 70

MISRACH, RICHARD
The Sky Book. Santa Fe: 2000. V. 68
Telegraph 3 a.m. Berkeley: 1974. V. 70

MISS Flora McFlimsey's Halloween. New York: 1972. V. 73

MISS Lovemouse's Letters. London: 1896. V. 72

MISSION San Xavier Del Bac Arizona. New York. V. 69

MISSIONARY Narratives. Dublin: 1830. V. 71

MISSIRINI, MELCHIOR
Del Tempio Eretto in Possagno da Antonio Canova Esposizione. Venice: 1833. V. 70; 72

MISSISSIPPI. HIGH COURT OF ERRORS AND APPEALS - 1839
Reports of Cases Argued and Determined. Philadelphia: 1839. V. 69

MISSISSIPPI. LAWS, STATUTES, ETC. - 1852
Laws of the State of Mississipi, Passed at a Called Session. Jackson: 1852. V. 72

MISSON DE VALBOURG, HENRI
Memoires et Observations Faites par un Voyageur en Angleterre. Amsterdam: 1698. V. 72

MISSOURI BOTANICAL GARDEN
Eighth Annual Report. St. Louis: 1897. V. 72

MISSOURI PACIFIC RAILWAY
Facts About Kansas. St Louis: 1903. V. 70

MISSOURI STATE CONVENTION
Journal and Proceedings of the Missouri State Convention, Held at Jefferson City and St. Louis March 1861. St. Louis: 1861. V. 70

MISSY, JEAN ROUSSET DE
The History of Cardinal Alberoni: Chief Favourite of their Catholick Majesties ad Universal Minster of the Spanish Monarchy.... London: 1719. V. 72

THE MISTAKEN Evil. 1797. V. 71

MR. Buchanan's Administration on the Eve of the Rebellion. New York: 1866. V. 70

MISTRAL, GABRIELA
Desolacion. New York: 1922. V. 69

MISTRAL, MAGALI
Magali. London ad Draguignan: 1977. V. 70

MISTRY, ROHINTON
Such a Long Journey. New York: 1991. V. 70; 72
Swimming Lessons. Boston: 1989. V. 70

MITCHARD, JACQUELYN
The Deep End of the Ocean. New York: 1996. V. 68; 70; 71

MITCHEL, EMERSON BLACKHORSE
Miracle Hill: The Story of a Navaho Boy. Norman: 1967. V. 69

MITCHEL, JOHN
Jail Journal. Dublin: 1854. V. 71

MITCHEL, O.
The Planetary and Stellar Worlds; a Popular Exposition of the Great Discoveries and Theories of Modern Astronomy. New York: 1848. V. 68
The Planetary and Stellar Worlds: a Popular Exposition of the Great Discoveries and Theories of Modern Astronomy in a Series of Ten Lectures. New York: 1859. V. 73

MITCHELL, ADRIAN
Poems. London: 1946. V. 70

MITCHELL, ANNE M.
The Cash-Boy's Trust. New York: 1872. V. 72

MITCHELL, B. R.
Abstract of British Historical Statistics. Cambridge: 1962. V. 70

MITCHELL, BETH
Beginning at a White Oak: Patents and Northern Neck Grants of Fairfax County, Virginia. 1979. V. 72

MITCHELL, CHARLES F.
Building Construction and Drawing. First Stage (with) Building Construction...Stages 2, 3 and Honours. London: 1906. V. 68

MITCHELL, DEWEY
Skilled Defense. Cleveland: 1936. V. 71

MITCHELL, DUGALD
A Popular History of the Highlands and Gaelic Scotland From the Earliest Times Till the Close of the 'Forty-five. Paisley: 1900. V. 71

MITCHELL, EDWIN VALENTINE
Concerning Beards. Hartford: 1930. V. 70

MITCHELL, ELIZABETH HARCOURT
First Fruits. London: 1857. V. 69
Wild Thyme, Verses. London: 1861. V. 69

MITCHELL, F. S.
The Birds of Lancashire. London: 1885. V. 73

MITCHELL, FRANK
Navajo Blessingway Singer. Tucson: 1978. V. 69

MITCHELL, G. A. G.
Cardiovascular Innervation. Edinburgh: 1956. V. 68

MITCHELL, GEORGE
Blow My Blues Away. New York. V. 72
Blow My Blues Away. Baton Rouge: 1971. V. 68

MITCHELL, GLADYS
Churchyard Salad. London: 1969. V. 70; 71
Cold, Lone and Still. London: 1983. V. 70; 72
The Crozier Pharaohs. London: 1984. V. 71
The Death-Cap Dancers. London: 1981. V. 70; 72
Faintly Speaking. 1954. V. 72
Here Comes a Chopper. London: 1946. V. 69; 71
Here Lies Gloria Mundy. London: 1982. V. 68; 69
Lament for Leto. London: 1971. V. 70
Late, Late in the Evening. London: 1976. V. 70
Lovers Make Moan. London: 1981. V. 70
No Winding-Sheet. London: 1984. V. 73
Noonday and Night. London: 1977. V. 73
The Rising of the Moon. 1945. V. 72
The Rising of the Moon. London: 1945. V. 69
Say It with Flowers. New York: 1960. V. 72
Spotted Hemlock. London: 1958. V. 73
Tom Brown's Body. 1949. V. 72
Uncoffin's Clay. London: 1980. V. 70; 72
When Last I Died. New York: 1942. V. 69
Wraiths and Changelings. London: 1978. V. 73

MITCHELL, ISAAC
A Short Account of the Courtship of Alonzo and Melissa. Plattsburgh: 1811. V. 68; 71

MITCHELL, J. H.
Scenic Rambles through Nova Scotia. Halifax;: 1932. V. 73

MITCHELL, JAMES
The Portable Encyclopaedia; or a Dictionary of the Arts and Sciences.... London: 1831. V. 68

MITCHELL, JOHN EDWARD
Records Of The Royal Horse Artillery, From Its Formation To The Present Time. London: 1888. V. 72

MITCHELL, JOHN M.
The Herring. Its Natural History and National Importance. Edinburgh: 1864. V. 68

MITCHELL, JOSEPH
Bottom of the Harbor. Boston: 1959. V. 69; 71
The Bottom of the Harbor. New York: 1991. V. 69; 73
Joe Gould's Secret. New York: 1965. V. 71; 73
Old Mr. Flood. New York: 1948. V. 70; 72; 73

MITCHELL, K. W. S.
Tales from Some Eastern Jungles. 1928. V. 69

MITCHELL, LIGE
Diary Exploits of Jesse James and His Band of Border Train and Bank Robbers. Baltimore: 1914. V. 68

MITCHELL, LUCY M.
A History of Ancient Sculpture. London: 1883. V. 71

MITCHELL, MARGARET
Before Scarlett. (Girlhood Writings). Athens: 2000. V. 71

MITCHELL, MARGARET continued
Gone With the Wind. New York: 1936. V. 68; 73
Gone With The Wind. New York: 1938. V. 72
Gone With the Wind. London: 1939. V. 71
Von Winde Verweht. (Gone with the Wind). Hamburg & Leipzig: 1937. V. 68

MITCHELL, P.
Atlas of Alberta Lakes. Edmonton: 1990. V. 73

MITCHELL, PETER
Jan Van O. 1744-1808. Leigh-on-Sea: 1968. V. 72

MITCHELL, PETER CHALMERS
Centenary History of the Zoological Society of London. London: 1929. V. 68
My Fill of Days. London: 1937. V. 68; 70

MITCHELL, RUTH COMFORT
Army with Banners. New York: 1928. V. 72
Dust of Mexico. New York: 1941. V. 71

MITCHELL, SAMUEL AUGUSTUS
An Accompaniment to Mitchell's Reference and Distance Map of the United States. Philadelphia: 1834. V. 73
Mitchell's New General Atlas. Philadelphia: 1865. V. 72
Texas, Oregon and California. 1948. V. 68
Traveller's Guide through the United States. Philadelphia: 1832. V. 71

MITCHELL, SILAS WEIR
The Comfort of the Hills and Other Poems. New York: 1910. V. 73
The Comfort of the Hills and Other Poems. New York: 1911. V. 70
The Cup of Youth and Other Poems. Boston: 1889. V. 73
Fair in the Forest. Philadelphia: 1889. V. 73
Hugh Wynne, Free Quaker. New York: 1897. V. 68
Hugh Wynne, Free Quaker. New York: 1909. V. 72
The Madeira Party. New York: 1895. V. 70
Mr. Kris Kringle. Philadelphia: 1904. V. 70
New Samaria and the Summer of St. Martin. Philadelphia: 1904. V. 70
The Psalm of Death and other Poems. Boston: 1890. V. 73
Researches Upon the Venom of the Rattlesnake.. Washington: 1860. V. 70
The Tendon-Jerk and Muscle-Jerk in Disease and Especially in Posterior Sclerosis. 1886. V. 70; 73
The Wonderful Stories of Fuz-Buz the Fly and Mother Grabem The Spider. Philadelphia: 1867. V. 70

MITCHELL, SUSAN
Secret Springs of Dublin Song. 1918. V. 71

MITCHELL, SUSAN L.
Aids to the Immortality of Certain Persons in Ireland. 1913. V. 70

MITCHELL, THOMAS D.
The Good Physician...Materia Medical and Therapeutics...Medical Deptartment of Transylvania University. Lexington: 1842. V. 73

MITCHELL, THOMAS L.
Journal of an Expedition Into the Interior of Tropical Australia. London: 1848. V. 71

MITCHELL, W.
Gardens of Georgia. Atlanta: 1989. V. 68

MITCHELL, WILLIAM
General Greely. The Story of a Great American. New York: 1936. V. 73

MITCHELL, WILLIAM SMITH
Catalogue of the Incunabula in Aberdeen University Library. Edinburgh and London: 1968. V. 70

MITCHELL HEDGES, F. A.
Battling with Sea Monsters. 1930. V. 70

MITCHILL, SAMUEL L.
A Lecture on Some Parts of the Natural History of New Jersey, Delivered Before the Newark Mechanic Association for Mutual Improvement in the Arts and Sciences on Tuesday, June 3, 1828. New York: 1828. V. 71

MITCHINER, PHILIP H.
Medical Organization and Surgical Practice in Air Raids. London: 1939. V. 68

MITCHNER, STUART
Let Me Be Awake. New York: 1959. V. 69

MITFORD, A. B.
Tales of Old Japan. London: 1883. V. 70

MITFORD, BERTRAM
The Curse of Clement Waynflete: a Tale of Two Wars. London: 1894. V. 73
A Legacy of the Granite Hills. London: 1909. V. 73
Renshaw Fanning's Quest: a Tale of the High Veldt. London: 1894. V. 69
The Ruby Sword: a Romance of Baluchistan. London: 1899. V. 73
Seaford's Snake. London: 1912. V. 73
A Veldt Official: a Novel of Circumstance. London: 1899. V. 73
The Weird of Deadly Hollow: a Tale of the Cape Colony. London: 1899. V. 73

MITFORD, JESSICA
A Fine Old Conflict. London: 1977. V. 70; 73

MITFORD, JOHN
The Adventures of Johnny Newcome in the Navy. London: 1823. V. 68
A Treatise on the Pleadings in Suits in the Court of Chancery. New York: 1849. V. 68

MITFORD, MARY RUSSELL
The Friendships of Mary Russell Mitford as Recorded in Letters from her Literary Correspondents. London: 1882. V. 73
The Life Of Mary Russell Mitford, Authoress of "Our Village", etc. Related In A Selection From Her Letters To Her Friends. London: 1870. V. 72
Narrative Poems on the Female Character in the Various Relations of Life. London: 1813. V. 72
Our Village. London: 1893. V. 71
Poems. London: 1810. V. 72
Recollections Of A Literary Life; or Books, Places, and People. London: 1853. V. 71; 72

MITFORD, NANCY
Love in a Cold Climate. London: 1949. V. 70
The Pursuit of Love - a Novel. London: 1945. V. 68
The Water Beetle. London: 1962. V. 69

MITFORD, WILLIAM
The History of Greece. London: 1829. V. 70
Principles of Design in Architecture Traced Observations on Buildings. London: 1809. V. 73

MITSCH, E.
The Art of Egon Schiele. London: 1975. V. 72
The Art of Egon Schiele. New York: 1975. V. 69

MITSCHERLICH, ALEXANDER
Doctors of Infamy; The Story of the Nazi Medical Crimes. New York: 1949. V. 69

MITTEN, W.
An Enumeration of all the Species of Musci and Hepaticae Recorded from Japan. London: 1891. V. 72

MITTON, G. E.
Cornwall. 1915. V. 68
Jane Austen and Her Times. London: 1905. V. 68; 70

MIURA, EINEN
The Art of Marbled Paper, Marbled Patterns and How to Make Them. Tokyo: 1991. V. 70

MIVART, ST. G.
Birds: the Elements of Ornithology. 1892. V. 69
The Cat. London: 1881. V. 69
Lessons from Nature, as Manifested in Mind and Matter. London: 1876. V. 71
A Monograph of the Lories, or Brush-Tongued Parrots, Comprising the Family Loriidae. 1896. V. 69
On the Genesis of Species. 1871. V. 69
On the Genesis of the Species. London: 1871. V. 72

MIXSON, FRANK M.
Reminiscences of a Private. Columbia: 1910. V. 69; 70

MIZE, JOHNNY
How to Hit. New York: 1953. V. 69

M'KENDRICK, JOHN GRAY
Hermann Ludwig Ferdinand von Helmholtz. London: 1889. V. 68

M'MURTRIE, H.
Sketches of Louisville and Its Environs.... Louisville: 1819. V. 72

MNEMONIKA; or Chronological Tablets, Exhibiting, in a Methodical Manner, the Most Remarkable Occurrences. Baltimore: 1812. V. 71

MO, TIMOTHY
Brownout on Breadfruit Boulevard. 1995. V. 68
The Monkey King. London: 1978. V. 73
The Redundancy of Courage. London: 1991. V. 73

MOAT, T.
The Practical Proofs of the Soundness of the Hygeian Theory of Physiology.... London: 1833. V. 69

MOBERLY, HENRY
When Fur Was King. London: 1929. V. 69

MOBERLY, WALTER
The Rocks and Rivers of British Columbia. Vienna: 192-. V. 68

MOBIUS, AUGUST FERDINAND
Der Barycentrische Calcul. Leipzig: 1827. V. 68; 70

MOCHI, UGO
Hoofed Mammals of the World. New York: 1953. V. 72

MOCK, E.
Built in USA 1932-1944. New York: 1944. V. 69

MODEL, LISETTE
Lisette Model. New York: 1979. V. 68

MODERN American Stories. 1963. V. 70

THE MODERN Part of an Universal History, from the Earliest Accounts to the Present Time. London: 1708-1784. V. 69

A MODEST Defence of Gaming. London: 1754. V. 69

MODISETT, BILL
J. Evetts Haley A True Texas Legend. Midland: 1996. V. 72

MODJESKI & MASTERS
Gateway Bridge, Clinton, Iowa over the Mississippi River. Final Report to City of Clinton Bridge Commission. Harrisburg: 1957. V. 73

MODY, N. H. N.
A Collection of Nagasaki Colour Prints and Paintings Showing the Influence of Chinese and European Art on that of Japan. Rutland: 1969. V. 70

MOE, LOUIS
Brumle-Brumle og Andre Muntre Billedhistorier for Børn. København: 1921. V. 70
Tommy-Tatters and the Four Bears. New York: 1929. V. 73

MOENS, WILLIAM JOHN CHARLES
Through France and Belgium, by River and Canal, in the Stream Yacht "Ytene". London: 1876. V. 73

MOERAN, J. W. W.
Mcullagh of Aiyansh. London: 1922. V. 68

MOERENHOUT, JACQUES ANTOINE
The Inside Story of the Gold Rush. San Francisco: 1935. V. 68

MOERS, WALTER
The Thirteen 1/2 Lives of Captain Bluebeard. London: 2000. V. 68

MOES, ROBERT J.
The Zamorano Press and the Botica, California's First Medical Book. Los Angeles: 1988. V. 73

MOFFAT, GWEN
Space Below My Feet. London: 1961. V. 69
Survival Count. London: 1972. V. 69

MOFFAT, R. BURNHAM
The Barclays of New York: Who They are and Who They are Not- and Some Other Barclays. New York: 1904. V. 71

MOFFAT, ROBERT
Apprenticeship at Kuruman. London: 1951. V. 71
Missionary Labours and Scenes in South Africa. London: 1842. V. 71

MOFFAT, ROBERT SCOTT
The Economy of Consumption. London: 1878. V. 71

MOFFAT, WILLIAM
Shetland: The Isles of Nightless Summer. London: 1934. V. 71

MOFFETT, CLEVELAND
Through the Wall. New York: 1909. V. 69
True Detective Stores, from the Archives of the Pinkertons. New York: 1898. V. 73

MOFOLO, THOMAS
Chaka. London: 1931. V. 71

MOGG, EDWARD
London in Miniature, with the Surrounding Villages, an Entire New Plan.... London: 1828. V. 72
Mogg's New Picture of London; or Strangers' Guide to the British Metropolis.... 1843. V. 71

MOGGRIDGE, J. T.
Harvesting Ants and Trap-Door Spiders, with Supplement. 1873-1874. V. 73

MOGRIDGE, GEORGE
Loiterings Among the Lakes of Cumberland and Westmoreland. London: 1849. V. 71
Points and Pickings of Information About the Chinese. London: 1844. V. 71
Sergeant Bell and His Raree-Show. London: 1839. V. 73

MOHAMMED BEN ABOULA
Dessin I. Tangier: 1962. V. 68

MOHANTY, B. C.
Natural Dyeing Processes of India. Ahmedabad: 1987. V. 68

MOHNS, FRIEDRICH
Grund-riss der Mineralogie. Dresden: 1822-1824. V. 68

MOHOLY, LUCIA
A 100 Years of Photography. Middlesex: 1939. V. 68

MOHOLY-NAGY, LASZLO
Portrait of Eton. London: 1949. V. 68
The Street Markets of London. London: 1936. V. 68; 69; 71

MOHOLY-NAGY, S.
Carlos Raul Villa-Nueva and the Architecture of Venezuela. New York: 1964. V. 69; 72
Moholy-Nagy: Experiment in Totality, a Biography. New York: 1950. V. 68; 72
Native Genius in Anonymous Architecture. New York: 1957. V. 69; 72

MOHR, C.
Plant Life of Alabama.... Montgomery: 1901. V. 72

MOHRENHEIM, JOSEPH FREYHERN VON
Abhandlung uber die Entbindungskunst Uberhaupt, und Insebesondere von Den Leichten Naturalichen Geburten. Leipzig: 1803. V. 72

MOHS, FRIEDRICH
Treatise on Mineralogy.... Edinburgh: 1825. V. 68

MOIR, ANDREW
The Indictment, Trial and Sentence of Mess. T(homa)s K(innea)r, A(ndre)w B(eatso)n, and R(ober)t M(orto)n, before the Associate Synod, at the Instance of the Rev. Mr. Adam Gib. Edinburgh: 1768. V. 72

MOIR, DAVID MAC BETH
Domestic Verses. Edinburgh: 1871. V. 69
The Life of Mansie Wauch, Tailor in Dalkeith. Edinburgh: 1839. V. 68; 72

MOIR, JOHN
One Thing Needful; or Devout and Philosophical Exercises on Various Subjects. London: 1795?. V. 71

MOISEEV, P. A.
Soviet Fisheries Invesigations in the Northeast Pacific. Jerusalem: 1968. V. 70

MOISY, ALEXANDRE
Les Fontaines de Paris, Anciennes et Nouvelles. Paris: 1813. V. 70; 72

MOJTABAI, A. G.
Mundome. New York: 1974. V. 72

MOKLER, ALFRED J.
History of Natrona County, Wyoming, 1888-1922. Chicago: 1923. V. 71
Transitions of The West. Chicago: 1927. V. 72

MOLD, F. E.
Presenting the Fly to the Trout. 1967. V. 68

MOLDENKE, CHARLES
The New York Obelisk, Cleopatra's Needle.... New York: 1891. V. 73

MOLEMA, S. M.
The Bantu Past and Present. Capetown: 1963. V. 69

MOLENGRAFF, G. A. F.
Borneo-Expedition. Geological Explorations in Central Borneo (1893- 1894). Leiden & Amsterdam: 1902. V. 73

MOLESWORTH, MRS.
The Carved Lions. London: 1895. V. 68; 69; 72; 73
Christmas Tree Land. London: 1884. V. 70
The Cuckoo Clock. London: 1898. V. 68
Hoodie. London: 1897. V. 69
The Rectory Children. London: 1889. V. 68; 72
The Ruby Ring. London: 1904. V. 70
Us an Old-Fashioned Story. London: 1908. V. 68

MOLESWORTH, W. N.
The History of the Reform Bill of 1832. London: 1865. V. 68

MOLIERE, JEAN BAPTISTE POQUELIN DE
Oeuvres Completes de Moliere avec les notes to tous les commentateurs. Paris: 1824. V. 71
Oevres Completes de Moliere. Paris: 1868. V. 71

MOLINA, PEDRO
Manifesto y Sensilla Exposicion, que de su Conducta Poltica Durante el Tiempos de su Gobiemo, y al Renunciar por Tercera vez el Amando ante la H. Representacion de esta Provincia.... Colophon: 1824. V. 70

MOLL, HERMAN
A Set of Fifty new and Correct Maps of England and Wales. London: 1724. V. 68

MOLL, J. W.
Phytography as a Fine Art, Comprising Linnean Description.... Leyden: 1934. V. 72

MOLLHAUSEN, BALDUIN
Reis van den Mississippi Naar de Kusten van den Grooten Oceaan. Zutphen: 1858. V. 68

MOLLIEN, G.
Travels in Africa. London: 1825. V. 71
Travels in the Interior of Africa to the Sources of the Senegal and Gambia. London: 1820. V. 71

MOLLIEN, GASPAR
Travels I Africa. London: 1825. V. 72
Voyage Dans L'Interieur de L'Afrique, Aux Sources du Senegal et de la Gambie. Paris: 1820. V. 72

MOLLISON, DAVID
Liberty of the Press. Proceedings Before the Sheriff Court of Glasgow, and Circuit Court of Justiciary, in the Summary Process Raised at the Instance of Mr. Dugald Bannatyne.... Glasgow: 1811. V. 70

MOLLLEN, GASPAR
Voyage dans l'Interieur de l'Afrique, Aux Sources du Senegal et de la Gambie. Paris: 1820. V. 68

MOLLOY, J. FITZGERALD
Court Life Below Stairs or London Under the First Georges 1714-1760. (and) London Under the Last Georges 1760-1830. London: 1882-1883. V. 73
The Faiths of the Peoples. 1892. V. 69
The Life and Adventures of Edmund Kean, Tragedian 1787-1833. London: 1888. V. 69; 72
The Life and Adventures of Peg Woffington with Pictures of the Period in Which She Lived. London: 1884. V. 72

MOLLOY, P.
The Cry of the Fish Eagle. 1957. V. 70; 72

MOLNAR, FERENC
The Devil, a Tragedy of the Heart and Conscience. New York: 1908. V. 69

MOLNAR, FRANZ
The Guardsman. New York: 1924. V. 71

MOLONY, CHARTRES
Savinelli. New York: 1930. V. 70

MOLONY, EILEEN
Portraits of Mountains. London: 1950. V. 69

MOM, the Flag and Apple Pie. Garden City: 1976. V. 69

MOMADAY, N. SCOTT
The Ancient Child. New York: 1989. V. 71
Circle of Wonder. Santa Fe: 1994. V. 68
Colorado. Chicago: 1973. V. 69
House Made of Dawn. New York: 1968. V. 69; 70; 73
In the Bear's House. New York: 1999. V. 72
In the Presence of the Sun. New York. V. 73
In the Presence of the Sun. New York: 1992. V. 71
In the Presence of the Sun. Santa Fe: 1992. V. 73
In the Presence of the Sun/A gathering of Shields. Santa Fe: 1991. V. 72
The Journey of Tai-Me. Santa Barbara: 1967. V. 70
The Way to Rainy Mountain. Albuquerque: 1969. V. 73

MOMMAERTS, W. F. H. M.
Muscular Contraction. A Topic in Molecular Physiology. New York: 1950. V. 68

MOMMSEN, THEODOR
The History of Rome. London: 1868. V. 72

MONACO, DOMENICO
Specimens from the Naples Museum. London: 1884. V. 72

MONAGHAN, FRANK
French Travelers in the United States 1765-1932. New York: 1961. V. 68

MONAGHAN, JAY
The Book of the American West. New York: 1963. V. 69
Custer - The Life of George Armstrong Custer. Boston: 1959. V. 72
Lincoln Bibliography 1839-1939. Springfield: 1943. V. 70

MONARDES, NICHOLAS
Joyfull Newes Out of the Newe Founde Worlde Writte in Spanish by Nicholas Monardes Physician of Seville and Englished by John Frampton.... London: 1925. V. 68; 73

MONCK, FRANCES E. O.
My Canadian Leaves. London: 1891. V. 71

MONCRIEFF, A. R. HOPE
Bonnie Scotland. London: 1904. V. 71

MONCRIEFF, THOMAS CLARKSON
Proceedings of the General Court-Martial, Held at Mussleburgh on the 24th, 25th and 26th Days of September Last, for the Trial of Major Tho. Clarkson Moncrieff, of the First, or Berwickshire, Regiment by Orders of His Royal Highness, the Duke of York, Co. Edinburgh: 1807. V. 70

MONCRIEFF, WILLIAM THOMAS
The Pickwickians; or, the Peregrinations of Sam Weller. London: 1872?. V. 70
Sam Weller, or, The Pickwickians. London: 1837. V. 70
Songs, Duets, Choruses, &c, &c. London: 1822. V. 70
Tom and Jerry, or Life in London. New York: 1823. V. 73
Tom and Jerry; or, Life in London. London: 1826. V. 68

MONEY, EDWARD
Twelve Months With the Bashi-Bazouk. London: 1880. V. 71

MONEY, L. G. CHIOZZA
Riches and Poverty. London: 1905. V. 72

MONGEZ, M. A.
Histoire de la Reine Marguerite De Valois, Premiere Femme Du Roi Henri IV. Paris: 1777. V. 70; 72

MONICART, JEAN BAPTISTE DE
Versailles Immortalise Par Les Merveilles Parlantes des Batimens,.... Paris: 1720. V. 69; 72

MONIER, PIERRE
The History of Painting, Sculpture, Architecture, Graving and of Those Who Have Excelled in Them.... London: 1699. V. 72

MONIER DE CLAIRCOMBE, JEAN
A New and Universal Practice of Mercantile Arithmetick; in which, What has Hitherto Appear'd Obscure, is Explain'd by Such Easie and Familiar Rules, that the Learner May, Without Any Other Help, Arrive to a Perfect Understanding.... 1707. V. 70

MONK, CHARLES JAMES
The Golden Horn. London: 1851. V. 71

MONK, MARIA
Awful Disclosures, of Maria Monk, of the Hotel Dieu Nunnery of Montreal. New York: 1836. V. 69

MONK, SAMUEL
The Sublime. New York: 1935. V. 72

MONK, WILLIAM
Dr. Livingstone's Cambridge Lectures. Cambridge: 1858. V. 71

MONKHOUSE, ALLAN
Books and Plays. London: 1894. V. 68

MONKHOUSE, COSMO
The Earlier English Water-Colour Painters. London: 1890. V. 70

MONKHOUSE, W.
The Churches of York. London: 1843. V. 69

MONKS, JOHN
Brother Rat. New York: 1937. V. 71

MONNETTE, ORRA EUGENE
First Settlers of ye Plantations of Piscataway and Woodbridge, Olde East New Jersey 1664-1714. Los Angeles: 1930-1935. V. 71

MONNIER, HENRY
Le Tems. Paris: 1828. V. 73

MONOTYPE CORPORATION LTD., LONDON
Pastonchi: a Specimen of a Letter for the Use on the Monotype. Verona: 1928. V. 71
Pastonchi: a Specimen of a New Letter for the Use on the Monotype. London: 1928. V. 69

MONRO, ALEXANDER
The Anatomy of the Human Bones and Nerves, with a Description of the Human Lacteal sac and Duct by.... Edinburgh: 1828. V. 71
The Anatomy of the Human Bones, Nerves and Lacteal Sac and Duct. London: 1788. V. 68
History, Geography and Statistics of British North America. Montreal: 1864. V. 73
Observations on the Structure and Functions of the Nervous System. Edinbrugh: 1783. V. 68; 73
The Structure and Physiology of Fishes Explained.... Edinburgh: 1785. V. 73

MONRO, DONALD
Praelectiones Medicae Ex cronii Insituto. Annis 1774 et 1775 et Oratio Anniversaria.... London: 1776. V. 68; 71; 73

MONRO, HAROLD
Before Dawn (Poems and Impressions). London: 1911. V. 68
The Chapbook (A Monthly Miscellany). London: 1923. V. 73
THE Chapbook (A Monthly Miscellany) First Portfolio. London: 1919-1920. V. 73
The Chapbook (A Monthly Miscellany) Second Portfolio. London: 1920-1921. V. 73
The Chapbook (A Monthly Miscellany) Third Portfolio. London: 1922. V. 73
Children of Love. London: 1914. V. 71
Poems. London: 1906. V. 72
Real Property. London: 1922. V. 71
Trees. London: 1916. V. 70

MONRO, HENRY
Remarks on Insanity. Its Nature and Treatment. London: 1851. V. 72

MONRO, P. A. G.
Lumbar Intermediate Sympathetic Ganglia in Man. London: 1951. V. 68
Sympathectomy. An Anatomical and Physiological Study with Clinical Applications. London: 1959. V. 68

MONROE, DEBRA
The Source of Trouble. Athens: 1990. V. 71

MONROE, HORACE
Foulis Castle and the Monroes of Lower Iveagh. 1929. V. 70

MONROE, JAMES
A View of the Conduct of the Executive, in the Foreign Affairs of the United States, Connected with the Mission to the French Republic, during the Years 1794, 1795 and 1796. Philadelphia: 1797. V. 69; 72

MONROE, JOHN
The American Botanist, and Family Physician.... Wheelock: 1824. V. 68

MONSARRAT, NICHOLAS
H. M. Corvette. Philadelphia: 1943. V. 68

MONSELL, J. R.
Polichinelle Old Nursery Songs of France. London: 1928. V. 70

MONSON, R. A.
Across Africa on Foot. 1931. V. 70; 72

MONSTRELET, ENGUERRAND DE
The Chronicles. London: 1810. V. 73
The Chronicles. London: 1840. V. 73

MONTAGNA, W.
The Skin of Primates. 1959-1962. V. 73

MONTAGNE, PROSPER
Larousse Gastronomique. Paris: 1938. V. 72

MONTAGU, BARBARA
A Description of Millenium Hall and the Country Adjacent, Together with the Characters of the Inhabitants.... London: 1764. V. 73

MONTAGU, BASIL
The Opinions of Different Authors Upon the Punishment of Death. London: 1809. V. 70

MONTAGU, CHARLES
Works and Life of the Right Honourable Charles, Late Earl of Halifax. London: 1715. V. 69

MONTAGU, EDWARD PROUDFOOT
The Personal Narrative of the Escape (of the Author) (an English Prisoner of War) from the Citadel of Verdun. Beccles: 1849. V. 72

MONTAGU, ELIZABETH ROBINSON
An Essay on the Writings and Genius of Shakespear.... Dublin: 1769. V. 73
An Essay on the Writings and Genius of Shakespear.... London: 1772. V. 72
An Essay on the Writings and Genius of Shakespear.... Dublin: 1778. V. 73

MONTAGU, FREDERIC
Gleanings in Craven. 1838. V. 73

MONTAGU, G.
Dictionary of British Birds. 1831. V. 69
Ornithological Dictionary of British Birds. London: 1831. V. 72

MONTAGU, J. A.
A Guide to the Study of Heraldry. London: 1840. V. 68

MONTAGU, M. F. ASHLEY
Edward Tyson, M.D., F.R.S. 1650-1708. Philadelphia: 1943. V. 68

MONTAGU, MARY PIERREPONE WORTLEY
Letters and Works of.... London: 1837. V. 71
The Letters and Works of.... London: 1861. V. 73
Letters of the Right Honourable Lady M--y W---y M---e; Written During Her Travels in Europe, Asia and Africa.... London: 1763. V. 69; 73
Letters.... London: 1767. V. 73
Lettres.... Rotterdam: 1764-1768. V. 69
The Poetical Works of the Right Honorable Lady.... London: 1785. V. 69; 72; 73
The Poetical Works of the Right Honourable Lady.... London: 1768. V. 69
The Works. London: 1803. V. 73
The Works. London: 1817. V. 73

MONTAGU, RICHARD
Diatribae Upon the First Part of the Late History of Tithes. London: 1621. V. 72

MONTAGUE, C. E.
Action and Other Stories. London: 1928. V. 71
Rough Justice - A Novel. London: 1926. V. 72

MONTAGUE, EDWARD J.
The Heritage of the Desert. New York: 1910. V. 71

MONTAGUE, GEORGE W.
History and Genealogy of Peter Montague of Nansemond and Lancasater Counties, Virginia and Its Descendants 1621-1894. Amherst: 1894. V. 70

MONTAGUE, JOHN
The Dolmen Miscellany of Irish Writing. 1962. V. 69
The Great Cloak. Dublin: 1978. V. 71
Home Again. Belfast: 1967. V. 70
Patriotic Suite. Dublin: 1966. V. 69

MONTAGUE, JOSEPH
The Crater of Kala. New York: 1925. V. 70

MONTAIGNE, MICHEL DE
The Diary of Montaigne's Journey to Italy by Way of Switzerland and Germany in 1580 and 1581. London: 1929. V. 72
Essais. Paris: 1925. V. 72
Essays. London: 1800. V. 73
Essays. London: 1931. V. 68
Journal Du Voyage en Italie, par la Suisse & L'Allemagne en 1580 & 1581. Paris: 1774. V. 68

MONTALBANO, WILLIAM D.
Basilica. New York: 1998. V. 72
A Death in China. 1984. V. 69
Powder Burn. New York: 1981. V. 69; 71; 73
Trap Line. 1982. V. 68
Trap Line. New York: 1982. V. 69

MONTALE, EUGENIO
Mottetti: the Motets of Eugenio Montale in Italian. San Francisco: 1973. V. 69; 73
Mottetti/Motets. Iowa City: 1981. V. 73

MONTANA: *Its Story & Biography - A History of Aboriginal & Territorial Montana & Three Decades of Statehood.* Chicago: 1921. V. 72

MONTANA - *History, Resources, Possibilities, Exhibit at the World's Fair and a Description....* Butte: 1893. V. 68; 73

MONTANA *Genesis.* Missoula: 1971. V. 68

MONTANA, *the Magazine of Western History. Special Custer Edition.* 1966. V. 68

MONTCLOS, J. M. PEROUSE DE
Etienne-Louis Boulee (1728-1799) Theoretician of Revolutionary Architecture. London: 1974. V. 72

MONTECINO, MARCEL
The Crosskiller. New York: 1988. V. 68; 72

MONTEFIORE, CHARLOTTE
A Few Words to the Jews by One of Themselves. London: 1853. V. 69

MONTEFIORE, JOSHUA
Commercial and Notarial Precedents: Consisting of All the Most Approved Forms, Special and Common, Which are Required in Transactions of Business. London: 1802. V. 70
The Trader's and Manufacturer's Compendium. London: 1804. V. 68

MONTEFIORE, LEONARD ABRAHAM
Essays and Letters Contributed to Various Periodicals Between September 1877 and August 1879. Together with Some Unpublished Fragments. London: 1881. V. 72

MONTEIRO, JOACHIM JOHN
Angola; and the River Congo. London: 1875. V. 71

MONTEIRO, ROSE
Delagoa Bay Its Natives and Natural History.... London: 1891. V. 71

MONTELATICI, DOMENICO
Villa Borghese Fuori di Porta a Pinciann. Rome: 1700. V. 70; 72

MONTENARI, GIOVANNI
Del Teatro Olimpico di Andrea Palladio in Vicenza.... Padua: 1749. V. 72

MONTESINOS, FERNANDO
Memorias Antiquas, Historiales Del Peru. London: 1920. V. 71

MONTESQUIEU, CHARLES LOUIS DE SECONDAT, BARON DE LA BREDE
De L'Esprit des Loix.... Geneva: 1750. V. 72
De l'Esprit des Loix. Copenhague et a Geneve: 1759. V. 69
The Spirit of Laws. Dublin: 1792. V. 70
A View of the English Constitution. London: 1781. V. 68

MONTESSORI, MARIA
Il Metodo Della Pedagogia Scientifica Applicato All 'Educazione Infantile Nelle Case dei Bambini. 1909. V. 68; 73

MONTEVAL, MARION
The Klan Inside Out. Claremore: 1924. V. 68

MONTEZ, LOLA
The Arts of Beauty. London: 1858?. V. 68
The Arts of Beauty; or, Secrets of a Lady's Toliet, with Things to Gentlemen on the Art of Fascinating. New York: 1858. V. 73
Autobiography and Lectures of Lola Montez. London: 1858. V. 71

MONTFAUCON, BERNARD DE
L'Antiquite Expliquee, et Representee en Figures. Paris: 1719. V. 73
Antiquity Explained and Represented in Sculptures, by the Learned Father Montfaucon. London: 1721-1722. V. 70

MONTFORT, GUILLAUME
Traite Elementaire de l'Art d'Ecrie. Paris: 1800. V. 68

MONTGAILLARD, JEAN GABRIEL MAURICE ROCQUES, COMTE
State of France in May, 1794. (bound with) Continuation of the State of France... (bound with) The Necessity of Continuing the War and the Dangers of an Immediate Peace. London: 1794. V. 68

MONTGOMERY & CO.
Odds & Ends #7. Tools, Supplies, and Machinery for All Branches of the Mechanical Trades. New York: 1890. V. 72

MONTGOMERY, BERNARD L.
El Alamein to the River Sangro Eighth Army. 1946. V. 68

MONTGOMERY, FLORENCE
The Town-Crier; to Which is Added The Children with the Indian Rubber Ball.... London: 1874. V. 73

MONTGOMERY, H. H.
The History of Kennington and Its Neighbourhood, With Chapters on Cricket Past and Present. London: 1889. V. 71

MONTGOMERY, INA
John Hugh Allen of the Gallant Company: A Memoir by his Sister. London: 1919. V. 72

MONTGOMERY, JAMES
The Chimney-Sweeper's Friend and Climbing-Boys Album.... London: 1825. V. 71
Montgomery's Christmas Annual 1955. Philadelphia: 1955. V. 69
The Pelican Island and Other Poems. London: 1827. V. 68
Poetical Works of James Montgomery. 1867. V. 68
Prison Amusements and Other Trifles. London: 1797. V. 72
Prose, by a Poet. London: 1824. V. 71
Songs of Zion; Being Imitations of Psalms. London: 1822. V. 69; 72
The Wanderer In Switzerland, And Other Poems. Edinburgh: 1813. V. 71; 72
The West Indies and Other Poems. London: 1814?. V. 73
The World Before the Flood, a Poem. London: 1815. V. 71; 72

MONTGOMERY, L. M.
Emily Climbs. New York: 1925. V. 70; 72
The Selected Journals of...Volume I to IV 1889-1935. Toronto: 1985-1998. V. 72
Magic for Marigold. New York: 1929. V. 72
Mistress Pat. 1935. V. 69

MONTGOMERY, ROBERT
Oxford. Oxford: 1831. V. 72
Oxford. Oxford: 1834. V. 72
Poetical Trifles by a Youth. 1825. V. 68
A Universal Prayer: Death; A Vision of Heaven and a Vision of Hell. Boston: 1829. V. 73

MONTGOMERY, ROSS GORDON
Franciscan Awatovi: the Excavation and Conjectural Reconstruction of a 17th Century Spanish Mission Establishment at a Hopi Indian Town in Northeastern Arizona. Cambridge: 1949. V. 69; 70

MONTGOMERY, RUTHERFORD G.
High Country. New York: 1938. V. 69

MONTGOMERY, WALTER
Appomattox and the Return Home. Raleigh: 1938. V. 69
The Days of Old and the Years that are Past. Charlottesville?: 1939?. V. 69

MONTGOMERY WARD & CO.
Catalog #112. Spring and Summer 1930. Chicago: 1930. V. 72
Catalog #97. 1872-1922. Golden Jubilee. Chicago: 1922. V. 72
Seeds. Chicago: 1908. V. 72

MONTGOMERY OF ALAMEIN, BERNARD LAW MONTGOMERY, 1ST VISCOUNT
El Alamein to the River Sangro. Berlin: 1946. V. 71
Normandy to the Baltic 21 Army Group. 1946. V. 68

MONTHAN, DORIS
R. C. Gorman: a Retrospective. Flagstaff: 1990. V. 68
R. C. Gorman: the Lithographs. Flagstaff: 1978. V. 68; 69; 70; 72; 73

MONTHAN, GUY
Art and Indian Individualists, the Art of Seventeen Contemporary Southwestern Artists and Craftsmen. Flagstaff: 1975. V. 70; 73

MONTHERLANT, HENRY DE
Le Cardinal d'Espagne - Piece en Trois Actes. Paris: 1960. V. 70
La Deesse Cypris. Paris & Bordeaux: 1946. V. 70
Les Garcons. Paris: 1969. V. 70
Service Inutile. Paris: 1935. V. 70

MONTORGUEIL, G.
Jouons a Histoire!. Paris: 1908. V. 70
Louis XI. Paris: 1905. V. 69
Murat. Paris: 1903. V. 72
Paris Dansant. Paris: 1898. V. 68; 71

MONTROSS, LOIS SEYSTER
Among Those Present. New York: 1927. V. 71

MONTROSS, LYNN
Town and Gown. New York: 1923. V. 71

MONTULE, E.
Travels In Egypt, During 1818 and 1819. London: 1821. V. 72
A Voyage to North America and the West Indies in 1817. London: 1821. V. 71

MONVEL, JACQUES MARIE BOUTET DE
L'Amant Bourru, Comedie en Trois Actes et en Vers Libres. Paris: 1777. V. 70

MONYPENNY, WILLIAM FLAVELLE
The Life of Benjamin Disraeli Earl of Beaconsfield. London: 1910-1920. V. 71; 73
The Life of Benjamin Disraeli, Earl of Beaconsfield. New York: 1913. V. 70

MOODIE, J. W. D.
Ten Years in South Africa.... London: 1835. V. 70

MOODY, D. W.
The Life of A Rover. 1926. V. 72

MOODY, RALPH
The Dry Divide. New York: 1963. V. 69
Mary Emma and Company. New York: 1961. V. 69

MOODY, RICK
Demonology. London: 2000. V. 68
Garden State. Wainscott: 1992. V. 68
Garden State. Wainscott: 1993. V. 70
The Ice Storm. Boston: 1994. V. 68; 69; 71; 72; 73
The Ring of Brightest Angels Around Heaven. Boston: 1995. V. 70

MOODY, SKYE KATHLEEN
Blue Poppy. New York: 1997. V. 70
Rain Dance. New York: 1996. V. 70

MOODY, T. W.
A New History of Ireland. Volume III. 1982. V. 73
Queen's Belfast 1845-1949. 1959. V. 70

MOODY, WILLIAM VAUGHN
The Masque of Judgment. Boston: 1900. V. 69

MOOKERJEE, MOHINDRO NAUTH
The Memoir of the Late Honourable Justice Onnocool Chunder Mookerjee. Serumpore: 1873. V. 70

MOON, ANNA MARIA
Family Memorial. London: 1872. V. 72; 73
In Memoriam. The Rev. W. Leeves, Author of the Air of "Auld Robin Gray". London: 1873. V. 73

MOON, LORNA
Dark Star. Indianapolis: 1929. V. 72

MOON, SARAH
Still. Minneapolis: 2000. V. 68; 70

MOONEY, BOOTH
Here Is My Body. New York: 1952. V. 72

MOONEYHAM, LAURA G.
Romance, Language and Education in Jane Austen's Novels. 1988. V. 70

MOOR, BARTHOLOMAEI DE
Cogitationum De Instauratione Medicinae, ad Sanitatis.... Amsterdam: 1695. V. 71

MOOR, EDWARD
The Hindu Pantheon. Madras: 1864. V. 69

MOOR, J. F.
The Birth-place, Home, Churches, and Other Places Connected with the Author of The Christian Year. Winchester: 1867. V. 70

MOORAT, S. A. J.
Catalogue of Western Manuscripts on Medicine and Science in the Wellcome Historical Medical Library. London: 1962-1973. V. 68

MOORCOCK, MICHAEL
Stormbringer. London: 1965. V. 71

MOORCROFT, WILLIAM
Travels in the Himalayan Provinces. London: 1841. V. 71

MOORE, A. W.
The Alps in 1864. 1902. V. 68; 70; 73
The Alps in 1864. 1939. V. 68
The Alps in 1864. Oxford: 1939. V. 69

MOORE, ANNE
An Account of the Extraordinary Abstinence of Ann Moor(e) of Tutbury. Uttoxeter: 1810. V. 70

MOORE, ANNE CARROLL
The Art of Beatrix Potter. London: 1955. V. 69
A Century of Kate Greenaway. London: 1946. V. 68; 72

MOORE, BERTHA B.
Doctor Happy. Grand Rapids: 1938. V. 71

MOORE, BRIAN
Judith Hearne. London: 1955. V. 70; 72
Lies of Silence. London: 1990. V. 73
The Lonely Passion of Judith Hearne. Boston and Toronto: 1955. V. 69; 71
The Mangan Inheritance. Toronto: 1979. V. 72

MOORE, C. L.
Shambleau and Others. New York: 1953. V. 69; 70

MOORE, CHRISTOPHER
Practical Demon Keeping. London: 1992. V. 73

MOORE, CLAYTON
I Was that Masked Man. Dallas: 1996. V. 68

MOORE, CLEMENT CLARKE
Compendious Lexicon of the Hebrew Language. New York: 1809. V. 71
The Night Before Christmas. London: 1904. V. 69
The Night Before Christmas. New York: 1908. V. 71
The Night Before Christmas. New York: 1911. V. 72; 73
The Night Before Christmas. Philadelphia: 1918. V. 70
The Night Before Christmas. New York: 1930. V. 69; 73
The Night Before Christmas. Philadelphia: 1931. V. 70
The Night Before Christmas. Akron: 1932. V. 71
The Night Before Christmas. New York: 1944. V. 69
The Night Before Christmas. New York: 1949. V. 73
The Night Before Christmas. New York: 1951. V. 71
Twas the Night Before Christmas. Boston: 1912. V. 70
A Visit from Saint Nicholas. New York: 1862. V. 71
A Visit from Saint Nicholas. Boston: 1879. V. 69
A Visit from St. Nicholas. Windham: 1937. V. 73

MOORE, COLLEEN
The Enchanted Castle. New York: 1935. V. 73

MOORE, DANIEL C.
Stellate Ganglion Block. Springfield: 1954. V. 68; 72

MOORE, DAPHNE
In Nimrod's Footsteps. 1994. V. 68

MOORE, DAVID
Concise Notices of British Grasses Best Suited for Agriculture, With Preserved Specimens of Each Kind. Dublin: 1850. V. 69
Concise Notices of the Indigenous Grasses of Ireland, Best Suited for Agriculture, with Dried Specimens of Each Kind. Mullingar: 1843. V. 69

MOORE, DORIS LANGLEY
E. Nesbit. A Biography. Philadelphia and New York: 1966. V. 72

MOORE, EDWARD
Fables for the Female Sex. London: 1771. V. 72; 73
Fables for the Ladies.... Philadelphia: 1787. V. 73

MOORE, EDWARD A.
The Story of a Cannoneer Under Stonewall Jackson in Which is Told the Part Taken by the Rockbridge Arillery in the Army of Northern Virginia. Lynchburg: 1910. V. 69; 70

MOORE, F. FRANKFORT
The Sale of a Soul. London: 1895. V. 69

MOORE, F. J.
A History of Chemistry. London: 1939. V. 69

MOORE, FRANCIS
Vox Stellarum; or, a Loyal Almanack for...1789. 1789. V. 69

MOORE, FRANK
Women of the War; Their Heroism and Self-Sacrifice. Hartford: 1867. V. 70

MOORE, GEORGE
Aphrodite in Aulis. 1930. V. 69; 73
Aphrodite in Aulis. London: 1930. V. 71
Avowals. London: 1919. V. 71
The Brook Kerith. London: 1916. V. 68
The Brook Kerith. London: 1929. V. 68; 71
Confessions of a Young Man. 1904. V. 71
Flowers of Passion. 1878. V. 72
Hail and Farewell. 1911-1914. V. 69; 73
Hail and Farewell. 1925. V. 70
Hail and Farewell. London: 1925. V. 71
Heloise and Abelard. New York: 1921. V. 69; 73
Heloise and Abelard. (with) Fragments from Heloise. 1921. V. 71
In Single Strictness. 1922. V. 69
In Single Strictness. London: 1922. V. 71
Letters from George Moore to Ed. Dujardin 1886-1922. New York: 1929. V. 70
The Making of an Immortal. New York and London: 1927. V. 69; 71
Memoirs of My Dead Life. 1921. V. 69
Memoirs of My Dead Life of Galanteries, Meditations and Remembrances, Soliloquies or Advice to Lovers . . . London: 1921. V. 71
A Mummer's Wife. 1918. V. 70
Pagan Poems. London: 1881. V. 72
The Pastoral Loves of Daphnis & Chloe. 1924. V. 69
Peronnik the Fool. New York: 1926. V. 72
Peronnik The Fool. London: 1933. V. 69; 71
The Power of the Soul Over the Body, Considered in Relation to Health and Morals. London: 1845. V. 71
Sister Theresa. London: 1901. V. 69
Ulick and Soracha. 1926. V. 69; 73

MOORE, HENRY
Henry Moore on Sculpture. London: 1966. V. 70
Shelter Sketch Book. London. V. 73
Shelter Sketch Book. London: 1945. V. 69

MOORE, HONOR
Darling. New York: 2001. V. 72

MOORE, J. A.
The Frogs of Eastern New South Wales. New York: 1961. V. 72

MOORE, J. E. S.
The Maoiotic Process in Mammalia. London: 1906. V. 72
To the Mountains of the Moon. London: 1901. V. 71

MOORE, JAMES
Kilpatrick and Our Cavalry.... New York: 1865. V. 69; 71

MOORE, JAMES EDWARD
Orthopedic Surgery. Philadelphia: 1898. V. 69

MOORE, JOHN
A Journal During a Residence in France, From the Beginning of August to the Middle of December 1792. London: 1793. V. 69; 73
Mordaunt: Sketches of Life, Characters and Manners, in Various Countries.... London: 1800. V. 68; 72
The Post Captain; or the Wooden Walls Well Manned.... London: 1815. V. 72
A View of Society and Manners in France, Switzerland and Germany: With Anecdotes Relating to Some Eminent Characters. London: 1789. V. 68
A View Of Society and Manners In Italy. London: 1781. V. 72
A View of the Causes and Progress of the French Revolution. London: 1795. V. 69
Zeluco. London: 1789. V. 69; 72; 73

MOORE, JOHN H.
Albemarle Jefferson's County 1727-1976. Charlottesville: 1976. V. 72

MOORE, JOHN HAMILTON
The New Practical Navigator; Being an Epitome of Navigation.... Newburyport: 1800. V. 68

MOORE, JOHN T.
Tennessee: the Volunteer State 1796-1923. Chicago and Nashville: 1923. V. 69

MOORE, JOHN W.
History of North Carolina. Raleigh: 1900. V. 71

MOORE, JOSEPH
Eighteen Views Taken at and Near Rangoon, with Views in the Birman Empire.... London: 1825-1826. V. 69

MOORE, L. B.
The Oxford Book of New Zealand Plants. Wellington: 1978. V. 68; 70; 73

MOORE, LORRIE
Anagrams. New York: 1986. V. 68; 69; 71; 73
Birds of America. New York: 1998. V. 68; 69; 72
I Know Some Things: Stories About Childhood by Contemporary Writers. Boston: 1992. V. 69
Like Life. New York: 1990. V. 68; 69
Self-Help. New York: 1985. V. 68; 69; 70; 71; 73
Who Will Run the Frog Hospital?. New York: 1994. V. 69; 70
Who Will Run the Frog Hospital?. Madison: 1995. V. 70

MOORE, LOUIS T.
Stories Old and New of the Cape Fear Region. Wilmington: 1956. V. 72

MOORE, MARIANNE
The Absentee - a Comedy in Four Acts. New York: 1962. V. 70; 73
The Accented Syllable. New York: 1969. V. 68
Collected Poems. London: 1951. V. 70
Collected Poems. New York: 1951. V. 69
Collected Poems. New York: 1959. V. 72
The Complete Poems. New York: 1967. V. 68; 70; 73
The Complete Poems. New York: 1981. V. 68
Dress and Kindred Subjects. New York: 1965. V. 68; 73
A Face: a Poem by Marianne Craig Moore. Massachusetts: 1949. V. 68
Idiosyncrasy and Technique. Berkeley and Los Angeles: 1958. V. 68; 70
Letters from and to the Ford Motor Company. New York: 1958. V. 68; 69
Like a Bulwark. New York: 1956. V. 73
A Marianne Moore Reader. New York: 1961. V. 70; 72
O to be a Dragon. New York: 1959. V. 70; 72
Poems. London: 1921. V. 69; 70; 72; 73
Poetry and Criticism. Cambridge: 1965. V. 68; 73
Predilections. New York: 1955. V. 73
Selected Poems. London: 1935. V. 73
Selected Poems. New York: 1935. V. 69
Tell Me, Tell Me. New York: 1966. V. 68; 72; 73
Tipoo's Tiger. New York: 1967. V. 68
What Are Years: Poems. New York: 1941. V. 68

MOORE, MARINDA BRANSON
The Geographical Reader for the Dixie Children. Raleigh: 1863. V. 70

MOORE, MERRILL
The Noise that Time Makes. New York: 1929. V. 68
Poems from the Fugitive (1922-1926). New York: 1936. V. 69
Sonnets from New Directions. Norfolk: 1938. V. 68

MOORE, MILCAH MARTHA HILL
Miscellanies, Moral and Instructive in Prose and Verse.... Burlington: 1796. V. 71

MOORE, N. HUDSON
Old Glass. European and American. New York: 1924. V. 69

MOORE, NICHOLAS
The Anonymous Elegies and Other Poems. London: 1945. V. 68
The Glass Gower. London: 1944. V. 68

MOORE, OLIVE
Further Reflections on the Death of a Porcupine. London: 1932. V. 72
Repentance at Leisure. New York: 1930. V. 71

MOORE, PHIL H.
With Gun and Rod in Canada. Boston: 1922. V. 73
With Gun and Rod in Canada. London: 1922. V. 73

MOORE, R. C.
Treatise on Invertebrate Paleontology. Part H. Brachiopoda. New York: 1965. V. 68

MOORE, RICHARD
Important Notices of that Which Concerns the Pecuniary Credit of a State, and in Particular that of England. London. V. 68

MOORE, ROBERT A.
Ageing and Degenerative Diseases. Lancaster: 1945. V. 72

MOORE, ROBERT J.
Native Americans- A Portrait- The Art and Travels of Charles Bird King, George Catlin, And Karl Bodmer. New York: 1997. V. 71

MOORE, ROBIN
The French Connection. Boston: 1969. V. 68; 70; 71

MOORE, ROGER
Roger Moore as James Bond. London: 1973. V. 70

MOORE, ROY L.
History of Woodford County. Eureka: 1910. V. 68

MOORE, SAMUEL
An Accurate System of Surveying.... Litchfield: 1796. V. 68; 71

MOORE, SARAH L.
Merry Jingles. New York: 1901. V. 70

MOORE, SUSANNA
Sleeping Beauties. New York: 1993. V. 71

MOORE, T. V.
Memorial Discourse on the Death of General Robert E. Lee, Delivered by Request of the People of Nashville, in the First Presbyterian Church, on Sunday Afternoon October 23, 1870. Nashville: 1870. V. 69

MOORE, TEX
The West. 1935. V. 70

MOORE, THOMAS
British Ferns and Their Allies: an Abrigment of the Popular History of British Ferns.... London: 1873. V. 68
British Wild Flowers. 1867. V. 68

MOORE, THOMAS continued
Epistles, Odes and Other Poems. London: 1806. V. 72
Epitome of Gardening. Edinburgh: 1881. V. 70
Irish Melodies, Lalla Rookh, National Airs, Legendary Ballads, Songs &c., with a memoir by J. F. Waller. London. V. 71
Lalla Rookh, an Oriental Romance. London: 1817. V. 72
Lalla Rookh, an Oriental Romance. London: 1822. V. 73
Lalla Rookh, an Oriental Romance. London: 1858. V. 70; 71
Lalla Rookh, an Oriental Romance. London: 1861. V. 70
Lalla Rookh: an Oriental Romance. Boston: 1888. V. 68
The Loves of the Angels, a Poem. London: 1823. V. 68; 72; 73
Melodies. Philadelphia: 1821. V. 72
Memoirs of the Life of Richard Brinsley Sheridan. London. V. 69; 72
Memoirs of the Life of Richard Brinsley Sheridan. 1827. V. 69; 73
The Octavo Nature-Printed British Ferns. London: 1859-1860. V. 72; 73
Paradise and the Peri. London: 1860. V. 69; 72
The Poetical Works of Thomas Moore. 1868-1869. V. 69
Travels of an Irish Gentleman in Search of a Religion. Paris: 1833. V. 69

MOORE, THOMAS GEORGE
The Bachelor; a Novel. London: 1809. V. 73

MOORE, THOMAS STURGE
Armour for Aphrodite. 1929. V. 68; 71
Danae. London: 1903. V. 73
The Passionate Pilgrim and the Songs in Shakespeare's Plays. London: 1896. V. 73
The Vinedresser and Other Poems. London: 1899. V. 72

MOORE, VANDI
Brands on the Boswell. 1986. V. 68
Brands On the Boswell. Glendo: 1986. V. 71

MOORE, VIRGINIA
The Life and Eager Death of Emily Bronte. 1936. V. 70; 73

MOOREHEAD, W. K.
The Hopewell Mound Group of Ohio. 1922. V. 69
Narrative of Explorations in the New Mexico, Arizona, Indiana, Etc. Andover;: 1906. V. 69
The Stone Age in North America. Boston: 1910. V. 69

MOORE'S Mineral Springs. Winston-Salem: 1913. V. 73

MOORHEAD, MAX L.
The Apache Frontier. Norman: 1968. V. 72

MOORHOUSE, REED
The Ivory Gate. London: 1911. V. 69

MOORLAND, MAX L.
New Mexico's Royal Road, Trade and Travel on the Chihuahua Trail. Norman: 1958. V. 73

MOORMAN, JOHN J.
Mineral Springs of North America, How to Reach and How to Use Them. Philadelphia: 1873. V. 70
Virginia Springs With Their Analysis and Some Remarks on Their Character, Together with a Directory for the Use of the White Sulphur Water.... Philadelphia: 1847. V. 71
Virginia White Sulphur Springs, With the Analysis of Its Waters, the Diseases to Which They Are Applicable ad Some Account of Society and its Amusements at the Springs. Baltimore: 1873. V. 71

MOORMAN, MARY
The Early Years 1770-1803. London: 1957. V. 72
William Wordsworth - a Biography. The Early Years 1770-1803. Oxford: 1957. V. 71
William Wordsworth - a Biography. The Early Years. 1770-1803. The Later Years 1803-1850. Oxford: 1965. V. 70; 71; 72
William Wordsworth - a Biography. The Later Years 1803-1850. Oxford: 1966. V. 71; 72

MOORREES, COENRAAD F. A.
The Aleut Dentition. A Corelative Study of Dental Characteristics in an Eskimoid People. Cambridge: 1957. V. 68

MOORS, H. J.
With Stevenson in Samoa. London: 1910. V. 69; 71

MOOTOO, SHANI
Cereus Blooms at Night. New York: 1998. V. 72

MOOTZ, HERMAN E.
Pawnee Bill, A Romance of Oklahoma. Los Angeles: 1928. V. 71

MORA, GILLES
Walker Evans Havana 1933. New York: 1989. V. 68

MORA, JOSEPH
Californios: the Saga of the Hard-Riding Vaqueros, Americas First Cowboys. Garden City: 1949. V. 69
Trail Dust and Saddle Leather. New York: 1946. V. 69
The Year of the Hopi: Paintings and Photographs by Joseph Mora, 1904-1906. Washington: 1979. V. 69; 70

MORAES, DOM
A Beginning. 1957. V. 68; 71

MORAIS, HERBERT
The History of the Negro in Medicine. New York: 1969. V. 73

THE MORAL Miscellany; or a Collection of Select Pieces in Prose and Verse. London: 1778. V. 69

MORAN, ISABELO C.
Handbook of Legal Maxims. Mainla: 1955. V. 71

MORAN, JAMES
The Black Art. 1962-1965. V. 71
The Double Crown: a History of Fifty Years. London: 1974. V. 69
Heraldic Influence on Early Printers' Devices. London: 1978. V. 69
Printing Presses: History and Development from the Fifteenth Century to Modern Times. London: 1973. V. 69; 70
Printing Presses, History and Development from the Fifteenth Century to the Modern Times. Los Angeles & Berkeley: 1973. V. 68
Stanley Morison. His Typographic Achievement. London: 1971. V. 70

MORAN, PATRICK A.
Essays on the Origin, Doctrines, and Discipline of the Early Irish Church. 1864. V. 69

MORAN, PATRICK F.
The Analecta of David Rothe, Bishop of Ossory. 1884. V. 70

MORAND, FRANCOIS SAUEVEUR
Opuscule de Chirurgie. Paris: 1768-1772. V. 68

MORAND, PAUL
Black Magic. New York: 1929. V. 68
Closed All Night. London: 1924. V. 68
Paris de Nuit. Paris: 1933. V. 70

MORAND, S. F.
Opuscule de Chirurgie. Paris: 1768-1772. V. 73
Opuscules de Chirurgie. Premiere Partie (only). Paris: 1768. V. 72

MORANDI, GIAMBATTISTA
Historia Botanica Practica.... Milan: 1744. V. 68; 73

MORANG, ALFRED
Dane Rudhyar. Pioneer In Creative Synthesis. New York: 1939. V. 72

MORANT, G. F.
Game Preservers and Bird Preservers. Which are Our Friends?. 1875. V. 71

MORANT, GEORGE SOULIE DE
A History of Chinese Art from Ancient Times to the Present Day. New York. V. 73

MORATH, INGE
Portraits. New York: 1963. V. 69

MORAVETZ, BRUNO
The Big Book of Mountaineering. London: 1980. V. 69

MORAY BROWN, J.
Stray Sport. 1893. V. 69; 70; 72; 73

MORDECAI, SAMUEL
Richmond in By-Gone Days: Being Reminiscences of an Old Citizen. Richmond: 1856. V. 68; 71

MORDEN, W.
Our African Adventure. 1953. V. 70; 72; 73
Our African Adventure. London: 1954. V. 71

MORDEN, WILLIAM I.
Across Asia's Snows and Deserts. New York: 1927. V. 70

MORE Adventures of Rupert (1953 Annual). V. 73

MORE, ALEXANDER G.
Contributions Towards a Cybele Hibernica.... 1898. V. 71
Contributions Towards a Cybele Hibernica.... Dublin: 1898. V. 69
Contributions Towards a Cybele Hibernica.... London: 1898. V. 70

MORE Dick and Jane Stories. Chicago: 1934. V. 72

MORE, HANNAH
The Letters of Hannah More. London: 1925. V. 72
Ode to Dragon, Mr. Garrick's House-Dog, at Hampton. London: 1777. V. 70; 71
Sacred Dramas, Chiefly Intended for Young Persons.. Newark: 1806. V. 71
The Search After Happiness. Philadelphia: 1811. V. 73
Strictures on the Modern System of Female Education. 1799. V. 69
Strictures on the Modern System of Female Education. London: 1799. V. 73
Strictures on the Modern System of Female Education. Charlestown: 1800. V. 69; 73
Strictures on the Modern System of Female Education. Philadelphia: 1800. V. 69; 73
Sunday Reading. The Valley of Tears, A Vision. London: 1800. V. 70
Thoughts on the Importance of the Manners of the Great to General Society. London: 1788. V. 69
The Works. New York: 1855. V. 71

MORE, HENRY
Divine Dialogues, Containing Sundry Disquisitions and Instructions Concerning the Attributes and Providence of God. 1668. V. 72
Divine Dialogues, Containing Sundry Disquisitions and Instructions Concerning the Attributes and Providence of God. London: 1668. V. 68
Enchiridion Ethicum: an Account of Virtue: or Dr. Henry More's Abridgement of Morals Put Into English. New York: 1930. V. 73

MORE, JAMES F.
The History of Queens County, N.S. Halifax: 1873. V. 73

MORE, LOUIS TRENCHARD
The Life and Works of the Honourable Robert Boyle. London: 1944. V. 68; 72

MORE Tasty Dishes Made from Tested Recipes. London: 1915?. V. 68

MORE, THOMAS
A Fruteful and Pleasaunt Worke of the Best State of a Publique Wale, and of the Newe Yle Called Utopia. 1906. V. 73
Utopia. London: 1684. V. 73
Utopia. Dublin: 1737. V. 70; 73
Utopia. Glasgow: 1743. V. 69; 71
Utopia. Glasgow: 1762. V. 73
Utopia. London: 1808. V. 69
Utopia. Boston: 1878. V. 69
Utopia. Detroit: 1902. V. 69
Utopia. 1906. V. 71
Utopia. New York: 1934. V. 70

MOREAU, ADELE
L'Avenir Devoile Chiromancie, Nouvelle. Paris: 1869. V. 73

MOREAU, B.
Interieurs en Couleur Premiere Serie, Meubles, Decoration Teintures. Paris: 1920. V. 68

MOREAU, F. J.
A Practical Treatise on Midwifery: Exhibiting the Present Advanced State of the Science. Philadelphia: 1844. V. 71; 73

MOREAU, JACOB NICHOLAS
Memoire Contenant le Precis des Faites, Avec Leurs Pieces Justificatives.... Paris: 1756. V. 68

MOREAU DE LA SARTHE, JACQUES LOUIS
Histoire Naturelle De La Femme, Suivie d'un Traite d'Hygiene Appliquee a Son Regime Physique et Moral, Aux Differentes Epoques de La Vie. Avec Planches Gravees en Taille Douce. Paris;: 1803. V. 73

MOREAU-VAUTHIER, C.
The Technique of Painting. London: 1923. V. 72

MORECAMP, ARTHUR
Live Boys in the Black Hills or the Young Texan Gold Hunters. 1880. V. 68
Live Boys in the Black Hills; Or The Young Texas Gold Hunters.... Boston: 1880. V. 71
Live Boys, or Charley and Nasho in Texas. 1878. V. 68
Live Boys: Or Charley and Nasho in Texas. Boston: 1879. V. 71

MOREL, BERNARD
The French Crown Jewels. Antwerp: 1988. V. 72

MOREL, C.
Culture des Orchidees. 1855. V. 69

MOREL, JEAN MARIE
Theorie des Jardins. Paris: 1776. V. 68; 70; 72

MORELAND, A.
Through South Westland. London: 1911. V. 71

MORELLY
Code de la Nature, ou le Veritable Esprit de ses Loix, de Tout Neglige ou Meconnu. Paris or Liege?: 1755. V. 73

MORES, EDWARD ROWE
A Dissertation Upon English Typographical Founders and Foundries. New York: 1924. V. 69; 70

MORETON, C. O.
The Auricula, Its History and Character. London: 1964. V. 70
Old Carnations and Pinks. London: 1955. V. 68

MOREY, FRANK
A Guide to the Natural History of the Isle of Wight.... Newport and London: 1909. V. 70

MOREY, P.
Charpente de la Cathedrale de Messine.... Paris: 1841. V. 69

MORGAGNI, GIOVANNI BATTISTA
Adversaria Anatomica Omnia. Lugduni Batavorum: 1723. V. 68; 70; 73
Epistolae Anatomicae Duae Novas Observationes et Animadversiones Complectentes.... Venetiis: 1762. V. 68
Opuscula Miscellanea Quorum Non Pauca Nunc Primum Prodeunt, Tres in Partes opuscula. Neapoli: 1763. V. 68
The Seats and Causes of Disease Investigated by Anatomy in Five Books.... London: 1769. V. 68; 70; 73

MORGAN, ALFRED P.
How to Build a 20-foot Bi-Plane Glider. New York and London: 1912. V. 72

MORGAN, BERRY
Pursuit. Boston: 1966. V. 69

MORGAN, CARLISLE LEE
Basic Principles of Computed Tomography. Baltimore: 1983. V. 68

MORGAN, CHARLES
Liberties of the Mind. London: 1951. V. 70
The Mohawks: a Satirical Poem. London: 1822. V. 68
Six Philosophical Dissertations on the Mechanical Powers. Cambridge: 1770. V. 70

MORGAN, D. J.
The Official History of Colonial Development. Atlantic Highlands: 1980. V. 69

MORGAN, DALE
California As I Saw It. Los Gatos: 1960. V. 70
Jedediah Smith and His Maps of the American West. San Francisco: 1954. V. 73
Jedediah Smith and the Opening of the West. Indianapolis: 1953. V. 69; 70; 72; 73
The Overland Diary of James Prichard from Kentucky to California in 1849. Denver: 1959. V. 69
Overland in 1846 - Diaries and Letters of the California-Oregon Trail. Georgetown: 1963. V. 73
The Rocky Mountain Journals of William Marshal Anderson: the West in 1834. San Marino: 1967. V. 68; 73
Santa Fe and the Far West. Los Angeles: 1949. V. 73
The West of William H. Ashley...Recorded in the Diaries and Letters...1822-1838. Denver: 1964. V. 68; 73

MORGAN, DECK
Winter Carnival. New York: 1935. V. 72

MORGAN, GWENDA
Wood Engravings. Andoversford: 1985. V. 70; 72

MORGAN, H. W.
The New Irish Constitution, an Exposition and Some Arguments. London: 1912. V. 71

MORGAN, HILARY
Burne-Jones, the Pre-Raphaelties and Their Century. 1989. V. 68

MORGAN, JAMES MORRIS
Recollections of a Rebel Reefer. Boston: 1917. V. 69; 70; 73

MORGAN, JOHN
A Discourse Upon the Institution of Medical Schools in America.... Philadelphia: 1765. V. 70
Four Dissertations on the Reciprocal Advantages of a Perpetual Union Between Great Britain and Her American Colonies. Philadelphia: 1766. V. 68; 73
Lectures on Diseases of the Eye. 1839. V. 73

MORGAN, JOHN MINTER
The Revolt of the Bees. 1830. V. 71
The Revolt of the Bees. London: 1830. V. 68
The Revolt of the Bees. London: 1839. V. 71; 72
Tracts Originally Published at Various Periods from 1819 to 1838. London: 1850. V. 71

MORGAN, JOHN PIERPONT
Pictures in the Collection of J. Pierpont Morgan at Prince's Gate and Dover House, London. London: 1907. V. 72

MORGAN, JONNIE
History of Wichita Falls. Wichita Falls: 1931. V. 68; 73

MORGAN, LEWIS H.
The American Beaver and His Works. 1868. V. 68
The American Beaver and His Works. Philadelphia: 1868. V. 72
Houses and House Life of the American Aborigines. Washington: 1881. V. 69
The Indian Journals 1859-1863. Ann Arbor: 1959. V. 71
League of the So-De-No-Sau-Nee or Iroquis. New York: 1922. V. 70

MORGAN, LLOYD
The Springs of Conduct. London: 1885. V. 71

MORGAN, MARSHALL
The Battle of Franklin. Franklin: 1931. V. 69; 70

MORGAN, P. W.
History of Wyandotte County Kansas and Its People. Chicago: 1911. V. 68

MORGAN, SETH
Dead Man Walkin'. New York: 1990. V. 72

MORGAN, SYDNEY OWENSON
France. London: 1817. V. 68; 73
Italy. London: 1821. V. 69; 73
O'Donnel. London: 1814. V. 68; 72
Passages from My Autobiography. 1859. V. 70
Woman and Her Master. London: 1840?. V. 68; 69

MORGAN, THOMAS
The Moral Philosopher. London: 1737. V. 70
My Story of The Last Indian War in The Northwest. Grove: 1954. V. 72
Romano-British Mosaic Pavements. A History of their Discover and a Record and Interpretation of their Designs. London: 1886. V. 70; 72

MORGAN, THOMAS CHARLES
An Eulogium on Sir Samuel Romilly, Pronounced at the Royal Athenaeum of Paris, on the 26th of December 1818. London: 1819. V. 69
Sketches of the Philosophy of Morals. London: 1822. V. 68

MORGAN, THOMAS HUNT
A Critique of the Theory of Evolution. London: 1916. V. 72
The Physical Basis of Heredity. Philadelphia: 1919. V. 72
The Scientific Basis of Evolution. New York: 1932. V. 72
The Theory of the Gene. New Haven: 1928. V. 72

MORGAN, W. A.
The House on Sport. 1899. V. 73

MORGAN, WILLIAM
Additional Facts, Addressed to the Serious Attention of the People of Great Britain, Respecting the Expences of the War and the State of the National Debt. London: 1796. V. 72

MORGAN, WILLIAM continued
An Appeal to the People of Great Britain on the Present Alarming State of the Public Finances and of Public Credit. London: 1797. V. 72
A Comparative View of the Public Finances, from the Beginning to the Close of the Late Administration. London: 1801. V. 72
A Comparative View of the Public Finances from The Beginning to the Close of the Late Administration.... London: 1803. V. 72
Facts Addressed to the Serious Attention of the People of Great Britain Respecting the Expence of the War, and the State of the National Debt. London: 1796. V. 72
Illustrations of Masonry, by One of the Fraternity, Who Has Devoted 30 Years to the Subject. Batavia?: 1827. V. 68
Illustrations of Masonry, by One of the Fraternity, Who Has Devoted Thirty Years to the Subject. New York: 1827. V. 73
A Narrative of the Facts and Circumstances Relating to the Kidnapping and Presumed Murder of William Morgan.... Brookfield: 1827. V. 68
The Principles and Doctrine of Assurances, Annuities on Lives and Contingent Reversions, Stated and Explained. London: 1821. V. 70; 71
A Review of Dr. Price's Writings on the Finances of Great Britain. London: 1795. V. 72

MORGAN, WILLIAM H.
Personal Reminiscences of the War of 1861-1865. Lynchburg: 1911. V. 69; 70

MORGENSTEIN, GARY
Take Me Out to the Ballgame. New York: 1980. V. 68

MORIARTY, HENRIETTA M.
Fifty Plates of Greenhouse Plants, Drawn and Coloured from Nature. 1807. V. 73

MORICE, A. G.
Le Petit Catechisme a L'Usage des Sauvages Porteurs. Mission du Lac Stuart: 1891. V. 70

MORICE, JOHN
Catalogue of the Valuable Library of the Late John Morice, Esq.... London: 1844. V. 70

MORIER, JAMES
The Adventures of Hajji Baba of Ispahan in England. London: 1856. V. 68

MORIER, JAMES JUSTINIAN
A Journey through Persia, Armenia and Asia Minor. (with) A Second Journey through Persia, Armenia and Asia Minor, to Constantinople, Between the Years 1810 and 1816. London: 1812-1818. V. 71

MORIN, JEAN BAPTISTE
Nova Mundi Sublunari Anatomia. Paris: 1619. V. 68; 73

MORIS, GIUSEPPE GIACINTO
Flora Sardoa seu Historia Plantarum in Sardinia et Adjacentibus Insulis vel Sponte Nascentium vel ad Utilitatem Latius Excultarum. Torino: 1837-1859. V. 70

MORISON, DOUGLAS
Sketches of Scenes in Scotland, Drawn in Outline by Lieut. Col. Murray (of Ochtertyre). Perth. V. 72

MORISON, J. COTTER
Macaulay. London: 1885. V. 71

MORISON, J. EDGAR
Foetal and Neonatal Pathology. London: 1970. V. 68

MORISON, MARGARET COTTER
A Lonely Summer in Kashmir. London: 1904. V. 71

MORISON, SAMUEL ELIOT
Admiral of the Ocean Sea. A Life of Christopher Columbus. Boston: 1942. V. 73
The European Discovery of America. The Northern Voyages, A.D. 500- 1600. (with) The European Discovery of America. The Southern Voyages A.D. 1492-1616. New York: 1971-1974. V. 73
Harvard College in the Seventeenth Century. Cambridge: 1936. V. 72
The Life and Letters of Harrison Gray Otis, Federalist 1765-1848. Boston: 1913. V. 71
Massachusettensis de Conditoribut or the Builders of the Bay Colony. Boston: 1930. V. 71

MORISON, STANLEY
The Art of the Printer. London: 1925. V. 69
The Calligraphic Models of Ludovico Degli Arrighi, Surnamed Vicentino. Paris: 1926. V. 70
Fra Luca De Pacioli of Burgo S. Sepolcoro. New York: 1933. V. 70
A Handlist of the Writings of Stanley Morison. Cambridge: 1950. V. 70
John Fell 1745-1831. Cambridge: 1930. V. 72
John Fell, the University Press and the Fell Types. Oxford: 1967. V. 69
Letter Forms, Typographical and Scriptorial. New York: 1968. V. 70
Modern Fine Printing. An Exhibit of Printing Issued in England, the United States of America, France, Germany, Italy.... London: 1925. V. 70
On Learned Presses. Cambridge: 1955. V. 70
On Type Designs Past and Present. London: 1962. V. 70
Rationalism and the Novelty Appropriate in Display Advertising. London. V. 70
A Review of Recent Typography in England, the United States, France and Germany. London: 1927. V. 70
Some Fruits of Theosophy. The Origins and Purpose of the So-Called Old Catholic Church. London: 1919. V. 70
Talbot Baines Reed: Author, Bibliographer, Typefounder. 1960. V. 71
Talbot Baines Reed. Author, Bibliographer, Typefounder. Cambridge: 1960. V. 70
Type Designs of the Past and Present. London: 1926. V. 70
The Typographic Arts, Past, Present and Future. A Lecture Delivered at the College of Art, Edinburgh 17 Feb. 1944. Edinburgh: 1944. V. 70
The Typographic Arts. Two Lectures. London: 1949. V. 70

MORKEL, BILL
Hunting in Africa. 1980. V. 72

MORLAND, NIGEL
The Careless Hangman. New York: 1941. V. 68
The Clue of the Bricklayer's Aunt. New York: 1937. V. 68
The Corpse on the Flying Trapeze. 1941. V. 68
Murder at Radio City. 1939. V. 68

MORLEY, B. D.
Flowering Plants in Australia. Adelaide: 1983. V. 72; 73
Wild Flowers of the World. New York: 1970. V. 68

MORLEY, CHRISTOPHER DARLINGTON
Collected Works. New York: 1927. V. 73
Eumenides of Book-Collecting. New York: 1935. V. 71
Kitty Foyle. Philadelphia: 1939. V. 71
A Letter to Leonora. Chicago: 1928. V. 71
The Pallet Knife. New York: 1929. V. 73
Paumanok. Garden City: 1926. V. 71
Rare Books: an Essay. New York: 1935. V. 69
Sherlock Holmes and Dr. Watson. New York: 1944. V. 69
Where the Blue Begins. London: 1932. V. 70; 72

MORLEY, HENRY
Life of Henry Cornelius Agrippa...Commonly Known as a Magician. London: 1856. V. 69
Tales and Songs of Ireland and North of England.... 1890. V. 70

MORLEY, HILDA
A Blessing Outside Us. Woods Hole: 1976. V. 69

MORLEY, IRIS
The Proud Paladin. New York: 1936. V. 70

MORLEY, JOHN
Cheap and Profitable Manure, &c. Norwich: 1812. V. 73
An Essay on the Nature and Cure of Scrophulous Disorders Commonly Called the King's Evil.... London: 1777. V. 73

MORLEY, JOHN, ED.
English Men of Letters Series. London: 1895. V. 70

MORLEY, JOHN MORLEY, VISCOUNT
The Life of Richard Cobden. London: 1881. V. 71
The Life of William Ewart Gladstone. London: 1903. V. 71; 73
Recollections. London: 1917. V. 71
Rousseau. 1873. V. 71

MORNER, KAREL GUSTAV HJALMAR, GRAF VON
Miscellaneous Sketches of Contrasts Drawn by Hjalmar Morner. London: 1831. V. 69; 72

MOROGUES, SEBASTIEN FRANCOIS BIGOT, VICOMTE DE
Naval Tactics; or, a Treatise of Evolutions and Signals, with Cuts, Lately Published in France, for the Use of Cadets or Guard Marines, of the Academy at Brest.... London: 1767. V. 69

MOROZOV, S.
Soviet Photography: an Age of Realism. New York: 1984. V. 68

MORPHOLOGY of the Giant Panda.... Beijing: 1986. V. 68

MORRELL, DAVID
The Brotherhood of the Rose. New York: 1984. V. 68
First Blood. London: 1972. V. 68; 70; 72; 73
First Blood. New York: 1972. V. 68; 69; 71; 72; 73
Last Reveille. New York: 1977. V. 72
The League Of Night And Fog. New York: 1987. V. 72

MORRELL, ED
The Twenty-Fifth Man - The Strange Story of Ed Morrell, the Hero of Jack London's Star Rover. Montclair: 1924. V. 73

MORRELL, J.
Gentleman of Science, Early Years of the British Associaton for the Advancement of Science. Oxford: 1981. V. 72

MORRELL, J. B.
York Monuments. London. V. 72; 73

MORRELL, W. WILBERFORCE
The History and Antiquities of Selby. Selby: 1867. V. 73

MORRICE, F. L. H.
The Nightless North. Cambridge: 1881. V. 69

MORRILL, CLAIRE
A Taos Mosaic: Portrait of a New Mexico Village. Albuquerque: 1973. V. 69

MORRIS, ALEXANDER
The Treaties of Canada with the Indians of Manitoba and the North- West Territories, Including the Negotiations on Which they are Based and Other Information Relating Thereto. Toronto: 1880. V. 68

MORRIS, ANTHONY P.
Jack Simons, Detective. New York: 1902. V. 71

MORRIS, ARTHUR
Proceedings In an Action Brought by Arthur Morris, Esq. Against Sir Francis Burdett, Bar. in the Court of King's Bench, Before Lord Ellenborough and a Special Jury on the 22d of February, 1808.... London: 1811. V. 70

MORRIS, BEVERLEY R.
British Game Birds and Wildfowl. London: 1895. V. 70; 73

MORRIS, CHARLES
Finding the North Pole. 1909. V. 73

MORRIS, CORBYN
A Letter Balancing the Causes of the Present Scarcity of Our Silver Coin, and the Means of Immediate Remedy, and Future Prevention of This Evil. London: 1757. V. 70

A Letter from a By-Stander to a Member of Parliament; Wherein is Examined What Necessity There is for the Maintenance of a Large Regular Land- Force in this Island.... London: 1742. V. 70

MORRIS, DAVID A.
The Canadian Militia. From 1855 - an Historical Summary. Erin: 1983. V. 73

MORRIS, DONALD R.
Warm Bodies. New York: 1957. V. 68

MORRIS, EDMUND
Dutch. New York: 1999. V. 72

MORRIS, EDWARD
The Life of Henry Bell. 1844. V. 70
The Life of Henry Bell. London: 1844. V. 68

MORRIS, ETHELBERTA
Ameliaranne Bridesmaid. London: 1946. V. 70
Ameliaranne's Moving-Day. London: 1950. V. 70

MORRIS, FRANCIS ORPEN
A History of British Birds. 1870. V. 69
A History of British Birds. London: 1870. V. 70; 73
A History of British Birds. 1890. V. 69
A History of British Birds. London: 1895. V. 70
A History of British Birds. 1900. V. 69
A History of British Butterflies. London: 1870. V. 69; 70
A History of British Butterflies. 1876. V. 69
A History of British Butterflies. London: 1904. V. 70
A Natural History of British Moths. 1861-1870. V. 69
A Natural History of British Moths. London: 1872. V. 72

MORRIS, GOVERNEUR
Yellow Men and Gold. New York: 1911. V. 70

MORRIS, HENRY
The First Fine Silver Coinage of the Republic of San Serriffe: the Bird and Bull Press Commemorative 100 Coronas. Newtown: 1988. V. 70
Japonica: the Study and Appreciaton of the Art of Japanese Paper. North Hills: 1981. V. 72
Omnibus. 1967. V. 70; 72
Omnibus. North Hills: 1967. V. 69

MORRIS, J.
Makers of Japan. London: 1906. V. 71

MORRIS, J. P.
A Glossary of the Words and Phrases of Furness. London: 1869. V. 71

MORRIS, JOHN
Living With the Lepches. London: 1938. V. 71

MORRIS, LEOPOLD
Pictorial History of Victoria and Victoria County. Clemens: 1953. V. 69

MORRIS, LERONA ROSAMOND
Oklahoma Land of Opportunity. Guthrie: 1934. V. 72

MORRIS, LEWIS
The Papers of Lewis Morris, Governor of the Province of New Jersey from 1738 to 1746. New York: 1852. V. 72
Rhodd Meistr i'w Brentis. Carmarthen: 1812. V. 69

MORRIS, MARY
Nothing to Declare. Boston: 1988. V. 72
Vanishing Animals and Other Stories. Boston: 1979. V. 69; 72

MORRIS, MAURICE O'CONNOR
Rambles in the Rocky Mountains with a Visit to the Gold Fields of Colorado. London: 1864. V. 68

MORRIS, MAY
The Introductions to the Collected Works of William Morris. New York: 1973. V. 72

MORRIS, RICHARD
Essays on Landscape Gardening and on Uniting Picturesque Effect and Rural Scenery.... London: 1825. V. 68; 70; 72
Flora Conspicua; a Selection of the Most Ornamental Flowering, Hardy, Exotic and Indigenous Trees, Shrubs, and Herbaceous Plants.... 1826. V. 69
Flora Conspicua, a Selection of the Most Ornamental Flowering Hardy, Exotic and Indigenous Trees, Shrubs and Herbaceous Plants.... London: 1826. V. 72; 73

MORRIS, ROBERT
A Letter to Lord B-, with an Address to the Town. London: 1768. V. 68

MORRIS, T. A.
Miscellany: Consisting of Essays, Biographical Sketches and Notes of Travel. Cincinnati: 1854. V. 69

MORRIS, THOMAS
A House for the Suburbs, Socially and Architecturally Sketched. 1860. V. 68; 71
A House for the Suburbs: Socially and Architecturally Sketched. London: 1860. V. 69

MORRIS, W. P.
The Records of Patterdale. Kendal: 1903. V. 71

MORRIS, WILLIAM
An Address Delivered by William Morris at the Distribution of Prizes to Students of the Birmingham Municipal School of Art on Feb. 21, 1894. London: 1898. V. 70; 73
The Aims of Art. 1887. V. 72
The Aims of Art. London: 1887. V. 70
Architecture and History and Westminster Abbey. London: 1900. V. 68; 70; 72
Art and Its Producers. London: 1901. V. 70
Art and Socialism: a Lecture Delivered (January 23rd, 1884) before the Secular Society of Leicester...and Watchman: What of the Night?. London: 1884. V. 68
Art and the Beauty of the Earth. London: 1898. V. 69; 73
Art and the Beauty of the Earth. London: 1899. V. 70
A Book of Verse. London: 1980. V. 72
Chants for Socialists. No. I. The Day is Coming. London: 1885. V. 68; 69
Child Christopher and Goldilind the Fair. 1895. V. 71
The Decorative Arts; Their Relation to Modern Life and Progress.... London: 1878. V. 71
The Defence of Guenevere and Other Poems. London: 1858. V. 68; 72; 73
The Defense of Guenevere and Other Poems. London: 1904. V. 71
A Dream of John Ball and A King's Lesson. 1888. V. 71
A Dream of John Ball and A King's Lesson. London: 1888. V. 72
A Dream of John Ball and a King's Lesson. 1892. V. 73
A Dream of John Ball and a King's Lesson. London: 1903. V. 68
The Earthly Paradise. 1896-1897. V. 71
The Earthly Paradise. London: 1904. V. 71
The Earthly Paradise. 1993. V. 68
Four Letters. San Francisco: 1984. V. 68
Glass: Artifact and Art. Seattle and London: 1989. V. 69
Gothic Architecture: a Lecture for the Arts and Crafts Exhibition Society. 1893. V. 71
Hopes and Fears for Art. New York: 1901. V. 68
Letters on Socialism. 1894. V. 73
The Life and Death of Jason. London: 1867. V. 72
The Life and Death of Jason. London: 1882. V. 71
The Life and Death of Jason. London: 1882. V. 68
Love Is Enough; or the Freeing of Pharamond, a Morality. London: 1873. V. 72
News from Nowhere. New York: 1901. V. 68
Old French Romances Done Into English. London: 1896. V. 68; 72
Poems by the Way. London: 1891. V. 68; 73
Poems by the Way. New York: 1900. V. 68
The Roots of the Mountains Wherein is Told Somewhat of the Lives of Men of Burgdale their friends their Neighbours their Foemen and their Fellows in Arms.... London: 1890. V. 68; 71
The Roots of the Mountains, wherein is told somewhat of the lives of the men of Burgdale their friends, their neighbours, their foeman and their fellows in arms. London: 1893. V. 71
The Saga of Thorir. Cincinnati: 1903. V. 68
Sir Galahad. Chicago: 1904. V. 68; 71
Socialism, Its Growth and Outcome. London: 1893. V. 68
Socialist Diary. Iowa City: 1981. V. 73
The Story of Cupid and Psyche. London and Cambridge: 1974. V. 68
The Story of Sigurd the Volsung and the Fall of the Niblungs. London: 1876. V. 68
The Story of Sigurd the Volsung and The Fall of the Niblungs. London: 1877. V. 72
The Story of Sigurd the Volsung, and the Fall of the Niblungs. London: 1887. V. 68
The Sundering Flood. 1897. V. 71
A Tale of the House of the Wolfings and All the Kindreds of the Mark.... London: 1889. V. 68
Under an Elm Tree; or, Thoughts in the Country-Side. Aberdeen: 1891. V. 68; 72
The Well at the World's End. London, New York, and Bombay: 1896. V. 68; 72
William Morris By Himself. Designs And Writings. London: 1988. V. 72
The Wood Beyond the World. London: 1895. V. 68; 71
The World of Romance - Being Contributions to the Oxford and Cambridge Magazine 1856. London: 1906. V. 71

MORRIS, WILLIAM O'CONNOR
Ireland 1798-1898. 1898. V. 69

MORRIS, WILLIE
James Jones: a Friendship. Garden City: 1978. V. 68
My Dog Skip. New York: 1995. V. 68; 71; 73
A Prayer for the Opening of the Little League Season. New York: 1995. V. 71; 73

MORRIS, WRIGHT
About Fiction. New York: 1975. V. 72
A Cloak of Light. New York: 1985. V. 71
Collected Stories, 1948-1986. New York: 1986. V. 72
The Field of Vision. New York: 1956. V. 69
Fire Sermon. New York: 1971. V. 71
The Inhabitants. New York and London: 1946. V. 68; 71
My Uncle Dudley. New York: 1942. V. 70
War Games. Los Angeles: 1972. V. 68

MORRISON, A. J.
Travels in Virginia in Revolutionary Times. Lynchburg: 1922. V. 69

MORRISON, ARTHUR
Chronicles of Martin Hewitt. 1896. V. 71
Chronicles of Martin Hewitt. New York: 1896. V. 68
The Chronicles of Martin Hewitt. Boston: 1907. V. 69
The Green Eye of Goona. London: 1904. V. 70
The Hole in the Wall. London: 1902. V. 71

MORRISON, ARTHUR continued
The Red Triangle. Boston: 1903. V. 69
The Red Triangle. London: 1903. V. 70

MORRISON, C.
An Essay on the Relations Between Labour and Capital. London: 1854. V. 71
The Young Lady's Guide to Practical Arithmetic, Comprising a Great Variety of Curious and Interesting Facts, Taken from Commerce, Chronology, Geography and Other Sources.... Glasgow: 1820. V. 73

MORRISON, CHARLES E.
Highway Engineering. New York: 1908. V. 73

MORRISON, GEORGE ERNEST
An Australian in China Being the Narrative of a Quiet Journey Across China to Burma. London: 1895. V. 69

MORRISON, INGRAM & CO.
Illustrated Catalogue and Price List of Sanitary Appliances. Manchester: 1890. V. 68; 70

MORRISON, JAMES
A Complete Treatise on Practical Book-Keeping.... Edinburgh: 1810. V. 71
The Journal of James Morrison, Boatswain's Mate of the Bounty . . . London: 1935. V. 71

MORRISON, JIM
The Lords and New Creatures. New York: 1970. V. 69

MORRISON, MOLLY
These are Some of My Favorite Things. Gainesville: 1981. V. 72

MORRISON, ROBERT
A Grammar of the Chinese Language. Sermapore: 1815. V. 73

MORRISON, T. J.
The Cairn. New York: 1935. V. 70

MORRISON, TONI
Beloved. London: 1987. V. 73
Beloved. New York: 1987. V. 68; 69; 70; 71; 72; 73
Beloved. New York: 1995. V. 68
Birth of a Nation'Hood: Gaze, Script, and Spectacle in the O.J. Simpson Case. New York: 1997. V. 72
The Bluest Eye. New York: 1970. V. 70
The Bluest Eye. London: 1979. V. 73
Conversations with Toni Morrison. Jackson: 1994. V. 70
The Dancing Mind. New York: 1996. V. 72
Jazz. Franklin Center: 1992. V. 69; 70; 72
Jazz. London: 1992. V. 72
Jazz. New York: 1992. V. 69; 70; 72; 73
Lecture and Speech of Acceptance, Upon the Award of the Nobel Prize for Literature, Delivered in Stockholm on the Seventh of December, Nineteen Hundred and Ninety-Three. New York: 1994. V. 70; 72
Paradise. London: 1998. V. 72
Paradise. New York: 1998. V. 68; 69; 70; 71; 72; 73
Playing in the Dark. Cambridge, MA & London: 1992. V. 68; 69; 71; 72; 73
Playing in the Dark. New York: 1993. V. 70
Song of Solomon. New York: 1977. V. 68; 69; 70; 71; 72; 73
Song of Solomon. London: 1978. V. 72
Sula. London: 1974. V. 68; 70; 72; 73
Sula. New York: 1974. V. 68; 70; 72; 73
Tar Baby. Franklin Center, PA: 1981. V. 72
Tar Baby. New York: 1981. V. 68; 69; 70; 72; 73

MORRISON, WILLIAM B.
Military Posts and Camps in Oklahoma. Oklahoma City: 1936. V. 72

MORRISS, GILLIAN MARY
The Teratogenesis of Hypervitaminosis A. Cambridge: 1971. V. 68

MORRISSEY, DONNA
Kit's Law. 2000. V. 68

THE MORROW Anthology of Great Western Short Stories. New York: 1997. V. 72

MORROW, B. H.
A Dictionary of Landscape Architecture. Albuquerque: 1987. V. 68

MORROW, BRADFORD
A Bestiary. New York: 1990. V. 69; 73
Come Sunday. New York: 1988. V. 70
Conjunctions Nos. 1-14: a Complete Run of the Hardcover Editions of the Literary Journal. New York: 1981-1989. V. 70; 73
Danae's Progress. 1982. V. 73
Posthumes. Santa Barbara: 1982. V. 73
Trinity Fields. New York: 1995. V. 68

MORROW, ELIZABETH
Beast, Bird and Fish, An Animal Alphabet. New York: 1933. V. 73

MORROW, JAMES
This Is The Way The World Ends. New York: 1986. V. 72
Towing Jehovah. New York: 1994. V. 72
The Wine of Violence. New York: 1981. V. 68

MORROW, MABLE
Indian Rawhide, an American Folk Art. Norman: 1975. V. 69

MORROW, PRINCE ALBERT
Atlas of Skin and Venereal Diseases. New York: 1889. V. 68; 71; 73
A System of Genito-Urinary Diseases Syphilology and Dermatology by Various Authors. New York: 1895. V. 71

MORSCH, LUCILLE
Check List of New Jersey Imprints 1784-1800. Baltimore: 1939. V. 72

MORSE, DRYDEN P.
Congenital Heart Disease. Oxford: 1962. V. 68

MORSE, EDWARD S.
Japanese Homes and Their Surroundings. Boston: 1886. V. 73

MORSE, JEDIDIAH
The American Geography; or a View of the Present Situation of the United States of America. Elizabeth Town: 1789. V. 68; 72
The History of America, in Two Books. Philadelphia: 1790. V. 73

MORSE, OLIVER A.
A Vindication of the Claim of Alexander M. W. Ball, of Elizabeth, N. J. to the Authorship of the Poem, Rock Me to Sleep, Mother. New York: 1867. V. 72

MORSE, PETER
Jean Charlot's Prints. A Catalogue Raisonne. Honolulu: 1976. V. 68

MORSE, SAMUEL F. B.
The Present Attempt to Dissolve the American Union, A British Aristorcatic Plot. New York: 1862. V. 73

MORSE, SAMUEL FRENCH
Wallace Stevens - a Preliminary Checklist of His Published Writings: 1898-1954. New Haven: 1954. V. 71

MORSE, WILLIAM INGLIS
Acadiensia Nova. London: 1935. V. 73
The Land of the New Adventure (The Georgian Era in Nova Scotia). London: 1932. V. 69; 73
Pierre Du Gua Sieur de Monts Records: Colonial and "Saintongeois". London: 1939. V. 68; 73

MORSELS for Merry and Melancholy Mortals. Ipswich: 1815. V. 72

MORSON, IAN
Falconer and the Face of God. London: 1996. V. 70
Falconer and the Great Beast. London: 1998. V. 70
Falconer's Crusade. London: 1994. V. 70
Falconer's Judgement. London: 1995. V. 68; 70
A Psalm for Falconer. London: 1997. V. 70

MORSS, NOEL
Notes on the Archaeology of the Kaibito and Rainbow Plateaus in Arizona Report on the Explorations, 1927. Cambridge: 1931. V. 68; 73

MORTENSEN, ROBERT K.
In the Cause of Progress, A History of New Mexico Cattle Growers Association. Albuquerque. V. 71
In the Cause of Progress: a History of the New Mexico Cattle Growers' Association. 1983. V. 68

MORTENSEN, T.
Handbook of the Echinoderms of the British Isles. London: 1927. V. 68

MORTENSEN, WILLIAM
The Command to Look. San Francisco: 1937. V. 68
Monsters and Madonnas. San Francisco: 1936. V. 70

MORTIMER, CHARLES EDWARD
An Historical Memoir of the Political Life of John Milton. London: 1805. V. 73

MORTIMER, J. R.
Forty Years' Researches in British and Saxon Burial Mounds of East Yorkshire. London: 1905. V. 73

MORTIMER, JOHN
Collaborators. London: 1973. V. 72
Cotton from the Field to the Factory.... Manchester: 1894. V. 71
Felix in the Underworld. London: 1997. V. 73
(Industrial Lancashire. Some Manufacturing Towns and Their Surroundings). 1897. V. 71
The Mail Robbers. Philadelphia: 1830. V. 71
Murderers and Other Friends - Another Part of Life. London: 1994. V. 73
Rumming Park - a Comedy. London: 1948. V. 70
Rumpole of the Bailey. New York: 1991. V. 68; 71
Summer's Lease. London: 1988. V. 73
Titmuss Regained. London: 1990. V. 68; 73

MORTIMER, PENELOPE
Long Distance. Garden City: 1974. V. 72
The Pumpkin Eater. London: 1962. V. 71

MORTIMER, THOMAS
Every Man His Own Broker; or, a Guide to the Stock-Exchange. London: 1801. V. 68

MORTIMER, W. GOLDEN
History of Coca the divine plant of the Incas. San Francisco: 1974. V. 72
Peru. History of Coca. New York: 1901. V. 70

MORTLAKE, G. N.
Love Letters of a Japanese. London: 1910. V. 71

MORTON, ALVIN C.
Report on the Gauge for the St. Lawrence and Atlantic Rail-Road. Montreal;: 1847. V. 73

MORTON, DUDLEY J.
The Grampas' Toyshop. Milford: 1922. V. 71; 73
The Human Foot. Its Evolution, Physiology and Functional Disorders. New York: 1935. V. 68

MORTON, J.
Chrysanthemum Culture for America. New York: 1891. V. 68; 71

MORTON, J. B.
By the Way. London: 1931. V. 71

MORTON, JAMES
The Reform of Our National Schools. Glasgow: 1876. V. 70

MORTON, JESSIE D. M.
Clarkson Gray and Other Poems. London: 1867. V. 69

MORTON, JOHN
The Natural History of Northampton-shire; with Some Account of the Antiquities. London: 1712. V. 70
The Nature and Property of Soils; their Connexion with the Geological Formation on Which they Rest.... London: 1843. V. 68

MORTON, JOHN CHALMERS
The Prince Consort's Farms: an Agricultural Memoir. London: 1863. V. 71

MORTON, JOSEPH W.
Sparks From The Camp Fires or Tales of The Old Veterans. Philadelphia: 1893. V. 72

MORTON, LESLIE T.
Garrison and Morton's Medical Bibliography. London: 1954. V. 71
A Medical Bibliography (Garrison and Morton). London: 1970. V. 68

MORTON, NATHANIEL
New England's Memorial...The Planters of New England in America.... Newport: 1772. V. 73

MORTON, RICHARD
Opera Medica.... Lyons: 1737. V. 68

MORTON, SAMUEL GEORGE
Crania Aegyptiaca; or, Observations on Egyptian Ethnography Derived from Anatomy, History and the Monuments. Philadelphia: 1844. V. 70

MORTON, SARAH WENTWORTH
Beacon Hill. Boston: 1797. V. 72

MORTON, WILLIAM T. GREEN
A Memoir to the Academy of Sciences at Paris on a New Use of Sulphuric Ether. New York: 1946. V. 73
Statements Supported by Evidence of William T. G. Morton, M.D. on his Claim to the Discovery of the Anesthetic Properties of Ether, Submitted to the Honorable the Select Committee Appointed by the Senate of the United States. Washington: 1853. V. 68; 72

THE MORTONS of Bardom. A Lancashire Tale. London: 1863. V. 71

MORYSON, FYNES
An Itinerary Written by Fynes Moryson, Etc. London: 1617. V. 68

MOSAIC III/4: a Journal for the Compartive Study of Literature and Ideas. New Views of Franz Kafka. Manitoba: 1970. V. 70

MOSBY, JOHN S.
The Memoirs of Colonel John S. Mosby. Boston: 1917. V. 69; 70
Mosby's War Reminiscences and Stuart's Cavalry Campaigns. Boston: 1887. V. 68; 69
Stuart's Cavalry in the Gettysburg Campaign. New York: 1908. V. 69; 70

MOSCHELES, IGNACE
The Life of Beethoven, Including His Correspondence with His Friends.... London: 1841. V. 69

MOSEL, TAD
Other People's Houses. New York: 1956. V. 70

MOSELEY, BENJAMIN
Commentaries on the Lues Bovilla or Cow Pox. London: 1806. V. 68; 73
A Treatise on Sugar, with Miscellaneous Medical Observations. London: 1800. V. 72

MOSELEY, C.
A Century of Emblems. Aldershot: 1989. V. 70

MOSELEY, H. F.
Textbook of Surgery. St. Louis: 1952. V. 70; 71; 73

MOSELEY, JOSEPH
Political Elements or, the Progress of Modern Legislation. London: 1852. V. 71

MOSELEY, MABOTH
Irascible Genius. A Life of Charles Babbage, Inventor. London: 1964. V. 68

MOSELEY, MARY
The Bahamas Handbook. Nassau: 1926. V. 71

MOSELY, M. E.
The British Caddis Flies. 1939. V. 69
The British Caddis Flies (Trichoptera) A Collector's Handbook. London: 1939. V. 71
Insect Life and the Mangement of a Trout Fishery. 1926. V. 68

MOSER, BARRY
Engravings from Alice: through the Looking Glass and What Alice Found There. West Hatfield: 1982. V. 72
Fifty Wood Engravings. Northampton: 1978. V. 69; 73
Goudy Creek. Easthampton: 1976. V. 69
Men of Printing. Anglo-American Profiles. 1976. V. 72
No Shortcuts: an Essay on Wood Engraving. Iowa City: 2001. V. 69

MOSER, DON
The Peninsula, a Story of the Olympic Country in Words and Pictures. San Francisco: 1962. V. 72

MOSER, MAURICE
Stories from Scotland Yard. London: 1891. V. 68

MOSES, E., & CO.
The Library of Elegance. London: 1852. V. 68

MOSES, GRANDMA
My Life's History. New York: 1952. V. 69; 71

MOSES, HENRY
The Gallery of Pictures Painted by Benjamin West Est., Historical Painter to His Majesty.... London: 1811-1816. V. 68
Sketches of Shipping. London: 1837. V. 69

MOSES BEN MAIMON
More Nevuchim: Doctor Perplexorum. Basil: 1629. V. 73

MOSGROVE, GEORGE DALLAS
Kentucky Cavaliers in Dixie. Jackson: 1957. V. 69

MOSHER, WILLIAM
Chronological History of the Mosher Family, from the Seventeenth Century to the Present Date. Windsor: 1891. V. 73

MOSHIRI, G. A.
Constructed Wetlands for Water Quality Improvement. Boca Raton: 1993. V. 69

MOSKOWITZ, IRA
Patterns and Ceremonials of the Indians of the Southwest. New York: 1949. V. 69

MOSLEY, NICHOLAS
Hopeful Monsters. London: 1990. V. 68

MOSLEY, OSWALD
History of the Castle, Priory and Town of Tutbury, in the County of Stafford. London: 1832. V. 70

MOSLEY, WALTER
Black Betty. New York: 1994. V. 72
Devil in a Blue Dress. New York: 1990. V. 68; 69; 70; 71; 72
Gone Fishin'. Baltimore: 1997. V. 71
A Red Death. New York: 1991. V. 68; 69; 70; 71; 72
RL's Dream. New York: 1995. V. 72
White Butterfly. London: 1992. V. 69
White Butterfly. New York: 1992. V. 69; 70; 72
White Butterfly. New York: 1994. V. 68

MOSS, FRANK
Persecution of Negroes by Roughs and Policemen, in the City of New York, August 1900. New York: 1900. V. 71

MOSS, FREDERICK J.
Through Atolls and Islands, in the Great South Sea. London: 1889. V. 71

MOSS, G. LAWTON
How to Build Your Own Split Cane Fishing Rod. London: 1954. V. 72

MOSS, GEORGE H.
Another Look at Nauvoo to the Hook. Sea Bright: 1990. V. 72
Double Exposure. Early Stereographic Views of Historic Monmouth County, New Jersey and Their Relationship to Pioneer Photography. Sea Bright: 1971. V. 72
Nauvoo to the Hook. The Iconography of a Barrier Beach. Locust: 1964. V. 72
Steamboat to the Shore. A Pictorial History of the Steamboat Era in Monmouth County, New Jersey. Locust: 1966. V. 72

MOSS, STANLEY
Interviews and Encounters with Stanley Kunitz. New York: 1993. V. 69
Skull of Adam. New York: 1979. V. 73

MOSSE, A. H. E.
My Somali Book. 1913. V. 70; 73
My Somali Book. London: 1913. V. 69

MOSSER, M.
The Architecture of Western Gardens. Cambridge: 1991. V. 68

MOSSER, MARJORIE
Good Maine Food. New York: 1939. V. 68

MOSSMAN, ISAAC VAN DORSEY
A Pony's Express Mans' Recollection. Portland: 1955. V. 68; 73

MOSSMAN, SAMUEL
Gems Of Womanhood. London: 1870. V. 72
Our Australian Colonies. London. V. 71

MOSSO, ANGELO
Fatigue. London: 1915. V. 72

MOSSO, ANGELO continued
Life of Man on the High Alps. London: 1898. V. 71

MOTHER GOOSE
ABC Old Mother Goose. New York: 1912. V. 73
All through the Day the Mother Goose Way - Mother Goose's Children of Long Ago.... Philadelphia: 1921. V. 71
The Fanny Cory Mother Goose. New York: 1913. V. 71
Gems from Mother Goose: Little Jack Horner. New York: 1899. V. 73
The Golden Mother Goose ABC. Cincinnati: 1885. V. 71
The History of the Celebrated Mother Hubbard. New York: 1843-1853. V. 70
The Janet Deen Mother Goose. Philadelphia: 1945. V. 72
The Jessie Willcox Smith Mother Goose: a Carefull and Full Selection of Rhymes. New York: 1914. V. 72
The Jolly Jump-Ups Mother Goose Book. Springfield: 1944. V. 70
Little Folks Mother Goose. New York: 1931. V. 73
Maud Humphrey's Mother Goose. New York: 1891. V. 70
Mother Goose. Chicago: 1921. V. 68
Mother Goose. Garden City: 1924. V. 70
Mother Goose. Akron: 1934. V. 70
Mother Goose. Boston: 1940. V. 70
Mother Goose. New York: 1944. V. 70
Mother Goose. New York: 1945. V. 73
Mother Goose. New York: 1949. V. 72
Mother Goose and the Golden Egg. New York. V. 73
Mother Goose Ditties. New York: 1905. V. 71; 73
Mother Goose: 5 of Her Books. Akron: 1929. V. 70
Mother Goose for Grown Folks. New York: 1859. V. 68
Mother Goose for Grown Folks. New York: 1860. V. 68
Mother Goose...Her ABC. Akron;: 1946. V. 73
Mother Goose in Catland. London: 1920. V. 72
Mother Goose Melodies. New York: 1894. V. 71
Mother Goose Nursery Rhymes. New York: 1930. V. 70
Mother Goose Nursery Rhymes. Springfield: 1932. V. 71
Mother Goose Nursery Tales. London: 1935. V. 70
Mother Goose's Nursery Rhymes. London: 1900. V. 70
Mother Goose's Nursery Tales. London: 1923. V. 70
Mother Goose on Wheels. London: 1900. V. 72
Mother Goose, or The Old Nursery Rhymes. London: 1881. V. 69
Mother Goose Pantry Shelf. Kenosha: 1942. V. 71
Mother Goose Picture Book. Racine: 1932. V. 71
Mother Goose Pictures. Chicago: 1927. V. 68
Mother Goose Rhymes. Philadelphia: 1925. V. 70
Mother Goose Tells Time. New York: 1945. V. 70
Mother Goose; the Old Nursery Rhymes. London: 1913. V. 70; 72
Mother Goose. The Old Nursery Rhymes. London: 1952. V. 73
Mother Goose's Melodies. Philadelphia. V. 72
Mother Hubbard's Book of Rhymes. London: 1920. V. 70
The Old Fashioned Mother Goose Melodies. New York: 1879. V. 71
The Old Mother Goose Nursery Book. London: 1916. V. 71
Pictures from Mother Goose. New York: 1945. V. 70
The Real Mother Goose. Chicago: 1916. V. 73
Royal Mother Goose Chimes. New York: 1898. V. 71
The So Big Book of Mother Goose. New York: 1947. V. 70
The So-Long Mother Goose. Kenosha: 1945. V. 70
The Tall Book of Mother Goose. New York: 1942. V. 70
The Teenie Weenie Man's Mother Goose - The Most Complete Mother Goose Published in America.... Chicago: 1921. V. 72
Willy Pogany's Mother Goose. New York: 1928. V. 72

MOTHER Hubbard and Her Dog. New York: 1859-1865. V. 73

MOTHER Hubbard's Dog. New York: 1875. V. 71

MOTHER Hubbard's Nursery Rhymes. London: 1900. V. 72

MOTHER Purr and Family. London: 1890. V. 70

MOTHERBY, GEORGE
A New Medical Dictionary; or, General Repository of Physic.... London: 1785. V. 70; 72
A New Medical Dictionary; or, General Repository of Physic.... London: 1791. V. 73

MOTHERILL, JOHN
The Genuine Trial of John Motherill, for a Rape on the Body of Miss Catharine Wade, Daughter of Mr. Wade, Master of the Ceremonies at Brightelmstone, at the Assizes Held a East Grimstead, England, before Mr. Justice Ashurst.... Dublin: 1786. V. 71

THE MOTHER'S Book of Song. London: 1902. V. 72

THE MOTHER'S Gift. 1820. V. 73

MOTHER'S Little Rhyme Book. London: 1913. V. 70

MOTHERSHEAD, HARMON ROSS
The Swan Land and Cattle Company, Ltd. 1971. V. 68

MOTHERSOLE, JESSE
The Isles of Scilly, Their Story, Their Folk, and Their Flowers. 1910. V. 68

MOTHERWELL, ROBERT
Robert Motherwell Selected Prints 1961-1974. New York: 1974. V. 70

MOTION, ANDREW
Indepdendence: a Narrative Poems. Edinburgh: 1981. V. 68
Two Poems. Child Okeford: 1988. V. 70

MOTLEY, JAMES
Tales of the Cymry; with Notes (in Poetry and Prose) Illustrative and Explanatory. London: 1848. V. 73

MOTLEY, JOHN LOTHROP
The Rise of the Dutch Republic. New York: 1857. V. 73

MOTLEY, WILLARD
Knock On Any Door. New York: 1947. V. 71

MOTOR Days and Motor Ways. New York: 1912. V. 69

MOTORING in the Park. London and Glasgow: 1905. V. 69

MOTT, ABIGAIL FIELD
Observations on the Importance of Female Education and Maternal Instruction with Their Beneficial Influence on Society. New York: 1827. V. 68; 69; 72

MOTT, D. W.
Legends And Love of Long Ago. Los Angeles: 1929. V. 71

MOTT, FRANK L.
History of American Magazines. Cambridge: 1939-. V. 71

MOTT, GEORGE S.
The First Century of Hunterdon County, State of New Jersey. Flemington: 1878. V. 72

MOTTELAY, PAUL FLEURY
Bibliographical History of Electricity and Magnetism. New York: 1991. V. 69

MOTTEVILLE, FRANCOISE
Memoirs of the History of Anne of Austria, Wife to Lewis XII of France, and Regent of that Kingdom from His Death to the Accession of her Son Lewis XIV. London: 1726. V. 69; 73

MOTTLEY, JOHN
The History of the Life of Peter I, Emperor of Russia. London: 1739. V. 71

MOTTRAM, J. C.
Fly-Fishing, Some New Arts and Mysteries. V. 68; 73

MOTTRAM, RALPH HALE
Bumphrey's. London: 1934. V. 69
Castle Island. London: 1931. V. 70
The English Miss. London: 1928. V. 69
Strawberry Time and the Banquet: Two Stories. Waltham St. Lawrence: 1934. V. 71

MOTTRAM, WILLIAM
The True Story of George Eliot in Relation to "Adam Bede" Giving the Real Life History of the More Prominent Characters. London: 1905. V. 73

MOUAT, JAMES
The Rise of the Australian Wool Kings. London: 1892. V. 68

MOULAM, A. J. J.
Carneddau. London: 1966. V. 69

MOULE, HENRY
Self-Supporting Boarding Schools for Children of the Operative Classes. (with) Parochial Work for Clergy and Laity. London: 1856. V. 73

MOULES, LEONARD
Three Miles High. London: 1947. V. 69

MOULTON, FOREST RAY
Tuberculosis and Leprosy. Lancaster, PA: 1938. V. 71

MOULTON, GARY E.
Atlas of the Lewis and Clark Expedition. Lincoln: 1983. V. 68

MOULTON, ROBERT
Rock Climbing in Devonshire. London: 1966. V. 69

MOULTRIE, WILLIAM
Memoirs of the American Revolution, So Far As It Is Related to the States of North and South Carolina and Georgia.... New York: 1802. V. 68; 73

MOUNTENEY JEPHSON, A. J.
Emin Pasha and the Rebellion at the Equator. New York: 1890. V. 69

MOURLOT, FERNAND
Marc Chagall - The Lithographs. Volume II: 1957-1962. Monte Carlo: 1963. V. 69
Picasso Lithographs. Boston: 1970. V. 73

MOURNING DOVE
Co-Ge-We-A, the Half Blood. A Deception of the Great Montana Cattle Range.... Boston: 1927. V. 68
Coyote Stories. Caldwell: 1933. V. 68

MOUSLEY, WILLIAM
Moral Strength; or the Nature and Conquest of Evil Habits Considered. London: 1843. V. 70

MOUSSINAC, LEON
The New Movement in the Theatre. New York: 1967. V. 70

MOVING Picture Teddies. Chicago: 1907. V. 71

MOVIUS, HALLAM L.
The Irish Stone Age.... Cambridge: 1942. V. 70

MOWAT, FARLEY
My Discovery of America. Toronto: 1985. V. 70
Never Cry Wolf. Toronto: 1963. V. 71
A Whale for Killing. Toronto: 1972. V. 71

MOWERY, WILLIAM B.
The Silver Hawk. Garden City: 1929. V. 72

MOWRER, EDGAR ANSEL
This American World. London: 1928. V. 72

MOWRER, PAUL SCOTT
Poems Between Wars. Chicago: 1941. V. 68

MOXON, ELIZABETH
English Housewifery. London: 1789. V. 73
English Housewifery. London: 1808. V. 72

MOXON, JOSEPH
Mechanick Exercises on the Whole Art of Printing. London: 1962. V. 69

MOXON, THOMAS BOUCHIER
English Practical Banking. London: 1885. V. 68

MOYER, J. L.
The Landscape Lighting Book. New York: 1992. V. 68

MOYES, PATRICIA
Black Girl, White Girl. London: 1990. V. 72
Murder Fantastical. London: 1967. V. 70
Who Is Simon Warwick?. London: 1978. V. 70

MOYNE, LORD
Walkabout. London: 1936. V. 71

MOYSEY, ABEL
Forman. A Tale. London: 1819. V. 73

MOYZISCH, L. C.
Operation Cicero. London: 1950. V. 70

MOZART, LEOPOLD
Leopold Mozart's Hochfurstl. Salzburgischen Vice-Capellmeisters Grundliche Violinschule.... Augsburg: 1769. V. 73

MOZART, WOLFGANG AMADEUS
Missa Pro Defunctis. Requiem. Leipzig: 1800. V. 72; 73

MR. Bug Goes to Town. New York: 1941. V. 72

MR. Sun and Mrs. Moon. New York: 1902. V. 72

MRABET, MOHAMMED
The Beach Cafe and the Voice. Santa Barbara: 1980. V. 71; 73
The Big Mirror. Los Angeles: 1977. V. 71; 73
The Big Mirror. Santa Barbara: 1977. V. 69; 71; 73
The Big Mirror. London: 1989. V. 71
The Boy Who Set the Fire and Other Stories. Los Angeles: 1974. V. 69; 73
Hadidan Aharam. Los Angeles: 1975. V. 71
Harmless Poisons, Blameless Sins. Santa Barbara: 1976. V. 73
The Lemon. London: 1969. V. 71; 73
Look and Move On. Santa Barbara: 1976. V. 73
Look and Move On. London: 1989. V. 71
Love with a Few Hairs. 1967. V. 68
Love with a Few Hairs. London: 1967. V. 71; 73
Marriage with Papers. Bolinas: 1986. V. 71; 73
M'Hashish. San Francisco: 1969. V. 73

MRACEK, FRANZ
Atlas of Diseases of the Skin Including an Epitome of Pathology and Treatment. Philadelphia: 1900. V. 72

MRS. Josephine S. Williamson's Life and Missionary Labors in the Slums, Dives and Opium Joints of New York City.... New York: 1897. V. 72

MRS. Lovechild's Golden Present, For All Good Little Boys and Girls. 1815. V. 73

MRS. Lovechild's Golden Present, for All Good Little Boys and Girls. 1820. V. 68; 72

MRS. Lovechild's Golden Present, for All Good Little Boys and Girls. York: 1820. V. 72

MRS. Lovechild's Golden Present for All Good Little Boys and Girls. York: 1825. V. 72

MUDD, JOSEPH A.
With Porter in North Missouri. Washington: 1909. V. 69; 70

MUDD, WILLIAM S.
The Old Boat Rocker. NY: 1935. V. 72

MUDDIMAN, BERNARD
The Men of the Nineties. London: 1920. V. 72

MUDFORD, WILLIAM
Nubilia in Search of a Husband: Including Sketches of Modern Society and Interspersed with Moral and Literary Disquisition. London: 1809. V. 73

MUDGE, ENOCH
A System of Bible Class Instruction. Boston: 1829. V. 73

MUDGE, JEAN MCLURE
Chinese Export Porcelain In North America. NY: 1986. V. 72

MUDIE, ROBERT
The Air: the Earth: The Heaven: The Sea. London: 1835. V. 68
The Feathered Tribes of the British Islands. London: 1835. V. 73
The Feathered Tribes of the British Isles. London: 1841. V. 69
History of Hampshire. 1850. V. 70
The Natural History of Domestic and Wild Animals their Structure, Habits, Localities, Distribution and Influence on Human Society. London. V. 68
The Picture of Australia: Exhibiting New Holland, Van Diemen's Land and All the Settlements from the First at Sydney to the Last at Swan River. London: 1829. V. 70; 71
(The Seasons) Spring...; Summr...; Autumn..; Winter.... London: 1837. V. 68

MUDIE SMITH, R.
The Religious Life of London. London: 1904. V. 71

MUDRICK, M.
Jane Austen. Irony as Defense and Discovery. Princeton: 1952. V. 70

MUELLER, FERDINAND, BARON VON
Report on the Forest Resources of Western Australia. London: 1879. V. 71

MUELLER, HANS ALEXANDER
Woodcuts and Wood Engravings: How I Make Them. New York: 1939. V. 72

MUELLER, LISEL
The Private Life. Baton Rouge: 1976. V. 69; 72
Selected Later Poems Of Marie Luiee Kaechnitz. Princeton: 1980. V. 72
Waving from Shore. Baton Rouge: 1989. V. 69; 71

MUENSCHER, W. C.
Aquatic Plants of the United States. Ithaca: 1944. V. 68

MUENSTER, SEBASTIAN
Cosmographie Universalis Lib. VI In Quibus Iuxta Certioris Fidei Scriptorum Traditionem Describuntur, Omnium Habitabilis.... Basel: 1559. V. 69

MUHLEN, HERMINIA
Fairy Tales for Worker's Children. Chicago: 1925. V. 69

MUHLHAUSER, G. H. P.
The Cruise of the Amaryllis. London: 1924. V. 71

MUIR, ANDREW FOREST
Texas in 1837. Austin: 1958. V. 69

MUIR, ANN
Harvesting Colour. The Year in a Marbler's Workshop. Oldham: 1999. V. 70

MUIR, AUGUSTUS
The Ace of Danger. Indianapolis: 1927. V. 70

MUIR, EDWIN
Chorus of the Newly Dead: a Poem. London: 1926. V. 68
First Poems. London: 1925. V. 68
Journeys and Places. London: 1937. V. 68
Latitudes. 1924. V. 68
The Narrow Place: Poems. London: 1943. V. 68
Scottish Journey. London: 1935. V. 71
The Three Brothers. 1931. V. 68
Transition - Essays on Contemporary Literature. London: 1926. V. 68; 69
Variations on a Time Theme. London: 1934. V. 72
The Voyage and Other Poems. London: 1946. V. 68
We Moderns: Enigmas and Guesses. London: 1918. V. 71

MUIR, JOHN
Heaven on Earth: Explorations into the Wilderness Set Forth by John Muir. Austin: 1998. V. 68
My First Summer in the Sierra. Covelo: 1988. V. 72
Picturesque California and the Region West of the Rocky Mountains from Alaska to Mexico. New York and San Francisco: 1888. V. 73
Prevent the Destruction of the Yosemite Park. To the Members of Congress.... 1909. V. 73
A Thousand-Mile Walk to the Gulf. Boston: 1916. V. 70; 72
Travels in Alaska. Boston: 1915. V. 73
The Works of John Muir. Boston and New York: 1916-1924. V. 73
The Yosemite. New York: 1912. V. 72

MUIR, PERCY
English Children's Books 1600 to 1900. London: 1954. V. 68; 70
English Children's Books 1600-1900. London: 1979. V. 70
Points. London: 1934. V. 70
Points 1874-1930... (with) Points: Second Series 1866-1934. London: 1931. V. 71
Talks on Book-Collecting Delivered Under the Authority of the Antiquarian Booksellers' Association. London: 1952. V. 71
Victorian Illustrated Books. London: 1989. V. 70

MUIRHEAD, ARNOLD
Grace Revere Osler. A Brief Memoir. London: 1931. V. 68

MUIRHEAD, GEORGE
The Birds of Berwickshire, with Remarks on Their Local Distribution, Migration, and Habits, and Also on the Folk-lore, Proverbs, Popular Rhymes and Sayings Connected With Them. Edinburgh: 1889. V. 71

MUIRHEAD, JAMES P.
The Life of James Watt. London: 1858. V. 68; 71

MUIRHEAD, THORBURN
Strange to Relate. 1937. V. 69; 70; 72; 73

MUKES, IDA L.
Principles, Constitution and By-Laws of the Ethiopian Spiritualist Church Association of the United States of America. Indianapolis: 1920. V. 68

MUKHERJEE, BHARATI
The Holder Of The World. London: 1993. V. 72
The Holder of the World. New York: 1993. V. 72
Jasmine. New York: 1989. V. 73
Wife. Boston: 1975. V. 71

MULDOON, PAUL
Hay. London: 1998. V. 71
New Selected Poems 1968-1994. London: 1996. V. 71
Selected Poems 1968-1983. London: 1986. V. 69
Six Honest Serving Men. Oldcastle: 1995. V. 71; 73
To Ireland, I. Oxford: 2000. V. 71

MULFORD, ISAAC S.
A Civil and Political History of New Jersey: Embracing a compenious History of the State, from Its Early Discovery and Settlement by Europeans. Philadelphia: 1851. V. 72

MULFORD, PRENTICE
Prentice Mulford's Story - Life by Land And Sea, A Personal Narrative. New York: 1889. V. 68; 73

MULFORD, ROLAND J.
History of the Lawrenceville School 1810-1935. Princeton: 1935. V. 72

MULFORD, WILLIAM C.
Historical Tales of Cumberland County, New Jersey. Bridgeton: 1941. V. 72

MULGRAVE, CONSTANTINE JOHN PHIPPS, 2ND BARON
A Voyage Towards the North Pole, Undertaken by His Majesty's Command. London: 1774. V. 73

MULGRAVIA: a New Year's Annual for 1869. Hayle: 1869. V. 68

MULGREW, PETER
No Place for Men. London: 1964. V. 69

MULLALLA, JAMES
A View of Irish Affairs Since the Revolution of 1688 to the Close of the Parliamentary Session of 1795.... Dublin: 1795. V. 69; 73

MULLAN, BOB
The Enid Blyton Story. 1987. V. 72
The Enid Blyton Story. London: 1987. V. 69

MULLAN, JOHN
Report on the Construction of a Military Road from Fort Walla-Walla to Fort Benton. Washington: 1863. V. 71

MULLENS, JOSEPH
Twelve Months in Madagascar. London: 1875. V. 71

MULLER, F. MAX
The Science of Thought. London: 1887. V. 71

MULLER, FALK VON
Characteristics of Goethe, from the German of.... 1833. V. 70

MULLER, FRIEDRICH C. G.
Krupp's Steel Works. London: 1898. V. 71

MULLER, JOHN
Indian Tables for the Conversion of Indian Mun Into Factory and Bazar Manuals, Madras and Bombay Commercial Weight, Troy and Avoirdupois Weight.... Calcutta: 1836. V. 68

MULLER, K. O.
History of the Literature of Ancient Greece.... London: 1858. V. 71

MULLER, KENNETH J.
Neurobiology of the Leech. New York: 1981. V. 68

MULLER, MARCIA
Ask the Cards a Question. New York: 1982. V. 68; 69; 71
Beyond the Grave. New York: 1986. V. 69
The Cavalier in White. New York: 1986. V. 68
The Cheshire Cat's Eye. New York: 1983. V. 68; 71; 72
Edwin of the Iron Shoes. New York: 1977. V. 68
Eye of the Storm. New York: 1988. V. 68
Games to Keep the Dark Away. New York: 1984. V. 72
Leave a Message for Willie. New York: 1984. V. 68; 69; 71
The Legend of the Slain Soldiers. New York: 1985. V. 71; 72
The McCone Files. Norfolk: 1995. V. 69; 72
There's Nothing to Be Afraid Of. New York: 1985. V. 72

MULLER, WILHELM
Diary and Letters of Wilhelm Muller. Chicago: 1903. V. 69

MULLER, WILLIAM
Topographical and Military Description of Germany and the Surrounding Country. London: 1813. V. 70

MULLINS, EUSTACE
Murder by Injection. The Story of the Medical Conspiracy Against America. Staunton: 1988. V. 68

MULLINS, HELENE
Earthbound and Other Poems. New York: 1929. V. 71

MULLINS, JANET E.
Liverool Privateering 1756-1815. 1936. V. 73
Some Liverpool Chronicles. Liverpool: 1941. V. 73

THE MULTIPLICATION Table in Rhyme, for Young Arithmeticians. New York: 1843-1852. V. 71

MUMEY, NOLIE
Alexander Taylor Rankin 1803-1885. His Diary and Letters. Boulder: 1966. V. 69
Amos Stack (1822-1908) Forty-Niner: His Overland Diary to California.... Denver: 1981. V. 72
Anselm Holcomb Barker 1822-1895: Pioneer Builder and Early Settler of Auraria.... Denver: 1959. V. 72; 73
Barker's Diary 1822-1859 - Pioneer Builder and Early Settler of America. Denver: 1959. V. 69
Bloody Trails Along the Rio Grande, The Diary of Alonzo Ferdinand Ickis. Denver: 1958. V. 68; 70; 73
Calamity Jane 1852-1903 - A History of Her Life.. Denver: 1950. V. 72
Charles Preuss Maps of 1846. Denver: 1952. V. 68
Creede: History of a Colorado Silver Mining Town. Denver: 1949. V. 71
History of the Early Settlements of Denver (1599-1860). Glendale: 1952. V. 73
History of the Early Settlements of Denver 1599-1860. Glendale: 1972. V. 68; 73
Hoofs to Wings. The Pony Express, Dramatic Story of a Mail Service from East to West.... Boulder: 1960. V. 70
James Pierson Beckwourth 1856-1866; an Enigmatic Figure of the West. Denver: 1957. V. 72; 73
John Williams Gunnison (1812-1853). The Last of the Western Explorers. Denver: 1955. V. 70; 71
The Life of Jim Baker 1818-1898. Denver: 1931. V. 71
The Life of Jim Baker 1818-1898. New York: 1972. V. 68; 70
March of the First Dragoons to the Rocky Mountains in 1835.... Denver: 1952. V. 68; 73
March of the First Dragoons to the Rocky Mountains in 1835.... Denver: 1957. V. 71; 72
Old Forts and Trading Posts of the West. Denver: 1956. V. 68; 72; 73
Pioneer Denver, Including Scenes from Central City, Colorado City and Nevada City. Denver: 1948. V. 68; 70; 73
Poker Alice - Alice Ivers, Duffield, Tibbs Hucker (1851-1930). History of a Woman Gambler in the West. Denver: 1951. V. 70
Quarter Centenary of the Publication of Scientific Anatomy (1543- 1943): a Description of the Fabrica, with Reproductions of Some of the Illustrations. Denver: 1944. V. 70
A Reproduction of Alfred E. Mathews Pencil Sketches of Colorado.... Denver: 1961. V. 68; 73
Rocky Mountain Dick (Richard W. Rock). Stories of His Adventures in Capturing Wild Animals. Denver: 1953. V. 69
The Saga of Auntie Stone and Her Cabin with The Overland Diary of Elizabeth Parke. 1964. V. 69
The Singing Arrow. Denver: 1958. V. 69
The Ute War, a History of the White River Massacre. Boulder: 1964. V. 73

MUMEY, NORMA L.
Nolie Mumey, M.D. 1891-1984: Surgeon, Aviator, Philosopher and Humanitarian. Boulder: 1987. V. 70

MUMFORD, ERASMUS
A Letter to the Club at White's. London: 1750. V. 68

MUMFORD, JAMES G.
A Narrative of Medicine in America. Philadelphia: 1903. V. 73

MUMFORD, JERRY
A Dignified Requiem for a Necrophiliac. 1973. V. 71

MUMFORD, JOHN K.
Oriental Rugs. New York: 1900. V. 69; 72
Oriental Rugs. London: 1901. V. 72

MUMFORD, LEWIS
The Brown Decades - a Study of the Arts in America. New York: 1931. V. 69
Technics and Civilization. London: 1934. V. 71

MUMM, A. L.
Five Months in the Himalaya. 1909. V. 70
Five Months in the Himalaya. London: 1909. V. 71

MUMMERY, A. F.
Blackwell's Mountaineering Library. Oxford: 1936. V. 69
My Climbs in the Alps and Caucasus. London: 1895. V. 69; 72
My Climbs In the Alps and Caucasus. Lawrence: 1974. V. 69

MUNARI, BRUNO
Georgie Lost His Cap. London: 1945. V. 73

MUNBY, A. N. L.
The Cult of the Autograph Letter in England. London: 1962. V. 71

MUNBY, A. N. L
The Formation of the Phillips Library Between 1841 and 1872. Cambridge: 1956. V. 68

MUNBY, A. N. L.
Phillipps Studies. Cambridge: 1951-1960. V. 70
Portrait of an Obsession: the Life of Sir Thomas Phillipps, the World's Greatest Book Collector. London: 1967. V. 71
Some Caricatures of Book-Collectors. London: 1948. V. 71

MUNDEN, THOMAS SHEPHERD
Memoirs of Joseph Shepherd Munden, Comedian. by his Son. London: 1846. V. 71; 72

MUNDY, FRANCIS NOEL CLARKE
Needwood Forest. Lichfield: 1790. V. 72; 73

MUNDY, GODFREY CHARLES
Our Antipodes. London: 1852. V. 71

MUNDY, P.
The Vultures of Africa. London: 1992. V. 73

MUNDY, R. G.
English Delft Pottery. London: 1928. V. 72

MUNDY, RODNEY
Narrative of Events in Borneo & Celebes. London: 1848. V. 71

MUNDY, TALBOT
Cock O'the North. Indianapolis: 1929. V. 70
The Hundred Days and The Woman Ayisha. New York: 1931. V. 70
The Nine Unknown. 1924. V. 70
Purple Pirate. New York: 1943. V. 69

MUNK, J. A.
Arizona Sketches. New York: 1905. V. 71
Southwest Sketches. New York: 1920. V. 69
Story of the Munk Library of Arizoniana. Los Angeles: 1927. V. 68

MUNKITTRICK, RICHARD K.
Some New Jersey Arabian Nights. New York: 1892. V. 72

MUNN, H. WARNER
Tales of the Werewolf Clan. 1980. V. 70

MUNN, MARGARET CROSBY
Homage and Vision. New York: 1925. V. 69

MUNN, PAUL SANDBY
Landscape Figures, Sketched from Nature Intended for the Use of Amateurs and Young Students in Landscapes. London: 1816. V. 72

MUNNINGS, ALFRED
An Artist's Life. London: 1950-1952. V. 69
The Autobiography: An Artist's Life: Second Burst; The Finish. London: 1950-1952. V. 72
The Autobiography. An Artist's Life; Second Burst; The Finish. London: 1950-62. V. 70
Ballads and Poems; or, a Rhyming Succession of Rhyming Digression. London: 1957. V. 69; 70
Larkbarrow Farm: a Ballad of Exmoor. London. V. 69
Old Brandy and Cherry Bounce. London. V. 69
Pictures of Horses and English Life. London: 1939. V. 72
The Tale of Anthony Bell: a Hunting Ballad. London: 1921. V. 69

MUNRO, ALICE
Friend of My Youth. New York: 1990. V. 72
Friend of My Youth. Toronto: 1990. V. 69
The Love of a Good Woman. New York: 1998. V. 72
The Moons of Jupiter. New York: 1982. V. 72
The Progress of Love. Toronto: 1986. V. 69; 70
Selected Stories. New York: 1996. V. 68; 69
Who Do You Think You Are?. Toronto: 1978. V. 69

MUNRO, DAVID A., MRS.
The Doggie's Promenade. Akron: 1907. V. 69

MUNRO, ELSIE SMEATON
Topsy Turvy Tales. London: 1923. V. 73

MUNRO, HECTOR HUGH
Reginald. London: 1904. V. 68
A Saki Sampler. Harrisburg: 1945. V. 71
The Westminster Alice. 1902. V. 71
The Westminster Alice. London: 1902. V. 70
When William Came. London: 1914. V. 70

MUNRO, I. S. R.
The Fishes of New Guinea. Port Moresby: 1967. V. 68; 71

MUNRO, NEIL
The Clyde. River and Firth. London: 1907. V. 71

MUNRO, ROBERT
Prehistoric Scotland and its Place in European Civilisation. London: 1899. V. 71

MUNROE, KIRK
Dorymates A Tale of the Fishing Banks Illustrated. New York: 1890. V. 71

MUNSELL, A. H.
A Grammar of Color. Mittineague: 1921. V. 68

MUNSELL, M. E.
Flying Sparks as Told by a Pullman Conductor. Kansas City: 1914. V. 68

MUNSON, JOHN WILLIAM
Reminiscences of a Mosby Guerrilla. New York: 1906. V. 69

MUNSON, THOMAS VOLNEY
Foundations of American Grape Culture. Denison: 1909. V. 70

MUNTHE, AXEL
Letters from a Mourning City. London: 1887. V. 69
Vagaries. London: 1898. V. 69

MURAKAMI, HARUKI
Norwegian Wood. 2000. V. 68
Norwegian Wood. London: 2000. V. 70; 71; 73
A Wild Sheep Chase. London: 1989. V. 71
A Wild Sheep Chase. New York: 1989. V. 71

MURALT, BEAT LOUIS DE
Letters Describing the Character and Customs of the English and French Nations. London: 1726. V. 69

MURARO, MICHELANGELO
Veneitan Villas. Cologne: 1986. V. 73

MURAT, ACHILLE
A Moral and Political Sketch of the United States of North America. London: 1833. V. 73

MURBARAK, SCOTT J.
Compartment Syndromes and Volkmann's Contracture. Philadelphia: 1981. V. 71

MURBARGER, NELL
Sovereigns of the Sage. 1958. V. 69

MURCHISON, CHARLES
A Treatise on the Continued Fevers of Great Britain. London: 1862. V. 72

MURCHISON, RODERICK I.
The Silurian Region and Adjacent Countries of England and Wales Geologically Illustrated. London: 1839. V. 69

MURDIN, WILLIAM
A Collection of State Papers Relating to Affairs in the Reign of Queen Elizabeth from the Year 1571 to 1596. London: 1759. V. 68

MURDOCH, ALEX
Light without a Wick. A Century of Gas-Lighting 1792-1892. A Sketch of William Murdoch, the Inventor. Glasgow: 1892. V. 69

MURDOCH, B. J.
The Red Vineyard. Glasgow: 1949. V. 72

MURDOCH, BEAMISH
Epitome of the Laws of Nova Scotia. Halifax: 1832-1833. V. 68; 73
Epitome of the Laws of Nova Scotia. Holmes Beach: 1971. V. 68
A History of Nova Scotia, or Acadie. Halifax: 1865. V. 68
A History of Nova Scotia, or Acadie. Halifax: 1865-1867. V. 68; 73

MURDOCH, IRIS
An Accidental Man. London: 1971. V. 70
Ada or Ardor: a Family Chronicle. New York: 1969. V. 68
The Bell. London: 1958. V. 70; 72
The Black Prince. London: 1973. V. 70; 72; 73
The Book and the Brotherhood. London: 1987. V. 68
The Book and the Brotherhood. Franklin Center: 1988. V. 70
The Existentialist Political Myth. London: 1989. V. 70
The Existentialist Political Myth. West Midlands: 1989. V. 70
A Fairly Honourable Defeat. London: 1970. V. 70
The Flight from the Enchanter. London: 1956. V. 70; 73
The Good Apprentice. London: 1985. V. 68; 70
The Green Knight. London: 1993. V. 70
Henry and Cato. London: 1976. V. 70
The Italian Girl. London: 1964. V. 68; 71; 73
Jackson's Dilemma. London: 1995. V. 70
Joanna Joanna: a Play in Two Acts. London: 1994. V. 70
The Message to the Planet. London: 1989. V. 70
Metaphysics as a Guide to Morals. London: 1992. V. 70
The Nice and the Good. London: 1968. V. 70
Nuns and Soldiers. London: 1980. V. 70
The One Alone. London: 1995. V. 70; 72
The Overcrowded Barracoon and Other Articles. London: 1972. V. 70
The Philosopher's Pupil. London: 1983. V. 68
Reynolds Stone: an Address Given by Iris Murdoch in St. James's Church, Piccadilly, London on 20 July 1979. London: 1981. V. 70; 73
The Sacred and Profane Love Machine. London: 1974. V. 70
The Sandcastle. London: 1957. V. 70
Sartre. Cambridge: 1953. V. 69; 70
The Sea, The Sea. London: 1978. V. 70
A Severed Head. London: 1961. V. 70
A Severed Head. London: 1964. V. 70
Something Special: Four Poems and a Story. Helsinki: 1990. V. 70
The Sovereignty of Good Over Other Concepts. The Leslie Stephen Lecture, 1967. London: 1967. V. 73
Three Plays: The Black Prince: The Three Arrows: The Servants and the Snow. London: 1989. V. 68
The Time of the Angels. New York: 1966. V. 73
The Unicorn. London: 1962. V. 73
The Unicorn. London: 1963. V. 70; 71; 72
An Unofficial Rose. London: 1962. V. 68; 72; 73
An Unofficial Rose. New York: 1962. V. 73
An Unofficial Rose. London: 1963. V. 71

MURDOCH, IRIS continued
A Word Child. London: 1975. V. 68
A Year of Birds: Poems. Tisbury: 1978. V. 70
A Year of Birds: Poems. London: 1984. V. 70

MURDOCK, CHARLES
A Backward Glance at Eighty. San Francisco: 1921. V. 69

MURDOCK, HAROLD
Earl Percy Dines Abroad. Boston: 1924. V. 70

MURDOCK, JOHN R.
Arizona Characters in Silhouette. Tempe: 1933. V. 68; 73
Arizona Characters in Silhouette. 1939. V. 69
Constitutional Developmet of Arizona. 1930. V. 68

MURDOCK, JOYCE EMERSON PRESTON
Dark Deeds. London: 1895. V. 68
A Detective Triumphs. London: 1906. V. 68
From Clue to Capture. London. V. 70
From Clue to Capture. London: 1893. V. 68
Pound and Fettered. London: 1905. V. 68
Suspicion Aroused/In the Grip of the Law. London: 1892-1893. V. 68
Tracked to Doom. London: 1907. V. 68
Wanted. London: 1904. V. 68

MURFREE, MARY NOAILLES
The Mystery of Witch Face Mountain and Other Stories. Boston: 1895. V. 69
The Phantoms of the Foot-Bridge and Other Stories. New York: 1895. V. 70
Where the Battle Was Fought. Boston: 1885. V. 70

MURGER, HENRI
La Boheme. London: 1926. V. 73

MURPHY, ARTHUR
An Essay on the Life and Genius of Samuel Johnson, LL.D. London: 1793. V. 69; 71
An Essay on the Life and Genuis of Samuel Johnson. 1820. V. 72
The Life of David Garrick. 1801. V. 73
The Way to Keep Him. London: 1785. V. 69
The Works of Arthur Murphy. London: 1786. V. 69

MURPHY, BILL
The Red Sands of Santa Maria. New York: 1956. V. 72

MURPHY, DALLAS
Lover Man. New York: 1987. V. 68

MURPHY, DENIS
Our Martyrs: a Record of Those Who Suffered...Under the Penal Laws. 1896. V. 73
Our Martyrs: A Record of Those Who Suffered...Under the Penal Laws. London: 1896. V. 69

MURPHY, EDMUND
The Present State and Condition of Ireland, But More Especially the Province of Ulster, Humbly Represented to the Kingdom of England. London: 1681. V. 73
A Treatise on the Agricultural Grasses. Dublin: 1844. V. 69

MURPHY, G.
A Bibliography of English Character Books 1608-1700. Oxford: 1925. V. 70

MURPHY, J. B.
Stereo-Clinic - Hysterectomy for Pelvic Inflammatory Disease. (with) Arthoplasty for Ankylosis of the Knee. Baltimore: 1910. V. 71

MURPHY, J. M.
Rambles in North Western America. London: 1879. V. 71

MURPHY, JAMES
Plans, Elevations, Sections and Views of the Church of Batalha in the Province of Estremadura in Portugal.... London: 1795. V. 72

MURPHY, JOHN
Fifty Photographic Views of the Steamers of the Fall River Line. Boston: 1896. V. 68

MURPHY, JOHN BENJAMIN
Resection of Arteries and Veins Injured in Continuity...End-to-End Suture. New York: 1987. V. 73

MURPHY, MICHAEL
Golf in the Kingdom. New York: 1972. V. 70

MURPHY, R. CUSHMAN
Bird Islands of Peru. 1925. V. 72
Bird Islands of Peru. New York: 1925. V. 69; 70; 73
Oceanic Birds of South America. 1936. V. 69
Oceanic Birds of South America. New York: 1936. V. 68; 70; 73

MURPHY, SHIRLEY FORSTER
Our Homes and How to Make them Healthy. London: 1883. V. 68

MURPHY, WILLIAM M.
Prodigal Father: Life of John Butler Yeats. 1978. V. 69

MURR, CHRISTOPH GOTTLIEB VON
Beschreibung der Vornehmsten Merkwurdigkeiten in des H. R. Reichs freyen Stadt Nurnberg und auf der Hohen Schule zu Altdorf.... Nurnberg: 1778. V. 70

MURR, CHRISTOPHE THEOPHILE DE
Dissertatio de Corona Regum Italiae, Vulgo Ferrea Dicta. Munich: 1808. V. 72

MURRAY, A.
The Geographical Distribution of Mammals. 1866. V. 69; 73

MURRAY, A. H.
Journal of the Yukon 1847-1848. Ottawa: 1910. V. 71

MURRAY, A. S.
Greek Bronzes and Greek Terracotta Statuettes. London: 1899. V. 72
White Athenian Vases in the British Museum. London: 1896. V. 69

MURRAY, ALBERT
The Hero and the Blues. 1973. V. 68
The Hero and the Blues. Columbia, MO: 1973. V. 71
The Omni-Americans. New York: 1970. V. 72
Train Whistle Guitar. New York: 1974. V. 68; 69

MURRAY, ALEXANDER
Journal Du Yukon 1847-1848. Ottawa: 1910. V. 68

MURRAY, ALICE EFFIE
A History of Commercial and Financial Relations Between England and Ireland from the Period of the Restoration. 1903. V. 72

MURRAY, AMELIA M.
Letters from the United States, Cuba and Canada. New York: 1856. V. 69; 72

MURRAY, ANN
Mentoria; or the Young Ladies Instructor, in Familiar Conversations on Moral and Entertaining Subjects. London: 1778. V. 68

MURRAY, CHARLES A.
Travels in North America..a Summer Residence with the Pawnee Tribe of Indians. London: 1854. V. 68

MURRAY, CHARLOTTE
Earth's Messages. London. V. 69

MURRAY, DAVID
History of Education in New Jersey. Washington: 1899. V. 72
Museums Their History and Their Use. Staten Island: 2000. V. 68; 70; 71; 72

MURRAY, DAVID CHRISTIE
First Person Singular: a Novel. London: 1887. V. 68
In His Grip. London: 1907. V. 70
Joseph's Coat. London: 1889. V. 68

MURRAY, E. C. GRENVILLE
The Boudoir Cabal by Trois Etoiles. Leipzig: 1875. V. 73

MURRAY, EUSTACE C. GRENVILLE
The Roving Englishman. London: 1854. V. 68

MURRAY, F. S.
History of Ft. Huachuca. El Paso: 1972. V. 69

MURRAY, FRANCES ELIZABETH
Memoir of Le Baron Botsford, M.D. St. John: 1892. V. 73

MURRAY, GEORGE
An Introduction to the Study of Seaweeds. London: 1895. V. 68

MURRAY, GEORGE W.
A History of George W. Murray and His Long Confinement at Andersonville Georgia. Northampton: 1865?. V. 68

MURRAY, GRISELL BAILLIE
Memoirs of the Lives and Characters of the Right Honourable George Baillie of Jerviswood and of Lady Grisell Baillie. Edinburgh: 1822. V. 71

MURRAY, HENRY
A Game of Bluff. London: 1890. V. 68

MURRAY, HILDA
Flower Legends for Children. London. V. 72

MURRAY, HUGH
Historical Account of Discoveries and Travels in North America. London: 1829. V. 68
Narrative of Discovery and Adventure In Africa. Edinburgh: 1840. V. 72

MURRAY, J.
Economy of Vegetation.... London: 1838. V. 69
How to Live in Tropical Africa. London: 1895. V. 71

MURRAY, J. A.
The Avifauna of British India.... London: 1887-1890. V. 73

MURRAY, JAMES
Lectures to Lords Spiritual; or, an Advice to the Bishops, Concerning Religious Articles, Tithes and Church Power. London: 1774. V. 70
Sermons to Asses. London: 1768. V. 69

MURRAY, JOHN
Bath-Kol. A Voice from the Wilderness. Boston: 1783. V. 70
Bathymetrical Survey of the Scottish Fresh-Water Lochs During the Years 1897 to 1909. Edinburgh: 1910. V. 71
A Handbook Of Travel-Talk. London: 1856. V. 72
Murray's Handbook for Travellers In Switzerland. Part 1. Switzerland Without the Pennine Alps. London: 1892. V. 72
The Trial of Lieutenant General Sir John Murray, Bart, by a General Court Martial, held at Winchester on Monday the 16th of January 1815.... London: 1815. V. 70

MURRAY, JOHN A.
American Nature Writing. San Francisco: 1994. V. 70

MURRAY, JOHN FISHER
The World of London. 1844. V. 71

MURRAY, JOHN OGDEN
The Immortal Six Hundred: a Story of Cruelty to Confederate Prisoners of War. Winchester: 1905. V. 69; 70
The Immortal Six Hundred: a Story of Cruelty to Confederate Prisoners of War. Roanoke: 1911. V. 70

MURRAY, LINDLEY
English Exercises, Adapted to the Grammar Lately Published by L. Murray.... Newark: 1802. V. 72
An English Grammar: Comprehending the Principles and Rules of the Language.... New York: 1814. V. 69
The English Reader; or Pieces in Prose and Poetry, Selected from the Best Writers. Burlington: 1816. V. 72
The Power of Religion on the Mind, in Retirement, Affliction, and at the Approach of Death.... Trenton: 1795. V. 72

MURRAY, NICHOLAS
Notes Historical and Biographical, Concerning Elizabeth-Town, its Eminent Men, Chuches and Ministers. Elizabeth Town: 1844. V. 72
A Sermon Preached Nov. 30, 1837, in the First Presbyterian Church, Elizabeth-Town: Being the Day of Public Thaknsgiving (sic). Elizabeth-Town: 1838. V. 72

MURRAY, PAULI
Dark Testament and Other Poems. CT: 1970:. V. 72

MURRAY, ROBERT
The Theory and Practice of Ship-Building with Portions of the Treatise On Naval Architecture by Augustin C. Creuze. Edinburgh: 1861. V. 69

MURRAY, ROBERT A.
The Army on the Powder River. Bellevue: 1969. V. 72; 73
Fort Laramie Visions of A Grand Old Post. Fort Collins: 1974. V. 72
Military Posts in The Power River Country of Wyoming 1865-1894. Lincoln: 1968. V. 72

MURRAY, T. DOUGLAS
Sir Samuel Baker. London: 1895. V. 71

MURRAY, THOMAS BOYLES
A Notice of Ely Chapel, Holborn, with Some Account of Ely Palace.... London: 1840. V. 73
Pitcairn: The Island, The People and The Pastor. London: 1857. V. 72

MURRAY, W. H.
Mountaineering in Scotland. Dent: 1947. V. 71
Mountaineering in Scotland. London: 1947. V. 69
Rock Climbs. Glencoe and Ardgour. Edinburgh: 1949. V. 69
The Story of Everest. London: 1953. V. 69

MURRAY, W. H. H.
Daylight Land. Boston: 1888. V. 71
Daylight Land. London: 1888. V. 71

MURRAY'S Buckinghamshire Architectural Guide. London: 1948. V. 68; 71

MURRAY'S Handbook for Travellers in France. London: 1854. V. 68

MURRAY'S Handbook For Travellers in France. 1875-1892. V. 70

MURRAY'S Handbook for Travellers in Turkey in Asia, Including Constantinople the Bosphorus, Plain of Troy, Isles of Cyprus, Rhodes &c. 1878. V. 70

MURRAY'S Handbook for Sicily: Including Palermo, Messina, Catania, Syracuse, Etna and the Ruins of the Greek Temples. 1864. V. 70

MURRELL, WILLIAM
What to Do in Cases of Poisoning. London: 1883. V. 68

MURRY, ANN
Poems on Various Subjects. London: 1779. V. 69

MURRY, JOHN MIDDLETON
Between 2 Worlds. London: 1935. V. 72
D. H. Lawrence. Cambridge: 1930. V. 68; 72
Reminiscences of D. H. Lawrence. London: 1933. V. 72
Son of Woman. The Story of D. H. Lawrence. London: 1931. V. 72
Studies in Keats. London: 1930. V. 68

MURTADI, IBN GAPHIPHUS
L'Egypte de Mutadi fils du Gaphiphe, ou il Est Traite des Pyramides du Debordement du Nil, & des Autres Merveilles de Cette Province.... Paris: 1666. V. 70

MUSA Proterva: Love Poems of the Restoration. London and Bungay: 1902. V. 71

MUSAEUS
Hero and Leander. Waltham St. Lawrence: 1949. V. 70; 71

MUSGRAVE, AGNES
Cicely; or the Rose of Raby. London: 1795. V. 69

MUSGRAVE, RICHARD
Memoirs of the Different Rebellions in Ireland from the Arrival of the English; Also, a Particular Detail of that Which Broke Out the XXIIId of May, MDCCXCVIII.... Dublin: 1801. V. 69

MUSGRAVE, THOMAS
Castaway on the Auckland Isles. London: 1866. V. 71

MUSGRAVE, W. R.
Itinerary of My Tour from Southhampton to Cape Town. Folkestone: 1913. V. 71

MUSGRAVE, WILLIAM
Antiquitates Britanno-Belgicae, Praecipue Romanae Figuris Illustratae, Tribus voll. Comprehensae Quorum. Exeter: 1719. V. 70

MUSICAL Travels through England. London: 1776. V. 70

MUSICK, JOHN R.
Stories of Missouri. New York: 1897. V. 71

MUSIL, ROBERT
Prosa, Dramen, Spate Briefe. Hamburg: 1957. V. 71
Tabebucher, Aphorismen, Essays und Reden. Hamburg: 1955. V. 71
Young Torless. London: 1965. V. 72

MUSPRATT, JAMES SHERIDAN
Chemistry, Theoretical, Practical and Analytical.... Glasgow/Edinburgh/London: 1857-1860. V. 69
Chemistry Theoretical, Practical and Analytical.... London: 1860. V. 70

MUSSET, PAUL DE
The Last Abbe. Paris. V. 68; 71

MUSSOLINI, BENITO
Vivo De Arnaldo. Budapest: 1934. V. 70

MUSSON, SPENCER C.
Sicily. London: 1911. V. 72

MUSTON, ALEXIS
The Israel of the Alps, a History of the Persecutions of the Waldenses. London: 1852. V. 73

MUTHESIUS, H.
Die Schone Wohnung: Beispiele Neuer Deutscher Innenraume. Muchen: 1922. V. 72

MUTIS, JOSE CELESTINO
Flora de la Real Expedicion Botanica del Nuevo Reyno de Granada. Madrid: 1954. V. 73

MUTT, EUGENIE
Fairy Tales from Baltic Shores. New York: 1930. V. 72

MUTUAL Criticism. Oneida;: 1876. V. 68

MUYBRIDGE, EADWEARD
Animals in Motion. London: 1902. V. 68

MUYLDER, C. G. DE
The Neurility of the Kidney. Oxford: 1952. V. 68

MUYS, JOHANNES
Praxis Chirurgica Rationalis seu Obervationes Chirurgicae Secundum Solida Verae Philosophiae Fundamenta Resolutae Quinque Decades. Leiden: 1685. V. 68; 71; 73
Praxis Medico-Chirurgica Rationalis, seu Observationes Medico- Chirurgicae Decades XII. Naples: 1727. V. 72

M'WILLIAM, JAMES O.
Medical History of the Expedition to the Niger. London: 1843. V. 71

MY Aunt's Ball. New York: 1850-1868. V. 71

MY Best Detective Story. London: 1931. V. 68

MY Best Thriller. London: 1933. V. 68

MY Birthday. 1870. V. 73

MY Book of Funny Folk. London: 1920. V. 73

MY Dolly. New York: 1890. V. 70

MY Experiences in a Lunatic Asylum. London: 1879. V. 69

MY Favorite Receipts. New York: 1893. V. 72

MY First Book. London: 1894. V. 68

MY Indestructible Easy Reading and Pictures. Philadelphia. V. 68

MY Life Story by E. Lephant. New York: 1915. V. 70

MY Life Story by P. Puppy. New York: 1915. V. 69

MY Life Story. By Ted Bear. New York: 1915. V. 69

MY Mother. New York: 1869. V. 71

MY New Big Book Stories and Poems by Many Authors. London. V. 68

MY Own Annual 1848. A Gift Book for Boys and Girls. London: 1848. V. 73

MY Poetry Book. Philadelphia: 1934. V. 70

MY Railway ABC and a Pull Out Train. Dundee: 1912. V. 72

MY Rambles in the Enchanted Summer Land of the Great Northwest During the Tourist Season of 1881. Revised to March 1, 1883. Chicago: 1883. V. 68

MY Very Own ABC of Toys. New York: 1900. V. 69

MYERS, CHARLES E.
Memoirs of a Hunter: a Story of Fifty-Eight Years of Hunting and Fishing. Davenport: 1948. V. 68

MYERS, DWIGHT
In Celebration of the Book, Literary New Mexico. 1982. V. 70
In Celebration of the Book: Literary New Mexico. Albuquerque: 1982. V. 71

MYERS, FRANK
Prompt to Action, Atlanta Fire Department (Part 2). Atlanta: 1975. V. 69

MYERS, FRANK M.
The Comanches. Baltimore: 1871. V. 69; 70
The Comanches. Gaithersburg: 1987. V. 72

MYERS, GRACE WHITING
History of the Massachusetts General Hospital June 1872 to December 1900. Boston: 1929. V. 68; 71

MYERS, J. ARTHUR
Masters of Medicine. An Historical Sketch of the College of Medical Sciences University of Minestoa 1888-1966. St. Louis: 1966. V. 72

MYERS, JOHN MYERS
Doc Holliday. 1955. V. 68
The Last Chance: Tombstone's Early Years. New York: 1950. V. 69

MYERS, L. H.
The Pool of Vishnu. New York: 1940. V. 70

MYERS, OLIVER P.
Illustrated Animal Kingdom and Leading Curiosities of J. E. Warner & Co.'s Great Pacific Museum, Menagerie and Circus. Buffalo: 1872. V. 69

MYERS, ROBERT MANSON
Anna Seward. An Eighteenth Century Handelian. Williamsburg: 1947. V. 69; 73
Early Moral Criticism of Handelian Oratorio. Williamsburg: 1947. V. 69; 73

MYERS, TAMAR
Too Many Crooks Spoil the Broth. New York: 1994. V. 68

MYERS, WALTER DEAN
Fallen Angels. New York: 1988. V. 72
Majo and the Russians. New York: 1977. V. 72

MYERS, WILLIAM H.
Sketches of California and Hawaii by William H. Meyers, Gunner, U.S.N. San Francisco: 1970. V. 73

MYKEL, A. W.
The Windchime Legacy. New York: 1980. V. 68

MYLIUS, CHRISTIAN F.
Malerische Fussreise Durch das Sudliche Frankreich und Einen Theil von Ober-Italien. Carlsruhe: 1818-1819. V. 69
Malerische Fussreise Durch das Sudliche Frankreich und einen Theil von Ober-Italien. Carlsruhe: 1819. V. 72

MYLNE, ROBERT
Observations on Bridge Building and the Several Plans Offered for a New Bridge. London: 1760. V. 73
The Report of Robert Mylne, Engineer; on the Proposed Improvement of the Drainage and Navigation of the River Ouze.... Lynn: 1792. V. 71

MYNORS, R. A. B.
Durham Cathedral Manuscripts to the End of the Twelfth Century. Oxford: 1939. V. 70

MYNTER, HERMAN
Appendicitis and Its Surgical Treatment. Philadelphia: 1897. V. 71; 73

MYRICK, DAVID F.
San Francisco's Telegraph Hill. Berkeley: 1972. V. 70

MYRICK, HERBERT
Cache La Poudre; The Romance of a Tenderfoot in the Days of Custer. New York: 1905. V. 71; 72

MYRTLE, JOHN H.
The Humpty Dumpty Animal Book. London: 1904. V. 70

THE MYSTERY and Method of His Majesty's Happy Restauration, Laid Open to Publick View. London: 1683. V. 69

N

N., C.
Tears and Smiles through Them. London: 1831. V. 72

NABOKOV, PETER
Architecture of Acoma Pueblo. Santa Fe: 1986. V. 70

NABOKOV, VLADIMIR
Ada. London: 1969. V. 70
Ada. New York: 1969. V. 71
Bend Sinister. New York: 1947. V. 70
Camera Obscura. Stockholm: 1935. V. 69
Conclusive Evidence. New York: 1951. V. 69; 71; 73
La Course du Fou. Paris: 1934. V. 72
The Defense. New York: 1964. V. 71
Despair. New York: 1966. V. 69; 73
Details of a Sunset and Other Stories. London: 1976. V. 72
Le Don. (The Gift). Paris: 1967. V. 71
The Eye. New York: 1965. V. 71
Invitation to a Beheading. New York: 1959. V. 68; 69; 70; 71
Laughter in the Dark. Indianapolis and New York: 1938. V. 69; 71; 73
Lolita. New York: 1955. V. 70
Lolita. Paris: 1955. V. 71; 72; 73
Lolita. New York: 1958. V. 70
Lolita. Paris: 1958. V. 73
Lolita. Buenos Aires: 1959. V. 69
Lolita. London: 1959. V. 70; 71
Look at the Harlequins. New York: 1974. V. 70
Mary. New York: 1970. V. 73
Mashenka. (Mary). Berlin: 1926. V. 71
Nabokov's Dozen. Garden City: 1958. V. 69
Nabokov's Dozen. London: 1959. V. 71; 73
Nabokov's Quartet. New York: 1966. V. 71; 73
Nikolai Gogol. Norfolk: 1944. V. 69; 71
Nikolai Gogol. London: 1947. V. 68
Pale Fire. New York: 1962. V. 73
Pnin. London: 1957. V. 70
Poems and Problems. London: 1972. V. 71
The Real Life of Sebastian Knight. London: 1945. V. 70
A Russian Beauty and Other Stories. New York: 1973. V. 68
Speak, Memory: a Memoir. London: 1951. V. 70
The Waltz Invention. New York: 1966. V. 70; 73

NACHMANSON, D.
Metabolism and Function. New York: 1950. V. 68

NACK, CARL
Reichstift Neresheim. Eine Kurze Geschichte Dieser Benediktinerabtey in Schwaben und Beschreibung ihrer im Jahre 1792.... 1792. V. 70

NACLERIO, EMIL
Bronchopulmonary Diseases Basic Aspects, Diagnosis and Treatment. New York: 1959. V. 71; 73

NADAILLAC, JEAN FRANCOIS ALBERT DE POUGET, MARQUIS DE
Pre-Historic America. London: 1885. V. 71

NADEAU, REMI
Fort Laramie and the Sioux Indians. 1967. V. 68
The Water Seekers. Santa Barbara and Salt Lake: 1974. V. 68

NAEF, WESTON J.
Era of Exploration. 1975. V. 70
Era of Exploration. Boston: 1975. V. 73

NAESS, A.
Tirich Mir. The Norwegian Himalayan Expedition. 1952. V. 71

NAHAS, GABRIEL
Carbon Dioxide and Metabolic Regulations. New York: 1974. V. 72

NAHL, ARTHUR
Instructions in Gymnastics. San Francisco: 1863. V. 68

NAIPAUL, SEEPERSAD
The Adventures of Gurudeva and other stories. London: 1976. V. 72

NAIPAUL, SHIVA
Beyond the Dragon's Mouth. London: 1984. V. 71
The Chip-Chip Gatherers. London: 1973. V. 71

NAIPAUL, V. S.
Among the Believers. London: 1981. V. 70
Among the Believers. New York: 1981. V. 70
A Bend in the River. London: 1979. V. 70
A Bend in the River. New York: 1980. V. 72
Beyond Belief. New York: 1998. V. 70
The Enigma of Arrival. London: 1987. V. 73
The Enigma of Arrival. Middlesex: 1987. V. 71
The Enigma of Arrival. New York: 1988. V. 72
A Flag on the Island. London: 1967. V. 70; 71
A Flag on the Island. New York: 1968. V. 71; 73
Guerrillas. London: 1975. V. 71; 73
Guerrillas. New York: 1975. V. 70; 72
Half a Life. London: 2001. V. 69; 70; 72
A Home for Mr. Biswas. New York: 1983. V. 72
A House for Mr. Biswas. London: 1961. V. 68
A House for Mr. Biswas. London: 1962. V. 69
In a Free State. New York: 1971. V. 69
India: a Million Mutinies. London: 1990. V. 70; 73
Letters Between a Father and Son. London: 1999. V. 70
The Loss of El Dorado. London: 1969. V. 70; 71
The Middle Passage. New York: 1963. V. 70
Miguel Street. London: 1959. V. 68
Miguel Street. London: 1960. V. 69
The Mimic Men. London: 1967. V. 72
Mr. Stone and the Knights Companion. New York: 1963. V. 70
Mr. Stone and the Knights Companion. New York: 1964. V. 69

NAIPAUL, V. S. continued
The Mystic Masseur. London: 1957. V. 68; 72
The Mystic Masseur. New York: 1959. V. 69; 70
The Mystic Masseur. London: 1960. V. 69
The Overcrowded Barracoon. London: 1972. V. 70
The Return of Eva Peron, with The Killings in Trinidad. London: 1980. V. 70
A Turn in the South. Franklin Center: 1989. V. 69; 70
A Turn in the South. London: 1989. V. 70; 71
A Turn in the South. New York: 1989. V. 68; 70
A Way in the World. London: 1994. V. 70
A Way in the World. New York: 1994. V. 70; 72

NAIRN, KATHARINE
The Trial of Katharine Nairn and Patrick Ogilvie, for the Crimes of Incest and Murder. Edinburgh: 1765. V. 69

NAIRN, THOMAS
A Letter from South Carolina.... London: 1718. V. 68

NAISH, GEORGE P. B.
Nelson's Letters To His Wife and other Documents 1785-1831. London: 1958. V. 73

NAISMITH, W. W.
The Islands of Scotland (Excluding Skye). Edinburgh: 1934. V. 69
The Islands of Scotland (Excluding Skye). Edinburgh: 1952. V. 69

NAITHANI, B. D.
Flora of Chamoli. New Delhi: 1984. V. 70

NAKAO, S.
Living Himalayan Flowers. Tokyo: 1964. V. 68

NAKATOMI, K.
Textile Arts of India. Kokyo Hatanaka Collection. Kyoto: 1993. V. 69

NAKED Came the Manatee. New York: 1996. V. 68; 70

NALL, G. H.
The Life of the Sea Trout. 1930. V. 68

NAMEH, MIRAJ
Miraculous Journey of Mahomet. London: 1977. V. 72

NAMES Of the Streets, Lanes and Alleys in the Town of Boston, with an Index.... Boston: 1800. V. 71

NANCE, R. MORTON
Sailing Ship Models. London: 1949. V. 72
Sailing Ship Models. New York: 1949. V. 69

NANNI, GIOVANNI
Antiqvitatvm Italiae Ac Totivs Orbis. Antverpiae: 1552. V. 69; 73

NANSEN, FRIDTJOF
Farthest North. London: 1897. V. 68; 72
Farthest North. Westminster: 1897. V. 71
Fram Over Polhavet den Norshe Polarfaerd 1893-1896 Med at Tillaeg af Otto Sverdrup. Kristiania (Oslo): 1897. V. 70
Hunting and Adventure in the Arctic. London: 1925. V. 71
In Northern Mists. London: 1911. V. 71; 73

NAOGEORGUS, THOMAS
Reprint of the Popish Kingdome or Reigne of Antichrist Written in Latin Verse by.... London: 1880. V. 68

NAPIER, ALEXANDER
A Noble Book of Cookry for a Prynce Houssolde or eny Other Estately Houssolde. London: 1882. V. 68

NAPIER, CATHERINE
Woman's Rights and Duties Considered with Relation to Their Influence on Society and On Her Own Condition. London: 1840. V. 68

NAPIER, CHARLES JAMES
A Letter to the Right Hon. Sir J. Hobhouse, President of the Board of Control, on the Baggage of the Indian Army. London: 1849. V. 73

NAPIER, GERALDINE
Here Come the Brides. New York: 1966. V. 71

NAPIER, JOHN
The Construction of the Wonderful Canon of Logarithms.... Edinburgh and London: 1889. V. 71

NAPIER, ROBERT
Catalogue of the Works of Art Forming the Collection of Robert Napier of West Shandon, Dumbartonshire. London: 1865. V. 69; 72

NAPIER, ROBINA
Johnsoniana, Anecdotes of the Late Samuel Johnson.... London: 1884. V. 69

NAPIER, WILLIAM FRANCIS PATRICK
History of the War in the Peninsula and in the South of France. London: 1828-1840. V. 68
History of the War in the Peninsula and In the South of France. New York: 1882. V. 71

NAPOLEON I, EMPEROR OF THE FRENCH
Officer's Manual. Napoleon's Maxims of War. Richmond: 1862. V. 69; 70

NAPTON, WILLIAM B.
Over the Santa Fe Trail 1857. Santa Fe: 1964. V. 68; 70

NARAIN, RAM
The Tigress of the Harem. New York: 1930. V. 71

NARANJO-MORSE, NORA
Mud Woman. Tucson: 1992. V. 72

NARAYAN, R. K.
The Financial Expert. London: 1952. V. 73

NARDI, JACOPO
Le Historie della Citta di Fiorenza.... Lione: 1582. V. 72

NARDI, LUIGI
Descrizione Antiquaria...Architettonica con Rami dell'Arco di Augusto Ponte di Tiberio e Tempio Malatestiano di Rimino. Rimini: 1813. V. 72

NARES, EDWARD
Think's-I-To-Myself, a Serio-Ludicro, Tragico Tale.... London: 1811. V. 68; 73

NARES, GEORGE STRONG
Narrative of a Voyage to the Polar Sea During 1875-1876 in H.M. Ships Alert and Discovery.... London: 1878. V. 71

NARES, ROBERT
A Glossary; or, Collection of Words, Phrases, Names and Allusions of Customs, Proverbs, etc...in the Works of English Authors...Shakespeare.... London: 1867. V. 73

NARKISS, BEZALEL
Hebrew Illuminated Manuscripts. Jerusalem: 1974. V. 70

THE NARRATIVE Companion; or, Entertaining Moralist.... London: 1760. V. 71

A NARRATIVE Of an Explorer in Tropical South Africa: Being an Account of a Visit to Darmaraland in 1851.... London: 1889. V. 68

A NARRATIVE of Five Youth from the Sandwich Islands, Now Receiving an Education in this Country. New York: 1816. V. 71

NARRATIVE of Privations and Sufferings of United States Officers and Soldiers While Prisoners of War in the Hands of Rebel Authorities. Boston: 1866. V. 72

NARRATIVE of the North Polar Expedition: U.S. Ship Polaris, Captain Charles Francis Hall Comannding. Washington: 1876. V. 72

A NARRATIVE of the Preparations at Hatfield House, the Seat of the Most Noble the Marquess of Salisbury for their Majesties and the Royal Family to Review the Volunteer Crops and Militia of the County of Hartford on Friday 13th June 1800. London: 1818. V. 68

A NARRATIVE of the Visit of Mr. Henry Leslie's Choir to the International Exhibiton at Paris, 16th to 24th July, by a Member of the Choir. London: 1879. V. 71

NASATIR, A.
French Activities in California an Archival Calendar - Guide. New York: 1945. V. 70
A French Journalist in the California Gold Rush. Georgetown: 1964. V. 69

NASH, CHARLES EDWARD
Biographical Sketches of Gen. Pat Cleburne and Gen. T. C. Hindman. Little Rock: 1898. V. 69; 70

NASH, D. L.
Flora of Guatemala. Chicago: 1976. V. 72

NASH, FREDERICK
A Series of Views, Interior and Exterior of the Collegiate Chapel of St. George at Windsor. London: 1805. V. 68

NASH, JOHN
Bucks - Shell Guide. London: 1936. V. 69; 70
Cobden-Sanderson and the Doves Press. San Francisco: 1929. V. 70
Happy New Lear. London: 1957. V. 70
The Wood Engravings of John Nash. Liverpool: 1987. V. 70; 72

NASH, OGDEN
Happy Days. New York: 1933. V. 69
Hard Lines. New York: 1931. V. 68
Verses from 1929. Boston: 1959. V. 69

NASH, PAUL
Dorset. Shell Guide. 1936. V. 68
Room and Book. 1932. V. 72
Room and Book. London: 1932. V. 68; 69
Wood Engravings. A Catalogue of the Wood Engravings, Pattern Papers, Etchings and Engraving on Copper. Woodbridge, Suffolk: 1997. V. 68; 70; 71

NASH, RAY
Durer's 1511 Drawing of a Press and Printer. Cambridge: 1947. V. 70; 72

NASH, SARA M.
Ancestors and Descendants. Fountain Inn: 1972. V. 72

NASH, WALLIS
Two Years in Oregon. New York: 1882. V. 68

NASHE, THOMAS
Works.... Oxford: 1966. V. 68

NASHVILLE Fire Department Then and Now. 1976?. V. 69

NASIR, Y. J.
Wild Flowers of Pakistan. Karachi: 1995. V. 68

NASMITH, JAMES
An Examination of the Statutes Now in Force Relating to the Assize of Bread; with Remarks on the Bill Intended to be Brought into Parliament by the Country Bakers. Wisbech: 1800. V. 68

NASMYTH, JAMES
James Nasmyth, Engineer: an Autobiography. London: 1883. V. 71
The Moon: Considered as a Planet, a World and a Satellite. London: 1874. V. 68; 73

NASSAU, ROBERT HAMILL
Fetichism in West Africa. London: 1904. V. 69; 71
A History of the Presbytery of Corisco, Ogove River, West Coast of Africa, February 1888. Trenton: 1888. V. 72

NASSY, D.
Observations on the Cause, Nature and Treatment of the Epidemic Disorders Prevalent in Philadelphia. Philadelphia: 1793. V. 70; 71

NATHAN, DANIEL
The Golden Summer. Boston: 1953. V. 71

NATHAN, HANS
Dan Emmet And The Rise Of Early Negro Minstrelsy. Norman: 1962. V. 72; 73

NATHAN, ROBERT
Autumn. New York: 1921. V. 71; 72
The Fiddler in Barly. New York: 1926. V. 70
Heaven and Hell and the Megas Factor. 1975. V. 71
Jonah. New York: 1925. V. 69
Portrait of Jennie. New York: 1940. V. 72
Winter in April. New York: 1938. V. 68
Youth Grows Old. New York: 1922. V. 72

NATHANSON, E. M.
The Dirty Dozen. New York: 1965. V. 71; 72

NATION, EARL F.
An Annotated Checklist of Osleriana. 1976. V. 72

NATIONAL ASSOCIATION FOR THE VINDICATION OF SCOTTISH RIGHTS
Address to the People of Scotland and Statement of Grievances. Edinburgh: 1853. V. 68
Justice to Scotland. Report of the First Public Meeting of the National Association for the Vindication of Scottish Rights, Held in the Music Hall, Edinburgh, on the Evening of November 2, 1853. Right Hon. the Earl of Eglington.... Edinburgh: 1853. V. 68

NATIONAL CANNERS ASSOCIATION
Canner's Directory and List of Members of the Canning Machinery and Supplies Association. Washington: 1935. V. 68

NATIONAL COWBOY HALL OF FAME
Persimmon Hill. OKC: 1970-2000. V. 72

THE NATIONAL Cyclopaedia of American Biography. New York: 1893-1897. V. 70; 73

NATIONAL Encyclopaedia of Useful Things. London: 1847-1851. V. 72

THE NATIONAL Gallery of Pictures by the Great Masters, Presnted by Individuals or Purchased by Grant of Parliament. London: 1840?. V. 68

NATIONAL GALLERY OF PRACTICAL SCIENCE
Catalogue for 1833. London: 1833. V. 69

NATIONAL LIVESTOCK ASSOCIATION
Proceedings of the Sixth Annual Convention of the National Livestock Association Forth Worth, Texas, January 16, 17, 18 and 19.... Denver: 1900. V. 71
Proceedings of the Third Annual Convention Report and Annual Report of the.... Kansas City: 1903. V. 71

NATIONAL MARITIME MUSEUM
Concise Catalogue of Oil Paintings in the National Maritime Museum. Woodbridge: 1988. V. 69

NATIONAL Nursery Rhymes and Nursery Songs Set to Original Music.... London: 1870. V. 68

NATIONAL Oeconomy Recommended as the Only Means of Retrieving Our Trade and Securing Liberties, Occasioned by the Perusal of the Late Report of a Committee of the House of Commons Relating to the Army.... London: 1746. V. 72

NATIONAL RAILWAYS OF MEXICO
Facts and Figures about Mexico and Its Great Railway System, the National Railways of Mexico Traffice and Industrial Departments. Mexico City: 1911. V. 73

NATIONAL Regeneration, Social, Political and Military; Suggested by Prince de Joinville's Essai sur les Forces Navales de la France. London: 1844. V. 68

NATIONAL RETAIL DRY GOODS ASSOCIATION
Twenty-Five Years of Retailing 1911-1936. New York: 1936. V. 73

NATIONAL Unanimity Recommended; or, the Necessity of a Constitutional Resistance to the Sinister Designs of False Brethren.... London: 1742. V. 73

NATIONAL WOMAN SUFFRAGE AND EDUCATIONAL COMMITTEE
An Appeal to the Women of the United States. Hartford: 1871. V. 69

NATIVES of Lourenco Marques, Their Homes and Customs. Lourenco Marques: 1900. V. 72

NATTES, J. C.
Bath Illustrated by a Series of Views. London: 1806. V. 69
Practical Geometry, or an Introduction to Perspective. London: 1805. V. 72

THE NATURAL History of Birds. London: 1791. V. 73

A NATURAL History of Singing Birds.... Edinburgh: 1754. V. 73

THE NATURE of Nature. New York: 1994. V. 72

NATZLER, OTTO
Gertrud and Otto Natzler Ceramics. Los Angeles: 1968. V. 68

NAUBERT, CHRISTIANE BENEDICTE EUGENIE
Feudal Tyrants; or the Counts of Carlsheim and Sargans. London: 1806. V. 73
Herman of Unna: a Series of Adventures of the Fifteenth Century, In Which the Proceedings of the Secret Tribunal Under the Emperors Winceslaus and Sigismond.... London: 1794. V. 70
Walter de Monbary, Grand Master of Knights Templars. London: 1803. V. 69

NAUDE, GABRIEL
Advis Pour Dresser une Bibliotheque. Paris: 1627. V. 73

NAUGHTON, BILL
The Goalkeeper's Revenge and Other Stories. London: 1961. V. 69

NAUMOFF, LAWRENCE
Silk Hope, N.C. New York: 1994. V. 71

NAUNTON, ROBERT
Fragmenta Regalia, or Observations on the Late Queen Elizabeth, Her Times and Favourites. London: 1642. V. 73

NAVAJO SCHOOL OF INDIAN BASKETRY
Indian Basket Weaving. Los Angeles: 1903. V. 69

NAVARI, L.
The Bookseller's Art: Catalogues Issued by the Firm of J. Pearson & Co. London: 1991. V. 70

NAWRATH, ERNST A.
The Glories of Hindustan. London: 1935. V. 71

NAYAR, M. P.
Red Data Book of Indian Plants. Calcutta: 1987-1988. V. 70

NAYLOR, GILLIAN
William Morris by Himself. 2000. V. 68

NAYLOR, GLORIA
Linden Hills. New York: 1985. V. 68; 72
Mama Day. New York: 1988. V. 71
The Women of Brewster Place. New York: 1982. V. 69; 70; 71; 73

NAYLOR, THOMAS H.
The Presidio and Militia on the Northern Frontier of New Spain. Tucson: 1986. V. 68

NAZAROFF, MR.
Russian Missions into the Interior of Asia. London: 1823. V. 71

NEAGOE, PETER
Easter Sun. New York: 1934. V. 71

NEAL, AVON
Pigs and Eagles. North Brookfield: 1978. V. 70; 72

NEAL, DOROTHY JENSEN
Captive Mountain Waters. El Paso: 1961. V. 71

NEAL, JOSEPH C.
In Town and About or Pencillings and Pennings. Philadelphia: 1843. V. 68

NEAL, JULIA
By Their Fruits: The Story of Shakerism in South Union, Kentucky. Chapel Hill: 1947. V. 71

NEAL, LARRY
Hoodoo Hollerin' Bebop Ghosts. Washington DC: 1974. V. 72

NEALE, C. M.
An Index to Pickwick. London: 1897. V. 69

NEALE, EDWARD VANSITTART
The Analogy of Thoughts and Nature. London: 1863. V. 71

NEALE, FRANCIS
An Essay on Money-Lending.... London: 1826. V. 70

NEALE, FREDERICK ARTHUR
Narrative of a Residence at the Capital of the Kingdom of Siam.... London: 1852. V. 68; 73

NEALE, J. M.
A Carol: Good King Wenceslas. London: 1919. V. 72
Mediaeval Hymns and Sequences. London: 1851. V. 72

NEALE, JAMES
The Abbey Church of Saint Alban: Hertfordshire. 1878. V. 70

NEALE, JOHN MASON
Good King Wenceslas. A Carol . . . Birmingham: 1895. V. 71

NEALE, JOHN PRESTON
The History and Antiquities of the Abbey Church of St. Peter, Westminster.... London: 1818-1823. V. 71

NEALE, THOMAS
The Ruinous State of the Parish of Manea in the Isle of Ely, with the Causes and Remedy Of It, Humbly Represented in a Letter to Matt. Robinson Morris, Esq., Lord of the manor of Coveney with Manea. London?: 1748. V. 73

NEARING, SCOTT
Social Sanity. New York: 1913. V. 68

NEATE, W. R.
Mountaineering and Its Literature. Milnthorpe: 1978. V. 69
Mountaineering in the Andes. London: 1987. V. 69

NEBEL, FREDERICK
Fifty Roads to Town. Boston: 1936. V. 71; 73
Six Deadly Dames With Introduction By Robert J. Randisi. Boston: 1980. V. 72
Sleepers East. Boston: 1933. V. 73

NEBESKY-WOJKOWITZ, RENE DE
Oracles and Demons of Tibet. London: 1956. V. 71

THE NEBRASKA Brand Book Of Cattle and Horses. Lincoln: 1908. V. 68; 71

NECESSITY of an Incoporate Union Between Great Britain and Ireland Proved from the Situation of Both Kingdoms. London: 1799. V. 68

THE NECESSITY of Some of the Positive Institutions of Ch.....ty Consider'd. In a Letter to the Minister of Moffat. London: 1731. V. 68; 72

NECKER, JACQUES
A Treatise on the Adminstration of the Finances of France. London: 1785. V. 73

NEEDHAM, DOROTHY M.
Machina Carnis. Cambridge: 1971. V. 68

NEEDHAM, GEORGE C.
Street Arabs and Gutter Snipes. Boston: 1884. V. 68

NEEDHAM, J.
Studies of Trees.... London: 1890. V. 68

NEEDHAM, JOSEPH
Biochemistry and Morphogenesis. Cambridge: 1942. V. 68; 72
A History of Embryology. Cambridge: 1934. V. 68; 70

NEEDHAM, P.
Twelve Centuries of Bookbindings 400-1600. New York: 1979. V. 70
William Morris and the Art of the Book. London: 1976. V. 70

NEEDHAM, VIOLET
The Betrayer. London: 1950. V. 73

NEEL, JANET
Death on Site. London: 1989. V. 69

NEELE, GEORGE P.
Railway Reminiscences. London: 1904. V. 68

NEELEY, BILL
Quanah Parker and His People. Slaton: 1986. V. 69

NEELY, BARBARA
Blanche on the Lamb. New York: 1992. V. 68; 69; 71

NEFF, ANDREW
History of Utah 1847-1869. Salt Lake City: 1940. V. 70

NEFF, ROBERT
Blues. Boston: 1975. V. 68; 71

THE NEGRO Problem. A Series of Articles by Representative American Negroes of To=Day. New York: 1903. V. 68; 70; 73

THE NEGRO'S Friend, or The Sheffield Anti-Slavery Album. Sheffield: 1826. V. 71

NEHLS, EDWARD
D. H. Lawrence: a Composite Biography. Madison: 1957-. V. 72

NEHR, ELLEN
Doubleday Crime Club Compendium 1928-1991. Martinez: 1992. V. 70

NEHRLING, H.
The Plant World in Florida. New York: 1933. V. 68; 71; 73

NEHRU, J.
Toward Freedom. The Autobiography of Jawaharlal Nehru. New York: 1942. V. 71

NEIDER, CHARLES
The Authentic Death of Hendry Jones. New York: 1956. V. 70

NEIDHARD, CHARLES
An Answer to the Homoeopathic Delusions of Dr. Oliver Wendell Holmes. Philadelphia: 1842. V. 68

NEIGHBOR, ALFRED
The Apiary; or, Bees, Bee-Hives, and Bee Culture.... London: 1865. V. 68; 72

NEIHARDT, JOHN G.
Black Elk Speaks. New York: 1932. V. 70

NEIL, J. M.
Will James, the Spirit of the Cowboy. 1985. V. 68

NEIL, JAMES
Ray's From the Realm of Nature; or, Parables of Plant Life. London: 1890. V. 68

NEILL, A. S.
The Free Child. London: 1953. V. 68

NEILL, EDWARD D.
Dakotah Land and Dakotah Life with the History of the Fur Trade of the Extreme Northwest During the French and British Dominions. Philadelphia: 1859. V. 68
History of Ramsey County and the City of St. Paul Including the Explorers and Pioneers of Minnesota and Outlines of the History of Minnesota. Minneapolis: 1881. V. 68
History of Rice Country Including Explorers And Pioneers of Minnesota... Also Sioux Massacre of 1862. Minnesota: 1882. V. 72

NEILL, HUGH
The Practice in the Liverpool Opththalmic Infirmary, for the Year 1834.... London: 1835. V. 72

NEILL, JOHN
Outlines of the Arteries with Short Description. Philadelphia: 1945. V. 71
Outlines of the Nerves with Short Descriptions. Philadelphia: 1852. V. 71

NEILL, JOHN R.
The Scalawagons of Oz. Chicago: 1941. V. 73
The Wonder City of Oz. Chicago: 1940. V. 73

NEILSON, GEORGE
Annals of the Solway Until A.D. 1307. Glasgow: 1899. V. 71

NEILSON, HARRY B.
A Leap-Year's Proposal. London: 1889. V. 71

NEILSON, WILLIAM
An Introduction to the Irish Language. Dublin: 1808. V. 73

NEILSON, WILLIAM ALLEN
Webster's New International Dictionary of the English Language. Springfield: 1940. V. 69

NEIMAN, LEROY
Big-Time Golf. New York: 1991. V. 69
Big-Time Golf. New York: 1992. V. 72

NEIMARK, PAUL
She Lives!. Los Angeles: 1972. V. 68

NEKRASOVA, N.
Stikhotvoreniya...Izdanie Chetvertoe. St. Petersburg: 1674. V. 73

NELSON, B.
The Sulidae. 1978. V. 69

NELSON, E. C.
The Brightest Jewel, a History of the National Botanic Gardens, Glasnevin, Dublin. Kilkenny: 1987. V. 68

NELSON, FLORENCE
O Come to the Fair. A Child's Day at the Fair. New York: 1939. V. 73

NELSON, GEORGE
Display. New York: 1953. V. 72

NELSON, HORATIO
Nelson's Letters from the Leeward Islands and Other Original Documents in the Public Record Office and the British Museum. Waltham St. Lawrence: 1953. V. 71

NELSON, J. K.
Harry Bertoia Sculptor. 1970. V. 72

NELSON, JAMES
The Complete Murder Sampler. New York: 1946. V. 68

NELSON, JAMES G.
The Early Nineties - A View From the Bodley Head. Cambridge: 1971. V. 72

NELSON, JOHN
The History and Antiquities of the Parish of Islington, in the County of Middlesex. London: 1829. V. 72

NELSON, JOHN L.
Rhythm for Rain. Boston: 1937. V. 69

NELSON, MARGUERITE
Jill's Hollywood Assignment. New York: 1958. V. 71

NELSON, MARY CARROLL
The Legendary Artists of Taos. New York: 1980. V. 70
Masters of Western Art. New York: 1982. V. 69

NELSON, N. C.
Pueblo Ruins of the Galisto Basin, New Mexico. New York: 1914. V. 72

NELSON, O. N.
History of the Scandinavians and Successful Scandinavians in the United States. Minneapolis: 1900. V. 69

NELSON, PAUL
Cargo. Iowa City: 1972. V. 73

NELSON, R.
Reminiscences of the Right Rev. William Meade. Shanghai: 1873. V. 71

NELSON, RICHARD K.
Hunters of the Northern Ice. Chicago: 1969. V. 71

NELSON, ROBERT
An Address To Persons of Quality and Estate to Which is Added, an Appendix of some Original and Valuable Papers. London: 1715. V. 72
The Life Of Dr. George Bull, Late Lord Bishop Of St. David's. London: 1713. V. 72

NELSON, T., & SONS
The Isle of Wight. London: 1859. V. 68
Wonders of Nature. London: 1857. V. 68; 70

NELSON, T. H.
The Birds of Yorkshire. London: 1907. V. 69

NELSON, THOMAS
A Genealogical History of the Nelson Family. Kings Lynn: 1908. V. 68

NELSON, W.
Fishing in Eden. 1922. V. 68

NELSON, WILLIAM
Fifty Years of Historical Works in New Jersey. Paterson: 1898. V. 72
History of Paterson and Its Environs. (The Silk City). New York: 1920. V. 72
Illustrated Catalogue of New Jersey Memorabilia and Rare and Valuable Books and Documents Comprising the Extensive Library of the Late William Nelson.... New York: 1915. V. 72
The Laws Concerning Game. London In the Savoy: 1751. V. 73
New Jersey Biographical and Genealogical Notes. Newark: 1916. V. 72
The Office and Authority of a Justice of Peace; Collected Out of All the Books.... London: 1707. V. 69
Personal Names of Indians of New Jersey: Being a List of Six Hundred and Fifty Such Names, Gleaned Mostly from Indian Deeds of the Seventeenth Century. Paterson: 1904. V. 72
Records of the Paterson Fire Associaton 1821-1854. Paterson: 1894. V. 72
Some New Jersey Printers and Printing in the Eighteenth Century. Worcester: 1911. V. 72

NEMEROV, HOWARD
The Blue Swallows. Chicago: 1967. V. 68
By Al Lebowitz's Pool. New York: 1979. V. 73
Journal of the Fictive Life. New Brunswick: 1965. V. 69
The Painter Dreaming in the Scholar's House: a Poem. London: 1968. V. 68

NEMESIUS, BISHOP
The Nature of Man. 1636. V. 72

NEMIROVITCH DANTCHENKO, VLADIMIR
My Life in the Russian Theatre. London: 1937. V. 69

NENNIS, JOHN
Facetiae: Musarum Deliciae; or, The Muses Recreation . . . London. V. 71

NEPOS, CORNELIUS
De Vitis Excellentium Imperatorum. London: 1794. V. 72
The Life and Death of Pomponius Atticus.... London: 1677. V. 71

NEQUATEWA, EDMUND
Truth of a Hopi and Other Clan Stories of Shung Opovi. Flagstaff: 1936. V. 69

NERET, G.
Arts of the 20's: Painting, Sculpture, Architecture, Design, Theatre Design, Graphic Art, Photography, Film. New York: 1986. V. 72

NERMAN
Darlings of the Gods in Music Hall, Revue and Musical Comedy. London: 1929. V. 70

NERUDA, PABLO
Aqui Estoy. Paris: 1938. V. 69
La Barcarola. Buenos Aires: 1967. V. 69
Bestiario/Bestiario. New York: 1965. V. 68; 69
The Captain's Verses. New York: 1972. V. 72
New Poems (1968-1970). New York: 1972. V. 71
Splendor and Death of Joaquin Murieta. New York: 1972. V. 71
Tercera Residencia. Buenos Aires: 1947. V. 69
Toward the Splendid City. New York: 1974. V. 71
We Are Many. London: 1967. V. 72

NESBIT, EDITH
The Enchanted Castle. London: 1907. V. 70
Harvest Home Original Poems. London and New York. V. 68
The Incredible Honeymoon. London: 1921. V. 72
The Magic City. 1910. V. 73
The Magic City. London: 1910. V. 68; 72
The Magic World. London: 1912. V. 68; 71; 73
Oswald Bastable and Others. 1905. V. 68
Oswald Bastable and Others. London: 1905. V. 72
The Royal Children of English History. London: 1897. V. 71
A School Bewitched. 1985. V. 73
These Little Ones. London: 1909. V. 70
Wings and the Child, or, the Building of Magic Cities. Toronto: 1913. V. 69
The Would-Be-Goods. London: 1901. V. 72; 73

NESBIT, J. C.
On Agricultural Chemistry.... London: 1859. V. 70

NESBIT, WILBUR
In Tumbledown Town. Joliet: 1926. V. 71

NESBIT, WILBUR D.
The Jolly Kid Book. Chicago: 1911. V. 72
The Jolly Kid Book. Joliet: 1925. V. 70
The Jolly Kid Book. Joliet: 1926. V. 72
The Loving Cup. Original Toasts by Original Folks. Chicago: 1909. V. 69

NESBITT, P. H.
Starkweather Ruin. Beloit. V. 69

NESMEYANOVNA, TATYANA N.
Experimental Studies in Regeneration of Spinal Neurons. New York: 1977. V. 68

NESS, CHRISTOPHER
An Antidote Against Arminianism; or a Treatise to Enervate and Conflute all the Five Points Thereof.... Plymouth: 1819. V. 68

NESS, ELIOT
The Untouchables. New York: 1957. V. 68

NESS, F. C.
Practical Dope on the .22. 1955. V. 72

NETHERCOTE, H. O.
The Pytchley Hunt, Past and Present. 1888. V. 68

NETHERSOLE-THOMPSON, DESMOND
The Cairngorms, Their Natural History and Scenery. 1974. V. 73
The Cairngorms. Their Natural History and Scenery. London: 1974. V. 71

NETTLEFOLD, J. S.
Practical Housing. Letchworth: 1908. V. 71

NETTLETON, THOMAS
A Treatise of Virtue and Happiness. Glasgow: 1751. V. 69

NETTY and Her Sister, or, The Two Paths. New York: 1867. V. 68

NEUBERG, FREDERIC
Glass in Antiquity. London: 1949. V. 68; 72

NEUBERG, VICTOR B.
Lillygay: an Anthology of Anonymous Poems. Steyning: 1920. V. 71
Swift Wings: Songs in Sussex. Steyning: 1921. V. 71
The Triumph of Pan: Poems. London: 1910. V. 71

NEUER, R.
Ukiyo-E: 250 Years of Japanese Art. New York: 1979. V. 69; 72

NEUGEBAUER, O.
The Exact Sciences in Antiquity. Providence: 1957. V. 69

NEUGEBOREN, JAY
Corky's Brother. New York: 1969. V. 69; 72

NEUHAUS, E.
William Keith: The Man and the Artist. Berkeley: 1938. V. 69; 72

NEUMANN, ARTHUR H.
Elephant Hunting in East Equatorial Africa. London: 1898. V. 71

NEUMANN, GEORGE C.
History of Weapons of the American Revolution. London: 1967. V. 72

NEUMANN, ROBERT
The Queen's Doctor. New York: 1936. V. 70

NEVADA Historical Papers, 1913-1916. Carson City: 1917. V. 71

NEVE, ERNEST F.
Beynod the Pir Panjal. 1912. V. 69; 70
Beyond the Pir Panjal. London: 1912. V. 71

NEVE, PHILIP
Cursory Remarks on Some of the Ancient Poets, Particularly Milton. London: 1789. V. 73

NEVE, RICHARD
The City and Countrey Purchaser, and Builder's Dictionary; or, the Compleat Builder's Guide. London: 1703. V. 69; 70
The City and Countrey Purchaser and Builder's Dictionary; or the Compleat Builder's Guide. London: 1726. V. 68; 69; 71
The City and Country Purchaser's and Builder's Dictionary; or, the Complete Builder's Guide.... London: 1736. V. 68

NEVELSON, LOUISE
Dawns Dusks: Taped Conversations with Diana Mackown. New York: 1976. V. 68

NEVES, J. C.
The Palace and Gardens of Frontiers, Seventeenth and Eighteenth Century Portuguese Style. New York: 1995. V. 68

NEVILL, RALPH
Light Come, Light Go. Gambling - Gamesters - Wagers - The Turf. London: 1909. V. 70

NEVILLE, A. W.
The History of Lamar County (Texas). Paris: 1937. V. 73
The Red River Then and Now. Paris: 1948. V. 69

NEVILLE, ALEXANDER
Alexandri Nevylli Angli, De Furoribus Norfolciensium Ketto Duce , Liber Unus Eiusdem Norvicus. London: 1575. V. 70; 73

NEVILLE, HENRY
The Isle of Pines. Katoomba: 1991. V. 71
The Stage: Its Past and Present in Relation to Fine Art. London: 1875. V. 72

NEVILLE, JAMES M.
Ladies Under Glass. Philadelphia: 1938. V. 70

NEVILLE, MARGOT
Confession Of Murder. London: 1960. V. 72

NEVILLE, RICHARD
Play Power. London: 1970. V. 69

NEVINS, ALLAN
Civil War Books: a Critical Bibliography. Baton Rouge: 1970. V. 69
Fremont the West's Greatest Adventurer Being a Biography from Certain Hitherto Unpublished Sources. New York: 1928. V. 68
John D. Rockefeller: The Heroic Age of American Enterprise. New York: 1940. V. 69

NEVINS, FRANCIS M.
Royal Bloodline. 1974. V. 68

NEVINS, FRANCIS M., JR.
First You Dream Then You Die. New York: 1988. V. 71

NEVINSON, HENRY W.
The Dawn in Russia or Scenes in the Russian Revolution. 1906. V. 71

NEVIZANUS, GIOVANNI
Sylva Nuptiales.... Lyon: 1540. V. 69; 72

NEW American Cookery, or Female Companion.... New York: 1805. V. 69

A **NEW** and General Biographical Dictionary. London: 1784. V. 70

A **NEW** and Improved History and Description of the Tower of London. London: 1827. V. 71

THE **NEW** Apocalypse. 1940. V. 68

A **NEW** Book of Knowledge; Treating of Things, Whereof Some are Profitable, Some Precious, and Some Pleasant and Delightful. London: 1697. V. 69

A **NEW** Book of Natural History of Various Little Known British Birds for the Amusement of Good Children. Chelmesford: 1820. V. 73

THE **NEW** Brunswick City and Business Diectory 1888. York: 1888. V. 72

NEW Brunswick City Directory. 1886-1887. New Brunswick: 1886. V. 72

NEW Brunswick City Directory. 1893. New Brunswick: 1893. V. 72

NEW Brunswick Directory for 1880-1881. New Brunswick: 1880. V. 72

NEW Brunswick Directory for 1883-1884. New Brunswick: 1883. V. 72

NEW BRUNSWICK Herd Book, Containing.... Fredericton: 1898. V. 71

NEW BRUNSWICK
Journal of the House of Assembly of the Province of New Brunswick, for 1827, 1828 & 1829. Fredericton: 1829. V. 71

NEW, CHARLES
Life, Wanderings, and Labours in Eastern Africa. London: 1874. V. 71

THE **NEW** Crime Club Golden Book of Best Detective Stories. New York: 1934. V. 70

NEW Cyclopaedia of Botany and Complete Book of Herbs.... Huddersfield: 1880. V. 68

THE **NEW** Decameron. Oxford: 1925. V. 72

THE **NEW** Decorator's Hand-Book. (with) Second Part of Decorator's Hand-Book. Barnsley: 1900. V. 68

THE **NEW-ENGLAND** Primer, or an Easy and Pleasant Guide to the Art of Reading. Boston: 1836. V. 70

THE **NEW-ENGLAND** Primer, Restored. Trenton: 1846. V. 72

NEW ENGLAND ANTI-SLAVERY SOCIETY
Constitution of the New England Anti-Slavery Society; with an Address to the Public. Boston: 1832. V. 71

THE **NEW** English Theatre in Eight Volumes. (with) Volumes IX-(XI). London: 1776-1777. V. 71

THE **NEW** Fiction. Urbana: 1974. V. 72

THE **NEW** Gothic. New York: 1991. V. 70; 72

THE **NEW** Hampshire Business Directory for the Year Commencing April 1 1868.... Boston: 1868. V. 73

NEW Hampshire Women. Concord: 1895. V. 69

THE **NEW** Harrogate Guide. Harrogate: no date. V. 73

A **NEW** History of England from the Invasion of Julius Caesar to the End of George the IId. London: 1785. V. 70

NEW JERSEY. ARCHIVES - 1890
Archives of the State of New Jersey. Subset: Journal of the Governor and Council, 1682-1775. Trenton: 1890-1893. V. 72

NEW JERSEY. ARCHIVES - 1894
Archives of the State of New Jersey. Subset: Extracts from American Newspapers Relating to New Jersey. 1704-1782. 1894-1923. V. 72

NEW JERSEY. ARCHIVES - 1901
Archives of the State of New Jersey. Subset: Calendar of New Jersey Wills, Administrations, etc., 1670-1817. 1901-1949. V. 72

NEW JERSEY. CENTENIAL EXHIBITION - 1877
Report of the New Jersey Commissioners on the Centennial Exhibition. Trenton: 1877. V. 72

NEW JERSEY. GEOLOGICAL SURVEY - 1856
Second Annual Report of the Geological Survey of the State of New Jersey for the Year 1855. Trenton: 1856. V. 72

NEW JERSEY. GEOLOGICAL SURVEY - 1878
Report on the Clay Deposits of Woodbridge, South Amboy and Other Places in New Jersey, Together with Their Uses for Fire, Brick, Pottery, &c. Trenton: 1878. V. 72

NEW JERSEY. GOVERNOR - 1848
Selections from the Correspondence of the Executive of New Jersey, from 1776-1786. Newark: 1848. V. 72

NEW JERSEY. LAWS, STATUTES, ETC. - 1752
The Acts of the General Assembly of the Province of New Jersey from the Time of the Surrender of the Government to this Present Time. (with) The Acts of the General Assembly of the Province of New Jersey from the Year 1753.... Philadelphia: 1752. V. 70; 72; 73

NEW JERSEY. LAWS, STATUTES, ETC. - 1758
The Grants, Concessions and Original Constitutions, of the Province of New Jersey. The Acts Passed During the Proprietary Governments and Other Material Transactions. Philadelphia: 1758. V. 68; 70; 72; 73

NEW JERSEY. LAWS, STATUTES, ETC. - 1761
The Acts of the General Assembly of the Province of New Jersey, from the Time of the Surrender of the Government...to the Present Time. (with) The Acts of the General Assembly of the Province of New Jersey from the Year 1753.... Woodbridge: 1761. V. 68

NEW JERSEY. LAWS, STATUTES, ETC. - 1776
Acts of the General Assembly of the Province of New Jersey, from the Surrender of the Government to Queen Anne, on the 17th Day of April in the Year of Our Lord 1702 to the 14th Day of Janaury 1776. Burlington: 1776. V. 68; 69; 70; 72; 73

NEW JERSEY. LAWS, STATUTES, ETC. - 1800
Laws of the State of New Jersey Revised. New Brunswick: 1800. V. 68; 70; 72; 73
Laws of the State of New Jersey: Revised and Published, Under the Authority of the Legislature, by William Paterson. Newark: 1800. V. 70; 72

NEW JERSEY. LAWS, STATUTES, ETC. - 1811
Laws of the State of New Jersey. Trenton: 1811. V. 72

NEW JERSEY. LAWS, STATUTES, ETC. - 1821
Laws of the State of New Jersey. Trenton: 1821. V. 72

NEW JERSEY. LAWS, STATUTES, ETC. - 1833
A Compilation of the Public Laws of the State of New Jersey, Passed since the Revision in the Year 1820. Camden: 1833. V. 72

NEW JERSEY. LAWS, STATUTES, ETC. - 1847
Statutes of the State of New Jersey. Trenton: 1847. V. 72

NEW JERSEY. LEGISLATURE - 1873
Manual of the Legislature. State of New Jersey. Ninety-Seventh Session. Morristown: 1873. V. 72

NEW JERSEY. LEGISLATURE - 1874
Manual of the Legislature. State of New Jersey. Ninety-Eighth Session. Morristown: 1874. V. 72

NEW JERSEY. STATE GEOLOGIST - 1888
Final Report of the State Geologist...Topography, Magnetism, Climate. Trenton: 1888. V. 72

NEW JERSEY. STATE GEOLOGIST - 1889
Final Report of the State Geologist: Mineralogy, Botany, Zoology. Trenton: 1889. V. 72

NEW JERSEY. STATE GEOLOGIST - 1894
Report on Water-Supply, Water-Power, the Flow of Streams and Attendant Phenomena. Trenton: 1894. V. 72

NEW JERSEY. STATE GEOLOGIST - 1898
The Physical Geography of New Jersey. Trenton: 1898. V. 72

NEW Jersey. A Guide to Its Present and Past. New York: 1939. V. 72

NEW Jersey Almanac, for the Year of Our Lord 1832. Newark: 1831. V. 72

NEW Jersey Almanac, for the Year of Our Lord 1833. Newark: 1832. V. 72

THE **NEW** Jersey Almanac for the Year of Our Lord 1824. Elizabeth-Town: 1823. V. 72

THE **NEW** Jersey Almanac for the Year of Our Lord 1825. Elizabeth-Town: 1824. V. 72

NEW Jersey Almanac for the Year of Our Lord 1828. Newark: 1827. V. 72

NEW Jersey Almanac for the Year of Our Lord 1829. Newark: 1828. V. 72

NEW Jersey Almanac for the Year of Our Lord 1831. Elizabeth-Town: 1830. V. 72

NEW Jersey and Its Builders. 1925. V. 72

THE **NEW** Jersey Preacher; or Sermons on Plain and Practical Subjects. Trenton: 1813. V. 72

THE **NEW** Keepsake - A Christmas, New Year & Birthday Present for Persons of Both Sexes. London: 1931. V. 72

THE **NEW** London Cookery and Complete Domestic Guide. London: 1820. V. 72

THE **NEW** Metal Magnesium for Illuminating Purposes; Manufactured by the American Magnesium Company, 5 Liberty Square, Boston. Cambridge: 1865. V. 68

NEW Mexico: a Guide to the Colorful State. New York: 1940. V. 69

NEW Mexico: the Last Great West. Chicago: 1917. V. 73

NEW MEXICO
The Mines of New Mexico. Santa Fe: 1896. V. 69
New Mexico Territorial Bureau of Immigration. Report as to Socorro County. Santa Fe: 1881. V. 69
Register of Volunteer Officers Head-Quarters, Department of New Mexico, General Orders #21. Santa Fe: 1863. V. 72

NEW MEXICO. GOVERNOR
Report of the Governor of New Mexico. Washington: 1900. V. 68

NEW MEXICO TERRITORY
Letter from the Secretary of the Territory of New Mexico, Transmitting Copies of the Acts, Resolutions, etc. of that Territory. Washington: 1852. V. 69

NEW MEXICO WRITERS' GUILD
Over the Turquoise Trail. Number I. Volume I. Santa Fe: 1938. V. 71

A NEW Natural History: Intended as a Present for Good Boys and Girls. Otley: 1830. V. 68; 72

NEW Orleans Fire Department 1829-1984. Dallas: 1984. V. 69

NEW Photography: Lighting and Composition. New York: 1940. V. 68

THE NEW Picture Alphabet. Charlestown: 1854-1861. V. 71

NEW Picture Book. Greenfield: 1845. V. 73

THE NEW Riddle Book, for the Amusement and Instruction, of Little Misses and Masters. London: 1820. V. 68

THE NEW Rupert Book. (Annual 1951). London. V. 70

THE NEW Savoy. London: 1946. V. 70

THE NEW South Wales Calendar and General Post Office Directory, 1833. Sydney: 1833. V. 73

NEW Stories from the South. The Year's Best, 1987. Chapel Hill: 1987. V. 71

A NEW Survey of London; Fully Developing Its Antiquity.... London: 1853. V. 71

A NEW System of Agriculture; or, a Plain, Easy and Demonstrative Method of Speedily Growing Rich. London: 1755. V. 70

A NEW System of Patriot Policy. London: 1756. V. 70

NEW Wave Canada. Toronto: 1966. V. 69

THE NEW Whole Duty of Man, Containing the Faith as Well as Practice of a Christian.... Trenton: 1809. V. 72

THE NEW Year's Feast on His Coming Home. London: 1824. V. 72

THE NEW York Cries. New York: 1835. V. 73

NEW YORK. LAWS, STATUTES, ETC. - 1894
Facsimile of the Laws and Acts of the General Assembly for Their Majesties Province of New York. New York: 1894. V. 68

NEW YORK. MAYOR'S COURT
Arguments and Judgment of Mayor's Court of the City of New York, in a Cause Between Elizabeth Rutgers and Joshua Waddington. New York: 1784. V. 68

NEW YORK ACADEMY OF MEDICINE
Catalogue of an Exhibition of Early and Later Medical Americana. New York: 1926. V. 71

NEW YORK CENTRAL & HUDSON RIVER RAILROAD
Seen From the Car. 1902. V. 68

THE NEW York Cries, in Rhyme. New York: 1831. V. 70

NEW YORK FIRE DEPARTMENT
The Constitution and By-Laws of the Fire Department of the City of New York Which are Added, the Act of Incorporation and Laws of the Corporation and State Relating to Fires. New York: 1826. V. 72

THE NEW York Herald. New York: 1865. V. 70

NEW YORK HISTORICAL SOCIETY
Muster and Pay Rolls. New York: 1914. V. 72

NEW YORK MAGDALEN BENEVOLENT SOCIETY
Missionary Labors through a Series of Years Among Fallen Women by the.... New York: 1870. V. 72

NEW YORK NAUTICAL INSTITUTION AND SHIPMASTERS' SOCIETY
Constitution and By-Laws of the New York Nautical Institution and Shipmasters' Society. New York: 1821. V. 72

NEW York State Cabinet of Natural History. Albany: 1850. V. 70

NEW York State Woman Suffrage Party. Suffrage as a War Measure. New York: 1917. V. 70

NEWALL, D. J. F.
Sketches in Cashmere. Newport, IOW: 1882. V. 71

NEWALL, J. T.
The Eastern Hunters. 1866. V. 72
Hog Hunting in the East and Other Sports. 1867. V. 70; 72; 73

NEWARK INDUSTRIAL EXHIBITION
Report and Catalogue of the First Exhibition of Newark Industries, Exclusively. 1872. Newark: 1882. V. 72

NEWBERRY, CLARE TURLAY
Babette. New York: 1937. V. 70; 71; 73
Babette. London: 1938. V. 71
Cats - a Portfolio. Newberry: 1943. V. 70
Cats and Kittens. New York: 1956. V. 69; 70
Cousin Toby. New York: 1939. V. 70
Marshmallow. New York: 1942. V. 70

NEWBERRY, J. S.
Catalogue of Flowering Plants and Ferns of Ohio. Colubmus: 1860. V. 70
The Paleozoic Fishes of N. America. Washington: 1889. V. 72; 73

NEWBERY, FRANCIS
Observations on the Income Act; Particularly as It Relates to the Occupiers of Land.... London: 1801. V. 73

NEWBERY, JOHN
The Newtonian System of Philosophy Explained by Familiar Objects, in an Entertaining Manner, for the Use of Young Ladies and Gentlemen. Philadelphia: 1808. V. 71; 73

NEWBIGGING, THOMAS
Devices for Gas Illuminations in Celebration of the Jubilee Year of the Reign of Her Most Gracious Majesty, Queen Victoria. London: 1886. V. 69
King's Treatise on the Science and Practice of the Manufacture and Distribution of Coal Gas. London: 1878. V. 69

NEWBOLT, HENRY
Aladore. Edinburgh and London: 1914. V. 69
Drake's Drum and Other Songs of the Sea. London. V. 71
The Island Race. London: 1898. V. 72
Tide in Time in English Poetry. London and Edinburgh: 1925. V. 73

NEWBOLT, PETER
George Alfred Henty 1832-1902. A Bibliographical Study of His British Editions.... 1996. V. 73

NEWBY, ERIC
Grain Race - Pictures of Life Before the Mast in a Windjammer. London: 1968. V. 72
Great Ascents. London: 1977. V. 69

NEWBY, GEORGE
Pleasures of Melancholy, In Three Parts. Keswick. V. 72
Pleasures of Melancholy, in three parts. Keswick: 1842. V. 71

NEWCASTLE UPON TYNE GAS LIGHT CO.
Deeds, Rules and Regulations for the Settlement and Government of the Newcastle Upon Tyne Gateshead Union Gas Light Company. Newcastle: 1839. V. 69

NEWCASTLE, WILLIAM CAVENDISH, MARQUIS OF
Phanseys...Addressed to Margaret Lucas and Her Letters in Reply. London: 1956. V. 68; 70

NEWCOMB, CHARLES G.
The Smoke Hole. San Antonio: 1968. V. 69

NEWCOMB, FRANC JOHNSON
Hosteen Klah: Navaho Medicine Man and Sand Painter. Norman: 1964. V. 69; 72
Navaho Folk Tales. 1967. V. 68
Navaho Folk Tales. Santa Fe: 1967. V. 69
Navaho Neighbors. 1966. V. 69
Sandpaintings of the Navajo Shooting Chant. New York: 1937. V. 69

NEWCOMB, NORMA
An Angel in Love. New York: 1944. V. 71

NEWCOMB, RAYMOND LEE
Our Lost Explorers. Hartford: 1884. V. 71

NEWCOMB, REXFORD
Spanish Colonial Architecture in the United States. New York: 1937. V. 71

NEWCOMB, W. W.
German Artist on the Texas Frontier, Friedrich Richard Petri. Austin: 1978. V. 69
Indian Tribes of Texas. Waco: 1971. V. 70

NEWCOME, RICHARD
A Memoir of Gabriel Goodman, D.D....with Some Acount of Ruthin School and the Names of Its Most Eminent Scholars.... Ruthin: 1825. V. 73

NEWCOMEN SOCIETY
The Newcomen Society for the Study of the History of Engineering and Technology. Transactions. London: 1921-2000. V. 68

NEWDEGATE, CHARLES
A Letter to the Right Hon. H. Labouchere, M.P....On the Balance of Trade, Ascertained from the Market Value of All Articles Imported During the Last Four Years. London: 1849. V. 70

NEWELL, AUDREY
Murder is Not Mute. Philadelhia: 1940. V. 69

NEWELL, CICERO
Indian Stories. Boston: 1912. V. 72

NEWELL, PETER
The Hole Book. New York: 1908. V. 69; 70; 71
The Rocket Book. New York: 1912. V. 70; 71
The Slant Book. New York: 1910. V. 73
Topsys and Turveys. New York: 1893. V. 70
Topsys and Turveys - Number Two. 1894. V. 71; 72

NEWELL, ROBERT
Robert Newell's Memoranda: Travels in the Territory of Missourie: Travel to the Kayuse War.... Portland: 1959. V. 70

NEWELL, ROBERT HENRY
The Cloven Foot. New York: 1870. V. 68

THE NEWEST Keepsake for 1840. Norwch (sic): 1840. V. 71; 73

NEWHAFER, RICHARD
The Last Tallyho. New York: 1964. V. 68; 70; 71

NEWHALL, BEAUMONT
Photography at Mid-Century. Rochester: 1959. V. 68

NEWHALL, NANCY
Emerson: the Fight for Photography. New York: 1975. V. 68
Paul Strand - Photographs 1915-1945. New York: 1945. V. 68

NEWHOUSE, EDWARD
This is Your Day. New York: 1937. V. 68; 69

NEWHOUSE, V.
Wallace K. Harrison, Architect. New York: 1989. V. 68; 69; 72

NEWLANDS, JAMES
The Carpenter and Joiner's Assistant:. London. V. 72
The Carpenter and Joiner's Assistant. London: 1857-1860?. V. 68

NEWLANDS, JOHN A. R.
On the Discovery of the Periodic Law and on Relations Among the Atomic Weights. 1884. V. 69

NEWLIN, GEORGE
Everyone in Dickens. Westport: 1995. V. 70

NEWMAN, ARNOLD
Americans. 1992. V. 68
Artists: Portraits from Four Decades. Boston: 1980. V. 68
One Mind's Eye.... Boston: 1974. V. 68

NEWMAN, BERNARD
German Spy. New York: 1936. V. 70

NEWMAN, CHARLES
New Axis. Boston: 1966. V. 70

NEWMAN, FRANCIS WILLIAM
Anglo-Saxon Abolition of Negro Slavery. London: 1889. V. 71
Lectures on Political Economy. London: 1851. V. 71

NEWMAN, J. A.
The Autobiography of an Old Fashioned Boy. Oklahoma City: 1923. V. 68

NEWMAN, JACQUELINE M.
Chinese Cookbooks. New York: 1987. V. 68

NEWMAN, JEREMIAH WHITTAKER
The Lounger's Common-Place Book, or, Miscellaneous Anecdotes. London: 1796-1799. V. 69

NEWMAN, JOHN HENRY, CARDINAL
Apologia Pro Vita Sua: Being a Reply to a Pamphlet Entitled What, Then Does Dr. Newman Mean?. London: 1864. V. 68; 70; 72
Callista, a Sketch of the Third Century. London: 1856. V. 70
Discourses on the Scope and Nature of University Education Addressed to the Catholics of Dublin. Dublin: 1852. V. 70; 72
The Dream of Gerontius. London: 1866. V. 72
An Essay on the Development of Christian Doctrine. London: 1845. V. 70
Lectures on Justification. London: 1838. V. 70
Lectures on the Prophetical Office of the Church, Viewed Relatively to Romanism and Popular Protestantism. London: 1837. V. 70; 72
Letters of John Henry Newman. 1957. V. 68
Lyra Apostolica. Derby: 1836. V. 72
Memorials of the Past. Oxford: 1832. V. 72
Verses on Religious Subjects. Dublin: 1853. V. 72
Verses on Various Occasions. London: 1868. V. 72

NEWMAN, KIM
Anno Dracula. London: 1992. V. 68; 69; 72
The Night Mayor. London: 1989. V. 68
The Night Mayor. New York: 1990. V. 72

NEWMAN, RALPH GEOFFREY
Abraham Lincoln's Last Full Measure of Devotion. Chicago: 1981. V. 71; 73

NEWMAN, SHARON
The Wandering Arm. New York: 1995. V. 72

NEWMARCH, ROSA
Mary Wakefield, a Memoir. Kendal: 1912. V. 71; 72
The Russian Arts. London: 1916. V. 73

NEWMARCH, WILLIAM
On the Loans Raised by Mr. Pitt During the First French War, 1793- 1801; with some Statements in Defence of the Methods of Funding Employed. London: 1855. V. 73

NEWS From Afar, or, Missionary Varieties; Chiefly Relating to the Baptist Missionary Society.... London: 1830. V. 68; 73

NEWSOM, J. D.
Garde 'a Vous!. New York: 1928. V. 70

NEWSOM, S.
A Thousand Years of Japanese Gardens,. Tokyo: 1957. V. 72

NEWSTEAD, R.
Monograph of the Coccidae of the British Isles. London: 1901-1903. V. 69

NEWTON, ADDISON V.
The Saloon Keeper's Companion, and Book of Reference.... Worcester: 1875. V. 68

NEWTON, ALFRED EDWARD
The Catalogue of Rare Books, Original Drawings, Autograph Letters and Manuscripts.... 1941. V. 69
Derby Day and Other Adventures, Seventeen Essays. Boston: 1934. V. 69
End Papers, Literary Recreations. Boston: 1933. V. 69; 73
The Format of the English Novel. Cleveland: 1928. V. 71
The Greatest Book in the World and Other Papers. Boston: 1925. V. 69; 72
Rare Books, Original Drawings, Autograph Letters and Manuscripts.... New York: 1941. V. 70
This Book Collecting Game. Boston: 1928. V. 69; 71; 73
A Tourist in Spite of Himself. Boston: 1930. V. 69; 70

NEWTON, CHARLES THOMAS
Travels and Discoveries in the Levant. London: 1865. V. 69

NEWTON, D.
Art Styles of the Pauan Gulf. 1961. V. 69

NEWTON, EDWARD A.
Thomas Hardy, Novelist or Poet?. 1929. V. 72

NEWTON, ELIZABETH
A Great Mystery Solved.... London: 1878. V. 70

NEWTON, G. W.
A Treatise on the Growth and Future Management of Timber Trees. 1859. V. 69

NEWTON, HELMUT
Sleepless Nights. New York: 1978. V. 68
White Women. New York: 1976. V. 68; 71

NEWTON, HENRY
In Far New Guinea. London: 1914. V. 71

NEWTON, HUEY P.
Revolutionary Suicide. New York: 1973. V. 73

NEWTON, ISAAC
The Chronology of Ancient Kingdoms Amended. London: 1728. V. 70; 71; 73
The Correspondence of Isaac Newton. Volume V, 1709-1713. Cambridge: 1975. V. 72
Four Letters from Sir Isaac Newton to Doctor Bentley. London: 1756. V. 73
The Mathematical Principles of Natural Philosophy. London: 1729. V. 72
The Mathematical Works of Isaac Newton. Volume I. New York and London: 1964. V. 72
Philosophia Naturalis Principia Mathematica. Cambridge: 1713. V. 73
Philosophiae Naturalis Principia Mathematica. London: 1687. V. 68
Sir Isaac Newton's Principia Reprinted for Sir William Thomson and Hugh Blackburn. Glasgow: 1871. V. 69
A Treatise of the System of the World.... London: 1728. V. 72
Universal Arithmetick; or, a Treatise of Arithmetical Composition and Resolution. London: 1728. V. 69; 72

NEWTON, JAMES
A Complete Herbal. 1805. V. 69

NEWTON, JOHN
An Authentick Narraitve of Some Remarkable and Interesting Particulars in the Life of the Rev. Mr. John Newton. Hudson: 1805. V. 73
The Christian Character Exemplified, from the Papers of Mrs. Margaret Magdalen.... Trenton: 1808. V. 72

NEWTON, JOSEPH FORT
Lincoln and Herndon. 1910. V. 68

NEWTON, R. H.
Town and Davis, Architects: Pioneers in American Revivalist Architecture 1812-1870. 1942. V. 69; 72

NEWTON, RICHARD
The Jewish Tabernacle and Its Furniture, in Their Typical Teachings. New York: 1864. V. 71
University Education; or, an Explication and Amendment of the Statute Which, Under a Penalty Insufficient and Eluded, Prohibits the Admission of Scholars Going from One Society to Another.... London: 1733. V. 69

NEWTON, THOMAS WODEHOUSE LEGH, BARON
Lord Lyons: a Record of British Diplomacy. London: 1913. V. 71

NEWTON, VIRGINIUS
The Confederate States Ram Merrimac or Virginia. Richmond: 1907. V. 70

NEWTON, WILLIAM
The History and Antiquities of Maidstone.... London: 1741. V. 68; 70

NEWTON ROBINSON, CHARLES
The Viol of Love. London: 1895. V. 68

NEYT, F.
The Arts of the Benue, to the Roots of Tradition. Ottignies: 1985. V. 69

NEZ PERCE TRIBE
Noon Nee-Mee-Poo. (We, the Nez Perce). Lapwai: 1973. V. 70

NG, FAE MYENNE
Bone. New York: 1993. V. 68; 70

THE NIAGARA Book. Buffalo: 1893. V. 71

NIAS, J. B.
Dr. John Radcliffe a Sketch of His Life with an Account of His Fellows and Foundations. Oxford: 1918. V. 70; 72

NIATUM, DUANE
Drawings of the Song Animals. Duluth: 1991. V. 72
Songs for the Harvester of Dreams. Seattle: 1981. V. 69
Taos Pueblo. Greenfield: 1973. V. 68

NIBLETT, F. DRUMMOND
The Henry Irving Dream of Eugene Aram. London: 1888. V. 72

NICHOLAS, THOMAS
The History and Antiquities of Glamorganshire and Its Families. London: 1874. V. 68; 72

NICHOLL, EDITH M.
Observations of a Ranchwoman in New Mexico. New York: 1898. V. 70; 73
Observations of a Ranchwoman in New Mexico. Cincinnati: 1901. V. 68

NICHOLL, JOHN
Some Account of the Worshipful Company of Ironmongers. London: 1866-1916. V. 73

NICHOLLS, GEORGE
Poor Laws - Ireland. 1838. V. 70

NICHOLLS, J. F.
The Remarkable Life, Adventures and Discoveries of Sebastian Cabot, of Bristol, The Founder of Great Britain's Maritime Power, Discoverer of America and Its First Colonizer. London: 1869. V. 73

NICHOLLS, THOMAS
The Steam Boat Companion or Margate Isle of Thanet, Isle of Sheppy (sic) South End, Gravesend, and River Thames Guide.... London. V. 68; 70; 71; 72

NICHOLLS, W.
The History and Traditions of Mallerstang Forest and Pendragon Castle. Manchester: 1883. V. 71
The History and Traditions of Ravenstonedale, Westmorland. Manchester: 1877. V. 71
The History and Traditions of Ravenstonedale, Westmorland. Manchester: 1910. V. 71

NICHOLLS, W. H.
Orchids of Australia. Sydney: 1969. V. 68; 70

NICHOLS, ANNE
Abie's Irish Rose. New York: 1927. V. 70
Abie's Irish Rose. New York: 1937. V. 71

NICHOLS, B.
The Art of Flower Arrangement. New York: 1967. V. 68; 71
Down the Garden Path. London: 1932. V. 68; 71

NICHOLS, BEVERLEY
Cry Havoc!. London: 1933. V. 68; 70

NICHOLS, BEVERLY
Sunlight on the Lawn. New York: 1956. V. 69

NICHOLS, F. D.
Thomas Jefferson Landscape Architect. Charlottesville: 1978. V. 72

NICHOLS, FRANCIS H.
Through Hidden Shensi. London: 1902. V. 71

NICHOLS, FREDERICK DOVETON
The Early Architecture of Georgia. Chapel Hill: 1957. V. 68; 71

NICHOLS, GEORGE
Cellular Mechanisms for Calcium Transfer and Homeostasis. New York: 1971. V. 68

NICHOLS, GEORGE WASHINGTON
A Soldier's Story of His Regiment (61st Georgia) and Incidentally of the Lawton-Gordon-Evans Brigade, Army Northern Virginia. Jessup: 1898. V. 69; 70

NICHOLS, J. B.
Account of the Royal Hospital and Collegiate Church of St. Katharine, Near the Tower of London. London: 1824. V. 71

NICHOLS, J. T.
The Fresh-water Fishes of China. New York: 1943. V. 69; 71; 72; 73

NICHOLS, JAMES WILSON
Now You Hear My Horn. Austin: 1967. V. 69

NICHOLS, JOHN
American Blood. New York: 1987. V. 71
A Fragile Beauty. Salt Lake City: 1987. V. 71
A Ghost in the Music. New York: 1979. V. 70
In Praise of Mountain Lions. Albuquerque: 1984. V. 71
The Last Beautiful Days of Autumn. New York: 1982. V. 69; 71; 72
The Magic Journey. New York: 1978. V. 69; 71; 72
The Milagro Beanfield War. New York: 1974. V. 68; 71; 72; 73
The Milagro Beanfield War. New York: 1975. V. 73
The Milagro Beanfield War. New York: 1994. V. 71

If Mountains Die, A New Mexico Memoir. New York: 1979. V. 72
The New Mexico Trilogy. The Milagro Beanfield War. The Magic Journey. The Nirvana Blues. New York: 1974. V. 70
The Nirvana Blues. New York: 1981. V. 71; 72
The Sterile Cuckoo. New York: 1965. V. 68; 70; 71; 73
The Wizard of Loneliness. New York: 1966. V. 70

NICHOLS, JOHN G.
Ancient Allegorical, Historical and Legendary Paintings, in Fresco, Discovered in the summer of 1804, on the Walls of the Chapel of the Trinity.... London: 1838. V. 68; 73
The Armorial Windows of Woodhouse Chapel. London: 1860. V. 72

NICHOLS, MARGARET
Passing Dream. Philadelphia: 1942. V. 71

NICHOLS, ROBERT
Ardours and Endurances, also A Faun's Holiday and Poems and Phantasies. London: 1917. V. 72
The Assault and Other War Poems from "Ardours and Endurances". London: 1918. V. 72
Invocation: War Poems and Others. London: 1915. V. 72
The Smile of the Sphinx. 1920. V. 73

NICHOLS, ROSE STANDISH
Italian Pleasure Gardens. London: 1929. V. 70
Spanish and Portuguese Gardens. Boston: 1924. V. 68; 71; 73
Spanish and Portuguese Gardens. London: 1925. V. 70; 73

NICHOLS, T. L.
Esoteric Anthropology: a Comprehensive and Confidential Treatise on the Structure, Functions, Passional Attractions and Perversions, True and False Physical and Social Conditions.... New York: 1854. V. 68

NICHOLS, THOMAS NICKLE
What's In a Name?. London: 1859. V. 68

NICHOLSON, ASENATH
Nature's Own Book. New York: 1835. V. 68; 73

NICHOLSON, BEN
Ben Nicholson: Drawings, Paints, and Reliefs 1911-1968. New York and London: 1969. V. 69; 72

NICHOLSON, CORNELIUS
The Annals of Kendal. 1861. V. 71
A Descriptive Account of the Recently Discovered Roman Villa near Brading, Isle of Wight. London: 1880. V. 68

NICHOLSON, FRANCIS
Six Views of Fountains Abbey, in Yorkshire; Drawn from Nature and on Stone. London: 1825. V. 70

NICHOLSON, G.
The Illustrated Dictionary of Gardening. London: 1885-1889. V. 69

NICHOLSON, G. W. DE P.
The History of Biology. London: 1929. V. 68

NICHOLSON, G. W. L.
Canada's Nursing Sisters. Toronto: 1975. V. 73
The Fighting Newfoundlander. St. John's: 1969. V. 71

NICHOLSON, GEORGE
The Literary Miscellany; or Selections and Extracts, Classical and Scientific.... Poughmill, Ludlow: 1801. V. 73

NICHOLSON, H. A.
A Manual of Palaeontology, for the Use of Students.... Edinburgh: 1889. V. 70
A Monograph of the British Stromatoporoids. 1886-1892. V. 73

NICHOLSON, HAMLET
An Autobiographical And Full Historical Account Of The Persecution Of Hamlet Nicholson. Manchester: 1890. V. 72

NICHOLSON, HENRY ALLEYNE
Manual of Palaeontology for the Use of Students. Edinburgh: 1879. V. 68

NICHOLSON, J. H.
Our Improved Artificial Ear Drums. New York: 1884. V. 73

NICHOLSON, JAMES B.
A Manual of the Art of Bookbinding.... Philadelphia: 1856. V. 70; 73
A Manual of the Art of Bookbinding.... Philadelphia: 1902. V. 70; 72

NICHOLSON, JOHN
Airedale in Ancient Times, Elwood and Elvina. London: 1825. V. 71
By Horse, Stage and Packet. San Francisco: 1988. V. 69; 73
The Farmer's Assistant. Albany: 1814. V. 71
Poems of John Nicholson, The Airedale Poet. London: 1859. V. 71

NICHOLSON, JOSEPH SHIELD
A Treatise on Money and Essays on Monetary Problems. London: 1893. V. 73

NICHOLSON, JOSIAH WALKER
Crosby Garrett, Westmorland. 1914. V. 71

NICHOLSON, KENYON
The Barker. New York: 1925. V. 69
Eva the Fifth. The Odyssey of a Tom Show. New York: 1928. V. 71

NICHOLSON, MEREDITH
The House of a Thousand Candles. Indianapolis: 1905. V. 68

NICHOLSON, NIGEL
Harold Nicolson-21st November 1966. 1966. V. 72

NICHOLSON, NORMAN
The Fire of the Lord - a Novel. London: 1944. V. 69
Five Rivers. New York: 1943. V. 70; 71
A Match for the Devil. London: 1955. V. 71
The Old Man of the Mountains. London: 1946. V. 71
Rock Face. London: 1948. V. 68; 71
William Cowper. London: 1951. V. 71; 72
Wordsworth. London: 1949. V. 71

NICHOLSON, PETER
An Architectural and Engineering Dictionary.... London: 1835. V. 71
Practical Carpentry, Joinery and Cabinet Making.... London: 1845. V. 73
Practical Carpentry, Joinery and Cabinet-Making.... London: 1846. V. 68

NICHOLSON, RENTON
Dombey and Daughter: a Moral Fiction. London: 1848. V. 69

NICHOLSON, REYNOLD A.
Literary History Of The Arabs. London: 1923. V. 72

NICHOLSON, WILLIAM
An Almanac of Twelve Sports. 1898. V. 69
An Almanac of Twelve Sports. with words by Rudyard Kipling. London: 1898. V. 71
An Alphabet. Andoversford: 1978. V. 72
The British Encyclopedia, or Dictionary of Arts and Sciences. Philadelphia: 1816. V. 73
Clever Bill. New York: 1926. V. 68; 71
The English Historical Library. London: 1696. V. 72
The Wind Singer. London: 2000. V. 68

NICKALLS, JOSEPH
Report Upon the Consequences Which the New Cut, from Eau-Brink Would be Attended with No Drainage. London: 1793. V. 71

NICKLESS, WILL
Molepie. 1967. V. 72
The Nitehood. 1966. V. 72
Owlglass. 1964. V. 72

NICKSON, G.
A Portrait of Salmon Fishing. 1976. V. 68

NICOL, WALTER
The Forcing, Fruit and Kitchen Gardener. Edinburgh: 1809. V. 68
The Villa Garden Directory, or Monthly Index of Work to Be done in Town and Villa Gardens, Shrubbries (sic) and Parterres.... Edinburgh: 1810. V. 70

NICOLAI, GIAMBATTISTA
Nova Analyseos Elementa. Padua: 1786-1793. V. 73

NICOLE FRERES LTD.
Musical Box Manufacturers and Importers. Geneva: 1899. V. 68

NICOLL, ALLARDYCE
Masks, Mimes and Miracles. London: 1931. V. 70

NICOLL, M. J.
Nicoll's Birds of Eygt. London: 1930. V. 73

NICOLL, W. ROBERTSON
The Problem of Edwin Drood: a Study in the Methods of Dickens. London: 1912. V. 69

NICOLSON, BENEDICT
Joseph Wright of Derby, Painter of Light. 1968. V. 68

NICOLSON, HAROLD
The Age of Reason (1700-1789). London: 1960. V. 68
Diaries and Letters 1930-1962. London: 1966-1968. V. 68; 71

NICOLSON, J.
The History and Antiquities of the Counties of Westmorland and Cumberland. London: 1777. V. 71

NICOLSON, MARJORIE HOPE
Newton Demands the Muse, Newton's Optics and the Eighteenth Century Poets. Princeton: 1946. V. 72

NICOLSON, WILLIAM
Miscellany Accounts of the Diocese of Carlisle.... London: 1877. V. 71

NIDER, JOHANNES
Praeceptorum Divinae Legis, Sive Exposition Decalogi. Cologne: 1470. V. 68

NIEBAUER, ABBY
Three Windows: Poems. Woodside: 1980. V. 71

NIEBUHR, B.
The Greek Heroes. London: 1910. V. 73

NIEBUHR, CARSTEN
Description de l'Arabie d'Apres les Observations et Recherches Faites dans le Pays Meme. Copenhagen: 1773. V. 68

NIEDECKER, LORINE
The Granite Pail. Selected Poems. San Francisco: 1985. V. 69

North Central. London: 1968. V. 69

NIEHAUS, T. F.
Pacific States Wildflowers, Field Marks of Species Found in Washington, Oregeon, California and Adjacent Areas. Norwalk: 1984. V. 68

NIEREMBERG, JUAN EUSEBIO
Historia Naturae, Maxime Peregrinae, Libris XVI. Antwerp: 1635. V. 71; 73

NIERENDORF, KARL
Paul Klee: Paintings and Watercolors 1913 to 1939. New York: 1941. V. 72; 73

NIESSEN, S. A.
Batak Cloth and Clothing, a Dynamic Indonesian Tradition. 1993. V. 69
Motifs of Life in Toba Batak Texts and Textiles. Dordrecht: 1985. V. 69

NIETZSCHE, FRIEDRICH
Die Geburt der Tragodie aus dem Geiste der Muzik. (The Birth of Tragedy). Leipzig: 1872. V. 70
Gotzen-Dammerung, oder Wie man Mit Dem Hammer Philosophiert. (Twilight of the Gods). Leipzig: 1889. V. 70
Thus Spake Zarathustra. New York: 1964. V. 68

NIGERIA in Costume. London: 1968. V. 69

NIGGLI, I.
Swiss Cottages. Teufen. V. 72

THE NIGHT Before Christmas. Akron: 1905. V. 72
THE **NIGHT** Before Christmas. London: 1910. V. 73
THE **NIGHT** Before Christmas. Akron: 1920. V. 73
THE **NIGHT** Before Christmas. Akron: 1945. V. 73

NIGHT Before Christmas. Racine: 1947. V. 70; 73

A **NIGHT** of Wonders. London: 1906. V. 70

NIGHTINGALE, ANNA ELIZABETH
Gleanings from the South, East and West. London: 1843. V. 68; 70; 72

NIGHTINGALE, FLORENCE
Notes on Nursing: What It Is and What It Is Not. 1860. V. 73
Notes on Nursing; What It Is, and What It Is Not. London: 1860. V. 69
Notes on Nursing; What It Is and What It Is Not. New York: 1860. V. 71; 73
Notes on Nursing, What It Is and What It Is Not. London: 1960. V. 72

NIGHTINGALE, J.
The History and Antiquities of the Paraochial Church of St. Saviour, Southwark.... London: 1818. V. 71

NIGHTINGALE, JOSEPH
A Portraiture of Methodism; Being an Impartial View of the Rise, Progress, Doctrines, Discipline and Manners of the Wesleyan Methodists. London: 1807. V. 73

NIJINSKY, ROMOLA
The Last Years of Nijinsky. New York: 1952. V. 68

NIKELSBURGER, JACOB
Koul Jacob in Defence of the Jewish Religion.... New York: 1816. V. 69

NIKLAUS, THELMA
Harlequin Phoenix or The Rise and Fall of a Bergamask Rogue. London: 1956. V. 72

NIKULINSKY, PHILIPPA
Flowering Plants of the Eastern Goldfields of Western Australia. Perth: 1983. V. 72; 73

NILES, BLAIR
Free. London: 1930. V. 72
Strange Brother. New York: 1949. V. 72

NILES, JOHN JACOB
Singing Soldiers. New York: 1927. V. 70; 72

NILES, JOHN MILTON
History of South America and Mexico...to Which is Annexed, a Geographical and Historical View of Texas. Hartford: 1837. V. 68
A View of South America and Mexico, Comprising their History, the Political Conditions, Geography, Agriculture, Commerce &c. of the Republics of Mexico.... New York: 1825. V. 70

NILSSON, SVEN
The Primitive Inhabitants of Scandinavia. London: 1868. V. 68; 72

NIMMO, JOSEPH
Commerce Between the United States and Mexico. Washington: 1884. V. 71
Treasury Department Report on the Internal Commerce of the United States. Washington: 1885. V. 68
Uncle Sam's Farm - The Reclamation of the Arid Region of the United States by Means of Irrigation. Washington: 1890. V. 72

NIMMO, WILLIAM
History of Stirlingshire. London: 1817. V. 71
History of Stirlingshire. Stirling: 1817. V. 73

NIMROD, HARRY, PSEUD.
The Fudge Family in Washington. Baltimore: 1820. V. 68

NIMROD'S Hunting Tours, Interspersed with Charateristic Anecdotes, Sayings and Doings of Sporting Men.... 1903. V. 69

NIMS, FRANKLIN A.
The Phogographer and River 1889-1890: the Colorado Canon Diary.... Santa Fe: 1967. V. 70; 72

NIMS, JOHN FREDERICK
The Shape of Leaves. Chicago: 1997. V. 71
The Six-Cornered Snowflake. New York: 1991. V. 69; 71
The Stranger and the Cyclotron. 1940. V. 71

NIN, ANAIS
A Child Born Out of the Fog. New York: 1947. V. 68
Children of the Albatross. New York: 1947. V. 73
Cities of the Interior. Denver: 1961. V. 68; 71
D. H. Lawrence. An Unprofessional Study. Paris: 1932. V. 72
Delta of Venus: Erotica. New York: 1977. V. 72
The Diary of Anais Nin. New York: 1966-1969. V. 68; 70
The Diary of Anais Nin. New York: 1974. V. 73
The Diary of Anais Nin: 1931-1934. New York: 1966. V. 70
The Diary of Anais Nin. Together with a Photographic Supplement to the Diary of Anais Nin, NY. 1974. New York: 1966-1980. V. 73
The Diary of Anais Nin. Vol 6. New York: 1976. V. 72
The Early Diary of Anais Nin. New York: 1982. V. 73
The Four Chambered Heart. New York: 1950. V. 68; 73
Henry and June. San Diego: 1986. V. 73
The House of Incest. New York. V. 71
House of Incest. Paris: 1936. V. 68
Ladders to Fire. New York: 1946. V. 73
Linotte. The Early Diary of Anais Nin 1914-1920. New York: 1978. V. 73
The Novel of the Future. New York: 1968. V. 71
On Writing. New York: 1947. V. 68
Preface to Henry Miller's Tropic of Cancer. New York: 1947. V. 71
Solar Barque. 1958. V. 73
Unpublished Selections from the Diary. Athens: 1968. V. 73
Winter of Artifice. New York: 1942. V. 69
Winter of Artifice. Denver: 1961. V. 68
A Woman Speaks. The Lectures, Seminars and Interviews of Anais Nin. Chicago: 1975. V. 68; 72

1937 Cocktail Book (&) Cocktails and Other Mixed Drinks. Manila: 1937. V. 71

THE 1929 Christmas Tree Annual. 1929. V. 71

NINHAM, HENRY
Fifteen Etchings by the Late Henry Ninham. Norwich?: 1875. V. 69

NISBET, HUME
A Desert Bride: a Story of Adventure in India and Persia. London: 1895. V. 68
The Jolly Roger a Story of Sea Heroes and Pirates. London: 1893. V. 68
Where Art Begins. London: 1892. V. 69

NISBET, JACK
Sources of the River Tracking David Thompson Across Western North America. Seattle: 1994. V. 72

NISBET, JOHN
Our Forests and Woodlands. London: 1900. V. 70

NISHIKAWA, JOKEN
Zoho Kwai-Tsusho-Ko. Kyoto: 1708. V. 71

NISHIKAWA, Y.
Average Distribution of Larvae of Oceanic Species of Scombroid fishes 1956-1981. 1985. V. 72

NISSEN BUILDINGS LTD.
Memorandum Containing Information Concerning Nissen Huts.... Hoddesdon: 1939. V. 68

NISTER'S Holiday Annual for 1901. London. V. 69

NISTER'S Holiday Annual for 1903. London: 1903. V. 70

NISTER'S Holiday Annual for 1906. London: 1906. V. 69

NIVEN, DAVID
Go, Slowly, Come Back Quickly. Garden City: 1981. V. 73
The Moon's a Balloon. London: 1971. V. 68
Once Over Lightly. New York: 1951. V. 69

NIVEN, FREDERICK
Treasure Trail. New York: 1923. V. 70
Triumph. New York: 1934. V. 69

NIVEN, LARRY
World of Ptavvs. London: 1968. V. 71

NIVEN, W.
London City Churches Destroyed Since A.D. 1800 or Now Threatened. London: 1887. V. 68

NIX, EVETT DUMAS
Oklahombres: Particularly the Wilder Ones. St. Louis: 1929. V. 70; 72; 73

NIX, JOHN W.
The Tale of Two Schools and Springtown-Parker County. Fort Worth: 1945. V. 69

NIXON, FRANCIS RUSSELL
The Cruise of the Beacon. London: 1857. V. 71

NIXON, HOWARD
Bookbindings from the Library of Jean Grolier. A Loan Exhibiton. London: 1965. V. 70
The Gardyners Passetaunce (c. 1512). London: 1995. V. 70
Sixteenth Century Gold Tooled Bookbindings in the Pierpont Morgan Library. New York: 1971. V. 70

NIXON, JOHN
The Complete Story of the Transvaal. London: 1885. V. 71

NIXON, M.
Biology of Cephalopods. 1977. V. 72

NIXON, MIMA
Royal Palaces & Gardens. London: 1916. V. 70

NIXON, RICHARD MILHOUS
The Challenges We Face. New York: 1960. V. 71
The Inaugural Address of...Delivered at the Capitol/Washington, January 20, 1969. Worcester. V. 70; 71
The Memoirs of Richard Nixon. New York: 1978. V. 69; 71; 72
1999. New York: 1988. V. 72
Real Peace. New York: 1983. V. 69; 71
The Real War. London: 1960. V. 70
Six Crises. Garden City: 1962. V. 69; 71
Summons to Greatness. A Collage of Inspirational Thought and Practical Ideas from the Messages and Addresses of Richard Nixon. Washington: 1972. V. 71

NOAH'S Ark. London: 1910. V. 70
NOAH'S Ark. 1950. V. 71

NOAILLES, MARQUIS DE
What is Poland?. London: 1863. V. 68

NOAKES, V.
Edward Lear 1812-1888. New York: 1986. V. 68

NOBEL, The Man and His Prizes.... Amsterdam: 1962. V. 73

THE NOBILITY of Life, Its Graces & Virtues, Portrayed in Prose and Verse by the Best Writers. London: 1869. V. 68

NOBLE, A.
Siberian Days. 1928. V. 69

NOBLE, JOHN
Fiscal Legislation 1842-1865. London: 1867. V. 71
Illustrated Official Handbook of the Cape and South Africa. Cape Town/Johannesburg: 1893. V. 71
South Africa Past and Present. London: 1877. V. 71

NOBLE Lives of a Noble Race. Minneapolis: 1909. V. 70

NOBLE, LOUIS L.
After Icebergs with a Painter: a Summer Voyage to Labrador and Around Newfoundland. London: 1861. V. 70

NOBLE, MARK
Memoirs of the Protectoral House of Cromwell; Deduced from an Early Period and Continued Down to the Present Time.... London: 1787. V. 69

NOBLE, MARY E.
The Registers of the Parish of Askham in the County of Westmorland from 1566 to 1812. Kendal: 1897. V. 71
The Registers of the Parish of Askham in the County of Westmorland from 1566 to 1812. London: 1904. V. 71

NOBLE, PETER
British Ballet. London: 1949. V. 68

NOBLE, SAMUEL H.
Life and Adventures of Buckskin Sam. Rumford: 1900. V. 72

THE NOCTES Ambrosianae. Philadelphia: 1843. V. 69; 73

NODAL, JOHN H.
The Pictorial Record of the Royal Jubilee Exhibition. Manchester: 1888. V. 71

NODIN, JOHN
The British Duties of Customs, Excise &c.... London: 1792. V. 72

NODOT, FRANCOIS
Nouveaux Memoires de Mr. Nodot, ou Observations.... Amsterdam: 1706. V. 72

NOE, LOUIS PANTALEON AMEDEE DE
Memoires Relatifs A L'Expedition Anglaise. Paris: 1826. V. 71

NOEL, BAPTIST W.
Freedom and Slavery in the United States of America. London: 1863. V. 68
Notes of a Tour in Switzerland, in the Summer of 1847. London: 1848. V. 69; 72

NOEL, JOSEPH
Footloose In Arcadia. A Personal Record of Jack London, George Sterling, Ambrose Bierce. New York: 1940. V. 72

NOEL, RODEN
The Waternymph and the Boy: a Poem. 1997. V. 71

NOEL, THEOPHILUS
Autobiography and Reminiscences of Theophilus Noel. Chicago: 1904. V. 69; 70
A Campaign from Santa Fe to the Mississippi. Houston: 1961. V. 69; 70; 71
A Campaign from Santa Fe to the Mississippi. Raleigh: 1961. V. 70

THE NOISY Book. No. B278. London. V. 68; 71

NOLAN, EDWARD HENRY
Illustrated History Of The War Against Russia. London: 1855-1857. V. 72

NOLAN, FREDERICK
The Life and Death of John Henry Tunstall. Albuquerque: 1965. V. 71
The Lincoln County War, A Documentary History. Norman: 1992. V. 71
The West of Billy the Kid. Norman: 1998. V. 68; 73

NOLAN, JEANNETTE COVERT
New Days New Ways. New York: 1936. V. 72

NOLAN, OREN W.
Galloping Down the Texas Trail, Sketches of Texas Cowboys, Rangers, Sheriffs, Cattle Horses, Guns and Game. Oden: 1947. V. 69

NOLAN, WILLIAM F.
Logan's Run. New York: 1967. V. 69; 73

NOLL, ARTHUR HOWARD
General Kirby-Smith. Sewanee: 1907. V. 69; 70

NONA, FRANCIS
The Fall of the Alamo: an Historical Drama in Four Acts.... New York: 1879. V. 68

NOON, JEFF
Automated Alice. London: 1996. V. 68; 73
Pollen. London: 1995. V. 68
Vurt. London: 1993. V. 70
Vurt. New York: 1995. V. 72

NOON, WILLIAM T.
Joyce and Aquinas. New Haven: 1957. V. 69

NOONAN, T., & CO.
Illustrated Catalogue Barber's Supplies. Boston: 1898. V. 73

NOOTEBOOM, CEES
Rituals - a Novel. Baton Rouge: 1983. V. 71

NORBOURNE, PHILLIP
Journals of The Late Brevet Major Phillip Norbourne Hopkins Barber Written During The War with Mexico 1846. NY: 1936. V. 72

NORDAN, LEWIS
Music of the Swamp. Chapel Hill: 1991. V. 68; 71; 73
Welcome to the Arrow-Catcher Fair. Baton Rouge: 1983. V. 70; 73
Wolf Whistle. Chapel Hill: 1993. V. 71

NORDAU, MAX
The Drones Must Die. New York: 1897. V. 68

NORDEN, HERMANN
From Golden Gate to Golden Sun. London: 1923. V. 69; 71

NORDENSKIOLD, ADOLF ERIK
The Arctic Voyages of Adolf Erik Nordenskiold 1858-1879. London: 1879. V. 71
The Voyage of the Vega Round Asia and Europe. London: 1881. V. 71
The Voyage of the Vega Round Asia and Europe. New York: 1882. V. 73

NORDENSKIOLD, N. OTTO G.
Antarctica or Two Years Amongst the Ice of the South Pole. London: 1905. V. 71

NORDENSTAM, A.
Marine Isopoda of the Familes Serolidae, Idotheidae, Pseudidotheidae Arcturidae.... Stockholm: 1933. V. 73

NORDGAARD, JOHN
Statistics of Polk County, Wisconsin 1887. Osceola;: 1887. V. 73

NORDHOFF, CHARLES
The Hurricane. New York: 1936. V. 70
Men Without Country. Boston: 1942. V. 72

NORDHOFF, CHARLES BERNARD
The Hurricane. Boston: 1936. V. 71
Mutiny on the Bounty. Boston: 1932. V. 71
Northern California, Oregon and the Sandwich Islands. London: 1874. V. 71

NORDLAND, G.
Richard Diebenkorn. New York: 1987. V. 72

NORDNESS, LEE
Art USA Now. Lucerne: 1962. V. 69; 72

NORDSTROM, ESTER B.
Tent Folk fo the Far North. London: 1930. V. 71

NORDYKE, LEWIS T.
The Angels Sing. Clarendon: 1964. V. 69

NORFOLK & WESTERN RAILROAD
Private Telegraph Code of the Norfolk and Western Railroad. New York: 1895. V. 72

NORFOLK, HORATIO EDWARD
Gleanings in Graveyards: a Collection of Curious Epitaphs. 1861. V. 73

NORFOLK, LAWRENCE
Lempriere's Dictionary. London: 1991. V. 70; 73

NORMAN, A.
Gentlemen! The Queen!. 1926. V. 69

NORMAN, A. P.
Congenital Abnormalities in Infancy. Oxford: 1963. V. 68

NORMAN, D.
Alfred Stieglitz: An American Seer. New York: 1973. V. 68

NORMAN, DON CLEVELAND
The 500th Anniversary Pictorial Census of the Gutenberg Bible. Chicago: 1961. V. 70; 72

NORMAN, FRANCIS MARTIN
Martello Tower in China and the Pacific. London: 1902. V. 71

NORMAN, FRANK
Bang to Rights. London: 1958. V. 70
Bang to Rights. London: 1985. V. 68

NORMAN, HASKELL F.
One Hundred Books Famous in Medicine. New York: 1995. V. 69; 73

NORMAN, HENRY
The Peoples and Politics of the Far East. London: 1905. V. 69; 71
The Real Japan. London: 1892. V. 71

NORMAN, HOWARD
The Bird Artist. New York: 1994. V. 68; 69; 70; 71; 72
How Glooskap Outwits the Ice Giants. New York: 1989. V. 73
Kiss in the Hotel Joseph Conrad and Other Stories. New York: 1989. V. 68; 69; 72; 73
The Museum Guard. New York: 1998. V. 72
The Museum Guard. London: 1999. V. 72
The Northern Lights. New York: 1987. V. 68; 69; 71; 72
Northern Tales. New York: 1990. V. 72
The Owl-Scatterer. New York: 1986. V. 69
The Wishing Bone Cycle. New York: 1976. V. 69

NORMAN, J. R.
Squire. London: 1944. V. 68
A Systematic Monograph of the Flatfishes. London: 1934. V. 68

NORMAN, JEREMY
Morton's Medical Bibliography. 1991. V. 70

NORMAN, SYLVIA
The Letters of Thomas Jefferson Hogg to Jane Williams. London: 1934. V. 69

NORMANBY, CONSTANTINE HENRY PHIPPS, 1ST MARQUIS OF
The Contrast. London: 1832. V. 70; 72
A Year of Revolution. From a Journal Kept in Paris in 1848. London: 1857. V. 68; 72

NORMAN-NERUDA, LUDWIG
The Climbs of Norman-Neruda. London: 1899. V. 71

NORRIS, FRANK
Collected Letters. San Francisco: 1986. V. 73
Frank Norris of The Wave. Stories and Sketches from the San Francisco Weekly 1893-1897. San Francisco: 1931. V. 68
The Pit. New York: 1903. V. 71

NORRIS, JOHN
A Catalogue of the Pictures, Models, Busts &c. in the Bodleian Gallery. Oxford: 1840. V. 69; 72
A Collection of Miscellanies: Consisting of Poems, Essays, Discourses and Letters, Occasionally Written. London: 1692. V. 73
Practical Discourses.... London: 1707-. V. 72

NORRIS, KATHLEEN
Dakota, A Spiritual Geography. New York: 1993. V. 72
Margaret Yorke. Garden City: 1930. V. 71
Mystery House. New York: 1939. V. 70
Rose of the World. Garden City: 1924. V. 71

NORRIS, LESLIE
Ransoms. London: 1970. V. 68

NORRIS, RICHARD
The Physiology and Pathology of the Blood. London: 1882. V. 68

NORRIS, THOMAS WAYNE
A Descriptive and Priced Catalogue of Books, Pamphlets, and Maps Relating Directly or Indirectly to the History, Literature and Printing of California and the Far West. Formerly in the Collection of Thomas Wayne Norris. Oakland: 1948. V. 70

NORRIS, WILLIAM EDWARD
Adrian Vidal. London: 1890. V. 68

NORRIS, WILLIAM F.
System of Diseases of the Eye. Philadelphia: 1897. V. 72

NORRIS-NEWMAN, CHARLES L.
With the Boers in the Transvaal and Orange Free State in 1880-1. London: 1882. V. 71

NORSTOG, K. J.
The Biology of the Cycads. Ithaca: 1997. V. 68

NORTH AMERICAN LILY SOCIETY
Lily Yearbook. New York: 1948-1976. V. 69

NORTH Carolina Troops 1861-1865. Raleigh: 1966. V. 73

NORTH CAROLINA. LAWS, STATUTES, ETC. - 1862
Ordinances and Resolutions Passed by the State Convention of North Carolina First Session in May and June 1861. Raleigh: 1862. V. 69; 70

NORTH Dakota Brand Book, 1944. Bismark: 1944. V. 71

NORTH, ELISHA
Outlines of the Science of Life, Which Treats Physiologically of Both Body and Mind.... New York: 1829. V. 71

NORTH, GEORGINA
Illustrations of the Ballad of Auld Robin Gray. 1834. V. 70

NORTH, JOHN
Sherlock Holmes and the Arabian Princess. Romford, Essex: 1990. V. 71

NORTH, JOHN S.
The Last Great Adventure. New York: 1941. V. 69

NORTH, MARIANNE
Recollections of a Happy Life. (with) Some Further Recollections of a Happy Life. New York: 1894. V. 69
Some Further Recollections of a Happy Life. London: 1893. V. 72
A Vision of Eden, the Life and Work of.... 1993. V. 68

NORTH, ROGER
A Discourse of Fish and Fishponds. (with) The Gentleman Farmer; or, Certain Observations Made by an English Gentleman, Upon the Husbandry of Flanders.... London: 1713. V. 71
The Lives of the Right Hon. Francis North...The Hon. Sir Dudley North...and The Hon. and Rev. Dr. John North. London: 1826. V. 68; 72
A Treatise on Fish and Fish Ponds. London: 1822-1835. V. 71
A Treatise on Fish and Fish Ponds. London: 1832-1835. V. 68; 73

NORTH, STERLING
So Dear to My Heart. Garden City: 1947. V. 72

NORTH WEST TRANSPORTATION CO.
North-West Transportation Co. Ltd. Running Between Windsor, Sarania, Saulte Ste. Marie, Fort William, Port Arthur and Duluth. Season of 1898. Sarnia: 1898. V. 68

NORTHALL, WILLIAM KNIGHT
Before and Behind the Curtain; or, Fifteen Year's Observations Among the Theatres of new York. New York: 1851. V. 71

NORTHCOTE, JAMES
The Life of Sir Joshua Reynolds, Late President of the Royal Academy. London: 1819. V. 73
One Hundred Fables. 1828. V. 72
One Hundred Fables. London: 1828. V. 71
One Hundred Fables. London: 1829-1833. V. 72

NORTHEN, R. T.
Home Orchid Growing. New York: 1970. V. 68

THE NORTHERN Heroine. Being Authentic Memoirs of the Late Czarina of Russia. London: 1727. V. 69

NORTHERN Lights. New York: 1994. V. 72

NORTHERN NAVIGATION CO. OF ONTARIO
Lake Superior an Georgian Bay. 1909. V. 68

NORTHEY, W. BROOK
The Gurkhas. London: 1928. V. 71; 72

NORTHLEIGH, JOHN
The Parallel; or the New Specious Association an Old Rebellious Covenant. London: 1682. V. 71

NORTHROP, CLAUDIAN BIRD
Southern Odes, by the Outcast, A Gentleman of South Carolina. Charleston: 1861. V. 70

NORTHROP, W. B.
With Pen and Camera, Interviews with Celebrities. London: 1904. V. 70

NORTHUMBERLAND, ELIZABETH SEYMOUR PERCY, DUCHESS OF
A Short Tour Made in the Year One Thousand Seven Hundred and Seventy One. London: 1775. V. 73

NORTHUP, E. F.
Zero to Eighty: Being My Lifetime Doings, Reflections and Inventions.... Princeton: 1937. V. 72

THE NORTON BOOK of Autobiography. New York: 1998. V. 72

NORTON, ANDRE
At Sword's Points. New York: 1954. V. 68
Fur Magic. Hampton Falls: 1992. V. 70; 73
Shadow Hawk. New York: 1960. V. 73
Tales of the Witch World No. 3. 1990. V. 71
Tales of the Witch World No. 4 - the Turning: Storms of Victory. London: 1991. V. 69

NORTON, CAROLINE
The Lady of La Garaye. Cambridge: 1862. V. 69; 72
The Sorrows of Rosalie. London: 1829. V. 72
The Undying One and Other Poems. London: 1830. V. 73

NORTON, E. F.
The Fight For Everest: 1924. London: 1925. V. 72

NORTON, E. F.
The Climber's Fireside Book. London: 1964. V. 69
Climbing the Fish's Tail. London: 1958. V. 69
The Fight for Everest: 1924. London: 1925. V. 69
South Col. London: 1954. V. 69
To the Unknown Mountain. London: 1962. V. 69

NORTON, JOHN
The Journal of Major John Norton, 1816. Toronto: 1970. V. 73

NORTON, L. A.
Life and Adventures of.... 1887. V. 73
The Life and Adventures of.... Oakland: 1887. V. 70

NORTON, MARY
The Borrower's Afloat. London: 1959. V. 70; 73
The Borrowers Aloft. London: 1961. V. 73

NORTON, MATTHEW G.
The Mississippi River Logging Company. An Historical Sketch. 1912. V. 72

NORTON, OLIVE
Now Lying Dead. London: 1967. V. 71

NORTON, ROBERT
Elements of Diagnosis, General Pathology and Therapeutics. London: 1831-1832. V. 70

NORTON, ROY
The Boomers. New York: 1914. V. 69

NORTON, W. A.
The Autobiography of Elizabeth Squirrell of Shottisham, and Selections from Her Writings.... London: 1853. V. 70

NORVELL, SANDERS
Forty Years of Hardware. New York: 1924. V. 71

NORWOOD, BENJAMIN ROBERT
Old Caldwell - A Retrospect 1699-1926. Caldwell: 1927. V. 72

NOSTRADAMUS, MICHAEL
The Complete Fortune teller Being the Magic Mirror Of Michael Nostradamus Also the Infallible Divination by Means of Figures.... New York: 1900. V. 73

NOSTRAND, JEANNE VAN
Edward Vischer's Drawings of the California Missions 1861-1878. San Francisco: 1982. V. 73

NOT a Station but a Place. San Francisco: 1979. V. 70

NOT In Precious Metals Alone, A Manuscript History of Montana. Helena: 1976. V. 72

NOTES of a Journey from Cornhill to Cairo. New York: 1846. V. 68

NOTES on Louis XI. London: 1878. V. 71

NOTES on the Cape of Good Hope, Made During an Excursion in that Colony in the Year 1820. London: 1821. V. 69

NOTITIA Utraque (Dignitatum)cum Orientis tum Occidentis Ultra Arcadii Honoriique Caesarum Tempora.... Basel: 1552. V. 68

NOTT, ELIPHALET
Miscellaneous Works. Schenectady: 1810. V. 73

NOTT, J. C.
Indigenous Races of the Earth; or, New Chapters of Ethnological Enquiry. Philadelphia and London: 1857. V. 69; 71

NOTT, STANLEY C.
Chinese Jade Throughout the Ages. London: 1936. V. 72

NOTTER, FLORENCE L.
My Dollies. Chicago: 1920. V. 69

NOTTINGHAM, STRATTON
Wills and Administrations of Accomack County, Virginia 1663-1800. Cottonport: 1973. V. 72

NOURSE, ALAN E.
Trouble on Titan. Philadelphia: 1954. V. 69

NOURSE, TIMOTHY
Campania Felix or, a Discoure of the Benefits and Improvements of Husbandry.... London: 1700. V. 69

NOUVEAU Cours Complet d'Agriculture, Theorique et Pratique, Contenant la Grande et la Petite Culture, l'Economie Rurale et Domestique la Medecine Veterinaire, etc. ou Dictionnaire Raisonne et Universel d'Agriculture.... Paris: 1821-1823. V. 71

NOUVEAU Dictionnaire d'Histoire Naturelle, Appliquee Aux Arts Principalement a L'Agriculture et a L'Economie Rurale et Domestique. Paris: 1803-1804. V. 68; 72

NOUVEL Atlas Portatif Destine Principalment Pour L'Instruction De La Jeunesse.... Paris: 1790. V. 71

NOUVELLE Cuisiniere Canadienne.... Montreal: 1879. V. 70

NOVA, CRAIG
The Geek. New York: 1975. V. 68

NOVA Scotia for Beauty and Business. Halifax: 1923. V. 72

NOVA SCOTIA. LAWS, STATUTES, ETC. - 1851
The Revised Statutes of Nova Scotia. Halifax: 1851. V. 73

NOVELL-THURLOW, T. J.
Trade Unions Abroad and Hints for Home Legislation. London: 1870. V. 71

NOVICE, GEORGE WILLIAM
Lights in Art, a Review of Ancient and Modern Pictures. Edinburgh: 1874. V. 72

NOWELL-SMITH, SIMON
Wordsworth to Robert Graves and Beyond.... London: 1983. V. 72

NOWILL, SIDNEY EDWARD PAYN
The Mountains of My Life. London: 1954. V. 69

NOWN, GRAHAM
Elementary My Dear Watson. London: 1986. V. 71

NOYCE, WILLIAM
Poems. London: 1960. V. 68

NOYES, A. J.
In the Land of Chinook or the Story of Blaine County. 1917. V. 68; 72

NOYES, ALFRED
Ballads and Poems. Edinburgh and London: 1928. V. 73
Drake, an English Epic. Edinburgh and London: 1906-1908. V. 68
Poems. Edinburgh: 1904. V. 68
The Return of the Scare-Crow. London: 1929. V. 71
Voltaire. New York: 1936. V. 72

NOYES, GEORGE WALLINGFORD
The Religious Experience of John Humphrey Noyes. New York: 1923. V. 73

NOYES, JOHN H.
Confessions of John H. Noyes. New York: 1849. V. 73

NOYES, JOHN HUMPHREY
Male Continence. Oneida: 1877. V. 68
Mutual Criticism. Oneida: 1876. V. 68
Salvation from Sin, the End of Christian Faith. Oneida: 1876. V. 68

NOYES, T. R.
Report on the Health of Children in the Onedia Community. Oneida: 1878. V. 68

NUCK, ANTONIUS
Adenographia Curiosa et Uteri Foeminei Anatome Nova. Leyden: 1696. V. 70
De Ductu Salivali Novo, Saliva, Ductibus Oculorum Aquosis et Humore Oculi Aqueo. Leyden: 1685. V. 70
Sialographia, et Ductum Aquosorum Anatome Nova. Leyden: 1723. V. 70; 72

NUCKEL, O.
Destiny. A Novel in Pictures. New York: 1930. V. 71

NUGENT, NELL M.
Cavaliers and Pioneers: Abstracts of Virginia Land Patents and Grants 1622-1749. Richmond: 1992. V. 68
Cavaliers and Pioneers: Abstracts of Virginia Land Patents and Grants, 1623-1666. Baltimore: 1969. V. 72

NUGENT, ROBERT CRAGGS
Considerations Upon a Reduction of the Land Tax. London: 1749. V. 72
Farther Considerations Upon a Reduction of the Land-Tax: Together with a State of the Annual Supplies of the Sinking-Fund and of the National Debt.... London: 1751. V. 72

NUGENT, THOMAS
The Grand Tour; or a Journey through the Netherlands, Germany, Italy and France. London: 1778. V. 72
Travels, through Germany. London: 1768. V. 68; 70

NUGGET, PSEUD.
Australia and Her Treasures. London: 1852. V. 73

NULAND, SHERWIN B.
The Origins of Anesthesia. Birmingham: 1983. V. 72

NUMBER Five Joy Street. A Medley of Prose and Verse for Boys and Girls. London. V. 73

NUMBER Six Joy Street. A Medley of Prose and Verse for Boys and Girls. V. 72; 73

NUMBER 7 Joy Street. A Medley of Prose and Verse for Boys and Girls. Oxford: 1929. V. 73

NUMBERS. Cambridge: 1986. V. 71

NUNEZ CABECA DE VACA, ALVAR
The Narrative of Alvar Nunez Cabeza De Vaca. Barre: 1972. V. 69
Relacion of.... San Francisco: 1929. V. 73
Relation that Alvar Nunez Cabeca De Vaca Gave of What Befel the Armament in the Indias Whither Panphilo de Narvaez Went for Governor (from the Years 1527 to 1537).. San Francisco: 1929. V. 69

NUNIS, DOYCE B.
The Hudson Bay Company's First Fur Brigade to Sacramento Valley, Alexander McLeod's 1829 Hunt. Sacramento: 1968. V. 73
The San Francisco Vigilance Committee of 1856 - Three Views, William T. Coleman, William T. Sherman, James Omeara. Los Angeles: 1971. V. 71
Southern California's Spanish Heritage. Los Angeles: 1992. V. 68

NUNLIST, HUGO
Spitzbergen. London: 1966. V. 69

NUNN, KEM
Pomona Queen. New York: 1992. V. 72
Tapping the Source. New York: 1984. V. 68; 70; 72

NURNBERG, WALTER
Words in Their Hands: a Series of Photographs. 1964. V. 71

THE NURSERY ABC. London: 1900. V. 72

NURSERY Ditties. London: 1857. V. 72

NURSERY Games in Prose and Verse. London. V. 69

NURSERY Jingles. New York: 1882. V. 73

NURSERY Melodies or Pretty Rhymes in Easy Verse. New York: 1855. V. 71

NURSERY Rhymes. London: 1920. V. 73
NURSERY Rhymes. London: 1930. V. 70
NURSERY Rhymes. London: 1970. V. 71

NURSERY Rhymes And Proverbs. London. V. 72

NURSERY Rhymes Stories and Pictures. London: 1938. V. 71

NURSERY Songs. London: 1870. V. 73

NURSERY Tales. Philadelphia: 1904. V. 70

NURSEY, WALTER R.
The Legend and the Legacy of Pere Marquette. Chicago: 1897. V. 68

NUS.. Paris. V. 70

NUTT, DAVID
A Catalogue of Theological Books in Foreign Languages, Including the Sacred Writings.... London: 1857. V. 68; 70; 72

NUTT, THOMAS
Humanity to Honey Bees; or, Practical Direction for the Mangement of Honey-Bees Upon an Improved and Humane Plan.... Wisbech: 1834. V. 68; 72

NUTTALL, JEFF
Pig. London: 1969. V. 70

NUTTALL, T.
A Manual of the Ornithology of the United States and of Canada. Boston: 1940. V. 70

NUTTALL, THOMAS
A Journal of Travels in the Arkansas Territory, During the Year 1819.... Philadelphia: 1821. V. 72

NUTTING, C. C.
Barbados-Antigua Expedition. 1919. V. 69
Barbados-Antigua Expedition. Iowa City: 1919. V. 68

NUTTING, WALLACE
Wallace Nutting's Biography. Framingham: 1936. V. 69

NYE, NAOMI SHIHAB
Red Suitcase. Brockport: 1994. V. 68

NYE, ROBERT
Tales I Told My Mother. London: 1969. V. 68

NYE, WILBUR S.
Bad Medicine and Good - Tale of The Kiowas. Norman: 1962. V. 69; 72
Carbine and Lance: the Story of Old Fort Sill. Norman: 1937. V. 69
Plains Indian Raiders. Norman: 1968. V. 68; 72

O

O. C.'s Letters from the South, on Northern and Southern Views Respecting Slavery and the American Tract Society. New York: 1857. V. 70

OAKES, AUGUSTUS FREDERICK
Suggestions on the Exercise and Field Movements of Horse Artillery in India.... Madras: 1839. V. 72

OAKES, EDWIN STACEY
The Law of Organized Labor and Industrial Conflicts. Rochester: 1927. V. 71

OAKES, PHILIP
Unlucky Jonah. 1954. V. 69

OAKESHOTT, W.
Classical Inspiration in Medieval Art. London: 1959. V. 72

OAKLEY, R. R.
Treks & Palavers. London: 1938. V. 71

OAKLEY, VIOLET
The Holy Experiment. Philadelphia: 1922. V. 71
The Holy Experiment. Philadelphia: 1950. V. 72

OAKS, GEORGE WASHINGTON
Man of The West, Reminiscences of 1840-1917 - Recorded By Ben Jaastad, Editor and Annotated By Arthur Woodward. Tucson: 1956. V. 69; 72

OATES, CHARLOTTE MANN BEAUMONT
Miscellaneous Poems, Songs, and Rhymes. Bradford: 1898. V. 69

OATES, J. C. T.
Cambridge University Library: a History. Cambridge: 1986. V. 70

OATES, JOYCE CAROL
All the Good People I've Left Behind. Santa Barbara: 1979. V. 73
Angel Fire. Poems. Baton Rouge: 1973. V. 70
Angel of Light. New York: 1981. V. 72; 73
Anonymous Sins and Other Poems. Baton Rouge: 1969. V. 68; 70; 73
The Art of Matt Phillips. New York: 1980. V. 71
The Assassins. New York: 1975. V. 72
The Assignation. New York: 1988. V. 73
The Barrens. New York: 2001. V. 69; 72
Blonde. New York: 1999. V. 72
Blonde. Franklin Center: 2000. V. 70
Broke Heart Blues. New York: 1999. V. 72
By the North Gate. New York: 1963. V. 70; 73
Celestial Timepiece. Poems. Dallas: 1980. V. 70
Childwold. New York: 1976. V. 70; 72; 73
Crossing the Border. New York: 1976. V. 68; 70
Crossing the Border. London: 1978. V. 70
Cupid & Psyche. A Short Story. New York: 1970. V. 70; 73
Cybele. Santa Barbara: 1979. V. 70; 73
Daisy. Santa Barbara: 1977. V. 73
Do With Me What You Will. New York: 1973. V. 72
Dreaming America and Other Poems. 1973. V. 70
Expensive People. New York: 1968. V. 70; 73
The Fabulous Beasts. Poems. Baton Rouge: 1975. V. 70
Foxfire. Confessions of a Girl Gang. New York: 1993. V. 68; 70
Funland. Concord: 1983. V. 70
A Garden of Earthly Delights. New York: 1967. V. 73
Haunted. New York: 1994. V. 72
The Hostile Sun: the Poetry of D. H. Lawrence. Los Angeles: 1973. V. 70
The Hungry Ghosts: Seven Allusive Comedies. Los Angeles: 1974. V. 70
Invisible Woman: New and Selected Poems 1970-1982. Princeton: 1982. V. 70
The Lamb of Abyssalia. 1979. V. 70
Lives of the Twins. New York: 1987. V. 70
Love and Its Derangements. Baton Rouge: 1970. V. 70; 73
Luxury of Sin. Northridge: 1984. V. 70; 73
Marriages and Infidelities. New York: 1972. V. 70
Marriages and Infidelities. London: 1974. V. 73
Marya. A Life. Franklin Center: 1986. V. 73
A Middle-Class Education. New York: 1980. V. 70
Miracle Play. Los Angeles: 1974. V. 70
My Heart Laid Bare. New York: 1998. V. 72
Mysteries of Winterthurn. New York: 1983. V. 70
Mysteries of Winterthurn. Franklin Center: 1984. V. 70; 73
New Heaven, New Earth: the Visionary Experience in Literature. New York: 1974. V. 70
Night-Side: Eighteen Tales. New York: 1977. V. 70
Nightless Nights. Concord: 1981. V. 70; 73
On Boxing. Garden City: 1987. V. 70
The Poisoned Kiss and Other Stories from the Portuguese. New York: 1975. V. 69
Queen of the Night. Northridge: 1979. V. 70; 73
Season of Peril. Santa Barbara: 1977. V. 70
Sentimental Education. Los Angeles: 1978. V. 70
A Sentimental Education. New York: 1980. V. 70
Small Avalanches and Other Stories. Helsinki: 1989. V. 70
Son of the Morning. New York: 1978. V. 70; 73
Soul/Mate. New York: 1989. V. 70
The Step-Father. Northbridge: 1978. V. 70
Them. New York: 1969. V. 69
The Time Traveler. Northridge: 1987. V. 70
The Triumph of the Spider Monkey. Santa Barbara: 1976. V. 70
Twelve Plays. New York: 1991. V. 73
Unholy Loves. New York: 1979. V. 73
Upon the Sweeping Flood. New York: 1966. V. 70; 73
We Were the Mulvaneys. New York: 1996. V. 70
What I Lived For. New York: 1994. V. 70; 72
The Wheel of Love and Other Stories. New York: 1970. V. 70
The Wheel of Love and Other Stories. London: 1971. V. 68
Women in Love and Other Poems. New York: 1968. V. 70; 73
Women Whose Lives are Food, Men Whose Lives Are Money. Poems. Baton Rouge & London: 1978. V. 70
Wonderland. New York: 1971. V. 70
You Must Remember This. Franklin Center: 1987. V. 70; 73
Zombie. New York: 1995. V. 70

OATES, STEPHEN B.
Confederate Cavalry West of the River. Austin: 1961. V. 69; 72

OATMAN, EDWARD L.
Diagnostics of The Fundus Oculi. Troy, NY: 1920. V. 72

OBACH, EUGENE
Society for the Encouragement of Arts, Manufactures and Commerce. 1898. V. 71

O'BEIRNE, H. F.
Leaders and Leading Men of the Indian Territory. Chicago: 1891. V. 69

OBER, C. K.
Out of the Fog. A Story of the Sea. New York: 1911. V. 70

OBER, F. A.
A Guide to the West Indies and Bermuda. New York: 1908. V. 70
Travels in Mexico and Life Among the Mexicans. Boston: 1884. V. 71

OBERBECK, GRACE J.
History of La Crescenta - La Canada Valleys: a Story of Beginings Put Into Writing. Montrose: 1938. V. 68

OBERHOLSER, H. C.
The Bird Life of Texas. Austin: 1974. V. 73

OBLER, ARCH
Free World Theatre: Nineteen New Radio Plays. New York: 1944. V. 72

O'BRENNAN, MARTIN A.
O'Brennan's Antiquities. Dublin: 1858. V. 69

O'BRIAN, PATRICK
Blue at the Mizzen. London: 1999. V. 68; 71; 72
Caesar & Hussein. 1999. V. 71
Clarissa Oakes. 1992. V. 73
The Commodore. 1994. V. 68; 73
The Commodore. London: 1994. V. 71
Desolation Island. 1978. V. 73
Desolation Island. New York: 1979. V. 72
The Fortune of War. 1979. V. 73
The Fortune of War. London: 1979. V. 70; 71; 72
H.M.S. Surprise. London: 1973. V. 70
The Hundred Days. London: 1998. V. 68; 71; 72
The Hundred Days. New York: 1998. V. 68
The Ionian Mission. 1981. V. 73
The Ionian Mission. London: 1981. V. 71
Master and Commander. London: 1970. V. 70
The Mauritius Command. 1977. V. 73
The Mauritius Command. London: 1977. V. 70; 71; 72
Men-of-War. New York: 1995. V. 72
Pablo Ruiz Picasso. A Biography. London: 1976. V. 71
Post Captain. London: 1972. V. 70; 71
Post Captain. Philadelphia: 1972. V. 73
The Reverse of the Medal. 1986. V. 73
The Reverse of the Medal. London: 1986. V. 68; 71; 72
The Surgeon's Mate. London: 1980. V. 71
The Thirteen-Gun Salute. London: 1989. V. 68; 71
Treasons's Harbour. London: 1983. V. 72; 73
The Wine Dark Sea. London: 1993. V. 68; 70; 71
The Wine Dark Sea. London: 1997. V. 72
The Yellow Admiral. London: 1997. V. 68; 71; 72

O'BRIEN, CORNELIUS
Memoirs of Rt. Rev. Edmund Burke, Bishop of Zion, First Vicar Apostolic of Nova Scotia. Ottawa: 1894. V. 73

O'BRIEN, EDNA
August is a Wicked Month. London: 1965. V. 68
The High Road. London: 1988. V. 70; 73
James Joyce. 1999. V. 72
A Pagan Place. New York: 1970. V. 68
A Pagan Place. London: 1973. V. 71; 73
A Scandalous Woman - Stories. London: 1974. V. 68; 71
Wild Decembers. Boston: 2000. V. 72

O'BRIEN, FLANN
The Dalkey Archive. London: 1964. V. 69
Faustus Kelly - a Play in Three Acts. Dublin: 1943. V. 71
The Hard Life. London: 1961. V. 71; 73
The Hard Life. New York: 1962. V. 69
Myles - Portraits of Brian O'Nolan. London: 1973. V. 68
The Third Policeman. New York: 1967. V. 70

O'BRIEN, FREDERICK
White Shadows in the South Seas. New York: 1919. V. 72

O'BRIEN, GEOFFREY
Hardboiled America: The Lurid Years of Paperbacks. New York: 1981. V. 69

O'BRIEN, GEORGE
The Economic History of Ireland in the 17th Century. 1919. V. 70

O'BRIEN, JOHN
Leaving Las Vegas. Wichita: 1990. V. 70; 71
Leaving Las Vegas. Wichita: 1991. V. 70

O'BRIEN, LIAM
The Remarkable Mr. Pennypacker. New York: 1954. V. 69

O'BRIEN, MICHAEL J.
A Hidden Phase of American History: Ireland's Part in America's Struggle for Liberty. New York: 1921. V. 70

O'BRIEN, PATRICK
The Walker and Other Stories. New York: 1955. V. 68

O'BRIEN, TIM
Friends and Enemies. Arizona: 2001. V. 70; 71; 72; 73

O'BRIEN, TIM continued
Going After Cacciato. London: 1978. V. 68; 69; 71; 73
Going After Cacciato. New York: 1978. V. 69; 70; 72; 73
Going After Cacciato. Paris: 1990. V. 72
If I Die in a Combat Zone. 1973. V. 70
If I Die in a Combat Zone. London: 1973. V. 68; 73
If I Die in a Combat Zone. New York: 1973. V. 68; 72
If I Die in a Combat Zone. New York: 1989. V. 72
In the Lake of the Woods. Boston and New York: 1994. V. 68; 69; 70; 71; 72
Northern Lights. New York: 1975. V. 68; 69; 72; 73
The Nuclear Age. New York: 1985. V. 69; 70; 71; 72; 73
Speaking of Courage. Santa Barbara: 1980. V. 68; 70; 72; 73
The Things They Carried. Boston: 1990. V. 68; 69; 70; 71; 72; 73
The Things They Carried. Franklin Center: 1990. V. 68; 69
The Things They Carried. New York: 1990. V. 73
Tomcat in Love. Franklin Center: 1998. V. 71; 72
Tomcat in Love. New York: 1998. V. 68

O'BRIEN, WILLIAM, MRS.
Unseen Friends. London: 1912. V. 70

OBSERVATIONS of the Present Tything System.... London: 1822. V. 71

OBSERVATIONS on the Case Now Depending in Parliament, Respecting the Isle of Man, in Reference to the Statement and Appendix Circulated in Support of the Duke of Atholl's Petition. London: 1805. V. 73

OBSERVATIONS On the Conduct of Great Britain, with Regard to the Negociations and Other Transactions Abroad. London: 1729. V. 71

OBSERVATIONS On the Conduct of Great-Britain, in Respect to Foreign Affairs. London: 1742. V. 73

OBSERVATIONS on the Parables of Our Saviour. London: 1825. V. 72

OBSERVATIONS Upon a Late Pamphlet, intitled, Miscellaneous Thoughts &c. London: 1742. V. 73

OBSERVATIONS Upon the Four Gospels; Shewing Their Defects...Thereby Evincing the Necessity of Revising the Whole by Authority.... Geneva: 1789. V. 71

O'BYRNE, CATHAL
The Gaelic Source of the Bronte Genius. 1933. V. 70

O'BYRNE, JOHN
Pikes Peak or Bust and Historical Sketchers of The Wild West. Colorado Springs: 1922. V. 72

O'CALLAGHAN, JEREMIAH
Usury; or, Lending at Interest; Also the Exaction and Payment of Certain Church-Fees.... London: 1828. V. 70

O'CASEY, SEAN
The Flying Wasp. London: 1937. V. 70
Oak Leaves and Lavender. 1947. V. 69
The Story of the Irish Citizen Army. Dublin: 1919. V. 72
Windfalls. Stories, Poems and Plays. London: 1934. V. 71

THE OCEAN; A Description of Wonders and Important Products of the Sea. London: 1830. V. 68

OCEAN Liners of the Past. The Cunard White Star Quadruple Liner Queen Mary. London: 1972. V. 68

OCHINO, BERNARDINO
A Dialogue of Polygamy. (with) A Dialogue of Divorce. London: 1657. V. 71

OCHS, SIDNEY
Axoplasmic Transport and Its Relation to Other Nerve Functions. New York: 1982. V. 68

O'CIANAIN, TADHG
The Flight of the Earls. 1916. V. 70

O'COIGLY, JAMES
The Trial of James O'Coigly, Otherwise Called James Quigley, Otherwise Called James John Fivey, Arthur O'Connor, Esq., John Binns, John Allen and Jeremia Leary, for High Treason, Under a Special Commission, at Maidstone in Kent on Monday the Twenty-First. London: 1798. V. 68

O'CONAIRE, PADRAIC
Field and Fair; Travels with a Donkey in Ireland. Dublin and Cork: 1929. V. 73

O'CONNELL, CAROL
Mallory's Oracle. London: 1994. V. 68; 69; 70; 71; 72
Mallory's Oracle. New York: 1994. V. 68; 72; 73
The Man Who Cast Two Shadows. New York: 1995. V. 73
The Man Who Lied to Women. London: 1995. V. 68; 69; 70; 73

O'CONNELL, DANIEL
Correspondence of Daniel O'Connell the Liberator.... London: 1888. V. 71
A Full Report of the Proceedings of the Great Meeting of the Catholics of London, Held at Freemasons' Hall, on the fifteenth day of July 1839.... London: 1839. V. 73
Memoir of Ireland, Native and Saxon. 1844. V. 69

O'CONNELL, JEFFERY C.
The Irish in the Revolution and The Civil War.... Washington, D.C: 1903. V. 72

O'CONNELL, MARY
Living with Saints. New York: 2001. V. 69; 72

O'CONNELL, NICHOLAS
At the Fields's End. Seattle: 1987. V. 73

O'CONNOR, EDWIN
The Last Hurrah. Boston;: 1956. V. 70

O'CONNOR, FLANNERY
The Artificial Nigger and Other Stories. London: 1957. V. 68; 73
Everything that Rises Must Converge. New York: 1965. V. 69; 72
Everything that Rises Must Converge. New York: 1966. V. 69
A Good Man is Hard to Find. New York: 1955. V. 71
A Good Man is Hard to Find. London: 1968. V. 71
The Habit of Being. New York: 1979. V. 68; 72
Mystery and Manners - Occasional Prose. London: 1972. V. 71
Wise Blood. New York: 1952. V. 68; 69; 70; 71; 73
Wise Blood. London: 1955. V. 73

O'CONNOR, FRANK
Guests of the Nation. 1931. V. 71
Lords and Commons. Dublin: 1938. V. 69; 71
The Saint and Mary Kate. London: 1932. V. 68
A Short History of Irish Literature. New York: 1967. V. 72
Traveller's Samples: Stories and Tales. London: 1951. V. 70

O'CONNOR, G. B.
Elizabethan Ireland, Native and English. 1903. V. 69

O'CONNOR, JACK
Game in the Desert. 1993. V. 69; 70; 72; 73

O'CONNOR, LAUREL
Drinking with Twain. 1936. V. 70

O'CONNOR, MARTIN
An Account of the Nature and Conditions of a Charter, To Be Granted for the Working and Manufacturing Mines and Minerals in Ireland.... London: 1745. V. 73

O'CONNOR, P. F.
Shark!. 1954. V. 68

O'CONNOR, PHILIP
Memoirs of a Public Baby. London: 1958. V. 70

O'CONNOR, RICHARD
Pat Garrett. New York: 1960. V. 69

O'CONNOR, ROBERT
Buffalo Soldiers. New York: 1993. V. 69; 70; 71

O'CONNOR, ROGER
Chronicles of Eri: Being the History of the Gaal Sciot Iber; or The Irish People. 1822. V. 71

O'CONNOR, V. C. SCOTT
The Charm Of Kashmir. London: 1920. V. 72

O'CROULEY, DON PEDRO ALONSO
A Description of the Kingdom of New Spain. San Francisco: 1972. V. 68; 71; 72

O'CURRY, EUGENE
Lectures on the Manuscript Materials of Ancient Irish History. 1873. V. 69; 73

O'DAY, EDWARD F.
Claude Garamond and His Place in the Renaissance. Eugene: 1940. V. 68; 72

AN ODD Bestiary, or a Compendium of Instructive and Entertaining Descriptions of Animals, Culled from Five Centuries of Travelers' Accounts.... Williamsburg: 1982. V. 70

ODDY, JOSHUA JEPSON
A Sketch for the Improvement of Political, Commercial and Local, Interests of Great Britain.... London: 1810. V. 73

AN ODE Addressed to the Scotch Junto, and their American Commission, on the Late Quarrel Between Commissioner Ed-n and Commissioner J-hnst-ne.... London;: 1778. V. 73

ODEN, BILL
Early Days on the Texas-New Mexico Plains. Canyon: 1965. V. 68

ODES and Sonnets. London: 1859. V. 68

ODETS, CLIFFORD
Three Plays: Awake and Sing! Waiting for Lefty, Till the Day I Die. New York: 1935. V. 73

ODLUM, JEROME
Each Dawn I Die. Indianapolis/New York: 1938. V. 71

ODOM, ANNE
A Taste For Splendor. Russian Imperial and European Treasures. Alexandria: 1998. V. 72

ODOM, MARY MC CALEB
Lenare; a Story of the Southern Revolution and Other Poems. New Orleans: 1866. V. 69

O'DONNELL, ELIOT
Family Ghosts and Ghostly Phenomena. 1933. V. 69

O'DONNELL, FRANK HUGH
A History of the Irish Parliamentary Party. 1910. V. 70

O'DONNELL, LILLIAN
Death Schuss. New York: 1966. V. 69
The Sleeping Beauty Murders. New York: 1967. V. 69; 71

O'DONNELL, PEADAR
Adrigoole. London: 1929. V. 68

O'DONNELL, PETER
Cobra Trap. London: 1996. V. 71; 72; 73
Dead Man's Handle. London: 1985. V. 68
Dead Man's Handle. New York: 1986. V. 72; 73
Dragon's Claw. London: 1978. V. 68
Dragon's Claw. New York: 1985. V. 72
I, Lucifer. 1967. V. 68; 69
I, Lucifer. London: 1967. V. 68; 70
The Impossible Virgin. Garden City: 1971. V. 69
Last Day in Limbo. London: 1976. V. 70; 71
Merlin's Keep. 1977. V. 68
Modesty Blaise. London: 1965. V. 69; 71
Modesty Blaise: First American Edition Series 1-5. Park Forest: 1981-1984. V. 73
The Night of Morningstar. London: 1982. V. 68
The Night Of The Morningstar. New York: 1987. V. 72
Pieces of Modesty. New York: 1986. V. 70; 73
Sabre-Tooth. London: 1966. V. 70
The Silver Mistress. London: 1973. V. 68; 71; 73
The Silver Mistress. Cambridge, Mass: 1981. V. 68; 72
The Silver Mistress. New York: 1984. V. 73
A Taste for Death. London: 1969. V. 70
The Xanadu Talisman. London: 1981. V. 68

O'DONNELL, RED
Chet Atkins. Nashville: 1967. V. 70

O'DONOVAN, JOHN
The Economic History of Live Stock in Ireland. 1940. V. 69

O'DRISCOLL, W. JUSTIN
A Memoir of Daniel Maclise, R.A. 1871. V. 69

ODUM, H. T.
A Tropical Rain Forest.... Oak Ridge: 1970. V. 72

ODUM, HAROLD W.
The Negro and His Songs: a Study of Typical Negro Songs in the South. Chapel Hill: 1925. V. 69

OE, KENZABURO
Hiroshima Notes. Tokyo: 1981. V. 71
Japan, the Ambiguous and Myself. New York: 1995. V. 69
Nip the Buds, Shoot the Kids. London and New York: 1995. V. 69
Teach Us to Outgrow Our Madness. New York: 1994. V. 69

OEHLER, BEN GOTTLIEB F.
Description of a Journey and Visit to the Pawnee Indians - April 22- May 18, 1851 and a Description of the Manners and Customs of the Pawnee Indians. New York: 1914. V. 68; 73

OEHME, W.
Bold Romantic Gardens, the New World Landscapes of Oehme and Van Sweden. Reston: 1990. V. 68

OEHSER, PAUL H.
Sons of Science. New York: 1949. V. 68

OEMLER, MARIE CONWAY
Slippy McGee, Sometimes Known as the Butterfly Man. New York: 1920. V. 69
Two Shall Be Born. New York: 1922. V. 70

OENSLAGER, D.
Stage Design: Four Centuries of Science Invention. New York: 1975. V. 72

OETTINGER, M.
Folk Treasures of Mexico. New York: 1990. V. 69

OETZMANN, JOHN
The Town Mouse and Other Fables. London: 1875. V. 72

O'FAOLAIN, NUALA
My Dream of You. London: 2001. V. 71

O'FAOLAIN, SEAN
Bird Alone. 1936. V. 70
The Born Genius: A Short Story. Detroit: 1936. V. 72
The Collected Stories of.... 1980-1982. V. 69
De Valera, a New Biography. 1939. V. 70
King of the Beggars; A Life of Daniel O'Connell. New York: 1938. V. 70
Midsummer Night Madness and Other Stories. London: 1932. V. 69; 70; 73
A Nest of Simple Folk. London: 1933. V. 73
A Nest of Simple Folk. New York: 1934. V. 72
The Silver Branch, a Collection of the Best of Old Irish Lyrics. 1938. V. 69

O'FERRALL, CHARLES T.
Forty Years of Active Service. New York and Washington: 1904. V. 69; 70

OFFERS, SIBYLLE VON
Was Marilenchen Erlebte! (What Happened to Little Marlene). Eklingen: 1905. V. 70

OFFICER Buckle and Gloria. New York: 1995. V. 71

OFFICIAL Assignees. Reform in Bankruptcy. Remarks and Suggestions by an Accountant, Vide Mercator, Morning Herald July 19, 1838. London: 1841. V. 71

OFFICIAL Brand Book of the State of South Dakota. Pierre: 1937. V. 71

OFFICIAL Records Union and Confederate Armies. Series II. Washington: 1894. V. 71

OFFICIAL Report of the Battle of Chickamauga. Richmond: 1864. V. 69; 70

THE OFFICINA Bodoni: The Operation of the Hand-Press During the First Six Years of Its Work. Paris and New York: 1929. V. 71

OFFICINA BODONI
German Illumination. I. Carolingian Miniatures. II. Ottonian Miniatures. Florence: 1928. V. 70

OFFICINA BODONI, VERONA.
Pastonchi: a Specimen of a New Letter for Use on the Monotype. 1928. V. 68

OFFIT, SIDNEY
Only a Girl Like You. New York: 1972. V. 69

OFFUTT, CHRIS
The Good Brother. New York: 1997. V. 68; 72
Kentucky Straight. New York: 1992. V. 69; 70
Out of the Woods. New York: 1999. V. 70; 72; 73
The Same River Twice. NY: 1993. V. 73
Tar Pit Love, Lettered. Castle Rock: 2000. V. 70
Two-Eleven All Around. Santa Monica: 1998. V. 70; 73

O'FLAHERTY, DANIEL
General Jo Shelby. Undefeated Rebel. 1954. V. 68

O'FLAHERTY, JOHN T.
A Sketch of the History and Antiquities of the Southern Islands of Aran, Lying of the West Coast of Ireland.... Dublin;: 1824. V. 73

O'FLAHERTY, JOSEPH H.
The South Coast and Los Angeles. Los Angeles: 1992. V. 68

O'FLAHERTY, LIAM
The Black Soul. 1929. V. 69; 73
The House of Gold. 1929. V. 69
The Mountain Tavern, and Other Stories. London: 1929. V. 70
The Puritan. 1932. V. 70
Shame the Devil. 1934. V. 69
Skerrett. New York: 1932. V. 69; 71
Spring Sowing. London: 1924. V. 73
Thy Neighbors Wife. 1923. V. 71
Thy Neighbor's Wife. London: 1923. V. 69; 70
A Tourist's Guide to Ireland. 1929. V. 69
The Wild Swan and Other Stories. London: 1932. V. 69; 71; 73

O'GALLCHOBHAIR, PRIONNSIAS
A History of Ireland Under the Union 1801-1922. 1952. V. 70

OGDEN, ADELE
Russian Sea-Otter and Seal Hunting on the California Coast 1803-1841. 1933. V. 73

OGDEN, GEORGE
War Letters from the West. New Bedford: 1823. V. 73

OGDEN, HENRY ALEXANDER
Uniforms of the United States Army. New York: 1959. V. 72

OGDEN, J.
Yorkshire's River Derwent. 1974. V. 68

OGDEN, PETER SKENE
Traits of American Indian Life "By a Fur Trader.". San Francisco: 1933. V. 72

OGDEN, WILLIAM
Mercantile Architecture. London: 1892. V. 71

OGG, DAVID
England in the Reign of Charles II. Oxford: 1955. V. 73

OGILBY, J. D.
Edible Fishes and Crustaceans of New South Wales. Sydney: 1893. V. 68

OGILBY, JOHN
The Traveller's Pocket Book; or Ogilby and Morgan's Book of Roads. London: 1764. V. 73

OGILVIE, CAMPBELL P.
Argentina. London: 1910. V. 71

OGILVIE, GEORGE W.
Duckworth's Encyclopaedia of Useful Information and Atlas of the World. Rochdale: 1893?. V. 71

OGILVIE, W.
Lecture on the Yukon Gold Fields (Canada) Delivered at Victoria, B. C... Revised, Amplified, and Authorized by the Lecturer. Victoria: 1897. V. 71

OGILVIE, WILL
A Handful of Leather. London: 1928. V. 73
My Life in the Open. London: 1908. V. 69

OGILVIE-GRANT, W. E.
The Gun At Home and Abroad. British Game Birds and Wildfowl. London: 1912. V. 73

OGILVIE-GRANT, W. R.
General Index to a Hand-List of the Genera and Species of Birds. London: 1912. V. 73

OGILVIE-GRANT, W. R. continued
Guide to the Gallery of Birds in the Department of Zoology, British Musueum. London: 1910. V. 73
A Handbook to the Game Birds, 2 Volumes. 1896. V. 70; 71

OGLE, NATHANIEL
Marianne the Last of the Asmonean Princesses: a Historical Novel of Palestine. London: 1889. V. 68

OGLE, W.
Aristotle on the Parts of Animals. London: 1882. V. 68

O'GORMAN, H.
Mexican Flowering Trees and Plants. Mexico City: 1961. V. 68

O'GRADY, ROHAN
Pippin's Journal or Rosemary is for Remembrance. London: 1962. V. 72

O'HAIR, MADALYN
An Atheist Epic. Austin: 1989. V. 68

O'HANLON, JOHN
The Life of Saint Malachy O'Morgair. 1859. V. 69

O'HANLON, JOHN C.
Life and Scenery in Missouri, Reminiscences of a Missouri Priest. Dublin: 1890. V. 70

O'HANLON, REDMOND
No Mercy. New York: 1997. V. 72

O'HARA, CLEOPHAS C.
The Badland Formations of the Black Hills Region In South Dakota School of Mines Bulletin No. 9 Department of Geology. Rapid City: 1910. V. 71

O'HARA, FRANK
Lunch Poems. San Francisco: 1964. V. 71
Meditations in an Emergency. New York: 1957. V. 68

O'HARA, JOHN
Appointment in Samarra. New York: 1934. V. 70; 71; 73
The Big Laugh. New York: 1962. V. 72
The Cape Cod Lighter, A Collection Of 23 New Stories.. New York: 1962. V. 72
A Family Party. New York: 1956. V. 70
The Farmer's Hotel. New York: 1951. V. 69; 72
Files on Parade. New York: 1939. V. 71
From the Terrace. New York: 1958. V. 70
Hope of Heaven. New York: 1938. V. 71
Hope of Heaven. New York: 1946. V. 72
Ourselves to Know. New York: 1960. V. 70
Sermons and Soda-Water. New York: 1960. V. 71; 72
Sermons and Soda-Water. London: 1961. V. 71
Ten North Frederick. New York: 1955. V. 68; 70; 72

O'HARA, RUSSELL E.
The Kingdom of Dreams. New York: 1926. V. 70

O'HARE, KATE RICHARDS CUNNINGHAM
In Prison, Being a Report by...to the President of the United States as to the Conditions Under Which Women Federal Prisoners are Confined.... St. Louis: 1920. V. 72

OHASHI, S.
Japanese Floral Arrangement.... New York: 1937. V. 68

OHBA, H.
The Himalayan Plants. Tokyo: 1988. V. 68

O'HEGARTY, P. S.
A History of Ireland Under the Union 1801-1922. 1952. V. 70

O'HEYNE, JOHN
The Irish Dominicans of the 17th century. 1902. V. 69; 70

OHIO Archaeological and Historical Publications. Columbus: 1900-1913. V. 70

OHIO CARRIAGE MANUFACTURING CO., CINCINNATI
Split Hickory Vehicles, Oak Tanned Harness. Annual Catalog no. 33. 1907. V. 68

OHWI, J.
Flora of Japan. Washington: 1965. V. 73

OHWL, J.
Flora of Japan. Washington: 1984. V. 69

OINOPHILUS, BONIFACE
Ebrietatis Enconium. New York: 1910. V. 68

OISTROS, PSEUD.
Truffle Eater. London: 1933. V. 70

OKAMURA, O.
Fishes of the Okinawa Trough and the Adjacent Waters. Tokyo: 1984-1985. V. 72

O'KANE, MICHAEL M.
Woman's Place in the World. Dublin: 1913. V. 72

O'KANE, WALTER COLLINS
Sun in the City. Norman: 1950. V. 69

OKE, RICHARD
The Oxford University Dramatic Society Presents Hassan. Oxford: 1931. V. 70

O'KEEFE, JOHN
O'Keefe's Legacy to His Daughter, Being the Poetical Works of the Late John O'Keefe, Esq. the Dramatic Author. London: 1834. V. 72
Recollections of the Life of John O'Keefe. London: 1826. V. 72

O'KEEFE, RUFE
Cowboy Life. San Antonio: 1936. V. 68

O'KEEFE, TOM
The Art of Ray Swanson - Celebrating People and Lifestyles. Carefree: 1994. V. 69

O'KEEFFE, GEORGIA
Georgia O'Keeffe. New York: 1976. V. 68

OKELY, FRANCIS
Dawnings of the Everlasting Gospel-Light, Glimmering Out of a Private Heart's Epistolary Correspondence. Northampton: 1775. V. 68

OKEN, LOENZ
Elements of Physiophilosophy. London: 1847. V. 72

OKITO, PSEUD.
Quality Magic. London: 1921. V. 68

OKLAHOMA the Beautiful Land. Oklahoma City: 1943. V. 70

OKRI, BEN
Astonishing the Gods. London: 1995. V. 68; 72
Dangerous Love. London: 1996. V. 68
Incidents at the Shrine. London: 1986. V. 68

OKUSA, YEJITSU
Principal Teachings of the tRue Sect of Pure Land. Tokyo: 1910. V. 72

O'LAVERTY, JAMES
The History of the Parish of Holywood, from the Earliest Times, Being a Part of An Historical Account of the Diocese of Down and Connor, Ancient and Modern.... Belfast: 1885. V. 72

OLCOTT, FRANCES JENKINS
The Adventures of Haroun Er Raschid and Other Tales from the Arabian Nights. New York: 1923. V. 73

THE OLD Ballad of the Boy and the Mantle. 1900. V. 69

OLD Ballads, Historical and Narrative with Some of Modern Date. London: 1784. V. 72

THE OLD Ballads of the Babes in the Wood. London: 1972. V. 69

OLD Cambridge. A Series of Original Sketches with Descriptive LetterPress by W. B. Redfarn. Cambridge: 1876. V. 72

OLD Dame Trot and Her Comical Cat. New York: 1869. V. 71; 73
OLD Dame Trot and Her Comical Cat. New York: 1891. V. 72

OLD England: a Pictorial Museum of Regal, Ecclesiastical, Baronial, Municipal and Popular Antiquities. London: 1845. V. 69

OLD England's Worthies: a Gallery of Portraits.... London: 1847. V. 69

THE OLD Fairy Tales Comprising Hop-O'-My-Thumb and Beauty and the Beast. London: 1915. V. 73

THE OLD Fairy Tales Comprising Puss in Boots and Jack and the Bean-Stalk. London: 1915. V. 73

THE OLD Fairy Tales Comprising Valentine and Orson and Jack and the Bean-Stalk. London: 1920. V. 73

THE OLD Fashion Farmer's Motives for Leaving the Church of England, and Embracing the Roman Catholic Faith.... London?: 1778. V. 69

OLD Friends with New Faces. London: 1870. V. 68

OLD Gingerbread and the Schoolboys. London: 1858. V. 70

OLD King Cole and Other Nursery Rhymes. London: 1904. V. 72

OLD King Cole's Book of Nursery Rhymes. London: 1901. V. 73

THE Old Man Who Made the Dead Trees Blossom. Tokyo: 1910. V. 72

OLD Mother Hubbard. London: 1855. V. 69

OLD Mother Hubbard and Her Dog. 1918. V. 68

OLD Mother Hubbard and Her Wonderful Dog. Coppestown: 1828. V. 73

OLD Mother Mitten and Her Funny Kitten. New York: 1850-1852. V. 70

THE OLD Nursery Rhymes. London: 1933. V. 72

OLD Nursery Stories. New York: 1892. V. 70

THE OLD Nursery Stories and Rhymes. London. V. 72

OLD, Old Tales Retold. Chicago: 1923. V. 68

OLD Old Tales Retold: Eight Best Loved Folk Stories for Children. Chicago: 1922. V. 70

OLD Poor Robin. An Almanack.... London: 1789. V. 69

OLD Robin Gray. London: 1780?. V. 70

OLD Time Rhymes. London: 1915. V. 72

THE OLD West Master Index. Alexandria: 1980. V. 68

THE OLD Woman and Her Pig. London: 1890. V. 71

OLDE, P.
The Grevilles Book. Portland: 1995. V. 68

OLDENBERG, HERMANN
Buddha. London: 1904. V. 70

OLDENBURG, CLAES
Notes in Hand. London: 1971. V. 69
Proposals for Monuments and Buildings 1965-1969. Chicago: 1969. V. 72
Store Days. New York: 1967. V. 70; 72

OLDEROGGE, D.
Negro Art from the Institute of Ethnography, Leningrad. Prague: 1969. V. 69

OLDFELLOW, ALFRED
Uncle Nat; or, the Good Time Which George and Frank Had, Trapping, Fishing, Camping Out, etc. New York: 1865. V. 69

OLDFIELD, CLAUDE
The Beast. Belfast: 1936. V. 69; 70
A Hair Divides. London: 1930. V. 68
Julian Grant Loses His Way. London: 1933. V. 69
This Was Ivor Trent. London: 1935. V. 68
This Was Ivor Trent. New York: 1935. V. 70

OLDFIELD, EDMUND
A Topographical and Historical Account of Wainfleet and the Wapentake of Candelshoe in the County of Lincoln. London: 1829. V. 73

OLDFIELD, T. H. B.
The Representative History of Great Britain and Ireland. 1816. V. 71

OLDHAM, J.
English Blindstamped Bindings and Blind Panels of English Binders. Cambridge: 1952-1958. V. 70

OLDHAM, JOHN
Satyrs Upon the Jesuits: Written in the Year 1679...Together with the Satyr Against Vertue and Some Other Pieces by the Same Hand. London: 1681. V. 71
Satyrs Upon the Jesuits: Written in the Year 1679. (with) Poems and Translations. (with) Some New Pieces Never Before Publish'd. London: 1682. V. 69

OLDHAM, T.
On the Geological Structure of Part of the Khasi Hills, with Observations on the Meteorology and Ethnology of the District. Calcutta: 1854. V. 68

OLDMIXON, JOHN
The History of Addresses. London: 1709. V. 69; 72

OLDS, SHARON
The Wellspring. New York: 1996. V. 69

O'LEARY, A. E.
Rambles thro' Memory Lane with Characters I Knew. Richibutco;: 1937. V. 73

O'LEARY, ARTHUR
An Essay on Toleration; or, Mr. O'Leary's Plea for Liberty of Conscience. Philadelphia: 1785. V. 73
Miscellaneous Tracts...Containing. I. The Defence of the Divinity of Christ, and Immortality of the Soul...II. Loyalty Asserted....III. An Address to the Common People of Ireland, on Occasion of an Apprehended Invasion by the French and Spaniards.... London: 1782. V. 71

O'LEARY, PETER
Travels and Experiences in Canada, the Red River Territory and the United States. London: 1874. V. 73

OLINA, GIOVANNI PIETRO
Uccelliera Overo Discorso della Natura e Properieta di Diversi Uccelli, e in Particolare.... Rome: 1684. V. 72

OLIPHANT, J. ORIN
On the Cattle Rangers of the Oregon Country. Seattle: 1968. V. 71

OLIPHANT, LAURENCE
Episodes in a Life of Adventure or Moss From a Rolling Stone. Edinburgh: 1887. V. 71
The Land of Gilead with Excursions in Lebanon. Edinburgh: 1880. V. 69; 71
Minnesota and the Far West. Edinburgh: 1855. V. 71
Narrative of the Earl of Elgin's Mission to China and Japan in 1857, '58, '59. Edinburgh and London: 1859. V. 70; 71
Patriots and Filibusters or Incidents and Political and Exploratory Travel. Edinburgh: 1860. V. 69; 71
The Russian Shores Of The Black Sea In The Autumn of 1852. London: 1853. V. 72

OLIPHANT, MARGARET
The Autobiography and Letters. Edinburgh: 1899. V. 70
The Autobiography and Letters of Mrs. M. O. W. Oliphant. New York: 1899. V. 71; 73
The Makers of Florence: Dante, Giotto, Savanarola and Their City. London: 1877. V. 68
The Makers of Venice. London: 1892. V. 68
Mrs. Arthur. London: 1891. V. 68

OLIPHANT, NIGEL
A Diary of the Siege of the Legations in Peking During the Summer of 1900. London: 1901. V. 69

OLIVA, LEO E.
Soldiers on the Santa Fe Trail. Norman: 1967. V. 68

OLIVER, CHAD
Mists of Dawn. 1952. V. 73
Mists of Dawn. Philadelphia: 1952. V. 69

OLIVER, EDITH PATTON
Miss Anna. Oakbrook: 1967. V. 72

OLIVER, GEORGE
The History and Antiquities of the Town and Minster of Beverley, in the County of York. Beverley: 1829. V. 69

OLIVER, ISABELLA
Poems on Various Subjects. Carlisle: 1805. V. 73

OLIVER, JOHN R.
Article Thirty-Two. New York: 1931. V. 69
The Geology of St. Helena. 1869. V. 68

OLIVER, JOHN RATHBONE
Victim and Victor. New York: 1928. V. 71

OLIVER, MARY
House of Light. Boston: 1990. V. 69
The Leaf and the Cloud. Cambridge: 2000. V. 72
The Leaf and the Cloud. New York: 2000. V. 69
No Voyage and Other Poems. Boston: 1965. V. 69

OLIVER, PAUL
Aspects of the Blues Tradition. New York: 1970. V. 73
Screening the Blues. London: 1968. V. 71
The Story Of The Blues. Radnor: 1982. V. 72

OLIVER, PEARLEEN
A Brief History of the Colored Baptists of Nova Scotia 1782-1953. Halifax: 1953. V. 71

OLIVER, PETER
The Puritan Commonwealth...Government in Massachusetts...from Its Rise to the Abrogation of the First Charter. Boston;: 1856. V. 69

OLIVER, RICHARD ALDWORTH
Sketches in New Zealand. Martinborough: 1977. V. 71

OLIVER, SAMUEL PASFIELD
Madagascar: an Historical and Descriptive Account. London: 1886. V. 69
The True Story of the French Dispute in Madagascar. London: 1885. V. 71

OLIVER, STEPHEN
The Old English Squire, a Song: the Words by Stephen Oliver. 1838. V. 71

OLIVER, W. R. B.
New Zealand Birds. Wellington: 1930. V. 73

OLIVER, WILLIAM
A Practical Essay on the Use and Abuse of Warm Bathing in Gout Cases. Bath: 1753. V. 72

OLLANTA. *An Ancient Ynca Drama. Translated from the original Quicha.* London: 1871. V. 73

OLLIER, LOUIS XAVIER EDOUARD LEOPOLD
Trait Experimental et Clinique de la Regeneration des Os ed de la Production Ardificielle du Tissu Osseux. Paris: 1867. V. 72

OLLIVIER, C. P.
Traite de La Moelle Epiniere et de Ses Maladies, Ourvrage Couronne par La Societe Royale De Medecine de Marseille.... Paris: 1824. V. 70

OLLYFFE, GEORGE
An Essay Humbly Offer'd for an Act of Parliament to Prevent Capital Crimes, and Loss of Many Lives.... London: 1731. V. 69

OLMSTEAD, EDWARD
Clip-Joint. London: 1938. V. 72

OLMSTEAD, ROBERT
America by Land. New York: 1993. V. 72
Soft Water. New York: 1988. V. 72

OLMSTED, FRANCIS ALLYN
Incident of a Whaling Voyage. New York: 1841. V. 71

OLMSTED, FREDERICK LAW
A Journey in the Back Country. New York: 1861. V. 72
A Journey in the Seaboard Slave Slates. New York and London: 1856. V. 70
Journey through Texas; or a Saddle-Trip on the Southwestern Frontier.... New York: 1859. V. 69
The Papers of Frederick Law Olmsted. Baltimore;: 1983. V. 68
Walks and Talks of an American Farmer in England. New York: 1852. V. 68
Walks and Talks of an American Farmer in England. Columbus: 1859. V. 72

OLMSTED, J. M. D.
Francois Croll, Pioneer in Experimental Physiology and Scientific Medicine in 19th Century France. New York: 1944. V. 68; 72
Francois Magendie. Pioneer in Experimental Physiology and Scientific Medicine in XIX Century France. New York: 1944. V. 68

OLMSTED, T.
The Musical Olio.... New London: 1811. V. 68

OLNEY, AMSDEN & SONS
Olney, Amsden & Sons, London & Redditch, Manufacturers and Warehousemen. London: 1897. V. 68

OLNEY, P. J. S.
Wildfowl Paintings of Henry Jones. 1987. V. 69

O'LOCHLAINN, COLM
Irish Street Ballads. London: 1939. V. 69

OLSEN, D. B.
The Cat Wears a Noose. Garden City: 1944. V. 70
Cat's Claw. Garden City: 1943. V. 70
Cats Don't Smile. Garden City: 1945. V. 70
Gallows for the Groom. Garden City: 1947. V. 70

OLSEN, JACK
Night of the Grizzlies. New York: 1969. V. 68

OLSEN, JOHN
The Land Beyond Time. A Modern Exploration of Australia's Northwest Frontiers. Melbourne: 1984. V. 70

OLSEN, TILLIE
Silences. New York: 1978. V. 68; 72
Tell Me a Riddle. London: 1964. V. 68; 69
Tell me a Riddle. New York: 1969. V. 68
Tell Me a Riddle. New York: 1978. V. 73
Yonnondio from the Thirties. 1974. V. 68

OLSON, CHARLES
A Bibliography on America for Ed Dorn. San Francisco: 1964. V. 71
Causal Mythology. San Francisco: 1969. V. 68
Charles Olson in Connecticut; Last Lectures as Heard by John Cech, Oliver Ford, Peter Rittner. Iowa City: 1974. V. 73
The Distances: Poems. New York: 1960. V. 71
Maximus, from Dogtown - I. San Francisco: 1961. V. 73
The Maximus Poems. New York: 1960. V. 70; 71
The Maximus Poems. 1-10. (with) The Maximus Poems 11-22. Stuttgart: 1953-1956. V. 73
Maximus Poems IV, V, VI. London: 1968. V. 72
Mayan Letters. Palma de Mallorca: 1953. V. 73
O'Ryan 1 2 3 4 5 6 7 8 9 10. San Francisco: 1965. V. 70; 72
Proprioception. 1965. V. 71
Proprioception. San Francisco: 1965. V. 69
Some Early Poems. Iowa City: 1978. V. 70; 72
The Special View of History. Berkeley: 1970. V. 73

OLSON, JAMES R.
Ulzana. Boston: 1973. V. 69

OLSON, T. A.
Pollution and Marine Ecology. London: 1967. V. 72

OLSON, TOBY
Seaview. New York: 1982. V. 68

OLSSON, BENGT
Memphis Blues and Jug Bands. London: 1970. V. 73

OLUFSEN, O.
The Emir of Bokhara and His Country. Copenhagen: 1911. V. 71

O'MALLEY, BRIAN
The Animals of Saint Gregory. Rhandirmyn: 1981. V. 71

O'MALLEY, CHARLES D.
Andreas Vesalius of Brussels 1514-1564. 1964. V. 70; 73
Andreas Vesalius of Brussels, 1514-1564. Berkeley: 1964. V. 68

OMAN, CHARLES
A History of the Art of the Middle Ages. Boston and New York: 1924. V. 68

OMAN, JOHN CAMPBELL
The Brahmans, Theists and Muslims of India. London: 1907. V. 72

OMAR KHAYYAM
A New Translation of Omar Khayyam.... 1922. V. 71
The Quatrains of Omar Khayyam of Nishapur. Worcester: 1906. V. 69
The Golden Cockerel Rubaiyat. Waltham St. Lawrence: 1938. V. 70
Rubaiyat. London: 1872. V. 72
Rubaiyat. Boston: 1886. V. 68
Rubaiyat. New York: 1900. V. 71; 72
Rubaiyat. London: 1901. V. 69
The Rubaiyat. London and New York: 1903. V. 68; 70
Rubaiyat. London: 1909. V. 68; 71
The Rubaiyat. 1913. V. 73
Rubaiyat. London: 1915. V. 72
Rubaiyat. London: 1920. V. 68; 71
The Rubaiyat. Sydney: 1920. V. 68
Rubaiyat. New York: 1921. V. 69
The Rubaiyat. London: 1924. V. 68; 69; 70; 71
Rubaiyat. London: 1930. V. 73
Rubaiyat. London: 1930. V. 70
Rubaiyat. New York: 1932. V. 72
The Rubaiyat. 1935. V. 69
The Rubaiyat. Cleveland and New York: 1938. V. 72
The Rubaiyat. Leigh-on-Sea: 1944. V. 71

OMBROSI, LUCA
The Last of the Medici. Florence: 1930. V. 68
The Last of the Medici. Orioli: 1930. V. 71

O'MEARA, BARRY E.
Napoleon in Exile, or a Voice from St. Helena. 1822. V. 70
Napoleon in Exile; or, a Voice from St. Helena. London: 1822. V. 69

OMEROD, OLIVER
O Full True on Perfikler Okewut o Wat Me Un Maw.... Rochdale: 1864. V. 71

OMOND, G. W. T.
Bruges And West Flanders. London: 1906. V. 72

ON the Nursery Stairs. Akron: 1906. V. 69

ON the Origin of Sam Weller, and the Real Cause of the Success of the Posthumous Papers of the Pickwick Club. London: 1883. V. 69

ON the Plains-The Companion Library. Boston: 1897. V. 71

O'NAN, STEWART
The Circus Fire. New York: 2000. V. 70; 72
In the Walled City. Pittsburgh: 1993. V. 68; 69; 70; 72
The Names Of The Dead. New York: 1996. V. 72
A Prayer for the Dying. New York: 1999. V. 70; 72
Snow Angels. New York: 1994. V. 69; 71; 72
The Speed Queen. New York: 1997. V. 72
A World Away. New York: 1998. V. 72

ONCE Upon a Time. 1910. V. 70

ONDAATJE, MICHAEL
Anil's Ghost. London: 2000. V. 68
Anil's Ghost. New York: 2000. V. 70; 72
Anil's Ghost. Toronto: 2000. V. 68
Claude Glass. Toronto: 1979. V. 72
The Collected Works of Billy the Kid. New York: 1974. V. 72
Coming Through Slaughter. Toronto: 1976. V. 72
Coming Through Slaughter. New York: 1977. V. 72
Coming Through Slaughter. London: 1979. V. 68; 72
Coming through Slaughter. New York: 1979. V. 68; 71
The English Patient. London: 1992. V. 68; 70; 72; 73
The English Patient. New York: 1992. V. 69; 70; 72
The English Patient. Toronto: 1992. V. 68; 69; 70; 71; 72
The English Patient. Norwalk: 1999. V. 68
Handwriting. Toronto: 1998. V. 68; 73
Handwriting. New York: 1999. V. 72
In the Skin of a Lion. London: 1987. V. 70
In the Skin of a Lion. New York: 1987. V. 72
In the Skin of a Lion. Toronto: 1987. V. 72
In the Skin of a Lion. New York: 1988. V. 68; 71
Leonard Cohen. Toronto: 1970. V. 71; 72
Rat Jelly & Other Poems, 1963-1978. London: 1980. V. 72
Running in the Family. New York and London: 1982. V. 69; 72; 73
Running in the Family. Toronto: 1982. V. 69; 72
There's A Trick With a Knife I'm Learning to Do. Poems 1963-1978. New York: 1979. V. 68; 69

100 Years of Ranching King Ranch. Corpus Christi: 1959. V. 71

1.2.3.. London: 1910. V. 69

ONE Act Plays for Stage and Study. New York: 1931. V. 71

ONE in Twenty. Duke Narrative and Verse 1924-1945. Durham: 1945. V. 71

ONE Thousand and One Useful Recipes. San Francisco. V. 72

ONE, Two Three. London: 1895. V. 72

ONE Two Three Four. London: 1895. V. 73

O'NEAL, BILL
The Arizona Rangers. Austin: 1987. V. 68

O'NEAL, HANK
Berenice Abbott: American Photographer. New York: 1982. V. 70
A Vision Shared: a Classic Portrait of America and Its People 1935-1943. New York: 1976. V. 68; 72

O'NEAL, LILA M.
Textiles of Highland Guatemala. New York: 1966. V. 70

O'NEAL, WILLIAM
The Work of William Lawrence Bottomley in Richmond. Charlottesville: 1985. V. 70

O'NEALL, JOHN BELTON
The Negro Law of South Carolina.... Columbia: 1848. V. 71

ONEIDA COMMUNITY
Bible Argument; Defining the Relations of the Sexes in the Kingdom of Heaven. Worcester: 1850. V. 68

O'NEIL, HENRY
Lectures on Painting Delivered at the Royal Academy. London: 1866. V. 73
Lectures on Painting Delivered at the Royal Academy. 1886. V. 70

O'NEIL, JAMES B.
They Die But Once: the Story of a Tejano. New York: 1935. V. 69

O'NEIL, KERRY
Mooney Moves Around. New York: 1939. V. 70

O'NEILL, CHARLES
Chemistry of Calico Printing, Dyeing and Bleaching, Including Silken, Woollen and Mixed Goods, Practical and Theoretical.... Manchester: 1840. V. 71
A Dictionary of Calico Printing and Dyeing.... London: 1867. V. 71
The Textile Colourist; a Monthly Journal of Bleaching, Printing, Dyeing and Finishing Textile Fabrics.... Manchester: 1876-1877. V. 69

O'NEILL, EUGENE GLADSTONE
Ah, Wilderness. New York: 1933. V. 69
All God's Chillun Got Wings and Welded. New York: 1924. V. 73
Anna Christie. New York: 1930. V. 69
Beyond the Horizon. New York: 1920. V. 70
Collected Plays. New York: 1924. V. 68
Dynamo. New York: 1929. V. 68; 69; 70; 71; 73
The Emperor Jones. Cincinnati: 1921. V. 71
Gold. New York: 1920. V. 68
The Great God Brown Including the Fountain, the Dreamy Kid and Before Breakfast. London: 1926. V. 68
The Iceman Cometh. New York: 1946. V. 72; 73
Marco Millions. New York: 1927. V. 70
Mourning Becomes Electra. 1931. V. 69
Mourning Becomes Electra. New York: 1931. V. 68; 70; 71
Plays: First Series - The Straw, The Emperor Jones & Diff'rent. London: 1922. V. 68
Strange Interlude. New York: 1928. V. 69; 70; 73
Thirst, and Other One-Act Plays. Boston: 1914. V. 70
A Touch of the Poet. New Haven: 1957. V. 70

O'NEILL, JOHN P.
Manet 1832-1883. New York: 1983. V. 68

O'NEILL, PAUL
The Oldest City. (Together with) A Seaport Legacy. The Story of St. John's Newfoundland. Erin: 1975-1976. V. 70

O'NEILL, ROSE
The Kewpies and Dotty Darling. New York: 1912. V. 72
The Kewpies and the Runaway Baby. Garden City: 1928. V. 73

O'NEILL, T. K.
English Language Dictionaries 1604-1900. New York: 1988. V. 69

ONIONS, OLIVER
The Debit Account. London: 1913. V. 69

ONSLOW FORD, GORDON
Painting in the Instant. London: 1964. V. 69; 72

ONTYD, CONRAD G.
A Treatise on Mortal Diseases: Containing a Particular View of the Different Ways, In which They Lead to Death.... London: 1798. V. 73

ONWHYN, T.
Etiquette Illustrated. Or, Hints.... London: 1849. V. 73
Nothing to Wear, a Poem of Transatlantic Origin. London: 1859. V. 68

ONWUEJEOGWU, M.
An Igbo Civilization, Nri Kingdom and Hegemony. London and Benin City: 1981. V. 69

THE OPAL. New York: 1846. V. 70
THE OPAL. New York: 1847. V. 71

OPEN Your Eyes!. London: 1904. V. 72
THE OPEN Window. 1910-. V. 71
THE OPEN Window. The Second Volume April-September 1911. London: 1911. V. 69

OPIE, AMELIA
Temper, or Domestic Scenes: a Tale. London: 1812. V. 68; 72

OPIE, IONA
I Saw Esau - The Schoolchild's Pocket Book. London: 1992. V. 72
I Saw Esau - Traditional Rhymes of Youth. London: 1947. V. 72
The Lore and Language of Schoolchildren. Oxford: 1959. V. 72
A Nursery Companion. London: 1980. V. 72
A Nursery Companion. Oxford: 1980. V. 72
The Oxford Dictionary of Nursery Rhymes. Oxford: 1951. V. 69; 72
The Singing Game. London: 1985. V. 72
The Treasures Of Childhood. Books, Toys And Games From The Opie Collection. London: 1989. V. 72

OPIE, JOHN
Lectures on Painting, Delivered at the Royal Academy of Arts.... London: 1832. V. 68

OPIE, JOHN N.
A Rebel Cavalryman. Chicago: 1899. V. 70

OPLER, MORRIS EDWARD
Dirty Boy: a Jicarilla Tale of Raid and War. Menasha: 1938. V. 68; 73
Myths and Tales of Chiricahua Apache Indians. Chicago: 1942. V. 69

OPPE, A. P.
Alexander & John Robert Cozens. With A Reprint of Alexander Cozen's A New Method of Assisting The Invention In Drawing Original Compositions Of Landscape. London: 1952. V. 72
The Water-Colours of Turner, Cox and Dew Wint. 1925. V. 68

OPPEN, GEORGE
Alpine. Mt. Horeb: 1969. V. 73

OPPENHEIM, E. PHILLIPS
The Channay Syndicate. Boston;: 1927. V. 68
The Colossus of Arcadia. Toronto: 1938. V. 70
The Court of St. Simon. 1912. V. 71
Crooks in the Sunshine. London: 1932. V. 68; 70; 72
Crooks in the Sunshine. Boston: 1933. V. 68
Curious Happenings to the Rookie Legatees. London: 1937. V. 68
Curious Happenings to the Rookie Legatees. Boston: 1938. V. 68; 72
Envoy Extraordinary. Boston: 1937. V. 71
Expiation: a Novel of England and Our Canadian Dominion. London: 1887. V. 68
General Besserley's Puzzle Box. Boston: 1935. V. 68; 70
General Besserley's Second Puzzle Box. Boston: 1940. V. 70; 71
The Grassleyes Mystery. Boston: 1940. V. 70
Harvey Garrard's Crime. Boston: 1926. V. 68
The Lion and the Lamb. Boston: 1930. V. 70
The Man and His Kingdom. London: 1899?. V. 68
The Man from Sing Sing. New York: 1932. V. 68
The Man Who Changed His Plea. Boston: 1942. V. 68
The Man Without Nerves. Boston: 1934. V. 68
The Milan Grill Room. Boston: 1941. V. 68
A Pulpit in the Grill Room. Boston: 1939. V. 68
Spies and Intrigues, the Oppenheim Secret Service Omninbus. Boston: 1936. V. 70
The Strange Borders of Palace Crescent. Boston: 1934. V. 68

OPPENHEIM, L.
International Law, a Treatise. London: 1920. V. 71

OPPENHEIMER, JANE M.
New Aspects of John and William Hunter. London: 1946. V. 68

OPPENHEIMER, JOEL
Acts. Mt. Horeb: 1976. V. 73
Del Quien Lo Tomo; A Suite. Mt. Horeb: 1983. V. 73
The Dutiful Son. Highlands: 1956. V. 73
New Hampshire Journal. Mount Horeb: 1994. V. 71
New Hampshire Journal. Perry Township: 1994. V. 69; 73
New Spaces. Santa Barbara: 1985. V. 68; 71
Notes Towards the Definition of David. Mt. Horeb: 1984. V. 73
Sirventes on a Sad Occurrence. Mt. Horeb: 1967. V. 73
The Woman Poems. Indianapolis: 1975. V. 72

OPPENHEIMER, LEHMANN J.
The Heart of Lakeland. Manchester: 1908. V. 69; 71

OPPENLANDER, ELLA ANN
Dickens' All the Year Round. Descriptive Index and Contributor List. Troy: 1984. V. 68

OPPRESSION Unmasked: Being a Narrative of the Proceedings in a Case Between a Great Corporation and a Little Fishmonger. Dublin: 1784. V. 73

O'RAHILLY, T. F.
Danta Gradha. 1926. V. 69
Gadelica. A Journal of Modern Irish Studies. 1912-1913. V. 70

ORAM, SAMUEL MARSH
Poems: by the Late Mr. Samuel Marsh Oram.... London: 1794. V. 69

ORAM, WILLIAM
Precepts and Observations on the Art of Colouring in Landscape Painting. London: 1810. V. 69

ORCHARD, HARRY
The Confessions and Autobiography of Harry Orchard. New York: 1907. V. 68

ORCHIDS from the Botanical Register 1815-1847. Basel: 1991. V. 68

ORCI, LELIO
Freeze-Etch Histology. A Comparison Between Thin Sections and Freeze- Etch Replicas. Berlin: 1975. V. 68

ORCUTT, WILLIAM DANA
Dagger and Jewels. New York: 1931. V. 69
The Kingdom of Books. Boston: 1927. V. 69

ORCZY, EMMUSKA, BARONESS
The Case of Miss Elliott. London: 1921. V. 68
The Celestial City. New York: 1926. V. 72
Eldorado: A Story Of The Scarlet Pimpernel. London: 1913. V. 72
The Enchanted Cat (and Other Tales). London: 1895. V. 72
Lady Molly of Scotland Yard. London: 1910. V. 71
League of the Scarlet Pimpernel. NY: 1919. V. 72
The Old Man in the Corner. London: 1909. V. 68; 71
A Spy of Napoleon. London: 1934. V. 71
Unravelled Knots. 1926. V. 71

ORDERS in Council; or an Examination of the Justice...of the New Commercial Regulation. London: 1808. V. 72

ORD-HUME, ARTHUR W. J. G.
Clockwork Music. London: 1973. V. 72
The Musical Box. London: 1995. V. 72

OREGON. SUPREME COURT - 1939
The Supreme Court of the State of Oregon, October Term, 1939. 1939. V. 71

THE OREGON Trail, The Missouri to the Pacific Ocean. New York: 1939. V. 68; 69

OREGON WASHINGTON RAILROAD & NAVIGATION CO.
Twenty-five Reasons Why You Should Come to Western Washington. Seattle: 1911. V. 68

O'REILLY, HARRINGTON
Fifty Years on the Trail. London: 1889. V. 71

O'REILLY, HENRY
Settlement in the West. Sketches of Rochester.... Rochester: 1838. V. 68; 71

O'REILLY, MILES
The Life and Adventures, Songs, Services and Speeches of Private Miles O'Reilly. New York: 1864. V. 72

ORIBASIUS
Collectorvm Medicinalivm Libri XVII. Venetiis: 1554-1555. V. 69; 73

THE ORIGIN of Printing: In Two Essays. I. The Substance of Dr. Middleton's Dissertation on the Origin of Printing in England. II. Mr. Meerman's Account of the First Invention of the Art. London: 1774. V. 68

ORIGINAL American Folk Songs as Sung by the Glazier' Carolinians. Chicago: 1904. V. 68

THE ORIGINAL Instrument and Republican Scheme of Government, Under the Colour.... 1722. V. 71

ORIGO, IRIS
Leopardi - a Study of Solitude. London: 1953. V. 70
A Need to Testify.... London: 1984. V. 72

ORIOLO, PINO
Some Letters of Pino Orioli to Mrs. Gordon Crotch. Edinburgh: 1974. V. 71

ORLANDINO, NICOLAO
Historiae Soietatis Iesu.... Antwerp: 1620. V. 70

ORLEAN, SUSAN
The Bullfighter Checks Her Makeup. New York: 2001. V. 69; 72
The Orchid Thief. New York: 1998. V. 70; 72; 73

ORLICH, LEOPOLD VON
Travels in India. London: 1845. V. 71

ORME, EDWARD
An Essay on Transparent Prints and on Transparencies in General. London: 1807. V. 72

ORMSBY, JOHN
Autumn Ramblers in North Africa. London: 1864. V. 71

ORMSBY'S Pentographic Illustrations of the Holy Scripture.... New York: 1835. V. 73

ORNDUFF, DONALD R.
Casement of Juniata, as a Man and as a Stockman...One of a Kind. Kansas City: 1975. V. 69; 71

ORNSTEIN, MARTHA
The Role of the Scientific Societies in the Seventeenth Century. New York: 1913. V. 71

O'RORKE, T.
The History of Sligo: Town and County. 1890. V. 69

O'ROURKE, FRANK
Action at Three Peaks. New York: 1948. V. 73
High Dive. New York: 1954. V. 72; 73
The Last Round. New York: 1956. V. 73
Latigo. New York: 1953. V. 71
The Man who Found His Way. New York: 1957. V. 71
The Team. New York: 1949. V. 73

O'ROURKE, JOHN
The Centenary Life of O'Connell. Dublin: 1877. V. 71

OROZ, PEDRO
The Oroz Codex. Washington: 1972. V. 72

ORPEN, WILLIAM
The Outline of Art. New York and London: 1929. V. 70
Sir William Orpen. Artist & Man. London: 1934. V. 72

ORPHAN HOUSE OF CHARLESTON
By-Laws of the Orphan House of Charleston, South Carolina. Charleston: 1861. V. 69; 73

ORR, CLIFFORD
The Dartmouth Murders. 1929. V. 73
The Wailing Rock Murders. 1932. V. 73

ORR, H. WINNETT
A List of Books and Pamphlets on the History of Surgery and Orthopedic Surgery. The Collection of.... Lincoln: 1943. V. 70

ORR, MUNRO S.
The Alphabet Set Forth in Six and Twenty Pictures. London: 1931. V. 71

ORR, THOMAS
Life History of...Pioneer Stories of California and Utah. Placerville: 1930. V. 69

ORSINI, FELICE
The Austrian Dungeons in Itlay. London: 1856. V. 72

ORSINI, FULVIA
Carmina Novem Illustrium Feminarvm.... Antwerp: 1568. V. 68; 72

ORSTED, HANS CHRISTIAN
Selected Scientific Works of Hans Christian Orsted. Princeton: 1998. V. 69

ORTA, GARCIA DE
Dell'Historia de i Semplici Aromati, et Altre Cose, che Vengono Portate dall'Indie Orientali Pertinenti all'vso Della Medicina. Venice: 1589. V. 68

ORTH, S. P.
The Armies of Labor; a Chronicle of the Organized Wage-Earners. New Haven: 1921. V. 68
Our Foreigners: a Chronicle of Americans in the Making. New Haven: 1921. V. 68

ORTIZ, SIMON
After and Before the Lightning. Tucson: 1994. V. 69; 73
Men on the Moon. Tucson: 1999. V. 69
Woven Stone. Tucson: 1992. V. 72

ORTON, J. R.
Arnold and Other Poems. New York: 1854. V. 68

ORTON, JAMES
Amazon and the Andes; or Across the Continent of South America. New York: 1870. V. 69

ORTON, JOE
Head to Toe. New York: 1971. V. 71

ORWELL, GEORGE
Animal Farm. London: 1945. V. 69; 70
Animal Farm. New York: 1946. V. 69; 71; 73
Animal Farm. New York: 1954. V. 73
Burmese Days. London: 1935. V. 71
A Clergyman's Daughter. London: 1935. V. 73
The Collected Essays, Journalism and Letters of George Orwell. London: 1968. V. 71
Dickens, Dali and Others. New York: 1946. V. 69
Down and Out in Paris and London. London: 1933. V. 70
Down and Out in Paris and London. New York: 1933. V. 73
England Your England and Other Essays. London: 1953. V. 70; 71
The English People. London: 1947. V. 68; 71
Homage to Catalonia. London: 1938. V. 70
Homage to Catalonia. New York: 1952. V. 73
Hop-Picking. Kent: 1970. V. 72
James Burnham and the Managerial Revolution. 1946. V. 68; 71
James Burnham and the Managerial Revolution. London: 1946. V. 69; 70
Keep the Aspidistra Flying. London: 1936. V. 70
The Lion and the Unicorn. London: 1940. V. 72
The Lion and the Unicorn. Socialism and the English Genius. London: 1940-1941. V. 69
The Lion and the Unicorn. Socialism and the English Genius. London: 1941. V. 68; 71
Nineteen Eighty-Four. London: 1949. V. 68; 69; 70; 71
Nineteen Eighty-Four. New York: 1949. V. 69; 70; 72; 73
Nineteen Eighty-Four. Paris: 1950. V. 70
Politics and the English Language. Evansville: 1947. V. 68; 73
The Road to Wigan Pier. 1937. V. 69; 70
The Road to Wigan Pier. London: 1937. V. 70; 71; 73
Such Were the Joys. New York: 1952. V. 70
The War Commentaries. The War Broadcasts. 1985. V. 70

ORWIN, C. S.
The Reclamation of Exmoor Forest. 1929. V. 68

OSBALDESTON, SQUIRE
Squire Osbaldeston; His Autobiography. 1926. V. 68; 71

OSBECK, PETER
A Voyage to China and the East Indies. London: 1771. V. 71

OSBORN, ALBERT S.
Questioned Documents. Albany: 1929. V. 70
Questioned Documents. New York and London: 1929. V. 71

OSBORN, CAMPBELL
Let Freedom Ring. Tokyo: 1954. V. 72

OSBORN, H. F.
The Titanotheres of Ancient Wyoming, Dakota and Nebraska. Washington: 1929. V. 70

OSBORN, HENRY FAIRFIELD
From the Greeks to Darwin. New York: 1913. V. 68

OSBORN, JOHN JAY
The Paper Chase. Boston: 1971. V. 69

OSBORN, LAUGHTON
Handbook of Young Artists and Amateurs in Oil Painting, Being Chiefly a Condensed Compilation from the Celebrated Manual of Bouvier.... New York: 1845. V. 71

OSBORN, SHERARD
A Cruise in Japanese Waters. London: 1859. V. 71
Japanese Fragments. London: 1861. V. 71
Narratives of Voyage and Adventure. Edinburgh: 1865. V. 71
Stray Leaves from an Arctic Journal or Eighteen Months in the Polar Regions, in Search of Sir John Franklin's Expedition in the Years 1850-1851. New York: 1852. V. 73

OSBORNE, CATHERINE
Memorials of the Life and Character of Lady Osborne and Some of Her Friends.... Dublin;: 1870. V. 69

OSBORNE, CHARLES
Swansong: Poems. London: 1968. V. 69

OSBORNE, CHARLES FRANCIS
Historic Houses and Gardens- Palaces, Castle, Country Places and Gardens of the Old and New Worlds Described by Several Writers. Philadelphia: 1908. V. 72

OSBORNE, E. ALLEN
The Facts About a Christmas Carol. London: 1937. V. 68

OSBORNE, E. C.
Osborne's Guide to the Grand Junction, or Birmingham, Liverpool and Manchester Railway with the Topography of the Country. Birmingham: 1838. V. 68; 70
Osborne's Guide to the Grand Junction, or, Birmingham, Liverpool and Manchester Railway with the Topography of the Country. Birmingham: 1838. V. 72

OSBORNE, JOHN
The Entertainer. London: 1957. V. 73
Inadmissable Evidence: a Play. London: 1965. V. 70
Look Back in Anger. London: 1957. V. 71; 73
Time Present/The Hotel in Amsterdam. London: 1968. V. 69

OSCAR Wilde and the Grave of Shelley. Edinburgh: 1992. V. 73

OSCAR Wilde: Graham Hill: a Brief Friendship. Edinburgh: 1982. V. 73

OSGOOD, CORNELIUS
Blue and White Chinese Porcelain: a Study of Form. New York: 1956. V. 73

OSGOOD, ERNEST STAPLES
The Day of the Cattleman. Minnesota: 1929. V. 71
The Field Notes of Captain William Clark 1803-1805. New Haven: 1964. V. 70

OSGOOD, HENRY O.
So This is Jazz. Boston: 1926. V. 72

O'SHAUGHNESSY, ARTHUR
An Epic of Women and Other Poems. London: 1870. V. 72
Lays of France. London: 1872. V. 72
Music and Moonlight. London: 1874. V. 68; 69; 72
Songs of a Worker. London: 1881. V. 69

O'SHEA, M. V.
Tobacco and Mental Efficiency. New York: 1923. V. 72

OSKISON, JOHN M.
A Texas Titan, The Story of Sam Houston. Garden City: 1929. V. 70

OSLER, WILLIAM
Aequanimitas with Other Addresses to Medical Students. Philadelphia: 1906. V. 73
An Alabama Student and Other Biographical Essays. London: 1908. V. 73
Bibliotheca Osleriana. Oxford: 1929. V. 68; 70; 71; 73
Bibliotheca Osleriana. Montreal and London: 1969. V. 70; 71; 72; 73
Bibliotheca Osleriana. Montreal: 1987. V. 68
The Collected Essays. Birmingham: 1985. V. 69
The Growth of Truth as Illustrated in the Discovery of the Circulation of the Blood: Being the Harveian Oration Delivered at the Royal College of Physicians. London: 1906. V. 70
Incunabula Medica. 1923. V. 73
Incunabula Medica. London: 1923. V. 68
Incunabula Medica. Mansfield: 1994. V. 73
Michael Servetus. Baltimore: 1909. V. 68; 73
The Old Humanities and the New Science. An Address Before the Classical Association Oxford May 16, 1919. London: 1919. V. 73
On the Etiology and Diagnosis of Cerebro-Spinal Fever. London: 1899. V. 70
The Principles and Practice of Medicine. New York: 1892. V. 68; 69; 70; 73
The Principles and Practice of Medicine. Edinburgh: 1895. V. 70; 71
The Principles and Practice of Medicine. New York: 1897. V. 69
The Principles and Practice of Medicine. Edinburgh: 1898. V. 71; 73
The Principles and Practice of Medicine. Edinburgh: 1901. V. 70; 71; 73
The Principles and Practice of Medicine. New York: 1911. V. 73
The Principles and Practice of Medicine. New York: 1930. V. 71
The Student Life and Other Essays. London: 1928. V. 68
Thomas Lincare. Cambridge: 1908. V. 68

OSMOND, S.
Lousiana's Art Nouveau: the Crafts of the Newcomb Style. Gretna: 1976. V. 72

OSOFSKY, GILBERT
Harlem: The Making of a Ghetto, Negro New York 1890-1930. New York: 1966. V. 72

OSSENDOWSKI, F.
The Breath of the Desert. 1927. V. 70
Man and Mystery in Asia. 1924. V. 70; 72; 73
Slaves of the Sun. 1928. V. 70; 72; 73
Slaves of the Sun. London: 1928. V. 71

OSSOLI, SARAH MARGARET FULLER, MARCHESA D'
Life Without and Life Within; or, Reviews, Narratives, Essays and Poems. Boston: 1860. V. 72
Memoirs of Margaret Fuller Ossoli. Boston: 1852. V. 68
Woman in the Nineteenth Century, and Kindred Papers Relating to the Sphere, Condition, and Duties of Woman. Boston and New York: 1855. V. 69; 72; 73

OSTERVALD, JEAN FREDERIC
The Grounds and Principles of the Christian Religion, Explain'd in a Catechetical discourse for the Instruction of Young People. London: 1704. V. 70
The Grounds and Principles of the Christian Religion, Explain'd in a Catechetical Discourse for the Instruction of Young People. London: 1711. V. 69

OSTRANDER, ALSON
An Army Boy of the Sixties. A Story of the Plains. New York: 1924. V. 69

OSTRANDER, ISABEL
How Many Cards?. New York: 1920. V. 73
The Mathematics of Guilt. New York: 1926. V. 69; 73

OSTRANDER, TOBIAS
The Planetarium and Astronomical Calculator.... New York: 1832. V. 69

OSTRANSKY, LEROY
The Anatomy of Jazz. Seattle: 1960. V. 68

OSTROGA, YVONNE
Nos Bebes Chiens. Paris: 1924. V. 69

OSTROM, JOHN H.
Marsh's Dinosaurs. The Collection from Como Bluff. New Haven: 1999. V. 69

OSTROM, VINCENT
Water and Poltics: a Study of Water Policies and Administration in the Development of Los Angeles. Los Angeles: 1953. V. 68

OSTROVISKI, NICHOLAS
The Making of a Hero. New York: 1937. V. 70

OSTWALD, WILHELM
Colour Science. (with) The Ostwald Colour Album. London: 1931. V. 69

O'SULLIVAN, FLORENCE
The History of Kinsdale. 1916. V. 71

O'SULLIVAN, MAURICE
Twenty Years A-Growing. London: 1933. V. 70

O'SULLIVAN, SEAMUS
Facetiae et Curiosa: Being a Selection from the Notebook of the Late J. H. Orwell. 1937. V. 70
Personal Talk, a Book of Verses. 1936. V. 70
Poems 1930-1938. 1938. V. 70

O'SULLIVAN, VINCENT
The Next Room. Edinburgh: 1988. V. 73

O'SULLIVAN, WILLIAM
The Economic History of Cork City from the Earliest Times. 1937. V. 69

OSWALD, E. J.
By Fell and Fjord or Scenes and Studies in Iceland. London: 1882. V. 68

OSWALD, FELIX
Index of Potter's Stamps on Terra Sigillata "Samian Ware". East Bridgford: 1931. V. 73
Summerland Sketches, or Rambles in the Backwoods of Mexico and Central America. Philadelphia: 1880. V. 73

OSWALD, JOHN CLYDE
A History of Printing. New York and London: 1928. V. 69

OSWELL, W. EDWARD
William Cotton Oswell. London: 1900. V. 71

OSWESTRY SAVINGS' BANK
Rules and Regulations.... Oswestry: 1836. V. 71

OSWYN, POWYS
Ernest Milman: a Tale of Manchester Life. London: 1857. V. 68

OTERO, MIGUEL ANTONIO
The Mexican American: Otero, an Autobiographical Trilogy. New York: 1974. V. 68
My Life on the Frontier 1882-1897 - Death Knell of a Territory and Birth of a State. Albuquerque: 1939. V. 68; 73
My Nine Years as Governor of the Territory of New Mexico 1887-1906. Albuquerque: 1940. V. 70; 72; 73
The Real Billy the Kid. New York: 1936. V. 69

OTHELLO-Travestie...With Burlesque Notes, in the Manner of the Most Celebrated Commentators and Other Curious Appendices. London: 1813. V. 69

OTHEMAN, EDWARD
Memoir and Writings of Mrs. Hannah Maynard Pickard; Late Wife of Rev. Humphrey Pickard, A. M., Principal of the Wesleyan Academy at Mount Allison, Sackville, N.B. Boston: 1845. V. 73

THE OTHER End of the Couch. Poems for Gordon Cairnie. Cambridge: 1964. V. 68

THE OTHER Side of the Question; or An Attempt to Rescue the Characters of the Two Royal Sisters, Q. Mary and Q. Anne, Out of the Hands of the D-D of (Marlborough). London: 1742. V. 69

OTIS, D.
Decorating with Flowers. New York: 1978. V. 68

OTIS, FESSENDEN NOTT
Studies of Animals, with Instructions for the Lead Pencil and Crayon. New York: 1866. V. 73

OTIS, PHILO ADAMS
The First Presbyterian Church, a History of the Oldest Organization in Chicago.... Chicago: 1900. V. 70

OTLEY, JONATHAN
A Concise Description of the English Lakes, the Mountains in Their Vicinity and the Roads by Which They May be Visited. London: 1823. V. 71
A Descriptive Guide to the English Lakes and Adjacent Mountains.... Keswick: 1842. V. 71
A Descriptive Guide to the English Lakes and Adjacent Mountains.... Keswick: 1850. V. 71

THE OTTAWA Almanac 1875 and Dominion Guide, Containing a Calendar for the Year.... Ottawa: 1874. V. 73

OTTENBERG, SIMON
Masked Rituals of Afikpo: the Context of an African Art. Seattle: 1975. V. 69; 72

OTTER, WILLIAM
The Life and Remains of the Rev. Edward Daniel Clarke LL.D. 1824. V. 68

OTTESEN, C.
The Native Plant Primer. New York: 1995. V. 68

OTTEWILL, D.
The Edwardian Garden. New Haven;: 1989. V. 68

OTTLEY, ROI
White Marble Lady. New York: 1965. V. 72

OTTLEY, W. Y.
A Collection of Fac-Similes of Scarce and Curious Prints, by the Early Masters of the Italian, German and Flemish Schools.... London: 1826. V. 70
Engravings of the Most Noble Marquis of Stafford's Collection of Pictures in London.... 1818. V. 73

OTTO, ADOLPH WILHELM
Monstrorum Sexcentorum Descriptio Anatomica. Bratislava: 1841. V. 70

OTTO, WHITNEY
How to Make an American Quilt. New York: 1991. V. 71; 73

OTWAY, THOMAS
Works. London: 1926. V. 73

OUCHI, ED
'Til We See the Light of Hope. Vernon: 1979. V. 71

OUCHTERLONY, JOHN
Mineralogical Report Upon a Portion of the Districts of Nellore, Cuddapah and Guntoor. Madras: 1841. V. 68

OUDEMANS, C. A. J. A.
Enumeratio Systematica Fungorum. The Hague: 1919-1924. V. 71

OUGHTON, FREDERICK
Grinling Gibbons and the English Woodcarving Tradition. Stobart: 1979. V. 73

OUGHTRED, WILLIAM
Clavis Mathematicae Denuo Limata, Sive Potius Fabricata. Oxoniae: 1693. V. 72

OUR Champions: The Athletics/Phila 1902. Philadelphia: 1902. V. 72

OUR Children. London. V. 70

OUR Children's Times; or Sketches of the Past and Present; from the French Revolution of 1848 to the Fall of Sebastopol 1855. London: 1856. V. 68; 73

OUR Coal and Coal-Pits: the People in Them, and the Scenes Around Them. London: 1853. V. 71

OUR County and Its People. Boston: 1899. V. 73

OUR Darlings. 1916. V. 70

OUR Darlings (for 1936). London. V. 69

OUR English Home: Its Early History and Progress. Oxford and London: 1861. V. 68

OUR Exagmination Round His Factification for Incamination of Work in Progress. Paris: 1929. V. 68; 69; 72

OUR Family Physician.... Chicago: 1871. V. 71

OUR Kitty's ABC. New York: 1911. V. 73

OUR Little Bones Object Book. London: 1904. V. 72

OUR Living Painters; Their Lives and Works. London: 1859. V. 69

OUR Old Nursery Rhymes. London: 1911. V. 70; 71; 73

OUR Time Has Come: Mississippi Embraces Its Future. Jackson: 1988. V. 70

OUR Women in the War. The Lives They Lived: the Deaths They Died. Charleston: 1887. V. 69

OURSLER, GRACE
The Spider. New York: 1929. V. 70

OURSLER, WILL
Folio on Florence White. New York: 1942. V. 71
I Found Him Dead. New York: 1947. V. 72

OUSELEY, WILLIAM
Persian Miscellanies. London: 1795. V. 71

OUSLEY, CLARENCE
Galveston in Nineteen Hundred. Atlanta: 1900. V. 68

OUT and Away: a Posy of Travellers' Joy. London: 1919. V. 70

OUT of the West. Northridge: 1979. V. 69; 71; 73

THE OUTCAST Poets. Yonkers: 1947. V. 69

OUTCAULT, R. F.
My Resolutions - Buster Brown. New York: 1906. V. 70

OUTERBRIDGE, PAUL
A Singular Aesthetic. Santa Barbara: 1981. V. 68

OUTHIER, REGINALD
Journal d'un Voyage au Nord en 1736 & 1737. Paris: 1744. V. 70; 73

OUTHWAITE, IDA RENTOUL
A Bunch of Wild Flowers. Australia: 1933. V. 73
Fairyland. Melbourne: 1926. V. 71
The Little Fairy Sister. London: 1923. V. 71
The Little Green Road to Fairyland. London: 1922. V. 73

OUTLAND, CHARLES F.
Man-Made Disaster: the Story of St. Francis Dam; Its Place in Southern California's Water System, Its Failure and the Tragedy of March 12 and 13, 1928, in the Santa Clara Valley. Glendale: 1963. V. 70

OUTLINE of the Plan of Education Pursued at the Greenfield High School for Ladies, with a Catalogue for the Year 1831-1832. V. 73

OVED, MOSHEH
For the Sake of the Days. London: 1940. V. 71

OVENDEN, GRAHAM
Alphonse Mucha: Photographs. New York London: 1974. V. 68
The Art C...S. A Reply to the Critics of Mr. Peter Blake R.A. Bodmin, Cornwall: 1983. V. 70
The Illustrators of Alice. London: 1972. V. 69
Victorian Erotic Photography. London. V. 70

OVERELL, LILIAN
A Woman's Impressions of German New Guinea. London: 1923. V. 71

OVERFIELD, DONALD
Famous Flies and Their Originators. 1972. V. 68

OVERMAN, FREDERICK
The Manufacture of Iron, In All Its Various Branches.... Philadelphia: 1854. V. 69

OVERMIER, JUDITH A.
Books and Manuscripts of the Bakken. Metuchen: 1992. V. 72

OVERS, JOHN
Evenings of a Working Man, Being the Occupation of His Scanty Leisure. London: 1844. V. 68; 70

OVERTON, GRANT
American Nights Entertainment. New York: 1923. V. 72

OVERTON, ROBERT
A Case Around the World. London: 1900. V. 69; 73
A Round Dozen: Character Sketches. London: 1884. V. 68

OVIDIUS NASO, PUBLIUS
Amores. Verona: 1932. V. 71
Amores. Waltham St. Lawrence: 1932. V. 70; 71
Ovid's Epistles; with his Amours. London: 1748. V. 73
(Heroides) Epistolae. Auli Sabini ad Earum aliquot Responsiones (and other works). Parisiis: 1563. V. 72
Metamorphose. Amsterdam: 1650. V. 69
Metamorphoseon Libri XV. Frankfurt: 1543. V. 70
Metamorphoses. Verona: 1958. V. 73
Metamorphoses. Waltham St. Lawrence: 1958. V. 70
Metamorphoses D'Ovide en Rondeaux. Paris: 1676. V. 68
Metamorphoses in Fifteen Books. 1958. V. 71
Ovid's Metamorphoses Englished, Mytholgiz'd and Represented in Figures. London: 1640. V. 71
Ovyde Hys Booke of Methamorphose. Books X-XV. Boston and New York: 1924. V. 72
Operum Tom 2: Metamorphoseown Libri xv, sum notis selectis varior studio. Amsterdam: 1683. V. 71
Ovidio Istoric, Politico Morale. Venice: 1696. V. 70
Tales from Ovid. London: 1997. V. 69

OVINGTON, MARY W.
The Wall Came Tumbling Down. New York: 1947. V. 71

OVITT, MABLE
Golden Treasure. Dillon: 1952. V. 68; 69

OWEN, CHARLES
An Essay Towards a Natural History of Serpents: in two parts. London: 1742. V. 72

OWEN, COLLINSON
Zero. New York: 1927. V. 70

OWEN, DORA
The Book of Fairy Poetry. London: 1920. V. 70
The Book of Fairy Tales. London: 1920. V. 72

OWEN, GEORGE
The Taylors Cussion...Being a Facsimile Reproduction by PhotoLithgraphy.... 1906. V. 73

OWEN, GUY
Cape Fear Country and Other Poems. Lake Como, FL: 1958. V. 71
White Stallion and Other Poems. Winston-Salem: 1969. V. 71

OWEN, HAROLD
Journey from Obscurity: Wilfred Owen 1893-1918. London: 1963-1970. V. 69

OWEN, JOHN
Epigrammatum Joan. Owen Cambro-Britanni Oxoniensis... Amsterdam: 1647. V. 71
The Journals and Letters of Major John Owen, Pioneer of the Northwest 1850-1871. 1927. V. 68
The Journals and Letters of Major John Owen, Pioneer of the Northwest 1850-1871. New York: 1927. V. 70; 72; 73

OWEN, LEWIS
The Key of the Spanish Tongue or a Plaine and Easy Introduction Whereby a Man May in Very Short Time Attaine to the Knowledge and Perfection of that Language. London: 1605. V. 72; 73

OWEN, M. A.
Folk-Lore of the Musquakie Indians of North America. (and) Catalogue of Musquakie Beadwork and Other Objects in the Collection of the Folk-Lore Society. London: 1904. V. 69
Voodoo Tales. New York: 1893. V. 70; 71

OWEN, PETER
The Peter Owen Anthology. London: 1991. V. 73

OWEN, RICHARD
The Eye of the Gods. New York: 1978. V. 68
A History of British Fossil Mammals and Birds. 1846. V. 73
A History of British Fossil Mammals and Birds. New York: 1846. V. 68
Monograph of the Fossil Mammalia of the Mesozoic Formations. London: 1871. V. 68
On the Classification and Geographical Distribution of the Mammalia, Being the Lecture on Sir Robert Reade's Foudnation, Delivered Before the University of Cambridge, in the Senate House May 10, 1859. London: 1859. V. 72
On the Nature of Limbs. A Discourse Delivered on Friday, February 9 at an Evening meeting of the Royal Insitution of Great Britain. London: 1849. V. 68; 72
Palaeontology. Edinburgh: 1860. V. 68; 73
Palaeontology. Edinburgh: 1861. V. 69; 73

OWEN, ROBERT
An Address Delivered to the Inhabitants of New Lanark, on the First of January 1816 at the Opening of the Institution Established for the Formation of Character. London: 1817. V. 71
The Book of the New Moral World.... London: 1836. V. 71
Debate on the Evidences of Christianity.... Cincinnati: 1829. V. 71
Lectures on the Comparative Anatomy and Physiology of the Invertebrate Animals.... London: 1855. V. 70
Letters to the Human Race on the Coming Universal Revolution. London: 1850. V. 71
New View of Society; or, Essays on the Formation of the Human Character.... London: 1816. V. 69; 72
A New View of Society; or, Essays on the Formation of the Human Character.... London: 1817. V. 71
Observations on the Effect of the Manufacturing System.... London: 1817. V. 71
Outline of the Rational System of Society, Founded on Demonstrable Facts, Developing the First Principles of the Science of Human Nature.... London: 1841. V. 71
Palaeontology; or a Systematic Summary of Extinct Animals and Their Geological Relations. Edinburgh: 1860. V. 70

OWEN, ROBERT DALE
Footfalls on the Boundary of Another World. Philadelphia: 1860. V. 70; 72
Footfalls On the Boundary of Another World. London: 1861. V. 68
The Future of the North-West: in Connection with the Scheme of Reconstruction without New England. Philadelphia: 1863. V. 72
Hints on Public Architecture, Containing, Among Other Illustrations, Views and Plans of the Smithsonian Institution. New York: 1849. V. 68; 71
Labor: Its History and Prospects. New York: 1851. V. 71; 73
Popular Tracts. London: 1844. V. 71

OWEN, WILFRED
The Complete Poems and Fragments. London: 1983. V. 70
The Complete Poems and Fragments. New York and London: 1984. V. 69
Poems. London: 1920. V. 68

OWEN, WILLIAM FITZ WILLIAM
Narrative of Voyages to Explore the Shores of Africa, Arabia, and Madagascar. London: 1833. V. 71
Narrative of Voyages to Explore the Shores of Africa, Arabia, and Madagascar.... New York: 1833. V. 71

OWEN, WILLIAM MILLER
In Camp and Battle with the Washington Artillery of New Orleans. Boston: 1885. V. 69

OWENS, BILL
Suburbia. New York: 1999. V. 72; 73

OWENS, LOUIS
Nightland. New York: 1996. V. 72
Other Destinies. Norman: 1992. V. 72

OXBERRY, WILLIAM
The Actors Budget of Wit and Merriment, Consisting of Monologues, Prologues, Epilogues, Tales, Comic Songs, Rare and Genuine Theatrical Anecdotes, etc. London: 1820. V. 70

OXENHAM, E. J.
A Patch and a Pawn. London: 1940. V. 71
A Princess in Tatters. London. V. 68
The Testing of the Torment. London: 1925. V. 71; 73

OXENHAM, JOHN
Barbe of Grand Bayou. New York: 1903. V. 68
The Hidden Years. London: 1931. V. 69

THE OXFORD Book Of American Verse. New York: 1927. V. 72

THE OXFORD Book of Modern Verse 1892-1935. Oxford: 1936. V. 70

OXFORD Book of Poetry for Children. 1963. V. 73

THE OXFORD Book of Twentieth-Century Verse. London: 1973. V. 69

OXFORD Delineated; or a Sketch of the History and Antiquities, and a General Topographical Description. Oxford: 1831-1833. V. 70

OXFORD English Dictionary. Oxford: 1971. V. 73
OXFORD English Dictionary. New York: 1981. V. 69

OXFORD Poetry 1915. 1915. V. 72

OXFORD Poetry 1916. Oxford: 1916. V. 71

OXFORD Poetry 1923. Oxford: 1923. V. 70
OXFORD Poetry 1923. New York: 1924. V. 70

THE OXFORD Sausage. Oxford: 1780?. V. 73

THE OXFORD University and City Guide on a New Plan.... Oxford: 1835. V. 72

OXFORD UNIVERSITY
Parecbolae sive Excerpta e Corpore Statutorum Universitatis Oxoniensis. Oxonii: 1771. V. 73

OXFORD, UNIVERSITY OF
Academiae Oxoniensis Gratulatio Pro Exoptato Serenissimi Regis Guilielmi Ex Hibernia Reditu. Oxoniae: 1690. V. 71

OXLEY, JOHN
Journals of Two Expeditions Into the Interior of New South Wales. London: 1820. V. 71

OYLER, LESLIE MARY
The Children's Entente Cordiale or Fun in French and English. London: 1915. V. 69

OZANAM, JACQUES
Recreations Mathematical and Physical, Laying Down and Solving Many Profitable and Delightful Problems of Arithmetick.... London: 1708. V. 69

OZICK, CYNTHIA
Bloodshed and Three Novellas. New York: 1976. V. 73
The Cannibal Galaxy. New York: 1983. V. 71
The Pagan Rabbi. New York: 1971. V. 69; 71
Quarrel and Quandary. New York: 2000. V. 69
Trust. New York: 1966. V. 73

P

P., C.
The Sheepherd's New Kalender: or, The Citizens and Country Man's Daily Companion. London: 1700. V. 70

PABOR, WILLIAM E.
Colorado as an Agricultural State, Its Farms, Fields and Garden Lands. New York: 1883. V. 68; 73

PACCARD, A.
Traditional Islamic Craft in Moroccan Architecture. France: 1980. V. 72

PACEY, H. B.
Considerations Upon the Present State of the Wool Trade, the Laws Made Concerning the Article, and How Far the Same are Consistent with True Policy, and the Real Interest of the State. London: 1781. V. 70

PACHT, O.
Van Eyck and the Founders of Early Netherlandish Painting. London: 1994. V. 70

PACHYMERES, GEORGIUS
Michael Paleologus sive Historia Rerum a Michael Paleologo Ante Imperium & Imperio Gestarum. Rome: 1666. V. 70; 73

PACIAUDI, PAOLO MARIA
De Cultu S. Johannis Baptistae Antiquitiates Christianae. Rome: 1755. V. 73

PACIFIC ALASKA NAVIGATION CO.
Alaska, Washington, California. 1916. V. 68

PACIFIC COAST STEAMSHIP CO.
All About Alaska. 1888. San Francisco: 1888. V. 71

PACIFIC DOOR AND SASH CO.
Door and Sash List No. 23, Pacific Door and Sash Co. Los Angeles: 1923. V. 68

PACIFIC Fisherman's 1918 Salmon Canners' Directory. Seattle: 1918. V. 68

PACIOLI, LUCA
Divina Proportione.... Venice: 1509. V. 70

PACKARD, ALPHAEUS S.
Lamarck, the Founder of Evolution. London: 1901. V. 68

PACKARD, FRANCIS R.
The History of Medicine in the United States. Philadelphia: 1901. V. 68; 71
History of Medicine in the United States. New York: 1931. V. 70; 73
History of Medicine in the United States. New York: 1973. V. 71
Some Account of the Pennsylvania Hospital. Philadelphia: 1938. V. 73

PACKARD, FRANK L.
The Devil's Mantle. New York: 1927. V. 72
The Devil's Mantle. Toronto: 1927. V. 71
Jimmie Dale and the Blue Envelope Murder. Garden City: 1930. V. 68; 71
The Locked Book. New York: 1924. V. 69; 72
Tiger Claws. New York: 1928. V. 69

PACKARD, GAR
Southwest 1880 with Ben Wittick Pioneer Photographer of Indian and Frontier Life. Santa Fe: 1970. V. 69

PACKARD, J. F.
Stanley and the Congo.... Philadelphia: 1884. V. 71

PACKER, LONA MOSK
Christina Rossetti. Berkeley and Los Angeles: 1963. V. 72
The Rossetti-MacMillan Letters.... Berkeley and Los Angeles: 1963. V. 68

PACKER, THOMAS
The Dyer's Guide: Being a Compendium of the Art of Dyeing Linen, Cotton, Silk, Wool, Muslin, Dresses, Furniture &c. London: 1830. V. 68

PACOT, JEAN
Figures De La Passion de Notre Seigneur Jesus Christ. Paris: 1725. V. 71

PADDOCK, JUDAH
A Narrative of the Shipwreck of the Ship Oswego, on the Coast of Barbary, and of the Sufferings of the Master and the Crew While in Bondage Among the Arabs.... New York: 1818. V. 70

PADEN, IRENE
The Big Oak Flat Road - an Account of Freighting from Stockton to Yosemite Valley. San Francisco: 1955. V. 68; 73
Prairie Schooner Detours. New York: 1949. V. 68

PADGET, ABIGAIL
Child of Silence. New York: 1993. V. 69

PADGETT, ABIGAIL
Child of Silence. New York: 1993. V. 68; 71
Moonbird Boy. New York: 1996. V. 68
Strawgirl. New York: 1994. V. 71

PADGETT, LEWIS
The Brass Ring. New York: 1946. V. 69

PADGETT, RON
The Adventures of Mr. and Mrs. Jim and Ron. London: 1970. V. 69

PADILLA, V.
Southern California Gardens, an Illustrated History. Berkeley: 1961. V. 68; 71; 72; 73

PADMORE, GEORGE
The Gold Coast Revolution - the Struggle of an African People from Slavery to Freedom. London: 1953. V. 69
How Russia Transformed Her Colonial Empire - a Challenge to the Imperialist Powers. London: 1946. V. 69
Pan-Africanism or Communism?. London: 1956. V. 69

PAE, DAVID
The Coming Struggle Among the Nations of the Earth.... Philadelphia: 1861. V. 73

PAGAN, ISABELLE M.
The Gentleman in the Next House. London: 1900. V. 68

PAGANI, GIAN FILIBERTO
Le Pitture e Sculture di Modena.... Modena: 1770. V. 72

PAGANO, J.
The Condemned. New York: 1947. V. 71

PAGDIN, WILLIAM E.
The Story of the Weathercock. London: 1949. V. 72

THE **PAGE**. St. Albans: 1898. V. 69

PAGE, BRUCE
Philby: The Spy Who Betrayed A Generation. London: 1968. V. 72

PAGE, ELIZABETH
The Tree of Liberty. New York: 1939. V. 70; 73

PAGE, J. W.
An Exploration of Exmoor and the Highlands of West Somerset. 1890. V. 68

PAGE, JAKE
Shoot the Moon. Indianapolis: 1979. V. 71
Shoot the Moon. New York: 1979. V. 69

PAGE, JAMES MADISON
The True Story Andersonville Prison: a Defense of Major Henry Wirz. New York and Washington: 1908. V. 72

PAGE, MARCO
Fast Company. New York: 1938. V. 72

PAGE, ROBIN
The Fox and the Orchid. 1987. V. 68

PAGE, RUSSELL
The Education of a Gardener. London: 1962. V. 69

PAGE, SUSANNE
Hopi. New York: 1962. V. 72
Hopi. New York: 1982. V. 69

PAGE, THOMAS HYDE PAGE
Considerations Upon the State of Dover-Harbour, With Its Relative Consequence to the Navy of Great Britain. Canterbury: 1784. V. 72

PAGE, THOMAS N.
Social Life In Old Virginia, Before the War. New York: 1898. V. 73

THE **PAGEANT**. 1896. V. 68
THE **PAGEANT**. 1897. V. 68

PAGEANT of Japanese Art. Volume VI. Architecture and Gardens. Tokyo: 1952. V. 68

PAGEL, WALTER
William Harvey's Biological Ideas. Basel and New York: 1967. V. 68

PAGET, ARTHUR
The Paget Papers. Diplomatic and Other Correspondence, 1794-1807. London: 1896. V. 72

PAGET, GUY
Bad'uns to Beat. 1936. V. 68

PAGET, J. O.
The Art of Beagling. 1931. V. 68
Beagles and Beagling. 1923. V. 68

PAGET, STEPHEN
Experiments on Animals.... London: 1906. V. 68
John Hunter. Man of Science and Surgeon (1728-1793). London: 1897. V. 68

PAGET, THOMAS CATESBY, BARON
Miscellanies in Prose and Verse. London: 1741. V. 69

PAGET, VIOLET
The Golden Keys and Other Essays on the Genius Loci. London: 1925. V. 73

PAHER, STANLEY W.
Nevada: an Annotated Bibliography. Las Vegas: 1980. V. 68; 70; 73

PAIK, L. GEORGE
The History of Protestant Missions in Korea 1832-1910. Pyeng Yang, Korea: 1929. V. 69

PAILTHORPE, F. W.
Illustrations to Great Expectations. London: 1885. V. 69

PAIN, BARRY
The Memoirs of Constantine Dix. London: 1905. V. 73
Wilhelmina in London. London: 1906. V. 70

PAIN, C. EARNEST
Fifty Years on the Test. 1934. V. 68

PAIN, WILLIAM
The Practical House Carpenter. 1799. V. 72
The Practical House Carpenter. London: 1799. V. 70
The Practical House Carpenter. London: 1805. V. 71

PAINE, ALBERT BIGELOW
Captain Bill McDonald Texas Ranger, a Story of Frontier Reform. New York: 1909. V. 68; 73
Jan the Romantic: a Story of France. Philadelphia: 1929. V. 71
Mark Twain a Biography. New York: 1912. V. 68; 70
The Tent Dwellers. New York: 1908. V. 71

PAINE, BAYARD H.
Pioneers, Indians and Buffaloes. Curtis: 1935. V. 69; 72

PAINE, ROBERT TREAT
The Art and Architecture of Japan. 1960. V. 68

PAINE, THOMAS
Agrarian Justice, Opposed to Agrarian Law and to Agrarian Monopoly. London: 1797. V. 69
Common Sense: Addressed to the Inhabitants of America. Philadelphia: 1791. V. 69
Common Sense, Addressed to the Inhabitants of America. London: 1792. V. 69
The Decline and Fall of the English System of France. Paris: 1796. V. 69
Dissertation on the First Principles of Government. London: 1795?. V. 69
Droits de l'Homme.... Paris: 1791. V. 68; 70; 73
A Letter Addressed to the Abbe Raynal, on the Affairs of North America. London: 1795. V. 69
Letter Addressed to the Addressers, on the Late Proclamation. London: 1792. V. 69
A Letter to George Washington on the Subject of the Late Treaty Concluded Between Great Britain and the United States of America.... London: 1797. V. 69

PAINE, THOMAS continued
A Letter to Mr. Henry Dundas...In Answer to His Speech on the Late Excellent Proclamation. London: 1792. V. 73
A Letter to the Earl of Sherburne, Now Marquess of Lansdowne, On His Speech, July 10, 1782.... London: 1791. V. 69
Prospects of the War and Paper Currency of Great Britain. London: 1793. V. 69
Prospects on the Rubicon; or, an Investigation into the Causes and Consequences of the Politics to be Agitated at the Meeting of Parliament. London: 1787. V. 70
Reasons for Wishing to Preserve the life of Louis Capet. London: 1793. V. 69
Die Rechte des Menschen. Kopenhagen: 1793. V. 70; 73
Rights of Man. Part the Second. Dublin: 1792. V. 69
Rights of Man. Part the Second. London: 1792-1795. V. 69
Rights of Man.... Dublin?: 1791?. V. 69
Rights of Man.... London: 1795. V. 69
Les Sens Commun. Paris: 1791. V. 68
The Theological Works of Thomas Paine.... New York: 1835. V. 69; 71
Two Letters to Lord Onslow...and One to Mr. Henry Dundas...on the Subject of the Late Excellent Proclamation. London: 1792. V. 71
The Whole Proceedings on the Trial of an Information Exhibited ex- officio by the King's Attorney Against Thomas Paine for Libel.. London: 1793. V. 71
The Writings. New York: 1894-1899. V. 71

PAINE, TIMOTHY OTIS
Solomon's Temple and Capitol, Ark of the Flood and Tabernacle or the Holy Houses. Boston and New York: 1886. V. 71

THE PAINTER'S Primer; in Familiar Rhyme Without Notes Containing the Most Approved Methods for Beginners in the Art Progressively Laid Down and Peculiarly Adapted for the Purpose of a Vade Mecum to Practioners of Every Branch of Painting. Oxford: 1810. V. 72

PAIVA MANSO, VISCONDE DE
Memoria Sobre Lourenco Marques (Delagoa Bay). Lisbon: 1870. V. 71

PAKULA, MARVIN
Centennial Album of the Civil War. New York: 1960. V. 72

PALAHNIUK, CHUCK
Choke. London: 2001. V. 70
Fight Club. New York: 1996. V. 71
Invisible Monsters. New York: 1999. V. 69
Survivor. London: 1999. V. 70
Survivor. New York: 1999. V. 69

PALARDY, JEAN
The Early Oak Furniture of French Canada. Toronto: 1963. V. 72

PALATINE, FREDERICK MICHAEL DE DEUX PONTS, COUNT
An Exact Relation of the Siege of Prague.... London: 1743. V. 73

PALAZZOLI, D.
Man Ray Portfolio. Milano: 1982. V. 72

PALEY, FRANK
Rumble on the Docks. New York: 1953. V. 71; 72

PALEY, GRACE
Enormous Changes at the Last Minute. New York: 1973. V. 72
Enormous Changes at the Last Minute. New York: 1974. V. 68; 72
Enormous Changes at the Last Minute. London: 1975. V. 71

PALEY, WILLIAM
Natural Theology; or Evidences of the Existence and Attributes of the Deity, Collected from the Appearances of Nature. Oxford: 1828. V. 70
A View of the Evidences of Christianity. London: 1821. V. 68

PALFREY, JOHN G.
Compendious History of New England.... Boston: 1883. V. 71

PALGRAVE, FRANCIS TURNER
Amenophis and Other Poems Sacred and Secular. London and New York: 1892. V. 69
Essays on Art. London: 1866. V. 73
The Golden Treasury of Songs and Lyrics. New York: 1911. V. 73
The Golden Treasury of the Best Songs and Lyrical Poems in the English Language. Cambridge and London: 1861. V. 68
The Golden Treasury of the Best Songs and Lyrical Poems in the English Language. Cambridge & London: 1861-1965. V. 68

PALGRAVE, OLIVE H. COATES
Trees of Central Africa. Salisbury: 1956. V. 71

PALGRAVE, WILLIAM GIFFORD
Narrative of a Year's Journey through Central and Eastern Arabia. London: 1865. V. 68

PALISSY, BERNARD
Oeuvres...Revues sur les Exemplaires de la Bibliotheque du Rois.... 1777. V. 68

PALLADIN, V. I.
Palladin's Plant Physiology.... Philadelphia: 1926. V. 72

PALLADINO, L. B.
Indian and White in the Northwest; or, A History of Catholicity in Montana. Baltimore: 1894. V. 72
Indian and White in The Northwest or A History of Catholicity in Montana, 1831 - 1891. Baltimore: 1922. V. 72

PALLADIO, ANDREA
Architecture de Palladio...avec des notes d'Inigo Jones.... The Hague: 1726. V. 72
Iquatrolinbri dell'Architettura. Milan: 1968. V. 70

PALLAS, PETER SIMON
Flora Rossica Seu Stirpium Imperii Rossici per Europam et Asiam Indigenarum Descriptiones et Icones. St. Petersburg: 1784-1788. V. 68; 70; 73

PALLISER, FANNY MARRYAT
A History of Lace. London: 1865. V. 69

PALLISER, HUGH
An Authentic and Impartial Copy of the Trial of Sir Hugh Palliser, Vice Admiral of the Blue, Held on Board His Majesty's Ship the Sandwich, in Portsmouth Harbour on Monday, April 12, 1779.... Portsmouth: 1779. V. 70

PALLLISER, GEORGE
Modern Buildings, a new and valuable work by a well-known practical architect . . . New York: 1901. V. 70

PALMEDO, ROLAND
Skiing - the International Sport. New York: 1937. V. 68; 70

PALMER, A. H.
The Life of Joseph Wolf, Animal Painter. London: 1895. V. 72

PALMER, B. M.
The Oath of Allegiance to the United States, Discussed in Its Moral and Poltical Bearings. Richmond: 1863. V. 70

PALMER, DAVE RICHARD
The River and the Rock. The History of Fortress West Point 1775-1783. 1991. V. 68

PALMER, FREDERICK
Central America and Its Problems. London. V. 71
In the Klondyke. New York: 1899. V. 70

PALMER, GEORGE
Kidnapping in the South Seas. Edinburgh: 1871. V. 71

PALMER, H.
Mountaineering and Exploration in the Selkirks. 1914. V. 68; 70; 73

PALMER, H. E.
Two Fishers and Other Poems. London: 1918. V. 72
Two Foemen. London: 1920. V. 72
Two Minstrels. London: 1921. V. 72

PALMER, H. S.
The Ordnance Survey of the Kingdom; Its Objects, Mode of Execution, History and Present Condition. 1873. V. 71

PALMER, HARRY CLAY
Athletic Sports in America, England and Australia. Philadelphia: 1890. V. 68
Sights Around the World with the Base Ball Boys. Philadelphia. V. 70

THE PALMER House, Chicago. Chicago: 1876. V. 68

PALMER, J. H.
Historic Farmhouses in and Around Westmorland. Kendal: 1945. V. 71

PALMER, J. W.
The New and the Old: or California and India to Romantic Aspects. New York: 1859. V. 69

PALMER, JOHN
Les Mysteres de la Tour Noire.... Paris: 1799. V. 73

PALMER, JOHN WILLIAMSON
Folk Songs. New York: 1861. V. 70

PALMER, JOSEPH
A Four Months' Tour through France. London: 1776. V. 73

PALMER, RALPH S.
Handbook of North American Birds. New Haven: 1962-1988. V. 69; 73
Handbook of North American Birds. 1976-1988. V. 73
Handbook of North American Birds. New Haven: 1976-1988. V. 70
Maine Birds. Cambridge: 1949. V. 73

PALMER, RICHMOND
The Bornu Sahara and Sudan. London: 1936. V. 71

PALMER, SAMUEL
The General History of Printing, From Its First Invention in the City of Mentz.... London: 1732. V. 72
A General History of Printing, from the First Invention of It in the City of Mentz.... London: 1733. V. 68; 70; 73
The Life and Letters of Samuel Palmer. London: 1892. V. 71
Moral Essays on Some of the Most Curious and Significant English, Scotch and Foreign Proverbs. London: 1710. V. 71

PALMER, STUART
The Adventure of the Marked Man and One Other. Boulder: 1973. V. 71; 72
Cold Poison. New York: 1954. V. 72
The Monkey Murder and Other Hildegarde Withers Stories. New York: 1950. V. 71
The Puzzle of the Happy Hooligan. New York: 1941. V. 71
The Puzzle of the Red Stallion. New York: 1936. V. 71; 72
The Riddles of Hildegarde Withers. New York: 1947. V. 68; 69

PALMER, THOMAS
Universal Suffrage. Speech of Hon. Thomas W. Palmer, of Michigan, in the Senate of the United States, Friday February 6, 1885. Washington: 1885. V. 70

PALMER, W. T.
The Complete Hill Walker Rock Climber and Cave Explorer. London: 1934. V. 69
The English Lakes. London: 1908. V. 71
Tramping in Lakeland. London: 1934. V. 69

PALMER, WILLIAM
Origines Liturgicae, or Antiquities of the English Ritual.... Oxford: 1839. V. 70
Report of the Trial of William Palmer for Poisoning John Parsons Cook at Rugeley. London: 1856. V. 72

PALMERSTON, HENRY TEMPLE, VISCOUNT
Opinions and Policy of Viscount Palmerston: as Minister, Diplomatist and Statesman.... London: 1852. V. 71

PALMIERI, LUIGI
The Eruption of Vesuvius in 1872.... 1873. V. 68
The Eruption of Vesuvius in 1872.... London: 1873. V. 70

PALMQUIST, PETER E.
Photographers: a Sourcebook for Historical Research. Nevada City: 2000. V. 68

PALOMINO HORSE BREEDERS OF AMERICA
Palomino Official Stud Book and Registry - Volume I-II. Mineral Wells. V. 73

PALOU, FRANCISCO
Fray Francisco Palou Historical Memoirs of New California. Berekeley: 1926. V. 68; 73
Historical Memoirs of New California. Berkeley: 1926. V. 68
Life and Apostolic Labors of the Venerable Father Junipero Serra. Pasadena: 1913. V. 68

PALSEY, C. W.
Observations on Limes, Calcareous Cements, Mortars, Stuccos and Concrete and on Puzzolanas, Natural and Artificial, Together with Rules Deduced from Numerous Experiments for Making an Artificial Water Cement.... London: 1838. V. 68

PALTOCK, ROBERT
The Life and Adventures of Peter Wilkins. London: 1751. V. 70
The Life and Adventures of Peter Wilkins. Boston: 1835. V. 69

PALUD, A. M. LE.
The Yangtze Gorges. Shanghai. V. 71

PAMMEL, L. H.
Anatomical Characters of the Seeds of Leguminosae, Chiefly Genera of Gray's Manual. N.P: 1899. V. 72

PAN AMERICAN HEALTH ORGANIZATION
Life at High Altitudes. Proceedings of the Special Session Held During the Fifty Meeting of the PAHO Advisory Committee on Medical Research 15 June 1966. Washington: 1966. V. 68

PAN Pipes, a Book of Old Songs.... London: 1883. V. 71

PANASSIE, HUGUES
Hot Jazz. New York: 1936. V. 69; 71; 73
Le Jazz Hot. Paris: 1934. V. 68
Quand Mezzrow Enregistre. Paris: 1952. V. 68
The Real Jazz. New York: 1942. V. 73

PANCAKE, BREECE D'J
The Stories of Breece D'J Pancake. Boston: 1983. V. 72

PANCOAST, JOSEPH
A Treatise on Operative Surgery. Philadelphia: 1844. V. 68; 72; 73
A Treatise on Operative Surgery. Philadelphia: 1846. V. 71

PANHANDLE PLAINS HISTORICAL REVIEW
The Indian Campaign on the Staked Plains, 1874-1875 Entire Issue Of Panhandle Plains Historical Review, Vol XXXIV 1961. V. 72

PANIZZI, ANTHONY
British Museum. A Short Guide to that Portion of the Library of Printed Books Now Open to the Public. London: 1851. V. 73

PANKHURST, E. SYLVIA
The Suffragette Movement. London: 1931. V. 71; 73
The Suffragette Movement. New York: 1932. V. 71
The Suffragette. The History of the Women's Militant Suffrage Movement 1905-1910. London: 1911. V. 71

PANKLIBANON
The Panklibanon Show Room and Stove Grate Manufactory. London: 1848?. V. 68

PANKO, ANDREW
Niagara, St. Catharines and Toronto Electric Railway in Pictures. Niagara-on-the-Lake: 1984. V. 73

PANKOW, F. H. E.
The Mollusc Paramount. London: 1909. V. 68

PANNEKOEK, A.
Researches on the Structure of the Universe. Amsterdam: 1924-1929. V. 69

PANOFSKY, E.
Albrect Durer. Princeton: 1948. V. 69; 72

PANTOMIME Pictures. London: 1895. V. 73

PANTON, EDWARD
Speculum Juvenatutis; or a True Mirror, Where Errors in Breeding Noble and Generous Youth, with the Miseries and Mischiefs that Usually Attend It, are Clearly Made Manifest.... London: 1671. V. 73

PANYELLA, AUGUST
Folk Art of the Americas. New York: 1981. V. 71

PANZER, GEORG WOLFGANG
Faunae Insectorum Germanicae Initia Oder Deutschlands Insecten. Nurnberg: 1793-1808. V. 73

PAOLI, PAOLO ANTONIO
Avanzi delle Antichita Esistenti; a Pozzuoli Cuma e Baja. Naples: 1768. V. 70; 72
Rovine della Citta di Pesto, detta Ancora Posidonia. Rome: 1784. V. 70

PAOLOZZI, EDUARDO
The Metallization of a Dream. 1963. V. 71

PAPADAKI, S.
Oscar Niemeyer: Works in Progress. New York: 1956. V. 68; 72

PAPADOPOULO, ALEXANDRE
Islam and Muslim Art. London: 1980. V. 72

PAPERS in Penology. Elmira: 1891. V. 69

PAPERS Relative to the Mission of Hon. T. Butler King, to Europe. Milledgeville: 1863. V. 69; 70

PAPEZ, JAMES W.
Comparative Neurology. New York: 1929. V. 71

PAPILLON, JEAN BAPTISTE MICHEL
Traite Historique et Pratique de la Gravure en Bois. Paris: 1766. V. 69; 72

PAPPE, I.
Synopsis of Edible Fishes at the Cape of Good Hope. Cape Town: 1853. V. 70

PAPWORTH, JOHN BUONAROTTI
Essay on the Causes of the Dry Rot in Buildings, Contained in a Series of Letters Addressed to George Ernest James Wright, Esq. London: 1803. V. 68
Hints on Ornamental Gardening.... London: 1823. V. 68; 70
Rural Residences, Consisting of a Series of Designs for Cottages, Decorated Cottages, Small Villas and Other Ornamental Buildings.... London: 1818. V. 68; 70; 72

THE PARABLES of Our Lord. London: 1847. V. 68

THE PARABLES of Our Lord and Saviour Jesus Christ with Pictures by John Everett Millais. London: 1875. V. 68

PARACELSUS
Philosophiae Magnae... (with) Def Hocherfarhrnesten... (with) Astronomica et Astrologica.... Cologne: 1567. V. 71

PARADIN, CLAUDE
Symbola Herioca. Antverpiae: 1583. V. 70

PARADOXICAL Philosophy. London: 1878. V. 70

PARBURT, GEORGE R.
Anselmo: a Poem. San Francisco: 1865. V. 73

PARDIGON, C. F.
The Practice of War: Being a Treatise on a French Military Work Entitled Maxims, Counsels and Instructions on the Art of War, or Handbook for the Practice of War. Richmond: 1863. V. 69; 70

PARDOE, JULIA
Beauties of the Bosphorus.... London: 1850?. V. 69

PARDON, GEORGE FREDERICK
The Faces in the Fire: a Story for the Season. London: 1849?. V. 70; 73
A Handbook of Whist. London: 1862. V. 73

PARE, AMBROSE
The Workes of that Famous Chirurgion. London: 1634. V. 71

PARETSKY, SARA
Bitter Medicine. New York: 1987. V. 69; 70; 71
Deadlock. London: 1984. V. 72; 73
Deadlock. New York: 1984. V. 69; 70; 71
Deadlock. New York: 1994. V. 70
Indemnity Only. London: 1982. V. 69; 73
Indemnity Only. New York: 1982. V. 71
Killing Orders. New York: 1985. V. 68; 69; 70
Killing Orders. London: 1986. V. 70
Toxic Shock. London: 1988. V. 69
Tunnel Vision. New York: 1994. V. 73

PARGETER, EDITH
The Assize of the Dying. New York: 1958. V. 69
The Marriage of Meggotta. London: 1979. V. 69

PARHAM, EUGENE C.
Shop and Road Testing of Dynamos and Motors: a Practical Manual for the Testing Floor, the Car Barn and the Road. New York: 1901. V. 68

PARIS, JOHN AYRTON
Philosophy in Sport Made Science in Earnest.... London: 1827. V. 70
Philosophy in Sport Made Science in Earnest.... London: 1833. V. 71
Philosophy in Sport Made Science in Earnest.... London: 1857. V. 71

PARIS, LOUIS PHILIPPE ALBERT D'ORLEANS, COMTE DE
History of the Civil War in America. Philadelphia: 1875-1888. V. 73

PARK, E. A.
New Backgrounds for a New Age. New York: 1927. V. 72

PARK, EDGAR
The Merrie Adventures of Robin Hood and Santa Claus. Boston: 1922. V. 73

PARK, JOHN JAMES
The Topography and Natural History of Hampstead in the County of Middlesex. London: 1818. V. 71

PARK, MUNGO
Travels in the Interior of Africa, in the Years 1795, 1796 and 1797.... London: 1799. V. 70

PARK, ORLANDO
Sherlock Holmes, Esq. And John H. Watson, M. D.: An Encyclopedia Of Their Affairs. Evanston: 1962. V. 69; 72; 73

PARK, ROSWELL
An Epitome of the History of Medicine.... Philadelphia: 1897. V. 71; 73
A Treatise on Surgery by American Authors. Philadelphia: 1896. V. 68; 70; 71; 73

PARK, SUZAN LORI
Betting on the Dust Commander (Practice Makes Practice). New York. V. 69

PARK, THOMAS
Heliconia. London: 1815. V. 69

PARKE, THOMAS HEAZLE
My Personal Experiences in Equatorial Africa. London: 1891. V. 69; 71

PARKER, A. C.
The Code of Handsome Lake, the Seneca Prophet. 1913. V. 69

PARKER, AL
Baseball Giant Killers; the Spudders of the 20's. Quannah, TX: 1976. V. 72

PARKER, ALFRED BROWNING
You and Architecture: a Practical Guide to the Best Building. New York: 1965. V. 68; 69; 72

PARKER, ANN
Molas: Folk Art of the Cuna Indians. Barre: 1977. V. 71

PARKER, B.
A Book of Bears. 1906. V. 71
The Browns: a Book of Bears. 1910. V. 72
Larder Lodge. London: 1920. V. 73

PARKER, BARRETT
Collects and Prayers in Wartime. London: 1953. V. 70

PARKER, CHARLES ARUNDEL
The Ancient Crosses at Gosfroth, Cumberland. London: 1896. V. 71
The Gosforth District: Its Antiquities and Places of Interest. Kendal: 1904. V. 71
The Runic Crosses at Gosforth Cumberland Described and Explained. London: 1882. V. 71
The Story of Shelagh, Olaf Cuaran's Daughter. Kendal: 1909. V. 71

PARKER, DOROTHY
After Such Pleasures. New York: 1933. V. 68; 69
After Such Pleasures. New York: 1934. V. 68
Death And Taxes. New York: 1931. V. 72
Enough Rope. New York: 1926. V. 70
Not So Deep As A Well: Collected Poems. New York: 1936. V. 70
Sunset Gun. New York: 1928. V. 69

PARKER, E.
Fine Angling for Coarse Fish. 1955. V. 73
Shooting by Moor, Field and Shore. 1929. V. 70; 71

PARKER, F. H. M.
The Pipe Rolls of Cumberland and Westmorland 1222-1260. Kendal: 1905. V. 71

PARKER, FRED R.
Manuel Alvarez Bravo. Pasadena: 1971. V. 70

PARKER, G. H.
The Elementary Nervous System. Philadelphia: 1919. V. 68

PARKER, GILBERT
Donovan Pasha and Some People of Egypt. London: 1902. V. 70
The Lane that Had No Turning and Other Associated Tales Concerning the People of Pontiac. London: 1900. V. 69
The Money Master: Being the Curious History of Jean Jacques Barbille, His Labours, His Loves, and His Ladies. New York: 1915. V. 72

PARKER, GWENDOLYN
These Same Long Bones. Boston: 1994. V. 72

PARKER, H. C.
Laddow Area. Climbs on Gritstone. Birkenhead: 1956. V. 69

PARKER, JAMES
Conductor Generalis; or, the Office, Duty and Authority of Justices of the Peace, High Sheriffs.... Woodbridge: 1764. V. 70; 73
The Conductor Generalis; or the Office, Duty and Authority of Justices of the Peace, High Sheriffs.... New York: 1790. V. 73

PARKER, JAMES A.
The Western Highlands. Edinburgh: 1931. V. 69
The Western Highlands. Edinburgh: 1947. V. 69

The Western Highlands. Edinburgh: 1964. V. 69

PARKER, JOHN
The Early History and Antiquities of Wycombe, in Buckinghamshire. Wycombe: 1878. V. 71

PARKER, JOHN HENRY
The Archaeology of Rome. Oxford and London: 1874-1877. V. 68
A Glossary of Terms Used in Grecian, Roman, Italian and Gothic Architeture. Oxford: 1850. V. 72
A Guide to the Architectural Antiquities of the Neighbourhood of Oxford. Oxford: 1846-1860. V. 70

PARKER, JOHN P.
Sails of the Maritimes. 1960. V. 73

PARKER, JOSEPH
Weaver Stephen: Odds and Events in Religion. London: 1889. V. 68

PARKER, L. A.
The Fishing or Angling Arts and Artifices. Salisbury: 1948. V. 73
This Fishing, or Angling Arts and Artifices. 1948. V. 68

PARKER, LANGSTON
The Modern Treatment of Syphilitic Diseases, Both Primary and Secondary. London: 1845. V. 71

PARKER, MARY ANN
A Voyage Round the World. Sydney: 1991. V. 70

PARKER, MICHAEL
Hello Down There. New York: 1993. V. 69

PARKER, NATHAN HOWE
Iowa As It Is in 1855: a Gazetteer for Citizens and a Hand-Book for Emigrants. Chicago: 1855. V. 68
The Minnesota Handbook for 1856-1857. Boston: 1857. V. 73
Missouri Hand-Book, Embracing a Full Description of the State of Missouri.... Saint Louis: 1865. V. 68

PARKER, RICHARD
To-Day. New York: 1914. V. 71

PARKER, ROBERT B.
A Catskill Eagle. New York: 1986. V. 71
Crimson Joy. New York: 1988. V. 73
Death in Paradise. New York: 2001. V. 70
God Save the Child. 1974. V. 69
The Godwulf Manuscript. Boston: 1974. V. 69
Hugger Mugger. New York: 2000. V. 72
Introduction to Raymond Chandler's Unknown Thriller: The Screenplay of Playback. New York: 1985. V. 68; 69; 71; 73
The Judas Goat. Boston: 1978. V. 68; 69; 70; 71; 72; 73
Looking for Rachel Wallace. New York: 1980. V. 68; 69
Love and Glory. New York: 1983. V. 71; 72
Mortal Stakes. Boston: 1975. V. 69
Pale Kings and Princes. New York: 1987. V. 73
Parker On Writing. Northridge: 1985. V. 71; 72
Poodle Springs. New York: 1989. V. 72
The Private Eye in Hammett and Chandler. Northridge: 1984. V. 70; 71; 72
Promised Land. 1976. V. 71
Promised Land. Boston: 1976. V. 68; 69; 70
Promised Land. London: 1977. V. 70
A Savage Place. New York: 1981. V. 69
Surrogate. Northridge: 1982. V. 68; 69
Taming a Sea-Horse. New York: 1986. V. 73
Thin Air. New York: 1995. V. 72
Ticket to Oblivion. New York: 1950. V. 69
The Widening Gyre. New York: 1983. V. 71
Widow's Walk. New York: 2002. V. 72

PARKER, SOLOMON
Parker's American Sure Guide, or Ready Reckoner, Measurer and Calendar. Sag Harbor: 1808. V. 70

PARKER, T. JEFFERSON
Easy Street. Royal Oak: 2000. V. 71; 72
Laguna Heat. New York: 1985. V. 68

PARKER, T. JEFFERY
William Kitchen Parker, F.R.S. London: 1893. V. 68; 70

PARKER, THEODORE
The Great Battle Between Slavery and Freedom. Boston: 1856. V. 68
John Brown's Expedition Reviewed in a Letter from Rev. Theodore Parker at Rome to Francis Jackson, Boston. Boston: 1860. V. 73
The Trial of Theodore Parker, for the "Misdemeanor" of a Speech in Faneuill Hall Against Kidnapping, Before the Circuit Court of the United States, at Boston, April 3, 1855. Boston: 1855. V. 71

PARKER, THOMAS N.
An Essay on the Construction, Hanging and Fastening of Gates. London: 1804. V. 68; 70

PARKER, W. THORNTON
Notes Concerning Our North American Indians. Northhampton: 1918. V. 72

PARKER, WILLIAM FREDERICK
Daniel McNeill Parker, M.D. His Ancestry and a Memoir of His Life. Toronto: 1910. V. 73

PARKER, WILLIAM H.
Recollections of a Naval Officer 1841-1865. New York: 1883. V. 70
Recollections of a Naval Officer 1841-1865. New York: 1885. V. 69

PARKES, OCSAR
British Battleships 1860-1950. London: 1970. V. 69

PARKES, S.
The Chemical Catechism.... London: 1812. V. 69
The Chemical Catechism.... 1814. V. 68
The Chemical Catechism.... 1822. V. 68

PARKES, WILLIAM, MRS.
Domestic Duties, or Instructions to Young Married Ladies.... New York: 1840. V. 72

PARKHURST, JOHN
An Hebrew and English Lexicon. London: 1799. V. 69

PARKIN, ALFRED
Ambroise Pare. Durham. V. 72
Ambroise Pare. Durham: 1911. V. 68

PARKINS, W. H.
How I Escaped: a Novel. London: 1889. V. 68; 73

PARKINSON, C. NORTHCOTE
East and West & The Life and Times of Horatio Hornblower. London: 1970. V. 71

PARKINSON, J.
Organic Remains of a Former World. 1804. V. 69

PARKINSON, JAMES
The Chemical Pocket Book or Memoranda Chemica. London: 1801. V. 72; 72

PARKINSON, JOHN
The Dinosaur in East Africa. London: 1930. V. 68
Nowhere is Too Far. The Annals of the Cruising Club of America. New York: 1960. V. 68; 73
Outlines of Oryctyology. 1822. V. 69; 73
Paradisi in Sole Paradisus Terrestris or a Garden of All Sorts of Ple asant Flowers Which Our English Ayre Will Permitt to be Noursed Up. London: 1629. V. 68; 70; 73
Paradisi in Sole Paradisus Terrestris or a Garden of all Sorts of Ple asant Flowers Which Our English Ayre Will Permitt to be Noursed Up. London: 1904. V. 68

PARKINSON, NORMAN
Sisters Under the Skin. London: 1978. V. 68

PARKINSON, THOMAS
Flower Painting Made Easy. London: 1766. V. 69
Hart Crane & Yvor Winters - Their Library Correspondence. Berkeley/Los Angeles/London: 1978. V. 71

PARKMAN, FRANCIS
The California and Oregon Trail: Being Sketches of Prairie and Rocky Mountain Life. New York: 1849. V. 73
The Conspiracy of Pontiac and the Indian War After the Conquest of Canada. Boston: 1870. V. 68
The Discovery of the Great West. Boston: 1869. V. 72
A Half Century of Conflict. Boston: 1892. V. 68
History of the Conspiracy of Pontiac and the War of the North American Tribes Against the English Colonies. Boston: 1855. V. 68
The Journals of Francis Parkman. New York: 1947. V. 73
The Oregon Trail. New York: 1943. V. 68; 69
The Oregon Trail. Garden City: 1945. V. 69
The Works. Boston: 1897. V. 71
The Works. Boston: 1910. V. 68

PARKS, FANNY
Wanderings of a Pilgrim in Search of the Picturesque, During Four and Twenty Years in the East.... London: 1850. V. 68; 70

PARKS, GEORGE BRUNER
Richard Hakluyt and the English Voyages. New York: 1928. V. 68

PARKS, GORDON
In Love. Philadelphia: 1971. V. 72
A Poet and His Camera. New York: 1968. V. 72; 73
Whispers of Intimate Things. New York: 1971. V. 72

PARKS, JOSEPH H.
General Kirby Smith CSA. Baton Rouge: 1954. V. 68; 73

PARKS, STEPHEN
R. C. Gorman: a Portrait. Boston: 1983. V. 70; 72; 73

PARKYNS, MANSFIELD
Life in Abyssinia. London: 1853. V. 71

PARKYNS, THOMAS
Progymnasmata. London: 1727. V. 70

PARLIAMENTARY Blue Book: A Copy of the Roll of Freeholders of Every County in Scotland, As Last Made Up. London: 1820. V. 71

THE PARLIAMENTARY Gazetteer of England and Wales, Adapted to the New Poor-Law, Franchise, Muncipal and Ecclesiastical Arrangements.... London: 1845-1847. V. 71

THE PARLIAMENTARY Register, Containing a List of Twenty Four Parliaments from 1660 to 1741. London: 1741. V. 70

PARLOA, MARIA
The Appledore Cook Book: Containing Practical Receipts for Plain and Rich Cooking. Boston: 1872. V. 68; 70
Miss Parloa's Young Housekeepers. Boston: 1903. V. 68; 73

PARMENTER, CHRISTINE WHITING
So Wise We Grow. Boston: 1930. V. 73

PARNASSUS Biceps, or Several Choice Pieces of Poetry. 1656. London: 1927. V. 69; 72

PARNELL, EDWARD
Elements of Chemical Analysis: Inorganic and Orangic. London: 1842. V. 71

PARNELL, HENRY
A Collection of Valuable Receipts, in Various Branches of Domestic Economy. London: 1819. V. 69
A History of the Penal Laws Against the Irish Catholics, from the Treaty of Limerick to the Union. London: 1808. V. 69
On Financial Reform. London: 1830. V. 71
A Treatise on Roads; Wherein the Principles on Which Roads Should be Made are Explained and Illustrated, by the Plans, Specifications and Contracts made Use of by Thomas Telford, Esq. on the Holyhead Road. London: 1833. V. 72

PARNELL, R.
Prize Essay On The Fishes Of The District Of The Firth Of Forth. Edinburgh: 1838. V. 72; 73

PARNELL, THOMAS
Poems on Several Occasions. London: 1747. V. 71
Poems Upon Several Occasions. London: 1773. V. 68; 72
The Poetical Works. Glasgow: 1786. V. 68; 73
The Poetical Works. London: 1852. V. 72

PARNELL, WILLIAM
An Historical Apology for the Irish Catholics. Dublin: 1807. V. 69
Maurice and Berghetta; or, the Priest of Rahery. London: 1819. V. 69

PARR, BARTHOLOMEW
The London Medical Dictionary.... 1809. V. 72
The London Medical Dictionary.... London: 1809. V. 70

PARR, HARRIET
Hawksview: a Family History of Our Own Times. 1859. V. 71

PARR, SAMUEL
Characters of the Late Charles James Fox, Selected and in Part Written, by Philopatris Varvicensis. London: 1809. V. 72
A Free Translation of the Preface to Bellendenus; Containing Animated Strictures on the Great Political Characters of the Present Time. London: 1788. V. 69
A Spital Sermon, Preached at Christ Church, Upon Easter Tuesday April 15, 1800, to which are added Notes. London: 1801. V. 68

PARRA, NICANOR
Poems and Antipoems. New York: 1967. V. 71

PARRISH, ANNE
All Kneeling. New York: 1928. V. 70; 71; 73
The Story of Appleby Gapple. New York: 1950. V. 73

PARRISH, JOSEPH
Practical Observations on Strangulated Hernia, and Some of the Diseases of the Urinary Organs. Philadelphia: 1836. V. 69

PARRISH, MICHAEL T.
Confederate Imprints: a Bibliography of Southern Publications from Secession to Surrender. Austin and Katonah: 1988. V. 69

PARRISH, MORRIS L.
Victorian Lady Novelists: George Eliot, Mrs. Gaskell, the Bronte Sisters, First Editions from the Library at Dormy House, Pine Valley, New Jersey, Described with Notes. London: 1933. V. 73

PARROT, FRIEDRICH
Journey to Ararat. London: 1845. V. 71

PARRY, EDWARD
The Cambrian Mirror; or, the Tourist's Companion through North Wales.... 1851. V. 71

PARRY, EDWARD ABBOTT
Butterscotia or a Cheap Trip to Fairy Land. London: 1896. V. 68; 73
The First Book of Krab Christmas Stories for Young and Old. London: 1902. V. 69
The Scarlet Herring and Other Stories.... London: 1899. V. 68; 72; 73

PARRY, H. LLOYD
The Exeter Civic Seals. Exeter: 1909. V. 72

PARRY, HENRY
The Art of Bookbinding.... London: 1818. V. 73

PARRY, J. D.
An Historical and Descriptive Account of the Coast of Sussex, Brighton, Eastbourn, Worthing.... Brighton: 1833. V. 70; 72

PARRY, JUDGE
Don Quioxte of the Mancha Retold. 1900. V. 68

PARRY, WILLIAM EDWARD
Journal of a Second Voyage for the Discovery of a North West Passage from the Atlantic to the Pacific. London: 1824. V. 68; 73
Journal of A Voyage for the Discovery of a North-West Passage from the Atlantic to the Pacific. London: 1821. V. 69; 70; 71

PARRY, WILLIAM EDWARD continued
Journals of the First, Second and Third Voyages For the Discovery of a North-West Passages from the Atlantic to the Pacific.... London: 1828. V. 71
Letters Written During the Late Voyage of Discovery in the Western Arctic. London: 1821. V. 73

PARSHLEY, H. M.
A Bibliography of the North American Hemiptera-Heteroptera. Northampton: 1925. V. 72

PARSLOW, JOHN
Trial for Adultery, in Westminster Hall, on Wednesday, December 9, 1789, Before the Lord Kenyon, John Parslow, Esq. Plaintiff and Francis William Sykes, Esq. Defendant, for Criminal Conversation with the Plaintiff's Wife. London: 1789. V. 70

PARSON, WILLIAM
History, Directory and Gazetteer of the Counties of Cumberland and Westmorland.... Leeds: 1829. V. 71

PARSONS, BENJAMIN
The Mental and Moral Dignity of Woman. London: 1846. V. 72

PARSONS, C. S. M.
China Mending and Restoration. London: 1963. V. 72

PARSONS, CHUCK
The Capture of John Wesley Hardin. College Station: 1978. V. 72

PARSONS, ELSIE CLEWS
American Indian Life. New York: 1922. V. 69
Isleta Paintings. Washington: 1962. V. 70; 72; 73
Pueblo Indian Religion. Chicago: 1939. V. 68; 69; 70; 72; 73
Taos Pueblo. New York: 1970. V. 70
Taos Tales. New York: 1940. V. 72
Tewa Tales. New York: 1926. V. 70

PARSONS, JAMES
Philosophical Observations on the Analogy Between the Propagation of Animals and that of Vegetables. 1752. V. 69
Philosophical Observations on the Anaology Between the Propagation of Animals and That of Vegetables.... London: 1752. V. 70; 73

PARSONS, LEE
Pre-Columbian Art. The Morton D. May and the St. Louis Art Museum Collections. New York: 1980. V. 70

PARSONS, LUCY
Life of Albert R. Parsons with a Brief History of the Labor Movement. Chicago: 1903. V. 70

PARSONS, ROBERT
A Treatise of Three Conversions of England from Paganisme to Christian Religion. St. Omer: 1603. V. 69

PARSONS, S.
The Art of Landscape Architecture. 1915. V. 68

PARSONS, SAMUEL
Poetical Trifles, Being a Collection of Songs and Fugitive Pieces.... York: 1822. V. 69

PARSONS, THOMAS
Poems. Boston: 1854. V. 71

PARSONS, TYLER
Mormon Fanaticism Exposed. A Compendium of the Book of Mormon, or Joseph Smith's Golden Bible. Boston: 1841. V. 71

PARSONS, WILLIAM
Chronological Tables of Europe...on 46 Copper-Plates.... London: 1707. V. 69

THE PARTHENON. London: 1826. V. 73

A PARTICULAR Account of the Commencement and Progress of the Insurrection of the Negroes in St. Domingo, Which Began in August Last. 1791. V. 70

PARTINGTON, C. E.
National History and Views of London and Its Environs.... London: 1835. V. 71

PARTINGTON, J. R.
A History of Chemistry. New York: 1996. V. 69
A History of Greek Fire and Gunpowder. 1960. V. 70
A History of Greek Fire and Gunpowder. Cambridge: 1960. V. 73

PARTINGTON, S. W.
A Gossiping Guide to Shap and Haweswater. Manchester: 1923. V. 71

PARTNERS in Wonder. New York: 1971. V. 68

PARTON, JAMES
Eminent Women of the Age: Being Narratives of the Lives and Deeds of the Most Prominent Women of the Present Generation. Hartford: 1869. V. 72
Life and Times of Benjamin Franklin. New York: 1864. V. 73
Life of Andrew Jackson. Boston: 1860. V. 71

PARTRIDGE, ERIC
Literary Sessions. London: 1912. V. 68
The Shaggy Dog Story - Its Origin, Development and Nature. London: 1953. V. 71

PARTRIDGE, FRANCES
Everything to Lose - Diaries 1945-1960. London: 1985. V. 69
Julia - a Portrait of Julia Strachey by Herself and Frances Partridge. London: 1983. V. 68
Memories. London: 1981. V. 69

PARTRIDGE, HELEN
The Windy Hill. New York: 1936. V. 71

PARTRIDGE, JOHN
Merlinus Liberatus. Being an Almanack for...1789.... 1789. V. 69

PARTRIDGE, WILLIAM
A Practical Treatise on Dying of Woollen, Cotton and Skein Silk, the Manufacaturing of Broadcloth and Cassimere.... New York: 1823. V. 68; 70

PARTS of the Pacific. London: 1896. V. 68

PARVILLIERS, ADRIEN
The Devotions of the Stations of the Passion of Jesus Christ, Crucified, Which are Made in Jerusalem. Dublin?: 1796. V. 70

PASCAL, BLAISE
Pascal's Pensees. London: 1931. V. 72
Pensees. Paris: 1670. V. 73
Les Provinciales; or, the Mysterie of Jesuitisme...Displaying the Corrupt Maximes and Politicks of that Society. London: 1657. V. 71
Thoughts on Religion and Other Subjects. London: 1704. V. 71
Traitez de l'Equilibre des Liqueurs, et de la Pesanteur de la Masse de l'Air. Paris: 1663. V. 68; 70; 73

PASCOE, JOHN
Unclimbed New Zealand. London: 1950. V. 69

PASCOLI, LIONE
Vite de' Pittori, Scultori. Rome: 1732. V. 72

PASHLEY, ROBERT
Travels in Crete. Cambridge: 1837. V. 71

PASLEY, CHARLES W.
Observations on the Expediency and Practicability of Simplifying and Improving the Measures, Weights, and Money, Used in This Country.... London: 1834. V. 73

PASMORE, VICTOR
Burning Waters - Second Version: Visual and Poetical Images. London: 1995. V. 73

PASSEE, THOMAS EDMUND
An Epic on the Miserable State of the Island of Grenada, British West Indies. Grenada: 1883. V. 69

PASSERON, R.
Impressionist Prints. New York: 1974. V. 69; 72

PASSI, GIUSEPPE
I Donneschi Difetti Nell' Illustrissima Academia e Signori Rissourati di Padova & Informi di Tavenna l'Aggiuntoui in Questa Quarta Impressione.... Venise: 1618. V. 72

PASSMORE, N. I.
South African Frogs. Johannesburg: 1979. V. 69; 73

THE PASSPORTS Printed by Benjamin Franklin at His Passy Press. Ann Arbor: 1925. V. 69

PASTERNAK, BORIS
Doctor Zhivago. London: 1958. V. 68; 71
Doctor Zhivago. Milan: 1958. V. 69
Doktor Zhivago. Ann Arbor: 1958. V. 72
My Sister, Life and Other Poems. New York. V. 68

PASTEUR, LOUIS
Oeuvres de Pasteur. Paris: 1922-1939. V. 72
Studies on Fermentation, the Diseases of Beer, Their Causes and the Means of Preventing Them. London: 1879. V. 72

PASTON, GEORGE
Little Memoirs of the Nineteenth Century. London: 1902. V. 69

THE PASTOR Chief; or The Escape of the Vaudois. London: 1843. V. 70; 71

A PATCH-WORK Quilt of Favorite Tales. 1933. V. 69

PATCHEN, KENNETH
An Astonished Eye Looks Out of the Air. Waldport: 1945. V. 71
Before the Brave. New York: 1936. V. 71
But Even So. New York: 1968. V. 71
Cloth of the Tempest. New York: 1943. V. 71
Cloth of the Tempest. New York: 1948. V. 71
The Collected Poems of Kenneth Patchen. New York: 1968. V. 71
The Dark Kingdom. New York: 1942. V. 68; 71
The Dark Kingdom. New York: 1948. V. 69; 71; 73
Fables and Other Little Tales. Karlsruhe/Baden: 1953. V. 68; 71; 73
The Famous Boating Party. New York: 1954. V. 71
First Will and Testament. Norfolk: 1939. V. 71
Hallelujah Anyway. New York: 1966. V. 71
Hallelujah Anyway!. Grand Forks: 1974. V. 71
Hurrah for Anything. Poems and Drawings. Highlands: 1957. V. 73
The Journal of Albion Moonlight. New York: 1944. V. 68; 71
Kenneth Patchen: Painter of Poems. Washington: 1969. V. 71
The Love Poems of Kenneth Patchen. San Francisco: 1960. V. 71
Outlaw of the Lowest Planet. London: 1946. V. 71
Pictures of Life and Death. New York: 1946. V. 71
Poem-Scapes. Highlands: 1958. V. 69
Red Wine and Yellow Hair. New York: 1949. V. 68; 71

PATCHEN, KENNETH continued
See You in the Morning. New York: 1947. V. 71
Sleepers Awake. New York: 1946. V. 71
The Teeth of the Lion. Norfolk: 1942. V. 70; 71
They Keep Riding Down All the Time. New York: 1946. V. 71
To Say If You Love Someone. Prairie City: 1948. V. 70
When We Were Here Together. Norfolk: 1957. V. 71
Wonderings. New York: 1971. V. 68; 71

PATCHETT, ANN
The Magician's Assistant. New York: 1997. V. 72
The Patron Saint of Liars. Boston: 1992. V. 69

PATE, J. S.
The Biology of Australian Plants. Nedlands: 1981. V. 72

PATENT Artificial Slate Manufactory, Woodford Bridge, Essex, for Covering Roofs, Fronts of Houses and Ricks; also Water Pipes and Gutters. London: 1786?. V. 68

PATER, WALTER
Appreciations: with an Essay on Style. London: 1927. V. 70
Essays from The Guardian. London: 1920. V. 70
Gaston De Latour: An Unfinished Romance. London: 1922. V. 70
Greek Studies. London: 1895. V. 68
Greek Studies. London: 1925. V. 70
Imaginary Portraits. London: 1922. V. 70
Marius the Epicurean. London: 1913. V. 68
Marius the Epicurean. London: 1925. V. 70
Miscellaneous Studies: a Series of Essays. London: 1924. V. 70
Plato and Platonism: a Series of Lectures. London: 1893. V. 69
Plato and Platonism: a Series of Lectures. London: 1925. V. 70
The Renaissance: Studies in Art and Poetry. London: 1925. V. 70
The Renaissance: Studies in Art and Poetry. Verona: 1976. V. 70
Studies in the History of the Renaissance. London: 1873. V. 73

PATERNOSTER, SIDNEY
The Hand of the Spoiler. London: 1908. V. 70

PATERSON, A. B.
The Animals Noah Forgot. Sydney: 1933. V. 68

PATERSON, DANIEL
A New and Accurate Description Of All the Direct and Principal Cross Roads in England and Wales, and Part of the Roads of Scotland.. London: 1803. V. 70

PATERSON, DAVID
Colour-Matching on Textiles. 1901. V. 71
Textile Colour Mixing. 1915. V. 71

PATERSON, JAMES
A Practical Treatise on the Making and Upholding of Public Roads. Montrose: 1819. V. 72

PATERSON, M.
Mountaineering Below the Snow Line or the Solitary Pedestrian in Snowdonia and Elsewhere. London: 1886. V. 69

PATERSON, WILLIAM
An Enquiry into the State of the Union of Great Britain and the Past and Present State of the Trade and Publick Revenues Thereof. London: 1717. V. 72

PATEY, T.
One Man's Mountains. 1975. V. 68; 71
One Man's Mountains. 1978. V. 71; 73

THE PATHS Of Learning Strewed with Flowers, or English Grammar Illustrated. London: 1820. V. 73

PATHS of Resistance. The Art and Craft of the Political Novel. Boston: 1989. V. 72

PATISON, JANE M.
Gleanings Among the British Ferns. London: 1858. V. 69

PATMORE, BRIGIT
This Impassioned Onlooker. London: 1926. V. 72

PATMORE, COVENTRY
The Angel in the House. Book I. The Betrothal. Book II. The Espousals. London: 1858. V. 72
The Angel in the House. Book I. The Betrothal. Book II. The Espousals. (with) The Angel in the House. Part II. Book I. Faithful for Ever. Book II - The Victories of Love. London and Cambridge: 1863. V. 69; 71
The Angel in the House Book II. The Espousals. London: 1856. V. 71; 72
The Angel in the House: Books I and II. The First Editions Collated with His Original Holograph Manuscript. 1998. V. 68
The Angel in the House. The Bethrothal. (with) The Espousals. London: 1854-1856. V. 69; 71
The Angel in the House. The Betrothal. London: 1854. V. 72
The Children's Garland from the best poets. London: 1862. V. 71
Florilegium Amantis. London: 1879. V. 69
Odes. 1868. V. 72
Poems. (with) Tamerton Church-Tower and Other Poems. London: 1844. V. 69; 72
The Unknown Eros and Other Odes. Odes I-XXXI. 1877. V. 72
The Unknown Eros. I-XLVI. London: 1878. V. 72

PATMORE, D.
Colour Schemes for the Modern Home. London: 1936. V. 69

PATMORE, DEREK
Greek Horizons. Athens: 1946. V. 71
World Sadness. Ikaros, Athens: 1945. V. 73

PATON, A. A.
Highlands and Islands of the Adriatic. London: 1849. V. 71

PATON, ALAN
Cry, the Beloved Country. New York: 1948. V. 73
Cry, the Beloved Country. New York: 1950. V. 68
Cry, the Beloved Country. Franklin Center: 1978. V. 69
Too Late the Phalarope. New York: 1953. V. 68; 71

PATON, E. RICHMOND
The Birds of Ayrshire. London: 1929. V. 71

PATON, J. A.
Liverwort Flora of the British Isles. Colchester: 1999. V. 72

PATON, J. NOEL
Compositions From Shakespeare's Tempest. London and Edinburgh: 1877. V. 68
Spindrift. 1867. V. 72

PATON, JAMES
Scottish National Memorials. Glasgow: 1890. V. 69

PATON, MAGGIE WHITECROSS
Letters and Sketches From The New Hebrides. London: 1894. V. 72

PATRICK, CHANN
The House of Retrogression. New York: 1932. V. 73

PATRICK, DIANA
Vain Pantomine. New York: 1933. V. 71

PATRICK, JOHN
The Teahouse of the August Moon. New York: 1952. V. 73

PATRICK, Q.
Cottage Sinister. 1931. V. 68; 73
Death and the Maiden. 1939. V. 68
Death Goes to School. 1936. V. 73
File on Claudia Cragge. 1938. V. 73
File on Fenton and Farr. New York: 1937. V. 73
The Grindle Nightmare. 1935. V. 73
Return to the Scene. 1941. V. 68

PATRICK, SYMON
Advice to a Friend. London: 1673. V. 72

PATRICK, VINCENT
Pope of Greenwich Village. New York: 1979. V. 72

PATRIOTS and People. London: 1917. V. 70

PATTEN, C. J.
The Aquatic Birds of Great Britain and Ireland. 1906. V. 70

PATTEN, R. L.
George Cruikshank, a Re-Evaluation. Princeton: 1974. V. 72

PATTEN, WILLIAM
The Book of Baseball from the Earliest Day to the Present Season. New York: 1911. V. 70
Pioneering the Telephone in Canada. Montreal: 1926. V. 72

A PATTERN of Well-Constructed and Well-Governed Hospital; or, a Brief Description of the Building, and Full Relation of the Establishment Constitution, Discipline, Oeconomy and Administration of the Government of the Royal Hospital of Invalids. London: 1695. V. 69

PATTERSON, C. S.
Railway Accident Law, the Liability of Railways for Injuries to the Person. Philadelphia: 1886. V. 68
The United States and the States Under the Constitution. Philadelphia: 1904. V. 69

PATTERSON, EDNA B.
Nevada's Northeast Frontier. Sparks: 1969. V. 68; 71

PATTERSON, FRANK H.
Acadian Tatamagouche and Fort Franklin. Truro: 1947. V. 73

PATTERSON, GEORGE
A History of the County of Pictou, Nova Scotia. Montreal: 1877. V. 73

PATTERSON, HAYWOOD
Scottsboro Boy. Garden City: 1950. V. 68; 72

PATTERSON, HENRY
To Catch a King. London: 1979. V. 70

PATTERSON, ISABELLA INNIS
The Eppworth Case. New York: 1930. V. 70
The Standish Gaunt Case. New York: 1931. V. 70

PATTERSON, J. A.
The Gold Fields of Victoria in 1862.... Melbourne: 1863. V. 68

PATTERSON, J. B.
Life of Ma-Ka-Tai-Me-She-Kia-Kiak or Black Hawk. Boston: 1834. V. 70

PATTERSON, J. H.
In the Grip of the Nyika. 1909. V. 70
The Man-Eaters of Tsavo and Other East African Adventures. 1907. V. 73

PATTERSON, JAMES
Black Market. New York: 1986. V. 68
The Jericho Commandment. New York: 1979. V. 68; 70; 71
Kiss The Girls. Boston: 1994. V. 72
The Midnight Club. Boston: 1985. V. 70
The Midnight Club. Boston: 1989. V. 71; 73
The Thomas Berryman Number. Boston: 1976. V. 70; 71
Virgin. 1980. V. 71

PATTERSON, JOHN M.
The Dickens Fellowship (Philadelphia Branch) Offers the Trial of John Jasper for the Murder of Edwin Drood at the Academy of Music...April 29, 1914. Philadelphia: 1914. V. 69

PATTERSON, R. F.
Ben Jonson's Conversations with William Drummond of Hawthornden. London: 1923. V. 68; 71

PATTERSON, R. H.
Essays in History and Art. London: 1857. V. 69

PATTERSON, RICHARD NORTH
The Lasko Tangent. New York: 1979. V. 73
The Outside Man. Boston: 1981. V. 70; 71; 73
Protect and Defend. New York: 2000. V. 69; 72

PATTERSON, ROBERT
Narrative of the Campaign in the Valley of the Shenandoah in 1861. Philadelphia: 1865. V. 69; 70; 71
The Natural History of Insects Mentioned in Shakespeare's Plays. London: 1841. V. 68

PATTERSON, SAMUEL
Narrative of the Adventures and Sufferings of Samuel Patterson, Experienced in the Pacific Ocean and Many Other Parts of the World.... Palmer: 1817. V. 68

PATTERSON, SAMUEL W.
Horatio Gates. Defender of American Liberty. New York: 1941. V. 73

PATTERSON, W. B.
King James VI and I and the Reunion of Chrstiendom. Cambridge;: 1997. V. 73

PATTIE, JANE
Cowboy Spurs and Their Makers. College Station: 1991. V. 68

PATTILLO, T. R.
Moose Hunting, Salmon Fishing and Other Sketches of Sport. London: 1902. V. 73

PATTISON, ELIOT
The Skull Mantra. New York: 1999. V. 71
The Skull Mantra. London: 2000. V. 68; 69

PATTULLO, GEORGE
A Good Rooster Crows Everywhere. 1939. V. 69

PAUCKER, PAULINE
New Borders: the Working Life of Elizabeth Friedlander. Oldham: 1998. V. 71

PAUL, A.
Parcas Art and Architecture. Iowa City: 1991. V. 69

PAUL, ELLIOT
The Amazon. New York: 1930. V. 70
Desperate Scenery. London: 1955:. V. 72
Hugger-Mugger in the Louvre. New York: 1940. V. 73

PAUL, JOHN DEAN
Journal of a Party of Pleasure to Paris, in the Month of August, 1802.... London: 1803. V. 69
Journal of a Party of Pleasure to Paris, in the Month of August 1802.... London: 1814. V. 68

PAUL, PHYLLIS
We Are Spoiled. New York: 1934. V. 71

PAUL, W.
The Rose Garden. 1872. V. 73

PAULDING, JAMES KIRKE
The Backwoodsman. Philadelphia: 1818. V. 73
Westward Ho!. New York: 1832. V. 68; 71

PAULI, WOLFGANG
Uber den Zusammenhang des Abschlusses der Elektronengruppen im atom mit der Komplexstruktur der Spektren in Zeitschrift fur Physik. Berlin: 1925. V. 73

PAULIN, DOROTHY M.
The Gallovidian Annual 1935-1936. Dumfries: 1935. V. 73

PAULIN, TOM
The Strange Museum. London: 1980. V. 68

PAULKE, W.
Hazards in Mountaineering. London: 1973. V. 69

PAULLIN, CHARLES O.
Atlas of the Historical Geography of the U.S. Washington: 1932. V. 71
Commodore John Rodgers, Captain, Commodore and Senior Officer of the American Navy 1773-1838. Cleveland: 1910. V. 70

PAULSSON, T.
Scandinavian Architecture: Buildings and Society in Denmark, Finland, Norway and Sweden from the Iron Age Until Today. London: 1958. V. 69; 72

PAULUS AEGINETA
The Seven Books. London: 1844-. V. 68; 70
The Seven Books. London: 1844-1847. V. 68

PAUSE, WALTER
Salute the Mountains. London: 1926. V. 69

PAUTHIER, M. G.
Chine. Paris: 1839. V. 71

PAVEY, L. A.
Moving Pageant. London: 1935. V. 70

PAVIERE, S. H.
A Dictionary of Flower, Fruit and Still Life Painters. Leigh-on-Sea: 1962-1964. V. 70

PAVLOFF, P. A.
The Manchurian Reptilia and Amphibia, Based Upn Collections Stored in the M.R.S. Museum. Harbin: 1926. V. 72

PAVLOU, STEL
Decipher. London: 2001. V. 69

PAVLOV, IVAN PETROVICH
Die Arbeit der Verdauungsdrusen. Wiesbaden: 1898. V. 68
Lectures on Conditioned Reflexes. New York: 1928. V. 68; 71
Le Travail des Glandes Digestives Lecons Du Professeur J. P. Pavlov. Paris: 1901. V. 68
The Work of the Digestive Glands. London: 1902. V. 68; 70

PAVLOVICH, IVAN
The Better Government for the United Kingdom, as Suggested by Ivan Pavlovich. London: 1886. V. 71

PAVLOVSKY, B. V.
Decorative Arts of Industrial Urals. Moscow: 1975. V. 69; 72

PAXSON, FREDERIC L.
History of the American Frontier 1763-1893. Boston: 1924. V. 72

PAXSON, WILLIAM EDGAR
E. S. Paxson, Frontier Artist. Boulder: 1984. V. 69; 72

PAXTON, J. D.
Letters on Slavery: Addressed to the Cumberland Congregation, Virginia. Lexington: 1833. V. 68

PAXTON, JOSEPH
Magazine of Botany. London: 1836. V. 70

PAXTON, W. M.
The Marshall Family. Cincinnati: 1885. V. 69

PAYER, JULIUS
New Lands Within the Arctic Circle. New York: 1877. V. 69; 73

PAYES, RACHEL COSGROVE
O Charitable Death. Garden City: 1968. V. 71

PAYETTE, B. C.
The Oregon Country Under the Union Jack - a Reference Book of Historical Documents for Scholars and Historians. Canada: 1961. V. 68
Warbonnets and Epaulets. Montreal: 1970. V. 72

PAYN, JAMES
Fallen Fortunes; a Novel. London: 1888. V. 68
Found Dead. London: 1889. V. 68
Furness Abbey and Its Neighbourhood. London: 1865. V. 71
The Heir of the Ages. London: 1886. V. 73
The Heir of the Ages. London: 1888. V. 68
Married Beneath Him. London: 1908. V. 68
A Prince of the Blood. London: 1890. V. 68
Some Private Views. London: 1900. V. 68
Walter's Word. London: 1890. V. 68
The Youth and Middle Age of Charles Dickens.... London: 1883. V. 70

PAYNE, A. A.
A Handbook of British and Foreign Orders, War Medal and Decorations. Sheffield: 1911. V. 72

PAYNE, DANIEL A.
History of the African Methodist Church. Nashville: 1891. V. 69

PAYNE, DAVID
Confessions of a Taoist on Wall Street. Boston: 1984. V. 68; 69; 72
Early From the Dance. New York: 1989. V. 71
Ruin Creek. New York: 1993. V. 72

PAYNE, E. W., MRS.
Necessity and Contrivance; or, Food, Clothing and Shelter. 1853. V. 68

PAYNE, EDWARD BIRON
The Soul of Jack London. 1926. V. 73

PAYNE, EDWARD F.
The Charity of Charles Dickens. Boston: 1929. V. 69; 71

PAYNE, ELISABETH STANCY
Out of the Dusk. New York: 1934. V. 70

PAYNE, EMMY
Katy No-Pocket. Boston: 1944. V. 72

PAYNE, GORDON E.
Ridley: a Sketch-Book. Toronto: 1930. V. 73

PAYNE, JAMES
Book of Landcapes After Payne. London: 1799. V. 69

PAYNE, JOHN
Tables for Valuing Labor and Stores, by Weight or by Number. 1811. V. 72
Twelve Designs of Country Houses, of Two, Three and Four Rooms on a Floor, Proper for Glebes and Small Estates.... Dublin: 1757. V. 68; 70; 72

PAYNE, JOHN HOWARD
Clari; or, the Maid of Milan, an Opera, in Three Acts.... New York: 1823. V. 68
Home Sweet Home. Boston: 1881. V. 68
Memoirs of John Howard Payne, the American Roscius. London: 1815. V. 70

PAYNE, LAURENCE
Vienna Blood. London: 1984. V. 72

PAYNE, N. F.
Techniques for Wildlife Habitat Management of Wetlands. New York: 1992. V. 72

PAYNE, WILLIAM
Maxims for Playing the Game of Whist.... Winton: 1783. V. 72

PAYNE-GALLWEY, RALPH
The Book of Duck Decoys, Their Construction, Management and History. 1886. V. 70
High Pheasants in Theory and Practice. 1913. V. 71
Letters to Young Shooters. First Series. London: 1890. V. 69
Letters to Young Shooters. Three Volumes. 1899. V. 71
Letters to Young Shooters. Three Volumes. 1914. V. 71

PAYNE WESTBROOK, HENRIETTA
The West-Brook Drives. New York: 1902. V. 68

PAYSON, GEORGE
Golden Dreams And Leaden Realities. New York: 1853. V. 71

PAYTIAMO, JAMES
Flaming Arrow's People By an Acoma Indian. New York: 1932. V. 69; 71

PAYTON, CHARLES A.
Days Of A Knight. London: 1924. V. 72

PAYTON, WILLIAM
The Last Man Over the Trail. 1939. V. 68; 73

PAZ, OCTAVIO
Air Born/Hijos del Aire. Mexico City: 1979. V. 68; 69
Alternating Current. New York: 1973. V. 69
Eagle or Sun?. New York: 1973. V. 69
In the Light of India. New York: 1997. V. 69; 72
Stanzas for an Imaginary Garden. Tuscaloosa: 1990. V. 69; 73
Three Poems. New York: 1988. V. 69
Tres Poemas/Three Poems. 1987. V. 68

PEABODY, ELIZABETH P.
Holiness; or the Legend of St. George; a Tale from Spencer's Faerie Queene, by a Mother. Boston: 1836. V. 71; 73
Sabbath Lessons, or an Abstract of Sacred History; to which is Annexed, a Geographical Sketch of the Principal Places Mentioned in Sacred History. Salem: 1810. V. 68

PEABODY, FRANCIS WELD
Doctor and Patient. Papers on the Relationship of the Physician to Men and Institutions. NY: 1930. V. 72

PEACH, B. N.
The Silurian Rocks of Britain. Volume I. Scotland. Glasgow: 1899. V. 69; 73

PEACH, WILLIAM
Cwm Dhu; or, The Black Dingle: Windermere; The Curse of Earth; and other poems. London: 1853. V. 71

PEACHAM, HENRY
The Compleat Gentleman: Fashioning Him Absolute in the Most Necessary and Commendable Qualities Concerning Minde or Bodie that May Be Required in a Noble Gentleman. London: 1622. V. 71

PEACHEY, EMMA
The Royal Guide to Wax Flower Modelling. London: 1851. V. 72

PEACHEY, GEORGE C.
A Memoir of William and John Hunter. Plymouth: 1924. V. 68

PEACHUM, HENRY
Square Cups Turned into Round-Heads; or the Brownists Conviction. London: 1642. V. 73

PEACOCK, DOUG
Grizzly Years. New York: 1990. V. 69; 71; 73

PEACOCK, E. H.
A Game Book for Burma and Adjoining territories. 1933. V. 72; 73

PEACOCK, EDWARD
English Church Furniture Ornaments and Decorations At The Period Of The Reformation As Exhibited In A List Of The Goods Destroyed In Certain Lincolnshire Churches, A.D.1566. London: 1866. V. 72

PEACOCK, LUCY
The Adventures of the Six Princesses of Babylon, in Their Travels to the Temple of Virtue; an Allegory. London: 1785. V. 70
The Knight of the Rose. London: 1793. V. 69
The Little Emigrant, a Tale. London: 1799. V. 73

PEACOCK, MABEL
North Lincolnshire Dialcet. London: 1899. V. 73

PEACOCK, ROBERT BACKHOUSE
A Glossary of the Dialect of the Hundred of Lonsdale, North and South of the Sands, in the County of Lancaster.... London: 1869. V. 71

PEACOCK, THOMAS LOVE
Crotchet Castle. 1831. V. 71
The Genius of the Thames: a Lyrical Poem in Two Parts. London: 1810. V. 72
The Genius of the Thames, Palmyra and Other Poems. London: 1812. V. 72
Gryll Grange. 1861. V. 72
Gryll Grange. London: 1861. V. 70
Letters to Edward Hookham and Percy B. Shelley with Fragments of Unpublished Manuscripts. Boston: 1910. V. 71
Melincourt or Sir Oran Haut-ton. London: 1856. V. 68
Misfortunes of Elphin. London: 1829. V. 72
The Misfortunes of Elphin. Newtown: 1928. V. 71
Palmyra and Other Poems. London: 1806. V. 68; 72
Paper Money Lyrics and Other Poems. London: 1837. V. 72
The Philosophy of Melancholy: a Poem in Fourth Part.... London: 1812. V. 72
Rhododaphne; or the Thessalian Spell: a Poem. London: 1818. V. 72

PEACOCKE, ISABEL MAUD
My Friend Phil. London: 1915. V. 73

PEAKE, HAROLD
The Bronze Age and the Celtic World. 1922. V. 69; 73

PEAKE, JAMES
Rudiments of Naval Architecture; or, an Exposition of the Practical Principles of the Science in Its Application to Naval Construction.... London: 1851. V. 71

PEAKE, MERVYN
Captain Slaughterboard Drops Anchor. London: 1945. V. 68; 70; 71
Drawings. 1949. V. 68
Prayers and Graces: a Little Book of Extraordinary Piety. London: 1944. V. 68
Selected Poems. London: 1972. V. 69
Titus Groan. London: 1968. V. 69; 73

PEAKE, RICHARD BRINSLEY
The Characteristic Costume of France, from Drawings Made On the Spot.... London: 1819-1822. V. 69
Memoirs of the Colman Family, Including Their Correspondence with the Most Distinguished Personages of Their Time. London: 1841. V. 69; 72

PEARCE, DONN
Cool Hand Luke. New York: 1965. V. 71
Pier Head Jump. Indianapolis & New York: 1972. V. 73

PEARCE, JOSEPH P.
Merseyside to Windermere. Ormskirk: 1931. V. 71

PEARCE, MICHAEL
A Cold Touch of Ice. 2000. V. 68
Death of an Effendi. London: 1999. V. 68; 72
Dragonmans Story. 2000. V. 68
The Face In The Cemetery. London: 2001. V. 72
The Mamur Zapt and the Girl in the Nile. London: 1992. V. 70
The Mamur Zapt And The Men Behind. London: 1991. V. 70; 72
The Mamur Zapt and the Return of the Carpet. London: 1988. V. 70; 71; 72
The Mingrelian Conspiracy. London: 1995. V. 72
The Snake-Catcher's Daughter. London: 1994. V. 69

PEARCE, T. M.
Cartoon Guide of New Mexico. New York: 1939. V. 69
Lane of the Llano Being the Story of Jim Cook as Told to.... Boston: 1936. V. 69

PEARCE, THOMAS
The Idstone Papers, a Series of Articles and Desultory Observations on Sport and Things in General. London: 1872. V. 71

PEARCE, W. M.
The Matador Land and Cattle Company. Norman: 1964. V. 68; 71

PEARCE, WILLIAM
General View of the Agriculture in Berkshire.... London: 1794. V. 72

PEARCH, GEORGE
A Collection of Poems in Four Volumes. London: 1770. V. 70

PEARD, W.
A Year of Liberty; or Salmon Angling in Ireland from February 1 to November 1. 1867. V. 71

PEARS, EDWIN
Forty Years in Constantinople. London: 1916. V. 73

PEARS, EDWIN continued
Turkey and Its People. London: 1912. V. 71

PEARS, IAIN
The Bernini Bust. London: 1992. V. 72; 73
Death and Restoration. London: 1996. V. 71; 72
The Dream of Scipio. London: 2002. V. 72
Giotto's Hand. New York: 1994. V. 69; 73
The Immaculate Deception. London: 2000. V. 72
An Instance of the Fingerpost. London: 1997. V. 68; 72; 73
The Last Judgement. London: 1993. V. 70
The Titian Committee. New York: 1991. V. 72

PEARS, TIM
In a Land of Plenty. London: 1997. V. 68; 72
In the Place of Fallen Leaves. London: 1993. V. 68; 72; 73
A Revolution of the Sun. London: 2000. V. 68; 69; 73

PEARSALL, D. M.
Paleoethnobotany. A Handbook of Procedures. New York: 1989. V. 68

PEARSALL, W. H.
The Lake District. London: 1973. V. 71

PEARSE, ALFRED
Merrie England. London: 1928. V. 69

PEARSE, R. O.
Barrier of Spears. London: 1973. V. 69

PEARSON, ABEL
An Analysis of the Principles of the Divine Government, in a Series of on Some Other Interesting Subjects.... Athens: 1832-1833. V. 68

PEARSON, ALEXANDER
Annals of Kirkby Lonsdale and Lunesdale in Bygone Days. Kendal: 1930. V. 71
The Doings of a Country Solicitor. Kendal: 1947. V. 71

PEARSON, ANTHONY
The Great Case of Tithes Truly Stated. London: 1754. V. 73
The Great Case of Tithes Truly Stated. Dublin: 1756. V. 71

PEARSON, E. O.
The Insect Pests of Cotton in Tropical Africa. London: 1958. V. 72

PEARSON, H.
A Guide to Laddow. London: 1934. V. 69
Three Summers Among the Birds of Russian Lapland. London: 1904. V. 69

PEARSON, HENRY J.
Beyond Petsora Eastward. 1899. V. 68

PEARSON, HESKETH
Doctor Darwin. London: 1930. V. 68
George Bernard Shaw. A Full Length Portrait. New York: 1942. V. 70; 71

PEARSON, J., & CO.
First Editions of One Hundred Books Famous in the World's Literature. London: 1904. V. 70
Holograph Letters of, and Historical Documents Signed by the Rulers of Europe During Five Centuries on Sale by J. Pearson & Co. London: 1913. V. 70
One Hundred and Eighty-Eight Manuscripts, Bindings, Books and Autograph Letters, Including the Magnificent Calvilo Pontifical, Written and Illuminated in Spain. London: 1922. V. 70
Two Hundred Books from the Libraries of the World's Greatest Book Collectors. Grolier (1479-1565) to Beckford (1759-1844). London: 1909. V. 70
Very Choice Books Including and Extremely Important Series of Historical Bindings Together with Original and Illuminated Manuscripts. London: 1902. V. 70

PEARSON, J. MICHAEL
American Cut Glass for the Discriminating Collector. New York: 1965. V. 72

PEARSON, JAMES LARKIN
Fifty Acres and Other Selected Poems. Wilkesboro: 1937. V. 68

PEARSON, JIM BERRY
The Maxwell Land Grant. Norman: 1961. V. 68; 70

PEARSON, JOHN
An Exposition of the Creed by John, Lord Bishop of Chester. London: 1683. V. 70
The Life of Ian Fleming. London: 1966. V. 69

PEARSON, KARL
Two New Pedigrees of Muscular Dystrophy. 1933. V. 71

PEARSON, P. D.
Alvar Aalto and the International Style. New York: 1978. V. 69

PEARSON, RIDLEY
Probable Cause. New York: 1990. V. 71
The Seizing Of Yankee Green Mall. New York: 1987. V. 71; 72

PEARSON, T. GILBERT
Birds of America. New York: 1917. V. 73

PEARSON, T. R.
Call and Response. New York: 1989. V. 72

PEARSON, WILLIAM
Hunt the Man Down. New York: 1956. V. 68

PEARSON-ROGERS, H. W.
Guns This Way!. 1962. V. 71

PEARY, R. E.
Nearest the Pole. London: 1907. V. 71
Nearest the Pole. New York: 1907. V. 73
The North Pole. London: 1910. V. 71
The North Pole. New York: 1910. V. 69
Northward Over the Great Ice. London: 1898. V. 69
Northward Over the Great Ice. New York: 1898. V. 72

PEASCOD, BILL
Journey After Dawn. Milnthorpe: 1985. V. 69

PEASE, HOWARD
The Lord Wardens of the Marches of England and Scotland. London: 1913. V. 71

PEASE, ZEPHANIA WALTER
The Catalpa Expedition. New Bedford: 1897. V. 71

PEAT, FERN BISSEL
Mother Goose. Akron: 1929. V. 71
Rags. Akron: 1929. V. 70
Three Little Kittens. Akron: 1940. V. 71

PEATE, IORWERTH C.
Clock and Watch Makers in Wales. Cardiff: 1975. V. 70; 72

PEATTIE, DONALD CULROSS
Audubon's America. Boston: 1940. V. 70
The Bright Lexicon. New York: 1934. V. 70
Green Laurels. London: 1937. V. 68
A Natural History of Trees of Eastern and Central North America. Boston: 1950. V. 72
Port Of Call. New York: 1932. V. 72
Sons Of The Martin. New York: 1932,. V. 72
Toward the Nation. New York: 1942. V. 68

PECK, ANNIE S.
A Search for the Apex of America. New York: 1911. V. 71

PECK, DALE
Now It's Time to Say Goodbye. New York: 1998. V. 72

PECK, FRANCIS
Desiderata Curiosa. London: 1732-1735. V. 70

PECK, GEORGE WASHINGTON
Aurifodina; or Adventures in the Gold Region. New York: 1849. V. 71

PECK, J. M.
A Guide for Emigrants, Containing Sketches of Illinois, Missouri and the Adjacent Parts. Boston: 1837. V. 68; 71

PECK, O.
A Catalogue of the Nearctic Chalciidoides (Insecta: Hymenoptera). Ottawa: 1963. V. 72

PECK, RICHARD
A Year Down Yonder. New York: 2000. V. 70

PECK, ROBERT NEWTON
A Part of the Sky. New York: 1994. V. 72

PECK, SAMUEL MINTURN
Maybloom and Myrtle. Boston: 1910. V. 72

PECK, WILLIAM
A Topographical Account of the Isle of Axholme, Being the Divison of the Wapentake of Manley, in the County of Lincoln. 1815. V. 70

PECKHAM, G. W.
On the Instincts and Habits of the Solitary Wasps. Madison: 1898. V. 71

PECKHAM, JOHN F.
Adventures in Printing. Lunenburg: 1984. V. 69

PEDERSEN, JOHANNES
The Carlsberg Foundation. Copenhagen: 1956. V. 68

PEDLER, MARGARET
Desert Sand. Garden City: 1932. V. 71
Not Heaven Itself. New York: 1941. V. 71
To-Morrow's Tangle. New York: 1926. V. 71

PEDRANZAS, ALLAN
The Harry Chronicles. New York: 1995. V. 71

PEDRICK, GALE
Monastic Seals of the XIIIth Century. London: 1902. V. 72

PEEK A Boo Library. Newark: 1920. V. 70

THE PEEK-A-Boos at School. Springfield: 1929. V. 71

THE PEEK-A-Boos' Desert Island. London: 1927. V. 70

PEEK, CLIFFORD H.
Five Years...Five Countries...Five Campaigns. Munich: 1945. V. 73

PEEL, BRUCE BRADEN
A Bibliography of the Prairie Provinces to 1953. Toronto: 1956. V. 71

PEEL, C. V. A.
Somaliland. London: 1900. V. 71
Wild Sport in the Outer Hebrides. London: 1901. V. 68; 71

PEEL, FRANK
The Risings of the Luddites. Heckmondwike: 1880. V. 71
The Risings of the Luddites, Chartists & Plug-drawers. Heckmondwike: 1888. V. 71
The Risings of the Luddites, Chartists & Plug-drawers. Brighouse: 1895. V. 71

PEEL, ROBERT
Speech...in the House of Commons, August 10, 1842. London: 1842. V. 71
Speeches...During His Administration.... London: 1835. V. 71
The Substance of a Speech of Robert Peel, Esquire, in the House of Commons, on Thursday, the 14th of February 1799.... London: 1799. V. 69

A PEEP at the Various Nations of the World, with a Concise Description of the Inhabitants. Portland. V. 69

A PEEP at the Various Nations of the World. Concord: 1837. V. 69

A PEEP Into Fairyland. London: 1905. V. 73

PEEPS Into Fairyland. London: 1896. V. 70; 73

THE PEERAGE Chart for 1822. London: 1822. V. 72

PEERY, JANET
The Alligator Dance. Dallas: 1993. V. 69; 72
The River Beyond the World. New York: 1996. V. 70; 72

PEET, L. H.
Trees and Shrubs of Central Park. New York: 1903. V. 68

PEETERS, H. J.
American Hawking, A General Account of Falconry in the New World. 1970. V. 69; 73

PEGGE, SAMUEL
The Life Of Robert Grosseteste. London: 1793. V. 72

PEGGY.. London: 1919. V. 70

PEHNT, W.
German Architecture 1960-1970. New York: 1970. V. 69; 72

PEI, MARIO
One Language for the World. New York: 1958. V. 71; 73

PEICH, MICHAEL
The Red Ozier: a Literary Fine Press. History and Bibliography 1976- 1987. Council Bluffs: 1993. V. 73

PEIRCE, ISAAC
The Narraganset Chief; or the Adventures of a Wanderer. New York: 1832. V. 68

PEIRCE, KATHLEEN
Divided Touch, Divided Color. XII Poems. Iowa City: 1995. V. 73

PELECANOS, GEORGE P.
The Big Blowdown. New York: 1996. V. 70; 71; 72; 73
Down by the River Where the Dead Men Go. New York: 1995. V. 70; 71; 72; 73
A Firing Offense. New York: 1992. V. 68; 69; 70; 71; 72; 73
A Firing Offense. New York: 1994. V. 69
Hell To Pay. Tucson: 2002. V. 72; 73
King Suckerman. Boston: 1997. V. 68; 70; 72; 73
Nick's Trip. New York: 1993. V. 70
Right as Rain. Boston: 2000. V. 73
Right as Rain. Blakeney: 2001. V. 68; 69; 70; 71; 72; 73
Shame the Devil. Tucson: 1999. V. 68; 69; 70; 71; 73
Shame the Devil. Boston: 2000. V. 70; 72
Shoedog. New York: 1987. V. 72
Shoedog. New York: 1994. V. 69; 70; 71; 72; 73
The Sweet Forever. Boston: 1998. V. 70; 71; 72; 73
The Sweet Forever. Tucson: 1998. V. 68; 69

PELL, WILLIAM J.
Treatise on the Games of Dominoes. New York: 1844. V. 71

PELLEPORC, MARQUIS DE
Essai sur la Arithmetique de L'Horlogerie. Neuchatel: 1779. V. 70

PELLER, SIGISMUND
Quantitative Research in Human Biology and Medicine. Bristol;: 1967. V. 68

PELLETIER DE FREPILLON
Essai sur la Taille des Arbres Fruitiers. Paris: 1773. V. 70; 71

PELLICER, CARLOS
Mural Painting of the Mexican Revolution. Mexico City: 1960. V. 71

PELTON, JOHN COTTER
Life's Sunbeams and Shadows - Poems and Prose. San Francisco: 1893. V. 69

PELZER, LOUIS
The Cattlemen's Frontier, A Record of the Trans-Mississippi Cattle Industry.... Glendale: 1936. V. 71
Henry Dodge. Iowa City: 1911. V. 68

PEMBERTON, EBENEZER
A Funeral Sermon on the Death of that Learned and Excellent Divine the Reverend Mr. Samuel Willard, Pastor of a Church of Christ in Boston.... Boston: 1707. V. 68

Sermons and Discourses on Several Occasions. London: 1727. V. 73

PEMBERTON, HENRY
A View of Sir Isaac Newton's Philosophy. London: 1728. V. 71; 72

PEMBERTON, J. D.
Facts and Figures Relating to Vancouver Island and British Columbia, Showing What to Expect and How to Get There. London: 1860. V. 71

PEMBERTON, JOHN
A Letter on the River Wear Navigation Act, Addressed to John George Lambton, Esq. M.P.: (and) A Letter on Certain Clauses, proposed to be Introduced into the River Wear Navigation Act, by a Bill This Session of Parliament Addressed to Richard Wharton.... Sunderland: 1819. V. 73

PEMBERTON, JOHN C.
Pemberton, Defender of Vicksburg. Chapel Hill: 1945. V. 69; 70

PEMBERTON, MAX
The Gold Wolf. London: 1903. V. 69
Jewel Mysteries I Have Known from a Dealer's Notebook. London. V. 72
Mid and Thick Arrows. London: 1903. V. 69

PEMBERTON, T. EDGAR
Charles Dickens an the Stage: a Record of His Connection with the Drama as Playwright Actor and Critic. London: 1888. V. 70
Sir Charles Wyndam. A Biography. London: 1904. V. 71

PEMBROKE, HENRY HERBERT, 10TH EARL OF
Military Equitation; or, a Method of Breaking Horses and Teaching Soldiers to Ride. Sarum: 1778. V. 70

PEN and Camera. Milwaukee: 1890. V. 72

PENDLETON, NATHANIEL GREENE
Military Posts - Council Bluffs to the Pacific Ocean. Washington: 1842. V. 73

PENDER, ROSE
No Telegraph. London: 1879. V. 71

PENDER, WILLIAM DORSEY
The General to His Lady. The Civil War Letters of William Dorsey Pender to Fanny Pender. Chapel Hill: 1965. V. 70

PENDERED, MARY L.
John Martin, Painter: His Life and Times. London: 1923. V. 73

PENDEXTER, HUGH
The Red Road. Indianapolis: 1927. V. 69

PENDLETON, EDMUND
A Complication of Hearts: a Novel. London: 1893. V. 68

PENDLETON, JOHN
Our Railways. London: 1896. V. 70

PENE DU BOIS, WILLIAM
Bear Party. 1975. V. 72
Giant Otto and Otto at Sea. New York: 1936. V. 70
The 21 Balloons. New York: 1947. V. 72

PENFIELD, FREDERIC COURTLAND
The Motor That Went to Court. New York: 1909. V. 70

PENFIELD, WILDER
The Cerebral Cortex of Man, A Clinical Study of Localization of Function. New York: 1950. V. 72
Epilepsy and the Functional Anatomy of the Human Brain. Boston: 1954. V. 68
Epileptic Seizure Patterns. Springfield: 1957. V. 68; 70; 71; 73
The Excitable Cortex in Conscious Man. Liverpool: 1958. V. 68; 70; 72; 73
The Second Career with Other Essays and Addresses. Boston: 1963. V. 68; 70; 71
Speech and Brain Mechanisms. Princeton: 1959. V. 68; 70; 71; 73

PENFOLD, A. R.
The Eucalyptus, Botany, Cultivation, Chemistry and Utilization. London: 1961. V. 70

PENFOLD, CHARLES
A Practical Treatise on the Best Mode of Repairing Roads, with Some Observations Upon the Present System. Croydon: 1835. V. 72

PENGELLY, WILLIAM
A Memoir of William Pengelly, of Torquay, F.R.S., Geologist. London: 1897. V. 72

PENINOU, ERNEST P.
Directory of California Wine Growers and Wine Makers in 1860. Berkeley: 1967. V. 70
Winemaking in California. San Francisco: 1954. V. 68

PENINSULAR & ORIENTAL STEAM NAVIGATION CO.
Peninsular & Oriental Steam Navigation Company's Guide Book for Passengers. London: 1893. V. 68

PENLEY, AARON
Sketching from Nature in Water Colours. London: 1876. V. 73

PENMAN, SHARON KAY
Here Be Dragons. New York: 1985. V. 68; 69
The Sunne in Splendour. New York: 1982. V. 68; 71

PENN, I. GARLAND
The Afro-American Press and It's Editors. Springfield: 1891. V. 68

PENN, IRVING
Issey Miyake. Boston: 1988. V. 68
Moments Preserved. New York: 1960. V. 68; 73
Passage: a Work Record. New York: 1991. V. 73
Worlds in a Small Room. New York: 1974. V. 68; 73

PENN, WILLIAM
Correspondence Between William Penn and James Logan 1700-1750. Philadelphia: 1870. V. 68; 70
Fruits of Solitude, in Relfections and Maxims Relating to the Conduct of Human Life. London: 1775. V. 73
Quakerism, a New-Nick-Name for Old Christianity; Being an Answer to a Book, Entituled, Quakerism No Christianity.... London: 1673. V. 73
Tender Counsel and Advice, by Way of Epistle, To All Those Who Are Sensible of Their Day of Visitation. Philadelphia: 1783. V. 68; 71

PENNANT, THOMAS
The Additions to the Quarto Edition of the Tour in Scotland Etc. For the Accomodation of the Purchasers of the First and Second Editions. London: 1774. V. 70
Arctic Zoology. London: 1784-1787. V. 70; 73
British Zoology. London: 1812. V. 70
Indian Zoology. London: 1790. V. 73
The Literary Life of the Late Thomas Pennant, Esq. by Himself. London: 1793. V. 73
Some Account of London. London: 1813. V. 72
A Tour from Downing to Alston-Moor. London: 1801. V. 71
A Tour in Scotland, and a Voyage to the Hebrides. London: 1776. V. 72
Tours in Wales. London: 1810. V. 68
Tours in Wales. London: 1831. V. 69

PENNANT, WILLIAM
A Tour in Scotland, and Voyage to the Hebrides. London: 1774. V. 71
A Tour in Scotland and Voyage to the Hebrides. London: 1774-1776. V. 68

PENNEL, T. L.
Among the Wild Tribes of the Afghan Frontier. London: 1912. V. 69

PENNELL, ELIZABETH ROBINS
The Life of James McNeill Whistler. Philadelphia: 1908. V. 69
My Cookery Books. London: 1983. V. 68

PENNELL, F. W.
The Scrophulariaceae of the Western Himalayas. Philadelphia: 1943. V. 72

PENNELL, H. C.
Angler-Naturalist. 1863. V. 72

PENNELL, JOSEPH
The Adventures of an Illustrator, Mostly in Following His Authors in America & Europe. Boston: 1925. V. 69
A Canterbury Pilgriamge. London: 1885. V. 73
Joseph Pennell's Pictures of the Wonder of Work. London: 1916. V. 71
Lithography and Lithographers. New York and London: 1898. V. 69; 71
Pen Drawing and Pen Draughtsmen. New York: 1920. V. 68

PENNELL ELMHIRST, CAPTAIN
The Best Season on Record. London: 1885. V. 69

PENNER, JONATHAN
Private Parties. Pittsburgh: 1983. V. 69

PENNETHORNE, JOHN
The Geometry and Optics of Ancient Architecture. London and Edinburgh: 1878. V. 68; 70; 72

PENNEY, C. L.
List of Books Printed 1601-1700 in the Library of the Hispanic Society of America. New York: 1929. V. 70

PENNEY, D. W.
Art of the American Indian Frontier. Seattle: 1992. V. 69

PENNINGTON, JALK
The Battle of The Little Big Horn - A Comprehensive Study. El Segundo: 2001. V. 72

PENNINGTON, LADY
A Mother's Advice to her Absent Daughters: with an additional letter on the Management and Education of Infant Children. London: 1817. V. 71

PENNINGTON, MONTAGUE
Memoirs of the Life of Mrs. Elizabeth Carter, with New Edition of Her Poems. London: 1807. V. 68

PENNSYLVANIA. SHIP CANAL COMMISSION
Report...Respecting the Feasibility of a Ship Canal to Connect the Waters of Lake Erie and the Ohio River. Erie: 1891. V. 68

PENNSYLVANIA At Gettysburg: Ceremonies at the Dedication of the Monuments. Harrisonburg?: 1904. V. 68

PENNSYLVANIA SOCIETY
The Constitution of the Pennsylvania Society, for Promoting the Abolition of Slavery and the relief of free Negroes, Unlawfully Held in Bondage.... Philadelphia: 1787. V. 68; 72

PENNY & SON
Penny's Improved Commercial Pocket Book, with Almanack for 1839. London: 1838. V. 71

PENNY, ANNE
Poems, with Dramatic Entertainment. London: 1771. V. 69

PENNY, DAVID W.
Art of the American Indian Frontier; The Chandler-Port Collection. Seattle: 1992. V. 72

PENNY, F. E.
Southern India - Painted by Lady Lawley. London: 1914. V. 69

PENNYPACKER, MORTON
General Washington's Spies on Long Island and in New York. Brooklyn: 1939. V. 68; 71

PENROSE, CHARLES B.
The Rustler Business. Douglas: 1959. V. 71

PENROSE, CHARLES W.
The Mountain Meadows Massacre, Who Were Guilty of the Crime?. 1906. V. 68

PENROSE, JOHN
An Inquiry, Chiefly on Principles of Religion, the Nature and Discipline. London: 1820. V. 71

PENROSE, MATT R.
Pots 'O Gold. Reno: 1935. V. 68; 73

PENROSE, ROLAND
Scrap Book 1900-1981. London: 1981. V. 70

PENROSE, THOMAS
Poems by the Rev. Thomas Penrose, Late Rector of Beckington and Standerwick, Somersetshire. London: 1781. V. 70

PENROSE'S Pictorial Annual. London: 1920. V. 72
PENROSE'S Pictorial Annual. London: 1925. V. 72
PENROSE'S Pictorial Annual 1905-1906. London: 1906. V. 72
PENROSE'S Pictorial Annual 1909-1910. London: 1910. V. 72
PENROSE'S Pictorial Annual 1910-1911. London: 1910. V. 72
PENROSE'S Pictorial Annual 1911-1912. London: 1912. V. 72
PENROSE'S Pictorial Annual 1913-1914. London: 1914. V. 72

PENS, Inks and Inkstands, with Illustrations. London: 1858. V. 68

PENSEES Sur les Femmes et le Mariage. Kehl: 1782. V. 73

PENTECOST, HUGH
The Brass Chills. 1943. V. 73
Cancelled in Red. 1939. V. 73

PENTHER, JOHANN FRIEDRICH
Erster Theil einer Ausfuhrlichen Anleitung zur Burgerlichen Bau-Kunst Enthaltend ein Lexicon Architectonicum Oder Erklarungen der Ublichsten Deutscen, Frantzosischen, Italienische Kunst-Worter.... Augsburg: 1744. V. 68; 70

PENZER, NORMAN M.
An Annotated Bibliography of Sir Richard Francis Burton. London: 1923. V. 70
An Annotated Bibliography of Sir Richard Francis Burton. London: 1967. V. 70

PENZLER, OTTO
Dectectionary. 1971. V. 70

THE PEOPLE'S Answer to the Court Pamphlet Entitled A Short Review of the Political State of Great Britian. London: 1787. V. 69

THE PEOPLE'S Charter; Being the Outline of an Act to Provide for the Just Representation of the People of Great Britain and Ireland in the Commons' House of Parliament.... London: 1838. V. 69

PEPE, PHIL
The Yankees. Dallas: 1995. V. 68

PEPIN, JACQUES
Technique. New York: 1976. V. 70

PEPLER, HILARY DOUGLAS CLARK
Concerning Dragons. Ditchling: 1916. V. 70
Libellus Lapidum; the First Part of a Collection of Verses and Wood Engravings. Ditchling, Sussex: 1924. V. 73

PEPLOW, EDWARD H.
History of Arizona. New York: 1958. V. 69

PEPPER, ART
Straight Life. The Story of Art Pepper. New York: 1979. V. 69; 71

PEPPER, J. H.
Cyclopaedic Science Simplified. London: 1869. V. 68

PEPPER, JAMES
Letters - Raymond Chandler and James M. Fox. 1978. V. 70

PEPPER, WILLIAM
A Text-Book of the Theory and Practice of Medicine. Philadelphia: 1894. V. 68; 70

PEPPERRELL, WILLIAM
The Journal of Sir William Pepperell, Kept During the Expedition Against Louisbourg March 24 - August 22, 1745. Worcester: 1910. V. 73

PEPYS, SAMUEL
The Diary. 1928. V. 69
The Diary and Correspondence of Samuel Pepys, Secretary to the Admiralty in the Reigns of Charles II and James II. Philadelphia: 1855. V. 68
Everybody's Pepys. The Diary of Samuel Pepys 1660-1669. London: 1926. V. 71; 72
The Letters of Samuel Pepys and His Family Circle. Oxford: 1955. V. 72; 73
Memoires Relating to the State of the Royal Navy of England. London: 1690. V. 71

PEPYS, SAMUEL continued
Memoirs of Samuel Pepys.... London: 1828. V. 68; 72

PERAU, GABRIEL LOUIS CALABRE
Description Historique de l'Hotel Royal des Invalides.... Paris: 1756. V. 72

PERCEVAL, DON
Maynard Dixon Sketch Book. Flagstaff: 1967. V. 69; 71
A Navajo Sketch Book. Flagstaff: 1962. V. 69; 70

PERCHIK, SIMON
I Want My Music Bent. New Rochelle: 1989. V. 73

PERCIER, CHARLES
Palais, Maisons et Autres Edifices Modernes Dessines a Rome. Paris: 1798. V. 68

PERCIVAL, EMILY
The Diadem: a Souvenir for the Drawing Room and Parlor (for 1853). New York: 1852. V. 68

PERCIVAL, ROBERT
An Account of the Cape of Good Hope. London: 1804. V. 73

PERCY Anecdotes. London: 1850. V. 71

PERCY, THOMAS
Reliques of Ancient English Poetry. London: 1765. V. 73

PERCY, THOMAS, BP. OF DROMORE
Five Pieces of Runic Poetry. London: 1763. V. 69
Reliques of Ancient English Poetry. London: 1765. V. 72
Reliques of Ancient English Poetry. London: 1839. V. 72
Reliques of Ancient English Poetry. London: 1876. V. 71; 72

PERCY, WALKER
Bourbon. Winston-Salem: 1979. V. 71
Going Back to Georgia. 1978. V. 71
Going Back To Georgia. Athens, GA: 1991. V. 71
Lancelot. New York: 1977. V. 68
The Last Gentleman. New York: 1966. V. 68; 69; 70; 71; 72
The Last Gentleman. New York: 1971. V. 69
Lost in the Cosmos: the Last Self Help Book. New York: 1983. V. 68; 69; 73
Love in the Ruins. New York: 1971. V. 68; 69; 70; 72; 73
The Message in the Bottle. New York: 1975. V. 68; 70
The Movie-goer. New York: 1961. V. 69; 70; 73
The Movie-Goer. New York: 1962. V. 71
The Movie-Goer. London: 1963. V. 72
The Movie-Goer. Franklin Center: 1980. V. 70
Novel Writing in an Apocalyptic Time. New Orleans: 1986. V. 70
Questions They Never Asked Me. Northridge: 1979. V. 68
The Second Coming. New York: 1980. V. 68; 69; 71
The Second Coming. New York: 1989. V. 70; 71
The Thanatos Syndrome. Franklin Center: 1987. V. 71; 73
The Thanatos Syndrome. New York: 1987. V. 71; 72; 73

PERCY, WILLIAM ALEXANDER
In April Once. New Haven: 1920. V. 69

PERCYVALL, RICHARD
A Dictionarie in Spanish and English. London: 1623. V. 70

PEREFIXE, HARDOUIN DE BEAUMONT DE, ABP.
The Life of Henry the Fourth of France. Paris: 1785. V. 73

PEREIRE, A.
Gardens of France. New York: 1983. V. 68

PEREISTIANY, J. G.
The Social Institutions of the Kipsigis. London: 1939. V. 71

PERELMAN, S. J.
Chicken Inspector No. 23. New York: 1966. V. 71
The Dream Department. New York: 1943. V. 71
The Ill Tempered Clavichord. New York: 1952. V. 69; 70
Listen to the Mocking Bird. New York: 1949. V. 72
One Touch of Venus. Boston: 1944. V. 69
Perelman's Home Companion: A Collector's Item (The collector being S. J. Perelman) of 36 otherwise unavailable pieces by himself. New York: 1955. V. 70
The Rising Gorge. New York: 1961. V. 71
Strictly From Hunger. New York: 1937. V. 72

THE PERENNIAL; A collection of moral and religious poetry. Selected by the Editor of the Evergreen. London. V. 71

PERET, BENJAMIN
Death to the Pigs - Selected Writings of Benjamin Peret. London: 1988. V. 68

PEREZ DE LUXAN, DIEGO
Expedition into New Mexico Made by Antonio de Espejo 1582-1583. Los Angeles: 1929. V. 73

PEREZ DE RIBAS, ANDRES
History of the Triumphs of Our Holy Faith Amongst the Most Barbarous and Fierce Peoples of the New World. Tucson: 1999. V. 70

PEREZ-REVERTE, ARTURO
The Club Dumas. New York: 1996. V. 73
The Dumas Club. London: 1996. V. 72; 73
The Fencing Master. London: 1999. V. 68; 69
The Flanders Panel. New York: 1990. V. 68
The Flanders Panel. New York: 1994. V. 71
The Seville Communion. London: 1998. V. 69; 70; 71; 73
The Seville Communion. New York: 1998. V. 71

THE PERFECT Gentleman; or, Etiquette and Eloquence. New York: 1860. V. 69

PERIN, FLORENCE HOBART
The Optimist's Good Night. Boston: 1912. V. 69; 71

PERINE, EDWARD TEN BROECK
Here's to Broadway!. New York: 1930. V. 70; 71

THE PERIODICAL Press of Great Britain and Ireland; or an Inquiry into the State of the Public Journals.... London: 1824. V. 72

PERKINS, CHARLES ELLIOT
Family Letters, 1861-1869. Boston: 1949. V. 72
The Pinto Horse. Santa Barbara: 1927. V. 69

PERKINS, CORNELIA ADAMS
Saga of San Juan. San Juan: 1968. V. 69

PERKINS, E. E.
Treatise on Haberdashery and Hosiery, and General Drapery.... 1874. V. 71
Treatise on Haberdashery and Hosiery Including the Manchester, Scotch, Silk, Linen and Woollen Departments.... 1836. V. 71

PERKINS, E. E., MRS.
The Elements of Botany. London: 1837. V. 69

PERKINS, EDITH FORBES
Letters and Journals 1908-1925. Cambridge: 1931. V. 69; 72

PERKINS, ELIZABETH STEELE
Flora's Fancy Fete, or Floral Characteristics. Brighton. V. 69

PERKINS, F. B.
Charles Dickens: a Sketch of His Life and Works. New York: 1870. V. 70

PERKINS, GEORGE
Letters of Capt. Geo. Hamilton Perkins, U.S.N. Concord: 1886. V. 70

PERKINS, HENRY
A Catalogue of the Very Valuable and Important Library Formed by the Late Henry Perkins.... 1873. V. 70

PERKINS, JOHN
Floral Designs for the Table.... London: 1877. V. 68; 69

PERKINS, KENNETH
Ride Him, Cowboy. New York: 1923. V. 69; 70

PERKINS, MARGARET
Echoes of Pawnee Rock. Wichita: 1908. V. 69

PERKINS, MARY E.
Old Houses of the Antient Town of Norwich, 1660-1800. Norwich: 1895. V. 72

PERKINS, SAMUEL
A History of the Political and Military Events of the Late War Between the United States and Great Britain. New Haven: 1825. V. 72

PERKINS, SIMEON
The Diary of Simeon Perkins. Toronto: 1948-1978. V. 70; 71
The Diary of Simeon Perkins 1790-1796. Toronto: 1961. V. 68
The Diary of Simeon Perkins 1797-1803. Toronto: 1967. V. 68
The Diary of Simeon Perkins 1804-1812. Toronto: 1978. V. 73

PERLES, ALFRED
My Friend Henry Miller. London: 1955. V. 68
Round Trip. London: 1946. V. 71

PERLEY, SIDNEY
The Indian Land Titles of Essex County Massachusetts. Salem: 1912. V. 69

PERLMAN, BARBARA H.
Allan Houser. Japan: 1987. V. 71

PERNELL, ROBERT
The Diseases of the Children. New York: 1971. V. 73

PERON, EVA
La Razon de mi Vida. Buenos Aires: 1952. V. 71

PEROWNE, BARRY
Raffles of the Albany. London: 1976. V. 70

PERRAULT, CHARLES
Cinderella. New York: 1886?. V. 68; 71; 73
Cinderella. Adapted by John Fowles. London: 1974. V. 70
Cinderella, or, the Little Glass Slipper. Cooperstown: 1824. V. 71
Cinderella; or the Little Glass Slipper. Providence: 1830. V. 71
Cinderilla (sic).... Albany: 1810. V. 73
Les Contes. Paris: 1869. V. 71
Contes des Fees. Paris: 1825. V. 70
Deux Contes de Ma Mere Loye: La Belle au Bois Dormant & Le Petitit Chaperon Rourge. London: 1899. V. 68
Fairy Tales. London: 1913. V. 68; 70

PERRAULT, CHARLES continued
Fairy Tales. London: 1922. V. 72
The Fairy Tales. New York: 1922. V. 71; 73
Old Time Stories. New York: 1921. V. 73
The Original Story of Cinderella. London: 1921. V. 73
The Popular Story of Blue Beard. Cooperstown: 1839. V. 71
Puss in Boots, the Sleeping Beauty and Cinderella. New York and London: 1963. V. 72

PERRAULT, CLAUDE
A Treatise of the Five Orders of Columns in Architecture.... London: 1708. V. 70

PERREAU, ROBERT
An Authentic Account of the Particulars which Appeared on the Trials of Robert and Dan Perreau on Thursday the 2d, and Friday the 3d Instant, for a Forgery on Robert and Henry Drummond.. London: 1775?. V. 70

PERRENS, F. T.
Etienne Marcel. Prevot des Marchands (1354-1358). Paris: 1874. V. 73

PERRET, F. A.
The Eruption of Mt. Pelee 1929-1932. 1937. V. 69; 73
The Vesuvius Eruption of 1906.... Washington;: 1924. V. 70

PERRI, FRANCESCO
Enough of Dreams. New York: 1929. V. 71

PERRIN, H.
British Flowering Plants. London: 1914. V. 69

PERRIN, JEAN PAUL
Luther's Fore-Runners; or a Cloud of Witnesses, Deposing for the Protestant Faith. London: 1624. V. 73

PERRIN, JIM
Mirrors in the Cliffs. 1983. V. 69

PERRINE, FRED S.
Military Escorts on Santa Fe Trail. Reuen: 1927-1928. V. 72

PERROT, ARISTIDE MICHEL
Dictionnaire des Inventions, Decouvertes t Perfectionnemens d l'Industrie.... Paris: 1837. V. 72

PERROT, GEORGES
A History of Art in Ancient Egypt. London: 1883. V. 71
History of Art In Sardina, Judae, Syria, and Asia Minor. London: 1890. V. 72
History of Art Series. Art in Ancient Egypt. Art in Persia. Art in Sardinia, Judaea, Syria & Asia Minor. Art in Phrygia, India, Caria & Lycia. Art in Chaldaea & Assyria. London: 1883-. V. 71

PERRY, AMOS
Memorial of Zachariah Allen. 1795-1882. Cambridge: 1883. V. 72

PERRY, ANNE
Belgrave Square. New York: 1992. V. 71
Belgrave Square. New York: 1993. V. 71
Bethlehem Road. New York: 1990. V. 69; 71; 73
Bluegate Fields. New York: 1984. V. 69
Cain His Brother. London: 1995. V. 68
Callander Square. New York: 1980. V. 70; 71; 73
Cardington Crescent. New York: 1987. V. 69; 71; 73
Defend and Betray. New York: 1992. V. 68
Defend and Betray. London: 1994. V. 71
Highgate Rise. New York: 1991. V. 68; 70
The Hyde Park Headsman. New York: 1994. V. 71
Paragon Walk. New York: 1981. V. 72; 73
Pentecost Alley. New York: 1996. V. 71
Resurrection Row. New York: 1981. V. 69; 71
Silence in Hanover Square. New York: 1988. V. 73
A Sudden, Fearful Death. New York: 1993. V. 71
Traitors Gate. New York: 1995. V. 71

PERRY, B.
Landscape Plants for Western Regions.... Claremont: 1992. V. 68

PERRY, BELA C.
A Treatise on the Human Hair. New Bedford: 1859. V. 70; 72

PERRY, CARMEN
The Impossible Dream by the Rio Grande. San Antonio: 1971. V. 69

PERRY, CHARLES
Medieval Arab Cookery. Prospect. V. 72

PERRY, G. W.
Treatise on Turpentine Farming; Being a Review of Natural and Artificial Obstructions, with Their Results.... New Bern: 1859. V. 68

PERRY, GEORGE
A Bear's Life. 1985. V. 72
The Great British Picture Show. London: 1974. V. 69
Rupert - a Bear's Life. 1985. V. 71

PERRY, GEORGE SESSIONS
Hold Autumn in Your Hand. New York: 1941. V. 70; 71

PERRY, HENRY FALES
History of the Thirty-Eighth Regiment Indiana Volunteer Infantry. Palo Alto: 1906. V. 69; 70

PERRY, JOHN
An Account of the Stopping of Daggenham Breach.... London: 1721. V. 68; 71

PERRY, JOHN FRANKLIN
Kennel Secrets. Boston: 1893. V. 68

PERRY, M. C.
Narrative of the Expedition of an America Squadron to the China Seas and Japan. New York: 1962. V. 73

PERRY, THOMAS
Big Fish. New York: 1985. V. 68; 71
Blood Money. New York: 1999. V. 71
The Butcher's Boy. 1982. V. 69
Dance for the Dead. New York: 1996. V. 71
Island. New York: 1987. V. 71
Island. New York: 1988. V. 71
Metzger's Dog. New York: 1983. V. 69; 73
Vanishing Act. New York: 1995. V. 71; 72

PERRY, WILLIAM
The Royal Standard English Dictionary.... Worcester: 1788. V. 73

PERRY-AYSCOUGH, H. G. C.
With the Russians in Mongolia. London: 1914. V. 71

PERSAUD, T. V. N.
Advances in the Study of Birth Defects. Lancaster: 1979. V. 68

PERSHING, JOHN J.
My Experiences in the World War. New York: 1931. V. 68

PERSOON, C. H.
Synopsis Plantarum. 1805-1807. V. 72

PERTUSIER, CHARLES
Picturesque Promenades In and Near Constantinople. London: 1820. V. 71

PERTWEE, GUY
Scenes from Dickens for Drawing-Room and Platform Acting. London: 1912. V. 68

PERTWEE, ROLAND
Royal Heritage. Boston: 1931. V. 69
The Transactions of Lord Louis Lewis. London: 1917. V. 71

PERVIGILIUM VENERIS
Pervigilium Veneris. 1910. V. 68
Pervigilium Veneris. 1911. V. 70
Pervigilium Veneris...the Eve of Venus, in Latin and English. London: 1924. V. 68
Pervigilvm Veneris Incerti Auctoris Carmen de Vere: the Eve of Venus. Boston and New York: 1924. V. 72
The Vigil of Venus. London: 1912. V. 69
The Vigil of Venus. London: 1939. V. 71
The Vigil of Venus. Cummington: 1943. V. 68

PESKETT, S. JOHN
Murders at Turbot Towers. London: 1937. V. 73

PESTALOZZI, JOHANN
The Use of the Bean Table; or an Introduction to Addition, Subtraction and Numeration, with Visible Objects on the Princples of Pestalozzi. Dublin: 1820. V. 70

PESTAOVA, Z.
Bohemian Engraved Glass. Middlesex: 1968. V. 72

THE PET *Lamb*. London: 1870. V. 73

PETAU, PAUL
Explication de Plusieurs Antiquites, Recueillies par Paul Petau, Sonseiller au Parlement de Paris. Amsterdam: 1757. V. 72

PETAVIUS, DIONYSIUS
Opus de Doctrina Temporum. Antwerp: 1703. V. 73

PETER, J.
Aluminum in Modern Architecture. Louisville: 1956. V. 69; 72

PETER Pan *Pictures form Peter Pan in Kensington Garden*. London: 1907. V. 70

PETER Pan's *ABC*. London: 1914. V. 71

PETER PEREGRINUS
Epistle of Peter Peregrinus of Maricourt to Sygerus of Foncaucourt, Soldier, Concerning the Magnet. London: 1902. V. 70; 71

PETER Rabbit. 1913. V. 69
PETER Rabbit. Chicago: 1913. V. 70
PETER Rabbit. New York: 1917. V. 70
PETER Rabbit. Newark: 1920. V. 71
PETER Rabbit. New York: 1939. V. 70

THE PETER Rabbit *Story Book - A Treasury of Sunshine Stories for Children*. Philadelphia: 1920. V. 73

PETER Rabbit's *Box of Books*. Akron: 1938. V. 70

PETER Thompson *of Needwood Forest; or Industry Rewarded*. Wellington: 1824. V. 68; 72

PETERBOROUGH, EARL OF
An Account of the Earl of Peterborough's Conduct in Spain Chiefly Since the Raising the Siege of Barcelona. London: 1707. V. 71; 72

PETERKIN, JULIA
Black April. Indianapolis: 1927. V. 70; 73
Bright Skin. Indianapolis: 1932. V. 71
Roll, Jordan, Roll. London: 1934. V. 71; 73

PETERS - FRAZIER - FORMAN
Houses of Stone. New York: 1936. V. 69; 72

PETERS, CHARLES
The Girl's Own Indoor Book. Philadelphia: 1888. V. 68

PETERS, ELIZABETH
The Camelot Caper. New York: 1969. V. 69
Crocodile on the Sandbank. New York: 1990. V. 68; 71
The Deeds of the Disturber. 1988. V. 70
Die for Love. New York: 1984. V. 68
The Jackal's Head. New York: 1968. V. 68; 69
The Last Camel Died at Noon. London: 1991. V. 68
Legend in Green Velvet. New York: 1976. V. 69; 70
Lion in the Valley. New York: 1986. V. 69
The Murders of Richard III. New York: 1974. V. 68; 71
Naked Once More. New York: 1989. V. 72
The Seventh Sinner. 1972. V. 73
Street of the Five Moons. New York: 1978. V. 68; 69; 71
Summer of the Dragon. New York: 1979. V. 69; 70
The Walker in Shadows. New York: 1979. V. 68

PETERS, ELLIS
The Assize of the Dying. New York: 1958. V. 70
Black Is the Colour of My True Love's Heart. London: 1967. V. 68; 70; 72
City of Gold and Shadows. London: 1973. V. 68; 70; 72
Dead Man's Ransom. New York: 1984. V. 69
Death and the Joyful Woman. London: 1961. V. 70
Death to the Landlords!. London: 1972. V. 68; 70; 72
The Devil's Novice. London: 1983. V. 68; 69; 71
The Devil's Novice. New York: 1984. V. 73
Flight of a Witch. London: 1964. V. 69; 70
The Hermit of Eyton Forest. New York: 1988. V. 72
The Horn of Roland. London: 1974. V. 68; 70; 72
The Leper of St. Giles. New York: 1982. V. 68; 69; 71
The Marriage of Meggotta. London: 1979. V. 71
Monk's Hood. London: 1980. V. 71
Monk's Hood. New York: 1981. V. 68; 69; 71; 72
A Morbid Taste for Bones. London: 1977. V. 68; 69; 70; 71; 73
A Morbid Taste for Bones. New York: 1978. V. 70; 72
Mourning Raga. London: 1969. V. 68; 70
A Nice Derangement of Epitaphs. London: 1965. V. 70
One Corpse Too Many. London: 1979. V. 68; 69; 70; 71; 73
One Corpse Too Many. New York: 1980. V. 69; 72
The Pilgrim of Hate. London: 1984. V. 72
The Piper on the Mountain. London: 1966. V. 69
The Potter's Field. London: 1989. V. 68; 69; 73
A Rare Benedictine. London: 1988. V. 69; 72
The Rose Rent. London: 1986. V. 72
Saint Peter's Fair. London: 1981. V. 68; 69; 71; 73
Saint Peter's Fair. New York: 1981. V. 68; 69; 71; 72
The Sanctuary Sparrow. New York: 1983. V. 69; 71
The Summer of the Danes. New York: 1991. V. 71; 72
The Will and the Deed. London: 1960. V. 70

PETERS, FRED J.
Railroad, Indian and Pioneer Prints by N. Currier and Currier and Ives. New York: 1930. V. 70

PETERS, G. S.
The Comic Adventures of Old Mother Hubbard and Her Dog; Showing the Wonderful Powers, Which that Good Old Lady Possessed in the Education of Her Favorite Animal. Harrisburg: 1835-1840. V. 71

PETERS, HAROLD S.
The Birds of Newfoundland. St. Johns: 1951. V. 73

PETERS, HARRY T.
California on Stone. New York: 1976. V. 69
Currier & Ives, Printmakers to the American People. New York: 1942. V. 72

PETERS, J. A.
Catalogue of the Neotropical Squamata.. Washington: 1970. V. 69; 72

PETERS, J. T.
History of Fayette County, West Virginia. Parsons: 1972. V. 73

PETERS, MARGOT
Charlotte Bronte. 1973. V. 70

PETERS, PAUL
Stevedore. New York: 1934. V. 70

PETERS, WILLIAM E.
Syntax of the Latin Verb. 1898. V. 71

PETERSEN, KAREN DANIELS
Howling Wolf: a Cheyenne Warrior's Graphic Interpretation of His People. 1968. V. 68

PETERSEN, WILLIAM J.
Steamboating on the Upper Mississippi, the Water Way to Iowa. Iowa City: 1937. V. 73

PETERSHAM, MAUD
The Circus Baby. New York: 1950. V. 72
Miki and Mary: Their Search for Treasures. New York: 1934. V. 73

PETERSON, C. S.
Representative New Mexicans. Denver: 1912. V. 68

PETERSON, D. A.
The American Diceratheres. Pittsburgh: 1920. V. 68

PETERSON, HAROLD L.
American Indian Tomahawks. Gluckstadt, Germany. V. 71
American Indian Tomahawks. 1965. V. 72

PETERSON, L. A.
Edible Wild Plants of Eastern and Central North America. Norwalk: 1985. V. 68

PETERSON, LARRY LEN
Charles M. Russell Legacy. Helena: 1999. V. 68

PETERSON, O. A.
Description of New Carnivores from the Micoene of Western Nebraska. Pittsburgh: 1910. V. 68
A Revision of the Entelodontidae. Pittsburgh: 1909. V. 68; 71

PETERSON, R. T.
Sir Kenelm Digby. London: 1956. V. 68

PETERSON, ROBERT C.
The Science-Fictional Sherlock Holmes Edited by Robert C. Peterson. Denver: 1960. V. 72

PETERSON, ROBERT W.
Only the Ball was White. Englewood Cliffs: 1970. V. 70

PETERSON, ROGER TORY
A Field Guide to the Birds.... Boston and New York: 1934. V. 69; 70; 72; 73
A Field Guide to the Birds.... Boston: 1980. V. 70; 71
Field Guide to Western Birds. Boston: 1990. V. 71
Roger Tory Peterson Field Guides. Norwalk: 1984-1987. V. 73

PETERSON, SUSAN
The Living Tradition of Maria Martinez. New York: 1977. V. 69; 70
Pottery by American Indian Women - The Legacy of Generations. New York: 1997. V. 68

PETERSON, WILLIAM S.
A Bibliography of the Kelmscott Press. Oxford: 2000. V. 70

PETIEVICH, GERALD
Money Men and One Shot Deal. New York: 1981. V. 68
To Die In Beverly Hills. New York: 1983. V. 71
To Live and Die in L.A. New York: 1984. V. 71

PETIT, ANTOINE FRANCOIS
Catalogue des Livres de la Bibliotheque De feu Le Citoyen Antoine Francois Petit, Medecin.... Paris: 1796. V. 68

PETIT, JEAN LOUIS
Traite des Maladies Chirurgicales, et des Operations.... Paris: 1774. V. 70; 73
Traite des Maladies de Os, Dans Lequel on a Represente les Appareils & les Machines Qui Conviennent a Leur Guerison. Paris: 1758. V. 68

PETIT, PHILIP A. J.
The Royal Forests of Northamptonshire, a Study in Their Economy 1558- 1714. Gateshead. V. 73

PETIT, VICTOR
Habitations Champetres, Recueil de Maisons, Villas, Chalets, Pavillons, Kiosques, Parcs et Jardins. Paris: 1855. V. 68; 70

PETITOT, ENNEMOND ALEXANDRE
Suite de Douze Vases. Paris: 1770. V. 70; 72

PETO, GLADYS
Gladys Peto's Children's Book. New York. V. 71

PETO, S. MORTON
The Resources and Prospects of America: Ascertained During a Visit to the States in the Autumn of 1865. London and New York: 1866. V. 72

PETOFI, SANDOR
No English Horse - Poems. Draguignan: 1967. V. 70

PETRE, DIANA
The Secret Orchard of Roger Ackerley. London: 1975. V. 69

PETRIE, CONSTANCE CAMPBELL
Tom Petrie's Reminiscences of Early Queensland. Brisbane;: 1904. V. 71

PETRIE, WILLIAM MATTHE FLINDERS
Syria and Egypt from the Tell El Amarna Letters. London: 1898. V. 73

PETROFF, IVAN
Historical Sketch of Alaska. Minneapolis: 1890. V. 71

PETRONIUS
The Complete Works of Gaius Petronius. New York: 1932. V. 72
The Satyrical Works.... 1708. V. 72
The Satyrical Works.... London: 1708. V. 68

PETRONIUS continued
The Satyricon. 1933. V. 70

PETRUS DE PALUDE
Sermones Thesauri Novi de Sanctis. Nuremberg: 1496. V. 69

PETRY, ANN
The Common Ground. New York: 1964. V. 72
Country Place. Boston: 1947. V. 68
Miss Muriel and Other Stories. Boston: 1971. V. 71

PETTER, NICLAUS
Klare Onderrichtinge der Voortreffelijcke Worstel-Konst. Amsterdam: 1674. V. 68
Der Kunstliche Einger (i.e. Ringer). Amsterdam: 1674. V. 69; 73

PETTERSEN, C.
The Maya of Guatemala: Their Life and Dress. Guatemala City: 1977. V. 69

PETTIBONE, DANIEL
Pettibone's Economy of Fuel; or, Description of His Improvements of the Rarefying Air-Stoves, Grates, Tubes, Pipes, Cylinders, or Open Stoves.... Philadelphia: 1812. V. 70

PETTICOAT Loose, a Fragmentary Tale of the Castle. London: 1812. V. 68

PETTIE, GEORGE
A Petite Pallace or Pettie His Pleasure.... London: 1908. V. 72

PETTIGREW, JAMES JOHNSTON
Notes on Spain and the Spaniards, In the Summer of 1859, with a Glance at Sardinia. Charleston: 1861. V. 69

PETTIGREW, THOMAS JOSEPH
Bibliotheca Sussexiana. London: 1827-1839. V. 71

PETTIS, GEORGE H.
Kit Carson's Fight with the Comanche and Kiowa Indians. Santa Fe: 1908. V. 68

PETTY, GEORGE W.
In Camp with L Company. Second Regiment, New Jersey Volunteer Infantry. New York and Albany: 1899. V. 71

PETTY, WILLIAM
The Antient Right of the Commons of England Asserted; or a Discourse Proving by Records and the Best Historians.... London: 1680. V. 72
The Economic Writings. Cambridge: 1899. V. 71
The Political Anatomy of Ireland. London: 1691. V. 69
Political Arithmetick, or a Discourse Concerning the Extent and Value of Lands, People, Buildings.... London: 1691. V. 72
Several Essays in Political Arithmetick: the Titles of Which follow in the Ensuing Pages. London: 1699. V. 73
Sir William Petty's Political Survey of Ireland, with the Establishment of that Kingdom, When the Late Duke of Ormond was Lord Lieutenant.... London: 1719. V. 72
A Treatise of Taxes and Contributions. London: 1667. V. 73
A Treatise of Taxes and Contributions. London: 1679. V. 72

PETVIN, JOHN
Letters Concerning Mind. London: 1750. V. 70

PETYT, GEORGE
Lex Parliamentaria; or a Treatise of the Law and Custom of the Parliaments. London: 1748. V. 70

PEU, PHILLIPE
La Pratique Des Acouchemens. Paris: 1694. V. 70

PEUGENT, EUGENE
The Nature of Gunshot Wounds of the Abdomen and their Treatment. New York: 1874. V. 73

PEVSNER, NIKOLAUS
Academies of Art Past and Present. Cambridge: 1940. V. 70
The Anti-Rationalists. London: 1973. V. 72
The Buildings of England. London: 1951-1978. V. 70; 72
The Cathedrals of England. 1985. V. 68
The Englishness of English Art. London: 1956. V. 72
An Enquiry into Industrial Art in England. New York: 1937. V. 69; 72
High Victorian Design - a Study of the Exhibits of 1851. London: 1951. V. 71

PEYERO, JOHAN CONRADO
Meditatio de Valetudine Humana ad Obtinendum Doctoris Medicinae Titulum et Privelegia Procerum Nut Atque Decreto in Alma Rauracorum Academia die X Octorbirs MDCLXXXI Eruditorum Examini Proposita. Basel: 1681. V. 68; 72

PEYSSONNEL, CLAUDE DE
An Appendix to the Memors of Baron de Tott; Being a Letter from Mr. De Peyssonnel...to the Marquis of N****. London: 1786. V. 68

PEYTON, GREEN
Black Cabin. Boston: 1933. V. 69

PEYTON, JOHN ROWZEE
3 Letters from St. Louis. Denver: 1958. V. 69

PFAFF, OTTO
Buch und Bucheinband, eine Werbeschirft. Zur Ausstellung Kunsterische Bucheinbande der Werkstatten Burg giebichenstein Halle/Saale KunstGewerbeschule. Halle: 1926. V. 70

PFAUNDLER, MEINHARD VON
The Diseases of Children.... Philadelphia and London: 1912-1914. V. 69

PFEIFFER, BRUCE B.
Frank Lloyd Wright Drawings. New York: 1990. V. 68
Frank Lloyd Wright: in the Realm of Ideas. Carbondale: 1988. V. 68
Frank Lloyd Wright: Treasures of Taliesin. Fresno: 1985. V. 68

PFEIFFER, EMILY
Flying Leaves from East and West. London: 1885. V. 73

PFEIFFER, IDA
The Last Travels of Ida Pfeiffer. London: 1861. V. 71
Visit To Iceland And The Scandinavian North. London: 1852. V. 72
Visit to Iceland and the Scandinavian North. London: 1853. V. 73
Visit to the Holy Land, Egypt and Italy. London: 1852. V. 73

PHAEDRUS
Fabularum Aesopiarum Libri V. Amstelaedami: 1701. V. 71
A Poetical Translation of the Fables of Phaedrus. (by Christopher Smart). London: 1765. V. 71

PHANTASIEN zu Landlichen Verzierungen und Gartenbauden. Leipzig: 1800. V. 73

PHARALL, AISHIL
The Little Less. New York: 1926. V. 71

PHARIS, R. P.
Plant Growth Substances 1988. Berlin: 1990. V. 68

PHARMACOPOEIA Chirurgica or Formuae for the Use of Surgeons.... London: 1802. V. 69

PHELPS, CHARLES
Traumatic Injuries of the Brain and Its Membranes. New York: 1897. V. 68; 71; 73

PHELPS, ELIZABETH STUART
Sealed Orders. Boston: 1879. V. 69
A Singular Life. Boston: 1898. V. 68

PHELPS, WILLIAM
Calendarium Botanicum; or a Botanical Calendar.... London: 1810. V. 71

PHELPS, WILLIAM DANE
Alta California, 1840-1842. 1983. V. 68

THE PHILANTHROPE; after the Manner of a Periodical Paper. London: 1797. V. 70

PHILBRICK, NATANIEL
In the Heart of the Sea. London: 2000. V. 68; 73

PHILBRICK, NATHANIEL
In The Heart Of The Sea. New York: 2000. V. 72

PHILBRICK, W. R.
Shadow Kills. New York: 1985. V. 70

PHILBY, HARRY ST. JOHN BRIDGER
Arabian Jubilee. London: 1952. V. 71
A Pilgrim in Arabia. London: 1943. V. 70
A Pilgrim in Arabia. Waltham St. Lawrence: 1943. V. 71
A Pilgrim in Arabia. London: 1946. V. 71

PHILIDOR, FRANCOIS ANDRE DANICAN
Chess Analysed. London: 1750. V. 73
Chess Analysed. London: 1773. V. 73

PHILIP, ALEX J.
A History of Gravesend and Its Surroundings from Prehistoric Times. Wraysbury: 1954. V. 73

PHILIP, ALEXANDER J.
A Dickens Dictionary. London: 1909. V. 68
A Dickens Dictionary. London: 1928. V. 69
Dickens's Honeymoon and Where He Spent It. London: 1912. V. 69

PHILIP, ALEXANDER PHILIP WILSON
An Experimental Essay on the Manner in Which Opium Acts on the Living Body. Edinburgh: 1795. V. 68

PHILIP, GEORGE
Philips' Centenary Mercantile Marine Atlas. London: 1935. V. 70

PHILIP HARRIS & CO., LTD., BIRMINGHAM
Catalogue of Chemical and Physical Apparatus and Chemicals. 1889. V. 71

PHILIPP, ELLIOT E.
Scientific Foundations of Obstetrics and Gynaecology. London: 1977. V. 68

PHILIPPS, JOHN
The Case of the Controverted Election of Coventry, Reported by John Philipps, Barrister of the Inner Temple. London: 1784. V. 70

PHILIPS, CASPER JACOBSZ
Verzaameling van alle de Huizen en Prachtige Gebouwen langs de Keizers e Heere-Grachten der Stadt Amsterdam.... Amsterdam: 1768. V. 70

PHILIPS, CATHERINE C.
Jesse Benton Fremont - A Woman Who Made History. San Francisco: 1935. V. 70

PHILIPS, GEORGE
Lex Parliamentaria; or, a Treatise of the Law and Custom of the Parliaments of England. London: 1690. V. 70

PHILIPS, J.
Illustrations of the Geology of Yorkshire. Part I. and Part 2. 1835-1836. V. 73

PHILIPS, JOHN
Cyder. London: 1708. V. 69
Poems on Several Occasions. London: 1728. V. 72

PHILIPS, JUDSON
Hold'Em, Girls! The Intelligent Woman's Guide to Men and Football. New York: 1936. V. 69
Red War. New York: 1936. V. 69

PHILIPS, KATHERINE
Poems by.... London: 1667. V. 71

PHILLIPPS, A.
Pitcher-Plants of Borneo. Kota Kinabalu: 1996. V. 71

PHILLIPPS, FABIAN
The Antiquity, Legality, Reason, Duty and Necessity of Praemption and Pourveyance, for the King; or Compositions for His Pourveyance, as They Were Used and Taken for the Provisions of the Kings Houshold (sic).... London: 1663. V. 70

PHILLIPPS, THOMAS
Catalogue of the Mss. at Holkham. (with) Additional Mss. in the Possession of the Revd. Walter Sneyd, of Denton House, Oxon.... 1863. V. 70

PHILLIPPS-WOLLEY, C.
Big Game Shooting. 1894. V. 69; 70; 73
Big Game Shooting. London: 1894. V. 71
Big Game Shooting. 1901. V. 69
Big Game Shooting. 1902-1903. V. 70
Sport in the Crimea and the Caucasus. 1881. V. 73

PHILLIPS, A.
The Birds of Arizona. Tucson: 1964. V. 68

PHILLIPS, ARTHUR S.
My Wilderness Friends by Arthur S. Phillips, President of the Quequehan Fish and Game Club. Fall River: 1910. V. 73

PHILLIPS, C. E. L.
The Rothschild Rhododendrons, a Record of the Gardens at Exbury. New York: 1979. V. 68; 73

PHILLIPS, C. J.
The New Forest Handbook: Historical and Descriptive. Lyndhurst: 1876. V. 70

PHILLIPS, CARYL
Cambridge. New York: 1992. V. 72
Crossing the River. New York: 1994. V. 72
Higher Ground. New York: 1989. V. 72
A State of Independence. New York: 1986. V. 72

PHILLIPS, CATHERINE C.
Cornelius Cole - California Pioneer and United States Senator - A Study In Personality and Achievements Bearing Upon the Growth of a Commonwealth. San Francisco: 1929. V. 69
Coulterville Chronicle - the Annals of a Mother Lode. San Francisco: 1942. V. 68
Jessie Benton Fremont. San Francisco: 1935. V. 73

PHILLIPS, CHARLES
Samoa Past And Present. London. V. 72
The Speeches of Charles Phillips, Esq. Delivered at the Bar, and on Various Public Occasions, in Ireland and England. London: 1817. V. 68

PHILLIPS, COLES
A Young Man's Fancy. Indianapolis: 1912. V. 69

PHILLIPS, E. M.
The Gardens of Italy with Historical and Descriptive Notes. 1919. V. 69

PHILLIPS, G. F.
Practical Treatise on Drawing, and On Painting In Water Colours. London: 1839. V. 72
Principles of Effect and Colour, as Applicable to Landscape Painting. London: 1839. V. 69

PHILLIPS, GEORGE
Rudiments of Curvilinear Design. London: 1839. V. 68; 70; 72

PHILLIPS, GEORGE SEARLE
The Life, Character and Genius of Ebenezer Elliott the Corn Law Rhymer. London: 1850. V. 71

PHILLIPS, HENRY
The True Enjoyment of Angling. 1843. V. 68

PHILLIPS, HUGH
The Thames about 1750. London: 1951. V. 73

PHILLIPS, J. A.
Gold Mining and Assaying: a Scientific Guide for Australian Emigrants. London: 1852. V. 69

PHILLIPS, JAYNE ANNE
Black Tickets. New York: 1979. V. 68; 72
Black Tickets. London: 1980. V. 71
Counting. New York: 1978. V. 68
Fast Lanes. New York: 1984. V. 69; 73
How Mickey Made It. St. Paul: 1981. V. 68
Machine Dreams. New York: 1984. V. 72
Shelter. Boston: 1994. V. 72
Sweethearts. Carrboro: 1976. V. 68

PHILLIPS, JOHN
Illustrations of the Geology of Yorkshire. 1835-1836. V. 69
Letter and Representation to the Right Honourable the Lord Harcourt. 1721. V. 68
Letter and Representation to the Right Honourable the Lord Harcourt. 1921. V. 72
Manual of Geology: Theoretical and Practical. London: 1885. V. 69
The Rivers, Mountains and Sea-Coast of Yorkshire, with Essays on the Climate.... London: 1853. V. 68
Vesuvius. Oxford: 1869. V. 70

PHILLIPS, JOHN CHARLES
A Natural History of the Ducks. Boston and New York: 1922-1926. V. 69; 70; 73
Wenham Great Pond. Salem: 1938. V. 73

PHILLIPS, JOHN P.
A General History of Inland Navigation, Foreign and Domestic. London: 1792. V. 73

PHILLIPS, LIONEL, MRS.
Some South African Recollections. London: 1899. V. 69

PHILLIPS, MAUD GILLETTE
Law Unwrit. New York: 1925. V. 69

PHILLIPS, PAUL CHRISLER
The Fur Trade. Norman: 1961. V. 68; 70

PHILLIPS, PHILIP LEE
A List of Geographical Atlases in the Library of Congress. Washington: 1909-1920. V. 71
A List of Geographical Atlases in the Library of Congress. Washington: 1914-1920. V. 71
A List of Maps of America in the Library of Congress.... Washington: 1901. V. 71

PHILLIPS, PHILLIP
The Forth Bridge In Its Various Stages of Construction and Compared with the Most Notable Bridges in the World. Edinburgh: 1890. V. 73

PHILLIPS, RICHARD
A Letter to the Livery of London, Relative to the View of the Writer in Executing the Office of Sheriff. London: 1808. V. 69
The Sweepings of My Study. London;: 1824. V. 73

PHILLIPS, ROLAND ASHFORD
Golden Isle. New York: 1925. V. 70

PHILLIPS, SANDRA S.
Andre Kertesz: of Paris and New York. New York: 1985. V. 68

PHILLIPS, SCOTT
The Ice Harvest. Tucson: 2000. V. 73
The Walkaway. London: 2002. V. 72
The Walkaway. Tucson: 2002. V. 73

PHILLIPS, STEPHEN
Christ in Hades and Other Poems. London: 1896. V. 69
Eremus: a Poem. London: 1894. V. 72
The New Inferno. London: 1911. V. 68
Orestes and Other Poems. London: 1884. V. 72

PHILLIPS, T.
Africa, the Art of a Continent. Munich and New York: 1995. V. 69
Lectures on the History and Principles of Painting. London: 1833. V. 69; 71

PHILLIPS, TOM
A Humument. London: 1980. V. 69
A Humument. London: 1987. V. 71
A Humument. London: 1997. V. 70
Lesbia Waltz. London: 1971. V. 70
Works-Texts- to 1974. Stuttgart and Reykjavik: 1974. V. 69

PHILLIPS, V. T.
Guide to the Manuscript Colelctions in the Academy of Natural Sciences of Philadelphia. Philadelphia: 1963. V. 72

PHILLIPS, W.
A Manual of the British Discomycetes.... London: 1887. V. 72
An Outline of Mineralogy and Geology.... New York: 1816. V. 70

PHILLIPS, W. S.
Totem Tales. Chicago: 1896. V. 69

PHILLIPS, WALTER C.
Dickens, Reade and Collins, Sensation Novelists.... New York: 1919. V. 73

PHILLIPS, WATTS
MP, Showing How the Honourable Mr. Teddington Locke Was Not Returned for the Incorruptible Borough of Bubengrub. London: 1840. V. 69
The Model Republic; or, Cato Popps in Paris,. London: 1840. V. 70

PHILLLIPS, W. W. A.
Manual of the Mammals of Ceylon. Colombo: 1933. V. 70

PHILLPOTTS, EDEN
The Apes. New York: 1929. V. 70
The Banks of Colne: (The Nursery). New York: 1917. V. 72
Black, White and Brindled. London: 1923. V. 69
The Captain's Curio. New York: 1933. V. 68; 71
Children of the Mist. London: 1898. V. 69
A Clue from the Stars. New York: 1932. V. 71
A Deed Without a Name. New York: 1942. V. 70

PHILLPOTTS, EDEN continued
A Dish of Apples. London: 1921. V. 68
The Eden Phillpotts Calendar. London. V. 68
The Girl and the Faun. London: 1916. V. 69
The Girl and the Faun. London: 1917. V. 71
My Garden. London: 1906. V. 70
The Oldest Inhabitant. New York: 1934. V. 71
A Shadow Passes. New York: 1934. V. 70
Tryphena. New York: 1929. V. 72

THE PHILOBIBLION: a Monthly Bibliographical Journal.... New York: 1861-1863. V. 68

PHILOSOPHICAL Transactions Giving Some Accompt of Present Undertakings, Studies & Labours of the Ingenious in Many Considerable Parts of the World. Volume I. London: 1665-1666. V. 68

PHILOSTRATUS, L. FLAVIUS
The Two First Books of Philostratus Concerning the Life of Apollonius Tyaneus.... London: 1680. V. 72

PHILP, ROBERT KEMP
Enquire Within Upon Everything: to Which is Added Enquire Within Upon Fancy Needlework. London: 1871. V. 71
The History of Progress in Great Britain. 1859. V. 71
The History of Progress in Great Britain. London: 1859. V. 70
The Shopkeeper's Guide. 1853. V. 71

PHILPOT, GLYN
Glyn Philpot 1884-1937. London: 1951. V. 68

PHILPOTT, EDWARD
Crinoline from 1730 to 1864. London: 1864. V. 68

PHIN, JOHN
Open Air Grape Culture. New York: 1862. V. 68

PHINNEY, MARY A.
Allen-Isham Genealogy, Jirah Isham Allen, Montana Pioneer, Government Scout, Guide, Interpreter and Famous Hunter During Four Years of Indian Warfare in Montana and Dakota. Rutland, VT. V. 72

PHIPPS, JOSEPH
The Original and Present State of Man.... Philadelphia: 1783. V. 71

PHIPPS, POWNOLL W.
Records of the Churches, Rectory and Vicarage of Upton cum-Chalvey, Bucks. Slough: 1886. V. 71

PHIPSON, CECIL BALFOUR
The Redemption of Labour, or, Free Labour Upon Free Land. London: 1888-1892. V. 71

THE PH(O)ENIX: a Collection of Old and Rare Fragments.... New York: 1835. V. 71; 72

THE PHOENIX Bookshop. A Nest of Memories. Candia: 1997. V. 70

PHYSICK, J. F.
Catalogue of the Engraved Work of Eric Gill. London: 1963. V. 69; 72

PIATT, JOHN JAMES
Idyls and Lyrics of the Ohio Valley. London and New York: 1893. V. 69

PICARD LTD.
Album de Serrurerie Decorative. Paris: 1931. V. 69

PICART, BERNARD
A New Drawing Book of Modes. London: 1733. V. 69
Les Peintures de Charles Le Brun et d'Eustache Le Sueur qui Sont Dans l'Hotel du Chastelet, cy Devant la Maison du President Lambert. Paris: 1740. V. 72

PICASSO, PABLO
Desire Caught by the Tail. London: 1970. V. 70
The Four Little Girls. London: 1970. V. 70
A Retrospective. New York: 1980. V. 70
The Sculptor's Studio: Etchings by Picasso. New York: 1952. V. 71

PICCOLOMINI, ALESSANDRO
Notable Discours en Forme de Dialogue Touchant la Vraye et Prafaicte Amitie Duquel Toutes Personnes & Principalement Les Dames. Lyon: 1577. V. 68; 69

PICCOLPASSO, CIPRIANO
The Three Books of the Potter's Art. London: 1934. V. 69
The Three Books of the Potter's Art. London: 1980. V. 68

PICHON, THOMAS
Genuine Letters and Memoirs Relating to the Natural, Civil and Commercial History of the Islands of Cape Breton and Saint John. London: 1760. V. 68; 72
Lettres et Memories pour servir. L'Histoire Naturelle, Civile et Politque Du Cap Breton, depuis Son Etablessement Jusque. La Reprise de Cette Isle par les Anglois en 1758. La Haye & A. Londres: 1760. V. 73

PICKARD, KATE E. R.
The Kidnapped and the Ransomed. Syracuse: 1856. V. 68

PICKARD, TOM
The Order of Chance. London: 1971. V. 71

PICKEN, ANDREW
The Canadas, As They at Present Commend Themselves to the Enterprise of Emigrants, Colonists and Capitalists. London: 1832. V. 73

PICKEN, M.
City of Vancouver Terminus of the Canadian Pacific Railway. British Columbia Hand Book. Vancouver: 1887. V. 68

PICKERING & CHATTO
An Illustrated Catalogue of Old and Rare Books. 1902. V. 71

PICKERING, GEORGE
Westmorland, Cumberland, Durham and Northumberland Illustrated.... London: 1832. V. 71

PICKERING, H. G.
Angling of the Test or True Love Under Stress.... New York: 1936. V. 70

PICKERING, JOHN
A Vocabulary, or Collection of Works and Phrases. Boston;: 1816. V. 68

PICKERING, WILHELMINA
The Queen of the Goblins. London: 1892. V. 71

PICKET, ALBERT
The Juvenile Mentor or Select Readings. Wheeling: 1825. V. 71

PICKETT, A. ST. J.
The Sublime Tragedy of the Lost Cause, a Tragic Poem of the War. Columbus: 1884. V. 71

PICKETT, GEORGE E.
The Heart of a Solider, as Revealed in the Intimate Letters of George E. Pickett. New York: 1913. V. 70

PICKETT, LA SALLE CORBELL
Bugles of Gettysburg. Chicago: 1913. V. 69
What Happened to Me. New York: 1917. V. 70

PICKFORD, MARY
The Demi-Widow. Indianapolis: 1935. V. 70; 71

PICKTHALL, MARMADUKE
The Valley of the Kings. London: 1909. V. 70

PICON, GAETAN
Surrealists and Surrealism 1919-1939. New York: 1977. V. 70

PICTET, F. J.
Histoire Naturelle Generale et Particuliere des Insectes Neuropteres. Geneva: 1841-1845. V. 73

PICTON, THOMAS
A Letter Addressed to the Rt. Hon. Lord Hobart. London: 1804. V. 70

PICTORIAL History of England. London: 1838. V. 70

PICTORIAL Photography in America. New York: 1926. V. 70

PICTORIAL Records of The English In Egypt, With a Full and Descriptive Life of General Gordon the Hero of Khartoum. London. V. 72

THE PICTURE Alphabet or ABC in Rhyme. New Haven. V. 73

THE PICTURE Alphabet or Child's ABC. Portland: 1830. V. 73
THE PICTURE Alphabet or Child's ABC. Portland: 1865-1875. V. 69

A PICTURE Book for Little Children. Philadelphia: 1812. V. 70

THE PICTURE Book, or Familiar Objects Described. New Haven: 1840. V. 69

THE PICTURE Book: With Stories in Easy Words: for Litte Readers (First Series - No. 7). New York: 1856-1866. V. 73

PICTURE Encyclopedia. Tokyo: 1972. V. 72

PICTURE Gallery Annual. London: 1877. V. 72

THE PICTURE of Parliament; or a History of the General Election of 1802. London: 1802. V. 71

PICTURE of Scarborough for the Year 1824; Forming a Guide to that Favourite Watering-Place. Scarborough: 1824. V. 69

A PICTURE Story-Book. London. V. 70

PICTURES from Birdland. London: 1899. V. 72

PICTURES of Roman History. London: 1817. V. 69

PICTURES of Society. London: 1866. V. 68

PICTURES of the French: a Series of Literary and Graphic Delineations of French Character. London: 1840. V. 70

PICTURESQUE Excursions From Bridlington-Quay. Bridlington: 1836. V. 73

PICTURESQUE Riverside, California. Riverside: 1903. V. 68
PICTURESQUE Riverside, California. Riverside: 1910. V. 70

PIDGIN, CHARLES FELTON
The Chronicles of Quincy Adams Sawyer, Detective. Boston: 1912. V. 69; 73
The Further Adventures of Quincy Adams Sawyer and Mason Corner Folks. Boston: 1909. V. 69

PIELOU, E. C.
Biogeography. New York: 1979. V. 72

PIEPER, JOSEPH
Leisure - The Basis of Culture. New York: 1952. V. 72

PIEPER, R.
Chinesisches In Unkraut, Knospen, u. Bluten. Steyl: 1900. V. 72

PIER, ARTHUR STANWOOD
The Plattsburgers. Boston: 1917. V. 70

PIERCE, EDWARD L.
Memoir and Letters of Charles Sumner. Boston: 1881. V. 69

PIERCE, FRANK CUSHMAN
A Brief History of the Lower Rio Grande Valley. Menasha: 1917. V. 68; 69; 73

PIERCE, FREDERICK E.
Reminiscences of the Experiences of Company L, Second Regiment Massachusetts Infantry, U.S.V. in the Spanish American War. Greenfield: 1900. V. 73

PIERCE, GEORGE
Autumn's Bounty. San Antonio: 1972. V. 68

PIERCE, GEORGE F.
An Address on Female Education, Delivered in the Chapel of the Georgia Female College. Macon: 1839. V. 71

PIERCE, GERALD S.
Texas Under Arms - the Camp, Posts and Military Towns of the Republic of Texas 1836-1846. Austin: 1969. V. 69; 72

PIERCE, GILBERT A.
The Dickens Dictionary. Boston: 1872. V. 69
The Dickens Dictionary. London: 1878. V. 69; 71

PIERCE, N. B.
The California Vine Disease.... Washington: 1882. V. 70
The California Vine Disease.... Washington: 1892. V. 72

PIERCE, PARKER I.
Antelope Bill. Minnesota: 1962. V. 72

PIERCEALL, G. M.
Residential Landscapes, Graphics, Planning and Design. Reston: 1984. V. 68; 71

PIERCY, MARGE
Breaking Camp. Middletown: 1968. V. 73
Dance the Eagle to Sleep. Garden City: 1970. V. 73
Going Down Fast. New York: 1969. V. 73
Small Changes. Garden City: 1973. V. 73
Woman on the Edge of Time. New York: 1976. V. 72

PIERIS, P.
Guide to the Collections of the Colombo Museum, Ceylon. 1912. V. 69

PIERRE, BERNARD
A Mountain Called Nun Kun. London: 1955. V. 69

PIERRE DE LIMOGES
Libro del Occhio Morale et Spirituale Vulgare. Venice: 1496. V. 73

PIERS, HARRY
Robert Field, Portrait Painter in Oils, Miniature and Water-colours and Engraver. New York: 1927. V. 73

PIERS, JOHN
A Full and Accurate Report of the Trial of Sir John Piers, for Criminal Conversation with Lady Cloncurry. Dublin: 1807. V. 70

PIERSALL, JIM
Fear Strikes Out: the Jim Piersall Story. Boston: 1955. V. 71

PIERSON, FRANK R.
Cool Hand Luke. Burbank: 1966. V. 71

PIERSON, JOSIAH
Millenium, a Poem in Five Books. Rochester: 1831. V. 71

PIESSE, GEORGE WILLIAM SEPTIMUS
The Art of Perfumery. London: 1855. V. 68

PIFFARD, HENRY G.
A Practical Treatise on Diseases of the Skin. New York: 1891. V. 73

PIFFLE'S A B C Book of Funny Animals. Philadelphia: 1919. V. 70

PIGAL, EDME JEAN
Recueil e Scenes de Societe. Paris: 1822. V. 69

PIGONATI, ANDREA
Stato Presente Degli Antichi Monumenti Siciliana. 1767. V. 68

PIGOT & CO.
Royal National and Commercial Directory and Topography.... London: 1839. V. 73

PIGOT, R.
Twenty-five Years Big Game Hunting. 1928. V. 69; 70; 72; 73

PIGOTT, CHARLES
The Female Jockey Club, or a Sketch of the Manners of the Age. London: 1794. V. 68; 71
The Jockey Club, or a Sketch of the Manners of the Age. (with) Part the Second. (with) Part the Third. London: 1792. V. 73

PIGOTT, JOHN HUGH SMYTH
Catalogue of the Remaining Portion of the Valuable Library of.... London: 1853. V. 70

PIGOTT, N.
A Treatise of Common Recoveries, Their Nature and Use. London: 1739. V. 72

PIGOU, ARTHUR CECIL
The Economy and Finance of the War, Being A Discussion of the Real Costs of the War and the Way in Which They Should be Met. London: 1916. V. 71

PIKE, ALBERT
Lyrics and Love Songs. Little Rock: 1916. V. 73
Morals and Dogma of the Ancient and Accepted Scottish Rite of Freemasonry Prepared for the Supreme Council of the Thirty-Third Degree . . . Charleston: 1906. V. 71

PIKE, GRANVILLE ROSS
Dining Room and the Kitchen. The No. 1 Hard Cook Book. Fargo: 1889. V. 69

PIKE, JAMES
The Scout and Ranger: Being the Personal Adventures of Corporal Pike of the Fourth Ohio Cavalry. Cincinnati: 1865. V. 73
Scout and Ranger Being the Personal Adventures of James Pike of the Texas Rangers in 1859-1860. 1932. V. 68

PIKE, JOSEPH
An Epistle to the National Meeting of Friends in Dublin, Concerning Good Order and Discipline in the Church. Dublin: 1726. V. 73

PIKE, NICHOLAS
Sub-Tropical Rambles in the Land of the Aphanapteryx. London: 1873. V. 71

PIKE, WARBURTON
The Barren Ground of Northern Canada. New York: 1917. V. 70
The Barren Ground of Northern Canada. 1967. V. 70; 72; 73
Through the Subarctic Forest. 1967. V. 70; 72; 73

PIKE, ZEBULON MONTGOMERY
The Expeditions of Zebulon Montgomery Pike to Headwaters of the Mississippi River Through Louisiana Territory.... Minnesota: 1965. V. 71
Exploratory Travels - Pike's Exploration by the Order of the U. S. Government - to the Source of the Mississippi in 1805 through the Territory of Louisiana and Provinces of New Spain in 1806-1807. Denver: 1889. V. 70; 72
Exploratory Travels through the Western Territories of North America.... 1889. V. 68
The Journals of Zebulon Montgomery Pike with Letters and Related Documents. Norman: 1966. V. 70; 72; 73

PILATE, a Passion Play. Sussex: 1928. V. 69

PILBROW, RICHARD
Stage Lighting Design. The Art, the Craft, the Life. New York: 1997. V. 70

PILCHER, LEWIS A.
A List of Books by Some of the Old Masters of Medicine and Surgery. Brooklyn: 1918. V. 68

PILCHER, VELONA
The Searcher - a War Play. London: 1929. V. 69

PILE, C. C. R.
Cranbrook - a Waeldon Town. Cranbrook: 1955. V. 72

PILEGGI, NICHOLAS
Casino: Love and Honor in Las Vegas. New York: 1995. V. 71

PILES, ROGER DE
Nouveau Traite d'Anatomie Accomodee Aux Arts de Peinture et de Sculpture par Tortebat. Paris: 1799. V. 68; 73
Recueil de Divers Ouvrages sur la Peinture et le Coloris. Paris: 1755. V. 70

PILGER, JOHN
The Outsiders. London: 1985. V. 68

THE PILGRIM Fathers: a Journal of Their Coming in the Mayflower to New England and Their Life and Adventures There. Waltham St. Lawrence: 1939. V. 71

PILKINGTON, LIONEL SCOTT
Life and Eccentricities of Lionel Scott Pilkington, Alias Jack Hawley. Doncaster. V. 72

PILKINGTON, MARY
The Gentleman's and Connoisseur's Dictionary of Painters. London: 1770. V. 68
A Mirror for the Female Sex. Hartford: 1799. V. 73
A Mirror for the Female Sex. London: 1799. V. 68
Tales of the Hermitage. London: 1798. V. 68; 72

PILKINGTON, MATTHEW
A General Dictionary of Painters.... London: 1829. V. 69; 70
A Rational Concordance or an Index to the Bible. Nottingham: 1749. V. 73

PILLET, R. L.
Warshawksy: les Impressions de Paris. Paris: 1948. V. 72

PILLING, JAMES CONSTANTINE
Bibliography of the Iroquoian Languages. Washington: 1888. V. 68

PILLIPPS, HENRY
The Grandeur of the Law; or, an Exact Collection of the Nobility and Gentry of This Kingdom, Whose Honors and Estates Have by Some of Their Ancestors Been Acquired or Considerably Augmented.... London: 1684. V. 71

PILSBRY, H. A.
Catalogue of the Marine Mollusks of Japan.... Detroit: 1895. V. 69; 73

PIM, JAMES
Irish Railways. A Letter to the Right Hon. Frederic Shaw, M.P. London: 1839. V. 68

PINCHBECK, IVY
Women Workers and the Industrial Revolution 1750-1850. London: 1930. V. 71

PINCHON, EDGCUMB
Until I Find. New York: 1936. V. 71

PINCKNEY, GUSTAVUS M.
Life of John C. Calhoun. Charleston: 1903. V. 71

PINCKNEY, JOSEPHINE
My Son and Foe. New York: 1952. V. 71
Sea-Drinking Cities. New York and London: 1927. V. 70; 71; 73
Splendid in Ashes. New York: 1958. V. 71

PINCKNEY, MARIA HENRIETTA
The Quintessence of Long Speeches, Arranged as a Political Catehchism.... Charleston;: 1830. V. 73

PINDARUS
Carmina et Fragmenta. Oxoni: 1807. V. 68; 72
Carmina Juxta Exemplar Heynianum. London: 1821. V. 72
The Pythian, Nemean, and Isthmian Odes of Pindar. London: 1778. V. 71

PINELLI, MAFFEO
Bibliotheca Pinelliana. A Catalogue of the Magnificent and Celebrated Library of.... London: 1789. V. 70

PINERO, ARTHUR W.
Iris - a Drama in Five Acts. London: 1902. V. 69

PINGRE, ALEXANDRE GUY
Cometographie ou Traite Historique et Theorique des Cometes. Paris: 1783-1784. V. 71; 72

PINGRET, EDOUARD
Voyages de S. M. Louis Philippe Ier, Roi des Francais, au Chateau de Windsor.... Paris: 1846. V. 73

PINHEY, E.
A Descriptive Catalogue of the Odonata of the African Continent (Up to Dec. 1959). 1962. V. 69

PINKERTON, A. F.
Jim Cummings and the Great Adams Express Robbery. Chicago: 1887. V. 68

PINKERTON, ALLAN
Bank-Robbers and the Detectives. New York: 1882. V. 73
Criminal Reminiscences and Detective Sketches. New York: 1878. V. 73
The Detective and the Somnambulist - the Murderer of the Fortune Teller. Chicago: 1875. V. 73
A Double Life and the Detectives. New York: 1884. V. 73
The Gypsies and the Detectives. New York: 1879. V. 73
Model Town and Detectives. 1876. V. 73
Thirty Years a Detective. Philadelphia: 1884. V. 73

PINKERTON, JOHN
An Essay on Medals.... London: 1808. V. 72

PINKERTON, ROBERT
Russia; or Miscellaneous Observations on the Past and Present State of that Country and Its Inhabitants. London: 1833. V. 70

PINKS, WILLIAM J.
The History of Clerkenwell.... London: 1880. V. 69

PINKUS, HENRY
Prospectus of a New Agrarian System. London: 1840. V. 73

PINNER, ROBERT
Turkoman Studies I: Aspects of the Weaving and Decorative Arts of Central Asia. London: 1980. V. 69; 72

PINNOCK, WILLIAM
A Catechism of Conchology.... London: 1829. V. 68
Pinnock's Catechism of Zoology. Part VI. London: 1831. V. 68

PINSKY, ROBERT
An Explanation of America. Princeton: 1979. V. 69; 73
The Rhyme of Reb Nachman. Winnetka: 1998. V. 69; 73

PINTER, HAROLD
Betrayal. London: 1970. V. 68
The Birthday Party: a Play in Three Acts. London: 1959. V. 70
The Dwarfs. London: 1990. V. 70
The Early Poems. Warwick: 1992. V. 70
Family Voices: a Play for Radio. London: 1981. V. 69; 72
The French Lieutenant's Woman. A Screenplay. Boston-Toronto: 1981. V. 70
The French Lieutenant's Woman and Other Screenplays. London: 1982. V. 69
The Homecoming. London: 1966. V. 69
New Poems 1967 - a P.E.N. Anthology of Contemporary Poetry. London: 1968. V. 71
No Man's Land. London: 1975. V. 68
One for the Road. London: 1984. V. 72
Poems. London: 1968. V. 68; 69; 71; 73
The Screenplay of the French Lieutenant's Woman. Based on the novel by John Fowles, with a foreword by John Fowles. London: 1981. V. 69; 71
A Speech of Thanks. London: 1995. V. 68

PINTO, A. A. DE SERPA
How I Crossed Africa. London: 1881. V. 71

PINTURA
Cubana De Hoy. La Habana: 1944. V. 68

PIOCHE COMMERCIAL CLUB
The Heritage of the Desert. Pioche: 1924. V. 68

THE PIOUS
Child's Delight; or Some Helps to the Religion of Children and Their Knowledge of the Scripture. Coventury. V. 69

PIOZZI, HESTER LYNCH SALUSBURY THRALE
Anecdotes of the Late Samuel Johnson, LL.D. London: 1786. V. 69; 70; 72
Autobiography, Letters and Literary Remains. London: 1861. V. 69; 73
British Synonymy; or an Attempt at Regulating the Choice of Words in Familiar Conversation. London: 1794. V. 73
Dr Johnson's Mrs. Thrale, Autobiography, Letters and Literary Remains of Mrs. Piozzi, edited by A. Hayward QC., newly selected and edited with introductions and notes by J.H. Lobban. 1910. V. 72
Extracts from Mrs. Piozzi's Retrospections. Herford: 1804. V. 70
The Intimate Letters of Hester Piozzi and Penelope Pennington 1788- 1821. London: 1914. V. 69
Love Letters of Mrs. Piozzi Written When She Was Eighty to William Augustus Conway. London: 1843. V. 69
Observations and Reflections Made in the Course of a Journey through France, Italy and Germany. London: 1789. V. 69
Retrospection of a Review of the Most Striking and Important Events, Characters, Situations and Their Consequences Which the Last Eighteen Hundred Years Have Presented to the View of Mankind. London: 1801. V. 68; 69; 70; 72; 73
Thraliana, the Diary of Mrs. Hester Lynch Thrale (Later Piozzi) 1776- 1809. Oxford: 1951. V. 69; 72

PIP
and Squeak Annual, 1923. V. 69

PIP
and Squeak Annual 1924. V. 73

PIP
& Squeak Annual 1931. V. 69

THE PIPE-
Rolls, or Sheriff's Annual Accounts of the Revenues of the Crown for the Counties of Cumberland, Westmorland and Durham, during the Reigns of Henry II, Richard I, and John. Newcastle: 1848. V. 71; 73

PIPER, C. V.
Flora of the State of Washington. Washington: 1906. V. 70

PIPER, H. BEAM
Murder in the Gunroom. New York: 1953. V. 69; 70

PIPER, JOHN
Brighton Aquatints. London: 1939. V. 70
British Romantic Artists. London: 1942. V. 69

PIPER, MYFANWY
Reynolds Stone. London: 1951. V. 72
Sea Poems. London: 1944. V. 69
The Seducer - A Play in Two Acts.... London: 1958. V. 68

PIPER, WATTY
Eight Fairy Tales. New York: 1934-1938. V. 70
Folk Tales Children Love. New York: 1934. V. 69; 71; 73
The Little Engine that Could. New York: 1930. V. 70; 72
Mother Goose Rhymes. New York: 1940. V. 70

PIPES, WILLIAM H.
Say Amen, Brother! Old-Time Negro Preaching: A Study in American Frustration. New York: 1961. V. 72

PIRANDELLO, LUIGI
A Character in Distress. London: 1938. V. 69

PIRANESI, GIAMBATTISTA
Diverse Maniere d'Adornare i Cammini ed Orgni Altra Parte Degli Edifizi.... Rome: 1769. V. 72
Magnificenza di Roma. Milano: 1961. V. 72

PIROGOV, NIKOLAY IVANOVICH
(In Cyrillic) *Nachala Obshechey Voennolotevoy Khirurgii (The Principles of Military Field Surgery).* Dresden: 1865-1866. V. 71

PIRSIG, ROBERT M.
Zen and the Art of Motorcycle Maintenance. London: 1974. V. 69; 70; 71
Zen and the Art of Motorcycle Maintenance. New York: 1974. V. 68; 71; 72; 73

PIRTLE, CALEB
XIT: Being a New and Original Exploration, in Art and Words, Into the Life and Times of the American Cowboy. Birmingham: 1975. V. 69

PISO, WILLEM
Guilielmi Pisonis Medici Amstelaedamensis de Indiae de Indiae Utriusque re Naturalis et Medica Libri Quatuordeim. Amsterdam: 1658. V. 73

PISSARRO, LUCIEN
Notes on the Eragny Press, and a Letter to J. B. Manson. Cambridge: 1957. V. 70

THE PISTOLS
as a Weapon of Defence in the House and on the Road. New York: 1875. V. 71

PITCAIRNE, ARCHIBALD
Elementa Medicinae Physico-Mathematica Libris Duobus.... Venice: 1740. V. 72

PITMAN, BEN
Assassination of President Lincoln and the Trial of the Conspirators. Cincinnati & New York: 1865. V. 69

PITMAN, C. R. S.
A Game Warden Among His Charges. 1931. V. 69
A Guide to the Snakes of Uganda. London: 1974. V. 69

PITMAN, JOSEPH S.
Report of the Trial of Thomas Wilson Dorr, for Treason...together with The Sentence of the Court, and the Speech of Mr. Dorr Before Sentence. Providence: 1844. V. 69; 73

PITT, ROBERT
The Craft and Frauds of Physick Expos'd. London: 1703. V. 73

PITTER, RUTH
The Bridge: Poems 1939-1944. London: 1945. V. 69
First Poems. London: 1920. V. 71

PITTILOCH, ROBERT
Oppression Under the Colour of the Law, or, My Lord Hercarse His New Praticks As a Waymarke for Peaceable Subjects to be ware of Pleying with a hot Spirited Lord of the Session . . . Edinburgh: 1827. V. 71

PITT KETHLEY, FIONA
Gesta - Poems. London: 1986. V. 71
Private Parts. London: 1987. V. 71

PITTLE, CALEB
XIT - Being a New and Original Exploration, in Art and Words, into the Life and Times of the American Cowboy. Birmingham: 1975. V. 68

PITTMAN, PHILIP
The Present State of the European Settlements on the Mississippi. Cleveland: 1906. V. 71

PITT-RIVERS, A.
Antique Works of Art from Benin, Collected by Lieutenant General Pitt Rivers. London: 1900. V. 69
Excavations in Cranborne Chase, Near Rushmore on the Borders of Dorset and Wilts.... 1888-1905. V. 73

PITTS, CHARLES F.
Chaplains in Gray. Nashville: 1957. V. 69

PITTSBURGH PLATE GLASS CO.
Glass: History, Manufacturing and Its Universal Application. Pittsburgh: 1923. V. 68

PITZER, ROBERT C.
Three Frontiers, Memories and a Portrait of Henry L. Pitzer. Muscatine: 1935. V. 73

PIUS XI, POPE
Climbs on Alpine Peaks. 1923. V. 71; 73

PIZZEY, G.
A Field Guide to the Birds of Australia. Princeton: 1980. V. 73

PLACE Names and Places of Nova Scotia. Belleville: 1974. V. 73

PLACE, FRANCIS
Illustrations and Proofs of the Principle of Population: Including an Examination of the Proposed Remedies of Mr. Malthus.... London: 1822. V. 69

PLAGENS, P.
Sunshine Muse: Contemporary Art on the West Coast. New York: 1974. V. 72

THE PALIMPSEST of Gloria Patri. 1999. V. 69

PLAIN Directions for Reading the Holy Scriptures. London: 1771. V. 70

A PLAIN Guide to Baptism: Being a Short Treatise Upon the Subjects and Mode. Boston: 1832. V. 73

PLAIN Reasons Addressed to the People of Great Britain, Against the (Intended) Petition to Parliament from the Owners and Occupiers of Land in the County of Lincoln, for Leave to Export Wool. Leeds: 1782. V. 72

PLAISTED, ARTHUR H.
The Parsons and Parish Registers of Medmenham, Buckinghamshire. London: 1932. V. 71
The Plaisted Family of North Wilts. London: 1939. V. 71

THE PLAN and Section of the Boxes at the King's Theatre, Pantheon. With an Alphabetical List of the Subscribers. London: 1791. V. 70

PLANCHE, J. R.
The Conqueror and His Companions. London: 1874. V. 73
Descent of the Danube from Ratisbon to Vienna, During the Autumn of 1827. London: 1828. V. 69

PLANCHON, JULES EMILE
La Victoria Regia.... Ghent: 1850-1851. V. 69; 71; 73

PLANCK, MAX KARL ERNST LUDWIG
General Mechanics. London: 1933. V. 72
Treatise on Thermodynamics. New York and Bombay: 1903. V. 72

PLANS of the Lakes in Cumberland, Westmorland and Lancashire; together with Representations of the Different Seats Adjoining the Same.... Keswick: 1822. V. 73

PLANTE, DAVID
The Foreigner. New York: 1984. V. 70

THE PLATE-GLASS Book, Consisting of...Tables.... London: 1764. V. 69

THE PLATE-Glass Book: Consisting of the Following Authentic Tables. I. The Value of Any Lookingglass.... 1771. V. 71

PLATH, IONA
The Decorative Arts of Sweden. London: 1948. V. 72

PLATH, JAMES
Conversations with John Updike. Jackson: 1994. V. 72

PLATH, SYLVIA
Ariel. London: 1965. V. 69; 70
Ariel. New York: 1966. V. 68; 69; 71; 73
The Bed Book. London: 1976. V. 73
The Bed Book. New York: 1976. V. 73
The Bell Jar. London: 1962. V. 69; 70
The Bell Jar. London: 1964. V. 68
Collected Poems. London: 1981. V. 69
The Colossus. London: 1960. V. 70; 72
The Colossus. New York: 1962. V. 71; 73
Crossing the Water. New York: 1971. V. 71
Crystal Gazer. London: 1971. V. 73
A Day in June. Ely: 1981. V. 73
The Green Rock. Ely: 1982. V. 72
Letters Home - Correspondence 1950-1963. London: 1975. V. 72
Lyonnesse. London: 1971. V. 68
The Magic Mirror: a Study of the Double in Two of Dostoevsky's Novels. Llanwydden: 1989. V. 71
Three Women. London: 1968. V. 68
Three Women. 1970-1975. V. 71
Winter Trees. London: 1971. V. 70; 71

PLATINA, BARTOLOMEO
Opus, de Vita ac Gelis Summorum Pontificum ad Sixtum IV. Pont. Max. Deductum. 1664. V. 68; 72

PLATINA, GIOVANNI BATTISTA
De Vitis Pontificum Romanorum ad N. Iesu Christo Usque ad Paulum II. Venetum Papam. Longe Quam Antea Emendatior, Doctissimarumque Annotationum Onuphri Panuinii.... Lovanii (Louvain): 1572. V. 73

PLATO
Crito a Socratic Dialogue. Paris: 1926. V. 71
The Dialogues. Oxford: 1871. V. 72
The Dialogues of Plato. Oxford: 1925. V. 73
Lysis. London: 1930. V. 70
The Phaedo. Waltham St. Lawrence: 1930. V. 72
The Phaedo. Translated into English by Benjamin Jowett. London: 1930. V. 71
Phaedon; or, a Dialogue on the Immortality of the Soul. New York: 1833. V. 68
Plato His Apology of Socrates, and Phaedo or Dialogue Concerning the Immortality of Mans Soul, and Manner of Socrates His Death. London: 1675. V. 71
Platonis Dialogi V. Oxonii: 1752. V. 69
Plato's Works. 1904. V. 71
La Republica...Tradotta Dalla Lingua Greca Nella Thoscana.... Venice: 1554. V. 72
The Trial and Death of Societies. Verona: 1962. V. 70; 72

PLATT, CYNTHIA
Isadora Duncan & Gordon Craig. The Prose & Poetry of Action. London: 1988. V. 72

PLATT, EDWARD
The Masters of the Skies. London. V. 69

PLATT, JAMES
Platt's Essays. London: 1883-1884. V. 71

PLATT, KIN
The Kissing Gourami. New York: 1970. V. 71

PLATTER, FELIX
Observationum, in Hominis Affectibus Plerisqu, Corpori et Animo, Functionum Laesione, Dolore, Aliave Molestia & Vitio Incommodantibus, Libri Tres. Basel: 1614. V. 68; 70; 73

PLAUT, J. S.
Steuben Glass: a Monograph. New York: 1948. V. 69; 72

PLAUTUS, TITUS MACCIUS
Comedie de Plaute.... Paris: 1683. V. 72
Comoediae. Amsterdam: 1684. V. 72
(Opera). Paris: 1577. V. 73

PLAY TIME Circus - Three Dimensional Cut-Out Book. Springfield: 1932. V. 72

PLAYFAIR, A.
The Garos. London: 1909. V. 71

PLAYFAIR, JOHN
Illustrations of the Huttonian Theory of the Earth. Edinburgh: 1802. V. 70

PLAYFAIR, R. L.
The Fishes of Zanzibar. Kentfield: 1971. V. 69; 72; 73

PLAYFORD, JOHN
Vade Mecum, or the Necessary Companion. London: 1679. V. 73

A PLEA for Moderation. 1642. V. 68; 70

PLEASANTS, W. SHEPARD
The Stingaree Murders. New York: 1932. V. 69

A PLEASING Toy. Newport: 1837. V. 69

PLEASING Toy for Girl or Boy. Wendell: 1830. V. 73

PLEASONTON, AUGUSTUS JAMES
The Influence of the Blue Ray of the Sunlight and of the Blue Colour of the Sky, in Developing Animal and Vegetable Life.... Philadelphia: 1877. V. 68; 69

PLEASURE ABC and Reading Book.... London: 1938. V. 72

PLENN, J. H.
Mexico Marches. Indianapolis: 1939. V. 69
Saddle in the Sky: the Lone Star State. Indianapolis: 1940. V. 69

PLESCH, ARPAD
The Magnificent Botanical Library of the Stiftung fur Botanik. 1975-1976. V. 71
The Magnificent Botanical Library of the Stiftung fur Botanik. London: 1976. V. 68

PLESCH, JOHN
Physiology and Pathology of the Heart and Blood Vessels. London: 1937. V. 68

PLESKE, T.
Wissenschaftliche resultate der von N. M. Przewalski Nach Central- Asien Unternommen Reisen. St. Petersburg: 1889-1905. V. 73

PLETKA, PAUL
Pletka. Flagstaff: 1983. V. 68; 71; 73

PLETSCH, OSCAR
Schnick Schnack: Trifles for the Little Ones. London: 1867. V. 71

PLIMPTON, GEORGE
Out of My League. London: 1962. V. 69
The Rabbit's Umbrella. New York: 1955. V. 69

PLIMSOLL, SAMUEL
Cattle Ships. London: 1890. V. 69
Our Seamen. London: 1873. V. 68; 69

PLINIUS SECUNDUS, C.
Epistolae et Panegyricus. Parisiis: 1788. V. 71
Epistolae et Panegyricus Notis Illustrata. Oxonii: 1677. V. 72
Epistolarum Libri Decem (and Other Works). Basilea: 1521. V. 71
Epistolarum Libri X. 1790. V. 72
Epistolarum Libri X. London: 1790. V. 68
Histoire de la Peinture Ancienne, Extraite de l'Histoire Naturelle De Pline, Liv. XXXV. London: 1725. V. 68
Historie Naturelle de Pline.... Paris: 1829-1833. V. 68; 71
The Historie of the World, Commonly called the Naturall Historie.... London: 1634. V. 70; 73
The Natural History of Pliny. London: 1893-1898. V. 68
Naturalis Historiae. Venetiis: 1525. V. 71
Naturalis Historie Libri XXXVI. Paris: 1516. V. 68
Pliny's Panegyricke: a Speech in Senate Wherein Publike Thankes are Presented to the Emperoour Traian. Oxford: 1644. V. 71

PLOMER, HENRY RAUP
Wynkyn de Worde and His Contemporaries from the Death of Caxton to 1535. London: 1925. V. 69

PLOMER, WILLIAM
Address Given at the Memorial Service for Ian Fleming. 1964. V. 72
At Home - Memoirs. London: 1958. V. 68
The Case is Altered. London: 1932. V. 70
The Case is Altered. New York: 1932. V. 70
The Case is Altered. London: 1946. V. 68
Collected Poems. London: 1960. V. 72
Conversation with My Younger Self. 1963. V. 72
Conversation with My Younger Self. Ewelme: 1963. V. 68
A Dialogue. 1977. V. 72
The Family Tree. London: 1929. V. 69; 72
Notes for Poems. London: 1927. V. 72
Turbott Wolfe. London: 1925. V. 69

PLOT, ROBERT
The Natural History of Oxfordshire.... Oxford: 1705. V. 70
Natural History of Staffordshire.... Oxford: 1686. V. 68; 70

PLOWDEN, DAVID
Bridges. The Spans of North America. New York: 1974. V. 72
Floor of the Sky: the Great Plains. San Francisco: 1972. V. 69

PLOWDEN, EDMUND
Les Commentaries ou Reports...de Divers Cases Esteant Matters en Icy...(with) Un Report Fait per un Uncerteine Author del part de un Argument del Edmond Plowden.... London: 1588-1584. V. 70

PLOWDEN, FRANCIS
An Historical Letter to Rev. Charles O'Connor.. 1812. V. 70

PLUCHE, NOEL ANTOINE
Spectacle de la Nature; or Nature Display'd. London: 1736. V. 73

THE PLUMBER Painter and Glazier. London: 1882. V. 68

PLUMIER, CHARLES
L'Art de Tourner.... Paris: 1749. V. 73
L'Art De Tourner.... Leipzig: 1776. V. 72

PLUMMER, CAROLUS
Vitae Sanctorum Hiberniae. 1910. V. 70

PLUMMER, JOHN
The Glazier Collection of Illuminated Manuscripts. New York: 1968. V. 70

PLUMMER, T. ARTHUR
Frampton of The Yard. New York: 1935. V. 70

PLUMPTRE, JAMES
A Collection of Songs, Moral, Sentimental, Instructive and Amusing. Cambridge: 1805. V. 68
A Collection of Songs, Moral Sentimental, Instructive and Amusing. London: 1806. V. 72
Four Discourses on Subjects Relating to the Amusement of the Stage: Preached at Great St. Mary's Church, Cambridge, on Sunday September 25 and Sunday October 2, 1808.... Cambridge: 1809. V. 73

PLUNKET, DAVID
Life, Letters and Speeches of Lord Plunket. 1867. V. 73
The State of Ireland. London: 1880. V. 69

PLUNKET, FREDERICA
Here and There Among the Alps. London: 1875. V. 69

PLUNKETT, FRANCIS
As the Fool. 1935. V. 69

PLUNKETT, HARRIET M.
Women, Plumbers and Doctors; or Household Sanitation. New York: 1885. V. 69; 72

PLUNKETT GREENE, H.
Where the Bright Waters Meet. 1924. V. 68
Where the Bright Waters Meet. 1936. V. 73

PLURALITY of Worlds: Letters, Notes and Memoranda, Philosophical and Critical....* London: 1817. V. 69

PLUTA, M.
Advanced Light Microscopy. Amsterdam: 1988-. V. 70

PLUTARCHUS
The Lives of the Noble Grecians and Romanes. Oxford: 1928. V. 73
The Lives of the Noble Grecians and Romanes. London: 1929. V. 68; 69
Morallia. (Greek). Venice: 1509. V. 73
Les Oeuvres Morales de Plutarque.... Paris: 1606. V. 68
The Philosophie, Commonlie Called, the Morals Written by the Learned Philosopher Plutarch. London: 1603. V. 73
Plutarch's Lives. Liverpool: 1910. V. 69

POBJOY, H. N.
A History of Mirfield. Driffeld, Yorks: 1969. V. 73

A POCKET Hymn Book, Designed as a Constant Companion for the Pious. York: 1786. V. 73

THE POCKET Navigator, Consisting of a Collection of the Most Select Voyages. London: 1808. V. 72

POCOCK, ROGER
Following the Frontier. New York: 1903. V. 68

POCOCK, W. F.
Architectural Designs for Rustic Cottages, Picturesque Dwellings, Villas &c.... London: 1823. V. 70; 72

PODESCHI, JOHN B.
Books on the Horse and Horsemanship. 1981. V. 70
Books on the Horse and Horsemanship. Riding, Hunting, Breeding and Racing 1400-1941. A Catalogue. London: 1981. V. 73
Dickens and Dickensiana: A Catalogue of the Richard Gimbel Collection in the Yale University Library. New Haven: 1980. V. 68

PODMORE, FRANK
Mesmerism and Christian Science. A Short History of Mental Healing. Philadelphia: 1909. V. 71
Robert Owen: a Biography. London: 1923. V. 71

POE, EDGAR ALLAN
The Black Cat. Easthampton: 1984. V. 72
A Chapter on Autobiography. New York: 1926. V. 73
The Complete Works of Edgar Allan Poe. New York: 1908. V. 68; 69
The Conchologist's First Book; or A System of Testaceous Malacology.... Philadelphia: 1839. V. 68; 71; 72
The Conqueror Worm and other pieces in Graham's Magazine Volumes 22-23. Philadelphia: 1843. V. 73
Erstaunliche Geschichte und Unheimliche Begebenheiten. (Tales). Stuttgart: 1859. V. 71; 72
Eureka: a Prose Poem. New York. V. 71; 72
The Fall of the House of Usher. New York: 1931. V. 70
The Fall of the House of Usher. New York: 1985. V. 70; 72
The Fall of the House of Usher. New York: 1990. V. 69
Histoires Extraordinaires. (Tales translated by Baudelaire). Paris: 1934. V. 71; 72
The Journal of Julius Rodman. San Francisco: 1947. V. 70; 72
The Last Letters of Edgar Allan Poe to Sarah Whitman. New York: 1906. V. 73
The Masque of the Red Death and Other Tales. 1932. V. 70
Mesmerism In Articulo Mortis an Astounding and Horrifying Narrative, Shewing the Extraordinary Power of Mesmerism in Arresting the Progress of Death. London: 1846. V. 68; 69
The Murders in the Rue Morgue. Philadelphia: 1895. V. 71
The Murders in the Rue Morgue. New York: 1932. V. 69
The Murders in the Rue Morgue. Antibes: 1958. V. 72
The Narrative of Arthur Gordon Pym, of Nantucket. New York: 1838. V. 69; 72
The Poems. London: 1881. V. 72
Poems. East Aurora: 1901. V. 69
The Poetical Works. London. V. 71
The Poetical Works. New York: 1919. V. 69

POE, EDGAR ALLAN continued
The Raven. New York: 1845. V. 68; 71; 72; 73
The Raven. Philadelphia: 1870. V. 68
The Raven. London: 1899. V. 69
The Raven. London: 1901. V. 70
The Raven. Easthampton: 1986. V. 72
Tales. New York: 1845. V. 71; 72
The Tales and Poems.... London: 1884. V. 71; 72
Tales of Mystery and Imagination. London and New York. V. 73
Tales of Mystery and Imagination. London: 1919. V. 71
Tales of Mystery and Imagination. New York: 1923. V. 71
Tales of Mystery and Imagination. New York: 1928. V. 71
Tales of Mystery and Imagination. New York: 1930. V. 68
Tales of Mystery and Imagination. London: 1935. V. 72
Tales of Mystery and Imagination. New York: 1935. V. 69
Tales of Mystery and Imagination. New York: 1936. V. 71
Tamerlane and Other Poems. San Francisco: 1923. V. 70; 72
Tamerlane and Other Poems. London: 1931. V. 70
The Works of Edgar Allan Poe. Edinburgh: 1874-1875. V. 73
The Works of Edgar Allan Poe in Five Volumes. New York: 1903. V. 68
The Works of the Late Edgar A. Poe with Notices of His Life and Genius.... New York: 1850. V. 71; 72

POE, JOHN W.
The Death of Billy the Kid,. Boston: 1933. V. 71; 73

POE, SOPHIE A.
Buckboard Days. Caldwell: 1936. V. 70

POEL, JEAN VAN DER
Selections from the Smuts Papers. Cambridge: 1966. V. 71

POEMS.. New York: 1892. V. 70

POEMS and Translations. London: 1889. V. 68

POEMS Chiefly Lyrical, From Romances and Prose-Tracts of the Elizabethan Age: With Chosen Poems of Nicholas Breton. London: 1890. V. 71

POEMS for Alan Hancox. Andoversford: 1993. V. 68; 71

POEMS of Death. London: 1945. V. 72

POEMS of the Forces - the Fortune Forces Anthology. London: 1949. V. 71

POEMS of the Old South. Boston: 1877. V. 71

LA POESIE Symboliste - Trois Entretiens sur Les Temps Heroiques.... Paris: 1909. V. 71

POET Venturers: a Collection of Poems Written by Bristol School Boys and Girls. Bristol: 1938. V. 71

THE POETIC Gift; or Alphabet in Rhyme. New Haven: 1844. V. 69

POETICAL Alphabet. Lowell: 1848. V. 71

A POETICAL Description of Beasts, with Moral Reflections for the Amusement of Children. 1773. V. 73

A POETICAL Epistle from a Louse to Peter Pindar, Esq; or the Louse Banished From Court. Bath: 1787. V. 69

POETICAL Excursions in the Isle of Wight. London: 1777. V. 69

THE POETICAL Farrago; Being Miscellaneous Assemblage of Epigrams and Other Jeux d'esprit Selected from the Most Approved Writers. London: 1794. V. 68

THE POETICAL Miscellany: Consisting of Selected Pieces from the Works.... London: 1769. V. 68

POETRY.. Chicago: 1943. V. 69

POETRY of Mid-Century 1940/1960. Toronto: 1964. V. 69

THE POETRY of Song: Five Tributes to Stephen Sondheim. New York: 1992. V. 69

POETRY of the Anti-Jacobin.... London: 1801. V. 69; 72; 73

POETRY Of the Anti-Jacobin.... 1852. V. 73

POETS' CLUB
The Book of the Poets' Club. London: 1909. V. 68

POETS of Tomorrow - Third Selection. London: 1942. V. 69

POGANY, ELAINE
The Golden Cockerel. New York: 1938. V. 71

POGGI, MAURO
Alfabeto Di Lettere Iniziali...Incise Dall'Abate Lorenzo Lorenzi. Florence: 1730. V. 69

POGNON, EDMOND
Les Tres Riches Heures du Duc De Berry. New York: 1979. V. 70

POHANKA, BRIAN C.
Nelson A. Miles. A Documentary Biography of His Military Career 1861- 1903. 1985. V. 68

POHL, FREDERIK
Drunkard's Walk. 1960. V. 70
Jem. 1995. V. 71
Man Plus. 1976. V. 73

Man Plus. New York: 1976. V. 71
Prince Henry Sinclair. His Expeditions to the New World in 1398. New York: 1974. V. 73

POINT, NICOLAS
Wilderness Kingdom. Chicago: 1967. V. 68
Wilderness Kingdom. New York: 1967. V. 70

POINTER, LARRY
Harry Jackson. New York: 1981. V. 71

POINTS of Humour. London: 1823-1824. V. 68; 72

POIRET, J.
Histoire Philosophique, Litteraire, Economique des Plantes de l'Europe. 1825-1829. V. 69

POIRET, L'ABBE
Voyage en Barbarie ou Lettres Ecrites de l'Ancienne Numidie Pendent les Annees 1785 and 1786. Paris: 1789. V. 73

POLACK, JOEL SAMUEL
Manners and Customs of the New Zealanders. London: 1840. V. 71
New Zealand. London: 1839. V. 71

POLANSKI, ROMAN
Roman. New York: 1984. V. 73

POLEHAMPTON, ARTHUR
Kangaroo Land. London: 1862. V. 69; 71

POLENI, GIOVANNI
Exercitationes Vitruvianae Primae.... Padova: 1739-1741. V. 68; 70; 72

POLETIKA, PETER IVANOVICH
A Sketch of the Internal Condition of the United States of America and of Their Political Relations with Europe. Baltimore: 1826. V. 72

POLEY, ARTHUR F. E.
St. Paul's Cathedral, London, Measured, Drawn and Described. London: 1927. V. 72

POLICHINELLE Prenant Ses Vacances. Paris: 1845?. V. 72

POLING, JAMES
Esquire's World of Jazz. New York: 1962. V. 71

THE POLITE Academy; or School of Behaviour for Young Gentlemen and Ladies. London: 1823. V. 72

THE POLITE Lady; or a Course of Female Education in a Series of Letters, from a Mother to Her Daughter. Philadelphia: 1798. V. 73

POLITI, LEO
Little Pancho. New York: 1938. V. 68; 71
The Mission Bell. New York: 1953. V. 71
Mr. Fong's Toy Shop. New York: 1978. V. 69

THE POLITICAL Crisis or A Dissertation on the Rights of Man. London: 1791. V. 72

POLITICAL Dialogues Between the Celebrated Statues of Pasquin and Marforio at Rome...(with) Second Political Dialogues Between the Celebrated Statues of Pasquin and Marforio at Rome. London: 1736-1737. V. 73

THE POLITICAL Pilgrim's Progress. Newcastle-Upon-Tyne: 1839. V. 71

POLK, NOEL
An Anthology of Mississippi Writers. 1979. V. 70

POLK, STELLA GIPSON
Mason and Mason County: a History. Austin: 1966. V. 69

POLK, WILLIS
A Matter of Taste. San Francisco: 1979. V. 73

POLK'S Newton (New Jersey) Directory...1929-1930. New Brunswick: 1929. V. 72

POLLACK, PETER
Picture History of Photography, From the Earliest Beginnings to the Present Day. New York: 1969. V. 68

POLLARD, ALFRED WILLIAM
Bibliographica, Papers on Books, Their History and Art. London: 1895-1897. V. 70
Cobden-Sanderson and the Doves Press: the History of the Press and the Story of Its Types Told by Alfred W. Pollard.... San Francisco: 1929. V. 72

POLLARD, EDWARD ALFRED
The First Year of the War. Richmond: 1862. V. 69; 70
The First Year of the War In America. London: 1863. V. 73
Observations in the North: Eight Months in Prison and On Parole. Richmond: 1865. V. 69; 70
The Second Year of the War. Richmond: 1863. V. 73
Southern History of the War. New York: 1863-1866. V. 73

POLLARD, H. B. C.
Automatic Pistols. 1920. V. 70; 71
British and American Game Birds. New York: 1929. V. 69
British and American Gamebirds. 1945. V. 71
Game Birds. 1929. V. 70; 71
Game Birds and Game Bird Shooting. 1936. V. 70; 71
The Gun Room Guide. 1930. V. 71
The Mystery of Scent. 1937. V. 68
Shot-Guns. 1923. V. 71

POLLARD, H. B. C. continued
Wildfowl and Waders. Nature and Sport in the Coastlands. 1940. V. 71

POLLARD, JOHN G.
Virginia Born Presidents: Addresses Delivered on the Occasions of Unveiling the Busts of Virginia Born Presidents at Old Hall of the House of Delegates.... New York: 1932. V. 72

POLLARD, JOSEPH
The Land Of The Monuments. London: 1898. V. 72

POLLARD, JOSEPHINE
The Decorative Sisters. New York: 1881. V. 70; 71

POLLEN, a Novel in Black and White. London: 1933. V. 72

POLLEY, JOSEPH BENJAMIN
A Soldier's Letters to Charming Nellie. New York: 1908. V. 69; 70

POLLOCK, CHANNING
The Enemy. New York: 1925. V. 70
The House Beautiful. New York: 1931. V. 70; 71

POLLOCK, FITZWILLIAM THOMAS
Wild Sports of Burma and Assam. 1900. V. 70; 73
Wild Sports of Burma and Assam. London: 1900. V. 71

POLLOCK, FREDERICK
A Digest of the Law of Partnership. St. Louis: 1878. V. 72
Essays in Jurisprudence and Ethics. London;: 1882. V. 73
Principles of Contract at Law and In Equity. Cincinnati: 1881. V. 68

POLLOCK, W. H.
Jane Austen, Her Contemporaries and Herself, an Essay in Criticism. London: 1899. V. 73

POLLOK, ROBERT A. M.
The Course of Time. A Poem. Concord: 1836. V. 72

POLO, MARCO
The Book of Ser Marco Polo the Venetian Concerning the Kingdoms and Marvels of the East. New York: 1903. V. 68
The Description of the World. London: 1938. V. 72

POLOVTSOFF, A.
The Land of Timur. London: 1932. V. 71

POLSON, ALEXANDER
Scottish Witchcraft Lore. Inverness: 1932. V. 70; 71

POLSON, ARCHER
Law and Lawyers: or, Sketches and Illustrations of Legal History and Biography. London: 1840. V. 73

POLSON NEWMAN, E. W.
The Middle East. London: 1926. V. 71

THE POLITICAL Drama Nos. 1-38. London: 1834. V. 70

POLUNIN, O.
Flowers of Europe, a Field Guide. London: 1969. V. 68; 73

POLWHELE, RICHARD
Poems Chiefly by Gentlemen of Devonshire and Cornwall. Bath: 1792. V. 68; 69
Traditions and Recollections, Domestic, Clerical and Literary. London: 1826. V. 70

POLYBIUS
The Histories. London: 1889. V. 72
The History of Polybius the Megalopolitan. London: 1634. V. 71

POMEROY, JOHN N.
A Treatise on the Law of Riparian Rights. St. Paul: 1887. V. 72

POMEROY, SETH
The Journals and Papers of Seth Pomeroy. New York: 1926. V. 72

POMET, PIERRE
A Compleat History of Druggs.... London: 1725. V. 72
A Compleat History of Druggs.... London: 1737. V. 73

POMEY, FRANCOIS ANTOINE
Indiculus Universalis; or, the Universe in Epitome. 1769. V. 71

POMFRET, JOHN
Miscellany Poems on Several Occasions. London: 1707. V. 69
Poems Upon Several Occasions. London: 1736. V. 73

POMPADOUR, JEANNE ANTOINETTE POISSON, MARQUISE DE
Catalogue des Livres de la Bibliotheque de feue Madame la Marquise de Pompadour, Dame du Palais de la Reine. Paris: 1765. V. 70

POND, FRED E.
The Life and Adventures of "Ned Buntline" With Ned Buntline's Anecdote of Frank Forster.... New York: 1919. V. 70

PONGE, FRANCIS
The Voice of Things. New York: 1972. V. 68

PONICSAN, DARRYL
The Last Detail. New York: 1970. V. 71

PONS, MAURICE
Mademoiselle B. New York: 1974. V. 69; 71; 73

PONSONBY, ARTHUR
Scottish and Irish Diaries from the 16th to the 19th Century. 1927. V. 70

PONSOT, MARIE
The Green Dark. New York: 1990. V. 69

PONTA, GIOACHINO
Il Trionfo Della Vaccinia, Poema. Parma: 1810. V. 68

PONTEY, WILLIAM
The Forest Pruner; or Timber Owner's Assistant.... Huddersfield: 1805. V. 71
The Forest Pruner; or Timber Owner's Assistant.... London: 1808. V. 70
The Profitable Planter. Huddersfield: 1808. V. 69
The Profitable Planter. London: 1814. V. 70; 71

PONTING, TOM C.
Life of Tom Candy Ponting- An Autobiography. Evanston: 1952. V. 71

PONTOPPIDAN, ERICH
The Natural History of Norway. London: 1755. V. 68; 70; 73
The Natural History of Norway. 1765. V. 73

THE POOH Corner Cook Book. London: 1980. V. 72

POOL, J. L.
Acoustic Nerve Tumors. Early Diagnosis and Treatment. Springfield: 1970. V. 71
The Early Diagnosis and Treatment of Acoustic Nerve Tumors. Springfield: 1957. V. 71
The Neurological Institute of New York 1909-1974. 1975. V. 73
The Neurosurgical Treatment of Traumatic Paraplegia. Springfield: 1951. V. 73

POOLE, A. F.
Ospreys, a Natural and Unnatural History. Cambridge: 1989. V. 72

POOLE, B. W.
The Science of Pattern Construction for Garment Makers. 1930. V. 68

POOLE, BRAITHWAITE
Statistics of British Commerce. London: 1852. V. 71

POOLE, E.
Silent Storms. London: 1927. V. 73

POOLE, EDMUND DUVAL
Annals of Yarmouth and Barrington (Nova Scotia) in the Revolutionary War. Yarmouth: 1899. V. 73

POOLE, ERNEST
Danger. New York: 1923. V. 69
His Family. New York: 1917. V. 71

POOLE, GEORGE AYLIFFE
A History of Ecclesiastical Architecture in England. London: 1848. V. 73

POOLE, MATTHEW
Synopsis Criticorum Aliorumque S. Scriptuare Interpretum. London: 1669-1676. V. 72

POOLE, MONICA
Wood Engravings of John Farleigh. London: 1985. V. 72

POOLE, RICHARD
Memoranda Regarding the Royal Lunatic Asylum, Infirmary and Dispensary of Montrose, with Observations on some Other Institutions of a Like Nature.... Montrose: 1841. V. 73

POOLE, SOPHIA
The Englishwoman in Egypt: Letters from Cairo.... London: 1844. V. 72

POOLE, STANLEY LANE
Cairo. Sketches of Its History, Monuments and Social Life. London: 1893. V. 68; 72

POOR, HENRY V.
Money and Its Laws: Embracing a History of Monetary Theories and a History of the Currencies of the United States. New York: 1877. V. 73

POOR, J. M.
Plants that Merit Attention. Volume II. Shrubs. Portland: 1996. V. 68

POOR, M. C.
Denver, South Park and Pacific. Denver: 1949. V. 69

POORE, BEN PERLEY
The Federal and State Constitutions, Colonial, Charters and Other Organic Laws of the United States. Washington: 1878. V. 71

POOR'S Directory of Railway Officials and Railway Directors. New York: 1886. V. 70

POORTVLIET, RIEN
Dutch Treat. The Artist's Life, Written and Painted by Himself. New York: 1981. V. 69

POPE, ALEXANDER
The Dunciad. London: 1729. V. 69; 72; 73
An Epistle from Mr. Pope to Dr. Arbuthnot. London: 1734. V. 70
Essai sur l'Homme.... A Lausanne & a Geneve: 1745. V. 69
Letters of Mr. Alexander Pope, and Several of His Friends. London: 1737. V. 70
Letters of Mr. Pope and Several Eminent Persons, from the Year 1705 to 1711 (from the Year 1711 &c). London: 1735. V. 69
Miscellaneous Poems and Translations. London: 1712. V. 68; 73
Of the Characters of Women: an Epistle to a Lady. 1735. V. 72
Pope's Pastorals and a Discourse on Pastoral.... Naples: 1767. V. 68
The Poetical Works. Glasgow: 1785. V. 68; 73
The Poetical Works. London: 1852. V. 72

POPE, ALEXANDER continued
Pope's Own Miscellany. London: 1935. V. 70
Pope's Pastorals and a Discoure on Pastoral.... Naples: 1767. V. 73
Pope's Poetical Works. London: 1849. V. 68
The Rape of the Lock. London: 1798. V. 69
The Rape of the Lock. London: 1896. V. 70
The Works. London: 1718. V. 72
The Works. London i.e. The Hague: 1720. V. 69
The Works. London: 1740-1741. V. 69
The Works. London: 1770. V. 70; 73
The Works. London: 1824. V. 73
The Works. London: 1847. V. 72

POPE, C. H.
China's Animal Frontier. New York: 1940. V. 73
The Reptiles of China.... New York: 1935. V. 69

POPE, CLARENCE
Oil Scout in the Permian Basin 1924-1960. El Paso: 1972. V. 69

POPE, DUDLEY
Ramage's Trial. London: 1984. V. 69

POPE, FRANKLIN LEONARD
Evolution of the Electric Incandescent Lamp. Elizabeth: 1889. V. 69

POPE, JESSIE
Three Jolly Anglers. London: 1914. V. 71

POPE, MARY
Novel Dishes for Vegetarian Households. Bradford & London: 1893. V. 68

POPE, WALTER
The Wish. London: 1710. V. 73

POPPING, J. F.
Orbis Illustratus Seu Nova Historico-Politico-Geographica. Razeburg: 1668. V. 72

PORCHE, FRANCOIS
Charles Baudelaire. London: 1928. V. 68

PORCHER, FRANCIS PEYRE
Resources of the Southern Fields and Forests.... Charleston: 1863. V. 69; 70
Resources of the Southern Fields and Forests.... Charleston: 1869. V. 68; 72; 73

PORCHER, FREDERICK ADOLPHUS
A Memoir of Gen. Christopher Gadsden, Read Before the South Carolina Historical Society. Charleston: 1878. V. 68

PORCHER, JEAN
The Rohan Book of Hours. New York: 1959. V. 70

PORSILD, A. E.
Botany of Southeastern Yukon, Adjacent to the Canal Road. Ottawa: 1951. V. 72
The Vascular Plants of the Western Canadian Arctic Archipelago. Ottawa: 1955. V. 72

PORTA, GIOVANNI BATTISTA DELLA
Della Fisonomia dell'Huomo...Libri Sei. Padoua: 1613. V. 68; 70; 73
Structure and Control of the Melanocyte. Berlin: 1966. V. 68

PORTAL, ABRAHAM
Nuptial Elegies. London: 1774. V. 73

PORTAL, ANTOINE
Historie de l'Anatomie et de la Chirurgie.... Paris: 1770-1773. V. 68; 70; 73

PORTAL, GERALD
The British Mission to Uganda. London: 1894. V. 71; 72

PORTEOUS, CRICHTON
Pioneers of Fertility. London. V. 71; 72

PORTER, ANNA
Hidden Agenda. Toronto: 1985. V. 72

PORTER, ANNA MARIA
Don Sebastian; or the House of Braganza. London: 1809. V. 68; 72
The Hungarian Brothers. London: 1807. V. 68
The Recluse of Norway. London: 1814. V. 73
Roche-Blance; or the Hunters of the Pyrenees. A Romance. London: 1822. V. 68; 72

PORTER, BURTON B.
One of the People, His Own Story. 1907. V. 68; 73

PORTER, CLYDE
Matt Field on the Santa Fe Trail. Norman: 1960. V. 70

PORTER, COLE
Cole Porter Song Book. New York: 1959. V. 70

PORTER, DAVID D.
Naval History of the Civil War. New York: 1886. V. 70

PORTER, DOROTHY
Early Negro Writing 1760-1837. Boston: 1971. V. 72

PORTER, EDWIN H.
The Fall River Tragedy. Fall River: 1893. V. 69; 72
The Fall River Tragedy. Portland: 1985. V. 70

PORTER, ELIOT
American Places. New York: 1981. V. 70; 72
American Places. New York: 1983. V. 68
Birds of North America. New York: 1972. V. 70; 73
Eliot Porter's Southwest. New York: 1985. V. 72
Forever Wild: the Adirondacks. New York: 1966. V. 71
Intimate Landscapes. New York: 1979. V. 68
The Place No One Knew: Glen Canyon on the Colorado. San Francisco: 1966. V. 69; 72

PORTER, EUGENE O.
San Elizario: a History. Austin: 1973. V. 69

PORTER, GENE STRATTON
Her Father's Daughter. Garden City: 1921. V. 71
Michael O'Halloran. Garden City: 1915. V. 70
Music of the Wild. Garden City: 1910. V. 73

PORTER, GEORGE RICHARDSON
The Progress of the Nation, in Its Various Social and Economical Relations.... London: 1851. V. 71

PORTER, HENRY M.
Pencillings of an Early Western Pioneer. Denver: 1929. V. 69; 71

PORTER, J. L.
The Giant Cities Of Bashan: And Syria's Holy Places. London: 1865. V. 72

PORTER, JANE
The Pastor's Fire-Side. London: 1817. V. 70
The Pastor's Fire-Side. London: 1849. V. 70
Thaddeus of Warsaw. London: 1819. V. 73

PORTER, JOHN W.
A Record of Events in Norfolk County, Virginia, From April 19th, 1861 to May 10th, 1862. Portsmouth: 1892. V. 72

PORTER, JOSEPH G.
Paper Medicine Man, John Gregory Bourke and His American West. Norman: 1986. V. 72

PORTER, KATHERINE ANNE
A Christmas Story. 1958. V. 68
The Collected Essays. New York: 1970. V. 68; 69; 72
The Collected Stories of.... New York: 1965. V. 69; 73
A Defense of Circe. New York: 1955. V. 68
Flowering Judas. New York: 1936. V. 69; 73
Hacienda. New York: 1934. V. 72
Katherine Anne Porter's French Song-Book. Paris: 1933. V. 69; 73
The Leaning Tower and Other Stories. New York: 1944. V. 68; 70; 71
Noon Wine. Detroit: 1937. V. 68
Pale Horse, Pale Rider. New York: 1939. V. 70
Ship of Fools. Boston: 1962. V. 68; 70; 71; 73

PORTER, LUTHER H.
Wheels and Wheeling. An Indespensable Handbook for Cyclists. Boston: 1892. V. 68; 71

PORTER, MILLIE JONES
Put Up or Shutup. Dallas: 1950. V. 71

PORTER, R.
The Pleasures of Home, with Other Poems. London: 1821. V. 69

PORTER, ROBERT KER
The Travelling Sketches in Russia and Sweden, During the Year 1805, 1806, 1807 and 1808. London: 1809. V. 73

PORTER, RUFUS
A Select Collection of Valuable and Curious Arts and Interesting Experiments. Concord: 1826. V. 68

PORTER, WILLIAM SYDNEY
Cabbages and Kings. New York: 1904. V. 70; 71; 72
Heart of the West. New York: 1907. V. 71
Strictly Business: More Stories of the Four Million. New York: 1910. V. 71
The Voice of the City. New York: 1908. V. 68
Waifs and Strays. Garden City: 1917. V. 70; 71
Whirligigs. New York: 1910. V. 68

PORTER, WILLIAM WARREN
Engravings from Drawings of.... London: 1806. V. 69

PORTEUS, STANLEY D.
The Psychology of a Primitive People. London: 1931. V. 71

PORTIS, CHARLES
True Grit. New York: 1968. V. 70; 71; 73

PORTLAND, DUKE OF
Fifty Years and More of Sport in Scotland. 1923. V. 70
Fifty Years and More of Sport in Scotland. 1933. V. 70; 72
The Red Deer of Langwell and Braemore. 1935. V. 70

PORTLOCK, J. E.
Report on the Geology of the Country of Londonderry, and Parts of Tyrone and Fermanagh. Dublin: 1843. V. 69; 73
A Rudimentary Treatise on Geology; for the Use of Beginners. London: 1859. V. 71

PORTRAIT and Biographical Album of Lenawee County, Michigan. Chicago: 1888. V. 73

PORTRAIT and Biographical Record of Denver, and Vicinity, Colorado. Chicago: 1898. V. 69

PORTRAITS from North American Indian Life. New York: 1972. V. 68

PORTSMOUTH POLICE RELIEF ASSOCIATION
Police Blue Book. Portsmouth: 1915. V. 68

POSEY, WALTER B.
The Presbyterian Church in the Old Southwest. 1778-1838. Richmond: 1952. V. 73

POSEY, WILLIAM CAMPBELL
The Eye and Nervous System. Philadelphia: 1906. V. 73

POSNANSKY, F. R. A. I.
Tihuanacu: The Cradle of American Man. New York: 1945. V. 73

POSNER, DONALD
Antoine Watteau. New York: 1984. V. 73

POSNER, MICHAEL I.
Chronometric Explorations of Mind. 1978. V. 68

POST, C. C.
Ten Years a Cowboy. Chicago: 1898. V. 68; 72

POST, EMILY
The Personality of a House: the Blue Book of Home Design and Decoration. London: 1930. V. 72

POST, KEN
Revolution, Socialism and Nationalism in Vietnam. Belmont: 1989-1990. V. 68

POST, MELVILLE DAVISSON
The Bradmoor Murder. 1929. V. 71
The Corrector of Destinies. 1908. V. 71
The Corrector of Destinies. New York: 1908. V. 69
The Man of Last Resort or the Clients of Randolph Mason. 1897. V. 71
The Methods Of Uncle Abner. Boulder: 1974. V. 72
Monsieur Jonquelle Perfect of Police of Paris. 1923. V. 71
Monsieur Jonquelle: Perfect Of Police Paris. New York: 1923. V. 70; 72
The Mystery at the Blue Villa. New York: 1919. V. 71
The Nameless Thing. New York: 1912. V. 71
The Revolt of the Birds. New York: 1927. V. 71; 72
The Silent Witness. 1930. V. 71
The Sleuth of St. James's Square. 1920. V. 71
The Sleuth of St. James's Square. 1921. V. 71
Uncle Abner. New York: 1918. V. 68
Uncle Abner, Master of Mysteries. 1918. V. 71
Walker of the Secret Service. 1924. V. 71

THE POST Office - a Review of the Activities of the Post Office. London: 1934. V. 68

POSTGATE, RAYMOND
The Ledger Is Kept. London: 1953. V. 72
Verdict Of Twelve. Garden City: 1940. V. 72

POSTL, KARL
The Americans as They Are; Described in a Tour through the Valley of the Mississippi. London: 1828. V. 68
Life in the New World; or Sketches of American Society.... New York: 1844. V. 68

POSTLETHWAITE, JOHN
The Geology of the English Lake District. Carlisle: 1906. V. 71
Mines and Mining in the (English) Lake District. Leeds: 1877. V. 71
Mines and Mining in the (English) Lake District. Leeds: 1889. V. 71
Mines and Mining in the (English) Lake District. Whitehaven: 1913. V. 71

POSTLETHWAYT, JAMES
The History of the Public Revenue, from the Revolution in 1688 to Christmas 1753.... London: 1759. V. 72

POSTLETHWAYT, MALACHY
Great Britain's True System; Wherein is Clearly Shown. I. That an Increase of the Public Debts and Taxes Must, in a Few Years, Prove the Ruin of the Monied, the Trading, and the Landed Interests. II. The Necessity of Raising the Supplies to Carry on War. London: 1757. V. 72

POSTON, CHARLES D.
Apache Land. San Francisco: 1878. V. 71

POTOCKI, JOSEPH
Sport in Somaliland. 1988. V. 69

POTOCKI DE MONTALK, GEOFFREY WLADYSLAW VAILE
Dogs' Eggs - a Study in Powysology: Part One. Draguignan: 1972. V. 70
The Fifth Columnist - a Short Story. Draguignan: 1960. V. 70
The Jinx. Draguignan: 1972. V. 72
Mel Meum. Draguignan: 1959. V. 70
Our Verdict. Draguignan: 1973. V. 70
Poem for Christmas. London: 1931. V. 70
Prison Poems. London: 1933. V. 70
Snobbery with Violence. London: 1932. V. 68; 70
Social Climbers in Bloomsbury Done from the Life. London: 1939. V. 70
The Whirling River. Dorchester, Dorset: 1964. V. 70
Whited Sepulchres - Being an Account of My Trial and Imprisonment for a Parody of Verlaine and Some Other Verses. London: 1936. V. 70

POTOK, CHAIM
The Chosen. New York: 1967. V. 71
Wanderings: Chaim Potok's History of the Jews. New York: 1978. V. 70; 72

POTT, PERCIVAL
The Chirurgical Works. London: 1779. V. 68
Some Few General Remarks on Fractures and Dislocations. London: 1769. V. 68; 71
A Treatise on Ruptures. London: 1756. V. 72

POTTER & CO.
The Dryden Ranges for Anthracite or Bituminous Coal....(with) The Dunkirk Ranges...(with) The Triumph Wrought Iron Furnaces. New York: 1890?. V. 68

POTTER, ALFRED CLAGHORN
The Librarians of Harvard College 1667-1877. Cambridge, Mass: 1897. V. 72

POTTER, BEATRIX
The Complete Tales. London: 1989. V. 71
Dear Ivy, Dear Jane. Letters from Beatrix Potter. Toronto: 1977. V. 68
The Fairy Caravan. London: 1952. V. 69
Ginger and Pickles. New York. V. 68; 70
Ginger and Pickles. London: 1909. V. 69
Jemima Puddle-Duck. London: 1908. V. 71; 72
The Journal of Beatrix Potter from 1881 to 1897. London: 1966. V. 71; 72
Peter Rabbit Goes to Market. 1920. V. 69
Peter Rabbit Runs Away. 1920. V. 69
The Peter Rabbit Story Book. Philadelphia: 1920. V. 69
The Pie and the Patty-pan. London: 1905. V. 69; 70
The Pie and the Patty-Pan. London: 1926. V. 69
Sister Anne. Philadelphia: 1932. V. 68
The Sly Old Cat. London: 1971. V. 69
The Story of a Fierce Bad Rabbit. London: 1906. V. 70; 71
The Story of a Fierce Bad Rabbit. London: 1918. V. 69
The Story of Miss Moppet. London: 1906. V. 73
The Story of Miss Moppet. London: 1916. V. 68; 70
The Story of Miss Moppet. London: 1917. V. 69
The Story of Peter Rabbit. New York: 1915. V. 69
The Tailor of Gloucester. London: 1902. V. 68; 69
The Tailor of Gloucester. London: 1903. V. 68; 71
The Tailor of Gloucester. London: 1968. V. 69; 70
The Tale of Benjamin Bunny. London: 1904. V. 73
The Tale of Jemima Puddle-Duck. London: 1908. V. 68; 69
The Tale of Jemima Puddle-Duck. London: 1910. V. 69
The Tale of Jemima Puddle-Duck. London: 1995. V. 69
The Tale of Johnny Town Mouse. Londo (sic): 1918. V. 71
The Tale of Little Pig Robinson. London: 1930. V. 73
The Tale of Little Pig Robinson. Philadelphia: 1930. V. 70
The Tale of Mr. Jeremy Fisher. London: 1907. V. 68
The Tale of Mr. Tod. London: 1912. V. 71; 72
The Tale of Mrs. Tittlemouse. London: 1910. V. 69
The Tale of Mrs. Tittlemouse. 1979. V. 68
The Tale of Mrs. Tittlemouse. London: 1979. V. 69
The Tale of Peter Rabbit. Philadelphia. V. 69
The Tale of Peter Rabbit. London: 1903. V. 73
The Tale of Peter Rabbit. Philadelphia: 1916. V. 69
The Tale of Peter Rabbit. Chicago: 1918. V. 69
The Tale of Peter Rabbit. New York: 1920. V. 69
The Tale of Peter Rabbit. Chicago: 1925. V. 69
The Tale of Peter Rabbit. Kingston: 1995. V. 69
The Tale of Pigling Bland. London: 1913. V. 70; 71; 72
The Tale of Squirrel Nutkin. London: 1903. V. 68
The Tale of Squirrel Nutkin. London: 1910. V. 69
The Tale of the Faithful Dove. London: 1956. V. 71
The Tale of the Faithful Dove. London: 1971. V. 69; 71
The Tale of the Flopsy Bunnies. London: 1909. V. 71; 72
The Tale of Timmy Tiptoes. London: 1911. V. 68; 71; 72
The Tale of Tom Kitten. London: 1907. V. 69; 71; 72
The Tale of Tom Kitten. London: 1910. V. 69
Wag by Wall. Boston: 1944. V. 69
Wag By Wall. Boston: 1967. V. 69

POTTER, DENNIS
The Changing Forest - Life in the Forest of Dean Today. London: 1962. V. 69
The Singing Detective. London: 1986. V. 72

POTTER, EDMUND
Practical Opinions Against Partnership with Limited Liability, in a Letter to a Friend. (with) The Law of Partnership. London: 1855. V. 71

POTTER, F. SCARLETT
Melcomb Manor. London: 1875. V. 68

POTTER, G. W.
Random Recollections of Hampstead. Hampstead: 1907. V. 71

POTTER, IRVING W.
The Place of Version in Obstetrics. St. Louis: 1922. V. 72

POTTER, JACK
Cattle Trails of the Old West. Clayton: 1925. V. 71

POTTER, JACK continued
Cattle Trails of the Old West. Clayton: 1939. V. 68; 69; 71
Lead Steer and Other Tales. Clayton: 1939. V. 69; 71

POTTER, JERRY ALLEN
Dalhart Windberg, Artist of Texas. Austin: 1984. V. 69

POTTER, JOHN
Archaeologia Graeca; or the Antiquities of Greece. London: 1728. V. 73
Archaeologia Graeca; or the Antiquities of Greece. Edinburgh: 1827. V. 69
Archaeologica Graeca, Sive Veterum Graecoru, Praecipue Vero Atheniensium.... Lugduni Batavorum: 1702. V. 73

POTTER, NATHANIEL
A Memoir on Contagion More Especially as It Respects the Yellow Fever, Etc. Baltimore: 1818. V. 73

POTTER, PARACLETE
Every Man His Own Lawyer or the Clerk and Magistrate's Assistant. Poughkeepsie: 1827. V. 70

POTTER, STEPHEN
Pedigree: Words from Nature. London: 1973. V. 70

POTTER, THEODORE
The Autobiography of Theodore Edgar Potter. Ann Arbor: 1978. V. 68

POTTINGER, HENRY
Flood, Fell and Forest. 1905. V. 73

POTTLE, FREDERICK ALBERT
James Boswell the Earlier Years 1740-1769. 1966. V. 68
The Literary Career of James Boswell, Being the Bibliographical Materials for a Life of Boswell. London: 1967. V. 68

POUCHER, W. A.
The Alps. London: 1983. V. 69
A Camera in the Cairngorms. London: 1947. V. 69
Escape to the Hills. London: 1943. V. 69
Lakeland Scrapbook. 1950. V. 68; 73
The Magic of the Dolomites. London: 1951. V. 69
The Magic of Skye. 1949. V. 68
The Magic of Skye. London: 1949. V. 71
The North-Western Highlands. London: 1954. V. 71
Scotland through the Lens. London: 1943. V. 69

POULNIN, N.
Introduction to Plant Geography and Some Related Sciences. London: 1960. V. 72

POULTNEY, EVAN
An Appeal to the Creditors of the Bank of Maryland and the Public Generally. Baltimore: 1835. V. 72

POUND, ARTHUR
Johnson of the Mohawks. New York: 1930. V. 73

POUND, DOROTHY SHAKESPEAR
Etruscan Gate: a Notebook with Drawings and Watercolors. Exeter: 1971. V. 68

POUND, EZRA LOOMIS
ABC of Economics. London: 1933. V. 68
ABC of Reading. London: 1934. V. 68; 73
Active Anthology. London: 1933. V. 68; 69; 72; 73
The Autobiographical Outline. New York: 1980. V. 73
Cantos LII-LXXXI. 1940. V. 70
Cantos LXXII & LXXIII. Milano: 1983. V. 73
The Cantos of. 1954. V. 72
Canzoni. London: 1911. V. 70
Cathay. New York: 1993. V. 69
Certain Noble Plays of Japan: From the Manuscripts of Ernest Fenollosa, chosen and finished by Ezra Pound. Dundrum: 1916. V. 70
Certain Radio Speeches of Ezra Pound from the Recordings and Transcriptions of His Wartime Broadcasts 1941-1943. Amsterdam: 1975. V. 70
The Classic Anthology Defined by Confucius. London: 1955. V. 68
Collected Early Poems. 1977. V. 70
The Collected Poems of Ezra Pound. New York: 1927. V. 68
A Draft of XXX Cantos. New York: 1933. V. 72
A Draft of Cantos. XXXI-XLI. 1935. V. 70
Drafts & Fragments of Cantos CX-CXVII. New York: 1968. V. 69; 70; 71; 72; 73
Drafts and Fragments of Cantos CX-CXVII. London and Iowa City: 1969. V. 71
Drafts and Fragments of Cantos CX-CXVII. New York: 1969. V. 71
Drafts and Fragments of Cantos CX-XCVII. London and Iowa City: 1968-1969. V. 69
EP to LU: Nine Letters Written to Louis Untermeyer. Bloomington: 1963. V. 68
Essays of Ezra Pound. New York: 1954. V. 70
Etre Citoyen Romain etait un Privilege/Etre Citoyen Moderne est une Calamite. Liege: 1965. V. 71
Exultations. London: 1909. V. 69
Ezra Pound: a Collection of Essays to be Presented to Ezra Pound on His Sixty-Fifth Birthday. London: 1950. V. 68
The Fifth Decade of Cantos. 1937. V. 70
Forked Branches. 1985. V. 71
Forked Branches. Iowa City: 1985. V. 73
Gaudier-Brzeska: a Memoir. Hessle: 1960. V. 68
Homage to Sextus Propertius. 1934. V. 70
Hugh Selwyn Mauberley. London: 1920. V. 68
Imaginary Letters. Paris: 1928. V. 73
Imaginary Letters. Paris: 1930. V. 69
Indiscretions: or, Une Revue de Deux Mondes. Paris: 1923. V. 72
Letters. New York: 1994. V. 72
The Letters of Ezra Pound 1907-1941. New York: 1950. V. 68; 72
A Lume Spento and Other Early Poems. London: 1965. V. 68
A Lume Spento and Other Early Poems. New York: 1965. V. 71
Lustra. 1916. V. 70
Make It New: Essays. London: 1934. V. 68
Pavannes and Divisions. New York: 1918. V. 68; 69; 70; 72; 73
Personae of Ezra Pound. London: 1909. V. 73
Personae: The Collected Poems of Ezra Pound. New York: 1926. V. 68; 73
The Pisan Cantos. New York: 1948. V. 73
The Pisan Cantos. 1949. V. 70
The Pisan Cantos. London: 1949. V. 68
Polite Essays. London: 1937. V. 68; 72
Pound/Joyce: the Letters of Ezra Pound to James Joyce, with Pound's Essays on Joyce. New York: 1967. V. 68
Provenca. Boston: 1910. V. 69; 70; 73
Quia Pauper Amavi. London: 1919. V. 69; 70; 71
Rene Crevel (an Essay). Paris: 1992. V. 68
Ripostes of Ezra Pound. London: 1912. V. 73
Rock Drill. 85-95 de Los Cantares. Milan: 1955. V. 68; 71
The Seafarer. Frankfurt am Main: 1965. V. 71
Section: Rock Drill. New York: 1956. V. 72
Selected Poems. London: 1928. V. 73
Seventy Cantos. London: 1950. V. 70; 71
The Spirit of Romance. London: 1952. V. 68
Thrones. New York: 1959. V. 72
Thrones - 96-109 de los Cantares. Milano: 1959. V. 71
What Is Money For?. London: 1939. V. 68

POUQUEVILLE, F. C. H. L.
Travels in Greece and Turkey, Comprehending a Particular Account of the Morea, Albania &c. London: 1820. V. 68

POUSMA, RICHARD H.
He Who Always Wins and Other Navajo Campfire Stories. Grand Rapids: 1934. V. 69

POVERMAN, C. E.
On the Edge. Princeton: 1997. V. 72

POWDERLY, T. V.
Thirty Years of Labor. Columbus: 1889. V. 68

POWDERLY, TERENCE
The Path I Trod. New York: 1940. V. 71

POWE, JOHN HARRINGTON
Reminiscences and Sketches of Confederate Times. Columbia: 1909. V. 69

POWEL, DAVID
The Historie of Cambria, Now Called Wales.... London: 1584. V. 69

POWELL, A. CLAYTON
Riots and Ruins. NY: 1945. V. 72

POWELL, ANTHONY
The Acceptance World. London: 1955. V. 68; 70; 71; 73
Afternoon Men. London: 1931. V. 71
Afternoon Men, Venusberg, from a View to a Death, Agents and Patients. London: 1931-1936. V. 69
At Lady Molly's. London: 1957. V. 70
Books Do Furnish a Room. London: 1971. V. 71
Casanova's Chinese Restaurant. London: 1960. V. 70
The Fisher King. London: 1986. V. 71
Hearing Secret Harmonies. London: 1975. V. 73
John Aubrey and His Friends. London: 1948. V. 71
The Kindly Ones. London: 1962. V. 70
O, How the Wheel Becomes It!. London: 1983. V. 71
A Reference for Mellors. London: 1964. V. 68
A Reference for Mellors. London: 1994. V. 73
The Soldier's Art. London: 1966. V. 69; 70; 73
Temporary Kings. Boston: 1973. V. 71; 73
To Keep the Ball Rolling: the Memoirs of Anthony Powell. London: 1976-1982. V. 71
The Valley of Bones. London: 1964. V. 70; 73
Venusberg. London: 1932. V. 71
What's Become of Waring?. London: 1939. V. 69

POWELL, BADEN
A General and Elementary View of the Undulatory Theory. London: 1841. V. 68
An Historical View of the Progress of the Physical and Mathematical Sciences. London: 1834. V. 68
Observations for Determining the Refractive Indices for the Standard Rays of the Solar Spectrum in Various Media. (with) Second Supplement. Oxford: 1838-1839. V. 69

POWELL, CUTHBERT
Twenty Years of Kansas City's Livestock Trade and Traders. Kansas City: 1893. V. 71

POWELL, DAWN
The Bride's House. New York: 1929. V. 69; 71; 73

POWELL, DAWN continued
A Cage for Lovers. Boston: 1957. V. 73
Jig Saw: A Comedy. New York: 1934. V. 70
My Home is Far Away. New York: 1944. V. 70

POWELL, DONALD M.
New Mexico and Arizona in the Serial Set 1846-1861. Los Angeles: 1970. V. 68

POWELL, E. ALEXANDER
The Last Frontier. New York: 1912. V. 71

POWELL, ELLIS T.
The Evolution of the Monkey Market (1385-1915).... London: 1915. V. 71

POWELL, ENOCH
Dancer's End. The Wedding Gift. Two Books of Poems. London: 1951. V. 70

POWELL, FRED WILBUR
Hall Jackson Kelley Prophet of Oregon. Portland: 1917. V. 70

POWELL, H. M. T.
The Santa Fe Trail to California. San Francisco: 1931. V. 72

POWELL, IDA F.
A Master of Destiny: Victor Tremaine. Boston: 1939. V. 70

POWELL, J. ENOCH
The House of Lords in the Middle Ages. London: 1968. V. 68

POWELL, J. H.
Phases of Thought and Feeling. Poems and Lyrics. 1857. V. 71

POWELL, JOHN J.
The Golden State and Its Resources. San Francisco: 1874. V. 70

POWELL, JOHN WESLEY
Down the Colorado. Diary of First Trip through the Grand Canyon. New York: 1969. V. 68; 69
The Exploration of the Colorado River. Chicago: 1957. V. 69

POWELL, LAWERENCE CLARK
The Manuscripts. A Descriptive Catalogue.... Los Angeles: 1937. V. 72

POWELL, LAWRENCE CLARK
Southwestern Books- A Reader's Guide to the Heartland of New Mexico and Arizona. Albuquerque: 1963. V. 71

POWELL, MICHAEL
Death in the South Atlantic: the Last Voyage of the Graf Spree. New York: 1967. V. 70
A Life in Movies. London: 1986. V. 69; 70
A Life In Movies. New York: 1987. V. 69
200,000 Feet: the Edge of the World. New York: 1938. V. 73

POWELL, PADGETT
Edisto. London: 1984. V. 69; 71
Edisto. New York: 1984. V. 68; 69; 71

POWELL, PETER J.
Sweet Medicine, the Continuing Role of the Sacred Arrows, the Sun Dance and the Sacred Buffalo Hat in Northern Cheyenne History. Norman: 1969. V. 72
Sweet Medicine, The Continuing Role of The Sacred Arrows, The Sun Dance, and The Sacred Buffalo Hat in Northern Cheyenne. Vol I-II. Norman: 1979. V. 72

POWELL, RICHARD
Proceedings of A General Court Martial Held at the Horse-Guards, on the 24th and 27th of March, 1792, for the Trail of Capt. Richard Powell, Lieut. Christopher Seton, and Lieut. John Hall, of the 54th Regiment of Foot.... London: 1809. V. 73

POWELL-COTTON, P. H. G.
A Sporting Trip through Abyssinia. London: 1902. V. 72
In Unknown Africa. London: 1904. V. 71

POWER, D'ARCY
William Harvey. London: 1897. V. 68; 71; 72

POWER, DAVID
On the Responsibilties of Employers. London: 1849. V. 69

POWER, JOHN
A Handy-Book About Books for Book-Lovers, Book-Buyers and Booksellers. London: 1870. V. 71
Law as to Cemeteries, Undertakers, Embalmers and Burials in the State of New York. Albany: 1901. V. 73

POWER, KEVIN
Heidegger My Way and Scarcely: a Long Poem. Amsterdam: 1982. V. 71
Work in Progress. London: 1977. V. 70

POWER, MARGUERITE
The Keepsake for 1851. London: 1851. V. 71
The Keepsake for 1852. London: 1852. V. 71

POWER, RHODA
How It Happened. Myths and Folk Tales. 1930. V. 68

POWER, SUSAN
The Grass Dancer. London: 1994. V. 72
The Grass Dancer. New York: 1994. V. 72

POWERS, RICHARD
The Gold Bug Variations. New York: 1991. V. 68; 70
The Gold Bug Variations. London: 1992. V. 68; 69; 72
Operation Wandering Soul. New York: 1993. V. 70
Prisoner's Dilemma. New York: 1988. V. 70; 71; 72
Three Farmers On Their Way to a Dance. 1985. V. 68; 69
Three Farmers on Their Way to a Dance. New York: 1985. V. 70; 71; 73
Three Farmers on Their Way to a Dance. London: 1988. V. 69; 72

POWERS, TIM
The Anubis Gates. 1989. V. 71
The Anubis Gates. Shingletown: 1989. V. 69
Night Moves. 1986. V. 73
The Skies Discrowned. 1993. V. 71

POWERS, W. P.
Some Annals of the Powers Family. Los Angeles: 1924. V. 68

POWLEY, MARY
Echoes of Old Cumberland. Poems and Translations. London: 1875. V. 69

POWYS, JOHN COWPER
Confessions of Two Brothers. Rochester: 1916. V. 71
Dorothy M. Richardson. London: 1931. V. 68
Ducdame. 1925. V. 71
In Denfense of Sensuality. New York: 1930. V. 68
The Meaning of Culture. London: 1930. V. 71
The Owl, the Duck and Miss Rowe! Miss Rowe!. Chicago: 1930. V. 70
Porius. A Romance. 1951. V. 71
Rodmoor. New York: 1916. V. 71
Visions and Revisions - a Book of Literary Devotions. New York: 1915. V. 71
Wolf Solent. London: 1929. V. 71

POWYS, LLEWELYN
The Book of Days of Llewelyn Powys. Waltham St. Lawrence: 1937. V. 68
Dorset Essays. London: 1935. V. 68
Glory of Life. Waltham St. Lawrence: 1934. V. 68
Impassioned Clay. London: 1931. V. 71
Now that the Gods are Dead. New York: 1932. V. 69
The Twelve Months. London: 1936. V. 71
The Verdict of Bridlegoose. London: 1927. V. 71

POWYS, THEODORE FRANCIS
Christ in the Cupboard. 1930. V. 71
Christ in the Cupboard. London: 1930. V. 72
Collected Poems. London: 1979. V. 71
The Dewpond. London: 1928. V. 68; 71
Fables. London: 1929. V. 69
Goat Green. London: 1937. V. 71
The House with the Echo. London: 1928. V. 68; 71
The Key of the Field. London: 1930. V. 68
Mark Only. London: 1924. V. 68; 71
Soliloquies of a Hermit. London: 1918. V. 71
Three Short Stories. 1971. V. 72
The Two Thieves. London: 1932. V. 68
Uncle Dottery, a Christmas Story. Cleverdon, Bristol: 1931. V. 68
When Thou Was Naked. Waltham St. Lawrence: 1931. V. 70

POYNTER, BEULAH
Mad Folly: A Love Story. New York: 1937. V. 72
Murder on 47th Street. Garden City: 1931. V. 68

POYNTER, F. N. L.
Medicine and Culture. London: 1969. V. 72

POZZO, ANDREA
Rules and Examples of Perspective Proper for Painters and Architects.... London: 1725. V. 71

THE PRACTICAL Cabinet-Maker. London: 1870?. V. 68

THE PRACTICAL Carver and Gilders' Guide and Picture Frame Makers' Companion...The Restoration of Oil Paintings, Cleaning Old Engravings &c.... Cirencester: 1875. V. 71

PRACTICAL Receipts and Useful Hints for a Young Wife or Inexperienced Housekeeper. Norwich: 1834. V. 71

PRADHAN, U. C.
100 Beautiful Himalayan Orchids and How to Grow Them. West Bengal: 1997. V. 68

PRAED, ROSA
Affinities: a Romance of To-Day. London: 1886. V. 68
The Romance of a Station. London: 1889?. V. 68

PRAED, WILLIAM MACKWORTH
The Poems. London. V. 68

PRAED, WINTHROP MACKWORTH
The Poems. London: 1864. V. 72
Poems. Boston: 1909. V. 72
The Poetical Works of Winthrop Macworth Praed. New York: 1844. V. 72

PRAEGER, ROBERT LLOYD
Irish Topographical Botany. 1901. V. 69; 73
Open Air Studies in Botany: Sketches of British Wild Flowers in their Homes. 1897. V. 69
A Tourist's Flora of the West of Ireland. Dublin: 1909. V. 72

PRAEGER, ROBERT LLOYD continued
The Way That I Went, an Irishman in Ireland. 1937. V. 69; 73
The Way That I Went, an Irishman in Ireland. London: 1939. V. 70
The Way That I Went, an Irishman in Ireland. 1947. V. 69

PRAEGER, S. ROSAMUND
How They Came Home from School. London: 1911. V. 71
Wee Tony. A Day in His Life. London: 1913. V. 71

PRAIRIE BIRD
The Trapper's Bride; or Spirit of Adventure. Cincinnati: 1860. V. 68

PRALL, ROBERT
This Is Costello. New York: 1951. V. 72

PRAMPOLINI, IDA RODRIGUEZ
El Surrealismo y el Arte Fantastico de Mexico. Mexico: 1969. V. 70

PRANG'S Standard Alphabets. Boston: 1886. V. 68

PRATCHETT, TERRY
Feet of Clay. London: 1996. V. 72

PRATER, DONALD
A Ringing Glass - the Life of Rainer Maria Rilke. Oxford: 1986. V. 71

PRATT, A. E.
To the Snows of Tibet, Through China. London: 1892. V. 71
Two Years Among New Guinea Cannibals. London: 1906. V. 71

PRATT, ALICE DAY
The Homesteaders Portfolio. New York: 1922. V. 71

PRATT, AMBROSE
The Counterstroke. New York: 1907. V. 69

PRATT, ANNE
The British Grasses and Sedges. London: 1859. V. 70
Chapters on the Common things of Sea-side. London: 1850. V. 68
The Ferns of Great Britain and their Allies the Club Mosses, Pepperworts and Horsetails. London: 1873. V. 72
The Ferns of Great Britain and their Allies the Club-Mosses, Pepperworts and Horsetails. London: 1861. V. 70
The Flowering Plants, Grasses, Sedges and Ferns of Great Britain and Their Allies the Club Mosses, Horsetails &c. London: 1899-1905. V. 68
Flowers and Their Associations. London: 1840. V. 68; 71; 73

PRATT, CHARLES
An Inquiry into the Nature and Effect of the Writ of Habeas Corpus, the Great Bulwark of British Liberty, Both at Common Law, and Under the Act of Parliament. London: 1758. V. 73

PRATT, D.
The Photographic Eye of Ben Shahn. Cambridge: 1975. V. 68; 69

PRATT, DANIEL
Autobiography of Daniel Pratt, Jr. A.A.S. of Boston, Formerly of Prattville, Chelsea, Mass. Boston: 1855. V. 68

PRATT, JULIUS HOWARD
Reminiscences, Personal and Otherwise. 1910. V. 69

PRATT, M. B.
Shade and Ornamental Trees of California. Sacramento: 1922. V. 68

PRATT, S. J.
Catalogue of a Highly Interesting and Valuable Collection of Autograph letters, in the Finest Preservation Including...Royal Letters of Great Rarity...Most Interesting Letters of Literary Men from the Joint Collections of S. J. Pratt & Dr. Mavor.... London: 1853. V. 70

PRATT, SAMUEL JACKSON
Pity's Gift: a Collection of Interesting Tales, to Excite the Compassion of Youth for the Animal Creation. London: 1798. V. 71
Pity's Gift: a Collection of Interesting Tales, to Excite the Compassion of Youth for the Animal Creation. London: 1801. V. 73

PRAUSER, H.
The Actinomycetales. Jean: 1970. V. 72

PRAZ, MARIO
An Illustrated History of Interior Decorations From Pompeii To Art Nouveau. New York: 1987. V. 72

PRECIS Historique de la Vie de Mad. La Comtesse Du Barry.... Paris: 1774. V. 73

PREJEVALSKY, NIKOLAI M.
Mongolia. London: 1876. V. 71

PRELUTSKY, JACK
The Random House Book of Poetry for Children. New York: 1983. V. 70

PREMINGER, OTTO
Preminger. New York: 1977. V. 70

PREMORD, C. L.
Reflections on Communities of Women and Monastic Institutions, By a Friend of Religious and Civil Liberty. Taunton: 1815. V. 72

PRENDERGAST, JOHN P.
The Cromwellian Settlement of Ireland. London: 1865. V. 69

PRENTICE, ARCHIBALD
History of the Anti-Corn-Law League. London: 1853. V. 71

PRENTICE, WALTER J.
My Adventures with the Coalie's Baby. London: 1923. V. 68

PRENTIS, JOHN H.
The Case of Doctor Horace. New York: 1907. V. 69; 70

PRESCOTT, GEORGE B.
The Speaking Telephone, Talking Phonograph and Other Novelties. New York: 1878. V. 70

PRESCOTT, J. E.
The Register of the Priory of Wetheral. London: 1897. V. 71
The Statutes of the Cathedral Church of Carlisle. London: 1903. V. 71

PRESCOTT, JOHN R.
Camden on the Coast of Maine and Its Advantages for Summer Homes. Providence: 1900. V. 70

PRESCOTT, WILLIAM HICKLING
History of the Conquest of Mexico. Philadelphia: 1873. V. 71
History of the Conquest of Mexico. London: 1878. V. 71
The History of the Conquest of Mexico. Philadelphia: 1900-1920. V. 69
The History of the Conquest of Mexico. New York: 1920. V. 69
History of the Conquest of Peru. London: 1847. V. 70
History of the Reign of Ferdinand and Isabella. New York: 1967. V. 70
History of the Reign of Philip the Second, King of Spain. Boston: 1855-1858. V. 68
Prescott's Works. Philadelphia: 1870. V. 72

PRESCOTT-ALLEN, C.
The First Resource, Wild Species in the North American Economy. New Haven: 1986. V. 72

A PRESENT For a Good Little Boy. London: 1860. V. 73

A PRESENT for a Little Boy. London: 1806. V. 70

THE PRESENT Interest of the People of Great Britain, at Home and Abroad, Consider'd: In a Letter to a Member of Parliament. London: 1742?. V. 73

THE PRESENT State of Europe; or the Historical and Political Mercury; Giving an Account of All the Public and Private Occurrences for the Month of August 1690. London: 1690. V. 69

THE PRESENT State of the Stage in Great Britain and Ireland.... London: 1758. V. 71

PRESHAW, G. W.
Banking Under Difficulties, or Life on the Goldfields of Victoria, New South Wales and New Zealand. Melbourne: 1888. V. 69

PRESIDENTIAL Cook Book. New York: 1904. V. 72; 73

PRESLAND, JOHN
Satni. A Tragedy. London: 1929. V. 71

PRESSFIELD, STEVEN
The Legend of Bagger Vance. New York: 1996. V. 70

PRESTON, ARTHUR
The Valley of the Monquis. New York: 1927. V. 69

PRESTON, CHLOE
Dumpty Dumpties. London: 1920. V. 70
Nursery Rhymes. London. V. 69
The Peek-a-Boos in Winter. London: 1911. V. 72

PRESTON, JACK
Heil! Hollywood. Chicago: 1939. V. 69; 73

PRESTON, RICHARD A.
Royal Fort Frontenac. Toronto: 1958. V. 73

PRESTON, TOM
The Peek-A-Boo Japs. London: 1912. V. 72

PRESTRUD, EARL
Bishop's Wildfowl. St. Paul: 1948. V. 70; 72; 73

PRETTY Polly. 1895. V. 73
PRETTY Polly. London: 1897. V. 68; 73

PRETTY Rhymes About Birds and Animals, for Little Boys and Girls. New York: 1849-1856. V. 71

PRETTY Tales; or, Stories for Youth. Derby: 1835. V. 72

PRETTYMAN, W. S.
Indian Territory. Norman: 1957. V. 72

PREVOST, ANTOINE FRANCOIS, CALLED PREVOST D'EXILES
Histoire de Manon Lescaut et du Chevalier des Grieux. Paris: 1934. V. 71
Histoire Du Chevalier des Grieux et de Manon Lescaut. Paris: 1942. V. 68
Histoire Generale des Voyages. Le Haye: 1747-1777. V. 71
Manon Lescaut. London: 1928. V. 73

PREVOST, FLORENT
Histoire Naturelle d'Oiseaux d'Europe (Passereaux). Paris: 1864. V. 70; 73

PREVOST, GEORGE
Some Account of the Public Life of the Late Lieutenant-General Sir George Prevost, Bart. London: 1823. V. 73

PRIANESI, GIAMBATTISTA
Diverse Maniere d'Adornare i Cammini ed Ogni Altra Parte Degli Edifizi.... Rome: 1769. V. 70

PRICE, ANTHONY
Colonel Butler's Wolf. London: 1972. V. 69; 71
The Hour of the Donkey. London: 1980. V. 69; 71
The Stalker. New York: 1971. V. 72
Tomorrow's Ghost. London: 1979. V. 69; 71; 73

PRICE, BYRON
Erwin E. Smith, Cowboy Photographer - Imagining the Open Range. Fort Worth: 1968. V. 69

PRICE, C. V.
The Merchantile Agency's Legal Guide for the Dominion of Canada. Montreal: 1868. V. 71

PRICE, CAROL ANN
Early El Paso Artists. El Paso: 1983. V. 70

PRICE, CON
Trails I Rode. Pasadena: 1947. V. 71

PRICE, DOUGHBELLY
Short Stirrups. Los Angeles: 1960. V. 68; 70; 73

PRICE, E. CURMIE
The State of the Union. Surrey: 1970. V. 72

PRICE, EDWARD
Norway. Views of Wild Scenery and Journal. 1834. V. 72
Norway. Views of Wild Scenery and Journal. London: 1834. V. 68; 71

PRICE, EUGENIA
Don Juan McQueen. Philadelphia: 1974. V. 68

PRICE, EVADNE
Enter Jane. London: 1937. V. 69
Jane the Sleuth. London: 1939. V. 69
One Woman's Freedom. New York: 1932. V. 72

PRICE, F. G. HILTON
The Signs of Old Lombard Street.... London: 1887. V. 71

PRICE, FRANCIS
The British Carpenter. London: 1735. V. 68
A Series of Particular and Useful Observation Made with Great Diligence and Care, Upon the Admirable Structure, the Cathedral Church of Salisbury.... London: 1753. V. 68; 70; 72
A Treatise on Carpentry. London: 1733. V. 68

PRICE, FRANCIS COMPTON
Facsimile of a Heraldic MS entitled "The Names and Armes of Them that Hath Beene Alldermen of the Ward of Alldersgate...". London: 1878. V. 73

PRICE, GEORGE F.
Across The Continent With The Fifth Cavalry. New York: 1959. V. 72

PRICE, HUMPHREY
Reasons in Support of an Extension of the Elective Franchise to the Working Classes. London: 1836. V. 71

PRICE, J.
The Buyers' Manual and Business Guide.... San Francisco: 1872. V. 73

PRICE, J. E.
A Description of the Remains of Roman Buildings Near Brading, Isle of Wight. London: 1880. V. 68
A Description of the Roman Tesselated Pavement Found in Bucklersbury; with Observations of Analogous Discoveries. Westminster: 1870. V. 70
Roman Antiquities Illustrated by Remains Recently Discovered on the Site of the National Safe Deposit Company's Premises, Mansion House, London. London: 1873. V. 71

PRICE, JAMES L.
Jungle Jim: the Autobiography of James L. Price. Garden City: 1941. V. 71

PRICE, JOHN D.
The Mystery and Method of His Majesty's Happy Restauration, Laid open to Publick View by John Price, D.D.... London: 1683. V. 72

PRICE, JULIUS MENDER
From the Arctic Ocean to the Yellow Sea. London: 1892. V. 71
The Land of Gold. London: 1896. V. 69; 73

PRICE, LUXOR
The Quoks. London: 1925. V. 68

PRICE, MARY
Treasury of Great Recipes. New York: 1965. V. 72; 73

PRICE, R. N.
Holston Methodism: from Its Origin to the Present Time. Nashville: 1904-1914. V. 72

PRICE, REYNOLDS
Back Before Day. Rocky Mount: 1989. V. 68; 70; 73
Blue Calhoun. New York: 1992. V. 71
Clear Pictures. New York: 1989. V. 70; 72
The Collected Stories. New York: 1993. V. 68; 71
A Common Book. Essays 1954-1987. New York: 1987. V. 68
Country Mouse, City Mouse. Rocky Mount, NC: 1981. V. 71
The Dream of a House. Winston-Salem: 1977. V. 71
An Early Christmas. Rocky Mount: 1992. V. 68
The Foreseeable Future. New York: 1991. V. 68
A Generous Man. New York: 1966. V. 68; 70
Good Hearts. New York: 1988. V. 68; 71
Home Made. Rocky Mount: 1990. V. 70; 73
House Snake. Northridge: 1987. V. 70; 71
Kate Vaiden. New York: 1986. V. 68; 70; 72
Late Warning. Four Poems. New York: 1968. V. 70
Learning a Trade. Durham: 1998. V. 71
A Long and Happy Life. New York: 1962. V. 70; 71; 72; 73
Love and Work. New York: 1968. V. 68; 70
Mustian. Two Novels and a Story Complete and Unabridged, A Generous Man. A Chain of Love. A Long and Happy Life. New York: 1983. V. 71
The Names and Faces of Heroes. New York: 1963. V. 70; 72; 73
Oracles. Durham: 1977. V. 70; 73
Permanent Errors. New York: 1970. V. 69; 71
The Promise of Rest. New York: 1995. V. 68; 72
Roxanna Slade. New York: 1998. V. 72
The Surface of Earth. New York: 1975. V. 68; 70
The Tongues of Angels. New York: 1990. V. 68
The Use of Fire. New York: 1990. V. 68

PRICE, RICHARD
Additional Observations on the Nature and Value of Civil Liberty and the War with America. London: 1777. V. 73
The Breaks. New York: 1983. V. 72
A Discourse on the Love of Our Country, Delivered on Nov. 4, 1789, at the Meeting-Huse in the Old Jewry, to the Society for Commemorating the Revolution in Great Britain. London: 1789. V. 73
Four Dissertations. I. On Providence. II. On Prayer, etc. London: 1767. V. 69
Four Dissertations. I. On Providence. II. On Prayer. III. On the Reasons for Expecting the Virtuous Men Shall Meet After Death in a State of Happiness. IV. on the Importance of Christianity, the Nature of Historical Evidence and Miracles. London: 1777. V. 70
Freedomland. New York: 1998. V. 72
Ladies' Man. Boston: 1978. V. 68; 72; 73
Observations on Reversionary Payments.... London: 1772. V. 68; 72
Observations on Reversionary Payments.... London: 1773. V. 70
Observations on Reversionary Payments.... London: 1792. V. 68
Observations on the Nature of Civil Liberty, the Principles of Government and the Justice and Policy of the War with America. London: 1776. V. 73
Observations on the Nature of Civil Liberty, the Principles of Government, and the Justice and Policy of the War with America. (with) Additional Observations on the Nature and Value of Civil Liberty.... London: 1776-1770. V. 73
A Review of the Principal Questions and Difficulties in Morals. London: 1758. V. 72
A Review of the Principal Questions and Difficulties in Morals. London: 1769. V. 71
The Wanderers. Boston: 1974. V. 68; 70; 71; 72

PRICE, S. GOODALE
Saga of The Hills, An Illustrated Story of The Last Frontier. Hollywood: 1940. V. 72

PRICE, SAMMY
Boogie-Woogie Land. New York: 1944. V. 69; 71

PRICE, TAFF
Lures for Game, Coarse and Sea Fishing. 1972. V. 68

PRICE, VINCENT
I Like What I Know. Garden City: 1959. V. 73

PRICE, W. SALTER
My Third Campaign in East Africa. London: 1890. V. 71

PRICE, WILLARD
The Negro Around the World. New York: 1925. V. 72

PRICE JONES, CECIL
Red Blood Cell Diameters. London: 1933. V. 68

PRICES Of Carpenters Work, Submitted to the Public. London: 1796. V. 73

THE PRICES of Journeymen's Measured Work, Revised and Corrected by the Committee of Master Carpenters, and Agreed to at a General Meeting of the Trade. London: 1810. V. 73

PRICHARD, HESKETH
November Joe: Detective of the Woods. Boston: 1913. V. 69; 70
Sport in Wildest Britain. 1921. V. 71

PRICHARD, JAMES COWLES
Researches Into the Physical History of Mankind. London: 1826. V. 71
A Treatise on Insanity and Other Disorders Affecting the Mind. Philadelphia: 1837. V. 73

PRICHARD, K.
Don Q's Love Story. New York: 1925. V. 70

PRICHARD, KATHERINE SUSANNAH
Coonardoo. New York: 1930. V. 71

THE PRIDE of Peter Print; or Proverbs. Cooperstown: 1842. V. 73

PRIDE, W. F.
The History of Fort Riley. 1926. V. 72

PRIDEAUX, HUMPHREY
Ecclesiastical Tracts Formerly Published: I. The Validity of the Orders of the Church of England. II. The Justice of the Present Establish'd Law...III. An Award of King Charles the First, &c. London: 1716. V. 70
The True Nature of Imposture Fully Display'd in the Life of Mahomet. London: 1697. V. 73
The True Nature of Imposture Fully Display'd in the Life of Mahomet. London: 1723. V. 73

PRIDEAUX, JOHN
A Synopsis of Councels. Oxford: 1654. V. 73

PRIDEAUX, MATHIAS
An Easy and Compendious Introduction for Reading All Sorts of Histories. Oxford: 1648. V. 69
An Easy and Compendious Introduction for Reading all Sorts of Histories. Oxford: 1664. V. 71

PRIDEAUX, S. T.
Aquatint Engraving. A Chapter in the History of Book Illustration. London: 1909. V. 70

PRIDEAUX, TOM
Love or Nothing. The Life and Times of Ellen Terry. New York: 1975. V. 70; 72

PRIDHAM, CHARLES
Kossuth and Magyar Land. London: 1851. V. 71

PRIEST, ALFRED
The Hare and Three Leverets. Norwich: 1848. V. 70

PRIEST, JOSIAH
American Antiquities and Discoveries in the West.... Albany: 1833. V. 68
The Anti-Universalist, or, History of the Fallen Angels of the Scriptures.... Albany: 1837. V. 68; 71
The Anti-Universalist, or the Fallen Angels of the Scriptures.... New York: 1837. V. 69
Slavery, As It Relates to the Negro, or African Race, Examined in the Light of Circumstances, History and the Holy Scriptures.... Albany: 1843. V. 71

PRIESTLEY, HERBERT INGRAM
Tristan De Luna - Conquistador of the Old South - a Study of Spanish Imperial Strategy. Glendale: 1936. V. 69

PRIESTLEY, JOHN BOYNTON
Albert Goes Through. London: 1933. V. 69
Angel Pavement. London: 1930. V. 71; 72
Benighted. London: 1927. V. 72
Brief Diversions, Being Tales Travesties and Epigrams. Cambridge: 1922. V. 71
Dangerous Corner. New York: 1932. V. 69
English Journey. London: 1934:. V. 72
Faraway. New York: 1932. V. 70
I'll Tell You Everything. New York: 1933. V. 70
Journey Down a Rainbow. London: 1955. V. 73
The Town Major of Miraucourt. London: 1930. V. 68
A Visit to New Zealand. London: 1974. V. 71
Wonder Hero. London: 1933. V. 71

PRIESTLEY, JOSEPH
A Descriptive System of Biography; with a Catalogue of All the Names Inserted In It.... Philadelphia: 1803. V. 68
A Discourse on Occasion of the Death of Dr. Price, Delivered at Hackney, on Sunday, May, 1, 1791. London: 1791. V. 69
Disquisitions Relating to Matter and Spirit. London: 1777. V. 73
Experiments and Observations on Different Kinds of Air. London: 1775-1777. V. 72
Forms of Prayer and Other Offices, for the Use of Unitarian Societies. Birmingham: 1783. V. 69
The History and Present State of Discoveries Relating to Vision, Light and Colours. London: 1772. V. 73
The History and Present State of Electricity, with Original Experiments. London: 1767. V. 68; 71; 73
Lectures on History and General Policy.... Philadelphia: 1803. V. 73
Letters to a Philosophical Unbeliever. Birmingham: 1787. V. 73

PRIESTLEY, RAYMOND E.
Antarctic Adventure. London: 1914. V. 71

PRIESTMAN, AUSTIN
Child Verses & Poems. London. V. 71

PRIETO, GREGORIO
Paintings and Drawings. London: 1947. V. 68

PRIM, PETER
Peter Prim's Pride, or Proverbs, That Will Suit the Young, or the Old. London: 1810. V. 71

PRIMARY Colors. New York: 1996. V. 72

PRIMAVERA: Poems by Four Authors. Oxford: 1890. V. 73

PRIME, CECIL
Lords and Ladies. London: 1960. V. 68

PRIME, SAMUEL IRENAEUS
Travels in Europe and the East: a Year in England, Scotland, Ireland, Wales, France, Belgium, Holland.... New York: 1861. V. 73

PRIME, W.
I Go A-Fishing. 1873. V. 73

THE PRIMER More Ample and in a New Order, Containing the Three Offices of the Virgin Mary in Latin and English.... Rouen: 1684. V. 73

PRIMROSE, JAMES
Animadversiones in Theses, Quas Pro Circulatione Sanguinis in Academia Ultrajectensi De. Henricus Le Roy.... Leiden: 1640. V. 70

PRIN, ALICE
Kiki's Memoirs. Paris: 1930. V. 71; 72

PRINCE EDWARD ISLAND
The Acts of the General Assembly of Prince Edward Island. Charlottetown: 1857. V. 71

PRINCE, F. T.
Afterword on Rupert Brooke. London: 1976. V. 73
Drypoints of the Hasidim. London: 1975. V. 73

PRINCE, JOHN
Dammonii Orientales Illustres; or, the Worthies of Devon. Plymouth: 1810. V. 73

PRINCE, L. BRADFORD
A Concise History of New Mexico. Cedar Rapids: 1912. V. 68
A Concise History of New Mexico. Cedar Rapids: 1914. V. 69
Historical Sketches of New Mexico from the Earliest Records to the American Occupation. New York/Kansas City: 1883. V. 73
New Mexico's Struggle for Statehood. Santa Fe: 1910. V. 72
Old Fort Marcy - Santa Fe, New Mexico Historical Sketch and Panomaic View of Santa Fe and Its Vicinity. Santa Fe: 1912. V. 72
Spanish Mission Churches of New Mexico. Cedar Rapids: 1915. V. 69

PRINCE, NANCY
A Narrative of the Life and Travels. Boston: 1850. V. 73

PRINCE, SAMUEL HENRY
Catastrophe and Social Change. New York: 1920. V. 73

PRINCE, THOMAS
The Vade Mecum for America.... Boston: 1732. V. 68

THE PRINCE With the Long Nose. London: 1870. V. 68

THE PRINCESSE Cloria; or, the Royal Romance. London;: 1665. V. 73

THE PRINCIPLES of Harmonious Colouring, in Oil, Water and Photographic Colours.... London: 1859. V. 68

PRING, JAMES HURLEY
A Memoir of Thomas Chard, D.D. Suffragan Bishop, and the Last Abbot of Ford Abbey Dorsetshire; Late in the County of Devon. London: 1864. V. 73

PRING, JOSEPH
Particulars of the Grand Suspension Bridge, Erected Over the Straits of Menai...Designed by and Built Under the Immediate Direction of Thomas Telford, Esq. Bangor: 1826. V. 70

PRINGLE, E. L. L.
Pennington's Butterflies of Southern Africa. Cape Town: 1994. V. 69

PRINGLE, EDWARD J. •
Slavery in the Southern States. Cambridge: 1852. V. 68

PRINGLE, ELIZABETH
Chronicles of Chicora Wood. New York: 1922. V. 70
A Woman Rice Planter. New York: 1914. V. 70; 71

PRINGLE, JOHN
A Discourse on the Theory of Gunnery. London: 1778. V. 69
Observations on the Diseases of the Army.... Philadelphia: 1812. V. 68; 70; 73

PRINGLE, O. M.
Magic River Deschutes. 1911. V. 68

PRINGLE, TERRY
The Preacher's Boy. Chapel Hill: 1988. V. 68

PRINGLE, THOMAS
The Autumnal Excursion; or Sketches in Teviotdale; with Other Poems. Edinburgh and London: 1819. V. 72
Ephemerides; or, Occasional Poems written in Scotland and South Africa. London: 1828. V. 72
The Poetical Works of Thomas Pringle. London: 1838. V. 72

PRINGLE PATTISON, A. SETH
The Philosophical Radicals and Other Essays. London: 1907. V. 71

PRINS Lennarts ABC-Bok. Stockholm: 1912. V. 71

PRINSEP, HENRY THOBY
Note on the Historical Results, Deductible from Recent Discoveries in Afghanistan. London: 1844. V. 71; 73

A PRINTER'S Christmas Books. 1959. V. 71

PRIOR, JIM
A Balance of Power. London: 1986. V. 69

PRIOR, MATTHEW
The Hind and the Panther Transvers'd To the Story of the Country- Mouse and the City Mouse. London: 1687. V. 70; 72
Poems on Several Occasions. London: 1718. V. 70; 71; 72
Poems on Several Occasions. London: 1733. V. 69
Poems Upon Several Occasions. Edinburgh: 1773. V. 73
The Poetical Works. London: 1779. V. 73
The Poetical Works. London: 1835. V. 72
Selected Poems. London:: 1889. V. 68; 72

PRIOR, R. C. ALEXANDER
Ancient Danish Ballads Translated from the Originals. London: 1860. V. 69

PRIOR, THOMAS
A List of the Absentees of Ireland, and the Yearly Value of Their Estates and Incomes Spent Abroad. Dublin: 1729. V. 73

PRISCIANUS
Opera. Venice: 1488. V. 73
Prisciani Grammatici Caesariensis Libri Omnes. Venetiis: 1527. V. 69; 73

PRISCILLA CLUB OF THE FIRST CONGREGATIONAL CHURCH, BERKELEY
Priscilla Cook Book. Berkeley: 1923. V. 72

THE PRISONER of Zenda. Los Angeles: 1937. V. 73

PRITCHARD, ANDREW
A History of Infusoria, Living and Fossil.... London: 1841. V. 72
The Microscopic Cabinet of Select Animated Objects. London: 1832. V. 68
The Microscopic Cabinet of Select Animated Objects. Lincolnwood: 1987. V. 68; 71; 73
Notes on Aquatic Microscopic Subjects of Natural History.... London: 1854. V. 68; 70

PRITCHARD, H. HESKETH
Hunting Camps In Wood And Wilderness. London: 1910. V. 72
Through Trackless Labrador. London: 1911. V. 72

PRITCHARD, JAMES A.
The Overland Diary of James A. Pritchard from Kentucky to California in 1849.... Denver: 1959. V. 71

PRITCHETT, R. T.
Historical Smokiana. London: 1890. V. 72
Pen and Pencil Sketches of Shipping and Craft All Around the World. London: 1899. V. 72

PRITCHETT, V. S.
A Careless Widow. New York: 1989. V. 68; 69
It May Never Happen. London: 1945. V. 68
Mr. Beluncle. London: 1951. V. 69
New York Proclaimed. London: 1965. V. 68; 70
The Turn of the Years: The Seasons' Course: Selected Engravings by Reynolds Stone: as Old as the Century. London: 1982. V. 70

PRITT, T. E.
Yorkshire Trout Flies. 1998. V. 68; 73

THE PRIVILEDGES of the Citizens of London: Contained in the Charters.... London: 1682. V. 73

PRIZE Stories 1986. Garden City: 1986. V. 72

PRIZE Stories 1987. Garden City: 1987. V. 72

PRIZE Stories 2001. The O. Henry Awards. New York: 2001. V. 69

PRIZE Stories: The O. Henry Awards 1962. New York: 1962. V. 69

PRIZE Writing, an Original Collection of Writings of Past Winners of the Booker Prize. London: 1989. V. 68

PROCEEDINGS of a General Court Martial, Held in the Orderly Room at the Barracks in Colchester, On Seven Officers of the West Kent Regiment of Militia.... London: 1807. V. 70

PROCEEDINGS of a Public Meeting Held at the Freemason's Hall on the 18th June 1824 for Erecting a Monument to the Late James Watt. London: 1825. V. 71

PROCEEDINGS of Sundry Citizens of Baltimore, Convened for the Purpose of Devising the Most Efficient Means of Improving the Intercourse Between that City and the Western States. Baltimore: 1827. V. 73

PROCEEDINGS of the First Convention of the Industiral Workers of the World. NY: 1905. V. 73

PROCEEDINGS of the Public Meeting Held at Freemason's Hall, on the 18th June, 1824, for Erecting a Monument to the Late James Watt. London: 1824. V. 73

THE PROCEEDINGS Upon the Bill of Divorce Between His Grace the Duke of Norfolke (1655-1701) and the Lady Mary Mordant (Later Germain 1655-1701).... London: 1700. V. 73

LE PROCES sans Fin ou l'Histoire de John Bull.... Londres: 1753. V. 70

PROCOPIUS OF CESAREA
The Secret History of the Court of the Emperor Justinian. London: 1674. V. 71

PROCTER, ADELAIDE ANNE
The Complete Works. London: 1905. V. 70
Legends and Lyrics. Boston: 1866. V. 68
Legends and Lyrics. London: 1866. V. 68; 70
Legends and Lyrics. A Book of Verses. (and) Legends and Lyrics. Second Volume. London: 1861-1863. V. 71

PROCTER, E. H.
The Rabbits' Day in Town. London: 1908. V. 69

PROCTER, GIL
Panchita. San Antonio: 1960. V. 71

PROCTER, RICHARD WRIGHT
The Barber's Shop. Manchester: 1856. V. 68

PROCTOR, EDNA DEAN
The Song of the Ancient People. Boston: 1893. V. 70

PROCTOR, FRANK
Fox Hunting in Canada. Toronto: 1929. V. 71

PROCTOR, G. R.
Ferns of Puerto Rico and the Virgin Islands. New York: 1989. V. 69

PROCTOR, MAURICE
The Devil Was Handsome. London: 1961. V. 71

PROCTOR, RICHARD A.
The Moon, Her Motions, Aspect, Scenery and Physical Condition. New York: 1902. V. 69
Other Worlds than Ours. New York: 1902. V. 72
Our Place Among Infinities. New York: 1879. V. 72
Saturn and Its System; Containing Discussions of the Motions (Real and Apparent) and Telescopic Appearance or the Planet Saturn.... London: 1865. V. 72
Wages and Wants of Science Workers. London: 1876. V. 70
Watched by the Dead. London: 1887. V. 70

PROCTOR, ROBERT
An Index of German Books 1501-1520 in the British Museum. London: 1954. V. 70

PROCTOR, SAMUEL D.
The Young Negro in America, 1960-1980. NY: 1966. V. 72

PROFFITT, NICHOLAS
Gardens of Stone. New York: 1983. V. 72

PROGRESS. Commerce. 1893. London: 1893. V. 71

PROGRESSIVE Men of the State of Montana. Chicago: 1902. V. 71

PROGULSKE, DONALD R.
Yellow Ore, Yellow Hair, Yellow Pine. Brookings: 1974. V. 72

PROKOSCH, FREDERIC
The Assassins. New York: 1936. V. 71

PROLUSIONES Academiae Praemis Annuis Dignitatae et in Curia Cantabrigiensi Recitatae Coffmitis Maximis A.D. MDCCCXLIII. Cambridge: 1843. V. 73

PROLUSIONES Subsicivae (cover title). London: 1894. V. 71

PRONZINI, BILL
Blowback. New York: 1977. V. 69; 72
Blue Lonesome. New York: 1995. V. 69; 71; 72
Carpenter and Quincannon Professional Detective Services. Norfolk: 1998. V. 70
Case File. New York: 1983. V. 72
Cat's Paw. Richmond: 1983. V. 70
Freebooty. Indianapolis: 1976. V. 72
Hoodwink. New York: 1981. V. 72
Invitation To Murder. Arlington Heights: 1991. V. 72
The Jade Figurine. Indianapolis: 1972. V. 68; 72
A Killing in Xanadu. Richmond: 1980. V. 69; 71
Labyrinth. New York: 1980. V. 72
Masques. New York: 1981. V. 73
Panic. New York: 1972. V. 68; 72
Scattershot. New York: 1982. V. 72
She Who Sleeps. New York: 1928. V. 68
Six-Gun in Cheek. Minneapolis: 1997. V. 68
The Snatch. New York: 1971. V. 72
Snowbound. New York: 1974. V. 68
Spadework. Norfolk: 1996. V. 68; 70; 72
The Stalker. New York: 1971. V. 68; 73
Starvation Camp. Garden City: 1984. V. 69; 71
Twospot. New York: 1978. V. 72
Undercurrent. New York: 1973. V. 72
The Vanished. New York: 1973. V. 72
Wildfire. Indianapolis: 1978. V. 68

PROPERT, J. L.
A History of Miniature Art. London and New York: 1887. V. 69; 72

PROPERT, W. A.
The Russian Ballet 1921-1929. 1931. V. 68
The Russian Ballet in Western Europe 1909-1920. London: 1921. V. 73
The Russian Ballet in Western Europe 1909-1920. New York: 1921. V. 70; 72

PROPPER, MILTON
Hide the Body. New York: 1939. V. 69

PROSCH, THOMAS W.
McCarver and Tacoma. Seattle: 1906. V. 70

PROSE, e Versi per Onorare la memoria di Livia Doria Caraffa...di Alcuni Rinomati Autori. Parma: 1784. V. 68; 70

PROSE, FRANCINE
Animal Magnetism. New York: 1978. V. 68
Blue Angel. New York: 2000. V. 72
The Glorious Ones. New York: 1974. V. 72
The Lives of The Muses. Nine Women and The Artists They Inspired. New York: 2002. V. 73

PROSEK, JAMES
The Complete Angler. A Connecticut Yankee Follows in the Footsteps of Isaac Walton. 1999. V. 68

PROSPECTUS of the First Complete and Uniform Edition of the Various Memoirs of the Life of Samuel Johnson, with Numerous Annotations and Embellishments. London: 1834. V. 69

PROSSER, ELEANOR B.
Fables for You. London. V. 68

PROSSER, GEORGE FREDERICK
The Antiquities of Hampshire. Guildford: 1842. V. 73
Select Illustrations of Hampshire Comprising Picturesque Views of the Seas of the Nobility and Gentry, Lodge Entrances &c. (bound with) The Antiquities of Hampshire. 1832-1842. V. 70
Select Illustrations of the County of Surrey.... London: 1828. V. 68

PROSSER, HENRY
A Short Description of Parish Church of the Blessed Virgin Mary, in Guildford, in the County of Surrey. Guildford: 1836. V. 68; 70

PROTESTANT EPISCOPAL CHURCH. BOOK OF COMMON PRAYER
The Book of Common Prayer, and Administration of the Sacraments and Other Rites and Ceremonies, as Revised and Proposed to the Use of the Protestant Episcopal Church, at a Convention...held in Philadelphia...1785. Philadelphia: 1786. V. 68; 70

PROUDFIT, ALEXANDER
The Faithful Pastor...First Presbyterian Church in Newburyport, Oct. 4th, 1827. Newburyport: 1828. V. 72

PROUDFIT, DAVID LAW
Love Among the Gamins, and Other Poems. New York: 1877. V. 70

PROULX, E. ANNIE
Accordion Crimes. London: 1996. V. 68
Accordion Crimes. New York: 1996. V. 68; 69; 70; 72; 73
Accordion Crimes. London: 1998. V. 68
Brokeback Mountain. London: 1998. V. 70; 72
Close Range. New York: 1993. V. 72
Close Range. New York: 1999. V. 69; 70; 71; 72; 73
The Complete Dairy Foods Cookbook. Emmaus: 1982. V. 69
The Gardener's Journal and Record Book. Emmaus: 1983. V. 68; 72
Heart Songs. New York: 1988. V. 68; 69; 70; 71; 72; 73
Heart Songs. London: 1995. V. 72
Making the Best Apple Cider. Charlotte: 1980. V. 71
Postcards. New York: 1992. V. 68; 69; 70; 73
Postcards. London: 1993. V. 68; 72
The Shipping News. New York: 1993. V. 68; 69; 70; 71; 72; 73

PROUST, MARCEL
47 Lettres Inedites De Marcel Proust A Walter Berry. Paris: 1930. V. 73
L'Indifferent. New York: 1991. V. 73
A Vision of Paris. New York: 1963. V. 68

PROUT, SAMUEL
Facsimiles of Sketches Made in Flanders and Germany and Drawn on Stone by Samuel Prout. London: 1833. V. 68; 72
Hints on Light and Shadow, Composition, etc., as applicable to landscape Painting. London: 1876. V. 72

PROUTY, OLIVE HIGGINS
Conflict. Boston: 1927. V. 69; 71
Now, Voyager. Boston: 1941. V. 71; 72
White Fawn. Boston: 1931. V. 70

THE PROVIDENCE Selection of Hymns, Supplementary to Dr. Watts.. Providence: 1820. V. 73

PROVIDENCE
The City Hall, Providence. Corner-stone Laid June 24 1875. Dedicated November 14 1878 Providence Rhode Island.... Providence: 1878. V. 71

PROVIS, JOHN
Tables of the Most Useful Kind, to Facilitate Business in Several Branches of the Copper Trade, Never Before Printed.... Truro: 1801. V. 70

PROVISO LAND COMPANY
A Home at Maywood, the Place to Live. 1906. V. 68

PROVO: Pioneer Mormon City. Portland: 1942. V. 68; 73

PROWELL, SANDRA WEST
By Evil Means. New York: 1992. V. 69
By Evil Means. 1993. V. 69
By Evil Means. New York: 1993. V. 68; 71
The Killing of Monday Brown. New York: 1994. V. 71

PROWSE, D. W.
History of Newfoundland, from the English, Colonial and Foreign Records. London: 1895. V. 69

PROWSE, WILLIAM JEFFERY
Nicholas's Notes, and Sporting Prophecies, with Some Miscellaneous Poems.... London: 1870. V. 68

PRUCHA, FRANCIS PAUL
Broadax and Bayonet - The Role of The United States Army in The Development of The Northwest 1815-1860. Wisconsin: 1953. V. 72
A Guide to The Military Posts of The United States 1789-1895. Milwaukee: 1966. V. 72
Indian Peace Medals in American History. Lincoln: 1971. V. 72

PRUCHINCKI, SUZANNE SMITH
Charlotte Bronte and Mary Taylor, Early Feminists. 1999. V. 70; 73

PRUDENTIUS, AURELIUS
Aurelii Prudentii Clementis Quae Extant. Nicolaus Heinsius Dan. Fil. Amsterdam: 1667. V. 71
Opera. Interpretatione et Notis Illustravit Stephanus Chamillard, E. Soc. Jesu. . . Paris: 1687. V. 71
Quae Exstant. Amstelodami: 1667. V. 70; 73

PRUDHOMME, LOUIS MARIE
Les Crimes des Reines de France, Depuis le Commencement de la Monarchie jusqu'a Marie Antoinette. Paris: 1791. V. 68

PRUIETT, MOMAN
Moman Pruiett Criminal Lawyer. Oklahoma City: 1944. V. 70

PRULLER, WILHELM
Diary of a German Soldier. London: 1963. V. 72

PRYCE, JOHN
The Ancient British Church. 1878. V. 69

PRYCE, W. T. R.
Samuel Roberts Clock Maker. Cardiff: 1985. V. 70

PRYCE-TANNATT, E.
How to Dress Salmon Flies. 1977. V. 68

PRYNNE, J. H.
Into the Day. Saffron Walden: 1972. V. 71
News of Warring Clans. London: 1977. V. 71

PRYNNE, WILLIAM
The Aphorismes of the Kingdome. London: 1642. V. 68
Aurum Reginae; or a Compendious Tractate and Chronological Collection of Records in the Tower and Court of Exchequer Concerning Queen Gold.... London: 1668. V. 72
The Doome of Cowardize and Treachery, or a Looking Glasse for Cowardly or Corrupt Governours, and Souldiers.... London: 1643. V. 69
A Gospel Plea (interwoven with a rational and legal) for the Lawfulnes and Continuance of the Ancient Settled Maintenance and Tenthes of the Ministers of the Gospel.... London: 1653. V. 72
A Legall Vindication Of the Liberties of England Against Illegall Taxes and Presented Acts of Parliament Lately Enforced on the People.... London: 1649. V. 72

PRYOR, A. R.
A Flora of Hertfordshire. 1887. V. 69

PRYOR, SARA
My Day. Reminiscences of a Long Life. New York: 1909. V. 69; 70
Reminiscences of Peace and War. New York: 1904. V. 69; 70

PRZIBRAM, HANS
Embryogeny. An Account of the Laws Governing the Development of the Animal Egg as Ascertained through Experiment. Cambridge: 1908. V. 68

PS and QS. (P's and Q's). Boston: 1828. V. 68

PSALMANAZAR, GEORGE
An Historical and Geographical Description of Formosa, an Island Subject to the Emperor of Japan. London: 1704. V. 72

PTOLEMAEUS, CLAUDIUS
La Geografia. Venice: 1547-1548. V. 72; 73
Geografia cioe Descrittione Universale Della Terra.... Venice: 1598-1597. V. 73

THE PUBLIC Buildings of Westminster. London: 1831. V. 71

PUBLIC Eating: Oxford Symposium. 1991. V. 72

PUBLIC School Verse. Volume III: 1921-1922. 1923. V. 70

PUCK Annual 1927. V. 69

PUCKETT, J. L.
History of Oklahoma and Indian Territory and Homeseekers Guide. Vinita, OK: 1906. V. 72

PUCKETT, NEWBELL N.
Folk Beliefs of the Southern Negro. Chapel Hill: 1926. V. 71

PUCKLE, JAMES
The Club: in a Dialogue Between Father and Son. London: 1817. V. 68; 72
England's Path to Wealth and Honour; in a Dialogue Between and Englishman and a Dutchman. London: 1750. V. 71

PUCKLER MUSKAU, H. VON
Briefe Eines Verstorbenen, Ein Fragmentarisches Tagebuch aus England, Wales, Irland und Frankreich.... Stuttgart: 1831. V. 72

PUDNEY, JOHN
Beyond this Disregard. London: 1943. V. 68; 71
Commemorations. Poems. London: 1948. V. 68
South of Forty. London: 1943. V. 68; 71

PUFFENDORF, SAMUEL, FREIHERR VON
Of the Law of Nature and Nations. Oxford: 1703. V. 70; 73

PUGET SOUND NAVIGATION CO.
Puget Sound Summer Resorts. Seattle. V. 68

PUGH, EDWARD
Cambria Depicta: a Tour through North Wales. London: 1816. V. 70

PUGH, EDWIN
The Dickens Originals. London: 1912. V. 69
Tony Drum, a Cockney Boy. London: 1898. V. 69

PUGH, JOHN
A Treatise on the Science of Muscular Action. London. V. 70; 72
A Treatise on the Science of Muscular Action. 1970. V. 71

PUGHE, WILLIAM OWEN
The Cambrian Biography; or Historical Notices of Celebrated Men.... London: 1803. V. 72

PUGIN, AUGUSTUS CHARLES
Gothic Furniture. London: 1827. V. 68

PUGIN, AUGUSTUS WELBY NORTHMORE
An Apology for the Revival of Christian Architecture in England. London: 1843. V. 68; 73
Contrasts: or, a Parallel Between the Noble Edifices of the Middle Ages and Corresponding Buildings of the Present Day.... London: 1841. V. 68
Fifteenth and Sixteenth Century Ornaments. Edinburgh: 1843. V. 73
The Present State of Ecclesiastical Architecture in England. London: 1843. V. 73
Specimens of Gothic Architecture: Selected from Various Antient Edifices in England.... London: 1823. V. 71
A Treatise on Chancel Screens and Rood Lofts, Their Antiquity, Use and Symbolic Signification. London: 1851. V. 68; 72; 73
The True Principles of Pointed, or Christian Architecture. (with) An Apology for the Revival of Christian Architecture in England. London: 1853-1843. V. 73

PUGSLEY, WILLIAM
Bunker Hill: Last of the Lofty Mansions. Los Angeles: 1977. V. 68

PUIG, MANUEL
Betrayed by Rita Hayworth. New York: 1971. V. 69
Blood of Requited Love. New York: 1984. V. 68; 69; 72; 73
Buenos Aires Affair. New York: 1976. V. 68; 69; 72
Eternal Curse on the Reader of These Pages. New York: 1982. V. 69
Kiss of the Spider Woman. New York: 1979. V. 68; 69; 71; 73

PUISEUX, PIERRE
Atlas Photographique de la Lune. Paris: 1896-1910. V. 73

PULLAN, MATILDA MARIAN CHESNEY
The Lady's Manual of Fancy-Work: a Complete Instructor in Every Variety of Ornamental Needle-Work. New York: 1859. V. 72

PULLEN, H. F.
The Pullen Expedition in Search of Sir John Franklin the Original Diaries, Log and Letters of Commander W.J.S. Pullen. Toronto: 1979. V. 68

PULLEN, H. W.
The Fight at Dame Europa's School, Showing How the German Boy Thrashed the French Boy. The True Story About the Fight at Dame Europa's School; How the French Boy Began the Fight. Dame History's Tale of St. George. 1870-1871. V. 73

PULLEN-BURRY, B.
From Halifax to Vancouver. London: 1912. V. 73

PULLEYN, WILLIAM
The Etymological Compendium, or, Portfolio of Origins and Inventions . . . London: 1853. V. 71

PULLEYNE, DOUGLAS, MRS.
Spring Sorrel. New York: 1926. V. 69

PULLING, FREDERIC SANDERS
The Life and Speeches of the Marquis of Salisbury. London: 1885. V. 71

PULLMAN, PHILIP
The Amber Spyglass, His Dark Materials III. London: 2000. V. 68; 71
The Amber Spyglass. His Dark Materials III. New York: 2000. V. 69; 73
Galatea. London: 1978. V. 68; 69; 73
The Golden Compass. New York: 1995. V. 68; 71
Northern Lights. 1995. V. 70

PULMAN, G. P. R.
The Vade Mecum of Fly-Fishing for Trout. 1851. V. 68; 73

PULSZKY, THERESA
Tales and Traditions of Hungary. Redfield: 1852. V. 73

PULTENEY, WILLIAM
The Budget Opened. London: 1733. V. 73
Considerations on the Present State of Public Affairs and the Means of Raising the Necessary Supplies. London: 1779. V. 68; 70; 73

PULTON, FERDINANDO
A Collection of Sundrie Statutes, Frequent in Use; with Notes in the Margent and References to the Booke Cases and Bookes of Entries and Registers.... London: 1618. V. 72
De Pace Regis...a Treatise Declaring Which be the Great and Generall Offences of the Realme, and the Chiefe Impediments of the Peace of the King.... London: 1609. V. 72

PUNCH, W. T.
Keeping Eden, a History of Gardening in America. Boston: 1992. V. 68

PUNCTUATION *Personified: or Pointing Made Easy.* London: 1825-1827. V. 70

PUNK *Rock - 100 Nights at the Roxy.* London: 1978. V. 71

PURCHAS, SAMUEL
The Purchas Handbook. Studies of the Life Times and Writings of Samuel Purchas, 1577-1626. London: 1997. V. 73

PURCHASE, WILLIAM R.
Practical Masonry, A Guide to the Art of Stone Cutting.... London: 1904. V. 68

PURDEE, HOWELL
Pat Cleburne, Confederate General. Hillsboro: 1973. V. 70
Pat Cleburne: Confederate General. Tuscaloosa: 1977. V. 70

PRUDENT Paulina. London: 1905. V. 72

PURDON, WILLIAM
Report to the Secretary of State for India on the Navigation of the Punjab Rivers, with Description and Drawings of the Navigatonal Steam Boats Recommended. London: 1860. V. 72

PURDY, AL
Love in a Burning Building. Toronto and Montreal: 1970. V. 73

PURDY, JAMES
Cabot Wright Begins. New York: 1964. V. 70
Children Is All. New York: 1961. V. 70
The Color of Darkness: Eleven Stories and Novella. New York: 1957. V. 70
Don't Call Me by My Right Name and Other Stories. New York: 1956. V. 69; 70
Eustace Chisholm. New York: 1967. V. 70
The House of the Solitary Maggot. Garden City: 1974. V. 70
I Am Elijah Thrush. Garden City: 1972. V. 70
Jeremy's Version. Part One of Sleepers in Moon-Crowned Valleys. Garden City: 1970. V. 70
Lessons and Complaints. New York: 1978. V. 70; 73
Malcolm. New York: 1959. V. 70
Mr. Evening: a Story and Nine Poems. Los Angeles: 1968. V. 70
Mourners Below. 1981. V. 72
The Nephew. New York: 1960. V. 70
On the Rebound: a Story and Nine Poems. Los Angeles: 1970. V. 69
63: Dream Palace. New York: 1956. V. 70

PURDY, RICHARD LITTLE
Thomas Hardy: a Bibliographical Study. London: 1954. V. 72

PUREY-CUST, A. P.
The Heraldry of York Minister. Leeds: 1890-1896. V. 72

PURPURA, DOMINICK P.
The Thalamus. New York: 1966. V. 68

PURRY, JEAN P.
Description of the Province of South Carolina, Drawn Up at Charles Town in September 1731. Washington: 1837. V. 68

PURSH, F.
Flora Americae Septentrionalis, or a Systematic Arrangement and Description of the Plants of North America.... London: 1816. V. 70
Journal of Botanical Excursion in the Northeastern Parts of the States of Pennsylvania and New York, During the Year 1807. Philadelphia: 1896. V. 68

PURVIANCE, LEVI
The Biography of Elder David Purviance.... Dayton: 1848. V. 68; 69; 73

PURVIANCE, ROBERT
A Narrative of Events Which Occurred in Baltimore Town During the Revolutionary War. Baltimore: 1849. V. 73

PURVIS, J. B.
Through Uganda to Mount Elgon. London: 1909. V. 71

PUSEY, E. B.
The Real Presence of the Body and Blood of Our Lord Jesus Christ. Oxford: 1857. V. 68

PUSEY, WILLIAM
The History of Dermatology. Springfield: 1933. V. 71

THE PUSHCART Prize XIV. 1989. V. 72

PUSHKIN, ALEKSANDR SERGEEVICH
The Captain's Daughter. New York: 1971. V. 70; 72
Eugene Onegin. New York: 1964. V. 70; 73
The Golden Cockerel. New York: 1938. V. 72
The Golden Cockerel. New York: 1950. V. 69; 73
The Prose Tales of.... London: 1894. V. 69
Skazka os Tsare Saltane...(The Tale of Tsar Saltan). St. Petersburg: 1905. V. 69
The Tale of the Golden Cockerel. Waltham St. Lawrence: 1936. V. 70
Volbga (bylina of Volga). Petrograd: 1904. V. 69

PUSS in Boots. London: 1870. V. 73
PUSS in Boots. London: 1898. V. 69
PUSS in Boots. 1900. V. 71
PUSS in Boots. New York: 1907. V. 72
PUSS in Boots. New York: 1910. V. 69
PUSS in Boots. London: 1915. V. 71
PUSS in Boots. 1920. V. 69

PUSS In Boots. New York: 1934. V. 70; 72; 73

PUSS in Boots. Boston: 1947. V. 69; 73

PUTMAN, GEORGE HAVEN
Some Memories of The Civil War. New York: 1928. V. 72

PUTNAM, ELIZABETH
Mrs. Putnam's Receipt Book: and Young Housekeeper's Assistant. Boston: 1850. V. 68
Mrs. Putnam's Receipt Book and Young Housekeeper's Assistant. Boston: 1857. V. 70

PUTNAM, FRANK W.
The Plasma Proteins. New York: 1960. V. 68

PUTNAM, GEORGE H.
Books and Their Makers During the Middle Ages. New York and London: 1896-1897. V. 69
A Prisoner of War in Virginia 1864-1865. New York: 1912. V. 68; 73

PUTNAM, J. WESLEY
Playthings of Desire. New York: 1924. V. 71

PUTNAM, NINA WILCOX
Sunny Bunny. Chicago: 1918. V. 70

PUTNAM, SAMUEL
Evaporation - a Symposium: Poems and Prose. Winchester: 1923. V. 68

PUTNAM'S Library of Choice Stories. Sea Stories. New York: 1858. V. 73

PUTT, CHARLES
Essay on Civil Policy, or the Science of Legislation: Comprising the Origin and Nature of Government, Religion, Laws, Population, Wealth and Happiness. London: 1830. V. 70

PUTTICK & SIMPSON
Bibliotheca Americana. A Catalogue of Books Relating to the History and Literature of America. London: 1861. V. 70
Catalogue of a Collection of Curious and Interesting Books, Voyages and Travels, Memoirs, Criminal History...& Literary Curiosities...Early Playing Cards Including Specimens of the Greatest Rarity.... London: 1865. V. 70
Catalogue of a Collection of Rare and Curious Books and Books in Miscellaneous Literature, Natural History, the Sciences, Early Voyages, &c., Including a Selection of Duplicates from the Library of a Nobleman.... London: 1860. V. 70
Catalogue of a Large Collection of Miscellaneous Books, Consisting of Selections from Various Private Libraries, Amongst which are...Early Versions of the Scriptures in English.... London: 1861. V. 70
Catalogue of a Very Large and Interesting Collection of Engravings of Every Period and School, the Remaining Stock of an Eminent Printseller.... London: 1865. V. 70
Catalogue of an Important Assemblage of State Papers and Documents, Enriched with Numerous Royal and Other Autographs.... London: 1852. V. 70
Catalogue of an Interesting and Valuable Collection of Autograph Letters and Other Historical Documents; Including Sixty Five Original Warrants of Kings Henry VII and VIII; Forty-Seven Beautiful Letters of King Charles I...&c. London: 1852. V. 70
Catalogue of an Interesting Assemblage of Miscellaneous Property, Chiefly Removed from the Residence of Gentleman at Bayswater, Consisting of...Curious Books, Engravings...Watercolour Drawings...Sixty Pictures.... London: 1865. V. 70
Catalogue of Highly Interesting and Valuable Autograph Letters, English and Foreign...Including Those of Kings and Queens of England...Oliver Cromwell, Richard Cromwell (Rariss). Regicides and Parliamentarians. London: 1853. V. 70

PUXLEY, W. LAVALLIN
Green Islands in Glittering Seas. London: 1925. V. 71

PUYDT, EMILE DE
Les Orchidees.... Paris: 1880. V. 68; 71; 73

PUZO, MARIO
Fools Die. New York: 1978. V. 68
The Fortunate Pilgrim. New York: 1965. V. 71
The Godfather. London: 1969. V. 73
The Last Don. New York: 1996. V. 69

PYATT, EDWARD
A Climber in the West Country. London: 1970. V. 69

PYE, DANIEL
Pacific Heights. Los Angeles: 1987. V. 70

PYE, HENRY JAMES
Alfred; an Epic Poem, in Six Books. London: 1801. V. 70; 71; 72

PYE, JOHN
Notes and Memoranda Respecting the Liber Studiorum of J.M.W. Turner. London: 1879. V. 73
Patronage of British Art, an Historical Sketch.... London: 1845. V. 70; 71; 73

PYE, VIRGINIA
Half Term Holiday. London: 1943. V. 69

PYLE, HILARY
James Stephens: His Work and an Account of His Life. 1965. V. 69; 73

PYLE, HOWARD
Catalogue of Pictures by Howard Pyle. Wilmington;: 1926. V. 73
Howard Pyle's Book of Pirates. New York: 1921. V. 69
Howard Pyle's Book of the American Spirit. New York: 1923. V. 73
The Merry Adventures of Robin Hood. New York: 1883. V. 71
The Story of Champions of the Round Table. New York: 1907. V. 70
The Story of King Arthur and His Knights. New York: 1903. V. 72
The Story of King Arthur and His Knights. New York: 1909. V. 70
The Story of Sir Launcelot and His Companions. New York: 1907. V. 70

PYLE, KATHARINE
Where the Wind Blows Being Ten Fairy-Tales from Ten Nations.... New York: 1902. V. 71

PYLE, ROBERT MICHAEL
The Thunder Tree. Boston, New York: 1993. V. 72
Wintergreen. New York: 1986. V. 69

PYM, BARBARA
Excellent Women. London: 1952. V. 68; 71
A Few Green Leaves. London: 1980. V. 68
Less than Angels. London: 1955. V. 68
The Sweet Dove Died. London: 1978. V. 70
An Unsuitable Attachment. London: 1982. V. 71; 72

PYM, HORACE
Chats in the Book-room. Brasted, Kent: 1896. V. 70

PYNCHON, THOMAS
The Crying of Lot 49. Philadelphia: 1966. V. 68; 69; 70; 71; 72; 73
The Crying of Lot 49. New York: 1982. V. 70
Entropy. 1983. V. 71
Gravity's Rainbow. London: 1973. V. 69; 71
Gravity's Rainbow. New York: 1973. V. 68; 69; 70; 71; 72; 73
Mason & Dixon. New York: 1997. V. 69; 70; 71; 72
Mortality and Mercy in Vienna. London: 1970. V. 70
The Secret Integration. London: 1980. V. 70
Slow Learner. Boston: 1984. V. 69; 70
Slow Learner. Boston: 1990. V. 69
The Small Rain. London: 1982. V. 68
V. London: 1963. V. 68; 69; 70; 71
V. Philadelphia: 1963. V. 68; 69; 70; 72; 73
Vineland. Boston: 1990. V. 69; 70; 73

PYNE, GEORGE
A Rudimentary and Practical Treatise on Perspective for Beginners.... London: 1857. V. 68

PYNE, JAMES BAKER
The Lake Scenery of England. 1859. V. 71

PYNE, WILLIAM HENRY
Book with Groups of Figures (by Pyne) for Decorating Landscapes. London: 1798. V. 68; 69
On Rustic Figures in Imitation of Chalk. London: 1813. V. 69
The Twenty Ninth of May: Rare Doings at the Restoration.... London: 1825. V. 72

PYPER, ANDREW
Lost Girls. London: 2000. V. 68; 69

PYPER, GEORGE
The Romance of an Old Playhouse. Salt Lake City: 1928. V. 68; 70; 73

PYROTECHNICA Loyolana, Ignatian Fireworks, or the Fiery Jesuits Temper and Behaviour. London: 1667. V. 71

Q

QOYAWAYMA, POLINGAYSI
No Turning Back: a True Account of a Hopi Indian Girls' Struggle to Bridge the Gap Between the World of Her People and the World of the White Man. Albuquerque: 1964. V. 69

QUADRI, ANTONIO
La Piazza di San Marco in Venezia. (bound with) Il Canale Grande di Venezia. Venice: 1831-1828. V. 70

QUAIFE, MILO MILTON
Forty Six Year: the Published Writings of...1910-1955. Detroit: 1956. V. 69
The Indian Captivity of O.M. Specner. 1917. V. 68

QUAIN, JONES
The Viscera of the Human Body: Including the Organs of Digestion, Respiration, Secretion and Excretion in a Series of Plates. 1840. V. 72
The Viscera of the Human Body; Including the Organs of Digestion, Respiration, Secretion and Excretion in a Series of Plates. London: 1840. V. 70

QUAIN, RICHARD
The Anatomy of the Arteries of the Human Body With Its Applications to Pathology and Operative Surgery in Lithographic Drawings.... London: 1844. V. 68

QUAINT London: Describing a Number of Interesting Relics. London: 1870. V. 68; 71

QUALTROUGH, EDWARD F.
The Boat Sailer's Manual. New York: 1886. V. 73

QUAMMEN, DAVID
Natural Acts. New York: 1985. V. 70; 72
To Walk the Line. New York: 1970. V. 70; 73
Wild Thoughts from Wild Places. New York: 1998. V. 72

QUARENGHI, GIACOM
Fabbriche e Disegni.... Milan: 1821. V. 68; 70; 72

QUARITCH, BERNARD
A Catalogue of Books and Manuscripts Issued to Commemorate the One Hundredth Anniversary of the Firm of Bernard Quaritch 1847-1947. London: 1947. V. 70; 72
A Catalogue of Fifteen Hundred Books Remarkable for the Beauty of the Age of their Bindings.... London: 1889. V. 73
A Catalogue of Illuminated and Other Manuscripts Together with Some Works on Palaeography. London: 1931. V. 70
Contributions Towards a Dictionary of English Book-Collectors as Also of Some Foreign Collectors Whose Libraries Were Incorporated in English Collections.... London: 1892-1921. V. 71
A Rough List of Valuable, Rare and Curious Books from Various Libraries. London: 1870. V. 70

QUARITCH, WALES H. G.
Towards Angkor. London: 1937. V. 71

QUARLES' Emblems. London: 1886. V. 72

QUARLES, FRANCIS
Argalus and Parthenia. 1726. V. 72
Emblems. London: 1861. V. 70

THE QUARTO. An Artistic, Literary & Musical Quarterly. London: 1896-1898. V. 72

QUATREMER DE QUINCY, ANTOINE CHRYSOSTOME
Le Jupiter Olympien, ou l'Art de la Sculpture Antique Considere Sous un Nouveau Point de Vue.... Paris: 1814. V. 70; 72

QUAYLE, ANN
Bearing Up: a Sampling of Memories. 1995. V. 68

QUAYLE, ERIC
The Collector's Book of Children's Books. 1971. V. 72
The Collector's Book of Detective Fiction. London: 1972. V. 70; 71; 72
Old Cook Books. London: 1978. V. 70
Old Cook Books. New York: 1978. V. 70

QUEBEC BRIDGE & RAILWAY CO.
The Quebec Bridge, the Longest Single Span Bridge in the World Crossing the St. Lawrence River Seven Miles Above Quebec, Canada. Boston: 1907. V. 68

QUEBEDEAUX, RICHARD
Prime Sources of California and Nevada Local History: 151 Rare and Important City, County and State Directories 1850-1906. Glendale: 1992. V. 68

QUEEN, ELLERY, PSEUD.
Adventure of the Last Man Club. 1940. V. 73
The Adventure of the Murdered Millionaire. 1942. V. 73
The Adventures of Ellery Queen. 1934. V. 73
Calamity Town. Boston: 1942. V. 73
Calender of Crime. Boston: 1952. V. 73
Cat of Many Tails. Boston: 1949. V. 68; 71; 73
Challenge to the Reader. New York: 1938. V. 73
The Chinese Orange Mystery. 1934. V. 73
Detective Short Stories. London: 1948. V. 68
The Detective Short Story. Boston: 1942. V. 73
The Detective Short Story. 1969. V. 73
The Devil to Pay. 1938. V. 73
The Door Between. 1937. V. 71
The Dragon's Teeth. 1939. V. 69; 73
The Dragon's Teeth. New York: 1939. V. 70
The Egyptian Cross Mystery. 1932. V. 71
Ellery Queen, Master Detective. New York: 1941. V. 68
Ellery Queen's Calendar of Crime. Boston: 1952. V. 70
An Exhibition on the Occasion of the Opening of the Ellery Queen Collection. Austin: 1959. V. 68
The Female of the Species: The Great Women Detectives. Boston: 1943. V. 71
The Finishing Stroke. 1958. V. 73
The Glass Village. Boston: 1954. V. 70
The Four of Hearts. 1932. V. 71
The Four of Hearts. 1938. V. 69
The Four of Hearts. New York: 1938. V. 71
The Fourth Side of the Triangle. New York: 1966. V. 73
The French Powder Mystery. 1930. V. 73
The French Powder Mystery. New York: 1931. V. 71
The Golden Eagle Mystery. New York: 1942. V. 69
The Greek Coffin Mystery. New York: 1932. V. 68
Halfway House. New York: 1936. V. 69
The King is Dead. Boston: 1952. V. 73
Ladies in Crime. London: 1947. V. 68
The Misadventures of Sherlock Holmes. Boston: 1944. V. 68; 73
The Murderer is a Fox. Boston: 1945. V. 73
The New Adventures of Ellery Queen. 1940. V. 73
The New York Murders: an Ellery Queen Omnibus. Boston: 1953. V. 71
The Origin of Evil. Boston: 1951. V. 71
Queen's Quorum. Boston: 1951. V. 69
Queen's Quorum. New York: 1969. V. 70; 72
Rogues' Gallery. London: 1947. V. 68
The Roman Hat Mystery. 1929. V. 73
The Roman Hat Mystery. 1979. V. 69
The Scarlet Letters. Boston: 1953. V. 73
Sherlock Holmes Versus Jack the Ripper. London: 1967. V. 69; 73
The Siamese Twin Mystery. 1953. V. 73
Sporting Blood. The Great Sports Detective Stories. Boston: 1942. V. 72
Sporting Detective Stories. London: 1946. V. 68
A Study in Terror. New York: 1966. V. 73
Ten Days Wonder. Boston: 1948. V. 71; 73
There Was an Old Woman. Boston: 1943. V. 68; 69
To the Queen's Taste. London: 1949. V. 68
The Tragedy of Errors. Norfolk: 1999. V. 71

QUEEN Mab's Fairy Realm. London: 1901. V. 68; 71

QUEEN Summer or the Journey of the Lily and the Rose. London: 1891. V. 70

QUEENS of Literature of the Victorian Era. London: 1886. V. 73

QUEENS of the Circulating Library. London: 1950. V. 70

QUEER Characters. London: 1870. V. 73

QUEIROZ, ECA DE
The City and the Mountains. London: 1955. V. 71; 73
The Sweet Miracle. London: 1905. V. 71

QUEKETT, JOHN
Lectures on Histology, Delivered at the Royal College of Surgeons of England in the Session 1850-1851. London: 1850-1851. V. 71
A Practical Treatise on the Use of the Microscope. 1848. V. 69
A Practical Treatise on the Use of the Microscope. London: 1855. V. 73
A Practical Treatise on the Use of the Microscope. Lincolnwood: 1987. V. 68

QUELUS, D. DE
Histoire Naturelle du Cacao, et du Sucre, Divise en Deux Traitez qui Contiennent Plusieurs Faits Nouvea.... Amsterdam: 1720. V. 72

QUENEAU, RAYMOND
Between Blue and Blue - a Sort of Novel. London: 1967. V. 71

QUENNELL, PETER
Masques and Poems. Waltham St. Lawrence: 1922. V. 72
Poems. New York. V. 72

QUENTIN, PATRICK
File on Claudia Cragge. New York: 1938. V. 69
The Ordeal of Mrs. Snow. London: 1961. V. 73
The Ordeal of Mrs. Snow. 1962. V. 73
The Ordeal of Mrs. Snow. New York: 1962. V. 68; 71
The Ordeal of Mrs. Snow. New York: 1963. V. 72
A Puzzle for Fools. 1936. V. 73
Puzzle for Players. 1938. V. 68; 73
Puzzle for Players. New York: 1938. V. 69; 73
Puzzle for Wantons. New York: 1945. V. 68

QUERO, J. C.
Clofeta. Check-List of the Fishes of the Eastern Tropical Atlantic. Portugal: 1990. V. 69

QUERRY, RON
The Death of Bernadette Lefthand. Santa Fe: 1993. V. 69

QUERRY, RONALD B.
Growing Old at Willie Nelson's Picnic. College Station: 1983. V. 71

QUESNAY, FRANCOIS
Traite de la Gangrene.... Paris: 1771. V. 72
Traite de la Suppuration. Paris: 1749. V. 72

QUETELET, M. A.
A Treatise on Man and the Development of His Faculties. Edinburgh: 1842. V. 68

QUIA Amore Langueo. Colophon: 1902. V. 69

QUICK, DOROTHY
The Fifth Dagger. New York: 1947. V. 68; 72

QUIGGIN, A. HINGSTON
Haddon the Head Hunter. Cambridge: 1942. V. 68

QUILLER COUCH, ARTHUR THOMAS
The Astonishing History of Troy Town. by Q. London: 1888. V. 71
Green Bays: Verses and Parodies. London: 1893. V. 69
IA. London: 1896. V. 69
In Powder and Crinoline. London: 1913. V. 68
Nicky-Nan, Reservist. London: 1915. V. 68
The Sleeping Beauty and Other Fairy Tales. London. V. 70
The Sleeping Beauty and Other Fairy Tales from the Old French. London: 1910. V. 68; 73
The Sleeping Beauty and Other Fairy Tales from the Old French. New York: 1910. V. 72
The Sleeping Beauty and Other Fairy Tales from the Old French. London: 1922. V. 72
Virgil, an Address to the Boys of Sevenoaks School. Cambridge: 1930. V. 70

QUILLET, CLAUDE
Callipaedia &c. London: 1709. V. 71
Callipaedia; or the Art of Getting Pretty Children. London: 1710. V. 68; 72

QUILLET, CLAUDIUS
Callipaedia, a Poem in Four Books with Some Other Pieces. 1963. V. 68; 70

QUILLINAN, EDWARD
The King: the Lay of a Papist. 1829. V. 72

QUILLINAN, EDWARD continued
Woodcuts and Verses (Used at the Lee Priory Press). Kent: 1820. V. 68; 72

QUILTER, HARRY
Preferences in Art, Life and Literature. London: 1892. V. 70

QUIN, EDWARD
An Historical Atlas; in a Series of Maps of the World as Known at Different Periods; Constructed Upon an Uniform Scale and Coloured According to the Political Changes of Each Period. London: 1830. V. 70

QUIN, JAMES
The Life of Mr. James Quin, Comedian. London: 1887. V. 72

QUIN, MICHAEL J.
A Steam Voyage Down the Danube, with Sketches of Hungary, Wallachia, Servia and Turkey. London: 1835. V. 71; 73

QUIN, MIKE
On the Drumhead. San Francisco: 1948. V. 68; 69

QUIN, SHIRLAND
Dark Heritage. Boston: 1931. V. 71

QUIN, TARELLA
Gum Tree Brownie and Other Faerie Folk of the Never Never. Melbourne/Sydney/Adelaide: 1907. V. 71

QUINBY, J.
Catalogue of Botanical Books in the Collection of Rachel McMasters Miller Hunt. Pittsburgh: 1958-1961. V. 68; 71

QUINBY, JANE
Beatrix Potter. New York: 1954. V. 69

QUINCY, JOSEPH
Speech of the Hon...in the House of Representatives of the U.S. January 14, 1811 on the Passage of the Bill to Enable the People of the Territory of Orleans, to Form a Constitution and State Government, and for the Admission of such State into the Union. Baltimore: 1811. V. 70

QUINDLEN, ANNA
Object Lessons. New York: 1991. V. 72
One True Thing. New York: 1994. V. 70; 72

QUINIER, A.
Fournitures Pour la Marine A. Quinier 86 Rue St. Antoine, Paris, Specialite d' Armement pour la Navigation de Plaisance Tarif - Album.... Paris: 1879. V. 72

QUINN, ARTHUR HOBSON
Edith Wharton. New York: 1938. V. 70

QUINN, DANIEL
Ishmael. New York: 1992. V. 70; 72

QUINN, SEABURY
The Phantom Fighter. Sauk City: 1966. V. 72

QUINN, VERNON
War-Paint and Power-Horn On The Old Santa Fe Trail. New York: 1929. V. 72

QUINTILIAN, MARCUS FABIUS
(De Institute Oratoria). Florence: 1515. V. 73
The Declamations of Quintilian, Being an Exercitation or Praxis Upon His XII Books.... London: 1686. V. 71
Epitome Institutionum Oratoriarum. Parisiis: 1549. V. 72
Institutiones Oratorie ac Declamationes Rursus Summa Accuratione.... Paris: 1531. V. 73
Oratoris Eloquentissimi, de Instiutione Oratoria Libri XII.... Paris: 1549. V. 73
Quintilianus (Institutiones Oratoriae) Cum Commento. Venice: 1498. V. 73

QUINTUS CURTIUS
Quintus Curtius His History of the Wars of Alexander. London: 1714. V. 70; 71

QUINTUS SMYRNAEUS
Paralippomeni D'Omero. Modena: 1815. V. 68

QUIZEM, CALEB
Annals of Sporting. London: 1809. V. 68

R

R. & J. BECK, LTD.
Illustrated Catalogue of Microscopes, Object Glasses and Apparatus. Factory - Lister Works, Kentish Town. Part I. 1894. V. 71

R., G.
Alick's Adventures. New York: 1902. V. 70

RAB and His Friends. Chicago: 1908. V. 70

RAB, FORDHAM
Guide to Law of the Sea. New York: 1937. V. 70

RABAN, JONATHAN
For Love & Money. London: 1987. V. 73

The Society of the Poem. London: 1971. V. 73

RABAN, ZEEV
The Song of Solomon. Jerusalem: 1930. V. 70

RABE, DAVID
Streamers. New York: 1977. V. 68; 69

RABE, PETER
Anatomy of a Killer. New York: 1960. V. 69; 70; 72
Black Mafia. Greenwich: 1974. V. 72
Blood on the Desert. Greenwich: 1958. V. 71
Bring Me Another Corpse. Greenwich: 1959. V. 71; 72
Mission For Vengeance. Greenwich: 1958. V. 72
Time Enough To Die. Greenwich: 1959. V. 72

RABELAIS, FRANCOIS
Gargantua and Pantagruel. London: 1904. V. 71
Gargantua and Pantagruel: The Five Books Newly Translated into English by Jacques LeClercq.... New York: 1936. V. 73
Les Oeuvres. Amsterdam: 1663. V. 70; 73
The Whole Works. 1708. V. 72
Works. London: 1693-1694. V. 68
The Works. London: 1784. V. 73
The Works. 1901. V. 71; 72
Works. London: 1904. V. 73
The Works of Mr. Francis Rabelais Doctor in Physick.... London: 1921. V. 70

RABMANN, HANS RUDOLF
Ein Neuw, Lustig, Ernsthafft, Poetisch Gastmal und Gesprach Zweyer Bergen in der Loblichen Eydgnosschaffe und im Berner Gibiet Gelegen. Bern: 1606. V. 68

RACCOLTA di Tutte le Verdute che Esistevano nel Gabinetto del Duca Della Torre Rappresentanti l'Eruzioni del Monte Vesuvio. Naples: 1805. V. 68

RACCONTO Delle Sontuose Esequie Fatta alla Serenissima Isabella reina di Spagna nella Chiesa Maggiore della Citta di Milano il Giorno XXII. Milan: 1645. V. 68 70

RACH WOLSKI, OZELIA
The Desert Whispers. Philadelphia: 1942. V. 70

RACINE, JEAN
Oeuvres. Paris: 1810. V. 70

RACINE, JEAN BAPTISTE
Oeuvres Completes de Jean Racine. Paris: 1811. V. 69

RACINE WAGON AND CARRIAGE CO.
Illustrated Catalogue of the Leading Styles of Buggies, Carriages, Road Wagons, Spring Wagons, etc. 1896. 1896. V. 68

RACINET, ALBERT
L'Ornement Polychrome. Paris: 1872. V. 68

RACINET, M. A.
Le Costume Historique, Cinq Cents Planches, Trois Cents en Couleurs, or et Argent. Deux Cents en Camaieu. Paris: 1888. V. 68

RACKHAM, ARTHUR
The Allies' Fairy Book.... London. V. 70
The Arthur Rackham Fairy Book. 1933. V. 72
The Arthur Rackham Fairy Book. London: 1933. V. 70; 73
Arthur Rackham's Book of Pictures. London: 1913. V. 72
Arthur Rackham's Book of Pictures. New York: 1913. V. 68
Arthur Rackham's Book of Pictures. 1923. V. 70
Arthur Rackham's Book of Pictures. New York: 1960. V. 70
Some British Ballads. New York: 1919. V. 71

RACKHAM, BERNARD
A Book of Porcelain. London: 1910. V. 72

RACZ, ISTVAN
Art Treasures of Medieval Finland. London: 1962. V. 72

RADAU, MICHAEL
Orator Extemporaneus, seu Artis Oratoriae Breviarium.... Amsterdam: 1673. V. 73

RADBILL, SAMUEL X.
Bibliography of Medical Ex Libris Literature. Los Angeles: 1951. V. 68; 73

RADCLIFF, EBENEZER
A Funeral Oration for His Most Sacred Majesty King George the Second. London: 1760. V. 73

RADCLIFFE, ANN
The Italian, or Confessional of the Black Penitents. London: 1811. V. 70
A Journey Made in the Summer of 1794, through Holland the Western Frontier of Germany, with a return Down the Rhine, to Which are Added, Observations During a Tour to the Lakes of Lancashire, Westmoreland and Cumberland. London: 1795. V. 73

RADCLIFFE, CHARLES BLAND
Vital Motion as a Mode of Physical Motion. London: 1876. V. 68

RADCLIFFE, JOHN
Bibliotheca Chethamensis; Sive Bibliothecae Publicae Mancuniensis ab Humfredo Chetham, Armigero, Fundatae Catalogus Exhibens Libros in Varias classes Pro Varietate Argumenti Distributos. Manchester: 1791-1883. V. 70

RADCLIFFE, W.
Fishing from the Earliest Times. 1921. V. 68; 73

RADCLYFFE, C. R. E.
Big Game Shooting in Alaska. London: 1904. V. 69; 71

RADCLYFFE, C. W.
The Palace of Blenheim. Oxford: 1842. V. 70

RADDALL, THOMAS H.
The Markland Sagas. Liverpool: 1934. V. 70
West Novas. A History of the West Nova Scotia Regiment. Liverpool: 1947. V. 73

RADER, PAUL
Big Bug. New York: 1932. V. 69

RADFORD, DOLLIE
The Young Gardeners' Kalendar. London: 1904. V. 68

RADICAL Monday. A Letter from Bob in Botham to His Cousin Bob in the Country, Containing an Account of that Glorious Day!!. Newcastle-upon-Tyne: 1821. V. 73

RADIN, PAUL
The Story of the American Indian. Garden City: 1937. V. 69

RADLEY, SHEILA
Death and the Maiden. London: 1978. V. 69

RADSTOCK, WILLIAM WALDEGRAVE, 1ST BARON
The British Flag Triumphant!. London: 1806. V. 70

RAE, COLIN
Malaboch. London: 1898. V. 71

RAE, ISOBEL
The Anatomist. London: 1964. V. 68

RAE, JOHN
Granny Goose. Joliet: 1926. V. 71
Lucky Locket. Minneapolis: 1928. V. 73

RAE, W. FRASER
Newfoundland to Manitoba. London: 1881. V. 73

RAE BROWN, CAMPBELL
Very Long Odds and a Strange Finish. London: 1893. V. 68

RAFFALOVICH, ANDRE
The Thread and the Path. London: 1895. V. 69

RAFFEL, DAWN
In the Year of Long Division. New York: 1995. V. 72

RAFFERTY, T. N.
The Artificial Pheumothorax in Pulmonary Tuberculosis Including.... New York: 1944. V. 71

RAFFLES, SOPHIA
Memoir of the Life and Public Service of Sir Thomas Stanford Raffles. London: 1830. V. 71
Memoirs of the Life and Public Services of Sir Thomas Stamford Raffles, Particularly in the Government of Java 1811-1816. London: 1835. V. 71

RAFINESQUE, C. S.
Ancient History, or Annals of Kentucky.... Frankfort: 1824. V. 72
Autikon Botanikon, Icones Plantarum Select.... Philadelphia: 1815-1840. V. 70
The Complete Writings.... New York...London: 1864. V. 73
A Life of Travels and Researches in North America and South Europe, or Outlines of the Life, Travels and Researches.... Philadelphia: 1836. V. 70
A Monograph of the Fluviatile Vivalve Shells of the River Ohio.... Philadelphia: 1832. V. 68; 71; 73
New Genera and Species of Trees and Shrubs of North America, and Other Regions of the Earth.... Jamaica Plains: 1943. V. 72

RAGGE, D. R.
Grasshoppers, Crickets and Cockroaches of the British Isles. London: 1965. V. 70

RAGGUAGLIO Delle Nozze Della Maesta di Filippo Quinto e di Elisabetta Farnese...Celebre in Parma l'Anno 1714. Parma: 1717. V. 68; 70

RAGLAND, J. FARLEY
Rhymes of the Times. New York: 1946. V. 70

RAGUE, KATE
Jane Austen. Paris: 1914. V. 70; 73

RAGUENET, A.
Materials and Documents of Architecture and Sculpture. Chicago: 1925. V. 71

RAHIR, EDOUARD
La Bibliotheque de Feu Edoaurd Rahir Ancien Libraire. Paris: 1930. V. 73

RAHT, CARLYSLE G.
The Romance of Davis Mountains and Big Bend Country: a History. El Paso: 1919. V. 69; 70

RAIBAUD, B. L.
Traite de la Garantie des Matieres et Ouvrages d'or et d'Argent. 1825. V. 68

RAIKES, THOMAS
A Portion of the Journal...from 1831 to 1847. London: 1856-1857. V. 68

RAILWAY Alphabet. London. V. 73

A RAILWAY Book for Girls and Boys. London: 1925. V. 72

THE RAILWAY Train. London: 1905. V. 73

RAILWAYS and the Board of Trade. London: 1845. V. 71

RAINE, CRAIG
The Electrification of the Soviet Union. London: 1986. V. 69

RAINE, KATHLEEN
Cecil Collins. Ipswich: 1979. V. 70
City of Imagination. London: 1991. V. 71
Collected Poems 1935-1980. London: 1981. V. 70
From Blake to a Vision. Yeats Papers XVII. Dublin: 1979. V. 71
India Seen Afar. Bideford: 1990. V. 70; 71
The Inner Journey of the Poet and Other Papers. London: 1982. V. 70
Living With Mystery. Poems 1987-91. Ipswich: 1992. V. 70
The Presence. Poems 1984-87. Ipswich: 1987. V. 70; 71
Selected Poems. Ipswich: 1988. V. 70
Stone and Flower. Poems 1935-1943. London: 1943. V. 68; 71
The Year One. London: 1952. V. 71

RAINE, MACLEOD
Cattle. Garden City: 1930. V. 71

RAINE, NORMA REILLY
Tugboat Annie. New York: 1934. V. 69; 72

RAINE, WILLIAM MAC LEOD
Cattle, Cowboys and Rangers. New York: 1930. V. 69
The Dam Yank. Boston: 1942. V. 69
Glory Hole. Boston: 1952. V. 69
The Highgrader. New York: 1915. V. 69; 70
Moran Beats Back. Boston: 1939. V. 70
Troubled Waters. Garden City: 1925. V. 69

RAINERIUS DE PISIS
Pantheologia, Sive Summa Universae Theologiae. Nuremberg: 1477. V. 69

RAINES, C. W.
Bibliography of Texas, Being a Descriptive List of Books, Pamphlets, and Documents Relating to Texas...Since 1536.... Austin: 1934. V. 70

RAINEY, GEORGE
The Cherokee Strip. 1925. V. 71
The Cherokee Strip. Enid: 1933. V. 70
No Man's Land, The Historic Story of A Landed Orphan. Enid: 1937. V. 71; 72

RAINEY, GEORGE, MRS.
In Memory. Enid: 1949. V. 68

RAINOLDES, JOHN
The Overthrow of Stage-Plays, by the Way of Controversie Betwixt D. Gager and D. Rainoldes. Middelburg: 1599. V. 71
The Summe of the Conference Beteene John Rainoldes and John Hart.. Londini: 1584. V. 73

RAINSFORD, W. S.
The Land of the Lion. 1909. V. 72

RAISTRICK, ARTHUR
A History of Lead Mining in the Pennines. London: 1965. V. 71
Quakers in Science and Industry. London: 1950. V. 70; 72

RAIT, JAMES
The Relative Value of Round and Sawn Timber.... London: 1862. V. 70

RAIZIZUN, MAY MARTINEZ
Ninos Alegres. Dallas: 1942. V. 71

RAJAN, B.
Focus One. London: 1945. V. 70

RAK, MARY K.
A Cowman's Wife. Boston: 1934. V. 71
A Cowman's Wife. Boston: 1936. V. 71

THE RAKE'S Adventures; or a Trip through the Bills of Mortality Wherein Are Related the Several Remarkable and Humorous Passages that Occur'd to the Author. London: 1731?. V. 73

RAKOCY, WILLIAM
...For Art Anything. 1972. V. 70; 72; 73
Ghosts of Kingston and Hillsboro New Mexico: a Pictorial Documentary of the Great Black Range Country. 1983. V. 70; 72; 73

RAKOSI, CARL
The Collected Prose of Carl Rakosi. Orono: 1983. V. 68; 71

RALEIGH, MICHAEL
A Body in Belmont Harbor. New York: 1993. V. 68; 69; 71

RALEIGH, WALTER
An Aridgement of Sir Walter Raleigh's History of the World in Five Books. London: 1698. V. 68
Judicious and Select Essayes and Observations...Upon the First Invention of Shipping (by Sea). London: 1650. V. 69
The Letters of Sir Walter Raleigh (1879-1922). New York: 1926. V. 68; 72

RALFS, J.
The British Desmidieae. 1848. V. 73

RALPH, J.
Our Great West. New York: 1893. V. 69

RALPH, JAMES
The Other Side of the Question: or an Attempt to Rescue the Characters of the Two Royal Sisters, Q. Mary and Q. Ann, Out of the Hands of the D-D of (Marlborough). London: 1742. V. 72
The Taste of the Town; or, a Guide to All Publick Diversions.... London: 1731. V. 69; 70

RALPH, JULIAN
On Canada's Frontier. New York: 1892. V. 68; 73

RALPH Walker, Architect of Voorhees Gmelin: Walker Voorhees Walker Foley; Smith Voorhees Walker Smith and Smith. New York: 1957. V. 68; 72

RAMADHANA SENA
A Dictionary in Persian and English, with the Pronunciation of Persian Words in the Roman Character. Calcutta: 1841. V. 71

RAMASWAMY, CAVELLY VENKATA
A Digest of the Different Castes of India, with Account of Them. Madras: 1837. V. 68

THE RAMBLE in the Woods; or a Dialogue on Man And Animals. New Haven: 1829. V. 71

RAME, DAVID
The Sun Shall Greet Them. New York: 1941. V. 69

RAMEY, W. SANFORD
Kings of The Battlefield. Philadelphia: 1887. V. 72

RAMMELL, THOMAS WEBSTER
Report to the General Board of Health on a Preliminary Inquiry into the Sewerage, Drainage and Supply of Water, and the Sanitary Condition of the Inhabitants of the City and Borough of Salisbury, in the County of Wilts. London: 1851. V. 73

RAMMOHUN ROY, RAJA
Kane Upanishad. Calcutta: 1816. V. 71

RAMON Y CAJAL, SANTIAGO
Degeneration and Regeneration of the Nervous System. London: 1928. V. 68
Histology. Baltimore: 1933. V. 68; 73
Recollections of My Life. Philadelphia: 1937. V. 73
Studies on Vertebrate Neurogenesis. Springfield: 1960. V. 68

RAMOS, GRACILIANO
Anguish. New York: 1946. V. 69

RAMPA, T. LOBSANG
The Third Eye: The Autobiogrpahy of a Tibetan Lama. Garden City: 1957. V. 69

RAMSAY, A. C.
The Old Glaciers of Switzerland and North Wales. London: 1860. V. 69

RAMSAY, ALLAN
Christ's - Kirk on the Green. Edinburgh: 1718. V. 68
The Gentle Shepherd. Edinburgh: 1808. V. 68
Poems on Several Occasions. Aberdeen: 1776. V. 73
The Tea-Table Miscellany. Glasgow: 1871. V. 68; 72

RAMSAY, DAVID
The History of the Revolution in South Carolina, from a British Province to an Indepdendent State. Trenton: 1785. V. 68

RAMSAY, EDWARD BANNERMAN
Reminiscences of Scottish Life and Character. Edinburgh: 1872. V. 68

RAMSAY, GEORGE
A New Dictionary of Anecdotes, Illustrative of Character and Events from Genuine Sources. London: 1822. V. 70

RAMSAY, SMITH W.
In Southern Seas. London: 1924. V. 71

RAMSAY, WILLIAM
Elaminthologia (in Greek), or, some Physical Considerations of the Matter, Orgination and Several Species of Wormes, Macerating and Direfully Cruciating Every Part of the Bodies of Mankind.... London: 1668. V. 68; 73

RAMSAYE, TERRY
A Million and One Nights: the History of the Motion Picture. New York: 1926. V. 69; 70; 71; 73

RAMSBOTTOM, RICHARD
Fractions Anatomized; or, the Doctrine of Parts Made Plain and Easy to the Meanest Capicity. London: 1762. V. 68

RAMSDEN, J.
The Bronte Homeland; or Misrpheresentations Rectified. 1897. V. 73

RAMSEY, FREDERIC
Been Here and Gone. London: 1960. V. 73
Been Here and Gone. New Brunswick: 1960. V. 73
Jazzmen. New York: 1939. V. 70; 72; 73

RAMSEY, JOHN G. M.
Annals of Tennessee to the End of the Eighteenth Century.... Charleston: 1853. V. 68
Annals of Tennessee to the End of the Eighteenth Century.... Philadelphia: 1853. V. 71; 73

RANCE, PATRICK
Great British Cheese Book. London: 1982. V. 72

RAND, A. L.
The Distribution and Habits of Madagascar Birds.... London: 1936. V. 69

RAND, AYN
Atlas Shrugged. New York: 1957. V. 68; 69; 73
Atlas Shrugged. New York: 1967. V. 71
The Ayn Rand Letter. Palo Alto: 1979. V. 69
Capitalism: the Unknown Ideal. New York: 1966. V. 68; 69; 71
For the New Itellectual. New York: 1961. V. 70
The Fountainhead. Indianapolis and New York: 1943. V. 68; 71; 72
The Fountainhead. London: 1947. V. 73
Night of January 16th. New York: 1961-1968. V. 69
Philosophy: Who Needs It?. Indianapolis: 1982. V. 69
The Virtue of Selfishness. New York: 1961-1964. V. 69
We the Living. New York: 1936. V. 72; 73

RAND, EDWARD SPRAGUE
The Rhododendron and American Plants.... Boston: 1871. V. 68; 72; 73

RAND MC NALLY & CO.
Libby's Atlas of the World. Chicago: 1891. V. 71

RAND, MC NALLY & CO.
Rand, McNally & Co.'s Pictorial Chicago and Illustrated World's Columbian Exposition. Chicago: 1893. V. 70

RAND MC NALLY & CO.
Universal Atlas of the World. Chicago: 1898. V. 71
A Week at the Fair, Illustrating the Exhibits and Wonders of the World's Columbian Exposition. Chicago: 1893. V. 70

RAND, OLIVE
A Vacation Excursion from Massachusetts Bay to Puget Sound by O.R. Manchester: 1884. V. 68; 73

RANDALL, ALICE
The Wind Done Gone. Boston/New York: 2001. V. 69; 72

RANDALL, DAVID A.
The Adventure of the Notorious Forger. San Francisco: 1978. V. 70

RANDALL, E. O.
The Master Pieces of the Ohio Mound Builders - the Hilltop Fortifiations Including Fort Ancient. Columbus: 1908. V. 69
The Masterpieces of the Ohio Mound Builders. 1916. V. 69

RANDALL, J. T.
Nature and Structure Of Collagen. London: 1953. V. 68

RANDALL, JANE
When Toys Could Talk. Akron: 1934. V. 70

RANDALL Jarrell 1914-1965. New York: 1967. V. 68

RANDALL, JOHN
Our Coal and Iron Industries, and the Men WHo Have Wrought in Connection With Them - The Wilkinsons.... Barrow-in-Furness: 1917. V. 70

RANDALL, L. M. C.
Medieval and Renaissance Manuscripts in the Walters Art Gallery. Volume II: France 1420-1540. Parts I and II. Baltimore & London: 1992. V. 70

RANDALL, MARGARET
Giant of Tears. New York: 1959. V. 71

RANDALL, WALTER C.
Nervous Control of the Heart. Baltimore: 1965. V. 68

RANDALL MAC IVER, DAVID
Mediaeval Rhodesia. London: 1906. V. 71

RANDISI, ROBERT J.
The Eyes Have It. New York: 1984. V. 69; 70
Mean Streets. New York: 1986. V. 70

RANDLE, E. H.
Characteristics of the Southern Negro. New York and Washington: 1910. V. 72

RANDOLF, MARION
Grim Grow the Lilacs. New York: 1941. V. 72

RANDOLPH, FRANCIS LEWIS
Studies for a Byron Bibliography. Lititz: 1979. V. 72

RANDOLPH, J.
A Memoir on the Life and Character of Philip Syng Physick, MD. Philadelphia: 1839. V. 73

RANDOLPH, L. F.
Garden Irises. St. Louis: 1959. V. 68

RANHOFER, CHARLES
Epicurean. New York: 1971. V. 69; 73

RANJITSINHJI, K. S.
The Jubilee Book of Cricket. Edinburgh and London: 1898. V. 70

THE RANK and Talent of the Time. London: 1861. V. 71

RANKE, LEOPOLD
The History of the Popes, Their Church and State, in the 16th and 17th Centuries. Philadelphia: 1844. V. 71
The Popes of Rome: Their Ecclesiastical and Political History During the Sixteenth and Seventeenth Centuries. London: 1866. V. 73

RANKEN, W. H. L.
The Dominion of Australia. London: 1874. V. 69; 71

RANKIN, ARTHUR E.
Livingstone Returned. NY: 1955. V. 72

RANKIN, DANIEL JAMES
The Zambesi Basin and Nyassaland. Edinburgh: 1893. V. 69; 71

RANKIN, DANIEL S.
Kate Chopin and Her Creole Stories. Philadelphia: 1932. V. 69

RANKIN, IAN
The Black Book. London: 1993. V. 69; 70
The Black Book. New York: 1993. V. 70
The Black Book. New York: 1994. V. 69
The Black Foot. New York: 1994. V. 68
Blood Hunt. London: 1995. V. 70; 73
Dead Souls. London: 1999. V. 69; 70; 71; 72
Death is Not the End. London: 1998. V. 70; 72
The Falls. London: 2001. V. 69; 72
The Flood. Edinburgh: 1986. V. 70; 71
The Hanging Garden. London: 1998. V. 69; 70; 71
Hide and Seek. London: 1991. V. 68; 69; 70; 72; 73
Knots and Crosses. London: 1987. V. 71; 73
Knots and Crosses. New York: 1987. V. 71
Rebus: the Early Years. London: 1999. V. 69; 70; 71
Resurrection Men. London: 2001. V. 71; 72
Set in Darkness. London: 2000. V. 68
Strip Jack. London: 1992. V. 68; 69; 70; 71; 72
Strip Jack. New York: 1994. V. 69
Watchman. New York: 1991. V. 69; 70; 71; 72; 73
Westwind. London: 1990. V. 70
Witch Hunt. London: 1993. V. 70
Wolfman. London: 1992. V. 73

RANKIN, M. WILSON
Reminiscences of Frontier Days. Boulder: 1935. V. 72
Reminiscences of Frontier Days. Denver: 1938. V. 72

RANKIN, REGINALD
The Royal Ordering of Gardens. London: 1909. V. 68
A Tour in the Himalayas and Beyond. London: 1930. V. 71

RANKINE, DAVID
A Popular Exposition of the Effect of Forces Applied to Draught. Glasgow: 1828. V. 71

RANKINE, W. J. M.
A Manual of Applied Mechanics. London: 1868. V. 73

RANNEY, AMBROSE L.
Eye Strain in Health and Disease. Philadelphia: 1897. V. 71; 73

RANNIT, ALEKSIS
Signum et Verbum. New Rochelle: 1981. V. 73

RANSOM, HARRY H.
Texas Quarterly: Image of Mexico, the General Motors of Mexico Collection of Mexican Graphic Art. 1969. V. 70
Texas Quarterly: Image of Mexico: The General Motors of Mexico Collection of Mexican Graphic Art. Austin: 1969. V. 71

RANSOM, JOHN CROWE
Chills and Fever. New York: 1924. V. 68; 70
Grace After Meat. London: 1924. V. 70
Selected Poems. New York: 1945. V. 69; 70
Two Gentlemen in Bonds. New York: 1927. V. 68; 70
The World's Body. New York: 1938. V. 70

RANSOM, WILL
Private Presses and Their Books. New York: 1929. V. 69

RANSOME, ARTHUR
Aladdin and His Wonderful Lamp. London: 1919. V. 72
The Big Six. London: 1940. V. 71
The Book of Friendship. London And Edinburgh. V. 73
Coot Club. 1944. V. 72
Great Northern?. London: 1947. V. 70; 71
Missee Lee. London: 1941. V. 73
Missee Lee. 1947. V. 72
Old Peter's Russian Tales. London: 1927. V. 71
Pigeon Post. London: 1936. V. 71
Pigeon Post. 1953. V. 71
Secret Water. London: 1940. V. 71
Secret Water. 1955. V. 71
The Soldier and Death. London: 1945. V. 68
Swallowdale. London: 1931. V. 73
We Didn't Mean to Go to Sea. London: 1937. V. 70; 71
We Didn't Mean to Go to Sea. 1947. V. 72
Winter Holiday. London: 1933. V. 71
Winter Holiday. 1946. V. 73

RAPAHEL SANZIO D'URBINO
Imagines Veteris ac Novi Testamenti. Roma: 1675. V. 73

THE RAPE: A Poem Humbly Inscribed to the Ladies. London: 1768. V. 73

RAPED on the Railway. London: 1899. V. 70

RAPELJE, GEORGE
A Narrative of Excursions, Voyages and Travels, Performed at Different Periods in America, Europe, Asia and Africa. New York: 1834. V. 69

RAPHAEL, FREDERICK
Obbligato. London: 1956. V. 72

RAPHAEL, JOHN R.
Through Unknown Nigeria. London. V. 71

RAPHAEL, S.
The Oak Spring Garden Library. Volume I. An Oak Spring Sylva. Upperville: 1989. V. 68

RAPHAEL'S Witch!!!. London: 1850. V. 69

RAPHAEL'S LTD., HATTON GARDEN
Catalogue. London: 1911. V. 71

RAPHAELSON, SAMSON
Accent on Youth and White Man. New York: 1935. V. 71
The Human Nature of Playwriting. New York: 1949. V. 68; 71
Skylark. New York: 1939. V. 73
Young Love. New York: 1928. V. 71

RAPHALL, M. J.
Bible View of Slavery. A Discourse Delivered at the Jewish Synagogue Bnai Jeshurum New York. New York: 1861. V. 68

RAPIER, RICHARD C.
Remunerative Railways for New Countries, with Some Account of the First Railway in China. London: 1878. V. 68

RAPIN, H.
La Sculpture Decorative Moderne. (with) Sculpture Decorative a L'Expositon des Arts Decoratifs de 1925. Paris. V. 71

RAPIN, RENE
The Modest Critick; or, Remarks Upon the Most Eminent Historians, Antient and Modern.... London: 1689. V. 68

RAPOPORT, EDA
The Raven. New York: 1939. V. 69

RAPOU, A.
Typhoid Fever and Its Homoeopathic Treatment. Cincinnati: 1853. V. 71

RARE Old Chinese Porcelains Collected by Sir William Bennett. London: 1910. V. 72

RAREY, J. S.
The Modern Art of Taming Wild Horses. Columbus: 1857. V. 68

RASCOE, BURTON
Belle Starr: The Bandit Queen. New York: 1941. V. 69

RASHLEIGH, PHILIP
Specimens of British Minerals, Selected from the Cabinet of Philip Rashleigh.... London: 1797-1802. V. 70

RASK, ERASMUS
A Grammar of the Icelandic of Old Norse Tongue. London: 1843. V. 68; 73

RASKIN, SAUL
Land of Palestine. New York: 1947. V. 70

RASMUSSEN, KNUD JOHAN VICTOR
Greenland by the Polar Sea. The Story of the Thule Expediton from Melville Bay to Cape Morris Jessup. London: 1921. V. 71

RASMUSSEN, THEODORE ANDREW
The Principal Nervous Pathways. Neurological Charts and Schemas with Explanatory Notes. New York: 1933. V. 72

RASPE, RUDOLF ERICH
Original Travels and Surprising Adventures of Baron Munchausen. Boston: 1889. V. 71
The Singular Adventures of Baron Munchausen. New York: 1952. V. 68
The Surprising Adventures of Baron Munchausen. London: 1895. V. 73
The Surprising Travels and Adventures of Baron Munchausen. London: 1902. V. 70; 71
The Travels of Baron Munchausen. New York: 1929. V. 68

RASSWEILER, HENRY H.
Portfolio of Life; or, a Popular Study of the House in Which We Live. Fully Illustrated with a Complete Set of Anatomical Plates and Manikins. Chicago: 1891. V. 72

RASTELL, JOHN
The Four Elements. 1971. V. 71
Les Termes de la Ley; or, Certaine Difficult and Obscure Words and Termes of the Common Lawes and Statutes of this Realme Now in Use Expounded and Explained. London: 1642. V. 73

RATCHFORD, FANNY
Between the Lines. Letters and Memoranda Interchanged by H. Buxton Forman and Thomas J. Wise. Austin: 1945. V. 70
The Brontes Web of Childhood. New York: 1941. V. 70; 73
The Story of Champ D'asile as Told by Two of the Colonists. Dallas: 1937. V. 73

RATCLIFF, CARTER
John Singer Sargent. New York: 1982. V. 73

RATCLIFFE, BILL
Utah II. Portland: 1981. V. 69

RATCLIFFE, DOROTHY UNA
Dale Dramas. London: 1923. V. 71
Nightlights. London: 1929. V. 71

RATFORD, JENKIN
The Trial of Jenkin Ratford, One of the British Seamen Who Were Taken Out of the American Frigate Chesapeake, When Searched by the Leopard Man of War.... Glasgow: 1807. V. 70

RATH, E. J.
Elope If You Must. New York: 1926. V. 71
The Flying Courtship. New York: 1928. V. 71; 72
When the Devil Was Sick. New York: 1926. V. 72

RATH, VIRGINIA
Epitaph for Lydia. Garden City: 1942. V. 69

RATHBONE, PERRY T.
Westward the Way. St. Louis: 1954. V. 68

RATHBONE, R.
Unit Jewellery. London: 1921. V. 71

RATHBONE, RICHARD A.
Death in the Drawing Room. New York: 1954. V. 69

RATHBORNE, AARON
The Svrveyor in Foure Books. London: 1616. V. 71

RATHBUN, M. J.
The Cancroid Crabs of America of the Families Euryalidae, Portunidae, Atelecyclidae, Cancridae and Xanthidae. Washington;: 1930. V. 71
The Grapsoid Crabs of America. Washington: 1918. V. 71
The Oxystomatous and Allied Crabs of America. Washington: 1937. V. 73
The Spider Crabs of America. Washington: 1925. V. 69
The Trapsoid Crabs of America. Wasington: 1937. V. 73

RATHMANN, PEGGY
Officer Buckle and Gloria. New York: 1995. V. 72

RATTENBURY, JOHN
Memoirs of a Smuggler.... Sidmouth: 1837. V. 72

RATTENBURY, RICHARD C.
Packing Iron- Gun Leather of the Frontier West. Millwood, NY: 1993. V. 71

RATTI, ABATE ACHILLE
Climbs on Alpine Peaks. London: 1923. V. 69

RATTIGAN, TERENCE
The Deep Blue Sea - a Play. London: 1952. V. 69
French without Tears - a Play in Three Acts. London: 1937. V. 69
Separate Tables - Two Plays. London: 1955. V. 69; 73
The Winslow Boy - a Play in Four Acts. New York: 1948. V. 69

RATTRAY, ALEXANDER
Vancouver Island and British Columbia. London: 1862. V. 71

RATTRAY, J.
A Revision of the Genus Coscinodiscus and Some Allied Genera. Edinburgh: 1889. V. 73

RATTRAY, R. S.
Ashanti Law and Constitution. Oxford: 1929. V. 69
Hausa Folk-Lore, Customs, Proverbs, Etc. Oxford: 1913. V. 71

RAUCH, FRANCOIS ANTOINE
Regeneration de la Nature Vegetale, ou Recherches sur les Moyens de Recreer, dans tous Les Climats, Les Anciennes Temperatures et l'Ordre Primitif des Saisons.... Paris: 1818. V. 69

RAUCHER, HERMAN
Summer of '42. New York: 1971. V. 71

RAUCOURT DE CHARLEVILLE, ANTOINE
A Manual of Lithography, or a Memoir on the Lithographical Experiments Made in Paris.... London: 1820. V. 68; 72
Memoire sur les Experiences Lithographiqes (sic) Faites a l'Ecole Royale des Ponts et Chaussees de France; ou Manuel Theorique et Pratique du Dessinateur et de l'Imprimeur Lithographes. Toulon: 1819. V. 68; 72

RAUH, W.
Bromeliads for Home, Garden and Greenhouse. 1979. V. 73
Bromeliads for Home, Garden and Greenhouse. Poole: 1979. V. 68

RAULSTON, MARION C.
Memories of Owen Hymprey Churchill and His Family. 1950. V. 68; 71

RAUSING, G.
The Bow. 1967. V. 69

RAUTHMEL, RICHARD
The Roman Antiquities of Overborough. London: 1746. V. 71
The Roman Antiquities of Overborough. Kirkby Lonsdale: 1824. V. 71

RAVATON, HUGUES
Chirurgie D'Armee ou Traite des Plaies d'armes a feu, Et d'Armes Blanches avec des Observations sur ces Maladies.... Paris: 1768. V. 73

RAVEL, JEROME
Raoul, or the Magic Star.... New York: 1849. V. 70

RAVEN, CHARLES E.
English Naturalists from Neckam to Ray, a Study of the Making of the Modern World. Cambridge: 1947. V. 72
John Ray, Naturalist. Cambridge: 1942. V. 68
John Ray, Naturalist. Cambridge: 1950. V. 68

RAVEN, P. H.
The Genus Epilobium (Onagraceae) in Australasia.... Christchurch: 1976. V. 72

RAVEN, SIMON
Brother Cain. London: 1959. V. 72
Close of Play. London: 1962. V. 70
Doctors Wear Scarlet - a Romantic Tale. London: 1966. V. 73

RAVENEL, BEATRICE ST. JULIEN
Architects of Charleston. Charleston: 1945. V. 71
A Sketch of the History of South Carolina to the Close of the Proprietary Government by the Revolution of 1719. Charleston: 1856. V. 71

RAVENEL, HENRY WILLIAM
The Private Journal of Henry William Ravenel 1859-1887. Columbia: 1947. V. 68

RAVENHILL, A.
The Native Tribes of British Columbia. Victoria: 1938. V. 69

RAVEN-HILL, L.
The Butterfly. London: 1893. V. 71

RAVISIUS, TEXTOR
De Memorabilibus et Claris Mulieribus Aliquot Diversorum Scriptorum Opera. Parisiis: 1521. V. 69; 72

RAWLE, E. J.
Annals of the Ancient Royal Forest of Exmoor. Taunton: 1893. V. 68

RAWLING, C. J.
History of the First Regiment Virginia Infantry. Philadelphia: 1887. V. 71

RAWLINGS, MARJORIE KINNAN
Cross Creek. New York: 1942. V. 69; 70
Cross Creek Cookery. New York: 1942. V. 69; 73
The Marjorie Rawlings Reader. New York: 1956. V. 69
The Sojourner. New York: 1953. V. 69; 70
The Yearling. New York: 1938. V. 71; 72; 73
The Yearling. New York: 1939. V. 70
The Yearling. New York: 1940. V. 71; 73
The Yearling. New York: 1946. V. 68

RAWLINSON, GEORGE
Ancient Egypt. The Story of The Nations Series. London: 1895. V. 72

RAWLINSON, W. G.
The Water-Colours of J. M. W. Turner. London. V. 72

RAWNSLEY, HARDWICK DRUMMOND
The Book of Bristol Sonnets. London: 1877. V. 71
Flower-Time in the Oberland. Glasgow: 1904. V. 71
Harvey Goodwin, Bishop of Carlisle. London: 1896. V. 71; 72
Henry Whitehead 1825-1896. A Memorial Sketch. Glasgow: 1898. V. 71; 72
Literary Associations of the English Lakes. Glasgow: 1894. V. 71
Poems at Home and Abroad. Glasgow: 1909. V. 71
The Resurrection of Oldest Egypt. Laleham: 1904. V. 71
The Resurrection of Oldest Egypt. Staines: 1904. V. 71
Sonnets Round the Coast. London: 1887. V. 71
The Undoing of Harcla: a Ballad of Cumberland. London: 1892. V. 71
Valete. Glasgow: 1893. V. 71

RAWORTH, TOM
Lion Lion. London: 1970. V. 71
A Serial Biography. London: 1969. V. 68

RAWSON, CLAYTON
The Footprints on the Ceiling. 1939. V. 73
The Great Merlini. Boston: 1979. V. 70; 72
The Headless Lady. 1940. V. 71
Spots Before Your Eyes. New York: 1939. V. 70

RAWSON, GEOFFREY
Pandora's Last Voyage. London: 1963. V. 72

RAWSTONE, J. G.
An Account of the Regiments of Royal Lancashire Militia, 1759 to 1870. Lancaster: 1874. V. 70

RAY, ANTHONY
English Delftware Titles. 1973. V. 71

RAY, CLARENCE E.
The Alabama Wolf - Rube His Despearate Gang of Highwaymen. Chicago. V. 68
The Dalton Brothers in Their Oklahoma Cave. Chicago. V. 68
Famous American Scouts - Lives of Daniel Boone, Kit Carson, Davy Crockett, Wild Bill, and Others. Chicago. V. 72
The Oklahoma Bandits - the Daltons. Chicago. V. 68

RAY, D. J.
Artists of the Tundra and the Sea. Seattle: 1961. V. 69
Eskimo Masks; Art and Ceremony. Seattle: 1967. V. 69

RAY, JAMES
A Compleat History of the Rebellion, from its first Rise, in 1745, to its total Suppression at the glorious Battle of Culloden, in April 1746. . . 1757. V. 71

RAY, JOHN
Catalogus Plantarum Angliae, et Insularum Adjaentium.... London: 1670. V. 68
Catalogus Plantarum Circa Cantabrigiam Nascentium.... Cambridge: 1660. V. 72
A Compleat Collection of English Proverbs.... 1768. V. 72
Historia Plantarum Species Hactenus Editas Aliasque Insuper Multas Noviter Inventas & Descriptas Complectens. 1686-. V. 69
Methodus Plantarum Emendata et Aucta. Amsterdam: 1703. V. 69
Miscellaneous Discourses Concerning the Dissolution and Changes of the World. London: 1692. V. 68
Philosophical Letters Between the Late Learned Mr. Ray and Several of His Ingenious Correspondents, Natives and Foreigners. London: 1718. V. 69; 70; 72
Stiripium Europaearum Extra Britannias Nascentium Sylloge. 1694. V. 69
Synopsis Methodica Stirpium Britannicarum; tum Indigenis tum in Agris Cultis Locis Suis Dispositis.... Londini: 1724. V. 69
Travels through the Low Countries, Germany, Italy and France. 1738. V. 69
Travels through the Low-Countries, Germany, Italy and France.... London: 1738. V. 72

RAY, MAN
Man Ray: the Photographic Image. Woodbury: 1980. V. 72

RAY, OPHELIA
Daughter of the Tejas. Greenwich: 1965. V. 69

RAY, P. ORMAN
The Repeal of the Missouri Compromise. Cleveland: 1909. V. 68

RAY, SHEILA
The Blyton Phenomenon. London: 1982. V. 69

RAY SOCIETY
Reports on the Progress of Zoology and Botany 1841-1842. Edinburgh: 1845. V. 72

RAYMER, ROBERT GEORGE
Montana: the Land and the People. Chicago: 1930. V. 72; 73

RAYMOND, ANTONIN
Architectural Details. New York: 1938. V. 71

RAYMOND, CHARLES A.
Perversions Exposed and Mis-Statements Corrected. Edgefield: 1854. V. 68

RAYMOND, DEREK
Not Till the Red Fog Rises. London: 1994. V. 73

RAYMOND, DORA NEILL
Captain Lee Hall of Texas. Norman: 1940. V. 69

RAYMOND, ERNEST
Mary Leith. New York: 1932. V. 70
Morris in the Dance. London: 1927. V. 69; 73

RAYMOND, JEAN PAUL
Beyond the Threshold. Plaistow: 1929. V. 70

RAYMOND, MARTHA GOULD
The Ebell Club of Anaheim: Its History November 1907-July 1946. Placentia: 1947. V. 68

RAYNAL, GUILLAUME THOMAS FRANCOIS
Histoire du Stadhouderat Depuis son Origine Jusqu'a Present.... 1750. V. 72
The History of the Parliament of England. London: 1751. V. 71
A Philosophical and Political History of the Settlements and Trade of the Europeans in the East and West Indies. London: 1776. V. 70
A Philosophical and Political History of the Settlements and Trade of the Europeans in the East and West Indies. Edinburgh: 1782. V. 70; 72
A Philosophical and Political History of the Settlements and Trade of the Europeans in the East and West Indies. London: 1788. V. 72

RAYNAL, MAURICE
Matisse, Munch, Rouault, Fauvism, Expressionism. Geneva: 1950. V. 72

RAYNAL, PAUL
The Unknown Warrior. New York: 1928. V. 69

RAYNE, M. L., MRS.
What Can a Woman Do or Her Position in the Business and Literary World. Detroit: 1884. V. 71
What Can a Woman Do; or Her Position in the Business and Literary World. Petersburgh: 1893. V. 73

RAYNER, CLAIRE
The Enemy Below. New York: 1957. V. 68

RAYNER, ROBERT M.
Wagner and Die Meistersinger. London: 1940. V. 69

REA, C.
British Basidiomycetae, a Handbook to the Larger British Fungi. Cambridge: 1922. V. 72

READ, BENJAMIN M.
Guerra Mexico-Americana. Santa Fe: 1910. V. 70; 72; 73
Illustrated History of New Mexico. Santa Fe: 1912. V. 68; 73

READ, BILL
The Days of Dylan Thomas. London: 1964. V. 72

READ, CHARLES H.
The Waddesdon Bequest. London: 1902. V. 72

READ, COLIN
The Rebellion of 1837 in Upper Canada a Collection of Documents. Toronto: 1985. V. 68

READ, FLORENCE MATILDA
The Story of Spelman College. Atlanta: 1961. V. 68

READ, HERBERT
Ambush. London: 1930. V. 70
Anarchy and Order - Essays in Politics. London: 1954. V. 72
Arp. London: 1968. V. 72
Art and Industry: the Principles of Industrial Design. New York: 1938. V. 72
Art and Society. London;: 1937. V. 71
Collected Essays in Literary Criticism. London: 1938. V. 69
The Green Child. London: 1947. V. 70
Lord Byron at the Opera - a Play for Broadcasting. North Harrow: 1963. V. 68
Marino Marini: the Complete Works. New York. V. 68
Pursuits and Verdicts. Edinburgh: 1983. V. 70

READ, JOHN
The Alchemist in Life, Literature and Art. London: 1947. V. 68; 70
Prelude to Chemistry. London: 1936. V. 72
Prelude to Chemistry. London: 1939. V. 68; 70

READ, MISS
Village School and Village Diary. London: 1955-1957. V. 73

READ, OPIE
An Arkansas Planter. Chicago and New York: 1896. V. 68

READ, PIERS PAUL
Alive. The Story of the Andes Survivors. London: 1974. V. 70

READ, SYLVIA
The Poetical Ark; a Collection of Thirty Verses by Sylvia Read.... London: 1946. V. 68

READ-To-Me Storybook. New York: 1947. V. 73

READE, ALEYN LYELL
Johnsonian Gleanings. New York: 1968. V. 73

READE, AMYE
Slaves of the Sawdust. London: 1892. V. 68

READE, B.
Aubrey Beardsley. New York: 1967. V. 69; 72

READE, CHARLES
Charles Reade's Novels. London: 1896-1904. V. 73
Christie Johnstone. London: 1853. V. 73
Christie Johnstone. Boston: 1855. V. 73
The Cloister and the Hearth; a Tale of the Middle Ages. London: 1882. V. 73
Clouds and Sunshine and Art. Boston: 1855. V. 73
The Course of True Love Never Did Run Smooth. London: 1857. V. 73
The Eighth Commandment. London: 1860. V. 73
Foul Play. London: 1868. V. 73
Griffith Gaunt; or, Jealousy. London: 1882. V. 73
Griffith Gaunt; or Jealousy. London: 1887. V. 73
Hard Cash; a Matter of Fact Romance. London: 1863. V. 73
It Is Never Too Late to Mend. London: 1856. V. 73
It Is Never Too Late to Mend. London: 1857. V. 73
It's Never To Late to Mend. London: 1890. V. 73
The Jilt and Other Stories. London: 1884. V. 73
Love Me Little, Love Me Long. London: 1859. V. 73
Peg Woffington. London: 1853. V. 73
A Perilous Secret. London: 1884. V. 73
A Perilous Secret. London: 1891. V. 73
Singleheart and Doubleface: a Matter of Fact Romance. London: 1884. V. 73
A Terrible Temptation: a Story of the Day. London: 1871. V. 73
Trade Malice; a Personal Narrative; and the Wandering Heir.... London: 1875. V. 73
White Lies: a Story. London: 1857. V. 73

READE, COMPTON
Charles Reade: Dramatist, Novelist and Journalist. New York: 1887. V. 73
The Smith Family: Being a Popular Account of Most Branches of the Name However Spelt.... 1904. V. 70

READE, COMPTON, MRS.
The Maid O' the Mill. London: 1887. V. 72

READE, WILLIAM WINWOOD
The Martyrdom of Man. London: 1872. V. 70; 72

THE READER, or Extracts In Prose and Verse from English and American Authors. Boston: 1838. V. 70

READING, PETER
Shitheads. London: 1989. V. 68

READING Philip Roth. New York: 1988. V. 73

READING Races; or, the Berkshire Beauties. Reading: 1777. V. 69

REAGAN, RONALD
An American Life. New York: 1990. V. 68; 69; 71; 72
Speaking My Mind: Selected Speeches. New York: 1989. V. 71
Speaking My Mind: Selected Speeches. London: 1990. V. 71
Where's the Rest of Me?. New York: 1965. V. 69; 71

REAGE, PAULINE
Story of O. New York: 1965. V. 73

REANEY, PERCY H.
A Grammar of the Diaect of Penrith. Manchester: 1927. V. 71

REASONS Against the Intended Bill for Laying Some Restraint Upon the Liberty of the Press Wherein All the Arguments Yet Advanced by the Promoters of It are Unanswerably Answered. London: 1772. V. 70; 72

REASONS Against the Repeal of the Usury Laws. London: 1825. V. 70

REASONS Attempting to Shew the Necessity of the Proposed Cut from Eau Brink to Lynn; with Extracts from the Reports of Engineers and Other Writers on the Subject.... London: 1793. V. 72

REASONS for a Limited Exporation of Wool. Oxford: 1677. V. 70

REASONS for the Establishing and Further Encouragement of St. Luke's Hospital for Lunaticks.... London: 1822. V. 69

REAUMUR, RENE ANTOINE FERCHAULT DE
Art de Faire Eclorre et D'Elever en Toite Saison des Oiseau Domestiques de Toute Especes, Soit par Le Moyen de La Chaleur du Fumier.... Paris: 1751. V. 68
Memoires Pour Servir a l'Histoire des Insectes. Paris: 1734-1742. V. 70

REAVIS, LOGAN URIAH
A Change of National Empire; or Arguments in Favor of the National Capital from Washington City to the Mississippi Valley. St. Louis: 1869. V. 70

REBUFFAT, GASTON
Between Heaven and Earth. London: 1970. V. 69
Men and the Matterhorn. 1967. V. 68
The Mont Blanc Massif. 1974. V. 68; 71
The Mont Blanc Massif. London: 1974. V. 69
Mont Blanc to Everest. London: 1956. V. 69
On Ice and Snow and Rock. London: 1971. V. 69
On Snow and Rock. London: 1963. V. 69
On Snow and Rock. London: 1967. V. 69
Starlight and Storm. 1956. V. 68
Starlight and Storm. London: 1956. V. 69
Starlight and Storm. London: 1968. V. 69

RECENT Expeditions to Eastern Polar Seas. London: 1882. V. 73

RECENT Polaroid Color Photography: One of a Kind. Boston: 1979. V. 68

RECHY, JOHN
City of the Night. New York: 1963. V. 73

RECIPES for the Colour, Paint, Varnish, Oil, Soap and Drysaltery Trades. London: 1902. V. 68

RECKITT, WILLIAM
Some Account of the Life and Gospel Labours of William Reckitt. London: 1776. V. 69

RECLUS, E.
The Earth, a Descriptive History of the Phenomena of the List of the Globe. London: 1877. V. 70

RECORD of the Celebration Of...the Introduction of the Art of Printing Into Aberdeen by Edward Raban. Aberdeen: 1922. V. 70

THE RECORD of the First Presbyterian Church of Morristown, N.J. Jan. 1880-Dec. 1885. Morristown: 1885. V. 72

RECORDS of the Past: Being English Translations of the Assyrian and Egyptian Monuments. London. V. 71

THE RECREATION. Edinburgh: 1848. V. 68; 70

RECTOR, MARGARET
Cowboy Life on the Texas Plains - the Photographs of Ray Rector. College Station: 1982. V. 69

RECUEIL D'Estampes Representant les Differents Evenemens de la Guerre qui a Procure l'Independence aux Etats unis de l'Amerique. Paris: 1784?. V. 71

THE RED Indian. New York: 1931. V. 69

RED Riding Hood. New York: 1915. V. 70

RED-Riding Hood. London: 1950. V. 72

REDDELL, J. H.
The True State of the British Nation, as to Trade, Commerce &c. Clearly Pourtrayed.... London: 1817. V. 72

REDDICK, ALLEN
The Making of Johnson's Dictionary 1746-1773, a Study. 1990. V. 68

REDDING, J. SAUNDERS
The Lonesome Road: The Story of the Negro's Part in America. Garden City: 1958. V. 72

REDE, WILLIAM LEMAN
Peregrinations of Pickwick.... Philadelphia: 1837. V. 70

REDEMPTION and Sale of the Land-Tax. Thoughts on the Interesting Subject; and Remarks on the Original Act Passed for that Purpose in June 1798.... London: 1799. V. 73

REDFERN, PERCY
The Story of the C.W.S. The Jubilee History of the Co-Operative Wholesale Society Limited 1863-1913. Manchester: 1913. V. 68

REDFERN, RON
Corridors of the Time: 1,700,000,000 Years of Earth at Grand Canyon. New York: 1980. V. 71

REDFIELD, ISAAC F.
Leading American Cases and Notes Upon the Law of Wills. Boston: 1874. V. 68

REDFIELD, JAMES
The Celestine Prophecy. New York: 1994. V. 68

REDFIELD, R.
The Folk Culture of Yucatan. Chicago: 1941. V. 69

REDFORD, POLLY
The Christmas Bower. London: 1969. V. 68

REDFORD, ROBERT
The Outlaw Trail; a Journey through Time. New York: 1978. V. 69

REDGRAVE, MICHAEL
The Aspern Papers: A Play Adapted from Henry James' Story. London: 1959. V. 71
Water Music for a Botanist. Cambridge: 1929. V. 70

REDGRAVE, RICHARD
An Elementary Manual of Colour; with a Catechism.... London: 1855. V. 68

REDGRAVE, SAMUEL
A Descriptive Catalogue of the Historical Collection of Water-Colour Paintings in the South Kensington Museum. London: 1876. V. 68
A Descriptive Catalogue of the Historical Collection of Water-Colour Paintings in the South Kensington Museum. London: 1877. V. 68; 72

REDGROVE, PETER
The Collector and Other Poems. London: 1960. V. 68
Work in Progress. London: 1968. V. 68

REDI, FRANCESCO
Bacco in Toscana. Ditirambo...con le Annotazioni. Florence: 1685. V. 68; 70; 73
Esperienze Intorno all Generazione Degli'Insetti Fatte da.... Florence: 1668. V. 68; 69
Experimenta Circa Generationem Insectorum ad Nobilissimum Virum Carolum Dati. Amsterdam: 1671. V. 68
Experiments on the Generation of Insects. Chicago: 1909. V. 68; 70; 72
Opere di Francesco Redi Gentiluomo Aretino.... Venice: 1740-1765. V. 68
Osservazioni Intorno Agli Animali Viventi che si Trovano Negli Animali Viventi. Florence: 1684. V. 68
Osservazioni Intorno Alle Vipere. 1664. V. 72

REDL, HARRY
The World of De Grazia: an Artist of the American Southwest. Phoenix: 1981. V. 69

REDLICH, JOSEF
Local Government in England. London: 1903. V. 71

REDMAN, WILLIAM
The Jeweller's Guide and Handy Reference Book. Bradford: 1883. V. 71

REDMAYNE, R. A. S.
The Colliery Manager's Pocket Book, Almanac and Diary, for the Year 1905. 1905. V. 71

REDMOND, CHRISTOPHER
In Bed With Sherlock Holmes: Sexual Elements In Arthur Conan Doyle. Toronto: 1984. V. 72

REDMOND, PATRICK
Puppet Show. 2000. V. 68
The Wishing Game. London: 1999. V. 69; 70; 73

REDOUTE, P. J.
A Redoute Treasury. New York: 1986. V. 68
Roses. 1954-1956. V. 69
The Roses. Koln: 1999. V. 68

REDPATH, JAMES
The Roving Editor; or Talks with Slaves in the Southern States. New York: 1859. V. 68

REECE, MAYNARD
The Waterfowl Art of Maynard Reece. New York: 1984. V. 68

REECE, ROBERT
Night Bombing with the Bedouins, by One of the Squadron. Boston and New York: 1919. V. 73

REED, A. W.
Wonder Tales of Maoriland. Wellington: 1954. V. 68

REED, BYRON
The Byron Reed Collection of Important American Coins and Manuscripts. New York: 1996. V. 70

REED, C. A.
American Ornithology for the Home and School. Worcester: 1901-1904. V. 70

REED, C. F.
Selected Weeds of the United States. Washington: 1970. V. 72

REED, E. T.
Tails with a Twist. London. V. 69

REED, EDWARD
Japan. London: 1880. V. 71

REED, I.
Bibliotheca Reediana. A Catalogue of the Curious and Extensive Library of the Late Isaac Reed, Esq. of Staple Inn.... London: 1807. V. 70

REED, ISHMAEL
The Before Columbus Foundation Poetry Anthology. New York: 1992. V. 69
Chattanooga. New York: 1973. V. 72; 73
Conjure. Amherst: 1972. V. 68; 73
The Last Days of Louisiana Red. New York: 1974. V. 73
Mumbo Jumbo. Garden City: 1972. V. 70
The Terrible Twos. New York: 1982. V. 72

REED, JEREMY
Blue Rock. London: 1987. V. 72
The Lipstick Boys. London: 1984. V. 73

REED, JOHN
Insurgent Mexico. New York: 1914. V. 70; 72
Ten Days that Shook the World. London: 1926. V. 69

REED, PHILIP
The Seven Voyages of Sinbad the Sailor from the Arabian Nights Entertainments. Park Ridge, IL: 1939. V. 72

REED, REBECCA THERESA
Six Months in a Convent, or, the Narrative of.... Boston: 1835. V. 68

REED, TALBOT BAINES
A History of the Old English Letter Foundries. Folkestone: 1974. V. 70

REED, WALT
Harold von Schmidt Draws and Paints the Old West. Flagstaff: 1972. V. 69; 70
John Clymer: an Artist's Rendezvous with the Frontier West. Flagstaff: 1976. V. 69; 71

REED, WILLIAM
Olaf Wieghorst. Flagstaff: 1969. V. 69; 70; 72
Olaf Wieghorst. Flagstaff: 1981. V. 68

REED, WILLIAM HOWELL
Hospital Life in the Army of the Potomac. Boston: 1866. V. 71

REED, WILLIS
A Will To Win: The Comeback Year. Englewood Cliffs: 1973,. V. 72

REEDSTROM, ERNEST L.
Bugles, Banners and War Bonnets. Caldwell: 1977. V. 72

REES, ARTHUR J.
The Hand in the Dark. 1929. V. 73
Love Me Anise. New York: 1938. V. 69
The Moon Rock. 1922. V. 73
The Pavilion by the Lake. New York: 1930. V. 68; 70; 72

REES, FRED A.
On Peak, Pyramid and Prairie. London. V. 69

REES, J. D.
H.R.H. The Duke of Clarence and Avondale in Southern India. 1891. V. 69; 70; 73

REES, ROSEMARY
Sackcloth for Susan. New York: 1941. V. 71

REESE, DAVID MEREDITH
A Brief Review of the First Annual Report of the American Anti-Slavery Society, with the Speeches Delivered at the Anniversary Meeting May 6th, 1834 Addressed to the People of the United States. New York: 1834. V. 71
Phrenology Known by its Fruits, Being a Brief Review of Doctor Brigham's Late Work Entitled Observations on the Influence of Religion Upon the Health and Physical Welfare of Mankind. New York: 1836. V. 68; 70; 71; 73
A Plain and Practical Treatise on the Epidemic Cholera as it Prevailed in the City of New York in the Summer of 1832. New York: 1833. V. 73

REESE, LIZETTE WOODWORTH
Little Henrietta. New York: 1927. V. 70

REEVE, ARTHUR B.
Craig Kennedy Listens In. New York: 1923. V. 69; 73
Craig Kennedy Stories. New York: 1919. V. 69
The Golden Age of Crime. New York: 1931. V. 70; 71; 72
Guy Garrick - an Adventure with a Scientific Gunman. New York: 1914. V. 70
Pandora. New York: 1926. V. 68; 69; 73
The Silent Bullet. New York: 1917. V. 68

REEVE, CHRISTOPHER
The Toasted Blonde. New York: 1930. V. 73

REEVE, CLARA
Fatherless Fanny or Memoirs of a Little Mendicant and Her Benefactors. London: 1825. V. 68; 72
The Old English Baron. Dublin: 1801. V. 73

REEVE, D. C.
A Guide to Rock Climbing in Hong Kong. Hong Kong: 1968. V. 69

REEVE, HENRY, ED.
St. Petersburg and London in the Years 1852-1864. London: 1887. V. 70

REEVE, L.
Elements of Conchology.... 1860. V. 69

REEVE, MARY ANNE
Lays from the West. Odiham: 1865. V. 69

REEVE, TAPPING
The Law of Baron and Femme. New Haven: 1816. V. 68; 69; 72

REEVES, ELIZABETH
A House for Emily. New York: 1941. V. 71

REEVES, FRANK
A Century of Texas Cattle Brands. Fort Worth: 1936. V. 69; 71

REEVES, JAMES
Maildun, the Voyager. 1971. V. 69
Rhyming Will. London: 1967. V. 73
Titus in Trouble. London: 1959. V. 68

REEVES, JOSEPH
The History and Topography of Westbromwich, and Its Vicinity. London: 1837. V. 71

REEVES, ROBERT
Cellini Smith: Detective. 1943. V. 68; 73
Dead and Done For. 1939. V. 73

REFLECTIONS on the Short History of Standing Armies in England in Vindication of His Majesty and Government. London: 1699. V. 70

REFT Rob; or, the Witch of Scot-Muir, Commonly Called Madge the Snoober. London: 1817. V. 72

REGAN, C. TATE
Biologia Centrali Americana: Pisces. 1906-1908. V. 73
Biologia Centrali Americana: Pisces. 1972. V. 69
Biologia Centrali-Americana: Pisces. Lochem: 1972. V. 72
Fishes. London: 1914. V. 71; 72

REGAN, JOHN W.
Sketches and Traditions of the Northwest Arm.... Halifax: 1909. V. 73

THE REGISTER Of The Victoria Cross. Cheltenham: 1981. V. 72

REGIUS, CAROLUS
Orator Christianus in Quo Primu de Concioatore Ipso, tum in Concione, Demum de Cocionantis Prudentia et Industria Agitur. Cologne: 1613. V. 73

REGO, A. DA SILVA
Documents on the Portuguese in Mozambique and Central Africa 1497- 1840. Lisbon: 1962. V. 71

REHBERG, FREDERICK
Emma Hamilton's Attitudes. Cambridge: 1990. V. 71

REHDER, A.
Manual of Cultivated Trees and Shrubs, Hardy in North America Exclusive of the Subtropical and Warmer Temperate Regions. New York: 1940. V. 68

REHLAN, ANTHONY
A Short History of Brighthelmston with Remarks on Its Air and an Analysis of Its Waters. 1829. V. 72
A Short History of Brighthelmston with Remarks on Its Air and an Analysis of Its Waters. Brighton: 1829. V. 71

REICH, SHELDON
Zuniga Sculptor: Conversations and Interpretations. Tucson: 1980. V. 70; 71

REICHARD, GLADYS A.
Melanesian Design; a Study in Wood and Tortoiseshell Carving. New York: 1969. V. 69
Navaho Religion - a Study of Symbolism. New York: 1950. V. 69; 70
Navaho Religion - a Study of Symbolism. 1963. V. 69; 72
Navajo Medicine Man: Sandpaintings and Legends of Miguelito. New York: 1939. V. 69
Navajo Shepherd and Weaver. New York: 1936. V. 69; 73
Sandpaintings of the Navajo Shooting Chant. New York: 1937. V. 69
Social Life of the Navajo Indians with Some Attention to Minor Ceremonies. New York: 1928. V. 69
The Story of the Navajo Hail Chant. New York: 1944. V. 69

REICHARDT, J.
Cybernetics, Art and Ideas. 1971. V. 72

REICHENBACH KLINKE, H.
The Principal Diseases of Lower Vertebrates. 1965. V. 73
The Principal Diseases of Lower Vertebrates. London: 1965. V. 69

REICHERT, E. T.
A Biochemic Basis for the Study of Problems of Taxonomy, Heredity, Evolution, Etc.... Washington: 1919. V. 70
The Differentiation and Specificity of Starches in Relation to Genera, Species, Etc.... Washington: 1913. V. 70

REICHLER, MAX
Jewish Eugenics and Other Essays: Three Papers Read Before the New York Board of Jewish Ministers, 1915. New York: 1916. V. 70

REICHS, KATHY
Deja Dead. New York: 1997. V. 69

REID, ALEC
All I Can Manage, More than I Could. Dublin: 1968. V. 71

REID, ANDREW
The New Liberal Programme. London: 1886. V. 68

REID, ANTHONY
A Checklist of the Book Illustrations of John Buckland Wright. Pinner: 1968. V. 68

REID, B. L.
The Man from New York. John Quinn and His Friends. New York: 1968. V. 72

REID, ERSKINE
The Dramatic Peerage, 1891. Personal Notes and Professional Sketches of the Actors and Actresses of the London Stage. London: 1890. V. 72

REID, FORREST
Apostate. London: 1926. V. 68; 71
Apostate. London: 1937. V. 73
Apostate. London: 1947. V. 71
At the Door of the Gate. London: 1915. V. 73
The Bracknels; a Family Chronicle. London: 1911. V. 73
Demophon: a Traveller's Tale. London: 1927. V. 68; 73
A Garden by the Sea. Dublin: 1918. V. 68; 73
The Gentle Lover. London: 1913. V. 73
Illustrators of the Sixties. London: 1928. V. 68; 71; 72
The Kingdom of Twilight. London: 1904. V. 73
Pender Among the Residents. London: 1922. V. 68; 73
Pirates of the Spring (and) A Garden by the Sea. Dublin. V. 71
Private Road. London: 1940. V. 68; 71
Retrospective Adventures. London: 1941. V. 68; 71; 72
The Spring Song. London: 1916. V. 73
W. B. Yeats: a Critical Study. 1915. V. 69; 73
W. B. Yeats: a Critical Study. London: 1915. V. 68; 73
W. B. Yeats a Critical Study. 1935. V. 70
Walter de la Mare. A Critical Study. London: 1929. V. 68; 71

REID, J. A.
Anopheline Mosquitoes of Malaya and Borneo. Malaya: 1968. V. 72
The Collected Papers of J. A. Reid. 1938-1970. V. 72

REID, JESSE WALTON
History of the Fourth Regiment of S. C. Volunteers, from the Commencment of the War Until Lee's Surrender. Greenville: 1892. V. 69; 70

REID, JOHN
Anopheline Mosquitoes of Malaya and Borneo. Malaya: 1968. V. 71
Clyde-Style Flies and Their Dressings, with Some Hints on Their Use. 1971. V. 73
Essays on Hypochondriasis and Other Nervous Affections. London: 1823. V. 68; 73
The Spring Song. London: 1916. V. 68

REID, JOHN P.
A Law of Blood: the Primitive Law of the Cherokee Nation. New York: 1970. V. 70

REID, MAYNE
The Scalp Hunters; or Romantic Adventures in Northern Mexico. London: 1851. V. 70
The White Chief. A Legend of Northern Mexico. London: 1855. V. 70

REID, SAMUEL C.
The Scouting Expeditions of McCulloch's Texas Rangers. Austin: 1935. V. 68

REID, STUART J.
The Prime Ministers of Queen Victoria. London: 1890-1895. V. 71; 73

REID, T. W.
Life, Letters and Friendships of Richard Monckton Milnes, First Lord Houghton. New York: 1891. V. 69

REID, THOMAS
An Inquiry into the Human Mind. London: 1769. V. 69
Treatise on Clock and Watch Making, Theoretical and Practical. Philadelphia: 1832. V. 69

REID, WEMYSS
Charlotte Bronte. A Monograph. 1877. V. 70; 73
Charlotte Bronte. A Monograph. London: 1877. V. 73
Life of William Edward Forster. London: 1888. V. 71
Memoir and Correspondence of Lyon Playfair, First Lord Playfiar of St. Andrews. London: 1899. V. 71; 72

REIDE, THOMAS
A Treatise on the Duty of Infantry Officers and the Present System of Military Discipline. London: 1795. V. 70

REID GIRARDOT, MARION
Red Eagle of the Medicine Way. Boston;: 1922. V. 70

REIGART, JOHN FRANKLIN
The Life of Robert Fulton. Philadelphia: 1856. V. 68; 72

REILLY, HELEN
The Canvas Dagger. New York: 1956. V. 69
Death Demands an Audience. Garden City: 1940. V. 70
File on Rufus Ray. London: 1937. V. 73
The Line-Up. New York: 1934. V. 70
Mr. Smith's Hat. Garden City: 1936. V. 70
Murder in Shinbone Alley. New York: 1940,. V. 68
Murder in the Mews. New York: 1931. V. 68

REILLY, JOHN M.
Twentieth Century Crime and Mystery Writers. New York: 1985. V. 70

REILLY, ROBIN
Wedgewood. London: 1989. V. 71

REIN, J. J.
Japan: Travels and Researches. (with) The Industries of Japan. New York: 1888-1889. V. 70

REINERS, P.
The Springs of Virginia, Life, Love and Death at the Waters 1775- 1900. Chapel Hill: 1941. V. 72

REINES, THOMAS
Syntagma Inscriptionum Antiquarum Cumprimis Romae Veteris, Quarum Omissa est Recensio in Vasto Jani Gruteri Opere Cuius.... Leipzig: 1682. V. 72

REINHARDT, JOHANN CHRISTIAN
A Collection of Swiss Costumes in Miniature. London: 1822. V. 69

REINHARDT, KARL HEINRICH LEOPOLD
*Lettres sur Dresde a Madame *** Contenant une Esquisse, de ce Que elle Ville Offre de Plus Remarquable aux Etrangers.* Berlin: 1800. V. 68; 70

REINNEL, F.
The Masons, Bricklayers, Plasterers, and Slaters' Assistant.... London: 1873. V. 68; 69

REINZER, FRANZ
Meteorologia Philosohico-Politica. Augsburg: 1709. V. 71

REISER, ANTON
Albert Einstein. A Biographical Portrait. New York: 1930. V. 73

REISNER, MARY
Shadows on the Wall. New York: 1943. V. 70; 73

REISNER, ROBERT
Bird. The Legend of Charlie Parker. New York: 1962. V. 68; 69

REISS, R. A.
Report upon the Atrocities Committed by the Austro-Hungarian Army During the First Invasion of Serbia. London: 1916. V. 72

REISS, W.
Blackfeet Indians. St. Paul: 1935. V. 68

REITLINGER, GERALD
A Tower Of Skulls. A Journey Through Persia and Turkish Armenia. London: 1932. V. 72

REITLINGER, H. C.
Old Master Drawings. London: 1922. V. 72

REITZENSTEIN, JOSEPHINE VON
The Enchanted Fountain. London: 1945. V. 69

RELANDER, CLICK
Drummers and Dreamers. Caldwell: 1956. V. 68

RELHAN, R.
Flora Cantabrigiensis. Cambridge: 1785. V. 72
Flora Cantabrigiensis. 1802. V. 72
Flora Cantabrigiensis (Supplementum). Cambridge: 1785-1786. V. 69

REMAINES, Concerning Britaine: but Especially England and the Inhabitants Thereof. London: 1614. V. 73

REMARKS on Some Paragraphs in the Fourth Volume of Dr. Blackstone's Commentaries on the Laws of England. Philadelphia: 1773. V. 72

REMARKS on the Decison of the Appeal Court of South Carolina, in the Case of Wells and on the Abolition Movements at the North. Charleston;: 1845. V. 68

REMARKS on the Present State of the Coal Trade, with a Retrospective Glance at Its History, Addressed to the Marquis of Londonderry, K.D.B. Lord Lieutenant of the County of Durham. London: 1843. V. 73

REMARKS on the Result of an Ecclesiastical Council Which met at Dorchester, Mass., on November 16, 1773. Boston: 1774. V. 68

REMARKS on the Sentence Given in Favour of E----W----M---- and T---T----, Esqs. by the L---C---I at Paris. London: 1752. V. 69

REMARKS Upon Mr. Webber's Scheme and the Draper's Pamphlet. 1741. V. 71

REMARKS upon the Bank of England, with Regard More Especially to Our Trade and Government. London: 1705. V. 69

REMARQUE, ERICH MARIA
All Quiet on the Western Front. Boston: 1929. V. 73
All Quiet on the Western Front. London: 1929. V. 70
Arch of Triumph. New York: 1945. V. 71

REMARQUE, ERICH MARIA continued
Spark of Life. New York: 1952. V. 71
Three Comrades. Boston;: 1937. V. 69

REMARQUES Historiques et Critiques Faites dans un Voyage d'Italie en Hollande dans l'annee 1704. Cologne: 1705. V. 72

REMBADI, GEMMA MONGIARDINI
Pinocchio Under the Sea. New York: 1913. V. 70

REMBAR, CHARLES
The End of Obscenity. London: 1969. V. 73

REMBURG, JOHN
Charles Reynolds, Soldier, Hunter, Scout and Guide. Kansas City: 1931. V. 72

THE REMEMBRANCER, or Fragments for Leisure Hours. Philadelphia: 1840. V. 71

REMILINUS, JOHANN
A Survey of the Microcosme; or the Anatomy of the Bodies of Man and Woman. London: 1702. V. 68

REMINGTON, FREDERIC
The Collected Writings of.... New York: 1979. V. 72; 73
Crooked Trails. New York: 1898. V. 71
Frederic Remington: the American West. Kent: 1978. V. 70
Frederic Remington's Own West. New York: 1960. V. 68
Pony Tracks. New York: 1895. V. 68; 73
Pony Tracks. New York: 1923. V. 69
Pony Tracks. Columbus: 1951. V. 68; 71
Remington's Frontier Sketches. Chicago: 1898. V. 71; 73
Sundown Leflare. New York and London: 1899. V. 71

REMINGTON, JOHN STEWART
A Peep Into the Past. Kendal;: 1935. V. 71

REMISE, JAC
The Golden Age of Toys. Lausanne: 1967. V. 71

REMONDINO, P. C.
History of Circumcision from the Earliest Times to the Present. Philadelphia: 1900. V. 73

RENARD, MAURICE
New Bodies for Old, or, The Strange Experiments of Dr. Lerne. New York: 1923. V. 70

RENDELL, RUTH
Asta's Book. Bristol: 1993. V. 69
The Best Man to Die. Garden City: 1970. V. 68; 71
The Bridesmaid. London: 1989. V. 68; 73
The Bridesmaid. New York: 1989. V. 72
The Copper Peacock, and Other Stories. London: 1991. V. 73
The Crocodile Bird. London: 1993. V. 68; 73
The Crocodile Bird. New York: 1993. V. 72
A Dark-Adapted Eye. London: 1986. V. 73
A Demon in My View. London: 1976. V. 68; 71
The Face of Trespass. Garden City: 1974. V. 71
The Face of Trespass. London: 1974. V. 69; 71; 73
From Doon With Death. New York: 1964. V. 71
Gallowglass. London: 1990. V. 68
A Guilty Thing Surprised. London: 1970. V. 69
The House of Stairs. New York: 1989. V. 71
A Judgement in Stone. Garden City: 1978. V. 71
The Keys to the Street. London: 1996. V. 68; 73
Kissing the Gunner's Daughter. London: 1992. V. 68; 73
Live Flesh. London: 1986. V. 68; 73
Make Death Love Me. London: 1979. V. 69; 73
Matters of Suspense. Helsinki: 1986. V. 70
Means of Evil and Other Stories. London: 1979. V. 68; 71
Murder Being Once Done. London: 1972. V. 68; 71
No More Dying Then. London: 1961. V. 73
No More Dying Then. London: 1971. V. 72
One Across, Two Down. London: 1971. V. 69; 71; 73
The Reason Why, an Anthology of the Murderous Mind. London: 1995. V. 68
Road Rage. London: 1997. V. 73
The Secret House of Death. Garden City: 1969. V. 71
Shake Hands for Ever. London: 1975. V. 69
A Sight for Sore Eyes. London: 1998. V. 68
Simisola. London: 1994. V. 73
A Sleeping Life. New York: 1978. V. 71
Some Lie and Some Die. London: 1973. V. 69; 72
The Speaker of Mandarin. London: 1983. V. 69
Speaker of Mandarin. New York: 1983. V. 73
Talking to Strange Men. London: 1987. V. 68; 73
To Fear a Painted Devil. Garden City: 1965. V. 71
The Veiled One. London: 1988. V. 68; 73
Wolf to the Slaughter. 1967. V. 73
Wolf to the Slaughter. Garden City: 1968. V. 71

RENDINA, LAURA COOPER
Summer for Two. Boston: 1952. V. 71

RENDLE, A. B.
The Classification of Flowering Plants. Cambridge: 1953-1952. V. 68

RENDLE, B. J.
World Timbers. 1969. V. 73

RENEAULME, PAUL DE
Specimen Historiae Plantarum. Paris: 1611. V. 68; 72; 73

RENEHAN, LAURENCE F.
Collections of Irish Church History; Volume I. Archbishops. 1861. V. 69; 73

RENESSE, RUDOLF L. VAN
Optical Document Security. Boston: 1994. V. 68

RENN, LUDWIG
Death Without Battle. London: 1937. V. 69

RENNELL, JAMES
Memoir of a Map of Hindoostan; or the Mogul Empire.... London: 1792. V. 68

RENNER, A. L., PSEUD.
Sarah Bernhardt - Artist and Norman. New York: 1896. V. 70

RENNER, FREDERIC G.
Charles M. Russell - Paintings, Drawings and Sculpture in the Amon G. Carter Museum. Austin: 1966. V. 69
Charles M. Russell: Paintings, Drawings and Sculpture in the Amon Carter Museum. 1974. V. 71
Charles M. Russell: Paintings, Drawings and Sculpture in the Amon Carter Museum. New York: 1974. V. 69; 73
Paper Talk, Illustrated Letters of Charles M. Russell. Fort Worth: 1962. V. 68; 71

RENNER, GINGER
A Limitless Sky. The Work of Charles M. Russell. Flagstaff: 1986. V. 69

RENNIE, G. B.
Suggestions for the Improvement of the River Danube Between Isatcha and the Sulina Entrances. London: 1856. V. 72

RENNIE, J.
Insect Transformations. London: 1830. V. 72

RENNIE, JAMES
Alphabet of Angling. 1849. V. 68; 73
The Art of Preserving the Hair. London: 1825. V. 73

RENOIR, H.
Monograms and Ciphers. Edinburgh: 1870. V. 68

RENOIR, JEAN
Renoir, My Father. London: 1962. V. 73

RENOUARD, P. V.
History of Medicine from Its Origin to the Nineteenth Century, with an Appendix Containing a Philosophical and Historical Review of Medicine to the Present Time.... London: 1856. V. 68
History of Medicine...to the Nineteenth Century. Cincinnati: 1856. V. 70

THE RENOWNED History of Little Red Riding Hood. New York: 1967. V. 70

RENTON, A. H.
Observations on an Improved Oxyhydrogen Lime Light, as Adopted by the Lime Light Company. London: 1859. V. 69

RENTOUL, A. I.
Mollie's Staircase. Melbourne: 1906. V. 71; 73

RENTOUL, ANNIE R.
Elves and Fairies of Ida Rentoul Outhwaite. Melbourne: 1916. V. 70; 73
Fairyland. New York: 1929. V. 72
Fairyland. London: 1931. V. 71
The Lady of the Blue Beads. Melbourne: 1908. V. 69
The Little Green Road to Fairyland. London: 1922. V. 68

RENTOUL, J. N.
Growing Orchids. Portland and Melbourne: 1980-1985. V. 71

RENWICK, GEORGE
Romantic Corsica. London: 1909. V. 71

REPERTOIRE Medico-Chirurgical et Obstetrical. Brussels: 1836-1837. V. 72

THE REPETORY of Arts, Manufactures and Agriculture. London: 1818. V. 72
THE REPETORY of Arts, Manufactures and Agriculture. London: 1819. V. 72

A REPLY of a Member of Parliament to the Mayor of His Corporation. London: 1733. V. 68; 72

REPLY to the Charge of Fallacy, Brought Against the Exposition of the State of the Stamp Laws, Contained in the Law and Commercial Remembrancer for 1833. London: 1833. V. 71

REPORT of a Meeting Held 13th January 1839, at the London Tavern the Rt. Hon. Sir R. Wilmot Horton, Bart, in the Chair to Receive the Report of the Committee Appointed 12th October 1838 on Steam Communication with India via the Red Sea. London: 1839. V. 73

REPORT Upon the Claims of Mr. George Stephenson, Relative to the Invention of His Safety Lamp. Newcastle: 1817. V. 69

REPORTS of Tenant Farmers' Delegates on the Dominion of Canada as a Field for Settlement. Liverpool: 1880. V. 69

REPORTS of the Managers for the Poor of the Parish of Old Machar 1845-1846. Aberdeen: 1846. V. 73

A REPOSITORY of Music, Containing Elementary and Advanced Lessons.... Canterbury: 1880. V. 73

REPP, ED EARL
Suicide Ranch. New York: 1936. V. 70

REPPY, NELL
The Little Builders' ABC. New York: 1943. V. 71

THE REPROBATE'S Reward; or a Looking-Glass for Disobedient Children. Rhode Island: 1802. V. 73

REPRODUCTIONS of Thompson and West's History of Los Angeles County, California, with Illustrations. Berkeley: 1959. V. 73

REPS, JOHN
Cities on Stone: Nineteenth Century Lithograph Images of the Urban West. Fort Worth: 1976. V. 70

REPTON, HUMPHRY
The Landscape Gardening and Landscape Architecture of the Late Humphry Repton.... London: 1840. V. 68; 71; 73
Observations on the Theory and Practice of Landscape Gardening Including Some Remarks on Grecian and Gothic Architecture.... London: 1805. V. 70; 72
The Red Books. London: 1976. V. 68; 70
Variety; or a Collection of Essays Written in the Year 1787. London: 1788. V. 69

REQUA, RICHARD S.
Architectural Details: Spain and the Mediterranean.... Los Angeles: 1926. V. 69; 72

RERESBY, JOHN
The Memoirs of Sir John Reresby of Thrybergh, Bart, M.P. for York & c., 1634-1689. Written by Himself. London: 1875. V. 72

RERESBY, TAMWORTH
A Miscellany of Ingenious Thoughts and Reflections. London: 1721. V. 70

RESENDE, LUCA ANDREAS DE
Libri Quatuor de Antiquitatibus Lusitaniae, a Lucio Andea Resendio olim Inchoati et a Jac. Menoetio e Vasconcello.... Evora: 1593. V. 70; 72

RESIST Much, Obey Little. Some Notes on Edward Abbey. Salt Lake City: 1985. V. 72

RESPUBLICA Romana. Leiden: 1629. V. 69

RESPVESTA Theologica Acerca Del Abuso de Los Escotdados Dada Al Ilvstrissimo Y Excelentissimo Senor el Senor Don Andres Giron, Artobispo y Senor de Santiago.... Santiago: 1673. V. 69; 73

RESTE, BERNARD DE
Histoire des Peches des Decouvertes et des Establissmens des Hollandois dans les Mers du Nord. Paris: 1801. V. 73

RESTELI, ERNEST
Captain Knickerbocker. London: 1938. V. 73

RESTIF DE LA BRETONNE, NICHOLAS EDME
La Prevention Nationale, Action Adaptee a La Scene.... The Hague and Paris: 1784. V. 69
Sara. London: 1927. V. 72

RETI, L.
The Unknown Leonardo. New York: 1974. V. 69; 72

RETROSPECTIONS of Dorothea Herbert. 1929. V. 71

RETURN to Oasis. London: 1980. V. 70

RETZIUS, GUSTAF
Das Gehororgan der Wirbelthiere. Stockholm: 1881-1884. V. 72

REUTER, JOHANN
Neo-Confessarius Practice Instructus, Seu Methodus Rite Obeundi Munus Confesarii. Lovanii: 1772. V. 69

REUTER, ODO MORANNAL
Finlands Fiskar/the Fishes of Finland. Helsinki: 1883-1893. V. 73

REVELL, STANLEY
Not in Gallup. Oxford: 1988. V. 73

REVERDY, PIERRE
Selected Poems. New York: 1969. V. 68

REVERE, JOSEPH W.
Keel and Saddle: A Retrospect of Forty Years of Military and Naval Service. Boston: 1872. V. 72

THE REVIEW. A bi-monthly magazine of poetry and criticism. London: 1962. V. 71

REVIEW of the Quarterly Review; or, an Exposure of the Erroneous Opinions Promulgated in that Work on the Subject of Colonial Slavery.... London: 1824. V. 69

REX, Versus James Montague, W. L. Newman, John Nelson and Four Others. Report of the Trial of an Indictment Against the Defendants in Consequence of Their Having Cut through an Embankment at Grain Bridge for the Purpose of Restoring the Junction of the W. London: 1824. V. 70

REXROTH, KENNETH
The Collected Longer Poems of Kenneth Rexroth. New York: 1968. V. 71
The New British Poets. Verona: 1948. V. 70
One Hundred Poems from the French. Cambridge: 1972. V. 69; 71; 73
One Hundred Poems from the Japanese. 1955. V. 69
The Phoenix and the Tortoise. Norfolk: 1944. V. 68; 69; 71; 73

REY, C. F.
Unconquered Abyssinia. London: 1923. V. 71

REY, G.
The Matterhorn. 1907. V. 68; 70; 73
The Matterhorn. London: 1907. V. 69
The Matterhorn. 1913. V. 68
Peaks and Precipices. 1914. V. 68; 70; 73
Peaks and Precipices. London: 1914. V. 71

REY, H. A.
Humpty Dumpty and Other Mother Goose Songs. New York: 1943. V. 73

REY, H. L.
A Christmas Manger with Text from Mathew and Luke. Boston: 1942. V. 71

REYBAUD, HENRIETTE
The Old Convents of Paris. London: 1847. V. 68

REYNARD the Fox: a Renowned Apologue of the Middle Age, Reproduced in Rhyme. London: 1845. V. 72

REYNELL, CAREW
The True English Interest; or an Account of the Chief National Improvements; in Some Political Observations.... London: 1674. V. 73

REYNOLDES, EDWARD
A Treatise of the Passions and Faculties of the Soul of Man. London: 1647. V. 68

REYNOLDS, A. J.
From the Ivory Coast to the Cameroons. London: 1929. V. 71

REYNOLDS, A. M.
The Life and Work of Frank Holl. London: 1912. V. 73

REYNOLDS, BAILLE, MRS.
Accessory After the Fact. London: 1928. V. 70
The Affair at the Chateau. London: 1929. V. 70
Black Light. London: 1937. V. 70

REYNOLDS, BAILLIE, MRS.
It Is Not Safe to Know. New York: 1939. V. 68

REYNOLDS, BRUCE
Paris With the Lid Lifted. New York: 1927. V. 70; 72

REYNOLDS, CHARLES R.
American Indian Portraits from the Wanamaker Expedition of 1913. 1971. V. 69
American Indian Portraits from the Wanamaker Expedition of 1913. Brattleboro: 1971. V. 71

REYNOLDS, FREDERIC
The Keepsake for MDCCCXXIX. London: 1828. V. 70
The Keepsake for MDCCCXXX. London: 1829. V. 70
The Keepsake for MDCCCXXXII. London: 1831. V. 70
A Playwright's Adventures. London: 1831. V. 72

REYNOLDS, GEORGE WILLIAM
The Aloes of Tropical Africa and Madagascar. Mbabane: 1966. V. 70
The Steam Packet: a Tale of the River and the Ocean. London. V. 70

REYNOLDS, GEORGE WILLIAM MAC ARTHUR
Pickwick Abroad. A Companion to the Pickwick Papers. Philadelphia. V. 69
Pickwick Abroad, or the Tour in France. London: 1864. V. 69
Pickwick Abroad, or the Tour in France in Dicks English Library. London: 1890-1891. V. 69

REYNOLDS, HENRY
Memoir of James Prescott. Manchester: 1892. V. 70

REYNOLDS HISTORICAL LIBRARY
Rare Books and Collections of the Reynolds Historical Library. A Bibliography. Birmingham: 1968. V. 68

REYNOLDS, J. H.
The Naiad: a Tale. With Other Poems. London: 1816. V. 72
Peter Bell. A Lyrical Ballad. London: 1819. V. 72
Safie. An Eastern Tale. London: 1814. V. 72

REYNOLDS, JAMES
Andrea Palladio and the Winged Device. New York: 1948. V. 69; 72

REYNOLDS, JOHN
A Kansas Hell, or Life in the Kansas Penitentiary. Atchison: 1889. V. 71
The Twin Hells. Atchison: 1890. V. 71

REYNOLDS, JOSHUA
Johnson and Garrick. London: 1816. V. 68; 72
The Literary Works of Sir Joshua Reynolds, Kt.... London: 1819. V. 69; 72; 73
Portraits. Character Sketches of Oliver Goldsmith, Samuel Johnson, and David Garrick. London: 1952. V. 72
Seven Discourses Delivered in the Royal Academy by the President.... London: 1778. V. 70; 73
The Works Containing His Discourses, Idlers, a Journey to Flanders and Holland.. London: 1797. V. 73
The Works of Sir Joshua Reynolds.... London: 1797. V. 71

REYNOLDS, JULIA L.
No Answer? Poems. New York: 1937. V. 72

REYNOLDS, OSBORNE
Memoir of James Prescott. Manchester: 1892. V. 68; 72

REYNOLDS, SHERI
Bitterroot Landing. New York: 1994. V. 70; 71; 73

REYNOLDS-BALL, EUSTACE A.
The City of the Caliphs. Boston: 1897. V. 71

REZAC, J.
Ninety Six Photographs. 1964. V. 68

REZNIKOFF, CHARLES
By the Well of Living and Seeing: New and Selected Poems 1918-1973. Los Angeles: 1974. V. 68
Five Groups of Verse. New York: 1927. V. 68
In Memoriam: 1933. New York: 1934. V. 68; 71
Inscriptions: 1944-1956. New York: 1959. V. 68
Jerusalem the Golden. New York: 1934. V. 68
Nine Plays. New York: 1927. V. 68; 69; 71
Separate Way. New York: 1936. V. 68; 71

RHAM, W. L.
The Dictionary of the Farm. London: 1844. V. 71

RHEAD, LOUIS
The Speckled Brook Trout. New York: 1902. V. 72

RHIND, WILLIAM
A History of the Vegetable Kingdom. London: 1872. V. 70; 73
The Natural History of the Feline Species. 1834. V. 69; 72
The Natural History of the Feline Species. Edinburgh: 1834. V. 69; 70; 73

RHOAD, A. O.
Santa Gertrudis Breeders' International Recorded Herds. Kingsville: 1953-1959. V. 71

RHOADES, A.
A Houseful of Rebels...an Account of Three Naughty Girls; and Their Adventures in Fairyland. Westminster: 1897. V. 69

RHOADS, DOROTHY
The Corn Grows Ripe. New York: 1956. V. 68

RHODE ISLAND. LAWS, STATUTES, ETC. - 1752
Acts and Laws of His Majesty's Colony of Rhode Island, and providence Plantations in New England in America from Anno 1745 to Anno 1752. Newport: 1752. V. 68

RHODE, JOHN
Body Unidentified. New York: 1938. V. 69
By Registered Post. London: 1952. V. 71
Dead of the Night. New York: 1942. V. 72
Death at the Helm. New York: 1941. V. 70
Death Invades the Meeting. London: 1944. V. 71
Death of Bridegroom. 1957. V. 72
Death on the Lawn. London: 1955. V. 72
Dr. Priestly Investigates. New York: 1930. V. 71
The Dovebury Murders. London: 1954. V. 72
The Elm Murder. 1939. V. 71
Hendon's First Case. New York: 1935. V. 68
The House on Tollard Ridge. New York: 1929. V. 69
Invisible Weapons. 1938. V. 71
The Last Suspect. New York: 1951. V. 71
Nothing But The Truth. London: 1947. V. 72
Open Verdict. London: 1956. V. 72
Poison for One. 1934. V. 71
The Secret of High Eldersham. New York: 1931. V. 70
The Shadow on the Cliff. New York: 1944. V. 69
Three Cousins Die. 1960. V. 71
The Tower of Evil. New York: 1938. V. 71
Tragedy at the Unicorn. 1928. V. 69
The Venner Crime. London: 1933. V. 71
The White Menace. 1926. V. 71

RHODE, WERNER
Gerd Winner Bilder 1970-1976. Berlin: 1976. V. 70

RHODES, DANIEL P.
A Pleasure-Book of Grindelwald. New York: 1903. V. 69

RHODES, DENNIS
Bookbindings and Other Bibliophily. Verona: 1994. V. 68

RHODES, EBENEZER
Peak Scenery, or Excursions in Derbyshire: Made Chiefly for the Purpose of Picturesque Observation. London: 1818-1823. V. 71; 72

RHODES, EUGENE MANLOVE
Beyond the Desert. Boston: 1934. V. 70
The Line of Least Resistance. Chico, CA: 1958. V. 72
The Little World of Waddies. Chico, CA: 1946. V. 68; 71
The Little World of Waddies. El Paso: 1946. V. 70; 72
The Trusty Knaves. Boston: 1933. V. 71

West is West. New York: 1917. V. 68

RHODES, FREDERICK LELAND
Beginning of Telephony. New York and London: 1929. V. 69

RHODES, MAY D.
The Hired Man on Horseback - My Own Story of Eugene Manlove Rhodes. Boston: 1938. V. 68; 71

RHYMERS' CLUB, LONDON
The Book of the Rhymers' Club. London: 1892. V. 69; 73
The Book of the Rhymers' Club; together with The Second Book of the Rhymers' Club. London: 1892-1894. V. 72
The Second Book of the Rhymers' Club. London: 1894. V. 70; 73

RHYMES for the Nursery. New Haven. V. 73
RHYMES for the Nursery. Concord: 1843. V. 69

RHYS, ERNEST
The English Fairy Book. London: 1916. V. 72
The Fiddler of Carne: a North Sea Winter's Tale. Edinburgh: 1896. V. 69
Letters from Limbo. London: 1936. V. 69
A New Book of Sense and Nonsense. London: 1928. V. 69
The Old Country: A Book of Love and Praise of England. London: 1929. V. 70

RHYS, GRACE
The Diverted Village: a Holiday Book. London: 1903. V. 69
In Wheelabout and Cockalone. London: 1918. V. 69
In Wheelabout and Cockalone. New York: 1918. V. 69

RHYS, JEAN
The Collected Stories. New York. V. 73
The Left Bank and Other Stories. New York and London. V. 73
My Day. New York: 1975. V. 73
Sleep It Off Lady. London: 1976. V. 71
Sleep It Off Lady. New York: 1976. V. 73
Tigers Are Better Looking. London: 1968. V. 72
Voyage in the Dark. New York: 1935. V. 69
Wide Sargasso Sea. London: 1966. V. 70; 71
Wide Sargasso Sea. New York: 1967. V. 73

RHYS, LLOYD
High Lights and Flights in New Guinea. London: 1942. V. 71

RIBBLESDALE, LORD
The Queen's Hounds and Staghunting Recollections. 1897. V. 68

RIBELIN, W. E.
The Pathology of Fishes. Madison: 1975. V. 69; 72; 73

RICARD, JAMES D.
The Catholic Church and the Kaffir. London and Dublin: 1880. V. 70

RICARDO, DAVID
The High Price of Bullion, a Proof of the Depreciation of Bank Notes. London: 1810. V. 73
Letters...to Thomas Robert Malthus 1810-1823. Oxford: 1887. V. 69
Proposals for an Economical and Secure Currency; with Observations on the Profits of the Bank of England, as They Regard the Public and the Proprietors of Bank Stock.... London: 1819. V. 73
On Protection to Agriculture. London: 1822. V. 69
On the Principles of Political Economy and Taxation. London: 1817. V. 68
On the Principles of Political Economy and Taxation. London: 1819. V. 68; 72
On the Principles of Political Economy and Taxation. London: 1821. V. 68
Reply to Mr. Bosanquet's Practical Observations on the Report of the Bullion Committee. London: 1811. V. 73

RICARDO, M.
Observations on the Advantages of Oil Gas Establishments. London: 1823. V. 69

RICAUT, PAUL
The Present State of the Greek and American Churches, Anno Christi 1678. London: 1679. V. 70

RICCI, BARTOLOMEO
Apparatvs Latinae Locvitionis. Argentorati: 1535. V. 71

RICCI, GASPARD
Guide de la Ville de Florence avec Description de la Galerie et du Palais Pitti Ornee u Vues et Statues. Florence: 1827. V. 70

RICCI, JAMES V.
One Hundred Years of Gynecology: 1800-1900. Mansfield Centre: 1999. V. 68

RICCI, MATTEO
De Christiniana Expeditiona Apvd Sinas. Augsburg: 1615. V. 71

RICCI, SEYMOUR DE
The Book Collector's Guide: a Practical Handbook of British and American Bibliograhy. Philadelphia and New York: 1921. V. 71
Census of Medieval and Renaissance Manuscripts in the United States and Canada. New York: 1935-1940. V. 70
English Collectors of Books and Manuscripts (1530-1930) and Their Marks of Ownership. 1930. V. 71

RICCIUTI, I. W.
New Orleans and Its Environs: the Domestic Architecture.... New York: 1938. V. 69

RICCOBONI, LEWIS
An Historical and Critical Account of the Theatres in Europe.... London: 1741. V. 71

RICE, A. H.
The Shenandoah Pottery. Strasburg: 1929. V. 70

RICE, ANNE
Beauty's Punishment. New York: 1984. V. 69
Beauty's Release. 1985. V. 70
Belinda. New York: 1986. V. 68; 71
Cry to Heaven. New York: 1982. V. 68
Exit to Eden. 1985. V. 73
Exit to Eden. New York: 1985. V. 68; 71; 72
The Feast of All Saints. New York: 1979. V. 71; 73
Interview with the Vampire. London: 1976. V. 68; 69; 71
Interview with the Vampire. New York: 1976. V. 68; 69; 71; 72; 73
Lasher. New York: 1993. V. 69
The Master of Rampling Gate. Wheeling: 1991. V. 71
Memnoch the Devil. New York: 1995. V. 72
Merrick. Franklin Center: 2000. V. 68
Pandora. New Orleans: 1998. V. 69
Pandora. New York: 1998. V. 72
The Queen of the Damned. New York: 1988. V. 68
Servant of the Bones. London: 1996. V. 70
Servant of the Bones. New York: 1996. V. 68; 71; 72
The Tale of the Body Thief. New York: 1992. V. 68; 72
Taltos. New York: 1994. V. 72
The Vampire Armand. London: 1998. V. 70
The Vampire Armand. New Orleans: 1998. V. 69
The Vampire Armand. New York: 1998. V. 72
The Vampire Chronicles. New York: 1990. V. 70
The Vampire Lestat. New York: 1985. V. 69; 71
Violin. London: 1997. V. 70
Violin. New York: 1997. V. 72

RICE, CLARA C.
Mary Bird In Persia. London: 1916. V. 72

RICE, CRAIG
The April Robin Murders. New York: 1958. V. 71
The Fourth Postman. New York: 1948. V. 72
The G-String Murders. New York: 1941. V. 70
Los Angeles Murders. New York: 1947. V. 71
The Lucky Stiff. NY: 1945. V. 72
My Kingdom for a Horse. New York: 1957. V. 68
The Name is Malone. New York: 1958. V. 69

RICE, ELMER
Street Scene. New York: 1929. V. 72
We, the People. New York: 1933. V. 68

RICE, ETHEL M.
Wiggle and Waggle: the Story of the Cuddley Kitten and Pedigreed Pup. New York: 1939. V. 70

RICE, HOWARD C.
Barthelemi Tardiveau - a French Trader in the West. Baltimore: 1938. V. 69

RICE, LEE M.
They Saddled the West. Cambridge: 1975. V. 73

RICE, NATHAN P.
Trials of a Public Benefactor, as Illustrated in the Discovery of Etherization. New York: 1859. V. 68

RICE, WILLIAM
Indian Game, from Quail to Tiger. 1884. V. 72; 73

RICH, ADRIENNE
Collected Early Poems, 1950-1970. New York: 1993. V. 69; 72
What Is Found There. Notebooks on Poetry and Politics. New York: 1993. V. 69; 72

RICH, ARNOLD R.
The Pathogenesis of Tuberculosis. Springfield: 1944. V. 71

RICH, CLAUDIUS JAMES
Narrative of a Journey to the Site of Babylon in 1811. London: 1839. V. 70
Narrative of a Residence in Koordistan. London: 1836. V. 71

RICH, W. H.
Feathered Game of New England. London: 1908. V. 73

RICHARD, EDOUARD
Acadia. Missing Links of a Lost Chapter in American History. New York: 1895. V. 71; 72

RICHARD, LOUIS CLAUDE MARIE
A Botanical Dictionary.... New Haven: 1817. V. 69

RICHARD, MARK
The Ice at the Bottom of the World. New York: 1989. V. 70

RICHARD Meier Architect 1964-1984. 1984. V. 69
RICHARD Meier Architect 1964-1984. New York: 1984. V. 72

RICHARD MELHUISH & SONS
Illustrated Catalogue of Tools, &c. 1891. V. 71

RICHARD-HENRY, PSEUD.
Misery Junction and Other Stage Stories. London: 1890?. V. 68

RICHARDS, ALUN
The Elephant You Gave Me. London: 1963. V. 68

RICHARDS, CLARICE E.
A Tenderfoot Bride. New York: 1920. V. 71

RICHARDS, FRANK
The Banishing of Billy Bunter. London: 1956. V. 70; 71
Big Chief Bunter. London: 1963. V. 70; 71
Billy Bunter Afloat. London: 1957. V. 70
Billy Bunter Among the Cannibals. London: 1950. V. 70
Billy Bunter and the Blue Mauritius. 1952. V. 71
Billy Bunter and the Blue Mauritius. London: 1952. V. 70
Billy Bunter at Butlin's. London: 1961. V. 70; 71
Billy Bunter Butts In. London: 1951. V. 70
Billy Bunter in Brazil. London: 1949. V. 70
Billy Bunter the Bold. London: 1954. V. 70; 71; 72
Billy Bunter the Hiker. London: 1958. V. 70
Billy Bunter's Banknote. London: 1948. V. 70
Billy Bunter's Bargain. London: 1958. V. 70
Billy Bunters Barring Out. London: 1948. V. 70
Billy Bunter's Beanfeast. London: 1952. V. 68; 70; 71
Billy Bunter's Benefit. 1950. V. 71
Billy Bunter's Benefit. London: 1950. V. 70
Billy Bunter's Bodyguard. London: 1962. V. 70; 71
Billy Bunter's Bolt. London: 1957. V. 70; 71
Billy Bunter's Bolt. New York: 1957. V. 70
Billy Bunter's Brain-Wave. London: 1953. V. 70
Billy Bunter's Double. London: 1955. V. 70
Billy Bunter's First Case. London: 1953. V. 70; 71
Billy Bunter's Treasure Hunt. London: 1961. V. 70; 71
Bunter Comes for Christmas. London: 1959. V. 70; 71
Bunter Does His Best?. London: 1954. V. 70
Bunter Keeps It Dark. London: 1960. V. 70; 71
Bunter Out of Bounds. London: 1959. V. 70; 71
Bunter The Bad Lad. London: 1960. V. 72
Bunter the Caravanner. London: 1962. V. 70; 71
Bunter the Sportsman. London: 1965. V. 70; 71
Bunter the Stowaway. London: 1964. V. 70; 71
Bunter the Ventriloquist. London: 1961. V. 70; 71
Bunter's Last Fling. London: 1965. V. 70; 71
Just Like Bunter. London: 1963. V. 70; 71
Lord Billy Bunter. London: 1956. V. 70; 71
Thanks to Bunter. London: 1964. V. 70; 71; 72

RICHARDS, G. H.
The New Zealand Pilot. London: 1859. V. 71

RICHARDS, GEORGE HALLAM
The Politics of Connecticut.... Hartford: 1817. V. 68

RICHARDS, J.
Lakes, Peaks and Passes. Barrow-in-Furness: 1870. V. 71

RICHARDS, J. M.
High Street. London: 1938. V. 69

RICHARDS, JOHN MORGAN
A Chronology of Medicine Ancient, Mediaeval, and Modern. London: 1880. V. 68

RICHARDS, KENT D.
Isaac I. Stevens, Young Man in a Hurry. Provo: 1979. V. 68

RICHARDS, LAURA
Five Mice. Boston: 1882. V. 70
Five Mice in a Mouse Trap by the Man in the Moon. Boston: 1880. V. 70
Julia Ward Howe 1819-1910. Boston: 1916. V. 69

RICHARDS, MEL
Peter Rabbit the Magician. 1942. V. 69

RICHARDS, NAT
Otis Dunn, Mannunter. Port Washington: 1974:. V. 72

RICHARDSON, A. E.
Monumental Classic Architecture in Great Britain and Ireland During the XVIIIth and XIXth Centuries. London: 1914. V. 71

RICHARDSON, A. H.
A Description of the Oxford Baths or School of Natation. Oxford: 1830. V. 68; 70; 72

RICHARDSON, ALBERT
Garnered Sheaves - from the Writing of Albert P. Richardson. Hartford: 1871. V. 70

RICHARDSON, BENJAMIN WARD
Disciples of Aesculapius.... London: 1900. V. 68

RICHARDSON, C. J.
The Englishman's House. London: 1898. V. 71
The Englishman's House from a Cottage to a Mansion. London: 1871. V. 73
Picturesque Designs for Mansions, Villas, Lodges &c.... London: 1870. V. 68
A Popular Treatise on the Warming and Ventilation of Buildings.... London: 1839. V. 68

RICHARDSON, CHARLES
A New Dictionary of the English Language.... London: 1844. V. 72

RICHARDSON, CHARLOTTE CAROLINE
Poems Written on Different Occasions. York: 1809. V. 69

RICHARDSON, DARRELL C.
Max Brand: the Man and His Work. Los Angeles: 1952. V. 69

RICHARDSON, DAVID
Richardson's Virginia and North Carolina Almanac for the Year of Our Lord 1862.... Richmond: 1861. V. 70
Southern Almanac for 1864. Lynchburg: 1863. V. 69; 70

RICHARDSON, DOROTHY M.
Honeycomb. London: 1917. V. 71
Interim. London: 1919. V. 71
Oberland. London: 1927. V. 71
Revolving Lights. London: 1923. V. 71

RICHARDSON, GEORGE
Engravings From the Works of Henry Liverseege, With A Memoir. London: 1875. V. 72

RICHARDSON, GEORGE W.
Speech of George W. Richardson of Hanover, in Committe of the Whole.... Richmond: 1862. V. 70

RICHARDSON, H.
A Monograph on the Isopods of North America. Washington: 1905. V. 72

RICHARDSON, H. D.
Facts Concerning the Natural History of Gigantic Irish Deer. 1846. V. 69

RICHARDSON, HENRY HANDEL, PSEUD.
The End of Childhood and Other Stories. London: 1934. V. 69
The Fortunes of Richard Mahony. London: 1930. V. 69

RICHARDSON, ISAAC
Memoir of Isaac Richardson, of Newcastle-Upon Tyne. London: 1841. V. 72; 73

RICHARDSON, J.
Furness Past and Present: Its History and Antiquities. Barrow-in-Furness: 1870-1880. V. 71

RICHARDSON, JAMES D.
A Compilation of the Messages and Papers of the Presidents 1789-1905. 1905-1906. V. 71

RICHARDSON, JOHN
An Account of the Life of That Ancient Servant of Jesus Christ, John Richardson. London: 1774. V. 72
Arctic Searching Expedition: a Journal of a Boat Voyage through Rupert's Land and the Arctic Sea.... London: 1851. V. 69; 71
Fauna Boreali-Americana; or the Zoology of the Northern Parts of British America.... London: 1831. V. 70; 73
Ichthyology of the Voyage of H.M.S. Erebus & Terror, Under the Command of Captain Sir James Clark Ross.... London: 1844-1848. V. 73
The Museum of Natural History. Glasgow: 1859-1862?. V. 70; 72
The Museum of Natural History. Glasgow: 1868. V. 70
The Museum of Natural History. Glasgow: 1870. V. 72
Report on the Ichthyology of the Seas of China and Japan. London: 1846. V. 73
Wallace Stevens: the Early Years 1879-1923. (with) Wallace Stevens: The Later Years 1923-1955. New York: 1986-1988. V. 68

RICHARDSON, JONATHAN
Traite de la Peinture. Amsterdam: 1728. V. 71
Two Discourses. I. An Essay on the Whole Art of Criticism as It Relates to Painting....II. An Argument in Behalf of the Science of a Connoisseur.... London: 1725. V. 72
The Works. Strawberry Hill: 1792. V. 69

RICHARDSON, JOSEPH
A Practical Treatise on Mechanical Denistry. Philadelphia: 1869. V. 69

RICHARDSON, MAURICE
The Exploits of Englebrecht abstracted from the Chronicles of the Surrealist Sportman's Club. London: 1950. V. 71

RICHARDSON, R. H.
Wickedness in High Places a Discourse Occasioned by the Bill for the Government of Kanzas and Nebraska.... Chicago: 1854. V. 73

RICHARDSON, ROBERT
Bellringer Street. Gollancz: 1988. V. 72
The Book of the Dead. London: 1989. V. 72
Travels Along the Mediterranean and Parts Adjacent; in Company with the Earl of Belmore. London: 1822. V. 71

RICHARDSON, RUPERT NORVAL
The Comanche Barrier to South Plains Settlement. Abilene: 1991. V. 69; 73
The Frontier of Northwest Texas 1846 to 1876: Advance and Defense by the Pioneer Settlers of the Cross Timbers and Prairies. Glendale: 1963. V. 70; 72; 73
The Greater Southwest. Glendale: 1934. V. 68

RICHARDSON, SAMUEL
Clarissa, or the History of a Young Lady.... London: 1748. V. 71
Clarissa, or the History of a Young Lady.... London: 1759. V. 69; 72; 73
The History of Sir Charles Grandison. London: 1754. V. 68
The History of Sir Charles Grandison. London: 1766. V. 73
The History of Sir Charles Grandison. London: 1770. V. 69
The History of Sir Charles Grandison. London: 1781. V. 69
The History of Sir Charles Grandison. London: 1796. V. 71
The History of Sir Charles Grandison. London: 1873. V. 68
The History of Sir Charles Grandison...(and) Clarissa.... Suffield: 1798. V. 71
The History of Sir William Harrington. London: 1772. V. 73
Pamela, or Virtue Rewarded. London: 1785. V. 72; 73
The Works. London: 1811. V. 72

RICHARDSON, SARAH
Literary Relics of the Late Joseph Richardson, Esq.... London: 1807. V. 68; 73

RICHARDSON, T. A.
The Art of Architectural Modelling in Paper. London: 1859. V. 68

RICHARDSON, THOMAS
Richardson's New Royal Battledore. Derby: 1830. V. 70

RICHARDSON, W. C. F.
India Rubber Jack. London: 1902. V. 70

RICHARDSON, WILLIAM
Anecdotes of the Russian Empire. London: 1784. V. 70
A Philosophical Analysis and Illustration of Some of Shakespeare's Remarkable Characters. London: 1774. V. 69
A Philosophical Analysis and Illustration of Some of Shakespeare's Remarkable Characters. London: 1775. V. 71

RICHARDSON, WILLIS
Plays and Pageants From the Life of the Negro. Washington, D.C: 1930. V. 72

RICHARDSON-GARDNER, ROBERT
A Trip to St. Petersburg. London: 1872. V. 73

RICHARDSON'S
Virginia and North Carolina Almanac, for the Year of Our Lord 1863.... Richmond: 1862. V. 70

RICHERAND, A.
Elements of Physiology. London: 1812. V. 68; 73

RICHEY, MATTHEW
A Memoir of the Late Rev. William Black, Wesleyan Minister. Halifax: 1838. V. 73

RICHIE, D.
The Masters' Book of Ikebana.... Tokyo: 1966. V. 68

RICHIE, MARY CHRISTINE
Major General Sir Geoffrey Twining K.C.M.G., C.B., M.V.O. Montreal & Toronto: 1922. V. 73

RICHLER, MORDECAI
The Acrobats - a Novel. London: 1954. V. 68
The Apprenticeship of Duddy Kravitz. Boston and Toronto: 1959. V. 71
Son of a Smaller Hero. London: 1955. V. 69

RICHMAN, IRVING
California Under Spain and Mexico 1535-1847. Boston and New York: 1911. V. 73
Rhode Island. A Study in Separation. Boston: 1905. V. 70

RICHMOND
& Danville Railroad Series No. 1. Land of the Sky, Views on the Western North Carolina R.R. New York: 1883. V. 73

RICHMOND,
Capital of Virginia: Approaches to Its History. Richmond: 1938. V. 73

RICHMOND, GRACE S.
Cherry Square. Garden City: 1926. V. 70
Red of the Redfields. Garden City: 1924. V. 69

RICHMOND
Howitzers in the War: Four Years Campaigning with the Army of Northern Virginia. Richmond: 1891. V. 69

RICHMOND, MARY L.
Shaker Literature: a Bibliogrpahy. Hancock: 1977. V. 72

RICHMOND & LENNOX, CHARLES LENNOX, 3RD DUKE OF
A Letter from His Grace the Duke of Richmond to Lieutenant Colonel Sharman, Chairman to the Committee of Correspondence Appointed by the Delegates of Forty-Five Corps of Volunteers.... London: 1792. V. 71

RICHMOND'S
Morris County (New Jersey) Directory, 1902-1903. Yonkers: 1902. V. 72

RICHTER & CO.
A Charming Colour Illustrated Catalogue Issued by Richter and Co., for Their Architectural Building Sets. 1895. V. 69

RICHTER, AUGUST GOTTLIEB
Chirugische Bibliothek. Gottingen und Gotha: 1771-1796. V. 72

RICHTER, CONRAD
Always Young and Fair. New York: 1947. V. 71; 72
A Country of Strangers. New York: 1996. V. 69
The Fields. New York: 1946. V. 72
The Free Man. New York: 1943. V. 72
The Light in the Forest. New York: 1942. V. 72
The Sea of Grass. 1937. V. 68
The Sea of Grass. New York: 1937. V. 73
A Simple Honorable Man. New York: 1962. V. 70
Tacey Cromwell. New York: 1942. V. 72

RICHTER, DR.
The Toy the Child Likes Best. London: 1888-1892?. V. 68

RICHTER, FRANCIS C.
Richter's History and Records of Base Ball: The American Nation's Chief Sport. Philadelphia: 1914. V. 70

RICHTER, GISELA M. A.
Catalogue of Engraved Gems of the Classical Style. New York: 1920. V. 71
The Metropolitan Museum of Art: the Sculpture and Sculptures of the Greeks. New Haven: 1930. V. 70

RICHTER, HANS
Hans Richter. London: 1971. V. 72

RICHTER, HENRY
Day-Light: a Recent Discovery in the Art of Painting; with Hints on the Philosophy of the Fine Arts.... London: 1817. V. 69; 72
Illustrations of the Works of Henry Richter, First Series. London: 1822. V. 72

RICHTHOFEN, WALTER BARON VON
Cattle-Raising On the Plains of North America. New York: 1885. V. 71

RICKARD, THOMAS ARTHUR
The Copper Mines of Lake Superior. New York: 1905. V. 73
The Romance of Mining. Toronto: 1944. V. 68
Through the Yukon to Alaska. San Francisco: 1909. V. 69; 73

RICKARDS, COLIN
Buckskin Frank Leslie Gunman of Tombstone. El Paso: 1964. V. 68

RICKARDS, CONSTANTINE GEORGE
The Ruins of Mexico. London: 1910. V. 70; 71

RICKENBACKER, EDWARD
Fighting the Flying Circus. New York: 1919. V. 68
Rickenbacker. Englewood Cliffs: 1967. V. 69

RICKER, JACKSON
Historical Sketches of Glenwood and the Argyles, Yarmouth County, Nova Scotia. Truro: 1941. V. 73

RICKETSON, SHADRACH
Means of Preserving Health and Preventing Diseases, Founded Principally on an Attention to Air and Climate, Drink, Food.... New York: 1806. V. 73

RICKETT, H. W.
Wild Flowers of the United States. New York: 1966-1973. V. 72; 73
Wild Flowers of the United States. Volume 1. The Northeastern States (in two parts). New York: 1966. V. 68; 69; 71; 72; 73
Wild Flowers of the United States. Volume 2. The Southeastern States. New York: 1967. V. 69; 71
Wild Flowers of the United States. Volume 3. Texas (in two parts). New York: 1969. V. 68; 69; 71; 73
Wild Flowers of the United States. Volume 4. The Southwestern States. (in 3 parts). New York: 1970. V. 68; 73
Wild Flowers of the United States. Volume 5. The Northwestern States (in 2 parts). New York: 1971. V. 68; 70; 73

RICKETTS, CHARLES
Beyond the Threshold. 1929. V. 68
Charles Ricketts R. A. - Sixty-Five Illustrations. London: 1933. V. 69
De La Typographie et de l'Harmonie de la Page Imprimee. Willim Morris et Son Influence sur les Arts et Metiers. London: 1898. V. 72
Oscar Wilde: Recollections.... London: 1932. V. 72
Unrecorded Histories. London: 1936. V. 68

RICKEY, DON
History of Custer Battlefield. Montana: 1967. V. 72

RICKMAN, PHILIP
A Bird Painter's Sketch Book. 1935. V. 69; 71
Bird Sketches and Some Field Observations. 1938. V. 69; 71
A Bird-Painters Sketch Book. London and New York: 1931. V. 72; 73

RICKMAN, THOMAS
An Attempt to Discriminate the Styles of Architecture in England, From the Conquest to the Reformation .... London: 1835. V. 70
An Attempt to Discriminate the Styles of Architecture in England, from the Conquest to the Reformation.... London: 1848. V. 71

RICKMERS, W. RICKMER
The Duab of Turkestan. Cambridge: 1913. V. 71

RICKOFF, REBECCA
Appleton's Chart Primer. Exercises in Reading at Sight and Language and Color Lessons for Beginners. New York: 1885. V. 71

RICKS, JOEL E.
The History of a Valley - Cache Valley, Utah-Idaho. Logan: 1956. V. 68; 73

RICKWORD, EDGELL
Behind the Eyes. London: 1921. V. 70
Twittingpan and Some Others. London: 1931. V. 70

RIDDELL, CHARLOTTE ELIZABETH
Mortomley's Estate. London: 1875. V. 68

RIDDELL, FLORENCE
Out of the Mist. New York: 1926. V. 71

RIDDELL, JAMES R.
Handbook of Medical Electricity and Radiology. Edinburgh: 1926. V. 68

RIDDELL, MRS.
A Bright Sunset. The Last Days of A Young Scottish Football Player (William Easton Riddell). London: 1886. V. 72

RIDDELL, ROBERT
The Carpenter and Joiner, Stair Builder and Hand-Railer. Edinburgh: c.1880. V. 70; 72
Handrailing Simplified: Being an Entirely New and Original System of Lines, Containing the Grand Problems.... Philadelphia: 1856. V. 68

RIDDELL, W. R.
Hieronymus Fracastorius and His Poetical and Prose Works on Syphilis. Toronto: 1928. V. 73
The Life of John Graves Simcoe, First Lieutenant-Governor of the Province of Upper Canada 1792-1796. Toronto: 1926. V. 73

A RIDDLE Book for the Use of Children. (No. 3). Concord: 1843. V. 69; 70

RIDDLES for the Nursery. New York: 1856-1866. V. 71

RIDE a Cock Horse to Banbury Cross. London: 1895. V. 70

RIDEAL, C. F.
Wellerisms. London: 1886. V. 69

RIDEAL, SAMUEL
The Relative Hygienic Values of Gas and Electric Lighting. London: 1908. V. 69

RIDEOUT, HENRY MILLER
William Jones Indian, Cowboy, American Scholor, and Anthropologist in the Field. NY: 1912. V. 72

RIDER, CARDANUS
Rider's British Merlin; for...1789. 1789. V. 69

RIDER, SARAH
The Misplaced Corpse. Boston: 1940. V. 70

RIDGE, A.
The Man Who Painted Roses. London: 1974. V. 72

RIDGE, JOHN ROLLIN
A Trumpet of Our Own. Yellow Bird's Essays on the North American Indian. San Francisco: 1981. V. 73

RIDGE, LOLA
Firehead. New York: 1929. V. 69; 71; 73

RIDGELY, DAVID
Annals of Annapolis, Comprising Sundry Notices of that Old City from the Period of the First Settlements in Its Vicinity in the Year 1649 and the War of 1812. Baltimore: 1841. V. 73

RIDGELY, R. S.
The Birds of South America. Austin: 1989-1994. V. 68

RIDGELY NEVITT, CEDRIC
American Steamships on the Atlantic. Newark: 1981. V. 68

RIDGEWAY, RICK
The Shadow of Kilimanjaro. New York: 1998. V. 72

RIDGEWAY, WILLIAM
A Report of the Trial of Edward Kearney for High Treason. (with) Trial of James Byrne. 1803. V. 71
A Report of the Trial of Walter Clare...High Treason. 1803. V. 71

RIDGWAY, R.
A Manual of North American Birds. Philadelphia: 1887. V. 72; 73

RIDGWAY, ROBERT
Color Standards and Color Nomenclature. Washington: 1912. V. 68; 72

RIDING, LAURA
Description of Life. New York: 1980. V. 68
Four Unposted Letters to Catherine. Paris: 1930. V. 70
The Life of the Dead. London. V. 69; 73
Life of the Dead. London: 1933. V. 69
Lives of Wives. London: 1939. V. 68
Poet: a Lying Word. 1933. V. 70
Poet: a Lying Word. London: 1933. V. 68
Progress of Stories. Deya, Majorca and London: 1935. V. 68; 71
Progress of Stories. New York: 1982. V. 68
Some Communications of Broad Reference. Northridge: 1983. V. 68
Though Gently. Deya, Majorca: 1930. V. 70
A Trojan Ending. 1937. V. 70

RIDINGS, P. SAM
The Chisholm Trail: A History of the World's Greatest Cattle Trail. Guthrie: 1936. V. 68; 69; 71; 72

RIDLAND, JOHN
Elegy for My Aunt. Omaha: 1981. V. 68

RIDLER, ANNE
Dies Natalis: Poems of Birth and Infancy. London: 1980. V. 72
A Dream Observed and Other Poems. London: 1941. V. 72
A Dream Observed and Other Poems. London: 1948. V. 68
Henry Bly and Other Plays. London: 1950. V. 72
Italian Prospect: Six Poems. Oxford: 1976. V. 68; 70; 72
The Jesse Tree: a Church Opera or Masque. 1970. V. 72
A Matter of Life and Death. Oxford: 1975. V. 72

RIDLER, ANNE continued
Poems. London: 1929. V. 70
The Shadow Factory: a Nativity Play. London: 1946. V. 68
Working for T. S. Eliot. 2000. V. 70
Working of T. S. Eliot. London: 2000. V. 69

RIDLEY, BROMFIELD L.
Battles and Sketches of the Army of Tennessee. Mexico: 1906. V. 69; 70

RIDLEY, H. N.
The Dispersal of Plants Throughout the World. Ashford: 1930. V. 72
Materials for a Flora of the Malayan Peninsula. Singapore: 1907-1908. V. 68

RIDLEY, S. O.
Challenger Voyage. Zoology. Part 59. Monaxonida. 1887. V. 73

RIDPATH, GEORGE
The Border-History of England and Scotland, Deduced from the Earliest Times to the Union of the Two Crowns. London: 1776. V. 73
The Scots Episcopal Innocence; or, the Judging of that Party with the Late King, His Present Majesty, the Church of England, and the Church of Scotland, Demonstrated. London: 1694. V. 70
The Stage Condemned, and the Encouragement Given to Immoralities and Profaneness of the Theatre, by the English Schools, Universities and Pulpits Censor'd.... London: 1698. V. 68

RIDSDALE, BENJAMIN
Scenes and Adventures in Great Namaqualand. London: 1883. V. 71

RIEDY, JAMES L.
Chicago Sculpture. 1981. V. 72

RIEFENSTAHL, LENI
Coral Gardens. London: 1978. V. 68
Coral Gardens. New York: 1978. V. 68
The Last of the Nuba. New York: 1973. V. 68
The Last of the Nuba. New York: 1973-1995. V. 69
The People of Kau. New York: 1976. V. 68

RIESZ, R. R.
Description and Demonstration of an Artificial Larynx. 1930. V. 68

RIGBY, CUTHBERT
From Midsummer to Martinmas. A West Cumberland Idyl. London: 1891. V. 71

RIGBY, EDWARD
An Essay on the Uterine Haemorrhage Which Precedes the Delivery of the Full-Grown Fetus. London: 1822. V. 70; 71

RIGG, J. LINTON
The Alluring Antilles A Cruising Guide To The West Indies. London: 1963. V. 72

RIGGE, HENRY FLETCHER
Cartmel Priory Church, North Lancashire. Cartmel: 1885. V. 71

RIGGS, LYNN
Green Grow the Lilacs. Norman: 1954. V. 69
Roadside. New York: 1930. V. 70; 71
Russet Mantle and the Cherokee Night. New York: 1936. V. 70; 71; 72

RIGGS, STEPHEN R.
Mary and I - Forty Years with the Sioux. Chicago: 1880. V. 73

RIGHTER, G. A.
Casting and Mixing Printers' Metals. Richmond: 1923. V. 72

RIGHTS, DOUGLAS L.
The American Indian in North Carolina. Winston Salem: 1957. V. 73
Voyage Down the Yadkin-Great Peedee River. Winston Salem: 1928. V. 73

RIGHYNI, REG
Salmon Taking Times. 1965. V. 68; 73

RIIS, JACOB A.
The Battle with the Slum. New York: 1902. V. 72; 73
The Making of an American. New York: 1901. V. 68

RIKHOFF, J.
Hunting the Big Cats. 1981. V. 73

RILEY, BRIDGET
Bridget Riley Ausgewahlte Gemalde/Selected Paintings 1961-1999. London: 1999. V. 69
The Eye's Mind: Bridget Riley. Collected Writings 1965-1999. London: 1999. V. 69

RILEY, C. V.
Insect Life, Devoted to the Economy and Life Habits of Insects, Especially in Their Relations to Agriculture. Washington: 1888-1890. V. 72

RILEY, FRANKLIN L.
General Robert E. Lee After Appomattox. New York: 1922. V. 70

RILEY, H. P.
Families of Flowering Plants of Southern Africa. Lexington: 1963. V. 72

RILEY, HENRY THOMAS
Chronica Monasterii S. Albani. Gesta Abbatum Monasterii Sancti Albani a Thoma Walsingham, Regnante Ricardo Secundo.... London: 1867-1869. V. 68

RILEY, JAMES
An Authentic Narrative of the Loss of the American Brig Commerce, Wrecked on the Western Coast of Africa, in the Month of August 1815.... New York: 1817. V. 72

RILEY, JAMES F.
The Mast Cells. Edinburgh: 1959. V. 68

RILEY, JAMES WHITCOMB
The Book of Joyous Children. New York: 1902. V. 69
A Childworld. Indianapolis and Kansas City: 1897. V. 70
An Old Sweetheart of Mine. Indianapolis: 1902. V. 73
Out to Old Aunt Mary's. Indianapolis: 1904. V. 73
The Raggedy Man. Indianapolis: 1907. V. 70
Rubaiyat of Doc Sifers. New York: 1897. V. 69

RILEY, L. W.
Aristotle Texts and Commentary to 1700 in the University of Pennsylvania Library. A Catalogue. Philadelphia: 1961. V. 68; 71

RILEY, MICHAEL
Conversation with Anne Rice. New York: 1996. V. 72

RILEY, VERNON
The Pigment Cell: Molecular, Biological and Clinical Aspects. New York: 1963. V. 68

RILEY, WILLIAM HARRISON
Strikes, Their Cause and Remedy. Leeds: 1871?. V. 70

RILING, RAY
Uniform and Dress of the Army and Navy of the Confederate States of America. Meriden: 1960. V. 73

RILKE, RAINER MARIA
Selected Poems. London: 1941. V. 69
Selected Poems. New York: 1981. V. 68

RIMBAUD, ARTHUR
Le Bateau Ivre. New York: 1992. V. 73
A Season in Hell. New York: 1986. V. 69; 70; 71; 72

RIMMER, ALFRED
About England with Dickens. London: 1883. V. 69

RIMMER, CAROLINE
Animal Drawing: a Series of 13 Plates with descriptive Text. Boston and New York: 1895. V. 71

RIMMER, RICHARD
Shells of the British Isles, Land and Freshwater. Edinburgh: 1907. V. 68

RIMMER, WILLIAM GORDON
Marshalls of Leeds, Flax-Spinners 1788-1886. 1960. V. 72

RINDER, EDITH WINGATE
The Shadow of Arvor: Legendary Romances and Folk-Tales of Brittany. Edinburgh. V. 69

RINDER, FRANK
Old World Japan. Legends of the Land of the Gods. London: 1895. V. 71

RINDFLEISCH, EDUARD
A Manual of Pathological Histology to Serve as an Introduction to the Study of Morbid Anatomy. London: 1872-1873. V. 68

RINEHART, MARY ROBERTS
The Amazing Interlude. Toronto: 1918. V. 70
The Circular Staircase. Indianapolis: 1908. V. 69
Dangerous Days. New York: 1919. V. 70
The Doctor. New York and Toronto: 1936. V. 72
I Take This Woman. New York: 1931. V. 70; 71
Kings, Queens, and Pawns. New York: 1915. V. 70
Miss Pinkerton. New York: 1932. V. 70
The Red Lamp. 1925. V. 70
The Red Lamp. New York: 1925. V. 68
The Romantics. New York: 1929. V. 70
This Strange Adventure. Garden City: 1929. V. 70
This Strange Adventure. New York: 1948. V. 71
Tish. Boston: 1916. V. 70; 71
Tish Marches On. New York: 1937. V. 71
Two Flights Up. Garden City: 1928. V. 70

RING, JOHN
A Translation of Anstey's Ode to Jenner to Which is added, a Compendium of Vaccination, Consisting of Two Tables, one Showing the Advantages of Vaccine Inoculation, the Other Containing Instructions for the Practice. London: 1804. V. 72

RING, RAY
Telluride Smile. New York: 1988. V. 68

RINGWALT, J. L.
Development of Transportation Systems in the U.S. from the Colonial Era to the Present Time.... Philadelphia: 1888. V. 69

RIO HORTEGA, PIO DEL
The Microscopic Anatomy of Tumors of the Central and Peripheral Nervous System. Springfield: 1962. V. 70; 71

RIOLAN, JEAN
Manuel Anatomique et Pathologique ou Abrege de Toute l'Anatomie & des Usages que l'on en Peut Tirer Pour le Connaissance & Pour la Guerison des Lamladies. Paris: 1653. V. 70
Opuscula Anatomica Nova Quae Nunc Primium in Lucem Prodeunt Instauratio Imagna Physicae & Medicinae.... London: 1649. V. 70

RIOU, STEPHEN
The Grecian Orders of Architecture Delineated and Explained from the Antiquities of Athens.... London: 1768. V. 70; 72

RIPLEY, CLEMENTS
Black Moon. 1933. V. 73

RIPLEY, GEORGE
A Farewell Discourse, Delivered to the Congregational Church in Purchase Street March 20, 1841. Boston: 1841. V. 71
The Latest Form of Infidelity Examined. A Letter to Mr. Andrews Norton.... Boston: 1839. V. 73
A Letter Addressed to the Congregational Church in Purchase Street (Boston). Boston: 1840. V. 68

RIPLEY, HENRY
The History and Topography of Hampson-on-Thames. London: 1884. V. 70

RIPLEY, JAMES
Select Original Letters on Various Subjects.... London: 1781. V. 73

RIPLEY, MARY CHURCHILL
The Oriental Rug Book. New York: 1904. V. 69; 73

RIPLEY, ROBERT
Believe It or Not! Omnibus. New York: 1934. V. 70

RIPLEY, S. DILLON
Ornithological Books in the Yale University Library.... New Haven: 1961. V. 70; 73
Rails of the World.... Boston: 1977. V. 68; 72; 73

RIPLEY, SHERMAN
The Raggedy Animal Book with Rimes (sic). Chicago: 1928. V. 73

RIPLEY, THOMAS
They Died with Their Boots On. New York: 1935. V. 73

RIPLEY, W. L.
Dreamsicle. Boston;: 1993. V. 69

RIPPEY, SARAH CORY
The Goody-Naughty Book. Chicago & New York: 1913. V. 68

RIPPINGALE, O. H.
Queensland and Great Barrier Reef Shells. Brisbane: 1961. V. 73

RIPPINGILLE'S ALBION LAMP CO.
Rippingille's Albion Cookers. Birmingham: 1907. V. 68

RISCHBIETH, H.
Dwarfism. London: 1912. V. 71

RISING, LAWRENCE
Proud Flesh. New York: 1924. V. 71

RISSIK, ANDREW
The James Bond Man. The Films of Sean Connery. London: 1983. V. 68

RISTER, CARL COKE
Border Captives. Norman: 1941. V. 69
Border Command, General Phil Sheridan in The West. Norman: 1944. V. 72
Comanche Bondage. Glendale: 1955. V. 70; 73
No Man's Land. Norman: 1948. V. 71
Southern Plainsmen. Norman: 1938. V. 72
The Southwestern Frontier 1865-1881. Cleveland: 1928. V. 68

RISTOW, WALTER W.
American Maps and Mapmakers: Commercial Cartography in the Nineteenth Century. Detroit: 1986. V. 70

RITA, ELIZA
The Ending of My Day. London: 1895. V. 68
The Laird o'Cockpen. London: 1894. V. 68

RITCH, W. G.
Inaugural Address of Hon. W. G. Ritch. Santa Fe: 1881. V. 68; 73

RITCHIE, ANNE ISABELLA THACKERAY
A Book of Sibyls. London: 1883. V. 69; 73
Records of Tennyson, Ruskin, Browning. New York: 1893. V. 71
The Works of Miss Thackeray. London: 1876-1886. V. 70

RITCHIE, C. I. A.
The British Dog. It's History of Earliest Times. 1981. V. 68

RITCHIE, DONALD
The Donald Ritchie Reader: 50 Years of Writing on Japan. Berkeley, CA: 2001. V. 71

RITCHIE, JAMES
The Influence of Man on Animal Life in Scotland. Cambridge: 1920. V. 71

RITCHIE, JAMES EWING
Here and There in London. London: 1859. V. 71
The Life and Times of Viscount Palmerston.... London: 1866-1867. V. 71
The Life and Times of William Ewart Gladstone. London: 1882. V. 71

RITCHIE, JEAN
Singing Family of the Cumberlands. New York: 1955. V. 69

RITCHIE, LEITCH
Scott and Scotland. London: 1835. V. 71
Windsor Castle and Its Environs. London: 1840. V. 73

RITCHIE, ROBERT W.
The Hell-Roarin Forty-Niners. New York: 1928. V. 68

RITCHIE, RUTH
Garner-Keene Familes of Northern Neck Virginia. Charlottesville: 1952. V. 72

RITCHIE, WARD
Armitage: His Loves and His May Lives by Ward Ritchie. Laguna Beach: 1982. V. 73
Ashendene and the Double Crown Club. Laguna Beach: 1979. V. 73
The Dohenys of Los Angeles. Los Angeles: 1974. V. 73
Jane Grabhorn: the Roguish Printer of the Jumbo Press by Ward Ritchie. Laguna Beach: 1985. V. 73
Jeffers: Some Recollections of Robinson Jeffers by Ward Ritchie. Laguna Beach: 1977. V. 73
Paul Landacre. San Francisco: 1982. V. 73
A Requiem for Laurence Clark Powell. Laguna Beach: 1986. V. 73
A Summer Sequence. Poems for Marka. Laguna Beach: 1981. V. 73

RITNER, JOSEPH
Vindicaton of General Washington from the Stigma of Adherence to Secret Societies. Harrisburg: 1837. V. 68

RITSON, JOSEPH
Ancient English Metrical Romances. Edinburgh: 1844. V. 70
The Caledonian Muse: a Chronological Selection of Scotish Poetry from the Earliest Times. London: 1821. V. 70
The Letters.... London: 1833. V. 72
Pieces of Ancient Popular Poetry.... London: 1791. V. 69
A Select Collection of English Songs in 3 Volumes. London: 1783. V. 68

RITTENHOUSE, JACK D.
American Horse Drawn Vehicles. Los Angeles: 1948. V. 68; 71
Cabezon: a New Mexico Ghost Town. Santa Fe: 1965. V. 69
Disturnell's Treaty Map. Santa Fe: 1965. V. 71
The Man Who Owned Too Much. Houston: 1958. V. 72
New Mexico Civil War Bibliography. Houston: 1961. V. 69
Outlaw Days at Cabezon, New Mexico. Santa Fe: 1964. V. 68
The Santa Fe Trail - a Historical Bibliography. Albuquerque: 1971. V. 68; 73
The Santa Fe Trail: a Historical Bibliography. Albuquerque: 1986. V. 71

RITTER, AUGUST
Elementary Theory and Calculation of Iron Bridges and Roofs. London: 1879. V. 73

RITTER, WILLIAM EMERSON
The Probable Infinity of Nature and Life. Boston: 1918. V. 72

RITTERBUSH, PHILIP C.
Overtures to Biology. New Haven: 1964. V. 68

RITTS, HERB
Notorious. Boston: 1992. V. 68

RITUALE Romanum, Contractum et Abreviatum in Usum Sacerdotum Missionum Hollandiae. Daventriae: 1841. V. 72

RITZ, CHARLES
A Fly Fisher's Life. 1959. V. 68; 73

RITZENTHALER, R.
Iroquois False-Face Masks. Milwaukee: 1969. V. 69
The Miller Collection, Assembly and Text By Robert E. Ritzenthaler, Artwork on Plates By W. Ben Hunt. Milwaukee: 1961. V. 72

RIVER, W. L.
Transit U.S.A. New York: 1940. V. 71

RIVERA, DIEGO
Portrait of America. New York: 1934. V. 68; 73

RIVERA, IGNACIO CHAVEZ
Coma, Sincope y Shock. Mexico: 1966. V. 71

RIVERIE, LAZARUS
The Compleat Practice of Physick.... London: 1655. V. 68

RIVERS of Great Britain, Rivers of the East Coast, Descriptive, Historical, Pictorial. London: 1892. V. 70; 73

RIVERS, W. H. R.
The History of Melanesian Society. Cambridge: 1914. V. 71
The Todas. London: 1906. V. 69

RIVERS, WILLIAM J.
A Sketch of the History of South Carolina to the Close of the Proprietary Government by the Revolution of 1719. Charleston: 1856. V. 73

RIVES, AMELIE
A Brother to Dragons ad Other Old Time Tales. London: 1896. V. 68
The Quick or the Dead?. London: 1889. V. 68
Virginia of Virginia: a Story. London: 1891. V. 68
The Witness of the Sun. London: 1889. V. 68

RIVES, WILLIAM C.
Correspondence, Albemarle County, Jan. 12, 1861. Wm. C. Rives and V. W. Southall Esquire. 1861. V. 69

RIVIERE, CHARLES
Vues de Londres, Dessinees d'Apres Nature et Lithographiees. Paris: 1862. V. 71

RIVINGTON, SEPTIMUS
The Publishing House of Rivington. London: 1894. V. 73

RIVINGTON, WALTER
The Medical Profession: Being the Essay...Awarded First Carmichael Prize, Royal College of Surgeons, Ireland. 1879. V. 70

RIVNAY, E.
Field Crop Pests in the Near East. Den Haag: 1962. V. 72

RIX, HERBERT
Prince Pimpernel. London: 1909. V. 70

RIZK, A. F. M.
Poisonous Plant Contamination of Edible Plants. Boca Raton: 1991. V. 68

ROACH, JOHN
The Thespian Preceptor, or, a Full Display of the Scenic Art.... London: 1807. V. 71

ROACH SMITH, CHARLES
Catalogue of the Museum of London Antiquities Collected by and the Property of, Charles Roach Smith. London: 1844. V. 70

ROAD Maps and Tour Book of Western North Carolina. Lynchburg: 1916. V. 73

ROADKILLS.. Easthampton: 1981. V. 71

ROADS, SAMUEL
The History and Traditions of Marblehead. Boston: 1880. V. 70
History and Traditions of Marblehead. Boston: 1881. V. 69

ROARK, GARLAND
Fair Wind to Java. Garden City: 1948. V. 69; 71

ROBARTS, EDITH
Gulliver in Giantland. London. V. 68
Gulliver in Liliput. London. V. 68

ROBB, BERNARD
Welcum Hinges. New York: 1942. V. 73

ROBB, CANDACE M.
The Apothecary Rose. New York: 1993. V. 70

ROBB, JOHN S.
Streaks of Squatter Life, and Far West Scenes. Philadelphia: 1847. V. 68; 71; 73

ROBBE-GRILLET, ALAIN
Pour un Nouveau Roman. Paris: 1963. V. 71

THE ROBBER Kitten. Philadelphia: 1904. V. 70; 73

ROBBINS, ARCHIBALD
A Journal Comprising an Account of the Loss of the Brig Commerce upon the Western Coast of Africa. Hartford: 1818. V. 72

ROBBINS, C. A.
The Unholy Three. 1917. V. 73

ROBBINS, CLIFTON
The Mystery of Mr. Cross. New York: 1933. V. 70

ROBBINS, HAROLD
A Stone for Danny Fisher. New York: 1952. V. 73

ROBBINS, HELEN H.
Our First Ambassador to China. London: 1908. V. 71

ROBBINS, LIONEL CHARLES
The Economic Basis of Class Conflict and Other Essays in Political Economy. London: 1939. V. 69

ROBBINS, LOUIS
Dutch Doll Ditties. New York: 1904. V. 70

ROBBINS, TOM
Another Roadside Attraction. Garden City: 1971. V. 69; 72; 73
Another Roadside Attraction. London & New York: 1973. V. 72; 73
Even Cowgirls Get the Blues. Boston: 1976. V. 69; 71; 72; 73
Fierce Invalids Home from Hot Climates. Franklin Center: 2000. V. 68; 70
Fierce Invalids Home from Hot Climates. London: 2000. V. 70
Jitterbug Perfume. New York: 1984. V. 72; 73
Skinny Legs and All. New York: 1990. V. 70; 72
Still Life with Woodpecker. New York: 1980. V. 70

ROBBINS, W. M.
African Art in American Collections. Washington: 1989. V. 69

ROBBINS, W. W.
The Botany of Crop Plants. Philadelphia: 1924. V. 72
Ethnobotany of the Tewa Indians. Washington: 1916. V. 68; 71

ROBE, WILLIAM LAMB
Miscellaneous Pieces in Verse; Written at Various Times on Different Subjects and on Several Occasions.... Dover: 1825. V. 69

ROBERT and Richard, or the Ghost of Poor Molly. 1796. V. 71

ROBERT Louis Stevenson, the Man and His Work. London: 1913. V. 68

ROBERT, N.
Variae ac Multiformes Florum Species: Diverses Fleurs. London: 1975. V. 68

ROBERT DIABLE
The Lyfe of Roberte the Deuyll. London: 1798. V. 73
Robert the Devil. Iowa City: 1981. V. 69; 73

ROBERT-DUMAS, CHARLES
Contes Bleus de Ma Mere-Grand. Paris: 1929. V. 69
Contes Mauves de Ma Mere-Grand. Paris: 1929. V. 69

ROBERT-HOUDIN, JEAN EUGENE
Card Sharpers, Their Tricks Exposed or the Art of Always Winning. London: 1891. V. 69

ROBERTI, JACQUES
Without Sin. New York: 1932. V. 69

ROBERTS, ALGERNON SYDNEY
Contributions to Orthopaedic Surgery. Philadelphia: 1898. V. 69

ROBERTS, B. H.
The Missouri Persecutions. (with) The Rise and Fall of Nauvoo. Salt Lake City: 1900. V. 70
The Mormon Battalion, Its History and Achievements. Salt Lake City: 1919. V. 69

ROBERTS, CECIL
Gone Rambling. London: 1935. V. 68

ROBERTS, CHARLES G. D.
Around the Camp-Fire. Toronto: 1896. V. 73
The Backwoodsman. London: 1909. V. 69
The Little People of Sycamore. Boston: 1919. V. 73
The Lord of the Air. Boston: 1927. V. 73
New Poems. London: 1919. V. 73

ROBERTS, DAN W.
Rangers and Sovereignty. San Antonio: 1914. V. 68; 73

ROBERTS, DAVID
The Military Adventures of Johnny Newcome, with an Account of His Campaigns on the Peninsula, and in Pall Mall.... London;: 1815. V. 73
The Town of Cambridge as It Out to be Reformed.. 1955. V. 71

ROBERTS, EDITH
Reap the Whirlwind. New York and Indianapolis: 1938. V. 70
Tamarack. New York: 1940. V. 69

ROBERTS, EDWARDS
With the Invader: Glimpses of the Southwest. San Francisco: 1885. V. 68

ROBERTS, ELDER B. H.
Missouri Persecutions. 1900. V. 68
The Rise and Fall of Nauvoo. 1900. V. 68

ROBERTS, ELIZABETH MADOX
Not by Strange Gods. New York: 1941. V. 68

ROBERTS, ERIC
Welzenbach's Climbs. Goring: 1980. V. 69

ROBERTS, F. H.
The Ceramic Sequence in the Chaco Canyon, New Mexico and Its Relation to the Cultures of the San Juan Basin. New York: 1991. V. 69

ROBERTS, FREDERICK SLEIGH
Forty-one Years in India From Subaltern to Commander-in-Chief. London: 1897. V. 71

ROBERTS, GEORGE
A Guide, Descriptive of the Beauties of Lyme-Regis.... Lyme: 1830. V. 70; 72
The Life, Progresses, and Rebellion of James, Duke of Monmouth &c. To His Capture and Execution: with a Full Account of the Bloody Assize and Copious Biographical Notices. London: 1844. V. 73

ROBERTS, GILLIAN
Caught Dead in Philadelphia. New York: 1987. V. 68; 69; 71
Philly Stakes. New York: 1989. V. 68

ROBERTS, HELEN H.
Basketry of the San Carlos Apache. New York: 1929. V. 69

ROBERTS, HENRY
The Dwellings of the Labouring Classes, Their Arrangement and Construction.... London: 1850. V. 71
The Dwellings of the Labouring Classes, Their Arrangement and Construction.... London: 1867. V. 68

ROBERTS, J.
Grayling Angler. 1982. V. 73

ROBERTS, J. D.
Insanity in the Colored Race. Goldsboro: 1883. V. 71

ROBERTS, JAMES A.
New York in the Revolution as Colony and State. Albany: 1898. V. 72

ROBERTS, JOHN
Fly Fishing for Grayling. 1999. V. 68; 73

ROBERTS, JOHN BINGHAM
The Cure of Crooked and Otherwise Deformed Noses. Philadelphia: 1889. V. 69
Notes on the Modern Treatment of Fractures. New York: 1899. V. 71

ROBERTS, JOHN M.
A Better Country. Charleston: 1810. V. 68

ROBERTS, JOSEPH
The Hand-Book of Artillery, for the Service of the United States. Charleston: 1862. V. 68

ROBERTS, KATE
Two Old Men and Other Stories. Newtown, Powys: 1981. V. 71

ROBERTS, KEITH
The Chalk Giants. London: 1974. V. 72
Kiteworld. London: 1985. V. 72

ROBERTS, KENNETH
Captain Caution: a Chronicle of Arundel. Garden City: 1934. V. 71; 73
Europe's Morning After. New York: 1921. V. 71
Lydia Bailey. Garden City: 1947. V. 70; 73
Oliver Wisell. New York: 1940. V. 70; 71
Rabble in Arms. Garden City: 1933. V. 70
Trending Into Maine. Boston: 1938. V. 71; 72

ROBERTS, LES
An Infinite Number of Monkeys. New York: 1987. V. 68; 70
Snake Oil. New York: 1990. V. 68

ROBERTS, M. F.
Alkaloids - Biochemistry, Ecology, and Medicinal Applications. New York: 1998. V. 68

ROBERTS, M. N.
Memory. Luba Art and the Making of History. New York and Munich: 1996. V. 69

ROBERTS, MARY
The Annals of My Village.... London: 1831. V. 68
The Conchologist's Companion.... London: 1824. V. 68
The Conchologist's Companion.... London: 1834. V. 68
A Popular History of Mollusca. London: 1851. V. 68; 70
A Popular History of the Mollusca. 1851. V. 69
Ruins and Old Trees Associated with Remarkable Events in English History. London: 1843. V. 68; 72
The Sea-Side Companion; or, Marine Natural History. London: 1835. V. 68

ROBERTS, MICHAEL
Poems. London: 1936. V. 68
T. E. Hulme. London: 1938. V. 72

ROBERTS, MORLEY
Painted Rock Tales and Narrative of Painted Rock, South Panhandle Texas.... Philadelphia: 1907. V. 69; 71
The Western Avernus or Toil and Travel In Further North America. London: 1896. V. 72

ROBERTS, ORLANDO W.
Narrative of Voyages and Excursions of the East Coast and in the Interior of Central America. Edinburgh: 1827. V. 71

ROBERTS, R.
The Rivers Side, or the Trout and Grayling and How to Catch Them. 1866. V. 68; 73

ROBERTS, RANDAL H.
Handicapped. London: 1896. V. 68

ROBERTS, RICHARD SAMUEL
A True Likeness. Chapel Hill: 1986. V. 70

ROBERTS, ROBERT
The House Servant's Directory, or a Monitor for Private Families.... Boston: 1828. V. 73

ROBERTS, S. C.
Doctor Watson. London: 1931. V. 70

ROBERTS, T. S.
The Birds of Minnesota. Minneapolis: 1932. V. 68; 69; 73

ROBERTS, THEODORE GOODRIDGE
The Golden Highlander or the Romantic Adventures of Alastair MacIver. Boston: 1929. V. 69

ROBERTS, VERNE L.
Bibliotheca Mechanica. New York: 1991. V. 73

ROBERTS, W.
Rare Books and Their Prices With Chapters on Pictures, Pottery, Porcelain and Postage Stamps. London: 1896. V. 71

ROBERTS, W. ADOLPHE
The American Parade-January 1926. New York: 1926. V. 72
Brave Mardi Gras: a New Orleans Novel of the '60s. Indianapolis: 1946. V. 68
Royal Street. A Novel of Old New Orleans. Indianapolis: 1944. V. 70
The Single Star. Indianapolis: 1949. V. 69

ROBERTS, WARREN
A Bibliography of D. H. Lawrence. Cambridge: 2001. V. 72

ROBERTSHAW, JAMES, & SONS
1913 Illustrated Catalogue of Window Blind Rollers and Fittings, Portiere Rods, Cornice Poles, Spring Rollers of Every description for Inside and Outside Blinds. Manchester: 1913. V. 68

ROBERTSON, ALEXANDER
The Life of Sir Robert Moray. London: 1922. V. 68; 70

ROBERTSON, ANNE S.
Birrens (Blatobulgium). Edinburgh: 1975. V. 70; 71

ROBERTSON, ARCHIBALD
A Topographical Survey of the Great Road from London to Bath and Bristol, with Historical and Descriptive Accounts of the Country, Towns, Villages, and Gentlemen's Seats on and adjacent to it. 1792. V. 72

ROBERTSON, BEN
Red Hills and Cotton: An Upcountry Memory. New York: 1942. V. 71
Travelers' Rest. Clemson, SC: 1938. V. 71

ROBERTSON, C. F.
Historical Review: Development of the Worland Valley, Washakie County, Wyoming. 1941. V. 68

ROBERTSON, D.
George Mallory. 1969. V. 68; 73

ROBERTSON, DAVID
Yosemite As We Saw It: a Centennial Collection of Early Writings and Art. Yosemite: 1990. V. 68

ROBERTSON, DEREK
A Studio Under the Sky. 2000. V. 69

ROBERTSON, DON
The Genuine Man. Bangor: 1987. V. 70
The Ideal Genuine Man. Bangor: 1987. V. 69; 73

ROBERTSON, ERIC SUTHERLAND
English Poetesses; a Series of Critical Biographies.... London, Paris, and New York: 1883. V. 69

ROBERTSON, FRANK C.
Boom Towns of the Great Basin. Denver: 1962. V. 69
Soapy Smith: King of the Frontier Con Men. New York: 1961. V. 69

ROBERTSON, GEORGE S.
The Kafirs Of The Hindukush. London: 1896. V. 72

ROBERTSON, JAMES
History of the Mission of the Secession Church to Nova Scotia and Prince Edward Island from Its Commencement in 1765. London: 1847. V. 73
History of the Mission of the Secession Church to Nova Scotia and Prince Edward Island from Its Commencement in 1765. Edinburgh: 1847. V. 71

ROBERTSON, JOHN
Animal Life on the Shores of the Clyde and Firth. Glasgow. V. 68; 70; 71
A General Treatise of Mensuration. London: 1779. V. 71

ROBERTSON, JOHN W.
Edgar A. Poe: a Study. San Francisco: 1921. V. 73
Francis Drake and Other Early Explorers Along the Pacific Coast. San Francisco: 1927. V. 68; 70; 73

ROBERTSON, KEVIN
The Perfect Shot. 2000. V. 69; 72; 73

ROBERTSON, NORMAN
The History of the County of Bruce and of the Minor Municipalities. Province of Ontario, Canada. (with) *The History of the County of Bruce and the Minor Municipalities Therein 1907-1968.* Toronto: 1969. V. 73

ROBERTSON, RICHARD T.
Neuroanatomical Research Techniques. London: 1978. V. 68

ROBERTSON, W.
Forest Sketches. 1865. V. 70

ROBERTSON, W. GRAHAM
Gold, Frankincense and Myrrh. And Other Pageants for a Baby Girl. London: 1907. V. 71; 73

ROBERTSON, WILLIAM
An Attempt to Explain the Words Reason, Substance, Person, Creeds, Orthodoxy, Catholic Church, Subscription, and Index.... London: 1768. V. 70
Collection de Differentes Especes de Serres Chaudes, Pour Forcer des Ananas, des Arbres Fruitiers.... London: 1798. V. 70; 72
An Historical Disquisition Concerning the Knowledge Which the Ancients Had of India, and the Progress of the Trade with that Country Prior to the Discovery of the Passage to it by the Cape of Good Hope. Philadelphia: 1792. V. 69
The History of America. London: 1803. V. 72
The History of Scotland During the Reigns of Queen Mary and King James VI. London: 1759. V. 72
Journal of a Clergyman During a Visit to the Peninsula in the Manner and Autumn of 1841. Edinburgh and London: 1845. V. 69; 71

ROBERTSON, WILLIAM PARRISH
A Visit to Mexico by the West India Islands, Yucantan and United States. London: 1853. V. 71

ROBESON, ESLANDA GOODE
Paul Robeson, Negro. London: 1930. V. 70; 72

ROBESON, KENNETH
The Land of Terror. 1933. V. 73
The Man of Bronze. 1933. V. 73
Quest of the Spider. 1933. V. 73

ROBESON, PAUL
Here I Stand. New York: 1958. V. 68; 72; 73

ROBICSEK, FRANCIS
The May Book of the Dead, the Ceramic Codex. The Corps Codex Style Ceramics of the Late Classic Period. Charlottesville: 1981. V. 69
The Smoking Gods: Tobacco in Maya Art, History and Religion. 1978. V. 70
The Smoking Gods: Tobacco in Maya Art, History and Religion. Norman: 1978. V. 69

ROBIDA, ALBERT
La Guerre au Vingtieme Siecle. Paris: 1887. V. 73

ROBIN Hood. London: 1820. V. 70
ROBIN Hood. Philadelphia: 1917. V. 69; 70; 71

THE ROBIN of Woodside Lodge. 1850. V. 72
THE ROBIN of Woodside Lodge. London: 1850. V. 68

THE ROBINS at Home. London. V. 70

ROBINS, DENISE
Heat Wave. New York: 1930. V. 70
Murder in Mayfair. London: 1935. V. 70

ROBINS, WILLIAM
Paddington: Past and Present. 1853. V. 71

ROBINSON, A. CUNINGHAM
Historical Record of the King's, Liverpool Regiment of Foot.... London: 1883. V. 70

ROBINSON, A. MARY F.
The Collected Poems, Lyrical and Narrative. London: 1902. V. 68

ROBINSON, AGNES M.
Emily Bronte. London: 1883. V. 70

ROBINSON, ALAN JAMES
A Fowl Alphabet. Easthampton: 1986. V. 72
Gamebirds and Waterfowl. Easthampton: 1980. V. 72
An Odd Bestiary or a Compendium of Instructive and Entertaining Descriptions of Animals.... Easthampton: 1982. V. 72
Roadkills: a Collection of Prose and Poetry. Easthampton: 1981. V. 72
Trout: Brook, Brown and Rainbow. Easthampton: 1986. V. 72

ROBINSON, ALFRED
Life in California During a Residence of Several Years in that Territory,. New York: 1846. V. 73
Life in California During a Residence of Several Years in that Territory. San Francisco: 1891. V. 70

ROBINSON, B. W.
With Shotgun and Rifle in North American Game Fields. 1925. V. 73

ROBINSON, BERT
The Basket Weavers of Arizona. Albuquerque: 1954. V. 69

ROBINSON, BLACKWELL P.
The History of Guilford County, N.C., USA to 1980. A.D. Jamestown?: 1981. V. 68

ROBINSON, C.
Skyscraper Style: Art Deco New York. New York: 1975. V. 69; 72

ROBINSON, C. W.
Life of Sir John Beverley Robinson. Toronto: 1904. V. 73

ROBINSON, CHANDLER A.
J. Evetts Haley and the Passing of the Old West. Austin: 1978. V. 68; 72
J. Evetts Haley; Cowman-Historian. El Paso: 1967. V. 71; 72

ROBINSON, CHARLES
The Four Champions of Great Britain and Ireland. London: 1905. V. 73
The Four Gardens. London: 1912. V. 71; 72
The Kansas Conflict. Lawrence: 1898. V. 70

ROBINSON, CHARLES HENRY
Hausaland. London: 1896. V. 71
Specimens of Hausa Literature. Cambridge: 1896. V. 71

ROBINSON, CHARLES N.
The British Tar in Fact and Fiction.... 1909. V. 68
Celebrities of The Army. London: 1900. V. 72

ROBINSON, CONWAY
An Account of Discoveries in the West Until 1519 and of Voyages to and Along the Atlantic Coast of North America from 1520-1573. Richmond: 1848. V. 71

ROBINSON, DOAN
History of South Dakota. Chicago: 1930. V. 72

ROBINSON, DUNCAN
William Morris, Edward Burne-Jones and the Kelmscott Chaucer. London: 1982. V. 70

ROBINSON, EDGAR E.
The Evolution of American Political Parties: a Sketch of Party Development. New York: 1924. V. 72

ROBINSON, EDWIN ARLINGTON
Amaranth. New York: 1934. V. 72
Cavender's House. London: 1930. V. 69
The Glory of the Nightingales. New York: 1930. V. 70

ROBINSON, EMMA
The Merry Wives of Stamboul; an Eastern Tale. London: 1846. V. 71

ROBINSON, FREDERIC WILLIAM
Owen - a Waif. London: 1870. V. 68
Owen - a Waif. London: 1881. V. 68
The Woman in the Dark. London: 1898. V. 68

ROBINSON, GEORGE
The Florence Baptistery Doors. London: 1980. V. 72

ROBINSON, GERALDINE
Three Kittens in a Boat. London: 1920. V. 70

ROBINSON, H. C.
The Birds of the Malay Peninsula.... London: 1927-1928. V. 73

ROBINSON, H. WHEELER
The Baptists of Yorkshire. London: 1912. V. 72

ROBINSON, HELEN M.
Fun Wherever We Are. Chicago: 1962. V. 71
Fun with Our Family. Chicago: 1962. V. 71
Think and Do Book for Use with Sally Dick and Jane. Chicago: 1962. V. 71

ROBINSON, HENRY
Englands Safety in Trades Encrease. Most Humbly Presented to the High Court of Parliament. London: 1641. V. 73

ROBINSON, HENRY CRABB
Diary, Reminiscences and Correspondence of Henry Crabb Robinson, Barrister-at-Law, F.S.A. London: 1869. V. 70; 71

ROBINSON, J. C.
Catalogue of the Soulages Collection...Exhibited at the Museum of Ornamental Art Marlborough House,. London: 1856. V. 72
Italian Sculpture of the Middle Ages and Period of the Revival of Art; a Descriptive Catalogue of the Works Forming the Above Section of the Museum.... London: 1862. V. 71

ROBINSON, JACKIE
Baseball Has Done It. Philadelphia: 1964. V. 69; 71; 72

ROBINSON, JACOB S.
A Journal of the Santa Fe Expedition Under Colonel Doniphan. Princeton: 1932. V. 68

ROBINSON, JOHN
A Guide to the Lakes, in Cumberland, Westmorland and Lancashire.... 1819. V. 72
Letter to Sir John Sinclair, Bart. 5th April 1794. London: 1794. V. 73

ROBINSON, JOHN HOVEY
A Brief Review of the Two Systems of Medical Practice Pursued at the Present Day. Bangor: 1844. V. 68

ROBINSON, JOHN ROBERT
The Last Earls of Barrymore 1769-1824. London: 1894. V. 72

ROBINSON, KIM STANLEY
Blue Mars. London: 1996. V. 70
Red Mars. 1993. V. 71
Red Mars. New York: 1993. V. 73

ROBINSON, LEIGH
The South Before and at the Battle of the Wilderness. Richmond: 1878. V. 69; 70

ROBINSON, LENNOX
The Irish Theatre. 1939. V. 69
Harvest and the Clancy Name. Dublin: 1911. V. 68

ROBINSON, LYNDA S.
Murder at the Feast of Rejoicing. New York: 1996. V. 68; 69
Murder at the God's Gate. New York: 1995. V. 68
Murder in the Place of Anubis. 1994. V. 69; 70
Murder in the Place of Anubis. New York: 1994. V. 68; 69; 71

ROBINSON, M. S.
Van De Velde Drawings. Cambridge: 1958. V. 70; 72

ROBINSON, MARIA ELIZABETH
The Wild Wreath. London: 1804. V. 73

ROBINSON, MARILYNNE
Housekeeping. New York: 1980. V. 68; 69; 72

ROBINSON, MARY
Lyrical Tales. London: 1800. V. 72
Memoirs of Mary Robinson Perdita from the Edition Edited by Her Daughter. London: 1894. V. 72

ROBINSON, P. F.
Rural Architecture; or, a Series of Designs for Ornamental Cottages. London: 1836. V. 69

ROBINSON, PETER
Gallows View. New York: 1987. V. 70
Past Reason Hated. Toronto: 1991. V. 71

ROBINSON, PETER FREDERICK
Vitruvius Britannicus: History of Woburn Abbey, Hatfield House, Hardwicke Hall and Cassiobury Park. London: 1847. V. 70

ROBINSON, PHIL
Noah's Ark; or Mornings in the Zoo. London: 1892. V. 68
The Poets and Nature. London: 1893. V. 68

ROBINSON, ROBERT
Black on Red: My 44 Years Inside the Soviet Union. Washington, D.C: 1988:. V. 72

ROBINSON, ROWLAND E.
Sam Lovel's Camp. Uncle Lisha's Friends Under Bark and Canvas. New York: 1889. V. 70

ROBINSON, SARA T. L.
Kansas: Its Interior and Exterior Life. Boston: 1856. V. 68

ROBINSON, THOMAS
The Common Law of Kent, or, the Customs of Gavelkind. London: 1741. V. 69
An Essay Towards a Natural History of Westmorland and Cumberland. London: 1709. V. 71
The Last Days of Bishop Heber. Madras: 1829. V. 71

ROBINSON, W.
Mushroom Culture: Its Extension and Improvement. London: 1870. V. 68

ROBINSON, W. R.
Robinson's Guide to Richmond.... Richmond: 1833. V. 71

ROBINSON, W. W.
Bombs and Bribery: The Story of the McNamara and Darrow Trials Following the Dynamiting in 1910 of the Los Angeles Times Building. Los Angeles: 1969. V. 68
The Indians of Los Angeles: Story of the Liquidation of a People. Los Angeles: 1952. V. 68
The Malibu- Southern California's Famous Ranch Its Romatic History and Present Charm. Los Angeles: 1958. V. 71; 73
Maps of Los Angeles. Los Angeles: 1966. V. 70; 73
Ranchos Become Cities. Pasadena: 1939. V. 68
Southern California Local History: a Gathering of the Writings of.... Los Angeles: 1993. V. 73

ROBINSON, WILL H.
Joe, a Pima Indian Boy. Phoenix: 1935. V. 69
The Story of Arizona. Phoenix: 1919. V. 69
Under Turquoise Skies: Outstanding Features of the Story of America's Southwest from the Days of the Ancient Cliff Dwellers to Modern Times. New York: 1928. V. 70; 72; 73

ROBINSON, WILLIAM
Alpine Flowers for English Gardens. London: 1870. V. 72; 73
The English Flower Garden and Home Grounds. London: 1893. V. 68; 71; 73
The English Flower Garden and Home Grounds. London: 1906. V. 68; 71
The English Flower Garden and Home Grounds. London: 1907. V. 69
The English Flower Garden and Home Grounds. New York: 1921. V. 68; 71
The Parks, Promenades and Gardens of Paris Decribed and Considered in Relation to the Wants of Our Own Cities and of Public and Private Gardens. London: 1869. V. 70; 72; 73
Tobacco: Its Ups and Downs in England, and How to Cultivate and Cure It in the West Indies. Trinidad: 1886. V. 70
The Wild Garden. London: 1895. V. 69

ROBINSON, WILLIAM H.
A Selection of Precious Manuscripts, Historic Documents & Rare Books, the Majority from the Renowned Collection of Sir Thomas Phillipps, BT. London: 1950. V. 70

ROBINSON, WILLIAM HEATH
Absuridities-A Book of Collected Drawings. London: 1934. V. 72
Behind the Scenes at Moss Bros. Coven Garden: 1936. V. 72
Bill the Minder. London: 1912. V. 69; 72
The Gentle Art of Excavating. Lincoln: 1938. V. 71
Heath Robinson Sees IZAL Made. Near Sheffield. V. 70
Heath Robinson's Book of Goblins. London: 1934. V. 71; 72
How to be A Motorist. London: 1939. V. 70
How to Make the Best of Things. London: 1940. V. 72
Peter Quip: In Search of a Friend. London: 1922. V. 70
Railway Ribaldry. 1935. V. 71
Railway Ribaldry Being 96 Pages of Railway Humor. London: 1935. V. 70
Thorncliffe Visited. Near Sheffield. V. 70

ROBINSON, WILLIAM M.
The Confederate Privateers. New Haven: 1928. V. 69; 72
The Confederate Privateers. New York: 1928. V. 70

ROBISON, JOHN
A Rudimentary Treatise on the Principles of Construction in the Carpentry and Joinery of Roofs Deduced from the Works of John Robison, Price and Tredgold. London: 1859. V. 68

ROBSON, G. C.
The Species Problem, an Introduction to the Study of Evolutionary Divergence in Natural Populations. Edinburgh: 1928. V. 72

ROBSON, JOHN
Three Early English Metrical Romances. London: 1842. V. 73

ROBSON, LEVEY & FRANKLYN
Specimens of Printing Types in the Office of Robson, Levey and Franklyn. London. V. 70

ROBSON, WILLIAM
The Old Play-Goer. London: 1854. V. 68

ROBY, J.
Traditions of Lancashire. London: 1843. V. 71

ROCCHEGIANI, LORENZO
Invenzioni Divere di Mobili ed Utensigli Sacri e Profani Raccolta ed Incise in 100 Tavole in Rame da Pietro Ruga.... Milano: 1811. V. 70; 72

ROCH, ANDRE
On Rock and Ice. London: 1947. V. 69

ROCHE, ARTHUR SOMERS
The Great Abduction. New York: 1933. V. 70
Loot. Indianapolis: 1916. V. 69
Plunder. Indianapolis: 1917. V. 69
The Sport of Kings. Indianapolis: 1917. V. 70

ROCHE, HARRIET A.
On Trek in the Transvaal. London: 1878. V. 71

ROCHE, P. K.
Plaid Bear and the Rude Rabbit Gang. New York: 1982. V. 72

ROCHE, REGINA MARIA
The Children of the Abbey; a Tale. 1850. V. 72

ROCHER, EMILE
La Province Chinoise du Yun-Nan. Paris: 1879-1880. V. 71

ROCHESTER, G. E.
The Return of Grey Shadow. V. 73

ROCHESTER, JOHN WILMOT, 2ND EARL OF
The Works.... London: 1714. V. 70; 73

ROCK, J. F.
The Ornamental Tree of Hawaii. Honolulu: 1917. V. 68

ROCK, JAMES L.
Southern and Western Texas Guide for 1878. St. Louis: 1878. V. 68; 73

ROCKEFELLER, JOHN D.
Random Reminiscences of Men and Events. Garden City: 1916. V. 69

ROCKER, RUDOLF
The Tragedy of Spain. New York: 1937. V. 73

ROCKEY, HOWARD
Honeymoon's End. New York: 1926. V. 73
This Woman. New York: 1924. V. 71

ROCKWELL, A. D.
Rambling Recollections - An Autobiography. New York: 1920. V. 72

ROCKWELL, NORMAN
My Adventures as an Illustrator. Garden City: 1960. V. 69; 71; 73
Willie Was Different. New York: 1969. V. 69

ROCKWELL, WILSON
Sunset Sope. True Epics of Western Colorado. Denver: 1956. V. 69
Uncompahgre Country. Denver: 1965. V. 69

ROCKWOOD, HARRY
Walt Wheeler, the Scout Detective. New York: 1884. V. 69

THE ROCKY Mountain Directory and Colorado Gazetteer for 1871, Comprising a Brief History of Colorado.... Denver: 1870. V. 71

RODALE, J. I.
The Complete Book of Composting. Emmaus: 1960. V. 68

RODD, T.
First Part of T. Rodd's Catalogue for 1817; Containing Several Curious and Scarce Books, In all Languages Now on Sale.. London: 1817. V. 70

RODDIS, LOUIS H.
A Short History of Nautical Medicine. New York: 1941. V. 71

RODENBAUGH, THEODORE F.
From Everglade To Cannon With The Second Dragoons... An Authentic Account of Service in Florida, Mexico, Virginia And The Indian Country... 1836-1875. New York: 1875. V. 72

RODGERS, JIMMIE, MRS.
Jimmie Rodgers' Life Story. Nashville: 1953. V. 69

RODGERS, MARY
Summer Switch. New York: 1982. V. 71

RODGERS, RICHARD
Carousel. New York: 1946. V. 72
Me and Juliet. New York: 1953. V. 69
South Pacific. New York: 1949. V. 72

RODICK, BURLEIGH CUSHING
My Own New England. New York: 1929. V. 68

RODING, JOHANN HEINRICH
Allgemeines Worterbuch der Marine in Allen Europaeischen Seesprachen Nebst Vollstaendigen Erklaerungen. Hamburg: 1794-1798. V. 71

RODITI, EDOUARD
The Disorderly Poet and Other Essays. Santa Barbara: 1975. V. 73
New and Old Testaments. New York: 1983. V. 73
Orphic Love. New York: 1986. V. 73

RODKER, JOHN
Adolphe 1920. 1929. V. 68
Collected Poems 1912-1925. Paris: 1930. V. 68
Hymns. London: 1920. V. 68; 73
Poems. London: 1914. V. 68

RODKINSON, MICHAEL L.
The History of the Talmud: from the Time of Its Formation about 200 B.C., Up to the Present Time. New York: 1903. V. 71

RODLICH, H. F.
Beschreibung Funf Verschiedener Arten Ziegelschneid Maschinen.... Dusseldorf: 1819. V. 68; 70; 72

RODMAN, SELDEN
Horace Pippin: the Artist as a Black American. Garden City: 1972. V. 69; 72
Lawrence - the Last Crusade. New York: 1937. V. 68
Horace Pippin. A Negro Painter in America. New York: 1947. V. 72
Tongues of Fallen Angels.... New York: 1974. V. 71; 73

RODOCANACHI, C. P.
Forever Ulysses. New York: 1938. V. 69

RODRIGUEZ, LUIS J.
Always Running: La Vida Loca, Gang Days in L.A. Willimantic: 1993. V. 68; 73

RODWELL & MARTIN
Rodwell and Martin's Drawing Book for 1822. 1821-1823. V. 73

RODWELL, G. F.
Etna. A History of the Mountain and of Its Eruptions. London: 1878. V. 70

ROE, FRANCIS M. A.
Army Letters From An Officer's Wife, 1871-1888. New York: 1909. V. 72

ROE, FRANK GILBERT
The Indian and the Horse. Norman: 1955. V. 70; 72
The Indian and the Horse. Norman: 1968. V. 69

ROE, RICHARD BAILLIE
Radiography, or a System of Easy Writing. London: 1821. V. 70

ROEBLING, WASHINGTON
Report of the Chief Engineer of the New York and Brooklyn Bridge, Jan. 1. 1877. Brooklyn: 1877. V. 68

ROEBLING'S SONS COMPANY
Construction of Parallel Wire Cables for Suspension Bridges. Trenton: 1925. V. 68

ROEDIGER, VIRGINIA MORE
Ceremonial Costumes of the Pueblo Indians. Berkeley. V. 68
Ceremonial Costumes of the Pueblo Indians. Berkeley: 1941. V. 69

ROENIGK, ADOLPH
Pioneer History of Kansas. 1933. V. 70
Pioneer History of Kansas. Lincoln KS: 1933. V. 72

ROER, HENRY S.
History of Norfolk Public Schools 1681-1968. Norolk: 1968. V. 71

ROERICH, NICHOLAS
Altai Himalaya. New York: 1929. V. 71

ROESCH, KURT
Sprig and Turfy. Mt. Vernon: 1938. V. 68

ROESSEL, ROBERT A.
Pictorial History of the Navajo from 1860-1910. 1980. V. 69

ROESSLIN, EUCHARIUS
De Partu Hominis, et Qua Circa Ipsum Accidunt. Venice: 1536. V. 68

ROETHEL, H. K.
Kandinsky: Catalogue Raisonne of the Oil Paintings. Volume I 1900- 1915. London: 1982. V. 72

ROETHKE, THEODORE
Collected Poems. Garden City: 1966. V. 73
The Collected Poems of Theodore Roethke. London: 1970. V. 68
I am! Says the Lamb. Garden City: 1961. V. 71
The Lost Son and Other Poems. New York: 1948. V. 68
The Lost Son and Other Poems. London: 1949. V. 68; 69
Open House. New York: 1941. V. 72
Praise to the End!. New York: 1951. V. 68; 69
Sequence, Sometimes Metaphysical. Poems. Iowa City: 1963. V. 69
The Waking: Poems 1933-1953. New York: 1953. V. 68

ROETHLISBERGER, MARCEL
Claude Lorrain. The Drawings. 1968. V. 73
Claude Lorrain, The Drawings. Berkeley: 1968. V. 69; 72

ROGER Eliot Stoddard at Sixty-Five, a Celebration. New York: 2000. V. 73

ROGER, SAMUEL
Italy. A Poem. London: 1854. V. 71

ROGERS, BEN
Murder at the Coffee Stall: A Story of Gang Vengeance. London: 1935. V. 72

ROGERS, BRUCE
Paragraphs on Printing Elicited from Bruce Rogers in Talks with James Hendrickson on the Functions of the Book Designer. New York: 1943. V. 70; 72
Report on the Typography of the Cambridge University Press, Prepared in 1917 at the Request of the Syndics by Bruce Rogers and Now Printed in Honour of His Eightieth Birthday. 1950. V. 71
Report on the Typography of the Cambridge University Press, Prepared in 1917 at the Request of the Syndics by Bruce Rogers and Now Printed in Honour of His Eightieth Birthday. Cambridge: 1973. V. 68

ROGERS, CHARLES
Boswelliana, the Commonplace Book of James Boswell, with a Memoir and Annotations by.... London: 1874. V. 68

ROGERS, D. B.
Prehistoric Man of the Santa Barbara Coast. Santa Barbara: 1929. V. 69

ROGERS, EDWARD COIT
Letters on Slavery, Addressed to the Pro-Slavery Men of America.... Boston: 1855. V. 73

ROGERS, FRANKE
Tea Kettle Cottage and the Hurricane. New York: 1958. V. 69

ROGERS, FRED B.
Bear Flag Lieutenant - The Life of Henry L. Ford (1822-1860). San Francisco: 1951. V. 72
Soldiers of the Overland, Being Some Account of the Services of General Patrick Edward Conner and His Volunteers in the Old West. San Francisco: 1938. V. 69

ROGERS, FREDERICK
English Mansions, Lodges, Villas etc. London: 1866. V. 68

ROGERS, G. E.
The Structure of the Hair Follicle with Special Reference to the Formation of Keratin. 1956. V. 68

ROGERS, H. A.
Views of Some of the Most Celebrated By-Gone Pleasure Gardens of London.... 1896. V. 71

ROGERS, HOWELL
Voyager's Medical Companion. Norwich: 1847. V. 71

ROGERS, J.
Sport in Vancouver and Newfoundland. 1912. V. 69; 70; 72; 73

ROGERS, JAMES EDWIN THOROLD
Six Centuries of Work and Wages. London: 1884. V. 71

ROGERS, JOHN
The Book of the Revelation of Jesus Christ.... New London: 1817. V. 68
Sport in Vancouver & Newfoundland. London: 1912. V. 71

ROGERS, JOHN C.
English Furniture. London: 1950. V. 72

ROGERS, JOHN WILLIAM
Finding Literature on the Texas Plains. Dallas: 1931. V. 68; 71; 73

ROGERS, PATTIANN
Firekeeper. New and Selected Poems. Minneapolis: 1994. V. 73
Legendary Performance. Memphis: 1987. V. 73

ROGERS, R. L.
History of the Lincoln and Welland Regiment. 1954. V. 73
History of the Lincoln and Welland Regiment. Ottawa: 1979. V. 68

ROGERS, ROBERT
A Concise Account of North America; Containing a Description of the Several British Colonies on that Continent, Including the Islands of Newfoundland, Cape Breton, &c.... Wakefield and New York: 1966. V. 73

ROGERS, ROSE ANNIE
The Lonely Island. London: 1926. V. 71

ROGERS, SAMUEL
An Epistle to a Friend, with Other Poems. London: 1798. V. 72
Human Life, a Poem. London: 1819. V. 70; 72
Human Life, a Poem. London: 1820. V. 72
Italy. London: 1830. V. 69; 70; 71; 72; 73
Italy. London: 1842. V. 70
Jacqueline; a Tale. London: 1814. V. 72
A Ode to Superstition, with some other Poems. London: 1786. V. 72
The Pleasures of Memory. London: 1792. V. 72
The Pleasures of Memory. London: 1793. V. 72
The Pleasures of Memory. London: 1810. V. 72
Poems. London: 1812. V. 72
Poems. London: 1816. V. 72
Poems. London: 1820. V. 72
Poems. London: 1822. V. 72
Poems. 1834. V. 70
Poems. London: 1834. V. 68
You Leave Me Cold!. New York: 1946. V. 69

ROGERS, THOMAS
The Faith, Doctrine and Religion, Possessed and Protected in The Realm of England, and Dominions of the Same.... Cambridge: 1675. V. 72

ROGERS, W. E.
Tree Flowers of Forest, Park and Street. 1935. V. 71; 73
Tree Flowers of Forest, Park and Street. New York: 1935. V. 68

ROGERS, W. G.
Wise Men Fish Here. The Story of Frances Steloff and the Gotham Book Mart. New York: 1965. V. 70

ROGERS, W. S.
A Book of Spectres. London: 1915. V. 69

ROGERS, WILL
The Illiterate Digest. New York: 1924. V. 71

ROGERSON, SIDNEY
Both Sides of the Road. A Book About Farming. London: 1949. V. 68; 73
Our Bird Book. London: 1947. V. 73

ROGET, P. M.
Animal and Vegetable Physiology Considered with Reference to Natural Theology. 1834. V. 69

ROGET, PETER M.
Animal and Vegetable Physiology Considered with Reference to Natural History. London: 1834. V. 68

ROGOSIN, DONN
Invisible Men: Life in Baseball's Negro Leagues. New York: 1983:. V. 72

ROH, FRANZ
German Art in the 20th Century. 1968. V. 69; 72

ROHDE, ELEANOR SINCLAIR
A Garden of Herbs. London: 1920. V. 71
Gardens of Delight. Boston: 1934. V. 68
Gardens of Delight. London: 1934. V. 70; 73
The Old English Gardening Books. London: 1924. V. 68; 69; 71; 73
The Old-World Pleasaunce - an Anthology. London: 1925. V. 70
The Scented Garden. London: 1931. V. 69
Vegetable Cultivation and Cookery. London: 1938. V. 70

ROHMER, ERIC
Six Moral Tales. New York: 1980. V. 69

ROHMER, SAX
The Bat Flies Low. Garden City: 1935. V. 73
Bimbashi Baruk of Egypt. 1944. V. 73
Bimbashi Baruk of Egypt. New York: 1944. V. 71
The Day the World Ended. Garden City: 1929. V. 68
The Day the World Ended. 1930. V. 73
The Day the World Ended. New York: 1930. V. 69; 70
The Dream Detective. New York. V. 69
The Drums of Fu Manchu. New York: 1939. V. 70; 71
Emperor Fu Manchu. Greenwich: 1959. V. 72
The Emperor of America. New York: 1929. V. 70
Fu Manchu's Bride. Garden City: 1933. V. 68
The Golden Scorpion. New York: 1920. V. 71; 73
The Green Eyes of Bast. New York: 1920. V. 68
The Island of Fu Manchu. New York: 1941. V. 71; 72; 73
The Mask of Fu Manchu. New York: 1932. V. 69
President Fu Manchu. New York: 1936. V. 68; 69; 70
The Return of Dr. Fu-Manchu. New York: 1918. V. 70
The Sax Rohmer Omnibus. New York: 1915. V. 68
Seven Sins. New York: 1943. V. 70
She Who Sleeps. New York: 1928. V. 69; 71
Sinister Madonna. London: 1956. V. 68; 70; 72
Sinister Madonna. New York: 1956. V. 69
The Wrath of Fu Manchu and Other Stories. London: 1973. V. 71
Yellow Shadows. London: 1925. V. 71
Yu'an Hee See Laughs. 1932. V. 73

ROIPHE, ANNE RICHARDSON
Long Division. New York: 1972. V. 72

ROJANKOVSKY, FEDOR
Daniel Boone, Historic Adventures of an American Hunter Among the Indians. London: 1931. V. 70

ROJAS, A. R.
California Vaquero. Fresno: 1953. V. 71
The Vaquero. Santa Barbara: 1964. V. 71

ROJO, DIOSDADO GARCIA
Catalogo de Incunables de la Biblioteca Nacional. Madrid: 1945. V. 70

ROLAND, A. E.
The Flora of Nova Scotia. Halifax: 1969. V. 73

ROLAND, ARTHUR
Farming for Pleasure and Profit. Dairy-Farming, Management of Cows.... London: 1879. V. 72

ROLAND DE LA PLATIERE, MARIE JEANNE PHILIPOU
An Appeal to Impartial Posterity, by Madame Roland, Wife of the Minister of the Interior.... London: 1796. V. 73

ROLEWINCK, WERNER
Fasciculus Temporum. Paris: 1523. V. 71

ROLFE, EDWIN
Permit Me Refuge. Los Angeles: 1955. V. 71

ROLFE, FREDERICK WILLIAM
Agricultural and Pastoral Prospects of South Africa. London: 1904. V. 71
Amico di Sandro.... 1951. V. 71
Amico di Sandro.... Harrow: 1951. V. 69
The Armed Hands and Other Stories and Pieces. London: 1974. V. 71; 72
Ballade of Boys Bathing. 1972. V. 71
The Bull Against the Enemy of the Anglican Race. London: 1929. V. 71
The Cardinal Prefect of Propaganda and Other Stories. London: 1957. V. 69; 71
Chronicles of the House of Borgia. London: 1901. V. 71
Chronicles of the House of Borgia. New York: 1901. V. 69; 71
Collected Poems. London: 1974. V. 71; 72
The Desire and Pursuit of the Whole. London: 1934. V. 69; 70; 71; 72
The Desire and Pursuit of the Whole. London: 1953. V. 71
The Desire and Pursuit of the Whole. New York: 1953. V. 69
Don Renato: an Ideal Content. London: 1963. V. 69; 71
Don Tarquinio; a Kataleptic Phantasmic Romance. London: 1905. V. 69; 71
Don Tarquinio; a Kataleptic Phantasmic Romance. London: 1957. V. 71
Frederick Rolfe and the Times 4-12 Feb. 1901. Edinburgh: 1977. V. 71
Hadrian the Seventh. London: 1904. V. 71; 72
Hadrian the Seventh. New York: 1925. V. 71
Hubert's Arthur. London: 1935. V. 69; 71
In His Own Image. London: 1901. V. 69; 71
In His Own Image. London: 1924. V. 71
A Letter from Baron Corvo to John Lane Relating to the Title-page Design for In His Own Image.... 1958. V. 71
Letters. 1960-1962. V. 71
The Letters of Baron Corvo to Kenneth Grahame. 1962. V. 71
Letters to C.H.C. Pirie Gordon. London: 1959. V. 69; 71
Letters to Grant Richards. 1952. V. 71
Letters to Harry Bainbride. 1977. V. 68; 71
Letters to Harry Bainbridge. London: 1977. V. 69
Letters to James Walsh. London: 1972. V. 68; 71
Letters to Leonard Moore. London: 1960. V. 71
Letters to R. M. Dawkins. London: 1962. V. 71
Nicholas Crabbe; Or, The One and the Many. London: 1960. V. 69; 71; 73
The Reverse Side of the Coin: Some Further Correspondence Between Frederick William Rolfe and Grant Richards. Edinburgh;: 1974. V. 71
Saint Thomas. Edinburgh: 1979. V. 71
Stories Toto Told Me. London: 1898. V. 69; 71
Tarcissus: the Boy Martyr of Rome in the Diocletian Persecution. 1972. V. 71
Three Tales of Venice. 1950. V. 71
The Venice Letters. London: 1974. V. 71
The Venice Letters. London: 1987. V. 71
The Weird of the Wanderer, Being the Papyrus Records of Some Incidents in One of the Previous Lives of Mr. Nicholas Crabbe. 1912. V. 71
Without Prejudice. One Hundred Letters. London: 1963. V. 68; 71; 73

ROLFE, R. A.
The Orchid Stud-Book.... Kew: 1909. V. 68; 73

ROLL, ERICH
An Early Experiment in Industrial Organisation, Being a History of the Firm of Boulton & Watt 1775-1805. London: 1930. V. 71

ROLLAND, GUY
Un Demi Siecle de Swing et de Jazz. Paris: 1986. V. 69

ROLLAND, ROMAIN
Annette and Sylvie. New York: 1925. V. 71
The Death of a World: Being Volume Four of the Soul Enchanted. New York: 1933. V. 71
The Game of Love and Death. New York: 1926. V. 69

ROLLE, RICHARD
English Writings of Richard Rolle. Oxford: 1931. V. 69

ROLLENHAGEN, GABRIEL
Nvclevs Emlematvm Selectissimorvm. (with) Selectorum Emblematum Centuria Secunda. Ultraiecti: 1613. V. 71

ROLLESTON, THOMAS WILLIAM HAZEN
Parsifal. London: 1912. V. 68; 70
Parsifal. New York: 1912. V. 72
The Tale of Lohengrin. London: 1913. V. 68; 70; 72
Tannhauser. London: 1911. V. 70

ROLLIN, CHARLES
Histoire Ancienne Des Egyptiens, Des Carthaginois, Des Assyriens, Des Babyloniens, Des Medes Et Des Perses, Des Macedoniens, Des Grecs. Paris: 1740. V. 72

ROLLINS, HYDER E.
A Gorgeous Gallery of Gallant Inventions (1578). Cambridge: 1926. V. 73

ROLLINS, PHILIP ASHTON
The Cowboy. New York: 1922. V. 68; 69; 71
The Discovery of the Oregon Trail, Robert Stuart's Narrative of His Overland Trip East from Asteria in 1812-1813. New York: 1935. V. 69
Jinglebob. New York: 1930. V. 71

ROLLINS, WILLIAM
The Shadow Before. New York: 1934. V. 72

ROLLINSON, JOHN K.
Wyoming Cattle Trails - History of the Migration of Oregon Raised Herds to Midwestern Markets. Caldwell: 1948. V. 69; 73

ROLLS, HENRY, MRS.
Legends of the North, or the Feudal Christmas: a Poem. London: 1825. V. 69

ROLPH, C. H.
The Trial of Lady Chatterley: Regina v. Penguin Books Ltd. London: 1961. V. 68; 71

ROLPH, J. ALEXANDER
Dylan Thomas: a Bibliography. London: 1956. V. 69

ROLPH, THOMAS
A Brief Account, Together with Observations, Made During a Visit in the West Indies and a Tour through the United States of America in Parts of the Years 1832-1833. Dundas: 1836. V. 72

ROLVAAG, O. E.
The Boat of Longing. New York: 1933. V. 70

ROMAIN, JAMES HAROLD
Gambling; or, Fortuna, Her Temple and Shrine. Chicago: 1891. V. 68

ROMAINE, LAWRENCE B.
A Guide to American Trade Catalogues. New York: 1960. V. 72; 73

THE ROMAN Senate. Dublin: 1818. V. 73

ROMAN, ALFRED
Military Operations of General Beauregard. New York: 1884. V. 69; 70; 72

THE ROMANCE of Oklahoma. Oklahoma City: 1920. V. 72

ROMANOFF, ALEXANDER
Steel and Jade. New York: 1927. V. 72

ROMAYNE, NICHOLAS
Dissertatio Inauguralis, de Puris Generatione. Edinburgh: 1780. V. 68

ROME DE L'ISLE, JEAN BAPTISTE LOUIS
Cristallographie, ou Description des Formes Propres a tous les Corps du Regne Mineral, dans lEtat de Combinaison Saline, Pierreuse or Metallique. Paris: 1783. V. 73
Versuch einer Crystallographie...aus dem Franzosischen Ubersetzt mit Ammerkungen und Zusatzen. Greifswald: 1777. V. 68

ROMER, A. S.
Bibliography of Fossil Vertebrates Exclusive of North America 1509- 1927. New York: 1962. V. 72

ROMERO, GEORGE
Martin. New York: 1977. V. 68

ROMERO, MATIAS
Coffee and India Rubber Culture in Mexico Preceded by Geographical and Statistical Notes on Mexico. New York and London: 1898. V. 69

ROMILLY, HENRY
The Punishment of Death, to Which is Appended His Treatise on Public Responsibility and Vote by Ballot. London: 1886. V. 73

ROMILLY, HUGH H.
From My Verandah in New Guinea. London: 1889. V. 71
The Western Pacific and New Guinea. London: 1886. V. 71

ROMILLY, SAMUEL
The Life of Sir Samuel Romilly, Written by Himself. London: 1842. V. 71; 72

ROMM, MICHAEL
The Ascent of Mount Stalin. 1936. V. 68; 71; 73
The Ascent of Mount Stalin. London: 1936. V. 69

ROMTVEDT, DAVID
Moon. Saint Paul: 1984. V. 70; 72

RONALDS, ALFRED
The Fly-Fisher's Entomology. 1883. V. 68; 69
The Fly-Fisher's Entomology. London: 1901. V. 69
The Fly-Fisher's Entomology. 1921. V. 68

RONALDSHAY, LAWRENCE JOHN LUMLEY DUNDAS, EARL OF
The Heart of Aryavarta. London: 1925. V. 71
India. London: 1924. V. 71
Lands of the Thunderbolt Sikhim, Chumbi & Bhutan. London: 1923. V. 71
Sport and Politics Under an Eastern Sky. Edinburgh: 1902. V. 71

RONAN, PETER
Historical Sketch of the Flathead Indian Nation from the Year 1813 to 1890. Helena: 1890. V. 73

RONDELS.. 1951. V. 68

RONNE, FINN
Antarctic Conquest. New York: 1949. V. 71

RONS, JAMES CAMPBELL
Autobiographical Sketch Of James Croll, With Memoir Of His Life And Work. London: 1896. V. 72

RONSARD, PIERRE DE
Choix de Sonnets. 1902. V. 73
Poemes de Pierre de Ronsard. Manteno: 1985. V. 68

ROOCHVARG, ALIDA
The Alida Roochvarg Collection of Books About Books. Newcastle: 1981. V. 71

ROOD, HENRY E.
The Company Doctor and American Story. New York: 1895. V. 71

ROOK, ARTHUR
Progress in the Biological Sciences in Relation to Dermatology. Cambridge: 1960-1964. V. 68

ROOKE, HAYMAN
Descriptions and Sketches of Some Remarkable Oakes, in the Park at Welbeck, in the County of Nottingham.... London: 1790. V. 69; 71

ROOME, WILLIAM J. W.
Can Africa Be Won?. London: 1927. V. 71

ROOPER, G.
Thames and Tweed. 1870. V. 68

ROOS, KELLEY
The Frightened Stiff. New York: 1942. V. 70

ROOSEBOOM, MARIA
Microscopium. Leiden: 1956. V. 68

ROOSES, MAX
Dutch Painters of the Nineteenth Century. London: 1898. V. 72

ROOSEVELT, ELEANOR
Christmas. New York: 1940. V. 69; 71; 73
Growing Toward Peace. New York: 1960. V. 68
The Moral Basis of Democracy. New York: 1940. V. 68; 73
On My Own, the Years Since the White House. New York: 1958. V. 72; 73
This I Remember. New York: 1949. V. 70; 72; 73
This is My Story. New York: 1937. V. 69; 71; 72

ROOSEVELT, FRANKIN DELANO
The Roosevelt Letters. London: 1949-1952. V. 72

ROOSEVELT, FRANKLIN DELANO
Addresses of Franklin D. Roosevelt, President of the United States from July 19 1940 to January 20, 1941. Washington: 1941. V. 68
On Our Way. New York: 1934. V. 69; 70; 71
The Public Papers and Addresses of Franklin D. Roosevelt. New York: 1938. V. 69; 71

ROOSEVELT, MRS. T.
Cleared for Strange Ports. New York: 1927. V. 71; 72; 73

ROOSEVELT, THEODORE
African Game Trails. 1910. V. 69; 70; 72
African Game Trails. London: 1910. V. 71
African Game Trails. New York: 1910. V. 68; 70; 71; 72
An Autobiography. New York: 1913. V. 68; 69; 71
An Autobiography. New York: 1914. V. 71
Big Game Hunting in the Rockies and on the Great Plains. New York: 1899. V. 68; 70; 72
California Addresses by President Roosevelt. San Francisco: 1903. V. 72
Colonial Policies of the United States. Garden City: 1937. V. 71
East of the Sun and West of the Moon. 1926. V. 69
Fear God and Take Your Own Part. New York: 1916. V. 68
History as Literature. New York: 1913. V. 68
Hunting Trips of A Ranchman. New York: 1885. V. 71
On My Own. London: 1959. V. 71
Outdoor Pastimes of an American Hunter. New York: 1905. V. 68; 72
Ranch Life and the Hunting Trail. London: 1888. V. 68
Ranch Life and the Hunting Trail. New York: 1888. V. 71
The Rough Riders. New York: 1899. V. 69; 70; 71
This I Remember. New York: 1949. V. 71
Trailing the Giant Panda. 1929. V. 69
Trailing the Giant Panda. New York: 1929. V. 72

ROOT, FRANK A.
The Overland Stage to California. Glorietta: 1971. V. 68

ROOT, HARMON KNOX
The People's Medical Lighthouse; a Series of Popular and Scientific Essays.... New York: 1854. V. 68

ROOT, HENRY
Henry Root - Surveyor, Engineer and Inventor - Personal History and Reminiscences. San Francisco: 1921. V. 69

ROOT, SIDNEY
Primary Bible Questions for Young Children. Atlanta: 1864. V. 71

ROPER, L.
The Gardens in the Royal Park at Windsor.... Garden City: 1959. V. 68

ROPER, MOSES
Narrative of the Adventures and Escape of Moses Roper, from American Slavery. Berwick-upon-Tweed: 1848. V. 69

ROPER, THERESA
Rebounding Vengeance. Newport?: 1919. V. 70

ROPS, FELICIEN
Bibliotheca Ropsica, ex Libris E. M. London: 1918. V. 70

ROQUEFUIL, CAMILLE DE
A Voyage Round the World Between the Years 1816-1819. London: 1823. V. 70

ROREM, NED
Paul's Blues. New York: 1984. V. 69; 73

RORER, SARAH TYSON
Mrs. Rorer's Philadelphia Cookbook. Philadelphia: 1886. V. 68

ROS, AMANDA M.
Fumes of Formation. Belfast: 1933. V. 70; 72

ROSA, SALVATOR
Serie di LXXXV Disegni in Varie Grandezze Composte dal Celebre Pittore Salvator Rosa Pubblicati e Incisi da Carlo Antonini.... Roma: 1780. V. 69

ROSBOROUGH, MARY FREELS
Don't You Cry For Me. New York: 1954. V. 72

ROSCOE, E. S.
Rambles with a Fishing Rod. 1883. V. 68; 73

ROSCOE, H. E.
Spectrum Analysis. Six Lectures Delivered in 1868 Before the Society of Apothecaries of London. London: 1873. V. 73

ROSCOE, J.
The Bakitara or Banyoro, the First Part of the Mackie Ethnological Expedition to Central Africa. Cambridge: 1968. V. 69

ROSCOE, JOHN
Twenty-Five Years in East Africa. Cambridge: 1921. V. 71

ROSCOE, MARY ANNE
Poems for Youth. London: 1820. V. 69

ROSCOE, THOMAS
The Novelist's Library. London: 1831-1833. V. 70
Rambles In France And Switzerland. London. V. 72
The Tourist In France. London: 1834. V. 72
Wanderings and Excursions in North Wales and Wanderings and Excursions in South Wales. London: 1837-1873. V. 73

ROSCOE, WILLIAM
Catalogue of the Genuine and Entire Collection of Prints, Books and Prints &c, the Property of William Roscoe, Esq. Which Will Be sold by Auction, by Mr. Winstanley, at His Rooms in Marble Street, Liverpool. Liverpool: 1816. V. 69; 70
The Life of Lorenzo De' Medici, Called the Magnificent. Philadelphia: 1803. V. 69

ROSCOE, WILLIAM CALDWELL
Violenzia; a Tragedy. London: 1851. V. 68

ROSCOMMON, WENTWORTH DILLON, EARL OF
Poems.... London: 1717. V. 69
The Works. Glasgow: 1753. V. 68; 73

ROSE, A. C.
The Widow's Souvenir: a Gift Book for Widows. New York: 1853. V. 70

ROSE, ALFRED
Register of Erotic Books. New York: 1965. V. 70

ROSE, DAN
The Ancient Mines of Ajo. Tucson: 1936. V. 68

ROSE, GEORGE
A Brief Examination into the Increase of the Revenue, Commerce and Manufactures, of Great Britain, from 1792 to 1799. London: 1799. V. 72
A Brief Examination into the Increase of the Revenue, Commerce and Navigation of Great Britain During the Administration of the Rt. Hon. William Pitt.... London: 1806. V. 72
Mrs. Brown and Disraeli. London: 1874. V. 68
Mrs. Brown at Brighton. London: 1875. V. 68
Mrs. Brown at Margate. London: 1874. V. 68
Mrs. Brown at the Paris Exhibition. London: 1878. V. 68
Mrs. Brown at the Play. London: 1870. V. 68
Mrs. Brown at the Sea-Side. London: 1867. V. 68
Mrs. Brown in London. London: 1867. V. 68
Mrs. Brown in London. London: 1869. V. 68
Mrs. Brown in the Highlands. London: 1869. V. 68
Mrs. Brown on Spelling Bees. London: 1876. V. 68
Mrs. Brown on the Alabama Claims. London: 1872. V. 68
Mrs. Brown on the Grand Tour. London: 1870. V. 68
Mrs. Brown on the Shah's Visit. London: 1873. V. 68
Mrs. Brown on the Tichborne Case. London: 1872. V. 68
Mrs. Brown Up the Nile. London: 1869. V. 68
Mrs. Brown's Christmas Box. London: 1869. V. 68
Mrs. Brown's Olliday Outins. London: 1871. V. 68
Mrs. Brown's Visit to the Paris Exhibition. 1867. V. 68
Observations on the Historical Work of the Late Rt. Hon. Charles James Fox, with a Narrative of the events which occurred in the enterprize of the Earl of Argyle, in 1685, by Sir Patrick Hume. London: 1809. V. 68; 71
Observations Respecting the Public Expenditure and the Influence of the Crown.... London: 1810. V. 72

ROSE Merton the Little Orphan. London: 1860. V. 72

ROSE, RICHARD
Governing Without Concensus: an Irish Perspective. Boston: 1971. V. 70

ROSE, VICTOR M.
The Life and Services of General Ben Mc Culloch. Austin: 1958. V. 68; 73

Ross' Texas Brigade. Louisville: 1881. V. 69; 70
Ross' Texas Brigade. Kennesaw, GA: 1960. V. 71

ROSE, WILLIAM STEWART
The Court and Parliament of Beasts Freely Translated.... London: 1819. V. 68

ROSEE, MADAME
The Handbook of Millinery. 1898. V. 71

ROSEN, GEORGE
The Reception of William Beaumont's Discovery in Europe. New York: 1942. V. 73

ROSEN, PETER
Pa-Ha-Sap-Pa - The Black Hills of South Dakota. St. Louis: 1895. V. 72

ROSEN, R. D.
Strike Three You're Dead. New York: 1984. V. 68; 69; 71; 72

ROSEN, RICHARD
Fadeaway. New York: 1986. V. 68

ROSENAU, H.
Boulee and Visionary Architecture, Including Boullee's Architecture, Essay on Art. London: 1976. V. 69; 72

ROSENBACH, ABRAHAM SIMON WOLF
A Book Hunter's Holiday: Adventures with Books and Manuscripts. Cambridge: 1936. V. 69
Books and Bidders. The Adventures of a Bibliophile. Boston: 1927. V. 73
An Introduction to Herman Melville's Moby Dick. New York: 1924. V. 71

ROSENBERG, BETTY
The Letter Killeth. Los Angeles: 1982. V. 72; 73

ROSENBERG, C. B. H. VON
Reistochten Naar De Geelvinkbaai op Niew-Guinea . . . Gravenhage: 1875. V. 71

ROSENBERG, C. G.
Jenny Lind: Her Life, Her Struggles, and Her Triumphs. New York: 1850. V. 71

ROSENBERG, F.
Big Game Shooting in British Columbia and Norway. 1928. V. 69; 70; 72; 73

ROSENBERG, HAROLD
Saul Steinberg. London: 1979. V. 71; 72

ROSENBERG, ISAAC
Moses. 1916. V. 72
Moses. London: 1916. V. 69
Night and Day. 1912. V. 72
Poems. London: 1922. V. 69; 72; 73
Youth. London: 1915. V. 69; 72; 73

ROSENBERG, PHILIP
Contract on Cherry Street. New York: 1975. V. 68

ROSENBLATT, JULIA CARLSON
Dining with Sherlock Holmes. Indianapolis: 1976. V. 71

ROSENBLITH, W. A.
Sensory Communication, Contributions to the Symposium on Principles of Sensory Communication. Cambridge and New York: 1961. V. 68; 71

ROSENBLUM, L. A.
Handbook of Squirrel Monkey Research. New York: 1985. V. 70

ROSENBLUM, R.
Cubism and Twentieth Century Art. New York: 1976. V. 69; 72

ROSENFIELD, JOHN
Extraordinary Persons: Works by Eccentric Non-Conformist Japanese Artists of the Early Modern Era (1580-1868) in the Collection of Kimiko and John Powers. Cambridge: 1999. V. 72; 73

ROSENGARTEN, DAVID
Red Wine With Fish. New York: 1989. V. 72

ROSENMULLER, ERNST FRIEDRICH KARL
View of Interesting Places in the Holy Land.... Philadelphia: 1840. V. 69

ROSENTHAL, HAROLD
Baseball Is Their Business. New York: 1952. V. 71

ROSENTHAL, M.
A Clinical Treatise on the Diseases of the Nervous System. New York: 1879. V. 71; 73

ROSES of Sharon. Poems chosen from the flower of ancient Hebrew Literature. London: 1937. V. 71

ROSES of Sharon. Poems Chosen from the Flower of Ancient Hebrew Literature. Waltham St. Lawrence: 1937. V. 71

ROSETT, JOSHUA
Intercortical Systems of the Human Cerebrum Mapped by Means of New Anatomic Methods. New York: 1933. V. 68

THE ROSETTE; a Juvenile Annual. Boston: 1846. V. 71

ROSEVEAR, D. R.
The Carnivores of West Africa. London: 1974. V. 73
The Rodents of West Africa. London: 1969. V. 72

ROSMAN, ALICE GRANT
Visitors to Hugo. New York: 1993. V. 69

ROSNEK, CARL
Skystone and Silver: the Collector's Book of Southwest Indian Jewelry. New York: 1976. V. 71

ROSNER, CHARLES
Printer's Progress: a Comparative Survey of the Craft of Printing 1851-1951. London: 1951. V. 69

ROSS, ALEXANDER
Adventures of the First Settlers on the Oregon or Columbia River. London: 1849. V. 68
Arcana Microcosmi; or, the Hid Secrets of Man's Body Discovered.... London: 1652. V. 72; 73
The Fur Hunters of the Far West: a Narrative of Adventures in the Oregon and Rocky Mountains. London: 1855. V. 68; 70
Helenore; or The Fortunate Shepherdess: A Poem in the Broad Scotch Dialect. Edinburgh: 1866. V. 70; 71

ROSS, BARNABY
Drury Lane's Last Case. New York: 1933. V. 73
The Tragedy of Z. New York: 1933. V. 73

ROSS, CHARLES H.
High Tide at Any Hour. 1879. V. 72
High Tide at Any Hour. London: 1879. V. 68

ROSS, CLYDE P.
Water-Supply Paper: the Lower Gila Region, Arizona. Washington: 1923. V. 71

ROSS, D. H.
Wrapped in Pride. 1998. V. 69

ROSS, EDMUND G.
History of the Impeachment of Andrew Johnson. Santa Fe: 1896. V. 73

ROSS, FREDERICK A.
A Sermon, on Intemperance, Delivered in the First Presbyterian Church in Knoxville, Tenneessee on the Evening of the Twelfth of October, 1829. Rogersville: 1830. V. 68

ROSS, J. L. W.
A Medical Student's Letters to His Parents. Toronto: 1909. V. 73

ROSS, JAMES
Handbook of the Diseases of the Nervous System. London: 1885. V. 68
They Don't Dance Much. Boston: 1940. V. 69

ROSS, JOHN
The Book of the Red Deer and Empire Big Game. 1925. V. 69; 70; 72; 73
The Book of the Red Deer and Empire Big Game. London: 1925. V. 71
The Last Voyage of Captain Sir John Ross, R.N. Knt. to the Arctic Regions.... London: 1835. V. 69
Narrative of a Second Voyage in Search of a North-West Passage. London: 1835. V. 69; 71
Narrative of a Second Voyage in Search of a North-West Passage. Paris: 1835. V. 71
On Communication to India, in Large Steam Ships, by the Cape of Good Hope. London: 1838. V. 69
A Treatise on Navigation by Steam.... London: 1828. V. 69
A Voyage of Discovery. London: 1819. V. 71

ROSS, MALCOLM
The Cape Fear. New York: 1965. V. 71
A Climber in New Zealand. London: 1914. V. 71

ROSS, MARTIN
Beggars on Horseback - A Riding Tour in North Wales. London: 1895. V. 72

ROSS, MARVIN C.
George Catlin: Episodes from Life Among the Indians and Last Rambles. 1959. V. 69
The West of Alfred Jacob Miller (1837).... Norman: 1951. V. 70; 72; 73
The West of Alfred Jacob Miller (1837).... Norman: 1968. V. 71

ROSS, RICHARD M.
The History of the First Battalion Cameron Highlanders of Ottawa (MG). Ottawa: 1946. V. 73

ROSS, ROBERT
Aubrey Beardsley. London: 1909. V. 72

ROSS, ROSELLE
Bruiny Bear...Who Wasn't Hungry. New York: 1945. V. 72

ROSS, W. STEWART
Woman: Her Glory, Her Shame and Her God. London: 1890. V. 68
Woman; Her Glory, Her Shame and Her God. London: 1894. V. 69

ROSS, WALTER
The Immortal. New York: 1958. V. 70

ROSS CRAIG, S.
Drawings of British Plants. London: 1948-1973. V. 71

ROSSE, ALBAN
The Island Spectres: and Something More, but Nothing Worse.. Birmingham: 1855. V. 71

ROSSE, HERMAN
Designs and Impressions. Chicago: 1920. V. 70

ROSSETTI, CHRISTINA
Commonplace, a Tale of To-Day and Other Stories. Boston: 1870. V. 68
Goblin Market. London: 1862. V. 68; 72
Goblin Market. London: 1875. V. 72
Goblin Market. London: 1893. V. 71; 72
Goblin Market. London: 1933. V. 68
Goblin Market. Philadelphia: 1933. V. 70
Goblin Market. London: 1939. V. 71
New Poems by Christina Rossetti Hitherto Unpublished or Uncollected. London and New York: 1896. V. 71; 72
A Pageant and Other Poems. Boston: 1881. V. 72
A Pageant and Other Poems. London: 1881. V. 68; 72
Poems. Boston: 1866. V. 72
Poems. London and New York: 1890. V. 72
Poems Chose by Walter de la Mare. Newtown: 1930. V. 68; 70
The Prince's Progress and Other Poems. London: 1866. V. 71; 72
Sing Song. London: 1872. V. 68; 72
Sing Song. London: 1880. V. 68
Sing Song. London: 1893. V. 69; 72
Speaking Likenesses. London: 1874. V. 68; 70; 71; 72
Time Flies: a Reading Diary. London: 1885. V. 73
Verses. 1893. V. 72
Verses Dedicated to Her Mother. London: 1847. V. 72

ROSSETTI, DANTE GABRIEL
Ballads and Narrative Poems. London: 1894. V. 71
Ballads and Sonnets. London: 1881. V. 71; 72
The Blessed Damozel. London: 1898. V. 68
The Blessed Damozel. Chapel Hill: 1937. V. 68
Dante and His Circle: with the Italian Poets Preceding Him. London: 1874. V. 72
Drawings of Rossetti. London: 1905. V. 68
The Early Italian Poets from Ciullo D'Alcamo to Dante Aligheri.... London: 1861. V. 68; 69; 71; 72; 73
Hand and Soul. 1895. V. 71; 73
Hand and Soul. Maastricht: 1928. V. 73
Letters from Dante Gabriel Rossetti to Algernon Charles Swinburne Regarding the Attacks Made Upon the Latter by Mortimer Collins and Upon Both by Robert Buchanan. London: 1921. V. 72
Poems. London: 1869. V. 72
Poems. London: 1870. V. 72
Poems. London: 1881. V. 72
The Poems of.... 1904. V. 68
A Rossetti Cabinet. London: 1991. V. 68
Sir Hugh the Heron. A Legendary Tale in Four Parts. London: 1843. V. 72

ROSSETTI, MARIA FRANCESCA
Exercises in Idiomatic Italian through Literal Translation from the English. London and Edinburgh: 1867. V. 72

ROSSETTI, WILLIAM MICHAEL
Bibliography of the Works of D. G. Rossetti. 1905. V. 68
Rossetti Papers 1862-1870. 1903. V. 68
Rossetti Papers 1862-1870. London: 1903. V. 73
Shelley's Prometheus Unbound. A Study of Its Meaning and Personages. 1886. V. 68
Swinburne's Poems and Ballads. A Criticism. London: 1866. V. 68

ROSSI, G. G. DE
Villa Pamphilia Ejusque Palatium.... Rome: 1690. V. 72

ROSSI, PAUL A.
The Art of the Old West. New York: 1971. V. 69

ROSS KING, W.
The Sportsman and Naturalist in Canada. 1866. V. 69; 70; 72; 73

ROSTAND, EDMOND
Cyrano de Bergerac. New York: 1954. V. 69

ROSTAND, ROBERT
The Killer Elite. New York: 1973. V. 69; 71

ROSTEN, NORMAN
Over and Out. New York: 1972. V. 69

ROSTER of Soldiers from North Carolina in the American Revolution. Durham: 1932. V. 70

ROSTINIO, PIETRO
Compendio di Tutta la Cirugia, Utilissimo ad Ogni Studioso di Quella & Sopra Modo Necessario. Venice: 1561. V. 69
Compendio Di Tvtta La Cirvgia.... Venice: 1630. V. 73

ROSTOW, WALTER
View from the Seventh Floor. New York: 1964. V. 70

ROTH, BARRY
An Annotated Bibliography of Jane Austen Studies 1973-1982. 1985. V. 70

ROTH, BERNARD
Dress: Its Sanitary Aspect. A Paper Read Before the Bright Social Union, January 30th 1860.... London: 1880. V. 72
The Treatment of Lateral Curvature of the Spine.... London: 1889. V. 70

ROTH, DAVID
Sacred Honor. A Biography of Colin Powell. Grand Rapids: 1993. V. 69

ROTH, HENRY
Mercy Of A Rude Stream. New York: 1994. V. 72
Nature's First Green. New York: 1979. V. 69; 71; 73

ROTH, HENRY LING
Crozet's Voyage to Tasmania. London: 1891. V. 71
The Natives of Sarawak and British North Borneo. London: 1896. V. 71
Oriental Silverwork. London: 1910. V. 72

ROTH, JOSEPH
The Ballad of the Hundred Days. New York: 1936. V. 69
Job - The Story of a Simple Man. London: 1932. V. 72

ROTH, PHILIP
American Pastoral. Boston/New York: 1997. V. 69; 70; 71; 72
American Pastoral. Franklin Center: 1997. V. 68; 69; 70
The Anatomy Lesson. New York: 1983. V. 70; 72
The Conversion of the Jews. Mankato: 1993. V. 70
The Counterlife. Franklin Center: 1986. V. 70
The Facts. New York: 1988. V. 70
The Ghost Writer. New York: 1979. V. 73
Goodbye, Columbus. Boston: 1959. V. 69; 73
Goodbye, Columbus. Franklin Center: 1978. V. 69; 70
The Great American Novel. New York: 1973. V. 70
His Mistress's Voice. Lewisburg: 1995. V. 71
The Human Stain. Boston/NY: 2000. V. 72
The Human Stain. Franklin Center: 2000. V. 68; 70
I Always Wanted You to Admire My Fasting; or Looking at Kafka. 1972. V. 69
I Married a Communist. Boston/New York: 1998. V. 72
Looking at Kafka. Helsinki: 1990. V. 71
Operation Shylock. Franklin Center: 1993. V. 69; 70
Operation Shylock. New York: 1993. V. 69; 70; 72
Portnoy's Complaint. New York: 1969. V. 69; 70; 72
The Professor of Desire. New York: 1977. V. 69
Sabbath's Theater. Boston/New York: 1995. V. 72
Shop Talk. Boston/New York: 2001. V. 69
When She Was Good. New York: 1967. V. 70
Zuckerman Unbound. New York: 1981. V. 70

ROTHENBERG, JEROME
Between - Poems 1960/1963. London: 1967. V. 68
Improvisations. 1991. V. 73
Narratives and Real Theater Pieces. Bretenoux: 1977. V. 70
A Seneca Journal. New York: 1978. V. 68; 71

ROTHENSTEIN, JOHN
Agustus John. London: 1944. V. 72
An Introduction to English Painting. London: 1933. V. 69
Turner. London: 1965. V. 69; 72
Victor Hammer: Artist and Craftsman. Boston: 1978. V. 70; 72

ROTHENSTEIN, WILLIAM
Men and Memories, Recollections 1872-1922. Since Fifty, Recollections 1922-1938. 1931-1939. V. 73
Twenty-Four Portraits. London: 1920-1923. V. 73

ROTHERAY, L.
Flora of Skipton and District. Skipton: 1900. V. 69

ROTHERHAM, JEREMIAH & CO.
Great Autumn Show. 14th, 15th and 16th September. 1896. V. 68

ROTHERY, AGNES
Into What Port?. New York: 1931. V. 70

ROTHERY, G. A.
A Diary of the Wreck of His Majesty's Ship Challenger. London: 1836. V. 71

ROTHMAN, SYDNEY
Physiology and Biochemistry of the Skin. Chicago: 1954. V. 68

ROTHSCHILD, M.
A Colour Atlas of Insect Tissues via the Flea. London: 1986. V. 70
Fleas, Flukes and Cuckoos. 1952. V. 69

ROTHSCHILD, NATHANIEL MAYER VICTOR, BARON
The History of Tom Jones, a Changeling. Cambridge: 1951. V. 71
The Rothschild Library: a Catalogue of the Collection of Eighteenth Century Printed Books and Manuscripts formed by Lord Rothschild. London: 1969. V. 70
Two Bindings by Roger Payne in the Library of Lord Rothschild. Cambridge: 1947. V. 68

ROTHSCHUH, KARL E.
History of Physiology. New York: 1973. V. 68

ROTHSTEIN, ARTHUR
Photojournalism. Philadelphia: 1965. V. 72

ROTHWELL, C. F. SEYMOUR
The Printing of Textile Fabrics; a Practical Manual on the Printing of Cotton, Woolen, Silk and Half Silk Fabrics. 1897. V. 71

ROTHWELL, SELIM
Scraps from an Artist's Sketch Book. Bolton: 1877. V. 70; 72

ROTTENBERG, D. A.
Neurological Classics in Modern Translation. New York: 1977. V. 73

ROUALT, GEORGES
Miserere. London: 1950. V. 69
Soliloques. Neuchatel: 1944. V. 69

ROUCHER, JEAN ANTOINE
Collection Universelle de Memoires Particuliers Relatifs a L'Histoire de France. Londres: 1785-1791. V. 70

ROUGHLEY, T. C.
Fishes of Australia and Their Technology. Sydney: 1916. V. 72; 73

ROUILLE, GUILLAUME
Prima (Secunda) Pars Promptvarii Iconvm Insigniorvm a Secvlo Hominum. Lvgdvni: 1553. V. 71

ROUND London. *An Album of Pictures from Photographs of the Chief Places of Interest In and Around London.* London: 1896. V. 71

A ROUND of Days Described in Original Poems by Some of Our Most Celebrated Poets and in Pictures by Eminent Artists. London: 1866. V. 68

ROUND-ABOUT Rhymes. London: 1909. V. 70

ROUNDELL, CHARLES, MRS.
Ham House, Its History and Art Treasures.... London: 1904. V. 68; 70

ROUQUETTE, LOUIS FREDERIC
The Great White Silence. New York: 1930. V. 69

ROURKE, CONSTANCE
Audubon. London: 1936. V. 68
Charles Sheeler: Artist in the American Tradition. New York: 1938. V. 68; 69; 72
Troupers of the Gold Coast or the Rise of Lotta Crabtree. New York: 1928. V. 71

ROURKE, THOMAS
Haven for the Gallant. London: 1936. V. 68
The Scarlet Flower. London: 1934. V. 73

ROUSE, ELIZABETH G.
Fifty Years in Richmond 1898-1948. Richmond: 1948. V. 70

ROUSH, JOHN H.
Antlers Afield. 1988. V. 73

ROUSSEAU, JEAN BAPTISTE
Pieces Interessantes et Peu Connues Pour Servir a l'Histoire. Brussel: 1781. V. 72

ROUSSEAU, JEAN-JACQUES
Collection Complete Des Oeuvres. Kehl: 1783-1789. V. 71
Les Confessions.... Geneva: 1782. V. 70; 72; 73
The Confessions.... London: 1938. V. 68
Discours sur l'Origine et les Fondemens de L'Inegalite Parmi Les Hommes. Amsterdam: 1755. V. 71
A Discourse.... London: 1760. V. 73
Dissertation on Political Economy: to Which is Added, a Treatise on the Social Compact.... Albany: 1797. V. 71
Letters on the Elements of Botany. 1787-1778. V. 69
Letters on the Elements of Botany Addressed to a Lady. London: 1787. V. 69
Lettres de Deux Amans, Habitans d'une Petite Ville au Pied des Alpes. Amsterdam: 1761. V. 72
Nouvelles Lettres.... Paris: 1789. V. 73

ROUSSEAU, MELLE M. V.
Contes De La Jeune Tante. Paris: 1657?. V. 72

ROUSSEAU, VICTOR
The Messiah of the Cylinder. Chicago: 1917. V. 68

ROUSSEL, NAPOLEON
Mon Voyage en Algerie Raconte a mes Enfans. Paris: 1840. V. 73

ROUSSELET, R. P. PACIFIQUE
Histoire et Description de l'Eglise Royale de Brou Elevee a Bourg en Bresse, sous les Ordres de Marguerte d'Aturice.... Paris: 1767. V. 68

ROUTLEDGE, SCORESBY, MRS.
The Mystery of Easter Island. London: 1919. V. 71

ROUTLEDGE, W. SCORESBY
The Akikuyu of British Africa. London: 1910. V. 71

ROUTLEDGE'S Coloured Picture Book. London: 1870. V. 73

ROUX, F.
John Gould's Birds of Europe. Paris: 2000. V. 68

ROVIROSA, JOSE N.
Pteridografía del Sur de Mexico.... Mexico: 1910. V. 68

ROWAN, A. B.
Lake Lore, or an Antiquarian Guide to Some of the Ruins and Recollections of Kilarney. 1853. V. 69; 73

ROWAN, CARL T.
South of Freedom. NY: 1952:. V. 72

ROWAN, JOHN J.
The Emigrant and Sportsman in Canada. London: 1876. V. 73

ROWBOTHAM, SAMUEL B.
Zetetic Astronomy, Earth Not a Globe: an Experimental Inquiry. London: 1873. V. 69

ROWE, ANNE
The Little Dog Barked. New York: 1942. V. 70

ROWE BROS. & CO. LTD.
List No. 90. Manufacturers of Sheet Lead, Lead Pipe...Wire, Plumber's and Tinmen's Solder. Trade Catalogue.... 1935. V. 71

ROWE, ELIZABETH
Devout Exercises of the Heart.... Dublin: 1771. V. 73
Friendship in Death: in Twenty Letters from the Dead to the Living. 1750. V. 69
Friendship in Death: in Twenty Letters from the Dead to the Living. Glasgow?: 1750. V. 68
Friendship in Death: in Twenty Letters from the Dead to the Living. London: 1784. V. 73
Friendship in Death: in Twenty Letters to which are added, Letters Moral and Entertaining.... London: 1745. V. 69; 72

ROWE, FREDERICK W.
A History of Newfoundland and Labrador. Toronto: 1980. V. 69

ROWE, HENRY K.
Tercentenary History of Newton 1630-1930. Newton: 1930. V. 71

ROWE, MIKE
Chicago Breakdown. New York: 1975. V. 69; 73

ROWE, NATHANIEL
The Tragedy of Jane Shore. London: 1714. V. 68; 72

ROWE, NICHOLAS
The Works. London: 1747. V. 69

ROWETT, W.
The Ocean Telegraph Cable.... London: 1865. V. 68

ROWLAND, BENJAMIN
The Art and Architecture of India. Buddhist. Hindu. Jain. 1967. V. 68

ROWLAND, HENRY
Physical Papers. Baltimore: 1902. V. 68

ROWLAND, KATE MASON
Life of George Mason 1725-1792. New York and London: 1892. V. 69

ROWLAND, LAURA J.
Rhinju. New York: 1994. V. 68

ROWLAND'S Kalydor. A Treatise on the Formation of the Skin, with Directions for Preserving It in a State of Health; Illustrative of the Salutary Properties of Rowland's Kalydor. London: 1840. V. 68

ROWLANDSON, THOMAS
The Amorous Illustrations. 1969. V. 72
An Excursion to Brightelmstone. London: 1790. V. 70
Loyal Volunteers of London and Environs. London: 1798-1799. V. 71
Medical Caricatures. New York: 1971. V. 71
The Rhedarium, for the Sale of All Sorts of Carriages, by Gregory Gigg. A New Book of Horses and Carriages. London: 1784. V. 70
The Watercolour Drawings of Thomas Rowlandson, from the Albert H. Wiggin Collection in the Boston Public Library. New York: 1947. V. 69

ROWLEY, CHARLES
Fifty Years of Work Without Wages.... London: 1912. V. 71

ROWLEY, G.
A History of Succulent Plants. Mill Valley: 1997. V. 69

ROWLEY, HUGH
Gamosagammon; or Hints on Hymen. For the Use of Parties about to Connubialize. London: 1871. V. 71
More Puniana; or Thoughts Wise and Other-Why's. A new collection of the best Riddles, Conundrums, Jokes, Sells, &c. London: 1875. V. 71

ROWLEY, JOHN
Taxidermy and Museum Exhibition. 1925. V. 71

ROWLING, J. K.
Harry Potter and the Chamber of Secrets. Bloomsbury: 1998. V. 71; 73
Harry Potter and The Chamber of Secrets. New York: 1999. V. 73
Harry Potter and the Goblet of Fire. London: 2000. V. 68; 70; 72; 73
Harry Potter and the Goblet of Fire. New York: 2000. V. 68; 73
Harry Potter and the Philosopher's Stone. Maryborough: 1997-1998. V. 70
Harry Potter and the Philosopher's Stone. Harry Potter and the Chamber of Secrets. Harry Potter and the Prisoner of Azkaban. Harry Potter and the Goblet of Fire. Bloomsbury: 1999-2000. V. 68; 73
Harry Potter and the Prisoner of Azkaban. London: 1999. V. 73
Harry Potter and the Prisoner of Azkaban. New York: 1999. V. 69; 70; 73
Harry Potter and the Sorcerer's Stone. New York: 1998. V. 70

ROWNEY & FORSTER
Rowney and Forster's Lithographic Drawing-Book. 1820. V. 73

ROWNING, J.
A Compendious System of Natural Philosophy.... 1759. V. 68

ROY, ARUNDHATI
The God of Small Things. London: 1997. V. 69; 70; 71; 73
The God of Small Things. New York: 1997. V. 68; 69; 70; 72

ROY, JAMES A.
Joseph Howe. A Study in Achievement and Frustration. Toronto: 1935. V. 72

ROY, JENNET
History of Canada for Use of Schools and Families. Montreal: 1850. V. 72

ROY, JULES
The Navigator. New York: 1955. V. 72

ROY, OLIVA FITZ
The Island of Birds. London: 1954. V. 68

ROYAL Blue Book, Fashionable Directory and Parliamentary Guide 1847. London: 1846. V. 71

ROYAL Blue Book Fashionable Directory; and Parliamentary Guide.... 1864. V. 71

THE Royal Cabinet Atlas, and Compendious Universal Gazetteer Of All Places In the Known World. London. V. 72

ROYAL COLLEGE OF PHYSICIANS
Certain Necessary Directions, as Well for the Cure of the Plague, as for Preventing the Infection; with Many Easie Medicines of Small Charge. London: 1636. V. 72
The Statutes of the Colledge (sic) of Physicians London: Worthy to be Perused by all Men.... London: 1693. V. 68; 73

ROYAL GEOGRAPHICAL SOCIETY
Journal 1869. London: 1869. V. 71
Royal Geographical Society Proceedings and Monthly Record of Geography. London: 1891. V. 72
Royal Geographical Society Proceedings and Monthly Record of Geography. London: 1892. V. 72

ROYAL HUMANE SOCIETY
Plan and Reports of Society Instituted at London in the Year MDCCLXXIV for the Recovery of Persons Apparently Drowned. 1775. V. 72

THE ROYAL Illuminated Book of Legends. Edinburgh: 1880. V. 73

ROYAL INSTITUTE OF BRITISH ARCHITECTS
Papers Read at the Royal Institute of British Architects. London: 1859-1865. V. 69

THE ROYAL Kalendar; or Complete and Correct Annual Register...for the Year 1788.... London: 1787-1788. V. 73

THE ROYAL Kalendar; or Complete and Correct Annual Register...for the Year 1793.... London: 1792-1793. V. 73

THE ROYAL Military Tournament. London: 1885. V. 69

ROYAL ONTARIO MUSEUM
English Silver. A Catalogue to an Exhibition of Seven Centuries of English Domestic Silver. Toronto: 1958. V. 73

THE ROYAL River: the Thames from Source to Sea, Descriptive, Historical, Pictorial. London: 1885. V. 72

ROYAL SCOTTISH ACADEMY GALLERIES
Catalogue of the Naval and Military Exhibition, Historic, Technical and Artistic Held in the Royal Scottish Academy Galelries, Edinburgh, Opened on Waterloo Day June 18, 1889. Edinburgh: 1889. V. 71

ROYAL SOCIETY OF ARTS
A List of the Society for the Encouragement of Arts, Manufactures and Commerce. London: 1757. V. 73

ROYAL SOCIETY OF LITERATURE IN THE UNITED KINGDOM
Essays by Divers Hands. Transactions, New Series, Volume 1. Oxford: 1921. V. 71

ROYAL SOCIETY OF LITERATURE OF THE UNITED KINGDOM
Essays by Divers Hands -Being the Transactions of the Royal Society of Literature of the United Kingdom: New Series, Volume VII. London: 1927. V. 72

ROYAL JUBILEE EXHIBITION, 1887. MANCHESTER
Textile Manufacturer. Royal Jubilee Exhibition Number. 1887. V. 71

ROYALL, ANNE NEWPORT
The Black Book or a Continuation of Travels in the United States. Washington City: 1828. V. 69
Sketches of History, Life, and Manners in the United States.... New Haven: 1826. V. 69; 72
The Tennessean, a Novel, Founded on Facts. New Haven: 1827. V. 69

ROYALL, WILLIAM L.
Some Reminiscences. New York: 1909. V. 69; 70

ROYAL MANUFACTURING CO., DETROIT
Illustrated Catalogue and Price List of Silverware. 1902. V. 70

ROYAL MILITARY EXHIBITION, 1890. LONDON
Official Catalogue and Guide. London: 1890. V. 71

ROYAL NAVAL EXHIBITION, 1891. LONDON
Official Catalogue and Guide. London: 1891. V. 71

ROYCE, JOSIAH
California - from the Conquest in 1846 to Second Vigilance Committee in San Francisco. Boston: 1886. V. 68; 73

ROYCE, SARAH
A Frontier Lady - Recollections of the Gold Rush and Early California. New Haven: 1932. V. 68

ROYDE SMITH, N. G.
Una and the Red Cross Knight and Other Tales from Spenser's Faery Queene. London: 1915. V. 69

ROYER-COLLARD, F. B.
Skeleton Clocks. London: 1969. V. 72

ROYS, RALPH L.
The Book of Chilam Balam of Chumayel. Norman: 1967. V. 71

ROZAN, S. J.
China Trade. New York: 1994. V. 68; 69; 70; 71
Concourse. New York: 1995. V. 69; 70; 71; 72; 73

ROZE, J. A.
Coral Snakes of the Americas. Malabar: 1996. V. 70

RUARK, ROBERT
The Horn of the Hunter. 1954. V. 70; 72; 73
I Didn't Know It Was Loaded. Garden City: 1948. V. 73
The Old Man and the Boy. New York: 1957. V. 73
The Old Man's Boy Grows Older. New York: 1961. V. 73
One for the Road. Garden City: 1949. V. 70; 73
Something of Value. Garden City: 1955. V. 68
Use Enough Gun. New York: 1966. V. 68; 70; 73
Use Enough Gun. 1967. V. 70; 72
Women. New York: 1967. V. 73

RUBAN, PETRUS
Album de 102 Reproductions de Reliures d'Art et de Demi-Reliures Fantaisie de Petrus Ruban. Paris: 1898. V. 70

RUBENS, CHARLES
The Dummy Library of Charles Dickens at Gad's Hill Place. 1934. V. 69

RUBENSTEIN, HELENA
Food for Beauty. New York: 1938. V. 72

RUBIN, STEVEN JAY
The Complete James Bond Movie Encyclopedia. Chicago: 1990. V. 69; 73
The Complete James Bond Movie Encyclopedia. Chicago: 1995. V. 72

RUBIN, WILLIAM S.
Dada and Surrealist Art. New York: 1968. V. 70

RUBINO, JANE
Death of a DJ. 1994. V. 68; 69; 71
Death of a DJ. Aurora: 1994. V. 70
Death of a DJ. Aurora: 1995. V. 69

RUBINSTEIN, L. J.
Tumors of the Central Nervous System. Washington: 1972. V. 71

RUBTSOV, I. A.
Fauna of the U.S.S.R. Diptera. Volume 6, Part 6. Blackflies (simuliidae). New Delhi: 1989. V. 72

RUBY, ROBERT H.
The Cayuse Indians, Imperial Tribesmen of Old Oregon. Norman: 1972. V. 72
The Chinook Indians, Traders of the Lower Columbia River. Norman: 1976. V. 72
Indian Slavery in the Pacific Northwest. Spokane: 1993. V. 68
Indians of the Pacific Northwest, a History. Norman: 1970. V. 72

RUCK, BERTA
The Disturbing Charm. New York: 1919. V. 71
The Mind of a Minx. New York: 1927. V. 71
Sleeping Beauty. New York: 1936. V. 69

RUCKER, C. WILBUR
A History of the Ophthalmoscope. Rochester: 1971. V. 72

RUCKER, MAUDE A.
The Oregon Trail and Some of Its Makers. New York: 1930. V. 71

RUD, ANTHONY
House of the Damned. New York: 1934. V. 69
The Stuffed Men. New York: 1935. V. 69

RUDALL, J. N., & SONS
American Municipal Bonds as Investments. London: 1874. V. 68

RUDBECK, O.
Reliquiae Rudbeckiana, Sive Camporum Elysiorum Libri Primi.... London: 1789. V. 69

RUDD, MARGARET CAROLINE
Facts; or a Plain and Explicit Narrative of the Case of Mrs. Rudd. London: 1775. V. 70
Mrs. Marg. Car. Rudd's Case Considered, Respecting Robert Perreau, in an Address to Henry Drummond, Esq. and the Gentlemen of the Jury.... London: 1776. V. 70

RUDDEKSDEKK, H. J.
Flora of Gloucestershire, Phanerogams, Vascular Cryptograms Charophyta. Cheltenham: 1948. V. 73

RUDDIMAN, THOMAS
Grammataical Exercises, on the Moods, Tenses and Syntax of the Latin Language. Charleston: 1823. V. 68

RUDDIMAN, WALTER
A Collection of Scarce, Curious and Valuable Pieces.... Edinburgh: 1773. V. 68

RUDGE, M. M.
Madam Pussy Purr. London: 1910. V. 73

RUDISILL, RICHARD
Mirror Image: the Influence of the Daguerreotype on American Society. Albuquerque: 1971. V. 70
Photographers of the New Mexico Territory 1854-1912. Santa Fe: 1973. V. 71

RUDOLPH, PRINCE
Travels In The East Including A Visit To Egypt And The Holy Land. London: 1884. V. 72

RUEFF, JACOB
De Conceptu. Et Generatione Hominis: de Matrice et Eivs Partibvs.... Frankfurt: 1587. V. 70; 73

RUESCH, HANS
The Racer. New York: 1953. V. 70

RUESTOW, EDWARD G.
The Microscope in the Dutch Republic. The Shaping of Discovery. Cambridge: 1996. V. 68

RUFF, MATT
Fool on the Hill. 1988. V. 70

RUFFHEAD, OWEN
A Complete Index to the Statutes at Large, From Magna Charta to the Tenth Year of George III.... London: 1772. V. 70

RUFFIN, EDMUND
Agricultural, Geological and Descriptive Sketches of Lower North Carolina and the Similar Adjacent Lands. Raleigh: 1861. V. 68
Anticipations of the Future to Serve as Lessons for the Present Time. Richmond: 1860. V. 69
The Farmer' Register, a Monthly Publication Devoted to the Improvement of the Practice, and Support of the Interests of Agriculture. Shellbanks: 1834-1836. V. 68

RUFFIN, FRANK G.
The Negro as a Political and Social Factor. Richmond: 1888. V. 68

RUFFINI, JOHN
Lorenzo Benoni or Passages in the Life of an Italian. Edinburgh: 1853. V. 68

RUFFNER, HENRY
Address to the People of West Virginia; Shewing that Slavery is Injurious to the Public Welfare.... Louisville: 1847. V. 71

RUFUS or the Red King. London: 1838. V. 68

RUFZ DE LAVISON, ETIENNE
Enquete sur le Serpent de la Martinique.... 1859. V. 70

RUGGLES BRISE, A. W.
Shooting Reminiscences in Essex & Elsewhere. 1930. V. 71

RUHEMANN, HELMET
The Cleaning of Paintings: Problems and Potentialities. London: 1968. V. 69; 72

RUIZ, JUAN
The Book of Good Love of the Archpriest of Hita, Juan Ruiz. New York: 1933. V. 69

RUKEYSER, MURIEL
Wake Island. New York: 1942. V. 68

RULE, WILLIAM H.
The Crusade. London: 1854. V. 70

THE RULES of Work, or, The Carpenters, in the Town of Boston. Charlestown: 1800. V. 70

RULFO, JUAN
The Burning Plain. Austin: 1967. V. 70

RUMNEY, A. WREN
Tom Rumney of Mellfell (1764-1835). Kendal: 1936. V. 71

RUMP. Or an Exact Collection of the Choycest Poems and Songs Relating to the Late Times. London: 1874. V. 72

RUMSEY, JAMES
A Short Treatise on the Application of Steam, Whereby is Clearly Shewn from Actual Experiments.... Philadelphia: 1788. V. 73

RUNCIMAN, JAMES
Skippers and Shellbacks. London: 1885. V. 68

RUNCIMAN, STEVEN
The Fall of Constantinople 1453. London: 1965. V. 70
The Medieval Manichee - a Study of the Christian Dualist Heresy. Cambridge: 1947. V. 70

RUNDALL, L. B.
The Ibex of Sha-ping and Other Himalayan Studies. 1915. V. 69; 70; 72; 73

RUNDELL, MARIA ELIZA
American Domestic Cookery.... New York: 1823. V. 71
Letters Addressed to Two Absent Daughters. London: 1814. V. 71
Mrs. Rundell's Domestic Cookery.... London: 1867. V. 68
Modern Domestic Cookery. London: 1853. V. 68
A New System of Domestic Cookery.... London: 1815. V. 72

RUNYON, DAMON
Furthermore. London: 1938. V. 69
Guys and Dolls. 1931. V. 73
Guys and Dolls. New York: 1931. V. 71
Guys and Dolls. Philadelphia: 1935. V. 73
In Our Town. New York: 1946. V. 73
Money from Home. 1935. V. 73
Take It Easy. 1938. V. 73
Take It Easy. New York: 1938. V. 70; 72

RUPERT 1949 Annual. London. V. 70

RUPORT, ARCH
The Art of Cockfighting. New York: 1949. V. 69

RUPPLI, MICHEL
The Prestige Label. A Discography. Westport: 1980. V. 69; 71

RURAL, A.
Contributions to Natural History Chiefly in Relation to the Food of the People. London: 1865. V. 68

RURAL Archiecture: Being a Series of Designs for Rural and Other Dwellings, from the Labourer's Cottage to the Small Villa and Farm House with Out-Buildings.... London: 1860. V. 68

RUSCA, LUIGI
Raccolta dei Disegni...Recueil des Dessins de Differens Batimens Construits a Saint-Peterbourg, et dans l'Interieur de l'Empire de Russie. St. Petersburg: 1810. V. 70; 72

RUSCELLI, GIROLAMO
La Prima (-Terza) Parte de' Secreti. Pesaro: 1562. V. 73

RUSCHA, EDWARD
Nine Swimming Pools and a Broken Glass. 1968. V. 68
Various Small Fires and Milk. 1964. V. 68

RUSCHENBERGER, W. S. W.
Elements of Conchology.... Philadelphia: 1847. V. 68
Narrative of a Voyage Round the World. London: 1838. V. 71
Three Years in the Pacific, Containing Notices of Brazil, Chile, Bolivia, Peru &c.... London: 1835. V. 73

RUSH, BENJAMIN
An Account of the Bilious Remitting Yellow Fever, as It Appeared in the City of Philadelphia in the Year 1793. Philadelphia: 1794. V. 73
Essays, Literary, Moral and Philosophical. Philadelphia: 1806. V. 68
Letters of Benjamin Rush. Princeton: 1951. V. 73
Medical Inquiries and Observations Upon the Diseases of the Mind. Philadelphia: 1812. V. 68; 72
Three Lectures Upon Animal Life, Delivered in the University of Pennsylvania. Philadelphia: 1799. V. 70

RUSH, JAMES
An Inquiry into the Use of the Omentum. Philadelphia: 1809. V. 68; 73
The Philosophy of the Human Voice; Embracing Its Physiological History.... Philadelphia: 1855. V. 68

RUSH, NORMAN
Mating. New York: 1991. V. 69; 71
Whites. New York: 1986. V. 69; 70; 71; 73

RUSH, OSCAR B.
The Open Range and Bunk House Philosophy. 1930. V. 72
The Open Range and Bunk House Philosophy. Colorado: 1930. V. 71

RUSH, RICHARD
Memoranda of a Residence at the Court of London. Philadelphia: 1833. V. 69; 71
Memoranda of a Residence at the Court of London, Comprising Incidents Official and Personal from 1819 to 1825. Philadelphia: 1845. V. 73

RUSH, W. M.
Wild Animals of the Rockies. 1942. V. 69; 70

RUSHBY, G. G.
No More the Tusker. 1965. V. 70

RUSHDIE, SALMAN
East, West. London: 1994. V. 68; 69; 70; 71; 72
East, West. New York: 1994. V. 69
Fury. London: 2001. V. 70; 72; 73
Fury. New York: 2001. V. 69; 72
Good Advice is Rarer than Rubies. 1994. V. 69
Good Advice is Rarer than Rubies. New York: 1995. V. 70
Grimus. London: 1975. V. 68; 69; 70
Grimus. New York: 1979. V. 68
Grimus. Woodstock: 1979. V. 71
The Ground Beneath Her Feet. London: 1999. V. 69; 70
The Ground Beneath Her Feet. New York: 1999. V. 68; 69; 72
Haroun and the Sea of Stories. 1990. V. 68; 71; 73
Haroun and the Sea of Stories. London: 1990. V. 68; 69; 70; 71
Haroun and the Sea of Stories. New York: 1991. V. 69
Imaginary Homelands. London/New York: 1991. V. 68; 69; 70; 72
The Jaguar Smile. A Nicaraguan Journey. New York: 1987. V. 69
Midnight's Children. London: 1981. V. 68; 69; 70; 73
Midnight's Children. New York: 1981. V. 69; 70
The Moor's Last Sigh. London: 1995. V. 68; 69; 70; 71; 73
The Moor's Last Sigh. New York: 1995. V. 68; 70
The Moor's Last Sigh. New York: 1996. V. 69; 72
The Satanic Verses. 1988. V. 73
The Satanic Verses. London: 1988. V. 68; 69; 70; 71
The Satanic Verses. New York: 1988. V. 69; 70
The Satanic Verses. New York: 1989. V. 68; 70; 73
Shame. London: 1983. V. 68; 69; 70; 71
Shame. New York: 1983. V. 69; 72
Two Stories. London: 1989. V. 73
The Wizard of Oz. London: 1992. V. 69

RUSHE, JAMES P.
Carmel in Ireland: the Irish Province of Discalced Carmelites 1625- 1896. 1903. V. 69

RUSHWORTH & DREAPER
Antique Musical Instruments and Historical Manuscripts. Liverpool. V. 72; 73

RUSHWORTH, JOHN
Historical Collection of Private Passages of State. London: 1659. V. 72

RUSK, RALPH LESLIE
The Literature of the Middle Western Frontier. New York: 1925. V. 68

RUSKIN, JOHN
Arrows of the Chace.... London: 1880. V. 69; 72
The Art of England. Lectures Given in Oxford. Orpington, Kent: 1883. V. 68
La Bible D'Amiens. Paris: 1910. V. 69; 71
The Collected Works. Orpington: 1880-1887. V. 71
The Crown of Wild Olives. London: 1866. V. 70
Dame Wiggins of Lee and Her Seven Wonderful Cats. London: 1885. V. 73
The Elements of Drawing in Three Letters to Beginners. London: 1857. V. 69; 73
The Elements of Drawing. (with) The Elements of Perspective. London: 1857-1859. V. 70
The Elements of Perspective. London: 1859. V. 68; 71
Elements of Perspective. London: 1978. V. 72
Giotto and His Works in Padua. London: 1854. V. 70; 72
Giotto and His Works in Padua. London: 1900. V. 68
The Harbours of England. London: 1877. V. 72
Kate Greenaway Pictures. London: 1921. V. 69
The King of the Golden River. London: 1851. V. 71
The King of the Golden River. 1907. V. 70
The King of the Golden River. London: 1932. V. 72
The King of the Golden River. London: 1939. V. 68
Lectures on Art Delivered Before the University of Oxford in Hilary Term, 1870. Oxford: 1870. V. 71; 72
Letters from John Ruskin to Rev. J. P. Faunthorpe, M.A. London: 1895-1896. V. 71
Letters of John Ruskin to Charles Eliot Norton. Boston: 1905. V. 71
Letters of John Ruskin to Charles Eliot Norton. London: 1905. V. 70
Letters on Art and Literature. 1894. V. 68
Modern Painters. Orpington: 1888. V. 70
Morning in Florence; Being Simple Studies of Christian Art, for English Travellers. Orpington: 1875. V. 69
Mornings in FLorence: Being Simple Studies of Christian Art, for English Travellers. Kent: 1889. V. 73
The Nature of Gothic. Hammersmith: 1892. V. 70
The Nature of Gothic. 1899. V. 68
Of Kings' Treasuries. 1902. V. 68
Of Kings' Treasuries. Edinburgh: 1902. V. 71
Of Queen's Gardens. 1902. V. 68
Of Queen's Gardens. Edinburgh: 1902. V. 71
The Oxford Museum. London: 1859. V. 70; 71
The Pleasures of England. Orpington: 1884. V. 71
Poems of John Ruskin. New York: 1882. V. 68
The Poems of John Ruskin. London: 1891. V. 70; 72; 73
The Political Economy of Art.... London: 1857. V. 68; 70; 71
Pre-Raphaelitism. London: 1851. V. 68
Salette and Elephanta: a Prize Poem. Oxford: 1839. V. 72
Sesame and Lilies. London: 1891. V. 72
The Seven Lamps of Architecture. 1849. V. 68
The Seven Lamps of Architecture. London: 1855. V. 71
The Seven Lamps of Architecture. New York: 1876. V. 71
The Seven Lamps of Architecture. London: 1905. V. 68
The Stones of Venice. London: 1858. V. 72
The Stones of Venice. (with) The Seven Lamps of Architecture. London: 1886. V. 68
The Storm Cloud of the Nineteenth Century. Sunnyside, Orpington, Kent: 1884. V. 68
The Story of Ida: Epitaph of an Etrurian Tomb. New York: 1883. V. 68
Studies in Both Arts. London: 1895. V. 70; 71; 72
Three Letters and an Essay on Literature 1836-1841. 1893. V. 68
Time and Tide, by Weare and Tyne. London: 1867. V. 71
Unto This Last. Four Essays on the First Principles of Political Economy. London: 1862. V. 70
Unto This Last. Four Essays on the First Principles of Political Economy. London: 1902. V. 68
Unto this Last. Four Essays on the First Principles of Political Economy. Hammersmith: 1907. V. 73
The Winnington Letters. Cambridge: 1969. V. 68
The Winnington Letters. London: 1969. V. 70; 71

RUSLING, JAMES F.
Across America: the Great West and the Pacific Coast. New York: 1875. V. 68

RUSS, CAROLYN H.
The Log of a Forty-Niner. Boston: 1923. V. 70

RUSS, JOANNA
The Zanzibar Cat. Sauk City: 1983. V. 70

RUSS, SIDNEY
Physics in Medical Radiology. London: 1928. V. 68

RUSSEL, JOHN
Letters from a Young Painter Abroad to His Friends in England. London: 1748. V. 69

RUSSELL, A.
The Salmon. 1864. V. 68; 73

RUSSELL, ALAN
The Forest Prime Evil. New York: 1992. V. 70

RUSSELL, ANDY
Trails of a Wilderness Wanderer. 1971. V. 69

RUSSELL, ANNETTE BEAUCHAMP
The April Baby's Book of Tunes. London: 1900. V. 69

RUSSELL, BERTRAND
The Analysis of Matter. London: 1927. V. 69
The Analysis of Matter. New York: 1927. V. 69
Has Religion Made Useful Contributions to Civilization?. London: 1930. V. 70
A History of Western Philosophy. New York: 1945. V. 69; 71
An Outline of Philosophy. London: 1927. V. 71
The Philosophy of.... London: 1918. V. 71
The Policy of the Entente 1904-1914. A Reply to Professor Gilbert Murray. London: 1914. V. 71
Roads to Freedom: Socialism, Anarchism and Syndicalism. London: 1918. V. 71
Sceptical Essays. New York: 1928. V. 72

RUSSELL, C. E. M.
Bullet and Shot in Indian Forest, Plain and Hill. 1900. V. 69; 70; 72; 73
Bullet and Shot in Indian Forest, Plain and Hill. London: 1900. V. 71

RUSSELL, CARL P.
Firearms, Traps and Tools of the Mountain Men. New York: 1967. V. 70; 73

RUSSELL, CHARLES E. B.
Manchester Boys. Sketches of Manchester Lads at Work and Play. Manchester: 1905. V. 71

RUSSELL, CHARLES MARION
Back Trailing on the Old Frontier. Great Falls, MT: 1922. V. 72
Charles M. Russell: Paintings, Drawings, and Sculpture in the Amon G. Carter Collection. Austin: 1966. V. 69
Frontier Omnibus. Helena: 1962. V. 72
Good Medicine: Memories of the Real West. Garden City: 1930. V. 69
Good Medicine, the Illustrated Letters of.... Garden City: 1930. V. 68; 71
More Rawhides. Great Falls: 1925. V. 68; 71
More Rawhides. Pasadena: 1946. V. 69
Rawhide Rawlins Rides Again or Behind the Swining Doors. Pasadena: 1948. V. 69
Rawhide Rawlins Stories. Great Falls: 1921. V. 68; 69
Rawhide Rawlins Stories. Pasadena: 1946. V. 68; 69; 71
Trails Plowed Under. New York: 1927. V. 68; 71
Trails Plowed Under. Garden City: 1940. V. 69

RUSSELL, CHARLOTTE MURRAY
Cook Up a Crime. New York: 1951. V. 72
Murder Steps In. New York: 1942. V. 69

RUSSELL, DON
Custer's Last or the Battle of the Little Big Horn. Fort Worth: 1968. V. 69
One Hundred and Three Fights and Skirmishes - The Story of General Reuben F. Bernard. Washington, DC: 1936. V. 70; 72

RUSSELL, ERIC FRANK
Men, Martians and Machines. London: 1955. V. 70
Wasp. New York: 1957. V. 72

RUSSELL, F. E.
Snake Venom Poisoning. Great Neck: 1983. V. 68

RUSSELL, FOX
Tricked: a Sporting and Military Novel. London: 1902. V. 68

RUSSELL, FRANCIS
A Collection of Statutes Concerning the Incorporation, Trade and Commerce of the East India Company and Government of the British Possessions in India.... London: 1786. V. 73

RUSSELL, FRANK
Art Nouveau Architecture. New York: 1979. V. 69; 72

RUSSELL, GEORGE W. E.
One Look Back. London: 1911. V. 71

RUSSELL, GEORGE WILLIAM
The Avatars. 1933. V. 69
The Candle of Vision. London: 1918. V. 69
Collected Poems. 1913. V. 69
Dark Weeping. London: 1929. V. 72
The Divine Vision and Other Poems. 1903. V. 69
The Divine Vision and Other Poems. New York: 1904. V. 70
The Earth Breath and Other Poems. New York: 1897. V. 68
The House of the Titans and Other Poems. 1934. V. 69
The Living Torch. New York: 1938. V. 68
Midsummer Eve. New York: 1928. V. 72
A Plea for Justice: Being a Demand for a Public Enquiry into the Attacks on Co-Operative Socieities in Ireland. Dublin: 1920. V. 71
Selected Poems. 1935. V. 69
Voices of the Stones. New York: 1925. V. 68

RUSSELL, HENRY
The Ruin of the Soudan Cause, Effect and Remedy. London: 1892. V. 69

RUSSELL, J.
Africa. London: 1814. V. 72

RUSSELL, J., & CO.
Catalogue and Price List J. Russell & Company, Wholesale Dealers in Hardware, Iron and Steel, Mill, Manufacturing and Railway Supplies and Mechanics' Tools.... Holyoke: 1901. V. 68; 73

RUSSELL, J. A.
Sanitary Houses. Two Lectures to Builders and Plumbers Delivered in the Hall of the Royal Scottish Society of Arts, Edinburgh 3rd-11th 1877. Edinburgh: 1878. V. 72

RUSSELL, J. H.
Cattle on the Conejo. Los Angeles: 1957. V. 68
Cattle on the Conejo. New York: 1957. V. 71

RUSSELL, J. RUTHERFORD
A Treatise on Epidemic Cholera. 1849. V. 72

RUSSELL, JAMES
A Treatise on Scrofula. Edinburgh: 1808. V. 69

RUSSELL, JESSE LEWIS
Behind These Ozark Hills History. Reminiscences, Traditions Featuring the Author's Family. New York: 1947. V. 69

RUSSELL, JESSIE
The Blinkin' o' the Fire and Other Poems. Glasgow: 1877. V. 69

RUSSELL, JIM
Bob Fudge, Texas Trail Driver, Montana Wyoming Cowboy 1862-1933. Denver: 1962. V. 73

RUSSELL, JOHN
Francis Bacon. Greenwich: 1971. V. 69
In Dark Places. New York: 1923. V. 70
Max Ernst: Life and Work. London: 1967. V. 69; 72
Max Ernst: Life and Work. New York: 1967. V. 70; 72; 73
The Nun of Arrouca, a Tale. London: 1822. V. 73

RUSSELL, JOHN SCOTT
Report of Observations on the Tidal Wave of the River Clyde; with Remarks on the State of the Channel and the Improvement of the Navigation. Glasgow: 1838. V. 73

RUSSELL, JONATHAN
The Whole Truth. Charles Town: 1809. V. 71

RUSSELL, JOSIAH COX
Dictionary of Writers of Thirteenth Century England. London: 1936. V. 70

RUSSELL, K. F.
British Anatomy 1525-1800. A Bibliography. Melbourne: 1963. V. 68; 73
British Anatomy 1525-1800, a Bibliography. Bury St. Edmunds: 1987. V. 70

RUSSELL, L. B.
Granddad's Autobiography. Comanche, TX: 1927-1930. V. 71

RUSSELL, M.
Polyneisa: a History of the South Sea Islands.... London: 1852. V. 68

RUSSELL, MICHAEL
History and Present Condition of the Barbary States. New York: 1835. V. 73
Palestine or the Holy Land; from the Earliest Period to the Present Time. Edinburgh: 1837. V. 72

RUSSELL, NORMA
A Bibliography of William Cowper to 1837. Oxford: 1969. V. 71

RUSSELL, OSBOURNE
Journal of a Trapper 1834-1943. Boise: 1921. V. 70

RUSSELL, P. E.
The English Intervention in Spain and Portugal in the Time of Edward III and Richard II. Oxford: 1955. V. 73

RUSSELL, RACHEL
Letters...from the Manuscript in the Library at Woburn Abbey. London: 1773. V. 73
Letters. London: 1852. V. 71

RUSSELL, RICHARD
De Tabe Glandulari sive De Usu Aquae Marinae in Morbis Glandularum Dissertatio. Oxford: 1750. V. 73
A Dissertation Concerning the Use of Sea Water in Diseases of the Glands &c.... Oxford: 1753. V. 70
A Dissertation on the Use of Sea-Water in the Diseases of the Glands, Particularly The Scurvy, Jaundice, Kings-Evil, Leprosy, and the Glandular Consumption. London: 1752. V. 73

RUSSELL, ROSS
Bird Lives! The High Life and Hard Times of Charlie Yardbird Parker. New York: 1973. V. 72

RUSSELL, SCOTT
Mountain Prospect. London: 1946. V. 69

RUSSELL, W.
Eccentric Personages. Memoirs of the Lives and Actions of Remarkable Characters. London: 1880. V. 73

RUSSELL, WILFRID
Flame of the Forest and Other Poems of India. Bombay: 1956. V. 68

RUSSELL, WILLIAM
Extraordinary Men: Their Boyhood and Early Life. London: 1854. V. 73
Recollections of a Detective Police Officer. London: 1856. V. 73

RUSSELL, WILLIAM CLARK
In the Middle Watch. London: 1887. V. 68
Is He the Man?. London: 1898. V. 68
The Last Entry. London: 1899. V. 68
An Ocean Tragedy. London: 1907. V. 68
Representative Actors. London: 1872. V. 72

RUSSELL, WILLIAM HOWARD
The Atlantic Telegraph. 1865. V. 69
The Atlantic Telegraph. London: 1866. V. 70
A Diary in the East During the Tour to the Prince and Princess of Wales. London: 1869. V. 68

RUSSEN, DAVID
Iter Lunare; or, a Voyage to the Moon. London: 1703. V. 70

RUSSIA Seu Moscovia Itemque Tartaria. Leiden: 1630. V. 69

THE RUSSIANS in California. San Francisco: 1933. V. 70

RUSSO, PASQUALAE
Twelve O'Clock Lunch. Chicago: 1923. V. 68

RUSSO, RICHARD
Empire Falls. New York: 2001. V. 72
Mohawk. New York: 1986. V. 69
Nobody's Fool. New York: 1993. V. 68; 69; 70; 72; 73
The Risk Pool. New York: 1988. V. 68

RUST, BRIAN
The American Dance Band Discography 1917-1942. New Rochelle: 1975. V. 70
American Record Label Book. New Rochelle: 1978. V. 72
The Dance Bands. London: 1972. V. 72
Jazz Records 1897-1931. Hatch End;: 1962. V. 73
Jazz Records 1932-1942. Hatch End: 1962. V. 73
The Victor Master Book Volume 2 (1925-1936). Stanhope: 1970. V. 72

RUST, GEORGE
A Letter of Resolution Concerning Origen and the Chief of His Opinions. London: 1661-1667. V. 70; 71

RUST, GRAHAM
The Painted House. New York: 1988. V. 72

RUTGERS, A.
Encyclopaedia of Aviculture. 1970-1977. V. 69; 73

RUTH, BABE, MRS.
The Babe and I. Englewood Cliffs: 1959. V. 69

RUTHERFORD, DOUGLAS
Grand Prix Murder. London: 1955. V. 72

RUTHERFORD, ERNEST
Radioactive Substances and Their Radiations. Cambridge: 1913. V. 68; 69

RUTHERFORD, GAY
Old Love for New. New York: 1938. V. 71

RUTHERFORD, JOHN
Rutherford's Border Hand-Book; being a Guide to the Remarkable Places, Picturesque Scenery, and Antiquities of the Border. Kelso: 1849. V. 71

RUTHERFORD, MARK
Miriam's Schooling, and Other Papers, by Mark Rutherford. London: 1890. V. 69

RUTHERFORD, SAMUEL
Joshua Redivivus; or, Three Hundred and Fifty-Two Religious Letters.... Glasgow: 1765. V. 69

RUTHERFURD, LORD
Catalogue of the Extensive and Valubable Library of the Late Right Hon. Lord Rutherfurd...which will be sold by Auction by Mr. T. Nisbet. Edinburgh: 1855. V. 72

RUTHERSON, ALBERT
Sitwelliana 1915-1927. London: 1928. V. 70; 73
Sixteen Designs for the Theatre. London: 1928. V. 70

RUTHLEY, CECILY M.
The Tale of the Tabby Twins. London: 1920. V. 70

RUTKOW, I. M.
The History of Surgery in the United States 1775-1900. San Francisco: 1988. V. 68

RUTLAND, JOHN HENRY MANNERS, 5TH DUKE OF
Journal of a Trip to Paris...July MDCCCXIV. (with) Journal of a Short Trip to Paris During the Summer of MDCCCXV. London: 1814-1815. V. 70
A Tour Through Part of Belgium and the Rhenish Provinces. London: 1822. V. 73

RUTLEDGE, ARCHIBALD
An American Hunter. New York: 1937. V. 71; 73
Bright Angel and Other Poems. Columbia: 1955. V. 71
Collected Poems. Charleston: 1925. V. 70
Everlasting Light and Other Poems. Athens: 1949. V. 70
Fireworks in the Peafield Corner. Clinton: 1986. V. 73
From the Hills to the Sea. Indianapolis: 1958. V. 71
From the Hills to the Sea. New York: 1958. V. 70
God's Children. New York: 1947. V. 70; 71
Home by the River. Indianapolis and New York: 1941. V. 70
Hunter's Choice. New York: 1946. V. 72
Peace in the Heart. New York: 1930. V. 70; 71
Veiled Eros. New York: 1933. V. 71

RUTLEDGE, JAMES E.
Sheet Harbour: a Local History. Halifax;: 1954. V. 73

RUTLEDGE, JOHN
A Defence Against Calumny; or Haman, in the Shape of Christopher Ellery, Esq.... Newport: 1803. V. 68

RUTLEDGE, JOHN JAMES
The Englishman's Fortnight in Paris; or the Art of Ruining Himself There in a Few Days. Dublin: 1777. V. 68

RUTLEDGE, MARYSE
The Silver Peril. New York: 1931. V. 68; 71

RUTSTRUM, CALVIN
Challenge of the Wilderness. Minneapolis: 1970. V. 73

RUTTER, ELDON
The Holy Cities of Arabia. London: 1928. V. 71

RUTTER, JOHN
Delineations of the North West Division of Somerset. Shaftesbury for the author: 1829. V. 70

RUTTER, OWEN
The First Fleet. The Record of the Foundation of Australia From Its Conception to the Settlement at Sydney Cove. London: 1937. V. 70; 71
The First Fleet: the Record of the Foundation of Australia from Its Conception to the Settlement at Sydney Cove. Waltham St. Lawrence: 1937. V. 71
The Song of Tiadatha. Salonica: 1919. V. 71
Through Formosa. London: 1923. V. 71
Triumphant Pilgrimage. London: 1937. V. 71
We Happy Few: an Anthology. Waltham St. Lawrence: 1946. V. 71

RUTTLEDGE, HUGH
Everest 1933. 1934. V. 68; 71
Everest 1933. London: 1934. V. 69
Everest: the Unfinished Adventure. 1937. V. 68; 71; 73
Everest: the Unfinished Adventure. London: 1937. V. 69

RUTTLEDGE, ROBERT F.
Ireland's Birds: Their Distribution and Migrations. 1967. V. 69; 73

RUTTY, JOHN
An Essay Towards a Natural, Experimental and Medicinal History of the Mineral Waters of Ireland. Dublin: 1757. V. 69

RUXNER, GEORG
Thurnierbuch. Frankfurt: 1578. V. 71

RUXTON, GEORGE FREDERICK
Adventures in Mexico and the Rocky Mountains. London: 1847. V. 73
Adventures in Mexico and the Rocky Mountains. New York: 1848. V. 72
Adventures In Mexico And The Rocky Mountains. London: 1849. V. 72
In the Old West. New York: 1916. V. 69
Life in the Far West. New York: 1849. V. 68
Ruxton of the Rockies. Autobiographical writings by Ruxton. Norman: 1950. V. 72

RUYL, BEATRICE BAXTER
Little Indian Maidens at Work and Play. London: 1909. V. 70

RUYSDALE, PHILIP
A Pilgrimage Over the Prairies. London: 1863. V. 70

RYAN, CLARE TALBOT
In Quest of the Perfect Bookplate. Claremont: 1933. V. 68

RYAN, FREDERICK W.
Malta, Painted by Vittorio Boron. London: 1910. V. 71

RYAN, HELEN CHANDLER
The Spanish American Song and Game Book. New York: 1942. V. 68

RYAN, JOHN
Irish Monasticism, Origins and Early Development. 1931. V. 69
The Preparation of Long-Line. Flax-Cotton and Flax-wool, by the Claussen's System of Bleaching Fibres, Yarns and Fabrics. London: 1852. V. 71

RYAN, M. E.
The Flue of the Gods. New York: 1909. V. 69

RYAN, NOLAN
Nolan Ryan's Pitcher's Bible. New York: 1991. V. 68

RYAN, WILLIAM BURKE
Infanticide: Its Law, Prevalence, Prevention and History. London: 1862. V. 69

RYAN, WILLIAM REDMOND
Personal Adventures in Upper and Lower California in 1848-1849; with the Author's Experiences at the Mines. London: 1850. V. 72

RYDBERG, P. A.
Flora of the Rocky Mountains and Adjacent Plains. New York: 1954. V. 72

RYDER, JOHN
Flowers and Flourishes Including a Newly Annotated Edition of A Suite of Fleurons. London: 1976. V. 71
Intimate Leaves from a Designer's Notebook: Essays. 1993. V. 71

RYE, ANTHONY
Gilbert White & His Selborne. London: 1970. V. 72

RYE, EDGAR
The Quirt and the Spur, Vanishing Shadows of the Texas Frontier. Chicago: 1909. V. 69; 71

RYE, GRAHAM
The James Bond Girls. London: 1995. V. 71

RYKWERT, JOSEPH
The Golden House. London: 1951. V. 72

RYLAND, ARTHUR
A Paper Containing Some Suggestions Connected with the Consolidation of the Statutes...Read at the Annual Provincial Meeting of the Metropolitan and Provincial Law Association Held at Birmingham on October 22 and 23, 1855. London: 1856. V. 73

RYLAND, ELIZABETH H.
King William Co., Virginia, from Old Newspapers and Files. Richmond: 1955. V. 68

RYLAND, GARNETT
The Baptists of Virginia 1699-1926. Richmond: 1955. V. 68; 71; 72

RYMILL, JOHN
Southern Lights. London: 1938. V. 71
Southern Lights. New York and London: 1939. V. 69; 72

RYMSDYK, JOHN
Museum Britannicum; or, a Display in Thirty Two Plates, in Antiquities, and Natural Curiosities.... London: 1791. V. 71

RYND, EVELYNE E.
Otherland. London: 1907. V. 72

RYNNING, THOMAS H.
Gun Notches: the Life Story of a Cowboy Soldier. New York: 1931. V. 69

RYSKIND, MORRIE
The Home Movie Scenario Book: with Twenty New Plots for Amateur Producer. New York: 1927. V. 73

RYUS, WILLIAM H.
The Second William Penn: a True Account of Incidents that Happened Along the Old Santa Fe Trail in the Sixties. Kansas City: 1913. V. 69; 72

RYVARDEN, L.
Genera of Polypores, Nomenclature and Taxonomy. Oslo: 1991. V. 70

RYVES, BRUNO
Anglia Ruina; or England Ruine.. London: 1647. V. 68; 72
Mercurius Rusticus; or, the Countries Complaint of the Barbarous Outrages Committed by the Sectaries of the Late Flourishing Kingdom. London: 1685. V. 68

S

S., C. S.
Sketches from Nature, Consisting of Original Pieces in Verse. Chelmsford: 1837. V. 73

S., H.
German Glory. London: 1742. V. 73

S. MAW & SONS
Book of Illustrations to S. Maw & Son's Quarterly Price-Current. London: 1869. V. 71

S., T.
A Faithful Account of the Sickness, Death and Burial of Capt. William Bedlow, who Dyed August the 20th and Was Buried August the 22d. 1680. London: 1680. V. 71

S. W. FRANCIS & CO. LTD.
Manufacturers of Improved Wood, Iron and Steel Revolving Shutters. Price List 1905. 1905. V. 71

SAABYE, SVEND
Lystfisker Liv. 1981. V. 68

SAARINEN, ALINE B.
Eero Saarinen on His Work. New Haven: 1962. V. 69

SABARTES, JAIME
Picasso Toreros. New York: 1961. V. 69

SABATHY-JUDD, LINDA
Moravians in Upper Canada: The Diary of the Indian Mission of Fairfield on the Thames 1792-1813. Toronto: 1999. V. 68

SABATINI, RAFAEL
Bellarion the Fortunate. Boston: 1926. V. 69
Captain Blood. Boston: 1922. V. 71
The Gamester. Boston: 1949. V. 69
Scaramouche. New York: 1923. V. 70
The Sea Hawk. London: 1915. V. 71
Turbulent Tales. London: 1946. V. 70

SABBATH Bells, Chimed By The Poets. London. V. 71; 72

SABELLI, HECTOR C.
Chemical Modulation of Brain Function - a Tribute to J. E. P. Toman. New York: 1973. V. 68

SABIN, EDWIN LEGRAND
Kit Carson Days (1809-1868): Adventures in the Path of Empire. New York: 1935. V. 68; 70; 72; 73

SABIN, J.
A Dictionary of Books Relating to America, from Its Discovery to the Present Time. New York: 1967. V. 70

SABINE, EDWARD
The North Georgia Gazette and Winter Chronicle. London: 1821. V. 73

SABINE, LORENZO
Biographical Sketches of Loyalists of the American Revolution, with an Historical Essay. Boston: 1864. V. 69; 73

SACCARDO, PIER ANDREA
Sylloge Fungorum Omnium Huusque Cognitorum. Ann Arbor: 1944. V. 70

SACCO, LUIGI
Trattato Di Vaccinazione con Osservazioni sul Giavardo e Vajuolo Pecorino. Milano: 1809. V. 68

SACHS, HANNS
Caligula. London: 1931. V. 72

SACHS, S.
Beschreibung Einer Neu Erfundenen Dach-Construction, zu Stadtischen und Landlichen Gebauden aller Art Anwendbar, Welche Nicht Bloss Sehr Wasserdicht und Dauerhaft.... Berlin: 1829. V. 68

SACHSE, JULIUS FRIEDRICH
The Music of the Ephrata Cloister Also Conrad Beissel's Treatise on Music. Lancaster: 1803. V. 71

SACK, JOHN
The Ascent of Yerupaja. London: 1954. V. 69

SACKHEIM, ERIC
The Blues Line. A Collection of Blues Lyrics. New York: 1969. V. 70; 72
The Silent Zero, in Search of Sound...an Anthology of Chinese Poems from the Beginning through the Sixth Century. New York: 1968. V. 69; 71

SACKLER, HARRY
Festival at Meron. New York: 1935. V. 69

SACKLER, HOWARD
The Great White Hope. 1968. V. 69; 72
The Great White Hope. New York: 1968. V. 71; 72

SACKS, B.
Be It Enacted: the Creation of the Territory of Arizona. Phoenix: 1964. V. 68

SACKS, OLIVER
The Island of a Colorblind. New York: 1997. V. 72
Seeing Voices. Berkeley: 1989. V. 68; 70
Uncle Tungsten: Memories of a Chemical Boyhood. New York: 2001. V. 70; 73

SACKVILLE, MARGARET
The Traveling Companion and Other Stories for Children. London: 1915. V. 69

SACKVILLE, N. V. STOPFORD
Drayton House, Northamptonshire, a Short Historical Account of Ownership Architecture and Contents. Kettering: 1939. V. 69

SACKVILLE WEST, EDWARD
The Ruin. London: 1926. V. 68
The Ruin. New York: 1927. V. 73
Simpson - a Life. London: 1931. V. 68
Thomas De Quincey. His Life and Work. New Haven: 1936. V. 71; 72

SACKVILLE-WEST, VICTORIA MARY
All Passion Spent. Garden City: 1931. V. 72
All Passion Spent. London: 1931. V. 72
Andrew Marvell. London: 1929. V. 72
Aphra Behn - The Incomparable Astrea. London. V. 72
Aphra Behn - The Incomparable Astrea. New York: 1928. V. 72
Challenge. New York. V. 72
Challenge. New York: 1923. V. 71
Chatterton: a Drama in Three Acts. Sevenoaks: 1909. V. 72
Collected Poems - Volume One. London: 1933. V. 68; 71; 72
Constantinople: Eight Poems. London: 1915. V. 72
Country Notes. 1939. V. 69

SACKVILLE-WEST, VICTORIA MARY continued
Country Notes. New York: 1940. V. 73
Country Notes in Wartime. London: 1940. V. 68; 70
The Dark Island. 1934. V. 68
The Dark Island. London: 1934. V. 69; 72
The Dark Island. Garden City: 1936. V. 72
Daughter of France - The Life of Anne Marie Louise d'Orleans, Duchesse de Montpensier, 1627-1693, La Grande Mademoiselle. Garden City: 1959. V. 72
Daughter of France - The Life of Anne Marie Louise d'Orleans, duchesse de Montpensier-1627-1693, La Grande Mademoiselle. London: 1959. V. 72
The Dragon in Shallow Waters. London: 1921. V. 72
The Dragon in Shallow Waters. New York: 1922. V. 72
The Easter Party. Garden City: 1953. V. 72
The Easter Party. London: 1953. V. 69; 72
The Edwardians. Garden City: 1930. V. 72
The Edwardians. London: 1930. V. 68; 70; 72; 73
The English Character - An Address to the Boys of Sevenoaks School by Mrs. Harold Nicolson (V. Sackville-West) on the Occasion of the Presentation of Prizes - 1 August 1928. Oxford: 1928. V. 72
Even More for the Garden. London: 1958. V. 72
Family History. Garden City: 1932. V. 72
Family History. London: 1932. V. 72
The Garden. Tonbridge: 1989. V. 72
Grey Wethers. London: 1923. V. 72
The Heir - A Love Story. Letchworth. V. 72
In Your Garden Again. London: 1953. V. 69; 72; 73
Joan of Arc. London: 1937. V. 72
King's Daughter. London: 1929. V. 69; 72
King's Daughter. New York: 1930. V. 72
Knole and the Sackvilles. London: 1922. V. 72
The Land. London: 1926. V. 72
The Marie Curie Hospital. London. V. 72
More for Your Garden. London: 1955. V. 69; 72; 73
No Signposts in the Sea. London: 1961. V. 69; 70; 72
Orchard and Vineyard. London: 1921. V. 72
Passenger to Tehran. London: 1926. V. 72; 73
Passenger to Tehran. New York: 1927. V. 72
Pepita. Garden City: 1937. V. 72
Pepita. London: 1937. V. 72; 73
The Persian Coat. London: 1924. V. 72
Phantom. London: 1924. V. 72
Poems of West and East. London: 1917. V. 72
Saint Joan of Arc. London: 1936. V. 72
Seducers in Ecuador. London: 1924. V. 69; 71; 72; 73
Seducers in Ecuador. New York: 1925. V. 72
Selected Poems. London: 1941. V. 69
Sissinghurst. London: 1931. V. 72
Sissinghurst. Stuart's Hill Cottage, Warli: 1933. V. 70
Sissinghurst Castle - An Illustrated Guide. Sissinghurst: 1963. V. 72
Solitude: A Poem. London: 1938. V. 69; 72
Some Flowers. London: 1937. V. 72
Thirty Clocks Strike the Hour and Other Stories. Garden City: 1932. V. 72
Twelve Days. An Account of a Journey Across the Bakhtiari Mountains in South-Western Persia. London: 1928. V. 70; 71; 72
Walter de la Mare and The Traveller. London: 1953. V. 72
The Women's Land Army. London: 1944. V. 72

SACRAMENTAL Exercises Selected from Different Authors. Bristol: 1822. V. 72

SACRAMENTO DEVELOPMENT ASSOCIATION
The Best Spot on Earth is in the Sacramento Valley, California. Sacramento: 1904. V. 68

SACROBOSCO, JOHANNES DE
Sphaera. Venetiis: 1586. V. 71

SAD Fate of Poor Robin. New York: 1865. V. 70
SAD Fate of Poor Robin. New York: 1867. V. 71

SA'DI
Select Fables from Gulistan or the Bed of Roses. London: 1774. V. 73

SADLEIR, MICHAEL
Bentley's Standard Novel Series - Its History and Achievement. Edinburgh: 1932. V. 69
Blessington D'Orsay - a Masquerade. London: 1933. V. 68
Desolate Splendour. London: 1948. V. 71
Fanny by Gaslight. New York: 1940. V. 71
Forlorn Sunset. New York: 1946. V. 68
Forlorn Sunset. London: 1947. V. 68; 69; 71
XIX Century Fiction: A Bibliographic Record. New York: 1969. V. 68
The Noblest Frailty. London: 1925. V. 71
Thackeray's Letters: a Review. 1947. V. 71
These Foolish Things. London: 1937. V. 68; 71
These Foolish Things. New York: 1937. V. 70; 71
Tommy 1916-1942. Oxford: 1943. V. 71
Trollope: a Bibliography. London: 1964. V. 70

SADLER, F. C.
Sketches at Lloyd's. London: 1925. V. 69; 71

SADLER, MARIE CHRISTINE
Mamma's Angel Child in Toyland. Chicago: 1915. V. 70

SADLER, THOMAS MICHAEL
A Refutation: of an Article in the Edinburgh Review (No. CII) Entitled Sadler's Law of Population and Disproof of Human Superfecundity. London: 1830. V. 70; 71

SAENGER, PAUL
Catalogue of Pre-1500 Western Manuscript Books in the Newberry Library. Chicago and London: 1989. V. 70

SAFER, J. F.
Spirals from the Sea, an Anthropological Look at Shells. New York: 1982. V. 69

SAFFERY, MARIA GRACE
Poems on Sacred Subjects. London: 1834. V. 69

SAFRONI MIDDLETON, A.
No Extradition. London: 1923. V. 70

SAGA of Inyo County. Covina: 1977. V. 68

SAGAN, FRANCOISE
Bonjour Tristesse. Paris: 1954. V. 69
Un Certain Sourire. Paris: 1956. V. 69

SAGE, ALISON
Rumpelstiltskin. New York: 1990. V. 70

SAGE, D.
Salmon and Trout. New York: 1902. V. 73

SAGE, RUFUS B.
Rocky Mountain Life; or Startling Scenes and Perilous Adventures in the Far West. Dayton. V. 68

SAGGITTARUS
The Blackness of My Skin and the Kinkiness of My Hair. Washington, D.C: 1972. V. 72

SAHAGUN, BERNARDINO DE
Historia General de Las Cosas de Nueva Espana. Mexico: 1938. V. 71

THE SAILOR Boy and Other Stories. New York: 1865-1867. V. 70; 73

THE SAILOR Boy, or, the First and Last Voyage of Little Andrew. Portland: 1830. V. 71

SAINSBURY, HESTER
Meanderlane. Tales. 1925. V. 70

SAINSBURY, WILLIAM NOEL
Original Unpublished Papers Illustrative of the Life of Sir Peter Paul Rubens, as an Artist and a Diplomatist. London: 1859. V. 73

SAINT AMAND, IMBERT DE
The Women of the Court of Louis XV. Boston: 1892. V. 68; 69; 72

SAINT ANDRE, NATHANIEL
A Short Narrative of an Extraordinary Delivery of Rabbets, Perform'd by Mr. John Howard, Surgeon at Guilford.... London: 1727. V. 68

SAINT AUBIN, AUGUSTIN
Mes Gens ou les Commissionnaires Ultramontains au Service de Qui Veut les Payer. Paris: 1766-1770. V. 69

SAINT AUBIN DE TERAN, LISA
Keepers of the House. London: 1982. V. 68; 69
The Tiger. London: 1984. V. 69

SAINT AUDE, MAGLOIRE
Parias. Port-au-Prince: 1949. V. 69
Veille. Port-au-Prince: 1956. V. 69

SAINT CLAIR, PHILIP
Frederic Remington - the American West. Kent: 1978. V. 70

SAINTE MARIE, COUNT
Algeria in 1845. A Visit to the French Possessions in Africa. London: 1846. V. 73

SAINT-EXUPERY, ANTOINE DE
Flight to Arras. New York: 1942. V. 69; 72
The Little Prince. New York: 1943. V. 68; 69; 71; 72
Night Flight. New York: 1932. V. 71; 72
Le Petit Prince. New York: 1943. V. 70
Wind, Sand and Stars. New York: 1939. V. 71

SAINT-GAUDENS, AUGUSTUS
The Reminiscences of Augustus Saint Gaudens. New York: 1913. V. 70; 72

SAINT GEORGE, GEORGE
The Sires and Sons from Albion Sprung. London: 1876. V. 73

SAINT GEORGE, JUDITH
So You Want to Be President!. New York: 2000. V. 70

SAINT GERMAN, CHRISTOPHER
The Dialogue in English Between a Doctor of Divinitie and a Student of Laws of England. London: 1613. V. 70; 72
An Exact Abridgement of that Excellent Treatise Called Doctor and Student. London: 1630. V. 70

SAINTHILL, RICHARD
The Old Countess of Desmond: an Inquiry. 1861-1863. V. 70

SAINT JOHN, CHARLES
Charles St. John's Note Books. 1901. V. 69
Natural History and Sport in Moray. 1882. V. 73
Natural History and Sport in Moray. Edinburgh: 1882. V. 72
Sketches of the Wild Sports and Natural History of the Highlands. London: 1878. V. 68; 71; 72
Wild Sports and Natural History of the Highlands. 1893. V. 73
Wild Sports and Natural History of the Highlands. 1919. V. 72; 73
Wild Sports and Natural History of the Highlands. 1927. V. 73

SAINT JOHN, CHRISTOPHER
Ethel Smyth- A Biography. London: 1959. V. 72

SAINT JOHN, DAVID
The Figure You. New York: 1998. V. 73

SAINT JOHN, HORACE, MRS.
Audubon. The Naturalist in the New World. London: 1856. V. 68
Audubon, the Naturalist of the New World. New York: 1856. V. 72

SAINT JOHN, J. A.
Egypt and Nubia. London. V. 72

SAINT JOHN, JOHN
To the War with Waugh. London: 1973. V. 69

SAINT JOHN, JUDITH
The Osborne Collection of Early Children's Books 1566-1910. Toronto: 1958-1975. V. 68

SAINT JOHN, MOLYNEUX
The Province of British Columbia, Canada. Montreal: 1886. V. 71

SAINT JOHN, PERCY B.
Mary Rock; or, My Adventures in Texas. London: 1860. V. 68
The Trapper's Bride: a Tale of the Rocky Mountains, with the Rose of Ouisconsin. London: 1845. V. 73

SAINT JOHN COOPER, HENRY
Carniss and Company. London: 1922. V. 69

SAINT LAMBERT, JEAN FRANCOIS, MARQUIS DE
Les Deux amis, Conte Iroguois. 1770. V. 70
Les Saisons Poeme. Paris: 1796. V. 69

SAINT-LAURENT, YVES
Images of Design 1958-1988. London: 1988. V. 72

SAINT LO, GEORGE
England's Interest; or a Discipline for Seamen; Wherein Is Proposed a Sure Method for Raising Qualified Seamen.... London: 1694. V. 69

SAINT MARTIAL, BLANCHE MARIA
Sursum Corda, Letters of the Countess De Saint Martial, in Religion, Sister Blanche, Sister of Charity of St. Vincent de Paul. New York: 1907. V. 72

SAINT MAUR, ALGERNON, MRS.
Impressions of a Tenderfoot During a Journey in Search of Sport in the Far West. London: 1890. V. 68

SAINT MORIEN, M. DE
La Perspective Aerienne, Soumise a des Principes Puises dans la Nature.... Paris: 1788. V. 72

SAINT PIERRE, JACQUES HENRI BERNARDIN DE
Paul et Virginie. Cambridge: 1906. V. 68; 71

SAINT QUENTIN, DOMINIQUE DE
A Poetical Chronology of the Kings of England. Reading: 1792. V. 72

SAINT QUINTIN, T. A.
Chances of Sports of Sorts. 1912. V. 72; 73

SAINT REAL, CAESAR VISCHARD DE
The Memoirs of the Dutchess Mazarine (Hortense Mancini). London: 1676. V. 72

SAINT YVES, CHARLES DE
A New Treatise of the Diseases of the Eyes. London: 1741. V. 72

SAKAMOTO, KAZUYA
Japanese Toys: Playing with History. Tokyo: 1965. V. 68; 70; 72; 73

SALA, GEORGE AUGUSTUS
Charles Dickens. London: 1870. V. 70
Robson: a Sketch. London: 1864. V. 70
Things I Have Seen and People I Have Known. London: 1894. V. 69
The Thorough Good Cook. London: 1895. V. 68
William Hogarth: Painter, Engraver and Philosopher.... London: 1866. V. 68; 72

SALAMAN, MALCOLM C.
F.L.Griggs. London: 1926. V. 72
The Great Painter-Etchers from Rembrandt to Whistler. London: 1914. V. 68
Modern Book Illustrators and Their Work. London: 1914. V. 73
Old English Mezzotints. London: 1910. V. 69; 72

SALAMANCA, J. R.
Lilith. New York: 1961. V. 71
The Lost Country. New York: 1958. V. 71

SALAMANDER.. London: 1947. V. 71

SALBOM, JOHANNES
Dissertatio medica Exhibins Spiritus Corporis Humani Pathologiam. Dorpati: 1691. V. 71

SALE, RICHARD
Benefit Performance. New York: 1946. V. 70; 72
Lazarus #7. 1942. V. 73
Not Too Narrow...Not Too Deep. 1936. V. 73
Passing Strange. 1942. V. 73

SALE BARKER, MRS.
Little Wide-Awake. London: 1879. V. 68; 72

THE SALEM Collection of Classical Sacred Musick; in Three and Four Parts.... Boston: 1806. V. 71

SALGADO, JOSE AUGUSTO
Bibliotheca Lusitana Escholida, ou Catalogo dos Escriptores Portuguezes. 1841. V. 70

SALINAS, PORFIRIO
Bluebonnets and Cactus; an Album of Southwestern Paintings by Porfirio Salinas. Austin: 1967. V. 70

SALINGER, JEROME DAVID
The Catcher in the Rye. Boston: 1951. V. 69; 70; 71; 73
The Complete Uncollected Short Stories of J.D. Salinger. 1974. V. 71
For Esme - with Love and Squalor and Other Stories. London: 1953. V. 69
Franny and Zooey. Boston and Toronto: 1961. V. 69; 72; 73
Franny and Zooey. New York: 1961. V. 73
Franny and Zooey. Taiwan: 1961. V. 69
Nine Stories. Boston: 1953. V. 68; 70; 71; 72; 73
Raise High the Roof Beam, Carpenters and Seymour. Boston: 1959. V. 70; 72; 73
Raise High the Roof Beam, Carpenters and Seymour, an Introduction. Boston: 1963. V. 73
Raise High the Roof Beam, Carpenters and Seymour An Introduction. London: 1963. V. 72
Raise High the Roof Beam, Carpenters and Seymour an Introduction. New York: 1963. V. 72
Twenty-Two Stories. 1998. V. 70; 71

SALISBURY, E.
Downs and Dunes, their Plant Life and Its Environment. London: 1952. V. 72

SALISBURY, HARRISON E.
The New Emperors. Boston: 1992. V. 71

SALISBURY, RICHARD ANTHONY
Icones Stirpium Rariorum Desciptionibus Illustratae. London: 1791. V. 69

SALISBURY, W.
The Botanist's Companion.... London: 1816. V. 69

SALIVET, LOUIS GEORGES ISAAC
Manuel du Tourneur. Paris: 1792-1796. V. 70

SALK, JONAS
Man Unfolding. New York: 1972. V. 68
Survival of the Wisest. New York: 1973. V. 69; 72; 73

SALKEY, ANDREW
A Quality of Violence. London: 1959. V. 69

SALLENGRE, ALBERT HENRI DE
Ebrietatis Encomium, or the Praise of Drunkenness, Wherein is Authentically, and Most Evidently Proved.... London: 1723. V. 68; 73

SALLIS, JAMES
Eye of the Cricket. Blakeney, Gloucestershire: 1997. V. 73
A Few Last Words. New York: 1970. V. 73
The Long Legged Fly. New York: 1992. V. 69; 70; 71; 73
Moth. NY: 1993. V. 73

SALLUSTIUS CRISPUS, C.
C. Crisp Sallustii Opera Quae Supersunt, Omnia. Glasgow: 1777. V. 73
Opera Quae Exstant. Londini: 1864. V. 72
Opera Quae Supersunt, Omnia.... Glasgow: 1777. V. 68
Opera Quae Supesunt, Omnia.... Glasgow: 1751. V. 73
Salustio con Alcune Altre Belle Cose, Volgareggiato per Agostino Ortica de la Porta. Venice: 1518. V. 73
The Works of the Famous Historian Caius Salustius Crispus.... London: 1687. V. 70

SALMASIUS, CLAUDIUS
Epistola ad Andream Colvium: Super Cap XI. Leiden: 1644. V. 72

SALMI, MARIO
Italian Miniatures. New York: 1954. V. 70

SALMON, ARTHUR L.
Matins, Noon Song and Vespers. London;. V. 71

SALMON, E. S.
A Monograph of the Erysiphaceae. New York: 1900. V. 71

SALMON, J. T.
The Native Trees of New Zealand. Wellington: 1980. V. 70

SALMON, THOMAS
A Critical Essay Concerning Marriage. London: 1724. V. 69; 72
Salmon's Geographical and Astronomical Grammar, Including the Ancient and Present State the World. London: 1785. V. 72

SALMON, WILLIAM
Doron Medicum; or a Supplement to the New London Dispensatory in III Books. London: 1683. V. 70
The Family Dictionary; or, Household Companion.... London: 1695. V. 69
The Family Dictionary; or, Household Companion.... London: 1696. V. 73
The London and Country Builder's Vade Mecum; or, the Complete and Universal Estimator. London: 1773. V. 68; 70; 72

SALMOND, J. B.
Henderson's Benefaction. A Tercentenary Acknowledgement of the University's Debt to Alexander Henderson. St. Andrews: 1942. V. 70

SALOMON, JULIAN HARRIS
The Book of Indian Crafts and Indian Lore. New York: 1928. V. 69

SALOMONS, DAVID
Reflections on the Operation of the Present Scale of Duty for Regulating the Importation of Foreign Corn Addressed to the Borders of Kent and Sussex Agricutlural Association. London: 1840. V. 70

SALOMONSEN, FINN
Gronlands Fugle. The Birds of Greenland. Copenhagen: 1950-1951. V. 70; 73

SALT, SARAH
Sense and Sensuality. New York: 1929. V. 71

SALT, W.
A Memorial of the Methodist New Connexion: Containing a Short Memoir of the Circuit Preachers, Who Died Prior to the Year 1823.... Nottingham: 1827. V. 73

SALTEN, FELIX
Bambi: A Life in the Woods. London: 1928. V. 72
Bambi: a Life in the Woods. New York: 1928. V. 71

SALTER, ELIZABETH
Will to Survive. London: 1958. V. 68

SALTER, JAMES
Burning the Days. New York: 1997. V. 70; 72; 73
Dusk. Berkeley: 1988. V. 69; 70; 72
Dusk. San Francisco: 1988. V. 70
Forgotten Kings. New York: 1998. V. 72
Light Years. New York: 1975. V. 70
Sheridan Lord, 1926-1994. New York: 1995. V. 72
Solo Faces. London: 1980. V. 69
A Sport and a Pastime. London: 1987. V. 72
Still Such. New York: 1992. V. 73

SALTER, JOHN
The Chrysanthemum: Its History and Culture. London: 1865. V. 69

SALTER, MARJORIE
Delightful Food. London: 1957. V. 68

SALTER, MARY JO
Henry Purcell in Japan. New York: 1985. V. 69; 71

SALTER, ROBERT BRUCE
Textbook of Disorders and Injuries of the Musculoskeletal System. Baltimore: 1970. V. 71
Textbook of Disorders and Injuries of the Musculoskeletal System. Baltimore: 1983. V. 70; 71

SALTER, THOMAS
Field's Chromatography; or Treatise on Colours and Pigments as Used by Artists. London: 1869. V. 68

SALTER, THOMAS FREDERICK
The Angler's Guide.... London: 1815. V. 72
The Angler's Guide.... London: 1825. V. 72

SALTERN, GEORGE
Of the Antient Lawes of Great Britaine. Seruato Ius, Metue Mortalis Deum. London: 1605. V. 70

SALTONSTALL, WILLIAM G.
Ports of Piscataqua. Cambridge: 1941. V. 69

SALTUS, EDGAR
The Ghost Girl. New York: 1922. V. 70

SALUSBURY, THOMAS
Mathematical Collections and Translations. 1967. V. 73

SALUTE to the 30's. New York: 1971. V. 68

SALVAGE, JEAN GALBERT
Anatomie Du Gladiateur Combattant, Applicable aux Beaux Arts ou Traite des os des Muscles, du Mecanisme des Mouvemens des Proportions et des Caracteres du Corps Human. Paris: 1812. V. 68

SALVERTE, EUSEBIUS
History of the Names of Men, Nations and Places in Their Connection with the Progress of Civilization. London: 1862. V. 68

SALZMAN, L. F.
Building in England Down to 1540. Oxford: 1952. V. 70

SALZMAN, MARK
Iron and Silk. New York: 1986. V. 71; 72
The Laughing Sutra. New York: 1991. V. 70; 72

SALZMANN, MAXIMILLIAN
The Anatomy and Histology of the Human Eyeball in the Normal State. Its Development and Senescence. Chicago: 1912. V. 72

SAMAHA, JOEL
Law and Order in Historical Perspective: the Case of Elizabethan Essex. New York and London: 1974. V. 71

SAMBUCUS, JOHANNES
Veterum Aliquot ac Recentium Medicorum Philosophorum que Icones. Amsterdam: 1615. V. 73

SAMMY and Dinah. 1920. V. 73

SAMMY Tickletooth. New York: 1863-1866. V. 71

SAMOUELLE, GEORGE
General Directions for Collecting and Preserving Exotic Insects and Crustacea.... London: 1826. V. 68

SAMPEY, JOHN R.
Southern Baptist Theological Seminary: the First Years 1859-1889. Baltimore: 1890. V. 72

SAMPSON, MARMADUKE B.
Rationale of Crime and Its Appopriate Treatment.... New York and Philadelphia: 1846. V. 69; 70

SAMS, C. WHITTLE
Battle of Manassas, July 21, 1861. Norfolk: 1900. V. 73

SAMS, CONWAY W.
The Conquest of Virginia: the Second Attempt...1606-1610. Norfolk: 1929. V. 71

SAMSON, GEORGE GORDON
How To Plan a House. London: 1910. V. 68

SAMSON, J.
The Grizzly Book. 1982. V. 69; 72

SAMUELS, E. A.
The Birds of New England and Adjacent States.... Boston: 1870. V. 68
The Birds of New England and Adjacent States.... Boston: 1872. V. 73
Ornithology and Oology of New England.... Boston: 1867. V. 70; 72
With Rod and Gun in New England and the Maritime Provinces. Boston: 1897. V. 73

SAMUELS, LEE
A Hemingway Check List. New York: 1951. V. 69

SAMUELS, PEGGY
Contemporary Western Artists. 1982. V. 72
The Illustrated Biographical Encyclopedia of Artists of the American West. Garden City: 1976. V. 72

SAN Francisco Album. New York: 1885. V. 68

SANBORN, E. I.
Eocene Flora of Western America. Washington: 1937. V. 72

SANBORN, FRANKLIN B.
Henry D. Thoreau. Boston: 1882. V. 68
The Personality of Thoreau. Boston: 1901. V. 68; 73

SANBORN, MARGARET
Robert E. Lee- A Portrait: 1807-1861. New York: 1966. V. 71

SANCHEZ, NELLIE VAN DE GRIFT
The Life of Robert Louis Stevenson. New York: 1920. V. 72

SANCHEZ, SONIA
Home Coming. Detroit: 1969. V. 68

SANCHEZ DE LA BROZAS, FRANCISCO
Franc. Sanctii ...Minerva, seu de Causis Linguae Latinae commentarius, . . Amsterdam: 1754. V. 71

SANCHO, IGNATIUS
Letters of the Late Ignatius Sancho, an African.... London: 1782. V. 73

SANCLEMENTE, ENRICO
De Vulgaris Aere Emendatione Libri Quatuor. Rome: 1793. V. 68

SAND, GEORGE, PSEUD. OF MME. DUDEVANT
Consuelo. London: 1847. V. 68
Consuelo. New York: 1889. V. 70
The Countess of Rudolstadt. London: 1851. V. 68
The Countess of Rudolstadt. London: 1876. V. 68
Les Dames Vertes. Paris: 1859. V. 68
Histoire Du Veritable Gribouille. 1881. V. 72
Histoire du Veritable Gribouille. London: 1881. V. 68
Impressions and Reminiscences. Boston: 1877. V. 69
Jean De La Roche. Paris: 1860. V. 72
Lelia. Paris: 1833. V. 70
Letters of George Sand. London: 1886. V. 70
Little Fadette. London: 1885?. V. 68
The Wings of Courage. London: 1911. V. 71

SANDAEUS, MAXIMILIAN
Conciones de Morte. Mogvntiae: 1624. V. 69

SANDBURG, CARL
Abraham Lincoln: the Prairie Years. New York: 1926. V. 69; 70

SANDBURG, CARL continued
Abraham Lincoln. The Prairie Years. & The War Years. New York: 1954. V. 71
Abraham Lincoln. The War Years. New York: 1939. V. 68; 69; 70; 73
Abraham Lincoln. The War Years. New York: 1960. V. 72
Always the Young Strangers. New York: 1953. V. 70
Cornhuskers. New York: 1918. V. 70
Lincoln Collector. The Story of Oliver R. Barrett's Great Private Collection. New York: 1949. V. 69; 70
Mary Lincoln: Wife and Widow. New York: 1940. V. 68; 72
Remembrance Rock. New York: 1948. V. 69; 70; 71
Selected Poems. New York: 1926. V. 70
Slabs of the Sunburst West. New York: 1922. V. 73
Smoke and Steel. New York: 1920. V. 68; 73
Steichen the Photographer. New York: 1929. V. 68; 70; 73
Storm Over the Land: a Profile of the Civil War. New York: 1942. V. 73
Wind Song. New York: 1960. V. 71; 73

SANDBY, ARTHUR
London in Miniature, a Peep at the Metropolis of Great Britain: in Letters from a Young Gentleman to His Sisters in the Country. London: 1814. V. 71

SANDBY, WILLIAM
The History Of The Royal Academy Of Arts. London: 1862. V. 72

SANDEMAN, CHRISTOPHER
Thyme and Bergamot. London: 1947. V. 70; 71

SANDEMAN, F.
By Hook and By Crook. 1892. V. 68

SANDEN, THOMAS
Three Discourses. I. On the Use of Books. II. On the Result and Effects of Study. 3. On the Elements of Literary Taste. London: 1802. V. 68

SANDER, NICHOLAS
Rise and Growth of the Anglican Schism. London: 1877. V. 70

SANDERS, ALVIN HOWARD
At the Sign of the Stock Yard Inn. Chicago: 1915. V. 69; 71
Red White and Roan. Chicago: 1936. V. 71

SANDERS, BARRY
Fourteen Ninety Two or Three. 1993. V. 73

SANDERS Complete List of Orchid Hybrids.... St. Albans: 1947. V. 68

SANDERS, DANIEL CLARKE
A History of the Indian Wars with the First Settlers of the United States to the Commencement of the Late War.... Rochester: 1828. V. 69; 73

SANDERS, DORI
Clover. Chapel Hill: 1990. V. 68; 72; 73
Clover. New York: 1993. V. 72

SANDERS, G. D.
Elizabeth Gaskell, with a Bibliography.... New Haven: 1929. V. 68; 70

SANDERS, GORDON E.
Oscar E. Berninghaus, Taos, New Mexico; Master Painter of American Indians and the Frontier West. Taos, NM: 1985. V. 72

SANDERS, J. MILTON
The Crystal Sphere; Its Forces and Its Being.... London: 1857. V. 68; 69

SANDERS, LAWRENCE
The Anderson Tapes. New York: 1970. V. 68; 71
The First Deadly Sin. New York: 1973. V. 68

SANDERS Orchid Guide. St. Albans. V. 72

SANDERS, RUTH MANNING
The Crochet Woman. New York: 1930. V. 71

SANDERS, WILLIAM P.
Days that Are Done. Los Angeles: 1915. V. 69

SANDERSON, C. M.
The Practical Breaking and Training of Gundogs. 1910. V. 71

SANDERSON, HENRY
Considerations on the Proposed Communications by a Navigable Canal, Between the Town of Sheffield and the Peak Forest Canal.... Sheffield: 1826. V. 68

SANDERSON, JAMES M.
The Langham Hotel Guide to London. London: 1867. V. 71

SANDERSON, JOHN
Biography of the Signers of the Declaration of Independence. Philadelphia: 1820-. V. 71

SANDERSON, NICHOLAS
The Elements of Algebra in Ten Books. Cambridge: 1740. V. 70

SANDERSON, PATRICK
The Antiquities of the Abbey or Cathedral Church of Durham.... Newcastle upon Tyne: 1767. V. 69

SANDERSON, ROBERT
Episcopacy (as established by law in England) not Prejudicial to Regal Power. 1683. V. 73
Nine Cases of Conscience: Occasionally Determined. London: 1685. V. 70

SANDFORD, E.
A Manual of Exotic Ferns and Selaginella Comprising Descriptions of Over One Thousand Species and Varieties.... London: 1882. V. 68; 70

SANDFORD, FRANCIS
The History of the Coronation of...James II and...Queen Mary.... London: 1687. V. 71

SANDFORD, JOHN
Mind Prey. New York: 1995. V. 70
Rules of Prey. New York: 1989. V. 68; 69; 71; 72
Shadow Prey. New York: 1990. V. 68
Silent Prey. New York: 1992. V. 68

SANDFORD, JOHN, MRS.
Woman, in Her Social and Domestic Character. London: 1831. V. 72

SANDLIN, TIM
Sex and Sunsets. London: 1987. V. 68
Sex and Sunsets. New York: 1987. V. 69
Western Swing. New York: 1988. V. 72

SANDOE, JAMES
Murder: Plain and Fanciful. 1948. V. 68

SANDOVAL, JUDITH HANCOCK
Historic Ranches of Wyoming. Casper: 1984. V. 73
Historic Ranches of Wyoming. 1986. V. 68

SANDOZ, MARI
The Cattlemen From The Rio Grande Across The Far Marias. New York: 1958. V. 71
Crazy Horse: The Strange Man of the Oglalas. New York: 1942. V. 72; 73
The Horsecatcher. Philadelphia: 1962. V. 73

SANDRART, JOACHIM VON
Iconologia Deorum, Oder Abbildung der Botter.... Nuremberg: 1680. V. 69

SANDS, BENJAMIN
Metamorphosis; or a Transformation of Pictures with Poetical Explanations, for the Amuseument of Young Persons. New York: 1816. V. 71

SANDS, DAVID
Journal of The Life and Gospel Labours of David Sands, With Extracts From His Correspondence. London: 1848. V. 72

SANDS, FRANK
A Pastoral Prince, The History and Reminiscences of J. W. Cooper. Santa Barbara: 1893. V. 71

SANDUSKY COUNTY PIONEER HISTORICAL ASSOCIATION
Yearbook Of The Sandusky County Pioneer Historical Association. Fremont, OH: 1916. V. 72

SANDWEISS, MARTHA
Laura Gilpin: an Enduring Grace. Fort Worth: 1986. V. 70

SANDY, ISABELLE
Andorra. Boston: 1924. V. 69

SANDY, STEPHEN
End of the Picaro. Pawlet: 1977. V. 68

SANDYS, EDWIN
A Relation of the State of Religion; and with What Hopes and Policies It Hath Beene Framed, and Is Maintained in the Severall States of These Westerne Partes of the World. London: 1605. V. 73

SANDYS, GEORGE
A Paraphrase Upon the Divine Poems. London: 1648. V. 69
A Paraphrase Upon the Psalmes of David and Upon the Hymnes Dispersed Throughout the Old and New Testaments. London: 1636. V. 69

SANDYS, WILLIAM
Christmastide: Its History, Festivities and Carols. London: 1852. V. 73
Christmastide: Its History, Festivities and Carols. London: 1860. V. 69
Specimens of Macaronic Poetry. London: 1831. V. 72

SANESI, ROBERT
Four Poems. Milan: 1988. V. 70

SANFORD, GEORGE B.
Fighting Rebels and Redskins, Experiences in The Army Life of Colonel George B. Sanford 1861-1892. Norman: 1969. V. 72

SANFORD, JOHN B.
The Old Man's Place. New York: 1935. V. 73

SANFORD, L. C.
The Water-Fowl Family. New York: 1903. V. 69

SANFORD, TERRY
Danger of Democracy: The Presidential Nominating Process. Boulder: 1981. V. 71

SANGER, GEORGE
Seventy Years a Showman. London: 1908. V. 72

SANGER, MARGARET
An Autobiography. New York: 1938. V. 70; 72
An Autobiography. London: 1939. V. 69
Motherhood in Bondage. New York: 1928. V. 68; 72
The Practice of Contraception, an International Symposium and Survey. Batlimore: 1931. V. 68; 72

SANGER, MARGARET continued
Woman and the New Race. New York: 1920. V. 68; 69; 71

SANGER, WILLIAM
The History of Prostitution, Its Extent Causes and Effects Throughout the World. New York: 1859. V. 69

SANGSTER, CHARLES
Hesperus and Other Poems. Montreal and Kingston: 1860. V. 73

SANGSTER, JOHN
The Rights and Duties of Property; with a Plan for Paying Off the Natioanl Debt. London: 1851. V. 71

SANQUIRICO, ALESSANDRO
Incoronazione di S.M.I.R.A Ferdinando I...a Re del Regno Lombardo- Veneto con Sacra Solenne Pompa Celebrata nell'Insigne Metropolitana di Milano.... Milan: 1838. V. 70
Raccolta di Varie Decorazioni Sceniche Invenate ed Esegnite per il R. Teatro alla Scala di Milano. Florence and Milan: 1827-1832. V. 72

SANSAY, LEONORA HASSALL
Secret History; or the Horrors of St. Domingo in a Series of Letters Written by a Lay at Cape Francois to Colonel Burr, Late Vice President of the United States. Philadelphia: 1808. V. 73

SANSOM, GEORGE S.
Climbing at Wasdale Before the First World War. Somerset: 1982. V. 71

SANSOM, WILLIAM
Fireman Flower and Other Stories. London: 1944. V. 70; 73
South: Aspects and Images from Corsica, Italy and Southern France: Stories. London: 1948. V. 70

SANSOME, ALFRED W.
Commemorative Record of the Scottish National Demonstration...Honour of Arthur James Balfour. 1890. V. 69; 73

SANSONE, ANTONIO
The Printing of Cotton Fabrics, Comprising Calico Bleaching, Printing and Dyeing. Manchester: 1887. V. 71
Recent Progress in the Industries of Dyeing and Calico Printing.... Manchester: 1895-1896. V. 71

SAN SOUCI, ROBERT D.
The White Cat. New York: 1990. V. 70

SANSOVINO, FRANCESCO
Del Secretartio. Libri VII. Venice: 1584. V. 69
Venetia, Cita Noblissima et Singolare. Venetia: 1581. V. 68

THE SANTA *Claus Picture Book.* New York: 1901. V. 73

SANTANGELO, ANTONIO
The Development of Italian Textile Design from the 12th to the 18th Century. 1964. V. 70

SANTAYANA, GEORGE
The Works. New York: 1936-1937. V. 73
The Works. New York: 1938. V. 70

SANTE FE RAILROAD
A Colorado Summer. 1913. V. 68

SANTE, LUC
The Factory of Facts. New York: 1998. V. 71

SANTEE, ROSS
Apache Land. New York: 1947. V. 69
Cowboy. New York: 1928. V. 69; 71
Hardrock and Silver Sage. New York and London: 1951. V. 73
Lost Pony Tracks. New York: 1953. V. 71
Men and Horses. New York: 1926. V. 71

SANTI, DOMENICO
Designs for Cartouches. Bologna. V. 68; 70

SANTIAGO, ESMERALDA
Las Mamis. Favorite Latino Authors Remember their Mothers. New York: 2000. V. 68

SANTORIO, SANTORIO
Medica Statica: Being the Aphorisms of Sanctorius. London: 1728. V. 68

SANTOS, RICHARD
Aguayo Expedition into Texas 1721. Austin: 1981. V. 69
Santa Anna's Campaign Against Texas. 1835-1836. Waco: 1968. V. 69

SANTOS-DUMONT, A.
My Air-Ships. New York: 1904. V. 72

SAPRI, PIETRO
The History of the Inquisition, Composed by the Reverend Father Paul Servita.... London: 1655. V. 68

THE SARAH-Ad; *or, a Flight for Fame.* London: 1742. V. 68

SARALAMP, P.
Medicinal Plants in Siri Ruckhachati Garden. 1996. V. 68

SARAMAGO, JOSE
All the Names. New York: 2000. V. 69
The Stone Raft. New York: 1995. V. 70
The Year of the Death of Ricardo Reis. New York: 1990. V. 70

SARAYNA, TORELLO
De Origine et Amplitudine Civitatis Veronae.... Verona: 1540. V. 70

SARBER, MARY A.
Photographs from the Border. El Paso: 1977. V. 69

SARDA, DANIEL
Conte de Maitre. London: 1927. V. 68
Conte de Maitre Esapapidour. 1927. V. 71; 73
Conte de Maitre Espapidour. New York: 1927. V. 71

SARG, TONY
Tony Sarg's Book for Children. New York: 1924. V. 70
Tony Sarg's Magic Movie Book With Ten Tales That Will Never Die.... New York: 1943. V. 72
Tony Sarg's New York. New York: 1927. V. 69
Tony Sarg's Treasure Book. New York: 1942. V. 73
Where is Tommy?. New York: 1932. V. 69

SARGANT, EDMOND BEALE
A Guide Book to Books. London: 1891. V. 73

SARGEANT, J.
Frank Lloyd Wright's Usonian Houses: the Case for Organic Architecture. New York: 1976. V. 68

SARGEANT, WINTHROP
Jazz Hot and Hybrid. New York: 1938. V. 68

SARGENT & CO.
Locks and Hardware, 1922. New Haven: 1922. V. 69

SARGENT, C. P.
Plantae Wilsonianae.... Portland: 1988. V. 68

SARGENT, HARRY R.
Thoughts Upon Sport. 1895. V. 68

SARGENT, JAMES
James Sargent's Descriptive Catalogue of Patent Magnetic Bank and Safe Locks, Manufactured at 62 Buffalo St., Rochester, N.Y. Rochester: 1867. V. 68

SARGENT, JEAN A.
Stones and Bones: Cemetery Records of Prince George's Co. Md. Bowie: 1984. V. 72

SARGENT, JOHN T., MRS.
Sketches and Reminiscences of the Radical Club of Chestnut Street, Boston. Boston: 1880. V. 68

SARGENT, WINTHROP
The Life and Career of Major John Andre. Boston: 1861. V. 73

SARLL, ANDREW
Double Entry Book-Keeping in Theory and Practice.... 1895. V. 71

SARMA, P.
The Freshwater Chaetophorales of New Zealand. Berlin: 1986. V. 73

SARNELLI, POMPEO
Le Guide des Etrangers.... Naples: 1702. V. 70; 72

SAROYAN, WILLIAM
The Assyrian and Other Stories. London: 1950. V. 73
The Daring Young Man on the Flying Trapeze. New York: 1934. V. 69
Days of Life and Death and Escape to the Moon. New York: 1970. V. 71
Dear Baby. New York: 1944. V. 69
Get Away Old Man. New York: 1944. V. 69
The Human Comedy. New York: 1943. V. 70; 72
Inhale and Exhale. London: 1936. V. 69
Peace, It's a Wonderful. New York: 1939. V. 69
A Special Announcement. New York: 1940. V. 69
Three Times Three. 1936. V. 69
The Time of Your Life. New York: 1939. V. 69
The Trouble with Tigers. New York: 1938. V. 72

SARPI, PAOLO
A Treatise of Matters Beneficiary...Wherein is Related...How the Almes of the Faithful Were Distributed in the Primitive Church. London: 1680. V. 71

SARRAUTE, NATHALIE
Portrait of a Man Unknown. New York: 1958. V. 69; 71

SARRIS, ANDREW
Confessions of a Cultist. New York: 1970. V. 72
The Films of Josef von Sternberg. New York: 1966. V. 70

SARRIS, GREG
Grand Avenue. New York: 1994. V. 72

SARS, GEORGE OSSIAN
On Some Remarkable Forms of Animal Life from the Great Deeps Off the Norwegian Coast. Christiania: 1872. V. 68

SARTIN, MAY
Encounter in April with Correspondence. Boston: 1937. V. 73

SARTON, GEORGE
Introduction to the History of Science. Baltimore: 1927-1948. V. 68; 73
Introduction to the History of Science. Baltimore: 1931. V. 68; 73

SARTON, GEORGE continued
Introduction to the History of Science. Washington: 1953. V. 73
Introduction to the History of Science. Baltimore: 1953-1967. V. 69

SARTON, MAY
Anger. New York: 1982. V. 68
Collected Poems 1930-1973. New York: 1974. V. 68
The Fur Person. New York: 1957. V. 69
The Fur Person. New York: 1978. V. 72
Journal of a Solitude. New York: 1973. V. 73
Miss Pickthorn and Mr. Hare. New York: 1966. V. 73
Mrs. Stevens Hears the Mermaids Singing. New York: 1965. V. 73
Mrs. Stevens Hears the Mermaids Singing. New York: 1974. V. 71
Plant Dreaming Deep. New York: 1968. V. 71; 73
Recovering: a Journal. New York: 1980. V. 70
A World of Light. New York: 1976. V. 73

SARTORIUS, CARL CHRISTIAN
Mexico. Landscapes and Popular Sketches. London: 1858. V. 69

SARTRE, JEAN-PAUL
Being and Nothingness. New York: 1956. V. 72
Intimacy and Other Stories. London: 1949. V. 68
Le Mur. Paris: 1939. V. 70
La Nausee. Paris: 1938. V. 72; 73

SASEK, MIROSLAV
This Is Israel. New York: 1962. V. 70

SASOWSKY, N.
The Prints of Reginald Marsh.... New York: 1976. V. 69

SASS, HENRY
A Journey to Rome and Naples, Performed in 1817.... New York: 1818. V. 70

SASS, HERBERT RAVENEL
A Carolina Rice Plantation of the Fifties. New York: 1936. V. 71

SASSOON, SIEGFRIED LORRAINE
Collected Poems. London: 1947. V. 72
Common Chords. Stanford: 1950. V. 72
Counter-Attack and Other Poems. London: 1918. V. 71
The Daffodil Murderer. London: 1913. V. 70
Emblems of Experience. Cambridge: 1951. V. 70
The Flower-Show Match and Other Pieces. London: 1941. V. 72; 73
The Heart's Journey. New York: 1927. V. 70
The Heart's Journey. London: 1928. V. 71
In Sicily. London: 1930. V. 71
Letters to a Critic. Conachar: 1976. V. 72
Letters to a Critic. London: 1976. V. 71
Memoirs of a Fox-Hunting Man. London: 1929. V. 69; 73
Memoirs of a Fox-Hunting Man. Memoirs of an Infantry Officer. Sherston's Progress. London: 1928-1936. V. 73
Memoirs of an Infantry Officer. London: 1930. V. 68; 69; 70; 71; 72; 73
Memoirs of an Infantry Officer. London: 1931. V. 68; 69
Memoirs of an Infantry Officer. New York: 1981. V. 70; 72
Meredith. London: 1948. V. 72
An Octave. 1966. V. 70; 72; 73
An Ode for Music. London: 1912. V. 73
The Old Century and Seven More Years. London: 1938. V. 72
The Old Huntsman and Other Poems. London: 1917. V. 72
The Old Huntsman and Other Poems. New York: 1918. V. 73
The Path to Peace, Selected Poems. Worcester: 1960. V. 71
Picture Show. Cambridge: 1919. V. 73
Poems. 1931. V. 70
Poems. 1958. V. 72
Poems Newly Selected 1916-1935. London: 1940. V. 72; 73
Prehistoric Burial. New York: 1932. V. 69
Rhymed Ruminations. London: 1940. V. 70; 72
Satirical Poems. London: 1926. V. 72
Selected Poems. London: 1925. V. 72
Sherston's Progress. London: 1936. V. 72
Siegfried's Journey, 1916-1920. London: 1945. V. 72
Something About Myself. Worcester: 1966. V. 68; 71
To My Mother. London: 1928. V. 70
Vigils. London: 1935. V. 72
The War Poems. London: 1919. V. 71; 72; 73

SATO, CHIEKO
Japanese Cooking Of All Kinds. Tokyo: 1956. V. 68

SATO, SHOZO
The Art of Arranging Flowers. New York: 1965. V. 70
The Art of Arranging Flowers. New York: 1966. V. 72

SATTERLEE, MARION P.
The Massacre of The Redwood Indian Agency On Monday, August 18, 1862. Minnesota: 1916. V. 72

SATTERTHWAIT, WALTER
At Ease with the Dead. New York: 1990. V. 68; 71
A Flower in the Desert. New York: 1992. V. 68
The Gold of Mayani, The African Stories of Walter Satterthwait. Gallup: 1995. V. 69; 70; 72; 73
The Hanged Man. New York: 1993. V. 71
Miss Lizzie. New York: 1989. V. 70
Wall of Glass. New York: 1987. V. 68; 69; 71; 72

SATURDAY Book - Eighty Year. London: 1948. V. 69

SAUDEK, JAN
The World of Jan Saudek. 1983. V. 68

SAUER, CARL
The Road to Cibola. Berkeley: 1932. V. 68

SAUER, G. C.
John Gould the Bird Man. Melbourne: 1982. V. 71; 73

SAULT Ste. Marie, Ontario. On the Banks of St. Mary's Rapids. The History of Lake Navigation. 1905. V. 70

SAUMAREZ, MAURICE DE
Bridget Riley. London: 1970. V. 72

SAUMIERES, JACQUES DE LANGLADE, BARON DE
New Memoirs and Characters of the Two Great Brothers, the Duke of Bouillon and Mareschal Turenne. London: 1693. V. 71

SAUNDERS, CHARLES FRANCIS
The Southern Sierras of California. Boston and New York: 1923. V. 68
The Southern Sierras of California. New York: 1924. V. 68; 73
The Story of Carmelita: Its Associations and Its Trees. Pasadena: 1928. V. 68

SAUNDERS, EDWARD MANNING
History of the Baptists of the Maritime Provinces. Halifax: 1902. V. 73
Three Premiers of Nova Scotia. The. Hon. J. W. Johnstone. The Hon. Joseph Howe. The Hon. Charles Tupper. Toronto: 1909. V. 73

SAUNDERS, F.
About Woman, Love and Marriage. New York: 1868. V. 72

SAUNDERS, FREDERICK
The Author's Printing and Publishing Assistant. London: 1839. V. 73
Our National Centennial Jubilee. Orations, Addresses and Poems Delivered on the Fourth of July, 1876, in the Several States of the Union. New York: 1877. V. 70

SAUNDERS, GEORGE
Civil War Land in Bad Decline. New York: 1996. V. 69
A Treatise on Theatres. London: 1790. V. 68; 70

SAUNDERS, H.
Manual of British Birds. 1899. V. 69

SAUNDERS, JOHN
The Tinker's Wig. Loughborough: 1947. V. 71

SAUNDERS, JOHN CUNNINGHAM
A Treatise on Some Practical Points Relating to the Diseases of the Eye.... London: 1811. V. 69; 72

SAUNDERS, JOHN S.
The Law of Pleading and Evidence in Civil Actions, Arranged Alphabeticaly.... Philadelphia: 1829. V. 72

SAUNDERS, LOUISE
The Knave of Hearts. New York: 1925. V. 68; 72; 73

SAUNDERS, MONTAGU
The Mystery in the Drood Family. Cambridge: 1914. V. 69

SAUNDERSON, NICHOLAS
The Elements of Algebra, in Ten Books. Cambridge: 1740. V. 72
Select Parts of Professor Saunderson's Elements of Algebra. London: 1756. V. 73

SAUNIER, CLAUDIUS
Treatise on Modern Horology in Theory and Practice. London: 1882. V. 72
Treatise on Modern Horology in Theory and Practice. London: 1952. V. 73

SAUSAGE and Meat Specialities. Chicago: 1938. V. 73

SAUSAGE Manual and Text Book. Chicago: 1934. V. 73

SAUSSURE, HORACE BENEDICT DE
Essais sur l'Hygrometrie. Neuchatel: 1783. V. 73

SAUVAGE, ELIE
The Little Gipsy. London: 1869. V. 72

A SAVAGE Club Souvenir. 1916. V. 73

SAVAGE, GEORGE
The Catholick Question at Boston; or an Attempt to Prove that a Calvinist is a Christian.... Boston: 1815. V. 71

SAVAGE, JUANITA
Spanish Rapture. New York: 1934. V. 70

SAVAGE, LES
The Doctor at Coffin Gap. Garden City: 1949. V. 69

SAVAGE, MARMION W.
The Falcon Family; or, Young Ireland. London: 1860. V. 68
My Uncle the Curate. London: 1865. V. 68

SAVAGE, MINOT JUDSON
Man Woman and Child. Boston: 1904. V. 72

SAVAGE, RICHARD
The Works of Richard Savage Esq.... London: 1777. V. 68

SAVAGE, RICHARD HENRY
An Awkward Meeting and Other Thrilling Adventures. London: 1899. V. 68
An Exile from London: a Novel. London: 1897. V. 68
The Flying Halcyon; a Mystery of the Pacific Ocean. London: 1894. V. 68
For Life and Love: a Story of the Rio Grande. London: 1894. V. 68
Her Foreign Conquest: a Novel. London: 1896. V. 68
His Cuban Sweetheart: a Novel. London: 1895?. V. 68
In the Old Chateau: a Story of Russian Poland. London: 1895. V. 68
The Little Lady of Lagunitas; a Franco-Californian Romance. London: 1893. V. 68
My Official Wife: a Novel. London: 1893. V. 68
The Princess of Alaska, a Tale of Two Countries. London: 1894. V. 68

SAVERIEN, ALEXANDRE
Dictionnaire Universel de Mathematique et de Physique, ou l'on Traite de l'Origine du Progres de ces Deux Scieneces & Des Arts qui en Dependent.... Paris: 1753. V. 73

SAVERY, THOMAS
The Miners' Friend, or, an Engine to Raised Water by Fire, Described and of the Manner of Fixing It in Mines.... London: 1910. V. 68

SAVIGNON, ANDRE
The Sorrows of Elsie. New York: 1927. V. 69
Sunken Gold. New York: 1925. V. 72

SAVILE, ALBANY
Thirty-Six Hints to Sportsmen. Ikehampton: 1822. V. 70

SAVILE, FRANK
The River of the Giraffe, a Chronicle of the Desert, Stream and Forest Shooting in the Southern Sudan. London: 1925. V. 69

SAVILE, HENRY
Rerum Anglicarum Scriptores Post Bedam Praecipui.... 1596. V. 68; 72

SAVILL, P.
Plantation Siviculture in Europe. Oxford: 1997. V. 72

SAVILLE, MALCOLM
All Summer through. London: 1951. V. 72
Christmas at Nettleford. 1953. V. 71; 73
Come to Cornwall. London: 1969. V. 69
Come to London. London: 1967. V. 71
Come to Somerset. London: 1970. V. 68
The Coronation Gift Book for Boys and Girls. 1952. V. 70; 72
Dark Danger. London: 1965. V. 71; 72
Diamond in the Sky. London: 1974. V. 70
Eat What You Grow. 1975. V. 71
The Elusive Grasshopper. 1954. V. 73
The Gay Dolphin Adventure. 1950. V. 73
Lone Pine Five. London: 1949. V. 68; 73
Lone Pine Five. 1957. V. 72; 73
Lone Pine Five. 1972. V. 72
Lone Pine Five. London: 1972. V. 70
Lone Pine London. 1957. V. 72
Lone Pine London. London: 1957. V. 70
The Luck of Sallowby. 1952. V. 72
Man with Three Fingers. 1971. V. 71
The Master of Maryknoll. 1950. V. 72
Mystery at Witchend. 1943. V. 73
Mystery at Witchend. London: 1944. V. 68
Mystery at Witchend. 1945. V. 72
Mystery at Witchend. 1957. V. 73
Mystery Mine. 1959. V. 71; 72; 73
Not Scarlet but Gold. London: 1962. V. 72
A Palace for the Buckinghams. 1963. V. 72
The Purple Valley. London: 1964. V. 68; 71
Redshank's Warning. 1948. V. 70
The Riddle of the Painted Box. 1947. V. 72
The Riddle of the Painted Box. London: 1947. V. 68
Saucers Over the Moor. 1955. V. 71; 73
Sea Witch Comes Home. London: 1960. V. 68; 69; 71
The Secret of Grey Walls. 1958. V. 73
The Secret of the Gorge. 1958. V. 71; 73
The Secret of the Gorge. London: 1958. V. 70
The Secret of the Hidden Pool. London: 1953. V. 72
See How It Grows. London: 1971. V. 68
Seven White Gates. London: 1944. V. 68; 70
Seven White Gates. 1950. V. 73
Seven White Gates. 1963. V. 72
The Sign of the Alpine Rose. London: 1974. V. 70
Small Creatures. 1959. V. 70
Spring Comes to Nettleford. London: 1954. V. 69
Strangers at Snowfell. 1949. V. 71
Susan, Bill and the Bright Star Circus. 1960. V. 73
Susan, Bill and the Pirates Bold. 1961. V. 72
Susan, Bill and the Vanishing Boy. 1955. V. 72
The Thin Grey Man. 1966. V. 72
Treasure at Amorys. 1964. V. 72
Treasure at Amorys. 1969. V. 72
Two Fair Plaits. 1948. V. 72
Where's My Girl?. 1972. V. 71; 72; 73
Where's My Girl?. New York: 1972. V. 69
Where's My Girl?. London: 1976. V. 70
Wings over Witchend. 1956. V. 73
Wonder Why Book of Exploring the Seashore. 1979. V. 68
Wonder Why Book of Exploring the Seashore. London: 1979. V. 70
Words for All Seasons. 1979. V. 72

SAVONAROLA, MICHELE
Practica Savonarolae de Febribus. Venice: 1543. V. 68; 73

SAVORY, CHARLES H.
The Paper Hanger, Painter, Grainer and Decorator's Assistant: Containing Full Information as to the Best Methods Practised in Paper Hanging, Panelling, Room Decoration.... 1878. V. 68

SAVORY, ISABEL
A Sportswoman in India. 1900. V. 69; 70; 72; 73
A Sportswoman in India. London: 1900. V. 69

SAVORY, T. H.
The Spiders and Allied Orders of the British Isles. 1935. V. 69

THE SAVOY. 1896. V. 70

SAVOY HOTEL CO.
London's Social Calendar. London: 1912. V. 71

SAWARD, BLANCHE C.
Decorative Painting: a Practical Handbook on Painting and Etching Upon Various Objects and Materials.... London: 1884?. V. 68

SAWYER, A. R.
Early Nasca Needlework. London: 1997. V. 69

SAWYER, CHARLES JAMES
A Dickens Library: Exhibition Catalogue of the Sawyer Collection of the Works of Charles Dickens.... London: 1936. V. 70

SAWYER, EDITH A.
A Romance of Fisherman's Island. Boston: 1899. V. 70

SAWYER, EUGENE T.
Life and Career of Tiburcio Vasquez, the California Bandit and Murderer. San Francisco: 1875. V. 68
The Life and Career of Tiburcio Vasquez the California Bandit and Murderer.... San Jose: 1875. V. 70
The Life and Career of Tiburcio Vasquez, the California Stage Robber. Oakland: 1944. V. 70; 72

SAWYER, F.
The Keeper of the Stream. 1952. V. 73

SAWYER, FRANK
Nymphs and the Trout. 1958. V. 68

SAWYER, LORENZO
Way Sketches: Containing Incidents of Travel Across the Plains from St. Joseph to California in 1850. New York: 1926. V. 68

SAWYER, RUTH
Herself, Himself and Myself. New York: 1917. V. 71

SAWYER, WILLIAM EDWARD
Electric Lighting by Incandescence, and Its Application to Interior Illumination. New York: 1887. V. 69

SAXBY, HENRY
The British Customs: Containing an Historical and Practical Account of Each Branch of that Revenue.... London: 1757. V. 72

SAXBY, JESSIE M. E.
Preston Tower; or, Will He No' Come Back Again?. Edinburgh: 1884. V. 68

SAXE, MAURICE, COMTE DE
Memoires sur l'Art de La Guerre de Maurice Comte De Saxe.... Dresden: 1757. V. 69
Mes Reveries Ouvrage Posthume du Maurice Comte de Saxe. Amsterdam and Leipzig: 1757. V. 71
Reveries, or Memoirs Upon the Art of the War. London: 1757. V. 71

SAXL, FRITZ
Catalogue of Astrological and Mythological Illuminated Manuscripts of the Latin Middle Ages. III, 2: Manuscripts in English Libraries. London: 1953. V. 70

SAXON, LYLE
Gumbo Ya-Ya. A Collection of Louisiana Folk Tales. Boston: 1945. V. 71

SAXTON, MARK
The Broken Circle. New York: 1941. V. 71

SAY, ALLEN
Grandfather's Journey. Boston: 1993. V. 70; 72

SAY, JEAN BAPTISTE
Lettres a M. Malthus, sur Differens Sujets d'Economie Politique.... Paris: 1820. V. 71

SAY, JEAN BAPTISTE continued
A Treatise on Political Economy; or the Production, Distribution and Consumption of Wealth. Philadelphia: 1853. V. 72

SAY, THOMAS
American Conchology or Descriptions of the Shells of North America.,. New Harmony: 1830-1838. V. 73
American Entomology. Boston. V. 69
American Entomology, or Descriptions of the Insects of North America. Philadelphia: 1825. V. 69
The Complete Writings of Thomas Say on the Entomology of North America. Philadelphia: 1891. V. 69

SAYE, JAMES HODGE
Memoirs of Major Joseph McJunkin. Greenwood: 1925. V. 68

SAYER, C.
Costumes of Mexico. London and Austin: 1985. V. 69

SAYER, FREDERIC
The History of Gibraltar and Of Its Political Relation to Events in Europe. London: 1865. V. 70

SAYERS, DOROTHY L.
An Account of Lord Mortimer Wimsey, the Hermit of the Wash.... Bristol: 1937. V. 68
Busman's Honeymoon. New York: 1937. V. 71
Clouds of Witness. London: 1926. V. 73
Even the Parrot. London: 1944. V. 68
In the Teeth of the Evidence. London: 1939. V. 69
Lord Peter Views the Body. London: 1928. V. 73
The Man Born to Be King. London: 1943. V. 68
The Omnibus of Crime. New York: 1929. V. 71
The Story of Adam and Christ. London: 1955. V. 70
Unnatural Death. London: 1927. V. 73
The Unpleasantness at the Bellona Club. London: 1928. V. 73
Whose Body?. 1923. V. 73

SAYLER, OLIVER M.
Max Reinhardt and His Theatre - the Morris Gest Edition. New York: 1926. V. 70

SAYLES, E. B.
The Cochise Culture. Globe: 1941. V. 68; 73

SAYLES, JOHN
Pride of the Bimbos. Boston: 1975. V. 69; 70; 72
Thinking in Pictures. Boston: 1987. V. 72
Union Dues. Boston: 1977. V. 70; 71; 72

SAYLOR, STEVEN
Arms of Nemesis. New York: 1992. V. 68; 69; 71; 73
Roman Blood. New York: 1991. V. 68; 69; 70; 71
The Venus Throw. New York: 1995. V. 72

SAYRES, WILLIAM C.
Sammy Louis. The Life History of a Young Micmac. New Haven: 1956. V. 73

SAYWELL, F. B.
The Clever Little Tailor or Seven at a Blow. London: 1928. V. 69

SCAMMON, C. M.
The Marine Mammals of the North-Western Coast of North America and the American Whale Fishery. Riverside: 1969. V. 70

SCANDELO, GULIELMO, PSEUD.
The Elements of the Science of Scandal.... London: 1814. V. 70

SCANES, ARTHUR E.
Golden Days and Silver Eves. London: 1880. V. 70

SCANGA, F.
Atlas of Electron Microscopy. Amsterdam: 1964. V. 68

SCANLAN, FITZGERALD EDWARD
A to Z Being Twenty Six Notes On A Soldier's Trumpet. London: 1876. V. 70; 72

SCANNELL, VERNON
The Fight. London: 1953. V. 72; 73
New and Collected Poems 1950-1980. London: 1980. V. 71

SCARBERRY, ALMA SIOUX
Rainbow Over Broadway. New York: 1936. V. 71

SCARBOROUGH, DOROTHY
Can't Get a Red Bird. New York: 1929. V. 69

SCARBOROUGH, ELIZABETH ANN
The Healer's War. New York: 1988. V. 69; 72

SCARGILL, WILLIAM PITT
Blue Stocking Hall. London: 1829. V. 68; 73

SCARLETT, ROGER
The Back Bay Murders. New York: 1930. V. 68

SCARPA, ANTONIO
Anatomicae Disquisitiones de Auditu et Olfactu.... Mediolani: 1794. V. 73
Practical Observations on the Principal Diseases of the Eyes.... London: 1806. V. 72
Tabulae Nevrologicae. Turin: 1794. V. 68

SCARROW, SIMON
Under the Eagle. 2000. V. 68

SCATTERGOOD, THOMAS
Memoirs of Thomas Scattergood. London: 1845. V. 72

SCENES from the Life of Nickleby Married. London: 1840. V. 69

SCHAACK, MICHAEL J.
Anarchy and Anarchists. Chicago: 1889. V. 68; 69; 71

SCHAAF, GREGORY
Hopi-Tewa Pottery - 500 Artist Biographies. Santa Fe: 1998. V. 69

SCHAARSCHMIDT RICHTER, I.
Japanese Gardens. New York: 1979. V. 68; 71

SCHABALIE, JOHN P.
The Wandering Soul; or, Dialogues between the Wandering Soul and Adam, Noah and Simon Cleophas. Winchester: 1841. V. 72

SCHAD, JOHANN ADAM XAVER
Effigies Ducum et Regum Hungariae. 1687. V. 69

SCHADAEUS, OSEAS
Summum Argentorantensium Templum.... Strassburg: 1617. V. 68

SCHADLER, K.
African Art in Private German Collections. Munich: 1973. V. 69
Ceramics from Black Africa and Ancient America, the Hans Wolf Collection-Zurich. Zurich: 1985. V. 69

SCHAEFER, JACK
Company of Cowards. Boston: 1957. V. 70
The Great Endurance Horse Race. Santa Fe: 1963. V. 68; 73
Monte Walsh. Boston: 1963. V. 71; 73
Shane. Boston: 1954. V. 69; 71
Shane and Other Stories. London: 1963. V. 69

SCHAEFFER, JACOB CHRISTIAN
Elementa Entomologica. Regensburg: 1766. V. 73
Fungorum Qui in Bavaria et Palatinatu Circa Ratisbonam Nascuntur.... Erlangae: 1800. V. 68; 71

SCHAEFFER, L. M.
Sketches of Travels in South America, Mexico and California. New York: 1860. V. 73

SCHAEFFER, SAMUEL BERNARD
Morning, Noon, Night. New York: 1937. V. 68; 70

SCHAEFFER, SUSAN FROMBERG
Falling. New York: 1973. V. 72

SCHAFER, EDWARD ALBERT
A Course of Practical Histology. London: 1877. V. 68

SCHAFF, PHILIP
The Creeds of Christendom. New York: 1887. V. 71
History of the Christian Church I-V (In Six Volumes). New York: 1910-1912. V. 73

SCHALDACH, W. J.
Fish by Schaldach. 1993. V. 73
Upland Gunning, Collected Etchings and Watercolors of Sport in the Field and Allied Subjects. New York: 1946. V. 72; 73

SCHALK, EMIL
Campaigns of 1862 and 1863. Philadelphia: 1863. V. 68

SCHAPERA, I.
The Bantu Speaking Tribes of South Africa. An Ethnographical Survey. Cape Town: 1946. V. 69

SCHARF, ALFRED
A Catalogue of Pictures and Drawings from the Collection of Sir Thomas Merton...at Stubbings House, Maidenhead. London: 1960. V. 69

SCHARF, GEORGE
A Descriptive and Historical Catalogue of the Collection of the Picures at Woburn Abbey. London: 1890. V. 72

SCHARF, JOHN THOMAS
History of Maryland from the Earliest Period to the Present Day. Baltimore: 1879. V. 73

SCHARY, DORE
Sunrise at Campobello. New York: 1958. V. 69

SCHATZ, AUGUST H.
Longhorns Bring Culture. Boston: 1961. V. 71

SCHATZ, J. J.
Alpine Wonderland. London: 1936. V. 69

SCHEDEL, HARTMANN
Liber Chronicarum. Nuremberg: 1493. V. 69
The Nuremberg Chronicle. New York: 1979. V. 70

SCHEER, FREDERICK
The Cape of Good Hope Versus Egypt; or, Political and Commercial Considerations on the Proper Line of Steam Communication with the East Indies. London: 1839. V. 73
The Letters of Diogenes to Sir Robert Peel, Bart. London: 1841. V. 71

SCHEFFERUS, JOHANNES
Histoire De La Laponie. A Paris: 1678. V. 71

SCHEHERAZADE.. Paris: 1930?. V. 72

SCHEIPS, PAUL J.
Albert James Myer, Founder of the Army Signal Corps: a Biographical Study. Washington: 1965. V. 69

SCHEITHAUER, W.
Hummingbirds. New York: 1967. V. 73

SCHELIHA, VIKTOR ERNST KARL RUDOLF VON
A Treatise on Coast-Defence; Based on the Experience Gained by Officers of the Corp of Engineers of the Army of the Confederate States.... London: 1868. V. 72

SCHELL, JONATHAN
The Fate of the Earth. New York: 1982. V. 71; 72

SCHENDEL, ARTHUR VAN
Tristan en Isolde. Utrecht: 1915. V. 73

SCHENECTADY Fire Department 1900-1980. Schenectady: 1980. V. 69

SCHENK, ABE
Let's Play Cowboy. Garden City: 1951. V. 70

SCHENK, PETER
Aan Den Hoog-Edel Welgeboren en Gestrengen Heere, Den Heere Joan Baron van Arnhem, Heere van Rozendael tot Harsio, Byzonderen Raad des Vorstendoms.... Amsterdam: 1700. V. 72

SCHENK DE REGNIERS, BEATRICE
The Giant Story. New York: 1953. V. 72

SCHENKMAN, J.
Pierrot. Amsterdam: 1910. V. 68

SCHERER, JOANNA COHAN
Indians - the Great Photographs that Reveal North American Indian Life, 1847-1929, from the Unique Collection of the Smithsonian Institution. New York: 1973. V. 68; 69

SCHERF, MARGARET
Always Murder a Friend. New York: 1948. V. 70

SCHERZER, KARL
Narrative of The Circumnavigation Of The Globe By The Austrian Frigate "Novara" (Commodore B. von Wullerstorf-Rubair). London: 1861. V. 72

SCHEUCHZER, JOHANN JAKOB
Herbarium Divluvianum. Lyon: 1723. V. 68; 72

SCHEZEN, ROBERTO
The Splendor Of France. Chateaux, Mansions, And Country Houses. New York: 1991. V. 72

SCHICKLER, DAVID
Kissing in Mahatten. New York: 2001. V. 69; 72

SCHIEDT, DUNCAN
The Jazz State of Indiana. Indianapolis: 1977. V. 68

SCHIEL, JACOB H.
Journey through the Rocky Mountains and the Humboldt Mountains to the Pacific Coast. Norman: 1959. V. 71

SCHIERBEEK, A.
Measuring the Invisible World. London: 1959. V. 68

SCHIFF, STUART
Whispers. 1984. V. 71

SCHILDER, F. A.
Ph. Dautzenerg's Collection of Cypraeidae. Brussels: 1952. V. 73

SCHILLER, ELLY
First Photographs of the Holy Land. (&) The First Photographs of Jerusalem the Old City. Jerusalem: 1978. V. 73

SCHILLER, J.
Alice's Adventures in Wonderland. 1990. V. 70

SCHILLER, JOHANN CHRISTOPH FRIEDRICH VON
The Piccolomini, or the First Part of Wallenstein. London: 1800. V. 73
Wilhelm Tell. Bielefeld, Leipzig und Berli: 1905. V. 68

SCHILLINGS, C. G.
With Flashlight And Rifle. London: 1906. V. 72

SCHILPP, PAUL A.
Albert Einstein: Philosopher-Scientist. Evanston: 1949. V. 69

SCHIMMEL & CO.
Schimmel & Co.'s Works. 1908. V. 70

SCHIMMELPENNINCK, MARY ANNE
Life of Mary Anne Schimmelpenninck, Author of Select Memoirs of Port Royal. Philadelphia: 1859. V. 70
The Principles of Beauty.... London: 1859. V. 72

SCHIMPER, W.
Monographie des Plante Fossiles du Gres Bigarre de la Chaine des Vosges. Leipzig: 1844. V. 68

SCHINDLER, SOLOMON
Dissolving Views in the History of Judaism. Boston: 1888. V. 69

SCHINKEL, CARL FRIEDRICH
Sammlung Architektonischer Entuwrfe Enthaltend Theils Wrke, Welche Ausgefuhrt Sind Theils Gegenstande Deren Ausfuhrung Beabsichtigt Wurde, Neue Vollstandige Ausgabe.... Berlin: 1858. V. 70

SCHIWETZ, BUCK
Texas' Buck Schiwetz. San Antonio: 1972. V. 69

SCHLECHTER, R.
The Orchidaceae of German New Guinea. Essendon: 1982. V. 73

SCHLEGEL, HERMAN
De Vogels Van Nederlandsch Indie/Les Oiseaux des Indes Neerlandaises. Leiden: 1863-1866. V. 72; 73

SCHLEICH, CARL LUDWIG
Those Were Good Days. London: 1935. V. 68

SCHLEIDEN, M. J.
The Plant; a Biography.... London: 1848. V. 69
Principles of Scientific Botany.... London: 1849. V. 70

SCHLEIFFER, H.
Sacred Narcotic Plants of the New World Indians. NY: 1973. V. 72

SCHLEINITZ, O. VON
Walter Crane. Bielefeld & Leipzig: 1902. V. 72

SCHLES, KEN
Invisible City. Pasadena: 1988. V. 73

SCHLESINGER, ARTHUR M.
History of U.S. Political Parties. New York: 1973. V. 68

SCHLEY, STURGES MASON
Deepening Blue. Garden City: 1935. V. 70

SCHLEY, WINFIELD SCOTT
Report of Winfield S. Schley, Commander U.S. Navy, Commanding Greely Relief Expedition of 1884. Washington: 1887. V. 69

SCHLICH, WILLIAM
Manual of Forestry. London: 1922. V. 70

SCHLICK, MARY DODDS
Columbia River Basketry. Seattle: 1994. V. 69; 72

SCHLIEMANN, HENRY
Ilios. Stadt und Land der Trojaner. Leipzig: 1881. V. 70
Ilios: the City and Country of the Trojans. New York: 1880. V. 70
Ilios...Country of the Trojans. New York: 1881. V. 69
Mycenae...Researches and Discoveries at Mycenae & Tiryns. New York: 1880. V. 70
Tiryns: The Prehistoric Palace. New York: 1885. V. 69
Troja: Results of the Latest Researches...On the Site of Homer's Troy. New York: 1884. V. 70

SCHLIPP, PAUL A.
Albert Einstein: Philosopher-Scientist. Evanston: 1949. V. 71

SCHLOSS, DAVID F.
Methods of Industrial Renumeration. New York: 1892. V. 70

SCHMALENBACH, W.
African Art. New York: 1954. V. 69
Kurt Schwitters. New York: 1967. V. 69; 73

SCHMALZ, JOHN BARNES
Nuggets from King Solomon's Mine. Newton: 1908. V. 69

SCHMECKEBIER, L. F.
Catalogue and Index of the Publications of the Hayden, King, Powell and Wheeler Surveys. Washington: 1904. V. 69

SCHMID, CHRISTOPHER
Easter Eggs and Robin Red Breast. Edinburgh: 1839. V. 72

SCHMID, JOHANNES
Spiegel der Anatomiae Darinnen die Sinnreiche, Kunstliche Auffschneidung.... Frankfurt: 1654. V. 70

SCHMIDT, ERICH F.
Time-Relations of Prehistoric Pottery Types in Southern Arizona. New York: 1928. V. 73

SCHMIDT, F. A.
Petrefacten-Buch. Stuttgart: 1846. V. 72
Petrefactenbuch Oder Allgemeine und Besondere Vertinerunskunde.... Stuttgart: 1855. V. 68

SCHMIDT, J. E.
Narcotics Lingo and Lore. Springfield: 1959. V. 72

SCHMIDT, RUDOLPH
Pain - Its Causation and Diagnostic Significance in Internal Diseases. London: 1908. V. 68

SCHMIDT PAULI, EDGAR VON
We Indians. New York: 1931. V. 69

SCHMIT, MINNA MOSCHEROSCH
Four Hundred Outstanding Women of the World and Costumology of Their Time. Chicago: 1933. V. 70

SCHMITT, M.
The Cattle Drives of David Skirk, from Texas to the Idaho Mines 1871 and 1873. Portland: 1956. V. 70

SCHMITT, MARTIN F.
The Cattle Drives of David Shirk, From Texas to the Idaho Mines, 1871 and 1873. Portland: 1956. V. 71
Fighting Indians of the West. New York: 1948. V. 69
General George Crook: His Autobiography. Norman: 1946. V. 73

SCHMITT, W. L.
The Marine Decapod Crustacea of California. Lochem: 1972. V. 73

SCHMITZ, CARL A.
Oceanic Art: Myth, Man and Image in the South Seas. New York: 1969. V. 73

SCHMITZ, H.
Encyclopedia of Furniture: an Outline History.... New York: 1963. V. 69

SCHNABEL, ERNST
Anne Frank: A Portrait in Courage. New York: 1958. V. 70

SCHNACKENBERG, GJERTRUD
The Lamplit Answer. New York: 1985. V. 69
Portraits and Elegies. New York: 1982. V. 69

SCHNEIDER, A.
A Text-Book of General Lichenology.... Binghamton: 1897. V. 72

SCHNEIDER, G.
The Book of Choice Ferns.... London and New York: 1892. V. 72

SCHNEIR, JACQUES
Sculpture in Modern America. Berkeley: 1948. V. 69; 72

SCHNITZER, EDWARD
Emin Pasha in Central Africa: Being a Collection of His Letters and Journals. London: 1888. V. 68

SCHNITZLER, ARTHUR
Casanova's Homecoming. London: 1922. V. 68
Rhapsody: a Dream Novel. New York: 1927. V. 71

SCHNORR VON CAROLSFELD, JULIUS
The New Testament in Eighty Pictures. Philadelphia: 1885. V. 69

SCHODDE, R.
Nocturnal Birds of Australia. Melbourne: 1980. V. 73

SCHOENBERG, WILFRED P.
Jesuit Mission Presses in the Pacific Northwest: a History and Bibliography of Imprints 1876-1899. Champoeg: 1957. V. 73

SCHOENBERGER, DALE T.
The Gunfighters. 1971. V. 69

SCHOENDOERFFER, PIERRE
Farewell to the King. New York: 1970. V. 68

SCHOENER, A.
Harlem On My Mind: Cultural Capital of Black America: 1900-1968. New York: 1968. V. 72

SCHOEPF, JOHANN DAVID
Reise Durch Einige der Mittlern und Sudlichen Vereinigten Nordamerikanischen Staaten Nach Ost-Florida und den Bahama-Insein Unternommen in den Jahren 1783 and 1784. Erlangen: 1788. V. 68; 71; 73

SCHOEPFLIN, JOHANN DANIEL
Vindiciae Typographicae. Argentorati: 1760. V. 71

SCHOFIELD, G. PEABODY
The Ups and Downs of the Royal Calpe Hunt. 1912. V. 68

SCHOFIELD, JOHN M.
Forty-Six Years in The Army. New York: 1897. V. 72

SCHOFIELD, LILY
Billy Ruddylox: an Ancient British Boy. New York. V. 70

SCHOLDER, FRITZ
Fritz Scholder - Paintings and Monotypes. Altadena: 1988. V. 70
Major Indian Paintings 1967-1977. Santa Fe: 1977. V. 69
Scholder/Indians. Flagstaff: 1972. V. 72

SCHOLES, PERCY A.
The Great Dr. (Charles) Burney, His Life, His Travels, His Work, His Family, His Friends. 1948. V. 73

SCHOMBURG, R. H.
Fishes of British Guiana. Volume I. Edinburgh: 1841. V. 69

SCHONFELDER, I.
Wild Flowers of the Mediterranean. Norwalk: 1990. V. 68

THE SCHOOL of Arts; or, Fountain of Knowledge. London: 1819. V. 69

SCHOOLCRAFT, HENRY ROWE
Archives of Aboriginal Knowledge...The History, Antiquities, Language.... Philadelphia: 1860. V. 70
Narrative of an Expedition through the Upper Mississippi to Itasca Lake.... New York: 1834. V. 73
Notes on the Iroquois. New York: 1846. V. 70
Summary Narrative of an Exploratory Expedition to the Sources of the Mississippi River in 1820.... Philadelphia: 1855. V. 70

THE SCHOOLMISTRESS, or Instructive and Entertaining Conversations Between a Teacher and Her Scholars. Dublin: 1824. V. 71

SCHOONOVER, CORTLANDT
Frank Schoonover: Illustrator of the North American Frontier. New York: 1976. V. 69; 73

SCHOONOVER, J. J.
The Life and Times - General John A. Sutter. Sacramento: 1895. V. 70

SCHOOR, GENE
Sugar Ray Robinson, World's Greatest fighter - Pound for Pound. New York: 1951. V. 72

SCHOPENHAUER, ARTHUR
Essays from the Parerga and Paralipomena. London: 1951. V. 71

SCHOPFER, W. H.
Plants and Vitamins. Waltham: 1943. V. 68

SCHORER, MARK
The World We Imagine - Selected Essays. New York: 1968. V. 68

SCHOTT, FRANCOIS
Italy, In Its Original Glory, Ruine and Revival, Being an Exact Survey of the Whole Geography and History of that Famous Country. London: 1660. V. 70

SCHOTTUS, FRANCISCUS
Itinerari Italiae Rerumque Romanorum. Antwerp: 1600. V. 68; 70

SCHOWCROFT, RICHARD
Children of the Covenant. Boston: 1945. V. 69

SCHRADER, JUSTUS
Observations et Historiae Omnes & singulae e Guillelmi Haravei Libello de Generatione Animalium Excerptae & in Accurratissimum Ordinem Redatae. Amsterdam: 1674. V. 70

SCHRAM, F. R.
Crustacea. New York: 1986. V. 73
Crustacea. Oxford: 1986. V. 73
Crustaceans and the Biodiversity Crisis. Leiden: 1999. V. 73

SCHRAMM, CARL CHRISTIAN
Abhandlung der Porte-Chaises Oder Trage-Sanfften Durch menschen Oder Thiere, in Allen Vier Theilen der Welt.... Nurnberg: 1737. V. 68
Historisher Schauplatz in Welchem die Merwurdigsten Brucken aus Allen vier Theilen der Welt.... Leipzig: 1735. V. 72

SCHRANTZ, WARD L.
Jasper County, Missouri, in the Civil War. Carthage: 1923. V. 68

SCHREIBER, CHARLOTTE
Lady Charlotte Schreiber's Journals. London: 1911. V. 72

SCHREIBER, MARIN H.
Last of a Breed- Portraits of Working Cowboys. Austin: 1982. V. 71

SCHREINER, CHARLES
A Pictorial History of the Texas Rangers. New York: 1928. V. 73
A Pictorial History of the Texas Rangers. Mountain Home: 1969. V. 69

SCHREINER, OLIVE
Dream Life and Real Life. A Little African Story. London: 1893. V. 71
Dreams. East Aurora: 1901. V. 71
The Story of an African Farm. London: 1889. V. 68; 70
The Story of an African Farm. Boston: 1893. V. 73
The Story of an African Farm. Westerham, Kent: 1961. V. 72
Trooper Peter Halket of Mashonaland. Boston: 1897. V. 69
Trooper Peter Halket of Mashonaland. London: 1897. V. 71

SCHREUDERS, PIET
Paperbacks, U. S. A. San Diego: 1981. V. 71

SCHRIER, A. M.
Behavior of Nonhuman Primates. New York: 1971. V. 72

SCHRODER, JOHN
Catalogue of Books and Manuscripts by Rupert Brooke, Edward Marsh and Christopher Hassall. Cambridge: 1970. V. 68; 69
Collecting Rupert Brooke. Cambridge: 1992. V. 70

SCHRODINGER, ERWIN
Space-Time Structure. Cambridge: 1950. V. 69

SCHROEDER VAN DER KOLK, J. L. C.
On the Minute Structure and Functions of the Spinal Cord and Medulla Oblongata, and on the Proximate Cause and Rational Treatment of Epilepsy. London. V. 71

SCHUBERT, GOTTHILF HEINRICH VON
Palatina. Stuttgart: 1868. V. 71

SCHUBERT, H.
Modern Theatres: Architecture, Stage Design, Lighting. New York: 1971. V. 68; 69; 72

SCHUCHERT, CHARLES
Biographical Memoir of Othniel Charles Marsh 1831-1899 In National Academy of Sciences of The United States of America Biographical Memoirs Volume XX - First Memoir. Washington, DC: 1939. V. 72

SCHUCHHARDT, C.
Schliemann's Excavations: an Archaeological and Historical Study. London: 1891. V. 70

SCHUH, R. T.
True Bugs of the World (Hemiptera Heteroptera).... Ithaca: 1995. V. 72

SCHULBE, ERNEST
Advanced Piping and Modelling. London: 1906. V. 68
Cake Decoration. London: 1905. V. 68

SCHULBERG, BUDD
The Harder They Fall. New York: 1947. V. 68; 69; 71; 72
Love, Action, Laughter. New York: 1990. V. 68
Waterfront. New York: 1955. V. 71
Waterfront. London: 1956. V. 68; 70
What Makes Sammy Run?. New York: 1941. V. 68

SCHULBERG, SONYA
They Cried a Little. New York: 1937. V. 71

SCHULIAN, D. M.
A Catalogue of Incunbula and Manuscripts in the Army Medica Library. New York: 1948. V. 68; 71

SCHULLER, GUNTHER
Early Jazz: Its Roots and Musical Development. New York: 1968. V. 73

SCHULTHESS, EMIL
Soviet Union. New York: 1971. V. 68

SCHULTZ, CHRISTIAN
Travels on an Inland Voyage Through the States of New York, Pennsylvania, Virginia, Ohio, Kentucky and Tennessee and through the Territories of Indiana. New York: 1810. V. 70; 72; 73

SCHULTZ, CHRISTOPH
Kurze Fragen Ueber die Christiche Glaubens-Lehre...Den Christlichen Glaubens-Schulern. Philadelphia: 1784. V. 73

SCHULTZ, JAMES W.
An Indian Winter or With the Indians in the Rockies. Boston: 1913. V. 68; 73

SCHULTZ, JOY
The West Still Lives - a Book Based on the Painings and Sculpture of Joe Ruiz Grandee. Dallas: 1970. V. 68; 73

SCHULTZ, L. P.
Fishes of the Marshall and Marianas Islands. Washington: 1953-1966. V. 70; 73

SCHULTZE, CARL EMIL
The Adventures of Foxy Grandpa. New York: 1900. V. 71

SCHULZ, ALBERT
An Essay on the Influence of Welsh Tradition upon the Literature of Germany, France and Scandinavia . . . Llandovery: 1841. V. 71
The Lay of the Last Minstrel. Edinburgh: 1854. V. 71

SCHULZ, BRUNO
The Collected Works of Bruno Schulz. London: 1998. V. 72

SCHULZ, CHARLES M.
Charlie Brown's All-Stars. Cleveland: 1966. V. 70
It's the Great Pumpkin Charlie Brown. Cleveland/New York: 1967. V. 72
Snoopy and the Red Baron. New York: 1966. V. 68; 71

SCHULZ, E. D.
Texas Wild Flowers. Chicago: 1928. V. 68

SCHULZ, J.
Venetian Painted Ceilings of the Renaissance. Berkeley: 1968. V. 69; 72

SCHULZ, PHILLIP STEPHEN
America the Beautiful Cookbook. 1990. V. 69

SCHUMACHER, F., & CO.
A Collection of Wall Coverings, Companion Fabrics and Borders. 1959. V. 68

SCHUMACHER'S Taliesin Line of Decorative Fabrics and Wallpaper Designed by Frank Lloyd Wright. Chicago: 1955. V. 68

SCHUMACHER'S Taliesin Line of Decorative Wallpapers. 1950. V. 68

SCHUMANN Album of Children's Pieces for Piano. London: 1913. V. 69

SCHUMANN, ELKA
Bread and Puppet: the Dream of the Dirty Woman. Newark: 1980. V. 69; 73

SCHURIG, MARTIN
Syllepsilogia Historico-Medica hoc est Conceptionis Mulierbris Consideratio Physico-medico-Forensis Qua Ejusdem Locus Organa Materia.... Dresden & Leipzig: 1731. V. 69

SCHURMAN, ANNA MARIA VAN
Dissertatio de Ingenii Muliebris ad Doctrinam & Meliores Litteras Aptitudine. Leiden: 1641. V. 72

SCHUSTER, CLAUD
Peaks and Pleasant Pastures. Oxford: 1911. V. 69

SCHUSTER, M. LINCOLN
Eyes on the World - a Photographic Record of History in the Making. New York: 1935. V. 68

SCHUSTER, R. M.
The Hepaticae and Anthocerotae of North America.... New York: 1969. V. 68

SCHUSTER, THOMAS E.
Printed Kate Greenaway. A Catalogue Raisonne. London: 1986. V. 69

SCHUTZ, JOHN A.
Thomas Pownall British Defender of American Liberty: a Study of Anglo American Relations in the Eighteenth Century. Glendale: 1951. V. 70; 72; 73

SCHUYLER, GEORGE
Slaves Today: A Story of Liberia. New York: 1931. V. 72

SCHUYLER, JAMES
Alfred & Guinevere. New York: 1958. V. 69
The Morning of the Poem. New York: 1980. V. 69

SCHWAB, JOHN CHRISTOPHER
The Confederate States of America 1861-1865. New York: 1901. V. 70

SCHWABACHER, E. K.
Arshille Gorky. New York: 1957. V. 69; 72

SCHWANTES, CARLOS A.
Railroad Signatures Across the Pacific Northwest. Seattle: 1993. V. 70

SCHWARTZ, DELMORE
Genesis. Book One. New York: 1943. V. 68
In Dreams Begin Responsibilities. 1938. V. 70
Shenandoah. Norfolk: 1941. V. 68
The World is a Wedding. 1948. V. 73
The World is a Wedding. Norfolk: 1948. V. 71

SCHWARTZ, HARRY W.
This Book Collected Racket: a Few Notes on the Abuses of Book Collecting. Chicago: 1937. V. 71

SCHWARTZ, J. H.
Orang-utan Biology. New York: 1988. V. 72

SCHWARTZ, JACOB
1100 Obscure Points: the Bibliographies of 25 English and 21 American Authors. 1931. V. 69

SCHWARTZ, JOHN BURNHAM
Reservation Road. New York: 1998. V. 72

SCHWARTZMAN, GREGORY
Phenomenon of Local Tissue Reactivity and Its Immunological, Pathological and Clinical Significance. New York: 1938. V. 68

SCHWARZENNEGER, ARNOLD
Arnold: the Education of a Body Builder. New York: 1977. V. 69; 71

SCHWATKA, FREDERICK
In the Land of the Cave and Cliff Dwellers. New York: 1893. V. 73

SCHWECHTEN, F. W.
Der Dom zu Meissen.... Berlin: 1823-1826. V. 70; 72

SCHWEIGER, WERNER
Wiener Werkstatte: Design in Vienna 1903-1932. New York: 1984. V. 72

SCHWEINFURTH, C.
Orchids of Peru. Chicago: 1958-1961. V. 73

SCHWEITZER, ALBERT
Albert Schweitzer. An Anthology. New York/Boston: 1947. V. 69; 71

SCHWENKE, FREDERICK
Designs for Decorative Furniture and Modern Chamber Arrangement.... London: 1882. V. 68

SCHWERDT, C. F. G. R.
Hunting, Hawking and Shooting. 1985. V. 69; 70; 71; 72; 73

SCHWERNER, ARMAND
Redspel/Eleven American Indian Adaptations. Mt. Horeb: 1974. V. 73

SCHWIEBERT, E.
Nymphs.... New York: 1973. V. 73

SCIASCIA, LEONARDO
The Council of Egypt. London: 1966. V. 69

LA SCIENCE du Salut, Renfermee Dans Ces Deux Paroles. Rouen: 1701. V. 69

THE SCIENCE-Fictional Sherlock Holmes. Denver: 1960. V. 72

SCIENTIFIC Past and Present.... Kyoto: 192-. V. 73

SCIESZKA, JOH
Math Curse. New York: 1995. V. 73

SCLATER, PHILIP LUTLEY
Argentine Ornithology, a Descriptive Catalogue of the Birds of the Argentine Republic.... London: 1888-1889. V. 73
Catalogue of a Collection of American Birds. London: 1862. V. 70; 73
A Monograph of the Jacamars and Puff-Birds; or Families Galbulidae and Bucconidae. London: 1879-1882. V. 73

SCLATER, W. L.
The Mammals of South Africa. 1900-1901. V. 73
The Mammals of South Africa. London: 1900-1901. V. 69

SCLICH, W.
Schlich's Manual of Forestry. London: 1906. V. 68

SCOGGAN, H. J.
The Flora of Canada. Ottawa: 1978-1979. V. 70

SCOGGINS, C. E.
John Quixote. Indianapolis: 1929. V. 71

SCOPES, JOHN T.
The Worlds Most Famous Court Trial - Tennessee Evolution. Cincinnati: 1925. V. 70

SCORESBY, WILLIAM
An Account of the Arctic Regions with a History and Description of the Northern Whale Fishery. Edinburgh: 1820. V. 73
The Arctic Regions and the Northern Whale Fishery. London: 1850. V. 68
Journal of a Voyage to the Northern Whale-Fishery.... Edinburgh;: 1823. V. 73
The Northern Whale-Fishery. London: 1840. V. 68
The Story of Dr. Scoresby the Arctic Navigator. London: 1886. V. 68

SCOT, THOMAS
The Highwaies of God and the King. London i.e. Holland: 1623. V. 73

SCOTT, A. M.
New and Interesting Desmids from the Southeastern States. Helsinki: 1957. V. 72

SCOTT, ALEXANDER JOHN
On the Academical Study of Vernacular Literature; an Inaugural Lecture Delivered in University College, London November 25, 1848. London: 1849. V. 73

SCOTT, CHARLES A.
My Unknown Friend. London: 1883. V. 70

SCOTT, CLEMENT WILLIAM
Round About the Islands; or Sunny Spots Near Home. London: 1874. V. 73

SCOTT, DANIEL
The Stricklands of Sizergh Castle. Kendal: 1908. V. 70

SCOTT, DAVID
The Engineer and Machinist's Assistant.... Glasgow: 1844-1847. V. 70
The Engineer and Machinist's Assistant.... Glasgow: 1847. V. 71
The Engineer and Machinist's Assistant.... Glasgow: 1849. V. 71

SCOTT, DOUG
Big Wall Climbing. New York: 1981. V. 69
The Shishapangma Expedition. Seattle: 1984. V. 69

SCOTT, DUNCAN CAMPBELL
The Makers of Canada. Toronto: 1912. V. 73

SCOTT, ERNEST
Australian Discovery by Sea. London: 1929. V. 69; 71

SCOTT, EVELYN
These Foolish Things. New York: 1929. V. 70
The Wave. New York: 1929. V. 68; 71

SCOTT, F. R.
Poems of French Canada. Burnaby: 1977. V. 68

SCOTT, FLORENCE JOHNSON
Royal Land Grants North of the Rio Grande 1777-1821. 1969. V. 69

SCOTT, G. C.
Fishing in American Waters. New York: 1869. V. 73

SCOTT, G. FIRTH
The Romance of Polar Exploration. London: 1907. V. 69; 71

SCOTT, GEORGE RYLEY
The History of Cockfighting. London: 1955. V. 69
Such Outlaws as Jesse James - a Cavalcade of American Desperado Gunmen. London: 1945. V. 68

SCOTT, GEORGE W.
The Black Hill Story. Fort Collins: 1953. V. 72

SCOTT, HUGH STOWEL
The Phantom Future. London: 1888. V. 73

SCOTT, J.
Piranesi. London: 1975. V. 69; 72

SCOTT, J. D.
Forests of the Night. 1959. V. 72

SCOTT, J. F.
The Scientific Work of Rene Descartes (1596-1650). London: 1952. V. 72

SCOTT, J. IRVING E.
Negro Students and Their Colleges. Boston: 1949:. V. 72

SCOTT, J. M.
Gino Watkins. London: 1935. V. 69
Sea-Wyf. New York: 1956. V. 72

SCOTT, J. S.
An Introduction to the Sea Fishes of Malaya. Kuala Lumpur: 1959. V. 73

SCOTT, JANE LAURA
'Round the World We Sail. Minneapolis: 1939. V. 71

SCOTT, JOANNA
The Closest Possible Union. New York: 1988. V. 71; 72
Fading, My Parmachene Belle. New York: 1987. V. 71; 72

SCOTT, JOB
Journal Of The Life And Travels Of Job Scott. Dublin: 1798. V. 72
Journal of The Life and Travels of Job Scott. Warrington: 1798. V. 72

SCOTT, JOHN
The House of Mourning, a Poem: with Some Smaller Pieces. London: 1817. V. 68; 72
Partisan Life with Colonel John S. Mosby. New York: 1867. V. 69; 70

SCOTT, JONATHAN
Tales, Anecdotes and Letters. Shrewsbury: 1800. V. 70

SCOTT, JOSEPH
The Art of Preserving the Loss of the Teeth, Familiarly Explained.... London: 1833. V. 68

SCOTT, JULIA H. KINNEY
Prize Tale. The Sacrifice, a Clergyman's Story. Hudson: 1837. V. 73

SCOTT, KELLY W.
Lariats and Chevrons or Corporal Jack Wilson, US LA RR. Guthrie: 1905. V. 68

SCOTT, MARY HURLBURT
The Oregon Trail through Wyoming. 1958. V. 68
The Oregon Trail through Wyoming. Aurora: 1958. V. 70

SCOTT, MARY MONICA MAXWELL
Abbotsford, the Personal Relics and Antiquarian Treasures of Sir Walter Scott. London: 1893. V. 70

SCOTT, MICHAEL
Tom Cringle's Log. 1833. V. 72
Tom Cringle's Log. London: 1833. V. 70

SCOTT, OLIVE RAY
Alice au pays des merveilles. Paris: 1937. V. 73

SCOTT, PATRICK GREIG
The Early Editions of Arthur Hugh Clough. New York and London: 1977. V. 72

SCOTT, PAUL
After the Funeral. London: 1979. V. 70
The Birds of Paradise. London: 1962. V. 71
The Corrida at San Feliu. London: 1964. V. 71
The Day of the Scorpion. London: 1968. V. 68
A Division of the Spoils. London: 1975. V. 68
The Jewel in the Crown. 1966. V. 68
Johnnie Sahib. 1952. V. 68
Johnnie Sahib. London: 1952. V. 70
Six Days in Marapore. Garden City: 1953. V. 71
Staying On. London: 1977. V. 68
The Towers of Silence. London: 1971. V. 68

SCOTT, PETER
Portrait Drawings. London: 1949. V. 72
Wild Chorus. 1939. V. 71
Wild Geese And Eskimos. A Journal Of The Perry River Expedition of 1949. London: 1951. V. 72

SCOTT, R. T. M.
The Nameless Ones. New York: 1947. V. 68

SCOTT, R. W.
The Alpine Flora of the Rocky Mountains. Salt Lake City: 1995. V. 68

SCOTT, ROBERT
A Regular Series of Chronology, from the Creation of the World to the Year 5813, Ending with the Autumnal Equinox A.D. 1810. Poughkeepsie: 1810. V. 73

SCOTT, ROBERT FALCON
The Voyage of the Discovery. London: 1905. V. 71
The Voyage of the Discovery. New York: 1905. V. 68
The Voyage of the Discovery. New York: 1969. V. 68

SCOTT, SAMUEL
A Diary of The Religious Exercises and Experiences of Samuel Scott. London: 1809. V. 72

SCOTT, SAMUEL H.
The Silver Ship. London: 1926. V. 71

SCOTT, SEPTIMUS E.
Bunny: a Visit to Bourneville. Bourneville: 1930. V. 69

SCOTT, SUTHERLAND
Blood in their Ink: the March of the Modern Mystery Novel. London: 1953. V. 69

SCOTT, SUTTON SELWYN
Southbooke. Columbus: 1880. V. 70

SCOTT, THOMAS
Robert Earle of Essex His Ghost Sent from Elizian: to the Nobility, Gentry and Communaltie of England. (and) A Postscript, or a Second Part of Robert Earle of Essex.... 1624. V. 73

SCOTT, W. B.
Freshwater Fishes of Canada. Ottawa: 1973. V. 70
The Mammalian Fauna of the White River Oligocene. Philadelphia: 1937-1941. V. 72

SCOTT, WALTER
The Abbot. Edinburgh: 1820. V. 68; 69; 71; 72; 73
Anne of Geierstein; or the Maiden of the Mist. Edinburgh: 1829. V. 68

SCOTT, WALTER continued
Ballads and Lyrical Pieces. Edinburgh: 1806. V. 70; 72
The Border Antiquities of England and Scotland. London: 1814-1817. V. 69; 70
Border Antiquities of England and Scotland. London: 1889. V. 72
The Centenary Garland: Being Pictorial Illustrations of The Novels of Sir Walter Scott, In Their Order of Publication. By George Cruickshank, And Other Artists Of Eminence. Edinburgh: 1871. V. 72
Chronicles of the Canongate. Edinburgh: 1827. V. 69; 71
Chronicles of the Canongate. Second Series. Edinburgh: 1828. V. 71
Demonology and Witchcraft. London: 1850. V. 72
An Essay of the Nature and Actions of the Subterranean...Invisible People. Edinburgh: 1815. V. 70
Familiar Letters of Sir Walter Scott. 1894. V. 68
The Field of Waterloo. Edinburgh: 1815. V. 70
The Fortunes of Nigel. Edinburgh: 1822. V. 68; 70; 72
Guy Mannering; or the Astrologer. Edinburgh: 1815. V. 73
Halidon Hill. Philadelphia: 1822. V. 70
Harold the Dauntless; a Poem, in Six Cantos. Edinburgh: 1817. V. 70
Ivanhoe. Edinburgh: 1820. V. 68; 73
Ivanhoe. New York: 1940. V. 69
Kenilworth; a Romance. Edinburgh: 1821. V. 68
The Lady of the Lake. Edinburgh: 1810. V. 70
The Lady of the Lake. Edinburgh: 1870. V. 70
The Lay of the Last Minstrel. London: 1805. V. 70
The Lay of the Last Minstrel. London: 1808. V. 68
The Lay Of The Last Minstrel. London: 1810. V. 72
The Lay of the Last Minstrel. Edinburgh: 1854. V. 71
Letter on Landscape Illustrations. 1832. V. 70
Letters On Demonology and Witchcraft. London: 1830. V. 70
Marmion. Edinburgh: 1808. V. 69; 70
Marmion. Edinburgh: 1811. V. 71
The Minstrelsy of the Scottish Border. Kelso: 1802. V. 70
The Monastery. Edinburgh: 1820. V. 72
Peveril of the Peak. Edinburgh: 1822. V. 68; 72
Quentin Durward, by the Author of Waverley Peveril of the Peak. Edinburgh: 1823. V. 68
Redgauntlet. Edinburgh: 1824. V. 68
Rokeby. Edinburgh: 1813. V. 70
Some Unpublished Letters of Walter Scott From The Collection In the Brotherton Library. Oxford: 1932. V. 72
Tales of a Grandfather Being Stories taken from Scottish History. . . Second Series. Edinburgh: 1829. V. 71
Tales of a Grandfather (History of Scotland). Edinburgh: 1842. V. 71
Tales of the Crusaders. Edinburgh: 1825. V. 68; 72
Trial of Duncan Terig Alias Clerk and Alexander Bane MacDonald, for the Murder of Arthur Davis. Edinburgh: 1831. V. 70
The Vision of Don Roderick. Edinburgh: 1811. V. 70
Waverley. Edinburgh: 1814. V. 70
Waverley Novels. Edinburgh: 1814-1832. V. 70
Waverley Novels. New York: 1828. V. 68
Waverley Novels. Edinburgh and London: 1829. V. 70
Waverley Novels. Edinburgh: 1829-1833. V. 73
The Waverley Novels. London: 1876. V. 70; 71
The Waverley Novels. Edinburgh: 1891-1892. V. 73
The Waverley Novels. 1904. V. 68
Waverley Novels. (with) Poetical Works. Edinburgh: 1848-1849. V. 68
Woodstock; or, the Cavalier. Edinburgh: 1826. V. 68; 72

SCOTT, WALTER SIDNEY
The Athenians. London: 1943. V. 71
The Athenians. Waltham St. Lawrence: 1943. V. 71
The Athenians. Waltham St. Lawrence: 1943-1944. V. 71
Harriet & Mary. London: 1944. V. 71
Harriet & Mary. Waltham St. Lawrence: 1944. V. 68; 71
Shelley at Oxford. The early correspondence of P. B. Shelley with his friend T. J. Hogg together with letters of Mary Shelley and T. L. Peacock and a hitherto unpublished prose fragment by Shelley. London: 1944. V. 71

SCOTT, WILLIAM
An Essay of Drapery or the Complete Citizen. Trading Justly, Pleasingly, Profitably. London: 1635. V. 69; 72
The House Book; or Family Chronicle of Useful Knowledge and Cottage Physician.... London: 1826. V. 72
Lessons in Elocution; or Miscellaneous Pieces in Prose and Verse. Edinburgh: 1779. V. 69
Picturesque Scenery in the County of Sussex, Sketched from Nature, Drawn on Stone.... London: 1821. V. 70

SCOTT, WILLIAM BELL
Antiquarian Gleanings in the North of England Being Examples of Antique Furniture, Plate, Church Decorations, Objects of Historical Interest etc. London. V. 70; 72
Gems of Modern Belgian Art.... London: 1872. V. 68
Gems of Modern French Art.... London: 1871. V. 68
Gems of Modern German Art. London: 1873. V. 68
Hades; or, the Transit; and the Progress of Mind. Two Poems. London: 1838. V. 72
Ornamental Designs for Silver and Gold Work, Die-sinkers, Enamellers, Modellers, Engravers &c. Edinburgh: 1871. V. 71
Poems. London: 1854. V. 72
A Poet's Harvest Home: Being One Hundred Short Poems. London: 1882. V. 72
A Poet's Harvest Home: Being One Hundred Short Poems with an Aftermath of Twenty-one Short Poems. London: 1893. V. 72
William Blake. Etchings from His Works. London: 1878. V. 69
The Year of the World: a Philosophical Poem on "Redemption from the Fall". Edinburgh: 1846. V. 72

SCOTT, WILLIAM BERRYMAN
A History of Land Mammals in the Western Hemisphere. New York: 1913. V. 73

SCOTT, WILLIAM F.
The Story of a Cavalry Regiment: the Career of the Fourth Iowa Veteran Volunteers. New York: 1893. V. 71

SCOTT, WINFIELD
Memoirs of Lieut.-General Scott, LL.D. New York: 1864. V. 70

SCOTT-GILES, C. W.
The Whimsey Family. London: 1977. V. 72; 73

SCOTTO, FRANCESCO
Itinerario d'Italia...in Questa Nuova Edizione.... Roma: 1737. V. 73

SCOVILL, EDWARD TRACY
In the Department of the Ancachs and Other Papers. Cleveland: 1909. V. 73

SCRIBNER, CHARLES
A Descriptive Catalogue of Original American Books.... New York: 1854. V. 73

SCRIMGEOUR, J. B.
Towards the Prevention of Fetal Malformation. Edinburgh: 1978. V. 68

SCRIPPS INSTITUTION OF OCEANOGRAPHY
Contributions (University of California, San Diego). La Jolla: 1959-1975. V. 73

SCRIPPS, JAMES E.
Five Months Abroad, or, the Observations and Experiences of an Editor in Europe. Detroit: 1882. V. 70

SCRIPTURAL Epitaphs. London: 1847. V. 69

THE SCRIPTURE Doctrine of Predestination, Election and Reprobation. Carmarthen: 1807. V. 68

SCRIPTURE Illustrations. London. V. 71

SCROPE, GEORGE POULETT
The Geology and Extinct Volancos of Central France. London: 1858. V. 70; 72

SCROPE, RICHARD
A Letter to --- ---, Esq. Occasioned by a Late Misrepresentation of the Circumstances of a Prosecution Commenced A.D. 1763.... Salisbury: 1773. V. 68; 72

SCROPE, W.
The Art of Deer Stalking. 1838. V. 70
The Art of Deer Stalking. 1847. V. 73
The Art of Deer Stalking. London: 1897. V. 71
Days and Nights Salmon Fishing in the Tweed. 1843. V. 73

SCRUTINIES. By Various Writers. London: 1928. V. 72

SCRUTON, WILLIAM
Birthplace of Charlotte Bronte. Leeds: 1884. V. 70; 73
Thornton and the Brontes. Bradford: 1898. V. 70

SCUDDER, S. H.
The Oldest Known Insect-Larva, Mormolucoides, Articulatus, From the Connecticut River Rocks. Boston: 1886. V. 72

SCUDGELL, SARAH
The Life of Richard Turpin, a Notorious Highwayman.... 1802. V. 71

SCULL, E. MARSHALL
Hunting in the Arctic and Alaska. Philadelphia: 1914. V. 69

SCULLY, MICHAEL
This is Texas: a Photographic Tour of the Greatest State. Austin: 1936. V. 68

SCULLY, REGINALD W.
Flora of County Kerry. 1916. V. 71

SCULLY STEEL & IRON CO.
Stock List, September and October 1899. Chicago: 1899. V. 68

SCULLY, VINCENT
American Architecture and Urbanism. London: 1969. V. 68; 69
American Architecture and Urbanism. New York: 1969. V. 72
Pueblo: Mountain, Village, Dance. New York: 1975. V. 69; 72
The Shingle Style: Architectural Theory and Design from Richardson to the Origins of Wright. New Haven: 1965. V. 68; 69; 72

SCULPTURA-Historico-Technica: or the History and Art of Ingraving. London: 1747. V. 70

SCULPTURE in Ceramics by Miro and Artigas. December 1956. New York: 1956. V. 69

SCULTETUS, JOHANN
Armamentarium Chirurgicum Renovatum & Auctum Triginta.... Amsterdam: 1669-1672. V. 70; 73
Armamentarium Chirurgicum XLIII. Venice. V. 70

SEABY, ALAN
British Ponies Running Wild and Ridden. London: 1936. V. 68

SEACOLE, MARY
Wonderful Adventures of Mrs. Seacole in Many Lands. London: 1857. V. 68

SEAGER, H. W.
Natural History in Shakespeare's Time.... London: 1896. V. 68; 70; 71

SEAGO, EDWARD
Tideline. London: 1948. V. 71; 72
With the Allied Armies in Italy. London: 1945. V. 71

SEAL and Salmon Fisheries and General Resources of Alaska. Washington: 1898. V. 70; 73

SEALE, DORIS
Blood Salt. Little Rock: 1989. V. 69

SEALY, GEORGE
An Address to the Public, Relative to a Late Trial, at Salisbury Assizes, in March 1774, on a Curious Information, the King at the Suit of Wm. Buckler, Esq. London: 1774. V. 71

SEAMAN, F.
Diterpenes of Flowering Plants. New York: 1990. V. 72

SEARCH the Scriptures; or a Reference to the Awful, Striking and Impressive Events of the Present Moment.... Sheffield: 1806. V. 68

SEARE, NICHOLAS
1339 or So. New York: 1975. V. 68

SEARIGHT, THOMAS B.
The Old Pike. A History of the National Road with Incidents, Accidents and Anecdotes Thereon. Uniontown: 1894. V. 70

SEARLE, MARK
Turn-Pikes and Toll Bars. London: 1930. V. 72

SEARS, A. T.
Chicago, Rock Island and Pacific Railway. Chicago: 1883. V. 69

SEARS, GEORGE WASHINGTON
Woodcraft by Nessmuk. New York: 1888. V. 68

SEARS, JOHN EDWARD
The Contractors', Merchants' and Estate Managers' Compendium and Catalogue. 20th Annual Issue. London: 1906. V. 68

SEARS, LOUIS MARTIN
John Slidell. Durham: 1925. V. 69; 70

SEARS, M.
Progress in Oceanography. Volume 4. Oxford: 1967. V. 73

SEARS, ROBERT
The Family Instructor, or Digest of General Knowledge. New York: 1860. V. 71

SEARS, W. H.
Notes From A Cowboy's Diary. Lawrence, KS. V. 71

SEATON, BENJAMIN M.
The Bugle Softly Blows. Waco: 1965. V. 69

SEAVER, EDWIN
The Company. New York: 1930. V. 71

SEAWELL, MARY WRIGHT
Our Father's Care. Richmond: 1864. V. 70

SEBALD, W. G.
Austerlitz. London: 2001. V. 71; 72
The Emigrants. London: 1996. V. 71
The Rings of Saturn. London: 1998. V. 72
The Rings of Saturn. New York: 1998. V. 72
Vertigo. London: 1999. V. 72

SEBASTIANUS, AUGUSTUS
De Literarum, Vocum, et Accentuum Haebraicorum Natura. Marburg: 1532. V. 73

SEBOLD, ALICE
The Lovely Bones. Boston: 2002. V. 73

SEBRIGHT, JOHN SAUNDERS
Observations Upon Hawking, Describing the Mode of Breaking and Managing the Several Kinds of Hawks Used in Falconry. London: 1826. V. 70

SECCOMBE, MAJOR
Funny Pictures. London: 1880. V. 72

A SECOND Holiday for John Gilpin; or a Voyage to Vauxhall; Where, though he had better Luck than before, he was far from being concerned. London: 1808. V. 71

A SECOND Letter from Wiltshire to the Monitor, on the Vindication of His Constitutional Principles. London: 1759. V. 73

SECRETAN, E.
Catalogue of the Celebrated Collection of Paintings. Paris: 1889. V. 72

SECRETS of the Dark Chamber - The Art of the American Daguerreotye. Washington: 1995. V. 70

SECUNDUS, JOANNES NICOLAI
Kisses. London: 1778. V. 71; 72
Kisses. London: 1790. V. 72

SEDBERGH School and Its Chapel. Leeds: 1895. V. 71

SEDDON, JOHN POLLARD
Memoir and Letters of the Late Thomas Seddon. London: 1858. V. 73

SEDELMAYR, JACOBO
Jacobo Sedelmayr: Missionary, Frontiersman, Explorer in Arizona and Sonora. 1955. V. 70; 72

SEDGEFIELD, W. J.
The Place-Names of Cumberland and Westmorland. Manchester: 1915. V. 71

SEDGWICK, ADAM
A Discourse on the Studies of the University. Cambridge: 1834. V. 68; 70; 71; 72
A Discourse on the Studies of the University. Cambridge: 1835. V. 73
A Memorial by the Trustees of Cowgill Chapel.... Cambridge: 1868. V. 68; 71
On the Classification and Nomenclature of the Lower Palaeozoic Rocks of England and Wales; on the Lower Palaeozoic Rocks.... 1852. V. 68

SEDGWICK, ANNE DOUGLAS
Philippa. Boston: 1930. V. 71
The Third Window. Boston: 1920. V. 70

SEDGWICK, CATHERINE MARIA
Hope Leslie; or Early Times in the Massachusetts. New York: 1862. V. 70
Letters from Abroad to Kindred at home. London: 1841. V. 71; 72
Live and Let Live; or Domestic Service. New York: 1837. V. 68
The Poor Rich Man and the Rich Poor Man. New York: 1836. V. 70

SEDGWICK, JANE MINOT
Songs from the Greek. London: 1896. V. 73

SEDGWICK, THEODORE
Thoughts on the Annexation of Texas to the United States. New York: 1844. V. 70
Thoughts on the Proposed Annexation of Texas. New York: 1844. V. 68

SEDGWICK, W. T., MRS.
Acoma, the Sky City, a Study in Pueblo Indian History and Civlization. Cambridge: 1926. V. 69

SEDLEY, CHARLES
Antony and Cleopatra. London: 1696. V. 71
The Miscellaneous Works of the Honourable Charles Sedley. London: 1702. V. 69
The Works in Prose and Verse. London: 1722. V. 68; 69; 72; 73

SEDZIWOJ, MICHAEL
A Philosophical Account of nature in General, and of the Generation of the Three Principles of Nature.... London: 1722. V. 73

SEEBOHM, C.
Private Landscapes, Creating Form, Vistas and Mystery in the Garden. New York: 1989. V. 68

SEEBOHM, HENRY
The Birds of Siberia. London: 1901. V. 73
The Geographical Distribution of the Family Charadriidae.... London: 1887-1888. V. 73
History of British Birds. 1896. V. 71
A Monograph of the Turdidae, or family of Thrushes. London: 1898-1902. V. 70; 72; 73
Siberia in Europe: a Visit to the Valley of the Petchora in North- East Russia.... London: 1880. V. 71

SEEING Colorado, a Book of Information 1911. V. 68

SEELEY, CHARLES
Pioneer Days in the Arkansas Valley in Southern Colorado and History of Bent's Fort. Denver: 1932. V. 73

SEELEY, JOHN ROBERT
Life and Times of Stein, or Germany and Prussia in the Napoleonic Age. 1878. V. 71

SEELEY, MABEL
The Crying Sisters. New York: 1939. V. 68
Eleven Came Back. New York: 1943. V. 69; 70; 72
The Listening House. 1938. V. 73
The Whispering Cup. Garden City: 1940. V. 70; 72

SEELEY, ROBERT BENTON
Memoirs of the Life and Writings of Michael Thomas Sadler. London: 1842. V. 71

SEFERIS, GEORGE
Collected Poems 1924-1955. London: 1969. V. 68
George Seferis to Henry Miller. Two Letters from Greece. New Haven & Athens: 1990. V. 73
The King of Asine and Other Poems. London: 1948. V. 68; 71
Three Secret Poems. Cambridge: 1969. V. 71

SEGA, JAMES
What is True Civilization, or Means to Suppress the Practice of Duelling, to Prevent, or to Punish, Crimes and To Abolish the Punishment of Death. Boston: 1830. V. 68

SEGAL, ERICH
Love Story. New York: 1970. V. 69; 71

SEGAL, GLUCKEL
The Life of Gluckel of Hamlin 1646-1724. New York: 1963. V. 72

SEGAL, LORE
Other People's Houses. London: 1965. V. 68

SEGALAT, ROGER JEAN
Album Eluard. Paris: 1968. V. 71

SEGAR, E. C.
Popeye: the Fighting Sailor Man. Racine: 1937. V. 73
Popeye with the Hag of the Seven Seas. Chicago: 1935. V. 72

SEGAR, WILLIAM
Original Institutions of the Princely Orders of Collars. Edinburgh: 1823. V. 72

SEGATO, GIROLAMO
Atlante Monumentale Del Basso e Dell' Alto Egitto.... Firenze: 1838. V. 69

SEGHERS, ANNA
The Revolt of the Fishermen. New York: 1930. V. 70

SEGUR, G. C.
Directions for the Use of Family Medicines. New York: 1841. V. 68

SEGUR, PHILIPPE, COMTE DE
Histoire de Napoleon et de la Grande Armie Pendant l'Annee 1812.... Bruxelles: 1825. V. 70
History of Russia and of Peter the Great. London: 1829. V. 70
Napoleon. Paris: 1913. V. 70

SEGUR, SOPHIE, COMTESSE DE
Old French Fairy Tales. Philadelphia: 1920. V. 73

SEIDEL BUGGY COMPANY
(Catalogue). 1915?. V. 68

SEIDEL, L.
Songs of Glory: the Romanesque Facades of Aquitaine. Chicago: 1981. V. 72

SEIDLER, TOR
The Dulcimer Boy. London: 1981. V. 69

SEIDLITZ, WOLDEMAR VON
History of Japanese Colour-Prints. London: 1910. V. 70

SEIGNOBOSC, FRANCOISE
Biquette - The White Goat. New York: 1953. V. 71
Franchette and Jeannot - a Little Story with Pictures. New York: 1937. V. 73
Noel for Jeanne Marie. New York: 1953. V. 73
The Things I Like. New York: 1960. V. 73
What Do You Want to Be?. New York: 1957. V. 73

SEITZ, A.
Macrolepidoptera of the World. Volume 13. African Butterflies. Stuttgart: 1925. V. 69

SEITZ, DON C.
Braxton Bragg, General of the Confederacy. Columbia: 1924. V. 70
The Buccaneers. New York: 1912. V. 70

SEITZ, JOHANN CHRISTIAN
Annus Tertius Saecularis Inventae Artis Typographicae. Harlemi: 1741. V. 71

SEIXAS, JAMES
Manual Hebrew Grammar for the Use of Beginners. Andover: 1833. V. 68; 71

SELBY, ANGELICA
In the Sunlight. London: 1892. V. 68

SELBY, CHARLES
Barnaby Rudge. London: 1841. V. 70

SELBY, HUBERT
Last Exit to Brooklyn. New York: 1964. V. 68; 71
Last Exit to Brooklyn. London: 1966. V. 71

SELBY, PRIDEAUX JOHN
A History of British Forest-Trees.... London: 1842. V. 70
Illustrations of British Ornithology. 1825-1833. V. 72; 73
Ornithology. Volume V. Gallinaceous Birds. Part III. Pigeons. Edinburgh: 1835. V. 68

SELDEN, JOHN
Marmora Arundelliana, sive Saxa Graece Incisa.... London: 1628. V. 68
Table-Talk: Being the Discourses...or His Sence of Various Matters of Weight and High Consequence.... 1689. V. 72
Titles of Honor. London: 1672. V. 71; 72

SELDES, GILBERT
The Future of Drinking. Boston: 1930. V. 72

SELDES, MARIAN
The Lovely Lion. 1967. V. 72

A SELECTION of Fac-Similes of Water-colour Drawings from the Works of the Most Distinguished British Artists. London: 1825. V. 69

SELECTION of Sixty Subjects from the Works of the Best Ancient & Modern Sculptors. London. V. 72

SELECTIONS of Hymns and Spiritual Songs...as Usually Sung at Camp Meetings.... New York: 1831. V. 73

SELER, EDUARD
Commentarios al codice Borgia. Mexico: 1963. V. 72

SELF Portrait: Book People Picture Themselves. New York: 1976. V. 72

SELF, WILL
Cock and Bull. London: 1992. V. 69
Cock and Bull. New York: 1992. V. 68
Cock and Bull. New York: 1993. V. 69
The Quantity Theory of Insanity. New York: 1995. V. 72
The Sweet Smell of Psychosis. London: 1996. V. 68
The Sweet Smell of Psychosis. New York: 1999. V. 72
Tough, Tough Toys for Tough, Tough Boys. New York: 1999. V. 72

SELFRIDGE, THOMAS O.
A Correct Statement of the Whole Preliminary Controversy Between Tho. O. Selfridge and Benj. Austin.... Charlestown: 1807. V. 71

SELIGMAN, B. Z.
Pagan Tribes of the Nilotic Sudan. London: 1932. V. 69

SELIGMANN, C. G.
The Veddas. 1911. V. 69

SELIGMANN, HERBERT J.
D. H. Lawrence. An American Interpretation. New York: 1924. V. 72

SELKIRK, JAMES
Recollections of Ceylon, After a Residence of Nearly 13 Years. London: 1844. V. 70

SELKIRK, THOMAS DOUGLAS, 5TH EARL OF
Observations on the Present State of the Highlands of Scotland, with a View of the Causes and Consequences of Emigration. Edinburgh: 1805. V. 71
Observations on the Present State of the Highlands of Scotland, with a view of the causes and probable consequences of emigration. London: 1805. V. 71
A Sketch of the British Fur Trade in North America with Observations Relative to the North-West Company of Montreal. London: 1816. V. 71

SELL, HENRY BLACKMAN
Buffalo Bill and the Wild West. New York: 1955. V. 69

SELLER, ALVIN V.
Classics of the Bar. Baxley: 1924. V. 71

SELLERS, ALVIN V.
The Loeb-Leopold Case: with Excerpts from the Evidence of the Alienists and Including the Arguments in the Court by Counsel for the People and the Defense. Brunswick: 1926. V. 70

SELLERS, CHARLES COLEMAN
Benedict Arnold, the Proud Warrior. New York: 1930. V. 70

SELLON, EDWARD
The Ups and Downs Of Life. Miami Beach: 1987. V. 72

SELOUS, EDMUND
The Bird Watcher in the Shetlands, with some notes on seals - and digressions. London: 1905. V. 71

SELOUS, FREDERICK COURTENEY
African Nature Notes and Reminiscences. 1908. V. 72
African Nature Notes and Reminiscences. London: 1908. V. 69
Big Game Hunting and Angling. 1914. V. 73
A Hunter's Wanderings in Africa. 1907. V. 72
A Hunter's Wanderings in Africa. London: 1907. V. 69
A Hunter's Wanderings in Africa. 1925. V. 72; 73
Recent Hunting Trips in British North America. 1907. V. 69; 70; 72
Recent Hunting Trips in British North America. London: 1907. V. 69
Sport and Travel East and West. 1900. V. 69; 70
Sunshine and Storm in Rhodesia. 1896. V. 72

SELVON, SAMUEL
Turn Again Tiger. New York: 1959. V. 69

SELWYN, WILLIAM
An Abridgement of the Law of Nisi Prius. Philadelphia: 1807. V. 69

SELWYN-BROWN, ARTHUR
The Physician Throughout the Ages. New York: 1928. V. 72
The Physician Throughout the Ages. New York: 1938. V. 69

SELYE, HANS
Annual Report on Stress. 1951-1955/56. Montreal & New York: 1951-1956. V. 72
The Physiology and Pathology of Exposure to Stress. Montreal: 1950. V. 72

SEMMES, RAPHAEL
The Cruise of the Alabama and the Sumter. London: 1864. V. 70
Memoirs of Service Afloat During the War Between the States. Baltimore: 1869. V. 70; 72
My Adventures Afloat. London: 1869. V. 72
Service Afloat and Ashore During the Mexican War. Cincinnati: 1851. V. 68
Service Afloat, or, the Remarkable Career of the Confederate Cruisers Sumter and Alabama.... Baltimore: 1887. V. 69

SEMON, R.
In the Australian Bush, and on the Coast of the Coral Sea.... London: 1899. V. 68; 69; 72

SEMPLE, GEORGE
A Treatise on Building Under Water. Dublin: 1774. V. 72

SEMPLE, JAMES ALEXANDER
Representative Women of Colorado. Denver: 1911. V. 68; 72
Representative Women of Colorado. Denver: 1914. V. 70

SEMPLE, ROBERT B.
A History of the Rise and Progress of the Baptists in Virginia. Richmond: 1810. V. 72
A History of the Rise and Progress of the Baptists in Virginia. Richmond: 1894. V. 68

SENAC, JEAN BAPTISTE DE
Traite des Causes, des Accidens, et de la Cure de la Peste, avec un Recueil d'Obwervations, et un de'tail Circonstancie des Precautions.... Paris: 1744. V. 69

SENCERT, L.
Wounds of the Vessels. London: 1918. V. 68

SENDAK, MAURICE
Caldecott & Co., Notes on Books and Pictures. New York: 1988. V. 72; 73
In the Night Kitchen. New York: 1970. V. 72
Nutshell Library. New York: 1962. V. 71; 73
The Nutshell Library. London: 1964. V. 72
Outside Over There. London: 1981. V. 71; 72
Outside Over There. New York: 1981. V. 72
Pictures. New York: 1971. V. 72
The Sign on Rosie's Door. London: 1969. V. 72
Some Swell Pup or Are You Sure You Want a Dog?. New York: 1976. V. 71; 73
Very Far Away. Kingswood, Surrey: 1963. V. 72
Where the Wild Things Are. New York: 1963. V. 69; 73

SENDIVOGIUS, MICHAEL
A New Light of Alchymie: Taken Out of the Fountaine of Nature and Manual Experience. London: 1650. V. 72

SENECA, LUCIUS ANNAEUS
Opera, quae Exstant, Integris Iusti Lipsii, J. Fred. Gronovii & Selectis Variorum Commentariis Illustrata. Amstelodami: 1672. V. 72
Opera Quae Extant Omnia. Parisiis: 1587. V. 72
Philosophi Opera, Quae Exstant Omnia. Antwerp: 1605. V. 71
Seneca's Morals by Way of Abstract. London: 1764. V. 73
Tragoediae. Venice: 1517. V. 68; 70
Tragoediae, cum Notis Th. Farnabii. Amsterdam: 1633. V. 72

SENEFELDER, ALOIS
The Invention of Lithography. New York: 1911. V. 70

SENGER, J. V.
Final Construction Report, Woodrow Wilson Memorial Bridge. Washington: 1961. V. 73

SENGHOR, LEOPOLD SEDAR
Poems. New York: 1996. V. 71; 72

SENGUERDIUS, WOLFERDUS
Tractatus Physicus de Tarantula, in Quo Praeter ejus Descriptionem.. Lugdvni Bat: 1668. V. 72

SENIOR, NASSAU WILLIAM
Political Economy. London: 1858. V. 71

SENIOR, WILLIAM
Near and Far: an Angler's Sketches of Home Sport and Colonial Life. London: 1890. V. 68
Waterside Sketches. 1885. V. 68

SENN, EDWARD L.
Deadwood Dick and Calamity Jane. Deadwood: 1939. V. 68
Wild Bill Hickok Prince of Pistoleers a Tale of Facts and Not Fiction and Romance. Deadwood: 1939. V. 68

SENN, NICHOLAS
Principles of Surgery. Philadelphia: 1890. V. 68

SENNERT, DANIEL
Epitome Librorum de Febribus. Wittenberg: 1634. V. 69; 72
Practicae Medicinae Liber Primus (Secundus) Daniele Sennerto. 1654. V. 68; 73

SENNETT, A. R.
Across The Great Saint Bernard. London: 1904. V. 72

SENSING, THURMAN
Champ Ferguson. Confederate Guerilla. Nashville: 1942. V. 69

SEPTEM *Illustrium Virorum Poemata.* Amstelodaimi: 1672. V. 71

SERANELLA, BARBARA
No Human Involved. New York: 1997. V. 72

SERANNE, ANN
America Cooks. New York: 1967. V. 68

SEREDY, KATE
The White Stag. New York: 1937. V. 73

SERGE, VICTOR
Birth of Our Power - Naissance de Notre Force. London: 1968. V. 68

SERGEANT, ADELINE
In Vallombrosa; a Sequence. London: 1899. V. 68

SERGEANT, ELIZABETH SHEPLEY
Shadow Shapes, the Journal of a Wounded Woman. Boston: 1920. V. 68

SERGEANT, JANE
Missionary Lays; and Other Poems. London: 1848. V. 69

SERGEANT, JOHN
Of Devotion. London: 1678. V. 68; 72

SERGEANT, PHILIP W.
Little Jennings and Fighting Dick Talbot. 1913. V. 70

A SERIES of 38 Fine Woodcuts Illustrating the Life of Christ, Printed in the 19th Century, But Perhaps from Original 15th Century Blocks. Apparently London: 1818. V. 71

A SERIOUS Address to the Inhabitants of Bristol, On the Subject of the Multiplicity of Religious Distinctions.... Bristol;: 1820. V. 70

SERLING, ROBERT
Something's Alive on the Titanic. New York: 1990. V. 68

SERLING, ROD
Patterns: Four Television Plays with the Author's Personal Commentaries. New York: 1957. V. 70
Twilight Zone Revisited. New York: 1964. V. 73

A SERMON Preach'd at the Cathedral Church of York, September the 22nd, 1745. On the Occasion of the Present Rebellion in Scotland. 1745. V. 72

SERMONS by Artists. Waltham St. Lawrence: 1934. V. 71

SERMONS or Homilies Appointed to Be Read in Churches in the Time of Queen Elizabeth of Famous Memory. L: 1825. V. 70

SERMONS Preached in Boston on the Death of Abraham Lincoln...with Funeral Services at Washington. Boston: 1865. V. 68

SERRES DE LA TOUR, ALPHONSE
Londres et ses Environs ou Guide des Voyageurs. Paris: 1788. V. 71

SERVEN, JAMES
Colt Firearms: 1836-1954. Santa Ana: 1954. V. 71
Colt Firearms (from 1836). 1981. V. 70; 72; 73

SERVETUS, MICHAEL
A Translation of His Geographical, Medical and Astrological Writings.... Philadelphia: 1953. V. 68

SERVICE, ROBERT WILLIAM
Ballads of a Cheechako. Toronto: 1909. V. 71

SERVISS, GARRETT PUTMAN
Other Worlds. New York: 1901. V. 72

SETCHELL, W. A.
American Samoa. Washington: 1924. V. 68

SETH, RONALD
The Executioners: The Story of SMERSH. New York: 1968. V. 68

SETH, VIKRAM
An Equal Music. Leicester: 1999. V. 68; 71
An Equal Music. London: 1999. V. 68; 72
An Equal Music. New York: 1999. V. 72
From Heaven Lake. London: 1983. V. 71
The Golden Gate. New York: 1986. V. 68
Riot at Misri Mandi. London: 1996. V. 72

SETH-SMITH, DAVID
Jolly Families. 1950. V. 72
Parrakeets: a Handbook to the Imported Species. 1903. V. 70

SETON, ANYA
Dragonwyck. Boston: 1944. V. 71

SETON, BRUCE
The Pipes of War. Glasgow: 1920. V. 68

SETON, ERNEST THOMPSON
The Arctic Prairies. A Canoe Journey of 2000 Miles in Search of the Caribou.... Toronto: 1911. V. 73
Lives of Game Animals. Boston: 1953. V. 71
Lives of the Hunted.... New York: 1901. V. 70
Monarch the Big Bear of Tallac. London: 1905. V. 73
The Preacher of Cedar Mountain. Santa Fe: 1943. V. 68
Two Little Savages, Being the Adventures of Two Boys Who Lived as Learned. London: 1904. V. 68
Wild Animals at Home. New York: 1913. V. 68
Wild Animals Ways. Garden City & New York: 1917. V. 73

SETON, JULIA M.
The Pulse of the Pueblo, Personal Glimpses of Indian Life. Santa Fe: 1939. V. 69

SETON KARR, H. W.
My Sporting Holidays. 1904. V. 69; 70; 72; 73

THE SETT, or Decreet Arbitral of King James the 6th of Blessed Memory. Edinburgh: 1683. V. 73

SETTE OF ODD VOLUMES
The Year-Boke of the Sette of Odd Volumes. An Annual Record of the Transactions of the Sette: Fifty Eighth Year 1935-1936. London: 1938. V. 70

SETTLE, MARY LEE
All the Brave Promises. New York: 1966. V. 73
Blood Tie. Boston: 1977. V. 69; 71
Celebration. New York: 1986. V. 68; 71
Charley Bland. New York: 1989. V. 71
Fight Night on a Sweet Saturday. New York: 1964. V. 68; 73
The Killing Ground. New York: 1982. V. 73
The Kiss of Kin. New York: 1955. V. 73

SETTLE, MARY LEE continued
Know Nothing. New York: 1960. V. 68
Know Nothing. London: 1961. V. 71
The Love Eaters. New York: 1954. V. 73
O Beulah Land. London: 1956. V. 72

SETTLE, WILLIAM A.
Jesse James Was His Name or Fact and Fiction Concerning the Careers of the Notorious James Brothers of the West. Columbia;: 1966. V. 68

SETZLER, FRANK
Peachtree Mound and Village Site, Cherokee County North Carolina. Washington: 1941. V. 73

SEUPHOR, M.
Piet Mondrian, Life and Work. New York. V. 69; 72

SEUTONIUS TRANQUILLUS, GAIUS
XII Caesares Io. Baptistate Egnatii Veneti De Romanis Principibus. Lugduni: 1551. V. 72

SEVEN Poets at Bank Street. New York: 1975. V. 69

SEVENTEEN Steps to 221b. London: 1967. V. 71

SEVENTH Day Baptists in Europe and America. Plainfield: 1910. V. 69

76 A Cook Book. Des Moines: 1891. V. 68

SEVERANCE, EMILY A.
Journal Letters...Quaker City 1867. Cleveland: 1938. V. 70

SEVERIN, MARK F.
Making a Bookplate. London: 1949. V. 71

SEVERN, JAMES
Colt Firearms (from 1836). 1981. V. 69

SEVERN, JOHN PERCY
The Adventures of Ariston. London: 1830. V. 73

SEVERN, JOSEPH
From the Life: Joseph Severn to John Taylor 21 January 1825. New Rochelle: 1997. V. 73

SEVIGNE, MARIE DE RABUTIN-CHANTAL, MARQUISE DE
The Letters. Philadelphia: 1927. V. 68; 70

SEWALL, RICHARD
The Life of Emily Dickinson. New York: 1974. V. 73

SEWALL, THOMAS
An Examination of Phrenology in Two Lectures Delivered to the Students of the Columbian College. Boston: 1839. V. 68; 70; 71; 73

SEWALL, WILLIAM W.
Bill Sewall's Story of T.R. New York: 1919. V. 68

THE SEWANEE Review. Sewanee: 1958. V. 69

SEWARD, A. C.
Catalogue of the Mesozoic Plants in the Department of Geology, British Museum, Natural History. London: 1894-1904. V. 69
Mesozoic Plants from Afghanistan and Afghan Turkistan. Calcutta: 1912. V. 72
A Summer in Greenland. Cambridge: 1922. V. 69; 71

SEWARD, ANNA
Letters...Written Between the Years 1784 and 1807. Edinburgh: 1811. V. 69; 72
Memoirs of the Life of Dr. Darwin, Chiefly During His Residence in Lichfield, with Anecdotes of His Friends, and Criticisms of His Writings. 1804. V. 73
The Poetical Works of Anna Seward, with Extracts from her Literary Correspondence. Edinburgh: 1810. V. 69

SEWARD, JOHN
Observations on the Re-building of London Bridge; Demonstrating the Practicability of Executing the Work in Three Flat Elliptical Arches of Stone.... London: 1824. V. 73

SEWARD, WILLIAM H.
An Autobiography.... New York: 1891. V. 71
The Works. Boston: 1887-. V. 71

SEWEL, WILLIAM
The History of the Rise, Increase and Progress of the Christian People Called Quakers. London: 1795. V. 72

SEWELL, ANNA
Black Beauty. Boston: 1890. V. 68
Black Beauty. London: 1912. V. 69
Black Beauty. New York: 1952. V. 70

SEWELL, BROCARD
Like Black Swans: Some People and Themes. London: 1982. V. 71

SEWELL, ELIZABETH MISSING
Impressions of Rome, Florence and Turin. London: 1862. V. 70
Journal Of A Summer Tour, From Ostend, Through Germany, Switzerland, And Part Of The Tyrol, To Genoa. London: 1852. V. 72
Ursula, a Tale of Country Life. London: 1858. V. 73

SEWELL, WILLIAM
Hawkstone: A tale of and for England in 184-. London: 1847. V. 70; 71

SEWELL, WILLIAM G.
The Ordeal of Free Labor in the British West Indies. New York: 1862. V. 68

SEXTON, ANNE
All My Pretty Ones. Boston: 1962. V. 71
Live or Die. Boston: 1966. V. 69; 73
Love Poems. Boston: 1969. V. 69
Selected Poems. London: 1964. V. 71
Selected Poems of Anne Sexton. Boston: 1988. V. 72
To Bedlam and Part Way Back. Boston: 1960. V. 69; 70
Transformations. Boston: 1971. V. 69; 71

SEXTON, E.
Count Me Among the Living. New York: 1946. V. 69

SEXTON, GROVE F.
The Arizona Sheriff, The Studebaker Corp. 1925. V. 71

SEXTON, JOHN
Quiet Light. Boston: 1990. V. 68

SEXTON, R. W.
The Logic of Modern Architecture: Exteriors and Interiors of Modern American Buildings. New York: 1929. V. 69; 72

SEYBOLT, PAUL S.
A Catalogue of the First Editions of First Books in the Collection of Paul S. Seybolt. Boston: 1946. V. 73

SEYDELL, MILDRED
Secret Fathers. New York: 1930. V. 72

SEYMOUR, A. B.
Host Index of the Fungi of North America. Cambridge: 1929. V. 68

SEYMOUR, BEATRICE KEAN
But Not for Love. London: 1930. V. 69

SEYMOUR, CHARLES
How the World Votes: the Story of Democratic Development in Elections. Springfield: 1918. V. 71

SEYMOUR, E. S.
Sketches of Minnesota - The New England of the West with Incidents of Travel in that Territory During the Summer of 1849. New York: 1850. V. 68; 73

SEYMOUR, FANNIE E.
Benjamin Seymour in Russia, England and America 1787-1817. Plymouth: 1940. V. 71

SEYMOUR, R.
Humorous Sketches. 1878. V. 70

SEYMOUR, RICHARD
The Court Gamester. London: 1722. V. 69
The Court Gamester. London: 1728. V. 69

SEYMOUR, WILLIAM H.
The Story of Algiers, Now Fifth District of New Orleans. 1896. V. 68

SHAARA, JEFF
Gods and Generals. New York: 1996. V. 70
The Last Full Measure. New York: 1998. V. 68; 70

SHAARA, MICHAEL
For Love of the Game. New York: 1991. V. 71
The Killer Angels. New York: 1974. V. 68; 69; 72

SHACHTMAN, MAX
Sacco and Vanzetti. Labor's Martyrs. New York: 1927. V. 68

SHACKLEFORD, GEOFF
The Riveria Country Club - a Definitive History. Pacific Palisades: 1995. V. 73

SHACKLEFORD, OTIS M.
Lillian Simmons, or the Conflict of Sections. Kansas City: 1915. V. 70

SHACKLETON, ERNEST HENRY
Last Antarctic Expedition. 1920. V. 71

SHACOCHIS, BOB
The Next New World. New York: 1989. V. 73
Swimming in the Volcano. London: 1993. V. 68; 73
Swimming in the Volcano. New York: 1993. V. 71

SHADOWS - Second Series. London. V. 71

SHADWELL, JOHN LANCELOT
A System of Political Economy. London: 1877. V. 71

SHADWELL, THOMAS
The Complete Works. London: 1927. V. 69; 72
The Lancashire Witches and Tegu O Divelly the Irish Priest. London: 1691. V. 69

SHAFER, ROBERT
The Conquered Place. New York: 1954. V. 72

SHAFFER, A. WEBSTER
In the Matter of the Official Irregularities and Malpractice in the Fourth Collection District of North Carolina. Raleigh: 1879. V. 71

SHAFFER, ANTHONY
How Doth the Little Crocodile?. New York: 1957. V. 70
Sleuth. New York: 1970. V. 72; 73

SHAFFER, NEWTON MELMAN
Brief Essays on Orthopaedic Surgery Including a Consideration of Its Relation to General Surgery, Its Future Demand, and Its Operative as Well As Its Mechanical Aspects.... New York: 1898. V. 69

SHAFFER, PETER
Amadeus. London: 1980. V. 72
Equus. London: 1973. V. 71
Five Finger Exercise - a Play in Two Acts and Four Scenes. London: 1958. V. 71

SHAFTESBURY, ANTHONY ASHLEY COOPER, 1ST EARL OF
Some Memoirs; or, a Sober Essay for a Just Vindication of the Right Honourable the Earl of Shaftesbury. 1681. V. 71

SHAFTESBURY, ANTHONY ASHLEY COOPER, 3RD EARL OF
Characteristicks of Men, Manners, Opinion Times.... 1737-1738. V. 73
Characteristicks of Men, Manners, Opinions, Times &c. London: 1733. V. 69

SHAGAN, STEVE
Save the Tiger. New York: 1972. V. 68

SHAHN, BEN
An Alphabet of Creation. New York: 1954. V. 69; 71

SHAIRP, J. C.
Charles the Twelfth, a Prize Poem. Recited in the Theatre, Oxford, June VIII MDCCXLII. Oxford: 1842. V. 72

SHAIRP, JOHN CAMPBELL
Culture and Religion. New York: 1878. V. 68
Culture and Religion in Some of Their Relations. Edinburgh: 1870. V. 68

SHAKESPEAR, H.
The Wild Sports of India. 1860. V. 72

SHAKESPEARE
Illustrated by an Assemblage of Portraits and Views.... London: 1793. V. 71

SHAKESPEARE, NICHOLAS
The Dancer Upstairs. London: 1995. V. 73
The High Flyer. London: 1993. V. 71
Vision of Elena Silvas. London: 1989. V. 71

SHAKESPEARE
Pictures No. 2. London: Sep. 1890. V. 69

SHAKESPEARE, WILLIAM
As You Like It. London: 1930. V. 70; 71; 72; 73
A Collection of Poems. London: 1709. V. 73
Comedies, Histories and Tragedies.... London: 1632. V. 70
The Comedies. The Tragedies. The Histories and Poems. London: 1915. V. 73
The Complete Works of William Shakespeare. London: 1953. V. 68
Cymbeline. A Tragedy. London: 1734. V. 73
The Dramatic Works. Hartford: 1836. V. 73
The Dramatic Works. London: 1848. V. 73
The Dramatic Works. London: 1899. V. 72
The Family Shakespeare.... London: 1820. V. 73
Hamlet. Utrecht: 1915. V. 73
Hamlet, Prince of Denmark. London. V. 68
Hamlet, Prince of Denmark. Boston: 1794. V. 73
Hamlet, Prince of Denmark. London: 1922. V. 72
Hamlet, Prince of Denmark. Santa Fe: 1949. V. 72
The Handy Volume Shakespeare. London: 1897. V. 73
Julius Caesar. London: 1688. V. 68; 72
King Henry the Fifth. Or the Conquest of France by the English. London: 1723. V. 73
The History of King Lear: a Tragedy. London: 1729. V. 68
The Library Shakespeare. London. V. 73
The London Shakespeare. 1958. V. 68
Love's Labour's Lost. London: 1735. V. 68
Lucrece. 1915. V. 70
Lucrece. Hammersmith: 1915. V. 71
The Merry Wives of Windsor. London: 1910. V. 71
A Midsummer Night's Dream. London: 1908. V. 72
A Midsummer Night's Dream. London: 1914. V. 72
Midsummer Night's Dream. London: 1919. V. 71
A Midsummer Night's Dream. New York: 1977. V. 72
The Passionate Pilgrim. 1896. V. 68; 70
The Pictorial Edition of Works of Shakespeare. London: 1838-1843. V. 73
The Plays. London: 1765. V. 68
The Plays. London: 1803-1804. V. 70
The Plays. London: 1807. V. 73
The Plays. Boston: 1813. V. 68
The Plays. London: 1823. V. 70; 71; 72
The Plays. London: 1826. V. 68
A Pleasant Comedy Called Love's Labour Lost. The Vale Shakespeare. London: 1901. V. 71
Poems. London: 1825. V. 68; 73
Poems and Sonnets. Waltham St. Lawrence: 1960. V. 70; 71
Romeo and Juliet. London. V. 71
Scenes from the Winter's Tale. 1866. V. 72
Shakespeare's Sonnets. London: 1899. V. 68
Shakespeare's the Tragedie of Cymbeline. Printed from the Folio of 1623. 1923. V. 72
Songs and Sonnets of Shakespeare. London. V. 69
Songs from Shakespeare's Plays. Verona: 1974. V. 71
Songs of Shakespeare. London: 1865. V. 68
Sonnets. New York: 1909. V. 68
Sonnets. 1948. V. 73
The Sonnets. Los Angeles: 1974. V. 73
The Sonnets. London: 1982. V. 71
The Swan Shakespeare. A Player's Edition. London: 1930. V. 71
The Tempest. London: 1827. V. 68
The Tempest. London: 1860. V. 73
The Tempest. London: 1908. V. 68
The Tempest. New York and London: 1911. V. 68
The Tempest. Montagnola: 1924. V. 73
The Tempest. London: 1926. V. 68; 70
The Tempest. London: 1975. V. 70
La Tempte. Paris: 1920. V. 69
The Tragedie of Anthony and Cleopatra. 1912. V. 70
The Tragedie of Jvlivs Caesar. 1913. V. 70; 71
The Tragedie of King Lear. London: 1924. V. 70
The Tragedie of King Lear. London: 1927. V. 73
The Tragedie of King Lear. Bangor: 1986. V. 72
The Tragedy of Coriolanus. 1914. V. 70
Twelfth Night. London: 1908. V. 68; 72
Twenty-Five Sonnets of Shakespeare. Stratford-on-Avon: 1922. V. 71
Venus and Adonis. Paris: 1930. V. 68
Venus and Adonis. Rochester: 1931. V. 72; 73
The Winter's Tale. New York: 1922. V. 73
The Works. London: 1709. V. 73
The Works. London: 1842-1844. V. 70
The Works. Leipzig: 1868. V. 73
The Works. 1881. V. 68
The Works. 1895. V. 68
The Works. London: 1922. V. 71
The Works. London: 1929. V. 71

SHAKING
Hands with Immortality, Encomiums for Vincent Starrett. 1975. V. 73

SHALER, N. S.
A Comparison of the Features of the Earth and Moon. Washington: 1903. V. 71

SHALER, NATHANIEL SOUTHGATE
American Highways, a Popular Account of Their Conditions and of the Means by Which They May Be Bettered. New York: 1896. V. 73
The Autobiography. Boston and New York: 1909. V. 68; 72

SHAMES, LAURENCE
The Big Time. New York: 1986. V. 68; 71
Florida Straits. New York: 1992. V. 68; 69; 71; 72
Scavenger Reef. New York: 1994. V. 68
Tropical Depression. New York: 1996. V. 72

SHAND, A. I.
Shooting. 1902. V. 71

SHAND, ALEXANDER INNES
Against Time. London: 1870. V. 73

SHAND, P. MORTON
A Book of French Wines. London: 1963. V. 71

SHANE, LESLIE
The Greek Anthology. 1929. V. 71

SHANGE, NTOZAKE
For Colored Girls Who Have Considered Suicide/When the Rainbow is Enuf. San Lorenzo: 1975. V. 71
For Colored Girls Who Have Considered Suicide/When the Rainbow is Enuf. New York: 1977. V. 72
Nappy Edges. New York: 1978. V. 68; 72

SHANGHAI ZIONIST ASSOCIATION
Three Asiatic Powers Complete World Endorsement of the Jewish National Movement. Shanghai: 1919. V. 70

SHANKS & CO.
Manufacturers of Sanitary Appliances, Bath & Bath Fittings, Lavatories.... London: 1886. V. 68

SHANKS, EDWARD
The Dark Green Circle. Indianapolis: 1936. V. 70

SHANLY, CHARLES D.
The Monkey of Porto Bello. New York: 1867. V. 72
The Truant Chicken. New York: 1867. V. 73

SHANLY, WALTER
Report of Walter Shanly, Esquire on the Ottawa Survey. Submitted to the Legislative Assembly for their Information. Toronto: 1858. V. 73

SHANNON, C. HAZELWOOD
The Pageant 1896-97. London: 1896. V. 69; 71

SHANNON, CARL
Lady that's My Skull. New York: 1947. V. 70

SHANNON, MICHAEL OWEN
Modern Ireland, a Bibliography on Politics, Planning, Research and Development. 1981. V. 69; 73

SHANNON, MONICA
Dobry. New York: 1934. V. 72

SHAPIRO, DAVID
Jasper Johns: Drawings 1954-1984. New York: 1984. V. 73

SHAPIRO, KARL
The Alphabet. New Rochelle: 1988. V. 73
A Bibliography of Modern Prosody. Baltimore: 1948. V. 69
On Reading Keats in War Time. New Rochelle: 1986. V. 73
16 Poems. 1962. V. 68
Trial of a Poet and Other Poems. New York: 1947. V. 71

SHAPIRO, MICHAEL EDWARD
Frederic Remington. London: 1991. V. 72

SHAPLAND, H. P.
Practical Decoration of Furniture. London: 1927. V. 72

SHAPTER, THOMAS
The Climate of the South of Devon; and Its Influence Upon Health. London: 1842. V. 69

SHARKEY, TERENCE
Jack The Ripper: 100 Years Of Investigation. New York: 1992. V. 72

SHAROV, A. G.
Phylogeny of the Orthopteroidea. Jerusalem: 1971. V. 72

SHARP, A. J.
The Moss Flora of Mexico. Bronx: 1994. V. 72

SHARP, D.
20th Century Architecture: Visual History. New York: 1991. V. 69; 72

SHARP, E. A.
Lyra Celtica. 1932. V. 69

SHARP, EVELYN
The Child's Christmas. London: 1906. V. 69; 72

SHARP, GRANVILLE
A Declaration of the People's Natural Right to a Share in the Legislature, Which is the Fundamental Principle of the British Constitution of State. London: 1774. V. 68; 72
Remarks Concerning the Encroachments on the River Thames near Durham Yard. London: 1771. V. 69

SHARP, HENRY
The Gun Afield and Afloat. 1904. V. 70; 71

SHARP, JAMES
Descriptions of Some of the Utensils in Husbandry, Rolling Carriages, Cart Rollers and Divided Rollers for Land or Gardens.... London: 1780. V. 71; 73

SHARP, JOHN
A Sermon Preach'd at the Coronation of Queen Anne, in the Abby-Church of Westminster, April xxiii, MDCCI. London: 1702. V. 72

SHARP, MARGERY
Miss Bianca. Boston: 1962. V. 73
Miss Bianca in the Orient. Boston: 1970. V. 73
The Rescuers. London: 1959. V. 73
The Turret. Boston;: 1936. V. 70

SHARP, SAMUEL
A Critical Enquiry into the Present State of Surgery. London: 1754. V. 70; 73
Letters from Italy, Describing the Customs and Manners of that Country, in the Years 1765 and 1766. 1766. V. 73
Letters from Italy, Describing the Customs and Manners of that Country in the Years 1765 and 1766. 1767. V. 72
A Treatise on the Operations of Surgery, with a Description and Representation of the Instruments Used in Performing Them.... London: 1739. V. 68
A Treatise on the Operations of Surgery, with a Description and Representation of the Instruments used in Performing Them.... London: 1769. V. 68

SHARP, THOMAS
Poems. London: 1922. V. 72
The Rubric in the Common Prayer and the Canons of the Church of England, So Far as They Relate to the Parochial Clergy, Considered. London: 1753. V. 73

SHARP, WILLIAM
Earth's Voices, Transcripts from Nature Sopistra and Other Poems. London: 1884. V. 69
The Human Inheritance, The New Hope, Motherhood. London: 1882. V. 69; 72
The Life and Letters of Joseph Severn. London: 1892. V. 73
Life of Robert Browning. London: 1890. V. 68; 72
Romantic Ballads and Poems of Phantasy. London: 1888. V. 69
Where the Forest Murmurs: Nature Essays. London: 1906. V. 69

SHARPE, ALFRED
The Backbone of Africa. London: 1921. V. 72

SHARPE, CUTHBERT
Memorials of the Rebellion of 1569.... London: 1840. V. 72

SHARPE, EDMUND
The Seven Periods of English Architecture, Defined and Illustrated. London: 1851. V. 68

SHARPE, JAMES BIRCH
A Manual of Percussion and Ausculation. New York: 1832. V. 70; 73

SHARPE, JOHN
The Church, a Poem. London: 1797. V. 73

SHARPE, P. B.
Complete Guide To Handloading. 1942. V. 70; 72; 73
The Rifle in America. 1947. V. 69

SHARPE, REGINALD
London and the Kingdom. A History Derived Mainly from the Archives at Guildhall in the Custody of the Corporation of the City of Lonon. London: 1894-1895. V. 71; 73

SHARPE, RICHARD BOWDLER
An Analytical Index to the Works of the Late John Gould, F.R.S. London: 1893. V. 72; 73
A Handbook to the Birds of Great Britain. 1896-1897. V. 69

SHARPE, SAMUEL
The History of Egypt; from the Earliest Times Till the Conquest by the Arabs A.D. 640. London: 1852. V. 73

SHARPE, TOM
Indecent Exposure. London: 1973. V. 70; 73
Porterhouse Blue. London: 1974. V. 70; 73

SHARPHAM, EDWARD
Cupid's Whirligig: a Play. Waltham St. Lawrence: 1926. V. 71

SHARROCK, J. T. R.
Scarce Migrant Birds in Britain and Ireland. 1974. V. 69; 71

SHASTRI, MAHAMAHOPADHYAYA HARAPRASAD
A Descriptive Catalogue of Sanskrit Manuscripts in the Government Collection Under the Care of the Asiatic Society of Bengal. Volume II. Vedic Manuscripts. Calcutta: 1923. V. 73
A Descriptive Catalogue of Sanskrit Manuscripts in the Government Collection Under the Care of the Asiatic Society of Bengal. Volume III. Smrti Manuscripts. Calcutta: 1925. V. 73

SHATNER, WILLIAM
Star Trek Memories. 1993. V. 71
Star Trek Memories. New York: 1993. V. 73

SHATTUCK, GEORGE C.
The Peninsula of Yucatan: Medical, Biological, Meteorological and Sociological Studies. Washington: 1933. V. 68

SHATTUCK, GEORGE CHEYNE
Three Dissertations on Boylston Prize Questions for the Years 1806 and 1807. Boston: 1808. V. 70; 71

SHAVER, J. M.
Ferns of Tennessee.... Nashville: 1954. V. 68

SHAW, C. JAMES
North From Texas - Incidents in the Early Life of a Range Cowman in Texas, Dakota, Wyoming 1852-1883. Evanston: 1952. V. 69

SHAW, CHARLES
Heaven Knows Mr. Allison. New York: 1952. V. 68; 69; 71

SHAW, CHARLES G.
Nightlife: Vanity Fair's Intimate Guide to New York After Dark. New York: 1931. V. 73

SHAW, CLEMENT B.
The Footprints of Music: the Tangible and Visible in the Art, Treated in the Soratic Method. Lawrenceburg: 1896. V. 73

SHAW, D. A.
Eldorado, or, California as Seen by a Pioneer 1850-1900. Los Angeles: 1900. V. 68

SHAW, EDWARD
Civil Architecture; or a Complete Theoretical and Practical System of Building. Boston: 1834. V. 69
The Medical Remembrancer. London: 1837. V. 70

SHAW, EYRE
Records of the London Fire Engine Establishment. London: 1870. V. 71

SHAW, F. G.
The Science of Fly Fishing for Trout. 1925. V. 68

SHAW, FRED
Fred Shaw's American Diadem. New York: 1860. V. 68

SHAW, FREDERICK B.
One Hundred and Forty Years of Service in Peace and War - History of The Second Infantry United States Army. Detroit: 1930. V. 72

SHAW, G.
General Zoology or Systematic History. London: 1803-1804. V. 72

SHAW, G. C.
The Chinook Jargon and How to Use It. Seattle: 1909. V. 69

SHAW, GEORGE
Gems and Pearls. Leeds: 1870. V. 73
General Zoology or Systematic Natural History. Volume 4, Part I. Pisces. London: 1803. V. 73
General Zoology or Systematic Natural History. Volume 4, Parts I & 2, Volume 5 Parts 1 and 2. Pisces. London: 1803-1804. V. 73
The Naturalist's Miscellany. London: 1790. V. 68
A Select Cabinet of Natural History.... London: 1820. V. 69

SHAW, GEORGE BERNARD
Androcles and the Lion, Overrule, Pygmalion. London: 1916. V. 69; 71
The Apple Cart. 1930. V. 68
The Apple Cart. London: 1930. V. 71
Bernard Shaw and Mrs. Patrick Campbell: Their Correspondence. New York: 1952. V. 68
Bernard Shaw Through the Camera. London: 1948. V. 70
Buoyant Billions. London: 1949. V. 70
The Complete Plays. 1931. V. 68
The Complete Plays. London: 1934. V. 73
The Complete Works of.... 1930-1932. V. 69; 73
Cymbeline Reinfinished, a Variation. 1937. V. 68
The Devil's Disciple. London: 1908. V. 73
Dramatic Opinions and Essays. London: 1907. V. 68
Dramatic Opinions and Essays. New York: 1907. V. 68
Fabian Essays in Socialism. London: 1889. V. 68; 69
Fabianism and the Empire: a Manifesto by the Fabian Society. London: 1900. V. 70
Immaturity. London: 1931. V. 68; 71
The Intelligent Woman's Guide to Socialism and Capitalism. London: 1928. V. 72; 73
The Intelligent Woman's Guide to Socialism and Capitalism. New York: 1928. V. 68
Irish Nationalism and Labour Internationalism. London: 1920. V. 72
The Irrational Knot. 1905. V. 68
The Legal Eight Hours Question. A Public Debate. 1891. V. 69
Love Among the Artists. Chicago: 1900. V. 69
My Dear Dorothea. 1956. V. 69
On Going to Church. East Aurora: 1896. V. 70
A Plan of Campaign for Labor. London: 1894. V. 70
Prefaces. 1934. V. 68
Pygmalion and Candida. Avon: 1974. V. 69
The Quintessence of Ibsenism. London: 1891. V. 69
The Quintessence of Ibsenism. London: 1913. V. 73
Saint Joan. London: 1924. V. 73
Saint Joan. With Stage Settings and Sketches by C. Ricketts. London: 1904. V. 71
The Sanity of Art. 1908. V. 68
The Sanity of Art: an Exposure of the Current Nonsense About Artists Being Degenerate. London: 1908. V. 69
Selected Passages from the Works, Chosen by Charlotte F. Shaw. London: 1912. V. 73
Shaw Gives Himself Away, an Autobiographical Miscellany. Newtown: 1939. V. 73
Sixteen Self Sketches. London: 1949. V. 70
Socialism and Superior Brains. London: 1910. V. 70
Socialism. The Fabian Essays. Boston: 1894. V. 68
Statement of the Evidence in Chief of George Bernard Shaw Before the Joint Committee on Stage Plays. 1909. V. 69
Three New Plays. New York: 1936. V. 68
Three Plays. New York: 1934. V. 68
Translations and Tomfooleries. London: 1926. V. 71; 73
An Unfinished Novel. London: 1958. V. 72
An Unsocial Socialist. London: 1887. V. 70; 71
An Unsocial Socialist. New York: 1900. V. 69
Widowers' Houses. London: 1893. V. 68; 69
The Works. London: 1930-1938. V. 72

SHAW, HENRY
A Booke of Sundry Draughtes. London: 1848. V. 69
Details of Elizabethan Architecture. London: 1834. V. 72
Details of Elizabethan Architecture. London: 1839. V. 73
Dresses and Decorations of the Middle Ages. London: 1843. V. 69
A Handbook of the Art of Illumination, As Practised During the Middle Ages. London: 1866. V. 72
History of U.S. Marine Corps Opertions in World War II. Nashville: 1994. V. 73

SHAW, HUGH ROBINSON
The Egyptian Enigma. 1881. V. 71

SHAW, IRWIN
The Assassin. New York: 1946. V. 73
The Gentle People. New York: 1939. V. 71
God Was Here but He Left Early. New York: 1973. V. 68; 73
Rich Man, Poor Man. New York: 1970. V. 68
Short Stories: Five Decades. New York: 1978. V. 73
Whispers in Bedlam. London: 1972. V. 69
The Young Lions. New York: 1948. V. 68; 69; 71

SHAW, JAMES
American Resources: Life, Labour and Travels. London: 1867. V. 72

SHAW, JAMES C.
Pioneering in Texas and Wyoming- Incidents in the Life of James C. Shaw. Orin, WY. V. 71

SHAW, JONATHAN
Recollections of Liverpool Cotton Brokers by One of Themselves. 1869. V. 71

SHAW, JOSEPH
Danger Ahead. 1932. V. 73
Derelict. New York: 1930. V. 73
The Hard-Boiled Omnibus. 1946. V. 69; 73
Parish Law; or, a Guide to Justices of the Peace, Ministers, Churchwardens, and All Others Concern'd in Parish Business.... London: 1755. V. 69
The Practical Justice of Peace; or, a Treatise Shewing the Present Power and Authority of that Officer. London: 1751. V. 69

SHAW, JOSEPH T.
The Hard Boiled Omnibus. 1946. V. 68

SHAW, LUELLA
True History of Some of the Pioneers of Colorado. Hotchkiss: 1909. V. 68; 73

SHAW, PETER
The Dispensatory of the Royal College of Physicians in Edinburgh. London: 1727. V. 73
A New Practice of Physic: Wherein the Various Diseases Incident to the Human Body are Orderly Described, their Causes Assign'd.... London: 1728. V. 73

SHAW, ROBERT
Visits To High Tartary, Yarkand, and Kashgar (Formerly Chinese Tartary) And Return Journey Over the Karakoram Pass. London: 1871. V. 72

SHAW, S.
A Tour to the West of England in 1788. London: 1789. V. 70; 72

SHAW, SAMUEL
Immanuel: or a Discovery of True Religion. (with) Voice of One Crying in a Wilderness. Boston: 1744-1746. V. 69

SHAW, SIMEON
History of Staffordshire Potteries; and the Rise and Progress of the Manufacture of Pottery and Porcelain.... Hanley: 1829. V. 69; 72
Nature Displayed in the Heavens, and on the Earth. 1823. V. 69

SHAW, THOMAS
A Victorian in Europe. Geelong: 1883. V. 73

SHAW, THOMAS EDWARD
More Letters from T. E. Shaw to Bruce Rogers. 1936. V. 73

SHAW, VIRGINIA WOODSON VENABLE
O, Call Back Yesterday. Detroit: 1936-1937. V. 68

SHAWN, WALLACE
Aunt Dan and Lemon: a Play. New York: 1985. V. 69
Marie and Bruce. New York: 1980. V. 69

SHAWVER, LONA
Chuck Wagon Windies. San Antonio: 1950. V. 69
Chuck Wagon Windles And The Range Poems of Walt Cousins. San Antonio: 1934. V. 71

SHAY, FRANK
A Treasury of Plays for Women. Boston: 1922. V. 70

SHAY, JONATHAN
Achilles in Vietnam. New York: 1984. V. 68

SHAYLOR, JOSEPH
The Pleasures of Literature and the Solace of Books. London: 1898. V. 69

SHEA, JOHN GILMARY
The Fallen Brave; a Biographical Memorial of the American Officers Who Have Given Their Lives for the Preservation of the Union. New York: 1861. V. 68
Perils of the Ocean and Wilderness, or Narratives of Shipwreck and Indian Captivity, Gleaned from Early Missionary Annals. Boston: 1886. V. 68

SHEARAR, JAMES
Prinkle and His Friends. London: 1877. V. 72

SHEARER, JOHN
I Wish I Had an Afro. New York: 1970. V. 72

SHEARER, JOHN E.
Fact and Fiction in the Story of Bannockburn. Stirling: 1909. V. 71

SHEARER, R. S.
Illustrated Tourists' Guide to Stirling, Cambuskenneth Abbey, Bannockburn, Bridge of Allan . . . Stirling: 1869. V. 71

SHEARING, JOSEPH
Aunt Beardie. New York: 1940. V. 69

SHEARMAN, WILLIAM
Observations Illustrative of the History and Treatment of Chronic Debility, the Prolific Source of Indigestion, Spasmodic Diseases and Various Nervous Affections. London: 1824. V. 73

SHEARN, W. B.
The Practical Fruiterer and Florist.... London: 1934. V. 70; 71

SHEARS, PHILIP J.
The Story of the Border Regiment 1939-1945. New York: 1948. V. 71

SHEATH BROTHERS
India Rubber, Gutta Percha and General Manufacturers & Patentees. General Catalogue. 1912. V. 71

SHEBBEARE, JOHN
Letters on the English Nation.... London: 1756. V. 73
Matrimony; a Novel. London: 1766. V. 69

SHEEHAN, NEIL
After the War Was Over. New York: 1992. V. 72
A Bright Shining Lie. John Paul Vann an American in Vietnam. New York: 1988. V. 69

SHEFFIELD and Rotherham Up-to-Date. 1897. V. 71

SHEFFIELD, F.
How I Killed the Tiger. 1902. V. 69

SHEFFIELD, JOHN BAKER HOLROYD, 1ST EARL OF
A Letter on the Corn Laws, and on the Means of Obviating the Mischiefs and Distress, Which are Rapidly Increasing. London: 1815. V. 71
Observations of the Manufactures, Trade and Present State of Ireland. London: 1785. V. 70
Observations on the Impolicy, Abuses and False Interpretation of the Poor Laws; and on the Reports of the Two Houses of Parliament. 1818. V. 72; 73
Remarks on the Deficiency of Grain, Occasioned by the Bad Harvest of 1799. London: 1800. V. 70

SHEFFY, LESTER F.
The Francklyn Land and Cattle Company, A Panhandle Enterprise, 1882- 1957. San Antonio: 1963. V. 71
Timothy Dwight Hobart, 1855-1935. Texas: 1950. V. 71

SHEILDS, DAVID
Heroes. New York: 1984. V. 71

SHELBY, GERTRUDE M.
Po' Buckra. New York: 1930. V. 73

SHELDON, CHARLES
The Wilderness of Denali, Explorations of a Hunter Naturalist in Northern Alaska. New York: 1930. V. 69
The Wilderness of the North Pacific Coast Islands.... New York: 1912. V. 69
The Wilderness of the Upper Yukon.... New York: 1911. V. 69; 70; 72; 73

SHELDON, FREDERICK M.
The Practical Colorist: a Pathfinder for the Printer. Burlington: 1900. V. 68

SHELDON, HAROLD P.
Tranquility Revisited. Lyon: 1989. V. 70; 72

SHELDON, J. M. A.
Concretions from the Champlain Clays of the Connecticut Valley. Boston: 1900. V. 72

SHELDON, SIDNEY
Windmills of the Gods. New York: 1987. V. 73

SHELDON, WILLIAM
Aerial Navigation and the Patent Laws. Boston: 1850. V. 68

SHELLABARGER, SAMUEL
Captain from Castile. Boston: 1945. V. 71
Prince of Foxes. Boston: 1947. V. 71

SHELLER, ROSCOE
Bandit to Lawman. Washington: 1966. V. 69

SHELLEY, MARY WOLLSTONECRAFT GODWIN
Frankenstein; or the Modern Prometheus. London: 1823. V. 73
Frankenstein; or the Modern Prometheus. Philadelphia: 1833. V. 70
Frankenstein; or the Modern Prometheus. New York: 1934. V. 69
Frankenstein; or the Modern Prometheus. West Hatfield: 1983. V. 68; 71
The Last Man. London: 1826. V. 73
Lodore. Brussels: 1835. V. 69
Lodore. London: 1835. V. 73
Rambles in Germany and Italy in 1840, 1842 and 1843. London: 1844. V. 71

SHELLEY, PERCY BYSSHE
Adonais; an Elegy on the Death of John Keats.... Pisa: 1821. V. 72
Adonais XLII. New Rochelle: 1990. V. 73
Alastor; or the Spirit of Solitude and Other Poems. London: 1816. V. 72
The Cenci. London: 1819. V. 72
The Cenci. London: 1821. V. 73
The Complete Poetical Works. Boston: 1901. V. 70
Essays, Letters from Abroad, Translations and Fragments. London: 1840. V. 73
Laon and Cythna; or, the Revolution of the Golden City, a Vision of the 19th century in the Stanza of Spenser. London: 1818. V. 72
The Masque of Anarchy. London: 1832. V. 69; 72
Ozymandias. New Rochelle: 1992. V. 73
Poems. London: 1901-1902. V. 68
Poetical Pieces, by the Late Percy Bysshe Shelley.... London: 1823. V. 72
Poetical Works. London: 1839. V. 73
The Poetical Works. Boston: 1855. V. 70
Poetical Works. London: 1967. V. 71
Posthumous Poems. London: 1824. V. 68; 72
Prometheus Unbound. London: 1820. V. 70; 71; 72; 73
Queen Mab. London: 1813. V. 72
Queen Mab. London: 1821. V. 71
Relics of Shelley. London: 1862. V. 73
The Revolt of Islam: a Poem in Twelve Cantos. London: 1818. V. 72
Rosalind and Helen. London: 1819. V. 70; 72; 73
Select Letters of Percy Bysshe Shelley. London: 1882. V. 73
Shelley's Lost Letters to Harriet. London: 1930. V. 72
The Works.... 1834. V. 73
Zastrozzi. Waltham St. Lawrence: 1955. V. 71

SHELLS and *Their Inmates.* London: 1841. V. 70

SHELLY, GEORGE F.
Early History of American Fork with Some History of A Latter Day. American Fork City: 1945. V. 68; 73

SHELTON, A. C.
Newfoundland Our North Door Neighbor. New York: 1943. V. 72

SHELTON, LOLA
Charles Marion Russell. New York: 1962. V. 69

SHENSTONE, WILLIAM
Men and Manners. Waltham St. Lawrence: 1927. V. 71
The Works in Verse and Prose. Edinburgh: 1768. V. 71
The Works in Verse and Prose. Dublin: 1777. V. 73
The Works, in Verse and Prose, of William Shenstone. London: 1777. V. 69

SHEPARD, ALAN
Moon Shot. The Inside Story of Man's Race to the Moon. Atlanta: 1994. V. 71

SHEPARD, ERNEST
Ben and Brock. London: 1965. V. 72
Betsy and Joe. London: 1966. V. 72
Drawn from Life. London: 1961. V. 70; 72

SHEPARD, ERNEST H.
Fun and Fantasy - a Book of Drawings. London: 1927. V. 73

SHEPARD, JIM
Flights. New York: 1983. V. 73

SHEPARD, LESLIE
John Pitts Ballad Printer of Seven Dials, London, 1765-1844. London: 1969. V. 72

SHEPARD, LUCIUS
Green Eyes. New York: 1984. V. 73
Green Eyes. London: 1986. V. 73

SHEPARD, PAUL
Nature and Madness. San Francisco: 1982. V. 72

SHEPARD, SAM
Five Plays. Chicago. Icarus's Mother. Red Cross Fourteen Hundred Thousand Melodrama Play. Cleveland: 1967. V. 69
Motel Chronicles. New York: 1982. V. 71
The Unseen Hand and Other Plays. Indianapolis: 1972. V. 71

SHEPHARD, ESTHER
Paul Bunyan. New York: 1924. V. 69

SHEPHEARD, P.
Modern Gardens. London: 1953. V. 69; 71

SHEPHEARD, WILLIAM
Of Corporations, Fraternities and Guilds. London: 1659. V. 70

SHEPHERD, F. J.
Sir William Osler Memorial Number. Montreal: 1920. V. 72

SHEPHERD, HENRY ELLIOT
The Life of Robert Edward Lee. New York and Washington: 1906. V. 69; 70

SHEPHERD, J. C.
Garden and Design. London: 1927. V. 69; 71; 73
Italian Gardens of the Renaissance. London: 1953. V. 70

SHEPHERD, JEAN
In God We Trust, All Others Pay Cash. Garden City: 1966. V. 70

SHEPHERD, MAJOR W.
Prairie Experiences in Handling Cattle and Sheep. London: 1884. V. 68

SHEPHERD, R. H.
The Bibliography of Dickens. London: 1880. V. 68

SHEPHERD, THOMAS H.
Metropolitan Improvements, or London in the Nineteenth Century... (with) London In Its Environs in the Nineteenth Century. London: 1829. V. 71
Modern Athens! Displayed in a Series of Views; or Edinburgh in the Nineteenth Century. London: 1831. V. 70

SHEPHERD, WILLIAM
Praire Experiences in Handing Cattle and Sheep. New York: 1885. V. 71

SHEPHERDSON, WILLIAM
Reminiscences of the Hull General Infirmary. London: 1873. V. 70

SHEPPERD, TAD
Pack and Paddock. New York: 1938. V. 70

SHEPPEY, THOMAS
Several Weighty Considerations Humbly Recommended to the Serious Perusal of All, but More Especially the Roman Catholicks of England. London: 1679. V. 71

SHERBORN, C. D.
Index Animalium sive Index Nominum.... London: 1922-1933. V. 69
An Index to the Generic and Trivial Names of Animals, Described by Linneaus in the 10th and 12 Editions of His "Systema Nature". London and Manchester: 1899. V. 72
Where is the - Collection? An Account of the Various Natural History Colelctions Which Have Come Under the Notice of the Compiler Between 1880 and 1939. Cambridge: 1940. V. 72

SHERER, JOHN
The Gold Finder of Australia.. London: 1853. V. 69

SHERER, MOYLE
Notes and Reflections During A Ramble In Germany. London: 1826. V. 72
Scenes and Impressions in Egypt and Italy. London: 1825. V. 73

SHERER, MOYLE continued
Tales of the Wars of Our Times, by the Author of Recollections of the Peninusla. London: 1829. V. 68

SHERIDAN, CAROLINE HENRIETTA
Aims and Ends; and Oonagh Lych. London: 1833. V. 69

SHERIDAN, CHARLES FRANCIS
Observations on the Doctrine Laid Down by Sir William Blackstone; Respecting the Extent of the British Parliament.... Dublin: 1779. V. 70
Some Observations on a Late Address to the Citizens of Dublin, with the Citizens of Dublin, with Thoughts on the Present Crisis. Dublin: 1797. V. 69

SHERIDAN, EDWARD
A Report on the Trial of Edward Sheridan M.D. upon an Indictment for a Misdemeanor, at the Bar of the King's Bench, on Thursday and Friday, the 21st and 22nd Days of Nov. 1811. Dublin: 1811. V. 70

SHERIDAN, FRANCES
The Discovery: a Comedy in Five Acts. London: 1924. V. 70; 72; 73
The History of Nourjahad. London: 1767. V. 71

SHERIDAN, P. H.
Outline Descriptions of The Posts In the Military Division of The Missouri Accompanied By Tabular List of Indian Superintendencies, Agencies and Fort Reservations and A Summary of Certain Indian Tribes. Fort Collins: 1972. V. 72
Personal Memoirs of P. H. Sheridan. New York: 1888. V. 68; 69; 70; 72
Personal Memories of.... Wilmington: 1992. V. 69
Records of Engagements With Hostile Indians With The Military Division of The Missouri From 1868-1882. Bellevue, NE: 1969. V. 72

SHERIDAN, RICHARD BRINSLEY BUTLER
The Critic, or, a Tragedy Rehearsed. London: 1808. V. 72
An Ode to Scandal, Together with a Portrait. Stratford-upon-Avon: 1927. V. 72
The Rivals. London: 1953. V. 72
The School for Scandal. London. V. 71
The School for Scandal. London: 1911. V. 73
The School for Scandal. Oxford: 1934. V. 73

SHERIDAN, THOMAS
British Education; or, the Source of the Disorders of Great Britain. London: 1769. V. 69
The Life of the Rev. Dr. Jonathan Swift, Dean of St. Patrick's, Dublin. London: 1734. V. 73

SHERILL, C. O.
Notes on Cordage. Ft. Leavenworth: 1909. V. 72

SHERINGHAM, GEORGE
Design in the Theatre. London: 1927. V. 70

SHERINGHAM, H. T.
The Book of the Fly Rod. 1931. V. 68; 73

SHERLOCK, HERBERT
Black Power Snapshots. Huntington: 1946. V. 68; 73

SHERLOCK, MARTIN
Nouveles Lettres d'un Voyageur Anglois. Londres: 1780. V. 69

SHERLOCK, RICHARD
The Practical Christian; or, the Devout Penitent. London: 1713. V. 69

SHERLOCK, WILLIAM
A Letter from the Lord Bishop of London, to the Clergy and People of London and Westminster, on Occasion of the Earthquakes. York?: 1776?. V. 73
A Practical Discourse Concerning Death. Edinburgh: 1775. V. 69

SHERMAN, CINDY
The Hasselblad Award 1999: Cindy Sherman. Sweden: 2000. V. 68

SHERMAN, FRANK E.
An Atlas of Congenital Heart Disease Compiled from the Museum of Congenital Heart Disease at Children's Hospital of Pittsburgh. London: 1963. V. 68

SHERMAN, FREDERICK BARREDA
From the Guadalquivir to the Golden Gate by Way of Lima, Baltimore, New York, Newport, Washington, London, Paris and Cuajiniquilapa.... Mill Valley;: 1977. V. 70

SHERMAN, JAMES E.
Ghost Towns and Mining Camps of New Mexico. Norman: 1975. V. 68
Ghost Towns of Arizona. 1969. V. 69

SHERMAN, JOHN
Speech of Hon. John Sherman, of Ohio, on Emancipation as a Compensation for Military Service Rendered by Slaves. Washington: 1864. V. 70

SHERRIFF, R. C.
Journey's End. London: 1930. V. 71; 73

SHERRINGTON, CHARLES
The Endeavour of Jean Fernel. Cambridge: 1946. V. 68; 71; 73
The Grain and Its Mechanism. The Rede Lecture Delivered Before the University of Cambridge 5 December 1933. Cambridge: 1933. V. 72
The Integrative Action of the Nervous System. London: 1906. V. 68
The Integrative Action of the Nervous System. London: 1911. V. 70
The Integrative Action of the Nervous System. New Haven: 1920. V. 73
Reflex Inhibition as a Factor in the Co-Ordination of Movements and of Postures. 1913. V. 68
Selected Writings of Sir Charles Sherrington. London: 1939. V. 68

SHERRY, CHRISTOPHER
The Glasgow Botanic Gardens. Glasgow: 1902. V. 69

SHERRY, NORMAN
The Life of Graham Greene. Volume One 1904-1939. Volume Two: 1939- 1955. 1994. V. 70

SHERWELL, SAMUEL
Old Recollections of an Old Boy. New York: 1923. V. 69

SHERWOOD, BOB
Hold Everything. New York: 1929. V. 70

SHERWOOD, H. H.
Electro-Galvanic Symptoms, and Electro-Magnetic Remedies, in Chronic Diseases of the Class Hypertrophy.... New York: 1837. V. 73

SHERWOOD, ISAAC R.
An Appeal for Free Ireland: Speech in the House of Representatives Jan. 5th 1920. Washington: 1920. V. 69

SHERWOOD, MARY MARTHA BUTT
The Monk. London: 1855?. V. 68
The Re-Captured Negro. Wellington, Salop: 1819-1821. V. 68
The Traditions, a Legendary Tale.... London: 1795. V. 73

SHERWOOD, ROBERT
Abe Lincoln in Illinois. New York: 1939. V. 71
Idiot's Delight. New York: 1936. V. 69
The Petrified Forest. New York: 1935. V. 69; 71; 72
The Queen's Husband. New York: 1928. V. 71
The Road to Rome. New York: 1927. V. 71
Waterloo Bridge. New York: 1930. V. 71

SHERWOOD, W. E.
Oxford Rowing. London: 1900. V. 70
Oxford Rowing. Oxford: 1900. V. 72

SHEWRING, W. H.
The Water Meads: Stories. Ditchling: 1927. V. 73

SHIEL, M. P.
Best Short Stories. London: 1948. V. 70
Prince Zaleski. London: 1895. V. 71
Say Au R'Voir, but Not Goodbye. London: 1933. V. 69; 73
The Young Men are Coming. New York: 1937. V. 70

SHIEL, ROGER R.
Early to Bed And Early to Rise, Twenty Years in Hell With The Beef Trust, Facts Not Fiction. Indianapolis: 1909. V. 71

SHIELD, WILLIAM
The Woodman, a Comic Opera as Performed with Universal Applause at the Theatre Royal Covent Garden..., Composed Chiefly by Wilm. Shield. London: 1791. V. 70

SHIELDS, CAROL
The Box Garden. New York: 1996. V. 71
A Celibate Season. New York: 1999. V. 72
Flatties: Their Various Forms and Uses. Toronto: 1997. V. 68; 72
Happenstance. Toronto: 1980. V. 70; 72
Larry's Party. 1997. V. 71
Larry's Party. London: 1997. V. 72; 73
The Orange Fish. Toronto: 1989. V. 72
The Orange Fish. New York: 1990. V. 68
The Republic Of Love. Toronto: 1992. V. 72
Small Ceremonies. New York: 1996. V. 71
The Stone Diaries. New York: 1993. V. 68; 71
The Stone Diaries. Toronto: 1993. V. 71; 72; 73
The Stone Diaries. New York: 1994. V. 68; 69; 71; 72
The Stone Diaries. Toronto: 1994. V. 68
Swann. New York: 1987. V. 70; 71; 72
Various Miracles. London: 1994. V. 68; 72; 73

SHIELDS, G. O.
The Big Game of North America. 1890. V. 69; 70; 73
The Big Game of North America. Chicago and New York: 1890. V. 68; 70
The Blanket Indian Of The Northwest. New York: 1921. V. 72
Cruising in the Cascades. Chicago/New York: 1889. V. 70

SHIELS, GEORGE
Professor Tim and Paul Twyning. 1927. V. 69; 73

SHIIMBUN, ASAHI
Francois Marie Banier Tokyo 2000. 2000. V. 70

SHILLABER, C. P.
Photomicrography in Theory and Practice. New York: 1949. V. 71

SHILLIBEER, JOHN
A Narrative of the Briton's Voyage. Taunton: 1817. V. 71

SHILLITOE, THOMAS
Journal of the Life, Labours, and Travels of Thomas Shillitoe. London: 1839. V. 72

SHILTON, RICHARD PHILLIPS
The History of Southwell, in the County of Nottingham, Its Hamlets and Vicinage.... Newark: 1818. V. 70

SHIMPEI, KUSANO
Frogs & Others. New York: 1968. V. 71

SHINEDLING, ABRAHAM I.
West Virginia Jewry: Origins and History 1850-1958. Philadelphia: 1963. V. 70

SHINKLE, JAMES D.
Fort Sumner of the Basque Redondo Indian Reservation. Roswell: 1965. V. 69

SHINN, CHARLES H.
Graphic Description of Pacific Coast Outlaws. 1958. V. 68
The Story of the Mine as Illustrated by the Great Comstock Lode of Nevada. New York: 1896. V. 70

SHINN, EVERETT
The Sermon on the Mount. Philadelphia: 1946. V. 70

SHINN, G. HAZEN
Shoshonean Days: Recollections of a Residence of Five Years Among the Indians of Southern California 1885-1889. Glendale: 1951. V. 70

SHINWELL, EMANUEL
Lead with the Left - My First Ninety-Six Years. London: 1981. V. 68
Shinwell Talking - a Conversational Biography to Celebrate His Hundredth Birthday. London: 1984. V. 68

SHIPP, JOHN
The Military Bijou; or the Contents of a Soldier's Knapsack, Being the Gleanings of Thirty-Three Years' Active Service. London: 1831. V. 68

SHIPPEY, LEE
If We Only Had Money. Boston: 1939. V. 69

THE SHIP'S Bell. Baltimore: 1927. V. 71

SHIPTON, CLIFFORD K.
National Index of American Imprints through 1800: the Short-Title Evans. 1969. V. 69

SHIPTON, E.
Mountains of Tartary. 1951. V. 71; 73
That Untravelled World. 1969. V. 73
The Untravelled World. 1986. V. 73

SHIPTON, ERIC
The Mount Everest Reconnaissance Expedition 1951. London: 1952. V. 69
The Mount Everest Reconnaissance Expedition 1951. London: 1953. V. 69
Mountain Conquest. London: 1967. V. 69

SHIRAKAWA, Y.
Himalayas. 1986. V. 68

SHIRATA, SHIRO
The Alps. Berlin: 1985. V. 69

SHIRLEY, EDWARD
Jack Frost and Other Merry Sprites. 1907. V. 71

SHIRLEY, GLENN
Born to Kill - He Blazed a Trail of Death and Terror Across Fourteen States. Derby: 1963. V. 68; 72
Guardian of the Law - The Life and Times of William Matthew Tilghman 1854-1924. Austin: 1988. V. 68
Guardian of the Law. The Life and Times of William Matthew Tilghman (1854-1924). Austin: 2000. V. 68
Heck Thomas: Frontier Marshal, the Story of a Real Gunfighter. Philadelphia: 1962. V. 69; 72; 73

SHIRLEY, JAMES
The Doubtful Heir.... London: 1652. V. 72
The Doubtful Heir.... London: 1952. V. 70

SHIRLEY, JOHN
The Golden Gleanings; Being Sketches of Female Character from Bible History. London: 1863. V. 69; 73

SHIRLEY, KAY
The Book of Blues. New York: 1965. V. 72

SHIRLEY, T.
A Philosophical Essay: Declaring the Probable Causes Whence Stones are Produced in the Greater World.... London: 1672. V. 68

SHIRLEY Temple Song Album. No. 2. New York: 1936. V. 70

SHIRLEY-SMITH, RICHARD
The Wood Engravings of Richard Shirley Smith. Cambridge: 1994. V. 71

SHIROKOGOROFF, S. M.
Social Organization of the Northern Tungus.... New York: 1979. V. 69

SHIRREFFS, GORDON D.
The Secret of the Spanish Desert. Philadelphia and New York: 1964. V. 73

SHIRREFS, ANDREW
Poems, Chiefly in the Scottish Dialect. Edinburgh: 1790. V. 68; 72

SHIVERS, LOUISE
Here to Get My Baby Out of Jail. New York: 1983. V. 69; 71; 73

SHOBERL, FREDERIC
Forget me Not: a Christmas, New Year's and Birthday Present for 1829. Philadelphia: 1828. V. 71

Forget Me Not; a Christmas, New Year's and Birthday Present for 1843. London: 1842. V. 70

SHOBERL, FREDERICK
Forget Me Not; a Christmas and New Year's Present for 1829. London. V. 69

SHOCKING Calamnity! Particulars of the Tragical Death of Mrs. Ann Taylor, her Son William Francis Taylor - Mrs. Elizabeth Brewer - Mr. Patrick Jackson and Wife, and Miss Eliza Palfrey, Who Fell Victims to the Awful Conflagration in Broad Street, Boston. Boston: 1821. V. 68

SHOCKLETON, JANE
Facts and Fancies, in prose and verse. By Jenny Wren. London: 1864. V. 71

SHOEMAKER, F. C.
Missouri Day by Day. Jefferson: 1943. V. 70

SHOLOKHOV, MIKHAIL
Harvest on the Don. New York: 1961. V. 71

THE SHOOTING Star. London: 1961. V. 68

THE SHOPKEEPER Turned Sailor; or the Folly of Going Out of Our Element. London: 1796. V. 68

SHORE, HENRY N.
The Flight of the Lapwing: a Naval Officer's Jottings in China, Formosa and Japan. London: 1881. V. 70

SHORE, W. TEIGNMOUTH
Charles Dickens and His Friends. London: 1909. V. 69

A SHORT Account of the Late Application to Parliament Made by the Merchants of London Upon the Neglect of their Trade, with Substance of the Evidence Thereupon.... London: 1742. V. 73

SHORT, BOB, PSEUD.
Hoyle Abridged; or, Short Rules for Short Memories at the Game of Whist. London: 1818. V. 72

SHORT, FRANK
The Making of Etchings. London: 1898. V. 68

SHORT, LUKE
And the Wind Blows Free. New York: 1945. V. 69
Coroner Creek. New York: 1946. V. 71
Play a Lone Hand. Boston: 1951. V. 69

SHORT Stories of Latin America. New York: 1963. V. 69

THE SHORT Story: 25 Masterpieces. New York: 1979. V. 70

SHORT, THOMAS
The Natural, Experimental and Medicinal History of the Mineral Waters of Derbyshire, Lincolnshire and Yorkshire, Particularly Those of Scarborough. London: 1734. V. 73
The Natural Experimental and Medicinal History of the Mineral Waters of Derbyshire, Lincolnshire and Yorkshire...(with) An Essays Towards a Natural, Experimental and Medicinal History of the Principle Mineral Waters of Cumberland, Northumberland.... London: 1734-1740. V. 73

SHORTER, CLEMENT
The Brontes Life and Letters. London: 1908. V. 70; 73
Charlotte Bronte and Her Circle. London: 1896. V. 70; 72; 73

SHORTHOUSE, JOSEPH HENRY
John Inglesant: a Romance. Birmingham: 1880. V. 73

SHOT on Patrol. A True Incident of the Present War. London: 1900. V. 70

SHOVE, FREDEGOND MAITLAND
Fredegond and Gerald Shove. 1952. V. 71

SHOWALTER, NOAH D.
Atlas of Rockingham Co., Virginia. Harrisonburg: 1939. V. 72

SHREVE, ANITA
The Pilot's Wife. Boston: 1998. V. 71

SHREVE, F.
Vegetation and Flora of the Sonoran Desert. Stanford: 1964. V. 69

SHREWSBURY, CHARLES TALBOT, 19TH EARL OF
Meliora; or, Better Times to Come. London: 1852-1853. V. 71

SHRIBER, IONE SANDBERG
A Body for Bill. New York: 1942. V. 68

SHUAIB, L.
Wildflowers of Kuwait. London: 1995. V. 72

SHUEY, WILLIAM
A Manual of the United States Brethren Publishing House: Historical and Descriptive. Dayton: 1892. V. 71

SHUFELDT, R. W.
Chapters on the Natural History of the United States. New York: 1897. V. 68
The Myology of the Raven (Corvus Corax Sinuatus) a Guide to the Study of the Muscular System in Birds. London: 1890. V. 73
Reports of Explorations and Surveys to Ascertain the Practicability of a Ship-Canal Between the Atlantic and Pacific Oceans by Way of the Isthmus. Washington: 1872. V. 69

SHULDHAM, E. B.
Pictures from Birdland, with Rhymes by E.B.S. London: 1899. V. 73

SHULMAN, ALIX KATES
Memoirs of an Ex-Prom Queen. New York: 1972. V. 73

SHULMAN, IRVING
Cry Tough!. New York: 1949. V. 71
The Short End of the Stick and Other Stories. Garden City: 1959. V. 71
The Velvet Knife. Garden City: 1959. V. 69

SHULMAN, JULIUS
Photography of Architecture and Design. New York: 1978. V. 72

SHULMAN, KENNETH
Workshop in Hydrocephalus. Philadelphia: 1965. V. 71

SHULMAN, NEIL
Finally...I'm a Doctor. New York: 1976. V. 68; 69
What? Dead, Again?. Baton Rouge: 1979. V. 68; 69

SHUMAKER, WALTER A.
A Treatise on the Law of Partnership. St. Paul: 1901. V. 71

SHUMWAY, GEORGE
Conestoga Wagon 1750-1850 - Freight Carrier for 100 Years of America's Westward Expansion. New York: 1964. V. 73

SHUPTRINE, HUBERT
Jericho. The South Beheld. Birmingham: 1974. V. 68

SHURE, DAVID S.
Hester Bateman. Queen of English Silversmiths. London: 1959. V. 72

SHURTLEFF, HAROLD R.
The Log Cabin Myth: a Study of the Early Dwellings of the English Colonists in North America. Cambridge: 1939. V. 72

SHURTLEFF, NATHANIEL B.
A Topographical and Historical Description of Boston. Boston: 1871. V. 71

SHUTE, E. L.
Over the Hills. London: 1888. V. 68
What the Toys Did! A Dream Told in Verse. London: 1904. V. 72

SHUTE, HENRY A.
Brite and Fair - a Sequel to the Real Diary of a Real Boy. Peterborough: 1968. V. 73
The Real Diary of a Real Boy. Peterborough: 1967. V. 73

SHUTE, NEVIL
No Highway. New York: 1948. V. 71
On the Beach. London: 1957. V. 69; 71; 72
On the Beach. New York: 1957. V. 70
On the Beach. London: 1958. V. 68
The Rainbow and the Rose. London: 1958. V. 71
Slide Rule. The Autobiography of an Engineer. New York: 1954. V. 73
Stephen Morris. London: 1961. V. 71
Stephen Morris. New York: 1961. V. 71
Trustee from the Toolroom. London: 1960. V. 69

SHVIDKOVSKY, O. A.
Building in the U.S.S.R. 1917-1932. London: 1971. V. 69

SIBBES, RICHARD
The Soul's Conflict and Victory Over Itself by Faith. (with) The Bruised Reed and Smoking Flax. A Fountain Sealed. A Description of Christ. London: 1837-1838. V. 68; 72

SIBLEY, AGNES MARIE
May Sarton. New York: 1972. V. 70

SIBLEY, C. G.
Distribution and Taxonomy of Birds of the World. New Haven: 1990. V. 73

SIBLEY, HENRY C.
Iron Face, The Adventures of Jack Frazer, Frontier Warrior, Scout and Hunter. Chicago: 1950. V. 72

SIBLEY, ROBERT
America's Answer to the Russian Challenger. San Francisco: 1931. V. 71

SIBLY, E.
A Key to Physic, and the Occult Sciences.... London: 1794. V. 69
A Key to Physic, and the Occult Sciences... The Whole Forming an Interesting Supplement to Culppeer's Family Physician.... London: 1800. V. 73
A New and Complete Illustration of the Occult Sciences of the Art of Fortelling Future Events and Contingencies, by the Aspects, Positions and Influences of the Heavenly Bodies. London: 1784?. V. 69

SIBTHORP, JOHN
Florae Graecae Prodromus: Sive Plantarum Omnium Enumeratio.... London: 1806-1816. V. 70

SICHEL, JULIUS
Spectacles: Their Uses and Abuses in Long and Short Sightedness: and the Pathological Conditions Resulting from their Irrational Employment.... Boston: 1850. V. 73

SICK, H.
Birds in Brazil, a Natural History. Princeton: 1933. V. 73

SIDDONS, ANNE RIVERS
John Chancellor Makes Me Cry. Garden City: 1975. V. 73

SIDDONS, G. S.
The Cabinet Maker's Guide; or Rules and Instructions in the Art of Varnishing, Dying, Staining, Japanning, Polishing, Lackering and Beautifying Wood, Ivory, Tortoisehell and Metal with Observations on Their Management and Application. 1830. V. 71

SIDDONS, HENRY
Virtuous Poverty, a Tale. London: 1804. V. 73

SIDDONS, SARAH
The Story of Our First Parents; Selected from Milton's Paradise Lost.... London: 1822. V. 69

SIDEWALK.. Edinburgh: 1960?. V. 72

SIDGWICK, A., MRS.
The Children's Book of Gardening. London: 1913. V. 71

SIDGWICK, FRANK
Frank Sidgwick's Diary - and Other Material Relating to A. H. Bullen and the Shakespeare Head Press. Oxford: 1975. V. 68

SIDGWICK, HENRY
The Elements of Politics. London: 1891. V. 73
The Principles of Political Economy. London: 1887. V. 71

SIDNEY, ALGERNON
The Essence of Algernon Sidney's Work on Government. London: 1795. V. 73

SIDNEY, PHILIP
Astrophel and Stella. London: 1931. V. 70; 71; 72
The Countess of Pembroke's Arcadia. 1613. V. 73
The Countess of Pembroke's Arcadia. Countess: 1638. V. 73
The Lad Philisides, Being a Selection of Songs, Pastoral Eclogues & Elegies.... 1988. V. 71

SIDNEY, S.
The Three Colonies of Australia: New South Wales, Victoria, South Australia. Their Pastures, Copper Mines and Gold Fields. New York: 1859. V. 69

SIEBECK, RUDOLF
Guide Pratique du Jardinier Paysagiste. Paris: 1863. V. 70; 72

SIEBERT, I.
North American Indian Art. London: 1967. V. 69

SIEGEL, C.
Structure and Form in Modern Architecture. New York: 1962. V. 68; 69; 72

SIEGEMUND, JUSTINE D.
Die Konigl. Preusiche und Chur-Brandenb. Hof-Wehe-Mutter. Berlin: 1756. V. 70; 73

SIEM, CONRAD
The Future of Port Clarence as a Fishing and Whaling Port. Nome: 1907. V. 68

SIEMENS, WERNER VON
Personal Recollections. London: 1903. V. 70

SIENKIEWICZ, HENRYK
The Deluge. 1991. V. 68; 69
The Trilogy - The Duluge (2 Vols); Fire In The Steppe; With Fire and Sword. 1991-1992. V. 72
With Fire And Sword. New York: 1991. V. 72

SIERRA CLUB
The Sierra Club Bulletin 1893-1905. San Francisco: 1950. V. 68

SIERRA LEONE COMPANY
Substance of the Report Delivered by the Court of Directors of the Sierra Leone Company, to the General Court of Proprietors..1794. (with) Substance of the Report....1795. Philadelphia: 1795. V. 68

SIESJO, B. K.
Ion Homeostasis of the Brain. Copenhagen: 1971. V. 72

SIEVIER, ROBERT STANDISH
The Autobiography. London: 1906. V. 70

SIGAL, CLANCY
Zone of the Interior. New York: 1976. V. 72

SIGERIST, HENRY
The Great Doctors. New York: 1958. V. 68; 70; 71; 73

SIGNATURES.. Northridge: 1991. V. 70

SIGNIFICANT War Scenes by Battlefront Artists 1941-1945. 1951. V. 71

SIGOURNEY, LYDIA HUNTLEY
Letters to Young Ladies. Hartford: 1835. V. 68
Pocahontas, and other poems. London: 1841. V. 69; 71
Poems. Boston: 1827. V. 72
Poems. Philadelphia: 1834. V. 69; 72
Poems for the Sea. Hartford: 1850. V. 68
The Religious Souvenir for 1840 Republished for 1845. Hartford: 1845. V. 71

SILBERSTEIN, SOLOMON J.
The Jewish Problem and Theology in General. New York: 1904. V. 71

SILER, JENNY
Easy Money. New York: 1998. V. 73

SILIUS ITALICUS
The Second Punic War, Between Hannibal and the Romanes, the whole Seventeen Books.... London: 1672. V. 68; 73

SILKE, JOHN J.
Kinsale: Spanish Intervention in Ireland at the End of the Elizabethan Wars. 1970. V. 69

SILKO, LESLIE MARMON
Almanac of the Dead. New York: 1991. V. 68; 71; 72
Ceremony. New York: 1977. V. 68; 70; 73
Rain. New York: 1996. V. 73
Storyteller. New York: 1981. V. 68
Yellow Woman and A Beauty of the Spirit. New York: 1996. V. 70; 72; 73

SILLIMAN, B.
Professor Silliman's Report Upon the Oil Property of the Philadelphia and California Petroleum Company of Philadelphia, Situated in Santa Barbara and Los Angeles Counties, California. Philadelphia: 1865. V. 68
The World of Science Art and Industry Illustrated, for Examples in the New York Exhibition 1853-1854. New York: 1854. V. 73

SILLITOE, ALAN
The Broken Chariot. London: 1998. V. 73
The Loneliness of the Long Distance Runner. New York: 1960. V. 71
The Ragman's Daughter. London: 1976. V. 71
Saturday Night and Sunday Morning. 1958. V. 73
Saturday Night and Sunday Morning. London: 1958. V. 71

SILLITOE, P.
Made in Niugini. London: 1988. V. 69

SILSBEE, MARIANNE
Memory and Hope. Boston: 1851. V. 70

SILVA, ERCOLE
Dell'Arte dei Giardini Inglesi. Milan: 1801. V. 68; 70; 72

SILVA, P. C.
Catalogue of the Benthic Marine Algae of the Indian Ocean. Berkeley: 1996. V. 73

SILVA, TONY
A Monograph of Macaws and Conures. 1993. V. 72
A Monograph of Macaws and Conures. London: 1993. V. 70; 73

SILVER, ARTHUR P.
Farm-Cottage, Camp and Canoe in Maritime Canada, or the Call of Nova Scotia to the Emigrant and Sportsman. London: 1908. V. 73

THE SILVER Fairy Book. London: 1899. V. 70
THE SILVER Fairy Book. London: 1922. V. 71

THE SILVER Penny, for the Amusement and Instruction of Good Children. York: 1817. V. 68

SILVER, S. W., & CO.
S. W. Silver and Co.'s Handbook for Australia and New Zealand.... 1874. V. 71

SILVERBERG, ROBERT
The Mound Builders of Ancient America. Greenwich: 1968. V. 69
Nightstand. 1959. V. 71
Other Dimensions: Ten Stories of Science Action. New York: 1973. V. 68
The Pueblo Incident. New York: 1970. V. 69

SILVERSTEIN, SHEL
A Light in the Attic. New York: 1981. V. 69
Take Ten. Tokyo: 1955. V. 71

SILVESTER, PETER J.
A Left Hand Like God. A History of Boogie-Woogie Piano. New York: 1988. V. 72; 73
A Left Hand Like God. A History of Boogie-Woogie Piano. New York: 1989. V. 71

SILVESTRE, ARMAND
Le Conte de L'Archer. Paris: 1883. V. 69
La Plante Enchantee. Paris: 1896. V. 70

SIM, T. R.
The Forests and Forest Flora of the Colony of the Cape of Good Hope. Aberdeen: 1907. V. 69

SIMENON, GEORGES
Across the Street. London: 1954. V. 71
Act of Passion. New York: 1952. V. 71
Affairs of Destiny. New York: 1944. V. 71
Danger Ahead. London: 1955. V. 70
Inspector Maigret and the Burglar's Wife. Garden City: 1956. V. 71
Inspector Maigret and the Killers. Garden City: 1954. V. 69
Inspector Maigret and the Strangled Stripper. Garden City: 1954. V. 70
The Little Saint. New York: 1965. V. 68
Maigret and Monsieur Charles. London: 1972. V. 71
Maigret and Monsieur Charles. London: 1973. V. 69
Maigret and Monsieur Labbe. New York: 1942. V. 68; 69
Maigret and the Burglar's Wife. London: 1955. V. 69; 71
Maigret and the Flea. London: 1971. V. 71
Maigret and the Flea. London: 1972. V. 69
Maigret and the Gangsters. London: 1974. V. 71
Maigret and the Loner. London: 1975. V. 71
Maigret and the Man on the Boulevard. London: 1975. V. 70
Maigret and the Millionaires. London: 1974. V. 71
Maigret and the Nahour Case. London: 1967. V. 71
Maigret and the Saturday Caller. London: 1964. V. 71
Maigret and the Spinster. 1977. V. 70
Maigret and the Wine Merchant. London: 1971. V. 71
Maigret Goes to School. London: 1957. V. 70
Maigret Hesitates. London: 1970. V. 71
Maigret in New York's Underworld. Garden City: 1955. V. 70
Maigret Loses His Temper. London: 1965. V. 69; 73
Maigret on the Defensive. London: 1966. V. 71
Maigret Travels South. New York: 1940. V. 68; 71
Maigret's Memoirs. London: 1963. V. 71
The Negro. London: 1959,. V. 71; 72
The Novel of a Man. New York: 1964. V. 71
The Patience of Maigret. New York: 1940. V. 70; 71
The Shadow Falls. London: 1945. V. 68
The Shadow Falls. London: 1951. V. 68
The Short Cases of Inspector Maigret. New York: 1959. V. 73
The Son. London: 1958. V. 71
The Strangers in the House. London: 1951. V. 68; 70
Tropic Moon. New York: 1943. V. 68; 70

SIMEON, JOHN
Catalogue of the Valuable and Very Choice Library of the Late Sir John Simeon, Bart, M.P.... London: 1871. V. 70

SIMIC, CHARLES
Austerities. New York: 1982. V. 68
On the Music of the Spheres. New York: 1996. V. 73
The Pieces of the Clock Lie Scattered. Syracuse: 1997. V. 69; 73
Return to a Place Lit by a Glass of Milk. New York: 1974. V. 68
Three Poems. Syracuse: 1998. V. 69; 73
Unending Blues. San Diego: 1986. V. 73
Wendy's Pinball. Poems. East Hampton: 1996. V. 69; 73

SIMINGTON, ROBERT C.
The Civil Survey A.D. 1654-1656, County of Meath. 1940. V. 70
The Civil Survey A.D. 1654-1656, County of Waterford. 1942. V. 70
The Civil Survey A.D. 1654-1656, County of Tipperary. 1931-1934. V. 70

SIMKINS, CLEVELAND S.
Functional Human Anatomy. Dubuque: 1949. V. 71

SIMKINS, FRANCIS BUTLER
The Women of the Confederacy. Richmond & New York: 1936. V. 69; 70

SIMMONDS, A. J.
On the Big Range, A Centennial History At Cornish and Trenton, Cache County, Utah, 1870-1970. 1970. V. 71

SIMMONDS, P. L.
A Dictionary of Useful Animals and Their Products. London: 1883. V. 68

SIMMONS, AMELIA
American Cookery, or the Art of Dressing Viands, Fish, Poultry and Vegetables and the Best Modes of Making Pastes, Puffs, Pies, Tarts, Puddings, Custards, and Preserves.... Northampton: 1798. V. 73
American Cookery, or the Art of Dressing Viands, Fish, Poultry and Vegetables and the Best Modes of Making Pastes, Puffs, Pies, Tarts, Puddings, Custards and Preserves.... Brattleborough: 1814. V. 69; 71

SIMMONS, CHARLES
Wrinkles. New York: 1978. V. 68

SIMMONS, DAN
Carrion Comfort. 1989. V. 70
Carrion Comfort. Arlington Heights: 1989. V. 68
Children of the Night. 1992. V. 70
Children of the Night. New York: 1992. V. 73
The Hollow Man. 1992. V. 70
Lovedeath. 1993. V. 70
Phases of Gravity. 1989. V. 70
Song of Kali. 1985. V. 70
Song of Kali. New York: 1985. V. 68; 69
Summer Sketches. 1992. V. 70

SIMMONS, ERNEST J.
Leo Tolstoy. London: 1949. V. 68

SIMMONS, J. C.
Southern Methodists on the Pacific Coast. Nashville: 1886. V. 68

SIMMONS, JAMES
Constantly Singing. Belfast: 1980. V. 70

SIMMONS, MARC
Albuquerque, a Narrative History. Albuquerque: 1982. V. 71
Border Comanches - Seven Spanish Colonial Documents 1785-1819. Santa Fe: 1967. V. 69; 73
Spanish Government in New Mexico. Albuquerque: 1968. V. 68

SIMMONS, MARK
The Sena Family: Blacksmiths of Santa Fe. Santa Fe: 1981. V. 70

SIMMONS, NOAH
Heroes and Heroines of the Fort Dearborn Massacre. Lawrence: 1896. V. 68; 71

SIMMONS, OWEN
The Book of Bread. London: 1903. V. 70

SIMMONS'S COURT COSTUMIERS
(Catalogue). London: 1895. V. 68
SIMMS, F. W.
Public Works of Great Britian. London: 1846. V. 68
SIMMS, HENRY H.
Life of John Taylor: the Story of a Brilliant Leader in the Early Virginia State Rights School. Richmond: 1932. V. 68
SIMMS, JUDGE ORLAND
Cowpokes Nesters and So Forth. Austin: 1970. V. 71
SIMMS, WILLIAM GILMORE
Charlemont; or the Pride of the Village. New York: 1856. V. 70
The Damsel of Darien. Philadelphia: 1839. V. 70
Eutaw. New York: 1856. V. 70
Forayers; or, the Raid of the Dog Days. New York: 1855. V. 70
Life in America; or the Wigwam and the Cabin. Aberdeen: 1848. V. 71
The Lily and the Totem, or, the Huguenots in Florida. New York: 1850. V. 70
Sack and Destruction of the City of Columbia. Columbia: 1865. V. 69; 70
Vasconselos. New York: 1857. V. 70
War Lyrics and Songs of the South. London: 1866. V. 69
SIMON, ANDRE
Bibliotheca Vinaria. London: 1979. V. 69
Bottlescrew Days. Boston: 1927. V. 72
SIMON, CLAUDE
The Flanders Road. New York: 1961. V. 69; 71; 73
SIMON, FRANK B.
Letters on Sport in Eastern Bengal. 1886. V. 69
SIMON, GEORGE T.
The Best of the Music Makers. Garden City: 1979. V. 69
Glenn Miller and His Orchestra. New York: 1974. V. 68; 69
SIMON, INGO
Roving Shafts. Waltham St. Lawrence: 1924. V. 71
SIMON, JOHN
Three Speeches on the General Strike. London: 1926. V. 72
SIMON, JULES
L'Ouvriere. Paris: 1861. V. 72
SIMON, NEIL
Barefoot in the Park. New York: 1964. V. 68; 69; 70; 71
Brighton Beach Memoirs. New York: 1984. V. 69
California Suite. New York: 1977. V. 69
Come Blow Your Horn. Garden City: 1963. V. 69
God's Favorite. New York: 1975. V. 69
I Ought to Be in Pictures. New York: 1980. V. 69
Last of the Red Hot Lovers. New York: 1970. V. 69
The Odd Couple. New York: 1966. V. 70; 71
Promises, Promises. New York: 1969. V. 71
Three from the Stage. Franklin Center: 1995. V. 68; 69
SIMON, RACHEL
Little Nightmares, Little Dreams. Boston: 1990. V. 68; 71
SIMOND, LOUIS
Journal of a Tour and Residence in Great Britain, During the Years 1810 and 1811. Edinburgh: 1815. V. 71
Journal of a Tour and Residence in Great Britain, During the Years 1810 and 1811. London: 1815. V. 69
Journal of a Tour and Residence in Great Britain, During the Years 1810 and 1811. New York: 1815. V. 70
SIMONDS, JOHN
The Story of Manual Labor. Chicago: 1887. V. 68
SIMONS, DAN
Song of Kali. New York: 1985. V. 71
SIMONS, MINOT
Vexed Questions. Cleveland: 1913. V. 73
SIMONTON, IDA VERA
Hell's Playground. New York: 1925. V. 71
SIMPER, PAUL
The Saint: From Big Screen To Small Screen And Back Again. London: 1997. V. 71; 72
SIMPKIN, R.
The Royal Military Tournament. London: 1888. V. 72
SIMPKINSON, JOHN N.
The Washingtons, a Tale of a Country Parish in the 17th Century. London: 1860. V. 70
SIMPLE Simon. New York: 1897. V. 71; 73
SIMPLE Simon. London and Montreal: 1907. V. 69
SIMPSON, ALEXANDER
The Life And Travels of Thomas Simpson, the Arctic Discoverer. London: 1845. V. 70
SIMPSON, ANNA PRATT
Problems Women Solved. San Francisco: 1915. V. 73

SIMPSON, CHARLES
The Harboro' Country. 1927. V. 68
SIMPSON, CHRISTOPHER
A Compendium; or, Introduction to Practical Musick. London: 1714. V. 73
SIMPSON, E. B.
The R. L. Stevenson Originals. 1912. V. 68
SIMPSON, FRED M.
Drawing Room Dulogues. London: 1894. V. 68
SIMPSON, G. G.
American Mesozoic Mammalia. New Haven: 1929. V. 70
The Beginning of the Age of Mammals in South America. New York: 1948. V. 70
British Antarctic Expedition 1910-1913. Meteorology. Calcutta: 1919-1923. V. 70
SIMPSON, HAROLD B.
Frontier Forts of Texas. Waco: 1966. V. 72
Gaines' Mill to Appomatox. Waco: 1963. V. 69; 70
Hood's Texas Brigade. Waco: 1953. V. 69
Hood's Texas Brigade. Waco: 1970. V. 70
Hood's Texas Brigade. Hillsboro: 1974. V. 70
SIMPSON, HELEN
The Woman on the Beast. Garden City: 1933. V. 70
SIMPSON, HENRY I.
The Emigrant's Guide to the Gold Mines. Haverford: 1978. V. 68
SIMPSON, J.
The Wild Rabbit in a New Aspect, or Rabbit Warrens That Pay. A Record of.... 1895. V. 71
SIMPSON, J. PALGRAVE
The Lily of Paris; or the King's Nurse. London: 1851. V. 73
SIMPSON, JAMES
A Visit to Flanders, in July 1815, Being Chiefly an Account of the Field of Waterloo. Edinburgh;: 1815. V. 71
SIMPSON, JAMES HERVEY
Navaho Expedition. Norman: 1961. V. 72
Navaho Expedition. Norman: 1964. V. 72
SIMPSON, JAMES Y.
Archaeological Essays. Edinburgh: 1872. V. 70
SIMPSON, JEFFERY
Officers and Gentlemen, Historic West Point in Photographs. New York: 1982. V. 72
SIMPSON, JOHN
Complete System of Cookery. London: 1816. V. 70
SIMPSON, LESLEY BYRD
The Encomienda in New Spain: Forced Native Labor in the Spanish Colonies 1492-1550. Berkeley: 1929. V. 68
SIMPSON, MONA
Anywhere But Here. New York: 1986. V. 72
Anywhere but Here. New York: 1987. V. 68; 71; 72
The Lost Father. New York: 1992. V. 72
A Regular Guy. New York: 1996. V. 72
SIMPSON, N. D.
A Bibliographical Index of the British Flora.... Bournemouth: 1960. V. 71
SIMPSON, R. R.
Shakespeare and Medicine. Edinburgh: 1962. V. 71
SIMPSON, R. W.
History of Old Pendleton Disrict: with a Genealogy of the Leading Families of the District. Anderson: 1913. V. 71
SIMPSON, SPENCER
The Four Dead Men. 1937. V. 73
SIMPSON, THOMAS
The Doctrine of Annuities and Reversions, Deduced from General and Evident Principles; with Useful Tables, Shewing the Values of Single and Joint Lives &c at Different Rates of Interest. London: 1742. V. 70
SIMPSON, WILLIAM
Zenexton Ante-Pestilentiale. London: 1665. V. 69
SIMS, GEORGE
Biographs of Babylon. Life Pictures of London's Moving Scenes. London: 1902. V. 70
The Black Stain. 1907. V. 71
The End of the Web. London: 1976. V. 70
For Bibliophiles. 1961. V. 71
Hunters Point. London: 1973. V. 70
The Keys of Death. London: 1982. V. 70
The Last Best Friend. London: 1967. V. 70
My Life. Sixty Years' Recollections of Bohemian. London: 1917. V. 70
Rex Mundi. London: 1978. V. 70
Who is Cato?. London: 1981. V. 70
SIMS, JOHN
Dissertatio Medica Inauguralis, Quaedam de Cerebri Concussione Malisque Inde Oriundis.... Edinburgh: 1818. V. 71

SIMS, ORLAND L.
Gun-Toters I have Known. Austin: 1967. V. 72

SIMS, RICHARD
A Manual for the Genealogist, Topographer, Antiquary, and Legal Professor. London: 1856. V. 72

SIMSON, FRANK B.
Letters on Sport in Eastern Bengal. 1886. V. 70; 72; 73

SIMSON, JAMES
Charles Waterton. Edinburgh: 1880. V. 69; 71

SINBAD, a Dog's Life. London: 1931. V. 71

SINCLAIR, APRIL
Coffee Will Make You Black. New York: 1994. V. 71

SINCLAIR, ARCHIBALD
Swimming. London: 1893. V. 70

SINCLAIR, ARTHUR
Two Years on the Alabama. Boston: 1896. V. 69

SINCLAIR, BERTRAND W.
The Inverted Pyramid. Boston: 1924. V. 71

SINCLAIR, CATHERINE
Modern Society; or, the March of Intellect. London: 1865?. V. 68

SINCLAIR, G.
Useful and Ornamental Planting. London: 1832. V. 69

SINCLAIR, GEORGE
Satans Invisible World Discovered. Edinburgh: 1871. V. 73

SINCLAIR, HAROLD
The Horse Soldiers. New York: 1956. V. 69; 71; 73
Music Out of Dixie. New York and Toronto: 1952. V. 73

SINCLAIR, IAIN
Downriver. London: 1991. V. 68; 69; 72
Rodinsky's Room. London: 1999. V. 72

SINCLAIR, JOHN
The Code of Agriculture. London: 1817. V. 70
The Code of Agriculture. London: 1821. V. 72
The Code of Agriculture. London: 1832. V. 71
The Code of Agriculture. London: 1882. V. 69
The History of the Public Revenue of the British Empire. London: 1785. V. 72
Observations on the Report of the Bullion Committee.... London: 1810. V. 73
Observations on the Scottish Dialect. London: 1782. V. 70
This is Our Music. Detroit: 1965. V. 69

SINCLAIR, MAY
Tales Told by Simpson. New York: 1930. V. 71

SINCLAIR, UPTON
Between Two Worlds. New York: 1941. V. 69
A Captain of Industry. Girard: 1906. V. 69; 71
Clif, the Naval Cadet. New York: 1903. V. 68
Co-Op. A Novel of Living Together. New York: 1936. V. 69
Cruise of the Training Ship. New York. V. 68
The Fasting Cure. New York: 1911. V. 69
The Flivver King. London: 1938. V. 71
From Port to Port. New York: 1903. V. 68
The Journal of Arthur Stirling. New York: 1903. V. 69
The Jungle. New York: 1906. V. 68; 69; 71; 73
The Jungle. Toronto: 1906. V. 69
The Jungle. Baltimore: 1965. V. 68; 71
Marie Antoinette. New York: 1939. V. 69
The Moneychangers. New York: 1908. V. 68
Mountain City. New York. V. 70
O Shepherd, Speak!. New York: 1949. V. 69
One Clear Call. Monrovia: 1948. V. 69
The Overman. New York: 1907. V. 68
Presidential Mission. Monrovia: 1947. V. 69
The Way Out: What Lies Ahead for America. New York: 1933. V. 69
What God Means to Me. An Attempt at Working Religion. New York: 1936. V. 69
A World to Win. Monrovia: 1946. V. 69

SINCLAIR, W. A.
Diseases of Trees and Shrubs. Ithaca: 1987. V. 68

SINCLAIR, W. B.
The Grapefruit, Its Composition, Physiology and Products. Berkeley: 1972. V. 71

SINDERMANN, C. J.
Principal Diseases of Marine Fish and Shellfish. Volume 2. Diseases of Marine Shellfish. San Diego: 1990. V. 73

SINDING, PAUL C.
The Scandinavian Races. The Northmen: the Sea-King and Vikings. New York: 1877. V. 72

SING-a-Song of Sixpence. New York: 1871-1874. V. 71

SINGER, B.
Patent and Trade Marks of the World. Chicago: 1911. V. 73

SINGER, CHARLES
The Evolution of Anatomy. London: 1925. V. 68; 70
The Evolution of Anatomy. New York: 1925. V. 68; 71
From Magic to Science. London: 1928. V. 68
Galen on Anatomical Procedures.... London: 1956. V. 68
A History of Technology. London and New York: 1957-1959. V. 70; 71
Science and History: Essays on the Evolution of Scientific Thought and Medical Practice. London: 1953. V. 68
A Short History of Biology. Oxford: 1931. V. 68
A Short History of Science to the Nineteenth Century. Oxford: 1941. V. 68
Studies in the History and Method of Science. Oxford: 1917-1921. V. 68; 70
Studies in the History and Method of Science. Oxford: 1956. V. 73
Vesalius on the Human Brain. London: 1952. V. 68; 70; 73

SINGER, EDWARD
Fasciae of the Human Body and Their Relations to the Organs They Envelop. Baltimore: 1935. V. 72

SINGER, I. J.
The River Breaks Up. New York: 1938. V. 68

SINGER, ISAAC BASHEVIS
The Collected Stories. New York: 1982. V. 68
The Fearsome Inn. London: 1970. V. 68
The Image and Other Stories. New York: 1985. V. 69; 72
Lost in America. Garden City: 1981. V. 69; 71
The Magician from Lublin. New York: 1984. V. 72
One Day of Happiness. New York: 1982. V. 73
Reaches of Heaven. New York: 1980. V. 73
Satan in Goray. London: 1958. V. 72
Satan in Goray. New York: 1958. V. 70; 73
Shosha. New York: 1978. V. 69
Zlateh the Goat and Other Stories. New York: 1966. V. 69; 72; 73

SINGER, MARCUS
The Human Brain in Sagittal Section. Springfield: 1954. V. 68
The Human Brain in Sagittal Section. Springfield: 1964. V. 71

SINGER, SAMUEL WELLER
Catalogue of the...Extensive and Valuable Library Formed by the Late S. W. Singer, Esq.... London: 1860. V. 70
Shakespeare's Jest Book. Chiswick: 1814. V. 72
The Text of Shakespeare Vindicated from the Interpolations and Corruptions Advocated by John Payne Collier Esq. in His Notes and Emendations. London: 1853. V. 72

SINGH, K.
The Tiger of Rajasthan. 1959. V. 70; 72

SINGH, M.
Himalayan Art: Wall Painting and Sculpture in Ladakh, Lahaul and Spiti, The Siwalik Ranges, Nepal, Sikkim & Bhutan. 1968. V. 69; 72

SINGLETON, ESTHER
A Daughter of the Revolution. New York: 1915. V. 71
The Story of the White House. New York: 1907. V. 71
The Wild Flower Fairy Book. New York: 1905. V. 70

SINGLETON, JOHN
A Description of the West-Indies. London: 1776. V. 73

SINHA, RAJA KIRTYANAND
Purnea, a Shikar Land. Calcutta: 1916. V. 69

SINIGAGLIA, LEONE
Climbing Reminiscences of the Dolomites. 1896. V. 68; 70; 73
Climbing Reminiscences of the Dolomites. London: 1896. V. 69; 72

SINISTRARI, LUDOVICO MARIA
Demoniality. London: 1927. V. 69

SIODMAK, CURT
Donovan's Brain. New York: 1943. V. 68; 71

SIODMAK, KURT
F. P. I. Does Not Reply. 1933. V. 69

SIQUEREIROS, DAVID ALFARO
Asculto-Pintura: Cuarta Etapa Del Muralismo en Mexico. New York: 1968. V. 73

SIR Roger de Coverley. London: 1863. V. 68

SIRAT BANI HILAL
The Celebrated Romance of the Stealing of the Mare. London: 1892. V. 68; 71

SIREN, OSVALD
China and Gardens of Europe of the Eighteenth Century. New York: 1950. V. 69; 71; 73
China and Gardens of Europe of the Eighteenth Century. 1990. V. 73

SIRINGO, CHARLES ANGELO
A Cowboy Detective. Chicago: 1912. V. 71
A Cowboy Detective. New York: 1912. V. 68; 71
History of Billy the Kid. Austin: 1967. V. 69
A Lone Star Cowboy. Santa Fe: 1919. V. 68; 69; 71; 73
Riata and Spurs. Boston: 1927. V. 68; 70; 73

SIRINGO, CHARLES ANGELO continued
Riata and Spurs. Boston: 1931. V. 69
A Texas Cowboy. Chicago and New York. V. 72
A Texas Cowboy. 1886. V. 68
A Texas Cowboy. New York: 1950. V. 70; 72; 73

SIRLIN, J. L.
Biology of RNA. New York: 1972. V. 68

SISMONDE DE SISMONDI, JEAN CHARLES LEONARD
Political Economy and the Philosophy of Government.... London: 1847. V. 71

SISSON, EDGAR
One Hundred Red Days. A Personal Chronicle of the Bolshevik Revolution. New Haven: 1931. V. 68

SISTER Susie and the Twins. London: 1915. V. 73

THE SISTER'S Gift; or, the Bad Boy Reformed. London: 1826. V. 68

SITGREAVES, L.
Report of an Expedition Down the Zuni and Colorado Rivers. Washington: 1854. V. 68

SITTE, C.
The Art of Building Cities: City Building According to Its Artistic Fundamentals. New York: 1945. V. 72

SITTERSON, JOSEPH CARLYLE
The Secession Movement in North Carolina. Chapel Hill: 1939. V. 69

SITWELL, EDITH
Alexander Pope. London: 1930. V. 73
The Atlantic Book of British and American Poetry. London: 1959. V. 71
Augustan Books of Modern Poetry. London: 1928. V. 73
The Canticle of the Rose. London: 1949. V. 71; 73
Children's Tales. London: 1920. V. 73
Clown's Houses. Oxford: 1918. V. 69; 73
The Collected Poems. London: 1930. V. 73
The Collected Poems. New York: 1954. V. 68
Collected Poems. London: 1957. V. 69; 70; 72
Elegy on Dead Fashion. London: 1926. V. 73
Epithalamium. London: 1931. V. 71; 73
Facade. London: 1922. V. 72; 73
Facade. London: 1972. V. 72
Five Poems. London: 1928. V. 73
Five Variations on a Theme. London: 1933. V. 69; 73
Gardeners and Astronomers. London: 1953. V. 69
Gold Coast Customs. London: 1929. V. 71
In Spring. London: 1931. V. 73
Jane Barston 1719-1746. London: 1931. V. 73
The Mother and Other Poems. Oxford: 1915. V. 72; 73
The Pleasures of Poetry. A Critical Anthology. London: 1930. V. 71
The Pleasures of Poetry. Second Series. London: 1931. V. 73
Poor Men's Music. London: 1950. V. 68
Poor Young People. London: 1925. V. 73
Popular Song. London: 1928. V. 70; 73
Rustic Elegies. London: 1927. V. 72; 73
Troy Park. London: 1925. V. 72
Twentieth Century Harlequinade. Oxford: 1916. V. 73
Victoria of England. London: 1936. V. 69
Wheels, An Anthology of verse 1916. Oxford: 1916. V. 71; 73
Wheels, An Anthology of Verse 1916. Oxford: 1917. V. 73
Wheels: a Second Cycle. 1917. V. 72
Wheels: A Second Cycle 1917. Oxford: 1917. V. 73
Wheels 1918. A Third Cycle. Oxford: 1917. V. 71
Wheels 1918. Third Cycle. Oxford: 1918. V. 73
Wheels 1919. Fourth Cycle. Oxford: 1919. V. 73
Wheels 1920. (Fifth cycle). London: 1928. V. 71
The Wooden Pegasus. Oxford: 1920. V. 73

SITWELL, GEORGE
The Barbons of Pulford in the Eleventh and Twelfth Centuries and Their Descendants. Scarborough: 1889. V. 72
On the Making of Gardens. London: 1909. V. 68; 69; 70; 71; 72
On the Making of Gardens. London: 1949. V. 68; 72; 73

SITWELL, H. D.
Crown Jewels and Other Regalia in the Tower of London. London: 1953. V. 72

SITWELL, OSBERT
All At Sea. London: 1927. V. 73
Argonaut and Juggernaut. London: 1919. V. 72; 73
At The House of Mrs. Kinfoot. London: 1921. V. 73
Before the Bombardment. London: 1926. V. 73
Brighton. 1935. V. 70
Collected Satires and Poems. London: 1931. V. 73
The Cyder Feast and Other Poems. London: 1927. V. 71
Dickens. London: 1932. V. 73
Discursions on Travel, Art and Life. London: 1925. V. 73
England Reclaimed. London: 1927. V. 73
Four Songs of the Italian Earth. Pawlet: 1948. V. 68
Laughter in the Next Room. London: 1949. V. 68
Left Hand, Right Hand! An Autobiography. London: 1945-1950. V. 73
National Rat Week. New York: 1957. V. 72
Out of the Flame. London: 1923. V. 70; 73
The People's Album of London Statues. London: 1928. V. 73
Rat Week: an Essay on the Abdication. London: 1986. V. 72
Three-Quarter Length Portrait of Michael Arlen. London: 1931. V. 73
Triple Fugue. London: 1924. V. 73
Who Killed Cock-Robin? Remarks on Poetry, on Its Criticism and as a Sad Warning, the Story of Eunuch Arden. London: 1921. V. 68
The Winstonburg Line. 1919. V. 70
The Winstonburg Line. London: 1919. V. 72; 73

SITWELL, SACHEVERELL
All Summer in a Day - an Autobiographical Fantasia. London: 1926. V. 71
Beckford and Beckfordism. London: 1930. V. 73
A Book of Towers and Other Buildings of Southern Europe. London: 1928. V. 73
The Cyder Feast and Other Poems. London: 1927. V. 73
Dance of the Quick and the Dead. London: 1936. V. 70
Doctor Donne and Gargantua. London: 1930. V. 73
Doctor Donne and Gargantua First Canto. London: 1921. V. 73
Doctor Donne and Gargantua Second Canto. London: 1923. V. 73
Doctor Donne and Gargantua Third Canto. Stratford-upon-Avon: 1926. V. 73
Exalt the Eglantine and Other Poems. London: 1926. V. 73
Far From My Home. Stories: Long & Short. London: 1931. V. 73
Fine Bird Books 1700-1900. London and New York: 1953. V. 68; 73
The Gothick North: a Study of Mediaeval Life, Art and Thought. London: 1929-1930. V. 73
Great Flower Books 1700-1900. London: 1956. V. 69
Mauretania. London: 1940. V. 73
The People's Palace. London: 1918. V. 70
The People's Palace. Oxford: 1918. V. 73
Poltergeists. London: 1940. V. 73
The Romantic Ballet in Lithograhs of the Time. London: 1938. V. 73
Southern Baroque Art. London: 1924. V. 73
Two Poems, Ten Songs. London: 1929. V. 68; 73

SIX Brave Explorers - a Pop-up Book. London: 1988. V. 69

SIX Months in a Convent, or the Narrative of Rebecca Theresa Reed, who Was Under the Influence of the Roman Catholics About Two Years.... Boston: 1835. V. 69

SIX One-Act Plays for Festivals. London: 1938. V. 71

SIZER, NELSON
Forty Years in Phrenology.... Boston: 1839. V. 68
Forty Years in Phrenology.... New York: 1892. V. 71

SJOQVIST, OLOF
Studies in Pain Conduction in the Trigeminal Nerve. Helsingfors: 1938. V. 68; 73

SJOSTEDT, BROR YNGVE
Wissenschaftliche Ergebnisse der Schwedischen Zoologischen Expedition Nach Dem Kilimandjaro.... Stockholm: 1910. V. 71

SJOSTEDT, Y.
Wissenschaftliche Ergebnisse der Schwedischen Zoologischen Expedition Nach Dem Kilimandjaro, dem Meru und den Umgebenden Massaisteppen Deutsch Ostafrikas 1905-1906. Stockholm: 1910. V. 73

SJOWALL, MAJ
The Abominable Man. New York: 1972. V. 72
The Laughing Policeman. 1970. V. 68
The Laughing Policeman. New York: 1970. V. 72
Murder At The Savoy. New York: 1971. V. 72
Roseanna. 1967. V. 68; 70
The Terrorists. New York: 1976. V. 72

SKAIFE, THOMAS
A Key to Civil Architecture; or the Universal British Builder. 1774. V. 73

SKARSTEN, M. O.
George Drouillard, Hunter and Interpreter for Lewis and Clark and Fur Trader, 1807-1810. 1964. V. 68
George Drouillard, Hunter and Interpreter for Lewis and Clark and Fur Trader, 1807-1810. Glendale: 1964. V. 70

SKEET, FRANCIS JOHN ANGUS
Stuart Papers, Pictures, Relics, Medals and Books in the collection of Miss Maria Widdrington. Leeds: 1930. V. 71; 72

SKEETE, THOMAS
An Exact Representation of the Very Uncandid and Extraordinary Conduct of Dr. John Coakley Lettsom, as Well Previous to as On the Day of Election for Physician to the Finsbury Dispensary with Some Remarks on the Establishment of the New Finsbury Dispensa. London: 1786. V. 70

SKELTON, BARBARA
Weep No More. London: 1989. V. 70

SKELTON, EDITH
The Crucial Test and Other Poems. London: 1889. V. 69

SKELTON, G.
Five Little Pigs. London: 1910. V. 68

SKELTON, JOHN
John Skelton: A Sculptor's Work 1950-1975. London: 1977. V. 72

SKELTON, JOSEPH
Engraved Illustrations of the Principal Antiquities of Oxfordshire. Oxford: 1823. V. 68; 73
Engraved Illustrations of the Principal Antiquities of Oxfordshire. Oxford: 1823-1827. V. 70

SKELTON, R. A.
Decorative Printed Maps of the 15th to 18th Centuries. London: 1952. V. 72
Decorative Printed Maps of the 15th to 18th Centuries. London: 1967. V. 72
A Description of Maps and Architectural Drawings in the Collection Made by William Cecil, first Baron Brughley now at Hatfield House. Oxford: 1971. V. 70
The Vinland Map and the Tartar Relation. London: 1965. V. 72

SKELTON, ROBIN
Inscriptions. Victoria: 1967. V. 70
Lens of Cyrstal: Poems. 1996. V. 71

SKELTON, W. C.
Reminiscences of Joe Bowman and the Ullswater Foxhounds. Kendal: 1923. V. 71

SKENE, ALEXANDER
Medical Gynecology. New York: 1896. V. 73

A SKETCH of the Times; or, Memoirs of Lord Derville. Dublin: 1781. V. 73

SKETCHES and Adventures in Madeira, Portugal and the Andalusias of Spain. New York: 1856. V. 68

SKETCHES and Recollections of Lynchburg. Richmond: 1858. V. 72

SKETCHES of Australian Life and Scenery. London: 1876. V. 68; 72

SKETCHES of the History, Genius, Disposition, Accomplishments, Employments, Customs, Virtues and Vices of the Fair Sex, in all Parts of the World. Gettysburg: 1812. V. 73

SKETCHES of the Inter-Mountain States - Utah, Idaho, Nevada 1847-1909. Salt Lake City: 1909. V. 68; 73

SKETCHLEY, ARTHUR
Mrs. Brown in the Highlands and Mrs. Brown in London. London. V. 70
Mrs. Brown's Christmas Box. London: 1869. V. 73

SKEY, FREDERIC C.
Operative Surgery. London: 1850. V. 68; 71

SKIDMORE, OWINGS & MERRILL
Architecture and Urbanism 1973-1983. London: 1983. V. 72
Architecture and Urbanism 1973-1983. New York/Stuttgart: 1983. V. 68; 69

SKINNER, ADA M.
A Child's Book of Country Stories. New York: 1935. V. 72
A Very Little Child's Book of Stories. New York: 1935. V. 70

SKINNER, EMORY F.
Reminiscences. Chicago: 1908. V. 68; 73

SKINNER, H. B.
The Female's Medical Guide and Married Woman's Adviser.... Boston: 1849. V. 73

SKINNER, HARRY H.
Jiu-Jitsu: A Comprehensive and Copiously Illustrated Treatise on the Wonderful Japanese Method of Attack and Self Defense. New York: 1904. V. 70

SKINNER, JOHN
Amusements of Leisure Hours; or Poetical Pieces, Chiefly in the Scottish Dialect. Edinburgh: 1809. V. 68; 72

SKINNER, JOHN C.
Murder in the Village. London: 1930. V. 73

SKINNER, M. F.
The Fossil Bison of Alaska and Preliminary Revision of the Genus. New York: 1947. V. 72

SKINNER, M. L.
Black Swans. London: 1925. V. 71

SKINNER, MARTYN
The Return of Arthur - A Poem in the Future. London: 1966. V. 71

SKINNER, STEPHANO
Etymologicon Linguae Anglicanae. London: 1671. V. 68

SKINNER, THOMAS
The Life of General Monk: Duke of Albemarle.... London: 1724. V. 72

SKODA, JOSEF
Auscultation and Percussion. Philadelphia: 1854. V. 70; 71; 73

SKREBNESKI, VICTOR
Skrebneski Portaits: a Matter of Record. Garden City: 1978. V. 68

SKRIMSHIRE, FENWICK
A Series of Popular Chymical Essays.... 1802. V. 73

SKUES, G. E. M.
The Chalk-Stream Angler. 1976. V. 68
Itchen Memories. 1951. V. 70; 73
Minor Tactics of the Chalk Stream. 1950. V. 73
Minor Tactics of the Trout Stream. 1924. V. 68; 73
Nymph Fishing for Chalk Stream Trout. 1939. V. 68; 69
Side-Lines, Side-Lights and Reflections. 1932. V. 73
Side-Lines, Side-Lights and Reflections. 1934. V. 73
Side-Lines, Side-Lights and Reflections. 1996. V. 68; 73
Silk, Fur and Feather. 1950. V. 73
The Way of a Trout with a Fly. 1921. V. 68; 73
The Way of a Trout with a Fly. 1928. V. 68
The Way of a Trout with a Fly. 1973. V. 73

SKUSE, E.
The Confectioners' Hand-Book and Practical Guide to the Art of Sugar Boiling.... London: 1883. V. 68

SKUTCH, A. F.
Life of the Woodpecker. Santa Monica: 1985. V. 72

SKVORECKY, JOSEF
The Mournful Demeanour of Lieutenant Boruvka. London: 1973. V. 72

SKVORESKY, JOSEF
Sins for Father Knox. London: 1989. V. 68

SKYRING, W. H.
Skyring's Builders' Princes: Calculated from the Prime Cost of Materials and Labour; the New Buildings' Act, List of Surveyors.... London: 1859. V. 68

SLACK, HARRY D.
Studies on Loch Lomond. 1957. V. 71

SLADDEN, DILNOT
The Spirit of Beauty. Canterbury: 1840. V. 69

SLADE, GURNEY
In Lawrence's Bodygaurd. New York: 1930. V. 69
In Lawrence's Bodyguard. London: 1931. V. 68

SLADE, J.
Colloquies: Imaginary Conversations Between a Phrenologist and the Shade of Dugald Stewart. London: 1838. V. 73

SLADEK, JOHN
Black Aura. London: 1974. V. 69

SLADEN, F. L. W.
The Humble Bee, Its Life History and How to Domesticate It.... London: 1912. V. 69

SLATE, G. L.
The Lily Yearbook of the North American Lily Society. 1950-1969. V. 71

SLATER, ELIZA
Little Princes. London: 1845. V. 69

SLATER, ISAAC
Slater's Royal National Commercial Directory of the Counties of Cumberland and Westmoreland ad the Cleveland District.... Manchester: 1876-1877. V. 71

SLATER, J. HERBERT
Book Collecting: a Guide for Amateurs. London: 1892. V. 71
Early Editions: a Bibliographical Survey of the Works of Some Popular Modern Authors. London: 1894. V. 71
How to Collect Books. London: 1905. V. 71

SLATER, JOHN M.
El Moro Inscription Rock in New Mexico. Los Angeles: 1961. V. 68

SLATIN, RUDOLF ANTON CARL, FREIHERR VON
Fire and Sword in the Sudan. Leipzig: 1896. V. 73
Fire and Sword in the Sudan. London: 1896. V. 72; 73

SLATTER, HENRY
The Oxford University and City Guide on a New Plan.... Oxford: 1835. V. 70

SLATTER, JOHN
El Morro - Inscription Rock New Mexico. Los Angeles: 1961. V. 68; 73

SLAUGHTER, FRANCES E.
The Sportswoman's Library. London: 1898. V. 71

SLAUGHTER, PHILIP
History of St. Mark's Parrish (Culpeper Co., Va.). Culpeper: 1900. V. 68
A Sketch of the Life of Randolph Fairfax.... Richmond: 1864. V. 69; 70

SLAVE Songs of the United States. New York: 1867. V. 72

SLAVERY. From the Hull Rockingham of January 31, 1824. Liverpool: 1824. V. 71

SLEEPING Beauty. New York: 1882?. V. 70

SLEIGH, WILLIAM CAMPBELL
The Grand Jury System Subversive of the Moral Interests of Society; a Letter to the Rt. Hon. Spencer H. Walpole, M.P. Secretary of State for the Home Department. London: 1852. V. 73

SLEMONS, J. MORRIS
John Whitridge Williams Academic Aspects.... Baltimore: 1935. V. 70; 71

SLESSER, MALCOLM
The Andes are Prickly. London: 1966. V. 69

SLESSOR, KENNETH
Earth Visitors. London: 1926. V. 71

SLEVIN, J. R.
A Handbook of Reptiles and Amphibians of the Pacific States. San Francisco: 1934. V. 72

SLINGSBY, JONATHAN
The Dead Bridal: a Venetian Tale of the 14th Century. London: 1856. V. 68
A Familiar Epistle to Robert J. Walker. London: 1863. V. 72

SLINGSBY, W. C.
Norway - the Northern Playground. Oxford: 1941. V. 69

SLOAN, JOHN
Introduction to American Indian Art. New York: 1931. V. 68; 73

SLOAN, JOHN ALEXANDER
North Carolina in the War Between the States. Washington: 1883. V. 69; 70
Reminiscences of the Guilford Grays, Co., B. 27th N.C. Regiment. Washington: 1883. V. 69; 70

SLOAN, RICHARD E.
Memories of an Arizona Judge. Stanford: 1932. V. 69

SLOAN, ROBERT E.
The Rainbow Route: an Illustrated History of the Silverton Railroad, the Silverton Northern Railroad and the Silverton, Gladstone and Northerly Railroad. Silverton: 1979. V. 68

SLOAN, SAMUEL
Sloan's Constructive Architecture. Philadelphia: 1866. V. 68; 73
Sloan's Constructive Architecture. Philadelphia: 1886. V. 70

SLOANE, HANS
An Account of a Most Efficacious Medicine for Sore Eyes. 1745. V. 69
A Voyage to the Island Madera, Barbados, Nieves, S. Christophers and Jamaica.... London: 1707-1725. V. 69

SLOANE, WILLIAM M.
Life of Napoleon Bonaparte. New York: 1896. V. 71

SLOSSON, ANNIE TRUMBULL
The China Hunters Club. New York: 1878. V. 71

SLOTKIN, RICHARD
The Fatal Environment - The Myth of The Frontier in The Age of Industrialization. NY: 1985. V. 72
Gunfighter Nation, The Myth of The Frontier in Twentieth Century America. New York: 1992. V. 72

SLOVENLY Peter or Cheerful Stories and Funny Pictures for Good Little Folks with Illustrations. Philadelphia. V. 71

SLOW, EDWARD
Wiltshire Rhymes. London: 1881. V. 68; 71

SLY Mike a Hungarian Story. Budapest: 1937. V. 73

SMALL, ANDREW
Interesting Roman Antiquities Recently Discovered in Fife. Edinburgh: 1823. V. 69

SMALL, AUSTIN J.
The Avening Ray. New York: 1930. V. 68

SMALL, GEORGE G.
Fred Douglass and His Mule; a Story of the War. New York: 1886. V. 73

SMALL, GEORGE W.
Bricktop's Songs, Recitations and Parlor Dramas. New York: 1886?. V. 68

SMALL, J. K.
Ferns of Florida.... New York: 1931. V. 72
Ferns of the Southeastern States. Lancaster: 1938. V. 68; 70
Ferns of the Southeastern States. New York: 1964. V. 69
Manual of the Southeastern Flora.... New York: 1933. V. 71

SMALL, T.
Houses of the Wren and Early Georgian Periods. London: 1928. V. 69; 72

THE SMALLEST English Dictionary in the World. Glasgow: 1900. V. 72

SMALLEY, EUGENE VIRGIL
The Great Northwest a Guide-Book and Itinerary. St. Paul: 1886. V. 71
History of the Northern Pacific Railroad. New York: 1883. V. 70

SMALLFIELD, W. E.
The Story of Renfrew, from the Coming of the First Settlers about 1820. Volume One. (all published). Renfrew: 1919. V. 73

SMALLWOOD, J. R.
The Book of Newfoundland. St. John's: 1937-1967. V. 72
The Book of Newfoundland. St. John's: 1968-1979. V. 72

SMART, B. H.
The Practice of Elocution, or a Course of Exercises for Acquiring the Several Requisites of a Good Delivery. London: 1876. V. 71

SMART, CHRISTOPHER
Poems. Princeton: 1950. V. 72
Poems on Several Occasions. London: 1752. V. 71
A Song to David with Other Poems. London: 1924. V. 71

SMART, ELIZABETH
Autobiographies. Vancouver: 1987. V. 70
By Grand Central Station I Sat Down and Wept. London: 1945. V. 73

SMART, HAWLEY
Beatrice and Benedick: a Romance of the Crimea. London: 1893. V. 68
Cecile, or Modern Idolaters. London: 1878. V. 68
From Post to Finish. London: 1884. V. 69
The Great Tontine. London: 1882?. V. 68
Play or Pay. London: 1878. V. 68
A Racing Rubber. London: 1896. V. 68
Two Kisses. London: 1876. V. 68

SMART, W. M.
Stellar Dynamics. Cambridge: 1938. V. 69

SMART, WILLIAM
Economic Annals of the Nineteenth Century 1801-1820 (and 1821-1830). London: 1910-1917. V. 68

SMEAD, W.
Land of the Flatheads. St. Paul: 1905. V. 68; 71

SMEATON, A. C.
The Builder's Pocket Manual, Containing the Elements of Building, Surveying and Architecture.... London: 1836. V. 68

SMEATON, G.
The Builder's Pocket Manual; or, Rules and Instructions in the Art of Carpentry, Joinery, Masonry and Bricklaying. London: 1825. V. 68

SMEATON, JOHN
An Experimental Enquiry Concerning the Natural Powers of Wind and Water to Turn Mills, and Other Machines, Depending on a Circular Motion. London: 1760. V. 73
Experimental Inquiry Concerning the Natural Powers of Wind and Water to Turn Mills and Other Machines Depending on a Circular Motion. London: 1796. V. 68
An Historical Report on Ramsgate Harbour; Written by Order of, and Addressed to the Trustees. London: 1791. V. 73
John Smeaton's Diary of His Journey to the Low Countries 1755 from the Original MS in the Library of Trinity House, London. Leamington Spa: 1938. V. 73
The Report of John Smeaton Engineer and F.R.S. Concerning the Practicability and Expence of Joining the Rivers Forth and Clyde.... Edinburgh: 1768. V. 72
A Report Relative to Tyne Bridge. Newcastle: 1772. V. 68
A Review of Several Matters Relative to the Forth and Clyde Navigation, as Now Settled by Act of Parliament, with Some Observations of the Reports of Mess. Brindley, Yeoman and Golburne (sic). Edinburgh: 1768. V. 72

SMEDLEY, AGNES
Daughter of Earth. New York: 1929. V. 72

SMEDLEY, FRANK E.
The Fortunes of the Colville Family, o, a Cloud and Its Silver Lining. London: 1856. V. 68

SMEDLEY, WILLIAM
Across the Plains in '62. Denver: 1962. V. 69

SMEE, ALFRED
Elements of Electro-Metallurgy, or the Art of Working in Metals by the Galvanic Fluid. (with) Preparing for Publication, and Intended as an Acompaniment to the Foregoing Work.... 1841. V. 68
Instinct and Reason: Deduced from the Electro-biology. London: 1850. V. 71

SMEETON, GEORGE
Doings in London or Day and Night Scenes of the frauds, frolics, manners and depravities of the Metropolis. London. V. 70; 71
Doings in London; or Day and Night Scenes of the Frauds, Frolics, Manners and Depravities of the Metropolis. 1849?. V. 71

SMELLIE, WILLIAM
The Philosophy of Natural History. Edinburgh: 1790-1799. V. 70; 73

SMET, PIERRE JEAN DE
Western Missions and Missionaries: a Series of Letters. New York: 1881. V. 70

SMILES, SAMUEL
A Boy's Voyage Round the World.... London: 1871. V. 71
A Boy's Voyage Round the World.... London: 1877. V. 71
George Moore, Merchant and Philanthropist. London: 1878. V. 71
George Moore, Merchant and Philanthropist. London: 1884. V. 71
The Huguenots; their Settlements, Churches and Industries in England and Ireland. London: 1867. V. 71
The Huguenots; their Settlements, Churches and Industries in England and Ireland. London: 1868. V. 71
The Huguenots: their Settlements, Churches and Industries in England and Ireland. London: 1869. V. 71
The Huguenots: Their Settlements, Churches and Industries in England and Ireland. London: 1881. V. 71
Industrial Biography: Iron Workers and Tool Makers. London: 1863. V. 71
Industrial Biography: Iron Workers and Tool Makers. London: 1886. V. 71
James Brindley and the Early Engineers. London: 1864. V. 71
James Nasmyth Engineer. London: 1883. V. 68
Jasmin: Barber, Poet, Philanthropist. London: 1891. V. 71
Josiah Wedgwood, F.R.S.: His Personal History. London: 1894. V. 71
Life and Labour or Characteristics of Men of Industry Culture and Genius. London: 1887. V. 73
Life Of A Scotch Naturalist. Thomas Edward, Associate of the Linnaean Society. London: 1876. V. 68; 71; 72
Life of a Scotch Naturalist. Thomas Edward, Associate of the Linnaean Society. London: 1877. V. 68
Life of a Scotch Naturalist. Thomas Edward, Associate of the Linnaean Society. London: 1884. V. 68
The Life of George Stephenson, Railway Engineer. London: 1857. V. 68; 71; 73
The Life Of George Stephenson, Railway Engineer. Edinburgh: 1999. V. 72
The Story of the Life of George Stephenson, Railway Engineer. London: 1862. V. 71

SMILES, SAMUEL continued
Men of Invention and Industry. London: 1884. V. 71
A Publisher and His Friends. London: 1891. V. 71
Self-Help; with Illustrations of Character and Conduct. London: 1859. V. 71; 73
Self-Help; with Illustrations of Character and Conduct. London: 1860. V. 71
Self-Help; with Illustrations of Character and Conduct. London: 1862. V. 71
Self-Help; with Illustrations of Conduct and Perserverance. London: 1887. V. 72
Thrift. London: 1875. V. 71
Thrift. London: 1877. V. 71

SMILEY, JANE
The Age of Grief. New York: 1987. V. 68; 70; 71; 73
The All-True Travels and Adventures of Lidie Newton. New York: 1998. V. 72
At Paradise Gate. New York: 1981. V. 68; 71; 72
Barn Blind. New York: 1980. V. 68; 72
Catskill Crafts. New York: 1988. V. 71; 72
Duplicate Keys. London: 1984. V. 68; 71
Duplicate Keys. New York: 1984. V. 68; 71; 72
The Greenlanders. New York: 1988. V. 68; 71; 72; 73
Horse Heaven. New York: 2000. V. 68
Moo. New York: 1995. V. 68; 71; 72
Ordinary Love and Good Will. New York: 1989. V. 68; 71; 72
A Thousand Acres. New York: 1991. V. 68; 69; 71; 72; 73

SMILEY, JOSEPH
Catskill Crafts. New York: 1988. V. 68

SMITH, A. C.
The Power of the Dog. 1900. V. 70

SMITH, A. C. H.
Orhast at Persepolis: an Account of the Experiment in Theatre. London: 1972. V. 70

SMITH, A. H.
A Catalogue of Sculpture at Woburn Abbey in the Collection of His Grace the Duke of Bedford. London: 1900. V. 68
English Place-Name Elements. 1956. V. 68
Mushrooms in Their Natural Habitats. Portland: 1949. V. 68; 71; 72
The North American Species of Pholiota. New York: 1968. V. 72
The Place-Names of Westmorland. Cambridge: 1967. V. 71

SMITH, A. L.
A Monograph of the British Lichens, a Descriptive Catalogue of the Species in the Department of Botany, British Museum. 1918-1926. V. 73

SMITH, A. M.
Sport and Adventure in the Indian Jungle. 1904. V. 69; 70; 72; 73

SMITH, ADAM
Essays on Philosophical Subjects. Dublin: 1795. V. 73
An Inquiry Into the Nature and Causes of the Wealth of Nations. London: 1776. V. 68; 70; 72
An Inquiry Into the Nature and Causes of the Wealth of Nations. London: 1791. V. 69; 70
An Inquiry into the Nature and Causes of the Wealth of Nations. London: 1806. V. 71
An Inquiry Into the Nature and Causes of the Wealth of Nations. Hartford: 1811. V. 68; 69; 71
An Inquiry Into the Nature and Causes of the Wealth of Nations. London: 1811. V. 71
An Inquiry into the Nature and Causes of the Wealth of Nations. London: 1812. V. 73
An Inquiry Into the Nature and Causes of the Wealth of Nations. London: 1826. V. 71
An Inquiry into the Nature and Causes of the Wealth of Nations. Oxford: 1880. V. 69; 71
The Theory of Moral Sentiments; or, an Essay Toward an Analysis of the Principles by Which Men Naturally Judge Concerning the Conduct and Character.... Dublin: 1777. V. 69

SMITH, ALBERT
Mont Blanc. London: 1860?. V. 68
The Natural History of the Ballet-Girl. London: 1847. V. 72
Novelty Fair or Hints for 1851. London: 1850. V. 70
The Pottleton Legacy, a Story of Town and Country Life. London: 1849. V. 70
The Story of Mont Blanc. London: 1854. V. 69; 72
The Struggles and Adventures of Christopher Tadpole at Home and Abroad. London: 1848. V. 70; 71

SMITH, ALEXANDER
Memoirs of the Life and Times of the Famous Jonathan Wild, Together with the History and Lives of Modern Rogues.... London: 1726. V. 73
A Summer In Skye. Edinburgh: 1880. V. 71

SMITH, ALICE R. HUGER
Charles Fraser. New York: 1924. V. 71
The Dwelling Houses of Charleston South Carolina. Philadelphia: 1917. V. 71

SMITH, ALPHONSO
O. Henry Biography. Garden City: 1916. V. 68

SMITH, AMANDA
An Autobiography. The story of the Lord's Dealings with Mrs. Amanda Smith the colored Evangelist. Chicago: 1893. V. 72

SMITH, APRIL
North of Montana. New York: 1994. V. 72

SMITH, ARTHUR H.
Chinese Characteristics. London: 1895. V. 72

SMITH, ASHLEY
Children With Fire and Other Stories. London: 1934. V. 70

SMITH, B.
European Vision and the South Pacific. New Haven: 1985. V. 69

SMITH, BENJAMIN
A Fugitive From Hell Fifteen Years An Outlaw. Joplin, MO: 1935. V. 71

SMITH, BERNARD BRYON
The Heart of The New Kansas - A Pamphlet Historical and Descriptive of Southwestern Kansas - vol 1. Great Bend: 1960. V. 72

SMITH, BETTY
A Tree Grows in Brooklyn. New York: 1943. V. 71

SMITH, C. H.
Alfred Russel Wallace, an Anthology of His Shorter Writings. Oxford: 1991. V. 68
The Natural History of the Human Species.... Edinburgh: 1848. V. 72

SMITH, C. L.
Estaurine Research in the 1980's. Albany: 1992. V. 73

SMITH, C. W.
Journal of a Trip to California. New York: 1920. V. 69
Thin Men of Haddam. New York: 1973. V. 68

SMITH, CARL
The Olive Trail. Broken Bow: 1973. V. 72

SMITH, CAROLINE ESTES
The Philharmonic Orchestra of Los Angeles "The First Decade" 1919- 1929. Los Angeles: 1930. V. 68

SMITH, CHARLES
The Ancient and Present State of the County and City of Waterford.... Dublin: 1746. V. 73
The Antient and Present State of the County Kerry. Dublin: 1746. V. 73
The Antient and Present State of the County of Down. Dublin: 1744. V. 72
Smith's New Pocket Companion to the Roads of England and Wales and Part of Scotland. London: 1826. V. 68; 72

SMITH, CHARLES A.
A Comprehensive History of Minnehaha County, South Dakota. Mitchell: 1949. V. 70

SMITH, CHARLES EDWARD
From the Deep of the Sea. Being the Diary of.... London: 1922. V. 73

SMITH, CHARLES ROACH
Catalogue of the Museum of London Antiquites Collected by and Property of Charles Roach Smith. 1854. V. 71
Illustrations of Roman London. London: 1859. V. 68

SMITH, CHARLES W.
Journal of a Trip Across the Continent from Weston, Mo. to Weber Creek, California in the Summer of 1850. New York: 1920. V. 70

SMITH, CHARLIE
Canaan. New York: 1984. V. 68; 69; 70; 71

SMITH, CHARLOTTE
Desmond. London: 1792. V. 73
Elegiac Sonnets. London: 1786. V. 69
Elegiac Sonnets. London: 1795. V. 69; 72; 73
Marchmont, a Novel. London: 1796. V. 69
The Old Manor House. London: 1793. V. 68; 72; 73

SMITH, CHARLOTTE CURTIS
The Old Cobblestone House: a Ghost Story. Rochester: 1917. V. 73

SMITH, CLARK ASHTON
Genius Loci and Other Tales. Sauk City: 1948. V. 71; 73
Other Dimensions. Sauk City: 1970. V. 69

SMITH, DAMA MARGARET
I Married a Ranger. Stanford: 1931. V. 69

SMITH, DANIEL E. HUGER
Mason Smith Family Letters 1860-1868. Columbia: 1950. V. 70

SMITH, DANIEL P.
Company K. First Alabama Regiment, or Three Years in the Confederate Service. Prattville: 1885. V. 69; 70

SMITH, DAVE
Mean Rufus Throw Down. Fredonia: 1973. V. 72
Onliness. Baton Rouge: 1981. V. 72

SMITH, DAVID EUGENE
History of Mathematics.... Boston: 1923-1925. V. 72
Rara Arithmetica. A Catalogue of the Arithmetics Written Before the Year MDCI.... Mansfield Centre: 1996. V. 73
Rara Arithmetica. (with) Addenda. Boston and London: 1908-1939. V. 69

SMITH, DAVID W.
Recognizable Patterns of Human Malformation. Philadelphia: 1970. V. 68

SMITH, DE COST
Red Indian Experiences. Caldwell: 1943. V. 69; 72

SMITH, DENIS E.
Leaves from a Physician's Journal. New York: 1867. V. 71

SMITH, DEXTER
Cyclopedia of Boston and Vicinity. Boston: 1886. V. 72

SMITH, DIANE SOLETHER
The Armstrong Chronicle, a Ranching History. Corona: 1986. V. 69

SMITH, DODIE
The Hundred and One Dalmations. London: 1956. V. 71

SMITH, E. BOYD
Chicken World. New York: 1910. V. 70; 73
The Early Life of Mr. Man. Boston: 1914. V. 71; 73
The Story of Our Country. New York: 1920. V. 70
The Story of Pocahontas and Captain John Smith. Boston: 1906. V. 71; 73

SMITH, E. E.
Children of the Lens. Reading: 1954. V. 70
First Lensman. 1950. V. 68
The Forests of Cuba. 1954. V. 70
Galactic Patrol. 1950. V. 68
Galactic Patrol. Reading: 1950. V. 71; 73
Gray Lensman. 1951. V. 70
Gray Lensman. Hicksville: 1962. V. 71; 73
Second Stage Lensmen. 1953. V. 68
Second Stage Lensmen. New York: 1990. V. 70
Subspace Explorers. 1965. V. 68
Triplanetary. 1948. V. 68
Triplanetary. Reading: 1950. V. 71
The Vortex Blaster. Hicksville: 1960. V. 71

SMITH, E. F.
Bacteria in Relation to Plant Diseases. Washington: 1905-1914. V. 72

SMITH, E. H.
A Discourse, Delivered April 11, 1798, at the Request and Before the New York Society for Promoting the Manumission of Slaves, and Protecting Such of them As Have Been or May be Liberated. New York: 1798. V. 71

SMITH, EDGAR C.
A Short History of Naval and Marine Engineering. Cambridge: 1938. V. 68

SMITH, EDGAR W.
Baker Street and Beyond.... New York: 1940. V. 69
Baker Street and Beyond.... Morristown: 1957. V. 69
The Long Road from Maiwand. 1940. V. 69
The Napoleon of Crime. 1953. V. 69
The Napoleon of Crime. Summit: 1953. V. 69
Profile by Gaslight. New York: 1944. V. 70

SMITH, EDMUND
Phaedra and Hippolitus. London: 1707. V. 68

SMITH, EDWARD
Foods. New York: 1873. V. 68

SMITH, ELIAS
The Life, Conversion, Preaching, Travels and Sufferings of Elias Smith. Portsmouth: 1816. V. 73

SMITH, ELIHU HUBBARD
American Poems, Selected and Original. Volume I. Litchfield: 1793. V. 69; 72; 73

SMITH, ELIZABETH
The Brethren: a Poem in Four Books. Birmingham: 1787. V. 69
Life Review'd; a Poem.... Exeter: 1780. V. 69
Life Review'd; a Poem.... Birmingham: 1783. V. 69

SMITH, ELIZABETH OAKES
Bertha and Lily; or the Parsonage of Beech Glen, a Romance. New York: 1854. V. 72
Woman and Her Needs. New York: 1851. V. 69
Woman and Her Needs. (with) Shadow Land; or, the Seer. New York: 1851-1852. V. 69

SMITH, ERASMUS
The Charter of King Charles II, Impowering Erasmus Smith Esq. to Erect Grammar Schools in the Kingdom of Ireland.... Dublin: 1724. V. 71

SMITH, ERNEST BRAMAH
English Farming and Why I Turned It Up. 1894. V. 68; 69
English Farming and Why I Turned It Up. London: 1894. V. 68
The Eyes of Max Carrados. 1923. V. 73
The Eyes of Max Carrados. London: 1923. V. 68; 71
The Eyes of Max Carrados. New York: 1924. V. 70
Kai Lung Beneath the Mulberry Tree. London: 1940. V. 68
Kai Lung Unrolls His Mat. Garden City: 1928. V. 69; 71
Kai Lung Unrolls His Mat. London: 1928. V. 68
Kai Lung's Golden Hours. London: 1922. V. 68
Kai Lung's Golden Hours. Garden City: 1923. V. 71
Kai Lung's Golden Hours. London: 1924. V. 72
Max Carrados Mysteries. 1927. V. 71
The Specimen Case. London: 1924. V. 71
The Specimen Case. 1925. V. 71
The Specimen Case. New York: 1925. V. 71
The Transmutation of Ling. London: 1911. V. 69; 70

SMITH, ERWIN E.
Life on the Texas Range. Austin: 1952. V. 69

SMITH, ESTHER RUTH
The History of Del Norte County California - Including the Story of Its Pioneers with Many of Their Personal Narratives. Oakland: 1953. V. 69

SMITH, ETHAN
Key to the Revelation. In Thirty-Six Lectures, Taking the Whole Book in Course. New York: 1833. V. 71

SMITH, FAY JACKSON
Father Kino in Arizona. Phoenix: 1966. V. 71

SMITH, FRANCIS HOPKINSON
Colonel Carter's Christmas. New York: 1903. V. 69
The Virginia Military Institute, Its Building and Rebuilding. Lynchburg: 1912. V. 69; 70

SMITH, FRANK
The Life and Work of Sir James Kay-Shuttleworth. London: 1923. V. 73

SMITH, FRANK MERIWEATHER
San Francisco Vigilante Committee of 156. San Francisco: 1883. V. 73

SMITH, FREDERICK
The Stone Ages in North Britain and Ireland. 1909. V. 69

SMITH, FREDERICK E.
The Devil Behind Me. London: 1962. V. 72

SMITH, G.
The Laboratory, or School of Arts: Containing a Large...Collection of Valuable Secrets, Experiments, and Manual Operations in Arts and Manufactures. London: 1799. V. 73

SMITH, G. ELLIOT
The Archaeological Survey of Nubia. Report for 1907-1908. Volume II: Report on the Human remains. Cairo: 1910. V. 68
The Arris and Gale Lectures on Some Problems Relating to the Evolution of the Brain. London: 1910. V. 68

SMITH, G. M.
Phytoplankton of the Inland Lakes of Wisconsin. Madison: 1920-1924. V. 72

SMITH, GEORGE
A Collection of Ornamental Designs After the Manner of the Antique.... London: 1812. V. 68
A Compleat Body of Distilling, Explaining the Mysteries of that Science.... London: 1725. V. 70
A Narrative of an Explorative Visit to Each of the Consular Cities of China and to the Islands of Hong Kong and Chusan, in Behalf of the Church Missionary Society.... London: 1847. V. 71
The Oldest London Bookshop, a History of Two Hundred Years.... London: 1928. V. 70
Smith's Cabinet-Maker's and Upholster's Guide, Drawing Book and Repository of New and Original Designs for Household Furniture and Interior Decoration. London: 1826. V. 68

SMITH, GEORGE A.
The Historical Geography Of The Holy Land. London: 1895. V. 72
The Rise, Progress and Travels of the Church of Jesus Christ of Latter-Day Saints...the Revelation on Celestial Marriage.... Salt Lake City: 1872. V. 71; 73

SMITH, GEORGE BARNETT
The Life of William Ewart Gladstone. London: 1880-1882. V. 71

SMITH, GEORGE G.
The Life and Times of George Foster Pierce. Nashville: 1888. V. 71

SMITH, GEORGE O.
Venus Equilateral. Philadelphia: 1947. V. 69

SMITH, GERRIT
John, Esq., Syracuse, Chairman of the Jersey rescue Committee. Peterboro: 1859. V. 73

SMITH, GOLDWIN
Irish History and Irish Character. 1862. V. 69; 73
Lectures and Essays. Toronto: 1881. V. 71
Reminiscences. New York: 1910. V. 71

SMITH, GRAHAM
King's Cutters. London: 1983. V. 70

SMITH, GREGOR IAN
The Adventures of Willie Whiskers. London: 1950. V. 69
Hilda. London: 1946. V. 69

SMITH, GUSTAVUS WOODSON
Confederate War Papers. New York: 1884. V. 69; 70

SMITH, H. ALLEN
Life in a Putty Knife Factory. Garden City: 1943. V. 69

SMITH, H. CLIFFORD
The Panelled Rooms. IV. London: 1915. V. 72

SMITH, H. E.
Reliquiae Isurianae: The Remains of the Roman Isurium.... London: 1852. V. 72

SMITH, H. LLEWELLYN
The Story of the Dockers' Strike Told by Two East Londoners. London: 1889. V. 71

SMITH, H. M.
The Fresh Water Fishes of Siam, or Thailand. Washington: 1945. V. 72
Handbook of Lizards, Lizards of the United States and Canada. Ithaca: 1946. V. 71
Synopsis of the Herpetofauna of Mexico. Augusta and North Bennington: 1971-1980. V. 69

SMITH, H. M. continued
Synopsis of the Herpetofauna of Mexico. Augusta and North Bennington: 1971-1993. V. 69

SMITH, H. MAYNARD
Inspector Frost's Jigsaw. 1929. V. 73

SMITH, HAL H.
The Story of Lac Ste. Claire. Detroit: 1939. V. 68

SMITH, HARRIET LUMMIS
Happy Days for Shut-Ins. Elgin: 1931. V. 73

SMITH, HARRY B.
A Sentimental Library Comprising Books Formerly Owned by Famous Writers, Presentation Copies, Manuscripts and Drawings. New York: 1914. V. 71

SMITH, HARRY W.
A Sporting Family of the Old South...Reminiscences of an Old English Sportsman. Albany: 1936. V. 73

SMITH, HENRY
Collections Relating to Henry Smith, Esq., Sometime Alderman of London...(with) The Decree, Deed of Uses and Will of Henry Smith. London: 1781. V. 73

SMITH, HENRY ECROYD
Reliquiae Isurianae; the Remains of the Roman Isurium.... London: 1852. V. 69

SMITH, HENRY H.
Anatomical Atlas Illustrative of the Structure of the Human Body.... Philadelphia: 1954. V. 68; 70

SMITH, HENRY NASH
Mark Twain San Francisco Correspondent. Selections from His Letters to the Territorial Enterprise 1865-1866. San Francisco: 1957. V. 68

SMITH, HENRY STOOKS
The Parliaments of England, from the 1st George I, to the Present Time. London: 1844-1847. V. 71

SMITH, HERBERT H.
Brazil and the Amazons and the Coast. New York: 1879. V. 68

SMITH, HERMON DUNLAP
The Des Plaines River 1673-1940. Lake Forest: 1940. V. 70

SMITH, HOMER
Black Man in Red Russia. Chicago: 1964. V. 72

SMITH, HOMER W.
Lectures on the Kidney. Porter Lectures Series IX Delivered at the University of Kansas School of Medicine. Lawrence: 1943. V. 70
The Physiology of the Kidney. New York: 1937. V. 68; 70; 71

SMITH, HORACE
Festivals, Games and Amusements, ancient and modern. London: 1831. V. 71
Horace in London: consisting of Imitations of the First Two Books of the Odes of Horace. . . London: 1813. V. 71
The Poetical Works now First Collected. London: 1846. V. 71
Rejected Addresses. London: 1890. V. 72
A Treatise on the Law of Negligence. St. Louis: 1886. V. 68

SMITH, HORATIO
Festivals, Games and Amusements. New York: 1833. V. 72
Festivals, Games and Amusements. New York: 1842. V. 69

SMITH, HUGH
Letters to Married Women, on Nursing and Management of Children. Philadelphia: 1792. V. 71; 73

SMITH, IAIN CRICHTON
The Long River. Edinburgh: 1955. V. 73

SMITH, J.
Ferns: British and Foreign.... London: 1866. V. 71

SMITH, J. CALVIN
Harper's Statistical Gazetteer of the World. New York: 1855. V. 73

SMITH, J. E.
Flora Britannica. 1800-1804. V. 69

SMITH, J. E. A.
The History of Pittsfield (Berkshire County)...1800-1876. Springfield: 1876. V. 71

SMITH, J. F.
White Pillars: Early Life and Architecture of the Lower Mississippi Valley Country. New York: 1941. V. 69; 72

SMITH, J. J.
A Catalogue of the Manuscripts in the Library of Gonville and Caius College, Cambridge. Cambridge: 1849. V. 70; 72

SMITH, J. L. B.
The Fishes of the Seychelles. Grahamstown: 1963. V. 72; 73
Ichthyological Papers 1931-1943. Grahamstown: 1969. V. 73
A Living Coelacanthid Fish from South Africa. Cape Town: 1939. V. 73
The Sea Fishes of Southern Africa. Cape Town: 1961. V. 73
Sea Fishes of Southern Africa. South Africa: 1965. V. 69

SMITH, J. P.
Upper Triassic Marine Invertebrate Faunas of North America. Washington: 1927. V. 72

SMITH, J. SUTCLIFFE
The Life Of William Jackson (of Masham). Leeds: 1926. V. 72

SMITH, J. TOULMIN
The Discovery of America by the Northmen in the Tenth Century. London: 1839. V. 73

SMITH, J. V. C.
Natural History of the Fishes of Massachusetts. Boston: 1843. V. 72

SMITH, JAMES
Rejected Addresses; or, the New Theatrum Poetarum. London: 1833. V. 71
Researches in Newer Pliocene and Post Tertiary Geology. Glasgow: 1862. V. 68; 70
The Tin Trumpet; or Heads and Tails, for the Wise and Waggish, to Which are Added, Poetical Selections by the Late Paul Chatfield. London: 1836. V. 70

SMITH, JAMES B.
Studies in the Adequqacy of the Constitution. Los Angeles: 1939. V. 73

SMITH, JAMES EDWARD
English Botany. London: 1846. V. 73
An Introduction to Physiological and Systematical Botany. Philadelphia: 1814. V. 73
A Sketch of a Tour on the Continent in the Years 1786 and 1787. London: 1793. V. 73

SMITH, JAMES ELISHAMA
The Little Book; or, Momentous Crisis of 1840.... London: 1840. V. 71

SMITH, JAMES F.
The History of Pugwash. 1978. V. 73

SMITH, JAMES WALTER
A Handy Book on the Law of Banker and Customer. London: 1894. V. 71
A Handy Book on the Law of Bills, Cheques, Notes and I O U's. London: 1871. V. 71

SMITH, JAY D.
Jack Teagarden. The Story of a Jazz Maverick. London: 1960. V. 69

SMITH, JESSIE WILCOX
A Child's Book of Old Verses. New York: 1935. V. 70
A Child's Stamp Book of Old Verses. New York: 1915. V. 70

SMITH, JOEL
Edward Steichen: the Early Years. New York: 1999. V. 68

SMITH, JOHN
The Complete Works of Captain John Smith. Williamsburg: 1986. V. 72; 73
Irish Diamonds; or a Theory of Irish Wit and Blunders.... London: 1847. V. 73
Monograph of the Stalactites and Stalagmites of the Cleaves Cove, Near Dalry, Ayrshire. 1894. V. 68
Polygamy Indefensible. Two Sermons Preached in the Parish-Church of Nantwich, in Cheshire, on Sunday the 10th of December, 1780. London: 1780. V. 68
Select Discourses: Treating I. Of the True Method of Attaining Divine Knowledge. II. Of Superstition. III. Of Atheism. IV. Of the Immortality of the Soul...IX Of the Conflicts and Conquests of a Christian. Edinburgh: 1756. V. 70
Select Views in Italy, with Topographical and Historical Descriptions in English and French. London: 1792-1796-. V. 69
Select Views in Italy.... London: 1796-1817. V. 70
A Treatise on the Growth of Cucumbers and Melons.... London: 1839. V. 68
True Travels, Adventures and Obervations of.... Richmond: 1819. V. 68

SMITH, JOHN L.
Antietam to Appomattox with 118th Pennsylvania Volunteers, Corn Exchange Regiment. Philadelphia: 1892. V. 69; 70

SMITH, JOHN S.
A Treatise on the Practice of the Court of Chancery. Philadelphia: 1842. V. 71

SMITH, JOHN THOMAS
Antiquities of Westminster. London: 1807-1809. V. 68; 71
A Book for a Rainy Day, or Recollections of the Events of the Years 1766-1833. London: 1905. V. 69
Etchings of Remarkable Beggars Itinerant Traders and.... London: 1815. V. 71
Mendicant Wanderers through the Streets of London, with Portraits.... Edinburgh: 1883. V. 71
The Streets of London, with Anecdotes of their More Celebrated Residents. London: 1849. V. 71
Vagabondiana; or Anecdotes of Medicant Wanders through the Streets of London; with Portraits of the Most Remarkable Drawn from Life. 1817. V. 69; 71

SMITH, JOSEPH
Bibliotheca Anti-Quakeriana: a Catalogue of Books Adverse to the Society of Friends. London: 1873. V. 72

SMITH, JOSEPH FIELDING
Essentials in Church History. 1940. V. 69

SMITH, JOSEPH W.
Gleanings from the Sea.... Andover: 1887. V. 71

SMITH, JULES ANDRE
In France with the American Expeditionary Forces. New York: 1919. V. 70

SMITH, JULIE
The Axeman's Jazz. 1991. V. 70
Death Turns a Trick. New York: 1982. V. 69
Huckleberry Fiend. New York: 1987. V. 71
New Orleans Mourning. New York: 1990. V. 69; 70; 71
Tourist Trap. New York: 1986. V. 71

SMITH, JUSTIN H.
Our Struggle for the 14th Colony: Canada and the American Revolution. New York and London: 1907. V. 69

SMITH, KATE
Living in a Great Big Way. New York: 1938. V. 72

SMITH, KAY NOLTE
The Watcher. New York: 1980. V. 69

SMITH, KENNETH G. V.
Insects and Other Anthropods of Medical Importance. London: 1973. V. 68

SMITH, L. B.
Begoniaceae, Part I: Illustrated Key. Part II: Annotated Species List. Washington: 1986. V. 72
The Bromeliads. South Brunswick: 1969. V. 68

SMITH, LEE
Bob, a Dog. Chapel Hill: 1988. V. 68
Family Linen. New York: 1985. V. 68
Fancy Strut. New York: 1973. V. 73
Oral History. New York: 1983. V. 69
Something in the Wind. New York: 1971. V. 71; 73

SMITH, LEMUEL
The History of Job: with Reflections Affording Comfort to the Disconsolate. Utica: 1806. V. 71

SMITH, LOGAN PEARSALL
A Portrait of Logan Pearsall Smith drawn from his Letters and Diaries. London: 1950. V. 72
Songs and Sonnets. London: 1909. V. 69; 71

SMITH, LUCY CAROLINE CUMMING
Lines. Brighton: 1883. V. 69

SMITH, M.
East Coast Marine Shells.... Ann Arbor: 1945. V. 72; 73

SMITH, M. H.
Sunshine and Shadows. Hartford: 1879. V. 70

SMITH, MARGARET
Hopi Girl. Stanford: 1931. V. 69

SMITH, MARGARET BAYARD
The First Four Years of Washington Society, Portrayed by the Family Letters of.... New York: 1906. V. 69

SMITH, MARTIN CRUZ
The Analog Bullet. New York: 1977. V. 70
Gorky Park. New York: 1981. V. 68; 69; 72
Havana Bay. New York: 1999. V. 72
Nightwing. New York: 1977. V. 69
Polar Star. New York: 1989. V. 72
Stallion Gate. London: 1986. V. 70
Stallion Gate. New York: 1986. V. 72

SMITH, MEREDITH J.
Marsupials of Australia. Melbourne: 1980. V. 70

SMITH, MIRIAM JEAN
History of Alexander Bettis and the History of Bettis Academy. 1951. V. 71

SMITH, MYRON J.
Cloak And Dagger Fiction: An Annotated Guide To Spy Fiction With An Introduction By Clive Cussler. Santa Barbara: 1982. V. 72

SMITH, NATHAN
Medical and Surgical Memoirs.... Baltimore: 1831. V. 68; 70; 71; 73
A Practical Essay on Typhus Fever. New York: 1824. V. 69; 73

SMITH, NOBLE
The Descriptive Atlas of Anatomy. London: 1880. V. 68

SMITH, NORA ARCHIBALD
Boys and Girls of Bookland. New York: 1923. V. 69; 70

SMITH, OLIVER
Outlines of Nature. New York: 1847. V. 73

SMITH, P. W.
The Fishes of Illinois. Urbana: 1979. V. 70

SMITH, PATTI
Babel. New York: 1978. V. 71; 73
Complete Lyrics, Refelections and Notes for the Future. New York: 1998. V. 69; 70
The Coral Sea. New York: 1996. V. 70
Early Work: 1970-1979. New York: 1994. V. 70; 72
Ha! Ha! Houdini!. New York: 1977. V. 71
Witt. New York: 1973. V. 71

SMITH, PAUL JORDAN
A Key to the Ulysses of James Joyce. Chicago: 1927. V. 71

SMITH, PERLEY
History of Port Hood and Port Hood Island with the Genealogy of the Smith Family 1610-1697. 1967. V. 73

SMITH, PHILIP
A History of the World, from the Creation to the Fall of the Western Roman Empire. New York: 1883. V. 71

SMITH, PINE TOP
5 Boogie Woogie Blues Piano Solos. New York: 1941. V. 72

SMITH, R. A.
A History of Dickinson County, Iowa Together with an Account of the Spirit Lake Massacre and the Indian Troubles on the Northwestern Frontier. Des Moines: 1902. V. 73

SMITH, R. B.
Life of Lord Lawrence (Governor-General of India). New York: 1883. V. 69

SMITH, R. S.
A Manual of Linear Perspective. New York: 1857. V. 73

SMITH, RICHARD
A Tour of Four Great Rivers. New York: 1906. V. 71

SMITH, RICHARD, BP. OF CHALCEDON
Florum Historiae Ecclesiasticae Gentis Anglorum. Parisiis: 1654. V. 73

SMITH, RICHARD H.
Expositions of Great Pictures. London: 1868. V. 72
Expositions of the Cartoons of Raphael. London: 1860. V. 70

SMITH, RICHARD MC ALLISTER
The Confederate First Reader.... Richmond: 1864. V. 69

SMITH, ROBERT
The Universal Directory for Taking Alive and Destroying Rats, and All Other Kinds of Four Footed and Winged Vermin. London: 1786. V. 69

SMITH, ROBERT ANGUS
Memoir of John Dalton and History of the Atomic Theory Up to His Time. London: 1856. V. 68

SMITH, ROSWELL CHAMBERLAIN
Louisiana English Grammar. Shreveport: 1865. V. 69; 70

SMITH, S. THEYRE
The Fairy Horn. London: 1883. V. 69

SMITH, SAMUEL
An Essay on the Causes of the Variety of Complexion and Figure in the Human Species. New Brunswick: 1810. V. 68
The History of the Colony of Nova Caesaria; or New Jersey.... Burlington: 1765. V. 68; 70; 71; 73

SMITH, SAMUEL F.
History of Newton, Massachusetts. Boston: 1880. V. 69

SMITH, SAMUEL STANHOPE
An Essay on the Causes and the Variety of Complexion and Figure in the Human Species. Philadelphia: 1787. V. 68
The Lectures, Corrected and Improved, Have Been Delivered for a Series of Years in the College of New Jersey; on the Subjects of Moral and Political Philosophy. Philadelphia: 1812. V. 69

SMITH, SCOTT
A Simple Plan. New York: 1993. V. 68; 72

SMITH, SID
Something Like a House. London: 2001. V. 71

SMITH, SIDNEY
The Mother Country; or, the Spade, the Wastes, and the Eldest Son. 1849. V. 71

SMITH, SOLOMON
The Theatrical Apprenticeship and Anecdotal Recollections of.... Philadelphia: 1846. V. 68
The Theatrical Apprenticeship and Anecdotal Recollections of.... Philadelphia: 1847. V. 71; 73
Theatrical Management in the West and South for Thirty Years. New York: 1868. V. 68

SMITH, STANLEY K.
Heart Throbs of the Halifax Horror. Halifax: 1918. V. 73

SMITH, STEVIE
Harold's Leap. London: 1950. V. 69; 73
The Holiday. London: 1949. V. 69
Mother, What is Man?. London: 1942. V. 69
Not Waving but Drowning. Poems. London: 1957. V. 73
Novel on Yellow Paper; or, Work It Out for Yourself. London: 1936. V. 69
Over the Frontier. London: 1938. V. 69
Tender Only to One: Poems and Drawings. London: 1938. V. 69

SMITH, STUART
The Yellow Wagtail. 1950. V. 69

SMITH, SYDNEY
The Letters of Peter Plymley, Essays and Speeches. London: 1852. V. 68
The Selected Writings of Sydney Smith. London: 1957. V. 69
The Works. London: 1840. V. 73
The Works. London: 1848. V. 72; 73
The Works, Including his contributions to the Edinburgh Review. London: 1860. V. 71

SMITH, SYDNEY GOODSIR
Cokkils. Edinburgh: 1953. V. 71
Fifteen Poems and a Play. Edinburgh: 1969. V. 71

SMITH, SYDNEY GOODSIR continued
Orpheus and Eurydice: a Dramatic Poem. Edinburgh: 1955. V. 71

SMITH, SYDNEY K.
Life, Army Record and Public Services of D. Howard Smith. Louisville: 1890. V. 70

SMITH, T. MURRAY
Safari Trail. 1965. V. 70; 72

SMITH, T. ROGER
Acoustics in Relation to Architecture and Building. London: 1878. V. 68

SMITH, T. WATSON
History of the Methodist Church Within The Territories Embraced in the Late Conference of Eastern British America, Including Nova Scotia, New Brunswick, Prince Edward Island and Bermuda. Halifax: 1877-1890. V. 68

SMITH, THOMAS
The Art of Drawing in Its Various Branches, Exemplified in a Course of 28 Progressive Lessons.... London: 1825. V. 68
An Attempt to Define Some of the First Principles of Political Econony. London: 1821. V. 71
The Chairman and Speaker's Guide.... London: 1831?. V. 71
The Common-wealth of England, and the Manner of Government Thereof. London: 1609. V. 68; 69; 72
The Common-wealth of England; and the Manner and Government Thereof. London: 1633. V. 69
The Common-wealth of England; and the Manner and Government Thereof. London: 1640. V. 70
De Republica Anglorum Libri Tres. Lug. Batavorum (Leiden): 1641. V. 73
The Miner's Guide; Being a Description and illustration of a Chart of Sections of the Principal Mines of Coal and Ironstone.... Birmingham: 1836. V. 71
The Miner's Guide, Being a Description and Illustration of a Chart of Sections of the Principal Mines of Coal and Ironstone.... Birmingham: 1846. V. 71
Scott's 900 - Eleventh New York United States Volunteer Cavalry Association. 1906. V. 68
Sporting Incidents in the Life of another Tom Smith, Master of Foxhounds.... London: 1867. V. 73
A Topographical and Historical Account of the Parish of St. Mary-Le- Bone. London: 1833. V. 71

SMITH, THOMAS B.
Little Mayflower Land. Halifax: 1900. V. 73

SMITH, THOMAS SOUTHWOOD
A Treatise on Fever. London: 1830. V. 70

SMITH, THORNE
Biltmore Oswald - The Diary of a Hapless Recruit. New York: 1918. V. 71
The Bishop's Jaegers. Garden City: 1932. V. 71
Rain in the Doorway. Garden City: 1933. V. 71
Topper: an Improbable Adventure. New York: 1926. V. 69

SMITH, W.
A Synopsis of the British Diatomaceae. 1835-1836. V. 73
A Synopsis of the British Diatomaceae. 1853-1856. V. 69

SMITH, W. ANDERSON
Benderloch; or Notes from the Western Highlands. Paisley: 1882. V. 68
Lewsiana or Life in the Outer Hebrides. London: 1875. V. 68
Loch Creran: Notes from the West Highlands. London: 1887. V. 68

SMITH, W. EUGENE
Minamata: the Story of the Poisoning of a City and of the People. New York: 1975. V. 68

SMITH, W. H. B.
The Book of Rifles. 1960. V. 72
The Book of Rifles. 1965. V. 72

SMITH, W. P.
A History and Description of the Baltimore and Ohio Rail Road. Baltimore: 1853. V. 73

SMITH, WALKER C.
The Everett Massacre. Chicago: 1917. V. 68; 69

SMITH, WALTER E.
Charles Dickens in the Original Cloth: a Bibliographical Catalogue of the First Appearance of His Writings in Book form in England.... Los Angeles: 1982-1983. V. 68; 70

SMITH, WATSON
Excavations in Big Hawk Valley, Wupatki National Monument, Arizona. Flagstaff: 1952. V. 73

SMITH, WHITE MOUNTAIN, MRS.
Indian Tribes of the Southwest. Palo Alto: 1933. V. 69; 71

SMITH, WHITNEY
Flags Through the Ages and Across the World. New York: 1975. V. 72

SMITH, WILBUR
Eagle in the Sky. Garden City: 1974. V. 71
Hungry As the Sea. Garden City: 1978. V. 69
The Train from Katanga. New York: 1965. V. 73

SMITH, WILLIAM
Annual Statement of the Trade and Commerce of Cinicinnati.... Cincinnati: 1855. V. 68
A Catalogue of the Works of Cornelius Visscher. Bungay: 1864. V. 71
The Diary and Selected Papers of Chief Justice William Smith 1784- 1793. Toronto: 1963-1965. V. 68
A Dissertation on the Nerves: Containing An Account I. Of the Nature of Man. II. Of the Nature of Brutes. III. Of the Nature and Connection of Soul and Body. IV. Of the Threefold Life of Man. V. Of the Symptoms, Causes, and Cure of All Nervous Diseases. London: 1768. V. 68; 70
Gravenhurst; or, Thoughts on Good and Evil. London: 1873. V. 71
An Historical Account of the Expedition Against the Ohio Indians. London: 1766. V. 68
The History of the Province of New York, from the First Discovery to the Year MDCCXXXII. London: 1757. V. 70
Strata Identified by Organized Fossils, Containing Prints on Colored Paper...(with) Stratigraphical System of Organized Fossils. London: 1816-1819. V. 68

SMITH, WILLIAM BENJAMIN
James Sidney Rollins. New York: 1891. V. 68; 73

SMITH, WILLIAM G.
Anger at Innocence. New York: 1950. V. 70

SMITH, WILLIAM HAWKES
Kenilworth Castle in the 16th, 18th and 19th Centuries, Displayed in Thirteen Lithographic Plates. Birmingham: 1821. V. 70

SMITH, WILLIAM JAY
The Spectra Hoax. Ashland: 2000. V. 71

SMITH, WILLIE
Music On My Mind. Garden City: 1964. V. 72

SMITH, WINIFRED E.
Little Horse. Edinburgh: 1938. V. 73

SMITH, ZADIE
White Teeth. London: 2000. V. 68; 70; 72
White Teeth. New York: 2000. V. 68; 69; 73

SMITH & WELLSTOOD, LTD.
Bonnybridge Price List and Illustrated & Descriptive Catalogue.... London: 1880?. V. 68

SMITHERMAN, GENEVA
Talkin and Testifyin: The Language of Black America. Boston: 1977. V. 72

SMITHERS, LEONARD
Catalogue of Rare Books Offered for Sale by Leonard Smithers.... London: 1896. V. 68

SMITHERS, R. H. N.
Check List of the Birds of Southern Rhodesia. 1957. V. 69; 70

SMITHSONIAN INSTITUTION
Smithsonian Contributions to Knowledge. Washington: 1854. V. 72

SMOLLETT, TOBIAS GEORGE
The Adventures of Ferdinand Count Fathom. London: 1800. V. 73
The Adventures of Peregrine Pickle. London: 1773. V. 69
The Adventures of Peregrine Pickle. 1776. V. 73
The Adventures of Peregrine Pickle. Harrisburgh: 1807. V. 69
The Adventures of Peregrine Pickle. Oxford: 1936. V. 72; 73
The Adventures of Roderick Random. London: 1792. V. 71
The Expedition of Humphry Clinker. Dublin: 1771. V. 69
The Expedition of Humphry Clinker. London: 1771. V. 72
The Expedition of Humphry Clinker. Dublin: 1781. V. 69
The Expedition of Humphry Clinker. London: 1792. V. 71
The Expedition of Humphry Clinker. London: 1793. V. 70
The History of England, from the Revolution in 1688, to the Death of George II. London: 1805. V. 68
Humphry Clinker. London: 1868. V. 68
The Miscellaneous Works. Edinburgh: 1806. V. 71; 73
The Miscellaneous Works. Edinburgh: 1811. V. 71
The Miscellaneous Works. London: 1850. V. 71
The Novels. Boston: 1926. V. 72; 73
Travels through France and Italy.... Dublin: 1766. V. 72
Travels through France and Italy.... London: 1766. V. 69; 70; 72
The Works. New York: 1902. V. 68; 70

SMOLNIKAR, ANDREAS BERNARDUS
Secret Enemies of True Republicanism.... Springhill: 1859. V. 73

SMUCKER, SAMUEL
Life Among the Mormons, or the Religious Social and Political History of the Mormons. New York: 1880. V. 68
The Life of Col. John Charles Fremont, and Adventures in Kansas, Nebraska, Oregon and California. New York: 1856. V. 70

SMYTH, C. PIAZZI
On an Equal-Surface Projection for Maps of the World, Its Application to Certain Anthropological Questions.... Edinburgh: 1870. V. 70

SMYTH, ELAINE
Plain Wrapper Press 1966-1988. An Illustrated Bibliography of the Work of Richard-Gabriel Rummonds. Austin: 1993. V. 73

SMYTH, GEORGE LEWIS
The Monuments and Geni of St. Paul's And Westminster Abbey:. London: 1826. V. 72

SMYTH, HENRY DE WOLF
Atomic Energy for Military Purposes.. Princeton: 1945. V. 72
A General Account of the Development of Methods of Using Atomic Energy for Military Purposes, Under the Auspices of the United States Government 1940-1945. Washington: 1945. V. 68; 70; 73

SMYTH, JAMES CARMICHAEL
An Account of the Experiment Made at the Desire of the Lords Commissioners of the Admiralty, on Board the Union Hospital Ship.... London: 1796. V. 70

SMYTH, PAUL
Thistles and Thorns: Abraham and Sarah at Bethel. Omaha: 1977. V. 70

SMYTH, PIAZZI
Our Inheritance in the Great Pyramid: Including All the Most Important Discoveries Up to the Present Time. London: 1874. V. 73

SMYTH, THOMAS
The Christian Doctrine of the Human Rights and of Slavery, in Two Articles from the Southern Presbyterian Review. Columbia: 1849. V. 68

SMYTH, W. H.
The Sailor's Word-Book. London: 1991. V. 68

SMYTH, WILLIAM
Lectures on History: Second and Concluding Series: on the French Revolution. London: 1848. V. 71

SMYTH, WILLIAM HENRY
Nautical Observation on the Port and Maritime Vicinity of Cardiff, with Occasional Strictures on the Ninth Report of the Taff Vale Railway Directors.... Cardiff: 1840. V. 70

SMYTHE, AUGUSTINE T.
The Carolina Low-Country. New York: 1931. V. 71

SMYTHE, FRANK S.
Again Switzerland. London: 1947. V. 69
An Alpine Journey. 1934. V. 68; 71; 73
A Camera in the Hills. London: 1939. V. 69
A Camera in the Hills. London: 1942. V. 69
Camp Six. London: 1956. V. 69
Climbs and Ski Runs. London: 1929. V. 69
Climbs and Ski Runs. London: 1931. V. 69
Kamet Conquered. 1932. V. 68; 71
The Kangchenjunga Adventure. London: 1931. V. 69
The Mountain Scene. London: 1938. V. 69
Mountains in Colour. London: 1949. V. 69
My Alpine Album. London: 1940. V. 69
Peaks and Valleys. London: 1938. V. 69
Rocky Mountains. London: 1948. V. 69
Snow on the Hills. London: 1946. V. 69
Snow on the Hills. London: 1948. V. 69
Swiss Winter. London: 1948. V. 69
The Valley of Flowers. 1938. V. 68; 71; 73

SMYTHE, GEORGE WALTER
Views and Description of the Late Volcanic Island (Graham Island) off the Coast of Sicily. London: 1832?. V. 70

SMYTHE, P. M.
The Diary of an All-Round Angler. 1956. V. 68

SMYTHE, WILLIAM E.
The Conquest of Arid America. New York: 1905. V. 71

SMYTHIES, BERTRAM EVELYN
The Birds of Borneo. Sabah: 1981. V. 68
Birds of Burma. Rangoon: 1940. V. 73
The Birds of Burma. 1953. V. 69
The Birds of Burma. London: 1986. V. 73

SNAITH, J. C.
Willow the King. The Story of a Cricket Match. London: 1899. V. 70

SNAITH, STANLEY
A Flying Scroll. London: 1928. V. 70

SNAPSHOTS.. Boston: 2000. V. 72

SNART, CHARLES
Practical Observations on Angling, in the River Trent. Newark: 1801. V. 72

SNEIDER, VERN
The Teahouse of the August Moon. New York: 1951. V. 70; 72
The Teahouse of the August Moon. London: 1952. V. 71

SNELGRAVE, WILLIAM
A New Account of Some Parts of Guinea, and the Slave Trade.... London: 1734. V. 69

SNELL, EDMUND
Kontrol. Philadelphia: 1928. V. 70
The White Owl. Philadelphia: 1930. V. 69; 70
The Z Ray. Philadelphia: 1932. V. 69

SNELLING, H. H.
A Dictionary of Photographic Art, Forming a Complete Encyclopedia of all the Terms.... New York: 1854. V. 68

SNELLING, WILLIAM J.
Truth, a Gift for Scribblers. Boston: 1832. V. 73

SNEPP, FRANK
Decent Interval. New York: 1977. V. 68

SNIDER, C. H. J.
The Glorious Shannon's Old Blue Duster and other Faded Flags of Fadeless Fame. Toronto: 1923. V. 73
In the Wake of the Eighteen Twelvers. Fights and Flights of Frigates and Fore-'n-afters in the War of 1812-1815 on the Great Lakes. London: 1913. V. 73
Under the Red Jack. Toronto: 1928. V. 73

SNODGRASS, R. E.
Principles of Insect Morphology. New York: 1935. V. 72

SNODGRASS, W. D.
After Experience. Poems and Translations. New York: 1968. V. 71
Autumn Variations. New York: 1990. V. 73
Heart's Needle. 1960. V. 70
If Birds Build with Your Hair. New York: 1979. V. 73
The Kinder Capers. New York: 1986. V. 73
Remains. Mt. Horeb: 1970. V. 73
Spring Suite. New York: 1994. V. 73

SNOHOMISH County, Washington. Everett: 1914. V. 73

SNOW, C. P.
The Affair. London: 1960. V. 71
A Coat of Varnish. Franklin Center: 1979. V. 72
A Coat of Varnish. London: 1979. V. 72
A Coat of Varnish. New York: 1979. V. 72
The Conscience of the Rich. London: 1958. V. 71
Corridors of Power. London: 1964. V. 71
Corridors of Power. New York: 1964. V. 72
Death Under Sail. London: 1932. V. 69; 71
Death Under Sail. London: 1936. V. 71
Death Under Sail. London: 1959. V. 71
Homecomings. London: 1956. V. 71
In Their Wisdom. London: 1974. V. 72
In Their Wisdom. New York: 1974. V. 72
Kinds of Excellence: the Kenneth Aldred Spencer Lecture Given on the Occasion of the Dedication of the Kenneth Spencer Research Library, November 8, 1968. Lawrence: 1970. V. 72
Last Things. London: 1970. V. 72
Last Things. New York: 1970. V. 72
The Malcontents. London: 1972. V. 72
The Malcontents. New York: 1972. V. 72
The Masters. London: 1951. V. 69; 71
New Lives for Old. London: 1933. V. 71
The New Men. London: 1954. V. 69; 70; 71
A Postscript to Science and Government. London: 1962. V. 71
Public Affairs. London: 1971. V. 72
The Realists: Portraits of Eight Novelists. 1978. V. 72
Richard Aldington: an Appreciation. London: 1938. V. 71
Science and Government. London: 1961. V. 71
The Search. London: 1934. V. 69; 71
The Search. Indianapolis and New York: 1935. V. 71
The Search. London: 1958. V. 71
The Sleep of Reason. London: 1968. V. 69; 72
The Sleep of Reason. New York: 1968. V. 72
Strangers and Brothers. London: 1972. V. 72
Strangers and Brothers. New York: 1972. V. 70; 72
Time of Hope. London: 1949. V. 71
Trollope. London: 1975. V. 72
The Two Cultures: a Second Look. Cambridge: 1964. V. 72
Two Cultures and the Scientific Revolution: the Rede Lecture. New York: 1959. V. 69
The Two Cultures and the Scientific Revolution: the Rede Lecture 1959. Cambridge: 1959. V. 71
Variety of Men. London: 1967. V. 72
Variety of Men. London: 1968. V. 72

SNOW, JACK
The Magical Mimics in Oz. Chicago: 1946. V. 73
The Shaggy Man Of Oz. Chicago: 1949. V. 73

SNOW White and the Seven Dwarfs. Dornach, near Basel: 1947. V. 68

SNOW, WILLIAM P.
Southern Generals, who They are and What They Have Done. New York: 1865. V. 72

SNOWDEN, KEIGHLEY
The Master Spinner. A Life of Sir Swire Smith, LLD., M.P. London. V. 72

SNOWDEN, PHILIP
Socialism and the Drink Question. London: 1908. V. 72

SNOWDEN WARD, H.
The Photogram 1894 and 1895. Volumes I and II. London. V. 70

SNOWMAN, A. KENNETH
Art of Carl Faberge. London: 1953. V. 72

SNYDER, CHARLES M.
The Flow in the Sapphire. New York: 1909. V. 68

SNYDER, CHARLES MC COY
The Bandit Bunny Alphabet and Other Stories. Philadelphia?: 1901. V. 71

SNYDER, DUKE
The Duke of Flatbush. New York: 1988. V. 69

SNYDER, GARY
All In The Family. Davis, CA: 1975. V. 72; 73
The Back Country. London: 1967. V. 69; 73
Earth House Hold. New York: 1969. V. 70; 73
Mountains and Rivers Without End. Washington: 1996. V. 71; 73
Myths and Texts. New York: 1960. V. 68
Myths and Texts. New York: 1978. V. 68; 72
No Nature. New York: 1992. V. 68; 72; 73
A Place In Space. Washington, D.C: 1995. V. 72; 73
A Range of Poems. London: 1966. V. 73
Regarding Wave. Iowa City: 1969. V. 69; 73
Regarding Wave. London: 1970. V. 71
Riprap. Ashland: 1959. V. 71; 73
Six Selections from Mountains and Rivers Without End. San Francisco: 1965. V. 69; 71
Song of Roland. New York: 1938. V. 72
Songs for Gaia. Port Townsend: 1979. V. 71; 73
True Night. N. San Juan: 1980. V. 72
Turtle Island. New York: 1974. V. 73

SNYDER, ROBERT
This is Henry, Henry Miller from Booklyn. Los Angeles: 1974. V. 70

SNYDER, T. E.
Annotated Subject-Heading Bibliography of Termites 1350 B.C to A.D. 1954. Washington: 1956. V. 72

SO Happy. New York: 1880. V. 70

SOAMES, HENRY
The Anglo-Saxon Church: Its History, Revenues and General Character. London: 1835. V. 70

SOANE, GEORGE
New Curiosities of Literature: and Book of the Months. London: 1849. V. 69
Specimens of German Romance. London: 1826. V. 73

SOANE, JOHN
Description of the Residence of John Soane, Architect.... London: 1830. V. 68
Plans, Elevations and Sections of Buildings.... London: 1788. V. 70; 72
A Statement of Facts Respecting the Designs of a New House of Lords, as Ordered by the Lords Committees and Humbly Submitted to the Considerations of Their Lordships.... London: 1799. V. 72

SOBEL, DAVA
Longitude. New York: 1995. V. 71

SOBERS, GARY
Bonaventure and the Flashing Blade. London: 1967. V. 68

SOBIESKI, JOHN
Lays of the Deer Forest. 1848. V. 70; 73
The Life and Personal Reminiscences of Colonel John Sobieski. Shelbyville, Ill: 1900. V. 71

SOBIESZEK, ROBERT A.
The Spirit of Fact: the Daguerreotypes...1843-1862. Boston: 1976. V. 68

SOBY, JAMES THRALL
Ben Shahn: His Graphic Art. New York: 1957. V. 69; 71

SOCIAL Architecture, or, Reasons and Means for the Demolition and Reconstruction of the Social Edifice. London: 1876. V. 71

SOCIETY of Chemical Industry in Basle. 1884-1934. Zurich. V. 71

A SOCIETY of Gentlemen. The Complete Farmer: or, A General Dictionary of Husbandry.... London: 1777. V. 70

SOCIETY FOR ENCOURAGEMENT OF ARTS, MANUFACTURERS & COMMERCE
Premiums Offered by the Society Instituted at London for the Encouragement of Arts, Manufactures and Commerce. London: 1772. V. 73

SOCIETY FOR PROMOTING CHRISTIAN KNOWLEDGE
An Account of Charity-Schools in Great Britain and Ireland.... London: 1711. V. 70
British Colonies in North America. The Maritime Provinces. London: 1848. V. 73

SOCIETY FOR THE DIFFUSION OF USEFUL KNOWLEDGE
Vegetable Substances: Materials of Manufactures. London: 1833. V. 68

SOCIETY FOR THE PREVENTION OF ACCIDENTS IN FACTORIES
Collection of Appliances and Apparatus for the Prevention of Accidents in Factories. Mulhouse: 1889. V. 71

SOCIETY OF ANTIQUARIES
List of Printed Books in the Library of the Society of Antiquaries of London. London: 1861. V. 70; 71

SOCIETY OF AUTHORS
The Cost of Production Being Specimens of the Pages and Type in More Common Use. London: 1889. V. 68

SOCIETY OF DILETTANTI
Antiquities of Ionia...Part the Fourth. London: 1881. V. 73
The Unedited Antiquities of Attica, Comprising the Architectural Remains of Eleusis.... London: 1817. V. 68; 70; 72

SOCIETY OF FRIENDS
The Annual Monitor...and or Obituary of the Members of the Society of Friends in Great Britain and Ireland. London: 1854-1898. V. 72

SOCIETY OF PRINTERS
A Testimonial Dinner to William Dana Orcutt, Book Designer and Typographer, First President of the Society of Printers. Boston: 1942. V. 70; 72

SOCIETY OF THE CINCINNATI
The Institution and Records of the New Hampshire Society of the Cincinnati. Concord: 1893. V. 73

SOCIOLOGICAL SOCIETY
Sociological Papers by Francis Galton, E. Westermarck, P. Geddes, E. Durkheim, Harold H. Mann and V.V. Branford. London: 1905. V. 71

SOEMMERING, SAMUEL THOMAS VON
De Basi Encephali et Originibus Nervorum Cranio Egredientium. Gottingen: 1778. V. 68; 73
De Corporis Humani Fabrica. Frankfurt: 1794-1801. V. 70
De Morbis Vasorum Absorbentium Corporis Humani. Utrecht: 1795. V. 70

SOEMMERING, SAMUEL THOMAS VON
Uber das Organ der Seele. Konigsberg: 1796. V. 68

SOGLOW, O.
Wasn't the Depression Terrible?. New York: 1934. V. 72

SOKAL, ROBERT R.
Biometry. The Principles and Practice of Statistics in Biological Research. New York: 1981. V. 68

SOLA, A. E. IRONMONGER
Klondyke: Truth and Facts of the New El Dorado. London: 1897. V. 71

SOLANAS, VALERIE
S.C.U.M. Manifesto. New York: 1968. V. 70
Scum Manifesto. New York: 1970. V. 68

SOLDATI, MARIO
The Capri Letters. London: 1955. V. 72
The Confession. London: 1958. V. 72

THE SOLDIER Panorama Book: a Novel Colour Book for Children. London. V. 70; 73

THE SOLDIER Turned Farmer. Portland: 1830. V. 68; 73

THE SOLDIER'S Companion.... London: 1800. V. 72

SOLDIERS Of the Empire. London. V. 73

SOLDIERS of the Queen Cavalry. London. V. 73

SOLDIERS of the Queen Infantry. London. V. 73

SOLENSTEN, JOHN
Good Thunder. Albany: 1983. V. 72

SOLEY, JOHN C.
Sources of Volcanic Energy. New York and London: 1924. V. 70

SOLIS Y RIBADENEYRA, ANTONIO DE
History of the Conquest of Mexico by the Spaniards. London: 1724. V. 73

SOLLID, ROBERTA BEED
Calamity Jane. Helena: 1958. V. 68

SOLLY, EDWARD
An Index of Hereditary English, Scottish, And Irish Titles of Honour. London: 1879. V. 72

SOLLY, N. NEAL
Memoirs of the Life of William James Miller's Native of Bristol, Landscape and Figure Painter. London: 1875. V. 73

SOLLY, SAMUEL
The Human Brain; Its Structure, Physiology and Diseases.... Philadelphia: 1848. V. 68; 71; 73

SOLMS-LAUBACH, H. GRAF ZU
Fossil Botany, Being an Introduction to Palaeophytology from the Standpoint of the Botanist. Oxford: 1891. V. 72

SOLOMON, CORINE V.
It's Who. New York: 1984. V. 72

SOLOMON Stone's Marvelous Mental Calculator. New York: 1880. V. 68

SOLON, M. L.
Ceramic Literature; an Analytical Index to the Works Published in all Languages on the History and Technology of Ceramic Art.... London: 1910. V. 69
History and Description of Italian Majolica. London: 1907. V. 72

SOLTAU, H. W.
The Holy Vessels and Furniture of the Tabernacle of Israel. London: 1860. V. 72

SOLZHENITSYN, ALEKSANDR
The Gulag Archipelago. New York: 1974. V. 73
One Day in the Life of Ivan Denisovich. New York: 1963. V. 73
The Russian Question At the End of the Twentieth Century. New York: 1995. V. 72

SOME Account of Suffragan Bishops In England. Bibliotheca Topographica Britannica No. XXVIII. London: 1785. V. 72

SOME Account of the Life and Religious Labours of Sarah Grubb. Dublin: 1792. V. 70

SOME Account of the Oxford University Press 1468-1921. Oxford: 1922. V. 70; 71

SOME Account of the Oxford University Press 1468-1921. Oxford: 1926. V. 70; 71

SOME Brief Memoirs of the Life of David Hall; with an Account of the Life of His Father, John Hall. London: 1799. V. 72

SOME British Ballads. London: 1919. V. 68; 73
SOME British Ballads. New York: 1920. V. 73

SOME Considerations Upon the Proceedings Against the King etc. 1648. V. 73

SOME Experiences of Boss Neff in the Texas and Oklahoma Panhandle. Denver: 1968. V. 68

SOME German Woodcuts of the Fifteenth Century. 1897. V. 71; 73

SOME Hawarden Letters 1878-1913. 1917. V. 68

SOME Imagist Poets. An Anthology. Boston and New York: 1915. V. 72

SOME Imagist Poets, 1916. Boston and New York: 1916. V. 72

SOME Imagist Poets, 1917. Boston and New York: 1917. V. 72

SOME Observations on the Assiento Trade, As It Has Been Exercised by the South Sea Company.... London: 1728. V. 69

SOME Particular Matter of Fact Relating to the Administration of Affairs in Scotland Under the Duke of Lauderdale. London: 1679. V. 68; 72

SOME Practical Remarks on the Effect of the Usury Laws on the Landed Interests, in a Letter to John Calcraft, Esq. M.P. London: 1826. V. 70

SOMEREN, V. D. VAN
A Bird Watcher in Kenya. 1958. V. 70; 72

SOMERVELL, JOHN
Isaac and Rachel Wilson, Quakers of Kendal 1714-1785. London: 1924. V. 71; 72
Some Westmorland Wills 1686-1738. Kendal: 1928. V. 71
Water-Power Mills of South Westmorland, on the Kent, bela and Gilpin and Their Tributaries. Kendal: 1930. V. 71

SOMERVILLE, ALEXANDER
The Autobiography of a Working Man. London: 1854. V. 71

SOMERVILLE, EDITH OENONE
French Leave. 1928. V. 68
Further Experiences of an Irish R. M. London: 1908. V. 69; 71; 73
In Mr. Knox's Country. London: 1915. V. 68
An Irish Cousin. 1905. V. 68
Mount Music. 1919. V. 68
Mount Music. London: 1919. V. 71
Notions in Garrison. 1941. V. 68
Sporting Works. New York: 1927. V. 70
The States through Irish Eyes. 1931. V. 68; 70
The States through Irish Eyes. London: 1931. V. 73

SOMERVILLE, IVAN
Scattered Death. New York: 1931. V. 68

SOMERVILLE, J. ALEXANDER
Man of Color, An Autobiography: A Factual Report on the Status of the American Negro Today. Los Angeles: 1949:. V. 72

SOMERVILLE, WILLIAM
The Chace. London: 1735. V. 73
The Chase; to which is annexed Field Sports. With a sketch of the author's life; including a preface . . . London: 1817. V. 71

SOMMER, ANNIE VAN
Daylight in the Harem, a New Era for Moselm Women. Edinburgh and London: 1911. V. 72

SOMMERFELD, ARNOLD
Atomic Structure and Spectral Lines. New York: 1923. V. 69

SOMMERS, LORD
The Judgment of Whole Kingdoms and Nations, Concerning the Rights, Power and Prerogative of the Kings and Rights, Privileges and Properties of the People.... London: 1771. V. 73

SOMNER, WILLIAM
The Antiquities of Canterbury. London: 1640. V. 70; 72
A Treatise of the Roman Ports and Forts of Kent.... Oxford: 1693. V. 70; 72
A Treatise on Gavelkind, Both Name and Thing. London: 1660. V. 72

SONAKUL, SIBPAN
Everyday Siamese Dishes. Bangkok: 1963. V. 68

SONDHEIM, STEPHEN
Sunday in the Park with George. New York: 1986. V. 69; 71
Sweeney Todd. New York: 1979. V. 69

SONETTI E' Canzoni di Diversi Antichi Autori Toscani in Dieci Libri Raccolte. Florence: 1527. V. 73

THE SONG-Singer's Amusing Companion. Boston: 1818. V. 68; 73

SONGS and Stories. Charlestown: 1857. V. 73

SONGS, Chorusses &c In Hide and Seek; or, the Slippers. London: 1789. V. 69

SONGS, Duets, Trios and Chorusses, in the Haunted Tower. London: 1790. V. 71

THE SONGS, German and English, as Sung by the Tyrolese Minstrels (The Rainer Family).... Edinburgh: 1828. V. 72

SONGS of the Tewa. New York: 1933. V. 69

THE SONGSTER'S Jewel. Durham: 1838. V. 68
THE SONGSTER'S Jewel. 1840. V. 73
THE SONGSTER'S Jewel. London: 1840. V. 68

SONNICHSEN, C. L.
Alias Billy the Kid. Albuquerque: 1955. V. 70; 72; 73
Billy King's Tombstone. Caldwell: 1942. V. 68; 69
Cowboys and Cattle Kings: Life on the Range Today. Norman: 1950. V. 68; 69; 71; 72
The Mescalero Apaches. Norman: 1958. V. 71
Pass of the North. El Paso: 1968. V. 70
Pass of the North. El Paso: 1980. V. 68
The State National Since 1881: the Pioneer Bank of El Paso. El Paso: 1971. V. 68
Ten Texas Feuds. Albuquerque: 1957. V. 69; 70; 71

SONS OF THE COPPER BEECHES
Leaves from the Copper Beeches. Narberth: 1959. V. 69
Leaves from the Copper Beeches. Philadelphia: 1959. V. 71
More Leaves from the Copper Beeches. Philadelphia: 1976. V. 71

SONTAG, J.
Hints for Non-Commissioned Officers on Actual Service. London: 1804. V. 70

SONTAG, SUSAN
Against Interpretation. New York: 1966. V. 71
Aids and Its Metaphors. New York: 1989. V. 72
The Benefactor. New York: 1963. V. 72
Brother Carl. New York: 1974. V. 72
Dancers on a Plane: Cage, Cunningham, Johns. London: 1989. V. 69; 71
Death Kit. New York: 1967. V. 71; 72
Duet for Cannibals. New York: 1970. V. 71; 72
I, Etcetera. New York: 1978. V. 71; 72
Illness as Metaphor. New York: 1978. V. 71; 72
In America. Franklin Center: 2000. V. 70
In America. New York: 2000. V. 71
A Susan Sontag Reader. New York: 1982. V. 71; 72
Under the Sign of Saturn. New York: 1980. V. 71; 72
The Volcano Lover. New York: 1992. V. 72
The Way We Live Now. London: 1991. V. 69; 70; 73

SOOS, TROY
Hunting a Detroit Tiger. New York: 1997. V. 71
Murder at Fenway Park. New York: 1994. V. 69; 70; 71

SOPER, EILEEN
Wild Encounters. London: 1957. V. 73

SOPHIA, PRINCESS
A Catalogue of the Library of Her Royal Highness the Princess Sophia. London: 1849. V. 70

SOPHOCLES
Antigone. Haarlem: 1975. V. 70
Oedipus the King. New York: 1955. V. 68
Tragediae Septem Cum Commentariis. Venice: 1502. V. 68; 72
The Tragedies of Sopocles. London: 1865. V. 73
(Greek title, then) Tragoediae Septem. Francofvrti: 1544. V. 71
Women of Trachis. London: 1956. V. 68

SOPWITH, T.
Account of the Museum of Economic Geology and Mining Records Office.... London: 1843. V. 71

SORBIERE, SAMUEL
Relation d'un Voyage en Angleterre, ou Sont Touchees Plusieurs, Chose Qui Regardent L'Estate des Sciences.... Cologne: 1669. V. 70; 73
Sorberiana ou Bon Mots, Recontres Agreables, pensees Judicieuses et Observations Curieuses. Cologne: 1669. V. 70
A Voyage to England, Containing Many Things Relating to the State of Learning, Religion and Other Curiosities of that Kingdom.... London: 1709. V. 70

SORDO, E.
Moorish Spain: Cordoba, Seville, Granada. New York: 1963. V. 68; 69

SOREL, M. C.
La Bibliotheque Francoise. Ou le Choix et l'Examen des Liures Francois Qui Traitent de l'Eloquence de la Philosophie de la Devotion & de la Conduite des Moeurs.... Paris: 1664. V. 70

SORENSON, ALFRED
Early History of Omaha: Walks and Talks Among the Old Settlers: a Series of Sketches in the Shape of a Connected Narrative of the Events and Incidents of Early times in Omaha, Together with a brief Mention of the Most Important Events of Later Years. Omaha: 1876. V. 68; 73

SORENSON, LORIN
The Ford Road. 75th Anniversary. Ford Motor Company 1903-1978. St. Helen: 1978. V. 68

SORLEY, CHARLES HAMILTON
The Letters of Charles Sorley. London: 1919. V. 68
Marlborough and Other Poems. Cambridge: 1916. V. 72

SORLEY, W. R.
On the Ethics fo Naturalism. Edinburgh and London: 1885. V. 71

SORREL, G. MOXLEY
Recollections of a Confederate Staff Officer. New York and Washington: 1905. V. 68; 70
Recollections of a Confederate Staff Officer. New York: 1917. V. 69

SORRENTINO, GILBERT
A Beehive Arranged on Humane Principles. New York: 1986. V. 73
The Sky Changes. New York: 1966. V. 68
Sulpicia Elegidia/Elegiacs of Sulpicia. Mt. Horeb: 1977. V. 73

SOSEKI, MUSO
Sun at Midnight. 1985. V. 71
Sun at Midnight. New York: 1985. V. 73

SOTHEBY & CO.
Catalogues of Oriental Manuscripts and Miniatures. London: 1967-1980. V. 70

SOTHEBY, CAROLINE BOWLES
Ellen Fitzarthur: a Metrical Tale. London: 1822. V. 72

SOTHEBY, S. LEIGH
Paper-Marks in the Early Block-Books of the Netherlands and Germany...the Types and Marks in Productions of the Press of Caxton.. (together with) Specimen of Mr. S. Leigh Sotheby's Principia Typographica. London: 1858. V. 70
Ramblings in the Elucidation of the Autograph of Milton. London: 1861. V. 72

SOTHEBY, WILLIAM
Oberon, a Poem from the German of Wieland. London: 1798. V. 72
A Tour through Parts of Wales, Sonnets, Odes and Other Poems. London: 1794. V. 72

SOTHERAN'S York Guide: Including a Description of the Public Buildings, Antiquities &c..in and About that Ancient City. York: 1799. V. 72

SOUEIF, AHDAF
Aisha. London: 1983. V. 70

SOULE, FRANK
The Annals of San Francisco. San Francisco/London: 1855. V. 73

SOULE, GARDNER
The Long Trail: How Cowboys and Longhorns Opened the West. New York: 1976. V. 70

SOULE, MAURICE
La Grand Adventure-LePoPee Du Comte De Raousset- Boulbon Au Mexique (1850-1854). Paris: 1926. V. 71

SOULSBY, B. H.
A Catalogue of the Work of Linnaeus.... London: 1933. V. 71

THE SOUND of Writing. New York: 1991. V. 70

THE SOUNDER Few. Athens: 1971. V. 72

SOUSA BOTELHO MOURAU E VASCONCELLOS, ADELAIDE MARIE EMILIE
Adele de Senage, ou Lettres de Lord Sydenham. Geneve & Paris: 1798. V. 72

SOUSA DE MACEDO, ANTONIO
Flores de Espana Excelenias de Portugal...Primera Parte.... Lisboa: 1631. V. 70

SOUSTELLE, JACQUES
Arts of Ancient Mexico. New York: 1967. V. 72

SOUSTER, RAYMOND
New Wave Canada. Toronto: 1966. V. 72

SOUTAR, WILLIAM
Collected Poems. London: 1948. V. 69

SOUTH CAROLINA
The Address of the People of South Carolina, Assembled in Convention to the People of the Slaveholding States of the United States. Charleston: 1860. V. 70
State Papers on Nullification: Including the Public Acts of the Convention of the People of South Carolina, Assembled at Columbia, November 19, 1832 and March 11, 1833.... Boston: 1834. V. 72

SOUTH DAKOTA
South Dakota - Constitutional Debates 1885. Volume I. Huron: 1907. V. 69

SOUTH KENSINGTON MUSEUM
Fifty Etchings of Objects of Art in the South Kensington Museum. 1867. V. 68
The Industrial Arts: Historical Sketches. Piccadily: 1876. V. 71

SOUTH, ROBERT
A Sermon Preached Before the Court at Christchurch Chappel in Oxford. Oxford: 1665. V. 73

SOUTH-WEST LANCASHIRE JOINT TOWN PLANNING ADVISORY COMMITTEE
The Future of Development of South-West Lancashire.The Report. Hodder & Stoughton, and Live: 1930. V. 73

SOUTHAM, B. C.
Jane Austen's Literary Manuscripts, a Study of the Novelist's Development through the Surviving Papers. 1964. V. 73

SOUTHCOTT, JOANNA
Answer to Five Charges in the Leeds Mercury, Four of Which are Absolutely False.... London: 1805. V. 69; 72
An Answer to Thomas Paine's Third Part of the Age of Reason. London: 1812. V. 73
The Book of Wonders, Marvellous and True. (and) The Second Book of Wonders, More Marvellous than the First. (and) The Third Book of Wonders Announcing the Coming of Shiloh; with a Call to the Hebrews...(and) the Fourth Book of Wonders.... London: 1813-1814. V. 69; 71

SOUTHERLAND, ELLEASE
Let the Lion Eat Straw. New York: 1979. V. 72

SOUTHERN Bivouac. Wilmington: 1992. V. 69

SOUTHERN DIRECTORY COMPANY
General Directory of the City, of Marshall for 1893. Marshall. V. 69

SOUTHERN Express Company. Instructions for the Use of Employees Only. Augusta: 1868. V. 68

SOUTHERN, JOHN
Thorburn's Birds and Mammals. 1986. V. 69
A Treatise Upon Aerostatic Machines. Birmingham: 1785. V. 68

THE SOUTHERN Literary Messenger. Richmond: 1839-1844. V. 72

SOUTHERN PACIFIC CO.
Guest Ranches, Southern Arizona. 1928. V. 68

SOUTHERN, TERRY
The Magic Christian. New York: 1960. V. 68; 69; 71
Now Dig This. New York: 2001. V. 69; 72

SOUTHEY, CAROLINE ANNE BOWLES
The Poetical Works of.... London: 1867. V. 69
The Widow's Tale; and Other Poems. London: 1822. V. 69

SOUTHEY, ROBERT
Carmen Triumphale, for the Commencement of the Year 1814. London: 1814. V. 72
Carmen Triumphale, For the Commencement of the Year, 1814.... London: 1821. V. 71
Joan of Arc. Bristol: 1796. V. 72
Joan of Arc. London: 1798. V. 72
The Lay of the Laureate. Carmen Nupitale. London: 1816. V. 72
The Life Of Nelson. London: 1881. V. 72
Poems. (with) Poems. Second Volume. Bristol: 1797. V. 68; 72
The Poetical Works. Collected by Himself. London: 1853. V. 72
Roderick, the Last of The Goths. London: 1818. V. 72
Sir Thomas More; or the Colloquies on the Progress and Prospects of Society. London: 1829. V. 73
A Vision of Judgement. London: 1821. V. 72

SOUTHEY, WILLIAM
The Poetical Works. Collected by himself. London: 1853. V. 71

SOUTHWART, ELIZABETH
Bronte Moors and Villages. London: 1923. V. 70

SOUTHWORTH, EMMA
The Deserted Wife. Philadelphia: 1855. V. 70
The Lost Heiress. Philadelphia: 1854. V. 70
Retribution. A Tale of Passion. Philadelphia: 1856. V. 70
The Three Beauties. Philadelphia: 1858. V. 70

SOUVENIR Album of the Great West. Columbus: 1892. V. 69

A SOUVENIR in Photogravure of the Upper Peninsula of Michigan. 1900. V. 68

SOUVENIR of Scotland, its Cities, Lakes and Mountains. London: 1897. V. 71

SOUVENIR Of the Alice in Wonderland Illuminated Garden at Happy Valley. Llandudno: 1950. V. 69

SOUVENIR of the Sister Counties of Southern California. Los Angeles: 1905. V. 68

SOUVENIR Santa Monica. Los Angeles: 1901. V. 68

SOUVESTRE, EMILE
An Attic Philosopher in Paris: or, A Peep at the World from a Garret. London: 1853. V. 71

SOVIET Photography. Moscow/Leningrad: 1939. V. 68

SOWELL, A. J.
Early Settlers and Indian Fighters of Southwest Texas. New York: 1964. V. 69

SOWERBY, A. DE C.
The Naturalist in Manchuria. Tientsin: 1922-1930. V. 73
Naturalist's Holiday by the Sea. London: 1923. V. 68
A Naturalist's Note-Book in China. Shanghai: 1925. V. 69
A Sportsman's Miscellany. 1917. V. 69
A Sportsman's Miscellany. Tientsin: 1917. V. 73

SOWERBY, G. B.
Companion to Mr. Kinglsye's Glaucus.... Cambridge: 1858. V. 68
A Conchological Manual. London: 1839. V. 68; 70
A Conchological Manual. 1846. V. 73
A Conchological Manual. London: 1846. V. 69
Illustrated Index of British Shells. 1887. V. 69
Popular British Conchology. 1854. V. 69
Popular British Conchology. London: 1854. V. 68; 70
Popular History of the Aquarium. London: 1857. V. 68

SOWERBY, GITHA
Childhood. London: 1907. V. 69; 70
The Gay Book. London: 1914. V. 70
Little Plays for Little People. London: 1910. V. 71
The Merry Book. London: 1911. V. 69
The Wise Book. London: 1906. V. 70

SOWERBY, JAMES
The Genera of Recent and Fossil Shells. 1820-1825-. V. 69

SOWERBY, JOHN EDWARD
British Wild Flowers. 1894. V. 69; 73
The Ferns of Great Britain... (with) The Fern Allies: a Supplement to the Ferns of Great Britain. London: 1855-1856. V. 71

SOYER, ALEXIS
The Modern Housewife, or Menagere. London: 1849. V. 68

SOYER, RAPHAEL
A Painter's Pilgrimage: an Account of a Journey. New York: 1962. V. 72
Self-Revealment: a Memoir. New York: 1969. V. 72

SOYINKA, WOLE
Art, Dialogue and Outrage. New York: 1994. V. 69
The Burden of Memory, The Muse of Forgiveness. New York: 1998. V. 72
Outsiders. Canton: 1999. V. 68
Poems from Prison. London: 1969. V. 68; 70
The Road. 1965. V. 70

SPACHI, ISARELIS
Gyneciorvm Sive De Muliervm Tvm Commvnibuvs, Tvm Gravidarvm, Parientivm, Et Pverperarum.... Argentinae: 1597. V. 70

SPADE and Pail Tales. London. V. 69

SPAHER, MICHAEL
A Survey of the Micrcosme; or the Anatomy of the Bodies of Man and Woman. London: 1702. V. 73

SPAIN and Spanish America in the Libraries of the University of California. New York: 1969. V. 70; 73

SPAIN, JOHN
Death is Like That. 1943. V. 73

SPALDING, ALBERT G.
America's National Game: Historic Facts Concerning the Beginning Evolution, Development and Popularity of Base Ball with Personal Reminiscences of its Vicissitudes, Its Victories and Its Votaries. New York: 1911. V. 70

SPALDING, ARTHUR WHITEFIELD
Origin and History of Seventh-Day Adventists. Washington: 1961-1962. V. 73

SPALDING, JAMES ALFRED
Dr. Lyman Spalding, the Originator of the United States Pharmacopoeia. Boston: 1916. V. 73

SPALDING, WILLIAM A.
History and Reminiscences: Los Angeles City and County California. Los Angeles: 1930. V. 73

SPALLANZANI, LAZZARO
Dissertations Relative to the Natural History of Naimals and Vegetables. London: 1789. V. 70
Opuscoli di Fisica Animale, e Vegetabile dell'.... Modena: 1776. V. 70
Tracts on the Nature of Animals and Vegetables. Edinburgh: 1799. V. 70
Tracts on the Nature of Animals and Vegetables. London: 1799. V. 72

SPALTEHOLZ, WERNER
Hand Atlas of Human Anatomy. Philadelphia. V. 71

SPANHEIM, FRIEDRIC
A Funeral Oration to the Sacred Memory of the Most Serene and Potent Mary II.... London: 1695. V. 68

SPARE, AUSTIN OSMAN
The Collected Works of Austin Osman Spare. His Art, Philosophy and Magic. No place noted: 1982. V. 70

SPARER, PHINEAS J.
Personality, Stress and Tuberculosis. New York: 1956. V. 71

SPARGO, JOHN
Elements of Socialism. A Textbook. New York: 1912. V. 68
The Socialism of William Morris. Westwood: 1908. V. 71

SPARK, MURIEL
The Ballad of Peckham Rye. 1960. V. 68
The Bronte Letters. 1954. V. 68
The Comforters. 1958. V. 68
Doctors of Philosophy. London: 1963. V. 69; 71
Emily Bronte. Her Life and Work. London: 1953. V. 69
The Fanfarlo and Other Verse. Ashford: 1952. V. 72
A Far Cry from Kensington. 1988. V. 68
A Far Cry from Kensington. London: 1988. V. 73
The French Window and the Small Telephone. 1993. V. 68
The Go-Away Bird and Other Stories. 1958. V. 68
John Masefield. 1953. V. 68
John Masefield. London: 1953. V. 69
Memento Mori. Philadelphia. 1959. V. 73
My Best Mary; the Selected Letters of Mary Wollstonecraft Shelley. London: 1953. V. 70
Not to Disturb. 1971. V. 68
The Portobello Road and Other Stories. Finland: 1990. V. 68
The Prime of Miss Jean Brodie. 1961. V. 68; 71
The Prime of Miss Jean Brodie. London: 1961. V. 70; 71

Robinson. 1958. V. 68
Tribute to Wordsworth: a Miscellany of Opinion for the Centenary of the Poet's Death. London: 1950. V. 70
Voices at Play. London: 1961. V. 70

SPARKE, ARCHIBALD
A Bibliography of the Dialect Literature of Cumberland Westmorland, and Lancashire North-of-the-Sands. Kendal: 1907. V. 71

SPARKS, DAVID S.
Inside Lincoln's Army - The Diary of Marsena Rudolph Patrick, Provost Marshall General, Army of The Potomac. NY: 1964. V. 72

SPARKS, JARED
The Life of Gouverneur Morris, with Selections from His Correspondence.... Boston: 1832. V. 71

SPARKS, TIMOTHY
Sunday Under Three Heads. London: 1836. V. 68

SPARKS, WILLIAM
The Apache Kid, a Bear Fight and Other True Stories of the Old West. Los Angeles: 1926. V. 68; 73

SPARLING, H. H.
Irish Ministrelsy. 1888. V. 70

SPARRMAN, ANDERS
A Voyage Round the World with Captain James Cook in H.M.S. Resolution. Waltham St. Lawrence: 1944. V. 71

SPARROW 61-72. Santa Rosa: 1991. V. 71

SPARROW, JOHN
Devotions Upon Emergent Occasion by John Donne.... Cambridge: 1923. V. 71
Grave Epigrams. Bembridge: 1974. V. 72
Grave Epigrams and Other Verses. Burford: 1981. V. 72
Line Upon Line; an Epigraphical Anthology. 1967. V. 71
Visible Words, a Study of Inscriptions In and as Books and Works of Art. Cambridge: 1969. V. 68

SPARROW, WALTER SHAW
British Sporting Artists From Barlow to Herring. London: 1922. V. 72
British Sporting Artists from Barlow to Herring. 1965. V. 68
John Lavery and His Work. London: 1911. V. 73
Women Painters of the World: from the Time of Caterina Vigri 1413-1463 to Rosa Bonehur and the Present Day. New York: 1905. V. 72

SPARROY, MASSICKS
The Listening Woman. Boston;: 1932. V. 68

SPATH, L.
Revision of the Jurassic Cephalopod Fauna of Kachh (Cutch). Calcutta: 1927-1933. V. 68

SPATZ, H. DONALD
Murder with Long Hair. New York: 1940. V. 71

SPAULDING, EDWARD SELDEN
Adobe Days Along the Channel. 1957. V. 69; 70; 72; 73
Adobe Days Along the Channel. Santa Barbara: 1957. V. 70
Borein's West. Santa Barbara: 1952. V. 69; 70; 72

SPAULL, HEBE
Women Peace-Makers. London: 1924. V. 72

THE SPEAKING Picture Book. 1890. V. 68

THE SPEAKING Toybook Reproducing the Voices of the Cock, the Goat, the Cat, the Bird, the Lamb, and the Cuckoo Dedicated to All Children by One who Loves Them. Germany: 1910. V. 73

SPEAKING with the Angel. London: 2000. V. 68

SPEAR, ELSA
Fort Phil Kearny Dakota Territory 1866-1868. Sheridan, WY: 1939. V. 72

SPEARE, DOROTHY
Spring on 52nd Street. New York: 1947. V. 71

SPEARS, JOHN R.
A History of the Mississippi Valley from Its Discovery to the End of Foreign Domination. New York: 1903. V. 70; 73
Illustrated Sketches of Death Valley and Other Borax Deserts of the Pacific Coast. Chicago and New York: 1892. V. 69; 70

SPEARS, RAYMOND S.
The River Prophet. Garden City: 1920. V. 70

SPECHT, R. L.
Records of American-Austrlian Scientific Expedition to Arnhem Land. 4. Zoology. Parkville: 1964. V. 72

SPECIMENS of the Yorkshire Dialect. York: 1820. V. 72

SPECK, F. G.
Family Hunting Territories and Social Life of Various Algonkian Bands of the Ottawa Valley. Ottawa: 1915. V. 73
Midwinter Rites of the Cayuga Long House. Philadelphia: 1949. V. 69
Penobscot Man. Philadelphia: 1940. V. 69

THE SPECTATOR. London: 1712-1715. V. 68
THE SPECTATOR. London: 1747. V. 69

THE SPECTATOR. London: 1803. V. 69
THE SPECTATOR. New York: 1826. V. 70
THE SPECTATOR. Boston: 1856. V. 70

SPECTRE, PSEUD.
Ye Vampyres!. London: 1875. V. 68

SPECULATOR Morum. Bibliotheca Arcana seu Catalogus Librorum Penetralium Being Brief Notices of Boks that Have Been Secretly Printed, Prohibited by Law, Seized Anathematised, Burnt or Bowdlerised. London: 1973. V. 70

SPEECE, CONRAD
The Mountaineer. Harrisonburg: 1818. V. 68; 69

SPEECH of the Royal Watchman in the Court of Common Pleas, the 7th of November 1812 on a Motion for a Rule to Shew Cause Why This Case Should Not Be Sent to Another Jury. London: 1812?. V. 68

THE SPEECHES at full Length of Mr. Van Ness, Mr. Caines, The Attorney General, Mr. Harrison and General Hamilton, in the Great Cause of the People Against Harry Croswell on an Indictment for a Libel on Thomas Jefferseon, President of the United States. New York: 1804. V. 68; 72; 73

SPEECHLY, WILLIAM
A Treatise on the Culture of the Vine; with New Hints on the Formation of Vineyards in England. (with) *A Treatise on the Culture of the Pine Apple, and the Management of the Hot-House.* London: 1821. V. 69

SPEED, ROBERT
The Counter-Scuffle. Whereunto Is Added the Counter-Rat. London: 1680. V. 72

SPEEDY, TOM
The Natural History of Sport in Scotland with Rod and Gun. 1920. V. 72
The Natural History of Sport in Scotland with Rod and Gun. London: 1920. V. 68
Sport in the Highlands and Lowlands of Scotland with Rod and Gun. 1884. V. 70; 72; 73
Sport in the Highlands and Lowlands of Scotland with Rod and Gun. London: 1886. V. 71

SPEER, EMORY
Lincoln, Lee, Grant and Other Biographical Addresses. New York: 1909. V. 69

SPEER, JOHN
History of Blanco County. Austin: 1965. V. 69
Life of General James H. Lane- The Liberator of Kansas. Garden City, KS: 1896. V. 71

SPEER, MARION A.
Western Trails. Huntington Beach: 1931. V. 71

SPEER, S. G.
UPASI 1893-1953. Coonoor: 1953. V. 72

SPEER, WILLIAM
An Humble Plea, Addressed to the Legislature of California, in Behalf of the Immigrants from the Empire of China to this State. San Francisco: 1856. V. 71

SPEERT, HAROLD
Iconographica Gyniatrica; a Pictorial History of Gynecology and Obstetrics. Philadelphis: 1973. V. 70

SPEICHER, JOHN
Looking for Baby Paradise. New York: 1967. V. 71; 72

SPEIGHT, HARRY
Kirkby Overblow and District. 1903. V. 72
Kirkby Overblow and District. London: 1903. V. 68

SPEISER, W.
Oriental Architecture in Colour. London: 1965. V. 69; 72

SPEKE, J. H.
Journal of the Discovery of the Source of the Nile. New York: 1864. V. 70

SPELMAN, HENRY
Villare Anglicum; or a View of All the Cities, Towns and Villages in England.... London: 1678. V. 73

SPELMAN, JOHN
Aelfredi Magni Anglorum Regis Invictissimi Vita Tribus Libris Comprehensa. Oxford: 1678. V. 72
Certain Considerations Upon the Duties Both of Prince and People. Oxford: 1642. V. 68

SPELMAN, W. W. R.
Lowestoft China. Norwich: 1905. V. 72

SPELTZ, ALEXANDER
The Coloured Ornament of All Historic Styles. Leipzig: 1914. V. 71
The Coloured Ornament of All Historical Styles. Leipzig: 1915. V. 71

SPENCE, GEORGE
The Equitable Jurisidiction of the Court of Chancery (England). Philadelphia: 1846. V. 71

SPENCE, JOSEPH
Anecdotes, Observations and Characters of Books and Men. London and Edinburgh: 1820. V. 68; 69; 72
Observations, Anecdotes and Characters of Books and Men Collected from Conversation. 1966. V. 72

SPENCE, WILLIAM
Britain Independent of Commerce; or, Proofs, Deduced from an Investigation Into the True Causes of the Wealth of Nations, That Our Riches.... London: 1807. V. 68

SPENCER, B.
The Twist in the Plotting. 1960. V. 69

SPENCER, BALDWIN
Across Australia. London: 1912. V. 69
Native Tribes of Central Australia. London: 1899. V. 69
The Native Tribes of Central Australia. London: 1938. V. 69
Native Tribes of the Northern Territory of Australia. London: 1914. V. 69
Wanderings in Wild Australia. London: 1928. V. 68; 70; 73

SPENCER, BRIAN A.
Prairie School Tradition: the Prairie Archives of the Milwaukee Art Center. New York: 1979. V. 68; 69; 72

SPENCER, CHARLES CHILD
The Rudiments of the Art of Playing the Pianoforte.... London: 1853. V. 68

SPENCER, CLAIRE
Gallows' Orchard. New York: 1930. V. 69; 70

SPENCER, CORNELIA PHILLIPS
The Last Ninety Days of the War in North Carolina. New York: 1866. V. 69; 70

SPENCER, EDMUND
Turkey, Russia and the Black Sea, and Circassia. London: 1855. V. 68; 72

SPENCER, ELIZABETH
Knights and Dragons. New York: 1965. V. 68; 70
The Night Travellers. New York: 1991. V. 71
Ship Island and Other Stories. New York: 1968. V. 68; 69
The Stories of Elizabeth Spencer. New York: 1980. V. 70

SPENCER, FREDERICK CHARLES
The Vale of Bolton; a Poetical Sketch; and other poems. London. V. 71

SPENCER, HERBERT
An Autobiography. London: 1904. V. 69; 71
An Epitome of Synthetic Philosophy. London: 1889. V. 71
Essays: Scientific and Speculative. London: 1868-1875. V. 71
The Nature and Reality of Religion. New York: 1885. V. 71
The Principles of Biology. London: 1864-1867. V. 72
The Principles of Psychology. London: 1870-1872. V. 69
The Principles of Sociology. New York: 1896. V. 70
Railway Morals and Railway Policy.... London: 1855. V. 73
Social Statics; or, the Conditions Essential to Human Happiness Specified.... London: 1868. V. 71
Works. New York: 1897. V. 70

SPENCER, HERBERT RITCHIE
William Harvey, Obstetric Physician and Gynaecologist, Being the Harveian Oration Delivered at the Royal College of Physicians, Oct. 18th, 1921. London: 1921. V. 68

SPENCER, JOHN
De Legibus Hebraeorum Ritualibus et Earum Rationibus Libri IV.... Cantabrigiae: 1727. V. 71; 72
A Discourse Concerning Prodigies, Wherein the Vanity of Presages by Them is Reprehended.... London: 1665. V. 69
Japan and the East. Northampton: 1986. V. 68

SPENCER, R. E.
Felicita. Indianapolis: 1937. V. 69
The Lady Who Came to Stay. New York: 1931. V. 69

SPENCER, REUBEN
The Home Trade of Manchester, with Personal Reminiscences and Occasional Notes. London: 1890. V. 71

SPENCER, ROY
D. H. Lawrence Country. London: 1979. V. 72

SPENCER, S. A.
The Greatest Show on Earth. Garden City: 1938. V. 68

SPENCER, SCOTT
Endless Love. New York: 1979. V. 72
Last Night at the Brain Thieves Ball. 1973. V. 70
The Rich Man's Table. New York: 1998. V. 72

SPENCER, STANLEY
Scrapbook Drawings. 1964. V. 71
Stanley Spencer - A Complete Catalouge of the Paintings. London: 1992. V. 72

SPENCER, SYDNEY
Mountaineering. London: 1930. V. 69
Mountaineering. London: 1934. V. 69

SPENDER, EMILY
Kingsford. London: 1886. V. 68

SPENDER, HAROLD
In Praise of Switzerland. London: 1912. V. 69
Story of the Home Rule Session. 1893. V. 69; 73

SPENDER, JOHN ALFRED
The Life of Sir Henry Campbell Bannerman. London: 1923. V. 71

SPENDER, STEPHEN
China Diary. London: 1982. V. 70; 71
Collected Poems 1928-1953. London: 1955. V. 70; 71
Dolphins. London: 1994. V. 69
The Edge of Being. London: 1949. V. 69

SPENDER, STEPHEN continued
The Generous Days. Boston: 1969. V. 73
The Generous Days. New York: 1971. V. 68; 70
Poems for Spain. London: 1939. V. 70; 73
Poems of Dedication. London: 1947. V. 71
Poems of Dedication. New York: 1947. V. 68; 70
Returning to Vienna 1947. Pawlet: 1947. V. 70; 73
Ruins and Visions - Poems. London: 1942. V. 68; 69
Ruins and Visions. Poems 1934-1942. New York: 1942. V. 68
The Still Centre. London: 1939. V. 69
The Temple. London: 1988. V. 71; 73
Twenty Poems. Oxford: 1930. V. 68; 72
Vienna. London: 1934. V. 68

SPENGLER, OSWALD
Man and Technics: A Contribution to a Philosophy of Life. New York: 1932. V. 72

SPENSER, EDMUND
Amoretti and Epithalamion. London: 1927. V. 70; 72
Epithalamion and Amoretti. London: 1903. V. 68; 70
The Faerie Queen, Disposed into XII Bookes.... London: 1609. V. 69
The Faerie Queene. (and) The Second Part of the Faerie Queene. London: 1590-1596. V. 73
The Faerie Qveen: the Shepheards Calendar; Together with the Other Works of England's Arch-Poet. London: 1611-1613. V. 71
Minor Poems. 1925. V. 68
Poems of Spenser.... London. V. 69
The Poetical Works. London: 1825. V. 72
The Poetical Works. London: 1839. V. 68; 72
The Poetical Works. London: 1852. V. 72
The Shepheard's Calendar. London: 1930. V. 68
The Shepheard's Calender. Twelve Aeclogues proportional to the Twelve Monethes . . . London: 1898. V. 71
The Works.... London: 1679. V. 73
The Works.... London: 1715. V. 72
Works.... London: 1856. V. 70
The Works.... Oxford: 1930. V. 73

SPERONE, SPERONI DEGLI ALVAROTTI
Dialogi...Nuovamente Ristamapti and Con Molta Diligenza and Corretti. Venice: 1543. V. 73

SPERRY, ARMSTRONG
One Day with Manu. Philadelphia: 1933. V. 73

SPEVACK, MARVIN
The Harvard Concordance to Shakespeare. Cambridge: 1973. V. 73

SPICE, R. P.
The Story of the Ryde Gas Arbitration. London: 1875. V. 69

SPICER, BART
Blues for the Prince. New York: 1950. V. 69

SPICER, EDWARD H.
Cycles of Conquest, the Impact of Spain, Mexico and the United States on the Indians of the Southwest 1533-1960. Tucson: 1962. V. 68

SPICER, HENRY
Sights and Sounds; the Mystery of the Day; Comprising an Enitre History of the American Spirit Manifestations. London: 1853. V. 68

SPICER, JACK
After Lorca. San Francisco: 1957. V. 71; 73
Billy the Kid. Stinson Beach: 1959. V. 69; 71

SPICER, JOHN L.
Correlation Methods of Comparing Idiolects in a Transition Area. 1952. V. 69

SPICER, W. R.
A Handbook of the Plants of Tasmania. Hobart: 1878. V. 73

SPIEGELBERG, FLORA
Princess Goldenhair and the Wonderful Flower. Chicago: 1915. V. 70

SPIEGELMAN, ART
The Complete Maus. New York: 1997. V. 68; 69
Maus: a Survivor's Tale. New York: 1986. V. 68; 71

SPIELBERG, STEVEN
Close Encounters of the Third Kind. New York: 1977. V. 68; 69

SPIELMAN, M. H.
Kate Greenaway. London: 1905. V. 71; 72

SPIELMANN, M. H.
Kate Greenaway. London: 1910. V. 69
The Love Family. London: 1909. V. 69
The Rainbow Book. Tales of Fun and Fancy. London: 1909. V. 73

SPIER, PETER
Noah's Ark. Garden City: 1977. V. 70

SPIERS, F. S.
The Microscope. Its Design, Construction and Applications. London: 1920. V. 68

SPIES, AUGUST
August Spies' Autobiography, His Speech to Court and General Notes. Chicago: 1887. V. 68

SPIGELGLASS, LEONARD
A Majority of One. New York: 1959. V. 69

SPIKER, S. H.
Berlin und Seine Umgebungen in Neunzehnten Jahhundert. Berlin: 1833. V. 70

SPIKY the Hedgehog. New York: 1938. V. 73

SPILLANE, MICKEY
The Big Kill. New York: 1951. V. 71
The Big Kill. London: 1952. V. 71
The By-Pass Control. New York: 1966. V. 71
Day of the Guns. New York: 1964. V. 68
The Deep. New York: 1961. V. 68; 71
The Delta Factor. New York: 1967. V. 71
I, the Jury. New York: 1947. V. 70
I, the Jury. London: 1952. V. 72
Kiss Me, Deadly. New York: 1952. V. 69; 70; 71; 72; 73
Kiss Me, Deadly. London: 1953. V. 72
The Last Cop Out. New York: 1973. V. 70; 71
The Long Wait. New York: 1951. V. 71
Me, Hood!. New York: 1969. V. 71
My Guin is Quick. New York: 1950. V. 71
One Lonely Night. New York: 1951. V. 68
Tomorrow I Die. New York: 1984. V. 68; 73
The Twisted Thing. New York: 1966. V. 71
Vengeance is Mine. New York: 1950. V. 69

SPILLER, BURTON L.
Firelight. New York: 1937. V. 70; 72

SPILLER, ROBERT E.
A Descriptive Bibliography Of The Writings Of James Fenimore Cooper. New York: 1934. V. 72

SPILSBURY, EDMUND GYBBON
Wire Tramways. Philadelphia: 1878. V. 68

SPINCKES, NATHANAEL
The Sick Man Visited.... London: 1712. V. 69
The Sick Man Visited.... London: 1744. V. 71

SPINDEN, H. J.
Maya Art and Civilization. Indian Hills: 1957. V. 69

SPINDLER, KARL
The Natural Son. A German Tale. London: 1835. V. 68

SPINELLI, MARCOS
Assignment Without Glory. Philadelphia: 1945. V. 70

SPINGARN, J. E.
A Renaissance Courtesy Book. Galateo of Manners and Behaviours. London: 1914. V. 69

SPINKE, JOHN
A Letter, Truly Representing a Matrimonial Case. London: 1711. V. 71

SPIRIT Mysteries Exposed, Being a Full and Plain Explanation of the Wonderful Feasts of the Davenport Brothers and other Mediums, with a History of Spirit Rapping and Explanation of the Means by Which Its Manifestations are Produced Etc. New York: 1871. V. 71

SPIRIT of Praise. London: 1867. V. 68

SPIRIT of the Soviet Union. Anti-Nazi Cartoons and Posters. London: 1942. V. 73

SPIRITUAL Communications and the Comfort They Bring.... Melbourne: 1873. V. 69

SPIRITUAL Quests. Boston: 1988. V. 72

SPITTAL, ROBERT
A Treatise on Auscultation, Illustrated by Cases and Dissections. Edinburgh: 1830. V. 68

SPITTLEHOUSE, JOHN
An Answer to One Part of the Lord Protector's Speech, or a Vindication of the Fifth Monarchy-Men. Livewel Chapman: 1654. V. 70

SPITZKA, EDWARD A.
A Study of the Brains of Six Eminent Scientists and Scholars Belonging to the American Anthropometric Society.... Philadelphia: 1907. V. 68; 71; 73

SPIVAK, JOHN L.
Georgia Nigger. New York: 1932. V. 72

SPIVEY, RICHARD L.
Maria. Flagstaff: 1979. V. 69; 71

SPIVEY, THOMAS SAWYER
The Seven Sons of Ballyhack. New York: 1911. V. 70

SPOCK, BENJAMIN
The Psychological Apsects of Pediatric Practice. New York: 1938. V. 71

SPOERRI, DANIEL
An Anecdoted Typography of Chance - Atlas Arkhive Four. London: 1995. V. 69

SPOERRI, JAMES FULLER
Catalog of a Collection of the Works of James Joyce Exhibited at the Newberry Library March 1 to March 26, 1948. Chicago: 1948. V. 68

SPOFFORD, HARRIET PRESCOTT
Ballads and Authors. Boston;: 1887. V. 69
In Titian's Garden and Other Poems. Boston: 1903. V. 68

SPON, JACOB
Traitez, Nouveaux & Curieux du Cafe, du The et du Chocolate.... Lyon: 1685. V. 70

SPOONER, LYSANDER
Address of the Free Constitutionalists to the People of the United States. Boston: 1860. V. 68
The Unconstitutionality of Slavery. Boston: 1853. V. 68

THE SPORTING Repository. London: 1822. V. 72

THE SPORTING Repository, Containing Horse-Racing, Hunting, Coursing, Shooting, Archery, Trotting and Tandem Matches, Cocking, Pedestrianism, Pugilism, Anecdotes on Sporting Subjects.... London: 1904. V. 73

THE SPORTSMAN'S Dictionary; or the Country Gentleman's Companion, in All Rural Recreations.... London: 1744. V. 73

THE SPORTSMAN'S Dictionary; or, the Gentleman's Companion for Town and Country. London: 1778. V. 73

SPORTSMAN'S Dictionary, or the Gentleman's Companion for Town and Country. London: 1792. V. 69; 72; 73

THE SPORSTMAN'S Vade-Mecum for the Himalayas. 1891. V. 70

SPOTTISWOODE, WILLIAM
A Tarantasse Journey through Eastern Russia in the Autumn of 1856. London: 1857. V. 69; 71

SPOTTS, DAVID L.
Campaigning With Custer. Lincoln: 1986. V. 72
Campaigning with Custer and the Nineteenth Kansas Volunteer Cavalry on the Washita Campaign 1868-1869. 1928. V. 68

SPOTTSWOOD, RICHARD K.
Ethnic Music on Records, Volume 1: Western Europe. Urbana: 1990. V. 72

SPRAGUE, J. T.
The Treachery in Texas, the Secession of Texas, and the Arrest of the United States Officers and Soldiers Serving in Texas. New York: 1862. V. 69; 70

SPRAGUE, KURTH
The Promise Kept. Austin: 1975. V. 70

SPRAGUE, MARSHALL
Money Mountain: the Story of Cripple Creek Gold. Boston: 1953. V. 73

SPRAGUE, P. E.
The Drawings of Louis Sullivan: A Catalogue of the Frank Lloyd Wright Collection at the Avery Architectural Library. Princeton: 1979. V. 68; 69; 72

SPRAGUE, W. B.
Letters from Europe in 1828. New York: 1828. V. 69

SPRAT, THOMAS
Histoire De La Conspiration Faite Contre Charles II.... Paris: 1685. V. 70
The History of the Royal Society of London for the Improving of Natural Knowledge. London: 1722. V. 70; 73
The History of the Royal Society of London, for the Improving of Natural Knowledge. London: 1734. V. 69
A Letter from the Bishop of Rochester to the Right Honourable The Earl of Dorset and Middlesex, Lord Chamberlain of His Majesties Household, Concerning His Sitting in the Late Ecclesiastical Commission. In the Savoy: 1688. V. 70
Observations on Monsieur de Sorbier's Voyage into England. London: 1665. V. 70
The Plague of Ahtens (sic) Which Happened in the Second Year of the Pelop-onnesian War. London: 1709. V. 70
A Relation of the Wicked Contrivance of Stephen Blackhead and Robert Young, Against the Lives of Several Persons by Forging an Association Under Their Hands. London: 1722. V. 70
A Sermon Preached at the Anniversary Meeting of the Sons of Clergy- Men in the Church of St. Mary-le-Bow Nov. VII 1678. London: 1678. V. 70
A Sermon Preached Before the King and Queen at Whitehal on Good Friday 1690. London: 1690. V. 70
A Sermon Preached Before the King at White-Hall December the 22 1678. London: 1678. V. 70
A Sermon Preach'd Before the Right Honourable Sir Henry Tulse, Lord Mayor and the Court of Alderman and the Citizens of the City of London on May the 29th 1684. London. V. 70
Sermons Preached on Several Occasions. London: 1697. V. 70
A True Account and Declaration of the Horrid Conspiracy Against the Late King, His Present Majesty and the Government.... London: 1685. V. 70; 73

SPRATT, GEORGE
Obstetric Tables. London: 1833. V. 72
Obstetric Tables. London: 1835. V. 73
Obstetric Tables. Philadelphia: 1847. V. 68
Obstetric Tables. Philadelphia: 1850. V. 72
Supplement to Obstetric Tables. London: 1835. V. 69

SPREAT, W.
Picturesque Sketches of the Churches of Devon Drawn from Nature...and on Stone. Exeter: 1842. V. 69; 72

SPRENGEL, KURT
An Introduction to the Study of Cryptogamous Plants. In Letters. London: 1807. V. 71; 73

SPRIGG, C. ST. JOHN
Death of an Airman. Garden City: 1935. V. 73

SPRING, AGNES WRIGHT
Buffalo Bill and His Horses. 1968. V. 68
Caspar Collins, The Life and Exploits of Indian Fighter of The Sixties. New York: 1927. V. 72
The Cheyenne And Black Hills Stage and Express Routes. Glendale: 1949. V. 72
70 Years Cow Country, Seventy Years, A Panoramic History of the Wyoming Stockgrowers Association Interwoven...Cattle Industry in Wyoming. Gillette: 1942. V. 71
William Chapin Deming of Wyoming, Pioneer Publisher, and State and Federal Officer - a Biography. Glendale: 1944. V. 68; 73

SPRING, GARDINER
Memoirs of the Rev. Samuel J. Mills, Late Missionary to the South Western Section of the United States and Agent of the American Colonization Society.... New York: 1820. V. 73

SPRINGER, F.
Some New American Fossil Crinoids. Cambridge: 1911. V. 71

SPRINGER, LEONARD A.
Oude Nederlandsche Tuinen. (with) De Oud-Hollandsche Tuinkunst. Haarlem: 1889. V. 68

SPRINGER, THOMAS GRANT
The Sword Peddler. New York: 1928. V. 71

SPRINGS, ELLIOTT WHITE
Contact. New York: 1930. V. 69

SPROUSE, MARTIN
Threat by Example: a Documentation of Inspiration. San Francisco: 1989. V. 70

SPRUNGER, S.
Orchids from Curtis's Botanical Magazine (1787-1949). Cambridge: 1986. V. 68; 71
Orchids from the Botanical Register 1815-1847. Basel: 1991. V. 71

SPRUNT, ALEXANDER
South Carolina Bird Life. Columbia: 1949. V. 68
South Carolina Bird Life. Columbia: 1970. V. 68

SPRUNT, JAMES
Derelicts. Wilmington: 1920. V. 69; 70
Tales and Traditions of the Lower Cape Fear 1661-1896. Wilmington: 1896. V. 69

SPRY, W. J.
The Cruise of Her Majesty's Ship "Challenger".... Toronto: 1877. V. 68

SPUDE, ROBERT
Central Arizona Ghost Towns. Las Vegas: 1978. V. 69

SPURGIN, FRED
Elfin Tales. London: 1920. V. 69

SPURLIN, CHARLES
Texas Veterans in the Mexican War. 1984. V. 69

SPURLING, R. GLEN
Lesions of the Cervical Intervertebral Disc. Springfield: 1956. V. 71

SPURR, JOSIAH E.
Economic Geology of the Georgetown Quadrangle (Together with the Empire District) Colorado. Washington: 1908. V. 69; 71; 73

SPURZHEIM, G.
Outlines of Phrenology; Being Also a Manuel (!) of Reference for the Marked Bust. Boston: 1833. V. 68
Outlines of Phrenology; being Also a Manuel (!) of Reference for the Marked Bust. Boston: 1834. V. 68

SPURZHEIM, JOHANN GASPAR
The Anatomy of the Brain, with a General View of the Nervous System. London: 1826. V. 69; 72
Examinations of the Objections Made in Britain Against the Doctrines of Gall and Spurzheim. Boston: 1833. V. 69
The Physiognomical System of Drs. Gall and Spurzheim.... London: 1815. V. 69

SPYRI, JOHANNA
Dora. Philadelphia. V. 70
Heidi. Philadelphia: 1922. V. 73

SQUIER, EMMA LINDSAY
The Bride of the Sacred Well and Other Tales of Ancient Mexico. New York: 1928. V. 70

SQUIER, EPHRAIM GEORGE
Nicaragua: Its People, Scenery, Monuments and the Proposed Interoceanic Canal.... New York: 1852. V. 71
The States of Central America; Their Geography, Topography Climate, Population, Resources, Productions, Commerce, Political Organization, Aborigines, etc.... London: 1858. V. 73

SQUIER, M. A.
Antiquities of the State of New York. Buffalo: 1851. V. 69

SQUILL, PHOSPHORUS, PSEUD.
The Devil at Oxford. Oxford: 1847. V. 73

SQUINTS through an Opera Glass. New York: 1850. V. 71

SQUIRE, J. C.
The Gold Tree. London: 1917. V. 68; 72
The Grub Street Nights Entertainments. London: 1924. V. 69; 73

SQUIRE, JACK C.
Socialism and Art. 1907. V. 71

SQUIRE, SAMUEL
An Enquiry into the Foundation of the English Constitution; or, an Historical Essay Upon the Anglo-Saxon Government both in Germany and England. London: 1753. V. 70

SQUIRES, W. AUSTIN
The 104th Regiment of Foot (The New Brunswick Regiment). 1803-1817. Fredericton: 1962. V. 72; 73

SQUIRES, W. H. T.
Unleashed at Long Last: Reconstruction in Virginia, April 9, 1865 January 26, 1970. Portsmouth VA: 1939. V. 72

STABLEFORD, BRIAN
The Empire of Fear. New York: 1988. V. 70

STABLES, GORDON
The Cruise of the Land Yacht Wanderer;; or Thirteen Hundred Miles in my Caravan. London: 1886. V. 71

STACEY, C. P.
The Canadian Army, 1939-1945 an Official Historical Summary. Ottawa: 1948. V. 68
The Canadians in Britain 1939-1944. (with) *From Pachino to Ortona.* (with) *Canada's Battle in Normady.* Ottawa: 1946. V. 68

STACEY, MAY HUMPHREYS
Uncle Sam's Camels: the Journal of...Supplemented by the Report of Edward Fitzgerald Beale (1857-1858). Cambridge: 1929. V. 73

STACK, AMOS
Amos Stack (1822-1908) Forty-Niner: His Overland Diary to California; a Pioneer Coloradan, Prominent Citizen, Jurist, Educator.... Denver: 1981. V. 70

STACKHOUSE, J.
Nereis Britannica.... Bath: 1801. V. 69

STACKHOUSE, P. J.
One Hundred Years with the Baptists of Amherst, N.S. 1810-1910. Amherst: 1931. V. 73

STACKHOUSE, THOMAS
A New History of the Holy Bible, from the Beginning of the World, to the Establishment of Christianity. London: 1752-1753. V. 69

STACPOOLE, FLORENCE
Handbook of Housekeeping for Small Incomes. Preston: 1900. V. 68

STAEL HOLSTEIN, ANNE LOUISE GERMAINE NECKER, BARONNE DE
Corinne ou l'Italie. Paris: 1819. V. 72
De La Litterature Consideree dans ses Rapports avec les Institutions Sociales.... Paris and London: 1812. V. 68
De l'Allemagne. Paris: 1813. V. 68
The Influence of the Passions Upon the Happiness of Individuals and of Nations. London: 1813. V. 69

STAEL HOLSTEIN, AUGUSTIN
Lettres sur l'Angleterre. Paris: 1825. V. 70

STAFFORD, BARBARA MARIA
Voyage into Substance; Art, Science, Nature, and the Illustrated Travel Account, 1760-1840. Cambridge, MA: 1984. V. 72

STAFFORD, CORA ELDER
My Pinocchio Art Book. Chicago: 1930. V. 71

STAFFORD, JEAN
The Catherine Wheel. New York: 1952. V. 71; 72
A Mother in History. New York: 1966. V. 71
The Mountain Lion. London: 1948. V. 72

STAFFORD, MAGDALEN
The Romance and Its Hero. London: 1859. V. 73

STAFFORD, MALLIE
The March of Empire through Three Decades Embracing Sketches of California History. San Francisco: 1884. V. 68; 73

STAFFORD, MURIEL
X Marks the Dot. New York: 1943. V. 68

STAFFORD, WILLIAM
All About Light: Poems. Athens: 1978. V. 68
Allegiances. New York: 1970. V. 68
Allegiances. New York: 1973. V. 68
Eleven Untitled Poems. Mt. Horeb: 1968. V. 68
Fin, Feather, Fur: Poems. Rexburg: 1989. V. 68
History Is Loose Again: Poems. Rexburg: 1991. V. 68
How To Fold Your Arms When It Rains: Poems. Lewiston: 1990. V. 68
Listening Deep. Great Barrington: 1984. V. 68
The Rescued Year: Poems. New York: 1966. V. 68; 71
Sometimes Like a Legend: Puget Sound Country: Poems. 1981. V. 68
Stories and Storms and Strangers: Poems. Rexburg: 1984. V. 68
Traveling through the Dark. New York & Evanston: 1962. V. 73
Weather: Poems. Mt. Horeb: 1969. V. 68
Wyoming Circuit: Poems. 1980. V. 68
You and Some Other Characters: Poems. Rexburg: 1987. V. 68

STAGG, JOHN
The Minstrel of the North: or, Cumbrian Legends. London: 1810. V. 71
Miscellaneous Poems. Wigton: 1807. V. 70
Miscellaneous Poems, some of Which are in the Cumberland and Scottish Dialects. Wigton: 1808. V. 69

STAGGE, JONATHAN
The Dogs Do Bark. New York: 1937. V. 68
The Scarlet Circle. New York: 1943. V. 68
Turn of the Table. New York: 1940. V. 70
The Yellow Taxi. New York: 1942. V. 68

STAHL, F. A.
Rolling Stones. Glendale: 1928. V. 68; 71

STAHL, P. J.
A Butterfly Chase. Strasburgh: 1869. V. 72
Little Rosy's Voyage of Discovery Undertaken in Company With Her Cousin Charley. London: 1868. V. 68

STAHL, WILLIAM C.
New Method for Plectrum Banjo. New York: 1920. V. 71

STAIR, J. B.
Old Samoa, or Flotsam and Jetsam from the Pacific Ocean. London or Oxford: 1897. V. 69

STALEY, EUGENE
History of the Illinois State Federation of Labor. Chicago: 1930. V. 68

STALLARD, H. B.
Radiant Energy as (a) a Pathogenic, (b) a Therapeutic Agent in Ophthaolmic Disorders. London: 1933. V. 71

STALLWORTHY, JON
The Astronomy of Love. 1961. V. 72
A Day in the City. 1967. V. 72
Hand in Hand. London: 1974. V. 72
Out of Bounds. London: 1963. V. 72
Positives. Dublin: 1969. V. 72
Root and Branch. London: 1969. V. 72

STAMPART, FRANZ
Prodromus Oder Vor-Licht des Eroffineten Schau-und Wunder-Prachtes.... Vienna: 1735. V. 72

THE STANBROOK Abbey Press Ninety-Two Years of Its History. Worcester: 1970. V. 70; 71

STANDAGE, H. C.
Decoration of Metal, Wood, Glass, Etc. New York: 1908. V. 68

STANDEN, MICHAEL
Over the Wet Lawn. Oxford: 1977. V. 71

STANDIFORD, LES
Done Deal. 1993. V. 70
Spill. New York: 1991. V. 68

STANDING, JULIET
Exordium: Daedalus Press 1968-1983. Wymondham: 1983. V. 70; 72

STANDING BEAR, CHIEF
My People, The Sioux. Boston: 1928. V. 72

STANDS IN TIMBER, JOHN
Cheyenne Memories. London: 1967. V. 72

STANESBY, SAMUEL
The Floral Gift. An Illuminated Souvenir. London. V. 71

STANFORD Short Stories 1964. Stanford: 1964. V. 72

STANFORD, ALFRED
Far Horizons. Adventures in Cruising by Members Of The Cruising Club Of America. London: 1971. V. 72

STANFORD, DON
The Red Car. New York: 1954. V. 71

STANFORD, J. K.
Ladies in the Sun. 1962. V. 69

STANFORD, P. THOMAS
The Tragedy of the Negro In America. Boston: 1898. V. 68; 69

STANGE, HUGH
After Tomorrow: a Play in Three Acts. New York: 1931. V. 71

STANHOPE, CHARLES, 3RD EARL OF
Considerations on the Means of Preventing Fraudulent Practices on the Gold Coin. London: 1775. V. 73

STANHOPE, HESTER
Memoirs as Related by Herself in Conversations with Her Physician.... London: 1845. V. 69; 71
The Nun Of Lebanon. The Love Affair of Lady Hester Stanhope and Michael Bruce. London: 1951. V. 72

STANHOPE, PHILIP HENRY, 5TH EARL OF
History of England from the Peace of Utrecht to the Peace of Aix-laChapelle. London: 1836-1838. V. 71; 73
Life of the Right Honourable William Pitt. London: 1879. V. 71

STANIFORTH, J. M.
Cartoons of the Welsh Coal Strike April 1st to Sept. 1st, 1898. Cardiff: 1898. V. 69

STANLEY, ARTHUR
Historical Memorials of Westminster Abbey. New York: 1888. V. 71

STANLEY, ARTHUR PENRHYN
The Gipsies: a Prize Poem, Recited in the Theatre, Oxford June 7, 1873. Oxford: 1837. V. 72
The Life and Correspondence of Thomas Arnold. London: 1844. V. 68; 72
The Life And Correspondence Of Thomas Arnold. London: 1868. V. 72
Sinai And Palestine In Connection With Their History. London: 1856. V. 72

STANLEY, DONALD
Holmes Meets 007. San Francisco: 1967. V. 69

STANLEY, EDWARD
Before and After Waterloo. Letters From Edward Stanley. London: 1907. V. 72
Thomas Forty. New York: 1947. V. 69
A Treatise on Diseases of the Bones. London: 1849. V. 72

STANLEY, EDWIN
Rambles in Wonderland. New York: 1878. V. 69

STANLEY, EDWIN J.
Life of Rev. L. R. Stateler; or, Sixty-five Years on the Frontier. Nashville: 1907. V. 73

STANLEY, F.
The Apaches of New Mexico. Pampa: 1962. V. 71
Ciudad Santa Fe. Denver: 1958. V. 70
The Civil War in New Mexico. Denver: 1960. V. 72
Clay Allison. 1956. V. 68
Desperadoes Of New Mexico. Denver: 1953. V. 71; 73
The Duke City; The Story of Albuquerque New Mexico 1706-1956. Pampa, TX: 1963. V. 72
E. V. Sumner, Major General US Army. 1797-1863. Borger: 1969. V. 72
Fort Bascom Commanche-Kiowa Barrier. Pampa: 1961. V. 71; 72
Fort Stanton, New Mexico. Pampa: 1964. V. 68
Fort Union (New Mexico). 1953. V. 71; 73
The Grant That Maxwell Bought. Denver: 1952. V. 71
The Jicarilla Apaches of New Mexico 1540-1967. Pampa: 1967. V. 71; 73
Jim Courtright: Two Gun Marshal of Fort Worth. Denver: 1957. V. 69
The Las Vegas New Mexico Story. Denver: 1951. V. 73
Longhair Jim Courtright - Two Gun Marshall of Fort Worth. Denver: 1957. V. 68; 73
No Tears for Black Jack Ketchem. Denver: 1958. V. 73
One Half Mile from Heaven or, the Cimarron Story. Denver: 1949. V. 73
Rodeo Town. Denver: 1953. V. 72
Satanta and The Kiowas. Borger: 1968. V. 72
Socorro, the Oasis. Denver: 1950. V. 68; 73

STANLEY, GEORGE F. G.
The War of 1812 Land Operations. Toronto: 1983. V. 72

STANLEY, H.
Chinese Manual. London: 1854. V. 68

STANLEY, HENRY MORTON
The Autobiography of Sir Henry Morton Stanley.... Boston: 1909. V. 71
The Congo and the Founding of Its Free State.... New York: 1885. V. 70; 71
Coomassie and Magdala: the Story of Two British Campaigns in Africa. New York: 1874. V. 70
The Exploration Diaries of H. M. Stanley. London: 1961. V. 71
How I Found Livingstone. New York: 1872. V. 73
How I Found Livingstone. London: 1874. V. 72
How I Found Livingstone. New York: 1887. V. 71
In Darkest Africa. London: 1890. V. 70; 72
In Darkest Africa. New York: 1890. V. 70; 71; 73
My Early Experiences in America and Asia. New York: 1895. V. 72
My Early Travels and Adventures in America and Asia. New York: 1905. V. 71
Through South Africa, Being an Account of His Recent Visit to Rhodesia, the Transvaal, Cape Colony and Natal.... London: 1898. V. 71
Through the Dark Continent. New York: 1878. V. 71
Through the Dark Continent. New York: 1879. V. 70
Through the Dark Continent. New York: 1979. V. 71

STANLEY, THOMAS
The History of Philosophy. London: 1656. V. 70

STANLEY, W. B.
Elephant Hunting in West Africa. London: 1929. V. 69

STANNARD, HENRIETTA ELIZA VAUGHAN PALMER
Army Society: Life in a Garrison Town. London: 1887. V. 68
Everybody's Favourite. London: 1899. V. 68
Into an Unknown World. London: 1899. V. 68
A Magnificent Young Man. London: 1897. V. 68
The Strange Story of My Life. London: 1898. V. 68

STANNARD, HENRY
Outdoor Common Birds.... London: 1890. V. 68

STANNARD, MARTIN
Evelyn Waugh: the Critical Heritage. London: 1984. V. 71

STANNUS, GRAYDON, MRS.
Old Irish Glass. London: 1921. V. 68; 72

STANSBERRY, DOMENIC
The Last Days of Il Duce. Sag Harbor: 1998. V. 73
The Spoiler. New York: 1987. V. 73

STANSBERY, LON R.
The Passing of the 3D Ranch. Tulsa: 1930. V. 69

STANSBURY, HOWARD
Exploration and Survey of the Valley of the Great Salt Lake of Utah.... Philadelphia: 1852. V. 68

STANSFIELD, ABRAHAM
Essays and Sketches; being a few selections from the prose writings of twenty years. Manchester: 1897. V. 71

STANSKY, PETER
Journal to a Frontier: Julian Bell and John Cornford: their Lives and the 1930's. V. 68

STANTON, CORALIE
The Adventures. New York: 1907. V. 68

STANTON, ELIZABETH CADY
Eighty Years and More (1815-1897) Reminiscences of.... New York: 1898. V. 69; 72

STANTON, IRVING
Sixty Years in Colorado - Reminiscences and Recollections of a Pioneer 1860. Denver: 1922. V. 69

STANTON, J. E.
By Middle Seas: Photographic Studies Reflecting the Architectural Motive of Various Cities on the Mediterranean. Los Angeles: 1927. V. 68

STANTON, ROBERT B.
Down the Colorado. Norman: 1965. V. 73
The Hoskaninni Papers: Mining in Glen Canyon 1897-1902. Salt Lake City: 1961. V. 68

STANTON, THEODORE
The Woman Question in Europe. London: 1884. V. 69; 70

STANTON, WILLIAM
Thetriad Society or Heaven and Earth Association. Hong Kong: 1900. V. 71

STANWOOD, AVIS A. BURNHAM
Fostina Woodman The Wonderful Adventurer. Boston: 1854. V. 69

STANYAN, ABRAHAM
An Account of Switzerland. London: 1714. V. 71

STAPLEDON, OLAF
Last and First Men - A Story of the Near and far future. London: 1930. V. 72
A Man Divided. London: 1950. V. 72
Nebula Maker. Hayes, Middlesex: 1976. V. 72
New Hope for Britain. London: 1939. V. 72
Odd John - A Story Between Jest and Earnest. London: 1935. V. 72
The Opening of the Eyes. London: 1954. V. 72
Sirius - A Fantasy of Love and Discord. London: 1944. V. 72
Star Maker. 1937. V. 73
Star Maker. London: 1937. V. 72
Waking World. London: 1934. V. 72

STAPLES, ROBERT
Agitation in Ireland, from a Landlord's Point of View. London: 1880. V. 69; 73

STAPLETON, A.
A History of the Lordship of Kings' Clipstone, or Clipstone in Sherwood, Nottinghamshire. Mansfield: 1890. V. 70

STARBUCK, EDITH
Crossing the Plains. Nashville: 1927. V. 70

STARFORTH, JOHN
The Architecture of the Park. Edinburgh: 1890. V. 72

STARK, A. W.
Instruction for Field Artillery.... Richmond: 1864. V. 69; 70

STARK, FREYA
Alexander's Path, from Cairia to Cilicia. 1958. V. 73
Baghdad Sketches. Baghdad: 1932. V. 72
Beyond Euphrates; Autobiography 1928-1933. London: 1951. V. 72
The Coast of Incense, Autobiography 1933-1939. London: 1953. V. 72
Ionia, A quest. London: 1954. V. 72
The Journey's Echo. Selections from Freya Stark, Foreword by Lawrence Durrell. London: 1963. V. 72
Space, Time and Movement in Landscape. London: 1969. V. 72
Traveller's Prelude, Autobiography 1933-1939.. London: 1950. V. 72
A Winter In Arabia. London: 1940. V. 72

STARK, JAMES A.
The Loyalists of Massachusetts and the Other Side of the American Revolution. Boston: 1907. V. 73

STARK, JAMES H.
Stark's Illustrated Bermuda Guide. Boston: 1890. V. 73

STARK, L. D.
Big Game Hunting on Three Continents. 1971. V. 70; 72; 73

STARK, R. M.
A Popular History of British Mosses.... London: 1860. V. 71

STARK, RICHARD
The Black Ice Score. London: 1986. V. 72
The Green Eagle Score. Greenwich: 1967. V. 72
The Jugger. New York: 1965. V. 69
Music of the Spanish Folk Plays in New Mexico. Santa Fe: 1969. V. 73
The Outfit. London: 1988. V. 72
Slayground. New York: 1971. V. 73
The Sour Lemon Score. London: 1973. V. 73

STARK, SHARON SHEEBE
The Dealers' Yard. New York: 1985. V. 68; 71

STARKEY, JAMES
Twenty-Five Lyrics. Flansham: 1933. V. 68; 72

STARKIE, WALTER
Don Gypsy: Adventures with a Fiddle in Barbary, Andalusia and La Mancha. London: 1936. V. 71

STARKS, E. C.
Bones of the Ethmoid Region of the Fish Skull. Stanford: 1926. V. 71

STARKWEATHER, SAMUEL
A New and Familiar System of Arithmetic, for the Use of Schools. Cooperstown: 1815. V. 73

STARR, BELLA
Bella Starr, the Bandit Queen, or the Female Jesse James: a Full and Authentic History of the Dashing Female Highwayman.... Austin: 1960. V. 70; 72

STARR, EMMETT
History of the Cherokee Indian and Their Legend and Folklore. Oklahoma City: 1921. V. 70
History of the Cherokee Indians and Their Legends and Folk Lore. Millwood: 1977. V. 68

STARR, FREDERICK
Congo Natives. Chicago: 1912. V. 69
In Indian Mexico. Chicago: 1908. V. 70
Indians of Southern Mexico: An Ethnographic Album. Chicago: 1909. V. 70
Notes Upon the Ethnography of Southern Mexico. Davenport: 1900-1902. V. 69

STARR, JIMMY
Three Short Biers. Hollywood: 1945. V. 69

STARR, RICHARD
Nuzi: Report on the Excavations at Yorgan Tepa Near Kirkuk, Iraq Conducted by Harvard University in Conjunction with the American Schools of Oriental Research and the University Museum of Philadelphia 1927-1931. Cambridge: 1939. V. 69

STARR, STEPHEN Z.
The Union Cavalry in The Civil War. Baton Rouge. V. 72

STARR, WALTER A.
Guide to the John Muir Trail and the High Sierra Region. San Francisco: 1934. V. 68

STARRETT, AGNES
The Darlington Memorial Library: University of Pittsburgh. Pittsburgh: 1938. V. 70; 72

STARRETT, VINCENT
Bookman's Holiday. 1942. V. 73
The Casebook of Jimmy Lavender. 1944. V. 73
Coffins for Two. 1924. V. 73
Coffins for Two. Chicago: 1924. V. 68; 70
An Essay on Limited Editions. 1939. V. 73
14 Great Detective Stories. 1928. V. 73
Midnight and Percy Jones. 1936. V. 73
Murder in Peking. 1946. V. 73
Murder in Peking. New York: 1946. V. 70
Murder on B Deck. 1929. V. 73
Oriental Encounters. Chicago: 1938. V. 68; 69; 70; 71; 73
Persons from Porlock. Chicago: 1923. V. 71
The Private Life of Sherlock Holmes. New York: 1933. V. 68
The Private Life of Sherlock Holmes. Chicago: 1960. V. 70
The Quick and the Dead. Sauk City: 1965. V. 73
Seaports in the Moon. 1928. V. 73
221B: Studies in Sherlock Holmes. New York: 1940. V. 68; 70

THE STARS and Bars. Richmond: 1923. V. 70

STASHOWER, DANIEL
The Adventure of the Ectoplasmic Man. New York: 1985. V. 71
Elephants In The Distance. New York: 1989. V. 72

STATE HISTORICAL SOCIETY OF NORTH DAKOTA
Collections of The State Historical Society of North Dakota Vol 1. Bismarck: 1906. V. 72

STATE HISTORICAL SOCIETY OF WISCONSIN
Collections. Madison: 1905. V. 72

THE STATE of Justice Impartially Considered. By the Civil, Natural and National Law. London: 1732?. V. 72

THE STATE of the Nation, with Respect To Its Public Funded Debt, Revenue, Appointed by the House of Commons to Examine and State the Total Amount of the Public Debts. London: 1798. V. 72

THE STATE of Wisconsin: Embracing Brief Sketces of the History, Position, Resources and Industries. Madison: 1876. V. 71

A STATEMENT of the Claims Delivered to the Commissioners Named and Appointed In and by an Act of Parliament...entitled An Act for Inclosing Lands in the Parishes of Yaxham, Westfield, Whinebergh and Garvestone, in the County of Norfolk. Dereham: 1810. V. 72

STATHAM, NICHOLAS
(Abridgment of Laws). Rouen: 1490. V. 70

A STATISTICAL Inquiry Into the Condition of the People of Colour, of the City and Districts of Philadelphia. Philadelphia: 1849. V. 71

STATON, FRANCES M.
A Bibliography of Canadiana. Toronto: 1965. V. 73

THE STATUTES at Large Concerning Elections of Members to Serve in the House of Commons; Concerning a Compleat Collection of All the Acts of Parliament Now in Force, Which relate Thereto, Continued to the End of the Last Session of Parliament 1734. London: 1734. V. 70

STAUFFACHER, FRANK
Art in Cinema: a Symposium on the Avant Garde Together with Program Notes and References for Series One in Art in Cinema. San Francisco: 1947. V. 71

STAUNTON, HOWARD
The Chess Player's Handbook. London: 1847. V. 72

STAUNTON, MICHAEL
Case for Ireland: a Speech Delivered (to) the Dublin Political Union. 1931. V. 69

STAWELL, MAUD MARGARET KEY
My Days with the Fairies. London: 1913. V. 72

STEAD, CHRISTINA
Letty Fox: Her Luck. London: 1947. V. 72

STEAD, D. G.
General Report upon the Fisheries of British Malaya. Sydney: 1923. V. 72; 73

STEAD, WILLIAM T.
Portraits and Autographs. London: 1891. V. 70

STEADMAN, RALPH
America. San Francisco: 1974. V. 68
Between the Eyes. London: 1984. V. 68
Dogs Bodies. 1970. V. 68; 71
The Dogs Bodies Portfolio. Lexington: 2000. V. 72
Gonzo the Art. London: 1998. V. 68; 72
The Grapes of Ralph - Wine According to Ralph Steadman. London: 1992. V. 68
Little.com. London: 2000. V. 69
Sigmund Freud. New York and London: 1979. V. 69; 70; 72

STEARN, WILLIAM T.
The Australian Flower Paintings of Ferdinand Bauer. London: 1976. V. 69; 73
A Taxonomic and Historical Survey of the Genus Paeonia in Greece. Kifisia: 1984. V. 68

STEARNE, JOHN
The Death and Burial of John Asgill, Esq. with Some other Verses Occasion'd by His Books. Dublin: 1702. V. 68

STEBBING, E. P.
Jungle By-Ways in India. 1911. V. 72; 73
A Manual of Elementary Forest Zoology for India. Calcutta: 1908. V. 72

STEBBING, HENRY
Remains; or Fragments of Poems. London: 1825. V. 73

STEBBING, R. R.
Challenger Voyage. Zoology. Part 67. Amphipoda. 1888. V. 73

STEBBING, THOMAS R. R.
The Naturalist of Cumbrae. A True Story. Being the Life of David Robertson. London: 1891. V. 71; 72

STEBBING, W.
Analysis of Mr. Mill's System of Logic. London: 1864. V. 71

STEBBINS, G. B.
Facts and Opinions Touching the Real Origin, Character and Influence of the American Colonization Society.... Boston;: 1853. V. 71

STEBBINS, G. L.
Flowering Plants, Evolution Above the Species Level. Cambridge: 1974. V. 72

STEBBINS, H. M.
Pistols; A Modern Encyclopedia. 1961. V. 71

STEBBINS, R. C.
Amphibians and Reptiles of Western North America. New York: 1954. V. 72

STEBER, RICK
Where Rolls the Oregon. Union, Oregon: 1985. V. 72

STECK, FRANCIS BORGIA
Motolinia's History of the Indians of New Spain. Washington: 1951. V. 71; 72

STECKBECK, JOHN S.
Fabulous Redmen. The Carlisle Indians and Their Famous Football Teams. Harrisburg: 1951. V. 68

STECKMESSER, KENT
The Western Hero in History and Legend. Norman: 1965. V. 72

STEDMAN, EDMUND CLARENCE
An American Anthology 1787-1900. Cambridge: 1900. V. 71
Poets of America. Cambridge: 1885. V. 71

STEDMAN, J. G.
Narrative of a Five Years Expedition Against the Revolted Negroes of Surinam in Guinea on the Wild Coast of South America from the Years 1772 to 1777.... Barre: 1971. V. 69

STEEDMAN, CHARLES J.
Bucking the Sagebrush. New York: 1904. V. 69; 71

STEEDMAN, ROBERT D.
Thomas Bewick 1753-1828. Newcastle upon Tyne: 1978. V. 72

STEEGE, L. C.
Stone Artifacts of the Northwestern Plains. Colorado Springs: 1961. V. 69

STEEL, DAVID
The Ship-Master's Assistant and Owner's Manual.... London: 1801. V. 71
Steel's Naval Chronologist of the War, From Its Commencement in Feb. 1793 to its Conclusion in 1801. London: 1802?. V. 73

STEEL, FLORA ANNIE
English Fairy Tales. London: 1922. V. 72
English Fairy Tales. London: 1927. V. 73
In the Permanent Way, and Other Stories. London: 1898. V. 69

STEEL, JOHN H.
An Analysis of the Mineral Waters of Saratoga and Ballston, with Practical Remarks on Their Use.... Saratoga Springs: 1825. V. 71; 73

STEEL, KURT
Judas, Incorporated. Boston: 1939. V. 70
Madman's Buff. Boston: 1941. V. 68; 72

STEELE, EDWARD DUNSHA
Edward Dunsha Steele 1829-1865, Pioneer, School Teacher, Cabinet- Maker and Musician; a Diary of His Journey from Lodi Wisconsin, Across the Plains to Boulder, Colorado in the Year 1859. Boulder: 1960. V. 70

STEELE, J. W.
New Guide To the Pacific Coast, Santa Fe Route, California, Arizona, New Mexico, Colorado and Kansas. Chicago: 1893. V. 68

STEELE, JAMES COLUMBUS
Sketches of the Civil War, Especially of Companies A, C and H from Iredell County, N.C. and the 4th Regimental Band. And Also a Memorial of the Author by Mrs. W. A. Eliason. Statesville: 1931. V. 70
Sketches of the Civil War, Especially of the Companies A, C. and H. from Iredell County, N.C. and the 4th Regimental Band. Statesville: 1921. V. 69

STEELE, JAMES W.
The Sons of The Border Sketches of The Life and People of The Far Frontier. Topeka: 1873. V. 72

STEELE, JOHN
Across the Plains in 1850. Chicago: 1930. V. 71

STEELE, MATTHEW F.
American Campaigns. Washington: 1909. V. 69

STEELE, RICHARD
The Antidote in a Letter to a Free-Thinker. (with) The Antidote Number II. London: 1719. V. 70; 73
The Christian Hero.... London: 1741. V. 73
The Crisis: or a Discourse Representing the Most Authentic Record.... London: 1714. V. 72
The Romish Ecclesiastical History of Late Years. London: 1714. V. 69
The State of the Case Between the Lord Chamberlain of His Majesty's Household and the Governor of the Royal Company of Comedians. London: 1720. V. 72
The Tender Husband; or, the Accomplish'd Fools. London: 1705. V. 68; 72

STEELE, ROBERT
The Revival of Printing, a Bibliographical Catalogue of Works.... London: 1912. V. 68; 71

STEELE, WILBUR DANIEL
The Man Who Saw Through Heaven and Other Stories. New York: 1927. V. 69
Sound of Rowlocks. New York: 1938. V. 69

STEELE, ZADOCK
The Indian Captive; or a Narrative of the Captivity and Sufferings of Zadock Steele. Montpelier: 1818. V. 73

STEELL, WILLIS
Isidra. Boston: 1888. V. 70

STEEN, JAMES ELDER
Illustrated Souvenir of Winnipeg. Winnipeg: 1903. V. 73

STEEN, MARGUERITE
Matador. Boston: 1934. V. 69
Oakefield Plays. London: 1932. V. 71
Unicorn. New York: 1932. V. 70

STEENSTRUP, J. J. S.
Om Forplantning og Udvirling Gjennem Vexlende Generationsraekker. Copenhagen: 1842. V. 73
On the Alternation of Generations; or the Propagation and Development of Animals through Alternate Generations.... London: 1845. V. 69; 72

STEEPLE, E. W.
Island of Skye. Edinburgh: 1931. V. 69
Island of Skye. Edinburgh: 1935. V. 69
Island of Skye. Edinburgh: 1954. V. 69

STEESE, EDWARD
Ephemerae: Poems of Edward Steese. Princeton: 1951. V. 68
First Snow. New York: 1954. V. 68
Spring Night: a Review of Youth. London: 1927. V. 68

STEEVENS, GEORGE WARRINGTON
From Capetown to Ladysmith. Edinburgh: 1900. V. 71

STEEVES, HARRY R.
Good Night, Sheriff. New York: 1941. V. 73

STEEVES, HELEN HARPER
The Story of Moncton's First Store and Storekeeper. St. John: 1924. V. 72; 73

STEFANSSON, VILHJALMUR
Adventures in Error. New York: 1936. V. 73
Arctic Manual.... New York: 1944. V. 71
The Friendly Arctic, The Story of Five Years in Polar Regions. London: 1921. V. 72
My Life With The Eskimos. London: 1913. V. 72
Not By Bread Alone. New York: 1946. V. 72

STEFFEN, RANDY
The Horse Soldier - Volume 1. Norman: 1977. V. 69
The Horse Soldier: the United States Cavalryman: His Uniforms, Arms, Accoutrements and Equipment. Volume II. Norman: 1978. V. 69

STEFFY, J. RICHARD
Wooden Ship Building and the Interpretation of Shipwrecks. London: 1998. V. 69

STEGNER, PAGE
Catching the Light: Remembering Wallace Stegner. 1996. V. 70

STEGNER, WALLACE
All the Little Live Things. New York: 1967. V. 69; 71
Angle of Repose. Garden City: 1971. V. 68; 69; 71; 72; 73
Beyond the Hundredth Meridian. Boston: 1954. V. 68; 69; 73
The Big Rock Candy Mountain. New York: 1943. V. 69
The Big Rock Candy Mountain. Franklin Center: 1978. V. 69; 73
The City of the Living. Boston: 1956. V. 73
Crossing to Safety. Franklin Center: 1987. V. 69; 73
Crossing to Safety. New York: 1987. V. 69; 72
The Gathering of Zion. New York/Toronto/London: 1964. V. 68; 73
Joe Hill. New York: 1950. V. 69; 70
Marking the Sparrow's Fall. New York: 1998. V. 72
Mormon Country. New York: 1942. V. 69
The Potter's House. Muscatine: 1938. V. 71; 73
Recapitulation. Franklin Center: 1979. V. 69; 72
Remembering Laughter. Boston: 1937. V. 69; 70
A Shooting Star. New York: 1961. V. 71
The Spectator Bird. Franklin Center: 1976. V. 69; 70; 72
The Spectator Bird. Garden City: 1976. V. 68; 69
Stanford Short Stories. Stanford: 1964. V. 69
Where the Bluebird Sings To The Lemonade Springs. New York: 1992. V. 72
The Women on the Wall. Boston: 1950. V. 71; 72

STEIG, WILLIAM
Male/Female. New York: 1971. V. 72

STEIN, AARON MARC
Days of Misfortune. New York: 1949. V. 68
The Sun is a Witness. New York: 1940. V. 71
Up to No Good. New York: 1941. V. 70
We Saw Him Die. New York: 1947. V. 68

STEIN, AUREL
On Alexander's Track to the Indus. Peronslal Narrative of Explorations on the North-West Frontier of India. London: 1929. V. 73

STEIN, ELIZABETH P.
David Garrick, Dramatist. New York: 1938. V. 71

STEIN, GERTRUDE
An Acquaintance with Description. London: 1929. V. 73
The Autobiography of Alice B. Toklas. New York: 1933. V. 72
Brewsie and Willie. New York: 1946. V. 68; 73
Composition as Explanation. London: 1926. V. 71
An Elucidation. Paris: 1927. V. 71
Four in America. New Haven: 1947. V. 69; 72
Four Saints in Three Acts: an Opera to be Sung. New York: 1934. V. 73
Geography and Plays. Boston: 1922. V. 70; 72
The Making of Americans. New York: 1926. V. 69
The Making of Americans. New York: 1934. V. 72
The Making of Americans. Vermont: 1966. V. 70
Mrs. Reynolds (a novel) & Five Earlier Novelettes. New Haven, CT: 1952. V. 71
Paris France. New York: 1940. V. 71
Picasso. London: 1946. V. 73
Selected Writings of Gertrude Stein. New York: 1946. V. 69
Two (Hitherto Unpublished) Poems. New York: 1948. V. 69; 73
The World is Round. New York: 1939. V. 73

STEIN, JOEN
Money Matters. London: 1990. V. 70

STEIN, R. B.
Control of Posture and Locomotion. New York: 1973. V. 68

STEINBECK, ELAINE
Steinbeck. A Life in Letters. New York: 1975. V. 71

STEINBECK, JOHN ERNST
The Acts of King Arthur and His Noble Knights. New York: 1976. V. 68
America and Americans. New York: 1966. V. 68; 69; 70; 71
Bombs Away. New York: 1942. V. 68; 69; 71; 73
Burning Bright. New York: 1950. V. 68; 73
Cannery Row. London: 1945. V. 68; 69; 73
Cup of Gold. New York: 1929. V. 68; 73
Cup of Gold. New York: 1936. V. 68; 73
Cup of Gold. New York: 1939. V. 68; 71
East of Eden. London: 1952. V. 70
East of Eden. New York: 1952. V. 68; 69; 70; 71; 72; 73
The Forgotten Village. New York: 1941. V. 68; 71; 73
The Grapes of Wrath. London: 1939. V. 69
The Grapes of Wrath. New York: 1939. V. 68; 69; 70; 71; 72; 73
Grapes of Wrath. New York: 1940. V. 69
In Dubious Battle. New York: 1936. V. 68; 73
Journal of a Novel: the East of Eden Letters. New York: 1969. V. 68; 69; 71; 73
Letters to Elizabeth: a Selection of Letters from John Steinbeck to Elizabeth Otis. San Francisco: 1978. V. 68; 70; 71; 73
The Log from the Sea of Cortez. New York: 1951. V. 73
The Log From the Sea of Cortez. London: 1958. V. 73
The Long Valley. New York: 1938. V. 68; 69; 70; 72; 73
The Moon is Down. London: 1942. V. 70
The Moon is Down. New York: 1942. V. 68; 69; 70; 71; 73
Nothing So Monstrous. New York. V. 73
Nothing So Monstrous. New York: 1936. V. 68; 70; 71; 72
Of Mice and Men. London: 1937. V. 70
Of Mice and Men. New York: 1937. V. 68; 69; 72
Of Mice and Men. New York: 1970. V. 68; 69; 73
Once There Was a War. New York: 1958. V. 68; 69; 73
The Pastures of Heaven. New York: 1932. V. 71
The Pastures of Heaven. London: 1933. V. 71
The Pastures of Heaven. New York: 1935. V. 68
The Pearl. New York: 1947. V. 68; 69; 71
The Pearl. London: 1948. V. 69
The Red Pony. New York: 1945. V. 68; 70
A Russian Journal. New York: 1948. V. 68; 69; 73
Saint Katy the Virgin. Mount Vernon: 1936. V. 68; 72
St. Katy the Virgin. New York: 1936. V. 68; 73
Sea of Cortez. New York: 1941. V. 68; 72; 73
The Short Reign of Pippin IV. London: 1957. V. 70
The Short Reign of Pippin IV. New York: 1957. V. 68; 69; 70; 71; 73
Speech Accepting the Nobel Prize for Literature. New York: 1962. V. 68
Steinbeck a Life in Letters. New York: 1975. V. 70
Sweet Thursday. New York: 1953. V. 71; 73
Sweet Thursday. New York: 1954. V. 68; 69; 71
To a God Unknown. New York: 1933. V. 68; 69; 70
Tortilla Flat. London: 1935. V. 68
Tortilla Flat. New York: 1935. V. 68; 73
Tortilla Flat. New York: 1947. V. 68
Travels with Charley in Search of America. New York: 1962. V. 68; 69; 72; 73
De Vliegenvanger. (The Moon is Down). Utrecht: 1944. V. 68
The Wayward Bus. New York: 1947. V. 68; 69; 71
The Wayward Bus. New York: 1950. V. 69
The Winter of Our Discontent. London: 1961. V. 68
The Winter of Our Discontent. New York: 1961. V. 68; 69; 70; 71; 73
Zapata. London: 1991. V. 68; 69; 73

STEINBERG, SAUL
The Inspector. New York: 1973. V. 72
The Labyrinth. New York: 1960. V. 71

STEINBRUNNER, CHRIS
Detectionary. Lock Haven: 1972. V. 69; 73
Encyclopedia of Mystery and Detection. New York: 1976. V. 73

STEINEL, ALVIN
Histories of Agriculture in Colorado. Fort Collins: 1926. V. 71

STEINEM, GLORIA
Marilyn. New York: 1986. V. 73

STEINER, CHARLOTTE
Charlotte Steiner's ABC. New York: 1946. V. 70

STEINER, GEORGE
Tolstoy or Dostoevsky: an Essay in Contrast. London: 1959. V. 71; 72

STEINER, JOHANN FRIEDRICH RUDOLPH
Entwurf einer neuen Durchaus Feuevesten Bauart.... Weimar: 1803. V. 72

STEINGRUBER, JOHANN DAVID
Practische Burgerliche Baukunst Mit den Haupt-und Specialrissen und Gesimslehren.... Nuremberg: 1773. V. 68; 70; 72

STEINMETZ, CHARLES PROTEUS
Four Lectures on Relativity and Space. New York and London: 1923. V. 69

STEJNEGER, L.
Check List of North American Amphibians and Reptiles. Cambridge: 1943. V. 72
Herpetology of Japan and Adjacent Territory. Washington: 1907. V. 69
Notes on the American Soft-Shell Turtles with Special Reference to Amyda Agassizii. Cambridge: 1944. V. 72

STEM, THAD
The Animal Fair. Charlotte: 1960. V. 71
A Flagstone Walk. Charlotte: 1968. V. 71

STENHOUSE, T. B. H.
The Rocky Mountain Saints: a full...History of the Mormons. New York: 1873. V. 71

STENI, L.
Prelude to a Rope for Meyr. New York: 1928. V. 72

STENT, W. DREW
Egypt and the Holy Land in 1842, with Sketches of Greece, Constantinople, and the Levant. London: 1843. V. 73

STEP, E.
Bees, Wasps, Ants, and Allied Insects of the British Isles. 1932. V. 69

STEPHEN, A. M.
Hopi Journal. Mill Valley: 1999. V. 69
The Traditions of the Hopi. 1905. V. 69

STEPHEN, H. L.
State Trials, Political and Social. London: 1899-1902. V. 69

STEPHEN, JAMES
The Crisis of the Sugar Colonies, or, an Enquiry Into the Objects and Profitable Effects of the French Expedition to the West Indies and Their Connection.... 1802. V. 70
War in Disguise; or, the Frauds of the Neutral Flags. London: 1805. V. 68; 70; 73
War in Disguise; or the Frauds of the Neutral Flags. London: 1806. V. 70

STEPHEN, LESLIE
The Dictionary of National Biography. (with) The Concise Dictionary of National Biography. New York: 1973. V. 69; 72
English Utilitarians. London: 1912. V. 71
Life Of Henry Fawcett. London: 1886. V. 72
The Playground of Europe. London: 1904. V. 69
The Science of Ethics. London: 1882. V. 68; 71
The Science of Ethics. London: 1907. V. 71
Sir Leslie Stephen's Mausoleum Book. Oxford: 1977. V. 69
Sketches from Cambridge, by a Don. London and Cambridge: 1865. V. 73

STEPHEN, ROBERT W.
Texas Ranger Sketches. Dallas: 1972. V. 68

STEPHENS, ALEXANDER
Memoirs of John Horne Tooke. Interspersed with Original Documents. London: 1813. V. 72

STEPHENS, ALEXANDER H.
Constitutional View of the Late War Between the States. Philadelphia: 1868-1870. V. 69

STEPHENS, ANN SOPHIA
Fashion and Famine. New York: 1854. V. 70
Silent Struggles. Philadelphia: 1865. V. 70

STEPHENS, C. RALPH
The Fiction of Anne Tyler. Jackson: 1990. V. 68

STEPHENS, EDWARD
Authority Abused by the Vindication of the Last Years Transactions and the Abuses Detected. London: 1690. V. 70
Extracts from Sundry Publications and Essays on the Use and Application of Prepared Gypsum as a Manure. Dublin: 1811. V. 71

STEPHENS, F. DOUGLAS
Congenital Malformations of the Rectum, Anus and Genito-Urniary Tracts. Edinburgh: 1963. V. 68

STEPHENS, F. G.
Memorial of William Mulready. London: 1867. V. 72

STEPHENS, HIRAM B.
Jacques Cartier and His Four Voyages to Canada. Montreal: 1890. V. 73

STEPHENS, JAMES
The Crock of Gold. London: 1912. V. 72
The Crock of Gold. London: 1921. V. 73
The Crock of Gold. New York: 1922. V. 70
The Crock of Gold. London: 1926. V. 72
Etched in Moonlight. London: 1928. V. 70; 72
Green Branches. Dublin and London: 1916. V. 72
Hunger. Dublin: 1918. V. 68; 70
The Insurrection in Dublin. Dublin and London: 1904. V. 71
Irish Fairy Tales. 1923. V. 69
Julia Elizabeth: A Comedy. New York: 1929. V. 72
Letters on Imprisonment for Debt. London: 1773. V. 71

STEPHENS, JAMES continued
A Poetry Recital. London: 1925. V. 72
Reincarnations. 1918. V. 69
Theme and Variations. New York: 1910. V. 69

STEPHENS, JOHN
An Historical Discourse, Briefly Setting Forth the Nature of Procurations, and How They Were Anciently Paid.... London: 1661. V. 73

STEPHENS, JOHN LLOYD
Incidents of Travel In Central America, Chiapas, And Yucatan. London: 1841. V. 72
Incidents of Travel in Central America, Chiapas and Yucatan. New York: 1841. V. 69
Incidents of Travel in Central America, Chiapas and Yucatan. London: 1854. V. 71
Incidents of Travel in Yucatan. New York: 1843. V. 72
Incidents Of Travel In Yucatan. New York: 1860. V. 72

STEPHENS, KATE
American Thumb-Prints. Mettle of Our Men and Women. Philadelphia: 1905. V. 72

STEPHENS, LOUISE G.
Letters from an Oregon Ranch. Chicago: 1905. V. 70

STEPHENS, PHILIP
Catalogus Horti Botanici Oxoniensis. Oxford: 1658. V. 68; 72

STEPHENS, REED
The Man Who Tried to Get Away. 1990. V. 70

STEPHENS, ROBERT W.
Mannen Clements - Texas Gunfighter. Dallas: 1996. V. 68

STEPHENS, STEPHEN DE WITT
The Mavericks. American Engravers. New Brunswick: 1950. V. 71

STEPHENS, THOMAS
The Castle-Builders; or, the History of Williams Stephens, of the Isle of Wight, Esq., Lately Deceased. London: 1759. V. 73

STEPHENS, WALTER
Notes on the Mineralogy of Part of the Vicinity of Dublin. 1812. V. 69

STEPHENS, WINIFRED
The Soul of Russia. London: 1916. V. 73

STEPHENSON, ALAN M. G.
The Victorian Archbishops of Canterbury. 1991. V. 71

STEPHENSON, E. M.
T. S. Eliot and the Lay Reader. London: 1946. V. 71

STEPHENSON, GEORGE
A Description of the Safety Lamp, Invented by George Stephenson, and Now in Use in Killingworth Colliery. London: 1817. V. 69
Reports on the Formation of a Railway Between Lancaster and Carlisle (via Ulverston and Whitehaven) with Observations on the mode of Crossing Morecambe Bay. Whitehaven: 1837. V. 69
West Flanders Railways. Report of George Stephenson, Esq. with the Decree, Grant, Convention and the Statutes of the Company. September 1845. London: 1845. V. 68

STEPHENSON, J.
Medical Zoology and Mineralogy.... 1832. V. 73
Medical Zoology and Mineralogy.... London: 1832. V. 69

STEPHENSON, NEAL
The Diamond Age. New York: 1995. V. 69; 72
Zodiac. New York: 1988. V. 69

STEPHENSON, ROBERT
The Triumph of Science. Carnarvon: 1849. V. 73

STEPHENSON, SARAH
Memoirs of the Life, and Travels in the Service of the Gospel, of Sarah Stephenson. London: 1807. V. 68

STEPHENSON, T. A.
The British Sea Anemones. London: 1928-1935. V. 69; 73

STEPHENSON, TERRY E.
Caminos Viejos - Tales Found in the History of California of Especial Interest to Those Who Love the Valleys, The Hills and the Canyons of Orange County, Its Traditions and Its Landmarks. Santa Ana: 1930. V. 69
Don Bernardo Yorba. Los Angeles: 1963. V. 68

STERLING, BRUCE
The Artificial Kid. New York: 1980. V. 68; 69
Globalhead. 1992. V. 70
Heavy Weather. New York: 1994. V. 69
Holy Fire. New York: 1996. V. 69
Involution Ocean. New York: 1977. V. 71

STERLING, DOROTHY
We Are Your Sisters: Black Women in the Nineteenth Century. New York: 1984. V. 72

STERLING, GEORGE
The Evanescent City. San Francisco: 1916. V. 68

STERLING, JOHN
Fitzgeorge; a Novel. London: 1832. V. 69

STERLING, RICHARD
Our Own Second Reader; for the Use of Schools and Families. Greensboro: 1862. V. 69; 70

STERLING, WILLIAM W.
Trails and Trials of a Texas Ranger. 1959. V. 73
Trails and Trials of a Texas Ranger. Norman: 1959. V. 68

STERN, BERT
The Last Sitting. New York: 1982. V. 70

STERN, DANIEL
After the War. New York: 1967. V. 69
An Urban Affair. New York: 1980. V. 72

STERN, F. C.
A Study of the Genus Paeonia. London: 1946. V. 69; 71; 73

STERN, G. B.
Debonair. New York: 1928. V. 71
Oleander River. New York: 1937. V. 70

STERN, GERALD
Last Blue. New York: 1998. V. 73
Lovesick. New York: 1987. V. 69
Lucky Life. Boston: 1977. V. 69
Rejoicings. Poems 1966-1972. Los Angeles: 1984. V. 69
This Time. New and Selected Poems. New York: 1997. V. 69

STERN, JAMES
The Heartless Land. London: 1932. V. 71
The Hidden Damage. New York: 1947. V. 70
The Man Who Was Loved. London: 1952. V. 71

STERN, PHILIP VAN DOREN
The Greatest Gift. Philadelphia: 1944. V. 69

STERN, RUDI
Let There Be Neon. New York: 1979. V. 69; 72

STERNDALE, MARY
The Panorama of Youth. London: 1807. V. 69

STERNDALE, R. A.
Natural History of the Mammalia of India and Ceylon. Calcutta: 1884. V. 73

STERNE, EMMA GELDERS
All About Little Boy Blue. New York: 1924. V. 70
Drums of Monmouth. New York: 1935. V. 71

STERNE, LAURENCE
The Beauties of Sterne. London: 1782. V. 69
The Beauties of Sterne. London: 1787. V. 69
The Beauties of Sterne. London: 1793. V. 71
The Beauties of Sterne. London: 1809. V. 68
Letters from Yorick to Eliza. London: 1773. V. 71
Letters from Yorick to Eliza. London: 1775. V. 69
The Life and Letters of Laurence Sterne. London: 1911. V. 71
The Life and Opinions of Tristram Shandy, Gentleman. London: 1760-1767. V. 69
The Life and Opinions of Tristram Shandy, Gentleman. London: 1763-1767. V. 72
The Life and Opinions of Tristram Shandy, Gentleman. London: 1765-1769. V. 73
The Life and Opinions of Tristram Shandy, Gentleman. London: 1766. V. 73
The Life and Opinions of Tristram Shandy, Gentleman. Waltham St. Lawrence: 1929-1930. V. 72
The Life and Works of Laurence Sterne. New York: 1904. V. 72
A Sentimental Journey through France and Italy. 1769. V. 73
A Sentimental Journey through France and Italy. London: 1780. V. 73
A Sentimental Journey through France and Italy. 1794. V. 72
A Sentimental Journey through France and Italy. New York: 1884. V. 69
A Sentimental Journey Through France and Italy. London: 1910. V. 71
A Sentimental Journey through France and Italy. Reading, Berkshire: 1928. V. 72
A Sentimental Journey through France and Italy. Waltham St. Lawrence: 1928. V. 69
A Sentimental Journey through France and Italy. High Wycombe: 1936. V. 70
The Sermons of Mr. Yorick. London: 1760-1766. V. 71
Tristram Schandis. Leben und Meynungen. Hamburg: 1774. V. 69
Tristram Schandis Leben und Meynungen. Frankfurt und Leipzig: 1776-1777. V. 69
La Vie et Les Opinions de Tristram Shandy.... A Londres: 1784-1785. V. 71
The Works. London: 1783. V. 71; 72
The Works. 1790. V. 72
The Works. London: 1803. V. 73
The Works. London: 1815. V. 72; 73
The Works. London: 1819. V. 71
The Works. London: 1823. V. 70

STERNE, LOUIS
Seventy Years of an Active Life. London: 1912. V. 68; 73

STETTEN, PAUL VON
Erlauterungen der in Kupfer Gestochenen Vorstellungen, aus der Geschichte der Stadt Augsburg.... Augsburg: 1765. V. 70; 72

STEUART, HENRY
The Planter's Guide. Edinburgh: 1828. V. 70; 72
The Planter's Guide. New York: 1832. V. 68
The Planter's Guide. Edinburgh and London: 1848. V. 69; 70; 71; 72

STEUART, JOHN A.
The Immortal Lover: a Burns Romance. Philadelphia: 1919. V. 71

STEUART, WALTER
Collections and Observations Methodiz'd; Concerning the Worship, Discipline, and Government of the Church of Scotland. Edinburgh: 1709. V. 73

STEVEN, SHANE
Go Down Dead. New York: 1966. V. 69

STEVEN, WILLIAM
Letter Second to the Reverend William Fletcher, Author of the Late Publication, Intitled, The Scripture Loyalist.... Glasgow: 1798. V. 71

STEVENS, C. J.
The Cornish Nightmare. Maine: 1996. V. 72

STEVENS, CHARLES W.
Fly-Fishing in Maine Lakes; or Camp-Life in the Wilderness. Boston: 1881. V. 68; 73

STEVENS, F. L.
Through Merrie England. London: 1928. V. 71

STEVENS, FRANK E.
The Black Hawk War. Chicago: 1903. V. 69

STEVENS, GEORGE ALEXANDER
The Adventures of a Specialist; or, a Journey through London.... London: 1788. V. 72
The Dramatic History of Master Edward, Miss Ann and Others.... London: 1785. V. 69; 72
A Lecture on Heads. London: 1808. V. 69; 70; 72

STEVENS, GEORGE THOMAS
Functional Nervous Diseses their Causes and their Treatment. New York: 1887. V. 68; 71

STEVENS, HAZARD
The Life of Isaac Ingalls Stevens. Boston: 1901. V. 73

STEVENS, HENRY N.
Lewis Evans His Map of the Middle British Colonies in America. London: 1924. V. 70

STEVENS, JOAN
Mary Taylor, Friend of Charlotte Bronte. 1972. V. 70

STEVENS, JOHN
The Royal Treasury of England.... London: 1725. V. 72
The Spanish Libertines.... London: 1709. V. 72

STEVENS, JOHN W.
Leather Manufacture. London: 1891. V. 72

STEVENS, JOSEPH EARLE
Yesterdays in the Philippines. New York: 1898. V. 68

STEVENS, LINWOOD L.
Virgin Hannah. Philadelphia: 1977:. V. 72

STEVENS, P.
Stone Images of Esie. Ibadan: 1977. V. 69

STEVENS, SAMUEL
Letter from the Governor of the State of Maryland, Transmitting a Copy of an Act of the Legislature of Said State.... Washington: 1825. V. 73

STEVENS, SHANE
By Reason of Insanity. New York: 1979. V. 68
Dead City. New York: 1973. V. 68
Go Down Dead. New York: 1966. V. 69; 70; 71; 72

STEVENS, W. C.
Kansas Wild Flowers. Lawrence: 1948. V. 72; 73

STEVENS, WALLACE
The Auroras of Autumn. New York: 1950. V. 68; 69; 71; 73
The Collected Poems. London: 1935. V. 68
The Collected Poems. New York: 1954. V. 69
Description Without Place, a Poem. (in) The Sewanee Review. Volume LIII. Number 4. October-December 1945. Sewanee: 1945. V. 73
Harmonium. New York: 1923. V. 68
Harmonium. New York: 1931. V. 68; 69; 70; 73
Harmonium. Philadelphia: 1959. V. 73
Ideas of Order. New York: 1935. V. 68; 69; 71
Ideas of Order. New York: 1936. V. 68; 71
Letters of Wallace Stevens. New York: 1966. V. 68
The Man with the Blue Guitar and Other Poems. New York: 1937. V. 68; 69
The Man with the Blue Guitar Including Ideas of Order. New York: 1952. V. 68
Mattino Domenicale ed Altre Poesie. Turin: 1954. V. 68; 73
The Necessary Angel. New York: 1951. V. 68
The Necessary Angel. London: 1960. V. 68
Notes Toward a Supreme Fiction. Cummington: 1942. V. 68; 69; 73
Notes Toward a Supreme Fiction. Cummington: 1943. V. 68; 71
Opus Posthumous. London: 1959. V. 68
The Palm at the End of the Mind. New York: 1971. V. 69
Parts of a World. New York: 1942. V. 68
A Primitive Like an Orb. New York: 1948. V. 69; 70; 73
The Relations Between Poetry and Painting. New York: 1951. V. 73
Selected Poems. London: 1950. V. 73
Selected Poems. London: 1952. V. 68
Selected Poems. London: 1953. V. 68
Three Academic Pieces. The Realm of Resemblance, Someone Puts a Pineapple Together, Of Ideal Time and Choice. Cummington: 1947. V. 69

Transport to Summer. New York: 1947. V. 68; 71
Transport to Summer. New York: 1957. V. 73

STEVENS, WALTER B.
The Brown-Reynolds Duel. St. Louis: 1911. V. 68

STEVENS, WILLIAM
A System for the Discipline of the Artillery of the United States of America, or the Young Artillerist's Pocket Companion. New York: 1797. V. 71

STEVENSON, ADLAI
What I Think. New York: 1956. V. 68

STEVENSON, ALEXANDER F.
Battle of Stones River, Near Murfreesboro, Tenn. 1862...1863. Boston: 1884. V. 69

STEVENSON, B. F.
Cumberland Gap. Cincinnati: 1885. V. 69

STEVENSON, BILL
A Ray Bradbury File. London: 1977. V. 71

STEVENSON, BURTON E.
The House Next Door. New York: 1932. V. 68; 72

STEVENSON, D. A.
The World's Lighthouses Before 1820. London: 1959. V. 69

STEVENSON, D. E.
Crooked Adam. New York: 1942. V. 68

STEVENSON, DAVID
Sketch of the Civil Engineering of North America; Comprising Remarks on the Harbours, River and Lake Navigation, Lighthouses, Steam Navigation, Water-Works, Canals, Roads, Railways, Bridges and Other Works in that Country. London: 1838. V. 73

STEVENSON, J. A.
An Account of Fungus Exsiccati, Containing Material from the Americas. Lehre: 1971. V. 72

STEVENSON, JAMES H.
Boots and Saddles. A History of the First Volunteer Cavalry of the War (First New York Lincoln Cavalry). Harrisburg: 1879. V. 68
Songs and Poems of the Old West by an Old Cowboy. 1937. V. 68

STEVENSON, JOCELYN
Robin Hood: a High Spirited Tale of Adventure Starring Jim Henson's Muppets. New York: 1980. V. 71

STEVENSON, JOHN
Letters in Answer to Dr. Price's Two Pamphlets on Civil Liberty, &c with Some Remarks on the Parliamentary Debates of Last Session, as They Appeared in the Newspapers. London: 1778. V. 69

STEVENSON, JOHN HALL
Crazy Tales. London: 1769. V. 69

STEVENSON, MISS
Homely Musings. Kilmarnock: 1870. V. 69

STEVENSON, R. RANDOLPH
The Southern Side; or, Andersonville Prison. Baltimore: 1876. V. 69; 70

STEVENSON, RAY
Sex Pistols File. London: 1978. V. 72

STEVENSON, ROBERT LOUIS BALFOUR
Across the Plains. 1892. V. 68
Across the Plains. London: 1892. V. 69
Aes Triplex. New York: 1898. V. 68
The Amateur Emigrant from the Clyde to Sandy Hook. Chicago: 1895. V. 68
Ballads. London: 1890. V. 70; 71
The Beach of Falesa. New York: 1956. V. 73
The Black Arrow. New York: 1888. V. 71
The Black Arrow. New York: 1916. V. 73
The Body-Snatcher. New York: 1895. V. 70; 71
The Castaways of Soledad. Buffalo: 1928. V. 71
Catriona. London: 1893. V. 69; 70
A Child's Garden of Verses. London: 1885. V. 69; 72
A Child's Garden of Verses. London: 1896. V. 69
A Child's Garden of Verses. New York: 1905. V. 70; 72
A Child's Garden of Verses. Chicago: 1919. V. 70
A Child's Garden of Verses. Chicago: 1922. V. 71
A Child's Garden of Verses. Philadelphia: 1926. V. 70; 71
A Child's Garden of Verses. Chicago: 1928. V. 72
A Child's Garden of Verses. 1929. V. 70
A Child's Garden of Verses. Akron: 1930. V. 70
A Child's Garden of Verses. Chicago: 1930. V. 70
A Child's Garden of Verses. London: 1931. V. 71
A Child's Garden of Verses. Akron: 1940. V. 71
A Child's Garden of Verses. New York: 1944. V. 68; 69
A Child's Garden of Verses. New York: 1947. V. 71
A Child's Garden of Verses. London: 1960. V. 69
A Child's Garden of Verses. Chicago: 1981. V. 73
A Child's Garden of Verses. London: 1985. V. 71
A Christmas Sermon. San Francisco: 1928. V. 68
David Balfour. New York: 1924. V. 71; 72; 73
Dr. Jekyll and Mr. Hyde. London: 1948. V. 68; 73

STEVENSON, ROBERT LOUIS BALFOUR continued
The Ebb-tide. 1894. V. 68
Essays of Travel. London: 1905. V. 69; 71; 73
Familiar Studies of Men and Books. London: 1882. V. 68
Familiar Studies of Men and Books. London: 1888. V. 68
Father Damien, an Open Letter to the Reverend Doctor Hyde of Honolulu. Edinburgh: 1890. V. 68
Father Damien, an Open Letter to the Reverend Doctor Hyde of Honolulu. London: 1890. V. 68; 70
A Footnote to History. 1892. V. 68
The Hanging Judge. London: 1914. V. 68
Hitherto Unpublished Manuscripts. Boston: 1916. V. 71
In the South Seas: Being an Account of Experiences and Observations in the Marquesas, Paumotus and Gilbert Islands in the Course of Two Cruises, on the Yacht Casco (1888) and the Schooner Equator (1889). London: 1900. V. 69
Island Nights' Entertainments. London: 1893. V. 68; 71
An Island Voyage. The St. Martin's Illustrated Library of Standard Authors. London: 1912. V. 71
The Jolly Jump-Ups: a Children's Garden of Verses. Springfield: 1946. V. 72
Kidnapped. London: 1886. V. 68; 71; 72
Kidnapped. New York: 1913. V. 73
Kidnapped. New York: 1938. V. 69
The Letters. New Haven: 1994. V. 72
The Letters to His Family and Friends. London: 1900. V. 71; 72
A Lodging for the Night. Eat Aurora: 1902. V. 69
A Lowden Sabbath Morn. London: 1898. V. 69
The Master of Ballantrae. 1889. V. 68
The Master of Ballantrae. London: 1889. V. 71; 73
Memoirs of Himself. Philadelphia: 1912. V. 71
More New Arabian Nights: the Dynamiter. London: 1885. V. 71
A Mountain Town in France. New York and London: 1896. V. 68
Napa Wine. San Francisco: 1974. V. 72
New Arabian Nights. London: 1882. V. 68
New Arabian Nights. London: 1885. V. 68
New Arabian Nights. London: 1890. V. 68
On the Choice of a Profession. 1916. V. 69
On the Choice of a Profession. London: 1916. V. 68
Poems. London: 1913. V. 68; 70
Prayers Written at Vailima. London: 1910. V. 72
Prince Otto - A Romance. London: 1885. V. 71
Prince Otto: a Romance. London: 1886. V. 68
R. L. S. TO J. M. Barrie. A Vailima Portrait (in the Form of a Letter). San Francisco: 1962. V. 73
Records of a Family of Engineers. London: 1912. V. 69
Select Essays of Robert Louis Stevenson. Virginibus Puerisque, Crabbed Age and Youth, An Apology for Idlers and Walking Tours. Bangor: 1937. V. 68
The Silverado Squatters. London: 1883. V. 68
Songs with Music from A Child's Garden of Verses. London: 1918. V. 70
A Stevenson Medley. London: 1899. V. 68
Strange Case of Dr. Jekyll and Mr. Hyde. 1886. V. 68
Strange Case of Dr. Jekyll and Mr. Hyde. New York: 1887. V. 69
The Strange Case of Dr. Jekyll and Mr. Hyde. New York: 1929. V. 70
Three Short Poems. Chicago: 1902. V. 70
Travels with a Donkey in the Cevennes. London: 1879. V. 69
Travels with a Donkey in the Cevennes. London: 1931. V. 72; 73
Travels with a Donkey in the Cevennes. London: 1967. V. 68
Treasure Island. London. V. 72
Treasure Island. New York: 1911. V. 70; 71; 73
Treasure Island. New York: 1927. V. 70
Treasure Island. New York: 1932. V. 68
Treasure Island. New York: 1941. V. 69
Treasure Island. New York: 1942. V. 69
Treasure Island and Kidnapped. London. V. 70
Two Mediaeval Tales. New York: 1930. V. 72
Vailima Letters. London: 1895. V. 70
The Waif Woman. 1916. V. 69
The Waif Woman. London: 1916. V. 71
Weir of Hermiston. 1896. V. 68
Weir of Hermiston. London: 1896. V. 71
The Works.... Edinburgh: 1895-1903. V. 68
The Wrecker. 1892. V. 68
The Wrecker. London Paris and Melbourne: 1892. V. 69

STEVENSON, SARAH HACKETT
Boys and Girls in Biology.... New York: 1875. V. 69

STEVENSON, WILLIAM G.
Thirteen Months in the Rebel Army; Being a Narrative of Personal Adventures in the Infantry Ordnance, Cavalry, Courier and Hospital Services. New York: 1863. V. 68; 73

STEVENSON-HAMILTON, L.
The Low-Veld: Its Wild Life and Its People. 1929. V. 72; 73

STEWART, A. E.
Round the World with Rod and Rifle. 1936. V. 69; 70; 73
Tiger and Other Game. 1927. V. 72; 73

STEWART, A. F.
Paintings, Drawings and Prints in the Collection.... London: 1920. V. 69

STEWART, A. T.
Catalogue of the...Collection of Paintings, Sculptures and Other Objects of Art. New York: 1887. V. 73

STEWART, AGNES M.
Stories of Richard Coeur de Lion, for the Instruction and Amusement of Young People. Dublin: 1847. V. 68

STEWART, ALVAN
A Legal Argument Before the Supreme Count of the State of New Jersey, at the May Term, 1845 at Trenton, for the Deliverance of 4000 Persons from Bondage. New York: 1845. V. 70

STEWART, ANGUS
Snow in Harvest. London: 1969. V. 71

STEWART, BERTRAM
The Library and the Picture Collection of the Port of London Authority. London: 1955. V. 71

STEWART, C. J.
A Catalogue of the Library Collected by Miss Richardson Currer, at Eshton Hall, Craven, Yorkshire. London: 1833. V. 72

STEWART, CATHERINE POMEROY
So Thick the Fog. New York: 1944. V. 69; 71

STEWART, CECIL
Topiary. An Historical Diversion, with colour-engravings by Peter Barker-Mill. London. V. 71

STEWART, CHARLES EDWARD
A Collection of Trifles in Verse. Sudbury: 1797. V. 69

STEWART, DAVID
Sketches of the Characters, Manners and Present State of the Highlanders of Scotland; with Details of the Military Service of the Highland Regiments. Edinburgh: 1825. V. 71

STEWART, DESMOND
The Round Mosaic. London: 1965. V. 71

STEWART, DONALD OGDEN
Mr. and Mrs. Haddock Abroad. New York: 1924. V. 72
Perfect Behavior: A Guide for Ladies and Gentlemen in All Social Crises. New York: 1922. V. 72

STEWART, DUGALD
Elements of Philosophy of the Human Mind. London: 1792. V. 71
Elements of the Philosophy of the Human Mind. Albany: 1822. V. 71

STEWART, EDGAR I.
Custer's Luck. Norman: 1955. V. 72

STEWART, ELIZABETH M.
Original Poetry, for Young Persons. London: 1846. V. 69

STEWART, FRANK
Cross Country with Hounds. 1936. V. 70
Hark to Hounds. 1937. V. 70
Hunting Countries. 1935. V. 70

STEWART, GEORGE R.
Earth Abides. New York: 1949. V. 68; 72
Pickett's Charge. Boston: 1959. V. 73
Take Your Bible In One Hand; The Life of William Henry Thomas, Author of a Whaleman's Adventures On Land and Sea. San Francisco: 1939. V. 71

STEWART, HERBERT LESLIE
The Irish in Nova Scotia. Annals of the Charitable Irish Society of Halifax (1786-1836). Kentville: 1950. V. 73
The Irish in Nova Scotia: Annals of the Charitable Irish Society of Novia Scotia (1786-1836). Kentville: 1949. V. 72

STEWART, J.
Orchids of Africa, a Select Review. Johannesburg: 1981. V. 69

STEWART, J. I. M.
Our England Is a Garden and Other Stories. London: 1979. V. 71
Shakespeare's Lofty Scene. London: 1971. V. 68

STEWART, JAMES
The Trial of James Stewart in Aucham in Duror of Appin, for the Murder of Colin Campbell of Glenure, Esq. Factor for His Majesty on the Forfeited Estate of Ardshiel, etc. Edinburgh: 1753. V. 69; 70

STEWART, JIMMY
Jimmy Stewart and His Poems. New York: 1989. V. 69; 71; 72

STEWART, JOHN
Dalhousie No. 7 Stationary Hospital. Halifax: 1915?. V. 72

STEWART, K. M.
Palaeocology and Palaeoenvironments of Late Cenozoic Mammals. Toronto: 1996. V. 68

STEWART, KENSEY JOHNS
A Geography for Beginners. Richmond: 1864. V. 69; 70

STEWART, MARGARET
The Way to Wonderland. London: 1920. V. 72

STEWART, MARY
This Rough Magic. London: 1964. V. 68

STEWART, P. M.
Tales of Travel and Sport. 1940. V. 72; 73

STEWART, ROY P.
The Turner Ranch. Master Breeder of the Hereford Line. 1916. V. 68
The Turner Ranch- Master Breeder of the Hereford Line. Oklahoma City: 1961. V. 71

STEWART, THOMAS GRAINGER
An Introduction to the Study of the Diseases of the Nervous System Being Lectures Delivered in the University of Edinburgh During the Tercentenary Year. Edinburgh: 1884. V. 68; 70; 71

STEWART, VIRGINIA
45 Contemporary Mexican Artists: a Twentieth Century Renaissance. Stanford: 1952. V. 71

STEWART, W. C.
The Practical Angler. 1857. V. 68; 73

STEWART, WILLIAM
A Letter to the Reverend Professor Campbell, Whereto Is Subjoin'd Remarks on His Vindication of the Apostles from Enthusiasm and on His Preface Thereto.... Glasgow: 1731. V. 68

STEWART, WILLIAM H.
A Pair of Blankets. New York: 1911. V. 69; 70

STEWART-BROWN, R.
The Tower Of Liverpool With Some Notes On The Clayton Family. London: 1910. V. 72

STEWARTON
The Secret History of the Court and Cabinet of St. Cloud.... London: 1806. V. 68

STEYAERT, MARTIN
In Propositionibus Damnatis Annotationes Omnes Jam Collectae.... Lovanii: 1736. V. 69

STEYERMARK, J. A.
Contributions to the Flora of Venezuela. Chicago: 1951-1952. V. 70

STICKLEY, GUSTAV
Craftsman Homes. New York: 1909. V. 68; 69; 72
More Craftsman Homes. New York: 1912. V. 68; 69; 72

STIEGLITZ, ALFRED
Georgia O'Keefe a Portrait. New York: 1978. V. 68; 69; 70; 72

STIEHL, HENRY
The Life of a Frontier Builder - Autobiography of Henry (Shorty) Stiehl. Salt Lake City: 1941. V. 73

STIERLIN, HENRI
Art of the Aztecs and Its Origins. New York: 1982. V. 71
Art of the Incas and Its Origins. New York: 1984. V. 71
Art of the Maya from the Olmees to the Toltec-Maya. New York: 1981. V. 71

STIFTER, ADALBERT
Pictures of Life. London: 1852. V. 68

STIGAND, CHAUNCEY HUGH
The Game of British East Africa. London: 1909. V. 71

STILES, EZRA
A History of Three of the Judges of King Charles I. Major-General Whaley, Major-General Goffe, and Colonel Dixwell.... Hartford: 1794. V. 70

STILES, HELEN E.
Pottery of the American Indians. New York: 1939. V. 73

STILGEBAUER, EDWARD
The Star of Hollywood. Cleveland/New York: 1929. V. 72

STILL *Wild.* New York: 2000. V. 72

STILL, JAMES
Early Recollections and Life of Dr. James Still. Philadelphia: 1877. V. 73
Hounds on the Mountain. Lexington: 1965. V. 69; 73

STILLINGER, JACK
Keats and Me. New Rochelle: 1986. V. 73

STILLINGFLEET, BENJAMIN
Miscellaneous Tracts Relating to Natural History, Husbandry and Physick. London: 1775. V. 71

STILLINGFLEET, EDWARD
Origines Britannicae; or, the Antiquities of the British Churches. London: 1837. V. 73

STILLMAN, CHAUNCEY DEVEREUX
Charles Stillman. 1810-1875. New York: 1956. V. 70

STILLMAN, J. D. B.
The Horse in Motion. Boston: 1882. V. 68

STILLWELL, LEANDER
The Story of the Common Soldier, or Army Life in the Civil War 1861- 1865. Erie: 1920. V. 70

STILLWELL, MARGARET BINGHAM
The Awakening Interest in Science During the First Century of Printing 1450-1550. New York: 1970. V. 69
Noah's Ark in Early Woodcuts and Modern Rhymes. New York: 1942. V. 68
The Pageant of Benefit Street Down through the Years. Providence: 1945. V. 68

STILTON, W.
A View of the Life of King David. London: 1765?. V. 70

STIMPSON, CHARLES
Stimpson's Boston Directory. Boston: 1840. V. 68

STIMSON, DOROTHY
The Gradual Acceptance of the Copernican Theory of the Universe. New York: 1917. V. 71

STIMSON, H. K.
From the Stage Coach to the Pulpit. St. Louis: 1874. V. 69

STIMSON, LEWIS ATTERBURY
A Treatise on Fractures. Philadelphia: 1883. V. 69

STINE, HANK
The Prisoner 2: A Day in the Life. London: 1979. V. 71

THE STING *of the Wasp....* San Francisco: 1967. V. 71

STIRLING, AMELIA HUTCHINSON
The Reign of the Princess. London: 1899. V. 68

STIRLING, EDWARD
The Battle of Life. London: 1860?. V. 70
Martin Chuzzlewit. London: 1844. V. 70
The Pickwick Club; or, the Age We Live In!. London: 1837?. V. 70

STIRLING, EMMA M.
Our Children in Old Scotland and Nova Scotia. London: 1892. V. 73

STIRLING, JAMES HUTCHISON
Darwinianism: Workmen and Work. Edinburgh: 1894. V. 71

STIRLING, M. W.
Three Pictographic Autobiographies of Sitting Bull. City of Washington: 1938. V. 69

STIRLING, WILLIAM
Annals of the Artists of Spain. London: 1848. V. 69; 73
Outlines of Practical Histology: a Manual for Students. London: 1890. V. 68
Some Apostles of Physiology. London: 1902. V. 70; 72

STIRLING, WILLIAM ALEXANDER, EARL OF
Recreations with the Muses. London: 1637. V. 70

STIRNER, MAX
The Ego and His Own. New York: 1907. V. 68; 70

STISTED, GEORGIANA M.
The True Life Of Capt. Sir Richard F. Burton. London: 1896. V. 72

STITCH, S.
Made in U.S.A.: an Americanziation in Modern Art - the 50's and 60's. Berkeley: 1987. V. 72

STIX, HUGH
The Shell. New York: 1968. V. 72

STIX, THOMAS L.
Say it aint's so, Joe. New York: 1947. V. 69

STOBART, JOHN
American Maritime Paintings of John Stobart. New York: 1991. V. 69

STOCK, CECIL HADEN
A Treatise on Shoring and Underpinning and Generally Dealing with Ruinous and Dangerous Structures. London: 1902. V. 68

STOCK, DENNIS
Jazz Street. New York: 1960. V. 68

STOCK, JOSEPH
A Narrative of What Passed at Killalla, in the County of Mayo and the Parts Adjacent, During the French Invasion in the Summer of 1798. Dublin: 1800. V. 69

STOCKDALE, FREDERICK WILLIAM LITCHFIELD
Etchings...and Antiquities in the County of Kent. London: 1810. V. 70

STOCKDALE, JAMES
Annales Caermoelenses; or Annals of Cartmel. Ulverston: 1872. V. 71

STOCKDALE, JOHN
The Whole Proceedings on the Trial of an Information...Against John Stockdale; for a Libel on the House of Commons, Tried in the Court of King's Bench Westminster, on Wednesday the 9th of Dec. 1789. London: 1790. V. 70; 73

STOCKEL, H. HENRIETTA
Survival of the Spirit. Reno: 1993. V. 72

STOCKER, HARRY EMILIUS
A History of the Moravian Mission Among the Indians on the White River in Indiana. Bethlehem: 1917. V. 68

STOCKGROWER'S *Directory of Marks and Brands for the State of Montana, 1872-1900...Also A Complete Classified Directory of Sheep and Wool Growers.* Helena, MO: 1974. V. 71

STOCKLEY, C. H.
Big Game Hunting in the Indian Empire. 1928. V. 69; 70; 72; 73
Shikar. 1928. V. 72
Stalking in the Himalayas and Northern India. 1936. V. 70; 72; 73

STOCKLEY, CYNTHIA
Ponjola. New York: 1923. V. 70

STOCKLEY, V. M.
Big Game Shooting in India, Burma and Somaliland. 1913. V. 72; 73

STOCKLEY, V. M. *continued*
Big Game Shooting in India, Burma and Somaliland. London: 1913. V. 71

STOCKMEN'S Official Green Book Colorado 1919. V. 69

STOCKTON, ALFRED A.
The Judges of New Brunswick and Their Times. 1907. V. 73

STOCKTON, FRANK RICHARD
Amos Kilbright: His Adscititious Experiences, with Other Stories. London: 1888. V. 69
The Griffin and the Minor Canon. New York: 1963. V. 73

STOCKWELL, LA TOURETTE
Dublin Theatres and Theatre Customs 1637-1820. Kingsport: 1938. V. 71

STODDARD, ELLWYMN R.
Borderlands Sourcebook; A Guide to the Literature on Northern Mexican and the American Southwest. Norman, OK: 1983. V. 72

STODDARD, JOHN L.
Lectures: Supplementary Volume. 1911. V. 69

STODDARD, RICHARD HENRY
Abraham Lincoln. An Horation Ode. New York: 1865. V. 70
Songs of Summer. Boston: 1857. V. 73

STODDARD, SENECA RAY
Lake George (Illustrated) and Lake Champlain. also Saratoga Springs, Its Mineral Waters.... Great Falls: 1901. V. 71

STODDARD, W. S.
Adventure in Architecture: Building the New Saint John's.... New York: 1958. V. 68; 69

STODDART, JOHN
Remarks on Local Scenery and Manners in Scotland During the Years 1799 and 1800. London: 1801. V. 73

STODDART, THOMAS TOD
The Angler's Companion to the Rivers and Lochs of Scotland. 1853. V. 68; 73
The Angler's Companion to the Rivers and Lochs of Scotland. London: 1923. V. 71
Angling Reminiscences. 1837. V. 68; 73
Angling Reminiscences of the Rivers and Lochs of Scotland. London: 1887. V. 71
Angling Songs. With a Memoir by Anna M. Stoddart. London: 1889. V. 71; 72
The Art of Angling, as Practised in Scotland. Edinburgh: 1835. V. 72
Songs and Poems. 1839. V. 73

STODDART, W. H. B.
Mind and Its Disorders. London: 1908. V. 72

STOKE, WILL E.
Episodes of Early Days in Central and Western Kansas. Great Bend, KS: 1926. V. 71

STOKER, BRAM
Dracula. New York: 1947. V. 69
Dracula. New York: 1996. V. 71
Dracula's Guest. 1937. V. 70
The Mystery of the Sea. New York: 1902. V. 69; 71
Personal Reminiscences of Henry Irving. London: 1906. V. 71

STOKER, FRED
A Gardener's Progress. London: 1938. V. 70

STOKES, ADRIAN
The Quattro Cento - a Different Conception of the Italian Renaissance.... London: 1932. V. 72; 73

STOKES, FRANCIS G.
An Elegy Written in a Country Church Yard by Thomas Gray. (Bibliography). Oxford: 1929. V. 68

STOKES, GEOFFREY
The Beatles. London: 1981. V. 72

STOKES, GEORGE GABRIEL
On Light. Second Course, on Light as a Means of Investigation. London: 1885. V. 72

STOKES, HENRY SEWELL
Echoes of the War and Other Poems. London: 1855. V. 72

STOKES, MARGARET
Three Months in the Forests of France in Search of Vestiges of the Irish Saints. 1895. V. 71

STOKES, RICHARD L.
Merry Mount. New York: 1932. V. 70

STOKES, SEWELL
The China Cow and Other Stories. London: 1929. V. 72

STOKES, TERRY
Crimes of Passion. New York: 1973. V. 72

STOKES, VERNON
A Town Dog In The Country. London. V. 70; 72

STOKES, W. ROYAL
Swing Era New York. Philadelphia: 1994. V. 68

STOKES, WHITELY
The Old Irish Glosses at Wurzburg and Carlsruhe. Part I. 1887. V. 70; 71

STOKES, WHITLEY
The Tripartite Life of St. Patrick, with Other Documents Relating to Saint. 1887. V. 73

STOKES, WILLIAM
Diseases of the Heart and Aorta. Dublin: 1854. V. 68
A Treatise on the Diagnosis and Treatment of Diseases of the Chest. Philadelphia: 1837. V. 68; 73
A Treatise on the Diagnosis and Treatment of Diseases of the Chest. Philadelphia: 1844. V. 68; 70; 71
William Stokes: His Life and Work. 1898. V. 70

STOLBERG, BENJAMIN
The Story of the C.I.O. New York: 1938. V. 68

STOLL, MAXIMILIAN
Medecine Pratique de Maximilien Stoll, Medecin...Ouvrage.... Bordeaux: 1778. V. 68

STOLL, WILLIAM T.
Silver Strike, the True Story of Silver Mining in the Coeur d'Alenes. Boston: 1932. V. 69

STOLZE, R. G.
Ferns and Fern Allies of Guatamala. Chicago: 1976-1983. V. 69

STONE, A.
American Pep. New York: 1918. V. 68
A Synoptic Catalog of the Mosquitoes of the World. Washington: 1959. V. 72

STONE, EDWIN M.
Our French Allies...in the...American Revolution.... Providence: 1884. V. 69

STONE, ELIZABETH ARNOLD
Uinta County: It Place in History. 1924. V. 73
Uinta County: Its Place in History. Laramie: 1924. V. 69

STONE, FRANCIS
Picturesque Views of All the Bridges Belonging to the County of Norfolk. London: 1830-1832. V. 70

STONE, GEORGE CAMERON
A Glossary of the Construction, Decoration and Use of Arms and Armor in All Countries and in All Times. Portland: 1934. V. 68
A Glossary of the Construction, Decoration and Use of Arms and Armor in All Countries and in All Times. New York: 1961. V. 72

STONE, IRVING
The Agony and the Ecstasy. Garden City: 1961. V. 71
Depths of Glory. Franklin: 1985. V. 73
The Passions of the Mind. Garden City: 1971. V. 73

STONE, J. HARRIS
England's Riviera, a Topographical and Archaeological Description of Land's End, Cornwall and Adjacent Spots of Beauty and Interest. 1925. V. 68

STONE, JANET
Thinking Faces - Photographs 1953-1979. London: 1988. V. 72

STONE, JOHN A.
Put's Golden Songster - Containing the Largest and Most Popular Collections of California Songs Ever Published. San Francisco: 1858. V. 68

STONE, JOHN BENJAMIN
A Summer Holiday in Spain: Being a Series of Descriptive Letters of Ancient Cities and Scenery of Spain and of Life, Manners and Customs of Spaniards. London: 1876. V. 70

STONE, JULIUS F.
Canyon Country - the Romance of a Drop of Water and a Grain of Sand. New York/London: 1932. V. 69; 70

STONE, L.
Domesticated Trout. 1896. V. 68

STONE, MICHAEL
A Long Reach. New York: 1997. V. 70
The Low End of Nowhere. New York: 1966. V. 70

STONE, ORRA I.
History of Massachusetts Industries. Boston: 1930. V. 71

STONE, P.
Fishing for Big Chub. 1983. V. 73

STONE, PETER
A Guide to Coarse Fishing. 1964. V. 68

STONE, REYNOLDS
Boxwood. London: 1957. V. 69; 72
Engravings. Brattleboro: 1977. V. 69; 72
Reynolds Stone Engravings. London: 1977. V. 68; 69; 72
St. Mark's Gospel. London: 1951. V. 68
Wood Engravings of Thomas Bewick - Reproduced in Collotype. London: 1953. V. 69

STONE, ROBERT
Bear and His Daughter. Boston/New York: 1997. V. 72; 73
Children of Light. London: 1986. V. 70; 72; 73
Children of Light. New York: 1986. V. 70; 71; 73
Damascus Gate. Boston/New York: 1998. V. 70; 71; 72
Damascus Gate. Franklin Center: 1998. V. 71
Damascus Gate. London: 1998. V. 69; 71; 72
Dog Soldiers. Boston: 1974. V. 68; 69; 70; 71; 72; 73
A Flag for Sunrise. New York: 1981. V. 69; 70; 71
Hall of Mirrors. Boston: 1966. V. 72
A Hall of Mirrors. Boston: 1967. V. 69; 70; 71; 73

STONE, ROBERT *continued*
Outerbridge Reach. Franklin Center: 1992. V. 70; 72
Outerbridge Reach. New York: 1992. V. 70; 72
Paths of Resistance. Boston: 1989. V. 72

STONE, SOLOMON
Solomon Stone's Marvelous Mental Calculator. New York: 1880. V. 72

STONE, THOMAS
Observations on the Phrenological Development of Burke, Hare and Other Atrocious Murderers.... Edinburgh: 1829. V. 71
A Rejoinder to the Answer of George Combe, Esq. to "Observations on the Phrenological Development of Burke, Hare and Other Atrocious Murderers". Edinburgh: 1829. V. 71

STONE, W.
The Birds of Eastern Pennsylvania and New Jersey. Philadelphia: 1894. V. 73
The Birds of New Jersey, Their Nests and Eggs. Trenton: 1909. V. 68

STONE, WILBUR MACEY
Women Designers of Book-Plates. New York: 1902. V. 68

STONE, WILLIAM L.
The Life and Times of Sa-Go-Ye-Wat-Ha, or Red Jacket by the Late William L. Stone.... Albany: 1866. V. 73
Life of Joseph Brant - Thayendanegea. New York: 1838. V. 69; 72
Matthias and His Impostures; or, the Progress of Fanaticism. New York: 1835. V. 68

STONEHAM, C. T.
Wanderings in Wild Africa. 1936. V. 72; 73
Wanderings in Wild Africa. 1945. V. 70

STONEHOUSE, JOHN
New Tables, Shewing I. The Value of Any Quantity of Stock at any Price...II. What Interest is Made per cent per annum of any Purchase...III. The Number of Days from any Day in One Month to the Same in Any Other Month. IV. Of Interest at 3, 3 1/2.... London: 1760. V. 70

STONEHOUSE, JOHN HARRISON
Green Leaves: New Chapters in the Life of Charles Dickens. London: 1931. V. 68

STONEMAN, VERNON C.
John and Thomas Seymour, Cabinetmakers in Boston 1794-1816. Boston: 1959. V. 73

STONE MILLER, R.
To Weave for the Sun. Boston: 1992. V. 69

STONER, JAMES
Ancient Reliques; or, Delineations of Monastic, Catellated & Domestic Architecture. London: 1812. V. 69

STONES, GRAEME
The Parodies of the Romantic Age. London: 1999. V. 72

STONES, MARGARET
The Endemic Flora of Tasmania. 1967-1978. V. 73
The Endemic Flora of Tasmania. London: 1967-1978. V. 69; 70
The Endemic Flora of Tasmania. Part III. London: 1971. V. 70

STONEY, BARBARA
Enid Blyton - a Biography. London: 1974. V. 69

STONEY, SAMUEL GAIILARD
Black Genesis. New York: 1930. V. 73

STONG, PHIL
State Fair. New York: 1932. V. 71

STOOKEY, BYRON
Surgical and Mechanical Treatment of Peripheral Nerves. Philadelphia: 1922. V. 68; 70; 71
Trigeminal Neuralgia. Its History and Treatment. Springfield: 1959. V. 68; 70; 71

STOPES, MARIE CARMICHAEL
Contraception (Birth Control). Its Theory, History and Practice. London: 1923. V. 73
The Human Body. London: 1926. V. 68
Lord Alfred Douglas. London: 1949. V. 69; 72
Love Songs for Young Lovers. London: 1939. V. 68; 72
Truth About Venereal Disease. London: 1921. V. 70

STOPFORD, J. S. B.
The Arteries of the Pons and Medulla Oblongata in the Human Brain. 1917. V. 68

STOPPARD, TOM
Albert's Bridge and If You're Glad I'll Be Frank: Two Plays for Radio. London: 1969. V. 73
Artist Descending a Staircase (and) Where Are They Now?. London: 1973. V. 71
Dalliance and Undiscovered Country. London: 1986. V. 68
Every Good Boy Deserves Favour: a Play for Actors and Orchestra. (and) Professional Foul: a Play for Television. London: 1978. V. 71
Lord Malquist and Mr. Moon. London: 1966. V. 68; 73
Lord Malquist and Mr. Moon. New York: 1968. V. 68
On The Razzle. London: 1981. V. 73
The Real Inspector Hound. London: 1968. V. 70; 73
Rosencrantz and Guildenstern are Dead. 1967. V. 68
Rosencrantz and Guildenstern are Dead. London: 1967. V. 70; 73
Undiscovered Country. 1980. V. 68

STORCK, ANTHONY
An Essay on Medicinal Nature of Hemlock in Two Parts.... Edinburgh: 1762. V. 69; 72; 73
An Essay on the Medicinal Nature of Hemlock. London: 1762. V. 70

STORER, D. H.
A Report on the Fishes of Massachusetts. Boston: 1839. V. 72; 73
A Synopsis of the Fishes of North America. Cambridge: 1846. V. 69; 72

STORER, JAMES
Select Views of London and Its Environs.... London: 1804-1805. V. 69

STORER, JOHN SARGANT
The Antiquarian Itinerary, Comprising Specimens of Architecture, Monastic, Castellated and Domestic. London: 1815-1818. V. 73

STOREY, DAVID
Flight into Camden. London: 1960. V. 71
This Sporting Life. London: 1959. V. 71
This Sporting Life. London: 1960. V. 72; 73

STOREY, H.
Hunting and Shooting in Ceylon. 1907. V. 69; 70

STORIES from the New Yorker 1950-1960. London: 1961. V. 70

STORK, WILLIAM
An Account of East-Florida, with a Journal Kept by John Bartram of Philadelphia.... London: 1766. V. 70; 73

STORM, BARRY
Thunder Gods Gold. Tortilla Flat: 1945. V. 73

STORM, COLTON
A Catalogue of the Everett D. Graff Collection of Western Americana. Chicago: 1968. V. 72; 73

STORM, HANS OTTO
Full Measure. New York: 1929. V. 69

STORM, LESLEY
Head in the Wind. New York: 1928. V. 71

STORRS, RONALD
Orientations. London: 1937. V. 68

THE STORY of Little Black Sambo. New York: 1934. V. 73

STORY, ALFRED T.
The Life of John Linnell. London: 1892. V. 71

THE STORY Book: for Good Little Girls. (First Series - No. 5). New York: 1856-1866. V. 70

STORY, JACK TREVOR
The Trouble with Harry. London: 1949. V. 71

STORY, JOSEPH
Commentaries on Equity Pleadings and the Incidents Thereof, According to the Practice of the Courts of Equity of England and America. Boston: 1848. V. 71
Commentaries on the Constitution of the United States. Boston: 1833. V. 72
Discourse Pronounced Before the Phi Beta Kappa Society at the Anniversary Celebration on the Thirty-First Day of August, 1826. Boston: 1826. V. 72

THE STORY of a Troll-Hunt. Cambridge: 1904. V. 69

THE STORY of an English Village.... London: 1978. V. 68

THE Story of Jesus. London: 1938. V. 70

THE STORY of Little Jack Sprat. London: 1904. V. 72

THE STORY of Peter Rabbit. Kenosha: 1941. V. 71

THE STORY of Peter Rabbit. (together with) Dick Whittington and His Cat. Chicago: 1908. V. 69

THE STORY of Robin Hood. New York: 1895. V. 69

THE STORY of String and How It Grew. New York: 1916. V. 71

THE STORY Of Tabbykin Town in School and at Play. London: 1920. V. 73

THE STORY of the Norman Conquest. London: 1866. V. 72

THE STORY of the Three Little Kittens. New York: 1892. V. 71

THE STORY of Zelinda and the Monster; or, Beauty and the Beast. London: 1895. V. 68

STORY, T. W.
Notes on the Old Haworth Registers. Haworth: 1909. V. 70
Notes on the Old Haworth Registers. Haworth: 1925. V. 73

STORY, THOMAS
A Journal Of The Life of Thomas Storey. Newcastle upon Tyne: 1747. V. 72

STOSCH, PHILIPPE DE
Gemmae Antiquae...Pierres Antiques.... Amsterdam: 1724. V. 69; 72

STOTT, RAYMOND TOOLE
Maughamiana: The Writings of W. Somerset Maugham. London: 1950. V. 69

STOUGHTON, JOHN
The Palace of Glass and the Gathering of the People. London: 1851. V. 71

STOUT, A. B.
Papers Presented at the International Conference on Flower and Fruit Sterility...1926. New York: 1927. V. 68; 71

STOUT, HOSEA
On the Mormon Frontier - The Diary of Hosea Stout. Salt Lake City: 1964. V. 69

STOUT, JOSEPH A.
Oklahoma Cattlemen- An Association History. Stillwater: 1981. V. 71

STOUT, L. H.
Reminiscences of General Braxton Bragg. Hattiesburg: 1942. V. 69; 70

STOUT, REX
Alphabet Hicks. 1941. V. 69
And Be a Villain. New York: 1948. V. 68; 69; 70
And Four to Go. New York: 1958. V. 68; 69; 71
Before Midnight. New York: 1955. V. 68; 69; 70; 72; 73
The Best Families. New York: 1950. V. 70
The Black Mountain. New York: 1954. V. 68; 72
Black Orchids. New York: 1942. V. 70
The Broken Vase. London: 1942. V. 73
The Brownstone House of Nero Wolfe. Boston: 1983. V. 70
Champagne for One. New York: 1958. V. 68; 69; 70; 71
Champagne for One. London: 1959. V. 71
Curtains for Three. New York: 1951. V. 70
Death of a Doxy. New York: 1966. V. 68; 69; 70; 72; 73
Death of a Dude. New York: 1969. V. 68; 69; 70; 71; 72
The Doorbell Rang. New York: 1965. V. 68
Double for Death. New York: 1939. V. 68; 70; 71; 72
A Family Affair. London: 1976. V. 68
The Father Hunt. New York: 1968. V. 68; 69; 70; 72; 73
Fer-de-Lance. New York: 1934. V. 68; 69; 70; 73
Fer-De-Lance. New York: 1993. V. 72
The Final Deduction. New York: 1961. V. 68; 73
Forest Fire. 1933. V. 68; 69
Gambit. New York: 1962. V. 73
The Game of Croquet: Its Appointment and Laws. New York: 1968. V. 73
The Gazette: The Journal of the Wolfe Pack. 1979. V. 72
The Golden Spiders. London: 1954. V. 72
The Hand in the Glove. 1937. V. 69
If Death Ever Slept. New York: 1957. V. 70
In the Best Families. New York: 1950. V. 68; 73
Justice Ends at Home and Other Stories. New York: 1977. V. 69; 70; 71; 72; 73
Kings Full of Aces. New York: 1969. V. 71; 73
The League of Frightened Men. 1935. V. 68
The Mother Hunt. New York: 1963. V. 69
Mountain Cat. 1939. V. 69; 70
Murder by the Book. New York: 1951. V. 73
The Nero Wolfe Cook Book. New York: 1973. V. 68
Not Quite Dead Enough. New York: 1944. V. 69; 71; 72
Please Pass the Guilt. New York: 1973. V. 69; 70; 72
Please Pass the Guilt. London: 1974. V. 69
Prisoner's Base. New York: 1942. V. 69
Prisoner's Base. New York: 1952. V. 68; 70; 71
A Right to Die. New York: 1964. V. 68; 69; 70; 71; 72; 73
Royal Flush: a Nero Wolfe Omnibus. New York: 1965. V. 69; 71
The Rubber Band. 1936. V. 73
Rue Morgue No. 1. 1946. V. 68
The Second Confession. New York: 1949. V. 68; 70
The Silent Speaker. New York: 1946. V. 68; 69; 70; 71; 72
Three Aces. New York: 1971. V. 70
Three at Wolfe's Door. New York: 1960. V. 68
Three for the Chair. New York: 1957. V. 73
Three Trumps: a Nero Wolfe Omnibus. New York: 1973. V. 71
Too Many Clients. New York: 1960. V. 69; 71
Too Many Cooks. 1938. V. 68; 69
Too Many Cooks. New York: 1938. V. 69
Too Many Women. New York: 1947. V. 69; 70
Triple Zeck. New York: 1974. V. 69
Under The Andes. New York: 1984. V. 72
Where There's a Will. New York: 1940. V. 68

STOUT, WAYNE
Hosea Stout Utah's Pioneer Statesman. Salt Lake City: 1963. V. 68; 73

STOUT, WILLIAM
Autobiography of William Stout, of Lancaster. 1851. V. 72; 73

STOVER, D.
The Life of Sir Charles Linnaeus.... 1794. V. 69

STOW, HESTER H.
Greek Athletics and Festivals in the Fifty Century. New York: 1939. V. 68

STOW, JOHN
The Annales of England, Faithfully Collected Out of the Most Authenticall Authors, Records, and Other Monuments of Antiquitie, from the first Inhabitation Untill this Present Yeers 1592. London: 1592. V. 68
Survey of London, Written in the Year 1598 by John Stow, Now Edited by William J. Thoms of the Camden Society. London: 1842. V. 72
A Survey of the Cities of London and Westminster.... London: 1720. V. 68

STOW, W., MRS.
Probate Confiscation. Unjust Laws Which Govern Woman. 1877. V. 70

STOWE, HARRIET ELIZABETH BEECHER
La Cabane de l'Oncle Tom ou Les Noirs en Amerique. Paris: 1853. V. 68
Key to Uncle Tom's Cabin. Boston: 1853. V. 69
A Key to Uncle Tom's Cabin. London: 1853. V. 70; 71
Little Foxes, or, the Little Failings Which Mar Domestic Happiness. London: 1889. V. 68
The Minister's Wooing. New York: 1859. V. 70
Old Stories Told Anew. 1891. V. 73
Old Stories Told Anew. Uncle Tom's Cabin. London: 1891. V. 68
Palmetto Leaves. Boston: 1873. V. 69; 70; 71; 73
Religious Poems. Boston: 1867. V. 68; 70; 72
Sketches of American Life: a Companion to The Mayflower. London: 1855. V. 70
Sunny Memories of Foreign Lands. Boston: 1854. V. 68
Uncle Tom's Cabin. Boston: 1852. V. 68; 70; 72; 73
Uncle Tom's Cabin. London: 1852. V. 70; 71; 72; 73
Uncle Tom's Cabin. Boston: 1853. V. 72
Uncle Tom's Cabin. Boston and New York: 1891. V. 73
Uncle Tom's Cabin. London and Glasgow: 1900. V. 68
Uncle Tom's Cabin. New York: 1938. V. 70
Uncle Tom's Cabin. New York: 1983. V. 69

STOWE HOUSE
Catalogue of the Library Removed from Stowe House, Buckinghamshire, Catalogue of the Important Collection of Manuscripts from Stowe. London: 1849. V. 70

STOWE, JOHN
A Survey of London. London: 1890. V. 71

STOWE, LYMAN BEECHER
Booker T. Washington. Builder of a Civilization. 1916. V. 72

STOWELL, JAY S.
Methodist Adventures in Negro Education. New York and Cincinnati: 1922. V. 68

STOWERS, CARLTON
Careless Whispers. Dallas: 1986. V. 68

STRABO
Geographia cum Notis Casauboni et Aliorum. Amstelaedami: 1707. V. 72
Rerum Geographicarum Libri XVII. Graece et Latine. Oxford: 1807. V. 68

STRACEY, P. D.
Reade, Elephant Hunter. 1967. V. 69; 70; 72

STRACHAN, JAMES
A New Set of Tables, for Comprising the Weight of Cattle by Measurement.... Edinburgh: 1843. V. 71

STRACHER, ALFRED
Muscle and Nonmuscle Motility. New York: 1983. V. 68

STRACHEY, JOHN
Literature and Dialectical Materialism. New York: 1934. V. 72

STRACHEY, LYTTON
The Collected Works. London: 1948. V. 70
Elizabeth and Essex - a Tragic History. London: 1928. V. 70; 72
Ermyntrude and Esmeralda. London: 1969. V. 71
Portraits in Miniature and Other Essays. London: 1931. V. 69
Spectatorial Essays. London: 1964. V. 70

STRACHEY, RAY
Shaken by the Wind: a Story of Fanaticism. New York: 1928. V. 71

STRACHEY, RAYCHEL
Struggle, Stirring Story of Woman's Advance in England. New York: 1930. V. 72
Women's Suffrage and Women's Service. London: 1927. V. 72

STRACK, HENRY
Brick and Terra-Cotta Work During the Middle Ages and the Renaissance in Italy. Boston: 1914?. V. 68

STRADA, FAMIANUS
De Bello Belgico. Rome: 1700. V. 70

STRAHAN, KAY CLEAVER
The Desert Lake Mystery. Indianapolis: 1936. V. 68

STRAHAN, R.
Finches, Bowerbirds and Other Passerines of Australia. Sydney: 1996. V. 73

STRAHORN, CARRIE A.
Fifteen Thousand Miles By Stage- A Woman's Unique Experience During Thirty Years of Pathfinding and Pioneering from the Missouri to the Pacific and from Alaska to Mexico. New York: 1911. V. 71

STRAIGHT, SUSAN
Aquaboogie. Minneapolis: 1990. V. 69; 70
I Been in Sorrow's Kitchen and Licked Out all the Pots. New York: 1992. V. 68; 73

STRAKER, D. AUGUSTUS
The New South Investigated. Detroit: 1888. V. 68

STRALEY, JOHN
The Woman who Married a Bear. 1992. V. 70
The Woman Who Married A Bear. New York: 1992. V. 72

STRALEY, W.
Pioneer Sketches, Nebraska and Texas. Hico, TX: 1915. V. 69; 71

STRAND, J.
A Greene and Greene Guide. Pasadena: 1974. V. 69; 72

STRAND, MARK
The Continuous Life. Iowa City: 1990. V. 69; 73
The Continuous Life. New York: 1990. V. 68
Dark Harbor. New York: 1993. V. 73
Darker. New York: 1970. V. 73
89 Clouds. New York: 1999. V. 69; 73
The Monument. New York: 1978. V. 69; 73
The Planet of Lost Things. New York: 1982. V. 73
Prose. Four Poems. Portland: 1987. V. 69; 73
Sleeping with One Eye Open. Iowa City: 1964. V. 69; 73
The Story of Our Lives. New York: 1973. V. 69; 73
A Suite of Appearances. Portland: 1993. V. 73

STRAND, PAUL
Paul Strand - Sixty Years of Photographs. Millerton: 1976. V. 70
Photographs of Mexico. New York: 1940. V. 73
A Retrospective Monograph: the Years 1915-1946; The Years 1950-1968. 1972. V. 68
Time in New England. New York: 1950. V. 70

STRANG, JOHN
Germany in MDCCCXXXI. London: 1836. V. 70

STRANG, TOM
The Northern Highlands. Edinburgh: 1970. V. 69
The Northern Highlands. Edinburgh: 1975. V. 69

STRANG, WILLIAM
A Book of Giants. London: 1898. V. 73

STRANGE, E. H.
A Centenerary Bibliography of the Pickwick Papers. London: 1936. V. 69

STRANGE, EDWARD
The Colour-Prints of Hiroshige. London: 1925. V. 69; 72

STRANGE, JAMES
Records of Ft. St. George, James Strange's Journal and Narrative of the Commercial Expedition from Bombay to the North-West Coast of America. Madras: 1928. V. 68

STRANGE, JOHN STEPHEN
A Picture of The Victim. New York: 1940. V. 72
The Strangler Fig. Garden City: 1930. V. 71

STRANGE Secrets. London: 1890. V. 68

STRANGE, THOMAS ARTHUR
A Guide to Collectors. London: 1900. V. 68

THE STRANGER in Liverpool; or, an Historical and Descriptive View of the Town of Liverpool and Its Environs. Liverpool: 1816. V. 70

THE STRANGER'S Guide and Official Directory for the City of Richmond. Richmond: 1863. V. 69; 70

STRANGFORD, EMILY ANNE BEAUFORT SMYTHE, VISCOUNTESS
Egyptian Sepulchres and Syrian Shrines Including Some Stay in the Lebanon at Palmyra and in Western Turkey.... London: 1861. V. 68

STRANSKY, M. PAULO
Respublica Bojema, Descripta, Recognita, et Aucta. Leiden: 1643. V. 69

STRASBURGER, E.
Rambles on the Riviera. New York: 1906. V. 69; 70

STRATFORD, JENNY
The Bedford Inventories. The Worldly Goods of John, Duke of Bedford, Regent of France 1389-1435. London: 1993. V. 69; 70

STRATTON, A.
Sinan. New York: 1972. V. 72

STRATTON, ARTHUR
The Orders of Architecture, Greek Roman and Renaissance.... London: 1931. V. 70
Some XVIIIth Century Designs for Interior Decoration.... London: 1923. V. 70

STRATTON, CHARLES
An Account of the Life, Personal Appearance, Character and Manners of Charles Stratton.... New York: 1843. V. 72
The Life of General Tom Thumb. Troy: 1856. V. 71

STRATTON, CLARENCE
Swords and Statues. Philadelphia: 1937. V. 70; 71; 73

STRATTON, R. B.
Captivity of the Oatman Girls. Being an Interesting Narrative of Life Among the Apache and Mohave Indians.... San Francisco: 1935. V. 71

STRATTON, ROBERT BURCHER
The Heroes in Gray. Lyncburgh: 1894. V. 69; 70

STRATTON, ROY
One Among None: a Massachusetts State Police Mystery. New York: 1965. V. 70

STRAUB, PETER
Ghost Story. New York: 1979. V. 68; 71
Koko. New York: 1988. V. 71

STRAUS, RALPH
John Baskerville A Memoir. London: 1907. V. 72
Pengard Awake. New York: 1920. V. 68; 72
Robert Dodsley. Poet, Publisher and Playwright. London: 1910. V. 73
A Whip for the Woman. New York: 1932. V. 71

STRAUSBAUGH, P. D.
Flora of West Virginia. Morgantown: 1952-1964. V. 68

STRAUSS, E.
Sir William Petty, Portrait of a Genius. 1954. V. 69

STRAUSS, FREDERICK
Helon's Pilgrimage to Jerusalem: a Picture of Judaism in the Century Which Preceded the Advent of Our Saviour. Boston: 1835. V. 73

STRAUSS, WALTER L.
Chiaroscuro. New York: 1973. V. 72

STRAVINSKY, IGOR
Poetics of Music in the Form of Six Lessons. London: 1947. V. 71

STREAMER, D.
Ruthless Rhymes for Heartless Homes. London: 1899. V. 72

STREATEFEILD, N.
Tennis Shoes. 1948. V. 72

STREET, C. J. C.
Ireland in 1921. London: 1922. V. 71

STREET, G. S.
People and Questions. London: 1910. V. 69

STREET, GEORGE EDMUND
Some Account of Gothic Architecture in Spain. London: 1914. V. 69; 72

STREET, JULIAN
Mysterious Japan. Garden City: 1921. V. 72

STREET Pavements of All Kinds. Borough of Manhattan City of New York, January 1, 1916. New York: 1916. V. 73

STREETER, BEN J.
Prairie Trails and Cattle Towns. Boston: 1936. V. 71

STREETER, EDWARD
As You Were, Bill!. New York: 1920. V. 70

STREETER, EDWIN W.
Precious Stones and Gems. 1879. V. 68
Precious Stones and Gems. London: 1884. V. 71

STREETER, RUSSELL
Mirror of Calvinistic Fanaticism, or Jedediah Burchard & Co. During a Protracted Meeting of Twenty-six Days in Woodstock, Vermont. Woodstock: 1835. V. 71

STREETER, THOMAS WINTHROP
The Celebrated Collection of Americana Formed by.... New York: 1966-1970. V. 68

STREINNIUS, RICHARDUS
De Gentib. Et Familiis Romanorvm. Venitiis: 1571. V. 73

STREIT, CLARENCE KIRSHAM
Union Now. Washington: 1943. V. 71

STRELOW, MICHAEL
Kesey. Eugene: 1977. V. 69; 72

STRETE, CRAIG KEE
Burn Down the Night. 1982. V. 72

STRETTON, HENRY
Original Sketches, Drawn and Engraved on Stone. London: 1840. V. 73

STREVELL, CHARLES N.
As I Recall Them. 1943. V. 71

STRIBLING, T. S.
Birthright. New York: 1922. V. 71
Clues of the Caribbees. New York: 1929. V. 68; 69; 73
The Cruise of the Dry Dock. Chicago: 1917. V. 68

STRICKLAND, AGNES
Life of Mary Queen of Scots. London: 1873. V. 70
Old Friends and New Acquaintances. Second Series. London: 1861. V. 70
The Seven Ages of Woman and Other Poems. London: 1827. V. 69

STRICKLAND, JOSEPH
Documents and Maps on the Boundary Question Between Venezuela and British Guayana from the Capuchin Archives in Rome. Rome: 1896. V. 73

STRICKLAND, WILLIAM
Reports on Canals, Railway, Roads, and Other Subjects Made to "The Pennsylvania Society for the Promotion of Internal Improvements". Philadelphia: 1826. V. 68
Reports, Specifications and Estimates of Public Works in the United States of America.... London: 1841. V. 68

STRID, A.
Mountain Flora of Greece. Edinburgh: 1991. V. 72

STRIEBER, WHITLEY
The Hunger. New York: 1981. V. 68

STRIKER, FRAN
The Lone Ranger and the Outlaw Stronghold. New York: 1939. V. 69

STRINDBERG, AUGUST
The Son of a Servant. London: 1913. V. 71
Zones of the Spirit: a Book of Thoughts. London: 1913. V. 73

THE STING of the Wasp. San Francisco: 1967. V. 73

STRINGER, ARTHUR
Red Wine of Youth: a Life of Rupert Brooke. Indianapolis: 1948. V. 68
Without Warning. New York: 1924. V. 69
The Wolf Woman. Indianapolis: 1928. V. 70
The Woman Who Couldn't Die. Indianapolis: 1929. V. 70

STROBEL, MARION
Saturday Afternoon. New York: 1930. V. 72
Silvia's in Town. New York: 1933. V. 72

STRONG, A. B.
Illustrated Natural History of the Three Kingdoms.... New York: 1848. V. 72

STRONG, ARTURO CARRILLO
Corrido De Cocaine. Inside Stories of Hard Drugs Big Money and Short Lives. Tucson: 1990. V. 71; 73

STRONG, CHARLES S.
Private Secretary Plus. New York: 1938. V. 71

STRONG, D. E.
Catalogue of the Carved Amber in the Department of Greek and Roman Antiquities. London: 1966. V. 72

STRONG, L. A. G.
The Hansom Cab and the Pigeons, Being Random Reflections Upon the Silver Jubilee of King George V. Waltham St. Lawrence: 1935. V. 68; 73

STRONG, R. M.
A Bibliography of Birds with Special Reference to Anatomy, Behavior. Chicago: 1939-1946. V. 73

STRONG, R. P.
The African Republic of Liberia and the Belgian Congo.... New York: 1969. V. 68
Liberia. The African Republic of Liberia and the Belgian Congo.... Cambridge: 1930. V. 69

STRONG, ROY
Splendour at Court - Renaissance Spectacle and Illusion. London: 1973. V. 72

STRONG, S. ARTHUR
The Masterpieces in the Duke of Devonshire's Collection of Pictures. London: 1901. V. 69; 72

STRONG, TITUS
The Cypress Wreath or Mourner's Friend. Greenfield: 1828. V. 73

STRONG, TRACY
We Prisoners of War. New York: 1942. V. 69

STROTHER, D. H.
Illustrated Life of General Winfield Scott, Command-In-Chief of The Army in Mexico. New York: 1847. V. 72

STROTHER, EDWARD
Criticon Febrium; or a Critical Essay on Fevers, with the Diagnosticks and Methods of Cure. London: 1716. V. 69
An Essay on Sickness and Health.... London: 1725. V. 73

STROUD, DOROTHY
Capability Brown. London: 1950. V. 69; 72
Capability Brown. London: 1957. V. 72
Humphrey Repton. London: 1962. V. 69

STROUSE, NORMAN H.
The Silverado Episode. St. Helena, Calif: 1966. V. 72

STRUBE, SIDNEY
War Cartoons from the Daily Express. London: 1944. V. 71

STRUMPELL, ADOLF
A Text-Book of Medicine for Students and Practitioners. New York: 1896. V. 71

STRUTHER, JAN
Betsinda Dances and Other Poems. London: 1931. V. 68
Mrs. Miniver. London: 1939. V. 72
The Modern Struwwelpeter. London: 1936. V. 73
Sycamore Square. London: 1932. V. 72; 73

STRUTHERS, BURT
The Diary of A Dude Wrangler. New York: 1924. V. 71
Power River- Let'er Buck. New York. V. 71

STRUTHERS, JOHN
The History of Scotland, from the Union to the Abolition of the Heritable Jurisdictions in MDCCXLVIII. To which is subjoined . . . Glasgow: 1827. V. 71

STRUTT, ELIZABETH
The Feminine Soul: Its Nature and Attributes.... Boston: 1870. V. 72

STRUTT, JACOB GEORGE
Sylva Britannica; or Portraits of Forest Trees.... London: 1831-1836. V. 69; 72

STRUTT, JOSEPH
Clc. Camena Angel-Deod or the Sports and Pastimes of the People of England.... London: 1810. V. 70
Horda Angel-Cynnan; or a Compleat View of the Manners, Customs, Arms, Habits &c. of the Inhabitants of England. London: 1775-1776. V. 71
Sports and Pastimes of the People of England: Including Rural and Domestic Recreations, May-Games, Mummeries, Pageants.... London: 1810. V. 70

STRUVE, F. G. W.
Catalogus Novus Stellarum Duplicum et Multiplicum Maxima ex Parte in Specula Universitatis Caesarae Dorpatensis per Magnum Telescopium Achromaticum Franhoferi Detectarum. Dorpati: 1827. V. 73

STRUWWELPETER or Merry Stories and Funny Pictures. London: 1950. V. 70

STRYIENSKI, CASIMIR
La Galerie du Regent Philippe, Duc d'Orleans. Paris: 1913. V. 69; 72

STRYKER, ROY EMERSON
In This Proud Land: America 1935-1943 As Seen in the FSA Photographs. Greenwich: 1973. V. 68

STRYPE, JOHN
Historical Collections of the Life and Acts of the Reverend Father in God, John Aylmer, Lord Bishop of London n the Reign of Queen Elizabeth. London: 1701. V. 72

STUART, ALEX H.
A Narrative of the Leading Incidents of the Organization of the First Popular Movement in Virginia in 1865. Richmond: 1888. V. 70

STUART, ANDREW
Letters to the Right Honourable Lord Mansfield from Andrew Stuart. London: 1773. V. 69

STUART, C. M. VILLIERS
Gardens of Great Mughals. London: 1913. V. 72

STUART, ERSKINE
The Bronte Country. London: 1888. V. 73

STUART, ESME
The Good Old Days or Christmas Under Queen Elizabeth. London: 1876. V. 70

STUART, FRANCIS
Black List, Section H. Carbondale and Edwardsville: 1971. V. 72

STUART, GILBERT
A View of Society in Europe, in Its Progress from Rudeness to Refinement; or, Inquiries Concerning the History of Law, Government and Manners. Edinburgh: 1778. V. 69

STUART, GLORIA
March Fifteenth, Nineteen Eighty-Three. Laguna Beach: 1985. V. 73

STUART, GRANVILLE
Diary and Sketchbook of a Journey to America in 1866 and Return Trip Up the Missouri River to Fort Benton. Los Angeles: 1963. V. 68; 73
Forty Years On the Old Frontier As Seen By Granville Stuart, Goldminer, Trader, Merchant, Rancher, and Politician. Cleveland: 1925. V. 71

STUART, H. VILLIERS
Adventures Amidst the Equatorial Forests and Rivers of South America. London: 1891. V. 70

STUART, HENRY CLIFFORD
A Prophet in His Own Country. Being the Letters of Stuart X. Washington: 1916. V. 70; 73

STUART, JAMES
Poems on Various Subjects. Belfast: 1811. V. 69
Six Lectures to the Workmen of Crewe, Delivered in the Hall of the Crewe Mechanic's Institute in the Summer of 1868. Cambridge: 1869. V. 70

STUART, JESSE
Hold April. New York: 1962. V. 71
Mongrel Mettle. Richmond: 1944. V. 70
My Land Has a Voice. New York: 1966. V. 71

STUART, JOHN
Essays, Chiefly on Scottish Antiquities. Aberdeen: 1846. V. 72

STUART, MARTINUS COHEN
The Pilgrim Fathers' first Meeting for Public Worship in North America. Amsterdam: 1866. V. 73

STUART, MURIEL
Fool's Garden. London: 1936. V. 70

STUART, REGINOLD R.
Calvin B. West of the Umpqua- An Obscure Chapter in the History of Southern Oregon. San Francisco: 1961. V. 71

STUART, WILLIAM
Sketches of the Life of William Stuart. Bridgeport: 1854. V. 68

STUART, WILLIAM L.
Night Cry. New York: 1948. V. 71

STUART YOUNG, J. M.
Chits from West Africa. Stories and Sketches from the Tropics. London: 1923. V. 70
Osrac, The Self Sufficient, and Other Poems, with a Memoir of the Late Oscar Wilde. London: 1905. V. 70

STUBBE, HENRY
A Censure Upon Certain Passages Contained in the History of the Royal Society. Oxford: 1670. V. 73
The Miraculous Conformist; or an Account of Several Marvailous Cures Performed by the Stroaking of the Hands of Mr. Valentine Gratarick. Oxford: 1666. V. 70

STUBBES, PHILIP
Anatomy of Abuses. London: 1835. V. 72

STUBBES, PHILLIP
Anatomy of the Abuses in England in Shakespeare's Youth, A.D. 1583. London: 1877. V. 70

STUBBS, LAURA
Stevenson's Shrine, The Record of a Pilgrimage. London: 1903. V. 72

STUBBS, STANLEY A.
Bird's-Eye View of the Pueblos. Norman: 1950. V. 68

STUCK, HUDSON
The Ascent of Denali (Mount McKinley): a Narrative of the First Complete Ascent of the Highest Peak in North America. New York: 1914. V. 73

STUCKEY, CHARLES F.
Monet. A Retrospective. London: 1988. V. 72

STUCKEY, R.
The Lithographs of Stow Wengenroth 1931-1972. Boston: 1974. V. 69; 72

STUDDY, G. E.
Bonzo. Paris: 1932. V. 71
Bonzo and Us. London: 1931. V. 72
Bonzo's Annual. London: 1948. V. 74
Bonzo's Annual. London: 1949. V. 70
Bonzo's Annual. London: 1951. V. 70

STUDER, JACOB
The Birds of North America. Barre: 1977. V. 69

STUDIES; the Lancashire Domesday; Folios and Maps. London: 1987. V. 73

THE STUDIO. London: 1928. V. 68

THE STUDIO Year-Book of Decorative Art 1906. London: 1906. V. 68

STUKELEY, WILLIAM
Palaeographia Britannica; or Discourses on Antiquities That Relate to the History of Britian. Number III. London: 1752. V. 70
Palaeographia Sacra; or, Discourses on Monuments of Antiquity that Relate to Sacred History. London: 1736. V. 70

STURDEE, ALFRED B.
The Twin-Stern Steamer, with a Protected Propeller.... 1851. V. 70

STURDY, CARL
Society Doctor. New York: 1936. V. 71
Test Doctor. New York: 1938. V. 71

STURGE, JOSEPH
A Visit to the United States in 1841. London: 1842. V. 68

STURGEON, MARY
Michael Field. London: 1922. V. 73

STURGEON, THEODORE
More than Human. New York: 1978. V. 69
Sturgeon's West. Garden City: 1973. V. 71

STURGEON, WILLIAM
A Course of Twelve Elementary Lectures on Galvanism. London: 1843. V. 69

STURGES, JOCK
Jock Sturges: New Work 1996-2000. New York: 2000. V. 68

STURGIS, EDITH BARNES
My Busy Days; A Child's Verse. New York: 1908. V. 70

STURM, CHRISTOPHER CHRISTIAN
Reflections on the Works of God in Nature and Providence. London: 1805. V. 68

STURMEY, HENRY
The Cyclist Year Book for 1894. London: 1894. V. 69
The Cyclist Year Book for 1895. London: 1895. V. 69

STURO, ALFRED
The Batheaston Parnassus Fairs, a Manuscript Identified. San Francisco: 1936. V. 72

STURT, CHARLES
Two Expeditions into the Interior of Southern Australia, During the Years 1828, 1829, 1830 and 1831.... London: 1834. V. 71

STURT, GEORGE
The Journals. London: 1967. V. 70; 72

STUTZMAN, S. P.
The Horseman's Guide and Complete Farrier. Chillicothe: 1857. V. 68

STYFFE, KNUT
The Elasticity, Extensibility, and Tensile Strength of Iron and Steel. London: 1869. V. 68

STYLES, JOHN
Memoirs of the Life of the Right Honourable George Canning. London: 1828. V. 71

STYLES, SHOWELL
The Climber's Bedside Book. London: 1968. V. 69
First on the Summits. London: 1970. V. 69
The Moated Mountain. London: 1955. V. 69
The Mountaineer's Week-End Book. London: 1960. V. 69
Mountains of the Midnight Sun. London: 1954. V. 69
On Top of the World. London: 1967. V. 69

STYRON, WILLIAM
Admiral Robert Penn Warren and The Snows of Winter. Winston-Salem: 1978. V. 73
The Confessions of Nat Turner. New York: 1967. V. 68; 69; 70; 72; 73
Grateful Words About F. Scott Fitzgerald. 1997. V. 71
In the Clap Shack. New York: 1973. V. 71; 73
Inheritance of Night. Durham: 1993. V. 68
Lie Down in Darkness. Indianapolis: 1951. V. 68; 73
Lie Down in Darkness. Watertown: 1985. V. 71
Set This House on Fire. New York: 1960. V. 68; 70; 71; 72
Sophie's Choice. New York: 1973. V. 73
Sophie's Choice. Franklin Center: 1979. V. 73
Sophie's Choice. London: 1979. V. 73
Sophie's Choice. New York: 1979. V. 68; 69; 71; 72; 73
This Quiet Dust and Other Writings. New York: 1982. V. 68; 70; 71; 73
A Tidewater Morning. New York: 1982. V. 68
A Tidewater Morning. New York: 1993. V. 68; 72

SUCKLING, JOHN
A Ballad Upon a Wedding. London: 1927. V. 71
A Ballad Upon a Wedding. Waltham St. Lawrence: 1927. V. 68; 72
Fragmenta Aurea. London: 1646. V. 70; 71; 73
The Works. Dublin: 1766. V. 69; 72; 73
The Works. London: 1770. V. 70

SUCKOW, RUTH
The Folks. New York: 1934. V. 68

SUDAN Almanac 1912. London: 1912. V. 72

SUDERMANN, HERMANN
The Mad Professor. New York: 1928. V. 70
The Wife of Steffen Tromholt. New York: 1929. V. 71

SUDHOFF, KARL
Essays in the History of Medicine. New York: 1926. V. 68; 70; 71

SUE, EUGENE
The Refugees of Martinique. London: 1890?. V. 68

SUETONIUS TRANQUILLUS, GAIUS
XII Caesares. Lvgdvni;: 1558. V. 71

SUFFOLK, EDWARD HOWARD, 8TH EARL OF
Miscellanies in Prose and Verse, by a Person of Quality. London: 1725-1724. V. 70

THE SUFFOLK Garland; or, a Collection of Poems, Songs, Tales, Ballads, Sonnets and Elegies. Ipswich: 1818. V. 68; 71

SUFFOLK & BERKSHIRE, EARL OF
The Encyclopaedia of Sport. 1897. V. 69; 70; 72; 73

SUFLING, ERNEST R.
English Church Brasses From the 13th to the 17th Century. New York: 1910. V. 72

SUGDEN, EDWARD B.
A Practical Treatise of the Law of Vendors and Purchasers of Estates. Philadelphia: 1807. V. 68; 71

SUGG, MARIE JENNY
The Art of Cooking by Gas. London: 1890. V. 68

SUGG, WILLIAM T.
The Domestic Uses of Coal Gas, as Applied to Lighting, Cooking and Heating, Ventilation.... London: 1884. V. 69
Modern Street Lighting. London: 1887. V. 69

SUIDA, W. E.
Raphael. New York: 1948. V. 73

SUKENICK, RONALD
Up. New York: 1968. V. 72

SULEIMAN, HAMID
Miniatures of Babur-Nama. Tashkent: 1970. V. 72

SULLINS, D.
Recollections of an Old Man: Seventy Years in Dixie 1827-1897. Bristol: 1910. V. 73

SULLIVAN, BELLE SHAFER
The Unvanishing Navajos. Philadelphia: 1938. V. 69

SULLIVAN, EDMUND J.
The Kaiser's Garland. London: 1915. V. 70

SULLIVAN, FRANCIS STOUGHTON
An Historical Treatise on the Feudal Law, and the Constitutions and Laws of England, with a Commentary on Magna Charta and Necessary Illustrations of Many of the English Statutes. London: 1772. V. 68

SULLIVAN, FRANK S.
A History of Meade County, Kansas. Topeka: 1916. V. 71

SULLIVAN, JACK
Adios Old West. Cleveland: 1923. V. 72

SULLIVAN, JOHN
Letters and Papers of....Continental Army. Concord: 1930-1939. V. 70

SULLIVAN, JOHN B.
Life and Adventures of Broncho John- His First Trip Up The Trail By Himself. Valparaiso, IN. V. 71

SULLIVAN, JOHN L.
Report, on the Origin and Increase of the Paterson Manufactories, and the Intended Diversion of their Waters by the Morris Canal Company.... Paterson: 1828. V. 73

SULLIVAN, JOHN T.
Report of Historical and Technical Information Relating to the Problem of Inter-oceanic Communciation by Way of the American Isthmus. Washington: 1883. V. 70

SULLIVAN, LEON H.
Build Brother Build. Philadelphia: 1969:. V. 72

SULLIVAN, LOUIS
An Autobiography of an Idea. New York: 1926. V. 72
A System of Architectral Ornament. Chicago: 1964. V. 68; 69

SULLIVAN, MAURICE S.
Jedediah Smith, Trader and Trailbreaker. New York: 1936. V. 73
The Travels of Jedediah Smith.... Santa Ana: 1934. V. 68; 70; 73

SULLIVAN, ROBERT
A Dictionary of Derivations; or, an Introduction to Etymology; on a New Plan. Dublin: 1834. V. 70

SULLIVAN, VIRGINIA
Chaperoned. New York: 1939. V. 71

SULLIVAN, W. J.
Twelve Years in the Saddle for Law and Order on the Frontier of Texas. New York: 1966. V. 69

SULLIVANT, WILLIAM S.
The Musci and Hepaticae of the United States East of the Mississippi River. New York: 1856. V. 71; 73

SULLY, MAXIMILIEN DE BETHUNE, DUC DE
Memoires. London: 1745. V. 72

SULZBERGER, C. L.
The Resistentialists. New York: 1962. V. 70

SUMMER Rambles. London/Liverpool. V. 70

SUMMER, WILLIAM
Annual Catalogue of Southern and Acclimated Fruit Trees, Evergreens, Roses, Grape Vines, Rare Shrubs, &c. Columbia: 1860. V. 71
Descriptive Catalogue of Southern and Acclimated Fruit Trees, Evergreens, Roses, Grape Vines, Ornamental Trees, Shrubs &c. Columbia: 1861. V. 71

SUMMERHAYES, MARTHA
Vanished Arizona. Philadelphia: 1908. V. 72
Vanished Arizona. Salem: 1911. V. 71

SUMMERS, JAMES
The Rudiments of the Chinese Language with Dialogues, Exercises and a Vocabulary. London: 1864. V. 70; 72

SUMMERS, MONTAGUE
Covent Garden Drollery. 1927. V. 68
Covent Garden Drollery. London: 1927. V. 73
The History of Witchcraft and Demonology. London: 1926. V. 73
Malleus Maleficarum. London: 1928. V. 68
A Popular History of Witchcraft. London: 1937. V. 71
The Vampire in Europe. 1929. V. 68
Witchcraft and Black Magic. London: 1946. V. 68

SUMMERS, RICHARD
Vigilante: a Novel of San Francisco in the Lusty Fifties. New York: 1959. V. 70

SUMMERSETT, HENRY
Mad Man of the Mountain. London: 1799. V. 73

SUMMERSIDE, THOMAS
Anecdotes, Reminiscences and Conversations, of and with the Late George Stephenson, Father of Railways, Characteristically Illustrative of His Adroitness, Sarcasm, Benevolence and Intrepidity. London: 1878. V. 68

SUMMERSON, JOHN
Georgian London. London: 1945. V. 71

SUMNER, ANN
Luxury Sweetheart. New York: 1929. V. 69

SUMNER, CHARLES
Euology on Abraham Lincoln. Boston: 1865. V. 70
The Promises of the Declaration of Independence. Boston: 1865. V. 69
Speech of Hon. Charles Sumner, of Massachusetts, ont he Cession of Russian America to the United States. Washington: 1867. V. 71

SUMNER, DAVID
Alpine Country of the West. Portland: 1977. V. 69
Rocky Mountains. Portland: 1975. V. 69

SUMNER, L.
Birds and Mammals of the Sierra with Records from Sequoia and Kings Canyon National Parks. Berkeley: 1953. V. 73

THE SUN Princess Fairy Stories. London: 1930. V. 73

SUNDAY Reading for Good Children. 1865. V. 72

SUNDAY, WILLIAM E.
Gah Dah Gwa Shee. Pryor: 1953. V. 69

SUNDER, JOHN E.
Bill Sublette: Mountain Man. Norman: 1959. V. 70; 72; 73
The Fur Trade On the Upper Missouri 1840-1865. Norman: 1965. V. 71

SUNDERLAND, CHARLES SPENCER, 3RD EARL OF
Bibliotheca Sunderlandiana. Sale Catalogue.... London: 1881. V. 70

SUNDSTROEM, EDWARD S.
The Adrenal Cortex in Adaptation to Altitude, Climate and Cancer. Berkeley: 1942. V. 68
Studies on Adaptation of Man to High Altitudes. Berkeley: 1919. V. 72

A SUNNY Year Book for Sunny Children. Chicago: 1920. V. 71; 73

SUNSHINE on Daily Paths; or the Revelation of Beauty and Wonder in Common Things. Philadelphia: 1854. V. 68

SUPER, R. H.
The Publication of Landor's Works. London: 1954. V. 72

SURI, MANIL
The Death of Vishnu. New York: 2001. V. 69; 71; 72

THE SURPRISING, Unheard of and Never-to-be Surpassed Adventures of Young Munchausen. London: 1865. V. 71

SURTEES, ROBERT SMITH
The Analysis of the Hunting Field. 1846. V. 68; 70
The Analysis of the Hunting Field. 1903. V. 69
The Analysis of the Hunting Field. 1923. V. 73
Ask Mama. London: 1857-1858. V. 69; 72
Ask Mama. London: 1858. V. 73
Ask Mama. London: 1870. V. 71
Handley Cross; Hawbuck Grange; Plain or Ringlets? Mr. Sponge's Sporting Tour. Ask Mama. London: 1890. V. 68
Handley Cross, or Mr. Jorrock's Hunt. London: 1853-1854. V. 69
Hillingdon Hall. 1888. V. 68
Hillingdon Hall. London: 1888. V. 72
Hillingdon Hall. New York: 1931. V. 71
Hillingdon Hall. Mr. Facey Romford's Hounds. Mr. Sponge's Sporting Tour. Jorrock's Jaunts and Jollities. Plain or Ringlets. Handley Cross. Ask Mamma. V. 68
Hunting with Mr. Jorrocks. London: 1956. V. 72
Hunts with Jorrocks. London: 1908. V. 73
Jorrock's Jaunts and Jollities.... London: 1843. V. 69
Mr. Facey Romford's Hounds. London: 1864-1865. V. 69

SURTEES, ROBERT SMITH.
Mr. Sponge's Sporting Tour. London: 1860. V. 69

SURTEES, ROBERT SMITH
Mr. Sponge's Sporting Tour. 1888. V. 68
Soapey Sponge's Spoiting Tour. London: 1893. V. 68

SURVEY OF LONDON
Volume II. The Parish of Chelsea. Part III. London: 1921. V. 71
Volume VI. The Parish of Hammersmith. London: 1915. V. 71
Volume XIII. The Parish of St. Margaret, Westminster, Part II. Neighbourhood of Whitehall. Volume I. London: 1930. V. 71
Volume XIV. The Parish of St. Margaret, Westminster, Part III. (Neighbourhood of Whitehall, Volume II). London: 1931. V. 71
Volume XV. The Parish of All Hallows Barking. London: 1934. V. 71
SURVEY of London. London: 1900-2000. V. 73
Volume XXXV. The Theatre Royal Drury Lane and Royal Opera House Covent Garden. London: 1972. V. 71
Volume XXXVI. The Parish of St. Paul Covent Garden. London: 1970. V. 71
Volume XXXVII. Northern Kensington. London: 1973. V. 71
Volume XXXVIII. The Museums Area of South Kensington and Westminster. London: 1975. V. 71
Volume XL. The Grosvenor Estate in Mayfair, Part II. The Buildings. London: 1980. V. 71
Volume XLV. Knightsbridge. London: 2000. V. 71

A SURVEY of the National Debts, the Sinking Fund, the Civil List, and the Annual Supplies; Giving a Clear and Impartial Account of Our Present State with Regard to Publick Money. London: 1745. V. 72

SUSANN, JACQUELINE
Valley of the Dolls. New York: 1966. V. 69

SUSANNIS DE UTINO, MARQUARDUM DE
Tractatus De Iudaeis et Aliis Infidelibus Circa Concernentia Originem Contractuum.. Venice: 1558. V. 72

SUSKIND, PATRICK
Das Parfum. (Perfume). Zurich: 1985. V. 68
Perfume: the Story of a Murder. New York: 1986. V. 68; 70

SUSSEX Parish Churches &c. Specimens of Church Architecture Including Doorways, Windows, Fonts, Effigies &c. from the Original Etchings by a Local Artist. Brighton: 1874. V. 70

SUSUI, GIOVANNI BATTISTA
I Tre Libris...Della Inguistitia Del Duello, et Di Color, che Lo Permettono. Venice: 1558. V. 69

SUTCLIFF, ROSEMARY
The Silver Branch. London: 1957. V. 69
Sword at Sunset. London: 1963. V. 69
Sword at Sunset. New York: 1963. V. 70

SUTCLIFFE, HALLIWELL
My Moor & Fell in West Yorkshire: Landscapes and Langsettle Lore from West Yorkshire. London: 1899. V. 73

SUTHERLAND, ALEXANDER
Supplement to the Catalogue of the Sutherland Collection. London: 1838. V. 70

SUTHERLAND, DOUGLAS
Tried and Valiant. London: 1972. V. 70; 71; 72
The Yellow Earl. London: 1965. V. 70; 71

SUTHERLAND, JAMES
The Adventures of an Elephant Hunter. London: 1912. V. 71

SUTHERLAND, JOAN
Onslaught. New York: 1928. V. 69; 72

SUTHERLAND, WILLIAM
Handbook of Hardy Herbaceous and Alpine Flowers. London: 1871. V. 72

SUTHERLAND, WILLIAM GEORGE
Stencilling for Craftsmen.... Manchester: 1925. V. 68

SUTNAR, LADISLAV
Design. A-D. Gallery, New York Exhibition Jan 10-28,. 1947. V. 72

SUTRO, THEODORE
The Sutro Tunnel Company and Sutro Tunnel; Property, Income, Prospects and Pending Litigation: Report to the Stockholders. New York: 1887. V. 73

SUTTER, JOHANN AUGUST
The Diary of Johann August Sutter. San Francisco: 1932. V. 71
New Helvetia Diary; A Record of Events Kept By.... San Francisco: 1939. V. 71
Pioneers of the Scaramento. San Francisco: 1953. V. 69

SUTTER, JOHN A.
New Helvetia Diary. San Francisco: 1939. V. 70

SUTTON, ADAH LOUISE
The Teddy Bears. Akron: 1907. V. 72

SUTTON, ALFRED M.
Boardwork or the Art of Wigmaking. London: 1921. V. 71; 72

SUTTON, ALLAN
American Record Labels and Companies. Denver: 2000. V. 71; 72
Pseudonums on American Records (1892-1942). Denver: 2001. V. 71

SUTTON, AMOS
Hymns of the Divine Worship in the Oriya Language. Cuttack: 1844. V. 71

SUTTON, B. C.
The Coelomycetes. Kew: 1980. V. 73

SUTTON, D. A.
A Revision of the Tribe Antirrhineae. Oxford: 1988. V. 72

SUTTON, FRED E.
Hands Up! Stories of the Six-Gun Fighters of the Old West. Indianapolis: 1927. V. 70; 72; 73

SUTTON, R. L.
An African Holiday. St. Louis: 1924. V. 72
The Long Trek. 1930. V. 69

SUTTON, REMAR
Boiling Rock. New York: 1991. V. 71

SUTTON, S. L.
The Biology of Terrestrial Isopods. Oxford: 1984. V. 73

SUTTON MANNERS, D.
Black God. New York: 1934. V. 70

SUVATTI, C.
Fauna of Thailand. Bangkok: 1950. V. 69

SUYIN, HAN
A Many Splendoured Thing. London: 1942. V. 71
A Many Splendoured Thing. London: 1952. V. 70

SUYS, F. T.
Palais Massimi a Rome, Plans, Coupes, Elevations, Profiles, Voutes, Plafonds.... Paris: 1818. V. 68

SVEND WOHLERT, INC.
Danish Furniture. San Francisco: 1962. V. 68

SVETLOV, VALERIEN
Thamar Karsavina. 1922. V. 68

SVEVO, ITALO
The Hoax. New York: 1930. V. 69
The Nice Old Man and the Pretty Girl and Other Stories. London: 1930. V. 72

SWAAN, WIM
The Gothic Cathedral. London: 1969. V. 68; 69

SWADOS, FELICE
Reform School Girl (House of Fury). Chicago: 1948. V. 69

SWAIN, JOSEPH
Redemption, a Poem in Five Books. Charleston: 1819. V. 70; 73

SWAINSON, W.
The Natural History of Fishes, Amphibians and Reptiles. 1838-1839. V. 72; 73

SWALLOW, ALLAN
The Wild Bunch. Denver: 1966. V. 69

SWALLOW, G. C.
Geological Report of the Country Along the Line of the South-Western Branch of the Pacific Railroad, State of Missouri. St. Louis: 1859. V. 68

SWAMMERDAM, JAN
Bybel der Natuure...Biblia Naturae; Sive Historia Insectorum in Classes Certais Redacta.... London: 1758. V. 70

SWAN, ABRAHAM
The British Architect, or the Builder's Treasury of Stair Cases.... London: 1745. V. 70
The British Architect; or the Builder's Treasury of Stair-Cases.... London: 1858. V. 68

SWAN, JAMES
The Northwest Coast; or, Three Years' Residence in Washington Territory. New York: 1857. V. 70

SWAN, JOHN
Explanation of an Improved Mode of Tanning; Laid Down from Practical Results; Intended to Accompany the New Invented Barktrometer.... London: 1821. V. 71

SWAN, JOHN A.
A Trip to the Gold Mines of California in 1882. San Francisco: 1960. V. 68; 73

SWAN, JOSEPH
A Demonstration of the Nerves of the Human Body. London: 1834. V. 68

SWAN, KAY
Chicky-Chick-Chick. New York: 1927. V. 70

SWANEPOEL, D. A.
Butterflies of South Africa.... Cape Town: 1953. V. 72

SWANN, H. KIRKE
Nature in Acadie. London: 1895. V. 73
A Synopsis of Accipitres (Diurnal Birds of Prey).... London: 1921-1922. V. 73
A Synopsis of the Accipitres (Diurnal Birds of Prey).... London: 1922. V. 73

SWANN, W.
The Gothic Cathedral. 1969. V. 73

SWANSON, E. B.
A Century of Oil and Gas in Books. New York: 1960. V. 70

SWANSON, ELMER
Automatic Firearm Pistols. Weekhauken: 1955. V. 73

SWANWICK, CATHERINE
Richard Coeur de Lion, a Legendary Drama. London: 187?. V. 69

SWARBRICK, JOHN
Robert Adam & His Brothers. New York: 1915. V. 72

SWARTHOUT, GLENDON
The Shootist. New York: 1975. V. 68; 70
They Came to Cordura. New York: 1958. V. 68; 69; 71

SWARTWOUT, ANNIE FERN
Missie, an Historical Biography of Annie Oakley. Blanchester: 1947. V. 69

SWARTZ, O.
Flora Indiae Occidentalis aucta Atque Illustrata sive Descriptiones Plantarum in Prodromo Recensitarum. Erlangae: 1797. V. 68; 71
Nova Genera at Species Plantarum. New York: 1962. V. 72

SWAYSLAND, W.
Familiar Wild Birds. 1901. V. 69
Familiar Wild Birds. London: 1903. V. 68

SWAYZE, GEORGE B.
Yarb and Cretine or Rising from Bonds. Boston: 1906. V. 72

SWEANY, HENRY C.
Age Morphology of Primary Tubercles. Springfield, IL: 1941. V. 71

SWEDENBORG, EMANUEL
A Treatise on the Nature of Influx, or, of the Intercourse Between the Soul and Body. Boston: 1794. V. 71

SWEDIAUR, FRANCOIS XAVIER
Practical Observations on Venereal Complaints. New York: 1788. V. 70

SWEENEY, EDWIN R.
Cochise, Chiricahua Apache Chief. Norman: 1991. V. 72

SWEENEY, J. J.
African Negro Art (Exhibiton Catalogue). New York: 1935. V. 69
Joan Miro. Fotoscop. Visual Language. New York: 1970. V. 68

SWEENEY, J. J. continued
Museum of Modern Art - Alexander Calder. New York: 1943. V. 71

SWEENEY, ROBERT L.
Frank Lloyd Wright, an Annotated Bibliography. Los Angeles: 1978. V. 68

SWEET, A. E.
On a Mexican Mustang through Texas. London. V. 69
On a Mexican Mustang through Texas. Hartford: 1883. V. 70

SWEET, CHANNING F.
A Princeton Cowboy. Colorado Springs: 1961. V. 73
A Princeton Cowboy. 1967. V. 69

SWEET, HENRY
The Student's Dictionary of Anglo-Saxon. Oxford: 1928. V. 70

SWEET, R.
The British Warblers, an Account of the Genus Sylvia.... 1823. V. 73

SWEET, ROBERT
Flora Australasica; or a Selection of Handsome of Curious Plants, Natives of New Holland and the South Sea Islands. London: 1827-1828. V. 72; 73

SWEET, WILLIAM W.
Religon on the American Frontier. New York: 1964. V. 70

SWEETMAN, LUKE D.
Back Trailing on the Open Range. Caldwell: 1951. V. 68; 71

SWEETSER, M.
The Maritimes Provinces: a Handbook for Travellers. Boston and New York: 1890. V. 73

SWENSON, MAY
To Mix With Time. New and Selected Poems. New York: 1963. V. 72

SWERLING, JO
Kibitzer. New York: 1929. V. 70

SWETE, E. H.
Flora Bristoliensis. London and Bristol: 1854. V. 69

SWETT, JANE M.
Trial of Jane M. Swett, of Kennebunk, for Homicide.... Biddeford: 1867. V. 73

SWETT, JOHN A.
A Treatise on the Diseases of the Chest; Being a Course of Lectures Delivered at the New York Hospital. New York: 1852. V. 73

SWIETEN, GERALD VON
Commentaria in Hermanni Boerhaave Aphorismos De Cognoscendis et Curandis Morbis.... Venice: 1759-1764. V. 68; 71

SWIFT, DEANE
An Essay Upon the Life, Writings and Character of Dr. John Swift. London: 1755. V. 72

SWIFT, GRAHAM
Last Orders. London: 1996. V. 68; 69; 71; 72
Last Orders. New York: 1996. V. 69; 72
Learning to Swim and Other Stories. London: 1982. V. 71; 72
Out Of This World. London: 1988. V. 72; 73
Out of This World. New York: 1988. V. 71; 73
Shuttlecock. London: 1981. V. 71
The Sweet Shop Owner. London: 1980. V. 71
Waterland. 1983. V. 73
Waterland. London: 1983. V. 69; 71

SWIFT, HELEN
My Father And My Mother. Chicago: 1937. V. 71

SWIFT, HILDEGARDE HOYT
North Star Shining. New York: 1947. V. 70

SWIFT, JONATHAN
Captain Lemuel Gullivers Reise til Kjampernes Land Brobdignack... (Gulliver's Travels). Kjobenhavn: 1830. V. 71
A Catalogue of Books Belonging to Dr. Jonathan Swift. 1988. V. 69
A Catalogue of Books Belonging to Dr. Jonathan Swift. Cambridge: 1988. V. 72
Directions to Servants. Waltham St. Lawrence: 1925. V. 70; 71; 72
Gulliver v. Liliputu. (Gulliver in Lilliput). Osveta: 1956. V. 72
Gulliver's Travels. London: 1909. V. 68
Gulliver's Travels. New York: 1909. V. 70
Gulliver's Travels. London: 1912. V. 70
Gulliver's Travels. 1919. V. 69
(Gulliver's Travels): A Voyage to Brobdingnag Made by Lemuel Gulliver in the Year MDCCII. A Voyage to Lilliput Dr. Lemuel Gulliver MDCIC. New York: 1950. V. 69
Gulliver's Travels And Selected Writings In Prose & Verse. London: 1934. V. 69; 72
The History of the Four Last Years of the Queen. London: 1758. V. 69; 72
The Letters of Jonathan Swift to Charles Ford. 1935. V. 70
Miscellaneous Poems. Waltham St. Lawrence: 1928. V. 72
Miscellanies in Prose and Verse. London: 1713. V. 72
A New Journey to Paris; Together with Some Secret Transactions Between the Fr---h K--g, and an Eng---- Gentleman. London: 1711. V. 70
The Poetical Works. London: 1853. V. 72
The Right of Precedence Between Physicians and Civilians Enquir'd Into. London: 1720. V. 71
The Select Works. London: 1823. V. 72
Selected Essays. Waltham St. Lawrence: 1925. V. 72
The Sermons of the Reverend Dr. Jonathan Swift, Dean of St. Patrick's Dublin. Glasgow: 1763. V. 70
The Swearer's Bank; or Parliamentary Security for Establishing a New Bank in Ireland.... Dublin: 1720. V. 69
A Tale of a Tub. 1704. V. 70
A Tale of a Tub. London: 1704. V. 73
A Tale of a Tub. London: 1710. V. 69; 71; 72; 73
A Tale of a Tub. London: 1711. V. 71; 72
A Tale of a Tub. London: 1760. V. 73
A Tale of a Tub. London: 1781. V. 69
A Tale of a Tub. London: 1811. V. 70
Travels into Several Remote Nations of the World. London: 1726. V. 70
Travels into Several Remote Nations of the World. London: 1727. V. 73
Travels into Several Remote Nations of the World. London: 1747. V. 73
Travels Into Several Remote Nations of the World. London: 1798?. V. 73
Travels into Several Remote Nations of the World. London: 1840. V. 68
Travels into Several Remote Nations of the World. London: 1894. V. 68
Travels into Several Remote Nations of the World. Waltham St. Lawrence: 1925. V. 70
The Travels of Lemuel Gulliver. 1929. V. 71
Verses on the Death of Doctor Swift. London: 1739. V. 73
A Voyage to Lilliput and A Voyage to Brobdingnag Made by Lemuel Gulliver. New York: 1950. V. 68; 72
Voyages du Capitaine Gulliver, en Divers Pays Eloigne's.... La Haye: 1778. V. 69
The Works. 1760-1769. V. 71
The Works. Edinburgh: 1768. V. 70; 71; 72
The Works. Dublin: 1772. V. 71
The Works. London: 1801. V. 73
Works. Edinburgh: 1824. V. 70; 72
The Works. 1864. V. 71

SWIFT, L. H.
Botanical Bibliographies. Minneapolis: 1970. V. 68; 69; 71

SWINBORNE, FREDERICK PFANDER
Gustavus Adolphus: an Historical Poem and Romance of the Thirty Years War. London: 1884. V. 68

SWINBURNE, ALGERNON CHARLES
An Appeal to England Against the Execution of the Condemned Fenians. Manchester: 1867. V. 70
Atalanta in Calydon. London: 1865. V. 71; 72
Atalanta in Calydon. London: 1923. V. 68; 71
Bothwell: a tragedy. London: 1875. V. 72
The Brothers. 1889. V. 68
Charles Dickens. London: 1913. V. 68
Chastelard; a tragedy. London: 1865. V. 72
The Hepatologia; or the Seven Against Sense.... London: 1880. V. 72
Laus Veneris. London: 1948. V. 68
Laus Veneris. Waltham St. Lawrence: 1948. V. 71
Laus Veneris. Waltham St. Lawrence: 1950. V. 70
The Letters. London: 1918. V. 72
Letters on William Morris, Omar Khayyam and Other Subjects of Interest. 1910. V. 68
Letters to Victor Hugo by Algernon Charles Swinburne. London: 1917. V. 68
Love's Cross Currents. New York and London: 1905. V. 69; 72; 73
Lucretia Borgia. London: 1942. V. 68
Lucretia Borgia. Waltham St. Lawrence: 1942. V. 71
Note of an English Republican on the Muscovite Crusade. London: 1876. V. 68; 70; 72
A Note on Charlotte Bronte. London: 1877. V. 70
Ode on the Proclamation of the French Republic, September 4th 1870. London: 1870. V. 72
Pasiphae. London: 1950. V. 70
Pasiphae. Waltham St. Lawrence: 1950. V. 70; 72
Poems and Ballads. London: 1866. V. 69; 70; 71; 72
Poems and Ballads. London: 1889. V. 72
Poems and Ballads. Second Series. London: 1878. V. 72
Poems and Ballads. Third Series. London: 1889. V. 72
The Poetical Works. London: 1904. V. 71
Posthumous Poems. London: 1917. V. 71
The Queen Mother. Rosamond. London: 1860. V. 72
Rondeaux Parisiens. London: 1917. V. 68
Selected Poems. New York: 1928. V. 73
Selections from A. C. Swinburne. London: 1919. V. 73
The Sisters; a Tragedy. London: 1892. V. 72
A Song of Italy. London: 1867. V. 71
Songs Before Sunrise. London: 1871. V. 72
Songs Before Sunrise. London: 1909. V. 68; 69; 72
Songs of the Springtides. London: 1880. V. 71
The Springtide of Life. London: 1918. V. 68; 71
The Springtide of Life. London: 1925. V. 73
Wearieswa A Ballad. 1917. V. 68
William Blake. A Critical Essay. London: 1868. V. 73
A Year's Letters. Portland: 1901. V. 68

SWINBURNE, HENRY
A Briefe Treatise of Testaments and Last Willes, very Profitable to be Vnderstood of all the Subjects of this Realme of England.... London: 1611. V. 70
A Briefe Treatise of Testaments and Last Wils, Very Profitable to be Understood of all the Subjects of this Realme of England.... London: 1640. V. 70

SWINBURNE, JAMES
Population and the Social Problem. London: 1924. V. 71

SWINDELL, JOHN GEORGE
Rudimentary Treatise on Well-Digging, Boring and Pump-Work.... 1860. V. 71

SWINDEN, TOBIAS
An Enquiry into the Nature and Place of Hell. London: 1714. V. 68

SWINDLER, D. R.
Comparative Primate Biology. Volume I. Systematics, Evolution and Anatomy. New York: 1986. V. 72

SWINEY, G. C.
Historical Records of the 32nd (Cornwall) Light Infantry, Now the 1st Battalion Duke of Cornwall's L.I., from the Formation of the Regiment in 1702 down to 1892. London: 1893. V. 72

SWINGLE, CALVIN F.
Modern Locomotive Engineering with Questions and Answers. Chicago: 1908. V. 70

SWINGLER, W. H.
Painting for the Million and Property Owner's Companion of Useful Information. London: 1878. V. 68

SWINNERTON, FRANK
A Brood of Ducklings. Garden City: 1928. V. 71

SWINNERTON, JIMMY
Hosteen, Crochetty Or How a Good Heart Was Born. Palm Desert: 1965. V. 68

SWINTON, ALAN A. CAMPBELL
The Principles and Practice of Electric Lighting. London: 1884. V. 69

SWINTON, ARCHIBALD
Report of the Trial of Alexander Humphreys or Alexander, claiming the Title of Earl of Stirling, Before the High Court of Justiciary at Edinburgh, for the Crime of Forgery. Edinburgh: 1839. V. 72

SWINTON, G.
Sculpture of the Eskimo. Boston: 1972. V. 69
Sculpture of the Eskimo. London: 1972. V. 69; 72

SWINTON, JOHN
A Momentous Question. Philadelphia: 1895. V. 68
Striking for Life. Labor's Side of the Labor Question. 1894. V. 71

SWIRE, HERBERT
The Voyage of the Challenger. A Personal Narrative o the Historic Circumnavigation of the Globe in the Years 1872-1876. London: 1938. V. 68; 73

SWISTER, JAMES
How I Know Or Sixteen Years Eventful Experience. Cinncinnati: 1880. V. 71

SWITZER, S. L.
A Trolley Ride through Story Land. Chicago: 1915. V. 69

SWITZER, STEPHEN
An Introduction to a General System of Hydrostaticks and Hydraulicks, Philosophical and Practical. London: 1729. V. 72

SYDENHAM, THOMAS
Dissertatio Epistolaris ad Speclatissimum Dochissimumq: Virum Gulielmum Cole.... London: 1682. V. 68; 70
Dr. Sydenham's Compleat Method of Curing Almost all Diseases, and Description of their Symptoms to which are Now Added. London: 1695. V. 68; 70
The Entire Works. London: 1742. V. 72; 73
The Entire Works. London: 1769. V. 72
Opera Medica: Editio Novissima Variis Variorum.... Venetiis: 1735. V. 68
The Whole Works.... London: 1717. V. 73

SYDNEY HARBOUR BRIDGE ADVISORY BOARD
Report on Designs and Tenders Admitted in Connection with the Proposed Bridge Over Sydney Harbour to Connect Sydney with North Sydney. New South Wales: 1903. V. 68

SYKES, ARTHUR ASHLEY
A Second Letter to the Reverend Dr. Sherlock, Being a Reply to His Answer &c. London: 1717. V. 73

SYKES, CHRISTOPHER
Answer to Question 33. London: 1948. V. 72
High-Minded Murder. London: 1944. V. 72

SYKES, ELLA
Through Deserts and Oases of Central Asia. London: 1920. V. 71

SYKES, GEORGE
Handrailing Made Easy; or the Joiners' Practical Guide to Handrailing.... Kendal: 1886. V. 71

SYKES, GODFREY
A Westerly Trend...Being a Voracious Chronicle of More that Sixty Years of Joyous Wanderings, Mainly in Search of Space and Sunshine. Tucson: 1944. V. 69

SYKES, MARK MASTERMAN
A Catalogue of the Highly Valuable Collection of Prints, the Property of the Late Sir Mar Masterman Sykes. London: 1824. V. 71

SYKES, PERCY
A History of Afghanistan. London: 1940. V. 71
The Quest for Cathay. London: 1936. V. 71

SYLTHE, R. MARGARET
The Art of Illustration 1750-1900. London: 1970. V. 72

SYLVESTER, CHARLES
The Philosophy of Domestic Economy, as Exemplified in the Mode of Warming, Ventilating, Washing, Drying and Cooking and Various Arrangements Contributing to the Comfort and Convenience of Domestic Life.... Nottingham: 1819. V. 70

SYLVESTER, CHARLES H.
Journeys through Bookland. Chicago: 1913. V. 73
Manny and Co. A Christmas Story. Chicago: 1913. V. 73

SYME, JAMES
Contributions to the Pathology and Practice of Surgery. Edinburgh: 1848. V. 69
Excision with the Scapula. Edinburgh: 1864. V. 69
Observations on Clinical Surgery. Edinburgh: 1861. V. 69
On Diseases of the Rectum. Edinburgh: 1846. V. 69
On Stricture of the Urethra and Fistula in Perineo. Edinburgh: 1849. V. 69

SYMINGTON, ANDREW JAMES
Pen and Pencil Sketches of Faroe and Iceland with an Appendix.... London: 1862. V. 68

SYMINGTON, J.
In a Bengal Jungle. 1935. V. 72

SYMINGTON, J. A.
Bibliography of the Works of All Members of the Bronte Family and of Bronteana. 2000. V. 68; 70
Some Unpublished Letters of Walter Scott From the Collection in the Brotherton Library. Oxford: 1932. V. 71

SYMINGTON, JOHNSON
An Atlas of Skiagrams Illustrating the Development of the Teeth With Explantory Text. London: 1908. V. 68

SYMMONS, EDWARD
A Vindicaiton of King Charles; or, a Loyal Subjects Dury. 1648. V. 72

SYMON, J. D.
The Renaissance and Its Makers. London: 1913. V. 72

SYMONDS, ARTHUR
Notes on Joseph Conrad. London: 1926. V. 68

SYMONDS, EMILY MORSE
At John Murray's 1843-1892. London: 1932. V. 69; 72
Little Memoirs of the Eighteenth Century. New York: 1901. V. 72

SYMONDS, JOHN
The Great Beast. London: 1971. V. 70
Remarks Upon an Essay, Intituled, The History of the Colonization of the Free States of Antiquity.... London: 1778. V. 68

SYMONDS, JOHN ADDINGTON
The Autobiography of Benventuo Cellini. Garden City: 1946. V. 69
The Escorial. A Prize Poem Recited in the Theatre Oxford June 20, 1860. Oxford: 1860. V. 72
Fragilia Labilia.... London: 1884. V. 72
The Life of Benvenuto Cellini. London: 1888. V. 72
The Life Of Michangelo Buonarroti. London: 1893. V. 70; 72
Our Life in the Swiss Highlands. London: 1892. V. 69; 72
A Problem in Modern Ethics.... London: 1896. V. 69
Renaissance in Italy. London: 1897-1904. V. 73
Sir Philip Sidney. London and New York: 1886. V. 69

SYMONDS, R. W.
Masterpieces Of English Furniture and Clocks. London: 1940. V. 72
Old English Walnut and Lacquer Furniture.... London: 1923. V. 68

SYMONDS, ROBERT WEMYSS
Thomas Tompion. His Life and Work. London: 1951. V. 73

SYMONDS, W. S.
Records of the Rocks, or, Notes on the Geology, Natural History and Antiquities of North and South Wales, Devon and Cornwall. London: 1872. V. 72

SYMONS, A. J. A.
An Anthology of Nineties Verse. London: 1928. V. 70
A Bibliography of the First Editions of Books by William Butler Yeats. London: 1924. V. 70
An Episode in the Life of the Queen of Sheba. London: 1929. V. 71
H. M. Stanley. London: 1933. V. 68
The Quest for Corvo. London: 1934. V. 71; 72
The Quest for Corvo. London: 1952. V. 71

SYMONS, ARTHUR
Dante Gabriel Rossetti. Paris: 1909. V. 68
An Introduction to the Study of Browning. London: 1886. V. 68
An Introduction to the Study of Browning. London: 1906. V. 71
Parisian Nights: a Book of Essays. London: 1926. V. 68
The Romantic Movement in English Poetry. London: 1909. V. 69; 71
The Savoy: Illustrated Quarterly. London: 1896. V. 69; 73
Silhouettes. London: 1892. V. 70; 73
William Blake. London: 1970. V. 69

SYMONS, EDWARD
A Vindication of King Charles; or, a Loyal Subjects Duty. London: 1648. V. 70

SYMONS, G. J.
Report of the Lightning Rod Conference. London: 1882. V. 73

SYMONS, JELINGER
The Excise Laws Abridged and Digested Under their Proper Heads in Alphabetical Order.... London: 1775. V. 72

SYMONS, JULIAN
The Broken Penny. London: 1953. V. 68
Darkest Face. London: 1990. V. 68
The Modern Crime Story. Edinburgh: 1980. V. 70
The Name of Annabel Lee. London: 1983. V. 68
Playing Happy Families. London: 1994. V. 68
The Progress of a Crime. London: 1960. V. 69
The Progress Of A Crime. New York: 1960. V. 72
The Second Man - Poems. London: 1943. V. 68

SYMONS, THOMAS W.
Report of an Examination of the Upper Columbia River and the Territory in Its Vicinity. Washington: 1882. V. 71

SYMSON, WILLIAM
A New Voyage to the East Indies. London: 1715. V. 73

SYNGE, E.
Trefoil. London: 1868. V. 69

SYNGE, JOHN MILLINGTON
The Aran Islands. Dublin: 1907. V. 69
The Autobiography of J. M. Synge.... Dublin: 1965. V. 73
The Complete Works of.. 1911-1912. V. 69; 73
Deirdre of the Sorrows. New York: 1910. V. 70
A Few Personal Recollections, with Biographical Notes by John Masefield. Churchtown, Dundrum: 1915. V. 71
The Playboy of the Western World. Barre: 1970. V. 72
Queens. Mounrath, County Laois: 1986. V. 69
Riders to the Sea. 1969. V. 70
Some Letters of J. M. Synge to Lady Gregory and W. B. Yeats. 1971. V. 68
The Tinker's Wedding. 1907. V. 68

SYNGE, PATRICK M.
Plants with Personality. London: 1939. V. 70

SYNGE, WILLIAM W. FOLLETT
Tom Singleton, Dragoon and Dramatist. London: 1888. V. 68

SZABLOWSKI, JERZY
The Flemish Tapestries at Wawell Castle in Cracow, Treasures of King Sigismund Augustus Jagiello. Antwerp: 1972. V. 68

SZARKOWSKI, JOHN
Irving Penn. New York: 1984. V. 68
The Work of Atget. New York: 1981-1985. V. 70

SZECHENYI, Z.
Land of Elephants. 1935. V. 70

SZENT GYORGYI, ALBERT V.
On Oxidation, Fermentation, Vitamins, Health and Disease. Baltimore: 1939. V. 71

SZWEDZICKI, C.
Pueblo Indian Pottery. Nice: 1933. V. 69

SZWEYKOWSKI, J.
Atlas of Geographical Distribution of Spore-Plants in Poland. Series IV. Liverworts (Hepaticae). Poznan: 1962-1980. V. 72

T

TABERNAEMONTANUS, JACOBUS THEODORUS
Neuw Kreuterbuch, Mit Schonen, Kunstlichen und Leblichen Figuren Unnd Conterfeyten. Frankfurt am Mayn: 1588-1591. V. 71

TABOR, G.
Old Fashioned Gardening.... New York: 1913. V. 71

TABOR, J.
Land Surveying and Levelling for Farmers, Adapted for the Use of Schools. London: 1863. V. 70

TABOR, SILVER DOLLAR
Star of Blood. Denver: 1909. V. 68; 73

TACHARD, PERE GUY
Second Voyage du Pere Tachard et des Jesuites Envoyez par Le Roy Au Royaume de Siam. Paris: 1689. V. 71

TACITUS, CORNELIUS
Historiarum et Annalium Libri Qui Exstant, Iusti Lipsii Studio Emendati and Illustrati. Antwerp: 1574. V. 70; 72
Opera. Lvgdvni Batavorvm: 1640. V. 70
Opera Omnia. London: 1821. V. 72
Opera, Quae Exstant. Amstelodami: 1672. V. 70; 73
The Works of Cornelius Tacitus. London: 1850. V. 72

TAFFE, HENRY EDMUND
A Report of the Arguments and Judgment Upon the Demurrer, in the Case of Henry Edmund Taffe, Against the Right Hon. Wm. Downes, Lord Chief Justice of the King's Becnh, in Ireland, in Trinity, Michaelmas and Hilary Terms 1812 and 1813.... Dublin: 1815. V. 70

TAFFRAIL
Eurydice. London: 1953. V. 73
Fred Travis, A. B. London: 1939. V. 73

TAFT, L.
The History of American Sculpture. New York: 1930. V. 69; 72

TAFT, ROBERT
Photography and the American Scene. New York: 1938. V. 68; 69

TAFT, WILLIAM HOWARD
Ethics in Service. New Haven/London: 1915. V. 71
Political Issues and Outlooks. New York: 1909. V. 68

TAGG, TIMOTHY, PSEUD.
A Dialogue in Burlesque Verse, Between Parson Betty and Parson Bowman.... London: 1731. V. 69

TAGORE, RABINDRANATH
Fireflies. New York: 1929. V. 68
Gitanjali (Song Offerings). London: 1912. V. 70
Mashi and Other Stories. London: 1918. V. 71
Sacrifice and Other Plays. London: 1917. V. 71

TAIA, AGOSTINO
Descrizione del Palazzo Apostolico Vaticano. Roma: 1750. V. 70

TAIBO, PACO IGNACIO
Four Hands. New York: 1994. V. 71

THE TAILOR and the Elephant. Cincinnati: 1882. V. 71

TAINE, HIPPOLYTE ADOLPHE
English Positivism. London: 1870. V. 71
History of English Literature. London: 1877. V. 73
History of English Literature. Translated from the French by H. Van Laun. London: 1883. V. 71
History of English Literature.... London: 1890. V. 69

TAIT, J. H.
A Treatise on the Law of Scotland As Applied to the Game Laws, and Trout & Salmon Fishing. 1928. V. 71

TAKAGI, K.
Studies of the Gobioid Fishes in the Japanese Waters, on the Comparative Morphology.... 1963?. V. 73

TAKEMI, T. HASEGAWA
Herbal Medicine: Kampo, Past and Present. Tsumara Juntendo: 1985. V. 71

TAKEO CO., LTD.
Handmade Papers of the World. Tokyo: 1979. V. 72

TALBERT, B. J.
Examples of Ancient and Modern Furniture. London: 1876. V. 68

TALBOT, EDWARD ALLEN
Five Years' Residence in the Canadas: Including a Tour through Part of the United States of America in the Year 1823. London: 1824. V. 73

TALBOT, ELEANOR W.
My Lady's Casket of Jewels and Flowers for Her Adorning. Boston: 1885. V. 70
Wander-Eyes and What For. London: 1880. V. 70

TALBOT, FRANCIS X.
Saint Among the Hurons: the Life of Jean de Brebeuf. New York: 1949. V. 73

TALBOT, FREDERICK A.
Moving Pictures How They Are Made and Worked. Philadelphia: 1914. V. 69

TALBOT, HAKE
The Hangman's Handyman. 1942. V. 73

TALBOT, P. A.
In the Shadow of the Bush. London: 1912. V. 69
Life in Southern Nigeria, the Magic, Beliefs and Customs of the Ibibio Tribe.... London: 1923. V. 69

TALBOT, THEODORE
The Journals of Theodore Talbot 1843 and 1849-1852. Portland: 1931. V. 69

TALCOTT, DUDLEY VAILL
North of North Cape. The Arctic Voyages of The "Norkap II". London: 1936. V. 72

THE TALE of Bridget and the Bees. Poughkeepsie: 1935. V. 68

THE TALE of Peter Rabbit and Other Stories. Kenosha: 1946. V. 70

THE TALE of Peter Rabbit Animated!. New York: 1943. V. 70

THE Tale of Piggy the Pig. London: 1947. V. 71

TALES for Tinies. London: 1910. V. 72

TALES of a Parrot; Done into English.... London: 1792. V. 70

TALES of Heroism, and Record of Strange and Wonderful Adventures, Being a Collection and Register of Deeds of Bravery, Heroism and Devotion.... London: 1847. V. 69

TALES of Teddy (Bear). London: 1920. V. 72

TALFOURD, THOMAS NOON
Final Memorials of Charles Lamb.... London: 1848. V. 72
Three Speeches Delivered in the House of Commons in Favour of the Measure for an Extension of Copyright. London: 1840. V. 70
Vacation Rambles. London: 1851. V. 69
Vacation Rambles and Thoughts. London: 1845. V. 70; 72

TALIAFERRO, HARDEN E.
Fisher's River (North Carolina) Scenes and Characters. New York: 1859. V. 70

TALKING Up a Storm. Voices of the New West. Lincoln: 1994. V. 68; 72

TALKINGTON, HENRY L.
History of The Nez Perce Reservation and The City of Lewiston, Idaho in Idaho State Historical Society - Sixteen Biennial Report 1937-1938. Boise: 1938. V. 72

THE TALL Book of Nursery Rhymes. New York: 1944. V. 70

THE TALL T. New York: 1957. V. 73

TALLANT, ROBERT
Voodoo in New Orleans. New York: 1946. V. 69

TALLENT, A. E.
Black Hills or Last Hunting Ground of The Dakotahs. St. Louis: 1899. V. 72
Black Hills Or Last Hunting Grounds of The Dakotahs. 1974. V. 72

TALLENT, ANNIE D.
First Women In The Black Hills. Mitchell, SD: 1923. V. 72

TALLEY, MANSFIELD KIRBY
Portrait Painting in England: Studies in the Technical Literature Before 1700. 1981. V. 73

TALLEYRAND PERIGORD, CHARLES MAURICE DE, PRINCE DE BENEVENT
Memoir Concerning the Commercial Relations of the United States with England. London: 1806. V. 68

TALLIS, JOHN
British India. London: 1851. V. 72
London Street Views 1838-1840. Together with the revised and enlarged views of 1847. London: 1969. V. 71

TALLIS'S History and Description of the Crystal Palace and the Exhibition of the World's Industry in 1851. London and New York. V. 68

TALMAGE, T. DE WITT
More Crumbs Swept Up. London: 1876. V. 68

TALMUD
The Living Talmud: The Wisdom of the Fathers. New York: 1960. V. 69

TALWAR, P. K.
Commercial Sea Fishes of India. Calcutta: 1984. V. 73

TAMAS, ISTVAN
Sergeant Nikola. New York: 1942. V. 69

TAMBIMUTTU, M. J.
Fetscrift for Marianne Moore's Seventieth Birthday. London: 1966. V. 71
Out of This War. 1941. V. 71
Out of This War. London: 1941. V. 68

TAMMEN, H. H.
Gems of Colorado Scenery. Denver: 1905. V. 72

TAMPLIN, R. W.
Lectures on the Nature and Treatment of Deformities, Delivered at the Royal Orthopaedic Hospital Bloomsbury Square. Philadelphia: 1846. V. 73

TAMURA, T.
Art of the Landscape Garden in Japan. Tokyo: 1936. V. 69; 71; 73

TAN, AMY
The Bonesetter's Daughter. New York: 2001. V. 68
The Hundred Secret Senses. Franklin Center: 1995. V. 72
The Hundred Secret Senses. New York: 1995. V. 68; 72
The Joy Luck Club. New York: 1989. V. 68; 69; 70; 71; 72
The Kitchen God's Wife. New York: 1991. V. 69
The Moon Lady. New York: 1992. V. 69; 70; 72; 73

TANAKA, S.
Figures and Descriptions of the Fishes of Japan.... Tokyo: 1935-1958. V. 73

TANGYE, DEREK
A Drake at the Door. London: 1963. V. 73
A Gull on the Roof. 1961. V. 72
Jeannie. A Love Story. 1988. V. 72
Monty's Leap. 1993. V. 72

TANGYE, RICHARD
The Rise of a Great Industry. London: 1905. V. 71

TANIZAKI, JUNICHIRO
The Makioka Sisters. New York: 1957. V. 70

TANNER, CLARA LEE
Southwest Indian Craft Arts. Tucson: 1968. V. 69
Southwest Indian Painting. Tucson: 1957. V. 69; 70
Southwest Indian Painting: a Changing Art. Tucson: 1973. V. 69; 72

TANNER, EDWIN P.
The Province of New Jersey 1664-1738. New York: 1908. V. 71

TANNER, HENRY
Successful Emigration to Canada. Ottawa: 1885. V. 73

TANNER, HUDSON C.
The Lobby and Public Men from Thurlow Weed's Time. Albany: 1888. V. 72

TANNER, J. M.
A Biographical Sketch of James Jenson. Salt Lake City: 1911. V. 69

TANNER, THOMAS HAWKES
Memoranda on Poisons. London: 1862. V. 68

TANNER, WILLIAM
The Book of Bond or Every Man His Own 007. New York: 1965. V. 69

TANNER, WILLIAM R.
Reminiscences of the War Between the States. Cowpens: 1931. V. 69; 70
Reminiscences of the War Between the States. Cowpens: 1950. V. 69

TANNING, DOROTHEA
Ouvre-Tol. Milan. V. 70

TANSILLO, LUIGI
The Nurse, a Poem. Liverpool: 1800. V. 72

TANSLEY, A. G.
The British Islands and Their Vegetation. London: 1949. V. 70

TANSWELL, JOHN
The History and Antiquities of Lambeth. London: 1858. V. 71

TAPPAN, LEWIS
Narrative of the Late Riotous Proceedings Against the Liberty of the Press in Cincinnati. Cincinnati: 1836. V. 71; 73

TAPPLY, WILLIAM G.
Death at Charity's Point. New York: 1984. V. 68; 69
The Dutch Blue Error. New York: 1984. V. 69
The Dutch Blue Error. New York: 1985. V. 69; 72

TARAVAL, SIGISMUNDO
Indian Uprising in Lower California, 1734-1737. Los Angeles: 1931. V. 72

TARBELL, IDA M.
The History of the Standard Oil Company. New York: 1904. V. 71

TARBOTON, W.
Birds of Southern Africa, the Sasol Plates Collection. Cape Town: 1994. V. 68

TARBUCK, EDWARD L.
The Builder's Practical Director or Buildings for All Classes Containing Plans, Sections and Elevations for the Erection of Cottages.... Leipzig & Dresden: 1855-1858. V. 69; 71
The Encyclopaedia of Practical Carpentry and Joinery.... London: 1857-1859. V. 68

TARDEAU, AMBROISE
Etude Medico Legale sur les Attentats aux Moeurs. Paris: 1862. V. 68

TARDY, T. C.
Hot Springs, Bath County, Virginia, With Some Account of their Medicinal Properties.... Richmond: 1871. V. 71

TARG, WILLIAM
Bibliophile in the Nursery: a Bookman's Treasury of Collector's Lore on Old and Rare Children's Books. Cleveland and New York: 1957. V. 68; 69
Bouillabaisse for Bibliophiles. Cleveland and New York: 1955. V. 70

TARKINGTON, BOOTH
Alice Adams. Garden City: 1921. V. 70
Beauty and the Jacobin. New York: 1912. V. 70
Cherry. New York: 1903. V. 70
The Fascinating Stranger and Other Stories. Garden City: 1923. V. 71; 73
The Gentleman from Indiana. New York: 1899. V. 71
Harlequin and Columbine. Garden City: 1921. V. 69
Lady Hamilton and Her Nelson. New York: 1945. V. 71; 73
The Magnificent Ambersons. Garden City: 1918. V. 69; 71
Mary's Neck. Garden City: 1932. V. 71
Monsieur Beaucaire. New York. V. 70
Monsieur Beaucaire. New York: 1900. V. 71
Presenting Lily Mars. Garden City: 1933. V. 71
Seventeen. A Tale of Youth and Summer Time and the Baxter Family, Especially William. New York & London: 1916. V. 71
The Two Vanrevels. New York: 1902. V. 70
Wanton Mally. Garden City: 1932. V. 71
Women. Garden City: 1925. V. 69
Young Mrs. Greeley. Garden City: 1929. V. 71

TARLETON, BANASTRE
A History of the Campaigns of 1780 and 1781, in the Southern Provinces of North America. Dublin: 1787. V. 70
A History of the Campaigns of 1780 and 1781 in the Southern Provinces of North America. London: 1787. V. 68; 70; 73

TARN, NATHANIEL
Collected Poems 1934-1952. 1952. V. 70

TARN, W. W.
The Treasure of the Isle of Mist. New York: 1934. V. 71

TARPON Tales: Lost Stories and Research. Sanibel Island: 1990. V. 70

TARR, RALPH S.
Alaskan Glacier Studies of the National Geographic Society in the Yakutat Bay, Prince William Sound and Lower Copper River Regions. Washington: 1914. V. 68

TARRANT, JOHN
The Clauberg Trigger. London: 1978. V. 70

TARRANT, MARGARET
The Childrens' Year. London. V. 70
The Margaret Tarrant Nursery Rhyme Book. 1944. V. 72
The Margaret Tarrant Nursery Rhyme Book. New York: 1944. V. 70
The Margaret Tarrant Story Book. London: 1951. V. 70

TARTT, DONNA
The Secret History. New York: 1992. V. 69; 72; 73

TASHLIN, FRANK
The Bear that Wasn't. New York: 1946. V. 73

TASISTRO, LOUIS FITZGERALD
Etiquette of Washington; Setting Forth the Rules to Be Observed in Social Intercourse.... Washington City: 1866. V. 68

TASKER, J.
Savage Arena. 1982. V. 68; 73

TASSE, JOSEPH
Les Canadiens de l'Quest. Montreal: 1882. V. 72

TASSIN, NICOLAS
Carte Generalle de la Geographie Royalle (and) Cartes Generales de Toutes les Pronvinces de France et D'Espagne. Paris: 1655. V. 69; 72

TASSO, TORQUATO
Aminta, Favola Boscareccia. In Venezia: 1736. V. 71
Amintas a Dramtick Pastorial Written Originally in Italian.... London: 1737. V. 73
Gerusalemme Liberata. Lyon: 1581. V. 71
La Gerusalemme Liberata. Parigi: 1771. V. 70
La Gerusalemme Liberata. Parigi: 1785. V. 71
Godfrey of Bulloigne, or the Recouerie of Jerusalem. London: 1600. V. 71
Godfrey of Bulloigne; or the recovery of Jerusalem. London: 1687. V. 72

TASSONI, ALESSANDRO
La Secchia Rapita; or, the Rape of the Bucket; an Heroi-Comical Poem in Twelve Cantos. London: 1827. V. 68; 72

TATE, ALLEN
Christ and the Unicorn. West Branch: 1966. V. 73
The Forlorn Demon. Chicago: 1953. V. 68
The Hovering Fly and Other Essays. Cummington: 1949. V. 70
Memoirs and Opinions 1926-1974. Chicago: 1975. V. 68
Poems 1922-1947. New York: 1948. V. 68
A Southern Vanguard. New York: 1947. V. 70
Stonewall Jackson. The Good Soldier. New York: 1928. V. 70
Two Conceits for the Eye to Sing, if Possible. Cummington: 1950. V. 70

TATE, CHARLES SPENCER
Pickway - a True Narrative. 1905. V. 69

TATE, JAMES
Bewitched. Iowa City: 1989. V. 73
Bewitched. Llangynog: 1989. V. 73
Cages. Poems. Iowa City: 1966. V. 69; 73
Deaf Girl Playing. Cambridge: 1970. V. 73
If It Would All Please Hurry. A Poem. Amherst: 1980. V. 69; 73
Just Shades. Tuscaloosa: 1985. V. 69; 73
The Lost Pilot. New Haven & London: 1967. V. 73
Notes of Woe. Poems. Iowa City: 1968. V. 72; 73
Worshipful Company of Fletchers. Hopewell: 1994. V. 69

TATE, THOMAS
Drawing for Schools: Containing Expositions of the Method of Teaching Drawing in Schools.... London: 1854. V. 69

TATE, WILLIAM
The Counting-House Guide to the Higher Branches of Commercial Calculations.... London: 1858. V. 71

TATHAM, CHARLES HEATHCOTE
Etching, Representing the Best Examples of Ancient Ornamental Architecture, Drawn from the Originals in Rome and Other Parts of Italy During the Years 1794, 1795 and 7196. London: 1810. V. 68; 70
Etchings, Representing the Best Examples of Grecian and Roman Architectural Ornament.... London: 1826. V. 72

TATIN, A.
Principes Raisonnes et Pratiques de la Culture; des Arbres, Arbrisseaux et Arbustes, Fruitiers, d'Ornement.... Paris: 1811. V. 70

THE TATLER. London: 1713-. V. 68

THE TATLER, or Lucubrations of Isaac Bickerstaff Esq. London: 1764. V. 69

TATTERSALL, GEORGE
The Lakes of England. London: 1836. V. 69
Tablets of an Itinerant. London: 1836. V. 71

TATTERSALL, IVAN
The Avenging Brotherhood. Chicago: 1929. V. 70

TATUM, GEORGE B.
Penn's Great Town: 250 Years of Philadelphia Architecture. 1961. V. 69
Penn's Great Town: 250 Years of Philadelphia Architecture Illustrated in Prints and Drawings. Philadelphia: 1961. V. 68

TATUM, GEORGIA LEE
Disloyalty in the Confederacy. Chapel Hill: 1934. V. 69

TATUM, STEPHEN
Inventing Billy the Kid. Albuquerque: 1982. V. 68

TAUBES, FREDERIC
Paintings and Essays on Art. New York: 1950. V. 69; 72

TAULER, JOHN
The History and Life of the Reverend Dr. John Tauler of Strasbourg: with Twenty-Five of His Own Sermons. London: 1857. V. 72

TAUNT, HENRY W.
A New Map of the River Thames, from Thames Head to London.... Oxford: 1897. V. 70
Taunt's Map of the River Thames from Oxford to London. Oxford: 1877. V. 73

TAUNT, WILLIAM HENRY EDWARD
A New Map of the River Thames from Thames Head to London, from Enitrely New Surveys Finished During the Summer of 1878. Oxford: 1879. V. 73

TAUSSIG, FREDERICK J.
Abortion Its Prevention and Treatment. St. Louis: 1912. V. 68

TAUT, BRUNO
Alpine Architektur. Folkwang: 1919. V. 72

TAUVRY, DANIEL
A Treatise of Medicines Containing an Account of Their Chymical Principles.... London: 1700. V. 70

TAVANNES, JACQUES DE SAULX, COMTE DE
Memoires de Messire Jacques de Saulx, Comte de Tavannes, Lieutenant General des Arme'es du Roy. Paris: 1691. V. 71

TAXIDERMY, or the Art of Collecting, Preparing and Mounting Objects of Natural History. London: 1823. V. 69

TAYLER, JAMES
A Practical Treatise on Fly Fishing. 1888. V. 68
Red Palmer: a Practical Treatise on Fly Fishing. 1888. V. 73

TAYLER, WILLIAM
The History of the Taxation of England with an Account of the Rise and Progress of the National Debt. London: 1853. V. 71

TAYLOR, ALBERT PIERCE
Under Hawaiian Skies. Honolulu: 1922. V. 71

TAYLOR, ALFRED SWAINE
Taylor's Principles and Practice of medical Jurisprudence. London: 1956. V. 73

TAYLOR, ALISON G.
Simeon's Bride. London: 1995. V. 72

TAYLOR, ALRUTHEUS AMBUSH
The Negro in the Reconstruction of Virginia. Washington: 1926. V. 68

TAYLOR, ANN MARTIN
Maternal Solicitude for a Daughter's Best Interests. Philadelphia: 1816. V. 68; 69; 72

TAYLOR, ANNE
Press on Regardless. New York: 1956. V. 72

TAYLOR, ARCHER
The Proverb. Cambridge: 1931. V. 73

TAYLOR, ARTHUR
Notes and Tones. Leige: 1977. V. 69; 71

TAYLOR, BAYARD
Colorado: a Summer Trip. New York: 1867. V. 68; 73
Eldorado, or, Adventures in the Path of Empire: Comprising a Voyage of California. New York: 1850. V. 71
Northern Travel. Summer and Winter Pictures of Sweden, Lapland and Norway. London: 1858. V. 68; 72

TAYLOR, BENJAMIN F.
Pictures of Life in Camp and Field. Chicago: 1875. V. 72

TAYLOR, BRIAN
The Green Avenue: The Life and Writings of Forest Reid. 1980. V. 69

TAYLOR, CHARLES
A Familiar Treatise on Perspective.... London: 1816. V. 69

TAYLOR, CHARLES BENJAMIN
May You Like It. 1823-1824. V. 73
May You Like It. London: 1823-1824. V. 68

TAYLOR, CHARLES FAYETTE
On the Mechanical Treatment of Disese of the Hip-Joint. New York: 1873. V. 71

TAYLOR, D. K
Taylor's Thrilling Tales of Texas, Being the Experience of Drew Kirksey Taylor, Ex-Texas Ranger and Peace Officer on the Border of Texas. 1929. V. 69

TAYLOR, DAWSON
The Masters All About Its History, Its Records, Its Players, Its Remarkable Course and Even More Remarkable Tournament. South Brunswick and New York: 1973. V. 73

TAYLOR, DEEMS
Walt Disney's Fantasia. New York: 1940. V. 69

TAYLOR, E. H.
Contributions to the Herpetology of Thailand. 1958. V. 73
A Taxonomic Study of the Cosmopolitan Scincoid Lizards of the Genus Eumeces.... Lawrence: 1935. V. 70; 72

TAYLOR, ELIAS
An Essay and Familiar Treatise on the Art of Drawing In Perspective, Calculated for Young Students, and to be Acquired Without a Tutor. Brighton: 1831. V. 70

TAYLOR, ELIZABETH
Angel. London: 1957. V. 72
At Mrs. Lippincote's. London: 1945. V. 73
Authentic Memoirs of Mrs. Clarke.... London: 1809. V. 69; 73
A Game of Hide-and-Seek. London: 1951. V. 72
In a Summer Season. London: 1961. V. 68
The Wedding Group. London: 1968. V. 72; 73

TAYLOR, F.
Angling in Earnest. 1969. V. 68

TAYLOR, FRANCES
Eastern Hospitals and English Nurses: the Narrative of Twelve Months' Experience in the Hospitals of Koulali and Scutari. London: 1857. V. 70

TAYLOR, FRED
Reflections of a Countryman. 1982. V. 68

TAYLOR, FREDERICK WINSLOW
The Principles of Scientific Management. New York: 1911. V. 68; 72

TAYLOR, GEOFFREY
The Absurd World of Charles Bragg. New York: 1980. V. 73
A Dash of Garlic: Sonnets and Epigrams. Warminster: 1933. V. 72
Two Poems. 1932. V. 72

TAYLOR, GEORGE H.
Paralysis and Other Affections of the Nerves: Their Cure by Vibratory and Special Movements. New York: 1871. V. 71

TAYLOR, GEORGE WATSON
The Old Hag in a Red Cloak. London: 1801. V. 70

TAYLOR, GORHAM COFFIN
Notes of Conversations with a Volunteer Officer in the United States Navy, on the Passage of the Forts Below New Orleans, April 24, 1862 and Other Points of Service on the Mississippi River During the Year. New York: 1868. V. 69

TAYLOR, H. J., MRS.
Yosemite Indians and Other Sketches. San Francisco: 1936. V. 70; 72

TAYLOR, H. M.
Anglo Saxon Architecture. Cambridge: 1965. V. 70

TAYLOR, HERBERT
The Last Illness and Decease of His Royal Highness The Duke of York; Being a Journal of Occurrences Which took Place Between the 9th of June 1826, and the 5th of January 1827. London: 1827. V. 73

TAYLOR, INA
The Edwardian Lady. 1980. V. 69

TAYLOR, ISAAC
Designs for Shop-Fronts and Door Cases. London: 1785. V. 68; 70
Saturday Evening. 1832. V. 72
Scenes in Africa, for the Amusement and Instruction of Little Tarryat-Home Travellers. London: 1820. V. 72
Scenes in Africa, from the Amusement and Instruction of Little Tarry at Home Travellers. New York: 1827. V. 70
Scenes in Asia. London: 1821. V. 71
Scenes in British Wealth, in Produce, Manufactures and Commerce. London: 1825. V. 71

TAYLOR, J.
Decorations for Parks and Gardens. London: 1810. V. 68; 70

TAYLOR, J. C.
Fritz Scholder. New York: 1982. V. 69

TAYLOR, J. E.
Flowers: their Origin, Shapes, Perfumes and Colours. London. V. 72

TAYLOR, JAMES
A View of the Money System of England, from the Conquest.... London: 1828. V. 69

TAYLOR, JANE
City Scenes, or A Peep Into London. London: 1828. V. 72
The Contributions of Q. Q to a Periodical Work; with some Pieces Not Before Published. 1826. V. 69
Essays in Rhyme on Moral and Manners. London: 1816. V. 68
Hymns For Infant Minds. London: 1840. V. 72
Little Ann and Other Poems. London: 1882. V. 69
Little Ann and Other Poems. London: 1909. V. 69

TAYLOR, JEFFREYS
Old English Sayings Newly expounded, in Prose and Verse. London: 1827. V. 71

TAYLOR, JEREMY
The Architectural Medal. London: 1978. V. 72
(Greek Letter) A Discourse of the Liberty of Prophesying Shewing the Unreasonablenes (sic) of prescribing to Other Mens Faith and the Iniquity of Persecuting Differing Opinions. London: 1647. V. 70
A Dissuasive from Popery. To the People of England and Ireland. Together with 11 Additional Letters to Persons Changed in Their Religion.... London: 1686. V. 71
A Selection from His Works. Waltham St. Lawrence: 1923. V. 71
XXV Sermons Preached at Golden Grove. (with) XXVIII Sermons Preached at Golden Grove. (with) Clerus Domini; or a Discourse of the Divine Institution, Necessity Sacredness and Separation of the Office Ministerial. 1655. V. 71
XXVIII Sermons Preached at Golden Grove; Being the Summer Half Year, Beginning on Whit-Sunday and Ending the XXV Sunday After Trinity. London: 1651. V. 69
The Whole Works. London: 1859. V. 73

TAYLOR, JOHN
All the Workes.... London: 1630. V. 68; 70; 73
Geological Essays and Sketch of the Geology of Manchester and the Neighbourhood. London: 1864. V. 72
An Inquiry Into the Principles and Policy of the Government of the United States. Fredericksburg: 1814. V. 70; 72
Monsieur Tonson. Philadelphia: 1820?. V. 68
The Old, Old, Very Old Man, or the Age and Long Life of Thomas Parr.... London: 1774. V. 70; 71
The Old, Old, Very Old Man or the Age and Long Life of Thomas Parr.... London: 1794. V. 73
Verbum Sempiternae. Aberdeen: 1908. V. 69

TAYLOR, JOSEPH HENRY
Frontier and Indian Life and Kaleidoscopic Lives. Valley City: 1932. V. 72
Kaleidoscopic Lives. A Companion Book to Frontier and Indian Life. Washburn: 1902. V. 70

TAYLOR, JOSHUA C. •
Fritz Scholder. New York: 1982. V. 71

TAYLOR, JUSTICE HURD
Joe Taylor, Barnstormer. His Travels, Troubles and Triumphs During Fifty Years in Footlight Flashes. NY: 1913. V. 71

TAYLOR, KATHERINE AMES
Lights and Shadows of Yosemite: Being a Collection of Favorite Yosemite Views. San Francisco: 1926. V. 69

TAYLOR, L.
New Mexican Furniture 1660-1940. 1989. V. 69

TAYLOR, LONN
The American Cowboy. Washington: 1983. V. 69

TAYLOR, M.
Tables of Logarithms of All Numbers, from 1 to 101000; and of the Sines and Tangents.... London: 1792. V. 68

TAYLOR, MARY G.
The Teign; and the Legend of Sir Bryan of Tor Bryan; from a Devonshire Album. Teignmouth: 1856. V. 69

TAYLOR, MARY L.
The Tiger's Claw. 1946. V. 70
The Tiger's Claw. 1956. V. 69; 73

TAYLOR, MAXWELL
Swords and Plowshares: a Memoir. New York: 1972. V. 70; 72

TAYLOR, MORRIS F.
First Mail West. Albuquerque: 1971. V. 72

TAYLOR, PAUL BARTLETT
Tippletappleteven. New York: 1931. V. 70

TAYLOR, PETER
The Collected Stories of Peter Taylor. New York: 1969. V. 68; 69; 71; 73
Happy Families Are Alike. New York: 1959. V. 69; 71
Happy Families Are All Alike. New York: 1960. V. 69; 73
In the Tennessee Country. New York: 1994. V. 71; 73
A Long Fourth and Other Stories. New York: 1948. V. 73
Miss Leonora When Last Seen. New York: 1963. V. 71
The Old Forest and Other Stories. Garden City: 1985. V. 68; 69; 70; 71; 73
The Oracle at Stoneleigh Court. New York: 1993. V. 71
A Summons to Memphis. New York: 1986. V. 68; 71; 73
Tennessee Day in St. Louis. New York: 1957. V. 71
The Widows of Thornton. New York: 1954. V. 71
A Woman of Means. London: 1950. V. 69
A Woman of Means. New York: 1950. V. 69; 73

TAYLOR, PHOEBE ATWOOD
The Cape Cod Mystery. Indianapolis: 1931. V. 73
The Deadly Sunshade. New York: 1940. V. 68; 72
Death Lights a Candle. Indianapolis: 1932. V. 69

TAYLOR, PHOEBE ATWOOD continued
Murder at the New York World's Fair. New York: 1938. V. 73

TAYLOR, R. H.
The Airedale Fairy Stories. Keighley: 1926. V. 70

TAYLOR, R. V.
The Biographia Leodiensis; or Biographical Sketches of the Worthies of Leeds and Neighbourhood. London: 1865. V. 72

TAYLOR, RACHEL
Poems. London: 1904. V. 69

TAYLOR, REX
Michael Collins. London: 1958. V. 69

TAYLOR, ROBERT
Fiddle and Bow. Chapel Hill: 1985. V. 70

TAYLOR, ROBERT H.
Authors At Work: an Address Delivered by Robert H. Taylor at the Opening Exhibition of Literary Manuscripts at the Grolier Club, Together with a Catalogue of the Exhibition by Herman W. Liebert and Facsimiles of Many of the Exhibits. New York: 1957. V. 68

TAYLOR, ROBERT LEWIS
A Journey to Matecumbe. New York: 1961. V. 71
The Travels of Jaimie McPheeters. Garden City: 1958. V. 69

TAYLOR, ROBERT W.
A Clinical Atlas of Venereal and Skin Diseases, Including Diagnosis, Prognosis and Treatment. Philadelphia: 1889. V. 68; 70; 71

TAYLOR, SAMUEL
The Arte of Angling. 2000. V. 68
Sabrina Fair. New York: 1954. V. 71

TAYLOR, T. U.
The Chisholm Trail and Other Routes. San Antonio: 1936. V. 71
Jesse Chisholm. Bandera: 1939. V. 68; 71

TAYLOR, THOMAS
A-18. 1967. V. 68
A Dissertation on the Philosophy of Aristotle, in Four Books. London: 1812. V. 73
Two Orations of the Emperor Julian; one to the Sovereign Sun and the Other to the Mother of the Gods.... London: 1793. V. 73

TAYLOR, THOMAS E.
Running the Blockade. London: 1896. V. 71

TAYLOR, THOMAS J.
A History of the Tar River Association. 1923. V. 71

TAYLOR, TOM
Ballads and Songs of Brittany. London: 1865. V. 68
A Tale of Two Cities. London: 1860. V. 70

TAYLOR, W. B. SARSFIELD
A Manual of Fresco and Encaustic Painting Containing Ample Instructions for Executing Works of These Descriptions. London: 1843. V. 71
The Origin, Progress, and Present Condition of the Fine Arts in Great Britain and Ireland. London: 1841. V. 71

TAYLOR, W. COOKE
Ancient And Modern India. London: 1858. V. 72

TAYLOR, WALKER P.
Murder in the Flagship. New York: 1937. V. 72

TAYLOR, WALTER H.
Four Years with General Lee. New York: 1877. V. 69

TAYLOR, WILLIAM
California Life Illustrated. New York: 1858. V. 70

TAYLOR-HALL, MARY ANN
Come and Go. Molly Snow. New York: 1995. V. 73

TAYLOUR, B., MRS.
Japanese Gardens. 1912. V. 73

TCHERNAVIN, V.
Changes in the Salmon Skull. London: 1938. V. 72; 73

TCHERTKOFF, VLADIMIR
The Last Days of Tolstoy. London: 1922. V. 70

TEAGLE, MIKE
Death Over San Silvestro. New York: 1936. V. 68

TEAGUE, W. D.
Design This Day: the Technique of Order in the Machine Age. London: 1946. V. 69; 72

TEAKLE, THOMAS
The Spirit Lake Massacre. Iowa City: 1918. V. 71; 73

TEALE, T. PRIDGIN
Dangers to Health: a Pictorial Guide to Domestic Sanitary Defects. London: 1883. V. 71

TEALL, J. J. H.
British Petrography.... London: 1888. V. 69

TEARLE, JOHN
Mrs. Piozzi's Tall Young Beau, William Augustus Conway, a Biography. 1991. V. 69

TEASDALE, SARA
Stars To-Night. New York: 1930. V. 70

TEASDALE-BUCKELL, G. T.
The Complete Shot. 1907. V. 73

TEBBUTT, R.
A Guide or Companion to the Midland Counties Railway, Containing Its Parliamentary History, Engineering Facts.... Leicester: 1840. V. 73

TEDDIES.. New York: 1920. V. 70

THE TEDDY Bears Baking School. Philadelphia: 1906-1907. V. 69

TEDDY I Squeak. London. V. 68

TEDDY Tail's Annual 1936. V. 69

TEFERTILLER, CASEY
Wyatt Earp, the Life Behind the Legend. London: 1997. V. 68; 72

TEGETMEIER, W. B.
Horses, Asses, Zebras, Mules and Mule Breeding. 1895. V. 69
Horses, Asses, Zebras, Mules and Mule Breeding. London: 1895. V. 68
A Manual of Domestic Economy.... London: 1880. V. 68
Pheasants, Their Natural History and Practical Management. 1897. V. 73
Pheasants. Their Natural History and Practical Management. 1904. V. 71
The Scholars' Handbook of Household Management and Cookery. London: 1876. V. 68

TEGG, WILLIAM
Meetings and Greetings. The Salutations, Obeisances, Courtesies of Nations. London: 1877. V. 68

TEGGART, FREDERICK J.
Diary of Nelson Kingsley, A California Argonaut of 1849. Berkeley: 1914. V. 71
The Portola Expedition of 1769-1770. Berkeley: 1911. V. 72; 73

TEGNER, ESAIAS
Frithiof's Saga. A Legend of the North; translated from the Original Swedish by G. S. London: 1839. V. 71

TEGNER, H.
Wild Hares. 1969. V. 68

TEICHERT, C.
Devonian Rocks and Paleogeography of Central Arizona.... Washington: 1965. V. 72

TEIGNMOUTH, LORD
Memoirs of the Life, Writings and Correspondence of Sir William Jones. London: 1806. V. 70

TEISER, RUTH
Lawton Kennedy, Printer. Mountain View: 1988. V. 73
Lawton Kennedy, Printer. San Francisco: 1988. V. 72
Printing as a Performing Art. San Francisco: 1970. V. 70; 72

TELFORD, THOMAS
General Rules for Repairing Roads, Recommended, by the Parliamentary Commissioners for the Improvemet of the Mail Coach Road from London, by Coventry, to Holyhead, to the Turnpike Trustees Between London and Shrewsbury. London: 1820. V. 72

TELLEEN, MAURICE
Thinking Like a Prairie. Carrollton: 2001. V. 73

TELLER, SYDNEY A.
Synopsis of Social Studies of the Neighbourhood of the Irene Kaufmann Settlement. Pittsburgh: 1917. V. 70

TELLER, THOMAS
The Two Friends: or a Visit to the Seashore. New Haven;: 1844. V. 70

TELLIER, JULES
Abd-er-Rhaman in Paradise. Waltham St. Lawrence: 1928. V. 68; 71

TELLMAN, JOHN
Practical Hotel Steward. Chicago: 1900. V. 73

TEMMINCK, C. J.
Manuel D'Ornithologie Our Tableau Systematique des Oiseaux Qui se Trouvent en Europe. 1820-1835. V. 69

TEMPEL, E.
New Finnish Architecture. New York: 1968. V. 69

TEMPERANCE Cook Book: Being a Collection of Receipts for Cooking, From Which all Intoxicating Liquids are Excluded. Philadelphia: 1841. V. 68

TEMPEST, MARGARET
Curly Cobbler and the Happy Return. London: 1949. V. 70

TEMPLE, FREDERICK
The Relations Between Religion and Science. London: 1884. V. 68

TEMPLE, JAMES GRAHAM
The Scotch Forcing Gardener. Edinburgh: 1828. V. 68

TEMPLE, OLIVER P.
East Tennessee and the Civil War. Cincinnati: 1899. V. 69

TEMPLE, P.
The World at Their Feet. 1969. V. 68

TEMPLE, PEGGY
The Admiral and Others. New York: 1927. V. 71

TEMPLE, RALPH
Cuckoo Time. New York: 1945. V. 69

TEMPLE, RICHARD
Palestine Illustrated. London: 1888. V. 69; 71
Practice of Physic.... 1798. V. 72

TEMPLE, WILLIAM
Memoirs of the Life and Negotiations of Sir W. Temple. London: 1714. V. 72
Observations Upon the United Provinces of the Netherlands.... London: 1673. V. 72
Upon the Gardens of Epicurus, with Other 17th Century Garden Essays. London: 1908. V. 70

TEMPLETON, WILLIAM
The Millwright and Engineer's Pocket Companion, Being a Selection of Useful Practical Rules in Decimals, Geometry, Mensuration, Mechanical Powers, Water Wheels.... Liverpool: 1832. V. 71

TEMPSKY, GUSTAV FERDINAND VON
Mitla. A Narrative of Incidents and Personal Adventures on a Journey in Mexico, Guatemala, and Salvador in the Years 1853 to 1855. London: 1858. V. 69; 71

TEN Little Mulligan Guards. New York: 1874. V. 71

TEN Little Nigger Boys. Buffalo: 1910. V. 69
TEN Little Nigger Boys. London: 1919. V. 69
TEN Little Nigger Boys. London: 1920. V. 73

TEN Little Niggers. London: 1910. V. 73
TEN Little Niggers. New York: 1915. V. 73

TEN Merry Monkeys. Amsterdam: 1950. V. 70

TEN Tales. Huntington Beach: 1994. V. 69

TENANTS Law; or the Laws Concerning Landlords, Tenants and Farmers. London: 1768. V. 73

TENCH, WATKIN
Letters Written in France, to a Friend in London, Between the Month of November 1794 and the Month of May 1795. London: 1796. V. 73

TENGGREN, GUSTAF
The Lively Little Rabbit. New York: 1943. V. 70

TENNANT, EDWARD WYNDHAM
Worple Flit and Other Poems. Oxford: 1916. V. 72

TENNENT, GILBERT
Sermons on Important Subjects; Adapted to the Perilous State of the British Nation, Lately Preached in Philadelphia. Philadelphia: 1758. V. 68

TENNENT, JAMES E.
Ceylon: an Account.... London: 1859. V. 70
Sketches of the Natural History of Ceylon.... London: 1861. V. 69

TENNESSEE
Regulations Adopted for the Provisional Force of the Tennessee Volunteers, Together with the Act of Tennessee Legislature of 1861.... Nashville: 1861. V. 69

TENNEY, TOM
Mark Twain: a Reference Guide. Boston: 1977. V. 68

TENNIEL, JOHN
Cartoons from Punch. London. V. 73
Cartoons Selected From the Pages of Punch. London: 1901. V. 72

TENNYSON, ALFRED TENNYSON, 1ST BARON
Ballads, and Other Poems. London: 1880. V. 69
The Cup and the Falcon. London: 1884. V. 72
The Death of Oenone, Akbar's Dream, and Other Poems. London: 1892. V. 68; 69; 72
Demeter and Other Poems. London: 1889. V. 72
Dora. Boston: 1886. V. 68
Elaine. London: 1868. V. 73
Enid. London: 1868. V. 73
Enoch Arden. London: 1864. V. 68; 72
The Foresters, Robin Hood and Maid Marian. London: 1892. V. 72
Gareth and Lynette etc. London: 1872. V. 72
Geraint and Enid. London: 1906. V. 73
Guinevere. London: 1868. V. 73
Harold, a Drama. London: 1877. V. 72
The Holy Grail and Other Poems. London: 1870. V. 70; 72
Idylls of the King. 1859. V. 70
Idylls of the King. London: 1859. V. 68; 72
Idylls of the King. London: 1862. V. 72
Idylls of the King. London: 1869. V. 70; 72
Idylls of the King. London: 1906. V. 68
In Memoriam. London: 1850. V. 69
In Memoriam. London: 1851. V. 72
In Memoriam. London: 1900. V. 71
In Memoriam. London: 1933. V. 68; 70; 71
The Lady of Shalott. Oxford: 1986. V. 73
Life and Works. London: 1898-1899. V. 68
The Lotos Eaters. London: 1901. V. 69
The Lover's Tale. Boston: 1879. V. 70
The Lover's Tale. London: 1879. V. 73
Maud. London: 1855. V. 70; 72; 73
Maud. London: 1856. V. 72
Maud. London: 1861. V. 68; 70
Maud. London: 1866. V. 71
Maud. 1893. V. 71; 72
Maud. Hammersmith: 1893. V. 68
The May Queen. London: 1872. V. 73
Morte D'Arthur. London: 1912. V. 71; 72
A Poem, Which obtained the Chancellor's Medal at the Cambridge Commencement.... Cambridge: 1829. V. 68
Poems. London: 1833. V. 72
Poems. London: 1842. V. 72
Poems. London: 1857. V. 70
Poems. London: 1860. V. 68
Poems by Two Brothers. London: 1827. V. 72
Poems. MDCCCXXX. MDCCCXXXIII. 1862. V. 68; 70
The Poetical Works. Boston & New York. V. 70; 71
The Poetical Works of Alfred Tennyson, Poet Laureate. New York: 1870. V. 68
The Princess: a Medley. London: 1874. V. 72
A Selection From The Poems Of Alfred, Lord Tennyson. Garden City: 1944. V. 72
A Selection from the Works of Alfred Tennyson. 1866. V. 70
Tennyson's Suppressed Poems. New York and London: 1903. V. 72
Timbuctoo. Cambridge: 1829. V. 72
Tiresias and Other Poems. London: 1885. V. 72
Westminster Abbey. Funeral of the Right Honourable Lord Tennyson, Poet Laureate, on Wednesday, Oct. 12th, 1892 at 12.30 p.m. London: 1892. V. 69
The Works. London: 1870. V. 68
The Works. 1892-1900. V. 73
The Works. Boston: 1895. V. 68; 69
The Works. London: 1897. V. 68

TENNYSON, CHARLES
Collected Sonnets Old and New. London: 1880. V. 72
Small Tableaux. London: 1868. V. 72
Sonnets. London: 1864. V. 71
Sonnets, Lyrics and Translations. London: 1873. V. 72

TENNYSON, FREDERICK
Days and Hours. London: 1854. V. 72
Nine Poems. 1887-1888. V. 72
Poems of the Day of the Year. London: 1895. V. 72

TENNYSON, HALLAM
Alfred, Lord Tennyson, by His Son. London: 1897. V. 71; 72
Jack and the Bean Stalk. London: 1886. V. 69

TENNYSON, THE BROTHERS
Poems by Two Brothers. London and New York: 1893. V. 69

TENZING NORGAY, SHERPA
After Everest. London: 1977. V. 69

TEPPER, SHERI S.
Northshore. New York: 1987. V. 73

TERAMOTO, KAIYU
Nanban Torai Kibun. Tokyo: 1980. V. 73

TERAN, BOSTON
God Is a Bullet. New York: 1999. V. 70; 72

TERENTIUS AFER, PUBLIUS
Andria Oder Das Madchen von Andros. 1971. V. 68; 72
The Comedies of Terence. London: 1765. V. 68; 72
Comoediae. Londini: 1751. V. 72
Comoediae. Birmingham: 1772. V. 69
Comoediae sex ex recensione Heinsiana. Amsterdam. V. 71
Comoediae Sex, ex Recensione Heinsiana.... Amsterdam: 1651. V. 70; 72
Comoediae Sex.... Glasgow: 1742. V. 68; 73

TERENZIO, S.
The Prints of Robert Motherwell: a Catalogue Raisonne 1943-1984. New York: 1984. V. 69

TERHUNE, ANICE
The Boarder Up at Em's. New York: 1925. V. 70
The Eyes of the Village. New York: 1922. V. 71

TERNAN, TREVOR
The Story of the Tyneside Scottish. Newcastle-upon-Tyne. V. 71

TERRACE, VINCENT
The Complete Encyclopedia of Television Programs 1947-1976. New York: 1976. V. 69

TERRASSE, ANTOINE
Pierre Bonnard Illustrator - a Catalogue Raisonne. London: 1988. V. 73

TERRAY, LIONEL
Conquistadors of the Useless. 1963. V. 71
Conquistadors of the Useless. London: 1963. V. 69

TERRELL, J. C.
Reminiscenes of the Early Days of Fort Worth. Fort Worth: 1906. V. 68

TERRELL, JOHN U.
War For The Colorado River, 2 Volumes. Glendale: 1965. V. 71

TERRELL, MARY CHURCH
A Colored Woman in a White World. Washington: 1968. V. 71

TERRES, J. K.
The Audubon Society Encyclopedia of North American Birds. New York: 1980. V. 72

TERRY, ALFRED H.
The Field Diary of General Alfred H. Terry - The Yellowstone Expedition 1876. Bellevue, NE: 1969. V. 72

TERRY, ELLEN
The Russian Ballet. London: 1913. V. 70

TERRY, EZEKIEL
Narrative of the Adventures and Sufferings of Samuel Patterson, Experienced in the Pacific Ocean and Many Other Parts of the World, with an Account of the Feegee and Sandwich Islands. Palmer: 1817. V. 69; 71

TERRY, T. PHILIP
Terry's Mexico. Handbook for Travellers. City of Mexico: 1909. V. 73

TESNOHLIDEK, RUDOLF
The Cunning Little Vixen. New York: 1985. V. 71

TESSIER, THOMAS
Secret Strangers. Arlington Heights: 1992. V. 71

TESTELIN, LOUIS
Les Vertus Innocentes ou Leurs Simboles sous des Figures d'Enfans, Necessaires aux Amateurs de la Muette Poesie et de la Peinture Parlante. Paris: 1650. V. 69; 72

TESTINO, MARIO
Any Objections?. London: 1998:. V. 72

TETENYI, P.
Infraspecific Chemical Taxa of Medicinal Plants. New York: 1970. V. 72

TEVIS, JAMES H.
Arizona in the '50's. Albuquerque: 1954. V. 69

TEVIS, WALTER
Far From Home. Garden City: 1981. V. 68
The Hustler. New York: 1959. V. 69; 70; 71
The Hustler. London: 1960. V. 71
The Man Who Fell to Earth. Greenwich: 1963. V. 71

A TEWKESBURY Guide: Containing a Sketch of the History of the Borough; the Battle of Tewkesbury.... Tewkesbury: 1850. V. 69

TEXAS. WAR DEPARTMENT - 1839
General Regulations for the Government of the Army of the Republic of Texas. Houston: 1839. V. 70

A TEXTILE At Home with Harding, Whitman and Company and Their Allied Mills. Boston, NY and Philadelphia: 1902. V. 68

TEY, JOSEPHINE
The Daughter of Time. London: 1951. V. 72
The Daughter of Time. New York: 1952. V. 70
The Franchise Affair. New York: 1949. V. 71
Miss Pym Disposes. London: 1946. V. 73
Richard of Bordeaux: A Play in Two Parts. London: 1935. V. 71
A Shilling for Candles. New York: 1954. V. 71
The Singing Sands. London: 1952. V. 69; 72
To Love and Be Wise. London: 1950. V. 69

THACHER, JAMES
American Medical Biography. Boston: 1828. V. 68; 71
American Modern Practice; or a Simple Method of Prevention and Cure of Disease.... Boston: 1817. V. 68; 69
American Modern Practice or a Simple Method of Prevention and Cure of Diseases.... Boston: 1826. V. 73
An American New Dispensatory.... Boston: 1810. V. 72
An American New Dispensatory.... Boston: 1813. V. 72
The American Revolution, from the Commencement to the Disbanding of the American Army.... Cincinnati: 1859. V. 73
History of the Town of Plymouth from Its First Settlement in 1620 to the Year 1832 to the Present Time. Boston: 1832. V. 73
Military Journal During the American Revolutionary War from 1775 to 1783. Boston: 1823. V. 73
A Military Journal During the American Revolutionary War from 1775 to 1783.... Boston: 1827. V. 68; 73
Observations on Hydrophobia, Produced by the Bite of a Mad Dog, or Other Rabid Animal. Plymouth: 1812. V. 68; 73
A Practical Treatise on the Management of Bees.... Boston: 1829. V. 68

THACKERAY, WILLIAM MAKEPEACE
The Awful History of Bluebeard. New York: 1924. V. 73
Ballads. London: 1855. V. 72
Ballads. London: 1879. V. 70
The Book of Snobs. London: 1848. V. 73
Christmas Books. Mrs. Perkins's Ball; Our Street; Dr. Birch. London: 1857. V. 73
A Collection of Letters of W. M. Thackeray 1847-1855. London: 1887. V. 72
Doctor Birch and His Young Friends. London: 1849. V. 70; 72; 73
The English Humorists of the Eighteenth Century. London: 1853. V. 72
The English Humourists of the Eighteenth Century. London: 1858. V. 73
Etchings by the Late William Makepeace Thackeray, While at Cambridge.... London: 1878. V. 73

The History of Henry Esmond, Esq.... London: 1852. V. 73
The History of Pendennis. London: 1850. V. 73
The Irish Sketch-Book. London: 1843. V. 68
The Kickleburys on the Rhine. London: 1866. V. 73
The Letters and Private Papers of William Makepeace Thackeray. London: 1945-1946. V. 71
The Loving Ballad of Lord Bateman. London: 1839. V. 68
The Memoirs of Barry Lyndon. London: 1856. V. 68
Mr. Brown's Letters to a Young Man About Town. Cambridge: 1901. V. 70; 72
Mrs. Perkins's Ball. London: 1847. V. 73
The Newcomes. London: 1854. V. 71; 73
Notes of a Journey from Cornhill to Grand Cairo. New York: 1846. V. 70
Notes of a Journey from Cornhill to Grand Cairo. London: 1865. V. 73
Novels by Eminent Hands and Character Sketches. London: 1856. V. 73
On the Genius of George Cruikshank. London: 1884. V. 73
The Orphan of Pimlico, and Other Sketches, Fragments and Drawings. London: 1876. V. 68; 69; 72
Our Street. London: 1848. V. 73
The Paris Sketch Book. London: 1866. V. 73
Reading a Poem. New York: 1911. V. 69; 71; 73
Rebecca and Rowena. London: 1850. V. 68
The Rose and the Ring. London: 1855. V. 73
The Rose and the Ring. London: 1867. V. 73
The Rose and The Ring. New York: 1942. V. 69
Roundabout Papers. London: 1863. V. 73
The Second Funeral of Napoleon and the Chronicle of the Drum. London: 1841. V. 73
Sultan Stork; and Other Stories and Sketches. London: 1887. V. 68; 73
Vanity Fair. London. V. 71
Vanity Fair. London: 1848. V. 68; 69; 72; 73
Vanity Fair. London: 1913. V. 69
Vanity Fair. Oxford: 1931. V. 68
Virginians. London: 1857-1859. V. 73
The Virginians. London: 1858. V. 71; 73
The Virginians. London: 1858-1859. V. 68; 70; 71; 73
The Virginians. London: 1884. V. 71
The Works. London: 1879. V. 72
The Works. London: 1883-1886. V. 73
The Works. London: 1886-1891. V. 72
The Works. London: 1888. V. 71
The Works. London: 1901. V. 72
The Works. London: 1902-1903. V. 72
The Works. London: 1907-1913. V. 73
The Works. New York and London: 1910. V. 72
The Yellowplush Correspondence. Philadelphia: 1838. V. 68; 69

THE THAMES. Waterway of the World. 1893. V. 71

THARP, THEODORE A.
Cradled in a Storm: a Story of Gaunchester-Haugh. London: 1888. V. 68

THATCHER, B. B.
Indian Traits: Being Sketches of the Manners, Customs and Character of the North American Natives. New York: 1860. V. 73

THAUSING, MORIZ
Albert Durer. London: 1882. V. 70

THAXTER, CELIA
Drift-Weed. Boston: 1879. V. 70
An Island Garden. Boston and New York: 1894. V. 73

THAYER, E.
Family Memorial. Hingham: 1835. V. 70

THAYER, FRANK S.
Hoofs, Claws and Antlers of the Rocky Mountains by the Camera. Denver: 1894. V. 68

THAYER, G. H.
Concealing-Coloration in the Animal Kingdom, an Exposition of the Laws of Disguise through Color and Pattern. New York: 1909. V. 73

THAYER, HENRY
Descriptive Catalogue of Fluid and Solid Extracts, also Pills, Resinoids and Alkaloids, Prepared by Henry Thayer and Co.... Cambridgeport: 1877. V. 69

THAYER, JANE
The Blueberry Pie Elf. New York: 1961. V. 68

THAYER, JOHN
A Discourse, Delivered, at the Roman Catholic Church in Boston, on the 9th of May 1798.... Boston: 1798. V. 71

THAYER, LEE
The Affair at The Cedars. New York: 1921. V. 69
A Man's Enemies. New York: 1937. V. 69
Set a Thief. New York: 1931. V. 68
Within the Vault. New York: 1950. V. 69

THAYER, PHINEAS
Casey at the Bat. Chicago: 1912. V. 69; 72

THAYER, TIFFANY
The Cluck Abroad. Garden City: 1935. V. 71

THAYER, WILLIAM S.
Osler and Other Papers. Baltimore: 1931. V. 71

THEAL, GEORGE MC CALL
Documents Relating to the Kaffir War of 1835. London: 1912. V. 69

THE THEATRE of Love. I. Frederick and Harriet; or, the Discreet Parent. II. Miranda. III. Horatio. IV. Coredlia. V. The Cruel Father. VI. Clerimont. VII. The Lovers Quarrel. VIII. John and Joan. IX. Celia. X. Innocence in Distress. XI. The Rival Sisters. London: 1759. V. 73

THE THEATRICAL Olio, or Actor's Ways and Means.... London: 1820. V. 72

THEILHAVBER, FELIX
Judische Flieger im Weltkrieg. Berlin: 1924. V. 72

THELWALL, JOHN
Sober Reflections on the Seditious and Inflammatory Letter to the Right Hon. Edmund Burke, to a Nobel Lord. London: 1796. V. 70

THELWELL, MICHAEL
The Harder They Come. New York: 1980. V. 69; 72

THENARD, L. J.
Traite de Chimie Elementaire, Theorique et Pratique. Paris: 1813-1816. V. 68

THEOBALD, LEWIS
The Perfidious Brother. London: 1715. V. 70

THEOCRITUS
The Complete Poems. London: 1929. V. 70; 72
The Complete Poems. London: 1930. V. 71
Sixe Idyllia. New York: 1971. V. 70

THEOPHRASTUS
De Historia Plantarum Libri Decem. Amsterdam: 1644. V. 69; 73
Theophrasti Charateres Ethici, ex Recensione Petri Needham.... Glasgow: 1743. V. 68; 73

THEOPHYLACT, SAINT
(...) In Quatuor Euangelia Enarrationes Innumeris pene Locis Per Phil. Montanum Armentarianum.... Basiliae: 1554. V. 72

THEROUX, ALEXANDER
An Adultery. New York: 1987. V. 72
Three Wogs. Boston: 1972. V. 71

THEROUX, PAUL
The Black House. Boston: 1974. V. 68
The Black House. London: 1974. V. 68; 70
Chicago Loop. London: 1990. V. 70
A Christmas Card. Boston: 1978. V. 70
The Consul's File. Boston: 1977. V. 70; 71
The Consul's File. London: 1977. V. 70
Doctor Slaughter. London: 1984. V. 70
The Family Arsenal. Boston: 1976. V. 70
The Family Arsenal. London: 1976. V. 68; 70; 71
Fong and the Indians. Boston: 1968. V. 69; 70
Fong and the Indians. London: 1976. V. 70
Girls at Play. London: 1969. V. 70
The Great Railway Bazaar. Boston: 1975. V. 69
The Great Railway Bazaar. New York: 1975. V. 70
Half Moon Street. Boston: 1984. V. 68; 72
The Happy Isles of Oceania Paddling the Pacific. New York: 1992. V. 70
Hotel Honolulu. London: 2001. V. 70
Jungle Lovers. Boston: 1971. V. 69; 70
Jungle Lovers. London: 1971. V. 70; 73
The Kingdom by the Sea. Boston: 1983. V. 70; 71
London Snow: a Christmas Story. London: 1979. V. 70
Millroy the Magician. London: 1993. V. 70
The Mosquito Coast. London: 1981. V. 70
The Mosquito Coast. Boston: 1982. V. 68; 70
The Mosquito Coast. New York: 1982. V. 71
Murder in Mount Holly. London: 1969. V. 69
My Other Life. London: 1996. V. 70
My Secret History. London: 1989. V. 68; 70; 73
My Secret History. New York: 1989. V. 72
O-Zone. Franklin Center: 1986. V. 70
O-Zone. London: 1986. V. 70
O-Zone. New York: 1986. V. 72
The Old Patagonian Express. Boston: 1979. V. 71
The Old Patagonian Express. London: 1979. V. 68; 71
Picture Palace. Boston: 1978. V. 68; 70
Picture Palace. Franklin Center: 1978. V. 70
Picture Palace. London: 1978. V. 70; 71
Riding the Iron Rooster: by Train through China. London: 1988. V. 70
Sailing through China. London: 1983. V. 70
Sailing through China. Wilton, Salisbury, Wiltshire: 1983. V. 70
Saint Jack. Boston: 1973. V. 68; 69; 70; 71; 72
Saint Jack. New York: 1973. V. 70
The Shortest Day of the Year. Leamington Spa: 1986. V. 70
Sinning with Annie and Other Stories. Boston: 1972. V. 69; 70; 73
Sinning with Annie and Other Stories. 1975. V. 71
Sinning With Annie and Other Stories. London: 1975. V. 68; 70

Sunrise with Seamonsters. Boston: 1985. V. 72
To the Ends of the Earth: the Selected Travels of Paul Theroux. New York: 1990. V. 70
Waldo. Boston: 1967. V. 69; 71
Waldo. London: 1968. V. 70
The White Man's Burden. London: 1987. V. 70
World's End and Other Stories. London: 1980. V. 70

THESIGER, WILFRED
Arabian Sands. 1959. V. 70
The Danakil Diary - Journey through Abyssinia 1930-1934. London: 1996. V. 69

THESLEFF, S.
Motor Innervation of Muscle. London: 1976. V. 68

THE THESPIAN Dictionary; or, Dramatic Biography of the Present Age.... London: 1805. V. 72

THE THESPIAN Preceptor; or, a Full Display of the Scenic Art.... Boston: 1810. V. 68; 70

THICKNESSE, PHILIP
Useful Hints to Those Who Make the Tour of France, in a Series of Letters.... London: 1770. V. 69

THICKNESSE, RALPH
The Rights and Wrongs of Women. London: 1890. V. 69

THIENEMANN, FRIEDRICH
Systematische Darstellung der Fortpflanzung der Vogel Europa.... Leipzig: 1925-1938. V. 73

THIERRY, AUGUSTIN
History of the Conquest of England by the Normans; with Its causes and Consequences to the Present Time. 1840. V. 73

THIERS, M. A.
History of the Consulate and the Empire of France Under Napoleon. London: 1845-1862. V. 71

THIES, LOUIS
Catalogue of the Collection of Engravings Bequeathed to Harvard College by Francis Calley Gray. Cambridge: 1869. V. 71

THIGPEN, CORBETT H.
The Three Faces of Eve. New York: 1957. V. 69

THIOLLET, FRANCOIS
Nouveau Recueil de Menuiserie et de Decorations Interieures et Exterieures.... Paris: 1837. V. 68; 70; 72

THIRD Chapter of Accidents and Remarkable Events: Containing Caution and Instruction for Children. Philadelphia: 1807. V. 70

THIRKELL, ANGELA
Before Lunch. New York: 1940. V. 72
County Chronicle. New York: 1950. V. 73
Double Affair. London: 1957. V. 72
Love Among the Ruins. New York: 1948. V. 71
Marling Hall. New York: 1942. V. 71
Three Houses. London: 1931. V. 68
What Did It Mean. New York: 1954. V. 71

THIRTY Favorite Paintings by Leading American Artists. 1908. V. 69

THIS is Tomorrow. London: 1956. V. 73

THISELTON, WILLIAM MATHEW
National Anecdotes: Interspersed with Historical Facts.... London: 1812. V. 70

THISELTON DYER, T. F.
Folk-Lore of Women.... London: 1905. V. 73
Folk-Lore of Women.... Chicago: 1906. V. 69

THISTLETHWAITE, BERNARD
The Thistlethwaite Family. London: 1910. V. 71

THOBURN, JOSEPH B.
Oklahoma - A History of The State and Its People. New York: 1929. V. 72
A Standard History of Oklahoma. Chicago and New York: 1916. V. 70

THOBY MARCELIN, PHILIPPE
Canape Vert. New York: 1944. V. 69; 72
The Pencil of God. Boston: 1951. V. 69

THOENEN, EUGENE D.
History of the Oil and Gas Industry in West Virginia. Charleston: 1964. V. 68

THOM, ADAM
The Claims to the Oregon Territory Considered. London: 1844. V. 70; 72

THOM, C.
The Aspergilli. Baltimore: 1926. V. 68

THOM, WALTER
Pedestrianism; or, an Account of the Performances of Celebrated Pedestrians During the Last and Present Century.... Aberdeen: 1813. V. 71

THOMA, KURT H.
Clinical Pathology of the Jaws with a Histologic and Roentgen Study of Practical Cases. Springfield: 1934. V. 72
Traumatic Surgery of the Jaws Including First Aid Treatment. St. Louis: 1942. V. 72

THOMAS, ABEL
A Brief Memoir Concerning Abel Thomas. Philadelphia: 1824. V. 72

THOMAS, ALAN
Summer Adventure. London: 1933. V. 72

THOMAS, ALAN G.
Great Books and Book Collectors. London: 1975. V. 70; 71

THOMAS, ALFRED B.
Forgotten Frontiers, a Study of the Spanish Indian Policy of Don Juan Buatiste De Anza, Governor of New Mexico. Norman: 1932. V. 70
The Plains Indians and New Mexico 1751-1778. Albuquerque: 1940. V. 69

THOMAS, ANNIE
Walter Goring. London: 1875?. V. 68

THOMAS, ANTOINE LEONARD
Essay on the Character, Manners and Genius of Women in Differnet Ages. London: 1773. V. 68; 69; 72

THOMAS, ARAD
Pioneer History of Orleans Co., New York. Albion: 1871. V. 70

THOMAS, BERTRAM
Arabia Felix: Across The Empty Quarter of Arabia. London: 1932. V. 72

THOMAS, C. F. THEODORE
Theodore Thomas, a Musical Autobiography. Chicago: 1905. V. 69

THOMAS, CHARLES
Adventures and Observations on the West Coast of Africa, and Its Islands.... New York: 1860. V. 69

THOMAS, CLARENCE
General Turner Ashby, The Centaur of the South. Winchester: 1907. V. 69; 70

THOMAS, CRAIG
Firefox. London: 1977. V. 73
Rat Trap. London: 1976. V. 71; 73
Wolfsbane. London: 1978. V. 73

THOMAS, D. M.
Ararat. London: 1983. V. 70
D. M. Thomas. Berkhamstead: 1974. V. 70
In the Fair Field. Hereford: 1978. V. 70
Lilith-Prints. Cardiff: 1974. V. 70
Logan Stone. London: 1971. V. 70
News from the Front. Todmorden, Lancs: 1983. V. 70
Poetry in Crosslight. London: 1975. V. 70
The Shaft. Gillingham, Kent: 1973. V. 70
Two Voices. London: 1968. V. 70
The White Hotel. London: 1981. V. 70
The White Hotel. New York: 1981. V. 68; 71

THOMAS, DAVID
Travels through the Western Country in the Summer of 1816.... New York: 1819. V. 72

THOMAS, DAVID H.
The Anthropology of St. Catherine's Island. New York: 1979. V. 70

THOMAS, DAVIS
People of the First Man. New York: 1976. V. 71

THOMAS, DONALD
The Ripper's Apprentice. London: 1986. V. 72

THOMAS, DYLAN MARLAIS
Adventures in the Skin Trade. London: 1955. V. 69; 71; 73
A Child's Christmas in Wales. Norfolk: 1955. V. 69
A Child's Christmas in Wales. London: 1978. V. 72
Collected Poems 1934-1952. London: 1952. V. 69; 70; 72; 73
Conversations About Christmas. New York: 1954. V. 69; 73
Deaths and Entrances. London: 1946. V. 70
The Doctor and the Devils. 1953. V. 68
The Doctor and the Devils. London: 1953. V. 69
The Doctor and the Devils. London: 1966. V. 68
18 Poems. London: 1934. V. 72
18 Poems. London: 1942. V. 69
In Country Sleep. New York: 1952. V. 69; 71
Letters to Vernon Watkins. London: 1957. V. 69; 70; 72
Me and My Bike: an Unfinished Film Script. New York: 1965. V. 69
The Notebooks of Dylan Thomas. New York: 1966. V. 69
Poemas. Madrid: 1955. V. 68
The Poems of Dylan Thomas. 1971. V. 70
Poet in the Making; the Notebooks of Dylan Thomas. London: 1968. V. 69; 71
Portrait de l'Artiste en Jeune Chien. Paris: 1947. V. 68; 70; 71
Portrait of the Artist as a Young Dog. London: 1940. V. 69
Portrait of the Artist as a Young Dog. Norfolk: 1940. V. 69
A Prospect of the Sea. 1955. V. 70
A Prospect of the Sea and Other Stories and Prose Writings. London: 1955. V. 69
Quite Early One Morning: Broadcasts. London: 1954. V. 69; 70
Quite Early One Morning: Broadcasts. New York: 1954. V. 69
Selected Writings of Dylan Thomas. New York: 1946. V. 68
Twelve More Letters. 1970. V. 69
Twenty Years A-Growing. 1964. V. 68
Twenty-five Poems. 1936. V. 70
Twenty-Five Poems. London: 1936. V. 68; 71; 73
Under Milk Wood. 1954. V. 68
Under Milk Wood. London: 1954. V. 69; 70; 73
Under Milk Wood. 1958. V. 68
Under Milk Wood. London: 1958. V. 70; 71
Under Milk Wood. Leeds: 1985. V. 70
The World I Breathe. Norfolk: 1939. V. 69; 73

THOMAS, EBEN FRANCIS
The Rose Garden of Omar Khayyam. 1910. V. 71

THOMAS, EDGAR
The Lawes Resolutions of Womens Rights; or the Lawes Provision for Women. 1632. V. 72
The Lawes Resolutions of Womens Rights; or, the Lawes Provision for Women. London: 1632. V. 70

THOMAS, EDWARD
The Chessplayer. Andoversford: 1981. V. 72; 73
The Chessplayer. London: 1981. V. 71
The Childhood of Edward Thomas - A Fragment of autobiography. London: 1937. V. 72
Chosen Essays. Newtown: 1926. V. 70; 71; 73
Collected Poems. London: 1920. V. 70; 72
The Happy-Go-Lucky Morgans. London: 1913. V. 72; 73
The Heart of England. London: 1906. V. 68; 72
Last Poems. London: 1918. V. 72
Letters from Edward Thomas to Gordon Bottomley. London: 1968:. V. 72
Oxford. London: 1932. V. 69
Personal Letters. Andoversford: 2000. V. 68
Personal Letters. Risbury: 2000. V. 68
Poems. London: 1917. V. 72; 73
Selected Poems. Montgomeryshire: 1927. V. 72; 73
Six Poems. Flansham: 1917. V. 72
The Trumpet and Other Poems. London: 1940. V. 68
Two Poems. London: 1927. V. 72

THOMAS, ELLA M.
Virginia Women in Literature. Richmond: 1902. V. 72

THOMAS, ELTON
Douglas Fairbanks in Robin Hood. 1922. V. 70

THOMAS, EMORY H.
Confederate State of Richmond. Austin;: 1971. V. 69

THOMAS, FRANK
Sherlock Holmes, Bridge Detective. London: 1976. V. 70

THOMAS, GEORGE C.
Golf Architecture in America, Its Strategy and Construction. Los Angeles: 1927. V. 69

THOMAS, HELEN
As It Was. (with) World Without End. London: 1926-1931. V. 72
World Without End. London: 1931. V. 68

THOMAS, HENRY
Andres Brun, Calligrapher of Saragossa, Some Account of His Life and Work. Paris: 1928. V. 71
Early Spanish Bookbindings XI-XV Centuries. London: 1939. V. 70

THOMAS, HENRY DAVID
Cape Cod. Boston: 1865. V. 70

THOMAS, HERBERT
Classical Contributions to Obstetrics and Gynecology. Springfield: 1935. V. 68; 71; 73

THOMAS, ISAIAH
The History of Printing in America. Worcester: 1810. V. 69; 71; 73

THOMAS, J. B.
Hounds and Hunting through the Ages. 1937. V. 68

THOMAS, J. BISSELL
The Dragon Green. 1944. V. 71; 72

THOMAS, J. E.
The Harvester: a Book of Sacred Songs. Ft. Worth: 1900. V. 70

THOMAS, J. J.
The Illustrated Annual Register of Rural Affairs and Cultivator Almanac for the Year 1864.... Albany: 1864. V. 73

THOMAS, JAMES
Selections from the Original Contributions. Liverpool: 1889. V. 70

THOMAS, JENNIE
Biography and Early Life Sketch of the Late Abram Sortore Including His Trip to California and Back. Alexandria: 1909. V. 69

THOMAS, JERRY
The Bar-Tender's Guide, or How to Mix All Kinds of Plain and Fancy Drinks. New York: 1887. V. 69

THOMAS, JOHN
Walks in the Neighbourhood of Sheffield. (Second Series). Sheffield: 1844. V. 73

THOMAS, JOHN P.
Career and Character of General Micha Jenkins C.S.A. Columbia: 1903. V. 69
A Legal and Constitutional Argument Against the Alleged Judicial Right of Restraining the Publication of Reports of Judicial Proceedings, as Assumed in the King v. Thistlewood and Others, Enforced Against the Proprietor of the Observer by a Fine.... London: 1822. V. 68

THOMAS, JOSEPH L.
An Undergraduate's Trip to Italy and Attica. Oxford: 1881. V. 69

THOMAS, KENNETH
Portrait of Laurel. New York: 1943. V. 71

THOMAS, LESLIE
Midnight Clear. A Christmas Story. London: 1978. V. 71

THOMAS, MALCOLM
Churchill His Life & Times; A Churchill Anthology; Painting As A Pastime. London: 1962-1965. V. 72

THOMAS, MARGARET
An Anthology of Cambridge Women's Verse. London: 1931. V. 69

THOMAS, MAYNARD F.
How to Enjoy Detective Fiction. London: 1947. V. 68

THOMAS, O.
Catalogue of the Marsupialia and Monotremata in the Collection of the British Museum. 1888. V. 73

THOMAS, PHILIP E.
Memorial of the Baltimore and Ohio Railraod Company, for a Subscription to It's Stock. Washington: 1832. V. 73

THOMAS, R. S.
Autobiographies - Former Paths, The Creative Writer's Sucicide, No- One, A Year in Llyn. London: 1997. V. 68
Collected Poems 1945-1900. London: 1993. V. 68; 69; 72; 73
Destinations. Halford: 1985. V. 72
Das Helle Feld. London: 1995. V. 70
Ingrowing Thoughts. Bridgend: 1985. V. 72
Laboratories of the Spirit. 1976. V. 72
Later Poems. London: 1983. V. 72
The Mountains. New York: 1968. V. 70
Pieta. London: 1966. V. 71; 72
Poetry for Supper. London: 1958. V. 72
Poet's Meeting. Stratford-upon-Avon. V. 72
Poet's Meeting. Stratford-upon-Avon: 1983. V. 71
Selected Poems 1946-1968. London: 1973. V. 72
Song at the Year's Turning. Poems 1942-1954. London: 1955. V. 73
The Stones of the Field. Carmarthen: 1946. V. 73

THOMAS, RALPH
Serjeant Thomas and Sir J. E. Millais Bart. London: 1901. V. 72

THOMAS, ROSS
The Backup Men. New York: 1971. V. 69; 71; 73
Briarpatch. New York: 1984. V. 69; 70; 72
Cast a Yellow Shadow. New York: 1967. V. 68; 69; 70; 71; 72; 73
Chinaman's Chance. New York: 1978. V. 68; 69; 70; 71; 72
The Eighth Dwarf. New York: 1979. V. 68; 71; 72
The Fools in Town are On Our Side. London: 1970. V. 70; 72; 73
The Fools in Town Are On Our Side. New York: 1970. V. 70
The Fools in Town Are On Our Side. New York: 1971. V. 69
The Highbinders. New York: 1973. V. 69; 70
The Highbinders. London: 1974. V. 71; 72
The Highbinders. New York: 1974. V. 70; 73
If You Can't Be Good. New York: 1973. V. 68; 69; 70; 71
Missionary Stew. New York: 1983. V. 68; 71
Missionary Stew. London: 1984. V. 71; 72
The Money Harvest. New York: 1975. V. 68; 69; 71; 72; 73
The Mordida Man. New York: 1981. V. 69; 70; 71; 72
No Questions Asked. New York: 1976. V. 70; 71; 72
Out on the Rim. New York: 1987. V. 70; 71
The Porkchoppers. New York: 1972. V. 68; 69; 70; 71; 72
The Seersucker Whipsaw. New York: 1967. V. 68; 69; 70; 71; 72; 73
The Singapore Wink. 1969. V. 69
The Singapore Wink. London: 1969. V. 70
The Singapore Wink. New York: 1969. V. 69; 72
Spies, Thumbsuckers, etc. Northridge: 1989. V. 68; 69; 70; 71; 72
Twilight at Mac's Place. New York: 1990. V. 70; 71; 72; 73
Voodoo, Ltd. New York: 1992. V. 71; 72
Yellow-Dog Contract. New York: 1977. V. 68; 69; 71; 72; 73

THOMAS, VAUGHAN
Memorials of the Malignant Cholera in Oxford, MDCCCXXXII. Oxford: 1835. V. 72

THOMAS, WILLIAM
The Historye of Italye. London: 1561. V. 68; 70; 73

THOMAS A KEMPIS
The Christian Pattern Paraphras'd or the Book of the Imitation of Christ. London: 1697. V. 71
The Christian's Pattern; or A Treatise of the Imitation of Jesus Christ. London: 1702. V. 71
De Imitatione Christi. Antwerp: 1617. V. 72
De Imitatione Christi Libri Qvatvor Mvltiplici Lingva Nvnc Primo Pimpressi. Solisbaci in Bavaria: 1837. V. 72
An Extract of The Christian's Pattern; or a Treatise of the Imitation of Christ. London: 1741. V. 70
Imitation de Jesus Christ. Paris: 1881?. V. 71
Meditations on Our Lady. Ditchling, Sussex: 1929. V. 73
Of the Imitation of Christ, with the Book of the Sacrament. London: 1911. V. 71

THOMAS AQUANIS, SAINT
Praeclarissima Commentaria, in Libros Aristotelis Perihermenias et Posteriorum Analyticorum.... Venetiis: 1570. V. 69

THOMAS AQUINAS, SAINT
Sermones Valde pii et Docti Pro Dominicis et Festivis Diebus ex Bibliotheca Vaticana nunc Primum in Lecem Editi. Rome: 1571. V. 68; 72

THOMASON, CAROLINE WASSON
Youth of Color. New York: 1951. V. 72

THOMES, WILLIAM H.
The Bushrangers. Boston: 1866. V. 71
The Gold Hunter's Adventures; or, Life in Australia. Boston;: 1864. V. 71
On Land and Sea or California in the Years 1843, 1844 and 1845. Boston: 1884. V. 68

THOMPSON and West's History of Nevada. Berkeley: 1958. V. 70

THOMPSON, ALBERT W.
The Story of Early Clayton, New Mexico. Clayton: 1933. V. 71
They Were Open Range Days - Annals of a Western Frontier. Denver: 1946. V. 69; 70; 71; 73

THOMPSON, C. MILDRED
Reconstruction in Georgia: Economic, Social, Political 1865-1872. New York: 1915. V. 70

THOMPSON, C. V. R.
Trousers Will Be Worn. New York: 1941. V. 70

THOMPSON, CHARLES
Evidences in Proof of the Book of Mormon, Being a Divinely Inspired Record.... Batavia: 1841. V. 71

THOMPSON, CHARLES WILLIAM
Twelve Months in the British Legion. London: 1836. V. 73

THOMPSON, DANIEL P.
The Green Mountain Boys. London: 1840. V. 73

THOMPSON, D'ARCY W.
Day-Dreams of a School-Master. London. V. 71

THOMPSON, DAVID
History of the Late War, Between Great Britain and the United States of America. Niagara: 1832. V. 73

THOMPSON, DENMAN
The Old Homestead. New York: 1908. V. 71

THOMPSON, DUNSTAN
The Phoenix in the Desert - a Book of Travels. London: 1951. V. 71

THOMPSON, EDWARD
Collected Poems. London: 1930. V. 68
A Farewell to India. London: 1931. V. 70

THOMPSON, ELROY S.
History of Plymouth, Norfolk and Barnstable Counties, Massachusetts. New York: 1928. V. 68

THOMPSON, ERNEST
On Golden Pond. New York: 1979. V. 72

THOMPSON, EVELYN PROUTY
Manteca, Selected Chapters from Its History. Manteca: 1980. V. 71

THOMPSON, FRANCIS
The Collected Poetry. London: 1913. V. 71
New Poems. Westminster: 1897. V. 69
Poems. London: 1893. V. 72
Sister Songs. London: 1895. V. 72
Uncollected Verses. London: 1917. V. 68

THOMPSON, FRANCIS BENJAMIN ROSS
The Universal Decorator. London: 1859. V. 68

THOMPSON, GEORGE
Prison Life and Reflections; or, a Narrative of the Arrest, Trial, Conviction, Imprisonment in Missouri Penitentiary.... Hartford: 1851. V. 69

THOMPSON, GEORGE D.
Bat Masterson; The Dodge City Years in Fort Hays Kansas.... Topeka: 1943. V. 71

THOMPSON, H. S.
Ireland in 1839 and 1869. 1870. V. 71
Sub-Alpine Plants of the Swiss Woods and Meadows. 1912. V. 69

THOMPSON, H. V.
The European Rabbit.... Oxford: 1994. V. 72

THOMPSON, HENRY
The Diseases of the Prostate. London: 1873. V. 70

THOMPSON, HENRY continued
Food and Feeding. London: 1880. V. 68
Food and Feeding. London: 1891. V. 68

THOMPSON, HUNTER S.
The Curse of Lono. New York: 1983. V. 73
Fear and Loathing in America. New York: 2000. V. 69; 70; 72; 73
Fear and Loathing in America. New York: 2001. V. 68
Fear and Loathing in Las Vegas. New York: 1971. V. 69; 70; 71; 72; 73
Fear and Loathing in Las Vegas. New York: 1972. V. 68
Fear and Loathing on the Campaign Trail '72. New York: 1973. V. 73
Fear and Loathing on the Campaign Trail '72. San Francisco: 1973. V. 68; 69; 70; 72; 73
Golf Dreams. New York: 1996. V. 72
Hell's Angels: a Strange and Terrible Saga. New York: 1967. V. 73
Mistah Leary He Dead. San Francisco: 1996. V. 73
The Proud Highway. New York: 1997. V. 68; 71; 72; 73
The Rum Diary. New York: 1998. V. 72; 73
Screwjack. Santa Barbara: 1991. V. 72

THOMPSON, I. OWEN
Adventures And Day Dreams. Long Beach: 1913. V. 71

THOMPSON, J. E. S.
A Catalog of Maya Hieroglyphs. Norman: 1970. V. 69

THOMPSON, J. V.
A Catalogue of Plants Growing in the Vicinity of Berwick Upon Tweed. 1807. V. 69

THOMPSON, JAMES
Poems in the Scottish Dialect. Edinburgh: 1801. V. 71

THOMPSON, JERRY
Sabers on the Rio Grande. Austin: 1974. V. 69; 72

THOMPSON, JIM
The Alcoholics. New York: 1953. V. 68; 70
Bad Boy. New York: 1953. V. 69; 71; 73
Calendar of Annual Events in Oklahoma. Oklahoma: 1938. V. 73
Child of Rage. Los Angeles: 1991. V. 69; 70; 71; 73
The End Of The Book In American Stuff. New York: 1937. V. 72
4 Novels. London: 1983. V. 73
The Getaway. New York: 1959. V. 70
The Getaway. London: 1972. V. 70
Heed the Thunder. New York: 1946. V. 68; 69; 72; 73
The Killer Inside Me. New York: 1952. V. 68; 70; 73
The Killer Inside Me. London: 1973. V. 70
The Killer Inside Me. Los Angeles: 1989. V. 68; 69; 70; 71; 73
King Blood. New York: 1993. V. 70; 71; 73
Nothing More than Murder. New York: 1949. V. 69; 73
Now and On Earth. New York: 1942. V. 70
Now and On Earth. Belen: 1986. V. 69; 71; 73
Texas by the Tail. Greenwich: 1965. V. 69; 70; 73

THOMPSON, JOHN
The Life of John Thompson, a Fugitive Slave.... Worcester: 1856. V. 69

THOMPSON, JOHN CARGILL
The Boys' Dumas, G. A. Henty: Aspects of Victorian Publishing. Cheadle, Cheshire: 1975. V. 73

THOMPSON, JOHN E.
The Magnetic Properties of Materials. Cleveland: 1968. V. 70

THOMPSON, K. L.
Ameliaranne at the Zoo,. London: 1936. V. 70

THOMPSON, KAY
Eloise. New York: 1955. V. 73
Eloise at Christmastime. New York: 1958. V. 73
Eloise in Moscow. New York: 1959. V. 69; 70
Eloise in Paris. New York: 1957. V. 69; 70

THOMPSON, LAURA
The Hopi Way. Chicago: 1944. V. 69

THOMPSON, LEROY
Commando Dagger. The Complete Illustrated History. Boulder: 1985. V. 72

THOMPSON, MARY M.
Mallerstang. Appleby: 1965. V. 71

THOMPSON, NEIL BAIRD
Crazy Horse Called Them Walk-A-Heaps, The Story of The Foot Soldier in The Prairie Indian Wars. St. Cloud, MN: 1979. V. 72

THOMPSON, P.
The Cabinet-Maker's Sketch Book, a Series of Original Details for Modern Furniture. Glasgow and Edinburgh: 1852-1853. V. 68; 70

THOMPSON, PETER
Peter Thompson's Narrative of The Little Big Horn Campaign, 1876. Glendale: 1974. V. 72
Thompson's Narrative of the Little Bighorn Campaign 1876: a Critical Analysis of an Eyewitness Account of the Custer Debacle. 1974. V. 68

THOMPSON, PISHEY
The History and Antiquities of Boston, and the Villages of Skirbeck, Fishtoft, Freiston, Butterwick, Bennington, Leverton, Leake and Wrangle.... Boston: 1856. V. 73

THOMPSON, R. F.
Face of the Gods. New York: 1993. V. 69

THOMPSON, ROBERT
The Gardener's Assistant. London: 1859. V. 69
The Gardener's Assistant. London: 1878. V. 68

THOMPSON, RUPERT
The Insult. New York: 1996. V. 72

THOMPSON, RUTH PLUMLY
The Giant Horse of Oz. Chicago: 1928. V. 68; 70
The Gnome King of Oz. Chicago: 1927. V. 73
King Kojo. Philadelphia: 1938. V. 73
The Perhappsy Chaps. Chicago: 1918. V. 73
The Purple Prince of Oz. Chicago: 1932. V. 73

THOMPSON, SAMUEL
New Guide to Health; or Botanic Family Physician. Boston: 1822. V. 73

THOMPSON, SILVANUS P.
Dynamo-Electric Machinery: A Manual for Students of Electrotechnics. London and New York: 1888. V. 72
Dynamo-Electric Machinery: a Manual for Students of Electrotechnics. New York: 1892. V. 68
Gilbert of Colchester; an Elizabethan Magnetizer. London: 1891. V. 71

THOMPSON, SYLVIA
Chariot Wheels. Boston: 1929. V. 71
Summers Night. Boston: 1932. V. 72

THOMPSON, T.
A Collection of Songs, Comic, Satirical and Descriptive, Chiefly in theNewcastle Dialect, . . . Newcastle-upon-Tyne: 1827. V. 71

THOMPSON, THELMA
Bright Ramparts. New York: 1943. V. 71

THOMPSON, THEODORE
On Certain Changes in Sensation Associated with Gross Lesions of the Spinal Cord. 1906. V. 68

THOMPSON, THOMAS
History of the Royal Society.... London: 1812. V. 70

THOMPSON, VANCE
The Scarlet Iris. Indianapolis: 1924. V. 70

THOMPSON, VINCENT
St. Helier, the Hermit, a Poetic Vision. Jersey: 1834. V. 69

THOMPSON, W.
Sedbergh Garsdale and Dent. Leeds: 1892. V. 71
Sedbergh Garsdale and Dent. Leeds: 1910. V. 71

THOMPSON, W. N.
The Episcopal Registers of Carlisle. Part I. 1293-1300. Kendal: 1906. V. 71
The Episcopal Registers of Carlisle. Part II. 1300-1309. Kendal: 1909. V. 71
The Episcopal Registers of Carlisle. Part III 1292-1324. Kendal: 1913. V. 71

THOMPSON, W. R.
The Tachinids (Diptera) of Trinidad. 1961-1968. V. 70

THOMPSON, WADDY
Recollections of Mexico. New York and London: 1846. V. 68; 71

THOMPSON, WILLIAM
An Inquiry Into the Principles of the Distribution of Wealth Most Conducive to Human Happiness.... London: 1824. V. 73
An Inquiry into the Principles of the Distribution of Wealth Most Conducive to Human Happiness.... London: 1850. V. 73
Reminiscences of A Pioneer. San Francisco: 1912. V. 72

THOMPSON, WILLIAM TAPPEN
Major Jones' Chronicles of Pineville: Embracing Sketches of Georgia Scenes, Incidents and Characters. Philadelphia: 1879. V. 71

THOMPSON, WINFIELD
Lawson History of the America's Cup. Boston: 1902. V. 69

THOMS, HERBERT
Classical Contributions to Obstetrics and Gynecology. Springfield: 1935. V. 69

THOMSON, ALEX
An Enquiry into the Nature, Causes and Method of Cure, of Nervous Disorders. London: 1782. V. 68; 72

THOMSON, ANTHONY TODD
A Conspectus of the Pharmacopoeias of the London, Edinburgh and Dublin Colleges of Physicians.... London: 1810. V. 72

THOMSON, BASIL
Mr. Pepper Investigator. London: 1925. V. 68

THOMSON, C. LINKLATER
Jane Austen - A Survey. 1929. V. 70

THOMSON, CHARLES WYVILLE
Report on the Scientific Results of the Voyage of H.M.S. Challenger During the Years 1873-1876 Under the Command of Captain George S. Nares and the Late Captain Frank Tourle Thomson.... London: 1885. V. 71
The Voyage of the Challenger. London: 1877. V. 71

THOMSON, DAVID
African Wildlife in Art. 1991. V. 69
The British Standard and Mr. Smedley's Hydropathic Establishment. London: 1864. V. 73
Handby Book of the Flower Garden. London: 1868. V. 69; 70
Handy Book of the Flower Garden. London: 1887. V. 72

THOMSON, DAVID CLEGHORN
No Room at the Inn or, the Calling of the Bride. Edinburgh and London: 1928. V. 69
Oxford Poetry 1923. Oxford: 1923. V. 69

THOMSON, DON W.
Men and Meridians the History of Surveying and Mapping in Canada. Ottawa: 1966-1969. V. 69

THOMSON, H. DOUGLAS
Sherlock Holmes in Masters of Mystery. London: 1931. V. 68; 72

THOMSON, H. K.
Doenitz at Nuremberg: a Reappraisal, War Crimes and the Military Professional. New York: 1976. V. 71

THOMSON, J. ANSTRUTHER
Eighty Years Reminiscences. London: 1904. V. 72

THOMSON, J. B.
Joseph Thomson African Explorer. A Biography by His Brother with Contributions by Friends. London: 1896. V. 71

THOMSON, J. C.
Bibliographical List of the Writings of Algernon Charles Swinburne. 1905. V. 68
Bibliography of the Writings of Charles Dickens. Warwick: 1904. V. 68

THOMSON, J. J.
Recent Researches in Electricity and Magnetism Intended as a Sequel to Professor Clerk-Maxwell's Treatise on Electricity and Magnetism. Oxford: 1893. V. 68

THOMSON, J. M. ARCHER
Climbing in the Ogwen District. London: 1910. V. 69
The Climbs on Lliwedd. London: 1909. V. 69

THOMSON, J. W.
Lichens of the Alaskan Arctic Slope. Toronto: 1979. V. 72

THOMSON, JAMES
Britannia. A Poem. London: 1730. V. 69
The City of Dreadful Night and Other Poems. London: 1880. V. 72
The Poetical Works. London: 1847. V. 72
The Seasons. London: 1730. V. 69
The Seasons. Basil: 1769. V. 69
The Seasons. Glasgow: 1792. V. 71
The Seasons. London: 1802. V. 68
The Seasons. London: 1805. V. 72
The Seasons. London: 1821. V. 71
The Seasons. London: 1825. V. 69
The Seasons. London: 1859. V. 71
The Seasons. London: 1927. V. 68
The Seasons and The Castle of Indolence. London: 1841. V. 71
The Value and Importance of the Scottish Fisheries.... London: 1849. V. 68
Vane's Story. Weddah and Om-El Bonain and Other Poems. London: 1881. V. 72
A Voice from the Nile and Other Poems. London: 1884. V. 72
Winter. A Poem. London: 1726. V. 68

THOMSON, JOHN
The Letters of Curtius.... Richmond: 1804. V. 68
Street Incidents. London: 1881. V. 71
Tables of Interest at 3, 4, 4 1/2 and 5 per cent.... Edinburgh: 1783. V. 69

THOMSON, JOHN LEWIS
History of the War of the United States with Great Britain in 1812, and of the War with Mexico. Philadelphia: 1887. V. 69

THOMSON, JOSEPH JOHN
Applications of Dynamics to Physics and Chemistry. London and New York: 1888. V. 72
Cathode rays. In: The London, Edinburgh and Dublin Philosophical Magazine and Journal of Science, Fifth Series. Number CCLXIX, October 1897. London: 1897. V. 72
On the Charge of Electricity carried by the ions produced by Rontgen rays in: The London, Edinburgh and Dublin Philosophical Magazine and Journal of Science Fifth Series, Volume XLVI July-December 1898. London: 1898. V. 72

THOMSON, JUNE
The Secret Chronicles Of Sherlock Holmes. London: 1992. V. 72
The Secret Documents of Sherlock Holmes. London: 1997. V. 70; 73
The Secret Files of Sherlock Holmes. London: 1990. V. 70; 73
The Secret Journals of Sherlock Holmes. London: 1993. V. 69

THOMSON, MOLLY B.
The Three Little Pigs. England: 1948. V. 70

THOMSON, RICHARD
An Historical Essay on the Magna Charta of King John; to Which are Added, The Great Charter in Latin and English; The Charters of Liberties and Confirmations, etc. London: 1829. V. 70

THOMSON, RON
Mahohboh. Elephant and Elephant Hunting in South Central Africa. 1997. V. 70; 72; 73
The Wildlife Game. 1992. V. 70; 72; 73
The Wildlilfe Game. South Africa: 1992. V. 71

THOMSON, SAMUEL
A Narrative of the Life and Medical Discoveries of Samuel Thomson. Boston: 1822. V. 68
New Guide to Health or Botanic Family Physician. Brockville: 1831. V. 71
New Guide to Health, or Botanic Family Physician. (bound with) New Guide to Health or Botanic Family Physician. Boston: 1835. V. 71

THOMSON, SPENCER
Wanderings Among the Wild Flowers: How to See and How to Gather Them. London: 1857. V. 71
Wild Flowers: How to See and How to Gather Them. London: 1861. V. 72
Wild Flowers: Where to Find and How to Know Them. London: 1870. V. 72

THOMSON, THOMAS
On the Gaseous Combinations of Hydrogen and Carbon. Edinburgh: 1810. V. 68

THOMSON, W. G.
A History of Tapestry From the Earliest Times Until the Present Day. London: 1906. V. 72
A History of Tapestry from the Earliest Times Until the Present Day. London: 1930. V. 72

THOMSON, WILLIAM
Practical Treatise on the Cultivation of the Grape Vine. Edinburgh: 1862. V. 70
The Sizing of Cotton Goods, and the Causes and Prevention of Mildew. Manchester: 1877. V. 71
Tables for Facilitating Sumner's Method at Sea. London: 1876. V. 69

THON, MELANIE RAE
Girls in the Grass. New York: 1991. V. 68; 69; 71
Iona Moon. New York: 1993. V. 69
Meteors in August. New York: 1990. V. 69
Meteors in August. London: 1991. V. 69

THORBURN, A.
Birds of Prey. 1985. V. 72
Birds of Prey. Bures: 1985. V. 73
British Birds. 1915-1918. V. 69
British Birds. 1925. V. 69
British Mammals. 1920-1921. V. 69
Game Birds and Wild-Fowl of Great Britain and Ireland. London: 1923. V. 73

THORBURN, W. STEWART
A Guide to the Coins of Great Britain and Ireland, in Gold, Silver and Copper.... London: 1885. V. 68

THOREAU, HENRY DAVID
Autumn. Boston: 1892. V. 68
Cape Cod. Boston: 1865. V. 68; 72; 73
Cape Cod. Boston and New York: 1896. V. 69
Cape Cod. Portland: 1968. V. 68
Civil Disobedience. Boston: 1969. V. 69
Excursions. Boston: 1863. V. 68
The First and Last Journeys of Thoreau. Boston: 1905. V. 71
Huckleberries. Iowa: 1970. V. 73
The Journal of Henry D. Thoreau. New York: 1962. V. 68
Letters to Various Persons. Boston: 1865. V. 68; 72
A Plea for Captain John Brown. Boston: 1969. V. 72
Thoreau's Last Letter. Amenia: 1925. V. 68
Walden. Boston: 1854. V. 68; 70
Walden. Boston: 1909. V. 73
Walden. London: 1927. V. 70
Walden. Chicago: 1930. V. 73
Walden. Boston: 1936. V. 69; 73
Walden. New York: 1936. V. 69; 71
Walden (in German). Munich: 1897. V. 72
A Week on the Concord and Merrimack Rivers. Boston: 1868. V. 70
A Yankee in Canada. Boston;: 1866. V. 68

THOREK, PHILIP
Anatomy in Surgery. Philadelphia: 1951. V. 71

THORER, ALBAN
De Re Medica. Basileae: 1528. V. 71

THORESBY, RALPH
Ducatus Leodiensis; or the Topography of the Ancient and Populous Town and Parish of Leedes, and Parts Adjacent in the West Riding of the County of York. London: 1715. V. 69; 70; 73

THORGERSON, S.
Album Cover Album. New York: 1977. V. 72

THORIN, DUANE
A Ride to Panmunjom. Chicago: 1956. V. 69

THORINGTON, J. MONROE
A Survey of Early American Ascents in the Alps in the Nineteenth Century. New York: 1943. V. 69

THORIUS, RAPHAEL
Hymnus Tabaci; a Poem in Honour of Tabaco. London: 1651. V. 68

THORLEY, JOHN
Melisselogia (Greek Type), or the Female Monarchy. London: 1744. V. 68; 72

THORN, ISMAY
In and Out. London: 1884. V. 70

THORNBER, WILLIAM
An Historical and Descriptive Account of Blackpool and Its Neighbourhood.... Poulton: 1837. V. 71

THORNBURG, NEWTON
To Die in California. Boston: 1973. V. 68; 71

THORNBURY, WALTER
British Artists from Hogarth to Turner, Being a Series of Biographical Sketches. London: 1861. V. 73

THORNDIKE, RUSSELL
Doctor Syn. A Tale of the Romney Marsh. 1915. V. 73
Doctor Syn Returns. London: 1935. V. 69; 71; 73
The Forbidden Room. New York: 1933. V. 70
The Tragedy of Mr. Punch - a Fantastic Play in Prologue and One Act. London: 1923. V. 68

THORNE, EDWARD
Decorative Draperies and Upholstery. Grand Rapids: 1929. V. 69

THORNE, GUY
The Secret Service Submarine. London: 1915. V. 69

THORNE, JAMES
Handbook to the Environs of London, Alphabetically Arranged.... London: 1876. V. 68; 71
Rambles by Rivers. 1844-1845. V. 73
Rambles by Rivers - the Thames. 1849. V. 68

THORNICROFT, JANE
Stripey the Badger. London: 1935. V. 72

THORNTON, ABEL
The Life of Abel Thornton, Late of Johnston, R.I. Providence: 1828. V. 71

THORNTON, ERNEST
Leaves from an Afghan Scrapbook. London: 1910. V. 69

THORNTON, FRANK S.
History of the Escalon Community in California. 1964. V. 71

THORNTON, J. P.
The Sectional System of Gentlemen's Garment Cutting, Comprising Coats, Vests, Breeches, Trousers &c. London: 1894. V. 68; 69; 72

THORNTON, J. QUINN
The California Tragedy. Oakland: 1945. V. 71

THORNTON, LAWRENCE
Ghost Woman. New York: 1992. V. 72
Imagining Argentina. New York: 1987. V. 69; 72

THORNTON, MARY L.
A Bibliography of North Carolina 1589-1956. Chapel Hill: 1958. V. 68

THORNTON, PETER
Authentic Decor. the Domestic Interior 1620-1920. New York: 1984. V. 72

THORNTON, R.
A New Family Herbal.... 1810. V. 69

THORNTON, RICHARD H.
An American Glossary. Philadelphia and London: 1912,. V. 73

THORNTON, ROBERT JOHN
Elements of Botany. (with) The British Flora; or Genera and Species of British Plants. London: 1812. V. 70; 71

THORNTON, THOMAS
A Sporting Tour Through the Northern Parts of England and a Great Part of the Highlands of Scotland. 1896. V. 71

THORNTON, WILLIAM
Cadmus; or a Treatise on the Elements of Written Language. Philadelphia: 1793. V. 73
Political Economy: Founded in Justice and Humanity, in a Letter to a Friend. Washington City: 1804. V. 68; 71

THORNWELL, JAMES H.
The State of the Country: an Article Republished from the Southern Presbyterian Reivew. Columbia: 1861. V. 69; 70

THOROTON SOCIETY
Transactions of Thoroton Society: an Antiquarian Society for Nottingham and Nottinghamshire. Nottingham: 1898-1983. V. 72

THORP, JACK
Pardner of the Wind. Caldwell: 1944. V. 71
Pardner of the Wind. Caldwell: 1945. V. 73

THORP, JOHN
Letters of the Late John Thorp, of Manchester. Manchester: 1828. V. 72

THORP, JOSEPH
Early Days in the West Along the Missouri One Hundred Years Ago. Liberty: 1924. V. 68; 70; 73

THORP, N. HOWARD
Pardner of the Wind. Caldwell: 1945. V. 69
Songs of Cowboys. Boston: 1921. V. 68

THORP, RAYMOND
Bowie Knife. Albuquerque: 1948. V. 71; 73
Spirit Gun of the West. Glendale: 1957. V. 68

THORP, RODERICK
Nothing Lasts Forever. New York: 1979. V. 71

THORP, W. H.
John N. Rhodes, A Yorkshire Painter, 1809-1842. London: 1904. V. 72

THORPE, ADAM
The Ox-Bow's Heath. London: 1999. V. 73
Ulverton. London: 1992. V. 72

THORPE, CARLYLE
Journey to the Walnut Sections of Europe and Asia. 1923. V. 72

THORPE, ELPHINSTONE
Nursery Rhymes for Fighting Times. London: 1915. V. 68

THORPE, J. E.
Salmon Ranching. New York: 1980. V. 73

THORPE, W. A.
A History of English and Irish Glass. London: 1929. V. 68

THORSON, T. B.
Investigations of the Icthyofauna of the Nicaraguan Lakes. Lincoln: 1976. V. 69

THORTON, W. W.
The Law of Railroad Fences and Private Crossings. Indianapolis: 1892. V. 68

THORY, CLAUDE ANTOINE
Monographie ou Histoire Naturelle du Genre Groseillier.... Paris: 1829. V. 72

THOUGHTS On Non-Residence, Tithes, Inclosures, Rare Landlords, Rich Tenants, Regimental Chaplains, &c &c. London: 1800. V. 73

THOUGHTS on Public Prayer, and On Modern Infidelity. London: 1730. V. 70

THOUGHTS on the Importance of the Manners of the Great to General Society. Philadelphia: 1788. V. 71

THOUGHTS on Traits of the Ministerial Policy. London: 1843. V. 69

THRAPP, DAN L.
Al Sieber: Chief of Scouts. Norman: 1964. V. 69; 72
A Cavalryman In Indian Country. Ashland, OR: 1974. V. 72
The Conquest of Apacheria. 1967. V. 69
The Conquest of Apacheria. Norman: 1967. V. 72
General Crook and The Sierra Madre Adventure. Norman: 1972. V. 72
Victorio - And The Mimbres Apaches. Norman: 1974. V. 72

THRASHER, HARRIETTE F.
The Clan Chisholm and Allied Clans. New York: 1935. V. 72

THREE American Painters. Kenneth Noland, Jules Olitski, Frank Stella. Harvard: 1965. V. 70

THE THREE Bears. London: 1895. V. 72
THE THREE Bears. Dundee: 1926. V. 70
THE THREE Bears. 1938. V. 72

THE THREE Bears Model Cut-Outs. England: 1930. V. 70

THREE Famous New Songs Called Effects of Whisky. The Valley below. Larry O'Gaff. Paisley: 1820. V. 68; 72

THE THREE Good Friends: Lillie, Carrie, and Floss. New York: 1871-1874. V. 71

THREE Hundred and Fifty Tried and Tested Formulas by the Ladies of the Second Congregational Church, Biddeford, Maine. 1886. Biddeford: 1886. V. 70

THREE Hundred Things a Bright Boy Can Do. Philadelphia: 1910. V. 73

THREE Kittens in a Boat. London: 1930. V. 68

THREE Letters from Hell. Letters Reputedly in the Hand of the Whitechapel Murderer. 1988. V. 70

THREE Little Kittens. New York: 1875. V. 71
THE THREE Little Kittens. New York: 1890. V. 70
THREE Little Kittens. New York: 1908. V. 69
THE THREE Little Kittens. London: 1910. V. 71
THREE Little Kittens. Akron: 1940. V. 71

THREE Little Kittens and Mr. Fox. New York: 1863-1866. V. 71

THE THREE Little Pigs. Racine: 1933. V. 70

THREE Pieces of Advice, or, the Friend Indeed. Carmarthen: 1820. V. 68

THREE Wishes. New York: 1868-1874. V. 71

THE THRILLING Adventures of a New York Detective. New York: 1893. V. 70

THRILLS, Crimes and Mysteries. London: 1936. V. 68

THROCKMORTON, ROBERT
Columbus Ohio Division of Fire. Columbus?: 1979?. V. 69

THROOP, A. J.
Mound Builders of Illinois. East St. Louis: 1928. V. 69

THROUGH the Window. 1930. V. 71

THROWER, N. J. W.
Sir Francis Drake and the Famous Voyage 1577-1580. Berkeley: 1984. V. 68

THRUM, THOMAS G.
Hawaiian Folk Tales: a Collection of Native Legends. Chicago: 1907. V. 71
More Hawiian Folk Tales. Chicago: 1923. V. 71

THUBRON, COLIN
Distance. London: 1996. V. 73
Jerusalem. London: 1969. V. 72; 73
Journey into Cyprus. London: 1975. V. 69

THUCYDIDES
Peloponnesian War. Oxford: 1881. V. 68
Thucydides Translated into English.... Oxford: 1881. V. 70

THUDICHUM, J. L. W.
Spirit of Cookery. London: 1895. V. 73
Treatise on the Chemical Constitution of the Brain. 1962. V. 71

THUNBERG, CARL PETER
Flora Capensis.... Stuttgart: 1823. V. 72; 73
Resa uti Europa, Africa, Asia, Forratted Aren 1770-1779. Upsala: 1788-1793. V. 70

THURAH, LAURIDS DE
Hafina Hodierna...Ausfuhrliche Beschreibung der Koniglichen Residenz- und Haupstadt Copenhagen, Nebst Einer Erklarung Aller Merkwurdigkeiten.... Copenhagen: 1748. V. 70; 72

THURBER, JAMES
Alarms and Diversions. New York: 1957. V. 73
The Beast in Me ad Other Animals. New York: 1948. V. 68; 70; 73
Further Fables for Our Time. New York: 1956. V. 71; 73
My World - and Welcome To It. London: 1942. V. 68
People Have More Fun Than Anybody. New York: 1994. V. 69; 72
Selected Letters. Boston: 1981. V. 72
The 13 Clocks. New York: 1950. V. 70
Thurber's Men, Women and Dogs - A Book of Drawings. London: 1944. V. 72
The White Deer. New York: 1945. V. 68; 69; 71
The Wonderful O. New York: 1957. V. 71

THURMAN, HOWARD
Deep River. Reflections on the Religious Insight of Certain of the Negro Spirituals. New York: 1955. V. 70
Why I Believe There Is A God: Sixteen Essays By Negro Clergymen. Chicago: 1965. V. 72

THURMAN, WALLACE
The Blacker the Berry.... New York: 1929. V. 70

THURSTON, E.
Ethnographic Notes of Southern India. Madras: 1907. V. 69

THURSTON, E. TEMPLE
The Goose-Feather Bed. New York: 1927. V. 71; 72
The World of Wonderful Reality. New York: 1919. V. 70

THURSTON, G. P.
Antiquities of Tennessee and the Adjacent States. Cincinnati: 1890. V. 69

THURSTON, JOHN
Illustrations of Shakespeare, Comprised in Two Hundred and Thirty Vignette Engravings by Thompson, from Designs by Thurston. 1825. V. 73

THURSTON, ROBERT H.
Reports of the United States to the International Exhibiton Held at Vienna 1873.... Washington: 1876. V. 71

THWAITE, ANTHONY
Paeans for Peter Porter - a Celebration for Peter Porter on His Seventieth Birthday by Twenty of His Friends 16 February 1999. London: 1999. V. 70

THWAITES, REUBEN GOLD
Early Western Travels 1748-1846. Volume II. J. Long's Voyages. Cleveland: 1904. V. 69
Early Western Travels 1748-1846. Volume XVIII - Pattie's Personal Narrative, 1824-1830; Willard's Inland Trade with New Mexico, 1825. and Downfall of the Fredonian Republic and Malte-Brun's Account of Mexico. Cleveland: 1904. V. 69
Early Western Travels 1748-1846. Volumes XIV, XV, XVI, XVII. Account of an Expedition from Pittsburgh to the Rocky Mountains. Cleveland: 1905. V. 69
Early Western Travels: Volumes XIX & XX. Letters from the West - Sketch of a Journey - Commerce of the Prairies. Cleveland: 1905. V. 69
Historic Waterways. Chicago: 1888. V. 69
The Revolution on the Upper Ohio 1775-1777. Madison: 1908. V. 72; 73

THWING, EUGENE
The World's Best One Hundred Detective Stories. New York: 1929. V. 68

THYNNE, BERYL
The Shetland Sheepdog. 1916. V. 68

TIBULLUS, ALBIUS
Opera. Patavii: 1749. V. 71

TICE, CLARA
ABC Dogs. New York: 1940. V. 72

TICE, GEORGE A.
Photographs 1953-1973. New Brunswick: 1975. V. 70

TICE, HENRY A.
Early Railroad Days in Mexico. Santa Fe: 1965. V. 68; 73

TICE, JOHN H.
Over the Plains, on the Mountains; or Kansas, Colorado and the Rocky Mountains.... St. Louis: 1872. V. 68; 71

TICEHURST, C. B.
A History of the Birds of Suffolk. London: 1932. V. 73

TICEHURST, F. W.
Views of Battle Abbey. Battle: 1840. V. 70

TICK Tick. London: 1910. V. 73

TICK-Tock All Around the Clock. New York: 1917. V. 72

TICKELL, RICHARD
Catalogue of the Classical, Theological and Miscellaneous Library of the Late. Rev. Charles Drury...and also the Library of a Naturalist and Sportsman...Curious Books and Manuscripts from the Library of Richard Tickell.... London: 1869. V. 70
The Green Box of Monsieur de Sartine, Found at Mademoiselle du The's Lodgings. Dublin: 1779. V. 71
Probationary Odes for the Laureatship.... London: 1785. V. 73
The Wreath of Fashion, or, the Art of Sentimental Poetry. London: 1778. V. 73

TICKNOR, CAROLINE
Hawthorne and His Publisher. Boston and New York: 1913. V. 68

TICKNOR, GEORGE
The Life of William Hickling Prescott. Boston: 1804. V. 72
Life of William Hickling Prescott. London: 1864. V. 68

TIDCOMBE, M.
The Bookbindings of T. J. Cobden-Sanderson. A Study of His Work 18841893.... London: 1984. V. 70

TIDCOMBE, MARIANNE
The Doves Bindery. London: 1991. V. 73

TIDESTROM, I.
Elysium Marianum: Ferns and Fern Allies and Elysium Marianum: Evergreens. Washington: 1907-1908. V. 68

TIDYMAN, ERNEST
Line of Duty. Boston: 1974. V. 70
Shaft. New York: 1970. V. 69; 72
Shaft. London: 1971. V. 69
Shaft Among the Jews. New York: 1972. V. 70
Shaft Among the Jews. London: 1973. V. 69

TIEDMANN, FRIEDRICH
Das Hirn des Negers mit dem des Europaers und Orag-Outangs Verglichen. Heidelberg: 1837. V. 72

TIEPOLO, GIOVANNI DOMENICO
Via Crucis Novellamente Eretta nell'atrio del Santissimo Crocifisso della Chiesa Parrocchiale, e Collegiata di S. Polo. Venice: 1749. V. 72

TIFFANY STUDIOS
The Tiffany Studios Collection of Antique Chinese Rugs. New York: 1908. V. 72; 73

TIGER, PEGGY
The Life and Art of Jerome Tiger: War to Peace, Death of Life. Norman: 1980. V. 70; 71; 73

TIGER Tim's Annual 1924. 1924. V. 73

TIGHE, MARY
Psyche: or the Legend of Love. London: 1805. V. 72

TIGHE, WILLIAM
The Plants; a Poem, Cantos the Third and Fourth with Notes and Observations. London: 1811. V. 72

TIKADER, B. K.
The Fauna of India. Scorpions. Scorpionida: Arachnida. Volume III. Calcutta: 1983. V. 72

TILBURY DREDGING AND CONTRACTING CO., LTD.
A Review of 30 Years Work. London: 1918. V. 70

TILDEN, J. E.
The Algae and Their Life Relations.... Minneapolis: 1937. V. 72

TILDEN, JOSEPH
Joe Tilden's Recipes for Epicures. San Francisco: 1907. V. 68; 73

TILDEN, WILLIAM T.
Glory's Net. Garden City: 1930. V. 72

TILDESLEY, MIRIAM L.
Sir Thomas Browne: His Skull, Portraits and Ancestry. 1923. V. 70; 71

TILGHMAN, CHRISTOPHER
In a Father's Place. New York: 1990. V. 68
Mason's Retreat. New York: 1996. V. 68
The Way People Run. New York: 1999. V. 72

TILGHMAN, ZOE A.
Marshal of the Last Frontier: Life and Services of William Matthew (Bill) Tilghman. Glendale: 1949. V. 70
Marshal of the Last Frontier: Life and Services of William Matthew (Bill) Tilghman. Glendale: 1964. V. 69
Quanah - The Eagle of The Comanches. Oklahoma City: 1938. V. 72

TILLENT, LESLIE
Wind On The Buffalo Grass, The Indian's Own Account of The Battle At The Little Big Horn and The Death of Their Life On the Plains. New York: 1976. V. 72

TILLER, TERENCE
The Inward Animal. London: 1943. V. 68
Poems. London: 1941. V. 69

TILLESLEY, RICHARD
Animadversions Upon Mr. Seldens History of Tythes, and His Review Thereof: Before Which (in lieu of the two first Chapters Purposely Pretermitted) is Premised a Catalouge of 72 Authors, Before the Years 1215. London: 1621. V. 70

TILLETT, LESLIE
Wind on the Buffalo Grass: the Indian's Own Account of the Battle of the Little Big Horn River.... New York: 1976. V. 72

TILLEY, W. W.
One Hundred Masterpieces from the Collection of Dr. Walter A. Compton. New York: 1992. V. 69

TILLOTSON, F. H.
How to Be A Detective. Kansas City: 1909. V. 71

TILLOTSON, H. JOHN
Diseases of Men: Cause and Cure. Chicago: 1906. V. 71

TILLOTSON, M. R.
Grand Canyon Country. Stanford: 1929. V. 69

TILLY, WILLIAM
A Letter to a Worthy and Learned Gentleman in the Law, Concerning Some Passages of the Life and Death of Mrs. Sarah Tilly.... Oxford: 1739. V. 71

TILMAN, H. W.
The Ascent of Nanda Devi. 1937. V. 68
The Ascent of Nanda Devi. London: 1937. V. 69
The Ascent of Nanda Devi. 1973. V. 71
China to Chitral. London: 1950. V. 72
China to Chitral. 1951. V. 68
China to Chitral. Cambridge: 1951. V. 70
Mischief Among the Penguins. 1961. V. 68
Mischief Among The Penguins. London: 1961. V. 72
Mischief In Patagonia. Cambridge: 1957. V. 72
Mount Everest 1938. 1938. V. 68
Mount Everest 1938. 1948. V. 71; 73
Mount Everest 1948. 1948. V. 68
Nepal Himalaya. Description of Three Expeditions. 1942. V. 68
The Seven Mountain - Travel Books. London: 1983. V. 69
Snow on the Equator. 1937. V. 68
Two Mountains and a River. 1949. V. 68; 71; 73
When Men and Mountains Meet. 1946. V. 68; 69; 71

TILNEY, F.
The Brain from Ape to Man.... New York: 1928. V. 70
The Form and Functions of the Central Nervous System. New York: 1921. V. 68

TILTON, ALICE
The Hollow Chest. New York: 1941. V. 69; 72

TILY, JOSEPH
Select Orations Upon the Liberty and Peace of Europe. London: 1704. V. 72

TIMBS, JOHN
Abbeys, Castles and Ancient Halls of England And Wales. London: 1875. V. 71
Curiosities of London, Exhibiting the Most Rare and Remarkable Objects of Interest in the Metropolis.... London: 1867. V. 71
Eccentrics and Eccentricities. London: 1877. V. 73
London and Westminster...Strange Events, Characteristics and Changes of Metropolitan Life. London: 1868. V. 69
Predictions Realized in Modern Times. London: 1880. V. 73
Walks and Talks About London. London: 1865. V. 71
The Year Book of Facts in Science and Art. London: 1862-1871. V. 72

THE TIMES
Anthology of Ghost Stories. London: 1975. V. 69

TIMLIN, WILLIAM
The Ship That Sailed to Mars. London: 1923. V. 71
The Ship that Sailed to Mars. A Fantasy. New York: 1923. V. 69

TIMMONS, WILBERT H.
Morelos of Mexico: Priest Soldier Statesman. El Paso: 1970. V. 71

TIMPERLEY, C. H.
Encyclopaedia of Literary and Typographical Anecdote.... London: 1842. V. 73
The Printers' Manual... (bound with) Encyclopaedia of Literary and Typographical Anecdote.... London: 1838. V. 70

TIMPSON, THOMAS
Memoirs of Mrs. Elizabeth Fry.... London: 1847. V. 72

TINDALE, THOMAS KEITH
Handmade Papers of Japan. Rutland: 1952. V. 68

TINDALL, GEORGE B.
South Carolina Negroes 1877-1900. Columbia: 1952. V. 71

TINEL, J.
Nerve Wounds Symptomatology of Peripheral Nerve Lesions Caused by War Wounds. London: 1918. V. 68; 70; 71

TINER, FRANCIS
Old New Orleans. New York: 1931. V. 70

TINGLEY, ELBERT R.
Poco Loco: Sketches of New Mexico Life. Blair: 1900. V. 70

TINGRY, P. F.
The Painter and Varnisher's Guide. London: 1804. V. 68; 69
The Painter and Varnisher's Guide. London: 1816. V. 68; 69
The Painter and Varnisher's Guide; or a Treatise Both in Theory and Practice, on the Art of Making and Applying Varnishes.... 1816. V. 71

TINKER, CHAUNCEY BREWSTER
Addresses Commemorating the One Hundredth Anniversary of the Birth of William Morris Delivered Before the Yale Library Associates in the Sterling Memorial Library XXIX October MCMXXXIV. 1935. V. 70; 72

TINKER, EDWARD LAROCQUE
Corridos and Calaveras. Austin: 1961. V. 71
The Horsemen of the Americas and the Literature They Inspired. Austin: 1967. V. 70
Lafcadio Hearn's American Days. New York: 1924. V. 70
Lafcadio Hearn's American Days. London: 1925. V. 72

TINKER, EDWARD LAROQUE
The Horsemen of the Americas. New York: 1953. V. 69

TINKHAM, GEORGE
California Men & Events. Stockton: 1915. V. 71
History of San Joaquin County, California.... Los Angeles: 1923. V. 71

TINKLE, LON J.
Frank Dobie, the Makings of an Ample Mind. Austin: 1968. V. 70

TINLEY, G. F.
Colour Planning of the Garden. London: 1924. V. 69; 71

TINTIN
in America. London: 1978. V. 68

TINY
Tots ABC. London: 1902. V. 73
TINY Tots ABC. London: 1919. V. 72

TIP
Top Build a Motorcar. London: 1961. V. 72

TIPHAIGNE DE LA ROCHE, CHARLES FRANCOIS
Giphantia; or, a View of What Has Passed, What is Now Passing and During the Present Century, What Will Pass in the World. London: 1761. V. 70

TIPPETT, EDWARD D.
The Experience and Trials of Edward D. Tippett, Preceptor, or 44 Years of His Life. Washinbgton: 1833. V. 73

TIPPETT, MICHAEL
String Quartet III. London: 1948. V. 72

TIPPING, HENRY AVARY
English Homes. Period III. Volume I. Late Tudor and Early Stuart 1649-1714. 1929. V. 69
English Homes. Period IV Volume I. 1929. V. 69

TIPPING, HENRY AVRAY
Gardens Old and New: the Country House and Its Garden Environment. Volume I. London: 1914. V. 68
Gardens Old and New: The Country House and Its Garden Environment. Volume III. London: 1910. V. 68
Gardens Old and New: the Country House and Its Garden Environment. Volume III. London: 1916. V. 68

TISDALE, CELES
Betcha Ain't: Poems From Attica. New York: 1962. V. 72

TISSANDIER, GASTON
Marvels of Earth, Air and Water.... New York: 1880. V. 71
Marvels of Invention and Scientific Puzzles. London and New York: 1890. V. 68
Popular Scientific Recreations in Natural Philosophy.... London. V. 70

TISSOT, SAMUEL AUGUSTE ANDRE DAVID
Advice to the People in General, with Regard to Their Health.... Dublin: 1766. V. 73
An Essay on Bilious Fevers or the History of a Bilious Epidemic Fever at Lausanne in the Year 1755. London. V. 73
Practical Observations on the Small Pox, the Apoplexy, Dropsy and Nervous Cholic, in a Series of Letters to the Most Noble and Illustrious Albert Haller. Dublin: 1773. V. 73
Three Essays: First on the Disorders of People of Fashion Second on Diseases Incidental to Literary and Sedentary Persons Third On Onanism.... Dublin: 1772. V. 73
Traite des Nerfs et de Leurs Maladies. Lausanne: 1784. V. 68; 73

TISSOT, SIMON ANDRE
Advice to the People in General, with Regard to Their Health.... London: 1771. V. 69

TITFORD, WILLIAM JOWIT
Sketches Towards a Hortus Botanicus Americanus.... London: 1812. V. 69

TITIEV, MISCHA
Old Araibi, a Study of the Hopi Indians of Third Mesa. Cambridge: 1944. V. 72

TITON, JEFF TODD
Early Downhome Blues. Urbana: 1977. V. 69; 71

TIZZARD, SAMUEL
The New Athenian Oracle; or Ladies' Companion. Carlisle: 1806. V. 68; 69; 72

TO Remember Gregg Anderson: Tributes by Members at the Columbiad Club, the Rounce and Coffin Club, the Roxburghe Club and Zamorano Club. 1949. V. 68

TO Utah With The Dragoons & Glimpses of Life in Arizona & California 1858-1859. Salt Lake City: 1904. V. 72

TO You, Walt Whitman. New York: 1977. V. 72

TOBENKIN, ELIAS
City of Friends. New York: 1934. V. 71
Witte Arrives. New York: 1916. V. 68

TOCQUEVILLE, ALEXIS CHARLES HENRI MAURICE CLEREL DE, COMTE
Correspondence and Conversations of Alexis de Tocqueville with Nassau William Senior, from 1834 to 1859. London: 1872. V. 71
Democracy in America. London: 1835. V. 73

TOD, GEORGE
Plans, Elevations and Sections of Hot-Houses, Green-Houses, an Aquarium, Conservatories &c.... London: 1812. V. 68; 70; 72

TODD, ALPHEUS
Parliamentary Government in England.... London: 1892. V. 71

TODD, CHARLES
Search the Dark. 1999. V. 68
A Test of Wills. London: 1996. V. 68
A Test of Wills. New York: 1996. V. 68; 69; 70; 71; 73

TODD, CHARLES W.
Woodville; or, the Anchoret Reclaimed. Knoxville: 1832. V. 69

TODD, F. S.
Waterfowl, Ducks, Geese and Swans of the World. New York: 1979. V. 73

TODD, GEORGE T.
First Texas Regiment. Waco;: 1963. V. 70

TODD, JAMES HENTHORN
Descriptive Remarks on Illuminations in Certain Ancient Irish Manuscripts. 1869. V. 70
The History of the College of Bonhommes at Ashridge, in the County of Buckingham Founded in the Year 1276.... London: 1823. V. 68; 70; 72
Inaugural Address to the Members of the Royal Irish Academy April 14th 1856. 1856. V. 70

TODD, MABEL LOOMIS
A Cycle of Sonnets. Boston: 1896. V. 71

TODD, MARILYN
I, Claudia. London: 1995. V. 69

TODD, MARTHA GADDIS
Life and Letters of.... Chicago: 1940. V. 72

TODD, NICHOLAS H.
Poems and Plays. Sedbergh: 1917. V. 71

TODD, PETER
The Adventure Of Sherlock Holmes. New York: 1976. V. 72

TODD, RUTHVEN
The Acreage of the Heart. 1944. V. 68
Until Now. London: 1942. V. 68

TODD, THOMAS
The Gaugers' Useful Companion.... Manchester: 1841. V. 71

TODD, W. E.
The Birds of the Santa Marta Region of Colombia.... Pittsburgh: 1922. V. 73

TODD, W. E. C.
Birds of Western Pennsylvania. Pittsburgh: 1940. V. 72

TODD, W. H.
Tiger! Tiger!. 1927. V. 69; 70; 72
Work, Sport and Play. 1928. V. 70; 72; 73

TODHUNTER, ISAAC
An Elementary Treatise on the Theory of Equations with a Collection of Examples. London and New York: 1895. V. 69
A History of the Progress of the Calculus of Variations During the Nineteenth Century. Cambridge and London: 1861. V. 72
A History of the Theory of Elsasticity and of the Strength of Materials from Galilei to the Present Time. Cambridge: 1886-1893. V. 71

TODHUNTER, JOHN
An Essay in Search of a Subject. 1904. V. 70
Forest Songs - and Other Poems. London: 1881. V. 68

TODOD, CHARLES
A Test of Wills. New York: 1996. V. 69

TOEPFFER, RUDOLPHE
The Veritable History of Mr. Bachelor Butterfly. London: 1845. V. 68

TOIBIN, COLM
New Writing from Ireland. Winchester: 1994. V. 69
The Penguin Book of Irish Fiction. 2000. V. 69
The South. 1991. V. 72

TOLAND, JOHN
The Art of Governing by Partys.... London: 1701. V. 73
The Dillinger Days. London: 1963. V. 71
The Second Part of the State Anatomy &c. London: 1717. V. 69

TOLD, SILAS
An Account of the Life and Dealings of God with Silas Told, Late Preacher of the Gospel.... Salford: 1805. V. 69

TOLEDANO, RALPH DE
Nixon. New York: 1956. V. 69; 71

TOLET, FRANCOIS
Traite de La Lithotomie Ou de L'Extraction De La Pierre Hors de la Vessie. Paris: 1708. V. 71
A Treatise of Lithotomy; or, of the Extraction of the Stone Out of the Bladder. London: 1683. V. 68

TOLFREY, F.
Jones' Guide to Norway. 1994. V. 68; 73

TOLKIEN, JOHN RONALD REUEL
The Adventures of Tom Bombadil and Other Verses from the Red Book. London: 1962. V. 72
Beowulf the Monsters and the Critics. 1971. V. 73
Bilbo's Last Song. 1990. V. 71
Bilbo's Last Song. London: 1990. V. 69
The Book of Lost Tales I. London: 1983. V. 68
The Devil's Coach-Horses Contained in The Review of English Studies. Volume I. No. 3. London: 1925. V. 72; 73
Farmer Giles of Ham. London: 1949. V. 73
The Father Christmas Letters. Boston: 1976. V. 70; 71
The Father Christmas Letters. London: 1976. V. 71; 73
Finn and Hengest: the Fragment and the Episode. Boston: 1983. V. 71
Goblin Fleet contained in Fifty New Poems for Children, an Anthology. London: 1924. V. 73
Goblin Fleet contained in Oxford Poetry. 1915. V. 73
The Hobbit. London: 1937. V. 72; 73
The Hobbit. Boston: 1938. V. 73
The Hobbit. London: 1946. V. 73
The Hobbit. London: 1955. V. 71; 72
The Hobbit. 1961. V. 73
The Hobbit. Boston: 1966. V. 73
The Hobbit. London: 1966. V. 71
The Hobbit. London: 1980. V. 68
The Hobbit. Boston: 1984. V. 71
The Hobbit. Forestville: 1990. V. 71
The Hobbit and the Lord of the Rings Trilogy. London: 1977-1979. V. 73
The Lord of the Rings. London: 1954-1955. V. 70
The Lord of the Rings. London: 1956-. V. 72
The Lord of the Rings. London: 1966. V. 70
The Lord of the Rings: The Fellowship of the Ring. The Two Towers. The Return of the King. London: 1954-1955. V. 71
The Lord of the Rings: The Fellowship of the Ring, The Two Towers, The Return of the King. Boston: 1965. V. 73
Poems and Stories. London: 1980. V. 70
The Return of the King. 1967. V. 71
The Road Goes Ever On. Boston: 1967. V. 70
The Road Goes Ever On. London: 1968. V. 68; 70; 71; 72
The Silmarillion. Boston: 1977. V. 71
The Silmarillion. London: 1977. V. 69; 70
Smith of Wootton Major. London: 1967. V. 72
Some Contributions to Middle English Lexicography. London: 1925. V. 70
Tree and Leaf. Boston: 1965. V. 72

TOLKIN, MICHAEL
The Player. London: 1988. V. 68
Player. New York: 1988. V. 72

TOLLEMACHE, STANHOPE
British Trees with Illustrations. London: 1901. V. 73

TOLLER, ERNST
Pastor Hall and Blind Man's Buff. New York: 1939. V. 71

TOLLEY, A. T.
Roy Fuller: a Tribute. Ottawa: 1993. V. 71

TOLOMEI, CLAUDIO
Delle Lettere (Libri VII). Venice: 1558. V. 73

TOLSON, JOHN
Mr. Vice-Chancellors Speech to His Maiestie, at Christ Chruch in Oxford on New Yeares Day.... Oxford: 1643. V. 68; 72

TOLSON, MELVIN B.
Rendezvous with America. New York: 1944. V. 68

TOLSTOI, LEV NIKOLAEVICH
Anna Karenina. New York: 1886. V. 70
Anna Karenina. Moscow: 1933. V. 68; 69
Childhood, Boyhood, Youth. New York: 1972. V. 70; 72
Ivan Ilyitch and Other Stories. New York: 1887. V. 70; 73
The Kreutzer Sonata. New York: 1890. V. 70
Love Letters. London: 1923. V. 70; 71
Master and Man. London: 1895. V. 71
Resurrection. London: 1900. V. 72
Resurrection. New York: 1927. V. 70
Resurrection. New York: 1963. V. 68; 70
War and Peace. Glasgow: 1938. V. 69
War and Peace. London: 1971. V. 70
What to Do. New York: 1887. V. 68

TOM of Bedlam's Songs. San Francisco: 1931. V. 73

TOM Thumb. London: 1875. V. 69

TOM Thumb Alphabet. New York: 1870. V. 69

TOM Thumb's Alphabet. London: 1870. V. 73

TOM Thumb's Folio; or, a New Penny Play-Thing for Little Giants.... 1825. V. 68

TOM Thumb's Picture Alphabet: in Rhyme. New York: 1856-1866. V. 70; 71

TOM Tom was a Piper's Son. London: 1890. V. 72

TOMASI, L. T.
An Oak Spring Flora.... Upperville: 1997. V. 73

TOMBLESON, THOMAS
Tombleson's Thames. London: 1834. V. 71

TOMKIN, DIANA
22 Poems. Dublin: 1959. V. 72

TOMKINS, ISAAC
Thoughts Upon the Aristocracy of England. London: 1835. V. 71

TOMLINS, ELIZABETH SOPHIA
Rosalind de Tracey, a Novel, in Two Volumes. Dublin: 1799. V. 69

TOMLINSON, CHARLES
The Manufacture of a Pin.... London: 1868. V. 68; 69
Relations and Contraries. Aldington: 1951. V. 73

TOMLINSON, DAVID
African Wildlife in Art. 1991. V. 69; 70; 72; 73

TOMLINSON, HENRY MAJOR
All Hands!. London: 1937. V. 69
All Our Yesterdays. London: 1930. V. 68; 73
Mars His Idiot. London: 1935. V. 70
Thomas Hardy. New York: 1929. V. 70; 72
Tidemarks: Some Records of a Journey to the Beaches of the Moluccas and the Forest of Malaya in 1923. London: 1924. V. 70

TOMMASI, GIUGURTA
Dell'Historie di Siena. Venice: 1625-1626. V. 72

TOMMY Tatters. New York: 1879. V. 71

TOMMY Tucker's Stories: Tom Tucker. Philadelphia: 1865-1866. V. 71

TOMPKINS, C. B.
High Speed Computing Devices. New York: 1950. V. 71

TOMPKINS, E. P.
The Natural Bridge and Its Historical Surroundings. VA: 1939. V. 71

TOMPKINS, G. C.
A Compendium of the Overland Mail Company On the South Route 1858- 1861 and The Period Surrounding It. Shawnee Mission: 1985. V. 73

TOMS, W.
Thirty-Six New and Pracical Designs for Chairs Adapted for the Drawing and Dining Room, Parlour and Hall.... Bath. V. 70
Thirty-Six New and Practical Designs for Chairs Adapted for the Drawing and Dining Room, Parlour and Hall. Bath: 1830. V. 68; 72

TONER, J. M.
Address Before the Rocky Mountain Medical Association June 6, 1877. Washington: 1877. V. 71

TONER, JEROME
Rural Ireland, Some Of Its Problems. 1955. V. 69

TONEY, MARCUS B.
The Privations of a Private. Nashville: 1905. V. 68; 73
The Privations of a Private. Nashville and Dallas: 1907. V. 69; 70

TONEYAMA, KOJIN
The Popular Arts of Mexico. New York: 1974. V. 71

TONGE, THOMAS
Denver, by Pen and Picture. Denver: 1898. V. 68

THE TONGUE Cut Sparrow. Tokyo. V. 70
THE TONGUE Cut Sparrow. Tokyo: 1900. V. 72

TONGUES of Fallen Angels. New York: 1974. V. 69

TONKIN, A. J.
Wampens' Systems of Man Measuring and Form Fitting.... London: 1890. V. 70

TONNA, CHARLOTTE ELIZABETH
Derry, a Tale of the Revolution. London: 1833. V. 70
Posthumous and Other Poems. London: 1846. V. 69

TONNIES, FERDINAND
Warlike England As Seen by Herself. New York: 1915. V. 70

TONY and the Circus Boy. London. V. 70

TOOGOOD, CORA
A Child's Prayer. Philadelphia: 1925. V. 70

TOOKE, ANDREW
The Pantheon, Representing the Fabulous Histories of the Heathen Gods.... London: 1729. V. 69

TOOKE, JOHN HORNE
Epea Ptereonta or the Diversions of Purley. London: 1798-1805. V. 73
Letters Between the Rev. Mr. Horne, John Wilkes, Esq.... London: 1771. V. 71
An Oration Delivered by the Rev. Mr. Horne at a Numerous Meeting of the Freeholders of Middlesex, Assembled at Mile-End Assembly-Room March 30, 1770. London: 1770. V. 71

TOOKE, THOMAS
Considerations on the State of the Currency. London: 1826. V. 69
A History of Prices and Of the State of the Circulation (from 1793 to 1856). London: 1838-1857. V. 70
Thoughts and Details on the High and Low Prices of the Last Thirty Years. London: 1823. V. 71

TOOKER, E.
Lewis A. Morgan on Iroquois Material Culture. Tucson: 1994. V. 69

TOOLE, J. L.
Reminiscences, Related by Himself.... London: 1892. V. 68

TOOLE, JOHN KENNEDY
A Confederacy of Dunces. Baton Rouge: 1980. V. 71; 73
A Confederacy of Dunces. London: 1981. V. 70

TOOLEY, R. V.
English Books with Coloured Plates 1790-1860.... London: 1954. V. 71
Some English Books with Coloured Plates. London: 1935. V. 71

TOOMER, JEAN
Cane. New York: 1923. V. 70
Essentials. Definitions and Aphorisms. Chicago: 1931. V. 70; 71; 72

TOOR, FRANCES
A Treasury of Mexican Folkways. New York: 1947. V. 69

TOPFFER, RODOLPH
Rosa and Gertrude. And, My Uncle's Library. London: 1848. V. 68

TOPHAM, EDWARD
Letters from Edinburgh; Written in the Years 1774 and 1775.... London: 1776. V. 69
The Life of John Elwes, Esq. 1790. V. 69
The Life of Mr. Elwes, the Celebrated Miser. 1792. V. 71; 72
The Poetry of the World. London: 1788. V. 73
The Remarkable Life of John Elwes, Esq.... London: 1797. V. 70
The Remarkable Life of John Elwes, Esq.... London: 1845. V. 72

TOPHAM, W. F.
The Lakes of England. London: 1869. V. 70

TOPKINS, KATHARINE
Guadalcanal Diary. New York: 1943. V. 69

TOPLADY, AUGUSTUS
Historic Proof of the Doctrinal Calvinism of the Church of England. London: 1774. V. 73

TOPOGRAPHICAL Description of Texas to Which is Added an Account of the Indian Tribes. Waco: 1964. V. 73

TOPONCE, ALEXANDER
Reminiscences of Alexander Toponce Pioneer 1839-1923. Ogden: 1923. V. 68; 73

TOPOR, ROLAND
Stories and Drawings. London: 1968. V. 68

TOPP, C. BERESFORD
The 42nd Battalion, C.E.F. Royal Highlanders of Canada in the Great War. Montreal: 1931. V. 73

TOPP, CHESTER W.
Victorian Yellow-Backs and Paperbacks 1849-1905. Volume I. George Routledge. Denver: 1993. V. 70; 72; 73
Victorian Yellow-Backs and Paperbacks 1849-1905. Volume II. Ward and Lock. Denver: 1995. V. 70; 72; 73
Victorian Yellow-Backs and Paperbacks 1849-1905. Volume III. Hotten, Chatto and Windus. Denver: 1997. V. 70; 72; 73
Victorian Yellow-Backs and Paperbacks 1849-1905. Volume V. Macmillan and Co. and Smith, Elder and Co. Denver: 2001. V. 72

TOPP, CHESTER W. continued
Victorian Yellowbacks and Paperbacks 1849-1905. Volume I: George Routledge. Volume II: Ward and Lock. Denver: 1993-1995. V. 70
Victorian Yellowbacks and Paperbacks 1849-1905. Volume IV: Frederick Warne and Co and Sampson Low and Co. Denver: 1999. V. 70; 72

TORCHIANA, H. A.
California Gringos. San Francisco: 1930. V. 68; 72; 73

TORCZYNER, H.
Magritte: Ideas and Images. New York: 1977. V. 69; 72

TORME, MEL
The Other Side of the Rainbow with Judy Garland on Dawn Patrol. New York: 1970. V. 69

TORRENCE, BRUCE T.
Hollywood: the First Hundred Years. New York: 1982. V. 68

TORRENCE, RIDGELY
El Dorado; a Tragedy. New York and London: 1903. V. 73
Granny Maumee. The Rider of Dreams. Simon the Cyrenian. Plays for a Negro Theatre. New York: 1917. V. 72

TORRENS, HENRY D'OYLEY
Travels in Ladak, Tartary, and Kashmir. London: 1862. V. 69

TORRENTIUS, HERMANN
Dictionarium Poeticum, Elucidarius Carminum, Vulgo Inscriptum. Leyden: 1540. V. 73

TORRES, ISRAEL
Magnificent Obsession. In Quest of Mountain High Game. 1990. V. 69

TORREY, CHARLES T.
Home! or the Pilgrims Faith Revived. Salem: 1845. V. 68

TORREY, J.
A Compendium of the Flora of the Northern and Middle States.... New York: 1826. V. 72
A Flora of North America.... New York: 1838-1843. V. 72
A Flora of the State of New York.... Albany: 1843. V. 68

TORROJA, EDUARDO
The Structures of Eduardo Torroja: an Autobiography of Engineering Accomplishment. New York: 1958. V. 68; 69; 72

TORSELLINO, ORZAIO
Historia dell'origine e translatione della Santa Casa, della B. Vergine Mrie di Loreto. Venice: 1629. V. 72

TORY, GEOFFROY
L'Art and Science De la Vraye Proportion des Lettres Antique.... Paris: 1549. V. 70
Itinerarium Provinciarum Omnium Antonini Augusti.... Paris: 1512. V. 70; 72

TOSCHES, NICK
Hellfire: The Jerry Lee Lewis Story. New York: 1982. V. 72
Where Dead Voices Gather. Boston: 2001. V. 69; 72

TOTH, KARL
Woman and Rococo in France. Philadelphia: 1931. V. 70

TOTTENHAM, GEORGE L.
An Irish Board of Agriculture. 1898. V. 69

TOUHY, FRANK
Yeats. 1976. V. 70

TOULMIN, CAMILLA
Lays and Legends Illustrative of English Life. London: 1845. V. 73

TOULMIN, JOSHUA
Addresses to Young Men. London: 1803. V. 71

TOUR in Holland in the Year 1819. London: 1823. V. 69

A TOUR in Scotland in 1863. London: 1984. V. 69

A TOUR in Teesdale. York: 1803. V. 69

A TOUR in Teesdale, Including a Description of the Beauties of Rokeby, and Its Vicinity, Raby Castle, the Highly Romantic Walks and Picturesque Views Near Barnard Castle, the High Force, Caldron Snout &c. &c. 1824. V. 69

TOUR of Doctor Syntax through London; or the Pleasures and Miseries of the Metropolis. London: 1820. V. 68

A TOUR Through the Whole Island of Great Britain. London: 1769. V. 73

A TOUR to Great St. Bernard's and Round Mount Blanc. London: 1827. V. 68

TOURE, ASKIA MUHAMMAD
Songhai!. New York: 1972. V. 72

THE TOURIST'S Companion; Being a Concise Description and History of Ripon Studley Park, Fountains Abbey, Hackfall, Brimham Craggs, Boroughbridge, Aldborough, Plumpton Harrogate and Harewood House. Ripon: 1817. V. 69

TOURIST'S Guide to Scarborough and Its Neighbourhood. London. V. 68

TOURNEFORT, JOSEPH PITTON DE
Elemens de Botanique, ou Methode Pour Connitre les Plantes. Lyon: 1797. V. 70; 73

TOURNIER, MICHEL
The Erl-King. London: 1972. V. 70
Gemini. London: 1981. V. 71
The Ogre. New York: 1972. V. 68

TOURTEL, MARY
The Monster Rupert, a Story and Picture Book. 1953. V. 72

TOUSEY, THOMAS G.
Military History of Carlise and Carlisle Barracks. Richmond: 1939. V. 72

TOUSSAINT, FRANCOIS VINCENT
Manners. London: 1749. V. 70
Manners. 1752. V. 71
Manners. London: 1752. V. 69; 73
Manners. London: 1765. V. 69; 72

TOUSSAINT, FRANZ
The Garden of Caresses. Waltham St. Lawrence: 1934. V. 68; 71

TOUSSAINT-SAMAT, JEAN
Shoes That Had Walked Twice. Philadelphia: 1933. V. 69

TOVEY, DUNCAN C.
Gray and His Friends - Letters and Relics - in Great Part Hitherto Unpublished. Cambridge: 1890. V. 71

TOWBIN, ABRAHAM
The Pathology of Cerebral Palsy. Springfield: 1960. V. 68

TOWER, D. B.
Structure and Function of the Cerebral Cortex. Amsterdam: 1960. V. 68

TOWERS, JOHN
Polygamy Unscriptural; or Two Dialogues Between Philalethes and Monograms in Which the Principal Errors of the First and Second Editions of the Revd. Mr. M-D-N's Thelyphthora are Detected. London: 1781. V. 68

TOWERS, JOHNSON
Caesar's Commentaries of his War in Gaul; with an English Translation for Use of Schools. London: 1786. V. 71

TOWERS, JOSEPH
An Oration Delivered at the London Tavern on the Fourth of November, 1788, on Occasion of the Commemoration of the Revolution and the Completion of a Century from that Great Event.... London: 1788. V. 73

TOWLE, NANCY
Vicissitudes Illustrated, in the Experience of Nancy Towle, in Europe and America. Portsmouth: 1833. V. 68

TOWNE, ARTHUR E.
Old Prairie Days. Otsego: 1941. V. 68

TOWNE, CHARLES HANSON
The Rise and Fall of Prohibition: The Human Side of What the Eighteenth Amendment and the Volstead Act Have Done to the United States. New York: 1923. V. 71
The Shop of Dreams: A Tale of Love, Youth and Books. New York: 1939. V. 72

TOWNE, CHARLES WAYLAND
Cattle and Men. 1955. V. 68

TOWNE, ROBERT D.
The Teddy Bears at the Circus. 1907. V. 72
The Teddy Bears at the Circus. Chicago: 1907. V. 70
The Teddy Bears Come to Life. 1907. V. 72
The Teddy Bears Come to Life. Chicago: 1907. V. 70
The Teddy Bears in Hot Water. 1907. V. 72
The Teddy Bears in Hot Water. Chicago: 1907. V. 70
The Teddy Bears on a Lark. 1907. V. 72

TOWNER, DONALD
Creamware. London: 1978. V. 72

TOWNLEY, HOUGHTON
English Woodlands and Their Story. London: 1910. V. 70

TOWNLEY, RICHARD
A Journal Kept in the Isle of Man, Giving an Account of the Wind and Weather, and Daily Occurrences from Upwards of Eleven Months.... Whitehaven: 1791. V. 69

TOWNSEND, C. W.
The Birds of Essex County, Massachusetts. Cambridge: 1905. V. 73

TOWNSEND, E.
Acting Proverbs; or Drawing Room Theatricals. London: 1864. V. 68; 73

TOWNSEND, EDWARD DAVIS
The California Diary of General E. D. Townsend. 1970. V. 70

TOWNSEND, F.
Flora of Hampshire.... 1883. V. 69
Flora of Hampshire.... 1904. V. 69

TOWNSEND, F. TRENCH
Ten Thousand Miles of Travel, Sport and Adventure. London: 1869. V. 69; 70

TOWNSEND, JOHN
Memoirs of The Rev. John Townsend. Boston: 1831. V. 72

TOWNSEND, JOSEPH
A Journey through Spain in the Years 1786 and 1787. London: 1792. V. 70

TOWNSEND, PETER S.
Result of Observations Made Upon the Black Vomit, or Yellow Fever, at Havana and New York. New York: 1831. V. 68

TOWNSEND, R. T.
The Book of Gardens and Gardening. Garden City: 1924. V. 69; 71; 73

TOWNSEND, RICHARD H.
Original Poems. Baltimore: 1809. V. 68; 73

TOWNSEND, SHIPPIE
An Attempt to Illustrate the Great Subject of the Psalms.... Boston: 1773. V. 73

TOWNSEND, W. G. PAULSON
Modern Decorative Art in England. London: 1922. V. 72

TOWNSEND, WILLIAM H.
Lincoln and the Bluegrass. Lexington: 1955. V. 68; 69; 70

TOWNSEND, WILLIAM THOMPSON
The Cricket on the Hearth...Adapted from Charles Dickens' Popular Story. London: 1860. V. 70
The Cricket on the Hearth...adapted from Mr. Charles Dickens' Popular Story. London: 1873. V. 70

TOWNSHEND, R. B.
Last Memories of a Tenderfoot. London: 1926. V. 71
The Tenderfoot in New Mexico. London: 1923. V. 71
The Tenderfoot in New Mexico. London/New York: 1924. V. 71

TOWNSHEND, THOMAS
Poems. 1796. V. 72

TOWNSHIP Officer's and Young Clek's (sic) Assistant.... Columbus: 1826. V. 68

THE TOWNSHIP Officer's and Young Clerk's Assistant.... Columbus: 1832. V. 68

TOWNSON, ROBERT
Travels in Hungary, with a Short Account of Vienna in the Year 1793. London: 1797. V. 71

THE TOY Merchant. (plus) Lazy Peter's Troubles. Cincinnati: 1884. V. 71

THE TOY Book Present. 1868. V. 70

TOY Land; Trot's Journey and Other Poems and Stories. New York: 1882. V. 70; 73

TOYE, STANLEY
Cyanide. London: 1940. V. 69

TOYNBEE, ARNOLD
Lectures on the Industrial Revolution in England.... London: 1884. V. 71

TOYNBEE, PHILIP
The Barricades. London: 1943. V. 68

TOZER, HENRY FANSHAWE
The Islands of the Aegean. Oxford: 1890. V. 69; 71

TRACTATUS Diversi Super Maleficiis Nampe. Lugduni: 1555. V. 69; 73

TRACTENBERG, MARVIN
The Campanile of Florence Cathedral Giotto's Tower. New York: 1971. V. 70

TRACTS (Chiefly Rare and Curious Reprints) Relating to Northamptonshire. Northampton: 1870-1898. V. 73

TRACY, JACK
Subcutaneously, My Dear Watson. Bloomington: 1978. V. 71

TRACY, LOUIS
The Albert Gate Mystery. New York: 1904. V. 71
The Manning-Burke Murder. New York: 1930. V. 71
The Stowmarket Mystery. New York: 1904. V. 68
The Wooing of Esther Gray. London: 1902. V. 71

TRAHERNE, THOMAS
A Glimpse of Thomas Traherne: Texts Selected from the Centuries and Poems. 1978. V. 71

TRAILL, CATHERINE PARR
The Adventures of Little Downy: or, the History of a Field Mouse. London: 1832. V. 71
Canadian Wild Flowers. Montreal: 1869. V. 69
Studies of Plant Life in Canada: or Gleanings from Forest, Lake and Plain. Ottawa: 1885. V. 73

TRAILL, H. D.
The Life of Sir John Franklin. London: 1896. V. 73

TRAILL, SINCLAIR
Just Jazz 4. London: 1960. V. 69

TRAILL, THOMAS W.
Merchant Shipping Experiments on Steel. London: 1881. V. 68

TRAIN, ARTHUR
The Adventures of Ephraim Tutt. New York: 1930. V. 68
C Q, or in the Wireless House. New York: 1912. V. 68
Mr. Tutt Takes the Stand. New York: 1936. V. 68
No Matter Where. New York: 1933. V. 70
Old Man Tutt. New York: 1938. V. 68
Tutt for Tutt. New York: 1934. V. 71
When Tutt Meets Tutt. New York: 1927. V. 71

TRAIN, GEORGE FRANCES
Street Railways. London and Liverpool: 1860. V. 72

TRALBAUT, MARC EDO
Vincent Van Gogh. New York: 1969. V. 70

TRALL, R. THATCHER
New Hydropathic Cookbook. London: 1854. V. 68; 73
The Water-Cure Journal and Herald of Reforms, Devoted to Physiology, Hydropathy and the Laws of Life. New York: 1851-1852. V. 68

TRANSFERRING Papers. Manchester: 1882. V. 70

A TRANSLATION of the Memorial to the Sovereigns of Europe Upon the Present State of Affairs, Between the Old and the New World, Into Common Sense and Intelligible English. London: 1781. V. 70

TRANSYLVANIA UNIVERSITY
Catalogue of the Officers and Students of Transylvania University. Lexington: 1831. V. 68

TRAPIDO, BARBARA
Brother of the More Famous Jack. London: 1982. V. 72

TRAPIER, PAUL
The Gospel to be Given to Our Servants. Charleston: 1847. V. 68

TRAPROCK, WALTER E.
Sarah of the Sahara. New York: 1923. V. 69

TRASK, DAVID F.
A Bibliography of United States Latin American Relations Since 1810: a Selected List of Eleven Thousand Published References. Lincoln: 1968. V. 68

TRASK, JOHN B.
Report on the Geology of Northern and Southern California. Sacramento: 1856. V. 72

TRASK, KATRINA
The Little Town of Bethlehem. New York: 1929. V. 71

TRASK, LEONARD
A Brief Historical Sketch of the Life and Sufferings of Leonard Trask, the Wonderful Invalid. Portland: 1858. V. 71

TRATTINNICK, LEOPOLD
Fungi Austriaci, cum Descriptionibus ac Historia Naturali Ecompleta Oesterreichs Schwamme.... Wien: 1804-1805. V. 70

TRAUBEL, HORACE
At the Graveside of Walt Whitman, Harleigh, Camden, New Jersey, March 30th and Srigs of Lilac. Camden: 1892. V. 71

TRAUBEL, HORACE L.
Camden's Compliment to Walt Whitman. Philadelphia: 1889. V. 70
With Walt Whitman in Camden (March 28-July 14 1888). London: 1906. V. 71

TRAUTMAN, M. B.
The Fishes of Ohio. Columbus: 1957. V. 72; 73

TRAVELLERS Mounted Upon Curious and Wonderful Animals. New York: 1833. V. 73

THE TRAVELLER'S Guide Through Scotland. Edinburgh: 1824. V. 71

THE TRAVELLER'S Guide to Madeira and the West Indies.... Haddington: 1815. V. 70

TRAVELS in South-Eastern Asia.... Dublin: 1823. V. 69

TRAVELS in Southern Asia. Dublin: 1822. V. 71

TRAVELS Through The Alps Of Savoy. Edinburgh: 1843. V. 72

TRAVELS Through The Alps of Savoy. Edinburgh: 1900. V. 72

TRAVEN, B.
The Bridge in the Jungle. New York: 1938. V. 73
The Bridge in the Jungle. London: 1940. V. 73
The Creation of The Sun and The Moon. London: 1971. V. 73
The Death Ship. London: 1934. V. 73
The Death Ship. London: 1940. V. 69
Der Wobbly. Berlin: 1926. V. 73
March to the Monteria. New York: 1964. V. 73
The Night Visitor. London: 1967. V. 73
The Rebellion of the Hanged. 1952. V. 73
The Rebellion of the Hanged. London: 1952. V. 69
The Rebellion of the Hanged. New York: 1952. V. 70; 72
Der Shatz Der Sierra Madre. (The Treasure of the Sierra Madre). Berlin: 1927. V. 71
The Treasure of the Sierra Madre. London: 1934. V. 71; 73

TRAVER, ROBERT
Anatomy of a Murder. New York: 1958. V. 73
Small Town D. A. New York: 1954. V. 72
Trouble Shooter. New York: 1943. V. 73

TRAVERS, BENJAMIN
A Synopsis of the Diseases of the Eye, and Their Treatment.... London: 1824. V. 72

TRAVERS, GEORGIA
The Wily Woodchucks. New York: 1946. V. 70

TRAVERS, GRAHAM
Fellow Travellers. Edinburgh and London: 1896. V. 69

TRAVERS, P. L.
The Fox at the Manger. London: 1962. V. 72; 73

TRAVERS, P. L. continued
The Fox at the Manger. New York: 1962. V. 70
Happily Ever After. New York: 1940. V. 70
I Go by Sea, I Go by Land. London: 1941. V. 70
Mary Poppins. New York: 1934. V. 69
Mary Poppins in the Park. New York: 1952. V. 73

TRAVIS, HENRY
Moral Freedom Reconciled with Causation.. London: 1865. V. 71

TRAYLEN, CHARLES W.
The Wentworth Woodhouse Library. Catalogues 14 & 21. Guildford, Surrey: 1949-1951. V. 70

TRAYSER, DONALD G.
Barnstable. Three Centuries of a Cape Cod Town. Hyannis: 1939. V. 73

TREACY, SEAN
Shay Scally and Manny Wagstaff. London: 1976. V. 70

A TREASURY of Grimm and Andersen. London and Glasgow: 1957. V. 69

TREAT, LAWRENCE
B as in Banshee. New York: 1940. V. 68
T as in Trapped. New York: 1947. V. 68

TREATISE On the Manufacture, Imitation and Reduction of Foreign Wines, Brandies, Gins, Rums, Etc. Philadelphia: 1860. V. 70

TREDGOLD, THOMAS
Elementary Principles of Carpentry; a Treatise on the Pressure and Equilibrium of Beams.... London: 1820. V. 73
Elementary Principles of Carpentry, A Treatise on the Pressure and Equilibrium of Timber Framing.... 1853. V. 71
Elementary Principles of Carpentry Chiefly Composed from the Standard Work of Thomas Tredgold.... London: 1890. V. 68
Practical Strength of Cast Iron and Other Metals.... London: 1824. V. 73

TREDWELL, DANIEL M.
A Monograph on Privately Illustrated Books: a Plea for Bibliomania. Brooklyn: 1881. V. 71

TREECE, HENRY
Dylan Thomas, Dog Among the Fairies. London: 1949. V. 69

TREFFINGER, CAROLYN
Rag-Doll Jane. Akron: 1930. V. 73

TREFUSIS, VIOLET
Memoirs of an Armchair. London: 1960. V. 71

TREGASKIS, RICHARD
Vietnam Diary. New York: 1963. V. 72

TREGEAGLE of Dozmary Pool and Original Cornish Ballads.... Devonport: 1869. V. 71

TREGEAR, E.
The Maori Race. Wanganui: 1904. V. 69
The Maori Race. New York: 1973. V. 69

TREGGON & CO., LTD.
Zinc and Galvanized Iron Merchants and Manufacturers, Perforators, Galvanizers, Corrugators, and Contractors for Plain and Ornamental Zinc Roofing. London: 1887. V. 68

TRELAWNY, E. J.
Recollections of the Last Days of Shelley and Byron. London: 1858. V. 71

TRELEASE, W.
The Genus Phoradendron, a Monographic Revision. Urbana: 1916. V. 72
A Revison of the American Species of Epilobium Occuring North of Mexico. St. Louis: 1891. V. 72

TRELKER, A.
Hansje in Wonderland. Bussum: 1915. V. 71

TREMAIN, ROSE
Sacred Country. London: 1992. V. 73
The Way I Found Her. London: 1997. V. 73

TREMAYNE, PETER
Absolution by Murder. London: 1994. V. 70; 71

TREMAYNE, SYDNEY
Tatlings. Epigrams. London: 1922. V. 72

TREMBLEY, ABRAHAM
Memoires, Pour Servir a l'Histoire d'un Genre de Polypes d'eau Douce, a Bras en Forme de Cornes. Leiden: 1744. V. 70; 73

TREMEARINE, A. J. N.
The Ban of the Bori. London: 1968. V. 69
Hausa Superstitions and Customs, an Introduction to Folk-Lore and the Folk. London: 1913. V. 69
The Tailed Headhunters of Nigeria...and a Description of the Manners, Habits and Customs of the Native Tribes. London: 1912. V. 69

TREMEARNE, A. J. N.
The Tailed Head-Hunters of Nigeria. Philadelphia: 1912. V. 73

TRENCH, JOHN
Dishonoured Bones. London: 1954. V. 73

TRENHAILE, JOHN
Kyril. London: 1981. V. 71
Nocturne for the General. London: 1985. V. 71

TRENHOLM, GLADYS
A History of Fort Lawrence Times, Tides and Towns. Edmonton, Alberta: 1985. V. 71

TRENHOLM, VIRGINIA COLE
Footprints on the Frontier Saga of the La Ramie Region of Wyoming. Douglas: 1945. V. 73
The Shoshonis Sentinels of the Rockies. Norman: 1964. V. 72
Wyoming Blue Book. 1974. V. 68

TRENT, COUNCIL OF
Canones, et Decreta Sacro-Sancti Oecvmenici et Generalis Concilii Tridentini. Romae: 1564. V. 69; 73

TRENT, JOSEPH
An Inquiry into the Effects of Light in Respiration.... Philadelphia: 1800. V. 72

TREPTOW, OTTO
John Siberch. Johann Lair von Siegburg. Cambridge: 1970. V. 72

TRESSLER, D. K.
Marine Products of Commerce.... New York: 1923. V. 73

TREUTTNER, WILLIAM H.
The Natural Man Observed: a Study of Catlin's Indian Gallery. Washington: 1979. V. 70

TREVANIAN
The Eiger Sanction. New York: 1972. V. 68; 71; 72
The Loo Sanction. New York: 1973. V. 72
The Summer Of Katya. New York: 1983. V. 72

TREVELYAN, R. C.
Aftermath. London: 1941. V. 71

TREVERS, JOSEPH
An Essay to the Restoring of Our Decayed Trade. London: 1675. V. 73

TREVES, FREDERICK
The Riviera Of The Corniche Road. London: 1926. V. 72

TREVOR, ELLESTON
The Flight of the Phoenix. London: 1964. V. 69; 73
The Flight of the Phoenix. New York: 1964. V. 69

TREVOR, GLEN
Was It Murder?. 1933. V. 73

TREVOR, WILLIAM
Angels at the Ritz and Other Stories. London: 1975. V. 72; 73
The Boarding-House. London: 1965. V. 73
Collected Stories. London: 1993. V. 70
The Day We Got Drunk on Cake. London: 1967. V. 70
Dreaming. London: 1973. V. 70
Excursions in the Real World. London: 1993. V. 70
The Hill Bachelors. London: 2000. V. 70
The Last Lunch of the Season. London: 1973. V. 68
The Love Department. 1966. V. 70
The Love Department. New York: 1967. V. 70
Lovers of Their Time. London: 1978. V. 68; 73
Low Sunday. London: 2000. V. 70
Marrying Damian. London: 1995. V. 70
Other People's Worlds. London: 1980. V. 69; 73
A Writer's Ireland - Landscape in Literature. London: 1984. V. 73

TREVOR-BATTYE, AUBYN
Camping in Crete. 1913. V. 72
Ice-Bound On Kolguev. London: 1895. V. 72

TREVOR-ROPER, H. R.
The Letters of Mercurius. 1970. V. 73

TREZEVANT, D. H.
The Burning of Columbia, S.C. Columbia: 1866. V. 69

THE TRIAL in Ejectment Between Campbell Craig, lessee of James Annesley, Esq; and Others, Plaintiffs, and the Right Honourable Richard, Earl of Anglesey, Defendant...in Ireland. Dublin: 1744. V. 70

THE TRIALS of Chinko. 1910. V. 72

THE TRIALS of James, Duncan, and Robert M'Gregor, Three Sons of the Celebrated Rob Roy.... Edinburgh: 1818. V. 70

TRIANA, S. PEREZ
Down the Orinoco in a Canoe. London: 1902. V. 68

TRIBUTE to Kenneth Patchen. London: 1977. V. 71

TRIBUTES to Edward Johnston, Calligrapher. Kent: 1948. V. 69

TRIBUTES to Graham Greene, OM, CH, 1904-1911. At the Memorial Requiem Mass at Westminster Cathedral. 1992. V. 71

TRIBUTES to Graham Greene OM, CH, 1904-1991, at the Memorial Requiem Mass at Westminster Cathedral. London: 1992. V. 68

TRIED and True Recipes. The Home Cook Book. Orange: 1889. V. 69

TRIENENS, ROGER J.
Pioneer Imprints from Fifty States. Washington: 1973. V. 70; 72

TRIESCH, MANFRED
The Lillian Hellman Collection at the University of Texas. Austin: 1966. V. 68

TRIGG, ROBERTA
Haworth Idyll. A Fantasy. 1946. V. 73

TRIGGS, H. I.
Formal Gardens in England and Scotland. London: 1902. V. 69

TRIGGS, J. H.
History and Directory of Laramie City and History of Cheyenne and Northern Wyoming. Laramie: 1955. V. 68; 71

TRIGIANI, ADRIANA
Big Stone Gap. New York: 2000. V. 70

TRILLIN, CALVIN
U.S. Journal. New York: 1971. V. 72

TRILLING, LIONEL
Emma and the Legend of Jane Austen. New York: 1965. V. 73

TRILLIONS of Trilligs. 1977. V. 72
TRILLIONS of Trilligs. New York: 1977. V. 73

TRIMBLE, ISAAC P.
A Treatise on the Insect Enemies of Fruit and Fruit Trees. New York: 1865. V. 69

TRIMBLE, MARSHALL
CO Bar - Bill Owen Depicts the Historic Babbit Ranch. Flagstaff: 1982. V. 69; 70

TRIMBLE, WILLIAM TENNANT
The Trimbles and Cowens of Dalston, Cumberland. Carlisle: 1935. V. 71
The Trimbles & Cowens of Dalston, Cumberland. London: 1935. V. 72

TRIMEN, HENRY
A Systematic Catalogue of the Flowering Plants and Ferns...in Ceylon.... Colombo: 1885. V. 69

TRIMEN, ROLAND
Rhopalocera Africae Australis: a Catalogue of South African Butterflies. Cape Town: 1862-1866. V. 73

TRIMMER, SARAH
A Description of a Set of Prints of English History...(with) A Series of Prints of English History.. London: 1792. V. 68; 69
Some Account of the Life and Writings of Mrs. Trimmer.... London: 1814. V. 73

TRIMMER, SARAH KIRBY
A Series of Prints of English History. Part II: A Description of a Set of Pirnts (sic) of English History. London. V. 70

TRINAJSTIC, NENAD
Mathematical and Computional Concepts in Chemistry. Chicester: 1986. V. 71

TRINITY HOUSE
A Catalogue of Books, in the Library of the Honourable the Corporation of Trinity House. London: 1853. V. 70

TRINKA, ZENA
Medora. New York: 1940. V. 71
Out Where the West Begins. St. Paul: 1920. V. 70

TRINKAUS, CHARLES
In Our Image and Likeness: Humanity and Divinity in Italian Humanist Thought. London: 1970. V. 72

TRINKLER, EMIL
The Stormswept Roof of Asia. 1931. V. 69; 70; 72; 73

TRIONFETTI, GIOVANNI BATTISTA
Observationes de Ortu ac Vegetatione Plantarum cum Novarum Stirpium Historia Iconibus Illustrata. Rome: 1685. V. 68; 73

TRIP, TOM
The History of Giles Gingerbread. York: 1820. V. 71

TRIPE, ANDREW
Dr. Woodward's Ghost. Occasion'd by a Passage in Dr. Mead's Preface to His Treatise of the Small Pox and Measles, Severely Reflecting on the Gentleman's Memory. London: 1748. V. 70

TRIPLETT, FRANK
The Life, Times and Treacherous Death of Jesse James. Chicago: 1970. V. 69

TRIPON, JEAN BAPTISTE
Traite Elementaire de Topographie et de Lavis des Plans.... Paris: 1846. V. 72

TRIPP, F. E.
British Mosses, Their Homes, Structure, and Uses. London: 1874. V. 70

TRISMOSIN, SOLOMON
Splendor Solis. London: 1920. V. 69

TRISSINO, GIOVANNI GIORGIO
La Italia Liberata da Gotthi. Rome: 1547. V. 71

TRISTAN, FLORA
Promenades dans Londres. Londres: 1840. V. 70

TROCCHI, ALEXANDER
Cain's Book. New York: 1960. V. 69; 72
Man at Leisure. London: 1972. V. 68
Merlin. Paris: 1952-1953. V. 71

TROCHECK, KATHY HOGAN
Every Crooked Nanny. New York: 1992. V. 68; 69; 71

TROGLODYTE, A., PSEUD.
Mind! A Unique Review of Ancient and Modern Philosophy. London: 1901. V. 71

TROILI, GIULIO
Paradossi per Pratticare la Prospettiva Senza Saperla. Bologna: 1683. V. 73

TROLLOPE, ANTHONY
The American Senator. London: 1877. V. 72
The American Senator. London: 1915. V. 68
An Autobiography. Edinburgh and London: 1883. V. 70; 73
Ayala's Angels. London: 1884?. V. 68
The Barchester Novels of Anthony Trollope. Stratford-upon-Avon: 1929. V. 72
Barchester Towers. London: 1872. V. 68
The Belton Estate. London: 1868. V. 68
The Belton Estate. London: 1877. V. 68
Can You Forgive Her. London: 1883. V. 68
Castle Richmond. 1883. V. 68
The Chronicles of Barsetshire. London: 1878-1879. V. 73
Clergymen of the Church of England. London: 1866. V. 72
Cousin Henry. London: 1880. V. 68
Cousin Henry. London: 1883. V. 68
Doctor Thorne. London: 1866. V. 68
Doctor Thorne. London: 1867. V. 68
Dr. Wortle's School. London: 1881?. V. 68
Dr. Wortle's School. London: 1882. V. 68
The Duke's Children. London: 1880. V. 73
The Duke's Children. London: 1881. V. 68
The Eustace Diamonds. London: 1873. V. 73
The Eustace Diamonds. London: 1950. V. 69
Frau Frohmann and Other Stories. London: 1884. V. 68
Harry Heathcote of Gangoil. Leipzig: 1874. V. 73
Harry Heathcote of Gangoil. London: 1883. V. 68; 73
He Knew He Was Right. London: 1869. V. 71
He Knew He Was Right. London: 1880. V. 73
How the Mastiffs Went to Iceland. London: 1878. V. 73
Hunting Sketches. London: 1865. V. 68
Hunting Sketches. 1952. V. 68
Is He Popenjoy?. London: 1878. V. 68
Is He Popenjoy?. London: 1882. V. 68
John Calldigate. London: 1879. V. 73
The Kellys and the O'Kellys. London: 1878. V. 68
Lady Anna. London: 1874. V. 68
The Last Chronicle of Barset. London: 1867. V. 68; 70; 71; 73
The Last Chronicle of Barset. London: 1868. V. 73
The Letters of Anthony Trollope. Stanford, Calif: 1983. V. 72
The Life of Cicero. London: 1880. V. 68; 69; 71; 73
Lotta Schmidt and Other Stories. London: 1867. V. 73
The Macdermots of Ballycloran. London: 1869. V. 73
The Macdermots of Ballycloran. London: 1874. V. 68
The Macdermots of Ballycloran. London: 1877. V. 68
Marion Fay. London: 1883. V. 73
Marion Fay. London: 1902. V. 68
Mr. Scarborough's Family. London: 1885. V. 73
Mr. Scarborough's Family. London: 1907. V. 68
New South Wales and Queensland. London: 1875. V. 68; 73
The Noble Jilt; a Comedy. London: 1923. V. 73
North America. London: 1862. V. 70
North America. New York: 1862. V. 72
Orley Farm. London: 1866. V. 73
Orley Farm. London: 1882. V. 68
Phineas Finn, the Irish Member. London: 1884?. V. 68
Phineas Redux. London: 1875. V. 68
Phineas Redux. London: 1884?. V. 68
The Prime Minister. London: 1877. V. 68
The Prime Minister. London: 1878. V. 68
Rachel Ray. London: 1868. V. 72
Ralph the Heir. London: 1873. V. 68
Ralph the Heir. London: 1882. V. 68
Sir Harry Hotspur of Humblethwaite. 1871. V. 72
Sir Harry Hotspur of Humblethwaite. London: 1871. V. 70
Sir Harry Hotspur of Humblethwaite. London: 1877. V. 68
The Small House at Allington. London: 1864. V. 73
Tales of All Countries. London: 1867. V. 68
Tales of All Countries. London: 1875. V. 68
Tales of All Countries. London: 1877. V. 68
Thackeray. London: 1879. V. 68
Thackeray. New York: 1879. V. 69; 71; 73
The Three Clerks. London: 1865. V. 72

TROLLOPE, ANTHONY continued
Travelling Sketches. London: 1866. V. 68; 72
The Vicar of Bullhampton. London: 1870. V. 73
The Vicar of Bullhampton. London: 1882. V. 68
The Warden. London: 1878. V. 68
The Way We Live Now. London: 1911. V. 68
The West Indies and the Spanish Main. London: 1860. V. 73
The Works. New York: 1903. V. 70

TROLLOPE, FRANCES MILTON
Costumbres Familiares de Los Americanos del Norte, Obra Escrita en Ingles por Mistress Trollope...(Domestic Manners). Paris: 1835. V. 68
Domestic Manners of the Americans. London and New York: 1832. V. 68; 69; 70; 72; 73
Domestic Manners of the Americans. Barre: 1959. V. 69
Jessie Phillips. London: 1844. V. 73
The Mother's Manual or Illustrations of Matrimonial Economy: an Essay in Verse. London: 1833. V. 70
Petticoat Government. London: 1857. V. 70
The Widow Barnaby. Paris: 1841. V. 70

TROLLOPE, JOANNA
The Choir. London: 1988. V. 69
Eliza Stanhope. London: 1978. V. 72; 73
Parson Harding's Daughter. London: 1979. V. 71; 73

TROLLOPE, THOMAS ADOLPHUS
La Beata. London: 1884. V. 68
Beppo the Conscript. London: 1874. V. 68

THE TROLLOPIAN. A Journal of Victorian Fiction. Berkeley and Los Angeles. V. 70

TROMHOLT, SOPHUS
Under the Rays of the Aurora Borealis; in the Land of the Lapps and Kavens. Boston: 1885. V. 70

TROOPERS West Military And Indian Affairs On The American Frontier. San Diego: 1970. V. 72

TROT'S Journey Pictures, Rhymes and Stories. New York: 1880. V. 70

TROTSKY, LEON
The Permanent Revolution. London: 1940. V. 70

TROTTER, A. F., MRS
Old Cape Colony. London: 1903. V. 72

TROTTER, COUTTS
The Principles of Currency and Exchanges Applied to The Report from the Select Committee of the House of Commons, Appointed to Inquire into the High Price of Gold Bullion &c.... London: 1810. V. 73

TROTTER, JACQUELINE T.
Valour and Vision - Poems of the War 1914-1918. London: 1923. V. 72

TROTTI, LAMAR
Hudson's Bay Company. Hollywood: 1940. V. 72

TROUBRIDGE, LADY
Bric-a-Brac. London: 1895. V. 69

TROUGHTON, R. ZOUCH S.
Nina Sforza. A Tragedy in Five Acts. London: 1855. V. 71

TROUPE, QUINCY
Embryo. New York: 1972. V. 72

TROUSSEAU, A.
Treatise on Therapeutics. New York: 1880. V. 71

TROUT, KILGORE
Venus on the Half Shell. New York: 1975. V. 73

TROW, M. J.
The Adventures of Insepctor Lestrade. London: 1985. V. 69; 73
Lestrade and the Brother of Death. London: 1988. V. 73
Lestrade and the Leviathan. London: 1987. V. 73
Lestrade and the Ripper. London: 1988. V. 73

TROWBRIDGE, JOHN TOWNSEND
A Home Idyl and Other Poems. Boston: 1881. V. 68
Lucy Arlyn. Boston: 1866. V. 68
The Poetical Works of John Townsend Trowbridge. Boston: 1903. V. 71

TROWELL, M.
African Arts and Crafts. Their Developments in the School. London: 1937. V. 69
Classical African Sculpture. New York: 1964. V. 69
Tribal Crafts of Uganda. 1953. V. 69

TROXELL, HAROLD C.
Flood in La Canada Valley, California, January 1, 1934. Washington: 1937. V. 68

TRUANT Peter. New York: 1867?. V. 70
TRUANT Peter. New York: 1876?. V. 70

TRUBLET DE VILLEJEGU, JACQUES JEROME ANTOINE
Relation Detailee de la Campagne de M. le Commandeur de Suffren, dans l'Indie du 1 er Juin 1782 au 29 Septembre Suivant. Port Louis: 1783. V. 73

TRUCHESSIAN GALLERY
Summary Catalogue of the Pictures Now Exhibiting at the Truchessian Gallery, New Road, Opposite Portland Place. 1804?. V. 70

TRUDEAU, GARRY
Doonesbury Deluxe. New York: 1987. V. 71
Planet Doonesbury. Kansas City: 1997. V. 71

A TRUE and Faithful Account of the Several Informations Exhibited to the Honourable Committee Appointed by the Parliament to Inquire into the Late Dreadful Burning of the City of London. London: 1667. V. 69

A TRUE Authentick, and Impartial History of the Life and Glorious Actions of the Czar of Muscovy.... London: 1725?. V. 73

TRUE, CHARLES FREDERICK
Covered Wagon Pioneers. Madison: 1966. V. 68

TRUE, FREDERICK W.
Whalebone Whales of the Western North Atlantic. Washington: 1904. V. 69

A TRUE State of the Case Between Capt. H---h and Mr. P---e. Wherein the Sufferings of an Injured Lady are Faithfully Related. London: 1750. V. 70

TRUE Story of the Spoilt Frock. New York: 1864. V. 71

THE TRUE Tom Double; or, an Account of Dr. Davenants' Late Conduct and Writings, Particularly with Relation to the XIth Section of His Essays on Peace at Home and War Abroad. London: 1704?. V. 73

TRUELOVE, DAME
Truelove's Tales.... 1837. V. 71

TRUEMAN, HOWARD
Early Agriculture in the Atlantic Provinces. Monton: 1907. V. 73

TRUETTNER, WILLIAM H.
The Natural Man Observed: a Study of Catlin's Indian Gallery. Kent: 1979. V. 68

TRUEX, RAYMOND C.
Detailed Atlas of the Head and Neck. New York: 1948. V. 71

TRUFFAUT, FRANCOIS
The Films in My Life. New York: 1978. V. 69
Hitchcock/Truffaut. New York: 1967. V. 70

TRUMAN, BEN C.
Occidental Sketches. San Francisco: 1881. V. 68; 73
Tiburcio Vasquez: the Life, Adventures and Capture of the Great California Bandit and Murderer. Los Angeles: 1941. V. 73

TRUMAN, EDWIN
History of Ilkeston; together with Shipley, Kirk Hallam, West Hallam, Dale Abbey and Cossall. Ilkeston: 1880. V. 72

TRUMAN, HARRY
Memoirs. Year of Decisions. Garden City: 1955. V. 71
Memoirs. Year of Decisions and Years of Trial and Hope. Garden City: 1955-1956. V. 69; 71
Mr. Citizen. New York: 1960. V. 73
Mr. President. The First Publication from the Personal Diaries, Private Letters, Papers and Revealing Interviews of Harry Truman. New York: 1952. V. 70

TRUMBLE, ALFRED
In Jail with Charles Dickens. New York: 1896. V. 69

TRUMBO, DALTON
Johnny Got His Gun. Philadelphia: 1939. V. 71

TRUMBULL, COLONEL
Catalogue of Paintings of Colonel Trumbull, Including Nine Subjects of the American Revolution.... New York: 1831. V. 73

TRUMBULL, HENRY CLAY
The Blood Covenant. New York: 1885. V. 69

TRUSCOTT BOAT MFG. CO.
Pleasure Craft and Marine Motors. Annual Catalogue. St. Joseph: 1898. V. 72
Truscott Boats 1903-1904. New York: 1970. V. 70

TRUSLER, JOHN
The Art of Carving Excerpted from a Work Entitled The Honours of the Table (1788). 1932. V. 71
Hogarth Moralized: a Complete Edition.... London: 1831. V. 73
Life; or the Adventures of William Ramble, Esq.... London: 1793. V. 73

TRUSS, SELDON
Number Naught. New York: 1930. V. 69
Turmoil at Brede. New York: 1931. V. 70; 71

TRUST, ESTELLE
Anne Bronte. Dallas: 1954. V. 70; 73

TRYON, GEORGE W.
Manual of Conchology; Structural and Systematic. Philadelphia: 1888-1910. V. 68; 71
Structural and Systematic Conchology.... Philadelphia: 1882-1884. V. 69; 73

TRYON, R. M.
Ferns and Allied Plants, with Special Reference to Tropical America. New York: 1982. V. 69

TRYON, THOMAS
The Other. New York: 1971. V. 68; 69; 71

TSCHOPIK, HARVEY
Navaho Pottery Making. Cambridge: 1941. V. 69

TSCHUDI, F. VON
Nature in the Alps. 1856. V. 69; 70; 72; 73

TSENG, C. K.
Common Seaweeds of China. Beijing: 1983. V. 73

TSE-TUNG, MAO
Selected Works. Peking: 1967. V. 72

TSHIRKY, OSCAR
Cook Book by Oscar of the Waldorf. Chicago: 1986. V. 73

TSVELEV, N. N.
Grasses of the Soviet Union. New Delhi: 1983. V. 69

TUCK, DONALD H.
The Encyclopedia of Science Fiction. 1974-1978. V. 68

TUCKER, BENJAMIN
Observations on a Pamphlet Which Has been Privately Circulated Said to be A Concise Statement of Facts, and the Treatment Experienced by Sir Home Popham, Since His Return from the Red Sea. London: 1805. V. 70

TUCKER, BENJAMIN R.
Instead of a Book by a Man Too Busy to Write One. A Fragmentary Exposition of Philosophical Anarchism. New York: 1897. V. 68; 69; 73

TUCKER, E. S.
The Book of Pets. New York: 1893. V. 70

TUCKER, GEORGE
Essays on Various Subjects of Taste, Morals and National Policy. Georgetown: 1822. V. 70
The Theory of Money and Banks Investigated. Boston: 1839. V. 70

TUCKER, JOHN
Kanchenjunga. London: 1955. V. 69

TUCKER, JOSIAH
Four Letters on Important National Subjects, Addressed to the Right Honourable the Earl of Shelburne. Gloucester: 1783. V. 70
A Letter to a Friend Concerning Naturalizations.... London: 1753. V. 69
Letter to Edmund Burke, Esq.; Member of Parliament for the City of Bristol.... Glocester: 1775. V. 73

TUCKER, KERRY
Still Waters. New York: 1991. V. 71

TUCKER, MARWOOD
Michael Tressider. London: 1872. V. 68

TUCKER, NATHANIEL
The Bermudian: a Poem. London: 1774. V. 70

TUCKER, PATRICK T.
Riding the High Country. Caldwell: 1923. V. 68
Riding the High Country. Caldwell: 1933. V. 71

TUCKER, ST. GEORGE
Blackstone's Commentaries. Philadelphia: 1803. V. 70
A Dissertation on Slavery; with a Proposal for the Gradual Abolition of It, in the State of Virginia. Philadelphia: 1796. V. 68; 71

TUCKER, WILLARD D.
Gratiot Co., Michigan: Historical, Biographical, Statistical. Saginaw: 1913. V. 71

TUCKER, WILLIAM
The Family Dyer and Scourer.... Hartford: 1831?. V. 71

TUCKERMAN, E.
An Enumeration of North American Lichens.... Cambridge: 1845. V. 72

TUCKERMAN, HENRY
The Optimist. New York: 1801. V. 73

TUCKERMAN, HENRY T.
Book of the Artists. American Artists Life, Comprising Biographical and Critical Sketches. New York: 1867. V. 70

TUCKETT, HARVEY G.
Practical Remarks on the Present State of Life Insurance in the United States. Philadelphia: 1851. V. 71
Where to Go, and What to Pay: a Hand-Book to All the World's Fair to be Held in the Palace of Glass, May 1851.... Philadelphia: 1851. V. 71

TUCKEY, J. K.
Narrative of an Expedition to Explore the River Zaire, usually called the Congo, in South Africa in 1816. New York: 1818. V. 72

TUDOR, BETHANY
Samantha's Surprise. Philadelphia: 1964. V. 73
Skiddycock Pond. Philadelphia: 1965. V. 73

TUDOR, EMMA
October Dawn. Cambridge: 1926. V. 69

TUDOR, TASHA
Alexander the Gander. New York: 1939. V. 71
Amanda and the Bear. New York: 1951. V. 73
Around the Year. New York: 1957. V. 71
A Book of Christmas. 1979. V. 73
The County Fair. New York: 1940. V. 71
The Doll's Christmas. New York: 1950. V. 70
Dorcas Porkus. New York: 1942. V. 71
First Delights - A Book About the Five Senses. New York: 1966. V. 71
Linsey Woolsey. New York: 1946. V. 70; 73
Pumpkin Moonshine. New York: 1938. V. 73
Rosemary for Remembrance. New York: 1981. V. 71
Snow Before Christmas. New York: 1941. V. 70; 71
Take Joy! The Tasha Tudor Christmas Book. Cleveland: 1966. V. 71
The Tasha Tudor Sketchbook Series Family and Friends.... Richmond: 1995. V. 72
Tasha Tudor's Bedtime Book. New York: 1977. V. 71
Tasha Tudor's Favorite Christmas Carols. New York: 1978. V. 72
Tasha Tudor's Favorite Stories. Philadelphia: 1965. V. 71
Thistly B. New York: 1949. V. 70
A Time To Keep: the Tasha Tudor Book of Holidays. Chicago: 1977. V. 71; 72

TUDOT, EDMOND
Vues du Chateau de Veauce. 1850. V. 70

TUER, ANDREW WHITE
Bygone Beauties: a Select Series of Ten Portraits of Ladies of Rank and Fashion.... London: 1883. V. 68
Forgotten Children's Books. London: 1898-1899. V. 70
History of the Horn-Book. London: 1897. V. 70
London Cries.... 1883. V. 71
Old London Street Cries, and the Cries of Today. London: 1885. V. 71
Pages and Pictures from Forgotten Children's Books. London: 1898. V. 70; 72
Pages and Pictures from Forgotten Children's Books. London: 1898-1899. V. 69; 71
Quads for Authors, Editors and Devils. London: 1884. V. 69; 70
Stories from Old Fashioned Children's Books. London: 1899-1900. V. 71
Stories from Old Fashioned Children's Books. London: 1900. V. 73

TUFFY and Merboo. London and Edinburgh: 1904. V. 68

TUFNELL, EDWARD CARLTON
Character, Object and Effects of Trades' Unions; with Some Remarks on the Law Concerning Them. London: 1834. V. 68

TUKE, SAMUEL
Memoirs of The Life of Stephen Crisp, With Selections From His Works. York: 1824. V. 72

TULL, JETHRO
Horse Hoeing Husbandry; or, an Essay on the Principles of Vegetation and Tillage. London: 1751. V. 70

TULLIS, JULIE
Clouds from Both Sides. London: 1986. V. 69

TULLY, JIM
Biddy Borgan's Boy. New York: 1942. V. 73
The Bruiser. New York: 1936. V. 73

TUMBLE Down Pictures. London: 1898. V. 73

TUNBERG, KARL
While the Crowd Cheers. New York: 1935. V. 72

TUNG, C.
Soochow Gardens. 1979. V. 73

TUNIS, EDWIN
Indians. Cleveland and New York: 1959. V. 72

TUNIS, W. E.
Tunis's Geographical and Pictorial Guide to Niagara Falls and Route Book to Montreal, Quebec, Saratoga and the White Mountains. Niagara Falls: 1855. V. 73

TUNNARD, WILLIAM H.
A Southern Record. The History of the Third Regiment of Louisiana Infantry. Baton Rouge: 1866. V. 69

TUNNEY, GENE
A Man Must Fight. Boston and New York: 1932. V. 71

TUNSTALL, BRIAN
William Pitt, Earl of Chatham. London: 1937. V. 73

TUOHEY, GEORGE V.
A History of the Boston Base Ball Club . . . Being a Testimonial to the Players of the 1897 Team.... Boston: 1897. V. 70

TUOHY, FRANK
The Ice Saints. London: 1964. V. 73

TUPPER, ANSEL
Two Eagles/Dos Aguilas: The Natural World of the United States-Mexico Borderlands. Los Angeles: 1994. V. 68

TUPPER, MARTIN FARQUHAR
Proverbial Philosophy: a Book of Thoughts and Arguments. London: 1838. V. 72
Rides and Reveries of the late Mr. Aesop Smith. London: 1858. V. 71
Sacra Poesis. London: 1832. V. 72
Stephan Langton; or the Days of King John. Guildford: 1922. V. 68; 73
Stephan Langton; or the Days of King John. Guildford: 1925?. V. 68
Stephan Langton; or the Days of King John. Guildford: 1930?. V. 68

TURBERVILLE, A. S.
A History of Welbeck Abbey and Its Owners. London: 1938-1939. V. 70
Johnson's England: an Account of the Life and Manners of His Age. London: 1952. V. 70

TURENNE, LOUIS DE LA TOUR D'AUVERGNE, PRINCE OF
Theses ex Universa Philosophia. 1679. V. 71

TURENNE, RAYMOND
The Last of the Mammoths. London: 1907. V. 70

TURGENEV, IVAN SERGEEVICH
Fathers and Sons. New York: 1867. V. 72
Fathers and Sons. New York: 1951. V. 72
A Month in the Country. London: 1981. V. 72
Smoke: a Russian Novel. London: 1882. V. 68
The Torrents of Spring. Westport: 1976. V. 70; 72

TURGOT, E. F.
Memoire Instructif sur la Maniere de Rassembler, de Preparer, de Conserver et d'Envoyer les Diverses Curiosites d'Historie Nataurelle.... Lyons: 1758. V. 73

TURING, ALAN MATHISON
Solvable and unsolvable problems in Science News 31. Melbourne: 1954. V. 72

THE TURKISH Jester; or, the Pleasantries of Cogia Nasr Eddin Effendi. Ipswich;: 1884. V. 73

TURMAN, NORA M.
The Eastern Shore of Virginia 1603-1964. Onancock: 1964. V. 68

TURNBULL, GAEL
Circus: Poems. Malvern: 1984. V. 71

TURNBULL, ROBERT
A Visit to the Philadelphia Prison; Being an Accurate and Particular Account of the Wise and Humane Administration Adopted in Every Part of that Building.... London: 1797. V. 68; 70; 73

TURNBULL, W. P.
The Birds of East Pennsylvania and New Jersey. Glasgow: 1869. V. 70; 72

TURNBULL, WILLIAM PEVERIL
Chessman in Action. London: 1914. V. 68

TURNER, A. LOGAN
Sir William Turner Professor of Anatomy and Principal and Vice-Chancellor of the University of Edinburgh. London: 1919. V. 71; 72
The Skiagraphy of the Accessory Nasal Sinuses. New York: 1912. V. 71

TURNER, ALFORD E.
The Earps Talk. College Station: 1980. V. 69

TURNER, AMBROSE TRUSSWELL
Hardwycke Annals, Co. Derby. 1905. V. 70
Hardwycke Annals, Co. Derby. London: 1905. V. 72

TURNER, AVERY, MRS.
These High Plains. Amarillo: 1941. V. 70

TURNER, B. J.
Evolutionary Genetics of Fishes. New York: 1984. V. 73

TURNER, COLIN
In Search of Shergar. London: 1984. V. 68

TURNER, DANIEL
Syphilis. A Practical Dissertation on the Venereal Diseases. London: 1724. V. 73

TURNER, DAWSON
Account of a Tour in Normandy.... London: 1820. V. 69; 72
Catalogue of the Manuscript Library of the Late Dawson Turner.... London: 1859. V. 70
Outlines in Lithography, from a Small Collection of Pictures. Yarmouth: 1840. V. 70; 72

TURNER, EDWARD
Ned Turner's Clown Joke Book. New York: 1870. V. 69

TURNER, ELIZABETH
The Daisy; or Cautionary Stories in Verse. Philadelphia: 1808. V. 73

TURNER, ERNEST
Hints for Househunters and Householders. London: 1883. V. 68
Hints to Househunters and Householders. London: 1884. V. 71

TURNER, FREDERICK JACKSON
The Significance of the Frontier in American History. Madison: 1894. V. 73

TURNER, G. GREY
The Hunterian Museum Yesterday and Tomorrow. London: 1946. V. 68

TURNER, GEORGE EDGAR
Victory Rode the Rails, the Strategic Place of Railroads in the Civil War. Indianapolis: 1953. V. 68

TURNER, J. E. CARRINGTON
Man Eaters and Memories. 1959. V. 70

TURNER, J. HORSFALL
Haworth Past and Present, a History of Haworth, Stanbury and Oxenhope. Brighouse: 1879. V. 73

TURNER, J. W.
Novel Musical Grammar. Boston: 1887. V. 72

TURNER, JOHN P.
The Northwest Mounted Police, 2 Vols. Ottawa: 1930. V. 72

TURNER, JOSEPH MALLORD WILLIAM
A Collection of Thirty Three Copper Plate Engravings from Whitaker's History of Richmondshire.... London: 1823. V. 73
Liber Fluviorum; or River Scenery of France. London: 1853. V. 72
Liber Studiorum. London. V. 72
The Sunset Ship - the Poems of J. M. W. Turner. Lowestoft, Suffolk: 1966. V. 71
The Turner Gallery: a Series of 120 Engravings. New York: 1880. V. 71

TURNER, L. E.
The Great Age of the Microscope. The Collection of the Royal Microscopical Society through 150 Years. Bristol: 1989. V. 71

TURNER, MORRIE
Nipper's Secret Power. Philadelphia: 1971. V. 72

TURNER, NAT
The Confessions of Nat Turner.... Baltimore: 1831. V. 69

TURNER, NICHOLAS
An Essay on Draining and Improving Peat Bogs; in Which their Nature and Properties are Fully Considered. London: 1784. V. 73

TURNER, R.
An Easy Introduction to the Arts and Sciences; Being A Short, but Comprehensive System of Useful and Polite Learning, Divided into Lessons. London: 1791. V. 73

TURNER, RICHARD
The Young Geometrician's Companion.... London: 1787. V. 71

TURNER, ROBERT
Ars Notaria: the Notary Art of Solomon, Shewing the Cabbalistic Key of Magical Operations, the Liberal Sciences, Divine Revelation and the Art of Memory.... London: 1657. V. 72
Maria Stuarta, Regina Scotiae.... Cologne: 1627. V. 68

TURNER, SAMUEL
My Climbing Adventures in Four Continents. 1911. V. 68; 70
My Climbing Adventures in Four Continents. London: 1913. V. 69
Siberia: a Record of Travel, Climbing and Exploration. London: 1905. V. 70; 72

TURNER, THOMAS, & CO.
Handicrafts that Survive. Sheffield: 1902-1903. V. 68

TURNER, TIMOTHY G.
Bullets, Bottles and Gardenias. Dallas: 1935. V. 69

TURNER, W.
Challenger Voyage. Parts 29 and 47. Human Crania and Other Bones of the Skeletons Collected. Parts 1-2. 1884-1886. V. 73

TURNER, W. J.
The Man Who Ate the Popomack - a Tragi-Comedy of Love in Four Acts. Oxford: 1922. V. 69
Marigold - an Idyll of the Sea. London: 1926. V. 69
Mozart. The Man And His Works. London: 1938. V. 72
New Poems. London: 1928. V. 68

TURNER, WILLIAM
The Ceramics of Swansea and Nantgarw: A History of the Factories. London: 1897. V. 72
The Comparative Osteology of Races of Men. Edinburgh: 1884-1886. V. 68
Lectures on the Comparative Anatomy of te Placenta. Edinburgh: 1876. V. 68

TURNEY HIGH, HARRY HOLBERT
The Flathead Indians of Montana.... Menasha: 1937. V. 68

TURNOR, CHRISTOPHER HATTON
Astra Castra Experiments and Adventures in the Air. London: 1865. V. 73

TURNOR, LEWIS
History of the Ancient Town and Borough of Hertford. Hertford: 1830. V. 72

TURNOR, THOMAS
The Case of the Bankers and Their Creditors. 1675. V. 71

TUROW, SCOTT
Burden of Proof. 1990. V. 70
The Laws of Our Fathers. New York: 1996. V. 72
Presumed Innocent. New York: 1987. V. 68; 71; 72; 73

TURPIN, RICHARD
The Trial of Notorious Highwayman Richard Turpin, at York Assizes, on 22d Day of March, 1739.... York: 1739. V. 69

TURRONI, AGOSTINO
La Origine di Molte Citta del Mondo, e Particolarmanete di Tutta Italia.... Viterbo: 1619. V. 68; 70

TURTON, THOMAS
Thoughts on the Admission of Persons Without Regard to Their Religious Opinions to Certain Degrees in the Universities of England.... London: 1835. V. 70

TURTON, WILLIAM
The Tryal of William Turton, Esq. for the Murder of John Holloway, at the Assizes Held at Oxford, on Thursday, the Seventeenth Day of July, 1755. London: 1755. V. 69

TURTON, ZOUCH H.
To the Desert and Back; or, Travels in Spain, the Barbary States, Italy, etc. in 1875-1876. London: 1876. V. 73

TUSON, EDWARD WILLIAM
The Dissector's Guide; or Student's Companion. Boston: 1844. V. 68; 71

TUSSAUD, MARIE
Memoirs of Madame Tussaud: Her Eventful History. London: 1878. V. 68

TUSSER, THOMAS
Five Hundred Points of Good Husbandry.... London: 1812. V. 69

TUTEN, FREDERIC
Tintin in the New World. New York: 1993. V. 68

TUTHILL, C.
The Tres Alamo Site on the San Pedro River, Southeastern Arizona. 1947. V. 69

TUTHILL, LOUISA C.
History of Architecture, from the Earliest Times.... Philadelphia: 1848. V. 68; 70; 73
The Young Lady at Home and in Society. New York: 1869. V. 69; 72

TUTIN, J. R.
A Concordance to Fitzgerald's Translation of the Rubaiyat of Omar Khayyam. London: 1900. V. 69

TUTIN, T. G.
Flora Europaea. Cambridge: 1964-1980. V. 70

TUTTLE, CHARLES RICHARD
General History of the State of Michigan.... Detroit: 1873. V. 69

TUTTLE, HUDSON
Blossoms of our Spring. London: 1864. V. 71

TUTTLE, MARGARETTA
Feet of Clay. New York: 1923. V. 70

TUTTLE, RUSSELL H.
Paleoanthropology - Morphology and Paleoecology. The Hague: 1975. V. 68

TUTTLE, SARAH
Conversations on the Choctaw Mission.... Boston: 1830. V. 68; 69; 72

TUTUOLA, AMOS
The Brave African Huntress. New York: 1958. V. 71
My Life in the Bush of Ghosts. London: 1954. V. 73
My Life in the Bush of Ghosts. New York: 1954. V. 71
The Palm-Wine Drinkard. London: 1952. V. 73
The Palm-Wine Drinkard and His Dead Palm-Wine Tapster in the Dead's Town. New York: 1953. V. 69

'TWAS the Night Before Chrsitmas. Racine: 1940. V. 70; 73

THE TWELVE Months of the Year with a Picture for Each Month - Adapted to Northern Latitudes. Concord: 1837. V. 70

25 NON-ROYALTY One-Act Plays for All-Girl Casts. New York: 1942. V. 72

TWENTY-Five Years of Industrial Unionism. Chicago: 1930. V. 68

TWENTY-Seven Prints of Natural History.... London: 1802. V. 71

TWICE 1 are 2. London: 1920. V. 72

TWIGGY by Twiggy. New York: 1968. V. 68

TWINING, HENRY
The Elements of Picturesque Scenery, or Studies of Nature Made in Travel with a View to Improvement in Landscape Painting. London: 1853-1856. V. 72
On the Philosophy of Painting: a Theoretical and Practical Treatise.... London: 1849. V. 69

THE TWINS. 1890. V. 70

TWISLETON, TOM
Poems in the Craven Dialect. Settle: 1869. V. 69

TWISS, HORACE
The Carib Chief: a Tragedy in Five Acts. London: 1819. V. 73
The Public and Private Life of Lord Chancellor Eldon. London: 1844. V. 71; 72

TWISS, RICHARD
A Tour in Ireland in 1775. London: 1776. V. 71

TWITCHELL, RALPH EMERSON
The History of The Military Occupation of New Mexico From 1846-1851. Denver: 1909. V. 72
The Leading Facts of New Mexican History. Cedar Rapids, IA: 1911-1917. V. 72
The Leading Facts of New Mexican History. London: 1963. V. 68
The Military Occupation of New Mexico 1846-1851. Denver: 1909. V. 70; 72
The Spanish Archives of New Mexico. Cedar Rapids, IA: 1914. V. 72

THE TWO Friends or the Dying Fawn: a Tale.... London: 1832. V. 73

200 Poems by the Idaho Poet, Author, Editor and Printer. 1922?. V. 70

TWO Weeks of Hawaiian History. Honolulu: 1893. V. 68

TWOPENY, RICHARD ERNEST NOWELL
Town Life in Australia. London: 1883. V. 69; 71

TWOPENY, WILLIAM
English Metal Work: Ninety Three Drawings. London: 1904. V. 68; 72

TWYMAN, MICHAEL
Lithography 1800-1850. London: 1970. V. 69
Printing 1770-1970: an Illustrated History of Its Development and Uses in England. London: 1970. V. 69

TYACKE, SARAH
London Map-Sellers 1660-1720. Tring: 1978. V. 70

TYAS, ROBERT
Favourite Field Flowers; or Wild Flowers of England. London: 1848-50. V. 70
Flowers and Heraldry; or, Floral Emblems and Heraldic Figures.... London: 1851. V. 70

TYERMAN, L.
The Life and Times of the Rev John Wesley, M.A. founder of the Methodists. New York: 1872. V. 71

TYLER, ANNE
The Accidental Tourist. London: 1985. V. 69
The Accidental Tourist. New York: 1985. V. 68; 69; 70; 71; 72; 73
Back When We Were Grownups. London: 2001. V. 70
Breathing Lessons. Franklin Center: 1988. V. 68; 69; 70; 71; 73
Breathing Lessons. New York: 1988. V. 68; 69; 70; 71; 72
Celestial Navigation. New York: 1974. V. 68; 69; 70; 71; 72; 73
The Clock Winder. New York: 1972. V. 68; 70
The Clock Winder. London: 1973. V. 71; 72
Dinner at the Homesick Restaurant. New York: 1982. V. 68; 70; 71; 72
Earthly Possessions. London: 1977. V. 68; 71
Earthly Possessions. New York: 1977. V. 68; 69; 70; 71
If Morning Ever Comes. New York: 1964. V. 69; 71; 73
Ladder of Years. Franklin Center: 1995. V. 68; 69
Ladder of Years. New York: 1995. V. 68; 70; 71; 72
Morgan's Passing. New York: 1980. V. 68; 70; 71; 72; 73
A Patchwork Planet. New York: 1998. V. 68; 71; 72
Saint Maybe. Franklin Center: 1991. V. 68; 71
Saint Maybe. New York: 1991. V. 68; 69; 70; 71; 72; 73
Searching for Caleb. New York: 1976. V. 68; 69; 70; 71; 72
A Slipping-Down Life. New York: 1970. V. 68; 69; 70; 71; 73
A Slipping-Down Life. London: 1983. V. 68
The Tin Can Tree. New York: 1964. V. 70
The Tin Can Tree. New York: 1965. V. 68; 71
The Tin Can Tree. London: 1966. V. 70; 71
To Eudora Welty, for Showering Us With Gifts. 1984. V. 69
Tumble Tower. New York: 1993. V. 70; 71
A Visit with Eudora Welty. Chicago: 1980. V. 70
Your Place is Empty. Concord: 1992. V. 70

TYLER, EPHRAIM D.
Tyler's Poems: Poems of Every Day Life. Shreveport: 1936. V. 70

TYLER, GEORGE
Whatever Goes Up - the Hazardous Fortunes of a Natural Born Gambler. Indianapolis: 1934. V. 68; 70

TYLER, HAMILTON A.
Pueblo Gods and Myths. Norman: 1964. V. 69

TYLER, MASON W.
Recollections of the Civil War. New York: 1912. V. 69

TYLER, MOSES COIT
A History of American Literature 1607-1765. New York: 1880. V. 70
Literary History of the American Revolution 1763-1783. New York: 1897. V. 70

TYLER, PARKER
The Will of Eros - Selected Poems 1930-1970. Los Angeles: 1972. V. 68

TYLER, R.
Audubon's Great National Work The Royal Octavo Editions of the Birds of America. Austin: 1993. V. 70

TYLER, RON
Alfred Jacob Miller; Artist On the Oregon Trail. Fort Worth: 1982. V. 71; 72
The Mexican War - a Lithographic Record. Austin: 1973. V. 73
Posada's Mexico. Washington: 1979. V. 73

TYLER, WILLIAM
An Inquiry, Historical and Critical into Evidence Against Mary Queen of Scots.... Edinburgh: 1767. V. 69

TYLOR, A.
Colouration in Animals and Plants. London: 1886. V. 70

TYLOR, EDWARD B.
Anahuac; or Mexico and the Mexicans, Ancient and Modern. London: 1861. V. 69
Anahuac; or Mexico and the Mexicans, Ancient and Modern. London: 1961. V. 71

TYMMS, W. R.
The Art of Illuminating. London: 1866. V. 70
The Art of Illuminating. London: 1987. V. 72

TYNAC, FRANCAISE
Wallpaper. A History. New York: 1982. V. 72

TYNAN, KATHARINE
Irish Poems. 1913. V. 69
Shamrocks. London: 1887. V. 68

TYNAN, PATRICK J. P.
The Irish National Invincibles and Their Times. 1896. V. 70; 71

TYNDALE, WALTER
An Artist in Italy. London: 1913. V. 72
Below The Cataracts. London: 1907. V. 72
Egypt. London: 1912. V. 68

TYNDALL, JOHN
Address Delivered Before the British Association Assembled at Belfast with Additions. London: 1874. V. 72
Essays on the Floating Matter of the Air in Relation to Putrefaction and Infection. London: 1881. V. 69; 72
Faraday as a Discoverer. London: 1868. V. 70; 72
Fragments of Science for Unscientific People: a Series of Detached Essays, Lectures and Reviews. London: 1871. V. 72
The Glaciers of the Alps. London: 1860. V. 73
The Glaciers of the Alps. Boston: 1861. V. 73
The Glaciers of the Alps. London: 1896. V. 69
Lessons in Electricity at the Royal Insitution 1875-1876. London: 1876. V. 71
Mountaineering in 1861. A Vacation Tour. 1862. V. 68; 70; 73
New Fragments. London: 1892. V. 72
Notes on Light. London: 1869. V. 70
Researches on Diamagnetism and Magne-Crystallic Action, Including the Question of Diamagnetic Polarity. London: 1870. V. 68
The Study of Physics. 1854. V. 68; 70; 73

TYRELL, HENRY
The Doubtful Plays of Shakespeare; being all the dramas attributed to the muse of the world's greatest poet . . . London. V. 71

TYRELL, J. B.
Documents Relating to the Early History of Hudson Bay. Toronto: 1931. V. 71

TYRELL, JAMES WILLIAMS
Across the Sub-Arctics of Canada. London: 1898. V. 71

TYRIE, DAVID
The Trial of David Tyrie, for High Treason, at the Assize at Winchester, Held by Adjournment on Saturday, August the 10th, 1782.. London: 1782. V. 70

TYRMAND, LEOPOLD
The Seven Long Voyages. London: 1959. V. 71

TYRRELL, CHRISTINA
Success: And How He Won It. London: 1876. V. 73

TYRRELL, H.
History of Russia, from the Foundation of the Empire: to the War With Turkey in 1877-1878. London: 1880. V. 71
Tallis's History of England for the Young. London: 1855. V. 69

TYRRELL, JAMES WILLIAMS
Across the Sub-Arctics of Canada. London: 1898. V. 69

TYRRELL, MABEL L.
The Forgotten Hills. London: 1936. V. 70

TYRWHITT, JANICE
Bartlett's Canada. Toronto: 1968. V. 73

TYRWHITT, R. ST. JOHN
A Handbook of Pictorial Art.... Oxford: 1868. V. 73

TYRWHITT, THOMAS
Substance of a Statement Made to the Chamber of Commerce, Plymouth on Tuesday the 3rd Day of November 1818.... Plymouth-Dock: 1819. V. 70; 72

TYSON, A. G.
An Essay on the Poetic and Musical Customs of the Ancients; with Original Poems on Her Majesty Queen Victoria's Visit to Castle Howard...and Other Interesting Subjects. 1852. V. 72

TYSON, EDWARD
Orang-Outang, sive Homo Sylvestris; or, the Anatomy of a Pygmie Compared with that of a Monkey, an Ape and a Man. London: 1699. V. 68
A Philological Essay Concerning the Pygmies of the Ancients. London: 1894. V. 68

TYSON, IAN
The Life and Times of Baby Woojams. London: 1980. V. 70
Transliniations. London: 1979. V. 70

TYSSEN, SAMUEL
Catalogue of the Entire Museum, of the Late Samuel Tyssen, esq. F.A. S. of Narborough-Hall in the County of Norfolk.... London: 1802. V. 68; 72

TYTLER, CHRISTINA CATHERINE FRASER
Songs in Minor Keys. London: 1881. V. 69

TYTLER, PATRICK FRASER
Historical Notes on the Lennox or Darnley Jewel, the Property of the Queen. London: 1843. V. 68; 72
Historical View of the Progress of Discovery on the More Northern Coasts of America.... Edinburgh and London: 1832. V. 73

TYTLER, SARAH
Jane Austen and Her Works. London: 1884. V. 70; 73
Noblesse Oblige: an English Story of To-day. London: 1890. V. 68
The Songstress of Scotland. London: 1871. V. 71

TYTLER, WILLIAM
An Inquiry, Historical and Critical into the Evidence Against Mary Queen of Scots. Edinburgh: 1767. V. 69; 72; 73

TZARA, TRISTAN
Midis Gagnes - Poemes. Paris: 1939. V. 71

U

UDALL, SHARYN ROHIFSEN
Modernist Paintings in New Mexico 1913-1935. Albuquerque: 1984. V. 70

UDELL, JOHN
Journal of John Udell Kept During a Trip Across the Plains, Containing an Account of the Massacre of a Portion of His Party by the Mohave Indians in 1858. Suisun: 1952. V. 68

UDRY, JANICE MAY
Danny's Pig. New York: 1960. V. 73
The Moon Jumpers. London: 1979. V. 72

UHDE, WILHELM
Picasso et la Tradition Francaise. Notes sur la Peinture Actuelle. Paris: 1928. V. 73

UHLMAN, FRED
Reunion. London: 1971. V. 69

UKERS, WILLIAM H.
All About Coffee. New York: 1935. V. 69
Romance of Coffee. New York: 1948. V. 70

ULANOV, BARRY
Duke Ellington. New York: 1946. V. 70; 71

ULLMAN, JAMES RAMSEY
The Age of Mountaineering. London: 1956. V. 69
Americans on Everest. London: 1965. V. 69
Straight Up. New York: 1968. V. 69

ULLOA, ANTONIO DE
A Voyage to South-America.... Dublin: 1765. V. 73

ULMANN, DORIS
A Book of Portraits of the Faculty of the Medical Department of the Johns Hopkins University Baltimore. Baltimore: 1922. V. 70

ULMER, ULRICUS
Fraternitas Cleri. Ulm: 1480. V. 69

ULRICH, CHARLES
On The Little Big Horn - A Comedy Drama of The West In Four Acts. Chicago: 1907. V. 72

UMFREVILLE, EDWARD
The Present State of Hudson's Bay. London: 1790. V. 68; 70; 73

UMLAUFT, F.
The Alps. 1889. V. 70; 73

UNCLE *Blunder's Studio.* London: 1943. V. 69

UNCLE *Jock's Book of New Nursery Rhymes.* London: 1903. V. 68; 71; 73

UNCLE *Oojah's Big Annual c. 1928.* London. V. 69

UNCLE MILTON
Bennie and Jennie. New York: 1907. V. 70
The Sunbonnet Twins. New York: 1907. V. 70

UNDERHILL, DANIEL C.
Underhill's New Table Book; or, Tables of Arithmetic Made Easier. New York: 1850-1856. V. 70

UNDERHILL, EVELYN
Jacopone Da Todi Poet and Mystic 1228-1306. London: 1919. V. 72

UNDERHILL, GEORGE F.
The Helterskelter Hounds on Mr. Flopkin's Sporting Memoirs. London: 1894. V. 68

UNDERHILL, HAROLD A.
Deep-Water Sail. Glasgow: 1952. V. 73

UNDERHILL, RUTH MURRAY
First Penthouse Dwellers of America. New York. V. 69
Hawk Over Whirlpools. New York: 1940. V. 69
Singing for Power: The Song Magic of the Papago Indians of Southern Arizona. Berkeley: 1938. V. 69

UNDERWOOD, J. CABANISS
Gilbert; Or, Then and Now. A Thrilling Story of the Life and Achievements of a Virginia Negro. Philadelphia: 1902. V. 69

UNDERWOOD, MICHAEL
Death by Misadventure. London: 1960. V. 68

UNDERWOOD, THOMAS
The Snarlers, A Poem. London: 1768. V. 71

UNDERWOOD, TIM
Fear Itself, the Horror Fiction of Stephen King. 1982. V. 73

UNDSET, SIGRID
Kristin Lavransdatter. New York: 1937. V. 73
The Master of Hestviken. New York: 1934. V. 70
The Master of Hestviken. New York: 1952. V. 71
The Wild Orchid. New York: 1931. V. 70

UNGER, DOUGLAS
Leaving the Land. New York: 1984. V. 71

UNGERER, TOMI
Adelaide. New York: 1959. V. 70

THE UNION Army, a History of Military Affairs in the Loyal States 1861-1865....
Wilmington: 1997-1998. V. 69

UNION BANK OF LOS ANGELES
Kaspare Cohn: a Commemorative Tribute to the Founder. Los Angeles: 1964. V. 68

THE UNION Jacks. London: 1904. V. 68

UNION PACIFIC RAILROAD
Nebraska, Its Resources and Attractions. Omaha: 1902. V. 70

UNION STEAMSHIP CO.
Standing Orders of the Union Steamship Company of British Columbia, Limited. Vancouver. V. 68

UNION SWITCH & SIGNAL CO.
A Catalogue of Devices and Their Parts Manufactured by the Union Switch and Signal Co., General Office and Works, Swissvale, Pa. Buffalo: 1894. V. 73

UNITED CATTLE AND HORSE GROWER'S ASSOCIATION OF IDAHO
1916 Brand Book. MacKay: 1916. V. 68; 71

UNITED SOVIET SOCIALIST REPUBLIC
Report of Court Proceedings in the Case of the Anti-Soviet Trotskyite Centre Heard Before the Military Collegium of the Supreme Court of the U.S.S. R. Moscow January 23-30, 1937. Moscow: 1937. V. 69

UNITED STATES. ARMY - 1829
A System of Exercise and Instruction of Field Artillery, Including Manoeuvres for Light or Horse Artillery. Boston: 1829. V. 72

UNITED STATES. BUREAU OF AMERICAN ETHNOLOGY - 1886
Fourth Annual Report 1882-1883. Washington: 1886. V. 71

UNITED STATES. BUREAU OF AMERICAN ETHNOLOGY - 1903
Twentieth Annual Report...1898-1899. Washington: 1903. V. 71

UNITED STATES. BUREAU OF AMERICAN ETHNOLOGY - 1916
Twenty-Ninth Annual Report 1907-1908. Washington: 1916. V. 71

UNITED STATES. BUREAU OF AMERICAN ETHNOLOGY - 1919
Thirty-Third Annual Report...1911-1912. Washington: 1919. V. 71

UNITED STATES. BUREAU OF AMERICAN ETHNOLOGY - 1928
Annual Report...1919-1924. Washington: 1928. V. 71

UNITED STATES. BUREAU OF FISHERIES - 1905
Bulletin of...1904. Washington: 1905. V. 72

UNITED STATES. BUREAU OF FISHERIES - 1940
Bulletin of.... Washington: 1940. V. 72

UNITED STATES. BUREAU OF MINE OFFICIALS - 1931
Safety: Life and Limb, Dollars and Cents. Chicago?: 1931?. V. 73

UNITED STATES. BUREAU OF THE BUDGET - 1962
The Budget of the United States Government for the Fiscal Year Ending June 30 1963. Washington: 1962. V. 69

UNITED STATES. CIRCUIT COURT - 1891
The Edison Incandescent Lamp Case. Full Text of Judge Wallace's Opinion in the Case of the Edison Electric Light Company Against the United States Electric Lighting Company...in the U.S. Circuit Court, New York City, July 14, 1891. New York: 1891?. V. 69

UNITED STATES. COMMERCE DEPARTMENT. BUREAU OF CENSUS - 1919
Religious Bodies, 1916. Washington: 1919. V. 69

UNITED STATES. CONGRESS - 1792
Journal of the Senate of the United States of America, Being the First Session of the Second Congress, Begun and Held at the City of Philadelphia, October 24th 1791. Philadelphia: 1792. V. 72

UNITED STATES. CONGRESS - 1804
Acts Passed at the First Session of the Eighth Congress of the United States of America...in the Year 1803. Washington: 1804. V. 68

UNITED STATES. CONGRESS - 1834
American State Papers-documents, Legislative and Executive, of the Congress of the United States, in relation to the Public Lands. Washington: 1834. V. 72
The Debates and Proceedings in the Congress of the United States.... Washington: 1834. V. 73

UNITED STATES. CONGRESS - 1867
Condition of the Indian Tribes: Report of the Joint Special Committee Appointed Under Joint Resolution of March 3D, 1865. With an Appendix. Washington: 1867. V. 72

UNITED STATES. CONGRESS - 1939
Congressional Documents on Florida Ship Canal. Washington: 1939. V. 68

UNITED STATES. CONGRESS. HOUSE OF REPRESENTATIVES - 1796
A Bill to Ascertain and Fix the Military Establishment of the United States. Philadelphia: 1796. V. 69; 70; 72

UNITED STATES. CONGRESS. HOUSE OF REPRESENTATIVES - 1805
Report of the Committee Appointed the Twelfth of November Last on so Much of the Message of the President...Form of Government of the Territory of Louisiana. Washington: 1805. V. 72

UNITED STATES. CONGRESS. HOUSE OF REPRESENTATIVES - 1832
Executive Documents Printed by Order of the House of Representatives.... Washington: 1832. V. 68

UNITED STATES. CONGRESS. HOUSE OF REPRESENTATIVES - 1850
Report of the Naval Committee to the House of Representatives, August 1850 in Favor of the Establishment of a Line of Mail Steamships to the Western Coast of Africa, and thence Via the Mediterranean to London.... Washington: 1850. V. 73

UNITED STATES. CONGRESS. HOUSE OF REPRESENTATIVES - 1946
Laws Relating to the Physically Handicapped. Washington: 1946. V. 72

UNITED STATES. CONGRESS. SENATE - 1791
Journal of the Senate of the United States of America, Being the First Session of the Second Congress, Begun and Held at the City of Philadelphia, October 24th, 1791. Philadelphia: 1792. V. 68

UNITED STATES. CONGRESS. SENATE - 1908
A Company for Breeding Horses on the Crow Indian Reservations Montana, the Survey & Allotment of Indian Lands Within the Limits of the Crow. Washington: 1908. V. 70

UNITED STATES. DEPARTMENT OF AGRICULTURE - 1936
The Western Range, Letter from The Secretary of Agriculture. Washington, DC: 1936. V. 71

UNITED STATES. DEPARTMENT OF COMMERCE - 1917
Circular of the Bureau of Standards #70. Materials for the Household. Washington: 1917. V. 73

UNITED STATES. DISTRICT COURT - 1813
Cases Decided in the District and Circuit Court of the United States for the Pennsylvania District, and also a Case Decided in the District Court of Massachusetts, Relative to the Employment of British Licences on Board of Vessals of the United States. Philadelphia: 1813. V. 68

UNITED STATES. FISH COMMISSION - 1894
Bulletin...for 1893. Washington: 1894. V. 72

UNITED STATES. FISH COMMISSION - 1896
Bulletin....for 1895. Washington: 1896. V. 72

UNITED STATES. FISH COMMISSION - 1898
Bulletin...for 1897. Washington: 1898. V. 72

UNITED STATES. FISH COMMISSION - 1899
Bulletin...for 1898. Washington: 1899. V. 72

UNITED STATES. FISH COMMISSION - 1901
Bulletin...for 1899. Washington: 1901. V. 72

UNITED STATES. GEOGRAPHICAL SURVEYS WEST OF THE 100TH MERID
Report Upon the United States Geographical Surveys West of the One Hundredth Meridian...Volume VII. Archaeology. Washington: 1879. V. 73
Report Upon United States Geographical Surveys West of the One Hundredth Meridian. Washington: 1879-1889. V. 70
United States Explorations and Surveys West of the One Hundredth Meridian. Volume 5. Zoology. Washington: 1875. V. 73

UNITED STATES. GEOLOGICAL AND GEOGRAPHICAL SURVEY - 1877
Ninth Annual Report of the United States Geological and Geographical Survey of the Territories, Embracing Colorado and Parts of Adjacent Territories Being a Report of Progress of the Exploration for the Year 1875. Washington: 1877. V. 73

UNITED STATES. GEOLOGICAL AND GEOGRAPHICAL SURVEY - 1882
Bulletin of the Unitd States Geological and Geographical Survey of the Territories: Volume VI. Washington: 1882. V. 68

UNITED STATES. GEOLOGICAL AND GEOGRAPHICAL SURVEY - 1883
Twelfth Annual Report of the United States Geological and Geographical Survey of the Territories: a Report of Progress of the Exploration in Wyoming and Idaho for the Year 1878 in Two Parts...Part II. Washington: 1883. V. 73

UNITED STATES. INTERIOR DEPARTMENT - 1930
Federal Irrigation Projects. Washington: 1930. V. 68

UNITED STATES. INTERIOR DEPARTMENT - 1950
A Survey of the Recreational Resources of the Colorado River Basin. Washington: 1950. V. 70

UNITED STATES. LAWS, STATUTES, ETC. - 1790
An Act for Giving Effect to the Several Acts Therein mentioned in Respect to the State of North Carolina. New York: 1790. V. 73

UNITED STATES. LAWS, STATUTES, ETC. - 1791
Acts Passed at the First (Second, Third) Session of the Congress of the United States. Philadelphia: 1791. V. 69

UNITED STATES. LAWS, STATUTES, ETC. - 1795
Laws of the United States of America. Volume I (all published). Containing the Federal Constitution: the Acts of the Sessions of the First and Second Congress.... Boston: 1795. V. 69; 72

UNITED STATES. LAWS, STATUTES, ETC. - 1804
Acts Passed at the Fist Session of the Eighth Congress of the United States of America...in the Year 1803. Washington: 1804. V. 72

UNITED STATES. NAVY DEPARTMENT - 1830
Register of the Commissioned and Warrant Offices of the Navy of the United States; Including Officers of the Marine Corps &c. for the Year 1830. City of Washington: 1830. V. 73

UNITED STATES. NAVY DEPARTMENT - 1878
Report of the Secretary of the Navy for 1878. Washington: 1878. V. 73

UNITED STATES. NAVY DEPARTMENT - 1880
Report of the Secretary of the Navy for 1879. Washington: 1880. V. 73

UNITED STATES. NAVY DEPARTMENT - 1882
Report of the Secretary of the Navy for 1882. Washington: 1882. V. 73

UNITED STATES. NAVY DEPARTMENT - 1884
Report of the Secretary of the Navy for 1884. Washington: 1884. V. 73

UNITED STATES. NAVY DEPARTMENT - 1887
Report of the Secretary of the Navy for 1887-1888. Washington: 1888. V. 73

UNITED STATES. OFFICE OF PRICE ADMINISTRATION - 1944
OPA Is Our Battle Line: Handbook for War Price and Rationing Boards. Washington: 1944. V. 73

UNITED STATES. OFFICE OF THE BUDGET - 1962
The Budget of the United States Government for the Fiscal Year Ending June 30, 1963. Washington: 1962. V. 73

UNITED STATES. PATENT OFFICE - 1857
Report of the Commissioner of Patents for the Year 1856: Agriculture. Washington: 1857. V. 73

UNITED STATES. PATENT OFFICE - 1858
Report of the Commissioner of Patents for the Year 1857: Agriculture. Washington: 1858. V. 73

UNITED STATES. PRESIDENT - 1795
A Message of the President of the United States, to Congress, Relative to France and Great Britain: Delivered December 5, 1793. Philadelphia: 1795. V. 72

UNITED STATES. PRESIDENT - 1823
Message from the President of the United States to Both Houses of Congress at the Commencement of the First Session of the Eighteenth Congress. (together with) Documents Accompanying the Message of the President.... Washington: 1823. V. 73

UNITED STATES. PRESIDENT - 1829
Message from the President of the United States, to...the Twenty- First Congress December 8, 1829. Washington: 1829. V. 71

UNITED STATES. PRESIDENT - 1841
Attorney General, Construction of Public Laws. Message from the President of the U.S. Washington: 1841. V. 72

UNITED STATES. PRESIDENT - 1848
Messages of the President of the United States with the Correspondence...on the Subject of the Mexican War. 1848. V. 69

UNITED STATES. PRESIDENT - 1849
Message from the President of the United States to the Two Houses of Congress at the Commencement of the First Session of the Thirty-First Congress. Washington: 1849. V. 69

UNITED STATES. PRESIDENT - 1850
Message From The President (Millard Filmore)...Dec 2, 1850...Printed for the Senate. Washington, DC: 1850. V. 72

Message from the President of the United States, Transmitting Information...on the Subject of California and New Mexico. Washington: 1850. V. 69

UNITED STATES. PRESIDENT - 1860
Message of the President of the United States Communicating in Compliance with a Resolution of the Senate Information in Relation to the Massacre at Mountain Meadows and Other Massacres in Utah Territory. Washington: 1860. V. 68

UNITED STATES. PRESIDENT - 1866
Message of the President of the United States, and Accompanying Documents, to the Two Houses of Congress at the Commencement of the Second Session of the Thirty-Ninth Congress. Washington: 1866. V. 73

UNITED STATES. PRESIDENT - 1869
Message From The President of The United States to The Two Houses of Congress at The Commencement of the 3rd Session of the 40th Congress. Washington, DC: 1869. V. 72

UNITED STATES. PRESIDENT - 1961
Inaugural Addresses of the Presidents of the United States from George Washington 1789 to John F. Kennedy 1961. Washington: 1961. V. 70

UNITED STATES. SANITARY COMMISSION - 1865
Narrative of the Privations and Sufferings of United States Offcers and Soldiers While Prisoners of War in the Hands of the Rebel Authorities.... Boston: 1865. V. 73

UNITED STATES. SUPREME COURT - 1857
Report of the Decision of the Supreme Court of the United States and the Opinions of the Judges Thereof, in the Case of Dred Scott versus John F. A. Sandford, December Term, 1856. Washington: 1857. V. 68; 69; 70

UNITED STATES. TREASURY DEPARTMENT - 1793
Sundry Statements, by the Secretary of the Treasury. In Conformity with the Resolution of the House of Representatives of the 23d of January 1793. Philadelphia: 1793. V. 73

UNITED STATES. TREASURY DEPARTMENT - 1794
Summary Statement of the Receipts and Expenditures of The United States, from the Commencement of the Present Government to the end of the Year One Thousand Seven Hundred and Ninety-Three. Philadelphia: 1794. V. 73

UNITED STATES. TREASURY DEPARTMENT - 1795
Report of the Secretary of the Treasury, Read in the House of Representatives of the United States, January 19th 1795. Philadelphia: 1795. V. 73

UNITED STATES. WAR DEPARTMENT - 1850
Reports of the Secretary of War, with Reconaissances of Routes from San Antonio to El Paso. Washington: 1850. V. 69; 73

UNITED STATES. WAR DEPARTMENT - 1857
Senate Report of Explorations and Surveys to Ascertain the Most Practicable and Economical Route for a Railroad from the Mississippi River to the Pacific Ocean 1854-1855. Washington: 1857. V. 70

UNITED STATES. WAR DEPARTMENT - 1858
Reports of Explorations and Surveys to Ascertain the Most Practicable and Economical Route for a Railroad from the Mississippi River to the Pacific Ocean. Fishes. Washington: 1858. V. 73

UNITED STATES. WAR DEPARTMENT - 1864
Letter of the Secretary of War, Transmitting Report on the Organization of the Army of the Potomac, and Of It's Campaigns in Virginia and Maryland, Under the Command of Maj. Gen. George B. McClellan from July 26 1861 to November 7, 1862. Washington: 1864. V. 73

UNITED STATES. WAR DEPARTMENT - 1919
Manual of Neuro-Surgery Authorized by the Secretary of War. Washington: 1919. V. 68; 70

UNITED STATES ANTI-MASONIC CONVENTION
The Proceedings of the United States Anti-Masonic Convention, Held at Philadelphia, September 11, 1830. Philadelphia: 1830. V. 70

UNITED STATES ASTRONOMICAL EXPEDITON 1849-1852.
The U. S. Naval Astronomical Expedition to the Southern Hemisphere, During the Years 1849-1850-1851-1852. Washington: 1855. V. 70

UNITED STATES NAVAL ACADEMY
Regulations of the U.S. Naval Academy as Approved by the. Secretary of the Navy. Washington: 1869. V. 71

UNITED STATES NAVAL ASTRONOMICAL EXPEDITION, 1849-1852
The U.S. Naval Astronomical Expedition to the Southern Hemisphere During the Years 1849-50-51-52. Washington: 1855. V. 72

UNITED STRIKE COMMISSION
Report on the Chicago Strike of June-July 1894. Washington: 1895. V. 68

THE UNIVERSAL Songster, or Museum of Mirth...Ancient and Modern Songs. London: 1875. V. 71

UNIVERSITY OF CALIFORNIA
Publications in Zoology. Volume 22. Berkeley: 1921-1923. V. 73
Publications in Zoology. Volume 4. Berkeley: 1907-1908. V. 73
Publications in Zoology. Volume 8. Berkeley: 1914-1916. V. 73
Publications in Zoology. Volume 9. Berkeley: 1911-1913. V. 73

THE UNIVERSITY of Charleston Appalachian Gold Medallion Honoring Eudora Welty. Charleston: 1987. V. 70

THE UNIVERSITY Printing Houses at Cambridge from the Sixteenth to the Twentieth Century. 1962. V. 71

UNRAU, JOHN D.
The Plains Across the Overland- Emigrants And The Trans-Mississippi West 1840-60. Urbana: 1979. V. 68; 71

UNSWORTH, BARRY
Morality Play. London: 1995. V. 70; 72

UNSWORTH, WALT
Because It Is There. London: 1968. V. 69

UNTERMEYER, LOUIS
Including Horace. New York: 1919. V. 68
Love Sonnets. New York: 1964. V. 69

UNWIN, W. C.
Illustrations and Dissections of the Genera of British Mosses. Lewes: 1878. V. 69

UP DE GRAFF, F. W.
Head-Hunters of the Amazon. London: 1923. V. 69
Head-Hunters of the Amazon. New York: 1923. V. 69

UPDIKE, DANIEL BERKELEY
Printing Types, their History, Form and Use; a Study in Survivals. Cambridge: 1962. V. 69

UPDIKE, JOHN
The Afterlife. Leamington Spa: 1987. V. 70
The Afterlife. New York: 1994. V. 69; 70
The Alligators. Mankato: 1990. V. 72
Americana and Other Poems. New York: 2001. V. 68; 69; 71; 72
Assorted Prose. New York: 1965. V. 71; 73
Bech: A Book. New York: 1970. V. 73
Bech at Bay. New York: 1998. V. 69; 72
Bech is Back. New York: 1982. V. 68; 72; 73
The Beloved. Northridge: 1982. V. 73
Brazil. Franklin Center: 1994. V. 68; 71
Brazil. New York: 1994. V. 71; 72; 73
Buchanan Dying. New York: 1974. V. 68; 70
The Carpentered Hen and Other Tame Creatures. New York: 1958. V. 70
The Carpentered Hen and Other Tame Creatures. New York: 1982. V. 68
The Centaur. New York: 1963. V. 72

UPDIKE, JOHN *continued*
Collected Poems. New York: 1993. V. 72
The Complete Henry Bech. New York: 2001. V. 68; 70; 71
The Coup. London: 1978. V. 70
The Coup. New York: 1978. V. 68; 69; 70
Couples. London: 1968. V. 71
Couples. Cambridge: 1976. V. 70
The Dance of the Solids. New York: 1969. V. 70
Gertrude and Claudius. London: 2000. V. 70
Gertrude and Claudius. New York: 2000. V. 68; 69; 70
Getting Older: Three Stories. Helsinki: 1986. V. 70
A Good Place. 1973. V. 73
The Haunted Major. Hopewell: 1999. V. 72
Hawthorne's Creed. New York: 1981. V. 70
Hoping for a Hoopoe. London: 1959. V. 68; 70
Hub Fans Bid Kid Adieu. Northridge: 1977. V. 69
In Memoriam Felis Felis. Leamington Spa: 1990. V. 73
In the Beauty of the Lilies. Franklin Center: 1996. V. 69; 72
In the Beauty of the Lilies. New York: 1996. V. 72
In the Cemetery High Above Shillington. A Poem. Concord: 1995. V. 73
The Indian. Marvin: 1971. V. 71
Just Looking. New York: 1989. V. 69; 70; 72
Licks of Love. New York: 2000. V. 68; 69; 70; 72
Licks of Love. Norwalk: 2000. V. 68
Love Factories. Helsinki: 1993. V. 72
The Lovelorn Astronomer. Boston: 1978. V. 73
Marry Me. New York: 1976. V. 71
Memories of the Ford Administration. New York: 1992. V. 68; 70; 72
Midpoint and Other Poems. London: 1969. V. 73
Midpoint and Other Poems. New York: 1969. V. 68; 72; 73
A Month of Sundays. New York: 1974. V. 69
A Month of Sundays. New York: 1975. V. 70; 73
More Matter. New York: 1999. V. 69; 73
Museums and Women and Other Stories. New York: 1972. V. 68; 70; 73
The Music School. New York: 1966. V. 70
The Music School. London: 1967. V. 69
Odd Jobs. Essays and Criticism. New York: 1991. V. 70
Of the Farm. New York: 1965. V. 68; 73
Of the Farm. London: 1966. V. 73
People One Knows: Interviews with Insufficiently Famous Americans. Northridge: 1980. V. 70; 73
Picked-Up Pieces. New York: 1975. V. 73
Pigeon Feathers. Franklin Center: 1981. V. 69
Poem Begun on Thursday October 14, 1993 at O'Hare Airport, Terminal 3, Around Six O'Clock P.M. Louisville: 1994. V. 72
The Poorhouse Fair. New York: 1959. V. 68; 69; 71; 72; 73
Problems. New York: 1979. V. 73
Query. 1974. V. 71
Rabbit at Rest. New York: 1990. V. 68; 69; 70; 71; 72; 73
Rabbit is Rich. New York: 1981. V. 69; 72; 73
Rabbit Redux. New York: 1971. V. 68; 69; 71; 72
Rabbit, Run. New York: 1960. V. 68; 71; 72
Rabbit, Run. London: 1964. V. 69
Roger's Version. Franklin Center: 1986. V. 70; 71
Roger's Version. New York: 1986. V. 68; 70; 72
S. New York: 1988. V. 69; 72
The Same Door. New York: 1959. V. 69
Self-Consciousness. New York: 1989. V. 70; 71; 72; 73
Six Poems. 1973. V. 69; 71
A Soft Spring Night in Shillington. Northridge: 1986. V. 71
Talk from the Fifties. Northridge: 1979. V. 73
Telephone Poles and Other Poems. New York: 1963. V. 71; 73
Telephone Poles and Other Poems. 1964. V. 73
Three Illuminations in the Life of an American Author. New York: 1979. V. 68; 70; 72; 73
Tossing and Turning. New York: 1977. V. 70
Toward the End of Time. Franklin Center: 1997. V. 70; 71; 72
Toward the End of Time. New York: 1997. V. 70; 72
Trust Me. New York: 1987. V. 69; 72
Verse. New York: 1965. V. 71
Warm Wine. New York: 1973. V. 70
The Witches of Eastwick. Franklin Center: 1984. V. 70; 73
The Witches of Eastwick. New York: 1984. V. 70; 71; 72; 73

UPDIKE, WILLIAM
An Address to the People of Rhode Island; Proving that more than Eight Millions of the Public Money has Been Wasted by the Present Administration. Providence: 1828. V. 73

UPFIELD, ARTHUR W.
The Bachelor's of Broken Hill. 1950. V. 73
The Bachelors of Broken Hill. London: 1958. V. 70
The Battling Prophet. London: 1956. V. 73
The Body at Madman's Bend. 1963. V. 73
The Bone is Pointed. 1938. V. 73
The Bone is Pointed. Sydney and London: 1938. V. 70
Bony and the Black Virgin. London: 1959. V. 70
Bony and the Kelly Gang. London: 1960. V. 70; 73
Bony and the White Savage. London: 1961. V. 73
Bony Buys a Woman. London: 1957. V. 70; 73
Breakaway House. 1987. V. 73
Bushranger of the Skies. 1987. V. 73
The Devil's Steps. 1946. V. 73
The Great Melbourne Cup. Watson Bay: 1996. V. 70; 73
Gripped by Drought. 1980. V. 73
Gripped by Drought. Missoula: 1990. V. 70
The House of Cain. 1929. V. 73
The House of Cain. San Francisco: 1983. V. 69; 70
Journey to the Hangman. 1959. V. 73
Journey to the Hangman. Garden City: 1959. V. 71
The Lake Frome Monster. London: 1966. V. 73
Madman's Bend. London: 1963. V. 70; 73
The Man of Two Tribes. 1956. V. 73
Mr. Jelly's Business. 1937. V. 73
The Mountains Have a Secret. New York: 1948. V. 70
The Murchison Murders. 1934. V. 73
The Murchison Murders. 1987. V. 73
The Murchison Murders. Miami Beach: 1990. V. 70
Murder Down Under. New York: 1943. V. 68
Murder Must Wait. 1953. V. 73
The Mystery of Swordfish Reef. 1939. V. 73
A Royal Abduction. London: 1932. V. 73
A Royal Abduction. Belen: 1984. V. 70
The Sands of Windee. London: 1931. V. 70
Valley of Smugglers. 1960. V. 73
Venom House. 1952. V. 73
Venom House. Garden City: 1952. V. 68
The Widows of Broome. 1950. V. 73
The Will of the Tribe. 1962. V. 73
The Will of the Tribe. New York: 1962. V. 70
Winds of Evil. 1937. V. 73
Wings Above the Claypan. New York: 1943. V. 71; 73

UPHAM, CHARLES WENTWORTH
Life Explorations and Public Services of John Charles Fremont. Boston: 1856. V. 72

UPHAM, MR.
Mr. Upham's Speech On The Extension Of Slavery: Together With The Ordinance of 1787. Salem: 1849. V. 72

UPSHUR, GEORGE L.
As I Recalled The - Memories of Crowded Years. New York: 1936. V. 69

UPTON, BERTHA
The Adventures of Two Dutch Dolls and a Golliwogg. Boston: 1895. V. 72; 73
The Golliwogg's Bicycle Club. London: 1896. V. 70; 73
The Golliwogg's Christmas. London: 1907. V. 72
The Golliwogg's Circus. London: 1903. V. 70; 73
The Golliwogg's Desert Island. London: 1906. V. 73
The Golliwogg's Fox-Hunt. London: 1905. V. 70
The Vege-men's Revenge. London: 1897. V. 71

UPTON, BREVET
The Military Policy of The United States. Washington, DC: 1904. V. 72

UPTON, FLORENCE
The Adventures of Borbee and the Wisp. London: 1908. V. 71
The Adventures of Two Dutch Dolls and a Golliwogg. London: 1895. V. 73
Golliwogg In The African Jungle. London: 1909. V. 72
The Golliwogg In War!. London: 1899. V. 71
The Golliwogg's Auto-Go-Cart. London: 1901. V. 72
The Golliwogg's Desert Island. London: 1906. V. 70; 72

UPTON, ROBERT
Dead on the Stick. New York: 1986. V. 71

UPWARD, ALLEN
The Club of Masks. Philadelphia: 1926. V. 73
The Prince of Balkistan. London: 1897. V. 68

UPWARD, EDWARD
In the Thirties. London: 1962. V. 73
The Scenic Railway. London: 1997. V. 72; 73

URBANITZKY, ALFRED VON
Electricity in the Service of Man.... London: 1890. V. 71

URCIANUS, P.
Quaestiones excerpte ex explanatione . . . Perugia: 1619. V. 71

URE, DAVID
The History of Rutherglen and East-Kilbride. Published with a view to promote the study of antiquity and natural history. Glasgow: 1793. V. 71

URE, GEORGE, & CO. LTD.
Ornamental and General Iron Founders, Bonnybridge Foundry. Glasgow: 1885. V. 68

URIS, LEON
The Angry Hills. New York: 1955. V. 70; 71; 72; 73
Battle Cry. 1953. V. 69
Battle Cry. New York: 1953. V. 73

URIS, LEON *continued*
Exodus. Garden City: 1958. V. 71
Topaz. New York: 1967. V. 71; 72

URLICH, MATHIAS
Schrift und Druck-Proben der Buchdruckerey von Mathias Urlichs in Aachen. 1823. V. 73

URQUHART, FRED
The Clouds are Big with Mercy: Short Stories. Glasgow: 1946. V. 68
The Ploughing Match: The Collected Stories: Volume Two. London: 1968. V. 68

URQUHART, J. W.
Electric Light, Its Production and Use. 1883. V. 71

URQUHART, JANE
The Whirlpool. Toronto: 1986. V. 72
The Whirlpool. London: 1989. V. 68

URQUHART, THOMAS
The Life and Death of the Admirable Crichtoun from the Original Text of the Discovery.... London: 1927. V. 69

URQUHART, WILLIAM POLLARD
Life and Times of Francesco Sforza, Duke of Milan. Edinburgh and London: 1852. V. 69
Some Thoughts on Natural Theology, Suggested by a Work entitled "Vestiges of the Natural History of Creation". London: 1849. V. 72

URREA, LUIS ALBERTO
Across the Wire. New York: 1990. V. 71; 72

URWICK, THOMAS A.
Records of the Family of Urswyk, Urswick, or Urwick. 1893. V. 71
Records of The Family of Urswyk, Urswick, or Urwick. Edited by Rev. William Urwick...with illustrations by W. H. Urwick. St Albans: 1893. V. 72

U.S. *Infantry Tactics, for the Instruction, Exercise and Maneuvers, of the Soldier, Line of Skirmishers, and Battalion; for the Use of the Colored Troops of the United States Infantry....* Washington: 1863. V. 69

USDIN, EARL
Neuropsycho-pharmacology of Monoamines and Their Regulatory Enzymes. New York: 1974. V. 68

THE USEFUL Arts and Manufactures of Great Britain. London: 1848. V. 71

THE USEFUL Arts and Manufactures of Great Britain. (Second Selection). London: 1850. V. 71

THE USEFUL Arts Employed in the Construction of Dwelling Houses. London: 1851. V. 68; 71

THE USEFUL Arts Employed in the Production of Clothing. London: 1844. V. 68

THE USEFUL Arts Employed in the Production of Food. London: 1850. V. 68

THE USEFUL Letter Writer, Comprising a Succinct Treatise on the Epistolary Art; and Forms of Letters for All the Ordinary Occasions of Life. New York: 1844. V. 73

THE USEFULLNESS of the Stage to Religion and To Government.... London: 1738. V. 69

USHER, JAMES W.
An Art Collector's Treasures. London: 1916. V. 72

USINGER, R. L.
Aquatic Insects of California.... Berkeley: 1956. V. 72

USSHER, ARLAND
The Face and Mind of Ireland. 1950. V. 69

USSHER, J.
A Method for Meditation; or a Manual of Divine Duties, Fit for Every Christians Practice. London: 1651. V. 69
The Power Communicated by God to the Prince and the Obedience Required of the Subject. London: 1688. V. 72

USSHER, RICHARD
Neo-Malthusianism; an Enquiry Into that System with Regard to Its Economy and Morality. London: 1897. V. 71

USSHER, RICHARD J.
The Birds of Ireland. 1900. V. 70

USTINOV, PETER
House of Regrets: a Tragi-comedy in Three Acts. London: 1943. V. 70

UTAH, A Guide to the State. New York: 1941. V. 68

UTLEY, ROBERT M.
The American Heritage History of the Indian Wars. New York: 1977. V. 68
Custer And The Great Controversy. Los Angeles: 1962. V. 72
Fort Union and the Santa Fe Trail: a Special Study of Santa Fe Trail Remains at and Near Fort Union National Monument, New Mexico. Santa Fe: 1959. V. 70
Frontier Regulars to United States Army and The Indian 1866-1890. New York: 1973. V. 72
High Noon in Lincoln County - Violence on the Western Frontier. Albuquerque: 1987. V. 68; 73

UTTERSON, SARAH ELIZABETH
Tales of the Dead. London: 1813. V. 69

UTTLEY, ALISON
Fuzzypeg Goes to School. London: 1938. V. 73
Fuzzypeg Goes to School. 1955. V. 72

Fuzzypeg Goes to School. London: 1955. V. 68
Fuzzypeg's Brothers. London: 1971. V. 70; 72
Going to the Fair. London: 1951. V. 72
Grey Rabbit and the Circus. 1961. V. 73
Grey Rabbit and the Circus. London: 1961. V. 68; 72
Grey Rabbit and the Wandering Hedgehog. 1950. V. 73
Grey Rabbit and the Wandering Hedgehog. London: 1950. V. 68
Grey Rabbit's May Day. London: 1963. V. 72
Hare and Guy Fawkes. 1956. V. 71; 73
Hare and the Rainbow. 1975. V. 72
Hare Goes Shopping. London: 1965. V. 69
The Knot Squirrel Tied. London: 1937. V. 71
Little Grey Rabbit Goes to the North Pole. London: 1970. V. 70; 71
Little Grey Rabbit's Christmas. London: 1939. V. 71
Little Grey Rabbit's Paint-Box. 1970. V. 72
Little Grey Rabbit's Pancake Day. London: 1967. V. 72
A Little Grey Rabbit's Pancake Day. London: 1967. V. 68
Little Grey Rabbit's Party. 1936. V. 71; 73
Little Grey Rabbit's Party. London: 1937. V. 70
Little Grey Rabbit's Spring-Cleaning Party. London: 1972. V. 69
Little Grey Rabbit's Valentine. 1953. V. 72
Little Grey Rabbit's Valentine. London: 1953. V. 68
Little Grey Rabbit's Washing Day. London: 1942. V. 68
Moldy Warp the Mole. London: 1940. V. 72
Snug and Serena Meet a Queen. London: 1950. V. 72
Snug and Serena Pick Cowslips. London. V. 68; 72
The Squirrel, the Hare and the Little Grey Rabbit. London: 1934. V. 69
The Stuff of Dreams. London: 1953. V. 72
Toad's Castle. London: 1951. V. 69
Wise Owl's Story a Little Grey Rabbit Book. London: 1935. V. 70

UWINS, DAVID
Modern Maladies, and the Present State of Medicine, the Anniversary Oration Delivered March 9, 1818, Before the Medical Society of London. London: 1818. V. 70

UZANNE, OCTAVE
The Book-Hunter in Paris.... London: 1893. V. 73
Le Calendrier de Venus. Paris: 1880. V. 69
The French Bookbinders of the Eighteenth Century. Chicago: 1904. V. 70; 73
The Frenchwoman of the Century. London: 1886. V. 70

V

VACARESCO, HELENE
The Bard of the Dimbovitza, Romanian Folk Songs... (with) Second Series. London: 1892-1894. V. 69; 72

VACHELL, HORACE ANNESLEY
The Enchanted Garden. London: 1929. V. 72
Some Happenings. New York: 1918. V. 71
Sport and Life On the Pacific Slope. London: 1908. V. 70

VACHER, FRANCIS
Engravers & Engraving. Manchester: 1887. V. 72

VACHER, SYDNEY
Fifteenth Century Italian Ornament Chiefly Taken from Brocades and Stuffs, Found in Pictures in the National Gallery. London: 1886. V. 68; 73

VACHSS, ANDREW
Choice of Evil. New York: 1999. V. 68
Flood. New York: 1985. V. 68; 71
Hard Candy. New York: 1989. V. 71
Sacrifice. New York: 1991. V. 71
Strega. New York: 1987. V. 68; 71

VACUUM BRAKE CO.
The Vacuum Automatic Brake. Engineers: Alfred L. Sacre and James Gresham. London: 1890?. V. 68

VAENIUS, ERNESTUS
Tractatus Physiologicus De Pulchritudine. Justa Ea Quae De Sponsa in Canticis Canticorum Mystice Pronunciantur. Bruxellis: 1662. V. 71

VAGO, C.
Invertebrate Tissue Culture. New York: 1971-1972. V. 68

VAGTBORG, H.
The Baboon in Medical Research.... Austin: 1965-1967. V. 68

VAHEY, JOHN H.
Spies in Ambush. London: 1934. V. 70

VAILLANCOURT, EMILE
The History of the Brewing Industry in the Province of Quebec. Montreal: 1940. V. 73

VAILLANT, GEORGE C.
Indian Arts in North America. New York: 1939. V. 69

VAILLANT, SEBASTIEN
Botanicon Pariesiense ou Denombrement par Ordre Alphabetique des Plantes, qui se Trouvent aux Environs de Paris.... Leiden and Amsterdam: 1727. V. 72; 73

VALE, BENJAMIN
A Lecture on Ancient Druidism. Burslem: 1824. V. 70

VALE, W. H.
Fugitive Pieces. Maidstone: 1871. V. 70

VALENCIENNES, P. H.
Elemens de Perspective Pratique, a l'Usage des Artistes, Suivis de Reflexions et Conseil a un Elee sur la Peinture.... Paris: 1800. V. 69

VALENTI Angelo: Author, Illustrator, Printer. 1976. V. 70

VALENTIA, GEORGE ANNESLEY, VISCOUNT
Voyages and Travels to India, Ceylon, the Red Sea, Abyssinia and Eygpt in the Years 1802, 1803, 1804, 1805 and 1806. London: 1809. V. 72

VALENTINE and Orson. 1850. V. 72

VALENTINE, CHARLES R.
Butter Making. London: 1889. V. 68; 69

VALENTINE, M. S.
The Mock Auction. Ossawatomie Sold, a Mock Heroic Poem. Richmond: 1860. V. 68

VALENTINE, MRS.
Games for Family Parties and Children. London and New York: 1875. V. 69

VALENTINO, RUDOLPH
My Private Diary. New York: 1929. V. 69; 73

VALERIUS FLACCUS, CAIUS
Argonavtica and Orpheus, Argonautica. Venitiis: 1523. V. 73

VALERIUS MAXIMUS, GAIUS
Exempla Quattuor and Viginti Nuper Inventa Ante Caput De Omnibus (and) Plutarchi Cheronei Parallela Addita Propter Materiae Similitudinem. Florence: 1526. V. 71

VALERO, WAYNE
The Collector's Guide to Clive Cussler. Kearney: 2000. V. 70

VALERY, PAUL
Dialogues. New York: 1956. V. 68
Eupalinos, or the Architect. London: 1932. V. 68; 70
The Graveyard by the Sea. Vancouver: 1938. V. 68
Introduction to the Method of Leonardo Da Vinci. London: 1929. V. 70; 72
Moralites. Paris: 1932. V. 68
Narcisse. Anvers: 1926. V. 70
Variation sur Une Pensee annotee par l'auteur. Liege: 1930. V. 72
Variety: Second Series. New York: 1938. V. 68

VALIN, JONATHAN
Dead Letter. New York: 1981. V. 68; 71; 72
Final Notice. New York: 1980. V. 69; 71
Fire Lake. New York: 1987. V. 71
The Lime Pit. New York: 1980. V. 69; 70; 71

VALLA, LORENZO
Laurentii Vallae cum Graecae tum Latinae Linguae Doctissimi Elegantiarum Libri Sex Ualde Utiles. Gyberti Longolii & Ioannis Raenerii.... Basle: 1543. V. 73

VALLANCE, WILLIAM HOWARD AYMER
The Old Colleges of Oxford their Architectural History Illustrated and Described. London: 1912. V. 68; 72

VALLEE, RUDY
Vagabond Dreams Come True. New York: 1930. V. 68

VALLEJO, CESAR
Twenty Poems of Cesar Vallejo. Madison: 1962. V. 69

VALLEMONT, PIERRE LE LORRAIN
Curiositez de la Nature et de l'Art sur la Vegetation, ou L'Agriculture et le Jardinage dans leur Perfection.... Paris: 1709. V. 70; 71

VALLENTIN, ELINOR FRANCES
Illustrations of the Flowering Plants and Ferns of the Falkland Islands. London: 1921. V. 69; 70; 72

VALLERY RADOT, R.
La Vie de Pasteur. Paris: 1900. V. 68

VALLIER, D.
Braque: L'Oeuvre Grave: Catalogue Raisonne. Lausanne: 1982. V. 72
Henri Rousseau. New York: 1962. V. 69; 72

VALLISNIERI, ANTONIO
Istoria Della Generazione dell'uomo, e Degli Animali.... Venice: 1721. V. 70
Opere Fisico-Mediche.... Venice: 1733. V. 70

VALPY, R. V.
Poetical Chronology of Ancient and English History with Historical and Explanatory Notes. Reading: 1804. V. 71

VALUABLE Secrets Concerning Arts and Trades; or, Approved Directions, from the Best Artists.... Dublin: 1778. V. 68

VALUABLE Secrets Concerning Arts and Trades; or Approved Directions, from the Best Artists. Norwich: 1795. V. 69

VALUABLE Secrets in Arts and Trades etc. 1790?. V. 69

VALUABLE Secrets in Arts, Trades &c. New York: 1809. V. 68
VALUABLE Secrets in Arts, Trades &c. New York: 1816. V. 69

VALVASSORI, GALDINO E.
Tomography and Cross Sections of the Ear. Philadelphia: 1975. V. 68

VAN RAALTE & SONS
Illustrated Price List for the Year 1871 of Havana Cigars and Manila Cheroots. London: 1871. V. 68

VAN ALLSBURG, CHRIS
Bad Day at Riverbend. Boston: 1995. V. 70
The Garden of Abdul Gasazi. Boston: 1979. V. 70; 72
Jumanji. Boston: 1981. V. 68; 70; 72; 73
Just a Dream. Boston: 1990. V. 70
The Polar Express. Boston: 1985. V. 70; 73

VAN ANTWERP, WILLIAM C.
A Collector's Comment on His First Editions of the Works of Sir Walter Scott. San Francisco: 1932. V. 70

VANARDY, VARICK
The Girl by the Roadside. New York: 1917. V. 71; 72

VAN ARMAN, DEREK
Just Killing Time. New York: 1992. V. 69

VAN ASH, CAY
Master of Villainy: a Biography of Sax Rohmer. 1972. V. 73
Master of Villainy: a Biography of Sax Rohmer. London: 1972. V. 70

VANCE, JACK
Bad Ronald. 1982. V. 71
Chateau d'If. 1990. V. 70
The Dying Earth. New York: 1950. V. 69
The Dying Earth. 1994. V. 70
Emphyrio. New York: 1969. V. 71
The Man in the Cage. New York: 1960. V. 71
The Man in the Cage. 1983. V. 71
Throy: Cadwall III. 1992. V. 70
To Live Forever. 1956. V. 69
To Live Forever. 1995. V. 70
Vandals of the Void. Philadelphia: 1953. V. 69
When the Five Moons Rise. 1992. V. 70

VANCE, JOHN HOLBROOK
The Fox Valley Murders. 1966. V. 71
The Fox Valley Murders. Indianapolis: 1966. V. 72

VANCE, LOUIS JOSEPH
Cynthia-of the-Minute. New York: 1911. V. 70
The Dead Ride Hard. Philadelphia: 1926. V. 69
The Lone Wolf Returns. New York: 1923. V. 72
The Lone Wolf's Son. New York: 1931. V. 69; 70
The Lone Wolf's Son. Philadelphia: 1931. V. 68

VANCE, ZEBULON BAIRD
The Duties of Defeat. An Address Delivered Before the Two Literary Societies of the University of North Carolina June 7th 1866. Raleigh: 1866. V. 70

VANCOUVER, GEORGE
A Voyage of Discovery to the North Pacific Ocean and Round the World.... London: 1798. V. 73

VANDAM, ALBERT D.
An Englishman In Paris.(Notes and Recollections). London: 1892. V. 72

VANDEBURG, MILLIE BIRD
The Door to the Moor. Philadelphia: 1925. V. 70

VANDELEUR, SEYMOUR
Campaigning on the Upper Nile and Niger. 1898. V. 69

VAN DE LINDE, GERARD
Bookkeeping and Other Papers. London: 1904. V. 71

VANDEN AVONT, PIERRE
Livres de Satyres et Grotesses. Antwerp: 1650. V. 70

VAN DENBURGH, ELIZABETH DOUGLAS
My Voyage in the United States Frigate "Congress". New York: 1913. V. 73

VAN DENHOLM, CARL
Notices and Voyages of the Famed Queque Mission to the Pacific Northwest. Portland: 1956. V. 68; 73

VAN DER BURG, A. R.
School of Painting for the Imitation of Woods and Marbles, as Taught and Practised by A R. and P. Van der Burg. London: 1936. V. 68

VAN DER BURG, P.
School of Painting for the Imitation of Woods and Marbles. London: 1908. V. 68

VANDERCOOK, JOHN W.
Murder in Fiji. Garden City: 1936. V. 73

VAN DER ELSKEN, E.
Eye Love You. 1977. V. 68

VANDERGRIFT, MARGARET
The Absent Minded Fairy for Boys and Girls. Philadelphia: 1884. V. 70

VANDERHAEGHE, GUY
Homesick. Toronto: 1989. V. 71
Things as They Are?. Toronto: 1992. V. 70

VANDERPOEL, EMILY NOYES
Chronicles of a Pioneer School from 1792 to 1833 Being the History of Miss Sarah Pierce and Her Litchfield School. Cambridge: 1903. V. 68; 70

VAN DER ZWAN, N.
Madagascar. The Zebu as Guide through Past and Present. Berg en Dal: 1998. V. 69

VAN DE WATER, FREDERIC F.
Alibi. Garden City: 1930. V. 72
Glory Hunter - A Life of General Custer. New York: 1934. V. 72
Glory Hunter: a Life of General Custer. New York: 1963. V. 69

VANDIVER, CLARENCE
The Fur Trade and Early Western Exploration. Cleveland: 1929. V. 70

VANDIVER, FRANK
Ploughshares into Swords. Austin: 1952. V. 69; 70
Rebel Brass. The Confederate Command System. Baton Rouge: 1956. V. 69

VAN DOREN, MARK
Collected and New Poems 1924-1963. New York: 1963. V. 73
Collected Poems 1922-1938. New York: 1939. V. 69
The Country Year. Poems. New York: 1946. V. 68
Humanity Unlimited. Williamsburg VA: 1950. V. 72
That Shining Place. New York: 1969. V. 73
Windless Cabins. New York: 1940. V. 70

VAN DRUTEN, JOHN
After All. New York: 1931. V. 72
There's Always Juliet. New York: 1932. V. 71
Young Woodley. New York: 1929. V. 71

VAN DUZER, WINIFRED
The Good Bad Girl. New York: 1926. V. 72

VAN DYKE, H. B.
The Physiology and Pharmacology of the Pituitary Body. Chicago: 1936-1939. V. 68

VAN DYKE, HENRY
Redemption. 1983. V. 72

VANE, BARON
Across the Threshold. Middletown: 1917. V. 70

VAN EEDEN, FREDERICK
Little Johannes. London: 1895. V. 69

VAN EVRIE, J. H.
Negroes and Negro Slavery: the First an Inferior Race: the Later Its Normal Condition. New York. V. 70

VAN GELDEREN, D. M.
Conifers. Portland: 1989. V. 71

VAN GIESON, JUDITH
North of the Border. 1988. V. 69
Raptor. New York: 1990. V. 68; 69; 70; 71
The Wolf Path. New York: 1992. V. 69

VAN GREENAWAY, PETER
Manrissa Man. London: 1982. V. 70

VAN GULIK, ROBERT
The Chinese Bell Murders. London: 1958. V. 68; 69; 70
The Chinese Bell Murders. New York: 1958. V. 69
The Chinese Gold Murders. London: 1959. V. 70
The Chinese Gold Murders. New York: 1961. V. 73
The Chinese Lake Murders. London: 1960. V. 69
The Chinese Lake Murders. New York: 1960. V. 68
The Chinese Lake Murders. New York: 1962. V. 71
The Chinese Maze Murders. 1956. V. 68
The Chinese Maze Murders. The Hague and Bandung: 1956. V. 69; 70; 73
The Chinese Maze Murders. London: 1962. V. 70
The Emperor's Pearl. London: 1963. V. 68; 69
The Given Day. Kuala Lumpur: 1964. V. 69; 73
The Given Day. 1984. V. 68
The Given Day. San Antonio: 1984. V. 69; 70
The Haunted Monastery - a Chinese Detective Story. Kuala Lumpur: 1961. V. 69
The Haunted Monastery - a Chinese Detective Story. London: 1963. V. 69; 73
Judge Dee at Work. London: 1967. V. 69; 70; 71; 72
Labyrinth in Lang-Fang. 1957. V. 68
The Lacquer Screen. London: 1962. V. 69; 70
The Lacquer Screen. London: 1964. V. 68; 69; 72; 73
The Lacquer Screen. New York: 1969. V. 68; 69
The Lore of the Chinese Lute. Tokyo: 1940. V. 69; 70
The Monkey and the Tiger. London: 1965. V. 68; 69
The Monkey and the Tiger. New York: 1965. V. 68; 71
Necklace and Calabash. London: 1967. V. 70; 72
Necklace and Calabash. New York: 1971. V. 69; 71
The Phantom of the Temple. London: 1966. V. 68
Poets and Murder. London: 1968. V. 68; 69; 70; 72; 73
Poets and Murder. New York: 1968. V. 68
The Red Pavilion. Kuala Lumpur: 1961. V. 68; 70; 72
The Red Pavilion. London: 1964. V. 69; 70; 73
The Red Pavilion. New York: 1964. V. 72
The Red Pavilion. New York: 1968. V. 68
Sexual Life in Ancient China. Leiden: 1961. V. 72
Vier Vingers. 1964. V. 68
Vier Vingers (Four Fingers). Amsterdam: 1964. V. 71; 72
The Willow Pattern. London: 1965. V. 72
The Willow Pattern. New York: 1965. V. 68

VAN HALEN, DON JUAN
Narrative of...Imprisonment in the Dungeons of the Inquisition at Madrid, and his Escape in 1817 and 1818. London: 1827. V. 72; 73

VAN HARE, G.
Fifty Years of a Showman's Life, or the Life and Travels of Van Hare. London: 1888. V. 72
Fifty Years of a Showman's Life, or the Life and Travels of Van Hare. London: 1893. V. 70

VAN HISE, C. R.
The Geology of the Lake Superior Region. Washington: 1911. V. 71; 73

VAN HOLST, H. V.
Modern American Homes. Chicago: 1913. V. 72

VAN HORNE, THOMAS B.
History of the Army of the Cumberland. Cincinnati: 1875. V. 71

VANISHING Pictures - a Novel Colour Book with Changing Pictures and Verses. London: 1895. V. 71

VAN LENNEP, H. C. ROETERS
A Catalogue of the Valuable and Extensive Collection of Shells formed by.... London: 1876. V. 68

VAN LHIN, ERIK
Battle on Mercury. Philadelphia: 1953. V. 69

VAN METER, BENJAMIN F.
Genealogies and Sketches of Some Old Families. Louisville: 1901. V. 69

VAN METER, DAVID L.
Elko, Nevada. A History of the World Famous Saddlemaker. 1984. V. 68

VAN MOE, E. A.
The Decorated Letter, from the VIIIth to the XIIth Century. Paris: 1950. V. 69; 72

VAN NOSTRAND, JEANNE
A Camera in the Gold Rush. San Francisco: 1946. V. 73
The First Hundred Years of Painting in California. San Francisco: 1980. V. 73

VAN NOSTRAND, JEROME
The First Hundred Years of Painting in California 1775-1875. San Francisco: 1980. V. 69

VAN OSDEL, A. L.
Historic Landmarks. 1915?. V. 69
Historic Landmarks in the Great Northwest, Being A History of Early Explorers and Fur Traders with a Narrative of their Adventures in the Wilds of the Great Northwest Territory. 1951. V. 70

VAN RAVENSWAAY, C.
Drawn from Nature, the Botanical Art of Joseph Prestle and His Sons. Washington: 1984. V. 69

VAN RENSSELAER, MARIANA GRISWOLD
Henry Hobson Richardson and His Works. Boston and New York: 1888. V. 71

VAN RENSSELAER, STEPHEN
American Firearms. An Histology of American Gunsmiths, Arms Manufacturers and Patentees with Detailed Descriptions of their Arms. (also)....The Colt Supplement. Watkins Glen: 1947-1948. V. 73

VAN SCHREEVEN, WILLIAM J.
Revolutionary Virginia: the Road to Independence. Charlottesville: 1973. V. 73

VAN SICKLE, V. A.
The Wrong Body. New York: 1937. V. 70

VANSITTART, NICHOLAS
Certain Ancient Tracts, Concerning the Management of Landed Property Reprinted. London: 1767. V. 69
Substance of Two Speeches, Made by the Right Hon. N. Vansittart, on the 7th and 13th of May, 1811, in the Committee of the Whole House of Commons, to which the Report of the Bullion Committee was Referred. London: 1811. V. 73

VAN TASSEL, C. S.
Picturesque Northwestern Ohio and Battle Grounds of the Mumee Valley. Bowling Green and Toledo: 1900. V. 71

VAN TRAMP, JOHN C.
Prairie and Rocky Mountain Adventures. Columbus: 1869. V. 69
Prairie and Rocky Mountain Adventures. Columbus: 1870. V. 69

VAN UDEN, N.
Alcohol Toxicity in Yeasts and Bacteria. Boca Raton: 1989. V. 68

VAN VALKENBURGH, HELEN
Myself and I. Chicago: 1918. V. 73

VAN VECHTEN, CARL
Nigger Heaven. New York: 1926. V. 71

VAN VLEET, A.
The Ohio Justice and Township Officers Assistant. Lebanon: 1821. V. 68

VAN VOGT, A. E.
Destination: Universe!. New York: 1952. V. 69
Out of the Unknown. 1948. V. 69
Slan. Sauk City: 1946. V. 69

VAN WALLEGHEN, MICHAEL
The Wichita Poems. Iowa City: 1973. V. 73

VAN WINKLE, HENRY EDWARD
Rombert: a Tale of Carolina. New York: 1835. V. 70

VAN WOERKOM, DOROTHY
The Rat, the Ox and the Zodiac: a Chinese Legend. New York: 1976. V. 70

VAN ZILE, EDWARD S.
Perkins, the Fakeer: a Travesty on Reincarnation. New York: 1903. V. 71

VAN ZYLE, JON
Best of Alaska, the Art of Jon Van Zyle. Minneapolis: 1990. V. 73

VARD, KENNETH
Liners In Art. London: 1990. V. 72
Liners in Art. Southampton: 1990. V. 70

VARDILL, ANNA JANE
Poems and Translations, from the Minor Greek Poets. London: 1809. V. 69

VAREKMAP, MARJOLEIN
Francesco:. Groningen: 1987. V. 71

VARGAS LLOSA, MARIO
The Time Of The Hero. New York: 1960. V. 72
The Time of the Hero. New York: 1966. V. 68; 69; 70; 71

VARILLAS, ANTOINE
La Pratique de l'Education des Princes. Amsterdam: 1684. V. 69

VARIN, AMEDEE
Papillons Metamorphoses Terrestres des Peulpes de L'Air. Paris: 1852. V. 73

VARLEY, JOHN
Titan, Wizard and Demon. New York: 1979-1984. V. 73

VARLO, CHARLES
The Essence of Agriculture.... London: 1786. V. 70; 73
Nature Display'd, a New Work. London: 1793. V. 69

VARMAN, D. P.
The Northanger Set of the Jane Austen Horrid Novels. London: 1968. V. 73

VARNEDOE, K.
Vienna 1900: Art, Architecture and Design. 1986. V. 69; 72

VARRO MARCUS TERENTIUS
Opera Omnia Quae Extant. Durdrechti: 1619. V. 72

VARTEMA, LUDOVICO DI
The Nauigation and Voyages of Lewis Wertomannus....in the yeere of Our Lorde 1503. Edinburgh: 1884. V. 71

VASARELY, VICTOR
Fondation Vasarely. Aix-en-Provence: 1975. V. 72
The Vasarely Didactic Museum at the Gordes Chateau. Vaucluse: 1976. V. 72

VASARI, GIORGIO
Choice Observations Upon the Art of Painting. Together with Vasari's Lives of the Most Eminent Painters.... London: 1719. V. 68; 73

VASEY, GEORGE
Illustrations of North American Grasses. Washington: 1891-1893. V. 70
The Philosophy of Laughter and Smiling. London: 1877. V. 71

VASSE, LOYS
In Anatomen Corporis Humani Tabulae Quatuor.... Venice: 1549. V. 68; 73

VASSILIKOS, VASSILIS
Z. New York: 1968. V. 71

VASSOS, JOHN
Kubla Khan. New York: 1933. V. 71
Phobia. New York: 1931. V. 69; 70
Ultimo: An Imaginative Narration of Life Under the Earth with Projections by John Vassos and text by Ruth Vassos. NY: 1930. V. 72

VASSOS, RUTH
Humanities. New York: 1935. V. 69

VATTEL, M. D.
The Law of Nations; or Principles of the Law of Nature.... Northampton: 1805. V. 68

VAUCANSON, JACQUES DE
Le Mecanisme du Fluter Automate Presentee a Messieurs de l'Academie Royale des Sciences. Paris: 1738. V. 72

VAUGHAN, HAROLD S.
Congenital Cleft Lip, Cleft Palate and Associate Nasal Deformaties. Philadelphia: 1940. V. 71

VAUGHAN, J. B.
Vaughan's Selected Songs. Athens: 1901. V. 73

VAUGHAN, JAMES D.
The Silver Trumpet for Revivals, Sunday Schools, Conventions and General Religious Work and Worship. Lawrenceburg: 1908. V. 72

VAUGHAN, JANET M.
The Effects of Irradiation on the Skeleton. Oxford: 1973. V. 68

VAUGHAN, KEITH
Journal and Drawings 1939-1965. London: 1966. V. 69
Journals - 1939-1977. London: 1989. V. 73

VAUGHAN, ROBERT
The Age of Great Cities; or, Modern Society Viewed In Its Relation to Intelligence, Morals and Religion. London: 1843. V. 71
British Antiquities Revived, or a Friendly Contest Touching the Soveraignty of the Three Princes of Wales in Ancient Times. Bala: 1834. V. 72

VAUGHAN, T. W.
Recent Madreporaria of the Hawaiian Islands and Laysan. Washington: 1907. V. 72

VAUGHAN, WARREN T.
Strange Malady: The Story of Allergy. New York: 1941. V. 70

VAUGHAN, WILLIAM
Memoir of William Vaughan, Esq. F.R.S. with Miscellaneous Pieces Relative to Docks, Commerce, Etc. (with) Reasons in Favour of the London Docks. London: 1839. V. 73

VAUGHAN WILLIAMS, URSULA
Silence and Music. London: 1959. V. 71

VAUGHN, J. W.
The Battle of Platte Bridge. Norman: 1963. V. 72
Indian Fights - New Facts on Seven Encounters. Norman: 1966. V. 72
The Reynold's Campaign on Power River. Norman: 1961. V. 72
With Crook At The Rosebud. Harrisburg: 1955. V. 72
With Crook at the Rosebud. 1956. V. 68
With Crook at the Rosebud. Harrisburg: 1956. V. 69

VAUGHN, ROBERT
Then And Now or Thirty-Six Years In The Rockies. Minnesota: 1900. V. 72

VAUMORIERE, PIERRE D'ORTIGUE
The Grand Scipio, an Excellent New Romance.... London: 1660. V. 73

VAURIE, C.
The Birds of the Palearctic Fauna. 1959-1965. V. 73
The Birds of the Palearctic Fauna. (Volume II). London: 1965. V. 69
Tibet and Its Birds. 1972. V. 72

VAUX, CALVERT
Villas and Cottages: a Series of Designs Prepared for Execution in the U.S. New York: 1857. V. 70
Villas and Cottages: a Series of Designs Prepared for Execution in the U.S. New York: 1869. V. 69; 72

VAVRA, ROBERT
Bulls of Iberia: Life and Death of the Fighting Bull. Sevilla: 1972. V. 72
Curro: Reflections of a Spanish Youth. Sevilla: 1975. V. 72

VAWDRY, ELLEN GEORGINA
Mulgravia; a New Year's Annual for 1869. Hayle: 1868 or 1869. V. 73

VEBLEN, THORSTEIN
Absentee Ownership and Business Enterprise in Recent Times. The Case of America. New York: 1923. V. 72
The Ecology and Biogeography of Nothofagus Forests. New Haven: 1996. V. 72
The Higher Learning in America: a Memorandum on the Conduct of Universities by Business Men. New York: 1918. V. 69; 71; 73
The Theory of the Leisure Class; an Economic Study of Institutions. London: 1905. V. 71

VECELLIO, CESARE
Habitit Antichi et Moderni di Tutto il Mondo, di Nuovo Accresciuti di Molte Figure. Venice: 1598. V. 69

VEDEY, JULIEN
Band Leaders. London: 1950. V. 72

VEE, JAY
Wild Oats. Topeka: 1914. V. 70

VEECK, BILL
Veeck - as in Wreck, the Autobiography. New York: 1962. V. 69; 72

VEEN, OCTAVIO VAN, KNOWN AS OTTO VAENIUS
Quinti Horatii Flacci Emblemata. Antwerp: 1612. V. 69

VEGETIUS, FLAVIUS RENATUS
Institutions Militaires. Paris: 1743. V. 73

VEHLING, JOSEPH DOMMERS
Apicius: Cookery and Dining in Imperial Rome. Chicago: 1936. V. 68
Platine and the Rebirth of Man. Chicago: 1941. V. 68

VEILLETTE, JOHN
Early Indian Village Churches. Vancouver: 1977. V. 68

VEITCH, JAMES, & SONS
A Manaul of Orchidaceous Plants. 1887-1894. V. 69
A Manual of Orchidaceous Plants Cultivated Under Glass in Great Britain. Amsterdam: 1963. V. 69; 72

VEITCH, JAMES H.
Hortus Veitchii.... London: 1906. V. 69; 71; 73
A Traveller's Notes, or Notes of a Tour Through India, Malaysia, Japan, Corea.... Chelsea: 1896. V. 68; 70; 73

VEITCH, JOHN
The Feeling for Nature in Scottish Poetry. London: 1887. V. 71

VELARDE, PABLITA
Old Father the Story Teller. Globe: 1960. V. 69

VELDE, BRAM VAN
Bram Van Velde. New York: 1962. V. 72; 73

VELIE, ALAN R.
Four American Indian Literary Masters. Norman: 1982. V. 68

VELIKOVSKY, IMMANUEL
Worlds in Collison. New York: 1950. V. 70

VELLEY, T.
Coloured Figures of Marine Plants Found off the Southern Coast of England.... Bath: 1795. V. 69

VELNET, MARY
An Affecting History of the Captivity and Suffering of.... Boston: 1804?. V. 68

VELPEAU, ALFRED ARMAND LOUIS MARIE
De L'Operation du Trepan dans les Plaises de Tete. Paris: 1834. V. 68
An Elementary Treatise on Midwifery; or Principles of Tikology and Embryology. Philadelphia: 1831. V. 70; 71; 73
Surgical Clinic of La Charite. Boston: 1866. V. 68; 70; 71; 73

VELTER, JOSEPH M.
Arctic S. O. S. New York: 1935. V. 69

VENABLE, ABRAHAM S.
Building Black Business: An Analysis and a Plan. New York: 1972. V. 72

VENABLES, L. S. V.
Birds and Mammals of Shetland. London: 1955. V. 71

VENABLES, ROBERT
The Experienced Angler.... London: 1825. V. 69; 73

VENEGAS, MIGUEL
Histoire Naturelle et Civile de la Californie.... Paris: 1767. V. 70
Juan Maria de Salvatierra of the Company of Jesus; Missionary of the Province of New Spain and Apostoli Conquerer of the Californias. Cleveland: 1929. V. 68

VENEMA, REINI
Bloemen Alphabet. Rotterdam: 1930. V. 68

VENIAMINOV, I.
Wegweiser Zum Himmelreich, Oder Vortrage zur Behlehrung der Neugetausten Schriften in Russichen Amerika, Von I. Veniaminoff...Nebst Einem Auszuge Aus Seinen Missionsberichten. Odessa: 1848. V. 70

VENN, T. W.
Cochin - Malabar, Palms and Pageants. Calicut. V. 72

VENNER, NORMAN
Brief Candle. Indianapolis: 1928. V. 70

VENNER, THOMAS
Via recta ad Vitam Longam. London: 1650. V. 68

VENNER, TOBIAS
Via Recta Ad Vitam Longam. London: 1650. V. 70

VENNING, MARY ANNE
Rudiments of Conchology. London: 1837. V. 68; 70

VENNOR, H. G.
Our Birds of Prey, or the Eagles, Hawks and Owls of Canada. Montreal: 1876. V. 69

VENTRETTI, FRANCESCO
Del Modo di Trovare La Fisica Proporzione. Verona: 1768. V. 69

THE VENTURE, an Annual of Art and Literature. London: 1903. V. 70

VER Beck's Bears in Mother Goose Land. London: 1918. V. 72
VER Beck's Bears in Mother Goose Land. New York: 1918. V. 71
VER Beck's Book of Bears. Philadelphia: 1906. V. 72

VER BECK, FRANK
The Little Lost Bear. London: 1915. V. 68

VERDELLE, A. J.
The Good Negress. Chapel Hill: 1995. V. 70

VERDIZOTTI, GIOVANNI MARIO
Cento Favole Morali De i Piu Illustri Antichi & Moderni Autori Greci & Latini. Venice: 1586. V. 72

VERDOORN, F.
Plants and Plant Science in Latin America. 1945. V. 69; 73
Plants and Plant Science in Latin America. New York: 1945. V. 72

VERE Foster's Simple Lessons in Water Colour. Marine. London: 1885. V. 71

VERE, FRANCIS
The Commentaries of Sir Frances Vere. Cambridge: 1657. V. 73

VERGA, GIOVANNI
Cavalleria Rusticana. New York: 1928. V. 71
Little Novels of Sicily. New York: 1925. V. 71
Little Novels of Sicily. Oxford: 1925. V. 71
Mastro-Don Gesualdo. New York: 1923. V. 71
Mastro-Don Gesualdo. London: 1925. V. 71

VERGENNES, CHARLES GRAVIER, COMTE DE
Memoire Historique et Politique sur la Louisiane. Paris: 1802. V. 68

VERGILIUS, POLYDORUS
De Gli Inventori Delle Cose Libri Otto. In Fiorenza: 1587. V. 71
A Pleasant and Compendious History of the First Inventors and Instituters of the Most Famous Arts, Misteries, Laws, Customs and Manners in the Whole World.... London: 1686. V. 71

VERGILIUS MARO, PUBLIUS
The Aeneid. London: 1794. V. 70
The Aeneid. London: 1952. V. 71; 73
Appendix Cum Supplemento Multorum Antehac Nunquam Excusorum Poematum Veterum Poetarum. Lvgdvni: 1573. V. 71
Bucolica, Georgica, et Aeneis. Birmingham: 1757. V. 72
Bucolica, Georgica et Aeneis. Birminghamiae: 1771?. V. 72
Bucolica, Georgica et Aeneis. Argentorati: 1789. V. 72
The Bucolicks of Vergil. Oxford: 1820. V. 70; 71
Bucolicorum Eclogae Decem. The Buccolicks of Virgil. London: 1749. V. 73
Les Bucoliques. Paris: 1951. V. 72
(Codex Mediceus). P. Vergili Maronis Codex Antiqvissimvs. Florentiae: 1741. V. 71
L'Eneide di Virgilio Del Commendatore Annibal Caro.... Padoa: 1608. V. 69
Georgica/Les Georgiques. Paris: 1937-. V. 72
Georgica/Les Georgiques. Paris: 1937-1950. V. 68
Georgicorum Libri Quatuor. The Georgicks of Virgil: Bucolicorum Eclogne Decem. The Buccolicks of Virgil. London: 1741-1749. V. 69
The Georgics of Virgil. Dublin: 1834. V. 72
The Georgics of Virgil. Ithaca: 1966. V. 68
Opera. Leipzig: 1596. V. 68
Opera. Londini: 1687. V. 72
Opera. Leeuwarden: 1717. V. 68
Opera. London: 1753. V. 69
Opera. St. Andrews: 1799. V. 68
Opera, Pristino Nitori Restituta, Cum Notis & Variis Lectionibus Ex Codicibus and Optimis Exemplaribus. Parisiis: 1790. V. 71
Opera Virgiliana cum Decem Commentis Docte et Familiariter Exposita. Lyons: 1529. V. 69
The XII Aenedis of Virgil, the Most Renowned Laureat Prince of Latine-Poets. London: 1632. V. 71
Virgil's Aeneis, Translated into Scottish Verse. Edinburgh: 1710. V. 72
The Works. London: 1650. V. 71
The Works. London: 1709. V. 73
The Works. London: 1716. V. 71
The Works. London: 1731. V. 69
The Works. Glasgow: 1769. V. 73

VERGNAUD, N.
L'Art de Creer les Jardins. Paris: 1839. V. 68; 70; 72

VERHAEREN, EMILE
Five Tales. New York: 1924. V. 72
Les Heures Claires. Bruxelles: 1896. V. 69
Les Petits Vieux. 1901. V. 71; 73
Poems of Emile Verhaeren. London: 1915. V. 69

VERHEYEN, PHILIP
Corporis Humani Anatomiae Liber Primus in Quo Tam Veteru.... Brussels: 1710. V. 68; 73

VERITY, FRANK T.
Flats, Urban Houses and Cottage Homes. London: 1906. V. 68; 71

VERLAINE, PAUL
Fetes Galantes. 1944. V. 72
Sagesse. London: 1944. V. 68

VERMEULEN, JAN
De Picturis et Imaginibus Sacris.... Louvain: 1570. V. 72

VERNE, JULES
Adrift in the Pacific. London: 1889. V. 69
Around The World In Eighty Days. London: 1876. V. 72
The Barsac Mission: Into the Niger Bend and The City in the Saraha. Westport CT: 1960. V. 70
Caesar Cascabel. New York: 1890. V. 69; 71; 73
De La Terre a La Lune. Paris: 1865. V. 70
From the Earth to the Moon and Around the Moon. New York: 1970. V. 73
The Fur Country; or, Seventy Degrees North Latitude. London: 1874. V. 71
The Fur Country; or, Seventy Degrees North Latitude. New York: 1876. V. 73

VERNE, JULES continued
Into the Niger Bend. Westport: 1960. V. 69
A Journey to the Centre of the Earth. Boston. V. 71
A Journey to the Centre of the Earth. New York: 1874. V. 69
Meridiana, or Adventures in South Africa. New York: 1874. V. 71; 73
Michael Strogoff. New York: 1927. V. 70; 71; 73
The Mysterious Island. New York: 1918. V. 71
The Tour of the World in 80 Days. London: 1888. V. 68
A Voyage Round the World. South America. London and New York: 1876. V. 71

VERNER, COOLIE
The Northpart of America. Toronto: 1979. V. 69

VERNER, ELIZABETH O'NEILL
Other Places. Columbia: 1946. V. 71
Prints and Impressions of Charleston. Columbia: 1939. V. 71

VERNER, GERALD
The Crooked Circle. New York: 1937. V. 68; 73

VERNER, W.
My Life Among the Wild Birds in Spain. 1909. V. 72
Sketches in The Soudan. London: 1886. V. 72

VERNET, CARL
Cris de Paris Dessines d'Apres Nature. Paris: 1820. V. 73

VERNEY, FRANCES PARTHENOPE
The Grey Pool and Other Stories. London: 1891. V. 68; 73

VERNON, C. W.
Bicentenary Sketches and Early Days of the Church in Nova Scotia. Halifax: 1910. V. 72
Bicentenary Sketches. And Early Days of the Church in Nova Scotia. Halifax: 1911. V. 73
Cape Breton, Canada. Toronto: 1903. V. 73

VERNON, CHRISTOPHER
Considerations for Regulating the Exchequer, in the More Timely Answering, Better Husbanding, and More Orderly and Safe Conduct of the Revenues of the Crown.... London: 1642. V. 72

VERNON, EDWARD
Admiral V----n's Opinion on the Present State of the British Navy in a Letter to the Secretary of the Same Board. London: 1744. V. 71
Original Papers Relating to the Expedition to Carthagena. London: 1744. V. 69; 71
Some Seasonable Advice from an Honest Sailor, to Whom It Might Have Concerned, for the Service of the C(row)n and C(ountr)y. London: 1746. V. 71

VERNON, GRENVILLE
The Image in the Path. New York: 1927. V. 70

VERNON, H. M.
Variation in Animals and Plants. New York: 1902. V. 68

VERNON, I. R.
The Harvest Of A Quiet Eye. Leisure Thoughts For Busy Lives. London. V. 72

VERNON, JOSEPH S.
Along the Old Trail. Cimarron: 1910. V. 71

VERNON-COLE, WILLIS
Constanza. New York: 1927. V. 70

VERON, J. E. N.
Corals of Australia and the Indo Pacific. Honolulu: 1993. V. 72; 73

VERONA, GUIDO DA
Mimi Bluette. New York: 1929. V. 71

VERPLANCK, JAMES DE LANCEY
A Country of Shepherds. Boston: 1934. V. 69

VERRI, ALESSANDRO
The Roman Nights; or, Dialogues at the Tombs of Scipios. London: 1798. V. 71

VERRILL, A. E.
Monograph of the Shallow-Water Starfishes of the North Pacific Coast from the Arctic Ocean to California. 1914. V. 69

VERRILL, A. HYATT
The Inquisition. New York: 1931. V. 70

VERSAILLES *Illustrated, or Divers Views of the Several Parts of the Royal Palace of Versailles....* London: 1726. V. 72

VERSCHOYLE, DEREK
The English Novelists - a Survey of the Novel by Twenty Contemporary Novelists. London: 1936. V. 69

VERSES *for Children of The Sort You Can Read to Them....* London. V. 70

VERSOR, JOHANNES
Dicta Vesoris super Septem Tractatus Magistri Petri Hispani cum Textu. 1489-1492. V. 72

VERTES, MARCEL
Art and Fashion. New York: 1944. V. 69
Variations. Drawings, Water Colors, Etchings and Lithographs. Greenwich: 1916. V. 69

VERTOT, RENE AUBERT DE
A Critical History of the Establishment of the Bretons Among the Gauls and of their Dependence Upon the Kings of France and Dukes of Normandy. London: 1722. V. 70; 72
Histoire des Revolutions de Portugal. Paris: 1711. V. 70; 72
The History of the Revolutions of Portugal. London: 1735. V. 72
The History of the Revolutions of Portugal. Glasgow: 1750. V. 69

VERTUE, GEORGE
Medals, Coins, Great Seals, Impressions, from the Elaborate Works of Thomas Simon, Chief Engraver of the Mint to K. Charles. London: 1753. V. 71

VERY, JONES
Essays and Poems. Boston: 1839. V. 69
Poems. Boston and New York: 1883. V. 68

VERZURE, MADAME DE
Reflexions Hazardees d'Une Femme Ignorante.... Amsterdam: 1766. V. 69

VESALIUS, ANDREAS
Anatomia. Venice: 1604. V. 70
Anatomische Erklarung der Original-Figuren von Andreas Vesal, Samt Einer Anwendung der Winslowischen Zergliederungslehre in Sieben Buchern. Langoldstadt: 1783. V. 68
De Humani Corporis Fabrica Libri Septem. Bruxelles: 1964. V. 71
Epitome. Madrid. V. 70; 72
Librorum Andreae Vesalii Bruxellensis De Humani Corporis Fabrica Epitomes.... Amstelodami: 1642. V. 73
Zergliederung des Menschilichen Coerpers...Die Figuren von Titian Arzeichnet. Augsburg: 1723. V. 70

VESEY, FRANCIS
Case Upon the Will, of the Late Peter Theullusson, Esq. London: 1799. V. 70

VESEY FITZGERALD, B.
The Book of the Horse. 1949. V. 68

VESPUCCI, AMERIGO
The Letter of Amerigo Vespucci Describing His Four Voyages to the New World 1497-1504. San Francisco: 1926. V. 72

VESSEY, J.
The Rescue, a Narrative of Facts and Statements. Lincoln: 1854. V. 73

VEST, GEORGE
Man's Best Friend. A Plea to a Jury. New York: 1920. V. 72

VESTAL, STANLEY
Bigfoot Wallace. Boston: 1942. V. 68; 69; 73
Fandango: Ballads of the Old West. Boston: 1927. V. 73
Joe Meek. Caldwell: 1952. V. 69
Kit Carson: the Happy Warrior of the Old West. Boston: 1928. V. 69
The Missouri. New York: 1945. V. 69
New Sources of Indian History 1850-1891, The Ghost Dance - The Prairie Sioux. Norman: 1934. V. 72
The Old Santa Fe Trail. Boston;: 1939. V. 73
Short Grass Country. 1941. V. 69
Sitting Bull: Champion of the Sioux. A Biography. Boston and New York: 1932. V. 69; 72
War Path and Council Fire. New York: 1948. V. 72
Warpath - The True Story of The Fighting Sioux Told In A Biography of Chief White Bull. Boston: 1934. V. 72

VESTRIS, LUCIA
Memoirs of the Life, Public and Private Adventures of Madame Vestris.... London: 1836. V. 69

VETALAPANCAVIMASTI
Vikram and the Vampire or Tales of Hindu Devilry. London: 1893. V. 73

VETROMILE, EUGENE
The Abnakis and Their History or Historical Notices on the Aborigines of Acadia. New York: 1866. V. 73

VETTIER, JACQUES
Big Game Hunting in Asia, Africa and Elsewhere. 1993. V. 69; 70; 72; 73

VIAGGIO Pittoresco Alla Vallombrosa. Florence: 1819. V. 70

VIALA, P.
American Vines. San Francisco: 1903. V. 70

VIALLA DE SOMMIERES, L. C.
Voyage Historique et Politique au Montenegro. Paris: 1820. V. 72

VIAN, BORIS
Heartsnatcher. London: 1968. V. 69

VICARS, JOHN
England's Worthies. London: 1845. V. 72
Jehovah-Jireh. God in the Mount. Or, Englands Parliamentarie- Chronicle. London: 1644. V. 70; 72

VICARY, M.
Pencillings in Poetry. London: 1857. V. 73

VICARY, THOMAS
The Anatomie of the Bodie of Man. 1930. V. 72
The Anatomie of the Bodie of Man. Oxford: 1930. V. 70

VICK, JAMES
Vick's Illustrated Monthly Magazine. Rochester: 1878-1889. V. 69

VICKERS, HUGO
The Private World Of The Duke and Duchess Of Windsor. NY: 1995. V. 72

VICKERS, ROY
Best Dective Stories of Roy Vickers. London: 1965. V. 72; 73
The Department of Dead Ends. 1947. V. 73
The Department of Dead Ends. London: 1949. V. 69
Double Image. London: 1955. V. 73
Lord Roberts - the Story of His Life. London: 1914. V. 68
Murder Will Out. London: 1950. V. 69; 71; 73
Seven Chose Murder. London: 1959. V. 68; 69; 71; 73

VICKERS, W. B.
History of the City of Denver, Arapahoe County, and Colorado. Chicago: 1880. V. 71

VICO, E.
Augustarum Imagines Aereis Formis Expressae. Vinegia: 1558. V. 68
Four Candlesticks. Rome: 1552. V. 72

VICQ-D-AZYR, FELIX
Planches pour Les Oeuvres de Vicq-D'Azyr Recueillies et Publiees Avec des Notes et un Discours sur sa Vie et ses Ouvrages. Paris: 1805. V. 70

THE VICTIM in Five Letters to Adolphus. London: 1809. V. 69; 73

VICTOR, BENJAMIN
The Widow of the Wood. London: 1755. V. 71; 73

VICTOR, SEXTUS AURELIUS
Historiae Romanae Compendium Interpretatione et Notis Illustravit anna Tanaqvilli Fabri Filia. Paris: 1681. V. 68; 73

VICTOR TALKING MACHINE COMPANY OF CANADA
His Master's Voice, Victor Records. 1929. Montreal: 1929. V. 73

VICTORIA, QUEEN OF GREAT BRITAIN
Leaves from the Journal of our Life in the Highlands, from 1848 to 1861. London: 1868. V. 70; 71; 72
Leaves from the Journal of Our Life in the Highlands, from 1848 to 1861. (with) More Leaves from the Journal of a Life in the Highlands from 1862 to 1882. London: 1868-1884. V. 68; 72

VIDA, MARCO GIROLAMO, BP. OF ALBA
Christiados Libri Sex. Cremonae: 1535. V. 71
The Game of Chess. London: 1921. V. 68
Vida's Art of Poetry. London: 1742. V. 69; 72

VIDAL, DOMINGO
Tratato de las Enfermedades de Ojos Para Instruccion de los Alumnos del Real Colegio de Cirugia de Barcelona. Barcelona: 1785. V. 70

VIDAL, GORE
At Home. New York: 1988. V. 68
The Best Man - a Play About Politics. Boston;: 1960. V. 72
Death Before Bedtime. New York: 1953. V. 69
Death Before Bedtime. New York: 1990. V. 71
Death in the Fifth Position. New York: 1952. V. 69
Death in the Fifth Position. London: 1954. V. 73
Death in the Fifth Position. New York: 1991. V. 71
Death Likes It Hot. New York: 1954. V. 69
Death Likes It Hot. London: 1955. V. 73
Death Likes It Hot. New York: 1990. V. 71
Empire. Franklin Center: 1987. V. 70
The Essential Gore Vidal. New York: 1999. V. 72
An Evening with Richard Nixon. New York: 1972. V. 70
In a Yellow Wood. New York: 1947. V. 69; 70
The Judgment of Paris. New York: 1952. V. 69; 70; 71
Julian. Boston: 1964. V. 73
Julian. London: 1964. V. 69
Kalki. Franklin Center: 1978. V. 70
Kalki. New York: 1978. V. 69; 72
Lincoln. New York: 1984. V. 70; 73
Myra Breckinridge. Boston: 1968. V. 70; 71
Rocking the Boat. Boston: 1962. V. 70
A Search for the King. New York: 1950. V. 69; 70; 71
The Season of Comfort. New York: 1949. V. 71
The Smithsonian Institution. London: 1998. V. 68; 69
A Star's Progress. New York: 1950. V. 73
A Thirsty Evil. New York: 1956. V. 70
A Thirsty Evil. 1968. V. 68
Two Sisters. Boston: 1970. V. 71
Visit to a Small Planet. Boston: 1957. V. 73
Washington, D.C. Boston: 1967. V. 69
Williwaw. New York: 1946. V. 69

VIDALL, W.
The Historie of the Life and Death of Mary Stuart, Queene of Scotland. London: 1636. V. 72

VIDARI, GIOVANNI MARIA
Il Viaggio in Pratica, o sia Istruzione Generale, e Ristretta per Tutte Quelle Persone. Venice: 1730. V. 69

VIDOCQ, EUGENE FRANCOIS
Histoire de Vidocq, Chef de la Brigade De La Surete. Paris: 1830. V. 69

VIDOR, KING
King Vidor on Film Making. New York: 1972. V. 73

A Tree is a Tree. New York: 1953. V. 71

LA VIE de Londres Cotes Riants. Paris: 1900. V. 71

VIEILLOT, LOUIS J. P.
Songbirds of the Torrid Zone. 1979. V. 69
Songbirds of the Torrid Zone. Kent: 1979. V. 73

VIELE, EGBERT L., MRS.
Following The Drum. New York: 1858. V. 72

VIELE, TERESA
Following the Drum. New York: 1858. V. 69; 72

VIERECK, GEORGE SYLVESTER
The House of the Vampire. New York: 1907. V. 70
Songs of Armageddon and Other Poems. New York: 1916. V. 68

VIERTEL, PETER
White Hunter Black Heart. New York: 1953. V. 70

VIEUSSENS, RAYMOND
Neurographia Universalis. Frankfurt (und Ulm): 1690. V. 68; 71; 73

VIEUSSEUX, A.
History of Switzerland.... London: 1846. V. 69; 72

VIEYRA, D. I.
Fill 'er Up: an Architectural History of America's Gas Stations. New York: 1979. V. 69; 72

VIGNAUD, JEAN
Venus. Indianapolis: 1929. V. 71; 72

VIGNE, GODFREY THOMAS
Travels in Kashmir, Ladak, Iskardo. London: 1842. V. 69

VIGNIER, NICOLAS
L: a Bibliotheque Hisoriale.... Paris: 1588. V. 70

VIGNOLA, GIACOMO BAROZZIO DA
Reigles des Cinq Ordres d'Architecture. Paris. V. 68; 70
Reigles des Cinq Ordres d'Architecture. Paris: 1780. V. 70

VIGNOLES, CHARLES
Two Reports, Addressed to the Liverpool and Manchester Railway Company, on the Projected North Line of Railway from Liverpool to the Manchester, Bolton and Bury Canal, Near Manchester, Exhibiting the Extent of its Cuttings and Embankings.... Liverpool: 1835. V. 68

VIGNOLES, OLINTHUS
Life of Charles Blacker Vignoles, Soldier and Civil Engineer. 1889. V. 69

VIGNOLI, GIOVANNI
De Columna Imperatoris Antonini Pii Dissertatio. Rome: 1705. V. 70

VIGOR, WILLIAM, MRS.
Letters from a Lady, Who Resided Some Years in Russia, to Her Friends in England. London: 1775. V. 69

VIGOUREUX, CLARISSE
Parole de Providence et Melanges. Paris: 1847. V. 72

THE VILLAGE Voice Anthology 1956-1980. New York: 1982. V. 72

VILLAIN, ABBE ESTIENNE FRANCOIS
Histoire Critique de Nicolas Flamel et de Pernelle sa Femme. Paris: 1761. V. 73

VILLANI, GIOVANNI
Croniche di Messer.... Venice: 1537. V. 70

VILLARD, HENRY SERRANO
Hemingway in Love and War. New York: 1996. V. 69
Hemingway In Love and War.... 1989. V. 69; 72

VILLARD, LEONIE
Jane Austen, a French Appreciation. London: 1924. V. 70; 73

VILLEGAS, FRANCISCO DE QUEVEDO
Visions of Dom Francisco De Quevedo Villegas, Knight of the Order of Saint James. London: 1678. V. 69

VILLER, FREDERICK
The Black Tortoise: Being the Strange Story of Old Frick's Diamond. London: 1901. V. 70

VILLIERS DE L'ISLE-ADAM, JEAN MARIE MATHIAS PHILIPPE
Claire Lenoir. New York: 1925. V. 70

VILLIERS STUART, C. M.
Spanish Gardens, Their History, Types and Features. New York: 1929. V. 69

VILLON, FRANCOIS
The Lyrical Poems of Francois Villon. New York: 1979. V. 70
Oeuvres. Les Lais Le Testament, Poesies Diverses, Le Jargon. Maastricht: 1929. V. 73

VINCE, SAMUEL
The Elements of the Conic Sections, Adapted to the Use of Students in Philosophy. Cambridge: 1800. V. 68

VINCENT, ADRIAN
19th Century Maritime Watercolours. London: 1989. V. 70; 72

VINCENT, C. W.
Chemistry, Theoretical, Practical and Analytical, as Applied to the Arts and Manufactures.... London: 1879. V. 69

VINCENT, CHARLES
Histoire de la Chaussure, de la Cordonnerie et des Cordonniers Celebres d'Antiquite. Paris: 1861. V. 71

VINCENT, HOWARD, MRS.
China To Peru, Over The Andes. London: 1894. V. 72

VINCENT, JAMES
The Castle of the Appennines. (with) *Female Intrepidity, or the Heroic Matron.* London: 1805. V. 68

VINCENT, JOHN
Fowling, a Poem. London: 1808. V. 73

VINCENT, STEPHEN
O California!: Nineteenth and Early Twentieth Century California Landscapes and Observations. San Francisco: 1990. V. 68

A VINDICATION of the Forceps Described and Recommended by Dr. Leake; in Which, the Injudicious and Illiberal Remarks on the Subject, Signed Thomas Denman, are Examined and Refuted. London: 1774. V. 69

VINE, FREDERICK T.
Saleable Shop Goods for Counter-Tray and Window. 1898. V. 71
Savoury Pastry. Savoury Dish and Raised Pies, Pork Pies, Patties, Vol-au-Vents.... London: 1900. V. 68

VINGT-CINQ Costumes Pour Le Theatre. Paris: 1927. V. 68

VINGUT, GERTRUDE FAIRFIELD
Irene; or the Autobiograhy of an Artist's Daughter. And Other Tales. Boston: 1853. V. 71

VINJE, A. O.
A Norseman's View of Britain and the British. Edinburgh: 1863. V. 68

VINOGRADOV, A. P.
The Elementary Chemical Composition of Marine Organisms. New Haven: 1953. V. 73

THE VINTAGE Book of African American Poetry. New York: 2000. V. 69; 72

VINTON, STALLO
John Colter, Discoverer of Yellowtone Park. New York: 1926. V. 73

VINYCOMB, JOHN
Fictitious and Symbolic Creatures in Art.... 1906. V. 71

VIOLA, HERMAN
The Indian Legacy of Charles Bird King. New York: 1976. V. 68

VIOLET, THOMAS
A True Narrative of Som (sic) Remarkable Proceedings Concerning the Ships Samson, Salvadore and George, and Severall Other Prize-Ships.... London: 1653. V. 71

VIOLLET LE DUC, EUGENE EMMANUEL
Dictionnarie de l'Architecture. Paris: 1854-1868. V. 68

VIRCHOW, RUDOLF
Cellular Pathology as Based Upon Physiological and Pathological Histology. New York: 1860. V. 68; 70
Die Cellular Pathologie in Ihrer Begrundung auf Physiologische und Pathologische Gewebelehre. Berlin;: 1858. V. 69

VIRDEN, KATHARINE
The Thing in the Night. Garden City: 1930. V. 71

VIRGINIA. CONSTITUTIONAL CONVENTION - 1861
Rules and Articles for the Government of the Army of Virginia. Richmond: 1861. V. 70

VIRGINIA. HOUSE OF DELEGATES - 1865
Journal of the House of Delegates of the State of Virginia for the Session of 1864-1865. Alexandria: 1865. V. 72

VIRGINIA. LAWS, STATUTES, ETC. - 1785
The Articles of Confederation; The Declaration of Rights; The Constitution of the Commonwealth and the Articles of the Definitive Treaty of America. Richmond: 1785. V. 68

VIRGINIA. LAWS, STATUTES, ETC. - 1813
Acts Passed at a General Assembly of the Commonwealth of Virginia, Begun and Held at the Capitol in the City of Richmond...1813. Richmond: 1813. V. 72

VIRGINIA. LAWS, STATUTES, ETC. - 1817
Acts Passed at a General Assembly of the Commonwealth of Virginia. Richmond: 1817. V. 72

VIRGINIA. LAWS, STATUTES, ETC. - 1819
The Revised Code of the Laws of Virginia: Being a Collection of All Such Acts of the General Assembly. Richmond: 1819. V. 70

VIRGINIA. LAWS, STATUTES, ETC. - 1849
Code of Virginia. Richmond: 1849. V. 71

VIRGINIA. LAWS, STATUTES, ETC. - 1862
Acts of the General Assembly of the State of Virginia...1862. (with) *Acts...1863...and The New Constitution of Virginia....* Richmond: 1862-1863. V. 71

VIRGINIA COMPANY OF LONDON
The Records of the Virginia Company of The Court Book, from the Mss. Washington: 1906. V. 71

VIRGINIA NATIONAL GUARD
Historical and Pictorial Review: National Guard of the Commonwealth of Virginia. Baton Rouge: 1940. V. 72

VIRTUE & CO.
Virtue's Household Physician. London: 1930?. V. 68

VISHNIAC, ROMAN
A Vanished World. New York: 1983. V. 68

VISIAK, E. H.
The Animus against Milton. Derby: 1945. V. 72
Buccaneer Ballads. London: 1910. V. 73
E. H. Visiak. London: 1986. V. 70

THE VISION and the Creed of Piers Ploughman.... London: 1842. V. 72

VISIT of a London Exquisite to His Maiden Aunts in the Country. London: 1859. V. 68

A VISIT to the Country. London: 1873. V. 73

A VISIT to the Tower, Being an Account of Several Birds and Beasts. 1820. V. 73

THE VISITATION Of The Country Palatine Of Duresme, Taken by Richard St. George,. Sundeland. V. 72

THE VISITING Day. A Novel. London: 1768. V. 73

THE VISITOR'S Guide to Places Worth Seeing in London a Handbook to the Great Metropolis. London: 1862. V. 71

VISSCHER, L. L. B.
Tenting Tonight on the Old Camp Ground. 1917. V. 68

VITA Beati P. Ignatii Loyolae, Societatis Jesu Fundatoris. London: 1609. V. 72

VITRUVIUS, MARCUS POLLIO
L'Architettura di M. Vitruvio Pollione Colla Traduzione Itlaiana e Comento Del Marchese Berardo Galiani. In Napoli: 1758. V. 71
Architecture Generale de Vitruve. Reduite en Abrege par Mr. Perrault. Amsterdam: 1691. V. 70
The Architecture in Ten Books. London: 1826. V. 68
The Architecture of Marcus Vitruvius in Ten Books. London: 1860. V. 68
De Architectura Libri Decem. Como: 1521. V. 72
De Architectura Libri Decem. Amsterdam: 1649. V. 68; 70; 72
De Architectura Libri Decem. Berlin: 1800. V. 68

VITRY, JACQUES DE
The Exempla or Illustrative Stories from the Sermones Vulgares. London: 1890. V. 70

VITTORINI, ELIO
In Sicily. Norfolk: 1949. V. 68

VIVES, JUAN LUIS
De L'Ufficio del Marito, Como si Debba Portare Verso la Moglie. De l'Istitione de la Femina Christiana, Vergine, Maritata, o Vedova. Venizia: 1546. V. 70

VIVIAN, H. HUSSEY
Notes of a Tour in America from August 7th to November 17th 1877. London: 1878. V. 68; 73

VIVIAN, IMOGEN HOLBROOK
A Biographical Sketch of the Life of Charles Algernon Sidney Vivian Founder of the Order of Elks. San Francisco: 1904. V. 69

VIVIAN, MARTHA CAMPBELL
Down the Avenue of Ninety Years Reminiscences of Martha Campbell Vivian. 1924. V. 68

VIZETELLY, HENRY
Extracts Principally from the English Classics, Showing that the Legal Suppression of M. Zola's Novels Would Logically Involve the Bowdlerization of some of the Greatest Works in English Literature. London: 1888. V. 71
Paris in Peril. London: 1882. V. 70; 72

VLIET, RUSS
Manual of Woodslore Survival As Developed at Philmont. Cimmaron. V. 73

VOCH, LUKAS
Abhandlung von der Perspektivkunst.... Augusburg: 1780. V. 72

VOET, LEON
The Plantin Press (1555-1589): a Bibliography of the Works Printed and Published by Christopher Plantin at Antwerp and Leiden. Amsterdam: 1980. V. 70

VOGE, CECIL I. B.
The Chemistry and Physics of Contraceptives. London: 1933. V. 73

VOGEL, HERMANN
The Chemistry of Light and Photography. New York: 1875. V. 69

VOGEL, VIRGIL J.
American Indian Medicine. Norman: 1970. V. 72

VOGT, C.
The Natural History of Animals (Class Mammalia). 1887. V. 73

VOGT, EVON Z.
Navaho Means People. Cambridge: 1951. V. 70; 72; 73

THE VOICE of the People: a Collection of Addresses to His Majesty and Instructions to Members of Parliament by Their Constituents upon the Unsuccessful Management of the Present War Both at Land and Sea. London: 1756. V. 70

VOICE of the Turtle. New York: 1994. V. 72

VOICES from the Moon. San Diego: 1995. V. 70; 73

VOICES Louder than Words. New York: 1991. V. 72

VOIGT, CYNTHIA
Dicey's Song. New York: 1982. V. 72

VOINOVA, A. I.
Semi-Precious Stones. New York: 1931. V. 69

VOLANT, F.
Memoirs of Alexis Soyer; with Unpublished Receipts and Odds and Ends of Gastronomy. London: 1859. V. 68

VOLCK, ADELBERT J.
Confederate War Etchings. Philadelphia: 1880-1890. V. 69; 70

VOLEBELLE, G.
Progetto di Riduzione...Delle Due Case di Proprieta.... Cittadella: 1803. V. 68

VOLKEL, L.
Ueber die Wegfuhrung der Kunstwerke aus den eroberten Landern Nach Rom. eine Vorlesung in der Casselischen Alterthumer Gersellschaft gehalten. Leipzig: 1798. V. 70

VOLKHOVSKY, FELIX
A China Cup and Other Stories for Children. London: 1892. V. 68

VOLLIER, GASTON
A History of Dancing from the Earliest Ages to Our Own Times.... 1898. V. 70

VOLLMANN, WILLIAM T.
An Afghanistan Picture Show, Or, How I Saved The World. New York: 1992. V. 72
Butterfly Stories. London: 1993. V. 68
Butterfly Stories. New York: 1993. V. 71
Fathers and Crows. London: 1992. V. 69
The Ice Shirt. New York: 1990. V. 69
The Rainbow Stories. London: 1989. V. 69; 73
The Rainbow Stories. New York: 1989. V. 69
The Rifles. London: 1994. V. 71
Rifles. New York: 1994. V. 73
Thirteen Stories and Thirteen Epitaphs. London: 1991. V. 69; 71
You Bright and Risen Angels. London: 1987. V. 68; 69; 71
You Bright and Risen Angels. New York: 1987. V. 68; 70

VOLNEY, CONSTANTINE FRANCOIS
Common Sense; or Natural Ideas Opposed to Supernatural. Philadelphia: 1795. V. 69; 71
Oeuvres Completes.... Paris: 1821. V. 72

VOLPINI, GIUSEPPE
Opere Medico-Pratiche Filosofice.... Parma: 1726. V. 70

VOLTAIRE, FRANCOIS MARIE AROUET DE
The Age of Lewis (Louis) XIV. London: 1752. V. 72
Babouc; or, the World As It Goes.... London: 1754. V. 70
Candide. London: 1898. V. 71
Candide. New York: 1928. V. 70
Candide. London: 1939. V. 69; 71
Candidus. Edinburgh: 1761. V. 70
Elemens de la Philosophie de Neuton (sic). Amsterdam: 1738. V. 72
The General History and State of Europe from the Time of Charlemain to Charles V. London: 1754. V. 70
La Henriade. Paris: 1770. V. 72
Histoire De la Guerre de Mil Sept Cent Quarante & Un. Amsterdam: 1755. V. 71
Letters Concerning the English Nation. London: 1733. V. 69; 72
Letters Concerning the English Nation. 1741. V. 72
Letters Concerning the English Nation. London: 1741. V. 73
Memoirs of the Life of Voltaire. London: 1784. V. 69
The Philosophical Dictionary for the Pocket. London: 1765. V. 72
The Philosophical Dictionary. Glasgow: 1766. V. 69
A Philosophical Dictionary from the French of.... Boston: 1881. V. 69
La Philosophie de L'Histoire. Geneva: 1765. V. 68
The Princess of Babylon. London: 1927. V. 71; 73
Therese: a Fragment. Cambridge: 1981. V. 69
Zadig and Other Romances. London: 1929. V. 68

VOLUPSA: The Song of the Sybil. Iowa City: 1968. V. 73

VON ARNIM, ELIZABETH
The Enchanted April. Garden City: 1923. V. 71

VON BAYROS, MARQUIS
The Amorous Drawings. New York: 1968. V. 72

VON BECKERATH, HERBERT
In Defense of the West: a Political and Economic Study. Durham: 1942. V. 73

VON BRAUN, WERNHER
First Men to the Moon. New York: 1960. V. 70

VON ERDBERG, E.
Chinese Influence on European Garden Structures. Cambridge: 1936. V. 69; 71; 73

VON GRIMMELSHAUSEN, JOHANN JAKOB CHRISTOFFEL
The Adventures of Simplicissimus. New York: 1981. V. 71

VON HAGEN, VICTOR WOLFGANG
The Aztec and Maya Papermakers. New York: 1944. V. 69; 70; 72

VON HEFELE, REV.
The Life of Cardinal Ximenez. London: 1860. V. 72

VON HEINE GELDERN, R.
Indonesian Art, a Loan Exhibition from the Royal Indies Institute. New York: 1948. V. 69

VON HOLST, H.
Constitutional and Political History of the U.S. Chicago: 1877-1892. V. 71

VON HOLST, H. V.
Modern American Homes. Chicago: 1913. V. 69

VON HUTTEN, BARONESS
Mag Pye. New York: 1917. V. 71
Mice for Amusement. New York: 1934. V. 71

VON KEYSERLING, EDOUARD, COUNT
Tides. New York: 1929. V. 70

VON KOLNITZ, A. H.
Cryin' in De Wilderness. Charleston: 1937. V. 73

VON LIEBIG, BARON
Letters on Modern Agriculture. 1859. V. 71

VONNEGUT, KURT
Bagombo Snuff Box. New York: 1999. V. 68; 69; 72
Between Time and Timbuktu. New York: 1972. V. 68; 70; 72; 73
Bluebeard. Franklin Center: 1987. V. 68; 70; 71
Bluebeard. New York: 1987. V. 70; 72
Breakfast of Champions. London: 1973. V. 73
Breakfast of Champions. New York: 1973. V. 68; 73
Cat's Cradle. New York: 1963. V. 73
Deadeye Dick. New York: 1982. V. 70; 72; 73
Galapagos. Franklin Center: 1985. V. 69; 70
Galapagos. New York: 1985. V. 70; 73
God Bless You Mr. Rosewater, or Pearls Before Swine. New York: 1956. V. 70; 71
God Bless You Mr. Rosewater, or Pearls Before Swine. New York: 1965. V. 69; 72; 73
Histoire du Soldat. 1997. V. 71
Hocus Pocus. Franklin Center: 1990. V. 70
Hocus Pocus. New York: 1990. V. 69
Jailbird. Franklin Center: 1979. V. 70; 73
Jailbird. New York: 1979. V. 68; 70
Mother Night. Greenwich: 1962. V. 73
Mother Night. New York: 1966. V. 73
Mother Night. London: 1968. V. 72
Nothing is Lost Save Honor. Jackson: 1984. V. 70; 73
Palm Sunday. 1981. V. 71
Palm Sunday. New York: 1991. V. 73
Player Piano. New York: 1952. V. 69; 71; 73
The Sirens of Titan. New York: 1957. V. 69
The Sirens of Titan. New York: 1959. V. 73
Slapstick. 1976. V. 72; 73
Slapstick. Franklin Center: 1976. V. 70; 73
Slapstick. New York: 1976. V. 69; 72
Slaughterhouse-Five. New York: 1969. V. 69; 71; 72; 73
Slaughterhouse-Five. London: 1970. V. 70
Slaughterhouse-Five. Franklin Center: 1978. V. 69; 71
Sun Moon Star. New York: 1980. V. 69; 73
Timequake. London: 1997. V. 72
Timequake. New York: 1997. V. 68; 69; 72
Wampeters, Foma and Granfalloons. New York: 1974. V. 70; 72
Welcome to the Monkey House. New York: 1968. V. 70; 71
Welcome to the Monkey House. London: 1969. V. 72

VON NEUMANN, JOHN
Theory of Games and Economic Behavior. Princeton: 1944. V. 72

VON RANKE, LEOPOLD
A History of England, Principally in the 17th Century. Oxford: 1875. V. 71

VON STERNBERG, JOSEF
Fun in a Chinese Laundry. New York: 1965. V. 69

VOORHEES, IKE
Personal Recollections of Pioneer Life. Cheyenne: 1920. V. 73

VORSE, MARY HEATON
The Ninth Man. New York: 1920. V. 69

VOSBURGH, W. S.
Cherry and Black. New York: 1916. V. 69

VOSE, RUBEN
Wealth of the World, Displayed. New York: 1859. V. 73

VOSPER, FRANK
Love from a Stranger: a Play in Three Acts. London: 1936. V. 70

VOSSIUS, GERARDUS JOANNES
De Historicis Latinis Libri III. Lugduni Batavorum: 1651. V. 72
De Universae Mathesis Natura & Constitutione Liber.... Amsterdam: 1650. V. 72

VOTH, H. R.
The Oraibi Oaqol Ceremony. 1903. V. 69

VOTH, H. R. continued
The Oraibi Powamu Ceremony. Chicago: 1901. V. 69
The Oraibi Summer Snake Ceremony. Chicago: 1903. V. 69
The Traditions of the Hopi. Chicago: 1905. V. 69

VOUET, SIMON
Livre de Divers Grotesques Peintes dans le Cabinet et Bains de la Reyne Regente, au Palais Royal par Simon Vouet. Paris: 1647. V. 72

VOX Cleri pro regi; or the Rights of the Imperial Soveraignty of the Crown of England Vindicated. London: 1688. V. 70

THE VOYAGE of Commodore Anson Round the World. Dublin: 1825. V. 69

A VOYAGE through the Island of the Pacific Ocean. Dublin: 1824. V. 70

VOYAGES and Travels Mainly During the 16th and 17th Centuries. London: 1903. V. 72

VREDENBURG, EDRIC
My Book of Favourite Fairy Tales. London: 1921. V. 70
My Book of Mother Goose Nursery Rhymes. Philadelphia: 1927. V. 71
Tinker, Tailor. London. V. 73
Tinker, Tailor. London: 1914. V. 70; 71

VRIES, HUGO DE
Intracellular Pangenesis Including a Paper on Fertilization and Hybridization.... Chicago: 1910. V. 71; 72

VUES des Palais, Batimens Celebres, Places, Mascarades, et Autres Beautes singulieres de la Ville de Venise. Leiden;: 1762. V. 68

VUILLIER, GASTON
A History of Dancing from the Earliest Ages to Our Own Times. New York: 1897. V. 69

VULLEUMIER, F.
High Altitude Tropical Biogeography. New York: 1986. V. 68

VULLIAMY, B. L.
Some Considerations on the Subject of Public Clocks, Particularly Church Clocks, with Hints for Their Improvement. London: 1828. V. 73

VYNER, ROBERT
Notitia Venatica. 1871. V. 68

VYSE, CHARLES
The Key to the Tutor's Guide; or the Arithmetician's Repository. London: 1791. V. 69
The Tutor's Guide, Being a Complete System of Arithmetic.... London: 1793. V. 71

W

W., H.
The Unlawfulness of Polygamy Evinced; or Observations Occasioned by the Erroneous Interpretations of the Passages of the New Testament, Respecting the Laws of Marriage, Lately Published in a Treatise on Female Ruin. London: 1780. V. 68

WAAGEN, G. F.
Treasures of Art in Great Britain; Being an Account of the Chief Collections of Paintings, Drawings, Sculptures, Illuminated Mss. &c. (with) Galleries and Cabinets of Art in Great Britain.... London: 1854-1857. V. 71

WABASH RALROAD CO.
Lake and Sea. St. Louis: 1900-1905?. V. 70

WACHER, JOHN
Pleasures Without Change. London: 1947. V. 71

WADA, TSUNASHIRO
Minerals of Japan.... Tokyo: 1904. V. 68

WADD, WILLIAM
Cases of Diseased Bladder and Testicle Illustrated With Etchings. London: 1815. V. 70; 71
Comments on Corpulency Lineaments of Leanness Mems on Diet and Dietetics. London: 1829. V. 73
Mems. Maxims and Memoirs. London: 1827. V. 71
Nugae Carnorae; or Epitaphian Memntos (In stone cutters verse) of the Medici Family of Modern Times. London: 1827. V. 73

WADDELL, HELEN
The Abbe Prevost. A Play. London: 1933. V. 68; 71

WADDELL, L. AUSTINE
Lhasa and Its Mysteries. London: 1906. V. 73

WADDINGTON'S Guide to Belfast and North of Ireland. York: 1908. V. 69

WADE, ALLAN
A Bibliography of the Writings of W. B. Yeats. London: 1968. V. 72

WADE, BRENT
(Company Man). Dreams of Horn, Dreams of Ivory. Chapel Hill: 1992. V. 68

WADE, EDWIN L.
America's Lost Expediton: The Thomas Keam Collection of Hopi Pottery from the Second Hemenway Expedition 1890-1894. Phoenix: 1980. V. 70

WADE, H. T.
With Boat and Gun in the Yangtze Valley. Shanghai: 1910. V. 72

WADE, HENRY
Constable Guard Thyself!. London: 1934. V. 73
The Duke of York's Steps. London: 1932. V. 73
The Dying Alderman. London: 1930. V. 73
A Dying Fall. London: 1955. V. 70; 71; 73
Here Come's The Copper. London: 1938. V. 73
Policeman's Lot. London: 1933. V. 73
Policeman's Lot. London: 1935. V. 73

WADE, JOHN
The Black Book; or, Corruption Unmasked!. London: 1820. V. 73
The Extraordinary Black Book.... London: 1831. V. 68
Junius, including Letters by the Same Writer Under Other Signatures.... London: 1850. V. 68
A Political Dictionary; or, Pocket Companion; Chiefly Designed for the Use of Members of Parliament, Whigs, Tories, Loyalists, Magistrates, Clergymen, Half-Pay Officers.... London: 1821. V. 69
Women, Past and Present. London: 1865. V. 69; 72

WADE, KATHLEEN
Crime At Gargoyles. London: 1947. V. 70

WADE, MURRAY
Legislative Sketches of 1903. Portland: 1903. V. 73

WADE, P.
Every Australian Bird Illustrated. London: 1975. V. 72

WADE, R. T.
The Triassic Fishes of Brookvale, New South Wales. London: 1935. V. 73

WADSLEY, OLIVE
Serenade. London: 1931. V. 69

WADSWORTH, EDWARD
Sailing Ships and Barges of the Western Mediterranean and Adriatic Sea. London: 1926. V. 70

WADSWORTH, L. A.
Mystery at the Black Cat. New York: 1941. V. 72

WADSWORTH, WALLACE
The Modern Story Book. 1931. V. 71

WAFER, LIONEL
A New Voyage and Description of the Isthmus of America. London: 1699. V. 71

WAGENSEIL, JOHANN CHRISTOPHOR
Tel Ignea Satanae.... Altdorf: 1681. V. 70

WAGER, V. A.
Frogs of South Africa, Their Fascinating Life Stories. Craighall: 1986. V. 72

WAGG, HENRY J.
A Chronological Survey of Work for the Blind. London: 1932. V. 71

THE WAGGON Load of Money. York: 1820. V. 72
THE WAGGON Load of Money. 1825. V. 73

WAGNER, ANTHONY
Heralds Of England. A History of The Office and College of Arms. London: 1967,. V. 72

WAGNER, BRUCE
Force Majeure. New York: 1991. V. 71
I'm Losing You. New York: 1996. V. 71

WAGNER, CONSTANCE
The Major Has 7 Guests. New York: 1940. V. 70

WAGNER, COSIMA
Cosima Wagner's Diaries 1869-1877 and 1878-1883. New York and London: 1978-1980. V. 68

WAGNER, G.
The Bantu of North Kavirondo. London: 1949-1956. V. 69

WAGNER, GEOFFREY
Wyndham Lewis - A Portrait of the Artists as the Enemy. London: 1957. V. 72

WAGNER, GLENDOLIN DAMON
Blankets and Moccasins. Caldwell: 1933. V. 72
Old Neutriment. Boston: 1934. V. 72
Old Neutriment. 1973. V. 72

WAGNER, HENRY RAUP
Alphonse Pinart - Journey to Arizona in 1876. Los Angeles: 1962. V. 69
Bullion to Books; the Fifty Years of Buisness and Pleasure. Los Angeles: 1942. V. 68
The Cartography of the Northwest Coast of America to the Year 1800. Berkeley: 1937. V. 73
The Life and Writings of Bartolome de las Casas. Albuquerque: 1967. V. 71
Peter Pond, Fur Trader and Explorer. New Haven: 1955. V. 68; 73
The Plains and the Rockies. San Francisco: 1921. V. 69
The Plains and the Rockies. San Francisco: 1937. V. 68; 69; 71
The Plains and the Rockies. Columbus: 1953. V. 69
The Plains and the Rockies. San Francisco: 1982. V. 68
Sir Francis Drake's Voyage Around the World. San Francisco: 1926. V. 70
Sir Francis Drake's Voyage Around the World. Amsterdam: 1969. V. 72; 73

WAGNER, HENRY RAUP continued
Spanish Explorations in the Strait of Juan De Fuca. Santa Ana: 1933. V. 68; 70
The Spanish Southwest 1542-1794. Albuquerque: 1937. V. 72
The Spanish Southwest 1542-1794. New York: 1967. V. 68
Spanish Voyages to the Northwest Coast of America. San Francisco: 1929. V. 70
Spanish Voyages to the Northwest Coast of America in the Sixteenth Century. Amsterdam: 1966. V. 68

WAGNER, LINDA W.
Sylvia Plath: The Critical Heritage. London: 1988. V. 71

WAGNER, MORITZ
The Tricolor on the Atlas; or, Algeria and the French Conquest. London: 1854. V. 68

WAGNER, RICHARD
The Rhinegold and the Valkyrie. London/New York: 1910. V. 69
Richard Wagner Parsifal Kalendar fur 1921. Berlin: 1920. V. 73
The Ring of the Nibelung. New York. V. 70
Wagner's Ring of the Nibelung. New York: 1939. V. 71
Siegfried & the Twilight of the Gods. London/New York: 1911. V. 69
The Tale of Lohengrin Knight of the Swan.... London: 1913. V. 70
Tannhauser. London: 1911. V. 70; 72
The Valkyrie. London: 1882. V. 71
Die Walkure. The Valkyrie. Mainz: 1882. V. 70

WAGNER, SALLIE R.
Yazz: Navajo Painter. Flagstaff: 1983. V. 68; 69

THE WAGON Boy; or Trust in Providence. New York: 1840. V. 70

WAGSTAFFE, WILLIAM
A Comment Upon the History of Tom Thumb. London: 1711. V. 73
A Letter to Dr. Freind: Shewing the Danger and Uncertainty of Inoculating the Small. London: 1722. V. 73
Miscellaneous Works of Dr. William Wagstaffe, Physician to St. Bartholomew's Hospital . . . London: 1726. V. 70; 71

WAHBA, MAGDI
Johnsonian Studies, Including a Bibliography of Johnsonian Studies 1950-1960. Cairo: 1962. V. 69; 72

WAHL, ALBERTA HUGHES
Handsome, but Dead. New York: 1942. V. 70

WAHL, JAN
Pleasant Fieldmouse. London: 1969. V. 72

WAI-CHUEN, PETER YUNG
Photographic Interpretation of Autumn Floods. Hong Kong: 1989. V. 70; 72

WAIN, HARRY
The Story Behind the Word. Springfield: 1958. V. 69

WAIN, JOHN
Hurry on Down. London: 1953. V. 68; 69
The Seafarer. London: 1980. V. 68

WAIN, LOUIS
Big Dogs, Little Dogs, Cats and Kittens. London. V. 70
Catland. London: 1901. V. 70
Flossy and Fluffy. London: 1919. V. 73
Louis Wain's Annual, 1901. London: 1901. V. 70
Louis Wain's Annual, 1902. London: 1902. V. 70
Louis Wain's Cats. London: 1983. V. 69
Louis Wain's Painting Book. London: 1912. V. 70; 73
Louis Wain's Summer Book. London: 1906. V. 72
Music in Pussytown. London: 1920. V. 73
Pa Cats Ma Cats and Their Kittens. London: 1901. V. 70; 73
Pussy Cat's ABC. London: 1916. V. 70
Somebody's Pussies. London: 1925. V. 70; 72

WAINEWRIGHT, THOMAS GRIFFITHS
Essays and Criticisms: Now First Collected.... London: 1880. V. 70

WAINWRIGHT, A.
A Bowland Sketchbook. Kendal: 1981. V. 69
The Central Fells. Kentmere: 1958. V. 69; 71
The Central Highlands. Scottish Mountain Drawings, Vol. 4. Kendal: 1977. V. 69; 71
A Dales Sketchbook. Kendal: 1976. V. 69
The Eastern Fells. Book One. Kentmere: 1956. V. 69; 71
The Eastern Highlands. Scottish Mountain Drawings, Vol. 5. Kendal: 1978. V. 69; 71
An Eden Sketchbook. Kendal: 1980. V. 69; 71
Ex-Fell Wanderer. Kendal: 1987. V. 69; 71
The Far Eastern Fells. Book Two. Kentmere: 1957. V. 69; 71
Fell Wanderer. Kendal: 1966. V. 69; 71
Fellwalking With a Camera. Kendal: 1988. V. 69; 71
Fellwalking with Wainwright. London: 1984. V. 71
A Furness Sketchbook. Kendal: 1978. V. 69; 71
Kendal in the Nineteenth Century. Kendal: 1977. V. 69; 71
Lakeland Mountain Drawings. Volume I. Kendal: 1980. V. 69
Lakeland Mountain Drawings. Volume II. Kendal: 1981. V. 69
Lakeland Mountain Drawings. Volume III. Kendal: 1982. V. 69; 71
Lakeland Mountain Drawings. Volume IV. Kendal: 1983. V. 69; 71
Lakeland Mountain Drawings. Volume V. Kendal: 1984. V. 69; 71
A Lakeland Sketchbook. Kendal: 1969. V. 69
A North Wales Sketchbook. Kendal: 1982. V. 69
The North-Western Highlands. Scottish Mountain Drawings. Vol 2. Kendal: 1976. V. 69; 71
The Northern Fells. Kentmere: 1962. V. 69; 71
The Northern Highlands. Scottish Mountain Drawings, Volume 1. Kendal: 1974. V. 69; 71
Old Roads of Eastern Lakeland. Kendal: 1985. V. 69; 71
The Outlying Fells. Kendal: 1974. V. 69; 71
A Peak District Sketchbook. Kendal: 1984. V. 69
Pennine Way Companion. Kendal: 1968. V. 71
A Pennine Journey. London: 1986. V. 69
A Pennine Journey. London: 1987. V. 69
Pennine Way Companion. Kendal: 1968. V. 69
A Ribble Sketchbook. Kendal: 1980. V. 69
A Second Dales Sketchbook. Kendal: 1978. V. 69
A Second Furness Sketchbook. Kendal: 1979. V. 69; 71
A Second Lakeland Sketchbook. Kendal: 1970. V. 71
The Southern Fells. Kentmere: 1960. V. 69; 71
A Third Lakeland Sketchbook. Kendal: 1971. V. 69; 71
Wainwright in Lakeland. Kendal: 1983. V. 71
Wainwright in Lakeland. Kendal: 1985. V. 69; 71
Wainwright in the Limestone Dales. London: 1991. V. 69
Wainwright on the Lakeland and Mountain Passes. London: 1989. V. 69
Wainwright on the Pennine Way. London: 1985. V. 69
Wainwright's Coast to Coast Walk. London: 1987. V. 69; 71
Walks from Ratty. London: 1978. V. 69
Walks in Limestone Country. Kendal: 1970. V. 69
Walks on the Howgill Fells and Adjoining Fells. Kendal: 1972. V. 69
Welsh Mountain Drawings. Kendal: 1981. V. 69
The Western Highlands. Kendal: 1976. V. 69
Westmorland Heritage. Kendal: 1975. V. 69; 71
A Wyre Sketchbook. Kendal: 1982. V. 69

WAINWRIGHT, CHARLES
A Diary of Battle, The Personal Journal of Colonel Charles S. Wainwright, 1861-1865. New York: 1962. V. 72

WAISTELL, CHARLES
Designs for Agricultural Buildings, Including Labourers' Cottages, Farmhouses and Out-Offices.... London: 1827. V. 68

WAIT, BENJAMIN
Letters from Van Dieman's Land, Written During Four Years Imprisonment for Political Offences Committed in Upper Canada. Buffalo: 1843. V. 68

WAITE, E. R.
Fishes. Adelaide: 1916. V. 72
A Monograph and Four Papers, Mostly of Fishes, from the Australian and New Zealand Regions. 1897-1916. V. 73
Scientific Results of the Trawling Expedition of H.M.C.S. "Thetis". Sydney: 1899. V. 73

WAKE, HENRY THOMAS
All the Monumental Inscriptions in the Graveyards of Brigham and Bridekirk, Near Cockermouth, in the County of Cumberland from 1666 to 1876. Cockermouth: 1878. V. 71

WAKE, WILLIAM
The Missionarie's Arts Discovered.... London: 1688. V. 70

WAKEFIELD, BENJAMIN
The Warbling Muses, or Treasure of Lyric Poetry. London: 1749. V. 68; 73

WAKEFIELD, DAN
All Her Children. Garden City: 1976. V. 72
New York in the 50's. Boston: 1992. V. 68
Starting Over. New York: 1973. V. 72
Under the Apple Tree. New York: 1982. V. 68

WAKEFIELD, DANIEL
Public Expenditure Apart from Taxation, or, Remarks on the Inadequate and Excessive Pay of Public Servants. London: 1834. V. 71

WAKEFIELD, H. R.
Imagine a Man with a Box. London: 1931. V. 68

WAKEFIELD, MARY
Jacobite Essays. Kendal: 1922. V. 71

WAKEFIELD, PRISCILLA
Excursions in North America, Described in Letters from a Gentleman and His Young Companion to Their Friends in England. London: 1806. V. 68

WAKEFIELD, ROBERT
Schwiering and the West. Aberdeen: 1973. V. 69

WAKEFORD, EDWARD
Memorial Exhibition. Edward Wakeford. A.R.A. (1914-1973). London: 1973. V. 73

WAKEMAN, FREDERIC
The Hucksters. New York: 1946. V. 70

WAKEMAN, GEOFFREY
Functional Developments in Bookbinding. Kidlington/Oxford/Newcastle: 1993. V. 71
The Literature of Letterpress Printing 1849-1900: a Selection. Kidlington: 1986. V. 71
Victorian Book Illustration: the Technical Revolution. London: 1973. V. 71

WAKEMAN, JOHN
World Film Directors. 1890-1985. New York: 1987. V. 70

WAKOSKI, DIANE
Coins and Coffins. New York: 1962. V. 69
Dancing on the Grave of a Son of a Bitch. Los Angeles: 1972. V. 73
Dancing on the Grave of a Son of a Bitch. Los Angeles: 1973. V. 72
The Diamond Merchant. Cambridge: 1968. V. 73
The Motorcycle Betrayal Poems. New York: 1971. V. 71; 73
Smudging. Los Angeles: 1972. V. 73

WALCOT, WILLIAM
Architectural Water Colours and Etchings of W. Walcot. London: 1919. V. 72

WALCOTT, C. D.
Cambrian Brachiopoda. Washington: 1912. V. 70

WALCOTT, DEREK
The Arkansas Testament. New York: 1987. V. 69
The Caribbean Poetry...and the Art of Romare Bearden. New York: 1983. V. 73
Dream on Monkey Mountain. New York: 1970. V. 72
The Fortunate Traveller. New York: 1981. V. 68; 69
In a Green Night. London: 1962. V. 69; 70
The Joker of Seville and O Babylon!. New York: 1978. V. 69; 72
Poems of the Caribbean. New York: 1983. V. 69; 71; 72
The Sea at Dauphin. 1958. V. 69
Sea Grapes. New York: 1976. V. 72
Selected Poems. New York: 1964. V. 69; 73
The Star-Apple Kingdom. New York: 1979. V. 68
Tiepolo's Hound. London: 2000. V. 70

WALCOTT, MACKENZIE, E. C.
Scot-Monasticon, The Ancient Church of Scotland. London: 1874. V. 71

WALCOTT, MARY V.
North American Wild Flowers. Washington: 1925. V. 71

WALD, PAUL
The Twelve Days Campaign of the Fifth Regiment Pennsylvania Militia.... Allentown: 1862. V. 69

WALDBERG, PATRICK
Marino Marini: Complete Works. New York: 1970. V. 73

WALDEN, B. M.
Wild Flowers of Hong Kong Around the Year.... Hong Kong: 1977. V. 72

WALDMAN, DIANE
Joseph Cornell. New York: 1977. V. 69; 72

WALDO, EDNA LA MOURE
Dakota - An Informal Study of Territorial Days, Gleaned From Contemporary Newspapers. Bismarck: 1936. V. 72

WALDO, FULLERTON
Down the Mackenzie, through the Great Lone Land. New York: 1923. V. 73
Grenfell: Knight-Errant of the North. Philadelphia: 1924. V. 72

WALDRON, GEORGE
The History and Description of the Isle of Man.... London: 1744. V. 72

WALDROP, HOWARD
Them Bones: a Dozen Tough Jobs. 1989. V. 70

WALDSTEIN, CHARLES
Herculaneum: Past, Present and Future. London: 1908. V. 70

WALE, W. H. JAMES
Bookbindings and Rubbings of Bindings in the National Art Library South Kensington Muuseum. London: 1898-1894. V. 73

WALEY, ARTHUR
Chinese Poems.... London: 1946. V. 70
An Introduction to the Study of Chinese Painting. 1923. V. 73

WALFORD, L. A.
Marine Game Fishes of the Pacific Coast from Alaska to the Equator. Berkeley: 1937. V. 73

WALFORD, LUCY BETHIA
Dick Netherby. London: 1891?. V. 68
Troublesome Daughters. London: 1891?. V. 68

WALGAMOTT, CHARLES S.
Six Decades Back. Caldwell: 1936. V. 70

WALK, CHARLES E.
The Silver Blade. Chicago: 1908. V. 70

WALKER & CLELAND
Farms and City and Country Residences, for Sale by Walker and Cleland, No. 23 Court Street, Boston. Boston: 1855?. V. 71

WALKER, A.
Analysis of a Course of Lectures in Natural and Experimental Philosophy. London: 1804. V. 69

WALKER, A. EARL
A Follow-Up Study of Head Wounds in World War II. Washington;: 1961. V. 68
A History of Neurological Surgery. Baltimore: 1951. V. 68; 70; 71

WALKER, ADAM
A Journal of Two Campaigns of the Fourth Regiment of U.S. Infantry, in the Michigan and Indiana Territories, Under the Command of Col. John P. Boyd and Lt. Col. James Miller, During the Yers 1811 and 1812. Kenne: 1816. V. 72

WALKER, ALEXANDER
Beauty. London: 1852. V. 68; 69
Beauty Illustrated by an Analysis and Classification of the Beauty in Woman. London: 1852. V. 72
Disblair 1634-1884, or An Old Oak Panel and Something Thereon. Aberdeen: 1884. V. 71
Woman Physiologically Considered, As to Mind, Morals, Marriage, Matrimonial Slavery, Infidelity and Divorce. London: 1840. V. 69

WALKER, ALICE
Anything We Love Can Be Saved. New York: 1997. V. 73
The Color Purple. New York: 1982. V. 68; 69; 70; 71; 72; 73
The Color Purple. 1985. V. 72
The Color Purple. London: 1986. V. 73
Finding the Green Stone. New York: 1991. V. 73
Good Night Willie Lee, I'll See You in the Morning. New York: 1978. V. 73
Good Night, Willie Lee, I'll See You in the Morning. New Haven: 1979. V. 70
Good Night, Willie Lee, I'll See You in the Morning. New York: 1979. V. 68; 69
Good Night Willie Lee, I'll See You in the Morning. London: 1987. V. 73
Her Blue Body Everything We Know. New York: 1991. V. 73
Horses Make a Landscape Look More Beautiful. New York: 1984. V. 73
In Love and Trouble. New York: 1973. V. 73
In Love and Trouble. London: 1984. V. 73
In Search of Our Mothers' Gardens. New York: 1983. V. 73
Living by the Word. New York: 1988. V. 72; 73
Meridian. New York: 1970. V. 72
Meridian. London: 1971. V. 68; 73
Meridian. London: 1976. V. 73
Meridian. New York: 1976. V. 69; 70; 71; 73
Possessing the Secret of Joy. New York: 1992. V. 68; 70; 71; 72; 73
Revolutionary Petunias. New York: 1970. V. 70; 71; 72; 73
Revolutionary Petunias. London: 1988. V. 73
The Same River Twice. New York: 1996. V. 73
The Temple of My Familiar. New York: 1989. V. 68; 69; 73
The Temple of My Familiar. San Diego: 1989. V. 72
The Third Life of Grange Copeland. New York: 1970. V. 69; 71; 72; 73
To Hell with Dying. New York: 1988. V. 73
Warrior Marks. New York: 1993. V. 71
The Way Forward is With a Broken Heart. New York: 2000. V. 70; 73
You Can't Keep a Good Woman Down. New York: 1981. V. 73

WALKER, ANTHONY
Eyphka, Eyphka. The Virtuous Woman Founder Her Loss Bewailed and Character Exemplified in a Sermon Preached at Felsted in Essex, April 30 1678. London: 1678. V. 73

WALKER, ARTHUR N.
The Holcombe Hunt. 1937. V. 70; 72

WALKER, BETTINA
Songs and Sonnets. London: 1893. V. 69

WALKER, C. F.
Brown Trout and Dry Fly Natural and Artificial. 1955. V. 68; 73
Chalk Stream Flies. 1953. V. 68; 73
Lake Flies and Their Imitation. 1960. V. 68; 73
Old Flies in New Dresses. 1898. V. 73

WALKER, C. IRVINE
The Life of Lieutenant General Richard Heron Anderson of the Confederate State Army. Charleston: 1917. V. 69
Rolls and Historical Sketch of the Tenth Regiment, South Carolina Volunteers. Charleston: 1881. V. 69; 70

WALKER, D. GREER
Malformations of the Face. Edinburgh: 1961. V. 68

WALKER, D. S.
Oriental Rugs of the Hajji Babas. New York: 1982. V. 72

WALKER, DAVID H.
Pioneers of Prosperity. San Francisco: 1895. V. 68

WALKER, DONALD
British Manly Exercises: in Which Rowing and Sailing Are Now First Described.... Philadelphia: 1836. V. 69

WALKER, E. P.
Mammals of the World. Baltimore: 1964. V. 70

WALKER, EDWARD
Explorations in the Biology of Language. Sussex: 1978. V. 68

WALKER, EDWIN C.
The Ethics of Freedom. New York: 1913. V. 68

WALKER, F.
Catalogue of the Specimens of Heteropterous Hemiptera in the Collection of the British Museum. 1867-1873. V. 69

WALKER, FRANCIS A.
History of The Second Army Corps in The Army of The Potomac. New York: 1891. V. 72

WALKER, FRANKLIN
The Seacoast of Bohemia. San Francisco: 1966. V. 73

WALKER, GEORGE
The Art of Chess-Play: a New Treatise on the Game of Chess. 1846. V. 72
The Costume of Yorkshire. London: 1814. V. 69
Cribbage Made Easy. New York: 1875. V. 69
The Vagabond; or, Practical Infidelity. Harrisonburg: 1814. V. 71

WALKER, GERALD
Cruising. New York: 1970. V. 71

WALKER, HOVENDEN
A Journal: or Full Account of the Late Expedition to Canada. London: 1720. V. 68

WALKER, J. A.
The History of Penrith. Penrith: 1857. V. 71
The History of Penrith, from the Earliest Period to the Present Time. Penrith: 1858. V. 71

WALKER, J. HUBERT
Mountain Days in the Highlands and Alps. London: 1937. V. 69; 71
On Hills of the North. Edinburgh: 1948. V. 69
Walking In the Alps. Edinburgh: 1951. V. 69

WALKER, JAMES SCOTT
An Accurate Description of the Liverpool and Manchester Rail-way, the Tunnel, Bridges and Other Works Throughout the Line.... Liverpool: 1830. V. 71; 73

WALKER, JAN
The Singular Case of the Duplicate Holmes. Romford, Essex: 1994. V. 71

WALKER, JOEL P.
A Pioneer of Pioneers - Narrative of Adventures Thro' Alabama, Florida, New Mexico, Oregon, California. Los Angeles: 1953. V. 68; 73

WALKER, JOHN
The Academic Speaker; or, a Selection of Parliamentary Debates, Orations.... London: 1789. V. 69
An Attempt Towards Recovering an Account of the Numbers and Sufferings of the Clergy of the Church of England, Heads of Colleges, Fellows, Scholars &c. 1714. V. 72
The National Gallery Of Art. Washington. One Thousand Masterpieces. New York: 1974. V. 72
The Philosophy of the Eye.... 1837. V. 73

WALKER, JONATHAN
Trial and Imprisonment of Jonathan Walker, at Pensacola, Florida, for Aiding Slaves to Escape from Bondage with an Appendix.... Boston: 1846. V. 70; 72; 73

WALKER, JOSEPH COOPER
Historical Memoir on Italian Tragedy, from the Earliest Period to the Present Time.... London: 1799. V. 70

WALKER, JUDSON ELLIOTT
Campaigns of General Custer in the North-West, and the Final Surrender of Sitting Bull. New York: 1881. V. 73

WALKER, MARGARET
For My People. New Haven: 1942. V. 69; 70; 72
For My People. New York: 1992. V. 72

WALKER, MARY
Letters from the Duchess de cruі and Others, on Subjects Moral and Entertaining, Wherein the Character of the Female Sex.... London: 1777. V. 73

WALKER, MARY ADELAIDE
Eastern Life and Scenery with Excursions in Asia Minor, Mytilene, Crete and Roumania. London: 1886. V. 69

WALKER, MARY E.
Hit. New York: 1871. V. 68

WALKER, MARY WILLIS
The Red Scream. New York: 1994. V. 68; 69; 70; 71; 72; 73
Under the Beetle's Cellar. New York: 1995. V. 70; 73
Zero at the Bone. London: 1991. V. 69
Zero at the Bone. New York: 1991. V. 68; 69; 70; 71; 73

WALKER, OBADIAH
Of Education. Especially of Young Gentlemen. Oxford: 1683. V. 69

WALKER, R.
The Flora of Oxfordshire and Its Contiguous Counties.... Oxford: 1833. V. 69
Rod Building for Amateurs. 1952. V. 73

WALKER, RALPH
The Fly in the Amber: Comments on the Making of Architecture. New York: 1957. V. 68; 69; 72
Ralph Walker, Architect of Voorhees Gmelin; Walker Voorhees Walker Foley; Smith Voorhees Walker Smith and Smith. New York: 1957. V. 69

WALKER, RICHARD
Memoirs of Medicine, Including a Sketch of Medical History.... London: 1799. V. 72

WALKER, STANLEY
Mrs. Astor's Horse. New York: 1935. V. 72

WALKER, STELLA
British Sporting Art in the Twentieth Century. 1989. V. 68

WALKER, T. B.
Personal Recollections of The Campaigns in Abyssinia, 1868, And Afghanistan, 1872 - General Custer's Last Campaign, 1876 And The Hawaiian Rebellion. 1895. Honolulu: 1931. V. 72

WALKER, T. D.
Residential Landscaping I and II. West Lafayette and Mesa: 1982-1983. V. 71

WALKER, THOMAS
Aristology; or the Art of Dining. 1965. V. 71

WALKER, WALTER
A Dime to Dance By. New York: 1983. V. 68

WALKER, WILLIAM
Memoirs of the Distinguished Men of Science of Great Britain Living in the Years 1807-1808. London: 1862. V. 68; 70
Memoirs of the Distinguished Men of Science of Great Britain Living in the Years 1807-1808. 1862. V. 72

WALKINGAME, FRANCIS
The Tutor's Assistant: Being a Compendium of Arithmetic and A Complete Question Book. York: 1797. V. 70; 72
The Tutor's Assistant; Being a Compendium of Arithmetic and a Complete Question Book.... York: 1800. V. 69

WALKS with Mamma, or Stories in Words of One Syllable. London: 1824. V. 70

WALL, BERNHARDT
Following General Sam Houston, 1793-1863. Limerock: 1935. V. 69

WALL, DAVID
Rondoy. London: 1965. V. 69

WALL, DOROTHY
Stout Fellows: Chum, Angelina Wallaby, Um-Pig and Flip. Sydney: 1936. V. 73

WALLACE, A.
Darwinism. London: 1889. V. 73

WALLACE, ALFRED RUSSEL
Darwinism. An Exposition of the Theory of Natural Selection.... London: 1889. V. 68; 72
Darwinism. An Exposition of the Theory of Natural Selection.... London: 1897. V. 72
The Geographical Distribution of Animals with a Study of the Relations of Living and Extinct Faunas.... London: 1876. V. 72
Island Life; or the Phenomena and Causes of Insular Faunas and Floras.... London: 1880. V. 72
The Malay Archipelago: the Land of the Orang-Utan and the Bird of Paradise. London: 1869. V. 71; 72
Man's Place in the Universe. London: 1903. V. 72
My Life: a Record of Events and Opinions. London: 1905. V. 72
A Narrative of Travels on the Amazon and Rio Negro. London: 1853. V. 72
A Narrative of Travels on the Amazon and Rio Negro. London: 1889. V. 69; 72
Natural Selection and Tropical Nature. 1891. V. 69
Social Environment and Moral Progress. London: 1913. V. 71
Studies Scientific and Social. London: 1900. V. 72

WALLACE, ALFRED RUSSELL
Tropical Nature and Other Essays. London: 1878. V. 69; 72

WALLACE, D. MAC KENZIE
Russia. London: 1877. V. 69; 72

WALLACE, DAVID FOSTER
The Broom of the System. New York: 1987. V. 69; 72
Girl with Curious Hair. New York: 1989. V. 68; 69; 71; 72
Infinite Jest. Boston: 1996. V. 68; 69; 70; 73

WALLACE, DAVID RAINS
The Klamath Knot. San Francisco: 1983. V. 69; 72

WALLACE, DILLON
The Lure of the Labrador Wild: The Story of the Exploring Expedition Conducted by Leonidas Hubbard, Jr. New York, Toronto: 1905. V. 71
The Testing of Jim MacLean: A Tale of the Wilds of Labrador. New York, Chicago: 1924. V. 71

WALLACE, EDGAR
Bones in London. London: 1921. V. 69
The Day of Uniting. 1930. V. 71
The Day of Uniting. New York: 1930. V. 70; 73
The Death Safe. 1933. V. 73
The Devil Man. New York: 1931. V. 70
Diane of Kara-Kara. Boston: 1924. V. 70
The Flying Squad. New York: 1929. V. 68; 71
The Four Just Men. London: 1905. V. 68; 69
The Ghost of Down Hill. New York: 1929. V. 70
The Green Ribbon. Garden City: 1930. V. 69
Gunman's Bluff. Garden City: 1929. V. 69; 70
The Hand of Power. New York: 1930. V. 68; 70; 73
Jack O'Jugment. London: 1920. V. 69
The Law of the Three Just Men. Garden City: 1931. V. 68
The Murder Book of J. G. Reeder. New York: 1929. V. 69
The People of the River. London: 1912. V. 69
The Silver Key. New York: 1930. V. 69
The Stretelli Case and Other Mystery Stories. Cleveland and New York: 1930. V. 69
White Face. New York: 1931. V. 68; 69; 71

WALLACE, EDGAR *continued*
Writ in Barracks. London: 1900. V. 69; 73

WALLACE, ERNEST
Ranald S. MacKenzie On The Texas Frontier. Lubbock: 1964. V. 72

WALLACE, FRANK
A Stuart Sketch Book. 1542 to 1746. 1933. V. 69; 70; 73

WALLACE, FREDERICK WILLIAM
Captain Salvation. New York: 1925. V. 69
The Romance of a Great Port. The Story of Saint John New Brunswick. St. John: 1935. V. 73
Roving Fishermen: An Autobiography Recounting Personal Experiences.... Gardenvale, Quebec: 1955. V. 71
The Shack Locker: Yarns of the Deep Sea Fishing Fleets. Montreal and Toronto: 1916. V. 71
Under Sail in the Last of the Clippers. Glasgow: 1936. V. 73

WALLACE, GEORGE S.
Cabell County Annals and Familes. Richmond: 1935. V. 73
Huntington through Seventy-Five Years. Huntington: 1947. V. 73

WALLACE, H. F.
Big Game. 1934. V. 72
Stalks Abroad. 1908. V. 72; 73

WALLACE, HAROLD
Stalks Abroad, Being Some Account of the Sport Obtained During a Two Years' Tour of the World. London: 1908. V. 69

WALLACE, HENRY A.
Democracy Reborn. New York: 1944. V. 70

WALLACE, IRVING
The Chapman Report. New York: 1960. V. 69

WALLACE, IVY L.
Pookie Believes in Santa Claus. 1957. V. 73

WALLACE, LEW
Ben-Hur. London: 1892. V. 71
Ben-Hur. New York: 1903. V. 69; 71
Lew Wallace - an Autobiography. New York: 1902. V. 69
The Prince of India or Why Constantinople Fell. New York: 1893. V. 73

WALLACE, MAC KENZIE
Russia. London: 1905. V. 73

WALLACE, MARGARET
Emblems of Nature. Coupar-Angus: 1875. V. 69

WALLACE, MICHELE
Black Macho and the Myth of the Super Woman. New York: 1979. V. 72

WALLACE, RANDALL
So Late Into the Night. Garden City: 1963. V. 68

WALLACE, ROBERT
Characteristics of the Present Politial State of Great Britain. London: 1758. V. 72
A Dissertation on the Numbers of Mankind in Antient and Modern Times.... Edinburgh: 1753. V. 70
Various Prospects of Mankind, Nature and Providence. London: 1761. V. 69

WALLACE, ROBERT C.
A Few Memories of A Long Life. Fairfield: 1988. V. 72

WALLACE, SUSAN E.
The Land of the Pueblos. New York: 1888. V. 69

WALLACE, W. STEWART
Documents Relating to the North West Company. Toronto: 1934. V. 71

WALLACE, WILLARD M.
Soul of the Lion - Biography of General Joshua L. Chamberlain. Edinburn: 1960. V. 72

WALLACE, WILLIAM CLAY
The Structure of the Eye with Reference to Natural Theology. New York: 1836. V. 72

WALLACE, WILLIAM S.
Antoine Robidoux, 1794-1866. Los Angeles. V. 71

WALLACE-DUNLOP, M. A.
Glass in the Old World. London: 1882. V. 72

WALLANT, EDWARD LEWIS
The Pawnbroker. New York: 1961. V. 71
The Tenants of Moonbloom. New York: 1963. V. 69

WALLAS, ADA
Before the Bluestockings. London: 1929. V. 71

WALLER, EDMUND
The Works in Verse and Prose. Published by Mr. Fenton. London: 1730. V. 71; 73

WALLER, ERIC
Bibliotheca Walleriana. Stockholm: 1955. V. 69

WALLER, HORACE
The Last Journals of David Livingstone in Central Africa, from 1865 to His Death. London: 1874. V. 69

WALLER, IRENE
Thread: an Art Form. 1973. V. 68

WALLER, JAMES
The Everlasting Hills. London: 1939. V. 69

WALLER, JOHN
Fortunate Hamlet. London: 1941. V. 73
Golden Hair and The Two black Hawks. London: 1971. V. 70
Middle East Anthology. London: 1946. V. 68

WALLER, PICKFORD
Bookplates by Pickford Waller. Bognor, Sussex: 1916. V. 70

WALLER, ROBERT
Shadow of Authority. London: 1956. V. 70; 71

WALLER, ROBERT JAMES
Bridges of Madison County. 1992. V. 68; 70
The Bridges of Madison County. New York: 1992. V. 68; 69; 71; 72; 73

WALLERIUS, JOHANN GOTTSCHALK
Mineralogia, Eller Mineralriket. Stockholm: 1747. V. 68
Mineralogie, ou Description Generale des Substances du Regne Mineral. 1753. V. 68

WALLING, R. A. J.
The Corpse in the Coppice. New York: 1935. V. 68
The Corpse with the Blistered Hand. 1939. V. 73
The Corpse with the Eerie Eye. 1942. V. 73
The Corpse with the Eerie Eye. New York: 1942. V. 69
The Corpse with the Floating Foot. New York: 1936. V. 70
The Corpse with the Red-Headed Friend. New York: 1939. V. 68
The Corpse Without a Clue. New York: 1944. V. 68
In Time for Murder. New York: 1933. V. 69
The Late Unlamented. London: 1948. V. 68
Stroke of One. 1931. V. 68

WALLIS, GEORGE
The Art of Preventing Diseases and Restoring Health.... London: 1793. V. 70

WALLIS, GEORGE A.
Cattle Kings of the Great Plains. Dallas: 1957. V. 71

WALLIS, JOHN
Grammatica Lingaue Anglicanae.... London: 1765. V. 72
A Treatise of Algebra, Both Historical and Practical. London: 1685. V. 71

WALLIS, JONNIE LOCKHART
Sixty Years on the Brazos. Los Angeles: 1930. V. 73

WALLIS, MICHAEL
Pretty Boy; The Life and Times of Charles Arthur Floyd. New York: 1992. V. 72

WALLIS, N.
The Carpenter's Treasure, a Collection of Designs for Temples. London: 1795. V. 68; 70; 72

WALLIS, RUTH SAWTELL
Too Many Bones. 1943. V. 73

WALLS, J. G.
Encyclopedia of Marine Invertebartes. Neptune City: 1982. V. 73

WALMSLEY, HUGH MULLENEUX
Branksome Dene; a Sea Tale. London: 1873. V. 68

WALMSLEY, LEO
So Many Loves - an Autobiography. London: 1944. V. 68

WALPERS, GUILIELMO GERARDO
Annales Botanices Systematicae. Leipzig: 1848-1871. V. 72

WALPOLE, HORACE
Anecdotes of Painting in England. London: 1876. V. 71
Anecdotes of Painting in England.... London: 1826-1828. V. 73
The Castle of Otranto, a Gothic Story. London: 1782. V. 71; 73
The Castle of Otranto, a Gothic Story. London: 1791. V. 69
The Castle of Otranto, a Gothic Story. Parma: 1791. V. 68
The Castle of Otranto. A Gothic Story. Berlin: 1794. V. 69
A Catalogue of the Classic Contents of Strawberry Hill, Collected by Horace Walpole. 1842. V. 70
A Catalogue of the Royal and Noble Authors of England, Scotland and Ireland; with Lists of Their Works. London: 1806. V. 69
A Catalogue of the Royal and Noble Authors of England, with a List of Their Works. Edinburgh: 1796. V. 70
A Catalogue of the Royal and Noble Authors of England.... 1758. V. 69; 70; 72
A Catalogue of the Royal and Noble Authors. (with) Memoirs of the Reign of King George the Second. (with) The Letters of Horace Walpole. London: 1806. V. 73
A Description of the Villa...at Strawberry Hill Near Twickenham, Middlesex, with an Inventory of the Furniture, Pictures, Curiosities &c. Strawberry Hill;: 1784. V. 72
Essay on Modern Gardening. Strawberry Hill: 1785. V. 68
Essay on Modern Gardening. Canton: 1904. V. 69; 71
Historic Doubts on the Life and Reign of King Richard the Third. London: 1768. V. 69; 72
The Impenetrable Secret.... Farmington: 1939. V. 68
Journal of the Printing Office at Strawberry Hill, Now First printed from the MS. of Horace Walpole. London: 1923. V. 70
The Letters. Edinburgh: 1906. V. 73

WALPOLE, HORACE continued
Letters from the Hon. Horace Walpole to George Montagu, Esq. from the year 1736, to the year 1770... London: 1818. V. 71; 72
Letters from the Hon. Horace Walpole, to the Rev. William Cole, and others; from the year 1745, to the year 1782. London: 1818. V. 71
The Letters.... London: 1861-1866. V. 69
Letters.... London: 1880. V. 68; 72
Memoires of the Last Ten Years of the Reign of George the Second. London: 1822. V. 73
Memoirs of the Reign of King George the Second. London: 1847. V. 71
The Mysterious Mother: a Tragedy. Dublin: 1791. V. 72
Strawberry Hill, the Renowned Seat of Horace Walpole. Mr. George Robins is Honoured by Having Been Selected by the Earl of Waldegrave to Sell by Public Competition, the Valuable Contents of Strawberry Hill...Monday the 25th day of April 1843.... London: 1842. V. 73
Walpoliana. London: 1799. V. 69
The Works of Horace Walpole, the Earl of Orford. London: 1798. V. 70; 71

WALPOLE, HUGH
Above the Dark Circus. London: 1931. V. 71
Above the Dark Tumult. Garden City: 1931. V. 70
All Souls' Night - A Book of Stories. London: 1933. V. 72
The Apple Trees: Four Reminiscences. Waltham St. Lawrence: 1932. V. 71
Captain Nicholas. Garden City: 1934. V. 71
Captain Nicholas. London: 1934. V. 71
The Fortress. London: 1931. V. 71
Harmer John. London: 1926. V. 71
The Joyful Delaneys, a Novel. London: 1938. V. 70
Judith Paris. New York: 1931. V. 71
A Prayer for My Son. London: 1936. V. 69; 70
Reading. London: 1926. V. 70
Roman Fountain. London: 1940. V. 71
The Sea Tower. London: 1939. V. 70
Seven Pillars of Wisdom: T. E. Lawrence in Life and Death. London: 1985. V. 68
An Unworldly Story. New York: 1926. V. 69
Vanessa. London: 1933. V. 71
Wintersmoon. London: 1928. V. 71
The Wooden Horse. London: 1909. V. 72

WALPOLE, ROBERT
A Letter to the Right Honourable Robert Wapole, Esq. Occasioned by His Late Promotion to the Offices of First Lord of the Treasury and Chancelor of the Exchequer. London: 1716. V. 70
A Short History of the Parliament. 1713. V. 72
Some Considerations Concerning the Publick Funds, the Publick Revenues, and Annual Supplies, Granted by Parliament. London: 1735. V. 68; 72

WALPOLE, SPENCER
A History of England from the Conclusion of the Great War in 1815. London: 1878-1880. V. 71

WALPOLE BOND, J.
A History of Sussex Birds. 1938. V. 69

WALSDORF, J. J.
Julian Symons: a Bibliography. 1996. V. 70

WALSER, RICHARD
The Black Poet: Being the Remarkable Story (partly told by himself) of George Moses Horton a North Carolina Slave. New York: 1966. V. 71

WALSH, C.
Early Days on the Western Range - a Pastoral Narrative. Boston: 1917. V. 69

WALSH, J. C.
The Invincible Irish. New York: 1919. V. 70

WALSH, J. H.
The Dog in Health and Disease. 1867. V. 68; 70
The Dogs of the British Islands. 1872. V. 68
The English Cookery Book. London: 1859. V. 68

WALSH, J. M.
Spies in Spain. London: 1937. V. 73

WALSH, RAY
The Mycroft Memoranda. London: 1984. V. 70

WALSH, RICHARD J.
Kiddie-Kar Book. Philadelphia: 1920. V. 69; 73
The Making of Buffalo Bill. New York: 1928. V. 69

WALSH, ROBERT
The American Review of History and Politics...Of Literature and State Papers. Philadelphia: 1811-1812. V. 71

WALSH, THOMAS
Dangerous Passenger. Boston and Toronto: 1959. V. 73

WALSH, VICOMTE
Lettres sur l'Angleterre ou Voyage dans la Grande Bretagne en 1829. Paris: 1830. V. 70

WALSH, WILLIAM
A Dialogue Concerning Woman Being a Defense of Sex, Written to Eugenia. London: 1691. V. 69; 72

WALSHAM, HUGH
The Rontgen Rays in the Diagnosis of Diseases of the Chest. London: 1906. V. 68

WALSINGHAM, LORD
Hit and Miss. A Book of Shooting Memories. 1927. V. 71

WALTER, BAKER
Chocolate-Plant (Theobroma Cacao) and Its Products. Dorchester: 1891. V. 72

WALTER, J.
Luger. 1986. V. 71

WALTER, J. CONWAY
Records Historical and Antiquarian, of Parishes Round Horncastle. Horncastle: 1904. V. 70
Records of Woodhall Spa and Neighbourhood.... Horncastle: 1899. V. 70; 71

WALTER, JOHANN GOTTLIEB
Tabulae Nervorum Thoracis et Abdominis. Berlin: 1783. V. 70

WALTER, RICHARD
A Voyage Round the World in the Years 1740, 1741, 1742, 1743, 1744... Compiled From His Papers and Materials by Richard Walter. London: 1828. V. 72
A Voyage Round the World. In the Years MDCCXL, I, II, III, IV. London: 1767. V. 72

WALTERS, J. CUMING
Clues to Dickens's Mystery of Edwin Drood. London: 1905. V. 69
The Complete Edwin Drood. London: 1912. V. 69

WALTERS, L. D'O.
The Year's at the Spring. London: 1920. V. 69; 71; 73

WALTERS, LORENZO D.
Tombstone's Yesterday. Tucson: 1928. V. 70

WALTERS, MINETTE
The Breaker. London: 1998. V. 68; 69
The Dark Room. London: 1995. V. 68; 69
The Dark Room. New York: 1995. V. 73
The Dark Room. New York: 1996. V. 69
The Echo. London: 1997. V. 68; 69; 71; 72
The Ice House. London: 1992. V. 69
The Ice House. New York: 1992. V. 68; 69; 71; 73
The Scold's Bridle. Bristol: 1994. V. 68; 69; 70; 71; 73
The Scold's Bridle. London: 1994. V. 68; 69; 70; 71; 72; 73
The Scold's Bridle. New York: 1994. V. 71; 73
The Sculptress. London: 1993. V. 68; 69; 70; 71; 72; 73
The Sculptress. New York: 1993. V. 68; 69; 71; 73

WALTERS, S. M.
The European Garden Flora.... Cambridge: 1989. V. 71

WALTERSKIRCHEN, KATALIN DE
Maurice de Vlaminck: Catalogue Raisonne de l'Oevure Grave. Paris: 1974. V. 72

WALTHAM, JAMES
Classic Salmon Flies. The Francis Francis Collection. 1983. V. 68; 73

WALTHER, THOMAS
Other Pictures: Anonymous Photographs from the Thomas Walther Collection. Santa Fe: 2000. V. 68

WALTON, BRYCE
Sons of the Ocean Deep. Philadelphia: 1952. V. 69

WALTON, EDA LOU
Dawn Boy: Blackfoot and Navajo Songs. New York: 1926. V. 68; 69

WALTON, ELIJAH
English Lake Scenery. 1876. V. 72
English Lake Scenery. London: 1876. V. 71

WALTON, EVANGELINE
The Virgin and the Swine. New York: 1936. V. 70

WALTON, HANES
Black Political Parties: An Historical and Political Analysis. New York: 1972. V. 72

WALTON, IZAAK
Compleat Angler. London: 1876. V. 69
The Compleat Angler. 1897. V. 69
The Compleat Angler. London: 1929. V. 68
The Compleat Angler. London: 1931. V. 68; 69; 70; 71
The Compleat Angler. New York: 1948. V. 69
The Compleat Angler. 1976. V. 68
The Complete Angler. London: 1784. V. 69
The Complete Angler. London: 1792. V. 73
The Complete Angler. 1808. V. 68; 73
The Complete Angler. London: 1808. V. 69
The Complete Angler. London: 1825. V. 68
Complete Angler. London and Glasgow: 1826. V. 69
The Complete Angler. London: 1836. V. 73
The Complete Angler. London: 1844. V. 68
The Complete Angler. New York: 1848. V. 68; 69
The Complete Angler. 1853. V. 73
The Lives of Dr. Donne, Sir Henry Wotton, Mr. Richard Hooker, Mr. George Herbert, Dr. Sanderson. London: 1847. V. 72
The Lives of Dr. John Donne; Sir Henry Wotton; Mr. Richard Hooker; Mr. George Herbert and Dr. Robert Sanderson.... York: 1796. V. 73

WALTON, IZAAK continued
The Lives Of Mr. Richard Hooker, Mr. George Herbert, And Dr. Robert Sanderson. London: 1847. V. 72
Waltoniana. London: 1878. V. 72

WALTON, W. M.
Life and Adventures of Ben Thompson. Houston: 1954. V. 69
Life and Adventures of Ben Thompson the Famous Texan. Austin: 1956. V. 70; 73

WALZER, R.
Galen on Medical Experience. London: 1944. V. 68

WAMBAUGH, JOSEPH
The Choirboys. New York: 1975. V. 69
The New Centurions. Bston: 1970. V. 69
The Onion Field. New York: 1973. V. 69

WAMPEN, HENRY
Mathematical Instruction in Constructing Models, for Draping the Human Figure. 1853. V. 73
Mathematical Instruction, in Constructing Models, for Draping the Human Figure. London: 1853. V. 69

WANDREI, DONALD
The Eye and the Finger. 1944. V. 69
Poems for Midnight. Sauk City: 1964. V. 69

WANG, F.
Cycads in China. Guangzhou: 1996. V. 72

WANG, G. H.
The Neural Control of Sweating. Madison: 1964. V. 68

WAR PICTURES by British Artists. London: 1942. V. 70; 72

WARBURTON, ELIOT
The Crescent and the Cross, or the Romance and Realities of Eastern Travel. London: 1845. V. 70
Hochelaga; or England in The New World. London: 1846. V. 72
Hochelaga; or, England in the New World. London: 1847. V. 68

WARBURTON, JOHN
Vallum Romanum; or, the History and Antiquities of the Roman Wall, Commonly Called the Picts Wall, in Cumberland and Northumberland.... London: 1753. V. 71

WARBURTON, PETER EGERTON
Journey Across the Western Interior of Australia. London: 1875. V. 69; 71

WARBURTON, R. E. EGERTON
Hunting Songs. London: 1925. V. 73

WARBURTON, ROBERT
Eighteen Years in the Khyber 1879-1898. 1900. V. 73

WARBURTON, STANLEY
An Avatar in Vishnu Land. New York: 1928. V. 68

WARD, ARTEMUS
Encyclopedia of Food. New York: 1929. V. 70
The Grocer's Companion and Merchant's Hand-Book. Boston: 1883. V. 73
The Grocers' Hand-Book and Directory for 1883. Philadelphia: 1883. V. 69

WARD BROTHERS
Souvenir of Minneapolis. Columbus: 1885. V. 71

WARD, C.
Royal Gardens. London: 1912. V. 73

WARD, C. OSBORNE
The Ancient Lowly. Chicago: 1907. V. 73
A History of Ancient Working People. Washington: 1889. V. 71

WARD, CAROLINE
Marco Visconti: a Romance of the Fourteenth Century.... London: 1836. V. 69

WARD, CATHARINE GEORGE
Tales of the Glen, etc. London: 1813. V. 69

WARD, DALLAS T.
The Last Flag of Truce. Franklinton: 1915. V. 69; 70

WARD, EDWARD
A Collection of Historical and State Poems, Satyrs, songs and Epigrams.. London: 1717. V. 71
Hudibras Revivivus; or, a Burlesque Poems on the Times. London: 1705-1707. V. 69
Nuptial Dialogues and Debates; or, a Useful Prospect of the Felicities and Discomforts of a Marry'd Life. London: 1710. V. 69; 72
Nuptial Dialogues and Debates; or a Useful Prospect of the Felicities and Discomforts of a Marry'd Life.... London: 1723. V. 72
The Secret History of the Calves-Head Club, Complt. London: 1705. V. 71

WARD, EVELYN D.
The Children of Bladensfield. New York: 1978. V. 70

WARD, FAY E.
The Cowboy at Work. New York: 1958. V. 69

WARD, FRANCIS
An Account of Three Camp-Meetings, Held by the Methodists, at Sharon, in Litchfield County, Connecticut, at Rhinebeck, in Cutchess County, and at Petersburgh, in Rensselaer County, New York State. Brooklyn: 1806. V. 71

WARD, FRANCIS KINGDON
Plant Hunter's Paradise. 1938. V. 68

WARD, FREDERICK
Riverlisp: Black Memories. New York: 1974. V. 72

WARD, GENEVIEVE
Memoir of Ginerva Guerrabella. New York: 1863. V. 72

WARD, H. G.
Mexico in 1827. London: 1828. V. 70

WARD, H. L. D.
Catalogue of Romances in the Department of Manuscripts in the British Museum. London: 1961-1962. V. 70

WARD, H. M.
The Ginger-Bear Plant and the Organisms Composing It.... London: 1892. V. 72

WARD, HENSHAW
Charles Darwin. The Man and His Warfare. London: 1927. V. 68

WARD, J.
Workmen and Wages At Home and Abroad, or The Effects of Strikes, Combinations and Trades' Unions. London: 1868. V. 71

WARD, J. H.
Steam for the Million. New York: 1860. V. 69

WARD, JAMES
Colour Decoration of Architecture, Treating on Colour and Decoration of the Interiors and Exteriors of Buildings.... London: 1913. V. 72

WARD, JOHN
The Lives of the Professors of Gresham College.... London: 1740. V. 71
Nelson, the Latest Settlement of the New Zealand Company. London: 1842. V. 68; 72
The Young Mathematician's Guide. London: 1719. V. 69; 73

WARD, JOHN MONTGOMERY
Base-Ball. How to Become a Player with the Origin, History and Explanation of the Game. Philadelphia: 1888. V. 68; 70

WARD, LESTER F.
Glimpses of the Cosmos. New York: 1913-1917. V. 69

WARD, LYND
The Biggest Bear. Boston: 1952. V. 73
God's Man. New York: 1929. V. 69
God's Man. New York: 1933. V. 68
Madman's Drum. London: 1930. V. 70; 71
Madman's Drum. New York: 1930. V. 68; 70; 72
One of Us. The Story of John Reed. New York: 1935. V. 72
Wild Pilgrimage. New York: 1932. V. 73

WARD, MARY
The Miscroscope. London: 1869. V. 68

WARD, MARY AUGUSTA ARNOLD
Helbeck of Bannisdale. London: 1898. V. 71
The History of David Grace. London: 1892. V. 73
The Marriage of William Ashe. London: 1905. V. 70; 71
Unitarians and the Future. London: 1894. V. 69

WARD, MICHAEL
In This Short Span. London: 1972. V. 69
Mountain Medicine. London: 1975. V. 69
The Mountaineer's Companion. London: 1966. V. 69

WARD, NED
The London-Spy Compleat. London: 1924. V. 69; 72; 73

WARD, R.
The Buxton, Matlock and Castleton Guide. Wirksworth: 1818. V. 70; 72

WARD, ROBERT
Anima'dversions of Warre; or, a Militarie Magazine of the Truest Rules, and Ablest Instructions, for the Managing of Warre. London: 1639. V. 68

WARD, ROBERT ARTHUR
A Treatise on Investments: Being a Popular Exposition of the Advantages and Disadvantages of Each Kind of Investment and Of its Liability to Depreciation and Loss. London: 1852. V. 73

WARD, ROBERT PLUMER
De Vere; or the Man of Independence. London: 1827. V. 68; 72
Tremaine, or the Man of Refinement. London: 1825. V. 68; 72; 73

WARD, ROWLAND
Records of Big Game. 1819,. V. 73
Records of Big Game. 1903. V. 72; 73
Records of Big Game. 1910. V. 69; 70; 72
Records of Big Game. 1914. V. 69; 70; 72; 73
Records of Big Game. 1928. V. 69; 70; 72; 73
The Sportsman's Handbook to Practical Collecting and Preserving Trophies. 1891. V. 69; 70; 72; 73
The Sportsman's Handbook to Practical Collecting and Preserving Trophies. 1911. V. 69; 70; 73
The Sportsman's Handbook to Practical Collecting and Preserving Trophies. 1923. V. 69; 70; 72; 73

WARD, THOMAS
England's Reformation (from the Time of K. Hery VIII to the End of Oates's Plot). London: 1715. V. 69

WARD, VAUGHN
I Always Tell the Truth (Even If I Have to Lie to Do It!). Greenfield Center: 1990. V. 68

WARD, W. H.
A History of the Manor and Parish of Iver. London: 1933. V. 71

WARD, WILLIAM
A View of the History, Literature and Religion of the Hindoos.... London: 1817. V. 69
A View of the History, Literature, and Religion of the Hindoos.... Hartford: 1824. V. 69

WARDEN, ERNEST
Thrilling Tales of Kansas 1861-1932. Wichita: 1932. V. 73

WARDEN, FLORENCE
The Mystery of Dudley Horne. London: 1899. V. 68
A Wild Wooing. London: 1894. V. 68
A Woman's Face. London: 1890. V. 68

WARDEN, R. D.
C. M. Russell - Boyhood Sketchbook. 1972. V. 70

WARDEN, WILLIAM
Letters Written On Board His Majesty's Ship the Northumberland, and at Saint Helena.... London: 1816. V. 70

WARDER, T. B.
The Battle of Young's Branch; or, Manassas Plain, Fought July 21, 1861.... Richmond: 1862. V. 69

WARDLE, THOMAS
Royal Commission on Technical Instruction. Report on the English Silk Industry. London: 1885. V. 71
Silk: Its Entomology, Industry and Manufacture as Exemplified at the Royal Jubilee Exhibition. London: 1887. V. 71

WARDROP, A. E.
Days and Nights with Indian Big Game. 1923. V. 70; 72; 73
Modern Pig Sticking. 1914. V. 70; 72; 73
Modern Pig Sticking. London: 1914. V. 69

WARDROP, JAMES
The Morbid Anatomy of the Human Eye. London: 1834. V. 73

WARE, GILBERT
William Hastie: Grace Under Pressure. New York: 1984. V. 72

WARE, HENRY
Papers on the Diaries of William Nicolson, Sometime Bishop of Carlisle. Kendal: 1905. V. 71

WARE, WILLIAM
Pictures of European Capitals. London: 1852?. V. 68; 73
Probus; or Rome in the Third Century. New York: 1838. V. 68; 73

WAREING, CHARLES
Bugles for Beiderbecke. London: 1958. V. 73

WARFIELD, EDGAR
A Confederate Soldier's Memoirs. Richmond: 1936. V. 69; 70

WARFIELD, JOSHUA D.
The Founders of Anne Arundel and Howard Counties, Maryland. Baltimore: 1905. V. 71

WARHOL, ANDY
America. New York: 1985. V. 73
Exposures. New York: 1979. V. 68; 69; 72
Flash, November 22, 1963. New York: 1968. V. 70
The Philosophy of Andy Warhol. New York: 1975. V. 72; 73

WARING AND GILLOW
Decorative Contracts. London: 1907. V. 68
Italian Art. London: 1906. V. 72

WARING, R. A.
Su-Lin, the Real Story of a Baby Giant Panda. New York: 1937. V. 72

WARING, S.
The Wild Garland. London: 1827. V. 71

WARK, ROBERT R.
Drawings of Thomas Rolandson in the Huntington Collection. San Marino: 1975. V. 70

WARMAN, CY
Frontier Stories. New York: 1898. V. 73
Snow on Headlights. New York: 1899. V. 68

WARMESTRY, THOMAS
A Convocation Speech...Against Images, Altars, Crosses, the New Canons and the Oath &c. London: 1641. V. 70; 72

WARN, REUBEN HENRY
The Sheet Metal Worker's Instructor. London: 1884. V. 71
The Sheet Metal Worker's Instructor. 1890. V. 71

WARNER, ANNE
Your Child and Mine. Boston: 1909. V. 71

WARNER, CHARLES DUDLEY
Backlog Studies. Boston: 1873. V. 68
Charles Dickens. An Appreciation. Newark: 1913. V. 69
Complete Writings of Charles Dudley Warner. Hartford: 1904. V. 68

WARNER, FERDINANDO
A Full and Plain Account of the Gout, From Whence Will Be Clearly Seen, the Folly or the Baseness, of All Pretenders to the Cure of It.... London: 1768. V. 73
Memoirs of the Life of Sir Thomas More.... London: 1758. V. 73

WARNER, J. J.
An Historical Sketch of Los Angeles County, California: from the Spanish Occupancy, by the Founding of the Mission San Gabriel Archangel Sept. 8, 1771 to July 4, 1876. Los Angeles: 1876. V. 70
An Historical Sketch of Los Angeles County, California: from the Spanish Occupancy, by the Founding of the Mission San Gabriel Archangel Sept. 8, 1771 to July 4, 1876. Los Angeles: 1936. V. 68; 69

WARNER, OPIE L.
A Pardoned Lifer- Life of George Sontag, Forgotten Member of The Notorious Evane-Sontag Gang. San Bernardino: 1909. V. 71

WARNER, P. F.
Cricket Reminiscences with Some Review of the 1919 Season. London: 1920. V. 72
Imperial Cricket. 1912. V. 69

WARNER, RICHARD
Excursions from Bath. Bath: 1801. V. 68; 70; 72
An Illustration of the Roman Antiquities Discovered at Bath. Bath: 1797. V. 68; 70

WARNER, ROBERT
Select Orchidaceous Plants. Jacksonville: 1975. V. 73

WARNER, SYLVIA TOWNSEND
Azrael and Other Poems. 1978. V. 71
Elinor Barley. 1930. V. 71
Elinor Barley. London: 1930. V. 73
Mr. Fortune's Maggot. London: 1927. V. 72
A Spirit Rises. London: 1962. V. 71
The True Heart. London: 1929. V. 71
The Week-End Dickens. London: 1932. V. 69

WARNS, MELVIN OWEN
The Nevada Sixteen National Banks and Their Mining Camps. Washington: 1974. V. 69

WARREN, C. HENRY
Tide's Ending. London: 1950. V. 71

WARREN, CHARLES
The Supreme Court in United States History. Boston: 1924. V. 71
The Supreme Court in United States History. Boston: 1926. V. 72

WARREN, CHARLES MARQUIS
Deadhead. New York: 1949. V. 69

WARREN COMMISSION
The Official Warren Commission Report on the Assassination of President John F. Kennedy. Garden City: 1964. V. 68; 69; 71

WARREN, E. PRIOLEAU
The Wanderings Of The Beetle. London. V. 72

WARREN, EARL
The Public Papers of Chief Justice. New York: 1959. V. 69

WARREN, EDWARD H.
Shakespeare in Wall Street. Boston: 1929. V. 69

WARREN, ELIZA SPAULDING
Memories of the West. Portland: 1917. V. 68

WARREN, ELIZABETH
Spiritual Thrift. London: 1647. V. 68

WARREN, F. E.
The Liturgy and Ritual of the Celtic Church. 1881. V. 69
The Manuscript Irish Missal Belonging to the President and Fellows of Corpus Christi College, Oxford. 1879. V. 70

WARREN, G. K.
Report on Bridging the Mississippi River Between Saint Paul, Minnesota and St. Louis, Missouri. Washington: 1878. V. 73

WARREN, GEOFFREY C.
Elixir of Life (Uisge Beatha) being a Slight Account of the Romantic Rise to fame of a great House. Dublin: 1925. V. 72

WARREN, GEORGE
A Disquisition on the Nature and Properties of Living Animals. London: 1828. V. 73

WARREN, HENRY M.
To and From. Philadlephia: 1908. V. 68

WARREN, J. M.
The Frontal Granular Cortex and Behaviour. New York: 1964. V. 68

WARREN, J. MASON
Rhinoplastic Operations. Boston: 1840. V. 73
Surgical Observations with Cases and Observations. Boston: 1867. V. 68; 70; 71; 73

WARREN, JANE S.
The Morning Star: History of the Children's Missionary Vessel and of the Marquesan and Micronesian Missions. Boston: 1860. V. 70; 72

WARREN, JOHN COLLINS
The Healing of Arteries After Ligatures in Man and Animal. New York: 1886. V. 70
A Letter Addressed to a Republican Member of the House of Representatives of the State of Massachusetts on the Subject of a Petition for a New Incorporation.... Boston: 1812. V. 70
Physical Education and the Preservation of Health. Boston: 1846. V. 71

WARREN, JOSEPH
The General. New York: 1927. V. 71
Revenge. New York: 1928. V. 69; 71; 73

WARREN, KATHERINE BREHME
The Neuron. Cold Spring Harbor Symposia on Quantitative Biology. New York: 1952. V. 68

WARREN, MAUD R.
Tales Told by the Gander. London: 1922. V. 72

WARREN, MRS.
Time Thrift; or, All Hours Turned to Good Account. London: 1851. V. 68

WARREN, ROBERT PENN
All the King's Men. New York: 1946. V. 70; 71; 73
All the King's Men. New York: 1960. V. 68
All the King's Men. Franklin Center: 1977. V. 69
All the King's Men. 1989. V. 70; 72
At Heaven's Gate. New York: 1943. V. 69; 70; 72
At Heaven's Gate. New York: 1949. V. 72
Ballad of a Sweet Dream of Peace: a Charade for Peace. Dallas: 1980. V. 71; 72
Band of Angels. New York: 1955. V. 68; 70
Being Here. Poetry 1977-1980. New York: 1980. V. 68
The Cave. New York: 1959. V. 73
Chief Joseph of the Nez Perce. New York: 1983. V. 72; 73
Flood. New York: 1964. V. 69
Fugitives. New York: 1928. V. 72
The Gods of Mount Olympus. New York: 1959. V. 69; 71
Incarnations: Poems 1966-1968. New York: 1968. V. 69
Jefferson Davis Gets His Citizenship Back. Lexington: 1980. V. 69
John Brown: The Making of a Martyr. New York: 1929. V. 70
New and Selected Poems 1923-1985. Franklin Center: 1985. V. 68
New and Selected Poems 1923-1985. New York: 1985. V. 68; 71
Now and Then. Poems 1976-1978. New York: 1978. V. 71; 73
Or Else-Poem/Poems 1968-1974. New York: 1974. V. 71
A Place to Come To. New York: 1977. V. 68
A Plea in Migration: Modern Poetry and the End of the Era. Macon: 1966. V. 69
Promises. Poems 1954-1956. New York: 1957. V. 71; 73
Remember the Alamo!. New York: 1958. V. 70; 71; 73
Selected Poems. 1923-1943. New York: 1947. V. 72
Selected Poems 1923-1975. New York: 1976. V. 69
Selected Poems: New and Old, 1923-1966. New York: 1966. V. 71
Who Speaks for the Negro?. New York: 1965. V. 69
Wilderness. New York: 1961. V. 70
William Faulkner and His South. 1951. V. 73

WARREN, SAMUEL
Ten Thousand a Year. Edinburgh and London: 1841. V. 68; 71; 73
Works. Edinburgh and London: 1854. V. 73

WARTIME Harvest. 1943. V. 68

WARTON, JOSEPH
An Essay on the Genius and Writings of Pope. London: 1762. V. 69

WARTON, THOMAS
An Enquiry into the Authenticity of the Poems Attributed to Thomas Rowley. London: 1782. V. 69
The History and Antiquities of Kiddington.... London: 1815. V. 68
Observations on the Fairy Queen of Spenser. London: 1762. V. 69
Poems. London: 1777. V. 71
The Poems on Various Subjects.... London: 1791. V. 71
Specimen of a History of Oxfordshire. London: 1783. V. 68; 72

WARWICK, COUNTESS OF
Warwick Castle and Its Earls, from Saxon Times.... New York and London: 1905?. V. 69

WARWICK, PHILIP
Memoires of the Reign of King Charles I...Together with a Continuation to the Happy Restauration of King Charles II. London: 1709. V. 71

WASHBOURN, JOHN
Bibliotheca Gloucestrensis; a Collection of Scarce and Curious Tracts.... Gloucester: 1825. V. 70; 72

WASHBURN, ROBERT COLLYER
The Jury of Death. Garden City: 1930. V. 69; 71; 73

WASHBURNE, MARION F.
Old Fashioned Fairy Tales. Chicago: 1927. V. 68

WASHINGTON, BOOKER T.
The Future of the American Negro. Boston: 1899. V. 68; 70
The Future of the American Negro. Boston: 1900. V. 72
The Man Farthest Down. London: 1912. V. 71
My Larger Education, Being Chapters from My Experience. London: 1911. V. 70
The Negro and the Solid South. Cheyney: 1900. V. 70
The Negro in the South. Philadelphia: 1907. V. 69
Tuskegee and Its People: Their Ideals and Achievements. New York: 1906. V. 68; 70
Up from Slavery. New York: 1901. V. 69; 71; 72
Up From Slavery. New York: 1970. V. 72
Working with the Hands. New York: 1904. V. 71; 72

WASHINGTON, BUSHROD
Reports of Cases Argued and Determined in the Court of Appeals of Virginia.... Richmond: 1798-1799. V. 73

WASHINGTON, GEORGE
Letters from His Excellency George Washington to Arthur Young, Esq., FRS.... London: 1801. V. 68
A Message of the President of the United States, to Congress Relative to France and Great Britain: Delivered December 5, 1793. Philadelphia: 1795. V. 68
Washington's Monuments of Patriotism. Philadelphia: 1800. V. 73

WASHINGTON, H. A.
The Virginia Constitution of 1776. Richmond: 1852. V. 70

WASMANN, ERICH
Modern Biology and the Theory of Evolution. London: 1910. V. 69

WASSERMAN, JACOB
Kerkhoven's Third Existence. New York: 1934. V. 69

WASSERSTEIN, WENDY
The Heidi Chronicles and Other Plays. New York: 1990. V. 71
The Sisters Rosensweig. New York: 1993. V. 71

WASSON, A. GORDON
The Hall Carbine Affair. A Study in Contemporary Folklore. New York: 1948. V. 73

WASSON, R. GORDON
Maria Sabina and Her Mazatec Mushroom Velada. New York: 1974. V. 70; 71

WATCH & Clock Makers' Handbook, Dictionary and Guide. London: 1938. V. 72

THE WATER-Colours of Turner, Cox & De Wint. London: 1925. V. 72

WATERFIELD, MARGARET
Flower Grouping in English, Scotch and Irish Gardens. London: 1907. V. 70

WATERHOUSE, BENJAMIN
A Prospect of Exterminating the Small-Pox.... Boston: 1800. V. 68; 73
A Synopsis of a Course of Lectures, on the Theory and Practice of Medicine. Boston: 1786. V. 68

WATERHOUSE, JOSHUA
Narrative of the Murder of the Late Rev. J. Waterhouse; with a Full Report of the Trial, Confession and Execution of the Murderer (Joshua Slade) and a Biography and Anecdotes of Mr. Waterhouse and of Slade. Huntingdon: 1827. V. 72

WATERMAN, CATHARINE H.
The Book of Parlour Games. Philadelphia: 1853. V. 71

WATERMAN, T. H.
The Physiology of Crustacea. New York: 1960-1961. V. 73

THE WATERS of the Earth. London: 1840. V. 68

WATERS, C. E.
Ferns, a Manual for the Northeastern States.... New York: 1903. V. 72; 73

WATERS, FRANK
Book of the Hopi. New York: 1963. V. 69; 72
Brave Are My People. Sante Fe: 1993. V. 71
The Colorado. New York: 1946. V. 69
Flight from Fiesta. Santa Fe: 1986. V. 71
Leon Gaspard. Flagstaff: 1964. V. 69
The Man Who Killed the Deer. Denver: 1950. V. 69
Masked Gods. Navaho and Pueblo Ceremonialism. 1950. V. 68
Masked Gods: Navaho and Pueblo Ceremonialism. Albuquerque: 1950. V. 69; 73

WATERS, T. FRANK
Candlewood. Salem: 1909. V. 68

WATERS, THOMAS
The Reflections of a Policeman. Boston: 1856. V. 71

WATERS, WILLARD O.
Franciscan Missions of Upper California as Seen by Foreign Visitors and Residents: a Chronological List of Printed Accounts 1786-1848. Los Angeles: 1954. V. 73

WATERS, WILLIAM
A Short Account of the Christian Experience and Ministerial Labours of William Waters. Alexandria: 1806. V. 68

WATERSCAPES, Landscapes. East Hampton: 1999. V. 71

WATERSTON, JOHN JAMES
On the physics of media that are composed of free and perfectly elastic molecules in a state of motion. London: 1892. V. 72

WATERTON, CHARLES
Essays on Natural History, Chiefly Ornithology. Second Series.... London: 1844. V. 68
Essays on Natural History...Second Series. (with) Essays...Third Series. London: 1851-1858. V. 71

WATERTON, CHARLES continued
Letters of Charles Waterton of Walton Hall, Near Wakefield, Naturalist, Taxidermist.... London: 1955. V. 68
Wanderings in South America. London: 1828. V. 68; 71
Wanderings in South America. London: 1893. V. 72

WATERWORTH, W.
Origin and Developments of Anglicanism, or a History of the Liturgies, Homilies, Articles, Bibles, Principles and Governmental System of the Church of England. London: 1854. V. 68

WATHEN, DAVID
Harehunters. 1951. V. 68

WATHEN, JONATHAN
The Conductor and Containing Splits; or, a Description of Two Instruments, for the Safer Conveyance and More Perfect Cure of Fractured Legs.... London: 1781. V. 72

WATHERSTON, JAMES H.
The Gold Valuer: being a Table for Ascertaining the Value of Gold.... London: 1852. V. 71

WATKINS, FRANCIS
A Popular Sketch of Electro-Magnetism, or Electro-Dynamics.... 1856. V. 71

WATKINS, FRANCIS N.
A Catalogue of the Descendants of Thomas Watkins of Chickahomony, Virginia. Henderson: 1899. V. 73

WATKINS, GEORGE
The Mill Engine. Newton Abbot: 1970. V. 70

WATKINS, JOEL-PETER
Harms Way. Santa Fe: 1994. V. 72

WATKINS, JOHN
Memoirs of the Public and Private Life of R. B. Sheridan. 1817. V. 69

WATKINS, LOUISE WARD
Henry Edwards Huntington, a Character Sketch of a Great Man. Gardenia: 1928. V. 71

WATKINS, PAUL
Archangel. New York: 1995. V. 71
Calm at Sunset, Calm at Dawn. Boston: 1989. V. 68
Night Over Day Over Night. New York: 1988. V. 68; 69; 70
The Promise of Light. London: 1992. V. 68

WATKINS, PSEUD.
Hada, the Hindu; and Other Tales. Glasgow: 1883. V. 68

WATKINS, SAM. R.
Co. Aytch, Maury Grays, First Tennessee Regiment; or Side Show of the Big Show. Chattanooga: 1900. V. 69; 70

WATKINS, T. H.
The Grand Colorado: The Story of a River and Its Canyons. Palo Alto: 1969. V. 69

WATKINS, VERNON
Selected Verse Translations. London: 1977. V. 70

WATKINS-PITCHFORD, DENYS
The Little Grey Men. New York: 1949. V. 70

WATNEY, BERNARD
English Blue and White Porcelain of Eighteenth Century. London: 1979. V. 72
Longton Hall Porcelain. London: 1957. V. 72

WATNEY, VERNON J.
Cornbury and the Forest of Wychwood. London: 1910. V. 72

WATROUS, ANSEL
History of Larimer County, Colorado. 1911. V. 68

WATSON, A.
An Illustrated Catalog of the Neotropic Arctiinae Types in the United States National Museum (Lepidoptera Arctiidae). Washington: 1971-1973. V. 72

WATSON, A. E. T.
King Edward VII as a Sportsman. 1911. V. 70; 71
Racecourse and Covert Side. London: 1882. V. 69

WATSON, ARTHUR C.
The Long Harpoon, a Collection of Whaling Anecdotes. New Bedford: 1929. V. 69

WATSON, COLIN
Bump in the Night. New York: 1961. V. 69
Coffin Scarcely Used. London: 1958. V. 70
Hopjoy Was Here. London: 1962. V. 70; 73
The Puritan. 1966. V. 73

WATSON, DAVID
A Directory, Containing the Names, Occupations and Residence of the Inhabitants of Concord Centre Village. Concord: 1850. V. 73

WATSON, DAVID K.
The Constitution of the United States: Its History, Application and Construction. Chicago: 1910. V. 69

WATSON, DONALD
One Pair of Eyes. 1994. V. 69; 70

WATSON, DOUGLAS
The Founding of the First California Missions by Junipero.... San Francisco: 1934. V. 70
Traits of American Indian Life. San Francisco: 1933. V. 68; 73
West Wind, The Life Story of Joseph Reddedord Walker, Knight of the Golden Horseshoe. 1934. V. 69

WATSON, E. C.
Reproductions of prints, drawings and paintings of interest in the history of physcis. In American Journal of Physics Volume XXI 1953. V. 72

WATSON, E. L. GRANT
Daimon. London: 1925. V. 71

WATSON, FRANCIS
The Virgin King. New York: 1936. V. 70

WATSON, FREDERICK
The Animal World Display'd or the Nature and Qualities of Living Creatures Described.... London: 1755. V. 68
A Century of Gunmen - a Study in Lawlessness. London: 1931. V. 73

WATSON, G. N.
A Treatise on the Theory of Bessel Functions. Cambridge: 1922. V. 73

WATSON, GEORGE
The Roxburghshire World-book. Cambridge: 1923. V. 70; 71

WATSON, GEORGIA MITCHELL
So We Bought a Poets' Shrine: Incidents from years spent in the first home of Walt Whitman. New York: 1955. V. 72

WATSON, J.
Poachers and Poaching. 1891. V. 71

WATSON, J. N. P.
Lionel Edwards, Master of the Sporting Scene. 1986. V. 68

WATSON, JAMES
The History of the Art of Printing. Edinburgh: 1713. V. 72; 73

WATSON, JAMES D.
The DNA Story. San Francisco: 1981. V. 68

WATSON, JOHN
The History and Aquatints of the Parish of Halifax, in Yorkshire.... London: 1775. V. 70

WATSON, JOHN B.
Behaviorism. London: 1930. V. 71

WATSON, LARRY
Montana. 1948. V. 70
Montana 1948. Minneapolis: 1993. V. 68; 69; 70

WATSON, LYDIA
Our Homeward Way. New York: 1959. V. 72

WATSON, R. M. F.
Closeburn. Glasgow: 1901. V. 71

WATSON, RICHARD
Chemical Essays. London: 1787. V. 69
The Christian Panoply: Containing and Apology for the Bible, in a Series of Letters.... Shepherd's Town: 1797. V. 71

WATSON, SOLOMON
Report of the Trial Which Took Place at Clonmel Assizes for the County of Tipperary, on Thursday the 4th of August 1806. Wherein Charles Mac Carthy Esq. was Plaintiff and Solomon Watson, Banker in Clonmel, was defendant. Dublin: 1807. V. 70

WATSON, THOMAS
Lectures on the Principles and Practice of Physic: Delivered at King's College. Philadelphia: 1852. V. 72
Lectures on the Principles and Practice of Physic, Delivered at King's College. Philadelphia: 1858. V. 68; 69; 73

WATSON, VIRGINIA
With Cortes the Conqueror. Philadelphia: 1917. V. 73

WATSON, W. J.
Bridge Architecture. Cleveland: 1927. V. 70
Bridge Architecture. New York: 1927. V. 72

WATSON, W. M.
Life and Adventures of Ben Thompson. Austin: 1956. V. 68

WATSON, WILLIAM
A Delineation of the Strata of Derbyshire, Forming the Surface from Bolsover in the East to Buxton in the West.... Sheffield: 1811. V. 70
The Eloping Angels. London: 1893. V. 73
Epigrams of Art, Life and Nature. Liverpool: 1884. V. 69; 72
Excursions in Criticism: Being Some Prose Recreations of a Rhymer. London: 1893. V. 69
The Great Japan Exhibition. The Art of the Edo Period 1600-1868. London: 1981. V. 72
New Poems. Greenfield and London: 1902. V. 72
Pencraft: a Plea for the Older Ways. London: 1917. V. 69
Poems. London: 1892. V. 72
The Prince's Quest and Other Poems. London: 1880. V. 72

WATT, GEORGE
Essay on Dental Surgery for Popular Reading. Cincinnati: 1856. V. 71

WATT, ROBERT
Bibliotheca Britannica; Or a General Index to British and Foreign Literature. In two parts; - Authors and Subjects. Edinburgh: 1824. V. 72

WATT, ROBERT continued
Cases of Diabetes, Consumption &c. with Observations on the History and Treatment of Disease in General. Edinburgh: 1808. V. 73
A Summary Practical Elucidation of National Economy, in Support of Direct Taxation and Direct Assessment. Edinburgh: 1848. V. 71

WATTERS, FANNY C.
Plantation Memories of the Cape Fear River Country. Asheville: 1944. V. 68

WATTERSTON, GEORGE
Letters from Washington, on the Constitution and Laws.... Washington: 1818. V. 69

WATTEVILLE, V. DE
Out in the Blue. 1937. V. 69; 70; 72
Speak to the Earth. 1936. V. 69

WATTS, ALARIC A.
The Poetical Album: and Register of Modern Fugitive Poetry. Boston: 1828. V. 68

WATTS, DIANA
The Renaissance of the Greek Ideal. London: 1914. V. 72

WATTS, ELIZABETH
The Orchard and Fruit Garden. London: 1884?. V. 68
Poultry: an Original and Practical Guide to Their Breeding, Rearing and Feeding and Exhibiting. London: 1870?. V. 68
Vegetables and How to Grow Them. London: 1887. V. 68

WATTS, GEORGE FREDERICK
Exhibition Catalogue of the Works of, Together with the Late Frederick Sandys and Also the Design for the National Memorial to Queen Victoria by Thomas Brock, at the Royal Academy of Arts (Winter Exhibition), 1905. V. 68

WATTS, ISAAC
Divine Songs for Children...To Which is Added, Dr. Watts' Plain and Easy Catechisms. New Haven: 1819. V. 70
Horae Lyricae. Poems, Chiefly of the Lyric Kind. London: 1770. V. 73
A New Essay on Civil Power in Things Sacred; or an Enquiry After an Established Religion.... London: 1739. V. 71
The Psalms of David, Imitated in the Language of the New Testament. London: 1792. V. 73

WATTS, WILLIAM
An Essay on the Means And Expediency of Elevating the Profession of the Educator in the Estimation of the Public. Brimingham: 1840. V. 69

WATTS-DUNTON, THEODORE
The Coming of Love and Other Poems. London and New York: 1898. V. 72
The Coming of Love, Rhona Boswell's Story, and Other Poems. London and New York: 1899. V. 69
Jubilee Greeting at Spithead to the Men of Greater Britain. London and New York: 1897. V. 69; 73

WAUGH, ALEC
The Fatal Gift - a Novel. London: 1973. V. 68
The Lonely Unicorn - a Novel. London: 1922. V. 69
Unclouded Summer: a Love Story. London: 1948. V. 70
A Year to Remember - a Reminiscence of 1931. London: 1975. V. 68

WAUGH, ARTHUR
A Hundred Years of Publishing. London: 1930. V. 70

WAUGH, AUBERON
Consider the Lilies. London: 1968. V. 72

WAUGH, EVELYN
Basil Seal Rides Again. Boston: 1963. V. 69; 73
Basil Seal Rides Again. London: 1963. V. 68; 69; 70; 73
Black Mischief. London: 1932. V. 69; 71; 73
Brideshead Revisited. Boston: 1945. V. 69; 71; 72
Brideshead Revisited. London: 1945. V. 69
Brideshead Revisited. Boston: 1946. V. 69
Brideshead Revisited. London: 1960. V. 69
The Diaries of Evelyn Waugh. London: 1976. V. 68
A Handful of Dust. London: 1934. V. 69
A Handful of Dust. New York: 1934. V. 73
A Handful of Dust. London: 1948. V. 69
Helena. London: 1950. V. 68; 69; 72
The History of Mr. Polly. London: 1910. V. 69
The Holy Places. London: 1952. V. 68; 69
The Holy Places. London: 1953. V. 73
Labels: a Mediterranean Journal. London: 1930. V. 73
The Letters of Evelyn Waugh. London: 1980. V. 68; 72; 73
A Little Learning. London: 1964. V. 69; 73
A Little Order. Boston: 1977. V. 69
The Loom of Youth. London: 1917. V. 71
Love Among the Ruins. London: 1953. V. 69; 70; 71
Love Among the Ruins. London: 1962. V. 69
The Loved One. London: 1948. V. 68; 69; 72; 73
Men at Arms, Officers and Gentlemen, Unconditional Surrender. Boston: 1952-. V. 69
Men at Arms: Officers and Gentlemen, Unconditional Surrender. London: 1952-1961. V. 69
Mr. Loveday's Little Outing and Other Sad Stories. London: 1936. V. 70
Ninety-Two Days. London: 1934. V. 69
Officers and Gentlemen. 1955. V. 69
Officers and Gentlemen. London: 1955. V. 68
The Ordeal of Gilbert Pinfold. London: 1953. V. 70
The Ordeal of Gilbert Pinfold. London: 1957. V. 68; 69
P.R.B. An Essay on the Pre-Raphaelite Brotherhood 1847-1854. 1982. V. 68
PRB. An Essay on the Pre-Raphaelite Brotherhood 1847-1854. Westerham: 1982. V. 73
Put Out More Flags. London: 1942. V. 69
Remote People. London: 1931. V. 69
Robbery Under the Law: the Mexican Object-Lesson. London: 1939. V. 69
Scoop. London: 1933. V. 69; 71
Scott King's Modern Europe. 1947. V. 69; 71
Scott King's Modern Europe. London: 1947. V. 69
A Tourist in Africa. London: 1960. V. 70
Unconditional Surrender - the Conclusion of Men at Arms and Officers and Gentlemen. London: 1961. V. 68; 71
Vile Bodies. London: 1930. V. 69; 72
Waugh in Abyssinia. London: 1936. V. 73
When the Going Was Good. London: 1946. V. 69; 71; 72
Wine in Peace and War. 1947. V. 73
Wine in Peace and War. London: 1947. V. 70; 71; 72
Wine in Peace and War. London: 1948. V. 69
Work Suspended. London: 1942. V. 73
Work Suspended. London: 1948. V. 69

WAUGH, HILLARY
Madam Will Not Dine Tonight. New York: 1947. V. 71

WAUGH, JOSEPH LAING
Thornhill and Its Worthies. Dumfries. V. 71

WAUGH, LORENZO
Autobiography of.... Oakland: 1883. V. 69

WAUGH, NORA
Corsets and Crinolines. London: 1954. V. 69

WAVLE, ARDRA
Here They Are. Boston: 1940. V. 71

WAY, THOMAS E.
Frontier Arizona. New York: 1960. V. 69
Sgt. Fred Platten's Ten Years On The Trail Of The Redskins. Williams, AZ: 1959. V. 72

THE WAY to True Happinesse, Leading to the Gate of Knowledge. London: 1640. V. 69

WAYLAND, FRANCIS
The Elements of Political Economy. Boston: 1843. V. 71

WAYLAND, JOHN W.
The Valley of Turnpike, Winchester to Staunton and Other Roads. Winchester: 1967. V. 70

WAYLETT, RICHARD
Jock and Some Others. London: 1920. V. 69

WAYMAN, JOHN HUDSON
A Doctor on the California Trail: The Diary of Dr. John Hudson Wayman.... Denver: 1971. V. 70; 72; 73

WE Asked Gwendolyn Brooks About the Creative Environment in Illinois. 1967?. V. 68

WE HAPPY Few. An Anthology. London: 1946. V. 71

WEADOCK, JACK
Dust of the Desert. New York: 1936. V. 69

THE WEALTH of Great Britain in the Ocean.... London: 1749. V. 71

WEAR, BRUCE
The Bronze World of Frederic Remington. Tulsa: 1966. V. 70

WEARE, T. W.
Some Remarks Upon the Church of Great Haseley..Together with Extracts from Delafield's Ms. in the Bodleian Library entitled "Notitia Hasleiana". Oxford: 1848. V. 72

WEARIN, OTHA DONNER
Clarence Arthur Ellsworth, Artist of the Old West 1885-1964. Shenandoah: 1967. V. 73

WEATHERFORD, W. D.
Lawlessness or Civilization, Which?. 1917. V. 68

WEATHERILL, RICHARD
The Ancient Port of Whitby and Its Shipping. Whitby: 1908. V. 69

WEATHERLY, FREDERICK EDWARD
How and There: a Book of Transformation Pictures. London: 1894. V. 70
The Land of Little People. London: 1886. V. 70
The Old Woman Who Lived in a Shoe. London: 1890. V. 70
Punch and Judy and Some of Their Friends. London: 1885. V. 70

WEATHERS, BECK
Left for Dead. New York: 2000. V. 70

WEAVER, C. E.
Paleontology of the Jurassic and Cretaceous of West Central Argentina. Seattle: 1931. V. 69; 70

WEAVER, LAWRENCE
Cottages, Their Planning, Design and Materials. London: 1926. V. 73
Lutyens Houses and Gardens. London: 1921. V. 70
The Scottish National War Memorial. The Castle, Edinburgh. A Record and Appreciation. London. V. 71

WEAVER, MICHAEL S.
Water Song. Charlottesville: 1985. V. 72

WEAVER, RAYMOND
Herman Melville: Mariner and Mystic. New York: 1921. V. 73

WEAVER, WILLIAM
Catalogue of the Wheeler Gift of Books, Pamphlets and Periodicals in the Library of the American Institute of Electrical Engineers.... New York: 1909. V. 72
Catalogue of the Wheeler Gift of Books, Pamphlets and Periodicals in the Library of the American Institute of Engineers. Mansfield: 1998. V. 69

WEAVING, WILLOUGBY
The Star Fields and Other Poems. Oxford: 1916. V. 73

WEBB, CHARLES
The Graduate. New York: 1963. V. 69; 72

WEBB, CLIFFORD
A Jungle Picnic. London: 1934. V. 69

WEBB, DANIEL
An Inquiry Into the Beauties of Painting and into the Merits of the Most Celebrated Painters, Ancient and Modern. London: 1760. V. 69; 71

WEBB, EDITH BUCKLAND
Indian Life at the Old Missions. Los Angeles: 1952. V. 68

WEBB, HENRY LAW
The Silences of the Moon. London: 1911. V. 69

WEBB, J. B., MRS.
The Life and Adventures of Charles Durand; Shewing the Manners and Customs of Eastern Nations. London: 1860. V. 73

WEBB, J. J.
The Guilds of Dublin. London: 1929. V. 71

WEBB, JAMES
A Country Such as This. Garden City: 1983. V. 68

WEBB, JAMES JOSIAH
Adventures in the Santa Fe Trade 1844-1847. Glendale: 1931. V. 69

WEBB, JEAN FRANCIS
Forty Brothers. Menasha: 1934. V. 73

WEBB, KAYE
Impressions - Being the House Organ of the Hazell-Sun Group. Aylesbury: 1949-. V. 69

WEBB, M. I.
Michael Rysbrack Sculptor. London: 1954. V. 68

WEBB, MARIA
The Fells of Swarthmoor Hall. 1867. V. 71
The Fells of Swarthmoor Hall. London: 1867. V. 72
The Penns and Peningtons of the Seventeenth Century. Bishopsgate: 1867. V. 73
The Penns and Peningtons of the Seventeenth Century. London: 1867. V. 71
The Penns and Peningtons of The Seventeenth Century. London: 1891. V. 72

WEBB, MARION ST. JOHN
The Flower Fairies. London: 1923. V. 72
The House Fairies. London: 1925. V. 72
The Orchard Fairies. London: 1925. V. 73
The Seed Fairies. London: 1920. V. 73
The Wild Fruit Fairies. London: 1925. V. 72

WEBB, MARY
Armour Wherein He Trusted. London: 1929. V. 71
Gone to Earth. London: 1917. V. 69

WEBB, P. B.
Iter Hispaniense, or a Synopsis of Plants Collected in the Southern Provinces of Spain and in Portugal.... Paris and London: 1838. V. 72

WEBB, R. H.
Flora Hertfordiensis. London: 1849-1851. V. 69

WEBB, SAMUEL
History of Pennsylvania Hall, Which Was Destroyed by a Mob, on the 17th of May 1838. Philadelphia: 1838. V. 70; 72

WEBB, SIDNEY
How to Pay for the War: Being Ideas Offered to the Chancellor of the Exchequer by the Fabian Research Department. London: 1917:. V. 72
Soviet Communism: a New Civilisation?. Edinburgh: 1935. V. 71
Soviet Communism; a New Civilisation?. London: 1936. V. 71

WEBB, THOMAS SMITH
The Miniature Monitor: Containing All the Monitorial Instructions in Blue Lodge Masonry.... Chicago: 1864. V. 71

WEBB, TODD
Georgia O'Keeffe: the Artist's Landscape. Pasadena: 1984. V. 68; 70

WEBB, W. E.
Buffalo Land. Cincinnati: 1872. V. 68

WEBB, W. W.
A Complete Account of the Origin and Progress of the Clifton Suspension Bridge, Over the River Avon. Bristol: 1865. V. 69

WEBB, WALTER PRESCOTT
Flat Top- A Story of Modern Ranching. El Paso: 1960. V. 71
The Great Plains. Boston: 1931. V. 71
The Handbook of Texas- 2 Volumes. Austin: 1952. V. 71
The Texas Rangers. Boston: 1925. V. 71
The Texas Rangers. Boston: 1935. V. 69

WEBB, WILLIAM
Dweller at the Source. New York: 1973. V. 69

WEBBER, CHARLES WILKINS
The Hunter Naturalist, Romance of Sporting; or, Wild Scenes and Wild Hunters. Philadelphia: 1851. V. 69
Jack Long; or, Shot in the Eye. New York: 1846. V. 73
Old Hicks the Guide; or Adventures in the Camanche Country, in Search of a Gold Mine. New York: 1848. V. 73
Old Hicks the Guide; or, Adventures in the Comanche Country in Search of a Gold Mine. New York: 1868. V. 68

WEBBER, EVERETT
Bound Girl. New York: 1949. V. 72

WEBBER, IRMA
It Looks Like This-A Point-of-View Book. New York: 1949. V. 70

WEBBER, WINSLOW L.
Books About Books a Bio-Bibliography for Collectors. Boston: 1937. V. 71

WEBER, BRUCE
Bear Pond. Boston: 1990. V. 68
Bruce Weber. New York: 1988. V. 70

WEBER, CARL J.
A Bibliography of Jacob Abbott. Waterville: 1948. V. 69
Fore-edge Painting: a Historical Survey of a Curious Art in Book Decoration. New York: 1966. V. 70
Thomas Hardy In Maine. Keepsake No. 16 of The Southworth-Anthoensen Press. Portland, Maine: 1942. V. 72
A Thousand and One Fore-edge Paintings. Waterville: 1949. V. 71

WEBER, DAVID
The Californios Versus Jedediah Smith, 1826-1827, A New Cache of Documents. Spokane: 1990. V. 71
The Extranjeros, Selected Documents From the Mexican Side of the Santa Fe Trail, 1825-1828. Santa Fe: 1967. V. 71

WEBER, DAVID J.
The Mexican Frontier: 1821-1846: The American Southwest Under Mexico. Albuquerque: 1982. V. 70
Richard H. Kern; Expeditionary Artist in the Far Southwest, 1848- 1853. Albuquerque: 1985. V. 72
The Taos Trappers. Norman: 1971. V. 69

WEBER, FRANCIS J.
Zamorano Club Biographies and Memorial Tributes 1956-1997. Los Angeles: 1998. V. 73

WEBER, FRIEDRICH CHRISTIAN
The Present State of Russia. London: 1723-1722. V. 68

WEBER, I. M. ERICH
Practical Cake and Confectionary Art Pra-Ca-Coa.... Dresden-Austria/Chicago: 1921. V. 69

WEBER, JOSEPH
Memoirs of Maria Antoinetta, Archduchess of France and Navarre. 1805. V. 70

WEBER, M.
The Fishes of the Indo-Australian Archipelago. Leiden: 1911-1962. V. 68; 71
The Fishes of the Indo-Australian Archipelago. Leiden: 1962. V. 73
The Fishes of the Indo-Australian Archipelago. Leiden: 1964. V. 72; 73

WEBER, MAX
Cubist Poems. London: 1914. V. 71

WEBER, N. F.
The Art of Babar. New York: 1989. V. 69; 71

WEBSTER, ALEXANDER
Calculations, with the Principles and Data on which they are Instituted: Relative to a Late Act of Parliament, Intituled, an Act for Raising and Establishing a Fund for a Provision for the Widows and Children of the Ministers of the Church. Edinburgh: 1748. V. 70

WEBSTER, BEN
Mrs. Sarah Gamp's Tea and Turn Out. London: 1846. V. 70

WEBSTER, DANIEL
A Memorial to the Congress of the United States, on the Subject of Restraining the Increase of Slavery in the New States to be Admitted to the Union. Boston: 1819. V. 73
Speech Delivered by...at Niblos Saloon in New York on the 15th March 1837. New York: 1837. V. 68
Speech of Daniel Webster, War with Mexico. Boston: 1848. V. 68
Speech of Hon. Daniel Webster on Mr. Clay's Resolutions in the Senate of the United States March 7, 1850. Washington: 1850. V. 68
The Works of Daniel Webster. Boston: 1851. V. 68; 69; 71

WEBSTER, DAVID
The Angler and the Loop-Rod. 1885. V. 68

WEBSTER, DORIS
Consider the Consequences. New York: 1930. V. 71

WEBSTER, HENRY KITCHELL
The Beginners. Indianapolis: 1927. V. 71
Who is the Next?. 1931. V. 73
Who is the Next?. Indianapolis: 1931. V. 70

WEBSTER, JOHN
The Displaying of Supposed Witchcraft. London: 1677. V. 73
The Duchess of Malfi. London: 1945. V. 70; 71
Metallographia; or an History of Metals. 1671. V. 68

WEBSTER, JOHN CLARENCE
Catalogue of the John Clarence Webster Canadiana Collection (Pictorial Section) New Brunswick Museum. Saint John: 1939-1949. V. 73
The Forts of Chignecto. A Study of the Eighteenth Century Conflict Between France and Great Britain in Acadia. Shediac: 1930. V. 73
The Life of Thomas Pichon. Halifax: 1937. V. 73
Those Crowded Years 1863-1944 an Octogenarian's Record of Work. Shediac: 1944. V. 68
Wolfiana. A Potpourri of Facts and Fantasies, Culled From Literature Relating to the Life of James Wolfe.... 1927. V. 73

WEBSTER, JOHN W.
A Manual of Chemistry, on the Basis of Professor Brande's.... Boston: 1829. V. 73

WEBSTER, KIMBALL
The Gold Seekers of '49. Manchester: 1917. V. 70; 73

WEBSTER, MARIE D.
Quilts. Their Story and How to Make Them. Garden City: 1915. V. 68

WEBSTER, NOAH
An American Dictionary of the English Language. New York: 1828. V. 70; 72
A Collection of Essays and Fugitive Writings on Moral, Historical, Political and Literary Subjects. Boston: 1790. V. 71; 73
A Compendious Dictionary of the English Language. New Haven: 1806. V. 72
A Dictionary for Primary Schools. New York and New Haven: 1833. V. 68
A Dictionary for Primary Schools. New York: 1845?. V. 68

WEBSTER, WILLIAM
The Description and Use of a Complete Sett or Case of Pocket Instruments.... 1739. V. 71

WEBSTER, WILLIAM BULLOCK
Ireland Considered as a Field for Investment or Residence. Dublin: 1853. V. 69

WEBSTER, WILLIAM HENRY BAYLEY
The Recurring Monthly Periods and Periodic System of the Atmospheric Actions.... London: 1857. V. 73

WECHSBERG, JOSEPH
Dining at the Pavillion. Boston: 1962. V. 72

WECK, ANTON
Der Chur-Furstlichen Sachsischenweitberuffenen Residenzund Haupt- Vestung Dresden Beschreib und Vorstellung.... Nuremberg: 1680. V. 72

WEDDELL, ALEXANDER W.
Richmond Virignia in Old Prints. 1737-1887. Richmond: 1932. V. 72

THE WEDDING-Day: a Poem. Oxford: 1771. V. 73

WEDDLE, ROBERT S.
Plow-Horse Cavalry. Austin: 1974. V. 72

WEDGEWOOD, C. V.
Velvet Studies. London: 1946. V. 68

WEDGWOOD, WILLIAM B.
Wedgewood's Science of Numbers. New York: 1838. V. 68

WEDGWOOD BROWN, W.
Catalogue of Birds, Bassed on the Collection in the Sudan Government Museum. 1926-1931. V. 70

WEDL, CARL
Rudiments of Pathological Histology. London: 1855. V. 71

WEDMORE, FREDERICK
Dream of Provence (Orgeas and Miradou). London: 1905. V. 68
Etching in England. London: 1895. V. 72
To Nancy. London: 1905. V. 68

WEED, LEWIS H.
A Reconstruction of the Nuclear Masses in the Lower Portion of the Human Brain-Stem. Washington: 1914. V. 68

WEEDEN, HOWARD
Bandanna Ballads: Including "Shadows on the Wall". New York: 1901. V. 68
Shadows on the Wall. Huntsville: 1899. V. 73

WEEDON, L. L.
Come and Go in Fairyland: a Surprise Picture Book for Children. London: 1905. V. 70; 72
The Land of Long Ago: A Visit to Fairyland with Humpty Dumpty. London. V. 73
Up and Down: a Book of Changing Pictures. London: 1910. V. 72

THE WEEK-END Book. Bloomsbury: 1931. V. 70

WEEKS, A. G.
Massasoit of the Wampanoags. Fall River: 1920. V. 69

WEEKS, DONALD
Corvo. London: 1971. V. 71
Frederick Rolfe's Reviews of Unwritten Books.... Edinburgh: 1986-1988. V. 71
Frederick William Rolfe and Artists' Models. Edinburgh: 1981. V. 71
Frederick William Rolfe and Editors. Edinburgh: 1984. V. 71
Frederick William Rolfe and Editors. Edinburgh: 1994. V. 71
Fredercik William Rolfe, Christchurch and The Artist. Edinburgh: 1980. V. 71
Frederick William Rolfe, the 1903 Conclave and Hartwell de la Garde Grissell. Edinburgh: 1982. V. 71

WEEKS, EDWARD P.
A Treatise on the Law of Depositions, Comprising Abstracts of the Statutory Law Pertaining Thereto. San Francisco: 1880. V. 70

WEEMS, MASON LOCKE
God's Revenge Against Murder, or the Drown'd Wife, a Tragedy. Philadelphia: 1808. V. 73
The Life of Washington. Avon: 1974. V. 70; 72
The Philantropist; or a Good Twenty-Five Cents Worth of Political Love Powder, for Honest Adamites and Jeffersonians. Dumfries: 1799. V. 71

WEES, FRANCES S.
The Maestro Murders. 1931. V. 73

WEESE, ARTHUR
Skulpture and Malerei in Frankreich im XV und XVI Jahrhundert. Potsdam: 1927. V. 68

WEGG-PROSSER, FRANCIS RICHARD
Galileo and His Judges. London: 1889. V. 72

WEGMAN, WILLIAM
Fay. New York: 1999. V. 68
Little Red Riding Hood. New York: 1993. V. 68
Mother Goose. New York: 1996. V. 68
William Wegman. Tokyo/Kyoto: 1997. V. 68

WEGNER, ROBERT
Bibliography on Deer and Deer Hunting. 1992. V. 72

WEHR, JULIAN
Animated Nursery Tales. New York: 1943. V. 70
The Animated Picture Book of Alice in Wonderland. New York: 1945. V. 70
The Cock, the Mouse, and the Little Red Hen. New York: 1946. V. 71
Jack and the Beanstalk. New York: 1944. V. 72
Puss in Boots. New York: 1944. V. 70
Snow White. New York: 1945. V. 73

WEIBEL, ADELE COULIN
Two Thousand Years of Textiles. New York: 1952. V. 69

WEIBERT, HENRY
Sixty-Six Years in Custer's Shadow. Billings: 1985. V. 72

WEIDEMAN, JEROME
Tenderloin. New York: 1961. V. 69

WEIDENREICH, FRANZ
Apes, Giants and Man. Chicago: 1946. V. 68

WEIDMAN, JEROME
Fiorello!. New York: 1960. V. 70

WEIDMAN, JOHN
Assassins. New York: 1991. V. 73

WEIDMANN, F. C.
Der Costum-Ball am Schlusse des Carnevals 1826 bey.... Vienna: 1826. V. 70

WEIDNER, JOHANN LEONHARD
Hispanicae Dominations Arcana. Lugd. Batavor: 1643. V. 71

WEIGALL, ARTHUR
Burning Sands. New York: 1921. V. 72

WEIGALL, ROSE
A Brief Memoir of the Princess Charlotte of Wales.... London: 1874. V. 68

WEIGEL, JOHN C.
Letter to Carl Sandburg After Reading His Autobiography Always the Young Strangers Published on his 75th Birthday January 6, 1953. New York: 1968. V. 68; 70; 72

WEIGHTMAN, A. E.
Heraldry in the Royal Navy. Aldershot: 1957. V. 72

WEIGHTMAN, R. H.
Communication of R. H. Weightman and Accompanying Memorial of the Legislature of New Mexico, Setting Forth Sundry Grievances, and Calling Upon Congress for their Correction. Washington: 1850. V. 73
Speech of...Vindicatory of the Course of Governor James S. Calhoun, of New Mexico and the Character of the People of that Country. Washington: 1852. V. 73

WEIGL, BRUCE
Executioner. Tucson: 1976. V. 71

WEIGLE, MARTA
The Lore of New Mexico. Albuquerque: 1988. V. 68; 73

WEIL, ERNST
Catalogue of Books, Manuscripts, Photographs and Scientific Instruments Fully Described and Offered for Sale by Ernst Weil 1943-1965. Mansfield: 1995. V. 70

WEIL, JAMES L.
Keats Bound on Board the Maria Crowther. New Rochelle: 1986. V. 73
Two Poems to Two Prints. New Rochelle: 1987. V. 73
Uses. New Rochelle: 1974. V. 73

WEINBAUM, STANLEY G.
The Red Peri. Reading: 1952. V. 69

WEINBERGER, BERNHARD WOLF
Dental Bibliography: a Reference Index to the Literature of Dental Science and Art as Found in the Libraries of the New York Academy of Medicine and Bernhard Wolf Weinberger. 1929-1932. V. 69
An Introduction to the History of Dentistry with Medical & Dental Chronology & Bibliographic Data. St. Louis: 1948. V. 71; 72

WEINER, LAWRENCE
Having from Time to Time a Relation To. Amsterdam: 1973. V. 70

WEINGARDEN, L. S.
Louis H. Sullivan: the Banks. 1987. V. 72
Louis H. Sullivan: the Banks. Cambridge: 1987. V. 68

WEINREICH, MAX
Hitler's Professors. The Part of Scholarship in Germany's Crime Against the Jewish People. New York: 1946. V. 70

WEINZWEIG, JOHN
John Weinzweig, His Words and His Music as Heard at Convocation on June 11, 1982 in Convocation Hal, University of Tornto. Grimsby: 1982. V. 73

WEIR, HARRISON
Our Cats and All About Them. 1892. V. 68

WEIR, L. H.
Parks, a Manual of Municipal And County Parks.... New York: 1928. V. 69; 71

WEIR, THOMAS
Camps and Climbs in Arctic Norway. London: 1953. V. 69

WEIR, W. R.
Ayres' Cricket Companion 1921. London: 1921. V. 68

WEIR, WILLIAM
Sixty Years in Canada. Montreal: 1903. V. 73

WEIRD Islands. London: 1921. V. 72

WEISBORD, VERA BUCH
A Radical Life. Bloomington: 1977. V. 72

WEISMAN, JOHN
Evidence. New York: 1980. V. 68

WEISMANN, A.
Studies in the Theory of Descent.... London: 1882. V. 69

WEISMANN, FRIEDRICH LEOPOLD AUGUST
Essays Upon Heredity and Kindred Biological Problems.... Oxford: 1889. V. 72
Essays Upon Heredity and Kindred Biological Problems.... Oxford: 1891-1892. V. 72

WEISS, E. R.
Weiss Types for Advertising and Display. London. V. 72

WEISS, H. B.
The Pioneer Century of American Entomology. 1981. V. 72
Thomas Say, Early American Naturalist. Springfield: 1931. V. 72

WEISS, PETER
The Persecution and Assassination of Jean Paul Marat.... New York: 1965. V. 71

WEISSENBORN, HELLMUTH
Fantasy. 1978. V. 71
Fantasy. London: 1978. V. 68
Raven the Rascal - A Nature Story. London: 1946. V. 68

WEISSL, AUGUST
The Mystery of the Green Car. London: 1913. V. 73

WEITLANER JOHNSON, I.
Design Motifs on Mexican Indian Textiles. Graz: 1976. V. 69

WEIZMANN, CHAIM
Trial and Error: The Autobiography of.... New York: 1949. V. 70

WELCH, CHRISTOPHER
Six Lectures on the Recorder and Other Flutes in Relation to Literature. London: 1911. V. 69

WELCH, D'ALTE A.
Bibliography of American Children's Books Printed Prior to 1821. Worcester: 1963-1967. V. 72

WELCH, DENTON
Brave and Cruel and Other Stories. London: 1948. V. 70; 72
The Denton Welch Journals. London: 1952. V. 70
Dumb Instrument: Poems and Fragments. London: 1976. V. 70
I Left My Grandfather's House. London: 1958. V. 68; 70
In Youth Is Pleasure. London: 1944. V. 68; 70; 71; 72
A Last Sheaf. London: 1951. V. 70
A Lunch Appointment. 1993. V. 73
A Lunch Appointment. London: 1993. V. 70
Maiden Voyage. London: 1943. V. 69; 70; 72; 73
A Voice through a Cloud. London: 1950. V. 70

WELCH, EMILY S.
A Biographical Sketch: John Sedgewick, Major General. New York: 1899. V. 72

WELCH, J. J.
A Text Book of Naval Architecture for the Use of the Officers of the Royal Navy. London: 1901. V. 68

WELCH, JAMES
The Death of Jim Loney. New York: 1979. V. 68; 72
Fools Crow. New York: 1986. V. 68; 70; 73
The Heartsong of Charging Elk. New York: 2000. V. 71; 72
The Indian Lawyer. New York: 1990. V. 70; 71
Killing Custer. New York: 1994. V. 71
Riding the Earthboy 40. New York and Cleveland: 1971. V. 68; 70; 73
Winter in the Blood. New York: 1974. V. 70; 71; 72; 73

WELCH, LEW
Courses: No Credit, No Blame, No Balm. San Francisco: 1968. V. 71

WELCH, SPENCER GLASGOW
A Confederate Surgeon's Letters to His Wife. New York & Washington: 1911. V. 69; 70

WELCH, W. H.
Mosses of Indiana. Indianapolis: 1957. V. 72

WELCH, WILLIAM
Papers and Addresses by William Welch. Baltimore: 1920. V. 73

WELCH, WILLIAM HENRY
Contributions to the Science of Medicine Dedicated by His Pupils on the Twenty-Fifth Anniversary of His Doctorate. Baltimore: 1900. V. 71

WELCHMAN, EDVARDO
XXXIX Articuli Ecclesiae Anglicana, Textibus Sacrae Scripturae et Patrum Primaevorum Testimoniis Confirmati.... Oxonii: 1793. V. 69

WELD, CHARLES R.
Last Winter In Rome. London: 1865. V. 72

WELD, CHARLES RICHARD
A History of the Royal Society. London: 1848. V. 68; 70

WELD, EDWARD F.
The Ransomed Bride: a Tale of the Inquisition. New York: 1846. V. 73

WELD, JOHN
Don't You Cry for Me. New York: 1940. V. 69

WELD, THEODORE DWIGHT
American Slavery as It Is: Testimony of a Thousand Witnesses. New York: 1839. V. 72

WELDON & CO.
Weldon's Guide to Folding Finger Napkins. (with Weldon's Guide to Folding Serviettes). London: 1890?. V. 68

WELDON, FAY
Darcy's Utopia. London: 1990. V. 72; 73
The Heart of the Country. London: 1987. V. 73
The Life and Loves of a She-Devil. New York: 1984. V. 72
Moon Over Minneapolis. London: 1991. V. 73
Remember Me. London: 1976. V. 73
Splitting. London: 1995. V. 72
Wolf, the Mechanical Dog. London: 1988. V. 70

WELFORD, RICHARD GRIFFITHS
The Impolicy of the Present High Duties on Tobacco.... London: 1848. V. 71

WELL Dressed Lines. Stripped from the Reels of Five New Englanders. New York: 1962. V. 69

WELLBELOVED, CHARLES
Devotional Exercises for the Use of Young Persons. York: 1826. V. 69

WELLCOME HISTORICAL MEDICAL LIBRARY
A Catalogue of Printed Books in the Wellcome Historical Medical Library. London: 1962-1966. V. 69
Catalogue of Printed Books. Volumes I-IV. London: 1962-1995. V. 70

WELLCOME HISTORICAL MEDICAL MUSEUM
Lister Centenary Exhibition Handbook. London: 1927. V. 68

WELLCOME LIBRARY
Catalogue of Western Manuscripts on Medicine and Science in the Wellcome Historical Medical Library. London: 1962-1973. V. 72

WELLES, ALBERT
American Family Antiquity. New York: 1880. V. 69

WELLES, C. M.
Three Years' Wanderings of a Connecticut Yankee, in South America, Africa, Australia and California with Descriptions of the Several Countries, Manners, Customs and Conditions of the People.... New York: 1860. V. 69

WELLES, ORSON
Mr. Arkadin. New York: 1956. V. 71

WELLESLEY, DOROTHY
The Annual - Being a Selection from Forget-Me-Nots, Keepsakes and other Annuals of the Nineteenth Century. London. V. 72
A Broadcast Anthology of Modern Poetry. London: 1930. V. 69; 72
Desert Wells. London: 1946. V. 71
Far Have I Travelled. London: 1952. V. 72
Lost Planet and Other Poems. London: 1942. V. 69; 71

WELLESLEY, RICHARD COLLEY, MARQUIS
Primitiae et Reliquiae. London: 1840. V. 73

WELLINGTON, ARTHUR, DUKE OF
Civil Correspondence and Memoranda of Field Marshal Arthur, Duke of Wellington. 1860. V. 70

WELLMAN, F. L.
Tropical American Plant Disease. 1972. V. 72

WELLMAN, M. W.
Giant in Gray. New York: 1949. V. 70
Twice in Time. 1957. V. 73

WELLMAN, PAUL I.
Angel with Spurs. Philadelphia and New York: 1942. V. 73
The Callaghan Yesterday and Today. Encinal. V. 71
The Comancheros. Garden City: 1952. V. 70; 71; 72; 73
Death on the Prairie. New York: 1934. V. 69; 72
The Iron Mistress. Garden City: 1951. V. 71
The Trampling Herd: The Story of the Cattle Range in America. New York: 1939. V. 69

WELLMAN, WILLIAM A.
Go, Get 'em!. Boston: 1918. V. 71

WELLS, C.
Six Years in the Malay Jungle. London: 1925. V. 69

WELLS, CAROLYN
Anything But the Truth. Philadelphia: 1925. V. 68
The Bumblepuppy Book. Covent Garden: 1903. V. 70; 73
The Furthest Fury. Philadelphia: 1924. V. 68; 72
Gilt Edged Guilt. Philadelphia: 1938. V. 68
The Happychaps. New York: 1908. V. 71
Horror House. Philadelphia: 1931. V. 68
The Merry-Go Round. New York: 1901. V. 70
Seven Ages of Childhood. New York: 1909. V. 70; 73
Sleeping Dogs. Garden City: 1929. V. 70
The Technique of the Mystery Story. Springfield: 1913. V. 70

WELLS, CHARLES
Joseph and His Brethren, a Scriptural Drama: in Two Acts. London and New York: 1824. V. 72

WELLS, CHARLES KNOX POLK
Life and Adventures of Polk Wells the Notorious Outlaw. 1907. V. 70
Life and Adventures of Polk Wells...the Notorious Outlaw. Halls: 1907. V. 73

WELLS, CHARLES WESLEY
Frontier, Life, Sketches And Incidents Of Homes In The West. Cincinnati: 1902. V. 72

WELLS, DAVID A.
Robinson Crusoe's Money; or the Remarkable Financial Fortunes and Misfortunes of a Remote Island Community. New York: 1876. V. 73

WELLS, EDMUND
Argonaut Tales - Stories of the Gold Seekers and Indian Scouts of Early Arizona. New York: 1927. V. 68; 73

WELLS, EDWARD
The Young Gentleman's Astronomy, Chronology and Dialling, Containing Such Elements of the Said Arts or Sciences, as are Most Useful and Easy to Be Known. London: 1718. V. 69

WELLS, EDWARD LAIGHT
Hampton and His Cavalry in '64. Richmond: 1899. V. 69; 70
Hampton and Reconstruction. Columbia: 1907. V. 69

WELLS, ERNEST
The Scarlet City: Being the Adventures of John Franklyn and His Friend Anthony Fuller.... London: 1899. V. 69

WELLS, EVELYN
Hatshepsut. Garden City: 1969. V. 73

WELLS, GEOFFREY H.
The Works of H. G. Wells - a Bibliography, Dictionary and Subject- Index 1887-1925. London: 1926. V. 68

WELLS, HERBERT GEORGE
The Autocracy of Mr. Parham. Garden City: 1930. V. 70
The Autocracy of Mr. Parham. London: 1930. V. 69
The Country of the Blind. Waltham St. Lawrence: 1939. V. 71
Experiment in Autobiography: Discoveries and Conclusions of a Very Ordinary Brain (since 1866). London: 1934. V. 70; 73
The First Men in the Moon. London: 1901. V. 69
The First Men in the Moon. London: 1904. V. 73
The Food of the Gods and How It Came to Earth. London: 1904. V. 68; 69
In the Days of the Comet. London: 1906. V. 68; 70; 73
In the Days of the Comet. New York: 1906. V. 73
The Invisible Man. London: 1897. V. 71
The Invisible Man. 1898. V. 73
The Island Of Dr. Moreau. London: 1896. V. 69; 73
The King Who Was a King. Garden City: 1929. V. 70
Love and Mr. Lewisham. London and New York: 1900. V. 71
Men Like Gods. London: 1923. V. 70
Mr. Blettsworthy on Rampole Island. Garden City: 1928. V. 70
Mr. Britling Sees it Through. Chicago. V. 70
The New Machiavelli. London: 1911. V. 71
The Plattner Story. London: 1897. V. 69
Russia in the Shadows. London: 1920. V. 68; 70; 71
The Secret Places of the Heart. London: 1922. V. 70
Select Conversations with an Uncle. 1895. V. 71
Select Conversations with an Uncle (Now Extinct) and Two Other Reminiscences. London: 1895. V. 69; 73
Stalin-Wells Talk. London: 1934. V. 70
The Stolen Bacillus. London: 1895. V. 68; 71
Tales of Space and Time. New York: 1899. V. 72
Tales of Space and Time. London and New York: 1900. V. 71
The Time Machine. London: 1895. V. 71
The War in the Air. 1908. V. 71
The War in the Air. London: 1908. V. 68; 70
The War of the Worlds. 1918?. V. 73
The War of the Worlds and The Time Machine. New York: 1964. V. 69
When the Sleeper Wakes. 1899. V. 71; 73
When the Sleeper Wakes. New York: 1899. V. 71
The Wonderful Visit. London: 1895. V. 73
The Work, Wealth and Happiness of Mankind. Garden City: 1931. V. 68; 69
The Works of H. G. Wells. London: 1924. V. 69; 71
The Works of H. G. Wells. New York: 1924-1927. V. 72
The World of William Clissold. London: 1926. V. 68; 70; 73
A Year of Prophesying. London: 1924. V. 69

WELLS, IVERSON C.
The Crime Trust or the Mystery of the Invisible Hand. Chicago: 1911. V. 69

WELLS, JAMES M.
With Touch of Elbow or Death Before Dishonor. Philadelphia: 1909. V. 69

WELLS, JANE
The Year-Book of Natural History, for Young Persons. London: 1842. V. 68

WELLS, JOHN
An Epitome of Perspective. 1817. V. 71

WELLS, POLK
Life and Adventures of Polk Wells, the Notorious Outlaw. 1907. V. 68

WELLS, ROBERT
Cakes and Buns. Manchester: 1898. V. 68
Toffy and Sweets: How to Make Them; or, the Art of Sugar Boiling Made Easy. Manchester: 1893. V. 73

WELLS, ROLLA
Episodes of My Life. St. Louis: 1933. V. 69; 71

WELLS, ROSEMARY
Forest of Dreams. New York: 1988. V. 73

WELLS, SAMUEL
The History of the Drainage of the Great Level of the Fens, Called Bedford Level, with the Constitution and Laws of the Bedford Level Corporation. London: 1828-1830. V. 71; 73

WELLS, WILLIAM CHARLES
Two Essays: One Upon Single Vision with Two Eyes; the Other on Dew. A Letter to the Right Hon. Lloyd Lord Kenyon and an Account of a Female of the White Race of Mankind, Part of Whose Skin Resembles that of a Negro.... London: 1818. V. 72

WELLS, WILLIAM V.
Life and Public Services of Samuel Adams. Boston: 1865. V. 71

WELSEY, IRMA H.
Hardesty Family America. Charlotte: 1981. V. 72

WELSH, IRVINE
The Acid House. New York: 1995. V. 69
Ecstasy. London: 1996. V. 71; 72
Filth. London: 1998. V. 68; 71; 72
Marabou Stork Nightmares. London: 1995. V. 70
Marabou Stork Nightmares. New York: 1996. V. 69
Past Tense. South Queensberry: 1992. V. 71; 72
Trainspotting. London: 1993. V. 71

WELTY, EUDORA
Acrobats in a Park. Northridge: 1980. V. 70
The Bride of the Innisfallen and Other Stories. New York: 1955. V. 70; 71; 72; 73
Bye-Bye Brevoort. Jackson: 1980. V. 69; 70
The Collected Stories. New York and London: 1980. V. 70; 71; 73
The Complete Works of.... Kyoto: 1988. V. 70
A Curtain of Green. Garden City: 1941. V. 69; 70; 72
Delta Wedding. New York: 1946. V. 68; 69; 70; 71; 73
The Eye of the Story. New York: 1977. V. 73
The Eye of the Story. New York: 1978. V. 68; 70; 73
Fairy Tale of the Natchez Trace. Jackson: 1975. V. 69; 70; 71; 72; 73
The First Story. 1999. V. 70
A Flock of Guinea Hens Seen from a Car. New York: 1970. V. 70
The Golden Apples. New York: 1949. V. 68; 70; 73
The Golden Apples. London: 1950. V. 70
Henry Green. Austin: 1961. V. 73
Ida M'Toy. 1979. V. 70

WELTY, EUDORA continued
Ida M'toy. Urbana: 1979. V. 73
In Black and White. Northridge: 1985. V. 68; 70
John Rood. Exhibition of Recent Sculpture. New York: 1958. V. 69
The Key. Garden City: 1941. V. 68; 70
The Little Store. Newton: 1985. V. 70
Losing Battles. New York: 1970. V. 68; 69; 70; 71; 72; 73
Losing Battles. London: 1982. V. 73
Moon Lake and Other Stories. Franklin Center: 1980. V. 73
Morgana: Two Stories from The Golden Apples. 1988. V. 70
Music from Spain. Greenville: 1948. V. 68; 69; 70; 73
One Time, One Place: Mississippi in the Depression. A Snapshot Album. New York: 1971. V. 70; 73
One Writer's Beginnings. Cambridge: 1984. V. 68; 70; 71; 73
The Optimist's Daughter. New York: 1972. V. 68; 70; 71; 72; 73
The Optimist's Daughter. London: 1973. V. 69
The Optimist's Daughter. Franklin Center: 1980. V. 69; 70; 71
A Pageant of Birds. New York: 1974. V. 70; 73
Photographs. 1989. V. 70
Photographs. Franklin Center: 1989. V. 69
Photographs. Jackson & London: 1989. V. 68; 71; 73
Places in Fiction. New York: 1957. V. 69; 70; 72; 73
The Ponder Heart. London: 1954. V. 70
The Ponder Heart. New York: 1954. V. 70; 71; 73
Retreat. 1981. V. 70; 73
The Robber Bridegroom. Garden City: 1942. V. 68; 69; 70
The Robber Bridegroom. New York: 1987. V. 70
The Robber Bridegroom. West Hatfield: 1987. V. 70; 72; 73
The Shoe Bird. New York: 1964. V. 70; 71; 73
Short Stories. New York: 1949. V. 70
Some Notes on Time in Fiction. 1973. V. 71
Some Notes On Time in Fiction. Jackson: 1973. V. 73
A Sweet Devouring. New York: 1969. V. 70
Thirteen Stories by Eudora Welty. New York: 1965. V. 70
Three Papers on Fiction. Northampton: 1962. V. 70
Welty: an Exhibition at the Mississippi State Historical Museum, Jackson, Mississippi. Jackson: 1977. V. 73
White Fruitcake. New York: 1980. V. 70
The Wide Net and Other Stories. New York: 1943. V. 70; 73
The Wide Net and Other Stories. New York: 1947. V. 70
Women!! Make Turban in Own Home!. 1979. V. 69; 70

WELTY, RAYMOND L.
The Policing Of The Frontier By The Army 1860-70 In Kansas Historical Quarterly, Vol VII. Topeka: 1938. V. 72
The Policing Of The Frontier By The Army 1860-70 In The Kansas Historical Quarterly, Vol VIII#1-4, 1938. V. 72

WELWOOD, JAMES
Memoirs of the Most Material Transactions in England for the Last Hundred Years, Preceding the Revolution in 1688.. London: 1718. V. 72

WEMMER, C. M.
Biology and Management of the Cervidae. 1987. V. 69; 70; 73

WEMYSS, FRANCIS
The Theatrical Biography of Eminent Actors and Authors. New York: 1836. V. 72

WEMYSS, THOMAS
Pictures of War; from Authentic Narratives.... Edinburgh: 1817. V. 70

WENDELIN, MARCUS FREDERICK
Contemplationum Physicarum Sectio I (and II). (with) Admiranda Nili. Commentatione Philologica, Historica, Physica, & Hieroglypica ex CCCXVIII. Cambridge: 1648. V. 72

WENDELL
Berry. Confluence: 1991. V. 70

WENDEN, NADINE
The Freckle Faced Bear. New York: 1936. V. 71

WENGER, R.
Wegner's Bibliography on Deer and Deer Hunting. Deforest;: 1992. V. 70

WENIGER, D.
Cacti of the Southwest, Texas, New Mexico, Oklahoma, Arkansas, and Louisiana. Austin: 1970. V. 68; 73

WENTWORTH, EDWARD N.
America's Sheep Trails, History, Personalities. Ames: 1948. V. 68; 71

WENTWORTH, FRANK L.
Aspen on the Roaring Fork. Lakewood: 1952. V. 73
The Jolly Rover. Iowa City: 1931. V. 73
On the Road With Lizzie. Iowa City: 1930. V. 73

WENTWORTH, JOSIE A.
Janie Ellice's Recipes 1846-1859. London: 1974. V. 70

WENTWORTH, JUDITH ANNE DOROTHEA WENTWORTH BLUNT-LYTTON
Thoroughbred Racing Stock and Its Ancestors. London: 1938. V. 72

WENTWORTH, M. D.
Forged in Strong Fires, The Life & Experiences of John Edward Dalton, As Told By John Edward Dalton. Caldwell: 1948. V. 71

WENTWORTH, PATRICIA
Account Rendered. Philadelphia: 1940. V. 70
Beggar's Choice. Philadelphia: 1931. V. 68
The Black Cabinet. New York: 1926. V. 68
The Catherine Wheel. Philadelphia: 1949. V. 72
The Devil's Wind. London: 1912. V. 72
The Devil's Wind. New York: 1912. V. 69
The Gazebo. Philadelphia: 1958. V. 68
A Marriage Under the Terror. London: 1910. V. 69
Miss Silver Comes to Stay. Philadelphia: 1948. V. 68
Silence in Court. Philadelphia: 1945. V. 69

WENTWORTH, THOMAS
The Office and Duty of Executors. Philadelphia: 1832. V. 69

WENTZ, ROBY
The Grabhorn Press. A Biography. San Francisco: 1981. V. 73

WENZELL, A. B.
The Passing Show. 1900. V. 72

WERDERMANN, E.
Brazil and Its Columnar Cacti. Pasadena: 1942. V. 68

WERNE, FERDINAND
Expedition to Discover the Sources of the While Nile, in the Years 1840, 1841. London: 1849. V. 71

WERNER, A.
The Natives of British Central Africa. London: 1906. V. 69

WERNER, ABRAHAM GOTTLOB
A Treatise on the External Characters of Fossils. Dublin: 1805. V. 73
Von den Ausserlichen Kennzeichen der Fossilien. Leipzig: 1774. V. 68; 73

WERNER, ARNO
One Man's Work: a Lecture. 1982. V. 71

WERNER, HERMAN
On the Western Frontier with the United States Cavalry Fifty Years Ago. 1934. V. 68; 72

WERNER, JANE
The Giant Golden Book of Elves. New York: 1951. V. 70
Walt Disney's Alice in Wonderland Finds the Garden of Live Flowers retold by Jane Werner. New York: 1951. V. 70

WERNER, WILLIAM
The Evolution of the Boston Fire Department 1678-1977. Dallas: 1977?. V. 69

WERSTEIN, IRVING
Marshal Without a Gun: Tom Smith. New York: 1959. V. 69

WERTHAM, FREDRIC
Seduction of the Innocent. London: 1955. V. 70

WESCHER, H.
Collage. New York: 1968. V. 69; 72

WESCOTT, GLENWAY
The Babe's Bed. 1930. V. 71
The Babe's Bed. Paris: 1930. V. 72
The Bitterns. A Book of Twelve Poems. Evanston;: 1920. V. 73
Images of Truth. New York: 1962. V. 71

WESENBERG-LUND, C.
Plankton Investigations fo the Danish Lakes. Copenhagen: 1908. V. 68; 73

WESLEY, CHARLES H.
Negro Labor in the United States 1850-1925: A Study in American Economic History. New York: 1927. V. 69

WESLEY, JOHN
The Almost Christian: A Sermon (on Acts 26.28) Preached at St. Mary's Oxford, Before the University on July 25, 1741. London: 1741. V. 70
Christian Perfection. A Sermon (on Phil. 3.12), Preached by John Wesley, M.A. Fellow of Lincoln-College Oxford. London: 1741. V. 70
A Collection of Hymns, for the Use of the People Called Methodists. London: 1782. V. 69
A Dialogue Between a Predestinarian and His Friend. London: 1741. V. 70
Primitive Physick; or an Easy and Natural Method of Curing Most Diseases. London: 1772. V. 68
Sayings and Portraits of John Wesley. London: 1924. V. 72
The Scripture Doctrine Concerning Predestination, Election and Reprobation. London: 1741. V. 70
Serious Considerations on Absolute Predestination. Bristol: 1741. V. 70

WESLEY, MARCY
Second Fiddle. New York: 1989. V. 73

WESLEY, MARY
Harnessing Peacocks. London: 1985. V. 71
Jumping the Queue. London: 1983. V. 71

WESLEY, SAMUEL
Poems on Several Occasions. Cambridge: 1743. V. 68; 73

WESLEY, W. H.
Map of the Moon...Based on the Fiducial Measures of A. S. Saunder and J. Franz. London: 1935. V. 71

WESSEL, JOHN
This Far, No Further. New York: 1996. V. 73

WESSON, MARIANNE
Render Up the Body. London: 1997. V. 69; 73

WEST Cork Resource Study. 1963. V. 70

WEST, BENJAMIN
Christ Rejected, Catalogue of the Picture Representing the Above Subject.... London: 1814. V. 69
A Discourse Delivered to the Students of the Royal Academy. London: 1793. V. 71; 72
Sale Catalogue West's Gallery, No. 14, Newman Street, Oxford Street. London: 1821. V. 69

WEST by One and by One by the Scowrers and Molly Maguires of An Francisco. San Francisco: 1965. V. 71

WEST, CHARLES
Lectures on the Diseases of Infancy and Childhood. London: 1865. V. 70
The Story of My Life. London: 1859. V. 68

WEST, DOROTHY
The Living is Easy. Boston: 1948. V. 72

WEST, G. T. W.
Rock Climbs on the Mountain Limestone of Derbyshire. Manchester: 1961. V. 69

WEST, GILBERT
A Defence of the Christian Revelation, On Two Very Important Points.... London: 1748. V. 70

WEST, HERBERT FAULKNER
A Stephen Crane Collection. Hanover: 1948. V. 70

THE WEST Indian; or, the Happy Effects of Diligence and Self Control: Exemplified in the History of Philip Montague. Wellington: 1872. V. 70

WEST, J. W.
Sketches of Our Mountain Pioneers. Lynchburg: 1925. V. 68

WEST, JANE
A Tale of the Times. London: 1799. V. 73

WEST, JESSAMYN
The Friendly Persuasion. New York: 1945. V. 70; 73

WEST, JOHN BURNARD
High Altitude Physiology. Stroudsburg: 1981. V. 68

WEST, JOHN C.
A Texan in Search of a Fight - The Diary and Letter of a Private Soldier in Hood's Texas Brigade. Waco: 1901. V. 70; 73
A Texan in Search of A Fight- The Diary and Letters of a Private Soldier in Hood's Texas Brigade. Waco: 1969. V. 71

WEST Laurel Hill Cemetery. Philadelphia: 1928. V. 72

WEST, MAE
Goodness Had Nothing to do With It. New York: 1959. V. 73

WEST, MICHAEL
Claire de Lune and Other Troubadour Romances. St. Albans. V. 71

WEST, NATHANAEL
A Cool Million. New York: 1934. V. 68; 69; 70; 71; 73
A Cool Million. London: 1954. V. 69
The Day of the Locust. New York: 1939. V. 71
The Day of the Locust. London: 1951. V. 68
Miss Lonelyhearts. New York: 1933. V. 69; 73
Nathanael West: Novels and Other Writings. New York: 1997. V. 68; 71

WEST, PAUL
Bela Lugosi's White Christmas. New York: 1972. V. 69
Caliban's Filibuster. Garden City: 1971. V. 72
Doubt and Dylan Thomas. St. John's: 1970. V. 71
I'm Expecting to Live Quite Soon. New York: 1970. V. 72
The Pearl and the Pumpkin. New York: 1904. V. 71
The Women Of Whitechapel And Jack The Ripper. New York: 1991. V. 72
Words for a Deaf Daughter. New York: 1970. V. 72

WEST, REBECCA
Black Lamb and Grey Falcon. London: 1941. V. 73
Black Lamb and Grey Falcon. New York: 1943. V. 68
The Meaning of Treason. London: 1952. V. 69; 73
The Return of the Soldier. London: 1918. V. 71
The Strange Necessity - Essays and Reviews. London: 1928. V. 71; 73
War Nurse: The True Story of a Woman Who Lived, Loved and Suffered on the Western Front. New York: 1930. V. 72

WEST, S. J.
The Daughters of Merville. London: 1860. V. 70

WEST, THERESA JOHN CORNWALLIS
Frescoes and Sketches from Memory. London: 1855. V. 68

WEST, THOMAS
The Antiquities of Furness. London: 1774. V. 71
The Antiquities of Furness. Ulverston: 1805. V. 71; 72
The Antiquities of Furness. Beckermet: 1977. V. 71
A Guide to the Lakes.... London: 1778. V. 71
A Guide to the Lakes.... Kendal: 1780. V. 71
A Guide to the Lakes.... London: 1784. V. 69
A Guide to the Lakes.... London: 1789. V. 71; 73
A Guide to the Lakes.... London: 1796. V. 72; 73
A Guide to the Lakes.... London: 1799. V. 71
A Guide to the Lakes.... Kendal: 1802. V. 71
A Guide to the Lakes.... Kendal: 1812. V. 71
A Guide to the Lakes.... Kendal: 1821. V. 71; 72

WEST VIRGINIA. LAWS, STATUTES, ETC. - 1863
Acts of the Legislature of West Virginia at Its First Session, Commencing June 20th, 1863. Wheeling: 1863. V. 69; 70

WEST VIRGINIA WRITERS' PROJECT
My Memory Book. Charleston: 1940. V. 69

WEST, W.
Fresh Water Algae from Burma, Including a few From Bengal and Madras. Calcutta: 1907. V. 73
A Monograph of the British Desmidiaceae. London: 1904-1923. V. 73

WEST, WILLIAM
Cornered. New York: 1964. V. 72
Tavern Anecdotes and Reminiscences of the Origin of Signs, Clubs, Coffee Houses, Streets, City Companies, Wards &c. 1825. V. 71

WESTALL, R.
Illustrations of the Bible. London: 1835. V. 71

WESTALL, WILLIAM
As a Man Sows. 1894. V. 73
A Series of Views of the Lakes of Cumberland and Westmorland. London: 1819-1820. V. 69
Two Pinches of Snuff. London: 1890. V. 68
Views of the Lake and of the Vale of Keswick. London: 1820. V. 68; 72

WESTBROOK, ROBERT
The Magic Garden of Stanley Sweetheart. New York: 1996. V. 73

WESTBY, SELMER
Christopher Isherwood: a Bibliography 1923-1967. Los Angeles: 1968. V. 71

WESTCOTT, HENRY P.
Hand Book of Cadinghead Gas. Erie: 1916. V. 72

WESTELL, W. PERCIVAL
The Book of the Animal Kingdom. London: 1910. V. 69

WESTER, P. J.
The Food Plants of the Philippines. Manila: 1924. V. 72

WESTERMAN, J. F. C.
The Antarctic Treasure. London: 1929. V. 69

WESTERMAN, PERCY F.
The Submarine Hunters. London: 1918. V. 69
With Beattie Off Jutland. London: 1918. V. 69

WESTERMANN, G. E. G.
The Jurassic of the Circum Pacific. Cambridge: 1992. V. 72

WESTERMARCK, E.
The Belief in Spirit in Morocco. 1920. V. 69
Ritual and Belief in Morocco. London: 1926. V. 69

WESTERMEIER, CLIFFORD
Colorado's First Portrait, Scenes by Early Artists, 500 Drawings, Sketches, Engravings and Lithographs. Albuquerque: 1970. V. 68

WESTERN, CHARLES CALLIS
Observations on the Speech of the Right Hon. W. Huskisson in the House of Commons, Tuesday, the 11th of June 1822 on Mr. Western's Motion Concerning the Resumption of Cash Payments.... London: 1823. V. 70

WESTERN North Carolina R.R. Scenery. Land of the Sky. Portland: 1885. V. 73

WESTERN SURVEY COMPANY
New Meixco; the Last Great West. Chicago: 1917. V. 70

WESTERNERS. CHICAGO CORRAL
Chicago Westerners' Brand Book 1944. Chicago: 1946. V. 72
Chicago Westerners' Brand Book 1945-1946. Chicago: 1947. V. 72
Chicago Corral of Westerners' Brand Book Vol XXI 1964-1965. Chicago: 1965. V. 72
The Chicago Corral of Westerners' Brand Book Vol XXIII 1966-1967. Chicago: 1967. V. 72
Chicago Western Brand Book 1968-1969. Chicago: 1969. V. 72

WESTERNERS. DENVER POSSE
Brand Book. Denver: 1950. V. 69
Denver Westerners' Brand Book 1950. Volume VI. Denver: 1951. V. 69
Denver Westerners' Brand Book Volume VII. Denver: 1952. V. 69
Denver Westerns' Brand Book. Volume IX. Denver: 1954. V. 69
Denver Westerners' Brand Book. Volume X. Denver: 1955. V. 69
Denver Westerners' Brand Book. Volume XI. Denver: 1956. V. 69
Denver Westerners' Brand Book. Volume XII. Denver: 1957. V. 69
Denver Westerners' Brand Book. Volume XIV. Denver: 1958. V. 69
The 1960 Brand Book. Boulder: 1961. V. 69; 71
Denver Westerners' 1961 Brand Book. volume XVII. Boulder: 1962. V. 69
1968 Brand Book. Volume XXIV. Denver: 1969. V. 69

WESTERNERS. LOS ANGELES CORRAL
The Westerners' Brand Book Vol 1. Los Angeles: 1947. V. 72
Westerners' Brand Book, Book IV. Los Angeles: 1951. V. 72
Brand Book 6. Los Angeles: 1956. V. 68
Westerners Brand Book. Book Eight. Los Angeles: 1959. V. 70
The Westerners Brand Book. Book Nine. Los Angeles: 1961. V. 70
Brand Book 12. Los Angeles: 1966. V. 68
The Westerners Brand Book: Book Ten. Los Angeles: 1963. V. 73

WESTERNERS. SAN DIEGO CORRAL
Brand Book 1. San Diego: 1969. V. 70
The San Diego Corral of Westerners' Brand Book #2. San Diego: 1971. V. 71

WESTFALL, CAROLL W.
In this Most Perfect Paradise: Alberti, Nicholas V. and the Invention of Conscious Urban Planning in Rome, 1447-1455. University Park and London: 1974. V. 68

WESTGARD, A. L.
Tales of a Pathfinder. New York: 1920. V. 70

WESTLAKE, DONALD E.
Anarchaos. New York: 1967. V. 72
Bankshot. New York: 1972. V. 69
The Busy Body. New York: 1966. V. 70
Butcher's Moon. New York: 1974. V. 71
Dancing Aztecs. New York: 1976. V. 69; 70
Enough. New York: 1977. V. 69
Ex Officio. 1970. V. 70
Help I am Being Held Prisoner. New York: 1974. V. 70; 73
High Jinx. Miami Beach: 1987. V. 71
I Gave at the Office. New York: 1971. V. 69
A Jade in Aries. London: 1973. V. 71
Jimmy the Kid. New York: 1974. V. 70; 73
Killing Time. New York: 1961. V. 70; 73
Killy. New York: 1963. V. 68
Murder Among Children. New York: 1967. V. 70
One of Us Is Wrong. New York: 1986. V. 70
The Rare Coin Score. London: 1984. V. 71
Somebody Owes Me Money. New York: 1969. V. 69; 70; 72
The Spy in the Ointment. New York: 1966. V. 69; 70; 72; 73
361. New York: 1962. V. 69; 70
Two Much!. New York: 1975. V. 69; 70
What's the Worst that Could Happen?. New York: 1996. V. 72

WESTMACOTT, CHARLES MOLLOY
Catalogue of an Extremely Interesting Assemblage of Autograph Letters...the Collection of C. M. Westmacott.... London: 1852. V. 70

WESTMORELAND, WILLIAM C.
A Soldier Reports. Garden City: 1976. V. 68

WESTON, BRETT
A Personal Selection. Carmel: 1986. V. 68
Photographs from Five Decades. Millerton: 1980. V. 68

WESTON, CHRIS
California and the West. New York: 1940. V. 69

WESTON, EDWARD
California and the West. New York: 1940. V. 68; 70; 73
The Cats of Wildcat Hill. New York: 1947. V. 68; 70
Edward Weston. New York: 1932. V. 68; 73
50 Photographs. New York: 1947. V. 68
My Camera on Point Lobos. Boston: 1950. V. 68; 70
My Camera on Point Lobos. Yoesmite: 1950. V. 68
Seeing California with Edward Weston. 1939. V. 68

WESTON, GEORGE
The Apple Tree Girl. Philadelphia: 1918. V. 72

WESTON, HAROLD
The Patchwork Madonna. New York: 1929. V. 69

WESTON, MARY
A Short Account of Mary Weston, Jun. Late of Upton in the County of Essex, Particularly the Favoured State of Her Mind During Her Last Illness. London: 1799. V. 72

WESTON, STEPHEN
A Chinese Poem, Inscribed on Porcelain, in the Thirty-Third Year of the Cycle, A.D. 1776. 1816. V. 73
A Chinese Poem, Inscribed on Porcelain, in the Thirty-Third Year of the Cycle A.D. 1776. London: 1816. V. 68; 72

WESTPHAL, R.
Plein Art Painters of California: the North. Irvine: 1986. V. 69; 72

WESTPHALL, VICTOR
Mercede Reales; Hispanic Land Grants of the Upper Rio Grande Region. Albuquerque: 1983. V. 72

WESTROPP, M. S. DUDLEY
Irish Glass. London: 1920. V. 72

WESTWOOD, JENNIFER
Tales and Legends. 1971. V. 68

WESTWOOD, JOHN OBADIAH
The Art of Illuminated Manuscripts. London: 1988. V. 70

WESTWOOD, T.
Bibliotheca Piscatoria. A Catalogue of Books on Angling, the Fisheries and Fish-Culture.... London: 1883. V. 70

WETMORE, HELEN CODY
Last of the Great Scouts, the Life Story of Col. W. F. Cody "Buffalo Bill" as Told by His Sister. Chicago & Duluth: 1899. V. 68; 69; 72

WETTSTEIN, RICHARD
Ergebnisse der Botanische Expedition der Kaiserlichen Akademie der Wissenschaften nach Sudbrasilien 1901. Wien: 1908-1931. V. 70

WEVER, E. G.
The Amphibian Ear. Princeton: 1985. V. 72

WEWITZER, ROBERT
A Theatrical Pocket Book, or Brief Dramatic Chronology, from the Earliest Periods of History. London: 1814. V. 70

WEXLEY, JOHN
They Shall Not Die. New York: 1934. V. 70

WEYD, ERNEST
California and Its Resources. London: 1858. V. 69

WEYLLAND, JOHN MATTHIAS
Round the Tower; or the Story of the Londo City Mission. London: 1875. V. 71

WEYMAN, STANLEY
My Lady Rotha; a Romance. London: 1894. V. 69
The New Rector. London: 1893. V. 68
The Red Cockade. London: 1895. V. 69
Shrewsbury: a Romance. London: 1898. V. 69

WHALEN, PHILIP
Memoirs of an Interglacial Age. San Francisco: 1960. V. 72

WHALEY, MARCELLUS S.
The Old Types Pass. Gullah Sketches of the Carolina Sea Islands. Boston: 1925. V. 71

WHALLEY, JOYCE IRENE
A History of Children's Book Illustration. London: 1988. V. 68; 70

WHALLEY, THOMAS SEDGWICK
Edwy and Edilda; a Tale in Five Parts. London: 1779. V. 70

WHARFDALE; or, a Description of the Several Delightful Features of the Extensive, Splendid and Fascinating Valley, Interspersed with other Topographical Illustrations of Its Towns and Villages. Otley: 1813. V. 69

WHARFIELD, A. B.
Cooley - Army Scout, Arizona Pioneer, Wayside Host, Apache Friend. El Cajon: 1966. V. 72
With Scouts And Cavalry At Fort Apache. Tucson: 1965. V. 72

WHARTON, CLARENCE R.
Satanta. The Great Chief of the Kiowas and His People. 1935. V. 68
Texas Under Many Flags. 1930. V. 69

WHARTON, EDITH
The Age of Innocence. New York: 1920. V. 69
The Age of Innocence. Avon: 1973. V. 70
Artemis to Actaeon. London: 1909. V. 69
Artemis to Actaeon. New York: 1909. V. 69; 73
A Backward Glance. New York: 1934. V. 70
The Book of the Homeless. New York: 1916. V. 73
The Buccaneers. New York: 1938. V. 70
Certain People. New York: 1930. V. 71
Crucial Instances. New York: 1901. V. 71; 72
The Custom of the Country. New York: 1913. V. 71
The Decoration of Houses. New York: 1897. V. 70
The Decoration of Houses. London: 1907. V. 70
The Descent of Man. New York: 1904. V. 70
Edith Wharton's Library. Settrington: 1999. V. 68
Ethan Frome. New York: 1911. V. 68; 70; 73
Ethan Frome. New York: 1939. V. 69
French Ways and Their Meaning. New York: 1919. V. 68; 72
The Fruit of the Tree. New York: 1907. V. 68; 72
Ghosts. New York: 1937. V. 71
The Glimpses of the Moon. New York: 1922. V. 70
The Glimpses of the Moon. New York: 1994. V. 69; 72
Here and Beyond. New York: 1926. V. 70
The House of Mirth. London: 1905. V. 70
The House of Mirth. Leipzig: 1906. V. 70
Hudson River Bracketed. New York: 1929. V. 70; 71
In Morocco. New York: 1920. V. 71
Italian Backgrounds. New York: 1905. V. 70; 72
Italian Backgrounds. London: 1934. V. 71; 73
Italian Villas and Their Gardens. New York: 1904. V. 70
Madame de Treymes. London: 1907. V. 71
Madame De Treymes. New York: 1907. V. 68
The Marne. New York: 1918. V. 69; 70
The Marriage Playground. New York: 1928. V. 69; 71

WHARTON, EDITH continued
A Motor-Flight through France. New York: 1908. V. 71
New Year's Day. New York: 1924. V. 71
New Year's Day. New York: 1934. V. 71
The Old Maid. New York: 1924. V. 71
The Reef. New York: 1912. V. 68
Sanctuary. New York: 1903. V. 71
A Son at the Front. New York: 1923. V. 70; 71
The Valley of Decision. New York: 1902. V. 68; 70
Xingu and Other Stories. New York: 1916. V. 69

WHARTON, FRANCIS
A Treatise on the Criminal Law of the United States. Philadelphia: 1857. V. 71

WHARTON, G.
Errors of Observation. 1957. V. 69

WHARTON, GEORGE
The Works of the Late Most Excellent Philosopher and Astronomer Sir George Wharton. London: 1683. V. 70; 72

WHARTON, H. M.
War Songs and Poems of the Southern Confederacy 1861-1865. 1904. V. 68; 70; 73

WHARTON, J. E.
History of the City of Denver...to Which is added a Full and Complete Business Directory. Denver: 1909. V. 69

WHARTON, JAMES B.
Squad. New York: 1928. V. 70

WHARTON, JOHN
The Virginia Wreath, or Original Poems. Winchester: 1814. V. 72

WHARTON, WILLIAM
Birdy. London: 1979. V. 68; 69
Birdy. New York: 1979. V. 69; 70; 72; 73
Dad. New York: 1981. V. 72
Ever After. New York: 1995. V. 72
Houseboat on the Seine. New York: 1996. V. 72
A Midnight Clear. New York: 1982. V. 72

WHAT Is Good Iron and How Is It to be Got?. London: 1862. V. 71

WHATELEY, RICHARD
Memoirs of Richard Whateley, Archbishop of Dublin. London: 1864. V. 71

WHATELEY, THOMAS
Observations on Modern Gardening. Dublin: 1770. V. 70
Observations on Modern Gardening. London: 1770. V. 69; 71
Observations on Modern Gardening. London: 1777. V. 71

WHATELY, RICHARD
A Charge Delivered to the Clergy of the Dioceses of Dublin and Glandalagh...Visitation in July, 1840. 1840. V. 70
Essays on Some of the Difficulties in the Writings of the Apostle Paul. 1828. V. 69
Introductory Lectures on Political Economy...with Remarks on Tithes and On Poor Laws and On Penal Colonies. London: 1855. V. 68
Thoughts and Apophthegms from the Writings of.... Philadelphia: 1856. V. 72
The Use and Abuse of Party-Feeling in Matters of Religion Considered in Eight Sermons Preached Before the University of Oxford in the Year MDCCCXXII at the Lecture Founded by the Late Rev. John Bampton.... Oxford: 1822. V. 73

WHATMORE, D. E.
H. Rider Haggard: a Bibliogrpahy. London: 1987. V. 70

WHEAT, CARL IRVING
Books of the California Gold Rush. San Francisco: 1949. V. 68
Mapping the Transmississippi West 1540-1861. San Francisco: 1957-1963. V. 68; 73
The Maps of The California Gold Region 1848-1857. San Francisco: 1942. V. 73
The Maps of the California Gold Region 1848-1857. 1995. V. 70
The Maps of the California Gold Region 1848-1857. Storms-Mansfield: 1995. V. 68
The Pioneer Press of California. Oakland: 1948. V. 68

WHEAT, MARGARET M.
Survival Arts of the Primitive Painters. Reno: 1967. V. 72

WHEATCROFT, RACHEL
Siam and Camboida in Pen and Pastel with Excursions in China and Burmah. London: 1928. V. 71

WHEATER, W.
A Record of the Services of the Fifty-First (Second West York) The King's Own Light Infantry Regiment, with a List of Officers from 1755-1870. London: 1870. V. 72

WHEATHERLEY, HENRY
A Treatise on the Art of Boiling Sugar, Crystallizing, Lozenge Making, Comfits, Gum Goods and Other Processes for Confectionery, etc. Philadelphia: 1865. V. 68

WHEATLAND, DAVID P.
The Apparatus of Science at Harvard 1765-1800. Cambridge: 1968. V. 72

WHEATLEY, DENNIS
Curtain of Fear. London: 1953. V. 70
Desparate Measures. London: 1974. V. 69
Herewith the Clues. 1939. V. 71
Herewith the Clues. London: 1939. V. 70; 73
The Malinsay Massacre. London: 1938. V. 70; 73
Murder Off Miami. 1936. V. 71
Murder Off Miami. London: 1936. V. 68; 70; 73
They Found Atlantis. Philadelphia: 1936. V. 69; 73
Vendetta in Spain. London: 1961. V. 69
Who Killed Roger Prentice?. London: 1937. V. 73

WHEATLEY, RICHARD
Cathedrals and Abbeys in Great Britian and Ireland. New York: 1890. V. 71

WHEELER, A.
The Westmorland Dialect, with the Adjacency of Lancashire and Yorkshire in Four Familiar Dialogues.... Kendal: 1821. V. 71

WHEELER, C. A.
Sportascrapiana. London: 1868. V. 68

WHEELER, DOROTHY M.
The Three Little Pigs. London: 1955. V. 70

WHEELER, GERVASE
The Choice of a Dwelling. London: 1872. V. 68

WHEELER, HOMER
The Frontier Trail: Or From Cowboy To Colonel. Los Angeles: 1923. V. 72

WHEELER, J. TALBOYS
An Analysis And Summary Of The Historical Geography Of The Old And New Testaments. London: 1860. V. 72

WHEELER, JOHN H.
Historical Sketches of North Carolina. Philadelphia: 1851. V. 72

WHEELER, JOSEPH
Campaigns of Wheeler and His Cavalry 1862-1865.... Atlanta: 1899. V. 68
Revised System of Cavalry Tactics, for the Use of the Cavalry and Mounted Infantry. Mobile: 1863. V. 69; 70

WHEELER, KATE
Not Where I Started From. Boston: 1993. V. 72

WHEELER, MONROE
A Typographical Commonplace Book. New York: 1932. V. 68

WHEELER, OLIN D.
Lewis and Clark: Centennial Exposition. 1905. V. 68
Wonderland 1901. St. Paul: 1901. V. 72

WHEELER, OWEN
The War Office Past and Present. London: 1914. V. 71

WHEELER, W. H.
The Drainage of Fens and Low Lands by Gravitation and Steam Power. London: 1888. V. 71
A History of the Fens of South Lincolnshire, Being a Description of the Rivers Witham and Welland and Their Estuary.... Boston: 1897. V. 71

WHEELOCK, JOHN HALL
The Bright Doom: a Book of Poems. New York: 1927. V. 68

WHEELS: An Anthology of Verse. Oxford: 1917. V. 70

WHEELS; A Third Cycle. Oxford: 1918. V. 70

WHEELS.. 1919. V. 70
WHEELS. 1921. V. 70

WHEELS; a Fourth Cycle. Oxford: 1919. V. 70

WHEELWRIGHT, HORACE WILLIAM
Bush Wanderings of a Naturalist, or, Notes on the Field Sports and Fauna of Australia Felix, by an Old Bushman. London: 1864. V. 70

WHEELWRIGHT, MARY C.
Emergence Myth According to the Hanelthnayhe or Upward-Reaching Rite. Santa Fe: 1949. V. 69
Hail Chant and Water Chant. Santa Fe: 1946. V. 69
Myth of Sontso (Big Star). New York: 1940. V. 69
Tleji or Yehbechai Myth. 1938. V. 69
Wild Chant and Father Chant. 1946. V. 69

WHELAN, EDWARD
The Union of the British Provinces. Charlottetown: 1865. V. 68; 73

WHELAN, PETER
The Numismatic Dictionary, or, Collection of the Names of All Coins Known.... London: 1858. V. 68

WHELEN, T.
Small Arms Design and Ballistics. 1945. V. 69; 70; 72; 73

WHELEN, TOWNSEND
Wilderness Hunting and Wildcraft. Marshallton: 1927. V. 70

WHELER, GEORGE
A Journey into Greece...In Company of Dr. Spon of Lyons.... Cademan, Kettlewell: 1682. V. 70

WHELLAN, WILLIAM
The History and Topography of the Counties of Cumberland and Westmoreland.... Pontefract: 1860. V. 71

WHELTON, PAUL
Death and the Devil. Philadelphia: 1944. V. 69

WHERRY, GEORGE
Alpine Notes and the Climbing Foot. Cambridge: 1896. V. 68; 69

WHEWELL, W.
A General Method of Calculating the Angles Made by Any Planes of Crystals, and the Laws According to Which they Are Formed. 1825. V. 68

WHEWELL, WILLIAM
Astronomy and General Physics Considered with Reference to Natural Theology. London: 1839. V. 72
A Dialogue on the Plurality of Worlds; Being a Supplement to the Essay on that Subject. London: 1855. V. 72
Lectures on Systematic Morality Delivered in Lent Term, 1846.. London: 1846. V. 73
The Mechanics of Engineering Intended for Use in Universitities, and in Colleges of Engineers. Cambridge: 1841. V. 73
Of the Plurality of Worlds: an Essay. London: 1854. V. 72

WHIDDEN, D. G.
History of the Town of Antigonish. Wolfville: 1934. V. 73

WHIG Fraud and English Folly!. London: 1831. V. 68

WHILDIN, J. K.
Memoranda on the Strength of Materials Used in Engineering Construction. New York: 1867. V. 71

WHILEY, CECIL
Leaves of Gold. London: 1951. V. 69

WHILLANS, DON
Portrait of a Mountaineer. London: 1971. V. 69

WHIMPER, EDWARD
Thirty Prints of Holy Places Mentioned in the Holy Scriptures, Illustative of the Fulfilment of Prophecy. London: 1850. V. 68

WHIPPLE, ALLEN O.
The Evolution of Surgery in the United States. Springfield: 1963. V. 71

WHIPPLE, GEORGE C.
Typhoid Fever Its Causation, Transmission and Prevention. New York: 1908. V. 71

WHIPPLE, HENRY BENJAMIN
Lights and Shadows Of A Long Episcopate Being Reminiscences And Recollections of The Right Reverend Henry Benjamin Whipple, D. D., LLd Bishop Of Minnesota. New York: 1899. V. 72

WHIPS and Scorpions. Specimens of Modern Satiric Verse 1914-1931. London: 1932. V. 71

WHIPSAW, FRED
The Diamond of Evil. London: 1902. V. 69; 70

WHISTLER, HUGH
Popular Handbook of Indian Birds. 1949. V. 72
Popular Handbook of Indian Birds. 1963. V. 69

WHISTLER, JAMES ABBOT MC NEILL
The Gentle Art of Making Enemies. London: 1890. V. 69
Mr. Whistler's Ten O'Clock. London: 1888. V. 72
Mr. Whistler's Ten O'Clock Together With Mr. Swinburne's Comment and Mr. Whister's Reply. Chicago: 1904. V. 71
Ten O'Clock - A Lecture. Maine: 1916. V. 72

WHISTLER, LAURENCE
Armed October and Other Poems. London: 1932. V. 71
Oho!. London: 1946. V. 71; 73
Pictures on Glass. 1972. V. 73
The Work of Rex Whistler. London: 1960. V. 70
The World's Room. The Collected Poems. London: 1949. V. 71

WHISTON, WILLIAM
Astronomical Principles of Religion, Natural and Reveal'd. London: 1717. V. 70
A New Theory of the Earth, from Its Original, to the Consummation of All Things. London: 1696. V. 68
A Vindication of the Sibylline Oracles. London: 1715. V. 69

WHITAKER, A. J.
Souvenir of the Bell Tellephone Memorial and Bell Homestead, Brantford, Canada. Brantford: 1945. V. 73

WHITAKER, HAROLD
A Descriptive List of Maps of Northumberland 1576-1900. London: 1949. V. 70

WHITAKER, J. I. S.
The Birds of Tunisia, Being a History of the Birds Found in the Regency of Tunis. London: 1905. V. 73

WHITAKER, JOHN
The Genuine History of the Britons Asserted Against Mr. Macpherson. London: 1773. V. 73

WHITAKER, JOSEPH
A Descriptive List of the Deer Parks and Paddocks of England. 1892. V. 70; 72

WHITAKER, RALPH
Song of the Outriggers. 1968. V. 68

WHITE, ADAM
A Popular History of British Crustacea.... London: 1857. V. 68; 70

WHITE, ALAIN
The Stapelieae. Pasadena: 1933. V. 69; 71; 73
The Stapelieae. Pasadena: 1937. V. 69; 71; 73
The Succulent Euphorbieae (Southern Africa). Pasadena: 1941. V. 69; 72

WHITE, ALMA
The Titanic Tragedy - God Speaking to the Nations. Bound Brook: 1912. V. 69

WHITE & Parlby Illustrated Catalogue of Architectural Enrichments. Part 3. London: 1850. V. 70

WHITE, ANNE H.
The Uninvited Donkey. New York: 1957. V. 73

WHITE, ANTONIA
Diaries. London: 1991-1992. V. 71
Frost in May. London: 1933. V. 69; 73
Living with Minka and Curdy - a Marmalade Cat and His Siamese Wife. London: 1970. V. 71
The Lost Traveller. London: 1950. V. 72
Minka and Curdy. London: 1957. V. 71
The Sugar House. London: 1952. V. 73

WHITE, ARTHUR SILVA
From Sphinx To Oracle, Through The Libyan Desert to The Oasis Of Jupiter Ammon. London: 1899. V. 72

WHITE, BAILEY
Mama Makes Up Her Mind. New York: 1993. V. 70; 73

WHITE, BERTRAM
The Miracle of Haworth. 1937. V. 73

WHITE, C. S.
The People's Songster. Indianapolis: 1992. V. 68

WHITE, CHARLES
An Account of the Regular Gradation in Man and in Different Animals and Vegetables and from the Former to the Latter. London: 1799. V. 70; 73
London's Markets by Underground. 1875. V. 71
On the Regeneration of Animal Substances. Warrington: 1785. V. 69
A Treatise on the Management of Pregnant and Lying-in Women, and the Means of Curing.... Worcester: 1793. V. 68; 70; 72

WHITE, CHARLES A.
Report on the Geological Survey of the State of Iowa. Des Moines: 1870. V. 70

WHITE, COLIN
Emund Dulac. New York: 1976. V. 72

WHITE, DALE
Fast Draw Tilghman. New York: 1959. V. 69

WHITE, DIANA
The Descent of Ishtar. Hammersmith: 1903. V. 68

WHITE, EDGAR
Sati the Rastifarian. New York: 1973. V. 72

WHITE, EDMUND
The Beautiful Room. London: 1988. V. 70
The Farewell Symphony. New York: 1997. V. 72
The Flaneur. London and New York: 2001. V. 69

WHITE, EDWARD LUCAS
Helen. New York: 1925. V. 69

WHITE, ELIJAH VIERS
History of the Battle of Ball's Bluff. Leesburg: 1902. V. 69; 70

WHITE, ELLEN G.
The Spirit of Prophecy. The Great Controversy Between Christ and Satan. Battle Creek: 1870-1884. V. 71

WHITE, ELWYN BROOKS
Charlotte's Web. New York: 1945. V. 70
Charlotte's Web. 1952. V. 71
Charlotte's Web. London: 1952. V. 70; 72
Charlotte's Web. New York: 1952. V. 68; 69; 70; 71; 73
The Elephant and the Kangaroo. New York: 1947. V. 71
The Fox of Peapack. New York: 1938. V. 70; 71
The Geese. Newton: 1985. V. 71
The Lady is Cold. New York: 1929. V. 70
Letters of E. B. White. New York: 1976. V. 68; 69; 71; 72; 73
One Man's Meat. New York: 1944. V. 69
Poems and Sketches of E. B. White. New York: 1981. V. 68; 71; 72
The Points of My Compass. London: 1963. V. 71
The Second Tree from the Corner. New York: 1954. V. 71
Stuart Little. New York: 1945. V. 69; 71; 72
Stuart Little. London: 1946. V. 70
Stuart Little in the Schoolroom. New York: 1962. V. 70; 71
A Subtreasury of American Humor. New York: 1941. V. 71; 72
The Wild Flag. Boston: 1946. V. 68; 70

WHITE, ERIC
100 Years of Brentford. 1985. V. 70

WHITE, ERIC W.
Images of H.D. London: 1976. V. 71
Stravinsky's Sacrifice to Apollo. London: 1930. V. 72

WHITE, F. LE GRIX
Forgotten Seigneurs of the Alenonnais, by One Who Has raked Them Out from the Dust of Ages. 1880. V. 70

WHITE, FLORENCE
Good Things in England. London: 1933. V. 70

WHITE, FRANCIS BUCHANAN E.
The Flora of Perthshire. London: 1898. V. 71

WHITE, G. W.
The Flora of Bristol. Bristol and London: 1912. V. 69

WHITE, GEORGE FRANCIS
Views in India, Chiefly Among the Himalaya Mountains.... London: 1838. V. 69

WHITE, GEORGE S.
Memoir of Samuel Slater, the Father of American Manufactures. Philadelphia: 1836. V. 68

WHITE, GILBERT
The Natural History and Antiquities of Selborne. London: 1813. V. 69; 70; 71
Natural History and Antiquities of Selborne. London: 1877. V. 68
The Natural History and Antiquities of Selborne. London: 1890. V. 68; 70
The Natural History of Selborne. London and New York: 1900. V. 70
The Natural History of Selborne. New York: 1972. V. 71
A Naturalist's Calendar, with Observations in Various Branches of Natural History.... London: 1795. V. 70
The Works in Natural History.... 1802. V. 69

WHITE, GLEESON
Children's Books and Their Illustrators. London: 1897-1898. V. 68
Garde Joyeuse. a Handfull of Pleasant Delights from Overseas Plucked by Gleeson White. London: 1890. V. 70

WHITE, GRACE MILLER
The Shadow of the Sheltering Pines: a New Romance of the Storm Country. New York: 1919. V. 71

WHITE, GWEN
A World of Pattern. London: 1957. V. 70

WHITE, HENRY
Geology, Oil Fields, and Minerals of Canada West.... Toronto: 1865. V. 73
A Sailor-Boy's Voyage from England to Japan.... London: 1862. V. 69; 71

WHITE, HENRY KIRKE
Clifton Grove a Sketch in Verse with other Poems. London: 1803. V. 72
The Remains.... London: 1811. V. 68

WHITE, J. H.
Breakfast-Table Science. London: 1844. V. 70

WHITE, JAMES
Ancestry, Early Life, Christian Experience & Extensive Labours of Elder James White and His Wife, Mrs. Ellen G White. Battle Creek: 1880. V. 71
My Clonmel Scrapbook. 1907. V. 70
Robert Burns: a Memoir. London: 1859. V. 68

WHITE, JAMES C.
Pain, Its Mechanisms and Neurosurgical Control. Springfield: 1955. V. 68

WHITE, JOHN
The American Drawings of John White 1577-1790. London: 1964. V. 69
Art's Master-Piece, or a Companion for the Ingenious of Either Sex. London: 1720. V. 69; 72
An Essay on the Formation of Harbours of Refuge, and the Improvement of the Navigation of Rivers, and Sea Ports.... London: 1840. V. 73
Rural Architecture: Illustrated in a New Series of Designs.... Glasgow: 1845. V. 71
Some Account of the Proposed Improvement of the Western Part of London, by the Formation of Regent's Park,....(with) Brief Remarks on the Proposed Regent's Canal. London: 1815. V. 71; 73

WHITE, JOSH
Josh White Signs. Music of the New World. London: 1961. V. 72

WHITE, K.
Wild Orchids in Nepal, the Guide to the Himalayan Orchids of the Tribhuvan Rajpath and Chitwan Jungle. Bangkok: 2000. V. 72

WHITE, KATHRYN
Love's Echo. Philadelphia: 1940. V. 70

WHITE KNIGHTS LIBRARY
Catalogue of that Distinguished and Celebrated Library, Containing Numerous Very Fine and Rare Specimens from the Presses of Caxton, Pyson and Wynkyn de Worde &c. London: 1819. V. 70

WHITE, LESLIE A.
Lewis Henry Morgan. The Indian Journals 1859-1862. 1959. V. 68
Pioneers in American Anthropology: the Bandelier-Morgan Letters 1873- 1883. Albuquerque: 1940. V. 73

WHITE, LIONEL
Death of a City. New York: 1970. V. 73
To Find a Killer. New York: 1954. V. 70
Hijack. New York: 1969. V. 71
Steal Big. Greenwich: 1960. V. 72

WHITE, LONNIE J.
Hostiles and Horse Soldiers, Indian Battles And Campaigns in The West. Boulder: 1972. V. 72

WHITE, LYNN
Medieval Technology and Social Change. Oxford: 1962. V. 72

WHITE, MICHAEL C.
A Brother's Blood. 1996. V. 68; 70
A Brother's Blood. New York: 1996. V. 69; 70; 72
A Brother's Blood. London: 1997. V. 68

WHITE, MINOR
Mirrors, Messages, Manifestations. New York: 1969. V. 70

WHITE, NEWMAN I.
American Negro Folk Songs. Cambridge: 1928. V. 68; 72

WHITE, NEWPORT B.
The Red Book of Ormond. 1932. V. 69; 73

WHITE, OWEN P.
The Autobiography of a Durable Sinner. New York: 1942. V. 68; 73
A Frontier Mother. New York: 1929. V. 71
Just Me and Other Poems. El Paso: 1924. V. 71
Lead and Likker. New York: 1932. V. 69

WHITE, P.
Observations Upon the Present State of the Scotch Fisheries, and the Improvement of the Interior Part of the Highlands. Edinburgh: 1791. V. 68

WHITE, PATRICK
The Aunt's Story. London: 1948. V. 68; 70
The Aunt's Story. New York: 1948. V. 69
The Aunt's Story. London: 1958. V. 70
The Eye of the Storm. London: 1973. V. 71
Four Plays. 1965. V. 68
Happy Valley. London: 1939. V. 68; 70; 71
The Living and the Dead. New York: 1941. V. 72
The Living and The Dead. London: 1962. V. 72
Memoirs of Many in One. London: 1986. V. 70; 73
Riders in the Chariot. London: 1961. V. 68; 71
The Tree of Man. New York: 1955. V. 68; 70; 72
Voss. London: 1957. V. 72

THE WHITE Problem in America by the Editors of Ebony. Chicago: 1966. V. 72

WHITE, RANDY WAYNE
Batfishing in the Rainforest. Lyons and Burford: 1991. V. 71
Batfishing in the Rainforest. New York: 1991. V. 68; 71
Captiva. New York: 1996. V. 70; 72
The Heat Islands. New York: 1992. V. 68; 69; 71
The Man Who Invented Florida. New York: 1993. V. 69
Sanibel Flats. New York: 1990. V. 70
Sanibel Flats. New York: 1992. V. 70
Shark River. New York: 2001. V. 72

WHITE, ROBB
Surrender: Action in the Philippine Islands During World War II. Garden City: 1966. V. 68; 69
Up Periscope. Garden City: 1956. V. 68

WHITE, ROBERT
Atlas Ouranios, the Coelestial Atlas; or a New Ephemeris for... 1789.... 1789. V. 69
(Greek text) Or, a Survey of the Heavens. London: 1681. V. 73

WHITE, S. E.
The Land of Footprints. 1918. V. 73

WHITE, STEPHEN
Apologia Pro Hibernia Adversus Cambri Calumnias. Dublin: 1849. V. 70
Higher Authority. New York: 1994. V. 71
Private Practices. New York: 1992. V. 71; 73

WHITE, STEWART EDWARD
Secret Harbour. New York: 1926. V. 69

WHITE, TERENCE HANBURY
The Age of Scandal - an Excursion through a Minor Period. London: 1950. V. 71
The Book of Merlyn - the True Last Chapter of The Once and Future King. 1977. V. 72
England Have My Bones. London: 1936. V. 68; 71
The Goshawk. London: 1951. V. 68; 71
The Green Bay Tree, or, the Wicked Man Touches Wood. Cambridge: 1929. V. 70; 71
The Ill-Made Knight. London: 1942. V. 71
Loved Helen and Other Poems. London: 1929. V. 70
The Scandalmonger. London: 1952. V. 73
They Winter Abroad - a Novel. London: 1932. V. 73
The Witch in the Wood. London: 1940. V. 71

WHITE, WALKER
Flight. New York: 1926. V. 70

WHITE, WALTER
Holidays in Tyrol. London: 1876. V. 69
Holidays in Tyrol. Leipzig: 1881. V. 69
A Rising Wind. Garden City: 1945. V. 72
To Mont Blanc and Back Again. London: 1854. V. 68

WHITE, WILLIAM
Emanuel Swedenborg: His Life and Writings. London: 1868. V. 72
Furness Folk and Facts. Kendal: 1930. V. 71
The History and Directory of the Towns and Principal Villages in the County of Lincoln.... 1826. V. 71
History, Gazetteer and Directory of Lincolnshire, and the City and Diocese of Lincoln.... Sheffield: 1842. V. 70
History, Gazetteer and Directory of Lincolnshire and the City and Diocese of Lincoln.... Sheffield: 1856. V. 70
History, Gazetteer, and Directory of the West-Riding of Yorkshire.... Sheffield: 1837-1838. V. 70

WHITE, WILLIAM, & CO.
The Stranger's Guide to the Principal Objects of Curiosity, to be Found in the Port of Kingston-Upon-Hull. Hull: 1826. V. 69

WHITE, WILLIAM CHARLES
Chinese Jews. New York: 1966. V. 70; 72
Chinese Temple Frescoes: a Study of Three Wall Paintings of the Thirteenth Century. Toronto: 1940. V. 69

WHITE, WILLIAM HALE
The Autobiography of Mark Rutherford, Dissenting Minister. London: 1881. V. 73

WHITE, WILSON
Long Life. Norfolk: 1969. V. 71

WHITECAR, WILLIAM B.
Four Years Aboard the Whaleship. Philadelphia: 1864. V. 73

WHITECHURCH, VICTOR
Murder at the Pageant. New York: 1931. V. 73

WHITEFIELD, CHRISTOPHER
Mr. Chambers and Peresphone: a Tale. Waltham St. Lawrence: 1937. V. 71

WHITEFIELD, GEORGE
Journal of a Voyage from London to Savannah in Georgia. London: 1739. V. 70
A Short Account of God's Dealings with the Reverend Mr. George Whitefield, A.B. Late of Pembroke College, Oxford. London: 1740. V. 69

WHITEHALL in Cumberland. London: 1865. V. 71

WHITEHEAD, ALFRED NORTH
An Enquiry Concerning the Principles of Natural Knowledge. Cambridge: 1919. V. 69
Principia Mathematica. Cambridge: 1910. V. 70; 72
Treatise on Universal Algebra; with Applications. Cambridge: 1898. V. 73

WHITEHEAD, CHARLES
The Adventures of Gerard, the Lion Killer. New York: 1858. V. 69
The Life and Times of Sir Walter Raleigh.... London: 1854. V. 73

WHITEHEAD, COLSON
The Intuitionist. New York: 1999. V. 71; 72; 73

WHITEHEAD, G.
In the Nicobar Islands. London: 1924. V. 69

WHITEHEAD, G. K.
Deer and Their Management in the Deer Parks of G. B. and Ireland. 1950. V. 72; 73
The Deer of Great Britain and Ireland. 1964. V. 69; 73
Deer of the World. 1972. V. 69; 72; 73
Deer of the World. London: 1972. V. 70
Deer of the World. New York: 1972. V. 69; 70; 73
The Deerstalking Grounds of Great Britain and Ireland. London: 1960. V. 71; 73

WHITEHEAD, HENRY S.
Jumbee and Other Uncanny Tales. 1944. V. 69

WHITEHEAD, J., & SON
Views of Appleby & District. Appleby: 1910. V. 71

WHITEHEAD, JESSUP
Steward's Handbook and Dictionary. Chicago: 1903. V. 73
Steward's Handbook and Guide to Party Catering. Chicago: 1889. V. 70

WHITEHEAD, P. J. P.
Chinese Natural History Drawings Selected from the Reeves Collection in the British Museum. London: 1974. V. 73
Forty Drawings of Fishes made by the Artists Who Accompanied Captain James Cook. 1968. V. 72
Forty Drawings of Fishes Made by the Artists Who Accompanied Captain James Cook on His Three Voyages to the Pacific. London: 1968. V. 73

WHITEHEAD, WILLIAM
The Goat's Beard, a Fable. London: 1777. V. 69

WHITEHILL, WALTER MUIR
Museum of Fine Arts, Boston. A Centennial History. Cambridge: 1970. V. 71

WHITEHORN, KATHARINE
Observations. London: 1970. V. 69

WHITEHOUSE, J. HOWARD
Ruskin and Brantwood. An Account of the Exhibition Rooms. Cambridge: 1937. V. 71; 72

WHITEHURST, J.
An Inquiry into the Original State and Formation of the Earth. 1786. V. 69

WHITELAW, G.
Raquel Forner. Buenos Aires: 1980. V. 72

WHITELAW, JAMES
An Essay on the Population of Dublin. Dublin: 1805. V. 73

WHITELAW, WILLIAM MENZIES
The Maritimes and Canada Before Confederation. Toronto: 1934. V. 73

WHITELEY, WILLIAM
Illustrated Book of Fashion for the Spring and Summer Seasons 1890. London: 1890. V. 68

WHITELOCKE, R. H.
Sprains and Allied Injuries of Joints. London: 1909. V. 69

WHITEMAN, BETTY BLUE
Honyocker's Heritage - a History of Rickey and Community. Rickey: 1981. V. 68

WHITEMAN, ROBIN
The Cadfael Companion. New York: 1995. V. 71

WHITESIDE, J.
Shappe in Bygone Days. Kendal: 1904. V. 71

WHITFIELD, CHRISTOPHER
Lady from Yesterday. Waltham St. Lawrence: 1939. V. 71
Together and Alone: Two Short Novels. Waltham St. Lawrence: 1945. V. 71

WHITFIELD, HENRY
Sigismar. London: 1799. V. 73

WHITFIELD, RAOUL
Danger Circus. New York: 1933. V. 71
Death in a Bowl. New York: 1931. V. 73
Green Ice. New York: 1930. V. 73
The Virgin Kills. New York: 1932. V. 73

WHITFIELD, S.
Magritte. London: 1992. V. 72

WHITFORD, H. N.
The Forests of the Philippines. Manila: 1911. V. 70

WHITFORD, WILLIAM CLARKE
Colorado Volunteers in the Civil War. The New Mexico Campaign. Denver: 1906. V. 69

WHITHARD, PHILIP
Illuminating and Missal Painting on Paper and Vellum. London: 1909. V. 72

WHITING, JOHN
Persecution Exposed, in Some Memoirs Relating To The Sufferings of John Whiting. London: 1791. V. 72

WHITING, PERRY
Perry Experiences of a Pioneer. Los Angeles: 1930. V. 71

WHITLEY, EDYTHE JOHNS RUCKER
Sam Davis Confederate Hero 1842-1863. Nashville: 1947. V. 69; 70

WHITLING, HENRY JOHN
Pictures of Nuremberg: and Rambles in the Hills and Valleys of Franconia. London: 1850. V. 73

WHITLOCKE, M.
A Garland of Wild Poesy Comprising Tales, Sketches, Incidents &c. Dumfries: 1878. V. 69

WHITMAN, ALFRED
Samuel Cousins. London: 1904. V. 72

WHITMAN, JAMES
Canada. A Ballad in Three Parts. Halifax: 1885. V. 73

WHITMAN, ROYAL
Clinical Lessons in Orthopaedic Surgery. New York: 1900. V. 71

WHITMAN, SARAH HELEN
Edgar Poe and His Critics. New York: 1860. V. 69; 72
Hours of Life and Other Poems. Providence: 1853. V. 68

WHITMAN, STEPHEN
Here's Luck: A Social Footnote. New York: 1931. V. 72

WHITMAN, W. F.
Five Decades with Tropical Fruit.... Englewood: 2001. V. 72

WHITMAN, WALT
After All, Not to Create Only. Boston: 1871. V. 70; 71; 73
American Bard Being the Preface to the First Edition of Leaves of Grass Now Restored to Its Native Verse Rhythms and Presented as a Living Poem. Santa Cruz: 1981. V. 70
American Primer. Boston: 1904. V. 70; 73
As a Strong Bird on Pinions Free, and Other Poems. Washington: 1872. V. 71; 72; 73
Autobiographia or the Story of a Life. New York: 1892. V. 71
Calamus. A Series of Letters Written During the Yars 1868-1880. Boston: 1897. V. 70
Complete Poems and Prose.... Camden: 1888. V. 68; 71
Complete Poetry and Selected Prose and Letters. London: 1938. V. 72
Complete Prose Works. Philadelphia: 1892. V. 71
The Complete Writings of Walt Whitman.... New York & London: 1902. V. 71
Democratic Vistas. Washington: 1871. V. 68; 71; 72
An 1855-1856 Notebook Toward the Second Edition of Leaves of Grass. Carbondale: 1959. V. 71

WHITMAN, WALT continued
Franklin Evans. New York: 1842. V. 70
The Gathering of Forces. New York: 1920. V. 71
Good-bye My Fancy. Philadelphia: 1891. V. 71; 73
I Sit and Look Out. Editorials from the Brooklyn Daily Times. New York: 1932. V. 71
Leaves of Grass. Brooklyn: 1855. V. 70
Leaves of Grass. Brooklyn: 1856. V. 71; 72; 73
Leaves of Grass. Boston: 1860-1861. V. 68; 69; 71
Leaves of Grass. Camden: 1876. V. 70; 71; 72
Leaves of Grass. Camden: 1882. V. 73
Leaves of Grass. Philadelphia: 1889. V. 71
Leaves of Grass. Philadelphia: 1891-1892. V. 71
Leaves of Grass. New York: 1942. V. 69; 70; 73
Leaves of Grass. Mount Vernon: 1950. V. 70; 72
Leaves of Grass - The First (1955) Edition. New York: 1959. V. 72
Leaves of Grass Imprints. American and European Criticisms on "Leaves of Grass". Boston: 1860. V. 70
Leaves of Grass, Including Sands at Seventy, Good Bye My Fancy, Old Age Echoes and a Backward Glance o'er Travel'd Roads. Boston: 1898. V. 73
Leaves of Grass. With Sands at Seventy & a Backward Glance O'er Travel'd Roads. Philadelphia: 1889. V. 68; 72
Letters Written by Walt Whitman to His Mother 1866-1872. New York: 1936. V. 71
November Boughs. Philadelphia: 1888. V. 68; 71
November Boughs. London: 1889. V. 68
Overhead the Sun: Lines from Walt Whitman. New York: 1969. V. 69
Poems by Walt Whitman. London: 1868. V. 68
Selected Poems. New York: 1892. V. 68; 69; 71
Song of the Open Road. New York: 1990. V. 69; 72
Specimen Days and Collect. Philadelphia: 1882-1883. V. 68; 70; 71; 72
Specimen Days in America. London: 1887. V. 71
Two Rivulets. Camden: 1876. V. 70; 71; 72
Walt Whitman in Camden: a Selection of Prose from Specimen Days. Camden: 1938. V. 68; 73
Walt Whitman's Backward Glances. Philadelphia: 1947. V. 71
Walt Whitman's Diary in Canada with Extracts From Other of His Diaries and Literary Note-Books. Boston: 1904. V. 68; 71
Walt Whitman's Memoranda During the War Written on the Spot in 1863- 1865. Camden: 1875-1876. V. 71; 72
Walt Whitman's Workshop. A Collection of Unpublished Manuscripts. Cambridge: 1928. V. 71
The Wound Dresser. Boston: 1898. V. 70; 71

WHITMAN, WILLIAM
Navaho Tales. Boston: 1923. V. 69

WHITNEY, A. D. T., MRS.
Just How: A Key to the Cook-Books. Boston: 1887. V. 68; 73

WHITNEY, CASPAR
Jungle Trails and Jungle People. New York: 1905. V. 69

WHITNEY, COURTNEY
MacArthur. His Rendezvous with a History. New York: 1956. V. 69; 71

WHITNEY, HARRY
Hunting with the Eskimos.... 1910. V. 73

WHITNEY, HELEN HAY
The Bed-time Book. New York: 1909. V. 72
Some Verses. London: 1898. V. 69

WHITNEY, J. D.
The Climatic Changes of Later Geological Times.... 1882. V. 69

WHITNEY, J. PARKER
Reminiscences of a Sportsman. New York: 1906. V. 70; 71

WHITNEY, JOSIAH DWIGHT
The Yosemite Guide-Book: a Description of the Yosemite Valley and the Adjacent Region of the Sierra Nevada, and of the Big Trees of California. Cambridge: 1869. V. 70

WHITNEY, PARKHURST
Time Exposure. New York: 1931. V. 72

WHITNEY, PHYLLIS A.
Emerald. Garden City: 1983. V. 72
Rainsong. Garden City: 1984. V. 72
Step to the Music. New York: 1953. V. 69
Vermilion. Garden City: 1981. V. 72

WHITRIDGE, ISAAC FLETCHER
Whitridge's Northern Miscellany. Carlisle: 1847-1848. V. 71

WHITTAKER, EDMUND TAYLOR
A History of the Theories of Aether and Electricity. London: 1951-1953. V. 72

WHITTAKER, FREDERICK
A Complete Life of General George A. Custer. Lincoln: 1993. V. 72
A Popular Life Of General George A. Custer. New York: 1876. V. 72

WHITTAKER, MILO LEE
Pathbreakers & Pioneers of the Pueblo Region Comprising a History of Pueblo From the Earliest Times. np: 1917. V. 71

WHITTELL, H. M.
Literature of Australian Birds. Mansfield: 1993. V. 68
The Literature of Australian Birds. Mansfield: 1994. V. 73

WHITTEMORE, EDWARD
Quin's Shanghai Circus. New York: 1974. V. 71; 72
Sinai Tapestry. New York: 1977. V. 68

WHITTEMORE, LOREN R.
An Illustrated History of Ranching in the Pikes Peak Region. 1967. V. 68

WHITTIER, CHARLES COLLYER
The Descendants of Thomas Whittier and Ruth Green of Salisbury and Haverhill, Massachusetts. Rutland: 1937. V. 68; 73

WHITTIER, JOHN GREENLEAF
At Sundown. Cambridge: 1890. V. 68
At Sundown. London: 1892. V. 69
Ballads of New England. Boston: 1870. V. 68
Maud Miller. Boston: 1867. V. 68
Moll Pitcher, a Poem. Boston: 1832. V. 69
Narrative of James Williams, an American Slave, Who Was for Several Years a Driver on a Cotton Plantation in Alabama. New York: 1838. V. 68; 73
The Panorama and Other Poems. Boston: 1856. V. 70
Prose Works. Boston: 1872. V. 70
Snow-Bound. Boston: 1866. V. 71
Snow-Bound. Boston: 1906. V. 73
Snow-Bound. New York: 1930. V. 69

WHITTING, P. D.
Byzantine Coins. London: 1973. V. 72

WHITTINGTON And His Cat. Baltimore: 1837. V. 71

WHITTINGTON, HARRY
The Devil Wears Wings. New York: 1960. V. 69; 71
God's Back Was Turned. Greenwich: 1961. V. 70; 71
Guerrilla Girls. New York: 1961. V. 71
Journey into Violence. New York: 1961. V. 71
The Naked Jungle. New York: 1955. V. 71
Nita's Place. New York: 1960. V. 71
Slay Ride for a Lady. Kingston: 1950. V. 69; 70
Strangers on Friday. New York: 1959. V. 70
Strictly for the Boys. New York: 1959. V. 71
Strip the Town Naked. New York: 1960. V. 70
Temptations of Valerie. New York: 1957. V. 71
Web of Murder. Greenwich: 1958. V. 70; 71
The Wild Seed. New York: 1956. V. 70; 71

WHITTINGTON PRESS
A Miscellany of Type. Andoversford: 1990. V. 72

WHITTLESEY, CHARLES
Ancient Mining on the Shores of Lake Superior. Washington: 1863. V. 68

WHITTOCK, NATHANIEL
The Decorative Painters' and Glaziers' Guide.... London: 1827. V. 68; 70
The Decorative Painters' and Glaziers' Guide.... London: 1841. V. 69

WHITTOCK, TREVOR
A Reading of the Canterbury Tales. Cambridge: 1968. V. 69

WHITTON, R. W.
Hardwick's Traders' Check-Book; or Desk Companion for Checking Invoices.... 1867. V. 71

WHITWORTH, CHARLES
An Account of Russia as It Was in the Year 1710. 1758. V. 72

WHITWORTH, GEOFFREY
The Art of Nijinsky. 1913. V. 68

WHITWORTH, LAURA A.
Spes mea Christus. Boston: 1885. V. 69

WHITWORTH, ROBERT
A Report and Survey of the Canal, Proposed to Be Made on One Level, from Waltham Abbey to Moorfields. London: 1774. V. 72

WHO Burnt Columbia?. Charleston: 1873. V. 70

WHO Shall Make the Law Makers?. London: 1854. V. 70

THE WHOLE Art of Bookbinding.... Oswestry: 1811. V. 73

THE WHOLE Art of Dress! or, the Road to Elegance and Fashion, at the Enormous Saving of Thirty Per Cent!!!. 1830. V. 72

WHOM to Marry and How to Get Married! Or, The Adventures of a Lady in Search of a Good Husband. London. V. 71

WHO'S Who in Cumberland and Westmorland. 1937. V. 71

WHO'S Who In Cumberland and Westmorland. London: 1937. V. 72

WHO'S Who in New Jersey. Atlantic City: 1925. V. 69

WHO'S Who in the Pacific Southwest: A Compilation of Authentic Biographical Sketches of Citizens of Southern California and Arizona. Los Angeles: 1913. V. 68

WHO'S Who in Tony Sarg's Zoo. Springfield: 1937. V. 73

WHO'S Who In Yorkshire. North and East Ridings. Hereford: 1935. V. 72

WHYBROW, P. J.
Fossil Vertebrates of Arabia. New Haven: 1999. V. 70; 72

WHYMPER, CHARLES
Egyptian Birds. 1909. V. 69
Egyptian Birds for the Most Part Seen in the Nile Valley. London: 1909. V. 73

WHYMPER, EDWARD
The Ascent of the Matterhorn. 1880. V. 73
The Ascent of the Matterhorn. London: 1880. V. 69; 72
A Guide to Chamonix and the Range of Mont Blanc. London: 1901. V. 69; 72
How to Use the Aneroid Barometer. 1891. V. 68; 70
Scrambles Amongst The Alps. Philadelphia. V. 72
Scrambles Amongst the Alps. 1871. V. 68; 70; 73
Scrambles Amongst the Alps. London: 1871. V. 69
Scrambles Amongst the Alps. 1880. V. 68
Scrambles Amongst the Alps. 1900. V. 68; 70
Travels Amongst the Great Andes of the Equator. 1892. V. 68; 70; 73
Travels Amongst the Great Andes of the Equator. London: 1892. V. 69; 70; 72
Travels Amongst the Great Andes of the Equator. New York: 1892. V. 73
Travels Amongst the Great Andes of the Equator and Supplementary Appendix to Travels Amongst the Green Andes of the Equator. London: 1891-1892. V. 72

WHYMPER, F.
The Fisheries of the World. London: 1883. V. 71
The Sea: Its Stirring Story of Adventure, Peril and Heroism. London. V. 72
The Sea: Its Stirring Story of Adventure, Peril and Heroism. London. V. 70

WHYMPER, FREDERICK
Travel and Adventure in the Territory of Alaska. New York: 1869. V. 70
Travels and Adventure in the Territory of Alaska. London: 1868. V. 71

WHYTE, ALEXANDER
Characters and Characteristics of William Law, Nonjuror and Mystic. London: 1895. V. 69

WHYTE, FREDERIC
Actors of the Century. London: 1898. V. 72

WHYTE, J. H.
Church and State in Modern Ireland 1923-1970. 1971. V. 70

WHYTE, JON
Indians in the Rockies. 1985. V. 68

WHYTE, LANCELOT LAW
Aspects of Form. A Symposium on Form in Nature and Art. London: 1951. V. 68

WHYTE, SAMUEL
Miscellanea Nova. Dublin: 1800. V. 69; 73
A Miscellany, Containing, Amidst a Variety of Other Matters Curious and Interesting, Remarks on Boswell's Johnson, with Considerable Additions.... Dublin;: 1799. V. 73

WHYTE MELVILLE, GEORGE JOHN
Cerise. London: 1882. V. 68
General Bounce or the Lady and the Locusts. London: 1855. V. 68; 72
The Gladiators: a Tale of Rome and Judaea. Leipzig: 1864. V. 70
Good for Nothing or All Down Hill. London: 1878?. V. 68
Holmby House: a Tale of Old Northamptonshire. London: 1870. V. 68
The Interpreter: a Tale of the War. London: 1875. V. 68
Kate Coventry: an Autobiography. London: 1872. V. 68
Katerfelto: a Story of Exmoor. London: 1876. V. 68
Market-Harborough; or, How Mr. Sawyer Went to the Shires. London: 1876. V. 68
Riding Recollections. London: 1880. V. 68
Roy's Wife. London: 1879. V. 68
Sarchedon: a Legend of the Great Queen. London: 1872. V. 68
Satanella: a Story of Punchestown. London: 1884. V. 68
Songs and Verse. London: 1885?. V. 68
Sporting Songs and Verses. 1926. V. 68
Tilbury Nogo; or, Passages in the Life of an Unsuccessful Man. London: 1867. V. 68
The True Cross. London: 1884. V. 68
Uncle John. London: 1882. V. 68

WHYTT, ROBERT
An Essay on the Vital and Other Involuntary Motions of Animals. Edinburgh: 1751. V. 70; 73
An Essay on the Vital and Other Involuntary Motions of Animals. Edinburgh: 1763. V. 69
Observations on the Nature, Causes and Cure of Those Diseases Which Have Been Commonly Called Nervous, Hypochondriac or Hysterical.... Edinburgh: 1767. V. 72

WICKHAM, J. D. C.
Records by Spade and Terrier. Bath: 1915. V. 72

WICKS, FREDERICK
Golden Lives: the Story of a Woman's Courage. Edinbrugh: 1891. V. 68

WICQUEFORT, ABRAHAM DE
Advis Fidele aux Veritables HolIndois.... The Hague: 1673. V. 69

WIDDESS, J. D. H.
An Account of the Schools of Surgery, R.C.S. Dublin 1789-1948. 1949. V. 70

WIDDICOMBE, TOBY
A Reader's Guide To Raymond Chandler. Westport: 2001. V. 72

WIDEMAN, JOHN EDGAR
Brothers and Keepers. New York: 1984. V. 69; 72
Damballah. London: 1984. V. 72
Fatheralong. New York: 1994. V. 72
A Glance Away. New York: 1967. V. 69; 73
Hiding Place. London: 1984. V. 70; 72
Hiding Place and Damballah. New York: 1981. V. 69
The Lynchers. New York: 1973. V. 72
Philadelphia Fire. New York: 1990. V. 69
Reuben. New York: 1987. V. 72
Sent for You Yesterday. New York: 1983. V. 69
The Stories of John Edgar Wideman. New York: 1992. V. 68; 72
Two Cities. Boston/New York: 1998. V. 72

THE WIDOW of Kent; or, the History of Mrs. Rowley. London: 1788. V. 69

WIDOWS' Traps and Maidens' Tricks. New York: 1872?. V. 71

WIEBE, EDWARD
The Paradise of Childhood: a Manual for Self Instruction in Friedrich Froebel's Educational Principles. Springfield: 1887. V. 72

WIEBEN, JULIUS HENRICUS
Dissertatio Medica Inauguralis de Haemoptysi.... Utrect: 1772. V. 72

WIED, MAXIMILIAN, PRINZ VON
People of the First Man, Life Among the Plains Indians in Their Final Days of Glory. New York: 1976. V. 69
Travels In Brazil, in 1815, 1816, and 1817. London: 1820. V. 69

WIEDERSEIM, GRACE G.
The Tiny Tots. New York: 1909. V. 71

WIEDEWELT, JOHANNES
Samling af Aegyptiske og Romerske Oldsager, I Deel. Copenhagen: 1786. V. 70; 72

WIEGHORST, OLAF
Olaf Wieghorst Retrospective. Tucson: 1981. V. 69
Wieghorst: Dean of Western Painters. Tulsa: 1982. V. 68

WIEGLEY, RUSSELL F.
History of The United States Army. New York: 1967. V. 72

WIEL, H. J. VAN DER
Inheritance of Glioma. Amsterdam: 1960. V. 68

WIELAND, G. R.
The Cerro Cuadrado Petrified Forest. Washington: 1935. V. 68

WIENER, LEO
Mayan and Mexican Origins. Cambridge: 1926. V. 71

WIENER, NORBERT
Cybernetics of Control and Communication in the Animal and the Machine. Paris: 1948. V. 72
Cybernetics of Control and Communication in the Animal and the Machine. Cambridge and New York: 1961. V. 69

WIENERS, JOHN
The Hotel Wentley Poems. San Francisco: 1958. V. 73
Nerves. London: 1970. V. 72

WIESE, KURT
Buddy the Bear. New York: 1936. V. 73
Liang & Lo. Garden City: 1930. V. 70

WIESEL, ELIE
All Rivers Run to the Sea. New York: 1995. V. 69
Night. London: 1960. V. 70
One Generation After. London: 1971. V. 72

WIESNER, DAVID
The Three Pigs. New York: 2001. V. 73

WIFFEN, JEREMIAH HOMES
Verses Written in the Portico of the Temple of Liberty, at Woburn Abbey, On Placing Before It the Statues of Locke and Erskine in the Summer 1835. London: 1836. V. 73

WIGGIN, KATE DOUGLAS
The Arabian Knights: Their Best Known Tales. New York: 1909. V. 73
A Child's Journey with Dickens. New York: 1912. V. 69
Mother Carey's Chickens. Boston: 1911. V. 72
Penelope's English Experiences (in England and Scotland). Boston: 1900. V. 71
Rebecca of Sunnybrook Farm. Boston: 1903. V. 69; 71
Rebecca of Sunnybrook Farm. New York: 1917. V. 71
Timothy's Quest, a Story for Anybody, Young or Old, Who Cares to Read It. London: 1892. V. 69

WIGGINS, I. L.
A Flora of the Alaskan Arctic Slope. Toronto: 1962. V. 72
Flora of the Galapagos Islands. Stanford: 1971. V. 71

WIGGINS, JOHN
A Letter to the Abesentee Landlords of the South of Ireland; on the Means of Tranquillising their Tenantry, and Improving Their Estates. London: 1822. V. 73
The Practice of Embanking Lands from the Sea.... 1852. V. 71

WIGGINS, MARIANNE
Went South. New York: 1980. V. 72

WIGHT, JOHN
Mornings at Bow Street. (with) *More Mornings at Bow Street.* London: 1824-1827. V. 68; 73
Mornings at Bow Street.... London: 1875. V. 68
Sunday in London, Illustrated in Fourteen Cuts, by George Cruikshank.... London: 1833. V. 68

WIGHT, R.
Spicilegium Neilgherrense, or a Selection of Neilghherry Plants. Madras: 1846-1851. V. 73

WIGLEY, THOMAS B.
The Art of the Goldsmith and Jeweller.... London: 1898. V. 71

WIGMORE, J. H.
Science and Learning in France, with a Survey of Opportunities for American Students in French Universities.... Chicago: 1917. V. 69

WIJDEVELD, H. T.
The Life Work of the American Architect Frank Lloyd Wright. Santpoort: 1925. V. 68
The Life Work of the American Architect Frank Lloyd Wright. New York: 1965. V. 68
The Wendingen: the Early Work of the Great Architect Frank Lloyd Wright. New York: 1994. V. 68

WIJNBLAD, CARL
Ritningar pa Waningshus Fyratio of Sten, Och Trettio af Trad.... Stockholm: 1782. V. 72

WILBER, C. D.
The Great Valleys and Prairies of Nebraska and the Northwest. Omaha: 1881. V. 73

WILBERFORCE, ROBERT
The Life of William Wilberforce. (with) *The Correspondence of....* London: 1838-1840. V. 71

WILBERFORCE, WILLIAM
A Practical View of the Prevailing Religious System of Professed Christians, in the Higher and Middle Classes in this Country, Contrasted with Real Christianity. London: 1797. V. 73

WILBERT, C. D.
The Great Valleys and Prairies of Nebraska ad the Northwest. Omaha: 1881. V. 68

WILBUR, MARGUERITE E.
The Indian Uprising in Lower California, 1734-1737, As Described by Father Sigismundo Taraval. Los Angeles: 1931. V. 71
A Pioneer of Sutter's Fort 1846-1850. The Adventures of Heinrich Lienhard. Los Angeles: 1941. V. 70
Raveneau De Lussan - Buccaneer of the Spanish Main and Early French Filibuster of the Pacific. Cleveland: 1930. V. 69

WILBUR, RICHARD
Ceremony and Other Poems. New York: 1950. V. 68
Elizabeth Bishop: A Memorial Tribute. New York: 1982. V. 72
The 1996 Frost Medal Lecture. 1997. V. 73

WILCE, J. W.
How to Enjoy Football. Columbus: 1923. V. 68

WILCHILSEA, ANNE FINCH, COUNTESS OF
Miscellany Poems on Several Occasions. London: 1713. V. 70

WILCOX, ARTHUR
Moon Rocket. London Edinburgh: 1946. V. 73

WILCOX, DONALD E.
Damn Right I've Got the Blues. San Francisco: 1993. V. 72

WILCOX, ELLA WHEELER
Custer and Other Poems. Chicago: 1896. V. 72
New Thought Pastels. Holyoke MA: 1906. V. 72
Poems of Pleasure. London: 1911. V. 68
Poems of Passion and Pleasure. London. V. 71

WILCOX, JAMES
Modern Baptists. New York: 1983. V. 69

WILCOX, R. TURNER
The Mode in Hats and Headdress. New York: 1952. V. 73

WILCOX, W. D.
Camping in the Canadian Rockies. 1896. V. 68; 70
Camping in the Canadian Rockies. 1898. V. 73
The Rockies of Canada. 1900. V. 68; 70; 73

WILD, CHARLES
Twelve Etched Outlines, Selected from the Architectural Sketches Made in Belgium, Germany and France. (with) *Twelve Etched Outlines....* London: 1833-1836. V. 68

THE WILD Girl of the Wood. London: 1812. V. 68

WILD, JOHN
The History of Castle Bytham: Its Ancient Fortress and Manor, Its Feudal Lords, Vaudey Abbey &c. Stanford: 1871. V. 70

WILD, JUSTUS
England As It Is, and As It Might and Ought to Be. London: 1852. V. 73

WILDE, JOHN
1985: a Collaboration. Mount Horeb: 1992. V. 71
The Story of Jane and Joan. Mt. Horeb: 1977. V. 69

WILDE, OSCAR
After Reading. Letters of Oscar Wilde to Robert Ross. London: 1921. V. 68
The Ballad of Reading Gaol. London: 1898. V. 68; 69; 71; 72; 73
The Ballad of Reading Gaol. 1994. V. 71
The Ballad of Reading Gaol. Virginia Water: 1999. V. 73
The Birthday of the Infanta. Paris: 1928. V. 72
Children in Prison, and Other Cruelties of Prison Life. London: 1898. V. 69; 73
The Decay of Lying. New York: 1902. V. 68
The Duchess of Padua. London: 1908. V. 72
Extracts from the Poems of Oscar Wilde. London: 1980. V. 71
The Fisherman and His Soul. San Francisco: 1939. V. 70; 72
For Love of the King - A Burmese Masque. London: 1922. V. 68; 72
The Happy Prince. London: 1905. V. 69
The Happy Prince. London: 1910. V. 70; 71
The Happy Prince. London: 1913. V. 72
The Happy Prince. London: 1920. V. 73
The Happy Prince. London: 1970. V. 70
A House of Pomegranates. London: 1891. V. 68; 73
An Ideal Husband. 1899. V. 71
Intentions, the Decay of Lying, Pen, Pencil and Poison, the Critic as Artist, the Truth of Masks. London: 1891. V. 68
Lady Windermere's Fan A Play About A Good Woman. London: 1893. V. 68
The Letters of Oscar Wilde. London: 1962. V. 68
Lord Arthur Savile's Crime and Other Stories. London: 1891. V. 68
The Picture of Dorian Gray. Paris. V. 73
The Picture of Dorian Gray. London: 1891. V. 70
The Picture of Dorian Gray. New York: 1957. V. 69
Poems. London: 1881. V. 69; 72
Poems. Boston: 1882. V. 73
Poems, together with His Lecture on the English Renaissance (now first published). 1903. V. 72
Ravenna. Oxford: 1878. V. 68; 72
Salome. New York. V. 69
Salome. London: 1907. V. 72
Salome. Boston: 1912. V. 68
Salome. Paris: 1923. V. 73
Salome. San Francisco: 1927. V. 73
Salome. New York: 1938. V. 70; 71
Salome. New York: 1945. V. 68
Sixteen Letters from Oscar Wilde. London: 1930. V. 68
Sixteen Letters from Oscar Wilde. New York: 1930. V. 72
The Sphinx. London: 1894. V. 69
The Sphinx. London: 1920. V. 71
A Woman of No Importance. London: 1894. V. 72
The Woman's World. London: 1887. V. 71
The Young King and Other Stories. London: 1946. V. 72
The Young King and Other Tales by Oscar Wilde. New York: 1962. V. 68; 69

WILDE, PERCIVAL
Design for Murder. New York: 1941. V. 69
Inquest. New York: 1940. V. 68
P. Moran, Operative. New York: 1947. V. 68
Rogues in Clover. 1929. V. 73

WILDER, ALEXANDER
History of Medicine. New Sharon: 1901. V. 69

WILDER, DWIGHT
Life and Letters of Wilder Dwight. Boston: 1891. V. 71

WILDER, F. W.
The Modern Packing House. Chicago: 1905. V. 70

WILDER, L. B.
Adventures with Hardy Bulbs. New York: 1936. V. 71
Colour in My Garden. Garden City: 1918. V. 69

WILDER, LAURA INGALLS
By the Shores of Silver Lake. New York: 1939. V. 71
Little Town on the Prairie. New York: 1941. V. 68
The Shores of Silver Lake. New York: 1939. V. 72

WILDER, M. P.
The Horticulture of Boston and Vicinity. Boston: 1881. V. 69; 72

WILDER, MITCHELL A.
Santos; the Religious Art of New Mexico. Colorado Springs: 1943. V. 69; 72

WILDER, THORNTON
The Alcestiad. 1962. V. 69
American Characteristics and Other Essays. New York: 1979. V. 73
The Angel that Troubled the Waters. London: 1928. V. 72
The Angel that Troubled the Waters. New York: 1928. V. 73
The Bridge of San Luis Rey. London: 1927. V. 72
The Bridge of San Luis Rey. New York: 1927. V. 73
The Bridge of San Luis Rey. London: 1941. V. 69
The Cabala. New York: 1926. V. 73
The Eighth Day. New York: 1967. V. 68; 73
Heaven's My Destination. New York: 1935. V. 73
The Ides of March. New York: 1948. V. 70; 73
The Long Christmas Dinner and Other Plays in One Act. New York and New Haven: 1931. V. 69; 73
Lucrece. Boston;: 1933. V. 73

WILDER, THORNTON continued
The Merchant of Yonkers. New York: 1939. V. 70; 71; 72; 73
Our Town. New York: 1938. V. 69; 71; 73
Our Town. Avon: 1974. V. 68; 69; 71; 73
The Woman of Andros. London: 1930. V. 72

WILDFIRE, WALTER, PSEUD.
The Comet. Boston: 1811-1812. V. 69

WILDING, LAWRENCE
Storm Star. London: 1929. V. 73

WILDRIDGE, T. TINDALL
Grotesque in Church Art. London. V. 72

WILDSCHUT, WILLIAM
Crow Indian Beadwork - a Descriptive and Historical Study. New York: 1959. V. 68; 73

WILEY, HARVEY W.
Foods and Their Adulteration. Philadelphia: 1907. V. 69

WILEY, SAMUEL T.
Biographical and Historical Cyclopedia of Westmoreland County, Pennsylvania. Philadelphia: 1890. V. 70

WILFRED'S Annual 1924. V. 69

WILFRED'S Annual 1932. V. 69

WILFRED'S Annual 1936. V. 69

WILHELM, BENJAMIN
The Ready Reckoner, at Rate Per Centage, in a Compendium of Federal Money.... Dayton: 1827. V. 68

WILHELM, CROWN PRINCE
From My Hunting Day-Book. 1912. V. 70

WILHELM, THOMAS
A Military Dictionary and Gazetteer Comprising Ancient and Modern Military Technical Terms. Phila: 1881. V. 72

WILHELMINA, CONSORT OF FRIEDRICH MARGRAVINE
Memoirs of Frederica Sophia Wilhelmina, Princess Royal of Prussia, Margravine of Bareith. London: 1812. V. 72

WILIMOVSKY, N. J.
Environment of the Cape Thompson Region, Alaska. Washington: 1966. V. 70; 72

WILKES, CHARLES
Narrative of the United States Exploring Expedition, During the Years 1838, 1839, 1840, 1841, 1842. London: 1852. V. 73

WILKES, JOHN
The History of England from the Revolution to the Accession of the Brunswick Line. London: 1768. V. 69
A Letter to the Right Honourable William Lord Mansfield... Upon Some Star Chamber Proceedings...Against the Publishers of the Extraordinary North Britton. London: 1768. V. 71
The North Briton. London: 1763. V. 73

WILKES, MAURICE
The Preparation of Programs for an Electronic Digital Computer. Cambridge: 1951. V. 69

WILKESON, SAMUEL
A Concise History of the Commencement, Progress and Present Condition of the American Colonies in Liberia. Washington: 1839. V. 68

WILKIE, D.
Gentians. London: 1936. V. 72
Gentians. London: 1950. V. 72; 73

WILKINS, CHARLES
The History of the Literature of Wales from the year 1300 to the year 1650. Cardiff: 1884. V. 71

WILKINS, G. L.
Catalogue and Historical Account of the Sloane Shell Collection. 1953-1957. V. 73

WILKINS, HENRY
Suite de Vues Pittoresques des Ruines Pompeii et un Precis Historique de Ville. Rome: 1819. V. 70

WILKINS, JAMES F.
An Artist on the Overland Trail - the 1849 Diary and Sketches of James F. Wilkins. San Marino: 1968. V. 73

WILKINS, JOHN
An Essay Towards a Real Character and a Philosophical Language. 1668. V. 72
Mathematicall Magic or the Wonders that May be Performed by Mechanicall Geometry. London: 1648. V. 71

WILKINS, MARY E.
The Long Arm and Other Detective Tales. London: 1895. V. 68; 72

WILKINS, THURMAN
Thomas Moran - Artist of the Mountains. Norman: 1966. V. 69; 70; 72

WILKINS, W. H.
The Love of an Uncrowned Queen; Sophie Dorothea, Consort of George I and Her Correspondence with Philip Christopher Count Konigsmarck. London: 1900. V. 72

WILKINS, WILLIAM
The Antiquities of Magna Graecia. Cambridge: 1807. V. 70; 72

WILKINS, WILLIAM GLYDE
Charles Dickens in America. New York: 1911. V. 69
First and Early American Editions of the Works of Charles Dickens. Cedar Rapids: 1910. V. 68
Some Letters of Charles Dickens. Pittsburgh: 1907. V. 69

WILKINSON, E. S.
Shanghai Birds. Shanghai: 1929. V. 73

WILKINSON, FRANK
Yorkshire Limestone. Bradford: 1968. V. 69

WILKINSON, GEORGE HUTTON
The Old Inmates of Harperley Park 1858. Cambridge: 1859. V. 70

WILKINSON, HARRISON
The Principles of an Equitable and Efficient System of Finance, Founded Upon Self-Evident, Universal and Invariable Principles.... London: 1820. V. 72

WILKINSON, J.
The Narrative of a Blockade Runner. New York: 1877. V. 69

WILKINSON, J. G.
Manners and Customs of the Ancient Eygptians. New York: 1878. V. 71

WILKINSON, J. V. S.
The Lights of Canopus. London. V. 72

WILKINSON, JANET W.
Sketches and Legends Amid the Mountains of North Wales, in Verse. London: 1840. V. 69

WILKINSON, JOHN GARDNER
On Colour and the Necessity for a General Diffusion of Taste. London: 1858. V. 68

WILKINSON, JOSEPH
Select Views in Cumberland, Westmoreland and Lancashire. London: 1810. V. 72

WILKINSON, NEVILE R.
To All and Singular. 1925. V. 69

WILKINSON, R.
Switzerland With its Subjects And Allies, Drawn From The Best Authorities. London: 1794. V. 72

WILKINSON, ROBERT
Londina Illustrata. Graphic and Historic Memorials of Monasteries, Churches, Chapels, Schools, Charitable Foundations, Palaces, Halls, Courts, Processions, Places.... London: 1834. V. 71

WILKINSON, SYLVIA
Cale. Boston: 1970. V. 71; 73
Moss on the North Side. Boston: 1966. V. 73

WILKINSON, T. J.
The Falcon. Thirsk: 1889-1891. V. 69

WILKINSON, TATE
Memoirs of His Own Life. York: 1790. V. 70; 72

WILKINSON, THOMAS
Tours to the British Mountains, with the Descriptive Poems of Lowther, and Emont Vale. London: 1824. V. 71

WILKS, SAMUEL
Lectures on Diseases of the Nervous System Delivered at Guy's Hospital. London: 1883. V. 68

WILLANS, GEOFFREY
How to Be Topp. London: 1954. V. 70
Whizz for Atomms It's that Irrepressible School-Boy Nigel Molesworth of St. Custards Again. London: 1956. V. 70

WILLARD, CHARLES DWIGHT
The Free Harbor Contest at Los Angeles. Los Angeles: 1899. V. 69
A History of the Chamber of Commerce of Los Angeles, California, from Its Foundation, September 1888 to the Year 1900. Los Angeles: 1899. V. 73

WILLARD, EMMA
Last Leaves of American History.... New York: 1849. V. 71
Morals for the Young; or, Good Principles Instilling Wisdom. New York: 1857. V. 71

WILLARD, JAMES F.
The Trans-Mississippi West - Papers Read at a Conference Held at the University of Colorado June 18-June 21, 1929. Boulder: 1930. V. 69

WILLARD, JOHN
The Charles M. Russell Book. Seattle: 1970. V. 69; 71

WILLARD, NANCY
Childhood of the Magician. New York: 1973. V. 70
The Lively Anatomy of God. New York: 1967. V. 68
Pish, Posh said Hieronymus Bosch. New York: 1991. V. 70
A Visit to William Blake's Inn: Poems for Innocent and Experienced Travelers. New York: 1981. V. 68; 70

WILLARD, SIMON
The Columbian Union, Containing General and Particular Explanations of Government.... Albany: 1815. V. 73

WILLARD, THEODORE A.
The Lost Empires of the Itzaes and Mayas. An American Civilization, Contemporary with Christ, Which Rivaled the Culture of Egypt. Glendale: 1933. V. 71

WILLCOCKS, T.
Flora Poetica; or, Poetry of Flowers. Devonport: 1835. V. 71

WILLCOX, A. R.
Rock Paintings at the Drakensberg. London: 1956. V. 69

WILLEFORD, CHARLES
The Burnt Orange Heresy. New York: 1971. V. 69
A Charles Willeford Omnibus. London: 1991. V. 69
Cockfighter. Chicago: 1962. V. 68; 69; 70; 71; 73
Cockfighter Journal. Santa Barbara: 1989. V. 69; 70; 71; 72; 73
The Difference. Tucson: 1999. V. 71; 72
Everybody's Metamorphosis. Miami Beach: 1988. V. 72
Everybody's Metamorphosis. Missoula: 1988. V. 69
A Guide for the Undehemorrhoided. Boynton Beach: 1977. V. 68; 69; 70; 71
High Priest of California. New York: 1953. V. 71
High Priest of California & Wild Wives. New York: 1956. V. 71; 72; 73
Honey Gal. New York: 1958. V. 68; 70; 72
I Was Looking for a Street. Woodstock: 1988. V. 68; 69; 71
Kiss Your Ass Goodbye. Miami Beach: 1987. V. 69; 72; 73
Kiss Your Ass Goodbye. London: 1989. V. 69; 70; 71
The Machine in Ward Eleven. New York: 1963. V. 68; 69; 71; 72; 73
Miami Blues. New York: 1984. V. 72
New Forms Of Ugly. Miami Beach: 1987. V. 72
New Hope for the Dead. New York: 1985. V. 69; 72
Off the Wall. Montclair: 1980. V. 69; 71
The Outcast Poets. Yonkers: 1947. V. 69
Proletarian Laughter. Yonkers: 1948. V. 72; 73
The Shark-Infested Custard. Novato: 1993. V. 72
Sideswipe. New York: 1987. V. 71; 72; 73
The Way We Die Now. Hastings-On-Hudson: 1988. V. 68; 69; 70; 71; 72; 73
The Way We Die Now. New York: 1988. V. 71; 72; 73
Whip Hand. Greenwich: 1961. V. 68; 69; 70
The Woman Chaser. Chicago: 1960. V. 68; 69; 71

WILLEMIN, NICOLAS XAVIER
Monumens Francais Inedits Pour Servir a l'Histoire des Arts Depuis le Vie Siecle Jusqu'au Commencement du XVIIe.... Paris: 1806-1839. V. 69; 72

WILLERT, JAMES B.
Little Big Horn Diary Chronicle of The 1876 Indian War. La Mirada, CA: 1977. V. 72
March of The Columns Chronicle of The 1876 Indian War, June 27- September 16, 1876. El Segundo: 1994. V. 72
To The Edge of Darkness - A Chronicle of The 1876 Indian War. El Segundo: 1998. V. 72

WILLHEIM, DONALD A.
Operation: Phantasy. New York: 1967. V. 71

WILLIAM, HARRISON
Intruder in the Dust. New York: 1948. V. 70

WILLIAM, TERRY TEMPEST
Pieces of White Shell. New York: 1984. V. 69

WILLIAMS, A. B.
Game Trails in British Columbia. 1925. V. 72
Shrimps, Lobsters and Crabs of the Atlantic Coast of the Eastern United States, Maine to Florida. Washington: 1984. V. 73

WILLIAMS, A. D.
Spanish Colonial Furniture. Milwaukee: 1941. V. 69

WILLIAMS, AMELIA W.
The Writings of Sam Houston: 1821-1847. Austin: 1938-1943. V. 69

WILLIAMS, ANNA
Miscellanies in Prose and Verse. London: 1766. V. 69

WILLIAMS, ARCHIBALD
Petrol Peter. London: 1906. V. 71

WILLIAMS, BEN AMES
Leave Her To Heaven. Boston: 1944. V. 71
Small Town Girl. New York: 1935. V. 70

WILLIAMS, BENJAMIN SAMUEL
Choice Stove and Greenhouse Flowering Plants. (and) Choce Stove and Greenhouse Ornamental Leaves Plants. London: 1883-1876. V. 69
Choice Stove and Greenhouse Ornamental-Leaves Plants.... London: 1870. V. 69
The Orchid Grower's Manual. Weinheim: 1961. V. 72
The Orchid Grower's Manual. Lehre: 1973. V. 71; 73
The Orchid Grower's Manual. London: 1894. V. 69
Select Ferns Lycopods: British and Exotic. London: 1873. V. 71; 72

WILLIAMS, BRAD
A Borderline Case. New York: 1960. V. 71

WILLIAMS, C. K.
A Dream of Mind. New York: 1992. V. 69
Flesh and Blood. New York: 1987. V. 73
Helen. Washington: 1991. V. 73
The Lark. The Thrush. The Starling. Providence: 1983. V. 73
Misgivings: My Mother, My Father, Myself. New York: 2000. V. 69
Poems 1963-1983. New York: 1988. V. 69
Repair. New York: 1999. V. 69
The Vigil. New York: 1907. V. 69

WILLIAMS, C. R., MRS.
Tales National and Revolutionary. Providence: 1830. V. 69

WILLIAMS, CATHERINE READ ARNOLD
Original Poems, on Various Subjects. Providence: 1828. V. 73

WILLIAMS, CHANCELLOR
The Raven. Philadelphia: 1943. V. 69

WILLIAMS, CHARLES
Aground. New York: 1960. V. 68; 71
All Hallows' Eve. London: 1945. V. 71
Arthurian Torso Containing the Posthumous Fragment of the Figure of Arthur.... London: 1948. V. 69
The Big Bite. New York: 1956. V. 71
Dead Calm. New York: 1963. V. 68
Descent into Hell. London: 1937. V. 69
Divorce. London: 1920. V. 73
The House of the Octopus. 1945. V. 68
The House of the Octopus. London: 1945. V. 70; 71
Le Mare Aux Diams. Paris: 1956. V. 70
The Long Saturday Night. Greenwich: 1962. V. 70
Man in Motion. London: 1959. V. 71; 72
A Myth of Shakespeare. London: 1936. V. 70
The Place of the Lion. London: 1947. V. 69
Religion and Love in Dante - the Theology of Romantic Love. London: 1941. V. 72
River Girl. New York: 1951. V. 70
Scorpion Reef. New York: 1955. V. 71
Shadows of Ectasy. London: 1933. V. 69
Silvershell, or the Adventures of an Oyster. London: 1857. V. 68; 70
Taliessin through Logres. London: 1938. V. 68; 73
Thomas Cranmer of Canterbury. 1936. V. 68
Thomas Cranmer of Canterbury. London: 1936. V. 72
Witchcraft. London: 1941. V. 72

WILLIAMS, CHARLES THEODORE
Aero-Therapeutics or the Treatment of Lung Diseases by Climate. London: 1894. V. 68

WILLIAMS, CHAUNCEY PRATT
Lone Elk. The Life Story of Bill Williams; Trapper and Guide of the Far West. 1935-1936. V. 68
Lone Elk, The Life Story of Bill Williams, Trapper and Guide of the Far West. Denver: 1935-1936. V. 70

WILLIAMS, CICELY
Zermatt Saga. London: 1964. V. 69

WILLIAMS, CLARENCE
Clarence Williams Presents a Boogie Woogie and Blues Folio. New York: 1940. V. 72

WILLIAMS, DAVID
Damned by Destiny. Brighton: 1982. V. 69
Divided Treasure. London: 1987. V. 72
The History of Monmouthshire.... London: 1796. V. 68
Treasure in Oxford. London: 1988. V. 72
Treasure in Roubles. London: 1986. V. 72
Wedding Treasure. London: 1985. V. 70; 71

WILLIAMS, EDWARD
Poems, Lyric and Pastoral. London: 1794. V. 69

WILLIAMS, EMLYN
The Corn is Green. New York: 1941. V. 71
George. An Early Autobiography. London: 1961. V. 70

WILLIAMS, ERIC
Land. 1996. V. 71

WILLIAMS, ERNEST
The Fireman's Aid.... Lynn: 1922. V. 69

WILLIAMS, F. L.
Matthew Fontaine Maury, Scientist of the Sea. New Brunswick: 1963. V. 73

WILLIAMS, FREDERICK S.
The Midland Railway: Its Rise and Progress. London: 1878. V. 70

WILLIAMS, FREDERICK SMEETON
The Wonders of the Heavens. London: 1852. V. 72

WILLIAMS, G. C.
Lady Anne Clifford, Countess of Dorset, Pembroke and Montgomery 15901676. Her Life, Letters and Work.... Kendal: 1922. V. 71

WILLIAMS, GEORGE W.
History of the Negro Troops in the War of the Rebellion, 1861-1865. New York: 1888. V. 69

WILLIAMS, H.
The Geology of Crater Lake National Park, Oregon.... Washington: 1942. V. 70

WILLIAMS, H. L.
Great Houses of America. New York: 1966. V. 69

WILLIAMS, H. NOEL
The Pearl of Princesses: The Life of Marguerite D'Angouleme, Queen of Navarre. London: 1916. V. 72

WILLIAMS, H. T.
Window Gardening Devoted Specially to the Culture of Flowers and Ornamental Plants for Indoor Use and Parlor Decoration. New York: 1872. V. 71

WILLIAMS, H. W.
Select Views in Greece. London: 1829. V. 69

WILLIAMS, HARCOURT
Tales from Ebony. 1934. V. 68; 71

WILLIAMS, HARLEY
Don Quixote of the Microscope. London: 1954. V. 68

WILLIAMS, HARRY
Texas Trails, Legends of the Great Southwest. San Antonio: 1932. V. 68

WILLIAMS, HEATHCOTE
Falling for a Dolphin. London: 1990. V. 71

WILLIAMS, HELEN
A Search for Freedom. Sea Breeze: 1898. V. 73

WILLIAMS, HELEN MARIA
Peru, a Poem. London: 1784. V. 73

WILLIAMS, HENRY T.
The Pacific Tourist: Williams' Illustrated Trans-Continental Guide of Travel from the Atlantic to the Pacific Ocean. New York: 1878. V. 69

WILLIAMS, HENRY W.
On the Treatment of Iritis Without Mercury. Boston: 1856. V. 72

WILLIAMS, HERBERT
H. B. Williams' Song and Joke Book. 1871. V. 71

WILLIAMS, HERMANN WARNER
The Civil War: The Artists Record. Boston: 1961. V. 72

WILLIAMS, IOLA A.
Points in Eighteenth Century Verse: a Bibliographer's and Collector's Scrapbook.... London: 1934. V. 70

WILLIAMS, IOLO A.
Seven XVIIIth Century Bibliographies. 1924. V. 71

WILLIAMS, ISAAC
The Cathedral, or the Catholic and Apostolic Church in England. Oxford: 1838. V. 69

WILLIAMS, J. E.
Letter to A. B. J., Author of the Pamphlet Entitled The Union As It Was and the Constitution As It Is. New York: 1863. V. 70

WILLIAMS, J. P.
Alaskan Adventure. 1955. V. 69; 70; 72

WILLIAMS, J. R.
Cowboys Out Our Way. New York: 1951. V. 71; 72
Out Our Way. New York: 1943. V. 68; 71

WILLIAMS, JOHN
An Apology for the Pulpits: Being in Answer to a Late Book Intituled, Good Advice to the Pulpits. Together with an Appendix. London: 1688. V. 70
Early Spanish Manuscript Illumination. New York: 1977. V. 70
An Enquiry into the Truth of the Tradition, Concerning the Discovery of America by Prince Madog ab Owen Gwynedd, about the Year 1170. 1791. V. 72
The Natural History of the Mineral Kingdom, Relative to the Strata of Coal, Mineral.... Edinburgh: 1810. V. 68

WILLIAMS, JOHN A.
The Angry Black. New York: 1962. V. 72
The Junior Bachelor Society. Garden City: 1976. V. 73
The Man Who Cried I Am. Boston: 1967. V. 72
Sissie. New York: 1963. V. 71; 72

WILLIAMS, JOHN AMBROSE
Memoirs of John Philip Kemble, Esq.... London: 1817. V. 72

WILLIAMS, JOHN B.
The New Zealand Journal 1842-1844. Salem: 1956. V. 70

WILLIAMS, JOHN CAMP
An Oneida Printer, William Williams, Printer, Publisher, Editor. New York: 1906. V. 69

WILLIAMS, JOHN H.
St. Peter's Street Northampton. Excavations 1973-1976. Northampton: 1979. V. 73

WILLIAMS, JOHN S.
History of the Invasion and Capture of Washington and of the Events Which Preceded and Followed. New York: 1857. V. 71

WILLIAMS, JONATHAN
Amen Huzza Selah. Highlands: 1960. V. 69; 71
Amen Huzza Selah. Karlsruhe-Durlach: 1960. V. 73
Aposiopeses (Odds and Ends). Minneapolis: 1988. V. 73
Druopaedia; or a New and Interesting View of the Druidical System of Education.... Leominster: 1823. V. 70
Elegies and Celebrations. Highlands: 1962. V. 70
Elite/Elate Poems: Selected Poems 1971-1975. 1979. V. 73
Elite/Elate Poems: Selected Poems 1971-1975. Highlands: 1979. V. 69
Epitaphs for Lorine. Pentland: 1973. V. 73
In the Azure Over the Squalor.... 1983. V. 73
In the Field At the Solstice. Seven Epitaphs for His Friends by Jonathan Williams, Highlands, North Carolina December 22, 1976. Champaign: 1976. V. 73
Lines About Hills Above Lakes: Postals. Fort Lauderdale: 1964. V. 73
The Loco Logodaedalist in Situ - Selected Poems 1968-1970. London: 1971. V. 69
Lullabies Twisters Gibbers Drags. Bloomington: 1967. V. 73
Paean to Dvorak, Deemer & McClure. San Francisco: 1996. V. 73
Pairidaeza. Dentdale, Cumbria: 1975. V. 69; 73
Portrait Photographs. Frankfort: 1979. V. 69
Red/Gray. Black Mountain College: 1952. V. 73
Ripostes. Aspen/Stuttgart: 1968. V. 72
Sharp Tools for Catullan Gardens. Bloomington: 1968. V. 69; 72
Strung Out with Elgar On a Hill. Urbana: 1970. V. 73
Twelve Jargonelles from the Herbalist's Notebook 1965. Bloomington: 1965. V. 73

WILLIAMS, JOSHUA
A Treatise on the Law of Personal Property. Philadelphia: 1891. V. 70

WILLIAMS, JOY
The Changeling. Garden City: 1978. V. 72
State of Grace. Garden City: 1973. V. 68; 72

WILLIAMS, MARGERY
The Velveteen Rabbit. Garden City: c. 1923. V. 70
The Velveteen Rabbit. New York: 1974. V. 73
The Velveteen Rabbit. London: 1991. V. 69

WILLIAMS, MARY FLOYD
History of the San Francisco Committee of Vigilance of 1851 - a Study of Social Control on the California Frontier in the Days of the Gold Rush. Berkeley: 1921. V. 69

WILLIAMS, MILLER
Halfway from Hoxie. New York: 1973. V. 72

WILLIAMS, O. W.
Pioneer Surveyor Frontier Lawyer. El Paso: 1966. V. 68; 69; 70

WILLIAMS, ORLO
Life and Letters of John Rickman. London: 1911. V. 72

WILLIAMS, OTIS
Temptations. New York: 1988. V. 73

WILLIAMS, RENWICK
The Authentic Trial of Renwick Williams, for Assaulting Miss Ann Porter on the Night of the 18th of January, 1790.... London: 1790. V. 70

WILLIAMS, ROBERT FOLKSTONE
Strawberry Hill: an Historical Novel. London: 1847. V. 72

WILLIAMS, S. W.
The Middle Kingdom, A Survey of the Geography, Government, Literature, Social Life, Arts and History of the Chinese Empire and Its Inhabitants. New York: 1889. V. 69

WILLIAMS, SAMUEL
Six Wood-Blocks to Illustrate McQuinn's Description of Three-Hundred Animals. 1812. V. 69

WILLIAMS, SAMUEL COLE
Adair's History of the American Indians. Johnson City: 1930. V. 73
Early Travels in the Tennessee Country 1540-1800. Johnson City: 1928. V. 71; 73
History of the Lost State of Franklin. New York: 1933. V. 73
Tennessee During the Revolutionary War. Nashville: 1944. V. 71; 73

WILLIAMS, SIDNEY
The Murder of Miss Betty Sloane. New York: 1935. V. 69

WILLIAMS, STEPHEN W.
American Medical Biography, or Memoirs of Eminent Physicians Embracing Principally Those Who Have Died since the Publication of Dr. Thacher's Work.... Greenfield: 1845. V. 68; 71; 73
American Medical Biography, or Memoirs of Eminent Physicians, Embracing Principally Those who Have Died Since the Publication of Dr Thacher's Work.... 1845. V. 70

WILLIAMS, TALIESIN
Cardiff Castle: a Poem. Merthyr-Tydfil: 1827. V. 68; 72; 73
Iolo Manuscripts. Liverpool: 1888. V. 73

WILLIAMS, TENNESSEE
Baby Doll. New York: 1956. V. 68; 69; 70; 71; 73
Baby Doll. London: 1957. V. 69; 71
Battle of Angels. Murray: 1945. V. 69; 71; 73
Blue Mountain Ballads/Cabin. New York: 1946. V. 71
Camino Real. New York: 1953. V. 69
Cat on a Hot Tin Roof. New York: 1955. V. 70
Cat on a Hot Tin Roof. London: 1956. V. 69; 70; 71
Collected Stories. New York: 1985. V. 73
The Eccentricities of a Nightingale and Summer and Smoke. New York: 1964. V. 71
Eight Mortal Ladies Possessed. New York: 1974. V. 69; 73
The Glass Menagerie. New York: 1945. V. 68; 69; 70; 71; 73
Hard Candy. New York: 1959. V. 70
In The Bar of a Tokyo Hotel. New York: 1969. V. 72
In the Winter of Cities. New York: 1956. V. 73
In the Winter of Cities. Norfolk: 1956. V. 69; 71

WILLIAMS, TENNESSEE continued
The Knightly Quest. New York: 1966. V. 68; 69; 70; 71
Memoirs. Garden City: 1975. V. 69; 71; 73
The Milk Train Doesn't Stop Here Anymore. New York: 1964. V. 69
The Milk Train Doesn't Stop Here Anymore. Norfolk: 1964. V. 72
Moise and the World of Reason. New York: 1975. V. 68; 71
Moise and the World of Reason. London: 1976. V. 73
The Mutilated. New York: 1967. V. 72
The Night of the Iguana. New York: 1962. V. 68; 71
Orpheus Descending. New York: 1958. V. 69; 70
Period of Adjustment. London: 1960. V. 73
Period of Adjustment. London: 1961. V. 69
The Roman Spring of Mrs. Stone. New York: 1950. V. 69; 70; 71
The Rose Tattoo. New York: 1950. V. 70
Selected Plays. Franklin Center: 1980. V. 69; 70; 71; 73
Steps Must be Taken. New York: 1980. V. 69; 70
A Streetcar Named Desire. New York: 1947. V. 68; 69; 72
A Streetcar Named Desire. London: 1949. V. 69
A Streetcar Named Desire. New York: 1982. V. 69; 72
Suddenly Last Summer. New York: 1958. V. 71; 73
Summer and Smoke. London: 1952. V. 69
Sweet Bird of Youth. New York: 1959. V. 71; 73
Tennessee Williams' Letters to Donald Windham 1940-1965. Verona: 1976. V. 70; 73
The Theatre of Tennessee Williams. New York: 1971-1981. V. 69; 71
Un Tramway Nomme Desir. Paris: 1949. V. 69
27 Wagons Full of Cotton and Other One Act Plays. London: 1949. V. 69
Vieux Carre. New York: 1979. V. 69; 73
Where I Live. New York: 1978. V. 69; 72

WILLIAMS, TERRY TEMPEST
Coyote's Canyon. Salt Lake City: 1989. V. 71
Desert Quartet. An Erotic Landscape. 1995. V. 71
LEAP. New York: 2000. V. 71
Pieces of White Shell. New York: 1984. V. 69; 70; 73
Refuge. New York: 1991. V. 69; 71; 73
An Unspoken Hunger. New York: 1994. V. 71; 72

WILLIAMS, THEO
Prophetic Mystery, or the Man who Lives In Hell. Chicago: 1897. V. 71

WILLIAMS, THOMAS
Ceremony of Love. Indianapolis: 1955. V. 72
The Negro in American Politics. Pittsburgh: 1860. V. 68

WILLIAMS, VALENTINE
The Clue of the Rising Moon. Boston: 1935. V. 70
The Crouching Beast. Boston: 1928. V. 70
The Curiosity of Mr. Treadgold. Boston: 1937. V. 68
Dead Man Manor. Boston: 1936. V. 68
The Man with the Clubfoot. New York: 1918. V. 68
The Man With The Clubfoot. Boston: 1931. V. 72
The Mysterious Miss Morrisot. Boston: 1930. V. 72
The Mystery of the Gold Box. Boston: 1932. V. 70
The Orange Divan. Boston: 1923. V. 68; 70
The Portcullis Room. Boston: 1934. V. 71
The Spider's Touch. Boston: 1936. V. 71

WILLIAMS, VIOLET M.
Ten Little Nigger Boys. London: 1950. V. 69; 73

WILLIAMS, W.
An Essay on Halifax. Halifax: 1761. V. 69

WILLIAMS, W. H.
Facsimiles of Feoffments of Land and Other Ancient Documents Relating to the Parish Church of St. Peter.... London: 1913. V. 71

WILLIAMS, W. M.
The Sociology of and English Village - Gosforth. London: 1956. V. 71

WILLIAMS, W. MATTIEU
A Vindication of Phrenology. London: 1894. V. 69

WILLIAMS, W. W.
I, the King. New York: 1924. V. 69

WILLIAMS, WALTER
The State of Missouri: an Autobiography. Columbia: 1904. V. 68

WILLIAMS, WILLIAM
Journal of the Life, Travels and Gospel Labours of William Williams. Cincinnati: 1828. V. 68
My Summer in the Alps. New York: 1914. V. 68

WILLIAMS, WILLIAM CARLOS
The Autobiography of William Carlos Williams. New York: 1951. V. 68
The Broken Span. 1941. V. 70
The Broken Span. Connecticut: 1941. V. 72
The Build-Up. New York: 1952. V. 68
The Clouds, Aigeltinger, Russia &c. 1948. V. 68; 69; 73
The Clouds, Aigeltinger, Russia &c. Aurora: 1948. V. 73
The Collected Poems 1909-1939 and 1939-1962. 1986. V. 70
The Complete Collected Poems 1906-1938. New York: 1938. V. 72
The Desert Music and Other Poems. New York: 1954. V. 69; 73
A Dream of Love: a Play in Three Acts and Eight Scenes. New York: 1948. V. 70
The Gift, a Poem. 1957. V. 68
Go Go. New York: 1923. V. 73
Imaginations. New York: 1970. V. 69
In the Money: White Mule - Part II. Norfolk: 1940. V. 72
Journey to Love: Poems. New York: 1955. V. 68
The Knife of the Times and Other Stories. Ithaca: 1932. V. 71
Life Along the Passaic River. Norfolk: 1938. V. 70
Paterson. New York: 1946-1958. V. 70; 71; 73
The Pink Church. Columbus: 1949. V. 70
Selected Essays of William Carlos Williams. New York: 1954. V. 69
The Selected Letters of.... New York. V. 71
Two Drawings and Two Poems. 1937. V. 68; 69; 73
A Voyage to Pagany. New York: 1928. V. 73
White Mule. Norfolk: 1937. V. 72
William Carlos Williams, John Sanford: a Correspondence. Santa Barbara: 1984. V. 69
The William Carlos Williams Reader. New York: 1966. V. 73

WILLIAMS-ELLIS, CLOUGH
Architect Errant. London: 1971. V. 72
Portmeirion - the Place and Its Meaning. London: 1963. V. 71

WILLIAMSON, ALEX
Journeys in North China, Manchuria and Eastern Mongolia. London: 1870. V. 70

WILLIAMSON, C. N., MRS.
Name The Woman. London: 1924. V. 72

WILLIAMSON, CHARLES
Description of the Genessee Country, Its Rapidly Progressive Population and Improvements.... Albany: 1798. V. 68

WILLIAMSON, G. C.
Daniel Gardner, Painter in Pastel and Gouache. 1921. V. 70
George Third Earl of Cumberland (1558-1605). His Life and Voyages. A Study From Original Documents. Cambridge: 1920. V. 71; 72
The Keats Letters, Papers and Other Relics in the Hampstead Public Library. London: 1914. V. 72
Lady Anne Clifford, Countess of Dorset, Pembroke & Montgomery, 1590-1676. Kendal: 1922. V. 70; 72
Murray Marks and His Friends. London: 1919. V. 73

WILLIAMSON, GEORGE
Letters Respecting the Watt Family. Greenock: 1840. V. 71
Memorials of the Lineage, Early Life, Education and Development of the Genius of James Watt. Edinburgh: 1856. V. 69

WILLIAMSON, GEORGE M.
Catalogue of Books Letters and Manuscripts Written by Walt Whitman in the Library of George M. Williamson. Jamaica, N.Y: 1903. V. 71

WILLIAMSON, HAROLD F.
Winchester, the Gun that Won the West. Washington: 1952. V. 72

WILLIAMSON, HENRY
A Clear Water Stream. 1958. V. 68
The Dream of Fair Women. London: 1931. V. 69
The Innocent Moon. London: 1961. V. 68
It Was the Nightingale. London: 1962. V. 68
Linhay on the Downs. London: 1929. V. 68
The Old Stag and Other Hunting Stories. London: 1933. V. 71
Richard Jefferies - Selections of His Work, with Details of His Life and Circumstance, His Death and Immortality. London: 1937. V. 68
Some Nature Writers and Civilization. Oxford: 1960. V. 70
The Village Book. 1930. V. 70

WILLIAMSON, HUGH
The History of North Carolina. Philadelphia: 1812. V. 68; 73

WILLIAMSON, HUGH ROSS
A Wicked Pack of Cards. London: 1961. V. 70

WILLIAMSON, J.
Ferns of Kentucky. Louisville: 1878. V. 69; 72

WILLIAMSON, JACK
The Humanoids. New York: 1949. V. 69
The Legion. Reading: 1952. V. 71

WILLIAMSON, JAMES A.
The Voyages of the Cabots and the English Discovery of North America Under Henry VII and Henry VIII. London: 1929. V. 73

WILLIAMSON, JAMES J.
Mosby's Rangers: a Record of the Operations of the Forty-Third Battalion of Virginia Cavalry from Its Organization to the Surrender. New York: 1896. V. 70
Mosby's Rangers: A Record of the Operations of the Forty-Third Battalion of Virginia Cavalry from Its Organization to the Surrender. New York: 1909. V. 69

WILLIAMSON, KEN
This is Jazz. London: 1960. V. 70

WILLIAMSON, THAMES
Beginning at Dusk: An Interlude. 1935. V. 72
Hunky. New York: 1929. V. 70

WILLIAMSON, THAMES continued
The Woods Colt. New York: 1933. V. 70

WILLIAMSON, THOMAS
The Complete Angler's Vade Mecum. 1808. V. 68; 73
The Complete Angler's Vade-Mecum. London: 1808. V. 69
Illustrations of Indian Field Sports.... Westminster: 1892. V. 69
Oriental Field Sports. London: 1819. V. 73

WILLIAMSON, WILLIAM
Description of the Tumulus, Lately Opened at Gristhorpe, Near Scarborough.... Scarborough: 1834. V. 70

WILLIAMSON, WILLIAM CRAWFORD
Reminiscences of a Yorkshire Naturalist. London: 1896. V. 68; 72

WILLIAMS-TREFFGARNE, W. H.
The Festival and Other Poems. London: 1927. V. 73

WILLIAMS-WOOD, CYRIL
Staffordshire Pot Lids and Their Potters. London: 1972. V. 72

WILLICH, A. F. M.
The Domestic Encyclopedia; or, a Dictionary of Facts.... Philadelphia: 1804-1803. V. 68
Lectures on Diet and Regimen.... London: 1799. V. 69

WILLICH, CHARLES M.
Popular Tables Arranged in New Form, Giving Information at Sight for Ascertaining, According to the Carlisle Table of Mortality, the Value of Lifehold, Leasehold and Church Property.... London: 1853. V. 71

WILLINGHAM, CALDER
End as a Man. New York: 1947. V. 69
End as a Man. London: 1952. V. 68
Natural Child. New York: 1952. V. 73
Reach to the Stars. New York: 1951. V. 73

WILLINS, EDWARD PRESTON
Some of the Old Halls and Manor-Houses in the County of Norfolk. 1890. V. 73

WILLIS, B.
Earthquake Conditions in Chile. Washington: 1929. V. 70; 72
East African Plateaus and Rift Valleys. Washington: 1936. V. 70; 72
Index to the Stratigraphy of North America. Washington: 1912. V. 70

WILLIS, BROWNE
Notitia Parliamentaria; or an History of the Counties, Cities and Boroughs in England and Wales. (with) Notitia Parliamentaria: Containing an Account of the First Returns and Incorporations of the Cities, Towns and Boroughs. 1730. V. 72
Notitia Parliamentaria; or, an History of the Counties, Cities and Boroughs in England and Wales. (with) Notitia Parliamentaria: Containing an Account of the First Returns and Incorporations of the Cities, Towns and Boroughs. London: 1730. V. 70

WILLIS, CECIL
The Nature of Agistment Tithe of Unprofitable Stock Illustrated in the Case of the Vicar of Holbeach, as Decreed by the Right Honourable lrd Chief Parker, Baron Smythe &c.... London: 1778. V. 70

WILLIS, CONNIE
Doomsday Book. 1992. V. 69

WILLIS, IRENE COOPER
The Authorship of Wuthering Heights. London: 1936. V. 70

WILLIS, NATHANIEL PARKER
American Scenery. London: 1840-1842. V. 69; 73
American Scenery. Barre: 1971. V. 69
Canadian Scenery. London: 1842. V. 68; 72
Canadian Scenery. Toronto: 1967. V. 73

WILLIS, R. A.
The Borderland of Embryology and Pathology. London: 1962. V. 68

WILLIS, THOMAS
The Anatomy of the Brain and Nerves. Montreal: 1965. V. 73
Cerebri Anatome: Cui Accessit Nervorum Descriptio et Usus. London: 1664. V. 68; 70
De Anima Brutorum Quae Hominis Vitali ac Sensitiva est Exercitationes Duae, Prior Physiologica Ejusdem Naturam.... Oxonii: 1672. V. 73
De Anima Brutorum Quae Hominis Vitalis ac Sensitiva est, Exercitationes Duae, Prior Physiologica Ejusdem Naturum.... London: 1672. V. 68; 70
De Anima Brutorum Quae Hominis Vitalis Ac Sensitiva...with Pharmaceutica Rationalis, Sive Diatriba de Medicametorum Operationibus in Humano Corpore. with Opus Posthumum Pharmaceutica Rationalis. Lugduni: 1676. V. 70
Diatribe Duae Medico-Philosophicae. Amstelodami: 1663. V. 68
Opera Omnia Nitidius Quam Anquam Hactenus Edita.... Amsterdam: 1682. V. 70; 71; 73

WILLIS, W. H.
Poet's Wit and Humour. London: 1882. V. 70

WILLIS, WILLIAM G.
Charles the First: an Historical Tragedy. Edinburgh and London: 1873. V. 72

WILLIS BUND, J. W.
Salmon Problems. London: 1885. V. 73

WILLISTON, SAMUEL W.
American Permian Vertebrates. Chicago: 1911. V. 68

WILLIUS, F. A.
Cardiac Classics. A Collection of Classic Works on the Heart and Circulation with Comprehensive Biographic Accounts of the Authors. St. Louis: 1941. V. 71; 73

WILLMORE, GRAHAM
Confusion Worse Confounded; or the Statutes at Large in 1852. London: 1852. V. 73

WILLOCK, COLIN
The Gun-Punt Adventure. 1958. V. 71

WILLOCKS, TIM
Bloodstained Kings. London: 1995. V. 73
Bloodstained Kings. New York: 1997. V. 72
Green River Rising. London: 1994. V. 68

WILLOUGHBY, CHARLES A.
MacArthur 1941-1951. New York: 1954. V. 69

WILLOUGHBY, J.
Progress of Education in Nova Scotia During Fifty Years and Lights and Shadows in the Life of an Old Teacher. Halifax;: 1884. V. 72

WILLOUGHBY, JOHN C.
East Africa and Its Big Game. London: 1889. V. 71

WILLOUGHBY, MALCOM F.
Yankton Yacht and Man-of-War. Cambridge, Mass: 1935. V. 72

WILLS, A.
The Eagles Nest in the Valley of Sixt: a Summer Home Among the Alps, Together with Some Excursion Among the Great Glaciers. 1860. V. 68; 70
Wanderings Among the High Alps. Oxford: 1937. V. 69

WILLS, GEORGE S. V.
A Manual of Vegetable Materia Medica. London: 1884. V. 70

WILLS, HELEN
Fifteen-Thirty: The Story of a Tennis Player. New York: 1937. V. 72

WILLS, JAMES
Lives of Illustrious and Distinguished Irishmen from the Earliest Times to the Present Period. 1843-1847. V. 71

WILLS, JOHN R.
Carleton; or Duty and Patriotism. A Tale of the American Revolution. London: 1841. V. 73

WILLS, MARK
History of the Persecutions Endured by the Protestants of the South of France. London: 1821. V. 72

WILLS, ROYAL BARRY
Houses for Homemakers. New York: 1945. V. 71

WILLS, SAMUEL
To Devonia; and Other Poems. London: 1862. V. 73

WILLS, THOMAS
Remarks on Polygamy &c in Answer to the Rev. Mr. M-D-N's Thelypthora (sic). London: 1781. V. 68

WILLS, WILLIAM
An Essay on the Principles of Circumstantial Evidence, Illustrated by Numerous Cases. Philadelphia: 1852. V. 68

WILLS, WILLIAM HENRY
Old Leaves: Gather from Household Words. London: 1860. V. 70
Sir Roger de Coverley. London: 1851. V. 70

WILLSON, BECKLES
The Life and Letters of James Wolfe. London: 1909. V. 73

WILLSON, CLAIR EUGENE
Mimes and Miners: a Historical Study of the Theater in Tombstone. Tucson: 1935. V. 69

WILLSON, DIXIE
Honey Bear. Chicago: 1923. V. 73

WILLSON, H. BOWLBY
The Science of Ship-building, Considered in Relation to the Laws of Nature. 1863. V. 72
The Science of Ship-Building, Considered in Relation to the Laws of Nature. London: 1863. V. 68

WILLY, HERR
All About Piping. London: 1896. V. 68

WILLYAMS, COOPER
The History of Sudeley Castle in Gloucestershire. London: 1791. V. 68; 70
A Voyage Up the Mediterranean in His Majesty's Ship the Swiftsure. London: 1802. V. 73

WILMARTH, M. G.
Lexicon of Geologic Names of the United States (Including Alaska). Washington: 1938. V. 70; 72

WILME, B. P.
A Manual of Writing and Printing Characters. London: 1845. V. 72

WILMERDING, J.
Fritz Scholder. Paintings ad Monotypes. Altadena: 1988. V. 69
Winslow Homer. New York: 1972. V. 72; 73

WILMOT, JOHN
The Poetical Works of John Wilmot, Earl of Rochester. Manchester: 1933. V. 70; 71

WILMOT, S. EARDLEY
The Life of an Elephant.... London: 1912. V. 69

WILSON, A.
The Foresters: a Poem, Descriptive of a Pedestrian Journey to the Falls of Niagara.... West Chester: 1838. V. 70; 72
Sport and Service in Assam and Elsewhere. 1924. V. 69; 70; 72; 73

WILSON, A. N.
Daughters of Albion. 1992. V. 72
The Healing Art. London: 1980. V. 72
Kindly Light. London: 1979. V. 72
The Streets of Pimlico. London: 1977. V. 70; 73
Unguarded Hours. London: 1978. V. 72

WILSON, A. PHILIPS
A Treatise on Febrile Diseases.... Hartford: 1809. V. 68

WILSON, ADELAIDE
Historic and Picturesque Savannah. Boston: 1889. V. 71

WILSON, ADRIAN
The Design of Books. London: 1967. V. 71
A Medieval Mirror: Speculum Humanae Salvationis 1324-1500. Berkeley/Los Angeles/London: 1984. V. 69

WILSON, ALBERT
The Flora of Westmorland. 1938. V. 71
The Flora of Westmorland. London: 1938. V. 70

WILSON, ALEXANDER
American Ornithology; or the Natural History of the Birds of the United States. New York and Philadelphia: 1828-1829. V. 68; 69; 70
American Ornithology; or the Natural History of the Birds of the United States. Edinburgh: 1831. V. 70
American Ornithology; or the Natural History of the Birds of the United States. London: 1832. V. 73
American Ornithology; or the Natural History of the Birds of the United States. New York: 1877. V. 70

WILSON, ALEXANDER JOHNSTONE
The Resources of Modern Countries.... London: 1878. V. 71

WILSON, ANDREW
A Healthy Home and How to Attain It. London: 1898. V. 68
A Voyage Round the Coasts of Scotland and the Isles. Edinburgh: 1842. V. 68

WILSON, ANGUS
Emile Zola. New York: 1952. V. 72
Hemlock and After. London: 1952. V. 69
The Middle Age of Mrs. Eliot. 1958. V. 69
The Middle Age of Mrs. Eliot - a Novel. London: 1958. V. 72

WILSON, ANNE NEVILLE
Daily Meditations And Readings For The Young. Kirkby Lonsdale: 1835. V. 72
A Mother's Stories For Her Children. Kirkby Lonsdale: 1838. V. 72

WILSON, ARNOLD
A Dictionary of British Military Painters. Leigh-on-Sea: 1972. V. 72

WILSON, ARTHUR
The History of Great Britain; Being the Life and Reign of King James the First, Relating to What Passed from His First Access to the Crown Till his Death. London: 1653. V. 68; 72

WILSON, AUGUSTA JANE EVANS
Vashti; or, Until Death Us Do Part. New York: 1869. V. 70

WILSON, AUGUSTUS, MRS.
Parson's Memorial and Historical Library Magazine. St. Louis: 1885. V. 71

WILSON, B. R.
Australian Shells. Rutland: 1972. V. 72

WILSON, BECKLES
The Great Company. Toronto: 1899. V. 68

WILSON, CHARIS
California and the West. Millerton: 1978. V. 68
Nudes: Rembrance. 1977. V. 68
Through Another Lens: My Years With Edward Weston. New York: 1998. V. 70

WILSON, CHARLES
Nighwatcher. 1990. V. 69

WILSON, CHARLES BRANCH
The Copepods of the Woods Hole Region Massachusetts. Washington: 1932. V. 68

WILSON, CHRIS
The Myth of Santa Fe. Albuquerque: 1997. V. 68

WILSON, CLAUDE
Mountaineering. London: 1893. V. 69

WILSON, COLIN
Man without a Shadow - the Diary of an Existentialist. London: 1963. V. 72
The Outsider. Boston: 1956. V. 71
The Outsider. London: 1956. V. 69
Ritual in the Dark. London: 1960. V. 70

WILSON, DANIEL
The Archaeology and Prehistoric Annals of Scotland. Edinburgh: 1851. V. 71
Caliban: The Missing Link. London: 1873. V. 71; 72
The Substance of a Conversation with John Bellingham, the Assassin of the Late Right Hon. Spencer Perceval on Sunday May 17, 1812, the Day Previous to His Execution, Together with Some General Remarks. London: 1812. V. 70

WILSON, DAVID M.
The Bayeux Tapestry: the Complete Tapestry in Color. New York: 1985. V. 70

WILSON, E.
Birds of the Antarctic. New York: 1968. V. 73

WILSON, E. B.
An Atlas of the Fertilization and Kayokinesis of the Ovum. New York: 1895. V. 68

WILSON, E. B., MRS.
Cabin Days in Wyoming. Lusk: 1939. V. 73

WILSON, E. H.
If I Were To Make a Garden. Boston: 1931. V. 73
The Lilies of Eastern Asia, a Monograph. Boston: 1929. V. 71
Plant Hunting. Boston: 1927. V. 69; 70
Plantae Wilsonianae. Portland: 1988. V. 69

WILSON, EARL B.
Sugar and Its Wartime Controls 1941-1947. New York: 1947. V. 68

WILSON, EDMUND
Apologies to the Iroquois. New York: 1960. V. 68
The Boys in the Back Room: Notes on California Novelists. San Francisco: 1941. V. 68; 72
Christmas Delirium. 1955. V. 69
Letters on Literature and Politics 1912-1972. New York: 1977. V. 69
Memoirs of Hecatae County. Garden City: 1945. V. 72
Poets, Farewell!. New York: 1929. V. 68
The Thirties: From the Notebooks and Diaries of the Period. New York: 1980. V. 71
To the Finland Station. New York: 1940. V. 73
The Triple Thinkers - Twelve Essays on Literary Subjects. London: 1952. V. 68
Wilson's Christmas Stocking. 1953. V. 69
The Wound and the Bow. London: 1942. V. 69

WILSON, EDMUND BEECHER
The Cell in Development and Heredity. New York: 1925. V. 72
The Cell in Development and Inheritance. New York: 1906. V. 72

WILSON, EDWARD
An Unwritten History, A Record From The Exciting Days Of Early Arizona. Santa Fe: 1966. V. 71

WILSON, EDWARD O.
Consilience. New York: 1998. V. 72

WILSON, ELIZA
New Zealand and Other Poems. London: 1851. V. 73

WILSON, ERASMUS
Hufeland's Art of Prolonging Life. Boston: 1854. V. 73

WILSON, F. PAUL
Implant. New York: 1995. V. 72
The Keep. New York: 1981. V. 72
The Select. New York: 1994. V. 72
The Tomb. 1984. V. 73
Wheels Within Wheels. New York: 1978. V. 71

WILSON, FRANK
Cecil the Camel. London: 1948. V. 69

WILSON, FRANK I.
Sketches of Nassau. To Which is Added the Devil's Ball-alley; an Indian Tradition. Raleigh: 1864. V. 69

WILSON, G.
Memoir of Edward Forbes. London: 1861. V. 69

WILSON, G. W.
Photographs of English and Scottish Scenery...Blair-Athole. Aberdeen: 1866. V. 70
Photographs of English and Scottish Scenery...Scottish Abbeys. London: 1818. V. 70

WILSON, GEORGE
Cyril, a Poem in Four Cantos and Minor Poems. Leeds: 1834. V. 69
Electricity and the Electric Telegraph; Together with the Chemistry of the Stars.... London: 1852. V. 68

WILSON, GILBERT
The Hidatsa Earthlodge. New York: 1934. V. 68

WILSON, H. SCHUTZ
Alpine Ascents and Adventures; or, Rock and Snow Sketches. London: 1878. V. 69; 72

WILSON, H. W.
The Flag to Pretoria. London: 1900-1901. V. 69
Ironclads in Action: a Sketch of Naval Warfare from 1855 to 1895. Boston and London: 1896. V. 70

WILSON, HARRIET
Memoirs Of.... London: 1825. V. 70; 72
Our Nig, Our Sketches from the Life of a Free Black.... Boston: 1859. V. 70

WILSON, HARRY LEON
Professor How Could You!. New York: 1924. V. 70
So This is Golf. New York: 1923. V. 69; 71
The Spenders: a Tale of the Third Generation. Boston: 1902. V. 73

WILSON, HELEN
Brave Days: Pioneer Women of New Zealand. Wellington: 1939. V. 72

WILSON, HENRY
An Account of the Pelew Islands Situated in the Western Part of the Pacific Ocean. Dublin: 1788. V. 71
Leybourn's Dialling Improved; or the Whole Art Perform'd. 1721. V. 72
Leybourn's Dialling Improved; or, the Whole Art Perform'd. London: 1721. V. 68
Wilson's Wonderful Characters.... Halifax: 1857. V. 71
Wonderful Characters.... 1830-. V. 71

WILSON, HURLEY
A Retrospective Exhibition. Kansas City: 1985. V. 69

WILSON, ISAAC
Miscellanies, in Prose and Verse.... Kingston-upon-Hull: 1829. V. 69

WILSON, J. D. B.
The Southern Highlands. Edinburgh: 1949. V. 69

WILSON, J. OLIVER
Birds of Westmorland and the Northern Pennines. London: 1933. V. 71

WILSON, JAMES
A Complete Dictionary of Astrology.... London: 1830. V. 73
A Guide through the District of the Lakes in the North of England.... Malvern. V. 71
The Monumental Inscription of the Churchyard, and Cemetery, of S. Michael's, Dalston, Cumberland. Dalston: 1890. V. 71
The Parish Registers of Dalston, Cumberland. Dalston: 1893-1895. V. 71
Pharmacopoeia Chirurgica.... Philadelphia: 1818. V. 71; 73
The Register of the Priory of St. Bees. London: 1915. V. 71
The Rod & The Gun. 1840. V. 68; 71
The Victoria History of the County of Cumberland. London: 1901-1905. V. 71

WILSON, JAMES ANDREW
James Andrew Wilson - Life, Travels and Adventures. Austin: 1927. V. 70

WILSON, JAMES C.
Three-Wheeling through Africa. Indianapolis: 1936. V. 69
A Treatise on the Continued Fevers. New York: 1881. V. 71

WILSON, JAMES G.
Teratology, Principles and Techniques. Chicago: 1965. V. 68

WILSON, JAMES GRANT
The Life and Letters of Fitz-Green Halleck. New York: 1869. V. 69
Personal Recollections of The War of The Rebellion - Addresses Delivered Before The New York Commandery of The Loyal Legion of The United States, 1883-1891. New York: 1891. V. 72
Thackeray in the United States 1852-1853, 1855-1856. New York: 1904. V. 72

WILSON, JESSIE AITKEN
Memoir of George Wilson; by His Sister. London: 1862. V. 71

WILSON, JOB
An Inquiry into the Nature and Treatment of the Prevailing Epidemic Called Spotted Fever. Boston: 1815. V. 73

WILSON, JOHN
Lights and Shadows of Scottish Life, a Selection from the Papers of the Late Arthur Austin. Edinburgh: 1822. V. 68; 72
The Political State of Scotland.... London: 1831. V. 70
Reproduction of Thompson and West's History of Los Angels County, California. Berkeley: 1959. V. 70
The Rod and the Gun. 1840. V. 73
A Synopsis of British Plants in Mr. Ray's Method. Newcastle: 1744. V. 69
The Works. London: 1855. V. 71

WILSON, JOHN LEIGHTON
A Grammar of the Mpongwe Language, With Vocabularies. New York: 1847. V. 68

WILSON, JOHN M.
The Rural Cyclopedia; or a General Dictionary of Agriculture, and of Arts, Sciences, Instruments.... Edinburgh: 1851. V. 72

WILSON, JOHN MACKAY
Tales of the Borders, and of Scotland. Gateshead-on-Tyne. V. 71
Wilson's Tales of the Borders and of Scotland. Edinburgh: 1857. V. 73
Wilson's Tales of the Borders and of Scotland. London: 1887-1888. V. 73

WILSON, JOHN MORGAN
Simple Justice. New York: 1966. V. 72
Simple Justice. New York: 1996. V. 69

WILSON, JOHN P.
Merchants Guns and Money: the Story of Lincoln County and Its Wars. Santa Fe: 1987. V. 73

WILSON, JOSEPH
Memorabilia Cantabrigiae; or an Account of the Different Colleges in Cambridge.... London: 1803. V. 73

WILSON, JOSEPH T.
Black Phalanx; a History of the Negro Soldiers of the United States in the Wars of 1775-182, 1861-1865. Hartford: 1890. V. 70

WILSON, KEN
The Big Walks. London: 1980. V. 69
Classic Rock. London: 1978. V. 69

WILSON, LANFORD
The Hot L Baltimore. New York: 1973. V. 72

WILSON, LAURA
Watt Matthews of Lambshead. Austin: 1989. V. 69

WILSON, MARCIUS
The Drawing Guide: A Manual of Instruction in Industrial Drawing.... New York: 1873. V. 70

WILSON, MARGARET
One Came Out. New York: 1932. V. 71

WILSON, MONA
Jane Austen and Some Contemporaries. 1938. V. 73
The Life of William Blake. London: 1927. V. 70; 71; 72

WILSON, NEILL C.
Silver Stamped - the Career of Death Valley's Hell Camp Old Panamint. New York: 1937. V. 68; 69; 73
Treasure Express: Epic Days of the Wells Fargo. New York: 1936. V. 68; 69; 73

WILSON, O. MEREDITH
The Denver and Rio Grande Project 1870-1901. Salt Lake City: 1982. V. 69

WILSON, OLIVER
Alice's Adventures in Wonderland - A Survey of the Important Editions and Issues of One of the Outstanding Rarities. Seattle: 1937. V. 68

WILSON, R. A.
My Stalking Memories. Christchurch: 1961. V. 73

WILSON, R. G.
Bromeliads in Cultivation. Coconut Grove: 1963. V. 68

WILSON, R. L.
Buffalo Bill's Wild West - an American Legend. New York: 1998. V. 73
Colt. An American Legend. The Official History of Colt Firearms from 1836 to the Present. 1983. V. 68
The Colt Heritage. New York: 1979. V. 70
The Peacemakers - Arms and Adventures in the American West. New York: 1992. V. 68; 73
Short Ravelings from a Long Yarn, or Camp and March Sketches of the Santa Fe Trail. Santa Ana: 1936. V. 68; 71; 73

WILSON, RICHARD
Studies and Designs by Richard Wilson, Done at Rome 1752. Oxford: 1811. V. 69; 71; 72

WILSON, ROBERT
Blood is Dirt. London: 1997. V. 70
Boiler and Factory Chimneys. 1899. V. 71
British Traditional Colours. London: 1937. V. 70
The Company of Strangers. London: 2001. V. 69; 70; 71; 72
A Darkening Stain. 1998. V. 68
A Darkening Stain. London: 1998. V. 69; 70; 71; 72; 73
The Interest and Trade of Ireland Consider'd.... Dublin: 1732. V. 73
Narrative of Events During the Invasion of Russia by Napoleon. London: 1860. V. 69
A Small Death in Lisbon. London: 1999. V. 70; 71; 73

WILSON, ROBERT A.
Gertrude Stein: a Bibliography. New York: 1974. V. 72
Michael and the Lions. New York: 1980. V. 68

WILSON, ROMER
All Alone. The Life and Private History of Emily Jane Bronte. London: 1928. V. 73
The Life and Private History of Emily Bronte. New York: 1928. V. 68

WILSON, RUFUS ROCKWELL
A Noble Company of Adventures. New York: 1908. V. 68; 73
Out of the West. 1933. V. 68

WILSON, SLOAN
A Summer Place. New York: 1958. V. 71; 72

WILSON, SUSANNAH
Familiar Poems, Moral and Religious. London: 1814. V. 69

WILSON, T.
An Archaeological Dictionary; or Classical Antiquities of the Jews, Greeks and Romans.... London: 1783. V. 71

WILSON, THOMAS
The Christian Psalmodist: Being a Collection of Psalms, Hymns and Songs. Chicago: 1872. V. 70
A Descriptive Catalogue of the Prints of Rembrandt. London: 1836. V. 71
Distilled Spirituous Liquor the Bane of the Nation.... London: 1736. V. 69
The Many Advantages of a Good Language to Any Nation; with an Examination of the Present State of Our Own.... London: 1724. V. 69
The Pitman's Pay, and Other Poems. London: 1874. V. 68
Sacra Privata. The Private Meditations and Prayers of the Right Revered Thomas Wilson, D.D. Lord Bishop of Sodor and Man. Cork: 1806. V. 72

WILSON, THOMAS, BP. OF SODER AND MAN
The Knowledge and Practice of Christianity Made Easy to the Meanest Capacities.... London: 1781. V. 73

WILSON, WILBERT R.
Travels of the 20th Century and Beyond. New York: 1971. V. 72

WILSON, WILLIAM
Bryologia Britannica. London: 1855. V. 70
Gathered Together. Poems. London: 1860. V. 70

WILSON, WILLIAM CARUS
The Friendly Visitor. Volume III - New Series. London: 1853. V. 71
The Friendly Visitor. Volume XXIX. London: 1847. V. 71
The Friendly Visitor. Volume XXXII. Kirkby Lonsdale: 1850. V. 71

WILSON, WILLIAM S.
Why I Don't Write Like Franz Kafka. New York: 1977. V. 72

WILSON, WOODROW
The New Freedom. New York and Garden City: 1913. V. 71
When a Man Comes to Himself. New York: 1915. V. 69; 71

WILSON BAREAU, J.
Correspondence and Conversation: Manet by Himself. Boston: 1995. V. 72

WILSTACH, FRANK J.
The Plainsman Wild Bill Hicock. Garden City: 1937. V. 69
Wild Bill Hickok. Garden City: 1926. V. 69

WILSTACH, PAUL
Thais. Indianapolis: 1911. V. 70

WILTON, GEORGE
Fingerprints - History, Law and Romance. London: 1938. V. 68

WILTSEE, ERNEST A.
Gold Rush Steamers of the Pacific. San Francisco: 1938. V. 68; 73
The Pioneer and the Pack Mule Express.... San Francisco: 1931. V. 73

WILTZ, CHRIS
The Killing Circle. New York: 1981. V. 72

THE WIMP and the Woodle and Other Stories. Los Angeles: 1935. V. 71; 73

WINANS, WALTER
The Art of Revolver Shooting. 1901. V. 70; 72; 73
Hints on Revolver Shooting. 1904. V. 69
The Modern Pistol and How to Shoot It. 1919. V. 69
The Sporting Rifle. 1908. V. 73

WINANT, L.
Firearms Curiosa. 1956. V. 69; 70; 72; 73

WINCHELL, A. N.
Elements of Optical Mineralogy. New York: 1947. V. 68

WINCHELL, N. H.
The Aborigines of Minnesota. St. Paul: 1911. V. 69

WINCHELSEA, HENEAGE FINCH, 2ND EARL OF
A True and Exact Relation of the Late Prodigious Earthquake and Eruption of Mount Aetna, or, Monte-Gibello.... London: 1669. V. 70

THE WINCHESTER Guide; or a Description of the Curiosities and Antiquities of that Ancient City. Winton: 1780. V. 70; 72; 73

WINCHESTER, ELHANAN
The Three Woe Trumpets of Which the First and Second are Aleready Past and the Third Is Now Begun. New York: 1811. V. 73

WINCHILSEA, ANNE KINGSMILL FINCH, COUNTESS OF
Miscellany Poems, on Several Occasions. London: 1713. V. 69

WINCKELMANN, JOHANN JOACHIM
Critical Account of the Situation and Destruction by the First Eruptions of Mount Vesuvius of Herculaneum, Pomepii and Stabia.... 1771. V. 71
Critical Account of the Situation and Destruction by the First Eruptions of Mount Vesuvius of Herculaneum, Pompeii and Stabia.... London: 1771. V. 72
Geschichte der Kunst des Alterthums. Dresden: 1764. V. 72

WINDELER, BERNARD
Sailing-Ships and Barges of the Western Mediterranean and Adriatic Seas. 1926. V. 71

WINDELER, ROBERT
Links with a Past: the First 100 Years of the Los Angeles Country Club 1897-1997. Los Angeles: 1997. V. 73

WINDER, RICHARD
Reminiscences of an Engineer ar Home and Abroad. Louth: 1890. V. 71

WINDHAM, DONALD
Tanaquil. New York: 1977. V. 71; 73

WINDHORST & CO.
The Primo Incandescent Gasoline RC Lamps and Portable Machines. St. Louis: 1911. V. 71

WINDLE, BERTRAM
The Wessex of Thomas Hardy. London: 1902. V. 71

WINDLE, WILLIAM F.
Biology of Neuroglia. Springfield: 1958. V. 68
The Spinal Cord and its Reactions to Traumatic Injury. New York: 1980. V. 68

THE WINDSOR Guide; Containing a Description of the Town and Castle; the Present State of the Paintings and Curiosities in the Royal Apartments.... Windsor: 1786. V. 73

WINDUS, JOHN
A Journey to Mequinez; the Residence of the Present Emperor of Fez and Morocco. London: 1725. V. 71

WINDUS, THOMAS
A New Elucidation of the Subjects on the Celebrated Portland Vase, Formerly Called the Barberini.... London: 1845. V. 68

WINES, ENOCH COBB
Report on the International Penitentiary Congress of London, Held July 3-13, 1872.... Washington: 1873. V. 69

WINFIELD, R. D.
Night Frost. London: 1992. V. 71

WINFREY, OPRAH
Journey to Beloved. New York: 1998. V. 73

WING, JOHN
A Plain Elementary and Practical System of Natural Experimental Philosophy.... Philadelphia: 1809. V. 71

WING, TYCHO
Olympia Domata; or, an Almanack for...1789, etc. 1789. V. 69

WING, VINCENT
Astronomia Britannica; in Qua Per Novam, Concinnioremq.... Londini: 1669. V. 73

WINGATE, EDMUND
An Exact Abridgement of all Statutes in Force and Use; Upon the 4th Day of January in the Year of Our Lord 1641/42. London: 1655. V. 72
An Exact Abridgment of all Statutes in Force and In Use from the Beginning of Magna Charta, Until 1689. London: 1708. V. 68

WINGATE, GEORGE W.
Through the Yellowstone Park on Horseback. New York: 1886. V. 68

WINGET, DON H.
Anecdotes of Buffalo Bill - That Have Never Been Seen in Print. Chicago: 1927. V. 73
Anecdotes of Buffalo Bill - the Original Boy Scout. Clinton: 1912. V. 73

WINGFIELD, LEWIS
Notes on Civil Costume in England from the Conquest to the Regency. London: 1884. V. 70

WINGFIELD, MARSHALL
A History of Caroline County, Virginia. Richmond: 1924. V. 68

WINGFIELD, R. D.
Frost at Christmas,. Markham, Ontario: 1984. V. 68; 71; 72; 73
Frost at Christmas. London: 1989. V. 71
Hard Frost. London: 1995. V. 69; 71; 73
Night Frost. London: 1992. V. 69; 71; 73
A Touch of Frost. Toronto: 1987. V. 68; 72; 73
A Touch of Frost. Hassocks, Suffex: 1998. V. 71
Winter Frost. London: 1999. V. 71

WINGLER, HANS M.
The Bauhaus. Weimar, Dessau, Berlin, Chicago. Cambridge: 1969. V. 68

WINGRAVE, MARION M.
The May Blossom, or, the Pictures and Her People. London: 1881. V. 72

WINKELMANN, R. K.
Nerve Endings in Normal and Pathologic Skin. Springfield: 1960. V. 68

WINKLER, ANGELINA VIRGINIA
The Confederate Capital and Hood's Texas Brigade. Austin: 1894. V. 69; 70

WINKLER, C.
The Central Course of Nervus Octavus and Its Influence on Motility. Amsterdam: 1907. V. 68

WINKLER, EDWARD
Pharmaceutische Waarenkunde Oder Handatlas der Pharmakologie, Enthaltend Abbildungen Aller Wichtigen Pharmaceutischen.... Leipzig: 1852. V. 71

WINKLER, WILLIAM
Journal of the Secession Convention of Texas 1861. Austin: 1912. V. 70

WINKS, WILLIAM EDWARD
Lives of Distinguished Shoemakers. Portland: 1849. V. 70

WINN, ARTHUR T.
The Registers of the Parish Church of Sedbergh, Co. York 1594-1800. Sedbergh: 1911. V. 71

WINN, GODFREY
Dreams Fade. London: 1928. V. 71

WINNING, HASSO VON
Pre-Columbian Art of Mexico and Central America. New York. V. 70; 71
Pre-Columbian Art of Mexico and Central America. New York: 1968. V. 72; 73

WINSEMIUS, PIERIUS
Sirius. Franekerae: 1638. V. 71

WINSER, HENRY JACOB
The Greath Northwest, a Guide-Book and Itinerary for the Use of Tourists and Travelers over the lines of the Northern Pacific Railroad, the Oregon Railway and Navigation Company and the Oregon and California Railroad. St. Paul: 1888. V. 70
The Official Northern Pacific Railroad Guide for the Use of Tourists and Travelers Over the Lines of the Northern Pacific Railroad and Its Branches.... St. Paul: 1894. V. 68

WINSHIP, AMY DAVIS
My Life Story. Boston: 1920. V. 72

WINSHIP, GEORGE PARKER
The Journey of Coronado 1540-1542. New York: 1904. V. 69
Printing in the Fifteen Century. Philadelphia: 1940. V. 73

WINSLOW, ANN
Trial Balances. New York: 1935. V. 72

WINSLOW, ARTHUR
History of the Fifth Division. Luxembourg: 1918. V. 68

WINSLOW, C. M.
The Architecture and the Gardens of the San Diego Exposition. San Francisco: 1916. V. 69

WINSLOW, CHARLES F.
Attraction and Repulsion: the Radical Principles of Energy, Discussed in Their Relations to Physical and Morphological Developments. Philadelphia: 1869. V. 71

WINSLOW, DON
California Fire and Life. New York: 1999. V. 72
A Cool Breeze on the Underground. New York: 1991. V. 68; 69; 70; 71; 72
A Long Walk Up the Water Slide. New York: 1994. V. 69; 70; 73
The Trail to Buddha's Mirror. New York: 1992. V. 68
Way Down on the High Lonely. New York: 1993. V. 68; 69; 70; 73

WINSLOW, MARJORIE
Mud Pies and Other Recipes. New York: 1961. V. 73

WINSLOW, OLA ELIZABETH
American Broadside Verse from Imprints of the 17th and 18th Centuries. New Haven: 1930. V. 70

WINSLOW, STEPHEN N.
Biographies of Successful Philadelphia Merchants. Philadelphia: 1864. V. 71

WINSOR, JUSTIN
Cartier to Frontenac. Boston: 1894. V. 72
Christopher Columbus and How He Received and Imparted the Spirit of Discovery. Boston: 1892. V. 73
Narrative and Critical History of America. Boston: 1884-1889. V. 70
Narrative and Critical History of America. Boston and New York: 1889. V. 73

WINSTANLEY, HAMLET
The Knowsley Gallery, Being a Series of Engravings.... London: 1820. V. 72

WINSTON, ROBERT W.
High Stakes and Hair Triggers. The Life of Jefferson Davis. New York: 1930. V. 69

WINTER, DOUGLAS E.
Revelations. Baltimore: 1997. V. 69

WINTER, KEITH
The Shining Hour: a Play in Three Acts. Garden City: 1934. V. 69

WINTER, MILO
Billy Popgun. Boston: 1912. V. 70

WINTER, WILLIAM
Henry Irving. New York: 1885. V. 71

WINTER, WILLIAM WEST
Millions in Motors: a Big Business Story. New York: 1924. V. 69

WINTERICH, JOHN T.
An American Friend of Dickens. New York: 1933. V. 69
Books and the Man. New York: 1929. V. 69

WINTERNITZ, EMMANUEL
Leonardo da Vinci as a Musician. New Haven: 1981. V. 72
Musical Instruments of the Western World. London. V. 72

WINTERNITZ, MILTON CHARLES
Collected Studies on the Pathology of War Gas Poisoning. New Haven: 1920. V. 73

THE WINTER'S Wreath for MDCCCXXXI. London: 1831. V. 70

WINTERS, JOHN D.
The Civil War in Louisiana. Baton Rouge: 1963. V. 69

WINTERS, YVOR
Collected Poems. London: 1963. V. 71

WINTERSON, JEANETTE
Art and Lies. London: 1994. V. 68; 69; 71; 73
Art Objects - Essay on Ecstasy and Effrontery. London: 1995. V. 68
Boating for Beginners. London: 1985. V. 73
Gut Symmetries. London: 1997. V. 68; 73
Oranges are Not the Only Fruit. London: 1985. V. 71
Oranges are Not the Only Fruit. London: 1985. V. 70; 72
Oranges Are Not the Only Fruit. New York: 1985. V. 72
Oranges are Not the Only Fruit. New York: 1987. V. 69; 72

The Passion. Boston: 1987. V. 70
The Passion. New York: 1988. V. 70
Sexing the Cherry. London: 1989. V. 70; 72; 73
Written on the Body. London: 1992. V. 68; 70; 72

WINTHER, OSCAR O.
The Old Oregon Country - a History of Frontier Trade, Transportation and Travel. Bloomington: 1950. V. 69

WINTHROP, ROBERT C.
Life and Letters of John Winthrop, Governor of the Massachuseets Bay Company. Boston: 1869. V. 70

WINTHROP, WILLIAM
Military Law. Washington: 1886. V. 73

WINTON, F. R.
Modern Views on the Secretion of Urine. London: 1956. V. 68

WINWAR, FRANCES
Pagan Interval. Indianapolis: 1929. V. 68

WINWARD, WALTER
Rough Deal. London: 1977. V. 72

WIRE, HAROLD CHANNING
Indian Beef. New York: 1940. V. 72

WIRSUNG, CHRISTOPH
Ein New Artzney Buch. Neustadt an der Hardt: 1588. V. 73

WIRT, ELIZABETH WASHINGTON, MRS.
Flora's Dictionary. Baltimore: 1837. V. 71

WIRTZUNG, CHRISTOPHER
The General Practise of Physicke, Conteyning all Inward and Outward Parts of the Body.... London: 1617. V. 68

WISCHANATH, L.
Atlas of Livebearers of the World. Neptune City: 1993. V. 73

WISCHNITZER, R.
Architecture of the European Synagogue. Philadelphia: 1964. V. 69; 72

WISDOM In Miniature; or, the Young Gentleman and Lady's Pleasing Instructor.... Coventry: 1797. V. 71

WISE, ARTHUR
The Death's Head. London: 1962. V. 70
The Little Fishes. London: 1961. V. 70

WISE, EDWARD
The Law Relating to Riots and Unlawful Assemblies.... London: 1848. V. 71
The Remarkable Tryal of Thomas Chandler, late of Clifford's Inn, London, Gent. Reading: 1751. V. 70

WISE, H. D.
Tigers of the Sea. New York: 1937. V. 72

WISE, HENRY A.
Los Gringos. New York: 1849. V. 68
Los Gringos. New York: 1850. V. 68; 73
Seven Decades of the Union: the Humanities and Materialism Illustrated by a Memoir of John Tyler. Philadelphia: 1872. V. 72
Territorial Government and the Admission of New States Into the Union: a Historical and Constitutional Treatise. Richmond: 1860. V. 70

WISE, ISAAC M.
Judiasm: Its Doctrines and Duties. Cincinnati: 1872. V. 71
Report of Committe on Testimonial to the Rev. Dr. Isaac M. Wise, Including an Account of the Celebration April 6, 1889. Cincinnati: 1889. V. 68

WISE, JENNINGS CROOPER
The Long Arm of Lee, or, the History of the Artillery of the Army of Northern Virginia. Lynchburg: 1915. V. 69; 70; 72

WISE, JOHN S.
The End of an Era. Boston: 1899. V. 69
The End of an Era. Boston: 1901. V. 70

WISE, MARJORIE
English Village Schools. London: 1931. V. 69

WISE, R.
A Fragile Eden. Princeton: 1998. V. 72

WISE, THOMAS
An Apology for the Business of Pawn-Broking. London: 1744. V. 70

WISE, THOMAS JAMES
A Bibliography of the Writings in Prose and Verse of Algernon Charles Swinburne. London: 1927. V. 72
A Bibliography of the Writings in Verse and Prose of George Gordon Noel, Baron Byron.... Dawsons: 1963. V. 72
The Bronte Family: a Bibliography of the Writings in Prose and Verse. London: 1917. V. 68; 71; 73
The Bronte Family: a Bibliography of the Writings in Prose and Verse. 1965. V. 70; 73
A Bronte Library: a Catalogue of the Printed Manuscripts and Autograph Letters by Members of the Bronte Family. 1929. V. 73
John Ruskin and Frederick Denison Maurice on Notes on the Construction of Sheepfolds. 1896. V. 68

WISE, THOMAS JAMES continued
A Landor Library: a Catalogue of Printed Books, Manuscripts and Autograph Letters. London: 1928. V. 72
A Shelley Library: a Catalogue of Printed Books, Manuscripts, and Autograph Letters by Percy Bysshe Shelley, Harriet Shelley and Mary Wollstonecraft Shelley, Collected by Thomas James Wise. London: 1924. V. 72

WISEMAN, RICHARD
Eight Chirurgical Treatises on These Following Heads. I. of Tumours. II. Of Ulcers. III. Of diseases of the Anus. IV. Of the King's Evil. V. Of Wounds. VI. of Gun-shot Wounds. VII. Of Fractures and Luxations. VIII. Of the Lues Venerea. London: 1719. V. 68; 71; 73

WISLIZENUS, F. A.
A Journey to the Rocky Mountains in the Year 1839. St. Louis: 1912. V. 70
Memoir of a Tour to Northern Mexico Connected with Col. Doniphan's Expedition in 1846.... Washington: 1848. V. 69

WISNANT, CHARLEEN
Red Clay Reader, Volumes 1-7. Charlotte: 1965. V. 71

WISNIEWSKI, DAVID
Golem. New York: 1996. V. 73

WISSLER, CLARK
Costumes of the Plains Indians. New York: 1915. V. 69
Indian Cavalcade, or Life on the Old Time Indian Reservations. 1938. V. 68
Indians of the United States. New York: 1940. V. 69
North American Indians of the Plains. New York: 1934. V. 69
Population Changes Among the Northern Plain Indians. New Haven: 1936. V. 69

WISS SOHNE, G. B.
Musterbuch der Fabricate in Klein-Schmalkalden in Thuringen.... Saalfeld: 1869. V. 70

WISTAR, CASPAR
A System of Anatomy for the Use of Students of Medicine. Philadelphia: 1811-1814. V. 69; 71; 73
A System of Anatomy for the Use of Students of Medicine. Philadelphia: 1830. V. 73

WISTAR, ISAAC JONES
Autobiography of Isaac Jones Wistar 1827-1905. Philadelphia: 1914. V. 70

WISTER, OWEN
Lady Baltimore. New York: 1906. V. 69; 72; 73
The Virginian. New York: 1902. V. 70
The Virginian. New York: 1904. V. 73
The Virginian. New York: 1911. V. 69
The Virginian. Los Angeles: 1951. V. 68
When the West Was West. New York: 1928. V. 69

WITH Gun and Rod in India. New Delhi: 1956. V. 69

WITH the Engine Driver. London: 1930. V. 72

WITHAM, H.
Observations on Fossil Vegetables. Edinburgh: 1831. V. 68

WITHERBY, H. F.
The Handbook of British Birds. London: 1938-41. V. 70
The Handbook of British Birds. London: 1949. V. 70; 73

WITHERING, WILLIAM
An Arrangement of British Plants. Birmingham: 1796. V. 71; 73
A Botanical Arrangement of All the Vegetables Growing in Great Britian. Birmingham: 1776. V. 69

WITHEROW, THOMAS
Derry and Enniskillen in the Year 1689. 1885. V. 69

WITHERS, ALEXANDER SCOTT
Chronicles of Border Warfare, or a History of the Settlement by the Whites, of North Western Virginia.... Cincinnati: 1903. V. 70; 72; 73

WITHERS, JOHN
The Dutch Better Friends than the French, to the Monarchy, Church and Trade of England. London: 1713. V. 70

WITHERS, PHILIP
Alfred or a Narrative of the Daring and Illegal Measures to Suppress a Pamphlet Intituled Strictures on the Declaration of Horne Tooke, Esq.... London: 1789. V. 73

WITHERS, W.
The Acacia Tree.... 1842. V. 69

WITHERS, WILLIAM BRAMWELL
The History of Ballarat, from the First Pastoral Settlement to the Present Time. Ballarat: 1887. V. 70; 72

WITHERSPOON, JOHN
A Serious Inquiry into the Nature and Effects of the Stage. New York: 1812. V. 69

WITKIN, JOEL PETER
The Bone House. Santa Fe: 1998. V. 68; 72
Joel Peter Witkin: Photographs. Pasadena: 1985. V. 68

WITKIN, LEE
The Photograph Collector's Guide. Boston: 1979. V. 73

WITTE, HENNING
Memoriae Medicourm Nostri Seculi Clarissimorum Renovaiate Decas Prima. Frankfurt am Main: 1676. V. 73

WITTER, DEAN
Shikar. 1961. V. 70; 72
Shikar. San Francisco: 1961. V. 69

WITTGENSTEIN, LUDWIG
Notebooks 1914-1916. Oxford: 1961. V. 70

WITTHAUS, R. A.
Medical Jurisprudence, Forensic Medicine and Toxicology. New York: 1894. V. 72

WITTIE, ROBERT
(Greek text) Or, a Survey of the Heavens. London: 1681. V. 68

WITTKOWER, R.
Art and Architecture in Italy 1600-1750. Baltimore: 1958. V. 69; 72
Palladio and Palladianism. New York: 1974. V. 69

WITTLIFF, WILLIAM D.
William D. Wittliff and The Encino Press. Dallas: 1989. V. 71

WITTMAN, SALLY
Plenty of Pelly and Peak. New York: 1980. V. 73

WITTMER, P.
Caillebotte and His Garden at Yerres. New York: 1991. V. 71; 73

WITWER, H. C.
The Leather Pushers. New York: 1921. V. 70

THE WIZARD of Oz. Akron: 1944. V. 69

WODARCH, C.
Introduction to the Study of the Conchology. London: 1832. V. 68

WODEHOUSE, PELHAM GRENVILLE
Aunt's Aren't Gentlemen. London: 1974. V. 70
Bachelors Anonymous. London: 1973. V. 70
Big Money. Garden City: 1931. V. 70
Bill the Conqueror. London: 1924. V. 73
Bill the Conqueror. New York: 1924. V. 69
Cocktail Time. London: 1958. V. 71
The Code of Woosters. London: 1938. V. 71
The Coming of Bill. 1920. V. 71
The Coming of Bill. London: 1920. V. 68
The Crime Wave at Blandings. New York: 1937. V. 70
The Crime Wave at Blandings. New York: 1973. V. 73
Do Butlers Burgle Banks?. London: 1968. V. 70
Eggs, Beans and Crumpets. New York: 1940. V. 69; 72
A Few Quick Ones. New York: 1959. V. 69
French Leave. London: 1955. V. 69
Full Moon. Garden City: 1947. V. 70
Full Moon. London: 1947. V. 68; 70
The Gold Bat. London: 1904. V. 71
He Rather Enjoyed It. New York: 1925. V. 70; 73
The Head of Kay's. Black Boys' Library Series. London: 1924. V. 72
How Right You Are, Jeeves. New York: 1960. V. 69
The Ice in the Bedroom. New York: 1961. V. 70
Indiscretions of Archie. New York: 1921. V. 68
Indiscretions of Archie. 1967. V. 68
The Intrusion of Jimmy. 1910. V. 68; 69
The Intrusion of Jimmy. New York: 1910. V. 70
Jeeves and the Tie That Binds. New York: 1971. V. 70
Jeeves in the Offing. London: 1960. V. 70
Jill the Reckless. London: 1921. V. 68; 71
The Little Nugget. New York: 1914. V. 70
The Luck of the Bodkins. London: 1935. V. 71
The Mating Season. London: 1949. V. 70
The Mating Season. New York: 1949. V. 71
Money in the Bank. London: 1946. V. 69
Mostly Sally. 1923. V. 68
Mulliner Nights. Garden City: 1933. V. 72
Pearls, Girls and Monty Bodkin. London: 1972. V. 70
Picadilly Jim. 1917. V. 68
Plum Pie. New York: 1967. V. 69
The Prince and Betty. 1912. V. 68; 69
Psmith in the City. London: 1934. V. 70
Quick Service. London: 1940. V. 71
Service with a Smile. London: 1961. V. 68
Service with a Smile. London: 1962. V. 70
The Small Bachelor. London: 1927. V. 68
Spring Fever. London: 1948. V. 70
Stiff Upper Lip Jeeves. London: 1963. V. 70
Summer Moonshine. New York: 1937. V. 69
Sunset At Blandings. London: 1977. V. 68; 70
The Swoop! and Other Stories. New York: 1979. V. 72
Thank You, Jeeves!. Boston: 1934. V. 71
Uncle Dynamite. London: 1948. V. 70
Uncle Fred in the Springtime. London: 1939. V. 68
Uncle Fred in the Springtime. New York: 1939. V. 69

WODZICKI, K. A.
Introduced Mammals of New Zealand. 1950. V. 69; 70; 72; 73

WOEIROT, PIERRE
Pinax Iconicus Antiquorum ac Variorum in Sepulturis Rituum ex Lilio Gregorio (Gyraldio) Excerpta.... Lyon: 1556. V. 69

WOELFER, A. M.
Die Architectur Nebst Verzierungen aus dem Gebiete der Schonen Kunste Alterer und Neuerer Zeit. Gotha: 1826. V. 70

WOERDEMAN, M. W.
Experimental Embryology in the Netherlands 1940-1945. New York and Amsterdam: 1946. V. 68

WOHLBRG, MEG
Jody's Wonderful Day. New York: 1945. V. 70

WOHLVERDIENTE Ehren-Seule dem Weyland Durchlauchtigsten Fursten und Herrn Ernst Hertzogen zu Sachsen Julich Cleve und Bergk.... Gotha: 1678. V. 68; 70; 72

WOIWODE, LARRY
Beyond the Bedroom Wall. New York: 1975. V. 73
Born Brothers. New York: 1988. V. 73
Papa John. New York: 1981. V. 72
What I'm Going to Do. New York: 1969. V. 71

WOJNAROWICZ, DAVID
David. Close to the Knives. New York: 1991. V. 72

WOLCOT, ALEXANDER
The Convention Bill, an Ode. 1795. V. 72
The Convention Bill, an Ode. London: 1795. V. 68

WOLCOT, JOHN
Bozzy and Piozzi, or the British Biographers, A Town Eclogue. London: 1786. V. 71
Odes to Mr. Paine, author of the "Rights of Man", on the Intended Celebration of the Downfall of the French Empire.... London: 1791. V. 68
A Poetical and Congratulatory Epistle to James Boswell, Esq. and On His Journal of a Tour to the Hebrides. London: 1786. V. 71
The Works of Peter Pindar, Esq. London: 1812. V. 72; 73

WOLCOTT, OLIVER
An Address, to the People of the United States, on the Subject of the Report of a Committee of the House of Representatives, Appointed to Examine...Whether Monies Drawn from the Treasury, Have Been Faithfully Applied.... Boston: 1802. V. 69

WOLCOTT, ROGER
Poetical Meditations, Being the Improvement of Some Vacant Hours.... New London: 1725. V. 68

WOLF, ADOLF HUNGRY
The Blood People, a Division of the Blackfoot Confederacy. New York: 1977. V. 72

WOLF, GARY K.
Killerbowl. Garden City: 1975. V. 72
Who Censored Roger Rabbit?. New York: 1981. V. 70; 72
Who P-P-P-Plugged Roger Rabbit?. New York: 1991. V. 72

WOLF, JOSEPH
The Life and Habits of Wild Animals. London: 1874. V. 72; 73
Pheasant Drawings. Kingston upon Hull: 1988. V. 70; 73

WOLF, K.
Fish Viruses and Fish Viral Diseases. Ithaca: 1988. V. 73

WOLFE, BERTRAM D.
Portrait of Mexico. New York: 1937. V. 71

WOLFE, GENE
The Urth of the New Sun. New York: 1987. V. 73

WOLFE, GEOFFREY
Bad Debts. New York: 1969. V. 71

WOLFE, GEORGE HOOPER
I Drove Mules On The C and O Canal. Williamsport, MD: 1969. V. 72

WOLFE, HUMBERT
ABC of the Theatre. London: 1932. V. 72
The Craft of Verse. New York: 1928. V. 68; 72
Cursory Rhymes. London: 1927. V. 71
Homage to Meleager. London: 1930. V. 72
The Uncelestial City. London: 1930. V. 68

WOLFE, MICHAEL
The Chinese Fire Drill. New York: 1975. V. 72
Man on a String. New York: 1975. V. 72

WOLFE, RICHARD
Louis Herman Kinder and Fine Bookbinding in America. 1985. V. 71
Louis Herman Kinder and Fine Bookbinding in America. Newtown: 1985. V. 73
The Role of the Mann Family of Dedham, Massachusetts in the Marbling of Paper in the Nineteenth Century America and in the Printing of Music, the Making of Cards and Other Book Trade Activities. 1981. V. 71
The Role of the Mann Family of Dedham, Massachusetts in the Marbling of Paper in the Nineteenth-Century American and in the Printing of Music. London: 1981. V. 73

WOLFE, SUSAN
The Last Billable Hour. New York: 1989. V. 68; 69; 70

WOLFE, THOMAS CLAYTON
From Death to Morning. New York: 1935. V. 70; 71; 73
From Death to Morning. London: 1936. V. 69; 73
Gentleman of the Press: a Play. Chicago: 1942. V. 68; 73
The Hills Beyond. New York and London: 1941. V. 69; 73
The Hound of Darkness. 1986. V. 68
Look Homeward, Angel. New York: 1929. V. 71; 73
Look Homeward, Angel. London: 1930. V. 73
Mannerhouse: A Play in a Prologue and Three Acts. New York: 1948. V. 71
The Mountains. Chapel Hill: 1970. V. 71
Of Time and the River. London: 1935. V. 73
Of Time and the River. New York: 1935. V. 69; 71; 72; 73
The Short Novels of Thomas Wolfe. New York: 1961. V. 73
The Story of a Novel. New York: 1936. V. 70; 71; 73
The Web and the Rock. New York and London: 1939. V. 73
The Web and the Rock. London: 1947. V. 68
The Years Wandering in Many Lands and Cities. New York: 1949. V. 70
You Can't Go Home Again. New York: 1940. V. 73

WOLFE, TOM
The Bonfire of the Vanities. Franklin Center: 1987. V. 69; 70; 71
The Bonfire of the Vanities. New York: 1987. V. 68; 71
The Bonfire of the Vanities. London: 1988. V. 73
The Electric Kool-aid Acid Test. New York: 1968. V. 70; 72; 73
From Bauhaus to Our House. New York: 1981. V. 69; 71; 72; 73
Hooking Up. Franklin Center: 2000. V. 68; 70
A Man in Full. Franklin: 1998. V. 70
A Man in Full. New York: 1998. V. 70
Mauve Gloves & Madmen, Clutter & Vine. New York: 1976. V. 70
The Painted Word. New York: 1975. V. 73
The Pump House Gang. New York: 1968. V. 70
The Purple Decades. New York: 1982. V. 69; 72
Radical Chic and Mau-Mauing the Flak Catchers. New York: 1970. V. 70; 71; 72

WOLFENDEN, GEORGE
The House In Spitalfields. London: 1937. V. 72

WOLFENSBERGER, ARNOLD
Theory of Silk Weaving. New York: 1897. V. 71

WOLFENSTINE, MANFRED
The Manual of Brands and Marks. 1970. V. 68
The Manual of Marks & Brands. Norman: 1970. V. 71

WOLFERT, IRA
American Guerilla in the Philippines. New York: 1945. V. 71
Tucker's People. New York: 1943. V. 69; 71

WOLFF, HAROLD G.
Headache and Other Head Pain. New York: 1948. V. 68

WOLFF, JEREMIAS
Dem Durchleuchtigsten Fursten und Herrn Ferdinand, Herzogen in Schlesien zu Jagar dess Heyl. Rom. Reichs Fursten und Regiereren des Hausses Lobkowiz.... Augsburg: 1700. V. 70; 72

WOLFF, JULIAN
Practical Handbook of Sherlockian Heraldry. New York: 1955. V. 71
A Ramble in Bohemia. New York: 1957. V. 71
The Sherlockian Atlas. New York: 1952. V. 69; 71

WOLFF, TOBIAS
Back in the World. Boston: 1985. V. 68; 70; 72
The Barracks Thief. New York: 1984. V. 68
The Barracks Thief. London: 1987. V. 72
Hunters in the Snow. London: 1982. V. 71
In Pharaoh's Army. Memories of the Lost War. New York: 1994. V. 68; 72
In the Garden of North American Martyrs. New York: 1981. V. 69; 70
The Liar. Vineburg: 1989. V. 71; 72
The Night in Question. New York: 1996. V. 68
The Other Miller. Derry & Ridgewood: 1989. V. 71
Rumours. London: 1975. V. 70
This Boy's Life. New York: 1989. V. 68; 69; 72; 73
This Boy's Life. Stanford: 1989. V. 71
The Title Story from the Night in Question. New York: 1996. V. 71
Ugly Rumours. London: 1975. V. 73

WOLFSON, THERESA
The Woman Worker and Trade Unions. New York: 1926. V. 72

WOLLASTON, A. F. R.
Life of Alfred Newton. London: 1921. V. 68

WOLLASTON, WILLIAM
The Religion of Nature Delineated. London: 1725. V. 68; 69; 70

WOLLE, F.
Diatomaceae of North America. Bethlehem: 1890. V. 69
Diatomaceae of North America. Bethlehem: 1894. V. 69; 72
Fresh Water Algae of the United States.... Bethlehem: 1887. V. 70

WOLLE, MURIEL SIBELL
The Bonanza Trail: Ghost Towns and Mining Camps of the West. Bloomington: 1953. V. 72; 73
Montana Pay Dirt: a Guide to the Mining Camps of the Treasure State:. Denver: 1963. V. 68; 69; 70; 72; 73
Stampede to Timberline: The Ghost Towns and Mining Camps of Colorado. 1957. V. 69

WOLLSTONECRAFT, MARY
Letters to Imlay. London: 1879. V. 68; 72
Letters Written During a Short Residence in Sweden, Norway and Denmark. London: 1796. V. 70; 72
Letters Written During a Short Residence in Sweden, Norway and Denmark. London: 1802. V. 68
The Love Letters of...to Gilbert Imlay.... London: 1908. V. 72
Original Stories from Real Life.... London: 1791. V. 73
A Vindication of the Rights of Women.... London: 1792. V. 68; 70; 72

WOLOSHUK, NICHOLAS
Edward Borein: Drawings and Paintings of the Old West. Flagstaff: 1968. V. 69; 70; 72
Edward Borein: Drawings and Paintings of the Old West - Volume II - The Cowboys. Santa Fe: 1974. V. 68

WOLPE, BERTHOLD
Schmuckstucke und Marken. Frankfurt am Main: 1938. V. 70

WOLSELEY, GARNET, VISCOUNT
The Story of a Soldier's Life. Westminster: 1903.,. V. 73

WOLSTENHOLME, G. E. W.
Ciba Foundation on the Cerebrospinal Fluid Production, Circulation and Absorption. Boston: 1958. V. 72

WOLSTENHOLME, GORDON
The Royal College of Physicians of London Portraits. London: 1964. V. 71; 73
The Royal College of Physicians of London: Portraits. Catalogues I and II. London and Amsterdam: 1977. V. 72

WOLVERTON'S Atlas of Monmouth County, New Jersey.... Lincroft: 1986. V. 71

WOLZOGEN, ALFRED V.
Aus Schinkel's Nachlass. Reisetagebucher, Briefe und Aphorismen.... Berlin: 1862-1864. V. 68

WOMACK, JACK
Ambient. New York: 1987. V. 69
Going Going Gone. New York: 2000. V. 72

WOMAN'S CHRISTIAN ASSOCIATION OF SIOUX CITY, IOWA
Cookery. Sioux City: 1883. V. 71

WOMEN.. New York: 1948. V. 68

WOMEN; Obsolete Ideas. In Six Letters.... Sherborne: 1805. V. 69

WOMEN OF THE KU KLUX KLAN, INC.
Outline of Principles and Teachings. Little Rock: 1923. V. 69

THE WONDERFUL City of Carrie Van Wie. San Francisco: 1963. V. 73

THE WONDERFUL Wonder of Wonders; Being an Accurate Description of the Birth, Education, Manner of Living, Religion, Politicks, Learning, Etc. of Mine A--se. Dublin: 1721. V. 69

WONDERLAND Annual 1924. V. 69

WONDERS of Nature; Our Animal Friends; Baby Animals. 1982-. V. 72

WONDERS of the Waters. London: 1842. V. 68

WONG QUINCEY, J.
Chinese Hunter. 1939. V. 69; 70; 72; 73
Chinese Hunter. New York: 1939. V. 69; 70; 73

WOOD, A. B.
Fifty Years of Yesterdays. Gering, TX: 1945. V. 71

WOOD, BASIL
Stereometry; or, the Art of Solids Demonstrated Arithmetically, and by the Line of Numbers.... London: 1707. V. 69

WOOD, BEATRICE
I Shock Myself - the Autobiography of Beatrice Wood. San Francisco: 1988. V. 70

WOOD, BUTLER
Charlotte Bronte 1816-1916. London: 1917. V. 73
Charlotte Bronte 1816-1916. London: 1918. V. 70

WOOD, C. A.
An Introduction to the Literature of Vertebrate Zoology. London: 1931. V. 70; 72
An Introduction to the Literature of Vertebrate Zoology Based Chiefly on the Titles in the Blacker Library of Zoology.... Cambridge: 1992. V. 73
An Introduction to the Literature of Verterate Zoology, Based Chiefly on the titles in the Blacker Library of Zoology..., The Bibliotheca Olseriana and Other Libraries of McGill University, Montreal. Cambridge: 1993. V. 69

WOOD, CHRISTOPHER
James Bond and Moonraker. London: 1979. V. 73

WOOD, DEAN EARL
The Old Santa Fe Trail From The Missouri River. Kansas City: 1951. V. 71
The Old Santa Fe Trail from the Missouri River. Kansas City: 1955. V. 70

WOOD, EDWARD F. R.
Sailing Days at Mattapoisett 1870-1960. New Bedford: 1961. V. 69

WOOD, EDWARD J.
The Wedding Day In All Ages and Countries. New York: 1869. V. 73

WOOD, EDWARD S.
Arsenic as a Domestic Poison. 1884. V. 68

WOOD, ELLEN PRICE
East Lynne. Leipzig: 1861. V. 70
East Lynne. London: 1861-1862. V. 73

WOOD, ERSKINE
Days With Chief Joseph. Portland. V. 72

WOOD, ESTHER
Belinda Blue. New York and Toronto: 1940. V. 69

WOOD, EVELYN
The Crimea in 1854, and 1894. London: 1895. V. 70

WOOD, GEORGE B.
Introductory Lectures and Addresses on Medical Subjects Delivered Chiefly Before the Medical Classes of the University of Pennsylvania. Philadelphia: 1859. V. 73
A Treatise on the Practice of Medicine. Philadelphia: 1858. V. 73

WOOD, GEORGE H.
Twenty Woodcuts. Manchester: 1927. V. 72

WOOD, GRANT
Catalogue of a Loan Exhibition of Drawings and Paintings by Grant Wood. Chicago: 1935. V. 69

WOOD, H. C.
A Contribution to the History of the Fresh Water Algae of North America. Washington: 1873. V. 70; 73

WOOD, H. S.
Shikar Memories. 1934. V. 70; 72; 73
Shikar Memories. Burma: 1934. V. 69

WOOD, H. TRUEMAN
Colonial and Indian Exhibition. Reports on the Colonial Sections of the Exhibition. London: 1887. V. 71

WOOD, H. WELLINGTON
Base Ball Thrillers of the National Game. Philadelphia: 1914. V. 69

WOOD, HARVEY
Personal Recollections of Harvey Wood. Pasadena: 1955. V. 68; 73

WOOD, HENRY
Change of the American Notes: in Letters from London to New York. New York: 1843. V. 70

WOOD, HENRY FREEMAN
The Englishman of the Rue Cain. London: 1907. V. 68

WOOD, HORATIO CURTIS
Nervous Diseases and Their Diagnosis: a Treatise Upon the Phenomena Produced by Diseases of the Nervous System.... Philadelphia: 1887. V. 68

WOOD, ISAAC
Some Account of the Shrewsbury House of Industry, Its Establishment and Regulations.... Shrewsbury: 1791. V. 73

WOOD, JOHN
The Daguererreotype - a Sesquicentennial celebration. Iowa City: 1989. V. 70
A Manual of Perspective...for the Use of Amateurs. Worcester: 1849. V. 71

WOOD, JOHN DENNISTOUN
The Laws of the Australian Colonies as to the Administration and Distribution of the Estate of Deceased Persons. London: 1884. V. 70

WOOD, JOHN GEORGE
Animate Creation.... New York: 1885. V. 69
Bees: the Habits, Management and Treatment. London: 1877?. V. 68
Common British Beetles. London: 1881. V. 68
The Common Moths of England. London: 1892. V. 68
The Common Moths of England. London: 1898. V. 68
The Common Objects of the Country. London: 1865?. V. 68
Common Objects of the Microscope.... London: 1900. V. 68
The Common Objects of the Sea-Shore. London: 1857. V. 68
The Common Objects of the Sea-Shore. London: 1859. V. 68
The Common Objects of the Sea-Shore. London: 1875?. V. 68
The Common Objects of the Sea-Shore. London: 1896. V. 68
The Common Objects of the Sea-Shore. London: 1897?. V. 68
Common Objects of the Sea-Shore. London: 1904. V. 72
The Common Objects of the Sea-Shore. London: 1905. V. 68
The Fresh and Salt-Water Aquarium. London: 1868. V. 68
Half Hours with a Naturalist. London: 1889. V. 68
The Illustrated Natural History. London: 1863. V. 72
Lane and Field. London: 1884. V. 68
Out of Doors. London: 1891. V. 68
The Principal Rivers of Wales Illustrated.... London: 1813. V. 72
The Principles and Practice of Sketching Landscape Scenery from Nature.... London: 1816. V. 68

WOOD, LAWSON
Gran' Pop's Annual. (Number 1). London: 1935. V. 70; 73
Lawson Wood's Annual. London: 1951. V. 71
Lawson Wood's Fun Fair. London: 1931. V. 72
Lawson Wood's Merry Monkeys. London. V. 72
Meddlesome Monkeys. London: 1952. V. 72
Mischief Makers. London: 1952. V. 72
Mrs. Bear. London. V. 72
Poplar Gran'Pop. London: 1952. V. 72
Prehistoric Proverbs. London: 1907. V. 72
The Tootle Bird and the Brontos. Buffalo;: 1907. V. 70

WOOD, LEONARD
Chasing Geronimo - The Journal of Leonard Wood May-September 1886. 1970. V. 72

WOOD, M. E.
Laurence and Eleanor Hutton, Their Books of Association. New York: 1905. V. 68

WOOD, MARGUERITE
Foreign Correspondence with Marie de Lorraine Queen of Scotland. Edinburgh: 1923-1925. V. 69; 70

WOOD, N.
Taos Pueblo. New York: 1989. V. 69

WOOD, NANCY
War Cry on a Prayer Feather. New York: 1979. V. 68

WOOD, NICHOLAS
A Practical Treatise on Rail-Roads and Interior Communication in General. London: 1825. V. 72
A Practical Treatise on Rail-roads and Interior Communication in General. London: 1831. V. 68

WOOD, NORMAN B.
Lives of Famous Indian Chiefs. Aurora: 1906. V. 72

WOOD, P.
Thoughts on Beagling. 1938. V. 68

WOOD, R. COKE
Stockton Memories, a Pictorial History of Stockton, California. Fresno: 1977. V. 71

WOOD, ROBERT
The Ruins of Balbec, Otherwise Heliopolis in Coelosyria. London: 1757. V. 68
The Ruins of Palmyra, Otherwise Tedmor, in the Desart. London: 1753. V. 68; 70; 72

WOOD, ROBERT L.
Across the Olympic Mountains. London: 1967. V. 69

WOOD, RUTH KEDZIE
The Tourist's Maritime Province's. New York: 1915. V. 73

WOOD, S. V.
A Monograph of the Crag Mollusca. 1850-1860. V. 73

WOOD, SALLY S. K.
Ferdinand and Elmira: a Russian Story. Baltimore: 1804. V. 71; 73

WOOD, SILAS
A Sketch of the First Settlement of the Several Towns on Long Island with Their Political Condition, to the End of the American Reovlution.... Brooklyn: 1865. V. 68

WOOD, THEODORE
The Rev. J. G. Wood. His Life and Work. London: 1890. V. 68

WOOD, W. A. R.
A History of Siam. Bangkok: 1933. V. 71

WOOD, W. B.
The Civil War in The United States. New York: 1905. V. 72

WOOD, WALTER E.
Venezuela; or, Two Years on the Spanish Main.... Middleborough: 1896. V. 69; 71

WOOD, WILLIAM
The Bow-Mans Glory; or Archery Revived. London: 1682. V. 69
Index Entomologicus; or a Complete Illustrated Catalogue.... 1852. V. 69
Select British Documents of the Canadian War of 1812. Toronto: 1920-1928. V. 73

WOOD, WILLIAM NATHANIEL
Reminiscences of Big I. Charlottesville: 1909. V. 69; 70

WOODALL, E.
Charles Darwin. London: 1884. V. 73

WOOD ALLEN, MARY
What a Young Girl Should Know. Philadelphia: 1905. V. 69

WOODARD, JOHN
Select Cases and Consultations, Physick by the Late Eminent John Woodward, M.D. London: 1757. V. 73

WOODBURN, SAMUEL
The Lawrence Gallery 9th and 10th Exhibitions Only. London: 1836. V. 69; 72

WOODBURY, R. B.
The Ruins of Zaculeu Guatemala. Richmond: 1953. V. 69

WOODCOCK, A. W.
Golden Days. Salisbury, MD: 1951. V. 72

WOODCOCK, GEORGE
Henry Walter Bates, Naturalist of the Amazons. London: 1969. V. 68
William Godwin - A Biographical Study. London: 1946. V. 72

WOODEHOSE, ROBERT
A Treatise on Astronomy Theoretical and Practical. Cambridge: 1821-1823. V. 69

WOODFORD, JACK
Sin and Such: an Unconventional Novel. New York: 1936. V. 71

WOODFORDE, CHRISTOPHER
A Pad in the Straw - Stories. London: 1952. V. 68

WOODFORDE, J.
A Catalogue of the Indigenous Phenogamic Plants Growing in the Neighbourhood of Edinburgh; and of Certain Species of the Class Cryptogamia. Edinburgh: 1824. V. 69

WOODFORDE, JAMES
The Diary of a Country Parson. London: 1924. V. 71
The Diary of a Country Parson. Oxford: 1924. V. 70
The Diary of a Country Parson 1758-1802. Oxford: 1968. V. 68

WOODGATES, WILLIAM
Rays of Knowledge; or, Book of Information and Amusement; Comprising (in the Form of Question and Answer).. London: 1846. V. 73

WOODHOUSE, ADRIAN
Angus McBean. London: 1982. V. 68

WOODHOUSE, RICHARD
Note on Notices. New Rochelle: 1993. V. 73
Something Given: Notes on Keats's "Mode of Writing Poetry". New Rochelle: 1990. V. 73

WOODHOUSE, S. C.
Cats at School. London: 1911. V. 71
Miss Bounce. London: 1903. V. 70
Two Cats at Large: a Book of Surprises. London: 1910. V. 73

WOODLIEF, ANN
In River Time. The Way of the James. Chapel Hill: 1985. V. 68

WOODRELL, DANIEL
Muscle for the Wing. New York: 1988. V. 68; 71; 72
The Ones You Do. New York: 1992. V. 70
Tomato Red. 1998. V. 68; 70
Tomato Red. New York: 1998. V. 72
Under the Bright Lights. New York: 1986. V. 68; 69; 71

WOODRUFF, HALE
Hale Woodruff. 50 Years of His Art. New York: 1979. V. 72

WOODRUFF, MICHAEL F. A.
The Transplantation of Tissues and Organs. Sringfield: 1960. V. 68

WOODRUFF, WILLIAM EDWARD
With the Light Guns in '61-65: Reminiscences of Eleven Arkansas, Missouri and Texas Light Batteries in the Civil War. Little Rock: 1903. V. 69; 70

WOODS, ALICE
Edges. Indianapolis: 1902. V. 73

WOODS, FREDERICK
A Bibliography of the Works of Sir Winston Churchill. London: 1963. V. 70

WOODS, H.
A Monograph of the Cretaceous Lamellibranchia of England. 1899-1913. V. 69

WOODS INVESTMENT COMPANY OF COLORADO
Gold Fields of Cripple Creek. Denver: 1901. V. 70

WOODS, J.
The Tourist's Flora. London: 1850. V. 69; 73

WOODS, JAMES
California Recollections - Recolelctions of Pioneer Work in California. San Francisco: 1878. V. 68; 73
Recollections of Pioneer Work in California. San Francisco: 1878. V. 68

WOODS, JULIAN EDMUND TENISON
A History of the Discovery and Exploration of Australia.... London: 1865. V. 71

WOODS, LAWRENCE M.
British Gentlemen in the Wild West. The Era of the Intensely English Cowboy. 1989. V. 68

WOODS, MARGARET LOUISA
Lyrics and Ballads. London: 1889. V. 69

WOODS, MATTHEW
Rambles of a Physician or a Midsummer Dream. Philadelphia: 1889. V. 73

WOODS, PAULA L.
Inner City Blues. New York: 1999. V. 69

WOODS, REX
Bricks and Hearts. London: 1933. V. 70

WOODS, SARA
Malice Domestic. London: 1962. V. 71
The Taste of Fears. London: 1963. V. 68
This Little Measure. London: 1964. V. 68

WOODS, STUART
Chiefs. 1981. V. 68
Chiefs. New York: 1981. V. 69
Run Before the Wind. New York: 1983. V. 68; 69; 71

WOODSON, CARTER G.
The Negro in Our History. Washington: 1927. V. 68
The Negro in Our History. Washington, D.C: 1945. V. 72

WOODSON, R. E.
Flora of Panama. St. Louis: 1943-1978. V. 69

WOODVILLE, WILLIAM
Observations on the Cow Pox. London: 1800. V. 73

WOODWARD, A.
A Review of Uncle Tom's Cabin; or an Essay on Slavery. Cincinnati: 1853. V. 72

WOODWARD, A. S.
Catalogue of the Fossil Fishes in the British Museum. 1889-1901. V. 73
Catalogue of the Fossil Fishes in the British Museum. London: 1889-1901. V. 68
Outlines of Vertebrate Palaeontology for Students of Zoology. Cambridge: 1898. V. 68

WOODWARD, ALICE B.
Blackie's Model Readers. Book 1. London: 1905. V. 73

WOODWARD, ARTHUR
A Brief History of Navajo Silversmithing. Flagstaff: 1938. V. 69

WOODWARD, ASHBEL
Life of General Nathaniel Lyon. Hartford: 1862. V. 72

WOODWARD, CHARLES
A Familiar Introduction to the Study of Polarized Light.... 1851. V. 71

WOODWARD, DAVID
Slavery; its Origin, Progress and Effects. Boston: 1856. V. 71

WOODWARD, H. S.
History of the Geological Society of London. 1907. V. 73
History of the Geological Society of London. London: 1907. V. 69

WOODWARD, HELEN
Beauty, and Other Poems. Exeter: 1874. V. 69

WOODWARD, HORACE BOLINGBROKE
Reynold's Geological Atlas of Great Britain.... 1850?. V. 71

WOODWARD, J.
An Essay Toward a Natural History of the Earth and Terrestrial Bodies. London: 1695. V. 69

WOODWARD, JOHN
The Life and Adventures of Don Bilioso de L'Estomac. London: 1719. V. 73
Select Cases and Consultations, Physick by the Late Eminent John Woodward M.D.... London: 1757. V. 71; 73
The State of Physick and of Diseases; with an Inquiry into the Causes of the Late Increased of Them.... London: 1718. V. 71; 73

WOODWARD, JOSIAH
An Account of the Societies for the Reformation of Manners, in London and Westminster and Other Parts of the Kingdom. London: 1699. V. 73

WOODWARD, RICHARD
An Argument in Support of the Right of the Poor in the Kingdom of Ireland, to a National Provision.... Dublin: 1772. V. 69
The Present State of the Church of Ireland. 1864. V. 70

WOODWARD, W. E.
Bread & Circuses. New York: 1925. V. 68

WOODWARD, WOODY
Jazz Americana. Los Angeles: 1956. V. 72

WOODWORTH, MARGUERITE
History of the Dominion Atlantic Railway. 1936. V. 71
History of the Dominion Atlantic Railway. Kentville: 1936. V. 73

WOODWORTH, SAMUEL
The Champions of Freedom or the Mysterious Chief, a Romance of the Nineteenth Century. New York: 1816. V. 73
The Poems, Odes, Songs and Other Metrical Effusions. New York: 1818. V. 73

WOOLEY, C. LEONARD
The Wilderness of Zin. London: 1936. V. 73

WOOLEY, L. H.
California 1849-1913, or the Rambling Sketches and Experiences of Sixty-Four Years' Residence in that State. Oakland: 1913. V. 69

WOOLF, CECIL
A Bibliography of Frederick Rolfe, Baron Corvo. London: 1972. V. 69
The Clerk Without a Benefice: a Study of Fr. Rolfe, Baron Corvo's Conversion and Vocation. 1964. V. 71
Corvo 1860-1960: A Collection of Essays by Various Hands to Commemorate the Centenary of the Birth of Fr. Rolfe, Baron Corvo. Aylesford: 1961. V. 69; 71

WOOLF, DOUGLAS
The Hypocritic Days. Mallorca: 1955. V. 68
Ya! & John-Juan. New York: 1971. V. 73

WOOLF, LEONARD
Downhill All the Way...An Autobiography of the Years 1919 to 1939. London: 1967. V. 70; 71

WOOLF, VIRGINIA
Beau Brummell. New York: 1930. V. 69; 72
Between the Acts. London: 1941. V. 69; 70; 73
Between the Acts. New York: 1941. V. 69; 72
Between the Acts. London: 1974. V. 73
The Captain's Death Bed and Other Essays. 1950. V. 68
The Captain's Death Bed and Other Essays. London: 1950. V. 69; 72; 73
The Captain's Death Bed and Other Essays. New York: 1950. V. 69; 71; 72
Collected Essays. London: 1966-1967. V. 71
The Common Reader. London: 1925. V. 69; 70; 71; 72
The Common Reader. and The Common Reader Second Series. London: 1925-1932. V. 70
The Common Reader. First and Second Series Combined in One. New York: 1948. V. 70
The Common Reader: Second Series. London: 1932. V. 71
The Death of the Moth. London: 1942. V. 69
The Death of the Moth. New York: 1942. V. 69; 72
The Diaries of Virginia Woolf. London: 1977-1984. V. 69; 70
The Essays of Virginia Woolf. London: 1986-1994. V. 69
Flush: a Biography. London: 1933. V. 69; 71
Flush: A Biography. New York: 1933. V. 72
Granite and Rainbow. London: 1958. V. 69; 72
Granite and Rainbow. New York: 1958. V. 69; 71; 73
Haunted House. London: 1943. V. 69
A Haunted House. London: 1944. V. 70
Jacob's Room. Richmond: 1922. V. 69
Jacob's Room. New York: 1923. V. 71; 72
A Letter to a Young Poet. London: 1932. V. 68; 69; 72
Letters. London: 1956. V. 70
The Letters of Virginia Woolf. London: 1975-1980. V. 68; 69; 70
The London Scene. Five Essays. New York: 1975. V. 72
Mr. Bennett and Mrs. Brown. London: 1924. V. 69
Mrs. Dalloway. London: 1925. V. 69
Mrs. Dalloway. New York: 1925. V. 70
Mrs. Dalloway's Party. London: 1973. V. 73
The Moment and Other Essays. London: 1947. V. 69; 71
The Moment and Other Essays. New York: 1948. V. 68; 72
Moments of Being - Unpublished Autobiographical Writings. Sussex: 1976. V. 70
Monday or Tuesday. New York: 1921. V. 70; 72
Monday or Tuesday. Richmond: 1921. V. 69
Night and Day. London: 1919. V. 69
Orlando. London: 1928. V. 70; 72
Orlando. New York: 1928. V. 68; 69; 70; 71
The Pargiters - the Novel-Essay Portion of the Years. New York: 1977. V. 70
A Reflection of the Other Person. The Letters of Virginia Woolf 1921- 1931. London: 1978. V. 72
Reviewing. London: 1939. V. 69; 72; 73
A Room of One's Own. London: 1929. V. 69; 70; 73
A Room Of One's Own. New York: 1929. V. 72
Stephen versus Gladstone. Cambridge: 1967. V. 72
Street Haunting. San Francisco: 1930. V. 69; 70; 71
Three Guineas. London: 1938. V. 69; 70; 71; 72; 73
To the Lighthouse. London: 1927. V. 69; 70; 72
To the Lighthouse. New York: 1927. V. 68; 69; 72
To the Lighthouse, the Original Holograph Draft. London: 1983. V. 72
Virginia Woolf and Lytton Strachey. Letters. London: 1956. V. 69
The Virginia Woolf Reader. San Diego: 1985. V. 69; 72
The Voyage Out. London: 1915. V. 69; 72
The Voyage Out. 1920. V. 69
The Voyage Out. London: 1920. V. 72
The Voyage Out. New York: 1920. V. 72
The Voyage Out. New York: 1926. V. 70; 73
Walter Sickert: a Conversation. London: 1934. V. 68; 69
The Waves. London: 1931. V. 68; 69; 72
The Waves. New York: 1931. V. 68; 72
A Writers Diary. London: 1953. V. 69; 73
The Years. London: 1937. V. 68; 69; 70; 72; 73
The Years. New York: 1937. V. 72

WOOLGAR, WILLIAM
Youth's Faithful Monitor; or, The Young Man's Best Companion. London: 1770. V. 69

WOOLLCOTT, ALEXANDER
Shouts and Murmurs. Echoes of a Thousand and One First Nights. New York: 1922. V. 71
The Wollcott Reader. New York: 1935. V. 68

WOOLLEY, A.
The Fly Fisher's Flies. 1938. V. 68

WOOLLEY, H.
The Piggy Wiggies. London: 1948. V. 73

WOOLLEY, LELL HAWLEY
California 1849-193; or the Rambling Sketches and Experiences of Sixty-Four Years Residence in that State. Oakland: 1913. V. 71

WOOLLEY, ROGER
Modern Trout Fly Dressing. 1932. V. 68; 73

WOOLMAN, JOHN
Serious Considerations on Various Subjects of Importance. London: 1773. V. 70; 73
The Works of John Woolman. Philadelphia: 1774. V. 69; 72
The Works of John Woolman in Two Parts. Philadelphia: 1775. V. 68; 72
The Works Of...In Two Parts. Philadelphia: 1818. V. 72

WOOLMER, HOWARD
A Checklist of the Hogarth Press, 1917-1946. 1986. V. 70

WOOLNER, THOMAS
My Beautiful Lady. London: 1863. V. 68
My Beautiful Lady. London: 1866. V. 68

WOOLNOUGH, C. W.
The Art of Marbling, as Applied to Book Edges and Paper, Containing Full Instructions for Executing British, French, Spanish and Italian, Nonpareil, etc., etc.... London: 1853. V. 70
The Whole Art of Marbling, as Applied to Paper Book-Edges etc. London: 1881. V. 68; 73

WOOLRICH, CORNELL
After-Dinner Story. New York and Philadelphia: 1944. V. 68; 71
Angels of Darkness. New York: 1978. V. 68; 69; 71; 72
Beyond the Night. New York: 1959. V. 68; 69; 71; 72
The Black Angel. New York: 1943. V. 70
The Black Curtain. New York: 1941. V. 68; 70
The Black Path of Fear. New York: 1944. V. 68; 72
The Blue Ribbon. Philadelphia: 1949. V. 68; 69; 71; 72
Bluebeard's Seventh Wife. New York: 1952. V. 68
The Bride Wore Black. New York: 1940. V. 68
Cover Charge. 1926. V. 69
Cover Charge. New York: 1926. V. 68
The Dancing Detective. London: 1948. V. 73
The Dark Side of Love. New York: 1964. V. 68
Darkness at Dawn. Carbondale: 1985. V. 73
Dead Man Blues. Philadelphia/New York: 1948. V. 70; 71
Deadline at Dawn. Philadelphia: 1944. V. 68; 71; 72
Deadline at Dawn. London: 1947. V. 70
Death Is My Dancing Partner. New York: 1959. V. 68; 69; 71; 72; 73
The Doom Stone. New York: 1960. V. 69; 71; 72; 73
The Fantastic Stories of Cornell Woolrich. Carbondale: 1981. V. 68
Fight. New York: 1950. V. 72
First You Dream, Then You Die. New York: 1988. V. 72
4 by Cornell Woolrich. The Bride Wore Black. Phantom Lady. Rear Window. and Waltz into Darkness. London: 1983. V. 69; 73
Hotel Room. New York: 1958. V. 68; 69
Manhattan Love Song. 1932. V. 73
Marihuana. New York: 1941. V. 73
Marihuana. New York: 1951. V. 68; 69
Night Has a Thousand Eyes. New York: 1945. V. 68; 69; 71
Nightmare. New York: 1956. V. 68; 72
Nightwebs. New York: 1971. V. 68; 69; 70
Phantom Lady. Philadelphia: 1942. V. 68; 71; 72; 73
Rendezvous in Black. New York: 1948. V. 69
Savage Bride. New York: 1950. V. 68
Six Nights of Mystery. New York: 1950. V. 72
Somebody on the Phone. Philadelphia: 1950. V. 68
Strangler's Serenade. New York: 1951. V. 68; 73
The Ten Faces of Cornell Woolrich. London: 1966. V. 69; 73
Violence. New York: 1958. V. 68; 72
Waltz Into Darkness. Philadelphia: 1947. V. 69; 70
You'll Never See Me Again. New York: 1951. V. 68; 69
A Young Man's Heart. New York: 1930. V. 73

WOOLSON, ABBA GOOLD
Woman in American Society. Boston: 1873. V. 68; 70

WOOLSON, CONSTANCE F.
For the Major, a Novelette. New York: 1883. V. 70

WOOLWICH ROYAL MILITARY ACADEMY
Records of the Royal Military Academy. Woolwich: 1851. V. 71

WOOSTER, D.
Alpine Plants. London: 1872. V. 69
Alpine Plants. 1874. V. 69

WOOTON, HENRY
Reliquiae Wottoniae; or a Collection of Lives, Letters, Poems.... London: 1672. V. 69

WORCESTER, D. C.
The Philippine Islands and Their People. New York: 1899. V. 69
The Philippines Past and Present. New York: 1914. V. 69
The Philippines Past and Present. New York: 1914-1930. V. 69

WORCESTER, DONALD E.
The Apaches: Eagles of the Southwest. Norman: 1979. V. 69

WORCESTER, J. E.
Gazetteer of the United States Abstracted from the Universal Gazetteer. Andover: 1818. V. 68

WORCESTER, NOAH
The Substance of a Pamphlet Entitled A Solemn Review of the Custom of War, Showing the War is the Effect of Popular Delusion and Proposing a Remedy. 1816. V. 71

WORCESTER, SAMUEL A.
Cherokee Hymn Book. Philadelphia: 1877. V. 71

A WORD of Advice to the Reformers in General, and to Those of Birmingham in Particular. Birmingham: 1819. V. 68

WORDS from the House of the Dead, Prison Writings from Soledad. Greenfield Center: 1971. V. 68

WORDSWORTH, CHRISTOPHER
Greece: Pictorial Descriptive and Historical. 1844. V. 69

WORDSWORTH, DOROTHY
Journals of Dorothy Wordsworth. London: 1941. V. 71; 72
Journals of Dorothy Wordsworth. London: 1970. V. 70
Journals of Dorothy Wordsworth: 2 Vols. London: 1952. V. 73
Recollections of a Tour Made in Scotland A.D. 1803. Edinburgh: 1874. V. 71

WORDSWORTH, ELIZABETH
St. Christopher and Other Poems. London: 1890. V. 69

WORDSWORTH, G. G.
Some Notes on the Wordsworths of Peniston and Their Aumbry. Ambleside: 1929. V. 71; 72

WORDSWORTH, WILLIAM
A Description of the Scenery of the District of the Lakes. Windermer. V. 71
Descriptive Sketches. London: 1793. V. 72
Ecclesiastical Sketches. London: 1822. V. 71; 72; 73
An Evening Walk. An Epistle. London: 1793. V. 72
The Excursion, Being a Portion of the Recluse, a Poem. London: 1814. V. 72
The Excursion, Being a Portion of The Recluse, a Poem. London: 1820. V. 70; 71
The Excursion, Being a Portion of the Recluse, a Poem. London: 1832. V. 71
A Guide through the District of the Lakes in the North of England, Etc. London: 1951. V. 69
Guide to the Lakes. London: 1906. V. 71
The Letters Of William And Dorothy Wordsworth. London: 1935-1939. V. 70; 72
The Letters of William and Dorothy Wordsworth. Oxford: 1935-1939. V. 70; 71
The Letters Of William And Dorothy Wordsworth. London: 1978. V. 72
The Letters of William and Dorothy Wordsworth. III. Oxford: 1978. V. 71
Lyrical Ballads and a Few Short Poems. London: 1798. V. 72
Lyrical Ballads, with Other Poems. London: 1800. V. 68; 72
Lyrical Ballads with Pastoral and Other Poems. London: 1802. V. 72
Memorials of a Tour on the Continent, 1820. London: 1822. V. 72
Poems. London: 1807. V. 70
Poems. London: 1902. V. 72
Poems by William Wordsworth Including Lyrical Ballads and the Miscellaneous Pieces of the Author. (with) Poems by William Wordsworth; Including the River Duddon; Vaudracour and Julia; Peter Bell; the Waggoner; a Thanksgiving Ode.... London: 1815-1820. V. 72
Poems, Chiefly of Early and Late Years; Including The Borders, a Tragedy. London: 1842. V. 70; 72
Poems for the Young. London: 1863. V. 70; 71
Poems in Two Volumes. London: 1807. V. 72
Poems; Including Lyrical Ballads. London: 1815. V. 72
The Poetical Works. London. V. 72
The Poetical Works. London: 1836. V. 71
The Poetical Works. London: 1836-1851. V. 69
The Poetical Works. London: 1849. V. 69
The Poetical Works. London: 1857. V. 72
The Poetical Works. London: 1864. V. 71
The Poetical Works. Oxford: 1967. V. 72
The Prelude, or Growth of a Poet's Mind. London: 1850. V. 71; 72
The Prelude, or Growth of a Poet's Mind. London: 1925. V. 71
The Prose Works. London: 1876. V. 72
The Recluse. London: 1888. V. 71; 72
The Ruined Cottage and the Pedlar. Ithaca: 1979. V. 71
The Sonnets of William Wordsworth Collected in One Volume. London: 1838. V. 71; 72
The White Doe of Rylstone; or the Fate of the Nortons. London: 1815. V. 69; 72
Wordsworth's Poems for the Young. 1863. V. 72
Yarrow Revisited. London: 1835. V. 68; 72; 73

WORK, JOHN
The Journal of John Work, a Chief-Trader of the Hudson's Bay Co., During His Expedition from Vancouver to the Flatheads and Blackfeet of the Pacific Northwest. Cleveland: 1923. V. 71
The Journal of John Work, January to October 1835. Victoria: 1945. V. 70

WORK, JOHN WESLEY
Folk Song of the American Negro. Nashville: 1915. V. 69; 71

WORK, MONROE
A Bibliography of the Negro in Africa and America. New York: 1965. V. 72

THE WORKINGMAN'S Guide and Laborer's Friend and Advocate. San Francisco: 1886. V. 73

WORKMAN, BENJAMIN
Gauging Epitomized. Philadelphia: 1788. V. 68; 73

WORKMAN, FANNY BULLOCK
Ice Bound Heights of the Mustagh. 1908. V. 68; 70; 73

WORKMAN, FANNY BULLOCK continued
In the Ice World of Himalaya. London: 1900. V. 68; 70; 73
Peaks and Glaciers of Nun Kun. New York: 1909. V. 70; 72

WORKMAN, JAMES
Political Essays. Alexandria: 1801. V. 70

WORKS, JOHN D.
Courts and Their Jurisdiction. Cincinnati: 1894. V. 72

WORLD Design Science Decade 1965-1975. Carbondale: 1963-1967. V. 70

THE WORLD Displayed, or a Curious Collection of Voyages and Travels.... Philadelphia: 1795. V. 68

THE WORLD Famous Williams Colored Singers. 1915. V. 69

WORLD Film Directors. 1890-1985. New York: 1987-1988. V. 72

A WORLD of Pleasure. Paul Whiteman. Chesterfield. V. 69

THE WORLD Turned Upside Down; or, No News and Strange News. York: 1820. V. 72; 73

WORLD War II In Asia And the Pacific And The War's Aftermath.... Westport: 1998. V. 72

WORLD-Wide Fables. New York: 1874. V. 71

THE WORLD'S Best Fairy Stories. London: 1913. V. 69

WORLDS of Childhood. Boston: 1989. V. 72

WORLIDGE, J.
Dictionarium Rusticum, Urbanicum & Botanicum; or a Dictionary of Husbandry, Gardening, Trade, Commerce and All Sorts of Country Affairs. 1717. V. 70
Systema Horti-Culturae; or the Art of Gardening. London: 1682. V. 73
Systema Horticulturae; or the Art of Gardening. London: 1700. V. 69
Vinetum Britannicum; or a Treatise of Cider and Such Other Wines and Drinks. London: 1676. V. 69

WORMALD, FRANCIS
Collected Writings. London: 1984. V. 72

WORNUM, RALPH N.
Some Account of the Life and Works of Hans Holbein. London: 1867. V. 70

WORSDELL, W. C.
Principles of Plant Teratology. London: 1915-1916. V. 73

WORSHAM, JOHN HENRY
One of Jackson's Foot Cavalry: His Experience and What He Saw During the War 1861-1865. New York: 1912. V. 69

WORSLEY, FRANK ARTHUR
Under Sail in the Frozen North. London: 1927. V. 71

WORSLEY, T. C.
Fellow Travellers - a Memoir of the Thirties. London: 1971. V. 70

WORSLEY-GOUGH, BARBARA
Lantern Hill. London: 1957. V. 72

WORSNOP, THOMAS
The Prehistoric Arts, Manufactures, Works, Weapons, Etc. of the Aborigines of Australia. South Australia: 1897. V. 70; 72; 73

WORTHINGTON, JOHN COTTON
Proceedings of a General Court Martial Held on Major Worthington, of the Sussex Fencible Cavalry. Hereford: 1800?. V. 69

WORTMAN, TUNIS
A Treatise Concerning Political Enquiry and the Liberty of the Press. New York: 1800. V. 71

WORTS, GEORGE F.
Dangerous Young Man. New York: 1940. V. 70

WOTTON, HENRY
The Elements of Architecture. London: 1903. V. 69
Letters of Sir Henry Wotton to Sir Edmund Bacon. London: 1661. V. 70

WOTTON, WILLIAM
Reflections Upon Ancient and Modern Learning. London: 1694. V. 68
Reflections Upon Ancient and Modern Learning. London: 1705. V. 69

WOTY, WILLIAM
The Shrubs of Parnassus. London: 1760. V. 69

WOUK, HERMAN
The Caine Mutiny. New York: 1951. V. 71
The Caine Mutiny. New York: 1952. V. 71
The Caine Mutiny. Franklin Center: 1977. V. 68
The Caine Mutiny Court Martial. New York: 1954. V. 69; 71
Inside, Outside. Boston: 1985. V. 68; 69
Marjorie Morningstar. Garden City: 1955. V. 68; 71
This is My God. Garden City: 1959. V. 70
War and Remembrance. Boston: 1978. V. 70
The Winds of War. Boston: 1971. V. 70
Youngblood Hawke. Garden City;: 1962. V. 68

WRAGG, ARTHUR
Jesus Wept - A commentary in black-and-white on ourselves and the world to-day. London: 1935. V. 72; 73

WRANGHAM, FRANCIS
The British Plutarch.... London: 1816. V. 71

WRAXALL, LASCELLES
Life in the Sea, or the Nature and Habits of Marine Animals. London: 1860. V. 68

WRAXALL, NATHANIEL
Historical Memoirs of My Own Time. London: 1815. V. 69
Memoirs of the Kings of France, of the Race of Valois.... London: 1777. V. 73

WRAY, MARY
The Ladies Library. London: 1714. V. 70
The Ladies Library. London: 1772-1773. V. 68; 70; 72

WREDE, PATRICIA C.
Snow White and Rose Red. New York: 1989. V. 73

THE WREN Society. Oxford: 1924-1943. V. 71

WREN, LASSITER
The Second Baffle Book. New York: 1929. V. 68

WREN, PERCIVAL CHRISTOPHER
Beau Geste. New York: 1926. V. 70
Beau Sabreur. New York: 1927. V. 70
Beau Sabreur. New York: 1928. V. 68
Mysterious Waye. New York: 1930. V. 69; 71; 73

WRIGHT & DITSON
Wright & Ditson's Catalogue of Sporting Goods and Games for In and Outdoors (for 1893). Boston;: 1893. V. 69

WRIGHT, A. E.
Principles of Microscopy. London: 1906. V. 73

WRIGHT, A. M. R.
Sons of the Sea. London: 1928?. V. 71

WRIGHT, ALAN
Bingo and Babs. London. V. 69
Comic Sport and Pastime. London: 1904. V. 72
Tony Twiddler, His Tale. Philadelphia: 1920. V. 70

WRIGHT, ALBERT HAZEN
Our Georgia Florida Frontier. The Okefinokee Swamp Its History and Cartography. New York: 1945. V. 68

WRIGHT, ANDREW
Court-Hand Restored. London: 1818. V. 68
Court-Hand Restored. London: 1877. V. 70

WRIGHT, ANNE
The Observing Eye; or, Letters to Children on the Three Lowest Divisions of Animal Life. London: 1875. V. 68

WRIGHT, AUSTIN TAPPAN
Islandia. New York: 1942. V. 69

WRIGHT, BARTON
Hopi Material Culture; Artifacts Gathered by H. R. Voth in the Fred Harvey Collection. Flagstaff: 1979. V. 68; 73
Kachinas: a Hopi Artist's Documentary. Flagstaff: 1973. V. 69; 71
Kachinas: a Hopi Artist's Documentary. Flagstaff: 1974. V. 69
Kachinas of the Zuni. 1985. V. 71
Kachinas of the Zuni. Flagstaff: 1985. V. 69
The Unchanging Hopi: an Artist's Interpretation in Scratch-Board Drawings and Text. 1976. V. 70; 72; 73

WRIGHT, C.
Poussin: Painting - a Catalogue Raisonne. New York: 1984. V. 69; 72

WRIGHT, CALEB
Historic Incidents and Life in India.... Chicago: 1867. V. 69
India and Its Inhabitants. Cincinnatti: 1856. V. 69

WRIGHT, CECIL
Words of the Earth. 1960. V. 68

WRIGHT, CHARLES
Colophons. Poems. Iowa City: 1977. V. 73
The Dreams Animal. Toronto: 1968. V. 69
Five Journals. New York: 1986. V. 73
Hard Freight. Middletown: 1973. V. 68
The Messenger. New York: 1963. V. 73
The Venice Notebook. Boston: 1971. V. 68; 69; 71; 73
Xionia. Iowa City: 1990. V. 71; 72; 73
Yard Journal. Poem. Richmond: 1986. V. 69; 73
Zone Journals. New York: 1988. V. 68

WRIGHT, DARE
The Lonely Doll. New York: 1916. V. 70
The Lonely Doll. Garden City: 1957. V. 70

WRIGHT, E. W.
Lewis & Dryden's Marine History of the Pacific Northwest. New York: 1961. V. 69; 72

WRIGHT, EDGAR
The Representative Old Cowboy, Ed Wright. np: 1954. V. 71

WRIGHT, EDWARD
Some Observations Made in Travelling through France, Italy &c. in the Years 1720, 1721 and 1722. London: 1764. V. 69; 73

WRIGHT, ELIZABETH
Independence In All Things, Neutrality in Nothing - The Story of A Pioneer Journalist of The American West. San Francisco: 1973. V. 72

WRIGHT, ELIZUR
Perforations in the Later-Day Pamphlets by One of the Eighteen Millions of Bores. No. 1 Universal Suffrage. Capital Punishment-Slavery. Boston: 1850. V. 70

WRIGHT, ERIC
Smoke Detector. Toronto: 1984. V. 72

WRIGHT, ESTHER CLARK
The Loyalists of New Brunswick. Fredericton: 1950. V. 73
The Loyalists of New Brunswick. Fredericton: 1955. V. 73

WRIGHT, FRANCES
A Few Days in Athens, Being the Translation of a Greek Manuscript Discovered in Herculaneum. London: 1822. V. 72
Views of Society and Manners in America.... New York: 1821. V. 68; 69; 70; 72

WRIGHT, FRANK LLOYD
An Autobiography. London: 1932. V. 69
An Autobiography. London: 1938. V. 68
An Autobiography. New York: 1943. V. 68
An Autobiography. London: 1977. V. 68
Buildings, Plans and Designs. New York: 1963. V. 68
The Disappearing City. New York: 1932. V. 68
Drawings for a Living Architecture. New York: 1959. V. 70; 72; 73
The Early Work. New York: 1968. V. 68
Frank Lloyd Wright Collected Writings. Volume 2. 1930-1932. New York: 1992. V. 68
Frank Lloyd Wright Collected Writings. Volume IV. 1939-1949. New York: 1994. V. 68
The Future of Architecture. New York: 1953. V. 72; 73
Genius and Mobocracy. New York: 1949. V. 68
The Japanese Print: an Interpretation. Chicago: 1912. V. 68
The Japanese Print: an Interpretation. New York: 1967. V. 68
The Life Work of the American Architect Frank Lloyd Wright. Santpoort: 1925. V. 68; 70; 73
The Living City. New York: 1958. V. 68
The Natural House. New York: 1954. V. 68
An Organic Architecture: The Architecture of Democracy. Cambridge: 1977. V. 68
Schumacher's Taliesin Line of Decorative Wallpapers. 1955. V. 68
The Story of the Tower. New York: 1956. V. 68
When Democracy Builds. Chicago: 1945. V. 68

WRIGHT, G. ERNEST
Biblical Archaeologist Reader. #1-4. Missoulu: 1975. V. 73

WRIGHT, G. N.
An Historical Guide to Ancient and Modern Dublin. 1821. V. 69
Scenes in Ireland. 1834. V. 69; 73

WRIGHT, GEORGE
The Gentleman's Miscellany.... Exeter: 1797. V. 69; 73

WRIGHT, GEORGE N.
The Life and Reign of William the Fourth. London: 1837. V. 71
The Life and Reign of William the Fourth. London: 1840. V. 71

WRIGHT, H. E.
The Quaternary of the United States.... Princeton: 1965. V. 72

WRIGHT, HAROLD BELL
Helen of the Old House. New York: 1921. V. 70
The Winning of Barbara Worth. Chicago: 1911. V. 73

WRIGHT, HENRY G.
Headaches their Causes and Their Cure. Philadelphia: 1867. V. 71

WRIGHT, I. L.
The Remarkable Tale of a Whale. Chicago: 1920. V. 72
Trails to Wonderland. London. V. 69

WRIGHT, ISAAC
Wright's Family Medicine, or System of Domestic Practice. Maryville: 1977. V. 68

WRIGHT, J.
A Monograph on the British Carboniferous Crinoidea. 1950-1960. V. 69; 73

WRIGHT, J. C.
The Story of the Brontes. 1925. V. 70; 73

WRIGHT, J. E. B.
Mountain Days in the Isle of Skye. London: 1934. V. 69; 71

WRIGHT, JAMES
The Green Wall. New Haven: 1957. V. 73

WRIGHT, JOHN
The Privilege of Man. Second Part. Stokesley: 1857. V. 72

WRIGHT, JOHN H.
Compendium of the Confederacy. Wilmington: 1989. V. 68; 73

WRIGHT, JOSEPH
The English Dialect Dictionary; Being the Complete Vocabulary of all Dialect Words Still in Use, or Known to Have Been in Use During the Last Two Hundred Years. Oxford: 1898-1905. V. 73
The English Dialect Dictionary Being the Complete Vocabulary of all Dialect Words Still in use, or Known to Have Been in Use During the Last Two Hundred Years. London: 1961. V. 70

WRIGHT, JOSHUA G.
Address Delivered at the Celebration of the Battle of Moore's Creek Bridge, February 27th 1857. Wilmington: 1857. V. 68

WRIGHT, JULIA MC NAIR
Complete Home. Philadelphia: 1879. V. 70
Grosvenor's Daughter. New York: 1893. V. 70

WRIGHT, KENNETH
The Mysterious Planet. Philadelphia: 1953. V. 69

WRIGHT, L. B.
The Arts in America: the Colonial Period. New York: 1966. V. 69; 72

WRIGHT, L. R.
Sleep While I Sing. New York: 1986. V. 71
The Suspect. New York: 1985. V. 71; 72

WRIGHT, LAURIE
Fats in Fact. Chigwell: 1992. V. 68; 70
King Oliver. Chigwell: 1987. V. 68
Mr. Jelly Lord. Chigwell: 1980. V. 68; 70
Okeh Race Records 8000 Series. Chigwell: 2001. V. 70; 73

WRIGHT, LOUIS B.
The First Americans in North Africa: William Eaton's Struggle for a Vigorous Policy Against the Barbary Pirates, 1799-1805. Princeton: 1945. V. 71

WRIGHT, M. O.
Flowers and Ferns in their Haunts. New York: 1901. V. 72

WRIGHT, OLGIVANNA LLOYD
Our House. New York: 1959. V. 68; 71

WRIGHT, ORLANDO
Maxims, Epigrams and Poetry. York: 1871. V. 69

WRIGHT, PHILIP
Old Farm Implements. London: 1961. V. 72

WRIGHT, R. G.
The Ducks of India; Their Habits, Breeding Grounds and Migrations, Together with the Other Useful Information for the Sportsman and Observer.... London: 1925. V. 68

WRIGHT, R. R.
The Encyclopaedia of the African Methodist Episcopal Church. Philadelphia: 1947. V. 70

WRIGHT, RICHARD
The Colour Curtain. London: 1956. V. 72
Native Son. New York: 1940. V. 71; 72
Native Son: a Play. New York: 1941. V. 69; 70
The Outsider. New York: 1953. V. 70
The Outsider. London: 1954. V. 72
12 Million Black Voices. A Folk History of the Negro in the United States. New York: 1941. V. 72

WRIGHT, ROBERT M.
Dodge City, the Cowboy Capital and the Great Southwest. Wichita: 1913. V. 71
Dodge City, the Cowboy Capital and the Great Southwest. 1930. V. 69

WRIGHT, RUTH
Tourist Third. Philadelphia: 1933. V. 71

WRIGHT, S. FOWLER
The Adventures of the Blue Room. London: 1945. V. 68
Deluge. New York: 1928. V. 69
Elfwin. New York: 1930. V. 72
The Island of Captain Sparrow. New York: 1928. V. 72
Poets of Merseyside - An Anthology of Present-day Liverpool Poetry. Westminster: 1923. V. 72

WRIGHT, SOLOMON ALEXANDER
My Rambles- As East Texas Cowboy, Hunter, Fisherman, Tie-Cutter. Austin: 1942. V. 71

WRIGHT, STEPHEN
Going Native. New York: 1994. V. 71
M31: a Family Romance. New York: 1988. V. 73
Meditations in Green. New York: 1983. V. 69; 72; 73

WRIGHT, T.
A Monograph of the British Fossil Echinodermata from the Cretaceous Formations. 1864-1908. V. 69; 73
A Monograph of the British Fossil Echinodermata from the Cretaceous Formations. Volume I. The Echinoidea. 1864-1882. V. 69
Monograph on the Lias Ammonites of The British Isles. 1878-1886. V. 69

WRIGHT, THOMAS
The Advantages and Method of Watering Meadows by Art.... Cirencester: 1790. V. 71
The Anglo-Latin Satirical Poets and Epigrammatists of the Twelfth Century. London: 1872. V. 68; 73

WRIGHT, THOMAS continued
Autobiography of Thomas Wright, of Birkenshaw in the County of York 1736-1797. London: 1864. V. 73
Caricature History of the Georges; or, Annals of the House of Hanover. London: 1876. V. 73
The Celt, The Roman, And The Saxon. London: 1852. V. 72
Essays on Archaeological Subjects and on Various Questions Connected with the History of Art, Science, and Literature in the Middle Ages. London: 1861. V. 68
History of Ireland from the Earliest.... London: 1880. V. 71
The Latin Poems Commonly Attributed to Walter Mapes. London: 1841. V. 73
The Life Of Daniel Defoe. London: 1894. V. 72
The Life of Sir Richard Burton. 1906. V. 72
A Short Address to the Public on the Monopoly of Small Farms, a Great Cause of the Present Scarcity and Dearness of Provisions. London: 1795. V. 73
A Treatise, Shewing the Possibilitie and Conueniencie of the Reall Presence of Our Sauiour in the Blessed Sacrament.... Antwerp: 1596. V. 70

WRIGHT, WALTER P.
Alpine Flowers and Rock Gardens Illustrated in Colour, with Notes on alpine Plants at Home.... 1924. V. 70

WRIGHT, WILLARD HUNTINGTON
The Benson Murder Case. New York: 1926. V. 68
The Bishop Murder Case. New York: 1929. V. 68; 70; 73
The Canary Murder Case. New York: 1927. V. 69
The Casino Murder Case. New York: 1934. V. 69
The Dragon Murder Case. New York: 1933. V. 69; 73
The Garden Murder Case. New York: 1935. V. 68; 70
The Gracie Allen Murder Case. New York: 1938. V. 69; 71; 73
The Greene Murder Case. London: 1928. V. 73
The Greene Murder Case. New York: 1928. V. 68
The John Riddell Murder Case. New York: 1930. V. 70
The Kennel Murder Case. New York: 1933. V. 68
The Kidnap Murder Case. New York: 1936. V. 68
Philo Vance Murder Cases. New York: 1936. V. 68
The Scarab Murder Case. New York: 1930. V. 69; 70
The Winter Murder Case. New York: 1939. V. 70

WRIGHT, WILLIAM
An Address to Persons Afflicted with Deafness.... London: 1820. V. 71
The Brontes in Ireland, or Facts Stranger than Fiction. New York: 1893. V. 70
The Brontes in Irleand or Facts Stranger than Fiction. London: 1894. V. 73
Catalogue of the Valuable Library and Collection of Engaved and Other Portraits, and Autograph Letters, the Property of the Well-Known Amateur William Wright. (with) *Catalogue of the Original Manuscripts of Charles Dickens and Wilkie Collins....* London: 1899-1890. V. 70
Dan de Quille of the Big Bonanza. San Francisco: 1980. V. 73
The Emperor of the Hittites. London: 1884. V. 71
A History of the Comstock Mines - Mineral and Agricultural Resources of the Silver Land. Virginia, Nevada: 1889. V. 68; 73

WRIGHTE, WILLIAM
Grotesque Architecture, or Rural Amusements Consisting of Plans, Elevations and Sections for Huts, Retreats, Summer and Winter Hermitages, Terminaries, Chinese, Gothic and Natural Grottos.... London: 1790. V. 68; 72

WRIGHTSON, THOMAS
An Enquiry into the Analytical Mechanism of the Internal Ear. London: 1918. V. 68

WRIGHTSON'S *Triennial Directory of Birmingham, Including an Alphabetical List of the Inhabitants of the Town, a Complete Classification of Trades.* Birmingham: 1825. V. 68

WRITERS at Work. 1984. V. 72

THE WRITER'S Forum. Brockport: 1975. V. 72

THE WRITINGS and World of Mary Butts - a Conference. Davis: 1984. V. 69

WRIXON, HENRY
Jacob Shumate or the People's March; a Voice from the Ranks. London: 1903. V. 71

WROE, RICHARD
A Sermon Preached at Bowden in Cheshire April 6, 1691. At the Funeral of the Right Honourable Mary Countess of Warrington.... London: 1691. V. 70; 72

WRONECKI, D.
New York. 1949. V. 68

WRONG, GEORGE M.
A Canadian Manor and Its Seigneurs. The Story of a Hundred Years 1761-1861. Toronto: 1926. V. 73

WROTH, LAWRENCE C.
The Early Cartography of the Pacific. New York: 1944. V. 69

WROTH, PEREGRINE
Clinical Aphorisms: a Contribution Towards the History and Treatment of the Endemic Bilious Fever of the Eastern Shore of Maryland.... Chestertown: 1842. V. 72

WROTH, W.
Christian Images in Hispanic New Mexico. 1982. V. 69
Images of Penance, Images of Mercy; Southwestern Santos in the Late Nineteenth Century. Norman: 1991. V. 68; 69

WROTH, WARWICK
Cremorne and Later London Gardens. London: 1907. V. 71

WROTTESLEY, JOHN
Thoughts on Government and Legislation. London: 1860. V. 70

WULFF, LEE
Leaping Silver: Words and Pictures on the Atlantic Salmon. New York: 1940. V. 70; 73

WURLITZER, RUDOLPH
Flats. New York: 1970. V. 69
Nog. New York: 1968. V. 69; 72
Slow Fade. New York: 1984. V. 69; 72

WURTENBERGER, F.
Mannerism: the European Style of the 16th Century. New York: 1963. V. 69; 72

WYATT, CLAUDE W.
British Birds. London: 1899. V. 70; 73

WYATT, HORACE M.
Alice in Motorland. (Second Series). London: 1905. V. 70
Malice in Kulturland. New York: 1917. V. 70

WYATT, LEO
A Suite of Little Alphabets Engraved in Wood.... 1988. V. 71

WYATT, M. DIGBY
The Industrial Arts of the Nineteenth Century. London: 1851. V. 71

WYATT, R. B. HERVEY
William Harvey (1578-1657). London: 1924. V. 68

WYATT, T.
A Manual of Conchology.... New York: 1838. V. 69

WYATT, THOMAS
Memoirs of the Generals, Commodores and Other Commanders Who Distinguished Themselves in the American Army and Navy During the Wars of the Revolution and 1812. Philadelphia: 1848. V. 72

WYATT, WOODROW
Into the Dangerous World. London: 1952. V. 72

WYBURN-MASON, ROGER
The Vascular Abnormalities and Tumours of the Spinal Cord and Its Membranes. London: 1943. V. 68

WYCHERLEY, WILLIAM
Miscellany Poems; as Satyrs, Epistles, Love Verses, Songs, Sonnets &c. London: 1704. V. 71; 73
Plays. London: 1735. V. 70

WYCOFF, E.
Bilbliographical Contributions from the Lloyd Library, Cincinnati, Ohio. Cincinnati: 1911-1913. V. 69

WYETH, B. J.
Christina's World. Boston: 1982. V. 69; 72

WYETH, JOHN ALLAN
Life of General Nathan Bedford Forrest. New York: 1899. V. 69; 70
Life of General Nathan Bedford Forrest. New York and London: 1901. V. 70
A Textbook on Surgery. New York: 1887. V. 68; 71; 73
That Devil Forrest. Life of General Nathan Bedford Forest. New York: 1959. V. 71
With Sabre and Scalpel: the Autobiography of a Soldier and Surgeon. New York: 1914. V. 70

WYETH, NATHANIEL J.
The Correspondence and Journals of...1831-1836. Eugene: 1899. V. 68; 73

WYKES, ALAN
The Pen-Friend. London: 1950. V. 72

WYLD, JAMES
The Great Western, Cheltenham and Great Western, and Bristol and Exeter Railway Guides.... London: 1839. V. 70

WYLDE, JAMES
The Book of Trades. London and Edinburgh: 1874. V. 71

WYLIE, DONOVAN
32 Counties: Photographs of Ireland by Donovan Wylie.... London: 1989. V. 69; 72

WYLIE, ELINOR
Collected Poems of Elinor Wylie. New York: 1932. V. 69
Mortal Image. London: 1927. V. 68
Nets to Catch the Wind. New York: 1921. V. 73
The Orphan Angel. New York: 1926. V. 73
Trivial Breath. London: 1928. V. 70
The Venetian Glass Nephew. New York: 1925. V. 68; 70

WYLIE, JAMES
The Homestead Grays. New York: 1977. V. 69

WYLIE, PHILIP
The Best of Crunch and Des. New York and Toronto: 1954. V. 73
Corpses at Indian Stones. New York: 1943. V. 72
The Smiling Corpse. 1935. V. 71; 73

WYLIE, W. L.
Nature's Laws and the Making of Pictures. London: 1963. V. 68

WYLLIE, JOHN
The Disorders of Speech. Edinburgh: 1894. V. 68

WYMAN, LELAND C.
Beautyway- A Navajo Ceremonial Texts Recorder Translated by Father Barnard Haile and Maude Oakes. New York: 1957. V. 71
Blessing Way. Tucson: 1970. V. 69
The Mountainway of the Navajo with a Myth of the Female Branch. Tucson: 1975. V. 69
Navaho Upward-Reaching Way: Objective Behavior, Raitionale and Sanction. 1943. V. 69
The Sandpaintings of the Kayenta Navaho. 1952. V. 69
The Windways of the Navaho. 1962. V. 69

WYMAN, PARTRIDGE & CO.
The Story of Progress in the Dry Goods Trade. Minneapolis: 1897. V. 68

WYMAN, WALKER D.
The Wild Horse of the West. Caldwell: 1945. V. 69

WYNDHAM, CHARLES
Sketches of Cockermouth Castle, in the County of Cumberland. Carlisle: 1845. V. 71

WYNDHAM, G.
The Ballad of Mr. Rook. London: 1902. V. 72

WYNDHAM, H. S.
The Annals of Covent Garden Theatre from 1732 to 1897. 1906. V. 68

WYNDHAM, HENRY PENDRUDDOCK
A Gentleman's Tour through Monmouthshire and Wales, in the Months of June and July 1774. London: 1781. V. 68; 69

WYNDHAM, JOHN
Chocky. London: 1968. V. 71
Consider Her Ways and Others. London: 1961. V. 70; 71
The Day of the Triffids. Garden City: 1951. V. 71
Foul Play Suspected. London: 1935. V. 70
The Midwich Cuckoos. 1957. V. 70
The Outward Urge. London: 1959. V. 70
Re-Birth. New York: 1955. V. 71
Trouble with Lichen. London: 1960. V. 70

WYNDHAM, RICHARD
A Book of Towers and Other Buildings of Southern Europe. 1928. V. 73

WYNN, OWEN
The Ties of Kindred; or, Read at Eventide. London: 1858. V. 68

WYNNE, A. B.
On the Geology of the Salt Range in the Punjab. Calcutta: 1878. V. 68

WYNNE, ANTHONY
The Blue Vesuvius. Philadelphia: 1931. V. 73
The Dagger. 1934. V. 68
Death of a Banker. Philadelphia: 1934. V. 70
The Fourth Finger. Philadelphia: 1929. V. 69
The Green Knife. Philadelphia: 1932. V. 73
The Horseman of Death. Philadelphia: 1928. V. 69
The Sign of Evil. Philadelphia: 1925. V. 73
Sinners Go Secretly. London: 1927. V. 73

WYNNE, DAVID
Sculpture of David Wynne 1968-1974. London: 1974. V. 72

WYNNE, ELISABETH
The Wynne Diaries 1789-1784; 1794-1798; 1798-1820. London: 1935-. V. 72

WYNNE, FRANCES
Whisper!. London: 1890. V. 69

WYNNE, JAMES
Private Libraries of New York. New York: 1860. V. 71

WYNNE, PAMELA
Ashes of Desire. New York: 1926. V. 71
A Little Flat in the Temple. Garden City: 1930. V. 71
Penelope Finds Out. New York: 1927. V. 70

WYNNE EDWARDS, V. C.
Animal Dispersion in Relation to Social Behaviour. New York: 1962. V. 72

WYNNTON, PATRICK
The Black Turret. Indianpolis: 1925. V. 69

WYNTER, ANDREW
Our Social Bees; or Pictures of Town and Country. London: 1861. V. 71

WYNTER, JOHN
Cyclus Metasyncriticus; or, an Essay on Chronic Diseases, the Methods of Cure. London: 1725. V. 68

WYNTER BLYTH, M. A.
Butterflies of the Indian Region. 1957. V. 68

WYOMING - A *Guide to Its History, Highways and People.* New York: 1941. V. 68; 71

WYOMING Platt County Heritage. Mardeline: 1981. V. 68

WYOMING STOCK GROWERS' ASSOCIATION
Cattle Brands Published by the Wyoming Stock Growers' Association. Chicago: 1883. V. 73

WYSE, HENRY T.
Modern Type Display and the Use of Type Ornament. Edinburgh: 1911. V. 71

WYSONG, THOMAS T.
The Rocks of Deer Creek: Harford, Co., Maryland. Baltimore: 1879. V. 71

WYSS, JOHANN DAVID
The Swiss Family Robinson; or, Adventures of a Father and Mother and Four Sons on a Desert Island. New York: 1832. V. 68

WYTFLIET, C.
Description Ptolemaicae Avgmentvm, Sive Occidentis Notita brevi Commentario Illustrata, et Hac Secunda Editione Magna Sui Parte Aucta.... Lovanii: 1598. V. 70

WYVILL, CHRISTOPHER
A Letter to the Right Hon. William Pitt, by the Rev. Christopher Wyvill, Late Chairman of the Committee of Association of the County of York. York: 1793. V. 73
Papers and Letters Chiefly Respecting the Reformation of Parliament. Richmond: 1816. V. 68
A State of the Representation of the People of England, on the Principles of Mr. Pitt in 1785.... York: 1794. V. 68

X

XAVIER, MARY, SISTER
Father Jaillet, Saddlebag Priest of the Nueces. 1948. V. 69

XENOPHON
The Banquet of Xenophon. Glasgow: 1750. V. 71
The Ephesian Story. Waltham St. Lawrence: 1957. V. 68
The Expedition of Cyrus Into Persia; and the Retreat of the Ten Thousand Greeks. London: 1776. V. 71
L'Opere Morali. Venice: 1547. V. 68; 72
Xenophon's Ephesian History; or the Love Adventures of Abrocomas and Anthia. London: 1727. V. 69
Xenophon's History of the Affairs of Greece, in Seven Books. (with) Kurou Paideia; or, the Institution and Life of Cyrus the Great. London: 1685. V. 71

XIMINEZ, SATURNINO
Asia Minor in Ruins. London: 1925. V. 71

XINGJIAN, GAO
Soul Mountain. New York: 2000. V. 71

XIPHILINUS, JOANNES
Dionis Nicaei, Rerum Romanarum a Pompeio Magno. Paris: 1551. V. 72
Rervm Romanarvm A Pompeio Magno Ad Alexandrvm . . . Epitome. Lvgdvni: 1559. V. 73

Y

YABLON, G. A.
A Bronte Bibliography. 1978. V. 70; 73

YACHTING Badminton Library. London: 1894. V. 68

YADAMSUREN, U.
National Costumes of the M.P.R. Ulan Bator: 1967. V. 70; 72

YALE UNIVERSITY
Catalogue of Books in the Library of Yale College. New Haven: 1823. V. 72

YAMANAKA K.
Jiu-Jutsu or Jiu-Do: Selection from Kodokwan Method. Cleveland: 1918. V. 70

YANG LING LIN
The Three-Fold San-Tsze-King or the Triliteral Classic of China as Issued. London: 1856. V. 73

THE YANKEE in London; or a Short Trip to America. Philadelphia: 1826. V. 71

YANKEE Ship Sailing Cards. Boston: 1948. V. 69

YAPP, G. W.
Art Industy: Metal Work. London: 1875. V. 71

YARBOROUGH, STEVE
Two Dogs. Candia: 2000. V. 71

YARBROUGH, STEVE
The Oxygen Man. Denver: 1999. V. 70
Two Dogs. Candia: 2000. V. 70; 73

YARN, NANCY
Let It Rain. 1981. V. 72

YARRELL, WILLIAM
A History of British Birds. London: 1836-1839. V. 73
A History of British Birds. London: 1837-1843. V. 69
A History of British Birds. London: 1843. V. 73
A History of British Birds. London: 1845. V. 69
A History of British Birds. London: 1871-1884. V. 72; 73
A History of British Birds. 1876-1885. V. 69
A History of British Birds. (with) A History of British Fishes. 1836-1843. V. 71
A History of British Fishes. 1836-1839. V. 72
A History of British Fishes. London: 1836-1839. V. 70
A History of British Fishes. 1841. V. 68; 72; 73
A History of British Fishes. London: 1859. V. 69
On the Growth Of The Salmon In Fresh Water. 1839. V. 72; 73

YATES, CHRISTOPHER
Casting at the Sun. 1986. V. 69
A Passion for Angling. 1993. V. 68

YATES, DORNFORD
Adele and Co. New York: 1931. V. 68
Blind Corner. 1927. V. 73
Gale Warning. London: 1939. V. 68
She Painted Her Face. New York: 1937. V. 68

YATES, EDMUND
Edmund Yates: His Recollections and Experiences. London: 1884. V. 70
The Forlorn Hope. London: 1872. V. 68
The Yellow Flag. London: 1875?. V. 68

YATES, ELIZABETH HALL
Shore Excursion. Philadelphia: 1936. V. 72

YATES, FREDERICK HENRY
Mr. Yates' New Entertainment. London: 1827. V. 73

YATES, MARGARET
The Hush-Hush Murders. New York: 1937. V. 70

YATES, RICHARD
Disturbing the Peace. New York: 1975. V. 70
The Easter Parade. New York: 1976. V. 70
Eleven Kinds of Loneliness. Boston: 1962. V. 70
A Good School. New York: 1978. V. 70
Lie Down in Darkness. Watertown: 1985. V. 69
Revolutionary Road. Boston: 1961. V. 72
A Special Providence. New York: 1969. V. 70; 72
Young Hearts Crying. New York: 1984. V. 70

YATES, W. W.
The Father of the Brontes. Leeds: 1897. V. 70

YATMAN, MATTHEW
A Familiar Analysis of the Fluid Capable of Producing the Pheneomena of Electricity and Galvanism.... 1810. V. 69

YATO, TAMOTSU
Young Samurai: Bodybuilders of Japan. New York: 1967. V. 68

YE GESTES of Ye Ladye Anne: A marvelous and comfortable tayle. London. V. 71

YEADON, RICHARD
The Amenability of Northern Incendiaries As Well to Southern as to Northern Laws, Without Prejudice to the Right of Free Discussion.... Charleston: 1835. V. 68

YEAGER, A. H.
Jacob Klodsloe, One of the Nobobides: How He Came Home from the War. 1899. V. 68

YEAGER, BUNNY
How I Photograph Nudes. New York: 1965. V. 70

THE YEAR That's Awa'. Waes me for Prince Charlie. A Man Without a Wife. Blythe, Blythe, an' Merry aer We. The Irish Farmer. Kelvin Grove. The Dashing white Sergeant. London: 1829. V. 68; 72

YEARSLEY, ANN
Earl Goodwin, an Historical Play. London: 1791. V. 69
Poems on Several Occasions. London: 1785. V. 69
Poems on Various Subjects.... London: 1787. V. 69

YEATES, JOHN
Michael Lyne, Sporting Artist. 1992. V. 68

YEATS is Dead!. New York: 2001. V. 69

YEATS, JACK BUTLER
Ah Well: a Romance in Perpetuity. London: 1942. V. 70; 73
The Careless Flower. 1947. V. 69
In Sand: a Play with the Green Wave. Dublin: 1964. V. 69
Life in the West of Ireland. Dublin & London: 1912. V. 73

YEATS, JOHN
The Growth and Vicissitudes of Commerce from B.C. 1500 - A.D. 1789. (with) A Manual of Recent and Existing Commerce from the Year 1789 to 1872.... London: 1872. V. 71

YEATS, JOHN BUTLER
J. B. Yeats: Letters to His Son W. B. Yeats, and Others 1869-1922. London: 1944. V. 73
Letters to His Son W. B. Yeats and Others 1869-1922. 1944. V. 70

YEATS, WILLIAM BUTLER
Autobiographies, Reveries Over Childhood and Youth. and The Trembling of the Veil. 1926. V. 69; 73
A Book of Images. London: 1898. V. 70
The Bounty of Sweden: a Meditation, and a Lecture Delivered Before the Royal Swedish Academy and Certain Notes by William Butler Yeats. Dublin: 1925. V. 73
The Cat and the Moon and Certain Poems. Dublin: 1924. V. 72; 73
The Celtic Twilight. Men and Women, Dhouls and Faeries. London: 1893. V. 68
Collected Plays. 1934. V. 70
The Collected Plays. 1952. V. 68
The Collected Plays. New York: 1953. V. 68
The Countess of Kathleen and Various Legends and Lyrics. London: 1892. V. 72
The Cutting of an Agate. New York: 1912. V. 68; 70
The Cutting of an Agate. London: 1919. V. 68; 70
Deirdre. Stratford-upon-Avon: 1914. V. 69
Dramatis Personae. Dublin: 1935. V. 70; 72
Dramatis Personae. London: 1936. V. 70
Dramatis Personae. New York: 1938. V. 68
Early Poems and Stories. New York: 1925. V. 72
Eight Poems. London: 1916. V. 71
Essays. 1924. V. 69
Essays. London: 1924. V. 70
Essays and Introductions. London: 1961. V. 72; 73
Explorations. London: 1962. V. 69; 72
A Full Moon in March. London: 1935. V. 72
The Herne's Egg. 1938. V. 68; 71
The Herne's Egg. London: 1938. V. 73
The Herne's Egg and Other Plays. New York: 1938. V. 68; 69; 73
The Hour Glass, Cathleen Ni Houlihan, The Pot of Broth. 1904. V. 68
Ideas of Good and Evil. London: 1907. V. 70
In the Seven Woods: Being Poems Chiefly of the Irish Heroic Age. Dublin: 1903. V. 73
Irish Fairy Tales. London: 1892. V. 73
The King of the Great Clock Tower, Commentaries and Poems. Dublin: 1934. V. 72
The King's Threshold. Stratford-upon-Avon: 1911. V. 69
The Land of Heart's Desire. 1894. V. 68
The Land of Heart's Desire. London: 1894. V. 72
The Land of Heart's Desire. Portland: 1903. V. 72
The Land of Heart's Desire. London: 1912. V. 69
Last Poems and Two Plays. Dublin: 1939. V. 72
Letters on Poetry from W. B. Yeats to Dorothy Wellesley. London: 1940. V. 69
Michael Robartes and the Dancer. London: 1920. V. 72
New Poems. Dublin: 1938. V. 72
October Blast. Dublin: 1927. V. 72
On the Boiler. Dublin: 1938. V. 68
On the Boiler. Dublin: 1939. V. 68; 70
A Packet for Ezra Pound. Dublin: 1929. V. 70; 72; 73
Pages from a Diary Written in Nineteen Hundred and Thirty. Dublin: 1944. V. 69
Per Amica Silentia Lunae. New York: 1918. V. 71
The Player Queen. 1922. V. 68
The Player Queen. London: 1922. V. 69
Plays and Controversies. New York: 1924. V. 69; 71
Plays for An Irish Theatre. London: 1911. V. 73
Plays in Prose and Verse. New York: 1924. V. 69
Poems. London: 1899. V. 71
Poems, 1899-1905. London: 1906. V. 71
Poems and Ballads of Young Ireland 1888. Dublin: 1888. V. 72
The Poems of W. B. Yeats. London: 1949. V. 69
Poems of W. B. Yeats. San Francisco: 1990. V. 69; 73
Poems Written in Discouragement 1912-1913. Dundrum: 1913. V. 72
Responsibilities and Other Poems. London: 1916. V. 72
Responsibilities: Poems and a Play. Dundrum: 1914. V. 72
The Secret Rose. London: 1897. V. 72
Seven Poems and a Fragment. Dublin: 1922. V. 72
Sophocles' King Opedipus; a Version for the Modern Stage. London: 1928. V. 73
Stories of Michael Robartes and His Friends. 1931. V. 68
Stories of Red Hanrahan and the Secret Rose. London: 1927. V. 73
The Tables of the Law and Adoration of the Magi. London: 1904. V. 69
The Tower. London: 1928. V. 70; 72; 73
The Trembling of the Veil. London: 1922. V. 68; 69; 70
Two Plays for Dancers. 1919. V. 68
The Variorum Edition of the Poems of W. B. Yeats. New York: 1957. V. 73
The Variorum Edition of the Poems of W. B. Yeats. New York: 1966. V. 69
A Vision. London: 1925. V. 70
A Vision. New York: 1938. V. 73
The Wanderings of Oisin and Other Poems. London: 1889. V. 72; 73
Wheels and Butterflies. London: 1934. V. 68
Where There Is Nothing: Being Volume One of Plays for an Irish Theatre. London: 1903. V. 70
The Wild Swans at Coole. Dublin: 1917. V. 72
The Wild Swans at Coole. London: 1919. V. 72; 73
The Wind Among the Reeds. London: 1899. V. 73
The Winding Stair. New York: 1929. V. 70
The Winding Stair and Other Poems. London: 1933. V. 72; 73
Words for Music Perhaps and Other Poems. Dublin: 1932. V. 69; 72; 73
The Words Upon the Window Pane. 1934. V. 68

YEATS, WILLIAM BUTLER continued
The Words Upon the Window Pane. Dublin: 1934. V. 73
The Yeats Reader. New York: 1997. V. 72

YEIGH, FRANK
5,000 Facts About Canada. Toronto: 1912. V. 73

YELD, GEORGE
Scrambles In The Eastern Graians 1878-1897. London: 1900. V. 72

YELLOW Book. London and New York: 1894-1897. V. 69; 72; 73

YELSEW, JEAN
Mountaineers; or Bottled Sunshine for Blue Mondays. Nashville: 1902. V. 68

THE YELVERTON Marriage Case, Thelwall V. Yelverton, Comprising an Authentic and Unabridged Account of the Most Extraordinary Trial of Modern Times.... London: 1861. V. 72

YELVERTON, THERESE
Zanita: a Tale of the Yo-semite. New York: 1872. V. 68

YENSER, STEPHEN
Clos Camardon. New York: 1985. V. 73

YEOMAN, THOMAS
The Report...Concerning the Drainage of the North Level of the Fens, and the Outfal of the Wisbeach River. 1769. V. 72
The Report...Concerning the Drainage of the North Level of the Fens, and the Outfal of the Wisebeach River. London: 1769. V. 68

YERBY, FRANK
The Foxes of Harrow. New York: 1946. V. 71
Goat Song. New York: 1967. V. 72
Griffin's Way. New York: 1962. V. 72

YERKES, R. M.
The Great Apes, a Study of Anthropoid Life. New Haven: 1929. V. 68; 71

YERRINTON, JAMES M. W.
Report of the Case of Geo. C. Hersey, Indicted for the Murder of Betsy Francis Tirrell, Before the Supreme Judicial Court of Massachusetts. Boston: 1862. V. 68

YESTERYEARS and Pioneer - a History of Wheatland County, Montana. Harlontown: 1972. V. 68

YETTE, SAMUEL F.
The Choice: The Issue of Black Survival in America. New York: 1971. V. 72

YEVTUSHENKO, YEVGENY
Bratsk Station. Garden City: 1967. V. 69
The Bratsk Station. London: 1967. V. 71
A Precocious Autobiography. New York: 1963. V. 71
Selected Poems. Baltimore: 1962. V. 69
Selections from the Bratsk Hydrolectric Station and Other Poems. New York: 1965. V. 69
Stolen Apples. Garden City: 1971. V. 71
Wild Berries. New York: 1984. V. 68

YOAKUM, H.
History of Texas from Its First Settlement in 1685 to Its Annexation. Austin: 1935. V. 69

YONGE, C. MAURICE
The Sea Shore. London: 1949. V. 68
The Seas. London: 1944. V. 68
The Seas. London: 1947. V. 68
The Seas. London: 1963. V. 68
Thomas Alan Stephenson 1898-1961. London: 1962. V. 68

YONGE, CHARLOTTE MARY
Beechcroft at Rockstone. London: 1888. V. 68; 72
Countess Kate. Leipzig: 1864. V. 70
The Dove in the Eagle's Nest. London: 1866. V. 68; 72
Heartsease. London: 1855. V. 71
Heartsease. New York: 1855. V. 68
History of Christian Names. London: 1863. V. 68
The History of Sir Thomas Thumb. Edinburgh: 1855. V. 73
Hopes and Fears; or Scenes from the Life of a Spinster. London: 1860. V. 71
The Little Duke, or, Richard the Fearless. London: 1854. V. 72
Love and Life an Old Story in Eighteenth Century Costume. London: 1880. V. 68; 72
The Trial: More Links of the Daisy Chain. London: 1864. V. 68
Two Penniless Princesses. London: 1891. V. 68
The Two Sides of the Shield. London: 1885. V. 73

YONGE, JAMES
The Journal of James Yonge (1647-1721). London: 1965. V. 71

YONGE, WILLIAM
Sedition and Defamation Display'd: in a Letter to the Author of the Craftsman. London: 1731. V. 71

YORDAN, PHILIP
Man of the West. New York: 1955. V. 69

YORE, CLEM
Hard Country and Gold. New York: 1935. V. 69

YORINKS, ARTHUR
Hey, Al. New York: 1986. V. 71

YORK, AGNES
Father Bear, Mother Bear and Baby Bear to Read and Color. Cleveland: 1932. V. 73

YORKINS, ARTHUR
The Miami Giant. New York: 1995. V. 72

YORKSHIRE. Progress. 1893. Commerce. 1893. V. 71

YORKSHIRE, West Riding, Contiguous to Wetherby, the Fine Residential, Agricultural and Sporting Property "The Ainsty Estate". 1931. V. 71

YORKSHIRE EXHIBITION OF ARTS AND MANUFACTURES
Official Catalogue. Leeds: 1875. V. 71

YORKSHIRE RAMBLERS' CLUB
Journal. Volume I. No. 1-3. Leeds: 1899-1901. V. 69

YOSEMITE National Park. 1912. V. 68

YOSHITARO, TAKEUCHI
A Graphic History of the Japanese Theatre. Tokyo: 1935. V. 68

YOST, KARL
A Bibliography of the Published Works of Charles M. Russell. Lincoln: 1971. V. 68; 71
A Bibliography of the Works of Edna St. Vincent Millay. New York: 1937. V. 73
Charles M. Russell the Cowboy Artist: a Bibliography. Pasadena: 1948. V. 70; 72

YOST, NELLIE SNYDER
Boss Cowman- The Recollections of Ed Lemmon 1857-1946. Lincoln: 1969. V. 71

YOUATT, WILLIAM
The Horse; with a Treatise on Draught; and Copious Index. London: 1831. V. 72

YOUMANS, EDWARD L.
The Hand-Book of Household Science. New York: 1857. V. 68

YOUNG Pegasus: Prose and Verse. New York: 1926. V. 72

YOUNG, A.
The Angler's and Sketcher's Guide to Sutherland. Edinburgh: 1881. V. 73

YOUNG, AL
Sitting Pretty. New York: 1976. V. 72
Who is Angelina. New York: 1974. V. 72

YOUNG, ALEXANDER
Very Important Collection of Modern Pictures and Water-Colour Drawings. 1910. V. 72

YOUNG, AMELIA
Madame Young's Guide to Health; Her Experience and Practice for Nearly Forty Years; a True Family Herbal.... Rochester: 1858. V. 71

YOUNG, ANDREW
The Bird Cage. London: 1926. V. 71
Collected Poems. London: 1936. V. 71
The New Shepherd. London: 1931. V. 71
Speak to the Earth. London: 1939. V. 71
Thirty-One Poems. 1922. V. 68
Winter Harvest. London: 1993. V. 71

YOUNG, ARCHER
Travels During the Years 1787, 1788 and 1789. Bury St. Edmunds: 1792. V. 72

YOUNG, ART
The Best of Art Young. New York: 1936. V. 70

YOUNG, ARTHUR
The Autobiography of Arthur Young, with Selections from His Correspondence. London: 1898. V. 71
The Farmer's Guide in Hiring and Stocking Farms. London: 1770. V. 73
The Farmer's Kalendar; or a Monthly Directory for All Sorts of Country Business.... London: 1771. V. 73
The Farmer's Tour through the East of England. London: 1771. V. 73
General View of the Agriculture of Lincolnshire. 1808. V. 73
An Idea of the Present State of France, and of the Consequences of the Events Passing in that Kingdom.... London: 1795. V. 69
Political Essays Concerning the Present State of the British Empire; Particularly Respecting. London: 1772. V. 69
A Tour in Ireland; with General Observations on the Present State of that Kingdom; Made in the Years 1776, 1777 and 1778. And Brought Down to the End of 1779. London: 1780. V. 68
Travels During the Years 1787, 1788 and 1789. Bury St. Edmunds: 1792. V. 68
Travels During the Years 1787, 1788 and 1789. Dublin: 1793. V. 70
Travels During the Years 1787, 1788 and 1789. London: 1794. V. 73

YOUNG, BENNETT H.
Confederate Wizards of the Saddle. Boston: 1914. V. 69; 70

YOUNG, BETTY LOU
Rustic Canyon and the Story of the Uplifters. Santa Monica: 1975. V. 73

YOUNG, C. G.
The Stalk-Eyed Crustacea of British Guiana, West Indies and Bermuda. London: 1900. V. 73

YOUNG, CHARLES
Dangers of the Trail in 1868, a Narrative of Actual Events. Geneva: 1912. V. 73

THE YOUNG Child's ABC or First Book. New York: 1820. V. 71

YOUNG, CHRISTIE T.
The Black Princess and Other Fairy Tales. London: 1916. V. 70

THE YOUNG Clergyman. Cambridge: 1828. V. 72

YOUNG, DAVID
Observations Upon Fire, with a View to the Best and Most Expeditious Methods of Extinguishing It, Upon a New Plan, With or Without Water. Edinburgh: 1784. V. 71

YOUNG, E. RYERSON
Three Arrows. The Young Buffalo Hunter. London: 1932. V. 73

YOUNG, EDWARD
The Centaur Not Fabulous. London: 1755. V. 69
The Complaint; or Night Thoughts, a Poem. London: 1819. V. 68
The Complaint, and the Consolation; or, Night Thoughts. London: 1797. V. 69
The Complaint; or Night Thoughts, a Poem. 1819. V. 72
The Ferns of Wales. Neath: 1856. V. 69
The Force of Religion; or Vanquish'd Love. London: 1714. V. 70
Information for Immigrants Relative to the Prices of Land, the Staple Products, Facilities of Access to Market, Cost of Farm Stock, Kind of Labor in Demand in Western and Southern States.... Philadelphia: 1871. V. 70
Love of Fame, the Universal Passion. London: 1728. V. 69
Love of Fame, the Universal Passion. London: 1730. V. 73
Poems on Several Occasions. Glasgow: 1771. V. 73
Poetical Works. London: 1834. V. 68; 72
The Works of the Author of the Night Thoughts. London: 1767. V. 69

YOUNG, ELLA
Poems by Ella Young. Dublin: 1906. V. 70

YOUNG England's Pictorial Library: Courtship, Marriage and Pic-Nic Dinner of Cock Robin and Jenny Wren. Otley. V. 70; 73

YOUNG England's Pictorial Library: Mother Hubbard. London: 1840. V. 71; 73

YOUNG, ERIC BRETT
THe Murder at Fleet. Philadelphia: 1928. V. 70

YOUNG, ERNEST A.
Walt Wheeler, the Scout Detective. New York: 1884. V. 73

YOUNG, FILSON
The Happy Motorist. London: 1906. V. 68

THE YOUNG Folks Birthday Book. New York: 1902. V. 70

YOUNG, FRANCIS BRETT
Blood Oranges. Kensington: 1932. V. 70
The Happy Highway. New York: 1940. V. 70

YOUNG, FRANK C.
Echoes from Arcadia - Story of Central City, As Told by One of The Clan. Denver: 1903. V. 69

YOUNG, G. O.
Alaskan-Yukon Trophies Won and Lost. Huntington: 1947. V. 69

YOUNG, G. W.
Collected Poems. 1936. V. 68

YOUNG, GEOFFREY WINTHROP
April and Rain. London: 1923. V. 69
Mountain Craft. London: 1934. V. 69
Mountain Craft. London: 1954. V. 69
Snowdown Biography. London: 1957. V. 69

YOUNG, GEORGE
A Treatise on Opium, Founded Upon Practical Observations. London: 1753. V. 73

YOUNG, GEORGE R.
On Colonial Literature, Science and Education.... Halifax: 1842. V. 73

YOUNG, GORDON
Hurricane Williams. Indianapolis: 1922. V. 72

YOUNG, HARRY
Hard Knocks - a Life Story of the Vanishing West. Chicago: 1915. V. 70

YOUNG, HERBERT V.
They Came to Jerome. 1972. V. 69

YOUNG, HUGH
Hugh Young. A Surgeon's Autobiography. New York: 1940. V. 71

YOUNG, J. Z.
Anatomy of the Nervous System of Octopus Vulgaris. 1971. V. 72

YOUNG, JAMES HARVEY
The Medical Messiahs. A Social History of Health Quackery in TwentiethCentury America. 1967. V. 71
The Toadstool Millionaires. A Social History of Patent Medicines in America before Federal Regulation. 1961. V. 71

YOUNG, JAMES KELLY
A Practical Treatise on Orthopedic Surgery. Philadelphia: 1894. V. 69

YOUNG, JAMES REID
Scottish Mountaineering Club Guide. Edinburgh: 1929. V. 69

YOUNG, JENNIE J.
The Ceramic Art: a Compendium of the History and Manufacture of Pottery and Porcelain. New York: 1878. V. 73

YOUNG, JESSE BOWMAN
The Battle of Gettysburg. New York and London: 1913. V. 69; 70

YOUNG, JOHN
A Criticism on the Elegy Writtin in a Country Church-Yard. Edinburgh: 1810. V. 68; 72
Essays and Addresses. Glasgow: 1904. V. 68
The Letters of Agricola, on Principles of Vegetation and Tillage. Halifax: 1822. V. 73
A Series of Designs for Shop Fronts and Entrances to Buildings Public and Private. London: 1835. V. 70; 71; 72

YOUNG, JOHN R.
Memoirs of John R. Young - Utah Pioneer 1847. Salt Lake City: 1920. V. 70

YOUNG, L. D.
Reminiscences of a Soldier of the Orphan Brigade. Paris: 1918?. V. 69

THE YOUNG Lady's Book. A Manual of Elegant Recreations, Arts, Sciences and Accomplishments. London: 1859. V. 73

THE YOUNG Lady's Toliet. Ohio: 1841. V. 68

YOUNG, LAMBTON J. H.
Sea Fishing as a Sport.... London: 1865. V. 68

YOUNG, LYMAN
Tim Tyler in the Jungle. Chicago: 1935. V. 70

YOUNG, M. J.
Familiar Lessons in Botany with Flora of Texas, Adapted to General Use in the Southern States. New York: 1873. V. 69

THE YOUNG Man's Magazine, Containing the Substance of Moral Philosophy and Divinity.... Philadelphia: 1784. V. 71

YOUNG, MARGUERITE
Harp Song for a Radical. New York: 1999. V. 69; 72

THE YOUNG Naturalist, a New Hitory of Foreign and British Beasts. Chelmsford: 1815. V. 71

YOUNG, OTIS E.
The First Military Escort on the Santa Fe Trail.... Glendale: 1952. V. 68; 73
The West of Philip St. George Cooke 1809-1895. Glendale: 1955. V. 72

THE YOUNG Painter's Assistant in the Art of Drawing, a New Drawing Book.... 1753. V. 73

YOUNG, PHILIP
The Hemingway Manuscripts: an Inventory. University Park and London: 1969. V. 69

YOUNG, ROBERT FITZGIBBON
Comenius in England. The Visit of Jan Amos Komensky (Comenius). London: 1932. V. 71

YOUNG, ROBERT W.
The Navaho Language. 1943. V. 69

YOUNG, S. GLENN, MRS.
Life and Exploits of S. Glenn Young - World Famous Law Enforcement Officer. Herrin: 1924. V. 70

YOUNG, S. O.
A Thumb-Nail History of the City of Houston, Texas. Houston: 1912. V. 68
True Stories of Old Houston and Houstonians. Galveston: 1913. V. 68

YOUNG, S. P.
The Wolves of North America. Washington: 1944. V. 69

THE YOUNG Sailor; or the Sea-Life of Tom Bowline. New York: 1855. V. 68

YOUNG, SAMUEL
A Treatise on Internal Navigation, Explaining the Principles by Which Canals and Their Appendages are Laid Out.... New York: 1817. V. 73

YOUNG, SIDNEY
The Annals of the Barber-Surgeons of London. London: 1890. V. 68

YOUNG, STARK
Feliciana. New York: 1935. V. 72
So Red the Rose. New York: 1934. V. 72

YOUNG, THOMAS
Narrative of a Residence on the Mosquito Shore. London: 1842. V. 71

THE YOUNG Traveller's Delight.... Chelmsford: 1815. V. 71

YOUNG, W. E.
Shark! Shark!. New York: 1933. V. 70

YOUNG, WHITNEY
Beyond Racism. New York: 1969. V. 68

YOUNG, WILLIAM
Amativeness, or the Confessional. Philadelphia: 1853. V. 73
Considerations Which May Tend to Promote the Settlement of Our New West-India Colonies. London: 1764. V. 71
The Spirit of Athens.... London: 1777. V. 73

YOUNG BEAR, RAY
Black Eagle Child. Iowa City: 1992. V. 72
Remnants of the First Earth. New York: 1996. V. 72

YOUNGBLOOD, BONNEY
An Economic Study of a Typical Ranching Area On The Edwards Plateau of Texas. College Station, TX: 1922. V. 71

YOUNGER, C.
Ireland's Civil War. 1968. V. 69

YOUNGER, JOHN
River Angling for Salmon and Trout. 1864. V. 73

YOUNGHUSBAND, FRANCIS
The Epic of Mount Everest. London: 1974. V. 69
Everest: The Challenge. London: 1936. V. 69
The Heart of a Continent. 1904. V. 69; 70; 72; 73
The Heart of Nature or the Quest for Natural Beauty. London: 1921. V. 69
Kashmir. London: 1933. V. 72

YOUNGHUSBAND, G. J.
The Relief of Chitral. London: 1895. V. 70

YOUNGMAN, W. E.
Gleanings from Western Prairies. Cambridge: 1882. V. 70

YOUNG OTIS, E.
The First Military Escort on The Santa Fe Trail, 1829, From Journals and Reports of Major Bennett Riley and Lieutenant Philip St. George Crook. Glendale: 1952. V. 72

YOUNGPRAPPAKORN, P.
A Color Atlas of Diseases of the Crocodile. 1995. V. 72

YOUNT, GEORGE C.
George C. Yount and His Chronicles of the West. Denver: 1966. V. 72

THE YOUTH'S Cabinet of Nature, for the Year.... New York: 1814. V. 73

YRIATE, CHARLES
Florence: Its History.... London: 1882. V. 71

YUKON GOLD COMPANY
An Abridged History with Illustrations of the Operations of the Yukon Gold Company June 1911. New York: 1911. V. 68

YULE, HENRY
A Narrative of the Mission Sent by the Governor General of India to the Court of Ava in 1855. Calcutta: 1858. V. 70

YVES Saint Laurent: Images of Design 1958-1988. London: 1988. V. 68

Y-WORTH, WILLIAM
Cerevisiarii Comes; or, the New and True Art of Brewing. London: 1692. V. 69

Z

ZABOR, RAFI
The Bear Comes Home. New York: 1997. V. 69
The Bear Comes Home. New York: 1997-1998. V. 69

ZABRE, ALFONSO T.
Guide to the History of Mexico: a Modern Interpretation. Mexico: 1935. V. 68

ZABRISKIE, GEORGE A.
Bon Vivant's Companion. Ormond Beach: 1933. V. 72
The Pathfinder. Ormond Beach: 1947. V. 73

ZACCHIROLI, FRANCESCO
Versi. Venezia: 1781. V. 73

ZACHARIAS, GERHARD
The Satanic Cult. London: 1980. V. 71

ZADOR, A.
Revival Architecture in Hungary; Classicism and Romanticism. Budapest: 1985. V. 69

ZAEHNSDORF, JOSEPH W.
The Art of Bookbinding: a Practical Treatise. London: 1890. V. 69

ZAHN, JOHANN
Specula Physico-Mathematico-Historica Notabilium ac Mirablium Siendorum.... Nuremberg: 1696. V. 68

ZAHN, WILHELM
Ornamente Aller Klassichen Kunst-Epochen Nach den Orignialien in inhren Eigenthumlichen Farben. Berlin: 1849. V. 68; 70; 72

ZAMACOIS, EDUARD
Roots. New York: 1929. V. 72

ZAMORANO CLUB
Zamorano Choice II: Selections from the Zamorano Club's Haja Volante 1967-1993. Los Angeles: 1996. V. 73
Zamorano Club 1929. Los Angeles: 1929. V. 73

ZAMYATIN, YEVGENY
We. London: 1970. V. 70

ZANETTI, ANTONIO MARIA
Varie Pitture a Fresco de Principali Maestri Veneziani.... Venice: 1760. V. 69

ZANGWILL, ISRAEL
The Big Bow Mystery. Chicago and New York: 1895. V. 69; 70
Chosen Peoples: the Hebraic Ideal Versus the Teutonic. London: 1918. V. 71
The King of Schnorrers, Grotesques and Fantasies. London: 1894. V. 70

ZANOTTI, EUSTACHIO
Trattato Teorico-Pratico di Prospecttiva.... Bologna: 1766. V. 72

ZAOROWSKY, JEROME
Secreta Monita Societatis Jesu. The Secret Instructions of the Jesuits. London: 1746. V. 70

ZAPATA, GIOVANNI BATTISTA
Li Maravigliosi Secreti di Medicina e Chirvrgia, Nvovamente Ritrovati per Guaire Ogni Sorte d'Infirmita. Venice: 1586. V. 70

ZAPF, HERMANN
Hermann Zapf and His Design Philosophy. Chicago: 1987. V. 73
Pen and Graver. New York: 1952. V. 73

ZAPF'S Civilite Disclosed. Northampton: 1995. V. 69

ZARA, LOUIS
Blessed is the Man. New York: 1935. V. 71
Give Us This Day. New York: 1936. V. 71

ZATTA, ANTONIO
Catalogo di Libri Latini e Italiani, Che Trovansi Vendibili Ne Negozio.... Venice: 1791-1790. V. 72

ZAWADIWSKY, CHRISTINE
The World at Large. Madison: 1978. V. 70; 72

ZEIGLER, WILBUR G.
Heart of the Alleghanies or Western North Carolina.... Raleigh: 1883. V. 73

ZEILLER, MARTIN
Topographia Galliae. Frankfurt: 1655-1661. V. 71
Topographia Germaniae Inferioris. Frankfurt: 1659. V. 71

ZEISBERGER'S Indian Dictionary - English, German, Iroquois - the Onondaga and Algonquin, the Delaware. Cambridge: 1887. V. 73

ZEISLER, ERNEST BLOOMFIELD
Baker Street Chronology: Commentaries on the Sacred Writings of Dr. John H. Watson. New York: 1983. V. 69

ZEISLER, SIGMUND
Reminiscences of the Anarchist Case. Chicago: 1927. V. 68

ZEISLOFT, IDELL E.
The New Metropolis. 1600. Memorable Events of Three Centuries - 1900. New York: 1899. V. 70

ZEISS, CARL
A Spectacle of Spectacles. Jena: 1988. V. 68

ZELAYETA, ELENA
Elena's Fiesta Recipes. Los Angeles: 1952. V. 69

ZELAZNY, ROGER
Blood of Amber. New York: 1986. V. 69
The Guns of Avalon. New York: 1972. V. 71
Nine Princes in Amber. New York: 1972. V. 68

ZEMACH, MARGOT
Duffy and the Devil - a Cornish Tale. New York: 1973. V. 72

ZENDRINI, BERNARDINO
Trattato della Chinachina. Venice: 1715. V. 72

ZENGER, JOHN PETER
The Trial of John Peter Zenger, of New York, Printer Who Was Tried and Acquitted for Printing and Publishing, a Libel Against the Government. London: 1752. V. 70

ZENKER, E. V.
Anarchism. London: 1898. V. 68

ZETLAND, LAWRENCE JOHN LUMLEY DUNDAS, 2ND MARQUIS OF
A Wandering Student in the Far East. Edinburgh and London: 1908. V. 68

ZEUNER, F. E.
A History of Domesticated Animals. 1963. V. 69

ZEVI, BRUNO
Frank Lloyd Wright's Fallingwater: La Casa Sulla Cascata di Frank Lloyd Wright. Milan: 1965. V. 68
The Modern Language of Architecture. 1978. V. 68

ZEYHER, J. M.
Beschreibung der Gartenanlagen zu Schwetzingen. Mannheim: 1825. V. 68

ZHADANOV, V. M.
The Study of Influenza. Bethesda: 1960. V. 72

ZIAUDDIN, M.
A Monograph on Moslem Calligraphy. Calcutta: 1936. V. 72

ZIEGLER, RICHARD
Judith the Widow of Bethulia: the Drawings and Script of Richard Zeigler. London: 1946. V. 70; 72

ZIEMANN, HUGO
Cabinet Cook Book. Springfield: 1901. V. 73

ZIENKOWICZ, LEON
Les Costumes du Peuple Polonais, suivis d'une Description Exacte de ses Moeurs.... Paris: 1841. V. 69

ZIGLIARA, F. THOMA MARIA
Summa Philosophica in Usum Scholarum. Parisiis/Lugduni: 1898. V. 68

ZIGROSSER, CARL
The Expressionsts: A Survey of Their Graphic Art. New York: 1957. V. 70; 72

ZIMMER, GEORGE F.
K-7 Spies at War. New York: 1934. V. 70

ZIMMER, J. T.
Catalogue of the Edward E. Ayer Ornithological Library. 1990. V. 73

ZIMMERMAN, BRUCE
Crimson Green. New York: 1994. V. 71

ZIMMERMAN, WILLIAM
Waterfowl of North America. Louisville: 1974. V. 69

ZIMMERMANN, HENRY
Zimmermann's Captain Cook. An Account of the Third Voyage of Captain Cook Around the World. Toronto: 1930. V. 73

ZIMMERMANN, JOHNANN GEORG
An Essay on National Pride.. London: 1771. V. 73

ZINBERG, LEN
Walk Hard, Talk Long. Indianapolis: 1940. V. 68

ZINZERLING, JUSTUS
Itinerarium Galliae...Cum Appendice, De Burdigala. Amsterlodami: 1649. V. 71
Jodoci Sinceri Itinerarium Galliae.... Amsterdam: 1655. V. 68; 70

ZIRNGIBL, M. A.
African Weapons. Passau: 1980. V. 69

ZOGBAUM, RUFUS F.
Horse, Foot & Dragoons, Sketches of Army Life At Home and Abroad. New York: 1888. V. 72

ZOLA, EMILE
L'Assommoir. London: 1928. V. 73
L'Assomoir. Philadelphia: 1879. V. 69
The Attack on the Mill. London: 1895. V. 71; 73
Doctor Pascal, or Life and Heredity. London: 1893. V. 69; 73
The Fortune of the Rougons. London: 1889. V. 71
Money. London: 1894. V. 71
The Soil (La Terre). London: 1888. V. 69

ZOLLINGER, JAMES PETER
Sutter: The Man and His Empire. New York: 1939. V. 69

ZONCA, VITTORIO
Novo Teatro di machine et edificii Per Varie et Sicure Operationi Co le Lor Figure Tagliate in Rame e la Dichiaratione.... Padua: 1607. V. 68

ZOOLOGICAL SOCIETY OF LONDON
Proceedings. London: 1830-1918. V. 70; 73

ZOSIMUS
The New History of Count Zosimus.... London: 1684. V. 71

ZOUCHE, ROBERT CURZON, BARON
Armenia; a Year at Erzeroom and on the Frontiers of Russia, Turkey, and Persia. London: 1854. V. 68

ZSAMBOKI, JANOS
Emblemata, et Aliquot Nummi Antiqui Operis Loan. Leiden: 1599. V. 70

ZSIGMONDY, EMIL
In the High Mountains. 1992. V. 68; 70

ZUKOFSKY, LOUIS
A 1-12. Ashland: 1959. V. 68
After I's. Pittsburgh: 1964. V. 71
Anew: Poems. Prairie City: 1946. V. 68
Bottom: On Shakespeare. Austin: 1963. V. 69; 71; 72
I's (pronounced eyes): poems. New York: 1963. V. 68
Initial: a Poem. New York: 1970. V. 68
An Objectivists Anthology. Dijon: 1932. V. 68
Prepositions - the Collected Critical Essays. London: 1967. V. 71
16 Once Published: Poems. Edinburgh: 1962. V. 68
Some Time. Short Poems. Stuttgart: 1956. V. 73
A Test of Poetry. New York: 1964. V. 71

ZULCH, KLAUS J.
Otfrid Foerster - Physician and Naturalist November 9, 1873 - June 15, 1941. Berlin: 1969. V. 68

ZUMAGLINO, VITTORIO
Cento Istantanee. Milano: 1936. V. 70

ZURCHER, F.
Volcanoes and Earthquakes. Philadelphia: 1869. V. 70

ZWEIFACH, BENJAMIN W.
Annotated Bibliography on Shock 1950-1962. Washington: 1963. V. 72
Annotated Bibliography on Shock 1962-1964. Washington: 1966. V. 72

ZWEIG, ARNOLD
The Case of Sergeant Grischa. New York: 1929. V. 69

ZWEIG, STEFAN
Letter from an Unknown Woman. New York: 1932. V. 71

ZWINGER, ANN
A Conscious Stillness. New York: 1982. V. 72

ISBN 0-7876-9086-4